The Travellers' DICTIONARY OF QUOTATION

The Travellers' DICTIONARY OF QUOTATION

Who Said What, About Where?

Edited by Peter Yapp

Routledge & Kegan Paul
London, Boston, Melbourne and Henley

First published in 1983
by Routledge & Kegan Paul plc
39 Store Street, London WC1E 7DD,
9 Park Street, Boston, Mass. 02108, USA,
296 Beaconsfield Parade, Middle Park,
Melbourne, 3206, Australia, and
Broadway House, Newtown Road,
Henley-on-Thames, Oxon RG9 1EN
Set in Baskerville
and printed in Great Britain by
Billing & Sons Ltd, Worcester.

Library of Congress Cataloging in Publication Data

The Travellers' dictionary of quotation.
Includes indexes.
1. Quotations about places. 2. National characteristics—Quotations, maxims, etc. I. Yapp, Peter.
PN6084.P55T72 1983 082 8223026

ISBN 0-7100-0992-5

Contents

For J. Y.

Acknowledgments

So many people have been drawn into this black hole that I cannot thank them all individually here. I hope they know how grateful I am. Special thanks must go first to Justin Wintle, but for whom *The Travellers' Dictionary* would not have been begun, and without whose advice it would never have been completed, inasmuch as it has been. I am indebted for their skills and patience to all those who have worked on production at Routledge & Kegan Paul, and elsewhere, especially to Jennifer Martin for her typescript, and to Carol Gardiner for copy-editing beyond the call of duty. In Cambridge Tristram Riley-Smith and Mark Padmore were foremost among those who helped me to check references and suggested more material for inclusion; and it is a further pleasure to thank Hugh Brogan, Anna Caldwell, Anthony Cornish, Lissa Demetriou, Stephanie Herman, Dr Theo Hoppen, Alan McConnell, David Phillips, Arnold Rattenbury, John Scotney, Jenny Speller, Nadra Woosnam-Mills, Peter Wilson, Ailian Wyn, and in New Zealand, James McNeish, Tony Simpson, and Christopher and Sonja Pinfield. And I would like to thank Mary Cohen, Katharine Barker and Michael Percival for help with the index. This book would have been far less of a pleasure to compile without the collections and staff of the London Library.

For permission to quote extensively from works which are still in copyright I make grateful acknowledgment as follows:

Extracts from *The Letters of Henry Adams*, Volume I, edited by Worthington C. Ford. Copyright 1930 by Worthington C. Ford. Copyright © renewed 1958 by Emily E.F. Lowes. Reprinted by permission of Houghton Mifflin Company. From *The Letters of Henry Adams*, Volume II, edited by Worthington C. Ford. Copyright 1938 by Worthington C. Ford. Copyright © renewed 1966 by Emily E.F. Lowes. Reprinted by permission of Houghton Mifflin Company. Extracts from James Agate's *Ego 3* to *Ego 9* are reprinted by permission of George G. Harrap & Co. Ltd.; from Jonathan Aitken's *Land of Fortune*, by permission of the author; from Patrick Anderson's *Poem of Canada*, and *Search Me*, by permission of Orlando Gearing; from John Arlott's 'Brighton' and 'Leslie Thomas's' [John Arlott's] 'Basingstoke' both from *Landmarks*, edited by John Arlott and G. Rostrevor Hamilton, and published by Cambridge University Press in 1943, by permission of the author. Lines from W.H. Auden's 'O Beautiful City of Brussels', copyright by the Estate of W.H. Auden, are reprinted by permission of Edward Mendelson, not to be reprinted without written permission. Excerpts from W.H. Auden's 'Dover', 'Night Mail' and the complete poem 'Brussels in Winter', copyright 1938, 1940, 1945, and renewed 1968 by W.H. Auden, are reprinted from W.H. Auden's *Collected Poems*, edited by Edward Mendelson, by permission of Random House, and by permission of Faber & Faber Ltd from *Collected Shorter Poems* by W.H. Auden. 'A Voyage, V – Macao', copyright 1945, and renewed 1973 by W.H. Auden, reprinted from W.H. Auden, *Collected Poems*, edited by Edward Mendelson, by permission of Random House Inc., and by permission of Faber & Faber Ltd from *Journey to a War*, 1939/1973, by W.H. Auden and Christopher Isherwood; extracts from Maurice Baring's *Round the World in Any Number of Days*, by permission of the Trustees of the Estate of Maurice Baring; lines from two poems by George Barker, by permission of the author; from *Away from it All* by Cedric Belfrage, published by Victor Gollancz in 1936, by permission of the author; from Hilaire Belloc's *Hills and the Sea*, published by Methuen & Co. Ltd, reprinted by permission of Associated Book Publishers Ltd; from Hilaire Belloc's *The Path to Rome*, published by George Allen & Unwin (Publishers) Ltd, reprinted by permission of the publisher; from Hilaire Belloc's *Places*, published by Cassell & Co. Ltd, reprinted by permission of A.D. Peters & Co. Ltd; extracts from 'The South Country', 'A Moral Alphabet', 'The Modern Traveller', and 'New Cautionary Tales', from Hilaire Belloc's *Complete Verse*, published by Gerald Duckworth and Co. Ltd, are reprinted by permission of the publisher, and A.D. Peters & Co. Ltd; extract from *John Brown's Body*, by Stephen Vincent Benét, from *The Selected Works of Stephen Vincent Benét*, Holt Rinehart & Winston, Inc., Copyright renewed, 1955, 1956, by Rosemary Carr Benét. Reprinted by permission of Brandt & Brandt Literary Agents, Inc. 'American Names' by Stephen Vincent Benét, from *The Selected Works of Stephen Vincent Benét*, Holt Rinehart & Winston, Inc. Copyright, 1927, by Stephen Vincent Benét, Copyright renewed, 1955, by Rosemary Carr Benét. Reprinted by permission of Brandt & Brandt Literary Agents, Inc.; 'The Golden Corpse' by Stephen Vincent Benét, from *The Selected Works of Stephen Vincent Benét*, Holt Rinehart & Winston, Inc., Copyright, 1925, by Stephen Vincent Benét; Copyright renewed, 1953, by Rosemary Carr Benét; Reprinted by permission of Brandt & Brandt Literary Agents, Inc.; Extract from 'American Lights Seen from Off Abroad', from *Short Poems* by John Berryman, Copyright © 1958, by John Berryman, reprinted by permission of Farrar, Strauss & Giroux, Inc.; extracts from *The Journals of Arnold Bennett*, published by Cassell & Co. Ltd, by permission of Madame V.M. Eldin; four lines from *The Complete Clerihews of E. Clerihew Bentley* (1981), reprinted by permission of Oxford University Press; lines from Sir John Betjeman's *Collected Poems of John Betjeman*, published by John Murray Ltd, and from the same author's *A Nip in the Air*, published by John Murray in 1974, by permission of the publisher; the poem 'Who took away our counties', is reprinted by permission of Sir John Betjeman; 'Canada, Case History, 1945', from *Ghost in the Wheels: The Selected Poems of Earle Birney*, is reprinted by permission of the Canadian publishers, McLelland & Stewart Ltd, Toronto; 'In Bloody Orkney', from *Bawdy Barrack-Room Ballads*, edited by Hugh de Witt, is reprinted by permission of Tandem Publishing Ltd (W.H. Allen); extracts from *The Face of Spain*, by Gerald Brenan, published by Turnstile Press, are reprinted by permission of C. & J. Wolfers Ltd; 'The Moorland Map', by Ivor Brown, is reprinted by permission of

A.D. Peters Ltd; extracts from *First Russia, then Tibet*, and *The Road to Oxiana*, by Robert Byron, both published by Macmillan, are reprinted by permission of A.D. Peters & Co. Ltd; lines from 'The Wayzgoose' by Roy Campbell are reprinted by permission of the Executors of the Roy Campbell Estate, and Jonathan Cape Ltd; from Roy Campbell's *Collected Poems*, published by The Bodley Head in 1961, lines from 'The Golden Shower', 'Colloquy of the Sphinx and the Soldier', 'The Hoopoe', 'On the Architect's Designs for the Escurial', 'Fishing Boats in Martigues', 'Flowering Rifle', and 'Toledo', are reprinted by permission of Miss Teresa Campbell; lines from 'Rounding the Cape', and 'Tristan da Cunha', from *Selected Poems by Roy Campbell*, edited by J.M. Lalley, and published by The Bodley Head in 1968, are reprinted by permission of Miss Teresa Campbell, Francisco Campbell Custodio, and A.D. Donker (Pty) Ltd; extracts from *Point of Departure*, by James Cameron, published by Arthur Barker, are reprinted by permission of David Higham Associates Ltd, on behalf of the author; lines from G.K. Chesterton's 'Me Heart', 'The World State', 'The Secret People', 'The Judgement of England', and 'The Napoleon of Notting Hill', are reprinted by permission of Dodd, Mead & Company, Inc. from *The Collected Poems of G.K. Chesterton*, Copyright 1932 by Dodd, Mead & Company. Copyright renewed 1959 by Oliver Chesterton. Chesterton's *Collected Poems* were published in England by Methuen & Co., and the extracts are used here by permission of Miss D.E. Collins and A.P. Watt & Co.; 'Haworth in May', by Wilfred Rowland Childe, from his *Selected Poems*, published by Thomas Nelson & Sons Ltd, in 1936, are reprinted by permission of the publishers; lines from 'Galway Bay' by Arthur Colahan are reprinted by permission of Box & Cox Publications Ltd; 'Oh Canada', Copyright © 1965 by John Robert Colombo, is used with permission of the author; extracts from *Ideas and Places* by Cyril Connolly, published by George Weidenfeld & Nicolson Ltd, are reprinted by permission of Deborah Rogers Ltd; extracts from the *Journals of Captain Cook*, edited by J.C. Beaglehole (and including extracts from Journals by David Samwell, and William Wales, published with them), are reprinted by permission of the Hakluyt Society; 'Cambridgeshire' by Frances Cornford, from her *Collected Poems*, published by the Cresset Press, in 1954, is reprinted by permission of Cresset Press, now part of Hutchinson Publishing Group; from songs by Noel Coward, lines from 'Fête Galante', from *On With the Dance*, words and music by Noel Coward, © 1926 Ascherberg Hopwood & Crew Ltd (Chappell Music Ltd), published in the USA by Chappell & Co. Inc., from 'The Stately Homes of England', from *Operette*, words and music by Noel Coward, © 1938 Chappell & Co. Ltd. Copyright renewed, published in the USA by Chappell and Co. Inc.; from 'There are Bad Times Just Around the Corner', from *The Globe Revue*, words and music by Noel Coward, © 1952 by Chappell & Co. Ltd, copyright renewed, published in the USA by Chappell & Co. Inc., International copyrights secured, all rights reserved, used by permission; from 'Mad Dogs and Englishmen', from *Words and Music*, words and music by Noel Coward, © 1932 Chappell & Co. Ltd, © 1931 (Renewed) Warner Bros Inc., All rights reserved. Used by Permission; from *Complete Poems by e.e. cummings*, edited by George James Firmage, and published by Granada Publishing Ltd, lines from 'Thanksgiving, 1956', 'O to be in finland', and the complete poems 'Paris: this april sunset completely utters', 'next to of course god america i', 'who knows if the moon's a balloon', and 'the Cambridge ladies who live in furnished souls', are reprinted by permission of the publisher; in the USA the lines from 'Thanksgiving, 1956' and from 'O to be in finland', copyright respectively © 1957, and 1950 by e.e. cummings, are reprinted from his volume *Complete Poems 1913–1962*, by permission of Harcourt Brace Jovanovich, Inc.; 'Paris; this April sunshine completely utters', 'who knows if the moon's', and 'the Cambridge ladies who live in furnished souls' are reprinted from *Tulips and Chimneys* by e.e. cummings, by permission of Liveright Publishing Corporation. Copyright 1923, 1925 and renewed 1951, 1953 by e.e. cummings. Copyright © 1973 by Nancy T. Andrews. Copyright © 1973, 1976 by George James Firmage; 'next to of course god America i' is reprinted from *IS 5 Poems by e.e. cummings*, by permission of Liveright Publishing Corporation. Copyright 1926 by Horace Liveright. Copyright renewed 1953 by e.e. cummings; lines from 'Pennsylvania Places', from *Late Lark Singing* by T.A. Daly, are reprinted by permission of Harcourt Brace Jovanovich, Inc.; lines from 'Identity Card', from *The Selected Poems of Mahmoud Darwish*, edited and translated by Ian Wedde and Fawwaz Tuqan, and published by Carcanet Press Ltd in 1973, are reprinted by permission of the publisher; 'Gwalia Deserta, No: XV', by Idris Davies, from his *Collected Poems*, Published by J.D. Lewis & Sons Ltd, Gomer Press, 1972, are reprinted by permission of the publisher; four lines from 'Thoughts on Death' by Clarence Day, Copyright 1928 by Clarence Day, and renewed 1956 by Mrs Clarence Day, are reprinted from *The Best of Clarence Day*, by permission of Alfred A. Knopf, Inc.; lines from *I Hear America Swinging*, Copyright © 1974, by Peter de Vries, are reprinted by permission of the author; extracts from *The Pilgrim Edition of the Letters of Charles Dickens*, Vols 1 and 2 edited by Madeline House and Graham Storey (1965; 1969) vol. 3 edited by Madeline House, Graham Storey and Kathleen Tillotson (1974) and vol. 4 edited by Kathleen Tillotson and Nina Burgis (1977); © Oxford University Press, Reprinted by permission of Oxford University Press; extracts from *Alone* by Norman Douglas, reprinted by permission of the Society of Authors as the literary representative of the Estate of Norman Douglas; lines from 'Canterbury' from 'Canterbury and Other Poems', by Basil Dowling 1949, are reprinted by permission of the author; 'Nemea', is reprinted by permission of Faber & Faber Ltd, and Viking Penguin Inc., from *Collected Poems* by Lawrence Durrell, edited by James A. Brigham, Copyright 1980 by Lawrence Durrell; and excerpts from *Sicilian Carousel* by Lawrence Durrell, Copyright © 1977 by Lawrence Durrell, are reprinted by permission of Faber & Faber Ltd, and Viking Penguin Inc.; Excerpts from 'The Waste Land' and 'The Hollow Men', in *Collected Poems, 1909–1962*, by T.S. Eliot, copyright 1936, by Harcourt Brace Jovanovich, Inc; copyright © 1963, 1964 by T.S. Eliot are reprinted by permission of Faber & Faber Ltd, and Harcourt Brace Jovanovich, Inc.; 'Chelsea in Winter', from *Londoners* by Gavin Ewart, published by William Heinemann Ltd, is reprinted by permission of the author and publisher; and *Haiku: the Wit and Wisdom of Cyril Connolly*, by Gavin Ewart, by permission of the author; lines from 'I'm older than you, please listen', from *Strange Rendezvous*, and 'Album Leaves', from *Dominion*, both by A.R.D. Fairburn, are reprinted from his *Collected Poems*, published by Pegasus Press Ltd, by permission of the publisher and Miss Dinah Holman on behalf of the Estate of A.R.D. Fairburn; Duncan Fallowell has kindly allowed me to include his observation on Penang; excerpts from *Behind God's Back*, by Negley Farson, published by Victor Gollancz, are reprinted by permission of A.D. Peters & Co.

Ltd; extracts from *The Travellers Tree*, and *A Time of Gifts*, by Patrick Leigh Fermor, published by John Murray Ltd, are reprinted by permission of the publisher; extracts from Ford Madox Ford's *Return to Yesterday*, published by Victor Gollancz, are reprinted by permission of David Higham Associates Ltd; extracts from essays by E.M. Forster, 'India Again', 'The United States', 'Ferney', and 'London is a Muddle', all included in *Two Cheers for Democracy*, published by Edward Arnold Ltd, in 1951, and copyright 1951 by E.M. Forster, renewed 1979 by Donald Parry, are reprinted by permission of Edward Arnold Ltd, and Harcourt Brace Jovanovich, Inc.; extracts from 'New Hampshire', 'Once by the Pacific', 'Birches', 'The Gift Outright', and 'North of Boston', from *The Poetry of Robert Frost*, edited by Edward Connery Lathem. Copyright 1916, 1928, © 1969 by Holt Rinehart & Winston. Copyright 1942, 1944, © 1956 by Robert Frost. Copyright © 1970 by Lesley Frost Ballantine. Reprinted by permission of Holt Rinehart & Winston, Publishers, the Estate of Robert Frost, and Jonathan Cape Ltd; 'For Travelers Going Sidereal' from *Robert Frost: Poetry and Prose* edited by Edward Connery Lathem and Lawrance Thompson. Copyright © 1972 by Holt, Rinehart & Winston. Reprinted by permission of Holt Rinehart & Winston, Publishers; extract from 'The Lambeth Walk', by Noel Gray and Douglas Furber, © 1937 by Cinephonic Music Co. Ltd, 37 Soho Square, reprinted by permission of Campbell Connelly & Co. Ltd; extracts from *The Dragon and the Lotus* by Crosbie Garstin, published by William Heinemann Ltd, reprinted by permission of Tessa Sayle; 'Northumberland' by Wilfred Wilson Gibson, reprinted by permission of Michael Gibson; lines from 'Just One Glimpse', 'Lesbos', and 'Connemara' from *Collected Poems* by Oliver St John Gogarty, published by Constable and Co. Ltd, and Devin Adair Company, are reprinted by permission of Mr Oliver D. Gogarty and Devin Adair Company, Old Greenwich Ct. Copyright © 1954 by Oliver St John Gogarty, reserved 1982; lines from *Verse and Worse*, and *The Motley Muse*, by Harry Graham, published by Edward Arnold (Publishers) Ltd, are reprinted by permission of the publisher; excerpts from *Journey Without Maps* by Graham Greene, copyright 1936 by Graham Greene, All rights reserved, reprinted by permission of William Heinemann/The Bodley Head, Laurence Pollinger Ltd, and Viking Penguin, Inc.; 'Scarred Landscape', from *'Scars'* by Bryn Griffiths, published by J.M. Dent & Sons, 1969, is reprinted by permission of the author; excerpts from *Inside U.S.A.* by John Gunther, Copyright 1946, 1947 by John Gunther. Copyright 1947 by the Curtis Publishing Company, from *Inside Africa* by John Gunther. Copyright 1953, 1954 © 1955 by John Gunther, from *Inside South America* by John Gunther, Copyright © 1966, 1967 by John Gunther, are reprinted by permission of Harper & Row, Publishers, Inc.; lines from 'English pleasures', 'The Carved Stone', 'Cathedral Bourges', and the poems 'Albert Memorial', and 'Zoo', from *Collected Poems and Epigrams* by G. Rostrevor Hamilton, published by William Heinemann Ltd, in 1958, are reprinted by permission of the publisher; from songs by Oscar Hammerstein II, lines from 'Ol' Man River' from *Showboat*, Music by Jerome Kern, Words by Oscar Hammerstein II, Copyright © 1927 by T.B. Harms Company, Copyright renewed. (C/O The Welk Music Group, Santa Monica, CA 90401) Used by permission. All rights reserved. International Copyright Secured. And by permission of Chappell Music Ltd; from 'The Last Time I Saw Paris' Music by Jerome Kern, Words by Oscar Hammerstein II, copyright © 1940 T.B. Harms Company. Copyright renewed. (C/O The Welk Music Group, Santa Monica, CA 90401) Used by permission. All rights reserved. International Copyright Secured; and used by permission of Chappell Music Ltd; from 'Kansas City' from *Oklahoma*, Music by Richard Rodgers, Words by Oscar Hammerstein II, Copyright © 1943 Williamson Music Co., British Publisher Williamson Music Ltd, Copyright renewed, International Copyright Secured. All Rights Reserved, used by permission of Chappell Music company, Inc., and Chappell Music Ltd; from *The Complete Poems of Thomas Hardy*, edited by James Gibson, published by Macmillan Publishing Co. Inc. in 1978, lines from 'Wessex Heights', 'Moments of Vision', and 'The Marble-streeted Town' are used by permission of the publishers; extract from 'Manhattan' by Lorenz Hart, © copyright Edward B. Marks Music Corporation. Used by Permission; lines from *Dunciad Minor*, by A.D. Hope, published by Melbourne University Press in 1970, are reprinted by permission of Curtis Brown (Aust) Pty Ltd, Sydney; and from 'Australia', in A.D. Hope's *Collected Poems, 1930–1970*, by permission of Angus and Robertson (UK) Ltd; extracts from *The Journals and Papers of Gerard Manley Hopkins*, edited by Humphrey House and Graham Storey, 1959, are reprinted by permission of Oxford University Press; lines from 'A Shropshire Lad' – Authorised Edition – from *The Collected Poems of A.E. Housman*. Copyright 1939, 1940, © 1965 by Holt, Rinehart & Winston. Copyright © 1967, 1968 by Robert E. Symons are reprinted by permission of Holt Rinehart & Winston, Publishers, of the Society of Authors as the literary representative of the Estate of A.E. Housman, and Jonathan Cape Ltd, publishers of A.E. Housman's *Collected Poems*; extracts from *Beyond the Mexique Bay* by Aldous Huxley, copyright 1934, © 1962 by Aldous Huxley, are reprinted by permission of Harper & Row, Publishers, Inc., of Mrs Laura Huxley, and Chatto & Windus Ltd; excerpts from *Goodbye to Berlin* by Christopher Isherwood, Copyright © 1939 by Christopher Isherwood, reprinted by permission of the Hogarth Press, and Candida Donadio and Associates, Inc., on behalf of the author; and extracts from *The Condor and the Cows*, copyright 1947 by Christopher Isherwood, reprinted by permission of Curtis Brown London Ltd, and Candida Donadio & Associates, Inc., on behalf of the author; excerpts from *The Letters of Henry James*, edited by Leon Edel are reprinted by permission of Alexander R. James, and Macmillan, London and Basingstoke, and J. Fraser Cocks III, Curator, Special Collections, Colby College, Waterville, Maine; lines from 'Antrim' copyright 1931 and renewed 1959 by Robinson Jeffers, and 'The Eye', copyright 1941, 1944 and renewed 1969, 1972 by Donnan Jeffers and Garth Jeffers, are reprinted from *Selected Poetry of Robinson Jeffers*, by permission of Random House, Inc.; 'Welsh and Proud of It', by Gareth Jones, is reprinted by permission of the author; 'Secular Litany' from *Imaginary Islands* by M.K. Joseph, is reprinted by permission of Mrs M.J. Joseph; excerpts from *The Letters of James Joyce*, edited by Stuart Gilbert, copyright © 1957 by The Viking Press, Inc., from *The Letters of James Joyce II*, edited by Richard Ellmann. Copyright © 1966 by F. Lionel Munro as Executor of the Estate of James Joyce; from *The Letters of James Joyce, III*, edited by Richard Ellmann. Copyright © 1966 by F. Lionel Munro as Executor of the Estate of James Joyce, are reprinted by permission of Viking Penguin, Inc., and Faber & Faber Ltd; excerpt from 'Gas from a Burner' by James Joyce, from *The Portable James Joyce*, edited by Harry Levin, Copyright 1946, 1947 by the Viking Press, Inc., Copyright renewed 1974, 1975 by the Viking Press, Inc., reprinted by permission of Viking Penguin, Inc.; verses from Joyce's Letters, and 'Gas from a Burner' from *Pomes Penyeach* are reprinted in England by permission of the Society of Authors as the Literary Representative of the Estate of James Joyce; lines from Jack Judge and Harry Williams, 'It's a Long Way to Tipperary', © 1912 by B. Feldman & Co. Ltd, are reproduced by permission of EMI Music Publishing Ltd; excerpts from *The Collected Works of C.G. Jung*, translated by R.F.C. Hull, Bollingen Series XX, Vol. 10, *Civilization in Transition*, Copyright © 1964, 1970 by Princeton University Press, are reprinted by permission of Princeton University Press, and Messrs Routledge & Kegan Paul Ltd; verses by Rudyard Kipling, copyright 1908, 1910, 1911, and 1913 by Rudyard Kipling and copyright 1917 by Doubleday & Company, Inc. from *Rudyard Kipling's Verse: Definitive Edition*, are reprinted by permission of The National Trust, Macmillan London Ltd, and Doubleday & Company, Inc.; excerpts from *Something of Myself* by Rudyard Kipling, Copyright 1937 by Caroline Kipling, are reprinted by permission of The National Trust, Macmillan London Ltd, and Doubleday & Company, Inc.; from *Letters: Rudyard Kipling to Rider Haggard*, edited by Morton N. Cohen, published by Hutchinson Ltd, are reprinted by permission of The National Trust; excerpts from *From Tideway to Tideway, Letters to the Family,* and *From Sea to Sea*, by Rudyard Kipling, are reprinted by permission of The National Trust and Macmillan London Ltd; excerpts from books by James Kirkup, *These Horned Islands*, published by William Collins Sons & Co. Ltd in 1962, *Japan Behind the Fan*, published by J.M. Dent, 1970, *Heaven Hell and Hara-Kiri*, by Angus & Robertson, 1974, *One Man's Russia*, Phoenix House, 1968, and *Streets of Asia*, J.M. Dent, 1969, are reprinted by kind permission of James Kirkup; lines from *The Whitsun Weddings*, by Philip Larkin, are reprinted by permission of Faber & Faber Ltd; excerpts from *The Collected Letters of D.H. Lawrence,* edited by H.T. Moore, copyright © 1962 by Angelo Ravagli and C. Montegue Weekley, as Executors of the Estate of Frieda Lawrence Ravagli, from *Phoenix: The Posthumous Papers by D.H. Lawrence*, edited by Edward McDonald, Copyright 1936 by Frieda Lawrence, Copyright renewed, 1964, by the Estate of Frieda Lawrence, and from *The Complete Poems of D.H. Lawrence*, edited by Vivian da Sola Pinto and F. Warren Roberts, copyright © 1964, 1971 by Angelo Ravagli and C.M. Weekley, as Executors of the Estate of Frieda Lawrence Ravagli, are reprinted by permission of Lawrence Pollinger Ltd. the Estate of Frieda Lawrence Ravagli, and Viking Penguin, Inc.; excerpt from *Seven Pillars of Wisdom*, by T.E. Lawrence, Copyright 1926, 135 by Doubleday & Company, Inc., reprinted by permission of the publisher, and in England by permission of the Seven Pillars Trust and Jonathan Cape Ltd; excerpts from Stephen Leacock's works, *My Discovery of England, Sunshine Sketches of a Little Town, Humor: Its Theory and Technique,* and *Behind the Beyond*, are reprinted by permission of Dodd, Mead & Company, The Bodley Head, and McLelland & Stewart Ltd; lines from 'Paris Day by Day', by Richard Le Gallienne, are reprinted by permission of the Society of Authors as the Literary Representative of the Estate of Richard Le Gallienne; excerpts from *Canada Made Me*, by Norman Levine, copyright 1958 by Norman Levine, first published by Putnam, 1958, first Canadian edition by Deneau & Greenberg, 1979, are reprinted with the permission of the author and Virginia Barber Literary Agency, Inc., New York; excerpts from *The Changing Sky,* by Norman Lewis, published by Jonathan Cape Ltd, in 1959, are reprinted by permission of Richard Scott Simon Ltd, on behalf of the author; from poems by Vachel Lindsay, lines from 'Niagara' copyright 1917 by Macmillan Publishing Co., Inc., renewed 1945 by Elizabeth C. Lindsay, from 'Yet Gentle Will the Griffin Be', copyright 1914 by Macmillan Publishing Co., Inc., renewed 1942 by Elizabeth C. Lindsay, from 'The Golden Whales of California', copyright 1920 by Macmillan Publishing Co., Inc., renewed 1948 by Elizabeth C. Lindsay, and from 'Springfield Magical', 'The Gospel of Beauty', 'Kansas', 'The City that Will Not Repent', and 'To Reformers in Despair', all from *Collected Poems* of Vachel Lindsay, New York, Macmillan, 1925, are reprinted with permission of Macmillan Publishing Co., Inc.; lines from 'Caracas', from *Notebook* by Robert Lowell, Copyright © 1967, 1968, 1969, 1970 by Robert Lowell, are reprinted by permission of Farrar, Strauss & Giroux, Inc., and Faber & Faber Ltd; lines from *England Day By Day*, by E.V. Lucas and C.L. Graves, are reprinted by permission of Associated Book Publishers Ltd; lines from 'Drop-out in Edinburgh', by Norman McCaig, from *The World's Room*, are reprinted by permission of the author, and Hogarth Press; lines from 'New Guinea', 'The True Discovery of Australia', and 'Envoi', from James McAuley's *Collected Poems 1936–1970* are reprinted with the permission of Angus & Robertson (UK) Ltd; extracts from *On The Contrary*, by Mary McCarthy, Copyright © 1946, 1947, 1949, 1950, 1951, 1952, 1953, 1954, 1955, 1958, 1959, 1960, 1961 by Mary McCarthy, are reprinted by permission of Farrar, Strauss & Giroux Inc., and the author; extracts from *The Complete Poems of Hugh McDiarmid* (C.M. Grieve), edited by Michael Grieve and William Aitken, published by Martin, Brian & O'Keeffe, London, namely lines from 'Scotland', 'North of the Tweed', 'Separation', 'Towards a New Scotland, IV', and 'Towards a New Scotland, VII', and 'Glasgow', are reprinted by permission of Mrs Valda Grieve and Mr Michael Grieve; from poems by Louis MacNeice, lines from 'Birmingham', 'Eclogue from Iceland', 'Valediction', 'The Hebrides', 'Letter to Graham and Anne Shepherd', 'Autumn Journal', 'The Closing Album, I', 'The Closing Album, IV', 'Street Scene', 'Relics', 'Mahabalipuram', 'Letter from India', 'Autumn Sequel', and 'Goodbye to London', all from *The Collected Poems of Louis MacNeice*, are reprinted by permission of Faber & Faber Ltd; extract from 'Lines on the Occasion of Her Majesty's Visit to Canada' 1959, by John Masefield, are reprinted by permission of the Society of Authors, as the Literary Representative of the Estate of John Masefield; excerpts from the travel books of W. Somerset Maugham, *Don Fernando*, copyright 1935 by W. Somerset Maugham, *On a Chinese Screen*, copyright 1922 by W. Somerset Maugham, and *The Gentleman in the Parlour*, copyright 1930 by Doubleday & Company, Inc., copyright 1926 by International Management Company, Inc., are reprinted by permission of the Estate of the late W. Somerset Maugham, Doubleday & Company, Inc., and William Heinemann Ltd; excerpts from *Letters from the Field: 1925–75* by Margaret Mead, Volume 52 in World Perspectives planned and edited by Ruth Nanda Anshen, Copyright © 1977 by Margaret Mead, are reprinted by permission of Harper & Row, Publishers, Inc.; excerpts from Howard C. Horsford (ed.), *Journal of a Visit to Europe and the Levant: October 11, 1856 to May 6, 1857*, by Herman Melville, Copyright 1955 by Princeton University Press, are reprinted by permission of Princeton University Press; lines from Alice Duer Miller's *The White Cliffs*, © 1940, renewed © 1967, by Alice Duer Miller, are reprinted by permission of Methuen & Co. Ltd, and Coward, McCann & Geoghegan, Inc.; excerpts from *The Air Conditioned Nightmare*, by Henry Miller, copyright 1945 by New Directions Publishing Corporation, are reprinted by permission of New Directions and William Heinemann Ltd; extracts from Lady Mary Wortley Montagu's *Complete Letters*, edited by Robert Halsband, and published by Oxford University Press, 1965–7, are reprinted by permission of the editor; lines from 'Spenser's Ireland' from *Collected Poems* of Marianne Moore, copyright 1941 and renewed 1969 by Marianne Moore, are reprinted by permission of Macmillan Publishing Co. Inc., and Faber & Faber Ltd; lines from 'The Hubbub of the Universe', from *Translations from the Chinese* by Christopher Morley, are reprinted by permission of Harper & Row, Inc.; excerpts from *Places*, by James (now Jan) Morris, published by Faber & Faber in 1972, and from *Travels*, 1976, by the same author and publisher, are reprinted by permission of A.D. Peters & Co. Ltd; excerpts from *Oxford* by the same author are reprinted by permission of Faber & Faber Ltd; excerpts from *In Search of Scotland* by H.V. Morton, copyright 1929, 1930, by H.V. Morton, copyright renewed 1957, 1958 by H.V. Morton, are reprinted by permission of Dodd, Mead & Company, Inc., and Eyre Methuen & Co. Ltd; excerpts from *Scottish Journey* by Edwin Muir are reprinted by permission of Mainstream Publishing Co. (Edinburgh) Ltd; lines from 'A Sough O' War' from *Hamewith and Other Poems*, by Charles Murray, published by Constable & Co. Ltd, are reprinted by permission of J.C. and A. Steuart, W.S., on behalf of the family of the late Dr Charles Murray; excerpts from *The Middle Passage*, by V.S. Naipaul, published by André Deutsch in 1962, are reprinted by permission of the publisher, and Gillon Aitken, on behalf of the author; the following poems, and extracts from poems by Ogden Nash, are reprinted by permission of Little, Brown & Company, and Curtis Brown Ltd, New York; 'Geographical Reflection' from *Hard Lines*, copyright 1931 by Ogden Nash; from 'Kipling's Vermont', 'Is It True What They Say About Dixie, or Is It Just The Way They Say It', and 'The Dust Storm, or I've Got Texas in my Lungs', from *The Private Dining Room*, copyright 1935 by Ogden Nash; from *Many Long Years Ago*, lines from 'A Bas Ben Adhem', and 'These Latins', both copyright 1931 by Ogden Nash, and 'A Brief Guide to New York', copyright 1940 by Ogden Nash; from *I'm A Stranger Here Myself*, 'The Neighbors', 'The Japanese', 'The Northerners', from 'Fellow Creatures', copyright 1935 by Ogden Nash, first appeared in *Saturday Evening Post*, and 'England Expects', copyright 1936 by The Curtis Publishing Co., first appeared in the *Saturday Evening Post*; from *Good Intentions*, 'Don't Shoot Los Angeles' and 'Ask Daddy, He Won't Know', copyright 1942 by Ogden Nash; from *Versus*, lines from 'Martha's Vineyard', copyright 1945 by Ogden Nash, first appeared in the *New Yorker*; and from *Everyone but Thee and Me*, 'The Azores', 'Amsterdam Rotterdam and the Hague', 'Morocco', 'Madeira', and 'City Greenery', copyright © 1962 by Ogden Nash; lines from 'The Heights of Macchu Pichu', from *Selected Poems of Pablo Neruda*, translated by Ben Belitt, © 1961 by Grove Press, Inc., are reprinted by permission of Grove Press, Inc.; 'Ireland, Ireland', from *The Selected Poems of Henry Newbolt*, published by Hodder & Stoughton in 1981 is reprinted by permission of Peter Newbolt; lines from 'The Barrel Organ', from *Collected Poems*, Volume I, by Alfred Noyes, are reprinted by permission of William Blackwood & Sons; excerpts from *Homage to Catalonia* by George Orwell, copyright 1952, 1980 by Sonia Brownell Orwell, are reprinted by permission of Harcourt Brace Jovanovich, Inc., the Estate of the late Sonia Brownell Orwell, and Martin Secker & Warburg Ltd; lines from 'There'll Always Be an England', by Ross Parker and Hughie Charles, © 1939 by Dash Music Co. Ltd, 37 Soho Square, London, are reprinted by permission of Campbell Connelly and Co. Ltd; excerpts from *The Most of S.J. Perelman* by S.J. Perelman, 1978, © 1930–1958 by S.J. Perelman, are reprinted by permission of Simon & Schuster, a Division of Gulf & Western Corporation and A.D. Peters & Co. Ltd; lines from 'Towards the Last Spike', from *The Collected Poems of E.J. Pratt*, edited by Northrop Frye, published by The Macmillan Company of Canada, in 1958, are reprinted by permission of Sandra A. Djwa for Viola and Claire Pratt and the Pratt Estate; 'Quite So', by A.G. Prys-Jones is reprinted by permission of the author; extracts from *A Superficial Journey Through Tokyo and Peking* by Peter Quennell are reprinted by permission of Faber & Faber Ltd; lines from 'Ode Upon Ekington Bridge', from *'Q' Anthology*, by Sir Arthur Quiller Couch, published by J.M. Dent & Sons, in 1948, are reprinted by permission of Messrs Monro Pennefather & Co.; excerpts from *Arabia Through the Looking Glass* by Jonathan Raban are reprinted by permission of William Collins Sons & Company Ltd; for permission to include 'Lake Huron', 'Lake Erie', and 'Lake Superior' from *Poems* by James Reaney, ed. by Germaine Warkentin, copyright, Canada, by New Press, Toronto, 1970, thanks are due to the author and his literary agent, Sybil Hutchinson; extracts from the journal of Samuel Rogers are reprinted by permission of Faber & Faber Ltd, from *Italian Journal* by Samuel Rogers, edited by J.R. Hale; extracts from *The Valley of the Assassins*, 1934, *Travellers Prelude*, 1950, *Beyond Euphrates*, 1951, *The Coasts of Incense*, 1953, and *Dust in the Lion's Paw*, 1961,by Freya Stark are reprinted by permission of John Murray (Publishers) Ltd; extracts from *The Waveless Plain* by Walter Starkie are reprinted by permission of John Murray (Publishers) Ltd; lines from *The Land* by Vita Sackville-West are reprinted by permission of William Heinemann Ltd; excerpts from 'Chicago' in *Chicago Poems*, 'Slants at Buffalo, New York' in *Cornhuskers*, 'Pennsylvania', 'Omaha', and 'The Sins of Kalamazoo' in *Smoke and Steel*, and 'The Windy City' in *Slabs of the Sunburnt West*, all by Carl Sandberg, are reprinted by permission of Harcourt Brace Jovanovich, Inc.; copyright 1916, 1918 by Holt Rinehart & Winston, Inc., copyright 1920, 1922 by Harcourt Brace Jovanovich, Inc., copyright 1944, 1946, 1948, 1950 by Carl Sandberg; extracts from *Blue Skies, Brown Studies*, by William Sansom, published by the Hogarth Press, © William Sansom, 1961, are reprinted by permission of Elaine Greene Ltd; lines from 'The Scholar Farmer', from *In Cap and Bells* by Sir Owen Seaman are reprinted by permission of The Bodley Head Ltd; two lines from 'The Law of the Yukon' from *The Collected Poems of Robert Service* are reprinted by permission of Dodd, Mead & Company, Inc., and Ernest Benn Ltd; extracts from *Escape with Me* by Osbert Sitwell are reprinted by permission of Macmillan London Ltd, and David Higham Associates Ltd; lines from 'Five Visions of Captain Cook' from *One Hundred Poems* by Kenneth Slessor, 1944, are reprinted by permission of Angus & Robertson (UK) Ltd; extracts from *The Letters of Sydney Smith* edited by Nowell C. Smith, 1953, are reprinted by permission of Oxford University Press; lines from 'Kynd Kittock's Land' from *Collected Poems* by Sydney Goodsir Smith are reprinted by permission of John Calder (Publishers) Ltd; lines from 'Stonehenge' from *Collected Poems of Sir John Squire* are reprinted by permission of Macmillan, London and Basingstoke; 'Vor a Gauguin Picture zu Singen', from *Gemixte Pickles* by Kurt M. Stein, copyright 1927 by Pascal Covici (Publisher) Inc., is used by permission of Crown Pulishers, Inc.; extracts from *Travels with Charley* by John Steinbeck, copyright

© 1961, 1962 by Curtis Publishing Co., Inc. copyright 1962 by John Steinbeck, are reprinted by permission of Viking Penguin, Inc., and William Heinemann Ltd; lines from 'Meet Me in St Louis, Louis' by Andrew B. Sterling and Kerry Mills, © 1945 by Shawnee Press, Inc. USA are reproduced by permission of Shawnee Press, Inc. EMI Music Publishing Ltd, and J. Albert & Son Pty Ltd; lines from 'O Florida Venereal Soil', 'Boston Without a Notebook', 'The Man With the Blue Guitar', 'Arcades of Philadelphia the Past', 'Variations on a Summer Day', 'Lunar Paraphrase', 'Arrival at the Waldorf' and 'The River of Rivers in Connecticut', all from *The Collected Poems of Wallace Stevens*, are reprinted by permission of Alfred A. Knopf, Inc., and Faber & Faber Ltd; excerpts from *Cities* by Arthur Symons, published by J.M. Dent & Sons, in 1903 are reprinted by permission of Mr H.F. Read; lines from 'In Our Land' reprinted by permission of The Revd. Harold M. Telemaque; excerpts from *Letters and Papers of W.M. Thackeray* edited by G.N. Ray, published by Oxford University Press, are reprinted by permission of Mrs Belinda Norman-Butler; excerpts from *The Great Railway Bazaar* by Paul Theroux, Copyright © 1975 by Paul Theroux, and *The Old Patagonian Express* by Paul Theroux, Copyright © 1979 by Cape Cod Scrivenors Company, are reprinted by permission of Houghton Mifflin Company and Gillon Aitken, on behalf of the author; excerpts from *Dylan Thomas: Selected Letters*, edited by Constantine Fitzgibbon, published by J.M. Dent in 1967 are reprinted by permission of David Higham Associates Ltd; 'Welsh History' from *Song at the Year's Turning*, 1956 and 'The Small Window' from *Selected Poems*, 1946–1968, 1973, both by R.S. Thomas, are reprinted by permission of Granada Publishing Ltd; lines from 'Ali Gharbi', 'The River Front, Kut', and 'Damascus Orchards', from *Collected Poems*, 1930, and 'East River, Brooklyn' from *One Hundred Poems*, 1944, both by Edward Thompson, are reprinted by permission of A.D. Peters & Co. Ltd; 'The Indian Scene' by Harold Hugh Tilley, from *Poems from India*, edited by R.N. Currey and R.V. Gibson, 1946, is reprinted by permission of the author; excerpts from *East To West*, 1958 and *Between Niger and Nile*, 1965 by Arnold Toynbee are reprinted by permission of Oxford University Press; extracts from *The Lost World of the Kalahari* by Laurens Van der Post, published by Hogarth Press in 1958, are reprinted by permission of the author and publisher; 'Farewell to New Zealand' by Wynford Vaughan Thomas, fom *The New Oxford Book of Light Verse* edited by Kingsley Amis, is reprinted by permission of the author; extracts from the unpublished Journal of John Webster are printed by kind permission of Peter Cleverly; excerpts from *The White Tribes of Africa* by Richard West, published by Jonathan Cape Ltd, in 1965, are reprinted by permission of A.D. Peters & Co. Ltd; lines from 'Whim Wham Land' are reprinted by permission of 'Whim Wham'; excerpts from *Europe Without Baedeker* by Edmund Wilson, copyright © 1947, 1966 by Edmund Wilson, copyright renewed © 1975 by Elena Wilson, are reprinted by permission of Farrar Strauss & Giroux, Inc.; excerpts from *Red Rumba* by Nicholas Wollaston, published by Hodder & Stoughton in 1962 are reprinted by permission of John Farquharson Ltd, on behalf of the author; excerpts from *Asia Gods and Cities* by George Woodcock, published by Faber & Faber Ltd, in 1966 © George Woodcock, are reprinted by permission of Anthony Sheil Associates Ltd, on behalf of the author; a line from 'All Things Can Tempt Me', copyright 1912 by Macmillan Publishing Co., Inc., renewed 1940 by Bertha Georgie Yeats; lines from 'September 1913' copyright 1916 by Macmillan Publishing Co., Inc., renewed 1944 by Bertha Georgie Yeats; and lines from 'Under Ben Bulben' are all reprinted by permission of Macmillan Publishing Co., Inc., and of M.B. Yeats, Anne Yeats, and Macmillan London Ltd, from *Collected Poems by W.B. Yeats*, © 1940 by Georgie Yeats, renewed 1968 by Bertha Georgie Yeats, Michael Butler Yeats and Anne Yeats; 'London Fog' from *The Silent Traveller in London* by Chiang Yee is reproduced by permission of The Hamlyn Publishing Group Ltd; and 'Beaulieu River' from *Complete Poems* by Andrew Young, published by Martin Secker & Warburg Ltd, is reprinted by permission of the publishers.

In spite of extensive efforts to locate them, the holders of some copyrights have proved elusive. It is hoped that omissions can be rectified in a future edition.

Introduction

In this book I have tried to combine the stimulus of an anthology with the usefulness of a work of reference. 'Who said what about where?' is a general question with innumerable particular answers: some thousands of them are here. The reader who wants to verify a well known quotation about place or race will, I hope, find it here, together with much that may be less familiar. The book has been compiled for all those who are curious as to the opinions of others on the world around them, and for anyone who looks on the global village of today, and wonders how its scattered hamlets struck observers in times gone by. To this end I have selected observations as variously as possible, ranging in time as well as space, to indicate that styles of perception change as well as places; mixing description with reaction, balancing delight with disgust, and including the odd alongside the witty or the wise. Topographical material contrasts with historical or political comments, today's epigram with the more leisured pace of old travellers. The quotations have been drawn mainly from English language sources, from the fifteenth century to the present day, from the literature of travel, from letters and diaries, verse and song, history, fiction, journalism and drama. The world-reflecting world of books is itself so vast that a work of this size cannot be comprehensive: I am conscious of its shortcomings and omissions, and shall be grateful to readers whose enthusiasm or irritation impel them to suggest passages which might appear in any future editions – from the celebrated poem I should have known, to the most local of epigrams to which only luck could have led me. Though so many of the more vivid comments seem to be pejorative, I hope this book will be seen as the celebration of human idiosyncrasy confronting its environment that it is intended to be, and that the reader who encounters an author here for the first time in extract may be tempted to seek out his or her work to explore at length.

A NOTE ON ARRANGEMENT

The quotations are arranged alphabetically under existing countries, and entries for such supra-national features as continents and oceans appear at appropriate points in this sequence. Outlying territories, islands, etc., usually appear under their own headings. Each national entry begins with quotations about the country as a whole, and continues with those about its people(s). This division sometimes appears arbitrary, but seems useful. Quotations about places and features within the country follow, again arranged alphabetically. Where a region and a town have the same name, any regional material is placed first. Quotations about streets, buildings, etc., follow general material on the town concerned. Within each sub-heading the quotations are in chronological order, to give some sense, especially in the longer entries, of changing conditions.

Sections on the whole earth, the sun, moon, and universe, are placed at the end of the book.

A few anomalies which elude this classification have been dealt with as follows: (1) Some currently divided nations have been treated as entities, because older quotations are usually about the people as a whole; thus: *Ireland, Germany, Korea,* etc. More local quotations under these headings carry a note indicating their current status: under *Ireland* 'Northern' indicates that the quotation concerns part of the UK, under *Germany*, 'GDR' that a town is now in East Germany. (2) Under *India* appear also the minor states of that sub-continent, and a heading for *British Raj*. (3) Quotations about the Jewish people appear under *Israel and Palestine*. This is not intended to imply that all Jewish people are either Israelis or Zionists. (4) Comparisons between European peoples appear under *Europe*. Other comparisons are indicated by cross-references in the indexes.

In all but a few elusive cases, quotations have been sourced and dated. The date is that of the observation, if known, otherwise that of publication. I have followed familiar spellings in headings, but names within quotations are as spelt by their authors.

Quotations from works of fiction have been distinguished by an asterisk. Extracts from plays usually indicate the character speaking.

Note: The book's classification is *de facto*, and where sovereignty is disputed, the sympathies of compiler and publisher should not necessarily be deduced from the arrangement.

Points of View

POINTS OF VIEW: FOR

To lie about a far country is easy.
Amharic Proverb

When a traveller returneth home, let him not leave the countries where he hath travelled altogether behind him.
Francis Bacon, *Essays,* 1597-1625

Intending to present the World to the World in the most certaine view, I thought a world of Authors fitter for that purpose, then any One Author writing of the World.
Samuel Purchas, *Hakluytus Posthumus, or, Purchas his Pilgrimes,* 1625, The First Booke, Chapter 1

In travelling we visit *names* as well as places.
William Hazlitt, *Notes of a Journey through France and Italy,* 1826

My voyages (in paper boats) among savages often yield me matter for reflection at home.
Charles Dickens, 'Medicine Men of Civilisation', in *The Uncommercial Traveller,* 1861

The difference between landscape and landscape is small, but there is a great difference between the beholders.
Ralph Waldo Emerson, *Essays – Nature,* 1844

Un paysage quelconque est un état de l'âme.
– (Any sort of landscape is a condition of the soul.)
H.F. Amiel, *Journal Intime,* 31 October 1852

I am one of those for whom the visible world exists, very actively; and, for me, cities are like people, with souls and temperaments of their own, and it has always been one of my chief pleasures to associate with the souls and temperaments congenial to me among cities.
Arthur Symons, *Cities,* 1903

It is delightful to read on the spot the impressions and opinions of tourists who visited a hundred years ago, in the vehicles and with the aesthetic prejudices of the period, the places which you are visiting now. The voyage ceases to be a mere tour through space; you travel through time and thought as well.
Aldous Huxley, *Along the Road,* 1925

Countries, like people are loved for their failings.
F. Yeats Brown, *Bengal Lancer,* 1930

A city is the face wherein a nation's character may be read.
Oliver St John Gogarty, *As I Was Going Down Sackville Street,* 1937

Syllables are always superior to sights.
John Robert Colombo, Letter, 13 April 1982

POINTS OF VIEW: AGAINST

Who that is besy to mesure and compace
The hevyn and erth and all the worlde large
Descrybynge the clymatis and folke of every place
He is a fole and hath a grevous charge,
Without avauntage. . . .
Alexander Barclay, *The Ship of Folys,* 1509

It was the saying of a great Emperour, that he had rather go fifty miles to heare a wise man, than five to see a faire City.
James Howell, *Instructions for Forren Travell,* 1650

But damn description, it is always disgusting.
Lord Byron, Letter to Francis Hodgson, 6 August 1809

These are dangerous times to libel a man in, much more a world.
John Keats, Letter to Georgiana Keats, 13–28 January 1820

For, it must always be remembered that his impressions are not produced by the observation of a series of details considered one after another, – the only method in which a reader can view them, – but are stamped upon his mind and feelings, at the moment, by the whole in combination. The process of reading a description, in short, is like that of taking a telescope to pieces, and looking at the distant object through each separate lens, – instead of making them all bear upon one another by appropriate adjustments in the tube.
Captain Basil Hall, *Travels in North America,* 1829

When I wish to be misinformed about a country I ask a man who has lived there thirty years.

Lord Palmerston, quoted in A.P.Thornton, *The Imperial Idea and its Enemies,* 1959

I doubt whether I ever read any description of scenery which gave me an idea of the place described.

Anthony Trollope, *Australia and New Zealand,* 1873

It is a delicate matter to indulge in platitudes about a city.

John Buchan, *The African Colony,* 1903

The Muses care so little for geography.

Oscar Wilde, *'Sententiae'* (from reviews of the 1880s), in E.V. Lucas (ed.), *A Critic in Pall Mall,* 1918

A place has almost the shyness of a person, with strangers; and its secret is not to be surprised by a too direct interrogation.

Arthur Symons, *Cities,* 1903

Happy is the country that has no geography.

Saki [H.H. Munro], *The Unbearable Bassington,* 1912

For every traveller who has any taste of his own, the only useful guide-book will be the one which he himself has written.

Aldous Huxley, *Along the Road,* 1925

The idea of national characteristics has been greatly overdone.

Stephen Leacock, *Humour,* 1935

Oh S. the sights are worse than the journeys.

Sybille Bedford, *The Sudden View – A Mexican Journey,* 1953

A

ABU DHABI

Someone in Abu Dhabi must have bought the idea of New York on the strength of getting picture postcards of the place from a holidaying friend: the entire city had the appearance of something obtained ready-made in bulk. Twenty-eighth to Fortieth Street, please, from Park Avenue to the East River Drive. The condition of Abu Dhabi was so evidently mint that it would not have been surprising to see adhering to the buildings bits of straw and polystyrene from the crates in which they had been packed.

Jonathan Raban, *Arabia through the Looking Glass,* 1979

No Medici would ever have committed Abu Dhabi.

Ibid.

ADRIATIC

Far, far from here,
The Adriatic breaks in a warm bay
Among the green Illyrian hills; . . .
And there, they say, two bright and aged snakes,
Who once were Cadmus and Harmonica,
Bask in the glens or on the warm sea-shore,
In breathless quiet, after all their ills.

Matthew Arnold, *Empedocles on Etna,* 1852

AEGEAN SEA

A sea dangerous and troublesome to sayle through, in regard of the multitude of Rockes, and Ilands, every where dispersed. Insomuch, that a man is proverbially said to sayle in the Aegean Sea, that is encumbred with difficulties.

George Sandys, 1610, in *Purchas his Pilgrimes,* 1625

I still sigh for the Aegean. Shall you not always love its bluest of waves & brightest of all skies?

Lord Byron, Letter to Edward Daniel Clarke, 26 June 1812

AFGHANISTAN

The Afghans are such a savage set.

Emily Eden, Letter, 3 October 1841, in *Letters from India,* 1872

For fifty years Afghanistan has inspired the British people with a feeling of almost superstitious apprehension . . . It is only with the greatest reluctance that Englishmen can be persuaded to have anything to do with so fateful a region . . . In the history of most conquering races is found some spot that has invariably exposed their weakness like the joints in armour of steel. Afghanistan has long been the Achilles' heel of Great Britain in the East. Impregnable elsewhere, she has shown herself uniformly vulnerable here.

Hon. G.N. Curzon, *Russia in Central Asia,* 1889

. . . that same elusive smell which has pervaded the whole journey since we first met it at the Afghan frontier, and which now, in its overwhelming sweetness, brought the minarets of Herat before my eyes again. It emanated from clusters of small yellow-green flowers,[1] which are unnoticeable from a distance, but which, if I ever smell them again, will remind me of Afghanistan as a cedar wardrobe reminds me of childhood.

Robert Byron, *The Road to Oxiana,* 1937

[1] Flowers of the oleaster tree.

A kind of footnote to Persia.

John Gunther, *Inside Asia,* 1939

The Afghan official smiled at the three Western correspondents arriving at Kabul airport and said: 'Welcome to Afghanistan. Which hotel would you like to stay in tonight before you are expelled tomorrow?'

Richard Banforth, *The Times,* 5 January 1980

The attitude of all honest Afghans to Soviet troops is that of sincere hospitality and profound gratitude.

Tass, quoted, *Observer,* 'Sayings of the Week', 16 March 1980

Pathans

Except at harvest-time, when self-preservation enjoins a temporary truce, the Pathan tribes are always engaged in private or public war. The life of the Pathan is thus full of interest.

Sir Winston Churchill, *The Malakand Field Force,* 1898

Kabul

Kabul for the most part has an easy unpretentious character, as of a Balkan town in the good sense of the term. It clusters round a few bare rocky hills which rise abruptly from the verdant plain and act as defences. Snow-mountains decorate the distance, the parliament sits in a corn-field, and long avenues shade the town's approaches . . . One feels that perhaps Afghanistan has struck the mean for which Asia is looking. Even the most nationalist of them makes a pleasant contrast with the mincing assertiveness of the modern Persian.

Robert Byron, *The Road to Oxiana*, 1937

Kunduz

There is a proverb which says a visit to Kunduz is tantamount to suicide.

Ibid.

AFRICA

See also under individual countries

Ex Africa semper aliquid novi.

There is always something new from Africa. Proverbial from Pliny: Unde etiam vulgare Graeciae dictum 'semper aliquid novi Africam adferre'.

Whence it is commonly said among the Greeks that 'Africa always offers something new.'

Pliny the Elder, *Historia Naturalis,* II, viii, 42, *c.* AD77

A foutra for the world, and worldlings base!
I speak of Africa and golden joys.

William Shakespeare, *King Henry IV,* part 2, *c.* 1597–8

Some write that Africa was so named by the Grecians because it is without colde. For the Greek letter Alpha or A signifieth privation, voyd or without: and Phryce signifieth colde. For in deed although in the stead of Winter they have a cloudy and tempestuous season, yet is it not colde, but rather smoothering hote, with hote showres of raine also, and somewhere such scorching windes, that what by one meanes and other, they seeme at certaine times to live as it were in fornaces, and in maner already halfe way in Purgatorie or hell. Gemma Phrisius writeth that in certaine parts of Africa as in Atlas the greater, the aire in the night season is seene shining, with many strange fires and flames rising in maner high as the Moone: and that in the element are sometime heard as it were the sound of pipes, trumpets and drummes: which noises may perhaps be caused by the vehement and sundry motions of such firie exhalations in the aire, as we see the like in many experiences wrought by fire, aire and winde.

Richard Hakluyt, *Principal Navigations . . . of the English Nation*, 1598–1600

We carry within us the wonders we seek without us:
There is all Africa and her prodigies in us.

Sir Thomas Browne, *Religio Medici*, 1643

Nor could his eye not ken . . .
Mombasa and Quiloa and Meilind,
And Sofala, through Ophir, to the realm
Of Congo and Angola further south.

John Milton, *Paradise Lost*, 1667

So geographers in Afric-maps
With savage-pictures fill their gaps;
And o'er unhabitable downs
Place elephants for want of towns.

Jonathan Swift, *On Poetry*, 1733

Plains immense
Lie stretch'd below, interminable meads,
And vast savannas, where the wandering eye,
Unfixt, is in a verdant ocean lost.
Another Flora there, of golden hues,
And richer sweets, beyond our garden's pride,
Plays o'er the fields, and showers with sudden hand
Exuberant Spring: for oft these valleys shift
Their green-embroidered robe to fiery brown,
And swift to green again, as scorching suns,
Or streaming dews, and torrent rains, prevail.
Along these lonely regions, where, retired
From little scenes of art, great Nature dwells
In awful solitude, and nought is seen
But the wild herds, that own no master's stall,
Prodigious rivers roll their fattening seas:
On whose luxuriant herbage, half-conceal'd,
Like a fallen cedar, far diffused his train,
Cased in green scales, the crocodile extends
The flood disparts: behold, in plated mail
Behemoth rears his head! Glanced from his side,
The darted steel in idle shivers flies:
He fearless walks the plain, or seeks the hills;
Where, as he crops his varied fare, the herds,
In widening circle round, forget their food,
And at the harmless stranger wondering gaze.

James Thomson, *The Seasons – Summer,* 1727

Heart-formed Africa.

William Blake, *The Song of Los – Africa,* 1795

Afric is all the sun's, and as her earth
Her human clay is kindled. Full of power
For good or evil, burning from its birth,
The Moorish blood partakes the planet's hour,
And like the soil beneath it will bring forth.

Lord Byron, *Don Juan*, 1819–24

I sometimes wish that I was the Owner of Africa – to do at once – what Wilberforce will do in time – viz – sweep Slavery from her desarts – and look upon the first dance of their Freedom.

Lord Byron, *Detached Thoughts*, 1821–2

All I can add in my loneliness is, may Heaven's rich blessing come down on every one – American English or Turk – who will help to heal this running sore of the world.

David Livingstone, Letter to *New York Herald*, 1 May 1872

The education of the world is a terrible one, and it has come down with relentless vigour on Africa from the most remote times! What the African will become after this awfully hard lesson is learned, is among the future developments of Providence. When He, who is higher than the highest, accomplishes His purposes, this will be a wonderful country, and again something like it was of old, when Zerah and Tirhaka flourished, and were great.

David Livingstone, *Last Journals* (11 November 1870), 1874

In region of the unknown, Africa is the absolute.

Victor Hugo, before 1885, quoted in H.W. Nevinson, *A Modern Slavery*, 1906

'That's my dream,' he said, pointing to the map of Africa, 'all red.'

Cecil Rhodes, quoted William Plomer, *Cecil Rhodes*, 1933

In Africa think big.

Cecil Rhodes, attrib.

My motto is – Equal rights for every civilised man south of the Zambesi. What is a civilized man? A man, whether white or black, who has sufficient education to write his name, has some property, or works. In fact, is not a loafer.

Cecil Rhodes, in William Plomer, *ibid.*

In Africa moisture is everything.

James Bryce, *Impressions of South Africa*, 1897

Oh Africa, mysterious land!
Surrounded by a lot of sand
And full of grass and trees,
And elephants and Africanders,
And politics and salamanders
And native rum in little kegs
And savages called Tuaregs . . .
And tons of diamonds, and lots
Of nasty, dirty Hottentots
And coolies coming from the East,
And serpents, seven yards long at least
And lions, that retain
Their vigour, appetites, and rage
Intact, to an extreme old age,
And never lose their mane . . .
Vast continent! Whose cumbrous shape
Runs from Bizerta to the Cape.

Hilaire Belloc, *The Modern Traveller*, 1898

Fatal Africa! One after another, travellers drop away. It is such a huge continent, and each of its secrets is environed by so many difficulties, – the torrid heat, the miasma exhaled from the soil, the noisome vapours enveloping every path, the giant cane-grass suffocating the wayfarer, the rabid fury of the native guarding every entry and exit, the unspeakable misery of the life within the wild continent, the utter absence of every comfort, the bitterness which each day heaps upon the poor white man's head, in that land of blackness, the sombrous solemnity pervading every feature of it, and the little – too little – promise of success which one feels on entering it.

Sir Henry Morton Stanley, *Autobiography*, 1909

Never take a cold bath in Africa, unless ordered to do so by a doctor.

William Henry Cross, MD in *Hints to Travellers*, 1906

I thought for some reason even then of Africa, not a particular place, but a shape, a strangeness, a wanting to know. The unconscious mind is often sentimental; I have written 'a shape', and the shape, of course, is roughly that of the human heart.

Graham Greene, *Journey without Maps*, 1936

To the words 'South Africa' my reaction, I find, is immediate: Rhodes and the British Empire and an ugly building in Oxford and Trafalgar Square. After 'Kenya' there is no hesitation: 'gentleman farmers, aristocracy in exile and the gossip columns.' 'Rhodesia' produces: 'failure, Empire Tobacco', and 'failure' again.

Ibid.

Africa, amongst the continents, will teach it to you: that God and the Devil are one, the majesty coeternal, not two uncreated but one uncreated, and the Natives neither confounded the persons nor divided the substance.

Karen Blixen, *Out of Africa*, 1937

This Continent of Africa has a terribly strong sense of sarcasm.

Denys Finch-Hatton, Remark, quoted by Karen Blixen, *ibid.*

Life in Africa is like in a ship – and the white men are the passengers.

Negley Farson, *Behind God's Back*, 1940

In Africa it is always five minutes to twelve.
Anon, quoted Lord Hemingford, *Nationalism in Africa*, 1954

The darkest thing about Africa has always been our ignorance of it.
George H.T. Kimble, 'Africa Today: the Lifting Darkness', *Reporter*, 15 May 1951

One of Nasser's chief associates, who yields to no one in his hatred of colonialism, . . . said that the two things that counted most in Black Africa were 'the germ' and 'happiness'.
John Gunther, *Inside Africa*, 1955

Africa obliterates; she does not remember.
Elspeth Huxley, *Four Guineas*, 1954

Little old cousin, if you want to go into the blue in Africa, always pick your companions only from among men you have known for at least five years. And the chances are, even then, that you will pick the wrong one.
Advice quoted by Laurens van der Post, *The Lost World of the Kalahari*, 1958

Night silence in Africa always holds the far sea-sound of urgent stars.
Laurens van der Post, *The Lost World of the Kalahari*, 1958

The wind of change is blowing through this continent, and whether we like it or not this growth of national consciousness is a political fact. We must all accept it as a fact and our national policies must take account of it.
Harold Macmillan, Speech to both houses of the South African Parliament, February 1960

Africa used to be known as the white man's grave; one might also think of it as his cradle. People always talk of their travels in Africa as a journey back.
Richard West, *The White Tribes of Africa*, 1965

Nothing in Africa is adjacent to anywhere.
James Cameron, *Point of Departure*, 1967

*Hobbies – have you read Thomas Hobbies? He was right, life in Africa is nasty, British, and short.
'Mwase', in Paul Theroux, *Jungle Lovers*, 1971

Once you have been to Africa the bug gets into your system.
Edward Heath, *Travels, People and Places in My Life*, 1977

African time is behind time.
John Heilpern, *Conference of the Birds*, 1977

Africa has for the last few years, been regarded in the West much as we regard our weather – a phenomenon so unpredictable that everybody talks about it, but nobody does anything about it.
Lord Chalfont, 'Who Will Reap the African Whirlwind?', *The Times*, 29 May 1978

We fear Africa because, when we leave it alone, it works.
Patrick Marnham, *Fantastic Invasion*, 1980

No known existing governmental system works in Africa.
Nigerian political observer, quoted Patrick Marnham, *ibid.*

East Africa

There is one phrase that indelibly haunts all East African conversation, that epitomizes everything in the East African soul – the Swahili words: 'Bado kidogo'. They mean: 'Not Just Yet'. It is more futile than *mañana*, slightly more optimistic than Maybe. All will come, but Not Just Yet.
James Cameron, *Point of Departure*, 1967

Rift Valley

It makes the Grand Canyon of the Colorado look like a line scratched with a toothpick.
John Gunther, *Inside Africa*, 1955

North Africa

Sahara Desert

Man eats you; the desert does not.
Arab proverb, quoted by Richard Burton, *Abeokuta and the Cameroons Mountains*, 1863

So, where our wide Numidian wastes extend,
Sudden the impetuous hurricanes descend,
Wheel through the air, in circling eddies play,
Tear up the sands, and sweep whole plains away.
The helpless traveller with wild surprise,
Sees the dry desert all around him rise,
And, smothered in the dusty whirlwind, dies.
Joseph Addison, *Cato*, 1713

The climate of Sahara is . . . day after day, sunstroke after sunstroke with a frosty shadow between.
Ralph Waldo Emerson, *Journals*, 1859

The country which is the prison-wall of our race.
Hilaire Belloc, *Esto Perpetua*, 1906

Taken in reasonably small doses, the Sahara exhilarates, like alcohol. Too much of it, however (I speak, at any rate, for myself), has the depressing effect of the second bottle of Burgundy.

Aldous Huxley, *Do What You Will*, 1929

Practically all communication in the Sahara is by way of the oases; one travels like a golf ball, hopping from green to green.

John Gunther, *Inside Africa*, 1955

Every oasis is an island that has water inside it but not round it.

Arnold Toynbee, *Between Niger and Nile*, 1965

West Africa

Others seek out to *Africk's* Torrid Zone,
And search the burning Shores of *Serralone*:
There in unsufferable Heats *they fry*,
And run vast Risques to see the Gold, *and die.*
The harmless Natives basely they trepan,
And barter Baubles for the *Souls of Men*;
The Wretches they to Christian Climes bring o'er,
To serve worse Heathens than they did before.
The Cruelties they suffer there are such,
Amboyna's nothing, they've outdone the *Dutch.*

Daniel Defoe, *Reformation of Manners, a Satyr*, 1702

Anti-Paradise.

Richard Burton, *Abeokuta and the Cameroons Mountains*, 1863

There is no place where a wife is so much wanted as in the Tropics; but then comes the rub – how to keep the wife alive.

Richard Burton, *Wanderings in West Africa*, 1863

I told him I intended going to West Africa and he said 'When you have made up your mind to go to West Africa the very best thing you can do, is to get it unmade again and go to Scotland instead; but if your intelligence is not strong enough to do so, abstain from exposing yourself to the direct rays of the sun, take 4 grains of quinine every day for a fortnight before you reach the Rivers, and get yourself some introductions to the Wesleyans: they are the only people on the Coast who have got a hearse with feathers.'

Mary Kingsley, *Travels in West Africa*, 1897

'Why did I come to Africa?' thought I. 'Why! who would not come to its twin brother Hell itself for all the beauty and charm of it!'

Ibid.

Coast of woeful retrospection, as 'White Man's Grave' renowned –
So its evil reputation throughout all the world is found.
Of the men who ventured thither, risking life in countless ways,
Few returned with health uninjured in the former tragic days.

Death! – it lurked around the white men, daily hovered overhead,
Frolicked in their food and water, menaced them asleep in bed,
Laid in wait on each occasion when all thought of it had fled;
Many who at dawn were robust in the evening time were dead.

Death by savage spear and juju, death by fever swift and hot,
Death that came with ample warning, or in forms expected not;
Death that took its toll of thousands of the young and strong and brave –
Builders of the British Empire in this famous 'White Man's Grave' . . .

Allister Macmillan, F.R.G.S., 'Land of the Black Man', in *The Red Book of Africa*, 1920

It is not the fully conscious mind which chooses West Africa in preference to Switzerland.

Graham Greene, *Journey without Maps*, 1936

It would not be rash to say that there is far less anguish about race – with all the concomitant boredom and hysteria – in West Africa than in West London.

Richard West, *The White Tribes of Africa*, 1965

Negro peoples

Some negroes who believe the Resurrection, think that they shall rise white.

Sir Thomas Browne, *Christian Morals* (before 1682), 1716

He seems to belong to one of those childish races which, never rising to man's estate, fall like worn-out links from the great chain of animated nature.

Richard Burton, *First Footsteps in East Africa*, 1856

Their tears lie high; they weep like Goanese.

Richard Burton, *Lake Regions of Central Africa*, 1860

The accusing conscience is unknown to him. His only fear after committing a treacherous murder is that of being haunted by the angry ghost of the dead; he robs as one doing a good deed, and he begs as if it were his calling. His depravity is of the grossest: intrigue fills up the moments not devoted to intoxication.

Richard Burton, *Lake Regions of Central Africa*, 1860

The African is nearly as strong physically as the European, and, as a race, is wonderfully persistent among the nations of the earth. Neither the diseases nor the ardent spirits which proved so fatal to the North American Indians, seem capable of annihilating the negroes. Even when subjected to that system so destructive to human life, by which they are torn from their native soil, they spring up irrepressibly and darken half the new continent. They are gifted by nature with physical strength capable of withstanding the sorest privations, and a light-heartedness which, as a sort of compensation, enables them to make the best of the worst situations. It is like that power which the human frame possesses of withstanding heat . . . The Africans have wonderfully born up under unnatural conditions that would have proved fatal to most races.

David and Charles Livingstone, *Narrative of an Expedition to the Zambesi and Its Tributaries*, 1865

The Negro, thanks to his temperament, appears to make the greatest amount of happiness out of the smallest capital.

Ralph Waldo Emerson, *Journals*, October 1866

African negroes are incomprehensible people, and they cannot be judged by the ordinary rules of human nature.

Sir Samuel Baker, *Ismailia*, 1874

The African race has had about the worst set of conditions possible to bring out the higher powers of man. He has been surrounded by a set of terrific natural phenomena, combined with a good food supply and a warm and equable climate.

Mary Kingsley, *West African Studies*, 1899

Negroes, who are prodigiously malleable, oftener than not become what people think, or want, or fear them to be.

André Gide, *Travels in the Congo*, 1930

The disaster of the man of colour lies in the fact that he was once enslaved. The disaster and the inhumanity of the white man lies in the fact that somewhere he has killed man.

Franz Fanon, *Black Skin White Masks*, 1970

ALBANIA

Viola: What Country (Friends) is this?
Captain: This is Illyria Ladie.
Viola: And what should I do in Illyria?

William Shakespeare, *Twelfe Night*, *c.* 1601–2

Land of Albania! where Iskander rose,
Theme of the young, and beacon of the wise,
And he his namesake, whose oft-baffled foes
Shrunk from his deeds of chivalrous emprize:
Land of Albania! let me bend mine eyes
On thee, thou rugged Nurse of savage men!
The Cross descends, thy Minarets arise,
And the pale Crescent sparkles in the glen,
Through many a cypress-grove within each city's ken.

Lord Byron, *Childe Harold's Pilgrimage*, Canto the Second, 1812

In Moscow and Prague and Sofia and Bucharest the statues of Stalin were carted away; in Tirana, on the contrary, the massive concrete images of the great man were not only rooted to the ground, but garlanded with flowers. It was the perfect, the text-book case of human bloody-mindedness adopted as a national principle.

James Cameron, *Point of Departure*, 1967

Albanians

Thei be white people, thei be strong and use a lyfe pastorall. Thei have myghtie dogges, thei do honor moche the olde men, and whan thei dye burye ther tresure with them and for this cause thei be but poore and because thei have nothing proper but live in comon.

Roger Barlow, *A Brief Summe of Geographie*, *c.* 1540

A country rarely visited from the savage character of the natives.

Lord Byron, Letter to Henry Drury, 3 May 1810

Fierce are Albania's children, yet they lack
Not virtues, were those virtues more mature.
Where is the foe that ever saw their back?
Who can so well the toil of War endure?
Their native fastnesses not more secure
Than they in doubtful time of troublous need:
Their wrath how deadly! but their friendship sure,
When Gratitude, or Valour bids them bleed –
Unshaken rushing on where'er their Chief may lead.

Lord Byron, *Childe Harold's Pilgrimage*, Canto the Second, 1812

Women of, at Himare/Khimara

'Heavens!' said I, surprised out of my wonted philosophy of travel, which ought not to exclaim at anything, 'how can you make your women such slaves?' 'O Signore,' said Anastasio, 'to you as a stranger, it must seem extraordinary; but the fact is, we have no mules in Khimara, that is the reason why we employ a creature so inferior in strength as a woman is (un animale tanto poco capace); but there is no remedy, for mules there are none, and women are next best to mules. Vi assicuro, Signore, although certainly far inferior to mules, they are really better than asses, or even horses.' That was all I got for my interference.

Edward Lear, 23 October 1848, *Journals of a Landscape Painter in Albania, Illyria, Etc.*, 1852

ALGERIA

Algiers alone possesses any power, and they are brave.
Thomas Jefferson, Letter to James Monroe, February 1785

Algerians

These are the cruell pirates of *Argeire*,
That damned traine, the scum of *Affrica*,
Inhabited with stragling Runnagates,
That make quick havock of the Christian blood.

Christopher Marlowe, *Tamburlaine*, part 1, *c.* 1587

These Algerians have the foolish conceits of other Mahumetans, some also more proper, that Fooles and Dwarfes are Saints, their Morabutes to be inspired and to consult with God, the Viands set on Sepulchres weekly to be eaten by the soules; and if sicke persons offer there any thing which a beast eateth, that the disease is derived to it; that the head-ach is lessened with rolling a Goats or sheeps head on the Roofe; that it is not lawfull to buy in May, nor to bring in at doore Garleeke or Broomes, but (if there be need of them) at the Roofe; that it is a meritorious worke to prostitute their Wives to the Morabutes, and that the same men bugger with beasts; shaving, washing (though in the Sea) clenseth sinnes; that (Sodomiticall) sinnes against Nature are vertues. But to bedew the Garment in making urine, to let paper lye on the ground, the Alcoran to be touched or seene of one not Mahumetan, to fart in Sala (or Prayer time,) or then to defend a mans selfe . . . or to bleed, or sneeze, or spit, to wipe the buttockes except with the left finger, to drink out of a smacking narrow mouthed pot, to locke the Bed-chamber by night, to stampe on the Earth when they play at ball, to write with a Pen (for they use Reeds) to eate Snailes taken out of the fields (reputed holy) to touch money before they have said their Morning Prayers, to hold the Alcoran beneath the girdle, to have printed Bookes, or Pictures of men or beasts; to admit Christians or women to their Mesquits, to use Bels, to exchange a Christian captive for a Turke, to breech children with Rods (they whip the sole of the foot with a Whip) these are all sinnes and enormities at Algier. They beleeve that on their Easter mid-night all waters are asleepe, and hee which can get that sleepe shall be a happie man.

J.B. Gramaye, *Relations of . . . Algiers*, 1619, in *Purchas his Pilgrimes*, 1625

Algerians became French before they became Algerian.
General Augustin Guillaume, quoted John Gunther, *Inside Africa*, 1955

Algiers

Shee is scituated upon the Mediterranean Sea, upon the hanging of a Mountaine environed with strong Walls, Ramperds, Ditches, Platformes, and Bulwarks, in forme almost three-square; the largenesse which goeth towards the Sea side stretcheth narrowly almost unto the highest part, whereas there is a great building made in forme of a Citadell, to command the Towne and entrie of the Haven. As for the buildings being beyond the Pallace Royall, are very faire Houses belonging to particular men, with a great number of Bathes and Cookes houses. The places and streetes are so well ordained, that every one in his Occupation apart: there are about three thousand Hearthsteeds. At the bottome of the Citie which is towards the North joyning to the Walles, which are beaten with the Surges of the Sea in a great place, is by great Artifice and subtill Architecture builded their principall and head Mosquee; and a little below that is the Arcenall, which is the place into which are hailed up, and trimmed the Gallies and other vessels. This Citie is very Merchant-like, for that she is situated upon the Sea, and for this cause marveilously peopled, for her bignesse: she is inhabited of Turkes, Moores, and Jewes in great number, which with marveilous gaine exercise the Trade of Merchandise, and lend out money at Usury.

Nicholas Nicholay, in *Purchas his Pilgrimes*, 1625

Leaving it in the distance the town looked like a sloping rock, covered with bird lime.

Herman Melville, *Journal of a Visit to Europe and the Levant*, 26 November 1856

The sun beams down on Algiers – but the inhabitants do not smile back. It is a surly city, harrowed by the stresses of over-population and under-employment; with the architecture of Cannes, but the atmosphere of Aberdeen. During the day the cafés are thronged with all male, typically Arab society. At night, the city, responsive to President Boumédienne's own personal brand of puritanism, closes down like wartime Toronto on a Sunday.

Alistair Horne, *A Savage War of Peace*, 1977

Salah

Salah, an ancient fortress town in open desert, a town sometimes buried completely by sandstorms. . . . The market place was almost deserted, yet it was a large town. When I asked a man who spoke French where everyone was, he replied: 'Cultivating their gardens,' and gave me a huge smile.

John Heilpern, *Conference of the Birds*, 1977

Tamanrasset

I am never going to stand in line waiting for the first tickets to the moon. I have already seen the moon. That is, I have seen Tamanrasset in the Sahara.

John Gunther, *Inside Africa*, 1955

Timgad

Timgad impresses me more powerfully with the past than any other place I know.

Hilaire Belloc, *Many Cities*, 1928

Oran

Oran, city of half-castes and mean whites on the eternal fringe of things.

Osbert Sitwell, *Escape with Me*, 1939

Algerian Sahara – the Tuareg

These nobles are tall men, with a splendid bearing, and the combination of white hood and blue veil makes them resemble armoured, helmeted creatures out of science fiction. They look like blue bullets with a blunt white trip.

John Gunther, *Inside Africa*, 1955

AMERICA

See also entries for individual countries and South and Central America

Seneca the tragedian hath these verses:
– Venient annis
Saecula seris, quibus Oceanus
Vincula rerum laxet, et ingens
Pateat Tellus, Tiphysque novos
Detegat orbes; nec sit terris
Ultima Thule:
[There shall come a time when the bands of ocean shall be loosened, and the vast earth shall be laid open; another Tiphys shall disclose new worlds, and lands shall be seen beyond Thule:] a prophecy of the discovery of America.

Francis Bacon, *Essays*, 1597-1625

But let that man with better sense advize
That of the world least part to us is red;
And daily how through hardy enterprize
Many great regions are discovered,
Which to late age were never mentioned
Who ever heard of th'Indian Peru?
Or who in venturous vessel measured
The Amazon huge river, now found trew?
Or fruitfullest Virginia who did ever view?

Yet all these were when no man did them know,
Yet have from wisest ages hidden been;
And later times thinges more unknowne shall show.
Why then should witless man so much misweene
That nothing is but that which he hath seene?
What if within the Moones faire shining sphere,
What if in every other starre unseene
Of other worlds he happily should heare,
He wonder would much more; yet such to some appeare.

Edmund Spenser, *The Fairie Queene*, 1589

And who, in time, knows whither we may vent
The treasure of our tongue? To what strange shores
This gain of our best glory shall be sent
To enrich unknowing nations with our stores?
What worlds in th' yet unformed Occident
May come refined with accents that are ours?

Or who can tell for what great work in hand
The greatness of our style is now ordained?
What powers it shall bring in, what spirits command?
What thoughts let out, what humours keep restrained?
What mischief it may powerfully withstand,
And what fair ends may thereby be attained?

Samuel Daniel, *Musophilus*, 1599

. . . O my America! my new-found-land,
My kingdome, safeliest when with one man man'd,
My Myne of precious stones, My Emperie,
How blest am I in thus discovering thee!
To enter in these bonds is to be free;
Then where my hand is set, my seal shall be. . . .

John Donne, *To His Mistris Going to Bed*, *c.* 1593-6

I am of his mind, that Columbus did not find out America by chance, but God directed him at that time to discover it: it was contingent to him, but necessary to God.

Robert Burton, *Anatomy of Melancholy*, 1621

In the beginning all the world was America.

John Locke, *Two Treatises of Government*, 1690

The Muse, disgusted at an Age and Clime,
Barren of every glorious Theme,
In distant Lands now waits a better Time,
Producing Subjects worthy Fame: . . .

Westward the Course of Empire takes its Way;
The four first Acts already past,
A fifth shall close the Drama with the Day;
Time's noblest Offspring is the last.

George Berkeley, *On the Prospect of Planting Arts and Learning in America*, 1725

Landing on this great continent is like going to sea.

Hector St John de Crèvecoeur, *Letters from an American Farmer*, 1782

I called the New World into existence to redress the balance of the Old.

George Canning, Speech, 12 December 1826

*I hold, as some have done before me, that the human mind degenerates in America and that the superiority of the white race, such as it is, is only kept up by intercourse with Europe.

Thomas Love Peacock, *Gryll Grange*, 1860

The Discovery of America was the occasion of the greatest outburst of cruelty and reckless greed known in history.

Joseph Conrad, 'Geography and Some Explorers', 1924, in *Last Essays*, 1926

America was too big to have been discovered all at one time. It would have been better for the graces if it had been discovered in pieces about the size of France and Germany at a time.

Samuel Butler, *Further Extracts from Notebooks*, 1934

ANDAMAN ISLANDS

In those isles are many manners of folk of divers conditions. In one of them is a manner of folk of great stature, as they were giants, horrible and foul to the sight; and they have but one eye, and that is in the midst the forehead. They eat raw flesh and raw fish. In another isle are foul men of figure without heads, and they have eyes in either shoulder one, and their mouths are round shaped like a horseshoe, y-midst their breasts. In another isle are men without heads; and their eyes and their mouths are behind in their shoulders. In another isle is a manner of folk that has a plat face, without nose or eyes; but they have two small holes instead of eyes, and they have a plat mouth, lipless. In another isle are foul men that have the overlip so great that, when they sleep in the sun, they cover all the visage with that lip. In another isle are folk of little stature, as they were dwarfs; and they are somewhat more than pigmies. They have no mouth, but they have instead of their mouth a little hole, and therefore, when they shall eat, them behoves suck it with a reed or a pipe. Tongues have they none; and therefore they speak not, but hiss and make signs as monkeys do, ilk one til other, and ilk one of them wots well what other means. In another isle are folk whose ears are so syde that they hang down to their knees. In another isle are folk that have feet like horse, and on them they will run so swythe that they will overtake wild beasts and slay them to their meat through swiftness of foot. In another isle are folk which go on their hand and on their feet, as they were four-footed beasts; and they are rough and will climb into trees als lightly as they were apes. There is another isle where folk are that are both men and women, and have members of both the tane and the tother, and ilk one of them has a pap on the ta side. And when they use the member of men, they get childer; and when they use the member of women they bear childer. Another isle there is where the folk go on their knees wonderfully, . . . and they have on either foot eight toes. Yet is there another isle where the folk have but a foot, and that foot is so broad that it will cover all the body and ombre it from the sun. And upon this foot will they run so fast that it is wonder to see. Also there is another isle where the folk live all with the savour of a manner of apple; and if they tharned that savour, alsone they should die. Many other maner folk there are in other isles thereabouts which were too long to tell all.

John Mandeville, *The Book of John Mandeville*, *c.* 1360

They call those Ilands the Ilands of Andemaon, and they call their people Savage or wilde, because they eate one another: also these Ilands have warre one with another, for they have small Barkes, and with them they take one another, and so eate one another: and if by evill chance any Ship bee lost on those Ilands, as many have beene, there is not one man of those ships lost there that escapeth uneaten or unslaine. These people have not any acquaintance with any other people, neither have they trade with any, but live onely of such Fruites as those Ilands yeeld.

Caesar Frederick, *Indian Observations*, *c.* 1567, in *Purchas his Pilgrimes*, 1625

ANGOLA

The Countrie is Champain plaine, and drie blacke earth, and yeeldeth verie little Corne, the most of any thing that it yeeldeth is Plantons, which the Portugals call Baynonas, and the Moores call them Mahonge, and their Wheate they call Tumba, and the Bread Anov; and if you will buy any bread of them, you must say Tala Cune aven tumbola gimbo, that is, give me some bread, here is money. Their money is called Gull ginbo, a shell of a fish that they finde by the shoare side. . . . The Moores of Angolo are as blacke as Jet; they are men of good stature, they never take but one Wife, whom they call Mocasha. These Moores doe cut long streakes in their faces, that reach from the top of their eares to their chinnes. The women doe weare shels of fishes on their armes, and on the small of their legges. The Law amongst them, is, that if any More doe lie with an others wife, hee shall lose his eares for his offence. These Moores doe circumcize their children, and give them their names, as wee doe when we baptize. Angola may very easily be taken, for the

Portugals have no Forts to defend it of any strength.

Anthony Knivet, 1601, in *Purchas his Pilgrimes*, 1625

As for the interior of Angola if Eden sent up so quickly such a rush of rank vegetation our progenitor must have found sufficient occupation in dressing it.

David Livingstone, Letter to Arthur Tidman, 12 October 1855

'Dombe'

This Province is called, Dombe, and it hath a ridge of high Serras, or Mountaines, that stretch from the Serras, or Mountaines of Cambambe, wherein are Mines; and lye along that Coast South and by West. Here is great store of fine Copper, if they would worke in their Mines: but they take no more then they weare for a braverie. The men of this place weare skinnes about their middles, and beads about their neckes. They carrie Darts of Iron, and Bow and Arrowes in their hands. They are beastly in their living, for they have men in womens apparell whom they keepe among their wives.

Their women weare a Ring of Copper about their neckes, which weigheth fifteene pound at the least, about their armes little Rings of Copper, that reach to their elbowes, about their middles a cloth of the Insandie Tree, which is neither spunne nor woven, on their legs Rings of Copper, that reach to the calves of their legs.

Andrew Battell, *Strange Adventures*, in *Purchas his Pilgrimes*, 1625

ANGUILLA

Dear island of such poor beauty,
meekly waiting to rebel.

John Updike, Letter from Anguilla, 1968, *Picked Up Pieces*, 1976

A long, low coral formation of thirty-four square miles, it seems from the air a cloud shadow, or a shadow image of St Martin, which lies twelve miles to the south, and whose green mountains loom dramatically in the view from Anguilla.

Ibid.

ANTARCTICA

Lands doomed by nature to everlasting frigidness and never once to feel the warmth of the suns rays, whose horrible and savage aspect I have no words to describe; such are the lands we have discovered, what may we expect those to be which lie more to the South, for we may reasonably suppose we have seen the best as lying more to the North, whoever has resolution and perseverance to clear up this point by proceeding farther than we have done, I shall not envy him the honour of the discovery but I will be bold to say that the world will not be benefited by it.

Captain James Cook, *Journal*, February 1775

The Ice in some other of the loose fields appeared like Corral rocks, honey combed and as it were rotten and exhibited such a variety of figures that there is not an animal on Earth that was not in some degree represented by it.

Ibid., 26 December 1772

Polar exploration is at once the cleanest and most isolated way of having a bad time which has been devised.

Apsley Cherry-Garrard, Introduction to *The Worst Journey in the World*, 1922

There is something extravagantly insensate about an Antarctic blizzard at night. Its vindictiveness cannot be measured on an anemometer sheet. It is more than just wind: it is a solid wall of snow moving at gale force, pounding like surf.

Richard E. Byrd, *Alone*, 1938

Whenever Admiral Byrd was asked what men missed most on Antarctic expeditions, he would reply with the single word, 'temptation'.

Paul Siple, *90° South*, 1959

and Arctic

The Arctic and Antarctica are poles apart.

Charles Neider, *Antarctica*, 1973

The South Pole

Great God! this is an awful place.

Robert Falcon Scott, *Journal*, 17 January 1912

ARABIA

See also entries for individual countries

This lond of promesse hathe in the orient arabia which is devided in iii partes, arabia deserta, arabia petrea and arabia felix. Arabia petrea is by egipt, and arabia felix is on the southside of thes to the occient see, and hathe on the orient the persian see and on the ponyent the red see. Hit is called felix for the aromatikes that bee in it, and it is the best and richest lond in the woorlde. Pretea begynneth at the red se where is the port ailon in the land of the idumeos, where is the citie precia.

Roger Barlow, *A Brief Summe of Geographie*, *c.* 1540

Araby the blest.

John Milton, *Paradise Lost*, book 4, 1667

In the vacant space between Persia, Syria, Egypt, and Aethiopia, the Arabian peninsula may be conceived as a triangle of spacious but irregular dimensions. . . . Far the greater part has been justly stigmatized with the epithets of the *stony* and the *sandy*. Even the wilds of Tartary are decked by the hand of nature with lofty trees and luxuriant herbage; and the lonesome traveller derives a sort of comfort and society from the presence of vegetable life. But in the dreary wastes of Arabia, a boundless level of sand is intersected by sharp and naked mountains, and the face of the desert, without shade or shelter, is scorched by the direct and intense rays of a tropical sun. Instead of refreshing breezes, the winds, particularly from the south-west, diffuse a noxious and even deadly vapour; the hillocks of sand which they alternately raise and scatter are compared to the billows of the ocean; and whole caravans, whole armies, have been lost and buried in the whirlwind. The common benefits of water are an object of desire and contest; and such is the scarcity of wood that some art is requisite to preserve and propagate the element of fire. Arabia is destitute of navigable rivers, which fertilise the soil and convey its produce to the adjacent regions; the torrents that fall from the hills are imbibed by the thirsty earth; the rare and hardy plants, the tamarind or the acacia, that strike their roots into the clefts of the rocks, are nourished by the dews of the night; a scanty supply of rain is collected in cisterns and aqueducts; the wells and springs are the secret treasures of the desert; and the pilgrim of Mecca, after many a dry and sultry march, is disgusted by the taste of the waters, which have rolled over a bed of sulphur or salt. Such is the general and genuine picture of the climate of Arabia.

Edward Gibbon, *The Decline and Fall of the Roman Empire*, 1776-88

Two chiefly are the perils of Arabia, famine and the dreadful-faced harpy of their religion, a third is the rash weapon of every Ishmaelite robber. . . . Here is a dead land, whence, if he die not, he shall bring home nothing but a perpetual weariness in his bones. The Semites are like to a man sitting in a cloaca to the eyes, and whose brows touch heaven.

Charles M. Doughty, *Travels in Arabia Deserta*, 1888

Beauty is the natural gift, to desert man and desert beast, only of peninsular Arabia.

Wilfred Scawen Blunt, Diary, 11 February 1897, *My Diaries*, 1919

Noteworthy is that opinion maintained by some scholars, that the huge and mostly waste Arabian Peninsula has been the prehistoric Nest.

Charles M. Doughty, *Travels in Arabia Deserta*, Preface to 3rd edn, 1921

Travel in Arabia in the best circumstances, with a train of servants, good riding-beasts, tents, and your own kitchen, is a trying experience.

T.E. Lawrence, Introduction to Charles M. Doughty, *Travels in Arabia Deserta*, 1921

What has chiefly remained with me from that winter, apart from the beauty of the valley-pictures that lie deep in my mind, is the *intimacy* with a world so strange and remote: it amounts almost to an annihilation of time, for the then scarcely visited smaller valleys of the Hadhramaut seemed to be separated by centuries rather than by space from the life of Europe; I thought constantly of some illuminated manuscript, roughly painted with draped sandalled figures and crowded backgrounds of towns, coming suddenly awake and living and moving beyond its frame; and the history of the Middle or even of the Dark Ages will never again be mere history to me, since I have lived in it and known what it has been. Its difference from our world went far deeper than outward circumstances: it went beyond its permanent insecurity, which is now no longer a stranger in Europe: it was perhaps the *acceptance* of insecurity as the foundation of life.

Freya Stark, *The Coasts of Incense*, 1953 – of 1938

Arabia is like a huge rough-hewn paving-stone which has been slightly tilted so as to dip towards the south-east.

Arnold Toynbee, *East to West*, 1958

Arabia Felix

The people of this countre be heery, for almost al ther bodie is covered with heere. In this contrey thei lie with ther mothers and systers and take as many wifes as thei lyste and the women as many men as thei wil, and when won goes to lie with her he levith his staf at the dore and that is a token that whosoever cometh after shud not come in. Thes be idolatours and dothe honour the sonne.

Roger Barlow, *A Brief Summe of Geographie*, *c.* 1540

Arabs

The nature of the Arabs is not unlike to the jackals; for when any of them hear the shot of a harquebuss, they presently turn back with such speed, as if the fiends of the infernal court were broken loose at their heels.

William Lithgow, *Rare Adventures and Painfull Peregrinations*, 1614/32

An Arab is a man who will pull down a whole temple to have a stone to sit on.

Proverb, quoted John Gunther, *Inside Africa*, 1955

One of that saintly, murd'rous brood,
To carnage and the Koran giv'n,
Who think through unbelievers' blood
Lies their directest way to Heav'n.

Thomas Moore, *The Fire-Worshippers – Lallah Rookh*, 1817

There is in these Arabians such a facility of mind, that it seems they only lack the occasion to speed in any way of learning; – that were by an easy imitation.

Charles M. Doughty, *Travels in Arabia Deserta*, 1888

Semites had no half-tones in their register of vision. They were a people of primary colours, or rather of black and white, who saw the world always in contour. They were a dogmatic people, despising doubt, our modern crown of thorns. They did not understand our metaphysical difficulties, our introspective questionings. They knew only truth and untruth, belief and unbelief, without our hesitating retinue of finer shades. . . . Their thoughts were at ease only in extremes. They inhabited superlatives by choice. Sometimes inconsistents seemed to possess them at once in joint sway; but they never compromised: they pursued the logic of several incompatible opinions to absurd ends, without perceiving the incongruity.

They were a limited, narrow-minded people, whose inert intellects lay fallow in incurious resignation. Their imaginations were vivid, but not creative. . . . The least morbid of peoples, they had accepted the gift of life unquestioningly as axiomatic. To them it was a thing inevitable, entailed on man, a usufruct beyond control. Suicide was a thing impossible, and death no grief.

They were a people of spasms, of upheavals, of ideas, the race of the individual genius. Their movements were the more shocking by contrast with the quietude of every day, their great men greater by contrast with the humanity of their mob. Their convictions were by instinct, their activities intuitional. Their largest manufacture was of creeds: almost they were monopolists of revealed religions.

T.E. Lawrence, *Seven Pillars of Wisdom*, 1926

I have never been able to appreciate and never encourage this curious Arab weakness for vaunting an obsequious desire to please. Another national characteristic, somewhat akin to this, is the constant anxiety to be the announcer of good or pleasing news – in the hope of reward. It is less objectionable, of course, and has an intelligible basis of origin, but it has a tendency in Arabia to discourage the purveying of true news which is more important and to encourage exaggeration or even suppression of material facts. But the East in general has no squeamishness about working for rewards. What else indeed should one work for? The philosophy of Arabia is definitely materialistic both in its metaphysics and its ethics.

H.St J.B. Philby, *The Empty Quarter*, 1933

Islam is the enemy of the tree, as it is the enemy of all patient and continuous human effort.

Hilaire Belloc, *Places*, 1942

All that is best in the Arabs has come to them from the desert: their deep religious instinct, which has found expression in Islam; their sense of fellowship, which binds them as members of one faith; their pride of race; their generosity and sense of hospitality; their dignity and the regard they have for the dignity of others as fellow human beings; their humour, their courage and patience, the language which they speak and their passionate love of poetry. But the Arabs are a race which produces its best only under conditions of extreme hardship and deteriorates progressively as living conditions become easier.

Wilfred Thesiger, *Arabian Sands*, 1959

Give us the job, and we will finish the tools.

Paraphrase of Sir Winston Churchill, quoted by John Gunther, as widespread opinion of Arab craftsman skills, *Inside Africa*, 1955

I shook hands with a friendly Arab . . . I still have my right hand to prove it.

Spike Milligan, *A Dustbin of Milligan*, 1962

Bedouin

The Badoies are wild men, amongst whom is no civill societie, no truth nor civilitie used: They worship Mahomet, and are very bad Moores, above all other People they are given to Stealths and Rapine; they eate raw flesh, and drinke milke; their habit is vile and filthy, they are greatly endued with swiftnesse and nimblenesse; they fight on foote and horse-backe, their weapons are Darts, they never have peace with their Neighbours, but continually have warre, and fight with every one.

Don John de Castro, 1541, in *Purchas his Pilgrimes*, 1625

The Wild Arabs . . . will traverse burning sands barefooted, to receive the last breath of some kind relation or friend, . . . teach their children at the earliest period resignation and fortitude, and . . . always keep alive a spirit of emulation amongst them! They are the boldest people in the world, yet are endued with a tenderness quite poetic, and their kindness extends to the brute creation by which they are surrounded. For myself I have the greatest affection and confidence in these people; besides, I admire their diamond eyes, their fine teeth, and the grace and agility (without capers), which is peculiar to them alone.

Lady Hester Stanhope, Letter to Mr Webb, October 1827, in Charles Meryon, *Memoirs of the Lady Hester Stanhope*, 1845

One who has never met an Arab in the desert can have no conception of his terrible appearance. The worst pictures of the Italian bandits or Greek mountain robbers I ever saw are tame in comparison . . . The celebrated Gasperini, who ten years ago kept in terror the whole country between Rome and Naples . . . and told me he could not remember how many murders he had committed, . . . looked civil and harmless compared with a Bedouin of the desert. The swarthy complexion of the latter, his long beard, his piercing coal-black eyes, half-naked figure, an enormous sword slung over his back, and a rusty matchlock in his hand, make the best figure for a painter I ever saw; but happily he is not as bad as he looks to be.

John Lloyd Stephens, *Incidents of Travel in Egypt, etc.*, 1837

The want of foresight is an anomalous part of the Bedouin's character, for it does not result either from recklessness or stupidity. I know of no human being whose body is so thoroughly the slave of mind as the Arab. His mental anxieties seem to be for ever torturing every nerve and fibre of his body, and yet, with all this exquisite sensitiveness to the suggestions of the mind, he is grossly improvident.

A.W. Kinglake, *Eothen*, 1844

Like most other *beau ideals*, this in regard to tent-dwelling Arabs would flatten down sadly by close acquaintance. Pshah! The Bedawin are mere barbarians – rough when rational, and in all else coarse and vulgar.

W.M.Thomson, *The Land and the Book*, 1859

To glance at the genuine son of the desert is to take the romance out of him for ever – to behold his steed is to long in charity to strip his harness off and let him fall to pieces.

Mark Twain, *The Innocents Abroad*, 1869

The life in the desert is better than any, *if there were not the Beduw*, is said proverbially by the oases' Arabians.

Charles M. Doughty, *Travels in Arabia Deserta*, 1888

The Bedu were odd people. For an Englishman, sojourning with them was unsatisfactory unless he had patience wide and deep as the sea. They were absolute slaves of their appetite, with no stamina of mind, drunkards for coffee, milk or water, gluttons for stewed meat, shameless beggars of tobacco. They dreamed for weeks before and after their rare sexual exercises, and spent the intervening days titillating themselves and their hearers with bawdy tales. Had the circumstances of their lives given them opportunity they would have been sheer sensualists. Their strength was the strength of men geographically beyond temptation: the poverty of Arabia made them simple, continent, enduring. If forced into civilized life they would have succumbed like any savage race to its diseases, meanness, luxury, cruelty, crooked dealing, artifice; and, like savages, they would have suffered them exaggeratedly for lack of inoculation.

T.E. Lawrence, *Seven Pillars of Wisdom*, 1926

The rearing of the camel is in this environment the predestined life to which every man-child is born. He is her parasite: her milk provides almost all his food and drink, her wool his shelter and clothing. Life is the quest for green pastures, rain the gift of God, and lightning man's pillar of fire. The great changing world without; the rise and fall of kingdoms; science and art and learning; spiritual forces at work for human betterment – 'the oppositions of science falsely so-called' and immoral systems making for human degradation; the welter of races, tongues and classes – of these he is unaware. They have no meaning, and therefore no existence for him. He follows the primitive life his fathers have led for ten thousand years, and his sons must live for as long to come. He abjures the soft and sedentary ways of life; his code knows only pitiless ferocity for his enemies, and for his friends the heights and depths of human courage and the milk of human kindness.

Bertram Thomas, *Arabia Felix*, 1932

ARCTIC

The great open spaces of the North are God's sanatorium.

Jessica Borthwick, Interview in the *Bioscope*, 7 May 1914

The North is the only place where Nature can still claim to rule, the only place as yet but little vexed by man. All over the globe there spread his noisy failures; the North alone is silent and at peace. Give man time and he will spoil that too.

Stephen Leacock, *My Discovery of the West*, 1937

The Northeast Passage

Truely this way consisteth rather in the imagination of Geographers, than allowable either in reason, or approved by experience, as well it may appeare by the dangerous trending of the Scythish Cape set by Ortelius under the 80 degree North, by unlikely sailing in the Northerne sea alwayes clad with yce and snow, or at the least continually pestred therewith, if happily it be at any time dissolved: besides bayes and shelfes, the water waxing more shallow towards the East, that we say nothing of the foule mists and darke fogs in the cold clime, of the little power of the Sunne to cleare the aire, of the uncomfortable nights, so neere the Pole, five moneths long.

Richard Willes, 1576, in Richard Hakluyt, *Principal Navigations . . . of the English Nation*, 1598–1600

The North Pole

Still pressing on, beyond Tornea's lake,
And Hecla flaming through a waste of snow,
And farthest Greenland, to the Pole itself,
Where, failing gradual, life at length goes out,
The Muse expands her solitary flight;
And, hovering o'er the wild stupendous scene,
Beholds new seas beneath another sky.
Throned in his palace of cerulean ice,
Here Winter holds his unrejoicing court;
And through his airy hall the loud misrule
Of driving tempest is for ever heard.
Here the grim tyrant meditates his wrath;
Here arms his winds with all-subduing frost;
Moulds his fierce hail, and treasures up his snows,
With which he now oppresses half the globe.

James Thomson, *The Seasons – Winter*, 1726

Parry, my man! has thy brave leg
Yet struck its foot against the peg
On which the world is spun?
Or hast thou found No Thoroughfare
Writ by the hand of Nature there
Where man has never run! . . .

O come and tell us what the Pole is –
Whether it singular or sole is, –
Or straight, or crooked bent, –
If very thick, or very thin, –
Made of wood – and if akin
To those there be in Kent.

Thomas Hood, *Ode to Captain Parry*, 1825

ARGENTINA

See also under Patagonia

It is the United States of the Southern Hemisphere.

James Bryce, *South America*, 1912

Did not a friend of mine in Buenos Aires once begin an anecdote with the immortal opening: 'As we were driving to the revolution . . . '.

Philip Guedalla, *Argentine Tango*, 1932

Argentina of the pampas, Argentina of the enormous plains, Argentina flowing out into the morning beyond the hills like a sea beyond capes . . . Argentina without towns, with few roads, with fences straight and wide apart as meridians on a map . . . It is a country in which the distances from house to house are too great for the barking of dogs even on the stillest night, a country in which the cocks crow only twice because there is no answer. It is a country so level that even time has no hold upon it and one century is like another; a country so empty that the watchers at night put their eyes along the ground to see the circle of the horizon; a country in which the sky is so huge that men plant islands of eucalyptus over their houses to be covered from the blue . . . It is . . . the country in which the green goes on and on like water, and the gulls follow the plough as seagulls follow ships – the country in which the women are always together under the dark trees in the evening, their faces fading into loneliness with the night.

Archibald MacLeish, writing anonymously in *Fortune*, 1938

Argentina is more like Australia than it is like Peru.

J.H. Ferguson, *Latin America*, 1968

This country of the future whose future, somehow, never becomes a present.

Brian Crozier, 'Latin American Journey', *Encounter*, December 1964

The sadness of Argentina is hard to define. It is not new – Argentine intellectuals were analysing that strangest expression of it, the Tango, thirty years ago.

John Mander, 'Mexico City to Buenos Aires', *Encounter*, September 1965

A shadow state gripped by psychoses because the world has passed it by.

John Gunther, *Inside South America*, 1967

In Argentina today the Citizens Advice Bureau would be a subversive organisation.

Perico Rodriguez, Argentinian exile, quoted by Alan Road, *Observer Magazine*, 24 May 1981

Argentinians

The Natives feed most on Beef half-raw without Bread or Salt, and in such quantities that they throw themselves naked into cold water, that they may retain the natural Heat within their Entrails to help Digestion; and sometimes they lie down with their Stomachs in hot Sand: but their Gluttony in devouring so much raw flesh fills them so with Worms that they seldom live till 50 years old.

Captain Woodes Rogers, *A Cruising Voyage Round the World*, 1712 – of 1708, near Buenos Aires

The absence of gentlemen by profession appears to an Englishman something strange.

Charles Darwin, *Journal . . . During the Voyage . . . of H.M.S. Beagle*, 1832–6

One doubts whether there yet exists a definite Argentine type. They have ceased to be Spaniards without becoming something new of their own. They seem to be a nation in the making, not yet made.

James Bryce, *South America*, 1912

The Argentines have everything but themselves.

John Gunther, quoting a local quip, *Inside South America*, 1967

What exists here is a ludicrous form of nationalism. Our entire country is imported. Everyone here is really from somewhere else.

Jorge Luis Borges, quoted by Alastair Reid, *New Yorker*, 7 August 1978

Some thirty years ago Borges remarked that the Argentine is not a citizen but an individual – that he lacks any idea of the nation he resides in, and views it as a territory that, owing to its wealth, can be exploited rapidly. To my mind, this is a noteworthy comment on the Argentine problem.

Jacobo Timerman, 'Reflections (Argentina)' *New Yorker*, 20 April 1981

An Argentine is an Italian who speaks Spanish, thinks he's French, but would like to be English.

Old Saying, quoted by Frank Taylor, *Sunday Telegraph*, 4 April 1982

Gaucho women

The habits of the women are very curious; they have literally nothing to do; the great plains which surround them offer them no motive to walk, they seldom ride, and *their* lives certainly are very indolent and inactive. They have all, however, families, whether married or not; and once when I enquired of a young woman employed in nursing a very pretty child, who was the father of the 'creatura' she replied, 'Quien sabe?'

Captain F.B. Head, *Rough Notes . . . across the Pampas and the Andes*, 1827

Buenos Aires

Buenos Aires is far from being an agreeable residence for those who are accustomed to English comfort. The water is extremely impure, scarce, and expensive. The town is badly paved and dirty, and the houses are the most comfortless abodes I ever entered. The walls, from the climate, are damp, mouldy, and discoloured. The floors are badly paved with bricks, which are generally cracked, and often in holes. The roofs have no ceiling, and the families have no ideas of warming themselves, except by drinking hot maté, or by huddling round a fire of charcoal, which is put outside the door until the carbonic acid gas has rolled away. Some of the principal families of Buenos Aires furnish their rooms in a very expensive but comfortless manner; they put down upon the brick floor a brilliant Brussels carpet, hang a lustre from the rafters, and place against the damp wall which they whitewash, a number of tawdry North American chairs. They get an English pianoforte, and some marble vases, but they have no idea of grouping their furniture into a comfortable form: the ladies sit with their backs against the walls without any apparent means of enjoying themselves; and when a stranger calls upon them, he is much surprised to find that they have the uncourteous custom of never rising from their chairs.

Ibid.

Not even the approach by sea to Alexandria or to the mouth of the Hooghly below Calcutta, is duller than that to Buenos Aires.

James Bryce, *South America*, 1912

Everybody seems to have money, and to like spending it, and to like letting everybody else know that it is being spent . . . Nowhere in the world does one get a stronger impression of exuberant wealth and extravagance . . . They are a type of our time, in their equal devotion to business and pleasure, the two and only deities of this latest phase of humanity.

Ibid.

He had a lot of stocks and shares
And half a street in Buenos Aires.
But this pronunciation varies,
Some people call it Bu-enos Airés.

Hilaire Belloc, *About John, – New Cautionary Tales*, 1930

It is not, one feels, for nothing that it was named Buenos Aires, since the airs are admirable and every air a tango.

Philip Guedalla, *Argentine Tango*, 1932

Large cities are often spoken of as being 'international', but I suppose that Buenos Aires must be the most truly international city in the world. Its population – at any rate in the business sections of town – appears to be a three-part mixture of British, German and Latin (Italian almost as much as Spanish). Its banks and offices have a definitely British atmosphere; they recall the solid solvent grandeur of Victorian London. Many of its restaurants are German, they have the well-stocked gemuetlichkeit of pre-1914 Munich and Berlin. Its boulevards and private mansions belong to the Paris of forty years ago.

But this does not mean that Buenos Aires and its inhabitants have no national character. Quite the reverse. For these foreign elements have been blended and transformed into something indigenous, immediately recognisable, unique. Many cities are big in actual acreage, but Buenos Aires, more than any other I have seen, gives you the impression of space. Space for the sake of space. Space easily, casually afforded. Space squandered with a sort of imperial magnificence. You feel here an infinite freedom of elbow-room which corresponds naturally to the expanse of the nearby estuary and the ocean, and to the vastness of the surrounding plains. The other characteristic is weight. The public buildings are laden with ponderous statuary; their arches, doorways and staircases are wide and massive. The people, despite their briskness and usually good proportions, seem curiously heavy and earthbound. Their faces, regardless of racial origin, have a placid, somewhat bovine expression. This is hardly surprising, considering the amount of meat they eat.

Christopher Isherwood, *The Condor and the Cows*, 1949

The history of Buenos Aires is written in its telephone directory. Pompey Romanov, Emilio Rommel, Crespina D.Z de Rose, Ladislao Radziwil, and Elisabeta Marta Callman de Rothschild – five names taken at random from among the R's – told a story of exile, disillusion and anxiety behind lace curtains.

Bruce Chatwyn, *In Patagonia*, 1977

The city kept reminding me of Russia – the cars of the secret police bristling with aerials; women with splayed haunches licking ice-cream in dusty parks; the same bullying statues, the pie-crust architecture, the same avenues that were not quite straight, giving the illusion of endless space and leading out into nowhere.

Tsarist rather than Soviet Russian. Bazarov could be an Argentine character, *The Cherry Orchard* is an Argentine situation. The Russia of greedy kulaks, corrupt officials, imported groceries and landowners asquint to Europe.

I said as much to a friend.

'Lots of people say that,' he said. 'Last year an old White *emigrée* came to our place in the country. She got terrifically excited and asked to see every room. We went up to the attics and she said: "Ah! I knew it! The smell of my childhood!"

Ibid.

Buenos Aires is at first glance, and for days afterwards, a most civilized ant-hill. It has all the elegance of the old world in its buildings and streets, and in its people all the vulgarity and frank good health of the new world . . . I had expected a fairly prosperous place, cattle and gauchos, and a merciless dictatorship; I had not counted on its being charming, on the seduction of its architecture, or the vigour of its appeal. . . . The pink-flowered 'drunken branch' trees of the pampas grew in the parks, but the parks were English and Italian, and this told in their names, Britannia Park, Palermo Park. The downtown section was architecturally French, the industrial parts German, the harbour Italian. Only the scale of the city was American; its dimensions, its sense of space, gave it a familiarity.

Paul Theroux, *The Old Patagonian Express*, 1979

The Recoleta cemetery

It is cheaper to live extravagantly all your life than to be buried in Recoleta.

Anon., *Buenos Aires through Bifocals*, quoted by John Gunther, *Inside South America*, 1967

The cemetery is a sort of Mayfair of the dead, the most expensive real estate in Buenos Aires.

Robert Robinson, article in *The Times*, 22 July 1978

Andes Mountains

crossing the Cordillera between Argentina and Chile

'What a magnificent view!' said I to one of my Cornish companions, whose honest heart and thoughts were always faithful to Old England. 'What thing can be more beautiful?' I added. After smiling for some seconds he replied, 'Them things, Sir, that do wear caps and aprons.'

Captain F.B.Head, *Rough Notes . . . across the Pampas and the Andes*, 1827

ASCENSION

The dreariness of this island surpassed all the horrors of Easter Island and Tierra del Fuego, even without the assistance of snow. It was a ruinous heap of rocks.

George Forster, *A Voyage Round the World*, 1777

Imagine smooth conical hills of a bright red colour, with their summits generally truncated, rising separately out of a level surface of black rugged lava. A principal mound in the centre of the island, seems the father of the lesser cones. It is called Green Hill; its name being taken from the faintest tinge of that colour, which at this time of the year is barely perceptible from the anchorage. To complete the desolate scene, the black rocks on the coast are lashed by a wild and turbulent sea.

Charles Darwin, *Journal . . . During the Voyage . . . of H.M.S. Beagle*, 1832–6

The little island is fitly entered in the British Navy List as a commissioned ship.

George Baden Powell, *Orient Line Guide*, 1885

ASIA – EAST – ORIENT

The farther I journey towards the West, the more convinced I am that the wise men came from the East.

William Davy, King's Sargeant, 1762, quoted in Woolrych, *Lives of Eminent Sergeants at Law*, 1869

Europe is but a molehill; there never have existed mighty empires, there never have occurred great revolutions, save in the East, where live six hundred millions of men – the cradle of all religions, the birth-place of all metaphysics.

Napoleon Bonaparte, in *Table Talk and Opinions of Napoleon the First*, 1868

The Asiatics are not qualified to be republicans, but they have the liberty of demolishing despots, which is the next thing to it.

Lord Byron, *Journal*, November 1813

The East is a career.

Benjamin Disraeli, *Tancred*, 1847

Oriental scenes look best in steel engravings.

Mark Twain, *The Innocents Abroad*, 1869

I can only trust this book may deter others from following my example, and shall then have some satisfaction in knowing that its pages have not been written in vain.

M. Victor Meignan concludes his amusing work 'De Paris à Pékin par terre,' thus:–

'N'allez pas là! C'est la morale de ce livre!'

Let the reader benefit by our experience.

Harry de Windt, *From Pekin to Calais by Land*, 1889

Ship me somewhere East of Suez, where the best is like the worst,
Where there aren't no Ten Commandments, an' a man can raise a thirst.

Rudyard Kipling, *Mandalay*, 1890

*Asia is not going to be civilized after the methods of the West. There is too much Asia and she is too old.

Rudyard Kipling, 'The Man Who Was', in *Life's Handicap*, 1891

Now it is not good for the Christian's health to hustle the Aryan brown,
For the Christian riles, and the Aryan smiles and he weareth the Christian down;
And the end of the fight is a tombstone white with the name of the late deceased,
And the epitaph drear: 'A Fool lies here who tried to hustle the East.'

Rudyard Kipling, *The Naulakha* (Chapter heading), 1892

The East looks to itself; it knows nothing of the greater world of which you are a citizen, asks nothing of you and of your civilization.

Gertrude Bell, *Safar Nameh – Persian Pictures*, 1894

The attraction of the East for the West is after all nostalgia; it is as if, when we are awakened by dreams, we remember that forgotten country out of which we came. We came out of the East, and we return to the East; all our civilisation has been but an attempt at forgetting, and, in spite of that long attempt, we still remember . . . Its attraction is like the attraction of those women whom it is impossible to live with or without.

Arthur Symons, *Cities*, 1903

The East is not for me – the sensuous spiritual voluptuousness, the curious sensitiveness of the naked people, their black bottomless, hopeless eyes – and the heads of elephants and buffaloes poking out of primeval mud – the queer noise of tall metallic palm trees: *ach!* – altogether the tropics have something of the world before the flood – hot dark mud and the life inherent in it: makes me feel rather sick. But wonderful to have known.

D.H. Lawrence, Letter to Lady Cynthia Asquith, 30 April 1922

*'Can you always tell when a stranger is a friend?'
'Yes.'
'Then you are an Oriental.'

E.M.Forster, *A Passage to India*, 1924 – Aziz to Fielding

There is no silence in the East.

W. Somerset Maugham, *The Gentleman in the Parlour*, 1930

In England, Nature seems a tender mother, but East of Suez, she changes her sex and she becomes Siva, Lord of Change and Destroyer of names and Forms – Destroyer, that is, of ignorance.

F. Yeats Brown, *Bengal Lancer*, 1930

To travel in Europe is to assume a foreseen inheritance; in Islam, to inspect that of a close and familiar cousin. But to travel in farther Asia is to discover a novelty previously unsuspected and unimaginable. It is not a question of probing this novelty, of analysing its sociological, artistic, or religious origins, but of learning, simply, that it exists. Suddenly, as it were, in the opening of an eye, the potential world – the field of man and his environment – is doubly extended. The stimulus is inconceivable to those who have not experienced it.

Robert Byron, *First Russia then Tibet*, 1933

Asiatics seem in general to have less stamina than westerners; they lack solidity, they lack shoulders.

John Gunther, *Inside Asia*, 1939

I thought of a quotation from Confucius . . . 'The gentleman behaves in harmony, but never conforms; the man of small character does conform, but never behaves in harmony.'

This small quotation from the analects of Confucius is one which, unwittingly, I carried in my heart all through my life; until I came to the streets of Asia and realized that my soul is an Oriental's.

James Kirkup, *Streets of Asia*, 1969

ATLANTIC OCEAN

I do not mean to be disrespectful but the attempt of the Lords to stop the progress of reform reminds me very forcibly of the great storm of Sidmouth, and of the conduct of the excellent Mrs Partington on that occasion. In the winter of 1824 there set in a great flood upon that town – the tide rose to an incredible height – the waves rushed in upon the houses – and everything was threatened with destruction. In the midst of this sublime storm, Dame Partington, who lived upon the beach, was seen at the door of her house with mop and pattens, trundling her mop and squeezing out the sea-water, and vigorously pushing away the Atlantic Ocean. The Atlantic was roused. Mrs Partington's spirit was up; but I need not tell you that the contest was unequal. The Atlantic Ocean beat Mrs Partington. She was excellent at a slop or a puddle, but she should not have meddled with a tempest.

Sydney Smith, *Speech at Taunton, on the Reform Bill*, October 1831

I think it possible I may forget the sensations with which I watched the long course of the gigantic Mississippi; the Ohio and the Potomac may mingle and be confounded with other streams in my memory, I may even recall with difficulty the blue outline of the Alleghany mountains, but never, while I remember anything, can I forget the first and last hour of light on the Atlantic.

Mrs Frances Trollope, *Domestic Manners of the Americans*, 1832

aboard the Great Western, 20 September 1838
I continued my position, and holding on by a rope attached to the hind mast, read the opening scene of the Talisman, in Sir Walter Scott's Tales of the Crusaders. The imagination was transported in an instant to the calm, sultry desert regions of the Dead Sea, while the reader was careering amidst the Atlantic billows, and fanned by an equinoctial gale. The enjoyment was exquisite.

The scene in the saloon was not so sublimely captivating.

George Combe, *Notes During a Phrenological Visit*, in 1838–40, 1841

*On, on, on, over the countless miles of angry space roll the long, heaving billows. Mountains and caves are here, and yet are not; for what is now the one, is now the other; then all is but a boiling heap of rushing water. Pursuit, and flight, and mad return of wave on wave, and savage struggle, ending in a spouting up of foam that whitens the black night; incessant change of place, and form, and hue; constancy in nothing but eternal strife; on, on, on, they roll, and darker grows the night, and louder howls the wind, and more clamorous and fierce become the million voices in the sea.

Charles Dickens, *Martin Chuzzlewit*, 1844

How in all wonder Columbus got over,
That is a marvel to me, I protest,
Cabot, and Raleigh too, that well-read rover,
Frobisher, Dampier, Drake, and the rest.
Bad enough all the same,
For them that after came,
But, in great Heaven's name,
How *he* should ever think
That on the other brink
Of this huge waste terra firma should be,
Is a pure wonder I must say to me . . .

How a man should ever hope to get thither,
E'en if he knew of there being another side;
But to suppose he should come any whither,
Sailing right on into chaos untried,
Across the whole ocean,
In spite of the motion,
To stick to the notion
That in some nook or bend
Of a sea without end
He should find north and South Amerikee.
Was a pure madness as it seems to me.

Arthur Hugh Clough, (untitled), 1852–3

Atlantic is the sieve through which only or chiefly the liberal, bold, *America-loving* part of each city, clan, or family pass hither.

Ralph Waldo Emerson, *Journals*, 1856

DISAPPOINTED WITH THE ATLANTIC
On the journey over Mr Wilde did not attain, it appears, to very great popularity among the passengers. Before the ship had been five days out he said to a gentleman with whom he was promenading the deck (and this gentleman kindly retailed the conversation to the writer), 'I am not exactly pleased with the Atlantic. It is not so majestic as I expected. I would like to see the ship's bridge carried away.'

New York World, 3 January 1882

Disappointing.

Oscar Wilde, Letter to George Alexander, September 1894

The Atlantic Ocean is geographically a misnomer, socially and politically a dwindling superstition . . . Ocean forsooth! this little belt of blue water that we cross before we know where we are, at a single hop-skip-and-jump! From north to south perhaps, it may still count as an ocean.

William Archer, *America Today*, 1900

The Atlantic Ocean is the only really convenient way of disposing of old razor blades.

James Agate, *Ego* (9 May 1934), 1935

and Mediterranean
The Atlantic seemed, as it still seems to me, a mere obstacle to human intercourse, so opposite to the Mediterranean's ballroom floor meant for perambulation.

Freya Stark, *Beyond Euphrates*, 1951

South Atlantic Ocean

While sailing a little south of the Plata on one very dark night, the sea presented a wonderful and most beautiful spectacle. There was a fresh breeze, and every part of the surface, which during the day is seen as foam, now glowed with a pale light. The vessel drove before her bows two billows of liquid phosphorous, and in her wake she was followed by a milky train. As far as the eye reached, the crest of every wave was bright and the sky above the horizon, from the reflected glare of these livid flames, was not so utterly obscure as over the vault of the heavens.

Charles Darwin, *Journal . . . During the Voyage . . . of H.M.S. Beagle*, 1832–6

AUSTRALIA

This large and hitherto almost unknown Tract of Land is situated so very advantageously in the richest Climates of the World, the Torrid and Temperate Zones; having in it especially all the Advantages of the Torrid Zone, as being known to reach from the Equator itself (within a Degree) to the Tropick of Capricorn and beyond it; that in coasting round it, which I design'd by this Voyage, if possible; I could not but hope to meet with some fruitful Lands, Continent, or Islands, or both, productive of any of the rich Fruit, Drugs, or Spices (perhaps Minerals also, &c.) that are in the other Parts of the Torrid Zone, under equal Parallels of Latitude; at least a Soil and Air capable of such, upon transplanting them hither, and Cultivation.

William Dampier, *A Voyage to New Holland, in 1699*, 1703–9

Farewell Australia! you are a rising child, and doubtless some day will reign a great princess in the South; but you are too great and ambitious for affection, yet not great enough for respect. I leave your shores without sorrow or regret.

Charles Darwin, *Journal . . . During the Voyage . . . of H.M.S. Beagle*, 1832–6

Now Father, I think this is the Promised Land, but there are faults in it.

Emigrant's Letter in the *Bradford Observer*, 7 December 1848

Earth is here so kind that just tickle her with a hoe and she laughs with a harvest.

Douglas William Jerrold, *A Man Made of Money*, 1849

I sing of a commodity, it's one that will not fail yer,
I mean the common oddity, the mainstay of Australia;
Gold it is a precious thing, for commerce it increases,
But stringy bark and green hide can beat it all to pieces.

Chorus:
Stringy bark and green hide, that will never fail yer,
Stringy bark and green hide, the mainstay of Australia . . .

New chums to this golden land, never dream of failure,
Whilst you've got such useful things as these in fair Australia,
For stringy bark and green hide will never, never fail yer,
Stringy bark and green hide is the mainstay of Australia.

George Chanson, *The Sydney Songster* No.1, 1866

Sons of the South, make choice between
(Sons of the South, choose true)
The Land of Morn and the Land of E'en
The Old Dead Tree and the Young Tree Green
The Land that belongs to the lord and Queen
And the Land that belongs to you.

Henry Lawson, *A Song of the Republic*, 1887

I found myself in a new land with new smells and among people who insisted a little too much that they also were new.

Rudyard Kipling, *Something of Myself*, 1937 – of 1891

and New Zealand

Australia and New Zealand are not likely to change very much. They can go little further, for they have nowhere to go. Things are already fixed in grooves here, and the grooves are pretty shallow. I think they would do better on the long run, if there were no such thing as steamers or rapid communication. They might then develop character.

Henry Adams, Letter to Henry Cabot Lodge, 4 August 1891

Duchess of Berwick: It must be so pretty with all the dear little kangaroos flying about. Agatha has found it on the map. What a curious shape it is! Just like a large packing case. However, it is a very young country, isn't it?

Oscar Wilde, *Lady Windermere's Fan*, 1892

Australia is the best place in the world (taking it all round) for the rank and file, and for the rank and file of art and letters no less than of trade and labour.

Francis Adams, *The Australians*, 1893

Cecily: Well, he said at dinner on Wednesday night, that you would have to choose between this world, the next world, and Australia.
Algernon: Oh, well! The accounts I have received of Australia and the next world are not particularly encouraging. This world is good enough for me, Cousin Cecily.

Oscar Wilde, *The Importance of Being Earnest*, 1895

Australian history is almost always picturesque; indeed it is so curious and strange that it is itself the chiefest novelty the country has to offer, and so it pushes the other novelties into second and third place. It does not read like history, but like the most beautiful lies; and all of a fresh new sort, no mouldy old stale ones. It is full of surprises and adventures, and incongruities and incredibilities; but they are all true, they all happened.

Mark Twain, *More Tramps Abroad*, 1897

October was close at hand, spring was come. It was really spring – everybody said so; but you could have sold it for summer in Canada, and nobody would have suspected.

Ibid.

Australia, *n.* A country lying in the South Sea whose industrial and commercial development has been unspeakably retarded by an unfortunate dispute among geographers as to whether it is a continent or an island.

Ambrose Bierce, *The Cynic's Word Book*, 1906

The Australian, one hundred to two hundred years hence, will still live with the consciousness that, if he only goes far enough back over the hills and across the plains, he comes in the end to the mysterious half-desert country where men have to live the lives of strong men. And the life of that mysterious country will affect Australian imagination much as the life of the sea has affected that of the English. It will always be there to help the Australian to form his ideals; and one knows of no land where they have a more definite ideal than in Australia, or where the whole people, men, women, and even youngsters, are more consciously employed in working it out.

C.E.W. Bean, *The Dreadnought of the Darling*, 1911

I had no idea that it was a kind of glorified French Riviera.

Alfred Viscount Northcliffe, *My Journey Round the World*, 1923 – of 1921

If you want to know what it is to feel the 'correct' social world fizzle to nothing, you should come to Australia. It is a weird place. In the *established* sense it is socially nil. Happy-go-lucky, don't-you-bother, we're-in-Australia. But also there seems to be no inside life of any sort: just a long lapse and drift. A rather fascinating indifference, a *physical* indifference to what we call soul or spirit. It's really a weird show. The country has an extraordinary hoary, weird attraction. As you get used to it it seems so *old*, as if it had missed all this Semite-Egyptian-Indo-European vast era of history, and was coal age, the age of great ferns and mosses. It hasn't got a consciousness, just none – too far back. A strange effect it has on me. Often I hate it like poison, then again it fascinates me, and the spell of its indifference gets me. I can't quite explain it: as if one resolved back almost to the plant kingdom, before souls, spirits and minds were grown at all: only quite a live energetic body with a weird face.

D.H. Lawrence, Letter to Catherine Carswell, Wyewurk, 22 June 1922

*That curious sombreness of Australia, the sense of oldness, with the forms all worn down low and blunt, squat. The squat-seeming earth. And then they ran at last into real country rather rocky, dark old rocks, and sombre bush with its different pale-stemmed dull-leaved gum trees standing graceful, and various healthy-looking undergrowth, and great spiky things like zuccas. As they turned south they saw tree ferns standing on one knobbly leg among the gums, and among the rocks ordinary ferns and small bushes spreading in glades and sharp hill-slopes. It was virgin bush, and as if unvisited, lost, sombre, with plenty of space, yet spreading grey for miles and miles, in a hollow towards the west. Far in the west, the sky having suddenly cleared, they saw the magical range of the Blue Mountains. And all this hoary space of bush between. The strange, as it were, *invisible* beauty of Australia, which is undeniably there, but which seems to lurk just beyond the range of our white vision. You feel you can't *see* – as if your eyes hadn't the vision in them to correspond with the outside landscape. For the landscape is so unimpressive, like a face with little or no features, a dark face. It is so aboriginal, out of our ken, and it hangs back so aloof.

D.H.Lawrence, *Kangaroo*, 1923

*The soft, blue, humanless sky of Australia, the pale unwritten atmosphere of Australia. *Tabula rasa*. The world a new leaf. And on the new leaf nothing.

Ibid.

Nobody in England or America has any idea of the intensity of the servant problem in the southern hemisphere.

Dame Nellie Melba, *Melodies and Memories*, 1925

It is all so like Britain; there is the same living spirit of freedom, mysteriously stifled and frustrated, not by a simple organised tyranny, but by a complex of obscurantisms.

H.G.Wells, *Travels of a Republican Radical in Search of Hot Water.*, 1939

A Nation of trees, drab green and desolate grey
In the field uniform of modern wars,
Darkens her hills, those endless, outstretched paws
Of Sphinx demolished or stone lion warn away.

They call her a young country, but they lie:
She is the last of lands, the emptiest,
A woman beyond her change of life, a breast
Still tender, but within the womb is dry.

Without songs, architecture, history:
The emotions and superstitions of younger lands.
Her rivers of water drown among inland sands,
The river of her immense stupidity

Floods her monotonous tribes from Cairns to Perth.
In them at last the ultimate men arrive
Whose boast is not: 'we live' but 'we survive',
A type who will inhabit the dying earth.

And her five cities, like five teeming sores,
Each drains her: a vast parasite robber-state
Where second-hand Europeans pullulate
Timidly on the edge of alien shores.

Yet there are some like me turn gladly home
From the lush jungle of modern thought, to find
The Arabian desert of the human mind,
Hoping, if still from the deserts the prophets come,

Such savage and scarlet as no green hills dare
Springs in that waste, some spirit which escapes
The learned doubt, the chatter of cultured apes
Which is called civilization over there.

A.D. Hope, *Australia*, 1939

Where once was a sea is now a salty sunken desert,
A futile heart within a fair periphery;
The people are hard-eyed kindly, with nothing inside them,
The men are independent but you could not call them free.

James McAuley, *Envoi*, 1938, in *Under Aldebaran*, 1946

'The place, my lord, is much like Gideon's fleece
The second time he laid it on the ground;
For by the will of God it has remained
Bone-dry itself, with water all around.

Yet as a wheel that's driven in the ruts,
It has a wet rim where the people clot
Like mud; and though they praise the inner spaces,
When asked to go themselves, they'd rather not.

The men are brave, contentious, ignorant;
The women very much as one expects.
For their religion, I must be excused,
Having no stomach to observe their sects.

You must be wary in your conversation;
For, seeing them thumb-high, you might suppose
They recognised their stature, but beware!
Their notion of themselves is grandiose.

And you will often find, although their heads
Are like a berry on a twig of bones,
They speak as Giants of the South Pacific
And treat the islands as their stepping stones . . .

Mentally they're still in Pliocene,
A flat terrain impermeably dense;
And will be so, until volcanic mind
Arches its back at brute indifference . . .

A man of even middling parts will look
So tall, he may forget his real status,
And play the sorry fable of the frog
Who burst his belly with his own afflatus.

James McAuley, *The True Discovery of Australia*, 1944, in *Under Aldebaran*, 1946

We have to remind ourselves that geographically we are Oriental, we are not European. We are an island just off the south-east coast of Asia, and are part of the Oriental world. There our fate is set. We are there geographically and there we will stay. We are not bound up with the fate of Europe but with the fate of Asia.

Rt Rev. E.H. Burgmann, January 1946, quoted in F.K.Crowley (ed.), *Modern Australia in Documents*, 1973

In a land of rolling plains and wide blue skies, a race of cheerful agoraphobes grew up in little weather-sealed boxes.

Robin Boyd, *Australia's Home*, 1952

The immense cities lie basking on the beaches of the continent like whales that have taken to the land again.

Arnold Toynbee, *East to West*, 1958

Above all Australia is Australian. It is indeed an astonishing thing how strong a character Australia has – so strong that the ever-continuing waves of British migrants have no impact on it but are ruthlessly bent to its pattern. It is a character immediately recognisable in her soldiers as in her poets, in her politicians as in her cricketers – rough rather than tough, kindly but not tolerant, a generous, sardonic, sceptical but surprisingly gullible character, quick to take offence and by no means unwilling to give it, always ready for a fight but just as ready to help a fellow-creature in distress. Its worst faults are aggressiveness, which leads easily to violence in word and deed, and a dreadful complacency; its greatest virtues courage and a certain downright honesty which at least says what it thinks. It is indeed very much the character of John Bull as imagined by foreigners in the eighteenth and nineteenth centuries.

John Douglas Pringle, *Australian Accent*, 1958

I like to think of it as the only Anglo-Saxon country with Mediterranean qualities.

Ibid.

When the first highway robbery in Australia occurred, David Collins, the Judge-Advocate, is said to have considered it 'one step towards refinement' and 'at least a manly method of taking property'.

Russell Ward, *The Australian Legend*, 1958, quoting *Australian Encyclopaedia*, 1926

There is a strange quality in the Australian landscape. To a European and especially an English eye it is, at first, lacking in freshness and greenness; the light is too harsh, the trees too thin and sparse, the ground too hard and there are no soft outlines anywhere. Desiccation seems to be the theme, a pitiless drying-out of all sap and moisture, and monotonous is the favourite adjective for the bush: monotonous and therefore worthless. It is a country for the ants. But then on closer acquaintance one begins to perceive that, very silently and slowly, life is going on here at another level: the embattled young sapling that looks so gnarled and old is full of strength, its tiny flowers are a gay miniature of larger flowers, and its leaves, when burnt or crushed, release a smell as pungent as a lemon's. Dead fallen trees, it is true, give a graveyard appearance to the ground and the prevailing colour of the scrub is greenish grey. But then unexpectedly a flock of pink galahs will perch on the bare branches, or one catches sight of the wattle in flower and it is more gold than gold can ever be, a clear leaping colour in a field of grey. The bell-bird's single note is a small bell sounding against utter silence, and the fungus, pushing up through the cracked brown clay, is a dome of bright scarlet. These things, however, have to be discovered. Nothing is at once revealed. You must walk for miles alone and gradually the feel of the bush begins to seep into the mind, its immense stillness and quietness; and out of that austerity it is a wonderful thing to see a wild animal start up and bound away, or to come on a group of herons fishing in a water-hole. There is nothing menacing in the bush – even the snakes will always avoid you if they can – and nearly always overhead there is the pale blue sky. Like the bush itself it has a kind of implacable indifference but it is not oppressive. One feels very well in this dry air.

Alan Moorhead, *The Fatal Impact*, 1966

This country is a rim containing people round a withered hub.

Elspeth Huxley, *Their Shining Eldorado*, 1967

In Australia there is no such thing as constructive criticism.

George Mikes, *Boomerang – Australia Rediscovered*, 1968

There are many non-intellectual countries; Australia is one of the few anti-intellectual ones.

Ibid.

Australia spent the first half of the century as a farm for the British. Now it looks as though we may spend the second half as a quarry for the Japanese.

Gough Whitlam, quoted in Jonathan Aitken, *Land of Fortune*, 1971

Possums and parrots are protected in Australia, but mugs are not.

Sir Arthur Fadden, former Federal Treasurer, quoted Jonathan Aitken, *Land of Fortune*, 1971

I think I might like Australia; but I have met so many Australians everywhere but in Australia whose sole desire is to make good, by which they mean to make enough not to have to return home, except on holiday, and preferably as celebrities, that I accept their evidence.

George Gale, 'I Like it Here', *Spectator*, 23 September 1978

The world's wildest island.

Airline Advertisement, 1980

Australia is an outdoor country. People only go inside to use the toilet. And that's only a recent development.

Barry Humphries, quoted by Peter Nichols, in interview with Stephen Pile, *Sunday Times*, 11 January 1981

KOALA TRIANGLE, a mysterious zone in the Southern Hemisphere where persons of talent disappear without trace.

Barry Humphries, Glossary entry in *A Nice Night's Entertainment*, 1982

Australians

The children born in these colonies, and now grown up, speak a better language, purer, and more harmonious, than is generally the case in most parts of England. The amalgamation of such various dialects assembled together, seems to improve the mode of articulating the words.

James Dixon, *Narrative of a Voyage*, 1822

And lo! a transport comes in view
I hear the merry motley crew,
Well skill'd in pocket to make entry,
Of Dieman's Land the elected Gentry,
And founders of Australian Races. –
The Rogues! I see it in their faces!
Receive me Lads! I'll go with you,
Hunt the black swan and kangaroo,
And that New Holland we'll presume
Old England with some elbow-room.

S.T. Coleridge, *The Delinquent Travellers*, 1824

Even among male Australians there is a taciturnity proceeding from natural diffidence and reserve, not from any want of mental resources; this led one of their more lively countrymen to observe, 'that they could do everything but speak.'

G. Bennett, *Wanderings in New South Wales*, 1834

I must say somewhere, and may as well say here as elsewhere, that the wonders performed in the way of riding, driving, fighting, walking, working, drinking, love-making, and speech-making, which men and women in Australia have told me of themselves, would have been worth recording in a separate volume, had they been related by any but the heroes and heroines themselves. But reaching one as they do always in the first person, these stories are soon received as works of a fine art much cultivated in the colonies, for which the general phrase of 'blowing' has been created. When a gentleman sounds his own trumpet, he 'blows.' The art is perfectly understood and appreciated among those who practise it . . . They blow a good deal in Queensland; – a good deal in South Australia. They blow even in poor Tasmania. They blow loudly in New South Wales, and very loudly in New Zealand. But the blast of the trumpet as heard in Victoria is louder than all the blasts, – and the Melbourne blast beats all the other blowing of that proud colony. My first, my constant, my parting advice to my Australian cousins is contained in two words – 'Don't blow.'

Anthony Trollope, *Australia and New Zealand*, 1873

A community of speculators, overlying convicts.

Unidentified evening paper, quoted by H.E. Watts, *Orient Line Guide*, 1885

The average Australian boy is a cheeky brat with a leaning towards larrikinism, a craving for cigarettes, and no ambition beyond the cricket and football field; he regards his parents with contempt, takes it for granted that his mother mostly talks nonsense or 'rot' when she talks to him – and he doesn't always hesitate to tell her so.

The average Australian youth is a weedy individual with a weak, dirty, and contemptible vocabulary, and a cramped mind devoted to sport; his god is a two-legged brute with unnaturally developed muscles and no brains.

The average Australian man has not been developed yet.

Henry Lawson, *Our Countrymen*, 1893

. . . met my friend Harry Brand, just back from Australia, where he has been Governor of a colony. He found it dull work among people without literature, art, or culture of any kind, except a taste for bad music.

Wilfred Scawen Blunt, Diary, 18 May 1899, *My Diaries*, 1919

'Tis the duty of Australians, in the bush and in the town
To for ever praise their country but to run no other down;
Not to start at every nothing with the boast that bluffs and halts
But to love their young Australia and explain away her faults . . .

We can worship foreign talent – give our money, hearts and hands
While we send our own, embittered, to win bread in foreign lands.
We are great to men who pedal, men who kick or bat the ball
While our duty to the stranger is Australia's over all . . .

'Tis our duty when he's foreign, and his English very young,
To find out and take him somewhere where he'll hear his native tongue

To give him our last spare moment, and our pleasures to defer –
He'll be father of Australians, as our foreign fathers were!

Henry Lawson, *The Duty of Australians*, 1909

The Anzacs of the First World War

. . . the finest body of young men ever brought together in modern times. For physical beauty and nobility of bearing they surpassed any men I have ever seen; they walked and looked like kings in old poems, and reminded me of a line in Shakespeare:

'Baited like eagles having lately bathed.'

. . . there was no thought of surrender in these marvellous young men; they were the flower of the world's manhood, and died as they had lived, owning no master on this earth.

John Masefield, *Gallipoli*, 1916

Australians have sought average satisfaction for average people – an excellent aim which becomes delusive only when it is pretended that the average is 'divine'. They have said, 'Seek ye first a high standard of comfort, and the Kingdom of God shall be added unto you.' What they have really wanted is the high standard of comfort. Perhaps Tocqueville was right when he reflected that democratic nations 'will cultivate the arts which make life easy, in preference to the arts whose object is to adorn it.'

Sir Keith Hancock, *Australia*, 1930

Far in the South, beyond the burning line,
Where Gulliver, that much-wrecked mariner,
Described their customs, such as then they were,
And found them, like their manners, somewhat coarse,
The yahoos live in slavery to the horse.
And since, though little altered from that time,
Great Britain gave them trade and beer and crime
And politics and healthy out-door games,
Now they wear clothes, and some can write their names.
A sort of costive English, too, they speak,
And sweat, and drink, and quarrel round the week;
And what they earn in their own time they spend
On their four-footed masters each week-end.

A.D. Hope, *Dunciad Minor, An Heroick Poem*, Book i, pub. 1970

What has happened to the spirit, the gusto, the faith? The twentieth century seems to have tamed and deadened and cheapened the Australian character. The frustrated old man's lament – an old head on young shoulders – has come to unnatural life. The Wild Colonial Boy is selling used cars.

Robin Boyd, *Australia's Home*, 1952

But perhaps the majority (i.e. male) Australian approach to articulation is best indicated by a generalisation: utterance is better not done at all; but, if it is done, when it is done, it were well it were done slowly and flatly and expressionlessly, to betoken that the subject, any subject, is hardly worth talking about.

Brian Fitzpatrick, *The Australian Commonwealth*, 1956

We Australians often display a certain queasiness in recalling our founding fathers.

Russell Ward, *The Australian Legend*, 1958

Nordic Man's inborn honesty is not, I suppose, greater in Australia than it is in his original habitat; but in Australia, if he does turn predatory, he preys on the shark's scale and not on the parrot fish's.

Arnold Toynbee, *East to West*, 1958

The Australian story is something like a fun-fair. The same things happen again and again. Ferris wheels go round and round, hurdy-gurdies grind out the same tunes, swings and see-saws move up and down. Everyone appears to have something to spend. Worries are left behind and troubles are forgotten. People press from one sideshow to another, eager to sample everything. The biggest crowds throng around the lucky dips where anyone may draw a winning ticket. From outside the scene appears featureless and dull. The shouts and laughter are too carefree and light-hearted. Apart from the showmen no one seems more important than anyone else. What is the purpose of it all? How can a fun-fair give a young nation an inspiring history?

Douglas Pike, *Australia, The Quiet Continent*, 1962

It is often said that Scandinavians find the achievement of plenty linked with mediocrity, and a general absence of extremes, so dull that many of them either take to drink or commit suicide. Australians are more apt to commit smugness.

Elspeth Huxley, *Their Shining Eldorado*, 1967

The question of whether any Australians today have convict ancestry is now somewhat academic. If they have, it is a most encouraging sign for the future of the human race.

John Fisher, *The Australians*, 1968

If you find an Australian indoors, it's a fair bet that he will have a glass in his hand.

Jonathan Aitken, *Land of Fortune*, 1971

Aborigines

The Hodmadods of Monomatapa, though a nasty People, yet for wealth are Gentlemen to these.

William Dampier, *A New Voyage Round the World*, 1697 – of 1688

What their absolute colour is, is difficult to say, they

were so completely covered with dirt, which seemed to have stuck to their hides from the day of their birth, without their once having attempted to remove it. I tried indeed by spitting upon my finger and rubbing, but altered the colour very little, which as nearly as might be resembled chocolate.

Sir Joseph Banks, *Journal of the Rt Hon. Sir Joseph Banks*, 1768–71 (1770)

They may appear to some to be the most wretched people upon Earth, but in reality they are far more happier than we Europeans; being wholly unacquainted not only with the superfluous but the necessary Conveniences so much sought after in Europe, they are happy in not knowing the use of them. They live in a Tranquillity which is not disturb'd by the Inequality of Condition: The Earth and sea of their own accord furnishes them with all things necessary for life, they covet not Magnificent Houses Household-stuff &c, they live in a warm and fine Climate and enjoy a very wholsome air, so that they have very little need of Clothing and this they seem to be fully sencible of, for many to whom we gave Cloth &c to, left it carelessly upon the Sea-beach and in the woods as a thing they had no manner of use for. In short they seemed to set no Value upon any thing we gave them, nor would they ever part with any thing of their own for any one article we could offer them; this in my opinion argues that they think themselves provided with all the necessarys of Life and that they have no superfluities.

Captain James Cook, *Journal*, August 1770

The women suffer'd every part to be examined without the least appearance of bashfulness, and the men absolutely play with their Penis as a child would with any bauble or a man twirl about the key of his watch, while conversing with you. Their manner of making the natural evacuations also show that they are either destitute of all sense of shame or at least that they are under no restraint amongst each other, for the men never changed their posture on making water and would sometimes not move their legs out of the way but suffer the Urine to run down upon them.

William Anderson, *Journals*, 29 January 1777

I would walk thirty miles to see a stuffed one

Mark Twain, *More Tramps Abroad*, 1897

Aborigines, *n.* Persons of little worth found cumbering the soil of a newly discovered country. They soon cease to cumber; they fertilize.

Ambrose Bierce, *The Cynic's Word Book*, 1906

An Aboriginal's luck starts to run out on the day he is born.

Jonathan Aitken, *Land of Fortune*, 1971

Cities

Australians themselves have a saying that when a stranger arrives in Perth, the first question he is asked is, 'Where do you come from?'; in Adelaide, 'What church do you belong to?'; in Melbourne, 'What school were you at?'; in Sydney, 'How much money have you got?'; while in Brisbane they merely say. 'Come and have a drink.'

John Douglas Pringle, *Australian Accent*, 1958

Compared with their own past relations to each other Brisbane falls backwards, Sydney falls apart, Melbourne moves forward to stay where it is, Adelaide goes ahead.

Donald Horne, *The Lucky Country*, 1964

Adelaide

Adelaide takes a lot of pride in the purity of its origins. This was not a penal settlement so there were never any convicts here. No Irish settlers ever came here and there was no invasion of American servicemen to corrupt us here during the war. You see, Adelaide was founded by, and is still run by, a lot of religious Scotsmen – when I said that to an American visitor the other day he interrupted me with, 'Good God – not as bad as that!'

Sir Thomas Playford, former Premier of South Australia, quoted by Jonathan Aitken, *Land of Fortune*, 1971

Alice Springs

I was taken to Alice Springs which I wanted to see because it was so isolated. It was a centre for agriculture and inhabited chiefly by sheep owners. I was shown a fine gaol where I was assured that the cells were comfortable. In reply to my query as to why, I was told: 'Oh, because all the leading citizens at one time or another are in gaol.' I was told that, expectedly and regularly, whenever possible, they stole each others' sheep.

Bertrand Russell, *Autobiography*, 1969 – of 1950

Alice – small though it may be – is a lovable town, with a sharp profile and marked personality, so rare among Australian towns. The place has a charm and atmosphere quite of its own. Alice Springs was the second place in Australia where I felt: this is an indigenous growth, a true Australian town belonging to Australia alone which could not be anywhere else. (The second place, you notice: nothing will induce me to say whether Sydney or Melbourne was the first.)

George Mikes, *Boomerang – Australia Rediscovered*, 1968

Ballarat

Ballarat . . . struck me with more surprise than any other city in Australia. It is not only its youth . . . but that a town so well built, so well ordered, endowed with present advantages so great in the way of schools, hospitals, libraries, hotels, public gardens, and the like, should have sprung up so quickly, with no internal advantages of its own other than that of gold. The town is very pleasant to the sight, which is, perhaps, more than can be said for any other 'provincial' town in the Australian colonies.

Anthony Trollope, *Australia and New Zealand*, 1873

Barrier Reef

So cook made choice, so Cook sailed westabout,
So men write poems in Australia.

II

Flowers turned to stone! Not all the botany
Of Joseph Banks, hung pensive in a porthole,
Could find the Latin for this loveliness,
Could put the Barrier reef in a glass box
Tagged by the horid Gorgon squint
Of horticulture. Stone turned to flowers
It seemed – you'd snap a crystal twig,
One petal even of the water-garden
And have it dying like a cherry-bough.

They'd sailed all day outside a coral hedge,
And half the night . . .

Kenneth Slessor, 'Five Visions of Captain Cook' in *One Hundred Poems*, 1944

Broken Hill

After many years Providence, desiring to show regard for New South Wales, and to exhibit a loving interest in its welfare which should certify to all nations the recognition of that colony's conspicuous righteousness and distinguished well-deserving, conferred upon it that treasury of inconceivable riches, Broken Hill; and South Australia went over the border and took it, giving thanks.

Mark Twain, *More Tramps Abroad*, 1897

Broken Hill is not just a closed shop but a closed city.

Elspeth Huxley, *Their Shining Eldorado*, 1967

Blue Mountains/Great Dividing Range

Accurately named. 'My word?' as the Australians say, but it was a stunning colour, that blue. Deep, strong, rich, exquisite; towering and majestic masses of blue – a softly luminous blue, a smouldering blue, as if vaguely lit by fires within. It extinguished the blue of the sky – made it pallid and unwholesome, whitey, and washed out. A wonderful colour – just divine.

A resident told me that those were not mountains; he said they were rabbit-piles; and explained that long exposure and the over-ripe condition of the rabbits was what made them look so blue. The man may have been right, but reading of books of travel has made me distrustful of gratis information furnished by unofficial residents of a country.

Mark Twain, *More Tramps Abroad*, 1897

The Outback / Bush Country

A poor dried-up land afflicted only by fever and flies.

Matthew Flinders, *Voyage to Terra Australis 1801–3*, 1814

'Sunny plains!' Great Scott! – those burning wastes of barren soil and sand
With their everlasting fences stretching out across the land!
Desolation where the crow is! Desert where the eagle flies
Paddocks where the luny bullock starts and stares with reddened eyes;
Where, in clouds of dust enveloped, roasted bullock-drivers creep
Slowly past the sun dried shepherd dragged behind his crawling sheep.
Stunted peak of granite gleaming, glaring like a molten mass
Turned from some infernal furnace on a plain devoid of grass . . .
Bush! where there is no horizon! where the buried bushman sees
Nothing – Nothing! but the sameness of the ragged stunted trees!
Lonely hut where drought's eternal – suffocating atmosphere –
Where the God-forgotten hatter dreams of city life and beer . . .
Land of day and night – no morning freshness and no afternoon
When the great white sun in rising brings the summer heat in June
Dismal country for the exile, when the shades begin to fall
From the sad heart-breaking sunset, to the new chum worst of all . . .

Henry Lawson, *Up the Country*, 1892

By homestead, hut and shearing-shed
  By railroad, coach, and track –
By lonely graves where rest our dead,
  Up-country and Out-Back.
To where beneath the clustered stars
  The dreamy plains expand –
My home lies wide a thousand miles
  In the Never-Never Land.

Henry Lawson, *The Never-Never Land*, 1901

Out on the wastes of the Never Never –
That's where the dead men lie!

There where the heat waves dance for ever –
That's where the dead men lie! . . .
Where brown Summer and Death have mated –
That's where the dead men lie! . . .
Moneygrub, as he sips his claret,
Looks with complacent eye,
Down at his watch-chain, eighteen carat –
There, in his club, hard by
Recks not that every link is stamped with
Names of the men whose limbs are cramped with
Death where the dead men lie.

Bancroft Henry Boake, *Where the Dead Men Lie*, 1913

Fremantle

Fremantle is the least attractive of ports. You are not meant to stay there. You are meant to go on to Perth . . . It struck me as being . . . rather like a Russian provincial town; this is not odd, because Russia is a country of colonists.

Maurice Baring, *Round the World in any Number of Days*, 1913

Hobart

Man's love first found me; man's hate made me Hell;
  For my babes' sake I cleansed those infamies.
Earnest for leave to live and labour well,
  God flung me peace and ease.

Rudyard Kipling, *The Song of the Cities*, 1893

It was at Hobart that we struck the head of the procession of Junior Englands. We were to encounter other sections of it in New Zealand, presently, and others later in Natal. Wherever the exiled Englishman can find in his new home resemblances to his old one, he is touched, to the marrow of his being; the love that is in his heart inspires his imagination, and these allied forces transfigure those resemblances into authentic duplicates of the revered originals. It is beautiful, the feeling which works this enchantment, and it compels one's homage; compels it, and also compels one's assent – compels it always – even when, as happens sometimes, one does not see the resemblances as clearly as does the exile who is pointing them out.

Mark Twain, *More Tramps Abroad*, 1897

Launceston, Tasmania

Launceston is built in a broad hollow between two hills, sloping down to the Tamar. It is like a quiet, decent, English country town.

Thomas Arnold, Letter to Jane Arnold, 13 January 1850

Launceston is another of those Betjeman towns with which Australia is so well endowed. Victoriana is everywhere. Buildings in alternate layers of cream and liver-red like a Neapolitan ice, their waywardly pitched roofs flounced with ornament and frilled with scrolls; balconies also full of scroll-work; tortured brick, unexpected turrets, multi-coloured tiles, heavy colonnades, thick vaulted doorways, potted palms in dark lobbies; an overgrown English country town. The narrowish streets are packed with people, the women mostly wearing gloves.

Elspeth Huxley, *Their Shining Eldorado*, 1967

Melbourne

Imagine a huge chessboard flung on to the earth, and you have what is the true and characteristic Melbourne.

Francis Adams, *The Australians*, 1893

Greeting! Nor fear nor favour won us place,
  Got between greed of gold and dread of drouth,
Loud-voiced and reckless as the wild tide-race
  That whips our harbour-mouth!

Rudyard Kipling, *The Song of the Cities*, 1893

Sometimes in dreams the fancy creates a composite, coloured photograph of a town, a place, or a house. The dreamer notices the difference of the component parts, but accepts the whole as correct . . . So it was to a certain degree with my impression of Melbourne. I saw it as a huge city in the Midlands of England, or the Five Towns, but the buildings were more perpendicular, the streets more rectangular, all was larger and more symmetrical, and there was a multitude of tramcars.

But these large, tall, black, square buildings were set in a soft, tepid, luminous air: pearly pink and grey . . . unlike anything in modern Europe – a dreamlike contrast.

When the fancy creates a place it forgets the necessary changes in background: air, sky and light. This is true of dreams . . .

Maurice Baring, *Round the World in Any Number of Days*, 1913

Lord Northcliffe was asked what impressions he had formed during his stay in Melbourne. 'One of the most striking things I have noticed,' said he, 'is the amazing tallness of the people. At the reception given to me by the newspaper proprietors I felt like a dwarf among giants. There were some tremendous men there. Why, look at your Lord Mayor, Councillor Swanson. What height is he? I should certainly say that you have the biggest Lord Mayor in the Empire. Yet he is quite small compared to some of the men I have met.'

Alfred Viscount Northcliffe, Interview in *Melbourne Herald*, 16 September 1921, quoted from *My Journey Round the World*, 1923

It is very Parisian.

Ibid.

One of the stock Sydney jokes is of the census-taker who enquired; 'How many children have you, ma'am?' 'Two living and three in Melbourne.'

Elspeth Huxley, *Their Shining Eldorado*, 1967

The Yarra River (Melbourne)
The Yarra, . . . Melbournians will tell you is the only river in the world that runs upside down – it looks so brown and muddy.

Elspeth Huxley, *Their Shining Eldorado*, 1967

Toorak (Melbourne)
Sing a song of Melbourne
Money by the sack
Twenty thousand squatters
Squatting in Toorak

Heaven all around them
Hear the angels sing
Strictly no admittance here
God save The King!

'A former vice chancellor of Melbourne University', quoted Jonathan Aitken, *Land of Fortune*, 1971

If Queen Victoria were still alive, not only would she approve of Melbourne, she would probably feel more at home there than in any other city of her former Empire.

Jonathan Aitken, *Land of Fortune*, 1971

New South Wales

On the whole, from what I heard, more than what I saw, I was disappointed in the state of society. The whole community is rancorously divided into parties on almost every subject. Among those, who from their station in life ought to be the best, many live in such open profligacy that respectable people cannot associate with them. There is much jealousy between the children of the rich emancipist, and the free settlers, the former being pleased to consider honest men as interlopers. The whole population, poor and rich, are bent on acquiring wealth: amongst the higher orders, wool and sheep-grazing form the constant subject of conversation. There are many serious drawbacks to the comfort of a family, the chief of which, perhaps, is being surrounded by convict servants.

Charles Darwin, *Journal . . . During the Voyage . . . of H.M.S. Beagle*, 1832–6

The number of sheep at these stations will generally indicate with fair accuracy the mode of life at the head station. A hundred thousand sheep and upwards require a professed man-cook and a butler to look after them; forty thousand sheep cannot be shorn without a piano; twenty thousand is the lowest number that renders napkins at dinner imperative. Ten thousand require absolute plenty, meat in plenty, tea in plenty, brandy and water and colonial wine in plenty, but do not expect champagne, sherry, or made dishes, and are supposed to be content with continued mutton or continued beef – as the squatter may at the time be in the way of killing sheep or oxen.

Anthony Trollope, *Australia and New Zealand*, 1873

It is a country that is rich in mines, wool-ranches, trams, railways, steam-ship lines, schools, newspapers, botanical gardens, art galleries, libraries, museums, hospitals, learned societies; it is the hospitable home of every species of culture and of every species of material enterprise, and there is a church at every man's door and a race-track over the way.

Mark Twain, *More Tramps Abroad*, 1897

Perth

Most cities use the rivers on which they lie primarily as highways and sewers. Perth is the only modern city I can recall that puts first the uses of embellishment, as Venice must once have done.

Elspeth Huxley, *Their Shining Eldorado*, 1967

Attitudes die hard . . . not only in the East. A new friend told me in Perth: 'What do you mean by saying that we were not a convict settlement? We are a convict-settlement even today. Easterners dump their rejects on us. The days of colonization are not over yet. The rest of Australia is becoming a colony of America and Japan. Why, they say that even the Church of England is being replaced by the Church of America. But *we* are not in danger, we won't become a colony of America and Japan. We are going to remain a colony of the rest of Australia!

George Mikes, *Boomerang – Australia Rediscovered*, 1968

Port Headland

Breaking a glass in the north-west is rather like belching in Arabia, for it appears to be done as a mark of appreciation or elation. In Port Headland, happiness comes smithereen-shaped.

Jonathan Aitken, *Land of Fortune*, 1971

Queensland

The countrey tho in general well enough clothd, appeared in some places bare; it reesembled in my imagination the back of a lean Cow, covered in general with long hair, but nevertheless where her scraggy hip bones have stuck out farther than they ought, accidental rubbs and knocks have intirely bard them of their share of covering.

Sir Joseph Banks, *Journal*, 25 April 1770

The subject of heat is one of extreme delicacy in Queensland, as indeed it is also in the other colonies. One does not allude to heat in a host's house any more than to a bad bottle of wine or an ill-cooked joint of meat. You may remark that it is very cool in your friend's verandah, your friend of the moment being present, and may hint that the whole of your absent friend's establishment is as hot as a furnace; but though you be constrained to keep your handkerchief to your brow, and hardly dare to walk to the garden gate, you must never complain of the heat then and there. You may call an inn hot, or a court-house, but not a gentleman's paddock, or a lady's drawing-room. And you should never own to a musquito.

Anthony Trollope, *Australia and New Zealand*, 1873

Rockhampton

Rockhampton . . . is so hot that people going from it to an evil place are said to send back to earth for their blankets, finding that evil place to be too chilly for them after the home they have left.

Anthony Trollope, *Australia and New Zealand*, 1873

Sydney

Where Sydney Cove her lucid bosom swells,
And with wide arms the indignant storm repels;
High on a rock amid the troubled air
Hope stood sublime, and waves her golden hair; . . .
'Hear me,' she cried, 'ye rising realms! record
Time's opening scenes, and Truth's prophetic word.–
There shall broad streets their stately walls extend,
The circus widen and the crescent bend;
There, ray'd from cities o'er the cultured land,
Shall bright canals and solid roads expand.–

There the proud arch, colossus-like bestride
Yon glittering streams, and bound the chafing tide;
Embellish'd villas crown the landscape-scene.
Farms wave with gold, and orchards blush between.–
There shall tall spires, and dome-capt towers ascend,
And piers and quays their massy structures blend;
While with each breeze approaching vessels glide,
And northern treasures dance on every tide!' –
Then ceased the nymph – tumultuous echoes roar,
And Joy's loud voice was heard from shore to shore –
Her grateful steps descending press'd the plain,
And Peace, and Art, and Labour, join'd her train.

Erasmus Darwin, *Visit of Hope to Sidney Cove*, near Botany Bay, written to accompany Wedgwood's Medallions made from clay from Sydney Cove, 1789

In the evening I walked through the town, and returned full of admiration for the whole scene. It is a most magnificent testimony to the power of the British nation. Here, in a less promising country, scores of years have done many times more than an equal number of centuries have effected in South America. My first feeling was to congratulate myself that I was born an Englishman. Upon seeing more of the town afterwards, perhaps my admiration fell a little; but yet it is a fine town.

Charles Darwin, *Journal . . . During the Voyage . . . of H.M.S. Beagle*, 1832–6

There is something of shame-facedness, a confession of provincial weakness, almost an acknowledgement that they ought not to be proud of a thing so insignificant, in the tone in which you are asked whether, upon the whole, you do not think Sydney Harbour rather pretty. Every Sydney man and every Sydney woman does ask you the question, . . . but it is asked in Sydney with bated breath, and with something of an apology, 'Of course you have been bothered out of your life about our harbour; – but it is pretty, don't you think so?' It is so inexpressibly lovely that it makes a man ask himself whether it would not be worth his while to move his household goods to the eastern coast of Australia, in order that he might look at it as long as he can look at anything.

Anthony Trollope, *Australia and New Zealand*, 1873

Greeting! My birth-stain have I turned to good;
  Forcing strong wills perverse to steadfastness:
The first flush of the tropics in my blood,
  And at my feet Success!

Rudyard Kipling, *The Song of the Cities*, 1893

'It is beautiful, of course it's beautiful – the harbour; but that isn't all of it, it's only half of it; Sydney's the other half, and it takes both of them together to ring the supremacy-bell. God made the harbour, and that's all right, but Satan made Sydney.'

Citizen of Sydney, quoted by Mark Twain, *More Tramps Abroad*, 1897

Sydney, that's set in beauty
  Sydney with health aglow –
No glimmering sense of duty
  To the great land that made her so –
In one thing standing lonely
  (To sum up the bitter whole)
Not the most soulless – *the only*
  City without a soul . . .
She has had her years to learn wisdom
  Great chances to rise or fall –
She, of Australian cities
  The least Australian of all!
Greedy, luxurious, corrupting
  Her sisters one by one –

She must take the fifth place humbly
For her Octopus days are done.

Henry Lawson, *The Spirit of Sydney*, 1910

*Night came on, and Somers sat on his tub of a summer-house looking at the lights glittering in the various hollows down to the water, and the light-houses flashing in the distance, and ship lights on the water, and the dark places thinly sprinkled with lights. It wasn't like a town, it was like a whole country with towns and bays and darknesses. And all lying mysteriously within the Australian underdark, that peculiar lost, weary aloofness of Australia. There was the vast town of Sydney. And it didn't seem to be real, it seemed to be sprinkled on the surface of a darkness into which it never penetrated.

D.H. Lawrence, *Kangaroo*, 1923

*It was all London without being London. Without any of the lovely old glamour that invests London. This London of the Southern Hemisphere was all, as it were, made in five minutes, a substitute for the real thing. Just a substitute – as margarine is a substitute for butter.

Ibid.

My impression of Australia is that there is too much amusement here. We have nothing like it at home.

Alfred Viscount Northcliffe, *My Journey Round the World* (September 1921), 1923

Sydney is exactly like Manchester except that you have the Pacific Ocean at the bottom of Market Street instead of the Irwell.

Neville Cardus, Remark, 1952

It's part San Francisco. A bit of England. The flavor of New York.

Airline Advertisement, 1980

Sydney Harbour
. . . The finest harbour in the world . . .

Captain Arthur Philip, *The Voyage of Governor Philip to Botany Bay*, 1790 – of c. 1788

Sydney Opera House
The greatest public-relations building since the pyramids.

Billy Wentworth, Sydney MP and minister, quoted Jonathan Aitken, *Land of Fortune*, 1971

It is like nuns in a rugger scrum.

Anon.

Tasmania

Now the Tasmanians declare themselves to be ruined, and are not slow to let a stranger know that the last new name given to the island is that of 'Sleepy Hollow.' When the stranger asks the reason of this ruin, he is told that all the public money has gone with the convicts, and that – the rabbits have eaten up all the grass. The rabbits, like the sheep, have been imported from Europe, and the rabbits have got ahead of the sheep. 'If it was not that this is Sleepy Hollow,' they say, 'we should stir ourselves and get rid of the rabbits. But it is Sleepy Hollow, and so we don't.'

Anthony Trollope, *Australia and New Zealand*, 1873

You know, of course, that the Tasmanians, who never committed adultery, are now extinct.

W. Somerset Maugham, *The Bread-Winner*, 1930

Tasmania, of course, gave up any idea of seceding from Australia; perhaps because it has, in fact, seceded. It did not secede politically . . . Tasmania seceded first of all geologically.

George Mikes, *Boomerang – Australia Rediscovered*, 1968

Mount Wellington, near Hobart

Mount Wellington, nearly 5000 feet high, is just enough of a mountain to give excitement to ladies and gentlemen in middle life.

Anthony Trollope, *Australia and New Zealand*, 1873

Western Australia

An ingenious, but sarcastic Yankee, when asked what he thought of Western Australia, declared that it was the best country he had ever seen to run through an hour-glass.

Anthony Trollope, *Australia and New Zealand*, 1873

Come to Western Australia. Relax in a State of Excitement.

Tourist slogan for the state, quoted by Minister of Tourism for Western Australia on the BBC *World at One* programme, 12 July 1979

West Point – Tasmania

The main reason we need a casino here is to keep the boys and girls out of real trouble. In some of these quiet sleepy little villages they're shockers! Not only do we have the highest illegitimacy rate in Australia, we have incest, sodomy, rape by 12-year-old boys, – the lot. These larrikins get up to some stuff, my word they do. The sooner a bit of modern progress cools them off a bit the better.

West Point hotel manager, quoted Jonathan Aitken, *Land of Fortune*, 1971

AUSTRIA

Habsburg Empire

Bella Gerant alii; tu, felix Austria, nube:
Nam quae Mars aliis, dat tibi regna Venus,

(Fight those who will, let well-starred Austria wed,
And conquer kingdoms in the marriage-bed.)

Sometimes attributed to Matthias Corvinus of Hungary, d. 1490, but probably sixteenth century. Quoted and translated in Sir William Stirling Maxwell, *Cloister Life of Charles V*, 1852

and the Orient
Östlich von Wien, fängt der Orient an.
East of Vienna, the orient begins.

Prince Metternich, attrib.

Pure Austria too – whose hist'ry nought repeats
But broken leagues and subsidiz'd defeats.

Thomas Moore, *The Fudge Family in Paris*, 1818

O daughter of pride, wasted with misery
  With all the glory that thy shame put on
  Stripped of thy shame, O daughter of Babylon.
Yea, whose be it, yea, happy shall he be,
That as thou hast served us hath rewarded thee.
  Blessed, who throweth against war's boundary stone
  Thy warrior brood, and breaketh bone by bone
Misrule thy son, thy daughter Tyranny.
That landmark shalt thou not remove for shame,
  But sitting down there in a widow's weed
Wail: for what fruit is now of thy red flame?
  Have thy sons too and daughters learnt indeed
  What thing it is to weep, what thing to bleed?
Is it not thou that now art but a name.

A.C. Swinburne, 'The Burden of Austria', 1866, *Songs of Two Nations*

I left Austria with feelings of utter disgust and dislike. They are a stupid, stolid, disobliging grasping lot. There is no place in the world where you pay so high and get so little, even of common politeness, in return, as in Germany.

Lilian Leland, *Travelling Alone, A Woman's Journey Round the World*, 1890

The situation in Germany is serious but not hopeless; the situation in Austria is hopeless but not serious.

Viennese saying, 1930s

The Old Hapsburg Empire – Pola and Istria
I hate this Catholic country with its hundred races and thousand languages, governed by a parliament which can transact no business and sits for a week at the most, and by the most physically corrupt royal house in Europe. Pola is a back-of-God-speed place – a naval Siberia – 37 men o' war in the harbour, swarming with faded uniforms. Istria is a long boring place wedged into the Adriatic peopled by ignorant Slavs who wear little red caps and colossal breeches.

James Joyce, Letter to Mrs William Murray, 1904

Austria is queer – seems to have gone quite void. It's like being at the centre of a vital vacuum. The people are healthy, rather handsome, and don't seem to care about a thing – a void, where caring is concerned. Most queer! But the peasants look unpleasant and stink of greed. – This queer vacuum is the centre of Europe. I wonder what wind will whirl in to fill it up . . . California on a small scale. *L'ideale del vuoto.*

D.H. Lawrence, Letter to Mabel Luhan, Villach, 25 August 1927

The chief crop of provincial Austria is – scenery.

John Gunther, *Inside Europe*, 1938 edn

Austria is Switzerland, speaking pure German and with history added.

J.E. Morpugo, *The Road to Athens*, 1963

Little Austria, a torso from which all four limbs have been amputated, is running merrily about in its self-propelled invalid chair.

Arthur Koestler, 'The Lion and the Ostrich', *Encounter*, July 1963

Over the centuries Austria has produced more than its share of historical events.

Travel Advertisement, 1980

We practise active neutrality.

Chancellor Bruno Kreisky, attrib.

Austrians

It is not from Austria that one can write with vivacity, and I am already infected with the Phlegm of the Country. Even their Amours and their Quarrels are carry'd on with a surprizing temper, and they are never lively but upon points of ceremony. There, I own, they shew all their passions.

Lady Mary Wortley Montagu, Letter to Mrs T . . . 1, 26 September 1716

The Austrian youth of rank or condition are in general insupportable. Distinguished only by pride, ignorance, and illiberality; regarding themselves as superior to every other European nation, because their sovereign is titular head of the German Empire; altogether destitute of improvement, commonly haughty and assuming;

they want equally the inclination and the requisites to be agreeable in society . . . They imitate the French manners; but possess neither the urbanity, the vivacity, nor the elegant levity of France. Though coxcombs, they are not amusing ones, and in cultivation of mind they are totally deficient.

Sir N.W. Wraxall, *Memoirs of the Courts of Berlin*, etc., 1779

The Austrians do not appear to me to have that decided national character of countenance which I had expected. I do not remark the thick upper lip – &c. The Mixture of Hungarians have crossed the breed.

Washington Irving, *Journal*, 1822

Czernowitz

He then recounted what the theatre meant to him in his native town, (Czernowitz, Eastern Austria) when he was a schoolboy. He said it coloured his whole life. They did everything very badly, and he saw everything. He said: 'couldn't *walk* to that theatre. I had to run there.'

Czernowitz is a small town, but it had a municipal Academy of Music, and the Director of the Academy wrote a serious opera. Nobody outside Czernowitz wanted to produce it; but Czernowitz wanted to produce it, and did. After the first performance (or the 2nd or 3rd) the Burgomaster came onto the stage amid terrific applause and presented to the composer 1,000 gold ducats in the name of the town. Fancy such a thing in England!

Arnold Bennett, *Journal*, 17 July 1925, quoting Rudolf Kommer

Durrenstein

The old castle of Durnstein where Richard Coeur de Leon was confined. I suppose you know the romantic story of his captivity; . . . [the castle] is built round the very peak of a high craggy rock, among stern dark mountains, and gloomy forests; with the Danube sweeping along below it. In one part of the ruins is the sweetest dark dungeon you can imagine; cut out of the solid rock; in which I'll warrant Richard was often put on bread and water, when he happened to be a little restive. I never saw a finer castle for a heroine to be confined in, or a ghost to haunt . . .

Washington Irving, Letter to Susan Storrow, 10 November 1822

Mayerling

Mayerling . . . is an absolute waste of time.

Charles Graves, *The Rich Man's Guide to Europe*, 1966

Salzburg

The inhabitants of the city have a most whimsical custom (I mean those who have the means of satisfying their caprice); when in good health and spirits, they fix on their future burial-places, and having selected snug and suitable spots, have their portraits painted, and placed over their graves; to me it seemed as if this absurdity could not be surpassed.

Michael Kelly, *Reminiscences*, 1826

The scenery around is wonderful. There must be about a dozen 10,000ft. mountains in the region. But we soon tired of this imposing, picturesque scenery. It is as if it was done on purpose – some *tour de force* of a creator.

Arnold Bennett, *Journal*, 15 July 1925

As well as changing the entire world for the better, the advent of Wolfgang Amadeus Mozart came as close as anything in recent times to modifying the static perfection of Salzburg's architecture. Every second building now sports an elaborate plaque identifying it as the site of his birth, or of his wife's sister's death, or of his mother's brother's nephew's friend's dachshund's first litter.

Mozart's departure, which occurred soon after his arrival, was the last event for a long time. During the nineteenth century, Salzburg's main achievement was to become, at long last, part of Austria. Meanwhile boredom thinned the population by 75 per cent. Salzburg was becoming an empty theatre.

Clive James, 'Postcard from Salzburg', *Observer*, 21 October 1979

Semmering

All around Semmering there are mountain peaks. On every peak there has been placed a pimple – a chapel, a Kaiserstein, a monastery, a cable-railway station. Cable-railways and chair-lifts move up and down the steepest mountain-sides with the legless motion of slow spiders. Man is everywhere. Sometimes, mother-loving, it looks as though he must put a nipple on every white breast pointing Godwards: sometimes, more patriarchally, he sets up a steeple to mark the skywish of his curious spirit. Whether this merits applause or the dunce's cap is debatable: what cannot be doubted is the achievement itself, whatever the motives are.

William Sansom, *Blue Skies, Brown Studies*, 1961

Styria (now in part Yugoslavian)

As much as the Country is agreeable in its Wildness; as much are the Inhabitants savage & deform'd & monstrous in their Appearance. Very many of them have ugly swelld Throats: Idiots & Deaf People swarm in every Village; & the general Aspect of the People is the most shocking I ever saw. One wou'd think, that as this was the great Road, thro which all the barbarous Nations made their Irruptions into the Roman Empire, they always left here the Refuse of their Armies before they entered into the Enemies Country; and that from thence the present Inhabitants are descended. Their dress is scarce European as their Figure is scarce human.

David Hume, Letter to John Home of Ninewells, 28 April 1748

Tyrol

The country is wonderful. Mountains holding up cups of snow to the fiery sun, who glares on them in vain. The peasantry are a noble race; pious, and with a strong smell . . . Meran is southern in heat and luxury of growth of all kinds of fruits. The cicada goes all day like a factory wheel – poetic simile! The flies sting, and the sun is relentless. I begin to understand why Daphne fled into a laurel from the fiery fellow. Still, I like the sun, as you do. This land abounds in falling waters, brooks, torrents, all ice cold. We drank at the wells every ten minutes, sat over the brooks naked legged, dipped our heads desperately. There are crucifixes at every fifty yards. You go to a well and the pipe through which the water flows is through the body of a Christ. Hear you a droning noise on the wind, it issues from a body of peasants mumbling their rosaries as they march to work.

George Meredith, Letter to Frederick A. Maxse, 26 July 1861

Vienna

Wien the metropolitan City of Austria, is a famous fort against the Turkes. . . . It is dangerous to walke the streetes in the night, for the great number of disordered people, which are easily found upon any confines, especially where such an army lieth neere, as that of Hungary, governed by no strict discipline.

Fynes Moryson, *An Itinerary*, 1617

The streets are very close and so narrow one cannot observe the fine fronts of the Palaces, tho many of them very well deserve observations, being truly magnificent, all built of fine white stone and excessive high. The Town being so much too little for the number of the people that desire to live in it, the Builders seem to have projected to repair that misfortune by claping one Town on the top of another, most of the houses being of 5 and some of them of 6 storys. You may easily imagine that the streets being so narrow, the upper rooms are extream Dark, and what is an inconveniency much more intolerable in my Opinion, there is no house that has so few as 5 or 6 familys in it. The Apartments of the greatest Ladys and even of the Ministers of state are divided but by a Partition from that of a Tailor or a shoe-maker, . . . Those that have houses of their own let out the rest of them to whoever will take 'em; thus the great stairs (which are all of stone) are as common and as dirty as the street. 'Tis true when you have once travelled through them, nothing can be more surprizingly magnificent than the Apartments. They are commonly a suitte of 8 or 10 large rooms, all inlaid, the doors and windows richly carved and Gilt, and the furniture such as is seldom seen in the Palaces of sovereign Princes in other Countrys: the Hangings of the finest Tapestry of Brussells, prodigious large looking glasses in silver frames, fine Japan Tables, the Beds, Chairs, Canopys and window Curtains of the richest Genoa Damask or Velvet, allmost cover'd with gold Lace or Embrodiery – the whole made Gay by Pictures and vast Jars of Japan china, and almost in every room large Lustres of rock chrystal . . . I must own I never saw a place so perfectly delightful as the Fauxbourgs of Vienna. It is very large and almost wholly compos'd of delicious Palaces.

Lady Mary Wortley Montagu, Letter to Lady Mar, 8 September 1716

A Woman till 5 and thirty is only look'd upon as a raw Girl and can possibly make no noise in the World till about forty. I don't know what your Ladyship may think of this matter, but tis a considerable comfort to me to know that there is upon Earth such a paradise for old Women, and I am content to be insignificant at present in the design of returning when I am fit to appear no where else.

Lady Mary Wortley Montagu, Letter to Lady Rich, 20 September 1716

Few European cities offer more resources to the stranger who does not place his felicity in absolute dissipation.

Sir N.W. Wraxall, *Memoirs of the Courts of Berlin, etc.*, 1779

The streets of Vienna are not pretty at all, God knows; so narrow, so ill built, so crowded, many wares placed upon the ground where there is a little opening, seems a strange awkward disposition of things for sale; and the people cutting wood in the streets makes one half wild when walking; it is hardly possible to pass another strange custom, borrowed from Italy I trust, of shutting up their shops in the middle of the day; it must tend, one would think, but little to the promotion of that commerce which the sovereign professes to encourage, and I see no excuse for it *here* which can be made from heat, gaiety, or devotion.

Hester Lynch Piozzi, *Observations . . . in the Course of a Journey*, 1789

I have no notion that Vienna . . . can be a very wholesome place to live in; the double windows, double feather-beds, &c. in a room without a chimney, is surely ill contrived; and sleeping smothered up in down so, like a hydrophobous patient in some parts of Ireland, is not *particularly* agreeable, though I begin to like it better than I did. All external air is shut out in such a manner that I am frighted lest, after a certain time, the room should become like an exhausted receiver, while the wind whirls about the street in such a manner, that it is displeasing to put out one's head.

Ibid.

This is one of the most perplexing cities that I was ever in. It is extensive, irregular, crowded, dusty, dissipated, magnificent, and to me disagreeable. It has immense palaces, superb galleries of paintings, several theatres, public walks, and drives crowded with equipages. In short, everything bears the stamp of luxury and ostentation; for here is assembled and concentrated all the wealth, fashion, and nobility of the Austrian empire, and every one strives to eclipse his neighbour. The gentlemen all dress in the English fashion, and in walking the fashionable lounges you would imagine yourself surrounded by Bond Street dandies. The ladies dress in the Parisian mode, the equipages are in the English style though more gaudy; with all this, however, there is a mixture of foreign costumes, that gives a very motley look to the population in the streets. You meet here with Greeks, Turks, Polonaise, Jews, Sclavonians, Croats, Hungarians, Tyroleans, all in the dress of their several countries; and you hear all kinds of languages spoken around you . . . here the people think only of sensual gratifications.

Washington Irving, Letter to his sister,
10 November 1822

A clever thing said by Lord Dudley, on some Vienna lady remarking impudently to him, 'What wretchedly bad French you all speak in London!' 'It is true, Madame (he answered), we have not enjoyed the advantage of having the French twice in our capital.'

Thomas Moore, Diary, 5 July 1829

We had heard of Vienna being a rival of Paris. . . . We found Vienna a small city that fringed off into Shantyville.

Lilian Leland, *Travelling Alone, A Woman's Journey Round the World*, 1890

. . . The mirage of Vienna.

William Sansom, *Blue Skies, Brown Studies*, 1961

Whiffs of incense, hot plaster, and Egyptian-smelling cigarettes seem to be the prevalent smells. Coffee, whipped cream, hockish white wine, paprika and, curiously, boiled beef (*Beinfleisch*) are the tastes. (The Schnitzel, as we know, hardly tastes of anything, unless it is a Kaiserschnitzel, larded with ham and Emmentaler cheese.) Mix into these colours and smells the rumble of motor traffic and the grinding of trams, and the sound of the last piece of music, great or small that you heard in this most musical city of *Eroica* or *Schmaltz*; add the omnipresence of glittering gaswork-heavy baroque *Prunk*; place these impressions against miles and miles of pavement and caryatid-encrusted nineteenth century building, and sprinkle with the sense that although few people are rich there is a feeling somewhere of ease in most pockets – at least wine and beer and black coffee are cheap – and you will begin to feel some of the quality of this monstrously pleasant mirage. *Prunk* is a nice word, used for a show-room in a palace; 'pride' and 'hunk' combine in our ear to give a phonetically exact description of baroque.

Ibid.

I had heard someone say that Vienna combined the splendour of a capital with the familiarity of a village. In the Inner City, where crooked lanes opened on gold and marble outbursts of Baroque, it was true; and in the Kärntnerstrasse or the Graben, after I had bumped into three brand-new acquaintances within a quarter of an hour, it seemed truer still, and parts of the town suggested an even narrower focus. There were squares as small and complete and as carefully furnished as rooms. Façades of broken pediment and tiered shutter enclosed hushed rectangles of cobble; the drip of icicles eroded gaps in the frozen scallops of the fountains; the statues of archdukes or composers presided with pensive nonchalance; and all at once, as I loitered there, the silence would fly in pieces when the initial clang from a tower routed a hundred pigeons crowding a Palladian cornice and scattered avalanches of snow and filled the geometric sky with wings. Palace succeeded palace, casemented arches sailed across the streets, pillars lifted their statues; ice-fettered in their pools, tritons floundered beneath a cloudy heaven and ribbed cupolas expanded by the score. The greatest of these, the dome of the Karlskirche, floated with a balloon's lightness in an enclosing hemisphere of snow and the friezes that spiralled the shafts of the two statue-crowned guardian columns – free-standing and as heavily wrought as Trajan's – gained an added impromptu spin when they vanished half-way up in a gyre of flakes.

Patrick Leigh Fermor, *A Time of Gifts*, 1977

The nostalgic city with a streak of gentle hopelessness, where Freud discovered sex. Baroque Vienna knows that an illusion which makes you happy is better than a reality which makes you sad.

Alan Whicker, in William Davis (ed.), *The Best of Everything*, 1980

Vienna has a population of about one and a half million in a country of about seven and a half million, and is thus affectionately known as the *Wasserkopf*, the hydrocephalus.

Sue Masterman, 'Long Faces in Harry Lime Country', *The Times*, 19 March 1980

AZORES (Portugal)

An Azore is an isle volcanic
Whose drivers put me in a panic.
The English expression 'Slow down, please,'
Means, 'Step on the Gas!' in Portuguese.
An Azore is a beauty spot?
I don't know whether it is or not
While racing around it hell-for-leather
My eyelids were always jammed together.

Ogden Nash, *Everyone But Thee and Me*, 1964

Fayal

They plant abundance of potatoes by the express command of the government, and sell them very cheap, because they do not like to eat them.

George Forster, *A Voyage Round the World*, 1777

Flores

It seemed only a mountain of mud standing up out of the dull mists of the sea. But as we bore down on it the sun came out and made it a beautiful picture – a mass of green farms and meadows that welled up to a height of fifteen hundred feet, and mingled its upper outlines with the clouds. It was ribbed with sharp, steel ridges, and cloven with narrow cañons, and here and there on the heights, rocky upheavals shaped themselves into mimic battlements and castles; and out of rifted clouds came broad shafts of sunlight, that painted summit, and slope, and glen, with bands of fire, and left belts of sombre shade between. It was the aurora borealis of the frozen pole exiled to a summer land!

Mark Twain, *The Innocents Abroad*, 1869

Pico

The isle of Pico has its name from the peak or high mountain upon it, which is frequently capt with clouds, and serves the inhabitants of Fayal nearly the same purpose as a barometer.

George Forster, *A Voyage Round the World*, 1777

B

BAHAMAS

Paradise Island

They say the Shah had people killed. Well, we don't care about that as long as he doesn't do it here. We have a history of receiving criminals here.

Assistant Manager of the Paradise Island Hotel, quoted by Sally Quinn in *The Guardian*, 19 May 1979

BAHRAIN

That famous Iland Baharem, . . . where they fish for Pearles foure moneths in the yeere; to wit, in June, July, August, September. And here are the best Pearles, which are round and Orient.

Joseph Salbancke, Letter to Sir Thomas Smith, 1609, in *Purchas his Pilgrimes*, 1625

BALTIC SEA

The Balticke Sea, so called because it is compassed by the Land, as it were with a girdle.

Fynes Moryson, *An Itinerary*, 1617

BANGLADESH

Chittagong

I have never seen so lovely a place to look at, nor one so loathsome to live in.

John Beames (1878), *Memoirs of a Bengal Civilian*, 1961

You up-country fellows never see rain like we have here. It begins early in the morning before daybreak on the first of the month, and when you go to bed on the 31st it is still drizzling on in the same remorseless way. Your boots grow a crop of mould every night. My beloved books, the only things that keep me going, are losing their bindings, and curling up into limp masses of pulp. The green mould crops out all over the damp unwholesome walls, rank weeds grow up all the hillsides, and the rain carves out great gutters ending in a moraine of muddy, fetid slush at the bottom. Whatsoever things are loathsome, whatsoever things are slimy, whatsoever things are stinking, sickening, ghastly oozy, decaying, and decayed, morbiferous, faeculent, miasmatic, malarious, and repulsive – these things abound. And over everything steadily, slowly, pitilessly, drenchingly, comes down by night and by day the dull, deadly rain like a pall covering the flaccid corpse of the soil.

John Beames, Letter, August 1878, in *Memoirs of a Bengal Civilian*, 1961

One of the ship's officers lurched towards me. He goggled for a moment out of a congested red face. 'Mister,' he said, 'Chittagong is the world's arse. Rectum bloody mundi!'

George Woodcock, *Asia, Gods and Cities*, 1966

A whole country in intensive care.

Trevor Fishlock, *The Times*, 19 March 1981

Dacca

The people of Dacca are an almost congenitally aggrieved race, rather like the French in Canada; their record, before and after independence, has been one of consistent complaint, always vocal and often violent.

George Woodcock, *Asia, Gods and Cities*, 1966

BARBADOS

This Illand is the Dunghill wharone England doth cast forth its rubidg: Rodgs and hors and such like peopel are those which are gennerally Broght heare. A rodge in England will hardly make a cheater heare; a Baud brought over puts on a demuor comportment, a whore if hansume makes a wife for sume rich planter.

Henry Whistler, *Journal*, 9 February 1655

The Virtue, which is too obdurate for Gold or Paper, shall melt away very kindly in a Liquid. The Island of *Barbadoes* (a shrewd People) manage all their Appeals to *Great Britain* by a skillful Distribution of Citron Water among the Whisperers about Men in Power.

Richard Steele, *The Spectator*, no. 394, 2 June 1712

Barbados and most of the other West Indian colonies appear externally to be governed on the model of England, but in reality they participate in a small degree in the genuine spirit of the mother-country.

They are practical republics, and present as faithful a picture of the petty states of old Greece, as the change of manners and religion will allow. There is the same equality amongst the free, the same undue conception of their own importance, the same restlessness of spirit, the same irritability of temper which has ever been the characteristic curse of all little commonwealths. The old remark, that the masters of slaves, if free themselves, are always the freest of the free, is as eminently true of them as it was of the citizens of Athens or Sparta; submission from those below them is so natural to them, that submission to any one above them seems unnatural.

H.N. Coleridge, *Six Months in the West Indies in 1825*, 1826

It is the waste land of the world that makes it picturesque. But there is not a rood of waste land in Barbados. It certainly is not the country for a gypsy immigration. Indeed, I doubt whether there is even room for a picnic.

The island is something over twenty miles long, and something over twelve broad . . . I was informed that the population was larger than that of China, but my informant of course meant by the square foot. He could hardly have counted by the square mile in Barbados.

And thus I was irresistibly made to think of the frog that would blow itself out and look as large as an ox.

Anthony Trollope, *The West Indies and the Spanish Main*, 1859

That prosperous and civilized little cane-garden.

Charles Kingsley, *At Last, A Christmas in the West Indies*, 1871

Looking backward we could almost see, suspended with the most delicate equipoise above the flat little island, the ghostly shapes of those twin orbs of the Empire, the cricket ball and the blackball.

Patrick Leigh Fermor, *The Traveller's Tree*, 1951

I see these ancestors of ours:
The merchants, the adventurers, the youngest sons of squires,
Leaving the city and the shires and the seaports,
Eager to establish a temporary home and make a fortune
In the new lands beyond the West, pawning perhaps
The old familiar acres or the assured competence;
Sturdy, realist, eager to win wealth from these Barbadoes
And to build, trade, colonize, pay homage to their king
And worship, according to the doctrines of the Church of England.

I see these ancestors of ours
Torn from the hills and dales of their motherland
Weeping, hoping in the mercy of time to return
To farm and holding, shuttle and loom, to return
In snow or rain or shine to humble homes, their own;
Cursing the day they were cheated by rebel standards
Or betrayed for their country's honour; fearing
The unknown land, the fever and the hurricane
The swamp and the jungle – all the traveller's tales.

I see them, these ancestors of ours:
Children of the tribe, ignorant of their doom, innocent
As cattle, bartered for, captured, beaten, penned
Cattle of the slave-ship, less than cattle:
Sold in the market-place, yoked to servitude;
Cattle, bruised and broken, but strong enough to plough
And, promised white man's heaven where they sing
Fill lamps with oil nor wait the bridegroom's coming;
Raise chorused voices in the hymn of praise.

Frank Collymore, *Triptych*, in John Figueroa (ed). *Caribbean Voices, – Dreams and Visions*, 1966

Let us thank now each polypite
Who laboured with all his tiny might
Through countless aeons till he made us
This little island home, Barbados.

Frank Collymore, *The Coral Polyp*, in *ibid.*

Bridgetown

Bridgetown, the metropolis of the island, is much like a second or third rate English town. It has none of the general peculiarities of the West Indies, except the heat. The streets are narrow, irregular, and crooked, so that at first a stranger is apt to miss his way. They all, however converge at Trafalgar Square, a spot which in Barbados is presumed to compete with the open space at Charing Cross bearing the same name. They have this resemblance, that each contains a statue of Nelson. The Barbadian Trafalgar Square also contains a tree, which is more than can be said for its namesake. It can make also this boast, that no attempt has been made within it which has failed so grievously as our picture gallery.

Anthony Trollope, *The West Indies and the Spanish Main*, 1859

Bridgetown is not a large place; ten minutes of slow walking brought us to the suburbs. It was evening and the hot air was perfectly still. We walked through a vertical stratification of sewage smells and flowers, through minglings of tuberose and stale fish. Gigantically tall thin palms, bending with their own lankiness, had been drawn, so it seemed, by a very vulgar but extraordinarily accurate and laborious artist – drawn in Indian ink, on the pale orange expanses of the West. There was a yelling of frogs; and the insects were like an invisible but ubiquitous orchestra, incessantly engaged in tuning up.

Aldous Huxley, *Beyond the Mexique Bay*, 1934

BELGIUM

The peopull in all thez kuntreiz, do loov to drink karows
and such az willnot do the same, thei kar not for A lows.

Thomas Whythorne, *Autobiography*, *c.* 1576

And now I have gained the cockpit of the Western world, and academy of arms for many years.

James Howell, *Vocall Forest*, *c.* 1640

as Old Austrian Netherlands
That most Popish, but unluckily whilst popish the most cultivated, the most populous and most flourishing of all countries, the Austrian Netherlands.

Edmund Burke, Letter to the Rev. Thomas Hussey, *c.* 9 December 1796

A country belonging to our Allies, and indeed a great deal more, which they who can speak no language but the new French, choose to call Belgium, but which neither by that name, nor with any certain bounds or limits is to be found in any Map . . . These new Appelations have been adopted in order to support the new System of giving to modern France the limits of antient Gaul.

Edmund Burke, Letter to French Laurence, 1 March 1797

A country which art seems to have endeavoured to render picturesque in proportion as it has been made otherwise by nature.

Robert Southey, Letter to Miss Barker, 10 October 1815

Imagine to yourself a succession of avenues with a Dutch spire at the end of each – and you see the road; – an accompaniment of highly cultivated farms on each side intersected with small canals or ditches – and sprinkled with very neat and clean cottages – a village every two miles – and you see the country – not a rise from Ostend to Antwerp – a molehill would make the inhabitants think that the Alps had come here on a visit – it is a perpetuity of plain & an eternity of *pavement* (on the *road*) but it is a country of great apparent comfort – and a singular though *tame* beauty.

Lord Byron, Letter to Augusta Leigh, 1 May 1816

The Belgian said that one of the worst names you could call any body (in Belgium, I think) was *un hibou quarré*. Lord Lansdowne owned he should not like to be called a *hibou quarré*.

Thomas Moore, Diary, 15 October 1833

Fine cities – admirable architects, far exceeding ours, both in their old and new buildings – good bakers – very ugly – stink of tobacco – horses all fat – soldiers little – inns dirty and very expensive; – better modern painters than we are . . .

I went to the Belgic Parliament. There was a pound short in the public accounts, and they were speaking about it . . .

All the great cities of Flanders are underpeopled.

Sydney Smith, Letter to Sir George Philips, 20 May 1837

If wood and stone can worship God per se, if he is adored *by* temples and not *in* temples, then is Belgium a right holy and religious nation.

M.F. Tupper, *Paterfamilias' Diary of Everybody's Tour*, 1856

I dislike Belgium, and think the Belgians, on the whole, the most contemptible people in Europe.

Matthew Arnold, Letter to Miss Arnold, 19 June 1859

La Belgique se croit toute pleine d'appas;
El dort. Voyageur, ne la réveillez pas.
(Belgium thinks herself very attractive. She is
asleep. Traveller, do not wake her.)

Charles Baudelaire, *Le Rêve Belge*, *c.* 1864

On me demande une épitaphe
Pour la Belgique morte. En vain
Je creuse, et je rue et je piaffe;
Je ne trouve qu'un mot: Enfin!

(They ask me for an epitaph for dead Belgium. In vain I rack my brains: I can find only one word: 'At last!')

Charles Baudelaire, Epitaphe pour la Belgique, *c.* 1864

The little white ewe lamb of Europe.

Father Vincent McNabb, *Open Letter* to the Kaiser, August 1914

and her former colony, Congo
It is the Congo that makes Belgium a first-class power; . . . Belgium is like an iceberg; the exposed fragment of motherland gets most of its weight, wealth, and substance from the huge submerged Congo mass underneath . . . To change the metaphor, the Congo is the Belgian ace of spades.

John Gunther, *Inside Africa*, 1955

Carr: The war itself had causes. I forget what they were, but it was in all the papers at the time. Something about brave little Belgium, wasn't it?
Tzara: Was it? I thought it was Serbia . . .
Carr: Brave little Serbia . . . ? No, I don't think so. The newspapers would never have risked calling the British public to arms without a proper regard for succinct alliteration.

Tom Stoppard, *Travesties*, 1975

Belgium suffers severely from linguistic indigestion.

R.W.G. Penn, 'Belgian with Tears', *Geographical Magazine*, March 1980

Belgians

old Austrian Netherlands

I have met with none who have escaped the impositions of the lower order of the people, and but few who have been wise enough even to perceive the artifices of the UPPER; . . . I must observe, therefore, that strangers, who are permitted to the *honour* of eating, and conversing, with the high and mighty people of the *Pais-bas*, should avoid playing with them; first, because they *understand play*; and secondly, because they do not *always*, as Englishmen do, *pay when they lose*. If, therefore, I can shew such who follow me, where *man-traps* are laid, and how they may be avoided, those who set their feet into them with their eyes open must not complain of the smart which may follow.

Philip Thicknesse, *A Journey through the Pais Bas, or Spanish Netherlands*, 1786

Ayant beaucoup cherché la raison de l'existence des Belges, j'ai imaginé qu'ils étaient peut-être d'anciennes âmes enfermées, pour d'horribles vices, dans les hideux corps qui sont leur image.

Un Belge est un enfer vivant sur la terre.

(After searching for a long time for a reason for the existence of the Belgians, I decided that perhaps they were ancient souls, shut up, for horrible vices, in hideous bodies fashioned in their own image.

A Belgian is a hell living on earth.)

Charles Baudelaire, *Pauvre Belgique*, *c.* 1864

Food

The food, as usual in Belgium, was of a nondescript occasional character; indeed I have never been able to detect anything in the nature of a meal among this pleasing people; they seem to pick and trifle with viands all day long in an amateur spirit: tentatively French, truly German, and somehow falling between the two.

Robert Louis Stevenson, *An Inland Voyage*, 1878

Alost / Aalst (Oost Vlanderen)

Alost a rather shabbily-flashy town. Indifference of Innkeepers noticeable and boldness of women. Unreasonable demands made by the postilions, and Wm. at the Inn door looked as fierce as Buonaparte.

Dorothy Wordsworth, *Journal*, 15 July 1820

Antwerp

At this day forsaken of Merchants, it lies overgrowne with grasse . . .

Fynes Moryson, *An Itinerary*, 1617

This goodly ancient City methinks looks like a disconsolate Widow, or rather some super-annuated Virgin, that hath lost her Lover, being almost quite bereft of that flourishing Commerce wherewith before the falling off the rest of the Provinces from *Spain* she abounded to the envy of all other Cities and Marts of *Europe*. There are few Places this side the *Alps* better built and so well streeted as this; and none at all so well girt with Bastions and Ramparts, which in some places are so spacious that they usually take the Air in Coaches upon the very Walls, which are beautified with divers rows of Trees and pleasant Walks. The Citadel here, tho' it be an addition to the stateliness and strength of the Town, yet it serves as a shrewd Curb unto her; which makes her chomp upon the Bit, and foam sometimes with anger, but she cannot help it.

James Howell, 'Letter to Sir James Crofts, 5 July 1619', *Epistolae Ho-Elianae, Familiar Letters*, 1645

View from the spire of the Vrou-Kirke

It is a very venerable fabrique, built after the Gotick manner, and especially the Tower, which is in truth of an excessive height: This I ascended, that I might the better take a view of the Country about it, which happning on a day when the sunn shone exceedingly hot, and darted the rayes without any interruption, afforded so bright a reflection to us who were above, and had a full prospect of both the Land and Water about it, that I was much confirm'd in my opinion of the Moones being of some such substance as this earthly Globe consists of; perceiving all the subjacent Country (at so smale an horizontal distance) to repercusse such a light as I could hardly looke against; save where the River, and other large water within our View appeard of a more darke & uniforme Colour, resembling those spotts in the Moone, attributed to the seas there &c according to our new Philosophy & the Phaenomenas by optical Glasses.

John Evelyn, *Diary*, 4 October 1641

Were any man to ask my advice upon the subject of retirement, I should tell him: By all means repair to Antwerp. No village amongst the Alps, or hermitage upon Mount Lebanon, is less disturbed: you may pass your days in this great city without being the least conscious of its sixty thousand inhabitants, unless you visit the churches.

William Beckford, *Dreams Waking Thoughts and Incidents*, 1783

This is a dismal heavy looking town – *so* melancholy!

Hester Lynch Piozzi, *Observations . . . in the Course of a Journey*, 1789

Ostade and Teniers were as much alive as they ever were, and even the Duke of Alva was still at home. The thirteenth century cathedral towered above a sixteenth century mass of tiled roofs, ending abruptly in walls and a landscape that had not changed. The taste of the town was thick, rich, like a sweet wine; it was mediaeval, so that Rubens seemed modern; it was one of the strongest and fullest flavours that ever touched the young man's palate; but he might as well have drunk out his excitement in old Malmsey, for all the education he got from it. Even in art, one can hardly begin with Antwerp Cathedral and the Descent from the Cross. He merely got drunk on his emotions, and had then to get sober as best he could.

Henry Adams, *The Education of Henry Adams*, 1906

Jones was at dinner the other night and heard a clergyman raving about Antwerp.

'You feel,' he said, 'under the spell of a certain painter – Rubens for instance. As you go about the streets you feel as though you might meet him at any corner.'

The hostess said, 'Ah, when we were there we went about in the trams.'

Samuel Butler, *Further Extracts from Note-books*, 1934

Antwerp I renamed Gnantwerp for I was devoured there by mosquitoes.

James Joyce, Letter to Harriet Shaw Weaver, Brussels, 24 September 1926

Brabant

The Sea lying upon this part of Brabant was of old firme land, joined to the continent, till many villages by divers floods (and seventeen parishes at once by a famous flood) were within lesse than 200. yeeres agoe swallowed up of the Sea, and for witnes of this calamity, divers Towers farre distant the one from the other, appeare in this Sea, and according to the ebbing and flowing, more or lesse seene, doe alwaies by their sad spectacle put the passengers in mind of that wofull event.

Fynes Moryson, *An Itinerary*, 1617

Bruges / Brugge

When you have seen what this town offers to the notice of a stranger, you will be, as I was, glad to quit it, for the inhabitants, (quite the reverse of their neighbours the French) are all shut up within their houses, and a stranger is apt at Bruges, to think himself in a city just depopulated by the plague.

Philip Thicknesse, *A Journey through the Pais Bas, or Austrian Netherlands*, 1786

One might fancy that as the city had been built so it had remained. . . . The general effect upon the mind can never be forgotten. The race of the Great and Powerful by whom the noble public edifices were raised has passed away, yet the attire, the staid motions and demeanour of the present inhabitants are accordant with the stateliness of former ages; and the City remains as if self-sustained – no new houses to be seen, no repairs going on! you might fancy that the sound of the Builder's hammer was never heard in these days!

Dorothy Wordsworth, *Journal*, 14 July 1820

In Brugès town is many a street
Whence busy life hath fled;
Where, without hurry, noiseless feet
The grass-grown pavement tread.
There heard we, halting in the shade
Flung from a Convent-tower,
A harp that tuneful prelude made
To a voice of thrilling power.

William Wordsworth, *Incident at Bruges*, 1828

In the market-place of Bruges stands the Belfry old and brown;
Thrice consumed and thrice rebuilded, still it watches o'er the town.

As the summer morn was breaking, on that lofty tower I stood,
And the world threw off the darkness, like the weeds of widowhood.

Thick with towns and hamlets studded, and with streams and vapors gray
Like a shield embossed with silver, round and vast the landscape lay.

At my feet the city slumbered. From its chimneys, here and there,
Wreaths of snow-white smoke ascending, vanished, ghost-like, into air.

Not a sound rose from the city at that early morning hour,
But I heard a heart of iron beating in that ancient tower . . . .

Visions of the day departed, snowy phantoms filled my brain;
They who live in history only seemed to walk the earth again . . .

Henry Wadsworth Longfellow, *The Belfry of Bruges*, 1845

The difference between Bruges and other cities is that in the latter you look about for the picturesque, while in Bruges, assailed on every side by the picturesque, you look curiously for the unpicturesque, and don't find it easily.

Arnold Bennett, *Journal*, 23 August 1896

Brussels

Brussels is the Paris of the Belgians and wants a little fire and Brimstone.

Robert Southey, Letter to Miss Barker, 1 October 1815

Brussels has been too much modernised, too much Frenchified in all respects. As a specimen of the leprous filthiness with which the French have infected these countries, I saw some toys in a shop window representing men with their loins ungirt, in the attitude of the *Deus Cacaturiens*, each with a piece of yellow metal, like a sham coin, inserted behind. The persons who exhibit such things as these for sale deserve the pillory or the whipping post.

Robert Southey, *Journal of a Tour in the Netherlands in the Autumn of 1815*, 1902

My impressions of this city are certainly anything but respectful. It has an absurd kind of Lilliput look with it. There are soldiers, just as in Paris, better dressed, and doing a vast deal of drumming and bustle; and yet, somehow, far from being frightened at them, I feel inclined to laugh in their faces. There are little Ministers, who work at their little bureaux; and to read the journals, how fierce they are! A great thundering *Times* could hardly talk more big . . . Think what a comfort it would be to belong to a little state like this; not to abuse their privilege, but philosophically to use it. If I were a Belgian I would not care one single fig about politics. I would not read thundering leading articles. I would not have an opinion. What's the use of an opinion here? Happy fellows! do not the French, the English, and the Prussians spare them the trouble of thinking, and make all their opinions for them. Think of living in a country, free, easy, respectable, wealthy, and with the nuisance of talking politics removed from out of it. All this might the Belgians have, and a part do they enjoy, but not the best part: no, these people will be brawling and by the ears, and parties run as high here as at Stoke Pogis or Little Pedlington.

W.M. Thackeray, *From Richmond to Brussels*, May 1844

'There was a sound of revelry by night
And Belgium's capital had gathered then her beauty and her
chivalry . . . !

But no sound of 'revelry' now, heaven knows. A more dull, humdrum place I never saw – though it seems a fine built place. Waterloo is some 8 miles off. Cannot visit it – & care not about it.

Herman Melville, *Journal of a Visit to London and the Continent, in 1849–50* (7 December 1849)

It is a white sparkling, cheerful, wicked little place, which however one finds rather good for one's spirits.

Matthew Arnold, Letter to Wyndham Slade, 28 July 1854

*A city that always makes me think of a whited sepulchre.

Joseph Conrad, *Heart of Darkness*, 1902

Wandering through cold streets tangled like old string,
Coming on fountains rigid in the frost,
Its formula escapes you; it has lost
The certainty that constitutes a thing.

Only the old, the hungry and the humbled
Keep at this temperature a sense of place,
And in their misery are all assembled;
The winter holds them like an Opera-House.

Ridges of rich apartments loom to-night
Where isolated windows glow like farms,
A phrase goes packed with meaning like a van,

A look contains the history of a man,
And fifty francs will earn a stranger right
To take the shuddering city in his arms.

W.H. Auden, *Brussels in Winter*, December 1938

O beautiful city of Brussels
With your parks and statues & boites,
Where they really know how to cook mussels,
And there's fucking á gauche et á droite;
For the sake of Breughel & Weyden,
For Rubens' wonderful cuisses,
In the name of Gudila the Maiden,
On behalf of the Manneken Pis,
Surrounded by glasses & dishes,
The pretty, the witty, the queer,
I offer you first my good wishes,
I wish you a happy New Year.

W.H. Auden, *Ode to the New Year*, 1939, first verse

The Parc

Numbers of statues decorate the place, the very worst I ever saw. These Cupids must have been erected in the time of the Dutch dynasty, as I judge from the immense posterior developments.

W.M. Thackeray, *From Richmond to Brussels*, May 1844

If any person wants to be happy I should advise the Parc. You sit drinking iced drinks and smoking penny cigars under great old trees. The band place, covered walks, etc., are all lit up. And you can't fancy how beautiful was the contrast of the great masses of lamplit foliage and the dark sapphire night sky, with just one blue star set overhead in the middle of the largest patch. In the dark walks, too, there are crowds of people whose faces you cannot see, and here and there a colossal white statue at the corner of an alley that gives the place a nice *artificial*, eighteenth century sentiment. There was a good deal of summer lightning blinking overhead, and the black avenues and white statues leap out every minute into short-lived distinctness.

Robert Louis Stevenson, Letter to his Mother, 25 July 1872

Flanders (in part France)

Flanders I liked because tis likest to England. the Inns were very unlike those at home being much cleaner & better served, so here I could not maintain my partiality with common justice; as to the civilizing any of that Nation it would imploy more ill spent time fruitlesly than any one has to spare, they are the only people I ever saw that was quite without a genious to be civil when they had a mind to be so.

Duchess of Queensbury, Letter to Jonathan Swift, 10 November 1733

I resolved to journey along with Quiet and Contentment for my companions. These two comfortable deities have, I believe, taken Flanders under their special protection; every step one advances discovering some new proof of their influence.

William Beckford, *Dreams Waking Thoughts and Incidents*, 1783

In Flanders fields the poppies blow
Between the crosses, row on row,
That mark our place; and in the sky
The larks, still bravely singing, fly
Scarce heard amid the guns below.

We are the Dead. Short days ago
We lived, felt dawn, saw sunset glow,
Loved and were loved, and now we lie
In Flanders field.

Take up our quarrel with the foe:
To you from failing hands we throw
The torch: be yours to hold it high.
If ye break faith with us who die,
We shall not sleep, though poppies grow
In Flanders field.

John McCrae, *In Flanders Fields, Punch*, 8 December 1915

Ghent / Gand

The prime for extent and fame, is Flanders, the chiefest Earldom in Christendom, which is three days' journey in length; *Ghent*, its Metropolis, is reputed the greatest Town of *Europe*, whence arose the Proverb, *Les flamens tient un Gan, qui tiendra Paris dedans.*

James Howell, 'A Survey of the Seventeen Provinces, Antwerp, 1 May 1622', *Familiar Letters*, 1645

Ghendt is an extravagant Citty of so vast a Circumference, that it is reported to be no lesse than 7 leagues in compasse; but there is not an halfe part of it now built; much of it remaining in feilds and desolate pastures, even within the Wales, which has marvailous strong Gates towards the West, and two faire Churches in one of which I heard a Sermon . . . The Ley and Scheld, meeting in this vast Citty divide it into 26 Ilands which are united togethere by many bridges somewhat resembling Venice.

John Evelyn, *Diary*, 8 October 1641

To one so far gone in the poetic antiquity, Ghent is not the most likely place to recall his attention; and I know nothing more about it, than that it is a large, ill-paved, dismal-looking city, with a decent proportion of convents and chapels, stuffed with monuments, brazen gates, and glittering marbles.

William Beckford, *Dreams Waking Thoughts and Incidents*, 1783

The buildings, streets, squares, all are picturesque; the houses, green, blue, pink, yellow, with richest ornaments still varying. Strange it is that so many and such strongly contrasted colours should compose an undiscordant whole.

Dorothy Wordsworth, *Journal*, 14 July 1820

Ghent has, I believe, been called a vulgar Venice. It contains dirty canals and old houses that must satisfy the most eager antiquary, though the buildings are not in quite so good preservation as others that may be seen in the Netherlands. The commercial bustle of the place seems considerable, and it contains more beershops than any city I ever saw.

W.M. Thackeray, *Little Travels and Roadside Sketches*, October 1844

A trifle of time in such a town as this is bewildering; it is like having to describe a curiosity shop.

M.F Tupper, *Paterfamilias' Diary of Everybody's Tour*, 1856

The Butter Market
I can hardly endure to call a place so dignified by such a name.

Dorothy Wordsworth, *Journal*, 15 July 1820

River Hans-sur-Lesse

Old Euclid may go the wall,
For we've solved what he never could guess
How the fish in the river are *small*
But the river they live in is Lesse.

Anon., in Rev. John Booth (ed.), *Epigrams*, 1863

Liège

Assassinations are very common, particularly in and about Liège, a city as replete with vice as it is with inhabitants.

Philip Thicknesse, *A Journey through the Pais Bas, or Spanish Netherlands*, 1786

Near Liège, the gradient being steep, we are pulled up to Hautpré by a rope; and soon coming to the top, have a grand view of the Belgian Birmingham, nearly as well supplied with tall chimnies, but more countryfied, and much prettier. Liège is quite an urbs in rure, – houses and manufactories dotted about among trees and hills, and winding streams, with turreted and spired and cupola'd churches here and there, picturesque enough. Within, however, most of the streets are narrow, wind-about and roughly trottoired – dirty withal and smelly; and the rapid Meuse, from thunder-showers I suppose, a river of mud.

M.F. Tupper, *Paterfamilias' Diary of Everybody's Tour*, 1856

Namur

At Namur we walked out by the light of a splendid full moon. We poked our way through the narrow streets to the bridge of the Sambre, then to that of the Meuse . . . Coleridge advanced towards the river with quiet expressions of enjoyment at the beauty around him. Wordsworth stepped quickly on, and said aloud, yet more to himself than to us –

'Ay, there it is – there's the bridge! Let's see how many arches there are – one, two, three,' and so on, till he counted them all, with the accuracy and hardness of a stone-cutter.

T.C. Grattan, *Beaten Paths and Those Who Trod Them*, 1862 – of June 1828

Ostend

You are nice and peevish, how long will you hold out thinke you? not so long as *Ostend*.

Mistress Birdlime to Mistress Justiniano, in Thomas Dekker and John Webster, *Westward Hoe*, 1607

(Ostend was under siege from 5 July 1601 to 15 September 1604, and 70,000 are said to have lost their lives before it was stormed.)

Art thou become a tragic stage, and more
Whence bravest wits, brave stories may begin
To show the world, more than the world would crave
How all thine intrench'd ground became one grave? . . .
At last, from threat'ning terror of despair,
Thine hemm'd defendants, with divided walls
Were forc'd to render; then came mourning care
Of mutual foes; for friends untimely falls:
Thus lost, and got, by wrong and lawless right,
My judgement thinks thee scarcely worth the fight.
But there's the question, when the muse hath done,
Whether the victor, or the vanquish'd won?

William Lithgow, *Rare Adventures and Painfull Peregrinations*, 1614/32

Were I to remain ten days in Ostend I should scarcely have one delightful vision; 'tis so unclassic a place! Nothing but preposterous Flemish roofs disgust your eyes when you cast them upwards: swaggering Dutchmen and mungrel barbers are the first objects they meet with below.

William Beckford, *Dreams Waking Thoughts and Incidents*, 1783

Passchendaele

The preparations for Passchendaele were a poem in mud cum blood-and-thunder. The appetite of the Teuton for this odd game called war – in which a dum-dum bullet is a foul, but a gas-bomb is O.K. – and British 'doggedness,' in the gentle art of 'muddling through', when other nations misunderstand British kindliness and get tough, made a perfect combination. If the Germans and the English had not been there, all the others would long before that have run away and the war been over.

These two contrasted, but as it were complementary types of *idée fixe*, found their most perfect expression on the battlefield, or battle-bog, of Passchendaele. The very name with its suggestion of *splashiness* and *passion* at once, was subtly appropriate. This nonsense could not have come to its full flower at any other place but at *Passchendaele*. It was pre-ordained. The moment I saw the name on the trench-map, intuitively I knew what was going to happen.

Wyndham Lewis, *Blasting and Bombardiering*, 1937

Spa

The town of *Spa* is situated in a stoney, mountainous country, on the banks of what in Summer, is a murmuring stream, but which in Winter is sometimes a rapid river; the air is good, and the environs, in general, are pleasant, though rude, and uncultivated, having much the appearance of a part of the globe, which has been broken up by earthquakes, or some violent convulsions of Nature. . . . You may easily imagine, therefore, that a spot like this, visited by all the world, and where gaming is tolerated, nay, *encouraged* by the first *magistrate of the principality*, that it is not only the resort of invalids, and people of real fashion, but of *counterfeit nobility* innumerable, and the outcasts, scum, and refuse of both sexes, from every nation. So that what with the real, and the *assumed badges* of distinction, to be seen at Spa, a stranger would be apt to think all the crown heads in Europe had sent their courtiers to drink the *Pohoun* water. . . .

Having mentioned above, that the *Pohoun* is the spring from which the bottled Spa-water is taken, it may be necessary to inform you, that there are near Spa, several other mineral springs, viz. the *Geronstere*, and about two miles from Spa, the *Sauveniere* and the *Tonnelet*, somewhat nearer; and all these waters are used by those who are within the reach of them. I cannot pretend to tell you what the healing powers of the last mentioned springs are; but I suppose there must be some *extraordinary virtue in the Geronstere water*, as it is exceedingly nauseous, and tastes and smells like rotten eggs, but it is perfectly clear.

Philip Thicknesse, *A Journey through the Pais Bas, or Austrian Netherlands*, 1786

As a town it astonished us both by its insignificance.

Matthew Arnold, Letter to Miss Arnold, 9 September 1860

Waterloo

The Plain at Waterloo is a fine one – but not much after Marathon & Troy – Cheronea – & Platea. — Perhaps there is something of prejudice in this – but I detest the cause & the victors – & the victory including Blucher and the Bourbons.

Lord Byron, Letter to John Cam Hobhouse, 16 May 1816

Stop! – for thy tread is on an Empire's dust!
An Earthquake's spoil is sepulchred below!
Is the spot marked with no colossal bust?
Nor column trophied for triumphal show?
None; but *the moral's truth* tells simpler so
As the ground was before, thus let it be; –
How that red rain hath made the harvest grow!
And is this all the world hath gained by thee,
Thou first and last of Fields! king-making Victory?

Lord Byron, *Childe Harold's Pilgrimage*, Canto the Third, 1816

We stood upon grass and corn fields where *heaps* of our countrymen lay buried beneath our feet. There was little to be seen; but much to be felt; – sorrow and sadness, and even something like horror breathed out of the ground as we stood upon it! . . . The ruins of the severely contested chateau of Hougamont had been ridded away since the battle, and the injuries done to the farm-house repaired. Even these circumstances, natural and trivial as they were, suggested melancholy thoughts, by furnishing grounds for a charge of ingratitude against the course of things, that was thus hastily removing from the spot all vestiges of so momentous an event.

Dorothy Wordsworth, *Journal*, 17 July 1820

prospect blank and cold
Of wind-swept corn that wide around us rolled,
In dreary billows, wood and meagre cot,
And monuments that soon must disappear;
Yet a dread local recompense we found;
While glory seemed betrayed, while patriot-zeal
Sank in our hearts, we felt as men *should* feel
With such vast hoards of hidden carnage near,
And horror breathing from the silent ground!

William Wordsworth, *After Visiting the Field of Waterloo, 1821*, 1822

In that world-earthquake, Waterloo!

Alfred Lord Tennyson, *Ode on the Death of the Duke of Wellington*, 1852

I have seldom been more interested. One has read the account of the battle so often, the area is so limited, and the main points of the battle so simple, that one understands it the moment one sees the place with one's eyes.

Matthew Arnold, Letter to Miss Arnold, 9 October 1860

Ypres

A soldier said to an old lady, 'So when we got to Wipers – ' '*Ypres*,' said the old lady. The soldier resumed: 'So when we got to Wipers – ' '*Ypres*,' said the old lady. The soldier heaved a sigh and began again: 'So when we got to Wipers – ' '*Ypres*,' said the old lady. 'Cor,' said the soldier, 'you ain't 'arf got 'iccups.'

J.B. Morton [?], quoted in James Agate, *Ego* 7, 1945

No Norman Keep, in ivy-clad decay was ever so romantic as Ypres, literally swarming with ghosts even at high noon (in the moonlight you could not tell which were the quick and which the dead), and looking as if Time, that does not hurry when making a ruin as a rule, had telescoped itself to make this one, Death having lent it a hand.

Wyndham Lewis, *Blasting and Bombardiering*, 1937

BELIZE (formerly British Honduras)

We remembered Captain Hampton's description before our arrival, and felt the point of his concluding remark, that Belize was the last place made.

J.L. Stephens, *Incidents of Travel in Central America, Chiapas and Yucatan*, 1841

If the world had any ends British Honduras would certainly be one of them.

Aldous Huxley, *Beyond the Mexique Bay*, 1934

One of the first things that strike the newcomer to Belize who has seen anything of life in the West Indies is the mysterious absence of anything that might come under the heading of having a good time.

Norman Lewis, *The Changing Sky*, 1959

Among the many self-deprecatory reports sponsored by the citizens of Belize is one that their town was built upon a foundation of mahogany chips and rum bottles.

Ibid.

Copan (ruins of)

The only sounds that disturbed the quiet of this buried city were the noise of monkeys moving among the tops of the trees, and the cracking of dry branches broken by their weight. They moved over our heads in long and swift processions, forty or fifty at a time, some with little ones wound in their long arms, walking out to the end of boughs, and holding on with their hind feet or a curl of the tail, sprang to a branch of the next tree, and, with a noise like a current of wind, passed on into the depths of the forest. It was the first time we had seen these mockeries of humanity, and, with the strange monuments around us, they seemed like wandering spirits of the departed race guarding the ruins of their former habitations.

J.L. Stephens, *Incidents of Travel in Central America, Chiapas and Yucatan*, 1841

The reader is perhaps curious to know how old cities sell in Central America. Like other articles of trade they are regulated by the quantity in the market, and the demand; but, not being staple articles, like cotton and indigo, they were held at fancy prices, and at that time were dull of sale. I paid fifty dollars for Copan. There was never any difficulty about price. I offered that sum, for which Don Jose Maria thought me only a fool; if I had offered more, he would probably have considered me something worse.

Ibid.

BERMUDA

The infamous Iland of Bermuda, notorious with unmercifull and incredible stormes of fearefull thunder and lightning.

George, Earl of Cumberland, 1596, in *Purchas his Pilgrimes*, 1625

The still-vext *Bermoothes.*

William Shakespeare, *The Tempest*, *c.* 1611–12.

They be so terrible to all that ever touched on them, and such tempests, thunders, and other fearefull objects are seene and heard about them, that they be called commonly, the Devils Ilands, and are feared and avoyded of all sea travellers alive, above any other place in the world . . . whereas indeed wee find them now be experience, to bee as habitable and commodious as most Countries of the same climate and situation: insomuch as if the entrance into them were as easie as the place it selfe is contenting, it had long ere this beene inhabited, as well as other Ilands . . .

The Bermudas bee broken Ilands, five hundred of them in manner of an Archipelagus . . . of small compasse, some larger yet then other, as time and the Sea hath wonne from them, and eaten his passage through, and all now lying in the figure of a Croissant, within the circuit of sixe or seven leagues at the most . . . These Ilands are often afflicted and rent with tempests, great strokes of thunder, lightning and raine in the extreamity of violence . . . sometimes fortie eight houres together: especially if the circle, which the Philosophers call Halo were (in our being there) seene about the Moone at any season, which bow indeed appeared there often, and would bee of a mightie compasse and breadth.

William Strachy, *A true Reportory of the Wracke and Redemption of Sir Thomas Gates*, 1610, in *Purchas his Pilgrimes*, 1625

The ilands of the Bermudaes, . . . Lieing thus together . . . become in forme not much unlike a reaper's sickle, being in their whole longitude from east to west not above twentye miles English: in the latitude (wher most extended) not fully two and a halfe: the surface and outward posture of the whole lieing altogether uneven, and distributed into smale hils and dales. As for the soyle, the inner-most part is of two sortes, either a white soft rock not much different from our English marle, or a craggie hard rock, whereof lime is made, the uppermost a light sandy mould, of coulour in some places whitish, in some redd and in others brown, the which by a naturall production affords great varietye of symples; many tall and goodly caedars, infinite store of palmitoes, numbers of mulberries, wild olives, very many, with divers others of unknowen both name and vertue.

Captain John Smith[?], *The Historye of the Burmudaes*, *c.* 1630

As for the health and generall salubritye of the place, I

doubt not to affirme, but that ther is not a part of the world that can excell it, fewe equall it. I deny not but that at the first entrance of newe commers, most of them for a while are troubled with a gentle flux . . .

For the serenitie, it may as truely be said of these Ilands, as ever it was of Rhodes, that there is noe one day throughout the yeare but that in some houre thereof the sunne lookes clearely and smilingly out upon them; stinckinge and infectious mists are never seen, nor the coffe and reumatic unknowen. For their temperature, it is admirable, noe colde ther is beyonde an English Aprill, nor heate much greater than a hott July in France. And thus haveinge presented you with the furniture and trimme of this little theatre . . .

Ibid.

Bermudas wall'd with Rocks, who does not know
That happy Island where huge Lemons grow,
And Orange Trees which golden fruit do bear,
Th'Hesperian Garden boasts of none so fair?
Where shining Pearl, Coral, and many a pound
On the rich shore, of Amber-greece is found:
The lofty Cedar which to Heaven aspires,
The Prince of Trees is fewel for their fires:
The smoak by which their loaded spits do turn
For incense, might on sacred Altars burn.
There private roofs on od'rous timber born,
Such as might Pallaces for Kings adorn:
The sweet *Palmettas*, a new Bacchus yield
With leaves as ample as the broadest shield:
Under the shadow of whose friendly boughs
They sit carrowsing, where their liquor grows: . . .
The naked rocks are not unfruitful there,
But at some constant seasons every year:
Their barren top with loucious food abound,
And with the eggs of various fowls are crown'd:
Tobacco is their worst of things which they
To English Land-lords as their Tribute pay:
Such is the mould, that the blest Tenant feeds
On pretious fruits, and payes his rent in weeds:
With candid Plantines, and the juicy Pine,
On choicest Melons and sweet Grapes they dine,
And with Potato's fat their wanton Swine:
Nature these Cates with such a lavish hand
Pours out among them, that our courser Land
Tastes of that bounty, and does cloath return,
Which not for warmth, but ornament is worn:
For the kinde Spring which but salutes us here
Inhabits there, and courts them all the year:
Ripe fruits and blossoms, on the same trees live,
At once they promise what at once they give:
So sweet the air, so moderate the clime,
None sickly lives, or dies before his time.
Heaven sure has kept this spot of earth uncurst
To shew how all things were created first: . . .

Edmund Waller, *The Battel of the Summer Islands*, Canto I, *Poems*, 1645

Where the remote Bermudas ride
In the ocean's bosom, unespied.

Andrew Marvell, *Bermudas*, *c.* 1650

It would take up too much of your Lordship's time minutely to describe the beauties of Bermuda, . . . But above all, that uninterrupted health and alacrity of spirit, which is the result of the finest weather and gentlest climate in the world, and which of all others is the most effectual cure for the cholic, as I am most certainly assured by the information of many very credible persons of all ranks who have been there.

George Berkeley, Letter to Lord Percival, 4 March 1722/3

I find Bermuda is a place where physicians order their patients when no other air will keep them alive.

Thomas Moore, Letter to his Mother, 10 September 1803

No, ne'er did the wave in its elements steep
  An island of lovelier charms;
It blooms in the giant embrace of the deep,
  Like Hebe in Hercules' arms.
The blush of your bowers is light to the eye,
  And their melody balm to the ear;
But the fiery planet of day is too nigh,
  And the Snow Spirit never comes here.

Thomas Moore, *The Snow Spirit*, *Poems relating to America*, 1806

There can be no place in the world as to which there can be less to be said than there is about this island. . . . If these be the veritable scenes of Prospero's incantations, I will at any rate say this – that there are now to be found stronger traces of the breed of Caliban than of that of Ariel. Strong, however, of neither; for though Caliban did not relish working for his master more keenly than a Bermudian of the present day, there was nevertheless about him a sort of energy which is altogether wanting in the existing islanders.

Anthony Trollope, *The West Indies and the Spanish Main*, 1859

Had America ever suffered from land hunger . . . she would have seized Bermuda long ago. Wise, she took it not with soldiers, but with tourists, and today she controls it with dollars and an air-base. There is nothing to be sorry about. The Bermudans stand on their tradition and their cash tills.

Cecil Roberts, *And So to America*, 1946

Bermuda is essentially a small town in a glamorous setting.

David Shelley Nicholl, Letter to *The Times*, 17 February 1978

A condensed place.

Suzannah Lissard, *New Yorker Magazine*, 16 April 1979

BAY OF BISCAY

In the Bay of Biscay, O!

Andrew Cherry (d.1812), attrib.

In Biscay's sleepless bay.

Lord Byron, *Childe Harold's Pilgrimage*, Canto the First, 1812

The same day, we were becalmed in the Bay of Biscay – a pleasant surprise. A calm in the Bay of Biscay, after what we had read and heard of it, sounded to us like repose in a boiling cauldron. But a calm, after all, is not repose: it is a very unresting and unpleasant thing, the ship taking a great gawky motion from side to side as if playing the buffoon; and the sea heaving in huge oily fields, like a carpet lifted.

Leigh Hunt, *Autobiography*, 1850 – of 1821

Have you ever been in a gale of wind off the Bay of Biscay? If not and you are fond of variety, it is really worth your while to take a trip to Lisbon or Madeira for the chance of meeting with one. Calculate your season well in December or January, when the south-wester has properly set in, and you will find it one of the finest and most uncomfortable things in the world. *My* gale lasted from Sunday till Wednesday evening, which is something long, perhaps, for amusement, but it gave ample scope for observation and philosophy.

H.N. Coleridge, *Six Months in the West Indies*, in 1825, 1826

To those whose health would be benefited by sea-sickness, I can safely recommend the ungentle exercise of the Bay of Biscay; – there is little chance of failure.

Michael Kelly, *Reminiscences*, 1826

An unrestful place for writing in.

Mary Kingsley, Letter, 1900

BLACK SEA

Othello: Like to the Ponticke Sea,
Whose Icie Current, and compulsive course,
Nev'r keepes retyring ebbe, but keepes due on
To the Proponticke, and the Hellespont:
Even so my bloody thoughts, with violent pace
Shall nev'r looke backe, nev'r ebbe to humble Love
Till that a capable, and wide Revenge
Swallow them up . . .

William Shakespeare, *Othello*, 1604–5

There's not a sea the passenger e'er pukes in
Turns up more dangerous breakers than the Euxine.

Lord Byron, *Don Juan*, 1819–24

Here is an authentic anecdote from Vienna. The French and English Plenipotentiaries urged how natural the arrangement would be that the Euxine should, like the American lakes, be common to both nations; to which Prince Gortschakoff answered that he should not object to that, were there only a Niagara at the Dardanelles.

Arthur Hugh Clough, Letter to Professor F.J. Child, 3 May 1855

BOLIVIA

Just as on no side has it anything that can be called a natural frontier, neither have its inhabitants any distinctive quality or character to distinguish them sharply from other peoples.

James Bryce, *South America*, 1912

Bolivia is the Switzerland of South America, a Republic without access to the sea. In shape it resembles the hall of a great hotel, a huge green carpet at the foot of a staircase that rises to a flat landing a good deal nearer the stars. Nine-tenths of the population live either at the top or half way down. . . .

Julian Duguid, *Green Hell*, 1931

Bolivia . . . is Peru exploded.

John Gunther, *Inside South America*, 1967

Whatever the Bolivian armed forces want, the country wants.

Local adage, quoted by John Gunther, *ibid.*

Lift the Anatolian plateau to about four times its actual altitude, and then shift it about twenty degrees nearer the Equator, and you have the Altiplano of Peru and Bolivia.

Arnold Toynbee, *East to West*, 1958

Paradoxically . . . Bolivia emerged in practice as a non-maritime Pacific State, . . . a remote mid-continental hinterland of extreme physical difficulty, its core secluded to the point of isolation within the lofty Andean cordilleras. . . . It has never been easy to find many Bolivians who have seen the sea.

Joan Valerie Fifer, *Bolivia: Land, Location, and Politics since 1825*, 1972

La Paz

To be enclosed between two lofty ranges and two deserts, to live at the bottom of a hole and yet be nearly as high above sea level as the top of the Rocky Mountains or the Jungfrau are strange conditions for a dwelling place. Nevertheless it was a place in which one might do much meditation.

James Bryce, *South America*, 1912

The altitude takes a savage toll of the Indians, who are the only people capable of surviving the rigours of the habitat at all; life expectancy on the *altiplano* is thirty-two years, and women of twenty-five, their faces ravaged, look seventy. A friend told me, driving near La Paz, 'You can live here three months without ever seeing a person smile.'

John Gunther, *Inside South America*, 1967

It was a city that seemed suited to ghastliness . . . It suffered itself from a sort of urban gangrene, and if any city looked blighted to the point of being wounded – it even had a scabrous cankered colour – it was La Paz. Its extreme ugliness was woeful enough to be endearing, and I found it on further inspection to be a likable place. It was a city of cement and stale bread, of ice storms that produced a Bulgarian aroma of wet tweeds, built above the timber line in a high pass in the Andes . . . it was hard to believe I was not in eastern Europe.

Paul Theroux, *The Old Patagonian Express*, 1979

Lake Titicaca (also borders Peru)

The lake waters below were pale blue like the cup of a blue poppy, and that the blue poppy is Tibetan seemed only right and sensible. Where else could it come from, with lamaseries on its shores confusing the two countries in our minds? Never before has one seen waters of such a colour.

Sacheverell Sitwell, *Golden Wall and Mirador*, 1961

BOTSWANA

Kalahari Desert

The miraculous thing about the Kalahari is that it is a desert only in the sense that it contains no permanent surface water. Otherwise its deep fertile sands are covered with grass glistening in the wind like fields of gallant corn. It has luxuriant bush, clumps of trees, and in places great strips of its own dense woods. It is filled too with its own varieties of game, buck of all kinds, birds and lion and leopard. When the rains come it grows sweet-tasting grasses and hangs its bushes with amber berries, glowing raisins, and sugared plums. Even the spaces between the satin grass are filled with succulent melons and fragrant cucumbers and in the earth itself bulbs, tubers, wild carrots, potatoes, turnips and sweet potatoes grow great with moisture and abundantly multiply. After the rains there is a great invasion of life from the outside world into a desert which produces such sweetness out of its winter travail of heat and thirst. Every bird, beast and indigenous being waits expectantly in its stony upland for the summer to come round. Then, as the first lightning begins to flare up and down below the horizon in the west as if a god walked there swinging a storm lantern to light his great strides in the dark, they eagerly test the winds with their noses. As soon as the air goes dank with a whiff of far-off water they will wait no longer. The elephant is generally the first to move in because he not only possesses the most sensitive nose but also has the sweetest tooth. Close on his heels follow numbers of buck, wildebeest, zebra, and the carnivorous beasts that live off them. Even the black buffalo emerges from the river-beds and swamps shaking the tsetse fly like flakes of dried clay from his coat, and grazes in surly crescents far into the desert. When this animal movement is at its height and all the signs confirm that a fruitful summer is at last established, the human beings follow.

Laurens van der Post, *The Lost World of the Kalahari*, 1958

BRAZIL

This Countrie is somewhat melancholicke, overflowne with many waters, as wel of maine Rivers, as from the Skie; in it is great store of raine chiefly in Winter, it is ful of great Woods that are greene all the yeere. It is a Hilly Countrie, especially toward the Sea Coast, and from Pernambuco unto the Captainship of the Holy Ghost, is verie scarce of stone; but from thence to Saint Vincent are verie rough and high Mountaines, of great Quarries of Rockie stone, the food and waters are generally healthfull, light, and of easie digestion. There are few Commodities for apparrell, because the Countrie yeeldeth nothing but Cotton-wooll, and of the rest the Countrie is plentifull: especially of Cattell and Sugars.

A Treatise of Brasil, written by a Portugal before 1601, in *Purchas his Pilgrimes*, 1625

It is now said, that there is a small slender vein of [gold] spread through all the country, at about twenty-four feet from the surface, but that this vein is too thin and poor to answer the expence of digging.

George Anson (Richard Walter and Benjamin Robins), *A Voyage Round the World, 1740–4*, 1748

It is lawful to wish . . . the Brazil as well as Mexico will homologize with us.

Thomas Jefferson, Letter to James Monroe, 1 December 1822

In England any person fond of natural history enjoys in his walks a great advantage, by always having something to attract his attention; but in these fertile climates, teeming with life, the attractions are so numerous, that he is scarcely able to walk at all.

Charles Darwin, *Journal . . . During the Voyage . . . of H.M.S. Beagle*, 1832–6

Hospitality is the greatest delay in Brazilian travel. It is the old style of Colonial greeting; you may do what you like, you may stay for a month, but not for a day.

Richard Burton, *Explorations of the Highlands of the Brazil*, 1869

There must, I believe, be some modification in the Brazilian Constitution before the nation can cease to be what the witty Frenchman termed it, 'un peuple prospectus.'

Ibid.

People who talk and write about the disorderly South American republics are fond of pointing to Brazil, that great, peaceful, progressive empire, as setting an example to be followed. An orderly country, yes, and the people in it steeped to their lips in every abominable vice!

W.H. Hudson, *The Purple Land*, 1885

I'm Charley's aunt from Brazil, where the nuts come from.

Brandon Thomas, *Charley's Aunt* (Lord Fancourt Babberley, Act 1), 1892

On the Portuguese of Brazil nature has bestowed nothing for which man cannot find a use.

James Bryce, *South America*, 1912

Delay in Brazil is a climate. You live in it. You can't get away from it. There is nothing to be done about it. It should, I think, be a source of pride to the Brazilians that they possess a national characteristic which it is absolutely impossible to ignore.

Peter Fleming, *Brazilian Adventure*, 1933

A little covey of rockets went up from somewhere in the town. They burst in a chorus of inoffensive plopping noises and left surprised balls of smoke hanging in the air. . . . Rockets are to the Brazilian calendar what exclamation marks are to the correspondence of a debutante.

Ibid.

*It's such a useless thing for a man to want to be: the p-p-president of Brazil.

Truman Capote, *Breakfast at Tiffany's*, 1958

A great country, administering every section of its great area, on paper.

V.S. Naipaul, *The Middle Passage*, 1962

The giant north-east is known as the land of *miseria morte*: the sorrows of death. It is one of the poorest places on earth.

James Cameron, *Daily Herald*, 24 June 1964, *What a Way to Run the Tribe*, 1968

The country has been nicely described as a continent with its colonies inside it.

John Gunther, *Inside South America*, 1967

Sociology is the art of saving Brazil quickly.

Mario de Andrade, quoted John Gunther, *ibid.*

We progress at night when the politicians sleep.

Brazilian saying, quoted John Gunther, *ibid.*

Brazilians

If the English are a nation of shopkeepers, what are we to say of the Portuguese?

Henry Walter Bates, *The Naturalist on the River Amazons*, 1863

In almost all cases of premeditated murder throughout Brazil, two of the active actors are a woman and a negro.

Richard Burton, *Explorations of the Highlands of the Brazil*, 1869

You cannot disillusion a Brazilian.

Peter Fleming, *Brazilian Adventure*, 1933

Foreigners say: 'A rich Brazilian is a monkey who fell out of a coconut tree into a Cadillac.'

Christopher Isherwood, *The Condor and the Cows*, 1949

Indians

The features exhibit scarcely any mobility of expression; this is connected with the apathetic and undemonstrative character of the race. They never betray, in fact they do not feel keenly, the emotions of joy, grief, wonder, fear, and so forth. They can never be excited to enthusiasm, but they have strong affections, especially those connected with the family . . . All the actions of the Indian show that his ruling desire is to be let alone . . .

Henry Walter Bates, *The Naturalist on the River Amazons*, 1863

Caraja Indians

Their features – though the type varies widely – suggest a Mongoloid variation on the conventional Red Indian of illustrations to Fenimore Cooper.

Peter Fleming, *Brazilian Adventure*, 1933

River Amazon

This river, . . . for the greatnesse, is called of many the Sweet Sea.

Robert Harcourt, 1608, in *Purchas his Pilgrimes*, 1625

In this River I continued tenne weekes, seeing the fashion of the people and Countrie there: This Countrie is altogether full of Woods, with all sorts of wilde Beasts: as Lions Beares, Woolves, Leopards, Baboones, strange Boores, Apes, Monkeies, Martines, Sanguines, Marmosets, with divers other strange beasts: also these Woods are full of Wild-fowle of all sorts, and Parrats more plentifull then Pidgeins in England, and as good meate, for I have eaten often of them. Also this Countrey is very full of Rivers, having a King over everie River. In this place is continuall Tempests, as Lightning, Thunder, and Raine, and so extreame, that it continues most commonly sixteene or eighteene houres in foure and twentie. There are many standing waters in this Countrie, which bee full of Aligators, Guianes, with many other severall water Serpents, and great store of fresh fish, of strange fashions. This Countrie is full of Muskitas, which is a small Flie, which much offends a Stranger comming newly into the Countrie . . .

The people are verie ingenious, craftie, and treacherous, verie light of foot, and good Bowemen, whose like I have never seene . . . The manner of their Lodging is this: they have a kinde of Net made of the rinde of a Tree which they call Haemac, being three fathome in length, and two in breadth, and gathered at both ends at length, then fastning either end to a Tree, to the full length about a yard and halfe from the ground, when hee hath desire to sleepe, hee creepes into it.

William Davies, 1608, in *Purchas his Pilgrimes*, 1625

Amazon Forest

The forest of the Amazons is not merely trees and shrubs. It is not land. It is another element. Its inhabitants are arborean; they have been fashioned for life in that medium as fishes to the sea and birds to the air. Its green apparition is persistent as the sky is and the ocean. In months of travel it is the horizon which the traveller cannot reach, and its unchanging surface, merged through distance into a mere reflector of the day, a brightness or a gloom, in his immediate vicinity breaks into a complexity of green surges; then one day the voyager sees land at last and is released from it.

H.M. Tomlinson, *The Sea and the Jungle*, 1912

The mind sees this forest better than the eye.

Ibid.

Jungles of the Araguaya River

Night in these jungles had a curious rhythm to it. It was as though one was in some nightmare engine-room, a vast place working quietly to some predestined purpose. There was a permanent regulated background of noise, as there is when you are in the presence of machines. The cicadas and the frogs laid measured strips of sound across the silence – monotonous, impersonal strips of sound with no end and no beginning, such as are produced by pressing a button.

Peter Fleming, *Brazilian Adventure*, 1933

Bahia

Bahia de todos los Santos lies in Lat 13 deg. S. It is the most considerable Town in Brazil, whether in Respect of the Beauty of its Buildings, its Bulk, or its Trade and Revenue. It has the Convenience of a good Harbour that is capable of receiving Ships of the greatest Burthen: the Entrance of which is guarded with a strong Fort standing without the Harbour, call'd St Antonio: . . . There are other smaller Forts that command the Harbour . . . There are in the Town 13 Churches, Chapels, Hospitals, Convents, besides one Nunnery . . . The Houses of the Town are 2 or 3 Stories high, the Walls thick and strong, being built with Stone, with a covering of Pantile; and many of them have Balconies. The principal Streets are large, and all of them pav'd or pitch'd with small Stones. There are also Parades in the most eminent Places of the Town, and many Gardens, as well within the Town as in the Out-parts of it, wherein are Fruit-trees, Herbs, Salladings, and Flowers in great Variety, but order'd with no great Care or Art.

William Dampier, *A Voyage to New Holland in 1699*, 1703–9

The land is one great wild, untidy, luxuriant hot-house, made by nature for herself, but taken possession of by man, who has studded it with gay houses and formal gardens. How great would be the desire in every admirer of nature to behold the scenery of another planet! yet, to every person in Europe, it may be truly said, that at the distance of only a few degrees from his native soil, the glories of another world are opened to him.

Charles Darwin, *Journal . . . During the Voyage . . . of H.M.S. Beagle*, 1832–6

The Bahiano holds himself the cream of Brazilian cream.

Richard Burton, *Explorations of the Highlands of the Brazil*, 1869

Here, far more than in Parisianized Rio, one finds the familiar features of a Portuguese town reproduced, irregular and narrow streets, houses, often high, roofed with red tiles, and coloured with all sorts of washes, pink, green, blue, and yellow . . . In Sao Paulo there are few negroes, in Rio not very many, but here in Bahia all the town seems black. One might be in Africa or the West Indies.

James Bryce, *South America*, 1912

forest nearby
Delight itself, however, is a weak term to express the feelings of a naturalist who, for the first time has wandered by himself in a Brazilian forest. The elegance of the grasses, the novelty of the parasitical plants, the beauty of the flowers, the glossy green of the foliage, but above all the general luxuriance of the vegetation, filled me with admiration. A most paradoxical mixture of sound and silence pervades the shady parts of the wood. The noise from the insects is so loud that it may be heard even in a vessel anchored several hundred yards from the shore; yet within the recesses of the forest a universal silence appears to reign. To a person fond of natural history, such a day as this brings with it a deeper pleasure than he can ever hope to experience again.

Charles Darwin, *Journal . . . During the Voyage . . . of H.M.S. Beagle*, 1832–6

Boa Vista – Roraima

Boa Vista is a preposterous city: separate huddles of shabby houses along wide streets that have been marked out according to the design of a master town-planner. Only, the streets have not yet been built, except in short, abrupt, and arbitrary stretches. The planners have planned for the year 2000, and what in that year will be magnificent avenues in the meantime connect nothing to nothing through red Brazilian dirt. One curious result is that though in terms of population Boa Vista is a small city, its distances are metropolitan, without the alleviation of a metropolitan bus service. Lamp-standards line the well-planned desolation, part of the promise of the future, and a number of grand buildings, among them an abattoir and a hospital, both uncommissioned, have been put up, awaiting the future and an increase of population, which at present consists mainly of civil servants administering one another and smugglers who keep the civil servants supplied; the Brazilian Government, for reasons of economy and convenience, tolerating smuggling in this territory.

V.S. Naipaul, *The Middle Passage*, 1962

Brasilia

The sight of it from a high floor of the Hotel Nacional is like a strident chord in a desert of silence. Everything about it is *insolite*: a building here, a building there, receding in a clear, hand-painted Daliesque perspective to an improbable horizon, very minute and distant. Red, red earth. Spectacular underpasses and flyovers and endless avenues of brilliant, contemporary lamp-posts which, at night, create an illusion of a vast, inhabited metropolis, instead of the inspired, under-populated lunacy one sees by day. Here and there, workmen are busy, encouraging the visitor to hope that one day, perhaps, Brasilia will be completed.

Brian Crozier, 'Latin American Journey', *Encounter*, December 1964

We drove through the impersonal and sinister streets of Brasilia, that terrifying preview of a collectivist future.

Arthur M. Schlesinger, *One Thousand Days*, 1965

Ega

Nearly all the enmities which arise amongst residents at Ega and other places are caused by disputes about Indian servants. No one who has lived only in old settled countries, where service can be readily bought, can imagine the difficulties and annoyances of a land where the servant class are ignorant of the value of money, and hands cannot be obtained except by coaxing them from the employ of other masters.

Henry Walter Bates, *The Naturalist on the River Amazons*, 1863

Madeira River

The pilot we engaged . . . called the Madeira the 'long cemetery'.

H.M. Tomlinson, *The Sea and the Jungle*, 1912

Algeria, Egypt, or New York . . . never betray to the traveller that our world is not a shapeless parcel of fields and buildings, tied up with by-laws, and sealed by the Grand Lama as his last act in the stupendous work of creation. There it is, an angular package in the sky, which the sun reads, and directs on its way to heaven in advance of its limited syndicate of proprietors.

Here on the Madeira I had a vision instead of the earth as a great and shining sphere. There were no fences and private bounds. I saw for the first time an horizon as an arc suggesting how wide is our ambit. That bare shoulder of the world effaced regions and constellations in the sky. Our earth had celestial magnitude. It was a warm, a living body.

Ibid.

Manaus

There was also a geographical snobbism on my part. To find myself in Manaus seemed to me so extraordinary an achievement as to make me truly famous in my own eyes.

Saul Steinberg, 'Chronology', of 1952, in Harold Rosenberg, *Saul Steinberg*, 1978

Para (forest near)

There is something in a tropical forest akin to the ocean in its effects on the mind. Man feels so completely his insignificance there, and the vastness of nature. A naturalist cannot help reflecting on the vegetable forces manifested on so grand a scale around him. A German traveller, Burmeister, has said that the contemplation of a Brazilian forest produced on him a painful impression, on account of the vegetation displaying a spirit of restless selfishness, eager emulation, and craftiness. He thought the softness, earnestness, and repose of European woodland scenery were far more pleasing, and that these formed one of the causes of the superior moral character of European nations.

Henry Walter Bates, *The Naturalist on the River Amazons*, 1863

Petropolis

It is no small matter to find within five hours of Rio de Janeiro a spot where appetite is European, where exercise may be taken freely, and where you enjoy the luxury of sitting in a dry skin.

Richard Burton, *Explorations of the Highlands of the Brazil*, 1869

Rio de Janeiro

Following a pathway, I entered a noble forest, and from a height of five or six hundred feet, one of those splendid views was presented, which are so common on this side of Rio. At this elevation, the landscape attains its most brilliant tint; and every form, every shade, so completely surpasses in magnificence all that the European has ever beheld in his own country, that he knows not how to express his feelings. The general effect frequently recalled to my mind the gayest scenery of the Opera House or the great theatres.

Charles Darwin, *Journal . . . During the Voyage . . . of H.M.S. Beagle*, 1832–6

There – we have discovered America! just like Columbus and Americus and all those others. We hunted about for it yesterday, and found it today, and so I suppose the country will promote us all.

Emily Eden, Letter, 16 November 1835, in *Letters from India*, 1872

More than two-thirds of the population are slaves, and there is hardly a pure *white* left. It is odd how short a time surprise lasts. The streets swarm with natives wearing the same quantity of clothing that Adam did when he left Paradise, and they are carrying weights and dragging carts and making an odd hallooing noise, rather a cheerful one, and are totally unlike anything we are in the habit of seeing, and yet the sight of all these undressed creatures is not startling after the first moment. They have come out of the pictures in 'Steadmans Surinam' and I have seen them all before.

Emily Eden, Letter, 17 November 1835, in *Letters from India*, 1872

He thought Rio Janeiro the best place in the world for a great capital city.

R.W. Emerson, quoting William Wordsworth in conversation, *English Traits*, 1856

That charming, but somewhat drowsy, dreamy, and do-little Capital . . .

Richard Burton, *Explorations of the Highlands of the Brazil*, 1869

It is hard for man to make any city worthy of such surroundings as Nature has given to Rio.

James Bryce, *South America*, 1912

Anyone might be excused for doubting Rio. Its air is heavy with unreality; and cautious travellers, habituated to landscapes couched in a more normal idiom, justifiably refuse to believe a word of it. The mountains alone, a palpable invention of some demented stage designer, would not convince a child; and at any moment visitors expect to walk clean through the whole extravagant device and come out on the other side to find a disillusioned stage-hand working the lights. . . . But . . . nobody has ever found it out. . . . The hand of Nature (powerfully aided by the hand of man) stuns new arrivals into a sort of happy dream where anything may happen. Suburban streets end suddenly against the grey flank of a lonely mountain that has somehow got forgotten in a residential neighbourhood; roads climb out of a shopping district into the dripping silence of a forest in the tropics, where the big lianas hang and unimagined flowers blaze in the shadow of the trees, and drivers of oncoming traffic are apt to be bewildered by enormous blue butterflies flapping slowly towards them; and a road-tunnel full of trams opens incredibly upon the sudden blue of unexpected bays that curve between a line of big Atlantic rollers and a tall plantation where the palms are full of enthusiasts watching American football.

Philip Guedalla, *Argentine Tango*, 1932

Looking down on the city from the Sugar Loaf, you are aware of conflict. Rio has edged in between the hills and the sea, and on that boldly chosen strip of land has met and trounced the jungle. She gleams up at you complacently, a successful opportunist.

Peter Fleming, *Brazilian Adventure*, 1933

The Rio de Janeirians have but one social fault. They are committed, heart and soul, therefore so are you, to photography.

Frank Lloyd Wright, *An Autobiography*, 1943

Rio de Janeiro is the world's most beautiful city and the worst thing that has ever happened to Brazilians.

Hernane Taveres de Sá, *The Brazilians, People of Tomorrow*, 1947

Rio is not a sexy town: it is a copulating town. . . . Going to bed with women is almost a national hobby with Brazilians; it is rather like cricket in England.

George Mikes, *Tango: A Solo Across South America*, 1961

On the top of Corcovado, a gigantic statue of Jesus, with outstretched arms, dominates the picture. ('Never has Christ blessed a happier and more lovable brothel,' as the local saying has it.)

Ibid.

São Paulo (formerly Santos)

Santos . . . alias Wapping in the Far West.

Richard Burton, *Explorations of the Highlands of the Brazil*, 1869

Several immense Madrids breaking half the horizon.

Rudyard Kipling, *Brazilian Sketches*, 1927

Sao Paulo is like Reading, only much further away.

Peter Fleming, *Brazilian Adventure*, 1933

The locomotive which pulls the rest of Brazil.

Local saying, quoted by John Gunther, *Inside South America*, 1967

Varzea Redonda (on the São Francisco River, near Tacaratu)

The law of genesis, or development, is here carried out with particular vigour; the sole métier is apparently père de famille – a man who has not his dozen is considered a poor devil.

Richard Burton, *Explorations of the Highlands of the Brazil*, 1869

BULGARIA

I could note litle but the strange abundance of Chattering Magpies and of scolding women to which Exercise theyr Language helps much and tis probable those mimick birds are decoyed hither by the Delight they have in the Musique . . . The women here do allmost all the worke, at lest theyr shares with the Men; having a masculine proportion apted for it. Theyr Habit is a kind of Gowne without Sleeves wrought round at the Bottome, as are also theyr smocks so ordering the length of Either that the works on both do appeare. They weare Sylver Rings almost on every finger Bracelotts of black and white Beads or Shells upon theyr wrists and great Collars of sylver Coines about theyr Necks.

Robert Bargrave, *Journal*, 1648–52

A Bulgarian village presents a coup d'oeil different from any thing of the kind I have ever seen. It has the appearance of a Gipsey Encampment. The houses are composed of wicker work, with clay plastered inside, sometimes also on the outside – the method is driving a number of stakes into the ground about a foot and a half apart and entertwining twigs in a basket – the wall thus formed is about six feet high on which the roof is raised sloping at the sides and ends. It is covered with straw held down by sticks. They do not use ropes – indeed as the grain is trodden out by oxen, the straw is broken short and cannot be used as in moister countries, when it is tough.

John Webster, *Notes of a Journey from Constantinople to London via Vienna . . .*, 1834

Princess Bibesco . . . was very amusing about Tsar Ferdinand of Bulgaria, whom she knew well and who she declared was the complete cynic. He never referred to his people in any other terms than '*mes bufles*' – my buffaloes.

Sir Robert Bruce Lockhart, *Diary*, 23 February 1933

They are a fine people with a *passion* for freedom: so great that it made them able to remain 500 years under the Turk and come out pure Bulger at the end.

Freya Stark, Letter, 24 March 1939, in *The Coasts of Incense*, 1953

Sofia

Nor hath it yet lost the old Grecian Civilitie, for of all the Cities I ever passed, either in Christendome or without, I never saw any where a stranger is less troubled either with affronts or gaping . . . The Jews and Christians here have the doors of their houses little above three feet high, which they told me was, that the Turks might not bring in their horses, who else would use them for stables in their travel; which I noted for a sign of greater slavery than in other places.

Henry Blount, *A Voyage into the Levant*, 1634

There is something dry, hot, and fierce in this place, which is at once ordinary, sordid, and almost startling. It is a place at once violent and sullen, in which everything is dusty and dingy and half-used or half-finished. Stones and building materials lie strewn in the streets, houses are being made and houses are falling into ruins; everything is crude, sordid, with a crudity and sordidness which are half-western and half-eastern, and made out of the worst elements of both. The houses are for the most part such houses as one might see in any small town in any country, but at a corner of the main street there is a mosque, and around the mosque something like a village fair.

Arthur Symons, *Cities*, 1903

A kind of mongrel East was visibly upon me, and I felt that it would be only one more step to Constantinople.

And yet that one step I realised, would mean everything. What is so disquieting in Sofia is that it lies between two civilisations, and that it is a kind of rag-heap for the refuse of both. The main street of Sofia is the most horrible street in Europe. You see first of all mere European frippery, tin pots and pans, scraps of leather, shoes and slippers hanging from nails in front of shops, gimcracks in china, knives, 'fancy articles,' none personal to the place; rows of second-hand books and pamphlets, mostly in Russian . . . and along with them, strung upon upright boards by strings, cheap photographs of actresses, Cavalieri, or Cleo de Merode, and sentimental German photographs; then stalls of fruit, powdered thick with dust, dust-covered loaves of bread, which looked like great stones, crescents of sausages, coloured greenish red, trays and dishes of hot messes cooked over little ovens in the road; but above all meat: carcasses stripped of the hide, with their tails still hanging, the horns and hide lying outside in the gutter; beasts hacked in two, from which joints are being cut; everywhere yellow meat hanging from chains; all smells and all colours, as of the refuse of a slaughter-house. Men pass you on the pavement carrying the bodies of dead beasts upon their shoulders; you see a huddle of bloodstained hides in a cart standing beside the pavement; ducks and chickens squeak and flutter as they writhe head downwards under men's arms. And there is a continual coming and going of peasants in ragged and coloured clothes, women and girls with negress-like faces, wearing Turkish trousers under a sort of apron, half-naked gipsy children darting hither and thither, merchants, casual Europeans, in bowlers and overcoats; and, all the time, the rattle of the electric trams in the street as they pass to and fro, with their mockery of progress, through this city of dust and rags.

Ibid.

BURMA

Pegu, the old kingdom of

By the helpe of God we came safe to Pegu, which are two Cities, the old and the new, in the old Citie are the Merchant strangers, and Merchants of the Countrie, for there are the greatest doings and the greatest trade. This Citie is not very great, but it hath very great Suburbs. Their houses be made with canes, and covered with leaves, or with straw, but the Merchants have all one house or Magason, which house they call Godon, which is made of brickes, and there they put all their goods of any value, to save them from the often mischance that there happen to houses made of such stuffe. In the new Citie is the Palace of the King, and his abiding place with all his Barons and Nobles, and other Gentlemen; and in the time that I was there, they finished the building of the new Citie: it is a great Citie, very plaine and flat, and foure square, walled round about with water, in which Ditches are many Crocodiles. It hath no Draw-bridges, yet it hath twenty Gates, five for every square on the Walls, there are many places made for Centinels to watch, made of Wood and covered or gilt with Gold, the Streets thereof are the fairest that I have seene, they are as streight as a line from one Gate to another, and standing at the one Gate you may discover to the other, and they are as broad as ten or twelve men many ride a-breast in them: and those Streets that be thwart are faire and large, these Streets, both on the one side and the other, are planted at the doores of the Houses with Nut trees of India, which make a very commodious shadow, the Houses be made of wood, and covered with a kind of tiles in forme of Cups, very necessary for their use: the Kings Palace is in the middle of the Citie, made in forme of a walled Castle, with ditches full of water round about it, the Lodgings within are made of wood all over gilded, with fine pinacles, and very costly worke, covered with plates of gold.

Caesar Frederick, *Eighteene Yeares Indian Observations*, 1567 in *Purchas his Pilgrimes*, 1625

Nothing happens in Burma, but then nothing is expected to happen.

Paul Theroux, *The Great Railway Bazaar*, 1975

Burmese

in Pegu (the old kingdom)

In Pegu, and in all the Countries of Ava, Langeiannes, Siam, and the Bramas, the men weare bunches or little round balls in their privie members: some of them weare two and some three. They cut the skinne and so put them in, one into one side and another into the other side; which they doe when they bee five and twentie or thirtie yeeres old, and at their pleasure they take one or more of them out as they thinke good. When they be married the Husband is for every Child which his Wife hath, to put in one untill hee come three, and then no more: for they say the women doe desire them. They were invented because they should not abuse the male sexe. For in times past all those Countries were so given to that Villanie, that they were very scarce of people . . . The bunches aforesaid bee of divers sorts: the least be as bigge as a little Walnut, and very round: the greatest are as bigge as a little Hens egge: some are of Brasse and some of Silver: but those of silver bee for the King and his Noblemen. These are gilded and made with great cunning, and ring like a little bell. There are some made of Lead, which they call Selwy, because they ring but little: and these be of lesser price for the poorer sort. The King sometimes taketh his out, and giveth them to his Noblemen as a great gift: and because he hath used them, they esteeme them greatly. They will put one in and heale up the place in seven or eight dayes.

Ralph Fitch, *The Voyage*, 1583–91, in *Purchas his Pilgrimes*, 1625

The Burman is a smiling obdurate humorist who shines in opposition. He is beginning to idealise the Irish. 'We are the Irish of the East,' he says.

H.G. Wells, *Travels of a Republican Radical in Search of Hot Water*, 1939

Kaw People

The Kaws stand out from among the others by reason of their fine physique and swarthy colour. The authorities, however, state that the darkness of their complexion is due for the most part to their dislike of the use of water.

W. Somerset Maugham, *The Gentleman in the Parlour*, 1930

Cosmin

Cosmin . . . is a very pretie Towne, and standeth very pleasantly, very well furnished with all things. The people be very tall and well disposed; the women white, round faced, with little eyes: the houses are high built, set upon great high posts, and they goe up to them with long Ladders for feare of the Tigres, which be very many.

Ralph Fitch, *The Voyage*, 1583–91, in *Purchas his Pilgrimes*, 1625

Mandalay

On the road to Mandalay
Where the flyin' fishes play,
An' the dawn comes up like thunder outer China 'crost
the Bay!

Rudyard Kipling, *Mandalay*, 1890

There is a marvellous Indo-Chinese-Transatlantic-British-cum-Gallic appearance about the city.

John Foster Fraser, *Round the World on a Wheel*, 1899

Mengon – near Amarapura

Then I went to see the great bell at Mengon. Here is a Buddhist convent and as I stood looking a group of nuns surrounded me . . . Their dark eyes were alert with covetousness and their smiles were mischievous. They were very old and they had no human ties or affections. They seemed to look upon the world with a humorous cynicism. They had lived through every kind of illusion and held existence in a malicious and laughing contempt. They had no tolerance for the follies of men and no indulgence for their weakness. There was something vaguely frightening in their entire lack of attachment to human things. They had done with love, they had finished with the anguish of separation, death had no terrors for them, they had nothing left now but laughter. They struck the great bell so that I might hear its tone; boom, boom, it went, a long, low note, that travelled in slow reverberations down the river, a solemn sound that seemed to call the soul from its tenement of clay, and reminded it that though all created things were illusion, in the illusion was also beauty; and the nuns, following the sound, burst into ribald cackles of laughter, hi, hi, hi, that mocked the call of the great bell. Dupes, their laughter said, dupes and fools. Laughter is the only reality.

W. Somerset Maugham, *The Gentleman in the Parlour*, 1930

Moulmein

Moulmein is situated up the mouth of a river which ought to flow through South America.

Rudyard Kipling, *From Sea to Sea*, 1889

In Moulmein, in Lower Burma, I was hated by large numbers of people – the only time in my life that I have been important enough for this to happen to me. I was sub-divisional police officer of the town, and in an aimless, petty kind of way anti-European feeling was very bitter. . . . As a police officer I was an obvious target and was baited whenever it seemed safe to do so.

George Orwell, *Shooting an Elephant*, 1936

Rangoon

The Government was contemplating the dispatch of an expedition to Burma, with a view to taking Rangoon, and a question arose as to who would be the fittest general to be sent in command of the expedition. The Cabinet sent for the Duke of Wellington, and asked his advice. He instantly replied, 'Send Lord Combermere.'

'But we have always understood that your Grace thought Lord Combermere a fool.'

'So he is a fool, and a d . . . d fool; but he can take Rangoon.'

G.W.E. Russell, *Collections and Recollections*, 1898

It seemed to me that Rangoon consisted chiefly of pawn-shops and pagodas.

John Foster Fraser, *Round the World on a Wheel*, 1899

En route to Rangoon

Then, a golden mystery upheaved itself on the horizon – a beautiful winking wonder that blazed in the sun, of a shape that was neither Muslim dome nor Hindu temple spire. It stood upon a green knoll, and below it were lines of warehouses, sheds, and mills. Under what new god, thought I, are we irrepressible English sitting now?

'There's the old Shway Dagon' (pronounced Dagone, *not* like the god in the Scriptures), said my companion. 'Confound it!' But it was not a thing to be sworn at. It explained in the first place why we took Rangoon, and in the second why we pushed on to see what more of rich or rare the land held. Up till that sight my uninstructed eyes could not see that the land differed much in appearance from the Sunderbuns, but the golden dome said: 'This is Burma, and it will be quite unlike any land you know about.' 'It's a famous old shrine o' sorts,' said my companion, 'and now the Tounghoo-Mandalay line is open, pilgrims are flocking down by the thousand to see it. It lost its big gold top – 'thing that they call a '*htee* – in an earthquake: that's why it's all hidden by bamboo-work for a third of its height. You should see it when it's all uncovered. They're regilding it now.'

Rudyard Kipling, *From Sea to Sea*, 1889

C

CAMBODIA/KAMPUCHEA

. . . the miles of lime-green mirrors for the sky that the rice-fields made on either side of the road leading northward, reflecting the images of castellated and turreted clouds, or a perfect blue vacancy, broken in some cases by the thin, shrill green shoots of the young rice, showing through them, as if the sky were bursting into bud.

Osbert Sitwell, *Escape with Me,* 1939

I have lived seventy-eight years without hearing of bloody places like Cambodia.

Sir Winston Churchill, 28 April 1953, remark quoted in Lord Moran, *Winston Churchill, The Struggle For Survival,* 1966

Westerners are always astonished that we Cambodians are not disturbed by our future in which China will play such a powerful role. But one should try to put himself in our place: in this jungle, which is the real world, should we, simple deer, interest ourselves in a dinosaur like China, when we are more directly menaced, and have been for centuries by the wolf and the tiger, who are Vietnam and Thailand?

Prince Norodum Sihanouk, 1961, quoted by Cynthia Frederick, in *Bulletin of Concerned Asian Scholars,* 2 (April–July) 1970

I have seen the past and it works.

Richard West, 'Sihanouk's Cambodia: Forward into the Past', *Sunday Times Magazine,* 8 September 1968

The country is so fertile that only war or grotesque mismanagement could produce real hunger and poverty.

Ibid.

Before the fall of Sihanouk it was the last paradise, the last paradise.

Helicopter pilot, quoted by Richard West, *Victory in Vietnam,* 1974

Cambodians

We are not just animals like buffalo or oxen to make rice. We make rice, but we have not to be like oxen and buffaloes but, er, a little better, ha ha – if possible – if possible.

Prince Norodom Sihanouk, Press Conference, Peking, 8 January 1979 (after the fall of the Pol Pot regime during the invasion of Cambodia by 'rebel forces' backed by Vietnam)

Angkor Thom, ruins of

All is now desolate, fantastic, and ambushed with ghosts; the erroneous opinions of archaeologists twitter among them like bats.

Rose Macaulay, *Pleasures of Ruins,* 1953

Angkor Wat

It calls you silently, irresistibly, day and night. People go out there alone, at all hours, and when met with are not communicative. Unable to sleep in the stifling small hours, I have wandered out along the causeway and up into the vast, still temple and met with other pyjamaed figures smoking their pipes apart and in silence on the moon-bathed heights of the Sanctuary.

Crosbie Garstin, *The Dragon and the Lotus,* 1928

Angkor, compared with Borobudur in Indonesia

Man is a born geometer. Even when he is expressing himself in curves, as he has done in the undulating roofs of Eastern Asia and in the flowing sculptures at Borubudur, his lines follow mathematical laws that are unknown to Nature; and he is frankly defying her when he works in rectangles. Angkor is perhaps the greatest of Man's essays in rectangular architecture that has yet been brought to light . . .

The Buddhist stupa at Borobudur in Central Java is a lyric poem in stone, flowing round the crown of a hill to the musical accompaniment of a jagged mountain range on one side and a green expanse of rice fields on the other. Angkor is not orchestral; it is monumental. It is an epic poem which makes its effect, like the Odyssey and like Paradise Lost, by the grandeur of its structure as well as by the beauty of the details. Angkor is an epic in rectangular forms imposed upon the Cambodian jungle.

Arnold Toynbee, *East to West,* 1958

Piranesi would have loved the place.

James Kirkup, *Streets of Asia,* 1969

Pailin

Pailin, *c'est le far ouest cambodgien!*

A Cambodian prince, in 1966, quoted by Milton Osborne, *Before Kampuchea,* 1979

Phnom Penh

Phnom-Penh was one of those synthetic Chinese towns with all the warm glitter so cheering to the hearts of Sunday night Coventry Street crowds. The Chinese are not interested in South-East Asian towns until they have reached on their own initiative a certain level of population and prosperity. They then descend like a flock of gregarious birds, galvanizing its life with their crow-like vitality. The feeble shoots of local culture wither away and what remains is a degenerate native slum round the hard, bright, self-contained Chinese core.

Norman Lewis, *A Dragon Apparent,* 1951

Phnom Penh struck one as a city almost entirely alien to the country of which it is the capital.

George Woodcock, *Asia, Gods and Cities,* 1966

I remember Phnom Penh as a city of broad streets, trees, flowers and flamboyants; serene and smiling people; of dusk at a café beside the river and after dark the floating dance halls where Vietnamese girls, insubstantial as shadows, swayed in the moonlight to music that I had never before heard or imagined. In the mornings I sat under the green awning at *La Paillotte* in the market place, drinking orange juice and bitter tea, watching the slow crowds by the foodstalls crammed with the abundance of a fertile land. There were Vietnamese lunches and French dinners and late at night a soft tap on the door from a barefoot girl who smiled as you unwound her from her sarong.

Richard West, *Victory in Vietnam,* 1974

If the charm of the city was provincial, there was charm nonetheless. Just how 'provincial' the city was in French terms I was not to realise until years later when I saw in southern France the models for the Post Office Square, the bars and cafes, the Magasin Modern that just occasionally had in stock the items one wanted to buy, and the villas of the French Quarter with their gravelled courtyards behind walls topped with iron spikes and bougainvillea.

Milton Osborne, *Before Kampuchea,* 1979

CAMEROUN

Farewell, Camaroons! Farewell, beautiful heights! where so many calm and quiet days have sped without sandflies or mosquitoes, or prickly heat. Adieu! happy rustic wilds! where I have spent so many pleasant weeks, even in West Africa. Adieu! and may adieu in this case bear all the significance of au revoir!

Richard Burton, *Abeokuta and the Camaroons Mountains,* 1863

Portuguese slave traders dominated the Cameroons first, and gave the country its name, from the piquantly edible prawns (*camaroes* in Portuguese) found in its clouded waters. Every time the Cameroons have become a political issue among the European powers, erudite wits have been unable to resist making a mild joke, to the effect that the Cameroons are prawns in the game.

John Gunther, *Inside Africa,* 1955

Mount Cameroun

It was impossible to hear, or make oneself heard at the distance of even a few paces, because of the shrill squeal of the wind, the roar of the thunder, and the rush of the rain on the trees round us. It was not like having a storm burst over you in the least; you felt you were in the middle of its engine-room when it had broken down badly. After half an hour or so, the thunder seemed to lift itself off the ground, and the lightning came in sheets, instead of in great forks that flew like flights of spears among the forest trees. The thunder, however had not settled things amicably with the mountain; it roared its rage at Mungo, and Mungo answered back, quivering with a rage as great, under our feet. One feels here, as if one were constantly dropping, unasked, and unregarded, among painful and violent discussions between the elemental powers of the Universe. Mungo growls and swears in thunder at the sky, and sulks in white mist all the morning, and then the sky answers back, hurling down lightnings and rivers of water, with total disregard for Mungo's visitors.

Mary Kingsley, *Travels in West Africa,* 1897

Yaounde

The 250 white people in this capital . . . seem always conscious of their good fortune in being stationed where a man can breathe.

Negley Farson, *Behind God's Back,* 1940

CANADA

Quelques arpens de neige.
(A few acres of snow)

Voltaire, *Candide,* 1759

Canada at this day is an exact picture of ancient Germany.

Edward Gibbon, *The Decline and Fall of the Roman Empire,* 1776-88

Respecting Canada, one or other of the two following will take place, *viz* if Canada should become populous, it will revolt; and if it does not become so, it will not be worth the expense of holding . . . But Canada *never will* be populous; neither is there any occasion for contrivances on one side or the other, for nature alone will do the whole . . . I would not, were I a European power, have Canada under the conditions that Britain must retain it, could it be given to me. It is one of those kind of dominions that is, and ever will be, a constant charge upon any foreign holder.

Thomas Paine, Letter to the Abbé Raynal, 1782

Every man of sense, whether in the Cabinet or out of it, knows that Canada must, at no distant period, be merged in the American Republic.

Edinburgh Review, 1825

British America appears to me not a bad country for a destitute man, or one who possesses health and strength, and nothing more, but who has been accustomed to bodily labour from his youth upwards.

Captain Basil Hall, *Travels in North America,* 1829

My eyes never rested on the Canada shore without my feeling how absurd it was that that poor country should belong to us, its poverty and hopeless inactivity contrasting, so much to our disgrace, with the prosperous activity of the opposite shore: – but here was the climax of absurdity, the prevention of a free traffic in butter and eggs.

Harriet Martineau, *Retrospect of Western Travel,* 1838

Few Englishmen are prepared to find it what it is. Advancing quietly; old differences settling down, and being fast forgotten; public feeling and private enterprise alike in a sound and wholesome state; nothing of flush or fever in its system, but health and vigour throbbing in its steady pulse: it is full of hope and promise.

Charles Dickens, *American Notes,* 1842

I must confess that in going from the States into Canada an Englishman is struck by the feeling that he is going from a richer country into one that is poorer, and from a greater country into one that is less.

Anthony Trollope, *North America,* 1862

The Great Lone Land.

Sir William Butler, Title of Book, 1872

Canada is a political expression.

Goldwin Smith, *Canada and the Canadian Question,* 1891

Canada is said to have got its name from the two Spanish words 'Aca' and 'Nada,' as signifying 'there is nothing here.'

R.B. Cunninghame Graham, *Mogreb-el-Acksa,* 1898

If Canada did not exist it would be to the interest of the United States to invent her.

James Bryce, quoted by H.A.L. Fisher, *An Unfinished Autobiography,* 1940

There is no mistaking the spirit of sane and realised nationality, which fills the land from end to end precisely as the joyous hum of a big dynamo well settled to its load makes a background to all the other shop noises.

Rudyard Kipling, *Letters to the Family,* 1907

Have you ever noticed that Canada has to deal in the lump with most of the problems that afflict us others severally? For example, she has the Double-Language, Double-Law, Double-Politics drawback in a worse form than South Africa, because, unlike our Dutch, her French cannot well marry outside their religion, and they take their orders from Italy – less central, sometimes, than Pretoria or Stellenbosch. She has, too, something of Australia's labour fuss, minus Australia's isolation, but plus the open and secret influence of 'Labour' entrenched, with arms, and high explosives on neighbouring soil. To complete the parallel, she keeps, tucked away behind mountains, a trifle of land called British Columbia, which resembles New Zealand; and New Zealanders who do not find much scope for young enterprise in their own country are drifting up to British Columbia already.

Ibid.

I don't even know what street Canada is on.

Al Capone, remark 1931, quoted in Roy Greenaway, *The News Game,* 1966

Canada is the linch-pin of the English-speaking world.

Sir Winston Churchill, Speech at Mansion House, 4 September 1941, in the presence of Mr Mackenzie King, Prime Minister of Canada

The long unguarded frontier, the habits and intercourse of daily life, the fruitful and profitable connexions of business, the sympathies and even the antipathies of honest neighbourliness, make Canada a binder together of the English speaking peoples. She is a magnet exercising a double attraction, drawing both Great Britain and the United States towards herself, and thus drawing them closer to each other.

Sir Winston Churchill, quoted in the *Oxford Junior Encyclopedia,* vol. 1

This is the case of a high-school land,
deadset in adolescence,
loud treble laughs and sudden fists,
bright cheeks, the gangling presence.
This boy is wonderful at sports
and physically quite healthy;
he's taken to church on Sunday still

and keeps his prurience stealthy.
He doesn't like books except about bears,
collects new coins and model planes
and never refuses a dare.
His uncle spoils him with candy of course,
yet shouts him down when he talks at table.
You will note he's got some of his French mother's
looks,
though he's not so witty and no more stable.
He's really much more like his father and yet
if you say so he'll pull a great face.
He wants to be different from everyone else
and daydreams of winning the global race.
Parents unmarried and living abroad,
relatives keen to bag the estate,
schizophrenia not excluded,
will he grow up before it's too late?

Earle Birney, *Canada: Case History,* 1945

I saw a great and wonderful country; a land containing in its soil everything that a man desires; a proper land, fit for proper men to live in and to prosper exceedingly.

Field-Marshal Lord Montgomery, Broadcast Message to the Peoples of Canada, September 1946, quoted in Montgomery's *Memoirs,* 1958

Canadian statesmen reconciled the irreconcilable when in the 1840's they joined dependence to independence . . . In every generation Canadians have had to rework the miracle of their political existence. Canada has been created because there has existed within the hearts of its people a determination to build for themselves an enduring home. Canada is a supreme act of faith.

A.R.M. Lower, *Colony to Nation,* 1946

You have to know a man awfully well in Canada to know his surname.

John Buchan, Lord Tweedsmuir, *Observer,* 'Sayings of the Week', 21 May 1950

What are you? . . . they ask, in wonder.
And she replies in the worst silence of her woods:
. . . I am the wind that wants a flag.
I am the mirror of your picture
until you make me the marvel of your life.

Patrick Anderson, *Poem of Canada, The White Centre,* 1946

The aloofness of Canada, not less inhabited perhaps, but so far less humanized than Asia, struck me with awe, and an immense admiration for the courage that had tackled it.

Freya Stark, *Beyond Euphrates,* 1951

And then, of course, there was *Nature,* the landscape, the geographical immensity, which Canadians talked about so much: the 'wild beast' they told you they tried unsuccessfully to domesticate in their backyards; the curious pressure of muskeg and tundra and forest they felt 'on their skulls'; the sense of being high up in the rigging of America, as the more fanciful might put it, and giddy with height – of playing lonely children's games in the attic of a populous house and always having to reach out along the horizontal beam of East and West, the roof misty above them, to make tenuous contact with anyone else. At first, anyway, this was simply bewilderment. All we knew was that, however 'young' the country might be, the landscape seemed old and violent and sad. In summer we staggered out of the boiling city; the landscape closed around us; we sank into it like peasants into a feather bed . . . And in winter the same valleys that had sucked us in tightened below our feet into fold upon fold of snow, flicking our shadows askew behind us, jerking our breath from our mouths, chapping our lips and crisping the corners of our eyes, and then hurling us up into immense depths of blue but icy sky.

Patrick Anderson, *Search Me,* 1957

Space enters the bloodstream . . . this is an immense country.

Report of the Royal Commission on Canada's Economic Prospects, The Gordon Commission, 1957

The wilderness remains a partner in the venture.

Ibid.

I wondered why I felt so bitter about Canada. After all, it was all part of a dream, an experiment that could not come off. It was foolish to believe that you can take the throwouts, the rejects, the human kickabouts from Europe and tell them: Here you have a second chance. Here you can start a new life. But no one ever mentioned the price one had to pay; how much of oneself you had to betray.

Norman Levine, *Canada Made Me,* 1958

I rang up an official in the Montreal Board of Trade. . . .

I wasn't in the man's office ten minutes before he began to lecture me on Canada. What did I mean by living away when Canada needed all her writers at home? I was in no mood for a sermon. And I thought I would gradually change the subject by asking him what did those advertisements BE A GOOD CANADIAN mean, put out by Seagrams. I had seen them again this morning on the streetcar. Before, they had a green parrot saying these words, now there were pictures of smiling bank-managers, smiling farmers, smiling salesmen. He stood up as if he was going to make a public speech. But he was betrayed by his physical presence: the round plump face, the glasses, the weak eyes, pink like a mouse, and the pot belly making his trouser seams fan out as if he was smuggling something inside. 'A Good Canadian is one who sees that he earns enough money . . . ' The voice drawled slowly on full of small-town wisdom, '. . . so that he is able to do the same things and live the same kind of life and maintain the standard of living that his friends are enjoying.'

Ibid.

The greatest single land under the sun,
The planet's greatest hope, her friends believe.

John Masefield, *Lines on the Occasion of Her Majesty's Visit to Canada*, 1959

and USA

Geography has made us neighbours. History has made us friends. Economics has made us partners. And necessity has made us allies. Those whom nature has so joined together, let no man put asunder.

John F. Kennedy, Address to the Canadian Parliament, Ottawa, 17 May 1961

Railways, as somebody once remarked, became the national genius.

Alistair Horne, *Canada and the Canadians*, 1961

The symbol of contemporary Canada is the beaver, that industrious rodent whose destiny it was to furnish hats that warmed better brains than his own.

Roy Daniells, in Julian Parks (ed.), *The Culture of Contemporary Canada*, 1957

Canada is really two countries held together by three nation-saving bywords – conservatism, caution and compromise – bequeathed to us by Britain.

William Toye, *A Book of Canada*, 1962

When I was in New York an editor told me that he and his associates had recently compiled a list of twelve books with which to start a publishing firm that was bound to fail. Leading the list of unreadables was: *Canada Our Good Neighbour to the North.*

Mordecai Richler, 'Quebec Oui, Ottawa Non', *Encounter*, December 1964

Canada could have enjoyed:
  English government,
    French culture,
      and American know-how.
Instead it ended up with:
  English know-how,
    French government,
      and American culture.

John Robert Colombo, *Oh Canada*, 1965

Canada can now be considered a major power. She rates it because she has a major sex-scandal . . . No country which wants to play a deciding role in international affairs can have any influence without a first-class sex-in-government crisis.

Art Buchwald, 'Sex and the Single Nation', in *Son of the Great Society*, 1967

The national voice in Canada is muted. To quote Hugh Hood . . . there cannot be an Uncanadian Activities Committee because 'Uncanadianism is almost the very definition of Canadianism.'

George Woodcock, *Canada and the Canadians*, 1970

When they had a competition to name Canada's first space satellite, the poet Leonard Cohen thought that even this prodigy should reflect the Canadian nature. They should call it, he suggested, *Ralph.*

Jan Morris, 'On the Confederation Special', *Travels*, 1976

Canada . . . has a balance of payments deficit bigger than any country on earth. . . . We have no policies, no convictions, and no future. The big question for this conference should be, Why don't we give the country to the Americans? They seem to want it much more than we do.

Dian Cohen, Speech at Duke of Edinburgh's Commonwealth Study Conference, Kingston, Ontario, reported in the *Montreal Gazette* Sunday Magazine, *Today*, 9 August 1980

Canadians

When the Canadians have a decent restaurant they will be nicer people, and when they are nicer people they will have a decent restaurant.

Samuel Butler, *Further Extracts from Note-books*, 1934

When I was there I found their jokes like their roads – very long and not very good, leading to a little tin point of a spire which has been remorselessly obvious for miles without seeming to get any nearer.

Ibid.

The energy and *joie de vivre* of the young country seems only to flourish in the towns. The country seems to rise on stepping stones not of its dead selves, but of its dead pioneers, and the first lot who do the cleaning and the real hard work seem usually to succumb: then their successors get on.

Freya Stark, Letter, 30 November 1928, in *Beyond Euphrates*, 1951

If we could get off by ourselves on a continental island, far away from the wicked Americans, all we should achieve would be to become a people like the Australians.

Frank Underhill, 'Notes on the Massey Report', *Canadian Forum*, xxxi, 1951–2

The Canadian is *not* an American – at least, not entirely, not yet.

Alistair Horne, *Canada and the Canadians*, 1961

You won't find any Canadians in the North; only mad dogs and Scotsmen.

Welsh scientist, remark quoted by Alistair Horne, *Ibid.*

A Canadian is somebody who knows how to make love in a canoe.

Pierre Berton, attrib. 1973

A North American who does not owe allegiance to the United States or Mexico.

George Woodcock, *The Canadians,* 1980

French Canadians

There can hardly be conceived a nationality more destitute of all that can invigorate and elevate a people than that which is exhibited by the descendants of the French in Lower Canada, owing to their retaining their peculiar language and manners. They are a people with no history and no literature.

Lord Durham, *Report on the Affairs of British North America,* 1839

Americans south of the Canadian border forget, or never knew, . . . that the French were the first Westerners.

Alastair Cooke, *Alastair Cooke's America,* 1973

Eskimoes

I was reminded . . . of a story Peter Scott had told me about the Eskimoes. After he had described some incident of the last war to them they had exclaimed with horror: 'But do you Europeans actually go out and kill people you've never met?'

Laurens van der Post, *The Lost World of the Kalahari,* 1958

British Columbia

The history of British Columbia proper is of the briefest possible kind.

S.W. Silver & Co's Handbook to Canada, 1881

on the Fraser River

It is impossible to convey an idea of the *luxe* of beautiful views there is in this country.

The Marchioness of Dufferin and Ava, *My Canadian Journal,* 6 September 1876, 1891

Such a land is good for an energetic man. It is also not so bad for the loafer.

Rudyard Kipling, Letters to the Family, 1908

You cross the Rocky Mountains from the prairies to British Columbia, and you are in a different place: you are in another country. I don't know how to say it strongly enough. Let me begin again. The Prairie Provinces are one place and British Columbia is another . . . a thing by itself: a vast Pacific Empire beside the sea. It is only the fact that it is as far from Europe as you can get that so long kept it out of history.

Stephen Leacock, *My Discovery of the West,* 1937

An ideal home for the human race not too cold, not too hot, not too wet, and not too dry, except in the hotels, a thing which time may remedy.

Ibid.

Calgary

and Toronto

Toronto stood recognisably for Empire; Calgary did not stand for anything much, except personal opportunity, . . . Toronto might seem a substitute for older societies, but Calgary was more like an alternative. It did not compete, it did not pretend, it was something different in kind. . . . As the city signs say to this day, 'The Car Park is temporarily Full' – and in that Temporarily, Calgary speaks.

Jan Morris, 'On the Confederation Special,' *Travels,* 1976 – of 1927

They say of Calgary that it's going to look really great when it finally gets uncrated.

Robert Fox, BBC Radio, March 1981

Chilcoot Pass

I was anxious to ascertain if the pass was really as heartbreaking as the pictures I had seen in the guide-books portraying it, and consulted an American gentleman who came up in the *Alert* with me, and who subsequently had been industriously earning a 'grub stake' by packing up to the summit. I simply asked him if it was as steep as represented. He had a wan, pale, drawn look, and after reflectively scratching his ear, he said, 'Wal, cap, I was *prepared* for it to be per-*pen*-dicular, but by G–d, I never thought it would *lean back.*'

J.H.E. Secretan, *To Klondyke and Back,* 1898

Dawson

It is in summer one of the prettiest places imaginable. Viewed from a distance on a still July day, the clean bright looking town and garden-girt villas dotting the green hills around are more suggestive of a tropical country than of a bleak arctic land. . . . Notwithstanding its remoteness Dawson may almost be called a gay place.

Harry de Windt, *From Paris to New York by Land,* 1904

Dawson City's streets are still partly paved with gold. Whenever repair or demolition work is proceeding on an old building the workmen adopt certain precautions dictated by enlightened self-interest. For example, if they are taking up a floor, they sweep the dirt between and beneath the boards into pans and wash it with care. For every now and then a speck or two of gold-dust is revealed. The workmen themselves always receive at least a share of this treasure trove and consequently the solicitude with which they treat dirt lying around the place is great. Sometimes their reward is on a splendid scale. When the old Bank of Commerce building—where Robert W. Service worked as a clerk before he became poet laureate of the Yukon—was reconstructed recently the men recovered from various cracks and crevices in the structure twenty-two ounces of pure gold.

Malcolm MacDonald, *Canadian North,* 1945

Most of the buildings have been part of Dawson since the gold rush. Easily half of them are boarded up and empty, and there is hardly one that does not slant crazily along the plank sidewalks. Perhaps half are log; the rest are frame with corrugated iron roofs. Their architecture is of that style familiar to students of the Old West—the school of the false front, the bay window, the fluted pillar and covered entrance, the scrolled cornice and ornamental balcony. But now the architecture mocks the visitor because it is crumbling away.

Street after street is lined with empty buildings: old hotels and gaming houses, deserted dance halls, saloons and grocery stores with rotting porticoes and sightless windows. Nature is not kind to frame buildings set in permafrost. There was once a flat little park built in Dawson. It stayed flat for a year, then took on the roller-coaster contours characteristic of the terrain. Even the occupied structures slump drunkenly because the ground on which they are built—frozen permanently for some two hundred feet down—continually heaves and sinks. . . .

Pierre Berton, *The Mysterious North,* 1956

Edmonton

It was the essential rawness of Edmonton that made it seem to conform more to my idea of a new Siberian city than anything else I had seen in Canada. . . . Exciting, perhaps even colourful, but tough; a city I would not like to be unemployed in. . . . It has the worst case of Los Angeles spread in all Canada.

Alistair Horne, *Canada and the Canadians,* 1961

Mount Eisenhower

You know, it's a very small peak, considering the Canadian terrain.

Douglas MacArthur, Remark, 1946, quoted by William Manchester from article by Faubion Bowers, *Esquire,* 1967, in *American Caesar,* 1979

Fort William and Port Arthur *(now Thunder Bay)*

When I say Fort William I include with it the adjoining city of Port Arthur. They ought to be joined and called Fwather, or Port Arthliam. One can't keep saying both. But under any name it is quite literally what you would call a *gigantic* place. It is drawn upon a big scale, as if a great hand had seized a pencil and marked out, in great bold strokes, vast empty squares, and streets as wide as fields. So big is the city that they haven't had time to fill in the houses. Later on, when they get time to put in lots of houses and buildings, it will be a fine city. At present it is all so spread out that a motor car looks lonely and a pedestrian like a solitary wanderer. There are great open spaces everywhere. Everything is planned to be a mile away from everything else.

Stephen Leacock, *My Discovery of the West,* 1937

Fredericton, Nova Scotia

Fredericton can only yet be rated as a village, but is laid off very well in large broad streets. . . .

George Ramsey, 9th Earl of Dalhousie, Journal, 24 October 1817

Fredericton is the unmarred and unscratched relic, the perfect museum piece, and with that final rarity in our time, a complete unconsciousness of itself, for it has never been discovered, extolled, or exploited by the traveller. . . . It is the Home Town as it should be, where men can sit and dream, as they must have dreamed in the Athens of Pericles.

Bruce Hutchinson, *The Unknown Dominion,* 1946

The Great Lakes

See also under USA

There is a quiet horror about the Great Lakes which grows as one revisits them. Fresh water has no right or call to dip over the horizon, pulling down and pushing up the hulls of big steamers; no right to tread the slow deep-sea dance-step between wrinkled cliffs; nor to roar in on weed and sand beaches between vast headlands that run out for leagues into haze and sea-fog. Lake Superior is all the same stuff as what towns pay taxes for, but it engulfs, and wrecks, and drives ashore, like a fully-accredited ocean – a hideous thing to behold in the heart of a Continent. Some people go sailing on it for pleasure, and it has produced a breed of sailors who bear the same relation to the salt-water variety as a snake-charmer does to a lion-tamer.

Rudyard Kipling, 'Cities and Spaces', in *Letters of Travel*, 1907

There is something ominous and unnatural about these great lakes. . . . The sea, very properly, will not be allowed in heaven. It has no soul. It is unvintageable, cruel, treacherous, what you will. But, in the end, – while we have it with us – it is all right; even though that all-rightness result, but, as with France, from the recognition of an age-long feud, and an irremediable lack of sympathy. But these monstrous lakes, which ape the ocean, are not proper to fresh water, or to salt. They have souls, perceptibly, and wicked ones.

Rupert Brooke, *Letters from America, 1913*, 1916

Lake Erie

Lake Erie is weary
Of washing the dreary
Crowds of the cities
That line her shores.
Oh, you know
The dirty people of Buffalo
And those of Cleveland
That must leave land
To see what the water's like.
And those that by bike,
Motor car, bus and screeching train
Come from London in the rain
To Port Stanley where they spend
The day in deciding whether Grand Bend
Might not have been a nicer place to go.
Up and down in thousands
They walk upon Lake Erie's sands.
Those in Cleveland say, 'Plainly,'
As they gaze across the waters
Where swim their sons and daughters,
'That distant speck must be Port Stanley.'
Those in Port Stanley yawn, 'Oh,
That lump in the mist
Over there really must
Be populous Cleveland in Ohio.'
But Lake Erie says, 'I know
That people say I'm shallow
But you just watch me when I go
With a thump
And a plump
At the Falls of Niagara into Lake Ontario.
When you see that you'll admit
That I'm not just a shallow nitwit
But a lake
That takes the cake
For a grand gigantic thunderous exit.'

James Reaney, *The Red Heart,* 1949

Lake Huron

Yoohoo Yoohoo
I'm blue, blue
Lake Huron.
By my shores
In fratricidal wars
Indians killed each other.
At Bayfield
The people stop
To see me slop
Against the pier.
At Grant Bend
The people tend
Instead to
Look at each other.
The Au Sable River and the Maitland
Flow into me.
They think I'm a sea
But haw haw
They're not through yet
For blue and wet
I flow into Lake St. Clair
And Lake St. Clair into Lake Erie
So very very weary
And Lake Erie into
Lake Ontario
Like a blue grain bag
At which that frowsy hag
Of a city Toronto nibbles.
And then the River St. Lawrence!
Whose waters resemble those
Dark barrelled waves that
Drowned the Duke of Clarence.
So haw haw you Maitland River
And you Au Sable one too.
For when you flow into me
You're not all through.

James Reaney, *The Red Heart,* 1949

Lake Ontario

It has the merit, from the shore, of producing a slight ambiguity of vision. It is the sea, and yet just not the sea. The huge expanse, the landless line of the horizon, suggest the ocean; while an indefinable shortness of pulse, a kind of fresh-water gentleness of tone, seem to contradict the idea. What meets the eye is on the scale of the ocean, but you feel somehow that the lake is a thing of smaller spirit. . . . The scene tends to offer, as one may say, a sort of marine effect missed. It has the blankness and vacancy of the sea, without that vast essential swell which, amid the belting brine, so often saves the situation to the eye.

Henry James, 'Niagara,' 1871, in *Portraits of Places,* 1883

Lake Superior

I am Lake Superior
Cold and grey.
I have no superior;
All other lakes

Haven't got what it takes;
All are inferior.
I am Lake Superior
Cold and grey.
I am so cold
That because I chill them
The girls of Fort William
Can't swim in me.
I am so deep
That when people drown in me
Their relatives weep
For they'll never find them.
In me swims the fearsome
Great big sturgeon.
My shores are made of iron
Lined with tough wizened trees.
No knife of a surgeon
Is sharper than these
Waves of mine
That glitter and shine
In the light of the Moon my mother
In the light of the Sun, my grandmother.

James Reaney, *The Red Heart*, 1949

Halifax

*As for Halifax, its well enough in itself, though no great shakes neither, a few sizeable houses, with a proper sight of small ones, like half a dozen old hens with their broods of young chickens; but the people, the strange critters, they are all asleep. They walk in their sleep, and talk in their sleep, and what they say one day they forget the next, they say they were dreamin.

T.C.Haliburton, *The Clockmaker, or the Sayings and Doings of Samuel Slick*, first series, 1836

Into the mist my guardian prows put forth,
  Behind the mist my virgin ramparts lie,
The Warden of the Honour of the North,
  Sleepless and veiled am I!

Rudyard Kipling, *The Song of the Cities*, 1893

Hudson's Bay (site of Churchill)

I never See such a Miserable Place in my life.

Captain James Knight, *Journal*, 16 July 1717

A gigantic natural refrigerator.

Alistair Horne, *Canada and the Canadians*, 1961

Kingston

It may be said of Kingston, that one half of it appears to be burnt down, and the other half not to be built up.

Charles Dickens, *American Notes*, 1842

Klondike River

This millionaire amongst rivers.

Malcolm MacDonald, *Canadian North*, 1945

Labrador

To be short, I believe that this was the land that God allotted to Caine.

Jacques Cartier, *The First Relation*, in Richard Hakluyt, *Principal Navigations . . . of the English Nation*, 1598–1600 – of 1534

  the dismal shore
Of cold and pitiless Labrador;
Where, under the moon, upon mounts of frost,
Full many a mariner's bones are tost.

Thomas Moore, *Written on Passing Deadman's Island, in the Gulf of St. Lawrence . . . September*, 1804

The Laurentian Shield

On the North Shore a reptile lay asleep—
A hybrid that the myths might have conceived
But not delivered, as progenitor
Of crawling, gliding things upon the earth.
She lay snug in the folds of a huge boa
Whose tail had covered Labrador and swished
Atlantic tides, whose body coiled itself
Around the Hudson Bay, then curled up north
Through Manitoba and Saskatchewan
To Great Slave Lake. In Continental reach
The neck went past the Great Bear Lake until
Its head was hidden in the Arctic Seas.
This folded reptile was asleep or dead:
So motionless she seemed stone dead—just seemed:
She was too old for death, too old for life,
For as if jealous of all living forms
She had lain there before bivalves began
To catacomb their shells on western mountains.
Somewhere within this life-death zone she sprawled,
Torpid upon a rock-and-mineral mattress.
Ice-ages had passed by and over her
But these, for all their motion, had but sheared
Her spotty carboniferous hair or made
Her ridges stand out like the spikes of molochs.
Her back grown stronger every million years,
She had shed water by the longer rivers
To Hudson Bay and by the shorter streams
To the great basins to the south, had filled
Them up, would keep them filled until the end
Of time.

E.J. Pratt, *Towards the Last Spike*, 1952

Manitoba

Manitoba may be regarded as the keystone of that

mighty arch of sister provinces which spans the continent from the Atlantic to the Pacific. It was here that Canada, emerging from her woods and forests, first gazed upon the rolling prairies and unexplored North-West, and learned, as by an unexpected revelation, that her historical territories of the Canadas, her eastern sea-boards of New Brunswick, Labrador, and Nova Scotia, her Laurentian lakes and valleys, corn lands and pastures, though themselves more extensive than half-a-dozen European kingdoms, were but the vestibules and ante-chambers to that till-then undreamed of dominion, whose illimitable dimensions alike confound the arithmetic of the surveyor and the verification of the explorer. It was hence that, counting her past achievements as but the preface and prelude to her future exertions and expanding destinies, she took a fresh departure, received the afflatus of a more imperial inspiration, and felt herself no longer a mere settler along the banks of a single river, but the owner of half a continent; and in the amplitude of her possession, in the wealth of her resources, in the sinews of her imperial might, the peer of any power on earth.

Marquess of Dufferin and Ava when Governor General, Speech at Winnipeg City Hall, 29 September 1877

When the province was created no doubt there existed special reasons why its bounds should be circumscribed. The patriotism of some at least of its earliest settlers was not exactly of the stamp calculated to inspire the utmost confidence either in its sincerity or its stability, and a limitation of its territory may fairly enough have been deemed advisable from motives of public policy.

S.W. Silver & Co.'s Handbook to Canada, 1881

Montreal

You cannot fancy you are in America; everything about it conveys the idea of a substantial, handsomely built European town, with modern improvements of half English, half French architecture.

Lieut. Col. B.W.A. Sleigh, *Pine Forests and Hacmatack Clearings*, 1853

Stowed away in a Montreal lumber room
The Discobolus standeth and turneth his face to the wall;
Dusty, cobweb-covered, maimed, and set at naught,
Beauty crieth in an attic and no man regardeth:
O God! O Montreal!

Samuel Butler, 'A Psalm of Montreal', in *Note-Books*, 1912

. . . a vague general impression that Montreal consists of banks and churches. The people of this city spend much of their time laying up their riches in this world or the next. Indeed, the British part of Montreal is dominated by the Scotch race; there is a Scotch spirit sensible in the whole place – in the rather narrow, rather gloomy streets, the solid, square, grey, aggressively pompous buildings, the general greyness of the city, the air of dour prosperity.

Rupert Brooke, *Letters from America, 1913*, 1916

I believed that Montreal was the largest inland seaport and the second biggest French city in the world, *but only because my geography books said so.*

Mordecai Richler, 'Quebec Oui, Ottawa Non', *Encounter*, December 1964

Montreal now surpasses San Francisco in my estimation as the most interesting North American city. . . . There is a swagger about the city which one used to find in San Francisco before it went limp in the early seventies.

Cal McCrystal, *Sunday Times*, 30 December 1979

New Brunswick

What was the secret behind all the great men that this tiny, rather backward corner of Canada had produced? In Fredericton, the capital of New Brunswick, I asked this of a dynamic, one-eyed British ex-Brigadier called Mike Wardell, a former lieutenant of Lord Beaverbrook, who had migrated, fairly late in life, in the reverse direction to the 'Beaver.'

'I can tell you exactly what makes them,' he replied, 'It's the challenge of having to creep out to the outhouse every winter's day at 30° below zero!'

Alistair Horne, *Canada and the Canadians*, 1961

New Brunswick, Ontario, and Hell
In that last speech – which was, I now see, a farewell – . . . [Lord Beaverbrook] explained how first New Brunswick had become too small for him, then Ontario too small for him, then London too small for him. 'They say,' he mused, 'that I may well find the same trouble with Hell.'

James Cameron, *Daily Herald*, 10 June 1964

Newfoundland

Now to certifie you of the fertilitie and goodnesse of the countrey, you shall understand that I have in sundry places sowen Wheate, Barlie, Rie, Oates, Beanes, Pease and seedes of herbes, kernels, Plumstones, nuts, all which have prospered as in England. The countrey yeeldeth many good trees of fruit, as Filberds in some places, but in all places Cherie trees, and a kind of Pearetree meet to graffe on. As for Roses they are as common as brambles here: Strawberies, Dewberies, and Raspis, as common as grasse. The timber is most

Firre, yet plentie of Pineapple trees: fewe of these two kindes meete to mast a ship of threescore and ten: but neere Cape Briton, and to the Southward, big and sufficient for any ship. There be also Okes and thornes, there is in all the countrey plentie of Birch and Alder, which bee the meetest wood for cole, and also willow, which will serve for many other purposes. As touching the kindes of Fish beside Cod, there are Herrings, Salmons, Thornebacke, Plase, or rather wee should call them Flounders, Dog fish, and other most excellent of tast called of us a Cat, Oisters, and Muskles, in which I have found pearles above 40. in one Muskle, and generally all have some, great or small. . . . There are also other kinds of Shel-fish, as limpets, cockles, wilkes, lobsters, and crabs: also a fish like a Smelt which commeth on shore, and another that hath the like propertie, called a Squid: these be the fishes, which (when I please to be merie with my old companions) I say, doe come on shore when I commaund them in the name of the 5. ports, and conjure them by such like words: These also bee the fishes which I may sweepe with brommes on a heape, and never wet my foote, onely pronouncing two or three wordes whatsoever they be appoynted by any man, so they heare my voyce: the vertue of the wordes be small, but the nature of the fish great and strange. . . . Nowe to let these merrie tales passe, and to come to earnest matters againe, you shall understand, that Newfoundland is in a temperate Climate, and not so colde as foolish Mariners doe say, who finde it colde sometimes, when plentie of Isles of yce lie neere the shore: but up in the land they shall finde it hotter than England in many parts of the countrey toward the South. . . . The countrey is full of little small rivers all the yeere long, proceeding from the mountaines, ingendred both of snow and raine . . . in some places or rather in most places great lakes with plentie of fish, the countrey most covered with woods of firre, yet in many places indifferent good grasse, and plentie of Beares every where.

Anthony Parkhurst (1578), in Richard Hakluyt, *Principal Navigations . . . of the English Nation,* 1598-1600

The next morning, being Sunday, and the fourth of August, the General [Sir Humphrey Gilbert] and his company, were brought on land by English merchants who showed unto us their accustomed walks unto a place they called the *Garden.* But nothing appeared more than nature itself without art, who confusedly hath brought forth roses abundantly, wild but odoriferous, and to sense very comfortable. Also the like plenty of raspberries which do grow in every place.

Edward Haie, *A Report of the Voyage . . . in the Year of Our Lord 1583 by Sir Humfrey Gilbert,* in Richard Hakluyt, *ibid.*

Although in cloathes, company, buildings faire,
With England, New-found-land cannot compare:
Did some know what contentment I found there,
Alwayes enough, most times somewhat to spare,
With little paines, lesse toyle, and lesser care,
Exempt from taxings, ill newes, Lawing, feare,
If cleane, and warme, no matter what you weare,
Healthy, and wealthy, if men carefull are,
With much – much more, then I will now declare,
(I say) if some wise men knew what this were,
(I doe beleeve) they'd live no other where.

Robert Hayman, 'A Skeltonicall continued rhyme in praise of my New-found-land,' in *Quodlibets,* 1628

We . . . were flying over a desolate expanse of rocks and great pools. 'Bloody country,' he ejaculated.

Lord Moran, quoting Winston Churchill, 2 December 1953, in *Winston Churchill, The Struggle for Survival,* 1966

North West Territories

'Distance!' said a Yankee traveller, when appealed to on the probable width of the apparently limitless expanse of rolling prairie which everywhere confronted him; 'distance! I should think so – distance till you can't see!'

S.W. Silver & Co.'s Handbook to Canada, 1881

Between Great Slave and Mackenzie Rivers
'Tain't nothin' but miles and miles of miles and miles.

American serviceman, quoted Malcolm MacDonald, *Canadian North,* 1945

Apparently we have administered these vast territories in an almost continuous state of absence of mind.

Prime Minister Louis S. St Laurent, Speech in the Canadian Parliament, 1953

Nova Scotia

. . . chill Nova Scotia's unpromising strand
Is the last I shall tread of American land.

Thomas Moore, *To the Boston Frigate, on Leaving Halifax . . . October,* 1804

It is a country in its infancy, shewing in every corner the promise of becoming one day a valuable and powerful state. But at present helpless and neglected by its Parent.

The people are very poor and indolent; fond of rum, they appear generally half drunk and wasting their time; they loiter about their houses and their field work and seem content in raising a sufficiency of potatoes for winter. But the country is capable of great improvement, and were proper encouragement held out, much good might result. They are all lairds, they pay no rent, and trifling local taxes. There is therefore no spur to industry, nor is there any example of Gentlemen Proprietors of land to give instruction towards the improvement of agriculture.

George Ramsey, 9th Earl of Dalhousie, *Journals*, 26 October 1817

*That dismal country, that's nothing but an iceberg aground.

T.C. Haliburton, *The Clockmaker*, 1836

Nova Scotia is very poor. Bangladesh on the St. Lawrence, some have called it.

Simon Winchester, 'Letter from America', *Daily Mail*, 21 May 1979

'Mariposa' = Orillia (Leacock's home town)

*I don't know whether you know Mariposa. If not it is of no consequence, for if you know Canada at all, you are probably well acquainted with a dozen towns just like it.

There it lies in the sunlight, sloping up from the little lake that spreads out at the foot of the hillsides on which the town is built. There is a wharf beside the lake, and lying alongside of it a steamer that is tied to the wharf with two ropes of about the same size as they use on the *Lusitania*. The steamer goes nowhere in particular, for the lake is land-locked and there is no navigation for the '*Mariposa Belle*' except to 'run trips' on the first of July and the Queen's Birthday, and to take excursions of the Knights of Pythias and the Sons of Temperance to and from the Local Option Townships. . . .

The town, I say, has one broad street that runs up from the lake, commonly called the Main Street. There is no doubt about its width. When Mariposa was laid out there was none of that shortsightedness which is seen in the cramped dimensions of Wall Street and Piccadilly. . . . On the Main Street itself are a number of buildings of extraordinary importance – Smith's Hotel and the Continental and the Mariposa House, and the two banks (the Commercial and the Exchange) to say nothing of McCarthy's Block (erected in 1878) and Glover's Hardware Store with the Oddfellows' Hall above it. Then on the 'cross' street that intersects Missinaba Street at the main corner there is the Post Office and the Fire Hall and the Young Men's Christian Association and the office of the Mariposa *Newspacket* – in fact to the eye of discernment a perfect jostle of public institutions comparable only to Threadneedle Street or Lower Broadway. On all the side-streets there are maple trees and broad sidewalks, trim gardens with upright calla lilies, houses with verandas which are here and there being replaced by residences with piazzas. . . .

Outside of Mariposa there are farms that begin well but get thinner and meaner as you go on and end sooner or later in bush and swamp and the rock of the north country. And beyond that again, as the background of it all, though it's far away, you are somehow aware of the great pine woods of the lumber country reaching endlessly into the north.

Stephen Leacock, *Sunshine Sketches of a Little Town*, 1912

Ontario

[Ontario has] no recognisable image, accurate or inaccurate. In the National Gallery, its portrait is a blur.

Bruce Hutchinson, *Canada, Tomorrow's Giant*, 1957

Ottawa

Ottawa is a small town with incongruously beautiful buildings crowning its insignificance.

The Marchioness of Dufferin and Ava, *My Canadian Journal*, 2 November 1872, 1891

I would not wish to say anything disparaging of the capital, but it is hard to say anything good of it. Ottawa is not a handsome city and does not appear destined to become one either.

Sir Wilfred Laurier, in *Wilfred Laurier on the Platform*, 14 May 1884

The nearest lumber village to the North Pole.

Goldwin Smith, *c.* 1880, in the *Bystander*

A sub-Arctic lumber village converted by royal mandate into a political cockpit.

Goldwin Smith, *c.* 1880, in the *Bystander*, quoted in Bruce Hutchinson, *Canada, Tomorrow's Giant*, 1957

It was still a small town. A safe provincial place overflowing with boys and girls from still smaller towns who come here to take unimaginative jobs in the Civil Service.

Norman Levine, *Canada Made Me*, 1958

The Prairies

The Prairie . . . is the High Veldt, plus Hope, Activity, and Reward.

Rudyard Kipling, *Letters to the Family*, 1907

'Take a good look at it, Mary,' Dad said quietly. 'You'll never see it this way again.'

I did as I was told. I looked at the tall grass and the pea-vine and the soft green silk of the wild barley, but the sad note in Dad's voice puzzled me. How could the prairie change? I wondered. I did not realise then what an instrument of change a plough is.

The trees and willows are gone now, grubbed out and burned, and the roses and wild mint have been ploughed under. Wheat now grows where the chock-cherries and the violets bloomed. The wind is still sweet, but there is no wildness in it and it no longer seems to have wandered a great way over the grass and trees and flowers. It now smells of dry straw and bread. The wild keen fragrance the wind knew in those days has gone for ever.

Mary Hiemstra, *Gully Farm*, 1955

between Winnipeg and Regina
These little towns do not look to the passer-by comfortable as homes. Partly, there is the difficulty of distinguishing your village from the others. It would be as bad as being married to a Jap.

Rupert Brooke, *Letters from America, 1913,* 1916

Quebec

I expected to find a contest between a government and a people: I found two nations warring in the bosom of a single state: I found a struggle, not of principles, but of races; and I perceived that it would be idle to attempt any amelioration of laws or institutions, until we could first succeed in terminating the deadly animosity that now separates the inhabitants of Lower Canada into the hostile divisions of French and English.

Lord Durham, *Report on the Affairs of British North America,* 1839

The national feud forces itself on the very senses, irresistibly and palpably, as the origin or essence of every dispute which divides the community; we discover that dissensions, which appear to have another origin, are but forms of this constant and all-pervading quarrel; and that every contest is one of French and English in the outset, or becomes so ere it has run its course.

Ibid.

It may be said . . . that the French were originally the whole, and still are the bulk of the population of Lower Canada; that the English are new comers, who have no right to demand the extinction of the nationality of the people, among whom commercial enterprise has drawn them. . . . If the disputes of the two races are irreconcileable, it may be urged that justice demands that the minority should be compelled to acquiesce in the supremacy of the ancient and most numerous occupants of the Province, and not pretend to force their own institutions and customs on the majority.

Ibid.

Their ultimate designs and hopes are equally unintelligible. Some vague expectation of absolute independence still seems to delude them.

Ibid.

André Malraux came to town to open a '*France in Canada*' exhibition. 'France needs you,' he told the sapient aldermen of the Montreal City Council. 'We will build the next civilization together.' Malraux added that he brought a personal message from General de Gaulle. It was that 'Montreal was France's second city. He wanted this message to reach you. . . . You are not aware of the meaning you have for France. There is nowhere in the world where the spirit of France works so movingly as it does in the Province of Quebec.'

Mordecai Richler, quoting Malraux, in 'Quebec Oui, Ottawa Non', *Encounter*, December 1964

Quebec City

Je suis un chien qui ronge son os;
Tout en rongeant je prends mon repos;
Un jour viendra qui n'est pas venu;
Ou je mordrai celui qui m'aura mordu.

Plaque on the wall of the Post Office building in Quebec City's 'upper town' – roughly translatable as: I am a dog that gnaws his bone / I crouch and gnaw it all alone / A time will come which is not yet / When I'll bite him by whom I'm bit.

We anchored at Quebec, which is a Strait of the said River of Canada, which is some three hundred pases broad: there is at this Strait on the North side a very high Mountayne, which falleth downe on both sides: all the rest is a levell and goodly Countrye, where there are good grounds full of Trees, as Okes, Cypresses, Birches, Firre-trees and Aspes, and other Trees bearing fruit, and wild Vines: So that in mine opinion, if they were dressed, they would be as good as ours. There are along the Coast of the said Quebec Diamants in the Rockes of Slate, which are better than those of Alonson.

Samuel Champlain, 1603, in *Purchas his Pilgrimes,* 1625

You ask after Quebec. Gen: Townsend says, it is much like Richmond-Hill, & the River as fine (but bigger) & the Vale as *riant,* as rich, & as well cultivated.

Thomas Gray, Letter to Thomas Wharton, 23 January 1760

The steeples of Quebec . . . covered with tin look like massive silver; grand and singularly striking at first sight.

George Ramsey, 9th Earl of Dalhousie, *Journal,* 1 July 1819

The Lower Town
I wish I could give a picture of this extraordinary mass of confusion, which is quite as irregular in shape, height, position and colour, as many of the extravagant parts of the Old town of Edinburgh. The roofs are very steep, being so constructed that the snow may be shelved off in winter; but are stuck full of storm-windows, galleries, platforms, cupolas and every kind of projection – really a very singular spectacle. About one quarter of these strangely jumbled abodes are covered at top with sheet tin, and some of them have their walls also plated in this manner. But the greater number are roofed after the ordinary fashion of American houses, with wooden shingles – and every house is painted, to protect it, I presume from the violent heat of the sun in summer. Be this as it may, the effect of the whole is very lively.

Captain Basil Hall, *Travels in North America,* 1829

The impression made upon the visitor by this Gibraltar of America: its giddy heights; its citadel suspended as it were, in the air; its picturesque steep streets and frowning gate-ways; and the splendid views which burst upon the eye at every turn: is at once unique and lasting. It is a place not to be forgotten or mixed up in the mind with other places, or altered for a moment in the crowd of scenes a traveller can recall.

Charles Dickens, *American Notes,* 1842

Nevertheless, and as a matter of course, I went to see the rock, and can only say, as so many have said before me, that it is very steep. It is not a rock which I think it would be difficult for any ordinary active man to climb, – providing, of course that he was used to such work.

Anthony Trollope, *North America,* 1862

Quebeck was surveyed and laid out by a gentleman who had been afflicted with the delirium tremens from childhood, and hence his idees of things was a little irreg'ler. The streets dont lead anywhere in partic'ler, but everywheres in gin'ral. The city is bilt on a variety of perpendicler hills each hill bein a trifle wuss nor t'other one. Quebeck is full of stone walls and arches, and citadels and things. It is said no foe could ever get into Quebec, and I guess they couldn't. And I don't see what they'd *want* to get in there for.

Charles F. Browne, 'Artemus Ward', *In Canada,* 1865

His first impression will certainly have been that not America, but Europe, should have the credit of Quebec. . . . As we rattled toward our goal in the faint raw dawn, and, . . . I began to consult the misty window-panes and descried through the moving glass little but crude, monotonous woods, suggestive of nothing that I had ever heard of in song or story, I felt that the land would have much to do to give itself a romantic air. And, in fact, the feat is achieved with almost magical suddenness. The old world rises in the midst of the new in the manner of a change of scene on the stage. The St. Lawrence shines at your left, large as a harbour-mouth, gray with smoke and masts, and edged on its hither verge by a bustling water-side *faubourg* which looks French or English, or anything not local that you please; and beyond it, over against you, on its rocky promontory, sits the ancient town, belted with its hoary wall and crowned with its granite citadel. Now that I have been here a while I find myself wondering how the city would strike one if the imagination had not been bribed beforehand. The place, after all, is of the soil on which it stands; yet it appeals to you so cunningly with its little stock of transatlantic wares that you overlook its flaws and lapses, and swallow it whole.

Henry James, 'Quebec,' 1871, in *Portraits of Places,* 1883

Quebec is the most interesting thing by much that I have seen on this Continent, and I think I would sooner be a poor priest in Quebec than a rich hog-merchant in Chicago.

Matthew Arnold, Letter to Walter Arnold, 28 February 1884

Quebec . . . ranks by herself among those Mother-cities of whom none can say, 'This reminds me.'

Rudyard Kipling, *Letters to the Family,* 1907

Is there any city in the world that stands so nobly as Quebec? . . . Quebec is as refreshing and definite after the other cities of this continent, as an immortal among a crowd of stockbrokers. . . . You are in a foreign land, for the people have an alien tongue, short stature, the quick, decided, cinematographic quality of movement, and the inexplicable cheerfulness, which makes a foreigner.

Rupert Brooke, *Letters from America, 1913,* 1916

Quebec is all steps and, at the bottom of the steps, poverty.

Norman Levine, *Canada Made Me,* 1958

Regina. Saskatchewan

Pile-of-Bones.

Nickname, 1882

St John's, Newfoundland

In trying to describe St. John's there is some difficulty in applying to it an adjective sufficiently distinctive and appropriate. We find other cities coupled with epithets which at once give their predominant characteristic: London the richest, Paris the gayest, St. Petersburg the coldest. In one respect the chief town of Newfoundland has, I believe, no rival: we may therefore call it the fishiest of modern capitals. Round a great part of the harbour are sheds, acres in extent, roofed with cod split in half, laid on like slates, drying in the sun, or rather in the air, for there is not much of the former to depend upon.

G.D. Warburton, *Hochelaga; or, England in the New World*, 1846

St Lawrence River

When Mrs. Brooke upon her Return to England from Quebec told Mr. Johnson that the Prospect *up* the River Saint Lawrence was the finest in the World – but Madam says he, the Prospect *down* the River St. Lawrence is I have a Notion the finest you ever saw.

Hester Lynch Thrale/Piozzi, *Thraliana*, 1777

Saskatchewan

The Lord said 'let there be wheat' and Saskatchewan was born.

Stephen Leacock, *My Discovery of America*, 1937

Lake Superior Country, and The North

The best that anyone could say of the place was that it was a 'sportsman's paradise,' which only means a good place to drink whisky in.

Stephen Leacock, *My Discovery of the West*, 1937

Toronto

The houses and stores at Toronto are not to be compared with those of the American towns opposite. But the Englishman has built according to his means – the American according to his expectations.

Captain Frederick Marryat, *A Diary in America*, 1839

The wild and rabid toryism of Toronto, is, I speak seriously, *appalling*.

Charles Dickens, Letter to John Forster, 12 May 1842

There is a Yankee look about the place . . . a pushing, thrusting, business-like, smart appearance.

Charles Mackay, *Life and Liberty in America, 1857-8*, 1859

The streets in Toronto are framed with wood, or rather planked, as are those of Montreal and Quebec; but they are kept in better order. I should say that the planks are first used at Toronto, then sent down by the lake to Montreal, and when all but rotted out there, are again floated off by the St. Lawrence to be used in the thoroughfares of the old French capital.

Anthony Trollope, *North America*, 1862

One must say something – *what* must one say about Toronto? What can one? What has anybody every said? It is impossible to give it anything but commendation. It is not squalid like Birmingham, or cramped like Canton, or scattered like Edmonton or sham like Berlin or hellish like New York or tiresome like Nice. It is all right. The only depressing thing is that it will always be what it is, only larger, and that no Canadian city can ever be anything better or different. If they are good they may become Toronto.

Rupert Brooke, *Letters from America, 1913*, 1916

To any Canadian from a distance, Toronto, Ontario's capital and metropolis is almost an alien city. He may well feel more at home in Boston or San Francisco. 'One of the worst blue-devil haunts on the face of the earth,' cried John Gaunt the Scottish immigrant poet in the days of the Family Compact. 'The city has more grasping, greedy, unctuous people in it than any other city in the world,' shouts Ralph Maybank of Winnipeg, in the Parliament of Canada.

Bruce Hutchinson, *The Unknown Country*, 1943

Returning to Toronto was like finding a Jaguar parked in front of the vicarage and the padre inside with a pitcher of vodka martinis reading Lolita.

Article in *Maclean's*, 3 January 1959

Drear but pompous, the city straggled down to its pallid lake, and the grid of streets downtown seemed to fade from sheer lack of spirit into the suburbs of the north. There was the statutory Anglican cathedral, of course, and the University stood ineffably Oxbridge in its green, and here and there neo-classical palaces of commerce, or finance loomed slightly embarrassed at intersections. Nobody, though, could call it a handsome city. It looked more or less like a bit of Birmingham, straightened out, drained of bawdy and homogenized – 'a nest', suggested the local writer, Jesse Edgar Middleton cosily, or perhaps despairingly, 'of British-thinking, British-acting people.'

Jan Morris, 'On the Confederation Special', *Travels*, 1976 – of 1927

Lord Bessborough, later Governor-General of Canada, once described Toronto as understanding two things perfectly – 'The British Empire and a good horse.'

Ibid.

ladies of Toronto
How famed is our city
For the beauty and talents

Of our ladies that's pretty
    And *chaste* in their *sentiments.*
'T.S.', Toronto, *Ode to the Ladies of the City of Toronto*, 21 January 1837

In reply to a question as to whether he did not think the Toronto ladies the handsomest in the world, he said that the ladies of every town he had been in were the handsomest in the world.
Oscar Wilde, quoted in *The Toronto Evening News*, 25 May 1882

Vancouver Island, British Columbian Indians, and some names

It is odd . . . that on the Island they have a whole lot of names . . . Indian names, with the 'U' pronounced out in full as 'You' – such as Ucluit, and Uquittit, and Ucheesit, and others I don't remember. British Columbian names are very easy: the natives' minds are simple; they had to have something they could say and remember. If they had named the other Canadian places they would have called Quebec, Oceit, and Montreat, Owatalotofit and Toronto, Dontmentionit.
Stephen Leacock, *My Discovery of the West*, 1937

Vancouver

Vancouver is an aged city, for only a few days previous to my arrival the Vancouver Baby – *i.e.* the first child born in Vancouver – had been married.
Rudyard Kipling, *Letters to the Family*, 1907

and Montreal, Quebec, and Toronto
Vancouver is a wonder city. There will be a million people in it in twenty years. It has the combined excellence of Nature's gift and man's handiwork. God did a lot for Montreal, but man didn't add to it. Quebec is historical and has a majesty of situation, but a lot of it is squalid. Toronto – I come from there myself, so I have the right to insult it – Toronto is a village and always will be, if it spreads out a hundred miles wide: the prairie cities are impressive in their isolation and extension – fill in houses and they will be wonderful – but Vancouver is wonderful right now.
Stephen Leacock, *My Discovery of the West*, 1937

Victoria

I remember . . . when one of us was sounding the praises of the Victoria climate, Sir John [Macdonald] agreed, but added as an aside, 'The day was always in the afternoon.'
Sir Joseph Pope, *Public Servant*, 1966 – of *c*. 1886

From East to West the circling word has passed,
    Till West is East beside our land-locked blue;
From East to West the tested chain holds fast,
    The well-forged link rings true!
Rudyard Kipling, *The Song of the Cities*, 1893

To realise Victoria you must take all that the eye admires most in Bournemouth, Torquay, the Isle of Wight, the Happy Valley at Hong-Kong, the Doon, Sorrento, and Camps Bay; add reminiscences of the Thousand Islands, and arrange the whole round the Bay of Naples, with some Himalayas for the background.

Real estate agents recommend it as a little piece of England – the island on which it stands is about the size of Great Britain – but no England is set in any such seas or so fully charged with the mystery of the larger ocean beyond.
Rudyard Kipling, *Letters to the Family*, 1907

Victoria was like a lying-down cow, chewing. She had made one enormous effort of upheaval. She had hoisted herself from a Hudson's Bay Fort into a little town and there she paused, chewing the cud of imported fodder, afraid to crop the pastures of the new world for fear she might lose the good flavour of the old to which she was so deeply loyal. Her jaws went on rolling on and on, long after there was nothing left to chew.
Emily Carr, *A Little Town and a Little Girl*, 1942

It was like Cheltenham with sea air. And not the Cheltenham that I knew but the Cheltenham of music-hall jokes: a comfortable old-people's home; women on bicycles; English tweed and woollens; quiet, retired, residential. But that was a first impression. Later one realized how much it belonged to the Coast. The heat, the slowness, the thick foliage, the bungalows with the nice drives, blossoms on the trees and blossoms on the sidewalk and roads, the large gardens, the blue mountains with snow on top across the water.

It was provincial middle-class English in exile.
Norman Levine, *Canada Made Me*, 1958

White Pass Railway, Yukon

The train begins to ascend, and its erratic movements are less conducive to discussion than reverie. For although the rails are smooth and level enough, the engine proceeds in a manner suggestive of a toy train being dragged across a nursery floor by a fractious child.
Harry de Windt, *From Paris to New York by Land*, 1904

Winnipeg

With the thermometer at 30 below zero and the wind

behind him, a man walking on Main Street in Winnipeg knows which side of him is which.

Stephen Leacock, *My Discovery of the West,* 1937

Yukon

Mosquitoes invariably swarm, and the Yukon specimen is so unequalled for size and ferocity that I once heard an old miner declare that this virulent insect was 'as big as a rabbit and bit at both ends.'

Harry de Windt, *From Paris to New York by Land,* 1904

This is the Law of the Yukon, that only the Strong shall thrive;
That surely the Weak shall perish, and only the Fit survive.

Robert William Service, 'The Law of the Yukon', *Songs of a Sourdough,* 1907

CANARY ISLANDS (Spain)

To speake somewhat of these Ilands, being called in olde time Insulae Fortunatae, by the meanes of the flourishing thereof, the fruitfullnesse of them doeth surely exceed farre all other that I have heard of: for they make wine better than any in Spaine, they have grapes of such bignesse, that they may bee compared to damsons, and taste inferiour to none: for sugar, suckets, rasins of the Sunne, and many other fruits, abundance: for rosine and rawe silke, there is great store, they want neither corne, pullets, cattell, nor yet wilde foule: they have many camels also which being young are eaten of the people for victuals, and being olde, they are used for caryage of necessaries.

Richard Hakluyt, *Principal Navigations and Discoveries of the English Nation,* 1598-1600

Tenerife

This Iland containeth 17 leagues in length, and the land lieth high in forme of a ridge of sowen lande in some part of England, and in the midst of the sayd place standeth a round hill called Pico Deteithe, situated in this sort. The top of this pike conteineth of heigth directly upward 15 leagues & more, which is 45 English miles, out of the which often time proceedeth fire and brimstone, and it may be about halfe a mile in compasse: the sayd top is in forme or likenesse of a caldron. But within two miles of the top is nothing but ashes and pumish stones: yet beneath that two miles is the colde region covered all the yere with snow, and somewhat lower are mighty huge trees growing, called Vinatico, which are exceeding heavy, and will not rot in any water, although they lie a thousand yeeres therein. . . . And beneath these sorts of trees are woods of Bay trees of 10 or 12 miles long, which is a pleasant thing to travel thorow, among the which are great numbers of small birds, which sing exceeding sweet.

Thomas Nichols, *A Description of the . . . Islands of Canaria, c.* 1550, in Richard Hakluyt, *Principal Navigations . . . of the English Nation,* 1598-1600

El Teide/Peak of Tenerife

In the said Iland is a marveilous high hill called the Pike, which is a far off more like a cloud in the aire, then any other thing: the hill is round and somewhat small at the top, it hath not bene knowen that ever any man could goe to the top thereof.

Walter Wren (1566), in Richard Hakluyt, *Principal Navigations . . . of the English Nation,* 1598-1600

The Mountaine which threatens the Skie.

Edward Terry, 1616, in *Purchas his Pilgrimes,* 1625

Doth not a Tenarif or higher Hill
Rise so high like a Rocke, that one might thinke
The floating Moone would shipwracke there and sinke?

John Donne, *The First Anniversary,* 1611

Like Teneriff or Atlas unremov'd:
His stature reach'd the Skie.

John Milton, *Paradise Lost,* 1667

Ah, Teneriffe!
Retreating Mountain!
Purple of Ages – pause for *you* –
Sunset – reviews her Sapphire Regiment –
Day – drops you her Red Adieu!

Still – Clad in your Mail of ices –
Thigh of Granite – and thew – of Steel –
Heedless-alike – of pomp – or parting

Ah, Teneriffe!
I'm kneeling – still –

Emily Dickinson (untitled), *c.* 1863

It displayed itself, as usual, as an entirely celestial phenomenon. A great many people miss seeing it. Suffering under the delusion that El Pico is a terrestrial affair, they look in vain somewhere about the level of their own eyes, which are striving to penetrate the dense masses of mist that usually enshroud its slopes by day, and then a friend comes along, and gaily points out to the newcomer the glittering white triangle somewhere near the zenith.

Mary Kingsley, *Travels in West Africa,* 1897

Suddenly the cloud-fringe parted and the Teide in all its wonder and symmetry blazed out against the sky. Binyon clutched Logan by the arm. 'Look at that!' he gasped, and then, after a pause added, 'Did Dante know about this?'

Robert Gathorne Hardy, *Recollections of Logan Pearsall Smith,* 1949 – of 1936

CAPE VERDE ISLANDS

These Ilands are held to bee scituate in one of the most unhealthiest Climates of the world, and therefore it is wisedome to shunne the sight of them, how much more to make abode in them?

Sir Richard Hawkins, 1593, in *Purchas his Pilgrimes,* 1625

Such a complaint I read of those islands of Cape Verde, fourteen degrees from the Equator, they do *male audire;* one calls them the unhealthiest clime of the world, for fluxes, fevers, frenzies, calentures, which commonly seize on seafaring men that touch at them, and all by reason of a hot distemperature of the air. The hardiest men are offended with the heat, and the stiffest clowns cannot resist it.

Robert Burton, *The Anatomie of Melancholie,* 1621

Porto Praya

The neighbourhood of Porto Praya viewed from the sea wears a desolate aspect. The volcanic fires of a past age, and the scorching heat of a tropical sun, have in most places rendered the soil unfit for vegetation. The country rises in successive steps of table-land, interspersed with some truncate conical hills, and the horizon is bounded by an irregular chain of more lofty mountains. The scene, as beheld through the hazy atmosphere of this climate, is one of great interest: if, indeed, a person fresh from sea, and who has just walked for the first time in a grove of cocoa-nut trees, can be a judge of anything but his own happiness.

Charles Darwin, *Journal . . . During the Voyage . . . of H.M.S. Beagle,* 1832-6

CARIBBEAN SEA

Blue water ends at Trinidad; there and from there onwards the sea is murky; opaque, dingy stuff the colour of shabby stucco, thick with mud sweeping down from the great continental rivers.

Evelyn Waugh, *Ninety-two Days,* 1934

The Caribbean has been described as Europe's other sea, the Mediterranean of the New World. It was a Mediterranean which summoned up every dark human instinct without the complementary impulses towards nobility and beauty of older lands, a Mediterranean where civilization turned satanic, perverting those it attracted. And if one considers this sea, which the tourist now enlivens with his fantastic uniform, as a wasteful consumer of men through more than three centuries . . . it would seem that simply to have survived in the West Indies is to have triumphed.

V.S. Naipaul, *The Middle Passage,* 1962

CAROLINE ISLANDS (US Trust Territory)

Yap

Yap, if I may use the expression, is 'the genuine article,' though curiously enough, I could discover no record of any books having been written on this enthralling subject and my information, other than that which I gathered from observation, was obtained from beachcombers of diverse nationalities who, for various reasons have drifted into this easy state of 'living for the day.'

Major R.V.C. Bodley, *A Japanese Omelette,* 1933

The people of Pelew . . . though they appeared to be philosophers in adversity, Stoics in pain, and Heroes in death, yet, in many of the more delicate feelings of the human breast, they possessed all the amiable tenderness of a woman.

George Keate, *An Account of the Pelew Islands composed from the Journals of Captain Henry Wilson, etc.,* 1788

Though the natives had not till now made . . . birds an article of food, yet when they went into the woods, they frequently eat their eggs; but they did not admire them for being newly laid; the luxury to them was, when they could swallow an imperfect chicken in the bargain.

Ibid

CENTRAL AFRICAN REPUBLIC

as French Equatorial African territory of Ubangi-Shari

The Commandant was a tired, bowed little man, old. . . . He sweated, and his blue veined hand shook as he wrote the visas – he obviously had 'the fever' – and, as he courteously handed them back, he said:

'*M'sieu et Madame* . . . French Equatorial is the most under-paid, under-staffed . . . and has the most abominable climate . . . of any territory in Africa. We welcome you.'

Negley Farson, *Behind God's Back,* 1940

Bangui

It was the only place in the world where I have seen almost the entire French community drunk at 10 o'clock in the morning.

Ibid.

At Bangui, when I tried to get some films developed, the photographer said: 'It is impossible. The water here is too hot. It would melt your films.'

Ibid.

CENTRAL AMERICA

See also under individual countries

This is the rock on which all the politicians of Central America split: there is no such thing as national feeling. Every state would be an empire; the officers of state cannot brook superiors; a chief of state cannot brook a president.

J.L. Stephens, *Incidents of Travel in Central America Chiapas and Yucatan,* 1841

These Central American Republics are queer concerns. I do not, of course precisely know what a last year's calf's ideas of immortal glory may be, but probably they are about as lucid as those of a Central American, in regard to a republican form of government.

Charles F. Browne, *Artemus Ward (His Travels) Among the Mormons* (1863), 1865

To understand European politics, one should read the history of Central America. . . . Central America, being just Europe in miniature and with the lid off, is the ideal laboratory in which to study the behaviour of the Great Powers.

Aldous Huxley, *Beyond the Mexique Bay,* 1934

The signs of Americanisation . . . run through Central America like an acne. The name-signs of towns have Pepsi in huge letters and the place-names in smaller lettering. It is as if they were all subsidiaries of Pepsi.

William McIlvanney, 'The Tartan Trail to Argentina', *Observer,* 28 May 1978

CEYLON/SRI LANKA

Towards the east from the land of Prester John is an isle mickle and large and good, the which is called Taprobane. And in that isle is a noble king and a rich, which is subject unto Prester John. This king is chosen by election. In this isle are two summers and two winters in a year and harvest also twice in the year. And all the times of the year are their gardens flourished and their meadows green. In this isle is good folk dwelling and reasonable; and there are many good Christian men among them that are so rich that they know none end of their goods. In old time, when men went from the land of Prester John unto this foresaid isle, they used such manner of ships that them behoved needs be in sailing thither twenty days; but in such manner of ships as men use now may sail it in seven days. And as they said they may oft-times see the ground of the sea in divers places, for it is not full deep.

John Mandeville, *The Book of John Mandeville, c.* 1360

This Ceylon is a brave Iland, verie fruitfull and faire; but by reason of continuall Warres with the King thereof, all things are verie deare: for he will not suffer any thing to be brought to the Castle where the Portugals be: wherefore oftentimes they have great want of victuals. . . . They be naked people all of them; yet many of them be good with their Pieces which be Muskets. When the King talketh with any man, hee standeth upon one legge, and setteth the other foot upon his knee with his Sword in his hand: it is not their order for the King to sit but to stand. . . . They are of the race of the Chingalayes, which they say are the best kind of all the Malabars. Their Eares are verie large; for the greater they are, the more Honourable they are accounted. Some of them are a spanne long. The Wood which they burne is Cinamon wood, and it smelleth verie sweet. . . . Their Women have a cloth bound about them from their middle to their knee: and all the rest is bare. All of them bee Blacke and but little, both Men and Women. Their Houses are verie little, made of the branches of the Palmer or Coco-tree, and covered with the leaves of the same tree.

Ralph Fitch, *The Voyage,* 1583-91, in *Purchas his Pilgrimes,* 1625

Wee passed faire by the faire Iland of Zeilaon where groweth the best Cinamon in the world, and affirmed none good elce where. Lindscoten commends it For the Fruitfullest, the most pleasant, and most Delicious Iland thatt is in all these parts of the world. This Morning wee saw a very high hill farre within the land, resembling somwhatt the Crowne of our now new fashion hatts. Whether this bee thatt called Adams peake I know nott.

Peter Mundy, *Travels in Europe and Asia,* 1637

What though the spicy breezes
  Blow soft o'er Ceylon's isle,
Though every prospect pleases
  And only man is vile:
In vain with lavish kindness
  The gifts of God are strown
The heathen in his blindness
  Bows down to wood and stone!

Reginald Heber, 'Before a Collection Made for the Society for Propagating the Gospel', *Poems,* 1842

There is so much vegetable luxuriance in Ceylon, that even the marrow in people's bones is vegetable marrow. My!

Edward Lear, Letter to Lord Carlingford, 28 March 1875

Ceylon is certainly the most interesting and beautiful

island we have seen, taking its many-sided interests into account. In one way Hawaii is grander, in another, Tahiti is more lovely; but Hawaii is a volcano and Tahiti a dream; while Ceylon is what I supposed Java to be, and it was not – a combination of rich nature and varied human interest, a true piece of voluptuous creativeness.

Henry Adams, Letter to Elizabeth Cameron, 8 September 1891

One of the charms of the island is its infinite variety. In the north, east, and south-east you get the flat, dry, hot low country with a very small rainfall which comes mainly in a month or so of the north-east monsoon. It is a land of silent, sinister, scrub-jungle, or of great stretches of sand broken occasionally by clumps of low blackish shrubs, the vast dry lagoons in which as you cross them under the blazing sun you continually see in the flickering distance the mirage of water, a great non-existent lake sometimes, surrounded by non-existent coconut trees or palmyra palms. That is a country of sand and sun, an enormous blue sky stretching away unbroken to an immensely distant horizon. Many people dislike the arid sterility of this kind of Asiatic low country. But I lived in it for many years, indeed for most of my time in Ceylon, and it got into my heart and my bones, its austere beauty, its immobility and unchangeableness except for minute modulations of light and colour beneath the uncompromising sun, the silence, the emptiness, the melancholia, and so the purging of the passions by complete solitude.

Leonard Woolf, *Growing*, 1961, of 1904-11

There is a widespread popular belief, no doubt fostered by obsolete geography books, that Ceylon's fame derives from her production of much of the world's tea crop. The notion is a completely erroneous one. The principal industry of the island is the manufacture of souvenir ebony elephants, cunningly constructed in such a way that the tusks and ears break off the moment one's ship is out of sight of land. This leaves the tourist with a misshapen chunk of wood that can be used effectively as either paperweight or missile, depending on his ability to adjust himself to local conditions.

S.J. Perelman, *Westward Ha!*, 1948

Ceylon has always given pleasure . . . even the sensible Dutch thought the shape of the place reminiscent of a dressed ham hanging from the rafters.

James Morris, 'Ceylon', *Places*, 1972

It was not a country where people raised their voices. They argued in whispers; catastrophe put them to sleep.

Paul Theroux, *The Great Railway Bazaar*, 1975

Adam's Peak

In that isle is a great mountain and even above on the top thereof is a great loch full of water. And men of that country say that Adam and Eve wept upon that hill a hundred year after that they were driven out of Paradise, and of their tears that they wept was that water gathered.

John Mandeville, *The Book of John Mandeville, c.* 1360

Colombo

I . . . was terribly oppressed by the damp heat of Colombo—a rice-field heat—which has made me think that if Bishop Heber had known more of the matter he would have made an improvement in his poetry, and would have altered it to: 'What though the ricey breezes, blow damp o'er Ceylon's isle!' Spice I know not, but Colombo is in a big rice-swamp, and I felt as though I were in a Turkish bath, and could not get out.

Henry Adams, Letter to Elizabeth Cameron, 8 September 1891

By midday in Colombo, the heat is so unbearable that the streets are empty save for thousands of Englishmen taking mad dogs for walks.

Spike Milligan, *A Dustbin of Milligan*, 1962

Nuwara Eliya

People who arrive here direct from home are very disappointed, for they want to know where the tropics are, and didn't expect they were coming to Scotland.

Alfred Viscount Northcliffe, *My Journey Round the World*, January 1922, 1923

Tangalla

If I had to show anyone what God can do in the way of tropical nights, I think I should take him to the Rest House verandah at Tangalla. . . . The ocean laps against the verandah. The evening air is warm and gentle. An enormous sky meets an enormous sea. The stars blaze in the sky and blaze in the sea. Every now and then—it seems almost at one's feet—a long, snake-like, black head rises out of the stars in the sea, remains for a moment motionless above the water looking at the stars in the sky, and then silently slides back into the sea. It seems incredibly mysterious, this black head emerging from the water to gaze at the stars in the sky, even though you knew it to be only a turtle coming to the surface to breathe. There is no sound in this melodrama of a tropical night except a faint lapping of the sea, and now and then a shivery stir of palm leaves. The sky, the sea, the stars, the turtles, the bay, the palms were so lusciously magnificent at

Tangalla Rest House that Nature seemed to tremble on the verge – I don't think she ever actually fell over the verge – of vulgarity.

Leonard Woolf, *Growing*, 1961 – of 1904–11

CHAD

Who holds Chad holds Africa.

French maxim, quoted by John Gunther, *Inside Africa*, 1955 ('Also Chad is the first fort for the defence of Cape Town'.)

Even the water is French.

Nigerian diplomat, quoted by Xan Smiley, *Spectator*, 26 April 1980

Njamena, formerly Fort Lamy

Fort Lamy, the capital of the Republic of Chad, lies at the desolate centre of the immense continent; and feels like it. It was the rainy season when I arrived, with a climate like hot Irish stew.

Richard West, *The White Tribes of Africa*, 1965

ENGLISH CHANNEL

Nay, I'll send printed scrolls beyond
To neighbours o'er the Herring Pond.

Thomas D'Urfey, *Pills to Purge Melancholy: Part ii, The Fable of the Lady, The Lurcher, and the Marrow-puddings*, 1661

What a cursed thing to live in an island, this step is more awkward than the whole journey.

Edward Gibbon, Letter to Lord Sheffield, 17 September 1783

I Was never before so Sea sick, nor was my Son. My Servant was very bad. Allmost all the Passengers were sick. It is a remarkable Place for it. We are told that many Persons Masters of Vessells and others who were never Sea sick before have been very bad in making this Passage.

John Adams, *Diary*, 23 October 1783

The streight that separates England, so fortunately for her, from all the rest of the world.

Arthur Young, *Travels . . . [in] . . . France*, 15 May 1787, 1792

Passage to Calais; 14 hours for reflection in a vehicle that does not allow one power to reflect.

Ibid., 5 June 1789

A mere strip of water, not much wider than an American river.

William Cobbett, *Rural Rides*, 1 September 1823

We . . . vomited as usual into the channel which divides Albion from Gallia. Rivers are said to run blood after an engagement; the Channel is discoloured, I am sure, in a less elegant and less pernicious way by English tourists going and coming.

Sidney Smith, Letter to Sir Wilmot-Horton, Bart, December 1835

Tut! the best thing I know between France and England is the sea.

Douglas Jerrold, *Wit and Opinions*, 1859 – before 1857

The pen refuses to describe the sufferings of some of the passengers during our smooth trip of ninety minutes: my own sensations were those of extreme surprise, and a little indignation, at there being no other sensations – it was not for *that* I paid my money.

Lewis Carroll, *Diary*, 13 July 1867

Shortly after quitting the wind-swept cliffs of Dover, as we were looking down on the tumbling waves, and enjoying the salt smell and keen spray that flew up towards the bows of the steamer, Tennyson said: 'They are swift, glittering deeps, sharp like the back of a fish,' and so they were.

Alfred Lord Tennyson, *A Memoir, by his Son*, 1897 – of 1869

It is the most marvellous sea in the world, – the most suited for these little adventures; it is crammed with strange towns, differing one from the other; it has two opposite peoples upon either side, and hills, and varying climates, and the hundred shapes and colours of the earth, here rocks, there sand, there cliffs, and there marshy shores. It is a little world. And what is more, it is a kind of inland sea.

Hilaire Belloc, *Hills and the Sea*, 1906

Oh, the Channel's as bright as a ball-room already,
And pilots are thicker than pilchards at Looe.

Rudyard Kipling, *Big Steamers*, 1911

That channel which so often has a guffaw up its sleeve.

James Joyce, Letter to Constantine P. Curran, 6 August 1937

If the Almighty were to rebuild the world and asked me for advice I would have English Channels round every country. And the atmosphere would be such that anything which attempted to fly would be set on fire.

Winston Churchill, Remark, 16 January 1952, quoted Lord Moran, *Winston Churchill, The Struggle for Survival*, 1966

It was like swimming in a dishwasher.

Sandra Blewett, long distance swimmer, quoted *Evening Standard*, 21 August 1979

Channel Tunnel (projected)

A tunnel underneath the sea, from Calais straight to Dover, Sir,
That qualmish folks may cross by land from shore to shore,
With sluices made to drown the French, if e'er they would come over, Sir,
Has long been talked of, till at length 'tis thought a *monstrous bore.*

Theodore Hook, *Bubbles of 1825,* 1825

Not for less love, all glorious France, to thee,
'Sweet enemy' called in days long since at end,
Now found and hailed of England sweeter friend,
Bright sister of our freedom now, being free;
Not for less love or faith in friendship we
Whose love burnt ever toward thee reprehend
The vile vain greed whose pursy dreams portend
Between our shores suppression of the sea.
Not by dull toil of blind mechanic art
Shall these be linked for no man's force to part
Nor length of years and changes to divide,
But union only of trust and lovely heart
And perfect faith in freedom strong to abide
And spirit at one with spirit on either side.

A.C. Swinburne, *The Channel Tunnel,* 3 April 1882

CHANNEL ISLANDS

Faire Jersey first of these heere scattred in the deepe,
Peculiarlie that boast'st thy double-horned sheepe:
Inferior nor to thee, thou Jernsey, bravelie crown'd
With rough-imbatteld rocks, whose venom-hating ground,
The hardned emerill hath, which thou abroad doost send:
Thou Ligon, her belov'd, and Serk, that doost attend
Her pleasure everie howre; as Jethow, them at need,
With phesants, fallow deere, and conies that doost feed:
Yee seaven small sister iles, and Sorlings, which to see
The halfe-sunk sea-man joyes, or whatsoe're you be,
From fruitfull Aurney, neere the ancient Celtick shore,
To Ushant and the Seames, whereas those nunnes of yore
Gave answers from their caves, and tooke what shapes they please:
Ye happie ilands set within the British seas.

Michael Drayton, *Poly-Olbion, The First Song,* 1612

Jersey

It hath thirteen parishes, little waste ground aboundance of Villags, and but one litle Towne called St Helier, plenty of Cider.

Peter Mundy, *Voyages,* 1625

You must know,
Sir, that *Verse* does not in this *Island grow*
No more than *Sack;* One lately did not fear
(Without the *Muses* leave) to plant it here.
But it produc'd such base, rough crabbed, hedge
Rhymes, as ev'en set the hearers *Ears* on *Edge,* . . .
Well, since the Soil then does not natu'rally bear
Verse, who (*a Devil)* should *import* it here?
For that to me would seem so strange a thing
As who did first *Wild Beasts* into *Islands* bring.

Abraham Cowley, 'An Answer to a Copy of Verses Sent into Jersey', in *Miscellanies,* 1656

Sark

Sark, fairer than aught in the world that the lit skies cover
Laughs inly behind her cliffs, and the seafarers mark
As a shrine where the sunlight serves, though the brown clouds hover,
Sark. . . .
Here earth lies lordly, triumphal as heaven is above her
And splendid and strange as the sea that upbears as an ark,
As a sign for the rapture of storm-spent eyes to discover,
Sark.

A.C. Swinburne, 'Insularum Ocelle', *A Century of Roundels,* 1883

CHILE

and see under Patagonia

The Country which doth most resemble Spaine and the Regions of Europe in all the West Indies, is the Realme of Chille, which is without the generall rule of these other Provinces, being seated within the burning Zone, and the Tropicke of Capricorne. This Land of it selfe is coole and fertile, and brings forth all kindes of fruits that bee in Spaine; it yeelds great abundance of bread and Wine, and abounds in Pastures and Cattell. The aire is wholesome and cleere, temperate betwixt heat and cold, Winter and Summer are very distinct, and there they find great store of very fine gold. Yet this Land is poore and smally peopled, by reason of their continuall warre with the Auricanos, and their Associates, being a rough people and friends to libertie.

Joseph Acosta, *c.* 1588, in *Purchas his Pilgrimes,* 1625

One of the best Countries that the Sun shineth on: for it is of a temperate climate, and abounding in all things necessarie for the use of man, with infinite rich Mynes of Gold, Copper, and sundry other mettals. The poorest houses in it, by report of their Inhabitants, have of their owne store, Bread, Wine, Flesh, and Fruit; which is so plentifull, that of their superfluitie they supplie other parts: sundrie kinds of cattell; as Horses, Goates, and Oxen brought thither by the Spaniards, are found in heards of thousands, wilde, and without owner; besides those of the Countrie, which are common to most parts of America: in some of which are found the Bezar stones, and those very good and great.

Sir Richard Hawkins, 1594, in *Purchas his Pilgrimes*, 1625

The host, talking about the state of Chile, as compared to other countries, was very humble: 'Some see with two eyes, and some with one, but for my part I do not think that Chile sees with any.'

Charles Darwin, *Journal . . . During the Voyage . . . of H.M.S. Beagle*, 1832-6

Of all the parts of South America that we visited, Southern Chile stands out to me as the land where one would choose to make a home.

James Bryce, *South America*, 1912

For further entertainment in the long evenings [at *The Times*] someone had invented a game – a competition with a small prize for the winner – to see who could write the dullest headline. It had to be a genuine headline, that is to say one which was actually printed in the next morning's newspaper. I won it only once with a headline which announced: 'Small Earthquake in Chile. Not many dead.'

Claud Cockburn, *In Time of Trouble*, 1956 – of *c.* 1930?

Chile is one of the most oddly shaped of nations, hanging down the west coast of South America like a bell rope full of knots and kinks.

John Gunther, *Inside South America*, 1967

You have to be thin to be a Chileno. Otherwise you fall off.

Remark made to John Gunther in Santiago, *ibid.*

Chile is God's mechanism for keeping Argentina from the Pacific.

Santiago saying, quoted by John Gunther, *ibid.*

Chile has an extraordinary history . . . because Chile was invented by a poet.

Pablo Neruda, Interview with Rita Guibert, Winter 1971, *Paris Review Interviews, Fifth Series*, 1981. (He refers to Don Alonso de Ercilla y Zuniga, author of *La Araucana*)

Chileans

Everyone is more European here than in Europe.

George Mikes, *Tango! A Solo Across South America*, 1961

Chilean women

It is said that the ladies of Chili never wash their faces; they merely add a fresh coat of powder.

Lilian Leland, *Travelling Alone, A Woman's Journey Round the World*, 1890

Arica

Arica in Chile is by report one of the sweetest places that ever the sun shined on.

Robert Burton, *Anatomie of Melancholie*, 1621

Arica, a small, clean town beside a high cliff. The mile-wide cliffs change colour from black to white as the birds fly away from them in an endless living cloud. They blot out the town, the liners, the horizon, and the sun. Out over the green waters they drive, in close formation, their wings touching. It looks as if an immense carpet with an all-over design of birds were suddenly unrolled into the sea.

Ludwig Bemelmans, *The Donkey Inside*, 1947

The Strait of Magellan

The Strait of Magellan is another case of Nature imitating Art. A Nuremberg cartographer, Martin Beheim, drew the South-West passage for Magellan to discover.

Bruce Chatwyn, *In Patagonia*, 1977

Santiago

The town is full of priests – the people are consequently indolent and immoral; but I certainly never saw more examples of the consequences of bad education, or a state of society more deplorable. The streets are crowded with a set of lazy indolent, bloated monks and priests, with their heads shaved in different ways, wearing enormous flat hats, and dressed, some in white serge cowls and gowns, and others in black. The men all touch their hats to these drones, who are also to be seen in the houses, leaning over the backs of their chairs, and talking to women who are evidently of the most abandoned class of society. The number of people of this description in Santiago is quite extraordinary. The lower rooms of the most reputable houses are invariably let to them, and it is really shocking beyond description, to see them sitting at their doors, with a candle in the back part of the room burning before sacred pictures and images.

Captain F.B. Head, *Rough Notes . . . across the Pampas and the Andes*, 1827

The English there, also, looked very pale and exhausted; and although they keep each other in countenance, it appeared to me that a strong dose of British wind, with snow and rain, and a few of what the Scotch call 'sour mornings,' would do them a great deal of good.

Ibid.

Valdivia

The town is situated on the low banks of the stream, and is so completely buried in a wood of apple-trees, that the streets are merely paths in an orchard.

Charles Darwin, *Journal . . . During the Voyage . . . of H.M.S. Beagle,* 1832-6

Valparaiso

Whoever called 'Valparaiso' the 'Valley of Paradise' must have been thinking of Quillota.

Charles Darwin, *Journal . . . During the Voyage . . . of H.M.S. Beagle,* 1832-6

Patagonian Chile

The sense of sublimity which the great deserts of Patagonia and the forest-clad mountains of Tierra del Fuego excited in me . . . has left an indelible impression on my mind.

Charles Darwin, *Journal . . . During the Voyage . . . of H.M.S. Beagle,* 1832-6

CHINA

This Countrie may bee said to excell in these particulers: Antiquity, largenesse, Ritchnesse, healthynesse, Plentifullnesse. For Arts and manner off governmentt I thinck noe Kingdome in the world Comparable to it, Considered alltogether.

Peter Mundy, *Travels in Europe and Asia,* 1637

The abominable Sin of Sodomy is tolerated here, and all over China, and so is Buggery, which they use both with Beasts and Fowls, in so much that Europeans do not care to eat Duck.

Alexander Hamilton, *A New Account of the East Indies,* 1727

China? There lies a sleeping giant. Let him sleep! For when he wakes he will move the world.

Napoleon, attrib.

Was there ever a day's *Universal* peace – except perhaps in China – where they have found out the miserable happiness of a stationary & unwarlike mediocrity?

Lord Byron, *Detached Thoughts,* 1821-2

China is an instance of a permanency without progression.

Samuel Taylor Coleridge, *Table Talk,* 1 January 1823

Why does the same dull current of ignoble blood creep through a thousand generations in China without any provision for its own purification, without the mixture of one drop from the fountains of goodness & glory? . . . they worship crockery gods . . . the summit of their philosophy and science is how to make tea. . . . The closer contemplation we condescend to bestow the more disgustful is that booby nation. The Chinese Empire enjoys precisely a mummy's reputation, that of having preserved to a hair for 3 or 4,000 years the ugliest features in the world. I have no gift to see a meaning in the venerable vegetation of this extraordinary people. They are not tools for other nations to use. . . .

But China, reverend dulness! hoary ideot! all she can say at the convocation of nations must be – 'I made the tea!' Egypt, Assyria, Persia, Palestine, polished Greece and haughty Rome have bequeathed us arts & institutions, the memory and the books of great men. . . . These nations have left ruins of noble cities as the skeleton and monument of themselves. China is her own monument.

R.W. Emerson, *Notebooks,* 1824

Oriental powers like China, incapable of a true civilisation, semi-refined in manners and mechanic arts, but incurably savage in the moral sense. . . .

Thomas de Quincey, *The Opium Question with China in 1840,* in *Works,* ed. Masson, 1890

Better fifty years of Europe than a cycle of Cathay.

Alfred Lord Tennyson, *Locksley Hall,* 1832

and Japan

Jealous China, dire Japan
With bewildered eyes I scan
– They are but dead seas of man.

Ages in succession find
Forms that change not, stagnant mind
And they leave the same behind.

James Montgomery, *A Voyage Round the World, Works,* 1841

In spite of the fact that China offers the unique example of a country that has simply lived to be conquered, mentally her masters have invariably become her pupils. Having ousted her from her throne as a ruler, they proceeded to sit at her feet as disciples. Thus they have rather helped than hindered her civilization.

Percival Lowell, *The Soul of the Far East,* 1888

Chinese society resembles some of the scenery in China. At a little distance it appears fair and attractive. Upon a nearer approach, however, there is invariably much that is shabby and repulsive, and the air is full of odours which are not fragrant. No photograph does justice to Chinese scenery, for though photography has been described as 'justice without mercy,' this is not true of Chinese photography, in which the dirt and smells are omitted.

Arthur H. Smith, *Chinese Characteristics,* 1894

. . .
Hanging upside down like rows of disgusting old rags
And grinning in their sleep.
Bats!

In China the bat is a symbol of happiness.

Not for me!

D.H. Lawrence, *Bat,* 1921

China may be regarded as an artist nation, with the virtues and vices to be expected of the artist: virtues chiefly useful to others, and vices chiefly harmful to oneself.

Bertrand Russell, *The Problem of China,* 1922

Every country expresses its destiny through its landscape; and in China, where distances are so huge and the extent of recorded history so imposing, one can see the beginning and end of the same movement, and too much history becomes no history at all.

Peter Quennell, *A Superficial Journey through Tokyo and Peking,* 1932

What is China, after all, but a Geographical Expression.

Sir John Simon, Remark to journalists in Geneva in 1933, during conflict between China and Japan, quoted in George Slocumbe, *A Mirror to Geneva,* 1937

When one is in China one is compelled to think about her, with compassion always, with despair sometimes, and with discrimination and understanding, very rarely. For one either loves or hates China. . . . If one comes to China, one feels engulfed, and soon stops thinking. One merely feels that she is there, a tremendous existence somewhat too big for the human mind to encompass, a seemingly inconsequential chaos obeying its own laws of existence.

Lin Yutang, *My Country and My People,* 1936

and Japan
China, as the years pass, is being eaten by Japan like an artichoke, leaf by leaf.

Sir Winston Churchill, Letter, 3 September 1937

One of the most astounding discoveries in history was made the other day when a group of American State Department people found a new country named Red China. For years there had been rumors that there was a country in the Far East with 800 million people. Yet no one in the United States would believe it.

But an expedition of Senators, led by Marco Fulbright, came across it accidentally while looking for a new route to North Vietnam.

When the existence of Red China was reported, a meeting of all the top policy people in the State Department was called. . . .

'I'm an old China hand, and I say there is no place called Red China. The only China is located on the island of Formosa.' . . .

'Does the CIA have anything on it?'

'No Sir. They're as much in the dark as we are. The French, the British, and the Canadians have all reported that they believe there is a Red China, but the Russians now claim it isn't there.'

The old China hand spoke up, 'Mr. Secretary, I believe we're only looking for trouble by following up the rumor. We already have a China. It's *our* kind of China. Another China would only mean trouble.'

'But,' said one of the other men, 'if the reports are true that this land mass contains 800 million people, won't we have to deal with it sooner or later? I think we should announce that we don't believe there is a Red China, but if there is, we intend to contain it, but not isolate it.' . . .

One of the advisers said,'Seventeen years ago, the American people didn't believe in Flying Saucers either. Perhaps we could announce the existence of Red China and flying saucers at the same time.'

Art Buchwald, 'Is there a Red China?,' in *Son of the Great Society,* 1967

The late Walter Lippmann, in one of his rare appearances on television – I believe it was his last – was asked at the end by a student what did he consider to be the worst catastrophe that could happen to the world. The clock ticked audibly as he thought for the longest time. Then he said, very slowly and emphatically: 'China – on the loose.'

Alistair Cooke, *The Americans,* 1979

When Moscow claimed in 1969 that China's northern frontier since the fourth century B.C. had been defined by the Great Wall and that areas north of the wall were not historically subject to Chinese sovereignty, a Chinese historian acidly commented, 'Where, one may ask, were the frontiers of the *Russian* state in the fourth century B.C.?'

David Bonavia, *The Chinese,* 1981

and Taiwan

I finally put forward the American position as: 'The United States acknowledges that all Chinese on either side of the Taiwan Straits maintain there is but one China. The United States Government does not challenge that position.' I do not think anything I did or said impressed Chou as much as this ambiguous formula with which both sides were able to live for nearly a decade.

Henry Kissinger, *White House Years,* 1979 – of 23 October 1971

Chinese

You can kill a Chinese peasant by letting him sit down.

Old Proverb, quoted by Denis Bloodworth, *Chinese Looking Glass,* 1967

These Catayans are men of a little stature, speaking much through the nose. And this is generall, that all they of the East have small eyes. They are excellent workmen in every Art: and their Physicians are well skilled in the Vertues of Herbs, and judge exactly of the Pulse; but use no Urinals, nor know any thing concerning Urine.

Friar William of Rubruck, 1253, in *Purchas his Pilgrimes,* 1625

The Inhabitants of those parts are exceeding wise and subtill, replenished with all kind of skill and cunning, insomuch that they disdaine the endeavours of all other Nations, in all kind of Arts, and Sciences: saying, that they only see with two Eyes, the Latines with but one eye, and that all other Nations are blind. And albeit they are exceeding sharpe-sighted in the exercise of all bodily workes and labours; yet is there not amongst them any knowledge of spirituall things; the men of that Countrey are not bold, or couragious, but more fearefull of death then befitteth such as beare Armes; yet are they very ingenious, and have oftener had victories of their enemies by Sea, then by Land. . . .

Anthony the Armenian, 1307, in *Purchas his Pilgrimes,* 1625

The Chinois are white (but neerer the South more browne) with thinne beards (some having none) with staring haires, and late growing; their haire wholly blacke; eyes narrow, of Egge forme, blacke and standing out: the nose very little, and scarcely standing forth; eares meane: in some Provinces they are square faced. Many of Canton and Quamsi Provinces on their little toes have two nailes, as they have generally in Cachin-china. Their women are all low, and account great beauty in little feet, for which cause from their infancy they bind them straight with clothes, that one would judge them stump-footed: this, as is thought, devised to make them housewives.

Father Ricii, *c.* 1579, in *Purchas his Pilgrimes,* 1625

between Macao and Tayphoo

The people there gave us a certaine Drinke called Chaa, which is only water with a kind of herbe boyled in itt. It must bee Drancke warme and is accompted wholesome.

Peter Mundy, *Travels in Europe and Asia,* 1637

The Chinese are very great Gamesters, and they will never be tired with it, playing night and day, till they have lost all their Estates; then it is usual with them to hang themselves.

William Dampier, *A New Voyage Round the World,* 1697 – of 1687

The Chinese are a civilized and hospitable people; complaisant to strangers and to one another; very regular in their manners and behaviour, and respectful to their superiors; but above all, their regard for their parents, and decent treatment of their women of all ranks, ought to be imitated, and deserve great praise. These good qualities are a natural consequence of the sobriety and uniformity of life, to which they have been long accustomed.

John Bell, *A Journey from St Petersburg to Pekin, 1719-22,* 1763

The calm and patient turn of the *Chinese,* on which they so much value themselves, and which distinguishes the Nation from all others, is, in reality the source of the most exceptionable part of their character; for it has been often observed by those who have attended to the nature of mankind, that it is difficult to curb the more robust and violent passions, without augmenting, at the same time, the force of the selfish ones: So that the timidity, dissimulation, and dishonesty of the *Chinese,* may, in some part, be owing to the composure, and external decency, so universally prevailing in that Empire.

George Anson (Richard Walter and Benjamin Robins), *A Voyage Round the World, 1740-4,* 1748

Capital punishments are rare in *China,* the effeminate genius of that nation, and their strong attachment to lucre, disposing them rather to make use of fines.

Ibid.

Cheating and Over-reaching seems to be the natural Bent and Genius of this People.

Salmon, *A New Geographical and Historical Grammar,* 1751

Johnson called the East-Indians barbarians. BOSWELL. 'You will except the Chinese, Sir?' JOHNSON. 'No, Sir.' BOSWELL. 'Have they not arts?'

JOHNSON. 'They have pottery.' BOSWELL. 'What do you say to the written character of their language?' JOHNSON. 'Sir, they have not an alphabet. They have not been able to form what other nations have formed.' BOSWELL. 'There is more learning in their language than in any other, from the immense number of their characters.' JOHNSON. 'It is only more difficult from its rudeness; as there is more labour in hewing down a tree with a stone than with an axe.'

James Boswell, *Life of Johnson* (8 May 1778), 1791

First China's sons, with early art elate,
Form'd the gay tea-pot, and the pictured plate;
Saw with illumin'd brow and dazzled eyes
In the red stove vitrescent colours rise;
Speck'd her tall beakers with enamell'd stars,
Her monster-josses, and gigantic jars;
Smear'd her huge dragons with metallic hues,
With golden purples, and cobaltic blue;
Bade on wide hills her porcelain castles glare,
And glazed pagodas tremble in the air.

Erasmus Darwin, *The Botanic Garden – The Economy of Vegetation*, 1791

The Government of China is purposely absurd but the people are reasonable in their views and conceptions.

G. Tradescant Lay, *The Chinese as they Are*, 1841

It seems quite useless to kill the Chinese. It is like killing flies in July.

Sidney Smith, Letter to Sir George Philips, 13 September 1842

It is well known to all who have taken any pains in studying the Chinese temper and character that obstinacy – obstinacy like that of mules – is one of its foremost features. And it is also known, by a multiplied experience, that the very greatest importance attaches in Chinese estimate to the initial movement. Once having conceded a point, you need not hope to recover your lost ground.

Thomas de Quincey, *The Chinese Question in 1857*, in *Works*, ed. Masson, 1890

Which I wish to remark, –
  And my language is plain, –
That for ways that are dark
  And for tricks that are vain
The heathen Chinee is peculiar
  Which the same I would rise to explain.

Bret Harte, *Plain Language from Truthful James*, Table Mountain, 1870

Why do Chinese never smile? Why do they look as if some one had sat upon their noses as soon as they were born, and they had been weeping bitterly over the calamity ever since?

Charles Kingsley, *At Last, A Christmas in the West Indies*, 1871

One needs more discretion than valor in dealing with the Chinese.

Thomas Stevens, *Around the World on a Bicycle*, 1887

The Chinaman bores one in a new way, as Dr Johnson said of the poet Gray.

Henry Adams, Letter to Charles Milnes Gaskell, 28 October 1888

The Chinaman is dreaded because of his power to underlive the white.

Lafcadio Hearn, Letter to Basil Hall Chamberlain, 2 May 1893

It is in his *staying qualities* that the Chinese excels the world.

Arthur H. Smith, D.D., *Chinese Characteristics*, 1894

They seem to be able to do almost everything by means of almost nothing, and this is a characteristic generality of their productions, whether simple or complex.

Ibid.

The history of foreign diplomacy with China is largely a history of attempted explanations of matters which have been deliberately misunderstood.

Ibid.

This was the first Chinese official we had met. . . . The commander watched us with dubious eye. Perhaps he had heard of a cycle in Cathay. But three of them was unprecedented.

John Foster Fraser, *Round the World on a Wheel*, 1899

In fact, when nature made the Chinaman, wishing to forestall the inventions of the future, she made an auto-laundry with the chemistry of digestion for a motor, and then covered the contrivance with a skin of cheap vellum.

T.G. Selby, *Chinaman at Home*, 1900

The Chinaman from early youth
Is by his wise preceptors taught
To have no dealings with the Truth,
In fact romancing is his 'forte.'
In juggling words he takes the prize,
By the sheer beauty of his lies.

Harry Graham, *China – Verse and Worse*, 1905

People say airily, 'The Chinese are so backward poor things'; my advice to such people is to go and see. They will find that the Chinese arrived at a certain point of civilisation centuries ago and remained there because they saw nothing in the progress of other countries which tempted them to imitate it. They anticipated our so-called civilisation and deliberately discarded it, since they did not consider that it would tend to greater happiness in the long run.

Maurice Baring, *What I Saw in Russia*, 1913

The Chinese constantly remind me of Oscar Wilde in his first trial when he thought wit would pull one through anything, and found himself in the grip of a great machine that cared nothing for human values. . . . I would do anything in the world to help the Chinese, but it is difficult. They are like a nation of artists with all their good and bad points. Imagine Gertler and [Augustus] John and Lytton set to govern the British Empire, and you will have some idea of how China has been governed for 2000 years.

Bertrand Russell, Letter to Ottoline Morrell, 1921, in *Autobiography*, 1968

The callousness of the Chinese is bound to strike every Anglo-Saxon. They have none of that humanitarian impulse which leads us to devote one per cent of our energy to mitigating the evils wrought by the other ninety-nine per cent.

Bertrand Russell, *The Problem of China*, 1922

The distinctive merit of our civilization, I should say, is the scientific method; the distinctive merit of the Chinese is a just conception of the ends of life.

Ibid.

But though the Chinese take such careful pains to avoid fatiguing your eye, with sure taste making the elaborateness of a decoration endurable by contrasting it with a plain surface, in the end weariness overcomes you. Their exuberance bewilders. You cannot refuse your admiration to the ingenuity with which they so diversify the ideas that occupy them as to give you an impression of changing fantasy, but the fact is plain that the ideas are few. The Chinese artist is like a fiddler who with infinite skill should play infinite variations upon a single tune.

W. Somerset Maugham, *On A Chinese Screen,* 1922

The Chinese, who know more about wisdom than any other race, designate the wise by a combination of the ideographs for wind and lightning.

Count Hermann Keyserling, *America Set Free,* 1930

Cruelty pervades the air of a Chinese town. The Chinese are grossly ignorant and self-satisfied, dependent on but contemptuous of the 'foreign devil,' venal and narrow minded, inveterate bigots. They have a long literature which instils official rectitude, and a long record of dishonest and greedy functionaries. . . . Life here is reduced to its lowest terms; every man attends to his own business, his family, his own comfort, his own pleasure, and takes his pet bird for an airing in the cool of the day. Amid the endless meddling of the modern world, perfect cynicism has much to recommend it.

Peter Quennell, *A Superficial Journey through Tokyo and Peking,* 1932

'Religion,' say the Russians, 'the opium of the people.' 'Opium,' assert Chinese cynics, 'the religion of the people.'

Edgar Snow, *Far Eastern Front,* 1934

The Chinese people take to indifference as Englishmen take to umbrellas, because the political weather always looks a little ominous for the individual who ventures too far out alone.

Lin Yutang, *My Country and My People,* 1936

All Chinese are Confucianists when successful, and Taoists when they are failures.

Ibid.

Our fellow-passengers . . . all had that gift (which the Chinese need and have, which the Russians need and lack) for making one cubic foot into two and turning the Black Hole of Calcutta into an only slightly overcrowded debating hall.

Peter Fleming, *News from Tartary,* 1936

A race of pragmatists.

Edgar Snow, *Red Star Over China,* 1937

Even so rigid a faith as Communism, if for the sake of convenience it had temporarily to be accepted, would find itself powerless to alter the national character: on the contrary, the national character would very soon modify Communism to suit itself, or even assimilate it, as it has always assimilated foreign conquerors.

Osbert Sitwell, *Escape with Me,* 1939

Who but the Chinese, seeking a name for the wild aborigines near the Tibetan border, would think to call them the '*Shy* people?' Who but the Chinese would name a city 'Nothing to Do,' simply because it was a lonely spot?

John Gunther, *Inside Asia,* 1939

One of the most eloquent foreigners in China told me, 'Opium to the Chinese is an extra hour of daylight.'

Ibid.

It was the Middle Ages with electric light and no Pope.

E.R. Dodds, *Missing Persons,* 1977 – of 1942

More people speak Chinese than any other language in the world.

Dr Frederick H. Jackson, 'Instruction in Chinese and Japanese in Secondary Schools,' in *The Annals of the American Academy of Political Sciences,* November 1964

The Chinese are only too often ready to sweep the dust of reality under the carpet of appearance.

Dennis Bloodworth, *Chinese Looking Glass,* 1967

While it is permissible for a Chinese hero to be a villain, it is not permissible for him to be a fool.

Ibid.

and the Japanese

We like the Chinese but we don't admire them.
We admire the Japanese but we don't like them.

Anon. American lady, quoted by Charles A. Fisher, *Three Times a Guest*, 1979

Masturbation has an adverse effect on general health and also decreases the revolutionary will.

Chinese booklet on puberty, quoted by Beverley Hooper, *Inside Peking*, 1979

I had no illusions about the system Chou represented nor did I doubt that in serving its purposes he could be as formidable a foe as he was fascinating an interlocutor. The new society in China had been achieved at an enormous, by my values exorbitant, price. The sacrifices in freedom, spontaneity, culture, family life, seemed to me to go beyond what any group of leaders have a moral right to impose on their people. The Chinese were cold-blooded practitioners of power politics, a far cry from the romantic humanitarians imagined in Western intellectual circles.

Henry Kissinger, *White House Years*, 1979

Their civilization is based on the most forthrightly materialistic value system in the history of mankind. If they see pie in the sky, they immediately start figuring out how to get it down onto the dinner table.

David Bonavia, *The Chinese*, 1981

Frankly speaking, it is difficult to trust the Chinese. Once bitten by a snake you feel suspicious even when you see a piece of rope.

The Dalai Lama, remark to journalist, quoted by John Blair, *Observer Colour Magazine*, 5 April 1981

Canton

I had taken one fair look at the city from the steamer, and threw up my cards. 'I can't describe this place, and besides, I hate Chinamen.'

'Bosh! It is only Benares, magnified about eight times. Come along.'

Rudyard Kipling, *From Sea to Sea*, 1889

Cequian/Sciauhin/Ciquion

This Citie, . . . is a type and representation of Venice.

Father Rogers, or Ruggerius, quoted in *Purchas his Pilgrimes*, 1625

Cheng Sha

The town is just like a mediaeval town – narrow streets, every house a shop with a gay sign hung out, no traffic possible except sedan chairs and a few rickshaws. The Europeans have a few factories, a few banks, a few missions and a hospital – the whole gamut of damaging and repairing body and soul by western methods.

Bertrand Russell, *Autobiography*, 1968 – of 1920

Chunking

A dank, fog-ridden, almost sunless city. ('When the sun shines in Chungking,' says the Chinese proverb, 'the dogs bark.')

E.R. Dodds, *Missing Persons*, 1977 – of 1942

I welcomed the spring in romantic Chungking,
I walked in her beautiful bowers,
In the light of the moon in the sunshine at noon
I savored the fragrance of flowers
(Not to speak of the slush, or the muck and the mush
That covers the streets and the alleys,
Or the reek of the swill as it seeps down the hill –
Or the odour of pig in the valleys. . . .)
Aromatic Chunking, where I welcomed the spring,
In a mixture of beauty and stenches,
Of flowers and birds with a sprinkling of turds,
And of bow-legged Szechuan wenches.

General Joe Stilwell, 'Lyric to Spring', in Letter to his wife, 21 March 1943, in Theodore H. White (ed.), *The Stilwell Papers*, 1948

Dzunchia

The fort was not a fort but a small dilapidated lamasery. Round this had sprung up a little warren of mud huts. . . . That was all there was to Dzunchia: an unsightly, unexpected cluster of walls and roofs which grew like a wart in the middle of a vast bare plain. The poor gesture which man had made towards establishing himself there, the dingy skeleton of domesticity, enhanced to an overpowering degree the desolation of the place. Dzunchia looked, felt, and smelt like the end of the world. . . .

It is always the way. The desert is clean and comfortable, and the Ritz is clean and comfortable; it is on the first of the stages from the desert to the Ritz that you find the real dirt, the real discomfort.

Peter Fleming, *News from Tartary*, 1936

The Great Wall of China

An Account of it would have been thought Fabulous, were not the Wall itself still extant.

Joseph Addison, *Spectator*, No. 415, 26 June 1712

I said I really believed I should go and see the wall of

China had I not children, of whom it was my duty to take care. 'Sir, (said he,) by doing so, you would do what would be of importance in raising your children to eminence. There would be a lustre reflected on them from your spirit and curiosity. They would be at all times regarded as the children of a man who had gone to view the wall of China. I am serious, Sir.'

James Boswell, *Life of Johnson* (10 April 1778), 1791

near Kalgan

The stones of which it is composed are so time-worn and moss-covered that it is almost impossible to say to what species they belong; they seemed mostly of one kind and extremely heavy. I managed to secure three small ones for paper weights, while Ivanoff and Kolestnikoff 'kept cave.'

Harry de Windt, *From Pekin to Calais by Land*, 1889

There in the mist, enormous, majestic, silent and terrible, stood the Great Wall of China. Solitarily, with the indifference of nature herself, it crept up the mountain side and slipped down to the depth of the valley. Menacingly, the grim watch-towers, stark and foursquare, at due intervals stood at their posts. Ruthlessly, for it was built at the cost of a million lives and each one of those great grey stones has been stained with the bloody tears of the captive and the outcast, it forged its dark way through a sea of rugged mountains. Fearlessly it went on its endless journey, league upon league to the farthermost regions of Asia, in utter solitude, mysterious like the great empire it guarded. There in the mist, enormous, majestic, silent, and terrible, stood the Great Wall of China.

W. Somerset Maugham, *On a Chinese Screen*, 1922

In a rash moment I promised to bring home some bricks from the Great Wall of China. The railway officials heard of my wish, and at once sent coolies to the Great Wall before I reached it. They brought back six bricks. I must keep my promise and shall transport these immense things to England. I think they will make a little curiosity for gardens. . . . They are three thousand years old, and six times the size of an ordinary modern English brick. Think of it!

Alfred Viscount Northcliffe, *My Journey Round the World* (November 1921), 1923

Of all man's work on earth, it alone could be seen from Mars.

John Gunther, *Inside Asia*, 1939

Hangchow/Hamceu/Hamcheu

Hamceu is the chiefe Citie of this Province: yea, in all this Kingdome, lesse perhaps somewhat in compasse of walles than Nanquin, but better peopled: no place in the Citie emptie, nor occupied with Gardens, but all builded, and all the Buildings almost with divers Stories, which in other Cities of China is not usuall. . . . The chiefe street is almost halfe a dayes Journey in length, and cannot be lesse then admirable. For whereas the Chinois use to erect triumphall Arches, as Monuments to wel-deserving Magistrates, and Ornaments to their Cities; this one street hath at least three hundred such . . . of massive stones and exceeding curious Workmanship, that if the Houses on both sides yeelded the like splendor, the World could not shew such a spectacle. But they occupie it all with shops, and build the most magnificence of their Houses inwards, and yet those not like the European Palaces.

There is also a Lake close to the Citie, which the eye can scarsly measure, which sliding into a Valley encompassing, embossed with divers Hillocks, hath given occasion to Art to shew her utmost in the adorning the same, beautifying all those spacious bankes with Houses, Gardens, Groves; a very Labyrinth to the bewitched eyes, not knowing whereat most in this Maze to bee most amazed, wherein most to delight. And in delights doe they spend their dayes, filling the Lake with Vessels, furnished with Feasts, Spectacles and Playes on the water. There is a pleasant Hill in the middle of the Citie, whereon is a faire Towre or Steeple, where they measure their houres by a strange device. Out of huge Vessels water droppeth from one to another, the lowest being very large, in the middle whereof is perpendicularly raysed a Rule, distinguished with houre-spaces, which by the ascent or descent of the water, divide the rising and declining day, and declare the houres. . . . From this Hill is a prospect over all the Citie. All the streets being set with Trees, make shew of pleasant Gardens. It is so full of Rivers, Lakes, Rils, Ponds, both in the Citie and Suburbs, as if a man would frame a Platonicall Idaea of elegancie to his minde.

Father Ricii, *c.* 1604, in *Purchas his Pilgrimes*, 1625

Hangkow, now Wuhan (the foreign community there)

The impression one has of Hangkow is that while one-half the settlement are standing on their dignity, the other half have considerable difficulty in standing at all. Hangkow is a thirsty place.

John Foster Fraser, *Round the World on a Wheel*, 1899

Harbin

(under Russian control)

I had obtained the impression that Harbin resembled one of those huge American cities that grow up in a night. I pictured to myself a town somewhat like Vienna, with asphalt pavement and electric light. On arriving all that I saw before me from the station was a sea of mud, deep, thick swamps, which did duty for roads, a few houses in the distance, and a certain amount of scaffolding. . . . I experienced a sinking sense of disappointment and echoed Faust's cry of disillusionment on seeing Helen of Troy, 'Is *this,*' I thought, 'the place that's launched a thousand ships?'

Hon. Maurice Baring, *What I Saw in Russia,* 1913 – of 1904

Harbin is now called the Chicago of the East. This is not a compliment to Chicago.

Ibid.

Honan, and the Yellow River

How wonderful are the works of God
At times among His people abroad –
Therefore, let us be careful of what we do or say
For fear God doth suddenly take our lives away
The province of Honan is about half the size of
Scotland
Dotted over with about 3000 villages, most grand;
And inhabited by millions of people of every degree
And these villages, and people, were transformed into a
raging sea.

William McGonagall, *The Great Yellow River Inundation in China,* 28 September 1887

Kweichow

Kweichow was a wild region of which it was said that it had not three feet of level ground or three fine days running or three dollars in anybody's pocket.

E.R. Dodds, *Missing Persons,* 1977

Khotan

Several mosques – larger, more solidly picturesque than heretofore – . . . though they did not prevent Khotan from suggesting a film set, at least made it suggest a more careful, expensive, and permanent film set than the other cases.

Peter Fleming, *News from Tartary,* 1936

Kwi-La-Shai (between Pekin and Kalgan)

Like many other beautiful things in this world, Kwi-La-Shai is best seen at a distance. . . .

It is called in China a 'village' which means that it is rather larger than Birmingham.

Harry de Windt, *From Pekin to Calais by Land,* 1889

Macao

Macao standeth at one end of a greatt Iland built on rising hills, some gardeins and trees among their houses making a pretty prospecte somwhatt resembling Goa, allthough not soe bigge; Their houses double tyled, and thatt plaistred over againe, for prevention of Hurracanes or violent wyndes thatt happen some Yeares, called by the Chinois Tuffaones, which is also the reason (as they say) they build no high towers Nor steeples to their Churches.

Beeffore Macao are many Ilands, some greater some lesse some inhabited, most part nott; high uneven land, no trees, much grasse and plenty of water springs; very stony, many great ones such as wee have in some part off the Westcountry, called Moorestones; Many China vessells passing to and Fro. . . .

Peter Mundy, *Travels in Europe and Asia,* 1637

I, therefore, after dinner went on shore to this miserable place, where there is a wretched ill-constructed fort belonging to the Portuguese, in which I saw a few sallow-faced, half-naked, and apparently half-starved creatures in old tattered coats that had once been blue, carrying muskets upon their shoulders, which, like the other accoutrements were of a piece with their dress. These wretches are honoured with a title of soldiers. Not only the men, but everything around, bespoke the acme of poverty and misery. Satisfied with what I had seen, and nothing tempted by a printed board indicating the house upon which it was fixed to be 'The British Hotel,' where was to be found 'elegant entertainment and comfortable lodging,' I did not even take a look within, but walked as fast as my legs could carry me back to the sea side. . . .

William Hickey, *Memoirs,* 1749-1809

The town is a bit of Medieval Portugal transported half the world away. People old Coimbra with Chinese and there you have it. The arcaded houses have flat, brown-tiled roofs and are painted all colours, cream, yellow, pink, blue and mauve. The narrow, cobbled alleys twist this way and that, up hill and down, past here a convent, there a grim wall, blank but for a single-barred air-hole, black as the pit inside. It is a relic of the yellow-slave traffic, a barracoon where the coolies were kept, awaiting shipment to the Chincha Isles, there to toil in misery till they died, shovelling guano for the Peruvian Government. . . . The whole place is a relic of old barbarism, the shell of former power. . . . At the top of an imposing flight of steps, like a huge cardboard silhouette reared against the sky, stands a curious monument, the Church of San Paulo. But there is no church; it was burnt down nearly a century ago; only the façade remains, with its gaping doors and curious carving of the Virgin treading on the heathen dragon, medieval ships and winged skeletons. It typifies Macao of to-day – a façade only.

Crosbie Garstin, *The Dragon and the Lotus,* 1923

A weed from Catholic Europe, it took root
Between some yellow mountains and a sea,
Its gay stone houses an exotic fruit
A Portugal-cum-China oddity

Rococo images of saint and Saviour
Promise its gamblers fortunes when they die,
Churches alongside brothels testify
That faith can pardon natural behaviour.

A town of such indulgence need not fear
Those mortal sins by which the strong are killed
And limbs and governments are torn to pieces.

Religious clocks will strike, the childish vices
Will safeguard the low virtues of the child
And nothing serious can happen here.

W.H. Auden, 'Macao', 1938, in *Journey to a War*, 1939. (But see James Kirkup below.)

It was unthinkable for anyone who had consumed as much pulp fiction as myself to put into Hong Kong without visiting Macao, widely acclaimed as the wickedest city in the East, and I lost no time in making the pilgrimage. . . . To it, the legend goes, gravitate the cutthroat, gambler, Jezebel, and drug addict, when the underworld finally closes its doors; whatever your whim, whether opium, fan-tan, or the sing-song girls, Macao waits to gratify it.

On the basis of an overnight sojourn, I can report that I found the Pearl of the Orient slightly less exciting than a rainy Sunday evening in Rochester.

S.J. Perelman, *Westward Ha!*, 1948

Well, it all depends upon what you mean by 'serious'.

James Kirkup, *Streets of Asia*, 1969

Manchuria

To my mind Manchuria is infinitely more beautiful in its leafless state than in summer. When the kowliang is cut the hidden undulations and delicate lines are revealed. It is a country of exquisite outlines. When one sees the rare trees, with their frail fretwork of branches standing out in dark and intricate patterns against the rosy haze of the wintry sunset, suffused and softened with innumerable particles of brown dust, one realises whence Chinese art drew its inspiration; one understands how the 'cunning worker in Pekin' pricked onto porcelain the colours and designs which make oriental china beautiful and precious.

Maurice Baring, *What I Saw in Russia*, 1913

Nanking

The Chinois affirme, that in Nanquin are eight hundred thousand housholds, foure and twentie thousand houses of Mandarines, sixtie two great market places; one hundred and thirtie shambles, each having eightie blockes; eight thousand streets, of which the sixe hundred principall have grates of Latten on both sides all alongst; two thousand three hundred Pagodes or Temples, one thousand of which are Monasteries of Religious persons, richly built, with Towres of sixtie or seventie Bells of Metall and Iron, which make a noise horrible to heare; thirtie Prisons great and strong, each having two or three thousand Prisoners, and an Hospitall. The houses of the Mandarines are of earth, encompassed with Walls and Ditches, with faire Bridges, and rich Arches. The principall Magistrates have high Towers with gilded pinacles, where are their Armories and Treasures. The Street-arches with their night shut Gates, their new and full Moone feasts, incredible fishings, their ten thousand Silke-loomes, one hundred and thirtie Gates in the strong wall, with as many Bridges over the ditch . . . twelve Fortresses with Bulwarkes and Towers, . . . I can but touch. The rarities of China, compared with the things seene at home, seeme doubtfull or incredible.

Fernan Mendez Pinto, 1542, in *Purchas his Pilgrimes*, 1625

Peking

To the South it is compassed with two walls high and strong, so broad that twelve Horses may easily runne abrest on the breadth without hindering one the other. They are made of Brickes, save that on the foot it stands all on huge stones, the midle of the wall is filled with Earth: the height farre exceeds those in Europe. To the North is but one wall. On these walls by night is kept as vigilant watch as if it were time of warre. . . .

The Kings Palace riseth within the inner Southerne wall, neere the City gates and extends to the Northerne wall, seeming to take up the whole Citie: the rest of the Citie running forth on both sides: It is some-what narrower then the Palace of Nanquin, but more goodly and glorious; that seeming by the Kings absence, as a carkasse without soule. Few of the Streets are paved with Bricke or Stone, so that in Winter dirt, and dust in Summer, are very offensive: and because it raineth there seldome, the ground is all crumbled into dust, and if any wind blow, it enters every Roome. To prevent which they have brought in a custom, that no man of whatsoever ranke goeth on foot or rideth without a Veile or Bonnet hanging to his brest, of that subtiltie that he may see, and yet the dust not annoy him: which also hath another commoditie that he may goe any whither unseene, so freed from innumerable tedious salutations, and also he spares attendance and cost.

Father Ricii, *c.* 1595, in *Purchas his Pilgrimes*, 1625

To describe the celestial capital is not difficult. One street is so exactly like another, that when you have seen a bit of the place you have seen the whole of it. The principal street of the Tartar city may be described in very few words. A broad, straggling thoroughfare, knee deep in dust, with low, tumble-down houses on either side, hidden at intervals by dirty canvas booths, wherein fortune-tellers, sellers of sweet-meats, keepers of gambling-hells, and jugglers ply their trade. Deep open cess-pools at every fifty yards; crowds of dirty, half-naked men and painted women; mandarins and palanquins preceded by gaudily-clad soldiers on horse-back and followed by a yelling rabble of men and boys, armed with flags, spears, and sticks, on foot; Tartar ladies in mule litters, hung with bells, and bright cloths; dark, savage-looking Mongolians from the desert, leading caravans of camels; Chinamen in grey, green, or heliotrope silk, Chinamen in rags, and Chinamen in nothing at all; water-carriers, soldiers, porters, sellers of fruit and ice, the latter coated with dust, like everything else, and looking singularly uninviting; Chow-chow and sweetmeat sellers; camels, mules, ponies, oxen carts thronging the ruined road-way; a deafening noise of bells, cymbals, shouting and cursing; indecency, and filth everywhere, with a dusty, gloomy glare over everything, even on the brightest day, while the air everywhere around is poisoned with the hot, sickly smell peculiar to Pekin. . . . We saw many curious sights, but most were of such a nature that I cannot describe them.

Harry de Windt, *From Pekin to Calais by Land,* 1889

If we, in England, must eat, according to the proverb, a peck of dirt before we die, I feel convinced that the inhabitants of Pekin swallow at least a hundredweight before their last hour. The dust of Pekin is, next to its smells, its greatest curse. . . . There is a saying, among the Chinese, that it will worm its way into a watch-glass.

Ibid.

Peking is one of those focal points which we set ourselves as a future destination.

Peter Quennell, *A Superficial Journey through Tokyo and Peking,* 1932

Peking – in this, as in several other ways, curiously resembling Oxford – can usually be relied upon to be characteristic.

Peter Fleming, *News from Tartary,* 1936

A huge city, a great metropolis set in a gold and sepia plain which extended to the shadow of lovely, blue hills lying light as veined bubbles upon the horizon.

Osbert Sitwell, *Escape with Me,* 1939

At five in the morning Peking has a disembodied air; its strange pearly quality achieves no sort of shape in the half-light; its outlines are blurred and misty; it is rather like existing within a seventeenth century Chinese water-colour. It is lovely, but eerie.

James Cameron, *Witness,* 1966

By the end of my first winter in Peking I had an insatiable craving for colour. . . . By the time my second winter came round my eye had become more discriminating. Now shades of grey looked beautiful in themselves: the shadows of bare trees against the earth, the darkness of bicycles and their riders against the lighter streets.

Beverley Hooper, *Inside Peking,* 1979

You know what this place needs – a few good paint salesmen.

Visiting Australian businessman, quoted by Beverley Hooper, *ibid.*

The Forbidden City

I have been fortunate enough to see the Forbidden City under snow, and it was a sight unforgettably lovely. The huge buildings floated upon clouds, were borne up by them. . . . The glory that shone from the ground (for it seemed now as if more light came up from the earth than down from the sky) imparted a brilliance beyond belief to the interiors, to the great red pillars, up the length of which golden dragons clawed their way, to doors and frescoed walls; and still more glittering was it outside, where it reverberated up against the flashing eaves which supported the quilted tents of snow covering the roofs. Below, the white terraces were now whiter still, beneath their soft loads of swansdown: and this expanse of whiteness still further exaggerated the size of hall and of court. Even the moats beyond were padded out of sight, the canals extinguished; and in the gardens, the dark foliage of cypress and cedar made startling patterns, of lace and fans and cubist needles, over the light ground. From the walk and round the top of the Guard-House, floating high above walls and roof – a walk like that in the gallery of an Italian Romanesque cathedral, just wide enough for one person – the more distant towers and gateways of the Forbidden City appeared sombre and isolated by this whiteness. . . . But astonishing as were the reversals of appearance undergone by the great buildings, it was the delicacy of the nearer details that, by this new emphasis placed upon them, triumphed; the flowers painted upon a shutter, the bird or crag upon a panel, were now luminous and melting as the snow itself.

Osbert Sitwell, *Escape with Me,* 1939

Shanghai

The walls are two miles compasse, the Suburbes contayne as many houses as the Citie; so that there are numbred fortie thousand Housholds, . . . the Territorie is an even Playne, and so cultivated that they seeme a Citie of Gardens, full also of Villages, Hamlets, Towers. . . . There are many good wits and Students, a good Ayre, and they live long, eightie, ninetie, and a hundred yeeres.

Father Ricii, *c.* 1610, in *Purchas his Pilgrimes,* 1625

Nevertheless, the tired or lustful business man will find here everything to gratify his desires. You can buy an electric razor, or a French dinner, or a well-cut suit. You can dance at the Tower Restaurant on the roof of the Cathay Hotel, and gossip with Freddy Kaufmann, its charming manager, about the European aristocracy, or pre-Hitler Berlin. You can attend race-meetings baseball games football matches. You can see the latest American films. If you want girls or boys, you can have them, at all prices, in the bath-houses and the brothels. If you want opium you can smoke it in the best company, served on a tray, like afternoon tea. Good wine is difficult in this climate, but there is whisky and gin to float a fleet of battleships. The jeweller and the antique dealer await your orders, and their charges will make you imagine yourself back on Fifth Avenue or in Bond Street. Finally, if you ever repent, there are churches and chapels of all denominations.

Christopher Isherwood, *Journey to a War,* 1939, with W.H. Auden, – of 1938

As Vincent Sheean once said, Shanghai is the city par excellence of two things, money and the fear of losing it.

John Gunther, *Inside Asia,* 1939

Shensi

The farms of Shensi may be described as slanting . . . There are few genuine mountains, only endless broken hills, hills as interminable as a sentence by James Joyce, and even more tiresome. Yet the effect is often strikingly like Picasso.

Edgar Snow, *Red Star Over China,* 1937

Sinkiang

In 1935 Sinkiang, if you substitute political for physical difficulties, shared with the peak of Everest the blue riband of inaccessibility.

Peter Fleming, *News from Tartary,* 1936

Shang Tu/Xanadu *(summer palace of Kubla Khan)*

In Xanadu did Kubla Khan
A stately pleasure-dome decree:
Where Alph, the sacred river, ran
Through caverns measureless to man
Down to a sunless sea.

Samuel Taylor Coleridge, *Kubla Khan,* 1816

Soochow

This Noble Mart is one of them whereof is the Proverbe, That which is in Heaven the Seat of the Blessed, that in Earth is named Suceu, and Hamceu: in splendour, wealth, frequencie remarkable. It is built in a calme freshwater River, and quite thorow one may goe, as in Venice, by Land or Water, but herein it excelleth Venice that the water is fresh. The streets and buildings stand upon piles of Timber, the Wares from Amacao and other parts are most sold here. It hath one gate to the Land, the other are water-wayes. The Bridges are innumerable, & Magnificent, Ancient, but of one Arch in those narrow Chanels.

Jesuit writer, *c.* 1541-1622, in *Purchas his Pilgrimes,* 1625

To be happy on earth one must be born in Soo Chow.

Chinese proverb

CITIES

God the first garden made, and the first city Cain.

Abraham Cowley, *The Garden – Essays in Verse and Prose,* 1668 – before 1667

The axis of the earth sticks out visibly through the center of each and every town and city.

O.W. Holmes, *The Autocrat of the Breakfast-table,* 1857-8

The test of civilization is the power of drawing the most benefit out of cities.

R.W. Emerson, *Journal,* 1864

God made the country and man made the town.

William Cowper, *The Task,* 1783 – the Sofa

God made the country, man the town; the devil the little country town.

Anon, quoted from East Anglian Daily Times, 20 May 1922, by Sir Gurney Benham, *Benham's Book of Quotations*

COLOMBIA

We occupy the centre of the universe and border upon every nation. Who else can claim as much? We possess two and a half million inhabitants scattered over a wide desert. One part is savage, another slave, and most are enemies each of the other, all have been corrupted by superstition and despotism. What a wonderful contrast to hold up to all the nations of the earth! Such is our situation; such is Colombia.

Simon Bolivar, Letter to General Santander, 23 December 1822

'And why did you come to visit such a region as this?' asked Bolivar, when dying, of a Frenchman, to whom in his last days, he was indebted for much. 'For freedom,' said the Frenchman. 'For freedom!' said Bolivar. 'Then let me tell you that you have missed your mark altogether; you could hardly have turned in a worse direction.'

Anthony Trollope, *The West Indies and the Spanish Main*, 1859

The President . . . resembled a typical French politician of the old school. . . . When we were presented I said that I must apologize for my ignorance about Colombia, since we had only arrived the afternoon before. His reply was, 'If you have been here twenty-four hours you already know more than most Colombians do.'

John Gunther, *Inside South America*, 1967, in conversation with President Valencia

The country is a mélange of Socrates and Jack the Ripper. An explanation may be that, for unknown reasons, but of which geography is certainly one, Colombia still represents the fundamental atavistic conflict, not yet resolved, between Spaniard and Indian, which is characteristic of much of the west coast of South America.

John Gunther, *Inside South America*, 1967

One of the men said, 'In Colombia we don't usually call the toilet the *escusado*, but the *chicago*, because the first ones imported into our country were made there, and had the name prominently engraved on the bowl.'

John Masters, *Pilgrim Son*, 1971

When Colombians spoke about the past I often had the sense of being in a place where history tended to sink, even as it happened, into the traceless solitude of autosuggestion.

Joan Didion, *The White Album*, 1979

Bogota

The ladies rarely go out. Domestic habits, joined to severe stomach-aches, caused by the garlic, tobacco, pork and chicha of which they partake very freely, cause them to be almost continually indisposed.

G. Mollien, *Travels in the Republic of Columbia in 1822–3*, 1824

The residential suburbs . . . extend for miles. . . . There are some fine houses, certainly, but the general effect is depressingly undistinguished. Nowhere could we see the least signs of a modern national style, even a bad one. The Spanish houses look more Californian than Spanish. And there are rows of bastard Tudor villas which must be amongst the ugliest things of their kind in the world. In the midst of this wild largely undeveloped country the British and American architects and their pupils have managed to create an oasis of respectable boredom, an atmosphere of stodgy security, which is as tame as anything in Greater London. . . .

A walk in the city . . . corrected many of our negative first impressions. Bogota's dullness is merely suburban; the centre of town is full of character and contrasts. In the strolling crowds, business suits mingle with blanket capes. Right around the corner from the U.S. drugstores you see Indian women sitting behind their wares on the sidewalk. If New York seems very near, so do the mountain villages.

Around the Plaza Bolivar are the steep narrow streets and massive mansions of the old colonial quarter, with their brown-tiled roofs, barred windows, carved doorways and deep sheltering eaves. We saw several modern apartment buildings of severe and beautiful design, and went into a church where there were wonderful old walnut altars. The slums are a warren of muddy lanes and wretched crumbling hovels, but some of these will shortly disappear; for Bogota is frantically busy tearing itself down and building itself up in preparation for the Pan-American Conference, early next year. . . .

Bogota is a city of conversation. As you walk along you have to keep skirting couples or small groups, all absorbed in excited talk. Some of them even stand out in the middle of the street, holding up the traffic. We suppose they are discussing politics. The cafés are crammed, too; and everybody has a newspaper, to quote from or simply wave in the air.

I have never seen so many bookshops anywhere.

Christopher Isherwood, *The Condor and the Cows*, 1949

This is a drab-looking city, in spite of its vivid environs, if only because most citizens wear dark clothes, and carry raincoats. A man who leaves his house in the morning without a raincoat is thought to be mad.

John Gunther, *Inside South America*, 1967

Would even its best friends claim that Bogota was especially *gay*? James Morris, when he was here, described Bogota as living 'in a kind of perpetual damp October.' That was unkind; but one knows how he felt. I, too, was oppressed by that sombre, apparently endless raincloud hanging from the peak of the Andes around which Bogota – at 8,000 feet – is spread out like a cloth. It never actually rains, and it's always about to rain – a most depressing combination.

John Mander, 'Mexico City to Buenos Aires', *Encounter*, September 1965

Bogota reminded us at times of a kind of Spanish-speaking Glasgow, not least in its heavy-lidded friendliness, a kind of take-a-drink-or-I'll-break-your-arm quality.

William McIlvanney, 'The Tartan Trail to Argentina', *Observer*, 28 May 1978

In retrospect Bogota seemed a cruel towering place, like an eagle's nest now inhabited by vultures and their dying prey.

Paul Theroux, *The Old Patagonian Express*, 1979

Cartagena

'It's a nice clean little town,' one of the ship's officers told us, as we approached down the long pale blue waterway and turned the point into the Boca Chica – the harbour entrance. The surface of the channel was littered with floating vegetable wreaths, some variety of water-hyacinth. When the rainy-season begins, they are swept out of the stagnant shallows of the rivers where they grow and away downstream into the ocean. You sometimes find live snakes still coiled about their roots. They give the place an air of melancholy. It is as though a mass funeral ceremony had just been performed for all the soldiers and pirates whose bones lie unburied in the bay.

Christopher Isherwood, *The Condor and the Cows*, 1949

Santa Martha

Santa Martha is a wretched village – a city it is there called, – at which we, with intense cruelty, maintain a British Consul, and a British post-office. . . . 'Every one of my predecessors here died of fever,' said the Consul to me, in a tone of triumph.

Anthony Trollope, *The West Indies and the Spanish Main*, 1859

Falls of Tequendama *(near Bogota)*

They are about thirteen miles from Bogota, at the edge of the plateau where the river drops 450 feet into the gorge below. This must be breathtaking in clear weather. But all we got were glimpses through the fog which kept rolling up the face of the precipice. Tequendama is a favourite spot for suicides – perhaps because there is something hypnotic about that great feather-bed of foam heaving over the rocks. A policeman with a dog is always on duty to prevent them. He sits forlornly beneath a palm-thatch shelter, with a pair of handcuffs dangling from his belt. Arturo asked him if he always knew which of the many visitors were planning to kill themselves. 'Almost always,' said the policeman: 'And when I don't, my dog does.'

Christopher Isherwood, *The Condor and the Cows*, 1949

COMOROS ISLANDS (France)

Exceeding full of people, which are Moores of tawnie colour and good stature, but they be very trecherous and diligently to be taken heed of.

Edmund Barker, in Richard Hakluyt, *Principal Navigations . . . of the English Nation*, 1598-1600

Anjuan Island *(formerly called Johanna)*

They spoke a strange jargon, intended as English, frequently repeating these words, 'Johanna man, Englishman, all a one brother come. Englishman very good man, drinkee de punch, fire de gun, beatee de French, very good fun.'

William Hickey, *Memoirs*, 1749-1809

On the 24th June, we anchored in the Bay of Johanna, one of the African Isles to the northward of Madagascar. It is a fertile little spot. We here met with plenty of refreshments, and very cheap. The oranges were remarkably fine: I took a good quantity of them: their beef is pretty good: Captain Walker purchased several bullocks for the ship's use and to supply our table. The inhabitants are very civil, but are said to be the greatest thieves in existence. We were much amused with the high titles assumed by them. The Prince of Wales honoured us with his company at breakfast, after which Mr Lewin one of our passengers, took him down to his cabin, where having a number of knick-knacks, he requested his royal highness to make choice of some article to keep in remembrance of him; when to Mr L's astonishment he fixed on a large mahogany book-case, which occupied one side of the cabin; and on being told that could not be spared, went away in high displeasure, refusing to accept anything else. The Duke of Buccleugh washed our linen. H.R.H. the Duke of York officiated as boatman, and a boy of fourteen, who sold us some fruit, introduced himself as the Earl of Mansfield. They seem very proud of these titles – . . . . These people are almost constantly at war with those of the adjacent Isles. Being in great want of gunpowder, they prevailed on Captain Walker to give them the quantity that would have been expended in the customary salutes.

Eliza Fay, *Original Letters from India* (15 February 1815), 1817

Mohilla or Molala

This Island is . . . faire, pleasant and leasurelye ascendinge land, open to an exceedinge highte, full of fruitfull greene Trees of severall sortes, as Coconutts, Plantaines, Lemons, oranges, etts. Also Papaes, of which latter some are soe perfectly round every way, as hardly to be discerned with a paire of Compasses, haveinge a hard shell, and within full of meat not unsavourie, some eight or nine inches about, some more, some lesse. The fairest and slekest Goates that I thinck are in any part of the world. Besides also, small Guinny henns, being black, speckled all over with small round white spotts. . . .

In my opinion it is a very prettie pleasant and fruitefull Island, as well for necessetye as delighte, full of shadie woods of strange Trees, Springs and Rilletts of Water. Heere are alsoe Crowes halfe white as our Pies are in England; also Batts, whose winges extend almost an English Yard, their bodyes in forme and Coulour like Foxes, though noe bigger then a great Ratt. Theie hang all daye on trees by certaine hookes att the end of their winges, with their heads downewards, 4 or 500 together, and att night fly abroad.

Comoro is a huge, highe, massie peece of land; but our Shipps never touched there, by reason of the treacherie of the Inhabitants, only at Johanna and Mohilla, where the people are more Civill, though all Mahometans.

Peter Mundy, *Travels in Europe and Asia*, 1628

COOK ISLANDS (New Zealand)

Takutea

Their superstition here exceeds that at Otaheite, for the whole inhabitants esteem themselves no less than Divinitys.

William Anderson, *Journal*, April 1777

CORSICA (France)

Empty my head of Corsica! Empty it of honour, empty it of humanity, empty it of friendship, empty it of piety. No! while I live, Corsica and the cause of the brave Islanders shall ever employ much of my attention, shall ever interest me in the sincerest manner.

James Boswell, Letter to Samuel Johnson, 26 April 1768

I had got upon a rock in Corsica, and jumped into the middle of life.

James Boswell, *Boswelliana*, 1874 (referring to his experiences, and the reputation he made out of his visit there, to the patriot General Paoli in 1765)

It is easier to deplore than to describe the actual condition of Corsica.

Edward Gibbon, *The Decline and Fall of the Roman Empire*, 1776-88

The inland mountain scenery is of the most magnificent character, but the coast or edges are not remarkable. The great pine forest of Bavella is I think one of the most wonderfully beautiful sights nature can produce. The extraordinary covering of verdure on all but the tops of granite mountains make Corsica delightful: such ilex trees and Chestnuts are rarely seen, and where they are not, a blaze of colour from wild flowers charms the foolish traveller into fits. The people are unlike what I expected, having read of 'revenge,' etc; they have the intelligence of Italians but not their vivacity: shrewd as Scotch, but slow and lazy and quiet generally. It must be added that a more thoroughly kindly and obliging set of people so far as I have gone, cannot easily be found. . . .

I should tell you the people nearly all dress in black, which makes a glumly appearance: the food is good generally, but partickly trout and lobsters: and the wine is delightful, and some well known landscape painters drink no end of it.

Edward Lear, Letter to Lady Waldegrave, 6 May 1868

I have never seen mountains that *looked* grander.

Edward Marsh, *A Number of People*, 1939

Corsicans

The Corsicans with all their resolution are afraid of bad weather to a degree of effeminacy. I got indeed a droll but just account of this from one of them. 'Sir,' said he, 'if you were as poor as a Corsican, and had but one coat, so that after being wet, you could not put on dry clothes, you would be afraid too.'

James Boswell, *Account of Corsica*, 1769

'The Corsicans,' said he, 'have a steady resolution that would amaze you. I wish you could see one of them die. It is a proverb among the Genoese, "The Corsicans deserve the gallows, and they fear not to meet it." There is a real compliment to us in this saying.'

Pasquale de Paoli, quoted by James Boswell, *Journal of a Tour to Corsica*, 1768

The Corsican, though so lazy in his own land, works well when away and makes an excellent policeman, warder or soldier, when the etiquette of idleness is relaxed.

Mrs E.R. Whitwell, *Through Corsica with a Paint-Brush*, 1908

Ajaccio

The town, huddled down low against the dark mountains, looked poor and squalid. And then, as we neared its long façade, and as the ship seemed to fly through the water with each flat square-windowed building marking its speed, that grey light showed clearly the scabrous texture of each wall, the cracked and peeled and stained surface of decay. Later when the sun had risen and I was warming over a glass of coffee on the Cours Napoleon, the sun threw into sharper definition the ulcerous scars, the gutter-soaked patches that smeared the walls of all those tall barrack-like buildings. The kerbs had fallen away, sand from the pavements had run out in rivulets onto the pocked carriageway of this the main street of the capital; no soft grasses and lichens pursued such decay, but instead only sand and powdered asphalt, giving, with their dull ochreous aridity the tone of the town, a town of huge barrack-buildings, dry palms and now leafless plane-trees, of Senegalese troops and occasional statues of Napoleon, of garbage in the streets and wide main square, of sand and the tricolour. Two main avenues converged on that immense sandy Place Diamant; along one, the Cours Napoleon, men in many clothes were already sipping their pastis and talking.

I was to know later that in these lines of cafés and bars there was no dancing, only pastis and cards, – this was much a garrison town, a port for sailors and land-locked soldiers upon which one could feel written in the sand and round the monuments and over the acres of blighted plaster the hideous word 'caserne.'

William Sansom, *South,* 1948

opposite the Hotel de Ville

Napoleon stood moveless in white marble, encircled in his grove of withered palms. Four lions slobbered at his feet, their mouths green with moss over which slow water trickled; it seemed that these lions, snub-faced as pekingese, dropped their saliva as the townsfolk themselves spat, with no ejaculatory effort – it was too hot – only leaning their heads aside and letting the saliva fall.

Ibid.

COSTA RICA

Who will put his capital into a country in which the President can pass any law he pleases on his own behalf?

Anthony Trollope, *The West Indies and the Spanish Main,* 1859

The only embarrassment in Costa Rica is the answer to the reason why. If you ask a Costan Rican why his country is so very different from the other republics of Central America he will at first pretend that he doesn't quite understand, and ask you to explain in what way it seems to differ. Then he will mumble something about the system of land tenure; there are very few big landowners and most of the coffee and banana plantations are in the form of small holdings. If you press him further, he will tell you that Costa Rica is poor in minerals, which meant that the early Spanish settlers had to get down to working the land instead of hoping for quick fortunes. But you know that there is something else at the back of his mind, something perhaps to do with the nature of the population, something more personal, something that he is possibly proud of, but something he feels may vex you. You persist, and finally he will clear his throat, and say, 'Well, of course, I'm no racist, but in Costa Rica we are white people, and . . . ' and discreetly he will begin to blush.

Nicholas Wollaston, *Red Rumba,* 1962

'Costa Rica is certainly civilized and democratic and prosperous, and all the things that we should like to be,' a slightly embittered Nicaraguan had said, 'but it is so dull. It is the Switzerland of Central America.' And then he added, as a malicious afterthought, 'The Costa Ricans – they have no hormones.'

Ibid.

Costa Rica is considered unique in Central America; prosperity has made it dull. . . . What is remarkable is its secularity. I was not prepared for this. . . . The Costa Rican's dislike of dictators had made him intolerant of priests. Luck and ingenuity had made the country prosperous, and it was small and self-contained enough to remain so.

The unambiguous wish in, say, geriatric parts of Florida (which Costa Rica much resembles) is to have comfort and the good life now, on earth. Only the poor peasant believes that he will become bourgeois in Heaven. A rising class wants its comforts on earth and has neither the time nor the inclination to be religious: this was obvious in Costa Rica. In time of crisis – sickness, collapse, the mortal wound – the Costa Rican would turn to the Church and demand a miracle, but middle-class people generally haven't the time to believe in miracles, and so, without consciously rejecting the Church, they seek answers in politics or business. It has made them fair, but boring.

Paul Theroux, *The Old Patagonian Express,* 1979

Women of Costa Rica

The women were humdrum in their appearance, as the men are in their pursuits. They are addicted to crinoline as is the nature of women in these ages; but so long as their petticoats stuck out, that seemed to be everything. In the Churches, they squat down on the ground, in lieu of kneeling, with their dresses and petticoats arranged around them, looking like huge turnips with cropped heads – like turnips that, by their persevering growth had got half their roots above the ground. Now women looking like turnips are not specially attractive.

Anthony Trollope, *The West Indies and the Spanish Main,* 1859

San José

The buildings of San José are all republican; there is not one of any grandeur or architectural beauty; and the churches are inferior to many erected by the Spaniards in the smallest villages. Nevertheless, it exhibited a development of resources and an appearance of business unusual in this lethargic country; and there was one house in the plaza which showed that the owner had been abroad, and had returned with his mind so liberalized as to adopt the improvements of other countries, and build differently from the custom of his fathers and the taste of his neighbours.

J.L. Stephens, *Incidents of Travel in Central America Chiapas and Yucatan*, 1841

When a man has travelled all the way to Costa Rica, he does expect something strange. He does not look to find everything as tame and flat and uninteresting as though he were riding into a sleepy little borough town in Wiltshire. . . . The houses are comfortable enough. They are built with very ordinary doors and windows, of one or two stories according to the wealth of the owners, and are decently clean outside, though apparently rather dirty within. The streets are broad and straight, being all at right angles to each other, and though not very well paved, are not rough enough to elicit admiration. There is a square, the plaza, in which stands the cathedral, the barracks, and a few of the best houses in the town. There is a large, and tolerably well-arranged market-place. There is a really handsome set of public buildings, and there are two moderately good hotels. What more can a man rationally want, if he travel for business? And if he travel for pleasure how can he possibly find less.

Anthony Trollope, *The West Indies and the Spanish Main*, 1859

Volcano of Cartago

We ascended on the south side by a ridge running east and west till we reached a high point, at which there was an immense gap in the crater impossible to cross. The lofty point on which we stood was perfectly clear, the atmosphere was of transparent purity, and looking beyond the region of desolation, below us, at a distance of perhaps two thousand feet, the whole country was covered with clouds, and the city at the foot of the volcano was invisible. By degrees the more distant clouds were lifted, and over the immense bed we saw at the same moment the Atlantic and Pacific Oceans. This was the grand spectacle we had hoped, but scarcely expected to behold. My companions had ascended the volcano several times, but on account of the clouds had only seen the two seas once before. The points at which they were visible were the Gulf of Nicoya and the harbour of San Juan, not directly opposite, but nearly at right angles to one another, so that we saw them without turning the body. In a right line over the tops of the mountains neither was more than twenty miles distant, and from the great height at which we stood they seemed almost at our feet. It is the only point in the world which commands a view of two seas; and I ranked the sight with those most interesting occasions, when from the top of Mount Sinai I looked out upon the Desert of Arabia, and from Mount Hor I saw the Dead Sea.

J.L. Stephens, *Incidents of Travel in Central America Chiapas and Yucatan*, 1841

CUBA

It is a good ilond and plentie of vitell but the land is somewhat montuos and asperous.

Roger Barlow, *A Brief Summe of Geographie, c.* 1540

Cuba alone seems at present to hold up a speck of war to us.

Thomas Jefferson, Letter to James Monroe, 11 January 1823

There are laws of political as well as physical gravitation, and if an apple, severed by the tempest from its native tree, cannot choose but fall to the ground, Cuba, forcibly disjoined from its own unnatural connexion with Spain and incapable of self-support, can gravitate only towards the North American Union.

John Quincey Adams, 1823

When first in the dim light of early morning I saw the shores of Cuba rise and define themselves from dark-blue horizons, I felt as if I sailed with Captain Silver and first gazed on Treasure Island. Here was a place where real things were going on. Here was a scene of vital action. Here was a place where anything might happen. Here was a place where something would certainly happen. Here I might leave my bones.

Winston Spencer Churchill, *My Early Life*, 1930

Cuba is communist, but being Cuban it simply hasn't paid its subscription.

American/Cuban woman, quoted Nicholas Wollaston, *Red Rumba*, 1962

Cuba, lying in the middle of the Caribbean, topographically like a large caterpillar but politically more like a Colorado beetle, may be a paradox, but certainly it is composed of millions of smaller paradoxes. It is a weird, effervescent mixture of blood and Coca-Cola, of violence and indolence, apathy and passion.

Nicholas Wollaston, *ibid.*

Of all the Republics the one that remains most in my mind is that of Cuba, if only because this was the first time I had met with Communism in a warm climate. Up to then I had associated People's Democracies with bleak November afternoons in Eastern Europe; it required the Caribbean to invest the faith with a redeeming fantasy. I remember I arrived at Havana airport in accidental company with a party of British shop-stewards, in whose honour the comrades had employed a small guitar orchestra to play what was generally believed in Cuba to be the British workers' anthem. I had never before heard the 'Red Flag' played as a cha-cha-cha. And when, shortly afterwards, the Cuban Militia band gave a formal State rendering of the 'Internationale' in calypso time, I realised that this was a deviation with which I, at least, could certainly live.

James Cameron, *What a Way to Run the Tribe,* 1968

Cubans

'I am Cuban,' he said, 'You know the type. We are very wild kind of men. All we are innerested in is dames and revolutions – OK?' He wriggled with self-delight.

Laurie Lee, *As I Walked Out One Midsummer Morning,* 1969

The Carretera Central

The Carretera Central runs the length of Cuba, a six-hundred-mile long ribbon of traffic, like an electric element, threaded through the country, with the current switched on.

Nicholas Wollaston, *Red Rumba,* 1962

Cien Fuegos

It is clean, prosperous, and quickly increasing. Its streets are lighted with gas, while those in Havana still depend upon oil-lamps. It has its opera, its governor's house, its alameda, its military and public hospital, its market-place, and railway-station; and unless the engineers deceive themselves, it will in time have its well.

Anthony Trollope, *The West Indies and the Spanish Main,* 1859

Havana

Havana . . . is the chiefest port that the king of Spaine hath in all the countreys of the Indies, and of greatest importance: for all the ships both from Peru, Hundur-as, Porto rico, S. Domingo, Jamaica, and all other places in his Indies, arrive there in their returne to Spaine, for that in this port they take in victuals and water, and the most part of their lading: here they meet from all the foresayd places alwayes in the beginning of May by the king's commandement: at the entrance of this port it is so narrow, that there can scarse come in two ships together, although it be above six fadome deep in the narrowest place of it. In the North side of the comming in there standeth a tower, in which there watcheth every day a man to descrie the sailes of ships which hee can see on the sea; and as many as he discovereth, so many banners he setteth upon the tower, that the people of the towne (which standeth within the port about a mile from the tower) may understand thereof. Under this tower there lieth a sandy shore, where men may easily go aland; and by the tower there runneth a hill along by the waters side, which easily with small store of ordnance subdueth the towne and port. The port within is so large that there may easily ride a thousand saile of ships without anker or cable, for no winde is able to hurt them.

John Chilton (1570), in Richard Hakluyt, *Principal Navigations . . . of the English Nation,* 1598-1600

The land over Havana maketh two small mountaines like a womans breasts or paps.

Richard Hakluyt, *Principal Navigations and Discoveries of the English Nation,* 1598-1600

The marks of the poynt of Havana be these, that on the East side it hath an hie blacke land, which is sloping to the sea, with a little white tower on the top thereof: and as thou goest into the port, thou must keepe neere the high blacke land, and when thou are hard to it, strike thy toppe sayles in signe of peace to the castle; least it shoote at thee.

A Ruttier for the West Indies, in Richard Hakluyt, *ibid.*

A Pennsylvanian with pouchy insomniac eyes warned me against Havana, staring gloomily out over the bright square. 'It's awful,' he said, 'the things they do. I've been in Paris, an' I can stand a lot, but these Cubans . . . the things they show you.' It was as if the world was being found out at last by even its most innocent inhabitants.

Graham Greene, *The Lawless Roads,* 1939

Its nightmare hotels are incomparable in size and ugliness, and its claim to be 'the Paris of the western hemisphere' is to some extent borne out in its lay-out and disposition. Rather, one should say, to *have* been the Paris.

Sacheverell Sitwell, *Golden Wall and Mirador,* 1961

near Havana
The outskirts of Havana are Florida again, only even more so.

Dane Chandos, *Isles to Windward,* 1955

CYPRUS

This Iland yeeldeth to no place in fruitfulness or pleasure, being inriched with Corne, Oile, Cheese, most sweet Porkes, Sheepe, (having tailes that weigh more than twenty pound) Capers (growing upon pricking bushes) Pomegranats, Oranges, and life fruites; Canes or Reedes of sugar, (which they beat in mils, drawing out a water which they seeth to make sugar,) with rich wines, (but gnawing or burning the stomacke) odoriferous Cipres trees, (whereof they make fiers,) store of Cotton and many other blessings of nature. . . . They sowe corne in the moneth of October, and reape it in Aprill. I know not how it comes to passe, that in this Iland of Venus, all fruites taste of salt, which Venus loved so well. And I thought that this was onely proper to the place at which we landed, where they make salt, till many Ilanders affirmed to me, that the very earth, the sweet hearbs, the beasts feeding there, and the fountaines of waters, had a naturall saltnes. The houses are built after the manner of Asia, of a little stone, one roofe high, and plaine in the top, which is plastered, and there they eate and sleepe in the open aire.

Fynes Moryson, *An Itinerary*, 1617

We departed to Cyprus . . . where wee found nothing to answere the famous Relations given by ancient Histories of the excellency of that Iland, but the name onely, (the barbarousnesse of the Turke, and Time, having defaced all the Monuments of Antiquitie) no shew of splendor, no habitation of men in fashion, nor possessors of the ground in a Principalitie; but rather Slaves to cruell Masters, or Prisoners shut up in divers prisons: so grievous is the burthen of that miserable people, and so deformed is the state of that Noble Realme. Notwithstanding, the Redemption of that place and people were most facile (being but foure thousand Turkes in the whole Iland.)

Sir Anthony Sherley, 1599, in *Purchas his Pilgrimes*, 1625

The greatest imperfection of this isle is scarcity of water, and too much plenty of scorching heat, and sandy grounds. The inhabitants are very civil, courteous, and affable; and notwithstanding of their delicious and delicate fare, they are much subject to melancholy, of a robust nature, and good warriors, if they might carry arms.

William Lithgow, *Rare Adventures and Painfull Peregrinations*, 1614–32

Cyprus remained in my mind . . . much as heaven does in the minds of respectable people, as a place I should shortly go to, though I made no preparations for getting there.

W.H. Mallock, *In an Enchanted Island*, 1889

History in this island is almost too profuse. It gives one a sort of mental indigestion.

Robert Byron, *The Road to Oxiana*, 1937

The affinity of the landscape is with Asia rather than the other Greek islands. The earth is bleached to whiteness; only a green patch of vines or a flock of black and tawny goats relieves its arid solitude. Trees were planted along the immaculate tarmac road that brought me from Larnaca to Nicosia, casuarinas and cypresses. But the wind has defeated them, a furious hot blast which gets up off the sea every afternoon and turns the countless water-wheels. These gaunt iron skeletons stand in groves on the outskirts of the towns; their choral creaking is the island's chief song. In the distance are always mountains. And over the whole scene hangs a peculiar light, a glaze of steel and lilac, which sharpens the contours and perspectives, and makes each vagrant goat, each isolated carob tree, stand out from the white earth as though seen through a stereoscope.

The prospect is beautiful in the abstract, but violent and forbidding as the home of man.

Ibid.

Cyprus combines everything that is hateful in the Orient and the Occident.

Osbert Sitwell, *The Four Continents*, 1954

Cyprus is rather a lovely, spare, big bland sexy island.

Lawrence Durrell, Letter to T.S. Eliot, 1954, in *Spirit of Place*, 1969

Cypriots

The people are generally strong and nimble, of great civility, hospitable to their neighbours, and exceedingly fond of strangers.

William Lithgow, *Rare Adventures and Painfull Peregrinations*, 1614–32

The Cypriotes are the most subtle and artful people in all the Levant, nor have they more veracity than their neighbours, so that their words are not to be depended upon, as they make use of all means that way to deceive. The women are little superior to their ancestors with regard to their virtue; and as they go unveiled, so they expose themselves in a manner that in these parts is looked on as very indecent. . . . They retain here the barbarous custom of the other eastern nations of treating their wives as servants.

Richard Pococke, *A Description of the East, and Some Other Countries*, 1743-5

What they are they were; and what they were they are – an indolent, careless and mimetic people, but without a spark of Turkish fire, without a touch of

Grecian taste. With neither beauty of body nor sense of beauty in mind—with neither personal restlessness nor pride of origin—with neither large aspirations nor practical dexterity of hand, they live on in a limpid state, like creatures of the lower types clinging to life for life's own sake; voluptuaries of the sun and sea; holding on by simple animal tenacity through tempests which have wrecked the nobler races of mankind.

W. Hepworth Dixon, *British Cyprus*, 1887

Realizing that they will never be a world power, the Cypriots have decided to settle for being a world nuisance.

George Mikes, quoted in *The Times*, 8 April 1980

Women of Cyprus

The common voice of the Levant allows that in face the women of Cyprus are less beautiful than their majestic sisters of Smyrna, and yet, says the Greek, he may trust himself to one and all the bright cities of the Aegean, and may still weigh anchor with a heart entire, but that so surely as he ventures upon the enchanted Isle of Cyprus, so surely will he know the rapture or the bitterness of Love. The charm, they say, owes its power to that which the people call the astonishing 'politics' (πολιτιχη) of the women, meaning, I fancy, their tact, and their witching ways; the word, however, plainly fails to express one half of that which the speakers would say. I have smiled to hear the Greek with all his plenteousness of fancy, and all the wealth of his generous language, yet vainly struggling to describe the ineffable spell which the Parisians dispose of in their own smart way, by a summary 'Je ne sçai quoi.'

A.W. Kinglake, *Eothen*, 1844

It would appear affectation in my readers to say, that they do not feel a desire to know whether the women at Cyprus retain any of those charms and of that amiability which once drew down the protection of the goddess of beauty on the isle. I reluctantly confess that the favours of that deity were no longer so manifest as of old. . . . The voices of the Cypriot women had something in them peculiarly dissonant, and they all seemed to speak in a false tone, nor did use ever make these shrill accents agreeable: They were not in general beautiful, nor was their dress graceful. . . . Seen from behind they resembled nothing so much as a horse in a mantua-maker's showroom, with a dress appended to it. In their habits they were indolent; they were not good, though niggardly housewives. . . . They rule their servants by caprice, and educate their children by fits of anger and indulgence.

Charles Lewis Meryon, *Travels with Lady Hester Stanhope*, 1846

Perhaps sexual starvation has a part to play in it, too. . . . I cannot suppress my feeling that had the Cypriot girls been just a shade less virtuous, the history of Cyprus would be less eventful and much happier.

George Mikes, 'Letter from Cyprus,' *Encounter*, March 1965

Famagusta

Famagusta, of which the sound is so strangely lovely, though when you visit it you find it to be an undistinguished Cotswold village which has been whitewashed.

Osbert Sitwell, *The Four Continents*, 1954

CZECHOSLOVAKIA

Bohemia, a desert country near the sea.

Stage direction to William Shakespeare, *The Winter's Tale*, *c.* 1610-11

Antigonus: Thou art perfect then, our ship hath toucht upon the Desarts of *Bohemia*.

William Shakespeare, *ibid.*

the frontier, near Comoda

When . . . that we might looke down the mountaines, into the fruitfull Land of *Bohem*, never did sight more rejoice us, the lower Hils being all full of Vineyards and the Vallyes corne and pasture, not an English mile distance, but a village every way; and 20. 30. or 40. es or stacks of corne which their barns cannot hold, in the space of every houres journey: in a word, every thing that belonged to the use and commodity of man was and is there, and all the delightful objects to satisfie every sence, is there abundantly so that nature seemed to make that country her store house or granary, for there is nothing wanting, except mens gratitude to God for such blessings.

John Taylor, *Taylors Travels to Bohemia*, in *All the Works of John Taylor*, 1630

The Kingdom of Bohemia is the most desart of any I have seen in Germany; the Villages so poor and the post houses so miserable, clean straw and fair Water are blessings not allways to be found and better Accomodation not to be hop'd. Tho I carry my own bed with me, I could not sometimes find a place to set it up in, and I rather chose to travel all night, as cold as it is, wrap'd up in my furs, then go into the common Stoves, which are fill'd with a mixture of all sorts of ill Scents.

Lady Mary Wortley Montagu, Letter to Lady Mar, 17 November 1716

Bohemia seems no badly-cultivated country; the ground undulates like many parts of Hertfordshire, and the property seems divided much in the same manner as about Dunstable.

Hester Lynch Piozzi, *Observations . . . in the Course of a Journey*, 1789

I am now in Bohemia a foreign Country of which I dare say you have no clear Ideas, but a confused Notion that it is uncultivated intellectually at least & where something new in Manners and Opinions may be seen – Your notions are not false. Bohemia may be considered as a sort of Back Settlement to Germany – The Natives speak a jargon of Wendish or Sklavonian Origin and do not even understand German – The land is thoroughly catholic And consistently with the present Maxims of imperial policy there reigns here a very egyptian Darkness.

Henry Crabb Robinson, Letter to his Brother, 20 October 1801

He who holds Bohemia holds mid-Europe.

Bismarck, attrib.

My dear old man, we made some new nations after the Peace that might well not have been created. A Czecho-Slovak is what came up and fermented after Austria putrified.

Rudyard Kipling, Letter to Rider Haggard, 7 May 1925

The belief that security can be obtained by throwing a small state to the wolves is a fatal delusion.

Winston Churchill, Statement to the Press, 21 September 1938 – in *The Gathering Storm*, 1948

However much we may admire a gallant little country, it is a very serious thing to commit the people of the British Empire to fighting for it.

Neville Chamberlain, Broadcast, 27 September 1938, quoted in Diary of Sir Robert Bruce Lockhart for that day

Almost everybody who visits Czechoslovakia returns to quote the old saying, 'Happy is the country that has no history.'

John Gunther, *Inside Europe*, 1938 edn

A weird upside-down country where you can find boilers stoked by economists, streets swept by men reading Henry James in English; where filing clerks rise early to write articles for learned journals abroad, and third-rate time-servers are chauffered around in black, bulbous, chrome-trimmed Tatra 603s straight out of a Fifties spy film; where millions of crowns per month are spent on maintaining little cordons of policemen and vehicles to disarm a handful of dangerous men whose only weapon is free conversation. Corruption is everywhere and bribes are part of the common currency. You bribe the butcher for meat, the mechanic for a spare part. In the upper reaches of this corruption – say, to get a better flat – you bribe the bureaucrats to tell you whom to bribe. To keep this ramshackle, profoundly flawed edifice upright requires one apparatchik for every twenty Czechoslovaks. . . . The question is whether the edifice will fall down before it blows up.

Tom Stoppard, 'Prague: The Story of the Chartists', *New York Review of Books*, 4 August 1977

and Hungary

The nationalist hatreds of these regions cannot be expressed in graphs and charts. They defy belief. I remember a young Hungarian's response to a proposal for a mutual ten per cent on Czech-Hungarian tariffs.

'What!' he exclaimed. 'Do you imagine we rate our hatred of the Czechs at only ten per cent!'

John Gunther, *Inside Europe*, 1938 edn

Czechs

The Czechs, I knew, were not everybody's people. Without ever taking much trouble to study them, foreigners of the upper classes, not excluding the English, regarded them as *petit-bourgeois* and boorish. But I had always liked them and admired their qualities. They were a fine people, hard-working, highly-educated, rational, efficient and full of the virtues, and the faults, of the Lowland Scots whom they resemble. I felt not only a deep sympathy but also a genuine affinity with them. It was far from being their own fault that so much sorrow and disaster had overtaken them.

R.H. Bruce Lockhart, *My Europe*, 1952

You can leave your country twice, or as many times as you have strength, to fight a foreign enemy. You can't do it to fight your own countrymen.

Jan Masaryk, quoted R.H. Bruce Lockhart, *ibid.*

'What nation has the largest cow in the world?'
'Czechoslovakia, of course.'
'Why?'
'Because its head is in Prague and it's milked in Moscow.'

Czechoslovakian joke, quoted R.H. Bruce Lockhart, *ibid.*

Be it in good or in bad times whenever the Czechoslovak people needed a helping hand, it was extended first of all by the Soviet Union.

Mr Vasil Bilak, Secretary, Czechoslovak Communist Party, *Observer* 'Sayings of the Week', 13 August 1978

and Eastern Europe generally

Tourists from the West have altered the face of the

Soviet bloc over the last ten years. 'We have a new upper class,' a Prague publican accusingly remarked, 'you – the westerners.'

Tim Garton Ash, *Spectator*, 29 September 1979

Bohemia

Bohemia is the most beautiful part of Czechoslovakia. The road from Prague passes through a rolling thickly wooded landscape, dotted with squat, rounded hills like the dumplings on a plate of Bohemian stew. The inhabitants of Bohemia are the least Bohemian people I have met.

Tim Garton Ash, *Spectator*, 29 September 1979

Brno

Brno is a vry nce cty, but we ddn't get a chance to spnd mch tme thre. . . . Thre are mny twns in Czechoslovakia wthout vwels, but Brno is the lrgest one of thm all.

Art Buchwald, *More Caviar*, 1958

Karlovy Vary (formerly Carlsbad)

*In Carlsbad you rise at five; the fashionable hour for promenade, when the band plays under the colonnade, and the Sprudel is filled with a packed throng over a mile long, being from six to eight in the morning. Here you may hear more languages spoken than the Tower of Babel could have echoed. Polish Jews and Russian princes, Chinese mandarins and Turkish pashas, Norwegians looking as if they had stepped out of Ibsen's plays, women from the Boulevards, Spanish grandees and English countesses, mountaineers from Montenegro, and millionaires from Chicago, you will find every dozen yards. Every luxury in the world Carlsbad provides for its visitors with the one exception of pepper. . . . Pepper, to the liver brigade that forms four-fifths of Carlsbad's customers is poison; and, prevention being better than cure, it is carefully kept out of the neighbourhood. 'Pepper parties' are formed in Carlsbad to journey to some place without the boundary, and there indulge in pepper orgies.

Jerome K. Jerome, *Three Men on the Bummel*, 1900

*Good Germans, when they die, go, they say, to Carlsbad, as good Americans to Paris. This I doubt, seeing that it is a small place, with no convenience for a crowd.

Ibid.

After a few days I noticed cracks in the balneatory co-existence. Many East Germans seemed to ignore the West Germans as they stood in line for their cup of warm water. The West Germans could easily be recognised by their loud voices, and often their women wore gold bracelets. The West Germans seemed somewhat guilty on seeing the East Germans in their cheap nylon shirts. The Czechs, who were the majority anyway, ignored the Russians, and the Russians ignored the Chinese. The Chinese ignored everybody. A few Arabs took no notice of the Jews who retaliated in kind. Only the East Germans and the Czechs and Slovaks carried the Party badge on their lapels. A Viennese couple fraternising with the comrades turned out to be members of Austria's very small Communist Party. Even some Hungarians from Budapest ignored the Hungarians from New York, possibly indicating a split in the world-wide Hungarian Secret Society. At the Colonnade, some Westerners felt lonely and lost, and they would furtively nod to other Westerners.

Joseph Wechsberg, *The Lost World of the Great Spas*, 1979

Prague

On the West side of the Molda is the Emperours Castle, seated on a most high Mountaine, in the fall whereof is the Suburbe called Kleinseit, or little side. From this Suburbe to goe into the City, a long stone bridge is to be passed over Molda, which runnes from the South to the North, and divides the suburbe from the City, to which as you goe, on the left side is a little City of the Jewes, compassed with wals, and before your eies towards the East, is the City called new Prage, both which Cities are compassed about with a third, called old Prage. So as Prage consists of three Cities, all compassed with wals, yet is nothing lesse then strong, and except the stinch of the streetes drive back the Turkes, or they meet them in open field, there is small hope in the fortifications thereof.

Fynes Moryson, *An Itinerary*, 1617

The Citty of *Prague* is almost circular or round, being divided in the middle by the River of *Moldove*, over which is a faire stone Bridge, of 600 paces over, and at each end a strong gate of stone: there is said to be in it of Churches & Chappels, 150. . . . and I was there at 4. severall sorts of divine exercises, *viz.* at good Sermons with the Protestants, at Masse with the Papists, and at a Lutherans preaching, & at the Jewes Synagog; 3 of which I saw and heard for curiosity, & the other for edification. The Jewes in *Prague*, are in such great numbers, that they are thought to be, of men, women, and children, betwixt 50. or 60000 who do all live by brocage and usury upon the Christians, and are very rich in mony and Jewels, so that a man may see 10, or 12 together of them, that are accounted worth 20. 30. or 40000.1. a piece; and yet the slaves goe so miserably attired, that 15. of them are not worth the hanging for their whole ward-ropes.

The Castle where the King and Queene doe keepe

their Court, is magnificent and sumptuous in building, strongly scituated and fortified by nature and art, being founded on a high hill, so that at pleasure it keepes the towne in command, and it is much more spacious in roomes for receipt in Gardens and Orchards, then the Towre of *London*. . . .

The Citty of *Prague* hath in it (by reason of the wars) thrice the number of its owne Inhabitants, and yet for all that, victuals is in such great plenty, that sixe men cannot eate three halfe penny worth of bread, and I did buy in the Market a fat Goose well roast for the valew of 9. pence English. . . .

John Taylor, *Taylors Travels to Bohemia*, in *All the Works of John Taylor*, 1630

Doctor Johnson was very angry with a gentleman at our house once, I well remember, for not being better company; and urged that he had travelled into Bohemia, and seen Prague: – 'Surely,' added he, 'the man who has seen Prague might tell us something new and something strange, and not sit silent for want of matter to put his lips in motion.'

Hester Lynch Piozzi, *Observations . . . in the Course of a Journey*, 1789

*It is the town that conceived the Reformation and hatched the Thirty Years' War.

Jerome K. Jerome, *Three Men on the Bummel*, 1900

Wherever you go in Prague, you will find a bastard kind of architecture, Renaissance crossed with Slavonic, which has little sense of design and no sense of decoration, except the overlaying of a plain surface with protruding figures. . . . And the taste of the people runs all to angles. Every square runs to lines of houses of irregular height, set irregularly; when a square is sub-divided, it is inset with a triangle; every corner is turned so as to make as many angles as possible. The pavement is mosaicked into squares and triangles, and these angles are carried into the sky. Spires bristle up from every church, and at the corners of every tower, and these spires, pointed, wedge-shaped, with an occasional bulbous dome, like the domes of Moscow, are set with a family of little spires growing out of them at alternate angles. They are seen, a mere suggestion, on the twelfth century church of St George, in the Hradcin; gradually the cluster of spires develops, century by century, until we come to the fifteenth century west façade of the Teyn Church and the corner towers of the Powder Gate. This detail, the only invention in architecture of the Bohemians, is typical of the people, so alive to the utility of straight lines, the emphasis of sharp angles, so insensitive to the gradual beauty of the curve, the more delicate harmonies of proportion. There is something in their way of building, fierce, violent, unrestrained, like the savagery of their fighting, of their fighting songs, of their fighting music. . . . And nothing is more curious than to contrast this fiery spirit, showing itself in energy of line and angularity of outline, with the gentleness, the soft colour, the placidity of the wide green spaces within the city, and the vast green plains and hillsides in whose midst the city has entrenched itself.

Arthur Symons, *Cities*, 1903

One might praise it even more for its individuality than for its beauty. It is a most *personal* town. I am not sure that you could say, were you to wake up of a morning in Prague and see it for the first time, 'This is Slavonic. This is the fruit of the Slav mind.' But I am quite sure one would say to oneself, if one saw Prague first suddenly, after having last contemplated a German city, 'This is certainly not German.'

Hilaire Belloc, *Places*, 1942

It was, I knew afresh, the most beautiful city after Edinburgh that I should ever see.

R.H. Bruce Lockhart, *My Europe*, 1952

Prague seemed – it still seems, after many rival cities – not only one of the most beautiful places in the world, but one of the strangest. Fear, piety, zeal, strife and pride, tempered in the end by the milder impulses of munificence and learning and *douceur de vivre*, had flung up an unusual array of grand and unenigmatic monuments. The city, however, was scattered with darker, more reticent, less easily decipherable clues. There were moments when every detail seemed the tip of a phalanx of inexplicable phantoms. This recurring and slightly sinister feeling was fortified by the conviction that Prague, of all my halts including Vienna itself, was the place which the word *Mitteleuropa*, and all that it implies, fitted most aptly. History pressed heavily upon it. Built a hundred miles north of the Danube and three hundred east of the Rhine, it seemed, somehow, out of reach; far withdrawn into the conjectural hinterland of a world the Romans never knew.

Patrick Leigh Fermor, *A Time of Gifts*, 1977

Sudeten Mountains

The Sudetenland is the last territorial claim I have to make in Europe.

Adolf Hitler, Speech, 26 September 1938

D

DENMARK

Hamlet: Denmark's a Prison.
Rosencrantz: Then is the World one.
Hamlet: A goodly one, in which there are many Confines, Wards, and Dungeons; *Denmarke* being one o'th'worst.
Rosencrantz: We thinke not so my Lord.
Hamlet: Why then 'tis none to you; for there is nothing either good or bad, but thinking makes it so: to me it is a prison.

William Shakespeare, *Hamlet, c.* 1600-1

Marcellus: Something is rotten in the State of Denmarke.

Ibid.

Hamlet: My Tables, my Tables; meet it is I set it downe,
That one may smile, and smile and be a Villaine;
At least I'm sure it may be so in Denmarke.

Ibid.

Denmarke, lying neere the Artick circle, must needs be subject to great cold, howsoever the mistie aire, caused by the frequent Iles, doth in some sort mitigate the extremity thereof.

Fynes Moryson, *An Itinerary,* 1617

The hoary winter here conceals from sight
All pleasing objects which to verse invite.
The hills and dales, and the delightful woods,
The flow'ry plains, and silver-streaming floods,
By snow disguis'd, in bright confusion lie,
And with one dazzling waste fatigue the eye.
No gentle breathing breeze prepares the spring,
No birds within the desert region sing.
The Ships, unmov'd, the boist'rous winds defy,
While rattling chariots o'er the ocean fly. . . .
O'er many a shining league the level main
Here spreads itself into a glassy plain:
There solid billows of enormous size,
Alps of green ice, in wild disorder rise.
And yet but lately I have seen ev'n here,
The winter in a lovely dress appear.
Ere yet the clouds let fall the treasur'd snow,
Or winds begin through hazy skies to blow,
At ev'ning a keen eastern breeze arose,
And the descending rain unsully'd froze.
Soon as the silent shades of night withdrew,
The ruddy morn disclos'd at once to view
The face of nature in a rich disguise,
And brighten'd ev'ry object to my eyes:
For ev'ry shrub, and ev'ry blade of grass,
And ev'ry pointed thorn, seem'd wrought in glass; . . .
When if a sudden gust of wind arise,
The brittle forest into atoms flies,
The crackling wood beneath the tempest bends,
And in a spangl'd show'r the prospect ends:
Or, if a southern gale the region warm,
And by degrees unwind the wintry charm,
The traveller a miry country sees,
And journies sad beneath the dropping trees.

Ambrose Philips, 'To the Earl of Dorset', 9 March 1709, *Tatler,* 7 May 1709

A Region which is the very reverse of Paradise. The seasons here are all of them unpleasant, and the Country quite destitute of Rural Charms. I have not heard a bird sing, nor a Brook murmur, nor a Breeze whisper, neither have I been blest with the sight of a Flowry Meadow, these two Years. Every wind here is a Tempest, and every Water a turbulent Ocean.

Ambrose Philips (?), *Spectator,* No. 393, 31 May 1712

The scenery of Denmark at its purest – and nowhere is it more exquisite than from Valdemar Castle to the further mouth of the Svendborg Sound – is built up on a system of infinite softness and sweetness. It consists of sinuous lines and modulated horizons, woods that now dip into the wave, now withdraw in curves to throw girdling shadows over lawn and meadow; a labyrinth of delicate waters that here wind in convoluted darkness, there spread a bosom of refulgence to the sky. The impression given by this characteristic elegance of the Danish landscape is fugitive and difficult to seize. It consists in a complicated harmony of lines for ever shifting and dissolving, while, over it-all, the polished lozenge of the beech-leaf, an heraldic sign incessantly recurrent, rules the composition in every variety of form and in every vicissitude of arrangement.

Edmund Gosse, *Two Visits to Denmark,* 1911 – of 1872

What strikes me now most as regards Denmark is the charm, beauty, and independence of the women. They go about freely, sit in cafés together, smoke without self-consciousness. They seem decidedly more independent than Englishwomen. The men have charm of manner, especially of voice and tone. The race is evidently receptive, and it must be beneficially influenced by the attractiveness of its women. On the other hand, Denmark struck both Rickards and me as being an unimportant and dull little country. Its villages were simply naught. They had nothing, except a material sufficiency—no beauty, no evidence of ancient traditions. The landscape also was practically everywhere negligible.

Arnold Bennett, *Journal,* 29 August 1913

Danes

With the Dane and the Dutchman I will not encounter, for they are simple honest men, that with *Danaus* Daughters doe nothing but fill bottomless tubs, & will be drunke & snort in the midst of dinner: he hurts himself only that goes thither, he cannot lightly be damnd, for the vintners, the brewers, the malt-men and ale-wives pray for him.

Thomas Nashe, *The Unfortunate Traveller,* 1594

The *Danes* that drench
Their cares in wine.

Ben Jonson, *Ode Allegorical,* prefixed to Hugh Holland, *Pancharis,* 1603

I do not see that they are good at imitating the inventions of other countries; and for inventing themselves, I believe none, since the famous Tycho Brahe, ever pretended to it.

Anon., *Account of Denmark as it was in the Year 1692,* 4th edn, 1738

They have true *Dutch* Shapes, and move very heavily. . . . Not many of them are happy in a bright Genius. . . . Their Vices are the same as their Nighbours, Intemperance and Drunkenness.

Thomas Salmon, *A New Geographical and Historical Grammar,* 1751

From every thing I have had an opportunity of observing, the danes are the people who have made the fewest sacrifices to the graces.

Mary Wollstonecraft, *Letters Written during a Short Residence in Sweden, &c.,* 1796

The Danes, in general, seem extremely averse to innovation, and, if happiness only consist in opinion, they are the happiest people in the world; for I never saw any so well satisfied with their own situation.

Ibid.

There is nothing of Hamlet in their character.

R.H. Bruce Lockhart, *My Europe,* 1952

Copenhagen

Copenhagen is the best-built city of the north; for although St Petersburg excels it in superb edifices, yet as it contains no wooden houses, it does not display that striking contrast of meanness and magnificence, but in general exhibits a more equable and uniform appearance. The town is surrounded towards the land with regular ramparts and bastions, a broad ditch full of water, and a few outworks: its circumference measures between four and five miles. The streets are well-paved, with a foot-way on each side, but too narrow and inconvenient for general use. The greatest part of the buildings are of brick; and a few of free-stone brought from Germany. The houses of the nobility are in general splendid, and constructed in the Italian style of architecture. The royal palace is a magnificent pile of building of hewn stone, the wings and stables of brick stuccoed. . . .

The busy spirit of commerce is visible in Copenhagen. The haven is always crowded with merchant-ships; and the streets are intersected by broad canals, which bring the merchandize close to the warehouses that line the quays. The city owes its principal beauty to a dreadful fire in 1728, that destroyed five churches and sixty-seven streets, which have since been rebuilt in the modern style. The new part of the town, raised by the late king Frederic V. is extremely beautiful: it consists of an octagon, containing four uniform and elegant buildings of hewn stone, and of four broad streets leading to it in opposite directions.

William Coxe, *Travels into Poland, Russia, Sweden, etc.,* 4th edn, 1792

I see here nothing but heaps of ruins and only converse with people immersed in trade and sensuality.

Mary Wollstonecraft, Letter to Gilbert Imlay, 6 September 1795

Our French companions complained of the bad taste by which every thing in Copenhagen is characterized. To our eyes, it seemed, indeed, that a journey from London to Copenhagen might exhibit the retrogression of a century; every thing being found, in the latter city, as it existed in the former a hundred years before. . . .

E.D. Clarke, *Travels in Various Countries,* 1824

Copenhagen . . . is as London might be if Hyde Park and St James's Park were arms of the sea and ocean-going steamers sailed up to the gardens of Buckingham Palace.

R.H. Bruce Lockhart, *My Europe,* 1952

Parliament Building

We stopped before the Danish Parliament to look again at the four massive sculptured figures above the entrance. I had always supposed that these huge

Grecian heads, each as ugly as Socrates, were symbolic of the burdens and responsibilities which lie heavily on the shoulders of politicians. The Chauffeur interrupted my thoughts with a chuckle: Do you know how we Danes have Christened these old gentlemen. We call them: 'Headache, Earache, Stomachache and Toothache.' I looked again and had to admit that the names fitted.

R.H. Bruce Lockhart, *My Europe*, 1952

Elsinore and Cronenburg Castle

This is a poore village, but much frequented by sea-faring men, by reason of the straight sea, called the Sownd; where the King of Denmark hath laid so great imposition upon ships and goods comming out of the Balticke sea, or brought into the same, as this sole profit passeth all the revenues of his Kingdome. . . . In respect of the Danes scrupulous and jealous nature, I did with great difficulty, (putting on a Merchants habite, and giving a greater reward then the favour deserved,) obtaine to enter Croneburg Castle, which was built foure square, and hath only one gate on the East side, where it lies upon the straight. Above this gate is a chamber in which the King useth to eat, and two chambers wherein the King and Queene lie apart. Under the fortification of the Castle round about, are stables for horses, and some roomes for like purposes. On the South-side towards the Baltich sea, is the largest roade for ships. And upon this side is the prison, and above it a short gallery. On the West side towards the village is the Church of the Castle, & above it a very faire gallery, in which the King useth to feast at solemne times. On the North side is the prospect partly upon the Iland, and partly upon the Narrow sea, which reacheth twenty foure miles to the German Ocean. And because great store of ships passe this way in great Fleets, of a hundreth more or lesse together: this prospect is most pleasant to all men, but most of all to the King, seeing so many shippes, whereof not one shall passe, without adding somewhat to his treasure.

Fynes Moryson, *An Itinerary*, 1617

His torpid mind I envy not
Though crown and kingdom were his lot
Who here, amid this morning balm
With Nature eloquently calm, –
With tender sky and tranquil sea,
Partook no inborn sympathy.

Robert Montgomery, 'Morning Scene at Elsinore', *Woman the Angel of Life*, 1833

To say that Elsinore is pretty would be fulsome; no Scandinavian country-town possesses any real charm of architecture or picturesque amenity, apart from its local position. This is a weak point of the country to the eye of the foreign visitor; the provincial town of Denmark, Sweden, or Norway being not merely without beauty or dignity, but without any appearance of antiquity. The meanness of such a place as Viborg, for instance a city no less ancient than Siena or York, is indescribable; it might have been jerry-built the year before yesterday. Successive wars no doubt have had something to do with this, and a wooden type of architecture more. But the absence of trees and gardens, the squalid bareness of the Danish streets, is extraordinary and can only be accounted for by believing the inhabitants insensible to what makes an English country-town attractive.

Edmund Gosse, *Two Visits to Denmark*, 1911

Zealand

Nor is Zealand of sufficient magnitude, to take away altogether the odious idea of restraint and confinement. In England, or Ireland, we wholly forget that we are in an island. Even in Sicily or in Sardinia, that impression might rarely occur to the mind. But Zealand, were I compelled to reside in it, I should consider only as an agreeable prison, the bars of which are not far enough removed from the eye, or the imagination, to enable an inhabitant to divest himself completely of recollections allied to captivity. Such at least, have been my feelings and reflections, on this capital and island.

Sir N.W. Wraxall, *A Tour Round the Baltic*, 1775 (1807 edn)

The Watteau-like character of Zealand. . . .

Edmund Gosse, *Two Visits to Denmark*, 1911

DJIBOUTI

Jibuti, white and neat and empty, looked as if it had just been washed and dumped out in the sun to dry.

Rosita Forbes, *From Red Sea to Blue Nile*, 1925

Jibuti is a strange remote place: situated on the equator, it yet has all the comforts and discomforts of a French provincial town. The buildings gleam white in the bright glaring air, but the faces of the people are dark. It is a black and white town with a thousand and one moods: the inhabitants are at once obsequious and impudent, laughing and sullen, contented and sad, rich and poverty-stricken, purse-proud and unassuming. It is a beautiful town! It is a horrible town! It is, above all, a hot town. . . . The air is like foul water. It is impossible to breathe: one gasps for air like a fish landed high and dry.

Ladislas Farago, *Abyssinia on the Eve*, 1935

DOMINICA

The Island of Dominica lieth Northwest and Southeast,

and upon the Northwest side it sheweth more high: and if you come neere it at full sea, it will shew like two Islands, but by comming neerer unto it, you shall perceive it to be but one: and upon the Southeast side you shall make or see a plaine and long point, and upon the same point appeareth a cliffe like to the cliffe of Cape Tiburon; and upon the North side a little from the land it sheweth like a little Island, and upon the top thereof is, as it were, an high steeple, and upon the nother side you shall perceive it like many white sheetes.

A Ruttier for the West Indies, in Richard Hakluyt, *Principal Navigations . . . of the English Nation*, 1598-1600

Dominica is one of the fayrest Islands of the West, full of hilles, and of very good smell.

René Laudonnière (1564), in Richard Hakluyt, *ibid.*

Now they say, that within this little while, they of Dominica did eate a Fryer, and that all they which did eate his flesh, had such a fluxe, that some dyed, and that therefore they have left eating humane flesh: and it may be, because instead of men, with lesse danger, they steale Kine and Mares, for the great quantitie there is of them, and with this they satisfie their raging appetite.

Antonio de Herrera, 1601, in *Purchas his Pilgrimes*, 1625

Roseau

It is impossible to conceive a more distressing sight. Every house is in a state of decadence. There are no shops that can properly be so called; the people wander about chattering, idle, and listless; the streets are covered with thick, rank grass; there is no sign either of money made, or of money making. Everything seems to speak of desolation apathy, and ruin. There is nothing, even in Jamaica, so sad to look at as the town of Roseau.

Anthony Trollope, *The West Indies and the Spanish Main*, 1859

The houses were built like chalets, and some had jutting, pillar-supported gables of trellis work, but most remarkable were the wooden houses built throughout of overlapping dark grey wooden shingles in the style of Bukovina. . . .

The gathering of buildings on this hill-top, the clean white-washed walls and the trees, the flags and towers, and the few acres of the roofs of Roseau possessed an engaging and a rather disarming quality. Altogether the capital was scarcely more than a village, an Antillean Cranford clustering gracefully on the edge of a blazing extent of water, and overshadowed by steep and enormous hills fleecy with every excess of tropical vegetation. If they escape the gloom and the ungainliness which is so often their lot, there is something delightfully comic about many of these little Caribbean towns. The fact that there is a town at all, especially an almost European town, in the middle of such violence of flora and the elements, seems as unnatural in effect as a swimmer remaining for long periods under water.

Patrick Leigh Fermor, *The Traveller's Tree*, 1951

DOMINICAN REPUBLIC

The one part of the West Indies where you are reasonably certain to meet no beggars is that country, politically so very highly suspect, in democratically minded circles, the Dominican Republic. And if this doesn't make begging a respectable profession, what will?

Dane Chandos, *Isles to Windward*, 1945

Santo Domingo

Santo Domingo was built by line and rule: the Houses of Stone very faire.

Gonzalo de Oviedo, 1525, in *Purchas his Pilgrimes*, 1625

Santo Domingo was Napoleon's Vietnam.

Alistair Cooke, *Alistair Cooke's America*, 1973

E

EASTER ISLAND

No Nation will ever contend for the honour of the discovery of Easter Island as there is hardly an Island in this sea which affords less refreshments and conveniences for Shiping than it does; Nature has hardly provided it with any thing fit for man to eat or drink, and as the Natives are but few and may be supposed to plant no more than sufficient for themselves, they cannot have much to spare to new comers.

Captain James Cook, *Journal,* 17 March 1774

The water was a very strong Mineral, had a thick green scum on the top, and stunk worse than that of Harrogate in Yorkshire.

William Wales, *Journal,* 15 March 1774

Easter Island has usually been described as bleak and treeless; but there are in fact flourishing Eucalyptus groves, so that at first sight the island seems like a tiny fragment of New South Wales moored in mid-ocean.

Claude Nigel Davies, *Voyagers to the New World,* 1979

Women of Easter Island

The women are not quite disagreeable.

John Reinhold Forster, *Observations Made During a Voyage Round the World,* 1778

ECUADOR

and Colombia and Venezuela

Ecuador is a monastery, Venezuela is a barracks, Colombia is a university.

Remark attributed to Simón Bolívar

'We are a small country, we have little more than three million people, and the Indians outnumber us ten to one. Most of our people cannot read or write; our records for the most part are unreliable and our statistics largely guesswork. . . . We have a revolution here every Thursday afternoon at half-past two and our Government is run like a night-club.'

Ludwig Bemelmans, *The Donkey Inside,* 1947

In eleven hours we . . . passed from the climate of Westmorland, through the climate of Ireland, to the climate of West Africa.

Arnold Toynbee, *East to West,* 1958

Ecuador is nice, in its tiny way.

V.S. Pritchett, quoted by Paul Theroux, *The Old Patagonian Express,* 1979

Guayaquil

And then there is the monument on the waterfront commemorating Bolivar's meeting here with San Martin, in 1822. As large as history, but somewhat weak at the knees, the figures of the Liberator and the Protector are exchanging a languid handshake. 'My dear,' Bolivar seems to be saying, 'you must be *dead.* Aren't those Peruvians *awful?'*

Christopher Isherwood, *The Condor and the Cows,* 1949

Visitors to Guayaquil are urged to raise their eyes, for on a clear day it is possible to see the snowy hood of Mount Chimborazo from the humid streets of this stinking city; and, if you look down, all you see is rats.

Paul Theroux, *The Old Patagonian Express,* 1979

Quito

Quito, the oldest city in the New World, is seemingly built over a sunken roller coaster. Up and down in wide curves and sudden drops go its streets and white houses; the base of one monument is above the spray of the fountain in the next plaza. It is at once like Tunis and like Bruges, and its near-by background of mountains reminds one of Innsbruck. . . .

It has been said of Quito that it had one hundred churches and one bathtub.

Ludwig Bemelmans, *The Donkey Inside,* 1947

A lieutenant was even more gloomy. . . . 'It is terrible here, Señor. First you must make love to this girl you want until your nose bleeds; second you must make love not only to her, but to her mother, her father, the butler, and the parrot, and in the end you always must marry her.'

Ibid.

The Quito telephone service is about as reliable as roulette.

Christopher Isherwood, *The Condor and the Cows,* 1949

The surroundings of Quito are like those of Sedbergh, on a rather larger scale.

Arnold Toynbee, *East to West,* 1958

People of Quito
On page 110 of a geography book that is used in the schools of Ecuador, written by Professor Juan Morales, the character of the natives of Quito is described in detail. I requested one of the pupils to translate the passage into English, and here is the paragraph verbatim:

'About the inhabitants of Quito: The character of his inhabitants is laughing, frank and sincere, noble and full of those qualities that are a gift and they are learned. Is besides extremely patriot and lofty and incontaminated by any moral misery, but we must call attention to a quality in this noble town that is called "Sal Quitena," is a quality that every Quiteno like to make joke of every word they talk and like to smile with their funny word.'

He forgot to say that they are also extremely generous, polite, hospitable to a fault, and proud.

Ludwig Bemelmans, *The Donkey Inside,* 1947

EGYPT

Thou trustest upon the staff of this bruised reed, even upon Egypt, on which, if a man lean, it will go into his hand, and pierce it.

The Bible, Old Testament, 2 Kings 18:21

Egypt is an acquired country, the gift of the river.

Herodotus, *History, c.*460 BC

How conveniently it stands upon a neck of land commanding both seas on either side, and embracing, as it were with two arms, Asia and Afric, besides the benefit of the famous river of Nilus.

Francis Bacon, *Of the True Greatness of the Kingdom of Britain, c.* 1606

Egypt is most fertile, the very garner of the universall World.

Fynes Moryson, *An Itinerary,* 1617

Egypt is a compound of black earth and green plants, between a pulverized mountain and a red sand.

Amr, Letter to the Caliph Omar, *c.* 643 AD, quoted Edward Gibbon, *The Decline and Fall of the Roman Empire,* 1776–88

The distant view of Mount Horeb again brought the flight of the children of Israel to my mind; and you may be sure, I did not wonder that they sought to quit the land of Egypt, after the various specimens of its *advantages* that I have experienced.

Eliza Fay, *Original Letters from India* (15 September 1779), 1817

Egypt is eager for France – only more, far more eager for G. Britain. The universal cry there – I have seen translations of 20 at least mercantile Letters in the Court of Admiralty here [Malta], all stating that the vox populi is – Engish, English, if we can! But *Hats,* at all events! – ('*Hats*' means Europeans in contradistinction to Turbans!) –

Samuel Taylor Coleridge, Letter to Robert Southey, 2 February 1805

Although there is a sameness in the character of the Egyptian scenery, it is such as is to be seen in no other land. The Libyan and Arabian chains of mountains, perfectly naked, stretch on each side of the Nile nearly to the first cataract, generally within a few miles of the river, and sometimes close to it, or forming its bank. At the foot of these naked masses of a light colour, often appear groups of the most vivid and beautiful verdure, the palm and sycamore spreading over some lonely cottage, a herd of goats and buffaloes winding their way, or a camel silently grazing. The utter barrenness and desolation that often encompass scenes and spots of exquisite fruitfulness and beauty, the tomb of the santon with its scanty shade, and the white minaret with its palm and cypress placed on the very verge of a boundless desert, or amidst a burning expanse of sand are almost peculiar to Egypt. Then you often pass from the rich banks of the Nile covered with lime and orange-trees, where groups of Orientals are seated luxuriously in the shade, into a wild and howling waste, where all, even the broken monuments of past ages, only inspires feelings of sadness and regret.

John Carne, *Letters from the East,* 1830

Arrival there after crossing the Sinai desert
The next day I entered upon Egypt, and floated along (for the delight was as the delight of bathing) through green wavy fields of rice, and pastures fresh and plentiful, and dived into the cold verdure of groves and gardens, and quenched my hot eyes in shade as though in a bed of deep waters.

A.W. Kinglake, *Eothen,* 1844 – of *c.* 1835

Egypt is not the country to go to for the recreation of travel. It is too suggestive and too confounding to be met but in the spirit of study. One's powers of observation sink under the perpetual exercise of thought.

Harriet Martineau, *Eastern Life, Past and Present,* 1848

That the sunset in Egypt is gorgeous, every body

knows; but I, for one, was not aware that there is a renewal of beauty, some time after the sun has departed and left all grey. This discharge of colour is here much what it is among the Alps, where the flame-coloured peaks become grey and ghastly as the last sunbeam leaves them. But here, every thing begins to brighten again in twenty minutes; – the hills are again purple or golden, – the sands orange, – the palms verdant, – the moonlight on the water, a pale green ripple on a lilac surface: and this after-glow continues for ten minutes, when it slowly fades away.

Ibid.

This country is a palimpsest, in which the Bible is written over Herodotus, and the Koran over that.

Lady Duff Gordon, *Letters from Egypt,* 1865

Egypt is henceforth part of Europe, not Africa.

The Khedive, Ismail, Speech at the Opening of the Suez Canal, 1869

Could anything be wilder insanity than leaving a country like ours to see this bareness of mud? – Look! there is some water, and see! there is a crowd of people. They have collected with a purpose of drowning themselves.

R.W. Emerson, Remark to his daughter, in Egypt, 1873

No country has more to offer the wearied Londoner.

Stanley Lane-Poole, *Cairo,* 1892

There is no country so easy to govern as Egypt is, given fair intelligence and perfect honesty in the governor.

Wilfred Scawen Blunt, Diary, 19 December 1895, *My Diaries,* 1919

All the same Egypt is better than opium. It soothes and smoothes one's creases out with the patient weight of a German philosopher trying to be intelligible. Hay and I ponder painfully over the strange state of mind which results from learning to regard Homer as a modern poet and Herodotus as a trivial Cook tourist.

Henry Adams, Letter to Elizabeth Cameron, 26 February 1898

Here is a country which is not a country but a longish strip of market-garden, nominally in charge of a government which is not a government but the disconnected satrapy of a half-dead empire, controlled pecksniffingly by a Power which is not a Power but an Agency, which Agency has been tied up by years, custom, and blackmail into all sorts of intimate relations with six or seven European Powers, all with rights and perquisites, none of whose subjects seem directly amenable to any Power which at first, second, or third hand is supposed to be responsible. That is the barest outline.

Rudyard Kipling, *Egypt of the Magicians,* 1913

I can't think much of a people who drew cats the same for four thousand years.

Field-Marshal Lord Kitchener, quoted by Vita Sackville-West, *Passenger to Teheran,* 1926

*'I've never travelled,' Dona Consolation blandly confessed, 'but I dare say, dear, that you can't judge Egypt by *Aida.*'

Ronald Firbank, *The Eccentricities of Cardinal Pirelli,* 1926

A phrase in the London paper caught my eye which beautifully summed up the English attitude. 'The most numerous party in the state,' it said, 'is the Wafdist. They count among their followers 90 per cent of the population . . . but it is not in any sense the true spokesman of the uncomprehending and largely illiterate Egyptian people.' One certainly could not accuse England of not carrying on the Nelson tradition with regard to Egypt.

Cedric Belfrage, *Away from it All,* 1936

Certain areas of Egypt are cultivated by irritation.

Schoolboy howler, quoted by John Gunther, *Inside Africa,* 1955

Egyptians

Their strength is to sit still.

The Bible, Isaiah, 30:7

Δειλοὶ πλεκειν τοι μηχανας Αιγυπτιοι.
– Truly at weaving wiles the Egyptians are clever.

Aeschylus, *Fragments,* Frag. 206

The Ayre of the Countrey is hot and unwholesome: and it rayneth here very seldome or never. And Raine is the cause of many Diseases in Egypt: for in raynie weather some of the Egyptians are subject unto dangerous Rheumes, and Fevers; and others unto a strange kind of swelling in their privy Members: which swelling the Physicians impute unto Salt Cheese and Beefe, which are the common Dyet of the Egyptians.

John Leo, on Africa, in *Purchas his Pilgrimes,* 1625

A boastful race, that in the vain abyss
Of fabling ages loved to lose their source,
And, with their river, traced it from the skies.

James Thomson, *Liberty,* 1734-6

The common People live Part of the Year on Cucumbers, and find no manner of Inconvenience from this kind of Food.

Thomas Salmon, *A New Geographical and Historical Grammar,* 1751

The Conversation turned on Eastern Literature And it

was interesting to me to perceive that G [Goethe] had a great Aversion to the Easterns. 'I do hate the Egyptians And all that are connected with them.' And he then added – 'And I am glad that I have something to hate – That is absolutely necessary, otherwise one is in danger of falling into the dull liberal habit of finding all things tolerable and good in their place – And that is the Ruin of all good Sentiments.'

Henry Crabb Robinson, Letter to his Brother, 3 June 1804

Any *Englishman* hearing a party of *Egyptian Arabs* in conversation, and being ignorant of their language, would suppose they were quarrelling.

E.D. Clarke, *Travels in Various Countries*, 4th edn, 1817

Nile boatmen

The crew were all alive, – kicking dust over one another on shore, leaping high in the water, to make a splash, and perpetrating all manner of practical jokes. We do not agree with travellers who declare it necessary to treat these people with coldness and severity, – to repel and beat them. We treated them as children; and this answered perfectly well.

Harriet Martineau, *Eastern Life, Past and Present*, 1848

If anyone tries to make you believe nonsense about 'civilization' in Egypt, laugh at it. The real life and the real people are exactly as described in that most veracious of books, the Thousand and One Nights.

Lady Duff Gordon, *Letters from Egypt*, 1865

Egyptian cavalry

As soldiers they lack both vices and virtues.

Sir Winston Churchill, *The River War*, 1899

Embalm, *v.t.*, To cheat vegetation by locking up the gases on which it feeds. By embalming their dead and thereby deranging the natural balance between animal and vegetable life, the Egyptians made their once fertile country barren and incapable of supporting more than a meagre crew.

Ambrose Bierce, *The Cynic's Word Book*, 1906

Dr Garnett . . . would say to you that the ancient Egyptians were the only really civilized race, for, when fires occurred in their great buildings, they organised environing cordons, not to put out the fires but to see that no cats re-entered their burning homes.

Ford Madox Ford, *Return to Yesterday*, 1932

'The only thing that grows in Egypt and stays in the country,' said my friend the university professor, 'is the population. We are a nation smothered by ourselves.' He paused with an ironic chuckle. 'One fault is that most of our four thousand villages do not have electric light. There is nothing for the people to do after sundown except have sexual intercourse.'

Make more land. Make fewer people. Either of these solutions would alleviate the problem, but neither is easy.

John Gunther, *Inside Africa*, 1955

Abu Simbel

The white-wash which Champollion (it is said) left on the face of the northernmost colossus has the curious effect of bringing out the expression of countenance, so as to be seen far off. Nothing can be more strange than so extremely distinct a revelation of a face, in every feature, perhaps a mile off. . . . The expression of this colossus is very agreeable; – it is so tranquil and cheerful.

Harriet Martineau, *Eastern Life, Past and Present*, 1848

The temple is very fine, and has the great merit of being no ruin, but a perfectly habitable place cut out of the rock, and very little injured by time. There was a party outside it clearing away the sand. There is a grave, too, where an English officer is buried who happened to die on board a passing steamer – 'a rotten place,' Laurie remarked, 'to bury an Englishman in.'

Wilfred Scawen Blunt, Diary, 8 November 1895, *My Diaries*, 1919

Alamein

Before Alamein we never had a victory. After Alamein we never had a defeat.

Winston Spencer Churchill, *The Hinge of Fate*, 1951

Alexandria

That Citie and Land standeth so lowe, that were it not for the Pharos, and some sight of the tops of the Palme trees, you may bee upon it before you bee aware; which is very dangerous for the ships that come thither; for in my time divers were cast away.

John Sanderson, 1585, in *Purchas his Pilgrimes*, 1625

The said citie of Alexandria is an old thing decayed or ruinated, having bene a faire and great citie neere two miles in length, being all vauted underneath for provision of freshwater, which water commeth thither but once every yeere, out of one of the foure rivers of paradise (as it is termed) called Nilus, which in September floweth neere eighteene foote upright higher then his accustomed manner, and so the banke being cut, as it were a sluce, about thirty miles from Alexandria, at a towne called Rossetto, it doth so come to the said Citie, with such aboundance, that barkes of twelve tunne doe come upon the said water, which water doth fill all the vauts, cesternes and wels in the said Citie, with very good water and doth so continue good, till the next yeere following: for they have there very litle raine or none at all, yet have they exceeding great dewes.

John Evesham (1586), in Richard Hakluyt, *Principal Navigations . . . of the English Nation,* 1598-1600

Alexandria . . . makes a fine appearance from the sea on a near approach; but being built on low ground, is, as the seamen say, 'very difficult to hit.'

Eliza Fay, *Original Letters from India* (20 July 1779), 1817

The work of fortification itself seems absurd, judging by the eye; for there appears nothing to take, and therefore nothing to defend. Except in the direction of the small and poor-looking town, the area within the new walls appears to contain little but dusty spaces and heaps of rubbish, with a few lines of sordid huts, and clumps of palms set down in the midst; and a hot cemetery or two with crumbling tombs. I have seen many desolate-looking places, in one country or another; but there is nothing like Alexandria, as seen from a height, for utter dreariness.

Harriet Martineau, *Eastern Life, Past and Present,* 1848

The appearance of Alexandria is highly interesting to a man who delights in commerce, or whose heart gladdens as he sees an embryo Europe about to be hatched in Africa; for instead of a rude but picturesque city, such as the Arabian tale would lead one to fancy would be a part of Egypt, he beholds a few narrow and uninteresting suburban streets surrounding a fine square of houses, built altogether in European style, and many of them the residences of the different consuls, bearing the ensigns of their respective nations. The square is very large, and from its shape and position would do credit to the fairest capital of Europe. A couple of trumpery fountains have lately been added, which however, I believe can seldom be induced to play.

Mansfield Parkyns, *Life in Abyssinia,* 1853

Alexandria. Seems Mcadamed with the ruins of thousand cities. Every shovel full of earth dug over. The soil, deep loam, looks historical. . . . Pompey's Pillar like a long stick of candy, well sucked.

Herman Melville, *Journal of a Visit to Europe and the Levant,* January 1857

The seventeenth- and eighteenth-century Turkish town

The best way of seeing it is to wander aimlessly about.

E.M. Forster, *Alexandria, a History and a Guide,* 1922

Modern Alexandria is scarcely a city of the soul. Founded upon cotton, with the concurrence of onions and eggs, ill built, ill planned, ill drained – many hard things can be said against it, and most are said by its inhabitants.

E.M. Forster, *Pharos and Pharillon,* 1923

The Alexandria I knew and loved belongs to the war-years. . . . She was then a towsled unsmartened sort of place, and the country surrounding her had a magic which has inevitably vanished. . . . I realised what was coming a few years back, when I paid a brief visit and lost my way as I came out of the new railway station. What a humiliating experience for the author of a Guide!

E.M. Forster, *Alexandria, a History and a Guide,* Preface to the 2nd edn, 1938

*Capitally, what is this city of ours? What is resumed in the word Alexandria? In a flash my mind's eye shows me a thousand dust-tormented streets. Flies and beggars own it today – and those who enjoy an intermediate existence between either.

Five races, five languages, a dozen creeds: five fleets turning through their greasy reflections behind the harbour bar. But there are more than five sexes and only demotic Greek seems to distinguish among them. The sexual provender which lies to hand is staggering in its variety and profusion. You would never mistake it for a happy place. . . . I remember Nessim once saying – I think he was quoting – that Alexandria was the great wine-press of love; those who emerged from it were the sick men, the solitaries, the prophets – I mean all who have been deeply wounded in their sex.

Lawrence Durrell, *Justine,* 1957

*Alexandria was still Europe – the capital city of Asiatic Europe, if such a thing could exist.

Lawrence Durrell, *Mountolive,* 1958

Like Algiers, and Tunis – or Leptis Magna and Cyrene – Alexandria was one of those grappling hooks that Europe cast upon Africa in a time of imperial expansion.

David Holden, *Encounter,* August 1963

. . . Alexandria out of season, when the city turns its back upon the sea, as a sheep puts its rump to a blizzard.

Ibid.

Legendary on the seafront; torpid in the centre; the vitality of Alexandria is all at the back. The pallor of this city is the pallor of a hiatus – a pause in history, at the point where civilizations meet. Europe has withdrawn from this African seaport, leaving nostalgia and bitterness behind: but from the back Egypt herself comes flooding in, like fresh blood into desiccated veins

– as though Maryut itself has burst its banks, and is inundating the city with muddy life. Baedeker's view and Durrell's music are both illusory now: today you must look at Alex out of the desert, and allow for a lot of noise.

James Morris, *Places,* 1972

Alexandrians

The Alexandrians have never been truly Egyptian.

E.M. Forster, *Alexandria, a History and a Guide,* 1922

Alexandria's people, a mixture of Greeks, various Levantines, Italians and Egyptians have in a way, untroubled minds. Those better off never think about anything except how to make money, which simplifies things. The others are, generally, thinking about where their next meal, if any, is coming from. . . . One day at the Union Club a grumpy Englishman told me that most Alexandrians were too poor to have any morals, and that the idea had never occurred to the others.

Albion Ross, *Journey of an American,* 1957

The Assuan Dam (and the Pyramids)

What a pity the pyramid-builders did not immortalize themselves in a more productive way. If they had thought of it, they could have used the Assuan granite on the spot for anticipating the building of the High Dam. Their architects and engineers would have been equal to this gigantic job; and then Egypt would have already enjoyed, for more than 4,500 years, the extra acreage that the High Dam is now going to give her. The Pharaohs of the Fourth Dynasty could have built the High Dam and have used its water-storage for the extension of cultivation. The one thing that they could not have done is to have used it for the generation of hydro-electric power.

Arnold Toynbee, *Between Niger and Nile,* 1965

Beni Hassan (on the Nile)

We stopped at Beni Hassan, but I did not go ashore, as I draw the line at tombs.

Wilfred Scawen Blunt, Diary, 15 November 1895, *My Diaries,* 1919

Cairo

This citie was edified by people that came out of troye with menelao when troye was destroyed.

Roger Barlow, *A Brief Summe of Geographie, c.* 1540

This little world, the great Cairo. . . .
This incorporate world of Grand Cairo, is the most admirable, and greatest city seen upon the earth. . . .
The Microcosmus of the greater world. . . .

William Lithgow, *Rare Adventures and Painfull Peregrinations,* 1614/32

The Inhabitants of Cairo are people of a merry, jocund, and cheerefull disposition, such as will promise much, but performe little.

John Leo, on Africa, in *Purchas his Pilgrimes,* 1625

I have found scarce any inconvenience from the heat, though all of our party, who have been in India, agree that they never felt the weather so oppressively hot as here; which proceeds from the terrible sandy deserts, that surround the town, causing the air to smell like hot bricks.

Eliza Fay, *Original Letters from India* (27 August 1779), 1817

I never saw a place I liked worse, nor which afforded less pleasure or instruction, than *Cairo;* nor antiquities which less answered their descriptions.

James Bruce, *Travels,* 1790

There is not perhaps upon earth a more dirty metropolis.

E.D. Clarke, *Travels in Various Countries,* 4th edn, 1817

One cannot find the comforts of an English breakfast at Cairo.

John Carne, *Letters from the East,* 1830

There are few gayer things in life, for one who chooses to be gay, than a visit to Cairo.

Harriet Martineau, *Eastern Life, Past and Present,* 1848

Cairo streets are wholly indescribable; their narrowness, antiquity, sharp lights, and arcades of gloom, carved lattices, mat awnings, mixture of hubbub and fatalist quietude in the people, to whom loss of sight appears a matter of course; the modes of buying and selling; – all are in my mind, but cannot be set down.

Ibid.

It seems one booth and Bartholomew Fair – a grand masquerade of mortality. – Several of the thoroughfares covered at vast heigth with old planks & matting, so that the street has the light of a closed verandah. In one case this matting extends from mosque to mosque, where they are opposite. The houses seem a collection of old orchestras, organs, proscenium boxes – or like masses of old furniture (grotesque) lumbering a garret & covered with dust. Lattice-work of the projecting windows. With little square hole, just large enough to contain the head. Curious aspect of women's faces peeping out. Most of the houses built of stone of a brownish white. Some of the streets of private houses are like tunnels from meeting overhead of projecting windows &c. Like night at noon. Sometimes high blank walls – mysterious passages, – dim peeps at courts & wells in shadow. Great numbers of uninhabited houses in the lonelier parts of the city. Their dusty, cadaverous ogerish look. Ghostly, & suggestive of all that is weird. Haunted houses & Cock Lanes. Ruined mosques, domes knocked in like stoven boats. Others, upper part empty & desolate with broken rafters & dismantled windows; (rubbish) below, the dirty rites of religion. Aspect of the thoroughfares like London streets on Saturday night. All the world gossiping & marketing, – but in picturesque costumes. Crookedness of the streets – multitudes of blind men – worst city in the world for them. Flies on the eyes at noon. Nature feeding on man. Contiguity of desert and verdure, splendor & squalor, gloom & gayety; numerous blind men going about led. Children opthalmick. Too much light and no defence against it. . . . Cairo nipped between two deserts – the one leading to Suez & the Red Sea, the other the Lybian Desert. – Dust colored city. The dust of ages.

Herman Melville, *Journal of a Visit to Europe and the Levant,* 3 January 1857

The Jewish Physician, in the story of the Humpback (Arabian Nights?) calls Cairo, 'The Mother of the World.'

Quoted Stanley Lane-Poole, *Cairo,* 1892

The upper classes are becoming daily less and less Oriental in outward appearance and habits, though it will take some time to Europeanise their minds. They dance with foreign ladies, wear Frankish clothes, smoke cigarettes, enjoy French plays, and, but for their Eastern habits of tyranny, peculation, insincerity, and corruption, they might for all the world be Europeans.

Stanley Lane-Poole, *ibid.*

The Nile does not change. Indeed I know of no place where everything changes as much as it does here, and nothing is ever changed. Curiously enough, Cairo reminds me of Mexico more than of anything else. You feel quite at home.

Henry Adams, Letter to Elizabeth Cameron, 3 February 1898

On our way back to Sheykh Obeyd we followed the Mokattam range to its extreme edge overlooking Cairo. The view of the vast city, half Oriental, half European, approached thus as we approached it from the desert, is, I think, the most astonishing in the world. We arrived after several days' wandering in an absolute waste, the last mile of the way being waster than all the rest . . . It is not until one is actually within twenty yards of the cliff's edge that one gets the slightest hint of the living world spread out close beneath one's feet, the immense city of Cairo, with its citadels and towers, and walls, and minarets stretching away for miles, the splendid ancient city, and beyond it, modern Cairo, with its turmoil of tramways, railroads, and other modernities, and yet further still the Nile and the Nile Valley, seven miles across, and green as a spinach bowl, with the yellow desert, far away in Africa with its Pyramids. The immediate foreground is dazzlingly white, a huge stone quarry, where men in gangs are at work like ants, quarrying the white limestone of which modern Cairo is being built. The sudden contrast brought tears into my eyes as sudden wonders are apt to do.

Wilfred Scawen Blunt, Diary, 9 December 1903, *My Diaries,* 1919

The general atmosphere of backsheesh and parasitism is appalling and turns one to stone. The wheedlers of Cairo are innumerable and seem to get bolder at every repulse. They are the modern examples of an Atreus. Your pocket is, as it were, the aim of an universal magnet. For myself, I used to find peace in my hotel-garden, where a stork, meandering slowly down the lawns, was my sole companion.

Richard Curle, *Wanderings,* 1920

Had I ever been in Egypt before? Yes, during the winter of 1948, in the time of the bad fat King. Had things improved? I told him honestly that they had indeed. Cairo had changed from a nineteenth-century French provincial capital surrounded by a casbah to a glittering modern city, only partially surrounded by a casbah.

Gore Vidal, *Reflections upon a Sinking Ship,* 1969

James Morris had been *The Times* correspondent in the Middle East, . . . Jan Morris . . . was revisiting Cairo for the first time since she had changed gender, and she was nervous about what Jan might see in James's city.

'I'm so frightened of going back to places and finding that I liked them better as I was than I do as I am.'

'It all must have been so different anyway, when you were here last. Two wars ago – or is it three or four? No Saudis, presumably. . . . Don't you find the city itself has changed so much that it's difficult to find your own landmarks in it?'

'Well, you see, I feel that *I*'ve changed so much more than Cairo has that it's really rather hard to tell.'

Jonathan Raban, *Arabia through the Looking Glass,* 1979

Shepherd's Hotel

As a whole this Shepherd's Hotel (or Zech's as it is called now,) is more like a pigstye mixed with a beargarden or a horribly noisy railway station than anything that I can compare it to.

Edward Lear, Letter to Lady Waldegrave, 9 March 1867

Edfu/Idfu

By the mellow light of the moon everything seemed magnified; the majestic proportions of the temple appeared more majestic, and the miserable huts around it still more miserable, and the past glory and the present ruin of this once most favored land rushed upon me with a force I had not felt even at the foot of the pyramids. If the temple of that little unknown city now stood in Hyde Park or the garden of the Tuileries, France, England, all Europe would gaze upon it with wonder and admiration; and when thousands of years shall have rolled away, and they too shall have fallen, there will be no monument of these proudest of modern cities, like this in the little town to Edfu, to raise its majestic head and tell the passing traveller the story of their former greatness.

John Lloyd Stephens, *Incidents of Travel in Egypt, etc.*, 1837

Heliopolis

Heliopolis is a humbug.

Anthony Trollope, Letter to Edmund Yates, 11 March 1858

Luxor, Karnak (formerly Thebes)

Hundred-gated City! thou
With gryphoned arch and avenue
For denizen giants, serve they now
But to let one mortal through?
Wide those streaming gates of war
Ran once with many a conqueror,
Horseman and chariot, to the sound
Of the dry serpent blazoning round
Theban Sesostris' dreaded name.
Where is now the loud acclaim?
Where the trample and the roll,
Shaking staid earth like a mole?

Sunk to a rush's sigh! – Farewell,
Thou bleached wilderness o'erblown
By treeless winds, unscythable
Sandbanks, with peeping rocks bestrown,
That for thy barrenness seem'st to be
The bed of some retreated sea!
City of Apis, shrine and throne,
Fare thee well! dispeopled sheer
Of thy mighty millions, here
Giant thing inhabits none
But vast Desolation!

George Darley, *Nepenthe*, *c.* 1839

Tombs of the Valley of the Kings
Every sarcophagus is broken and the bones of the kings of Egypt are scattered. In one I picked up a skull. I mused over it a moment, and handed it to Paul, who moralized at large. 'That man,' said he, 'once talked and laughed, and sang and danced, and ate macaroni.' Among the paintings on the walls was represented a heap of hands severed from the arms, showing that the hero of the tomb had played the tyrant during his brief hour on earth. I dashed the skull against a stone, broke it in fragments, and pocketed a piece as a memorial of a king. Paul cut off one of the ears, and we left the tomb.

John Lloyd Stephens, *Incidents of Travel in Egypt, etc.*, 1837

Denon, in his account of the expedition to Egypt, says that when the French soldiers first came in sight of Thebes, the whole army involuntarily threw down their arms and stood in silent admiration: a sublime idea whether true or not; but, I am inclined to think that the French soldiers would have thrown down their arms, and clapped their hands with much greater satisfaction, if they had seen a living city and a prospect of good quarters.

Ibid.

The Ramaseum
It is melancholy to sit on the piled stones amidst the wreck of this wonderful edifice, where violence inconceivable to us has been used to destroy what art inconceivable to us had erected. What a rebuke to the vanity of succeeding ages is here! What have we been about, to imagine men in those early times childish or barbarous, – to suppose science and civilisation reserved for us of these later ages, when here are works in whose presence it is a task for the imagination to overtake the eyesight!

Harriet Martineau, *Eastern Life, Past and Present*, 1848

Karnak
The close mass of Arab huts within the courts effectively prevent measurement, but by going in on all fours into these Arab huts, we saw a profusion of capitals which capped the columns which support them. Only utter barbarians would have dared to desecrate a temple of such splendour with mud huts. One wonders whether Ismail, the Khedive, knows of such things being done by these vile creatures. There was one – a greater than he – who did not disdain to use a scourge for lesser offences.

H.M. Stanley, *My Early Travels and Adventures* (December 1869), 1895

I have done Thebes somewhat hurriedly, it is true, but I have gone over it. Travellers no doubt, may wish to purchase mummies and other souvenirs here. If they but express a wish to buy, mummies by the wholesale, whole mummies, heads of mummies, hands, feet, limbs and trunks of mummies; human, animal, and bird mummies will be offered to them, until they will imagine that the vendors of them are themselves resurrected mummies.

Ibid.

Walking into Karnak was like walking into one of Piranesi's Prisons, solidified suddenly into stone, and grown to natural, nay to heroic size. Piled on fantastic ruin, obelisks pricked the sky; the colossal aisle soared, its base plunged in the deepest shadow, its head lifted to the moon; shafts of light struck the columns, lay in silver druggets across the floor. The black, enormous temple was shot through and through by those broad beams of light. Beyond the aisle, a vast space littered with fallen masonry lay open to the sky. Cavernous openings, porticos, colonnades, blocks of masonry; obelisks, statues of Pharaohs, some upright, some prone; and beyond them, beyond this magnificent desolation, shrilled the thin piping of the frogs. . . . It crushed the mind, since it was not the human mind that had conceived it as it now appeared, but such inhuman factors as time upon earth.

Vita Sackville-West, *Passenger to Teheran*, 1926

Nile

This river . . . comes out of Paradise and runs through the deserts of India, and then it sinks down into the earth and runs so under the earth a great country and comes up again under a mountain that hat Alloche, the which is betwixt India and Ethiopia, as it were five month journeys from the entry of Ethiopia. And then it runs all about Ethiopia and Mauretainia, and so all the length of Egypt to the city of Alexandria; and there it enters into the sea at the end of Egypt. About this river are great plenty of fowls that are called in the Latin Ciconie or Ibices.

John Mandeville, *The Book of John Mandeville, c.* 1360

As when old father *Nilus* gins to swell
With timely pride above the *Aegyptian* vale,
His fattie waves do fertile slime outwell,
And overflow each plaine and lowly dale:
But when his later spring gins to avale,
Huge heapes of mudd he leaves, wherein there breed
Ten thousand kindes of creatures, partly male
And partly female of his fruitfull seed;
Such ugly monstrous shapes elsewhere may no man reed.

Edmund Spenser, *The Faerie Queene,* Book 1, Canto 1, 1589

Nilus water I thinke also to be the profitablest and wholsomest in the World, by being both Bread and Drinke to them: for Bread there could be none without it; no rayne falling in Egypt to that purpose: yet I have seene it rayne there, but it hath beene very little, as it were a small showre, at a time this River doth cover the Land, and fatten it, whereby it fructifieth abundantly. It breedeth no manner of disease in the bodie, as divers other waters doe: it hurteth not to drinke thereof either troubled or cleere; for being brought to our Houses one mile and halfe or two miles off, it commeth in warmer then bloud, and troubled seeming sandy; standing all night in our Jarres of Earth, it is very cleere and coole in the morning, and so continueth in the House be the weather never so hot.

John Sanderson, *Sundrie the Personal Voyages . . .* , 1602 (1586), in *Purchas his Pilgrimes,* 1625

Anthony: The higher Nilus swels,
The more it promises: as it ebbes, the Seedsman
Upon the slime and Ooze scatters his graine,
And shortly comes to Harvest.
Lepidus: Y'have strange Serpents there?
Anthony: I *Lepidus.*
Lepidus: Your Serpent of Egypt, is bred now of your mud by the operation of your Sun: so is your Crocodile.

William Shakespeare, *Anthonie and Cleopatra, c.* 1606–7

the Brook that parts
Egypt from *Syrian* ground.

John Milton, *Paradise Lost,* 1667

As Nilus when he quits his sacred *Bed*
(But like a *Friend* he visits all the Land
With welcome *presents* in his hand). . . .

Abraham Cowley, 'The Plagues of Egypt', in *Pindarique Odes*, 1656

There is no country then where the government has more influence than in Egypt on agriculture, and as a result of that, on its people. . . . In Egypt government is everything. . . . Under a good administration the Nile gains on the desert; under a bad one the desert gains on the Nile.

Napoleon, translated from *Mémoires pour Servir à l'Histoire de France . . . écrits à Sainte-Hélène*, 1830 – before 1821

Son of the old moon-mountains African!
Chief of the Pyramid and Crocodile!
We call thee fruitful, and, that very while,
A desert fills our seeing's inward span;
Nurse of swart nations since the world began,
Art thou so fruitful? or dost thou beguile
Such men to honour thee, who, worn with toil,
Rest for a space 'twixt Cairo and Decan?
O may dark fancies err! they surely do;
'Tis ignorance that makes a barren waste
Of all beyond itself, thou dost bedew
Green rushes like our rivers, and dost taste
The pleasant sun-rise, green isles hast thou too,
And to the sea as happily dost haste.

John Keats, *Sonnet to the Nile,* 4 February 1818

It flows through old hushed Egypt and its sands
Like some grave mighty thought threading a

dream
And times and things as in that vision seem
Keeping along it their eternal stands, –
Caves, pillars, pyramids, the shepherd bands
That roamed through the young world, the glory extreme
Of high Sesostris, and that Southern beam
The laughing Queen that caught the world's great hands
Then comes a mightier silence, stern and strong
As of a world left empty of its throng,
And the void weighs on us; and then we wake
And hear the fruitful stream lapsing along
Twixt villages and think how we shall take
Our own calm journey on for human sake.

Leigh Hunt, *A Thought of the Nile*, 1818

For myself, being alone, and not in very good health, I had some heavy moments; but I have no hesitation in saying that, with a friend, a good boat well fitted up, books, guns, plenty of time, and a cook like Michel, a voyage on the Nile would exceed any travelling within my experience. The perfect freedom from all restraint, and from the conventional trammels of civilized society, form an episode in a man's life that is vastly agreeable and exciting. Think of not shaving for two months, of washing your shirts in the Nile, and wearing them without being ironed.

John Lloyd Stephens, *Incidents of Travel in Egypt, etc.*, 1837

Cataracts of

The Cataracts, or rather, if a citizen of a new world may lay his innovating hand upon things consecrated by the universal consent of ages, what we who have heard the roar of the Niagara would call simply the 'rapids.'

John Lloyd Stephens, *Incidents of Travel in Egypt, etc.*, 1837

Everywhere else, where a river flows through the centre of a valley, the land either slopes from the base of the hills down to the river, or it is level. In Egypt, on the contrary, the land rises from the mountains up to the banks of the Nile: and where, as usually happens, the banks are higher than the eye of the spectator on the deck of his boat, all view of the interior, as far as the hills is precluded. He sees nothing but the towns, villages, and palm-groves on the banks, and the mountains on the horizon. My attention had been directed upon this point before I went by the complaints of some readers of Eastern travel that, after all their reading, they knew no more what the Egyptian valley looked like than if it had never been visited. As this failure of description appeared to regard Egypt alone, there must be some peculiar cause for it: and thus we found it.

Harriet Martineau, *Eastern Life, Past and Present*, 1848

Nile country above Assuan

When we came out upon Mahatta, we were in Nubia, and found ourselves at once in the midst of the wilderness of which we had read so much in relation to the First Cataract. The Mississippi is wild: and the Indian grounds of Wisconsin with their wigwam camps, are wild: but their wildness is only that of primitive Nature. This is fantastic, – impish. It is the wildness of Prospero's island. Prospero's island and his company of servitors were never out of my head between Aswan and the next placid reach of the river above Philoe. – The rocks are not sublime: they are too like Titanic heaps of black paving-stones to be imposing otherwise than by their oddity: and they are strewn about the land and river to an excess and with a caprice which takes one's imagination quite out of the ordinary world. Their appearance is made the more strange by the cartouches and other hieroglyphic inscriptions which abound among them; – sometimes on a face above the river; sometimes on a mere ordinary block near the path; – sometimes on an unapproachable fragment in the middle of the stream.

Harriet Martineau, *Eastern Life, Past and Present*, 1848

To those who wish to be wise, to be healthful, to borrow one month of real pleasure from a serious life, I would say, come and see the Nile.

H.M. Stanley, *My Early Travels and Adventures* (December 1869), 1895

I come from mountains under other stars
Than those reflected in my waters here;
Athwart broad realms, beneath large skies, I flow,
Between the Libyan and Arabian hills,
And merge at last into the great Mid-Sea;
And make this land of Egypt. All is mine;
The palm-trees and the doves among the palms,
The corn-fields and the flowers among the corn,
The patient oxen and the crocodiles,
The ibis and the heron and the hawk,
The lotus and the thick papyrus reeds,
The slant-sailed boats that drift before the wind
Or up my rapids ropes hale heavily;
Yea, even all the massive temple-fronts
With all their columns and huge effigies,
The pyramids and Memnon and the Sphinx,
This Cairo and the City of the Greek
As Memphis and the hundred gated Thebes,
Sais and Denderah of Isis queen;
Have grown because I fed them with full life,
And flourish only while I feed them still. . . .

James Thomson ('B.V.'), *A Voice from the Nile and Other Poems*, 1884 (1881)

But I am left with the impression that the Nile itself, with its great flow of water and its ever green banks and eternal youth is the really interesting thing, far finer than its monuments. These are interesting as part of the river's history, not the Nile because of them.

Wilfred Scawen Blunt, Diary, 2 November 1895, *My Diaries,* 1919

Going up the Nile is like running the gauntlet before Eternity. Till one has seen it, one does not realise the amazing thinness of that little damp trickle of life that steals along undefeated through the jaws of established death. A rifle-shot would cover the widest limits of cultivation, a bow-shot the narrower.

Rudyard Kipling, *Egypt of the Magicians,* 1913

She went up the Nile as far as the first crocodile.

Samuel Butler, *Further Extracts from Note-books,* 1934

The alien and mysterious Nile, that gigantic serpent that winds so fabulously, so ungraspably, back through history.

Rose Macaulay, *Pleasures of Ruins,* 1953

This stupendous river, at once fixed and elastic, with its swampy roots and flowering Delta, has often been compared to a palm tree, but it more closely resembles the shaft of an oesophagus, or alimentary canal, through which the stuff of Egypt's life passes.

John Gunther, *Inside Africa,* 1955
(He cites Plato and Winston Churchill for the palm tree image.)

Philae *(now largely submerged)*

Perhaps the general monotony of the scenery on the Nile gives it a peculiar beauty; but I think it would be called beautiful anywhere, even among the finest scenes in Italy. It brought forcibly to my mind, but seemed to me far more lovely than, the Lake Maggiore, with the beautiful Isola Bella and Isola Madre. It is entirely unique, a beautiful *lusus naturae,* a little island about a thousand feet long and four hundred broad, rising in the centre of a circular bay, which appears to be cut off from the river, and forms a lake surrounded by dark sandstone rocks; carpeted with green to the water's edge, and covered with columns, propylons and towers, the ruins of a majestic temple. A sunken wall encircles it on all sides.

John Lloyd Stephens, *Incidents of Travel in Egypt, etc.,* 1837

Philae, as it is, is perhaps the one perfect thing in the world, and anything added to or taken from it would probably spoil it. So I trust they will leave it alone. At the same time if they would be content with banking the river to the natural height of the Nile at flood, I do not see that it need do a great harm. But of course they want more, and to make it the biggest engineering thing in the universe. The situation is tempting to an engineer, as the solid boulders of granite would make it an heroic bit of stonework.

Wilfred Scawen Blunt, Diary, 6 November 1895, *My Diaries,* 1919

Port Said (and the Nile Delta)

What an astoundingly different kind of landscape from that of Buckinghamshire.

Eric Gill, Letter to Graham Carey, 7 July 1937

There is nothing worthy of note about Port Said. It admits to a bad reputation and has, for its size, an even larger stock of improper photographs than Brussels or Buenos Aires. I am able to look after myself, but there is something objectionable in being accosted every five yards by a man who urges you to 'step inside' where he will show you some photographs that are 'very good.' I will only remark that if they are better than the ones in the windows they are probably very good.

Richard Curle, *Wanderings,* 1920

Pyramids

The name is derived from a flame of fire, in regard of their shape; broad below, and sharpe above, like a pointed Diamond. By such the ancient did expresse the originall of things, and that formelesse forme-taking substance. . . .

The greatest of the three, and chiefe of the Worlds seven wonders, being square at the bottome, is supposed to take up eight Acres of ground. Every square being three hundred single paces in length, the square at the top consisting of three stones onely, yet large enough for threescore to stand upon: ascended by two hundred and fiftie five steps, each step above three feet high, of a breadth proportionable. No stone so little throughout the whole, as to be drawne by our Carriages, yet were these hewen out of the Trojan mountaynes, farre off in Arabia, so called of the Captive Trojans, brought by Menelaus into Egypt, and there afterward planted. A wonder how conveyed hither: how so mounted a greater. Twentie yeares it was a building, by three hundred threescore and sixe thousand men continually wrought upon: who onely in Radishes, Garlicke, and Onions, are said to have consumed one thousand and eight hundred Talents. By these and the like Inventions exhausted they their Treasure, and employed the people, for feare lest such infinite wealth should corrupt their Successors, and dangerous idlenesse beget in the Subject and desire of innovation.

George Sandys, *Discourse,* 1610, in *Purchas his Pilgrimes,* 1625

The pyramids themselves, doting with age, have forgotten the names of their founders.

Rev. Thomas Fuller, *The Holy and the Profane State,* 1642

Th'Aegyptian Pyramids were first begun
Upon the same Designe with Babilon
T'avoyd an Inundation and Deliver
The Founders from the Deluge of their River.

Samuel Butler, *Poetical Thesaurus – History,* before 1680

Soldats! Du haut de ces monuments, quarante siècles vous regardent.
(Soldiers! From the summit of these monuments, forty centuries look upon you.)

Napoleon, Exhortation to his troops before the Battle of the Pyramids, 21 July 1798

What are the hopes of man? Old Egypt's King
  Cheops erected the first pyramid,
And largest, thinking it was just the thing
  To keep his memory whole and mummy hid;
But somebody or other rummaging,
  Burglariously broke his coffin's lid.
Let not a monument give you or me hopes,
Since not a pinch of dust remains of Cheops.

Lord Byron, *Don Juan,* 1819-24

When I was very young . . . I was often in time of night the victim of a strange kind of mental oppression. I lay in my bed perfectly conscious, and with open eyes, but without power to speak, or to move, and all the while my brain was oppressed to distraction by the presence of a single and abstract idea, – the idea of solid Immensity. . . . I could not of course find words to describe the nature of my sensations. . . . Well, now my eyes saw and knew, and my hands and my feet informed my understanding that there was nothing at all abstract about the great Pyramid – it was a big triangle, sufficiently concrete, easy to see, and rough to the touch; it could not, of course, affect me with the peculiar sensation I have been talking of, but yet there was something akin to that old night-mare agony in the terrible completeness with which a mere mass of masonry could fill and load my mind.

And Time too; the remoteness of its origin, no less than the enormity of its proportions, screens an Egyptian Pyramid from the easy and familiar contact of our modern minds; at its base the common Earth ends, and all above is a world, – one not created of God, – not seeming to be made by men's hands, but rather, the sheer giant-work of some old dismal age weighing down this younger planet.

Fine sayings! but the truth seems to be, after all, that the Pyramids are quite of this world; that they were piled up into the air for the realization of some kingly crotchets about immortality, – some priestly longing for burial fees; and that as for the building – they were built like coral rocks by swarms of insects, – by swarms of poor Egyptians, who were not only the abject tools and slaves of power, but who also eat onions for the reward of their immortal labours! The Pyramids are quite of this world.

A.W. Kinglake, *Eothen,* 1844 – of *c.* 1835

From Cairo to the Pyramids

The journey I find briefly set down in my pocket-book as thus: – Cairo Gardens – Mosquitoes – Women dressed in blue – Children dressed in nothing – Old Cairo – Nile, dirty water, ferry-boat – Town – Palm-trees, town – Rice fields – Maize fields – Fellows on Dromedaries – Donkey down – Over his head – Pick up pieces – More palm-trees – More rice-fields – Watercourses – Howling Arabs – Donkey tumbles down again – Inundations – Herons or cranes – Broken bridges – Sands – Pyramids. If a man cannot make a landscape out of *that* he has no imagination. Let him paint the skies very blue – the sands very yellow – the plains very flat and green – the dromedaries and palm-trees very tall – the women very brown, some with veils, some with nose-rings, some tattooed, and none with stays – and the picture is complete. You may shut your eyes and imagine yourself there. It is the pleasantest way, *entre nous.*

W.M. Thackeray, *Punch in the East,* 1845

Looking ahead in an hour or two, we saw the Pyramids. Fancy my sensations, dear M – –: two big ones and a little one –

! ! !

W.M. Thackeray, *Journey from Cornhill to Cairo,* 1845

Ascending the Pyramid, I could not but think of Waterloo Bridge in my dear native London – a building as vast and as magnificent, as beautiful, as useless, and as lonely. . . .

If I use in the above sentence the longest words I can find, it is because the occasion is great and demands the finest words the dictionary can supply. . . . The 19th of October was *Punch's Coronation;* I officiated at this august ceremony. To be brief . . . ON THE 19TH OF OCTOBER 1844, I PASTED THE GREAT PLACARD OF PUNCH ON THE PYRAMID OF CHEOPS. I did it. The fat Contributor did it. If I die it could not be undone. If I perish, I have not lived in vain.

If the forty centuries *are* on the summit of the Pyramids, as Bonaparte remarks, all I can say is, *I* did not see them. But *Punch* has really been there; this I swear. One placard I pasted on the first landing-place (who knows how long Arab rapacity will respect the sacred hieroglyphic?). One I placed under a great stone on the summit; one I waved in the air, as my Arabs raised a mighty cheer round the peaceful victorious banner; and I flung it towards the sky, which the Pyramid almost touches, and left it to its fate, to mount into the azure vault and take its place among the constellations.

W.M. Thackeray, *Punch in the East*, 1845

The mighty pyramids of stone
That wedge-like cleave the desert airs,
When nearer seen and better known,
Are but gigantic flights of stairs.

H.W. Longfellow, *The Ladder of St Augustine*, 1850

I resolved that morning not to be induced by any pleasure or triumph of the hour to tell people that it is very easy to go up and into the Pyramid. To determined and practised people it is easy; but not, probably, to the majority. I would not recommend any one to do it of whose nerve I was not sure. To the tranquil, the inside of the Pyramid is sufficiently airy and cool for the need of the hour. But it is a dreadful place in which to be seized with a panic: and no woman should go who cannot trust herself to put down panic by reason. There is absolutely nothing to fear but from one's self. . . .

Harriet Martineau, *Eastern Life, Past and Present*, 1848

In the hills, angular at their summits, with angular mounds at their bases, and angular caves in their strata, we could not but at once see the original of temples, pyramids, and tombs. Indeed, the pyramids look like an eternal fixing down of the shifting sand-hills which are here a main feature of the desert.

Ibid.

All things dread Time: but Time dreads the Pyramids.

Anon., quoted Harriet Martineau, *ibid.*

Pyramids from distance purple like mountains. Seem high and pointed, but flatten & depress you as you approach. Vapors below summits. . . . Looks larger midway than from top or bottom. Precipice on precipice, cliff on cliff. Nothing in Nature gives such an idea of vastness. A balloon to ascend them. View of persons ascending, Arab guides in flowing white mantles. Conducted as by angels up to heaven. Guides so tender. Resting. Pain in the chest. Exhaustion. Must hurry. None but the phlegmatic go deliberately. Old man with the spirits of youth – long looked for this chance – tried the ascent, half way – failed – brought down. Tried to go into the interior – fainted, – brought out – leaned against the pyramid by the entrance – pale as death. Nothing so pathetic. Too much for him; oppressed by the massiveness and mystery of the pyramids. I myself too. A feeling of awe & terror came over me. Dread of Arabs. Offering to lead me into a side-hole. The Dust. Long arched way, – then down as in a coal shaft. Then as in mines, under the sea. The stooping & doubling. I shudder at the idea of ancient Egyptians. It was in these pyramids that was conceived the idea of Jehovah. Terrible mixture of the cunning and awful. Moses learned in all the lore of the Egyptians. . . . When I was at top, thought it not so high – sat down on edge, looked below – gradual nervousness & final giddiness & terror. Entrance of pyramids like shoot for coal or timber. Horrible place for assassination. As long as earth endures some vestige will remain of the pyramids. . . . Arabs climb them like goats, or any other animal. Down one & up the other. Pyramids still loom before me – something vast, undefined, incomprehensible, and awful. Line of desert & verdure plainer than that between good & evil. An instant collision of alien elements. A long billow of desert forever hovers as in act of breaking, upon the verdure of Egypt. Grass near the pyramids, but will not touch them – as if in fear or awe of them. Desert more fearful to look at than ocean.

Herman Melville, *Journal of a Visit to Europe and the Levant*, 3 January 1857

Who shall doubt 'the secret hid
Under Cheops' pyramid'
Was that the contractor did
Cheops out of several millions?
Or that Joseph's sudden rise
To Comptroller of Supplies
Was a fraud of monstrous size
On King Pharaoh's swart Civilians? . . .

Rudyard Kipling, *A General Summary*, 1886

The Pyramids will not last a moment compared with the daisy.

D.H. Lawrence, *Etruscan Places*, 1932

A practical joke played on History.

Peter Forster, Letter to James Agate, 10 December 1946, quoted in James Agate, *Ego 9* 1948

Napoleon first demanded to know the measurement of the Great Pyramid: and then astonished his staff on their return from climbing to the top by pointing out that its cubic content would suffice to build a wall ten feet high and a foot thick entirely surrounding France. This is one way of bringing home its staggering bulk.

Julian Huxley, *From an Antique Land*, 1954

I could see the pyramids from the balcony on which I prepared this essay, and even from that comfortable distance, I could sense a miasma of horror that attended them, swirling down to the Sphinx in its bunker over the ridge. I have hated that plateau of the pyramids always: when I climbed to the top of the Great Pyramid once, its evil influence debilitated me there and then, and I was violently ill upon the summit.

Jan Morris, *Destinations*, 1980 (article of 1978)

They form the Hyde Park Corner of the Middle East.
Lawrence Durrell, *Radio Times*, 8-14 April 1978

There is something about the pyramids which is calculated to warm the cockles of the heart of any thoroughgoing gangster. It is easy to imagine Al Capone or Ronnie Kray being moved to tears by the sight of the Great Pyramid. Every single enormous block of it tells you that Mister Big was here.

Its shape, too, has a gangsterish simplicity. Cathedrals, mosques, castles feed the eye with detail. They invite one to exercise one's curiosity and intelligence. The Great Pyramid invites one to do nothing except acknowledge it. . . . Its sole interest lies in its size. It is a simple-minded megalomaniac's dream come true. All the subtlety of engineering which went into its construction – the levelling of the ground, the dizzying calculus of stress and weight and proportion – was dedicated to the service of a fantasy so crude that a human vegetable could have conceived it. It exists below the level of reason. Its contempt for money, labour, time, materials, its blind disregard of limitation or compromise, could be matched by any psychopath in a locked ward for the severely subnormal. All the Great Pyramid does is stand between you and the sun, like a mindless giant with his thumbs locked in his hip-pockets, saying, '*OK?*'
Jonathan Raban, *Arabia through the Looking Glass*, 1979

Rosetta

Rosetta is a most beautiful place, surrounded by groves of lemon and orange trees; and the flat roofs of the houses have gardens on them, whose fragrance perfumes the air. There is an appearance of cleanliness in it, the more gratifying to an English eye, because seldom met with in any degree, so as to remind us of what we are accustomed to at home.
Eliza Fay, *Original Letters from India*, (27 August 1779), 1817

All authors mention the beauty of its scenery, complaining only of the monotony and dulness of the city. At the time we saw it, no such complaint could be made. . . . From the different people by whom it was thronged, its streets resembled an immense masquerade. There was hardly a nation in the *Mediterranean* but might have been then said to have had its representative in *Rosetta;* and the motley appearance thus caused was further diversified by the addition of English ladies from the fleet and from the army, who, in long white dresses, were riding about upon the asses of the country.
E.D. Clarke, *Travels in Various Countries*, 4th edn, 1817

Mt Sinai

The account delivered gives us reason to imagine that the summit or scene where God appeared was shrouded from the hosts around; as the seventy elders only were permitted to behold 'the body of heaven in its clearness, the feet of sapphire,' etc. But what occasions no small surprise, at first, is the scarcity of plains, valleys, or open places, where the children of Israel could have stood conveniently to behold the glory on the Mount. From the summit of Sinai you see only innumerable ranges of rocky mountains. One generally places in imagination, around Sinai, extensive plains, or sandy deserts, where the camp of the hosts was placed, where the families of Israel stood at the doors of their tents, and the line was drawn round the mountain, which no one might break through on pain of death. But it is not thus: save the valley by which we approached Sinai, about half a mile wide, and a few miles in length, and a small plain we afterwards passed through, with a rocky hill in the middle, there appear to be few open places around the Mount. We did not, however, examine it on all sides. On putting the question to the superior of the convent, where he imagined the Israelites stood: everywhere, he replied, waving his hands about – in the ravines, the valleys, as well as the plains.
John Carne, *Letters from the East*, 1830

Can this naked rock have been the witness of that great interview between man and his Maker? . . . Among all the stupendous works of Nature, not a place can be selected more fitted for the exhibition of Almighty power. . . .

The level surface of the very top, or pinnacle, is about sixty feet square. At one end is a single rock about twenty feet high, on which, as said the monk, the spirit of God descended, while in the crevice beneath, his favored servant received the tables of the law.
John Lloyd Stephens, *Incidents of Travel in Egypt, etc.*, 1837

No one sings,
Descending Sinai.
Elizabeth Barrett Browning, *Aurora Leigh*, 1856

Like a vengeful dagger that was dipped in blood many ages ago, so sharp and defined and old pink-red in colour.
D.H. Lawrence, Letter to S.S. Koteliansky, 7 March 1922

The Sinai

The earth is so samely, that your eyes turn towards heaven—towards heaven, I mean in sense of sky. You look to the Sun, for he is your task-master, and by him you know the measure of the work that you have done, and the measure of the work that remains for you to do.

He comes when you strike your tent in the early morning, and then, for the first hour of the day, as you move forward on your camel, he stands at your near side, and makes you know that the whole day's toil is before you; then for a while, and a long while, you see him no more, for you are veiled and shrouded, and dare not look upon the greatness of his glory, but you know where he strides over head, by the touch of his flaming sword. No words are spoken, but your Arabs moan, your camels sigh, your skin glows, your shoulders ache, and for sights you see the pattern and the web of the silk that veils your eyes, and the glare of the outer light. Time labours on – your skin glows, your shoulders ache, your Arabs moan, your camels sigh, and you see the same pattern in the silk, and the same glare of light beyond; but conquering Time marches on, and by and by the descending sun has compassed the heaven, and now softly touches your right arm, and throws your lank shadow over the sand right along on the way for Persia. Then again you look upon his face, for his power is all veiled in his beauty, and the redness of flames has become the redness of roses: the fair, wavy cloud that fled in the morning now comes to his sight once more – comes blushing, yet still comes on – comes burning with blushes yet comes and clings to his side.

A.W. Kinglake, *Eothen,* 1844

In travelling from the Nile to Mount Sinai, the chief interest is in following the track of the Israelites; and the person one thinks of most is Moses.

Harriet Martineau, *Eastern Life, Past and Present,* 1848

Sir Frederick Henniker calls some of the Arabian scenery, 'the Alps stripped naked.' No description could better convey what we now saw.

Harriet Martineau, *Eastern Life, Past and Present,* 1848

That vast mountainous labyrinthine solitude of rainless valleys.

Charles M. Doughty, *Travels in Arabia Deserta,* 1888

The war has etched its picture over the face of the desert like a surrealist drawing. From the air over Sinai the whole conduct of the campaign is physically imprinted on the sand by the tank-tracks – a fantastically elaborate pattern of whorls and loops and intensely meaningful straight lines and sudden stops. It is the most extraordinarily effective record of an engagement I have ever seen, perhaps anyone has ever seen.

James Cameron, *Evening Standard,* 11 June 1967, in *What a Way to Run the Tribe,* 1968

Historically, the Sinai is a paradox. This seemingly worthless, underpopulated, undercultivated, static piece of gritty real estate has been the most besieged territory in the world—at last count, the battleground for at least fifty invading armies since recorded history began, surpassing even war-weary Belgium for the dubious title. It has been touched, in one way or another by most of Western and Near Eastern history, both actual and mythic, and its sand and rock have been sacred to disparate cultures. The reason for its historical stature is its strategic position between East and West; it is the land an army must invade, conquer, and occupy in order to seize a grander prize somewhere else. As a result of this unhappy situation, it has been occupied by some alien force ever since the Early Bronze Age, about five thousand years ago.

Burton Bernstein, *Sinai, the Great and Terrible Wilderness,* 1980

The Sphinx

Its head, neck, shoulders, and breast are still uncovered; its face, though worn and broken, is mild, amiable, and intelligent, seeming, among the tombs around it, like a divinity guarding the dead.

John Lloyd Stephens, *Incidents of Travel in Egypt, etc.,* 1837

You dare not mock at the Sphinx.

A.W. Kinglake, *Eothen,* 1844

. . . not a hideous compound animal, as it is when carved by an English stone mason for a park gate, but a sacred symbol of the union of the strongest physical with the highest intellectual power on earth.

Harriet Martineau, *Eastern Life, Past and Present,* 1848

Mrs Helen Bell, it seems was asked, 'What do you think the Sphinx said to Mr Emerson?' 'Why,' replied Mrs Bell, 'the Sphinx probably said to him, "You're another."'

R.W. Emerson, *Journal,* 1873

We . . . waited till the moon came up and wandered out among the huge straight slopes, and sat and looked at the Sphinx with her great lion paws that seem too big and give an extraordinary animal feeling to her: she is really more astonishing than any statue I have ever seen: in the moonlight now and then the shadow on her neck seemed to move, and if it had really done so I should hardly have been surprised. And as she is exactly the same colour, built of the actual desert, she seemed its very embodiment: also the embodiment of all life, rising from its huge animal foundations to the questioning human face, the chin just tilted up, as if it were looking out with immense courage and steadfastness into the spaces of the stars. All the miserable traffic of tourists and donkeys, and guides cannot spoil all this; and somehow it seemed merely suitable that eight or nine of them should fall off the pyramid and get killed every year: an offering in the old style.

Freya Stark, Letter, 7 June 1928, in *Beyond Euphrates*, 1951

The Minx by Spoonlight.

The Rev. W.A. Spooner, alleged Spoonerism, describing the most remarkable sight in Egypt, quoted Julian Huxley, *Memories*, 1970

Across the sands and burning flints,
The huge Gibraltar of the Bints
With half a lion for her crupper,
She who defies the worm and weevil,
With sands and seas and stars coaeval,
Sits with eternity at supper. . . .

Roy Campbell, 'The Colloquy of the Sphinx and the Soldier', *Talking Bronco*, 1946 (Campbell's note: The side view of the Sphinx is so like Gibraltar that she might be called the Gibraltar of the female sex. Bints = women.)

Suez

This is the Paradise of Thieves, I think the whole population may be divided into two classes of them; those who adopt force, and those who effect their purpose by fraud.

Eliza Fay, *Original Letters from India* (1 September 1779), 1817

Gulf of Suez

The beauty of the Gulf of Suez – and surely it is most beautiful – has never received full appreciation from the traveller. He is in too much of a hurry to arrive or to depart, his eyes are too ardently bent on England or India for him to enjoy that exquisite corridor of tinted mountains and radiant water. He is too much occupied with his own thoughts to realize that here, here and nowhere else, is the vestibule between the Levant and the Tropics.

E.M. Forster, *Pharos and Pharillon,* 1923

Suez Canal

And here not far from *Alexandria,*
Whereas the Terren and the red sea meet,
Being distant lesse than ful a hundred leagues,
I meant to cut a channel to them both,
That men might quickly sail to *India.*

Christopher Marlowe, *Tamburlaine,* Part ii, *c.* 1588

It cannot be made, it shall not be made; but if it were made there would be a war between England and France for the possession of Egypt.

Lord Palmerston, Speech, 1851

I have a very strong opinion that such a canal will not and cannot be made.

Anthony Trollope, *The West Indies and the Spanish Main,* 1859

You have it Madam.

Benjamin Disraeli, Letter to Queen Victoria, 24 November 1875, after buying Britain's shares in the Canal Company

*The French mind set the Egyptian muscle in motion and produced a dismal but profitable ditch.

Joseph Conrad, *An Outcast of the Islands,* 1896

The Ditch.

Anon., Traditional nickname

Has any one idea – apart, perhaps, from the discovery of the application of anaesthetics and of steam power and electricity, – done so much?

Alfred Viscount Northcliffe, *My Journey Round the World* (January 1922), 1923

During the last few weeks I have felt that the Suez Canal was flowing through my drawing room.

Lady Clarissa Eden, Remark at the time of the Suez crisis, 1956

Yam Suf (Ancient Lake Serbonis, near Damyât, formerly Damietta)

A gulf profound as that *Serbonian* Bog
Betwixt Damiata and mount Casius old,
Where Armies whole have sunk. . . .

John Milton, *Paradise Lost,* Book II, 1667

EQUATOR

and North Pole

Sydney Smith . . . told of Leslie, the Scotch philosopher, once complaining to him that Jeffrey had 'damned the North Pole.' Leslie had called upon Jeffrey just as the latter was going out riding to explain some point (in an article for the Edinburgh Review, I believe) concerning the North Pole; and Jeffrey, who was in a hurry, exclaimed impatiently, as he rode off, 'Oh, damn the North Pole!' This Leslie complained of to Sydney; who entered gravely into his feelings, and told him, in confidence, that he himself had once heard Jeffrey 'speak disrespectfully of the Equator.'

Thomas Moore, *Diary,* 6 April 1832

Closing in on the equator this noon. A sailor explained to a young girl that the ship's speed is poor because we are climbing up the bulge toward the centre of the globe, but that when we should once get over, at the equator, and start downhill, we should fly. . . .

Afternoon. Crossed the equator. In the distance it looked like a blue ribbon stretched across the ocean. Several passengers kodak'd it.

Mark Twain, *More Tramps Abroad*, 1897

There isn't a Parallel of Latitude but thinks it would have been the Equator if it had had its rights.

Mark Twain, 'Pudd'nhead Wilson's New Calendar,' in *ibid.*

In every book I ever read
Of travels on the Equator
A plague, mysterious and dread,
Imperils the narrator.

Hilaire Belloc, *The Modern Traveller*, 1898

between Honolulu and Fiji
Like so many things one has heard about a great deal, the equator is disappointing.

Alfred Viscount Northcliffe, *My Journey Round the World* (August 1921), 1923

in Kenya
That day we ate lunch by the road directly on the Equator, at 9,300 feet. There is a road sign there which is most exhilarating:

THE EQUATOR
Southern Hemisphere   Northern Hemisphere

Negley Farson, *Behind God's Back*, 1940

The equator is only kind to the lazy or the very wise.

Denis Saurat, *Watch Over Africa*, 1941

I agree with V. that it would be nice if they could designate the Equator by a row of red and green buoys encircling the globe, so that one knew exactly at what moment one had passed from the Northern into the Southern Hemisphere. Strange as it may seem I actually had this experience when visiting Uganda with the De La Warr mission in 1936. Across the dining-room floor at Government House, Entebbe, was drawn a broad green line, similar to those with which one marks out a hard tennis court. I was assured by the A.D.C. that this line marked the exact line of the Equator. Although to this day I am uncertain whether the A.D.C. was not making a mock of me, I accepted his statement with my wonted gullibility. I stepped with a great stride and without ceremony across the Equator, and then I stepped back again into the Northern Hemisphere. I then straddled the line, which gave me the impression of being titanic, bestriding the globe with all the majesty of Atlas, King of Mauretania and brother of Prometheus. It was a pleasurable experience. So when Hubrecht asked me whether this was the first occasion that I had crossed the line, I could reply with sincerity that I had already crossed it in Lady Mitchell's dining room. He imagined that I had not heard his question and assumed the expression of bored pity that one adopts towards the deaf.

Harold Nicolson, *Journey to Java*, 1957

EQUATORIAL GUINEA

Fernando Po

The Madeira of the Gulf of Guinea.
The Foreign Office Grave.

Nicknames quoted by Richard Burton, *Wanderings in West Africa*, 1863

Seen from the sea, or from the continent it looks like an immense single mountain that has floated out to sea . . . and anything more perfect than Fernando Po when you sight it, as you occasionally do from far-away Bonny Bar, in the sunset, floating like a fairy island made of gold or of amethyst, I cannot conceive. . . . Its moods of beauty are infinite; for the most part gentle and gorgeous, but I have seen it silhouetted hard against tornado-clouds, and grandly grim. . . . And as for Fernando Po in full moonlight – well there! you had better go and see it yourself.

Mary Kingsley, *Travels in West Africa*, 1897

The Bubis

The Bubis – as the inhabitants on Fernando Po are called, from a confusion arising in the minds of the sailors calling at Fernando Po, between their stupidity and their word Babi stranger which they use as a word of greeting – these Bubis are undoubtedly a very early African race. Their culture, though presenting some remarkable points, is on the whole, exceedingly low. They never wear clothes unless compelled to, and their language depends so much on gesture that they cannot talk in it to each other in the dark.

Mary Kingsley, *Travels in West Africa*, 1897

ETHIOPIA

The chiefe city of Ethiopia, where this great Emperor is resident, is called Amacaiz, being a faire city, whose inhabitants are of the colour of an Olive. There are also many other cities, as the city of Sava upon the river of Nilus, where the Emperour is accustomed to remaine in the Sommer season. There is likewise a great city named Barbaregaf, and Ascon, from whence it is said that the Queen of Saba came to Hierusalem to heare the wisdom of Salomon. This citie is but litle, yet very faire, and one of the chiefe cities in Ethiope. In this province are many exceeding high mountains, upon the which is said to be the earthly paradise: and some say that there are the trees of the Sunne and Moone, whereof the antiquitie maketh mention: yet that none can passe thither by reason of great deserts of an hundred daies journey.

Richard Eden, 1553, in Richard Hakluyt, *Principal Navigations . . . of the English Nation*, 1598-1600

There on the breezy summit spreading fair
For many a league; or on stupendous rocks,
That from the sun-redoubling valley lift,
Cool to the middle air, their lawny tops;
Where palaces, and fanes, and villas rise;
And gardens smile around, and cultured fields;
And fountains gush; and careless herds and flocks
Securely stray; a world within itself,
Disdaining all assault: there let me draw
Ethereal soul, there drink reviving gales,
Profusely breathing from the spicy groves,
And vales of fragrance; there, at distance hear
The roaring floods, and cataracts, that sweep
From disembowell'd earth, the virgin gold;
And o'er the varied landscape, restless, rove,
Fervent with life of every fairer kind:
A land of wonders! which the Sun still eyes
With ray direct, as of the lovely realm
Enamour'd, and delighting there to dwell.

James Thomson, *The Seasons – Summer*, 1727

I saw parch'd Abyssinia rouse and sing.

John Keats, *Endymion*, 1818

King Guigar lives in a little circular house built by Joas on the ruins of a part of the Palace. . . . There are still three large rooms, but full of dust and filth. The King occupies only one room . . . divided into two compartments by a white curtain. He asked me if I had ever seen a mansion like it. 'Yes,' I said, 'I have seen some in my country which resemble it a little.' 'What,' said King Guigar, 'do there still exist men able to build a house its equal?'

Samuel Gobat, *Journal*, 1830

It was between Axum and Adowa that Bruce witnessed the case of live-ox eating, which so affected his fame at home. Now, in a country where I have seen eaten and often partaken of flesh warm and quivering from the ox, actually moving in the hand, – where it is a custom also to eat the raw paunch and liver, with the gall-juice of the goat, and where the natives told me it was common for shepherds to cut a sheep's tail while alive and suck the fat out, filling the wound with salt for another occasion, – I can readily believe to have taken place what Bruce described, especially as he never insisted on its being a practice, but only an exceptional case.

Henry Dufton, *Narrative of a Journey through Abyssinia in 1862-3*, 1867

We met a German baron of the name of Dablin. . . . He heartily cursed the people, at which we did not marvel from the little we had seen of them. He uttered a truth which might serve as a caution to every traveller who enters the country. 'Abyssinia is a place to teach patience to a man who has it not, and take it away from him who has.'

Ibid.

The first thing probably that will strike the traveller in Abyssinia is the almost entire absence of high trees, except immediately surrounding the churches which, built on nearly all the conspicuous elevations, become from this fact, visible at great distances, and generally guide the wearied stranger to some hamlet in their neighbourhood. This, arising from the rank fertility of a burial ground, is attributed by the Abyssinians to the hallowing influence of celestial visitants.

Walter Chichele Plowden, *Travels in Abyssinia and the Galla Country*, 1868

The standard of St George was hoisted on the mountains of Rasselas.

Benjamin Disraeli, Speech proposing Vote of Thanks to Her Majesty's Forces, 2 July 1868

The magnificent scenery lightened the fatigue in no small way: for there can be no doubt that it is less tiring to march through a beautiful country than over a dead flat, although most of the men may be unconscious, or but half-conscious, of the reason for this difference. They swore at the mountain passes, while actually enjoying their grandeur. 'They tell us this is a table-land,' exclaimed one of the 33d, in climbing up the Alaji ascent. 'If it is, they have turned the table upside down, and we are scrambling up and down the legs.'

Clements R. Markham, *A History of the Abyssinian Expedition*, 1869

'We need European progress only because we are surrounded by it,' said the Ras. 'That is at once a benefit and a misfortune. It will expedite our development, but we are afraid of being swamped by it.'

Rosita Forbes, *From Red Sea to Blue Nile*, 1925, quoting remark by Ras Tafari, later Emperor Haile Selassie

Strategically, Abyssinia is like a porcupine bristling with quite exceptional difficulties.

Major-General J.F.C. Fuller, 'A Soldier-Journalist in Abyssinia', in *Abyssinian Stop Press*, 1936

I seemed to be travelling through a nightmarish land that only a god of hate or a mad god could have fashioned. The high plateau is seamed with vast crevices, so that Abyssinia seems a country that stops short suddenly after several miles of travel, to go on again hundreds of feet higher or lower. I remember my surprise at one point when I thought we were going along a plain slightly less barren than most, but suddenly saw that a hundred yards on our right was a sheer drop of about a thousand feet to another plain, out of which an amba of bare rock, hundreds of feet high, stuck up like a colossal tooth. On a later journey, an American colleague remarked that the scenery 'beats the Colorado canyon.'

Mortimer Durand, 'The Crazy War', in *Abyssinian Stop Press,* 1936

Ethiopia . . . a terrain of crag and precipice, where Nature seems to have lost her temper with the landscape or to have become demented. . . .

Ibid.

The Ethiopian highlands rise up from the wastes of equatorial Africa like an island from the sea. There they stand in lonely isolation, for the surrounding wilderness has cut them off from the outer world more effectually than the sea itself.

David Buxton, *Travels in Ethiopia,* 1949

This country often gives one an Orlando-like illusion of living through different centuries.

Dervla Murphy, *In Ethiopia with a Mule,* 1968

In Ethiopia one travels in broadened dimensions of both space and time. In terms of space, travel is not only horizontal but vertical. . . . Time is less tangible than space and more than merely three dimensional, so the contrasts are even greater. . . .

Paul B. Henze, *Travels in Ethiopia, 1969-72,* 1977

That shrewd old man Doctor Schweitzer once asked an Ethiopian visitor to his hospital whether his country had oil and on hearing that it had not said that in that case it might have a happy future.

Richard West, 'A Decade of Horrors', *Spectator,* 5 January 1980

Ethiopians

Can the Ethiopian change his skin, or the leopard his spots?

The Bible, Jeremiah 13:23

Avoid the Abyssinians as long as they avoid you.

Saying attributed to the Prophet Muhammad

The folk of that land will lightly be drunken, and they have little appetite to their meat; and they have commonly the flux; and they live but short time. And in that land are folk of divers shapes. For there are some that have but one foot; and they will run so fast upon that one foot that it is wonder to see. And that ilk foot is so mickle that it will cover and ombre all his body for the sun.

John Mandeville, *The Book of John Mandeville, c.* 1360

The Galla People

These Gallas inhabit in the Countries bordering to Magadoxo: they are a fierce Nation, they make warre with their Neighbours, and with all people, no more then onely to destroy them, and disinhabit the Countries: in the Countries where they overcome, they kill all the men, they geld the young men, the old women they kill, the young they keepe for their use and service.

Don John Bermudez, 1565, in *Purchas his Pilgrimes,* 1625

Encompassed on all sides by the enemies of their religion, the Aethiopians slept near a thousand years, forgetful of the world, by whom they were forgotten.

Edward Gibbon, *The Decline and Fall of the Roman Empire,* 1776-88

Nor have I been where men (what loss alas!)
Kill half a cow and turn the rest to grass.

Peter Pindar (pseud. of John Wolcot), *A Complimentary Epistle to James Bruce Esq., – Works* 1794

A damsel with a dulcimer
In a vision once I saw:
It was an Abyssinian maid,
And on her dulcimer she played,
Singing of Mount Abora.

Samuel Taylor Coleridge, *Kubla Khan,* 1816

'There are two sorts of Abyssinians,' continued Lady Hester; 'one with Greek features in bronze, and one of a pug breed. The first have a noble demeanour, are born to command, and have hands and feet so beautiful, that nature has nothing superior: their arms, when they expand them, fly open like an umbrella. . . . '

Charles Meryon, *Memoirs of the Lady Hester Stanhope,* 1845

Pride is not their only fault: they are deceitful, lying, insincere; their breasts are seldom stirred by generosity towards others, or in gratitude for benefits received; and, added to all, they are inhospitable, which in the estimation of even Mohammedans, whose ideas of morality and virtue are not as ours, is a great offence. Hospitality will redeem the character of an Arab, but an Abyssinian cannot even boast of this.

Henry Dufton, *Narrative of a Journey through Abyssinia in 1862-3,* 1867

The Abyssinian character has a strong dash of the

ancient Jewish in these things – their inveterate aversion to any change, their inconceivable love of litigation, and their wonderful obstinacy in trifles.

Walter Chichele Plowden, *Travels in Abyssinia and the Galla Country*, 1868

Galla Tribesmen

They plait their hair in tight plaits, commencing from the centre of the crown, and hanging round the head in thick masses. Their favourite ornaments are the entrails of cows, and, if possible, they are dirtier than the Abyssinians. A vile race of thieves and murderers.

Clements R. Markham, *A History of the Abyssinian Expedition*, 1869

No one who has any acquaintance with the Abyssinians can deny their desperate bravery; thieves and liars, brutal, savage, and untrustworthy they are by nature, but these evil national characteristics are to a great extent redeemed by the possession of unbounded courage, by a disregard of death, and by a national pride which leads them to look down with genuine contempt on every human being who has not had the good fortune to be born an Abyssinian.

Gerald H. Portal, *My Mission to Abyssinia*, 1892

I decided that many Abyssinians are honest with money, none with their thoughts.

Rosita Forbes, *From Red Sea to Blue Nile*, 1925

I have always thought it would be impossible to be an atheist in the desert. A cynic answered me 'Equally impossible to be a believer in Abyssinia.' I think, perhaps, that just as the boundless deserts give some of their greatness to the men who live in them, so the mountains narrow a man's outlook, shut him into a small world full of small interests. The eyes of the Abyssinian mountaineer are dull. You never see in them that splendid isolation, born of loneliness and a hundred-mile horizon. There is no mountain wisdom among them as there is desert wisdom among the Arabs. They are enemies of their rocks and crags and frightened of them, whereas the Bedouin is kin to his sands and friendly to all their moods. The difference may be due to the fact that the peasant Abyssinian is no traveller. A journey is a thief-haunted terror and two days away is 'far country,' nameless and without interest. For the desert Arab there are only two subjects of conversation – routes and wells. The Abyssinian talks food, money, and robbers.

Ibid.

When journalists visit Ethiopia I am afraid they regard us as a very picturesque but rather a contemptible people. They do not appreciate that while we are immensely proud of our ancient heritage there is a growing body of opinion in this country which is calling for the best of Western culture. The trouble is, we do not always *get* the best and we are only beginning to tell the good from the bad.

Emperor Haile Selassie of Ethiopia, Interview with Geoffrey Harmsworth, *Abyssinian Adventure*, 1935

If you want to insult an Ethiopian you will refer to him as an Abyssinian. It is like calling a Chinese a Chinaman. Ethiopia means 'Land of the Red Faces;' Abyssinian is a word originally applied by the Arabs to the Ethiopians and means 'Mongrel.' Although they are a mixed race, they naturally resent the use of this word.

Geoffrey Harmsworth, *ibid.*

The 'tame' European has always been a popular and valued institution in Ethiopia.

David Buxton, *Travels in Ethiopia*, 1949

The general characteristics of the people of Ethiopia make them ideally suited to the development of an excellent agricultural economy. They are intelligent, and physically well suited to the work involved. They have strong but not ponderous bodies and seem to be almost tireless, whether working in the fields or walking to and from the market. The high altitude would make such sustained exertion much more difficult for heavy men or those inclined to be fat or lazy.

Guide Book of Ethiopia, published by the Chamber of Commerce, Addis Ababa, 1954

They are a thin and nervous people with a curious mixture of darting quickness and gravity in their manners. One feels the emotional warmth of Africa here, the lingering handshake, the cool, smooth black hand in yours, inert, idle, unwilling to let go; and one observes the greetings and farewells among the Ethiopians themselves – the way the men very rapidly kiss one another alternately on either cheek, bobbing and ducking all the while. They repeat this process five or six times or more. . . .

These things are very strange, and they are made stranger by a certain feeling of hysteria in the atmosphere, an almost palpable tension. One feels that at any moment all this affection might turn into hate and violence. Europeans in Addis Ababa like to go down to the hot plains for their holidays, and there, they say, their nerves are calmer.

Alan Moorehead, *The Blue Nile*, 1962

Addis Ababa

It is to *Alice in Wonderland* that my thoughts recur in seeking some historical parallel for life in Addis Ababa. There are others: Israel in the time of Saul, the Scotland of Shakespeare's *Macbeth*, the sublime Porte as one sees it revealed in the despatches of the late eighteenth century, but it is in *Alice* only that one finds the peculiar flavour of galvanised and translated reality, where animals carry watches in their waistcoat pockets, royalty paces the croquet lawn beside the chief executioner, and litigation ends in a flutter of playing cards. . . . Addis Ababa is a new town; so new indeed, that not a single piece of it appears to be really finished.

Evelyn Waugh, 'A Coronation in 1930', in *When the Going Was Good*, 1946

Breathing, and occasional heart attacks caused by the rareified air are the only discomforts during the first few days.

Ladislas Farago, *Abyssinia on the Eve*, 1935

Addis Ababa was built less than fifty years ago, and to-day, in spite of the efforts of Haile Selassie, it is little more than an untidy conglomeration of stone and mud huts, roofed with thatch or corrugated iron. . . . But what Addis Ababa lacks in elegance, it makes up for in gilt. The court architect is a German (he is responsible for the gilt Lion of Judah at the station) and one is not surprised therefore to find a large equestrian statue of Menelik cast in gilt-bronze, and that the dome of Menelik's Mausoleum suggests an offshoot of the Reichstag. A new cathedral which has been many years in building (and is added to from time to time as fresh funds are forthcoming) is already showing similar Aryan tendencies. The parliament house, built at the Emperor's own expense, has deserted the traditions of Wilhelm II, and blossomed forth in the likeness of a modernistic scent factory with stainless steel embellishments. Most remarkable of all the buildings in Addis Ababa however, is the Gebbi. It was designed by a Frenchman who undoubtedly had the Petit Palais in mind at the outset, but allowed his ideas to run riot, with the sad result that the Gebbi now looks like a mixture of Earl's Court and the Alexandra Palace. It is a great entanglement of tin huts, look-out towers, courtyards, outbuildings, throne-rooms, barracks, sheds and stables, surrounded by a high wall which, in places, has completely collapsed.

Geoffrey Harmsworth, *Abyssinian Adventure*, 1935

There was a press bureau which you visited, as a sort of conventional rite, each morning. You waited for an hour or so in a bare room with a large map of Switzerland and a few Italian shipping posters on the walls. One day a wit marked Addis Ababa and Harar on the Swiss map, and you saw newcomers studying it with earnest, puzzled expressions, wondering why they had never noticed all those lakes before.

Patrick Balfour, 'Fiasco in Addis Ababa', in *Abyssinian Stop Press*, 1936

From the beginning there had been confusion about the Red Cross, since the sign had, from time immemorial in Abyssinia, denoted a house of ill-fame. (The Italians might, indeed, have justified their bombing of Red Cross units as a crusade of moral reform.) The old signs were quickly expunged. Nevertheless the opening of a resplendent central Red Cross office in the main street caused a certain misapprehension among the inhabitants, who thought at first that the Government was simply providing more up-to-date headquarters for a time-honoured pastime.

Ibid.

Addis Ababa . . . looks as if it had been dropped piecemeal from an aeroplane carrying rubbish.

John Gunther, *Inside Africa*, 1955

Other recently-modernised non-European capitals seem unreal too, and are all the more enchanting for that. Yet they are unreal only in relation to the Western visitor, whereas Addis Ababa is unreal in relation to Ethiopia. . . . To most foreigners familiar with the provinces, Addis seems like a fake jewel that has been hastily stuck in to the fabric of the Empire and that may fall off any day, since it represents a centralised administration unacceptable to millions of the Emperor's subjects.

Dervla Murphy, *In Ethiopia with a Mule*, 1968

The general impression that I received in those few moments between skimming over the Entoto Hills and landing at Bole on the other side of the city was of a hill station, like the ones I had seen in India, swollen to extraordinary proportions.

Duncan Forbes, *The Heart of Ethiopia*, 1972

As I returned through the iron gates into the private park in the centre of the city, and the gatekeeper bowed low as my car went past, I thought of the old Amharic proverb that seemed to sum up feudal Ethiopia on its painful journey into the twentieth century: 'He who bows lowest farts loudest.'

And then I thought of that other one, equally, and sometimes painfully applicable: 'Keep your mouth shut, or the flies will get in.'

Ibid.

Amba Geshen – Mount Amara

Nor where Abassin Kings their issue Guard,
Mount Amara (though this by some supposed
True Paradise) under the Ethiop line
By Nilus' head, enclosed with shining Rock
A whole day's journey high.

John Milton, *Paradise Lost*, Book 4, 1667

It was on Amba Geshen or Amara that all the princes of the blood royal of Abyssinia were confined, except the reigning sovereign; and the glowing description of this secluded royal abode given by the Spanish monk Ureta, and copied by old Purchas, led to its coming to the knowledge of Milton. . . . The description by Milton is quite correct. The rugged and difficult ascent from the Beshilo would be a good day's journey; and the beds of beautiful opal and chalcedony on the basalt may well entitle the scarped cliffs of Amba Geshen to be described as a shining wall. Dr Johnson appears also to have based his account of the beautiful valley in his story of Rasselas, on the tale told by Ureta, as quoted in Purchas. The real valley, or rather mountain of Rasselas, is Amba Geshen, within sight of Magdala; so that it was quite an allowable poetic licence for Mr Disraeli to talk of the English having planted the standard of St George on the mountains of Rasselas. But Ureta was an untrustworthy old romancer, and the true Amba Geshen, as described by more reliable authors, and as it really exists, is a dreary abode enough, with, however, a delightful climate.

Clements R. Markham, *A History of the Abyssinian Expedition*, 1869

The situation of Geshen was more melancholy than words can describe. How ironical that Milton should have chosen Geshen to be his Earthly Paradise.

Thomas Pakenham, *The Mountains of Rasselas*, 1959

Amhara Country

(between Tchelga and Genda)

Nature here appears always to put on a splendid robe, like a beautiful woman richly scented; for here the wild rose is more common than with us, and jessamine, honeysuckle, and other flowers abound: the number and variety of them covering the bushes and trees gave a gorgeous colouring to the landscape, that few artists would dare to put on canvas, for fear of seeming to overstep the bounds of truth.

Henry Dufton, *Narrative of a Journey through Abyssinia in 1862-3*, 1867

and Tigre

The Amhara plateau is Africa Felix; the Tigre plateau is a detached fragment of Arabia Deserta. . . . Tigre, like the rest of North Africa, belongs culturally to Western Asia. In fact, the frontier between Asia and Africa is delimited, not by the Suez Canal, but by the gorge of the River Takazze.

Arnold Toynbee, *Between Niger and Nile*, 1965

by the River Weri

Beech and I wandered up the stream and agreed that if only it were more accessible to civilization, this would be an almost perfect spot for a country house or a hunting lodge. A delightful climate, with exhilarating mountain air, magnificent scenery, with the bold outlines of the Temben range forming a background to woodland glades and clumps of splendid forest trees standing in a park of bright green turf, intersected by the sparkling waters of the Weri river, here rippling quietly over its bed of gravel, there tumbling, foaming, and rushing boisterously over an obstacle of grey granite boulders. How we longed for a trout-rod and a few small flies!

Gerald H. Portal, *My Mission to Abyssinia*, 1892

Asmara

A Transalpine European city overhanging the Red Sea.

Arnold Toynbee, *Between Niger and Nile*, 1965

Asmara was founded by the Italians seventy years ago and looks like a lost suburb of Milan.

Dervla Murphy, *In Ethiopia with a Mule*, 1968

Asmara, . . . when seen from the air, looks like a model city on a drawing-board. . . . The Italians designed the city as if land had been as scarce as in Italy itself.

Paul B. Henze, *Ethiopian Journeys, 1969-72*, 1977

Bale Province

During my time in Ethiopia a coloured map of J.R.R. Tolkien's 'Middle Earth' hung in the big grey stone house above Dincho which served as headquarters for the 'Proposed Bale Mountains National Park.' The PCVs who had put it up had in the same style lettered in 'Bale Mountains' before the vaguely Celtic 'Middle Earth' title so that on first glance the map appeared to be an official issuance. The better acquainted I became with Bale, the less whimsical I regarded this map.

Paul B. Henze, *Ethiopian Journeys, 1969-72*, 1977

Dessie

By switching off the current between eyes and brain it is possible eventually to derive some joy from Dessie.

Dervla Murphy, *In Ethiopia with a Mule*, 1968

Dessie is a puzzling place. The name, which means 'My Joy' in Amharic, seems peculiarly inappropriate.

Paul B. Henze, *Ethiopian Journeys, 1969-72*, 1977

Danakil Desert

The desert of Danakil is a part of the world that the Creator must have fashioned when he was in a bad mood.

Ladislas Farago, 'The "Busu Tshiki-Tshik"', in *Abyssinian Stop Press*, 1936

between Gondar and Aksum

On this road, a few miles to the north of Gondar, a gap opens in the hills round which the road is climbing, and through this gap there comes suddenly into view, to the north, a fantastic world of dizzy depths and heights and precipices and peaks. Here Nature has vied with Prospero in conjuring up the semblance of towers and palaces, and this pageant too, seems insubstantial when the hills shut out the view again as abruptly as they had opened it up. Was that brief vision really an illusion. . . . We begin to have doubts about the map's veracity, till suddenly Prospero's fantastic world reappears, and this time at point-blank range.

Arnold Toynbee, *Between Niger and Nile*, 1965

Harar

The town of Harar itself suddenly appeared beneath us, large, but completely walled, a neat and harmonious entity, as though placed intact on the hillside by a single hand. Here, for the first time in Abyssinia was a town, not a mere conglomeration of native hovels and European shacks. Here were streets: a bewildering network of them, high and narrow, but well-built and on a coherent plan. The houses were of mud, but they were architecture, not mere huts.

There was colour in the streets. The monotony of the Abyssinian dirty-white was broken by the deep reds and greens and purples of Moslem costume.

Patrick Balfour, 'Fiasco in Addis Ababa', in *Abyssinian Stop Press*, 1936

Lalibelah – Church of Mariam

Into Mariam, the church of the Virgin, with a lack of logic that is truly Abyssinian, only men are allowed.

'Why do you exclude women from the one church dedicated to a woman?' I asked the Chief Priest, who was attended by an acolyte with a fly whisk.

'It is the rule,' he said.

'What would happen if Mary appeared on earth, and wanted to enter her own house?'

The man of learning laughed. 'That is a very good joke! We should know her, of course,' he answered with the simplicity of a child.

Rosita Forbes, *From Red Sea to Blue Nile*, 1925

Massawa

The less said about Massowah the better. It was one of those dark patches in a special correspondent's experiences that are best forgotten. 'The Venice of the South' they call it.

Geoffrey Harmsworth, *Abyssinian Adventure*, 1935

Blue Nile (source of)

Half undressed as I was by the loss of my sash, and throwing my shoes off, I ran down the hill, towards the little island of green sods, which was about two hundred yards distant; the whole side of the hill was thick grown over with flowers, the large bulbous roots of which appearing above the surface of the ground, and their skins coming off on treading upon them, occasioned me two very severe falls before I reached the brink of the marsh; I after this came to the island of green turf, which was in the form of an altar, apparently the work of art, and I stood in rapture over the principal fountain which rises in the middle of it.

It is easier to guess than to describe the situation of my mind at that moment, – standing in that spot which had baffled the genius, industry, and inquiry of both ancients and moderns, for the course of near three thousand years. Kings had attempted this discovery at the head of armies, and each expedition was distinguished from the last, only by the difference of the numbers which had perished, and agreed alone in the disappointment which had uniformly, and without exception, followed them all. . . . Though a mere private Briton, I triumphed here, in my own mind, over Kings and their armies; and every comparison was leading nearer and nearer to presumption, when the place itself where I stood, the object of my vainglory, suggested what depressed my short-lived triumph. I was but a few minutes arrived at the sources of the Nile, through numberless dangers and sufferings, the least of which would have overwhelmed me but for the continual goodness and protection of Providence; I was, however, but then half through my journey, and all those dangers which I had already passed, awaited me again on my return. I found a despondency gaining fast upon me, and blasting the crown of laurels I had too rashly woven for myself.

James Bruce, *Travels to Discover the Source of the Nile*, 1790

Ogaden

Ogaden looks as if it had already been rent by war. There are deep ruptures in the ground that look like natural trenches but are only the result of the perpetual drought. Sometimes the ground is rocky, covered with sand, and cactuses are the only living things to be seen, sometimes it changes into a green paradise: but the luxuriant parts never extend for more than a few square miles, and the general impression one gets is desolation, sand desert follows on stony desert, bush on steppeland, at one place the grass grows as high as men, at another the ground is bare. In these pitiless surroundings live fierce men and wild beasts. Nature is not friendly to her European guests.

Ladislas Farago, *Abyssinia on the Eve*, 1935

In Ogaden diplomacy is unknown, and the tribes only argue with concrete things. For them the war is not a thing which might happen in the future, but an actuality, and they are not displeased, for they love fighting. They have neither imperialistic, nor patriotic aims; they just want to kill and it does not matter whom. If there is no one else a neighbouring tribesman will do, but they prefer Italians. . . . Death lurks behind every tree in Ogaden.

Ibid.

Semien

Semen, a Switzerland in miniature, is aptly described by an Abyssinian proverb – 'God has given mules, but no roads to ride on.'

Walter Chichele Plowden, *Travels in Ethiopia and the Galla Country*, 1868

The most marvellous of all Abyssinian landscapes opened before us, as we looked across a gorge that was clouded amethyst to the peaks of Simyen. A thousand thousand years ago when the old gods reigned in Ethiopia, they must have played chess with those stupendous crags, for we saw bishops' mitres cut in lapis lazuli, castles with the ruby of approaching sunset on their turrets, an emerald knight where the forest crept up on to the rock, and far away, a king, crowned with sapphire, and guarded by a row of pawns. When the gods exchanged their games for shield and buckler to fight the new men clamouring at their gates, they turned the pieces of their chessboard into mountains. In Simyen they stand enchanted, till once again the world is pagan and the Titans and the earth gods lean down from the monstrous cloud-banks to wager a star or two on their sport.

Rosita Forbes, *From Red Sea to Blue Nile*, 1925

Never have I seen such strange mountains. They look like peaks in a cartoon film.

Dervla Murphy, *In Ethiopia with a Mule*, 1968

EUROPE

See also under individual states

Dromio: . . . She is sphericall, like a globe: I could find out Countries in her.
Antipholus: In what part of her body stands *Ireland?*
Dromio: Marry sir in her buttockes, I found it out by the bogges.
Antipholus: Where *Scotland?*
Dromio: I found it by the barrennesse, hard in the palme of the hand.
Antipholus: Where *France?*
Dromio: In her forhead, arm'd and reverted, making warre against her heire.
Antipholus: Where *England?*
Dromio: I look'd for the chalkle Cliffes, but I could find no whitenesse in them. But I guesse, it stood in her chin by the salt rheume that ranne betweene *France*, and it.
Antipholus: Where *Spaine?*
Dromio: Faith I saw it not: but I felt it hot in her breth.
Antipholus: Where *America*, the *Indies?*
Dromio: Oh sir, upon her nose, all ore embellished with Rubies, Carbuncles, Saphires, declining their rich Aspect to the hot breath of Spaine, who sent whole Armadoes of Carrects to be ballast at her nose.
Antipholus: Where stood *Belgia*, the *Netherlands?*
Dromio: Oh sir, I did not looke so low.

William Shakespeare, *The Comedie of Errors, c.* 1592-3

But what speake I of Men, Arts, Armes? Nature hath yeelded her selfe to Europaean Industry. Who ever found out that Loadstone and Compasse, that findes out and compasseth the World? Who ever tooke possession of the huge Ocean, and made procession round about the vast Earth? Who ever discovered new Constellations, saluted the Frozen Poles, subjected the burning Zones? And who else by the Art of Navigation have seemed to imitate Him, which laies the beames of his Chambers in the Waters, and walketh on the wings of the Wind? And is this all? Is Europe onely a fruitfull Field, a well watered Garden, a pleasant Paradise in Nature? A continued Citie for Habitation? Queene of the World for power? A Schoole of Arts Liberall, Shop of Mechanicall, Tents of Military, Arsenall of Weapons and Shipping? And is shee but Nurse to Nature, Mistresse to Arts, Mother of resolute Courages and ingenious dispositions? Nay these are the least of her praises, or His rather, who hath given Europe more then Eagles wings, and lifted her up above the Starres. I speake it not in Poeticall fiction, or Hyperbolicall phrase, but Christian sincerity. Europe is taught the way to scale Heaven, not by Mathematicall principles, but by Divine veritie. Jesus Christ is their way, their truth, their life; who hath long since given a Bill of Divorce to ingratefull Asia where hee was borne, and Africa the place of his flight and refuge, and is become almost wholly and onely Europaean. . . . God himselfe is our portion, and the lot of Europes Inheritance, which hath made Nature an indulgent Mother to her, hath bowed the Heavens over her in the kindest influence, hath trenched the Seas about her in most commodious affluence, hath furrowed in her delightfull, profitable confluence of Streames, hath tempered the Ayre about her, fructified the Soyle on her, enriched the Mines under her, diversified his Creatures to serve her, and multiplied Inhabitants to enjoy her; hath given them so goodly composition of body, so good disposition of mind, so free condition of life, so happy successe in affaires; all these annexed as attendants to that true happinesse in Religions truth, which brings us to God againe, that hee may bee both Alpha and Omega in all our good.

Samuel Purchas, *Hakluytus Posthumus, or, Purchas his Pilgrimes,* 1625

Now Europe's balanc'd neither Side prevails,
For nothing's left in either of the Scales.

Alexander Pope, *The Balance of Europe,* 1711

It is the duty of a patriot to prefer and promote the exclusive interest and glory of his native country; but a philosopher may be permitted to enlarge his views, and to consider Europe as one great republic, whose various inhabitants have attained almost the same level of politeness and cultivation. The balance of power will continue to fluctuate, and the prosperity of our own or the neighbouring kingdoms may be alternately exalted or depressed; but these partial events cannot essentially injure our general state of happiness, the system of arts and laws, and manners, which so advantageously distinguish, above the rest of mankind, the Europeans and their colonies. The savage nations of the globe are the common enemies of civilized society; and we may inquire with anxious curiosity, whether Europe is still threatened with a repetition of those calamities which formerly oppressed the arms and institutions of Rome.

Edward Gibbon, *The Decline and Fall of the Roman Empire,* 1776-88

I am convinced that those societies (as the Indians) which live without government enjoy in their general mass an infinitely greater degree of happiness than those who live under the European governments. Among the former public opinion is in the place of law, and restrains morals as powerfully as laws ever did anywhere. Among the latter, under pretence of governing they have divided their nations into two classes, wolves and sheep. I do not exaggerate. This is a true picture of Europe. . . . It seems to be the law of our general nature in spite of individual exceptions, and experience declares that man is the only animal which devours his own kind, for I can apply no milder term to the governments of Europe, and to the general prey of the rich on the poor.

Thomas Jefferson, Letter to Edward Carrington, Paris, 16 January 1787

With all the defects of our constitutions, whether general or particular the comparison of our governments with those of Europe, are like a comparison of heaven and hell. England, like the earth, may be allowed to take the intermediate station.

Thomas Jefferson, Letter to Joseph Jones, Paris, 14 August 1787

Roll up that map; it will not be wanted these ten years.

William Pitt, Remark, on a map of Europe, after hearing the news of the Battle of Austerlitz, December 1805, quoted in Stanhope, *Life of Pitt,* 1862

Better fifty years of Europe than a cycle of Cathay.

Alfred Lord Tennyson, *Locksley Hall,* 1832

I remember being much amused last year, when landing at Calais, at the answer made by an old traveller to a novice who was making his first voyage. 'What a dreadful smell!' said the uninitiated stranger, enveloping his nose in his pocket handkerchief. 'It is the smell of the continent, sir,' replied the man of experience. And so it was.

Mrs Frances Trollope, *Paris and the Parisians in 1835,* 1836

There is not a nation in Europe but labours
To toady itself and to humbug its neighbours.

Rev. Richard Harris Barham, *The Auto-da-Fe,* Canto 2, *c.* 1840

Most persons are probably aware that Mahometans have a religious horror of bells, and, in countries under their domination, have never allowed of their introduction, even into Christian churches. It is not uncommon, by way of contempt, to designate Europe as the land of bells.

Charles Lewis Meryon, *Memoirs of the Lady Hester Stanhope,* 1845

Forget Europe wholly, your veins throb with blood,
To which the dull current in hers is but mud;
Let her sneer, let her say your experiment fails,
In her voice there's a tremble e'en now while she rails. . . .
O my friends, thank your god, if you have one, that he
'Twixt the Old World and you set the gulf of a sea.

J.R. Lowell, *A Fable for the Critics,* 1848

Can we never extract the tapeworm of Europe from the brain of our countrymen?

Ralph Waldo Emerson, *Conduct of Life: Culture,* 1860

We go to Europe to be Americanized.

Ibid.

L'Europe ennui.
– Europe is boring.

Alleged remark of Lady Hester Stanhope to Chateaubriand, quoted by H. O'Shea, *A Guide to Spain,* 1865

Nor red from Europe's old dynastic slaughterhouse
(Area of murder-plots of thrones, with scent left yet of
wars and scaffolds everywhere).

Walt Whitman, *Song of the Redwood Tree,* 1873

We are part of the community of Europe and we must do our duty as such.

William Ewart Gladstone, Speech at Carnarvon, 10 April 1888

Life in America is in most ways pleasanter, easier, simpler than in Europe. It floats in a sense of happiness like that of a radiant summer morning. But life in one of the great European centers is capable of an intensity, a richness blended of many elements which has not yet been reached in America. There are more problems in Europe calling for a solution; there is more passion in the struggles that rage round them; the past more frequently kindles the present in a glow of imaginative light. In whichever country of Europe one dwells, one feels that the other countries are near, that the fortunes of their people are bound up with the fortunes of one's own, that ideas are shooting to and fro between them.

James Bryce, *The American Commonwealth,* 1888

Sweden and Norway and Great Britain belong to our system; not to Eastern Europe. The Baltic separates, while the Atlantic only unites. Why it is so, I cannot conceive, but I begin to see that it was always so, and that somebody, at the beginning cut Europe in halves, once for all, along the Vistula.

Henry Adams, Letter to Elizabeth Cameron, 10 September 1901

The north is the place for men. Eden was there; and the four rivers of Paradise are the Seine, the Oise, the Thames, and the Arun; there are grasses there, and the trees are generous, and the air is an unnoticed pleasure. The waters brim up to the edges of the fields. But for this bare Tuscany I was never made.

Hilaire Belloc, *The Path to Rome,* 1902

The nether sky opens and Europe is disclosed as a prone and emaciated figure, the Alps shaping like a backbone, and the branching mountain-chains like ribs, the peninsular plateau of Spain forming a head. Broad and lengthy lowlands stretch from the north of France across Russia like a grey-green garment hemmed by the Ural mountains and the glistening Arctic Ocean.

The point of view then sinks downwards through space, and draws near to the surface of the perturbed countries, where the people, distressed by events which they did not cause, are seen writhing, crawling, heaving, and vibrating in their various cities and nationalities.

Thomas Hardy, *The Dynasts,* Stage Direction, 1904

A European State is only a State because it is a State of Europe.

Hilaire Belloc, *Hills and the Sea,* 1906

The only continent that has no wilderness.

James Bryce, *South America,* 1912

The lamps are going out all over Europe; we shall not see them lit again in our lifetime.

Edward, Viscount Grey of Fallodon, Remark, 3 August 1914, *Twenty-Five Years,* 1925

God damn the continent of Europe. It is of merely antiquarian interest. Rome is only a few years behind Tyre and Babylon. The negroid streak creeps northward to defile the Nordic race. Already the Italians have the souls of blackamoors. Raise the bars of immigration and permit only Scandinavians, Teutons, Anglo-Saxons and Celts to enter. France made me sick. Its silly pose as the thing the world has to save. I think it's a shame that England and America didn't let Germany conquer Europe. It's the only thing that would have saved the fleet of tottering old wrecks. My reactions were all philistine, anti-socialistic, provincial, and racially snobbish. I believe at last in the white man's burden. We are as far above the modern Frenchman as he is above the Negro. . . . We will be the Romans in the next generations as the English are now.

F. Scott Fitzgerald, Letter to Edmund Wilson, London, May 1921

Europe is so well gardened that it resembles a work of art, a scientific theory, a neat metaphysical system. Man has recreated Europe in his own image.

Aldous Huxley, *Do What You Will,* 1929

Europe is dangerously close to becoming a mere hyphen between America and Asia.

C.G. Jung, *The Rise of a New World,* 1930, trans. R.F.C. Hull

We are just a peninsula of Asia.

C.G. Jung, *The Tavistock Lectures,* 1935

To hell with Europe!

Senator Schall (of Minnesota), 1935, *Observer,* 'Sayings of our Times', 31 May 1953

Beyond and below Czechoslovakia lie the deep Balkans. They are, it has been said, a sort of hell paved with the bad intentions of the powers. The War was fought, remarked the Greek statesman Venizelos, to Europeanise the Balkans; what the War did, more or less, was Balkanise Europe.

John Gunther, *Inside Europe,* 1938 edn

Two or three winters ago a heavy storm completely blocked traffic across the Channel. 'CONTINENT ISOLATED,' the newspaper posters couldn't help saying.

Ibid.

Europe has lost her smile.

Norman Douglas, *An Almanac,* 1945

From Stettin, in the Baltic, to Trieste, in the Adriatic, an iron curtain has descended across the Continent. Behind that line lie all the capitals of the ancient states of Central and Eastern Europe – Warsaw, Berlin,

Prague, Vienna, Budapest, Belgrade, Bucharest, and Sofia. All these famous cities and the populations around them lie in the Soviet sphere, and all are subject in one form or another not only to Soviet influence, but to a very high and increasing measure of control from Moscow.

Sir Winston Churchill, Speech in the House of Commons, 1945

I am now going to say something that will astonish you. The first step in the re-creation of the European family must be a partnership between France and Germany. In this way only can France recover the moral and cultural leadership of Europe. There can be no revival of Europe without a spiritually great France and a spiritually great Germany.

Sir Winston Churchill, Speech at Zurich, 19 September 1946

We must build a kind of United States of Europe.

Ibid.

Baldwin thought Europe was a bore, and Chamberlain thought it was only a greater Birmingham.

Sir Winston Churchill, Remark quoted in Lord Moran, *Winston Churchill, The Struggle for Survival,* 1966 – of July 1953

Europe has what we do not have yet, a sense of the mysterious and inexorable limits of life, a sense, in a word, of tragedy, and we [Americans] have what they sorely need: a sense of life's possibilities.

James Baldwin, 'The Discovery of What it Means to be an American', *Nobody Knows my Name,* 1961

The immense popularity of American movies abroad demonstrates that Europe is the unfinished negative of which America is the proof.

Mary McCarthy, 'America the Beautiful: The Humanist in the Bathtub', *On the Contrary,* 1961

Our own concept of Europe has also sunk immeasurably. So many great cities, so many historic provinces, so many peoples have now been lost to Europe that she only survives as a fringe of the Atlantic. How much thinner is the blood that flows through her veins; how petty and small even General de Gaulle's most grandiose ambitions seem as compared with the community of ideas that once stretched from London to Warsaw.

Goronwy Rees, 'Diary from Berlin to Munich', *Encounter,* April 1964

When young and untravelled the English do not believe in the Continent at all. It is a sort of Fairy Tale.

William Golding, *The Hot Gates and Other Occasional Pieces,* 1965

As connoisseurs of the commonplace have been observing since Caesar, Western Europe has an appalling winter climate. It's a marvel that European civilization has survived it and shows that people are better when they are punished.

John Kenneth Galbraith, *Economics Peace and Laughter,* 1971

Time passes in America and Asia; in Europe, history occurs.

John Updike, 'Europe, Two Points on a Descending Curve', *Picked Up Pieces,* 1976

Danube

See how the wand'ring *Danube* flows,
Realms and religions parting!
A friend to all true *Christian foes,*
To *Peter, Jack* and *Martin.*
Now Protestant, and Papist now;
Not constant long to either;
At length an infidel does grow,
And ends his journey neither.

Anon, Attributed to Jonathan Swift in Charles Stokes Carey, *A Commonplace Book of Epigrams*

Europe: National Comparisons

Je parle espagnol à Dieu, italien aux femmes, français aux hommes et allemand à mon cheval.
(I speak Spanish to God, Italian to women, French to men, and German to my horse.)

Emperor Charles V, attributed

The Germans are said to woe like Lyons, rather by commanding than obsequiousness, the Italians like foxes stealing creeping into their sweet-hearts affections, the Spaniards like religious Friers, worshipping the idoll of beauty with astonishment. The French like Bees presently stinging. Of like variety of loves affections in divers Nations, these verses are vulgar: . . .

The Frenchman loves a nimble lasse,
that gently as you cast her lyes.
Spaniards love her, that like a glasse
darts beauty at him from her eyes.
Italians love a fearful wench,
that often flies from Venus sport.
To her that at the drinking bench
challengeth love, the Dutch resort.

Fynes Moryson, *An Itinerary,* 1617

It hath been an opinion, that the French are wiser than they seem, and the Spaniards seem wiser than they are.

Francis Bacon, *Essays,* 1597-1625

The Italian seems wise, and is wise; the Spaniard seems wise, and is a fool; the French seems a fool, and is wise; and the Englishman seems a fool, and is a fool.

Thomas Scott, *The Highwaies of God and the King*, 1623

The Italians are wise before the deed, the Germans in the deed, the French after the deed.
(Gli Italiani saggi innanzi il fatto, i Tedesci nel fatto, i francesi dopo il fatto.)

George Herbert, *Outlandish Proverbs*, 1640

England is a paradise for women, and hell for horses; Italy a paradise for horses, hell for women, as the diverb goes.

Robert Burton, *Anatomie of Melancholie*, 1621

The Italians most part sleep away care and grief, if it unseasonably seize upon them; Danes, Dutchmen, Polanders, and Bohemians, drink it down; our countrymen go to plays.

Ibid.

High-Dutch . . . a rough Language you know: which made the *Italian* tell a *German* Gentleman once, that *when God Almighty thrust* Adam *out of Paradise, he spake* Dutch; but the *German* retorted wittily, *Then, Sir, if God spake* Dutch *when* Adam *was ejected,* Eve *spake* Italian *when* Adam *was seduced.*

James Howell, 'Letter to Capt. J. Smith, at the Hague, Hamburgh, 22 October 1632', *Familiar Letters*, 1645

I feel not in myself those common antipathies that I can discover in others; those national repugnances do not touch me, nor do I hold with prejudice the French, Italian, Spaniard, or Dutch; but where I find their actions in balance with my countrymen's, I honour, love and embrace them in the same degree.

Sir Thomas Browne, *Religio Medici*, 1643

There was a *Spanish Doctor,* who had a fancy that *Spanish, Italian* and *French,* were spoken in *Paradise*, that God Almighty *commanded in Spanish,* the *Tempter perswaded in Italian,* and Adam *begged pardon in French.*

James Howell, *Instructions for Forren Travell*, 1650

The Scotch may be compared to a Tulip planted in dung but I never see a dutch man in his own house, but I think of a magnificent Egyptian Temple dedicated to an ox.

Oliver Goldsmith, Letter to The Reverend Thomas Contarine, Leyden, *c.* 6 May 1754

The English love their wives with much passion, the Hollanders with much prudence. The English when they give their hands, frequently give their hearts; the Dutch give the hand, but keep the heart wisely in their own possession. The English love with violence, and expect violent love in return; the Dutch are satisfied with the slightest acknowledgements, for they give little away. The English expend many of the matrimonial comforts in the first year; the Dutch frugally husband out their pleasures, and are always constant because they are always indifferent.

There seems very little difference between a Dutch bridegroom and a Dutch husband. Both are equally possessed of the same cool unexpecting serenity; they can see neither Elysium nor Paradise behind the curtain; and *Yiffraw* is not more a goddess on the wedding night, than after twenty years of matrimonial acquaintance. On the other hand, many of the English marry, in order to have one happy month in their lives; they seem incapable of looking beyond that period; they unite in hopes of finding rapture, and disappointed in that, disdain ever to accept of happiness.

Oliver Goldsmith, *The Citizen of the World*, 1760-1

It is a proverb in China that an European suffers not even his spittle to be lost.

Ibid.

I wish I had been born a Frenchman. – Frenchmen live as if they were never to die. Englishmen die all *their lives.*

Philip Thicknesse, *A Year's Journey through France and Spain*, 1789

In settling an island, the first building erected by a Spaniard will be a church; by a Frenchman, a fort; by a Dutchman, a warehouse; and by an Englishmen, an alehouse.

Francis Grose, *Provincial Glossary*, 1790

Providence has given to the French the empire of the land; to the English that of the sea; to the Germans that of – the air!

Jean Paul Friedrich Richter, as reported by Madame de Stael, quoted by T. Carlyle, 'Essays – Richter', *Edinburgh Review*, 1827

The French Courage proceeds from vanity – the German from phlegm – the English from coolness – the Dutch from obstinacy – the Russian from insensibility – but the Italian from *anger.*

Lord Byron, Letter to John Murray, 31 August 1820

The French have taste in all they do,
  Which we are quite without
For Nature, which to them gave goût
  To us gave only gout.

Thomas Lord Erskine, *Epigram*, before 1823

Condemn not in such haste
  To letters four appealing

Their 'goût' is only taste
The English 'gout' is feeling.

Anon., *Answer to Gout, ibid.*

Talked with a Spaniard, – who took me for an American, – of the English and French. He summed up what he had to say on their respective merits, in the following sentence of broken English, – 'I should like to hang de Englishman in de bowels of de Frenchman.' This sentiment will, I believe, express pretty accurately the feeling entertained towards us by a large portion of his countrymen.

Henry Matthews, *The Diary of an Invalid,* 1820

The Saxons and Prussians dislike each other as much as the English and French – The Saxons call the Prussians *Windbeutel* or wind bags.

The Saxons call the Bohemians Halters from their often using the word halter – an expletive – characterize the Bohemians as cheats & knaves.

They say the Poles are liars – are spendthrifts, idle & dirty – an irregular confused kind of housekeeping they call polish housekeeping – A chattering confused assembly they call a polish parliament.

Washington Irving, *Journal,* 1 January 1823, in Dresden, quoting his language teacher

The difference between the vanity of a Frenchman and an Englishman seems to be this: the one thinks everything right that is French, the other thinks everything wrong that is not English.

William Hazlitt, *Characteristics,* 1823

The English affect stimulant nourishment – beef and beer. The French, excitants, irritants – nitrous oxide, alcohol, champagne. The Austrians sedatives – hyoscyamus. The Russians, narcotics – opium, tobacco, and beng.

Samuel Taylor Coleridge, *Table Talk,* 30 April 1833

I could not help thinking, that as a race of females, the countenances both of the French and Italian women announced more pleasantness and reasonableness of intercourse, than those of my fair and serious countrywomen. The Frenchwoman looked as if she wished to please you at any rate, and to be pleased herself. She is too conscious; and her coquetry is said, and I believe with truth, to promise more than an Englishman would easily find her to perform: but at any rate she thinks of you somehow, and is smiling and good-humoured. An Italian woman appears to think of nothing, nor even of herself. Existence seems enough for her. But she also is easy of intercourse, smiling when you speak to her, and very unaffected. Now in simplicity of character the Italian appears to me to have the advantage of the English women, and in pleasantness of intercourse, both the Italian and French.

Leigh Hunt, *Autobiography,* 1850

Quand Italie sera sans poison,
France sans trahison,
Angleterre sans guerre,
Lors sera le monde sans terre.

(When Italy shall be without poison, France without treason, England without war, then the world shall have no earth.)

'Leigh's Observations', quoted by R.W. Emerson, from Southey, *Commonplace Book,* Third Series, ed. John Wood Warter, 1850

In the delegation of the parts of Jove to the races of men, one would say, that, the Greeks sprung from his eyes, the Germans from his brain, the Romans from his virility, the English from his hands.

Ralph Waldo Emerson, *Journals,* 1856

An English lady on the Rhine hearing a German speaking of her party as foreigners, exclaimed, 'No, we are not foreigners; we are English; it is you that are foreigners.' They tell you daily in London the story of the Frenchman and the Englishman who quarrelled. Both were unwilling to fight, but their companions put them up to it; at last it was agreed that they should fight alone, in the dark, and with pistols: the candles were put out, and the Englishman, to make sure not to hit any body, fired up the chimney, – and brought down the Frenchman.

Ralph Waldo Emerson, *English Traits,* 1856

When an Englishman has nothing to do, and a certain time to wait, his one recourse is to walk about. A Frenchman sits down and lights a cigar, an Italian goes to sleep, a German meditates, an American invents some new position for his limbs as far as possible asunder from that intended for them by nature, but an Englishman always takes a walk.

Anthony Trollope, *The West Indies and the Spanish Main,* 1859

Nothing can well be more different from anything else than the English from the French, so that, if you are acquainted with both nations, it may be said that on any special point your agreeable impression of the one implies a censorious attitude toward the other, and vice versa.

Henry James, *Occasional Paris,* 1877, in *Portraits of Places,*1883

As one nears Italy physical beauty comes running to meet one. At Nice I knew three lads like bronzes, quite perfect in form. English lads are chryselephantine. Swiss people are carved out of wood with a rough knife, most of them; the others are carved out of turnips.

Oscar Wilde, Letter to More Adey, March 1899

I knew a man once, a seafaring man, a Scotchman, who told me that the Northern people of Europe were bravest in an unexpected danger, but the Southern in a danger long foreseen. He said he had known many of both kinds, and had served under them and commanded them.

Hilaire Belloc, *Hills and the Sea,* 1906

Italians, and perhaps Frenchmen, consider first whether they like or want to do a thing and then whether, on the whole, it will do them any harm. Englishmen, and perhaps Germans, consider first whether they ought to like a thing and often never reach the questions whether they do like it and whether it will hurt. There is much to be said for both systems, but I suppose it is best to combine them as far as possible.

Samuel Butler, *Note-books,* 1912

There is no mistaking now that England represents in the world, and has represented for 300 years the great Christian democratic principle: and that Germany represents the Lucifer, the Satan, who has reacted directly against this principle. But the horrible obscene rats that will devour England and Germany both, these are our noble Allies, our greedy-mouthed, narrow-toothed France, our depraved Russia, our obscene little Belgium. And we give ourselves to be eaten by them.

D.H. Lawrence, Letter to Lady Ottoline Morrell, May 1916

You will always be fools; we shall never be gentlemen.

Quoted by Lord Fisher, in *The Times,* 16 June 1919, as the remark of a German naval officer to an English one. Lord Fisher commented: 'On the whole, I think I prefer to be the fool.'

When a German is confronted with something outside normal experience he sits down to study it, whereas an Englishman in the same situation sends for a policeman. The German is perfectly willing to believe that something he has not previously encountered in the world may nevertheless be as old as the world itself, whereas your Englishman, meeting something for the first time, imagines that it must be the first time the thing has happened. This explains why the Germans are a race of philosophers and the English a nation of cricketers.

James Agate, *Ego* (14 October 1932), 1935

The Frenches do not please the Germans,
Who call them names in hymns and sermons;
The Germans do not please the Frenches,
Who wish to shoot at them from trenches.
Now, anybody whom a German hates,
He presently exterminates,
But he who exterminates a French
Is never safe from Gallic revench,
But he who gets even with a German
Is obliterated like a vermin,
And so it goes on for ages and aeons
Between these neighboring Europeans.
I hope that such perpetual motion
Stays where it started, across the ocean.

Ogden Nash, 'Fellow Creatures, 1: The Neighbours', in *I'm a Stranger Here Myself,* 1938

People tell me the English win wars because they like musical comedy, and the Germans lose wars because they like music. I don't believe it.

James Agate, *Ego 8* (VJ Day, August 1945), 1946

The two countries which are the most difficult for British people to understand are the United States and France.

R.H. Bruce Lockhart, *My Europe,* 1952

The Western Front 1914-18

The time is gone, but the place remains, that strange over-populated city, five hundred miles long, by thirty wide, which Europe's youth inhabited for four unforgettable years. – After all, the Western Front was genuinely a *place,* however suddenly settled, however swiftly depopulated, with its own street-plan, place-names, backwaters, dangerous turnings, local patriotisms, and emotional geography; and because it was the place in which our European century was very largely made, its history, and the significance of its history for the homelands to which the settlers scattered, is still too dark, proximate, complex and rat-infested for us to face or understand.

John Keegan, *New Statesman,* 28 April 1978

F

FALKLAND ISLANDS / ISLAS MALVINAS

That of which we were almost weary ourselves, we did not expect any one to envy; and therefore supposed that we should be permitted to reside in *Falkland's Island,* the undisputed lords of tempest-beaten barrenness.

Samuel Johnson, *Thoughts on the late Transactions Respecting Falklands Islands,* 1771

A war declared for the empty sound of an ancient title to a Magellanick rock, would raise the indignation of the earth against us.

Ibid.

Never, perhaps, was any object, in itself abstractedly considered, less valuable nor less worthy of public attention than the Falkland Islands.

Sir Nathaniel Wraxall, *Historical Memoirs of My Own Time,* 1815

An undulating land, with a desolate and wretched aspect, is everywhere covered by a peaty soil and wiry grass, of one monotonous brown colour. Here and there a peak or ridge of grey quartz rocks breaks through the smooth surface. Every one has heard of the climate of these regions; it may be compared to that which is experienced at the height of between one and two thousand feet on the mountains of North Wales; having, however, less sunshine and less frost, but more wind and rain.

Charles Darwin, *Journal . . . During the Voyage . . . of H.M.S. Beagle,* 1832–6

The climate is extremely healthy, but the winds are so strong and incessant that everybody goes about stooping forward.

James Bryce, *South America,* 1912

One seemed to have reached the very end of the world. . . . I have seen many wild islands in many stormy seas, and some of them more bare and forbidding than this, but never any inhabited spot that seemed so entirely desolate and solitary and featureless. There was nothing for the eye to dwell upon, no lake, no river, no mountain – only scattered and shapeless hills, – a land without form or expression, yet with a certain simple and primitive beauty in the colours of the yellow grass and grey-blue rocks, shining through clear air, with the sea-wind singing over them. . . .

Anyone who today desires seclusion to think out a new philosophy might find this a fitting place of peace, if only he could learn to endure the perpetual drive of the wind.

James Bryce, *South America,* 1912

A windswept, treeless group in the South Atlantic, which are a British possession and which Argentina claims . . . Argentine nationalism is inflammatory on the issue. One little story goes back to Perón when all schools in Argentina, no matter of what nationality, had to have their instruction given in Spanish by Argentine teachers half the day. Perón visited St George's, the smart Anglo-American boys' school in Buenos Aires, and, entering a history class, asked a boy, 'To whom do the Islas Malvinas belong?'

'To England in the morning and to Argentina in the afternoon,' the boy replied. Even Perón smiled.

John Gunther, *Inside South America,* 1967

This has been a pimple on the ass of progress festering for 200 years, and I guess someone decided to lance it.

Alexander Haig, US Secretary of State, quoted by Peter Wilsher, *Sunday Times,* 4 April 1982, after Argentina invaded the Falklands

South Georgia (dependency of Falkland Islands)

The wild rocks raised their lofty summits till they were lost in the Clouds and the Vallies lay buried in everlasting snow. Not a tree or shrub was to be seen, no not even big enough to make a tooth-pick. I landed in three different places,–displayed our Colours and took possession of the Country in his Majesty's name under a descharge of small Arms. Our Botanists found here only three plants.

Captain James Cook, *Journal,* 17 January 1775

FAROE ISLANDS

Kirkiuboe (Kirkby)

The bonder . . . welcomed us in that queer northern manner I got used to after a little, as if he were thinking of anything else than us; nay rather, as if he were not quite sure if we were there or not. . . .

William Morris, *Journal of Travel in Iceland,* 11 July 1871

Thorshaven

Thorshaven . . . pleased me very much: certainly there was a smell of fish, and these creatures, or parts of them, from guts to gutted bodies, hung and lay about in many places; but there was no other dirt apparent; the houses were all of wood, high-roofed, with little white casements, the rest of the walls being mostly done over with Stockholm tar: every roof was of turf, and fine crops of flowery grass grew on some of them: the people we met were very polite, good-tempered and contented-looking: the women not pretty but not horrible either, and the men often quite handsome, and always carrying themselves well in their neat dresses; which include, by the by, skin shoes tied about the ankle with neat thongs: the men were often quite swarthy, and had a curious cast of melancholy in their faces, natural I should think to the dwellers in small remote islands.

William Morris, *Journal of Travel in Iceland*, 11 July 1871

FIJI

The scenery is very like the Virginian Alleghanies, if you would throw in a few fern-trees and palms and long pendent creepers.

Henry Adams, Letter to Elizabeth Cameron, 28 June 1891

Fiji was ceded to England by this king [Thakombau] in 1874. One of the gentlemen present at the governor's quoted a remark made by the king at the time of the cession – a neat retort, and with a touch of pathos in it, too. The English commissioner had offered a crumb of comfort to Thakombau by saying that the transfer of the kingdom to Great Britain was merely 'a sort of hermit-crab formality, you know.' 'Yes,' said poor Thakombau, 'but with this difference – the crab moves into an unoccupied shell, but mine isn't.'

Mark Twain, *More Tramps Abroad*, 1897

Tahiti was put on the map by Gauguin, Fiji by Qantas and Panam.

George Mikes, *Boomerang – Australia Rediscovered*, 1968

Greater Tasmania.

Tasmanian nickname, indicative of Tasmanian emigration there, quoted Jonathan Aitken, *Land of Fortune*, 1971

Wise visitors to Fiji break away from Paradise. It is not compulsory.

James Morris, 'Fiji', *Places*, 1972

There seem to be very few fools in the 300 islands: and so far as I could tell, not a single innocent.

Ibid.

Suva

Suva is a scrap of England dropped into space.

Henry Adams, Letter to Elizabeth Cameron, 16 June 1891

It was a hell of a way to have come to find anything so little like Fiji.

Cedric Belfrage, *Away from It All*, 1936

FINLAND

See also entry under Lapland

It is important to remember that in Finland the lavatory for men is called *Miehille*, and for women *Naiselle*. For a gentleman to say *Viekää minut Naiselle* ('Guide me to the women') is to court disaster; and in any case the beds are very lumpy.

Karl Baedeker, *Guide to Russia*, 1914

It was a severe land – or, as it seemed to us, a land of lines. At first hills were few and very slight, so that even the grey furrows seldom curved over a hillside, but cut straight lines through the level earth. Perfectly straight pines were the universal background – or rather they formed the backcloth to whatever *scena*, was shown – sometimes nearer, sometimes farther, but always pine-trees, and always severely perpendicular. When cut down their straight trunks formed the sides of the log huts, and their straight branches made hedges still and unyielding. Stiff and unyielding too, was the attitude of the Finns during those days of stress, and it was only by prefixing my Russian remarks with the assertion that I was English that I could induce them to understand me: but the farther we went from Russia, the more beautiful the country became, and the more easily were the Finns induced to smile. We passed through large forests of firs, by beautiful lakes and rivers with logs floating down them, by little wooden villages, the houses painted dull red, their windows and door-posts clean and white; a very pleasant country with its deep green trees, black pools and shadows, little hills, and small fields.

Denis Garstin, *Friendly Russia*, 1915

The South

A man flying over it (which I have not done) sees, I am told, such a mass of isolated water patches, from very large lakes to mere pools, that the thing looks under a morning summer sun like torn and ragged lace, supposing such lace to be green in colour and stretched over a shining surface of mirror.

Hilaire Belloc, *Places*, 1942

o to be in finland
now that russia's here.

e.e. cummings, *o to be in finland – XAIPE*, 1950

Finns

The peasants of Finland differ widely from the Russians in their look and dress: they have for the most part fair complexions, and many of them red hair: they shave their beards, wear their hair parted at the top, and hanging to a considerable length over their shoulders. We could not avoid remarking that they were in general more civilized than the Russians; and even in the smallest villages we were able to procure much better accommodations, than we usually met with in the largest towns which we had hitherto visited in this empire.

William Coxe, *Travels into Poland, Russia, Sweden, etc.*, 1792

A race of men very different in character and morals from the Swedes, namely the Finlanders; and as this race prevails among the inhabitants, a greater vivacity of spirit, a more irascible disposition, and a propensity to criminal actions begins to be manifested.

E.D. Clarke, *Travels in Various Countries*, 1824

We are doomed to be eternal sentinels, our periods of rest have not been long.

Anon. Finnish poet, quoted by Peter Ackroyd, *Spectator*, 8 March 1980

'Europeans speak of communism and we speak of communism,' a Finnish publisher said to me, 'but it is the difference between the young speaking of death and the old.'

Peter Ackroyd, *ibid.*

Helsinki

The appearance of the town is entirely modern, in some respects suggesting America rather than Europe. Many granite buildings erected since 1900 show a praiseworthy attempt at originality of style.

Karl Baedeker, *Russia with Teheran, Port Arthur, and Peking* 1914

I became aware at once of the translucent, transparent, pure, elusive, clean and clinical quality of Helsinki. I begin to hate the almost paralysing perfection of modern buildings, equipment, accommodation, accessories, service. At night it is a city of lighted glass blocks and boxes. After 8 p.m. on weekdays, and all day Sundays, the streets are virtually empty. Such abstraction numbs the heart, such empty perfection chills the soul.

James Kirkup, *One Man's Russia*, 1968

Korpikyla

This night we reached Korpikyla: not being able to find a human being, we began to suspect that the place was deserted; when our boatmen, knowing better where to look for the people, opened the door of one of the little steam-baths, for all the world like a cow-house, and out rushed men, women, and children, stark-naked, with dripping locks, and scorched skins, and began rolling about upon the grass.

E.D. Clarke, *Travels in Various Countries*, 1824

Turko / Abo

There is very little in Abo, which has entertained me in the survey, or can amuse you by the description. It is a wretched capital, of a barbarous province. The houses are almost all of wood; and the archiepiscopal palace, which has not even a single story, but may be called a sort of barrack, is composed of no better materials, except that it is painted red. I inquired if there was not any object in the university, meriting attention; but they assure me that it would be regarded as a piece of ridicule, to visit it on such an errand, there being nothing within its walls except a very small library, and a few philosophical instruments.

Sir N.W. Wraxall, *A Tour Round the Baltic*, 1775

FRANCE

France, mère des arts, des armes et des lois.
– France, mother of the arts, of arms, of law.

Joachim du Bellay, *Les Regrets*, ix, 1558

'Tis better using France than trusting France.

William Shakespeare, *Henry VI*, Part 3, *c.* 1589–92

That sweet enemy, France.

Sir Philip Sidney, 'Sonnet xli', *Astrophel and Stella*, 1591

What is there in *France* to bee learned more than in *England*, but falsehood in fellowship, perfect slovenrie, to love no man but for my pleasure, to sweare *Ah par la mort Dieu* when a mans hammes are scabd. For the idle Traveller, (I meane not for the Souldiour) I have knowen some that have continued there by the space of halfe a dozzen yeares, and when they come home, they have hid a little weerish leane face under a broad French hat, kept a terrible coyle with the dust in the streets in their long cloaks of gray paper, and spoke English strangely. Nought els have they profited by their travell, save learnt to distinguish of the true *Burdeaux* Grape, and know a cup of neate *Gascoigne*, from the wine of *Orleance*: yea and peradventure this also, to esteeme of the pox as a pimple, to weare a velvet patch on their face, and walke melancholy with their Armes folded.

Thomas Nashe, *The Unfortunate Traveller*, 1594

France, in her lunatique giddiness did hate
Ever our men, yea and our God of late;
Yet she relyes upon our Angels well,
Which nere returne; no more than they which fell.

John Donne, *Love's Warre*, *c.* 1594

Constance. France is a Bawd to Fortune. . . .

William Shakespeare, *King John*, *c.*, 1596–7

Methinks nobody should be sad but I:
Yet I remember, when I was in France,
Young gentlemen would be as sad as night,
Only for wantonness.

Ibid.

Parolles: France is a dog-hole. . . .

William Shakespeare, *All's Well That Ends Well*, 1602–3

Marry, in *Fraunce*, wee feare noe *bloud*, but wine;
Lesse danger's in her *Sword*, then in her *Vine*.

Richard Corbet, *A Letter Sent from Doctor Corbet to Master Ailesbury*, 9 December 1618

I am now upon the fair Continent of *France*, one of the Nature's choicest Masterpieces; one of *Ceres'* chiefest Barns for Corn; one of *Bacchus's* prime Wine-Cellars, and of *Neptunes's* best Salt-pits; a compleat self-sufficent Country, where there is rather a Superfluity than Defect of anything, either for Necessity or Pleasure, did the *Policy of the Country correspond with the Bounty of Nature, in the equal distribution of the Wealth amongst the Inhabitants*; for I think there is not upon the Earth a richer Country, and poorer People.

James Howell, 'Letter to My Father, from Rouen, 7 September 1619', *Familiar Letters*, 1645

France is a meadow that cuts thrice a year.

George Herbert, *Jacula Prudentum*, 1640

Eighteenth Century

Ungovern'd Passion settled first in *France*,
Where Mankind Lives in Haste, and Thrives by Chance,
A *Dancing Nation*, Fickle and Untrue:
Have oft undone themselves, and others too:
Prompt the Infernal Dictates to Obey,
And in Hell's Favour none more great than they.

Daniel Defoe, *The True-Born Englishman*, 1701

France, a Country which has Infected all the Nations of *Europe* with its Levity.

Joseph Addison, *Spectator*, No.435, 19 July 1712

Others import yet nobler arts from France,
Teach kings to fiddle, and make senates dance.

Alexander Pope, *The Dunciad*, 1728–43

The faithless vain disturber of mankind,
Insulting Gaul.

James Thomson, *The Seasons – Autumn*, 1730

The land where social Pleasure loves to dwell.

James Thomson, *Liberty*, 1734–6

France is so much improvd it is not to be known to be the same Country we pass'd through 20 year ago. Every thing I see speaks in praise of Cardinal Fleury; the roads are all mended and the greatest part of them pav'd as well as the streets of Paris, planted on both sides like the roads in Holland, and such good care taken against Robbers that you may cross the Country with your purse in your Hand. The French are more chang'd than their roads; instead of pale yellow Faces wrapp'd up in Blankets as we saw them, the Villages are all fill'd with fresh colour'd lusty peasants, in good Cloath and clean Linnen. It is incredible, the Air of plenty and content that is over the whole Country.

Lady Mary Wortley Montagu, Letter to her Husband, Dijon, 18 August 1739

. . . friendship in France as impossible to be attained as orange-trees on the mountains of Scotland; it is not the product of the climate. . . .

Lady Mary Wortley Montagu, Letter to Lady Pomfret, 12 July 1744

Let the French but have England, and they won't want to conquer it.

Horace Walpole, Letter to the Hon. H.S. Conway, 1 July 1745

Gay sprightly land of mirth and social ease
Pleas'd with thyself, whom all the world can please . . .
Theirs are those arts that mind to mind endear,
For honour forms the social temper here.
Honour, that praise which real merit gains,
Or even imaginary worth obtains,
Here passes current; paid from hand to hand
It shifts in splendid traffic round the land:
From courts to camps, to cottages it strays,
And all are taught an avarice of praise;
They please, are pleased, they give to get esteem,
Till, seeming blest, they grow to what they seem.

But while this softer art their bliss supplies
It gives their follies also room to rise;
For praise too dearly lov'd, or warmly sought,
Enfeebles all internal strength of thought, . . .
Hence ostentation here, with tawdry art,
Pants for the vulgar praise which fools impart;
Here vanity assumes her pert grimace,
And trims her robes of frize with copper lace,

Here beggar pride defrauds her daily cheer,
To boast one splendid banquet once a year;
The mind still turns where shifting fashion draws,
Nor weighs the solid worth of self applause.

Oliver Goldsmith, *The Traveller*, 1764

I shan't say any thing of France till I see thee & then – perhaps we may talk of Something else – .

David Garrick, Letter to the Rev. John Hoadly, July 1751

In this country nothing must be spared for the back – and if you dine on an onion, and lay in a garret seven stories high, you must not betray it in your cloaths, according to which you are well or ill look'd on.

Laurence Sterne, Letter to Mrs Sterne, Paris, 7 June 1762

They have not even the implements of cleanliness in this country.

Tobias Smollett, *Travels through France and Italy*, 1766

They order, said I, this matter better in France.

Laurence Sterne, *A Sentimental Journey through France and Italy*, 1768

In this whole kingdom there is no such thing as seeing a tree that is not well behaved. They are first stripped up and then cut down; and you would as soon meet a man with his hair about his ears as an oak or ash. As the weather is very hot now, and the soil chalk, and the dust white, I assure you it is very difficult, powdered as both are all over, to distinguish a tree from a hair-dresser. Lest this should sound like a travelling hyperbole, I must advertise your lordship, that there is little difference in their heights, for a tree of thirty years' growth being liable to be marked as royal timber the proprietors take care not to let their trees live to the age of being enlisted, but burn them, and plant others as often almost as they change their fashions. This gives an air of perpetual youth to the face of the country.

Horace Walpole, Letter to the Earl of Strafford, 8 September 1769

France is worse than Scotland in every thing but climate. Nature has done more for the French; but they have done less for themselves than the Scotch have done.

Samuel Johnson, in James Boswell, *Life of Johnson*, (1775), 1791

Nothing is more strictly true than, that France is *beguilt* and ****** all over.

Philip Thicknesse, *A Journey through the Pais Bas, or Spanish Netherlands*, 1786

France has undoubtedly more to apprehend from the ambition of her own rulers, than from that of any neighbour.

Arthur Young, *Travels . . . [in] . . . France*, 1792

A town is ever an accompanyment of a chateau in France, as it was formerly in most parts of Europe; it seems to have resulted from a feudal arrangement, that the Grand Seigneur might keep his slaves the nearer to his call, as a man builds his stables near his house.

Ibid., 13 August 1787

That power against which nature, not less than policy, has designed us to form a balance.

Edmund Burke, Speech in the House of Commons, February 1787

France has always more or less influenced manners in England: and when your fountain is choked up and polluted, the stream will not run long, or will not run clear with us, or perhaps with any nation.

Edmund Burke, *Reflections upon the Revolution in France*, 1790

And oh, fair France! though now the traveller sees
Thy three-striped banner fluctuate on the breeze;
Though martial songs have banished songs of love,
And nightingales desert the village grove,
Scared by the fife and rumbling drum's alarms,
And the short thunder, and the flash of arms; . . .
– Yet hast thou found that Freedom spreads her power
Beyond the cottage hearth, the cottage door;
All nature smiles, and owns beneath her eyes
Her fields peculiar and peculiar skies.

William Wordsworth, *Descriptive Sketches*, 1791–2, pub. 1793

Nineteenth Century

France standing on the top of golden hours
And human nature seeming born again.

William Wordsworth, *The Prelude*, 1799–1805

Since from cursed Gallia, o'er the nations flow
Freedom of guilt, – equality of woe;
Since thus she pours her bitterness o'er all
Let Gallia henceforth be translated Gall.

Anon., *On Gallia – The English Martial*, 1806

Bless you, you do not, *cannot* know
How far a little French will go;
For all one's stock, one need but draw
On some half-dozen words like these –
Comme ça – par-là – là-bas – ah ha!
They'll take you all through France with ease.

Thomas Moore, *The Fudge Family in Paris*, 1818

Who can help loving the land that has taught us
Six hundred and eighty-five ways to dress eggs?

Ibid.

Ask the travelled inhabitant of any nation, In what country on earth would you rather live? – Certainly in my own, where are all my friends, my relations, and the earliest and sweetest affections and recollections of my life. Which would be your second choice? France.

Thomas Jefferson, *Autobiography*, 1821

Never was there a country where the practise of governing too much had taken deeper root, and done more mischief.

Ibid.

There is something in the air of France that carries off the *blue devils*!

William Hazlitt, *Notes of a Journey through France and Italy*, 1826

French cooking comprehends English, and easily condescends to it; so that an Englishman finds himself better off in France than a Frenchman does in England.

Ibid.

The want of drains and sewers is the great defect of all the cities in France; and a tremendous defect it is. The people, who from their first breath of life have been obliged to accustom their senses and submit without struggle to the sufferings this evil entails upon them, – that people so circumstanced should have less refinement in their thoughts and words than ourselves, I hold to be natural and inevitable. Thus, you see, I have come round like a preacher to his text, and have explained, as I think, very satisfactorily, what I mean by saying that the indelicacy which so often offends us in France does not arise from any natural coarseness of mind, but is the unavoidable result of circumstances, which may, and doubtless will change, as the wealth of the country, and its familiarity with the manners of England increases.

Mrs Frances Trollope, *Paris and the Parisians in 1835*, 1836

France was long a 'Despotism tempered by Epigrams.'

Thomas Carlyle, *French Revolution*, 1837

Never go to France
Unless you know the lingo,
If you do, like me,
You will repent, by jingo.
Staring like a fool,
And silent as a mummy,
There I stood alone,
A nation with a dummy. . . .

Thomas Hood, *French and English*, 1839

France, famed in all great arts, in none supreme.

Matthew Arnold, *To a Republican Friend*, *c.* March 1848

In France, 'fraternity,' 'equality,' and 'indivisible unity' are names for assassination.

R.W. Emerson, *English Traits*, 1856

To change from England to France is almost the transition from one planet to another.

John W. Forney, *Letters from Europe*, 1867

France is not an enemy whom I despise, nor does it deserve I should.

Duke of Wellington, quoted, *Words of Wellington*, 1869

From Nice to Boulogne I was deeply struck with the magnificient order and method and decency and prosperity of France – with the felicity of *manner* in all things – the completeness of form.

Henry James, Letter to William James, 13 February 1870

We have come five hundred miles by rail through the heart of France. What a bewitching land it is! – What a garden! Surely the leagues of bright green lawns are swept and brushed and watered every day, and their grasses trimmed by the barber. Surely the hedges are shaped and measured, and their symmetry preserved, by the most architectural of gardeners. Surely the long straight rows of stately poplars that divide the beautiful landscape like the squares of a chequer-board are set with line and plummet, and their uniform height determined with a spirit-level. Surely the straight, smooth, pure white turnpikes are jackplaned and sandpapered every day. How else are these marvels of symmetry, cleanliness and order attained? It is wonderful. There are no unsightly stone walls, and never a fence of any kind. There is no dirt, no decay, no rubbish anywhere – nothing that even hints at untidiness – nothing that ever suggests neglect. All is orderly and beautiful – everything is charming to the eye.

Mark Twain, *The Innocents Abroad*, 1869

France . . . is justly said to be the mean term between the Latin and the German races.

Walter Bagehot, *Physics and Politics*, 1872

Every French road has a touch of despotism in it.

Anthony Trollope, *Australia and New Zealand*, 1873

All southern countries look a little false under the ground glass of incipient bad weather.

Henry James, *A Little Tour in France*, 1882

France has neither winter, summer, nor morals – apart from these drawbacks it is a fine country.

Mark Twain, *Notebook*, 1935 – before 1910

Twentieth Century

In fine art, France is a nation of born pedants.

G. Bernard Shaw, *Preface to Three Plays by Brieux*, 1909

Broke to every known mischance, lifted over all
By the light sane joy of life, the buckler of the Gaul;
Furious in luxury, merciless in toil,
Terrible with strength that draws from her tireless soil;
Strictest judge of her own worth, gentlest of man's mind,
First to follow Truth and last to leave old Truths behind –
France, beloved of every soul that loves its fellow-kind . . .

Rudyard Kipling, *France*, 1913

In France a servant works longer and harder than in England, but she is permitted the constant use of a soul.

Arnold Bennett, *Paris Nights*, 1913

He added – and how sincerely and with what passion – putting one hand on his chest and just bowing, that he loved and had loved France as he had never loved a woman.

Ford Madox Ford, *Return to Yesterday*, 1932, quoting Henry James, 14 August 1915

How beautiful the Republic was under the Empire.

Clemenceau, attrib.

France has always thought too much in terms of Europe.

H.G. Wells, *A Short History of the World*, 1922

You can always pick a fight in France by calling a man a vache.

Alfred Viscount Northcliffe, *My Journey Round the World*, 1923

*Everything is on such a clear financial basis in France. It is the simplest country to live in. No one makes things complicated by becoming your friend for any obscure reason. If you want people to like you, you have only to spend a little money.

Ernest Hemingway, *The Sun Also Rises*, 1926

France is the working model of Europe; like a clock with the clockwork showing clearly in a glass-case. There the movements occur rapidly, sharply, and logically, which appear elsewhere more slowly, more confusedly, and more at large. And French history exhibits a sort of extreme case of this process.

G.K. Chesterton, *Generally Speaking*, 1928

France, though armed to the teeth, is pacifist to the core.

Sir Winston Churchill, Speech in the House of Commons, 23 November 1932

They once said, or rather told us, every man has two countries; his own and France. That might be amended now to: every man has three countries – his own, France and the poorhouse.

Ernest Hemingway, *Esquire*, January 1934, in *By-Line*, 1968

I love France; and I am glad I saw it first when I was young. For if an Englishman has understood a Frenchman, he has understood the most foreign of foreigners. The nation that is nearest is now the furthest away. Italy and Spain, and rather especially Poland, are much more like England than that square stone fortress of equal citizens and Roman soldiers.

G.K. Chesterton, *Autobiography*, 1936

France is the most civilized country in the world and doesn't care who knows it.

John Gunther, *Inside Europe*, 1938 edn

All my life I have been grateful for the contribution France has made to the glory and culture of Europe – above all for the sense of personal liberty and the rights of man that has radiated from the soul of France.

Sir Winston Churchill, Speech in the House of Commons, 2 August 1944

France is a geographical necessity.

Sir Anthony Eden, quoted Lord Moran, *Winston Churchill, The Struggle for Survival*, 1966 (of February 1945) later amplified as:

The French are pretty hopeless, but France is a geographical necessity.

Sir Anthony Eden, Remark, 2 December 1953, quoted Lord Moran, *ibid.*

She must have a great Army; France without an Army is a cock without a comb.

Sir Winston Churchill, Remark, 9 July 1945, quoted Lord Moran, *ibid.*

France is an idea necessary to civilization.

Charles Morgan, Title of Lecture at the Royal Institution of Great Britain, 25 February 1941, in *Reflections in a Mirror*, 2nd Series, 1946

On ne peut rassembler les français que sous le coup de peur. On ne peut pas rassembler à froid un pays qui compte 265 spécialités de fromages.
(You can only unite the French through fear. You cannot simply bring together a country that has 265 kinds of cheese.)

General Charles de Gaulle, Speech, 1951

As Maxine du Camp has left on record in his memoirs, there is a book to be written under the title of 'The Influence of Rhetoric on the Misfortunes of France.'

R.H. Bruce Lockhart, *My Europe*, 1952

In Britain you have at all times only a very few men who are ever likely to become Prime Minister. Here in France we have about thirty men who not only can but do, in fact, become Prime Minister and, in order to enable them to do so, the Government changes every six months.

M. de Brèdevant, aircraft industrialist, Honfleur, quoted by R.H. Bruce Lockhart, *ibid.*

'There is a way of travelling cheaply in France,' he said. 'One simply gets on a train, sits down, in a first-class compartment, and falls asleep. There is a law in France that no first-class passenger asleep may be awakened by a conductor. They may awaken you in second or third class, but never in first. Considering that we are a republic we have more regard for privilege than any other nation on earth.'

Ludwig Bemelmans, *How to Travel Incognito*, 1952

The French will stay in Africa as long as France exists. But does France exist?

Abdel Krim, in conversation with Miss Dorothy Thompson, quoted John Gunther, *Inside Africa*, 1955

In France logic is applied logic.

William Sansom, *Blue Skies Brown Studies*, 1961

France has no friends, only interests.

General Charles de Gaulle, attrib.

An expensive minefield between Dover and the Spanish border.

Roger Bray, *Evening Standard*, 16 August 1979

France is the only country near enough for a British citizen to swim to.

Anon., 'French Leave', *The Sunday Times*, 30 December 1979

French

It is not the fashion for the maids in France to kiss before they are married.

William Shakespeare, *King Henry V*, *c.* 1598–9

rich, not gaudy;
For the apparel oft proclaims the man,
And they in France of the best rank and station
Are most select and generous, chief in that.

William Shakespeare, *Hamlet*, *c.* 1600–1, Polonius' advice to Laertes

Needy rather by negligence than want of means, as the French manner oftentimes is.

Francis Bacon, *Of the True Greatness of the Kingdom of Britain*, *c.* 1606

Tell me, if you be tyed like Apes to imitate their everchanging humours? and can draw from them (in any Art or cariage) a greater draught, than they draw from the Italian, for first they be Imitators, next Mutators; thirdly, Temptators; and lastly your Plantators, in all the varieties of vanity. . . .

Thus they fondly Write, thus they pratle, thus they sing, thus they Daunce, thus they brangle, thus they dally in capritziat humours, and thus they vary, in the fleering conceite of sa, sa, sa, sa, sa, far beyond the inconstancy of all female inconstancies. . . .

But to conclude this Epitome of France, three things I wish the way-faring man to prevent there: First, the eating of Victuals, and drinking of Wine without price making; least (when he hath done) for the stridor of his teeth his charges be redoubled. Next to choose his lodgings (if it fall out in any way-standing Taverne) far from palludiat Ditches, least the vehemency of chirking frogs, vexe the wish'd-for Repose of his fatigated body, and cast him in a vigilant perplexity.

And lastly, unlesse earley hee would arise, I never wish him to lye neere the fore-streetes of a Towne: because of the disturbant clamours of the Peasant samboies or nayle-woodden shoes: whose noyse like an aequivox, resembleth the clashing armour of Armies; or the clangour of the Ulyssen-tumbling Horse to fatall Troy.

William Lithgow, *Rare Adventures and Painfull Peregrinations*, 1614/32

The French are passing courtly, ripe of wit,
Kind, but extreme dissemblers; you shall have
A Frenchman ducking lower than your knee,
At th'instant mocking even your very shoe-ties:
To give the country due, it is on earth
A paradise; and if you can neglect
Your own appropriaments, but praising that
In others, wherein you excel yourself,
You shall be much belov'd there.

John Ford, *Love's Sacrifice*, 1633

The *French* are a free and debonair accostable People, both Men and Women. Among the one, at first entrance, one may have Acquaintance, and at first Acquaintance one may have Entrance; for the other, whereas the old rule was, that there could be no true Friendship without commessation of a bushel of salt, one may have enough there before he eat a spoonful with them.

James Howell, 'Letter to Mr T.W., 28 February 1634', *New Volume of Familiar Letters*, 1647

The old saying was, *Ayez le François pour ton amy, non pas pour ton Voisin:* Have the *Frenchman* for thy Friend, not for thy Neighbour.

James Howell, 'Letter to . . . the Lord R., 1 December 1643', *New Volume of Familiar Letters*, 1647

I have not yet seene in all this Country a man or woman with a pimpled red drunken face Nor a Puritan sqynt eye, very rarely. . . .

Richard Symonds, *Notebooks*, 1649, quoted in Peter Mundy, *Travels*, 1907 edn.

The present French is nothing but an old Gaul moulded into a new name: as rash he is, as head-strong, and as hair-brained. A nation which you shall win with a feather, and lose with a straw; upon the first sight of him you shall have him as familiar as your sleep, or the necessity of breathing. In one hour's conference you may endear him to you, in the second unbutton him, the third pumps him dry of all his secrets, and he gives them you as faithfully as if you were his ghostly father. . . . When you have learned this, you may lay him aside, for he is no longer serviceable. If you have any humour in holding him in a further acquaintance, (a favour which he confesseth, and I believe him, he is unworthy of) himself will make the first separation: he hath said over his lesson now unto you, and now must find out somebody else to whom to repeat it. Fare him well: he is a garment whom I would be loth to wear above two days together, for in that time he will be threadbare. . . . He is very kind-hearted to himself, and thinketh himself as free from wants as he is full; . . . himself is the only courtier and complete gentleman, but it is his own glass which he seeth in. Out of this conceit of his own excellency, and partly out of shallowness of brain, he is very liable to exceptions; . . . if you beat him into better manners, he shall take it kindly, and cry *Serviteur*, In this one thing they are wonderfully like the devil; meekness or submission makes them insolent; a little resistance putteth them to their heels, or makes them your spaniels. In a word . . . he is a walking vanity in a new fashion.

Peter Heylin, *Microcosmus*, 1652

There is no men in the world of a more insolent spirit where they do well or before they begin a matter, and more abject if they miscarry, then these people are.

Samuel Pepys, *Diary*, 30 September 1661

Gerrard: You know, to be a perfect *French*-man, you must never be silent, never sit still, and never be clean.
Martin: But you have forgot one main qualification of a true *French*-man, he should never be sound, that is, be very pockie too.

William Wycherley, *The Gentleman-Dancing-Master*, 1672

Eighteenth Century

A People who are taught to do any thing so it be with an Assurance.

Richard Steele, *Spectator*, No. 104, 29 June 1711

It would, indeed, be incredible to a Man who has never been in *France*, should one relate the extravagant Notion they entertain of themselves, and the mean Opinion they have of their Neighbours.

Joseph Addison, *Freeholder*, XXX, 2 April 1716

I shall not presume to take up any part of your time in describing the people of *France*, since they have been so excellently painted by *Julius Caesar*, near two thousand years ago: if there be any difference, they are obliged for it to the taylors and peruke-makers.

John Sican, Letter to Jonathan Swift, 20 October 1735

The French love show, but there is a meanness reigns through it all. . . . At dinner they give you three courses; but a third of the dishes is patched up with sallads, butter, puff-paste, or some such miscarriage of a dish.

Horace Walpole, Letter to Richard West, Paris, 21 April 1739

The French are the only people, except the Greeks, who have been at once philosophers, poets, orators, historians, painters, architects, sculptors and musicians. With regard to the stage, they have excelled even the Greeks who far excelled the English. And, in common life, they have, in great measure, perfected that art, the most useful and agreeable of any, *l'Art de Vivre*, the art of society and conversation.

David Hume, *Of Civil Liberty – Essays Moral and Political*, 1741

*But of all the People I ever saw, Heaven defend me from the *French*. With their damned prate and Civilities, and doing the Honour of their Nation to strangers (as they are pleased to call it) but indeed setting forth their own Vanity: they are so troublesome that I had infinitely rather pass my life with the *Hottentots* than set my Foot in Paris again. They are a nasty People, but their Nastiness is mostly *without*, whereas in *France*, and some other Nations that I won't name, it is all *within*, and makes them stink much more to my reason than that of *Hottentots* does to my Nose.

Henry Fielding, *Tom Jones*, 1749 (The Man on the Hill speaking)

I believe the ground work of my *ennui* is more to the eternal platitude of the French characters – little variety, no originality in it at all – than to any other cause – for they are very civil – but civility itself, in that uniform, wearies and bodders one to death.

Laurence Sterne, Letter to John Hall-Stevenson, 19 October 1762

Voltaire: You have the better government. If it gets bad, heave it into the ocean; that's why you have the ocean all about you. You are the slaves of laws. The French are slaves of men. In France every man is either an anvil or a hammer; he is a beater or must be beaten.
Boswell: Yet it is a light, a genteel hammer.
Voltaire: Yes, a pocket hammer. We are too mean for our governors to cut off our heads. We are on the earth; they trample us.

James Boswell, *Journal*, 27 December 1764, notes of conversation with Voltaire at Ferney

The first national peculiarity a traveller meets upon

entering that kingdom, is an odd sort of a staring vivacity in every eye, not excepting even the children; the people it seems have got it into their heads, that they have more wit than others, and so stare in order to look smart. . . .

Their civility to strangers is what they are chiefly proud of, and to confess sincerely, their beggars are the very politest beggars I ever knew; in other places a traveller is addressed with a piteous whine, or a sturdy solemnity, but a French beggar shall ask your charity with a very genteel bow, and thank you for it with a smile and a shrug. . . .

But their civility to strangers is not half so great as their admiration of themselves. Every thing that belongs to them and their nation is great; magnificent beyond expression; quite romantic! every garden is a paradice, every hovel a palace, and every woman an angel. They shut their eyes close, throw their mouths wide open, and cry out in rapture: Sacre! What beauty; O Ciel, what taste, mort de ma vie, what grandeur, was ever any people like ourselves; we are the nation of men, and all the rest no better than two-legged barbarians.

Oliver Goldsmith, *The Citizen of the World*, 1760–1

I hate the French because they are all slaves and wear wooden shoes.

Oliver Goldsmith, *Distresses of a Common Soldier*, 1760 – *Citizen of the World* 1762

They tell us a pleasant anecdote relating to Mr Sterne when he was at Paris: A French Gentleman asked him, If he had found in France no original characters that he could make use of in his history? *No*, replied he, *The French resemble old pieces of coin, whose impression is worn out by rubbing*.

London Chronicle, 16–18 April 1765

Nay, I don't pay homage to their authors. Every woman has one or two planted in her house, and God knows how they water them.

Horace Walpole, Letter to the Hon. Seymour Conway, 6 October 1765

If a Frenchman is admitted into your family, and distinguished by repeated marks of your friendship and regard, the first return he makes for your civilities is to make love to your wife, if she is handsome; if not, to your sister, or daughter, or niece. If he suffers a repulse from your wife, or attempts in vain to debauch your sister, or your daughter or your niece, he will, rather than not play the traitor with his gallantry, make his addresses to your grandmother; and ten to one but, in one shape or another, he will find means to ruin the peace of a family in which he has been so kindly entertained. . . .

If a Frenchman is capable of real friendship, it must certainly be the most disagreeable present he can possibly make to a man of a true English character. You know, Madam, we are naturally taciturn, soon tired of impertinence, and much subject to fits of disgust. Your French friend intrudes upon you at all hours: he stuns you with his loquacity; he teases you with impertinent questions about your domestic and private affairs; he attempts to meddle in all your concerns; and forces his advice on you with the most unwearied importunity. . . .

A French friend tires out your patience with long visits; and, far from taking the most palpable hints to withdraw when he perceives you uneasy, observes you are low spirited, and therefore he declares he will keep you company. This perseverance shews that he must either be void of all penetration, or that his disposition must be truly diabolical. Rather than be tormented with such a fiend, a man had better turn him out of doors, even though at the hazard of being run through the body.

Tobias Smollett, *Travels through France and Italy*, 1766

Of all the people I have ever known, I think the French are the least capable of feeling for the distresses of their fellow-creatures.

Ibid.

They have certainly got the credit of understanding more of love, and making it better than any other nation upon earth: but for my own part I think them arrant bunglers, and in truth the worst set of marksmen that ever tried Cupid's patience.
– To think of making love by *sentiments*!

Laurence Sterne, *A Sentimental Journey through France and Italy*, 1768

Your Idea of France exactly agrees with mine, their Politesse has reduced their Characters to such a sameness, that their Humours and Passions are so Curb'd by Habit, that when you have seen half a dozen French Men and Women you have seen the whole: in England (and I suppose in Denmark) every Man is a distinct Being, and requires a distinct Study to Investigate him; it is from this great Variety that our Comedies are less uniform than the French, and our Characters more Strong and Dramatic.

David Garrick, Letter to Helfrich Peter Sturz, 3 January 1769

Les Français seront toujours moitié tigres et moitié singes.
(The French will always be partly tigers and partly monkeys.)

Voltaire, Letter to Charles Joseph Panckoucke, 30 April 1777

Somebody complimented him [Dr Johnson] upon his Dictionary & mentioned the Ill Success of the French in a similiar Attempt. Why what would you expect says he of Fellows that eat Frogs.

Hester Lynch Thrale/Piozzi, *Thraliana*, 1777

The French are foppish, and will be foppish, no Philosophy can cure them.

Ibid., June 1777

There is nothing wanting to the character of a Frenchman that belongs to that of an agreeable and worthy man. There are only some trifles surpless, or that might be spared.

Benjamin Franklin, Letter to Josiah Quincy, 22 April 1779

I am afraid, said I, yesterday, to a French gentleman, the phrase which I used just now is not French. Monsieur, replied he, cette expression effectivement n'est pas Françoise, mais elle mérite bien de l'être.

John Moore, *A View of Society and Manners, in France, Switzerland, Germany, etc.*, 1779

A Frenchman not only means nothing beyond common civility, by the plentiful shower of compliments which he pours on every stranger; but also, he takes it for granted, that the stranger knows that nothing more is meant.

Ibid.

The Frenchman, easy, debonair, and brisk,
Give him his lass, his fiddle, and his frisk,
Is always happy, reign whoever may,
And laughs the sense of mis'ry far away.

William Cowper, *Table Talk*, 1782

The people at large view every object only as it may furnish puns and bons mots; and I pronounce that a good punster would disarm the whole nation were they ever so seriously disposed to revolt.

Thomas Jefferson, Letter to Mrs John (Abigail) Adams, 22 February 1787

I do not dislike the French from the vulgar antipathy between neighbouring nations, but for their insolent and unfounded airs of superiority.

Horace Walpole, Letter to Hannah More, 14 October 1787

Never let a Frenchman with whom you live, or with whom you travel, be master. An Englishman cannot possibly live twenty-four hours with a Frenchman who *commands*; he will try for that superiority; but by one single pointed resolution, shew him it must not be so, and he will give it up, and become an useful, and an agreeable companion.

Philip Thicknesse, *General Hints to Strangers who Travel in France*, 1789

Jealousy is scarce known in France. By the time the first child is born, an indifference generally takes place: the husband and wife have their separate acquaintance, and pursue their separate *amusements*, undisturbed by domestic squabbles. When they meet in the evening it is with perfect good humour, and, in general, perfect good breeding. – When an English wife plays truant, she soon becomes abandoned: it is not so with the French; they preserve appearances and proper decorum, because they are seldom attached to any particular man. While they are at their toilet they receive the visits of their male acquaintance, and he must be a man of uncommon discernment, who finds out who it is she prefers at that time. – In the southern parts of France, the women are in general very *free* and *easy* indeed.

Ibid.

Whenever you want honest information, get it from a French officer or a priest, provided they are on the *wrong* side of forty; but, in general, avoid all intimacy with either on the *right* side of thirty.

Ibid.

The irregular and lively spirit of the Nation has disgraced their liberty, and, instead of building a free constitution, they have only exchanged Despotism for Anarchy.

Edward Gibbon, Letter to Dorothea Gibbon, 18 May 1791

An ordinary Man asked our Curate – (who is himself, no *Extra* ordinary Man) if he did not think we should have a War? and if there is a War added the Fellow it will go hard with the *French*; for I was reading in the Bible this Morng. – Continued he; – & saw in the Prophet Isaiah these remarkable Words Mount Seir shall be laid low, by which no doubt is meant this new Republic of *France; Mounseer shall be laid low*: I suppose Isaiah must have meant *that*.

Hester Lynch Thrale/Piozzi, *Thraliana*, January 1793

All the affection I have for the French is for the whole nation, and it seems to be a little honey spread over all the bread I eat in their land.

Mary Wollstonecraft, Letter to Ruth Barlow, February 1793

I hate the shrugging dogs
I've liv'd amongst them, eat their frogs . . .

Peter Pindar [John Wolcot], *The Great Peter Despiseth French-men, – Lyric Odes for 1785*, xv – *Works*, 1794

There is no way of dealing with a Frenchman but to knock him down. To be civil to them is only to be laughed at, when they are enemies.

Horatio Viscount Nelson, Letter to Captain Louis, 4 August 1799

Nineteenth Century

N.B. The french like the Quakers do not like to be called Citizen by a Citizen.

Henry Crabb Robinson, Letter to his Brother, 22 September 1800

The pretensions of liberty are become a farce too egregious to be any longer a subject of Merriment – 'It is' said B. Constant 'founded in the character of the french – if they cannot be of one party they will be of the other – they are too vain to be neutral' – the remark appears to me to be very excellent – .

Henry Crabb Robinson, Letter to his Brother, 30 January 1804

It is easy to govern the French through vanity.

Napoleon Bonaparte, in J. Christopher Herold (ed.), *The Mind of Napoleon, 1955*

The French complain of everything, and always.

Napoleon I, *Maxims*, 1804–15

You must consider every man your enemy who speaks ill of your king . . . and you must hate a Frenchman as you hate the devil.

Horatio Viscount Nelson, quoted in Southey, *Life of Nelson*, 1813

The French! – vain, insolent, thoughtless, blood-thirsty, active & impetuous by Nature, so susceptible as to have their little reason always blinded by the bubble of Glory held before the mind's eye, a People who are brilliant without intensity, have courage without firmness, are polite without benevolence, & tender without heart; tall: fierce, & elegant in their looks; depraved, lecherous, & blasphemous in their feelings; mingling the most disgusting offices of Nature with the most elegant duties of Social Life. Good God! This is the being [Napoleon] & these are the people who are to be the instruments of liberty!

Benjamin Robert Haydon, *Diary*, 25 June 1815

I have just returned from seeing the French wounded received in their hospital; and could you see them laid out naked, or almost so . . . though wounded, exhausted, beaten, you would still conclude with me that these were men capable of marching unopposed from the west of Europe to the east of Asia. Strong, thickset hardy veterans, brave spirits, and unsubdued, as they cast their wild glance upon you . . . I must not have you to lose the present impression on me of the formidable nature of these fellows as exemplars of the breed in France. It is a forced praise; for from all I have seen, and all I have heard, of their fierceness, cruelty, and blood-thirstiness, I cannot convey to you my detestation of this race of trained banditti. By what means they are to be kept in subjection until other habits come upon them, I know not; but I am convinced that these men cannot be left to the bent of their propensities.

George Joseph Bell, Letter to Sir Walter Scott, Brussels, 2 July 1815

The fate of the French, after this day of decisive appeal, has been severe enough. . . . They submit with sad civility to the extortions of the Prussians and Russians, and avenge themselves at the expense of the English, whom they charge three prices for everything, because they are the only people who pay at all.

Sir Walter Scott, Letter to Joanna Baillie, Paris, 6 September 1815

*A Frenchman is born in harness, ready saddled, bitted, and bridled, for any tyrant to ride. He will fawn under his rider one moment, and throw him and kick him to death the next; but another adventurer springs on his back, and by dint of whip and spur on he goes as before.

Thomas Love Peacock, *Nightmare Abbey*, 1818

In all the every-day conveniences of life the French are unaccountably behind us.

Dorothy Wordsworth, *Journal*, 12 July 1820

It would seem, that a man's head was like a bowl, and that he came into the world, with a certain bias impressed upon it by the hand of nature herself. This bias in an Englishman's head disposes him to dislike every thing belonging to a Frenchman.

Henry Matthews, *Diary of an Invalid*, 1820

The French, in whom the lower forms of passion are constantly bubbling up from the shallow and superficial character of their feelings, have appropriated all the phases of passion to the service of trivial and ordinary life: and hence they have no language of passion for the service of poetry, or of occasions really demanding it.

Thomas de Quincey, 'London Reminiscences', *London Magazine*, 1823

The patriotic affection which that fickle nation are supposed to possess, . . . perhaps exists more in appearance than in reality, as wherever a Frenchman can do best, there he will settle.

Captain John Dundas Cochrane, *Narrative of a Pedestrian Journey through Russia, etc.*, 1824

A Frenchman's imagination . . . is always at the call of his senses. The latter have but to give him the hint, and the former is glad to take it.

William Hazlitt, *Notes of a Journey through France and Italy*, 1826

They over-ran Europe like tigers, and defended their

own territory like deer. They are a nation of heroes – on this side of martyrdom!

William Hazlitt, *Notes of a Journey through France and Italy*, 1826

The French physiognomy is like a telegraphic machine, ready to shift and form new combinations every moment. It is commonly too light and variable for repose; it is careless, indifferent, but not sunk in indolence, nor wedded to ease: as on the other hand, it is restless, rapid, extravagant, without depth or force. Is it not the same with their feelings, which are alike incapable of a habit of quiescence, or of persevering action or passion? It seems so to me. Their freedom from any tendency to drunkenness, to indulge in its dreamy stupor, or give way to its incorrigible excesses, confirms by analogy the general view of their character. I do not bring this as an accusation against them, I ask if it is not the fact; and if it will not account for many things observable in them, good, bad, and indifferent? In a word, mobility without *momentum* solves the whole riddle of the French character.

Ibid.

The familiarity of common servants in France surpasses the English at first; but it has nothing offensive in it, any more than the good natured gambols of and freedoms of a Newfoundland dog. It is quite natural.

Ibid.

'I have no fears for the French,' said Goethe; 'they stand upon such a height from a world-historical point of view, that their mind cannot by any means be suppressed.'

J.P. Eckermann, *Conversations of Goethe with Eckermann*, trans. Oxenford, 1874, – of 9 July 1827

Long straight lines of poplars delight the French; they suit the military turn of the nation, and resemble ranks of soldiers, into which they delight to form themselves, to their own impoverishment and to the great annoyance of their neighbours, for the acquisition of what they call glory.

T.J. Hogg, *Two Hundred and Nine Days on the Continent*, 1827

How much less of the *bear* there is in a Frenchman's ridicule than in that of an Englishman.

J.P. Cobbett, *Journal of a Tour in Italy, etc.*, 1830

Frenchmen are like grains of gunpowder – each by itself smutty and contemptible, but mass them together and they are terrible indeed.

Samuel Taylor Coleridge, *Table Talk*, 30 July 1831

Something of the monkey aspect inseparable from a little Frenchman.

Nathaniel Hawthorne, *Journals*, 5 July 1837

The Duke talked of the want of fuel in Spain, that the troops suffered, and that whole houses, so many to a Division, were pulled down regularly & paid for to get fuel. He said every Englishman goes to bed by night who has a home. He found Bivouacing was not suitable to the English character. He got drunk, & lay down under any hedge. Discipline was destroyed. But when he introduced tents, every Soldier belonged to his tent, & drunk or sober, he got to it before he went to sleep. Capital. I said, 'Your Grace, the French always bivouac.' 'Yes,' he replied, 'because French, Spanish, & all other nations lie anywhere. It is their habit. They have no homes.' Beautiful.

Benjamin Robert Haydon, *Diary*, 10–11 October 1839

The French army tailors are bad too: they make the coats too baboonish; but then they have a tail to them, a sort of something; it is at least the monkey who has seen the world.

Lady Hester Stanhope, in Charles Meryon, *Memoirs of the Lady Hester Stanhope*, 1845

The French character is indeed a character, stampt upon them from without. Their profoundest thoughts are *bons mots*. They are the only nation that ever existed, in which a government can be hist off the stage like a bad play, and in which its fall excites less consternation, than the violation of a fashion in dress.

J.C. and A. Hare, *Guesses at Truth*, 3rd edn, 1847

* . . . For this young man has a general impression that every foreigner is a Frenchman, and must be by the laws of nature.

Charles Dickens, *Dombey and Son*, 1847–8 (of Mr Towlinson, the footman)

You must by this time begin to see what people mean by placing France *politically* in the van of Europe; it is the intelligence of their *idea-moved masses* which makes them, politically, as far superior to the *insensible masses* of England as to the Russian serfs, and at the same time they do not threaten the educated world with the intolerable *laideur* of the well-fed American masses, so deeply antipathetic to continental Europe.

Matthew Arnold, Letter to his sister, 10 March 1848

I liked much what little I saw of the French people. They are accused of vanity; and doubtless they have it, and after a more obvious fashion than other nations; but their vanity, at least, includes the wish to please; other people are necessary to them; they are not wrapped up in themselves, not sulky; not too vain even to tolerate vanity. Their vanity is too much confounded with self-satisfaction. There is a good deal of touchiness, I suspect, among them – a good deal of ready-made heat, prepared to fire up in case the little commerce of flattery and sweetness is not properly carried on. But this is better than ill-temper, or than such egotism as is not to be appeased by anything short of subjection. On the other hand there is more melancholy than one could expect, especially in old faces. Consciences in the south are frightened in their old age, perhaps for nothing. In the north, I suspect, they are frightened earlier, perhaps from equal want of knowledge. The worst in France is (at least, from all that I saw), that *fine* old faces are rare. There are multitudes of pretty girls; but the faces of both sexes fall off deplorably as they advance in life; which is not a good symptom. Nor do the pretty faces, while they last, appear to contain much depth, or sentiment, or firmness of purpose. They seem like their toys, not to last, but to break up.

Leigh Hunt, *Autobiography*, 1850

I need not prove to you that the French *have* a national character. Nor need I try your patience with a likeness of it. I have only to examine whether it be a fit basis for national freedom. I fear you will laugh when I tell you what I conceive to be about the most essential mental quality for a free people whose liberty is to be progressive, permanent, and on a large scale; it is much *stupidity*. . . . I need not say that, in real sound stupidity, the English are unrivalled. . . . You don't want me to tell you that a Frenchman, – a real Frenchman – can't be stupid; *esprit* is his essence, wit is to him as water, *bons-mots* as *bons-bons*. He reads and he learns by reading; levity and literature are essentially his line.

Walter Bagehot, 'Letters on the French Coup d'Etat of 1851, III', *The Inquirer*, 20 January 1852

The French, said Napoleon, are *des machines nerveuses*.

Walter Bagehot, 'Letters on the French Coup d'Etat', in *ibid.*, 19 February 1852

The English have a scornful insular way
Of calling the French light . . .
We say the French are light, as if we said
The cat mews or the milch-cow gives us milk:
Say rather cats are milked, and milch-cows mew;
For what is lightness but inconsequence,
Vague fluctuation 'twixt effect and cause,
Compelled by neither? Is a bullet light,
That dashes from the gun-mouth, while the eye
Winks, and the heart beats one, to flatten itself
To a wafer on the white speck on a wall
A hundred paces off? Even so direct,
So sternly undivertible of aim,
Is this French people.
All idealists
Too absolute and earnest, with them all
The idea of a knife cuts real flesh;
And still, devouring the safe interval
Which Nature placed between the thought and act,
With those too fiery and impatient souls,
They threaten conflagration to the world
And rush with most unscrupulous logic on
Impossible practice. Set your orators
To blow upon them with loud windy mouths
Through watchword phrases, jest or sentiment,
Which drive our burley brutal English mobs
Like so much chaff, whichever way they blow, –
This light French people will not thus be driven.
They turn indeed; but then they turn upon
Some central pivot of their thoughts and choice,
And veer out by the force of holding fast. . . .
And so I am strong to love this noble France,
This poet of the nations, who dreams on
And wails on (while the household goes to wreck)
For ever, after some ideal good, –
Some equal poise of sex, some unvowed love
Inviolate, some spontaneous brotherhood,
Some wealth that leaves none poor and finds none tired,
Some freedom of the many, that respects
The wisdom of the few. Heroic dreams!
Sublime, to dream so; natural, to wake:
And sad, to use such lofty scaffoldings,
Erected for the building of a church,
To build, instead, a brothel . . . or a prison –
May God save France!

Elizabeth Barrett Browning, *Aurora Leigh*, 1856

At the table d'hôte of the inn . . . I first saw that repulsive type of French face. It is hard to seize what it is. The outline is oval but cut away at the jaws; the eyes are big, shallow-set, close to the eyebrows, and near, the upper lid straight and long, the lower brought down to a marked corner in the middle, the pupils large and clear; the nostrils prominent; the lips fleshy, long and unwaved, with a vertical curling at the end (in one case at any rate); the nose curved hollow or so tending; the head large; the skin fair – white and scarlet colour.

Gerard Manley Hopkins, *Journal*, 20 July 1868

The French are better *consumers* than we are. They will buy nothing which is not what they want, will buy no more than they want, and will take care that what they buy is fitted and finished in the precise manner which suits them best. The consequence is, that France, as a country, has a kind of finish which England lacks.

Walter Bagehot, 'One Difference Between England and France', *The Economist*, 12 September 1868

Frenchmen have never yet shown themselves able to bear exciting discussion.

Walter Bagehot, 'Do Conditions Requisite for a Stable Government Exist in France?', *The Economist*, 10 September 1870

The Paris Commune of 1871

What news from Paris! One hardly knows what to wish, except that the present generation of Frenchmen may pass clean away as soon as possible and be replaced by a better one. I am not sorry that the English sightseers who, with the national vulgarity, have begun to flock over to the show of fallen Paris and France, should be put to a little fright and inconvenience. One thing is certain, that miserable as it is for herself, there is no way by which France can make the rest of Europe so alarmed and uneasy as by a socialist and red republic. It is a perpetual flag to the proletaire class everywhere – the class which makes all governments uneasy.

Matthew Arnold, Letter to his mother, 20 March 1871

I assent to the common tradition that the French are a temperate people, so long as it is understood in this sense – that they eat no more than they want to. But their wants are very comprehensive.

Henry James, *From Normandy to the Pyrenees*, 1876, in *Portraits of Places*, 1883

In arriving from other countries one is struck with a certain want of dignity in the French face. I do not know, however, whether this is anything worse than the fact that the French face is expressive; for it may be said that in a certain sense, to express anything is to compromise with one's dignity, which likes to be understood without taking trouble. As regards the lower classes, at any rate, the impression I am speaking of always passes away; you perceive that the good looks of the French working people are to be found in their look of intelligence. These people in Paris strike me afresh as the cleverest, the most perceptive, and, intellectually speaking, the most humane of their kind. The Paris *ouvrier*, with his democratic *blouse*, his expressive, demonstrative, agreeable eye, his meagre limbs, his irregular, pointed features, his sallow complexion, his face at once fatigued and animated, his light, nervous organisation, is a figure that I always encounter with pleasure. In some cases he looks depraved and perverted, but at his worst he looks refined; he is full of vivacity of perception, of something that one can appeal to.

Henry James, *Occasional Paris*, 1877, in *Portraits of Places*, 1883

*'Is a Frenchman a man?' 'Yes.' '*Well*, den! Dad blame it, why doan' he *talk* like a man? You answer me *dat*!'

Mark Twain, *Huckleberry Finn*, 1884

I asked . . . [General Boulanger] . . . whether he intended to destroy liberty in France, to shut up the Chambers and make himself Dictator? intentions commonly attributed to him. To this he said that the idea was ridiculous. The French could never get on without talking, and a Parliament in some form they must have.

Wilfred Scawen Blunt, Diary, 19 May 1889, *My Diaries*, 191ᶜ

We distribute tracts, the French distribute medals.

George Moore, 'Meissonier and the Salon Julian', *Impressions and Opinions*, 1891

I feel as cold as a Frenchman.

Russian proverb, inspired by Napoleon's winter retreat from Moscow, 1812, quoted Harry de Windt, *From Pekin to Calais by Land*, 1889

At every interval of years I come back here with a wider experience of men and knowledge of races, and always the impression becomes stronger that, of all people in the world, the French are the most gratuitously wicked. They almost do me good. I feel it a gain to have an object of dislike.

Henry Adams, Letter to Elizabeth Cameron, 29 December 1891

I feel more and more convinced that Frenchmen think only with their nerves – and too much with the pudic nerve especially.

Lafcadio Hearn, Letter to Basil Hall Chamberlain, 6 February 1893

Twentieth Century

Note that the French for unemployed is not *hors d'oeuvre*.

E.V. Lucas and C.L. Graves, 'Solecisms to be Avoided', in *England Day by Day*, 1903

The French are a 'stuffy' nation; but they *do* hang their bedding out of the windows in the morning to air. This is more than can be said of the English.

Arnold Bennett, *Journal*, 16 March 1905

The natives here remark 'Mon Dieu!'
'Que voulez-vous?' 'Comment ça va?'
'Sapristi! Par exemple! Un peu!'
'Tiens donc! Mais qu'est que c'est que ça?'
They shave one portion of their dogs,
And live exclusively on frogs . . .
The closest scrutiny can find
No morals here of any kind.

Harry Graham, *France*, – *Verse and Worse*, 1905

Guillotine: *n.*, A machine which makes a French man shrug his shoulders with good reason. In his great work on *Devergent Lines of Racial Evolution*, the learned and ingenious Professor Brayfugle argues from the prevalence of this gesture – the shrug – among Frenchmen, that they are descended from turtles, and it is simply a survival of the habit of withdrawing the head inside the shell. It is with reluctance that I differ with so eminent an authority, but in my judgement . . . previously to the Revolution the shrug was unknown. I have not a doubt that it is directly referable to the terror inspired by the guillotine during the period of that instrument's awful activity.

Ambrose Bierce, *The Cynic's Word Book*, 1906

That enduring mystery of Europe, the French temper: whose aims and reticence, whose hidden enthusiasms, great range, effort, divisions, defeats, and resurrections must now remain the principal problem before my mind. . . . The French mind is the pivot on which Europe turns.

Hilaire Belloc, 'The First Day's March', *Hills and the Sea*, 1906

The vices and energy of this people are well known. They are perpetually critical of their own authorities, and perpetually lamenting the decline of their honour. There is no difficulty they will not surmount. They have crossed all deserts and have perfected every art. Their victories in the field would seem legendary were they not attested; their audacity whether in civil war or in foreign has permanently astonished their neighbours to the south, the east and the north. They are the most general in framing a policy and the most actual in pursuing it. Their incredible achievements have always the appearance of accidents. They are tenacious of the memory of defeats rather than of victories. They change more rapidly and with less reverence than any other men the external expression of their tireless effort, yet, more than any other men, they preserve – in spite of themselves – an original and unchanging spirit. Their boundaries are continually the same. They are acute and vivid in matters of reason, careless in those of judgement. A coward and a statesman are equally rare among them, yet their achievements are the result of prudence and their history is marked by a succession of silent and calculating politicians. Alone of European peoples the Gauls have, by a sort of habit, indulged in huge raids which seemed an expense of military passion to no purpose.

Hilaire Belloc, *Esto Perpetua*, 1906

The French are strangely unclub-able and unsocial.

Henry Adams, Letter to Charles Milnes Gaskell, 23 May 1907

We talk in a cant phrase of the Man in the Street, but the Frenchman is the man in the street. Things quite central for him are connected with these lamp-posts and pavements; everything from his meals to his martyrdoms.

G.K. Chesterton, *Tremendous Trifles*, 1909

German soldiers look at you as if they despised you, but French soldiers as if they despised you and themselves even more than you. It is a part, I suppose, of the realism of the nation which has made good at war and science and other things in which what is necessary is combined with what is nasty.

Ibid.

I would have loved it – without the French.

D.H. Lawrence, Letter to Catherine Carswell, 28 May 1920

The character of a nation, like its mind, is always determined, not by the masses of its citizens, but by a small minority of resolute and influential men. Nothing, for example, could be more absurd than the common notion that the French, as a people, are gallant, courageous and fond of hazard. The truth is that they are mainly dull shopkeepers and peace-loving peasants, and have been driven into all their wars of conquest by their masters, who are extraordinarily prehensile, and audacious.

H.L. Mencken, 'On the Nature of Man', in *Prejudices*, 4th Series, 1925

It seems to me the French are just worn out. And not nearly so much with the late great war, as with the pink nudities of women. The men are just worn out, making offerings on the shrine of Aphrodite, in elastic garters. And the women are worn out, keeping the men up to it. The rest is all nervous exasperation. And the table. One shouldn't forget that other four-legged mistress of man, more unwitherable than Cleopatra. The table. . . . But the Aphrodite, in a hard black hat opposite, when she has eaten herself also pink, is going to insist on further delights, to which somebody has got to play up. Weariness isn't the word for it.

D.H. Lawrence, 'Paris Letter – Laughing Horse', April 1926, *Phoenix*, 1936

Fifty million Frenchmen can't be wrong.

Attributed to Texas Guinan, *New York World-Telegram*, 21 March 1931

In a well-defined civilization with a solid historical background, such as for instance the French, you can easily discover the keynote of the French *esprit*: it is 'la gloire,' a most marked prestige psychology in its noblest as well as its most ridiculous forms. You find it in their speech, gestures, beliefs, in the style of everything, in politics, and even in science.

C.G. Jung, *The Complications of American Psychology* 1930

A Frenchman is at his very worst in uniform. . . .

How I hate the French police! And what rottenness there must be in a social system which needs or tolerates such law-keepers.

Eric Muspratt, *Wild Oats*, 1932

Oh, how I love humanity
With love so pure and pringlish
And how I hate the horrid French
Who never will be English.

G.K. Chesterton, *The World State*, 1932

The French . . . are a morbidly suspicious people.

Norman Douglas, *Looking Back*, 1933

One of my small daughters, bewildered, once said to us: 'But French people aren't *true*, are they?'

J.B. Priestley, *English Journey*, 1934

Sat on the verandah till 1.30 watching the moon make its way through the trees, and discussed all sorts of things. Said I accepted Nature and Metaphysics – 'Begad,' said George, 'you remind me of Carlyle' – but could not account for the meanness of the French.

James Agate, *Ego* (17 June 1932), 1935

For good or for ill the French people have been effective masters in their own house and have built as they chose upon the ruins of the old regime. They have done what they like. Their difficulty is to like what they have done.

Sir Winston Churchill, Letter, 18 September 1936

There's something Vichy about the French.

Ivor Novello, remark, 1941, quoted in Edward Marsh, *Ambrosia and Small Beer*, 1964

A Frenchman is first and foremost a *man*. He is likeable often just because of his weaknesses, which are always thoroughly human, even if despicable.

Henry Miller, 'Raimu', *The Wisdom of the Heart*, 1941

The Almighty in His infinite wisdom has not seen fit to create Frenchmen in the image of Englishmen.

Sir Winston Churchill, Speech in the House of Commons, 10 December 1942

The simple thing is to consider the French as an erratic and brilliant people, dressed either in blue blouses and berets or trick suits and Charvet ties, who have all the gifts except that of running their country.

James Cameron, *News Chronicle*, 18 January 1954, in *What a Way to Run the Tribe*, 1968

A bad liver is to a Frenchman what a nervous breakdown is to an American. Everyone has had one and everyone wants to talk about it.

Art Buchwald, *New York Herald Tribune*, 16 January 1958

Maybe the French will get a manned craft into space, if they can get a rocket strong enough to lift a bottle of wine.

David Brinkley, Newscast on NBC-TV, 15 December 1965

For two days now I have asked myself why the French frighten me. . . . In the last years I am timid as I walk along the lovely streets. It's as if all of France had become a too thin lady. Very thin ladies, any age, with hand sewing on them, have always frightened me. . . . The more bones that show on women the more inferior I feel.

Lillian Hellman, *An Unfinished Woman*, 1969

How lucky France was to have one foot in the Mediterranean; it modified the *acerbe* French northern character, and made the Midi a sort of filter, which admitted the precious influences which stretched back into pre-history.

Lawrence Durrell, *Sicilian Carousel*, 1977

They are children of this world, and they have the advantage of knowing it.

Conor Cruise O'Brien, *Observer*, 23 December 1979

French Women

I could heartily wish that there was an Act of Parliament for Prohibiting the Importation of *French* fopperies. The Female Inhabitants of our Island have already received very strong impressions from this ludicrous Nation . . . the whole Discourse and Behaviour of the *French* is to make the Sex more Fantastical, or (as they are pleased to term it,) more *awaken'd* than is consistent either with Virtue or Discretion.

Joseph Addison, *Spectator*, No. 45, 21 April 1711

There is a quality in which no woman in the world can compete with her, – it is in the power of intellectual irritation. She will draw wit out of a fool. She strikes with such address the chords of self-love, that she gives unexpected vigor and agility to fancy, and electrifies a body that appeared non-electric.

William Shenstone (before 1763), quoted in R.W. Emerson, *Letters and Social Aims*, 1876

A French woman is as great an adept at laughing an English woman into all contempt of fidelity to her husband, as married English women are in general, in preparing them during their first pregnancy, for the touch of the man-midwife, – and both from the same motive; i.e. to do as they have done, and bring all the sex upon a level.

Philip Thicknesse, *General Hints to Strangers who Travel in France*, 1789

The manners of the French women are fascinating, but I have never seen one yet without a beard which destroyed the effect of their sparkling eyes. As to their forms! – really, really, skeletons wrapped in lace and muslin and fringe.

Benjamin Robert Haydon, *Diary*, June 1814

The French ladies may be said rather to plaster than to paint.

Eliza Fay, *Original Letters from India* (28 June 1779), 1817

In France, when the heart of a woman sets sail,
On the ocean of wedlock its fortune to try,

Love seldom goes far in a vessel so frail,
But just pilots her off, and then bids her good-bye.

Thomas Moore, 'We May Roam through this World', *Irish Melodies*, 1807–35

The French women are often in the suburbs of beauty, but never enter the town.

Henry Luttrell, Remark to Thomas Moore, 13 June 1821

French woman dips into love like a duck into water, tis but a shake of the feathers & wag of the tail & all is well again but an English woman is like a heedless swan venturing into a pool who gets drowned.

Washington Irving, *Journal*, 1822

Landor . . . talks of hating all society. I told him that he reminded me of what I used to say – that I hated all Frenchwomen except all I had ever seen.

Henry Crabb Robinson, *Diary*, 17 September 1830

The French woman says, 'I am a woman and a Parisienne, and nothing foreign to me appears altogether human.'

Ralph Waldo Emerson, *Uncollected Lectures: Table Talk*, 1935

There is, in fact, no branch of human activity in which one is not liable, in France, to find a woman engaged. Women, indeed, are not priests; but priests are, more or less, women. They are not in the army, it may be said; but then they *are* the army.

Henry James, *A Little Tour in France*, 1882

The French bourgeois has everything in life to make him happy except beauty in his wife, and that is a dubious happiness.

Freya Stark, *Traveller's Prelude*, 1950

French Food

The French are commended and said to excell others in boyled meates, sawces and made dishes, vulgarly called Quelques choses, but in my opinion the larding of their meates is not commendable, whereby they take away all variety of taste, making all meates savor of Porke; and the French alone delight in mortified meates.

Fynes Moryson, *An Itinerary*, 1617

Their beef they cut out into such chops, that that which goeth there for a laudable dish, would be thought here a university commons new served from the hatch. A loin of mutton serves amongst them for three roastings, besides the hazard of making pottage with the rump. Fowl, also, they have in good plenty, . . . to say truth, that which they have is sufficient for nature and a friend, were it not for the mistress or the kitchen wench. I have heard much fame of the French cooks, but their skill lieth not in the neat handling of beef and mutton. They have (as generally have all this nation) good fancies, and are special fellows for the making of puff-pastes and the ordering of banquets. Their trade is not to fill the belly but the palate. . . . When you are risen, if you can digest the sluttishness of the cookery (which is most abominable at first sight) I dare trust you in a garrison.

Peter Heylin, *Microcosmus*, 1652

If hunger be the best sauce to meat, the French are certainly the worst cooks in the world; for what tables we have seen have been so delicately served, and so profusely, that, after rising from one of them, one imagines it impossible ever to eat again.

Thomas Gray, Letter to Richard West, 12 April 1739

The most exquisite diners of all nations say that the French are the most exquisite diners.

Walter Bagehot, 'One Difference Between France and England', *The Economist*, 12 September 1868

The French . . . have no notion of making the nourishment fit the clime.

Crosbie Garstin, *The Dragon and the Lotus*, 1928

The French do not understand cooking, only good cooking – this is where we score.

Cyril Connolly, 'England, Not My England', in *The Condemned Playground*, 1945

Italian cuisine merely presents Nature at its best. French cuisine is a challenge to Nature, it subverts Nature, it creates a new Nature of its own. It is an art.

Luigi Barzini, *The Italians*, 1964

Abbeville

Abbeville . . . a Towne that affords a most gracious aspect towards the hill from whence we descended; nor indeede dos it deceive the Eye, for it is handsomly built, and has many pleasant and useful streames passing through it, the maine river being the Somme which dos after wards discharge it selfe into the sea at St Valery almost in view of the Towne. . . . the Towne abounds in Gun-Smiths.

John Evelyn, *Diary*, November, 1643

*Was I in a condition to stipulate with death, as I am this moment with my apothecary, how and where I will take his glister – I should certainly declare against submitting to it before my friends; and therefore I never seriously think upon the mode and manner of this great catastrophe, which generally takes up and torments my thoughts as much as the catastrophe itself, but I constantly draw the curtain across it with the wish, that the *Disposer* of all things may so order it, that it happen not to me in my own house – but rather in some decent inn – at home, I know it, – the concern of my friends, and the last services of wiping my brows and smoothing my pillow, which the quivering hand of pale affection shall pay me, will so crucify my soul, that I shall die of a distemper which my physician is not aware of: but in an inn the few cold offices I wanted, would be purchased with a few guineas, and paid me with an undisturbed but punctual attention . . . but mark. This inn, should not be the inn at *Abbeville*.

Laurence Sterne, *Tristram Shandy*, Vol. vii, 1765

Abbeville . . . is the preface and interpretation of Rouen.

John Ruskin, *Praeterita*, 1885–9

Aigues Mortes

It can hardly be said to be alive, but if it is dead, it is very neatly embalmed.

Henry James, *A Little Tour in France*, 1882

Aigues Mortes presents quite the appearance of the walled town that a school-boy draws upon his slate, or that we see in the background of early Flemish pictures – a simple parallelogram, of a contour almost absurdly bare, broken at intervals by angular towers and square holes. . . . It is extraordinarily pictorial, and if it is a very small sister of Carcassonne, it has at least the essential features of the family. Indeed, it is even more like an image and less like a reality than Carcassonne.

Ibid.

Aix-les–Bains

. . . Arrived at Aix in Savoy, famous for its baths; which, as disagreeable things are generally the most salutary, ought, doubtless, to be of the greatest efficacy; for more uninviting objects one seldom meets with.

Advancing beneath a little eminence, partly rock, partly wall, we discovered the principal bath, filled with a blue reeking water, whose very steam is sufficient to seethe one, without further assistance.

William Beckford, *An Excursion to the Grande Chartreuse . . . in 1778*

Aix-les-Bains is a dirty longish village, approached by a beautiful walnut avenue set in the midst of gardens festooned with vineyards and surrounded by a craggy wall of mountains. Its main attraction is hot water.

M.F. Tupper, *Paterfamilias' Diary of Everybody's Tour*, 1856

Aix-en-Provence

The town was very clean; but so hot, and so intensely light, that when I walked out at noon it was like coming suddenly from the darkened room into crisp blue fire. The air was so very clear, that distant hills and rocky points appeared within an hour's walk; while the town immediately at hand – with a kind of blue wind between me and it – seemed to be white hot, and to be throwing off a fiery air from the surface.

Charles Dickens, *Pictures from Italy*, 1846

Alsace

Looking at a map of France, and reading histories of Louis XIV, never threw his conquest or seizure of Alsace into the light which travelling into it did: to cross a great range of mountains; to enter a level plain, inhabited by a people totally distinct and different from France, with manners, language, ideas, prejudices, and habits all different, made an impression of the injustice and ambition of such conduct, much more forcible than ever reading had done: so much more powerful are things than words.

Arthur Young, *Travels . . . [in] . . . France* (19 July 1789), 1792

Laissez les parler allemand, pourvu qu'ils sabrent en français.

Napoleon, attrib.

The plain of Alsace is to me one of the pleasantest anywhere, so genially productive, so well cultivated, and so cheerful, yet with the Vosges and the Black Forest and the Alps to hinder its being prosaic. . . . You know the people here are among the Frenchest of the French, in spite of their German Race and language. It strikes one as something unnatural to see this German town and German-speaking people all mad for joy at a victory gained by the French over other Germans. The fact speaks much for the French power of managing and attaching its conquests, but little for the German character.

Matthew Arnold, Letter to Miss Arnold, 25 June 1859

and Lorraine

We do not hesitate to say that as a general rule a nation gains, more man for man, by those districts of its country which supplement the weakness of its typical character than by those which are most characteristic and typical, so long as the former belong to it *willingly*, and really yield to it their characteristic genius and life. France needs German elements, so long as they embrace French rule gladly more probably than she needs any other elements of the national life. . . . Alsace and Lorraine are worth infinitely more in a moral point of view to France than they can be in a military point of view to Germany.

Walter Bagehot, 'Are Alsace and Lorraine Worth More to Germany or France?', *The Economist*, 24 September 1870

The Ballon d'Alsace is the knot of Europe.

Hilaire Belloc, *The Path to Rome*, 1902

The Alsatians do not sing as well as their storks.
Their storks are their statuettes.

Gertrude Stein, 'Accents in Alsace', *Geography and Plays*, 1922

Amboise

A little white-faced town, staring across an admirable bridge, and leaning, behind, as it were, against the pedestal of rock on which the dark castle masses itself. The town is so small, the pedestal so big, and the castle so high and striking, that the clustered houses at the base of the rock are like the crumbs that have fallen from a well-laden table.

Henry James, *A Little Tour in France*, 1882

The Chateau of Chanteloup
The Chateau of Chanteloup ought to be seen, as affording a superb specimen of the wretchedness of French taste.

Henry Matthews, *Diary of an Invalid*, 1820

Lake Annecy

There are one or two fine mountains in full view (7,000 ft. or so) but I found it impossible to be enthusiastic about lake scenery. It is like living in a picture postcard, especially when there is full sunshine.

Arnold Bennett, *Journal*, 6 September 1928

Antibes

There was no one at Antibes this summer except me, Zelda, the Valentinos, the Murphys, Mistinguett, Rex Ingram, Dos Passos, Alice Terry, the MacLeishes, Charlie Brackett, Maude Kahn, Esther Murphy, Marguerite Namara, E. Phillips Oppenheim, Mannes the violinist, Floyd Dell, Max and Crystal Eastman, ex-Premier Orlando, Etienne de Beaumont – just a real place to rough it, an escape from all the world.

F. Scott Fitzgerald, Letter to John Peale Bishop, Paris, September 1925

Arles

A European State is only a State, because it is a State of Europe. . . .

Now a man who recognises this will ask, 'Where could I find a model of the past of that Europe? In what place could I find the best single collection of all the forms which European energy has created, and of all the outward symbols in which its soul has been made manifest?' To such a man the answer should be given, 'You will find these things better in the town of *Arles* than in any other place.' A man asking such questions would mean to travel. He ought to travel to *Arles*.

Hilaire Belloc, *Hills and the Sea*, 1906

Avignon

L'Ile Sonnante
(The ringing island.)

Traditional, after Rabelais, or his imitators' *Cinquième Livre*, 1562 although it has been suggested that the Ile Sonnante of that book is not Papal Avignon, but Rome.

*Before I go further, let me get rid of my remark upon *Avignon*, which is this; That I think it wrong, merely because a man's hat has been blown off his head by chance the first night he comes to *Avignon*, – that he should therefore say, '*Avignon* is more subject to high winds than any town in all *France*:' for which reason I laid no stress upon the accident till I had inquired of the master of the inn about it, who telling me seriously it was so – and hearing, moreover, the windyness of *Avignon* spoke of in the country round about as a proverb – I set it down, merely to ask the learned what can be the cause.

Laurence Sterne, *Tristram Shandy*, Vol. vii, 1765

Avignon is remarkable for the number seven; having seven ports, seven parishes, seven colleges, seven hospitals, and seven monasteries; and I may add, I think, seven hundred bells, which are always making a horrid jingle; for they have no idea of ringing bells harmoniously in any part of France.

Philip Thicknesse, *A Year's Journey through France and Spain*, 1789

At Avignon I saw some large baths in the garden by the temple of Diana, built on the foundations of the old Roman ones. *Does anybody bathe here now?* we askt; for we could see no materials for the purpose.

No; the guide answered. *Before the Revolution, the rich used to bathe here; but they wanted to keep the baths to themselves; and the poor wanted to come too; and now nobody comes.*

What an epitome of a revolution!

J.C. and A. Hare, *Guesses at Truth*, 3rd edn, 1847

Palais des Papes
The Palais has little or no aesthetic interest. Its interest is archaeological and social. Only one open staircase.

All the many others, together with endless narrow corridors are cut in the thick walls (8 or 10 ft. thick), as it were secretly. And everywhere are little holes, through which everyone could be spied on by somebody else. An impression unpleasant, mean, and particularly mediaeval.

Arnold Bennett, *Journal*, 10 March 1926

The place is as intricate as it is vast, and as desolate as it is dirty. The imagination has, for some reason or other, to make more than the effort usual in such cases to restore and re-people it.

Henry James, *A Little Tour in France*, 1882

Bandol

I love this place more and more. One is conscious of it as I used to be conscious of New Zealand. I mean if I went for a walk there and lay down under a pine tree and looked up at the wispy clouds through the branches I came home plus the pine tree – don't you know? Here it's just the same.

Katherine Mansfield, Letter to J.M. Murry, October 1920

Les Baux

Les Beaux (this is where Dante got his idea of Hell Duncan said).

Virginia Woolf, *Diary*, 17 April 1928

Of the present inhabitants of Les Baux it were better not to speak.

Guide Book, quoted Rose Macaulay, *Pleasures of Ruins*, 1953

Bayonne

Bayonne is celebrated for its chocolate, hams, and the invention of the bayonet.

H. O'Shea, *A Guide to Spain*, 1865

Give me the back of the Bayonne.

Peter Forster, 'The Views that Please of the High Pyrenees', *Sunday Times*, 30 December 1979

Beaune

At Beaune . . . we found nothing good but the wine. . . .

Tobias Smollett, *Travels through France and Italy*, 1766

Beaune, a small French town surrounded only by Burgundy. Wine is so important in Beaune that they keep it in a museum.

Art Buchwald, *More Caviar*, 1958

Beauvais

Beauvais is called the *Pucelle* – yet, so far as I can see, she wears no stays – I mean, has no fortifications. . . .

Sir Walter Scott, *Diary*, 29 October 1826, in Lockhart, *Life of Scott*, 1838

Bernay

Dined, or rather starved, at Bernay, where for the first time I met with that wine of whose ill fame I had heard so much in England, that of being worse than small beer.

Arthur Young, *Travels . . . [in] . . . France* (19 May 1787), 1792

Berneval-sur-Mer

I am not responsible for the architecture of the chalet: all that I am responsible for at Berneval are the sunsets and the sea.

Oscar Wilde, Letter to Reginald Turner, Berneval, 31 July 1897

Besançon

He gave us a number of entertaining anecdotes about Besançon, his native town, from some of which it appeared that the ladies of that place were not the most virtuous in the world. The Marshall of the District was importuned to build a hospital to contain such unfortunate women as were diseased – 'In that case,' said the marshall 'we may as well erect a wall that shall encompass *the whole city*.'

Washington Irving, *Journal*, 21 May 1805

Besançon stands like a sort of peninsula in a horseshoe of river. . . . You will not learn from guide-books that the very tiles on the roofs seem to be of some quainter and more delicate colour than the tiles of all the other towns of the world; that the tiles look like the little clouds of some strange sunset, or like the lustrous scales of some strange fish. They will not tell you that in this town the eye cannot rest on anything without finding it in some way attractive and even elvish, a carved face at a street corner, a gleam of green fields through a stunted arch, or some unexpected colour for the enamel of a spire or dome.

G.K. Chesterton, *Tremendous Trifles*, 1909

Biarritz

The pleasant Brighton of Bayonne.

Richard Ford, *A Handbook for Travellers in Spain*, 1855

This wild, rocky little Gascon village.
H. O'Shea, *A Guide to Spain*, 1865

This place is more hellish than ever. *I*'m no Christian – Allah knows – but I feel like a Bunyan character in Vanity Fair. And yet *au fond*, they are no more than idle Englishry bent on having a good time: and apparently all-ignorant of the way to get it. Few Hebrews; and so far as I can make out, no Huns.
Rudyard Kipling, Letter to Rider Haggard, 31 March 1925

The Casino
The Casino, I hasten to add, has quite the air of an establishment frequented by gentlemen who look at ladies' windows with telescopes.
Henry James, *From Normandy to the Pyrenees*, 1876, in *Portraits of Places*, 1883

The Hotel du Palais
That Gilded Caravanserai of all the Unrealities.
Rudyard Kipling, Letter to Rider Haggard, 19 March 1925

Blois

The physicians of this place are as cheap as our English farriers, and generally as ignorant.
Joseph Addison, Letter to Mr Adams, December 1699

The chateau
The murders, or political executions perpetrated in this castle, though not uninteresting, were inflicted on, and by men that command neither our love nor our veneration. The character of the period, and of the men that figured in it, were alike disgusting. Bigotry and ambition, equally dark, insidious and bloody, allow no feelings of regret. The parties could hardly be better employed than in cutting each others' throats.
Arthur Young, *Travels . . . [in] . . . France* (11 September 1787), 1792

Bordeaux

Bordeaux is . . . dedicated to the worship of Bacchus in the most discreet form.
Henry James, *A Little Tour in France*, 1882

Bordeaux, the fourth city of France, and once, after London, York, and Winchester, of England, is no place for the sightseer; it is a climate, a rest-cure, a state of mind, whose principal charm is that there is nothing to see. . . .

For when we say there is nothing to see at Bordeaux, we mean that there is everything to feel, if we would enjoy the sensuous atmosphere of this Bristol three hundred and fifty miles south, an atmosphere witty, inquiring, earthy, a little complacent and provincial, the climate of eighteenth-century philosophers like Montesquieu, of its wise mayor who gave Shakespeare the idea for *The Tempest*, Michel de Montaigne, or of its last Roman Governor, whose vineyard at St Emilion is still famous as Chateau Ausone and who celebrated in one of his most charming poems the air of his native city, that green and yellow harmony of the South West, the climate of humanism.
Cyril Connolly, *Bordeaux*, 1951, in *Ideas and Places*, 1953

Boulogne

All I can say is that it is a large, old, fortified town, with more English in it than French.
Thomas Gray, Letter to Mrs Gray, his mother, 1 April 1739

The air of Boulogne encourages putrefaction.
Tobias Smollett, *Travels through France and Italy*, 1766

I was glad to see Boulogne, though I can scarcely tell why. . . .
Hester Lynch Thrale/Piozzi, *Observations . . . in the Course of a Journey*, 1789

It is well known that this place has long been the resort of great numbers of persons from England, whose misfortunes in trade, or extravagance in life, have made a residence abroad more agreeable than at home, It is easy to suppose that they find here a *level* of society that tempts them to herd in the same place.
Arthur Young, *Travels . . . [in] . . . France* (17 May 1787), 1792

Resurrection of many Irish friends whom I had thought no longer *above* the *world*: Tom Grady, who told me that there was some other region (unknown) to which those, who exploded at Boulogne, were blown. Told me of some half-pay English officers, who having exhausted all other means of raising the wind, at last levied subscriptions for a private theatre, and having announced the 'Forty Thieves' for the first representation, absconded on the morning of the day with the money.
Thomas Moore, *Journal*, 15 April 1822

Suppose us fairly now afloat,
Till Boulogne mouth receives our Boat.
But, bless us! what a numerous band
Of cockneys anglicise the strand!
Delinquent bankrupts, leg-bail'd debtors,
Some for the news, and some for letters –
With hungry look and tarnished dress,

French shrugs and British surliness.
Sick of the country for their sake
Of them and France *French leave* I take.

Samuel Taylor Coleridge, *The Delinquent Travellers*, 1824

You are going to Boulogne, the city of debts, peopled by men who never understood arithmetic.

Sydney Smith, Letter to Miss Lucie Austin, 22 July 1835

It is a strange, mongrel, merry place, this town of Boulogne. . . .

W.M.Thackeray, *The Paris Sketch Book*, 1840

I never saw a better instance of our countrymen than this place. Because it is accessible it is genteel to say it is of no character, quite English, nothing continental about it and so forth. It is as quaint, picturesque, good a place as I know; the boatmen and fishing-people quite a race apart, and some of their villages as good as the fishing-villages on the Mediterranean. The Haute Ville, with a walk all round it on the ramparts, charming. The country walks, delightful. It is the best mixture of town and country (with sea air into the bargain) I ever saw; everything cheap, everything good; and please God I shall be writing on those ramparts next July!

Charles Dickens, Letter, 1852, in Forster, *Life of Dickens*, 1872–3

Not but that Boulogne is a very interesting place, far more so than its popular characteristics had led me to expect: cockneyfied holidaymaking, the bankrupt's refuge, the worrying Douane halfway between London and Paris to be scuffled through and left behind as quickly as possible, the shabby French Brighton, the pestilential fishing town, these, with reminiscences of sea-sickness, and a welcome of exorbitant charges, amount to the common thoughts of ignorance respecting Boulogne.

M.F. Tupper, *Paterfamilias' Diary of Everybody's Tour*, 1856

Bourges

Bourges is a *ville de province* in the full sense of the term, especially as applied invidiously. The streets, narrow, tortuous, and dirty, have very wide cobblestone; the houses, for the most part, are shabby, without local colour. The look of things is neither modern nor antique – a kind of mediocrity of middle age. There is an enormous number of blank walls – walls of gardens, of courts, of private houses – that avert themselves from the street, as if in natural chagrin at there being so little to see. . . . In the course of six weeks spent *en province*, . . . I saw few places that had not more expression than Bourges.

Henry James, *A Little Tour in France*, 1882

The Cathedral
While here, a solid outer zone,
The hunched grey shoulders burdened rise,
As thrust and counter-thrust agreeing
Storm reluctant skies,
Within, the easy ascent of stone
Wins to such no-man's land of being
Matter might seem an exercise
For faith, spirit for seeing.

G. Rostrevor Hamilton, 'Cathedral: Bourges', *The Carved Stone*, 1952

Brittany

The Bretons are probably among the most conservative people in Europe; most Frenchmen consider them frankly pagan.

James Cameron, *Point of Departure*, 1967

Brittany and Anjou
One is haunted by the name Plantagenet there. The moment one enters Anjou, from which the family came, the broom begins, and Brittany seems all in flower with it, the furze mixed.

Matthew Arnold, Letter to his mother, 8 May 1859
(Broom = *Planta genista*)

Burgundy

Watrish *Burgundy*.

William Shakespeare, *King Lear*, *c.* 1605–6

Calais

When I am dead and opened, you shall find 'Calais lying in my heart.'

Mary Tudor/Queen Mary, Remark (before 1558), in Holinshed, *Chronicles*, 1577

Calais is an extraordinary well fortified Place consider'd in the old Castle, & new Citadell reguarding the Sea: the Haven consists of a long banke of Sand lying opposite to it: The Market-place and Church are very remarkable things, besides those reliques of our once dominion there, so as I remember there was engraven in stone upon the front of an ancient dwelling which was shew'd us, these words, God save the King, in English, together with the name of the Architect and date: The walls of the Towne are likewise very substantial, but the situation towards the Land not

Pleasant in the least, by reason of the Marishes and low-grounds about it.

John Evelyn, *Diary*, 11 November 1643

To speak sincerely, Calais surprised me more than anything I have seen since. . . . The farther I travel, the less I wonder at anything: a few days reconcile one to a new spot, or an unseen custom; and men are so much the same everywhere, that one scarce perceives any change of situation.

Horace Walpole, Letter to Richard West, 24 January 1740

Calais is a sort of enlarged King's Bench prison; the English fugitives live within *the rules*, and the French inhabitants make it a rule to oppress and distress them.

Philip Thicknesse, *A Year's Journey through France and Spain*, 1789

There is . . . something very pleasing in the manners and appearance of the people of Calais, that prepossesses you in their favour. A national reflection might occur, that when Edward III. took Calais, he turned out the old inhabitants, and peopled it almost entirely with our own countrymen; but unfortunately the manners are not English.

Mary Shelley, *History of a Six Weeks' Tour* (29 July 1814), 1817

Every one is struck with the excessive ugliness (if I may apply the word to any *human* creatures) of the fish-women of Calais, and *that* no one can forget. Here are dull shops, quiet streets, a large Cathedral, and a large *Place* or square with Town-hall.

Dorothy Wordsworth, *Journal*, 11 July 1820

It is an unsettled question with me whether I shall leave Calais something handsome in my will, or whether I shall leave it my malediction. I hate it so much, and yet I am always so very glad to see it, that I am in a state of constant indecision on this subject. . . . I know where it is beforehand, I keep a look out for it, I recognise its landmarks when I see any of them, I am acquainted with its ways, and I know – and I can bear – its worst behaviour.

Malignant Calais! Low-lying alligator, evading the eye-sight and discouraging hope! Dodging flat streak, now on this bow, now on that, now anywhere, now everywhere, now nowhere! In vain Cap Grinez, coming frankly forth into the sea, exhorts the failing to be stout of heart and stomach: sneaking Calais, prone behind its bar, invites emetically to despair. Even when it can no longer quite conceal itself in its muddy dock, it has an evil way of falling off, has Calais, which is more hopeless than its invisibility. The pier is all but on the bowsprit, and you think you are there – roll, roar, wash! – Calais has retired miles inland, and Dover has burst forth to look for it. It has a last dip and slide in its character, has Calais, to be especially commended to the infernal gods. Thrice accursed be that garrison-town, when it dives under the boat's keel and comes up a league or two to the right, with the packet shivering and spluttering and staring about for it!

Charles Dickens, 'The Calais Night Mail', in *The Uncommercial Traveller*, 1861

Calais is properly a Flemish, not French town . . . ; it has no wooden houses, which mark the essential French civic style, but only brick or chalk ones, with originally, most of them, good indented Flemish stone gables and tiled roofs. True French roofs are never tiled, but slated, and have no indented gables, but bold dormer windows rising over the front, never, in any pretty street groups of them, without very definite expression of pride. Poor little Calais had indeed nothing to be proud of, but it had a quaint look of contentment with itself on those easy terms; some dignity in its strong ramparts and drawbridge gates; and better than dignity, real power and service in the half-mile of pier, reaching to the low-tide breakers across its field of sand.

John Ruskin, *Praeterita*, 1885–9

Women of

'Tis said, fantastic ocean doth enfold
The likeness of whate'er on land is seen;
But if the Nereid sisters and their Queen,
Above whose heads the tide so long hath rolled,
The Dames resemble whom we here behold,
How fearful were it down through opening waves
To sink, and meet them in their fretted caves,
Withered, grotesque, immeasurably old,
And shrill and fierce in accent!

William Wordsworth, *Memorials of a Tour on the Continent*, 'Fish-Women on Landing at Calais', 1820, 1821

Cannes

*'Decent men don't go to Cannes with the – well with the kind of ladies you mean.' 'Don't they?' Strether asked with an interest in decent men that amused her. 'No; elsewhere, but not to Cannes. Cannes is different.'

Henry James, *The Ambassadors*, 1903

We went to Cannes. Its eccentric houses, villas, and toy palaces are nearly all built for pleasure; one could place the Pyramids, the Taj Mahal and Grant's Tomb into the center of it and they would scarcely be noticed.

Ludwig Bemelmans, *How to Travel Incognito*, 1952

Pleasure is still the biggest industry. Out-of-season Cannes feels not only empty, but strangely empty, a town waiting: and you realize that this is all really the stage, beautifully equipped, of an immense theatre where the protagonists pay to act. For finally it is the other visitors the visitor comes here to see.

William Sansom, *Blue Skies Brown Studies*, 1961

Carcassonne

Everything in the Cité is little; you can walk round the walls in twenty minutes. On the drawbridge of the chateau, which, with a picturesque old face, flanking towers, and a dry moat, is to-day simply a bare *caserne*, lounged half a dozen soldiers, unusually small. Nothing could be more odd than to see these objects enclosed in a receptacle which has much of the appearance of an enormous toy. The Cité and its population vaguely reminded me of an immense Noah's ark.

Henry James, *A Little Tour in France*, 1882

Carcassonne differs from other monumental towns in this: that it preserves exactly the aspect of many centuries up to a certain moment, and from that moment has 'set,' and has suffered no further change. . . .

No other town can present so vivid and clean-cut a fossil of the seven hundred years into which poured and melted all the dissolution of antiquity, and out of which was formed or crystallized the highly specialized diversity of our modern Europe.

Hilaire Belloc, *Hills and the Sea*, 1906

Chablais *(formerly Italian under the House of Savoy)*

Conversing with an inhabitant of the country, I asked him whether the people were contented and happy under the government of Sardinia; 'Oh yes,' said he, 'we are as happy as fish in a frying pan.'

Henry Matthews, *Diary of an Invalid*, 1820

Chalons *(and Lyons)*

Unless you would like to dwell on an enormous plain, with jagged rows of irregular poplars on it, that look in the distance like so many combs with broken teeth: and unless you would like to pass your life without the possibility of going up-hill, or going up anything but stairs: you would hardly approve of Chalons as a place of residence.

You would probably like it better, however, than Lyons. . . .

Charles Dickens, *Pictures from Italy*, 1846

Chantilly (the chateau of)

Chantilly! – magnificence is its reigning character; it is never lost. There is not taste or beauty enough to soften it into milder features. . . .

The labyrinth is the only complete one I have seen, and I have no inclination to see another: it is in gardening what a rebus is in poetry.

Arthur Young, *Travels . . . [in] . . . France* (25 May 1787), 1792

I cannot forbear mentioning the stables; one would think that Swift had been the architect; as the Hoynums of this prince are as magnificently lodged as any prince in Europe is. I really imagined the stables had been the chateau, and the chateau the stables.

Philip Thicknesse, *Observations on the Customs and Manners of the French Nation*, 1766

Chambéry

You know this town is very old and ill built, but is wholly inhabited by the poor Savoyard Nobillity, who are very well bred and extreamly carressing to strangers.

Lady Mary Wortley Montagu, Letter to her husband, 15 November 1741

Here is the most profound peace and unbounded plenty, that is to be found in any corner of the universe; but not one rag of money.

Lady Mary Wortley Montagu, Letter to Lady Pomfret, 3 December 1741

Chamberri, . . . is a little nasty old hole.

Horace Walpole, Letter to Richard West, 11 November 1739

Chamonix / Chamouni

See also under Mont Blanc

Last, let us turn to Chamouny that shields
With rocks and gloomy woods her fertile fields:
Five streams of ice amid her cots descend,
And with wild flowers, and blooming orchards blend; –
A scene more fair than what the Grecian feigns
Of purple lights and ever-vernal plains;
Here all the seasons revel hand in hand:
'Mid lawns and shades by breezy rivulets fanned,
They sport beneath that mountain's matchless height
That holds no commerce with the summer night.
From age to age, throughout his lonely bounds
The crash of ruin fitfully resounds;
Appalling havoc! but serene his brow,
Where daylight lingers on perpetual snow;
Glitter the stars above, and all is black below.

William Wordsworth, *Descriptive Sketches*, 1791–2, pub. 1793

The Arve at Chamonix
Thus thou Ravine of Arve – dark, deep Ravine –
Thou many-coloured, many-voiced vale,
Over whose pines, and crags, and caverns sail
Fast cloud shadows and sunbeams: awful scene,
Where Power in likeness of the Arve comes down
From the ice gulphs that gird his secret throne,
Bursting through these dark mountains like the flame
Of lightning thro' the tempest; – thou dost lie,
Thy giant brood of pines around thee clinging,
Children of elder time, in whose devotion
The chainless winds still come and ever came
To drink their odours, and their mighty swinging
To hear – an old and solemn harmony;
Thine earthly rainbows stretched across the sweep
Of the ethereal waterfall, whose veil
Robes some unsculptured image; the strange sleep
Which when the voices of the desart fail
Wraps all in its own deep eternity; –
Thy caverns echoing to the Arve's commotion,
A loud, lone sound no other sound can tame;
Thou art pervaded with that ceaseless motion,
Thou art the path of that unresting sound –
Dizzy Ravine!

Percy Bysshe Shelley, *Mont Blanc, Lines Written in the Vale of Chamouni*, July 1816

This place is altogether the Paradise of Wilderness.

Lord Byron, Letter to Augusta Leigh 14 September 1816

I remember at Chamouni – in the very eyes of Mont Blanc – hearing another woman – English also – exclaim to her party – 'did you ever see any thing more *rural*' – as if it was Highgate or Hampstead – or Brompton – or Hayes. – '*Rural*' quotha! – Rocks – pines – torrents – Glaciers – Clouds – and Summits of eternal snow far above them – and '*Rural!*'

Lord Byron, Letter to Augusta Leigh, 18 September 1816, *Alpine Journal*

O, Chamouni! thou fairy snow-clad maid,
(For to what else can I thy charms compare?)
And must I say farewell! – Alas! farewell
To those calm hours of solitary peace
In which alone, unheeded and unknown,
My eyes have revelled o'er thy naked form;
Where, hidden from the world, its noise and cares,
Between the rising of thy snowy breasts
A pillow and a resting place I found. . . .

Charles Tennant, *A Tour, etc.*, 1824

If one might suppose Nature studious to exhibit some favourite object with all possible advantages of position, and the happiest attendant circumstances, I should believe she had prepared the Vale of Chamouni for the perfect exhibition of Mont Blanc.

Sir T.N. Talfourd, *Vacation Rambles*, 1844

Every day here I seem to see further into nature and into myself – and into futurity.

John Ruskin, attrib.

Source of River Arveron
Pouring still, but I got out before dinner during a fine blink, which lasted just long enough to let me, by almost running, and leaping all the streams, reach the end of the pine wood next the source of the Arveron. There I had to turn to the left to the wooden bridge, when beheld a sight new to me; an avalanche had evidently taken place from the (upper) glacier into the very bed of the great cataract, and the stream was as nearly choked as could be with balls and ellipsoids of ice, from the size of its common stones, to that of a portmanteau, which were rolling down with it wildly generally swinging out and in of the water as it waved; but when they came to the shallow parts, tumbled and tossed over one another, and then plunging back into the deep water like so many stranded porpoises, spinning as they went down, and showing their dark backs with wilder swings after their plunge, – white, as they emerged, black, owing to their clearness as seen in the water; the stream itself of a pale clay-colour, opaque, larger by one half than ever I saw it, and running, as I suppose, not less than ten miles an hour; the whole mass, water and ice, looking like some thick paste full of plume, or ill-made pine-apple ice, with quantities of fruit in it, and the whole looking like a solid body; for the nodules of ice hardly changed their relative position during the quarter of a minute they were severally in sight, going down in a mass, thundering and rumbling against the piles of the bridge. It made me giddy to look at it; and the more, because, on raising the eye, there was always the great cataract itself startling one, as if it had just begun, and seeming to increase every instant, bounding and hurling itself hither and thither, as if it was striving to dash itself to pieces, not falling because it could not help it; and behind there was a fearful storm coming up by the Breven, its grisly clouds warping up, as it seemed, against the river and cataract, with pillars of hail behind.

John Ruskin, *Journal*, 17 June 1849, quoted in *Praeterita*, 1885–9

When the first sublime and overpowering impression of Chamonix and the majesty and gloom of its narrow valley wore off, it began to oppress me, and long before we got away I felt as if we were in a huge grave.

W.J. Stillman, *The Autobiography of a Journalist*, 1901 – of 1860

Powerful telescopes are numerous in Chamonix. These huge brass tubes, mounted on their scaffoldings, and pointing skyward from every choice vantage-ground, have the formidable look of artillery, and give the town the general aspect of getting ready to repel a charge of angels.

Mark Twain, *A Tramp Abroad*, 1880

Chartres

The place is pictorial, in a shabby, third-rate, poverty-stricken degree. . . . Most of the streets of Chartres are crooked lanes, winding over the face of the steep hill, the summit of the hill being occupied by half a dozen little open squares, which seem like reservoirs of the dullness and stillness that flow through the place. . . . Chartres gives us an impression of extreme antiquity, but it is an antiquity that has gone down in the world.

Henry James, *Chartres*, 1876, in *Portraits of Places*, 1883

All the steam in the world could not, like the Virgin, build Chartres.

Henry Adams, *The Education of Henry Adams*, 1906

We visited Chartres again on the way back to Paris – just before dark. We went into the Cathedral just in time to see the blue of heaven (but they'd lit a few electric beastly lights – I found a switch just near the west door and was bold and impudent enough – no vergers being visible – to jolly well turn all the lights of the nave out! It was grand, the church nearly dark, and only light coming through the West windows and the windows of the apse . . . then I turned them on again and we hastily departed.)

Eric Gill, Letter to the Rev. Desmond Chute, 24 January 1937

Châteaudun

Here is one of the prettiest views in the world . . . and a ruin of about four-score houses. . . . The inhabitants tell you that the fire which has been the occasion of it was put out by a miracle; and that in its full rage it immediately ceased at the sight of Him that in His lifetime rebuked the winds and waves with a look. He was brought hither in the disguise of a wafer, and was assisted, I don't question, with several tuns of water.

Joseph Addison, Letter to Mr Wortley Montagu, 23 July 1700

Chinon

Take a ramble through the gloomy picturesque old town. Houses projecting over the street, some of wood – some of stone with little tourelles at the corners. No lamps. Now and then a clatter of a pair of wooden shoes and a lantern approaches. Person in shade with strong light before puts one in mind of the line in fairy tale

Behind me night – before me day
That none may give my secret way

get into path winding up to old castle – lofty broken tower, with pinnacles – rising lastly on hill. Find ourselves on the brink of deep dark chasm or fosse – only aware of it by seeing at distance a dark shadowy bridge stretching across it to the town and wide arches of the bridge – catch glimpses of water far below with lights gleaming in it – we are now aware of the deep chasm which we were incautiously approaching. Walk to bridge. Dimly seen – no parapet – whitish path worn along the centre – deep chasms each side – town away below. River seen dimly winding – lights here and there in houses – distant bark of dogs. Cross the bridge to old tower of castle. Fearful lest dog should rush out of ruined arch way & startle me when on the dizzy pass of the bridge. Peter hesitates to cross as he hears steps approaching along the edge of the moat. a man passes him – he then crosses. Clock strikes 9 from old tower. vibrations of the clock.

All is indistinct and shadowy. Have never felt so impressed with awe and a kind of horror – on visting any ruin. The darkness of the night – a partial star light. The depth of the fosse the solitary ruin & the vast and uncertain prospect below of town and stream; gloomy landscape. . . .

Monday October 18
Get breakfast with some delay. Visited the Chateau of Chinon. Saw the place where we had felt such awe last night – looked quite difft by day.

Washington Irving, *Journal*, 17–18 October 1824

Combourg

To Combourg, the country has a savage aspect; husbandry not much further advanced, at least in skill than among the Hurons, which appears incredible amidst inclosures; the people almost as wild as their country, and their town of Combourg one of the most brutal filthy places that can be seen; mud houses, no windows, and a pavement so broken, as to impede all passengers, but ease none – yet here is a chateau, and inhabited; who is this Mons. de Chateaubriant, the owner, that has nerves strung for a residence amidst such filth and poverty?

Arthur Young, *Travels . . . [in] . . . France* (1 September 1788), 1792

Condom

*There's many a mile between Condom in Gascogne and Pussy in Savoiè.

Vladimir Nabokov, *Transparent Things*, 1972

Chateau de Coucy

Roi je ne suis
Prince ni comte aussi;
Je suis le Sire de Coucy.

Anon., quoted Henry James, *Portraits of Places*, 1883

Coutances

and Boston

I have rarely felt New England at its highest ideal power as it appeared to me, beautified and glorified, in the Cathedral of Coutances. Since then our ancestors have steadily declined and run until we have reached pretty nearly the bottom. They have played their little part according to the schedule. They have lost their religion, their art, and their military tastes. They cannot now comprehend the meaning of what they did at Mont St Michel. They have kept only the qualities which were most useful, with a dull instinct recalling dead associations. So we get Boston.

Henry Adams, Letter to Brooks Adams, 8 September, 1895

Dieppe

This Towne is situated betweene two Mountaines not unpleasantly; is washed on the north by our English Seas: The Port is commodious, but the entrance difficult: It has one very ample and faire streete, in which a pretty Church: In the afternoone I walked up the hill to view the Fort Pollet which consists of a strong Earth Worke and commands the Haven, as on the other side dos the Castle which is also well fortified with the Citadel before it; nor is the towne it selfe a little strong: This place exceedingly abounds in workemen that make and sell curiosities of Ivory and Tortoise shells, in which they turne and make many rare toyes; & indeed whatever the East Indys afford of Cabinets, Purcelan, natural and exotic rarities are here to be had with abundant choyce.

John Evelyn, *Diary*, 21 March 1644

This town presents a very agreeable and romantic appearance to strangers. It is cut up into a number of distinct divisions by canals, drawbridges, and bastions, as if to intercept the progress of an enemy. The best houses, too, are shut up in close courts and high walls on the same principle, that is, to stand a further siege in the good old times. There are rows of lime-trees on the quay, and some of the narrow streets running from it look like wells. This town is a picture to look at; it is a pity that it is not a nosegay, and that the passenger who ventures to explore its nooks and alleys is driven back again by 'a compound of villainous smells,' which seem to grow out of the ground. In walking the streets, one must take one's nose with one, and that sense is apt to be offended in France, as well as in Scotland. Is it hence called in French *the organ of sense?*

William Hazlitt, *Notes of a Journey through France and Italy*, 1826

Dunkirk

Here are gate-ways and drawbridges – a parade of strength with shabbiness and tendency to decay. Soldiers not spruce like ours, several washing their linen in the moats. *Dunkirk* is however a very pretty town.

Dorothy Wordsworth, *Journal*, 12 July 1820

Epernay

The country about Epernay seemed to me to have a charm of its own. It stretched away in soft undulations that were pricked all over with little stakes muffled in leaves. The effect, at a distance was that of vast surfaces, long, subdued billows, of pincushion. . . .

Henry James, *Rheims and Laon: A Little Tour*, 1877, in *Portraits of Places*, 1883

Fécamp

Maupassant was born here but his mother concealed the fact.

James Joyce, Letter to Harriet Shaw Weaver, Fécamp, 27 July 1925

Ferney-Voltaire *(en route from Geneva)*

Beautiful spot: the country here all so rich and so comfortably laid out; in short, so like England, with the addition of the romantic to the comfortable – a rare mixture.

Thomas Moore, *Journal*, 23 September 1819

Voltaire's house at

My hypochondria began to muse. I was dull to find how much this resembled any other house in the country.

James Boswell, *Journal*, 26 December 1764

So this was Ferney! This was the house that Voltaire built, these were the trees he planted. . . . Craning our noses to the left, we could see the chapel. It was a small and simple structure, and it looked a trifle *moisi*. I cannot think of the right English equivalent of 'moisi'. 'Mouldy' will not do. 'Moisi' must stand. After all, we are in France. That was always the advantage of Ferney – it was just in France, and Voltaire, who preferred a pop-hole to a moat, could be over the border into Switzerland if he felt nervous, and back again if his nerves relaxed or reversed. . . . Lucky, happy we, to get this last peep at one of the symbols of European civilization. Civilization. Humanity. Enjoyment. That was what the agreeable white building said to us, that was what we carried away. It was not a large building, and that has been part of the disaster. It was too small to cope with the modern world. A Ferney today would have to be enormous, with rolling staircases, and microphones, if it was to function proportionally, and if it was enormous, could it be Ferney? Even Voltaire felt that he saw too many people, and that the universe, though fortunately bounded by Russia, was upon too cumbrous a scale. He could just illuminate it, but only just, and he died without knowing that he was the last man who would ever perform such a feat, and that Goethe would die asking for more light. On the crest of a wave, Ferney sparkled. The boundaries of the universe were to expand bewilderingly, the common people were to neglect the pursuit of agriculture, and, worst of all, the human make-up was to reveal deadnesses, and depths which no acuteness could penetrate, and no benignity heal.

E.M. Forster, 'Ferney', 1940, *Two Cheers for Democracy*, 1951

Ferrieres

Ferrieres (which is the principal country seat of the Rothschilds in France) stands in splendid woods through which we drove for some two miles before reaching the chateau. The house itself is disappointing, '*une commode renversée*,' as Bismarck called it when he slept there during the Prussian occupation. . . . Inside it is like a monstrous Pall Mall club, decorated in the most outrageous Louis Philippe taste. . . .

Wilfred Scawen Blunt, Diary, 16 October 1892, *My Diaries*, 1919

Flavigny

As I came into Flavigny I saw at once that it was a place on which a book might easily be written, for it had a church built in the seventeenth century, when few churches were built outside great towns, a convent, and a general air of importance that made of it that grand and noble thing, that primary cell of the organism of Europe, that best of all Christian associations – a large village.

Hilaire Belloc, *The Path to Rome*, 1902

Fontainebleau

The King has humoured the genius of the place, and only made use of so much art as is necessary to help and regulate nature without reforming her too much.

Joseph Addison, Letter to William Congreve, December 1699

*All you need say of *Fontainebleau* (in case you are ask'd) is, that it stands about forty miles (south *something*) from *Paris*, in the middle of a large forest – That there is something great in it – That the king goes there once, every two or three years, with his whole court, for the pleasure of the chase. . . .

Laurence Sterne, *Tristram Shandy*, Vol. vii, 1765

The true reason of the monument's preservation is that it is too big to destroy. The later age has not the courage to raze it and parcel it and sell it, and give it to the poor. It is a defiance to the later age of the age departed. Like a gigantic idol, it is kept gilded and tidy at terrific expense by a cult which tempers fear with disdain.

Arnold Bennett, *Paris Nights*, 1913

The Forest of Fontainebleau

Without being informed, I knew that it was a great forest, because against the first trees there was a large board which said, 'General Instructions for reading the signposts in the forest,' and then a lot of details. No forest that was not a great forest, a mazy forest, and a dangerous forest to get lost in, would have had a notice board like that.

Ibid.

Glacier des Bossons

We saw this glacier, which comes close to the fertile plain, as we passed, its surface was broken into a thousand unaccountable figures: conical and pyramidical crystalizations, more than fifty feet in height, rise from its surface, and precipices of ice, of dazzling splendour, overhang the woods and meadows of the vale. This glacier winds upwards from the valley, until it joins the masses of frost from which it was produced above, winding through its own ravine like a bright belt flung over the black region of pines. There is more in all these scenes than mere magnitude of proportion: there is a majesty of outline; there is an awful grace in the very colours which invest these wonderful shapes – a charm which is peculiar to them, quite distinct even from the reality of their unutterable greatness.

Percy Bysshe Shelley, Letter to T.P. Esq. (22 July 1816), from *History of a Six Weeks' Tour, etc.*, 1817

The Grande Chartreuse

In our little journey up to the Grande Chartreuse, I do

not remember to have gone ten paces without an exclamation there was no restraining: not a precipice, not a torrent, not a cliff, but is pregnant with religion and poetry. There are certain scenes that would awe an atheist into belief, without the help of other argument. One need not have a very fantastic imagination to see spirits there at noon-day: you have Death perpetually before your eyes, only so far removed as to compose the mind without frighting it.

Thomas Gray, Letter from Turin, 16 November 1739

Grenoble

Now have I seen, in Graisivaudan's vale,
The fruits that dangle and the vines that trail,
The poplars standing up in bright blue air,
The silver turmoil of the broad Isère
And sheer pale cliffs that wait through Earth's long noon
Till the round Sun be colder than the Moon.

Mine be the ancient song of Travellers:
I hate this glittering land where nothing stirs:
I would go back, for I would see again
Mountains less vast, a less abundant plain,
The Northern Cliffs clean-swept with driven foam,
And the rose-garden of my gracious home.

James Elroy Flecker, *From Grenoble*, *c.* 1914

Joigny

*For JOIGNY – the less, I think, one says of it, the better.

Laurence Sterne, *Tristram Shandy*, Vol. vii, 1765

Juan-les-Pins

This is supposed to be the most popular 'rising' resort on the Riviera. . . . If Juan les Pins 'rises' any further, the beach, like New York, will have to rise upwards and be arranged somehow in two storeys.

Arnold Bennett, *Journal*, 1929, 1930

Languedoc

*There is nothing more pleasing to a traveller – or more terrible to travel-writers, than a large rich plain; especially if it is without great rivers or bridges; and presents nothing to the eye, but one unvaried picture of plenty; for after they have once told you that 'tis delicious! or delightful! (as the case happens) – that the soil was grateful, and that nature pours out all her abundance, &c. . . . they have then a large plain upon their hands, which they know not what to do with – and which is of little or no use to them but to carry them to some town; and that town, perhaps of little more, but a new place to start from to the next plain – and so on.

– This is most terrible work; judge, if I don't manage my plains better.

Laurence Sterne, *Tristram Shandy*, Vol. vii, 1765

Lanslebourg

The valley of the Lanneburg is itself, the most strange wild place you can conceive, in some parts grotesque, in others awfully terrible. The rocks rise around you so fantastically, that you might almost think yourself transported to a place which nature had made a repository of these stupendous productions, rather with a view of fixing them hereafter in appropriate situations, than of exhibiting them here.

Eliza Fay, *Original Letters from India*, (17 June 1779), 1817

La Rochelle

I do not find them so gentle and debonair to strangers, nor so hospitable as the rest of *France*; but I excuse them for it, in regard it is commonly so with all Republic and Hans Towns, whereof this smells very rank.

James Howell, 'Letter to Sir John North, Knight, from Rochel, 8 October 1620', *Familiar Letters*, 1645

La Rochelle . . . from the moment I entered . . . I perceived to be a fascinating little town, a most original mixture of brightness and dullness.

Henry James, *A Little Tour in France*, 1882

I won't throw you back by describing the horrors of the yellow and red muckings in the windows of *that* Cathedral. The Port with its fishing boats and mariners was the thing to see – and the arcaded, almost Spanish-style streets. Nice to notice how the *real* progress of civilization translates itself into improved sanitary plumbing. Four years ago I could have told you a lot about the W.C.'s of the La Rochelle inn and elsewhere. Now they are falling into line with the rest of their kind. And to think that twenty years ago I (and a few others) in automobile, braved all the horrors of the Unclean South just to make men a little purer and loftier in their habits! But as a race the Latin ought not to be trusted with plugs to pull etc., without an examination. Here's really valuable work for the League of Nations.

Rudyard Kipling, Letter to Rider Haggard, 19 March 1925

Lascaux

Lascaux is the Parthenon of prehistory.
Cyril Connolly, 'Dordogne', in *Ideas and Places*, 1953

Lille

Where everything appears to me just like England, at least, just by it.
Hester Lynch Piozzi, *Observations . . . in the Course of a Journey*, 1789

Limousin

Limousin, the country which has bred more popes and fewer lovers than any other in the world.
Jean Giraudoux, *Duel of Angels, [Pour Lucrèce]*, trans. Christopher Fry, 1953

Loire River

I should suppose the reputation of the Loire must have originated from persons who either had never seen it at all, or only below Angers, where in truth it merits every *éloge*. From that city to Nantes it is, probably, one of the finest rivers in the world, the breadth of the stream, the islands of woods, the boldness, culture, and richness of the coast, all conspire, with the animation derived from the swelling canvass of active commerce, to render that line eminently beautiful; but for the rest of its immense course, it exhibits a stream of sand; it rolls shingle through vales instead of water, and is an uglier object than I could possibly have conceived, unless I had actually seen it.
Arthur Young, *Travels . . . [in] . . . France* (1787–9), 1792

One of the most wonderful rivers in the world, mirroring from sea to source a hundred cities and five hundred towers.
Oscar Wilde, Letter to George Lewis Junior, November 1880

Chateaux of the Loire
An American woman, a tourist, a refugee from a conducted tour of the Chateaux de la Loire. She dismissed the historic safari with the words: 'Nothing but thick walls and running comment.'
Ludwig Bemelmans, *How to Travel Incognito*, 1952

Lourdes

At the end of the information given about a town in the guidebook you often find a mention of its speciality. For Lourdes, it says: *'Spécialité: Chocolat.'*
James Thurber, *My World and Welcome to It*, 1942

Lyons, and the rivers Rhône and Saône

We are at the ancient and celebrated Lugdunum, a city situated upon the confluence of the Rhone and Saone (Arar I should say) two people, who, though of tempers extremely unlike, think fit to join hands here, and make a little party to travel to the Mediterranean in company; the lady comes gliding along through the fruitful plains of Burgundy . . . ; the gentleman runs all rough and roaring down from the mountains of Switzerland to meet her; and with all her soft airs she likes him never the worse; she goes through the middle of the city in state, and he passes incog. without the walls, but waits for her a little below. The houses here are so high, and the streets so narrow, as would be sufficient to render Lyons the dismallest place in the world, but the number of people and the face of commerce diffused about it, are, at least, as sufficient to make it the liveliest.
Thomas Gray, Letter to Richard West, 18 September 1739

I will tell you truly my sentiments with respect to the south of France; which is, that *Lyons* is quite southward enough for an Englishman, who will, if he goes farther, have many wants which cannot be supplied.
Philip Thicknesse, *A Year's Journey through France and Spain*, 1789

Lyons is the Manchester of France; filled with a manufacturing, money-getting tribe, who wear their hearts in their purses. The sight of an Englishman is wormwood to them; and well it may, – for we seem to be travelling fast towards surpassing them even in their own staple manufacture.
Henry Matthews, *Diary of an Invalid*, 1820

At Lyons I saw this inscription over a door: *Ici on trouve le seul et unique dépôt de l'encre sans pareil et incorruptible* – which appeared to me to contain the whole secret of French poetry.
William Hazlitt, *Notes of a Journey through France and Italy*, 1826

Were you ever at Lyons? *That's* the place. It's a great Nightmare – a bad conscience – a fit of indigestion – the recollection of having done a murder. An awful place!
Charles Dickens, Letter to Count D'Orsay, 7 August 1844

What a city Lyons is! Talk about people feeling, at certain unlucky times, as if they had tumbled from the clouds! Here is a whole town that is tumbled, anyhow, out of the sky; having been first caught up, like other stones that tumble down from that region, out of fens and barren places, dismal to behold! The two great streets through which the two great rivers dash, and all the little streets whose name is Legion, were scorching, blistering, and sweltering. The houses, high and vast, dirty to excess, rotten as cheeses, and as thickly peopled. All up the hills that hem the city in, these houses swarm; and the mites inside were lolling out of the windows, and drying their ragged clothes on poles, and crawling in and out at the doors, and coming out to pant and gasp upon the pavement, and creeping in and out among huge piles and bales of fusty, musty, stifling goods; and living, or rather, not dying till their time should come, in an exhausted receiver. Every manufacturing town, melted into one, would hardly convey an impression of Lyons as it presented itself to me: for all the undrained, unscavengered qualities of a foreign town, seemed grafted, there, upon the native miseries of a manufacturing one; and it bears such fruit as I would go some miles out of my way to avoid encountering again.

Charles Dickens, *Pictures from Italy*, 1846

Beyond Lyons, we met on the road the statue of Louis XIV going to that city to overawe it with Bourbon memories. It was an equestrian statue, covered up, guarded with soldiers, and looking on that road like some mysterious heap. Don Quixote would have attacked it, and not been thought mad: so much has romance done for us. The natives would infallibly have looked quietly on. There was a riot about it at Lyons, soon after its arrival.

Leigh Hunt, *Autobiography*, 1850

The vast congeries of tall whity-brown houses.

M.F. Tupper, *Paterfamilias' Diary of Everybody's Tour*, 1856

Macon

Macon struck me, somehow, as suffering from a chronic numbness.

Henry James, *A Little Tour in France*, 1882

The Marne countryside

It is a miserable journey from Paris to Nancy, through that Marne country, where the country still seems to have had the soul blasted out of it, though the dreary fields are ploughed and level, and the pale wire trees stand up. But it is all void and null. And in the villages, the smashed houses in the street rows, like rotten teeth between good teeth.

D.H. Lawrence, 'A Letter from Germany' (written February 1924), *New Statesman and Nation*, 13 October 1924

Marseilles

between Aix and
We had a most delicious journey to Marselles through a Country sweetely declining to the South & Mediterranean Coasts, full of Vine-yards, & Olive-yards, Orange Trees, Myrtils, Pomegranads & the like sweete Plantations, to which belong innumerable pleasantly situated Villas, to the number of above 15 hundred; built all of Free-stone, and most of them in prospect shewing as if they were so many heapes of snow dropp'd out of the clowds amongst those perennial greenes.

John Evelyn, *Diary*, October 1644

Marseilles . . . is indeed a noble city, large, populous, and flourishing. The streets, for the most part, are open, airy, and spacious; the houses well built, and even magnificent. The harbour is an oval basin, surrounded on every side either by the buildings or the land, so that the shipping lies perfectly secure; and here is generally an incredible number of vessels. On the city side, there is a semicircular quay of free-stone, which extends thirteen hundred paces; and the space between this and the houses that front it, is continually filled with a surprising croud of people. The gallies, to the number of eight or nine, are moored with their sterns to one part of the wharf, and the slaves are permitted to work for their own benefit at their respective occupations, in little shops or booths which they rent for a trifle. There you see tradesmen of all kinds sitting at work, chained by one foot, shoemakers, tailors, silversmiths, watch and clockmakers, barbers, stocking-weavers, jewellers, pattern-drawers, scriveners, booksellers, cutlers, and all manner of shopkeepers. They pay about two sols a day to the king for this indulgence; live well, and look jolly.

Tobias Smollett, *Travels through France and Italy*, 1766

No place abounds more with dissolute persons of both sexes than Marseilles, and in the abundance of prostitutes, that appear in the streets, it is almost upon a par with London.

Henry Swinburne, 'A Journey from Bayonne to Marseilles', in *Travels in Spain in the Years 1775 and 1776*, 1783

The windows of our rooms are immediately overlooking the *quai*, a theatre of wares and traffick, which has more life, and less of the disgusting about it, than any other like object that I have ever looked on. The prospect is quite spirit-stirring. But, then, the sky under which all is going forward is delightfully clear; the sun is shining its brightest and serenest upon every thing in view; and the atmosphere is entirely free from that smoke in which the cities of England are everlastingly smothered. For a place of such trade, this city is surprisingly clean. The people, too, are good-looking. One would hardly believe, from merely English experience, that a large seaport could be so agreeable. The French have not much taste for *towns*; at least, their taste is not like ours: our French friends here marvel at our admiration of Marseilles, and seem to count the *cleanliness* of it as no weighty consideration in its favour.

J.P. Cobbett, *Journal of a Tour in Italy, etc.*, 1830

Much, however, I suppose, is to be excused in a population without fresh water, without cows, whose poultry comes from Nice, and whose butter is brought from Lyons. Let us earnestly hope that with irrigation and consequent fertility, the waters of the Durance may bring an influx of liberality to the dealings of the inhabitants of Marseilles.

Fanny Kemble (Mrs Butler), *A Year of Consolation*, 1847

These Marseillaise make Marseillaise hymns, and Marseilles vests, and Marseilles soap for all the world; but they never sing their hymns, or wear their vests, or wash with their soap themselves.

Mark Twain, *The Innocents Abroad*, 1869

Calvocoressi said that you can call a man anything in Marseilles except 'mobile'. Call a coachman a 'mobile' and he will get down from his box and try to kill you. The majority of the Marseillaise have of course no notion why they object to being called 'mobile'. The explanation is that during the Franco-German war Marseilles enrolled a regiment to go to the rescue of Paris. This *garde mobile* got as far as Avignon where, someone shouting 'Prussians', it threw down its arms and ran back home, Calvocoressi is a native of Marseilles.

Arnold Bennett, *Journal*, 18 October 1907

Everyone in Marseilles seemed most dishonest. They all tried to swindle me mostly with complete success.

Evelyn Waugh, *Diary*, December 1926

Nothing short of a recording angel could sum up the activities of the Vieux Port.

Eric Muspratt, *Wild Oats*, 1932

Martigny

I cannot help thinking that few people, unless they belong to the Antiquarian Society, find themselves within it with any other desire than to secure their means to departure. Its aspect is that of a decayed monastery: its shops, of which there is a row in a spectral kind of market-place, are about equal to those in Barmouth or Delgelly; and it seems to owe its life, as it certainly owes its trade, to the monks of St. Bernard, who at once dignify and grace its poor streets by their presence, like a kind of poetic Quakers. Else, it looks like a city – the phantasm of a city – in Hades . . . – and where pale ghosts may play at trades and offices.

Sir T.N. Talfourd, *Vacation Rambles*, 1844

Martigues

Around the quays, kicked off in twos
The Four Winds dry their wooden shoes.

Roy Campbell, 'Fishing Boats in Martigues', *Collected Poems*, 1961

Meillerie

Meillerie is indeed inchanted ground, were Rousseau no magician. Groves of pine, chestnut, and walnut overshadow it; magnificent and unbounded forests to which England affords no parallel. In the midst of these woods are dells of lawny expanse, inconceivably verdant, adorned with a thousand of the rarest flowers and odourous with thyme.

Percy Bysshe Shelley, Letter to T.P. Esq., 12 July 1816, from *History of a Six Weeks' Tour, etc.*, 1817

Mentone

Of *all the beasts* of countries I ever see, I reckon this about caps them. I also strongly notion that there ain't a hole in St. Giles's which isn't a paradise to this. How any professing Christian as has been in France and England can look at it, passes me. It is more like the landscape in Browning's *Childe Roland* than anything I ever heard tell on. A calcined, scalped, rasped, scraped, flayed, broiled, powdered, leprous, blotched, mangy, grimy, parboiled, country, *without* trees, water, grass, fields – *with* blank, beastly, senseless olives and orange-trees like a mad cabbage gone indigestible; it is infinitely liker hell than earth, and one looks for tails among the people. And such females, with hunched bodies and crooked necks carrying tons on their heads, and looking like Death taken seasick. Ar-r-r-r-r! Gr-r-r-rn!

Algernon Charles Swinburne, Letter to Pauline Trevelyan, 19 January 1861

Too shut in and befizzled a place for me.

Edward Lear, Letter to Chichester Fortescue, 13 November 1864

Mentone was of recent growth – the old settlement, Mentone of Symonds, proclaims its existence only by a ceaseless and infernal clanging of bells, rivalling Malta – no history, no character, no tradition – a mushroom town inhabited by shopkeepers and *hoteliers* who are there for the sole purpose of plucking foreigners: how should a youngster's imagination be nurtured in this atmosphere of savourless modernism? Then I asked myself: who comes to these regions, now that invalids have learnt the drawbacks of their climate? Decayed Muscovites, Englishmen such as you will vainly seek in

England, and their painted women-folk with stony, Medusa-like gambling eyes, a Turk or two, Jews and cosmopolitan sharks and sharpers, flamboyant Americans, Brazilian, Peruvian, Chilian, Bolivian rastaqueros with names that read like a nightmare (*see* 'List of Arrivals' in *New York Herald*) – the whole exotic riff-raff enlivened and perfumed by a copious sprinkling of *horizontales*.

Norman Douglas, *Alone*, 1921

Menton, the last sigh of France. . . .

William Sansom, *Blue Skies Brown Studies*, 1961

Mont Blanc

Hast thou a charm to stay the Morning Star
In his steep Course? So long he seems to pause
On thy bold awful Top, O Chamouny!
The Arve and Arveiron at thy Base
Rave ceaselessly; but thou, dread Mountain Form!
Risest from out thy silent Sea of Pines,
How silently! Around thee and above,
Deep is the Sky and black! transpicuous, black,
An ebon Mass! Methinks, thou piercest it,
As with a Wedge! – . . .
Rise, mighty Form! even as thou *seems't* to rise!
Rise, like a Cloud of Incense, from the Earth!

Thou kingly Spirit thron'd among the Hills,
Thou dread Ambassador from Earth to Heaven,
Great Hierarch! tell thou the silent Stars,
Tell the blue Sky, and tell the rising Sun,
Earth with her thousand Voices calls on God!

S.T. Coleridge, *Mont Blanc, the summit of the Vale of Chamouny, an Hour before Sunrise – An Hymn*, 1802

That very day,
From a bare ridge we also first beheld
Unveiled the summit of Mont Blanc, and grieved
To have a soulless image on the eye
That had usurped upon a living thought
That never more could be. The wondrous Vale
Of Chamouny stretched far below, and soon
With its dumb cataracts, and streams of ice,
A motionless array of mighty waves
Five rivers broad and vast, made rich amends,
And reconciled us to realities.

William Wordsworth, *The Prelude*, 1805 (Text of 1850)

from between Servoz and Chamouni

Mont Blanc was before us – the Alps, with their innumerable glaciers on high all around, closing in the complicated windings of the single vale – forests inexpressibly beautiful, but majestic in their beauty – intermingled beech and pine, and oak, overshadowed our road, or receded, whilst lawns of such verdure as I have never seen before occupied these openings, and gradually became darker in their recesses. Mont Blanc was before us, but it was covered with cloud; its base, furrowed with dreadful gaps, was seen above. Pinnacles of snow, intolerably bright, part of the chain connected with Mont Blanc, shone through the clouds at intervals on high. I never knew – I never imagined what mountains were before. The immensity of these aerial summits excited, when they suddenly burst upon the sight, a sentiment of extatic wonder, not unallied to madness. And remember, this was all one scene, it all pressed home to our regard and our imagination. Though it embraced a vast extent of space, the snowy pyramids which shot into the bright blue sky seemed to overhang our path; the ravine, clothed with gigantic pines, and black with its depth below, so deep that the very roaring of the untameable Arve, which rolled through it, could not be heard above – all was as much our own, as if we had been the creators of such impressions in the minds of others as now occupied our own. Nature was the poet, whose harmony held our spirits more breathless than that of the divinest.

Percy Bysshe Shelley, Letter to T.P. Esq., 22 July 1816, from *History of a Six Weeks' Tour, etc.*, 1817

Far, far above, piercing the infinite sky,
Mont Blanc appears, – still, snowy, and serene –
Its subject mountains their unearthly forms
Pile around it, ice and rock; broad vales between
Of frozen floods, unfathomable deeps,
Blue as the overhanging heaven, that spread
And wind among the accumulated steeps;
A desart peopled by the storms alone,
Save when the eagle brings some hunter's bone,
And the wolf tracks her there – how hideously
Its shapes are heaped around! rude, bare, and high,
Ghastly, and scarred, and riven. . . .
Thou hast a voice, great Mountain, to repeal
Large codes of fraud and woe; not understood
By all, but which the wise, and great, and good
Interpret, or make felt, or deeply feel. . . .
Mont Blanc yet gleams on high: – the power is there,
The still and solemn power of many sights,
And many sounds, and much of life and death.
In the calm darkness of the moonless nights,
In the lone glare of day, the snows descend
Upon that Mountain; none beholds them there,
Nor when the flakes burn in the sinking sun,
Or the star-beams dart through them: – Winds contend
Silently there, and heap the snow with breath
Rapid and strong, but silently! Its home
The voiceless lightning in these solitudes
Keeps innocently, and like vapour broods
Over the snow. The secret strength of things
Which governs thought, and to the infinite dome
Of heaven is as a law, inhabits thee!
And what wert thou, and earth, and stars, and sea,

If to the human mind's imaginings
Silence and solitude were vacancy?

Percy Bysshe Shelley, *Mont Blanc, Lines Written in the Vale of Chamouni*, July 1816

I am going to Chamouni (to leave my card with Mont Blanc). . . .

Lord Byron, Letter to Augusta Leigh, 27 August 1816

Mont Blanc is the monarch of mountains;
They crown'd him long ago
On a throne of rocks, in a robe of clouds,
With a diadem of snow.

Lord Byron, *Manfred*, 1816–17

from between La Vattay and Gex
. . . the sun was getting very low. It was just on the point of sinking when I ran on by myself, and at the turn of the road caught a sight of the stupendous Mont Blanc. It is impossible to describe what I felt. I ran like lightning down the steep road that led towards it, with my glass to my eye, and uttering exclamations of wonder at every step.

Thomas Moore, *Journal*, 22 September 1819

That scene – I have viewed it this evening again
By the same brilliant light that hung over it then –
The valley, the Lake in their tenderest charms –
Mont Blanc in his awfullest pomp – and the whole
A bright picture of Beauty, reclin'd in the arms
Of sublimity, bridegroom elect of her soul!
But where are the mountains that round me at first,
One dazzling horizon of miracles, burst?
Those Alps beyond Alps, without end swelling on
Like the waves of eternity – where are *they* gone?
Clouds – clouds – they were nothing but clouds after all!
That chain of Mont Blanc, which my fancy flew o'er,
With a wonder that nought on this earth can recall,
Were but clouds of the evening, and now are no more.
What a picture of Life's young illusions! Oh, Night,
Drop thy curtain at once, and hide *all* from my sight.

Thomas Moore, *Rhymes on the Road*, 1819

When Kemble was living at Lausanne, he used to feel rather jealous of Mont Blanc; he disliked to hear people always asking, 'How does Mont Blanc look this morning?'

Samuel Rogers, *Recollections of the Table Talk of Samuel Rogers, by the Rev. Alexander Dyce*, 1887

My favorite object.

Charles Tennant, *A Tour, etc.*, 1824

It was an image of immensity and eternity. Earth had heaved it from its bosom; the 'vast cerulean' had touched it with its breath. It was a meeting of earth and sky. Other peaked cliffs rose perpendicularly by its side, and a range of rocks, of red granite, fronted it to the north; but Mont-Blanc itself was round, bald, shining, ample, and equal in its swelling proportions – a huge dumb heap of matter. . . . There is an end here of vanity and littleness, and all transitory jarring interests. You stand as it were in the presence of the Spirit of the Universe, before the majesty of Nature, with her chief elements about you; cloud and air, and rock, and stream, and mountain are brought into immediate contact with primeval Chaos and the great First Cause.

William Hazlitt, *Notes of a Journey through France and Italy*, 1826

Let me confess, then, that the upper part of Mont Blanc, thus surveyed, seemd to me like nothing so much in nature or art as a gigantic twelfth-cake which a scapegrace of Titan's 'enormous brood' or 'younger Saturn,' had cut and slashed with wild irregularity, so as to leave the most tempting contrast between the thick crust of sugar and the deep brown indentations beneath it!

Sir T.N. Talfourd, *Vacation Rambles*, 1844

from the Col de Balme pass
Going by that Col de Balme pass, you climb up and up and up for five hours and more, and look – from a mere unguarded ledge of path on the side of the precipice – into such awful valleys, that at last you are firm in the belief that you have got above everything in the world, and that there can be nothing earthly overhead. Just as you arrive at this conclusion, a different (and oh Heaven! what a free and wonderful) air comes blowing on your face; you cross a ridge of snow; and lying before you (wholly unseen till then), towering up into the distant sky, is the vast range of Mont Blanc, with attendant mountains diminished by its majestic side into mere dwarfs tapering up into innumerable rude Gothic pinnacles; deserts of ice and snow; forests of firs on mountain sides, of no account at all in the enormous scene; villages down in the hollow, that you can shut out with a finger; waterfalls, avalanches, pyramids and towers of ice, torrents, bridges; mountain upon mountain until the very sky is blocked away, and you must look up, overhead, to see it. Good God, what a country Switzerland is, and what a concentration of it is to be beheld from that one spot!

Charles Dickens, Letter, 2 August 1846, in Forster, *Life of Dickens*, 1872–3

A highly intelligent Swiss guide once gazed with me upon the dreary expanse of chimney-pots through which the South-Western Railway escapes from this dingy metropolis. Fancying that I rightly interpreted his looks as symptomatic of the proverbial homesickness of mountaineers, I remarked with an appropriate sigh, 'That is not so fine a view as we have seen together from the top of Mont Blanc.' 'Ah, Sir!' was his pathetic reply, 'it is far finer!'

Leslie Stephen, *The Playground of Europe*, 1871

They had a beautiful view of Mont Blanc, A. saying it 'looked like a great cathedral with three naves.'

Alfred Lord Tennyson, *A Memoir, by his Son*, 1897 (of 1872)

It has lost the virginity of the snows: spinsters and curates climb it: its terrors are over.

Oscar Wilde, Letter to Reginald Turner, Gland, 20 March 1899

Too many eyes before mine have looked with awe upon Mont Blanc; too many hearts before mine have throbbed with deep emotion in the presence of the Sistine Madonna. Sights like these are like women of too generous sympathies: you feel that so many persons have found solace in their commiseration that you are embarrassed when they bid you, with what practised tact, to whisper in their discreet ears the whole tale of your distress. Supposing you were the last straw that broke the camel's back.

W. Somerset Maugham, *On a Chinese Screen*, 1922

Mont Canigou

The Roussillon depends upon the Canigou just as the Bay of Syracuse depends upon Etna or that of Naples upon Vesuvius and its familiar presence has sunk into the patriotism of the Roussillon people. . . . Yet it is the mountain which very many men who have hardly heard its name have been looking for all their lives. It gives as good camping as is to be had in the whole of the Pyrenees. I believe there is fishing, and perhaps one can shoot. Properly speaking there is no climbing in it; at least, one can walk up it all the way if one chooses the right path, but there is everything else men look for when they escape from cities. . . . From the summit the view has two interests – of colour and of the past. You have below you a plain like an inlaid work of chosen stones: the whole field is an arrangement of different culture and of bright rocks and sand; and below you, also in a curve, is all that coast which at the close of the Roman Empire was, perhaps, the wealthiest in Europe.

Hilaire Belloc, *Hills and the Sea*, 1906

Mont Cenis

(climbing from Susa)
The valley below us full of a sea of mist, reminding one of the deluge, and as if we were escaping out of it to the high places. . . .

Thomas Moore, *Journal*, 4 December 1819

We were capsized on the top. Very lucky it was so; and the carriage door so completely frozen that we were obliged to get out at the window – the guide and Cantonier began to fight, and the driver was by a process verbal put into prison, so doing while we had to march or rather flounder up to our knees nothing less in snow all the way down to Lancesbyburgh (sc. Lanslebourg) by the King of Roadmakers' Road, not the Colossus of Roads, Mr MacAdam, but Bonaparte, filled up by snow and only known by the precipitous zigzag.

J.M.W. Turner, Letter to James Holdworthy, 7 January 1826, describing incident of 14 January 1820

Montdidier

The little town on the hill . . . was called Montdidier. Many of the houses were in ruins from the War: new ones were being built everywhere. In some parts the original streets stood intact except for occasional shell and bullet marks: in others entire new blocks arose from the scattered ruins. It was strange to see a town's history so plainly marked upon it. One felt for it as for a crippled veteran.

Eric Muspratt, *Wild Oats*, 1932

Montdidier, like Rye, is a red-and-grey town huddled on a hill, which rises from a plain flat as the Sussex marshes and stretching away on all sides to the horizon. At the end of several of the quiet stone-paved streets you see nothing but the sky. The town has rampart walks and two ancient weather-beaten churches, begun in a spirit of magnificence and brought to completion long afterwards in humility.

Desmond MacCarthy, *Experience*, 1935

Montpellier

I find it much better to go twise to Montpellier then once to the other world.

John Locke, Letter to William Charleton, September 1678

I have been dangerously ill, and cannot think that the sharp air of Montpellier has been of service to me – and so my physicians told me when they had me under their hands for above a month – if you stay any longer here, Sir, it will be fatal to you – And why good people were you not kind enough to tell me this sooner?

Laurence Sterne, Letter to Mrs Fenton, 1 February 1764

The longer I stay at Montpellier, the less I like it. The inhabitants are characterized in the proverbs of their own country. – Pound seven Jews in a mortar, says one of these, and the juice will make one Montpelliard.

Henry Matthews, *Diary of an Invalid*, 1820

There are places that please, without your being able to say wherefore, and Montpellier is one of the number. . . . The place has neither the gaiety of a modern nor the solemnity of an ancient town, and it is agreeable as certain women are agreeable who are neither beautiful nor clever.

Henry James, *A Little Tour in France*, 1882

Montreuil

*There is not a town in all *France*, which in my opinion, looks better in the map, than MONTREUIL; – I own, it does not look so well in the book of post roads; but when you come to see it – to be sure it looks most pitifully.

Laurence Sterne, *Tristram Shandy*, vol. vii, 1765

It is unenlivened by those circumstances that render towns pleasant.

Arthur Young, *Travels . . . [in] . . . France* (18 May 1787), 1792

Moret

Moret is one of the deadest places I ever had tea in.

Arnold Bennett, *Paris Nights*, 1913

Napoule, *the Mistral there*

. . . it is a harsh philistine wind. . . .

Oscar Wilde, Letter to Reginald Turner, Napoule, 3 January 1899

Narbonne

This intricate, curious, but lifeless town.

Murray's Guide, *A Handbook for Travellers in France*, 1877

Narbonne is a *sale petite ville* in all the force of the term.

Henry James, *A Litttle Tour in France*, 1882

Nice

the view from

When I stand upon the rampart and look round me, I can scarce help thinking myself inchanted. The small extent of country which I see, is all cultivated like a garden. Indeed the plain presents nothing but gardens, full of green trees, loaded with oranges, lemons, citrons, and bergamots, which make a delightful appearance. If you examine them more nearly, you will find plantations of green pease ready to gather; all sorts of sallading, and pot herbs, in perfection; and plats of roses, carnations, ranunculas, anemonies, and daffodils, blowing in full glory, with such beauty, vigour, and perfume, as no flower in England ever exhibited.

Tobias Smollett, *Travels through France and Italy*, 1766

A place where I leave nothing but the air which I can possibly regret.

Ibid.

They quote to you the French translation of an epigram, made by some Turkish prince, who, after having lived at Nice for some time, notwithstanding his love of variety, is said to have exclaimed,

'Ah! quelle ville admirable que NICE:
On y *demeure* en dépit du *caprice*!'
Ah! what an admirable town is NICE
For there we *stay* in spite of our *caprice*!

J.P. Cobbett, *Journal of a Tour in Italy*, 1830

This place is so wonderfully dry that nothing can be kept moist. I never was in so dry a place in all my life. When the little children cry, they cry dust and not tears. There is some water in the sea, but not much: – all the wet-nurses cease to be so immediately on arriving: – Dryden is the only book read: – the neighbourhood abounds with Dryads and Hammer-dryads: and weterinary surgeons are quite unknown. It is queer place, – Brighton and Belgravia and Baden by the Mediterranean: odious to me in all respects but its magnificent winter climate. . . .

Edward Lear, Letter to Chichester Fortescue, 24 February 1865

I am alane myself, in Nice, they ca't, but damned, I think they micht as well ca't Nesty. The Pile-on, 's they ca't, 's aboot as big as the river Tay at Perth; and it's rainin' maist like Greenock. Dod, i've seen's had mair o' what they ca' the I-talian at Muttonhole. I-talian! I haenae seen the sun for eicht and forty hours.

Robert Louis Stevenson, Letter to Charles Baxter, 12 January 1883

Like another Poictesme, it is a place in which almost anything is more than likely to happen.

James Thurber, *My World and Welcome to It*, 1942

But it's nicer, much nicer in Nice.

Sandy Wilson, *The Boy Friend*, 1953

Nice is a feminine city, quite properly full of men.

William Sansom, *Blue Skies Brown Studies*, 1961

Nîmes

I took Wordsworth to see the exterior of both the Maison Carrée and the Arena. He acknowledged their beauty, but expressed no great pleasure. He says: 'I am unable from ignorance to enjoy these sights. I receive an impression, but that is all. I have no science, and can refer nothing to principle.' He was on the other hand delighted by two beautiful little girls near the Arena, and said: 'I wish I could take them to Rydal Mount.'

Henry Crabb Robinson, *Diary*, 3 April 1837

I was free to look about me at Nimes, and I did so with such attention as the place appeared to require. At the risk of seeming too easily and too frequently disappointed, I will say that it required rather less than I had been prepared to give.

Henry James, *A Little Tour in France*, 1882

The Maison Carrée
It is said, and I have felt the truth of it, in part, that there does not exist, at this day, any building, ancient or modern, which conveys so secret a pleasure, not only to the *connoisseur*, but to the clown also, whenever, or how often soever they approach it. The proportions and beauties of the whole building are so intimately united, that they may be compared to good breeding in men – it is what every body perceives, and is captivated with, but what few can define.

Philip Thicknesse, *A Year's Journey through France and Spain*, 1789

Normandy

Normandy has a bad reputation for rain and on that account is called the *pot de chambre* of France.

R.H. Bruce Lockhart, *My Europe*, 1952

The Normans
The little bullet-headed men, vivacious and splendidly brave, we know that they awoke all Europe, that they first provided settled financial systems and settled governments of land, and that everywhere, from the Grampians to Mesopotamia, they were like steel when all other Christians were like wood or like lead.

We know too that they were a flash. They were not formed or definable at all before the year 1000; by the year 1200 they were gone. Some odd transitory phenomenon of cross-breeding, a very lucky freak in the history of the European family, produced the only body of men who all were lords, and who in their collective action showed continually nothing but genius.

We know that they were the spear-head, as it were, of the Gallic spirit.

Hilaire Belloc, *Hills and the Sea*, 1906

Orléans

The Wine of this Place is so grosse & strong that the Kings Cupbearers are (as I was assurd) sworne never to give the King any of it: But it is else a very noble liquor, & much of it transported into other Countrys.

The Language for being here spoken with greate purity, as well for divers other Privileges, & the University, makes the Towne to be much frequented by strangers, especialy Germans; which causes the English to make no long sojourne here; but such as can drinke & debauch.

John Evelyn, *Diary*, 21 April 1644

Pamiers

Many vines about Pamiers, which is situated in a beautiful vale, upon a fine river. The place itself is ugly striking, and ill built; with an inn! Adieu, Mons. Gascit; if fate sends me to such another house as thine – be it in expiation for my sins!

Arthur Young, *Travels . . . [in] . . . France* (3 August 1787), 1792

Paris

Seventeenth Century

Paris vaut bien une messe.
(Paris is well worth a mass.)

Attributed either to Henri IV of France or to his minister Sully, in conversation with King Henry, *Caquets de l'Accouchée*, 1622

Paris I confesse is populous, a masse of poore people for lacques and pages, a nest of rogues, a tumultuous place, a noctuall den of theeves, and a confused multitude: Where contrariwise London is adorned with many grave, prudent and provident Senators, civill, well taught, and courteous people, and absolutely the best governed City on the whole face of the earth, as well by night, as by day, and nothing inferior in quantity to it.

William Lithgow, *Rare Adventures and Painfull Peregrinations*, 1614/32

I am now newly come to *Paris*, this huge Magazine of Men, the Epitome of this large populous Kingdom, and Rendezvous of all Foreigners. The Structures here are indifferently fair, tho' the Streets generally foul all the four Seasons of the year; which I impute first to the Position of the City, being built upon an Isle, (the Isle of *France*, made so by the branching and serpentine course of the River of *Seine*) and having some of her Suburbs seated high, the Filth runs down the Channel, and settles in many places within the body of the City, which lies upon a Flat; as also for a world of Coaches,

Carts, and Horses of all sorts that go to and fro perpetually, so that sometimes one shall meet with a stop half a mile long of those Coaches, Carts and Horses, that can move neither forward nor backward, by reason of some sudden Encounter of others coming a cross-way; so that often-times it will be an hour or two before they can disintangle. . . . Hence comes it to pass, that this Town (for Paris is a *Town*, a *City*, and an *University)* is always dirty, and 'tis such a Dirt, that by perpetual Motion is beaten into such a black unctuous Oil, that where it sticks no Art can wash it off some Colours; insomuch, that it may be no improper Comparison to say, That an ill Name is like the *Crot* (the *Dirt*) of *Paris*, which is indelible; besides, the Stain this Dirt leaves, it gives also so strong a scent, that it may be smelt many miles off, if the Wind be in one's Face as he comes from the fresh Air of the Country: this may be one cause why the Plague is always in some corner or other of this vast City, which may be call'd, as once Scythia was, *Vagina populorum*, or (as Mankind was call'd by a great Philosopher) a great Molehill of Ants: yet I believe this City is not so populous as she seems to be, for her Form being round (as the whole Kingdom is) the Passengers wheel about, and meet oftener than they use to do in the long continued Streets of *London.*

James Howell, 'Letter to Capt. Francis Bacon, from Paris, 30 March 1620', *Familiar Letters*, 1645

And truely Paris, comprehending the Suburbs is certainely for the material the houses are built with, and many noble and magnificent piles, one of the most gallant Cittys in the World, and best built: large in Circuit, of a round forme, infinitly populous; but situat in a botome environd with gentle declivities, which renders some places very durty, and makes it smell as if sulphure were mingled with the mudd: Yet it is pav'd with a kind of freestone of neere a foote square which renders it more easy to walke on then our pibbles of London.

John Evelyn, *Diary*, 24 December 1643

Paris, that huge (though durty) Theater of all Nations.

James Howell, *Instructions for Forren Travell*, 1650

Si le roi m'avoit donné
Paris sa grand' ville
Et qu'il me fallut quitter
L'amour de ma vie!

Je dirois au roi Henri
Reprenez votre Paris;
J'aime mieux ma vie, o gué,
J'aime mieux ma vie.

(If the king had given me his great town of Paris, but I had to give up the love of my life for it, I should say to King Henry, 'Take back your Paris: I prefer my life as it is.')

Old Song, quoted by Molière in *Le Misanthrope*, 1666

Paris . . . where nothing is more usual than for mean people to press into the presence and conversation of great men, and where modesty is so very scarce, that I think I have not seen a blush since my first landing at Calais.

Joseph Addison, Letter to Charles Montagu, 14 October 1699

Eighteenth Century

After having been accustomed to the gravity of Turks, I can scarce look with an easy and familiar aspect at the levity and agility of the airy phantoms that are dancing about me here, and I often think that I am at a puppet-shew amidst the representations of real life. I stare prodigiously, but no body remarks it, for every body stares here; staring is à-la-mode – there is a stare of attention and *intérêt*, a stare of curiosity, a stare of expectation, a stare of surprize, and it would greatly amuse you to see what trifling objects excite all this staring. This staring would have rather a solemn kind of air, were it not alleviated by grinning, for at the end of a stare there comes always a grin, and very often the entrance of a gentleman or lady into a room is accompanied with a grin, which is designed to express complacence and social pleasure, but really shews nothing more than a certain contortion of muscles that must make a stranger laugh really, as they laugh artificially. The French grin is equally remote from the chearful serenity of a smile, and the cordial mirth of an honest English horse-laugh. I shall not perhaps stay here long enough to form a just idea of French manners and characters, tho' this I believe would require but little study, as there is no great depth in either. It appears, on a superficial view, to be a frivolous, restless, agreeable people.

Lady Mary Wortley Montagu, Letter to Alexander Pope, October 1718

Paris is a huge round City, divided by the Seine, a very near relation (if we may judge from the resemblance) of your old acquaintance, that ancient river, the river Cam. Along it on either side runs a key of perhaps as handsome buildings, as any in the World. The view down which on either hand from the Pont Neuf is the charming'st Sight imaginable. There are infinite Swarms of inhabitants & more Coaches than Men. The Women in general dressed in Sacs, flat Hoops of 5 yards wide nosegays of artificial flowers, on one shoulder, and faces dyed in Scarlet up to the Eyes. The Men in bags, rollupps, Muffs and Solitaires.

Thomas Gray, Letter to Thomas Ashton, 21 April 1739

A professed Gamester being the most advantageous Character a Man can have at Paris.

Ibid.

Paris is the place in the world where, if you wish, you may best unite the *utile* and the *dulce*.

Lord Chesterfield, *Letters*, 30 April 1750

Les Parisiens passent leur temps à élever des statues et à les briser.
(Parisians spend their time erecting statues and smashing them.)

Voltaire, Letter, 1758, quoted in Adrien Lefort and Paul Buquet, *Les Mots de Voltaire*, 1886

However they may figure away, when they are from home, and make their boasting and vaunting of the elegance beauty and deliciousness of Paris, a good cleanly English stomach in passing through any of their streets, at first coming among them, would be apt to convince them of their nastiness, by not being able without being sick, to pass by so much carrion, hung up in their shops as eatable Victuals. It has been as much as I could do to forbear putting my head out at the coach window many a Time in the Streets, the principal streets of this glory of the world, to bring up the contents of my stomach, when I have passed by so much liver, lights and other offal, cut out in slices and sold on small tables in almost every street, whether it is for Dogs, Cats or themselves it is equally offensive: the monstrous black sausages, in great Guts or Bladders, hanging by many of their Shop windows: quantities of Sheep's heads boiled and partly dried in heaps on stalls, are all such odious and indelicate sights as would turn any other stomach but that of a Frenchman. All these delicacies and elegancies you perpetually encounter and while Monsieur le Parisien and Madame La Parisienne, with their heads most elegantly *frisez* and *poudrez* and their tails bedraggled and full of holes and all over rags cheapen with a watery mouth some of these *bons morceaux* without any difficulty, where all live alike, would perhaps, at a distance from home, equally turn up their noses at such rarities, and the indelicacy of English Roast Beef. Poverty, Rags, and a poor mean way of living are by no means the proper subject of Ridicule, when unavoidable; but when Vanity with a contempt for the manners of other people are joined to them, then surely there cannot be a more proper subject to laugh at.

Rev. William Cole, *A Journal of My Journey to Paris, in 1765*, 1931

*Crack, crack – crack, crack – so this is *Paris*! quoth I . . . – and this is *Paris*! – humph! – Paris! cried I, repeating the name the third time – The first, the finest, the most brilliant –

– The streets however are nasty;

But it looks, I suppose, better than it smells – crack, crack, – crack, crack – what a fuss thou makest! – as if it concern'd the good people to be inform'd, That a man with a pale face, and clad in black, had the honour to be driven into *Paris* at nine o'clock at night, by a postillion in a tawny yellow jerkin turned up with red calamanco – crack crack, – crack, crack – crack, crack – I wish thy whip –

– But 'tis the spirit of thy nation; so crack – crack on.

Ha! – and no one gives the wall! – but in the SCHOOL OF URBANITY herself, if the walls are besh-t – how can you do otherwise?

And prithee when do they light the lamps? What? – never in the summer months! – Ho! 'tis the time of sallads. – O rare! sallad and soup – soup and sallad – sallad and soup, *encore*.

– 'Tis *too much* for sinners.

Now I cannot bear the barbarity of it; how can that unconscionable coachman talk so much bawdy to that lean horse? don't you see, friend, the streets are so villainously narrow, that there is not room in all *Paris* to turn a wheel-barrow? In the grandest city of the whole world, it would not have been amiss, if they had been left a thought wider; nay were it only so much in every single street, as that a man might know (was it only for satisfaction) on which side of it he was walking.

One – two – three – four – five – six – seven – eight – nine – ten. – Ten cook's shops! and twice the number of barber's! and all within three minutes driving! one would think that all the cooks in the world on some great merrymeeting with the barbers by just consent had said – Come, let us all go live at *Paris*: the *French* love good eating – they are all *gourmands* – we shall rank high; if their god is their belly – their cooks must be gentlemen: and forasmuch as the *periwig maketh the man*, and the periwig-maker maketh the periwig – ergo, would the barbers say, we shall rank higher still. . . .

Laurence Sterne, *Tristram Shandy*, vol. vii, 1765

*The FRENCH are certainly misunderstood; – but whether the fault is theirs, in not sufficiently explaining themselves; or speaking with that exact limitation and precision which one would expect on a point of such importance, and which, moreover, is so likely to be contested by us – or whether the fault may not be altogether on our side, in not understanding their language always so critically as to know 'what they would be at' – I shall not decide; but 'tis evident to me, when they affirm, *'That they who have seen Paris, have seen every thing*,' they must mean to speak of those who have seen it by day light.

Ibid.

It is the ugliest beastly town in the universe.

Horace Walpole, Letter to Thomas Gray, 19 November 1765

*The people of Paris are much fonder of strangers that have money, than of those that have wit.

Oliver Goldsmith, *The Vicar of Wakefield*, 1766

So being in Paris where the Mode is to be sacredly

follow'd I was once very near making Love to my Friend's Wife.

Benjamin Franklin, Letter to Miss Mary Stevenson, 14 September 1767

Paris is, indeed, a place very different from the Hebrides, but it is to a hasty traveller not so fertile of novelty, nor affords so many opportunities of remark.

Samuel Johnson, Letter to James Boswell, 16 November 1775

The gay and thoughtless Paris is now become a furnace of politics. . . . Recollect the women of this capital, some on foot, some on horses, and some in carriages, hunting pleasure in the streets, in routs and assemblies, and forgetting that they have left it behind them in their nurseries; compare them with your own countrymen, occupied in the tender and tranquil amusements of domestic life, and confess that it is a comparison of Americans and Angels.

Thomas Jefferson, Letter to Mrs William Bingham, 11 May 1788

To a person of great fortune, in the *heyday* of life, Paris may be preferable even to *London*; but to one of my age and walk in life, it is, and was ten years ago, the least agreeable place I have seen in France. – Walking the streets is extremely dangerous, riding in them very expensive; and when those things which are worthy to be seen (and much there is very worthy) have been seen, the city of Paris becomes a melancholy residence for a stranger who neither plays at cards, dice, or deals in the principal manufacture of the city; i.e. *ready-made love*, a business which is carried on with great success, and with more decency, I think, than even in *London*. The English ladies are weak enough to attach themselves to, and love, *one* man. The gay part of the French women love none, but receive all, *pour passer le tems*. – The *English*, unlike the *Parisian* ladies, take pains to discover *who* they love; the French women to dissemble with those they hate.

Philip Thicknesse, *A Year's Journey through France and Spain*, 1789

I have been upon the full silly gape to find out things that I had not found before, as if a street in Paris could be composed of any thing but houses, or houses formed of any thing but brick or stone – or that the people in them, not being English, would be walking on their heads. I shall shake off this folly as fast as I can.

Arthur Young, *Travels . . . [in] . . . France* (25 May 1787), 1792

The opulence of the French capital arises from the defects of its government and religion.

Edward Gibbon, *Memoirs of his Life*, 1796

C'est la ville du monde où on peut le mieux se passer du bonheur.

(Of all towns in the world, it is the one where one can most easily do without happiness.)

Madame de Stael, quoted by Thomas Moore, *Journal*, 16 April 1823

Secrets travel fast in Paris.

Napoleon I, *Sayings of Napoleon*, 1895

Nineteenth Century

It was the subject of my perpetual dreams to render Paris the real capital of Europe. I sometimes wished it, for instance, to become a city with a population of two, three, or four millions – in a word, something fabulous, colossal, unexampled, until our days, and with public establishments suitable to its population.

Napoleon, quoted by Comte de Las Cases, *Journal . . . at St Helena*, 1824 – of 4 August 1816

Paris is a filthy hole.

Benjamin Robert Haydon, *Diary*, June 1814

At a distance it looks too much like a great rough stone quarry.

Samuel Rogers, *Italian Journal*, 30 August 1814

Paris is taken for the second time. I presume it, for the future, will have an anniversary capture.

Lord Byron, Letter to Thomas Moore, 7 July 1815

Oh Dick! you may talk of your writing and reading,
Your Logic and Greek, but there's nothing like feeding;
And *this* is the place for it, DICKY, you dog,
Of all places on earth – the head-quarters of Prog!

Thomas Moore, *The Fudge Family in Paris*, 1818

Where shall I begin with the endless delights
Of this Eden of milliners, monkies and sights –
This dear busy place, where there's nothing transacting
But dressing and dinnering, dancing and acting?

Ibid.

Winter *will* come, and then Paris is the devil.

Thomas Moore, Letter to Samuel Rogers, 17 July 1820

It is a charming place to play the fool in. But whatever superiority it may have over London is derived chiefly from its very inferiority of scale and grandeur . . . Every thing, in a word, that Paris contains, is *come-atable* at pleasure; and if you add, that there is no smoke, that a dollar will go as far as a guinea does in London, and that it has not, as far as I could see, the horrid nests of human vermin which are to be found in Wapping and St. Giles's; you will have said nearly all that can be said in its favour.

Henry Matthews, *Diary of an Invalid*, 1820

Fancy yourself in London with the footpath taken away, so that you are forced to walk along the middle of the streets with a dirty gutter running through them, fighting your way through coaches, waggons, and hand-carts trundled along by large mastiff-dogs, with the houses twice as high, greasy holes for shop-windows, and piles of wood, green-stalls, and wheel-barrows placed at the doors, and the contents of wash-hand basins pouring out of a dozen stories – fancy all this and worse, and, with a change of scene, you are in Paris. The continual panic in which the passenger is kept, the alarm and the escape from it, the anger and the laughter at it, must have an effect on the Parisian character, and tend to make it the whiffling, skittish, snappish, volatile, inconsequential, unmeaning thing it is. . . . The very walk of the Parisians, that light, jerking, fidgetting trip on which they pride themselves, and think it grace and spirit, is the effect of the awkward construction of their streets, or of the round, flat, slippery stones, over which you are obliged to make your way on tiptoe, as over a succession of stepping-stones, and where natural ease and steadiness are out of the question . . . Paris is a vast pile of tall and dirty alleys, of slaughter-houses, and barbers' shops – an immense suburb huddled together within the walls so close, that you cannot see the loftiness of the buildings for the narrowness of the streets, and where all that is fit to live in, and best worth looking at, is turned out upon the quays, the boulevards, and their immediate vicinity.

Paris, where you can get a sight of it, is really fine. The view from the bridges is even more imposing and picturesque than ours. . . . The mass of public buildings and houses, as seen from the Pont Neuf, rises around you on either hand, whether you look up or down the river, in huge, aspiring, tortuous ridges, and produces a solidity of impression and a fantastic confusion not easy to reconcile. The clearness of the air, the glittering sunshine, and the cool shadows add to the enchantment of the scene. In a bright day it dazzles the eye like a steel mirror. The view of London is more open and extensive; it lies lower, and stretches out in a lengthened line of dusky magnificence. After all, it is an ordinary town, a place of trade and business. Paris is a splendid vision, a fabric dug out of the earth, and hanging over it. . . . It looks like a collection of palaces, or of ruins!

William Hazlitt, *Notes of a Journey through France and Italy*, 1826

A loud modern New York of a place.

Ralph Waldo Emerson, *Journal*, July 1833

You, who have ever been to Paris, know;
And you who have not been to Paris – go!

John Ruskin, *A Tour through France*, 1835

I think every wife has a right to insist upon seeing Paris.

Sydney Smith, Letter to Countess Grey, 11 September 1835

Paris is very full. I look at it with some attention, as I am not sure I may not end my days in it. I suspect the fifth act of life should be in great cities; it is there in the long death of old-age, that a man most forgets himself and his infirmities; receives the greatest consolation from the attentions of friends, and the greatest diversion from external circumstances.

Sydney Smith, Letter to Mrs Austin, 11 October 1835

Southey read to me part of a pleasant letter to his daughter in which he said: 'I would rather live in Paris than be hanged, and could find quiet spots to reside in, in the country round. The people look comfortable and might be clean if they would, but they have a hydrophobia in all things but one. They use water for no other purpose than to mix with their wine – for which God forgive them.'

Henry Crabb Robinson, quoting Southey in his Diary, 6 October 1838

Everything is gay in Paris but childhood. . . . Why are the children so joyless? . . . Is it not that there are no firesides – no *homes*?

Sir T.N. Talfourd, *Vacation Rambles*, 1844

I cannot tell you what an immense impression Paris made upon me. It is the most extraordinary place in the World. I was not prepared for, and really could not have believed in, its perfectly direct and separate character. My eyes ached, and my head grew giddy, as novelty, novelty, novelty; nothing but strange and striking things; came swarming before me. I cannot conceive any place so perfectly and wonderfully expressive of its own character; its secret character no less than that which is on its surface; as Paris is. I walked about streets – in and out, up and down, backwards and forwards – during the two days we were there; and almost every house, and every person I passed, seemed to be another leaf in the enormous book that stands wide open there. I was perpetually turning over, and never coming any nearer the end. There never was such a place for a description.

Charles Dickens, Letter to Count D'Orsay, 7 August 1844

*'And how, my dearest Dombey, did you find that delightfullest of cities, Paris?' she asked, subduing her emotion.
'It was cold,' returned Mr Dombey.
'Gay as ever,' said Mrs Skewton, 'of course.'
'Not particularly. I thought it dull,' said Mr Dombey.
'Fie my dearest Dombey!' archly; 'dull!'

'It made that impression, upon me, madam,' said Mr Dombey with grave politeness. 'I believe Mrs Dombey found it dull too. She mentioned once or twice that she thought it so.'

'Why, you naughty girl!' cried Mrs Skewton, rallying her dear child, who now entered, 'what dreadfully heretical things have you been saying about Paris?'

Charles Dickens, *Dombey and Son*, 1847-8

We kept very still of course, and were satisfied with the *idea* of Paris.

Elizabeth Barrett Browning, Letter to Miss Mitford, 2 October 1846, on her honeymoon

Well, now we are in Paris and have to forget the 'belle chiese;' we have beautiful shops instead, false teeth grinning at the corners of the streets, and disreputable prints, and fascinating hats and caps, and brilliant restaurants, and M. le Président in a cocked hat and with a train of cavalry, passing like a rocket along the boulevards to an occasional yell from the Red. Oh yes, and don't mistake me! for I like it all extremely, it's a splendid city – a city in the country, as Venice is a city in the sea.

Elizabeth Barrett Browning, Letter, 1851

. . . fair fantastic Paris who wears boughs
Like plumes, as if man made them, – tossing up
Her fountains in the sunshine from the squares,
As dice i' the game of beauty, sure to win;
Or as she blew the down-balls of her dreams,
And only waited for their falling back,
To breathe up more, and count her festive hours.
The city swims in verdure, beautiful
As Venice on the waters, the sea-swan.
What bosky gardens, dropped in close-walled courts,
As plums in ladies' laps, who start and laugh:
What miles of streets that run on after trees,
Still carrying the necessary shops,
Those open caskets with the jewels seen!
And trade is art, and art's philosophy,
In Paris.

Elizabeth Barrett Browning, *Aurora Leigh*, 1856

Paris has attained to a most immaculate and extraordinary varnish of decency, no doubt; but it were folly if not sin to enquire further.

M.F. Tupper, *Paterfamilias' Diary of Everybody's Tour*, 1856

The new buildings I only half like. They make Paris, which used to be the most historical place in the world, one monotonous handsomer Belgravia. To be sure, there are a great many nooks into which the improvements have not penetrated, but all that most catches the eye has been rebuilt or made uniform. There is a barrack, mean and poor as any building in England, on the other side of the Seine, just opposite this hotel, where there used to be one of the most irregular picturesque groups of houses possible. And then I cannot get over their having pulled down the true cock-hatted Napoleon from the pillar in the Place Vendôme, and put up instead, a sort of false Roman emperor figure in imperial robes. But the shops are splendid, and for show, pleasure, and luxury this place is, and every day more and more, the capital of Europe; and as Europe gets richer and richer, and show, pleasure, and luxury are more and more valued, Paris will be more and more important, and more and more the capital of Europe.

Matthew Arnold, Letter to his mother, 12 April 1865

The old faubourgs where Revolution plotted are being torn out by the roots like so many poisonous fangs. . . .

John W. Forney, Letters from Europe, 1867

France elects its ruler in the streets of Paris.

Walter Bagehot, *The English Constitution*, 1867

Paris is France for the purpose of making a government, but it is not France for the purpose of keeping a government.

Walter Bagehot, 'Do Conditions Requisite for a Stable Government Exist in France?', *Economist*, 10 September 1870

I must say that my savageness against France goes no further than wishing that the new and gay part of Paris were battered down; not the poor working part, no, nor any of the People destroyed. But I wish ornamental Paris down, because then I think the French would be kept quiet till they had rebuilt it. . . . I believe it would be a good thing if the rest of Europe would take possession of France itself, and rule it for better or worse, leaving the French themselves to amuse and enlighten the world by their Books, Plays, Songs, Bon Mots, and all the Arts and Sciences which they are so ingenious in. They can do all things but manage themselves and live at peace with others: and they should themselves be glad to have their volatile Spirits kept in order by the Good Sense and Honesty which other Nations certainly abound in more than themselves.

Edward Fitzgerald, Letter to W.F. Pollock, 1 November 1870

Flu will have told you of our wonderfully interesting visit to the ruins of Paris. The ruin was far greater than I had any notion of, but the natural tendency of Paris to gaiety and splendour is indestructible, and the place is fast on the way to have all its old fascinations again. The French are certainly much subdued, and that improves them greatly as to external manner; within, I fancy, they deceive themselves and feed themselves on nonsense as much as ever.

Matthew Arnold, Letter to his mother, 13 August 1871

You may not like Paris, and if you are not extremely fond of her you will in all probability detest and abominate her. . . . But even if you don't like her, you must at any rate admit that there are certain matters that she understands to perfection, and that if . . . one allows these things to play a large part in his life, one inevitably comes to think that the problem of existence is solved more comfortably here than elsewhere. The French have always flattered themselves that they have gone further in the art of living, in what they call *l'entente de la vie*, than any other people and with certain restrictions the claim is just. So far as man lives in his senses and his tastes he certainly lives as well here as he can imagine doing; and so far as he lives by the short run, as it were, rather than the long, he is equally well off. They seem to me to understand the 'long run' much better in England. There, if you live by the year, or by the semi-decade, say, you are free to find yourself at all points in relation with the world's best things. But the merit of Paris is that you have not to look so far ahead, and that without heavy machinery, by the day, by the month, by the season, you are surprisingly comfortable. There is to be found here, in other words, a greater amount of current well-being than elsewhere.

Henry James, Letter to the *New York Tribune*, 11 December 1875

Of all great cities, Paris is the most tolerable in hot weather. It it true that the asphalt liquefies, and it is true that the brilliant limestone of which the city is built reflects the sun with uncomfortable fierceness. It is also true that of a summer evening you pay a penalty for living in the best-lighted capital in the world. The inordinate amount of gas in the streets makes the atmosphere hot and thick, so that even under the dim constellations you feel on a July night as if you were in a big music-hall. If you look down at such a time upon the central portions of Paris from a high window in a remoter quarter, you see them wrapped in a lurid haze, of the devil's own brewing.

Henry James, 'Rouen', 1876, in *Portraits of Places*, 1883

That huge pretentious caravansery called Paris.

Henry James, 'Rheims and Laon', 1877, in *Portraits of Places*, 1883

The Paris of 1878 cares apparently not one farthing about any kind of war whatsoever. Her voice is all for Peace, and for Business, wholesale or retail, on a strictly ready-money basis. I never knew this ingenious and persevering people to be hungrier than they now are after francs and centimes. It is only Glory which seems to be at a discount. They may have had enough of it, and to spare, eight years ago.

G.A. Sala, *Paris Herself Again*, 1879

I hold the Parisian Old Woman to be the most remarkable individual of her sex and age to be found in the whole world.

Ibid.

A week in Paris reduced me to the limpness and lack of appetite peculiar to a kid glove . . . .It's my belief there's death in the kettle there.

Robert Louis Stevenson, Letter to his parents, 1 May 1881

The Parisian travels but little, he knows no language but his own, reads no literature but his own, and consequently he is pretty narrow, and pretty self-sufficient. However, let us not be too sweeping; there are Frenchmen who know languages not their own: these are the waiters.

Mark Twain, *Paris Notes*, 1882

Beautiful city, the centre and crater of European confusion,
O you with your passionate shriek for the rights of an equal humanity,
How often your Re-volution has proven but E-volution
Roll'd again back on itself in the tides of a civic insanity!

Alfred Lord Tennyson, 'Beautiful City', *Demeter and Other Poems*, 1889

My great terror here is of getting run over. There is a continual rush of carriages, drays and omnibuses through these wide boulevards and avenues. A coachman never holds up for you. On the contrary he will whip up and drive right at you. I believe they try to run over you. You have to pay a fine of twenty-five dollars for the privilege of being run over, I am told. It is a luxury that only the rich can afford.

Lilian Leland, *Travelling Alone, A Woman's Journey Round the World*, 1890

Paris is the best summer watering-place in Europe. It is the only city in the world which understands the world and itself. That I hate it is of course; it hates itself; but it at least amuses the pair of us.

Henry Adams, Letter to Elizabeth Cameron, 12 September 1895

Paris is the middle-aged woman's paradise.

Arthur Wing Pinero, *The Princess and the Butterfly*, Act 1, 1896

Twentieth Century

Do not . . . allow yourself to be 'put off' by the

superficial and external aspect of Paris; or rather (for the *true* superficial and external aspect of Paris has a considerable fascination) by what I may call the superficial and external aspect *of* the superficial and external aspect of Paris.

Henry James, remark, *c.* 1900, quoted Edward Marsh, *A Number of People*, 1939

Paris is, and has known herself to be, the City-state of modern Europe.

Hilaire Belloc, *Paris*, 1900

She is the typical city of western civilization – I mean, her history at any moment is always a peculiarly vivid reflection of the spirit which runs through western Europe at the time. Paris has not been typical in the sense of being the average. If she has been the typical city of the west, it is rather in this sense, that on her have been focussed the various rays of European energy; that she has been the stage upon which the contemporary emotions of Europe have been given *personae* through whose lips they could find expression; and that she has time and time again been the laboratory wherein the problems that perplexed our civilization have always been analyzed and sometimes solved.

Ibid.

Peter the Great said of Paris that if he possessed such a town he would be tempted to burn it down, for fear it should absorb the rest of his empire.

Augustus Hare, *Paris*, 1900

*Strether had at this very moment to recognize the truth that wherever one paused in Paris the imagination reacted before one could stop it.

Henry James, *The Ambassadors*, 1903

seen from the Sacré Coeur Church

I then came out and surveyed Paris from the front. I could distinguish most of the landmarks – Notre Dame, Pantheon, Invalides, Gare d'Orléans, St Sulpice, and Louvre. Never before had I such a just idea of the immense size of the Louvre. I could also see the Opera, (that centre of *Paris qui s'amuse*) with its green roof (?copper). And it looked so small and square and ordinary. And I thought of the world-famed boulevards and resorts lying hidden round about there. And I thought: Is that all it is? For a moment it seemed impossible to me that, as a result of a series of complicated conventions merely, that collocation of stones, etc. (paving stones and building stones) could really be what it is – a synonym and symbol for all that is luxurious, frivolous, gay, vicious and artistic. I thought: 'Really, Paris is not Paris after all; it is only a collocation of stones.' The idea, though obvious enough, was very striking for a minute or two.

Arnold Bennett, *Journal*, 4 October 1903

Paris is my home, and I am not ashamed to own that, like most Parisians, I suffer, when abroad, from a nostalgia of the Boulevards that a traveller were perhaps better without.

Harry de Windt, *From Paris to New York by Land*, 1904

The veneer of Paris is the thinnest in the world.

Hilaire Belloc, *Hills and the Sea*, 1906

The living charm of the place, the sense – of which the first hour in Paris is enough to make the English traveller conscious – that a quicker, lighter, easier spirit vibrates there than elsewhere; the sense of being saved from the dulness of existence, and given a fresh start with a livelier, more flexible mind. . . .

Percy Lubbock, *Elizabeth Barrett Browning in her Letters*, 1906

If a man fell out of the moon into the town of Paris he would know that it was the capital of a great nation. If, however, he fell (perhaps off some other side of the moon) so as to hit the city of London, he would not know so well that it was the capital of a great nation; at any rate, he would not know that the nation was as great as it is.

G.K. Chesterton, *All Things Considered*, 1908

Though Paris is easily the most prejudiced, old-fashioned, obsolete minded city in the west of Europe, yet when she produces great men, she certainly does not do it by halves. Unfortunately there is nothing she hates more than a Frenchman of genius. . . . To suppose that they know a great Frenchman when they see him . . . is contrary to all experience. They never know until the English tell them.

G. Bernard Shaw, *Three Plays By Brieux*, Preface, 1909

Every public man who fell ill at Paris was liable to stories about him. It was generally attributed either to delirium tremens or adultery.

Wilfred Scawen Blunt, quoting George Wyndham, Diary, 21 February 1910, *My Diaries*, 1919

Nobody who has not lived intimately in and with Paris can appreciate the unique savour of that word *femmes*.

Arnold Bennett, *Paris Nights*, 1913

It was raining. The boulevard was a mirror. And along the reflecting surface of this mirror cab after cab, hundreds of cabs, rolled swiftly. Dozens and dozens were empty, and had no goal; but none would stop. They all went ruthlessly by with offensive gestures of disdain. Strangers cannot believe that when a Paris cabman without a fare refuses to stop on a wet night, it is not because he is hoping for a client in richer furs, or because he is going to the stables, or because he has earned enough that night, or because he has an urgent appointment with his enchantress – but simply from malice. Nevertheless this is a psychological fact which any experienced Parisian will confirm. On a wet night the cabman revenges himself on the *bourgeoisie*, though the base satisfaction may cost him money.

Ibid.

*Paris, the very Vanity Fair of mundane pleasure.

Stephen Leacock, *Behind the Beyond*, 1919

*Quiet, conservative people in Paris like to get to bed at three o'clock; after all, what is the use of keeping late hours and ruining one's health and complexion? If you make it a strict rule to be in bed by three, you feel all the better for it in the long run – health better, nerves steadier, eyes clearer, and you're able to get up early – at half-past eleven – and feel fine.

Ibid.

Paris is a nasty city.

D.H. Lawrence, Letter to Cecily Lambert Minchin, November 1919

*Paris rawly waking, crude sunlight on her lemon streets. Moist pith of farls of bread, the froggreen wormwood, her matin incense, court the air. Belluomo rises from the bed of his wife's lover's wife, the kerchiefed housewife is astir, a saucer of acetic acid in her hands. In Rodot's Yvonne and Madeliene newmake their tumbled beauties, shattering with gold teeth *chaussons* of pastry, their mouths yellowed with the *pus* of *flan breton*. Faces of Paris men go by, their wellpleased pleasers, curled conquistadores.

James Joyce, *Ulysses*, 1922

Paris is a hostile brilliant alien city.

Virginia Woolf, Letter to Gwen Raverat, 8 April 1925

Paris;this April sunset completely utters;
utters serenely silently a cathedral

before whose upward lean magnificent face
the streets turn young with rain,

spiral acres of bloated rose
coiled within cobalt miles of sky
yield to and heed
the mauve
                    of twilight (who slenderly descends,
daintily carrying in her eyes the dangerous first stars)
people move love hurry in a gently

arriving gloom and
see!(the new moon
fills abruptly with sudden silver
these torn pockets of lame and begging colour)while
there and here the lithe indolent prostitute
Night,argues

with certain houses

e.e. cummings, *& [And]*, 1925

Paris is still monumental and handsome. Along the rivers where its splendours are, there's no denying its man-made beauty. The poor, pale little Seine runs rapidly north to the sea, the sky is pale, pale jade overhead, greenish and Parisian, the trees of black wire stand in rows, and flourish their black wire brushes against a low sky of jade-pale cobwebs, and the huge dark-grey palaces rear up their masses of stone and slope off towards the sky still with a massive, satisfying suggestion of pyramids. There is something noble and man-made about it all.

My wife says she wishes that grandeur still squared its shoulders on the earth. . . .

Well, she can have it. At least, she can't. The world has lost its faculty for splendour, and Paris is like an old, weary peacock, that sports a bunch of dirty twigs at its rump, where it used to have a tail. Democracy has collapsed into more and more democracy, and men, particularly Frenchmen, have collapsed into little, rather insignificant, rather wistful, rather nice, and helplessly commonplace little fellows, who rouse one's mother-instinct, and make one feel they should be tucked away in bed and left to sleep, like Rip van Winkle, till the rest of the storm's rolled by.

D.H. Lawrence, 'Paris Letter – Laughing Horse', April 1926, *Phoenix*, 1936

The characteristic thing about Paris is not so much the extent, – though that is vast, as the overwhelming variety of its reputation. It has become so overlaid with successive plasterings of paste and proclamation that it has come to resemble those rotten old houses one sometimes sees during their demolition, whose crumbling frame of walls is only held together by the solid strata of wall-papers.

What after all these years can we say about Paris? There is one word 'bogus', which I have heard used a great deal with various and often inconsistent implications. It seems to me that this scrap of jargon, in every gradation of meaning, every innuendo, every allusion and perversion, and 'bluff' it is capable of bearing, gives a very adequate expression of the essence of modern Paris.

Paris is bogus in its lack of genuine nationality. No one can feel a foreigner on Monte Carlo, but Paris is cosmopolitan in the diametrically opposite sense, that it makes everyone a foreigner. London, deficient as it is in all the attributes which make a town habitable, is at least British. It is our own family skeleton in our own cupboard. Bath and Wells and Birmingham are all implied in London in a way in which Tours or Tarascon or Lyons are not implicit in Paris; the febrile ardours of French provincial life, the tenacity and avarice and logic and militancy of the French character, seem out of place and improbable in the French capital. And sensitive Frenchmen confess to a feeling of awkwardness there. . . . It is in Paris that money must be made, but it is best spent in the provinces.

Evelyn Waugh, *Labels*, 1930

The Latin Quarter is in fact a very grave, silent, and austere region. But it has its Bohemian fringes – and a non-Anglo-Saxon population bred to survive such dissipations as are there to be found. Anglo-Saxons are not so bred. They resemble the populations of Central Africa succumbing before the clothing, gin, and creeds of white men. That in the bulk. There are, of course, individuals who survive.

Ford Madox Ford, *Return to Yesterday*, 1932

The Paris slums are a gathering place for eccentric people – people who have fallen into solitary half-mad grooves of life and given up trying to be normal or decent. Poverty frees them from normal standards of behaviour just as money frees people from work.

George Orwell, *Down and Out in Paris and London*, 1933

Paris is like myself a haughty ruin or if you like a decayed reveller.

James Joyce, Letter to Harriet Shaw Weaver, Paris, 1 May 1935

The last time I saw Paris,
Her heart was warm and gay,
I heard the laughter of her heart
In every street café.

Oscar Hammerstein II, *The Last Time I Saw Paris*, 1940

I have lived half my life in Paris, not the half that made me, but the half in which I made what I made.

Gertrude Stein, *An American and France*, 1940

I've been to Paris France and I've been to Paris Paramount. Paris Paramount is better.

Ernst Lubitsch, quoted Leslie Halliwell, *The Filmgoers Book of Quotes*, 1979

The character exists, unquestionably, who managed to have a rip-roaring time in Paris in the summer of 1947, but who he is, where he did so, and how he found the inclination, I cannot imagine. To my way of thinking, it was one of the more woeful locales west of Shanghai; the food scarcity was acute, the cost of living was astronomical, and a pall of futility and cynicism hung over the inhabitants. Physically, to be sure, the city was completely unchanged; it was still the most beautiful capital on earth, but it was mere architecture, a series of superb vistas forsaken by the spirit that had once animated it. There were streets, indeed whole quarters, devoid of any sign of life and business appeared to be at a complete standstill. Everywhere you went, you sensed the apathy and bitterness of a people corroded by years of enemy occupation.

S.J. Perelman, *Westward Ha!*, 1948

If you are lucky enough to have lived in Paris as a young man, then wherever you go for the rest of your life, it stays with you, for Paris is a moveable feast.

Ernest Hemingway, Letter to a friend, 1950

Paris is an air and a scent and a state of mind.

James Cameron, *News Chronicle*, 18 January 1954

Paris seems to be full of American girls who are hiding from their mothers.

James Thurber, *Credos and Curios*, 1962

Parasites are residents of Paris.

Art Linkletter, *A Child's Garden of Misinformation*, 1965

Livid Daylight. The French naturalistic novelists were always talking about '*un jour blafard.*' You will find in them such descriptions as '*Un jour blafard était tamisé au travers les rideaux de guipure sale.*' You have to spend a winter in Paris really to know what this *jour blafard* is. It is what you get most of the time. I have composed a short poem on the subject:

HIVER PARISIEN
Le jour blafard
Donne le cafard.

Edmund Wilson, *Europe without Baedeker*, 2nd edn, 1967, *Notes from a European Diary*, 1963–4

Paris is what is left of France if provincialism is taken away.

Peter Nichols, *Italia, Italia*, 1973

The yellow gas has made way for a whitish-blue electricity, the city itself becoming much darker and blacker. The trees have been driven increasingly off the streets and avenues; the boulevards extérieurs have become roaring express-ways, no longer suited to the imprudent night-walker, 'candidat au surin', and among which even the prostitutes, Les Amazones, have become motorized. In fact a symbol of the quadruple degradation of a city of one-time human proportions.

The becs de gaz were the first to go, but their disappearance was not entirely disastrous, as they were often adequately replaced by the orange clusters of electric globes such as decorated the Rond Point or the Concorde, thus allowing Paris still to retain its character as a constellation of many waxy moons.

Richard Cobb, *Times Literary Supplement*, 2 September 1977

Can there be any doubt that what visitors to Paris are

really looking for is . . . the Parisian him (or elle) self? The sort of fellow who, when asked the way to the Church of St Sulpice, directs you to the Crazy Horse Inn.

And long may he flourish. A touch of masochism never harmed anybody. . . . An encounter with a perverse Parisian is unique to the victim. It's pure gold, tourist-wise. He doesn't mug you, as in London, or nick your handbag from a scooter, as in Rome, or feed you dog meat, as in Singapore. The Frenchman is simply irritable, negative. They call it *'s'en foutism.'* . . .

Paris is in fact a northern place and finds its true self in the autumn and winter. When in April, a Mediterranean awning is unravelled above the trottoirs in defiance of geographical realities, the natives instantly go out of sorts. . . . They don't really like it here, forever dreaming of *Tremping* their *sabots* in the *bouse de vache* (steeping clogs in cow dung). Those who do well retire to their hamlet in the Massif Central. Those who don't stay to breed Parisians.

Denis Herbstein, 'Putting Paris Right', *Sunday Times*, 30 December 1979

Nostalgia is the city's cheapest commodity and everyone foreign gets it for free.

'Taki', *Spectator*, 28 June 1980

Districts and Details

Eiffel Tower
I ought to be jealous of that tower. She is more famous than I am.

Gustave Eiffel, attrib.

It seems to be saying perpetually; 'I am the end of the nineteenth century; I am glad they built me of iron; let me rust.' . . . It is like a passing fool in a crowd of the University, a buffoon in the hall; for of all the things that Paris has made, it alone has neither wits nor soul.

Hilaire Belloc, *Paris*, 1900

Bois de Boulogne
I will not describe the *Bois de Boulogne*. I cannot do it. It is simply a beautiful, cultivated, endless, wonderful wilderness.

Mark Twain, *The Innocents Abroad*, 1869

Les Halles
The Halles – the heart and the life-blood of Paris, the very essence of Parisian vitality and humour, sensuality, sexuality, generosity, vinous appetite, nocturnal sociability and ordered anarchy.

Richard Cobb, *Times Literary Supplement*, 2 September 1977

Quartier Montparnasse
I asked him [Somerset Maugham] if he liked the Quartier Montparnasse and he said, 'Yes; the atmosphere of it is rather like Oxford.'

Arnold Bennett, *Journal*, 3 March 1905

Pau

Pau, of whom her native Bearnais said that the year had eight months of winter and four of inferno.

Richard Burton, *Wanderings in West Africa*, 1863

and Biarritz
Soft, relaxing, *most* English Pau, full of elderly birds with doubtful lungs in plus fours! . . . And here at Biarritz is pure Philistia and wealth and comforts accumulated on fatted comforts.

Rudyard Kipling, Letter to Rider Haggard, 25 March 1925

Perpignan

Perpignan is a villainous ugly town, on the skirts of an extensive flat, that has just olive woods enough to make a tolerable appearance from the ramparts . . . a most disagreeable town, and, to a curious traveller, destitute of every kind of recommendation.

Henry Swinburne, *Travels through Spain in the Years 1775 and 1776*, 1783

The Pont du Gard

The hugeness, the solidity, the unexpectedness, the monumental rectitude of the whole thing leave you nothing to say – at the time – and make you stand gazing. You simply feel that it is noble and perfect, that it has the quality of greatness. . . . I remained there an hour, and got a complete impression. . . . It came to pass that I discovered in it a certain stupidity, a vague brutality. That element is rarely absent from great Roman work, which is wanting in the nice adaptation of the means to the end. The means are always exaggerated; the end is so much more than attained. The Roman rigidity was apt to overshoot the mark, and I suppose a race which could do nothing small is as defective as a race that can do nothing great. Of this Roman rigidity the Pont du Gard is an admirable example. It would be a great injustice, however, not to insist upon its beauty – a kind of manly beauty, that of an object constructed not to please, but to serve, and impressive simply from the scale on which it carries out this intention.

Henry James, *A Little Tour in France*, 1882

Of all the monuments which antiquity has left to mark this particular countryside of Europe, the most impressive, the most permanently enormous in the memory of those who have seen it, is the Pont du Gard. . . . When one sees the thing all that is said of it comes true. Its isolation, its dignity, its weight, are all three awful. It looks as though it had been built long before all record by beings greater than ourselves, and were intended to stand long after the dissolution of our petty race. One can repose in it. I confess to a great reluctance to praise what has been praised too much; but so it is. A man, suffering from the unrest of our time, might do worse than camp out for three days, fishing and bathing under the shadow of the Pont du Gard.

Hilaire Belloc, *Many Cities*, 1928

'But I thought you hated old monuments,' I said. Raoul looked at me scornfully. 'That is science!' he said coldly. 'It is not art but science, sir. It is a Roman triumph of the plumber's science. I always take my apprentices out there. It is their first lesson in plumbing. Now the Pont du Gard I love and know well.'

'But it is beautiful, no?'

'It is practical, sir,' said Raoul firmly.

Lawrence Durrell, 'Laura, a Portrait of Avignon', 1961 – in *Spirit of Place*, 1969

Provence

and Languedoc

Provence is a pleasant country, well cultivated; but the inns are not so good here as in Languedoc, and few of them are provided with a certain convenience which an English traveller can very ill dispense with. Those you find are generally on the tops of the houses, exceedingly nasty; and so much exposed to the weather, that a Valetudinarian cannot use them without hazard of his life. At Nismes in Languedoc, where we found the temple of Cloacina in a most shocking condition, the servant-maid told me her mistress had caused it to be made on purpose for the English travellers; but now she was very sorry for what she had done, as all the French who frequented her house, instead of using the seat, left their offerings on the floor, which she was obliged to have cleaned three or four times a day. This is a degree of beastliness which would appear detestable even in the capital of North Britain.

Tobias Smollett, *Travels through France and Italy*, 1766

Provence . . . the land where the silver-grey earth is impregnated with the light of the sky.

Henry James, *A Little Tour in France*, 1882

There is the first time we go abroad, and the first time we go to Provence.

Cyril Connolly, *Enemies of Promise*, 1938

In winter the Mistral cuts the whole Midi down to size.

Cyril Connolly, *The Evening Colonnade*, 1973

Provençal

The Provençal is all alive, and feels his nerves agitated in a supreme degree by accidents and objects that would scarce move a muscle or a feature in the phlegmatic natives of more northern climes; his spirits are flurried by the slightest sensations of pleasure or of pain, and seem always on the watch to seize the transient impressions of either; but to balance this destructive propensity, nature has wisely rendered it difficult for those impressions to sink into their souls; they easily receive, but as easily discard and forget, thus daily offering a surface smoothed afresh for new pains and pleasures to trace their light affections upon. But this by no means excludes warm attachments and solid friendships; when time and habit afford leisure for the impression to penetrate deep enough, it will, no doubt, acquire and retain as firm a hold in their breast as in any other, and perhaps be stamped with still greater warmth and energy.

Henry Swinburne, 'A Journey from Bayonne to Marseilles', in *Travels through Spain in the Years 1775 and 1776*, 1783

The Provençal language . . . is a most disagreeable jargon, as unintelligible even to those who understand French as to those who do not, and delighting in intonations of the voice, which always reminded me of a crying child.

Charles Lewis Meryon, *Travels with Lady Hester Stanhope*, 1846

Pyrenees

compared with the mountains of Wales

They are not so high and hideous as the *Alps*; but for our Mountains in *Wales*, as *Eppint* and *Penminmaur*, which are so much cry'd up among us, they are *Molehills* in comparison of these; they are but *Pigmies* compar'd to *Giants*, but *Blisters* compar'd to *Imposthumes*, or *Pimples* to *Warts*. Besides, our Mountains in *Wales* bear alway something useful to Man or Beast, some Grass at least; but these uncouth huge monstrous Excrescences of Nature bear nothing (most of them) but craggy Stones: the Tops of some of them are blanched over all the Year long with Snows; and the People who dwell in the Valleys, drinking for want of other this Snow-Water, are subject to a strange Swelling in the Throat, called *Goytre*, which is common among them.

James Howell, 'Letter to Sir J.H., from Lyons, 6 November 1621', *Familiar Letters*, 1645

Il n'y a plus de Pyrénées.*

(There are no more Pyrenees.)

Louis XIV to his grandson, the Duke of Anjou, on his accession to the Spanish throne in 1700, according to Voltaire, *Siècle de Louis XIV*, 1752, but probably a paraphrase of the Spanish Ambassador's compliment to Louis on that occasion.

What parts gay FRANCE from sober SPAIN?
A little rising Rocky Chain.
Of Men born South or North o'th Hill,
Those seldom move; these ne'er stand still.

Matthew Prior, *Alma*, Canto II, 1715–18

These mountains are of such an enormous height, as well as extent, that they seem as if they were formed even by nature to divide nations. . . . Indeed the extensive plains on both sides these lofty mountains (so unusual in the southern parts of Europe) would almost make one suspect that nature herself had been exhausted in raising such an immense pile, which, as if it were the backbone of an huge animal, was made to hold, and bind together, all the parts of the western world.

Philip Thicknesse, *A Year's Journey through France and Spain*, 1789

'The Pyrenean boundary,' says the Duke of Wellington, 'is the most vulnerable frontier of France, probably the only vulnerable one.'

Richard Ford, *Gatherings from Spain*, 1846

Africa begins at the Pyrenees.

Alexandre Dumas, attrib., before 1870

It is a romantic country, a land of cape and sword, a land of pretty women, and heady wines. . . . Rostand lives there, and George Gissing died there, than which I could wish no better epigrammatic description of this district.

Robert Harborough Sherard, *My Friends the French*, 1909

the snow-lit
Sharp annunciation of the Pyrenees.

Louis MacNeice, *Autumn Journal*, 1938

The mountains seemed wilder than the Alps, lapped round with forests rather than pastures – stretches of uninhabited lands, more like Asia: we left them with that Pisgah feeling all travellers know, of a view seen, not visited, not forgotten.

Freya Stark, *Traveller's Prelude*, 1950

Rheims

(*Mem.* – Must see *Rheims*, much fam'd, 'tis said,
For making Kings and gingerbread.)

Thomas Moore, *The Fudge Family in Paris*, 1818

As you draw near to Rheims the vineyards become sparser, and finally disappear, a fact not to be regretted, for there is something incongruous in the juxtaposition of champagne and gothic architecture.

Henry James, 'Rheims and Laon, A Little Tour', 1877, in *Portraits of Places*, 1883

It has a prosperous, modern, mercantile air. The streets look as if at one time, M. Haussmann, in person, may have taken a good deal of exercise in them; they prove however, that a French provincial town may be a wonderfully fresh, clean, comfortable-looking place.

Ibid.

Rheims! What do I say to Rheims? I say nothing at all, I have no words. . . . Rheims, the highest leaping flame of all the Gothic fires – a great fire which curled round the very throne of God – it was alive, it burned, it sparkled, it laughed. I am punished indeed – well are we served! We deserve nothing else. We have made the houses of God mere quarries for sightseers. . . . The thing was a mystery and we measured it. It was a great shout and we sat and listened. And now we are indignant. . . . God has found a whip of German guns wherewith to deprive the money changers of the temples of France. Why should Paris be indignant? What was Rheims to it? A blooming museum – a kind of provincial branch of the Louvre. I do not care. The sculptures of Rheims are gone. Good. If we cannot construct a Christian Europe in this age, we certainly are not fit to be the guardians of the evidence of the Christian Europe of the past. The whole thing should be wiped out. It would be completely just. When we want an altar we can build one. And when God has finished with the whip He will discard it.

Eric Gill, Letter to André Raffalovich, 24 September 1914

the fruit market

The fruit market, in particular, is superior to every thing of the kind; but I will not tantalize you by saying any more on that subject, unless you were near enough to *eat* a bottle of champagne, in the way that God gives it.

Philip Thicknesse, *A Year's Journey through France and Spain*, 1789

River Rhône

As I have seen a great part of the course of this river, I cannot but think it has been guided by the particular hand of Providence. It rises in the very heart of the Alps, and has a long valley that seems hewn out on purpose to give its waters a passage amidst so many rocks and mountains which are on all sides of it. This brings it almost in a direct line to Geneva. It would there overflow all the country, were there not one particular cleft that divides a vast circuit of mountains, and conveys it off to Lyons. From Lyons there is another great rent, which runs across the whole country in almost another straight line, and, notwithstanding the vast height of the mountains that rise about it, give it the shortest course it can take to fall into the sea. Had such a river as this been left to itself to have found its way out from among the Alps, whatever windings it had made it must have formed several little seas, and have laid many countries under water before it had come to the end of its course.

Joseph Addison, *Remarks on Several Parts of Italy, in the Years 1701, 1702, & 1703*, 1705

By the blue rushing of the arrowy Rhone.
. . . where the swift Rhone cleaves his way between
Heights which appear as lovers who have parted
In hate, whose mining depths so intervene,
That they can meet no more, though broken-hearted. . . .

Lord Byron, *Childe Harold's Pilgrimage*, Canto the Third, 1816

Swift Rhone! thou wert the *wings* on which we cut
A winding passage with majestic ease
Between thy lofty rocks.

William Wordsworth, *The Prelude*, 1805, Text of 1850

and other rivers

The French rivers partake of the national character. Many of them look broad, grand and imposing; but they have no depth. And the greatest river in the country, the Rhone, loses half its usefulness from the impetuosity of the current.

J.C. and A. Hare, *Guesses at Truth*, 3rd edn, 1847

Thou Royal River, born of sun and shower
  In chambers purple with the Alpine glow,
  Wrapped in the spotless ermine of the snow
  And rocked by tempests! – at the appointed hour
Forth, like a steel-clad horseman from a tower,
  With clang and clink of harness dost thou go
  To meet thy vassal torrents, that below
  Rush to receive thee and obey thy power.
And now thou movest in triumphal march,
  A king among the rivers! On thy way
  A hundred towns await and welcome thee;
Bridges uplift for thee the stately arch
  Vineyards encircle thee with garlands gay
  And fleets attend thy progress to the sea!

Henry Wadsworth Longfellow, *To the River Rhône*, 1876

at Tarascon

The big brown flood, of uncertain temper, which has never taken time to forget that it is the child of the mountain and the glacier, and that such an origin carries with it great privileges.

Henry James, *A Little Tour in France*, 1882

The Rhône is the river of Angels.

Robert Louis Stevenson, Letter to W.H. Low, March 1886

Delta of the Rhône

The delta of the Rhône is something quite different from the rest of France. It is a wedge of Greece and of the East thrust into the Gauls. It came north a hundred years ago and killed the monarchy. It caught the value in, and created, the great war song of the Republic.

Hilaire Belloc, *The Path to Rome*, 1902

The Riviera

I had my father's love of solidity and soundness, – of unveneered, unrouged, and well-finished things; and here on the Riviera there were lemons and palms, yes, – but the lemons pale, and mostly skin; the palms not much larger than parasols; the sea – blue, yes, but its beach nasty; the buildings pompous, luxurious, painted like Grimaldi, – usually broken down at the ends and in the middle, having sham architraves daubed over windows with no glass in them; the rocks shaly and ragged, the people filthy; and over everything, a coat of plaster dust.

John Ruskin, *Praeterita*, 1885–9

I took in the section from Genoa to Marseilles, an enormous stretch of country, and wondered: what has this coast ever produced in the way of thought or action, of great men or great women? There is Doria at Genoa, and Gaby Deslys at Marseilles; that may well exhaust the list. Ah, and half-way through, a couple of generals, born at Nice; and the delicious Fragonard at Grasse. It is really an instructive phenomenon, and one that should appeal to students of Buckle – this relative dearth of every form of human genius in one of the most favoured regions of the globe. Here, for unexplained reasons, the Italian loses his better qualities; so does the Frenchman. Are the natives descended from those mysterious Ligurians? Their reputation was none of the best; they were more prompt, says Crinagoras, in devising evil than good.

Norman Douglas, *Alone*, 1921

The Riviera Hinterland

A lavender-hemmed rocky chaos with airies over torrents.

Tourist brochure, quoted by William Sansom, *Blue Skies Brown Studies*, 1961

Route from Rouen to Paris

They vaunt much of the *Lower Road* from Rouen to

Paris; but is not so fine as that from Dieppe to Rouen. You have comparatively few trees, the soil is less fertile, and you are (nearly the whole way) tantalized with the vast, marshy-looking plains of Normandy, with the Seine glittering through them like a snake, and a chain of abrupt chalky hills, like a wall or barrier bounding them. There is nothing I hate like a distant prospect without any thing interesting in it – it is continually dragging the eye a wearisome journey, and repaying it with barrenness and deformity. Yet a Frenchman contrived to make a paneygeric on this scene, after the fashion of his countrymen, and with that sort of tripping jerk which is peculiar to their minds and bodies – '*Il y a de l'eau, il y a des bois, il y a des montagnes, il y a de la verdure,*' &c. It is true, there were all these things in the abstract, or as so many detached particulars to make a speech about, which was all that he wanted. A Frenchman's eye for nature is merely *nominal.*

William Hazlitt, *Notes of a Journey through France and Italy*, 1826

Rouen

They are right to have country villas – to get out of this great ugly, stinking close, and ill built town, which is full of nothing but dirt and industry. What a picture of new building does a flourishing manufacturing town in England exhibit!

Arthur Young, *Travels . . . [in] . . . France* (9 August 1788), 1792

and Geneva and Pisa
Rouen, Geneva and Pisa have been tutresses of all I know, and were mistresses of all I did, from the first moments I entered their gates.

John Ruskin, *Praeterita*, 1885–9

etcetera
Rouen is the rainiest place getting
Inside all impermeables, wetting
Damp marrow in drenched bones.
Midwinter soused us coming over Le Mans
Our inn at Niort was the Grape of Burgundy
But the winepress of the Lord thundered over that grape of Burgundy
And we left in a hurgundy
(Hurry up Joyce, it's time!).

I heard mosquitoes swarm in old Bordeaux
So many!
I had not thought the earth contained so many
(Hurry up, Joyce, it's time).

Mr Anthologos, the local gardener,
Greycapped, with politeness full of cunning
Has made wine these fifty years
And told me in his southern French
Le Petit vin is the surest drink to buy
For if 'tis bad
Vous ne l'avez pas payé
(Hurry up, hurry up, now, now, now!).

But we shall have great times,
When we return to Clinic, that waste land
O Esculapios!
(Shan't we? Shan't we? Shan't we?)

James Joyce, Letter to Harriet Shaw Weaver, Arcachon, 15 August 1925

St Denis

St Denys is a towne considerable onely for its stately Cathedrall, and Dormitory of the French Kings who lye there inhum'd, as ours at Westminster: Not omitting the Treasury esteemed one of the richest in Europe.

John Evelyn, *Diary*, 17 November 1643

St Germain en Laye

If dulness inspires literary activity (which I deny) no better place of course could be found. . . . It is as Americans say 'the limit' of provincial seclusion. It ensures quiet to the extent that motors are discouraged from crossing its drowsy streets. One has heard that the Mayor of St Germain did on a notable occasion lay his bulky form prone in the dust so as to compel a 'scorcher' who was approaching *à toute vitesse* to slacken speed. . . .

Robert Harborough Sherard, *My Friends the French*, 1909

St Malo

A place of very great Strength and traffique, there being the most, the fairest and biggest Shipping, that I thinck are in any other port of Fraunce. . . . Also, notwithstandinge the extraordinary strength of the place, being built on a Rock, strongly walled, fortefied and guarded with great vigillancie, there are twenty-four mungrell Doggs, whoe every night are sent out of the Gates with their keeper, and all night long course to and froe about the walls, killinge and teareinge any liveinge Creature they encounter withall, be it man or beast, haveing att my being there torne one man to peices, and Cattle. Theis in the morninge first enter in att the opening of the gates and last that goe forth att their Closeing in the Eveninge.

Peter Mundy, *Voyages*, 1625

This Town of *St Malo* hath one rarity in it; for there is

here a perpetual Garison of *English*, but they are of *English* Dogs, which are let out in the Night to guard the Ships, and eat the Carrens up and down the Streets, and so they are shut up again in the Morning.

James Howell, 'Letter to My Cousin W. Vaughan Esq, from St Malo, 25 September 1620', *Familiar Letters*, 1645

St Tropez (and Hyères)

I went to Hyères and St. Tropez, both of which were bosh.

Edward Lear, Letter to Lady Waldegrave, 11 December 1866

Savoy

The worst wayes that ever I travelled in all my life in the Sommer were those betwixt Chamberie and Aiguebelle, which were as bad as the worst I ever rode in England in the midst of Winter: insomuch that the wayes of Savoy may be proverbially spoken of as the Owles of Athens, the peares of Calabria, and the Quailes of Delos. . . . On every Alpe I saw wonderfull abundance of pine trees, especially about the toppe, and many of them of a very great height; and betwixt the toppe and the foote there are in many of those mountains wilde Olive-trees, Chesnut-trees, Walnut-trees Beeches, Hasel-trees, &c. The whole side of many a hill being replenished with all these sorts of trees. . . . The countrey of Savoy is very cold, and much subject to raine, by reason of those clouds, that are continually hovering about the Alpes, which being the receptacles of raine do there more distill their moisture, then in other countries.

I observed an admirable abundance of Butter-flies in many places of Savoy, by the hundred part more then ever I saw in any countrey before, whereof many great swarmes, which were, (according to my estimation and coniecture) at the least two thousand, lay dead upon the high waies as we travelled.

When I came to Aiguebelle I saw the effect of the common drinking of snow water in Savoy. For there I saw many men and women have exceeding great bunches or swellings in their throates, such as we call in latin *strumas*, as bigge as the fistes of a man, through the drinking of snow water, yea some of their bunches are almost as great as an ordinary foot-ball with us in England. These swellings are much to be seen amongst these Savoyards, neither are all the *Pedemontanes* free from them.

Thomas Coryat, *Crudities*, 1611

Wall'd by the cloud-capt Alps on every side,
The plenteous vales of SAVOY guarded seem
From the fierce inroad of Ambition's tide,
When neighbouring powers unsluice its wasteful
stream.

Anna Seward, *Alpine Scenery*, 1785

Savoy . . . may be considered as the vestibule of the Alps. . . .

Lady Morgan, *Italy*, 1820

Souillac

Souillac is a little town in a thriving state, having some rich merchants. . . . It is not in the power of an English imagination to figure the animals that waited upon us here, at the Chapeau Rouge. Some things that called themselves by the courtesy of Souillac women, but in reality walking dung-hills.

Arthur Young, *Travels . . . [in] . . . France* (9 June 1787), 1792

Souillac is the only small town of the region to make an appeal to the mind.

Cyril Connolly, 'Dordogne', in *Ideas and Places*, 1953

Sologne

The miserable province of Sologne, which the French writers call the *triste* Sologne.

Arthur Young, *Travels . . . [in] . . . France* (31 May 1787), 1792

Somme

Mondrian on the other side of the carriage was gazing wrapt onto the Somme country as we sped past it on our way to Calais. It was September 21st 1938. The grass was lush and green, the poplars were green and soft, the sky was evening yellow, sunlight, a green peace lay over the marshy land. 'How beautiful, how peaceful it is,' I thought, 'and you see Mondrian does not hate green or the country. His eyes are full of its marvel.' 'Isn't it wonderful,' he murmured. 'Yes, it is,' I said.

'Look' he continued, 'how they pass, they pass, they pass, cutting the horizon, here, and here, and here,' . . . I realized that what delighted him were the telegraph poles – the vertical that cut the horizontal of the horizon.

Winifred Nicholson, quoted in *Studio International*, December 1966

Strasbourg

The Cathedral
That hallow'd spire which rises to the skies,
Fills ev'ry heart with rapture and surprise;

Approach the temple – round its rev'rend base
Vile traffic shops God's edifice disgrace.
Are there still Goths in this enlightened age
Who dare oppose and scorn the sacred page?
Who by one impious act at once express
Their want of virtue, taste and righteousness?

David Garrick, *Upon Seeing Strasbourg Cathedral, Extempore by a Stranger*, 1764

The tower at Strasburg is red, and has a singular appearance. The fortifications here, in time of peace, have an effect like the stillness of death.

William Hazlitt, *Notes of a Journey through France and Italy*, 1826

Toulon

Toulon is a considerable place, even exclusive of the basin, docks, and arsenal, which indeed are such as justify the remark made by a stranger, when he viewed them, 'The king of France (said he) is greater at Toulon than at Versailles.'

Tobias Smollett, *Travels through France and Italy*, 1766

Toulouse

The circumference of the city is about four miles: its streets are roomy, and houses well constructed; some of them are grand and spacious, but there is a gloominess in the colour of the brick with which they are built, and a want of motion in the streets, that casts a damp upon my spirits, and excites ideas of misery.

Henry Swinburne, 'A Journey from Bayonne to Marseilles', in *Travels in Spain in the Years 1775 and 1776*, 1783

The oddity is that the place should be both animated and dull. A big, brown-skinned population, clattering about in a flat, tortuous town, which produces nothing whatever that I can discover.

Henry James, quoting his notebook, *A Little Tour in France*, 1882

Tours

Balzac says in one of his tales that the real Tourangeau will not make an effort, or displace himself even, to go in search of a pleasure. . . .

Henry James, *A Little Tour in France*, 1882

Trouville

When I got there I knew it at once – not from any specific book or painting, but from a whole temper or even genre of art. There lay the long empty foreshore, with only a few shrimp-catchers knee-deep in its sand pools; and there along the boardwalk strolled a group of those that Boudin loved, blurred and shimmery in flowered cottons; and the beach was lined with a gallimaufry of villas, gabled, pinnacled, or preposterously half-timbered; and three fishing boats with riding sails chugged away off-shore; and over it all, over the sands, and the estuary, and the distant promontory of Le Havre, there hung a soft impressionist light, summoned out of moist sunshine, high rolling clouds and the reflection of the sea. I knew the scene at once, from Monet and Bonnard and Proust. The English were the modern inventors of the salt-water resort, and made it fashionable to frequent the beaches; but the French first saw the beauty of the seaside scene, and transmuted into art all its perennial sights – the slant of that white sail, the stoop of that child beside his sand castle, the preen of the great ladies along the promenade.

This particular aesthetic was born in Trouville. It was among the earliest of the French seaside resorts, for a time it was the grandest, and at the back of our minds it is half familiar to us all.

James Morris, 'Trouville', *Places*, 1972

Troyes

The suburbs of Troyes were destroyed, and the town itself dirty and uninviting. . . . A curious instance of French vanity occurred on leaving this town. Our *voiturier* pointed to the plain around, and mentioned, that it had been the scene of a battle between the Russians and the French. 'In which the Russians gained the victory?' – 'Ah, no, Madame,' replied the man, 'the French are never beaten.' 'But how was it then,' we asked, 'that the Russians had entered Troyes soon after?' – 'Oh, after having been defeated, they took a circuitous route, and thus entered the town.'

Mary Shelley, *History of a Six Weeks' Tour* (14 August 1814), 1817

Fontaine de Vaucluse

I have seen Vaucluse and am disappointed. A huge cavern yawning at the foot of a perpendicular wall of bare rocks, and a large body of water issuing through the chinks of the stone, from an unfathomable pool that fills the cave, are undoubtedly bold, horrid, features of nature; but I have seen the like in many mountainous countries in much greater perfection: here is not a single tree, not a bush to enliven the dull uniformity of the cliff, nor any lofty barrier of rock, over which the stream may rush in grand cascades; the landscape is dreary and frightful without romantic beauty.

Henry Swinburne, 'A Journey from Bayonne to Marseilles', in *Travels through Spain in the Years 1775 and 1776*, 1783

Set off in a cabriolet to Vaucluse. . . . Wordsworth was strongly excited, predetermined to find the charm of interest, and he did. There is no verdure, but perhaps on looking more closely Petrarch may not have praised his retreat either for shady groves or meadows – and the stream of the Sorgues is eminently beautiful. The rocks are almost sublime, at least very romantic. Having taken a luncheon at the mouth of the cavern we ascended the heights above, and Wordsworth made a longer ramble among the rocks behind the fountain.

Henry Crabb Robinson, *Diary*, 2 April 1837

Versailles

Outre la passion, je n'ai jamais vu de chose plus triste. (Apart from passion, I have never seen anything more sad.)

Madame de Maintenon, late seventeenth century, quoted by Richard Ford, *A Handbook for Travellers in Spain*, 1855

The great front is a lumber of littlenesses, composed of black brick, stuck full of bad old busts, and fringed with gold rails. The rooms are all small, except the great gallery, which is noble, but totally wainscoted with looking-glass. The garden is littered with statues and fountains, each of which has its tutelary deity. In particular, the elementary god of fire solaces himself in one. In another, Enceladus, in lieu of a mountain, is overwhelmed with many waters. There are avenues of water-pots, who disport themselves much in squirting up cascadelins. In short, 'tis a garden for a great child. Such was Louis quatorze, who is here seen in his proper colours, where he commanded in person, unassisted by his armies and generals, and left to the pursuit of his own puerile ideas of glory.

Horace Walpole, Letter to Richard West, 1739

An amazing pile of building.

Philip Thicknesse, *Observations on the Customs and Manners of the French Nation*, 1766

The Chateau has a look of ruined splendour, and the Town of desolate devastation. Painted ceilings faded! Crimson tapestry torn! Gold friezes brown with age, and every thing wearing an appearance as if a thousand years ago there had been a nightly tournament, and that since it had sunk & withered under the stroke of a mighty enchanter.

The Palace of Versailles in its glory must have been a gleaming jewel. Invention seems to have been wracked to find excuses for new habitations. I wonder they did not build a room for the king's right hand and a room for his left, a room in short for every action of his body and every conception of his mind.

Benjamin Robert Haydon, *Diary*, 17 June 1814

The palace is a huge heap of littleness. . . . It ought to be one of the most striking effects of human power and art. I doubt whether there be anywhere any single architectural composition of equal extent . . . yet there are a dozen country houses of private individuals in England alone which have a greater air of majesty and splendour than this huge quarry.

T.B. Macaulay, *Journal*, 2 February 1839, in *Life and Letters*, by G.O. Trevelyan, 1876

Versailles! It is wonderfully beautiful! You gaze, and stare, and try to understand that it is real, that it is on the earth, that it is not the garden of Eden – but your brain grows giddy, stupefied by the world of beauty around you, and you half believe you are the dupe of an exquisite dream. The scene thrills one like military music!

Mark Twain, *The Innocents Abroad*, 1869

The other day I went out to Versailles and passed an hour or two in the gardens of the Petit Trianon. Versailles was actually most beautiful in its desertion. Certainly it is not a religious repose, but it is painfully human and pessimistic.

Henry Adams, Letter to Elizabeth Cameron, 3 August 1896

Versailles was, in practical function, a vast dormitory for the French nobility.

John Kenneth Galbraith, *Economics, Peace, and Laughter*, 1971

Villefranche

Villefranche's weather is naval, and queerly changeable: one week American ships will be there, in the next week, Greek, French, Argentinian, British – and the streets will for the period take on the clothes and songs and customs of the crews ashore. Villefranche is so small that the effect becomes fantastic – like a house changing its whole furniture once a week.

William Sansom, *Blue Skies Brown Studies*, 1961

Vosges

I am a tall tree in the Vosges!

Albert Schweitzer, quoted by Hermann Hagedorn, *Prophet in the Wilderness*, 1948

G

GABON

I am faint-hearted enough to hope that our next journey together may not be over a country that seems to me to have been laid down as an obstacle race-track for Mr. G.F. Watts's Titans, and to have fallen into shocking bad repair.

Mary Kingsley, *Travels in West Africa*, 1897

Sierra del Cristal (from the Ogowe River)

The majesty and beauty of the scene fascinated me, and I stood leaning with my back against a rock pinnacle, watching it. Do not imagine it gave rise, in what I am pleased to call my mind, to those complicated poetical reflections natural beauty seems to bring out in other people's minds. It never works that way with me; I just lose all sense of human individuality, all memory of human life, with its grief and worry and doubt, and become part of the atmosphere.

Mary Kingsley, *Travels in West Africa*, 1897

Rembwe River

By daylight the Rembwe scenery was certainly not so lovely, and might be slept through without a pang. It had monotony, without having enough of it to amount to grandeur.

Mary Kingsley, *Travels in West Africa*, 1897

The Fan Tribesmen

The Fan is full of fire, temper, intelligence, and go; very teachable, rather difficult to manage, quick to take offence, and utterly indifferent to human life. I ought to say that other people, who should know him better than I, say he is a treacherous, thievish, murderous cannibal. I never found him treacherous; but then I never trusted him. . . . The cannibalism of the Fans, although a prevalent habit, is no danger, I think, to white people, except as regards the bother it gives one in preventing one's black companions from getting eaten. The Fan is not a cannibal from sacrificial motives like the negro. He does it in his common sense way. Man's flesh, he says, is good to eat, very good, and he wishes you would try it. Oh dear no, he never eats it himself, but the next-door town does. He is always very much abused for eating his relations, but he really does not do this. He will eat his next door neighbour's relations and sell his own deceased to his next door neighbour in return; but he does not buy slaves and fatten them up for his table as some of the Middle Congo Tribes I know of do. He has no slaves, no prisoners of war, no cemeteries, so you must draw your own conclusions. No, my friend, I will not tell you any cannibal stories.

Mary Kingsley, *Travels in West Africa*, 1897

Lambaréné

I asked our pilot what Lambaréné was like. He replied in succinct Engish, 'It stinks.' I asked the Negro official representing Air France what it was like. He replied with the utmost sincerity, 'It is purgatory on earth, monsieur.'

John Gunther, *Inside Africa*, 1955

GALAPAGOS ISLANDS (Ecuador)

Chatham Island

Nothing could be less inviting than the first appearance. A broken field of black basaltic lava, thrown into the most rugged waves, and crossed by great fissures, is everywhere covered by stunted, sun-burnt brushwood, which shows little signs of life. . . . The dry and parched surface, being heated by the noonday sun, gave to the air a close and sultry feeling, like that from a stove; we fancied even that the bushes smelt unpleasantly. . . . The brushwood appears, from a distance, as leafless as our trees during winter; and it was some time before I discovered that not only almost every plant was now in full leaf, but that the greater number were in flower.

Charles Darwin, *Journal . . . During the Voyage . . . of H.M.S. Beagle*, 1832–6

GAMBIA

'Gambia' is said to mean clear water, surely a misnomer, it is as muddy as the Mersey.

Richard Burton, *Wanderings in West Africa*, 1863

The Gambia is one of the most oddly shaped countries in the world; it looks like an earthworm, and fits around the Gambia River like a long, tight, wrinkled sleeve.

John Gunther, *Inside Africa*, 1955

Gambia is more English than England, more English even than India.

Richard West, *The White Tribes of Africa*, 1965

Gambia is a country with eight barristers and no psychiatrists. When the British ambassador had to choose which project to support with a grant, he invited suggestions and was asked to make a contribution to the mental hospital, which had few modern facilities. He donated some cricket equipment. The British influence continues, in particular the links between politics and the law. Each of the country's eight barristers has at one time wanted to enter politics, and in so small a country there is only one political post that a lawyer trained in London considers to be worth his attention, the presidency. But all eight lawyers have been frustrated in this ambition, because, ever since independence, the office of president has been filled by a veterinary surgeon whose great achievement has been to authorize an entirely new Gambian industry – package tourism.

Patrick Marnham, *Fantastic Invasion*, 1980

Gambians

Stokes told us that notwithstanding the country of Gambo is so unhealthy, yet the people of that place live very long, so as the present King there is 150 years old, which they count by Raynes, because every year it rains continually four months together. He also told us that the Kings there have above 100 wives apiece, and offered him the choice of any of his wifes to lie with, and so he did Captain Holmes.

Samuel Pepys, *Diary*, 16 January 1662

Mandingo People

The Mandingos themselves, which are the Naturall Inhabitants, are perfectly blacke, living a most idle life, except two moneths of the yeare, in their Seed-time and harvest; wandering up and downe at other times from one to another, having little knowledge, to hunt, fish, or fowle, how soever both Woods and Waters abound in Game, the Beasts and Fowles (as Guinnie Hens and Partridges) resorting to their very doores. In the heate of the day they passe the time in companies chatting under the shady Trees, having one Game with some thirtie stones and holes cut in a piece of Wood, performed by a kind of counting.

Richard Jobson, 1620–1, in *Purchas his Pilgrimes*, 1625

Banjul (formerly Bathurst)

Bathurst . . . I thought an aged fogy.

Richard Burton, *Wanderings in West Africa*, 1863

Another half hour placed before us Bathurst in full view. It suggested somewhat the idea of a small European watering-place, and contains barely 5,000 souls. The site has none of those undulations which render a place picturesque; everything is horizontal, straight-lined, and barely above sea level. Beginning from the westward are a few detached houses, a colonial hospital, a military ditto, the Governor's quarters, large barracks – upon whose turret floated, or rather depended the flag of St George, the market, the slaveyard, and the esplanade, behind whose line of trees lay the mass of the settlement. The houses might be those of Byculla, Bombay – in fact they date from the same epoch – large, uncompact tenements, washed glistening white or yellow, with slates, tiles, or shingles, which last curl up in the sun like feathers. Further on are heaps of native huts, like beehives, or a crowded rickyard, rising from swamp and sand, and terminating abruptly up the river. There is an Octagon, not a concert-room or chapel, but a coal-depot, and there are two one-gun martello towers at the angles of the fort looking towards the town, which may relieve the view, but which look anything but dangerous. A nearer glance shows the house walls stained and gangrened with mildew; a fearful vegetation of Guinea grass, palms, plantains, cotton trees and caoutchouc figs, which at a distance resemble whitethorns, occupies every inch of soil, and the inundations of the river sometimes find their way into the ground floor. In fact, the island and settlement of St Mary (of old a cemetery) seem to be selected for unhealthiness, for proximity to mud, mangrove, miasma, and malaria.

Ibid.

The Bathurstian sharks are vivacious.

Ibid.

To those who would retain the Gambia, I wish nothing worse than a year's residence, or, rather, confinement there.

Ibid.

. . . The hawks flapping heavily over Bathurst, a long low backcloth of houses and trees along a sandy beach; a swarm of figures in the native quarter like flies on a piece of meat; the not being able to land because of yellow fever; the sense of isolation that the woman had as she went off to join her husband in the quarantined town; this was more really the Coast . . .

Graham Greene, *Journey Without Maps*, 1936

Mr. Greene was never one to look at the world through rose-tinted spectacles, but even so there is something grotesque about this description. The imagery of the flies on the meat gives him away. So might Graham Greene describe a cluster of angels in Paradise.

Richard West, *The White Tribes of Africa*, 1965

GERMANY

Seventeenth Century

Germany is the Queene of all other Provinces, the Eagle of all Kingdomes, and the Mother of all Nations.

Thomas Coryat, *Crudities*, 1611

Through all Germany they lodge betweene two fetherbeds (excepting Sweitzerland, where they use one bed under them, and are covered with woollen blankets) and these fetherbeds for softnesse and lightnesse are very commodious, for every winter night the servants are called into the warme stove, whereof such fethers as are reserved, they pull the fethers from the quill, using onely the softest of them for making of beds. The bed lying under is great and large, and that above is narrow and more soft, betweene which they sleepe aswell in Summer and Winter. This kind of lodging were not incommodious in Winter, if a man did lie alone: but since by the high way they force men to have bedfellowes, one side lies open to the cold, by reason that the upper bed is narrow, so as it cannot fall round about two, but leaves one side of them both open to the wind and weather. But in Summer time this kind of lodging is unpleasant, keeping a man in a continuall sweat from head to foote. Yet in Country Villages, and many parts of Saxony, passengers have no cause to complaine of this annoyance, since all without exception, rich and poore, drunken and sober, take up their lodging among the Cowes in straw, where sometimes it happens, that hee who lying downe had a pillow of straw under his head, when hee awaketh finds the same either scattered or eaten by the Cowes.

Fynes Moryson, *An Itinerary*, 1617

Germany cut into so many Principalties, into so many *Hansiatique* and *Imperiall* Townes, *is like a great River sluced into sundry Channels, which makes the maine streame farre the weaker*, the like may be said of *Italy*.

James Howell, *Instructions for Forren Travell*, 1650

Eighteenth Century

Since our leaving Prague we have seen nothing but a great variety of winter pieces, so that all the account I can give you of the country is that it abounds very much in snow . . . scarce any thing we meet with, except our sheets and napkins, that is not white.

Joseph Addison, Letter to Mr Stepney, 3 January 1703

'Tis impossible not to observe the difference between the free Towns and those under the Government of absolute Princes (as all the little Sovereigns of Germany are). In the first there appears an air of Commerce and Plenty. The streets are well built and full of people neatly and plainly dress'd, the shops loaded with Merchandize, and the commonalty clean and cheerful. In the other, a sort of shabby finery, a Number of dirty people of Quality tawder'd out, Narrow nasty streets out of repair, wretchedly thin of Inhabitants, and above halfe of the common sort asking alms. I can't help fancying one under the figure of a handsome clean Dutch Citizen's wife and the other like a poor Town lady of Pleasure, painted and riban'd out in her Head dress, with tarnish'd silver lac'd shoes, and a ragged under petticoat, a miserable mixture of Vice and poverty.

Lady Mary Wortley Montagu, Letter to Lady Bristol, Nuremberg, 22 August 1716

O'er vast Germania, the ferocious nurse
Of hardy men and hearts affronting death.

James Thomson, *Liberty*, 1734–6

A Scots baron cannot do better than travel in Germany. When he goes to Italy and France, he lives with artificial men cooped up in towns, and formed in such a manner that Nature is quite destroyed. Yet is an art so agreeable substituted in its place that these people feel themselves happy, although the true manly character is melted into elegant ease. If the Scots baron were to pass all his life abroad, he would not perceive his imbecility more than they do. But as he must return to his own country, let him not render himself unfit for it. Let him go and visit the German courts, where he can acquire French and polite manners, and at the same time be with people who live much in the same style that he must do at home. He may thus learn to support his character with dignity, and upon his paternal estate may have the felicity of a prince. Let him make a tour into the delicious countries of the south, to enrich his mind with a variety of brilliant ideas, and to give his manners a still finer polish. But let him not stay there too long. Let him not remain in the Italian sun till his Caledonian iron is melted.

James Boswell, *Journal*, 27 September 1764

The most civilized nations of modern Europe issued from the woods of Germany, and in the rude institutions of those barbarians we may still distinguish the original principles of our present laws and manners.

Edward Gibbon, *The Decline and Fall of the Roman Empire*, 1776–88

To be an Englishman is in Germany to be an angel – they almost worship you.

S.T. Coleridge, Letter to Thomas Poole, 26 October 1798

Nineteenth Century

Why did I come to Germany? Did I anticipate the German philosophy? Could I foresee in what connections I should fall? Had I any preacquaintance with the easy free active animated life of a german University? Had I any knowledge of the excellencies of the German Characters of the congenial habits & manners of its people? Nothing of the sort I came to Germany because I did not know what to do with myself in England.

Henry Crabb Robinson, Letter to his brother, 27 November 1803

The only Country in which a man dare exercise his *reason* without being thought to have lost his wits & be out *of his Senses*.

S.T. Coleridge, Letter to Charles Augustus Tulk, September 1817

Learned, indefatigable, deep-thinking Germany.

Thomas Carlyle, *Sartor Resartus*, 1836

Deutschland, Deutschland über Alles, über Alles in der Welt.

A.H. Hoffman von Fallersleben, *Deutschlandlied*, 1841

My companion in the carriage, Mr de Porbeck, an officer in the Baden army, . . . gave me some scraps of information about what may be called German politics, some of which I was not prepared for . . . He told me that there is a great and growing desire on the part of the smaller States to form one nation with one or other of the great Powers, and that before long they would all be thus absorbed by their own desire. I said surely none of them could desire to belong to Austria. He said this feeling was more prevalent in the north, and he thought eventually all the Rhenish and Protestant States, Baden, Nassau, Wurtemberg, Saxony, would be united to Prussia; that the first war which broke out would produce this revolution; that the fate of the Catholic parts of Germany might be different: that Bavaria might survive, and possibly unite other provinces to herself. But as to Austria, he was convinced that the death of Metternich would be the signal for a great movement in that country; that everything was preparing for it, and that event would bring the projects which were spreading more and more every day to maturity . . . there is also a great wish to have colonies and a navy, all of which he deems feasible, and says Prussia is already beginning to build ships of war. Whether there is truth in all this, or these are my friends's reveries, I know not; but as I had never before heard of such aspirations, I was struck by what he told me. We had a great deal of talk besides about the condition of the people, and he expressed with some pride his satisfaction that while they had nothing of the grandeur of English opulence to boast of, they had not the afflicting spectacle of English misery and destitution . . . There is certainly a degree of social equality which is very foreign to our habits, and yet it is not subversive of the respect which is due from persons in one station to those in another. To me it has nothing offensive. I see it as a trait of national character and manners.

Charles Greville, *A Journal of the Reign of Queen Victoria*, 5 July 1843

Setzen wir Deutschland, so zu sagen, in den Sattel! Reiten wird es schon können.

(Let us put Germany, so to speak, in the saddle! You will see that she can ride.)

Otto von Bismarck, Speech in the Parliament of the Confederation, 11 March 1867

The keeping a country in such beautiful order as Germany exhibits, has a wise practical side to it, too, for it keeps thousands of people in work and bread who would otherwise be idle and mischievous.

Mark Twain, *A Tramp Abroad*, 1880

*In Germany one breathes in love of order with the air, in Germany the babies beat time with their rattles . . .

Jerome K. Jerome, *Three Men on the Bummel*, 1900

*For in Germany there is no nonsense talked about untrammelled nature. In Germany nature has got to behave herself, and not set a bad example to the children.

Ibid.

Germany, the diseased world's bathhouse.

Mark Twain, *Autobiography*, 1906–10

Twentieth Century

I have suffered from the tightness, the domesticity of Germany. It is our domesticity which leads to our conformity, which chokes us. The very agricultural landscape here, and the distinct paths, stifles me. The very oxen are dull and featureless, and the folk seem like tables of figures.

D.H. Lawrence, Letter to Edward Garnett, April 1913

We have loved your burgs, your pines' green moan,
Fair Rhine-stream, and its storied towers;
Your shining souls of deathless dowers
Have won us as they were our own.

Thomas Hardy, *England to Germany in 1914*, *Moments of Vision*, 1917

German genius has a hypnotising power over half-baked souls and half-lighted minds. There is an immense force of suggestion in highly-organised mediocrity. Had it not hypnotised half Europe?

Joseph Conrad, 'Poland Revisited', 1915, in *Notes on Life and Letters*, 1921

In two years or ten years Germany will have found her Masaryk and her Benes and be on her way to recovery.

H.G. Wells, Article, 3 November 1923, in *A Year of Prophesying*, 1925

Germany will be either a world power or will not be at all.

Adolf Hitler, *Mein Kampf*, 1925–6

In the sphere of force, human records contain no manifestation like the eruption of the German volcano. For four years Germany fought and defied the five continents of the world by land, sea, and air . . . Surely, Germans, for history it is enough! Is this the end? Is it merely to be a chapter in a cruel and senseless story? . . . Will our children bleed and gasp again in devastated lands? Or will there spring from the very fires of conflict that reconciliation of the three giant combatants which would unite their genius and secure to each in safety and freedom a share in rebuilding the glory of Europe?

Sir Winston Churchill, *The World Crisis*, part II, 1927

In Germany it is the 'Idea' that is impersonated by everybody. There are no ordinary human beings, you are 'Herr Professor,' or 'Herr Geheimrat,' 'Herr Oberrechnungsrat,' and even longer things than that. Sometimes the German idea is right and sometimes it is wrong, but it never ceases to be an idea, whether it belongs to the highest philosophy, or is merely a foolish bias. Even when you die in Germany, you don't die in mere human misery, you die in the ideal form of 'Hausbesitzersgattin,' or something of the sort.

C.G. Jung, *The Complications of American Psychology*, 1930

Germany was the first country to experience the miracles worked by democracy's ghost, the State.

C.G. Jung, *Psychology and National Problems*, Lecture, 14 October 1936

The Germany praised by the pro-Germans is much nastier than the Germany abused by the anti-Germans.

G.K. Chesterton, *As I Was Saying*, 1936

These big, over-grown, bullying modern States were not the product of long time (the only true maker of States) but are all rapid imitations. They breed nothing but evil continually. It was a very bad day for the Germans when they were tempted to follow this novel fashion to which they are unsuited and in which they are now trapped.

Hilaire Belloc, *Places*, 1942

Germany . . . is a land of ghosts which have never been exorcised.

Goronwy Rees, 'Diary, from Berlin to Munich', *Encounter*, April 1964

The new Germany . . . is stunning. The place looks upholstered.

Patrick O'Donovan, 'How the Queen won Germany', *Observer*, 28 May 1978

J'aime tellement l'Allemagne que je suis heureux qu'il y en a deux.
(I love Germany so much I am glad there are two of them.)

François Mauriac, quoted by Roger Berthoud in *The Times*, 14 October 1978

Germans

Sixteenth and Seventeenth Centuries

A valiant and stowt nation in good aksions . . . for although the Germans and Almans be but blunt and riud, and also geven to delyt in their dayly drink to much, yet thoz fawts be not so hurtfull to otherz, neyther do giyv kaws of offens to otherz more then them selvz, az the forsaid vises and other vyses which I kowld nam that be in the french, Italiens, and Spanyardz. and bekawz that owr English nasion kam owt of Germany . . . I will Kommend the plainez of the Germans befor the dissimulasion of the iij nation afforsaid.

Thomas Whythorne, *Autobiography*, *c.* 1576

Germans are honest men.

William Shakespeare, *Merry Wives of Windsor*, *c.* 1600–1

A man is in almost as high proportion to a knave in England, as a Knight in Germany, for there a Gentleman is called a Youngcur, and a Knight is but a Youngcurs man, so that you shall have a scurvy Squire command a Knight to hold his stirrop.

John Taylor, *Taylor's Travells to Hamburgh in Germany*, 1616

And to say this truth, the Germans are in high excesse subject to this vice of drinking, scarce noted with any other nationall vice, so that as their Doctors and Artisans, affecting the knowledge onely of one science, or manuall art, doe become excellent therein, so this nation in generall, and every part or member thereof, practising night and day the faculty of drinking, become strong and invincible professors therein.

Fynes Moryson, *An Itinerary*, 1617

The German's wit is in his fingers.
(Les Allemands ont l'esprit aux doigts.)

George Herbert, *Outlandish Proverbs*, 1640

The old *Germans* seemed to have some reason in their custom, not to execute any great resolutions which had not been twice debated and agreed at two several assemblies, one in an afternoon, and t'other in a morning; because, they thought, their counsels might want vigour when they were sober, as well as caution when they had drunk.

Sir William Temple, *Observations upon the United Provinces of the Netherlands*, 1672

When you with Hogh Dutch Heeren dine,
Expect false Latin and Stum'd wine:
They never tast who always drink,
They always talk, who never think.

Matthew Prior, *On this Passage in the Scaligeriana*, *c.* 1687

Les Allemans ne se soucient pas quel Vin ils boivent pourveu que ce soit Vin, ni quel Latin ils parlent pourveu qu ce soit Latin.
(The Germans don't care what wine they drink, so long as it is wine, nor what Latin they speak, so long as it is Latin.)

J. Scaliger, *Scaligeriana, ou Bons Mots, Rencontres Agreables, etc.*, 1695

Eighteenth Century

Drunk'nness, the Darling Favourite of Hell,
Chose *Germany* to Rule; and Rules so well,
No Subjects more obsequiously obey,
None please so well, or are so pleas'd as they.
The cunning Artist manages so well,
He lets them Bow to Heav'n, and Drink to Hell.
If but to Wine and him they Homage pay,
He cares not to what Deity they Pray,
What God they worship most, or in what way.
Whether by *Luther*, *Calvin*, or by *Rome*,
They sail for Heav'n, by Wine he steers them home.

Daniel Defoe, *The True-Born Englishman*, 1701

Germany is undoubtedly a very fine Country, full of industrious honest People, & were it united it would be the greatest Power that ever was in the World. The common People are, here, almost everywhere, much better treated & more at their ease, than in France; and not very much inferior to the English, notwithstanding all the Airs the latter give themselves.

David Hume, Letter to John Home of Ninewells, 7 April 1748

They began by being commentators, and tho' they have given many instances of their industry, they have scarce afforded any of genius. If criticism would have improved the taste of a people, the Germans would have been the most polite nation alive.

Oliver Goldsmith, *An Enquiry into the Present State of Polite Learning in Europe*, 1759

Some nations, and the Germans in particular, have ever discovered a greater propensity to increase the language of science than to extend its discoveries.

Oliver Goldsmith, in *Monthly Review*, October 1763

I was enlivened by seeing the hearty Germans.

James Boswell, *Journal*, 6 July 1764

. . . the old observation, That the German genius lyes more in the back than in the brain.

Tobias Smollett, *Travels through France and Italy*, 1766

Pray tell *Townley* (with my Love to him), that I never, since I left England, till now, have regal'd Myself with a good house of Office, or as he calls it, a *Conveniency* – the holes in Germany are generally too large, & too round, chiefly owing I believe to the broader bottoms of the Germans, for they are *swingers* indeed all thro' Bavaria – We have a little English Gentleman with us, who Slipt up to the Middle of one of the holes & we were some Minutes before we could disEngage him. – in short you may assure Townley, (Who loves to hear of the state of these Matters) that in Italy the People *do their Needs*, in Germany they *disEmbogue*, but in England (& in England only) they *Ease* themselves.

David Garrick, Letter to George Garrick, Munich, 5 August 1764

To solicit by labour what might be ravished by arms was esteemed unworthy of the German spirit.

Edward Gibbon, *The Decline and Fall of the Roman Empire*, 1776–88

Love is the vital air of my Genius, & I have not seen one human Being in Germany, whom I can conceive it *possible* for me to *love* – no, not one. To my mind they are an unlovely Race, these Germans!

S.T. Coleridge, Letter to Mrs S.T. Coleridge, 10 March 1799

Nineteenth Century

Again on the Subject of Morals – Germany is certainly not arrived at that pitch of depravity which prevails in England – I believe we have here much fewer acts of notorious & gross dishonesty – Bankruptcy is very rare comparatively – Swindling of all Sorts is by no means reduced to such an Art. But amongst those called persons of honour & character there is a want of delicacy & liberality which I think is more striking than in England – The English travellers of my Acquaintance give a bad character of their Merchants – There is a sort of sly tricking among them & in common Life Meannesses which in England would be scouted – So that I am disposed to apply to the Germans what I have often observed of the Dissenters They wont do dishonest tricks but damed dirty ones.

Henry Crabb Robinson, Letter to his brother, Frankfurt, 22 March 1801

travelling by water between Mainz and Cologne
We took our place in the *diligence-par-eau* for Cologne . . . nothing could be more horribly disgusting

than the lower order of smoking, drinking Germans who travelled with us; they swaggered and talked, and what was hideous to English eyes, kissed one another . . .

Mary Shelley, *History of a Six Weeks' Tour* (4 September 1814), 1817

The *Germans* in *Greek*
Are sadly to seek,
Not five in five score,
But ninety-five more:
All, save only *Herman*,
And *Herman*'s a *German*.

Richard Porson, parodying an ancient epigram of Phocylydes, quoted E.D. Clarke, *Travels in Various Countries*, 4th edn, 1818

. . . Germany whose somewhat tardy millions
Have princes who spur more than their postillions.

Lord Byron, *Don Juan*, 1819–24

In many of the towns upon the Rhine, as Cologne, Bonn, Coblentz &c., a traveller finds the bed, which is prepared for his repose, open at the feet, as well as at the head; and when he asks the reason of this strange custom, he is told that the 'German gentlemen go to bed in their boots.'

E.D. Clarke, *Travels in Various Countries*, 1824

There is a nimiety – a too-muchness – in all Germans. It is the national fault.

Samuel Taylor Coleridge, *Table Talk*, 2 June 1834

The Germans are a singular people. Without much solidity in their opinions they indulge in a considerable range of thought and combine with it a sense of refined enjoyment of the essence of beauty in the world both moral and physical which makes them as writers generally pleasing, sometimes unintelligible.

Charles Francis Adams, *Diary*, 27 July 1834

Next to the favour and good opinion of my own countrymen, I value, above all price, the esteem of the German people. I honor and admire them past all expression. I know them to be, in their great mental endowments and cultivation, the chosen people of the Earth . . .

Charles Dickens, Letter to J.H. Kuenzel, 13 September 1841

The Germans cannot even do *simplicity* without a flourish.

Thomas Hood, Letter to C.W. Dilke, 12 July 1836

I think the German men kiss each other so because, thanks to dirt, there is no *fair sex* there.

Thomas Hood, Letter to John Wright, 13 July 1837

How all Germany can sleep in such short and perilous beds, with an eiderdown feather bed outside to be kicked off in the middle of the night, and with both extremities frozen while the middle is red hot, I cannot understand: this whole people illustrate the prophet's image of lying on a bed too short for them and with a coverlid that will not cover them.

M.F. Tupper, *Paterfamilias' Diary of Everybody's Tour*, 1856

The German and Irish millions, like the Negro, have a great deal of guano in their destiny. They are ferried over the Atlantic, and carted over America to ditch and to drudge, to make corn cheap, and then to lie down prematurely to make a spot of green grass on the prairie.

R.W. Emerson, *Fate – The Conduct of Life*, 1860

Wit requires delicate handling; the Germans generally touch it with gloved hands. Sarcasm is with them too often a sabre, not a rapier, hacking the victims, where a thrust would suffice.

G.H. Lewes, *The Life and Works of Goethe*, 2nd edn, 1864

The good-will of the Germans certainly diminishes as they become more of a political nation, and get imbued with all the envy, hatred, and malice of political striving.

Matthew Arnold, Letter to his mother, 23 July 1865

Excessively good people are, – speaking socially, – angular. Take, for instance, the Prussians; they are saints compared with the French. They have every sort of excellence; they are honest, sober, hard-working, well-instructed, brave, good sons, husbands, and fathers; and yet all this is spoilt by one single fault – they are insupportable. Laugh at the French, abuse them as one may, it is impossible to help liking them. Admire, respect the Prussians as one may, it is impossible to help disliking them. I will venture to say it would be impossible to find 100 Germans born south of the Main who would declare, on their honour, that they prefer a Prussian to a Frenchman. The only Prussian I ever knew who was an agreeable man was Bismarck. All others with whom I have been thrown – and I have lived for years in Germany – were proud as Scotchmen, cold as New Englanders, and touchy as only Prussians can be. I once had a friend among them. His name was Buckenbrock. Inadvertently I called hin Butterbrod. We have never spoken since.

Henry Labouchere, *Diary of the Besieged Resident in Paris*, 1871

The average German would much rather loll around, sipping wine or beer, and smoking cigarettes, than impel a bicycle across a continent.

Thomas Stevens, *Around the World on a Bicycle*, 1887

Twentieth Century

*The German citizen is a soldier, and the policeman is his officer . . . 'You get yourself born,' says the German Government to the German citizen, 'we do the rest. Indoors and out of doors, in sickness and in health, in pleasure and in work, we will tell you what to do, and we will see to it that you do it. Don't worry yourself about anything.'

Jerome K. Jerome, *Three Men on the Bummel*, 1900

*The Germans are a good people. On the whole, the best people perhaps in the world; an amiable, unselfish, kindly people. I am positive that the vast majority of them go to Heaven. Indeed, comparing them with the other Christian nations of the earth, one is forced to the conclusion that Heaven will be chiefly of German manufacture. But I cannot understand how they get there. That the soul of any single German has sufficient initiative to fly up by itself and knock at St Peter's door, I cannot believe. My own opinion is that they are taken there in small companies, and passed in under the charge of a dead policeman.

Jerome K. Jerome, *Three Men on the Bummel*, 1900

They are *of necessity* histrionic. Note I do not say it is a vice of theirs. It is a necessity of theirs, an appetite. They must see themselves on a stage . . . they *must* be play-actors to be happy and therefore to be efficient; and if I were Lord of Germany, and desired to lead my nation and to be loved by them, I should put great golden feathers on my helmet, I should use rhetorical expressions, spout monologues in public, organise wide cavalry charges at reviews, and move through life generally to the crashing of an orchestra. For by doing this even a vulgar, short, and diseased man, who dabbled in stocks and shares, and was led by financiers, could become a hero and do his nation good.

Hilaire Belloc, *The Path to Rome*, 1902

*'Do you imply that we Germans are stupid, Uncle Ernst?' exclaimed a haughty and magnificent nephew. Uncle Ernst replied, 'To my mind. You use the intellect, but you no longer care about it. That I call stupidity.'

E.M. Forster, *Howard's End*, 1910

One can imagine the hogs with their cigars (I think of Prussians whom I know somewhat) reading up a bit of *Zarathustra* in the evening to buck them up for a jolly day with bombs on unfortified towns, massacres of women and old men, destruction of an university or so, . . . but alas – the beasts are brave and victorious.

James Elroy Flecker, Letter to Frank Savery, 4 September 1914

That promised land of steel, of chemical dyes, of method, of efficiency; that race planted in the middle of Europe, assuming in grotesque vanity the attitude of Europeans among effete Asiatics or barbarous niggers; and, with a consciousness of superiority freeing their hands from all moral bonds, anxious to take up, if I may express myself so 'the perfect man's burden.'

Joseph Conrad, 'Poland Revisited, 1915', in *Notes on Life and Letters*, 1921

Germans are the ideal servants, I think, and they are so lasting. They don't ladder at once like the English kind.

Katherine Mansfield, Letter to the Countess Russell, 26 April 1922

The Germans are most curious. They love things just because they think they have a sentimental reason for loving them – *das Heimatland, der Tannenbaum, das Brünnele, das Bächlein* – the very words send a German into a swoon of love, which is as often as not entirely false. They make up their feelings in their heads while their *real* feelings go all wrong. That's why Germans come out with such startling and really silly bursts of hatred. It's the result of never living from their *real* feelings, always from the feelings they invent in their heads. And that's why, as a bourgeois crowd they are so monstrously ugly. My God, how ugly they can be! . . . And it's because they *never* live direct from their spontaneous feeling; except in the matter of eating and drinking, God help us!

D.H. Lawrence, Letter to G. Orioli, Baden-Baden, July 1929

I gained a great regard and admiration for the qualities of the German people. If a man begs his bread from one end to another of any country, he may claim to know something about the nature of its people. In fact, I don't think there is any better way of getting to know any people's nature. So I think there are few peoples, if any, with such kindliness and intelligence.

Eric Muspratt, *Wild Oats*, 1932

As far back as 1918 . . . I had caught hold of certain collective dreams of Germans which convinced me that they portrayed the beginning of a national regression analogous to the regression of a frightened and helpless individual, becoming first infantile, and then primitive or archaic. I saw Nietzsche's 'blond beast' looming up, with all that it implies. I felt sure that Christianity would be challenged and that the Jews would be taken to account.

C.G. Jung, *Psychology and National Problems*, Lecture, 14 October 1936

An immense responsibility rests upon the German people for this subservience to the barbaric idea of autocracy. This is the gravamen against them in history – that, in spite of all their brains and courage, they worship Power, and let themselves be led by the nose.

Sir Winston Churchill, *Great Contemporaries*, 1937

The German people are an orderly, vain, deeply sentimental and rather insensitive people. They seem to feel at their best when they are singing in chorus, saluting, or obeying orders. Obeying orders is their ruling passion. . . . They are now obeying the orders of a triumvirate of certifiable lunatics.

H.G. Wells, *Travels of a Republican Radical in Search of Hot Water*, 1939

But the Germans who matter, those under forty years of age, have been brought up in the belief that Great Britain is their hereditary enemy. Nothing but a sound thrashing will convince them of that error.

Field Marshal Lord Milne, *Evening Standard, c.* 1939, quoted M. Bateman (ed.), *This England – Selections from the New Statesman*, 1969

One could almost believe that in this people there is a peculiar sense of life as a mathematical problem which is known to have a solution.

Isak Dinesen, *Letters from a Land at War*, March–April 1940, *Daguerrotypes*, 1979

The people of Germany are just as responsible for Hitler as the people of Chicago are for the *Chicago Tribune.*

Alexander Woollcott, Remark on radio programme, *People's Platform*, 23 January 1943 (Woollcott's last words; he died a few hours after speaking them and collapsing at the microphone. The subject of the forum was 'Is Germany Incurable?')

The proud German army in its sudden collapse, sudden crumbling and breaking up, has once again proved the truth of the saying 'The Hun is always either at your throat or at your feet.'

Sir Winston Churchill, Speech to US Congress, 19 May 1943

German: a good fellow maybe; but it is better to hang him.

Russian proverb

The modern Germans . . . have approached the civilization of France as a jumped-up and ambitious tradesman approaches an artist or an aristocrat – now flattering it, now striving to humiliate or corrupt it, and proving always their sense of its inherent superiority . . . it is the fate of the Germans that their materialism always curdles their mysticism, their philosophy is corrupted in action by their terror of being despised.

Charles Morgan, *Reflections in a Mirror*, 1944

*How appallingly thorough the Germans always managed to be, how emphatic! In sex no less than in war – in scholarship, in science. Diving deeper than anyone else and coming up muddier.

Aldous Huxley, *Time Must Have a Stop*, 1944

The Germans in the 19th century developed a tradition, a philosophy of life and art, barbarous, grandiose, phoney. Wagner was both cause and effect of this repulsive process which ended in the apogee and apotheosis of human bestiality and degradation, Hitler and the Nazis.

Leonard Woolf, *Beginning Again*, 1964

The trouble is perhaps that there has been simply too much fuss about the Germans. We all need a rest and nobody more so than the Germans themselves.

John Mander, in *Encounter*, April 1964

The East Germans manage to combine a Teutonic capacity for bureaucracy with a Russian capacity for infinite delay.

Goronwy Rees, 'Diary from Berlin to Munich', *Encounter*, April 1964

German Language

I pray in German because that language is so energetic and expressive.

Signora Rosalba Carriera, Remark, 1740, quoted Joseph Spence, *Anecdotes*,

Nature seems to have dropped an acid into the language, when a-forming, which curdled the vowels, and made all the consonants flow together.

Samuel Taylor Coleridge, *Table Talk*, 7 July 1832

Seldom my goosequill of goose from Germany, fatted in England
(Frolicsome though I have been) have I tried on Hexameter knowing
Latin and Greek are alone its languages. We have a measure
Fashion'd by Milton's own hand, a fuller, a deeper, a louder.
Germans may flounder at will over consonant vowel and liquid
Liquid and vowel but one to a dozen of consonants, ending
Each with a verb at the tail, heavy as African ram's tail, . . .

W.S. Landor, *English Hexameters – Last Fruit from an Old Tree*, 1853

Whenever the literary German dives into a sentence, that is the last you are going to see of him till he emerges on the other side of his Atlantic with his verb in his mouth.

Mark Twain, *A Connecticut Yankee in King Arthur's Court*, 1889

The great majority of Germans, realizing the practical impossibility of talking their language with any degree of success, abandon it altogether, and communicate with one another on brass bands. German sounds better on a band, but not much.

Frank Richardson, *Love and All About It*, 1908

I never could learn their beastly language, nor will I till the Emperor William comes over here with his army.

Sir Winston Churchill, quoted by Wilfred Scawen Blunt, Diary, 30 January 1912, *My Diaries*, 1919

German Food

But now to close up all, I will relate what rare dyet . . . we had in our journey in *Germany*: . . . at our suppers at a table square, and so broad, that two men can hardly shake hands over it, we being some twelve about it. Our first dish being a raw Cabbadge, of the quantity of halfe a pecke, cut and chopped small, with the fat of resty bacon powred upon it in stead of oyle, which dish must be emptied before we could get any more: Our second dish perhaps a pecke of boyld apples & hony, the Apples being boyled skins, cores, stalkes and all: Thirdly 100. Gudgeons newly taken perhaps, yet as salt as if they had beene three years pickled, or twice at the East Indies, boyld with scayles, guts and all, and buried in Ginger like sawdust: a fresh pike as salt as brine, boyld in flat milke, with a pound of Garlicke. This was the manner of the most part of our dyet; and if we did aske them why they did salt their meate so unseasonable, there answer was, that their beere could not be consumed, except their meate were salted extraordinarily.

John Taylor, *Taylors Travels to Bohemia*, in *All the Works of John Taylor*, 1630

Strong beer, a liquor extracted with very little art from wheat or barley and *corrupted* . . . into a certain semblance of wine, was sufficient for the gross purposes of German debauchery. But those who had tasted the rich wines of Italy, and afterwards of Gaul, sighed for that more delicious species of intoxication.

Edward Gibbon, *The Decline and Fall of the Roman Empire*, 1766–88

I beg to offer the reader a formula I invented, which will teach him (should he ever come to Germany) what to expect. The simple rule is this: – Let him taste the dish, and if it be not sour, he may be quite certain that it is greasy.

Sir F.B. Head, *Bubbles from the Brunnens of Nassau*, 1834

The Germans are exceedingly fond of Rhine wines; they are put up in tall, slender bottles, and are considered a pleasant beverage. One tells them from vinegar by the label.

Mark Twain, *A Tramp Abroad*, 1880

*Think of the man who first tried German sausage.

Jerome K. Jerome, *Three Men in a Boat*, 1889

*There is this advantage about German beer: it does not make a man drunk as the word drunk is understood in England. There is nothing objectionable about him; he is simply tired. He does not want to talk; he wants to be let alone, to go to sleep; it does not matter where – anywhere.

Jerome K. Jerome, *Three Men on the Bummel*, 1900

Aachen / Aix-la-Chapelle

The market-place is a fine old Square; but at Aix-la-Chapelle there is always a mighty preponderance of poverty and dullness, except in a few of the shewiest of the streets, and even there, a flashy meanness, a slight patchery of things falling to pieces is everywhere visible. The way to the Fountain is through piazzas with stalls and shops; most of the latter were unoccupied, and had their window-shutters closed. The horrid stench of these far-famed waters, would of itself as one might think, have excluded both sellers and buyers; but in wealthier times there can have been no lack of either; or the shops would never have been made. . . .

Dorothy Wordsworth, *Journal*, 20 July 1820

The Redoutensaal

But to proceed to the grand saloon, or rendezvous of vice. This is a splendid room, lined with mirrors, with a ceiling beautifully and richly carved. In festive time this room is applied to the purposes of balls and concerts, and then glitters with the stars of royalty; but now it exhibited a motley crew, crowding around the well-baited trap, which, when it catches one, is sure to entice another miscalculating victim, like the deceitful birdcage-trap, which, having inveigled, closes upon the little flutterer; with this difference, however, that the man-trap is always baited, always set.

Charles Tennant, *A Tour, etc.*, 1824

Alt Breisach

*Of old, Alt Breisach, a rocky fortress with the river now on one side of it and now on the other – for in its inexperienced youth the Rhine never seems to have been quite sure of its way, – must, as a place of residence, have appealed exclusively to the lover of change and excitement. Whoever the war was between, and whatever it was about, Alt Breisach was bound to be in it. Everybody besieged it, most people captured it; the majority of them lost it again; nobody seemed able to keep it. Who he belonged to, and what he was, the dweller in Alt Breisach could never have been quite sure.

Jerome K. Jerome, *Three Men on the Bummel*, 1900

Altona

Altona is a large town; bearing the same relation to

Hamburgh, as Islington to London. But it belongs to the King of Denmark – & the Hamburghers (they say) named it for that reason, Altona – which in low German signifies, Too near.

S.T. Coleridge, Letter to Mrs S.T. Coleridge, 8 November 1798.

Augsburg

We dined and rambled about this renowned city in the cool of the evening. The colossal paintings on the walls of almost every considerable building gave it a strange air, which pleases upon the score of novelty. Having passed a number of streets decorated in this exotic manner, we found ourselves suddenly before the public hall, by a noble statue of Augustus, under whose auspices the colony was formed. Which way soever we turned, our eyes met some remarkable edifice, or marble bason into which several groups of sculptured river-gods pour a profusion of waters. These stately fountains and bronze statues, the extraordinary size and loftiness of the buildings, the towers rising in perspective, and the Doric portal of the town-house, answered in some measure the idea Monfaucon gives us of the scene of an ancient tragedy. Whenever a pompous Flemish painter attempts a representation of Troy or Babylon, and displays in his back-ground those streets of palaces described in the Iliad, Augsburg or some rich city, may easily be traced. Sometimes a corner of Antwerp discovers itself; and sometimes. above a Corinthian portico, rises a Gothic spire: . . .

William Beckford, *Dreams Waking Thoughts and Incidents*, 1783

This old town . . . is renowned for wig makers, pits, water works, and dancing ladies, who are by no means scrupulous on the point of exhibiting their legs.

Michael Kelly, *Reminiscences*, 1826

The town is antique, full of frescoes, gables, roof-windows, and architectural Ghentisms: decorated withal by plenty of bronze fountains, full of naked boys and equally natural Venuses; but – oftentimes very far from tasteful as to their waterworks, as travellers may remember.

M.F. Tupper, *Paterfamilias' Diary of Everybody's Tour*, 1856

Bad Ems

A small village, . . . composed of hovels for its inhabitants, and, comparatively speaking, palaces for its guests, is pleasantly enough situated on the bank of a stream of water, (the Lahn), imprisoned on every side by mountains which I should think very few of its visitors would be disposed to scale . . . I . . . remarked some stiff, formal little walks, up and down which many well-dressed strangers were slowly promenading . . . This mixture of sickness and finery – this confusion between the hectic flush and red and white ribands – in short, this dance of death, is not the particular sort of folly I am fond of . . . I was glad enough to leave dukes and duchesses, princes and ambassadors (whose carriages I saw standing in the one single narrow street), to be cooped up together in the hot, expensive little valley of Ems, – an existence, to my humble taste, not altogether unlike that which the foul witch, Sycorax, inflicted upon Ariel when . . . she left him hitched in a cloven pine.

Sir F. B. Head, *Bubbles from the Brunnens of Nassau*, 1934

Baden-Baden

This little town is a curious compound of rural life, German country-townishness, watering-place incitements, court stateliness, antient mouldering towers, old houses and new, and a life and chearfulness over all. We had a laughable scramble in the street among a drove of pigs, hastening to their several homes at the sound of the horn, a sight which had several times diverted us in passing through town or village in our voitures. But this was our only personal rencontre.

Dorothy Wordsworth, *Journal*, 29 July 1820

The society is extremely promiscuous, and completely democratic in its character, nevertheless perfectly respectable in appearance and behaviour. The locality is charming, the open booths round the garden exhibiting every variety of merchandise, and the numerous tables in the open air round which little parties are sitting, talking, drinking, eating, and smoking, while others are parading up and down, present a scene of remarkable gaiety, and when the concert began all the world flocked into the magnificent rooms, where everybody ranges about from high to low without paying anything. The early hour admits of children being there, and the little wretches are scampering about in great numbers. All the time the *rouge-et-noir* and *roulette* are going on, with crowds round the tables, but not much money staked. I found at last some people I knew . . . It is wonderful how glad one is to see anybody in such a solitude of unknown faces.

Charles Greville, *A Journal of the Reign of Queen Victoria*, 3 July 1843

*The prettiest town of all places where Pleasure has set up her tents.

W.M. Thackeray, *The Newcomes*, 1853–5

Morally Baden is delicious. The females one sees, are enough to make one's hair stand out in all directions.

Henry Adams, Letter to Charles Milnes Gaskell, 25 August 1867

The shop-keeper there swindles you if he can, and insults you whether he succeeds in swindling you or not . . . It is an inane town, filled with sham, and petty fraud, and snobbery, but the baths are good . . . I fully believe I left my rheumatism in Baden-Baden. Baden-Baden is welcome to it. It was little, but it was all I had to give. I would have preferred to leave something that was catching, but it was not in my power.

Mark Twain, *A Tramp Abroad*, 1880

Of all the great watering-places, the name of Baden Baden still seems to trumpet loudest. It sounds a queen-emperorship – Baden of All the Badens; Baden! Baden! *Baden*! it shouts.

William Sansom, *Blue Skies Brown Studies*, 1961

One is left with a strong impression that Baden-Baden was built on undelivered faeces.

Alex Comfort, *The Anxiety Makers*, 1967

Bavaria

Bavaria is too humid, too green and lush, and mountains *never* move – they are *always* there. They go all different tones and colours – but still, they are always there.

D.H. Lawrence, Letter to A.W. McLeod, May 1913

Bavarians say that the difference between a rich farmer and a poor farmer is that the poor farmer cleans his Mercedes himself.

J.W. Murray, *Observer*, 17 June 1979

Berlin

This place recalls to the beholder at every step, the image, genius, and the actions of the reigning Sovereign. It is a species of mirror, in which Frederic is perpetually seen, either as the General, the Architect, or the Master. Peter the Great is not more constantly present to the imagination at Petersburgh, than is the present King of Prussia at Berlin . . . If however, Berlin strikes by its regularity and the magnificence of its public buildings, it impresses not less forcibly with a sentiment of melancholy. It is neither enriched by commerce, enlivened by the general residence of the Sovereign, nor animated by industry, business and freedom. An air of silence and dejection reigns in the streets, where at noon-day scarcely any passengers are seen except soldiers. The population, much as it has augmented during the present reign, is still very unequal to the extent and magnitude of the city. Ostentation and vanity, more than utility or necessity, seem to have impelled Frederic to enlarge and embellish his capital. The splendid fronts of the finest houses, frequently conceal poverty and wretchedness . . . We are at first disappointed, and then disgusted with this deception

Sir N.W. Wraxall, *Memoirs of the Courts of Berlin, etc.*, 1779

Public courtezans are more numerous here than in any town in Europe, in proportion to the number of inhabitants. They appear openly at the windows in the day-time, beckon to passengers as they walk in the streets, and ply for employment in any way they please, without disturbance from the magistrate.

It seems to be a received opinion here, that the peace and happiness of the community are not interrupted by this species of licentiousness; or perhaps it is believed, that an attempt to restrain it would be attended with consequences worse than the thing itself. Therefore nobody is allowed to molest or abuse those who have chosen this for a trade, and as little attention is paid to customers, who frequent the chambers of these ladies, as if they stept into any other house or shop, to purchase any other commodity

Another species of debauchery is said to prevail in this capital. – I imagine, however, that what is related on that nauseous subject is greatly exaggerated.

John Moore, *A View of Society and Manners in France, Switzerland, Germany, etc.*, 1779

If a city may be called perfect in a proportion to its external convenience, if making houses to hold many people, keeping infection away by cleanliness, and ensuring security against fire by a nice separation of almost every building from almost every other; if uniformity of appearance can compensate for elegance of architecture, and space make amends for beauty, *Berlin* certainly deserves to be seen, and he who planned it, to be highly commended . . . and with this well-earned praise I am most willing to quit it. It is the first place of any consequence I have felt in a hurry to run away from.

Hester Lynch Thrale/Piozzi, *Observations . . . in the Course of a Journey*, 1789

The villages round Berlin do not announce a great & wealthy metropolis, nor is it to be expected as this city has been literally *forced* into its present, vast size.

Henry Crabb Robinson, Letter to his brother, 15 April 1802

Many parts of it are handsomely built, especially what may be termed the court end; but every building, from the palace to the meanest hut, is built of brick plastered over. In short, Berlin is all show, a forced place, having little commerce, and less content; no smiling faces – no mediocrity, that happiest of all conditions. Berlin contains nothing but the most hardened military despots, and is, in short, a mere Court; though it contains two hundred thousand inhabitants. I saw no modes of gaining a livelihood, or even of passing time honestly. Billiards, cards, and dice, succeed to the spectacle of the parade, and the streets present nothing but sentinels on guard.

Captain John Dundas Cochrane, *Narrative of a Pedestrian Journey through Russia, etc.*, 1824

The country round Berlin, the Mark of Brandenberg, is bitter, bad, deep sand almost a desert; I don't wonder the Great Frederick wanted something better.

Thomas Hood, Letter to his wife, 25 October 1836

We like our Berlin immensely – an ugly place it must be to anyone who comes to it hipped or solitary, or what is worse, with a disagreeable companion. But, to make a very novel quotation – 'the mind is its own place' and can make a pretty town even of Berlin. The day seems too short for our happiness and we both of us feel that we have begun life afresh – with new ambition and new powers. I say so much to you because I know you have a friendly interest in me and to that extent I am not afraid of incurring the fatality which the Germans seem still to believe in. When any one is spoken of as being very happy they say 'Unberufen' – meaning 'Don't talk of it or their happiness will vanish.'

It is distressing to see the multitude of soldiers here – to think of the nation's vitality going to feed 300,000 puppets in uniform. In the streets one's legs are in constant danger from officers' swords.

George Eliot, Letter to John Chapman, 9 January 1854

and Potsdam

The amount of art lavished on the whole region of Potsdam is marvellous; some of the tops of the palaces were like forests of statues, and they were all over the gardens, set on pedestals. In fact, the two principles of Berlin architecture appear to me to be these. On the house-tops, wherever there is a convenient place, put up the figure of a man; he is best placed standing on one leg. Wherever there is room on the ground, put either a circular group of busts on pedestals, in consultation, all looking inwards – or else the colossal figure of a man killing, about to kill, or having killed (the present tense is preferred) a beast; the more pricks the beast has, the better – in fact a dragon is the correct thing, but if that is beyond the artist, he may content himself with a lion or a pig. The beast-killing principle has been carried out everywhere with a relentless monotony, which makes some parts of Berlin look like a fossil slaughter-house.

Lewis Carroll, *Diary*, July 1867

In Berlin you meet so many broad-shouldered stunted privates, and so many gaunt, whiskered and tight-waisted officers in tunics, *pickelhaubes*, and red-striped trousers (and all seemingly with pokers down their backs underneath their tunics), that you begin to think after a while that these must form the normal garb of the population, and that the few people in civilian costume whom you come across are strangers like yourself.

G.A. Sala, *Paris Herself Again*, 1879

*Berlin is a disappointing town; its centre over-crowded, its outlying parts lifeless; its one famous street, Unter den Linden, an attempt to combine Oxford Street with the Champs Elysées, singularly unimposing, being much too wide for its size . . . In the Berlin cafés and restaurants the busy time is from midnight on till three. Yet most of the people who frequent them are up again at seven. Either the Berliner has solved the great problem of modern life, how to do without sleep, or, with Carlyle, he must be looking forward to eternity.

Jerome K. Jerome, *Three Men on the Bummel*, 1900

A student at twenty takes easily to anything, even to Berlin.

Henry Adams, *The Education of Henry Adams*, 1906

He said that in Berlin, if you wanted to make a scandal in the theatre, you had to have a mother committing incest with *two* sons; one wasn't enough.

Arnold Bennett, *Journal*, 17 July 1925, quoting Rudolf Kommer

*From my window, the deep solemn massive street. Cellar-shops where the lamps burn all day, under the shadow of top-heavy balconied façades, dirty plaster frontages embossed with scroll-work and heraldic devices. The whole district is like this: street leading into street of houses like shabby monumental safes crammed with the tarnished valuables and second-hand furniture of a bankrupt middle class.

Christopher Isherwood, 'A Berlin Diary, 1930', in *Goodbye to Berlin*, 1939

*To-night, for the first time this winter, it is very cold. The dead cold grips the town in utter silence, like the silence of intense midday summer heat. In the cold the town seems actually to contract, to dwindle to a small black dot, scarcely larger than hundreds of other dots, isolated and hard to find, on the enormous European map. Outside, in the night, beyond the last new-built blocks of concrete flats, where the streets end in frozen allotment gardens, are the Russian plains. You can feel them all round you, to-night, creeping in upon the city, like an immense waste of unhomely ocean – sprinkled with leafless copses and ice-lakes and tiny villages which are remembered only as the outlandish names of battlefields in half-forgotten wars. Berlin is a skeleton which aches in the cold: it is my own skeleton aching. I feel in my bones the sharp ache of the frost in the girders of the overhead railway, in the ironwork of balconies, in bridges, tramlines, lamp-standards, lat-

rines. The iron throbs and shrinks, the stone and the bricks ache dully, the plaster is numb.

Berlin is a city with two centres – the cluster of expensive hotels, bars, cinemas, shops round the Memorial Church, a sparkling nucleus of light, like a sham diamond, in the shabby twilight of the town; and the self-conscious civic centre of buildings round the Unter den Linden, carefully arranged. In grand international styles, copies of copies, they assert our dignity as a capital city – a parliament, a couple of museums, a State bank, a cathedral, an opera, a dozen embassies, a triumphal arch; nothing has been forgotten. And they are all so pompous, so very correct – all except the cathedral, which betrays, in its architecture, a flash of that hysteria which flickers always behind every grave, grey Prussian façade. Extinguished by its absurd dome, it is, at first sight, so startlingly funny that one searches for a name suitably preposterous – the Church of the Immaculate Consumption.

But the real heart of Berlin is a small damp black wood – the Tiergarten. At this time of the year, the cold begins to drive the peasant boys out of their tiny unprotected villages into the city, to look for food, and work. But the city, which glowed so brightly and invitingly in the night sky above the plains, is cold and cruel and dead. Its warmth is an illusion, a mirage of the winter desert. It will not receive these boys. It has nothing to give. The cold drives them out of its streets, into the wood which is its cruel heart. And there they cower on benches, to starve and freeze, and dream of their far-away cottage stoves.

Christopher Isherwood, 'A Berlin Diary, Winter 1932–3', in *Goodbye to Berlin*, 1939

There was a reasonable amount of destruction.

Sir Winston Churchill, Remark on visiting Berlin, 16 July 1945, in Lord Moran, *Winston Churchill, The Struggle for Survival*, 1966

I think it is a character in Jean Giraudoux's *Siegfried et le Limousin* who remarks that there is more mystery and terror in a single pine tree in the streets of Berlin at midday than in an entire French forest at midnight.

Claud Cockburn, *In Time of Trouble*, 1956

All free men, wherever they live, are citizens of Berlin, and therefore, as a free man, I take pride in the words, '*Ich bin ein Berliner.*'

John Fitzgerald Kennedy, Speech at Rudolf Wilde Platz, Berlin, 26 June 1963

The Berlin Wall

The Wall is a kind of masterpiece of the squalid, the cruel and the hideous, the most naked assertion one could find anywhere that life was not intended to be anything but nasty, brutish, and short. It is quite incredibly ugly, being built of a kind of porous concrete brick that is altogether greyer darker deader, less responsive to light and shade than any material has any right to be.

Goronwy Rees, 'Diary from Berlin to Munich', *Encounter*, April 1964

Coblenz

'Tis a mean, dirty assemblage of plaistered houses, striped with paint, and set off with wooden galleries, in the beautiful taste of St. Giles's. Above on the rock stands the palace of the Elector, which seems to be remarkable for nothing but situation.

William Beckford, *Dreams Waking Thoughts and Incidents*, 1783

Junction of the Rhine and the Moselle

The view is magnificent, especially when you command that 'Meeting of the Waters,' whence the city derives its name. The junction, indeed, is rather like an ill-assorted marriage, for the two rivers, in spite of their nominal union, seem mutually inclined to keep themselves to themselves. But so it is in life. I could name more than one couple, where, like the Rhine and the Moselle, the lady is rather yellow and the gentleman looks blue.

Thomas Hood, *Up the Rhine*, 1840

Inhabitants of Coblenz

In spite of all their sentimentality there is no *feeling* . . . Damn their sentimental tenderness – where is the practical? . . .

They *are* a heartless race set on the bawbees from high to low. Indeed, in a thousand things, language & all, I could fancy myself again, as when a boy, in Dundee. They have *some* of the virtues, all the vices, & most of the peculiarities of the Scotch. Above all they are dreadfully beastly filthy horribly dirty and *nasty*. . . . Then they are stupid and like all stupid people intensely obstinate. . . . They do not often show themselves drunk; but between wine and smoke their heads are in a continual *muddle*.

Thomas Hood, Letter to Charles Wentworth Dilke, 17 January 1836

And I like some of the people too – that is to say the peasants. I admire their industry, frugality, & content and cheerfulness – they are better *to the eye* too. But I detest the townspeople.

Ibid.

At Coblenz – at the precise junction of the Moselle – what regale myself with but Moselle? – The wine is bluish – at least *tinged* with blue – and seems a part of the river after which it is called.

Herman Melville, *Journal of a Tour to London and the Continent* (10 December 1849), 1849–50

The fashionable quarter of Coblenz is Portland Place-ish: elsewhere the town being old quaint middle-agey, grey roofed in round slates like fish-scales, and with here and there a toy minaret or spire.

M.F. Tupper, *Paterfamilias' Diary of Everybody's Tour*, 1856

Coburg

They say this City was of old called Cotburg, that is, the City of dirt, and the dirty streets well deserve the name. Here one of the Dukes of Saxony called of Coburg kept his Court, and our Host told us that his Dutchesse for adultery was then bricked up in a wall, the place being so narrow, as shee could onely stand, and having no dore, but onely a hole whereat they gave her meat. The building of the City was very base of timber and clay.

Fynes Moryson, *An Itinerary*, 1617

Cologne

It is the ugliest, dirtiest town I ever yet saw. There is neither form nor comeliness belonging to it. The great church itself is mere heaps upon heaps, a vast, misshaped, or rather no-shaped building, with no regularity or proportion within or without: many of the stones broken, the windows dusty and full of cobwebs, and the pavement less clean than that of many English stables.

John Wesley, Letter to Mrs Susanna Wesley, 28 June 1738

From thence he was drawn onwards to Cologne,
  A city which presents to the inspector
Eleven thousand maidenheads of bone,
The greatest number flesh hath ever known.

Lord Byron, *Don Juan*, 1819–24

The houses of Cologne are very old, overhanging and uncouth; – the streets narrow – gloomy in the chearfulest of their corners or openings; yet oftentimes pleasing. Windows and balconies make a pretty show of flowers; and birds hang on the outside of houses in cages. These sound like chearful images of active leisure: but with such feeling it is impossible to walk through these streets; yet it is pleasing to note how quietly a dull life may be varied, and how innocently; though, in looking at the plants, which yearly put out their summer blossoms to adorn these decaying walls and windows, I had something of the melancholy which I have felt on seeing a human being gaily dressed – a female tricked out with ornaments, while disease and death were on her countenance.

Dorothy Wordsworth, *Journal*, 21 July 1820

In Koln, a town of monks and bones,
And pavements fang'd with murderous stones
And rags and hags, and hideous wenches;
I counted two and seventy stenches,
All well defined, and several stinks!
Ye nymphs that reign o'er sewers and sinks,
The River Rhine, it is well known,
Doth wash your city of Cologne;
But tell me Nymphs, what power divine
Shall henceforth wash the river Rhine?

S.T. Coleridge, *Cologne*, 1828

Cologne . . . is in size considerable, in aspect unpromising, & in smell odious.

W.M. Thackeray, Letter to Mrs Carmichael-Smyth, 6–7 September 1830

I have seen the famous Cathedral, which is a fine building, but not half finished, and as such, an uncomfortable sight, for it looks like a broken promise to God.

Thomas Hood, *Up the Rhine*, 1840

You'll see old Cologne, – not the sweetest of towns, -
Wherever you follow your nose you will shock it;
And you'll pay your three dollars to look at three
  crowns, -
Take care of your pocket! – take care of your pocket!

Thomas Hood, *Ye Tourists and Travellers*, 1840

Is it not a strange bit of compensation, that a city immortalized for stenches by Coleridge and Byron, should have since redeem'd its character by an equally immortal scent?

M.F. Tupper, *Paterfamilias' Diary of Everybody's Tour*, 1856

We spent an hour in the cathedral, which I will not attempt to describe further than by saying it was the most beautiful of all the churches I have ever seen, or can imagine. If one could imagine the spirit of devotion embodied in any material form, it would be in such a building.

Lewis Carroll, *Diary*, July 1867

Constance

A fair apple to look at, but full of dust and ashes: a whitened sepulchre, beautiful outside, but its inside death and decay.

M.F. Tupper, *Paterfamilias' Diary of Everybody's Tour*, 1856

Coswig (GDR)

About noon I arrived at Coswig, the residence of the Prince of Zerbst, who is a strange, wrong-headed being. He has got his troops, forsooth, to the number of 150 foot and 30 horse, and, during the last war, he took a fancy that the King of Prussia was coming to attack him. So he put in readiness his little battery of cannon, and let out his 180 to make head against the armies of Frederick . . . The appearance of his little dirty town, his castle, and his sentinels with sentry-boxes painted in lozenges of different colours, like the stockings of Harlequin, diverted me a good deal.

James Boswell, *Journal*, 24 September 1764

Drachenfels

The castled crag of Drachenfels
Frowns o'er the wide and winding Rhine,
Whose breast of waters broadly swells
Between the banks which bear the vine;
And hills all rich with blossomed trees,
And fields which promise corn and wine,
And scattered cities, crowning these,
Whose fair white walls along them shine,
Have strewed a scene which I should see
With double joy, wert *thou* with me.

And peasant girls, with deep blue eyes
And hands which offer early flowers,
Walk smiling o'er this Paradise;
Above, the frequent feudal towers
Through green leaves lift their walls of gray;
And many a rock which steeply lowers,
And noble arch in proud decay,
Look o'er this vale of vintage-bowers;
But one thing want these banks of Rhine, –
Thy gentle hand to clasp in mine!

Lord Byron, *Childe Harold's Pilgrimage*, Canto the Third, 1816

The Drachenfels Group, beautiful as it is, is soon used up. . . .

Matthew Arnold, Letter to his mother, 23 July 1865

Dresden (GDR)

I am charmed with this city; with its environs, its society, and with its general aspect. The sandy plains of Brandenburgh are here exchanged for a rich, finely undulated, and populous country, covered with marks of opulence, industry, and freedom. Instead of the melancholy and deserted magnificence of Berlin, we find here a smaller capital, less regular in its construction; but cheerful, elegant, and in a situation the most picturesque. It retains indeed, in many parts, the frightful vestiges of bombardments, conflagrations, and ravages, principally inflicted by Frederic, during the course of the late war. Never perhaps, was any situation, politically considered, more unfortunate than that of Dresden. All the local or physical advantages which the Saxon capital enjoys, are dearly purchased by its exposed position.

Sir N.W. Wraxall, *Memoirs of the Courts of Berlin, etc.*, 1779

This really does seem a very charming town; the streets well built and spacious; the shops full of goods, and the people willing to shew them; and if they *do* cut all their wood before their own doors, why there is room to pass here without brawling and bones-breaking, which disgusts one so at Vienna; it seems lighter too here than there; I cannot tell why, but every thing looks clean and comfortable, and one feels *so much at home* . . . The architecture is truly hideous, but no ornaments are spared . . .

Hester Lynch Piozzi, *Observations . . . in the Course of a Journey*, 1789

The city has its public buildings partly in the style of Blenheim, partly in that of Bow Church, if you know those monuments; but the effect is very fine; and the town proper is a real German town of high old houses, not like Berlin, a handsomer Bond Street, all new.

Matthew Arnold, Letter to Miss Arnold, 4 December 1885

*Dresden, perhaps, is the most attractive town in Germany; but it is a place to be lived in for a while rather than visited. Its museums and galleries, its palaces and gardens, its beautiful and historically rich environment, provide pleasure for a winter, but bewilder for a week. It has not the gaiety of Paris or Vienna, which quickly palls; its charms are more solidly German and more lasting. It is the Mecca of the musician . . .

Jerome K. Jerome, *Three Men on the Bummel*, 1900

Frankfurt-am-Main

The streets of Frankfort are spacious and well-paved; the houses stately, clean and convenient; . . . The houses are of brick, but have a better appearance than brick-houses in general, owing chiefly to their being covered with a kind of reddish stucco, which is come into use here of late, and, it is believed, will render the buildings more durable. The fronts of many of the finest are also adorned with bas reliefs of white stucco, in imitation of marble. These white ornaments, on the red ground, form too strong a contrast, and do not please an eye fond of simplicity. But the Germans, in general, have a taste for showy ornament in their dress, furniture, and houses.

John Moore, *A View of Society and Manners in France, Switzerland, Germany, etc.*, 1779

The Gazetteers . . . call it an ancient, rich, free, commercial, imperial Stadt or Town . . . Imprimis, then it is *ancient*: That is the Streets are narrow & wretchedly paved the Houses lofty, & irregularly built, the Churches mean & the whole without either dignity or beauty excepting one broad place which is called the Zeil or strait line, tho' it is unluckily rather crooked . . .

it is rich and commercial – And in this charackter it holds a distinguished Rank in the Cities of the Empire . . . In the language of the Saints tho' not precisely in their Sense Frankfort is a dark Town there are but Two Coffee Houses and they take no News Papers but the ffrench and german Journals of the Town . . .

Henry Crabb Robinson, Letter to his brother, 29 July 1800

When God made Frankfurt-am-Main, he shat a lump of concrete.

Gunther Grass, quoted by Nigel Dennis, in *New York Review of Books*, 23 November 1978, reviewing Grass's *The Flounder*

Skyscrapers (most of them banking headquarters) sprouted all over Frankfurt; the town was dubbed 'Mainhattan' and 'Bankfurt.'

Gale Wiley, *International Herald Tribune*, 6 February 1979

Göttingen

The town itself is beautiful, and pleases most when looked at – backwards.

Heinrich Heine, *The Hartz Journey*, 1824, in *Pictures of Travel*, trans. Charles Godfrey Leland, 1866

Hamburg

Hamburg, where the people after dinner, warmed with drinke, are apt to wrong any stranger, and hardly indure an English-man in the morning when they are sober.

Fynes Moryson, *An Itinerary*, 1617

The stately river of Elbe is the best neighbour they have, and the branches and arms of it run through most of their streets by their doors, to the great advantage of their commerce; . . . It may be said of this towne, that God hath witheld nothing for them for their good. They have plenty of provisions, health, profit and pleasure, to their full contentment, in a peacable and just government, with freedom, strength in their magazines, fortifications, and bodies of men for their defence and protection, conveniences for their habitation and commerce, and, which is above all, a liberty to know the will of, and to worship God, for the health of their own souls.

Bulstrode Whitelocke, *Journal of the Swedish Embassy in 1653 and 1654*, edn of 1855

Hamburg is an ill, close-built town, swarming with inhabitants; and, from what I could learn, like all the other free towns, governed in a manner which bears hard on the poor, whilst narrowing the minds of the rich; the character of the man is lost in the hamburger.

Mary Wollstonecraft, *Letters Written During a Short Residence in Sweden, &c.*, 1796

The Streets narrow and stinking, without any appropriate path for the foot-passengers – the Gable Ends of the Houses, all towards the street; some in the ordinary Triangular form . . . – but most of them . . . notched and *shapified* with more than Chinese Grotesqueness. – Above all, both here and at Altona, I was struck with the *profusion* of windows – so large & so many that the Houses look all Glass. Mr Pitt's tax would greatly improve the Architecture of Hamburgh; but the Elbe & the Country round will be still more benefited by the last Conflagration. For it is a foul City!

I moved on & crossed a multitude of ugly Bridges, the water intersecting the City every where & furnishing to an Architect the *capabilities* of all that is beautiful & magnificent in human Edifices – such it might have been; it might have been more than the rival of Venice; & it is – Huddle and Ugliness, Stink and Stagnation!

S.T. Coleridge, Letter to Thomas Poole, 26 October 1798

In the shops (except the established booksellers and stationers) I have constantly observed a disposition to cheat, and take advantage of our ignorance of the language and money . . .

I am informed that it is the boast and glory of these people to cheat strangers, that when a feat of this kind is successfully performed the man goes from his shop into his house, and triumphantly relates it to his wife and family. The Hamburgh shopkeepers have three sorts of weights, and a great part of their skill, as shopkeepers consists in calculating upon the knowledge of the buyer, and suiting him with scales accordingly.

Dorothy Wordsworth, *Journal*, 26 and 28 September 1798

It is a *sad* place. In this epithet you have the soul and essence of all the information which I have been able to gather.

William Wordsworth, Letter to Thomas Poole, 3 October 1798

Hameln

This made me think upon that miraculous passage in *Hamelen*, . . . which was thus (nor would I relate it to you were there not some ground of truth of it.) The said Town of Hamelen was annoy'd with Rats and Mice; and it chanc'd, that a pied-coated Piper came thither, who convenanted with the chief Burgers for such a Reward, if he could free them quite from the said

Vermin, nor would he demand it till a twelvemonth and a day after. The agreement being made, he began to play on his Pipes, and all the Rats and the Mice follow'd him to a great Lough hard by, where they all perish'd; so the Town was infected no more. At the end of the year the said Piper return'd for his reward; the Burgers put him off with slightings and neglect, offering him some small matter; which he refusing, and staying some days in the Town, one *Sunday* morning at high Mass, when most people were at Church, he fell to play on his Pipes, and all the Children up and down follow'd him out of the Town, to a great Hill not far off, which rent in two, and open'd, and let him and the children in, and so clos'd up again. This happen'd a matter of 250 years since; and in that Town they date their bills and bonds, and other instruments in Law to this day, from the year of the going out of their Children: Besides, there is a great Pillar of stone at the foot of the said Hill, whereon this story is engraven.

James Howell, 'Letter to Mr E.P., 1 October 1643', *Familiar Letters*, 1645

Hamelin town's in Brunswick
By famous Hanover city;
The river Weser, deep and wide,
Washes its wall on the southern side;
A pleasanter spot you never spied.

Robert Browning, 'The Pied Piper of Hamelin', *Dramatic Lyrics*, 1842

Hanover

Hanover . . . presents the image of departed greatness; palaces without inhabitants, a capital without trade, and an Electorate without a Sovereign. It is principally by the recollection of what it was, that Hanover continues to interest an ordinary traveller.

Sir N.W. Wraxall, *Memoirs of the Courts of Berlin, etc.*, 1779

Description is not my Fort; but descriptions of Towns & Cities – I abhor even to *read* them! – Besides, I saw nothing particular in Hanover – it is a neat town, well-lighted, neither handsome or ugly, about the size of Taunton, (perhaps a little larger) & contains about 16,000 Inhabitants. *It being the seat of the Government*, the Inhabitants, at least the Gentry, dance & game & commit adultery, – there is a Tobacco Manufacture & a *Library with some curious books*. – (N.B. – I hold the *last line* for a master-piece of informative & discriminative Description).

S.T. Coleridge, Letter to Mrs S.T. Coleridge, 10 March 1799

*To Hanover one should go, they say, to learn the best German. The disadvantage is that outside Hanover, which is only a small province, nobody understands this best German. Thus you have to decide whether to speak good German and remain in Hanover, or bad German and travel about.

Jerome K. Jerome, *Three Men on the Bummel*, 1900

Heidelberg

The air agrees wonderful well with me, I praise God; and yet did I never behold town better suited for the wealth of physicians than Heydleberge.

Sir Henry Wotton, Letter to Edward Wotton, 15 December 1589

Heidelberg . . . in respect to its Situation is perhaps the most beautiful Town, unquestionably the most beautiful University I ever saw – Indeed it is in this respect so superior to Jena that he who has loved Jena for its beauty & comes to Heidelberg will forget the object of his former attachment as quickly as Romeo forgot his former Love on beholding Juliet.

Henry Crabb Robinson, Letter to his brother, 22 October 1804

Parties of students were to be seen in all quarters of the groves and gardens – I am sorry, however, to say, that their appearance was not very scholar-like. They wear whatever wild and coarse apparel pleases them – their hair long and disorderly – or rough as a water-dog – throats bare – or with a black collar – and often no appearance of a shirt. Every one has his pipe – and they all talk loud and boisterously. A Tavern is near the castle, where are all temptations to lounging and pleasure; no doubt preferred by the majority of these youths to the free gifts of garden and grove, and nature's prodigal wealth . . .

Dorothy Wordsworth, *Journal*, 27 July 1820

Fill me the beaker!
Now, Rhine and Nekkar
Health to ye both, ye noble streams!
Yours is a power
To wing the hour
High above wisdom's heavy dreams.
Germans! beer-drinking
Tobacco-stinking
Gladly, how gladly! I resign
All you are worth
From South to North
For this fresh air and fragant wine.

W. S. Landor, 'Garden at Heidelberg', in *Last Fruit from an Old Tree*, 1853

Heidelberg Castle
The Lear of inanimate nature.

Mark Twain, *A Tramp Abroad*, 1880

Because I was there first conscious of beauty; because

there I knew the first glow of the acquisition of knowledge (each book I read was an extraordinary adventure); because there I first knew the delight of conversation (oh, those wonderful commonplaces which each boy discovers as though none had discovered them before); because of the morning stroll in the sunny Anlage, the cakes, and coffee which refreshed my abstemious youth at the end of a strenuous walk, the leisurely evenings on the castle terrace, with the smoky blue haze over the tumbled roofs of the old town below me; because of Goethe and Heine and Beethoven and Wagner and (why not?) Strauss with his waltzes, and the beer-garden where the band played and girls with yellow plaits walked sedately; because of all these things – recollections which have all the force of the appeal of sense – to me not only does the word *plain* mean everywhere and exclusively the valley of the Rhine; but the only symbol for happiness I know is a wide prospect all golden in the setting sun, with a shinning stream of silver running through it, like the path of life, or like the ideal that guides you through it, and far away the grey towers of an ancient town.

W. Somerset Maugham, *On a Chinese Screen*, 1922

Heligoland

This Iland hath onely one Port capeable of some sixe ships, in the forme of the Moone decreasing, and lying open to the East. On the North side is a great Rocke, and the rest of the shore is all of high Cliffes. It is subject to the Duke of Holste, and by that title to the King of Denmarke; but the inhabitants are so poore, as they yeeld no other tribute then stones for the Dukes building. It is in circuit some three miles and hath about one hundred Families.

Fynes Moryson, *An Itinerary*, 1617

Hohenlinden

On Linden, when the sun was low,
All bloodless lay the untrodden snow,
And dark as winter was the flow
Of Iser, rolling rapidly.

But Linden saw another sight
When the drum beat at dead of night,
Commanding fires of death to light
The darkness of her scenery . . .

Then shook the hills with thunder riven
Then rushed the steed to battle driven,
And louder than the bolts of heaven
Far flashed the red artillery

But redder yet that light shall glow
On Linden's hills of stained snow,
And bloodier yet the torrent flow
Of Iser, rolling rapidly.

Thomas Campbell, 'Hohenlinden', *Poems*, 1803

Holstein

That which offered the greatest novelty to our party, was the loud and incessant chorus of myriads of frogs, the whole way from Lubeck to Eutin. To call it croaking, would convey a very erroneous idea of it, because it is really harmonious; and we gave to these reptiles the name of *Holstein nightingales* . . . The noise of any one of them singly, as we sometimes heard it near the road, was, as usual, disagreeable, and might be compared to the loudest quacking of a duck; but when, as it generally happened, tens of thousands, nay millions, sang together, it was a choral vibration, varied only by cadences of sound, something like those produced upon musical glasses; and it accorded with the uniformity which twilight cast over the woods and waters.

E.D. Clarke, *Travels in Various Countries*, 1824

Homburg

Do you know Homburg at all? it's very pretty – German pretty – and is cool and shady and comfortable generally, and still amusing enough, in spite of the death and burial of the gaming. The Kursaal stands there like a great cavernous tomb – a tomb, however in which they have concerts, a reading room and a café.

Henry James, Letter to Sarah Butler Wister,
10 August 1873

Kassel / Cassell

Cassell is to be seen rapidly only – there is a mixture of meanness & poverty with taste and splendour which is to me at least disgusting even to painfulness . . . In Cassell . . . are whole streets uniformly built the rooms lofty the Windows large the door spacious the steps wide, in short all that we find in the modern houses of persons in a comfortable situation in life, but the walls are unwashed, the windows broken the steps unswept and the people who inhabit them little better than our poor – You must I think have felt the same thing in seeing the inferior streets of Bath.

Henry Crabb Robinson, Letter to his brother,
15 June 1801

River Lahn (and Langen Schwalbach, scenery between)

On quitting the Lahn, the beauty of the scenery

dwindles like a flower for the want of *watering*, and you enter on a lumpy-bumpy-humpy country.

Thomas Hood, *Up the Rhine*, 1840

Leipsig (GDR)

We crossed part of that flat which surrounds Leipsic – what an immense flat it is! An ocean of sand literally stretching beyond the reach of the eye. It seems to have been intended for the grand armies of Europe to decide their differences on. That is to say, if Nature or Providence ever intended to form convenient plains for wholesale butcheries.

Thomas Hood, Letter to C.W. Dilke, 26 December 1836

Lübeck

The Citie is compassed with a double wall, one of bricke and narrow, the other of earth and broad, fastned with thicke rowes of willowes. But on the North side and on the South-east side there were no walles, those parts being compassed with deepe ditches full of water. On the South-east side the water seemeth narrow, but is so deepe, as ships of a thousand tunne are brought up to the Citie to lie there all winter, being first unladed at Tremuren the Port of the City lying upon the Baltick Sea. To this Port one mile distant from Lubeck we came in three houres, each man paying for his Coach five Lubeck shillings, and foure for our dinner, and returned back the same night to Lubeck. The building of this City is very beautifull, all of bricke, and it hath most sweete walkes without the walles. The Citizens are curious to avoid ill smels, to which end the Butchers have a place for killing their beasts without the walles upon a running streame. Water is brought to every Citizens houses by pipes, and all the Brewers dwelling in one street have each of them his iron Cock, which being turned, the water fals into their vessels. Though the building of this town be of the same matter as that of the neighbouring townes, yet it is much preferred before them, for the beautie and uniformitie of the houses; for the pleasant gardens, faire streets, sweete walkes without the walles, and for the Citizens themselves, who are much commended for civility of manners, and the strict execution of Justice. The poore dwell in the remote streets out of the common passages. . . . The forme of this Citie is like a lozing, thicke in the midst, and growing narrower towards the two ends.

Fynes Moryson, *An Itinerary*, 1617

Upon the view of the whole town it seemed a pleasant and noble city. It is of great antiquity, freedom, privileges, trade, polity, and strength, few in these parts exceeding it; not unhealthful in the situation, beautiful in the buildings, profitable in the commerce, strong in the fortifications, and rich in the inhabitants.

The streets are large and fair, kept clean and sweet; the houses built of brick, generally uniform, most in the frontispieces, and covered with tile; at the entry into them, usually the first and lower room is largest, paved with Orland stone, full of streaks of red and white, and some with black and white rich marble. In this first room they use to set their best household stuff, as the chief room for entertainment; yet they will also in some part of the room have a partition with boards, above a man's height, for a kitchen, where they dress meat and hang their bacon and other provision, which are not out of sight nor smell; and here also, in this room, some of their goods of merchandise are placed; but the better sort keep their houses more neat, and have kitchens and larders out of view. In the second storey are ordinarily the lodging-rooms and some for entertainment; the third and fourth stories are granaries and storehouses, which they hold better for such uses than cellars, and lower rooms which they say cause damage to the commodities.

The country about, for a league, and in some parts two leagues or more, belongs to the city, is within their jurisdiction and is fruitful and pleasant, sweetly watered by the Trave, adorned by the groves and meadows and many pleasant summer-houses for the recreation of the citizens.

Bulstrode Whitelocke, *Journal of the Swedish Embassy in 1653 and 1654*, edn of 1855

Magdebourg (GDR)

The forme of this City is like a Moone increasing.

Fynes Moryson, *An Itinerary*, 1617

Mannheim

Five winter days at Mannheim shall I be,
And in my lines that city shan't you see?
Shall not the Elector Palatine be prais'd
And to the skies his noble court be rais'd?
No, faith, my friend, to be exceeding plain,
Such scurvy courts deserve no tuneful strain.
Raise it? Why, faith, I'd raise it to the skies,
As the bold eagle made the tortoise rise -
That he might let it drop upon the stones,
And to a jelly bruise its flesh and bones.

James Boswell, *Journal*, 6 November 1764

This is generally reckoned one of the most beautiful cities in Germany. The streets are all as straight as arrows, being what they call *tirées au cordeau*, and intersect each other at right angles. This never fails to please at first, but becomes sooner tiresome than a town built with less regularity. When a man has walked through the town for half a forenoon, his eyes search in vain for variety; the same objects seem to move along with him, as if he had been all the while a ship-board.

John Moore, *A View of Society and Manners in France, Switzerland, Germany, etc.*, 1779

Manheim is a splendid town, both from its admirable buildings and the glossy neatness of the houses. They are too fine to live in, and seem only made to looked at. Would that one of the streets could be set down in Waterloo-place!

William Hazlitt, *Notes of a Journey through France and Italy*, 1826

Mecklenberg

The idea of a fashionable Bathing place in Mecklenburg! – How can people pretend to be fashionable or to bathe out of England!

Jane Austen, Letter to Francis Austen, 25 September 1813

Munich

Avenues of broad white houses,
Basking in the noontide glare; –
Streets, which foot of traveller shrink from,
As on hot plates shrinks the bear; –

Elsewhere lawns, and vista'd gardens,
Statues white, and cool arcades,
Where at eve the German warrior
Winks upon the German maids; –

Such is Munish: – broad and stately,
Rich of hue, and fair of form;
But, towards the end of August,
Unequivocally *warm*.

Charles Stuart Calverley, 'Dover to Munich', from *Verses and Translations*, 1861

It's a singular place, and one difficult to write of with a serious countenance. It has a fine lot of old pictures, but otherwise is a nightmare of pretentious vacuity: a city of chalky stucco – a Florence and Athens in canvas and planks. To have come thither from Venice is a sensation!

Henry James, Letter to his parents, Heidelberg, 15 September 1872

Art Nouveau . . . was born in Munich. Its parent on the male side was Japanese, on the female side a bastard descendant of William Morris via Maple. It was brought up in Germany, fostered by what are called *decadent* artists. These are artists whose works are a mixture of beer and sausage and Aubrey Beardsley.

Maurice Baring, *Round the World in Any Number of Days*, 1913

In Munich one always has a sense that just over the mountains there is always a way of escape from all German problems, to the lands where the lemons grow.

Goronwy Rees, 'Diary from Berlin to Munich', *Encounter*, April 1964

Nassau

From its hills burst mineral streams of various descriptions, and besides the Selters or Seltzer water, which is drunk as a luxury in every quarter of the globe, there are bright, sparkling remedies, prescribed for almost every disorder under the sun: – for instance, should our reader be consumptive, or, what is much more probable be dyspeptic, let him hurry to Ems; if he wishes to instil iron into his system, and to brace up his muscles, let him go to Langen-Schwalbach; if his brain should require calming, his nerves soothing, and his skin softening, let him glide onwards to Schlangenbad – the serpent's bath; but if he should be rheumatic in his limbs, or if mercury should be running riot in his system, let him hasten, 'body and Bones' to Wiesbaden, where, they say, by being parboiled in the Kochbrunnen (boiling spring), all his troubles will evaporate.

Sir F.B. Head, *Bubbles from the Brunnens of Nassau*, 1834

River Neckar

The Neckar is in many places so narrow that a person can throw a dog across it, if he has one.

Mark Twain, *A Tramp Abroad*, 1880

Nieder Selters

No writer can possibly do justice to that place unless every line of his description contains, at least once, the word . . . bottle. The moralists of Nieder-Selters preach on bottles. Life, they say, is a sound bottle, and death a cracked one – thoughtless men are empty bottles – drunken men are leaky ones; and a man highly educated, fit to appear in any country and in any society, is, of course, a bottle corked, rosined, and stamped with the seal of the Duke of Nassau.

Sir F.B. Head, *Bubbles from the Brunnens of Nassau*, 1834

Nonnewerth

Between the two white breasts of her we love
A dewy blushing rose will sometimes spring;
Thus Nonnewerth like an enchanted thing
Rises mid-stream the crystal depths above.

George Meredith, *Pictures of the Rhine*, IV, 1849

Nuremberg

Nuremberg a Town remarkable for its Mechanical Productions – And for its proverbially bad constitution. . . . It is the great Toy Shop of almost all Europe And almost exclusively by the Manufactury of Nick-Nacks arose some Centuries since to the rank of one of the first Cities in Europe. It is now a striking picture of fallen & falling Greatness. . . . In what respects ingenuity & fineness of Work, the Nurenbergers are still the most dextrous & expert in Europe: Their productions in Brass, their children's toys &c are still unrivalled. . . . But as the Nurenbergers are true Goshamites or as the classical phrase here is Abderites – & the great rule of their Conduct is to stand still while the Rest of the World is in progress, their Manufactures remain as they were, still of great excellence, but from the change of taste of less demand – The Birmingham Wares are peculiarly injurious to them – The Town is in its exterior very unpleasant Vast houses without beauty & almost all painted on the outside – Its Theatre wretchedly supplied with actors And its women notoriously & universally ugly – I hope you will not impute to personal resentment, my unfriendly description, When I state as one of the memorable Anecdotes of my Journey that I was here arrested on Suspicion of being either a Highwayman or a forger I can't tell which.

Henry Crabb Robinson, Letter to his brother, July 1802

We were informed that there is not a single English resident in all Nuremburg. It is a dull old town.

Lady Londonderry, *Visit to the Courts of Vienna, Constantinople, etc.*, 1844

In the valley of the Pegnitz, where across broad meadow-lands
Rise the blue Franconian mountains, Nuremberg the ancient, stands.

Quaint old town of toil and traffic, quaint old town of art and song,
Memories haunt thy pointed gables like the rooks that round them throng;

Memories of the Middle Ages, when the emperors, rough and bold,
Had their dwelling in thy castle, time-defying, centuries old; . . .

Here, when Art was still religion, with a simple, reverent heart,
Lived and laboured Albrecht Durer, the Evangelist of Art; . . .

Through these streets so broad and stately, these obscure and dismal lanes,
Walked of yore the Mastersingers, chanting rude poetic strains. . . .

Here Hans Sachs, the cobbler-poet, laureate of the gentle craft
Wisest of the Twelve Wise Masters, in huge folios sang and laughed. . . .

Not thy council, not thy Kaisers, win for thee the world's regard;
But thy painter, Albrecht Durer, and Hans Sachs, thy cobbler-bard.

Thus, O Nuremberg, a wanderer from a region far away,
As he paced thy streets and court-yards, sang in thought his careless lay:

Gathering from the pavement's crevice, as a floweret of the soil,
The nobility of labor, – the long pedigree of toil.

Henry Wadsworth Longfellow, *Nuremberg*, 1844

and comparison with Carcassone

I think Carcassone for the Middle Age of Knights and Crusaders, and Nuremberg for that of Burghers and Guilds, are the most perfect things imaginable. The outside decoration of the houses is all preserved, and of the churches likewise; every image seems in its place; and you cannot go a yard without finding a house with a statue or a decorated projecting window that compels you to stand still and get the snow down your neck while you look at it.

Matthew Arnold, Letter to his daughter, 6 March 1886

*Nuremberg, if one expects a town of mediaeval appearance, disappoints. Quaint corners, picturesque glimpses, there are in plenty; but everywhere they are surrounded and intruded upon by the modern, and even what is ancient is not nearly so ancient as one thought it was. After all, a town, like a woman, is only as old as it looks; and Nuremberg is still a comfortable-looking dame, its age somewhat difficult to conceive under its fresh paint and stucco in the blaze of the gas and the electric light. Still, looking closely, you may see its wrinkled walls and grey towers.

Jerome K. Jerome, *Three Men on the Bummel*, 1900

Nuremberg consists of a large luxury hotel run by the American army and a large luxury courthouse, everything else a waste of corpse-scented rubble with a handful of middle-aged middle-class Germans in Homburg hats picking their way through the ruins. We drove to the Sports Palace which is intact but probably due for demolition – typical modern functional magnificence designed for mass parades, now full of German Jews in American uniforms photographing one another in the act of giving the Nazi salute from Hitler's rostrum.

Evelyn Waugh, *Diary*, 31 March 1946

Potsdam (GDR)

and see under Berlin

Many causes, physical as well as moral, conduce to render Potsdam gloomy and cheerless. The local position is in itself destitute of natural gaiety or beauty. A sandy, barren soil, on which only the fir loves to run up or to thrive, is an inherent and irremediable defect. It is even adverse to the genius of architecture: for so loose is the ground, that it appears to be incapable of long sustaining the incumbent weight of any very large, or heavy structure: a deformity visible in various parts of the city, where the buildings have sunk at the foundation.

Sir N.W. Wraxall, *Memoirs of the Courts of Berlin, etc*, 1779

So great an air of melancholy pervades the place, that it seems a fitter residence for the dead than the living.

Captain John Dundas Cochrane, *Narrative of a Pedestrian Journey through Russia, etc.*, 1824

Everything about Potsdam smacks of the Great little Frederic, but nothing is more striking than the superabundance of statues. They *swarm!* – there is a whole garrison turned into marble, or stone, good, bad, and indifferent. They are as numerous in the gardens as the promenaders; there is a Neptune group, for example, without even the apology of a pond. The same at Sans Souci – in fact, everywhere. The effect, to my taste, is execrable or ridiculous. Solitude and stillness seem the proper attributes of a statue. We have no notion of marbles mobbing.

Thomas Hood, Letter to C.W. Dilke, 26 December 1836

Sans Souci
Sans Souci inspired me with an appropriate feeling; for I left it without caring for it.

Thomas Hood, *Up the Rhine*, 1840

Prussia

La guerre est l'industrie nationale de la Prusse.
(War is the national industry of Prussia.)

Comte de Mirabeau, attributed, *c.* 1788

The Prussian monarchy itself, sometimes reminds me of a vast prison.

Sir N.W. Wraxall, *Memoirs of the Courts of Berlin, etc.*, 1779

The transition from ease and opulence to extreme poverty is remarkable on crossing the line between the Dutch and Prussian territories. The soil and climate are the same; the governments alone differ. With the poverty the fear also of slaves is visible in the faces of the Prussian subjects. There is an improvement, however in the physiognomy, especially could it be brightened up.

Thomas Jefferson, *Memoranda on a Tour from Paris to Amsterdam, etc.*, 1 April 1788

Most mild and saintly Prussia – steep'd to th' ears
In persecuted Poland's blood and tears,
And now with all her harpy wings outspread
O'er severed Saxony's devoted head!

Thomas Moore, *The Fudge Family in Paris*, 1818

The only way to treat a Prussian is to step on his toes until *he* apologises.

Bavarian proverb

Regensberg / Ratisbon

. . . such an idle sneaking place,
Where vice and folly hide their face
And in a troublesome disguise
The wife seems modest, husband wise.
For pleasure here has the same fate
Which does attend affaires of State,
The Plague of Ceremony infects,
Ev'n in Love, the softer Sex;
Who an essential will neglect
Rather than loose the least respect.
With regular approach we Storm,
And never visit but in form,
That is, sending to know before
At what o'Clock they'll play the whore.
The nymphs are constant, Gallants private,
One scarce can guess who 'tis they drive at.
This seems to me a scurvy fashion,
Who have been bred in a free nation
With liberty of Speech, and passion.
Yet I cannot forbear to Spark it,
And make the best of a bad market.

George Etherege, *Epistle to My Lord Middleton*, from Ratisbon, January 1686

Rhine

There is a very strange custome observed amongst the Germanes as they passe in their boates betwixt Mentz and Colen, and likewise betwixt Colen and the lower parts of the Netherlands. Every man, whatsoever he be, poore or rich, shall labour hard when it commeth to his turne, except he doth either by friendship, or some small summe of money redeeme his labour. For their custome is, that the passengers must exercise themselves with oares and rowing *alternis vicibus*, a couple together. So that the master of the boate (who me thinkes in honestie ought either to doe it himselfe, or to procure some others to doe it for him) never roweth but when his turne commeth. This exercise, both for recreation and health sake I confesse is very convenient for man. But to be tied unto it by way of a strict necessity, when one payeth well for his passage, was a thing that did not a little distaste my humour.

Thomas Coryate, *Crudities*, 1611

Adieu to thee, fair Rhine! How long delighted
The stranger fain would linger on his way!
Thine is a scene alike where souls united,
Or lonely Contemplation thus might stray;
And could the ceaseless vultures cease to prey
On self-condemning bosoms, it were here,
Where Nature, nor too sombre, nor too gay,
Wild, but not rude, awful yet not austere,
Is to the mellow Earth as Autumn to the year.

Adieu to thee again! a vain adieu!
There can be no farewell to scene like thine;
The mind is coloured by thy every hue;
And if reluctantly the eyes resign
Their cherished gaze upon thee, lovely Rhine!
'Tis with the thankful glance of parting praise;
More mighty spots may rise – more glaring shine,
But none unite, in one attaching maze,
The brilliant, fair, and soft, – the glories of old days.

The negligently grand, the fruitful bloom
Of coming ripeness, the white city's sheen,
The rolling stream, the precipice's gloom,
The forest's growth, and Gothic walls between, -
The wild rocks shaped, as they had turrets been,
In mockery of man's art; and these withal
A race of faces happy as the scene,
Whose fertile bounties here extend to all,
Still springing o'er thy banks, though Empires near
them fall.

Lord Byron, *Childe Harold's Pilgrimage*, Canto the Third, 1816

Ye glorious Gothic scenes! how much ye strike
All phantasies, not even excepting mine.
A grey wall, a green ruin, rusty pike
Make my soul pass the equinoctial line
Between the present and past worlds and hover
Upon their airy confine half-seas-over.

Lord Byron, *Don Juan*, 1819–24

The part of the Rhine down which we now glided is that so beautifully described by Lord Byron in his third canto of *Childe Harold*. . . . We were carried down by a dangerously rapid current, and saw on either side of us hills covered with vines and trees, craggy cliffs crowned by desolate towers, and wooded islands, where picturesque ruins peeped from behind the foliage, and cast the shadows of their forms on the troubled waters, which distorted without deforming them. We heard the songs of the vintagers, and if, surrounded by disgusting Germans, the sight was not so replete with enjoyment as I now fancy it to have been; yet memory, taking all the dark shades from the picture, presents this part of the Rhine to my remembrance as the loveliest paradise on earth.

Mary Shelley, *History of a Six Weeks' Tour*, 1817

I cannot express to you how much I am delighted with these beautiful and romantic scenes. Fancy some of the finest parts of the Hudson embellished with old towns, castles, and convents, and seen under the advantage of the loveliest weather, and you may have some idea of the magnificence and beauty of the Rhine.

Washington Irving, Letter to his sister, Mrs Sarah Van Wart, 2 September 1822

How many thousands and hundreds of thousands of English, with their mouths, eyes, and purses wide open, have followed each other, in mournful succession, up and down the Rhine. . . .

Sir F.B. Head, *Bubbles from the Brunnens of Nassau*, 1834

Especially last year, when I came up the Rhine, I felt almost that I had seen gnomes and fairies – the people at work on the face of the mountains looked so *distinct* and yet so *small*, they appeared literal dwarfs – for want of that medium mistiness which ordinarily signifies distance. The only conviction you had, sensually, of their being remote was from the silence: you saw, but you could not hear, the blows of their pickaxes etc. The effect is really miraculous.

Thomas Hood, Letter to Charles Wentworth Dilke, 20 June 1836

The Rhine is like an army Tailor, it gains immensely by contracting.

Sydney Smith, Letter to the Hon. Caroline Fox, 28 May 1837

In short, . . . if you, or any of your friends ever suffer from hypochondriasis, weak nerves, – melancholy – morbid sensibility – or mere ennui – let me advise you and them, as you value your lives, health, and spirits – your bodies and your minds – to do as we have done, and go UP THE RHINE.

Thomas Hood, *Up the Rhine*, 1840

. . . across the broad stream of the Rhine,
The full moon cast a silvery zone;
And methought as I gazed on its shine,
'Surely that is the Eau de Cologne.'
I inquired not the place of its source,
If it ran to the east or the west;
But my heart took a note of its course
That it flow'd towards Her I love best,
Like those wandering thoughts of my own,

And the fancy such sweetness possess'd
That the Rhine seemed all Eau de Cologne!
Thomas Hood, *To ***** with a Flask of Rhine Water*, 1840

The lordly, lovely Rhine.
Thomas Campbell, *The Child and the Hind*, 1841

With regard to the scenery, I was disappointed in particular spots, but very well pleased on the whole. The beauties of the Rhine are not near so striking as I fancied they were; the scenery of the Wye is infinitely finer; in fact, there is not a single object of grandeur, but it is all excessively pretty; the river itself is noble. . . . A man in the steamboat, who was evidently concocting a journal, very sensibly copied out what he wanted to describe from Murray's handbook; probably he could not do better.
Charles Greville, *A Journal of the Reign of Queen Victoria*, 20–22 June 1843

Saw Drachenfels & the Seven Mountains, & Rolandseck, & the Isle of Nuns. The old ruins & arch are glorious – but the river Rhine is not the Hudson.
Herman Melville, *Journal of a Visit to London and the Continent* (11 December 1849), 1849–50

The beautifulest river on earth I do believe; – and my first idea of a World-river. It is many fathoms deep, broader twice over than the Thames here at high water; and rolls along, mirror-smooth (except that, in looking close, you will find ten thousand little eddies in it), voiceless, swift, with trim banks, through the heart of Europe, and of the Middle Ages, wedded to the Present Age: such an image of calm *power* (to say nothing of its other properties) I find I had never seen before.
Thomas Carlyle, Letter to R.W. Emerson, 13 May 1853

Men there are bold enough to stay from church on Sundays, to dine at their clubs without leave, to light cigars in their own parlours, and to insist upon brandy-and-water before they go to bed; but where is the man who can tell his wife and daughters that it is quite unnecessary that they should go up the Rhine!
Anthony Trollope, *Travelling Sketches*, 1866

Beetling brows with ivy grown
Frowning heights of mossy stone;
Turret, with its flaunting flag
Flung from battlemented crag
Dungeon-keep and fortalice
Looking down a precipice
O'er the darkly glancing wave
By the Lurline-haunted cave;
Robber haunt and maiden bower
Home of Love and Crime and Power, –
That's the scenery, in fine,
Of the Legends of the Rhine.
Bret Harte, *The Legends of the Rhine*, c. 1880

The Rhine is of course tedious, the vineyards are formal and dull, and as far as I can judge, the inhabitants of Germany are American.
Oscar Wilde, Letter to Robert Ross, July 1889

The Rhein is most awfully German. It makes me laugh. It looks fearfully fit for the theatre.
D.H. Lawrence, Letter to A.W. McLeod, Trier, May 1912

When you think about the defence of England you no longer think of the chalk cliffs of Dover. You think of the Rhine. That is where our frontier lies to-day.
Stanley Baldwin, Speech in the House of Commons, 30 July 1934

The Rhine . . . seems to me one of the few really ugly rivers in the world . . .
Leonard Woolf, *Downhill All the Way*, 1967

The principal artery of capitalism in Europe.
Richard West, *Victory in Vietnam*, 1974

Rhineland etc.

The Rhine is still the Rhine, the great divider. You feel it as you cross. The flat, frozen, watery places. Then the cold and curving river. Then the other side, seeming so cold, so empty, so frozen, so forsaken. The train stands and steams fiercely. Then it draws through the flat Rhine plain, past frozen pools of flood-water, and frozen fields, in the emptiness of this bit of occupied territory.

Immediately you are over the Rhine, the spirit of place has changed. There is no more attempt at the bluff of geniality. The marshy places are frozen. The fields are vacant. There seems no-body in the world. It is as if life had retreated eastwards. As if the Germanic life were slowly ebbing away from contact with western Europe, ebbing to the deserts of the east. And there stand the heavy, ponderous, round hills of the Black Forest, black with an inky blackness of Germanic trees, and patched with a whiteness of snow. They are like a series of huge involved black mounds, obstructing the vision eastwards. You look at them from the Rhine plain, and you know that you stand on an actual border, up against something.

The moment you are in Germany, you know. It feels empty, and somehow, menacing.
D.H. Lawrence, 'A Letter from Germany', *New Statesman and Nation*, 13 October 1924, *Phoenix* 1936

Salzig (scenery of the Rhine, near)

Here nature, by combining all her choicest beauties, and exhibiting them in one view and through the brightest colouring, had so outrivalled her own works that even nature seemed unnatural.

Charles Tennant, *A Tour, etc.*, 1824

Saxony (en route to Ballenstedt)

Saxony is a flat Country rich to the agricultural, poor to the picturesque Eye.

Henry Crabb Robinson, Letter to his brother, 6 July 1801

This day I had a pleasant drive between Meissen and Dresden. We went along the side of the Elbe. On each side of the river were beautiful rising grounds covered with vines. Pray may we not have the same in Scotland? Surely our climate differs little from that of Saxony. I saw too, here and there, old castles, Heerschaften's houses, seats of gentlemen. It pleased me. It was Scottish.

James Boswell, *Journal*, 8 October 1764

The being served at every inn, since we came into Saxony, upon Dresden china, gives one an odd feel somehow.

Hester Lynch Piozzi, *Observations . . . in the Course of a Journey*, 1789

Stuttgart

*Stuttgart is a charming town, clean and bright, a smaller Dresden. It has the additional attraction of containing little that one need to go out of one's way to see: a medium-sized picture gallery, a small museum of antiquities, and half a palace, and you are through with the entire thing and can enjoy yourself.

Jerome K. Jerome, *Three Men on the Bummel*, 1900

Trier

The valley all along coming is full of apple trees in blossom, pink puffs like the smoke of an explosion, and then bristling vine sticks, so that the hills are angry hedgehogs.

D.H. Lawrence, Letter to Frieda Lawrence, Trier, 8 May 1912

A. called the Basilica, 'The ideal Methodist Chapel.'

Alfred Lord Tennyson, *A Memoir, by his Son*, 1897

Weimar (GDR)

It is a very queer little place, although called the 'Athens of Germany' on account of the great poets who have lived here. . . . Fancy a little quiet town without cabs, omnibuses, very few carts, and scarcely a carriage – with no gas lights for the streets, which are lighted (in winter only) by oil lamps, strung across the streets on a cord. These, which are rare, give so little light that when ladies go to the theatre they take a servant with them to carry a lantern. – But though the town is quiet and queer, it is very agreeable, as the Park is within five minutes walk of even the most distant parts, and the Park is something like Kensington Gardens with a river running through it, and with rocky paths and winding ways.

G.H. Lewes, Letter to Charles and Thornton Lewes, 27 September 1854

Westphalia

Thy bread, Westphalia, thy brown bread I sing,
Bread which might make the dinner of a king;
Though one of those whom Englishmen call dogs,
One whose nice palate had been us'd to frogs
Could not, forsooth, digest a stuff so coarse,
But called it good provision for his horse.
An etymologist, who pokes his nose
Into dark holes which Time has wish'd to close,
May learn that 'Niccol' was the horse's name,
Hence the bread's title, 'Bon pour Niccol,' came.

James Boswell, *Journal*, 20 October 1764

Well may all writers agree in celebrating the miseries of Westphalia! well may they, while the wretched inhabitants, uniting poverty with pride, live on their hogs, with their hogs, and like their hogs, in mud-walled cottages, a dozen of which together is called by courtesy a village, surrounded by black heaths, and wild uncultivated plains, over which the unresisted wind sweeps with a velocity I never yet was witness to, and now and then exasperated perhaps by solitude, returns upon itself in eddies terrible to look on.

Hester Lynch Piozzi, *Observations . . . in the Course of a Journey*, 1789

Wiesbaden

Looking down upon it from the Platte, this town or city is about three-quarters of an English mile square, one quarter of this area being covered with a rubbishy old, the remainder with a staring, formal, new town, composed of streets of white stone houses, running at right angles to each other. As I first approached it, it appeared to me to be as hot, as formal, and as uninteresting a place as ever I beheld. . . .

The town of Wiesbaden is evidently one which does not appreciate the luxury of 'home sweet home!' for it is built not for itself, but for strangers; and though most people admire the size of the buildings, yet, to my mind, there is something very melancholy in seeing houses so much too fine for the style of inhabitants to whom they belong. A city of lodging houses, like an army of mercenaries, may to each individual be a profitable speculation, but no brilliant uniform, or external show, can secretly compensate for the want of national self-pride, which shines in the heart of a soldier, standing under his country's colours, or in the mind of a man living consistently in his own little home. . . . However, certainly the inhabitants of Wiesbaden do not seem to view the subject at all in this point of view, for they all talk with pride of their fine new town, and strut about their large houses like children wearing men's shoes, ten times too big for their feet.

Sir F.B. Head, *Bubbles from the Brunnens of Nassau*, 1834

There would be no end in stating what the Wiesbaden water is said to be good for; a much simpler course is to explain, that doctors do agree in saying, that it is *not* good for complaints where there is any disposition to inflammation or regular fever, and that it changes consumption into – death.

Ibid.

In describing the taste of the mineral water of Wiesbaden, were I to say, that while drinking it, one hears in one's ears the cackling of hens, and that one sees feathers flying before one's eyes, I should certainly grossly exaggerate; but when I declare that it exactly resembles very hot chicken broth, I only say what Dr Granville said, and what in fact everybody says, and must say, respecting it; and certainly I do wonder why the common people should be at the inconvenience of making bad soup, when they can get better from nature's great stock-pot – the Koch-brunnen of Wiesbaden. . . . One would think that . . . the chickens would at last be boiled to rags.

Ibid.

Wittenberge (GDR)

It is proverbially said, that a man shall meet nothing at Witteberg, but whores, students, and swine, to which purpose they have these two Verses:

> Had Witeberg no swine, if no whores were,
> Nor Phoebus traine, I pray you what is there?

Whence may be gathered that the Citizens have small trafficke, living only upon the Schollers, and that the streets must needs be filthy.

Fynes Moryson, *An Itinerary*, 1617

This court is much like the residence of an old British baron.

James Boswell, *Journal*, 30 September 1764

Worms

Worms, a fine old place, though greatly shrunken and decayed in respect of its population; with a picturesque old cathedral standing on the brink of the Rhine, and some brave old churches shut up, and so hemmed in and overgrown with vineyards that they look as if they were turning into leaves and grapes.

Charles Dickens, Letter to John Forster, *c.* 7 June 1846

Of Worms the characteristic is rather the preservation of what was domestic and familiar among western Germans before the new industrial transformation. It is a town the old houses of which recall, as vividly as a well-acted play or a well-written historical novel, the German culture of the highest German time; lovable, familiar, a little confused, but at ease and confident of itself.

Hilaire Belloc, *Many Cities*, 1928

GHANA

There is no part of the world, I may assert, where there is a worse feeling between black and white than upon the Gold Coast. The arrogance *de part et d'autre* is most comical to a stranger. There are about 100 Europeans in the land: amongst these there are many excellent fellows, but – it is an unpleasant confession to make – the others appear to me inferior to the Africans, native as well as mulatto. The possibility of such a thing had never yet reached my brain: at last, in colloquy with an old friend upon the Coast, the idea started up, and after due discussion we adopted it. I speak of *morale*; in intellect the black race is palpably superior, and is fast advancing in the path of civilisation. It cries for 'regular lawyers', and is now beginning, even at the out-stations to file schedules of bankruptcy.

Richard Burton, *Wanderings in West Africa*, 1863

It is a land of laughing people, very hospitable people. That's what the tourist posters proclaim. They forgot to add that pussy is cheap here, the liquor is indifferent, and the people suffer from a thousand diseases.

Kofi Awoonor, *This Earth, My Brother*, 1971

Accra

Accra . . . is one of the five West Coast towns that look well from the sea. The others don't look well from anywhere. . . . What there is of beauty in Accra is oriental in type. Seen from the sea, Fort St. James on the left and Christiansborg Castle on the right, both almost on shore level, give, with an outcrop of sandy dwarf cliffs, a certain air of balance and strength to the town, though but for these and the two old castles,

Accra would be but a poor place and a flimsy, for the rest of it is a mass of rubbishy mud and palm-leaf huts, and corrugated iron dwellings for the Europeans.

Corrugated iron is my abomination. I quite understand it has points, and I do not attack from an aesthetic standpoint. It really looks well enough, when it is painted white. There is, close to Christiansborg Castle, a patch of bungalows and offices for officialdom and wife that from a distance in the hard bright sunshine looks like an encampment of snow white tents among the coco palms, and pretty enough withal. . . . The main street of Accra is remarkable. The untidy, poverty-stricken native houses or huts are no credit to their owners, and a constant source of anxiety to a conscientious sanitary inspector. Almost every one of them is a shop, but this does not give rise to the animated commercial life one might imagine, owing, I presume, to the fact that every native inhabitant of Accra who has any money to get rid of is able recklessly to spend it in his own emporium. For these shops are of the store nature, each after his kind, and seem homogeneously stocked with tin pans, loud-patterned basins, iron pots, a few rolls of cloth, and bottles of American rum. After passing these there are the Haussa lines, a few European houses, and the cathedral; and when nearly into Christiansborg, a cemetery on either side of the road. That to the right is the old cemetery, now closed. . . . Opposite to it is the cemetery now in use, and I remember well my first visit to it under the guidance of a gloomy Government official, who said he always walked there every afternoon, 'so as to get used to the place before staying permanently in it.'

Mary Kingsley, *Travels in West Africa*, 1897

Accra is not what you would call a tidy town. But few cities in Africa are more interesting. The sewers are mostly open drains, like those in pre-war Teheran, and it has no traffic lights. . . . It looks like a collection of tin hovels, interspersed with dilapidated frame buildings and tawdry hole-in-the-wall shops under mouldy arcades. The first impression a visitor is apt to get is of an almost desperate physical squalor, together with a contrary note of extreme animation. The streets are thronged with people in their Roman-like togas. The airport and its hotel and restaurant look like a prodigious crazy dance hall in Harlem. I saw no sight in Africa more exhilarating.

John Gunther, *Inside Africa*, 1955

Earthquake of 1938

There was plenty of irony in that topsy-turvy night. Accra, like most British colonial seats, is a horrible site of pomposity and poverty. Vast, vulgarly ostentatious Government buildings – totally unnecessary in grandeur – lording it over a warren of native wattle huts. And what happened in the earthquake was that the mud-and-wattle native dwellings stood the strain much better than the European buildings. The huts heaved and swayed, ending up at impossible angles – but most of them stood up. Whereas, with the European buildings, the façades, and all the stone-gingerbread icing, fell off. The streets were cluttered with Grecian ruins.

Negley Farson, *Behind God's Back*, 1940

Coomasie (and the Ashanti)

Their capital was a charnel house; their religion a combination of cruelty and treachery; their policy the natural outcome of their religion.

Lord Wolseley, quoted in Henry Morton Stanley's *Autobiography*, 1909 – of 1873–4

GIBRALTAR

Cede to Spain Gibraltar, and the Mediterranean becomes a pool, a mere pond, on which the Spaniards can navigate at their pleasure. Deprive yourselves of this commanding station, and the states that border on that sea will no longer look to England for the maintenance of its free navigation.

Charles James Fox, Speech in the House of Commons, 12 December 1782

Gibraltar is not merely a post of pride; it is a post of power, of connection, and of commerce; one which makes us invaluable to our friends and dreadful to our enemies.

Edmund Burke, Speech in the House of Commons, 12 December 1782

Gibraltar is another instance of national ill-policy. A post which in time of peace is not wanted, and in time of war is of no use, must at all times be useless. Instead of affording protection to a navy, it requires the aid of one to maintain it. To suppose that Gibraltar commands the Mediterranean, or the pass into it, or the trade of it, is to suppose a detected falsehood; because though Britain holds the post she has lost the other three, and every benefit she expected from it. And to say that all this happens because it is besieged by land and water, is to say nothing, for this will always be the case in time of war, while France and Spain keep up superior fleets, and Britain holds the place. So that, though, as an impenetrable inaccessible rock, it may be held by the one, it is always in the power of the other to render it useless and excessively chargeable. . . . The short way to reduce Gibraltar is to attack the British fleet: for Gibraltar is dependent on a fleet for support, as a bird is on its wings for food, and when wounded there, it starves.

Thomas Paine, Letter to the Abbé Raynal, 1782

The dirtiest and most detestable spot in existence.
Lord Byron, Letter to John Hanson, 7 August 1809

In talking after dinner of sailing &c., Fox was describing the sea as he had once seen it, all in flames round the ship in passing through the Gut of Gibraltar; 'an inflammation in the bowels,' said Luttrell.
Thomas Moore, *Diary*, 7 October1826

England, we love thee better than we know -
And this I learned, when after wandering long
'Mid people of another stock and tongue,
I heard again thy martial music blow
And saw thy gallant children to and fro
Pace, keeping ward at one of those huge gates,
Which, like twin giants watch the Herculean straits:
When first I came in sight of that brave show,
It made my very heart within me dance,
To think that thou thy proud foot should'st advance
Forward so far into the mighty sea;
Joy was it, and exultation to behold
Thine ancient standard's rich emblazonry,
A glorious picture by the wind unrolled.
Richard Chenevix Trench, *The Story of Justin Martyr, &c.*, 1835

Suppose all the nations of the earth to send fitting ambassadors to represent them at Wapping or Portsmouth Point, with each under its own national signboard and language, its appropriate house of call, and your imagination may figure the Main Street of Gibraltar.
W.M. Thackeray, *Journey from Cornhill to Cairo*, 1845

. . . this great blunderbuss – which we seized out of the hands of the natural owners a hundred and forty years ago, and which we have kept ever since tremendously loaded and cleaned and ready for use.
Ibid.

Gibraltar seemed to me to be a place where no one would live but from necessity. Provisions and the necessaries of life of all kinds were exceedingly dear. The meat was poor and lean; vegetables were scarce; and servants, from the plenty of bad wine, were always drunk. Out-door amusements on a rock, where half the accessible places are to be reached by steps only, or where a start of a horse would plunge his rider over a precipice, must be, of course, but few.
Charles Lewis Meryon, *Travels of Lady Hester Stanhope*, 1846

The British houses, the rent of which is very dear, are built on the stuffy Wapping principle, with a Genoese exterior; all is brick and plaster and woodwork, cribbed and confined, and filled with curtains and carpets, on purpose to breed vermin and fever in this semi-African hotbed; calculated to let in the enemy, heat, so that Nelson, who dearly as he loved the 'old Rock,' hoped that all the small houses at its back might be burnt; 'perhaps if half the town went with them it would be better.'
Richard Ford, *A Handbook for Travellers in Spain*, 3rd edn, 1855

Entered the Strait of Gibraltar at 4. P.M. Mountainous & wild-looking coast of Africa – forsaken barbarous. 'Apes Mountain' nearly opposite Gibraltar. 'Pillar of Hercules.' Tarifa, small village, – white. Insular Rock. Sunset. Rock strongly lit, all the rest in shade. England throwing the rest of the world in shade.
Herman Melville, *Journal of a Visit to Europe and the Levant*, 24 November 1856

It rises like a monstrous monolith, a fragment of some shattered world dropped here by chance, and not ill-compared, by a foreign writer, to a gigantic granite sphinx, whose shoulders, groins and croup would lie towards Spain with the long, broad, loose, flowing, and undulating outlines, like those of a lion asleep, and whose head, somewhat truncated, is turned towards Africa, as if with a dreamy and steadfast deep attention.
H. O'Shea, *A Guide to Spain*, 1865

It . . . is suggestive of a 'gob' of mud on the end of a shingle.
Mark Twain, *The Innocents Abroad*, 1869

The greatest drawback to the charms of Gibraltar has seemed to us to be the difficulty of leaving it. It is a beautiful prison.
Augustus Hare, *Wanderings in Spain*, 1885

A place as unlike Spain as it is possible to imagine.
Ibid.

Gibraltar on a spring day, all in pastel shades, like the back-drop for a musical comedy. . . .
H.L. Mencken, 'The Shrine of Mnemosyne', in *Prejudices*, 4th Series, 1925

'And is that really Gibraltar?'
'Yes Madam.'
'Thank you so much. I understand that when we land there I must on no account miss seeing the Rock'.
D.H. Ghilchik, caption to cartoon, *Punch*, 25 July 1934

A current gag in the Madrid cafés is to pass round in a conspiratorial way, little packets which when opened reveal a tiny stone and a note saying: 'Patriots! Spain has regained the Rock! This bit is your share.'
James Cameron, *News Chronicle*, 1 March 1954, in *What a Way to Run the Tribe*, 1968

Gibraltar. . . . The drab British fortress that dangles from the Spanish mainland like an uncomfortable earring. . . . As an incitement to Anglophobia, Gibraltar has few rivals in continental Europe; atmospherically it is a successful blend of reform school, naval base, and Cornish seaside resort, and thus exemplifies the uncanny skill with which the British contrive to export their least likable features intact. It has fish, chips, and policemen in conical helmets; and the fact that it is frequently shrouded in mist provides a final touch of nostalgia for the Englishman abroad. They call it 'The Rock', a nickname it appropriately shares with Alcatraz.

Kenneth Tynan, 'The Rising Costa del Sol', 1963, in *Tynan Right and Left*, 1967

GREAT BRITAIN: ENGLAND

Sixteenth and Seventeenth Centuries

. . . Deare countrey! O! how dearely deare
Ought thy remembraunce and perpetuall band
Be to thy foster Childe, that from thy hand
Did commun breath and nouriture receave.
How brutish is it not to understand
How much to her we owe, that all us gave;
That gave unto us all what ever good we have.

Edmund Spenser, *The Faerie Queene*, Book 2, 1589

Holland: . . . Well, I say, it was never merrie world in England, since Gentlemen came up.

William Shakespeare, *Henry the Sixth*, part 2, *c.* 1589–92

This royall Throne of Kings, this sceptred Isle,
This earth of Majesty, this seate of Mars,
This other Eden, demy paradise,
This Fortresse built by Nature for her selfe,
Against infection, and the hand of warre:
This happy breed of men, this little world,
This precious stone, set in the silver sea,
Which serves it in the office of a wall,
Or as a Moate defensive to a house,
Against the envy of lesse happier Lands,
This blessed plot, this earth, this Realme, this England,
This Nurse, this teeming wombe of Royall Kings, . . .
This Land of such deere souls, this deere-deere Land,
Deere for her reputation through the world,
Is now leas'd out (I dye pronouncing it)
Like to a Tenement or pelting Farme.
England bound in with the triumphant sea,
Whose rockie shore beates backe the envious siedge
Of watery Neptune, is now bound in with shame,
With Inky blottes, and rotten Parchment bonds.
That England, that was wont to conquer others,
Hath made a shamefull conquest of it selfe.

William Shakespeare, *Richard the Second*, *c.* 1595–6

This England never did, nor never shall
Lye at the proud foote of a Conqueror,
But when it first did helpe to wound it selfe.
Now, these her Princes are come home againe,
Come the three corners of the world in Armes,
And we shall shocke them: Naught shall make us rue,
If England to it selfe, do rest but true.

William Shakespeare, *King John*, *c.* 1596–7

For the air is most temperate and wholesome, sited in the midst of the temperate Zone, subject to no storms and tempests as the more Southern and Northern are; but stored with infinite delicate fowl. For water it is walled and guarded with the Ocean most commodious for traffick to all parts of the world, and watered with pleasant fishfull and navigable rivers, which yield safe havens and roads, and furnished with shipping and Sailors, that it may rightly be termed the Lady of the Sea. That I may say nothing of healthful Baths and of Meres stored with both fish and fowl; the earth fertile of all kind of grain, manured with good husbandry, rich in mineral of coals, tin lead copper, not without gold and silver, abundant in pasture, replenished with cattle both tame and wild (for it hath more parks than all Europe besides), plentifully wooded, provided with all complete provisions of War, beautified with many populous Cities, fair Boroughs, good Towns, and well-built Villages, strong Munitions, magnificent Palaces of the Prince, stately houses of the Nobility, frequent Hospitals, beautiful Churches, fair Colleges, as well in other places as in the two Universities, which are comparable to all the rest in Christendom, not only in antiquity, but also in learning, buildings and endowments. As for Government, Ecclesiastical and Civil, which is the very soul of a kingdom, I need to say nothing, when as I write to home-born, and not to strangers.

William Camden, *Remaines Concerning Britain*, 1610

Britaine's a world
By it selfe, and we will nothing pay
For wearing our owne Noses.

William Shakespeare, *Cymbeline*, *c.* 1609–10

Hath Britaine all the Sunne that shines?

Ibid.

Of Albions glorious Ile the wonders whilst I write,
The sundry varying soyles, the pleasures infinite,
(Where heate kills not the cold, nor cold expells the heat,
The calmes too mildly small, nor winds too roughly great,
Nor night doth hinder day, nor day the night doth wrong.
The summer not too short, the winter not too long)
What helpe shall I invoke to ayde my Muse the while?

Michael Drayton, *Poly-Olbion, The First Song*, 1612

This is the most famous Iland of all the World, . . .
Fynes Moryson, *An Itinerary*, 1617

This Isle is a mere bedlam, and therein,
We all lye raving, mad in every sinne.
Michael Drayton, *Elegy, to My Noble Friend Master William Browne, of the evill time*, after 1613

The trivial prophecy, which I heard when I was a child, and queen Elizabeth was in the flower of her years, was,

When hempe is sponne
England's done:

Whereby it was generally conceived, that after the princes had reigned which had the principal letters of that word *hempe* (which were Henry, Edward, Mary, Philip, and Elizabeth), England should come to utter confusion; which, thanks be to God, is verified only in the change of the name; for that the King's style is now no more that of England, but of Britain.
Francis Bacon, *Essays*, 1597–1625

And now last, this most happy and glorious event, that this island of Britain, divided from all the world, should be united in itself.
Francis Bacon, *Advancement of Learning*, Book 2, 1605

When was there contract better driven by *Fate*?
Or celebrated with more truth of state?
The world the temple was, the priest a king,
The spoused paire two realmes, the sea the ring.
Ben Jonson, *Epigramme*, On the Union, (before) 1616

Idleness is the *malus genus* of our nation.
Robert Burton, *Anatomie of Melancholie*, 1621

It is true, that as every member of the bodie hath somewhat eminent, whereby it is serviceable to the whole; so every Region excelleth all others in some peculiar Raritie, which may be termed extraordinary respectively, though otherwise most common and ordinary in its owne place. So our England in the naturall temper, accidental want of Wolves, artificiall Rings of Bels, Sheepe not at all or seldome drinking, Lands and Waters turning Wood in some parts to Stone, Wonders of the Peke and other parts, doth not degenerate from nature, but hath a peculiar nature, almost miraculous to other Countries, as the naturall Wonders of their Regions are to us.
Samuel Purchas, 'To the Reader', *Hakluytus Posthumus, or Purchas his Pilgrimes*, 1625

O England! full of sin, but most of sloth;
Spit out thy phlegm, and fill thy breast with glory:
Thy gentry bleats, as if thy native cloth
Transfus'd a sheepishness into thy story:
Not that they all are so; but that the most
Are gone to grass, and in the pasture lost.
George Herbert, *The Church-Porch*, 1633

The dominion of the sea, as it is an ancient and undoubted right of the crown of England, so it is the best security of the land. The wooden walls are the best walls of this kingdom.
Thomas Coventry, Lord Keeper of the Great Seal, 17 June 1635

England is a prison for men, a paradise for women, a purgatory for servants, a hell for horses.
Thomas Fuller, quoted as a proverb, in *Holy State*, 1642

All places, all airs make unto me one country; I am in England, everywhere, and under any meridian.
Sir Thomas Browne, *Religio Medici*, 1642

Let not England forget her precedence of teaching nations how to live.
John Milton, *The Doctrine and Discipline of Divorce*, Preface, 1644

Methinks I see in my mind a noble and puissant nation rousing herself like a strong man after sleep, and shaking her invincible locks. Methinks I see her as an eagle mewing her mighty youth, and kindling her undazzled eyes at the full midday beam.
John Milton, *Areopagitica*, 1644

Oh Thou, that dear and happy Isle,
The Garden of the World ere while,
Thou *Paradise* of four Seas,
Which *Heaven* planted us to please,
But, to exclude the World, did guard
With watry if not flaming Sword;
What luckless Apple did we tast,
To make us Mortal, and The Wast?
Andrew Marvell, *Upon Appleton House, to my Lord Fairfax*, c. 1650, st. xli

Ah! la perfide Angleterre!
Jacques Bossuet, Sermon on the Circumcision, Metz, 1652, quoted by Napoleon when shipped to St Helena

Whether this portion of the world were rent
By the rude ocean from the continent,
Or thus created, it was sure designed
To be the sacred refuge of mankind.
Edmund Waller, *Paneygeric to My Lord Protector*, *c.* 1655

Rome, though her Eagle through the world had flown
Could never make this island all her own.
Ibid.

Where shall I find the noble *British* Land?
Lo, I at last a *Northern Spec* espie,
Which in the *Sea* does lie,
And seems a *Grain* o' th' *Sand*!
For this will any *sin*, or *Bleed*?
Of *Civil Wars* is this the *Meed*?

And is it this, alas, which we
(Oh *Irony* of *Words*!) do call *Great Britannie*?

Abraham Cowley, 'The Ecstasie', in *Pindarique Odes*, 1656

England may not unfitly be compared to a house, not very great, but convenient; and the several shires may properly be resembled to the *rooms* thereof.

Thomas Fuller, *The History of the Worthies of England*, 1662

England is a good land, and a bad people.
This is a French proverb.

Ibid.

England were but fling,
Save for the crooked stick and the grey goose wing.

England would be worthless without archery, quoted by Thomas Fuller, in *ibid.*

Freedom! which in no other land will thrive,
Freedom! an English subject's sole prerogative.

John Dryden, *Threnodia Augustalis*, 1685

Eighteenth Century

'Tis for the honour of England, that all Europe should know that we have blockheads of all ages.

William Congreve, *The Way of the World*, 1700

'Tis Liberty that crowns Britannia's Isle
And makes her barren rocks and her bleak mountains smile.
Others with towering piles may please the sight,
And in their proud aspiring domes delight,
A nicer touch to the stretched canvas give
Or teach their animated rocks to live:
'Tis Britain's care to watch o'er Europe's fate,
And hold in balance each contending state
To threaten bold, presumptuous kings with war,
And answer her afflicted neighbour's prayer.

Joseph Addison, *Letter from Italy to the Right Honourable Lord Halifax*, 1701

Farewell false friends, farewell ill wine
Farewell all women with design
Farewell all pocky cheating punks
Farewell lotteries, farewell banks
And *England*, I, in leaving thee
May say farewell to poverty.
  Adieu, where'er I go I'm sure to find
  Nothing so ill as that I leave behind

Farewell nation without sense
Farewell exchequer without pence;
Farewell army with bare feet
Farewell navy without meat;
Farewell writing, fighting beaus
And farewell, useless plenipoes
  Adieu, etc.

. . .

Adieu once more, Britannia fare thee well;
And if all this won't mend thee,
May the D—— triumph in your spoil
May beggary run throughout your isle
And no one think it worth his while
  To take up to defend thee.

Thomas Brown, *A Farewell to Poor England, in the Year 1704*

Rejoice, O Albion! severed from the world,
By Nature's wise indulgence.

John Philips, *Cider*, 1708

It is the great Advantage of a trading Nation that there are few in it so dull and heavy, who may not be placed in Stations of life which may give them an Opportunity of making their Fortunes.

Joseph Addison, *Spectator*, no. 21, 24 March 1711

I never will call it *Britain*, pray don't call it *Britain*.

Jonathan Swift, *Journal to Stella*, November 1711

The *English* Summer is pleasanter than that of any other Country in *Europe*, on no other account, but because it has greater mixture of Spring in it.

Joseph Addison, *Spectator*, no. 393, 31 May 1712

We have in *England* a particular Bashfulness in every thing that regards Religion. A well-bred Man is obliged to conceal any Serious Sentiment of this Nature, and very often to appear a greater Libertine than he is, that he may keep himself in Countenance among the Men of Mode.

Joseph Addison, *Spectator*, no. 458, 15 August 1712

Supper was no sooner served in, than he took occasion, from a Shoulder of Mutton they lay before us, to cry up the Plenty of *England*, which would be the happiest Country in the World, provided we would live within ourselves. Upon which, he expatiated on the Inconveniencies of Trade, that carried from us the Commodities of our Country, and made a Parcel of Upstarts as rich as Men of the most ancient Families of England. He then declared frankly, that he had always been against all Treaties and Alliances with Foreigners: *Our Wooden Walls*, says he, *are our Security, and we may bid Defiance to the whole World, especially if they should attack us when the Militia is out.* I ventured to reply, that I had as great an Opinion of the *English* Fleet as he had; but I cou'd not see how they could be pay'd and mann'd and fitted out, unless we encouraged Trade and Navigation.

Joseph Addison, *Freeholder*, XXII, 5 March 1716

The truth is, our symptoms are so bad that, notwithstanding all the care and vigilance of the legislature, it is to be feared that the final period of our state approaches. Strong constitutions, whether politic or natural, do not feel light disorders. But when they are sensibly affected, the distemper is for the most part violent, and of an ill prognostic. Free governments like our own were planted by the Goths in most parts of Europe; and, though we all know what they are come to, yet we seem rather disposed to follow their example than to profit by it.

God grant the time be not near when men shall say: 'This island was once inhabited by a religious, brave, sincere people, of plain uncorrupt manners, respecting inbred wealth rather than titles and appearances, asserters of liberty, lovers of their country, jealous of their own rights, and unwilling to infringe the rights of others; improvers of learning and useful arts, enemies to luxury, tender of other men's lives and prodigal of their own; inferior in nothing to the old Greeks or Romans, and superior to each of those people in the perfections of the other. Such were our ancestors during their rise and greatness; but they degenerated, grew servile flatterers of men in power, adopted Epicurean notions, became venal, corrupt, injurious, which drew upon them the hatred of God and man, and occasioned their final ruin.'

George Berkeley, *An Essay Towards Preventing the Ruin of Great Britain*, 1721

O fruitful Britain! doubtless thou wast meant
A nurse of *fools*, to stock the continent.

Rev. Edward Young, LL.D., *Love of Fame*, 1725

They are ill friends to England, who strive to write a history of her nudities, and expose, much less recommend her wicked part to posterity.

Daniel Defoe, *A Tour through the Whole Island of Great Britain*, 1724–7

Heavens! what a goodly prospect spreads around,
Of hills, and dales, and woods, and lawns, and spires,
And glittering towns, and gilded streams, till all
The stretching landscape into smoke decays!
Happy Britannia! where, the Queen of Arts,
Inspiring vigour, Liberty abroad
Walks, unconfined, even to thy farthest cots,
And scatters plenty with unsparing hand.
Rich is thy soil and merciful thy clime;
Thy streams unfailing in the Summer's drought;
Unmatch'd thy guardian oaks; thy valleys float
With golden waves; and on thy mountains flocks
Bleat numberless, while, roving round their sides,
Bellow the blackening herds in lusty droves.
Beneath, thy meadows glow, and rise unquell'd
Against the mower's scythe. On every hand
Thy villas shine. The country teems with wealth;
And property assures it to the swain,
Pleased and unwearied in his guarded toil.
Full are thy cities with the sons of Art;
And trade and joy, in every busy street,
Mingling are heard: even Drudgery himself,
As at the car he sweats, or dusty hews
The palace-stone, looks gay. Thy crowded ports,
Where rising masts an endless prospect yield,
With labour burn, and echo to the shouts
Of hurried sailor, as he hearty waves
His last adieu, and, loosening every sheet,
Resigns the spreading vessel to the wind.
Bold, firm, and graceful are thy generous youth,
By hardship sinew'd, and by danger fired,
Scattering the nations where they go; and first
Or on the listed plain, or stormy seas.
Mild are thy glories too, as o'er the plans
Of thriving peace thy thoughtful sires preside;
In genius, and substantial learning, high;
For every virtue, every worth, renown'd;
Sincere, plain-hearted, hospitable, kind;
Yet like the mustering thunder, when provoked,
The dread of tyrants, and the sole resource
Of those that under grim Oppression groan. . . .
May my song soften, as thy daughters I,
Britannia, hail! for beauty is their own,
The feeling heart, simplicity of life,
And elegance, and taste: the faultless form,
Shaped by the hand of Harmony; the cheek,
Where the live crimson, through the native white
Soft-shooting, o'er the face diffuses bloom,
And every nameless grace; the parted lip,
Like the red rose-bud, moist with morning dew,
Breathing delight; and under flowing jet,
Or sunny ringlets, or of circling brown,
The neck slight-shaded, and the swelling breast;
The look resistless, piercing to the soul,
And by the soul inform'd, when, drest in love,
She sits high-smiling, in the conscious eye.
Island of bliss! amid the subject seas,
That thunder round thy rocky coasts, set up,
At once the wonder, terror, and delight,
Of distant nations, whose remotest shore
Can soon be shaken by thy naval arm;
Not to be shook thyself, but all assaults
Baffling, as thy hoar cliffs the loud sea wave.

James Thomson, *The Seasons – Summer*, 1727

Say, Britain, could you ever boast,
Three poets in an age at most?
Our chilling climate hardly bears
A sprig of bays in fifty years

Jonathan Swift, *On Poetry*, 1733

Pox on the modern phrase Great Britain, which is only to distinguish it from Little Britain, where old clothes and books are to be bought and sold.

Jonathan Swift, Letter to John Barber, 8 August 1738

When Britain first, at Heaven's command,
Arose from out the azure main,
This was the charter of the land,
And guardian angels sung this strain:

'Rule Britannia! rule the waves;
Britons never will be slaves.'

James Thomson, *Masque of Alfred*, 1740

That happiness you mention of England as an island, does not so much consist in the difficulty of an invasion from a foreign power, as from the difficulty which our own people have of flinging themselves into other hands.

Lady Oxford, Remark, *c.* 1740, in Joseph Spence, *Anecdotes*

How erring oft the judgment in its hate,
Or fond desire! Those slow-descending show'rs,
Those hov'ring fogs, that bathe our growing vales
In deep November (loath'd by trifling Gaul,
Effeminate), are gifts the Pleiads shed,
Britannia's handmaids. As the bev'rage falls,
Her hills rejoice, her vallies laugh and sing.
Hail noble Albion! where no golden mines,
No soft perfumes, nor oils, nor myrtle bow'rs,
The vig'rous frame and lofty heart of man
Enervate: round whose stern cerulean brows
White-winged snow, and cloud, and pearly rain,
Frequent attend, with solemn majesty:
Rich queen of mists and vapours!

John Dyer, *The Fleece*, 1757

Thou, heedless Albion, what, alas, the while
Dost thou presume? Oh, inexpert in arms,
Yet vain of Freedom, how dost thou beguile,
With dreams of hope, these near and loud alarms?
Thy splendid home, thy plan of laws renowned,
The praise and envy of the nations round,
What care hast thou to guard from Fortune's sway?
Amid the storms of war, how soon may all
The lofty pile from its foundations fall,
Of ages the proud toil, the ruin of a day! . . .

But what hath Force or War to do with thee?
Girt by the azure tide, and throned sublime
Amid thy floating bulwarks, thou canst see,
With scorn, the fury of each hostile clime
Dashed ere it reach thee. Sacred from the foe
Are thy fair fields: athwart thy guardian prow
No bold invader's foot shall tempt the strand:
Yet say, my country, will the waves and wind
Obey thee? Hast thou all thy hopes resigned
To the sky's fickle faith? the pilot's wavering hand? . . .

But if thy sons be worthy of their name,
If liberal laws with liberal arts they prize,
Let them, from conquest and from servile shame,
In Wars glad school their own protectors rise. . . .

Mark Akenside, *Ode, to the Country Gentlemen of England*, 1758

Dans ce pays-ci il est bon de tuer de temps en temps un amiral pour encourager les autres.
(In this country it is a good idea to kill an admiral every now and again in order to encourage the others.)

Voltaire, *Candide*, 1759

England, a happy land we know,
Where follies naturally grow,
Where without culture they arise
And tower above the common size;
England, a fortune-telling host
As numerous as the stars could boast;
Matrons, who toss the cup and see
The grounds of fate in grounds of tea;
Who, versed in every modest lore,
Can a lost maidenhead restore,
Or, if their pupils rather choose it,
Can show the readiest way to lose it.

Charles Churchill, *The Ghost*, 1762

Is this the land, where, mindful of her charge
And office high fair Freedom walked at large?
Where, finding in our laws a sure defence,
She mock'd at all restraints but those of sense?

Charles Churchill, *The Author*, 1763

Be England what she will,
With all her faults she is my country still.

Charles Churchill, *The Farewell*, 1764

Creation's mildest charms are there combin'd,
Extremes are only in the master's mind;
Stern o'er each bosom reason holds her state
With daring aims, irregularly great,
Pride in their port, defiance in their eye,
I see the lords of human kind pass by
Intent on high designs, a thoughtful band,
By forms unfashion'd, fresh from Nature's hand:
Fierce in their native hardiness of soul,
True to imagin'd right above controul,
While even the peasant boasts these rights to scan,
And learns to venerate himself as man.
Thine, Freedom, thine the blessings pictur'd here,
Thine are those charms that dazzle and endear;
Too blest indeed were such without alloy,
But fosterd even by Freedom ills annoy:
That independence Britons prize too high,
Keeps man from man, and breaks the social tie;
The self dependent lordlings stand alone,
All claims that bind and sweeten life unknown;
Here by the bonds of nature feebly held,
Minds combat minds, repelling and repell'd;
Ferments arise, imprison'd factions roar,
Represt ambition struggles round her shore
Till over-wrought the general system feels
Its motions stopt, or phrenzy fire the wheels.
Nor this the worst. As nature's ties decay
As duty, love and honour fail to sway,

Fictitious bonds, the bonds of wealth and law
Still gather strength, and force unwilling awe.
Hence all obedience bows to these alone,
And talent sinks, and merit weeps unknown;
Till Time may come, when, stript of all her charms,
The land of scholars, and the nurse of arms;
Where noble stems transmit the patriot flame
Where kings have toil'd, and poets wrote for fame;
One sink of level avarice shall lie,
And scholars, soldiers, kings, unhonour'd die.

Oliver Goldsmith, *The Traveller*, 1764

England and Scotland, union of

I breakfasted with Burnett on Scots oatmeal pottage and English porter. This is one of the best methods that can be taken to render the union truly firm.

James Boswell, *Journal*, 16 September 1764

I am attached to my country, because it is the land of liberty, cleanliness, and convenience.

Tobias Smollett, *Travels through France and Italy*, 1766

Ill fares the land, to hast'ning ills a prey,
Where wealth accumulates, and men decay;
Princes and lords may flourish, or may fade;
A breath can make them, as a breath has made;
But a bold peasantry, their country's pride,
When once destroy'd, can never be supplied.
A time there was, ere England's griefs began,
When every rood of ground maintain'd its man;
For him light labour spread her wholesome store,
Just gave what life requir'd, but gave no more;
His best companions, innocence and health;
And his best riches, ignorance of wealth.

Oliver Goldsmith, *The Deserted Village*, 1770

I said the history of England was so strange that if we had it not so well vouched as it is, it would hardly be credible. 'Sir,' said Mr. Johnson, 'if it were told as shortly, and with as little preparation for introducing the different events, as the history of the Jewish kings, it would be equally liable to objections of improbability.'

James Boswell, *Journal of a Tour to the Hebrides with Samuel Johnson* (1773), 1785

The way to ensure summer in England is to have it framed and glazed in a comfortable room.

Horace Walpole, Letter to the Rev. William Cole, 28 May 1774

To found a great empire for the sole purpose of raising up a people of customers, may at first sight appear a project fit only for a nation of shopkeepers. It is, however, a project altogether unfit for a nation of shopkeepers, but extremely fit for a nation whose government is influenced by shopkeepers.

Adam Smith, *Wealth of Nations*, 1775

England, Sir, is a nation which still, I hope, respects, and formerly adored, her freedom.

Edmund Burke, Speech on Conciliation with America, 22 March 1775

I never yet knew an instance of any general Temper in the Nation, that might not have been tolerably well traced to some particular persons. If things are left to themselves, It is my clear opinion, that a nation may slide down fair and softly from the highest point of Grandeur and prosperity to the lowest state of imbecility and meanness, without any ones making a particular period in this declension; without asking a question about it; or in the least speculating on any of the innumerable acts which have stolen in this silent and insensible revolution. Every event so prepares the Subsequent, that when it arrives, it produces no surprise nor any extraordinary alarm. I am certain that if pains, and great and immediate pains are not taken to prevent it, such must be the fate of this Country.

Edmund Burke, Letter to Lord Rockingham, 22/23 August 1775

Sir, it is not so much to be lamented that Old England is lost, as that the Scotch have found it.

Samuel Johnson, in Boswell, *Life of Johnson*, 15 May 1776

Our Empire is falling to pieces! we are relapsing to a little island. In that state, men are apt to inquire how great their ancestors have been; and, when a kingdom is past doing anything, the few, that are studious, look into the memorials of past time; nations, like private persons, seek lustre from their progenitors, when they have none in themselves, and the further they are from the dignity of their source.

Horace Walpole, Letter to the Rev. William Cole, 1 September 1778

Why weeps the muse for England? What appears
In England's case to move the muse to tears?

William Cowper, *The Expostulation*, March 1781

Without one friend, above all foes,
Britannia gives the world repose.

William Cowper, *To Sir Joshua Reynolds*, 1781

The sun of her glory is fast descending to the horizon. Her Philosophy has crossed the channel, her freedom the Atlantic, and herself seems passing to that awful dissolution whose issue is not given human foresight to scan.

Thomas Jefferson, *Notes on Virginia*, 1782

England, with all thy faults I love thee still.
My country!

William Cowper, *The Task, The Time Piece*, 1783

O, it's a snug little island!
A right little, tight little island!
Search the globe round, none can be found
So happy as this little island.

Thomas Dibdin, *The Snug Little Island*, 1797

Down the river did glide, with wind and with tide,
A pig with vast celerity;
And the Devil look'd wise as he saw how the while
It cut its own throat. 'There!' quoth he with a smile,
'Goes England's commercial prosperity!'

S.T. Coleridge, *The Devil's Thoughts*, 1799

Nineteenth Century

Britannia needs no bulwarks,
No towers along the steep;
Her march is o'er the mountain waves,
Her home is on the deep.
With thunders from her native oak
She quells the floods below,
As they roar on the shore
When the stormy winds do blow, –
When the battle rages loud and long
And the stormy winds do blow.

The meteor flag of England
Shall yet terrific burn,
Till danger's troubled night depart
And the star of peace return.
Then, then, ye ocean warriors!
Our song and feast shall flow
To the fame of your name,
When the storm has ceased to blow, –
When the fiery fight is heard no more,
And the storm has ceased to blow.

Thomas Campbell, 'Ye Mariners of England: A Naval Ode', *Morning Chronicle*, 1801

The whore and gambler, by the state
Licensed, build that nation's fate.
The harlot's cry, from street to street,
Shall weave old England's winding sheet.

William Blake, *Auguries of Innocence*, *c.* 1803

And did those feet in ancient time
Walk upon England's mountains green?
And was the holy lamb of God
On England's pleasant pastures seen?

And did the Countenance Divine
Shine forth upon our clouded hills?
And was Jerusalem builded here
Among these dark Satanic mills?

Bring me my bow of burning gold!
Bring me my arrows of desire!
Bring me my spear! O clouds, unfold!
Bring me my chariot of fire!

I will not cease from mental fight,
Nor shall my sword sleep in my hand,
Till we have built Jerusalem
In England's green and pleasant land.

William Blake, *From 'Milton' – Preface*, 1804

I travelled among unknown men,
In lands beyond the sea;
Nor, England! did I know till then
What love I bore to thee.

William Wordsworth, composed 1801, pub. 1807

It is not to be thought of that the Flood
Of British freedom, which, to the open sea
Of the world's praise, from dark antiquity
Hath flowed, 'with pomp of waters unwithstood,'
Roused though it be full often to a mood
Which spurns the check of salutary bands,
That this most famous stream in bogs and sands
Should perish; and to evil and to good
Be lost for ever. In our halls is hung
Armoury of the invincible Knights of old:
We must be free or die, who speak the tongue
That Shakespeare spake; the faith and morals hold
Which Milton held. – In every thing we are sprung
Of Earth's first blood, have titles manifold.

William Wordsworth, Sonnet, 1802 or 1803

Milton! thou shouldst be living at this hour:
England hath need of thee: she is a fen
Of stagnant waters: altar, sword, and pen,
Fireside, the heroic wealth of hall and bower,
Have forfeited their ancient English dower
Of inward happiness. We are selfish men;
Oh! raise us up, return to us again; . . .

William Wordsworth, London 1802, pub. 1807

An Englishman
Born in a land whose very name appeared
To license some unruliness of mind. . . .

William Wordsworth, *The Prelude*, 1805, text of 1850

England expects every man to do his duty.

Lord Nelson, Signal to the Fleet at the Battle of Trafalgar, 21 October 1805

England has saved herself by her exertions, and will, I trust, save Europe by her example.

William Pitt, Speech at the Lord Mayor's banquet at Guildhall, 9 November 1805

England has as great an idea of her own importance and power, as a one-eyed man has of the magnitude of his nose when the candle is on his blind side.

Robert Southey, *Letters from England, by Don Manuel Alvarez Espriella*, 1807

My native land – good-night!
Lord Byron, *Childe Harold*, Canto the First, 1812

Hail England, dear England, true Queen of the West
With thy fair swelling bosom and ever-green vest.
How nobly thou sittst in thine own steady light,
On the left of thee Freedom, and Truth on the right
While the clouds at thy smile, break apart and turn bright!
The Muses, full voiced, half encircle the seat,
And Ocean comes kissing thy princely white feet.
All hail! All hail!
All hail to the beauty immortal and free
The only true goddess that rose from the sea.
Leigh Hunt, 'National Song', in the *Examiner*, 25 June 1815

You were greatly offended with me for having called you a *nation of shopkeepers*. Had I meant by this that you were a nation of cowards, you would have had reason to be displeased; . . . but no such thing was ever intended. I meant that you were a nation of merchants, and that all your great riches, and your grand resources arose from commerce, which is true. What else constitutes the riches of England?
Napoleon, 30 May 1817, Barry O'Meara, *Napoleon in Exile, A Voice from St Helena*, 1822

Through many a storm
His isles had floated on the abyss of time;
For the rough virtues chose them for their clime.
Lord Byron, *The Vision of Judgement*, 1822
('his' refers to George III)

I've no great cause to love that spot of earth,
Which holds what might have been the noblest nation;
But though I owe it little but my birth,
I feel a mixed regret and veneration
For its decaying fame and former worth.
Seven years (the usual term of transportation)
Of absence lay one's old resentments level,
When a man's country's going to the devil.
Lord Byron, *Don Juan*, 1819–24

The English winter, ending in July
To recommence in August.
Ibid.

For 'tis a low, newspaper, humdrum, law-suit Country.
Ibid.

The great charm, however, of English scenery is the moral feeling that seems to pervade it. It is associated in the mind with ideas of order, of quiet, of sober well established principles, of hoary usage and reverend custom. Every thing seems to be the growth of ages of reverend and peaceful existence.
Washington Irving, *The Sketch Book of Geoffrey Crayon, Gent.*, 1820

England . . . a perpetual volume of reference wherein are recorded sound deductions from ages of experience.
Washington Irving, 'Rural Life in England', *The Sketch Book*, 1820

You say nothing of politics – but, alas! what can be said?
The world is a bundle of hay,
Mankind are the asses who pull,
Each tugs it a different way –
And the greatest of all is John Bull!
Lord Byron, Letter to Thomas Moore, 22 June 1821

Luttrell's idea of the English climate; 'On a fine day, like looking up a chimney; on a rainy day, like looking down it.'
Thomas Moore, *Diary*, 22 May 1828

If we were to prophesy that in the year 1930 a population of fifty millions, better fed, clad, and lodged than the English of our time, will cover these islands, that Sussex and Huntingdonshire will be wealthier than the wealthiest parts of the West Riding of Yorkshire now are, that cultivation, rich as that of a flower-garden, will be carried up to the very tops of Ben Nevis and Helvellyn, that machines constructed on principles yet undiscovered, will be in every house, that there will be no highways but railroads, no travelling but by steam, that our debt, vast as it seems to us, will appear to our great-grandchildren a trifling incumbrance, which might easily be paid off in a year or two, many people would think us insane.
T.B. Macaulay, *Southey's Colloquies on Society*, January 1830

An Englishman said to his friend at Florence, that when he approached England on leaving Italy, the sky appeared to come *nearer to the earth.*
J.P. Cobbett, *Journal of a Tour through Italy*, 1830

On my saying that I had come to take leave of him before he quitted England, he exclaimed, with much excitement – 'England is no longer a place for an honest man. I shall not live to find it so; you may.' He then broke out into the details of a very favourite superstition of his, that the middle of every century had always been marked by some great convulsion or calamity in this island.
Dr Robert Fergusson, 1831, quoted by J.G. Lockhart in *Life of Sir Walter Scott*, 1838

The democracy of England, before the Reform Bill, was

where it ought to be, in the corporations, the vestries, the joint-stock companies, &c. The power, in a democracy, is in focal points, without a centre; and in proportion as such democratical power is strong, the strength of the central government ought to be intense – otherwise the nation will fall to pieces.

Samuel Taylor Coleridge, *Table Talk*, 21 May 1832

There have been three silent revolutions in England: first, when the professions fell off from the Church; secondly when literature fell off from the professions; and, thirdly, when the press fell off from literature.

Samuel Taylor Coleridge, *Table Talk*, 21 April 1832

A power to which, for the purposes of foreign conquest and subjugation, Rome, in the height of her glory, is not to be compared; a power which has dotted over the surface of the whole globe with her possessions and military posts, whose morning drum-beat, following the sun, and keeping company with the hours, circles the earth with one continuous and unbroken strain of the martial airs of England.

Daniel Webster, Speech in the Senate on the President's Protest, 7 May 1834

In England the centralization of the government is carried to great perfection; the state has the compact vigour of one man, and its will puts immense masses in motion and turns its whole power where it pleases. But England, which has done such great things for the last fifty years, has never centralized its administration. Indeed, I cannot conceive that a nation can live and prosper without a powerful centralization of government. But I am of the opinion that a centralized administration is fit only to enervate the nations in which it exists, by incessantly diminishing their local spirit. Although such an administration can bring together at a given moment, on a given point, all the disposable resources of a people, it injures the renewal of those resources.

Alexis de Tocqueville, *Democracy in America*, 1835

The history of England is emphatically the history of progress.

T.B. Macaulay, 'History of the Revolution, by Sir James Mackintosh', July 1835, *Critical and Historical Essays*, 1843

Peace, Freedom, Happiness, have loved to wait
On the fair islands, fenced by circling seas;
And ever of such favoured spots as these
Have the wise dreamers dreamed, who would create
That perfect model of a happy state,
Which the world never saw. Oceana,
Utopia such, and Plato's isle that lay
Westward of Gades and the Great Sea's gate.
Dreams are they all, which yet have helped to make
That underneath fair polities we dwell,
Though marred in part by envy, faction, hate –
Dreams which are dear, dear England, for thy sake,
Who art indeed that sea-girt citadel,
And nearest image of that perfect state.

Richard Chevenix Trench, *England, – The Story of Justin Martyr, etc.*, 1835

The Continent will not suffer England to be the workshop of the world.

Benjamin Disraeli, Earl of Beaconsfield, Speech in the House of Commons, 15 March 1838

You ask me why, tho' ill at ease,
Within this region I subsist,
Whose spirits falter in the mist,
And languish for the purple seas.

It is the land that freemen till,
That sober-suited Freedom chose,
The land where, girt with friends or foes
A man may speak the thing he will;

A land of settled government,
A land of just and old renown,
Where Freedom slowly broadens down
From precedent to precedent;

Where faction seldom gathers head,
But by degrees to fulness wrought,
The strength of some diffusive thought
Hath time and space to work and spread.

Should banded unions persecute
Opinion, and induce a time
When single thought is civil crime,
And individual freedom mute;

Tho' Power should make from land to land
The name of Britain trebly great –
Tho' every channel of the State
Should fill and choke with golden sand –

Yet waft me from the harbour-mouth,
Wild wind! I seek a warmer sky,
And I will see before I die
The palms and temples of the South.

Alfred Lord Tennyson, *You Ask Me Why – Poems*, 1842

An English home – gray twilight poured
On dewy pastures, dewy trees
Softer than sleep – all things in order stored.
A haunt of ancient peace.

Alfred Lord Tennyson, *The Palace of Art*, 1842

To me it seems, that of all the lands I know . . . there is none in which mere wealth – mere unaided wealth, is held half so cheaply – none in which a poor devil of a millionaire without birth or ability, occupies so humble a place as in England.

A.W. Kinglake, *Eothen*, 1844

*'Well,' resumed their new friend, after staring at them intently during the whole interval of silence, 'how's the unnat'ral old parent by this time?' . . .

'You mean the old country?' he said.

'Ah,' was the reply. 'How's she? Progressing back'ards, I expect, as usual? Well! . . . '

Charles Dickens, *Martin Chuzzlewit*, 1844

The real policy of England – apart from questions which involve her own particular interest, political or commercial – is to be the champion of justice and right.

Lord Palmerston, Speech on the Polish question, 1846

So . . . I feel in regard to this aged England . . . pressed upon by transitions of trade and . . . competing populations, – I see her not dispirited, not weak, but well remembering that she has seen dark days before; – indeed, with a kind of instinct that she sees a little better in a cloudy day, and that, in storm of battle and calamity, she has a secret vigour and a pulse like a cannon.

R.W. Emerson, *English Traits*, Speech at Manchester, 1847

English Landscape

*Is there any in the world like it? To a traveller returning home it looks so kind – it seems to shake hands with you as you pass through it.

W.M. Thackeray, *Vanity Fair*, 1847

Is there any country in which polygamy is more frequent than in England.

J.C. and A. Hare, *Guesses at Truth*, 3rd edn, 1847

At present England is the country where that depth and inwardness of thought, which seems to belong to the Germanic mind, has assumed the distinct, outward, positive form of the Roman.

Ibid.

Under the Kings of the House of Stuart, she was a blank on the map of Europe. She had lost one class of energies, and had not yet acquired another.

T.B. Macaulay, *History of England*, 1849–61

In no country has the enmity of race been carried further than in England. In no country has that enmity been more completely effaced.

Ibid.

In English scenery I found my old friend 'pastoral' still more pastoral. It was like a breakfast of milk and cream after yesterday's wine.

Leigh Hunt, *Autobiography*, 1850

There are no countries in the world less known by the British than these selfsame British Islands.

George Borrow, *Lavengro*, Preface, 1851

Thank Him who isled us here, and roughly set
His Briton in blown seas and storming showers.

Alfred Lord Tennyson, *Ode on the Death of the Duke of Wellington*, 1852

. . . the elements, our good old and only unsubsidised allies. . . .

Richard Ford, *A Handbook for Travellers in Spain*, 1855

Poverty, the great crime, never to be pardoned in England. . . .

Ibid.

Seashel should be the arms of England.

Ralph Waldo Emerson, *Journals*, 1855

It is a nation conveniently small. Fontenelle thought that nature sometimes had a little affectation; and there is such an artificial completeness in this nation of artificers as if there were a design from the beginning to elaborate a bigger Birmingham.

R.W. Emerson, *English Traits*, 1856

England is the best of actual nations. It is no ideal framework, it is an old pile built in different ages, with repairs, additions, and makeshifts; but you see the poor best you have got. London is the epitome of our times, and the Rome of today.

Ibid.

England, an old and exhausted island, must one day be contented, like other parents, to be strong only in her children.

Ibid.

On English ground
You understand the letter . . . ere the fall,
How Adam lived in a garden. All the fields
Are tied up fast with hedges, nosegay-like;
The hills are crumpled plains, – the plains, parterres, –
The trees round, woolly, ready to be clipped;
And if you seek for any wilderness
You find, at best, a park. A nature tamed
And grown domestic like a barn-door fowl,
Which does not awe you with its claws and beak,
Nor tempt you to an eyrie too high up,
But which, in cackling, sets you thinking of
Your eggs to-morrow at breakfast, in the pause
Of finer meditation. . . .
Rather say,
A sweet familiar nature, stealing in
As a dog might, or child, to touch your hand
Or pluck your gown, and humbly mind you so

Of presence and affection, excellent
For inner uses, from the things without.

Elizabeth Barrett Browning, *Aurora Leigh*, 1856

God's finger touched but did not press
In making England!

Ibid.

Was this my father's England? the great isle?
The ground seemed cut up from the fellowship
Of verdure, field from field, as man from man;
The skies themselves looked low and positive,
As almost you could touch them with a hand,
And dared to do it, they were so far off
From God's celestial crystals; all things blurred
And dull and vague. Did Shakespeare and his mates
Absorb the light here? – not a hill or stone
With heart to strike a radiant colour up
Or active outline on the indifferent air!

Ibid.

'Darn your little island! When I was there I found it so little I was afeerd I should tumble off. Look you, siree! We've steam-boats enough at St Louis to tow Great Britain out into the Atlantic and stick her fast; – opposite New York Harbour.'

Anon. citizen of St Louis to immigrant from the old country, in Charles Mackay, *Life and Liberty in America, 1857–8*, 1859

Life is here fossilized in its greenest leaf. The man who died yesterday, or ever so long ago, walks the village-street today, and chooses the same wife that he married a hundred years since, and must be buried again, tomorrow, under the same kindred dust that has already covered him half a score of times,

Nathaniel Hawthorne, *Our Old Home*, 1863

The wildest things in England are more than half-tame.

Ibid.

If Britannia chills with tears and sighs the hearts of her sons home-returning, at any rate, with the same tenderness she consoles them under departure. Who ever landed at Southampton in other but the worst of weather? Who ever left Dover on a fine clear morning?

Richard Burton, *Wanderings in West Africa*, 1863

England, the mother of parliaments.

John Bright, Speech, Rochdale, 18 January 1865

Whereas in France, since the Revolution, a man feels that the power which represses him is the *State*, is *himself*, here a man feels that the power which represses him is the Tories, the upper class, the aristocracy, and so on; and with this feeling he can, of course, never without loss of self-respect accept a formal beating, and so the thing goes on smouldering. If ever there comes a more equal state of society in England, the power of the State for repression will be a thousand times stronger.

Matthew Arnold, Letter to his mother, 27 July 1866

Of all the sarse that I can call to mind,
England *doos* make the most onpleasant kind:
It's you're the sinner 'ollers, she's the saint;
Wut's good's all English, all thet isn't ain't;
Wut profits her is ollers right an' just,
An' ef you don't read Scriptur so, you must;
She's praised herself ontil she fairly thinks
There ain't no light in Natur when she winks; . . .
She's all thet's honest, honnable, an' fair,
An' when the vartoos died they made her heir.

James Russell Lowell, *The Biglow Papers: Mason and Slidell*, 1867

But that vast portion, lastly, of the working-class which . . . is now issuing from its hiding-place to assert an Englishman's heaven-born privilege of doing as he likes, and is beginning to perplex us by marching where it likes, meeting where it likes, bawling what it likes, breaking what it likes – to this vast residuum we may with great propriety give the name of Populace.

Thus we have got three distinct terms, Barbarians, Philistines, Populace, to denote roughly the three great classes into which our society is divided.

Matthew Arnold, *Culture and Anarchy*, 1869

England is a domestic country; there the home is revered, the hearth sacred.

Benjamin Disraeli, Speech, 3 April 1872

I must make my choice whether England should be free or sober. I declare, strange as such a declaration may sound, coming from one of my profession, that I should say it would be better that England should be free than that England should be compulsorily sober.

William Connor Magee, Bishop of Peterborough, Speech in the House of Lords, 2 May 1872

England is a country successful in politics.

Walter Bagehot, 'The Chances for a long Conservative Regime in England', 1874 (pub. posthumously, *Fortnightly Review*, 1 December 1878)

For England expects – I forbear to proceed,
'Tis a maxim tremendous, but trite.

Rev. Charles Lutwidge Dodgson, 'Lewis Carroll', *The Hunting of the Snark*, 1876

The characteristic danger of great nations, like the Romans or the English which have a long history of continuous creation, is that they may at last fail from not comprehending the great institutions which they have created.

Walter Bagehot, 'Lord Althorp and the Reform Act of 1832', *Fortnightly Review*, November 1876

The great characteristic of English scenery . . . I should call density of feature. There are no waste details; everything in the landscape is something particular – has a history, has played a part, has a value to the imagination.

Henry James, 'Abbeys and Castles', 1877, in *Portraits of Places*, 1883

In England, a couple of hours of fine weather, islanded in moisture, assert their independence and leave an uncompromised memory.

Henry James, 'English Vignettes', 1879, in *Portraits of Places*, 1883

It is one of the happiest characteristics of this glorious country that official utterances are always regarded as unanswerable.

W.S. Gilbert, *H.M.S. Pinafore*, Act II, 1878

We are part of the community of Europe, and we must do our duty as such.

William Ewart Gladstone, Speech at Caernarvon, 10 April 1888

Ever the faith endures,
England, my England: –
'Take and break us: we are yours,
England, my own!
Life is good and joy runs high
Between English earth and sky;
Death is death; but we shall die
To the song on your bugles blown, England.'

William Ernest Henley, *For England's Sake*, iii, *Pro Rege Nostro*, *c.* 1891

*Tartuffe has emigrated to England and opened a shop.

Oscar Wilde, *The Picture of Dorian Gray*, 1891

And what should they know of England who only England know?

Rudyard Kipling, *The English Flag*, 1891

The Mother of Colonies has a wonderful gift for alienating the affections of her own household by neglect.

Rudyard Kipling, *From Tideway to Tideway*, 1892

A little foggy island in the north-west corner of Europe, the witless mother of nations.

Francis Adams, *The Australians*, 1893 (of England at the time of the loss of the American colonies)

The British Empire is the great engine of evil for the weak races now existing in the world – not that we are worse than the French or Italians or Americans – indeed, we are less actively destructive – but we do it over a far wider area and more successfully. I should be delighted to see England stripped of her whole foreign possessions. We were better off and more respected in Queen Elizabeth's time, the 'spacious days', when we had not a stick of territory outside the British Islands, than now, and infinitely more respectable. The gangrene of colonial rowdyism is infecting us, and the habit of repressing liberty in weak nations is endangering our own. I should be glad to see the end.

Wilfred Scawen Blunt, Diary, 9 January 1896, *My Diaries*, 1919

God of our fathers, known of old,
Lord of our far-flung battle-line,
Beneath whose awful hand we hold
Dominion over palm and pine –
Lord God of hosts, be with us yet,
Lest we forget – lest we forget!

Rudyard Kipling, *Recessional*, 17 July 1897 (written to celebrate Queen Victoria's Diamond Jubilee)

Twentieth Century

*With England we ar-re on such terms as must plaze ivry Canajeen, but not on anny such terms as wud make anny Irishman think we ar-re on such terms as we ought not to be. In other wurruds, we cherish a deep animosity mingled with passionate love, such a feelin' as we must entertain to a nation with common impulses f'r th' same money an' a common language iv abuse.

Finley Peter Dunne, *Mr Dooley's Philosophy*, 1900 (Mr Dooley's paraphrase of the President's message)

It is beginning to be hinted that we are a nation of amateurs.

Earl of Roseberry, Rectorial address, Glasgow, 16 November 1900

England has imposed her idea upon all nations and to girdle the world with Brixton seems to be her ultimate destiny. And we, sitting on the last verge, see into the universal suburb, in which a lean man with glasses on his nose and a black bag in his hand is always running after his bus.

George Moore, Speech to Supporters of the Irish Literary Theatre, February 1900, in Lady Gregory (ed.), *Ideals in Ireland*, 1901

England is one of the weird mysteries of God's afterthought.

Henry Adams, Letter to John Hay, 4 December 1900

*England, where men and the sea interpenetrate, so to speak – the sea entering into the life of most men, and the men knowing something or everything about the sea. . . .

Joseph Conrad, *Youth*, 1902

Land of Hope and Glory, Mother of the free,
How shall we extol thee, who are born of thee?
Wider still and wider, shall thy bounds be set;
God who made thee mighty, make thee mightier yet.

A.C. Benson, Song from *Pomp and Circumstance*, by Sir Edward Elgar, 1902

The oligarchic character of the modern English commonwealth does not rest, like many oligarchies, on the cruelty of the rich to the poor. It does not even rest on the kindness of the rich to the poor. It rests on the perennial and unfailing kindness of the poor to the rich.

G.K. Chesterton, *Heretics*, 1905

I take England 'for better for worse'; that is the *only* way of making it better.

G.K. Chesterton, Letter to a stranger who asked his advice, *c.* 1909

It is . . . fiction that England never yields to threats. My experience is that when England has her face well slapped she apologizes, not before.

Wilfred Scawen Blunt, Diary, 19 August 1909, *My Diaries*, 1919

Take of English earth as much
As either hand may rightly clutch
In the taking of it breathe
Prayer for all who lie beneath . . .
Lay that earth upon thy heart,
And thy sickness shall depart!

Rudyard Kipling, 'A Charm', in *Rewards and Fairies*, 1910

The ripest fruit of time.

Henry James, Letter to Mrs J.L. Gardner, 3 September 1911

We are in for one of those evil spaces, subject to foreign insults and domestic misfortune, which invariably attach to nations when, for a period, they lose grip over their destiny.

Hilaire Belloc, and Cecil Chesterton, *The Party System*, 1911

Yes, English nature is too green, and that green too monotonous in shade and outline; it is (*entre nous*) a salad landscape; you may find pretty vignettes of the sugar-water type, but London alone is picturesque in the large sense of the word – London and Newcastle-on-Tyne.

Norman Douglas, *Siren Land*, 1911

Our England is a garden that is full of stately views.
Of border beds and shrubberies and lawns and avenues,
With statues on the terraces and peacocks strutting by;
But the Glory of the Garden lies in more than meets the eye. . . .

Our England is a garden, and such gardens are not made
By singing: – 'Oh how beautiful!' and sitting in the shade,
While better men than we go out and start their working lives
At grubbing weeds from gravel-paths with broken dinner-knives. . . .

Rudyard Kipling, *The Glory of the Garden*, 1911

Wake up England

George V, Title of 1911 reprint of speech made when Prince of Wales, 5 December 1901, on his return from Empire tour

A mere whale's back insecurely anchored in the Atlantic.

Arnold Bennett, *Paris Nights*, 1913

The Englishman's home is assuredly the most elaborate organisation for sustaining and reproducing life in the world.

Ibid.

Before the Roman came to Rye or out to Severn strode
The rolling English drunkard made the rolling English road
A reeling road, a rolling road, that rambles round the shire
And after him the parson ran, the sexton and the squire:
A merry road, a mazy road, and such as we did tread
The night we went to Birmingham by way of Beachy Head.

G.K. Chesterton, 'The Rolling English Road', *The Flying Inn*, 1914

If I should die, think only this of me:
That there's some corner of a foreign field
That is for ever England.

Rupert Brooke, *The Soldier*, 1914

'Oh that England of yours! It is an extraordinary land,' he said. 'We Russians have our priests, it is true, but you also have them in another form – in one form, rather – the conventions. Oh, the things I have seen in England, the silly little rules, even in the family. . . . '

Denis Garstin, *Friendly Russia*, 1915

Even a boiled egg tastes of mutton fat in England.

Norman Douglas, *Old Calabria*, 1915

*He was inordinately proud of England, and he abused her incessantly.

H.G. Wells, *Mr Britling Sees it Through*, 1916

Go anywhere in England where there are natural, wholesome, contented, and really nice English people; and what do you always find? That the stables are the real centre of the household.

George Bernard Shaw, *Heartbreak House*, 1919

I feel very sick with England. It is a dead dog that died of a love disease like syphilis.

D.H. Lawrence, Letter to S.S. Koteliansky, 10 November 1921

But you don't catch me going back on my whiteness and Englishness and myself. English in the teeth of all the world, even in the teeth of England. How England deliberately undermines England.

D.H. Lawrence, Letter to Lady Cynthia Asquith, 30 April 1922

England is the paradise of individuality, eccentricity, heresy, anomalies, hobbies, and humours.

George Santayana, 'The British Character', *Soliloquies in England*, 1922

The whole place is so large that there is no dust and so there not being that there is every occasion for no difference to be noticeable. This makes reading so necessary.

Nothing is perplexing if there is an island. The special sign of this is in dusting.

Gertrude Stein, 'England', *Geography and Plays*, 1922

England is not governed by logic, but by Acts of Parliament.

Anon. saying quoted in the Court of King's Bench, London, 13 April 1923

From Leith Hill, in Surrey, the Shoreham gap in the South Downs allows you to see the shining waters of the English Channel. Then, if you turn to the north, you may see, when London's smoke does not hide it, the low line of south Middlesex hills about Highgate. From Highgate Hill to Finchley is only an afternoon's walk, and from Finchley to Barnet is nothing: each of these is within easy view of the next. From Barnet Hill, again, Ridge Hill is well within sight, and from Ridge Hill you see in fair weather the Minster church of St Albans. Northward St Albans looks up to the white Chiltern wall, and on gaining the crest of that wall, by the Holyhead road, you see across the valley of the Ouse the low sky-line of the Cotswolds trailing away into the north-east. On days when the air has been well washed with rain you may just descry from a well-picked point on the top of the Cotswolds the darkling bulge of the Peak. The Peak looks westward on Snowdon, and winter climbers on Scawfell have seen the streaks of snow that mark the northern gullies of the Carnedds, Snowdon's neighbours across the Holyhead road. Scawfell is a morning's walk from Skiddaw, and from Skiddaw the Cheviots are easily seen. The Cheviots look on the Lammermuir Hills, the Lammermuir Hills on Arthur's Seat, and if you sit on Arthur's Seat and look north across the Forth, on any fine day, the Highland mountains form your horizon.

Get to know by heart the view, forward and back, from each link of this chain of dominant heights. Then stand at one of them, close your eyes, and call up, with all the force of your imagination, what you would see from each of the others. If you are well stirred by the joy of the game, you will find that the several clear pictures are fusing into one picture, scarcely less clear, of the whole length of the island. At last you have succeeded. You have rendered all England impossibly and beautifully small. You have made her almost as practicable an object of sense, and of sensuous love, as some garden in which you played as a boy.

C.E. Montague, *The Right Place*, 1924

My God, where are the men in England now? The place is one howling nursery.

D.H. Lawrence, Letter to Vere H.G. Collins, Spotorno, 17 November 1925

This island of ours is a ship. . . . There are never more than six weeks' supplies of consumable stores aboard her at one time.

Rudyard Kipling, Speech, Chamber of Shipping dinner, February 1925

The nations which have put mankind and posterity most in their debt have all been small states – Israel, Athens, Florence, Elizabethan England.

W.R. Inge, *The State Visible and Invisible – Outspoken Essays*, 2nd Series, 1922

In England, where the climate is detestable, we love the country so much that we are prepared, for the privilege of living in it, to get up at seven, summer and winter, bicycle, wet or fine, to a distant station, and make an hour's journey to our place of labour. In our spare moments we go for walking tours, and we regard caravanning as a pleasure.

Aldous Huxley, *Along the Road*, 1927

England's innermost truth and at the same time her most valuable contribution to the assets of the human family is the 'gentleman', rescued from the dusty chivalry of the early Middle Ages, and now penetrating into the remotest corner of modern English life. It is an ultimate principle that never fails to carry conviction, the shining armour of the perfect knight in soul and body, and the miserable coffin of poor natural feelings.

C.G. Jung, *The Complications of American Psychology*, 1930

'Ill fares the land, to hastening ills a prey
Where Wealth accumulates and Men decay.'
So rang of old the noble voice in vain
O'er the last peasants wandering on the plain.
Doom has reversed the riddle and the rhyme,
While sinks the commerce reared upon that crime.
The thriftless towns litter with lives undone,
To whom our madness left no joy but one;
And irony that glares like Judgement Day
Sees Men accumulate and Wealth decay.

G.K. Chesterton, *The Judgement of England*, 1932

The real tragedy of England as I see it, is the tragedy of

ugliness. The country is so lovely: the man-made England is so vile.

D.H. Lawrence, 'Nottingham and the Mining Countryside', *Adelphi*, June 1930 / *Phoenix*, 1936

The strangest country I ever visited was England; but I visited it at a very early age, and so became a little queer myself. England is extremely subtle; and about the best of it there is something almost secretive; it is amateur even more than aristocratic in tradition; it is never official.

G.K. Chesterton, *Autobiography*, 1936

I like practically all kinds of English weather except that particular sort of weather that is called 'a glorious day.'

Ibid.

I have watched this famous island descending incontinently, fecklessly, the stairway which leads to a dark gulf. It is a fine broad stairway at the beginning, but after a bit, the carpet ends. A little further on there are only flagstones, and a little further on still, these break beneath your feet.

Sir Winston Churchill, *While England Slept*, 1936

How is the Empire?

George V, attributed, last words, 1936

In England 'genius' is obliged to affect the methods of the quack in order to survive at all.

Wyndham Lewis, *Blasting and Bombardiering*, 1937

(1914) England was of course much like any other country, sound as a bell.

Ibid.

Breathes there a man with soul so fond
Who never to himself hath groaned,
etc., etc.

James Agate, *Ego 3*, 13 June 1937 (on returning to England from a visit to the USA)

England never leaves a country so crippled that she cannot do business with it.

Oliver St John Gogarty, *As I Was Going Down Sackville Street*, 1937

Living in England, provincial England, must be like being married to a stupid, but exquisitely beautiful wife.

Margaret Halsey, *With Malice Toward Some*, 1938

In England's case, uniquely, God and Mammon *are* one.

John Gunther, *Inside Europe*, 1938

The British Isles are islands. And, as the schoolboy put it in a famous definition, 'an island is a piece of land entirely surrounded by the British Navy.'

Ibid.

I think England is the very place for a fluent and fiery writer. The highest hymns of the sun are written in the dark. I like the grey country. A bucket of Greek sun would drown in one colour the crowds of colours I like trying to mix for myself out of a grey flat insular mud.

Dylan Thomas, Letter to Lawrence Durrell, December 1938

Whenever I think of Hell I cannot visualise it as a place of eternal fire, but as one of your English industrial towns on a day when the rain is pattering on the slate roofs and the wind is moaning up the street; a place where the horizon is bounded by dark factory chimneys, with crowds of women muffled up in waterproofs slipping in the puddles in their galoshes, with red noses peering out of heavy mufflers.

Colonel Bertolini, quoted Walter Starkie, *The Waveless Plain*, 1938

The Stately homes of England
How beautiful they stand,
To prove the upper classes
Have still the upper hand.

Noel Coward, 'The Stately Homes of England', *Operette*, 1938

There'll always be an England
While there's a country lane
Wherever there's a cottage small
Beside a field of grain.

Ross Parker and Hughie Charles, Song, 1939

The lion tried to show his teeth, and it was all bridgework.

John Gunther, *Inside Asia*, 1939 (quoting a friend on the decline in British prestige during the 1930s)

*England was like a rich man after a disastrous orgy who makes up to the household by chatting with them individually, when it is obvious to them that he is only trying to get back his self-respect in order to usurp his former power.

F. Scott Fitzgerald, *Tender is the Night*, 1939

The south-west wind roaring in from the Atlantic, . . . is, I think the presiding genius of England.

Hilaire Belloc, *Places*, 1940

We shall treat England like a beautiful flower, but we shan't water the pot.

Hermann Goering, *c.* 1940, attributed remark, quoted by Cyril Connolly, *Ideas and Places*, 1953

I am American bred
I have seen much to hate here – much to forgive

But in a world where England is finished and dead
I do not wish to live.

Alice Duer Miller, *The White Cliffs*, 1940

Let us therefore brace ourselves to our duties, and so bear ourselves that, if the British Empire and its Commonwealth last for a thousand years, men will say, 'This was their finest hour.'

Sir Winston Churchill, Speech delivered first to the House of Commons, 18 June 1940 and then broadcast

When I warned them [the French Government] that Britain would fight on alone whatever they did, their generals told their Prime Minister and his divided Cabinet: 'In three weeks England will have her neck wrung like a chicken.' Some chicken! Some neck!

Sir Winston Churchill, Speech to the Canadian Parliament, 30 December 1941

England is not the jewelled isle of Shakespeare's much-quoted passage, nor is it the inferno depicted by Dr Goebbels. More than either it resembles a family, a rather stuffy Victorian family, with not many black sheep in it but with all its cupboards bursting with skeletons. It has rich relations who have to be kowtowed to and poor relations who are horribly sat upon, and there is a deep conspiracy of silence about the source of the family income. It is a family in which the young are generally thwarted and most of the power is in the hands of irresponsible uncles and bedridden aunts. Still, it is a family. It has its private language and its common memories, and at the approach of an enemy it closes its ranks. A family with the wrong members in control – that, perhaps, is as near as one can come to describing England in a phrase.

George Orwell, 'England Your England', *The Lion and the Unicorn*, 1941

England is the most class-ridden country under the sun. It is a land of snobbery and privilege, ruled largely by the old and silly.

Ibid.

We mean to hold our own. I have not become the King's First Minister in order to preside over the liquidation of the British Empire.

Sir Winston Churchill, Speech at the Mansion House, 10 November 1942

In England it is bad manners to be clever, to assert something confidently. It may be your personal view that two and two make four, but you must not state it in a self-assured way, because this is a democratic country, and others may be of a different opinion.

George Mikes, *How to be an Alien*, 1946

In England everything is the other way round.

Ibid.

This island is almost made of coal and surrounded by fish. Only an organizing genius could produce a shortage of coal and fish in Great Britain at the same time.

Aneurin Bevan, Speech, quoted in Vincent Brome, *Aneurin Bevan*, 1953 – before 1947

... The general state of mind to which England was now reduced: a combination of competitive spitefulness with exasperated patience.

Edmund Wilson, *Europe Without Baedeker*, 1947

It is only in England that truth is made a basis of morality.

Freya Stark, *Traveller's Prelude*, 1950

You know why the sun never sets on the British Empire, don't you? – It doesn't trust it.

Gilbert Harding, quoted in Brian Masters's *Daily Telegraph* review, 11 January 1979, of *Gilbert Harding, a Candid Portrait*, by Wallace Rayburn – before 1960

It will be said of this generation that it found England a land of beauty and left it a land of beauty spots.

C.E.M. Joad, *Observer*, 'Sayings of Our Times', 31 May 1953

Great Britain has lost an Empire and has not yet found a role.

Dean Acheson, Speech at the Military Academy, West Point, 5 December 1962

England is, and always has been, a country infested with people who love to tell us what to do, but who very rarely seem to know what's going on.

Colin MacInnes, 'Pop Songs and Teenagers', *England Half England*, 1962

In the end it may well be that Britain will be honoured by the historians more for the way she disposed of an empire than for the way in which she acquired it.

David Ormsby Gore, *New York Times*, 28 October 1962

Britain today is suffering from galloping obsolescence.

Anthony Wedgwood Benn, *Observer*, 'Sayings of the Week', 2 February 1963

Perhaps the highest praise one can give a country is that it is possible to spend nearly sixty years in it from birth without ever really feeling one belongs. No one has ever said to me: 'Remember you're British!' Sometimes I think the England I know now is like a parent that has had a first stroke. Gentle, understanding, walking on eggshells, gazing with the unspoken resignation of those who have received their boarding cards – can this be the ferocious figure who tried to bend us to their will? 'I simply won't have it. . . . ' I think of the England of the 'thirties' in that way, an autocrat at the last gasp, Chamberlain in office, the City rattling its money-bags, the Establishment like a group of poker-faced prefects who know there is going to be a beating.

Cyril Connolly, 'This Gale-swept Chip', *Encounter*, July 1963

. . . The English climate when each season succeeds the other like a prisoner being re-arrested as he leaves the gaol.

Ibid.

Imperial Britain was the creation of a small, aristocratic class. It is not fashionable to say anything kind about that class, but the fact remains that the nation it governed *meant* something in the eyes of the world – something quite unique and rather marvellous. Whether the democratic Britain that has emerged since the war – or, if one insists, is emerging – will have any such meaning, is *the* question of British politics today. Little England might, in the end, be a perfectly decent place for little Englishmen to live in. For the rest of us, it would signify an irreparable loss.

Irving Kristol, 'The View from Miami', *Encounter*, November 1963

There'll always be an England, even if it's in Hollywood.

Bob Hope, Remark, attrib., 1960s

Our policy now can only be to sustain the fragments of what was once a glorious empire on which the sun used never to set and on which it now seldom rises.

Lord Beaverbrook, Remark on his eighty-fifth birthday, May 1964

What Athens was in the Roman Empire, England can and should be in the American Empire of the 1970's.

David Frost and Antony Jay, *To England with Love*, 1967

Britain is the society where the ruling class does not rule, the working class does not work and the middle class is not in the middle.

George Mikes, attrib.

To let: a valuable site at the crossroads of the world. At present on offer to European clients. Outlying portions of the estate already disposed of to sitting tenants. Of some historical and period interest. Some alterations and improvements necessary.

Alan Bennett, *Forty Years On*, 1969

It was not surprising that Britain had lost her way in the world during the sixties; man himself had lost his way, in the same decade, in the universe.

Bernard Levin, *The Pendulum Years*, 1970

A soggy little island huffing and puffing to keep up with Western Europe.

John Updike, 'London Life', 1969, *Picked Up Pieces*, 1976

America is a land whose center is nowhere; England one whose center is everywhere. In America every town has its Chamber of Commerce; here every shire has been the site of a poem.

Ibid.

England has the strictness and estranging quality of school. It is an old-fashioned place in which unpredictable suffering is part of the process of enlightenment. It keeps me hard at work because I find there is absolutely nothing else to do there.

Paul Theroux, 'Salad Days on the Sandwich Coast', in the *Guardian*, 11 August 1979

The English sense of humour is the most wonderful thing any nation can boast of; if Britain wants to survive as a leading industrial nation it must get rid of it without delay.

George Mikes, *English Humour for Beginners*, 1980

. . . These islands, whose raggedy outline appeared to be trying to resemble something – possibly a pregnant kangaroo in a chef's hat.

Russell Davies, *Sunday Times*, 18 May 1980
(Of a satellite picture of the British Isles during fine weather.)

English

Early

Penitus toto divisos orbe Britannos.
(The Britons, wholly sundered from all the world.)

Virgil, *Eclogues*, I, 1. 66, 42–37 BC

Anglica gens est optima flens et pessima ridens.
(The English race is the best at weeping and the worst at laughing.)

Medieval Latin proverb, quoted by Thomas Hearne, *Reliquiae Hearnianae*, edn of 1857

Non Angli, sed Angeli.
(Not Angles but Angels.)

Pope Gregory I, commenting on the beauty of English captives exposed for sale in Rome

My muse is rightly of the English straine,
That cannot long one fashion intertaine.

Michael Drayton, 'To the Reader of these Sonnets', *Idea*, 1594

It was always yet the trick of our English nation, if they have a good thing, to make it too common.

William Shakespeare, *King Henry IV*, Part 2, *c.* 1597–8

Rambours: That Iland of England breedes very valiant Creatures; their Mastiffes are of unmatchable courage.

Orleans: Foolish Curres, that runne winking into the mouth of a Russian Beare, and have their heads crusht like rotten Apples: you may as well say, that's a valiant Flea, that dare eate his breakfast on the Lippe of a Lyon.

Constable: Just, just: and the men doe sympathize with the Mastiffes, in robustious and rough comming on, leaving their Wits with their Wives: and then give them great Meales of Beefe, and Iron and Steele; they will eate like Wolves, and fight like Devils.

William Shakespeare, *Henry the Fift*, *c.* 1598–9

Seventeenth Century

Clown: It was the very day that young *Hamlet* was borne, hee that was mad, and sent into England.
Hamlet: I marry, why was he sent into England?
Clown: Why, because he was mad: hee shall recover his wits there; or if he do not, its no great matter there.
Hamlet: Why?
Clown: 'Twill not be seene in him, there the men are as mad as he.

William Shakespeare, *Hamlet*, *c.* 1600–1

Cassio: 'Fore Heaven: an excellent Song.
Iago: I learn'd it in England: where indeed they are most potent in Potting. Your Dane, your Germaine, and your swag-belly'd Hollander, (drinke hoa) are nothing to your English.
Cassio: Is your Englishman so exquisite in his drinking?
Iago: Why, he drinkes you with facillitie, your Dane dead drunke. He sweates not to overthrow your Almaine. He gives your Hollander a vomit, ere the next Pottle can be fill'd. . . .
Oh sweet England.

William Shakespeare, *Othello*, *c.* 1604–5

I know an Englishman,
Being flatter'd, is a lamb; threaten'd, a lion.

George Chapman, *Alphonsus, Emperar of Germany*, before 1636

Which Quintius in Livy said of the inhabitants of Peloponnesus may well be applied to us, we are *testudines testa sua inclusi*, like so many tortoises in our shells, safely defended by an angry sea, as a wall on all sides.

Robert Burton, *Anatomie of Melancholie*, 1621

Les anglais s'amusent tristement selon l'usage de leur pays.
(The English take their pleasures sadly after the fashion of their country.)

Maximilian de Bethune, Duc de Sully, *Memoirs*, *c.* 1630

An Englishman's house (home) is his castle.

Proverb, seventeenth century

We are Englishmen; that is one good fact.

Oliver Cromwell, Speech to Parliament, 22 January 1655

For we Englishmen being farre northerly, doe not open our mouthes in the cold air, wide enough to grace a Southern tongue; but are observ'd by all other nations to speak exceeding close and inward.

John Milton, *Of Education*, 1644

Lords and Commons of England, consider what Nation it is whereof ye are, and whereof ye are the governors: a Nation not slow and dull, but of a quick, ingenious, and piercing spirit, acute to invent, suttle and sinewy to discours, not beneath the reach of any point the highest that humane capacity can soar to.

John Milton, *Areopagitica*, 1644

For *Britain*, to speak a truth not often spoken, as it is a land fruitful enough of Men stout and courageous in War, so it is naturally not over-fertile of Men able to govern justly, prudently, in Peace, trusting only in their Mother Wit; . . . valiant indeed, and prosperous to win a field; but to know the end and Reason of winning, injudicious and unwise: in good or bad success alike unteachable. For the Sun which we want, ripens Wits as well as Fruits; and as Wine and Oyl are imported to us from abroad: so must ripe Understanding, and many civil Virtues, be imported into our minds from Foreign Writings, and examples of best Ages, we shall else miscarry still, and come short in the attempts of any great Enterprise.

John Milton, *History of England*, Book III, *The Digression*, 1670–1, printed 1681

Others may use the ocean as their road,

Only the English make it their abode,
Whose ready sail with ev'ry wind can fly,
And make a cov'nant with th'inconstant sky;
Our oaks secure, as if they there took root,
We tread on billows with a steady foot.

Edmund Waller, *Of a War with Spain and a Fight at Sea*, before 1664

But Lord, to see the absurd nature of Englishmen, that cannot forbear laughing and jeering at everything that looks strange.

Samuel Pepys, *Diary*, 27 November 1662

Give but an Englishman his whore and ease,
Beef and a sea-coal fire, he's yours for ever.

Thomas Otway, *Venice Preserved*, 1682

Eighteenth Century

He made her First-born Race to be so rude,
And suffer'd her to be so oft subdu'd:
By sev'ral Crowds of wand'ring Thieves o'er run,
Often unpeopl'd, and as oft undone.
While ev'ry Nation that her Powers reduc'd,
Their languages and Manners introduc'd.
From whose mix'd Relicks our Compounded Breed,
By Spurious Generation does succeed;
Making a Race uncertain and unev'n,
Deriv'd from all the Nations under Heav'n.

The *Romans* first with *Julius Caesar* came.
Including all the Nations of that Name,
Gauls, *Greeks*, and *Lombards*; and by Computation,
Auxiliaries, or Slaves of ev'ry Nation.
With *Hengist*, *Saxons*; *Danes* with *Sueno* came,
In search of Plunder, not in search of Fame.
Scots, *Picts*, and *Irish* from th'*Hibernian Shore*;
And Conqu'ring *William* brought the Normans o'er.

All these their Barb'rous Off-spring left behind,
The Dregs of Armies, they of all Mankind;
Blended with *Britains* who before were here,
Of whom the *Welsh* ha' blest the Character.

From this Amphibious Ill-born Mob began
That vain ill-natur'd thing, an English-man.
The Customs, Sir-names, Languages, and Manners,
Of all these Nations are their own Explainers:
Whose Relicks are so lasting and so strong,
They ha' left a *Shiboleth* upon our Tongue;

By which with easie search you may distinguish
Your *Roman-Saxon-Danish-Norman* English. . . .
These are the Heroes who despise the *Dutch*,
And rail at new-come Foreigners so much;
Forgetting that themselves are all deriv'd
From the most Scoundrel Race that ever liv'd
A horrid Crowd of Rambling Thieves and Drones;
Who ransack'd Kingdoms, and dispeopl'd Towns.
The *Pict*, and Painted *Britain*, Treach'rous *Scot*,
By Hunger, Theft, and Rapine, hither brought.
Norwegian Pirates, Buccaneering *Danes*,
Whose red-hair'd Off-spring ev'ry where remains.
Who join'd with *Norman-French* compound the Breed
From whence your True-Born Englishmen proceed.

And lest by Length of Time it be pretended,
The Climate may this Modern Breed ha' mended,
Wise Providence, to keep us where we are,
Mixes us daily with exceeding Care:
We have been *Europe*'s Sink, *the Jakes* where she
Voids all her Offal Out-cast Progeny.

Daniel Defoe, *The True-Born Englishman*, 1701

Wealth, howsoever got, in England makes
Lords of mechanics, gentlemen of rakes:
Antiquity and birth are needless here;
'Tis impudence and money makes a peer.

Ibid.

But English gratitude is always such,
To hate the hand which doth oblige too much.

Ibid.

For my own part I look upon it as a peculiar Blessing that I was born an *Englishman*. Among many other Reasons I think myself very happy in my Country, as the *Language* of it is wonderfully adapted to a Man who is sparing of his Words, and an Enemy to Loquacity. . . . The *English* delight in Silence more than any other *European* Nation.

Joseph Addison, *Spectator*, no. 135, 4 August 1711

There is no Humour in my Countrymen, which I am more enclined to wonder at, than their general thirst after News. There are about half a Dozen Ingenious Men, who live very plentifully upon this Curiosity of their Fellow-Subjects.

Joseph Addison, *Spectator*, no. 452, 8 August 1712

Liberty is the idol of the English, under whose banner all the nation lists.

Susannah Centlivre, *The Wonder*, 1714

*I cannot but conclude the bulk of your natives to be the most pernicious race of little odious vermin that nature ever suffered to crawl upon the surface of the earth.

Jonathan Swift, *Gulliver's Travels: Voyage to Brobdingnag*, 1726

The English abroad can never get to look as if they were at home. The Irish and Scotch, after being some time in a place, get the air of the natives; but an

Englishman, in any foreign court, looks about him as if he was going to steal a tankard.

Francis Lockier, Remark, *c.* 1730 in Joseph Spence, *Anecdotes*

Mr. Hooke used to say that there were three reasons why a man should choose to live in England: liberty, liberty, liberty!

Joseph Spence, *Anecdotes*, June 1729

Something there is in our climate and complexion that makes idleness nowhere so much its own punishment as in England, where an uneducated fine gentleman pays for his momentary pleasures with long and cruel intervals of spleen; for relief of which he is driven into sensual excesses that produce a proportionable depression of spirits, which, as it createth a greater want of pleasures, so it lessens the ability to enjoy them. There is a cast of thought in the complexion of an Englishman which renders him the most unsuccessful rake in the world. He is (as Aristotle expresseth it) at variance with himself. He is neither brute enough to enjoy his appetites, nor man enough to govern them.

George Berkeley, *Alciphron, or the Minute Philosopher*, 1732

Time was, a sober Englishman wou'd knock
His servants up, and rise by five a clock,
Instruct his Family in ev'ry rule,
And send his Wife to Church, his Son to school.
To worship like his Fathers was his care;
To teach their frugal Virtues to his Heir;
To prove, that Luxury could never hold;
And place, on good Security, his Gold.
Now Times are chang'd, and one Poetick Itch
Has seiz'd the Court and City, Poor and Rich:
Sons, Sires and Grandsires, all will wear the Bays,
Our wives read Milton, and our Daughters Plays,
To Theatres, and to Rehearsals throng,
And all our Grace at Table is a Song.

Alexander Pope, *Imitations of Horace*, Epistle II, 1737

The most remarkable thing I have observed since I came abroad, is, that there are no people so obviously mad as the English. The French, the Italians, have great follies, great faults; but then they are so national, that they cease to be striking. In England, tempers vary so excessively, that almost everyone's faults are peculiar to himself. I take this diversity to proceed partly from our climate, partly from our government: the first is changeable, and makes us queer; the latter permits our queernesses to operate as they please.

Horace Walpole, Letter to Richard West, 24 January 1740

It is said the wise *Italians* make this proverbial Remark on our Nation, *viz.* 'The English *feel*, but they do not *see*.' That is, they are sensible of Inconveniences when they are present, but do not take sufficient Care to prevent them: their natural Courage makes them too little apprehensive of Danger.

Benjamin Franklin, *Plain Truth, or Serious Considerations on the Present State of . . . Philadelphia, etc.*, 1747

It must be owned that the Graces do not seem to be natives of Great Britain; and I doubt the best of us here have more of rough than polished diamond.

P.D. Stanhope, Earl of Chesterfield, Letter to his son, 18 November 1748

*And yet as no Nation produces so many drunken Quarrels, especially among the lower People, than in *England*; (for, indeed, with them, to drink and to fight together are almost synonymous Terms), I would not methinks have it thence concluded that the *English* are the worst-natured People alive. Perhaps the Love of Glory only is at the bottom of this; so that the fair Conclusion seems to be, that our Countrymen have more of that Love and more of Bravery, than any other Plebeians.

Henry Fielding, *Tom Jones*, 1749

But to say truth, we are a declining people; destined, I fear, to absolute destruction. We have had our day.

Earl of Orrery, Letter to Thomas Carte, 5 August 1752

The people of England are never so happy as when you tell them they are ruined.

Arthur Murphy, *The Upholsterer*, 1758

When two Englishmen meet, their first talk is of the weather.

Samuel Johnson, *The Idler*, 1758

You cannot conceive how shamefully the mode here is a single life. One can scarce be in the company of a dozen men of circumstance and fortune, but what it is odds that you find on inquiry eleven of them are single. The great complaint is the excessive expensiveness of English wives.

Benjamin Franklin, Letter to his wife, 1760

When the men of this country are once turned of thirty, they regularly retire every year at proper intervals to lie in of the *spleen*.

Oliver Goldsmith, *The Citizen of the World*, 1760–1

Ask an Englishman what nation in the world enjoys most freedom, and he immediately answers, his own. Ask him in what that freedom principally consists, and he is instantly silent. This happy pre-eminence does not arise from the people's enjoying a larger share in legislation than elsewhere; for in this particular several states in Europe excel them; nor does it arise from greater exemption from taxes, for few countries pay more; it does not proceed from their being restrained by fewer laws, for no people are burdened with so many; nor does it particularly consist in the security of their property, for property is pretty well secured in every polite state of Europe.

How then are the English more free (for more free they certainly are) than the people of any other country, or under any other form of government whatever? Their freedom consists in their enjoying all the advantages of democracy with this superior prerogative borrowed from monarchy, *that the severity of their laws may be relaxed without endangering the constitution.*

Ibid.

The love of retreat and solitude, with which the English are reproached, never appears more conspicuously, than when they draw together in a multitude of five hundred persons.

David Hume, Letter to the Comtesse de Boufflers, 3 July 1763

Hastings: In truth, I have been often surprized, that you, who have seen so much of the world, with your natural good sense, and your many opportunities, could never yet acquire a requisite share of assurance.

Marlow: The Englishman's malady. . . .

Oliver Goldsmith, *She Stoops to Conquer*, 1773

There is another circumstance which the people of England have not only not attended to, but seem to be utterly ignorant of, and that is, the difference between permanent power and accidental power, considered in a national sense.

Thomas Paine, Letter to the Abbé Raynal, 1782

Il y a en Angleterre soixante sectes religieuses différentes, et une seule sauce.
(In England there are sixty different religious sects and only one sauce.)

Francesco Caracciolo, Neapolitan Ambassador to London, Remark, attributed, *c.* 1790

Je n'aime pas un pays où il y a plus d'apothecaires que de boulangers, et où l'on ne trouve de fruits mûrs que les pommes cuites. Les Anglaises sont belles, mais elles ont deux bras gauches.
(I can't love a country where there are more chemists than bakers, and no ripe fruit apart from baked apples. Englishwomen are beautiful, but they have two left hands.)

Antoine Rivarol, Letter to the Abbe de Villefort, 1795

Nineteenth Century

Not only England but every Englishman is an island. He has all the qualities of a poker except its occasional warmth. On the other hand, his casualness is attractive. It is pleasant to see things done without fuss. It is engaging to meet an Englishman, as I once did in Hamburg, who will casually discuss Plato's *Republic* for an hour then indolently rise and announce, 'I must be off; my boat leaves for India in half an hour.'

Karl August von Hardenberg, *Fragments*, 1800

The English never know when they are beaten.

Proverb, nineteenth century (Napoleon?)

I believe I have already told you that to express what we should call puritanism in language and excess of delicacy in matters of physical love – the Word *Englanderei* has been invented, i.e. an englishman.

Henry Crabb Robinson, Letter to his brother, 3 June 1804

The English migrate as regularly as rooks.

Robert Southey, *Letters from England, by Don Manuel Alvarez Espriella*, 1807

I no longer wonder why these people talk so much of the weather; they live in the most inconstant of all climates, against which it is so difficult to take any effectual precaution, that they have given the matter up in despair, and take no precautions at all. Their great poet, Milton, describes the souls of the condemned as being hurried from fiery into frozen regions: perhaps he took the idea from his own feelings on such a day as this, when, like me, he was scorched on one side and frost-bitten on the other; and, not knowing which of the two torments was the worst, assigned them to the wicked both in turn.

Ibid.

I have long been of the opinion that a British army could bear neither success nor failure.

Duke of Wellington, Dispatch to the Right Hon. J. Villiers, 31 May 1809

Your friend *Kolfkovsky* was with me yesterday – complaining of the English husbands & the restrictions upon their wives – with whom he appears to have made little progress – but lays it all upon the *husbands* – I was obliged to comfort him with the assurance that the fault was all his own – & that husbands and wives are much the same here as elsewhere – it was impossible to hear them so traduced with patience.

Lord Byron, Letter to Lady Melbourne, 2 May 1813

Englishmen see with their ears.

Antonio Canova, comment, *c.* 1815, quoted in John Russell, *Portrait of Logan Pearsall Smith*, 1950

Men of England, wherefore plough
For the lords who lay you low?

P.B. Shelley, Song, 'To the Men of England', 1819

You are not a moral people, and you know it
Without the aid of too sincere a poet.

Lord Byron, *Don Juan*, 1819–24

I have always found the English *baser* in some things than any other nation. – You stare – but it's true – as to *gratitude*; – perhaps – because they are prouder – & proud people hate obligations.

Lord Byron, Letter to John Murray, 22 July 1821

The English (it must be owned) are rather a foul-mouthed nation.

William Hazlitt, *Table Talk*, 1821–2

There are two things that an Englishman understands, hard words and hard blows. Nothing short of this (generally speaking) excites his attention or interests him in the least.

William Hazlitt, *Notes of a Journey through France and Italy*, 1826

The assertion of an abstract right is the idea uppermost in the minds of all English people. Unfortunately, when its attainment is worth any thing, their spirit of contradiction makes them ready to relinquish it; or when it costs them any thing, their spirit of self-interest deters them from the pursuit!

Ibid.

An Irishman fights before he reasons, a Scotchman reasons before he fights, an Englishman is not particular as to the order of precedence, but will do either to accommodate his customers.

Charles Caleb Colton, *Lacon*, 1825

Minds like ours, my dear James, must always be above national prejudices, and in all companies, it gives me pleasure to declare, that, as a people, the English are very little indeed inferior to the Scotch.

Christopher North (John Wilson), *Noctes Ambrosianae*, no. 28, October 1826

We know of no spectacle so ridiculous as the British public in one of its periodical fits of morality.

T.B. Macaulay, *On Moore's Life of Byron*, 1830

I hope we English will long maintain our *grand talent pour le silence*.

Thomas Carlyle, *Heroes and Hero-worship*, 1841

Of all the nations in the world, at present the English are the stupidest in speech, the wisest in action.

Thomas Carlyle, *Past and Present*, 1843

The English are a dumb people. They can do great acts, but not describe them. Like the old Romans, and some few others, *their* Epic Poem is written on the Earth's surface: England her Mark!

Ibid.

There is a peculiarity in the countenance, as everybody knows, which, though it cannot be described, is sure to betray the Englishman.

George Borrow, *The Bible in Spain*, 1843

How they hate us, these foreigners, in Belgium as much as in France! What lies they tell of us; how gladly they would see us humiliated! Honest folks at home over their port-wine say, 'Ay, ay, and very good reason they have too. National vanity, sir, wounded – we have beaten them so often.' My dear sir, there is not a greater error in the world than this. They hate you because you are stupid, hard to please, and intolerably insolent and air-giving. . . . This is why we are hated, for pride. . . . Of all European people, which is the nation which has the most haughtiness, the strongest prejudices, the greatest reserve, the greatest dulness? I say an Englishman of the genteel classes.

W.M. Thackeray, *Little Travels and Roadside Sketches*, October 1844

There is something odd in the disposition of an Englishman's senses. He sees with his fingers, and hears with his toes. Enter a gallery of pictures, you find all the spectators longing to become handlers. Go to hear an opera of Mozart's: your next neighbour keeps all the while kicking time . . . as if he could not kill it without.

J.C. and A. Hare, *Guesses at Truth*, 3rd edn, 1847

*Still, you know, I feel that a duty devolves upon me. And when a duty devolves upon an Englishman, he is bound to get out of it, in my opinion, in the best way he can.

Charles Dickens, *Dombey and Son*, 1847–8 (Cousin Feenix speaking)

*How hard it is to make an Englishman acknowledge that he is happy!

W.M. Thackeray, *Pendennis*, 1848

Good ale, the true and proper drink of Englishmen. He is not deserving of the name of Englishman who speaketh against ale, that is good ale.

George Borrow, *Lavengro*, 1851

Englishmen are not made of polishable substance.

Nathaniel Hawthorne, *Journals*, 13 February 1854

The Englishman is too apt to neglect the present good in preparing against the possible evil.

Washington Irving, 'English and French Character', *Wolfert's Roost*, 1855

John Bull, like the snail, loves to carry his native shell with him, irrespective of changes of climate or habits of different conditions and necessities.

Richard Ford, *A Handbook for Travellers in Spain*, 3rd edn, 1855

Spleen, an organ found in an Englishman, not found in the American, & differencing the two nations.

Ralph Waldo Emerson, *Journals*, 1855

Have you observed that nothing can be done in England without a dinner? . . . It is quite true what Frere says: 'An Englishman opens like an oyster, with a knife and fork; one never knows what is in a man till these two agents are in active employment.'

Sydney Smith, quoted by Lady Holland, *Memoir of Sydney Smith*, 1855

Steam is almost an Englishman. I do not know but they will send him to Parliament next, to make laws.

R.W. Emerson, *English Traits*, 1856

I find the Englishman to be him of all men who stands firmest in his shoes.

Ibid.

What we can we will be
Honest Englishmen.
Do the work that's nearest,
Though it's dull at whiles,
Helping, when we meet them,
Lame dogs over stiles.

Charles Kingsley, Letter to Thomas Hughes, August 1856

The Chinese, even in 1851, and in the council-chamber of the Emperor, settled it as the most plausible hypothesis that the English people had no territorial home, but made a shift (like some birds) to float upon the sea in fine weather, and in rougher seasons to run for 'holes'.

Thomas de Quincey, *The Chinese Question in 1857*

'Tis the hard grey weather
Breeds hard English men.

Charles Kingsley, 'Ode to the North-East Wind', *Andromeda and Other Poems* 1858

A settled and practical people are distinctly in favour of heavy relaxations, placid prolixities, slow comforts. A state between the mind and the body, something intermediate, half-way from the newspaper to a nap – this is what we may call the middle-life theory of the influential English gentleman – the true aspiration of the ruler of the world.

Walter Bagehot, *Estimates of Some Englishmen and Scotchmen*, 1858

The French wittily describe the English on a steamboat as each endeavouring to draw around himself an impassable space detaching him from his countrymen, in which he shall stand alone, clean & miserable.

Ralph Waldo Emerson, *Journals*, 1859

If an earthquake were to engulf England tomorrow, the English would manage to meet and dine somewhere among the rubbish, just to celebrate the event.

Douglas William Jerrold, Remark, quoted in Blanchard Jerrold, *Life of Douglas Jerrold*, 1859

The first word an Englishman learns in any language is that which signifies a determination to proceed.

Anthony Trollope, *The West Indies and the Spanish Main*, 1859

We have risen so high that we may almost boast to have placed ourselves above national glory. The welfare of the coming world is now the proper care of the Anglo-Saxon race.

Ibid.

An attempt to explain the web of prejudices tangled round the English character would be as fruitless as an effort to unravel the fibrous roots of the oak, its noble and appropriate emblem. Like them, they form part of its very existence; are fed by the same sap; and are perhaps as necessary to the growth and greatness of the branching structure above them. The main strength of a nation often consists in its prejudices. But that which gives strength does not always produce happiness.

T.C. Grattan, *Beaten Paths and Those Who Trod Them*, 1862

They say that two Englishmen, meeting in the desert would not speak unless they were introduced. The further I travel, the less true do I find this of Englishmen, and the more true of other people.

Anthony Trollope, *North America*, 1862

All English people, I imagine, are influenced in a far greater degree than ourselves by this simple and honest tendency, in cases of disagreement, to batter one another's persons; and whoever has seen a crowd of English ladies (for instance, at the door of the Sistine Chapel, in Holy Week) will be satisfied that their belligerent propensities are kept in abeyance only by a merciless rigor on the part of society. It requires a vast deal of refinement to spiritualize their large physical endowments.

Nathaniel Hawthorne, *Our Old Home*, 1863

I never stood in an English crowd without being conscious of hereditary sympathies. Nevertheless, it is undeniable that an American is continually thrown upon his national antagonism by some acrid quality in the moral atmosphere of England. These people think so loftily of themselves, and so contemptuously of everybody else, that it requires more generosity than I possess to keep always in perfectly good humour with them.

Ibid.

The Englishman, in so far as he is German, – and he is mainly German, – proceeds in the steady-going German fashion; if he were all German, he would proceed thus for ever, without self-consciousness or embarrassment; but, in so far as he is Celtic, he has snatches of quick instinct which often make him feel he is fumbling, show him visions of an easier, more dexterous behaviour, disconcert him and fill him with misgiving. No people, therefore, are so shy, so self-conscious, so embarrassed as the English, because two natures are mixed in them, and natures which pull them such different ways. The Germanic part, indeed, triumphs in us, we are a Germanic people; but not so wholly as to exclude hauntings of Celtism, which clash with our Germanism, producing, as I believe, our *humour*, neither German nor Celtic, and so affect us that we strike people as odd and singular, not to be referred to any known type, and like nothing but ourselves. 'Nearly every Englishman,' says an excellent and by no means unfriendly observer, George Sand, 'nearly every Englishman, however good looking he may be, has something singular about him, which easily comes to seem comic; – a sort of typical awkwardness (*gaucherie typique*) in his looks or appearance, which hardly ever wears out.'

Matthew Arnold, *The Study of Celtic Literature*, 1867

Of all nations in the world the English are perhaps the least a nation of pure philosophers.

Walter Bagehot, *The English Constitution*, 1867

We look on state action, not as our own action, but as alien action: as an imposed tyranny from without, not as the consummated result of our organised wishes. . . . The natural impulse of English people is to resist authority.

Ibid.

We are . . . a deferential nation, but we are deferential by imagination not by reason.

Ibid.

One has often wondered whether upon the whole earth there is anything so unintelligent, so unapt to perceive how the world is really going, as an ordinary young Englishman of our upper class.

Matthew Arnold, *Culture and Anarchy*, 1869

A race that binds
Its body in chains and calls them Liberty,
And calls each fresh link Progress.

Robert Buchanan, *Titan and Avatar*, (*A Choral Mystic*), 1871

The pleasantness of the English . . . comes in great measure from the fact of their each having been dipped into the crucible, which gives them a sort of coating of comely varnish and color. They have been smoothed and polished by mutual social attrition. . . . You see Englishmen here in Italy to a particularly good advantage. In the midst of these false and beautiful Italians they glow with the light of the great fact, that after all they love a bathtub and they hate a lie.

Henry James, Letter to Mrs Henry James Sr, 13 October 1869

An Englishman is, of course, the first of created beings; and he owes this pre-eminence in great degree to his remarkable powers of self-assertion. As an Italian visitor informed me, the great motto of the English race is 'Selelf' – a mysterious word, which, after some investigation, I discovered to be the Italian version of the title of Mr. Smiles's book, 'Self-Help.' Now 'selelf' means the power and the will of treading on any toes that are in your way.

Leslie Stephen, *The Playground of Europe*, 1871

The French have a notion that, go where you may, to the top of a pyramid or to the top of Mont Blanc, you are sure to meet an Englishman reading a newspaper.

Henry Labouchère, *Diary of the Besieged Resident in Paris*, 1871

*He's an Anglo-Saxon Messenger – and those are Anglo-Saxon attitudes.

Lewis Carroll, *Alice through the Looking-Glass*, 1872

Combativeness . . . lies deep in the English nature: and . . . has expressed itself in brutal and in noble forms ever since we were a nation. . . . It is not a love of gambling, but the hot desire to be on every side of every conflict, that leads all classes of Englishmen to the racecourse. This same spirit is that which has developed our unparalleled extent of trade.

Blanchard Jerrold, *London, a Pilgrimage*, 1872

An English crowd is almost the ugliest in the world: because the poorer classes are but copyists in costume of the rich. The exceptions are the followers of street trades – the costermongers, the orangewomen, and the tramps. The workman approximates his nearest to the cut of Poole. The English carpenter wears a black tail-coat – like the waiter, the undertaker, and the duke. Poor English women are ghastly in their patches trimmed in outlandish imitation of the fashions . . . in these base and shabby copyings of the rich, the poverty of the wearers has a startling, abject air. It is, as I heard a stranger remark, 'misery advertised.' . . . In England, all classes, except the agricultural, dress alike, – with a difference.

Ibid.

I set myself the task of raising my profession to the only standard which the English mind applies to everything – the standard of money.

Dion Boucicault, Letter to the Editor of the *New York Tribune*, 23 October 1873

For he might have been a Roosian
A French, or Turk, or Proosian,
Or perhaps I-ta-li-an!
But in spite of all temptations
To belong to other nations,
He remains an Englishman.

Sir William Schwenk Gilbert, *H.M.S. Pinafore*, 1878

He is an Englishman!
For he himself has said it,
And it's greatly to his credit,
That he is an Englishman!

Ibid.

We seem, as it were, to have conquered and peopled the world in a fit of absence of mind.

Sir J.R. Seeley, *The Expansion of England*, 1883

In no other country, I imagine, are so many people to be found doing the same thing, in the same way, at the same time. . . . I have not in the least learned what becomes of that explosive personal force in the English character which is compressed and corked down by social conformity. I look with a certain awe at some of the manifestations of the conforming spirit, but the fermenting idiosyncrasies beneath it are hidden from my vision.

Henry James, 'An English Easter', 1877, in *Portraits of Places*, 1883

An Englishman is never so natural as when he is holding his tongue.

Henry James, *The Portrait of a Lady*, 1881

Let the German touch hands with the Gaul,
And the fortress of England must fall;
And the sea shall be swept of her seamen,
And the waters they ruled be their graves
And Dutchmen and Frenchmen be freemen,
And Englishmen slaves. . . .
Our time once more is over,
Once more our end is near:
A bull without a drover
The Briton reels to rear
And the van of the nations is held by his betters
And the seas of the world shall be loosed from his fetters
And his glory shall pass as a breath
And the life that is in him be death;
And the sepulchre sealed on his glory
For a sign to the nations shall be
As of Tyre and of Carthage in story,
Once lords of the sea. . . .
. . . the people whose hope hath its anchor
Made fast in the sea.

A.C. Swinburne, 'A Word for the Nation', *A Midsummer Holiday*, 1884

Those things which the English public never forgives – youth, power, and enthusiasm.

Oscar Wilde, *The English Renaissance of Art*, Lecture, Chickering Hall, New York, 9 January 1882

I have trust in the reason of the English people (who have an inborn respect for law), when they have time to reason; I believe in 'our crown'd republic's crowning common-sense.'

Alfred Lord Tennyson, in conversation, 1887, *Alfred Lord Tennyson, A Memoir, by his Son*, 1897

An analysis of public opinion in Britain will distinguish three sets of persons – I do not call them classes, for they do not coincide with social grades – those who make opinion, those who receive and hold opinion, and those who have no opinions at all.

James Bryce, *The American Commonwealth*, 1888

You make our faults too gross, and thence maintain
Our darker future. May your fears be vain!
At times the small black fly upon the pane
May seem the black ox of the distant plain.

Alfred Lord Tennyson, 'To One Who Ran Down the English', *Demeter and Other Poems*, 1889

Britannia rules the waves,
As I have heard her say;
She frees whatever slaves
She meets upon her way.

A teeming mother she
Of Parliaments and Laws;
Majestic, mighty, free:
Devoid of common flaws. . . .

The Saxon and the Celt
She equitably rules;
Her iron rod is felt
By countless knaves and fools.

In fact mankind at large,
Black, yellow, white and red,
Is given to her in charge
And owns her as a head.

But every here and there –
Deny it if you can –
She breeds a vacant stare
Unworthy of a man:

A look of dull surprise;
A nerveless idle hand;
An eye which never tries
To threaten or command:

In short a kind of man,
If man indeed he be,

As worthy of our ban
As any that we see:

Unspeakably obtuse,
Abominably vain,
Of very little use,
And execrably plain.

J.K. Stephen, *On a Parisian Boulevard*, 1891

The English are a very practical people. They like expansion, but they like it in connection with practical business.

Cecil Rhodes, Speech to Shareholders of the Chartered Company, 18 January 1895

But it never really mattered till the English grew polite.

Rudyard Kipling, *Et Dona Ferentes*, 1896

There is nothing so bad or good that you will not find an Englishman doing it, but you will never find an Englishman in the wrong. He does everything on principle. He fights you on patriotic principles; he robs you on business principles; he enslaves you on imperial principles.

Bernard Shaw, *The Man of Destiny*, 1897

The English are mentioned in the Bible: 'Blessed are the meek, for they shall inherit the earth.'

Mark Twain, 'Pudd'nhead Wilson's New Calendar', in *More Tramps Abroad*, 1897

For Allah created the English mad – the maddest of all mankind!

Rudyard Kipling, *Kitchener's School*, 1898

When I come back from a spell in Africa, the thing that makes me proud of being one of the English is not the manners or customs up here, certainly not the houses or the climate; but it is the thing embodied in a great railway engine. I once came home on a ship with an Englishman who had been in South West Africa for seven unbroken years; he was sane, and in his right mind. But no sooner did we get ashore at Liverpool, than he rushed at, and threw his arms round a postman, to that official's embarrassment and surprise. Well, that is just how I feel about the first magnificent bit of machinery I come across: it is the manifestation of the superiority of my race.

Mary Kingsley, *West African Studies*, 1899

Twentieth Century

'Tis a trait iv us Anglo-Saxons that we look on an inimy as a target. If ye hit him ye get three good seegars.

Finley Peter Dunne, *Mr Dooley's Philosophy*, 1900

The well-bred Englishman is about as agreeable a fellow as you can find anywhere – especially, as I have noted, if he is an Irishman, or a Scotchman.

Finley Peter Dunne, *Mr Dooley Remembers*, 1963 – (Anthology of Pieces c. 1900)

The well-fed Englishman, though he lives and dies a schoolboy, cannot play. He cannot even play cricket or football: he has to work at them: that is why he beats the foreigner who plays at them. To him playing means playing the fool.

G. Bernard Shaw, Preface to *Three Plays for Puritans*, 1900

'Do you know, Grey, I have just been thinking that you have never been sufficiently grateful for having been born an Englishman. Just think for a moment,' he went on, 'what it is to have been born an Englishman, in England. Think how many millions of men there are in this world who have been born Chinese or Hindus, or Kaffirs; but you were not born any of these, you were born an Englishman. And that is not all. You are just over forty . . . and you have a clean, healthy body. Now think of the odds there are against anyone having those three things – to be born an Englishman, to be over forty, and to have a clean, healthy body. Why, the chances are enormous against it, and yet you have all three. What enormous chances there are against you having drawn all those prizes in the lottery of life, and yet you never think of them.'

'I could have hugged the poor old chap,' said Lord Grey. . . .

W.T. Stead, *Last Will . . . of C.J. Rhodes, . . . etc.*, 1902, quoting Rhodes

The England which occupied of the largest and greatest dominion which can rarely be. The Englishman works with a very powerful hands and the long legs and even the eminenced mind, his chin is strong as decerved iron. He are not allowed it to escape if he did seized something. Being spread his dominion is dreadfully extensive so that his countrymen boastfully say 'the sun are never sets on our dominions.' The Testamony of English said that he lost the common sense, he never any benefit though he had gained the complete world. The English are cunning institutioned to establish a great empire of the Paradise. The Englishman always said to the another nation, 'give me your land and I will give you my Testimony.' So it is not robbed but exchanged as the Englishman always confide the object to be pure and the order to be holy and they reproach him if any them are killed to death with the contention of other men. I shall continue the other time.

Douglas Sladen, *Queer Things About Japan*, 1903 quotes this as 'The Character of the Englishman', an anonymous Japanese essay

No one can understand the nature of England or of English politics who does not realize that this island of ours is and always has been covered with a kind of beautiful cloud. No one can be a good critic of England who does not understand fogs. And no one can be a really patriotic Englishman who does not like fogs. Of all national histories the history of England must be the hardest to write, for the English, with all their great epochs, not only did not know what they were doing, but, so far as one can make out, did not want to know what they were doing. They always did a thing in such a way that a hundred years afterwards it could be maintained that they had done the precise opposite. They always said a thing in such a way that it could mean something different. This was not craft. It was their ingrained poetry. . . . The English law, for instance, is uncommonly like an impressionist picture of a rainy day. The Code Napoleon is like a coloured photograph of Rome.

G.K. Chesterton, 'The English Way', *Daily News*, 16 March 1905

The English themselves hardly conceived their mind was either economical, sharp, or direct; but the defect that most struck an American was its enormous waste in eccentricity. Americans needed and used their whole energy, and applied it with close economy; but English society was eccentric by law and for the sake of eccentricity itself. . . . Eccentricity was so general as to become hereditary distinction. It made the chief charm of English society as well as its chief terror.

Henry Adams, *The Education of Henry Adams*, 1906

The English mind was like the London drawing-room, a comfortable and easy spot, filled with bits and fragments of incoherent furnitures, which were never meant to go together, and could be arranged in any relation without making a whole, except by the square room. Philosophy might dispute about innate ideas till the stars died out in the sky, but about innate tastes, no one, except perhaps a collie dog, has the right to doubt; least of all the Englishman, for his tastes are his being; he drifts after them as unconsciously as a honey-bee drifts after his flowers, and, in England, every one must drift with him.

Ibid.

Of course the horror of any reference to illegitimacy is a general English characteristic, which, as it is mainly confined to the middle classes, may, one suppose, be attributed to the hereditary objection of the Anglo-Saxons (from which those middle classes are largely, if not entirely recruited) to the bastardy of their Norman Conqueror.

Robert Harborough Sherard, *My Friends the French*, 1909

Bullied and ordered about, the Englishman obeys like a sheep, evades like a knave, or tries to murder his oppressor.

G. Bernard Shaw, 'Parents and Children', Preface to *Misalliance*, 1910

*The English have a proverb: 'Conscience makes cowboys of us all.'

'Saki', H.H. Munro, *Wratislav, The Chronicles of Clovis*, 1911

The English have no respect for their language and will not teach their children to speak it. . . . It is impossible for an Englishman to open his mouth without making some other Englishman despise him.

G. Bernard Shaw, Preface to *Pygmalion*, 1912

Curse the blasted jelly-boned swines, the slimy belly-wriggling invertebrates, the miserable sodding rotters, the flaming sods, the snivelling, dribbling, dithering, palsied pulseless lot that make up England today. They've got white of egg in their veins, and their spunk is that watery it's a marvel they can breed. . . . Why, why, why, was I born an Englishman! – my cursed, rotten-boned, pappy hearted countrymen, *why* was I sent to *them*. Christ on the cross must have hated his countrymen. 'Crucify me, you swine,' he must have said through his teeth.

D.H. Lawrence, Letter to Edward Garnett, 3 July 1912

It is when one comes to survey with a fresh eye the amusements of the English race that one realises the incomprehensibility of existence. Here is the most serious people on earth – the only people, assuredly, with a genuine grasp of the principles of political wisdom – amusing itself untiringly with a play-ball. The ball may be large and soft, as in football, or small and hard, as in golf, or small and very hard, as in billiards, or neither one thing nor the other, as in cricket – it is always a ball. Abolish the sphere, and the flower of English manhood would perish from ennui.

Arnold Bennet, *Paris Nights*, 1913

. . . BLESS ENGLAND, industrial island machine, pyramidal workshop, its apex at Shetland, discharging itself on the sea.

BLESS cold
magnanimous
delicate
gauche
fanciful
stupid
ENGLISHMEN.

Wyndham Lewis, Manifesto from *Blast*, 1914

The maxim of the British people is 'Business as usual.'

Sir Winston Churchill, Speech, Guildhall, London, 9 November 1914

Smile at us, pay us, pass us; but do not quite forget.
For we are the people of England, that never have
spoken yet.

G.K. Chesterton, *The Secret People – Poems*, 1915

Hector: And this ship that we are all in? This soul's prison we call England?
Captain Shotover: The captain is in his bunk, drinking bottled ditch-water; and the crew is gambling in the forecastle. She will strike and sink and split. Do you think the laws of God will be suspended in favour of England because you were born in it?
Hector: Well, I don't mean to be drowned like a rat in a trap. I still have the will to live. What am I to do?
Captain Shotover: Do? Nothing simpler. Learn your business as an Englishman.
Hector: And what may my business as an Englishman be, pray?
Captain Shotover: Navigation. Learn it and live; or leave it and be damned.

G. Bernard Shaw, *Heartbreak House*, 1916

It is a part of English hypocrisy – or English reserve – that, whilst we are fluent enough in grumbling about small inconveniences, we insist on making light of any great difficulties or griefs that may beset us.

Max Beerbohm, 'Books Within Books', *And Even Now*, 1920

An Englishman is a man who lives on an island in the North Sea governed by Scotsmen.

Philip Guedalla, *Supers and Supermen*, 1920

They are the only people who like to be told how bad things are – who like to be told the worst.

Sir Winston Churchill, Speech, 1921

That's the weakness of an Englishman; he can't keep up his resentments.

John Galsworthy, *A Family Man*, 1921

What governs the Englishman is his inner atmosphere, the weather in his soul. It is nothing particularly spiritual or mysterious. . . . His adventures are all external; they change him so little that he is not afraid of them. He carries his English weather in his heart wherever he goes, and it becomes a cool spot in the desert, and a steady and sane oracle amongst all the deliriums of mankind. Never since the days of Greece has the world had such a sweet, just, boyish master. It will be a black day for the human race when scientific blackguards, conspirators, churls, and fanatics manage to supplant him.

George Santayana, *Soliloquies in England*, 1922

*He spoke of the English, a noble race, rulers of the waves, who sit on thrones of alabaster, silent as the deathless gods. . . .

James Joyce, *Ulysses*, 1922

With all our faults, we transplant best.

Alfred Viscount Northcliffe, *My Journey Round the World*, 1923

The Duchesse asked the famous wit – 'in your opinion, what animal the most closely resembles man?' Montrond reflected for a minute, and then replied gravely, 'L'Anglais, Duchesse.'

Anon., *Uncensored Recollections*, 1924

*'We've been awfully British over it, but I suppose that's all right.' 'As we are British, I suppose it is.'

E.M. Forster, *A Passage to India*, 1924

In some pleasant parts of the south you may reasonably tremble for England. The life lived there, by nearly every one who has the power to live it if he chooses, is such that England only survives as a great figure in the world because by far the greater number of her people either cannot or will not live in that way.

C.E. Montague, *The Right Place*, 1924

The English behave badly out of shyness – same as a horse goes through a shop window because he thinks a wheel-barrow is a tiger, only question is *what* made him think that originally. Perhaps the early oppression of the Normans.

Rudyard Kipling, Letter to Rider Haggard, 11 April 1925

There is a mood of scared obstinacy in which the Anglo-Saxon becomes capable of almost any swift atrocity. He is rarely deliberately cruel, but he is easily clumsily and hotly cruel.

H.G. Wells, *A Year of Prophesying*, 1925

*Nearly all people in England are of the superior sort, superiority being an English ailment.

D.H. Lawrence, *The Last Laugh*, 1925

The English people on the whole are surely the *nicest* people in the world, and everyone makes everything so easy for everybody else, that there is almost nothing to resist at all.

D.H. Lawrence, *Dull London*, 1928

The Latin race in judgement sits
On us poor English hypocrites:
But did they share (what's no pretence)
Our moral doubts and diffidence,
Then in their pleasures could they be
From our hypocrisy so free?

G. Rostrevor Hamilton, 'English Pleasures', *Epigrams*, 1928

English civilization, or what passes for it, is so smug and hypocritical, so grossly Philistine, and at bottom so brutal, that every first-rate Englishman necessarily becomes an outlaw.

Clive Bell, *Civilization*, 1928

But after all, what would the English be without their sweet unreasonableness?

John Galsworthy, *The Roof*, 1929

Every Briton is at heart a Tory – especially every British Liberal.

Arnold Bennett, *Journal 1929*, 1930

It may be doubted whether nature intended the Englishman to be a money-making animal.

William Ralph Inge, quoted in Sir James Marchant, *Wit and Wisdom of Dean Inge*, 1927

There seems to the Englishman something contemptible in animosity against an opponent.

William Ralph Inge, Dean of St Paul's, *Labels and Libels*, 1929 (UK title, *Assessments and Anticipations)*

It is the strange craving of Anglo-Saxons to seem wickeder than they are.

Philip Guedalla, *The Missing Muse and Other Essays – Period Pieces*, 1929

Mad dogs and Englishmen go out in the mid-day sun;
The Japanese don't care to, the Chinese wouldn't dare to;
Hindus and Argentines sleep firmly from twelve to one,
But Englishmen detest a siesta.

Noel Coward, *Mad Dogs and Englishmen*, 1930

The English are not an inventive people; they don't eat enough pie.

Thomas A. Edison, *Golden Book*, April 1931

The English: Are they human?

Dr G.J. Renier, Title of Book, 1931

Those were, you know, the days when it was glorious to be an English boy. You had God always behind you. You owned half the globe; you were foremost in every manly pursuit; you were clean, sober, honest; you hated injustice; by a glance of your eye, you could reveal that any bully of a Hussar was actually the merest coward; you righted wrongs, succoured the oppressed. With your back to the wall you could stand against the swords of the officers of a whole foreign army.

Ford Madox Ford, *Return to Yesterday*, 1932 (speaking of Edwardian days)

The whole art of diplomacy is to mask one's intentions. And that is where the English excel. No one ever knows what *they* intend to do . . . because they never know themselves.

M. Sazonoff, Russian Foreign Minister, quoted R.H. Bruce Lockhart, *Memoirs of a British Agent*, 1932

What Anglo-Saxon can resist the certainty that he is raised above mankind by something that he cannot quite express.

Philip Guedalla, *Argentine Tango*, 1932

The Englishman, you see, divides the entire universe into things nice to know and things not nice to know – the only remaining category being things nice not to know.

James Agate, *Ego* (14 October 1932), 1935

The Englishman can get along with sex quite perfectly so long as he can pretend that it isn't sex but something else.

Ibid.

This habit of the English upper-middle class of immediately establishing a code of manners whenever a few of them are gathered together, and of requiring everybody else to subscribe to it, is very queer.

Edwin Muir, *Scottish Journey*, 1935

Three things to fear: the horns of a bull, the heels of a stallion, the smile of an Englishman.

Irish proverb, quoted by Oliver St John Gogarty, *As I Was Going Down Sackville Street*, 1937

The attitude of the English . . . toward English history, reminds one a good deal of the attitude of a Hollywood director toward love.

Margaret Halsey, *With Malice Toward Some*, 1938

It takes a great deal to produce ennui in an Englishman, and if you do, he only takes it as convincing proof that you are well-bred.

Ibid.

Let us pause to consider the English,
Who when they pause to consider themselves they get all reticently thrilled and tinglish,
Because every Englishman is convinced of one thing, viz:
That to be an Englishman is to belong to the most exclusive club there is: . . .
English people disclaim sparkle and verve,
But speak without reservations of their Anglo-Saxon reserve.
After listening to little groups of English ladies and gentlemen at cocktail parties and in hotels and pullmans, of defining Anglo-Saxon reserve I despair,

But I think it consists of assuming that nobody else is there. . . .
Anyhow, I think the English people are sweet,
And we might as well get used to them because when they slip and fall they always land on their own or someone else's feet.

Ogden Nash, 'England Expects', in *I'm a Stranger Here Myself*, 1938

After all, *we English* invented Godless commerce and godless politics – so we can't set up to judge Russia, and *we English* invented the 'superior race' doctrine (public school, Kipling, 'The Lesser Breeds,' . . . etc.) so we can't set up to judge Germany and Nazism. Comic the way we carry on and then accuse our neighbours of our own sins.

Eric Gill, Letter to Ralph Downes, 26 September 1939

The English have an extraordinary ability for flying into a great calm.

Alexander Woollcott, before 1944

Favourite place of the English – the last ditch!

Freya Stark, Letter, 23 May 1940, in *Dust in the Lion's Paw*, 1961

In intention, at any rate, the English intelligentsia are Europeanized. They take their cookery from Paris and their opinions from Moscow. In the general patriotism of the country they form a sort of island of dissident thought. England is perhaps the only great country whose intellectuals are ashamed of their own nationality.

George Orwell, 'England Your England', *The Lion and the Unicorn*, 1941

We have not journeyed across the centuries, across the oceans, across the mountains, across the prairies because we were made of sugar-candy.

Sir Winston Churchill, Speech to the Canadian Parliament at Ottawa, 30 December 1941

He was the worst kind of Englishman; he could not even cheat without being found out.

Norman Douglas, *An Almanac*, 1945

Britons never shall be slaves. What else are we?

Ibid.

What we consider rudeness is their form of good manners. In other countries, manners are intended to diminish social friction, to show people consideration and to make them feel at ease. In England it is the other way: good breeding is something you exhibit by snubbing and scoring off people.

Edmund Wilson, *Europe Without Baedeker*, 1947

Every little American is born with his nose poking west; every little Briton with his nose pointing everywhere.

USA saying, quoted as proverb *Benham's Book of Quotations*, 1948 edn

The English never draw a line without blurring it.

Sir Winston Churchill, Speech in the House of Commons, 16 November 1948

You can do wonders with an Englishman if you make him feel ashamed of himself.

Negley Farson, *Last Chance in Africa*, 1949

'You are foreigners?' he asked.
'Yes, we are English.'
'Well, I'm pleased to meet you. I have never met one of your nation before. They tell me that the English are a people who travel all over the world to laugh at other countries. That's fine. I thoroughly approve of it. I hope you are having a good laugh at us.'

Gerald Brenan, *The Face of Spain*, 1950

One can say of the more reticent British that, as you come to know them, some are discovered and some are found out.

Freya Stark, *Beyond Euphrates*, 1951

We spend our time creating a magnificent *average* type of Englishman, the finest intrument in this world: which we then fritter away because we have no *super average* to use him: none of our education sets out to produce great men.

Freya Stark, Letter, 9 February 1930, in *ibid.*

The British are never so formidable as when they are driven back upon their boyhood.

Charles Morgan, *Reflections in a Mirror*, 2nd series, 1946

*You never find an Englishman among the underdogs – except in England of course.

Evelyn Waugh, *The Loved One*, 1948

I think the British have the distinction above all other nations of being able to put new wine into old bottles without bursting them.

Clement Attlee, *Time*, 6 November 1950 (on rebuilt House of Commons)

There are bad times just around the corner,
The horizon's gloomy as can be;
There are black clouds over
The greyish cliffs of Dover,
And the rats are preparing to leave the BBC.
We're an unhappy breed
And very bored indeed
When reminded of something that Nelson said,

And while the press and the politicians nag nag nag
We'll wait until we drop down dead.

There are bad times just around the corner,
And the outlook's absolutely vile;
There are Home Fires smoking
From Windermere to Woking,
And we're *not* going to tighten our belts and smile smile smile.
At the sound of a shot
We'd just as soon as not
Take a hot-water bottle and go to bed:
We're going to *un*tense our muscles till they sag sag sag
And wait until we drop down dead.

Noel Coward, 'There are Bad Times just around the Corner', *Globe Revue*, 1952

Britons believe in right, they believe in justice, they believe in the ineluctable process of history, and they believe in keeping their bread buttered right side up.

John Gunther, *Inside Africa*, 1955

It seems to me that you can go sauntering along for a certain period, telling the English some interesting things about themselves, and then all at once it feels as if you had stepped on the prongs of a rake.

Patrick Campbell, *A Short Trot with a Cultured Mind: Let the English Alone*, 1956

We do not regard Englishmen as foreigners. We look on them only as rather mad Norwegians.

Halvard Lange, *Observer*, 'Sayings of the Week', 9 March 1957

The English find ill-health not only interesting but respectable and often experience death in the effort to avoid a fuss.

Pamela Frankau, *Pen to Paper*, 1961

The English may not like music, but they absolutely love the noise it makes.

Sir Thomas Beecham, *New York Herald Tribune*, 9 March 1961

No one can be as calculatedly rude as the British, which amazes Americans, who do not understand studied insult and can only offer abuse as a substitute.

Paul Gallico, *New York Times*, 14 January 1962

The average Englishman is . . . [an] attractive hybrid between a lion and an ostrich.

Arthur Koestler, 'The Lion and the Ostrich', *Encounter*, July 1963

It has to be admitted that we English have sex on the brain, which is a very unsatisfactory place to have it.

Malcolm Muggeridge, 'Ideas and Men', *New York Times*, 11 October 1964

I do not expect Continentals to understand this. But I do expect Englishmen and even Americans to understand it. We have ways of conducting our affairs which provide our society with huge reserves of energy when it is needed: in a crisis.

Henry Fairlie, 'On the Comforts of Anger', *Encounter*, July 1963

Cricket is a game which the English, not being a spiritual people, have invented to give themselves some conception of eternity.

Lord Mancroft, attrib.

Life as I discovered holds no more wretched occupation than trying to make the English laugh.

Malcolm Muggeridge, *Tread Softly for You Tread on My Jokes*, 1966

A people whose modest but confident boast is that they *always* let the horse go before shutting the stable door.

James Cameron, *Queen*, October 1963, *What a Way to Run the Tribe*, 1968

The English sent all their bores abroad, and acquired the empire as a punishment.

Edward Bond, *Narrow Road to the Deep North*, 1968

In England we never entirely mean what we say, do we? Do I mean that? Not entirely. And logically it follows that when we say we don't mean what we say, only then are we entirely serious.

Alan Bennett, *The Old Country* (Hilary speaking), 1977

Only in England would Donne's assertion that no man is an island have seemed a paradox and not a commonplace. Son of an island, each man is himself an island, secure in the certainty of his own boundaries. Things foreign break upon him like waves. . . .

When did this character differentiate itself from the German character, from the Germans who cannot go anywhere except as a gang? Geographical insularity, relatively early consolidation as a nation, an underlying Celtic pawkishness, a dash of French bitters via the Normans – whatever its cause, its enforcer is the public school system that tears a lad from his mother's still-foaming breast and plunges him into ice-water. To those prophets distressed by the possibility of test-tube conception and mechanized rearing, the British national character should be a great reassurance.

John Updike, 'London Life', 1969, in *Picked Up Pieces*, 1976

A newspaper reported a German diplomat, or government official remarking, as he watched the parade held by the British army during the Queen's visit to Germany in May 1978: 'You English are the only Prussians left.'

The trouble with the British is that we have not been told which game we are playing.

Sir James Goldsmith, Remark to David Frost on television, quoted by Richard Ingrams, *Goldenballs*, 1979

Connolly called the
British 'sheep with a nasty
side'. How very true!

Gavin Ewart, 'Haiku: The Wit and Wisdom of Cyril Connolly', *Quarto*, March 1980

I certainly do not want to marry a member of the British aristocracy, because I am not a necrophiliac.

'Taki', *Spectator*, 3 May 1980

Women

The wife of every Englishman is counted blessed.

Thomas Deloney, *Works*, *c.* 1593

'Fore Heaven. I wonder at the desperate valure
Of the bold *English* that they dare let loose
Their wives, to all encounters.

Ben Jonson, *Volpone*, 1606

Gerrard: Come dear Miss . . . for in talking of any thing else we lose time and opportunity: people abroad indeed say the *English* Women are the worst in the World in using an opportunity, they love tittle and Ceremony.

Hippolyta: 'Tis because I warrant opportunities are not so scarce here as abroad, they have more here than they can use: but let people abroad say what they will of *English* Women because they do not know 'em, but what say people at home?

William Wycherley, *The Gentleman-Dancing-Master*, 1672

Willmore: Faith Sir, I am of a Nation, that are of opinion a Woman's Honour is not worth guarding when she has a mind to part with it.

Aphra Behn, *The Rover, or the Banish'd Cavaliers*, 1677

Britannia's daughters, much more fair than nice.

Rev. Edward Young, *Love of Fame*, 1725

But what surprizes more than all the rest is, what I have just now been credibly informed by one of this country, 'Most ladies here, says he, have two faces; one face to sleep in, and another to shew in company: the first is generally reserved for the husband and family at home, the other put on to please strangers abroad: the family face is often indifferent enough, but the out-door one looks something better; this is always made at the toilet, where the looking-glass, and toad-eater sit in council and settle the complexion of the day.'

Oliver Goldsmith, *The Citizen of the World*, 1760–1

Blair asked him why he was fond of staying in England, as he surely could not like John Bull. 'Sir,' said he, 'I hate John Bull, but I love his daughters.'

James Boswell, *Boswell's London Journal*, 14 May 1763, quoting remark by James MacPherson, author of *Fingal*, 1736–96

In England, the garden of Beauty is kept
By a dragon of prudery placed within call;
But so oft this unamiable dragon has slept,
That the garden's but carelessly watched after all.
Oh! they want the wild sweet-briery fence,
Which round the flowers of Erin dwells,
Which warns the touch, while winning the sense,
Nor charms us least, when it most repels.

Thomas Moore, 'We May Roam through this World', *Irish Melodies*, 1807–35

Happy is England, sweet her artless daughters;
Enough their simple loveliness for me.
Enough their whitest arms in silence clinging:
Yet do I often warmly burn to see
Beauties of deeper glance . . .

John Keats, Sonnet, *Happy is England*, 1816

And English women, she thanked God and sighed,
(Some people always sigh in thanking God)
Were models to the universe.

Elizabeth Barrett Browning, *Aurora Leigh*, 1856

It strikes me that an English lady of fifty is apt to become a creature less refined and delicate, so far as her physique goes, than anything that we Western people class under the name of woman. She has an awful ponderosity of frame, not pulpy, like the looser development of our few fat women, but massive with solid beef and streaky tallow; so that (though struggling manfully against the idea) you inevitably think of her as made up of steaks and sirloins. When she walks, her advance is elephantine. When she sits down, it is on a great round space of her Maker's footstool where she looks as if nothing could ever move her. She imposes awe and respect by the muchness of her personality, to such a degree that you probably credit her with far greater moral and intellectual force than she can fairly claim. . . . Without anything positively salient, or actively offensive, or, indeed, unjustly formidable to her neighbors, she has the effect of a seventy-four gun ship in time of peace. . . . Yet somewhere in this enormous bulk, there must be hidden the modest, slender, violet-nature of a girl, whom an alien mass of earthliness has unkindly overgrown. . . . It is a pity that the English violet should grow into such an outrageously developed peony as I have attempted to describe. I wonder whether a middle-aged husband ought to be considered as legally married to all the accretions that have overgrown the slenderness of his bride, since he led her to the altar, and which makes her so much more than he ever bargained for! Is it not a sounder view of the case, that the matrimonial bond cannot be held to include the three-fourths of the wife that had no existence when the ceremony was performed? And, as a matter of conscience, and good morals, ought not an English married pair to insist upon the celebration of a Silver Wedding, at the end of twenty-five years, in order to legalize and mutually appropriate that corporeal growth, of which both parties have individually come into possession since they were pronounced one flesh?

Nathaniel Hawthorne, *Our Old Home*, 1863

The middle-class woman of England, as of America . . . think of her in bulk . . . is potentially the greatest money-spending machine in the world.

Harley Granville Barker, *The Madras House*, 1910

Language

So now they have made our English tongue a gallimaufry or hodgepodge of all other speeches.

Edmund Spencer, *The Shepherd's Calendar*, Letter to Gabriel Harvey, 1579

The English is rather a hissing than a harsh language, and perhaps this was the characteristic to which Charles V. alluded when he said it was fit to speak to birds in.

Robert Southey, *Letters from England, by Don Manuel Alvarez Espriella*, 1807

The world was made before the English language, and seemingly upon a different design.

Robert Louis Stevenson, attrib.

Is it affection or impotence of the English that they can make no attempt to pronounce any language but their own.

James Joyce, Letter to Stanislaus Joyce, 13 November 1906

When an Englishman travels abroad the greatest gift and contribution he takes with him is his language. You may take it from me that if I had not known English from the merciful spread of the language by the English traveller I wouldn't have written a word for print in my life.

Joseph Conrad, Letter to Hugh Walpole, 1908

The English language isn't up to what I think.

John Galsworthy, *Exiled*, 1929

I would make all boys learn English; and then I would let the clever ones learn Latin as an honour and Greek as a treat. But the only thing I would whip them for is not knowing English. I would whip them hard for that.

Sir Winston Churchill, *My Early Life*, 1930

But I'm not original. The only way I could truly say I was original is if I created the English language. I did, man, but they don't believe me.

Lenny Bruce, 'Performing and the Art of Comedy', in *The Essential Lenny Bruce*, 1973 – before 1966

Aberford

Thence to Aberford, whose beginning
Came from buying drink with pinning;
Poor they are and very needy
Yet of liquor too much greedy;
Have they never so much plenty,
Belly makes their purses empty.

Richard Brathwaite, *Barnabees Journall*, 1638

Adlestrop

Yes. I remember Adlestrop –
The name, because one afternoon
Of heat the express-train drew up there
Unwontedly. It was late June.

The steam hissed. Someone cleared his throat
No one left and no one came
On the bare platform. What I saw
Was Adlestrop – only the name

And willows, willow-herbs, and grass,
And meadowsweet, and haycocks dry,
No whit less still and lonely fair
Than the high cloudlets in the sky.

And for that minute a blackbird sang
Close by, and round him, mistier,
Farther and farther, all the birds
Of Oxfordshire and Gloucestershire.

Edward Thomas, 'Adlestrop' – *Poems*, 1917

Aldborough

For situation right safe and very pleasant within *Slaughden vale*, where from the East the sea, and from the West the river beateth. . . . Now it is an harbour verie commodious for sailers and fishermen, and thereby well frequented, and acknowledgeth the Ocean sea to bee favourable unto it, how spitefull soever and malicious it is to other townes in this coast.

William Camden, *Britain*, 1610
(Philemon Holland's translation)

I grant indeed that fields and flocks have charms
For him that grazes or for him that farms;
But when amid such pleasing scenes I trace
The poor laborious Natives of the place,

And see the mid-day sun, with fervid ray,
On their bare heads and dewy temples play;
While some, with feebler heads and fainter hearts,
Deplore their fortune, yet sustain their parts:
Then shall I dare these real ills to hide
In tinsel trappings of poetic pride?

No; cast by Fortune on a frowning coast,
Which neither groves nor happy valleys boast;
Where other cares than those the Muse relates,
And other Shepherds dwell with other Mates;
By such examples taught, I paint the Cot,
As Truth will paint it, and as Bards will not: . . .

Lo! where the heath, with withering brake grown o'er,
Lends the light turf that warms the neighbouring poor;
From thence a length of burning sand appears,
Where the thin harvest waves its wither'd ears;
Rank weeds, that every art and care defy,
Reign o'er the land, and rob the blighted rye;
There thistles stretch their prickly arms afar,
And to the ragged infant threaten war;
There poppies nodding, mock the hope of toil;
There the blue bugloss paints the sterile soil;
Hardy and high, above the slender sheaf,
The slimy mallow waves her silky leaf;
O'er the young shoot the charlock throws a shade,
And clasping tares cling round the sickly blade;
With mingled tints the rocky coasts abound,
And a sad splendour vainly shines around.

George Crabbe, *The Village*, 1783

All-Hallows-on-Sea

Allhallows-on-sea . . . looked . . . as though it was built for fun, and something happened to frighten the revellers away.

Norman Shrapnel, *A View of the Thames*, 1977

Ambleside

Ambleside looked excessively beautiful as we came out – like a village in another country.

Dorothy Wordsworth, *Journal*, 17 December 1801

Ambleside Waterfall

The different falls have as different characters; the first darting down the slate-rock like an arrow; the second spreading out like a fan – the third dashed into a mist – and the one on the other side of the rock a sort of mixture of all these. We afterwards moved away a space, and saw nearly the whole more wild, streaming silvery through the trees. What astonished me more than any thing is the tone, the coloring, the slate, the stone, the moss, the rock-weed; or, if I may so say, the intellect, the countenance of such places. The space, the magnitude of mountains and waterfalls are well imagined before one sees them; but this countenance or intellectual tone must surpass every imagination and defy any remembrance. I shall learn poetry here, and shall henceforth write more than ever, for the abstract endeavour of being able to add a mite to that mass of beauty which is harvested from these grand materials, by the finest spirits, and put into etherial existence for the relish of one's fellows. I cannot think with Hazlitt that these scenes make man appear little. I never forgot my nature so completely – I live in the eye; and my imagination, surpassed, is at rest.

John Keats, Letter to Thomas Keats, 25–27 June 1818

Ashurst Forest

On the road to Uckfield you cross Ashurst Forest, which is a heath with here and there a few birch scrubs upon it, verily the most villainously ugly spot I ever saw in England. This lasts you for five miles, getting, if possible, uglier and uglier all the way, till, at last, as if barren soil, nasty spewy gravel, heath and even that stunted, were not enough, you see some rising spots, which instead of trees, present you with black, ragged, hideous rocks. There may be Englishmen who wish to see the coast of *Nova Scotia*. They need not go to sea; for it is here to the life.

William Cobbett, *Rural Rides*, 8 January 1822

Avon

Who took away our counties
So rolling, wild, and wide,
And called them after posh hotels,
Thamesdown and Humberside?

And where on earth is Avon?
Can it be holding yet
The lovely limestone church towers
Of what was Somerset?

John Betjeman, in *Spectator*, 6 October 1979

River Avon

'You English boast so of the things you have got at home,' said she. 'Why, I have seen your River Avon that you make so much of. I stood by the Avon under Warwick Castle, and I said to my husband that it was a mighty small thing to be talked of at such a distance. Why, if I had been ten years younger, I could almost have jumped over it.'

I told her that I believe the Avon was not so

celebrated for the quantity of water in it as on some other accounts.

Harriet Martineau, *Retrospect of Western Travel*, 1838

Bagshot-Heath (and Windsor Forest)

Those that despise Scotland, and the north part of England, for being full of vast and barren land, may take a view of this part of Surrey, and look upon it as a foil to the beauty of the rest of England; . . . here is a vast tract of land, some of it within seventeen or eighteen miles of the capital city; which is not only poor, but even quite sterile, given up to barrenness, horrid and frightful to look on, not only good for little but good for nothing; much of it is a sandy desert, and one may frequently be put in mind here of Arabia Deserta, where the winds raise the sands so as to overwhelm whole caravans of travellers, cattle and people together; for in passing this heath, in a windy day, I was so far in danger of smothering with the clouds of sand, which were raised by the storm, that I cou'd neither keep it out of my mouth, nose, or eyes; and when the wind was over, the sand appear'd spread over the adjacent fields of the forest some miles distant, so as that it ruins the very soil.

Daniel Defoe, *A Tour through the Whole Island of Great Britain*, 1724–7

Banbury

The loud pure wives of Banbury.

Ben Jonson, *The Gypsies Metamorphos'd – a Masque*, 1621

In my progresse, travelling Northward . . .
To *Banbery* came I, O prophane one!
Where I saw a Puritane-one
Hanging of his Cat on Monday
For killing of a Mouse on Sunday.

Richard Brathwaite, *Barnabees Journall*, 1638

Barnet

This Barnet is a place of great resort,
And commonly, upon the market days,
Here all the country gentlemen appoint
A friendly meeting; some about affairs
Of consequence and profit – bargain, sale,
And to confer with chapmen; some for pleasure,
To match their horses, wager on their dogs,
Or try their hawks; some to no other end
But only meet good company, discourse,
Dine, drink, and spend their money.

Thomas Heywood, *The English Traveller*, *c.* 1633

Barnet . . . seemes to be a very sharpe aire, its a large place and the houses are made commodious to entertain the Company that comes to drink the waters, which certainly if they be at paines to go once and see would have but little stomach to drink them.

Celia Fiennes, *Journeys*, 1697

Basingstoke

Some word that teems with hidden meaning – like Basingstoke.

Sir W.S. Gilbert, *Ruddigore*, 1887

Of Basingstoke in Hampshire
The claims to fame are small: –
A derelict canal
And a cream and green Town Hall.

At each week-end the 'locals'
Line the Market Square,
And as the traffic passes,
They stand and stand and stare.

'Leslie Thomas [John Arlott]', 'Basingstoke', in *Landmarks*, ed. G. Rostrevor Hamilton and John Arlott, 1943

Bath

A common phrase long used here hath beene,
And by prescription now some credit hath:
That divers Ladies comming to the Bathe,
Come chiefely but to see, and to be seene.
But if I should declare my conscience briefely,
I cannot thinke that is their Arrant chiefely.
For as I heare that most of them have dealt,
They chiefely came to feele, and to be felt.

Sir John Harington, *Of going to Bathe*, *c.* 1590s

Seated it is low in a plaine, and the same not great; environed round with hilles almost all of one height, out of which certaine rilles of fresh river waters continually descend into the City, to the great commoditie of the Citizens. Within the Citie it selfe there buble and boile up three springs of hote water, of a blewish or sea colour, sending up from them thin vapours, and a kind of strong sent withall, by reason that the water is drilled and strained through veines of Brimstone and a clamy kind of earth called *Bitumen*. Which springs are very medicinable and of great vertue to cure bodies over-charged and benummed (as it were) with corrupt humors: For, by their heat they procure sweat, and subdue the rebellious stubbernesse of the said humors.

William Camden, *Britain*, 1610
(Philemon Holland's translation)

We came before night to the *Bath*. Where I presently stepped out with my landlord and saw the baths with people in them. They are not so large as I expected but yet pleasant and the town most of stone and clean though the streets generally narrow. I home. . . .

Up at 4 a'clock being by appointment called up to the Cross *Bath* where we were carried after one another myself and wife and Betty Turner *Willet* and *WH*. And by and by though we designed to have done before company came much company came very fine ladies and the manner pretty enough only methinks it cannot be clean to go so many bodies together in to the same water. Good conversation among them that are acquainted here and stay together. Strange to see how hot the water is and in some places though this is the most temperate bath the springs so hot as the feet not to endure. But strange to see what women and men herein that live all the season in these waters that cannot but be parboiled and look like the creatures of the Bath. Carried back wrap in a sheet and in a chair home and there one after another thus carried (I staying above two hours in the water) home to bed sweating for an hour and by and by comes music to play to me extraordinary good as ever I heard at London almost anywhere.

Samuel Pepys, *Diary*, 12–13 June 1668

Bath, where such crowds of you stew in so little a pipkin; where you broil upon the earth, parboil in the water, and breathe the composition of gun-powder; or were nothing extraordinary in your soil, your climate, or the season of the year, where you have pretty ladies enough to set you all on fire . . . for I hear you have a mint at the Bath for scandal, as we have here for money.

Thomas Brown, *Letter to His Honoured Friend Mr Baynard, at the Bath*, 6 July 1699

Bath, . . . which, more like a prison than a place of diversion, scarce gives the company room to converse out of the smell of their own excrements, and where the very city it self may be said to stink like a general common-shore.

Daniel Defoe, *A Tour through the Whole Island of Great Britain*, 1724–7

They may say what they will, but it does one ten times more good to leave Bath than to go to it.

Horace Walpole, Letter to George Montagu, 22 October 1766

Of all the gay Places the World can afford,
By Gentle and Simple for Pastime ador'd,
Fine Balls, and fine Concerts, fine Buildings, and Springs,
Fine Walks, and fine Views, and a Thousand fine Things,
Not to mention the sweet Situation and Air,
What Place, my dear Mother, with *Bath* can compare?
Let *Bristol* for Commerce and Dirt be renown'd,
At *Sal'sbury* Pen Knives and Scissars be ground;
The Towns of *Devizes*, of *Bradford*, and *Frome*,
May boast that they better can manage the Loom;
I believe that they may; – but the World to refine,
In Manners, in Dress, in Politeness to shine,
O Bath! – let the Art, let the Glory be thine.
I'm sure I have travell'd our Country all o'er
And ne'er was so civilly treated before; . . .
You never can go, my dear Mother, where you
So much have to see, and so little to do.

Christopher Anstey, *The New Bath Guide*, 4th edn, 1767

Yet in searching about I had better Success,
For I got to a Place where the Ladies undress:
Thinks I to myself, they are after some Fun,
And I'll see what they're doing as sure as a Gun;
So I peep'd at the Door, and I saw a great Mat
That cover'd a Table, and got under that;
And laid myself down there, as snug and as still,
(As a body may say) like a Thief in a Mill:
And of all the fine Sights I have seen, my dear Mother,
I never expect to behold such another:
How the Ladies did giggle and set up their Clacks,
All the while an old Woman was rubbing their Backs!
Oh 'twas pretty to see them all put on their Flannels,
And then take the Water, like so many Spaniels.
And tho' all the while it grew hotter and hotter,
They swam, just as if they were hunting an Otter;
'Twas a glorious Sight to behold the Fair Sex
All wading with Gentlemen up to their Necks,
And view them so prettily tumble and sprawl
In a great smoaking Kettle as big as our Hall:
And To-Day many Persons of Rank and Condition
Were boil'd by Command of an able Physician: . . .
But what is surprizing, no Mortal e'er view'd
Any one of the Physical Gentlemen stew'd;
Since the Day that King BLADUD first found out the Bogs,
And thought them so good for himself and his Hogs,
Not one of the Faculty ever has try'd
These excellent Waters to cure his own Hide.

Ibid.

*The same artist who planned the Circus, has likewise projected a Crescent; when that is finished, we shall probably have a Star; and those who are living thirty years hence, may, perhaps, see all the signs of the Zodiac exhibited in architecture at Bath . . . but the rage of building has laid hold on such a number of adventurers, that one sees new houses starting up in every out-let and every corner of Bath; contrived without judgment, executed without solidity, and stuck together with so little regard to plan and propriety, that the different lines of the new rows and buildings interfere with, and intersect one another in every different angle of conjunction. They look like the wreck of streets and squares disjointed by an earthquake, which hath broken the ground into a variety of holes and hillocks; or, as if some Gothic devil had stuffed them altogether in a bag, and left them to stand higgledy piggledy, just as chance directed. What sort of a monster Bath will become in a few years, with those growing excrescences, may be easily conceived: but the want of beauty and proportion is not the worst effect of these new mansions; they are built so slight, with the soft crumbling stone found in this neighbourhood, that I shall never sleep quietly in one of them, when it blowed (as the sailors say) a cap-full of wind.

Tobias Smollett, *Humphrey Clinker*, 1771
('Matthew Bramble's' comments)

*Instead of that peace, tranquility, and ease, so necessary to those who labour under bad health, weak nerves, and irregular spirits; here we have nothing but noise, tumult, and hurry; with the fatigue and slavery of maintaining a ceremonial, more stiff, formal, and oppressive, than the etiquette of a German elector. A national hospital it may be, but one would imagine that none but lunatics are admitted.

Ibid.

They were disputing what to call the new Buildings here by the Crescent – & what were their Merits; – a Gentleman observed they were *good to break the Wind* which blew so strong from that Corner: Let us then said Mr James call them *Cardamum Buildings.*

Hester Lynch Thrale/Piozzi, *Thraliana*,
5 November 1787

The very idea of going to Bath at full season, when I cannot take a glass of water but in a crowd, frightens me so much, that I am sure the crowd would do me more *harm* than the waters would do me *good.*

Edmund Burke, Letter to William Windham,
9 January 1797

and Bristol

King Bladud once perceived his hogs
A wallowing in these steaming bogs,
From whence arise salubrious springs,
Twice honour'd by the best of kings.

He drove them hence in mighty wrath,
And built the stately town of Bath: –
The hogs thus banish'd by their prince,
Have liv'd in Bristol ever since.

Impromptu by an Alderman at a public dinner in Bath at which members of the Bristol Corporation were present, ed. Charles Stokes Carey, *A Commonplace Book of Epigrams*, 1872

The first view of Bath in fine weather does not answer my expectations; I think I see more distinctly through rain. The sun was got behind everything, and the appearance of the place from the top of Kingsdown was all vapour, shadow, smoke, and confusion.

Jane Austen, Letter to Cassandra Austen,
5 May 1801

I hate Bath. There is a stupid sameness, notwithstanding the beauties of its buildings.

Benjamin Robert Haydon, *Diary*, August 1809

In such a place as Bath, *any* little *lion* makes a stir.

Thomas Moore, *Diary*, 19 March 1819

To me, one of the most disagreeable places in the world.

Sydney Smith, Letter to Edward Davenport, 1820

*'Anybody here?' inquired Dowler, suspiciously.
'Anybody! The *elite* of Ba—ath. Mr Pickwick, do you see the lady in the gauze turban?'
'The fat old lady?' inquired Mr Pickwick, innocently.
'Hush, my dear sir — nobody's fat or old in Ba—ath. . . . '

Charles Dickens, *The Posthumous Papers of the Pickwick Club*, 1837

*'Have you drank the waters, Mr Weller?' inquired his companion, as they walked towards the High Street.

'Once,' replied Sam.

'What did you think of 'em, sir?'

'I thought they wos particklery unpleasant,' replied Sam.

'Ah,' said Mr John Smauker, 'you disliked the killibeate taste, perhaps?'

'I don't know much about that 'ere,' said Sam, 'I thought they'd a wery strong flavour o' warm flat irons.'

Ibid.

The great metropolis of that second-class gentility with which watering-places are chiefly populated.

Nathaniel Hawthorne, *Our Old Home*, 1863

Like a queen enchanted who may not laugh or weep
Glad at heart, and guarded from change and care like ours,
Girt about with beauty by days and nights that creep
Soft as breathless ripples that softly shoreward sweep,
Lies the lovely city whose grace no grief deflowers.
Age and grey forgetfulness, time that shifts and veers,
Touch not thee, our fairest, whose charm no rival nears
Hailed as England's Florence of one whose praise gives grace,
Landor, once thy lover, a name that love reveres:
Dawn and noon and sunset are one before thy face. . . .
City lulled asleep by the chime of passing years
Sweeter smiles thy rest than the radiance round thy peers;

Only love and lovely remembrance here have place
Time on thee lies lighter than music on men's ears;
Dawn and noon and sunset are one before thy face.

A.C. Swinburne, 'A Ballad of Bath', *Poems and Ballads*, 3rd Series, 1889

Not but what Bath beguiles me. Taste and measure
Of biscuit-coloured stone in curve and square,

The inference that life is either leisure
Or convalescence and that self-respect
Is not so much a duty as a treasure

And that due exercise of intellect
Denotes the gentleman and that, as Lord
Chesterfield put it, for the Life Correct

Each action at the ball or at the board
Or doubtless in the bed should always be
In minuet time: all this can afford

Me gentle pleasure, though not for long. For me
The Eighteenth Century, like Ovid's Rome,
Makes a fine show for sightseers to see

But never a context where I feel at home.
But let me take my Bath this winter day
In would-be minuet time through the foam

And steam of many bodies, a mixed display
Of history where the age of different ages
Seems relative. . . .

Louis MacNeice, *Autumn Sequel*, Canto XXI, 1953

Proud city of Bath, with your crescents and squares
Your hoary old Abbey and playbills and chairs,
Your plentiful chapels where preachers would preach
(And a different doctrine expounded in each)
Your gallant assemblies where squires took their daughters,
Your medicinal springs where their wives took the waters,
The terraces trim and the comely young wenches,
The cobbled back streets with their privies and stenches –
How varied and human did Bath then appear
As the roar of the Avon rolled up from the weir.

In those days no doubt there was not so much taste
But now there's so much it has all gone to waste
In working out methods of cutting down cost –
So that mouldings, proportion and texture are lost
In a uniform nothingness. (This I first find
In the terrible 'Tech' with its pointed behind.)
Now houses are 'units' and people are digits
And Bath has been planned into quarters for midgets.
Official designs are aggressively neuter
The Puritan work of an eyeless computer.
Goodbye to old Bath! We who loved you are sorry
They're carting you off by developer's lorry.

John Betjeman, 'The Newest Bath Guide', in *A Nip in the Air*, 1947

The Abbey Church
These walls, so full of monument and bust
Show how Bath waters serve to lay the dust.

Dr Harrington, attrib.

Battle

This town of Battle is remarkable for little now, but for making the finest gun-powder, and the best perhaps in Europe.

Daniel Defoe, *A Tour through the Whole Island of Great Britain*, 1724–7

Beaconsfield

. . . Beaconsfield, where Chesterton sat on his R.C.

Dylan Thomas, Letter to Vernon Watkins, 27 July 1944

Beaulieu River

Largest of Forest snakes, by heath and scrog
It stretches in its blue sky-borrowed coat,
For while its tail trails in a cotton bog
It grips with foaming mouth the Solent's throat.

Andrew Young, *Beaulieu River*, in *Speak to the Earth*, 1939

Beckenham

When you get to Beckenham, which is the last parish in Kent, the country begins to assume a cockney-like appearance; all is artificial, and you no longer feel any interest in it.

William Cobbett, *Rural Rides*, 6 September 1823

Bedford

How applicable is the G.I.'s description of Bedford – a cemetery with traffic lights.

Anon. letter-writer, in James Agate, *Ego 8*, 1946

Bedfordshire

Fat folk (whose collops stick to their sides) are generally lazy, whilst leaner people are of more activity.

Thus fruitful countries (as this is for the generality thereof) take to themselves a writ of ease; the principal cause why Bedfordshire affords not any trades peculiar to itself.

Thomas Fuller, *History of the Worthies of England*, 1662

Berkshire

Berkshire . . . may be fancied in a form like a lute lying along, whose belly is towards the west, while the narrow neck or long handle is extended towards the east.

Thomas Fuller, *History of the Worthies of England*, 1662

Beverley

The town did not please me quite so well as formerly – It appeared so diminutive; and, when I found that many of the inhabitants had lived in the same houses ever since I left it, I could not help wondering how they could thus have vegetated, whilst I was running over a world of sorrow, snatching at pleasure, and throwing off prejudices.

Mary Wollstonecraft, Letter to Gilbert Imlay, 14 June 1795

Saw the Minster – a pretty, clean building, but injured very much with Grecian architecture.

Dorothy Wordsworth, *Journal*, 26 July 1802

Bexhill

Filthy hole, dull and, I gather, purseproud.

James Agate, *Ego 2* (21 August 1934), 1936

Birmingham

What wilt thou doe, black *Vulcans* noysey Towne,
Old *Bremigham?* lowd Fame to thee affords
A title from the *Make*, not *Use* of *Swords*.

Abraham Cowley, *The Civil War*, Book ii. *c.* 1643

The longest chapter in *Deuteronomy* has not curses enow for an Anti-Bromingham.

John Dryden *To The Reader – Absalom and Achitophel*, 1681

Sheffield and Birmingham, whose redd'ning fields,
Rise and enlarge their suburbs.

John Dyer, *The Fleece*, 1757

Queen of the sounding Anvil! Aston thee,
And Edgebaston, with hospitable Shade
And rural Pomp invest. O! warn thy Sons,
when, for a Time, their Labours they forget,
With no licentious Boldness to invade
These peaceful Solitudes.

Richard Jago, *Edge-hill*, 1767

Far resounding BIRMINGHAM, the boast,
The growing LONDON of the MERCIAN realm;
. . . the town, the mart
Of rich inventive Commerce. Science there
Leads her enlighten'd sons, to guide the hand
Of the prompt artist, and with great design
Plan the vast engine, whose extended arms,
Heavy and huge, on the soft-seeming breath
Of the hot steam, rise slowly; – till, by cold
Condens'd, it leaves them soon, with clanging roar,
Down, down, to fall precipitant. . . .
our second London. . . .
While neighbouring cities waste the fleeting hours,
Careless of art, and knowledge, and the smile
Of every Muse, expanding BIRMINGHAM,
Illum'd by intellect, as gay in wealth,
Commands her aye-accumulating walls,
From month to month, to climb the adjacent hills;
Creep on the circling plains, now here, now there,
Divergent – change the hedges, thickets, trees,
Upturn'd, disrooted, into mortar'd piles,
The street elongate, and the statelier square.

Anna Seward, *Colebrook Dale*, *c.* 1784

Birmigham was less agreeable than I left it 13 years ago, but far grander; the People more rich and more insolent of Course – God send 'em ten times more so! They will not now shew their Manufactures.

Hester Lynch Thrale/Piozzi, *Thraliana*, September 1787

I am still giddy, dizzied with the hammering of presses, the clatter of engines, and the whirling of wheels; my head aches with the multiplicity of infernal noises, and my eyes with the light of infernal fires, – I may add, my heart also, at the sight of so many human beings employed in infernal occupations, and looking as if they were never destined for anything better. Our earth was designed to be a seminary for young angels, but the devil has certainly fixed upon this spot for his own nursery-garden and hot-house. . . . When we look at gold, we do not think of the poor slaves who dug it from the caverns of the earth; but I shall never think of the wealth of England, without remembering that I have been in the mines. Not that the labourers repine at their lot; it is not the least evil of the system, that they are perfectly well satisfied to be poisoned mind and body. . . . I cannot pretend to say, what is the consumption here of two-legged beasts of labour; commerce sends in no returns of its killed and wounded. Neither can I say that the people look sickly, having seen no other complexion in the place than what is composed of oil and dust smoke-dried. Every man whom I meet stinks of train-oil and emery. Some I have seen with red eyes and green hair; the eyes affected by the fires to which they are exposed, and the hair turned by the brass works. You would not however, discover any other resemblance to a triton in them for water is an element with the use of which, except to supply steam engines, they seem to be unacquainted.

The noise of Birmingham is beyond description; the hammers seem never to be at rest. The filth is sickening. . . . It is active and moving, a living principle of mischief, . . . I feel as if my throat wanted sweeping like an English chimney. Think not, however, that I am insensible to the wonders of the place.

Robert Southey, *Letters from England, by Don Manuel Alvarez Espriella*, 1807

There are, I can well believe, thousands to whom Birmingham is another name for domestic peace, and for a reasonable share of sunshine. But in my case, who have passed through Birmingham a hundred times, it always happened to rain, except once; and that once the Shrewsbury mail carried me so rapidly away, that I had not time to examine the sunshine, or see whether it might not be some gilt Birmingham counterfeit; for you know, men of Birmingham, that you *can* counterfeit – such is your cleverness – all things in heaven and earth, from Jove's thunder-bolts down to a tailor's bodkin.

Thomas de Quincey, *Autobiography*, 1834–53

*They came from Birmingham, which is not a place to promise much, you know, Mr Weston. One has not great hopes from Birmingham. I always say there is something direful in the sound.

Jane Austen, *Emma*, 1816 (Mrs Elton)

*Men of Birmingham or Manchester, – hard men, seemingly knit up in one thought, whose talk is of free trade.

Charlotte Bronte, *The Professor*, 1847

This is next to Liverpool the finest of the manufacturing towns: the situation high and good, the principal street capital, the shops good, cabs splendid, and the Music Hall unequalled by any Greek building in England that I have seen.

Matthew Arnold, Letter to his wife, 2 December 1851

Then came the journey up to London through Birmingham and the Black District, another lesson which needed much more to be rightly felt. The plunge into darkness lurid with flames; the sense of unknown horror in this weird gloom which then existed nowhere else, and never had existed before, except in volcanic craters; the violent contrast between this dense, smoky, impenetrable darkness, and the soft green charm that one glided into, as one emerged – the revelation of an unknown society of the pit – made a boy uncomfortable, though he had no idea that Karl Marx was standing there waiting for him. . . . The Black District was a practical education, but it was infinitely far in the distance. The boy ran away from it, as he ran away from everything he disliked.

Henry Adams, *The Education of Henry Adams*, 1906

It is a disgusting town with villas and slums and ready-made clothes shops and Chambers of Commerce.

Evelyn Waugh, *Diary*, 11 September 1925

Behind him the streets run away between the proud glass of shops,
Cubical scent-bottles artificial legs arctic foxes and electrical mops,
But beyond this centre the slumward vista thins like a diagram:
There, unvisited, are Vulcan's forges who doesn't care a thinker's damn.

Splayed outwards through the suburbs houses, houses for rest
Seducingly rigged by the builder, half-timbered houses with lips pressed
So tightly and eyes staring at the traffic through bleary haws
And only a six-inch gap of the racing earth in their concrete claws;
In these houses men as in a dream pursue the Platonic Forms
With wireless and cairn terriers and gadgets approximating to the fickle norms
And endeavour to find God and score one over the neighbour
By climbing tentatively upward on jerry-built beauty and sweated labour.

Louis MacNeice, *Birmingham*, October 1933

Birmingham is not at first sight the most attractive of English cities. . . . To the traveller going north, after the ancient splendours of Warwick and the eighteenth century elegance of Leamington, the place appears as the beginning of a new and sinister world, the frontier station of the Land of Mordor.

E.R. Dodds, *Missing Persons*, 1977

between Birmingham and Wolverhampton

The face of the country as we advanced was more hideous than can be described, uncultivated, black and smoking. I asked the coachman from whence the smoke proceeded, and he told me the whole earth beneath us was on fire; some coal-mines had taken fire many years ago, and still continued to burn. 'If you were to travel this road by night, sir,' said he, 'you would see the whole country a-fire, and might fancy you were going to hell!'

Robert Southey, *Letters from England, by Don Manuel Alvarez Espriella*, 1807

Blackpool

Though about fifty houses grace the sea-bank, it does not merit the name of a village, because they are scattered to the extent of a mile. About six of these front the sea, with an aspect exactly west, and are appropriated for the reception of company; the others, which are the dwellings of the inhabitants, chiefly form the background.

Anon., *A Guide to all the Watering and Sea-bathing Places*, c. 1810

Blackpool is an ugly town, mean in its vastness, but its dancing-halls present a beautiful spectacle. . . . This is the huge flower that springs from the horrid bed of the factory system. Human creatures are half-timers for this; they are knocked up at 5.30 A.M. in winter for this; they go on strike for this; they endure eleven months and three weeks for this. They all earn their living by hard and repulsive work, and here they are in splendour! They will work hard at joy till they drop from exhaustion.

Arnold Bennett, *Paris Nights*, 1913

*I don't like the place – can't stand it at any price. Without its blatancy it would be a bleak and miserable thing huddled in front of a grey and uninspiring sea. With it, it is the crown of a crazy, cowardly age that can't bear to be alone, or to be still, or to be silent.

Howard Spring, *My Son, My Son*, 1938

Blenheim House

See, Sir, see here's the grand approach;
This way is for his Grace's coach;
There lies the bridge, and here's the clock;
Observe the lion and the cock,
The spacious court, the colonnade,
And mark how wide the wall is made!
The chimneys are so well design'd
They never smoke in any wind,
The gallery's contriv'd for walking,
The windows to retire and talk in!
The council chamber for debate, –
And all the rest are rooms of state.
Thanks Sir, cry'd I: 'tis very fine
But where d'ye sleep, or where d'ye dine?
I find by all you have been telling
That 'tis a house, but not a dwelling.

Anon., in *The English Martial*, 1806

The Minnows, as through this vast arch they pass
Cry – How like *Whales* we look! Thanks to your *Grace*.

Anon., 'On Viewing the Bridge at Blenheim', *The English Martial*, 1806

A quarry of stone that looked at a distance like a great house.

Horace Walpole, Letter to George Montagu, 20 May 1736

We went to Blenheim and saw all Vanbrugh's quarries, all the acts of parliament and gazettes on the duke in inscriptions, and all the old flock chairs, wainscot tables, and gowns and petticoats of queen Anne, that old Sarah could crowd among blocks of marble. It looks like the palace of an auctioneer, who has been chosen king of Poland, and furnished his apartments with obsolete trophies, rubbish that nobody bid for, and a dozen pictures, that he had stolen from the inventories of different families. The place is as ugly as the house, and the bridge, like the beggars at the old duchess's gate, begs for a drop of water, and is refused.

Horace Walpole, Letter to George Montagu, 19 July 1760

Blenheim Park

Its natural features are not striking; but Art has effected such wonderful things that the uninstructed visitor would never guess that nearly the whole scene was but the embodied thought of a human mind. A skilful painter hardly does more for his blank sheet of canvass, than the landscape-gardener, the planter, the arranger of trees, has done for the monotonous surface of Blenheim; making the most of every undulation; flinging down a hillock, a big lump of earth out of a giant's hand, wherever it was needed; putting in beauty as often as there was a niche for it; opening vistas to every point that deserved to be seen, and throwing a veil of impenetrable foliage around what ought to be hidden; – and then, to be sure, the lapse of a century has softened the harsh outline of man's labors, and has given the place back to Nature again with the addition of what consummate science could achieve. . . . Positively, the garden of Eden cannot have been more beautiful than this private garden of Blenheim.

Nathaniel Hawthorne, *Our Old Home*, 1863

Do not you remember the story my father used to tell us, when we were children, of how his friend, the old Duke of Marlborough went to dine with a neighbour, a poor clergyman, whose house was small, and whose fires were low, and whose dinner was bad, and when the Duke drove back to Blenheim, and entered that magnificent hall, he said with a plaintive sigh, 'Well! home is home, be it never so homely?'

Emily Eden, Letter, 13 March 1840, in *Up the Country*, 1866

Bodmin

Bodmin, which (by illusion if not etymology) a man might, not unaptly, turn into Badham; for of all the towns in Cornwall, I hold none more healthfully situated than Saltash, or more contagiously than this. . . . Their back houses, of more necessary than cleanly service, as kitchens, stables, etc., are climbed into by steps, and their filth by every great shower washed down through their houses into the streets.

Richard Carew, *A Survey of Cornwall*, late sixteenth century

Ill-built, yet not worse built than situated, being shadowed by a hill to the south; and to complete the list of ill contrivances, their water is brought through the common burial place.

Robert Southey, *Letters from England, by Don Manuel Alvarez Espriella*, 1807

Bognor

Then madly, gladly out to Sea we thrust,
Gainst windes and stormes and many a churlish Gust:
By *Kingston chappell*, and by *Rustington*,
By little *Hampton*, and by *Middleton*,
To *Bognores* fearefull Rockes, which hidden lie
Two miles into the Sea, some wet, some dry.

John Taylor, *A Discovery by Sea*, 1623

Bugger Bognor.

George V, attributed, *c.* 1928
(on being told, when very ill, that he would soon be well enough to go there)

Boston

Solid men of Boston make no long orations;
Solid men of Boston drink no long potations;
Solid men of Boston go to bed at sundown;
Never lose your way like the loggerheads of London.

Anon., 'Billy Pitt and the Farmer', in *Debrett's Asylum for Fugitive Pieces*, 1786

The whole scene made an odd impression of bustle, and sluggishness, and decay, and a remnant of wholesome life; and I could not but contrast it with the mighty and populous activity of our own Boston, which was once the feeble infant of this old English town; – the latter, perhaps, almost stationary ever since that day, as if the birth of such an offspring had taken away its own principle of growth. I . . . began to feel at home in this good old town, for its very name's sake, as I never had before felt, in England.

. . . The crooked streets and narrow lanes reminded me much of Hanover-street, Ann-street, and other portions of the North End of our American Boston, as I remember that picturesque region in my boyish days. It is not unreasonable to suppose that the local habits and recollections of the first settlers may have had some influence on the physical character of the streets and houses, in the New England metropolis; at any rate, here is a similar intricacy of bewildering lanes, and numbers of old, peaked and projecting-storied dwellings, such as I used to see there. It is singular what a home-feeling, and sense of kindred, I derived from this hereditary connection and fancied physiognomical resemblance between the old town and its well-grown daughter, and how reluctant I was, after chill years of banishment, to leave this hospitable place, on that account. . . .

One thing more; – they have a Bunker Hill in the vicinity of their town; and (what could hardly be expected of an English community) seem proud to think that their neighbourhood has given name to our first, and most widely-celebrated, and best-remembered battle-field.

Nathaniel Hawthorne, *Our Old Home*, 1863

St. Botolph's Town! Hither across the plains
And fens of Lincolnshire, in garb austere
There came a Saxon monk, and founded here
A priory, pillaged by marauding Danes,
So that thereof no vestige now remains;
Only a name, that spoken loud and clear,
And echoed in another hemisphere,
Survives the sculptured walls, and painted panes.
St. Botolph's Town! Far over leagues of land
And leagues of sea looks forth its noble tower,
And far around the chiming bells are heard:
So may that sacred name for ever stand
A landmark, and a symbol of the power
That lies concentred in a single word.

Henry Wadsworth Longfellow, *Boston*, 1876

Oh, Boston, Boston, thou hast nought to boast on
But a grand sluice and a high steeple
And a coast as fools are lost on.

Anon.

Bournemouth

Bournemouth on the Sea is a very stupid place; a great moorland covered with furze and low pine woods comes down to the sea-shore, and breaks down towards it in a long sweep of cliff, half sand, half mud.

Matthew Arnold, Letter to his youngest sister, 1849

I decided absolutely against Bournemouth. It was symbolic that I couldn't even get China tea there.

Arnold Bennett, *Journal*, 29 December 1909

I advise you never to come here for a holiday. The

place exists for the sick. They hide the fact as far as possible, but it's like a huge hospital. At every turn you come across invalids being pushed or pulled along. Quite a nice place of course, everything arranged for the comfort of the invalid, sunny sheltered corners and the like, but pah – I shall be glad when I get away.

D.H. Lawrence, Letter to Jessie Chambers, January 1912

Bournemouth is one of the few English towns that one can safely call 'her'.

John Betjeman, *First and Last Loves*, 1960

Bowes (Yorkshire)

At Bowes begins the great grazing country for children. – It is the cheapest part of England, and schools for boys have long been established here, to which tradesmen and even some parents of higher order who think money better than learning, send their children from all the great towns, even from the western provinces, – but London supplies the greater number.

Robert Southey, *Letters from England, by Don Manuel Alvarez Espriella*, 1807

Brentford

Luke:
And pleasure stol'n being sweetest, apprehend
The rapture of being hurried in a Coach
To Brainford, Staines, or Barnet.

Massinger, *The City Madam*, 1658

Brandford's Tedious town,
For dirty streets and white-leg'd chickens known.

John Gay, *An Epistle to the Right Hon. The Earl of Burlington – A Journey to Exeter*, *c.* 1715

Even as thro' Brentford Town, a town of mud,
A herd of bristly swine is pricked along.

James Thomson, *Castle of Indolence*, 1748

The Jews offered my Lord Godolphin, to pay five hundred thousand pounds (and they would have made it a million), if the government would allow them to purchase the town of Brentford, with leave of settling there entirely, with full privileges of trade, &c. The agent from the Jews said, that the affair was already concerted with the chiefs of their brethren abroad; that it would bring the richest of their merchants hither, and of course an addition of above twenty millions of money to circulate in the nation. Lord Molesworth was in the room with Lord Godolphin, when this proposal was made, and as soon as the agent was gone, pressed him to close in with it. Lord Godolphin was not of his opinion. He foresaw, that it would provoke two of the most powerful bodies in the nation, the clergy and the merchants; he gave other reasons too against it, and in fine it was dropped.

Francis Lockier, quoted in Joseph Spence, *Anecdotes*, *c.* 1730

No persons are more solicitous about the preservation of rank than those who have no rank at all. Observe the humurs of a country Christening, and you will find no court in Christendom so ceremonious as the 'quality' of Brentford.

William Shenstone, *Of Men and Manners*, in *Essays on Men and Manners*, – *Works*, 1764 – before 1763

I once reminded him that when Dr Adam Smith was expatiating on the beauty of Glasgow, he had cut him short by saying, 'Pray, Sir, have you ever seen Brentford?' and I took the liberty to add, 'My dear Sir, surely that was *shocking*.' 'Why, then, Sir, (he replied), YOU have never seen Brentford.'

James Boswell, *Life of Johnson*, 1783

Bridgnorth

All on one side like Bridgnorth election.

Shropshire proverb

*'We must all be on one side, like the 'andle of a tin-pot or like Bridgnorth election.'

R.S. Surtees, *Handley Cross*, 1843

Bridlington

Bridlington – is as though somebody had uprooted Hackney Wick and planked it down on Canvey Island. . . . Nothing to do, and nothing to see except ex-repertory actresses trundling about on bicycles.

James Agate, *Ego 9* (29–30 April 1946), 1948

Brighton

Bright Helmston, commonly called Bredhemston, a poor fishing town, old built, and on the very edge of the sea. . . .

The sea is very unkind to this town, and has by its continual encroachments so gain'd upon them, that in a little time more they might reasonably expect it would eat up the whole town, above 100 houses having been devoured by the water in a few years past; they are now obliged to get a brief granted them, to beg money all over England, to raise banks against the water; the expence of which, the brief expresly sayd, will be eight thousand pounds; which if one were to look on the town, would seem to be more than all the houses in it are worth.

Daniel Defoe, *A Tour through the Whole Island of Great Britain*, 1724–7

Till lately it had the name of Brighthelmstone; but, like low persons rising to eminence, who are often ashamed of their origin, it has now assumed the title of Brighton; which certainly has a more genteel sound. . . .

Anon., *A Guide to all the Watering and Sea-bathing Places*, *c.* 1810

*They must all go to Brighton. That is the place to get husbands.

Jane Austen, *Pride and Prejudice*, 1813 (Lydia)

Come to Brighton, my dear fellow . . . let us be off tomorrow; we'll eat currant-tart, and live in chintz and salt-water.

Beau Brummell, remark, *c.* 1810, to Cecil Jenkinson, later Lord Liverpool, recalled in Captain Jesse's *Life of Brummell*, 1844

At brighthelmstone – (I love orthography at length). . . .

Lord Byron, *Detached Thoughts*, 1821–2

As I had not been out of Town for 2 Years or changed the scene my mind became rusty. I had a longing for the Sea shore, a thing I was always accustomed to. I took a place outside & rushed down to Brighton. I rolled in the Sea, shouted like a Savage, & laved my sides like a Bull in a June meadow, – dived, swam, floated, & came out quite refreshed. Brighton will always keep its superiority from its southern situation.

Benjamin Robert Haydon, *Diary*, September 1826

Brighton . . . is still very gay, and full of balls.

Samuel Rogers, Letter to Thomas Moore, 29 January 1829

Sea without ships and, without trees, land
Three miles of glare and a beach without sand.

Horace Smith, quoted in Henry Crabb Robinson, *Diary*, 12 November 1843

*Brighton, a clean Naples with genteel lazzaroni – . . . Brighton, that always looks brisk, gay and gaudy, like a harlequin's jacket. . . .

W.M. Thackeray, *Vanity Fair*, 1847

This (looking from Brighton Pier) is not a grand sea: only an angry curt sea. It seems to *shriek* as it recoils with its pebbles along the beach.

Alfred Lord Tennyson, in Edward Fitzgerald, *Some Recollections of Tennyson's Talk*, *c.* 1852–3

Tell me why on Brighton church you see
  A golden shark display'd?
Unless 'twere aptly meant to be
  An Emblem of its trade?
Nor can the truth so well be told
  In any other way
Brighton's the shark that lives on gold
  The company its prey.

Anon., *Epigrams Ancient and Modern*, ed. Rev. J. Booth, 1863

Brighton makes me bilious.

Matthew Arnold, Letter to his mother, 17 May 1867

I haven't made a study of the question, but I certainly think it is high time Brighton was relieved.

Horatio Bottomley, Remark when questioned on the Jewish National Home, December 1918

This thought came to me standing in a Brighton street the other day from which one sees the downs. Mankind was fuming & fretting & shouldering each other about; the down was smoothly sublime. But I thought this street frenzy is really the better of the two – the more courageous. One must put up a fight against passive turf, with an occasional snail, & a swell in the ground which it takes 2,000 years to produce. But I daresay the thought was forced upon me: I much prefer the downs myself.

Virginia Woolf, *Diary*, 26 August 1922

The sole thing I object to in Brighton is the penny-in-the-slot machines on the piers. Brighton has character, as the man who made its fame had character – but *his* character was evil.

Arnold Bennett, *Journal 1929*, 1930

Brighton is living and dying to itself. My waiter at dinner last night said, 'You won't see me tomorrow, sir: I'm going for my summer holidays.' I asked where he was going. 'Brighton,' he replied.

James Agate, *Ego 5* (19 July 1942), at Brighton

From the tomb-like cold Pavilion,
Drawing Rooms and Dome,
Regency ghosts are sweeping
Through the town that was their home.

Do they see the plaster peeling,
The fly-blown fluted ceiling
Regency houses tumbled down,
Hove another, *nicer* town,
The Phaeton gone for the family car,
Electric light in the Oyster-bar,
And buses bluing the salt sea-air
Under the trees in Castle Square?

Would they sing to the swing of the dance band,
Sway to the play with the grand-stand,
Swerve in a curve at the ice-rink,
Savour the flavour of a soft drink,
Find this a madder, gladder revel
Than their elegant, arrogant dance with the Devil?

And would they return to Hell by way
Of Brighton beach on a summer's day?
Would they trip with trippers up-to-date
And, Regency ghosts immaculate,
Arm in arm, and devil-may-care
Past the whelk-stalls, through the profanity,
Step
down
the
steep
stone
stair
Into the huddle of hot humanity?

John Arlott, 'Brighton', in *Landmarks*, ed. G. Rostrevor Hamilton and John Arlott, 1943

a side street

*The Castle of this ogress and child-queller was in a steep by-street at Brighton; where the soil was more than usually chalky, flinty, and sterile, and the houses were more than usually brittle and thin; where the small front-gardens had the unaccountable property of producing nothing but marigolds, whatever was sown in them; and where snails were constantly discovered holding on to the street doors, and other public places they were not expected to ornament, with the tenacity of cupping glasses. In the winter-time the air couldn't be got out of the Castle, and in the summer-time it couldn't be got in.

Charles Dickens, *Dombey and Son*, 1847–8

Royal Pavilion

Brighton is a very pleasant place. For a *wen* remarkably so! The *Kremlin*, the very name of which has so long been a subject of laughter all over the country, lies in the gorge of the valley, and amongst the old houses of the town. The grounds, which cannot, I think, exceed a couple or three acres, are surrounded by a wall neither lofty nor good-looking. Above this rise some trees, bad in sorts, stunted in growth, and dirty with smoke. As to the 'palace' as the Brighton newspapers call it, the apartments appear to be all upon the ground floor; and when you see the thing from a distance, you think you see a parcel of *cradle-spits*, of various dimensions, sticking up out of the mouths of so many enormous squat decanters. Take a square box, the sides of which are three feet and a half, and the height a foot and a half. Take a large Norfolk-turnip, cut off the green of the leaves, leave the stalks 9 inches long, tie these round with a string three inches from the top, and put the turnip on the middle of the top of the box. Then take four turnips of half the size, treat them in the same way, and put them on the corners of the box. Then take a considerable number of bulbs of the crown-imperial, the narcissus, the hyacinth, the tulip, the crocus, and others; let the leaves of each have sprouted to about an inch, more or less according to the size of the bulb; put all these, pretty promiscuously, but pretty thickly on the top of the box. Then stand off, and look at your architecture. There! That's '*a Kremlin*!' Only you must cut some church-looking windows in the sides of the box. As to what you ought to put *into* the box, that is a subject far above my cut.

William Cobbett, *Rural Rides*, 10 January 1822

The Pavilion at Brighton is like a collection of stone pumpkins and pepper-boxes. It seems as if the genius of architecture had at once the dropsy and the *megrims*. Any thing more fantastical, with a greater dearth of invention, was never seen. The King's stud (if they were horses of taste) would petition against so irrational a lodging.

William Hazlitt, *Notes of a Journey through France and Italy*, 1826

Bristol

The City wholy Mercantile, as standing neere the famous *Severne*, commodiously for *Ireland* and the Western world: Here I first saw the manner of refining Suggar, & casting it into loaves, where we had collation of Eggs fried in the suggar furnace, together with excellent Spanish Wine; but what was most stupendious to me, was the rock of St. *Vincent*, a little distance from the Towne, the precipice whereof is equal to any thing of that nature I have seene in the most confragose cataracts of the *Alpes*.

John Evelyn, *Diary*, July 1654

The city . . . is in every respect another London that one can hardly know it to stand in the country no more then that. No carts it standing generally on *vaults* only dog carts.

Samuel Pepys, *Diary*, 13 June 1668

Bristol lyes low in a bottom the greatest part of the town, tho' one end of it you have a pretty rise of ground; . . . the buildings of the town are pretty high most of timber work, the streets are narrow and something darkish, because the roomes on the upper storys are moste jutting out, soe contracts the streete and the light; the suburbs are better buildings and more spacious streetes. . . .

This town is a very great tradeing citty as most in England, and is esteemed the largest next London; the river Aven that is flowed up by the sea into the Severn and soe up the Aven to the town, beares shipps and barges up to the key, where I saw the harbour was full of shipps carrying coales and all sorts of commodityes to other parts; the Bridge is built over with houses just as London Bridge is, but its not so bigg or long, there are 4 large arches here; they have little boates which are called Wherryes such as we use on the Thames, soe they use them here to convey persons from place to place; and in many places there are signes to many houses that are not Publick houses just as it is in London; the streetes are well pitch'd and preserved by their useing sleds to carry all things about.

Celia Fiennes, *Journeys*, 1698

The greatest inconveniences of Bristol, are, its situation, and the tenacious folly of its inhabitants.

Daniel Defoe, *A Tour through the Whole Island of Great Britain*, 1724–7

You come in sight of Bristol, the River winding at the bottom of steeper banks to the Town where you see twenty odd Pyramids smoking over the Town (which are Glasshouses) and a vast Extent of Houses red & white. You come first to Old Walls, & over a Bridge built on both sides like London bridge, and as much crowded, with a strange mixture of Seamen, women, children, loaded Horses, Asses, & Sledges with Goods dragging along, all together, without posts to separate them. From thence you come to a Key along the old Wall with houses on both sides, and in the middle of the street, as far as you can see, hundreds of Ships, their Masts as thick as they can stand by one another, which is the oddest & most surprising sight imaginable. This street is fuller of them, than the Thames from London Bridge to Deptford, & at certain times only, the Water rises to carry them out; so that at other times, a Long Street full of ships in the Middle & Houses on both sides looks like a Dream. Passing still along by the River you come to a Rocky way on one Side, overlooking green Hills on the other; On that rocky way rise several white Houses, and over them red rocks, and as you go further, more Rocks above rocks, mixd with green bushes, and of different colourd stone. This at a Mile's end, terminates in the House of the Hot well, whereabouts lye several pretty Lodging Houses open to the River with Walks of Trees. When you have seen the Hills seem to shut upon you & to stop any further way, you go into the House & looking out of the Back door, a vast Rock of 100 foot high, of red, white, green, blue & yellowish Marbles, all blotch'd & variegated strikes you quite in the face, & turning on the left, there opens the River at a vast depth below, winding in & out, & accompanied on both sides with a Continued Range of Rocks up to the Clouds, of a hundred Colours, one behind another, & so to the end of the Prospect quite to the Sea. But the Sea nor the Severn you do not see, the Rocks and River fill the Eye, and terminate the View, much like the broken Scenes behind one another in a Playhouse.

Alexander Pope, Letter to Martha Blount, ?19 November 1739

What friendship can'st thou boast? what honours claim?
To thee each stranger owes an injured name.
What smiles thy sons must in their foes excite –
Thy sons to whom all discord is delight;
From whom eternal mutual railing flows;
Who in each other's crimes their own expose;
Thy sons, though crafty, deaf to wisdom's call;
Despising all men and despised by all;
Sons, while thy cliffs a ditch-like river laves,
Rude as thy rocks and muddy as thy waves;
Of thoughts as narrow as of words immense;
As full of turbulence as void of sense.

Richard Savage, *London and Bristol Delineated*, 1743

I did go to Bristol, the dirtiest great shop I ever saw, with so foul a river, that, had I seen the least appearance of cleanliness, I should have concluded they washed all their linen in it, as they do at Paris.

Horace Walpole, Letter to George Montagu, 22 October 1766

Farewell, Bristolia's dingy piles of brick,
Lovers of mammon, worshippers of trick!
Ye spurned the boy who gave you antique lays,
And paid for learning with your empty praise.
Farewell, ye guzzling aldermanic fools,
By nature fitted for corruption's tools!
I go to where celestial anthems swell;
But you, when you depart, will sink to hell.
Farewell, my mother! – cease, my anguished soul,
Nor let distraction's billows o'er me roll!
Have mercy, Heaven, when I cease to live,
And this last act of wretchedness forgive.

Thomas Chatterton, *Last Verses*, 24 August 1770

We were by no means pleased with our inn at Bristol. 'Let us see now, (said I), how we should describe it.' Johnson was ready with his raillery. 'Describe it, Sir? – Why, it was so bad that Boswell wished to be in Scotland!'

James Boswell, *Life of Johnson* (May 1776), 1783

'Though I have the honour to represent Bristol, I should not like to live there; I should be obliged to be so much *upon my good behaviour*.'

Edmund Burke, quoted in Boswell, *Life of Johnson* (April 1779), 1783

A town remarkable for Burglary, and Turtle; every body's stomach is full of green fat, every bodies house is broken open; all this comes of not hanging people. It is seven years since any one was hung here. How can 100,000 people live together in peace upon such terms?

Sydney Smith, Letter to Lady Grey, 8 November 1828

Broadstairs (and Eastbourne compared)

Charles Dickens, . . . maketh oath and saith, That this Deponent hath been for many years last past in the custom and habit of making certain annual visits (to wit in the months of August, September and October) to a certain seaside dipping, bathing, or watering-place, much frequented by individuals of a lone and quiet temper, and by certain virtuous and monastic fishermen; as also by a gloomy and thoughtful race much given to contemplation and retirement, and commonly known as The Preventive Service – to wit, the Port, Landing, Village, hamlet or town of Broadstairs in the County of Kent. And this Deponent saith that the said Port, Landing, Village, hamlet or town of Broadstairs in the said county, was and is, and to the best of this Deponent's judgement and belief will always be, the chosen retreat and resort of jaded intellect and exhausted nature; being, as this Deponent further saith it is, far removed from the sights and noises of the busy world, and filled with the delicious murmur and repose of the broad ocean; the said broad ocean being (as this Deponent further saith and fearlessly asserteth) the finest feature (when you are off it) in the whole creation.

And this Deponent further saith, That he has been informed and verily believes that there are, roaming the world . . . certain persons, who by reason of their inability to appreciate the many excellencies and unequalled beauties of the said Port, landing, village, hamlet or town of Broadstairs, do falsely and heretically deny the same; and do annually repair to a certain sty, hole, den, and sink of deep disgust called Eastbourne, which, as this Deponent hath been informed and verily believes is a desolate and desert place, inhabited by gulls and sea-Mews, and excessively geological – in points of flints and chalk. And this Deponent further saith that the aforesaid sty, hole, den, and sink of deep disgust called Eastbourne, is, and was, and to the best of this Deponent's judgement and belief will always be, a kind of English Saint Helena, to which stern husbands banish their unwilling and reluctant wives.

Charles Dickens, Letter to W.C. Macready, 7 July 1842

Buckinghamshire

Buckinghamshire, bread and beef
Where if you beat a bush, 'tis odds you start a thief.

Quoted by Michael Drayton, *Poly-Olbion*, 1613–22

Bude

I hear that there are larger waves there than on any other part of the British coast: and must go thither and be alone with God.

Alfred Lord Tennyson, Remark, 1848, in *Alfred Lord Tennyson, a Memoir, by his Son*, 1897

Budleigh Salterton

Charles: You were feckless and irresponsible and morally unstable – I realized that before we left Budleigh Salterton.
Elvira: Nobody but a monumental bore would have thought of having a honeymoon at Budleigh Salterton.
Charles: What's the matter with Budleigh Salterton?
Elvira: I was an eager young bride, Charles – I wanted glamour, and music and romance – all I got was potted palms, seven hours of every day on a damp golf course and a three piece orchestra playing 'Merrie England'.

Noel Coward, *Blithe Spirit*, 1941

Burton on Trent

Say, for what were hop-yards meant
Or why was Burton built on Trent?

A.E. Housman, *A Shropshire Lad*, 1896

Bury St Edmunds

It is crouded with nobility and gentry, and all sorts of the most agreeable company; and as the company invites, so there is the appearance of pleasure upon the very situation; and they that live at Bury, are supposed to live there for the sake of it.

Daniel Defoe, *A Tour through the Whole Island of Great Britain, 1724–7*

From St Edmundsbury to Thetford I had been accompanied by a clergyman who gave me some account of the former town. He said St Edmundsbury had been called 'The Montpellier of England,' from its fine air, and dry soil, and except in particular cases is a most healthy situation. The exceptions are when the constitution labours under complaints of an asthmatic kind, or where there is a tendency to consumption, in such cases the air is too keen. He spoke of the society of the place as being genteel and sociable.

Joseph Farington, *Diary*, 16 August 1812

The Montpelier of England; a place no less remarkable for its ecclesiastical antiquities, than for the polished manners of its inhabitants, and the curious extraneous fossils found in its neighbourhood.

E.D. Clarke, *Travels in Various Countries*, 1824

Even at Ipswich, when I was praising *that place*, the very people of that town asked me if I did not think Bury St. Edmund's the nicest town in the world. Meet them wherever you will, they have all the same boast;

and indeed, as a town *in itself*, it is the neatest place that ever was seen.

William Cobbett, *Rural Rides – Easter Tour*, 22 March 1830

Buxton

Buxton . . . that most delicious fount,
Which men the second Bath of England doe account.

Michael Drayton, *Poly-Olbion*, 'The Sixe and Twentieth Song', 1622

Of Buxton; the wonder to me is that in a nation so full of chronical diseases as we are, such as our scorbuticks, rheumaticks cholicks, and niphriticks, there should be such a fountain of medicine sent from heaven, and no more notice taken of it, or care to make it useful.

Daniel Defoe, *A Tour through the Whole Island of Great Britain*, 1724–7

So in green vales amid her mountains bleak
Buxtonia smiles, the goddess-nymph of Peak;
Deep in warm waves, and pebbly baths she dwells,
And calls Hygeia to her sainted wells. . . .
– Oft by her bubbling founts, and shadowy domes,
In gay undress the fairy legion roams,
Their dripping palms in playful malice fill,
Or taste with ruby lip the sparkling rill;
Crowd round her baths, and, bending o'er the side,
Unclasp'd their sandals, and their zones untied,
Dip with gay fear the shuddering foot undress'd
And quick retract it to the fringed vest;
Or cleave with brandish'd arms the lucid stream,
And sob, their blue eyes twinkling in the steam. . . .
Here oft her lord surveys the rude domain,
Fair arts of Greece triumphant in his train; . . .
Relenting nature gives her hand to taste,
And health and beauty crown the laughing waste.

Erasmus Darwin, 'Economy of Vegetation', *The Botanic Garden*, 1791

From Matlock we proceeded through a scandalous country to Buxton. That any but felonious and larcenous culprits, sent there by order of a court of justice, should be found convened together in Buxton, is to me a matter of most profound astonishment. The water I maintain to be common water, of the same heat as is in general employed in the administration of pukes.

Sydney Smith, Letter to Mrs Beach, 16 June 1798

Cambridge

and the Ouse

Next these the plenteous Ouse came far from land,
By many a city and by many a towne,
And many rivers taking under hand
Into his waters, as he passeth downe,
The Cle, the Were, the Grant, the Sture, the Rowne.
Thence doth by Huntingdon and Cambridge flit,
My mother Cambridge, whom as with a Crowne
He doth adorne, and is adorn'd of it
With many a gentle Muse, and many a learned wit.

Edmund Spencer, *The Faerie Queene*, 1596

The Nursery of all my good breedinge.

Sir John Harington, Letter to Sir Robert Cecil, 7 June 1602

This City which being the other University of England, the other eie, the other strong-staie, as it were thereof, and a most famous mart and store-house of good literature and Godlinesse, standeth upon the river *Cam*, which after it hath in sporting wise besprinkled the West side thereof with many *Islets*, turning into the East, divideth it into two parts, and hath a bridge over it, whence arose this later name, *Cambridge*. Beyond the bridge is seene a large & ancient Castle, which seemeth now to have lived out his ful time, & *Maudlen College*. On this side the bridge, where standeth the greatest part by far of the City, you have a pleasant sight everywhere to the eie, what of faire streets orderly raunged, what of a number of churches, and of 16. Colledges, sacred mansions of the *Muses*, wherein a number of great learned men are maintained, and wherein the knowledge of the best arts, and the skil in tongues so flourish, that they may be rightly counted the fountaines of literature, religion, and all knowledge whatsoever, who right sweetly bedew and sprinkle, with most holesome waters the gardens of the Church and *Common-wealth* through England, Neither is there wanting any thing here, that a man may require in a most flourishing *Universitie*, were it not that the ayre is somewhat unhealthfull arising as it doth out of a fenny ground hard by. And yet peradventure, they that first founded an University in that place, allowed of *Platoes* judgement. For he, being of a very excellent and strong constitution of bodie chose out the *Academia*, an unholsome place of *Attica*, for to studie in, so that the superfluous rankenesse of bodie which might overlaie the minde, might bee kept under by the distemperature of the place. Neverthelesse, for all this, our forefathers, men of singular wisdome, dedicated this place . . . and beautified it with notable workes and buildings.

William Camden, *Britain*, 1610 (Philemon Holland's translation)

Thence to Cambridge, where the Muses
Haunt the Vine-bush, as their use is;
Like sparks up a Chimney warming
Or Flyes near a Dung-hill swarming
In a Ring they did inclose me
Vowing they would never lose me.
'Bout midnight for drinke I call S^{r}.

As I had drunk nought at all S^{r}.
But all this did little shame me
Tipsy went I, tipsy came I:
Grounds, greenes, groves, are wet and homely.
But the schollers wondrous comely.

Richard Brathwaite, *Barnabees Journall*, 1638

The Mercat place of Chambridg is very ample and remarkable for old *Hobsons* the pleasant Carriers beneficence of a fountaine: but the whole Towne situated in a low dirty unpleasant place, the streetes ill paved, the aire thick, as infested by the fenns. . . .

John Evelyn, *Diary*, 1 September 1654

Ye fields of *Cambridge*, our dear *Cambridge*, say,
Have ye not seen us walking every day?
Was there a *Tree* about, which did not know
The *Love* betwixt us two?
Henceforth, ye gentle Trees, for ever fade;
Or your sad Branches thicker join,
And into darksome shades combine;
Dark as the *Grave* wherein my *Friend* is laid.

Abraham Cowley, 'On the Death of Mr William Harvey', in *Miscellanies*, 1656

Oxford . . . having been a famous place before this present town of Cambridge in all probability was built, and whilst the brutest of all beasts, viz. Hogs and Pigs lay wallowing and grunting in the gronnae, mire, fennish places or sloughs (for from such a word, viz. gronna, Granta is thought to be derived) where the said Town now standeth.

Anthony à Wood, *History and Antiquities*, 1674

. . . sins of omission, which I think we at Cambridge call lounging. . . .

Elijah Fenton, Letter to William Broome, 23 May 1722

A Burston horse, and a Cambridge Master of Arts will give the way to nobody.

Thomas Fuller, *Gnomologia*, 1732

What to say about this Terra Incognita, I don't know; First then it is a great old Town, shaped like a Spider, with a nasty lump in the middle of it, & half a dozen scambling long legs: it has 14 Parishes, 12 Colledges, & 4 Halls. . . . The Masters of Colledges are twelve gray-hair'd Gentlefolks, who are all mad with Pride; the Fellows are sleepy, drunken, dull, illiterate Things; the Fellow-Com: are imitators of the Fellows, or else Beaux, or else nothing: the Pension: grave, formal Sots, who would be thought old; or else drink Ale, & sing Songs against the Excise. The Sizers are Graziers Eldest Sons, who come to get good Learning, that they may all be Archbishops of Canterbury. . . .

Thomas Gray, Letter to Horace Walpole, 31 October 1734

Hail, horrors, hail! ye ever gloomy bowers,
Ye gothic fanes, and antiquated towers
Where rushy Camus' slowly winding flood
Perpetual draws his humid train of mud.

Thomas Gray, *Hymn to Ignorance*, 1742

Let GRANTA boast the patrons of her name,
Each splendid fool of fortune and of fame:
Still of preferment let her shine the queen,
Prolific parent of each bowing dean:
Be hers each prelate of the pampered cheek,
Each courtly chaplain, sanctified and sleek:
Still let the drones of her exhaustless hive
On rich pluralities supinely thrive:
Still let her senates titled slaves revere
Nor dare to know the patriot from the peer;
No longer charm'd by Virtue's lofty song,
Once heard sage Milton's manly tones among
Where CAM, meandering thro' the matted reeds
With loitering wave his groves of laurel feeds.

Thomas Wharton, *The Triumph of Isis*, 1749

To GRANTA, sweet GRANTA, (where studious of Ease
Seven Years did I sleep, and then lost my Degrees).

Christopher Anstey, *The New Bath Guide*, 4th edn, 1767

I do not ask you if Cambridge has produced anything, for it never does.

Horace Walpole, Letter to the Rev. William Cole, 10 December 1775

I was the Dreamer, they the Dream; I roamed
Delighted through the motley spectacle;
Gowns, grave, or gaudy, doctors, students, streets,
Courts, cloisters, flocks of churches, gateways, towers:
Migration strange for a stripling of the hills,
A northern villager. . . .
The Evangelist St John my patron was:
Three Gothic courts are his, and in the first,
Was my abiding-place, a nook obscure:
Right underneath, the College kitchens made
A humming sound, less tuneable than bees,
But hardly less industrious; with shrill notes
Of sharp command, and scolding intermixed.
Near me hung Trinity's loquacious clock,
Who never let the quarters, night or day,
Slip by him unproclaimed, and told the hours
Twice over with a male and female voice.
Her pealing organ was my neighbour too;
And from my pillow, looking forth by light
Of moon or favouring stars, I could behold
The antechapel where the statue stood
Of Newton with his prism and silent face,
The marble index of a mind for ever
Voyaging through strange seas of Thought, alone.

William Wordsworth, *The Prelude*, 1805 (text of 1850)

I have other Reasons for not residing at Cambridge, I dislike it; I was originally intended for Oxford, my Guardians determined otherwise. I quitted the Society of my earliest associates, who are all '*Alumni*' of the latter, to drag on a weary term, at a place where I had many acquaintances, but few friends. I therefore can never consider *Granta* as my '*Alma Mater*' but rather as a *Nurse* of no very promising appearance, on whom I have been forced, against *her* inclination & contrary to mine. – My affection is in Consequence by no means *filial*.

Lord Byron, Letter to the Rev. Thomas Jones, 14 February 1807

from the vantage point of the University of Pest in Hungary
As soon as we . . . added that we were members of the University of Cambridge, we were amused by a question from the principal Lecturer, who came towards us with a large atlas in his hand, requesting that we would point out to him the situation of Cambridge; as neither he nor his fellow professors had ever heard of the existence of such a University!

E.D. Clarke, *Travels in Various Countries*, 1818

I was not train'd in Academic bowers,
And to those learned streams I nothing owe
Which copious from those twin fair founts do flow;
Mine have been any thing but studious hours.
Yet I can fancy, wandering 'mid thy towers,
Myself a nursling, Granta of thy lap
My brow seems tightening with the Doctor's cap,
And I walk *gowned*; feel unusual powers.
Strange forms of logic clothe my admiring speech,
Old Ramus' ghost is busy at my brain;
And my scull teems with notions infinite.
Be still, ye reeds of Camus, while I teach
Truths, which transcend the searching Schoolmen's vein,
And half had stagger'd that stout stagirite!

Charles Lamb, written at Cambridge, *Examiner*, 29 August 1819

Cambridge lies out of the way, on one side of the world.

William Hazlitt, 'Oxford', *London Magazine*, November 1823

I know not how it is, but I feel isolated here in the midst of society. The country is so disgustingly level, the revelry of the place so monotonous, the studies of the University so uninteresting, so much matter-of-fact.

Alfred Lord Tennyson, Letter to his aunt, Mrs Russell, 1828

I past beside the reverend walls
In which of old I wore the gown;
I roved at random through the town,
And saw the tumult of the halls;

And heard once more in college fanes
The storm their high-built organs make,
And thunder-music, rolling, shake
The prophets blazon'd on the panes;

And caught once more the distant shout,
The measured pulse of racing oars
Among the willows; paced the shores
And many a bridge, and all about

The same gray flats again, and felt
The same, but not the same; and last
Up that long walk of limes I past
To see the rooms in which he dwelt.

Alfred Lord Tennyson, *In Memoriam*, 1850

When I visited Cambridge, the nakedness of the land was too plainly visible under a sheet of snow, through which gutters and ditches ran, like ink, by the side of leafless sallows, which resembled huge pincushions stuck on posts. The town, however, made amends. . . .

Leigh Hunt, *Autobiography*, 1850

It seems so strange to be in a place of colleges that is not Oxford.

Matthew Arnold, Letter to his wife, 28 February 1853

Oxford lends sweetness to labour and dignity to leisure. When I say Oxford, I mean Cambridge, for a barbarian is not the least obliged to know the difference, and it suddenly strikes me as being both very pedantic and very good-natured in him to pretend to know it.

Henry James, *English Vignettes* 1879, in *Portraits of Places*, 1883

Oxford is on the whole more attractive than Cambridge to the ordinary visitor; and the traveller is therefore recommended to visit Cambridge first, or to omit it altogether if he cannot visit both.

Carl Baedeker, *Baedeker's Great Britain*, 1887

My first impression of the place was in December 1889 when I was examined for entrance scholarships. I stayed in rooms in the New Court [of Trinity College] and I was too shy to enquire the way to the lavatory, so that I walked every morning to the station before the examination began.

Bertrand Russell, *Autobiography*, 1967

Oxford men think they rule the world, and Cambridge men don't care a cent who does.

Bishop Creighton, attributed,

After Cambridge, blank, blank, blank.

Lytton Strachey, Letter to Leonard Woolf, 1905

I find Cambridge an asylum, in more senses than one.
A.E. Housman, remark on coming to Cambridge from London, *c.* 1911, quoted in F.T. Grant Richards, *Housman*, 1941

For Cambridge people rarely smile
Being urban, squat, and packed with guile.
Rupert Brooke, *The Old Vicarage, Grantchester*, 1912

I cannot bear its smell of rottenness, marsh-stagnancy. I get a melancholic malaria.
D.H. Lawrence, Letter to Bertrand Russell, March 1915

Perhaps Cambridge is too much of a cave.
Virginia Woolf, *Diary*, 23 June 1920

Three years I was at Cambridge, three quiet years with little of disturbance in them, moving slowly on like the sluggish Cam.
Jawaharlal Nehru, *An Autobiography*, 1936

*'The Other Town' could best be visited by night. So every evening, after supper, we wandered the cold foggy streets, away from the lights and the shops, down back alleys, to the water's edge. We leant over clammy stone parapets, in a state of trance-like fascination, auto-hypnotized by the tones of our own voices, and the ink-black movement of the stream. Sometimes, we dropped pennies into the water. One evening, I happened to read aloud the name under a fluttering gas-lamp; 'Garret Hostel Bridge.' 'The Rats' Hostel!' Chalmers suddenly exclaimed. We often conversed in surrealist phrases of this kind. Now we both became abnormally excited: it seemed to us that an all-important statement had been made. At last, by pure accident, we had stumbled upon the key-words which expressed the inmost nature of the other town. 'The Rats' Hostel,' we kept repeating to each other, as we hurried back to our rooms to discuss this astonishing revelation.
Christopher Isherwood, *Lions and Shadows*, 1938

*Spring and summer did happen in Cambridge almost every year.
Vladimir Nabokov, *The Real Life of Sebastian Knight*, 1945

Certainly I thought, Cambridge meant too much to Cambridge.
Kingsley Amis, 'No More Parades', *Encounter*, February 1964

Cambridge is the least damaging place in England in which not to be found funny.
Ibid.

I do not know if anyone will ever go to Cambridge in search of the imprints which the teat-cleats on my soccer-boots have left in the black mud before a gaping goal, or follow the shadow of my cap across the quadrangle to my tutor's stairs; but I know that I thought of Milton, and Marvell and Marlowe, with more than a tourist's thrill as I passed beside the reverend walls. Nothing one looked at was shut off in terms of time, everything was a natural opening into it. . . . I had no interest whatever in the history of the place, and was quite sure that Cambridge was in no way affecting my soul, although actually it was Cambridge that supplied not only the casual frame, but also the very colours and inner rhythms for my very special Russian thoughts.
Vladimir Nabokov, *Speak Memory*, 1967

Cambridge in August is an annexe of paradise.
Philip Howard, *The Times*, 8 August 1978

River Cam
The muddy waves of the Cam, (always fatal to Genius).
Lord Byron, Letter to Robert Charles Dallas, 12 August 1811

King's College Chapel
Mr Simeon . . . took me into King's College Chapel that celebrated building. He told me that he had lately compared the size of it with the dimensions of Noah's Ark as given in the Scripture, and found that the Ark was twice the length, and twice the breadth, and two-thirds the height of the Chapel. . . . He took me to the roof of the building and shewed me the admirable manner in which it was contrived so that stones two yards thick were in the center tapering off to not more than two feet. The whole roof is of stone unsupported by beams. – It remains perfect, there having been no decay. The principle upon which it is constructed has not been so far discovered as to enable anyone to imitate it. Sir Christopher Wren said that if He could be shown where *the first stone was laid*, He would execute one like it.
Joseph Farington, *Diary*, 13 September 1805

(and Westminster Abbey)
They dreamt not of a perishable home
Who thus could build. Be mine, in hours of fear
Or grovelling thought, to seek a refuge here;
Or through the aisles of Westminster to roam;
Where bubbles burst, and folly's dancing foam
Melts, if it cross the threshold; . . .
William Wordsworth, Ecclesiastical Sonnets, *c.* 1820

Peterhouse
At last you get into Cambridge, all bemudded & tired, with three wheels and a half to the coach, four horses lame, and two blind: the first thing that appears, is a row of Alms-houses, & presently on the right-hand

you'll see a thing like two Presbeyterian Meeting-houses with the backside of a little Church between them, & there you must find out by Sympathy, that this is Peter-house. . . .

Thomas Gray, Letter to Horace Walpole, 4 February 1735

Trinity College

Trinity is like a dead body in a high state of putrefaction. The only interest of it is in the worms that come out of it.

Lytton Strachey, Letter to a friend, 1903

Cambridgeshire

The north part of this county is lately much improved by draining, though the poorest sort of people will not be sensible thereof. Tell them of the great benefit to the public, because where a pike or a duck fed formerly, now a bullock or a sheep is fatted; they will be ready to return, that if they be taken in taking that bullock or sheep, the rich owner inditeth them for felons; whereas that pike or duck were their own goods only for their pains of catching them.

Thomas Fuller, *History of the Worthies of England*, 1662

For England's the one land, I know
Where men with Splendid Hearts may go;
And Cambridgeshire, of all England
The shire for Men who Understand.

Rupert Brooke, *The Old Vicarage, Grantchester*, 1912

The stacks, like blunt impassive temples, rise
Across flat fields against the autumnal skies,
The hairy-hooved horses plough the land,
Or as in prayer and meditation stand
Upholding square, primeval, dung-stained carts,
With an unending patience in their hearts.

Nothing is changed. The farmer's gig goes by
Against the horizon. Surely, the same sky,
So vast and yet familiar, grey and mild,
And streaked with light like music, I, a child,
Lifted my face from leaf-edged lanes to see,
Late-coming home, to bread-and-butter tea.

Frances Cornford, 'Cambridgeshire', *Different Days*, 1928

Canterbury

and Winchester

Canterbury is the higher rack, but Winchester is the better manger. – (W. Edington, bishop of Winchester, was the author of this expression, rendering this the reason of his refusal to be removed to Canterbury, though chosen thereunto. Indeed, though Canterbury be graced with a higher honour, the revenues of Winchester, lying entirely, are more advantageous to gather riches thereon. The proverb is appliable to those who prefer a wealthy privacy before a less profitable dignity.)

Thomas Fuller, *History of the Worthies of England*, 1662

But the great wealth and encrease of the city of Canterbury, is from the surprizing encrease of the hop-grounds all round the place; it is within the memory of many of the inhabitants now living, and that none of the oldest, neither, that there was not an acre of ground planted with hops in the whole neighbourhood, or so few as not to be worth naming; whereas I was assured that there are at this near six thousand acres of ground so planted, within a very few miles of the city; I do not vouch the number, and I confess it seems incredible, but I deliver it as I receiv'd it.

It is observ'd that the ground round this city proves more particularly fruitful for the growth of hops than of any other production, which was not at first known; but which, upon its being discover'd, set the world, speaking in the language of a neighbourhood, a digging up their grounds and planting; so that now they may say without boasting, there is at Canterbury the greatest plantation of hops in the whole island.

Daniel Defoe, *A Tour through the Whole Island of Great Britain*, 1724–7

This fine old town, or rather city, is remarkable of cleanliness and niceness, notwithstanding it has a cathedral in it.

William Cobbett, *Rural Rides*, 4 September 1823

Canvey Island

When Canvey, Albion's child in-iled richly lyes,
Which, though her lower scite doth make her seeme but
meane,
Of him as dearly lov'd as Shepey is or Greane,
And him as dearly lov'd: for when he would depart,
With Hercules to fight, she tooke it so to heart,
That falling low and flat, her blubbered face to hide,
By Thames shee welneere is surrounded every tyde:
And since of worldly state she never taketh keepe,
But onely gives her selfe, to tend, and milke her sheepe.

Michael Drayton, *Poly-Olbion*, 'The Nineteenth Song', 1622

Carlton (Leicestershire)

And as for *Carleton*, as one would say, the husbandmen's towne, . . . wherein (I wote not whether it be worth the relating) all in maner that are borne, whether it be by a peculiar propertie of the soile, or the water, or else by some other secret operation of nature, have an ilfavoured, untunable, and harsh maner of speech, fetching their words with very much adoe deepe from out of the throat, with a certaine kind of wharling.

William Camden, *Britain*, 1610
(Philemon Holland's translation)

Cerne Abbas

We went to see the phallic giant at Cerne Abbas. Two little girls with long bare legs sat on his testicles.

Evelyn Waugh, *Diary*, 9 August 1930

Chatsworth

When *Scotland*'s Queen, her native realms expell'd
In ancient *Chatsworth* was a captive held,
Had then the pile to its new charms arriv'd
Happier the captive than the Queen had liv'd!
What sighs in pity of her state could rise
That found the fugitive in paradise!

Anon. 'On the Duke of Devonshire's Seat in Derbyshire', *A Collection of Epigrams*, 1737

from a hill near Eyam
At about four miles distance, the eye perceives the palace of Chatsworth, rising, in golden beauty, from beneath its dark and pendant woods, which are flanked by a ridge of grey, stony, and bleak mountains. The epithet golden for Chatsworth, is, as to appearance, literally just, since the yellowish colour of the beautiful stone of which it is built, and the gilt window frames, make the edifice, even at that distance, when the sun shines upon it, seem as if it were built of pale gold.

Though Chatsworth has not apartments sufficiently spacious for a ducal palace, yet is its exterior the most elegantly magnificent I have ever beheld. Here are no wings or bow-windows, which, however internally pleasant, seem to me excrescent deformities on the outward appearance. Here is no frittering into parts, no obtrusive grandeur of appertaining offices, but the eye, at once, perceives one fair and perfect whole. Its mingled lightness and strength, the invariable result of exquisite proportion, recall to my memory Milton's description of Pandaemonium, whenever I first discern Chatsworth from the neighbouring hills:
Behold, out of the earth, a fabric large
Rise, like an exhalation!

Anna Seward, Letter, 13 February 1765, in 'Literary Correspondence', *Works*, 1810

Chatsworth is very magnificent, but I looked back with regret to the house in its unfinished state, when we lived in three spacious cheerful rooms, looking to the south, which are now quite useless, being gorgeously furnished with velvet and silk, and marble tables, but unoccupied, and the windows closed lest the sun should spoil the finery with which the rooms are decorated. The comfort we had then has been ill exchanged for the magnificence which has replaced it, and the Duke has made the house so large that he cannot afford to live in it, and never remains there above two or three months in the year.

Charles Greville, *A Journal of the Reign of Queen Victoria*, October 1843

Chelmsford

If any one were to ask me what in my opinion was the dullest and most stupid spot on the face of the Earth, I should decidedly say Chelmsford.

Charles Dickens, Letter to Thomas Beard, 11 January 1835

Cheltenham

I came to this Place last Thursday, & a damn'd dull Place it is, . . . I have drank the Waters & they agree very well with Me; but I have unfortunately got a Boil under the Wasteband of my Breeches, that greatly discomposes Me. & perhaps my Want of Relish for the Pleasures of Cheltenham may be chiefly owing to that.

David Garrick, Letter to Francis Hayman, 18 August 1746

Cheltenham is a clean small place. . . . There is a formality in the whole scene that is not pleasant.

J.M.W. Turner, *Diary of a Tour in Part of Wales*, 1792

Here lie I and my four daughters,
Killed by drinking Cheltenham waters.
Had we but stuck to Epsom salts,
We wouldn't have been in these here vaults.

Anon.

and Tunbridge Wells
*'This is the first October that she has passed in the country since her infancy. I do not call Tunbridge or Cheltenham the country. . . . '

Jane Austen, *Mansfield Park*, 1814

Cheltenham is a nasty, ill-looking place, half clown and half cockney. The town is one street about a mile long; but then, at some distance from this street, there are rows of white tenements, with green balconies, like those inhabited by the tax-eaters round London. Indeed this place appears to be the residence of an assemblage of tax-eaters. These vermin shift about between London, Cheltenham, Bath, Bognor, Brighton, Tunbridge, Ramsgate, Margate, Worthing, and other spots in England, while some of them get over to France and Italy; just like those body vermin of different sorts, that are found in different parts of the tormented carcasses at different hours of the day and night, and in different degrees of heat and cold. . . .

Cheltenham, . . . this resort of the lame and the lazy, the gormandising and guzzling, the bilious and the nervous. . . .

William Cobbett, *Rural Rides*, 17 November 1821

She amused me by saying that the streets of Cheltenham are notoriously unsafe. Foot passengers are perpetually killed by bicyclists. It is the rarest thing to motor through without being asked to take a corpse to the doctors.

Virginia Woolf, *Diary*, 19 February 1923
(quoting Mary K. Snowden)

River Cherwell

From Banbury, desirous to add knowledge
To zeal, and to be taught in Magdalen College,
The River Cherwell doth to Isis runne,
And bears her company to Abington.

John Taylor, *Thames and Isis*, 1632

at Oxford
All pensive from her osier-woven bow'r
CHERWELL arose. Around her darknening edge
Pale eve began the streaming mist to pour
And breezes fann'd by fits the rustling sedge.
She rose, and thus she cried in deep despair
And tore the rushy wreath that bound her streaming hair.

Ah! why, she cried, should ISIS share alone
The tributary gifts of tuneful fame!
Shall every song her happier influence own
And stamp with partial praise her favourite name?
While I, alike to these proud domes allied,
Nor hear the Muse's call, nor boast a classic tide. . . .

Lo! here no commerce spreads the fervent toil
To pour pollution o'ver my verdant tide;
The freshness of my pastures to defile,
Or bruise the matted groves that fringe my side:
But Solitude, on this sequester'd bank
Mid the moist lilies sits, attir'd in mantle dank.

Thomas Wharton, 'The Complaint of Cherwell', in *Poems*, 1777

Cheshire

The grasse and fodder there, is of that goodnesse and vertue that cheeses be made heere in great number of a most pleasing and deleicate tast, such as all England againe affourdeth not the like; no, though the best dayriwomen otherwise, and skilfullest in cheese making be had from hence. . . . Howsoever this region, in fertility of soile commeth behind many Countries in England, yet it hath alwaies bred and reared more Gentry than the rest.

William Camden, *Britain*, 1610
(Philemon Holland's translation)

Cheshire lieth in form of an axe, Wirral being the handle thereof. . . .

Thomas Fuller, *History of the Worthies of England*, 1662

Cheshire born, and Cheshire bred,
Strong in the arm, and weak in the head.

Anon., Old Rhyme

My lord Chancellor Ellesmere's saying of a man newly married; God send him joy, and some sorrow too, as we say in Cheshire.

Francis Bacon, *Apothegms*, before 1625, 'from Dr Rawley's Commonplace Book', *Works* 1859

The men of Ches-shire, chiefest for their place,
Of bone so bigge, as onely made for blowes,
Which for their faith are had in special grace,
And have beene ever fearefull to their foes.

Michael Drayton, *The Barons Warres*, 1603

Chester

. . . faire *Chester*, call'd of old
Carlegion; whilst proud *Rome* her conquests heere did hold
Of those her legions known the faithfull station then,
So stoutly held to tack by those neere *North-wales* men;
Yet by her owne right name had rather called bee,
As her the *Britaine* tearm'd the *Fortresse upon Dee*,
Then vainly shee would seeme a Miracle to stand,
Th'imaginary worke of some huge Giants hand.

Michael Drayton, *Poly-Olbion*, 1613–22

It is a very antient city, and to this day, the buildings are very old; nor do the Rows as they call them, add any thing, in my opinion to the beauty of the city; but just the contrary, they serve to make the city look both old and ugly: These Rows are certain long galleries, up one pair of stairs, which run along the side of the streets, before all the houses, tho' joined to them, and as is pretended, they are to keep the people dry in walking along. This they do indeed effectually, but then they take away all the view of the houses from the street, nor can a stranger, that was to ride thro' Chester, see any shops in the city; besides, they make the shops themselves dark, and the way in them is dark, dirty, and uneven.

Daniel Defoe, *A Tour through the Whole Island of Great Britain*, 1724–7

I was quite enchanted at Chester, so that I could with difficulty quit it. But the enchantment was the reverse of that of Circe; for so far was there from being any thing sensual in it, that I was *all mind.* I do not mean all reason only; for my fancy was kept finely in play. And why not? – If you please I will send you a copy or an abridgement of my Chester journal, which is truly a log-book of felicity.

James Boswell, Letter to Samuel Johnson, 7 November 1779, in *Life of Johnson*, 1783

I like this place much; but somehow I feel glad when I get among the quiet eighteenth century buildings, in cosy places with some elbow-room about them, after the older architecture. This other is bedevilled and furtive; it seems to stoop; I am afraid of trap-doors, and could not go pleasantly into such houses. I don't know how much of this is legitimately the effect of the architecture; little enough, possibly; possibly far the most part of it comes from bad historical novels and the disquieting statuary that garnishes some facades.

Robert Louis Stevenson, Letter to Mrs Sitwell, 8 August 1874

Chichester

This is but a little Citty encompassed with a wall, with 4 gates which casts the two streetes directly a cross each other and so lookes through from gate to gate, one Streete does; the other it seemes did so formerly, but in new building of some of their houses they have encroach'd into the Streete and so hinders the through visto, in midst of these 2 or 4 streetes divided by the Market place is a very faire Cross of Stone like a Church or greate arch, its pretty large and pirramydy form with severall Carvings.

Celia Fiennes, *Journeys*, *c.* 1685–96

While one half of Chichester goes to sleep, the other half goes on tiptoe for fear of waking 'em up.

Sussex proverb

It had simply never occurred to me before that day that towns could have a shape and be, like my beloved locomotives, things with character and meaning. If you had been drawing 'engines' for years and were then suddenly taken to such a city, you would instantly see what I mean. I had not been training myself to become an engineer, I had been training myself to see Chichester, the human city, the city of God, the place where life and work and things were all in one and all in harmony. That, without words, was how it seemed to me that day. It was not its picturesqueness; for Chichester is the least picturesque of cathedral cities. It wasn't its antiquity; for I had learned no history and age meant little to me. It was a town, a city, a thing planned and ordered – no mere congeries of more or less sordid streets, growing, like a fungus, wherever the network of railways and sidings and railway sheds would allow.

Eric Gill, *Autobiography*, 1940

Clifton

Clifton, in vain thy varied scenes invite –
The mossy bank, dim glade, and dizzy height;
The sheep that starting from the tufted thyme,
Untune the distant churches' mellow chime.

W.S. Landor, *An English Scene, Works*, 1846

Clunton (etc.)

Clunton and Clunbury,
    Clungunford and Clun,
Are the quietest places
    Under the sun.

Anon., old local saying

Colchester

This is a raged, factious Towne, & now swarming in Sectaries.

John Evelyn, *Diary*, 8 July 1656

Colebrook Dale

Scene of superfluous grace, and wasted bloom,
O, violated COLEBROOK! in an hour,
To beauty unpropitious and to song,
The Genius of thy shades, by Plutus brib'd,
Amid thy grassy lanes, thy woodwild glens,
Thy knolls and bubbling wells, thy rocks, and streams,
Slumbers! – while tribes fulginous invade
The soft, romantic, consecrated scenes;
Haunt of the wood-nymph, who with airy step,
In times long vanish'd through thy pathless groves
Rang'd; . . .
                    What, though to vulgar eye
Invisible, yet oft the lucid gaze
Of the rapt Bard, in every dell and glade
Beheld them wander; . . .
                    Now we view
Their fresh, their fragant, and their silent reign
Usurpt by Cyclops; – hear, in mingled tones,
Shout their throng'd barge, their pond'rous engines clang

Through thy coy dales; while red the countless fires,
With umber'd flames, bicker on all thy hills, . . .

See, in troops,
The dusk artificers, with brazen throats,
Swarm on thy cliffs, and clamour in thy glens,
Steepy and wild, unsuited to such guests.

Ah! what avails it to the poet's sense,
That the large stores of thy metallic veins
Gleam over Europe; transatlantic shores
Illumine wide; – . . .
Ah! the traffic rich,
With equal vantage might Britannia send
From regions better suited to such aims,
Than from her Colebrook's muse-devoted vales.

Anna Seward, *Colebrook Dale*, *c.* 1784

Colebrook Dale, that Tartarus in Tempe, which is in its Kind unequalled. We slept there; looked at the Iron Bridge with Admiration, and at the nightly Fires with Astonishment – artificial Stromboli! strange Imitation of Nature's Volcanoes long since seen by me in Italy – they put one in mind of Milton's 2d Book, where *Mammon* projects such Imitation; & 'twas the same industrious Spirit of Money-getting produced it here.

Hester Lynch Thrale/Piozzi, *Thraliana*, September 1791

Combe Florey

It is a land of plenty, and a beautiful, though somewhat moist, climate. . . . The common people are civil (very civil), drunken, wretched, and degraded. The farming is contemptible; the neighbourhood of gentlemen very dense in numbers. I have seen many civil gentleman-like persons, and many convex ladies.

Sydney Smith, Letter to the Archbishop of York, 22 August 1829

What an air it is. . . . Some of my Scotch friends, it is true, complain that it is too enervating; but they are but northern barbarians, after all, and like to breathe their air raw. We civilized people of the south prefer it cooked.

Sydney Smith, quoted in Lady Holland, *Memoir of Sydney Smith*, 1855

Corby

Corby was conceived in a blast furnace and its parents were Stewarts and Lloyds.

Local saying, quoted on *Newsnight*, BBC TV, 2 April 1980

Cornwall

Touching the temperature of Cornwall, the air thereof is cleansed, as with bellows by the billows.

Richard Carew, *A Survey of Cornwall*, late sixteenth century

This angle, which so shutteth them in, hath wrought many interchangeable matches with each other's stock, and given beginning to the proverb, 'that all Cornish gentlemen are cousins.'

Ibid.

I love thee Cornwall and will ever,
And hope to see thee once again!
For why? – thine equal knew I never
For honest minds and active men.

Thomas Freeman, *Encomion Cornubiae*, 1614

The Cornish being a race of men stout of stomach, mighty of body and limb, and that lived hardly in a barren country, and many of them could for a need live under-ground, that were tinners.

Francis Bacon, *History of King Henry VII*, 1622

There are more saints in Cornwall than there are in heaven.

Cornish proverb

The devil will not come into Cornwall for fear of being put into a pie.

Old Cornish saying, alluding to the doubtful ingredients of Cornish pies

In Cornwall are the best gentlemen.

Cornish proverb, quoted by George Borrow, *Lavengro*, 1851

From Padstow Point to Lundy Light
Is a watery grave by day and night.

Anon., old local saying

Blind as you accuse me of being to the beauties of Nature, I am wonderfully pleased with this country. Of her three dull notes, *Ground*, *Plants*, and *Water*, Cornwall possesses the first and last in very high perfection. . . . In *Plants* indeed we are deficient, and though all the Gentlemen now attend to Posterity, the Country will for a long time be very naked.

Edward Gibbon, Letter to J.B. Holroyd, 10 September 1773

Nothing can be more desolate than the appearance of this province, where most part of the inhabitants live in the mines. 'I never see the greater part of my parishioners,' said a clergyman here, 'till they come up to be buried.'

Robert Southey, *Letters from England, by Don Manuel Alvarez Espriella*, 1807

Some peculiarities of the Cornish people I had before & did now notice. They speak in a singing tone; and, as 'Yes sure' is always in the mouth of a Devonshire man, so when a Cornish man, in this part of the country at least, answers in the negative He does it with this repitition, 'No, No Sir. No.'

Joseph Farington, *Diary*, 31 August 1810

The utmost crag
Of Cornwall, and the storm-encompassed isles
Where to the sky the rude sea rarely smiles
Unless in treacherous wrath.

P.B. Shelley, Letter to Maria Gisborne, 1820

When I was in Cornwall it had blown a storm of wind and rain for days – all of a sudden fell into perfect calm; I was a little inland of the cliffs, when, after a space of perfect silence, a long roll of Thunder – from some wave rushing into a cavern, I suppose – came up from the Distance and died away. I never *felt* Silence like that.

Alfred Lord Tennyson, in Edward Fitzgerald, *Some Recollections of Tennyson's Talk*, *c.* 1852–3

Cornwall is not much to my taste, being as bleak as the bleakest parts of Scotland, and nothing like so pointed and characteristic.

Robert Louis Stevenson, Letter to Mrs Sitwell, August 1877

This Cornwall is very primeval: great, black, jutting cliffs and rocks, like the original darkness, and a pale sea breaking in, like dawn. It is like the beginning of the world, wonderful: and so free and strong.

D.H. Lawrence, Letter to Lady Cynthia Asquith, 7 February 1916

People say it is spoilt. I still think to catch a mackerel in a Cornish bay the greatest excitement under the moon.

Virginia Woolf, Letter to Hugh Walpole, 20 August 1928

Here in the late October light
See Cornwall, a pathetic sight,
Raddled, and put upon and tired
And looking somewhat over-hired
Remembering in the autumn air
The years when she was young and fair –
Those golden and unpeopled bays
The shadowy cliffs and sheep-worn ways
The white unpopulated surf
The thyme-and-mushroom scented turf
The slate-hung farms, the oil-lit chapels
Thin elms and lemon-coloured apples –
Going and gone beyond recall
Now she is free for 'One and All.'

One day a tidal wave will break
Before the breakfasters awake
And sweep the cara's out to sea,
The oil, the tar, and you and me
And leave in windy, criss-cross motion
A waste of undulating ocean
With, jutting out, a second Scilly
The isles of Roughtor and Brown Willy.

John Betjeman, 'Delectable Duchy', in *A Nip in the Air*, 1974

Cornishmen

They are valiant, hardie, wel pitcht in stature, brawny and strong limmed: such as for wrastling, (to speak nothing of that manly exercise, and feat of hurling the Ball which they use) so farre excell, that for light and cleane strength together, they justly win the prize and praise from other Nations, in that behalfe. . . . Now whether this firme and wel compact constitution of the Cornish-men which proceedeth from the temperature of heat and moisture, is to bee referred unto the breeding-west wind and the Westerne situation . . . or rather to some peculiar and speciall reason of aire and soile; it is not my purpose to search curiously.

William Camden, *Britain*, 1610 (Philemon Holland's translation)

The Cornish people still attract me. They have become detestable, I think, and yet they *aren't* detestable. They are of course, strictly *anti-social* and un-Christian. . . . Nevertheless the old race is still revealed, a race which believed in the darkness, in magic, and in the magic transcendency of one man over another, which is fascinating. Also there is left some of the old sensuousness of the darkness, a sort of softness, a sort of flowing together in physical intimacy, something almost negroid, which is fascinating.

But curse them they are entirely mindless, and yet they are living purely for social advancement. They ought to be living in the darkness and warmth and passionateness of the blood, sudden, incalculable. Whereas they are like insects gone cold, living only for money, for *dirt*. They are foul in this. They ought all to die.

Not that I've seen very much of them.

D.H. Lawrence, Letter to J.D. Beresford, 1 February 1916

Cotswold Hills

In these *Woulds* there feed in great numbers, flockes of sheepe long necked and square of bulke and bone, by reason (as it is commonly thought) of the weally and hilly situation of their pasturage: whose wool being most fine and soft is had in passing great account among all nations.

William Camden, *Britain*, 1610
(Philemon Holland's translation)

But *Cotswold*, be this spoke to th'onely praise of thee,
That thou of all the rest, the chosen soyle shouldst bee,
Faire *Isis* to bring-forth (the Mother of great *Tames*)
With those delicious Brooks, by whose immortal streames
Her greatnesse is begunne: so that our Rivers King,
When he his long Descent shall from his Bel-shires bring,
Must needs (Great Pastures Prince) derive his stem by thee,
From kingly *Cotswolds* selfe, sprung of the third degree:
As th'old worlds Heroes wont, that in the times of yore,
On Neptune, Jove, and Mars, themselves so highly bore.

Michael Drayton, *Poly-Olbion*, 1613–22

Coventry

Coventry, that do'st adorne
The countrey wherein I was borne,
Yet therein lyes not thy prayse,
Why should I crowne thy tow'rs with bayes:
'Tis not thy wall, me to thee weds
Thy ports, nor thy proud pyrameds,
Nor thy trophies of the bore,
But that shee which I adore,
Which scarce goodness selfe can payre,
First there breathing blest thy ayre; . . .
Deare citie, travelling by thee,
When thy rising spyres I see,
Destined her place of birth;
Yet me thinkes the very earth
Hallowed is, so farre as I
Can thee possibly descry:
Then thou dwelling in this place,
Hearing some rude hinde disgrace
Thy citie with some scurvy thing,
Which some jester forth did bring,
Speake these lines where thou do'st come,
And strike the slave for ever dumbe.

Michael Drayton, *A Hymne to his Ladies Birth-place*, 1619

Thence to Conventre, where 'tis said-a
Coventry blew is only made-a;
This I know not, for sure am I,
In no market bought I any;
Bacchus made me such a Scholer
Black or blew I knew no colour.

Richard Brathwaite, *Barnabees Journall*, 1638

Coventry is a large and populous city, and drives a very great trade; the manufacture of tammies is their chief employ, and next to that weaving of ribbons of the meanest kind, chiefly black. The buildings are very old, and in some places much decay'd; the city may be taken for the very picture of the city of London, on the south side of Cheapside before the Great Fire; the timber-built houses, projecting forwards and towards one another, till in the narrow streets they were ready to touch one another at the top.

The tale of the Lady Godiva, who rode naked thro' the High Street of the city to purchase her beloved city of Coventry exemption from taxes, is held for so certain a truth, that they will not have it questioned upon any account whatever; and the picture of the poor fellow that peep'd out of the window to see her, is still kept up, looking out of a garret in the High Street of the city: But Mr. Cambden says positively no body look'd at her at all.

Daniel Defoe, *A Tour through the Whole Island of Great Britain*, 1724–7

Coventry – disappointed me. It would seem decidedly odder if it didn't seem quite so new.

Henry James, Letter to William James, 26 April 1869

Cowes

Here ocean's breath comes mingled with the breeze,
And drives far off the bloated fiend, disease;
Here ocean's balm the sinking heart delights,
And drooping Britain to the shore invites. . . .
Here ocean's essence unpolluted reigns:
From Nature's vitals, and from Neptune's veins.
Here lusty health comes rushing day and night,
Unmixed as truth, and clear as morning light;
No foul infection mingles with the tide,
In healing virtue pure and virgin pride;
Along the tented shore shall beauty skim,
And bosom bright shall lave the lovely limb; . . .
No more to foreign baths shall Britain roam,
But plunge at Cowes, and find rich health at home.

'Sharpe', (not identified), quoted in Anon., *Guide to all the Watering and Seabathing Places*, *c.* 1810

It does not convey a very favourable impression on first entering it from the harbour, the streets being narrow, and not very clean.

Anon., *A Guide to all the Watering and Sea-bathing Places*, *c.* 1810

Cromer

It is an Ancient Market Towne that stands
Upon a lofty Cliffe of mouldring Sands:

The Sea against the Cliffes doth daily beate,
And every tyde into the Land doth eate.
The Towne is poore, unable by Expence,
Against the raging Sea to make defence:
And every day it eateth further in,
Still wasting, washing down the sand doth win,
That if some course be not tane speedily,
The Town's in danger in the Sea to lye.

John Taylor, *A Very Merry Wherry-Ferry-Voyage*, 1622

Cumberland

The Country although it be somewhat with the coldest, as lying farre North, and seemeth as rough by reason of hilles, yet for the variety thereof it smileth upon the beholders, and giveth contentment to as many as travaile it. For, after the rockes bunching out, the mountaines standing thicke together, rich of mettal mines, and betweene them great meeres stored with all kindes of wild-foule, you come to prety hilles good for pasturage and well replenished with flockes of sheepe; beneath which againe you meet with goodly plaines spreading out a great way, yeelding corne sufficiently. Besides all this the Ocean driving and dashing upon the shore affourdeth plenty of excellent good fish, and upbraideth, as it were, the Inhabitants there abouts, with their negligence, for that they practise fishing no more than they doe.

William Camden, *Britain*, 1610
(Philemon Holland's translation)

No, I cannot come to Cumberland. It is too green.

Piet Mondrian, Letter to Winifred Nicholson, 1938

Dartmoor

If we could make contours in hearts as we do in maps, to see their loves, we should learn what strange unexpected regions attain the deepest depth. Often we might discover that a place rather than a person holds the secret. It was so with my father. The wild country of Dartmoor, where he had walked as a small boy, was to him a dark and refreshing well, from which the water of his life was drawn.

Freya Stark, *Traveller's Prelude*, 1950

Dawlish

O Dawlish, though unclassic be thy name, . . .
To thee will I consign
Often the timid virgin, to thy pure
Encircling waves; to thee will I consign
The feeble matron; or the child on whom
Thou may'st bestow a second happier birth
From weakness unto strength. . . .

Dr Hugh Downman, *Infancy*, 1790

Over the hill and over the dale
And over the bourn to Dawlish –
Where Gingerbread Wives have a scanty sale
And gingerbread nuts are smallish.

John Keats (?), Letter to James Rice,
24 March 1818

Deal

What a very pitiful town Deale is. We went to Fullers (the famous place for ale); but they had none but what was in the fat. After that to Pooles, a tavern in the town, where we drank.

Samuel Pepys, *Diary*, 30 April 1660

Deal is a most villainous place. It is full of filthy-looking people. Great desolation of abomination has been going on here; tremendous barracks, partly pulled down and partly tumbling down, and partly occupied by soldiers. Everything seems upon the perish. I was glad to hurry through it, and to leave its inns and public-houses to be occupied by the tarred and trowsered, and blue-and-buff crew whose very vicinage I always detest.

William Cobbett, *Rural Rides*, 3 September 1823

Forest of Dean

This was a wonderfull thicke forrest, and in former ages so darke and terrible, by reason of crooked and winding waies, as also the grisly shade therein, that it made the inhabitants more fierce, and boulder to commit robberies . . . But since that rich Mines of Iron were heere found out, those thicke woods began to wax thin by little and little.

William Camden, *Britain*, 1610
(Philemon Holland's translation)

River Dean-Bourn

Dean-bourn, farewell; I never look to see
Deane, or thy warty incivility.
Thy rockie bottome, that doth teare thy streams
And makes them frantick, ev'n to all extreames;
To my content, I never sho'd behold,
Were thy streames silver, or thy rocks all gold.
Rockie thou art; and rockie we discover
Thy men; and rockie are thy wayes all over.
O men, O manners; Now, and ever knowne
To be *A Rockie Generation!*
A people currish; churlish as the seas;
And rude (almost) as rudest Salvages.

With whom I did, and may re-sojourne when
Rockes turn to Rivers, Rivers turn to Men.

Robert Herrick, *Dean-bourn, a rude River in Devon, by which sometimes he lived*, 1648

Derby

Now all the name and credit that it hath, ariseth of the *Assises* there kept for the whole shire, & by the best nappie ale, that is brewed there . . . This is the ancient and peculiar drinke of the Englishmen and Britans.

William Camden, *Britain*, 1610
(Philemon Holland's translation)

Derbyshire

See also under Peak District

. . . this strange, mountainous, misty, moorish, rocky, wild country . . . the craggy ascents, the rocky unevenness of the roade, the high peaks and the almost perpendicular descents . . .

Edward Browne, *Journal of a Tour in Derbyshire*, 1662

Indeed all Darbyshire is but a world of peaked hills which from some of the highest you discover the rest like steeples or tops of hills as thick as can be, and tho' they appear so close yet the steepness down and up takes up the time that you go it . . .

Celia Fiennes, *Journeys*, 1697

Derbyshire would. . . . afford excellent Scenery for an Old English Play in Times when Baron and Castle still existed.

Hester Lynch Thrale/Piozzi, *Thraliana*, February 1789

Nature, who never yet made a clever fellow, without making half a dozen blockheads by way of compensation, or a beautiful place without some correspondent desolation, made us refund on the road from Bakewell to Disley all the pleasure we had experienced at Buxton. I doubted very much at first in passing over this road whether I should put myself to death, or go to sleep, but during the debate I insensibly adopted the latter and so the matter was settled.

Sydney Smith, Letter to Mrs Beach, 1798

After a certain hour one can't live on the picturesque and extract essential nutriment from it. Here we are in a show region – rather too utterly one.

Henry James, Letter to Charles Eliot Norton, 1 June 1872

seen from the train
Bald moors; the strangest looking places. So solitary they might be 18th Century England, the valleys cut by a thread of water falling roughly from heights; great sweeps of country all sunny & gloomy with bare rocks against the sky, & then behold a row of east end slum houses, with a strip of pavement & two factory chimneys set down in the midst. The houses are all stone, bleak, soot-stained, different from our cottages; not cottages at all, but streets. Suddenly, in the palm of a wide valley you come on a complete town – gasworks, factories, & little streams made to run over stone steps & turn engines I supppose. Now & again no houses but wild moors, a thread of road, & farms set in the earth, uncompromising, since nothing like flowers, long grass, or hedges grow round them.

Virginia Woolf, *Diary*, 18 March 1921

Men of
Altogether the life here is so dark and violent; it all happens in the senses, powerful and rather destructive: no mind nor mental consciousness, unintellectual. These men are passionate enough, sensuous, dark – God, how all my boyhood comes back – so violent, so dark, the mind always dark and without understanding, the senses violently active. It makes me sad beyond words. These men whom I love so much – and the life has such a power over me – they understand mentally so horribly: only industrialism, only wages and money and machinery. They can't think anything else. All their collective thinking is in those terms only. They are utterly unable to appreciate any pure, ulterior truth: only this industrial-mechanical-wage idea. This they will act from – nothing else . . . One must . . . think beyond them, know beyond them act beyond them.

D.H. Lawrence, Letter to Lady Ottoline Morrell, Ripley, 27 December 1915

River Derwent (Cumbria)

Was it for this
That one, the fairest of all rivers, loved
To blend his murmurs with my nurse's song,
And, from his alder shades and rocky falls,
And from his fords and shallows sent a voice
That flowed along my dreams? For this didst thou
O Derwent! winding among grassy holms
Where I was looking on, a babe in arms,
Make ceaseless music that composed my thoughts
To more than infant softness, giving me
Amid the fretful dwellings of mankind
A foretaste, a dim earnest of the calm
That Nature breathes among the hills and groves.

William Wordsworth, *The Prelude*, 1805
(text of 1850)

River Derwent (Derbyshire)

by Derwent's Willowy dells;
Where by tall groves his foamy flood he steers

Through ponderous arches o'er impetuous wears,
By Derby's shadowy towers reflective sweeps,
And gothic grandeur chills his dusky deeps.

Erasmus Darwin, *The Botanic Garden*, 'Economy of Vegetation', 1791

where Derwent rolls his dusky floods
Through vaulted mountains, and a night of woods.

Erasmus Darwin, *The Botanic Garden*, 'The Loves of the Plants', 1789

Derwent Water, Winander

Derwent! Winander! Sweetest of all sounds
The British tongue e'er utter'd! Lakes that Heaven
Reposes on, and finds his image there
In all its purity, in all its peace!

W.S. Landor, 'Written at Hurstmonceaux, on reading a poem of Wordsworth's', in *Last Fruit from an Old Tree*, 1853

Devonshire

More discontents I never had
Since I was born, then here;
Where I have been, and still am sad,
In this dull *Devon-shire*:

Yet justly too I must confesse;
I ne'r invented such
Ennobled numbers for the Presse,
Then where I loath'd so much.

Robert Herrick, *Discontents in Devon*, 1648

Virgil, if now alive, might make additions to his 'Georgics' from the plough-practice in this country . . . And Queen Elizabeth was wont to say of their gentry, 'They were all born courtiers with a becoming confidence.'

Thomas Fuller, *History of the Worthies of England*, 1662

'Tis a good proverb the Devonshire people have; Walk fast in snow, In frost walk slow, and still as you go, Tread on your toe: When frost and snow are both together, Sit by the fire and spare shoe-leather.

Jonathan Swift, *Journal to Stella*, January 1711

If ever you draw my affections nearer Devonshire than the Bath, you will have cause to think your self very Powerfull; for there's no Journey I dread like it, not even to Rome, tho the Pope & Pretender are there. The last ten miles of Rock, between Marlborow & Bath almost killed me once, & I really believe the Alps are more passable than from thence to Exeter.

Alexander Pope, Letter to William Fortescue, 25 December 1738

Devonshire is certainly a fine country, but by no means deserving of the encomiums which are passed upon it; those travellers who praise it so highly must either have come from Cornwall, or have slept through Somersetshire. Its rivers indeed are beautiful, clear, vocal, stony streams, with old bridges dangerously narrow, and angles in them like the corners of an English mince pie, for the foot-passenger to take shelter in.

Robert Southey, *Letters from England, by Don Manuel Alvarez Espriella*, 1807

Being agog to see some Devonshire, I would have taken a walk the first day, but the rain wo^{d} not let me; and the second, but the rain wo^{d} not let me; and the third, but the rain forbade it – Ditto 4 – ditto 5 – ditto – So I made up my mind to stop in doors, and catch a sight flying between the showers; and behold I saw a pretty valley – pretty cliffs, pretty Brooks, pretty Meadows, pretty trees, both standing as they were created, and blown down as they are uncreated – The green is beautiful, as they say, and pity it is that it is amphibious – mais! but alas! the flowers here wait as naturally for the Rain twice a day as the Muscles do for the Tide, – so we look upon a brook in these parts as you look upon a dash in your Country – there must be something to support this, aye fog, hail, snow rain – Mist – blanketing up three parts of the year – This devonshire is like Lydia Languish, very entertaining when at smiles, but cursedly subject to sympathetic moisture. You have the sensation of walking under one great Lamplighter: and you can't go on the other side of the ladder to keep your frock clean, and cosset your superstition.

John Keats, Letter to John Hamilton Reynolds, 14 March 1818

The land imagery of the north of Devon is most delightful.

Samuel Taylor Coleridge, *Table Talk*, 26 September 1830

Men of

A Devonshirer standing on his native hills is not a distinct object – he does not show against the light – a wolf or two would dispossess him.

John Keats, Letter to Benjamin Bailey, Teignmouth, 13 March 1818

Doncaster

Doncaster . . . a large and faire Towne, famous for greate Wax-lights, & good stockings.

John Evelyn, *Diary*, 16 August 1654

It was at Doncaster on Wednesday morning last that I heard of the Duke of Wellington's death, which at first nobody believed, but they speedily telegraphed to

London, and the answer proved that the report was correct. Doncaster was probably the only place in the kingdom where the sensation caused by this event was not absorbing and profound; but there, on the morning of the St. Leger, most people were too occupied with their own concerns to bestow much thought or lamentation on this great national loss.

Charles Greville, *A Journal of the Reign of Queen Victoria*, 18 September 1852

The landlord of the Reindeer told us at length of the difficulties with the swell-rough in race-weeks, and it appeared that at these times a loaded revolver always formed part of his personal outfit. 'This place is simply hell,' he said. 'We have two policemen continually at the foot of the stairs, and at any moment eight more can be summoned in 15 seconds.'

Arnold Bennett, *Journal*, 2 August 1897

Dorchester (Dorset)

Dorchester is indeed a pleasant, agreeable town to live in, and where I thought the people seem'd less divided into factions and parties, than in other places; for though here are divisions and the people are not all of one mind, either as to religion, or politicks, yet they did not seem to separate with so much animosity as in other places: Here I saw the Church of England clergyman, and the Dissenting minister, or preacher drinking tea together, and conversing with civility and good neighbourhood, like catholick Christians, and men of a catholick and extensive charity: The town is populous, tho' not large, the streets broad, but the buildings old, and low; however there is good company and a good deal of it; and a man that coveted a retreat in this world might as agreeably spend his time, and as well in Dorchester, as in any town that I know in England.

Daniel Defoe, *A Tour through the Whole Island of Great Britain*, 1724-7

Dorset

On the south parte, where it carieth the greatest length, it lieth all open to the sea, bearing upon the British Ocean . . . for fifty miles together, or much thereabout. A fruitfull soile it is: the North part thereof being overspred with woods and forrests; from thence garnished with many a greene hill, whereon feede flocks of sheepe in great number with pleasant pastures likewise and fruitfull valleis bearing corne: it hath a descent even to the verie sea shore . . .

William Camden, *Britain*, 1610
(Philemon Holland's translation)

Rime Intrinsica, Fontmell Magna, Sturminister
  Newton and Melbury Bubb,
Whist upon whist upon whist drive, in Institute,
  Legion and Social Club.
Horny hands that hold the aces which this morning
  held the plough –
While Tranter Reuben, T.S. Eliot, H.G. Wells and
  Edith Sitwell lie in Mellstock Churchyard now.

John Betjeman, 'Dorset', in *Collected Poems*, 1958
(Note: The names in the last line of this stanza are put in not out of malice or satire but merely for their euphony.)

River Dove

The Dove is various in its dales, like a great genius.

Alfred Lord Tennyson, quoted in *Alfred Lord Tennyson, a Memoir, by his Son*, 1897

Dover

and Folkstone
There was a whale came down the flood;
Folsteners couldn't catch 'un
But Doverers dud.

Anon., old country rhyme

Dover is commonly termed a den of thieves; and I am afraid it is not altogether without reason it has acquired this appellation. The people are said to live by piracy in time of war, and by smuggling and fleecing strangers in time of peace; but I will do them the justice to say, they make no distinction between foreigners and natives. Without all doubt, a man cannot be much worse lodged and worse treated in any part of Europe; nor will he in any other place meet with more flagrant instances of fraud, imposition and brutality. One would imagine they had formed a general conspiracy against all those who either go to, or return from, the continent.

Tobias Smollett, *Travels through France and Italy*, 1766

There they will extort the money out of your pocket, in a more unreasonable and rude manner, than is usually taken by a highwayman.

Philip Thicknesse, *Observations on the Customs and Manners of the French Nation*, 1766

A Dover and its custom-house are most judiciously placed . . . to counteract the effects of a too excessive joy.

John Mayne, *Journal*, 8 March 1815

Don Juan now saw Albion's earliest beauties:
  Thy cliffs, *dear* Dover, harbour and hotel,
Thy customhouse with all its delicate duties,
  Thy waiters running mucks at every bell,
Thy packets, all whose passengers are booties

To those who upon land or water dwell,
And last, not least to strangers uninstructed,
Thy long, long bills, whence nothing is deducted.

Lord Byron, *Don Juan*, 1819–24

The Duke talked of the sea encroaching at Dover, and of the various plans to stop it. 'What! there are plans?' said Sir Astley [Cooper]. 'Yes, yes, there are as many Dover doctors as other doctors,' said he; and we all laughed.

Duke of Wellington, remarks, 11 October 1839, quoted Benjamin Robert Haydon, *Diary*, of that date

I particularly detest Dover for the self-complacency with which it goes to bed. It always goes to bed (when I am going to Calais) with a more brilliant display of lamp and candle than any other town.

Charles Dickens, 'The Calais Night Mail', in *The Uncommercial Traveller*, 1861

Dover and Calais. What mean, amorphous entrance portals to great kingdoms! Mere grimy untended back-doors!

Arnold Bennett, *Journal*, 23 October 1897

Steep roads, a tunnel through chalk downs, are the approaches;
A ruined pharos overlooks a constructed bay;
The sea-front is almost elegant; all the show
Has, inland somewhere, a vague and dirty root:
Nothing is made in this town.

A Norman castle, dominant, flood-lit at night,
Trains which fume in a station built on the sea,
Testify to the interests of its regular life:
Here dwell the experts on what the soldiers want,
And who the travellers are

Whom ships carry in or out between the lighthouses,
Which guard for ever the made privacy of this bay
Like twin stone dogs opposed on a gentleman's gate.
Within these breakwaters English is properly spoken,
Outside an atlas of tongues . . .

The Old Town with its Keep and Georgian houses
Has built its routine upon such unusual moments;
Vows, tears, emotional farewell gestures,
Are common here, unremarkable actions
Like ploughing or a tipsy song.

W.H. Auden, *Dover*, August 1937

Dover Castle, seen from Calais

. . . seeing far off in the west the coast of England like a cloud crested with Dover Castle, which was but like the summit of the cloud.

Dorothy Wordsworth, *Journal*, August 1802

Dover Beach

The sea is calm tonight.
The tide is full, the moon lies fair
Upon the straits; – on the French coast the light
Gleams and is gone; the cliffs of England stand,
Glimmering and vast, out in the tranquil bay.
Come to the window, sweet is the night-air!

Only, from the long line of spray
Where the sea meets the moon-blanch'd land,
Listen! you hear the grating roar
Of pebbles which the waves draw back, and fling
At their return, up the high strand,
Begin, and cease, and then again begin,
With tremulous cadence slow, and bring
The eternal note of sadness in.

Matthew Arnold, *Dover Beach*, 1867

Dover Cliff

Heere's the place: stand still: how fearefull
And dizie 'tis, to cast one's eye's so low,
The Crowes and Choughes, that wing the midway ayre
Shew scarce so grosse as Beetles. Halfe way downe
Hangs one that gathers Samphire: dreadfull Trade:
Me thinkes he seemes no bigger then his head.
The Fishermen, that walke upon the beach
Appeare like Mice: and yond tall Anchoring Barke,
Diminish'd to her Cocke: her Cocke, a Buoy
Almost too small for sight. The murmuring Surge,
That on th' unnumbred idle Pebbles chafes
Cannot be heard so high.

William Shakespeare, *King Lear*, *c.* 1605–6

The Cliff, to which Shakespeare gave his immortal name, is, as all the world knows, a great deal lower than his description implies. Our Dover friends, justly jealous of the reputation of their Cliff, impute this diminution of its consequence to its having fallen in repeatedly since the poet's time. I think it more likely, that the imagination of Shakespeare, writing perhaps at a period long after he may have seen the rock, had described it such as he conceived it to have been. Besides, Shakespeare was born in a flat country, and Dover Cliff is at least lofty enough to have suggested the exaggerated features to his fancy.

Sir Walter Scott, Diary, 9 November 1826, in Lockhart, *Life of Scott*, 1838

The Downs

Though I have now travelled the Sussex Downs upwards of thirty years, yet I still investigate that chain of majestic mountains with fresh admiration year by year.

Gilbert White, Letter to Daines Barrington, 9 December 1773, in *The Natural History of Selbourne*, 1789

The Weald is good, the Downs are best –
I'll give you the run of 'em, East to West.
Beachy Head and Winddoor Hill,
They were once and they are still.
Firle, Mount Caburn and Mount Harry
Go back as far as sums'll carry.
Ditchling Beacon and Chanctonbury Ring,
They have looked on many a thing,
And what those two have missed between 'em,
I reckon Truleigh Hill has seen 'em.
Highden, Bignor and Duncton Down
Knew Old England before the Crown.
Linch Down, Treyford and Sunwood
Knew Old England before the Flood;
And when you end of the Hampshire side –
Butser's as old as Time and Tide.
The Downs are sheep, the Weald is corn,
You be glad you are Sussex born!

Rudyard Kipling, 'The Run of the Downs', *Rewards and Fairies*, 1910

Those Downs moved me to write some verses called 'Sussex'. To-day, from Rottingdean to Newhaven is almost fully developed suburb, of great horror.

Rudyard Kipling, *Something of Myself*, 1937

And perhaps before and above and beyond all such things there were the Downs. If you have been a little child brought up in those hills and in those days, you will understand their immortal loveliness. If, in your childhood you have walked over them and in them and under them; if you have seen their sweeping roundness, and the mists on them; and the sheep, and the little farmsteads in the bottoms, then you will know what I am talking about – but not otherwise. No one who was not there as a child can know that heaven, no grownup can capture it.

Eric Gill, *Autobiography*, 1940

River Duddon

I seek the birthplace of a native Stream. –
All hail, ye mountains! hail, thou morning light!
Better to breathe at large on this clear height
Than toil in needless sleep from dream to dream:
Pure flow the verse, pure, vigorous, free and bright,
For Duddon, long-loved Duddon, is my theme.

William Wordsworth, *The River Duddon*, 1806–20 (pub. 1820)

Dunmow

The Dunmow Flitch
One Robert Fitz-Walter, a powerful baron in this county in the time of Hen. III. on some merry occasion, which is not preserv'd in the rest of the story, instituted a custom in the priory here; that whatever married man did not repent of his being marry'd, or quarrel, or differ and dispute with his wife, within a year and a day after his marriage, and would swear to the truth of it, kneeling upon two hard pointed stones in the church yard, which stones he caus'd to be set up in the priory church-yard, for that purpose: The prior and convent, and as many of the town as would, to be present: such person should have a flitch of bacon.

Daniel Defoe, *A Tour through the Whole Island of Great Britain*, 1724–7

Dunstable

As plain as Dunstable road – It is applied to things plain and simple, without either welt or guard to adorn them, as also to matters easy and obvious to be found out without any difficulty or direction. Such this road, being broad and beaten, as the confluence of many leading to London from the north and north-west parts of this land.

Thomas Fuller, *History of the Worthies of England*, 1622

Downright Dunstable.

Old proverb

There were some good walkers that walked in the king's high waye, ordinarilye, uprightlye, plaine Dunstable waye.

Hugh Latimer, sermon before King Edward VI, 15 March 1549

Durham

I do loathe cities – that's certain. I am in Durham at an Inn – & that too I do not like – & have dined with a large parcel of Priests all belonging to the Cathedral – thoroughly ignorant & hard-hearted. I have had no small trouble in gaining permission to have a few books sent to me 8 miles from the place, which nobody has ever read in the memory of man. – Now you will think what follows a Lie – & it is not. I asked a stupid haugthy fool, who is the Librarian of the Dean & Chapter's Library in this city, if he had Leibnitz. He answered – 'We have no Museum in this Library for natural curiosities; but there is a mathematical Instrument-seller in the town, who shews such animacula thro' a glass of great magnifying powers.' Heaven & Earth! – he understood the word '*live Nits*.'

S.T. Coleridge, Letter to Robert Southey, 25 July 1801

Grey towers of Durham! . . .
Well yet I love thy mixed and massive piles,
Half church of God, half castle 'gainst the Scot;
And long to roam these venerable aisles,
With records stored of deeds long since forgot.

Sir Walter Scott, *Harold the Dauntless*, Canto III, 1817

Eastbourne

Your humble servant has been at this gay place now for eight long days. He has been led out daily to an extremely stony beach and there spread out in the sun for three, four or five hours as it might be, and he has there inhaled sea air into such lung as Providence has spared him, sea air mingled with the taint of such crabs as have gone recently from here to that bourne from which no traveller returns.

H.G. Wells, Letter, 1893, in *Experiment in Autobiography*, 1934

Eastwood (Nottinghamshire)

The scene of my Nottingham-Derby novels all centres round Eastwood, Notts, (where I was born): and whoever stands on Walker Street, Eastwood, will see the whole landscape of Sons and Lovers before him: Underwood in front, the hills of Derbyshire on the left, the woods and hills of Annesley on the right. The road from Nottingham by Watnall, Moorgreen, up to Underwood and on to Annesley (Byron's Annesley) – gives you all the landscape of the White Peacock, Miriam's farm in Sons and Lovers, and the home of the Crich family, and Willy Water, in Women in Love.

The Rainbow is Ilkeston and Cossall, near Ilkeston, moving to Eastwood. And Hermione, in Women in Love, is supposed to live not far from Cromford. The short stories are Ripley, Wirksworth, Stoney Middleton, Via Cellia, ('The Wintry Peacock'). The Lost Girl begins in Eastwood – the cinematograph show being held in Langley Mill.

D.H. Lawrence, Letter to H.A. Piehler, 17 April 1925

Eckington Bridge

O pastoral heart of England! like a psalm
Of green days, telling with a quiet beat.

Sir Arthur Quiller Couch, 'Ode Upon Eckington Bridge, River Avon', *Poems and Ballads*, 1896

Edgehill

I went to see Edgehill where was the famous battle fought in Cromwells tyme; . . . the Ridge of hills runs a great length and so high that the land beneath it appears vastly distant, its a rich ground full of inclosures and lookes finely, tho' formidable to look down on it and turnes ones head round, the wind allwayes blows with great violence there because of the steepness of the hill, the top is a flatt full of Barrows and hills that are markes of a Camp and battles.

Celia Fiennes, *Journeys*, *c.* 1685–96

Ely

Of all the *Marshland* Iles, I *Ely* am the Queene:
For winter each where sad, in me lookes fresh and greene.
The Horse, or other beast, o'rway'd with his own masse,
Lies wallowing in my Fennes, hid over head in grasse:
And in the place where growes ranke Fodder for my Neat;
The Turffe which beares the Hay, is wondrous needfull Peat:
My full and batning earth, needs not the Plowmans paines;
The Rils which runne in me, are like the branched vaines
In humane Bodies seene; those Ditches cut by hand
From the surrounding *Meres*, to winne the measured land,
To those choyce waters, I most fitly may compare,
Wherewith nice women use to blanch their Beauties rare.

Michael Drayton, *Poly-Olbion*, 1612–22

The dirtyest place I ever saw, not a bitt of pitching in the streetes so its a perfect quagmire the whole Citty, only just about the Palace and Churches the streetes are well enough for breadth but for want of pitching it seemes only a harbour to breed and nest vermin in, of which there is plenty enough, so that tho' my chamber was near 20 stepps up I had froggs and slow-worms and snailes in my roome – but it cannot but be infested with all such things being altogether moorish fenny ground which lyes low; its true were the least care taken to pitch their streetes it would make it looke more properly an habitation for human beings, and not a cage or nest of unclean creatures, it must needs be very unhealthy, tho' the natives say much to the contrary which proceeds from custom and use, otherwise to persons born in up and dry countryes it must destroy them like rotten sheep in consumptions and rhumes.

Celia Fiennes, *Journeys*, 1697

As these fenns appear cover'd with water, so I observ'd too, that they generally at this latter part of the year appear also cover'd with foggs, so that when the Downs and higher grounds of the adjacent country were gilded by the beams of the sun, the Isle of Ely look'd as if wrapp'd up in blankets, and nothing to be seen, but now and then, the lanthorn or cupola of Ely Minster.

Daniel Defoe, *A Tour through the Whole Island of Great Britain*, 1724–7

I first walked round the beautiful cathedral . . . It is impossible to look at that magnificent pile without *feeling* that we are a fallen race of men. The cathedral would, leaving out the palace of the bishop, and the houses of the dean, canons, and prebendaries, weigh more, if it were put into a scale, than all the houses in the town, and all the houses for a mile round the neighbourhood if you exclude the remains of the ancient monasteries. You have only to open your eyes to be convinced that England must have been a far greater and more wealthy country in those days than it is in these days. The hundreds of thousands of loads of stone, of which this cathedral and the monasteries in the neighbourhood were built, must all have been brought by sea from distant parts of the kingdom. These foundations were laid more than a thousand years ago; and yet there are vagabonds who have the impudence to say that it is the Protestant religion that has made England a great country.

William Cobbett, *Rural Rides – Eastern Tour*, 28 March 1830

The Isle of Ely lying on the fens is like a starfish lying on a flat stone at low tide.

Hilaire Belloc, *Hills and the Sea*, 1906

I know not by what accident it was, but never had I come so nearly into the presence of the men who founded England. The isolation of the hill, the absence of clamour, and false noise, and everything modern, the smallness of the village, the solidity and amplitude of the homes, and their security, all recalled an origin.

Ibid.

Epping Forest

and the Rodings

The country on that side of Essex is called the Roodings, I suppose because there are no less than ten towns almost together, called by the name of Roding, and is famous for good land, good malt, and dirty roads; the latter indeed in winter are scarce passable for horse or man.

Daniel Defoe, *A Tour through the Whole Island of Great Britain*, 1724-7

Epping for butter justly fam'd
  And pork in sausage pop't;
Where winter time, or summer time,
  Pig's flesh is always *chop't.*

But famous more, as annals tell,
  Because of Easter chaser;
There every year, 'twixt dog and deer,
  There is a gallant race.

Thomas Hood, *The Epping Hunt*, 1829

Epsom

We got to Epsum by 8 a-clock to the Well, where much company; and ther we light and I drank the water; they did not, but doe go about and walk a little among the women, but I did drink four pints and had some very good stools by it.

Samuel Pepys, *Diary*, 14 July 1667

I'm told, you think to take a Step some
Ten Miles from Town, t'a Place call'd *Epsom.*

Alexander Pope, *An Epistle to Henry Cromwell, Esq.*, 1707

Essex

A country large in compasse, fruitfull, full of woods plentifull of Saffron, and very wealthy: encircled, as it were, on the one side with the maine sea, on the other with fish-full rivers, which also doe afford peculiar commodities in great abundance.

William Camden, *Britain*, 1610
(Philemon Holland's translation)

A fair county, bearing the full proportion of five and thirty miles square, plentifully affording all things necessary to man's subsistence, save that the eastern part is not very healthful in the air thereof.

Those parts adjoining to the sea are commonly called 'The hundreds of Essex,' and are very fruitful in cattle. However, the vulgar wits of this county much astonish strangers with the stock of poor people in these parts, five hundred cows, nine hundred sheep, which indeed are but five cows, and nine sheep, in this part of the county called The Hundreds.

Thomas Fuller, *History of the Worthies of England*, 1662

The bleak flat, sedgy shores of Essex shun,
Where fog perpetual veils the winter sun;
Though flattering Fortune there invite thy stay,
Thy health the purchase of her smiles must pay.

John Scott, *Eclogue II*, 1786

How unjust the world is to Essex.

Matthew Arnold, Letter to his wife, 28 February 1853

The deepest Essex few explore
Where steepest thatch is sunk in flowers
And out of elm and sycamore
Rise flinty fifteenth century towers.

John Betjeman, 'Essex', in *Collected Poems*, 1958

Essex Marshes – Barnstaple Hundred, Rochford Hundred and Dengy Hundred

All along this county it was very frequent to meet with men that had had from five or six to fourteen or fifteen wives; nay, and some more; and I was informed that in the marshes on the other side the river over against Candy Island, there was a farmer who was then living with the five and twentieth wife, and that his son who was but 35 years old, had already had about fourteen. . . . The reason, as a merry fellow told me, who said he had had about a dozen and a half of wives (tho' I found afterwards he fibb'd a little) was this; That they, being bred in the marshes themselves, and season'd to the place, did pretty well with it; but that they always went up into the hilly country, or to speak their own language, into the uplands, for a wife: That when they took the young lasses out of the wholesome and fresh air, they were healthy, fresh and clear, and well; but when they came out of their native air into the marshes among the fogs and damps, there they presently chang'd their complexion, got an ague or two, and seldom held it above half a year, or a year at most; and then, said he, we go to the uplands again, and fetch another so that marrying of wives was reckon'd a kind of good farm to them.

Daniel Defoe, *A Tour through the Whole Island of Great Britain*, 1724-7

Eton

Ye distant spires, ye antique towers,
That crown the wat'ry glade,
Where grateful Science still adores
Her HENRY'S holy Shade;
And ye, that from the stately brow
Of WINDSOR'S heights th'expanse below
Of grove, of lawn, of mead survey,
Whose turf, whose shade, whose flowers among
Wanders the hoary Thames along
His silver-winding way.

Thomas Gray, *Ode on a Distant Prospect of Eton College*, 1742

I could not live the life they live at Eton – nothing but dress and ridicule going forward – and I really believe their fondness for ridicule tends to make them affected – the women in their manners and the men in their conversation – for witlings abound – and *puns* fly about like crackers, tho' you would scarcely guess they had any meaning in them, if you did not hear the noise they create.

Mary Wollstonecraft, Letter to Everina Wollstonecroft, 9 October 1786

The battle of Waterloo was won on the playing fields of Eton.

Arthur Wellesley, Duke of Wellington, saying attributed by Montalembert, *De l'avenir politique de l'Angleterre*, 1856

Or:
The battle of Waterloo was won here.

Duke of Wellington, Remark while watching a cricket match at Eton, attrib.

Four hundred summers and fifty have shone on the meadows of Thames and died
Since Eton arose in an age that was darkness and shone by his radiant side
As a star that the spell of a wise man's word bade live and ascend and Abide . . .
And ever as time's flow brightened, a river more dark than the storm-clothed sea,
And age upon age rose fairer and larger in promise of hope set free
With England Eton her child kept pace as mistress of men to be.

A.C. Swinburne, 'Eton, An Ode', in *Astrophel and Other Poems*, 1894

Probably the Battle of Waterloo *was* won on the playing-fields of Eton, but the opening battles of all subsequent wars have been lost there.

George Orwell, 'England Your England', *The Lion and the Unicorn*, 1941

Eton College in the eighteen-seventies and eighties was a vast incubator dedicatedly engaged in the task of hatching out the future rulers of the greatest Empire the world has ever known.

Leonard Mosley, *Curzon, the End of an Epoch*, 1960

Exeter

It is of a circular (and therefore most capable) form, sited on the top of a hill, having an easy ascent on every side thereunto. This conduceth much to the cleanness of this city; Nature being the chief scavenger thereof, so that the rain that falleth there falleth thence by the declivity of the place. The houses stand sideways, backward into their yards, and only endways with their gables towards the street. The city therefore is greater in content than appearance, being bigger than it presenteth itself to passengers through the same.

Thomas Fuller, *History of the Worthies of England*, 1662

Exeter is an antient city, and has been so slow in adopting modern improvements that it has the unsavoury odour of Lisbon.

Robert Southey, *Letters from England, by Don Manuel Alvarez Espriella*, 1807

Exeter was spoken of yesterday as being a place in which there is much gossiping, & that, perhaps, more among the men than even the women. There are many men who have settled here with their families from motives of general economy & convenience, have no occupation, & exercise their minds in hearing and reporting occurrences, great & little as they arise.

Joseph Farington, *Diary*, 12 November 1810

Falmouth

To Flamouth; . . .
Whose entrance is from sea so intricatelie wound,
Her haven angled so about her harbrous sound,
That in her quiet bay a hundred ships may ride,
Yet not the tallest mast, be of the tall'st descri'd.

Michael Drayton, *Poly-Olbion*, 'The First Song', 1612

The Town contains many Quakers and salt-fish, the oysters have a taste of copper owing to the soil of a mining country, the women (blessed be the Corporation therefore!) are flogged at the cart's tail when they pick and steal, as happened to one of the fair sex yesterday noon, she was pertinacious in her behaviour and damned the Mayor. – This is all I know of Falmouth.

Lord Byron, Letter to Francis Hodgson, 25 June 1809

Farnham

I was bred at the plough-tail, and in the Hop-Gardens of Farnham in Surrey, my native place, and which spot, as it so happened, is the neatest in England, and I believe, in the whole world. All there is a garden. The neat culture of the hop extends its influence to the fields round about. Hedges cut with shears and every other mark of skill and care strike the eye at Farnham, and become fainter and fainter as you go from it in every direction.

William Cobbett, *A Year's Residence in the United States of America*, 1817-19

Oh terrible country! Like a giant hen run. Half built houses everywhere. Roads scratched. Heath sandy and mangy.

Virginia Woolf, *Diary*, 21 December 1920

Fen Country (Norfolk etc.)

They that inhabited this fennish country . . . were . . . called . . . *Fen-men*, or *Fen-dwellers*. A kinde of people according to the nature of the place where they dwell rude, uncivill, and envious to all others whom they call *Upland-men*: who stalking high upon stilts, apply their mindes to grasing, fishing, and fowling. The whole region it selfe, which in winter season and sometimes most part of the yeers is oveflowed by the spreading waters of the rivers *Ouse, Nen, Welland, Glene* and *Witham*, having not leades and sewers large enough to voide away: But againe when their streames are retired within their own channels, it is so plenteous and ranke of certaine fatte grasse and full hey, (which they call *Lid*) thet when they have mowen downe as much . . . as will serve their turnes, they set fire to the rest and burne it in November, that it may come up againe in greater abundance. At which time a man may see this fennish and moist tract on a light flaming fire all over every way, and wonder thereat. Great plentie it hath besides of turfe and sedge for the maintenence of fire: of reed also for to thatch their houses, yea and of alders, beside other waterie shrubs. But chiefly it bringeth forth exceeding store of willows. . . .

William Camden, *Britain*, 1610 (Philemon Holland's translation)

There's not a hill in all the view,
Save that a forked cloud or two
Upon the verge of distance lies
And into mountains cheats the eyes.
And as to trees the willows wear
Lopped heads as high as bushes are;
Some taller things the distance shrouds
That may be trees or stacks or clouds
Or may be nothing; still they wear
A semblance where there's nought to spare . . .
Here's little save the river scene
And grounds of oats in rustling green
And crowded growths of wheat and beans
That with the hope of plenty leans . . .
And muse and marvel where we may
Gain mars the landscape every day – . . .
And the horizon stooping smiles
Oer treeless fens of many miles.
Spring comes and goes and comes again
And all is nakedness and fen.

John Clare, *The Fens*, *c*. 1824-36

Miles and miles and miles of desolation!
Leagues on leagues on leagues without a change!

Sign or token of some eldest nation
Here would make the strange land not so strange
Time-forgotten, yea, since time's creation,
Seem these borders where the sea-birds range.
A.C. Swinburne, 'By the North Sea', III, *Studies in Song*, 1880

A land that is lonelier than ruin;
A sea that is stranger than death:
Far fields that a rose never blew in,
Wan waste where the winds lack breath;
Waste endless and boundless and flowerless
But of marsh-blossoms fruitless as free:
Where earth lies exhausted as powerless
To strive with the sea . . .

The pastures are herdless and sheepless
No pasture or shelter for herds:
The wind is relentless and sleepless,
And restless and songless the birds;
Their cries from afar fall breathless,
Their wings are as lightnings that flee;
For the land has two lords that are deathless:
Death's self, and the sea.
A.C. Swinburne, 'By the North Sea', *Studies in Song*, 1880

From a dyke near the Nene beyond Ely, looking out to sea
Nowhere that I have been to in the world, does the land fade into the sea so inconspicuously.

The coasts of western England are like the death of a western man in battle—violent and heroic. The land dares all, and plunges into a noisy sea. This coast of eastern England is like the death of one of these eastern merchants here—lethargic, ill-contented, drugged with ease. The dry land slips and wallows into a quiet, very shallow water; confused with a yellow thickness and brackish with the weight of inland waters behind. . . . One does not understand the Fens until one has seen that shore

Hilaire Belloc, *Hills and the Sea*, 1906

Flamborough Head

Flamborough Head. I said to one of the boatmen: 'I suppose this is where people fall off?' He replied, 'Odd times,' and went on sucking at his pipe.

James Agate, *Ego 2* (12 August 1934), 1936

Flodden (Northumberland)

Still from the sire, the son shall hear
Of the stern strife, and carnage drear,
Of Flodden's fatal field,
Where shivered was fair Scotland's spear
And broken was her shield!
Sir Walter Scott, *Marmion*, 1808

Flushing (and Falmouth)

The situation of Flushing most favourable for consumptive invalids on account of the mildness of atmosphere in this part, protected by Hills from the East & the North and fronting the South and the West. It has been called the Montpellier of England. The scenery has much of the *Lake* character.

Joseph Farington, *Diary*, 22 September 1810

Foston (Yorkshire)

When I began to thump the cushion of my pulpit, on first coming to Foston, as is my wont when I preach, the accumulated dust of a hundred and fifty years made such a cloud, that for some minutes I lost sight of my congregation.

Sydney Smith, quoted in Lady Holland, *Memoir of Sydney Smith*, 1855

Fowey

The late ingenious Captain Grose was so delighted with Fowey that he used to say, he found a haunch of venison every twenty yards.

Anon., *A Guide to all the Watering and Sea-bathing Places*, *c.* 1810

Fountains Abbey (Yorkshire)

Abbey! for ever smiling pensively,
How like a thing of Nature dost thou rise,
Amid her loveliest works! as if the skies,
Clouded with grief, were arched thy roof to be,
And the tall trees were copied all from thee!
Mourning thy fortunes,—while the waters dim
Flow like the memory of thy evening hymn;
Beautiful in thy sorrowing sympathy,
As if they with a weeping sister wept,
Winds name thy name!
But thou, though sad, art calm,
And time with thee his plighted troth hath kept;
For harebells deck thy brow, and at thy feet,
Where sleep the proud, the bee and redbreast meet,
Mixing thy sighs with Nature's lonely Psalm.
Ebenezer Elliott, 'Fountains Abbey', *Works*, 1840

Frome

This appears to be a sort of little Manchester. A very small Manchester, indeed; for it does not contain above ten to twelve thousand people, but it has all the *flash* of a Manchester, and the innkeepers and their people look and behave like the Manchester fellows. I was, I must confess, glad to find proofs of the irretrievable decay of the place. I remembered how ready the bluff manufacturers had been to *call in the troops* of various descriptions.

William Cobbett, *Rural Rides,* 2 September 1826

Gads Hill

On one of our Sunday walks Jones and my Cousin and I were at Gad's Hill. An American tourist came up and asked if that was Charles Dickens's house, pointing to it. I looked grave, and said, 'Yes, I am afraid it was,' and left him.

Samuel Butler, *Further Extracts from Note-books,* 1934

Glastonbury

So this is Glastonbury. A green hill far away
Round as a lost round table; not a breath
Disturbs the too green grass where these grey ruins say

No more if even so much as the Preacher saith.
Bedivere, Arthur, Lancelot, Guinevere,
They left their names, their mark, and the mark is
death.

No more or not so much. Arriving here
For the first time I feel a mild surprise
Not to feel more surprised . . .

Louis MacNeice, *Autumn Sequel,* 1953

Gloucestershire

Beleeve me noble Lord
I am a stranger heere in Gloustershire,
These high wilde hilles, and rough uneeven waies
Drawes out our miles, and makes them wearisome.

William Shakespeare, *Richard II, c.* 1595–6

Gloucestershire kindness [said to be giving away what you do not want].

Godmanchester

Farewell Godmanchester where I
Was deluded by a Fairy.

Richard Brathwaite, *Barnabees Journall,* 1638

Godstow

Thence to Godsto, with my Lovers
Where a tombe a strumpet covers;
Rosamund lies there interrd,
Flesh to dust and shades compared
Lye he'above, or lye she under
To be buried, is no wonder.

Richard Brathwaite, *Barnabees Journall,* 1638

Gotham (Nottinghamshire)

As wise as a man of Gotham.
– It passeth publicly for the periphrasis of a fool; and a hundred fopperies are feigned and fathered on the town-folk of Gotham.

Thomas Fuller, *History of the Worthies of England,* 1662

This village has no neighbourhood, and, in itself, no prospect.

Anna Seward, Letter, September 1767, in 'Literary Correspondence', *Works,* 1810

as a symbol for England
Far off (no matter whether East or West,
A real country, or one made in jest),
Not yet by modern Mandevilles disgraced
Nor by map-jobbers wretchedly misplaced,
There lies an island, neither great nor small,
Which, for distinction sake, I Gotham call . . .
Europe discover'd India first; I found
My right to Gotham on the self-same ground; . . .
With Europe's rights my kindreds rights I twine,
Hers be the Western World, be Gotham mine.
Rejoice, ye happy Gothamites, rejoice;
Lift up your voice on high, a mighty voice,
The voice of gladness; and on every tongue,
In strains of gratitude, be praises hung,
The praises of so great and good a king;
Shall Churchill reign, and shall not Gotham sing?

Charles Churchill, *Gotham,* Book 1, 1764

(The proverb 'As the Wise men of Gotham' is a very old one. Gotham was a village in Nottinghamshire, celebrated for the stupidity of its inhabitants, who were said to have tried to drown an eel.)

Grasmere

Grasmere was very solemn in the last glimpse of twilight; it calls home the heart to quietness.

Dorothy Wordsworth, *Journal,*16 May 1800

We then went to John's Grove, sate a while at first. Afterwards William lay, and I lay, in the trench under the fence – he with his eyes shut, and listening to the waterfalls and the birds. There was no one waterfall above another – it was a sound of waters in the air – the voice of the air. William heard me breathing and rustling now and then, but we both lay still, and unseen by one another; he thought that it would be as sweet thus to lie so in the grave, to hear the *peaceful* sounds of the earth, and just to know that our dear friends were near.

Dorothy Wordsworth, *Journal*, 29 April 1802

Spirit of Grasmere, bells of Ambleside,
  Sing you and ring you, water bells, for me;
    You water-colour waterfalls may froth.
Long hiking holidays will yet provide
  Long stony lanes and back at six to tea
    And Heinz's ketchup on the tablecloth.

John Betjeman, 'Lake District', in *Collected Poems*, 1958

Gravesend

This Gravesend is a *cursed biting* place; the chief dependence of the people being the advantage they make of imposing upon strangers. If you buy anything of them and give half what they ask, you pay twice as much as the thing is worth.

Benjamin Franklin, *Journal of a Voyage from London to Philadelphia*, 22 July 1726

Guildford

Blandford and Dorchester are clean; but I have never yet seen anything like the towns in Surrey and Hampshire. If a Frenchman, born and bred, could be taken up and carried blindfold to Guildford, I wonder what his sensations would be, when he came to have the use of his sight! Every thing near Guildford seems to have received an influence from the town. Hedges, gates, stiles, gardens, houses inside and out, and the dresses of the people. The market day at Guildford is a perfect *show* of cleanliness

William Cobbett, *A Year's Residence in the United States of America*, 1817–19

Greenwich

The most delightful spot of ground in Great Britain; pleasant by situation, those pleasures encreas'd by art, and all made compleatly agreeable by the accident of fine buildings, the continual passing of fleets of ships up and down the most beautiful river in Europe; the best air, best prospect, and the best conversation in England.

Daniel Defoe, *A Tour through the Whole Island of Great Britain*, 1724–7

'No place on earth (he cry'd) like Greenwich hill!'
Up starts a Palace, lo! th'obedient base
Slopes at its foot, the woods its sides embrace,
The silver Thames reflects its marble face.

Alexander Pope, *Imitations of Horace*, Epistle 1, 1738

If the Parks be 'the lungs of London' we wonder what Greenwich Fair is – a periodical breaking out, we suppose – a sort of spring rash.

Charles Dickens, 'Greenwich Fair', *Sketches by Boz*, 1836–7

Time's headquarters.

Norman Shrapnel, *A View of the Thames*, 1977

Gurnard's Head (Cornwall)

The place is indescribable – far better than the Lizard or Land's End, or St Ives, or indeed anywhere.

Virginia Woolf, Letter to Lytton Strachey, Zennor, 30 March 1921

Hadrian's Wall

There continueth a setled perswasion among a great part of the people there about, and the same received by tradition: that the Roman souldiers of the marches did plant heere every where in old time for their use, certaine medicinable herbes for to cure wounds: whence it is that some Empiricke practitioners of Chirurgery of Scotland, flocke hither every yeere in the beginning of summer to gather such Simples and wound herbes, the vertue whereof they highly commend as found by long experience, and to be of singullar efficacie.

William Camden, *Britain*, 1610 (Philemon Holland's translation)

Halifax

Not many ages since tooke it this name; whereas before time it was called *Horton* as some of the Inhabitants doe report, who tell this prety story also, touching the alteration of the name.

A certaine Clerke, as they call him, was farre in love with a maiden who when he might not have his purpose of her, for all the faire meanes and entisements hee could use, his love being turned unto rage (vilanous wretch that he was) cut off the maides head: which being hung afterwards upon an Eugh-tree, the common people counted as an halloed relique, untill it was rotten, yea and they came devoutley to visit it, and every one gathered and carried away with him a branch or sprig of the sayd tree. But after the tree was bare and nothing left but the very stock (such was the credulity of that time) it maintained the opinion of reverence and religion still. For the people were perswaded, that the little veines that are stretched out and spred betweene the barke and bodie of the eugh tree in manner of haires or fine threads, were the very haires indeed of the virgins head. Hereupon they that dwelt there about repaired on pilgrimage hither, and such resort there was unto it, that *Horton* being but a little village before, grew up to a great towne, and was called by a new name, *Halig-fax*, or *Hali-fex*, that is *Holy haire*. For the Englishmen dwelling beyond *Trent* called the haire of the head *Fax*.

William Camden, *Britain*, 1610
(Philemon Holland's translation)

The town of Halifax is as unlike any American town as possible.

John W. Forney, *Letters from Europe*, 1867

Hampshire

A happy country in the four elements, if culinary fire in courtesy may pass for one, with plenty of the best wood for fuel thereof. Most pure and piercing the air of this shire; and none in England hath more plenty of clear and fresh rivulets of troutful water; not to speak of the friendly sea conveniently distanced from London. As for the earth, it is both fair and fruitful, and may pass for an expedient betwixt pleasure and profit; where, by mutual consent, they are moderately accommodated.

Thomas Fuller, *History of the Worthies of England*, 1662

Hampton Court

Why come ye not to Court
To whyche Court?
To the Kynge's Courte
Or to Hampton Court?
The Kynge's Courte
Shulde have the excellence;
But Hampton court
Hath the preeminence.

John Skelton, *Why Come Ye Not to Court*, 1522–3

Wattkyn: Hath the Cardinall any gay mansion?
Jeffary: Grett palaces without comparison . . .
Most glorious of outwarde sight
And within decked poynt device
More like unto a Paradice
Than an earthly Habitacion.

William Roy, *Rede Me and Be Nott Wrothe*, 1528

A roiall palace of the kings, a worke in truth of admirable magnificence built out of the ground by *Thomas Wolsey*, Cardinall, in ostentation of his riches, when for very pride, being otherwise a very prudent man, he was not able to manage his minde.

William Camden, *Britain*, 1610
(Philemon Holland's translation)

Here *Britain's* Statesmen oft the Fall foredoom
Of Foreign Tyrants, and of Nymphs at home;
Here thou, Great *Anna!* whom three Realms obey,
Dost sometimes Counsel take – and sometimes Tea.

Alexander Pope, *The Rape of the Lock*, 1714

The place can be seen as a kind of early super-suburbia, a mammoth exercise in top executive-style river-living.

Here is another great royal boot that treads on London's snaking river. . . .

Norman Shrapnel, *A View of the Thames*, 1977

David Garrick's villa at Hampton

Soon after Garrick's purchase at Hampton Court he was showing Dr Johnson over the grounds, the house, Shakespeare's temple, &c. and concluded by asking him, 'Well, Doctor, how do you like all this?' 'Why, it is pleasant enough,' growled the Doctor, 'for the present; but all these things, David, make death very terrible.'

William Cooke, *The Life of Samuel Foote*, 1810 –
Garrick bought his villa in 1754

Harrogate

Haragate . . . is just by the Spaw, . . . its all marshy and wett and here in the compass of 2 miles is 4 very different springs of water; there is the Sulpher or Stincking spaw, not improperly term'd for the Smell being so very strong and offensive that I could not force my horse near the Well.

Celia Fiennes, *Journeys*, 1697

*Truly, after having considered all the parts and particulars of the place, I cannot account for the concourse of people one finds here, upon any other principle but that of caprice, which seems to be the character of our nation.

Harrigate is a wild common, bare and bleak, without tree or shrub, or the least signs of cultivation; and the people who come to drink the water, are crowded together in paltry inns, where the few tolerable rooms are monopolized by the friends and favourites of the house, and all the rest of the lodgers are obliged to put up with dirty holes, where there is neither space, air, nor convenience. My apartment is about ten feet square; and when the folding bed is down, there is just room sufficient to pass between it and the fire. One might expect, indeed, that there would be no occasion for a fire at Midsummer; but here the climate is so backward, that an ash tree, which our landlord has planted before my window, is just beginning to put forth its leaves; and I am fain to have my bed warmed every night.

Tobias Smollett, *Humphrey Clinker*, 1771
('Matthew Bramble's' comments)

Harrowgate seemed to be the most heaven-forgotten

country under the sun. When I saw it there were only nine mangy fir-trees there; and even they all leant away from it.

Sydney Smith, quoted in Lady Holland, *Memoir of Sydney Smith*, 1855

'The place thou seest,' the old man said
'Is not unknown to fame;
Though young in years 'tis widely known
And Harrogate its name.

The reason why it stands so high
Expos'd on every hand,
Is that health-giving fountains flow
From out the barren land.' . . .

'Most wonderful,' the stranger cried
'The Great Creator's plan;
How watchful is his providence!
How great his care of man!

Say canst thou tell me who he was
Who made these waters known
Is he forgot? or is he named?
With honour and renown?'

'Not quite forgot,' the old man said
'Not yet with great renown
This benefactor of mankind
Has to our days come down.

Sir William Slingsby was his name
A Warrior tried and brave
And centuries twain have passed away
Since he sunk to the grave . . .

A miry swamp, dirty and damp
Around was widely spread
And the spongy soil that ye passed with toil
Trembled beneath the tread.

None but the eye of the learned sage
Saw aught uncommon there;
Yet Slingsby, when he saw it rise
Deemed it had virtues rare.

With eager lip he bent to sip
The water as it ran;
At every taste more pleased was he
That sage, experienced man.

He bade the workmen cleanse the spring
And guard it round about
To keep the precious waters in
And vile pollution out.

He of its many virtues told
Almost beyond belief;
And sick and feeble came and drank
And many found relief.

And from such small beginning rose
The town thou seest around;
It started grew and widely spread
And who shall fix its bound?' . . .

To some the golden mine is given
To some the corn and wine;
But water, – peerless water!
O Harrogate, is thine!

William Grainge of Harrogate, *The Origin of Harrogate, a Ballad*, nineteenth century

Harrow School

It may be true or it may not that the Battle of Waterloo was won on the playing fields of Eton, but it is quite obvious that Abyssinia was lost on the playing fields of Harrow.

Clement Attlee, Remark at the time of the Hoare-Laval Pact, 1935
(Stanley Baldwin and Sir Samuel Hoare were old Harrovians.)

Hitler, in one of his recent discourses, declared that the fight was between those who have been through the Adolf Hitler schools and those who have been at Eton. Hitler has forgotten Harrow . . .

Sir Winston Churchill, Speech at Harrow, 18 December 1940

Hartlepool

The rocks, the sea, & the weather there more than made up to me the want of bread & the want of water, two capital defects, but of which I learned from the inhabitants not to be sensible. They live on the refuse of their own fish-market, with a few potatoes, & a reasonable quantity of Geneva, six days in the week, & I have nowhere seen a taller, more robust, or healthy race. every house full of ruddy broad-faced children. Nobody dies but of drowning or old age. Nobody poor but from drunkenness or mere laziness.

Thomas Gray, Letter to James Brown, 15 August 1765

Harwich

The towne is not great, but well peopled, fortified by Art and nature, and made more sensible by Queene Elizabeth. The salt water so creaketh about it, that it almost insulateth it, but thereby maketh the springs so brackish, that there is a defect of fresh water, which they fetch some good way off.

William Camden, *Britain*, 1610
(Philemon Holland's translation)

Harwich is noted for being the port where the packet-boats between England and Holland go out, and come in: The inhabitants are far from being fam'd for good usage to strangers, but on the contrary, are blamed for being extravagant in their reckonings, in the publick houses, which has not a little encourag'd the setting up of sloops, which they now call passage-boats, to Holland, to go directly from the river of Thames . . . The inhabitants seem warm in their nests.

Daniel Defoe, *A Tour through the Whole Island of Great Britain*, 1724–7

*Harwich is not a merry town, towards evening you might call it dull.

Jerome K. Jerome, *Three Men on the Bummel*, 1900

Hastings

The society at Hastings is gay, without profligacy.

Anon., *A Guide to all the Watering and Sea-bathing Places*, *c.* 1810

I have been here renewing my acquaintance with my old friend Ocean; and I find his bosom as pleasant a pillow for an hour in the morning as his daughter's of Paphos could be in the twilight. I have been swimming and eating turbot, and smuggling neat brandies and silk handkerchiefs, – and listening to my friend Hodgson's raptures about a pretty wife-elect of his, – and walking on cliffs, and tumbling down hills, and making the most of the '*dolce far-niente*' for the last fortnight.

Lord Byron, Letter to Thomas Moore, 3 August 1814

'Twas August – Hastings every day was filling –
Hastings, that 'greenest spot on memory's waste!'
With crowds of idlers willing or unwilling
To be bedipped – be noticed – or be braced,
And all things rose a penny in the shilling . . .

Thomas Hood, *A Storm at Hastings*, 1839

This is dull enough.

Arthur Hugh Clough, Letter to Charles Eliot Norton, 29 December 1859

Like all the larger English watering-places, it is simply a little London *super mare*.

Henry James, 'An English Winter Watering-Place', 1879, in *Portraits of Places*, 1883

Could not get in at Hastings where the architectural style, according to Leo, is divided between Early Wedding Cake and Late Water Closet.

James Agate, *Ego 2* (22 August 1934), 1936

Haworth

There is a spot, mid barren hills
  Where winter howls and driving rain;
But if the dreary tempest chills
  There is a light that warms again.

The house is old, the trees are bare
  Moonless above bends twilight's dome
But what on earth is half so dear –
  So longed for – as the hearth of home.

The mute bird sitting on the stone
  The dark moss dripping from the wall
The thorn-trees gaunt, the walks o'ergrown
  I love them – how I love them all.

Emily J. Bronte, *Remembrance of Haworth Parsonage*, 1834

There let me dwell, to busy life unknown
  Where Nature's charms promiscuously blend
To breathe the fragrance of the florid lawn
  And share the solace of a social friend.

Joseph Hardaker of Haworth, *On Leaving York*, quoted in J. Horsefall Turner (ed.), *A Yorkshire Anthology*, 1901

The crowded graveyard, the tall solemn trees,
The dark tower and the narrow climbing street,
At every turn the grim blue distances,
The gray roofs and the hill-winds blowing sweet –

Here at the world's end in this house of stone
Gazing upon the tombs and the far hills,
Lived Genius, daughter of the Air and Fire,
The lovely victim of the harsh world's ill.

Then afterward we found a long green dale
Walled up to heaven with all its scattered farms,
And lean fields parcelled out with dun stone walls
And ragged clouds piled on the moor's faint arms.

In the gray ash-tree sang the black-birds of May,
And a remote ancestral beauty blessed
The granges and the groves, the water troughs
Flooded with upland crystal, and caressed

The hillsides with a magic wing, and I
Was near to tears whene'er I thought of thee,
Most glorious of that cabined falcon-brood,
Virgin and poet, huntress, Emily . . .

Wilfred Rowland Childe, 'Haworth in May', *Selected Poems*, 1936

Enormously impressed with Haworth Parsonage – the only place of its kind which has not disappointed me. The day was dressed to suit, sombre and cheerless, and the brow on which the house stands was wind-swept and forbidding. The house is large enough to have permitted all that secrecy of composition. I was struck, as always on such occasions, by the deadness of it all.

James Agate, *Ego 2* (14 August 1935), 1936

Helvellyn

We accompanied John over the fork of Helvellyn on a day when light & darkness coexisted in contiguous masses, & the earth & sky were but *one!* Nature lived for us in all her grandest accidents.

S.T. Coleridge, Letter to Dorothy Wordsworth, *c.* 10 November 1799

Helvellyn slopes where Coleridge crept
And Southey sprang
Where Wordsworth hoisted up with ropes
Took out his fountain pen and sang.

Anon.

Herefordshire

This Country, besides that it is right pleasant, is for yeelding of corne, and feeding of cattaile, in all places most fruitfull, and therewith passing well furnished with all things necessary for man's life: in so much, as it would skorne to come behind any one country throughout all England for fertility of soile, and therefore say that for three W.W.W. wheat, woll and water, it yeeldeth to no shire of England

William Camden, *Britain,* 1610 (Philemon Holland's translation)

Herne Bay

Herne Bay. Hum. I suppose it's no worse than any other place in this weather – but it *is* watery, rather – isn't it? In my mind's eye I have the sea in a perpetual state of smallpox; and the chalk running downhill like town milk.

Charles Dickens, Letter to Douglas Jerrold, 13 June 1843

Hertfordshire

It is the garden of England for delight; and men commonly say, that such who buy a house in Hertfordshire, pay two years' purchase for the air thereof.

Thomas Fuller, *History of the Worthies of England*, 1662

The custom is in this part of Hertfordshire (and I am told it continues into Bedfordshire) to leave a *border* round the ploughed part of the fields to bear grass and to make hay from, so that, the grass being now made into hay, every corn field has a closely mowed grass walk about ten feet wide all round it, between the corn and the hedge. This is most beautiful! The hedges are now full of the shepherd's rose, honeysuckles, and all sorts of wild flowers; so that you are upon a grass walk, with this most beautiful of all flower-gardens and shrubberies on your one hand, and with the corn on the other. And thus you go from field to field (on foot or on horseback), the sort of corn, the sort of underwood and timber, the shape and size of the fields, the height of the hedge-rows, the height of the trees all continually varying. Talk of *pleasure-grounds* indeed! What that man ever invented, under the name of pleasure-grounds can equal these fields in Hertfordshire?

William Cobbett, *Rural Rides*, 24 June 1822

I had forgotten Hertfordshire,
The large unwelcome fields of roots
Where with my knickerbockered sire
I trudged in syndicated shoots . . .

Colour-washed cottages reed-thatched
And weather-boarded water mills,
Flint churches, brick and plaster patched,
On mildly undistinguished hills –

These still are there. But now the shire
Suffers a devastating change,
Its gentle landscape strung with wire,
Old places looking ill and strange.

One can't be sure where London ends,
New towns have filled the fields of root
Where father and his business friends
Drove in the Landaulette to shoot;

Tall concrete standards line the lane,
Brick boxes glitter in the sun:
Far more would these have caused him pain
Than my mishandling of a gun.

John Betjeman, 'Hertfordshire', in *Collected Poems*, 1958

High Wycombe

High Wycombe, as if the name was ironical, lies along the bottom of a narrow and deep valley, the hills on each side being very steep indeed . . . Wycombe is a very fine, and very clean market town; the people all looking extremely well; the girls somewhat larger featured and larger boned than those in Sussex, and not so fresh-coloured and bright-eyed. More like the girls of

America, and that is saying quite as much as any reasonable woman can expect or wish for.

William Cobbett, *Rural Rides,* 24 June 1822

Hinchinbrooke

Well! I saw Hinchinbrook this morning. Considering it is in Huntingdonshire, the situation is not so ugly or melancholy as I expected; but I do not conceive what provoked so many of your ancestors to pitch their tents in that triste country, unless the Capulets loved fine prospects. The house of Hinchinbrook is most comfortable, and just what I like; old, spacious, irregular, yet not vast or forlorn. I believe much has been done since you saw it – it now only wants an apartment, for in no part of it are there above two chambers together.

Horace Walpole, Letter to George Montagu, 31 May 1763

Hockley in the Hole

Wee came to *Hockley* in the *Hole*, so named of the miry way in winter time verie troublesome to travelers: For the old Englishmen our progenitors called deepe myre *Hock* and *Hocks*. So passing along fields smelling sweet in Sommer of the best beanes, which with their redolent savour do dull the quick sent of hounds and spaniels, not without fuming and chafing of hunters.

William Camden, *Britain,* 1610
(Philemon Holland's translation)

Holmwood

It is suggested that this place was in antient times so unpassable a wild, or overgrown waste, the woods so thick, and the extent so large, reaching far into Sussex, that it was the retreat for many ages of the native Britons who the Romans cou'd never drive out; and after that it was the like to the Saxons, when the Danes harrass'd the nation with their troops, and ravag'd the country, wherever they came; and on this account they retain here in memory the following lines.

This is Holmes Dale,
Never conquer'd, never shall.

But this is a piece of history, which I leave as I find it.

Daniel Defoe, *A Tour through the Whole Island of Great Britain,* 1724–7

Huddersfield (and Warrington)

If ever I wanted to make a serious study of my native country, I should flee from London and steep myself in Huddersfield and Warrington.

Arnold Toynbee, *East to West* 1958

Hull

Foure well built Gates, with bolts, & lockes, & bars,
For ornament or strength, in Peace or Wars:
Besides, to keepe their Foes the further out
They can Drowne all the Land three miles about.
'Tis plentifully serv'd with Flesh and Fish,
As cheape, as reasonable man can wish.
And thus by Gods grace, and mans industry,
Dame Nature, or mens Art doth it supply.
Some 10. yeeres since Fresh water there was scant,
But with much Cost they have suppli'd that want;
By a most ex'lent Water-worke that's made,
And to the Towne in Pipes it is convai'd,
Wrought with most Artificiall engines, and
Perform'd by th'Art of the Industrious hand
Of Mr *William Maultby*, Gentleman,
So that each man of Note there alwayes can
But turne a Cocke within his House, and still
They have Fresh-water alwayes at their will,
This have they all unto their Great Content,
For which, they each doe pay a yeerely Rent.
There is a Proverbe, and a Prayer withall,
That we may not to three strange places fall:
From *Hull,* from *Halifax,* from *Hell,* 'tis thus,
From all these three, *Good Lord deliver us.*
This praying Proverb's meaning to set downe,
Men doe not wish deliverance from the Towne:
The Town's nam'd *Kingston, Hul's* the furious River;
And from *Hull's* dangers, I say, *Lord deliver.*

John Taylor, *A Very Merry Wherry-Ferry-Voyage,* 1622

Hull a frightful, dirty, *brick-housey,* tradesmanlike, rich, vulgar place: yet the river, though the shores are so low that they can hardly be seen, looked beautiful with the evening lights upon it, and boats moving about.

Dorothy Wordsworth, *Journal,* 26 July 1802

It is a little city of London; streets, shops, everything like it; clean as the best parts of London and the people as bustling and attentive. The town of Hull is *surrounded* with commodious docks for shipping.

William Cobbett, *Rural Rides–Eastern Tour,* 19 April 1830

River Humber

The Humber rough and stout.

Edmund Spenser, *Astrophel,* 1586

Where Humber pours his rich commercial stream
There dwelt a wretch, who breath'd but to blaspheme.

William Cowper, *A Tale, founded on a Fact,* January 1779

and Humber Bridge

The bridge that goes from nowt to nowt.
A bridge too far.

Local Sayings, before the opening of the bridge, quoted *Time Magazine,* 15 June 1981

The Humber Bridge is the biggest pink elephant in history . . . it should have been finished in 1976 but it never was.

Anon Schoolboy, examination script, Hull, 1981

Huntingdon

All that I have yet seen of Huntingdon I like exceedingly. It is one of those pretty, clean, unstenched, unconfined places that tend to lengthen life and make it happy.

William Cobbett, *Rural Rides*, 22 January 1822

Ickworth

Ickworth bears the same proportion to the Coliseum as a currant dumplin does to the hunting pudding of the Pytchely Hunt boiled in a sixty gallon! Verily the place deserves a better house. House! my English education will hardly allow me to call it a house.

J. Spiller, Letter to John Soane, 1 September 1821

Ipswich

A faire towne resembling a City, situate in a ground somewhat low: which is the eie (as it were) of this shire, as having an haven commodious enough; fensed in times past with a trench and rampire, of good trade and stored with wares, well peopled and full of inhabitants, adourned with foureteene Churches, and with goodly, large, and stately aedifices. I say nothing of foure religious houses now overturned, and that sumptuous and magnificent Colledge which Cardinall *Wolsey*, a Butchers sonne of this place, heere began to build, whose vast minde reached alwaies at things too high.

William Camden, *Britain*, 1610
(Philemon Holland's translation)

I take this town to be one of the most agreeable placed in England, for families who have liv'd well, but may have suffered in our late calamities of stocks and bubbles, to retreat to, where they may live within their own compass

Daniel Defoe, *A Tour through the Whole Island of Great Britain*, 1724–7

. . . The Florence of Suffolk, called Ipswich . . .

Edward Fitzgerald, Letter to Frederick Tennyson, 10 December 1843

Ireby

One of those townlets in which every thing reminds us of the distance from the metropolis.

Robert Southey, *Letters from England, by Don Manuel Alvarez Espriella*, 1807

Kendal

that dale . . . where Kendale towne doth stand
For making of our cloth scarce match'd in all the land.

Michael Drayton, *Poly-Olbion*, 'The Thirtieth Song', 1622

The Town consists chiefly of three nearly parallel streets almost a mile long. Except these all the other houses seem as if they had been dancing a country-dance & were out: there they stand back to back, corner to corner, some up hill, some down, without intent or meaning.

Thomas Gray, *Journal*, Letter to Thomas Wharton, 9 October 1769

Kent

From the river *Darent* or *Dart* unto the mouth of *Medway*, the Tamis seeth nothing aboue him but little townes pleasantly seated, which to passe over in silence were no prejudice either of their fame or any thing els.

William Camden, *Britain*, 1610
(Philemon Holland's translation)

A knight of Cales, and a gentleman of Wales,
And a laird of the north countree;
A yeoman of Kent, with his yearly rent,
Will buy them out all three.

Traditional, quoted in Thomas Fuller, *History of the Worthies of England*, 1662

(Cales–Calais. Robert Earl of Essex made sixty knights, on his Calais expedition in 1596, some of whom were impecunious, and 'therefore queen Elizabeth was half offended with the earl for making knighthood so common'.)

Some hold, when hospitality died in England, she gave her last groan among the yeomen of Kent.

Thomas Fuller, *The Holy State and the Profane State*, 1642

I came back through a Country the best cultivated of any that in my life I had any where seene, every field lying as even as a bowling greene, & the fences, plantations and husbandrie in such admirable order, as infinitely delighted me, after the sad and afflicting specctacles & objects I was come from: observing almost every tall tree to have a Weather-cock on the top bough, & some trees halfe a dozen, I learned, that on a certain holy-day, the Farmers feast their Servants, at which solemnity they set up these Cocks in a kind of Triumph . . .

John Evelyn, *Diary*, March 1672

Pray, whenever you travel in Kentish roads, take care of keeping your driver sober.

Horace Walpole, Letter to Richard Bentley, 5 August 1752

Vanguard of Liberty, ye men of Kent,
Ye children of a Soil that doth advance
Her haughty brow against the coast of France . . .

William Wordsworth, *To the Men of Kent*, October 1803

On, on! through meadows managed like a garden,
A paradise of hops and high production;
For after years of travel by a bard in
Countries of greater heat but lesser suction,
A green field is a sight which makes him pardon
The absence of that more sublime construction,
Which mixes up vines, olives, precipices,
Glaciers, volcanoes, oranges, and ices.

Lord Byron, *Don Juan*, 1819–24

*Kent, Sir, – everybody knows Kent – Apples, cherries, hops and women.

Charles Dickens, *Pickwick Papers*, 1837 (Jingle)

Keswick

It was well knowen many yeeres agoe by reason of the mines of copper, . . . and is at this day much inhabited by Minerall men, who have heere there smelting house by *Derwent* side which with his forcible streame, and their ingenious inventions serveth them in notable steede for easie bellowes workes, hammer workes, forge workes, and sawing of boords, not without admiration of such as behold it.

William Camden, *Britain*, 1610 (Philemon Holland's translation)

If I cannot procure a suitable house at Stowey, I return to Cumberland & settle at Keswick – in a house of such prospect, that if, according to you & Hume, impressions & ideas *constitute* our Being, I shall have a tendency to become a God – so sublime & beautiful will be the series of my visual existence.

S.T. Coleridge, Letter to William Godwin, 21 May 1800

Keswick Lake

The Lake of Kewsick has this decided advantage over the others which we have seen, that it immediately appears to be what it is, . . . You do not wish it to be larger, the mirror is in perfect proportion to its frame.

Robert Southey, *Letters from England, by Don Manuel Alvarez Espriella*, 1807

Kew

Hail Kew! thou darling of the tuneful nine,
Thou eating-house of verse, where poets dine;
The groves of Kew, however misapplied,
To serve the purposes of lust and pride,
Were, by the greater monarch's care, designed
A place of conversation for the mind;
Where solitude and silence should remain,
And conscience keep her sessions and arraign.

Thomas Chatterton, *Kew Gardens*, 1770

So sits enthroned in vegetable pride
Imperial Kew by Thames's glittering side;
Obedient sails from realms unfurrow'd bring
For her the unnamed progeny of spring;
Attendant nymphs her dulcet mandates hear,
And nurse in fostering arms the tender year,
Plant the young bulb, inhume the living seed,
Prop the weak stem, the erring tendril lead;
Or fan in glass-built fanes the stranger flowers
With milder gales, and steep with warmer showers.
Delighted Thames through tropic umbrage glides
And flowers antarctic, bending o'er his tides;
Drinks the new tints, the sweets unknown inhales,
And calls the sons of science to his vales.
In one bright point admiring nature eyes
The fruits and foliage of discordant skies
Twines the gay forest with discordant bough,
And bends the wreath round George's royal brow.

Erasmus Darwin, *The Botanic Garden*, 'Economy of Vegetation', 1791

From Paradise Adam and Eve were shut out
As a punishment due to their sin
But here after nine should you loiter about
For your punishment you'd be shut in.

Anon., *On being locked in Kew Gardens which shut at nine*, Nineteenth century

Go down to Kew in lilac-time, in lilac-time, in lilac time
Go down to Kew in lilac-time (it isn't far from London!)
And you shall wander hand in hand with love in summer's wonderland;
Go down to Kew in lilac-time (it isn't far from London!).

Alfred Noyes, 'The Barrel Organ', *Collected Poems*, 1910

Kingsgate (between Margate and Broadstairs, Kent)

Here Seagulls scream and cormorants rejoice,
And Mariners tho' shipwreckt dread to land,
Here reign the blustring north and blighting east,
No tree is heard to whisper, bird to sing,
Yet nature cannot furnish out the feast,
Art he invokes new horrors still to bring.

Now mouldring fanes and battlements arise,
Arches and turrets nodding to their fall,
Unpeopled palaces delude his eyes,
And mimick desolation covers all.

Thomas Gray, *On Lord Holland's Villa at Kingsgate,* 1768

That half-crystallised nowhere of a place, Kingsgate.

D.H. Lawrence, Letter to Lady Cynthia Asquith, August 1913

Kingston

The purplish fields outside Kingston somehow reminded me of Saragossa. There is a foreign look about a town which stands up against the sunset, & is approached by a much trodden footpath across a field. I wonder why one instinctively feels that one is complimenting Kingston absurdly in saying that it is like a foreign town.

Virginia Woolf, *Diary,* 9 January 1915

Knutsford

For warmth give me red Knutsford: it glows like a firelit room full of old masters in heavy gilt frames; its mellow, settled habitableness the sum of all that men and women neither poor nor very rich could think of, in about nine hundred years, to make their town good to live in.

C.E. Montague, *The Right Place,* 1924

Lake District

Far from my dearest friend 'tis mine to rove,
Through bare grey dell, high wood, and pastoral cove;
Where Derwent rests, and listens to the roar
That stuns the tremulous cliffs of high Lodore;
Where peace to Grasmere's lonely island leads,
To willowy hedge-rows, and to emerald meads;
Leads to her bridge, rude church, and cottaged grounds,
Her rocky sheepwalks, and her woodland bounds;
Where, undisturbed by winds, Winander sleeps;
'Mid clustering isles, and holly-sprinkled steeps;
Where twilight glens endear my Esthwaite's shore,
And memory of departed pleasures, more.

William Wordsworth, *An Evening Walk,* 1787–9 (pub. 1793)

near Ullswater

When we were in the woods beyond Gowbarrow Park we saw a few daffodils close to the water-side. We fancied that the lake had floated the seeds ashore, and that the little colony had so sprung up. But as we went along there were more and yet more; and at last, under the boughs of the trees, we saw that there was a long belt of them along the shore, about the breadth of a country turnpike road. I never saw daffodils so beautiful. They grew among the mossy stones about and about them; some rested their heads upon these stones as on a pillow for weariness; and the rest tossed and reeled and danced, and seemed as if they verily laughed with the wind, that blew upon them over the lake; they looked so gay, ever glancing, ever changing. The wind blew directly over the lake to them. There was here and there a little knot, and a few stragglers a few yards higher up; but they were so few as not to disturb the simplicity, unity and life of that one busy highway.

Dorothy Wordsworth, *Journal,* 15 April 1802
(And hence William's 'I wandered lonely as a cloud', of 1804)

Waterfall dividing Great Robinson from Buttermere Halse Fell

The Thing repaid me amply it is a great Torrent from the Top of the Mountain to the Bottom the lower part of it is not the least Interesting, where it is beginning to slope to a level – the mad water rushes thro' its *sinuous* Bed, or rather prison of Rock, with such rapid Curves, as if it turned the Corners not from the mechanic force, but with foreknowledge, like a fierce & skilful Driver great Masses of Water, one after the other, that in twilight one might have feelingly compared them to a vast crowd of huge white Bears, rushing one over the other against the wind – their long white hair shattering abroad in the wind. The remainder of the Torrent is marked out by three great Waterfalls – the lowest apron-shaped, and though the Rock down which it rushes is an inclined Plane, it shoots off in such an independence of the Rock as shews that it's direction was given it by the force of the Water from above. The middle, which in peacable times would be two tinkling Falls, formed in this furious Rain one great *Water-wheel* endlessly revolving & double the size and height of the lowest – the third & highest is a mighty one indeed it is twice the height of both the others added together nearly as high as Scale Force but it rushes down an inclined Plane – and does not *fall,* like Scale Force however, if the Plane has been smooth, it is so near a Perpendicular that it would have *appeared* to fall – but it is indeed so fearfully savage, & black, & jagged, that it tears the flood to pieces – and one great black Outjutment divides the water, & overbrows & keeps uncovered a long slip of jagged black Rock beneath, which gives a marked *character* to the whole force. What a sight it is to look down on such a Cataract! – the wheels that circumvolve in it – the leaping up & plunging forward of that infinity of Pearls & Glass Bulbs – the continual *change* of the *Matter,* the perpetual

Sameness of the *Form* – it is an awful Image & Shadow of God & the World

S.T. Coleridge, letter to Sara Hutchinson, 25 August 1802

*'We have not quite determined how far it shall carry us,' said Mr Gardiner, 'but perhaps to the Lakes.'

No scheme could have been more agreeable to Elizabeth, and her acceptance of the invitation was most ready and grateful. 'My dear, dear aunt,' she rapturously cried, 'what delight! what felicity! You give me fresh life and vigour. Adieu to disappointment and spleen. What are men to rocks and mountains? Oh! what hours of transport we shall spend! And when we *do* return, it shall not be like other travellers, without being able to give one accurate idea of any thing. We *will* know where we have gone—we *will* recollect what we have seen. Lakes, mountains and rivers, shall not be jumbled together in our imaginations; nor, when we attempt to describe any particular scene, will we begin quarrelling about its relative situation. Let *our* first effusions be less insupportable than those of the generality of travellers.'

Jane Austen, *Pride and Prejudice*, 1813

'Mid rocks and ringlets, specimens and sighs,
On wings of rapture every moment flies.
He views Matilda, lovely in her prime,
Then finds sulphuric acid mix'd with lime!
Guards from her lovely face the solar ray,
And fills his pockets with alluvial clay.
Science and love distract his tortured heart,
Now flints, now fondness take the larger part,
And now he breaks a stone, now feels a dart.

Sydney Smith, Letter to the Rev. W. Vernon, July 1824 (on Mr and Mrs William Vernon passing their honeymoon at the Lakes)

Lancashire

The air thereof is subtil and piercing, being free from fogs saving in the mosses; the effects whereof are found in the fair complexions and firm constitutions of the natives therein, whose bodies are as able as their minds willing for any laborious employment.

Thomas Fuller, *History of the Worthies of England*, 1662

He that would take a Lancashire man
At any time or tide
Must bait his hook with a good egg-pie
Or an apple with a red side.

John Ray, *Compleat Collection of English Proverbs*, 1670

No extravagant fortunes have, in this century, been made by Englishmen in India but Lancashire has been a California.

Walter Bagehot, 'Lord Brougham', *National Review*, July 1857

Lancashire is a dreary county, (at least, except in its hilly portions,) and I have never passed through it without wishing myself anywhere but in that particular spot wherein I then happened to be.

Nathaniel Hawthorne, *Our Old Home*, 1863

Land's End

from the sea
The rocks at the Lands End in Cornwall were particularly recommended to our notice by the Bishop [John Fisher, Bishop of Salisbury] & Mrs Fisher, as being the finest specimens of rock that are to be found on this island.

Joseph Farington, *Diary*, 14 September 1809

The wildest most impressive place I ever saw on the coasts of Britain. A lighthouse rises on a detached rock some considerable space ahead; many detached rocks, of a haggard skeleton character, worn haggard by the wild sea, are scattered about between the lighthouse and end of the firm cliff; that cluster, where the lighthouse is, had seemed to me like the ruins of a Cathedral for some time. Very wild and grim, impressive in itself and as the notablest of British capes.

Thomas Carlyle, *Reminiscences of My Irish Journey in 1849*, 1882

Little Langdale

All at once, behold!
Beneath our feet, a little lowly vale,
A lowly vale, and yet uplifted high
Among the mountains; even as if the spot
Had been from eldest time, by wish of theirs
So placed, to be shut out from all the world!
Urn-like it was in shape, deep as an urn;
With rocks encompassed, save that to the south
Was one small opening, where a heath-clad ridge
Supplied a boundary less abrupt and close;
A quiet treeless nook, with two green fields.
A liquid pool that glittered in the sun,
And one bare dwelling; one abode, no more!
It seemed the home of poverty and toil,
Though not of want: the little fields made green
By husbandry of many thrifty years,
Paid cheerful tribute to the moorland house.
—There crows the cock, single in his domain:
The small birds find in spring no thicket there
To shroud them; only from the neighbouring vales

The cuckoo, straggling up to the hill tops,
Shouteth faint tidings of some gladder place.

William Wordsworth, *The Excursion*, 1814

Leamington Spa

*'And can you be a day, or even a minute,' returned the lady, slightly settling her false curls and false eyebrows with her fan, and showing her false teeth, set off by her false complexion, 'in the garden of what's-its-name—'

'Eden, I suppose, mama,' interrupted the younger lady scornfully.

Charles Dickens, *Dombey and Son*, 1847–8
(Mrs Skewton and her daughter speaking)

Persons who have no country-houses, and whose fortunes are inadequate to a London expenditure, find here, I suppose, a sort of town and country life in one . . . Whether in street or suburb, Leamington may fairly be called beautiful, and, at some points magnificent; but, by-and-by, you become doubtfully suspicious of a somewhat unreal finery; it is pretentious, though not glaringly so; it has been built with malice aforethought as a place of gentility and enjoyment. Moreover, splendid as the houses look, and comfortable as they often are, there is a nameless something about them, betokening that they have not grown out of human hearts, but are creations of a skilfully applied human intellect; no man has reared any one of them, whether stately or humble, to be his life-long residence, wherein to bring up his children who are to inherit it as a home. They are nicely contrived lodging houses, one and all.

Nathaniel Hawthorne, *Our Old Home*, 1863

After the Bay of Naples, Mount Aventine, and St Mark's Place, it felt like the first practical scene of a pantomime, after the transformation, and before the business begins.

John Ruskin, *Praeterita*, 1885–9

Leeds

Leeds is a large town, severall large streetes cleane and well pitch'd and good houses all built of stone, some have good gardens and steps up to their houses and walls before them; this is esteemed the wealthyest town of its bigness in the Country, its manufacture is the woollen cloth the Yorkshire Cloth in which they are all employ'd and are esteemed very rich and very proud; they have provision soe plentifull that they may live with very little expense and get much variety; here if one calls for a tankard of ale which is allwayes a groate—its the only dear thing all over Yorkshire, their ale is very strong—but for paying this groat for your ale you may have a slice of meate either hott or cold according to the tyme of day you call, or else butter and cheese gratis into the bargaine.

Celia Fiennes, *Journeys*, 1698

A large dingy town.

Horace Walpole, Letter to Richard Bentley,
August 1756

Wide around
Hillock and valley, farm and village, smile;
And ruddy roofs, and chimney-tops appear,
Of busy Leeds, up-wafting to the clouds
The incense of thanksgiving: all is joy;
And trade and business guide the living scene,
Roll the full cars, adown the winding Aire
Load the slow-sailing barges, pile the pack
On the long tinkling train of slow-pace'd steeds . . .
Thus all is here in motion, all is life:
The creaking wain brings copious store of corn;
The grazier's sleeky kine obstruct the roads;
The neat-dress'd housewives, for the festal board
Crown'd with full baskets in the field-way paths
Come tripping on; th'echoing hills repeat
The stroke of axe and hammer; scaffolds rise,
And growing edifices; heaps of stone,
Beneath the chisel, beauteous shapes assume
Of frieze and column. Some, with even line,
New streets are marking in the neighb'ring fields,
And sacred domes of worship . . .
Such was the scene
Of hurrying Carthage, when the Trojan chief
First view'd her growing turrets. So appear
Th'increasing walls of busy Manchester,
Sheffield and Birmingham, whose redd'ning fields
Rise and enlarge their suburbs.

John Dyer, *The Fleece*, 1757

The town where toiling, buying, selling
Getting and spending, poising hope and fear
Make but one season of the livelong year.

Hartley Coleridge, *From Country to Town*, July 1832

Amongst all others the vilest of the vile.

Barclay Fox, attrib.

Leicester

I went . . . to the old & raged city of *Leicester*, large, & pleasantly seated, but despicably built; the Chimnies flues like so many smiths forges: however famous for the Tombs of the Tyrant *Rich*: the Third, which is now converted to a cistern at which (I think) catell drink . . .

John Evelyn, *Diary*, 9 August 1654

Leicestershire

This Shire hath beene more famous from time to time by reason of the Earles thereof have beene notorious.

William Camden, *Britain*, 1610
(Philemon Holland's translation)

Bean-belly Leicestershire—
So called from the great plenty of that grain growing therein. Yea, those in the neighbouring counties use to say merrily, 'Shake a Leicestershire yeoman by the collar, and you shall hear the beans rattle in his belly;' but those yeomen smile at what is said to rattle in their bellies, whilst they know good silver ringeth in their pockets.

Thomas Fuller, *History of the Worthies of England*, 1662

This county is, (though not exquisitely) circular in form; whilst Leicester, the shire town, is almost the exact centre thereof; and the river Soare, diameter-like, divides it into two equal halves . . .

Ibid.

An open, rich but unpleasant country.

John Evelyn, *Diary*, August 1654

Leominster

Why don't you do as we do when things are at a standstill—go and take a city? Leominster is famous for its carpets; so is Cabul. Go and take Leominster.

The Hon. F.H. Eden, Letter, 9 September 1839,
in Emily Eden, *Letters from India*, 1872

Letchworth

Broadbent: Have you ever heard of Garden City?
Tim: (doubtfully) D'ye mane Heavn?
Broadbent: Heaven! No: it's near Hitchin.

Bernard Shaw, *John Bull's Other Island*, 1904

Lichfield

Ah, lovely Lichfield! that so long hast shone
In blended charms, peculiarly thine own;
Stately, yet rural; through thy choral day,
Though shady, cheerful, and though quiet, gay.

Anna Seward, *The Anniversary*, June 1769

We talked of change of manners. Dr. Johnson observed that our drinking less than our ancestors was owing to the change from ale to wine. 'I remember,' said he, 'when all the *decent* people in Lichfield got drunk every night, and were not the worse thought of. Ale was cheap, so you pressed strongly.'

James Boswell, *Journal of a Tour to the Hebrides with Samuel Johnson*, 1773 (1785)

Very little business seemed to be going forward in Lichfield. I found however two strange manufactures for so inward a place, sail-cloth, and streamers for ships; and I observed them making some saddle-cloths, and dressing sheep-skins; but upon the whole, the busy hand of industry seemed to be quite slackened. 'Surely, Sir,' said I, 'you are an idle set of people,' 'Sir, (said Johnson) we are a city of philosophers: we work with our heads, and make the boobies of Birmingham work for us with their hands.'

James Boswell, *Life of Johnson*, 23 March 1776

Has Beauty made thee its peculiar care,
Bade thee arise pre-eminently fair?
Or do remember'd days, that swiftly flew,
When life and all her blooming days were new,
To my thrill'd spirit emulously bring
Illusions brighter than the shining Spring?

Yet, independent of their glowing spell,
Around thy spires exclusive graces dwell;
For there alone the blended charms prevail
Of city stateliness, and rural dale.
High o'er proud towns where Gothic structures rise,
How rare the freshness of unsullied skies!
Oft cling to choral walls the mansions vile,
Unseemly blots upon the graceful pile!
Here not one squalid, mouldering cell appears,
To mar the splendid toil of ancient years;
But, from the basis to the stately height,
One free and perfect whole it meets the sight,
Adorn'd, yet simple, though majestic, light;
While, as around that waving basis drawn,
Shines the green surface of the level lawn,
Full on its breast the spiral shadows tall,
Unbroken, and in solemn beauty, fall.

Anna Seward, *Lichfield, an Elegy*, May 1781

Lincoln

There is a proverb, part of which is this,
They say that Lincoln was, and London is.

John Taylor, 'The Water Poet', in *A Very Merry Wherry-Ferry Voyage*, 1622

I lik'd the motion, and made haste away
To *Lincolne*, which was 50 mile, that Day:
Which City in the 3 King *Edwards* Raigne
Was th'onely staple, for this Kingdome's gaine
For Leather, Lead, and Wooll, and then was seene
Five times ten Churches there, but now Fifteene.
A brave Cathedral Church there now doth stand,
That scarcely hath a fellow in this Land:
Tis for a Godly use, a goodly Frame,
And beares that blessed Virgin *Maries* name.

Ibid.

Lincoln is an antient, ragged, decay'd and still decaying city; it is so full of the ruins of monasteries and religious houses, that, in short, the very barns, stables, out-houses, and, as they shew'd me, some of the very hog-styes, were built church fashion; that is to say, with stone walls and arched windows and doors.

Daniel Defoe, *A Tour through the Whole Island of Great Britain*, 1724–7

Passing through the Stone-Bow as the city gate close by is called, we ascended a street which grew steeper and narrower as we advanced; till at last it got to be the steepest street I ever climbed . . . Being almost the only hill in Lincolnshire the inhabitants seem disposed to make the most of it.

Nathaniel Hawthorne, *Our Old Home*, 1863

The Cathedral

The cathedral is, I believe, *the finest building in the whole world.*

William Cobbett, *Rural Rides*, 23 April 1830

I have been since Monday at Lincoln, hard worked, but *subsisting* on the Cathedral. Every evening as it grew dark I mounted the hill to it, and remained through the evening service in the nave or transepts, more settled and refreshed than I could have been by anything else.

Matthew Arnold, Letter to his mother, 25 November 1852

Lincolnshire

This county, in fashion, is like a bended bow, the sea making the back, the rivers Welland and Humber the two horns thereof, whilst Trent hangeth down from the latter like a broken string, as being somewhat of the shortest. Such persecute the metaphor too much, who compare the river Witham (whose current is crooked) unto the arrow crossing the middle thereof.

Thomas Fuller, *History of the Worthies of England*, 1662

Lincolnshire may be termed the aviary of England, for the wild-fowl therein.

Ibid.

One part is all fen or marsh grounds, and extends itself south to the Isle of Ely, and here it is that so vast a quantity of sheep are fed, as makes this county and that of Leicester an inexhaustible fountain of wool for all the manufacturing counties of England.

Daniel Defoe, *A Tour through the Whole Island of Great Britain*, 1724–7

Lincolnshire where hogs shite sope, and cows shite fire.

The inhabitants of the poorer sort washing their clothes with hogs-dung, and burning dried cow-dung for want of better fuel.

John Ray, *A Compleat Collection of English Proverbs*, 4th edn, 1768

A lover of the picturesque would as soon think of settling in Holland.

Nathaniel Hawthorne, *Our Old Home*, 1863

Littlehampton

Littlehampton, dark and amorphous like a bad eruption on the edge of the land . . . all these little amorphous houses like an eruption, a disease on the clean earth; and all of them full of such a diseased spirit, every landlady harping on her money, her furniture, every visitor harping on his latitude of escape from money and furniture.

D.H. Lawrence, Letter to Lady Cynthia Asquith, August 1915

Littlemore *(near Oxford)*

This little village serves to show
What lengths the pride of man will go;
For, in whatever state or place,
(As if contentment were disgrace,)
Ambition prompts us to desire
Another post a little higher.
Search this capacious globe all o'er
You still will wish *a little more.*

Dr Bacon, in Charles Stokes Carey (ed.), *A Commonplace Book of Epigrams*, 1872

Liverpool

So named as it is thought, of the water spreading it selfe in manner of a Poole: whence there is a convenient passage over into Ireland, and much frequented, and in that respect more notorious, than for any antiquity.

William Camden, *Britain*, 1610 (Philemon Holland's translation)

Its a very rich trading town the houses of brick and stone built high and even, that a streete quite through lookes very handsome, the streetes well pitched; there are abundance of persons you see very well dress'd and of good fashion; the streetes are faire and long, its London in miniature as much as ever I saw any thing.

Celia Fiennes, *Journeys*, 1698

This town is now become so great, so populous, and so rich, that it may be call'd the Bristol of this part of England: . . . This part of the town may indeed be called the New Liverpool, for that, they have built more than another Leverpool that way, in new streets, and fine large houses for their merchants: Besides this, they have made a great wet dock, for laying up their ships, and which they greatly wanted; for tho' the Mersey is a noble harbour, and is able to ride a thousand sail of ships at once, yet those ships that are to be laid up, or lye by the walls all winter, or longer, as sometimes may be the case; must ride there as in an open road, or (as the seamen call it), be haled a shore; neither which would be practicable in a town of so much trade; And in the time of the late great storm, they suffer'd very much on that account . . . This is still an encreasing flourishing town, and if they go on in trade, as they have done for some time, 'tis probable it will in a little time be as big as the city of Dublin.

Daniel Defoe, *A Tour through the Whole Island of Great Britain*, 1724–7

'What! do you hiss me?—hiss George Frederick Cooke?—you contemptible money-getters! you shall never again have the *honour* of hissing me! Farewell! *I* banish *you*!' And concentrating into one vast heap all the malice of his offended feelings, he added, after a pause of intense meaning *'There is not a brick in your dirty town but what is cemented by the blood of a negro*!'

George Frederick Cooke, quoted by Mrs Mathews, *Memoirs of Charles Mathews, Comedian*, 1838–9 – of 1806

It has lately been resolved upon to have a botanical garden here; a large sum has been raised for the purpose, and the ground purchased. 'It will be long,' said I to our friend, 'before this can be brought to any perfection.' 'Oh, sir,' said he, with a smile of triumph which it was delightful to perceive, 'you do not know how we do things at Liverpool. Money and activity work wonders . . . '

Robert Southey, *Letters from England, by Don Manuel Alvarez Espriella*, 1807

Liverpool a sort of ideal Wapping.

Benjamin Robert Haydon, *Diary*, December 1820

Mr Paulet of Liverpool told me that, in his experience, he found he could do without a fire in his house, about one day in the year.

Ralph Waldo Emerson, *Journals*, 1863

Liverpool, though not very delightful as a place of residence, is a most convenient and admirable point to get away from.

Nathaniel Hawthorne, *Our Old Home*, 1863

Liverpool! it means a Noise and a Struggle and a Fight. It means the Valley of the shadow of Cotton bales and Sugar bales and the outer darkness of brokers offices and bank vaults. A Liverpool Consulate! it means being bored, vexed, bullied, or toadied from morning to night by dense merchant captains, by conceited supercargoes, by greedy merchants furious lest they should lose the pelf of a venture by the delay of a stamp or a signature; by drunken sailors, by sallow men with inscrutable grievances, by mad wanderers with impracticable inventions, by every one who is in debt, and every one who is discontented.

G.A. Sala, *My Diary in America in the Midst of the War*, 1865

Solidity is written everywhere; every thing is built to last, from the immense docks themselves down to the burly frames of the men and the large feet of the women.

John W. Forney, *Letters from Europe*, 1867

*They call Liverpool the slum of Europe, said Mynors.

Arnold Bennett, *Anna of the Five Towns*, 1902

The folk that live in Liverpool, their heart is in their boots
They go to hell like lambs they do, because the hooter hoots.
Where men may not be dancin', though the wheels may dance all day;
And men may not be smokin'; but only chimneys may.

G.K. Chesterton, 'Me Heart', *The Flying Inn*, 1914

Regard the case of Liverpool, born a mud village in 1207. Even then nature had given her what is her fortune to-day. But it came in the form of a post-dated cheque; having it all the time in her pocket, she still could not cash it before the age of the large modern steamship.

C.E. Montague, *The Right Place*, 1924

No one goes to Liverpoool for pleasure.

Graham Greene, *Journey without Maps*, 1936

*He felt exhilarated and full of energy. It had to do, he thought, with some quality of the northern light: the blackened city seemed to sail in an ocean of white sky, perpetually racing before the wind.

Beryl Bainbridge, *Young Adolf*, 1978

You've got to be a comedian to live there.

Ken Dodd, Remark on 'Des O'Connor Tonight' – BBC2, 15 December 1980

Liverpool Cathedral

* . . . discussing the merits of the new cathedral, one third built, rising like an improbable airship out of the sunken graveyard. Last year it had been taller and the year before taller still.

'They keep knocking it down,' said Meyer, 'and starting all over again. Once it resembled a child's sandcastle. Whatever it is they're after it seems to evade them.' Soon, he fancied, the structure might escape altogether; bursting from its moorings, it would lift, zeppelin-shaped and pink as a rose, into the scudding clouds.

Beryl Bainbridge, *Young Adolf*, 1978

Liverpool Docks
They are built as if they were intended to endure as long as the Pyramids.

John Forney, *Letters from Europe*, 1867

The Lizard Lighthouse

It was a grand thing, through the thick and turbid atmosphere, to see the great fiery eye of the lighthouse at the Lizard Point: it looked like a good genius with a ferocious aspect. Ancient mythology would have made dragons of these noble structures, – dragons with giant glare, warning the seamen of the coast.

Leigh Hunt, *Autobiography*, 1850

London

See also districts, below, and entries under separate headings for outlying boroughs, Greenwich, Richmond, etc.

London, thou art of townes A *per se*.
Soveraign of cities, semeliest in sight,
Of high renoun, riches, and royaltie;
Of lordis, barons, and many a goodly knyght;
Of most delectable lusty ladies bright;
Of famous prelatis in habitis clericall;
Of merchauntis full of substaunce and of myght:
London, thou art the flour of Cities all.

Gemme of all joy, jasper of jocunditie,
Most myghty carbuncle of vertue and valour;
Strong Troy in vigour and in strenuyitie;
Of royall cities rose and geraflour;
Empresse of townes, exalt in honour;
In beawtie beryng the crone imperiall;
Swete paradise precelling pleasure;
London, thou art the flour of Cities all.

Above all ryvers thy Ryver hath renowne,
Whose beryall stremys, pleasaunt and preclare,
Under thy lusty wallys renneth down,
Where many a swanne doth swymme with wyngis fair;
Where many a barge doth saile, and row with are,
Where many a ship doth rest with toppe-royall.
O! towne of townes, patrone and not compare:
London, thou art the flour of Cities all.

William Dunbar, *To the City of London, c.* 1501
(According to James Kinsley, *Dunbar*, 1979, this poem is no longer considered to be by Dunbar.)

Sixteenth Century

People-pestered London.
Nicholas Grimald, *The Lover to his Dear*, before 1562

At length they all to mery *London* came,
To mery London, my most kyndly Nurse,
That to me gave this Lifes first native sourse.

Edmund Spenser, *Prothalamion*, 1596

Seventeenth Century

But London, the Epitome or Breviary of all Britain, the seat of the British Empire, and the *Kings of Englands chamber* . . . none hath better right to assume unto it the name of a *ship-rode*, or *Haven*, than our London. For, in regard of both Elements, most blessed and happy it is, as being situate in a rich and fertile soile, abounding with plentifull store of all things and on the gentle ascent and rising of an hill, hard by the *Tamis* side, the most milde Merchant, as one would say, of all things that the world doth yeeld: which swelling at certaine set houres with the Ocean-tides, by his safe and deepe chanell able to entertaine the greatest ships that be, daily bringeth so great riches from all parts, that it striveth at this day with the Mart-townes of Christendome for the second prise, & affoordeth a most sure and beautiful road for shipping. A man would say that seeth the shipping there, that it is, as it were, a very wood of trees disbransched to make glades and let in light: So shaded it is with masts and sailes.

William Camden, *Britain*, 1610
(Philemon Holland's translation)

Our scene is London, 'cause we would make known,
No country's mirth is better than our own

Ben Jonson, *The Alchemist*, Prologue, 1610

Fitzdottrell: But, these same Citizens, they are such sharks.

Ben Jonson, *The Divell is an Asse*, 1616

London's the dining-room of Christendom.

Thomas Middleton, *City Pageant*, 1617

Oh city, founded by Dardanian hands,
Whose towering front the circling realms commands,
Too blest abode! No loveliness we see
In all the earth, but it abounds in thee.

John Milton, *Elegia Prima ad Carolum Diodatum*, *c.*1627, William Cowper's translation, September 1791–February 1792

Behold now this vast city; a city of refuge, the mansion-house of liberty, encompassed and surrounded with His protection.

John Milton, *Areopagitica*, 1644

From the dull confines of the drooping West,
To see the day spring from the pregnant East,
Ravisht in spirit, I come, nay more, I flie
To thee, blest place of my Nativitie! . . .
O fruitfull Genius! that bestowest here

An everlasting plenty, yeere by yeere.
O *Place*! O *People*! Manners! fram'd to please
All *Nations, Customes, Kindreds, Languages*!
I am a free-born *Roman*; suffer then,
That I amongst you live a Citizen
London my home is: though by hard fate sent
Into a long and irksome banishment;
Yet since cal'd back; henceforward let me be,
O native countrey, repossest by thee!
For, rather then I'le to the West return,
I'le beg of thee first here to have mine Urn. . . .

Robert Herrick, 'His returne to London', *Hesperides*, 1648

Tell me, O tell, what kind of thing is *Wit*,
Thou who *Master* art of it . . .
London that vents of *false Ware* so much store,
In no *Ware* deceives us more.
For men led by the *Colour*, and the *Shape*,
Like *Zeuxes Birds* fly to the painted Grape;
Some things do through our Judgements pass
As through a *Multiplying Glass*.
And sometimes, if the *Object* be too far,
We take a *Falling Meteor* for a *Star*.

Abraham Cowley, 'Ode, of Wit', in *Miscellanies*, 1656

Some say, the the City is best situated, which resembleth a *Camels* back. who hath protuberances, and bunches, so a City should be seated upon rising ground or small Hillocks; It is the posture of *London*; for she is builded upon the flanks sides and tops of divers small Hillocks, lying near the Banks of a Noble River, and being encompassed about with delightful green Medows, and Fields on all sides; and she is in so fair a distance from the Sea, that no danger of forren invasion can surprize her, but she must have notice before: the nature of her Soyl is sandy, which is wholsemest for Habitation, and conduceth much to goodness of Air, the barrenness whereof, is made prolifical by art.

James Howell, *Londinopolis*, 1657

It is the second city in Christendom for greatness, and the first for good government. There is no civilized part of the world but it hath heard thereof, though many with this mistake, that they conceive London to be the country, and England but the city therein.

Thomas Fuller, *History of the Worthies of England*, 1662

Methinks already from this chymic flame
I see a city of more precious mould,
Rich as the town which gave the Indies name,
With silver paved and all divine with gold . . .

More great than human now, and more August,
Now deified she from her fires does rise:
Her widening streets on new foundations trust,
And opening, into larger parts she flies.

Before, she like some shepherdess did show
Who sat to bathe her by a river's side,
Not answering to her fame, but rude and low,
Nor taught the beauteous arts of modern pride.

Now like a maiden queen she will behold
From her high turrets hourly suitors come;
The East with incense, and the West with gold
Will stand like suppliants to receive her doom.

The silver Thames, her own domestic flood,
Shall bear her vessels like a sweeping train,
And often wind, as of his mistress proud,
With longing eyes to meet her face again.

John Dryden, *Annus Mirabilis*,1667 – of London after the Great Fire, 1666

methinks I see
The *Monster* London laugh at me, . . .
Let but thy wicked men from out thee go,
And all the fools that crowd thee so,
Even thou who didst thy Millions boast,
A Village less than *Islington* wilt grow,
A Solitude almost.

Abraham Cowley, 'Of Solitude', *Essays in Prose and Verse*, 1668

The air of this town without the pleasures of it is enough to infect Women with an aversion for the Country.

William Wycherley, *The Gentleman Dancing Master*, 1672

Mrs Pinchwife: Well, 'tis e'ne so, I have got the *London* disease, they call Love, I am sick of my Husband, and for my Gallant . . .

William Wycherley, *The Country-Wife*, 1675

London, you know, has a great Belly, but no palate, nor taste of right and wrong.

Thomas Hobbes, *Behemoth*, 1680

When I behold this town of *London*, said our contemplative traveller, I fancy I behold a prodigious animal. The streets are so many *veins*, wherein the people circulate. With what hurry and swiftness is the circulation of *London* performed. You behold, cry'd I to him, the circulation that is made in the heart of *London*, but it moves more briskly in the blood of the *citizens*: they are always in motion and activity. Their actions succeed one another with so much rapidity, that they begin a thousand things before they have finished one, and finish a thousand others before they may properly be said to have begun them.

They are equally incapable both of attention and patience, and tho' nothing is more quick than the effects of hearing and seeing, yet they don't allow themselves time either to hear or see; but, like moles, work in the dark, and undermine one another.

Thomas Brown, *Amusements Serious and Comical*, 1700

Eighteenth Century

London joyned with Westminster, which are two great cittyes but now with building so joyned it makes up but one vast building with all its suburbs.

Celia Fiennes, *The Journeys of Celia Fiennes*, c. 1701

If a man had the art of the second sight for seeing lies, as they have in Scotland for seeing spirits, how admirably he might entertain himself in this town, by observing the different shapes, sizes and colours of those swarms of lies which buzz about the heads of some people.

Jonathan Swift, *Examiner*, no. 15, 9 November 1710

Do you know that about our town we are mowing already and making hay, and it smells so sweet as we walk through the flowry meads; but the hay-making nymphs are perfect drabs, nothing so clean and pretty as further in the country. There is a mighty increase of dirty wenches in straw hats since I knew London.

Jonathan Swift, *Journal to Stella*, May 1711

May my enemies live here in summer!

Jonathan Swift, *Journal to Stella*, August 1711

London . . . a kind of *Emporium* for the whole Earth.

Joseph Addison, *Spectator*, no. 69, 19 May 1711

The Hours of the Day and Night are taken up in the Cities of *London* and *Westminster* by People as different from each other as those who are born in different Centuries. Men of Six a Clock give way to those of Nine, they of Nine to the Generation of Twelve, and they of Twelve disappear, and make Room for the fashionable World, who have made Two a Clock the Noon of the Day.

Richard Steele, *Spectator*, no. 454, 11 August 1712

Yes; thank my stars! as early as I knew
This Town, I had the sense to hate it too.

Alexander Pope, *The Second Satire of Dr John Donne . . . Versifyed*, 1713

Dear, damn'd, distracting Town, farewell!
Thy Fools no more I'll teize:
This Year in Peace, ye Critics, dwell,
Ye Harlots, sleep at Ease!

Alexander Pope, *A Farewell to London. In the Year 1715*

. . . this sinfull Sea Cole Town . . .

Lady Mary Wortley Montagu, Letter to Lady Mar, December 1724

It is the disaster of London, as to the beauty of its figure, that it is thus stretched out in buildings, just at the pleasure of every builder, or undertaker of buildings, and as the convenience of the people directs, whether for trade or otherwise; and this has spread the face of it in a most straggling confus'd manner, out of all shape, incompact and unequal; neither long nor broad, round or square; . . . one sees it, in some places, three miles broad, as from St George's in Southwark to Shoreditch in Middlesex: or two miles, as from Petersburgh House to Montague House; and in some places, not half a mile, as in Wapping; and much less as in Redriff . . .

We see several villages, formerly standing, as it were, in the country, and at a great distance, now joyn'd to the streets by continued buildings, and more making haste to meet in the like manner . . .

That Westminster is in a fair way to shake hands with Chelsea, as St. Gyles's is with Marybone; and Great Russell Street by Montague House, with Tottenham-Court: all this is very evident, and yet all these put together, are still to be called London: whither will this monstrous city then extend? and where must a circumvallation or communication line of it be placed?

Daniel Defoe, *A Tour through the Whole Island of Great Britain*, 1724–7

The city swarms intense. The public haunt,
Full of each theme, and warm with mix'd discourse,
Hums indistinct. The sons of riot flow
Down the loose stream of false enchanted joy
To swift destruction. On the rankled soul
The gaming fury falls; and in one gulf
Of total ruin, honour, virtue, peace,
Friends, families, and fortune, headlong sink.
Up springs the dance along the lighted dome,
Mix'd and evolved a thousand sprightly ways.
The glittering court effuses every pomp;
The circle deepens; beam'd from gaudy robes,
Tapers, and sparkling gems, and radiant eyes,
A soft effulgence o'er the palace waves;
While, a gay insect in *his* Summer shine,
The fop, light fluttering, spreads his mealy wings.

James Thomson, *The Seasons – Winter*, 1726

There, London's voice: 'Get money still!
And then let virtue follow if she will.'

Alexander Pope, *First Book of the Epistles of Horace*, 1738

But grant I may relapse, for want of Grace,
Again to rhime, can *London* be the Place?
Who there his Muse, or Self, or Soul attends?
In Crouds and Courts, Law, Business, Feasts and
Friends?
My Counsel sends to execute a Deed:
A Poet begs me, I will hear him read:
In Palace-Yard at Nine you'll find me there –
At Ten for certain, Sir, in Bloomsb'ry-Square –

Before the Lords at Twelve my Cause comes on –
There's a Rehearsal, Sir, exact at One. –
'Oh but a Wit can study in the Streets,
And raise his Mind above the Mob he meets.'
Not quite so well however as one ought;
A Hackney-Coach may chance to spoil a Thought,
And then a nodding Beam, or Pig of Lead,
God knows, may hurt the very ablest Head.
Have you not seen at Guild-hall's narrow Pass,
Two Aldermen dispute it with an Ass?
And Peers give way, exalted as they are,
Ev'n to their own S-r-v--nce in a Carr?
Go, lofty Poet! and in such a Croud,
Sing thy sonorous Verse – but not aloud.

Alexander Pope, *Imitations of Horace, The Second Epistle of the Second Book*, 1737

(Sir-reverence = excrement.)

Here malice, rapine, accident conspire,
And now a rabble rages, now a fire;
Their ambush here relentless ruffians lay,
And here the fell attorney prowls for prey:
Here falling houses thunder on your head
And here a female atheist talks you dead . . .
London! the needy villain's gen'ral home
The common shore of Paris and of Rome;
With eager thirst, by folly or by fate
Sucks in the dregs of each corrupted state
Forgive my transports on a theme like this
I cannot bear a French metropolis.

Samuel Johnson, *London*, 1738

**London*, the best Retirement of either Grief or Shame, unless the Persons of a very public Character; for here you have the Advantage of solitude without its Disadvantage, since you may be alone and in Company at the same time; and while you sit or walk unobserved, Noise, Hurry, and a constant Succession of Objects entertain the Mind . . .

Henry Fielding, *Tom Jones*, 1749

When we came upon Highgate Hill and had a view of London, I was all life and joy. I repeated Cato's soliloquy on the immortality of the soul, and my soul bounded forth to a certain prospect of happy futurity. I sung all manner of songs, and began to make one about an amorous meeting with a pretty girl, the burthen of which was as follows:

She gave me *this*, I gave her *that*;
And tell me, had she not tit for tat?

I gave three huzzas, and we went briskly in. . . .

The noise the crowd, the glare of shops and signs agreeably confused me. I was rather more wildly struck than when I first came to London. My companion could not understand my feelings. He considered London just as a place where he was to receive orders from the East India Company.

James Boswell, *Boswell's London Journal*, 19 November 1762

There is indeed a kind of character perfectly disguised, a perfect made dish, which is often found, both male and female, in London. This is most disgusting: plain nature is infinitely better. . . .

Ibid., 3 February 1763

That tiresome dull place! where all people under thirty find so much amusement.

Thomas Gray, Letter to Norton Nicholls, 19 November 1764

The noble spirit of the metropolis is the life-blood of the nation, collected at the heart.

Junius, *Letters*, no. 37, *c.* 1770

*London is literally new to me; new in its streets, houses, and even in its situation; as the Irishman said, 'London is now gone out of town.' What I left open fields, producing hay and corn, I now find covered with streets and squares, and palaces, and churches . . . Pimlico and Knightsbridge are now almost joined to Chelsea and Kensington, and if this infatuation continues for half a century, I suppose the whole county of Middlesex will be covered with brick.

Thomas Smollett, *Humphrey Clinker*, 1771
('Matthew Bramble's' comments)

*O Molly! what shall I say of London? All the towns that ever I beheld in my born-days, are no more than Welsh barrows and crumlecks to this wonderful sitty! Even Bath itself is but a sillitch, and in the naam of God – One would think there's no end of the streets, but the land's end. Then there's such a power of people, going hurry skurry! Such a racket of coxes! Such a noise, and haliballoo! So many strange sites to be seen! O gracious! my poor Welsh brain has been spinning like a top ever since I came hither! And I have seen the Park, and the paleass of Saint Gimses, and the king's and the queen's magisterial pursing, and the sweet young princes, and the hillyfents, and pye bald ass, and all the rest of the royal family.

Ibid. ('Win. Jenkins's' comments)

Hardcastle: I wonder why London cannot keep its own fools at home. In my time the follies of the town crept slowly among us, but now they travel faster than a stage-coach. Its fopperies come down, not only as inside passengers, but in the very basket.

Oliver Goldsmith, *She Stoops to Conquer*, 1773

I suggested a doubt, that if I were to reside in London, the exquisite zest with which I relished it in occasional visits might go off, and I might grow tired of it. JOHNSON. 'Why, Sir, you find no man, at all intellectual, who is willing to leave London. No, Sir, when a man is tired of London, he is tired of life; for there is in London all that life can afford.'

James Boswell, *Life of Johnson*, 29 September 1777

The chief advantage of London . . . is, that a man is always *so near his burrow.*

Mr Meynell, quoted in James Boswell, *Life of Johnson*, 1779

Where has commerce such a mart,
So rich, so thronged, so drained and so supplied
As London, opulent, enlarged, and still
Increasing London?

William Cowper, *The Task*, 'The Sofa', 1783

Oh thou, resort and mart of all the earth
Chequer'd with all complexions of mankind
And spotted with all crimes, in whom I see
Much that I love and more that I admire,
And all that I abhor; thou freckled fair
That pleasest and yet shock'st me. I can laugh
And I can weep, can hope and can despond
Feel wrath and pity when I think on thee!
Ten righteous would have saved a city once,
And thou hast many righteous. – Well for thee!
That salt preserves thee; more corrupted, else,
And therefore more obnoxious at this hour
Than Sodom in her day had pow'r to be
For whom God heard his Ab'ram plead in vain.

William Cowper, *The Task*, Book III – 'The Garden', 1783–4, pub. 1785

In London . . . you have plays performed by good actors. That, however, is, I think, the only advantage London has over Philadelphia.

Benjamin Franklin, Letter to Mrs Mary Hewson, 6 May 1786

There will soon be one street from London to Brentford; ay, and from London to every village ten miles round! Lord Camden has just let ground at Kentish Town for building fourteen hundred houses – nor do I wonder; London is, I am certain, much fuller than ever I saw it. I have twice this spring been going to stop my coach in Piccadilly, to inquire what was the matter, thinking there was a mob – not at all; it was only passengers.

Horace Walpole, letter to Miss Mary Berry, 8 June 1791

Nothing is certain in London but expense.

William Shenstone, Remark quoted in Isaac D'Israeli, *Curiosities of Literature*, 1791–3

What is London? Clean, commodious, neat; but, a very few things indeed excepted, an endless addition of littleness to littleness, extending itself over a great tract of land.

Edmund Burke, Letter to the Rev. Robert Dodge, 29 February 1792

Nineteenth Century

I have passed all my days in London, until I have formed as many and intense local attachments, as any of you mountaineers can have done with dead nature. The lighted shops of the Strand and Fleet Street, the innumerable trades, tradesmen and customers, coaches, waggons, playhouses, all the bustle and wickedness round about Covent Garden, the very Women of the Town, the Watchmen, drunken scenes, rattles, – life awake, if you awake, at all hours of the night, the impossibility of being dull in Fleet Street, the crowds, the very dirt and mud, the Sun shining upon houses and pavements, the print shops, the old book stalls, parsons cheap'ning books, coffee houses, steams of soups from kitchens, the pantomimes, London itself a pantomime and a masquerade, – all these things work themselves into my mind and feed me, without a power of satiating me. The wonder of these sights impels me into night-walks about her crowded streets, and I often shed tears in the Strand from fulness of joy at so much Life.

Charles Lamb, Letter to William Wordsworth, 30 January 1801

Nursed amid her noise, her crowds, her beloved smoke, – what have I been doing all my life, if I have not lent out my heart with usury to such scenes?

Charles Lamb, Letter to Thomas Manning, 15 February 1802

The City of London . . . exists by victories at sea . . .

Horatio Lord Nelson, Letter to A. Davidson, 9 July 1802

The fields from Islington to Marybone
  To Primrose Hill and Saint John's Wood,
Were builded over with pillars of gold;
  And there Jerusalem's pillars stood . . .

Pancras and Kentish Town repose
  Among her golden pillars high,
Among her golden arches which
  Shine upon the starry sky.

The Jew's-harp House and the Green Man,
  The Ponds where boys to bathe delight,
The fields of cows by Willan's farm,
  Shine in Jerusalem's pleasant sight . . .

What are those Golden Builders doing
  Near mournful ever-weeping Paddington,
Standing above that mighty ruin,
  Where Satan the first victory won . . .

Jerusalem fell from Lambeth's vale,
  Down thro' Poplar and Old Bow,

Thro' Malden and across the sea,
In war and howling, death and woe.

William Blake, *Jerusalem – To the Jews*, 1804–20

Dr Jenner observed to Lawrence that He could by smelling at His Handkerchief on going out of London ascertain when He came into an atmosphere untainted by *London air*. – His method was to smell at His Handkerchief occasionally, and while He continued within the *London atmosphere* He could never be sensible of any *taint* upon it; but, for instance, when he approached *Blackheath* & took his Handkerchief out of his pocket where it had not been exposed to the better air of that situation – His sense of smelling having become more pure He could perceive the taint. – His calculation was that the air of London affected that in the vicinity to the distance of 3 miles.

Joseph Farington, *Diary*, 17 February 1809

Now fixed amidst that concourse of mankind
Where Pleasure whirls about incessantly,
And life and labour seem but one, I filled
An idler's place; an idler well content . . .
Rise up, thou monstrous ant-hill on the plain
Of a too busy world! Before me flow
Thou endless stream of men and moving things!
Thy every-day appearance, as it strikes –
With wonder heightened, or sublimed by awe –
On strangers of all ages; the quick dance
Of colours lights and forms; the deafening din;
The comers and the goers face to face,
Face after face; the string of dazzling wares,
Shop after shop, with symbols, blazoned names,
And all the tradesman's honours overhead:
Here, fronts of houses, like a title-page,
With letters huge inscribed from top to toe,
Stationed above the door, like guardian saints;
There, allegoric shapes, female, or male,
Or physiognomies of real men.
Land-warriors, kings, or admirals of the sea,
Boyle, Shakespeare, Newton, or the attractive head
Of some quack-doctor, famous in his day.
Meanwhile the roar continues, till at length,
Escaped as from an enemy, we turn
Abruptly into some sequestered nook,
Still as a sheltered place, when winds blow loud!
At leisure thence, through tracts of thin resort,
And sights and sounds that come at intervals,
We take our way . . .
Conducted through those labyrinths, unawares,
To privileged regions, and inviolate,
Where from their airy lodges, studious lawyers
Look out on waters, walks, and gardens green.

William Wordsworth, *The Prelude*, 1805 (text of 1850)

To sleep in London, however, is an art which a foreigner must acquire by time and habit. Here was the watchman, whose business it is, not merely to guard the streets, and take charge of the public security, but to inform the good people of London every half hour of the state of the weather. For the first three hours I was told it was a moonlight night, then it became cloudy, and at half past three o'clock was a rainy morning; so that I was well acquainted with every variation of the atmosphere, as if I had been looking from the window all night long. A strange custom this, to pay men for telling them what the weather is every hour during the night, till they get so accustomed to the noise, that they sleep on and cannot hear what is said.

Robert Southey, *Letters from England, by Don Manuel Alvarez Espriella*, 1807

The single spot whereon were crowded together more wealth, more splendour, more ingenuity, more worldly wisdom, and, alas! more worldly blindness, poverty, depravity, dishonesty, and wretchedness, than upon any other spot in the whole habitable earth

Ibid.

As usual, the atmosphere has proved a complete malaria to me. How, indeed should it be otherwise, when it is a compound of fen-fog, chimney-smoke, smuts, and pulverized horse-dung! The little leisure I have is employed in blowing my nose, with interludes of coughing.

Robert Southey, Letter, July 1808

*I know not where the SUN receives the more marked insults than in *London*, either in the way of neglect or interruption, or open contempt of its use and importance in the scheme of things: – the MOON, poor thing! is not worthy of a thought; – though *Queen* of the *Night*, which latter has more votaries in London than any-where else, all the honours are transferred to the one without the smallest care or concern being expressed for the other – *Thinks-I-to-myself*, there are OTHER QUEENS OF THE NIGHT at London!

Edward Nares, *Thinks-I-to Myself*, 1811

London and the world is the only place to take conceit out of a man.

Lord Byron, Letter to Thomas Moore, 3 August 1814

Was für Plunder!
(What a place to plunder!)

Field Marshal von Blucher, on viewing London from St Paul's after the peace banquet at Oxford, 1814

Paris is the City of the Great King, London of the Great People. Paris strikes the vulgar part of us infinitely the most, but to a thinking mind London is incomparably the most delightful subject for contemplation.

Samuel Rogers, *Italian Journal*, 30 August 1814

There was no judging, and still less any enjoying of each other in that vortex of London, in which it is as impossible to find out real opinions and feelings as it is to tell the colours of a top that is spinning.

Thomas Moore, Letter to E.T. Dalton, Esq., 1815

From the author's own experience in almost every part of Europe, after all the tales he has heard of the danger of traversing this or that country, he can mention no place so full of peril as the environs of *London* . . .

E.D. Clarke, *Travels in Various Countries*, 1816

*Nobody is healthy in London, nobody can be.

Jane Austen, *Emma*, 1816 (Mr Woodhouse)

The Characteristic of London is that you never go where you wish, nor do what you wish, and that you always wish to be somewhere else than where you are.

Sydney Smith, Letter to Lady Grey, *c.* 1818

Go where we may, rest where we will,
Eternal London haunts us still.

Thomas Moore, *Rhymes on the Road, c.* 1820

The sun went down, the smoke rose up, as from
A half-unquenched volcano, o'er a space
Which well beseemed the 'devil's drawing room',
As some have qualified that wondrous place.
But Juan felt though not approaching home,
As one who, though he were not of the race,
Revered the soil, of those true sons the mother,
Who butchered half the earth and bullied t'other.

A mighty mass of brick and smoke and shipping,
Dirty and dusky, but wide as eye
Could reach, with here and there a sail just skipping
In sight, then lost amidst the forestry
Of masts, a wilderness of steeples peeping
On tiptoe through their sea coal canopy,
A huge, dun cupola, like a foolscap crown
On a fool's head – and there is London town!

Lord Byron, *Don Juan*, 1819–24

To our theme. The man who has stood on the Acropolis
And looked down over Attica, or he
Who has sailed where picturesque Constantinople is,
Or seen Timbuctoo, or hath taken tea
In small-eyed China's crockery-ware metropolis,
Or sat amidst the bricks of Nineveh
May not think much of London's first appearance –
But ask him what he thinks of it a year hence?

Ibid.

Hell is a city much like London
A populous and smoky city.

Percy Bysshe Shelley, *Peter Bell the Third*, 1819

An immense metropolis like London, is calculated to make men selfish and uninteresting. In their casual and transient meetings, they can but deal briefly in commonplaces. They present but the cold superfices of character – its rich and genial qualities have no time to be warmed into a flow.

It is in the country that the Englishman gives scope to his natural feelings. . . .

Washington Irving, 'Rural Life in England', *The Sketch Book of Geoffrey Crayon, Gent.*, 1820

All I can say is that standing at Charing Cross and looking east west north and south I can see nothing but dullness.

John Keats, Letter to Georgiana Keats, 13–28 January 1820

You are now
In London, that great sea, whose ebb and flow
At once is deaf and loud, and on the shore
Vomits its wrecks, and still howls on for more.
Yet in its depth what treasures!

Percy Bysshe Shelley, Letter to Maria Gisborne, July 1820

But what is to be the fate of the great wen of all? The monster, called by the silly coxcombs of the press, 'the metropolis of the empire?' What is to become of that multitude of towns that has been stuck up around it? . . .

The dispersion of the wen is the only real difficulty that I see in settling the affairs of the nation and restoring it to a happy state. But dispersed it *must* be; and if there be half a million, or more, of people to suffer, the consolation is, that the suffering will be divided into half a million parts.

William Cobbett, *Rural Rides*, 4 December 1821

Do, Graham, let me have a quiz,
Lord! what a Lilliput it is,
That little world of Mogg's! –
Are those the London Docks? – that channel,
The mighty Thames? – a proper kennel
For that small Isle of Dogs! –

What is that seeming tea-urn there?
That fairy dome, St. Paul's! – I swear,
Wren must have been a Wren! –
And that small stripe? – it cannot be
The City Road! – Good lack! to see
The little ways of men! . . .

Thomas Hood, *Ode to Mr Graham, the Aeronaut*, 1825

Augustus at Rome was for building renown'd
And of marble he left what but brick he had found:
But is not our Nash, too, a very great master
He found London Brick and he leaves it all plaster.

Anon., in *Quarterly Review*, xxxiv, 1826 – but had probably been printed earlier

London is the only place in which the child grows completely up into the man.

William Hazlitt, Essay 'On Londoners and Country People', *The Plain Speaker*, 1826

To London; where a world of living mind
In one dark fever of excess we find;
Where talent sparkles with incessant rays
And authors perish for the want of praise!

Robert Montgomery, *Oxford, a Poem*, 1831

One lady asked me very gravely, if we had left home in order to get rid of the vermin with which the English of all ranks were afflicted? 'I have heard from unquestionable authority,' she added, 'that it is quite impossible to walk through the streets of London without having the head filled.'

Mrs Frances Trollope, *Domestic Manners of the Americans*, 1832

There is a Stupidest of London men, actually resident, with bed and board of some kind, in London

Thomas Carlyle, *Biography*, 1832

. . . he who drinks a tumbler of London Water has literally in his stomach more animated beings than there are men, Women and Children on the face of the Globe.

Sydney Smith, Letter to Lady Grey, 19 November 1834

You may depend upon it, all lives out of London are mistakes, more or less grievous; – but mistakes.

Sydney Smith, Letter, 9 November 1837

Made up my journal, which had fallen somewhat behind. In this phantasmagorical place, the objects of the day come and depart like shadows.

Sir Walter Scott, Diary, 17 April 1828, in Lockhart, *Life of Scott*, 1838

It was a most heavenly day in May of this year (1800) when I first beheld and first entered this mighty wilderness, the city – no! not the city, but the nation – of London. Often since then, at distances of two and three hundred miles or more from this colossal emporium of men, wealth, arts, and intellectual power, have I felt the sublime expression of her enormous magnitude in one simple form of ordinary occurrence – viz., in the vast droves of cattle, suppose upon the great north roads, all with their heads directed to London, and expounding the size of the attracting body, by the never-ending succession of these droves, and the remoteness from the capital of the lines on which they were moving. A suction so powerful, felt along radii so vast, and a consciousness, at the same time, that upon other radii still more vast, both by land and by sea, the same suction is operating, night and day, summer and winter, and hurrying for ever into one centre the infinite means needed for her infinite purposes, and the endless tributes to the skill or to the luxury of her endless population, crowds the imagination with a pomp to which there is nothing corresponding upon this planet, either amongst the things that have been or the things that are.

Thomas de Quincey, *Autobiography*, 1834–53

No man was ever left to himself for the first time in the streets, as yet unknown, of London, but he must have been saddened and mortified, perhaps terrified, by the sense of desertion and utter loneliness which belongs to his situation. No loneliness can be like that which weighs upon the heart in the centre of faces never-ending, without voice or utterance for him; eyes innumerable, that have 'no speculation' in their orbs which *he* can understand; and hurrying figures of men and women weaving to and fro, with no apparent purpose intelligible to a stranger, seeming like a mask of maniacs, or, often-times, like a pageant of phantoms. The great length of the streets in many quarters of London, the continual opening of transient glimpses into other vistas equally far-stretching, going off at right angles to the one which you are traversing; and the murky atmosphere which, settling upon the remoter end of every long avenue, wraps its termination in gloom and uncertainty; all these are circumstances aiding that sense of vastness and illimitable proportions which for ever brood over the aspect of London in its interior.

Ibid.

Some new neighbours, that came a month or two ago, brought with them an accumulation of all the things to be guarded against in a London neighbourhood, viz., a pianoforte, a lap-dog, and a parrot.

Jane Welsh Carlyle, Letter to Mrs Carlyle, 6 May 1839

O LUD! O Lud! O Lud!
I mean of course that venerable town,
Mention'd in stories of renown
Built formerly of mud.

Thomas Hood, *Ode for the Ninth of November*, 1839

She [The Roman Catholic Church] may still exist in undiminished vigour, when some traveller from New Zealand shall, in the midst of a vast solitude, take his stand on a broken arch of London Bridge to sketch the ruins of St. Paul's.

T.B. Macaulay, 'Ranke's History of the Popes', *Essays*, October 1840

Traffic, to speak from knowledge but begun,
I saw, and travelling much, and fashion – Yea,
And if that Competition and Display
Make a great Capital, then thou art one, . . .

The stranger's fancy of the thing thou art
Is rather truly of a huge Bazaar,
A railway terminus, a gay Hotel,
Anything but a mighty Nation's heart.

Arthur Hugh Clough, *To the Great Metropolis*, April 1841

After roaming the streets of the capital a day or two, making headway with difficulty through the human turmoil and the endless lines of vehicles, after visiting the slums of the metropolis, one realizes for the first time that these Londoners have been forced to sacrifice the best qualities of their human nature, to bring to pass all the marvels of civilization which crowd their city; that a hundred powers which slumbered within them have remained inactive, have been suppressed in order that a few might be developed more fully and multiply through union with those of others . . . The brutal indifference, the unfeeling isolation of each in his private interest becomes the more repellent and offensive, the more these individuals are crowded together within a limited space. And, however much one may be aware that this isolation of the individual, this narrow self-seeking, is the fundamental principle of our society everywhere, it is nowhere so shamelessly barefaced, so self-conscious as just here in the crowding of the great city. The dissolution of mankind into nomads, of which each one has a separate principle, the world of atoms, is here carried out to its utmost extreme.

Friedrich Engels, *Condition of the Working Class in England in 1844*, English translation, New York 1887, London 1892

I am still indignant at this nasty place, London. . . . I smoked a pipe with Carlyle yesterday. We ascended from his dining room carrying pipes and tobacco up through two stories of his house, and got into a little dressing room near the roof: there we sat down: the window was open and looked out on nursery gardens, their almond trees in blossom, and beyond, bare walls of houses, and over these, roofs and chimneys, and roofs and chimneys, and here and there a steeple, and whole London crowned with darkness gathering behind like the illimitable resources of a dream. I tried to persuade him to leave the accursed den, and he wished – but – but – perhaps he didn't wish on the whole.

Edward Fitzgerald, Letter to Bernard Barton, 11 April 1844

*There was a dense fog too – as if it were a city in the clouds, which they had been travelling to all night up a magic beanstalk; and there was a thick crust upon the pavement, like oil-cake, which one of the outside (mad, no doubt) said to another (his keeper, of course) was Snow.

Charles Dickens, *Martin Chuzzlewit*, 1844

*She often looked with compassion, at such a time, upon the stragglers who came wandering into London, by the great highway hard by, and who, footsore and weary, and gazing fearfully at the huge town before them, as if foreboding that their misery there would be but as a drop of water in the sea, or as a grain of sea-sand on the shore, went shrinking on, cowering before the angry weather, and looking as if the very elements rejected them. Day after day, such travellers crept past, but always, as she thought, in one direction, – always towards the town. Swallowed up in one phase or another of its immensity, towards which they seemed impelled by a desperate fascination, they never returned. Food for the hospitals, the churchyards, the prisons, the river, fever, madness, vice and death, – they passed on to the monster, roaring in the distance, and were lost

Charles Dickens, *Dombey and Son*, 1847–8

Whoever examines the maps of London which were published towards the close of the reign of Charles the Second will see that only the nucleus of the present capital then existed. The town did not, as now, fade by imperceptible degrees into the country. No long avenues of villas, embowered in lilacs and laburnums, extended from the great centre of wealth and civilisation almost to the boundaries of Middlesex and far into the heart of Kent and Surrey. In the east, no part of the immense line of warehouses and artificial lakes which now stretches from the Tower to Blackwall had even been projected. On the west, scarcely one of those stately piles of building which are inhabited by the noble and wealthy was in existence; and Chelsea, which is now peopled by more than forty thousand human beings, was a quiet country village with about a thousand inhabitants. On the north, cattle fed, and sportsmen wandered with dogs and guns, over the site of the borough of Marylebone, and far the greater part of the space now covered by the boroughs of Finsbury and of the Tower Hamlets. Islington was almost a solitude; and poets loved to contrast its silence and repose with the din and turmoil of monster London. On the south the capital is now connected with its suburb by several bridges, not inferior in magnificence and solidity to the noblest works of the Caesars. In 1685, a single line of irregular arches, overhung by piles of mean and crazy houses, and garnished, after a fashion worthy of the naked barbarians of Dahomey, with scores of mouldering heads, impeded the navigation of the river.

T.B. Macaulay, *History of England*, 1849–61

Upon sallying out this morning encountered the old-fashioned pea soup London fog – of a gamboge color. It was lifted, however, from the ground & floated in mid air. When lower, it is worse.

Herman Melville, *Journal of a Tour to London and the Continent in 1849–50*, 24 November 1849

*This is a London particular. . . . A fog, miss.
Charles Dickens, *Bleak House*, 1852

I believe the parallelogram between Oxford-street, Piccadilly, Regent-street, and Hyde Park, encloses more intelligence and human ability, to say nothing of wealth and beauty, than the world has ever collected in such a space before.
Sydney Smith, quoted by Lady Holland, *Memoir of Sydney Smith*, 1855

To any one who has reached a very advanced age, a walk through the streets of London is like a walk in a cemetery. How many houses do I pass, now inhabited by strangers, in which I used to spend such happy hours with those who have long been dead and gone!
Samuel Rogers, *Table Talk*, 1856

Or I saw
Fog only, the great tawny weltering fog,
Involve the passive city, strangle it,
Alive, and draw it off into the void,
Spires, bridges, streets, and squares, as if a spunge
Had wiped out London, – or as noon and night
Had clapped together and utterly struck out
The intermediate time, undoing themselves
In the act. Your city poets see such things
Not despicable.
Elizabeth Barrett Browning, *Aurora Leigh*, 1856

London is the epitome of our times and the Rome of today.
R.W. Emerson, *English Traits*, 1856

The nation sits in the immense city they have builded, a London extended to every man's mind, though he live in Van Dieman's Land or Capetown.
Ibid.

The greatest benefit of London seems today to be this, that in such a vast number of persons and conditions, one can believe there is room for such people as we read of in novels to exist.
Ralph Waldo Emerson, *Journals*, 1859

Some years ago a famous and witty French critic was in London with whom I walked the streets. I am ashamed to say that I informed him (being in hopes that he was about to write some papers regarding the manners and customs of this country) that all the statues he saw represented the Duke of Wellington. That on the arch opposite Apsley House? The Duke in a cloak, and a cock-hat on horseback. That behind Apsley House in an airy fig-leaf of costume? the Duke again. That in Cockspur Street? the Duke with a pig-tail – and so on. I showed him an army of Dukes.
W.M. Thackeray, *Roundabout Papers*, 1860–3

Houses, churches, mix'd together;
Streets, unpleasant in all weather;
Prisons, palaces contiguous;
Gates, a bridge, the Thames irriguous;
Gaudy things enough to tempt you
Showy outsides, insides empty;
Bubbles, trades, mechanic arts
Coaches, wheelbarrows, and carts;
Warrants, baliffs, bills unpaid
Lords of laundresses afraid;
Rogues that nightly shoot men
Hangmen aldermen and footmen;
Lawyers, poets, priests, physicians,
Noble, simple, – all conditions:
Worth, beneath a threadbare cover,
Villany bedaubed all over;
Women, black red fair and grey,
Prudes, and such as never pray,
Handsome ugly, noisy, still,
Some that will not – some that will
Many a beau without a shilling,
Many a widow – not unwilling;
Many a bargain – if you strike it:
This is London – how d'ye like it?
Anon., 'Description of London', in *Epigrams Ancient and Modern* ed. Rev. John Booth, 1863

I had found it better than my dream; for there is nothing else in life comparable (in that species of enjoyment, I mean) to the thick, heavy, oppressive, sombre delight which an American is sensible of, hardly knowing whether to call it a pleasure or a pain, in the atmosphere of London. The result was, that I acquired a home-feeling there, as nowhere else in the world; though afterwards I came to have a somewhat similar sentiment in regard to Rome; and as long as either of those two great cities shall exist, the cities of the Past and of the Present, a man's native soil may crumble beneath his feet without leaving him altogether homeless upon earth.
Nathaniel Hawthorne, *Our Old Home*, 1863

From the Thames
It seems indeed as if the heart of London had been cleft open for the mere purpose of showing how rotten and drearily mean it had become . . . had I known nothing more of the world's metropolis I might have fancied that it had already experienced the downfall which I have heard commercial and financial prophets predict for it, within the century. And the muddy tide of the Thames, reflecting nothing, and hiding a million of unclean secrets within its breast – a sort of guilty conscience, as it were, unwholesome with the rivulets of sin that constantly flow into it – is just the dismal stream to glide by such a city.
Ibid.

. . . That mystery of the world's proudest city, amid

which a man so longs and loves to be; not, perhaps, because it contains much that is positively admirable and enjoyable, but because at all events the world has nothing better, the cream of external life is there, and whatever intellectual or merely material good we fail to find perfect in London, we may as well content ourselves to seek that unattainable thing no further on this earth.

Ibid.

Forget six counties overhung with smoke
Forget the snorting steam and piston stroke,
Forget the spreading of the hideous town;
Think rather of the pack-horse on the down,
And dream of London, small and white and clean,
The clear Thames bordered by its gardens green.

William Morris, *The Earthly Paradise*, 1868–70

Peebles Body (to townsman supposed to be in London): E-eh Mac! you're sune hume again.
Mac:E-eh, it's just a ruinous place that! Mun, a had na' been there abune two hoours when Bang went saxpence.

Becket Foster, a joke from *Punch*, 5 December 1868, with a drawing by Charles Keene. The story had been communicated to Keene by Foster, who had it from Sir John Gilbert

Up to this time I have been crushed under a sense of the mere magnitude of London – its inconceivable immensity – in such a way as to paralyse my mind for any appreciation of details. This is gradually subsiding; but what does it leave behind it? An extraordinary intellectual depression, as I may say, and an indefineable flatness of mind. The place sits on you, broods on you, stamps on you with the feet of its myriad bipeds and quadrupeds. In fine it is anything but a cheerful or a charming city. Yet it is a very splendid one. It gives you, here at the West End and in the City proper, a vast impression of opulence and prosperity.

Henry James, Letter to Alice James, 10 March 1869

*London is a roost for every bird.

Benjamin Disraeli, Earl of Beaconsfield, *Lothair*, 1870

*London, a nation, not a city.

Ibid.

Those who can and do work are emphatically London . . . London wears a dismal exterior to the eye of the foreigner, because all London is hard at work.

Blanchard Jerrold, *London, a Pilgrimage*, 1872

A completely representative London fog. It was choking; it made the eyes ache. It rolled into the house, as a visitor remarked, like a feather bed, at the heels of every arrival. For sky we had a deep yellow-orange roof across the street; and about the street red specks of light played, borne by lads and men whose voices seemed to reach us through woollen comforters. . . . Today I could tell my fellow traveller that he had at last seen one of those famous darknesses, which, in every stranger's mind are the almost daily mantle of the wonderful and wonder working Babylon.

Ibid.

I think it on the whole the best point of view in the world.

Henry James, Letter to Charles Eliot Norton, 13 November 1880

London is ugly, dusky, dreary, more destitute than any European city of graceful and decorative incident; . . . As you walk along the streets, having no fellow-pedestrians to look at, you look up at the brown brick house-walls, corroded with soot and fog, pierced with their straight stiff window-slits, and finished by way of a cornice, with a little black line resembling a slice of curbstone. There is not an accessory, not a touch of architectural fancy, not the narrowest concession to beauty. If I were a foreigner it would make me rabid; being an Anglo-Saxon, I find in it what Thackeray found in Baker-Street—a delightful proof of English domestic virtue, of the sanctity of the British home. There are miles and miles of these edifying monuments, and it would seem that a city made up of them should have no claim to that larger effectiveness of which I just now spoke. London, however, is not made up of them; there are architectural combinations of a statelier kind, and the impression moreover does not rest in details. London is pictorial in spite of detail—from its dark-green, misty parks, the way the light comes down leaking and filtering from its cloud-ceiling, and the softness and richness of tone, which objects put on in such an atmosphere as soon as they begin to recede. Nowhere is there such a play of light and shade, such a struggle of sun and smoke, such aerial gradations and confusions. To eyes addicted to such contemplations this is a constant diversion, and yet this is only part of it. What completes the effect of the place is its appeal to the feelings, made in so many ways, but made above all, by agglomerated immensity. At any given point, London looks huge; even in narrow corners you have a sense of its hugeness, and petty places acquire a certain interest from their being parts of so mighty a whole. Nowhere else is so much human life gathered together, and nowhere does it press upon you with so many suggestions. These are not all of an exhilarating kind; far from it. But they are of every possible kind, and that is the interest of London

Henry James, *An English Easter*, 1877 in *Portraits of Places*, 1883

*London, that great cesspool into which all the loungers of the Empire are irresistibly drained.

Sir Arthur Conan Doyle, *A Study in Scarlet*, 1887

In London I saw nothing good and constantly remembered that Ruskin had said to some friend of my father 'As I go to work at the British Museum, I see the faces of the people become daily more corrupt.'

W.B. Yeats, *Autobiography*, 1887

*It is my belief, Watson, founded upon my experience, that the lowest and vilest alleys of London do not present a more dreadful record of sin than does the smiling and beautiful countryside.

Sir Arthur Conan Doyle, 'The Copper Beeches', *The Adventures of Sherlock Holmes*, 1891

Your father began by saying that, as he walked thro' Eaton Square at night with Carlyle in the moonlight, Carlyle looked up at the houses round about and said, 'Acrid putrescence.'

Anne Thackeray Ritchie, Letter, 11 December 1895

London sits on my stomach like a Welsh rabbit at midnight.

Henry Adams, Letter to Elizabeth Cameron, 11 July 1895

Judging from the ordinary occupants of the streets, one is apt to think of London as a city solely made up of the acute, the knowing, the worldly, the blasé. But hidden away behind sunblinds in quiet squares and crescents, there dwells another vast population, seen in large numbers only at such times as this, an army of the Ignorantly Innocent, in whose sheltered seclusion a bus-ride is an event, and a day spent amongst the traffic of the West End an occasion long to be remembered.

Arnold Bennett, *Journal*, 22 July 1896

Jubilee Sunday – The streets decked out with scaffolding and red cloth. London architecture lends itself to these disguisements, as there is nothing to lose by being hidden.

Wilfred Scawen Blunt, Diary, 20 June 1897, *My Diaries*, 1919

Came home today. London nearly as bad as usual. Even to hate a town is bad. The same results – but diminished in virulence – as follow on hating a human being – morbid exaggeration of its désagréments, denigration of its good things – inward restlessness – nursing of malice and uncharitableness till they are cossetted into virtues – a miserable tossing to and fro between desire to do harm and inability to do it, and many other vicious things and tempers. Nevertheless I hate the place.

Stopford Brooke, *Diary*, 16 February 1899

Twentieth Century

For the first few days I thought it more dreadful than the monotony of the Bush, and more utterly hopeless, seeing that the Bush becomes settled and humanised, while London can only change with the changes of the centuries.

Henry Lawson, *Letters to Jack Cornstalk*, 1900

The imagination cannot conceive a viler criminal than he who should build another London like the present one, nor a greater benefactor than he who should destroy it.

G. Bernard Shaw, 'Maxims for Revolutionists', *Man and Superman*, 1901–3

Provided that the city of London remains as it is at present, the clearing-house of the world.

Joseph Chamberlain, Speech, Guildhall, 19 January 1904

And indeed it is impossible, without an effort to dissociate in our minds the idea of London from the idea of a vast cloud beneath a cloud as vast. The memory cannot otherwise conceive of all these gray buildings, of all these gray people. You do not, for instance, call up in your mind all the houses you would pass between Charing Cross and Knightsbridge: they fade into one mass, and because that mass is one you will never touch and finger, it seems cloudlike enough. But all the limitless stretches of roofs that you have never seen, the streets you will never travel, the miles and miles of buildings, the myriads of plane-trees, of almonds, of elms – all these appalling regions of London that to every individual of us must remain unknown and untraversed – all those things fuse in our minds into one cloud. And the Corporations, the Water Boards, the Dock Boards, the Railway Organisations, the bodies of men who keep the parks in order, the armies who sweep in the streets – all these are cloudlike too. They seem unnatural, all these things, and London itself is apt at times to seem unreal. So that when we come across a park with sharp folds in the land, sharp dips, sudden rises, it is almost astonishing that anything so natural and real should remain in the heart of this cloud beneath a cloud. For, little by little, the Londoner comes to forget that his London is built upon real earth: he forgets that under the pavements there are hills, forgotten water courses, springs and marshland.

And beneath and amongst all those clouds – thunderclouds, the cloud of buildings, the clouds of corporations, – there hurries still the great swarm of tiny men and women, each one hugging desperately his own soul, his own hopes, his own passions, his own individuality.

Ford Madox Ford, *The Soul of London*, 1905

London, that like a bowl of viscid human fluid, boils sullenly over the rim of its encircling hills and slops messily and uglily into the home counties.

H.G. Wells, *The Future of America*, 1906

London is never so overpowering as when the opening of the 'season' turns the provinces into a mere suburb of the sprawling Metropolis. She is not only too big for herself – so big, indeed, that she has no civic consciousness – but she is too big for England. She drains, impoverishes, debauches it. 'Sick of prey yet howling for more,' she fastens upon the national life like a vampire. She is more than the capital of the country; she is its incubus, its tyrant, its leech. Her lure is the more deadly for being irresistible, and her sway at once more despotic and more devitalizing for its very benignity. To one great department of thought and activity, indeed, her absolutism does not extend. She is no politician . . . London takes most things for granted, discounts the rest, and originates nothing. . . . She is the last city to set the Thames on fire.

Anon., *Nation*, 30 May 1908

Chief observation in London: that it is a city of very rich and very poor. The vastness of this rich quarter is astonishing. In Bond St, this morning the main thing to be seen was the well-groomed, physically fit male animal: a sort of physical arrogance with it. . . . It is almost disconcerting to think that all this vast idle class has to 'go' one day. The idlers in this hotel make an imposing array. Offensive, many of them.

Arnold Bennett, *Journal*, 2 January 1908

and Paris

London is far more difficult to see properly than any other place. London is a riddle. Paris is an explanation.

G.K. Chesterton, *All Things Considered*, 1908

London was unrivalled in its powers of assimilation – the great, easy-going, tolerant, loveable old dressing-gown of a place it was then. It was never more to be so.

Ford Madox Ford, *Return to Yesterday*, 1932
(of London on eve of the First World War)

I decided to go to London, for the purpose of hearing the Strand roar, which I think one does want, after a day or two of Richmond.

Virginia Woolf, *Diary*, 28 January 1915

London, the London before the war, flaunting its enormous glare, as of a monstrous conflagration up into the black sky – with its best Venice-like aspect of rainy evenings, the wet asphalted streets lying with the sheen of sleeping water in winding canals, and the great houses of the city towering all dark like empty palaces above the reflected lights of the glistening roadway.

Joseph Conrad, 'Poland Revisited', 1915, in *Notes on Life and Letters*, 1921

There is in the aspect of London a certain magnificence; the magnificence of weight, solidity, energy, imperturbability, and an unconquered continuance. It is alive from border to border, not an inch of it is not alive. It exists, goes on, and has been going on for so many centuries. Here and there a stone or the line of a causeway fixes a date. If you look beyond it you look into fog. It sums up and includes England. Materially England is contained in it, and the soul of England has always inhabited it as a body. We have not had a great man who has never lived in London.

London makes no display; it is there, as it has come, as fire and plagues have left it . . . the appeal of London is made by no beauty or effect in things themselves, but by the sense which it gives us of inevitable growth and impregnable strength, and by the atmosphere which makes and unmakes this vast and solid city every morning and every evening with a natural magic peculiar to it.

Arthur Symons, *London*, 1918

London is at its worst – a drunk charwoman with child by a pauper lunatic – that's my feeling, something lewd about it, as well as indecent and detestable.

Virginia Woolf, Letter to Molly MacCarthy, 4 December 1919

The climate of London and indeed of England generally is due to the influence of the Gulf Stream. The way it works is thus: The Gulf Stream, as it nears the shores of the British Isles and feels the propinquity of Ireland, rises into the air, turns into soup, and comes down on London. At times the soup is thin and is in fact little more than a mist: at other times it has the consistency of a thick Potage St. Germain. London people are a little sensitive on this point and flatter their atmosphere by calling it a fog: but it is not: it is a soup. . . .

The whole subject of daylight in the London winter is, however, one which belongs rather to the technique of astronomy than to a book of description. In practice daylight is but little used. Electric lights are burned all the time in all houses, buildings, railway stations and clubs. This practice which is now universally observed is called Daylight Saving.

Stephen Leacock, *My Discovery of England*, 1922

*If there is such a thing as a shell secreted by man to fit himself here we find it, on the banks of the Thames, where the great streets join and St. Paul's Cathedral, like the volute on the top of the snail shell, finishes it off.

Virginia Woolf, *Jacob's Room*, 1922

*The lamps of London uphold the dark as upon the points of burning bayonets.

Ibid.

Unreal City,
Under the brown fog of a winter dawn,
A crowd flowed over London Bridge, so many,
I had not thought death had undone so many.
Sighs, short and infrequent were exhaled

And each man fixed his eyes before his feet.
Flowed up the hill and down King William Street,
To where Saint Mary Woolnoth kept the hours
With a dead sound on the final stroke of nine.

T.S. Eliot, *The Waste Land*, 1922

London is enchanting. I step out upon a tawny coloured magic carpet, it seems, & get carried into beauty without raising a finger. The nights are amazing, with all the white porticoes & broad silent avenues. And people pop in & out, lightly, divertingly like rabbits; & I look down Southampton Row, wet as a seal's back or red & yellow with sunshine, & watch the omnibus going & coming, & hear the old crazy organs. One of these days I will write about London & how it takes up the private life & carries it on, without any effort. Faces passing lift up my mind; prevent it from settling.

Virginia Woolf, *Diary*, 5 May 1924

'London!' It has the sound of distant thunder.

James Bone, *The London Perambulator*, 1925

I don't know what London's coming to – the higher the buildings the lower the morals.

Noel Coward, *Law and Order – Collected Sketches and Lyrics*, 1928

The first half-hour in London after some years abroad is really a plunge in misery. The strange, the grey and uncanny, and almost deathly sense of *dulness* is overwhelming. Of course you get over it after a while and admit that you exaggerated. You get into the rhythm of London again and you tell yourself that it is *not* dull. And yet you are haunted, all the time, sleeping or waking, with the uncanny feeling: It is dull! It is all dull! The life here is one vast complex of dulness! I am dull! I am being dulled! My spirit is being dulled! My life is dulling down to London dulness.

D.H. Lawrence, *Dull London*, 1929

One of the charms of London is that there are no Londoners.

H.V. Morton, *In Search of Scotland*, 1929

A cockney in Canada was asked by a recruiting sergeant where he came from. He replied: 'London.' Said the sergeant: 'London what? London, Ontario? London, N.Y? London, Mass?' 'London the bl—dy world!' the recruit replied with ineffable disgust. That is how it feels to the born Londoner.

Ford Madox Ford, *Return to Yesterday*, 1932

Till that day I never noticed one of the worst things about London – the fact that it costs money even to sit down.

George Orwell, *Down and Out in Paris and London*, 1933

On Sunday last went up to Manchester for Paul Dehn's, my godson's, twenty-first birthday.
GODFATHER. Tell me, Paul, what in your view a young man should possess who intends to conquer London.
GODSON (after thinking). A fine mind and a hide like a rhinoceros.
GODFATHER. A fine skin and a mind like a rhinoceros would do you a lot more good.

James Agate, *Ego* (12 November 1933), 1935

The greatest target in the world, a kind of tremendous, fat, vulnerable cow tied up to attract the beast of prey. . . .

Sir Winston Churchill, Speech in the House of Commons, 1934

The flying peril is not a peril from which one can fly. We cannot possibly retreat. We cannot move London.

Sir Winston Churchill, Speech in the House of Commons, 28 November 1934

London has been cosmopolitanised, democratised, commercialised, mechanised, standardised, vulgarised, so extensively that one's pride in showing it to a foreigner is changed to a wholesome humility. One feels rather as Virgil may have felt in showing Hell to Dante.

It is a bright, cheerful, salubrious Hell, certainly. But still – to *my* mind – Hell.

Max Beerbohm, 'London Revisited', Broadcast, 29 December 1935, *Mainly on the Air*, 1946

London is a university with ten million graduates qualified to live and let live.

Oliver St John Gogarty, *As I Was Going Down Sackville Street*, 1937

The city has piled itself up like a geological series, and, perhaps, the process will continue until a skin of unsmashable glass is stretched over her, as in H.G. Wells's dream.

E.M. Forster, 'London is a Muddle', 1937, in *Two Cheers for Democracy*, 1951

Time has tamed me, and though it is not practicable to love such a place (one could as easily embrace both volumes of the telephone directory at once), one can love bits of it, and become interested in the rest.

Ibid.

London, that noble deer bayed and brought down, and torn in pieces; the city of lamentations, ruled by Lilliputians and exploited by Yahoos, whose splendid streets, once one of the splendours of Europe, are now fit only to serve as the promenades of pet dogs or as vast ashtrays for the stubs of a million typists. . . .

Evelyn Waugh, 'A Call to Orders', *Country Life*, 26 February 1938

I've just come back from three dark days in London, city of the restless dead. It really is an insane city, and filled me with terror. Every pavement drills through your soles to your scalp, and out pops a lamp-post covered with hair. I'm not going to London again for years; its intelligentsia is so hurried in the head that nothing stays there; its glamour smells of goat; there's no difference between good and bad.

Dylan Thomas, Letter to Vernon Watkins, 20 December 1938

Oh, London Fog, London Fog,
How many people have pierced the fog's special joys
You want to go East, find yourself West, mind in utter confusion.
This way, that way, all obscure – that is the road in fog.
Bumping shoulders, kicking heels, exclaiming merrily,
No distinction of fine and plain – that is the meeting in fog.
Morning and evening, best of all,
As if there, not there – that is the trees in fog.
I like their subtle, evasive manner
That's why I like to live in London fog for a long time.

Chiang Yee, *The Silent Traveller in London*, 1938

Paris, half angel, half Grisette,
I would that I were with thee yet;
But London waits me, like a wife,
London, the love of my whole life.

Richard Le Gallienne, *Paris Day by Day*

Last night London had its biggest blitz to date. From my attic window the view was one of beauty and awe. Against the glow of the distant fires the Odeon Cinema and other daytime-ugly buildings at Swiss Cottage stood out like the battlements of Elsinore. I could smell my neighbour's thorn and cherry-trees, now in full flower, drenched by the full moon. Presently I heard drops of what in that empty sky could not be water. It was shrapnel, and I wondered what Debussy would have made of this garden under that rain.

James Agate, *Ego 5*, 11 May 1941

London is a splendid place to live for those who can get out of it.

Lord Balfour of Burleigh, *Observer*, 'Sayings of the Week', 1 October 1944

A foggy, dead-alive city like a dying ant-heap. London was created for rich young men to shop in, dine in, ride in, get married in, go to theatres in, and die in as respected householders. It is a city for the unmarried upper class, not for the poor.

Cyril Connolly, 'England, Not My England', in *The Condemned Playground*, 1945

Between March and April when barrows of daffodils butter the pavement,
The colossus of London stretches his gaunt legs, jerking
The smoke of his hair back from his eyes and puffing
Smoke-rings of heavenward pigeons over Saint Paul's,
While in each little city of each individual person
The black tree yearns for green confetti and the black kerb for yellow stalls.

Louis MacNeice, *Street Scene*, c.1946

The ugliness and anarchy of this great sprawling city, grown up like a miners' town on the banks of the Yukon, appals me. Can a civilised people really live in this low squatters' settlement? Yet as the rain lifts, I become aware of the April light, as it falls on the elm trees with their young pointed leaves and their black, silky branches and stems. London is ugly and haphazard, I tell myself, because the English are not a race of city dwellers: they are countrymen who are trying to pretend that they are camping here provisionally

Gerald Brenan, *The Face of Spain*, 1950

London is chaos incorporated.

George Mikes, *Down with Everybody*, 1951

The English . . . are already hard to find in London. No one lives there who is not paid to do so. You will find strange faces and strange tongues in the streets; tourists in the hotels; and there are no private houses. Do I exaggerate? Perhaps there are still a score where more than a dozen can sit down to dinner. I do not pretend to be a popular man-about-town. My knowledge comes second-hand, but I believe that London society has ceased to exist; all hospitality is now commercial or official.

Evelyn Waugh, 'I See Nothing but Boredom . . . Everywhere', *Daily Mail*, 28 December 1959

Those who have never seen the inhabitants of a nineteenth-century London slum can have no idea of the state to which dirt, drink, and economics can reduce human beings.

Leonard Woolf, *Sowing*, 1960

A bit of experience is excellent: a man must knock around the world, or the West End of London.

David Pryce-Jones, *Owls and Satyrs*, 1961

London is a bad habit one hates to lose.

Anon. saying, quoted William Sansom, *Blue Skies Brown Studies*, 1961

Having left the great mean city, I make
Shift to pretend I am finally quit of her

Though that cannot be so long as I work.
  Nevertheless let the petals fall
  Fast from the flower of cities all.

When I first met her to my child's ear
She was an ocean of drums and tumbrils
And in my nostrils horsepiss and petrol.
  Nevertheless let the petals fall
  Fast from the flower of cities all.

Next to my peering teens she was foreign
Names over winking doors, a kaleidoscope
Of wine and ice, of eyes and emeralds.
  Nevertheless let the petals fall
  East from the flower of cities all.

Later as a place to live in and love in
I jockeyed her fogs and quoted Johnson:
To be tired of this is to be tired of life.
  Nevertheless let the petals fall
  Fast from the flower of cities all.

Then came the headshrinking war, the city
Closed in too, the people were fewer
But closer too, we were back in the womb.
  Nevertheless let the petals fall
  Fast from the flower of cities all.

From which reborn into anticlimax
We endured much litter and apathy hoping
The phoenix would rise, for so they had promised.
  Nevertheless let the petals fall
  Fast from the flower of cities all.

And nobody rose, only some meaningless
Buildings and the people once more were strangers
At home with no one, sibling or friend.
  Which is why now the petals fall
  Fast from the flower of cities all.

Louis MacNeice, *Goodbye to London*, 1962

I thought of London spread out in the sun
Its postal districts packed like squares of wheat.

Philip Larkin, *The Whitsun Weddings*, 1964

Fifty years ago in the City of London all day and all night long there fell a slow gentle rain of smuts, so that, if you sat writing by an open window, a thin veil of smuts covered the paper before you had finished a page. The City is, – or rather was, – one of the pleasantest of all London districts to live in. . . . No Londoner who has never lived east of Chancery Lane really knows what the essence of London is. I have lived in Kensington, Bloomsbury, Westminster and the City – I would give the palm to the City.

Leonard Woolf, *Beginning Again*, 1964

I came to London. It had become the centre of my world and I had worked hard to come to it. And I was lost. London was not the centre of my world. I had been misled; but there was nowhere else to go. It was a good place for getting lost in, a city no one ever knew, a city explored from the neutral heart outwards, until, after years, it defined itself into a jumble of clearings separated by stretches of the unknown, through which the narrowest of paths had been cut.

V.S.Naipaul, *An Area of Darkness*, 1964

An American in London, whether he has come here to work for Esso or to escape the draft, cannot but be impressed and charmed by the city. The monumentality of Washington, the thriving business of New York, the antique intimacy of Boston, plus a certain spacious and open feeling reminiscent of Denver and San Francisco – all these he finds combined for his pleasure. . . .

A city then, of sections, rather than layers, where latitude mitigates pressure.

John Updike, 'London Life', 1969, in *Picked Up Pieces*, 1976

By October of 1969 Funky Chic was flying through London like an infected bat, which is to say, silently, blindly, insanely, and at night, fangs afoam . . . but with an infallible aim for the main vein . . . much like the Sideburns Fairy, who had been cruising about the city since 1966, visiting young groovies in their sleep and causing them to awake with sideburns running down their jawbones.

Tom Wolfe, 'Funky Chic', in *Mauve Gloves and Madmen, Clutter and Vine*, 1976

When it's three o'clock in New York, it's still 1938 in London.

Bette Midler, quoted in *The Times*, 21 September 1978

Foreign visitors make the mistake of starting with London . . .

London should come last. You can't appreciate the complex metropolis until you know where so much of its energy comes from.

Londoners like to talk of their city as a great magnet, but the image of Dracula is equally accurate. It drains the rest of the country in the same way as the oil rigs are draining the North Sea. One goes there at last as Americans go to New York: to experience the shock of vitality from so many millions living together and to see the country in a melting pot.

W.J. Wetherby, *Guardian*, 22 August 1979

More than any other city in Europe, London is a show, living by bluff and display. People have always remarked upon its theatrical nature. . . . It is, surprisingly, a very volatile capital: the U.S. ambassador recently diagnosed it as manic-depressive, on top of the world one day, all despondency the next.

Jan Morris, *Destinations*, 1980

V.S.Pritchett . . . once wrote that the chief characteristic of London was *experience*.

Ibid.

'Do you know what Johnny Gielgud said to Steve Gordon when he told him he hadn't been to London yet? "Oh pity – you've missed it!" I know what he means.'

Dudley Moore, quoted by George Perry, 'How Dud Made Good', *Sunday Times Magazine*, 13 December 1981

Districts and Details

Albert Memorial

Immortal Albert, why this mortal strife
On thy memorial 'twixt Death and Life –
That all too deathless tinsel round thy head,
And round they feet those all too lifeless dead?

G. Rostrevor Hamilton, 'On the Albert Memorial', *Making*, 1926

A venerated Queen of Northern Isles reared to the memory of her loving Consort a monument whereat the nations stand aghast. Is this the reward of conjugal virtue? Ye husbands, be unfaithful.

Norman Douglas, *An Almanac*, 1945

Baker Street

Before I forget: of course I went to look at Baker Street, but I came back terribly disappointed. There is not the slightest trace of Sherlock Holmes there: it is a business thoroughfare of unexampled respectability, which serves no higher purpose than to lead to Regent's Park, which, after a long endeavour, it almost manages to achieve. If we also briefly touch upon its underground railway station, we have exhausted everything, including our patience

Karel Capek, *Letters from England*, 1925

Barnes

Barnes, a suburb which, aiming desperately at the genteel, achieves only a sordid melancholy. . . .

W. Somerset Maugham, *On a Chinese Screen*, 1922

Battersea

Go to Battersea to be cut for the simples.

Quoted in John Ray, *A Compleat Collection of English Proverbs*, 1670

Battersea is so far off, the roads so execrable, and the rain so incessant. I cannot bear to take my cab from London over Battersea Bridge, as it seems so absurd to pay eightpence for the sake of the half-mile on this side; but that half-mile is one continued slough, as there is not a yard of flagging, I believe, in all Battersea.

Matthew Arnold, Letter to his wife, December 1852

Belgravia

South of Hyde Park is the now popular district of Belgravia, wholly devoid of interest, and which none would think of visiting unless drawn there by the claims of society.

A.J.C. Hare, *Walks in London*, 7th edn, 1901

Bloomsbury

Oh, mine in snows and summer heats,
These good old Tory brick-built streets!
My eye is pleased with all it meets
    In Bloomsbury.

Wilfred Whitten, *Bloomsbury*, 1893

London is incredibly beautiful – not with the soft suburban beauty of Richmond: I find Bloomsbury fierce and scornful and stony hearted, but as I say, so adorably lovely that I look out of my window all day long.

Virginia Woolf, Letter to Katharine Arnold-Forster, 12 April 1924

Bond Street

Might not a Frenchman, whose residence in England had been limited to a very short period in the immediate neighbourhood of Bond-street, return to Paris, and declare upon his honour, that the English were too *gay*?

J.A. Anderson, *A Dane's Excursions in Britain*, 1809

I like to walk down Bond Street, thinking of all the things I don't want.

Logan Pearsall Smith, *Afterthoughts*, 1931

The British Museum

I came one morning in May 1883 and found the steps of the main entrance all covered with stuffed birds and beasts on their way to South Kensington. It was very droll and very pretty. They looked like the creatures coming out of the Ark.

Samuel Butler, *Further Extracts from Note-books*, 1934

Brunswick Square

*'No, indeed – *we* are not at all in a bad air. Our part of London is so very superior to most others! – You must not confound us with London in general, my dear sir. The neighbourhood of Brunswick Square is very different from all the rest. We are so very airy! I should be unwilling, I own, to live in any other part of the town; there is hardly any other that I could be satisfied to have my children in: – but *we* are so remarkably airy! Mr Wingfield thinks the neighbourhood of Brunswick Square decidedly the most favourable as to air.'

Jane Austen, *Emma*, 1816

Buckingham Palace
I must say, notwithstanding the expense which has been incurred in building the palace, no sovereign in Europe, I may even add, perhaps no private gentleman, is so ill lodged as the king of this country.
Duke of Wellington, Speech in the House of Lords, 16 July 1828

Camden Hill
You saw the moon from Sussex Downs,
A Sussex moon, untravelled still,
I saw a moon that was the town's
The largest lamp on Camden Hill.
G.K. Chesterton, *The Napoleon of Notting Hill*, Dedication, 1904

Chancery Lane
I could not bear to go down the dark narrow street of Chancery Lane It was as bad as a haunted place to pass & one dark night I decided to venture the risk of being lost rather than go down though I tried all my courage to go down to no purpose for I could not get it out of my head but that I should be sure to meet death or the devil if I did so I passed it & tried to find Fleet Street by another road but I soon got lost & the more I tried to find the way the more I got wrong so I offered a watchman a shilling to show me the way thither but he said he would not go for that & asked a half-a-crown which I readily gave him
John Clare, *Autobiography* – of 1824

Chelsea
It's a long pull down the King's Road and down
to the Pier Hotel
To the Thames where the turbulent seagulls
float backwards on the swell
As muffled in my dufflecoat
Unruffled in my dufflecoat
I walk the streets of Hell.

Intellectual introspective streets of the higher
income brackets
Trodden by Mr Eliot's feet and the leaders
of the rackets
Where artists in their dufflecoats
Feel smartest in their dufflecoats
Like cigarettes in packets.

The Carlyle statue, pondering, sits wrapped in
gloomy thought
And warns that Human Wisdom still may be
too dearly bought –
When duffle coat meets duffle coat
Each passes like a river boat
Towards its final port!
Gavin Ewart, 'Chelsea in Winter', *Londoners*, 1964

Chiswick
Sir Stephen Fox's house at Chiswick is the flower of all the private gentlemens palaces in England. Here when the late King William, who was an allowed judge of fine buildings, and of gardening also, had seen the house and garden, he stood still on the terras for near half a quarter of an hour without speaking one word, when turning at last to the Earl of Portland, the king said, This place is perfectly fine, I could live here five days.
Daniel Defoe, *A Tour through the Whole Island of Great Britain*, 1724–7

Moon at the full: a shrunken tide,
Fingering rapidly through these
Low channels that the mudbank hems,
Runs lucid, blotted with humped trees.

A boat slips out in the further side
Obscure, and cutting a trail of gems
Completes the ebony and argent frieze –
Africa, on Thames.
G. Rostrevor Hamilton, 'Night on Chiswick Eyot', *The Carved Stone*, 1952

The City
I . . . still think that a walk on the City pavement is one of the most romantic things in the world; the austere and unpretentious doors – the River Plate Company, or Burma Oil, or affairs in Argentine or Ecuador or Hudson's Bay – they jostle each other and lead away to strange places, and create a feeling of being all over the world at once among the messenger boys and top hats which were then still visible in Moorgate.
Freya Stark, *Traveller's Prelude*, 1950

Clapham
Clapham like every other city is built on a volcano.
G.K. Chesterton, *Autobiography*, 1936

Clifford's Inn
People when they want to get rid of their cats, and do not like killing them, bring them to the garden of Clifford's Inn, drop them there, and go away. In spite of all that is said about cats being able to find their way so wonderfully, they seldom do find it, and once in Clifford's Inn the cat generally remains there. The technical word among the laundresses in the inn for this is 'losing' a cat:

'Poor thing, poor thing,' said one old woman to me a few days ago, 'it's got no fur on its head at all, and no doubt that's why the people she lived with lost her.'
Samuel Butler, *Note-Books*, 1912

Constitution Hill and Shooter's Hill
Of public changes, good or ill,
I seldom lead the mooters,
But really Constitution Hill
Should change its name with Shooter's.
Thomas Hood, *On a Certain Locality*, 1842

(In 1842 Queen Victoria was twice shot at when driving along Constitution Hill, and two years earlier a similar attempt on her life had been made at the same place.)

Craven Street

At a dinner at Lincoln's Inn, at which Sir George Rose was present, James Smith (1775–1839) produced the following epigram:

In Craven Street, Strand, ten attorneys found
  place
And ten dark coal-barges are moored at its base;
Fly honesty, fly to some safer retreat,
There's *craft* in the river and *craft* in the street.

Sir George Rose immediately replied:

Why should honesty seek any safer retreat
From lawyers or barges, odd-rot 'em?
For the lawyers are just at the top of the street
And the barges are just at the bottom.

Aubrey Stewart (ed.), *A Collection of English Epigrams and Epitaphs*, 1897

Dockland

Down by the Docks is a region I would choose as my point of embarkation aboard ship if I were an emigrant. It would present my intention to me in such a sensible light; it would show me so many things to run away from.

Charles Dickens, 'Bound for the Great Salt Lake', in *The Uncommercial Traveller*, 1861

Downing Street

Downing Street . . . is assuredly the oddest street in the world (except Bow Street). Everything in Downing Street is significant, save the official residence of the Prime Minister, which, with its three electric bells and its absurdly inadequate area steps, is merely comic. The way in which the vast pile of the Home Office frowns down upon that devoted comic house is symbolic of the empire of the permanent official over the elected of the people.

Arnold Bennett, *Paris Nights*, 1913

Drury Lane

If I may be allowed to object against any thing you write . . . it shou'd be that Passage in yours, where you are pleas'd to call the Whores of *Drury*-Lane, the nymphs of *Drury*, I must owne it was some time before I cou'd frame to my self any plausible Excuse for this Expression: but Affection (which you know Sir, excuses all things) at last furnish'd me with one in your Justification; which I have here sent you, in Verse, that you may have at least some Rhyme to defend you, tho' you shou'd have no Reason.

If Wit or Critick blame the tender Swain,
Who stil'd the gentle Damsels in his Strain
The Nymphs of *Drury*, not of Drury-Lane;
Be this his Answer, and most just Excuse –
'Far be it, Sirs, from my more civill Muse,
Those Loving Ladies rudely to traduce.
Allyes and Lanes are Terms too vile and base,
And give Idea's of a narrow Pass;
But the well-worn Paths of the Nymphs of
  Drury
Are large & wide; *Tydcomb* and I assure ye.'

Alexander Pope, Letter to Henry Cromwell, 25 April 1708

Earl's Court

Earl's Court is usually a reliable, if seedy barometer of the changes in social and political pressure in the world beyond. When anything really important happens on some outcrop of the globe with an unpronounceable name, it will show up a few months later on the Earl's Court Road. The street swarms with Europe's latest arrivals.

Jonathan Raban, *Arabia Through the Looking Glass*, 1979

East End

*Over the pest-stricken regions of East London, sweltering in sunshine which served only to reveal the intimacies of abomination; across miles of a city of the damned, such as thought never conceived before this age of ours; above streets swarming with a nameless populace, cruelly exposed by the unwonted light of heaven; stopping at stations which it crushes the heart to think should be the destination of any mortal, the train made its way at length beyond the utmost limits of dread, and entered upon a land of level meadows, of hedges and trees, of crops and cattle.

George Gissing, *The Nether World*, 1889

*The East End is a vast city, as famous in its way as any the hand of man has made. But who knows the East End? It is down through Cornhill and out beyond Leadenhall Street and Aldgate Pump, one will say: a shocking place, where he once went with a curate; an evil plexus of slums that hide human, creeping things; where filthy men and women live on penn'orths of gin, where collars and clean shirts are decencies unknown, where every citizen wears a black eye and never combs his hair.

Arthur Morrison, *Tales of Mean Streets*, 1895

The horrible thing in East London is not what can be seen and smelt, but its unbounded and unredeemable extent. Elsewhere poverty and ugliness exist merely as a rubbish-tip between two houses, like an unsavoury nook, a cess-pool or unclean offal; but here are miles and miles of grimy houses, hopeless streets, Jewish shops, a superfluity of children, gin palaces and Christian shelters . . . miles and miles of grimy houses where the whole street consists of nothing but a vast horizontal tenement, factories, gasometers, railway lines, clayey patches of waste ground, storehouses for goods, and storehouses for human beings. . . .

And that is just the distressing thing about the East End – there is too much of it; and it cannot be re-shaped. . . . I wandered through streets whose names recalled Jamaica, Canton, India or Peking; all are alike, in all the windows there are curtains; it might even look quite nice if there were not five hundred thousand of such dwellings. In this overwhelming quantity it no longer looks like an excess of human beings, but like a geological formation; this black magma has been vomited up by factories; or it is a deposit of the merchandise which floats yonder along the Thames upon white ships; or it was piled up from soot and dust. Go and have a look at Oxford Street and Regent Street and the Strand, and see what fine houses people have built to hold goods, commodities, things; for the produce of man has its values. A shirt would lose in value if it were to be sold within such drab and plain walls; but man can live there, i.e. sleep, eat repulsive food, and beget children.

Karel Capek, *Letters from England*, 1925

When I made the obvious point about not bombing Rome because the Nazis didn't bomb Athens, whose buildings I said were the equivalent of Shakespeare's plays or Beethoven's symphonies, somebody shouted, 'Wot abaht the 'uman architecture of the Whitechapel Road?'

James Agate, *Ego 6*, 14 January 1943

Euston Station Arch

Walked & looked at the grand entrance to the Railway. It is extraordinary how decidedly the public have adopted Greek Architecture. Its simplicity, I take it, is suitable to English decision.

Benjamin Robert Haydon, *Diary*, 27 May 1838

Finsbury

Hugh: there are a knot of Clownes,
The Counsell of Finsbury, so they are y-styl'd
all the wise o' th' hundred.

Ben Jonson, *A Tale of a Tub*, 1633

Fleet Street and Charing Cross

I talked of the cheerfulness of Fleet Street owing to the constant quick succession of people which we perceive passing through it. JOHNSON. 'Why, Sir, Fleet-street has a very animated appearance; but I think the full tide of human existence is at Charing Cross.'

James Boswell, *Life of Johnson* (2 April 1775), 1779

The passion for crowds is nowhere feasted so full as in London. The man must have a rare *recipe* for melancholy who can be dull in Fleet Street.

Charles Lamb, 'The Londoner', *Morning Post*, 1 February 1802

Mr George Gardiner (Reigate, C.) said Fleet Street was a jungle where the law of the jungle no longer obtained. The beasts in it were no longer killing off each other; they were slowly strangling themselves.

Parliamentary Report, *The Times*, 19 May 1978

The Old Fleet River

To where Fleet-ditch with disemboguing streams
Rolls the large tribute of dead dogs to Thames.

Alexander Pope, *The Dunciad*, 1728

Goswell Road

*That punctual servant of all work, the sun, had just risen, and begun to strike a light on the morning of the thirteenth of May, one thousand eight hundred and twenty-seven, when Mr Samuel Pickwick burst like another sun from his slumbers, threw open his chamber-window, and looked out upon the world beneath. Goswell street was on his right hand – as far as the eye could reach, Goswell street extended on his left; and the opposite side of Goswell street was at his feet, Goswell street was over the way. 'Such,' thought Mr Pickwick, 'are the narrow views of those philosophers who, content with examining the things that lie before them, look not to the truths which are hidden beyond. As well might I be content to gaze on Goswell Street for ever, without one effort to penetrate to the hidden countries which on every side surround it.'

Charles Dickens, *The Posthumous Papers of the Pickwick Club*, 1837

Grosvenor Square

Soon as through Grosvenor's lordly square –
That last impregnable redoubt,
Where, guarded with Patrician care,
Primeval error still holds out –
Where never gleam of gas must dare
'Gainst ancient Darkness to revolt,
Nor smooth Macadam hope to spare
The dowagers one single jolt; –
Where, far too stately and sublime
To profit by the lights of time,
Let intellect march how it will,
They stick to oil and watchmen still.

Thomas Moore, *The Summer Fête*, 1831

Grubstreet (no longer there)

Originally the name of a street near Moorfields in London, much inhabited by writers of small histories, dictionaries, and temporary poems.

Samuel Johnson, *Dictionary of the English Language*, 1755

Hampstead

Hampstead indeed is risen from a little country village, to a city, not upon the credit only of the waters, 'tho 'tis apparent its growing greatness began there; but company increasing gradually, and the people liking both the place and the diversions together; it grew suddenly populous, and the concourse of people was incredible. This consequently raised the rate of lodgings, and that encreased buildings, till the town grew up from a little village, to a magnitude equal to some cities; nor could the uneven surface, inconvenient for building, uncompact, and unpleasant, check the humour of the town, for even on the very steep of the hill, where there's no walking twenty yards together, without tugging up a hill, or stradling down a hill, yet 'tis all one, the buildings encreased to that degree, that the town almost spreads the whole side of the hill.

On the top of the hill indeed, there is a very pleasant plain, called the Heath, which on the very summit, is a plain of about a mile every way; and in good weather 'tis pleasant airing upon it, and some of the streets are extended so far, as that they begin to build, even on the highest part of the hill. But it must be confest, 'tis so near heaven, that I dare not say it can be a proper situation, for any but a race of mountaineers, whose lungs have been so used to a rarify'd air, nearer the second region, than any ground for 30 miles round it. It is true this place may be said to be prepared for a summer dwelling, for in winter nothing that I know can recommend it.

Daniel Defoe, *A Tour through the Whole Island of Great Britain*, 1724–7

A steeple issuing from a leafy rise
With farmy fields in front, and sloping green,
Dear Hampstead is thy southern face serene
Silently smiling on approaching eyes.
Within, thine ever-shifting looks surprise, –
Streets, hills and dells, trees overhead, now seen,
Now down below, with smoking roofs between, –
A Village, revelling in varieties
Then northward what a range, – with heath and pond
Nature's own ground: woods that let mansions through,
And cottaged vales with pillowy fields beyond
And clump of darkening pines, and prospects blue
And that clear path through all, where daily meet
Cold cheeks, and brilliant eyes, and morn-elastic feet.

Leigh Hunt, 'Hampstead, vii, Description of the Village', *Examiner*, 12 November 1815

. . . bleak Hampstead's swarthy moor . . .

Thomas Babington Macaulay, 'The Armada – Friendship's Offering', 1833, *Lays of Ancient Rome*, 1848

Now if yer want a 'igh old time
Just take a tip from me.
Why 'Ampstead, 'appy 'Ampstead,
Is the place to 'ave a spree . . .

Oh 'Ampstead! 'Appy, 'appy 'Ampstead;
All the doners look so nice;
Talk about a Paradise.
Oh, 'Ampstead's very 'ard to beat.
If you want a beano its a fair old treat.

Albert Chevalier, *Oh! 'Ampstead!*, 1914 (music by John Crook)

On Saturday L. gave a lecture at Hampstead. Strange what a stamp Hampstead sets even on a casual gathering of 30 people; such clean, decorous, uncompromising, & high minded old ladies & old gentlemen; & the young wearing brown clothes, & thinking seriously, the women dowdy, the men narrow shouldered; bright fire & lights & books surround us, & everyone of course agreeing beforehand to what was said.

Virginia Woolf, *Diary*, 3 December 1917

The immaculate and moral heights of Hampstead.

Ibid., 15 November 1919

Harrods

Tragic to say it, Michael, but a certain element has crept into Her Majesty's lovely boutique. Strangely clad persons are in the real estate department, I don't want to say too much, but would the expression 'pyramid selling' mean anything to you?

Dame Edna Everage/Barry Humphries, Interview, *Boulevard*, December/January 1978–9

Heathrow Airport

I did not fully understand the dread term 'terminal illness' until I saw Heathrow for myself.

Dennis Potter, *Sunday Times*, 4 June 1978

Hornsey Road

An area which should be avoided if you happened to have a hangover.

Barry Newcombe, *Evening Standard*, 24 January 1978

Hyde Park

To Hide parke, where great plenty of gallants. And pleasant it was, only for the dust.

Samuel Pepys, *Diary*, 22 April 1664

What e'er you say, I know all beyond Hyde-Park's a desert to you.

George Etherege, *The Man of Mode*, 1676

And then in Hide-Park do repair
To make a dust and take no Air.

Thomas Shadwell, 'The Answer', *Poems on Affairs of State*, 1698

Hyde-Park – where horses have their diversion as well as men, and neigh and court their mistresses almost in as intelligible a dialect. Here people coach it to take the air, amidst a cloud of dust able to choak a foot-soldier, and hinder'd as from seeing those that come thither on purpose to shew themselves.

Thomas Brown, *Amusements Serious and Comical* VI – 'The Walks', 1700

Some time before I had come upon Zola seated on a public bench in Hyde Park. He had been gazing gloomily at the ground and poking the sand with the end of his cane. It had been at the time of his exile during the Dreyfus case and no gloom could have been greater than his. He said wearily: 'What was one to think of a country where nursemaids dressed their hair so carelessly that he had found as many as eighteen hairpins on one morning in front of one park bench? A city so improvident must be doomed.'

Ford Madox Ford, *Return to Yesterday*, 1931

Islington

Thy fields, fair Islington! begin to bear
Unwelcome buildings, and unseemly piles;
The streets are spreading, and the Lord knows where
Improvement's hand will spare the neighb'ring stiles:
The rural blandishments of Maiden Lane
Are ev'ry day becoming less and less,
While kilns and lime roads force us to complain
Of nuisances time only can suppress.
A few more years, and Copenhagen House
Shall cease to charm the tailor and the snob;
And where attornies' clerks in smoke carouse,
Regardless wholly of to-morrow's job,
Some Claremont Row, or Prospect Place shall rise,
Or terrace, p'rhaps, misnomered Paradise.

J.G./William Hone, *Table Book*, 1827–8

Kensington

Kensington, especially in a summer afternoon, has seemed to me as delightful as any place can or ought to be, in a world which, sometime or other, we must quit.

Nathaniel Hawthorne, *Our Old Home*, 1863

Lambeth

Any time you're Lambeth way
Any evening any day,
You'll find us all doin' the Lambeth walk.

Douglas Furber, Song, *The Lambeth Walk*, 1937

Lewisham

As he [James VI and I] was going through Lusen by Greenwich, he asked what town it was? They said Lusen. He asked a good while after, What town is this we are now in? They said, still 'twas Lusen. *On my so'l*, said the King, *I will be King of Lusen.*

Francis Bacon, *Apothegms*, before 1625, in Dr Tenison's *Baconiana*, 1679

London Bridge

London Bridge was made for wise men to pass over, and for fools to pass under.

Quoted in John Ray, *A Compleat Collection of English Proverbs*, 1670

London Bridge was built upon woolpacks.

Seventeenth-century saying

Lord's Cricket Ground

Of course, *Elysium* means 'Lord's'.

Rev. Pycroft, *The Cricket Field*, 1851

Lots Road

There are probably other streets as ugly, as utterly bereft of the romantic as Lots-road, Chelsea, but certainly nothing more desolating can exist in London . . . Some time before I reached it I heard a humming vibration which grew louder and more impressive as I approached . . . Then I came to a gigantic building, quite new to me – I had not suspected that such a thing was – a building which must be among the largest in London, a red brick building with a grandiose architectural effect, an overpowering affair, one of those affairs that man creates in order to show how small and puny he himself is . . . I hate to question people in the street, but curiosity concerning a marvel is like love, stronger than hate.

'That?' said the milkman peevishly. 'That's the generating station for the electric rilewys.'

'Which railways?' I asked.

'All of 'em,' said he. 'There's bin above sixty men killed there already.'

Arnold Bennett, *Paris Night*, 1913

The Monument

After dinner I sauntered in a pleasing humour to London Bridge, viewed the Thames's silver expanse and the springy bosom of the surrounding fields. I then went up to the top of the Monument. This is a most amazing building. It is a pillar two hundred feet high. In the inside, a turnpike stair runs up all the way. When I was about half way up, I grew frightened. I would have come down again, but thought I would despise myself for my timidity. Thus does the spirit of pride get the better of fear. I mounted to the top and got upon the balcony. It was horrid to find myself so monstrous a way up in the air, so far above London and all its spires. I durst not look round me. There is no real danger as there is a strong rail both on the stair and balcony. But I shuddered, and as every heavy waggon passed down Gracechurch Street, dreaded that the shaking of the earth would make the tremendous pile tumble to the foundation.

James Boswell, *Boswell's London Journal*, 2 April 1763

The National Gallery

This unhappy structure may be said to have everything it ought not to have, and nothing which it ought to have. It possesses windows without glass, a cupola without size, a portico without height, pepper-boxes without pepper, and the finest site in Europe without anything to show upon it.

All the Year Round, 1862

How often my Soul visits the National Gallery, and how seldom I go there myself!

Logan Pearsall Smith, *Afterthoughts*, 1931

Notting Hill

I was one day wandering about the streets in part of North Kensington, telling myself stories of feudal sallies and sieges, in the manner of Walter Scott, and vaguely trying to apply them to the wilderness of bricks and mortar around me. I felt that London was already too large and loose a thing to be a city in the sense of a citadel. It seemed to me even larger and looser than the British Empire. And something irrationally arrested and pleased my eye about the look of one small block of little lighted shops, and I amused myself with the supposition that these alone were to be preserved and defended, like a hamlet in a desert. I found it quite exciting to count them and perceive that they contained the essentials of a civilisation, a chemist's shop, a book-shop, a provision merchant for food and a public-house for drink. Lastly, to my great delight, there was also an old curiosity shop bristling with swords and halberds; manifestly intended to arm the guard that was to fight for the sacred street. I wondered vaguely what they would attack, or whither they would advance. And looking up, I saw, grey with distance, but still seemingly immense in altitude, the tower of the Waterworks close to the street where I was born. It suddenly occurred to me that capturing the Waterworks might really mean the military stroke of flooding the valley; and with that torrent and cataract of visionary waters, the first fantastic notion of a tale called *The Napoleon of Notting Hill* rushed over my head.

G.K. Chesterton, *Autobiography*, 1936

Norwood and Crystal Palace

On either side, east and south, the Norwood hills, partly rough with furze, partly wooded with birch and oak, partly in pure bramble copse, and rather steep pasture, rose with the promise of all the rustic loveliness of Surrey and Kent in them, and with so much of space and height in their sweep, as to give them some fellowship with hills of true hill-districts. Fellowship now inconceivable, for the Crystal Palace, without ever itself attaining any true aspect of size, and possessing no more sublimity than a cucumber frame between two chimneys, yet by its stupidity of hollow bulk dwarfs the hills at once; so that now one thinks of them no more, but as three long lumps of clay, on lease for building.

John Ruskin, *Praeterita*, 1885–9

The Old Kent Road

I own, I think it would be for the honour of the kingdom . . . to improve the avenue to London by the way of Kent-street, which is a most disgraceful entrance to such an opulent city. A foreigner in passing through this beggarly and ruinous suburb, conceives such an idea of misery and meanness, as all the wealth and magnificence of London and Westminster are afterwards unable to destroy.

Tobias Smollett, *Travels through France and Italy*, 1766

Oxford Circus

*The bus perplexed 'Circus'.

Robert Smith Surtees, *Mr Sponge's Sporting Tour*, 1853

Oxford Street

So then, Oxford Street, stony-hearted stepmother, thou that listenest to the sighs of orphans and drinkest the tears of children, at length I was dismissed from thee!

Thomas de Quincey, *Confessions of an English Opium Eater*, 1822

Thou lengthy street of ceaseless din,
  Like culprit's life extending,
In famed St Giles's doth begin,
  At fatal Tyburn ending.

John Wilson Croker, *c.* 1825

Pall Mall

In town let me live then, in town let me die
For in truth I can't relish the country, not I.
If one *must* have a villa in summer to dwell,
Oh give me the sweet shady side of Pall Mall.

Charles Morris, 'The Contrast', *Lyra Urbanica*, 1840

The Parks

It was a saying of Lord Chatham, that the parks were the lungs of London.

W. Windham, Speech in the House of Commons, 30 June 1808

. . . those vegetable puncheons
  Called parks, where there is neither fruit nor flower
Enough to gratify a bee's slight munchings.
  But after all it is the only 'bower'
(In Moore's phrase), where the fashionable fair
Can form a slight acquaintance with fresh air.

Lord Byron, *Don Juan*, 1819–24

That rather pitiful patch of country which the Anglo-Saxon bears with him like a captive into cities.

H.V. Morton, *In Search of Scotland*, 1929

Parliament Hill

At about 11 we went for a walk and lost ourselves. A very remarkable thing occurred. God took away Parliament Hill entirely for some time. It was very puzzling.

Evelyn Waugh, *Diary*, 24 June 1924

Houses of Parliament: Big Ben

As four o'clock sounded from Big Ben, Stanley opened his eyes and said 'What is that?' I told him it was four o'clock striking. 'Four o'clock?' he repeated slowly; 'how strange! So that is Time! Strange!'

Henry Morton Stanley, last words, recorded by Dorothy Stanley in her edition of his *Autobiography*, 1909

The party was to meet at the pier of the House of Commons, and go up the river in two steamers. As we did not know precisely where the pier was we stopped outside the House of Lords to ask a policeman.

Dialogue:

I. 'Can you tell me where I shall find the pier of the House of Commons?'

Policeman. 'No, sir, indeed, we have plenty of peers in the House of Lords, but I have never yet heard of a peer of the House of Commons.'

Wilfred Scawen Blunt, Diary, 17 June 1893, *My Diaries*, 1919

House of Commons

The best club in Europe.

Sir Winston Churchill, remark, quoted in Leon Harris, *The Fine Art of Political Wit*, 1965

House of Lords

The House of Lords is like a glass of champagne that has stood for five days.

Clement Attlee, remark, quoted *ibid.*

Petticoat Lane

I have already observed how strongly the general wearing of cast off clothes by our poorer countrymen and countrywomen had struck upon the mind of my fellow pilgrim. The sadness and meanness of the habit were impressed upon us scores of times during our wanderings; so that when, on a certain Sunday we turned into Petticoat Lane, we had the key to the activity of the clothes market of Lazarus. The lane clothes thousands at Epsom.

Blanchard Jerrold, *London, a Pilgrimage*, 1872

Piccadilly

Piccadilly! Shops, palaces, bustle and breeze,
The whirring of wheels and the murmur of trees;
By night or by day, whether noisy or stilly,
Whatever my mood is, I love Piccadilly.

Frederick Locker, 'Piccadilly', in *London Lyrics*, 1857

Piccadilly Circus

A distorted isochromal triangle, square to nothing of its surroundings . . . an impossible site on which to place any outcome of the human brain except possibly an underground lavatory.

Sir Alfred Gilbert, designer of Eros, attrib., *c.* 1890

*'In Londres,' said Kashkavar Jones, 'there is a bigger circus – the biggest circus in the world where everybody goes. It is called,' he said, 'Pic-a-dolly, I think.'

Caryl Brahms and S.J. Simon, *Six Curtains for Stroganova*, 1945

Portman Square

The Precints pure of Portman Square.

Hester Lynch Thrale/Piozzi, *An Ode to Society*, 1786

Primrose Hill

My father . . . proposed to take me to Primrose Hill. I had never heard of the place, and names have always appealed directly to my imagination. I was in the highest degree delighted, and could hardly restrain my impatience. As soon as possible, we set forth westwards, my hand in my father's, with the liveliest anticipations. I expected to see a mountain absolutely carpeted with primroses, a terrestrial galaxy like that which covered the hill that led up to Montgomery Castle in Donne's poem. But at length, as we walked from the Chalk Farm direction, a miserable acclivity stole into view – surrounded even in those days, on most sides by houses, with its grass worn to the buff by millions of boots, and resembling what I mean by 'the country' about as much as Poplar resembles Paradise. We sat down on a bench at its inglorious summit, whereupon I burst into tears, and in a heart-rending whisper sobbed, 'Oh! Papa, let us go home!'

Edmund Gosse, *Father and Son*, 1907

Putney Common

It was on Putney Heath that the celebrated Swedish botanist, Carl von Linne (better known by the latinised form of his name, Linnaeus), first saw the gorse, which was then unknown in his own northern country, and he was so struck with the sight of it, that he fell upon his knees and thanked God for having made anything so beautiful.

Gordon S. Maxwell, *The Author's Thames*, 1924

I must take a cottage on Putney Heath or Richmond Green, or some other wild and desolate place. . . .

Charles Dickens, Letter to Miss Burdett Coutts, 22 March 1842

Regent's Park

Living in Regent's Park. During a candle-lit dinner there comes a moment when one does not know whether a lion in the zoo, or the stomach of one's table partner, has just growled.

John Updike, 'London Life', 1969, in *Picked Up Pieces*, 1976

Regent Street

Nash planned to connect Carlton House, where the Prince Regent lived, with Regent's Park. His plan to-day is unrecognisable, but it made some progress, and I am old enough to remember what his Regent

Street looked like while it was still untouched. I wish it was there to-day, for a bad muddle, instead of a good one has superseded it. It was not great architecture, but it knew what it was doing, and where it was going; it was reasonable, and refined. Of course, it had to be scrapped. Greed moulds the landscape of London, as of other great cities, and the Regent street frontages were too valuable to be occupied by such lowly piles. Besides, they belong to the Crown, and the Crown seems even greedier and more unaesthetic than most landlords. So Nash went, and the present insipid mixture took his place.

If you want a muddle look around you as you walk from Piccadilly Circus to Oxford Circus. Here are ornaments that do not adorn, features that feature nothing, flatness, meanness, uniformity without harmony, bigness without size. Even when the shops are built at the same moment and by architects of equal fatuity, they manage to contradict one another. Here is the heart of the Empire, and the best it can do. Regent Street exhibits, in its most depressing aspect, the Spirit of London.

E.M. Forster, 'London is a Muddle', 1937, in *Two Cheers for Democracy*, 1951

St James's Palace and Greenwich Hospital

The English say that their palaces are like hospitals and their hospitals like palaces; and the exterior of St. James's and of Greenwich justifies the saying.

Robert Southey, *Letters from England, by Don Manuel Alvarez Espriella*, 1807

St Martin in the Fields

Opie was divorced from his first wife, and Godwin was an Infidel. They were walking together near St. Martin's Church. 'Ha!' said Opie, 'I was married in that church.' 'Indeed!' said Godwin, and 'I was christened in it.' 'It is not a good shop,' replied Opie, 'their work don't last.'

John Adolphus, Journal, 25 July 1842, in *Recollections of . . . John Adolphus, . . . by his daughter, Emily Henderson*, 1871

Southwark

In this *Burgh of Southwarke* . . . along the Tamis banke their runneth Westward a continued range of dwelling houses: where within our fathers remembrance was the *Bordello* or *Lupanarie*, for so the Latines terme those little roomes or secret chambers of harlots wherein they filthily prostituted their bodies to saile, because they after the maner of ravening she-wolves catch hold of silly wretched men and pluck them into their hooles. But these were prohibited by King Henry the Eighth, at which time England was growen to excessive lasciviousnesse and roiot; which in other nations are continued for gaine, under a specious shew of helping man's infirmity: Neither, of these strumpets and brothel-houses, doe I thinke that this place in our tongue tooke the name *Stewes*, but of those *Ponds* or *Stewes*, which are heere for to feed Pikes and Tenches fat, and to scoure them from the strong and muddy fennish tast. Heere have I seen pike-panches opened with a knife to shew their fatnesse: and presently the wide gashes and wounds come together againe by the touch of tenches, and with their gluttinous slime perfectly healed up. Among these buildings there is a place in maner of a Theater for baiting of Beares and Buls with Dogges.

William Camden, *Britain*, 1610
(Philemon Holland's translation)

A royal city were not London by.

Quoted by Daniel Defoe, *A Tour through the Whole Island of Great Britain*, 1724–7

The Strand

I have taken to dream of England again, and woke up in a fright last night because I could not find my way out of the Strand.

Emily Eden, Letter, 31 December 1841, in *Letters from India*, 1872

Streatham

Streatham does very well for a Summer Villa, but the Consciousness that one should hate to *dye* there, would make me *live* in it with a kind of odd Anxiety one knows not how to describe – *like being abroad.*

Hester Lynch Thrale/Piozzi, *Thraliana*, January 1788

Tottenham

And so he jogged to Tot'n'am Cross
  An ancient town well known
Where Edward wept for Eleanor
  In mortar and in stone.

Thomas Hood, *The Epping Hunt*, 1829

Tottenham Court Road (at the end of the Second World War)

A section that has been badly blasted, like the Tottenham Court Road, looks gruesome in the late-gathering darkness: its bare and wry trees with tufts of leaves at the tips of the branches like the legs and necks of plucked fowl; its masklike fronts of bombed-out houses, with their dark eye-sockets and gaping jaws. There is a peculiar desolation and horror about finding these carcases of streets unburied in the midst of an inhabited city.

Edmund Wilson, *Europe without Baedeker*, 1947

Trafalgar Square

If Nelson looks down on a couple of Kings,
  However it pleases the Loyals;
Tis after the fashion of nautical things
A Sky-scraper over the Royals.

Thomas Hood, *Epigram on the Arrangement of the Statues in Trafalgar Square*, 1844

Why are Trafalgar Square fountains like Government Clerks? –
Because they play from 10 till 4.

Punch, 17 July 1858

We live in Trafalgar Square with four Lions to guard us,
Fountains and statues all over the place!
The 'Metropole' staring us right in the face!
We own it's a trifle draughty – but we don't want to make no fuss!
What's good *enough* for Nelson is good *enough* for us.

Music Hall Tramp Song, quoted by Admiral of the Fleet Lord Fisher, *Memories*, 1919

The Tower of London

Is not this house as nigh heaven as my own?

Sir Thomas More, quoted in William Roper, *Life of More*, after 1535

A most famous and goodly Citadell, encompassed round with thicke and strong walles, full of loftie, and stately Turrets, fensed with a broade and deepe ditch, furnished also with an armorie or magazine of warlicke munition, and other buildings besides: so as it resembleth a big towne.

William Camden, *Britain*, 1610 (Philemon Holland's translation)

Ye towers of Julius, London's lasting shame
With many a foul and midnight murther fed.

Thomas Gray, *The Bard*, 1757

An Englishman cares nothing about the Tower, which to us is a haunted castle in dream-land.

Nathaniel Hawthorne, *Our Old Home*, 1863

I saw at once that the Tower was established on a firm basis. In the entire history of firm basises I don't find a basis more firmer than this one.

'You have no Tower in America?' said a man in the crowd who had somehow detected my denomination.

'Alars! No,' I anserd; 'we boste of our enterprise and improovements and yit we are devoid of a Tower. America, oh my onhappy country! thou has not got no Tower! It's a sweet Boon!'

Charles F. Browne ('Artemus Ward'), 'The Tower of London', *Punch*, 1766

And so I left the Tower. It is a solid and commandin edifis, but I deny that it is cheerful. I bid it adoo without a pang.

Charles F. Browne, *Artemus Ward in London*, 1867

I got to understand that when a Londoner says 'Have you seen the Tower of London?' the answer is 'No, and neither have you.'

Stephen Leacock, *My Discovery of England*, 1922

Underground: the Metropolitan Line

Here were a goodly place wherein to die –
Grown latterly to sudden change averse,
All violent contrasts fain avoid would I
On passing from this world into a worse.

Sir William Watson, 'The Metropolitan Underground Railway', in *Poems*, 1892

Wanstead Flats

*There is no other fair like Whit Monday's on Wanstead Flats. Here is a square mile or more of open land where you may howl at large; here is no danger of losing yourself as in Epping Forest; the public-houses are always with you; shows, shies, swings, merry-go-rounds, fried fish stalls, donkeys are packed closer than on Hampstead Heath; the ladies' tormentors are larger, and their contents smell worse than at any other fair. Also, you may be drunk and disorderly without being locked up, – for the stations won't hold everybody, – and when all else has palled, you may set fire to the turf.

Arthur Morrison, *Tales of Mean Streets*, 1895

The West End

A transit from the City to the West End of the Town is the last step of the successful trader, when he throws off his *exuviae*, and emerges from his chrysalis state into the butterfly world of high life. Here are the Hesperides whither the commercial adventurers repair, not to gather, but to enjoy their golden fruits.

Yet this metropolis of fashion, this capital of the capital itself, has the most monotonous appearance imaginable. – The streets are perfectly parallel and uniformly extended brick walls, about forty feet high, with equally extended ranges of windows and doors, all precisely alike, and without any appearance of being distinct houses. You would rather suppose them to be hospitals, arsenals, or public granaries, were it not for their great extent. . . .

The merchants of this modern Tyre, are indeed princes in their wealth, and in their luxury; but it is to be wished that they had something more of the spirit of princely magnificence, and that when they build palaces they would cease to use the warehouse as their model.

Robert Southey, *Letters from England, by Don Manuel Alvarez Espriella*, 1807

It is very strange out West, down Piccadilly, on Saturday morning. There are women such as I have never seen before, beautiful, flowing women, with a pride and grace you never meet in the provinces. The proud ruling air of these women of the stately West is astounding; I stand still and stare at them.

D.H. Lawrence, Letter to May Chambers Holbrook, 16 February 1909

Westminster Abbey

When I behold, with deep astonishment,

To famous Westminster, how there resorte,
Living in brasse, or stoney monument,
The princes and the worthies of all sorte;
Doe I not see reformde nobilitie,
Without contempt, or pride, or ostentation
And looke upon offencelesse majesty,
Naked of pomp, or earthly domination?
And how a play-game of a painted stone
Contents the quiet now and silent sprites,
Whome all the world, which late they stood upon
Could not content nor quench their appetites.
Life is a frost of cold felicitie
And death the thaw of all our vanitie.

T.B., *Christolero's Epigrams*, 1598

Mortality, behold and fear!
What a change of flesh is here!
Think how many royal bones
Sleep within these heaps of stones!
Here they lie had realms and lands,
Who now want strength to stir their hands.
Where from their pulpits sealed with dust
They preach, 'In greatness is no trust'.
Here's an acre sown indeed
With the richest, royall'st seed
That the earth did e'er suck in,
Since the first man died for sin.
Here the bones of birth have cried,
'Though gods they were, as men they died.'
Here are sands, ignoble things,
Dropt from the ruined sides of kings;
Here's world of pomp and state,
Buried in dust, once dead by fate.

Francis Beaumont, *On the Tombes In Westminster Abbey*, before 1616

When I am in serious Humour, I very often walk by my self in *Westminster* Abbey; where the Gloominess of the Place, and the Use to which it is applied, with the Solemnity of the Building, and the Condition of the People who lye in it, are apt to fill the Mind with a kind of Melancholy, or rather Thoughtfulness that is not disagreeable.

Joseph Addison, *Spectator*, 26, 30 March 1711

This great Magazine of Mortality.

Ibid.

He said . . . 'By God, I will not be buried in Westminster.' I asked him why not. He answered 'they do bury fools there.'

Sir Godfrey Kneller, remarks on his death-bed, November 1723 quoted by Alexander Pope, Letter to Lord Stafford, 6 July 1725

and St Paul's Cathedral

– Length'ning ayles, and windows that impart
A gloomy steady light to chear the heart,
Such as affects the soul, and which I see
With joy, celestial *Westminster*! in thee.
Not like Saint PAUL'S, beneath whose ample dome
No thought arises of the life to come.
For, tho' superb, not solemn is the place,
The mind but wanders o'er the distant space,
Where, 'stead of thinking on their God, most men
Forget his presence to remember *Wren*.

William Woty, *Church-Langton, c.* 1768

The moment I entered Westminster Abbey I felt a kind of awe pervade my mind which I cannot describe; the very silence seemed sacred.

Edmund Burke, Letter to Mr Michael Smith, in *A Sketch of the Life of Mr Burke*, 1798 – of *c.*1750

Westminster Abbey or Victory!

Horatio Viscount Nelson, quoted in Robert Southey, *Life of Nelson*, 1813 (at the battle of Cape St Vincent, 1797)

I am against stuffing Westminster Abbey with any one's statue till a hundred years or so have proved whether Posterity is as warm about a Man's Merits as we are. What a vast monument is erected to Cider Phillips – to Gay? – the last of whom I love, but yet would not interfere with the perfect Gothic of the Abbey to stick up his ugly bust in it.

Edward Fitzgerald, Letter to Frederick Tennyson, 15 August 1850

A pious Frenchman . . . in Westminster Abbey, knelt down to pray. The verger, who had never seen such a thing happen before, promptly handed him over to the police and charged him with 'brawling'. Fortunately the magistrate had compassion on the foreigner's ignorance, and even went the length of asking why he should not be allowed to pray in church. The reply of the verger was simple and obvious. 'If we allowed that,' he said, 'we should have people praying all over the place.' And to this day the rule in Westminster Abbey is that you may stroll about and look at the monuments; but you must not, on any account, pray.

G. Bernard Shaw, *Preface to Three Plays by Brieux*, 1909

*He was solidly dazed by Westminster Abbey, which is not unnatural since that Church became the lumber-room of the larger and less successful statuary of the eighteenth century.

G.K. Chesterton, *The Man who Knew too Much*, 1922

Holy Moses! Take a look!
Flesh decayed in every nook!
Some rare bits of brain lie here,
Mortal loads of beef and beer. . . .

Amanda Ros, 'Verses on Visiting Westminster Abbey', *Fumes of Formation*, 1933

Westminster Bridge, view from
Earth has not anything to show more fair:
  Dull would he be of soul who could pass by
  A sight so touching in its majesty:
This City now doth like a garment wear
The beauty of the morning; silent, bare,
  Ships, towers, domes, theatres, and temples lie
  Open unto the fields, and to the sky;
All bright and glittering in the smokeless air.
Never did sun more beautifully steep
  In his first splendour valley, rock, or hill;
Ne'er saw I, never felt, a calm so deep!
  The river glideth at his own sweet will:
Dear God! the very houses seem asleep;
  And all the mighty heart is lying still!
William Wordsworth, *Upon Westminster Bridge*, 1802

We took a walk in the town by moonlight & went to Westminster Bridge to see the River Thames I had heard large wonders about its width of water but I was dissapointed thinking I should have seen a freshwater sea when I saw it was less in my eye than Whittlesea Meer I was uncommonly astonished to see so many ladys as I thought them walking about the streets I expressed my surprise & was told they were girls of the town as a modest woman rarely venturd out by herself at nightfall.
John Clare, *Autobiography* – of March 1820

As late the Trades' Unions, by way of a show
O'er Westminster Bridge strutted five in a row
'I feel for the bridge,' whispered Dick, with a shiver
'Thus tried by the mob, it may sink in the river.'
Quoth Tom, a Crown lawyer, 'Abandon your fears.
As a bridge, it can only be tried by its piers.'
James Smith, *Comic Miscellanies in Prose and Verse*, 1841

Go on a bus-top across Westminster Bridge at night, go on any train leaving Charing Cross station, and you are confronted with a spectacle that surely calls for a sonnet-substitute. A spasm of hard-rock ecstasy perhaps? Ships, tower-blocks, domes, discos make a familiar daytime scene that each evening is recreated into something astonishing and mysterious. The embankments are looped with strings of light. All dolled up and nobody looking. Earth, and Wordsworth would have to admit it, has not anything to show more unfair.
Norman Shrapnel, *A View of the Thames*, 1977

Whitechapel
*'Not a wery nice neighbourhood this, sir,' said Sam, with a touch of the hat, which always preceded his entering into conversation with his master.

'It is not indeed, Sam,' replied Mr Pickwick, surveying the crowded and filthy street through which they were passing.

'It's a wery remarkable circumstance, sir,' said Sam, 'that poverty and oysters always seems to go together.'

'I don't understand you, Sam,' said Mr Pickwick.

'What I mean, sir,' said Sam, 'is, that the poorer a place is, the greater call there seems to be for oysters. Look here, sir; here's an oyster stall to every half-dozen houses. The street's lined vith 'em. Blessed if I don't think that ven a man's wery poor, he rushes out of his lodgings, and eats oysters in reg'lar desperation.'
Charles Dickens, *The Posthumous Papers of the Pickwick Club*, 1837

Wimbledon
Wimbledon is a dreary, high, bleak, windy suburb, on the edge of a threadbare heath.
Virginia Woolf, *Diary*, 30 January 1915

The Zoo
The human species you condemn?
Go see the creatures at the Zoo.
At least, if you are bored by them,
They may be entertained by you.
G. Rostrevor Hamilton, 'Zoo', *Epigrams*, 1928

Churchill . . . asked me what, in the case of the imminent war, the Zoo was arranging to do. When I told him that, *inter alia*, we planned to shoot any dangerous animals that might escape during a raid, he brooded silently and suddenly said, 'What a pity.' I was baffled and could only mutter, 'A pity, Mr Churchill?' There was a longer silence, as if wheels were revolving inside that splendid head and then he burst out in a blaze of Churchillian rhetoric: 'Imagine a great air-raid over this great city of ours – squadrons of enemy planes dropping their bombs on London, houses smashed into ruins, fires breaking out everywhere – corpses lying in the smoking ashes – and lions and tigers roaming the desolation in search of the corpses – and you're going to shoot them! What a pity! . . . '
Julian Huxley, *Memories*, 1970

When I find myself in a strange city, at a loose end, waiting as one does eternally in strange cities for a boat, a plane, or an interview – when time seems to stop and the universe seems to have dwindled to an unending series of hotel corridors, lavatories and lounges – I tend to go to the zoo. . . . You can learn a great deal about the character of a country or city by going to its zoo and studying its arrangement and the behaviour of the animals. The London zoo is an animal microcosm of London, and even the lions, as a rule, behave as if they had been born in South Kensington.
Leonard Woolf, *Downhill all the Way*, 1967

Longleat House

A verie faire, neat, and elegant house, in a foule soile,

which although once or twise it hath beene burnt, hath risen eftsoones more faire.

William Camden, *Britain*, 1610
(Philemon Holland's translation)

The house disappointed me. It is very perfect, too perfect, and, large as it is, it is lost in the size of the park. What makes it look dull is the uniform plate-glass which has been put in every window. It is astonishing how this destroys the beauty of old buildings. It is as though the eyes in a beautiful face had been put out and replaced with spectacles.

Wilfred Scawen Blunt, Diary, 15 August 1896,
My Diaries, 1919

Lowestoft

The unpleasant harbour of Lowestoft.

Hilaire Belloc, *Hills and the Sea*, 1906

Ludlow

The Towne doth stand most part upon an Hill,
Built well and fayre, with streates both large and wide:
The houses such, where straungers lodge at will.
As long as there the Councell lists abide,
Both fine and cleane the streates are all throughout,
With Condits cleere, and wholesome water springs:
And who that lists to walke the towne about,
Shall finde therein some rare and pleasant things:
But chiefly there the ayre so sweete you have,
As in no place ye can no better crave. . . .
Two Bayliefes rules, one yeere the Towne throughout,
Twelve Aldermen they have therein likewise:
Who doth beare sway, as turne doth come about,
Who chosen are, by oth and auncient guise.
Good lawes they have, and open space to pleade,
In ample sort, for right and Justice sake:
A Preacher too, that dayly there doth reade,
A Schoolemaster, that doth good schollers make.
And for the Queere, are boyes brought up to sing,
And to serve God, and doe none other thing.

Thomas Churchyard, *The Worthines of Wales*, 1587

Lulworth Castle

Drove to see Lulworth Castle. The wretched taste of the statues in the niches; the chapel on one side, the church on the other, and the castle . . . keeping the peace between them.

Thomas Moore, *Diary*, 22 July 1826

Lutterworth

Our next dayes stage was *Lutterworth*, a Towne
Not willing to be noted or set downe
By any Traveller; for, when w'had bin
Through at both ends, wee could not find an Inne.

Richard Corbet, *Iter Boreale*, 1647

Lyme

Lime, a seaport place open to the main ocean, and so high a bleak sea that to secure the Harbour for shipps they have been at a great charge to build a Mold from the town with stone, like a halfe moon, which they call the Cobb, its raised with a high wall and this runns into the sea a good compass, that the Shipps rides safely within it; when the tide is out we may see the foundations of some part of it; that is the tyme they look over it to see any breach and repaire it immediately, else the tide comes with so much violence would soone beate it down; there is some part of it low and only is to joyne the rest to the land, and at high water is all covered of such a depth of water that shipps may pass over it to enter the Cobb or Halfe Moone, which is difficult for foreigners to attempt, being ignorant, though its better than goeing round the other way, for those that know and do observe the tide; the Spring tides and on any storme does sometimes beate up and wash over the walls of the forte or castle into the court, and so runns into the town, though at other tymes when its the ordinary tide and calme sea, it is at least 300 yards from the banke on which the high wall is built.

Celia Fiennes, *Journeys*, *c.* 1685–96

Lytham St Annes

Monty regards my holiday rig of white duck with his usual well-bred disfavour.
J.A. When I am in Blackpool I dress like Blackpool.
Monty. Being at St Anne's is no excuse for dressing like St Anne.

James Agate, *Ego 2* (23 August 1935), 1936

Mablethorpe

How often, when a child, I lay reclined,
   I took delight in this locality!
Here stood the infant Ilion of the mind,
   And here the Grecian ships did seem to be.

And here again I come and only find
   The drain-cut levels of the marshy lea, –
Gray sand banks and pale sunsets – dreary wind
   Dim shores, dense rain and heavy clouded sea.

Alfred Lord Tennyson, *Mablethorpe*, 1837

O for a good Mablethorpe breaker!

Alfred Lord Tennyson, *A Memoir, by his Son*, 1897
(at Aberystwith in 1839)

Maidstone

Maidstone is a great oyster and typhoid centre – that is all I know.

Virginia Woolf, Letter to Barbara Begenel, 21 September 1922

Malvern

Those waters so famed by the great Dr Wall,
Consist in containing just nothing at all.

Anon., *Epigrams*, ed. Rev. John Booth B.A., 1863

It is a most beautiful place. O heaven, to meet the Cold Waterers (as I did this morning when I went out for a shower-bath) dashing down the hills, with severe expressions on their countenances, like men doing matches and not exactly winning! Then, a young lady in a grey polka going *up* the hills, regardless of legs; and meeting a young gentleman (a bad case, I should say) with a light black silk cap on under his hat, and the pimples of I don't know how many douches under that. Likewise an old man who ran over a milkchild rather than stop! – with no neckcloth, on principle; and with his mouth wide open, to catch the morning air.

Charles Dickens, Letter to John Forster, 1851, in Forster, *Life of Dickens*, 1872–3

And ah! that watery sky – greatest of England's glories! – so high and vast and various, so many-lighted and many-shadowed, so full of poetry and motion and of a strange affinity with the swarming detail of scenery beneath! Indeed what I have most enjoyed in England since my return – what has most struck me – is the light – or rather, if you please, the darkness: that of Du Maurier's drawings.

Henry James, Letter to William James, 13 February 1870

Malvern Hills

Mauborn hills or as some term them the English Alps.

Celia Fiennes, *Journeys*, *c*. 1685–96

Isle of Man

I mentioned a scheme which I had of making a tour to the Isle of Man, and giving a full account of it; and that Mr. Burke had playfully suggested as a motto,
'The proper study of mankind is MAN.'

James Boswell, *Life of Johnson*, 15 May 1776

The people here are the most good-natured I think I have ever met.

Gerard Manley Hopkins, *Journal*, 5 August 1872

Port Soderick

Again to Port Soderick. This time it was a beautiful day. I looked down from the cliffs at the sea breaking on the rocks at high-water of a spring tide – first, say, it is an install of green marble knotted with ragged white, then fields of white lather, the comb of the wave richly clustered and crisped in breaking, then it is broken small and so unfolding till it runs in threads and thrums twitching down the backdraught to the sea again.

Gerard Manley Hopkins, *Journal*, 19 August 1872

Manchester

I must tell,
How men of *Manchester* did use me well,
Their loves they on the tenter-hookes did racke,
Rost, boyl'd bak'd, too too much, white, claret, sacke,
Nothing they thought too heavy or too hot,
Canne follow'd Canne, and Pot succeeded Pot,
That what they could do, all they thought too little,
Striving in love the Traveller to whittle.
We went into the house of one *John Pinners*,
(A man that lives amongst a crue of sinners)
And there eight severall sorts of Ale we had,
All able to make one starke drunke or mad.
But I with courage bravely flinched not,
And gave the Towne leave to discharge the shot.
We had at one time set upon the Table,
Good Ale of Hisope, 'twas no Esope fable:
Then had we Ale of Sage, and Ale of Malt,
And Ale of Woorme-wood, that could make one halt,
With Ale of Rosemary, and Bettony,
And two Ales more, or else I needs must lye.
But to conclude this drinking Alye tale,
We had a sort of Ale, called Scurvy Ale.
Thus all these men, at their owne charge & cost,
Did strive whose love should be expressed most.
And farther to declare their boundlesse loves
They saw I wanted, and they gave me Gloves. . . .
O all you worthy men of *Manchester*,
(True bred bloods of the County *Lancaster*)
When I forget what you to me have done,
Then let me head-long to confusion runne.

John Taylor, *Taylor's Pennillesse Pilgrimage*, in *All the Works of John Taylor*, 1630

Manchester, one of the greatest, if not really the greatest meer village in England.

Daniel Defoe, *A Tour through the Whole Island of Great Britain*, 1724–7

Manchester is a horrid unfinished town.

Sydney Smith, Letter to Mrs Beach, 16 June 1798

I really could not go. *Think*, Sir, *Manchester*! – Besides, *you* would not be there.

Beau Brummell, remark to the Prince Regent on being ordered with his troops to quell Manchester riots in 1798, quoted in Captain J. Jesse, *The Life of Beau Brummell*, 1844

A place more destitute of all interesting objects than Manchester it is not easy to conceive. . . . Imagine this multitude crowded together in narrow streets, the houses all built of brick and blackened with smoke; frequent buildings among them as large as convents, without their antiquity, without their beauty, without their holiness; where you hear from within, as you pass along, the everlasting din of machinery; and where when the bell rings it is to call wretches to their work instead of their prayers. . . . Imagine this, and you have the materials for a picture of Manchester.

Robert Southey, *Letters from England, by Don Manuel Alvarez Espriella*, 1807

I am not happy in Manchester. The association of those hideous mill prisons for Children destroys my enjoyments in Society. The people are quite insensible to it, but how they can go on as they do in all their luxurious enjoyments with huge factories overhanging the sky is most extraordinary.

Benjamin Robert Haydon, *Diary*, June 1837

I once went to Manchester with a bourgeois, and spoke to him of the bad, unwholesome method of building, the frightful condition of the working-people's quarters, and asserted that I had never seen so ill-built a city. The man listened quietly to the end, and said at the corner where we parted: 'And yet there is a great deal of money made here; good morning, sir.'

Friedrich Engels, *The Condition of the Working Class in England*, 1844 (English translation not published until 1892)

*'Ah! but the Mediterranean!' exclaimed Coningsby 'What would I not give to see Athens!'

'I have seen it,' said the stranger, [Sidonia] slightly shrugging his shoulders; 'and more wonderful things. Phantoms and spectres! The Age of Ruins is past. Have you seen Manchester?'

Benjamin Disraeli, *Coningsby, or The New Generation*, 1844

I like the Manchester people, of whom I have been seeing a little, better than the Liverpudlians. They are more provincial perhaps, but have more character; are less men of the world, but more men of themselves.

Arthur Hugh Clough, Letter to T. Arnold Esq., 15 February 1849

If my impression has remained, and even waxed, that Manchester would be an ideal metropolis for a nation of deaf mutes, my other early impression, of its artistic and intellectual primacy, is sharply renewed and intensified. . . . The explanation of Manchester is twofold. First, its geographical situation, midway between the corrupting languor of the south and the too bleak hardness of the north. And, second, that it enjoys the advantages of a population as vast as that of London, without the disadvantages of either an exaggerated centralisation or of a capital. London suffers from elephantiasis, a rush of blue blood to the head, vertigo, imperfect circulation, and other maladies. Bureaucratic and caste influences must always vitiate the existence of a capital, and I do not suppose that any great capital in Europe is the real source of its country's life and energy. Not Rome, but Milan! Not Madrid, but Barcelona! Not St Petersburg, but Moscow! Not Berlin, but Hamburg and Munich! Not Paris, but the rest of France! Not London, but the Manchester area!

Arnold Bennett, *Paris Nights*, 1913

All Manchester streets are the same, & all strung with tramlines. These follow each other at a few yards distance, making the roads mechanical & unsociable. You hear bells striking all the time. Then there are no teashops, but great cafes; & no little shops, but all big drapers. We lodged (paying 18/– each for bed only) at the Queens Hotel, in a large square; but what's a square when the trams meet there? Then there's Queen Victoria, like a large tea cosy, & Wellington, sleek as a mastiff with paw extended; none of this was quite English, or at least London. The people were lower middle class, no sprinkling of upper class.

Virginia Woolf, *Diary*, 18 March 1921

The Manchester Guardian man came to the hotel, and I gave him tea. Then he took me out to see architecture. Damned little to see.

Arnold Bennett, *Diary*, 19 October 1927

In my time Manchester was a city of liberal culture, awareness and gaiety, which it owed almost entirely to the large infusion of German-Jewish brains and taste. Disaster having overtaken the cotton trade, this part of the community is now submerged. Metaphorically grass now grows in the streets of what was once a second capital, actually the famous Theatre Royal has become a picture-palace, and in the place of the cultured Jew reigns the cheap and flashy Yid.

James Agate, *Ego*, 1935

Manchester, the curse of the Ministry of Health, the despair of the architect, the salvation of the umbrella trade.

Manchester Guardian, 14 January 1941

He chose to live in Manchester, a wholly incomprehensible choice for any free human being to make.

Mr Justice Melford Stevenson, attributed, of a man in a divorce case, quoted in the *Daily Telegraph*, 11 April 1979, in an article marking M.S.'s retirement from the Bench

Mansfield

Thence to Mansfield, where I knew one
That was comely and a trew one
With her a nak'd compact made I,
Her long lov'd I, with her laid I
Towne and her I left, being doubtfull
Lest my love had made her fruitful.

Richard Brathwaite, *Barnabees Journall*, 1638

Margate

This towne much consists of Brewers of a certaine heady Ale; & deale much in mault, &c: for the rest tis raggedly built, & an ill haven, with a small fort of little concernment, nor is the Iland well disciplin'd, but as to the husbandry and rural part, far exceeding any part of England, & I think of the whole world for the accurate culture of their ground

John Evelyn, *Diary*, 21 May 1672

I went to Margate for a day: one would think, it was Bartholomew Fair that had *flown* down: From Smithfield to Kent in the London machine like my Lady Stuffdamask.

Thomas Gray, Letter to Norton Nicholls, 26 August 1766

and Ramsgate

When I was at Margate it was an Excursion of Pleasure to go to see Ramsgate. The Pier, I remember, was accounted a most excellent Piece of Stonework, and such I found it. . . . But you think Margate more lively – So is a Cheshire Cheese full of Mites more lively than a sound one, but that very liveliness only proves its Rottenness. I remember too that Margate, tho' full of Company, was generally fill'd with Such Company, as People who were Nice in the choice of their Company, were rather fearfull of keeping Company with. The Hoy went to London every Week Loaded with Mackarel and Herrings, and return'd Loaded with Company. The Cheapness of the Conveyance made it equally commodious for Dead Fish and Lively Company.

William Cowper, Letter to William Unwin, July 1779

Whate'er from dirty Thames to Margate goes;
However foul, immediately turns fair;
Whatever filth offends the London nose,
Acquires a fragrance soon from Margate air.

Anon., quoted in *A Guide to all the Watering and Sea-bathing Places*, *c.* 1810

On Margate beach, where the sick one roams,
And the sentimental reads;
Where the maiden flirts, and the widow comes –
Like the ocean – to cast her weeds, –
Where urchins wander to pick up shells,
And the Cit to spy at the ships, –
Like the water gala at Sadler's Wells, –
And the Chandler for watery dips.

Thomas Hood, *The Mermaid of Margate*, 1826

Margate in February is like Nugget City after the gold rush.

Lee Wilson, *Evening News*, 7 February 1979

Market Harborough

Am in Market Harborough where ought I to be – Gilbert.

G.K. Chesterton, Telegram to his wife, quoted in *Chesterton, An Anthology*, ed. D. B. Wyndham Lewis, 1957

(But W.R. Titterton, *G. K. Chesterton, A Portrait*, 1936 cites this, or perhaps another occasion, as 'Am in Manchester, where am I supposed to be?')

Marlborough

Before night came to *Marlborough* and lay at the *Hart* a good house and there a fair a pretty fair town for a street or two and what is most singular is their houses on one side having their penthouses supported with pillars which makes it a good walk.

Samuel Pepys, *Diary*, 15 June 1668

An ill-looking place enough.

William Cobbett, *Rural Rides*, 6 November 1821

Matlock

Here in wild pomp, magnificently bleak,
Stupendous Matlock towers amid the Peak;
Here rocks on rocks, on forests forests rise,
Spurn the low earth and mingle with the skies.
Great Nature, slumbering by fair Derwent's stream,
Conceived these giant mountains in a dream.

James Montgomery, Lines written on the wall of an alcove in the Heights of Abraham at Matlock, in the presence of, and quoted by E.Rhodes, *Peak Scenery or the Derbyshire Tourist*, 1824

Dennis: Death isn't like going away on holiday you know.
Canon Throbbing: Oh yes it is. It's going away for a long, long holiday to a place by all accounts every bit as nice as Matlock. For some of us, anyway.

Alan Bennett, *Habeas Corpus*, 1973

Melford (and Lavenham)

Yesterday we were away to Melford and Lavenham,

both exceptionally placid, beautiful old English towns. Melford scattered all round a big green, with an Elizabethan Hall and Park, great screens of trees that seem twice as high as trees should seem, and everything else like what ought to be in a novel, and what one never expects to see in reality, made me cry out how good we were to live in Scotland, for the many hundredth time. I cannot get over my astonishment – indeed it increases every day – at the hopeless gulf there is between England and Scotland, and English and Scotch. Nothing is the same; and I feel as strange and outlandish here as I do in France or Germany. Everything by the wayside, in the houses or about the people, strikes me with an unexpected unfamiliarity: I walk among surprises, for just where you think you have them, something wrong turns up.

Robert Louis Stevenson, Letter to his mother, 28 July 1873

Mentmore

I had slept at Mentmore on Friday night, the Meyer de Rothschild's place. . . . Mentmore is the grandest place possessed by any of the family; its magnificence surpasses belief. It is like a Venetian palace doubled in size, and all Europe has been ransacked to fill it with appropriate furniture. In the great hall hang three immense lamps, which formerly did actually belong to a doge of Venice. All the openings in this great hall are screened by hangings of Gobelins tapestry, and when you stand in the passage that runs around this hall from the top of the grand staircase, and look through the arcades across and down into the hall, it is like fairyland.

Matthew Arnold, Letter to his mother, 2 December 1863

Medway

Then came the Bride, the lovely *Medua* came
Clad in a vesture of unknowen geare,
And uncouth fashion, yet her well became;
That seem'd like silver, sprinckled here and theare
With glittering spangs, that did like stars appeare,
And wav'd upon, like water Chamelot,
To hide the metall, which yet every where
Bewrayd it selfe, to let men plainly wot,
It was no mortall worke that seem'd and yet was not.

Her goodly lockes adowne her backe did flow
Unto her waste, with flowres bescattered,
The which ambrosiall odours forth did throw
To all about, and all her shoulders spred,
As a new spring; and likewise on her hed
A Chapelet of sundry flowers she wore,
From under which the deawy humour shed,
Did tricle down her haire, like to the hore
Congealed litle drops, which doe the morne adore.

Edmund Spenser, *The Faerie Queene*, 1589–96

I envy you so noble a *Bath*, as the Medway.

Lord Byron, Letter to Edward Noel Long, 14 May 1807

Middlesex

This county is much infested with the mildew.

Thomas Fuller, *History of the Worthies of England*, 1662

All Middlesex is ugly, notwithstanding the millions upon millions it is continually sucking up from the rest of the kingdom.

William Cobbett, *Rural Rides,* 25 September 1822, 1830

An acre in Middlesex is better than a principality in Utopia.

T.B. Macaulay, Essay, 'Lord Bacon', July 1837

and Southgate

It is a pleasure to me to know that I was even born in so sweet a village as Southgate . . . Middlesex in general . . . is a scene of trees and meadows, of 'greenery' and nestling cottages; and Southgate is a prime specimen of Middlesex. It is a place lying out of the way of innovation, therefore it has the pure, sweet air of antiquity about it. . . .

Leigh Hunt, *Autobiography*, 1850

Midlands

Defiant disregard of appearances . . . is perhaps the worst trait of the Midland character.

Arnold Bennett, *Paris Nights*, 1913

When I am living in the Midlands.
That are sodden and unkind.

Hilaire Belloc, *The South Country*, *Verses, 1910*

When men offer thanks for the bounties
That they in their boyhood have known,
When poets are praising their counties,
What ought I to say of my own?

Its highways are crowded with lorries
And buses encumber its lanes;
Its hills are used chiefly as quarries,
Its rivers used chiefly as drains.

The country is all over-ridden
By townsmen, ill-mannered and proud,
And beauty, unless it is hidden,
Is trampled to death by the crowd.

Disforested, featureless, faded –
Describe me a place if you can
Where Man was by Nature less aided
Or Nature less aided by Man.

And yet, though I keep in subjection
My heart, as a rule, to my head.
I still feel a sneaking affection
For ———, where I was bred.

For still, here and there, is a village,
Where factories have not been planned,
There still are some acres of tillage,
Some old men still work on the land.

And how can I help but remember
The Midsummer meadows of hay,
The stubbles dew-drenched in September,
The buttercups golden in May?

For we who seek out and discover
The charms of my county can be
As proud as a plain woman's lover
Of beauties the world does not see.

Colin Ellis, 'Living in the Midlands', *Mournful Numbers*, 1932

Morecambe

Morecambe, . . . which salubrious resort combines, as the polite world knows, the wit of Paris with the elegance of pre-War Vienna, and adds to the virtues of Buda the vices of Pesth.

James Agate, *Ego 9* (6 May 1946), 1948

Newbury (Berkshire)

Newbery is a little town famous for makeing the best whipps.

Celia Fiennes, *Journeys*, *c*. 1685–96

Newcastle

To carry coals to Newcastle.

Proverb, sixteenth century

Bartervile: . . . Is not this Newcastle?
Lurchall: No covetous wretch: tis Hell, thy blacke-soules prison.

Thomas Dekker, *If this be not a Good Play, the Divell is in It*, 1612

I rode on to Newcastle. Certainly if I did not believe there was another world, I should spend all my summers here; as I know no place in great Britain comparable to it for pleasantness. But I seek another country, and therefore am content to be a wanderer upon the earth.

John Wesley, *Journal*, 4 June 1759

To be out of Hell, Newcastle certainly is the damnedest district of country anywhere to be found.

Henry Brougham, Letter to Thomas Creevey, 15 September 1813

The singular practice of engaging women as labourers to bricklayers and slaters impresses strangers with an unfavourable and erroneous idea of the delicacy and humanity of the inhabitants. As the gentlemen seem not to have sufficient gallantry to reform this abuse, we hope that the ladies will exert themselves successfully in abolishing a custom so disgraceful to the town.

E. Mackenzie, *A Description and Historical Account of . . . Newcastle upon Tyne*, 1827

Are they always like this? – living in the past?
Well, we've had a bigger ration of the past here than in most places.

Alan Plater, *Close the Coalhouse Door*, 1968

The New Brasilia.

T. Dan Smith, 1960s slogan for Newcastle, quoted by John Ardagh, *A Tale of Five Cities*, 1979

T. Dan Smith . . . said at one time that he wanted to make this city the 'Venice of the North, with ring roads instead of canals.'

Richard West, *An English Journey*, 1981

Newcastle under Lyme

That Thursday morne, my weary course I fram'd,
Unto a Towne that is Newcastle nam'd,
(Not that *Newcastle* standing upon *Tine*)
But this Towne scituation doth confine
Neere *Cheshire*, in the famous County *Stafford*,
And for their love, I owe them not a straw for't.

John Taylor, *The Pennyles Pilgrimage*, in *All the Works of John Taylor*, 1630

At Newcastle-under Line-a
There I trounc'd it in burnt wine-a;
None o'th wicked there remained
Weekly lectures were proclaimed:
Chastity they roughly handle
While blind zeale snuffs out the candle.

Richard Brathwaite, *Barnabees Journall*, 1638

and Newcastle on Tyne
Newcastle Underline where is the fine shineing Channell Coale, so the proverb to both the Newcastles of bringing Coales to them is a needless labour, one being famous for this coale thats cloven and makes white ashes, as is this, and the Newcastle on the Tyne is for the sea-coale that cakes and is what is common and famillier to every smith in all villages.

Celia Fiennes, *Journeys*, 1698

New Forest

From God and Saint King *Rus* did Churches take?
From Citizens town-court, and mercate place,
From farmer lands: *New forest*, for to make,
In Beaulew tract, where whiles the King in chase,
Pursues the hart, just vengeance comes apace,
And King pursues. Tirrell him seeing not,
Unwares him slew with dint of arrow shot.

John White, Bishop of Winchester, in William Camden, *Britain*, 1610 (Philemon Holland's translation)

My admiration of the Forest is great: it is true old wild English Nature, and then the fresh heath-sweetened air is so delicious. The Forest is grand.

Alfred Lord Tennyson, Diary, 2 September 1855, in *Alfred Lord Tennyson, a Memoir by his Son*, 1897

The chief difficulty is what to do with the great fir enclosures, the firs ought to be cut down, but there is nobody to buy them, and an ugly growth of them is creeping over the open spaces, self-sown. It ought to be put a stop to, or in fifty years' time the Forest will be like Woking cemetery.

Wilfred Scawen Blunt, Diary, 12 August 1896, *My Diaries*, 1919

Newhaven

Newhaven is spot & rash & pimple & blister; with the incessant cars like active lice.

Virginia Woolf, *Diary*, 10 September 1921

Newmarket

Being come to Newmarket in the month of Ocotber, I had the opportunity to see the horse-races; and a great concourse of the nobility and gentry, as well from London as from all parts of England; but they were all so intent, so eager, so busy upon the sharping part of the sport, their wagers and bets, that to me they seem'd just as so many horse-coursers in Smithfield, descending (the greatest of them) from their high dignity and quality, to picking one another's pockets, and biting one another as much as possible, and that with such eagerness, as that it might be said they acted without respect to faith, honour, or good manners.

Daniel Defoe, *A Tour through the Whole Island of Great Britain*, 1724–7

Norfolk

But the goodness of the ground a man may collect by this, that the inhabitants are of a passing good complexion: to say nothing of their exceeding wily wits, and the same right quicke in the insight of our common laws: in so much, as it is counted, as well now, as in times past, the onley country for best breed of Lawyers: so that even out of the meanest sort of the common people, there may be found not a few, who if their were nothing else to beare action, are able to fetch matter enough of wrangling controversies, even out of the very prickes, titles, and accents of the Law.

William Camden, *Britain*, 1610 (Philemon Holland's translation)

Norfolk Marshland, near Outfall of the Great Ouse
There's scarcely any soyle that sitteth by thy side,
Whose turfe so batfull is, or beares so deepe a swath;
Nor is there any marsh in all Great Britaine, hath
So many goodly seats, or that can truely show
Such rarities as I: so that all marshes owe
Much honour to my name, for that exceeding grace,
Which they receive by me, so soveraigne in my place.
Though Rumney, as some say, for finenesse of her grasse,
And for her daintie scite, all other doth surpasse:
Yet are those seas but poore, and rivers that confine
Her greatnesse but meane rills, be they compar'd with mine.
Nor hardly doth she tyth th'aboundant fowls and fish,
Which Nature gives to me, as I my selfe can wish.

Michael Drayton, *Poly-Olbion*, 'The Twentieth Song', 1622

Norfolk Coast
As I went by land from Yarmouth northward, along the shoar towards Cromer . . . I was surpris'd to see, in all the way from Winterton, that the farmers, and country people had scarce a barn, or a shed, or a stable; nay, not the pales of their yards, and gardens, not a hogstye, not a necessary-house, but what was built of old planks, beams, wales and timbers, &c. the wrecks of ships, and ruins of mariners and merchants' fortunes; and in some places were whole yards fill'd, and piled up very high with the same stuff laid up, as I suppos'd to sell for the like building purposes as there should be occasion.

Daniel Defoe, *A Tour through the Whole Island of Great Britain*, 1724–7

The Norfolk people are quick and smart in their motions and in their speaking. Very neat and *trim* in all their farming concerns, and very skilful. Their land is good, their roads are level, and the bottom of their soil is dry, to be sure; and these are great advantages; but they are diligent, and make the most of everything. Their management of all sorts of stock is most judicious; they are careful about manure; their teams move quickly; and, in short, it is a county of most excellent cultivators. . . . The great drawbacks on the beauty of these counties are, their flatness and their want of fine woods; but to those who can dispense with these, Norfolk, under a wise and just government, can have nothing to ask more than Providence and the industry of man have given.

William Cobbett, *Rural Rides*, 24 December 1821

Amanda: Have you known her long?
Elyot: About four months, we met in a house party in Norfolk.
Amanda: Very flat, Norfolk.

Noel Coward, *Private Lives*, 1930

Northampton

He that must eat a buttered faggot let him go to Northampton. Because it is the dearest town in England for fuel, where no coals can come by water, and little wood doth grow on land.

Thomas Fuller, *History of the Worthies of England*, 1662

Northampton stands on other men's legs.

Ibid. (in allusion to Northampton's shoe-making industry)

Northamptonshire

Northamptonshire full of love
Beneath the girdle and not above.

Anon, *c.* 1500

Sure I am there is as little waste ground in this, as in any county in England, . . . Northamptonshire being an apple, without core to be cut out, or rind to be pared away.

Thomas Fuller, *History of the Worthies of England*, 1662

Northamptonshire, . . . is a clay-pudding stuck full of villages.

Horace Walpole, Letter to George Montagu, 23 July 1763

By Langley Bush I roam, but the bush hath left its hill,
On Cowper Green I stray, tis a desert strange and chill,
And the spreading Lea Close oak, ere decay had
penned its will,
To the ax of the spoiler and self-interest fell a prey,
And Crossberry Way and old Round Oak's narrow
lane
With its hollow trees like pulpits I shall never see again,
Enclosure like a Buonaparte let not a thing remain,
It levelled every bush and tree and levelled every hill
And hung the moles for traitors – though the brook is
running still,
It runs a sicker brook, cold and chill. . . .

John Clare, *Remembrances*, from his manuscript book – *Poems*, 1908

Northumberland

in Northumberlonde
Where men sethe rushes in gruell.

Anon., *Hyckescorner*, *c.* 1510–12

The ground it selfe for the most part rough, & hard to be manured, seemeth to have hardened the inhabitants, whom the Scots their neighbours also made more fierce and hardy, while sometimes they keepe them exercised in warres, and other whiles, in time of peace intermingle their manners among them, so that by these meanes they are a most warlike nation, & excellent good light horsemen. And wheras they addicted themselves as it were wholy to *Mars* and Armes, there is not a man amongst them of the better sort, that hath not his little towre or pile.

William Camden, *Britain*, 1610 (Philemon Holland's translation)

I must not quit Northumberland without taking notice, that the natives of this country, of the antient original race or families, are distinguished by a shibboleth upon their tongues, namely a difficulty in pronouncing the letter *r*, which they cannot deliver from their tongues without a hollow jarring in the throat, by which they are plainly known, as a foreigner is, in pronouncing the *th*; This they call the Northumbrian *r*, and the natives value themselves upon that imperfection, because, forsooth, it shows the antiquity of their blood.

Daniel Defoe, *A Tour through the Whole Island of Great Britain*, 1724–7

Between our eastward and our westward sea
The narrowing strand
Clasps close the noblest shore fame holds in fee
Even where English birth seals all men free
Northumberland.

A.C. Swinburne, 'Northumberland', *A Channel Passage and Other Poems*, 1904

Heatherland and bent-land –
Black land and white,

God bring me to Northumberland,
The land of my delight.

Land of singing waters,
And winds from off the sea,
God bring me to Northumberland,
The land where I would be.

Heatherland and bent-land,
And valleys rich with corn,
God bring me to Northumberland,
The land where I was born

Wilfrid Wilson Gibson, *Northumberland*, before 1943

Norwich

So all sufficient in her selfe, and so complete is shee,
That if neede were, of all the Realme the mistresse shee might bee.

John Johnston, in William Camden, *Britain*, 1610 (Philemon Holland's translation)

That hospitable place to the industrious Dutch,
Whose skill in making stuffes, and workmanship is such,
(For refuge thither come) as they our ayd deserve,
By labour sore that live, whilst oft the English starve;
On roots, and pulse that feed, on beefe and mutton spare,
So frugally they live, not gluttons as we are.

Michael Drayton, *Poly-Olbion*, 'The Twentieth Song', 1622

Norwich is (as you please) either a city in an orchard or an orchard in a city, so equally are houses and trees blended in it; so that the pleasure of the country and populousness of the city meet here together. Yet, in this mixture, the inhabitants participate nothing of the rusticalness of the one, but altogether of the urbanity and civility of the other.

Thomas Fuller, *History of the Worthies of England*, 1662

Nottingham

In Nottamun Town not a soul would look up,
Not a soul would look up, not a soul would look down,
Not a soul would look up, not a soul would look down,
To tell me the way to Nottamun town.

Anon.

There wee crost *Trent*, and on the other side
Prayd to Saint *Andrew*: and up hill we ride.
Where we observ'd the cunning men, like moles,
Dwell not in howses, but were earth't in holes;
So they did not build upwards, but digg thorough,
As *Hermitts* caves, or *Conyes* do their Borough:
Great Underminers sure as any where;
Tis thought the Powder-Traitors practis'd there.
Would you not thinke the men stood on their heads,
When Gardens cover Howses there, like Leades;
And on the Chimneyes-topp the Mayd may know
Whether her Pottage boyls or not, below;
There cast in Hearbes, and Salt, or Bread; her Meate
Contented rather with the Smoake then Heate?
This was the Rocky-Parish; higher stood
Churches and Howses, Buildings stone and wood.

Richard Corbet, *Iter Boreale*, 1647

The town of Nottingham is situated upon the steep ascent of a sandy rock; which is consequently remarkable, for that it is so soft that they easily work into it for making vaults and cellars, and yet so firm as to support the roofs of those cellars two or three under one another; the stairs into which, are all cut out of the solid, tho' crumbling rock; and we must not fail to have it remembered that the bountiful inhabitants generally keep these cellars well stock'd with excellent ALE; nor are they uncommunicative in bestowing it among their friends, as some of our company experienc'd, to a degree not fit to be made matter of history.

Daniel Defoe, *A Tour through the Whole Island of Great Britain*, 1724–7

We dined at Nottingham yesterday. That town is finely situated: the rich valley below; the castle on an eminence so noble; the Collec-woods, the river, are beautiful objects; yet the town itself, at the distance of a mile or two, looks like an immense brick-hill, especially on one approach, being built on the side of a hill, with the red houses, tier above tier.

Anna Seward, Letter, September 1767, in 'Literary Correspondence', *Works*, 1810

That *political Pandemonium*, Nottingham.

Lord Byron, Letter to John M.B. Pigot, 18 August 1806

When I read Dickens on Victorian London I think of Nottingham in the twenties. . . . I had found a town as haunting as Berkhampstead. . . . Like the bar of the City Hotel in Freetown which I was to know years later it was the focal point of failure, a place undisturbed by ambition, a place to be resigned to, a home from home.

Graham Greene, *A Sort of Life*, 1971

Nottingham Castle: Mortimer's Hole

Without the castle, in the earth, is found
A cave, resembling sleepie Morpheus cell,
In strangė meanders wynding under ground,
Where darknesse seekes continually to dwell,
Which with such feare and horror doth abound,
As though it were an entrance into hell;

By architects, to serve the castle made
When as the Danes this iland did invade.

Now, on along the crankling path doth keepe,
Then, by a rocke, turnes up another way,
Rising tow'rds day, then falling tow'rds the deepe,
On a smooth levell then it selfe doth lay,
Directly then, then obliquely doth creepe,
Nor in the course keepes any certaine stay;
Till in the castle, in an odde by-place,
It casts the foule maske from its duskie face.

Michael Drayton, *The Barons Warres*, 1603

and its surroundings, Sherwood Forest and the River Trent

To Nottingham, the North's imperious Eye,
Which as a Pharus doth survey the soyle
Armed by Nature, danger to defie, . . .

Here all along, the flower-befilled vales,
On her cleere sands the silver Trent doth slide,
And to the medowes telling wanton tales,
Her crystall limbes lasciviously, in pride,
(As ravish'd with the inamor'd gales)
With often turnings casts from side to side;
As she were loth the faire sight to forsake,
And runne her selfe into the German Lake

And north from thence, rude Sherwood as she roves,
Casts many a long looke at those loftie tow'rs,
And with the thicknesse of her well-growne groves,
Shelters the towne from stormie winters show'rs,
In pleasant summer, and to shew her loves,
Bids it againe to see her shadie bow'rs;
Courting the castle, which as turning to her,
Smiles to behold th'inamor'd wood-nymph woo her.

Michael Drayton, *The Barons Wares*, 1603

Nottinghamshire (and Yorkshire)

Sights are thick sown in the counties of York and Nottingham: the former is more historic, and the great lords live at a prouder distance: in Nottinghamshire there is a very heptarchy of little kingdoms elbowing one another, and the barons of them want nothing but small armies to make inroads into one another's parks, murder deer, and massacre park-keepers.

Horace Walpole, Letter to Richard Bentley, August 1756

Odcombe (Somerset)

Yea, I hope my generall country of England shall one day say that *Odde-combe*, for one part of the word may truelie be so called: (for *Odd-Combe* consisteth of two words, odde, and combe, which latter word in the olde Saxon tongue signifieth besides the vertical point of a cocks head, the side of a Hill, because the east side of the hill whereon *Od-combe* standeth is very conspicuous, and seene afar off in the Country Eastward) for breeding an odde man, one that hath not his peere in the whole kingdom to match him.

Thomas Coryate, Letter to Sir Edward Phillips, 1615 (on himself and Odcombe)

Olney

But oh! wherever else I am accounted dull . . . let me pass for a genius at Olney!

William Cooper, Letter to William Unwin, 12 June 1782

Ormskirk

We passed through Ormskirk, a town chiefly famous for the preparation of a nostrum of more repute than efficacy against hydrophobia.

Robert Southey, *Letters from England, by Don Manuel Alvarez Espreilla*, 1807

Ottery St Mary

They tell us the name is deriv'd from the river Ottery, and that, from the multitude of otters found always in that river, which however to me seems fabulous; nor does there appear to be any such great number of otters in that water, or in the county about, more than is usual in other counties, or in other parts of the county about them; they tell us they send 20000 hogsheads of cyder hence every year to London, and which is still worse, that it is most of it bought there by the merchants to mix with their wines, which, if true, is not much to the reputations of the London vintners; but that by the by.

Daniel Defoe, *A Tour through the Whole Island of Great Britain*, 1724–7

River Ouse

and Crawley Brook, Bedfordshire

As crooked as Crawley brook. – This is a nameless brook arising about Woburn, running by Crawley, and falling immediately into the Ouse. But this proverb may better be verified of Ouse itself in this shire, more *meandrous* than *Meander*, which runneth above eighty miles in eighteen by land. Blame it not, if sensible of its sad condition, and presaging its fall into the foggy fens in the next county, it be loath to leave this pleasant place; as who would not prolong their own happiness.

Thomas Fuller, *History of the Worthies of England*, 1662

The Bailiff of Bedford is coming. – This proverb hath its original in this, but use in the next, county of Cambridge. The river Ouse running by is called the Bailiff of Bedford, who, swelling with rain, snow-water, and tributary brooks in the winter, and coming down on a sudden, arresteth the Isle of Ely with inundation. But I am informed that the drainers of the Fens have of late, with incredible care, cost, and industry, wrested the mace out of this Bailiff's hand, and have secured the county against his power for the future.

Ibid.

at Huntingdon
The River Ouze, I forget how they spell it, is the most agreeable Circumstance in this part of the World. . . . It is a noble Stream to bath in, and I shall make that use of it three times a Week, having introduced myself to it for the first time this Morning.

William Cowper, Letter to Joseph Hill, 24 June 1765

Oxford

When Oxford draws knife
England will be soon at strife.

Thomas Fuller, *History of the Worthies of England*, 1662
(Founded on a medieval rhyme:
Chronica si penses cum pungent Oxonienses
Post aliquot menses volat ira per Angliginenses.)

Oxford for learning, London for wit,
Hull for women, and York for a tit.

Anon., old rhyme.
(Tit in this context means a horse.)

Emperour of Germany: Trust me, Plantagenet these Oxford schooles
Are richly seated neere the river side:
The mountaines full of fat and fallow deere,
The batling pastures laid with kine and flocks,
The towne gorgeous with high built colledges,
And schollers seemely in their grave attire,
Learned in searching principles of art.
What is thy judgement, *Jacques Vandermast?*
Vandermast: That lordly are the buildings of the towne,
Spatious the rooms and full of pleasant walkes;
But for the doctors, how that they be learned,
It may be meanly, for ought I can heere.

Robert Greene, *The Honourable Historie of Frier Bacon and Frier Bungay*, before 1952

and River Cherwell
Therefore on either side she was sustained
Of two smal grooms, which by their names were hight
The Churne, and Charwell, two small streames which pained
Them selves her footing to direct aright,
Which fayled oft through faint and feeble plight:
But Thame was stronger and of better stay;
Yet seem'd full aged by his outward sight,
With head all hoary and his beard all gray,
Dewed with silver drops that trickle down alway.
And eke he somewhat seemed to stoupe afore,
With bowed backe, by reason of the lode,
And ancient heavy burden which he bore
Of that faire city wherein make abode
So many learned impes, that shoote abrode,
And with their branches spred all Britany,
No lesse than do her elder sisters broode.
Ioy to you both, ye double nursery
Of Arts, but Oxford thine doth *Thame* most glorify.

Edmund Spenser, *The Faerie Queene*, 1589–96

Where Cherwell is confluent with Isis, and pleasant Eights or Islets lye dispersed by the sundry disseverings of waters; there the most famous Universitie of OXFORD . . . sheweth it selfe aloft in a champion plaine. OXFORD, *I say, our most noble Athens, the Muses-seate, and one of Englands staies*; nay *The Sun, the Eye, and the Soule thereof*, the very Source and most cleere spring of good literature and wisdome: From whence, religion, civility and learning are spred most plenteouslie into all parts of the Realme. A faire and goodlie Citie, whether a man respect the seemly beautie of private houses or the statelie magnificence of publicke buildings, together with the wholesome site or pleasant prospect thereof. For, the hils beset with woods doe soe environ the plaine, that as on the one side they exclude the pestilent Southwinde, and the tempestuous West winde on the other, so they let in the cleering Eastern winde onely, and the Northeast winde with all, which free from all corruption.

William Camden, *Britain*, 1610
(Philemon Holland's translation)

and the Bodleian Library
Were I not a king, I would be a university man; and if it were that I must be a prisoner, if I might have my wish, I would have no other prison than this library, and be chained together with these good authors.

James VI and I, in Oxford, 1605, quoted, in translation from Sir Isaac Wake, *Rex Platonicus*, 1607

Hail Learnings *Pantheon*! Hail the sacred Ark
Where all the World of Science does embarque!
Which ever shalt withstand, and hast so long withstood
Insatiate times devouring Flood.
Hail Tree of Knowledge, thy leaves Fruit! which well
Dost in the midst of Paradise arise,
Oxford the Muses Paradise,
From which may never Sword the blest expell.
Hail Bank of all past Ages! where they lie

T'inrich with interest Posterity!
Hail Wits illustrious Galaxy!
Where thousand Lights into one brightness spread;
Hail living Univers'ty of the dead!

Unconfus' Babel of all Tongues, which e'er
The mighty Linguist Fame, or Time, the mighty Traveller,
That could speak, or this could hear.
Majestick Monument and Pyramide,
Where still the shapes of parted Souls abide
Embalm'd in verse, exalted Souls which now
Enjoy those Arts they woo'd so well below,
Which now all wonders plainly see
That have been, are, or are to be,
In the mysterious Librarie,
The Beatifick *Bodley* of the Deitie.

Abraham Cowley, 'Ode, Mr Cowley's Book presenting it self to the University Library of Oxford', in *Verses Written upon Several Occasions*, 1663

We came to Oxford, a very sweet place. . . . Oxford mighty fine place and well seated, and cheap entertainment.

Samuel Pepys, *Diary*, 9 June 1668

and Cambridge
Oxford to Him a dearer Name shall be
Than His own Mother University
Thebes did his Green unknowing Youth ingage
He chuses *Athens* in his Riper Age.

John Dryden, *Prologue to the University of Oxford*, 1676

No wonder that Oxford and Cambridge profound
In learning and science so greatly abound;
Since some carry thither a little each day,
And we meet with so few who bring any away.

Anon., *The Universities*

The King, observing with judicious eyes
The state of both his universities,
To Oxford sent a troop of horse, and why?
That learned body wanted loyalty;
To Cambridge, books, as very well discerning
How much that loyal body wanted learning.

Joseph Trapp, 'On George I's Donation of the Bishop of Ely's Library to Cambridge University', in Nichols, *Literary Anecdotes*, 1812–15

The King to Oxford sent a troop of horse
For Tories own no argument but force:
With equal skill to Cambridge books he sent
For Whigs admit no force but argument.

Sir William Browne, Reply to Trapp's epigram, 'The King observing with judicious eyes', in Nichols, *Literary Anecdotes*, 1812–15

Ye fretted pinnacles, ye fanes sublime,
Ye towers that wear the mossy vest of time:
Ye massy piles of old magnificence,
At once the pride of learning and defence;
Ye cloisters pale, that lengthening to the sight
To contemplation, step by step invite,
Ye high-arch'd walks, where oft the whispers clear
Of harps unseen have swept the poet's ear;
Ye temples dim, where pious duty pays
Her holy hymns of ever echoing praise;
Lo! your lov'd Isis, from the bordering vale,
With all a mother's fondness bids you hail! –
Hail Oxford, hail! of all that's good and great
Of all that's fair, the guardian and the seat;
Nurse of each brave pursuit, each generous aim
By truth exalted in the throne of fame!
Like Greece in science and in Liberty,
As Athens learn'd, as Lacedemon free!

Thomas Wharton, *The Triumph of Isis*, 1749

That nursery of nonsense and bigotry, Oxford.

Horace Walpole, Letter to George Montagu, 30 May 1751

I . . . lay at Oxford. As I was quite alone, I did not care to see anything; but as soon as it was dark, I ventured out, and the moon rose as I was wandering among the colleges, and gave me a charming venerable Gothic scene, which was not lessened by the monkish appearance of the old fellows stealing to their pleasures. . . . the whole air of the town charms me.

Horace Walpole, Letter to Richard Bentley, September 1753

I tried to work myself up to a little enthusiasm, and took a draught of the water of Isis so much celebrated in poetry, but all in vain.

James Boswell, *Journal*, 24 April 1763

To the University of Oxford I acknowledge no obligation; and she will as cheerfully renounce me for a son, as I am willing to disclaim her for a mother. I spent fourteen months at Magdalen College: they proved the fourteen months the most idle and unprofitable of my whole life.

Edward Gibbon, *Autobiography*, before 1794

as 'an English University'
A sanctuary in which exploded systems and obsolete prejudices find shelter and protection after they have been hunted out of every corner of the world.

Adam Smith, *Wealth of Nations*, 1776

I am sure if he found no muses there, he could pick up none at Oxford, where there is not so much as a bed-maker that ever lived in a muse's family.

Horace Walpole, Letter to the Earl of Strafford, 3 October 1782

Oxford, ancient Mother! . . . I owe thee nothing.
Thomas de Quincey, *Autobiography*, *c.* 1835 – of 1803 and later

Wordsworth sometimes, though in a fine way, gives us sentences in the style of school exercises – For instance,

The lake doth glitter
Small birds twitter &c.

Now, I think this is an excellent method of giving a very clear description of an interesting place such as Oxford is –

The Gothic looks solemn –
The plain Doric column
Supports an old Bishop & Crosier
The mouldering arch
Shaded o'er by a larch,
Lives next door to Wilson the Hosier.

Vice – that is, by turns –
O'er pale visage mourns
The black tassell trencher or common hat:
The Chauntry boy sings,
The Steeple-bell rings,
And as for the Chancellor – *dominat.*

There are plenty of trees,
And plenty of ease,
And plenty of fat deer for Parsons;
And when it is venison
Short is the benison, –
Then each on a leg or thigh fastens.

John Keats, Letter to John Hamilton Reynolds, September 1817

It was interesting to see the effect of habit at Oxford of meeting Classical people. Every body showed you Latin and Greek books to explain any question, as if they had been English. It seemed never to enter their conception that there were people in the World who knew nothing of the one or the other.
Benjamin Robert Haydon, *Diary*, August 1817

Ye sacred nurseries of blooming Youth!
In whose collegiate shelter England's Flowers
Expand, enjoying through their vernal hours
The air of liberty, the light of truth;
Much have ye suffered from Time's gnawing tooth:
Yet, O ye spires of Oxford! domes and towers!
Gardens and groves! your presence overpowers
The soberness of reason; till, in sooth,
Transformed, and rushing on a bold exchange
I slight my own beloved Cam, to range
Where silver Isis leads my stripling feet;
Pace the long avenue, or glide adown
The stream-like windings of that glorious street –
An eager Novice robed in fluttering gown!

William Wordsworth, *Oxford*, 30 May 1820

Upon beholding the masses of buildings at Oxford, devoted to what they call *'learning'*, I could not help reflecting on the drones that they contain and the wasps they send forth! However, malignant as some are, the great and prevalent characteristic is *folly*; emptiness of head, want of talent; and one half of the fellows who are what they call *educated* here are unfit to be clerks in a grocer's or mercer's shop.
William Cobbett, *Rural Rides*, 18 November 1821

We could pass our lives at Oxford without having or wanting any other idea – that of the place is enough. We imbibe the air of thought; we stand in the presence of learning. . . .

Let him then who is fond of indulging in dreamlike existence go to Oxford, and stay there. . . .
William Hazlitt, *Sketches of the Principal Picture Galleries*, 1824

*This Babylon of buried literature.
Thomas Love Peacock, *Crotchet Castle*, 1831

And how reposeful in the haunted spot
Where life is mental, and the world forgot!
Robert Montgomery, *Oxford, a Poem*, 1831

I came through Oxford. . . . There was a young fellow of about five-and-twenty, moustachioed and smartly dressed, in the coach with me. . . . The coach stopped to dine; and this youth passed half an hour in the midst of that city of palaces. He looked about him with his mouth open, as he re-entered the coach, and all the while that we were driving away past the Ratcliffe Library, the great court of All Souls, Exeter, Lincoln, Trinity, Balliol and St. John's. When we were about a mile on the road he spoke the first words that I had heard him utter. 'That was a pretty town enough. Pray, sir, what is it called?'
Thomas Babington Macaulay, Letter to Hannah M. Macaulay, 29 September 1832

Oh! Oxford, Oxford, vainly still endow'd
With wealth and ease to lift thee from the crowd,
With opportunities too richly blest,
Why with slow step still lag behind the rest?
When wilt thou cease, with all thy pompous plan,
To waste on mummies, what was meant for man –
With all thy learning when wilt thou decide
That to be useful it must be applied?
Lo! on a pile of dusty folio's thron'd,
Her Janus brows with dog-ear'd fools-cap crown'd,
Fenc'd with a footstool, that no step should go
Too rashly near, nor crush her gouty toe,
Obese Tuition sits, and ever drips
An inky slaver from her bloated lips!
Unwholesome vapours round her presence shed,
Dim ev'ry eye, and muddle ev'ry head,
Stunt the young shoots, which smil'd with promise once,

And breathe a deeper dulness on the dunce.
Oxford awake! The land hath borne too long
The senseless jingling of thy drowsy song. . . .

G.V. Cox, *Black Gowns and Red Coats*, 1834

It is, I am sure, so much better a place than Cambridge.

Arthur Hugh Clough, Letter to J.P. Gell, 8 April 1838

Much as I like, fond as I am of Oxford, . . . I verily believe that as a preliminary stage it would be far better to be at Stinkomalee (the London University acknowledges that agnomen I believe).

Arthur Hugh Clough, Letter to Rev. J.P. Gell, 25 November 1844

Oxford is a glorious place; godlike! at night I have walked round the colleges under the full moon, and thought it would be heaven to live and die here. The Dons are terribly majestic, and the men are men, in spirit as in name – they seem overflowing with generosity and good-nature. . . . I wonder how the examiners ever have the heart to pluck such men.

Edward Burne Jones, Letter to his family, 29 January 1853

The world, surely, has not another place like Oxford: it is a despair to see such a place and ever to leave it.

Nathaniel Hawthorne, *Notebooks*, 1856

Most interesting spot I have seen in England. . . . It was here I first confessed with gratitude my mother land, & hailed her with pride. . . . Old reef washed by waves & showing detached parts – so Oxford. . . . Learning lodged like a faun. Garden to every college. Lands for centuries never molested by labor. Sacred to beauty and tranquility. . . . Grass smooth as green baize of billiard table. – The picturesque never goes beyond this. – I know nothing more fitted by mild & beautiful rebuke to chastise the presumptuous ranting of Yankees.

Herman Melville, *Journal of a Visit to Europe and the Levant*, 2 May 1857

There is much to be said in favour of the University of Oxford. No one can deny to it very great and very peculiar merits. But certainly it is not an exciting place, and its education operates as a narcotic rather than as a stimulant. . . . Oxford, it has been said, 'disheartens a man early.'

Walter Bagehot, 'Mr Gladstone', *National Review*, July 1860

The home of dead languages and undying prejudices.

John Bright, quoted in C. Day Lewis and Charles Fenby, *Anatomy of Oxford*, 1938

To call a man a characteristically Oxford man remained in his opinion the highest compliment that could be paid to a human being.

Alfred E. Robins, *The Early Public Life of William Ewart Gladstone*, 1894, quoting Gladstone

I always like this place, and the intellectual life here is certainly much more intense than it used to be; but this has its disadvantages too, in the envies, hatreds, and jealousies that come with the activity of mind of most men.

Matthew Arnold, Letter to his mother, 14 May 1861

Beautiful city! so venerable, so lovely, so unravaged by the fierce intellectual life of our century, so serene!

'There are our young barbarians all at play!'

And yet, steeped in sentiment as she lies, spreading her gardens to the moonlight, and whispering from her towers the last enchantments of the Middle Age, who will deny that Oxford, by her ineffable charm, keeps ever calling us nearer to the true goal of all of us, to the ideal, to perfection, – to beauty in a word, which is only truth seen from another side. . . . Adorable dreamer, whose heart has been so romantic! who has given thyself so prodigally, given thyself to sides and heroes not mine, only never to the Philistines! home of lost causes, and forsaken beliefs, and unpopular names, and impossible loyalties!

Matthew Arnold, Preface to *Essays in Criticism*, 1865

and surrounding countryside

Runs it not here, the track by Childsworth Farm,
Past the high wood, to where the elm-tree crowns
The hill behind whose ridge the sunset flames?
The signal-elm that looks on Ilsey Downs,
The Vale, the three lone wears, the youthful Thames? –
This winter-eve is warm,
Humid the air; leafless yet soft as spring,
The tender purple spray on copse and briers;
And that sweet City with her dreaming spires,
She needs not June for beauty's heightening.

Matthew Arnold, *Thyrsis*, 1867

Perhaps none but Oxford men can know how much truth there really is in the praise I have given to Oxford for her sentiment. I find I am generally thought to have *buttered her up* to excess for the sake of parting good friends; but this is not so, though I certainly kept her best side in sight, and not her worst.

Matthew Arnold, Letter to his brother, 23 July 1867

I walked along, thro' the lovely Christ Church meadow, by the river side and back through the town. It was a perfect evening and in the interminable British twilight the beauty of the whole place came forth with magical power. There are no words for these colleges. As I stood last evening within the precincts of mighty Magdalen, gazed at its great serene tower and uncapped my throbbing brow in the wild dimness of its courts, I thought that the heart of me would crack with the fulness of satisfied desire. It is, as I say, satisfied desire that you feel here; it is your tribute to the place. You ask nothing more; you have imagined only a quarter as much. The whole place gives me a deeper sense of English life than anything yet. As I walked along the river I saw hundreds of the mighty lads of England, clad in white flannel and blue, immense, fair-haired, magnificent in their youth, lounging down the stream in their punts or pulling in straining crews and rejoicing in their godlike strength. When along with this you think of their haunts in the grey-green quadrangles, you esteem them as elect among men.

Henry James, Letter to William James, 26 April 1869

I . . . spent the afternoon in various college gardens. These same gardens are the fairest things in Oxford. Locked in their own ancient verdure, behind their own ancient walls, filled with shade and music and perfumes and privacy – with lounging students and charming children – with the rich old college windows keeping guard from above – they are places to lie down on the grass in forever, in the happy belief that the world is all an English garden and time a fine old English afternoon.

Ibid.

In my first term, I fell into the doctor's hands, and never escaped from them so long as I was an undergraduate. I well remember the decisive counsel of the first doctor whom I consulted. . . . 'What wine do you drink?' 'None.' 'Oh! that's all nonsense. You never will be able to live in this climate unless you drink port and plenty of it.' . . . but even port was powerless to keep me well at Oxford.

G.W.E. Russell, *One Look Back*, 1912 – of 1872

He used to express the view that an Oxford resident never dies, having never existed, but ceases.

Algernon Charles Swinburne, quoted Edmund Gosse, *Life of Swinburne*, 1917

Nothing *ever* happens here, I believe! There never *was* such a place for things not happening.

C.L. Dodgson (Lewis Carroll), Letter to Helen Feilden, 15 March 1873

Towery city and branchy between towers;
Cuckoo-echoing, bell-swarmed, lark-charmed,
  rook-racked, river-rounded;
The dapple-eared lily below thee; that country and
  town did
Once encounter in, here coped and poised powers;

Thou hast a base and brickish skirt there, sours
That neighbour-nature thy grey beauty is grounded
Best in; graceless growth, thou hast confounded
Rural rural keeping – folk, flocks and flowers.

Yet ah! this air I gather and release
He lived on; these weeds and waters, these walls are
  what
He haunted who of all men most sways my spirits to
  peace;

Of realty the rarest-veinèd unraveller; a not
Rivalled insight, be rival Italy or Greece;
Who fired France for Mary without spot.

Gerard Manley Hopkins, *Duns Scotus's Oxford*, 1879

I wish I could call Oxford the home of any language. It, or at least a majority of it, will have nothing to do with English or any other Teutonic tongue. . . . Their ignorance is not that negative darkness which consists in the mere absence of light. It is something positive, Egyptian darkness that may be felt. It is an aggressive contempt for all wise learning.

E.A. Freeman, Letter to J.S. Blackie, *c.* 1890

O stands for Oxford. Hail! salubrious seat
Of learning! Academical Retreat!
Home of my Middle Age! Malarial Spot
Which People call Medeeval (though it's not).
The marshes in the neighbourhood can vie
With Cambridge, but the town itself is dry,
And serves to make a kind of Fold or Pen
Wherein to herd a lot of Learned Men.
Were I to write but half of what they know,
It would exhaust the space reserved for 'O';
And, as my book must not be over big,
I turn at once to 'P', which stands for Pig.

Moral

Be taught by this to speak with moderation
Of places where, with decent application,
One gets a good, sound, middle-class education.

Hilaire Belloc, *A Moral Alphabet*, 1899

Not that I had any special reason for hating school. Strange as it may seem to my reader, I was not unpopular there. I was a modest, good-humoured boy. It is Oxford that has made me insufferable.

Sir Max Beerbohm, 'Going Back to School', *More*, 1899

Very nice sort of place, Oxford, I should think, for people that like that sort of place.

George Bernard Shaw, *Man and Superman*, 1903

Oxford! of whom the poet said
  That one of your unwritten laws is
To back the weaker side, and wed
  Your gallant heart to wobbling causes.

Sir Owen Seaman, 'The Scholar Farmer', *In Cap and Bells*, 1905

The clever men at Oxford
Know all that there is to be knowed,
But they none of them know one half as much
As intelligent Mr Toad.

Kenneth Grahame, *The Wind in the Willows*, 1908

*Yes certainly, it is this mild, miasmal air, not less than the grey beauty and gravity of the buildings, that has helped Oxford to produce, and foster eternally, her peculiar race of artist-scholars, scholar-artists. . . . Oxford, that lotus-land, saps the will-power, the power of action. But, in doing so, it clarifies the mind, makes larger the vision, gives, above all, that playful and caressing suavity of manner which comes of a conviction that nothing matters, except ideas, and that not even ideas are worth dying for, inasmuch as the ghosts of them slain seem worthy of yet more piously elaborate homage than can be given to them in their heyday. If the Colleges could be transferred to the dry and bracing top of some hill, doubtless they would be more evidently useful to the nation. But let us be glad there is no engineer or enchanter to compass that task. *Egomet*, I would liefer have the rest of England subside into the sea than have Oxford set on a salubrious level. For there is nothing in England to be matched with what lurks in the vapours of these meadows, and in the shadows of these spires – that mysterious, inenubilable spirit, spirit of Oxford. Oxford! The very sight of the word printed, or sound of it spoken, is fraught for me with most actual magic.

Sir Max Beerbohn, *Zuleika Dobson*, 1911

Noon strikes on England, noon on Oxford town,
Beauty she was statue cold – there's blood upon
her gown;
Noon of my dreams, O noon!
Proud and godly kings had built her long ago,
With her towers and tombs and statues all arow,
With her fair and floral hair and the love that lingers
there,
And the streets where the great men go.

James Elroy Flecker, *The Dying Patriot*, before 1915

Oxford is a noble university. It has a great past. It is at present the greatest university in the world: and it is quite possible that it has a great future. Oxford trains scholars of the real type better than any other place in the world. Its methods are antiquated. It despises science. Its lectures are rotten. It has professors who never teach and students who never learn. It has no order, no arrangement, no system. Its curriculum is unintelligible. It has no president. It has no state legislature to tell it how to teach, and yet – it gets there. Whether we like it or not, Oxford gives something to its students, a life and a mode of thought, which in America as yet we can emulate but not equal. . . .

These singular results achieved at Oxford are all the more surprising when one considers the distressing conditions under which the students work. The lack of an adequate building fund compels them to go on working in the same old buildings which they have had for centuries. The buildings at Brasenose College have not been renewed since the year 1525. In New College and Magdalen the students are still housed in the old buildings erected in the sixteenth century. At Christ Church I was shown a kitchen which had been built at the expense of Cardinal Wolsey in 1527. Incredible though it may seem, they have no other place to cook in than this and are compelled to use it today. . . .

Stephen Leacock, *My Discovery of England*, 1922

A painted lady, from whom Labour has nothing to expect.

James Ramsay Macdonald, quoted in *Anatomy of Oxford*, by C. Day Lewis and Charles Fenby, 1938

Oxford where they make the best shirts.

James Joyce, Letter to Valéry Larbaud, 30 July 1929

I had the idea that I must go to Oxford when I came back from India. . . . However it appeared that this was impossible. I must pass examinations not only in Latin, but in Greek. I could not contemplate toiling at Greek irregular verbs after having commanded British regular troops; so after much pondering I had to my keen regret to put the plan aside.

Sir Winston Churchill, *My Early Life*, 1930

*When the High Lama asked him whether Shangri-la was not unique in his experience, and if the Western world could offer anything in the least like it, he answered with a smile: 'Well, yes – to be quite frank, it reminds me very slightly of Oxford.'

James Hilton, *Lost Horizon*, 1933

Can one have nostalgia for a place one has never been to or at? My rare visits to Oxford prove that one can.

James Agate, *Ego 3*, 28 November 1936

From a purely tourist standpoint, Oxford is overpowering, being so replete with architecture and history and anecdote that the visitor's mind feels dribbling and helpless, as with an over-large mouthful of nougat.

Margaret Halsey, *With Malice Towards Some*, 1938

Oxford . . . has always produced the finest second-class brains in the world.

Leo Pavia, Letter to James Agate, quoted in Agate, *Ego 5*, 27 November 1940

London is heaven and Oxford seventh heaven.

Sir Isaiah Berlin, Letter to Freya Stark, 1944, quoted in Freya Stark, *Dust in the Lion's Paw*, 1961

There are few greater temptations on earth than to stay permanently at Oxford in meditation, and to read all the books in the Bodleian.

Hilaire Belloc, Interview with Cyril Clemens, in the *Mark Twain Journal*, quoted in Robert Speaight, *Life of Belloc*, 1957

Obsolete as books in leather bindings
Buildings in stone like talkative ghosts continue
Their well-worn anecdotes
As here in Oxford shadow the dark-weathered
Astrakhan rustication of the arches
Puts a small world in quotes:

While high in Oxford sunlight playfully crocheted
Pinnacles, ripe as corn on the cob, look over
To downs where once without either wheel or hod
Ant-like, their muscles cracking under the sarsen,
Shins white with chalk and eyes dark with necessity,
The Beaker people pulled their weight of God.

Louis MacNeice, *Relics*, *c.* 1946

In Oxford you may see it all – century by century, or face by face. She is an England in miniature: an essence of England, drawn from the wood.

James Morris, *Oxford*, 1965

There is scarcely a human activity that she has not enriched, from the art of nonsense to the ruling of the world.

Ibid.

Oxford city is sheer hell. Compared with N.Y., it's five times as crowded and the noise of the traffic is six times louder. Ironically enough, I had to leave New York and come to Oxford in order to get robbed.

W.H. Auden, Letter to Michael Newman, 1972

A sort of mist of homosexuality does hang over Oxford like the mist of the Thames Valley.

Charles Ritchie, *Appetite for Life, The Education of a Young Diarist, 1924–7*, 1978

There is an air of insubstantiality about it all. This is odd since the physical fact of the place is clearly the most important: the bridges, the libraries, the gardens and the quads are, as it were, the doughnut round the hole. But the old no longer seems old; it seems fake, or as flimsy as a sepia print. There is a curious tinniness about the 16th century colleges, and the 13th century walls – if you tapped them, they would ring. . . . Oxford is insubstantial because it lives off myths, it is a clutter of broken images.

Peter Ackroyd, *Spectator*, 10 November 1979

Oxford is a city where too many bells are always ringing in the rain.

Elmer Davies, quoted James Morris, *Oxford*, 1965

Magdalen Hall
There once was at Magdalen Hall
A man who knew nothing at all
He took his degree
At seventy-three
Which is youngish – for Magdalen Hall.

Anon.

Oxford Canal
When you have wearied of the valiant spires of this County Town,
Of its wide white streets and glistening museums, and black monastic walls,
Of its red motors and lumbering trams, and self-sufficient people,
I will take you walking with me to a place you have not seen –
Half town and half country – the land of the Canal.
It is dearer to me than the antique town: I love it more than the rounded hills:
Straightest and sublimest of rivers is the long Canal.
I have observed great storms and trembled: I have wept for fear of the dark.
But nothing makes me so afraid as the clear water of this idle canal on a summer's noon.
Do you see the great telephone poles down in the water, how every wire is distinct?
If a body fell into the canal it would rest entangled in those wires for ever, beween earth and air
For the water is as deep as the stars are high. . . .

James Elroy Flecker, *Oxford Canal*, before 1915

Trinity College
I must prefer to laugh at the tale of the absent-minded and undejected president of Trinity College, Oxford, who, when asked what the four statues on top of church tower represented, said, 'The Holy Trinity.' 'But there are four,' the GI objected. 'Of course,' the president explained. 'Three Persons and one God.'

Oliver St John Gogarty, *It isn't this time of year at all*, 1954

Oxted

Oxted is an exceptionally banal suburb of London.

Ford Madox Ford, *Return to Yesterday*, 1932

The Peak District

and Buxton
Though in the utmost Peake,
A while we doe remaine,
Amongst the mountaines bleake,
Expos'd to sleet and raine,
No sport our houres shall breake,
To exercise our vaine.

What though bright Phoebus beames,
  Refresh the southerne ground
And though the princely Thames
  With beauteous nymphs abound,
And by old Camber's streames
  Be many wonders found;

Yet many rivers cleare
  Here glide in silver swathes,
And what of all most deare,
  Buckston's delicious bathes,
Strong ale and noble cheare,
  T'asswage breeme winters scathes.

Those grim and horrid caves,
  Whose lookes affright the day,
Wherein nice nature saves,
  What she would not bewray,
Our better leasure craves,
  And doth invite our lay. . . .

Michael Drayton, *An Ode Written in the Peake*, 1606

There is a cave or hole within the ground, called, saving your reverence, *The Devils Arse*, that gapeth with a wide mouth, and hath in it many turnings and retyring roomes: wherein for sooth, *Gervase of Tilbury*, whether for want of knowing the truth, or upon a delight hee had in fabling, hath written that a Shepheard saw a verie wide and large Country with riverets and brookes running here and there through it, and huge pooles of dead and standing waters.

William Camden, *Britain*, 1610
(Philemon Holland's translation)

Cock-Lovell would needes have the *Divell* his guest
  And bade him into the Peake to dinner,
Where never the ffeind had such a feast
  Provided him yet at the charge of a sinner. . . .
All which devourd, he then, for a Close,
  Did for a full draught of Darby Call,
He heav'd the huge vessell up to his nose,
  And lefte not till he had druncke up all.
Then from the Table he gave a start
  Where banquet and wine were nothing scarce
All wch he blewe away with a fart,
  From when it was calld the *Devills arse*.
And there he made such a breach with the wind,
  The hole too standing open the while,
That the scent of the vapour, before, and behinde,
  Hath fouly perfumed most part of the Isle.
And this was Tobacco, the learned suppose:
  Which since, in Countrey, Court, and Towne,
In the Devils Glister-pipe smoakes at the nose
  Of Polcat, and Madam, of Gallant, and clown.

Ben Jonson, *The Gypsies Metamorphos'd, a Masque*, 1621

The peak of Derby being extraordinarily noted, I could not in my travels omit to visit it, especially upon the account of the dreadful cave, called the *Devil's Arse*, somewhat resembling that of Sybil's in Cuma, which I have mentioned before. It goes into a very deep descent; and out of it, at several times, issues a hollow whistling wind; and in it is heard, in still weather, a singing, or rather howling tone, which the vulgar, especially in Popish times, have taken for the noise of souls tormented, and fabled this an inlet into hell; when, by all the observations I could make, upon strict inquiry, it proceeded from no other than some springs of water that gushed out of the sides of the rock in the deep recess, and passed away by currents, and conveyances under ground to the neighbouring rivers, though Gervasius tells us a fabulous story, that it is an inlet into Fairy Land.

William Lithgow, *Rare Adventures and Painfull Peregrinations, 1614/32*

A countrey beyond comparison uglier than any other I have seen in England, black, tedious, barren, & not mountainous enough to please one with its horrors.

Thomas Gray, Letter to Thomas Wharton,
4 December 1762

Penryn

Penryn, whose ill-built and narrow streets seemed to have been contrived to make as many acute angles in the road, and take the traveller up and down as many steep declivities as possible in a given distance.

Robert Southey, *Letters from England, by Don Manuel Alvarez Espriella*, 1807

Penshurst

Thou art not, *Penshurst*, built to envious show,
  Of touch, or marble; nor canst boast a row
Of polish'd pillars, or a roofe of gold:
  Thou hast no lantherne whereof tales are told;
Or stayre, or courts; but stand'st an ancient pile,
  And these grudg'd at, art reverenced the while.
Thou joy'st in better markes, of soyle, of ayre,
  Of wood, of water; therein thou art faire. . . .
Now, *Penshurst*, they that will proportion thee
  With other edifices, when they see
Those proud, ambitious heaps, and nothing else,
  May say, their lords have built, but thy lord dwells.

Ben Jonson, 'To Penshurst', from *The Forrest*, before 1616

Peterborough

On the steeple we viewed the fenns of *Lincolnshire*, now much inclosd, & drained with infinite expense, and by many sluces, cutts, mounds, & ingenious Mills & like inventions: at which the Citty & Country about it consisting of a poore and very lazy sort of people, were much displeas'd.

John Evelyn, *Diary*, 30 August 1654

Petworth

The park is very fine, and consists of a parcel of those hills and dells which Nature formed here when she was in one of her most sportive modes. I have never seen the earth flung about in such a wild way as round about Hind-head and Blackdown; and this park forms a part of this ground.

William Cobbett, *Rural Rides*, 1 August 1823

The very flies at Petworth seem to know there is room for their existence, that the windows are theirs.

Benjamin Robert Haydon, *Diary*, 15 November 1826

Plymouth

Wee are now againe at Plymouth; quasi ply-mouth for wee do nothing but eate and scarce that: I think when wee came in the burghers tooke us for the spanish fleet for they have either hid or convayed all there mony. Never was extreame beggery so extreamely brave except when a company of mummers had lost theire box. I do not think that 77 Kelleys could distil 10 l. out of all the towne. He that hath supt and hath 2 or 3s. is a king; for none hath a crowne fayth; lands, jerkins, knighthoods, are reprobate pawnes and but for the much gay cloathes (which yet are much melted) I should thinke wee were in Utopia; all are so utterly coyneles.

John Donne, Letter, August 1597

A Plymouth Cloak – That is, a cane, or a staff, whereof this the occasion. Many a man of good extraction, coming home from far voyages, may chance to land here, and being out of sorts, is unable, for the present time and place, to recruit himself with clothes. Here (if not friendly provided) they make the next wood their draper's shop, where a staff cut out serves them for a covering.

Thomas Fuller, *History of the Worthies of England*, 1662

. . . the houses all built of this marble and the slatt at the top lookes like lead and glisters in the sun; there are noe great houses in the town; the streetes are good and clean, there is a great many tho' some are but narrow; they are mostly inhabitted with seamen and those which have affaires on the sea, for here up to the town there is a depth of water for shipps of the first rate to ride; its great sea and dangerous, by reason of the severall poynts of land between which the sea runs up a great way, and there are severall little islands alsoe, all which beares the severall tydes hard one against the other.

Celia Fiennes, *Journeys*, 1698

The harbour, full of three-deckers, presents a glorious sight; which an Englishman cannot look at without feeling that inward glorying and exultation of mind, which Longinus describes as the effect of the sublime. . . .

Every thing in this district savours of the sea. The inhabitants are a sort of amphibious race. The very coachman partook of the marine nature; and the slang peculiar to his calling was tempered with sea-phrases. The coach was to be *under-sail* at such an hour, and it was promoted from the neuter to the feminine gender. . . .

Henry Matthews, *The Diary of an Invalid*, 1820

Twice I have been at Plymouth, and twice I have been made feverish by the oppressiveness of its air, and I have heard people say the same thing; It enjoys one of the worst sanitary reputations of any place in England.

Matthew Arnold, Letter to his mother, 14 April 1862

If the world of romance be divided into provinces, each having its capital, Plymouth is certainly the capital of that region in the romantic world of England which concerns the sea.

Maurice Baring, *Round the World in Any Number of Days*, 1913

I reach the marble-streeted town,
Whose 'Sound' outbreathes its air
Of sharp sea-salts;
I see the movement up and down
As when she was there.
Ships of all countries come and go,
The bandsmen boom in the sun
A throbbing waltz;
The schoolgirls laugh along the Hoe
As when she was one.
I move away as the music rolls:
The place seems not to mind
That she – of old
The brightest of its native souls –
Left it behind!
Over this green aforedays she
On light treads went and came,
Yea, times untold;
Yet none here knows her history –
Has heard her name.

Thomas Hardy, *The Marble-Streeted Town*, 1914

Pontefract

Rivers:
O Pomfret, Pomfret! O thou bloody Prison!
Fatall and ominous to Noble Peeres:

William Shakespeare, *King Richard the Third*, *c.* 1592–3

Thence to Pomfret, as long since is
Fatall to our English Princes:
For the choicest Licorice crowned
And for sundry acts renowned;
A house in Pomret is not surer
Than the poor thorugh sloth securer.

Richard Brathwaite, *Barnabees Journall*, 1638

Pomffret . . . looks very finely in the approach; its built on a hill all of stone, its a very neate building and the streets well pitch'd and broad, the houses well built and looks more stately than any in York, only its not the tenth part so bigg, its a neate little town as I have seen. . . .

Provisions are very easy here, we had 2 or 3 pound of Codffish for a small matter and it was a large dish; the town is full of great Gardens walled in all round, on the outside of the town on the edge of the hill so the Gardens runns down a great way, you descend into them by severall stepps; its a fruitfull place fine flowers and trees with all sorts of fruite, but that which is mostly intended is the increasing of Liquorish, which the Gardens are all filled with, and any body that has but a little ground improves it for the produce of Liquorish, of which there is vast quantetyes, and it returns severall 100 pounds yearly to the towns.

Celia Fiennes, *Journeys*, 1697

Strange is it, proud Pontefract's borough should sully
Its fame by returning to parliament Gully
The etymological cause I suppose is
His breaking the bridges of so many noses.

Horace Smith, Epigram, *c.* 1832 –
The prize fighter John Gully was Pontefract's MP from 1832–7, when it was a 'Pocket Borough'

Porlock

Porlock! thy verdant vale so fair to sight,
Thy lofty hills which fern and furze imbrown,
The waters that roll musically down
Thy woody glens, the traveller with delight
Recalls to memory, and the channel gray
Circling its surges in thy level bay.
Porlock! I shall forget thee not,
Here by the unwelcome summer rain confined;
But often shall hereafter call to mind
How here, a patient prisoner, 't was my lot
To wear the lonely, lingering close of day,
Making my sonnet by the ale-house fire,
Whilst Idleness and Solitude inspire
Dull rhymes to pass the duller hours away.

Robert Southey, *Porlock*, *Sonnet XVI*, 9 August 1799

Portsmouth

At the very gullet, or mouth where the sea entreth in, our fore-fathers built a towne, and thereupon named it *Portsmouth*, that is, the mouth of the haven. A place alwaies in time of warre well frequented, otherwise little resort there is to it: as being more favourable and better affected to *Mars* and *Neptune*, than to *Mercurie*, that is to warre rather than to Traffique.

William Camden, *Britain*, 1610
(Philemon Holland's translation)

and Chatham
There is also this note to be put upon the two great arsenals of England, Portsmouth and Chatham; Namely, That they thrive by a war, as the war respects their situation (viz.) That when a war with France happens, or with Spain, then Portsmouth grows rich, and when a war with Holland, or any of the powers of the north, then Chatham and Woolwich, and Deptford are in request; but of this I shall speak again, when I come to speak of the like antithesis between Plymouth and the Humber, or Portsmouth and the Firth of Edinburgh.

Daniel Defoe, *A Tour through the Whole Island of Great Britain*, 1724–7

How many villages has that scene of all that is wicked and odious, Portsmouth, Gosport and Portsea; how many villages has that hellish assemblage beggared!

William Cobbett, *Rural Rides*, 19–23 November 1822

I was born at Portsmouth, an English Seaport town principally remarkable for mud, Jews, and Sailors. . . .

Charles Dickens, Letter to J.H. Kuenzel, July 1838

It was probably a mistake to stop at Portsmouth. . . . I was distressed to perceive that a famous seaport could be at once untidy and prosaic. Portsmouth is dirty, but it is also dull. It may be roughly divided into the dock-yard and the public-houses. . . . The dockyard eats up the town, as it were, and there is nothing left over but the gin-shops, which the town drinks up.

Henry James, 'English Vignettes', 1879, in *Portraits of Places*, 1883

Preston

Thus three nights was I staid and lodg'd in *Preston*,
And saw nothing ridiculous to jest on.

John Taylor, *Taylor's Pennilesse Pilgrimage*, in *All the Works of John Taylor*, 1630

Pudsey

When e'er a chap is short o' wit
An hezzn't much he cud say
He quists his nose, an girns a bit
An tries a fling at Pudsey

Noa daht ears summat grand e' this
An people cannot bud say
At all these sneers are weel desarv'd
If they are true o' Pudsey.

Anon., *Pudsey's Answer to Halifax*, nineteenth century

Quantocks

The little Toe of Quantock is better than the head and shoulders of Surry & Middlesex.

S.T. Coleridge, Letter to Thomas Poole, 16 June 1798

Ramsgate

Ramsgate, a small port, the inhabitants are mighty fond of having us call it Roman's-Gate; pretending that the Romans under Julius Caesar made their first attempt to land here, when he was driven back by a storm; but soon return'd, and coming on shore, with a good body of troops that beat back the Britains, and fortify'd his camp, just at the entrance of the creek, where the town now stands; all of which may be true for aught any one knows, but is not to be prov'd; either by them or any one else; and is of so little concern to us, that it matters nothing whether here or at Deal. . . .

Daniel Defoe, *A Tour through the Whole Island of Great Britain*, 1724–7

All our weather-sages assure us that the Weather has taken a turn, and that we shall have a Spell of the *right Ramsgate* – dry, bracing, cheerful.

S.T. Coleridge, Letter to James Gillman, 13 November 1825

Few of the principal bathing-places have anything worth looking at in the neighbourhood, and Ramsgate has less than most. . . . The sea is a grand sight, but it becomes tiresome and melancholy – a great monotonous idea; at least one thinks so when not happy. I was destined to see it grander, and dislike it more.

Leigh Hunt, *Autobiography*, 1850

Margate . . . I believe, is the *nom-de-plume* of Ramsgate.

Oscar Wilde, Letter to Leonard Smithers, 7 March 1898

When he felt his end was coming, Mostyn [Piggott] said to some brother Savages: 'I'm going down to Ramsgate to die.' And a flash of the old Mostyn broke out when he added: 'And a damned good place to die in!'

James Agate, *Ego*, 1935

Reculver

Reculver is poetical in the highest degree.

Benjamin Robert Haydon, *Diary*, 12 September 1832

Richmond

Richmond, ev'n now
Thy living landscape spreads beneath my feet,
Calm as the sleep of infancy, – the song
Of Nature's vocalists, the blossom'd shrubs,
The velvet verdure, and the overshadowing trees,
The cattle wading in the clear smooth stream,
And mirrored on its surface, its deep glow
Of sunset, the white smoke, and yonder church,
Half hid by the green foliage of the grove,
These are thy charms, fair Richmond, and through these,
The river wafting many a graceful bark,
Glides swiftly onwards like a lovely dream,
Making the scene a Paradise.

James Thomson, *Lines Written on Richmond Park*, – Although ascribed to Thomson on a board displayed in Richmond Park in the nineteenth century, these lines are probably by John Heneage Jesse, who died in 1874

Richmond Hill

Doctor Burney took an Italian Singing Girl lately come over to shew her Richmond Hill; She had lived two Years in Paris, and resolved not to talk like an Italian; – *Oh what a great Knock in the Eye*! exclaims She innocently.

Hester Lynch Thrale/Piozzi, *Thraliana*, September 1777

The three summits of human happiness are first the consciousness of having done your duty & the pious purity that comes over your soul. The next, success in great schemes, & the third is a lovely girl who loves you in the dining room of the Star & Garter at Richmond, sitting after dinner on your knee, with her heavenly bosom palpitating against your own, her arm round your neck playing with your hair, enough of consciousness to keep her cheeks blushing, her eyes lustrous, & her lip shining, and her form twining & bending, while you are sufficiently heated to be passionately alive to the ecstasy without having lost your senses from its excess – claret on the table and the delicious scene of Nature in Richmond Park beneath your open window, moaty, sunny, out of which rise the wandering voice of the cuckoo, moaning its distant echo, and the singing of the birds in the Groves, while the sun, who throws a silent splendour over all, sinks into the lower vaults & the whole sky is beginning to assume the tinged lustre of an afternoon.

Benjamin Robert Haydon, *Diary*, 2 June 1816

Sunday. Spent it at Richmond with dearest Mary. We were rather melancholy from the beauty of the scenery.

Benjamin Robert Haydon, *Diary*, 1 September 1822

With foreigners it passes pretty generally for a sample (the only one they see) of the rural villages of England; and yet it is no more like the real untrimmed genuine country than a garden is like a field. I do not say this in disparagement. Richmond is Nature in a Court dress, but still Nature – ay, and very lovely Nature too.

The principal charm of this smiling landscape is the river, the beautiful river, for the hill seems to me overrated. That celebrated prospect is, to my eye, too woody, too leafy, too green. There is a monotony of vegetation, a heaviness. The view was finer as I first saw it in February, when the bare branches admitted frequent glimpses of houses and villages.

But the river, the beautiful river, there is no overrating that. Brimming to its very banks of meadow, or of garden, clean, pure, and calm as the bright summer day, which is reflected in clearer brightness from its bosom; no praise can be too enthusiastic for that glorious stream. How gracefully it glides through the graceful bridge! Certainly the Thames is the pleasantest highway in his Majesty's dominions.

Mary Russell Mitford, *A Visit to Richmond*, 1832

Richmond on fine Saturdays is like a lime tree in full flower – suppose one were an insect sitting on the flower. All the others swarm & buzz, and burble. Being residents we don't, of course.

Virginia Woolf, *Diary*, 15 May 1920

Richmond Hill, the view from

Here let us sweep
The boundless landscape: now the raptured eye,
Exulting, swift to huge Augusta send,
Now to the sister hills that skirt her plain,
To lofty Harrow now, and now to where
Majestic Windsor lifts his princely brow,
In lovely contrast to this glorious view
Calmly magnificent, then will we turn
To where the silver Thames first rural grows. . . .
Enchanting vale! beyond whate'er the Muse
Has of Achaia or Hesperia sung!
O vale of bliss! o softly-swelling hills!
On which the *Power of Cultivation* lies
And joys to see the wonders of his toil.
Heavens! what a goodly prospect spreads around,
Of hills, and dales, and woods, and lawns, and spires,
And glittering towns, and gilded streams, till all
The stretching landscape into smoke decays!
Happy Britannia! where, the Queen of Arts,
Inspiring vigour, Liberty abroad
Walks, unconfined, even to thy farthest cots,
And scatters plenty with unsparing hand.

James Thomson, *The Seasons – Summer*, 1727

When walking with me in Richmond Park, he (Borrow) would frequently stop, look round, and murmur, 'Beautiful England!' and then begin to declare eloquently that there was not a country in the world to be compared with it.

Theodore Watts-Dunton, Introduction to George Borrow, *Wild Wales*, edn of 1906

Richmond Park is one of the few remaining parts of the old world of romance. The hills rise up and look on the great oaks writhing and twisting – the beeches are tremendous steel shafts – there are broad spaces and great fierce groves, where the pale deer flee, where, I vow, there are dryads and fauns, where you might find a Viking asleep, where there are outlaws and knights in armour and ladies who exist solely to be succoured. The ponds – the ponds are marvels. Do you know Maurice Hewlett's Forest Lovers? It is not nearly so good as Richmond Park.

D.H. Lawrence, Letter to Blanche Jennings, 6 March 1909

Rivers

Our flouds-queen Thames, for ships and swans is
crowned,
And stately Severne for her shoare is praysed,
The crystal Trent, for foords and fish renowned,
And Avons fame, to Albions cliffes is raysed,
Carlegion Chester vaunts her holy Dee,
Yorke many wonders of her Owse can tell,
The Peake her Dove, whose bankes so fertile bee,
And Kent will say, her Medway doth excell,
Cotswold commends her Isis to the Thame,
Our Northerne borders boast of Tweeds faire floud,
Our Westerne parts extoll their Wilis fame,
And the old Lea brags of the Danish bloud;
Arden's sweet Ankor, let thy glory bee,
That faire Idea onely lives by thee.

Michael Drayton, *Idea*, 1594

In Britaine here we find, our Severne, and our Tweed,
The tripartited ile doth generally divide,
To England, Scotland, Wales, as each doth keep her
side.
Trent cuts the land in two, so equally as tho
Nature it pointed-out, to our great Brute to show
How to his mightie sonnes the iland he might share.

Michael Drayton, *Poly-Olbion*, 'The Fifteenth Song', 1612

Rivers arise; whether thou be the Son,
Of utmost *Tweed*, or *Oose*, or gulphie *Dun*,
Or *Trent*, who like some earth-born Giant spreads
His thirty Armes along the indented Meads,
Or sullen *Mole* that runneth underneath,
Or *Severn* swift, guilty of Maidens death,
Or rockie *Avon*, or of Sedgie *Lee*,
Or Coaly *Tine*, or antient hallowed *Dee*
Or *Humber* loud that keeps the *Scythians* Name,
Or *Medway* smooth, or Royal Towred *Thame*.

John Milton, *At a Vacation Exercise*, 1627

Rochester

The town is large includeing the suburbs and all, for there is a large place before you pass the river, which washes quite round that side of the town to the Dock yards, that a mile from it, where are two large yards for building ships; I saw severall large shipps building others refitting; there was in one place a sort of arches like a bridge of brick-work, they told me the use of it was to let in the water there and so they put their masts in to season; besides this dock here are severall streetes of houses on this hill which is pretty high and just against Rochester, and on the hill you have the best prospect of the town and see severall good Churches in it, and the Castle which is a pretty little thing, just by the Medway, which runs along by it and so at foote of this hill in a round, and so onward to sea; there were severall shipps at anchor along the River; all behind the town is another hill which is covered with fine woods that looks very fine.

Celia Fiennes, *Journeys*, 1697

*We do not find from a careful perusal of Mr Pickwick's notes on the four towns, Stroud, Rochester, Chatham, and Brompton, that his impressions of their appearance differ in any material point from those of other travellers who have gone over the same ground. His general description is easily abridged.

'The principal production of these towns,' says Mr Pickwick, 'appear to be soldiers, sailors, Jews, chalk, shrimps, officers, and dockyard men. The commodities chiefly exposed for sale in the public streets are marine stores, hard-bake, apples, flat-fish, and oysters. The streets present a lively and animated appearance, occasioned chiefly by the conviviality of the military. It is truly delightful to a philanthropic mind, to see these gallant men staggering along under the influence of an overflow, both of animal and ardent spirits; more especially when we remember that the following them about, and jesting with them, affords a cheap and innocent amusement for the boy population. . . .

The consumption of tobacco in these towns (continues Mr Pickwick) must be very great: and the smell which pervades the streets must be exceedingly delicious to those who are extremely fond of smoking. A superficial traveller might object to the dirt which is their leading characteristic; but to those who view it as an indication of traffic and commercial prosperity it must be truly gratifying.

Charles Dickens, *The Posthumous Papers of the Pickwick Club*, 1837

Rochester Cathedral and Castle

*'Ah! fine place,' said the stranger, 'glorious pile – frowning walls – tottering arches – dark nooks – crumbling staircases – Old Cathedral too – earthy smell – pilgrims' feet worn away the old steps – little Saxon doors – confessionals like money-takers' boxes at theatres – queer customers those monks – Popes, and Lord Treasurers, and all sorts of old fellows, with great red faces, and broken noses, turning up every day – buff jerkins too – match-locks – Sarcophagus – fine place – old legends too – strange stories: capital.'

Charles Dickens, *The Posthumous Papers of the Pickwick Club*, 1837

Romney Marsh

In the Middle Ages they used to say: 'These be the four quarters of the world: Europe, Asia, Africa, and the Romney Marsh.' But that was before Columbus committed his indiscretion.

Ford Madox Ford, *Return to Yesterday*, 1932

River Rotha

The old rude church, with bare bald tower is here;
  Beneath its shadow high-born Rotha flows;
Rotha remembering well who slumbers near
  And with cool murmur lulling his repose.
Rotha, remembering well who slumbers near
  His hills, his lakes, his streams are with him yet.
Surely the heart that read her own heart clear
  Nature forgets not soon: 'tis we forget.

Sir William Watson, 'Wordsworth's Grave', in *Poems*, 1892

Runcorn

When it's raspberry time in Runcorn
In Runcorn, in Runcorn
The air is like a draught of wine
The undertaker cleans his sign
The Hull express goes off the line
When it's raspberry time in Runcorn.

Noel Coward, *Collected Sketches and Lyrics, Fête Galante*, 1923

Runnymede

Thou, who the verdant plain doth traverse here,

Whilst Thames among his willows from thy view
Retires. . . .
This is the place
Where England's ancient barons, clad in arms,
And stern with conquest, from the tyrant king
(Then rendered tame) did challenge and secure
The charter of thy freedom.

Mark Akenside, *Inscription for a Column at Runnymede – Poems*, 1772 – before 1770

(MAGNA CARTA, 15 JUNE 1215)
At Runnymede, at Runnymede,
What say the reeds at Runnymede?
The lissom reeds that give and take,
That bend so far, but never break.
They keep the sleepy Thames awake
With tales of John at Runnymede.
At Runnymede, at Runnymede,
Oh, hear the reeds at Runnymede: –
'You mustn't sell, delay, deny,
A freeman's right or liberty.
It wakes the stubborn Englishry,
We saw 'em roused at Runnymede!'
And still when Mob or Monarch lays
Too rude a hand on English ways,
The whisper wakes, the shudder plays,
Across the reeds at Runnymede.
And Thames, that knows the moods of kings,
And crowds and priests and suchlike things,
Rolls deep and dreadful as he brings
Their warning down from Runnymede!

Rudyard Kipling, *The Reeds of Runnymede*, 1911

Rutland

A Countrie nothing inferiour to Leicester-shire either if fruitfull qualitie of soile, or pleasantnesse, but in quantitie onelie, as being the least Countie of all England. For lying in forme almost round like a circle, it is in compasse so farre about, as a light horseman will ride in one day.

William Camden, *Britain*, 1610
(Philemon Holland's translation)

Love not thy selfe the lesse, although the least thou art,
What thou in greatnesse wantst, wise Nature doth impart
In goodnesse of thy soyle; and more delicious mould,
Survaying all this Isle, the Sunne did nere behold.
Bring forth the *British* Vale, and be it ne'er so rare,
But *Catmus* with that Vale, for richnesse shall compare:
What Forrest-Nymph is found, how brave so ere she be,
But *Lyfield* shewes her selfe as brave a Nymph as shee?
What River ever rose from Banke, or swelling Hill,
Then *Rutlands* wandring *Wash*, a delicater Rill?
Small Shire that can produce to thy proportion good,
One vale of speciall name, one Forrest, and one Flood.
O *Catmus*, thou faire Vale, come on in Grasse and Corne,
That *Bever* ne'r be sayd thy sister-hood to scorne,
And let thy *Ocham* boast, to have no little grace,
That her the pleased Fates, did in thy bosom place,
And *Lyfield*, as thou art a Forrest, live so free,
That every Forrest-Nymph may praise the sports in thee.
And downe to *Wellands* course, O *Wash*, runne ever cleere,
To honour, and to be much honoured by this Shire.

Michael Drayton, *Poly-Olbion*, 1612–21

Rutlandshire . . . indeed . . . is but the pestle of a lark, which is better than a quarter of some bigger bird, having the most cleanly profit in it; no place, so fair for the *rider*, being more fruitful for the *abider* therein.

Thomas Fuller, *History of the Worthies of England*, 1662

Rydale

We were overtaken by two soldiers on our return – one of them being very drunk we wished them to pass us, but they had too much liquor in them to go very fast so we contrived to pass them – they were very merry and very civil. They fought the mountains with their sticks. 'Aye' says one, 'that will fall upon us. One might strike over that etc.'

Dorothy Wordsworth, *Journal*, 1 December 1801

Rye

This southern shore, twinkling and twittering with a semi-foreign light, a kind of familiar *wink* in the air. . . . It's really meridional. It would – Rye would – remind you of Granada – more or less.

Henry James, Letter to A.F. de Navarro, 13 November 1900

At little, huddled, neighbourly Rye, even a white December sea-fog is a cosy and convenient thing.

Henry James, Letter to W.E. Norris, 23 December 1900

It is very neat and old-maidish and quiet and comfortable, and exactly the sort of place Henry James ought to live in.

Logan Pearsall Smith, Letter to Alys Russell, 21 October 1913

and Winchelsea
An historic patina covers their buildings more deeply than any others, in England at least. Indeed, I know of

no place save for Paris, where memories seem so thick on every stone.

Ford Madox Ford, *Return to Yesterday*, 1932

St Ives

I remember looking at St Ives – from the height of the bus stop at the Malakoff and further up from Tregenna Steps – it was the perfect picture-postcard. A piece of land flung out like a small bent finger into the Atlantic; the C of the harbour; the waves coming in like horizons in reverse; a few fishing boats; gulls; the lighthouse in the bay; the island criss-crossed like a hot cross bun; and the pretty little sand beaches. But in the back streets, in condemned cottages with the water tap outside and soapy water stagnant in the gutter, they were living on national assistance. Damp funeral cards. 'Bed and Breakfast' signs. The retired middle class on the terraces who came here with their savings and bought their graves. And the careless people who come to places like St Ives anxious for the new holiday encounter because they need for their existence – to feed their pretence of being 'a painter', 'a writer', – a lot of strangers passing through. Then shot through the poverty, the squalor, the boredom (like those fantastic balloon shapes that the wind makes blowing through the spokes of a wheel which has passed through fish slime) were the lyrical absurdities of the summer. When the stenographers and the typists and the art students came down. 'The Yellow Peril', 'The Black Tulip', 'The White Goddess', 'Sin on Stilts'; that fitted. Where Gladys Jenkins, Jean Middleton, Sheila O'Connor, Thelma Elkin would not. And swimming at night in the nude in the harbour. 'The Black Tulip' marching through Fore Street, her white panties at the end of a broom-stick; the all-night parties in cottages on the moors; the homosexuals down from London; the rats squeezing at night down the drains; the tiny rooms with the walls damp, the light from the gas bracket. . . .

But from a height how could one see this or guess it?

Norman Levine, *Canada Made Me*, 1958

Salisbury

So we came to *Salisbury*, and view'd the most considerable parts of that Citty, the Merkat place, which together with most of the streetes are Watred by a quick current & pure streame, running through the middle of them, but are negligently kept, when with small charge they might be purged, & rendred infinitely agreable, & that one of the sweetest Townes in *Europe*; but as 'tis now, the common buildings are despicable, & the streetes dirty.

John Evelyn, *Diary*, 21 July 1654

The Cathedral

Faire *Sarum's* Church, beside the stately tower,
Hath many things in number aptly sorted,
Answering the yeere, the month, weeke, day & houre,
But above all (as I have heard reported,
And to the view doth probably appeare)
A piller for each houre in all the yeere.
Further, this Church of *Sarum* hath beene found.
To keepe in singing service so good forme,
That most Cathedrall Churches have beene bound,
Themselves *ad usum Sarum* to conforme:
I am no Cabalist to judge by number,
Yet that this Church is so with pillers fill'd
It seemes to me to be the lesser wonder,
That *Sarums* Church is every hower pill'd.
And sith the rest are bound to *Sarums* use,
What marvell if they taste of like abuse?

Sir John Harington, *A Salisbury Tale*, late sixteenth century

As many days as in one year there be,
So many windows in one church we see;
As many marble pillars there appear,
As there are hours throughout the fleeting year;
As many gates as moons one year do view;
Strange tale to tell, yet not more strange than true.

Quoted in Daniel Defoe, *A Tour through the Whole Island of Great Britain*, 1724–7

The Cathedral . . . has been scraped inside and garnished from end to end. In another hundred years it will perhaps tone down again to beauty, but at present the black pillar stems, newly polished, have the effect of so many tall stove pipes. It was infinitely finer under the old whitewash, but the deans will have their way.

Wilfred Scawen Blunt, Diary, 14 August 1896, *My Diaries*, 1919

Sun and clouds lit up the cathedral at Salisbury. I had felt its beauty before; with Logan, I suddenly realized the truth, which he gave to me as the opinion of Sir Kenneth Clark, that this was the most perfect building in Northern Europe

'I once told Roger Fry that,' said Logan, 'and he got very angry because, as you probably know, he *hates* English art and didn't like to allow that any English building was supreme. But when I asked him what buildings in Northern Europe he preferred, all he could do was get very angry, and blurt out "St Paul's". I felt that I'd scored off him. Don't you think I had?'

Robert Gathorne Hardy, *Recollections of Logan Pearsall Smith*, 1949 (of 1930)

Sandwich

This is a sad old town all timber building, you enter by a gate and you go out of it by a gate, but its run so to decay that except one or two good houses its just like to drop down the whole town.

Celia Fiennes, *Journeys*, 1697

Sandwich . . . is a rotten borough. Rottenness, putridity is excellent for land, but bad for boroughs. This place, . . . is as villainous a hole as one could wish to see.

William Cobbett, *Rural Rides*, 3 September 1823

A really antique feeling about this place. Streets such as Delf street. Most curious the moment you begin really to think about it inquisitively. Happily a few barges get there still, up the stream, and seem to live in fields.

Arnold Bennett, *Journal*, 10 October 1926

Savernake Forest (Wiltshire)

Savernake Forest is not a toy place.

Richard Jefferies, 'A Summer Day in Savernake Forest', in the *Globe*, 1876

Scarborough

Scarborough warning: a word and a blow, but the blow first!

Quoted in *Poetical Sketches of Scarborough*, 1813
(Local saying, referring originally to Thomas Stafford's taking the Castle when taking part in Wyatt's rebellion, 1553.)

About a month or so from London I came down, sir,
I took a dismal lodging in a little borough town, sir,
Where people cleanse their skins by wading and by drink, sir,
And so of all impurities this borough is the sink, sir. . . .

Within this little borough there are houses great and small, sir,
And one much larger than the rest, they call it the town hall, sir,
A dingy looking place it is, but much in estimation, sir,
For there each seven years are made the pillars of the nation, sir.

Besides it is the awful place where justice holds her court, sir,
And underneath are cellars there for sherry and for port, sir,
So Magistrates and bottles being thus together joined, sir,
They seem to keep the proverb up, that justice should be blind, sir.

Anon., *Johnny Gilpin*, no. 2, 1800

The sons of pleasure fly to more genial climes, and court the breezes of the south: and, except those who are allured by connections, and swayed by local considerations, Scarborough contains, among its visitors, more votaries of health than of dissipation.

Anon., *A Guide to all the Watering and Sea-bathing Places*, c. 1810

O Scarbo! queen of sea-side joys,
Which no domestic care alloys,
Far from the petty jangling war
Of housemaid and of housekeeper!
Throned on thy cliffs, how proudly thou
Survey'st the varied scene below:
In curve exact thy mansions bending,
And to the watery marge descending: . . .
Thy temple, castle, double mole
Port, spa, and circling round the whole,
Of beauty and of strength the zone,
The ocean's azure girdle thrown!
Thy pleasures ever charm the young,
The morning stroll – stroll all day long:
Joy, triumph, health, at once they give,
To see, to conquer, and to live;
And *vidi, vici, vixi*, plain
Records the bright and brief campaign. . . .
Nor hither 'Squires alone resort
With water to dilute their port,
Walk off the aches which riding gave
And tip the go-by to the grave –
That only *port* they still would pass,
As *Time's* their only hated *glass*:
For Scarbro' parsons quit their church,
For Scarbro' schoolmasters their birch;
And York and Lancaster agree
To sip their amicable tea.

John B. Papworth, Francis Wrangham and William Combe, *Poetical Sketches of Scarborough*, 1813

Scarsdale

Scardale . . .
Which like her mistris Peake, is naturally enclind
To thrust forth ragged cleeves, with which she scattered lyes,
As Busie Nature here could not her selfe suffice,
Of this oft-altring earth the sundry shapes to show,
That from my entrance here, doth rough and rougher grow,
Which of a lowly dale although the name it beare,
You by the rocks might think that it a mountaine were
From which it takes the name of Scardale, which exprest,
Is the hard vale of rocks, of Chesterfield possest. . . .

Michael Drayton, *Poly-Olbion*, 'The Sixe and Twentieth Song', 1622

Scilly Isles

The rocks of Scilly, of which, what is most famous, is

their infamy, or reproach; Namely, how many good ships are, almost *continually* dash'd in pieces there, and how many brave lives lost, in spite of the mariners best skill, or the light-houses and other sea-marks best notice.

Daniel Defoe, *A Tour through the Whole Island of Great Britain*, 1724–7

Seaham (Stockton-on-Tees)

Upon this dreary coast, we have nothing but county meetings and shipwrecks; and I have this day dined upon fish, which probably dined upon the crews of several colliers lost in the late gales.

Lord Byron, Letter to Thomas Moore, 2 February 1815

River Severn

On the gentle Severn's sedgy bank.

William Shakespeare, I Henry IV, *c.* 1597–8

Swift Severn's flood;
Who then, affrighted with their bloody looks,
Ran fearfully among the trembling reeds.

Ibid.

As Severne lately in her ebbes that sanke,
Vast and forsaken leaves th'uncovered sands,
Fetching full tides, luxurious, high, and ranke,
Seemes, in her pride t'invade the neighb'ring lands,
Breaking her limits, covering all her banks,
Threat'neth the proud hills with her wat'rie hands;
As though she meant her empyrie to have,
Where even but lately she beheld her grave.

Michael Drayton, *The Barons Warres*, 1603

and Wye

Blessed is the eye
That is betwixt Severn and Wye.

Some will justly question the truth hereof. True it is, the eyes of those inhabitants are entertained with a pleasant prospect; yet such as is equalled by other places. But it seems this is a prophetical promise of safety to such that live secured within those great rivers, as if privileged from martial impressions. But alas! civil war is a vagrant, and will trace all corners. . . .

Thomas Fuller, *History of the Worthies of England*, 1662

Shanklin (Isle of Wight)

A very pretty place it is were it not for the bad Weather. Our window looks over the house tops and Cliffs onto the Sea, so that when the Ships sail past the Cottage chimneys you may take them for Weathercocks. We have Hill and Dale forest and Mead and plenty of Lobsters.

John Keats, Letter to Fanny Keats, 6 July 1819

Sheffield

A towne of great name (like as other small townes adjoyning) for the Smithes therein (considering there bee many iron mines there about) fortified also with a strong and ancient Castle.

William Camden, *Britain*, 1610
(Philemon Holland's translation)

SHEFFIELD, smoke-involv'd; dim where she stands
Circled by lofty mountains, which condense
Her dark and spiral wreaths to drizzling rains,
Frequent and sullied; as the neighbouring hills
Ope their deep veins, and feed her cavern'd flames; . . .
No aerial forms
On Sheffield's arid moor, or Ketley's heath,
E'er wove the floral crowns, or smiling stretch'd
The shelly scepter; – there no Poet rov'd
To catch bright inspirations. . . .

Anna Seward, *Colebrook Dale*, *c.* 1784

Sheffield, . . . is one of the foulest towns in England, in the most charming situation.

Horace Walpole, Letter to George Montagu, 1 September 1760

All the way along from Leeds to Sheffield it is coal and iron, and iron and coal. It was dark before we reached Sheffield; so that we saw the iron furnaces in all the horrible splendour of their everlasting blaze. Nothing can be conceived more grand or more terrific than the yellow waves of fire that incessantly issue from the top of these furnaces, some of which are close by the wayside. Nature has placed the beds of iron and the beds of coal alongside of each other, and art has taught man to make one to operate upon the other, as to turn the iron-stone into liquid matter, which is drained off from the bottom of the furnace, and afterwards moulded into blocks and bars, and all sorts of things. . . . This Sheffield and the land all about it, is one bed of iron and coal. They call it black sheffield, and black enough it is; but from this one town and its environs go nine-tenths of the knives that are used in the whole world.

William Cobbett, *Rural Rides – Northern Tour*, 31 January 1830

It might have been Pluto's own metropolis, shrouded in sulphurous vapour.

Nathaniel Hawthorne, *Our Old Home*, 1863

Sheffield, I suppose, could justly claim to be called the ugliest town in the Old World: its inhabitants, who want it to be pre-eminent in everything, very likely do make that claim for it.

George Orwell, *The Road to Wigan Pier*, 1937

Sherwood Forest

The Forest *Shirewood* . . . in ancient times overshadowed all the Country over with greene leaved branches, and the boughes and armes of trees twisted one within another so implicated the woods together, that a man could scarcely goe alone in the beaten pathes: But now the trees grow not so thicke, yet hath it an infinite number of fallow deere, yea and Stagges with their stately branching heads feeding within it.

William Camden, *Britain*, 1610
(Philemon Holland's translation)

Shooter's Hill (eleven miles out of London on the old Dover road)

Mrs Ann and I rode under the man that hangs upon Shooters hill; and a filthy sight it was to see how his flesh is shrunk to his bones.

Samuel Pepys, *Diary*, 11 April 1661

This is esteemed as a noted robbing place.

Celia Fiennes, *Journeys*, 1697

Shrewsbury

The Towne three parts, stands in a valley loe,
Three gates there are, through which you needs must
  passe.
As to the height of Towne the people goe:
So Castle seemes, as twere a looking glasse,
To looke through all, and hold them all in awe,
Treangle wise, the gates and Towne doth drawe:
But Castle hill spyes out each streate so plaine,
As though an eye on them did still remaine.

In midst of Towne, fower Parrish Churches are
Full nere and close, together note that right:
The vewe farre of, is wondrous straunge and rare,
For they doe seeme a true love knot to sight:
They stand on hill, as Nature wrought a Seate
To place them fower, in stately beautie greate:
As men devout to buyld these works tooke care,
So in these daies these Temples famous are.

Thomas Churchyard, *The Worthines of Wales*, 1587

He that takes a wife at Shrewsbury must carry her to Staffordshire, else she'll drive him to Cumberland.

Quoted in Thomas Fuller, *Gnomologia*, 1732

Shropshire

The peculiar flavour of the scenery has something to do with the absence of evolution; it was better marked in Egypt: it was felt wherever time-sequences became interchangeable. One's instinct abhors time. As one lay on the slope of the Edge, looking sleepily through the summer haze towards Shrewsbury or Cader Idris or Caer Caradoc or Uriconium, nothing suggested sequence.

Henry Adams, *The Education of Henry Adams*, 1906

Sidmouth

Sidmouth – which place I pronounce to be an imposture.

Sydney Smith, Letter to Lady Grey, 25 April 1831

At Sidmouth we are no farther from the sea than the focus of Rogers's voice. Nothing intervenes between us and the coast of France. The noise of persons chattering French on the opposite coast is heard. Flat fish and mackerel have been known to leap into the drawing-room; and in the dreadful storm of 1824 the four Miss Somebodies were taken out in the lifeboat without petticoats by men who, in the hurry of the occasion, were without small clothes.

Sydney Smith, Letter to Thomas Moore,
11 August 1831

Sittingbourne

This is a very good town for the road and travellers as you shall meete with, the Church is all built with flints headed so curiously that it looks like a glass and shines with the suns reflection.

Celia Fiennes, *Journeys*, 1697

Skiddaw

and other hills
Skiddaw, Lauuellin, and Casticand,
Are the highest hils in all England.

Anon., quoted William Camden, *Britain*, 1610
(Philemon Holland's translation)

and Scafell

If Skiddaw hath a cap,
Scruffell wots well of that.

These are two neighbour hills, the one in this country, the other in Annandale in Scotland. If the former be capped with clouds and foggy mists, it will not be long before rain falls on the other. It is spoken of such who must expect to sympathise in their suffering, by reason of the vicinity of their habitation.

Thomas Fuller, *History of the Worthies of England*,
1662

Pelion and Ossa flourish side by side,
Together in immortal books enrolled:
His ancient dower Olympus hath not sold;
And that inspiring Hill, which 'did divide
Into two ample horns his forehead wide,'
Shines with poetic radiance as of old;
While not an English mountain we behold
By the celestial Muses glorified.
Yet round our sea-girt shore they rise in crowds:
What was the great Parnassus' self to Thee,
Mount Skiddaw? In his natural sovereignty
Our British Hill is nobler far; he shrouds
His double front among Atlantic clouds,
And pours forth streams more sweet than Castaly.

William Wordsworth, Sonnet, 1801 (pub. 1815)

I have now spent a week alone at this place, walking for the most part of the time in a place so wild and solitary and awful that I think you would have knelt in your devotions. It was among some old oaks in a crevice of the great mountain of Skiddaw, a cataract, leaping with fury from rock to rock by my side. Only two little girls did I ever see there, and they stopped at the sight of me, and made me such long and low reverences, with looks so full of awe, that I began to think myself the deity of the place.

Samuel Rogers, Letter to Thomas Moore, 21 August 1812 (from Keswick)

I trace continuously the tacit reference in my Cumberland built soul to moorish Skiddaw and far-sweeping Saddle-back as the proper types of majestic form.

John Ruskin, *Praeterita*, 1885–9

Slough

Come, friendly bombs, and fall on Slough
It isn't fit for humans now,
There isn't grass to graze a cow
Swarm over, Death!

Come, bombs, and blow to smithereens
Those air-conditioned, bright canteens,
Tinned fruit, tinned meat, tinned milk, tinned beans
Tinned minds, tinned breath.

Mess up the mess they call a town –
A house for ninety-seven down
And once a week a half-a-crown
For twenty years. . . .

Come, friendly bombs, and fall on Slough
To get it ready for the plough.
The cabbages are coming now:
The earth exhales.

John Betjeman, *Collected Poems*, 1958

I see you come from Slough. It's a horrible place. You can go back there.

Mr Justice Melford Stevenson, attributed, to a man acquitted of rape, quoted in the *Daily Telegraph*, 11 April 1979, in an article marking M.S.'s retirement from the Bench

Somerset

Some thinke it was so called, for that the aire there, is so mild and summer-like. . . . And verily, howsoever in summertime it is a right summerlike country, yet surely, in winter it may worthily be called, a winterish Region, so wet and weely, so miry and moorish it is, to the exceeding great trouble and encombrance of those that travell in it.

William Camden, *Britain*, 1610 (Philemon Holland's translation)

In most parts of Sommer-setshire it is very fruitfull for orchards, plenty of apples and peares, but they are not curious in the planting the best sort of fruite, which is a great pitty; being so soone produced, and such quantetyes, they are likewise as careless when they make cider, they press all sorts of apples together, else they might have as good sider as in any other parts. . . .

Celia Fiennes, *Journeys*, *c.* 1685–96

From hence we proceeded to Taunton through a tract of country which for its fertility and beauty is the boast of the island. 'Ah, sir,' said a countryman who was on the coach beside us and heard us admiring it, 'we have a saying about these western parts,

Cornwall's as ugly as can be;
Devonshire's better certainly;
But Somersetshire is the best of the three,
And Somersetshire is the country for me.'

Robert Southey, *Letters from England, by Don Manuel Alvarez Espriella*, 1807

Should there not be a place in Somerset called Newton Bessell? The names certainly sound appropriately West Country.

Robin Lustig, *Observer*, 3 December 1978

Southampton

South-hampton . . . that is a very neat clean town and the Streets well pitch'd and kept so by their carrying all their carriages on sleds as they do in Holland, and permit no Cart to go about the town and keep it clean swept, this was formerly more strictly observed when the town was full of trade for it is a good Port, but now the trade has failed and the town almost forsooke and neglected; its a place of no strength now by reason of the Castle being ruined and the Fortifications neglected and the Gunns taken thence, tho' by most it is thought the best scituated port for shipps to ride and take their provision in, and so capable of tradeing, but the last 2 Reignes for near 40 year discourag'd it, being a proper place for the French to have seiz'd and secured for themselves.

Celia Fiennes, *Journeys*, *c.* 1685–96

Southampton is a truly antient town, for 'tis in a manner dying with age; the decay of the trade is the real decay of the town; and all the business of moment that is transacted there is the trade between us and the islands Jersey and Guernsey, with a little of the wine trade, and much smuggling: the building of ships is also much stopp'd of late; however, the town is large, has many people in it, a noble fair High-Street, a spacious key; and if its trade should revive, is able to entertain great numbers of people: There is a French church, and no inconsiderable congregation, which was a help to the town, and there are still some merchants who trade to Newfoundland, and to the Streights with fish; but for all other trade it may be said of Southampton as of other towns, London has eaten it up. The situation of the town, between two rivers was to its advantage formerly in point of strength, and the town was wall'd with a very strong wall, strengthen'd with a rampart, and a double ditch; but I do not hear that they were ever put to make much use of them.

Daniel Defoe, *A Tour through the Whole Island of Great Britain*, 1724–7

The air is soft and mild, and sufficiently impregnated with saline particles to render it agreeable, and even salutary, to those who cannot endure a full exposure to the sea, on a bleak and open shore.

Anon., *A Guide to all the Watering and Sea-bathing Places*, *c.* 1810

The Southampton and Redbridge Canal

Southampton's wise sons found the river so large,
Though 'twould carry a ship, 'twould not carry a
barge;
But soon this defect their sage noddles supplied,
For they cut a snug ditch to run close to its side:
Like the man, who, contriving a hole through his wall
To admit his two cats – the one great, t'other small,
When a great hole was made for great puss to pass
through,
Had a little hole cut for the little cat too.

Anon., in ed. Charles Stokes Carey, *A Commonplace Book of Epigrams*, 1872

Southend

At low water a stranger would suppose that the sea had totally abandoned the place.

Anon., *A Guide to all the Watering and Sea-bathing Places*, *c.* 1810

and Cromer

*'Ah!' said Mr Woodhouse, shaking his head and fixing his eyes on her with tender concern . . . , 'if you must go to the sea, it had better not have been to South End. South End is an unhealthy place. Perry was suprised to hear you had fixed upon South End.'

'I know there is such an idea with many people, but indeed it is quite a mistake, sir. – We all had our health perfectly well there, never found the least inconvenience from the mud; and Mr Wingfield says it is entirely a mistake to suppose the place unhealthy; and I am sure he may be depended on, for he thoroughly understands the nature of the air, and his own brother and family have been there repeatedly.'

'You should have gone to Cromer, my dear, if you went any where. – Perry was a week at Cromer once, and he holds it to be the best of all the sea-bathing places. A fine open sea, he says, and very pure air. And, by what I understand, you might have had lodgings there quite away from the sea – a quarter of a mile off – very comfortable. You should have consulted Perry.'

Jane Austen, *Emma*, 1816

The note of Southend is *pearl.*

James Agate, *Ego* (13 October 1932), 1935

Southport

Southport fascinates me. It was here that I first saw *The School for Scandal*, wore my first London-made suit, and had my first semi-serious illness, a fierce attack of tonsillitis, not improved when the young and pretty night-nurse jumped into bed with me, starched cuffs and all, and stayed there. I was nineteen, and such a hellish little prig that next morning I begged the doctor to send her away! My lecture on bad manners took place in the Congregational Church. It went off fairly well, though I hadn't reckoned on delivering it from the pulpit.

James Agate, *Ego 4*, 2 November 1938

Southwell

. . . your *cursed*, *detestable*, & *abhorred* abode of *Scandal*, *antiquated virginity*, & universal *Infamy*. . . .

Lord Byron, Letter to Elizabeth Pigot, 30 June 1807

Southwell was a detestable residence; thank St Dominic I have done with it, I have been twice within 8 miles of it, but could not prevail on myself to *suffocate* in its heavy atmosphere. . . . oh! the misery of doing nothing, but make *Love*, *enemies*, and *Verses*.

Lord Byron, Letter to Elizabeth Pigot, 26 October 1807

Southwold (Dunwich and Walberswick)

It is remarkable, that this town is now so washed away by the sea, that what little trade they have, is carry'd on by Walderswick, a little town near Swole, the vessels coming in there, because the ruines of Dunwich make the shore there unsafe and uneasie to the boats; from whence the northern coasting seamen a rude verse of their own using, and I suppose of their own making; as follows,

Swoul and Dunwich, and Walderswick,
All go in at one lousie creek.

This lousie creek, in short, is a little river at Swoul, which our late famous atlas-maker calls a good harbour for ships, and rendezvous of the royal navy; but that by the bye; the author it seems knew no better.

Daniel Defoe, *A Tour through the Whole Island of Great Britain*, 1724–7

Spalding

The town of Spalding is not large, but pretty well built and well inhabited; but for the healthyness or pleasantness of it, I have no more to say than this, that I was very glad when I got out of it, and out of the rest of the fen country; for 'tis a horrid air for a stranger to breathe in.

Daniel Defoe, *A Tour through the Whole Island of Great Britain*, 1724–7

Staffordshire

The North part is full of hils and no lesse fruitfull: the middle being watered with the river *Trent* is more plentifull, clad with woods and embrodered galantly with corne fields and medowes: as is the Southpart likewise which hath coles also digged out of the earth and mines of Iron. But whether more for their commoditie or hinderance, I leave to the inhabitants who doe, or shall best understand it.

William Camden, *Britain*, 1610
(Philemon Holland's translation)

No people whatever are esteemed more subtle.

Robert Plot, *The Natural History of Staffordshire*, 1686

This country is much for entertainments in every house you must eat and drinke.

Celia Fiennes, *Journeys*, 1698

The people of this county have been particularly famous, and more than any other county in England, for good footmanship, and there have been, and still are among them, some of the fleetest runners in England; which I do not grant to be occasion'd by any particular temperature of the air or soil, so much as to the hardy breed of the inhabitants, especially in the moorlands, or northern part of the county, and to their exercising themselves to it from their childhood; for running foot-races seems to be the general sport or diversion of the country.

Daniel Defoe, *A Tour through the Whole Island of Great Britain*, 1724–7

Stilton

Thence to Stilton, slowly, paced,
With no bloome nor blossome graced,
With no plums nor apples stored,
But bald, like an old mans forehead;
Yet with Innes so well provided,
Guests are pleased when they have tride it.

Richard Brathwaite, *Barnabees Journall, His Northerne Journey*, Third Part, 1638

Stilton, a town famous for cheese, which is call'd our English Parmesan, and is brought to table with the mites, or maggots round it, so thick, that they bring a spoon with them for you to eat the mites with, as you do the cheese.

Daniel Defoe, *A Tour through the Whole Island of Great Britain*, 1724–7

Stoke-on-Trent

The Potteries

North of a line drawn from the Wash to the beak of Carnarvon and due south of the Trent's source, lies a tract of country some seven miles long by four at its widest, bearing in shape a rough similarity to the contour of England less Cornwall and Devon. Its face is an unbroken alteration of hillock and valley, the highest hills scarcely reaching 300 feet, and in the whole of it there is no river broader than a brook.

This is the home of pottery. Five contiguous towns whose red-brown bricks have inundated the moorland like a succession of great lakes strung together by some St Lawrence of a main road, devote themselves with several smaller townships, to the manufacture, from their own and other clays of every sort of earthenware, China and Porcelain. In these parts, the sound of the shattering of an earthen vessel, elsewhere unpleasing to the housewife's ear, is music, for upon the frequency of such fractures all the world over, the welfare almost the very existence of the inhabitants, chiefly depends. The towns are mean and ugly in appearance – sombre, shapeless, hard-featured, uncouth; and the vaporous prison of their ovens and chimneys has soiled and shrivelled the surrounding greenness of Nature for there is no country lane within miles but what presents a gaunt travesty of rural charms. Nothing could be more prosaic than the aspect of the huddled streets;

nothing more seemingly remote from romance. Yet romance dwells even here, though unsuspected by its very makers – the romance which always attends the alchemic processes of skilled, transmuting labour. . . .

Here indeed is Nature repaid for some of her notorious cruelties. She imperiously bids man sustain and reproduce himself, and this is one of the places where in the act itself of obedience he insults and horribly maltreats her. To go out beyond the municipal confines where, in the thick of altercation the subsidiary industries of coal and iron prosper amid a wreck of verdure, ought surely to raise one's estimate not only of man, but of Nature: so thorough and ruthless is his havoc of her, and so indomitable her ceaseless recuperation. . . .

And if here man has made of the very daylight an infamy, he can boast that he adds to the darkest night the weird beauty of fire, and flame-tinted cloud. From roof and hill you may see on every side furnace calling furnace with fiery tongues and wreathing messages of smoke across the blue-red glow of acres of burning ironstone. The unique pyrotechnics of labour atoning for its grime!

Arnold Bennett, *The Potteries: A Sketch*, 1898

The stranger, unless he enters the district by night, cannot be absolutely carried away by his first sight of the Potteries.

Arnold Bennett, 'The People of the Potteries', *Cassell's Magazine*, January 1911

It is doubtful whether the people of Southern England have even yet realized how much introspection there is going on all the time in the Five Towns.

Max Beerbohm, *A Christmas Garland*, 1912

My native heath, thanks to the enterprise of London newspapers and the indestructibility of picturesque lies, has the reputation of being quite unlike the rest of England, but when I set foot in it after absence, it seems to me the most English piece of England that I ever came across. With extraordinary clearness I see it as absurdly, ridiculously, splendidly English. All the English characteristics are, quite remarkably, exaggerated in the Potteries. . . . We practise in the Potteries the fine old English plan of not calling things by their names. We are one town, one unseparated mass of streets. We are, in fact, the twelfth largest town in the United Kingdom (though you would never guess it). And the chief of our retail commerce and our amusements are congregated in the centre of our town, as the custom is. But do not imagine that we will consent to call ourselves one town. No! We pretend that we are six towns, and to carry out the pretence we have six town halls, six Mayors or chief bailiffs, six sanitary inspectors, six everything, including six jealousies.

Arnold Bennett, *Paris Nights*, 1913

Stonehenge

Some there are that thinke them to be no naturall stones heawen out of the rocke, but artificially made of pure sand, and by some glewie and unctuous matter knit and incorporate together. . . .

William Camden, *Britain*, 1610
(Philemon Holland's translation)

Now we were ariv'd at *Stone-henge*, Indeede a stupendious Monument, how so many, & huge pillars of stone should have been brought together, erected some, other Transverse on the tops of them, in a Circular *area* as rudly representing a Cloyster, or heathen & more natural Temple: & so exceeding hard, that all my strength with an hammer, could not breake a fragment. . . .

John Evelyn, *Diary*, July 1654

To *Stonehenge* over the plain and some prodigious great hills even to fright us. Came thither and them find as prodigious as any tales I ever heard of them and worth going this journey to see. God knows what their use was. They are hard to tell but yet may be told.

Samuel Pepys, *Diary*, 11 June 1668

To increase the wonder the story is that none can count them twice alike, they stand confused, and some single stones at a distance, but I have told them often and bring their number to 91.

Celia Fiennes, *Journeys*, *c*. 1685–96

The Druid's groves are gone – so much the better.
Stonehenge is not, but what the devil is it?

Lord Byron, *Don Juan*, 1819–24

The impression of its grandeur rather grew upon me, than struck me all at once; which I find is the course its effect takes with most people. Found some sensible Quakers there, with whom we had some conversation, and one of them mentioned his having lately taken an American gentleman there, making him keep his eyes shut till he got directly under the highest stones. But the American, on looking up, merely said, 'What do you mean by this?' and saw nothing wonderful in it. The same person, however, when they took him to Salisbury Cathedral, was overwhelmed with admiration and astonishment at it. The fact is, that *art* surprises the Americans; *nature* they have on the grandest scale themselves.

Thomas Moore, *Diary*, 7 September 1833

After dinner we walked to Salisbury Plain. On the broad downs, under the gray sky, not a house was visible, nothing but Stonehenge, which looked like a group of brown dwarfs in the wide expanse, – Stonehenge and the barrows, which rose like green bosses about the plain, and a few hayricks. On the top of a mountain, the old temple would not be more impressive. Far and wide a few shepherds with their flocks sprinkled the plain, and a bagman drove along the road. It looked as if the wide margin given in this crowded isle to this primeval temple were accorded by the veneration of the English race to the old egg out of which all their ecclesiastical structures and history had proceeded.

R.W. Emerson, *English Traits*, 1856

To Stonehenge, where we camped about half a mile from the stones under lee of a small plantation. The stones I found in possession when I arrived of American tourists, but even these could do little to injure the fine calm of the place, and they were soon gone, and about midnight I returned and went again in full solitude to the stones and spent an hour there alone, making incantations in the hope of raising some ghost of ancient times, but in vain, and though I repeated the Lord's Prayer backwards, nothing would come. Perhaps it was the fact that in order to do so without a book, I had first to repeat each sentence in its natural sequence, and this may have neutralized the spell. Then I lay down under one of the fallen blocks and dozed off for an hour or two, but still nothing. Stonehenge has much in common with primitive Egypt.

Wilfred Scawen Blunt, Diary, 18 August 1894, *My Diaries*, 1919

Observatory, altar, temple, tomb,
Erected none knows when by none knows whom,
To serve strange gods or watch familiar stars,
We drive to see you in our motor-cars
And carry picture-postcards back to town
While still the unsleeping stars look coldly down.

Sir John Squire, *Stonehenge*, before 1958

I wish I could bring Stonehenge to Nyasaland to show there was a time when Britain had a savage culture.

Dr Hastings Banda, *Observer*, 'Sayings of the Week', 10 March 1963

Stowe (and landscape gardening)

To build, to plant, whatever you intend,
To rear the Column, or the Arch to bend,
To swell the Terras, or to sink the Grot;
In all, let Nature never be forgot.
But treat the Goddess like a modest fair,
Nor over-dress, nor leave her wholly bare;
Let not each beauty ev'ry where be spy'd,
Where half the skill is decently to hide.
He gains all points, who pleasingly confounds,
Surprizes, varies, and conceals the Bounds.
Consult the Genius of the Place in all;
That tells the Waters or to rise, or fall,
Or helps th'ambitious Hill the heav'n to scale,
Or scoops in circling theatres the Vale,
Calls in the Country, catches opening glades,
Joins willing woods, and varies shades from shades,
Now breaks or now directs, th'intending Lines;
Paints as you plant, and, as you work, designs.
Still follow Sense, of ev'ry Art the Soul,
Parts answ'ring parts shall slide into a whole,
Spontaneous beauties all around advance,
Start ev'n from Difficulty, strike from Chance;
Nature shall join you, Time shall make it grow
A Work to wonder at – perhaps a STOW.

Alexander Pope, *Moral Essays, Epistle IV. To Richard Boyle, Earl of Burlington*, 1731

I do like the Albano glut of buildings, let them be ever so much condemned.

Horace Walpole, Letter to George Montagu, 22 July 1751

It puzzles much the sages' brains
Where Eden stood of yore;
Some place it in Arabia's plains
Some say it is no more
But Cobham can these tales confute
As all the curious know;
For he has prov'd beyond dispute
That paradise is *STOW*.

Anon., 'On Lord Cobham's Gardens', *The English Martial*, 1806

Stratford upon Avon

A proper little mercate town, beholden for all the beauty that it hath to two men there bred and brought up, namely *John of Stratford*, Archbishop of Canterburie who built the Church: and Sir *Hugh Clopton*, Major of London, who over *Avon* made a stone bridge supported with foureteene arches, not without exceeding great expenses.

William Camden, *Britain*, 1610 (Philemon Holland's translation)

The wretchedest old town I ever saw, which I intended for Shakspeare's sake to find snug, and pretty, and antique, not old.

Horace Walpole, Letter to George Montagu, 22 July 1751

The first view of the Avon and of the town where Shakespeare was born gave me those feelings which men of enthusiasm have on seeing remarkable places. Cicero had them when he walked at Athens.

James Boswell, Journal, 6 September 1769, *Boswell in Search of a Wife*, 1957

But my good Friend, would the Gentlemen do real honour, & Shew their Love to Shakespeare – let 'Em decorate Ye Town, (ye *happiest* & Why not ye *handsomest*, in England) let your Streets be well pav'd, & kept clean, do Something with ye delightful Meadow, allure Every body to Visit ye *holy Land*; let it be well lighted, & clean under foot, and let it not be said for Your honour, & I hope for Your Interest, that the Town, which gave Birth to the first Genius since the Creation, is the most dirty, unseemly, ill-pav'd, wretched-looking Town in all Britain.

David Garrick, Letter to William Eaves, 8 March 1771 (Eaves was Mayor of Stratford at the time)

To have seen Stratford on Avon and the Dresden Madonna, must be almost peace.

Emily Dickinson, Letter to Mr T.W. Higginson, 1878

The whole vicinage is instinct with Shakespeare.

John W. Forney, *Letters from Europe*, 1867

At Stratford . . . my enthusiasm hung fire in the most humiliating manner.

Henry James, Letter to William James, 26 April 1869

. . . None that hate
The commonweal whose empire sets men free
Find comfort there, where once by grace of fate
A soul was born as boundless as the sea
If life, if love, if memory now be thine
Rejoice that still thy Stratford bears thy sign.

A.C. Swinburne, *Stratford on Avon*, 27 July 1901

Hideous place on a Sunday. What needs my Shakespeare for his honoured bones? Certainly not a theatre looking like a barracks-cum-roadhouse.

James Agate, *Ego* (3 September 1933), 1935

All of Stratford in fact, suggests powdered history – add hot water and stir and you have a delicious, nourishing Shakespeare.

Margaret Halsey, *With Malice Toward Some*, 1938

In the early years of the war when Hitler was threatening to invade England, the authorities blanked out the names on signposts to confuse German paratroopers. So about a mile from Stratford there was a large sign that read as follows:

YOU ARE APPROACHING
XXXXXXXXX
UPON
XXXX
THE
BIRTHPLACE
OF
WILLIAM SHAKESPEARE.

William Golding, 'Shakespeare's Birthplace', in *The Hot Gates and Other Occasional Pieces*, 1965

Stratton (Cornwall)

Stratton, an Auntient towne off that County, Noted to have the best garlike in all those parts.

Peter Mundy, *Travels in Europe and Asia*, 1639

Strawberry Hill

Some talk of Gunnersbury,
For Sion some declare,
Some say, that with Chiswick House
No villa can compare;
But all the beaux of Middlesex,
Who know the country well
Say that Strawberry-hill, that Strawberry-hill
Does bear away the bell.

William Pulteney, Earl of Bath, Poem quoted in Horace Walpole's Letter to Richard Bentley, 17 July 1755

Strawberry Hill for me! I looked all over it: you know all the pictures, jewels, curiosities, were sold some ten years ago; only bare walls remain: the walls indeed here and there stuck with Gothic woodwork, and the ceilings with Gothic gilding, sometimes painted Gothic to imitate woodwork; much of it therefore in less good taste: all a Toy, but yet the Toy of a very clever man. The rain is coming through the Roofs, and gradually disengaging the confectionary Battlements and Cornices.

Edward Fitzgerald, Letter to Frederick Tennyson, 8 June 1852

Suffolk

A large country it is, and full of havens, of a fat and fertile soile, (unlesse it be Eastward) being compounded (as it is) of clay and marle: by meanes whereof there are in every place most rich and goodly corne fields, with pastures as battable, for grazing and feeding of cattell. And great store of cheeses are there made, which to the great commodity of the inhabitants are vented into all parts of England: Nay, into Germanie France and Spaine also, as *Pantaleon* the Phisitian writeth, who stucke not to compare these of ours for colour, and tast both with those of *Placentia*: but he was no dainty toothed scholar out of *Apicius* schoole. Neither be their wanting woods heere, which have beene more plentifull, and parkes; for many there are lying to Noble mens and Gentlemens houses replenished with game.

William Camden, *Britain*, 1610 (Philemon Holland's translation)

I have always found Suffolk farmers great boasters of

their superiority over others; and I must say that it is not without reason.

William Cobbett, *Rural Rides – Eastern Tour*, 22 March 1830

A line of distant hills is all we want in Suffolk. A landscape should have that image of futurity in it.

Edward Fitzgerald, Letter to Bernard Barton, 15 August 1845

Suffolk – land of uncomfortable beds, brown sherry, and perpendicular Gothic.

Norman Douglas, *Looking Back*, 1933

Surrey

A country it is not very large, yet wealthy enough, where it beareth upon Tamis, and lieth as a plaine and champion country: it yeeldeth corne meetely well, and forrage abundantly especially towards the South, where a continuall valley falling lowe by little and little, called in times past *Holmesdale* of the woods therein, runneth downe very pleasant to behold, by reason of the delectable variety of groves, fields and medowes. On each side there bee prety hills rising up a great way along in the country, parkes every where replenished with Deare, rivers also full of fish: whereby it affordeth for pleasure faire game of hunting, and as delightsome fishing. Likened it is by some unto a course freese garment with a greene gard, or to a cloath of great spinning and thin woven, with a greene list about it, for that the inner part is but barraine, the outward edge or skirt more fertile.

William Camden, *Britain*, 1610
(Philemon Holland's translation)

It may be allowed to be a square (besides its angular expiation in the south-west) of two-and-twenty miles; and is not improperly compared to a cinnamon tree, whose bark is far better than the body thereof; for the skirts and borders bounding this shire are rich and fruitful, whilst the ground in the inward parts thereof is very hungry and barren, though, by reason of the clear air and clean ways, full of many genteel habitations.

Thomas Fuller, *History of the Worthies of England*, 1662

This county of Surrey . . . has some of the very best, and some of the worst lands, not only in England, but in the world.

William Cobbett, *Rural Rides*, 25 September 1822

Miles of pram in the wind and Pam in the gorse track,
Coco-nut smell of the broom, and a packet of Weights
Press'd in the sand. The thud of a hoof on a horse-track
A horse-riding horse for a horse-track –
Conifer county of Surrey approached
Through remarkable wrought-iron gates.

John Betjeman, 'Pot Pourri from a Surrey Garden', in *Collected Poems*, 1958

Down the winding Surrey lanes, past the decorated pubs, and houses set back from the road, with a Bentley instead of a garden in front.

David Pryce-Jones, *Owls and Satyrs*, 1961

Sussex

See also under Downs

It hath few harbours, by reason that the sea is dangerous for shelves, and therefore rough, and troublous, the shore also it selfe full of rocks, and the South-west wind doth tyrannize thereon, casting up beach infinitely. The sea coast of this countrie, hath greene hils on it mounting to a greater height, called the *Downes*, which because they stand upon a fat chalke or kind of marle yeeldeth corne abundantly.

The middle track, garnished with medowes, pastures, corne-fields, and groves, maketh a very lovely shew. The hithermore and Northern side thereof is shaded most pleasantly with woods, like as in times past the whole country throughout, which by reason of the woods was hardly passable. . . . Many prety rivers it hath, but such as springing out of the North side of the shire forthwith take their course to the Ocean, and therefore not able to beare any vessel of burden. Full of iron mines it is in sundry places, where for the making and fining thereof, there bee furnaces on every side, and a huge deale of wood is yearely spent, to which purpose divers brookes in many places are brought to run in one chanell, and sundry medowes turned into pooles and waters, so that they might bee of power sufficient to drive hammer milles, which beating upon the iron, resound all over the places adjoyning. . . . Neither want here glasse-houses, but the glasse there made, by reason of the matter or making, I wot not whether, is nothing so pure and cleare, and therefore used of the common sort onely.

William Camden, *Britain*, 1610
(Philemon Holland's translation)

A Sussex man he won't be druv.

Old proverb, quoted Edmund Blunden, *A Selection of his Poetry and Prose*, 1950

If you love good roads, conveniences, good inns, plenty of postilions and horses, be so kind as never to go in Sussex. We thought ourselves in the northest part of England; the whole country has a Saxon air, and the inhabitants are savage, as if king George the second was the first monarch of the East Angles. Coaches grow there no more than balm and spices; we were forced to drop our postchaise, that resembled nothing so much as harlequin's calash, which was occasionally a chaise or a baker's cart. We journeyed over Alpine mountains, drenched in clouds, and thought of harlequin again, when he was driving the chariot of the sun through the morning clouds, and so was glad to hear the *aqua vitae* man crying a dram. At last we got to Arundel-castle, which was visibly built for defence in an impracticable country.

Horace Walpole, Letter to George Montagu, 26 August 1749

God gives all men all earth to love,
But, since man's heart is small,
Ordains for each one spot shall prove
Beloved over all.
Each to his choice, and I rejoice
The lot has fallen to me
In a fair ground – in a fair ground
Yea, Sussex by the sea!

Rudyard Kipling, *Sussex*, 1902

That part of England which is very properly called her Eden, that centre of all good things and home of happy men, the county of Sussex.

Hilaire Belloc, *Hills and the Sea*, 1906

No county has such a crowd of enthusiastic poets to sing its praise. But when I hear the word Sussex, the picture it evokes for me has nothing to do with any of that lyrical enthusiasm.

I see a third-class railway carriage on a Monday morning full of blue jackets. They are travelling to London from Portsmouth. We have just left Horsham. One of these is looking out of the window; he observes a man sitting on a stile. 'Nice easy job that bloke's got,' the sailor observes, 'watching the tortoises *flash* by.'

Maurice Baring, *Round the World in Any Number of Days*, 1913

The imitation countryside of Sussex.

James Cameron, *Point of Departure*, 1967

Swanage

To Swanage, – that neat little town, in whose bay
Fair Thetis shows off, in her best silver slippers.

Thomas Moore, *A Late Scene at Swanage*, before 1841

Tadcaster

Thence to Tadcaster, where stood reared
A fair Bridge, where no flood appeared
Broken Pavements, Beggars waiting
Nothing more than labour hating;
But with speed I hasten'd from them
Lest I should be thought one of them.

Richard Brathwaite, *Barnabees Journall – Northerne Journey, Third Part*, 1638

Tamworth

A fine pleasant trading town, eminent for good ale, and good company, of the middling sort.

Daniel Defoe, *A Tour through the Whole Island of Great Britain*, 1724–7

Taunton and Bristol

a train journey between

The day delicious, and, being quite alone, I had full enjoyment of the beautiful country through which (or rather over which) I flew. I remember a pretty scene in some ballet where the centre of the stage represented a river on which the hero of the tale sat in a boat, rowing away with all his might, and appearing to pass through a succession of beautiful rural scenery, which was effected of course, by the constant change of the back scene, and the appeareance of progress it gave to the boat. I wanted nothing but the sweet music that accompanied this delusion on the stage, to make the enjoyment of my real journey complete.

Thomas Moore, *Diary*, 6 August 1843

Tees

and Wharfe and Rhone Rivers

I have never cared to see the lower Rhone any more; and to my love of cottage rather than castle, added at this time another strong moral principle, than if ever one was metamorphosed into a river, and could choose one's own size, it would be out of all doubt more prudent and delightful to be Tees or Wharfe than Rhone.

John Ruskin, *Praeterita*, 1885–9

Teignmouth

He looked across the river stream;
A little town was there,
O'er which the morning's earliest beam
Was wandering fresh and fair;
No architect of classic school
Had pondered there with line and rule;
And stranger still, no modern master
Had wasted there his lath and plaster;
The buildings in strange order lay,
As if the streets had lost their way,
Fantastic, puzzling, narrow, muddy,
Excess of toil from lack of study,

Where fashion's very newest fangles
Had no conception of right angles.
But still about that humble place
There was a look of rustic grace;
'Twas sweet to see the sports and labours
And morning greetings of good neighbours,
The seamen mending nets and oars,
The matrons knitting at the doors,
The invalids enjoying dips,
The children launching tiny ships,
The beldames clothed in rags and wrinkles
Investigating periwinkles.

Winthrop Mackworth Praed, *Fragments of a Descriptive Poem*, March 1826

Tenterden

A singularly bright spot.

William Cobbett, *Rural Rides*, 31 August 1823

Tewkesbury

His wit is as thick as Tewkesbury mustard.

William Shakespeare, *Henry IV*, Part ii, *c.* 1597–8

The Mustard off this place (For want off other Matter) is much spoken off, Made upp in balles as bigge as henns egges, att 3d and 4d each, allthough a Farthing worth off the ordinary sort will give better content in my opinion, this being in sight and tast Much like the old dried thicke scurffe thatt sticks by the sides off a Mustard pott, but you may see whatt opinion will doe.

Peter Mundy, *Travels in Europe and Asia*, 1639

Gloucestershire. . . . Mustard. . . . The best in England (to take no larger compasse) is made at Tewkesberry. . . . Proverbs: 'He looks as if he had liv'd on Tewkesbury Mustard.' It is spoken partly of such who always have a sad severe and tetrick countenance . . . partly of such as are snappish, captious and prone to take exceptions where they are not given, such as will *crispare nasum*, in derision of what they slight or neglect.

Thomas Fuller, *History of the Worthies of England*, 1662

River Thames

Sweete *Themmes* runne softly, till I end my Song.

Edmund Spenser, *Prothalamium*, 1596

and Medway

It fortun'd then, a solemne feast was there
To all the Sea-gods and their fruitfull seede,
In honour of the spousals which then were
Betwixt the *Medway* and the *Thames* agreed.
Long had the *Thames* (as we in records reed)
Before that day her wooed to his bed;
But the proud Nymph would for no worldly meed,
Nor no entreatie to his love be led;
Till now at last relenting she to him was wed.

Edmund Spenser, *The Faerie Queene*, 1589–96

This is that *Isis*, which afterwards enterteineth *Tame*, and by a compound word is called *Tamisis*, Soveraigne as it were of all the Britain rivers in Britaine: of which a man may well and truely say, as ancient writers did of *Euphrates* in the East-part of the world: that it doth both Sow and Water the best part of Britain.

William Camden, *Britain*, 1610
(Philemon Holland's translation)

Then *Westminster* next the great *Tames* doth entertaine;
That vaunts her Palace large, and her most sumptuous Fane:
The Land's tribunall seate that challengeth for hers,
The crowning of our Kings, their famous sepulchers.
Then goes he on along by that more beauteous Strand,
Expressing both the wealth and bravery of the Land.
(So many sumptuous Bowres, within so little space,
The All-beholding Sun scarse sees in all his race.)
And on by *London* leads, which like a Crescent lies,
Whose windowes seem to mock the Star-befreckled skies;
Besides her rising Spyres, so thick themselves that show,
As doe the bristling reeds, within his Bank that growe.
There sees his crouded Wharfes, and people-pestred shores,
His Bosome over-spread, with shoales of labouring ores:
With that most costly Bridge that doth him most renowne,
By which he cleerely puts all other Rivers downe.

Michael Drayton, *Poly-Olbion*, 1612–22

But noble Thames, whilst I can hold a pen,
I will divulge thy Glory unto men.

John Taylor, *All the Works of John Taylor*, 1630

I send, I send here my supremest kiss
To thee my *silver-footed Thamasis*.
No more shall I reiterate thy Strand,
Whereon so many Stately Structures stand:
Nor in the summers sweeter evenings go,
To bath in thee (as thousand others doe.)
No more shall I along thy christall glide,
In Barge (with boughes and rushes beautifi'd)
With soft-smooth Virgins (for our chast disport)
To *Richmond*, *Kingstone*, and to *Hampton-Court*:
Never againe shall I with Finnie-Ore
Put from, or draw unto the faithfull shore:
And Landing here, or safely Landing there,
Make way to my *Beloved Westminster*:
Or to the *Golden-cheap-side*, where the earth
Of *Julia Herrick* gave to me my Birth.

May all clean *Nimphs* and curious water Dames,
With Swan-like-state, flote up & down thy streams:
No drought upon thy wanton waters fall
To make them Leane, and languishing at all.
No ruffling winds come hither to discease
Thy pure and *Silver-wristed Naides*.
Keep up your state ye streams; and as ye spring,
Never make sick your Banks by surfeiting.
Grow young with Tydes, and though I see ye never,
Receive this vow, *so fare-ye-well for ever*.

Robert Herrick, *His teares to Thamasis*, 1648

My eye descending from the Hill surveys
Where *Thames* amongst the wanton vallies strays.
Thames, the most lov'd of all the Oceans sons,
By his old Sire to his embraces runs,
Hasting to pay his tribute to the Sea
Like mortal life to meet Eternity.
Though with those streams he no resemblance hold,
Whose foam is Amber, and their Gravel Gold;
His genuine, and less guilty wealth t'explore,
Search not his bottom, but survey his shore;
O'er which he kindly spreads his spacious wing,
And hatches plenty for th'ensuing Spring.
Nor then destroys it with too fond a stay,
Like Mothers which their Infants overlay.
Nor with a sudden and impetuous wave,
Like profuse Kings resumes the wealth he gave.
No unexpected inundations spoil
The mowers hopes, nor mock the plowmans toil:
But God-like his unwearied Bounty flows;
First loves to do, then loves the Good he does.
Nor are his blessings to his banks confin'd,
But free, and common, as the Sea or Wind;
When he to boast, or to disperse his stores
Full of the tributes of his grateful shores,
Visits the world, and in his flying towers
Brings home to us, and makes both *Indies* ours;
Finds wealth where 'tis, bestows it where it wants,
Cities in deserts, woods in Cities plants.
So that to us no thing, no place is strange,
While his fair bosom is the worlds exchange.
O could I flow like thee, and make thy stream
My great example, as it is my theme!
Though deep, yet clear, though gentle, yet not dull,
Strong without rage, without o'erflowing full.

Sir John Denham, *The Thames from Cooper's Hill*, 1643 (text of 1668)

Ah, happy Isle, how art thou chang'd and curst,
Since I was born, and knew thee first!
When Peace which had forsook the World around,
(Frighted with noise and the shrill Trumpets sound)
Thee for a private place of rest,
And a secure retirement chose
Wherein to build her Halcyon Nest;
No wind durst stir abroad the Air to discompose.
When all the Riches of the Globe beside,
Flow's in to Thee with every Tide;
When all that Nature did thy Soil deny,
The growth was of thy fruitful Industry,
When all the proud and dreadful Sea,
And all his Tributary-Streams
A constant Tribute paid to Thee,
When all the liquid World was one extended *Thames*.

Abraham Cowley, *A Discourse by Way of Vision, Concerning the Government of Oliver Cromwell*, 1661

London . . . oweth its greatness, under God's divine providence to the well-conditioned river of Thames. . . . Hence it was that when King James, offended with the city, threatened to remove his court to another place, the Lord Mayor, boldly enough returned, 'that he might remove his court at his pleasure, but could not remove the river of Thames.'

Thomas Fuller, *History of the Worthies of England*, 1662

To set the Thames on fire.

Proverb, eighteenth century

In ev'ry Town, where *Thamis* rolls his Tyde,
A narrow Pass there is, with Houses low;
Where ever and anon, the Stream is ey'd,
And many a Boat soft sliding to and fro.
There oft are heard the Notes of Infant Woe,
The short thick Sob, loud Scream, and shriller Squawl:
How can ye, Mothers, vex your Children so?
Some play, some eat, some cack against the Wall,
And as they crouchen low, for Bread and Butter call.

And on the broken Pavement here and there,
Doth many a stinking Sprat and Herring lie;
A Brandy and Tobacco Shop is near,
And Hens, and Dogs, and Hogs are feeding by:
And here's a Sailor's Jacket hangs to dry:
At ev'ry Door are Sun-burnt Matrons seen,
Mending old Nets to catch the scaly Fry;
Now singing shrill, and scolding oft between,
Scolds answer foul-mouthed Scolds; bad Neighbour-hood I ween.

The snappish Cur, (the Passengers annoy)
Close at my Heel with yelping Treble flies;
The whimp'ring Girl, and hoarser-screaming Boy,
Join to the yelping Treble shrilling Cries;
The scolding Quean to louder Notes doth rise,
And her full Pipes those shrilling Cries confound:
To her full Pipes the grunting Hog replies;
The grunting Hogs alarm the Neighbours round,
And Curs, Girls, Boys, and Scolds, in the deep Base are drown'd.

Such place hath *Deptford*, Navy-building Town,
Woolwich and *Wapping*, smelling strong of Pitch;
Such *Lambeth*, Envy of each Band and Gown,
And *Twick'nam* such, which fairer Scenes enrich,

Grots, Statues, Urns, and *J——n's Dog and Bitch*:
Ne Village is without, on either side,
All up the silver *Thames*, or all a down;
Ne Richmond's self, from whose tall Front are ey'd
Vales, Spires, meandring Streams, and *Windsor's* tow'ry
Pride.

Alexander Pope, *Imitations of English Poets: Spenser: The Alley*, before 1709

I am cruel thirsty this hot weather. – I am just this minute going to swim. I take Patrick down with me to hold my nightgown, shirt and slippers, and borrow a napkin of my landlady for a cap. – So farewell till I come up; but there's no danger, don't be frighted – I have been swimming this half-hour and more; and when I was coming out I dived, to make my head and all through wet, like a cold bath; but as I dived, the napkin fell off and is lost, and I have that to pay for. O faith, the great stones were so sharp, I could hardly set my feet on them as I came out. It was pure and warm....

Jonathan Swift, *Journal to Stella*, June 1711

Then Commerce brought into the public Walk
The busy Merchant; the big Warehouse built;
Rais'd the strong Crane; choak'd up the loaded Street
With foreign Plenty; and thy Stream, O THAMES,
Large, gentle, deep, majestic, King of Floods!
Chose for his grand Resort. On either hand,
Like a long wintry Forest, Groves of Masts
Shot up their Spires; the bellying Sheet between
Possess'd the breezy Void; the sooty Hulk
Steer'd sluggish on; the splendid Barge along
Row'd, regular, to Harmony; around,
The Boat, light-skimming, stretch'd its oary Wings;
While deep the various Voice of fervent Toil
From Bank to Bank increased.

James Thomson, *The Seasons*, 1726

Glide gently, thus for ever glide,
O Thames! that other bards may see
As lovely visions by thy side
As now, fair river, come to me.
O glide, fair stream, for ever so,
Thy quiet soul on all bestowing,
Till all our minds for ever flow
As thy deep waters now are flowing.

William Wordsworth, *Remembrance of Collins*, 1789

When it is considered that all the filth of this prodigious metropolis is emptied into the river, it is perfectly astonishing that any people should consent to drink it. One week's expenses of the late war would have built an aqueduct from the Surrey hills, and an hundred fountains to have distributed its stores. The Thames water ferments and purifies itself: in its state of fermentation it is said to be inflammable.

Robert Southey, *Letters from England, by Don Manuel Alvarez Espriella*, 1807

where Thames is seen
Gliding between his banks of green,
While rival villas, on each side,
Peep from their bowers to woo his tide,
And like a Turk between two rows
Of Harem beauties, on he goes –
A lover, lov'd for ev'n the grace
With which he slides from their embrace.

Thomas Moore, *The Summer Fete*, 1831

I had already had a bit of a taste of drowning in the River Thames....

Leigh Hunt, *Autobiography*, 1850

The river had an awful look, the buildings on the banks were muffled in black shrouds, and the reflected lights seemed to originate deep in the water, as if the spectres of suicides were holding them to show where they went down. The wild moon and clouds were as restless as an evil conscience in a tumbled bed, and the very shadow of the immensity of London seemed to lie oppressively upon the river.

Charles Dickens, 'Night Walks', in *The Uncommercial Traveller*, 1861

Few European cities have a finer river than the Thames, but none certainly has expended more ingenuity in producing an ugly river-front. For miles and miles you see nothing but the sooty backs of warehouses, or perhaps they are the sooty fronts: in buildings so very expressionless it is impossible to distinguish. They stand massed together on the banks of the wide, turbid stream, which is fortunately of too opaque a quality to reflect the dismal image. A damp-looking, dirty blackness is the universal tone. The river is almost black and is covered with black barges; above the black house-tops, from among the far-reaching docks and basins, rises a dusky wilderness of masts. . . . The whole picture, glazed over with the glutinous London mist, becomes a masterly composition. But it is very impressive in spite of its want of lightness and brightness, and though it is ugly, it is not insignificant. Like so many of the aspects of English civilization that are untouched by elegance or grace, it has the merit of expressing something very serious. Viewed in this intellectual light, the polluted river, the sprawling barges, the dead-faced warehouses, the frowsy people, the atmospheric impurities, become richly suggestive. It sounds rather absurd to say so, but all this sordid detail reminds me of nothing else than the wealth and power of the British empire at large; so that a kind of metaphysical magnificence hovers over the scene, and supplies what may be literally wanting.

Henry James, 'London at Midsummer', 1877, in *Portraits of Places*, 1883

Every drop of the Thames is liquid 'istory.

John Burns, attributed by Sir Frederick Whyte

The Thames is the Melbourne Yarra on a larger scale and without the smell.

Henry Lawson, *Letters to Jack Cornstalk*, 1900

I walk my beat before London Town,
Five hours up and seven down.
Up I go till I end my run
At Tide-end-town, which is Teddington.
Down I come with the mud in my hands
And plaster it over the Maplin Sands.
But I'd have you know that these waters of mine
Were once a branch of the River Rhine,
When hundreds of miles to the East I went
And England was joined to the Continent. . . .

Rudyard Kipling, 'The River's Tale', from *Songs Written for C.R.L. Fletcher's 'A History of England'*, 1911

The river, that string on which is threaded what was once the pearl of cities.

Bill Grundy, *Evening Standard*, 9 May 1979

Thames Valley (people of)

The people be of good and honest conversation, true and faithfull to their frendis and cruell to their enemyes.

Roger Barlow, *A Brief Summe of Geographie*, *c.* 1540

Thanet

. . . that which maketh for the singular praise of the inhabitants of *Tenet*, those especially which dwell by the roads or harboroughs of *Margat*, *Ramsgate*, and *Brodstear* . . . [is that] . . . they are passing industrious, and as if they were *Amphibii*, that is, both *land-creatures and sea-creatures*, get their living both by sea and land, as one would say with both these elements: they be Fishermen and Plough-men: as well Husband-men as Mariners: and they that hold the plough-tails in earing the ground, the same hold the helme in steering the ship. According to the season of the yeare, they knit nets, they fish for Cods, Herrings, Mackarels, &c. they saile, and carry foorth Merchandise. The same againe dung and mannure their grounds, Plough, Sow, harrow, reape their Corne and they inne it. Men most ready and well appointed both for sea and land: and thus goe they round and keepe a circle in these their labours. Furthermore whereas that otherwhiles there happen shipwrackes heere (for there lie full against the shore those dangerous flat, shallows shelves and sands, so much feared of sailers, which they use to call, the *Goodwinsands*, *The Brakes*, *The four-foots*, *The Whitdick &c.*) these men are wont to bestir themselves lustily in recovering both ships, men, and Marchandise endangered.

William Camden, *Britain*, 1610
(Philemon Holland's translation)

Wet, as is common on chalky soils, is most favourable to its vegetation, and confirms the monkish proverb, which says,

When England wrings
The island sings.

Anon., *A Guide to all the Watering and Sea-bathing Places*, *c.* 1810

We have had east winds, and the cliffs are chalk cliffs, and Ramsgate is in the Isle of Thanet, and to the great charm of Nature – the sense of her inexhaustible variety, her infinity – east wind, chalk cliffs, and Thanet are all unfavourable. East wind makes the world look as if you saw it all before you, bare and sharp, cold and bright. Chalk cliffs add to the impression, with their pettiness and clearness; and Thanet, which has no trees and a wonderfully bright atmosphere, adds to it further. The charm and mystery of a broken, wooded, dark-stoned landscape under a south-west wind one can never get a sense of here. Still there is the sea, and that is something even for me. . . .

Matthew Arnold, Letter to his mother, 17 April 1863

I have only known too late, . . . the absolutely literal truth of Turner's saying, that the most beautiful skies in the world known to him were those of the Isle of Thanet.

John Ruskin, *Praeterita*, 1885–9

Torquay

and Torbay

The amphitheatre which surrounds the spacious basin now exhibits everywhere the signs of prosperity and civilization. At the northeastern extremity has sprung up a great watering place, to which strangers are attracted from the most remote parts of our island by the Italian softness of the air: for in that climate the myrtle flourishes unsheltered; and even the winter is milder than the Northumbrian April. The inhabitants are about ten thousand in number. The newly built churches and chapels, the baths and libraries, the hotels and public gardens, the infirmary and the museum, the white streets, rising terrace above terrace, the gay villas peeping from the midst of shrubberies and flower-beds, present a spectacle widely different from any that in the seventeenth century England could show. . . . Torbay, when the Dutch fleet cast anchor there, was known only as a haven where ships sometimes took refuge from the tempests of the Atlantic. Its quiet shores were undisturbed by the bustle either of commerce or of pleasure; and the huts of ploughmen and fishermen were thinly scattered over what is now the site of crowded marts and of luxurious pavilions.

T.B. Macaulay, *History of England*, 1849–61

Torquay lies in a very deep and well-sheltered spot.
And at first sight by strangers it won't be forgot;
Tis said to be the mildest place in all England
And surrounded by lofty hills most beautiful and grand. . . .

You do not wonder at Napoleon's exclamation
As he stood on the deck of the 'Bellerophon' in a fit of admiration
When the vessel was lying to windbound,
He exclaimed – 'Oh what a beautiful country!' his joy was profound.

William McGonagall, *Beautiful Torquay*, *Poetic Gems*, 1890

Henry Philpotts, Bishop of Exeter from 1830 to 1869, lived at a beautiful villa near Torquay, and an enthusiastic lady who visited him there burst into dithyrambics and cried, 'What a lovely spot this is bishop! It is so Swiss.' 'Yes, ma'am,' blandly replied old Harry of Exeter, 'it is very Swiss – only there is no sea in Switzerland, and there are no mountains here.'

G.W.E. Russell, *Collections and Recollections*, 1898

River Trent

And of the British floods, though but the third I be,
Yet Thames, and Severne both in this come short of me,
For that I am the mere of England, that divides
The north part from the south, on my so either sides,
That reckoning how these tracts in compasse be extent,
Men bound them on the north, or on the south of Trent.

Michael Drayton, *Poly-Olbion*, 'The Sixe and Twentieth Song', 1622

Tunbridge Wells

The ladies that appear here are indeed the glory of the place; the coming to the Wells to drink the water is a meer matter of custom; some drink, others do not, and few drink physically: But company and diversion is in short the main business of the place; and those people who have nothing to do any where else, seem to be the only people who have any thing to do at Tunbridge.

Daniel Defoe, *A Tour through the Whole Island of Great Britain*, 1724–7

You can't imagine how much people lye with one another here. I had the narrowest escape in the world.

William Mason, Letter to Thomas Gray, 10 September 1755

I am persuaded Mineral Waters, which are provided by Nature, are the best (perhaps the only real) remedies, particularly that of Tunbridge, of which I have a great Opinion.

Lady Mary Wortley Montagu, Letter to her husband, 12 November 1757

To Indolence, with heart serene,
Apollo dedicates the scene;
A mind that vacancy repels
Is best away from *Tunbridge Wells*.

George Hardinge, *Tunbridge Wells*, *c.* 1800

In looking back over '*the Wells*' I cannot but admire the operation of the gambling system. This little *toadstool* is a thing created entirely by the gamble.

William Cobbett, *Rural Rides*, 31 August 1823

My people are located at a place which is my abomination, viz. Tunbridge Wells . . . they are half killed by the tenuity of the atmosphere and the presence of steel more or less, in earth, air, and water.

Alfred Lord Tennyson, Letter to the Rev. R.J. Tennant, *c* 1840

Uckfield

Garry Essendine: So you've come all the way from Uckfield?
Roland Maule: It isn't very far.
Garry Essendine: I know, but it sort of sounds far, doesn't it?

Noel Coward, *Present Laughter*, 1947

Upper Lambourne

Up the ash tree climbs the ivy,
Up the ivy climbs the sun.
With a twenty thousand pattering
Has a valley breeze begun,
Feathery ash, neglected elder,
Shift the shade and make it run –

Shift the shade toward the nettles,
And the nettles set it free
To streak the stained Carrara headstone
Where, in nineteen-twenty-three,
He who trained a hundred winners
Paid the final Entrance Fee.

Leathery limbs of Upper Lambourne,
Leathery skin from sun and wind,

Leathery breeches, spreading stables,
  Shining saddles left behind,
To the down the string of horses
  Moving out of sight and mind.

Feathery ash in leathery Lambourne
  Waves above the sarsen stone,
And Edwardian plantations
  So coniferously moan,
As to make the swelling downland,
  Far surrounding, seem their own.

John Betjeman, 'Upper Lambourne', *Old Lights for New Chancels*, 1940

Uppingham

I went to *Uppingham* the Shire-towne of *Rutland*, pretty & well built of stone, which is a rarity in that part of *England*, where most of the rural parishes are but of mud, and the people living as wretchedly as in the most impoverish'd parts of *France*, which they much resemble being idle & sluttish: The Country, (especially Licester shire) much in Commune, the Gentry greate drinkers.

John Evelyn, *Diary*, August 1654

River Ure

We, who by our river dwell
Know her changeful beauty well;
Love her with a love allied
Half to fear and half to pride.
If Yorkshire lips triumphant claim
Storied honours for her name
Many a saddened homestead knows
The years her stream in 'freshet' rose
When strength and courage helpless stood
To watch the work of Ure in flood
So, glory of our northern dales
So, terror of our northern tales
Through rocky dell and purple moor
Fierce, bright, and lovely, flashes Ure.

Anon., 'The River Ure', *All the Year Round*, 1878

Walmer

It seems to me the healthiest spot I ever sojourned on – the Clay here covering the calcareous Subsoil with a thin coat, and here mingled with the Lime, attracts the crude dankness from the sea-fogs, yet without retaining it on the one hand or chilling the air by sudden evaporation on the other. For what is not taken up by the plants, is carried off by filtration downward. The number of young Sylvages, too, and of wooded and bushy Hollows and Bottoms, uneven as Quarries, and (duly magnified by and thro' the poetic Herschel of a '*picturesque eye*') romantically sublime and really quite pretty, can not but contribute to purify and inspirit the air. The sea-breezes, I suspect, quicken the olfactory nerves: for I never remember to have caught the fragrance from the Birches and the aroma from the young Pines & arbor vitae Shrubs so perceptibly as from Lord Liverpool's plantation on the side toward the Cliffs.

S.T. Coleridge, Letter to James Gillman, October 1822

'Twas thought the Queen would this year go
  To Brighton as she did the former;
She chang'd her mind, because we know
  Brighton is cold, the Duke's is *Walmer*.

Anon., *On the Queen's visit to Walmer Castle*, *c.* November 1842

Walsingham

In the wrackes of Walsingham
  Whom should I chuse
But the Queen of Walsingham
  To be guide to my muse;
Then thou Prince of Walsingham
  Graunt me to frame
Bitter plaintes to rewe thy wronge
  Bitter wo for thy name,
Bitter was it so to see
  The seely sheepe
Murdred by the ravening wolves
  While the sheephardes did sleep,
Bitter was it oh to vewe
  The sacred vyne,
While the gardiners plaied all close,
  rooted up by the swine,
Bitter bitter oh to behould
  The grasse to growe
Where the walles of Walsingham
  So stately did shewe,
Such were the workes of Walsingham
  While shee did stand,
Such are the wrackes as now do shewe
  Of that holy land.
Levell Levell with the ground
  The towres do lye,
Which with their golden glittering tops
  Pearsed once with the skye,
Wher were gates, no gates are now,
  The waies unknowen
Where the presse of peares did passe
  While her fame was blowen.
Oules do skrike wher the sweetest himnes
  Lately weer songe,
Toades and serpentes hold their dennes
  Wher the Palmers did thronge.

Weepe weepe o Walsingham
  Whose dayes ar nightes,
Blessings turned to blasphemies
  Holy deedes to dispites,
Sinne is wher our Ladie sate,
  Heaven turned is to Hell.
Sathan sittes wher our Lord did swaye;
  Walsingham oh Farewell.

Anon., perhaps Robert Southwell, sixteenth century

As you came from the holy land
Of Walsinghame
Mett you not with my true love
By the way as you came?

Sir Walter Raleigh, *As You Came*, *c.* 1700

River Wandle

The Wandal cometh in, the Mole's loved mate,
So amiable, so fair, so pure, so delicate.

Michael Drayton, *Poly-Olbion*, 1612–22

The blue transparent Vandalis.

Alexander Pope, *Windsor Forest*, 1713

Wansford (Northamptonshire)

I lay at the Swan in Wanstead-in-England, being a jest on a man makeing hay fell a sleep on a heap of it and a great storme washed the hay and the man into the River, and carry'd him to the Bridge, where he awoke and knew not where he was, called to the people in the grounds and told them he lived in a place called Wanstead in England, which goes for a jest on the men of Wanstead to this day.

Celia Fiennes, *Journeys*, 1698

Warminster

Warminster is a very nice town; everything belonging to it is *solid* and *good*. There are no villainous gingerbread houses running up, and no nasty, shabby-genteel people; no women trapesing about with showy gowns and dirty necks; no jew-looking fellows with dandy coats, dirty shirts and half heels to their shoes. A really nice and good town. It is a great corn-market, one of the greatest in Britain.

William Cobbett, *Rural Rides*, 3 September 1826

Warwick

The High Street

The street is an emblem of England itself. What seems new in it is chiefly a skilful and fortunate adaptation of what such a people as ourselves would destroy. The new things are based and supported on sturdy old things, and derive a massive strength from their deep and immemorial foundations, though with such limitations and impediments as only an Englishman could endure. But he likes to feel the weight of all the past upon his back; and, moreover, the antiquity that overburdens him has taken root in his being, and has grown to be rather a hump than a pack, so that there is no getting rid of it without tearing his whole structure to pieces. In my judgement, as he appears to be sufficiently comfortable under the mouldy accretion, he had better stumble on with it as long as he can. He presents a spectacle which is by no means without its charm for a disinterested and unencumbered observer.

Nathaniel Hawthorne, *Our Old Home*, 1863

Warwick is one of those towns of which there are not a few in England for the existence of which it is difficult to account. Why people should have gathered their dwellings together at this spot in sufficient numbers to make a large town is not easily discoverable. It has no trade, no manufactures, no Cathedral, no School, no centralizing attraction. How the people live there is a mystery. For visiting strangers can do little to support the inhabitants of such a place; and whence do the Warwickers get the money wherewith to pay each other?

Richard Grant White, *England Without and Within*, 1881

Warwick Castle

. . . perceiving as soon as I could perceive any political truth at all, that it was probably much happier to live in a small house, and have Warwick Castle to be astonished at, than to live in Warwick Castle and have nothing to be astonished at.

John Ruskin, *Praeterita*, 1885–9

Warwickshire

Upon the mid-lands now th'industrious Muse doth fall;
That shire which wee the hart of England well may
  call, . . .
Brave Warwick . . .
If there be vertue yet remaining in thy earth,
Or any good of thine thou breathd'st into my birth
Accept it as thine owne whilst now I sing of thee;
Of all thy later brood th'unworthiest though I bee.

Michael Drayton, *Poly-Olbion*, 'The Thirteenth Song', 1612

Does external nature and beauty influence the soul to good? You go about Warwickshire and fancy that from merely being born and wandering in those sweet sunny plains and fresh woodlands Shakspere must have drunk in a portion of that frank artless sense of beauty which lies about his works like a bloom or dew; but a Coventry riband-maker, or a slang Leamington squire, are looking on those very same landscapes too, and what do they profit?

W.M. Thackeray, *Journey from Cornhill to Cairo*, 1845

The Warwickshire scenery is incredibly rich and pastoral. The land is one teeming garden. It is in fact too monotonously sweet and smooth – too comfortable, too ovine, too bovine, too English, in a word. But in its way it's the last word of human toil. It seems like a vast show region kept up at the expense of the poor.

Henry James, Letter to William James, 26 April 1869

It is the core and centre of the English world; mid-most England, unmitigated England. The place has taught me a great many English secrets; I have interviewed the genius of pastoral Britain.

Henry James, 'In Warwickshire', 1877, in *Portraits of Places*, 1883

The Weald of Kent

The common saying goes, that on the hill
A man may lie in bed to work his farm,
Propping his elbows on his window-sill
To watch his harvest growing like a charm.
But the man who works the wet and weeping soil
Down in the weald, must marl and delve and till
His three-horse land, fearing nor sweat nor droil.
For through the winter he must fight the flood,
The clay, that yellow enemy, that rots
His land, sucks at his horses' hooves
So that his waggon plunges in the mud,
And horses strain, but waggon never moves;
Delays his plough, and holds his spud
With yeavy spite in trenching garden-plots,
The catchy clay, that does its utmost harm,
And comes into his house, to spoil
Even his dwelling, creeps into his bones
Before their time, and makes them ache,
Leaving its token in his husky tones; . . .
. . . only a bold man ploughs the Weald for corn,
Most are content with fruit or pasture, knowing
Too well both drought and winter's heavy going;
So the lush Weald today
Lies green in distance, and the horizon's sweep
Deepens to blue in woods, with pointed spire
Pricking the foreground by the village tiles,
And the hop-kiln's whitened chimney stares between
Paler and darker green of Kentish miles,
And rarely a patch of corn in metal fire
Burnished by sunset ruffles in the green;
But meadow, shaw, and orchard keep
The glaucous country like a hilly sea
Pure in its monotone.

V. Sackville-West, *The Land*, 1926

Wells

Wells itself is ideally situated, amid the hills which break away from the windy Mendips to the great Somerset level. A peaceful village, little more; and at a turn of the street, you come upon that glorious Cathedral, set amid surely the most beautiful Close that exists; the entrance at each corner through archways of grey crumbling stone. Anything like the Bishop's Palace I never saw. It is surrounded by a wall and a moat: the wall embattled and loop-holed, overgrown with ivy, and in places with peach and apricot; the entrance a drawbridge and portcullis; and the moat very wide, supplied with water that rushes into it foaming and roaring from St Andrew's well, a great spring coming somehow from the hidden depths of the Mendips. Swans and ducks swim about on the olive-green water. Close by is a walk shadowed by huge, dense elms, and all around are lawns, meadows, hills, rising to woodland and heath. A marvellous spot, civilized with the culture of centuries, yet quite unlike the trimness of other cathedral towns.

George Gissing, Letter to his brother, 4 August 1894

Wenlock Edge

On Wenlock Edge the wood's in trouble;
His forest fleece the Wrekin heaves;
The gale, it plies the saplings double,
And thick on Severn snow the leaves.

'Twould blow like this through holt and hanger
When Uricon the city stood:
'Tis the old wind in the old anger,
But then it threshed another wood.

Then, 'twas before my time, the Roman
At yonder heaving hill would stare:
The blood that warms an English yeoman,
The thoughts that hurt him, they were there.

There, like the wind through woods in riot,
Through him the gale of life blew high;
The tree of man was never quiet;
Then 'twas the Roman, now 'tis I.

The gale, it plies the saplings double,
It blows so hard, 'twill soon be gone:
To-day the Roman and his trouble
Are ashes under Uricon.

A.E. Housman, *A Shropshire Lad*, 1896

Westerham

Passing through Westerham today, I noted how the

statue of General Wolfe brandishing his sword looked exactly like Mozart conducting *Don Giovanni*.

James Agate, *Ego 3*, 17 July 1937

Westgate-on-Sea

Hark, I hear the bells of Westgate,
  I will tell you what they sigh,
Where those minarets and steeples
  Prick the open Thanet sky. . . .

Church of England bells of Westgate!
  On this balcony I stand,
White the woodwork wriggles round me,
  Clock towers rise on either hand.

For me in my timber arbour
  You have one more message yet,
'Plimsolls, plimsolls in the summer,
  Oh goloshes in the wet!'

John Betjeman, *Collected Poems*, 1958

Westmorland

Westmoreland, a country eminent only for being the wildest, most barren and frightful of any that I have passed over in England, or even in Wales it self.

Daniel Defoe, *A Tour through the Whole Island of Great Britain*, 1724–7

Weston-super-Mare

Bristolians want somewhere to take their ladies of a Sunday afternoon; here they can bask in the mud like so many hippopotami. The last time I visited Weston-super-Mare was on the day of the Coronation. . . . The town did its best to look festive for the occasion, achieving the standard of jubilation which one might expect at a Jewish funeral in New York.

Auberon Waugh, *Country Topics*, 1974

Wessex

There are some heights in Wessex, shaped as if by a
  kindly hand
For thinking, dreaming, dying on, and at crises when I
  stand,
Say, on Ingpen Beacon eastward, or on Wylls-Neck
  westwardly,
I seem where I was before my birth, and after death
  may be.

Thomas Hardy, *Wessex Heights*, 1896

Weymouth

and Brighton

One contemplates old Ocean here in Peace and Quietness; no Storm, no tossing, no raving; yet sometimes I fancy Him *shaved*, and long to see his hoary Beard at Brighthelmstone, where his Dignity & Sublimity, not his Delicacy and glassy Smoothness are to be admired.

Hester Lynch Thrale/Piozzi, *Thraliana*, 1783

Weymouth is altogether a shocking place, I perceive, without recommendation of any kind, & worthy only of being frequented by the inhabitants of Gloucester.

Jane Austen, Letter to Cassandra Austen, 14 September 1804

Widnes

They say that men become attached even to Widnes.

A.J.P. Taylor, *Observer*, 15 September 1963

Isle of Wight

The ground (to say nothing of the sea exceeding full of fish) consisteth of soile very fruitfull and is thankfull to the husbandmen, in so much as it doth affoord corne to be carried forth: breeding every where store of conies, hares, partridges and phesants. One little forrest it hath likewise, and two parks replenished with deere, for game and hunting pleasure. Through the mids thereof runs a long tract or chaine of hils, yeelding plentie of pasture and forrage for sheepe. The wooll of which, next unto that of Lempster and Cotteswold, is esteemed best and in speciall request with Clothiers, whereby there groweth to the inhabitants much gaine and profit: The North side is all over greene with meddows, pastures, and woods: the south side lieth wholly in maner bedecked with corne fields enclosed, where at each end the sea on the North side doth so inbosome, encroatch within it selfe, that it maketh almost two Ilands: & verily so the Ilanders call them: namely *Fresh-water Isle* which looketh West, and *Binbridge Isle*, Eastward. . . . The inhabitants of this Isle were wont merrily to make their boast, that their case was happier than all others, because they had neither hooded monks nor cavilling Lawyers, nor yet crafty foxes. . . .

Neither are there wanting for the defence of this Isle naturall fences. For encircled it is with a continuall ridge, and raunge as it were of craggy cliff; there are under the waters like wise hidden stones: and every where there lie against it, bankes and rockes perilous for sailors: but the most dangerous of all the rest are the *Needles*, so called because they are so sharpe, and the *Shingles*; which stand forth against the West angle of the Isle: as also the *Owers* and *Mixon* that lie before the

East. Besides these *The Brambles*, which are *Shelves* and perilous for Sailers, in the North Coast. Moreover if there be any place that seemeth open and meete for a landing place, the same by an old order and custom among them is piled with strong stakes driven and pitched deepe into the ground.

William Camden, *Britain*, 1610
(Philemon Holland's translation)

The Isle of Wight hath no monks, lawyers or foxes.

Quoted in John Ray, *Compleat Collection of English Proverbs*, 1670

On the road from Cowes to Newport I saw some extensive Barracks which disgusted me extremely with Government for placing such a Nest of Debauchery in so beautiful a place – I asked a man on the coach about this – and he said that the people had been spoiled – In the room where I slept at Newport I found this on the Window 'O Isle spoilt by the Mil*a*tary!' I must in honesty however confess that I did not feel very sorry at the idea of the Women being a little profligate.

John Keats, Letter to John Hamilton Reynolds, 17–18 April 1817

Wigton

Wigton, Dickens described as a place of little houses all in half-mourning, yellow stone or white stone and black, with the wonderful peculiarity that though it had no population, no business, and no streets to speak of, it had five linendrapers within range of their single window, one linendrapers next door, and five more linendrapers round the corner.

John Forster, *Life of Dickens*, 1872–3

Wilton House

If Wholsom Aire, Earth, woods, & pleasant Springs
Are Elements, whereby a house is grac'd:
If strong and stately built, contentment brings,
Such is the house of *Wilton*, and so plac'd.
There Nature, Art, Art Nature hath embrac'd;
Without, within, below, aloft, compleat:
Delight and state, are there so interlac'd
With rich content, which makes all good and great
The Hangings there, with Histories repleat,
Divine, profane, and Morall pleasures giving –
With worke so lively exquisite, and neat
As if mans Art made mortall creatures living,
In briefe, there all things are composed so well,
Beyond my pen to write, or tongue to tell.

John Taylor, *A Discovery by Sea, from London to Salisbury*, 1623, in *All the Works of John Taylor*, 1630

Wilton is the paradise of England with its three rivers, eternally beautiful and unchanged while its owners change and perish. One passes by and finds Herberts living there, happily idling their lives away, as one finds swallows year after year nesting in a village, and one imagines them to be the same Herberts, as one imagines the others to be the same swallows.

Wilfred Scawen Blunt, Diary, August 1897, *My Diaries*, 1919

Wiltshire

A pleasant county, and of great variety. I have heard a wise man say, that an ox left to himself would, of all England, choose to live in the north, a sheep in the south part hereof, and a man in the middle betwixt both, as partaking of the pleasure of the plain, and the wealth of the deep country.

Thomas Fuller, *History of the Worthies of England*, 1662

. . . to find the Proportion of the Downes of this Countrey to the Vales, I did divide Speeds Mappe of Wiltshire with a pair of Cizars, according to the respective Hundreds of Downes and Vale: And I weighed them in a Curious Ballance of a Goldsmith. . . .

John Aubrey, *The Naturall Historie of Wiltshire*, *c.* 1675

Wiltshire Downs

There is a freedom in this vastness, these open downs, which far surpasses the most picturesque of landscape where the traveller cannot quit the beaten path. It is an almost prairie-like solitude; the farmhouses are far between, and lie chiefly in the 'bottoms,' as the combes are called, so that one may pass them easily unnoticed; and the hamlets farther still, placed where some never-failing spring supplies man and beast with water. Water is as precious here as in the veritable deserts of the East. The shepherds are the only human beings to be seen.

Richard Jefferies, 'The Wiltshire Downs', in the *Graphic*, 1877

Winchester

Where I saw an ancient City, like a body without a soule: and I know not the reason of it, but for ought which I perceived, there were almost as many Parishes as people. I lodged at the signe of the Cocke, being recommended to the Host of the house, by a token from *Salisbury*, but mine Host dyed the night before I came, and I being weary, had more minde to goe to bed, then to follow him so long a journey, to doe my message, or deliver any commendations: but the whole City seemed almost as dead as mine Host.

John Taylor, *A Discovery by Sea, from London to Salisbury*, 1623

I was disappointed in Winchester: it is a paltry town, and small: king Charles the second's house is the worst thing I ever saw of Sir Christopher Wren, a mixture of a town-hall and an hospital; not to mention the bad choice of the situation in such a country; it is all *ups* that should be *downs*.

Horace Walpole, Letter to Richard Bentley, 18 September 1755

. . . the pleasantest Town I ever was in, and has the most reccomendations of any. There is a fine Cathedrall, which to me is always a source of amusement. . . . The whole town is beautifully wooded – From the Hill at the eastern extremity you see a prospect of Streets, and old Buildings mixed up with Trees. Then there are the most beautiful streams about I ever saw – full of Trout. . . . And what improves it all is, the fashionable inhabitants are all gone to Southampton.

John Keats, Letter to Fanny Keats, 28 August 1819

There is not one loom or any thing like manufacturing beyond bread and butter in the whole City.

John Keats, Letter to George and Georgiana Keats, 18 September 1819

The city is of course in one of the deepest holes that can be imagined. It never could have been thought of as a place to be defended since the discovery of gunpowder; and indeed, one would think that a very considerable annoyance might be given to the inhabitants even by the flinging of the flintstones from the hills down into the city.

William Cobbett, *Rural Rides*, 7 August 1823

Addressing a coachman by whose side I was sitting as we drove in a coach through that place . . . I asked him, 'What sort of a place is Winchester?' Answer: Debauched, sir, debauched, like all other Cathedral cities.

Alfred Lord Tennyson, in Arthur Coleridge, *Fragmentary Notes of Tennyson's Talk*, in Hallam Tennyson (ed.), *Tennyson and his Friends* 1911

Lake Windermere

I overlooked the bed of Windermere,
Like a vast river, stretching in the sun.
With exultation at my feet I saw
Lake islands, promontories, gleaming bays,
A universe of Nature's fairest forms
Proudly revealed with instantaneous burst,
Magnificent, and beautiful, and gay.

William Wordsworth, *The Prelude*, 1805 (text of 1850)

There are many disfigurements to this Lake – not in the way of land or water. No; the two views we have had of it are of the most noble tenderness – they can never fade away – they make one forget the divisions of life; age, youth, poverty and riches; and refine one's sensual vision into a sort of north star which can never cease to be open lidded and stedfast over the wonders of the great Power. The disfigurement I mean is the miasma of London. I do suppose it contaminated with bucks and soldiers, and women of fashion – and hatband ignorance. The border inhabitants are quite out of keeping with the romance about them, from a continued intercourse with London rank and fashion. But why should I grumble? They let me have a prime glass of soda water.

John Keats, Letter to Thomas Keats, 25–27 June 1818

Winchelsea (and Rye)

Henry James . . . only came to Winchilsea in the late autumn and winter. In that great square, round the great half-fallen church, the rain would run in light drifts. He would dig his cane point into the grass between the cobbles and exclaim: 'A Winchilsea day, my dear lady. A true Winchilsea day. . . . This is Winchilsea. . . . Poor but proud.' Waspishly patriotic we would point to the red-roofed pyramid across the marsh and exclaim:

'That's your Rye. It's *pouring* there. . . . Rye. . . . Not rich but dirty.'

These were the only occasions on which we stood up to the Master. And he never heard. He would scuttle off towards tea. . . .

Ford Madox Ford, *Return to Yesterday*, 1932

Windsor

Surely a Princes seat cannot lightly have a more pleasant site. For, from an high hill that ariseth with a gentle ascent, it enjoieth a most delightfull prospect round about. For right in the Front it overlooketh a vale lying out farre and wide, garnished with cornefields flourishing greene with medowes, decked with groves on either side and watered with the most mild and calme river Tamis. Behind it arise hils every where, neither rough nor over high, attired, as it were, with woods and even dedicated as one would say by nature to hunting game.

William Camden, *Britain*, 1610 (Philemon Holland's translation)

Windsor Castle

Meadows trim with daisies pied;
Shallow brooks and rivers wide;
Towers and battlements it sees

Bosomed high in tufted trees,
Where perhaps some beauty lies
The cynosure of neighboring eyes.
Hard by a cottage chimney smokes
From betwixt two aged oaks.

John Milton, *L'Allegro*, 1645

It is a castle for strength, a palace for state; and hath in it a college for learning, a chapel for devotion, and an almshouse (of decayed gentlemen) for charity. In this place most remarkable, the hall for greatness, Winchester tower for height, and the terrace on the north side for pleasure, where a dull eye may travel twenty miles in a moment.

Thomas Fuller, *History of the Worthies of England*, 1662

Thy Forests, *Windsor*! and thy green Retreats,
At once the Monarch's and the Muse's Seats.

Alexander Pope, *Windsor-Forest*, 1713

In talking of Windsor, Lady Lansdowne objected to the number of dirty houses that came up quite close to the Castle. This Lord John said he liked; it was feudal, and he preferred it much to the insulation of the great houses of the present day. Was at first inclined to agree with him, but on recollecting the dependence implied by this juxtaposition of the great and small, retracted my concurrence, and was all for the stand-off system of Lady Lansdowne; each rank in its own station.

Thomas Moore, *Diary*, 12 October 1837

Windsor stood out in the evening light: I think there can be no place like it – the eye-greeting burl of the Round Tower; all the crown-like medley of lower towers warping round; red and white houses of the town abutting on these, gabled and irregularly jut-jotted against them, making a third stage or storey.

Gerard Manley Hopkins, *Journal*, 21 August 1874

Windsor Castle is a stately pile from the outside, but in the interior that one sees the state apartments – are decidedly shabby, like a second class boarding house.

Lilian Leland, *Travelling Alone, A Woman's Journey Round the World*, 1890

St George's Chapel
When I first saw it, the pillars within had acquired, by time, a sombre hue, which accorded with the architecture; and the gloom increased its dimensions to the eye by hiding its parts; but now it all bursts on the view at once, and the sublimity has vanished before the brush and broom; for it has been white-washed and scraped till it is become as bright and neat as the pots and pans in a notable house-wife's kitchen – yes; the very spurs on the recumbent knights were deprived of their venerable rust, to give a striking proof that a love of order in trifles, and taste for proportion and arrangement are very distinct. The glare of light thus introduced entirely destroys the sentiment these piles are calculated to inspire; so that, when I heard something like a jig from the organ-loft, I thought it an excellent hall for dancing or feasting.

Mary Wollstonecraft, *Letters Written During a Short Residence in Sweden, etc.*, 1796

Windsor Forest
All hail! once pleasing, once inspiring Shade,
Scene of my youthful Loves, and happier hours!
Where the kind Muses met me as I stray'd,
And gently pressd my hand, and said, Be Ours!

Alexander Pope, *A Hymn Written in Windsor Forest*, 1717

Windsor Forest, . . . as bleak, as barren, and as villainous a heath as ever man set eyes on.

William Cobbett, *Rural Rides*, 1822

Woking

Our withdrawal to Woking was a fairly cheerful adventure. Woking was the site of the first crematorium, but few of our friends made more than five or six jokes about that.

H.G. Wells, *An Experiment in Autobiography*, 1934

Wolverhampton

Grim Wolverhampton lights her smouldering fires.

Anna Seward, *Colebrook Dale*, *c.* 1784

The vilest-looking town I ever saw.

Charles Greville, *A Journal of the Reign of Queen Victoria*, 24 June 1839

A three-day fiesta at Wolverhampton organised by the Council to publicise the town has ended with an enquiry into interdepartmental discord arising from the chief public relations officer's punching of the anti-vandalism officer.

Daily Telegraph, quoted in 'This England', *New Statesman*, 4 July 1980

Wolverton

Wolverton is a mid-nineteenth century railway town in Buckinghamshire, halfway between Oxford and Cambridge. There are hundreds of small hideous terrace houses in livid brick, a few chapels and railwaymen's clubs, humped in the flat countryside around the railway workshops and one of the most dangerous road bridges in the country. It is a prosperous Southern edition of the squalid Northern Industrial town. The failure to rebuild it is somehow indicative of what is wrong with our country. Poised as it is, midway between the University cities, and on the main line to London, with the M.1. only a few miles away, Wolverton seems like something out of *Fanny by Gaslight*, God knows what the North must be like, you feel, if Wolverton is like this.

John Vaizey, 'The Tragedy of Being Clever', *Encounter*, July 1963

Wookey Hole

To Wookey Hole this morning, a cave; it was not quite what I wanted to see, tho' very grim.

Alfred Lord Tennyson, Letter-Diary, August 1854, *Alfred Lord Tennyson, a Memoir by his Son*, 1897

Worcestershire

This County . . . hath so temperate an aire, and soile so favourable, that for healthfulnesse and plenty, it is not inferiour to their neighbour countries, and in one part for deinty cheese surpasseth them: yeelding such store of peares, as none other the like; and albeit they are not so pleasing to these deinty and delicate mouthes, yet out of their winish juice, they make a bastard kinde of wine called *Pyrry*, which they drinke very much, although it bee (as other drinkes of that kinde) both cold and full of winde. Neither is it if you respect waters, lesse pleasant and commodious: for in every place there be passing sweet rivers, which affoord in great abundance the most delicate kinds of fishes.

William Camden, *Britain*, 1610
(Philemon Holland's translation)

As I got into Worcestershire, I opened upon a landscape of country which I prefer even to Kent, which I had reckoned the most beautiful county in England: but this, with all the richness of Kent, is bounded with mountains.

Horace Walpole, Letter to Richard Bentley, September 1753

When the immense misty plain of hedges-checkered Worcesterhire lies steeped in the beautiful verdurous shades which seem to rise as an emanation from its meadows and farm-steads and parks, and the sky expands above it, tremendous and Turneresque, a chaos of rolling grey – a rain of silver, a heaven of tender distant blue – there is something to my eyes in a sight so wonderfully characteristic and national, so eloquent of the English spirit and the English past that I half expect to hear from a thousand throats a murmur of sympathy and delight. But as a general thing all the people I see here are as utterly indifferent or deeply insensible to the beauty of their country.

Henry James, Letter to Henry James Sr, 19 March 1870

The other afternoon I trudged over to Worcester – thro' a region so thicksown with good old English 'effects' – with elm-scattered meadows and sheep-cropped commons and the ivy-smothered dwellings of small gentility, and high-gabled, heavy-timbered, broken-plastered farm-houses, and stiles leading to delicious meadow-footpaths and lodge-gates leading to far-off manors – with all things suggestive of the opening chapters of half-remembered novels, devoured in infancy – that I felt as if I were pressing all England to my soul.

Ibid.

Worksop

Worksop, a towne well knowne for the liquorice that there groweth and prospereth passing well.

William Camden, *Britain*, 1610
(Philemon Holland's translation)

Worthing

Even I loved Worthing.

D.H. Lawrence, Letter to Lady Ottoline Morrell, 30 April 1915

Wotton-under-Weaver

Wotton-under-Weaver
Where God came never

– It is time that this old profane proverb should die in men's mouths for ever. . . . It seems [it] took its wicked original from the situation of Wotton, so covered with hills from the light of the sun, a dismal place, as report representeth it.

Thomas Fuller, *History of the Worthies of England*, 1662

River Wye

a few miles above Tintern Abbey

. . . again I hear
These waters, rolling from their mountain-springs
With a sweet inland murmur. – Once again
Do I behold these steep and lofty cliffs,
That on a wild secluded scene impress
Thoughts of more deep seclusion; and connect
The landscape with the quiet of the sky. . . .
Once again I see
These hedge-rows, hardly hedge-rows, little lines
Of sportive wood run wild: these pastoral farms,
Green to the very door; and wreaths of smoke
Sent up, in silence from among the trees! . . .
These beauteous forms,
Through a long absence, have not been to me

As is a landscape to a blind man's eye:
But oft, in lonely rooms, and 'mid the din
Of towns and cities, I have owed to them,
In hours of weariness, sensations sweet,
Felt in the blood, and felt along the heart;
And passing even into my purer mind,
With tranquil restoration: . . .
Nor less, I trust,
To them I may have owed another gift,
Of aspect more sublime; that blessed mood,
In which the burthen of the mystery,
In which the heavy and the weary weight
Of all this unintelligible world,
Is lightened. . . .

William Wordsworth, *Lines Composed a Few Miles Above Tintern Abbey*, 13 July 1798

I left Tintern and went to Windcliffe, from the summit of which there is a very fine view; but the Wye, instead of being an embellishment, is an eyesore in the midst of such scenery: it looks like a long slimy snake dragging its foul length through the hills and woods which environ its muddy stream.

Charles Greville, *A Journal of the Reign of Queen Victoria*, 4 July 1839

Yarmouth

Whose fishing through the realme, doth her so much renowne
Where those that with their nets still haunt the boundles lake,
Her such a sumptuous feast of salted herrings make,
As they have rob'd the sea of all his former store,
And past that very howre it could produce no more.

Michael Drayton, *Poly-Olbion*, 'The Twentieth Song', 1622

There did I see a Towne well fortifide,
Well govern'd, with all Natures wants supplide;
The situation in a wholesome ayre,
The buildings (for the most part) sumptuous, faire,
The people courteous, and industrious, and
With labour makes the Sea inrich the Land.
Besides (for ought I know) this one thing more,
The Towne can scarcely yeeld a man a Whore:
It is renowned for Fishing, farre and neere,
And sure in *Britaine* it hath not a Peere.

John Taylor, *A Very Merry Wherry-Ferry-Voyage*, 1622

Yarmouth resembles Genoa, in its narrow alleys full of shops, which extend from the Market to the Quay. . . .

E.D. Clarke, *Travels in Various Countries*, 1824

. . . went to a horrible place called Yarmouth. Half of it was just like Wembley. . . .

Evelyn Waugh, *Diary*, 9 September 1925

Yarrow

And is this – Yarrow? – *This* the Stream
Of which my fancy cherished,
So faithfully, a waking dream?
An image that hath perished!
O that some Minstrel's harp were near,
To utter notes of gladness,
And chase this silence from the air,
That fills my heart with sadness!

Yet why? – a silvery current flows
With uncontrolled meanderings;
Nor have these eyes by greener hills
Been soothed in all my wanderings.
And through her depths, Saint Mary's Lake
Is visibly delighted;
For not a feature of those hills
Is in the mirror slighted.

William Wordsworth, *Yarrow Visited*, September 1814

York

Now for the City: 'Tis of state and Port,
Where Emperors & Kings have kept their Court, . . .
'Tis large, 'tis pleasant and magnificent,
The North's most fertile famous ornament.

John Taylor, *A Very Merry Wherry-Ferry-Voyage*, 1622

For one of the Metropolis and the See of the Archbishop it makes but a meane appearance, the Streetes are narrow and not of any length, save one which you enter of from the bridge, that is over the Ouse which lookes like a fine river when full after much raine – it is but low in comparison with some rivers – it bears great Barges, it looks muddy; its full of very good fish we eate very good Cod fish and Salmon and that at a pretty cheape rate tho' we were not in the best inn for the Angel is the best, in Cunny Streete; the houses are very low and as indifferent as in any Country town, and the narrowness of the streetes makes it appear very mean. . . .

It looks better at the approach, because you see the towers off the gates and severall Churches in compassing the Minster and all the Windmills round the town, of which there are many; the River runns through the town and so its divided, the buildings look no better than the outskirts off London Wappen etc. The Bridge is fine arches and built on with houses, the Pavement which is esteemed the chiefe part of town, where the Market house and Town hall stands, is so mean that Southwarke is much before it. . . .

Celia Fiennes, *Journeys*, 1697

York is indeed a pleasant and beautiful city, and not at all the less beautiful for the works and lines about it being demolished, and the city, as it may be said, being laid open, for the beauty of peace is seen in the rubbish; the lines and bastions and demolished fortifications, have a reserved secret pleasantness in them from the contemplation of the publick tranquility, that outshines all the beauty of advanced bastions, batteries, cavaliers, and all the hard named works of the engineers about a city.

Daniel Defoe, *A Tour through the Whole Island of Great Britain*, 1724–7

I . . . have laid the foundation of many nervous complaints which will agitate me for the rest of my life – unless I am restored by the copious feeding and profound tranquility of Yorkshire.

I have taken a very pleasant house about a mile from York – just sufficient to enable me to stem the torrents of Tea by which I should at a nearer distance be overwhelmed.

Sydney Smith, Letter to Lady Caroline Lamb, 18 June 1809

My father once exclaiming to one of the principal tradesman there, 'Why, Mr Brown, your streets are the narrowest in Europe; there is not actually room for two carriages to pass.'

'Not room!' said the indignant Yorkist, 'there's plenty of room, Sir, and above an inch and a half to spare!'

Lady Holland, *Memoir of Sydney Smith*, 1855

There are more harlots in York than ever I saw elsewhere.

Evelyn Waugh, *Diary*, August 1926

York Minster

York Minster, with the sun new-washed for bed shining full on the west window, looked lovelier than I have ever seen it. Yellow, crisp, and *eatable*, like the crust of apple-pie.

James Agate, *Ego* (5 June 1932), 1935

Yorkshire

He is Yorkshire – said of a shrewd man.

Quoted in John Ray, *A Compleat Collection of English Proverbs*, 1670

The appellation 'Yorkshire *bite*;' the acute sayings ascribed to Yorkshiremen; and their quick manner I remember in the army. When speaking of what county a man was, one used to say, in defence of the party, 'York, but honest.' Another saying was, that it was a bare common that a Yorkshireman would go over without taking a bite. Every one knows the story of the gentleman who, upon finding that a boot-cleaner in the south was a Yorkshireman, and expressing his surprise that he was not become master of the inn, received for an answer, 'Ah, sir, but master is York too!' And that of the Yorkshire boy, who, seeing a gentleman eating some eggs, asked the cook to give him a little *salt*; and upon being asked what he could want with salt, he said; 'perhaps that gentleman may give me an egg presently.'

It is surprising what effect sayings like these produce upon the mind. From one end to the other of the kingdom Yorkshiremen are looked upon as being keener than other people; more eager in pursuit of their own interests; more sharp and more selfish. For my part, I was cured with regard to the *people* long before I saw Yorkshire. In the army, where we see men of all counties, I always found Yorkshiremen distinguished for their frank manners and generous disposition . . . and . . . I long ago made up my mind that this hardness and sharpness ascribed to Yorkshiremen arose from the sort of envy excited by that quickness, that activity, that buoyancy of spirits, which bears them up through adverse circumstances, and their consequent success in all the situations of life. They, like the people of Lancashire are just the reverse of being *cunning* and *selfish*; be they farmers, or be they what they may, you get at the bottom of their hearts in a minute. Everything they think soon gets to the tongue, and out it comes, heads and tails, as fast as they can pour it.

William Cobbett, *Rural Rides – Eastern Tour*, 19 April 1830

*A Yorkshireman, like a dragoon, is nothing without his horse.

Robert Smith Surtees, *Jorrocks's Jaunts and Jollities*, 1838, originally pub. in the *New Sporting Magazine*, between July 1831 and September 1834, no. 2, 'The Yorkshireman and the Surrey'

My living in Yorkshire was so far out of the way that it was actually twelve miles from a lemon.

Sydney Smith, quoted by Lady Holland, *Memoir of Sydney Smith*, 1855

Ah's Yorkshire! bi mi truly!
Ah is, Ah'm proud ti say;
Just try ya ti get ower mah,
Ye'll heve eneaf ti deah.
Ah's oppen-gobbed an' soft like;
Ah knaw mare than ah tell;
The fellah that wad bite mah
All seaf get bit his sel. Ah's Yorkshire.

Ah's Yorkshire! Ah's a plain stick,
What's that? It's been mi luck
Ti bi like monny a dahmond,
Covered at top wi muck.
Some fooaks weear t'muck at insard
Seeah deep its scarcely seen

Nooah's flood a pure soft watter
Wad scarcely wesh em clean. Ah's Yorkshire.

Ah's Yorkshire ti the back beean
Out-spokken, frank and free,
Ah hate a leear as Ah hate
Awd Nick, that tell'd first lee.
Ance Ah may be catch'd nappin,
We all may slip sum day
But twice if ye get ower mah,
Ah nivver mair al say, Ah's Yorkshire.

William Hall Burnett, *Ah's Yorkshire*, nineteenth century

More than any other county in England, Yorkshire retained a sort of social independence of London. Scotland itself was hardly more distinct. . . . To a certain degree, evident enough to Yorkshiremen, Yorkshire was not English – or was all England, as they might choose to express it.

Henry Adams, *The Education of Henry Adams*, 1906

I hold Yorkshire to be a mistake.

James Agate, *Ego 9* (6 May 1946), 1948

Our maps are music and our northern titles,
Like wind among the grass and heather, grieve.
Our maps are candid charts of desolation
And wear the Pennine weather on their sleeve.

There's Howl Moor, Wetshaw, Winterings and Gutters,
Mirk Fell and Dirty Pool and Hagworm Hill,
Fog Close, Cold Skye, Ravock, and Crooks Altar,
And Loups and Wham and Whaw and Rotten Gill.

Our maps are music and they sing the miners'
Old wrestle with the rocks for yield of lead:
There's Old Gang, Windegg, Eskeleth, and Crackpot,
And Racca Vein, forsaken. They are dead.

Our maps are music and they sing the farmers'
Long battle to wring fodder from the fell:
There's Stony Mea and Nettlepot and Sour Nook,
There's Pasture End and Halfpenny, and Farewell.

Ivor Brown 'The Moorland Map', in *Landmarks*, ed. G. Rostrevor Hamilton and John Arlott, 1943

Zennor

When we came over the shoulder of the wild hill above the sea, to Zennor, I felt we were coming into the Promised Land. I know there will be a new heaven and a new earth take place now: we have triumphed. I feel like a Columbus who can see a shadowy America before him: only this isn't merely territory, it's a new continent of the soul.

D.H. Lawrence, Letter to Lady Ottoline Morrell, 25 February 1916

A tiny granite village nestling under high shaggy moor-hills, and a big sweep of lovely sea beyond, such a lovely sea, lovelier even than the Mediterranean. . . . It is all gorse now, flickering with flower; and then it will be heather; and then, hundreds of fox gloves. It is the best place I have been in, I think.

D.H. Lawrence, Letter to J.M. Murry and Katharine Mansfield, Zennor, 5 March 1916

GREAT BRITAIN – SCOTLAND

Quhen Alysander oure kynge wes dede
Thtt Scotland led in luve and le,
Away wes sons of ale and brede,
Of wyne and wax, of gamyn and gle:
Oure gold wes changyd into lede,
Cryst, borne into virgynyte,
Succour Scotland, and remede
That stad is in perplexyte.

Andrew Wyntoun, *Cronykill*, *c.* 1400

The londe of scotlande hathe plenty of vytail and corne but not so abundant as is the realme of englande, for this lande is in many places steryll. The people be tall men and hardy but unfaythfull of promesse.

Roger Barlow, *A Brief Summe of Geographie*, *c.* 1540

He that will England win
Must with Scotland first begin.

Quoted in Edward Hall, *Chronicle*, 1548

There is not such a word
Spoke of in Scotland as this term of fear.

William Shakespeare, *I Henry IV*, *c.* 1597–8

Bishop of Ely: But there's a saying very old and true,
If that you will France win, then with Scotland first begin.
For once the Eagle (England) being in prey,
To her unguarded Nest, the Weazell (Scot)
Comes sneaking, and so sucks her Princely Egges,
Playing the Mouse in absence of the Cat,
To tame and havocke more then she can eate.

William Shakespeare, *Henry V*, *c.* 1598–9

Macduff: Stands Scotland where it did?
Rosse: Alas, poore Countrey,
Almost affraid to know it selfe. It cannot
Be call'd our Mother, but our Grave; where nothing
But who knows nothing, is once seen to smile.

William Shakespeare, *Macbeth*, *c.* 1605–6

Macduff: O Scotland, Scotland,
. . .
O Nation miserable!

Ibid.

Neither may I (abandoning eye-pleasing grounds)

seclude here that sudaick bottom, reaching thirty miles betwixt Perth and Montrose, involving the half of Angus, within a fruitful, populous, and nobilitate planure; the heart whereof saluting Glamis, kisseth Cowper: so likewise, as thrice-divided Lothian is a girnal of grain for foreign nations; and Fyfe, betwixt Crail and Largo, the Ceren trenches of a royal camp; the incircling coast, a nest of corporations; and meandering Forth, from tiptoed Snadoun, the prospicuous mirror for matchless majesty: even so is melting Tweed, and weeping Tiviot, the Egyptian strands that irriguate the fertile fields, which imbolster both bosoms, sending their bordering breath of daily necessaries to strengthen the life of Berwick.

William Lithgow, *Rare Adventures and Painfull Peregrinations*, 1614/32

Treacherous Scotland, to no interest true.

John Dryden, *Death of Oliver Cromwell*, 1658

A Scottish mist may wet an Englishman to the skin, – that is, 'small mischiefs in the beginning, if not seasonably prevented, may prove very dangerous.'

Thomas Fuller, *History of the Worthies of England*, 1662

. . . that *Northern* Land,
Where Day contending with approaching Night,
Assists the Hero with continu'd Light.

Edmund Waller, *On the Duke of Monmouth's Expedition into Scotland, in the Summer Solstice*, 1678

Indians assert that wheresoe'er they roam
If slain they reach again their native home.
If every nation held this maxim right
Not English bread would make a Scotchman fight.

Anon., from *A Collection of Epigrams*, 1707

First *younger Sister* to the Frozen Zone
Battered by Parent Natures constant Frown.
Adapt to Hardships, and cut out for Toil;
The *best worst Climate*, and the *worst best Soil*.
A rough, unhewn, uncultivated Spot,
Of old *so fam'd*, and *so of late forgot*:
NEGLECTED SCOTLAND shews her awful Brow,
Not always *quite so near* to Heaven as now.

Daniel Defoe, *Caledonia, A Poem in Honour of Scotland*, 1707

And here a while the Muse,
High hovering o'er the broad cerulean scene,
Sees Caledonia, in romantic view:
Her airy mountains, from the waving main,
Invested with a keen diffusive sky,
Breathing the soul acute; her forests huge,
Incult, robust, and tall, by Nature's hand
Planted of old; her azure lakes between,
Pour'd out extensive, and of watery wealth
Full; winding deep and green, her fertile vales;
With many a cool, translucent, brimming flood
Wash'd lovely, from the Tweed (pure *parent-stream*,
Whose pastoral banks first heard my Doric reed,
With, sylvan Jed, thy tributary brook)
To where the North-inflated tempest foams
O'er Orca's or Betubim's highest peak:
Nurse of the people, in Misfortune's school
Train'd up to hardy deeds; soon visited
By Learning, when before the Gothic rage
She took her western flight. A manly race,
Of unsubmitting spirit, wise and brave;
Who still through bleeding ages struggled hard. . . .
To hold a generous undiminish'd state;
Too much in vain! Hence of unequal bounds
Impatient, and by tempting glory borne
O'er every land, for every land their life
Has flow'd profuse, their piercing genius plann'd,
And swell'd the pomp of peace their faithful toil:
As from their own clear North, in radiant streams,
Bright over Europe bursts the Boreal Morn.

James Thomson, *The Seasons, – Autumn*, 1730

SCOTLAND! *thy weather's* like a *modish wife*!
Thy *winds* and *rains*, forever are at *strife*:
So, TERMAGANT, a while, her *Thunder* tries,
And, when she can no longer *scold* – she *cries*.

Aaron Hill, *Writ on a Window, in the Highlands of Scotland*, *c.* 1728

Mourn, hapless Caledonia, mourn
They banish'd peace, they laurels torn!
Thy sons, for valour long renown'd,
Lie slaughter'd on their native ground;
Thy hospitable roofs no more
Invite the stranger to the door;
In smoaky ruins sunk they lie,
The monuments of cruelty. . . .
Whilst the warm blood bedews my veins,
And unimpair'd remembrance reigns,
Resentment of my country's fate
Within my filial breast shall beat;
And, spite of her insulting foe,
My sympathizing verse shall flow,
'Mourn, hapless Caledonia, mourn
'Thy banish'd peace, thy laurels torn.'

Tobias Smollett, *The Tears of Scotland*, 1746

Shall I tire you with a description of this unfruitfull country? where I must lead you over their hills all brown with heath, or their valleys scarce able to feed a rabbet? Man alone seems to be the only creature who has arrived to the naturall size in this poor soil; every part of the country presents the same dismall landscape, no grove nor brook lend their musick to cheer the stranger, or make the inhabitants forget their poverty; yet with all these disadvantages to call him down to humility, a scotchman is one of the prowdest things alive.

Oliver Goldsmith, Letter to Robert Bryanton, Edinburgh, 26 September 1753

Oats – a grain which is generally given to horses, but in Scotland supports the people.

Samuel Johnson, *A Dictionary of the English Language*, 1755

Scotland suits my Fortune best & is the Seat of my principal Friendships but it is too narrow a Place for me, and it mortifies me that I sometimes hurt my friends.

David Hume, Letter to Adam Smith, 20 July 1759

'Mr Johnson, (said I) I do indeed come from Scotland, but I cannot help it.' I am willing to flatter myself that I meant this as a light pleasantry to soothe and conciliate him, and not as an humiliating abasement at the expence of my country. But however that might be, this speech was somewhat unlucky; for with that quickness of wit for which he was so remarkable, he seized the expression 'come from Scotland,' which I used in the sense of being of that country, and, as if I had said that I had come away from it, or left it, retorted, 'That, Sir, I find, is what a very great many of your countrymen cannot help.'

James Boswell, *Life of Johnson*, 16 May 1763

To that rare soil, where virtues clust'ring grow,
What mighty blessings doth not England owe!
What waggon-loads of courage, wealth, and sense,
Doth each revolving day import from thence!
To us she gives, disinterested friend!
Faith without fraud, and Stuarts without end.
When we prosperity's rich trappings wear,
Come not her generous sons and take a share?

Charles Churchill, *The Prophecy of Famine*, 1763

Sir Allan began to brag that Scotland had the advantage of England, by its having more water. 'Sir,' said Mr Johnson, 'we would not have your water, to take the vile bogs which produce it. You have too much. A man who is drowned has more water than either of us' – and then he laughed. (But this was surely robust sophistry; for the people of taste in England who have seen Scotland, own that its variety of rivers and brooks makes it naturally prettier than England in that respect.) 'Sir,' said Mr Johnson, pursuing his victory over Sir Allan, 'your country consists of two things: stone and water. There is indeed a little earth above the stone in some places, but a very little; and the stone is always appearing. It is like a man in rags; the naked skin is always peeping out.'

James Boswell, *Journal of a Tour to the Hebrides with Samuel Johnson*, 1773 (1785)

I had now travelled two hundred miles in Scotland and seen only one tree not younger than myself.

Samuel Johnson, *Journey to the Western Isles of Scotland*, 1775

A Scotchman must be a very sturdy moralist who does not love Scotland better than truth.

Ibid.

Seeing Scotland, Madam, is only seeing a worse England. It is seeing the flower gradually fade away to the naked stalk.

Samuel Johnson, in Boswell, *Life of Johnson*, 7 April 1778

I wondered not when I was told
The venal Scot his country sold:
I rather very much admire
How he could ever find a buyer.

Anon., from Nichol, *Select Collection of Poems*, 1780

From scenes like these old Scotia's grandeur springs,
That makes her loved at home, revered abroad:
Princes and lords are but the breath of kings,
An honest man's the noblest work of God.

Robert Burns, *The Cotter's Saturday Night*, 1785–6

SCOTLAND, my auld respected Mither!
Tho' whyles ye moistify your leather,
Till when ye speak, ye aiblins blether;
  Yet deil-mak-matter!
FREEDOM and WHISKY gang the gither,
  Tak aff your whitter.

Robert Burns, *The Authors Earnest Cry and Prayer . . . to the Scotch Representatives in the House of Commons*, 1786, last verse

Farewell, old Scotia's bleak domains,
Far dearer than the torrid plains,
Where rich ananas blow! . . .

Robert Burns, *The Farewell*, 1786

There was on a time, but old Time was then young,
  That brave Caledonia, the chief of her line,
From some of your northern deities sprung,
  (Who knows not that brave Caledonia's divine)
From Tweed to the Orcades was her domain,
  To hunt, or to pasture, or do what she would;
Her heavenly relations there fixed her reign,
  And pledged their godheads to warrant it good. –

A lambkin in peace, but a lion in war,
  The pride of her kindred the Heroine grew;
Her grandsire, old Odin, triumphantly swore,
  'Who e'er shall provoke thee th' encounter shall rue!'
With tillage or pasture at times she would sport,
  To feed her fair flocks by her green-rustling corn;

But chiefly the woods were her fav'rite resort,
Her darling amusement the hounds and the horn. –

Thus bold, independant, unconquer'd and free,
Her bright course of glory for ever shall run;
For brave Caledonia immortal must be,
I'll prove it from Euclid as clear as the sun:
Rectangle-triangle the figure we'll chuse,
The Upright is Chance, and old Time is the Base;
But brave Caledonia's the Hypothenuse,
Then, Ergo, she'll match them, and match them always.

Robert Burns, *Caledonia*, 1789

In Scotland's realm, where trees are few
Nor even shrubs abound;
But where, however bleak the view
Some better things are found.

William Cowper, *A Tale*, 1793

Scotland is the country above all others that I have seen, in which a man of imagination may carve out his own pleasures; there are so many *inhabited* solitudes.

Dorothy Wordsworth, *Journal*, August 1803

There are about four Things worth going into Scotland for, to one who has been in Cumberland & Westmoreland – the view of all the Islands at the Foot of Loch Lomond from the top of the highest Island, called Ince devannoc: 2. the Trossachs at the foot of Loch Ketterin 3. The Chamber & anti-chamber of the Falls of Foyers – (the Fall itself is very fine – & so after Rain is White water Dash – 7 miles below Keswick & very like it – & how little difference in the feeling a great real difference in height makes, you know as well as I – no Fall, of itself, perhaps can be worth going a long Journey to see, to him who has seen any Fall of Water, but the Pool, & whole Rent of the Mountain is truly magnificent –) 4th and lastly, the City of Edinburgh. – Perhaps, I might add Glen Coe: it is at all events a good Make-weight – & very well worth going to see, if a Man be a Tory & hate the memory of William the Third.

S.T. Coleridge, Letter to Robert Southey, 13 September 1803

Breathes there a man, with soul so dead,
Who never to himself hath said,
This is my own, my native land!
Whose heart hath ne'er within him burn'd
As home his footsteps he hath turn'd
From wandering on a foreign strand!. . . .

O Caledonia! stern and wild,
Meet nurse for a poetic child!
Land of brown heath and shaggy wood,
Land of the mountain and the flood,
Land of my sires! what mortal hand
Can e'er untie the filial band
That knits me to thy rugged strand!

Sir Walter Scott, *The Lay of the Last Minstrel*, 1805

There are two Scotch ladies staying here . . . to whom he may safely make love the ensuing winter: for love, tho' a very acute disorder in Andalusia, puts on a very chronic shape in these high northern latitudes; for first the lover must prove *metapheezically* that she ought to yeild; and then in the fifth or 6th year of courtship, or rather argument, if the summer is tolerably warm, and oatmeal plenty, the fair one yeilds.

Sydney Smith, Letter to Lady Holland, 21 September 1809

Caledonia's ours.
And well I know within that bastard land
Hath Wisdom's goddess never held command;
A barren soil, where Nature's germs, confined
To stern sterility can stint the mind;
Whose thistle well betrays the niggard earth.
Emblem of all to whom the land gives birth;
Each genial influence nurtured to resist;
A land of meanness, sophistry, and mist.

Lord Byron, *The Curse of Minerva*, 1811

When shall I see Scotland again? Never shall I forget the happy days I passed there amidst odious smells, barbarous sounds, bad suppers, excellent hearts, and most enlightened and cultivated understandings.

Sydney Smith, Letter to Francis Jeffrey, 27 March 1814

That knuckle-end of England, – that land of Calvin, oat-cakes, and sulphur.

Sydney Smith, quoted in Lady Holland, *Memoir of Sydney Smith*, 1855

A French writer mentions, as a proof of Shakespeare's attention to particulars, his allusion to the climate of Scotland in the words, 'Hail, hail, all hail!' – *Grèle, grèle, toute grèle.*

Thomas Moore, *Journal*, 16 April 1821

In the history of Scotland, too, I can find properly but one epoch: we may say it contains nothing of a world-interest at all but this Reformation by Knox. A poor barren country, full of continual broils, dissensions, massacrings; a people in the last state of rudeness and destitution, little better perhaps than Ireland at this day. Hungry, fierce barons, not so much as able to form any arrangement with each other *how to divide* what they fleeced from these poor drudges; but obliged, as the Columbian Republics are at this day, to make of every alteration a revolution; no way of changing a ministry but by hanging the old ministers on gibbets: this is a historical spectacle of no very singular significance! 'Bravery' enough, I doubt not; fierce fighting in abundance: but no braver or fiercer than of their old Scandinavian Sea-king ancestors; *whose* exploits we have not found worth dwelling on! It is a country as yet without a soul: nothing developed in it but what is rude, external, semi-animal. And now at the Reformation, the internal life is kindled, as it were, under the ribs of this outward material death.

Thomas Carlyle, *On Heroes, Hero-Worship, and the Heroic in History*, 1841

In my youth, a Highland gentleman measured his importance by the number of men his domain could support. After some time the question was, to know how many great cattle it would feed. Today we are come to count the number of sheep. I suppose posterity will ask how many rats and mice it can feed.

R.W. Emerson, *Lectures and Biographical Sketches*, 'The Man of Letters', 1863, quoting 'A Scotch Mountaineer'

Mutton old and claret good were Caledonia's forte,
Before the Southron taxed her drink and poisoned her
with port.

Charles Neaves (Lord Neaves), *Beef and Potatoes*, *Songs and Verses Social and Scientific*, 1875

Once you get the hang of it, and apprehend the type, it is a most beautiful and admirable little country – fit, for 'distinction' etc., to make up a trio with Italy and Greece.

Henry James, Letter to Miss Alice James, 15 September 1878

There is no special loveliness in that grey country, with its rainy, sea-belt archipelago; its fields of dark mountains; its unsightly places, black with coal; its treeless, sour, unfriendly-looking cornlands; its quaint, grey, castled city, where the bells clash of a Sunday, and the wind squalls, and the salt showers fly and beat. I do not even know if I desire to live there; but let me hear, in some far land, a kindred voice sing out, 'O why left I my hame?' and it seems at once as if no beauty under the kind heavens, and no society of the wise and good, can repay me for my absence from my country. And though I think I would rather die elsewhere, yet in my heart of hearts I long to be buried among good Scots clods. I will say it fairly, it grows on me with every year: there are no stars so lovely as Edinburgh streetlamps.

Robert Louis Stevenson, *The Silverado Squatters*, 1883

Gin danger's there, we'll thole our share,
Gie's but the weapons, we've the will,
Ayont the main, to prove again
Auld Scotland counts for something still.

Charles Murray, *A Sough o' War*, 1914

So this is your Scotland. It is rather nice, but dampish and Northern and one shrinks a trifle inside one's skin. For these countries one should be amphibian.

D.H. Lawrence, Letter to Hon. Dorothy Brett, 14 August 1926

Scotland is renowned as the home of the most ambitious race in the world.

Frederic Edwin Smith, Earl of Birkenhead, Rectorial Address, Aberdeen, 16 November 1928

How can one ever explain to the go-ahead west the charm of the shabby grey haphazard old land? It is partly the feeling that things just grow and are not made.

Freya Stark, Note of 17 February 1929, in *Beyond Euphrates*, 1951

Scotland is the best place in the world to take an appetite.

H.V. Morton, *In Search of Scotland*, 1929

In Ireland and in the mountains of Scotland the moonlight has a sharper edge to it. It suggests not the amusing playful fancies of the Saxon but the witch and warlock of the Celt. If you did see a fairy by Scotch moonlight, it would be on its way to steal a baby.

Ibid.

Scotland's cauld and grey, you say,
But it's no' ill to prove
Oor dourest hills are only
Rainbows at a'e remove.

Hugh MacDiarmid (C.M. Grieve), 'Scotland', from *To Circumjack Cencrastus*,1930

If there's a sword-like sang
That can cut Scotland clear
O' a' the warld beside
Rax me the hilt o't here,

For there's nae jewel till
Frae the rest o' earth its's free,
Wi' the starry separateness
I'd fain to Scotland gie. . . .

Hugh MacDiarmid (C.M. Grieve), 'Separatism', from *To Circumjack Cencrastus*, 1930

Let nae man think he can serve you, Scotland,
Withoot muckle trial and trouble to himsel'.
The slightest service to you compares
Wi' fetchin' a bit o' Heaven doon into Hell.

Let wha wad serve you reflect for a minute
On a' the thoosands that seemed to and failed to
– Only service demands heich qualities then
These coontless thoosands ne'er scaled to.

And even at the best hoo many folk coont
O' the least consequence to you since Time began.
Lightly to fancy he's o' the favoured few
Nearly aye disposes o' the claims o' a man.

Nay, fegs, it's wi' you as wi' a lion-cub
A man may fetch hame and can play wi' at first,
But if he has it lang, it grows up and syne
– Suddenly his fool's paradise is burst!

Hugh MacDiarmid (C.M. Grieve), 'Towards a New Scotland, VII', from *Stony Limits and Other Poems*, 1934

Most . . . small towns I have seen in Scotland are contentedly or morosely lethargic, sunk in a fantastic dullness broken only by scandal-mongering and such alarums as drinking produces; a dead silence punctuated by malicious whispers and hiccups.

Edwin Muir, *Journey into Scotland*, 1935

What I think is that it has suffered in the past, and is suffering now, from too much England.

A.G. Macdonell, *My Scotland*, 1937

I am one of those who always think it fun to be in Scotland.

Hilaire Belloc, *Places*, 1942

I went to Scotland and found nothing there that looks like Scotland.

Arthur Freed, defending studio production of the film *Brigadoon* 1950s

Scotland be Englishman's bush country.

A Northern Ghanaian Chief, quoted by John Gunther, *Inside Africa*, 1955

Land of the omnipotent No.

Alan Bold, 'A Memory of Death', in *A Perpetual Motion Machine*, 1969

Scots

Trust yow no Skott.

Andrew Boorde, Suffragan Bishop of Chichester, Letter to Thomas Cromwell, 1 April 1536

The devellysche dysposicion of a Scottysh man, not to love nor favour an Englishe man.

Ibid.

Only a few industrious Scots perhaps, who indeed are dispersed over the face of the whole earth. But as for them, there are no greater friends to Englishmen and England, when they are out on't, in the world, than they are. And for my own part, I would a hundred thousand of them were there [Virginia], for we are all one countrymen now, ye know, and we should find ten times more comfort of them there than we do here.

George Chapman, *Eastword Hoe*, 1605

Now as for the nobility and gentry of the kingdom, certainly, as they are generous, manly, and full of courage; so are they courteous, discreet, learned scholars, well read in the best histories, delicate linguists, the most part of them being brought up in France or Italy; that for a general complete worthiness, I never found their matches amongst the best people of foreign nations; being also good house-keepers, affable to strangers, and full of hospitality.

William Lithgow, *Rare Adventures and Painfull Peregrinations*, 1614/32

Had *Cain* been *Scot*, God would have chang'd his doom
Not forc'd him wander, but confin'd him home.
Like Jews they spread, and as infection fly,
As if the Devil had ubiquity.
Hence 'tis they live at Rovers, and defie
This or that place; Rags of Geography.
They're Citizens o' th' world; they're all in all,
Scotland's a Nation Epidemicall. . . .
A Scot, when from the gallows-tree got loose
Drops into Styx, and turns a Soland Goose.

J. Cleveland, *Poems*, 1647

A Scotsman and a Newcastle grind-stone travel all the world over. The Scots (gentry especially), when young, leave their native land (hard their hap if losers by the exchange), and travel into foreign parts, most for the maintenance, many for accomplishment. Now no ship sets safe to sea without a carpenter, no carpenter is able without his tools, no tools useful without a grind-stone no grind-stone, so good as those of Newcastle. . . .

Thomas Fuller, *History of the Worthies of England*, 1662

In every corner of the world you will find a Scot, a rat, and a Newcastle grindstone.

John Gibson Lockhart, *Life of Scott*, 1838, quoting the above as an old saying

A Scottish man is ay wise behind the hand.

Quoted in John Ray, *A Compleat Collection of English Proverbs*, 1670

Scotsmen ay reckon frae an ill hour.

Scottish proverb

Biting and Scratching is Scots folks' wooing.

John Ray, *Scottish Proverbs, in A Compleat Collection of English Proverbs, etc.*, 4th edn, 1768

For a misobliging word
She'll dirk her neighbour o'er the board.

If any ask her of her drift,
Forsooth, her nainself lives by theft.

Col. William Cleland, *Mock Poem on the Expedition of the Highland Host . . .* , 1678, in *A Collection of Poems and Verses*, 1697

Says God to the Hielandman, 'Quhair wilt thou now?'
'I will down to the Lowlands, Lord, and there steal a cow.'
'Ffy,' quod St. Peter, 'thou wilt never do weel,'
'An thou, but new made, so sune gais to steal.'
'Umff,' quod the Hielandman, and swore by yon kirk,
'So long as I may geir get to steal, will I nevir work.'

Aphra Behn, *Miscellanies*, 1685

A hardy Race, possess the stormy Strand,
And share the Moderate Bounties of the Land;
Fitted by Nature for the *Boistrous Clime*,
And larger Blessings will grow due by time.
The num'rous Off-spring, patient and sedate,
With Courage, *special to the Climate*, wait.
When *Niggard Nature* shal their *Nation* hear,
Shall smile, and pay them all the vast Arrear.
A *Manly Surliness*, with Temper mix'd,
Is on their meanest Countenances fix'd.
An awful Frown sits on their threatening Brow,
And yet the Soul's all smooth, and calm *below*;
Thinking in Temper, rather grave than Gay,
Fitted to govern, able to obey.
Nor are their Spirits *very soon* enflam'd
And if provok'd, not *very soon* reclaim'd.
Fierce when resolv'd, and fix'd as Bars of Brass,
And Conquest *through their Blood* can only pass.
In spight of *Coward Cold*, the Race is Brave,
In Action Daring, and in Council Grave;
Their haughty Souls in Danger always grow,
No Man *durst lead 'em* where they *durst not go*.
Sedate in Thought, and steady in Resolve,
Polite in Manners, and as Years Revolve;
Always secure their largest share of Fame,
And by their Courage keep alive their Name.

Daniel Defoe, *Caledonia*, 1707

In all my travels I never met with any one Scotchman but what was a man of sense: I believe every body of that country that has any, leaves it as fast as they can.

Francis Lockier, Remark, *c.* 1730, quoted Joseph Spence, *Anecdotes*, 1820

As to their Genius and Temper, they have certainly more Command of themselves in the Beginning of Life, and commit fewer Extravagancies in their Youth, than the *English* do: Their Frugality and Temperance deserves our Imitation, which is indeed the Foundation of that Discretion we observe in them, at a Time of Life when our young Gentlemen are half mad.

Thomas Salmon, *A New Geographical and Historical Grammar*, 1751

Really it is admirable how many Men of Genius this Country produces at present. Is it not strange, that at a time when we have lost our Princes, our Parliaments, our independent Government, even the Presence of our chief Nobility, are unhappy, in our Accent & Pronunciation, speak a very corrupt Dialect of the Tongue which we make use of; Is it not strange, I say, that, in these Circumstances, we shou'd really be the People most distinguish'd for Literature in Europe.

David Hume, Letter to Gilbert Elliot of Minto, July 1757

The Scots are poor, cries surly English pride;
True is the charge, nor by themselves denied.
Are they not then in strictest reason clear,
Who wisely come to mend their fortunes here?
If, by low, supple arts successful grown,
They sapp'd our vigour to increase their own;
If, mean in want, and insolent in power,
They only fawn'd more surely to devour,
Roused by such wrongs should reason take alarm,
And e'en the Muse for public safety arm:
But if they own ingenuous virtue's sway,
And follow where true honour points the way;
If they revere the hand by which they're fed,
And bless the donors for their daily bread,
Or by vast debts of higher import bound,
Are always humble, always grateful found;
If they, directed by Paul's holy pen,
Become discreetly all things to all men,
That all men may become all things to them,
Envy may hate, but justice can't condemn.
'Into our places, states, and beds they creep;'
They've sense to get what we want sense to keep.

Charles Churchill, *The Prophecy of Famine*, 1763

There is really in Scotland a species of low insidious wicked women worse than any creatures in the world.

James Boswell, *Boswell's London Journal*, 1 March 1763

Mr Ogilvie . . . observed that Scotland had a great many noble wild prospects. JOHNSON. 'I believe, Sir, you have a great many. Norway too, has noble wild prospects; and Lapland is remarkable for prodigious noble wild prospects. But, Sir, let me tell you, the noblest prospect which a Scotsman ever sees, is the high road that leads him to England!'

James Boswell, *Life of Johnson*, 9 July 1763

I sought for merit wherever it could be found; it is my boast that I was the first minister who looked for it, and found it, in the mountains of the north. I called it forth and drew into your service a hardy and intrepid race of men – men who, when left by your jealousy became a prey to the artifices of your enemies, and had gone nigh to have overturned the state in the war before last. These men in the last war were brought to combat on your side; they served you with fidelity, as they fought with valour, and conquered for you in every corner of the world.

William Pitt, Earl of Chatham, Speech, 1766

Much (said he,) may be made of a Scotchman, if he be *caught* young.

Samuel Johnson, in Boswell, *Life of Johnson*, 1772

The conversation then turned on atheism; on that horrible book, *Système de la Nature*; and on the supposition of an eternal necessity, without design, without a governing mind. JOHNSON. 'If it were so, why has it ceased? Why don't we see men thus produced around us now? Why, at least, does it not keep pace in some measure with the progress of time? If it stops because there is no need of it, then it is plain there is and ever has been an all-powerful intelligence. But stay!' said he with one of his satiric laughs. 'Ha! ha! ha! I shall suppose Scotchmen made necessarily, and Englishmen by choice.'

James Boswell, *Journal of a Tour to the Hebrides with Samuel Johnson*, 1773 (1785)

Come, let me know what it is that makes a Scotchman happy!

Samuel Johnson, quoted in James Boswell, *A Tour to the Hebrides*, 23 October 1773 (calling for a gill of whisky)

In Scotland & Wales there seems to much Affection, & much hatred of Course: much Sentiment one may call it – They have little to do, & cultivate such Refinements of Character for Amusement.

Hester Lynch Thrale/Piozzi, *Thraliana*, December 1789

The best way of giving you a just idea of the Scotch is to shew you in what they principally differ from the English. In the first place (to begin with their physical peculiarities) they are larger in body than the English, and the women in my opinion (I say it to my shame) handsomer than English women; their dialect is very agreeable. The Scotch certainly do not understand cleanliness. They are poorer than the English, they are cautious, and a discreet people. – They are very much in earnest in their religion, tho' less so than they were. In England I maintain that (except amongst Ladies in the middle class of life) there is no religion at all. The Clergy of England have no more influence over the people at large than the Cheesemongers of England have. In Scotland the clergy are extremely active in the discharge of their functions, and are from the hold they have on the minds of the people a very important body of men. The common people are extremely conversant with the Scriptures, are really not so much pupils, as formidable critics to their preachers; many of them are well read in controversial divinity. They are perhaps in some points of view the most remarkable nation in the world, and no country can afford an example of so much order, morality, oeconomy, and knowledge amongst the lower classes of Society. Every nation has its peculiarities, the very improved state of the common people appears to me at present to be the phoenomenon of this country.

Sydney Smith, Letter to Mrs Beach, 15 July 1798

Proud and erect the Caledonian stood,
Old was his mutton, and his claret good;
'Let him drink port,' the English statesman cried:
He drank the potion, and his spirit died.

John Home, *Epigram on Enforcement of High Duty on French Wines*, before 1808

Every Scottishman has a pedigree. It is a national prerogative, as unalienable as his pride and his poverty.

Sir Walter Scott, *Memior of the early life of . . . written by himself*, 26 April 1808

We spoke of national characters, national dislikes, etc. Coleridge playfully said: 'I always say a *Scotch* rascal,' as if the infamy lay in the being *Scotch*.

Henry Crabb Robinson, *Diary*, 30 March 1811

*It's ill taking the breeks off a Hielandman.

Sir Walter Scott, *Rob Roy*, 1817

and Irish

I will speak as far as I can judge on the Irish and Scotch – I know nothing of the higher Classes – yet I have a persuasion that there the Irish are victorious. As to the 'profanum vulgus' I must incline to the scotch. They never laugh – but they are always comparatively neat and clean. Their constitutions are not so remote and puzzling as the irish. The Scotchman will never give a decision on any point – he will never commit himself in a sentence which may be referred to as a meridian in his notion of things – so that you do not know him – and yet you may come in nigher neighbourhood to him than to the irishman who commits himself in so many places that it dazes your head. A Scotchman's motive is more easily discovered than an irishman's. A Scotchman will go wisely about to deceive you, an irishman cunningly. An Irishman would bluster out of any discovery to his disadvantage. A Scotchman would retire perhaps without much desire of revenge. An Irishman likes to be thought a gallous fellow. A Scotchman is contented with himself. It seems to me they are both sensible of the character they hold in England and act accordingly to Englishmen. Thus the Scotchman will become over grave and over decent and the Irishman over-impetuous. I like a Scotchman best because he is less of a bore – I like the

Irishman best because he ought to be more comfortable – the Scotchman has made up his Mind within himself in a Sort of snail shell wisdom – the Irishman is full of strong headed instinct – The Scotchman is farther in Humanity than the Irishman – there he will stick perhaps when the Irishman shall be refined beyond him – for the former thinks he cannot be improved the latter would grasp at it for ever, place but the good plain before him.

John Keats, Letter to Thomas Keats, 10–14 July 1818

The Scotch, whatever other talents they may have, can never condense; they always begin a few days before the flood, and come *gradually* down to the reign of George the third, forgetful of nothing but the shortness of human life, and the volatility of human attention.

Sydney Smith, Letter to Lady Holland, 1819

It requires a surgical operation to get a joke well into a Scotch understanding.

Sydney Smith, Remark quoted in Lady Holland, *Memoir of Sydney Smith*, 1855

I have been trying all my life to like Scotchmen, and am obliged to desist from the experiment in despair.

Charles Lamb, 'Imperfect Sympathies', in *Essays of Elia*, 1820–3

You must beware of indirect expressions before a Caledonian. Clap an extinguisher on your irony, if you are unhappily blessed with a vein of it.

Ibid.

If you unscotch us, you will find us damned mischievous Englishmen.

Sir Walter Scott, Letter to J.W. Croker, MP, 19 March 1826

The Scotch are a nation of gentlemen.

George IV, Saying according, to Sir Walter Scott, quoted in *Noctes Ambrosianae*, November 1830

*It is said that a Scotchman returning home, after some years residence in England, being asked what he thought of the English, answered: 'They hanno ower muckle sense, but they are an unco braw people to live amang;' which would be a very good story, if it were not rendered apocryphal, by the incredible circumstance of the Scotchman going back.

Thomas Love Peacock, *Crotchet Castle*, 1831

He said that he could never impress a Scotchman with any new truth: that they all required it to be spelled and explained away in old equivalent and familiar words or images. Had spoken to a Scotchman who sat next to him at dinner the day before, of a healthy book.

'Healthy, Sir, healthy did you say?'

'Yes.'

'I dinna comprehend. I have heard of a healthy man and of a healthy morning but never of a healthy book.'

S.T. Coleridge, quoted in *Letters Conversations and Recollections of S.T. Coleridge*, 1836

Spoke of the cold and calculating character of the Scotch; agreed that they were in this the same drunk or sober: their heads seemed always so full that they could not hold more; adding, 'We value the Scotch, without however liking them; and we like the Irish without however *over*valuing them.'

Ibid.

The Scots are steadfast – not their clime.

Thomas Campbell, *The Pilgrim of Glencoe*, 1842

I have made great investigations on the subject of the origin of the Scotch, and could prove . . . that they came originally from this country Lebanon. [Syria]

Lady Hester Stanhope, in Charles Meryon, *Memoirs of the Lady Hester Stanhope*, 1845

The truth was that, in all those qualities which conduce to success in life, and especially in commercial life, the Scot had never been surpassed; perhaps he had never been equalled. All that was necessary was that his energy should take a proper direction.

T.B. Macaulay, *History of England*, 1849–61

Nowhere beats the heart so kindly
As beneath the tartan plaid!

W.E. Aytoun, 'Charles Edward at Versailles', – *Lays of the Scottish Cavaliers and Other Poems*, 1849

In Scotland there is a rapid loss of all grandeur of mien and manners; a provincial eagerness and acuteness appear; the poverty of the country makes itself remarked, and a coarseness of manners; and, among the intellectual, is the insanity of dialectics.

R.W. Emerson, *English Traits*, 1856

I have been greatly disgusted with the appearance of the brave highlanders. They strike me as stupid, dirty, ignorant and barbarous. Their mode of life is not different from that of African negroes. Their huts are floorless except for earth; they live all together in them like pigs; there are no chimneys, hardly a window; no conveniences of life of any sort. Dirty, ragged, starved and imbruted, they struggle to cultivate patches of rocky ground where nothing can mature, and in wretched superstition and prejudice they are as deep sunk as their ancestors ever were.

Henry Adams, Letter to Charles Francis Adams, 3 September 1863

It seems that the Scots

Turn out much better shots
At long distance, than most Englishmen are;
But this we all knew
That a Scotchman could do
Make a small piece of metal go awfully far.

Charles Shirley Brooks (1815–74),
'On Scots Frugality', from *Punch*

Three failures and a fire make a Scotchman's fortune.

Alexander Hislop, *Proverbs of Scotland*, 1870

The happiest lot on earth is to be born a Scotsman. You must pay for it in many ways, as for all other advantages on earth. You have to learn the Paraphrases and the Shorter Catechism; you generally take to drink; your youth, as far as I can find out, is a time of louder war against society, of more outcry and tears and turmoil, than if you had been born, for instance, in England. But somehow life is warmer and closer; the hearth burns more redly; the lights of home shine softer on the rainy street. The very names, endeared in words and music, cling nearer round our hearts.

Robert Louis Stevenson, *The Silverado Squatters*, 1883

Scotchmen seem to think it's a credit to them to be Scotch.

Somerset Maugham, *A Writer's Notebook*, 1949
[1900]

Your proper child of Caledonia believes in his rickety bones that he is the salt of the earth. . . . He is the one species of human animal that is taken by all the world to be fifty per cent cleverer and pluckier and honester than the facts warrant. He is the daw with a peacock's tail of his own painting. He is the ass who has been at pains to cultivate the convincing roar of a lion.

T.W.H. Crosland, *The Unspeakable Scot*, 1902

*But all Scotchmen are not religious . . . some are theologians.

Gerald Bendall, *Mrs Jones's Bonnet*, 1907

You've forgotten the grandest moral attribute of a Scotsman, Maggie, that he'll do nothing which might damage his career.

Sir James M. Barrie, *What Every Woman Knows*, 1908

There are few more impressive sights in the world than a Scotsman on the make.

Ibid.

A young Scotsman of your ability, let loose upon the world with £300, what could he not do? It's almost appalling to think of; especially if he went among the English.

Ibid.

I've sometimes thought that the difference between the Scotch and the English is that the Scotch are hard in all other respects but soft with women, and the English are hard with women and soft in all other respects.

Ibid.

You come of a race of men the very wind of whose name has swept to the ultimate seas.

Sir James M. Barrie, Rectorial Address,
St Andrew's, 3 May 1922

There is no fear . . . that prohibition will be adopted there: and this from the simple reason that the Scotch do not drink. . . . Because they manufacture the best whiskey in the world, the Scotch, in popular fancy, are often thought to be addicted to the drinking of it. This is purely a delusion. During the whole of two or three pleasant weeks spent lecturing in Scotland, I never on any occasion saw whiskey made use of *as a beverage*. I have seen people take it, of course, as a medicine, or as a precaution, or as a wise offset against a rather treacherous climate; but as a beverage, never.

Stephen Leacock, *My Discovery of England*, 1922

God help England if she had no Scots to think for her!

George Bernard Shaw, *The Apple Cart*, 1929

Patriotism is the most abused of all the sentiments. In its best sense it expresses an animal instinct of self-preservation. In its worst it is tainted with material interests, and such sordid things as money and self-advancement. In the Englishman it manifests itself in a dumb contempt for everything that is not English. The Scot has a more practical patriotism. His contempt for foreigners includes the Englishman but is carefully concealed. His jingoism is confined to cheering Scotland at Twickenham. It is rather racial than local. It concerns Scotland hardly at all. Its aim is the glorification and self-satisfaction of the Scot in whatever part of the globe the impulse of self-advancement drives him.

R.H. Bruce Lockhart, *Memoirs of a British Agent*, 1932

I wad dae onything for you, Scotland, save
– Even tho' your true line should be wi' such –
Become like ninety per cent o' Scots;
That 'ud be askin' faur owre much!

Hugh MacDiarmid (C.M. Grieve) 'Towards a New Scotland, IV', from *Stony Limits and Other Poems*, 1934

It is a peculiar element in Scottish humour, as appreciated by Scotchmen, that the harder it is to see, the better it is esteemed. If it is obvious it is of less account. This rests on the intellectuality of the Scotch; having little else to cultivate, they cultivate the intellect. The export of brains came to be their chief item of commerce.

Stephen Leacock, *Humour*, 1935

Scottish streets are given an atmosphere of their own simply by the number of drunk people that one encounters in them. . . . Scottish people drink spasmodically and intensely, for the sake of momentary but complete release, whereas the English like to bathe and paddle about bucolically in a mild puddle of beer.

Edwin Muir, *Scottish Journey*, 1935

I think it possible that all Scots are illegitimate, Scotsmen being so mean and Scotswomen so generous.

Anonymous letter to James Agate, quoted in *Ego 2*, 19 March 1936

The background of the Highlander's life is dramatic. He was born on a stage of magnificent scenes. . . . Half the year is soft and scented and gay, and half is hard and cruel. Both are dramatic. There are no half tones. . . . It is all pure theatre.

Nature is heightened, made more vivid, more intense, by just that small iota which changes life into art. And, to match his background, the Highlander has changed himself, or been changed – for it is partly conscious, and partly subconscious – into a being who must live vividly and therefore artificially. . . . Once this fact is grasped, that the Highlander is an actor first, last, and all the time, everything about him becomes clear and consistent. . . . There was never a male panoply to equal for sheer theatricality the full-dress kilt. And its 'props' are on the same brilliant level of theatrical fantasy. Not even the most dashing Regency buck or Restoration fop ever thought of carrying more than one sword when he was entering society. The Highlander is incompletely dressed by his own standards unless he carries three, one on his right hip, one at his left side, and one in his stocking. . . . It is a male costume, the costume of a fighting man who is not concerned with manual labour. It is three swords that he carries, not three spades or three spanners.

A.G. Macdonell, *My Scotland*, 1937

It is never difficult to distinguish between a Scotsman with a grievance and a ray of sunshine.

P.G. Wodehouse, quoted in Richard Usborne, *Wodehouse at Work*, 1961

Abbotsford

etc.

A visit to Edinburgh . . . I have intended these thirty years, only for the purpose of seeing my dear Sir Walter's House and Home: and which I am glad to have seen as that of Shakespeare. I had expected to find a rather Cockney Castle: but no such thing: all substantially and proportionably built, according to the Style of the Country: the Grounds are simply laid out: the woods he planted well-grown, and that dear Tweed running and murmuring still – as on the day of his Death. I did not so much care for Melrose and Jedburgh, though his Tomb is there – in one of the half-ruined corners. Another day I went to the Trossachs, Katrine, Lomond, etc., which (as I expected) seemed much better to me in Pictures and Drop-scenes. I was but three days in Scotland, and was glad to get back to my own dull flat country, though I did worship the Pentland, Cheviot, and Eildon Hills, more for their Associations than themselves. They are not big enough for that.

Edward Fitzgerald, Letter to Fanny Kemble, 21 July 1874

Crowds of Scottish and American visitors stand gazing doubtfully at the rich harvest of mediaevalism, thinking that it would be a difficult place to live in; as, of course, it would. It fitted Walter Scott's mind as his clothes fitted his body.

H.V. Morton, *In Search of Scotland*, 1929

Abbotsford is a very strange house. It is a place certainly well-suited to be displayed, to astonish, to stagger, and to sadden; that it should ever have been lived in is the most astonishing, staggering, saddening thing of all. One feels, while wandering through it, that one is on the track of a secret more intimate than either Scott's biography or his written works can tell. . . . It is surely the saddest and strangest monument that Scott's genius created.

Edwin Muir, *Scottish Journey*, 1935

Aberdeen

Blyth Aberdeane, thow beriall of all tounis,
  The lamp of bewtie bountie and blythnes,
Unto the heaven ascendit thy renoun is
  Off vertew, wisdome and of worthines;
He nottit is thy name of nobilnes
Into the cuming of our lustie quein,
  The wall of welth, guid cheir and mirrines:
Be blyth and blisfull, burgh of Aberdein.

William Dunbar, *To Aberdein*, 1511
(Queen Margaret made a ceremonial entry into Aberdeen in May 1511)
(Beriall = beryl, crystal)

He is an Aberdeen's man, taking his word again. It seems the men of that town . . . have formerly been taxed for breach of promise. I hope if true . . . only of the old Aberdeen, now much decayed, and famous only for salmon-fishing. If of the new, then I believe it of the townsmen, not scholars living in the university.

Thomas Fuller, *History of the Worthies of England*, 1662

Next to Germans, the most ubiquitous people in the world are the Aberdonians.

James Bryce, *South America*, 1912

Aberdeen impresses the stranger as a city of granite palaces, inhabited by people as definite as their building material. Even their prejudices are of the same hard character. The beauty of Aberdeen is the beauty of uniformity and solidity. Nothing so time-defying has been built since the Temple of Karnak.

H.V. Morton, *In Search of Scotland*, 1929

Loch Achray

At the opening of the pass we climbed up a low eminence, and had an unexpected prospect suddenly before us – another lake, small compared with Loch Ketterine, though perhaps four miles long, but the misty air concealed the end of it. The transition from the solitary wildness of Loch Ketterine and the narrow valley or pass to this scene was very delightful: it was a gentle place, with lovely open bays, one small island, corn fields, woods, and a group of cottages. This vale seemed to have been made to be tributary to the comforts of man, Loch Ketterine for the lonely delight of Nature, and kind spirits delighting in beauty.

Dorothy Wordsworth, Journal, 27 August 1803

River Afton (*a tributary of the Nith, near Cumnock*)

Flow gently, sweet Afton, among thy green braes,
Flow gently, I'll sing thee a song in thy praise;
My Mary's asleep by thy murmuring stream,
Flow gently, sweet Afton, disturb not her dream.

Robert Burns, *Afton Water*, 1789

Ailsa Craig

Hearken thou craggy ocean pyramid,
Give answer by thy voice the Sea-fowls screams!
When were thy shoulders mantled in huge streams?
When, from the Sun, was thy broad forehead hid?
How long ist since the mighty Power bid
Thee heave to airy sleep from fathom dreams –
Sleep in the Lap of Thunder or Sunbeams,
Or when grey clouds are thy cold Coverlid –
Thou answerst not for thou art dead asleep
Thy life is but two dead eternities –
The last in Air, the former in the deep;
First with the Whales, last with the eagle skies –
Drown'd wast thou till an earth quake made thee steep,

Another cannot wake thy giant size!

John Keats, *To Ailsa Rock*, July 1818

Anoch

Anoch, a village in Glenmollison of three huts, one of which is distinguished by a chimney.

Samuel Johnson, *Journey to the Western Isles of Scotland*, 1775

Isle of Arran

Neither is there any isle like to it, for brave gentry, good archers, and hill-hovering hunters.

William Lithgow, *Rare Adventures and Painfull Peregrinations*, 1614/32

Ayr

It has certainly been a good Town, and much bigger than it is now: At present like an old Beauty, it shews the Ruins of a good Face; but is also apparently, not only decay'd and declin'd, but decaying and declining every Day.

Daniel Defoe, *A Tour through the Whole Island of Great Britain*, 1724–7

O Ayr, my dear, my native ground.

Robert Burns, *To the Rev. John M'Math . . .*, 17 September 1885

Auld Ayr, wham ne'er a town surpasses,
For honest men and bonny lasses.

Robert Burns, *Tam o'Shanter. A Tale*, 1791

The Bridges of Ayr

NEW BRIG

Auld Vandal, ye but show your little mense,
Just much about it wi' your scanty sense;
Will your poor, narrow foot-path of a street,
Where twa wheel-barrows tremble when they meet,
Your ruin'd formless bulk o' stane and lime,
Compare wi' bonie *Brigs* o' modern time?
There's men of taste wou'd tak the *Ducat-stream*,
Tho' they should cast the vera sark and swim,
Ere they would grate their feelings wi' the view
Of sic an ugly, Gothic hulk as you.

AULD BRIG

Conceited gowk! puff'd up wi' windy pride!
This mony a year I've stood the flood an' tide;
And tho' wi' crazy eild I'm sair forfairn,
I'll be a *Brig* when ye're a shapeless cairn!
As yet ye little ken about the matter,
But twa-three winters will inform ye better.
When heavy, dark, continued, a'-day rains
Wi' deepening deluges o'erflow the plains;
When from the hills where springs the brawling *Coil*,
Or stately *Lugar's* mossy fountains boil,
Or where the *Greenock* winds his moorland course,
Or haunted *Garpal* draws his feeble source,
Arous'd by blustering winds an' spotting thowes,
In mony a torrent down the snaw-broo rowes;
While crashing ice, borne on the roaring speat,
Sweeps dams, an' mills, an' brigs, a' to the gate;

And from *Glenbuck*, down to the *Ratton-key*,
Auld *Ayr* is just one lengthen'd, tumbling sea;
Then down ye'll hurl, deil nor ye never rise!
And dash the gumlie jaups up to the pouring skies,
A lesson sadly teaching, to your cost,
That Architecture's noble art is lost!

Robert Burns, *The Brigs of Ayr*, 1786

Burns's Cottage
We went to the cottage and took some Whisky. I wrote a sonnet for the mere sake of writing some lines under the roof – they are so bad I cannot transcribe them. The man at the cottage was a great bore with his anecdotes – I hate the rascal – his life consists in fuz, fuzzy, fuzziest. He drinks glasses five for the quarter and twelve for the hour – he is a mahogany-faced old Jackass who knew Burns. He ought to have been kicked for having spoken to him . . . Oh the flummery of a birthplace! Cant! Cant! Cant! It is enough to give a spirit the guts-ache. Many a true word they say, is spoken in jest – this may be because his gab hindered my sublimity: the flat dog made me write a flat sonnet.

John Keats, Letter to John Hamilton Reynolds, 13 July 1818

Ayrshire

Farewell old *Coila's* hills and dales,
Her healthy moors and winding vales;
The scenes where wretched Fancy roves,
Pursuing past, unhappy loves!
Farewell my friends! farewell, my foes!
My peace with these, my love with those –
The bursting tears my heart declare,
Farewell the bonie banks of *Ayr*!

Robert Burns, Song, 1786

On a sudden we turned a corner upon the immediate Country of Ayr – the sight was as rich as possible – I had no conception that the native place of Burns was so beautiful – the Idea I had was more desolate, his rigs of Barley seemed always to me but a few strips of Green on a cold hill – O prejudice! it was as rich as Devon – I endeavoured to drink in the Prospect, that I might spin it out to you, as the Silkworm makes silk from Mulberry leaves – I cannot recollect it Besides all the Beauty, there were the Mountains of Arran Isle, black and huge over the Sea.

John Keats, Letter to John Hamilton Reynolds, 11–13 July 1818

Birnam (and Dunsinane)

Macbeth: Till Byrnane wood remove to Dunsinane,
I cannot taint with Feare. . . .

William Shakespeare, *Macbeth, c.* 1605–6

Messenger: As I did stand my watch upon the Hill
I look'd toward Byrnane, and anon me thought
The Wood began to move. . . .
Within this three Mile may you see it comming.
I say, a moving Grove.

Ibid.

Bonhill (Leven Water)

*Above that house is a romantic glen or clift of a mountain, covered with hanging woods having at bottom a stream of fine water that forms a number of cascades in its descent to join the Leven; so that the scene is quite enchanting. A captain of a man of war, who had made the circuit of the globe with Mr.Anson, being conducted to this glen, exclaimed, 'Juan Fernandez, by God!'

Indeed, this country would be a perfect paradise, if it was not, like Wales, cursed with a weeping climate.

Tobias Smollett, *Humphrey Clinker*, 1771
('Matthew Bramble's' comments)

Border Country

This queer compromise between fairyland and battlefield which is the Border.

H.V. Morton, *In Search of Scotland*, 1929

Buckhaven (near East Wemyss)

. . . a miserable Row of Cottage-like Buildings. . . . Here we saw the Shore of the Sea cover'd with Shrimps, like the Ground cover'd with a thin Snow; and as you rode among them they would rise like a Kind of Dust, being scar'd by the Footing of the Horse, and Hopping like Grasshoppers.

Daniel Defoe, *A Tour through the Whole Island of Great Britain*, 1724–7

Caledonian Canal

I am very glad to have seen the Caledonian Canal, but don't want to see it again.

Matthew Arnold, Letter to his wife, 11 September 1882

Carse of Gowrie

And now the second soil for pleasure, is the platformed carse of Gowry, twelve miles long, (wheat, rye, corns, fruit-yards, being its only commodity), which I may term, for its levelled face, to be the garden of Angus, yea, the diamond-plot of Tay, or rather the youngest sister of matchless Piedmont; the inhabitants being only defective in affableness, and communicating courtesies of natural things, whence sprung this proverb, *The carles of the Carse.*

William Lithgow, *Rare Adventures and Painfull Peregrinations*, 1614/32

Cawdor

Call by the way at Cawdor the ancient seat of McBeth you know in Shakespear, there I saw the identical bed in which Tradition says king Duncan was murdered.

Robert Burns, Letter to Mr Gilbert Burns, 17 September 1787

Clyde (and Lanark)

The pleasant banks of Clyde,
Where orchards, castles, towns, and wood
Are planted by his side;
And chiefly Lanerk thou,
Thy country's laureat lamp,
In which this bruised body now
Did first receive the stamp.

William Lithgow, *Rare Adventures and Painfull Peregrinations*, 1614/32

A voyage down the Clyde is enough to make anybody happy: nowhere can the home tourist, at all events, behold, in the course of one day, such a succession and variety of beautiful, romantic, and majestic scenery.

J.G. Lockhart, *Life of Scott*, 1838

Clydesdale

Clydesdale . . . being the best mixed country for corns, meads, pasturage, woods, parks, orchards, castles, palaces, divers kinds of coal, and earth fewel, that our included Albion produceth; and may justly be surnamed the paradise of Scotland. Besides, it is adorned, on both borders along, with the greatest peers and nobility in the kingdom.

William Lithgow, *Rare Adventures and Painfull Peregrinations*, 1614/32

Crieff

Ye lover of the picturesque if ye wish to drown your grief
Take my advice and visit the ancient town of Crieff.

William McGonagall, 'Beautiful Crieff', *Poetic Gems*, 1890

Cromarty Firth

Cromarty Firth, noted for being the finest Harbour, with the least Business, of perhaps any in Britain.

Daniel Defoe, *A Tour through the Whole Island of Great Britain*, 1724–7

Cruachan

We thought it the grandest mountain we had seen, and on saying to the man who was with us that it was a fine mountain, 'Yes,' he replied, 'it is an excellent mountain.'

Dorothy Wordsworth, *Journal*, 31 August 1803

Culross

A Trading Town, as Trade must be understood in Scotland.

Daniel Defoe, *A Tour through the Whole Island of Great Britain*, 1724–7

Deeside

Here on fine days the Highlands wear a perpetual smile. It is true that there are wild places, but you are never quite deceived by them: you know that every pine-tree near Balmoral has a valet, and that no matter how cold the wind, how cruel the mountainside, how bleak the rolling moor, there is a hot bath at the end of every day. . . . There is a charm about Deeside which is the charm of an arm-chair after a storm.

H.V. Morton, *In Search of Scotland*, 1929

River Doon

Ye banks and braes o' bonny Doon,
How can ye bloom sae fresh and fair!

Robert Burns, *The Banks of Doon*, 1792

When I was sitting by the banks of Doon – I don't know why – I wasn't in the least spoony – not thinking of Burns (but of the lapsing of the Ages) – when all of a sudden I gave way to a passion of tears.

Alfred Lord Tennyson, in Edward Fitzgerald, *Some Recollections of Tennyson's Talk*, 1850

Drumlanrig Castle

Drumlanrig, like *Chatsworth* in *Darbyshire*, is like a fine Picture in a dirty Grotto, or like an Equestrian Statue set up in a Barn; 'tis environ'd with Mountains, and that of the wildest and most hideous Aspect in all the South of Scotland.

Daniel Defoe, *A Tour through the Whole Island of Great Britain*, 1724–7

This mansion is indeed very large; but to us it appeared like a gathering together of little things – the roof is broken into a hundred pieces, cupolas, etc., in the shape of casters, conjuror's balls, cups, and the like.

Dorothy Wordsworth, *Journal*, 19 August 1803

Dumfries

Dumfries is no agreeable place to them who do not love the bustle of a town that seems to be rising up to wealth.

Dorothy Wordsworth, *Journal*, 18 August 1803

Burns street . . . is a vile lane, paved with small, hard stones from side to side, and bordered by cottages, or mean houses of white-washed stone, joining one to another along the whole length of the street. With not a tree, of course, or a blade of grass between the paving-stones, the narrow lane was as hot as Tophet, and reeked with a genuine Scotch odor, being infested with unwashed children, and altogether in a state of chronic filth; although some women seemed to be hopelessly scrubbing the thresholds of their wretched dwellings. I never saw an outskirt of a town less fit for a poet's residence, or in which it would be more miserable for a man of cleanly predilections to spend his days.

Nathaniel Hawthorne, *Our Old Home*, 1863

Dumfriesshire

Dumfriesshire looks to the passer's eye like the classical incarnation of the trinity which Matthew Arnold disliked so much: Scotch drink, Scotch love and Scotch religion. It is solid, fertile and handsome. There may be found in certain districts of it, I have been told, a great number of people who look very like Burns. This fact has never been explained by historians as far as I know.

Edwin Muir, *Scottish Journey*, 1935

Dundee

The town is ill-built and is dirty beside
For with water its scantily, badly supplied
By wells, where the servants, in filling their pails
Stand for hours, spreading scandal, and falsehood and
tales
And abounds so in smells that a stranger supposes
The people are very deficient in noses
Their buildings, as though they'd been scanty of
ground
Are crammed into corners that cannot be found.
Or as though so ill built and contrived they had been,
That the town were ashamed they should ever be seen.
And their rooted dislike and aversion to waste
Is suffer'd sometimes to encroach on their taste,
For beneath a Theatre, or Chapel they'll pop
A saleroom, a warehouse, or mean little shop,
Whose windows, or rather no windows at all
Are more like so many holes in the wall.
And four churches together with only one steeple
Is an emblem quite apt of the thrift of the people. . . .
I've seen the Asylum they lately have made,
And approve of the plan, but indeed I'm afraid
If they send all the people of reason bereft
To this Bedlam, but few in the town will be left.
For their passions and drink are so terribly strong
That but few here retain all their faculties long.
And with shame I must own, that the females, I think
Are in general somewhat addicted to drink.

Thomas Hood, *Verse Letter to his Aunts*, December 1815

Welcome! thrice welcome! to the year 1893
For it is the year that I intend to leave Dundee
Owing to the treatment I receive
Which does my heart sadly grieve.
Every morning when I go out
The ignorant rabble they do shout
'There goes mad McGonagall'
In derisive shouts, as loud as they can bawl
And lifts stones and snowballs, throws them at me –
And such actions are shameful to be heard in the City
of Dundee.
And I'm ashamed Kind Christians to confess
That from the magistrates I can get no redress
Therefore I have made up my mind, in the year of 1893
To leave the ancient city of Dundee
Because the citizens and me cannot agree
The reason why? – because they disrespect me
Which makes me feel rather discontent.
Therefore to leave them I am bent
And I will make my arrangements without delay.
And leave Dundee some early day.

William McGonagall, *A New Year's Resolution to Leave Dundee*, 1893

The city of Dundee in the early thirties was a place of singular desolation. The whole of industrial Britain in those days was gripped in depression, even despair, and Dundee could have stood as a symbol of a society that had gone sour. It had, for a start, the air of a place that from the beginning of time had reconciled itself to an intrinsic ugliness. This struck me even in my youth as being odd, even anomalous, since of all cities in the kingdom Dundee had been placed with the greatest potential for grace and charm: it was set on a firth of breadth and grandeur; it was built around the slopes of a small mountain, the Law Hill; it backed on to a hinterland of fields and glens – at one time or another Dundee had the makings of a kind of Naples, which, forgetting the punitive nature of its climate, it geographically resembled. Even in those days I had known Naples; I would often look at that bleak Angus shore half-expecting singing fishermen, and hoping for a drift of Vesuvius smoke from the summit of the Law.

Dundee, however, had for generations dedicated itself to a kind of commercial single-mindedness that had come to fruition, in my day, in black and terrible industrial depression. Even then I felt the impact of its brutal melancholy, the façade of unparalleled charmlessness, an absence of grace so total that it was almost a thing of wonder.

James Cameron, *Point of Departure*, 1967

Dunfermline

The antient Town of *Dunfermling*, as I may say, in my Lord *Rochester's* Words, in *its full Perfection of Decay*. . . .

Daniel Defoe, *A Tour through the Whole Island of Great Britain*, 1724–7

Dunkeld

'Div ye ken Dunkeld?' he inquired.
'Right well,' I rejoined, 'one of the loveliest spots in all Scotland; charmingly situated on the Tay, amongst the first ridges of the Grampians, as you approach them from the noble Carse of Gowrie.'
'Ay, I see ye ken it weel,' continued he.

Alexander Mackay, *The Western World*, 1849

Little Dunkeld

O what a parish, what a terrible parish,
  O what a parish is Little Dunkel'!
They hae hangit the minister, drowned the precentor,
  Dung down the steeple and drucken the bell!

Anon.

Dunvegan Loch (Isay)

There is a beautiful little island in the Loch of Dunvegan, called Isay. MacLeod said he would give it to Mr. Johnson, on condition of his residing on it three months in the year, nay, one month. Mr Johnson was highly pleased with the fancy. I have seen him please himself with little things, even with mere ideas, as this was. He talked a great deal of this island – how he would build a house, how he would fortify it, how he would have cannon, how he would plant, how he would sally out and *take* the Isle of Muck; and then he laughed with a glee that was astonishing, and could hardly leave off. I have seen him do so at a small matter that struck him, and was a sport to no one else. MacLeod humoured Mr. Johnson finely as to his island; told him that as it was his practice in this country to name every man by his lands, he begged leave to drink him in that manner: '*Island Isay*, your health!' Ullinish, Talisker, and Mr. Macqueen all joined in their different manners, while Mr. Johnson bowed to each in excellent good humour.

James Boswell, *Journal of a Tour to the Hebrides with Samuel Johnson*, 1773 (1785)

Dunvegan (Isle of Skye)

Ane starke strengthe, biggit upon ane craig.

Donald Monro, *A Description of the Western Isles of Scotland, called Hybrides, c.* 1549

At Dunvegan I had tasted lotus, and was in danger of forgetting that I was ever to depart, till Mr. Boswell sagely reproached me with my sluggishness and softness.

Samuel Johnson, *Journey to the Western Isles of Scotland*, 1775

Ecclefechan

This unfortunate, wicked, little village.

Robert Burns, Letter to George Thomson, 7 February 1795

Edinburgh

Quhy will ye merchantis of renoun
Lat Edinburgh your nobill toun
For laik of reformatioun
The commone proffeitt tyine, and fame?
    Think ye not schame,
That onie uther regioun
Sall with dishonour hurt your name?

May nane pas throw your principall gaittis
For stink of haddockis and of scaittis,
For cryis of carlingis and debaittis,
For fensum flyttingis of defame;
    Think ye not schame,
Befoir strangeris of all estaittis
That sic dishonour hurt your name? . . .

Your burgh of beggeris is ane nest,
To schout thai swentyouris will not rest;
All honest folk they do molest,

Sa piteuslie thai cry and rame;
    Think ye not schame,
That for the poore hes nothing drest,
In hurt and sclander of your name?

Your proffeit daylie dois incres,
Your godlie workis les and les;
Through streittis nane may mak progres
For cry of cruikit, blind and lame;
    Think ye not schame,
That ye sic substance dois posses
And will not win ane bettir name? . . .

Thairfor strangeris and leigis triet,
Tak not over mekill for thair meit,
And gar your merchandis be discreit;
That na estortiounes be, proclame
    All fraud and schame;
Keip ordour and poore nighbouris beit,
That ye may gett ane bettir name.

William Dunbar, *To the Merchantis of Edinburgh*, c. 1500

. . . in a poem he called Edinborough the hart of Scotland Britaines other eye.

William Drummond, quoting Ben Jonson, *Ben Jonson's Conversations with W.D. of Hawthornden*, 1619

Tho' many Cities have more People in them, yet, I believe, this may be said with Truth, that in no City in the World so many People live in so little Room as at Edinburgh.

Daniel Defoe, *A Tour through the Whole Island of Great Britain*, 1724–7

I . . . am not sorry to have seen that most picturesque (at a distance) & nastiest (when near) of all capital Cities.

Thomas Gray, Letter to Thomas Wharton, c. 30 September 1765

Sir John Pringle observed that the manners of Edinburgh are very bad. That the people there have a familiarity, an inquisitiveness, a way of looking through one, that is extremely disagreeable. He is very right. But how can a man do who is to live amongst them? He must be exceedingly reserved, for, if he allows his vivacity to play, the sarcastical rogues will attack him; and should he, with the politeness well known abroad, show his displeasure, they would raise a hoarse laugh and never mind him. So that nothing less than a downright quarrel can make them understand that they have hurt him.

James Boswell, Journal, 3 September 1769, *Boswell in Search of a Wife*, 1957

*The city stands upon two hills, and the bottom between them; and, with all its defects, may very well pass for the capital of a moderate kingdom.

Tobias Smollett, *Humphrey Clinker*, 1771 ('Matthew Bramble's' comments)

. . . Which disputatious turn, by the way, is apt to become a very bad habit, making people often extremely disagreeable in company by the contradiction that is necessary to bring it into practice. . . . Persons of good sense, I have since observ'd, seldom fall into it, except lawyers, university men, and men of all sorts that have been bred at Edinborough.

Benjamin Franklin, *Autobiography*, 1771

Reikie, fareweel! I ne'er cou'd part
Wi' thee but wi' a dowy heart;
Aft frae the Fifan coast I've seen
Thee tow'ring on thy summit green;
So glowr the saints when first is given,
A fav'rite keek o' glore and heaven;
On earth nae mair they bend their ein,
But quick assume angelic mein;
So I on Fife wad glowr no more,
But gallop'd to Edina's shore.

Robert Fergusson, *Auld Reikie*, 1773

A city too well known to admit description.

Samuel Johnson, *Journey to the Western Isles of Scotland*, 1775

Edina! *Scotia's* darling seat!
  All hail thy palaces and tow'rs,
Where once beneath a Monarch's feet
  Sat Legislation's sov'reign pow'rs!
From marking wildly-scatt'red flow'rs,
  As on the banks of *Ayr* I stray'd,
And singing, lone, the ling'ring hours,
  I shelter in thy honor'd shade.

Here Wealth still swells the golden tide,
  As busy Trade his labours plies;
There Architecture's noble pride
  Bids elegance and splendor rise;
Here Justice, from her native skies,
  High wields her balance and her rod;
There Learning, with his eagle eyes,
  Seeks Science in her coy abode.

Robert Burns, *Address to Edinburgh*, 1786

Nae Heathen Name shall I prefix
  Frae Pindus or Parnassus;
AULD REEKIE dings them a' to sticks
  For rhyme-inspiring Lasses.

Robert Burns, *To Miss Ferrier*, 1787

No Smells were ever equal to Scotch Smells. It is the School of Physic; walk the Streets, and you would imagine that every Medical man had been administering Cathartics to every man woman and child in the Town. Yet the place is uncommonly beautiful, and I am in a constant balance between admiration and trepidation –

Taste guides my Eye, where e'er new beauties spread
While prudence whispers, 'Look before you tread.'

Sydney Smith, Letter to M.H. Beach, 30 June 1798

What a wonderful City Edinburgh is! – What alternation of Height & Depth! – a city looked at in the polish'd back of a Brobdignag Spoon, held lengthways – so enormously *stretched-up* are the Houses! – When I first looked down on it as the Coach drove in on the higher Street, I cannot express what I felt – such a section of a wasp's nest, striking you with a sort of bastard Sublimity from the enormity and infinity of it's littleness – the infinity swelling out the mind, the enormity striking it with wonder. I think I have seen an old Plate of Montserrat, that struck me with the same feeling – and I am sure, I have seen huge Quarries of Lime or Free-Stone, in which the Shafts or Strata have stood perpendicularly instead of horizontally, with the same high Thin Slices, & corresponding Interstices! – I climbed last night to the Crags just below Arthur's Seat, itself a rude triangle-shaped bare Cliff, & looked down on the whole City & Firth, the Sun then setting behind the magnificent rock, crested by the Castle – the Firth was full of Ships, & I counted 54 heads of mountains, of which at least 44 were cones or pyramids – the smoke rising up from ten thousand houses, each smoke from some one family – it was an affecting sight to me! – I stood gazing at the setting Sun, so tranquil to a passing Look, & so restless & vibrating to one who looks stedfast; & then all at once turning my eyes down upon the City, it & all it's smokes & figures became at once dipped in the brightest blue-purple – such a sight that I almost grieved when my eyes recovered their natural Tone!

S.T. Coleridge, Letter to Robert Southey,
13 September 1803

The old town, with its irregular houses, stage above stage, seen as we saw it, in the obscurity of a rainy day, hardly resembles the work of men, it is more like a piling up of rocks; and I cannot attempt to describe what we saw so imperfectly, but must say that, high as my expectations had been raised, the city of Edinburgh far surpassed all expectation.

Dorothy Wordsworth, *Journal*, 16 September 1803

Still on the spot Lord Marmion stay'd,
For fairer scene he ne'er survey'd.
When sated with the martial show
That peopled all the plain below,
The wandering eye could o'er it go,
And mark the distant city glow
With gloomy splendour red;
For on the smoke-wreaths, huge and slow,
That round her sable turrets flow,
The morning beams were shed,
And tinged them with a lustre proud,
Like that which streaks a thunder-cloud.
Such dusky grandeur clothed the height,
Where the huge Castle holds its state,
And all the steep slope down,
Whose ridgy back heaves to the sky,
Piled deep and massy, close and high,
Mine own romantic town!
But northward far, with purer blaze,
On Ochil mountains fell the rays,
And as each heathy top they kiss'd,
It gleamed a purple amethyst.
Yonder the shores of Fife you saw;
Here Preston-Bay and Berwick Law;
And broad between them roll'd,
The gallant Frith the eye might note,
Whose islands on its bosom float,
Like emeralds chased in gold.
Fitz-Eustace' heart felt closely pent;
As if to give his nature vent,
The spur he to his charger lent,
And raised his bridle hand,
And making demi-volte in air,
Cried, 'Where's the coward that would not dare
To fight for such a land!'

Sir Walter Scott, *Marmion*, 1808

It is the misfortune of Edinburgh men, that they see no fools and common persons (I mean, of clever men in Edinburgh).

Sydney Smith, Letter to J.A. Murray,
18 August 1813

Stately Edinburgh throned on crags.

William Wordsworth, *The Excursion*, 1814

*If I were to choose a spot from which the rising or setting sun could be seen to the greatest possible advantage, it would be that wild path winding around the foot of the high belt of semicircular rocks, called Salisbury Crags, and marking the verge of the steep descent which slopes down into the glen on the south-eastern side of Edinburgh. The prospect, in its general outline, commands a close-built, high-piled city, stretching itself out beneath in a form, which, to a romantic imagination, may be supposed to represent that of a dragon; now, a noble arm of the sea, with its rocks, isles, distant shores, and boundary of mountains; and now, a fair and fertile champaign country, varied with hill, dale, and rock, and skirted by the picturesque ridge of the Pentland mountains. But as the path gently circles around the base of the cliffs, the prospect, composed as it is of these enchanting and sublime objects, changes at every step, and presents them blended with, or divided from, each other, in every possible variety which can gratify the eye and the imagination. When a piece of scenery, so beautiful yet so varied – so exciting by its intricacy, and yet so sublime – is lighted up by the tints of morning or of evening, and displays all that variety of shadowy depth, exchanged with partial brilliancy, which gives character even to the tamest of landscapes, the effect approaches near to enchantment.

Walter Scott, *The Heart of Midlothian*, 1818

See yon hamlet, o'ershadowed with smoke;
See yon hoary battlement throned on the rock;
Even there shall a city in splendour break forth,
The haughty Dun-Edin, the Queen of the North;
There learning shall flourish, and liberty smile,
The awe of this world, and the pride of the isle.

James Hogg, *The Queen's Wake*, 1819

When I lived there, very few maids had shoes and stockings, but plodded about the house with feet as big as a family Bible, and legs as large as portmanteaus.

Sydney Smith, Letter to Lady Mary Bennet, 20 December 1820

Came to Edinburgh by night – astonished at the city next morning – wild dream of a great genius – finest city in Europe – may be in time in the world. . . . The only city in the World where the Parthenon might be erected with something of its ancient splendour.

Benjamin Robert Haydon, *Diary*, December 1820

This accursed, stinking, reeky mass of stones and lime and dung.

Thomas Carlyle, Letter to his brother John, 10 February 1821

Edinburgh alone is as splendid in its situation and buildings, and would have even a more imposing and delightful effect if Arthur's Seat were crowned with thick woods, and if the Pentland-hills could be converted into green pastures, if the Scotch people were French, and Leith-walk planted with vineyards.

William Hazlitt, *Notes of a Journey through France and Italy*, 1826

The impression *Edinburgh* has made upon us is very great; it is quite beautiful, totally unlike anything else I have seen; and what is even more, Albert, who has seen so much, says it is unlike anything *he* ever saw.

Queen Victoria, 1 September 1842, *Leaves from the Journal of Our Life in the Highlands*, 1868

Albert says that many of the people look like Germans.

Queen Victoria, 2 September 1842, *Leaves from the Journal of Our Life in the Highlands*, 1868

Who indeed, that has once seen Edinburgh, with its couchant rag-lion, but must see it again in dreams, waking or sleeping? My dear Sir, do not think I blaspheme when I tell you that your great London, as compared to Dun-Edin, 'mine own romantic town', is as prose compared to poetry, or as a great rumbling, rambling, heavy epic compared to a lyric, brief, bright, clear, and vital as a flash of lightning. You have nothing like Scott's monument, or if you had that, and all the glories of architecture assembled together, you have nothing like Arthur's Seat, and above all you have not the Scotch national character; and it is that grand character after all which gives the land its true charm, its true greatness.

Charlotte Brontë, Letter to W. Smith Williams, 1850

Pompous the boast, and yet a truth it speaks
A 'modern Athens,' – fit for modern Greeks.

James Hannay, in *The Edinburgh Courant*, 10 November 1860

Once upon a time it must have been an impressive and poetical place, but I should think always very doleful: the dolefulness remains, the poetry is pretty much gone.

William Morris, *Journal*, 7 July 1871

Every now and then as we went, Arthur's Seat showed its head at the end of a street. Now, today, the blue sky and the sunshine were both entirely wintry; and there was about the hill in these glimpses, a sort of thin, unreal, crystalline distinctness that I have not often seen excelled. As the sun began to go down over the valley between the new town and the old, the evening grew resplendent; all the gardens and low-lying buildings sank back, and became almost invisible in a mist of wonderful sun, and the castle stood up against the sky, as thin and sharp in the outline as a castle cut out of paper. Baxter made a good remark about Princes Street, that it was the most elastic street for length that he knew; sometimes it looks as it looked tonight, interminable, a way leading right into the heart of the red sundown; sometimes again, it shrinks together, as if for warmth, on one of the withering, clear, east-windy days, until it seems to lie underneath your feet.

Robert Louis Stevenson, Letter to Mrs Sitwell, 4 October 1873

. . . it is quite lovely – bits of it.

Oscar Wilde, Letter to E.W. Godwin, 19 December 1884

A place where it seems to me, looking back, it must be always autumn and generally Sunday.

R.L. Stevenson, *The Coast of Fife*, 1888

I saw rain falling and the rainbow drawn
On Lammermuir. Hearkening I heard again
In my precipitous city beaten bells

Winnow the keen sea wind. And here afar
Intent on my own race and place I wrote.

Robert Louis Stevenson, Prefatory verses, in *Weir of Hermiston*, 1896

and Dublin and New York

This place in which I find myself is the strangest mixture of Edinburgh and Dublin and New York and some other place I don't know.

Henry James, Remark during his last illness, 1916, quoted in H. Montgomery Hyde, *Henry James at Home*, 1969

Is there another city in the world which marches hand in hand with its past as does Edinburgh; which can look up from its modernity and see itself as it always was, upon a hill, intact, impregnable, and still in arms?

H.V. Morton, *In Search of Scotland*, 1929

Although Edinburgh is Scottish in itself, one cannot feel that the people who live in it are Scottish in any radical sense, or have any essential connection with it. They do not even go with it; they look like visitors who have stayed there for a long time. One imagines that not very long ago the real population must have been driven out, and that the people one sees walking about came to stay in the town simply because the houses happened to be empty. In other words, one cannot look at Edinburgh without being conscious of a visible crack in historical continuity. The actual town, the houses, streets, churches, rocks, gardens, are there still; but these exist wholly in the past. That past is a national past; the present, which is made up of the thoughts and feelings and prejudices of the inhabitants, their way of life in general, is as cosmopolitan as the cinema.

Edwin Muir, *Scottish Journey*, 1935

Edinburgh presents outwardly the face it had a hundred years ago, while within it is worm-eaten with all the ingenuity in tastelessness which modern resources can supply.

Ibid.

. . . well-set Edinburgh.

W.H. Auden, *Night Mail*, 1935

It has all the beauty of half a dozen sorts of beautiful city. The old town has the picturesqueness of Cracow in grey instead of in red. The squares and crescents of the new town are eighteenth century at its most elegantly dignified. Princes street and the Calton Hill are sheer magnificence. The view from George street over the Forth and the hills of the kingdom of Fife is pure San Francisco. And, as if that was not enough beauty and strangeness for one city, in the middle of it all is that incredible castle. To Edinburgh's beauty add Edinburgh's history. To both add her men of genius. Add her arts, her medicine, her schools; her law; her legends; her traditions. What other capital city in the world outside Rome and Athens can equal the result of all that heaping of treasure upon treasure? . . . Edinburgh has often been called the New Athens. It cannot be allowed to be a very happy description. . . . The framework is there, the city, the education, the history, all is there except the divine spark. Edinburgh is the greatest dead thing in the world. Athens was the greatest alive thing in the world.

A.G. Macdonell, *My Scotland*, 1937

Most of the denizens wheeze, sniffle, and exude a sort of snozzling whnoff whnoff, apparently through a hydrophile sponge.

Ezra Pound, quoted by Hugh McDiarmid (C.M. Grieve), as Epigraph to 'Edinburgh', *Lucky Poet*, 1943

This rortie wretched city . . .
And shall she get the richts o' it
A diadem for the brou?
Shall Scotland croun her ain again,
This ancient capital? –
Or sell the thing for scrap?
Or some yankee museum maybe?
I'll be here bidin the answer . . .
Here I be and here I drink,
This is mine, Kynd Kittock's land
For ever and aye while stane shall stand –
For ever and aye till the World's End.

Sydney Goodsir Smith, *Kynd Kittock's Land*, 1965

City of everywhere, broken necklace in the sun,
you are caves of guilt, you are pinnacles of jubilation.
Your music is a filigree of drumming.
You frown into the advent of heavenly hosts.
Your iron finger shatters sad suns –
they multiply in scatters, they swarm
on fizzing roofs. When the sea
breathes gray over you, you become
one lurking-place, one shifting of nowheres –
in it are warpipes and genteel pianos
and the sawing voices of lawyers. Your buildings
are broken memories, your streets
lost hopes – but you shrug off time, you set your face
against all that is not you.

Norman McCraig, 'Drop-Out in Edinburgh', *The World's Room*, 1974

Auld Reekie wins every time. The New Town looks pallid beside it, overawed despite itself, like some able and imaginative young executive, fresh from management training, outfaced by a criminal, self-made tycoon.

Jan Morris, 'A Northern Prodigy', *Travels*, 1976

The Castle

The Castle on a loftie Rocke is so strongly grounded,

bounded and founded, that by force of man it can never be confounded; the Foundation and Walls are unpenetrable, the Rampiers impregnable, the Bulwarkes invincible, no way but one to it is or can be possible to be made passable.

John Taylor, *Taylors Pennilesse Pilgrimage*, in *All the Works of John Taylor*, 1630

Edinburgh Castle . . . he owned was 'a great place.' But I must mention, as a striking instance of that spirit of contradiction to which he had a strong propensity, when Lord Elibank was some days after talking of it with the natural elation of a Scotchman, or of any man who is proud of a stately fortress in his own country. Dr. Johnson affected to despise it, observing that, 'it would make a good *prison* in ENGLAND.'

James Boswell, *Journal of a Tour to the Hebrides with Samuel Johnson*, 1773 (1785)

Ellisland (near Dumfries)

In this strange land, this uncouth clime,
A land unknown to prose or rhyme;
Where words ne'er crost the muse's heckles,
Nor limpet in poetic shackles;
A land that prose did never view it,
Except when drunk he stacher thro' it.

Robert Burns, *Epistle to Hugh Parker*, 1788

The whisky of this country is a most rascally liquor; and by consequence only drank by the most rascally part of the inhabitants.

Robert Burns, Letter to Mr John Tennant, 22 December 1788

Fife

There is also a Ferry at *Leith*, . . . but. . . . The Passengers are so often frighted, that I know several Gentlemen that would always choose to go round to the *Queens-Ferry*, rather than venture over at *Leith*; this, I suppose, gave beginning to that homely piece of Proverb Poetry, that

There is never a Laird in Fife,
But once a Year he would give his Estate for his Life.

Daniel Defoe, *A Tour through the Whole Island of Great Britain*, 1724–7

Forth Bridge

To see the Forth Bridge is rather like meeting a popular actress, but with this difference; it exceeds expectations.

H.V. Morton, *In Search of Scotland*, 1929

Fort William (waterfall nearby visible from window of Glenfinnan Inn)

Did you ever see a waterfall turned inside out, downside up? The south-wester is doing this to one opposite the window.

Arthur Hugh Clough, Letter to J.C. Shairp, 1 September 1847

Galloway (and Ayrshire, between)

A parcel of damn'd melancholy, joyless muirs.

Robert Burns, Letter to Mr Robert Cleghorn, 31 March 1788

Glamis

When you see it at a Distance, it is so full of Turrets and lofty Buildings, Spires and Towers, some plain, others shining with gilded Tops, that it looks not like a Town, but a City; and the noble Appearance seen through the long Vista's of the Park are so differing, that it does not appear like the same Place any two Ways together.

Daniel Defoe, *A Tour through the Whole Island of Great Britain*, 1724–7

Glasgow

and the Clyde
The Clyde made Glasgow and Glasgow made the Clyde.

Old saying

One of the inhabitants of St. Kilda, being some time ago wind-bound in the isle of Harris, was prevailed on by some of them that traded to Glasgow to go thither with them. . . . Upon his arrival at Glasgow he was like one that had dropped from the clouds into a new world, whose language, habit, &c., were in all respects new to him; he never imagined that such big houses of stone were made with hands; and for the pavements of the streets he thought it must needs be altogether natural, for he could not believe that men would be at the pains to beat stones into the ground to walk upon. He stood dumb at the door of his lodging with the greatest admiration; and when he saw a coach and two horses, he thought it to be a little house they were drawing at their tail, with men in it; but he condemned the coachman for a fool to sit so uneasy, for he thought it safer to sit on the horse's back. The mechanism of the coach's wheel and its running about, was the greatest of all his wonders.

When he went through the streets, he desired to have one to lead him by the hand. Thomas Ross . . . asked his opinion of the High Church? He answered that it was a large rock, yet there were some in St. Kilda much higher, but that these were the best caves he ever saw; for that was the idea which he conceived of the pillars and arches upon which the church stands. When they carried him into the church, he was yet more surprised, and held up his hands with admiration, wondering how it was possible for men to build such a prodigious fabric, which he supposed to be the largest in the universe. . . . When he heard the church bells ring he was under a mighty consternation, as if the fabric of the world had been in great disorder. . . . He longed to see his native country again, and passionately wished it were blessed with ale, brandy, tobacco, and iron, as Glasgow was.

Martin Martin, *A Description of the Western Islands of Scotland*, 1703

Glasgow is . . . the prettiest and most uniform Town that I ever saw; . . . there is nothing like it in Britain.

It has a spacious Carrifour, where stands the Cross; and in going round it, you have, by Turns, the View of four Streets, that in regular Angles proceed from thence. The Houses of these Streets are faced with Ashlar Stone, they are well sashed, all of one Model, and Piazzas run round them on either Side, which gives a good Air to the Buildings. There are some handsome Streets, but the extreme Parts of the Town are mean and disagreeable to the Eye.

Edward Burt, *Letters from a Gentleman in the North of Scotland*, 1754 – of *c.* 1730

This is wrote at a place which I shall ever hold in contempt as being filled with a set of unmannerly, low-bred, narrow-minded wretches; the place itself, however, is really pretty, and were the present inhabitants taken out and drowned in the ocean, and others with generous souls put in their stead, it would be an honour to Scotland.

David Boswell, Letter to James Boswell, Glasgow, 30 October 1767

*Glasgow, . . . to the best of my recollections and judgement, is one of the prettiest towns in Europe; and, without all doubt it is one of the most flourishing in Great Britain. In short, it is a perfect bee-hive in point of industry. It stands partly on a gentle declivity, but the greatest part of it is in a plain, watered by the river Clyde. The streets are open, straight, airy, and well paved; and the houses lofty, and well built of hewn stone . . . marks of opulence and independency appear in every quarter of this commercial city . . . a defect, not . . . easily remedied, is the shallowness of the river, which will not float vessels of any burthen within ten or twelve miles of the city; so that the merchants are obliged to load and unload their ships at Greenock, and Port-Glasgow, situated about fourteen miles nearer the mouth of the Frith, where it is about two miles broad.

Tobias Smollett, *Humphrey Clinker*, 1771 ('Matthew Bramble's' comments)

The City of Glasgow I take to be a very fine one – I was astonished to hear it was twice the size of Edinburgh – It is built of Stone and has a much more solid appearance than London.

John Keats, Letter to Thomas Keats, 10–14 July 1818

Glasgow fine streets, fires enormous, houses hot, same smell as Edinburgh, the look of manufacture and abomination. . . . Travelled all night, & on rolling over a bridge near Gretna Green into England all of us inside passengers gave three cheers.

Benjamin Robert Haydon, *Diary*, December 1820

Glasgow finer than any town I have seen in England except Oxford; but Edinburgh is the king and the Queen of Scotland.

Dorothy Wordsworth, *Journal*, 19 September 1822

The curses of Glasgow are, itch, punch, cotton, and metaphysics.

Sydney Smith, Letter to Sir George Philips, September 1838

Commercial capital of Britain, *this*.

Thomas Carlyle, *Reminiscences of My Irish Journey in 1849*, 1882

. . . went up the Clyde to Glasgow. Great excitement all along. Banks like tow-paths – narrow channel – immense steamer – green heights – received by acclamation – Lord Blantyre's place – opposite mud cottage – cattle tenders – women – face like cattle – places for building iron steamers.

Next morning went to old cathedral, – tombs, defaced inscriptions – others worn in flagging – some letters traced in moss – back of cathedral gorge and stream – Acropolis – John Knox in Geneva cap frowning down on the cathedral – dimness of atmosphere in keeping – all looked like picture of one of the old masters smoked by Time – Old buildings about the hill stone walls & thatch roof – solid and fragile – miserable poverty – look of the Middle Ages – west end & fine houses – the moderns – contemporary.

Herman Melville, *Journal of a Visit to Europe and the Levant*, October 1856

And without fear of contradiction I will venture to say
You are the second grandest city in Scotland at the
present day.

William McGonagall, 'Glasgow', *Poetic Gems*, 1890

Have you been to the Arran islands and seen a civilization entirely unspoiled by the factory system? Have you been to Glasgow and seen a civilization entirely unspoiled by religion?

Eric Gill, Letter to Geoffrey Keynes, 30 October 1919

'Heaven seems vera little improvement on Glesga,' a good Glasgow man is said to have murmured, after death, to a friend who had predeceased him. 'Man, this is no Heaven,' the other replied.

C.E. Montague, *The Right Place*, 1924

and Edinburgh
Glasgow plays the part of Chicago to Edinburgh's Boston. Glasgow is a city of the glad hand and the smack on the back; Edinburgh is a city of silence until birth or brains open the social circle. In Glasgow a man is innocent until he is found guilty; in Edinburgh a man is guilty until he is found innocent. Glasgow is willing to believe the best of an unknown quantity; Edinburgh, like all aristocracies, the worst!. . . .

Glasgow is a mighty and an inspiring story. She is Scotland's anchor to reality.

H.V. Morton, *In Search of Scotland*, 1929

It may be confidently maintained that here is the liveliest community in Scotland. This fantastic mixture of racial strains, this collection of survivors from one of the most exacting of social processes, is a dynamo of confident, ruthless, literal energy. The Glasgow man is downright, unpolished, direct, and immediate. He may seem to compare in that respect with the Aberdonian, but in him there is none of that queer Teutonic reserve, which is so apt to affect human intercourse with the native of Buchan. That he is a mighty man with his hands the world knows and acknowledges; that he is nearer the poet than his brothers in the other cities is less obvious, but equally true. He has the 'furious' quality of the Scot in its most extreme form. He can be terribly dangerous in revolt and as terribly strong in defence of his own conception of order. He hates pretence, ceremonial, form – and is at the same time capable of the most abysmal sentimentality. He is grave – and one of the world's most devastating humorists.

George Blake, *The Heart of Scotland*, 1934

Nobody will ever understand Glasgow who does not realise that it is a city which has risen to wealth with enormous rapidity. People often complain that in the world generally invention outruns the ability of human beings to adapt themselves to it, and to use it for the right ends. In a rapidly growing city the same thing happens with wealth; a number of people become rich in a very short time without any notion of how to spend their money even with ordinary selfish taste. This seems to have happened on a large scale in the United States before the present depression; and in its combination of riches and tastelessness upper-class Glasgow is very like the United States.

Edwin Muir, *Scottish Journey*, 1935

and Edinburgh
If one wanted a rough-and-ready generalisation to express the difference between a Glasgow man and an Edinburgh man, one might say that every Edinburgh man considers himself a little better than his neighbour, and every Glasgow man just as good as his neighbour.

Ibid.

The City of Dreadful Knights.

Saying quoted by Edward Marsh, *A Number of People*, 1939

Glasgow thinks nothing and is content to be
Just what it is, not caring or knowing what. . . .
The houses are Glasgow, not the people – these
Are simply the food the houses live and grow on
Endlessly, drawing from their vulgarity
And pettiness and darkness of spirit
– Gorgonising the mindless generations,
Turning them all into filthy property, . . .
Everything is dead except stupidity here

Where have I seen a human being looking
As Glasgow looks this gin-clear evening – with face and fingers
A cadaverous blue, hand-clasp slimy and cold
As that of a corpse, finger-nails grown immensely long
As they do in a grave, little white eyes, and hardly
Any face at all? Cold, lightning-like, unpleasant light, and blue
Like having one's cold-spots intoxicated with mescal.
Looking down a street the houses seem
Long pointed teeth like a ferret's over the slit
Of a crooked unspeakable smile, like the Thracian woman's
When Thales fell in the well, a hag
Whose soul-gelding ugliness would chill
To eternal chastity a cantharidized satyr;
And the smell reminds me of the *odeur de souris*
Of Balzac's Cousin Pons. All the strength seems
To leave my body as I look, and a deadly
Grey weariness falls over my thoughts like dust.
A terrible shadow descends like dust over my thoughts,
Almost like reading a *Glasgow Herald* leader,
Or any of our Anglo-Scottish daily papers. . . .

Hugh MacDiarmid, 'Glasgow', from *Lucky Poet*, 1943

In a city like Glasgow, all the upper class well-to-do, and professional people are nothing more than so many phagocytes feeding on the pus of an abscess.

Anon., quoted in *ibid.*

Bridge of the Clyde at Glasgow
As for the Bridge, which is a lofty, stately Fabrick; it stood out of the Water as naked as a Skeleton, and look'd somewhat like the Bridge over the *Mansanares* near Madrid, . . . of which a *French* Ambassador told

the People the King should either buy them a River, or sell their Bridge.

Daniel Defoe, *A Tour through the Whole Island of Great Britain*, 1724–7

Glencoe

Glen Coe interested me; but rather disappointed me – there was no *superincumbency* of Crag, the Crags not so bare or precipitous, as I had expected.

S.T. Coleridge, Letter to Mrs S.T. Coleridge, 2 September 1803

Glencoe itself is perfectly *terrible*. The pass is an awful place. It is shut in on each side by enormous rocks from which great torrents come rushing down in all directions. In amongst these rocks on one side of the pass (the left as we came) there are scores of glens, high up, which form such haunts as you might imagine yourself wandering in, in the very height and madness of a fever. They will live in my dreams for years – I was going to say as long as I live, and I seriously think so. The very recollection of them makes me shudder. . . . Well, I will not bore you with my impressions of these tremendous wilds, but they really are fearful in their grandeur and amazing solitude. Wales is a mere toy compared to them.

Charles Dickens, Letter to John Forster, 9 July 1841

In the Gaelic tongue, Glencoe signifies the Glen of Weeping: and in truth that pass is the most dreary and melancholy of all the Scottish passes, the very Valley of the Shadow of Death. Mists and storms brood over it through the greater part of the finest summer; and even on those rare days when the sun is bright, and when there is no cloud in the sky, the impression made by the landscape is sad and awful. The path lies along a stream which issues from the most sullen and gloomy of mountain pools. Huge precipices of naked stone frown on both sides. Even in July the streaks of snow may often be discerned in the rifts near the summits. All down the sides of the crags heaps of ruin mark the headlong paths of the torrents. Mile after mile the traveller looks in vain for the smoke of one hut, or for one human form wrapped in a plaid, and listens in vain for the bark of a shepherd's dog, or the bleat of a lamb. Mile after mile the only sound that indicates life is the faint cry of a bird of prey from some storm beaten pinnacle of rock. The progress of civilisation which has turned so many wastes into fields yellow with harvests or gay with apple blossoms, has only made Glencoe more desolate.

T.B. Macaulay, *History of England*, 1849–61

Along the road from Ballachulish where the river Coe pours into Loch Leven is a comfortable little village which boasts the most grotesque signpost in the British Isles:

THE VILLAGE OF GLENCOE
SCENE OF THE FAMOUS MASSACRE
TEAS AND REFRESHMENTS, TOBACCO AND CIGARETTES.

H.V. Morton, *In Search of Scotland*, 1929

Glenfalloch

At that point from which a step or two would have carried us out of sight of the green fields of Glenfalloch, being at a great height on the mountain, we sate down, and heard, as if from the heart of the earth, the sound of torrents ascending out of the long, hollow glen. To the eye all was motionless, a perfect stillness. The noise of waters did not appear to come this way or that, from any particular quarter: it was everywhere, almost, one might say, as if *exhaled* through the whole surface of the green earth. Glenfalloch, Coleridge has since told me, signifies the Hidden Vale; but Wm. says, if we were to name it from our recollections of that time, we should call it the Vale of Awful Sound.

Dorothy Wordsworth, *Journal*, 12 September 1803

Glen Shiel

We passed through Glen Shiel, with prodigious mountains on each side. We saw where the battle was in the year 1715. Mr Johnson owned he was now in a scene of as wild nature as he could see. But he corrected me sometimes in my observations. 'There,' said I, 'is a mountain like a cone.' 'No sir,' said he. 'It would be called so in a book; and when a man comes to look at it, he sees 'tis not so. It is indeed pointed at the top. But one side of it is much longer than the other.' Another mountain I called immense. 'No,' said he, 'but 'tis a considerable protruberance.'

James Boswell, *Journal of a Tour to the Hebrides with Samuel Johnson*, 1773 (1785)

Granton

Granton is a dull dull place with the slip-shod do-nothing air that hangs about a small port, though I suppose more is going on than seems to be: except for the steam-ferry . . . which is always coming and going, the same vessels seem as if they must always be lying in the same places, and the sailors loafing about look as if they had been 'struck so' with their hands in their pockets.

William Morris, *Journal*, 7 July 1871

Gretna Green

Gretna Green, upon a hill and among trees . . . sounds

well but it is a dreary place; the stone houses dirty and miserable, with broken windows. There is a pleasant view from the churchyard.

Dorothy Wordsworth, *Journal*, 17 August 1803

Hebrides

The north-west isles are of all others most capable of improvement by sea and land.

Martin Martin, *A Description of the Western Islands of Scotland*, 1703

Women were anciently denied the use of writing in the islands to prevent love-intrigues: their parents believed that nature was too skilful in that matter, and needed not the help of education; and therefore, that writing would be of dangerous consequence to the weaker sex.

Ibid.

Besides the ordinary rent paid by the tenant to his master, if a cow brought forth two calves at a time, which indeed is extraordinary, or an ewe two lambs, which is frequent, the tenant paid to the master one of the calves or lambs; and the master on his part was obliged, if any of his tenants' wives bore twins, to take one of them, and breed him in his own family. I have known a gentleman who had sixteen of these twins in his family at a time.

Ibid.

Or where the Northern Ocean, in vast whirls,
Boils round the naked, melancholy isles
Of farthest Thule, and th' Atlantic surge
Pours in among the stormy Hebrides;
Who can recount what transmigrations there
Are annual made? what nations come and go?
And how the living clouds on clouds arise –
Infinite wings! – till all the plume-dark air
And rude-resounding shore are one wild cry?

James Thomson, *The Seasons, Autumn*, 1730

When I was at Ferney in 1764, I mentioned our design to Voltaire. He looked at me as if I had talked of going to the North Pole, and said, 'You do not insist on my accompanying you?' 'No sir.' 'Then I am very willing you should go.'

James Boswell, *Journal of a Tour to the Hebrides with Samuel Johnson*, 1773 (1785)

I had desired to visit the Hebrides, or Western Isles of Scotland, so long, that I scarcely remember how the wish was excited.

Samuel Johnson, *Journey to the Western Isles of Scotland*, 1775

Of these islands it must be confessed, that they have not many allurements, but to the mere lover of naked nature. The inhabitants are thin, provisions are scarce, and desolation and penury give little pleasure.

Ibid.

A man of the Hebrides, for of the women's diet I can give no account, as soon as he appears in the morning, swallows a glass of whisky; yet they are not a drunken race, at least I never was present at much intemperance; but no man is so abstemious as to refuse the morning dram, which they call a *skalk*.

Ibid.

I never was in any house of the Islands, where I did not find books in more languages than one, if I staid long enough to want them.

Ibid.

Some of those islands might be considered as the hell of Great Britain, where all evil spirits should be sent.

Hector St John de Crèvecoeur, *Letters from an American Farmer*, 1782

From the lone shieling of the misty island
Mountains divide us, and the waste of seas –
Yet still the blood is strong, the heart is Highland,
And we in dreams behold the Hebrides!
Fair these broad meads, these hoary woods are grand
But we are exiles from our fathers' land.

Anon., *Canadian Boat Song* (from the Gaelic), *Blackwood's Edinburgh Magazine*, September 1829. (Possibly by David Macbeth Moir, but numerous other candidates have been suggested.)

On those islands
There is echo of the leaping fish, the identical
Sound that cheered the chiefs at ease from slaughter;
There is echo of baying hounds of a lost breed
And echo of MacCrimmon's pipes lost in the cave;
And seals cry with the voices of the drowned.
When men go out to fish, no one must say 'Good luck'
And the confidences told in a boat at sea
Must be as if printed on the white ribbon of a wave
Withdrawn as soon as printed – so never heard. . . .
On those islands
The fish come singing from the drunken sea,
The herring rush the gunwales and sort themselves
To cram the expectant barrels of their own accord –
Or such is the dream of the fisherman whose wet
Leggings hang on the door as he sleeps returned
From a night when miles of net were drawn up
  empty. . . .
  on those islands
Where a few surnames cover a host of people
And the art of being a stranger with your neighbour
Has still to be imported, death is still
No lottery ticket in a public lottery –
The result to be read on the front page of a journal –
But a family matter near to the whole family.

On those islands
Where no train runs on rails and the tyrant time
Has no clock-towers to signal people to doom
With semaphore ultimatums tick by tick,
There is still peace though not for me and not
Perhaps for long – still peace on the bevel hills
For those who can live as their fathers lived
On those islands.

Louis MacNeice, *The Hebrides*, 1937

Highlands

Speak weel o' the Hielands, but dwell in the Laigh.

Scottish proverb

Our Geographers seem to be almost as much at a loss in the Description of this North Part of *Scotland*, as the *Romans* were to conquer it; and they are oblig'd to fill it up with Hills and Mountains, as they do the inner Parts of *Africa*, with Lyons and Elephants, for want of knowing what else to place there.

Daniel Defoe, *A Tour through the Whole Island of Great Britain*, 1724–7

The Highlands . . . would be Italy, if they had but a climate, . . . there it is that the beauties of Scotland lie hid. of the Lowlands, which every true Scotsman celebrates as a Paradise, I shall only say, they are better than Northumberland . . . and the nearer they come to the Mountains the better they grow.

Thomas Gray, Letter to James Brown, 2 November 1765

I am return'd from Scotland charm'd with my expedition: it is of the Highlands I speak: the Lowlands are worth seeing once, but the Mountains are extatic, & ought to be visited in pilgrimage once a year. none but those monstrous creatures of God know how to join so much beauty with so much horror. . . . Italy could hardly produce a nobler scene, or a finer season. and this is so sweetly contrasted with that perfection of nastiness, & total want of accomodation, that Scotland only can supply.

Thomas Gray, Letter to William Mason, 8 November 1765

Some gentlemen of the neighbourhood came to visit my father. . . . One of them asked Dr Johnson how he liked the Highlands. The question seemed to irritate him, for he answered, 'How, sir, can you ask me what obliges me to speak unfavourably of a country where I have been hospitably entertained? Who *can* like the Highlands? I like the inhabitants very well.'

James Boswell, *Journal of a Tour to the Hebrides with Samuel Johnson*, 1773 (1785)

He that travels in the Highlands, may easily saturate his soul with intelligence, if he will acquiesce in the first account. The Highlander gives to every question an answer so prompt and peremptory, that skepticism itself is dared into silence, and the mind sinks before the bold reporter in unresisting credulity; but, if a second question be ventured, it breaks the enchantment; for it is immediately discovered, that what was told so confidently was told at hazard, and that such fearlessness of assertion was either the sport of negligence, or the refuge of ignorance.

Samuel Johnson, *Journey to the Western Isles of Scotland*, 1775

When death's dark stream I ferry o'er
A time that surely shall come;
In Heaven itself, I'll ask no more,
Than just a Highland welcome.

Robert Burns, *A verse . . . on taking Leave*, 2 September 1787

My heart's in the Highlands, my heart is not here;
My heart's in the Highlands a chasing the deer;
Chasing the wild deer, and following the roe;
My heart's in the Highlands, wherever I go. –

Farewell to the Highlands, farewell to the North;
The birth-place of Valour, the country of Worth:
Wherever I wander, wherever I rove,
The hills of the Highlands for ever I love. –

Farewell to the mountains high cover'd with snow;
Farewell to the Straths and green vallies below:
Farewell to the forests and wild-hanging woods;
Farewell to the torrents and loud-pouring floods. –

My heart's in the Highlands, my heart is not here,
My heart's in the Highlands a chasing the deer:
Chasing the wild deer, and following the roe;
My heart's in the Highlands, wherever I go. –

Robert Burns, *My Heart's in the Highlands*, 1790
(Burns notes, 'The first half-stanza of this song is old; the rest is mine.')

He who first met the Highlands' swelling blue
Will love each peak that shows a kindred hue,
Hail in each crag a friend's familiar face,
And clasp the mountain in his mind's embrace.
Long have I roamed through lands which are not mine,
Adored the Alp, and loved the Apennine,
Revered Parnassus, and beheld the steep
Jove's Ida, and Olympus crown the deep:
But 'twas not all long ages lore, nor all
Their nature held me in their thrilling thrall;
The infant rapture still survived the boy,
And Loch-nagar with Ida look'd o'er Troy,
Mix'd Celtic memories with the Phrygian mount,
And Highland linns with Castalie's clear fount.
Forgive me, Homer's universal shade!

Forgive me, Phoebus! that my fancy stray'd;
The north and nature taught me to adore
Your scenes sublime, from those beloved before.

Lord Byron, *The Island*, 1823

At present I am full of the Highlands which I had never seen till this year, except a glimpse of the outskirts of them which I got when a boy of eight years old. I have been up in Ross-shire, and a more impressive country I never saw. After being used to the Lake country, over which you could throw a pocket-handkerchief, the extent of the Highlands gives a sense of vastness; and then the desolation, which in Switzerland, with the meadows, industry, and population of the valleys, one never has; but in the Highlands, miles and miles and miles of mere heather and peat and rocks, and not a soul. And then the sea comes up into the land on the west coast, and the mountain forms are there quite magnificent. Norway alone, I imagine has country like it. Then also I have a great *penchant* for the Celtic races, with their melancholy and unprogressiveness.

Matthew Arnold, Letter to Lady de Rothschild, 25 September 1864

In the highlands, in the country places,
Where the old plain men have rosy faces
And the young fair maidens,
Quiet eyes.

Robert Louis Stevenson, *Songs of Travel*, 1896

There is still something of an Odyssey up there, in among the islands and the silent Lochs: like the twilight morning of the world, the herons fishing undisturbed by the water, and the sea running far in, for miles, between the wet trickling hills, where the cottages are low and almost invisible, built into the earth. It is still out of the world like the very beginning of Europe.

D.H. Lawrence, Letter to Else Jaffe, Newtonmore, 20 August 1926

With the exception of the North and South Poles, the Highlands of Scotland were the last portion of the earth's surface to be explored. . . . America was already an old country when the Highlands were discovered.

H.V. Morton, *In Search of Scotland*, 1929

Had you seen this road before it was made,
You would lift both your hands and bless General
Wade.

Anon., 'An Irish Ensign', quoted James Pettit Andrews, *Anecdotes*, 1789
(General Wade employed five hundred soldiers in road-making in the Highlands, 1726–9.)

Inchkenneth

I was very much taken with Inchkenneth. I said I was resolved to have it for an elegant retreat for our family during a month or two in summer. Sir Allan said, if he recovered it from the Duke of Argyll, I should have it on my own terms. I really indulged serious thoughts of buying it. My brother David always talked of purchasing an island. 'Sir,' said Mr. Johnson, 'so does almost every man, till he knows what it is.'

James Boswell, *Journal of a Tour to the Hebrides with Samuel Johnson*, 1773 (1785)

Inverary

Who'er he be that sojourns here,
I pity much his case,
Unless he come to wait upon
The Lord their God, his Grace.

There's naething here but Highland pride,
And Highland scab and hunger;
If Providence has sent me here,
'Twas surely in an anger.

Robert Burns, *Epigram*, 24 June 1787
(on the Inn at Inverary)

The town looked pretty when we drew near to it in connexion with its situation , different from any place I had ever seen, yet exceedingly like what I imagined to myself from representations in raree-shows, or pictures of foreign places (Venice for example) painted on the scene of a play-house, which one is apt to fancy are as cleanly and gay as they look through the magnifying-glass of the raree-show or in the candle-light dazzle of a theatre. . . .

At the beginning of this our second walk we passed through the town, which is but a doleful example of Scotch filth. . . . Smoke and blackness are the wild growth of a Highland hut: the mud floors cannot be washed, the door-steads are trampled by cattle, and if the inhabitants are not very cleanly it gives one little pain; but dirty people living in two-storied stone houses, with *dirty* sash windows, are a melancholy spectacle anywhere, giving the notion either of vice or the extreme of wretchedness.

Dorothy Wordsworth, *Journal*, 30 August 1803

Inverary Castle

Mr Johnson was much pleased with the remarkable grandeur and improvements about Inverary. He said, 'What I admire here is the total defiance of expense.'

James Boswell, *Journal of a Tour to the Hebrides with Samuel Johnson*, 1773 (1785)

Inverness

As *Cromwell's* Soldiers initiated them thus into the Arts and Industry of the Husbandman, so they left them the *English* Accent upon their Tongues, and they preserve it also to this Day; for they speak perfect *English*, even much better than in the most Southerly Provinces of *Scotland*; nay, some will say that they speak it as well as at *London*; though I do not grant that neither. It is certain they keep the Southern Accent very well, and speak very good *English*.

They have also much of the *English* Way of Living among them, as well in their Manner of Dress and Customs, as also of their Eating and Drinking, and even of their Dressing and Cookery, which we found here much more agreeable to *English* Stomachs than in other Parts of *Scotland*; all which, and several other Usages and Customs, they retain from the settling of Three Regiments of *English* Soldiers here, after they were disbanded, and who had, at least many of them, their Wives and Children with them.

Daniel Defoe, *A Tour through the Whole Island of Great Britain*, 1724–7

Hither the inhabitants of the inland parts come to be supplied with what they cannot make for themselves: Hither the young nymphs of the mountains and valleys are sent for education, and as far as my observation has reached, are not sent in vain.

Samuel Johnson, *Journey to the Western Isles of Scotland*, 1775

Inverness was a Saxon colony among the Celts, a hive of traders and artisans in the midst of a population of loungers and plunderers, a solitary outpost of civilisation in a region of barbarians. Though the buildings covered but a small part of the space over which they now extend; though the arrival of a brig in the port was a rare event; though the Exchange was the middle of a miry street, in which stood a market cross much resembling a broken milestone; though the sittings of the municipal council were held in a filthy den with a roughcast wall; though the best houses were such as would now be called hovels; though the best roofs were of thatch; though the best ceilings were of bare rafters; though the best windows were, in bad weather, closed with shutters for want of glass; though the humbler dwellings were mere heaps of turf, in which barrels with the bottoms knocked out served the purpose of chimneys; yet to the mountaineer of the Grampians this city was as Babylon or as Tyre. Nowhere else had he seen four or five hundred houses, two churches, twelve malt-kilns, crowded close together. Nowhere else had he been dazzled by the splendour of rows of booths, where knives, horn spoons, tin kettles, and gaudy ribands were exposed to sale. Nowhere else had he been on board one of those huge ships which brought sugar and wine over the sea from countries far beyond the limits of his geography.

T.B. Macaulay, *History of England*, 1849–61 – of 1689

I will arise now, and go to Inverness,
 And a small villa rent there, of lath and plaster built;
Nine bedrooms will I have there, and I'll don my native dress,
 And walk around in a damned loud kilt.
And I will have some sport there, when grouse come driven slow,
 Driven from purple hill-tops to where the loaders quail;
While midges bite their ankles, and shots are flying low,
 And the air is full of the grey-hen's tail.

Captain Harry Graham, 'The Cockney of the North', *The Motley Muse*, 1913

It is almost as though centuries of human history steam upward through the soil of Inverness. Like Edinburgh, Stirling, Dundee, and Perth, it has the appearance of having been founded by a member of the Royal Academy in a landscape mood.

H.V. Morton, *In Search of Scotland*, 1929

Iona

A nest of singing birds.

St Columba, before 597, attrib.

In Iona of my heart, Iona of my love, instead of monks' voices shall be lowing of cattle, but ere the world come to an end, Iona shall be as it was.

St Columba, attrib. prophecy, before 597, quoted by John Morrison, Forword to *Iona*, 1953

Indeed, the seeing of Mr Samuel Johnson at Icolmkill was what I had often imagined as a very venerable scene. A landscape or view of any kind is defective, in my opinion, without some human figures to give it animation. What an addition was it to Icolmkill to have the Rambler upon the spot! After we had landed I shook hands with him cordially.

James Boswell, *Journal of a Tour to the Hebrides with Samuel Johnson*, 1773 (1785)

Jura

The Paps of Jura
The unambiguity of these two hemispheres rising from the level plain of the sea adds a touch of human pathos to their majesty, and evokes with peculiar force the feeling that everyone must have had at moments in looking at nature: that it is a dumb living thing which has suffered for long ages an unjust but ordained imprisonment. The more strongly the forms of nature suggest some human association, the more deeply does one have this sense – whether real or illusory – of the imprisonment of nature. Such feelings are always mingled with sadness.

Edwin Muir, *Scottish Journey*, 1935

Loch Katrine

The whole lake appeared a solitude – neither boats, islands, nor houses, no grandeur in the hills, nor any loveliness in the shores. When we first came in view of it we had said it was like a barren Ulswater – Ulswater dismantled of its grandeur, and cropped of its lesser beauties.

Dorothy Wordsworth, *Journal*, 26 August 1803

The sun had been set for some time, when, being within a quarter of a mile of the ferryman's hut, our path having led us close to the shore of the calm lake, we met two neatly dressed women, without hats, who had probably been taking their Sunday evening's walk. One of them said to us, in a friendly and soft tone of voice, 'What! you are stepping westward?' I cannot describe how affecting this simple expression was in that remote place, with the western sky in front, *yet* glowing with the departed sun.

Dorothy Wordsworth, *Journal*, 11 September 1803

Then away to Loch Katrine in the summer time
and feast on its scenery most lovely and sublime;
There's no other scene can surpass it in fair Scotland
It's surrounded by mountains and trees most grand.

And as I gaze upon it let me pause and think
How many people in Glasgow of its water drink
That's conveyed to them in pipes from its placid lake
And are glad to get its water their thirst to slake.

William McGonagall, 'Loch Katrine', *Poetic Gems*, 1890

Kilmany

Bonny Kilmany in the County of Fife
Is a healthy spot to reside in to lengthen one's life.

William McGonagall, *Bonny Kilmany*, *c.* 1890

Kilmarnock (and Stewarton)

I'm now arrived – thanks to the gods! –
Thro' pathways rough and muddy,
A certain sign that makin' roads
Is no this people's study:
Altho' I'm no wi' scripture cram'd,
I'm sure the Bible says
That heedless sinners shall be damn'd,
Unless they mend their ways.

Robert Burns, *On Rough Roads*
(attributed to Burns, and dated October 1786 by Scott Douglas, who first published it in his 1877 edition of the poet's works, and ascribed this location. Later editors differ as to its date and authenticity.)

Leith

and golf there

*Hard by, in the fields called the Links, the citizens of Edinburgh divert themselves at a game called golf, in which they use a curious kind of bats, tipt with horn, and small elastic balls of leather, stuffed with feathers, rather less than tennis balls, but of a much harder consistence – This they strike with such force and dexterity from one hole to another, that they will fly to an incredible distance. Of this diversion the Scots are so fond, that when the weather will permit, you may see a multitude of all ranks, from the senator of justice to the lowest tradesman, mingled together in their shirts, and following the balls with the utmost eagerness – Among others, I was shewn one particular set of golfers, the youngest of whom was turned of fourscore – They were all gentlemen of independent fortunes, who had amused themselves with this pastime for the best part of a century, without having ever felt the least alarm from sickness or disgust; and they never went to bed, without having each the best part of a gallon of claret in his belly. Such uninterrupted exercise, co-operating with the keen air from the sea, must, without all doubt, keep the appetite always on edge, and steel the constitution against all the common attacks of distemper.

Tobias Smollett, *Humphrey Clinker*, 1771
('Jer. Melford's' comments)

Firth of Forth

When we came to Leith, I talked with perhaps too boasting an air, how pretty the Firth of Forth looked; as indeed, after the prospect from Constantinople, of which I have been told, and that from Naples, which I have seen, I believe the view of that Firth and its environs from the Castle Hill of Edinburgh is the finest in Europe. 'Ay,' said Dr. Johnson, 'that is the state of the world. Water is the same everywhere;

'Una est injusti caerula forma maris.'

I told him the port here was the mouth of the river or water of Leith. 'Not *Lethe*,' said Mr. Nairne. 'Why sir,' said Dr. Johnson, 'when a Scotchman sets out from this port for England, he forgets his native country.' NAIRNE. 'I hope, sir, you will forget England here.' JOHNSON. 'Then 'twill be still more Lethe.'

James Boswell, *Journal of a Tour to the Hebrides with Samuel Johnson*, 1773 (1785)

I was down at Leith in the afternoon. God bless me, what horrid women I saw; I never knew what a plain-looking race it was before. I was sick at heart with the looks of them. And the children, filthy and ragged! And the smells! And the fat black mud! . . . and yet the ships were beautiful to see as they are always; and on the pier there was a clean cold wind that smelt a little of the sea, though it came down the Firth, and the sunset had a certain *éclat* and warmth.

Robert Louis Stevenson, Letter to Mrs Sitwell, January 1876

Leven Water

On Leven's banks, while free to rove,
And tune the rural pipe to love;
I envied not the happiest swain
That ever trod the Arcadian plain.
Pure stream! in whose transparent wave
My youthful limbs I wont to lave;
No torrents stain thy limpid source;
No rocks impede thy dimpling course,
That sweetly warbles o'er its bed,
With white, round, polish'd pebbles spread;
While, lightly pois'd, the scaly brood
In myriads cleave thy crystal flood;
The springing trout in speckled pride;
The salmon, monarch of the tide;
The ruthless pike, intent on war;
The silver eel, and mottled par.
Devolving from thy parent lake,
A charming maze thy waters make,
By bowers of birch, and groves of pine,
And edges flower'd with eglantine.
Still on thy banks so gayly green,
May num'rous herds and flocks be seen,
And lasses chanting o'er the pail,
And shepherds piping in the dale,
And ancient faith that knows no guile,
And industry imbrown'd with toil,
And hearts resolv'd, and hands prepar'd,
The blessings they enjoy to guard.

Tobias Smollett, 'Ode to Leven Water', in *Plays and Poems*, 1777

Isle of Lewis

The natives are generally ingenious and quick of apprehension; they have a mechanical genius, and several of both sexes have a gift of poesy, and are able to form a satire or paneygeric *ex tempore* without the assistance of any stronger liquor than water to raise their fancy.

Martin Martin, *A Description of the Western Islands of Scotland*, 1703, of 1695

Ben Lomond

Leave Ben Lomond where it stands.

Scottish proverb

There was something in this mountain which disappointed me, – a want of massiveness and simplicity, perhaps from the top being broken into three distinct stages.

Dorothy Wordsworth, *Journal*, 25 August 1803

Loch Lomond

He heth intention to writt a fisher or Pastorall play & sett the stage of it in the Lowmond Lake.

William Drummond, 'Informations be Ben Johnston to W.D. when he came to Scotland upon Foot', 1619, *Ben Jonson's Conversations with W.D. of Hawthornden*, 1711 first published in part, full text 1842

*This country is justly stiled the Arcadia of Scotland; and I don't doubt but it may vie with Arcadia in every thing but climate.

Tobias Smollett, *Humphrey Clinker*, 1771 ('Matthew Bramble's' comments)

O ye'll tak' the high road, and I'll tak' the low road,
And I'll be in Scotland afore ye
But me and my true-love will never meet again,
On the bonnie, bonnie banks o' Loch Lomon'.

Anon., *The Bonnie Banks of Loch Lomon'* (attrib. to Lady John (i.e. Lady Alicia) Scott)

from the island of Inch-ta-vannach

We had not climbed far when we were stopped by a sudden burst of prospect, so singular and beautiful that it was like a flash of images from another world. We stood with our backs to the hill of the island, which we were ascending, and which shut out Ben Lomond entirely, and all the upper part of the lake, and we looked towards the foot of the lake, scattered over with islands without beginning and without end. The sun shone, and the distant hills were visible, some through sunny mists, others in gloom with patches of sunshine; the lake was lost under the low and distant hills, and the islands lost in the lake, which was all in motion with travelling fields of light, or dark shadows under rainy clouds. There are many hills, but no commanding eminence at a distance to confine the prospect, so that the land seemed endless as the water.

Dorothy Wordsworth, *Journal*, 25 August 1803

and Ben Lomond

The road to Tarbet is superb. It is on the very verge of the lake – hard, level, rocky, with low stone bridges constantly flung across it, and fringed with birch trees, just then budding into spring, behind which, as through a slight veil, you saw the huge shadowy form of Ben Lomond. It lifts its enormous but graceful bulk direct from the edge of the water without any projecting lowlands, and has in this respect much the advantage of Skiddaw. Loch Lomond comes upon you by degrees as you advance, unfolding and then withdrawing its conscious beauties like an accomplished coquet. You are struck with the point of a rock, the arch of a bridge, the Highland huts (like the first rude habitations of men) dug out of the soil, built of turf, and covered with brown heather, a sheep-cote, some straggling cattle feeding half-way down a precipice; but as you advance farther on, the view expands into the perfection of lake scenery. It is nothing (or your eye is caught by nothing) but water, earth and sky. Ben Lomond waves to the right, in its simple majesty, cloud-capt or bare, and descending to a point at the head of the lake, shews the Trossacs beyond, tumbling about their blue ridges like woods waving; to the left is the Cobler, whose top is like a Castle shattered in pieces and nodding to its ruin; and at your side rise the shapes of round pastoral hills, green, fleeced with herds, and retiring into mountainous bays and upland valleys, where solitude and peace might make their lasting home, if peace were to be found in solitude!

William Hazlitt, Letter to James Sheridan Knowles, 1822

Moray

The third, and beautiful soil, is the delectable planure of Moray, thirty miles long, and six in breadth; whose comely grounds, encircled with corns, plantings, pasturage, stately dwellings, over-faced with generous Octanian gentry, and topped with a noble earl, its chief patron, it may be called a second Lombardy, or pleasant meadow of the north.

William Lithgow, *Rare Adventures and Painfull Peregrinations*, 1614/32

Isle of Muck

A visit was paid by the laird and lady of a small island south of Sky, of which the proper name is Muack, which signifies swine. It is commonly called Muck, which the proprietor not liking, has endeavoured, without effect, to change to Monk. It is usual to call gentlemen in Scotland by the name of their possessions, as Raasay, Bernera, Loch Buy, a practice necessary in countries inhabited by clans, where all that live in the same territory have one name, and must be therefore discriminated by some addition. This gentleman, whose name, I think, is Maclean, should be regularly called Muck; but the appelation, which he thinks too coarse for his island, he would like still less for himself, and he is therefore addressed by the title of, Isle of Muck.

Samuel Johnson, *Journey to the Western Isles of Scotland*, 1775

Mull

Mull corresponded exactly with the idea which I had always had of it: a hilly country, diversified with heath and grass, and many rivulets. Dr Johnson was not in very good humour. He said it was a dreary country, much worse than Skye. I differed from him. 'Oh, sir,' said he, 'a most dolorous country!'

James Boswell, *Journal of a Tour to the Hebrides with Samuel Johnson*, 1773 (1785)

Ben Nevis

Yesterday . . . we went up Ben Nevis, the highest Mountain in Great Britain. . . . I am heartily glad it is done – it is almost like a fly crawling up a wainscot – Imagine the task of mounting 10 Saint Pauls without the convenience of Stair cases.

John Keats, Letter to Thomas Keats, 3 August 1818

Read me a lesson, muse, and speak it loud
  Upon the top of Nevis blind in Mist!
I look into the Chasms and a Shroud
  Vaprous doth hide them; just so much I wist
Mankind do know of Hell: I look o'erhead
  And there is sullen mist; even so much
Mankind can tell of Heaven: Mist is spread
  Before the Earth beneath me – even such
Even so vague is Man's sight of himself!
  Here are the craggy Stones beneath my feet;
Thus much I know, that a poor witless elf
  I tread on them; that all my eye doth meet
    Is mist and Crag – not only on this height,
    But in the world of thought and mental might.

John Keats, *On Ben Nevis*, 3 August 1818

Loch Ness

Beautiful Loch Ness
The truth to express . . .
Your scenery is romantic
With rocks and hills gigantic
Enough to make one frantic . . .
Oh beautiful Loch Ness!
I must sincerely confess
That you are most beautiful to behold
With your lovely landscape and water so cold.

William McGonagall, *Loch Ness*, *c.* 1890

Oban

At Oban of discomfort one is sure,
Little the difference whether rich or poor.

Arthur Hugh Clough, *Mari Magno, The Lawyer's Second Tale*, 1861

Orkneys

At oure landing the people fled from their poore

cottages, with shrikes and alarms, to warne their neighbours of enemies, but by gentle persuasions we reclamed them to their houses. It seemeth they are often frighted with Pirats, or some other enemies, that moove them to such sudden feare. Their houses are very simply builded with Pibble stone, without any chimneis, the fire being made in the middest thereof. The good man, wife, children, and other of their family eate and sleepe on the one side of the house, and the cattell on the other, very beastly and rudely in respect of civilitie. They are destitute of wood, their fire is turffes, and Cowshards. They have corne, bigge, and oates, with which they pay the Kings rent, to the maintenance of his house. They take great quantitie of fish, which they dry in the wind and Sunne. They dresse their meat very filthily and eate it without salt. Their apparell is after the rudest sort of Scotland. Their money is all base.

Dionise Settle (1577) in Richard Hakluyt, *Principal Navigations . . . of the English Nation*, 1598–1600

and Shetland Islands

Those north-western islands, in summer, are neither hot not cold, having a most wholesome and temperate air, and to yield abundance of corn, even more than sufficient for the inhabitants; which is yearly transported to the firm land, and sold. They have also a great store of good cattle, and cheap; and the best fish that the whole ocean yieldeth is upon the coasts of Orkney and Zetland.

In all these separated parts of the earth, (which of themselves, of old, made up a little kingdom), you shall always find strong March ale, surpassing fine aqua vitae, abundance of geese, hens, pigeons, partridges, muirfowl, mutton, beef, and termigants, with an infinite number of conies, which you may kill with a crossbow, or harquebuss, every morning, out of your chamber window, according to your pleasure in that pastime, which I have both practised myself, and seen practised by others; for they multiply so exceedingly, that they dig even under the foundations of dwelling-houses. . . . I have seldom seen, in all my travels, more toward and tractable people (I mean their gentlemen), and better housekeepers, than these Orcadians and Zetlanders are.

William Lithgow, *Rare Adventures and Painfull Peregrinations*, 1614/32

Ladykirk

The inhabitants are well proportioned, and seem to be more sanguine than they are.

Martin Martin, *A Description of the Western Islands of Scotland*, 1703

and Shetland Islands

What struck me in these islands was their bleakness, the number of ridiculous little churches, the fact that bogs do not require a level surface for their existence but can also run uphill, and that ponies sometimes have a black stripe like the wild ass; the local fashion of eating mutton chops and tea in the afternoons, and pronouncing words such as 'whatever' like 'quatever.' Nightmarish regions, swathed in boreal mists. . . . On returning to Deeside we felt as if we had entered the Tropics.

Norman Douglas, *Looking Back*, 1933 – of 1891

Orkney . . . represented the only desirable form of life that I found in all my journey through Scotland. . . . It has managed, as far as that is humanly possible, to have its cake and eat it. It has been saved by being just outside the circumference of the industrial world, near enough to know about it, but too far off to be drawn into it. Now it seems to me that this is the only way in which any community can achieve a partial salvation today and live a desirable life, surrounded by an industrial world.

Edwin Muir, *Scottish Journey*, 1935

This bloody town's a bloody cuss –
No bloody trains, no bloody bus,
And no one cares for bloody us,
In bloody Orkney

The bloody roads are bloody bad,
The bloody folks are bloody mad,
They'd make the brightest bloody sad
In bloody Orkney. . . .

Everything's so bloody dear,
A bloody bob for bloody beer,
And is it good, – no bloody fear,
In bloody Orkney. . . .

No bloody sport, no bloody games,
No bloody fun; the bloody dames
Won't even give their bloody names,
In bloody Orkney.

Best bloody place is bloody bed,
With bloody ice on bloody head,
You might as well be bloody dead,
In bloody Orkney.

Captain Hamish Blair, attrib. *In Bloody Orkney*, *c.* 1940

Orkney is one of the best regions in Britain for wind power.

Anthony Tucker, *Guardian*, 6 August 1979

Peeblesshire

Think of having been called Tweeddale, and being called PEEBLES!

Robert Louis Stevenson, Letter to Edmund Gosse, June 1882

Perth

This Town was unhappily for some time, the Seat of the late Rebellion; but I cannot say it was unhappy for the Town; For the Townsmen got so much Money by both Parties, that they are evidently enriched by it; and it appears not only by the particular Families and Persons in the Town, but by their publick and private Buildings which they have rais'd since that; as particularly a new *Tolbooth* or *Town-Hall*. . . . It seems a little Enigmatick to us in the South, how a Rebellion should enrich any Place.

Daniel Defoe, *A Tour through the Whole Island of Great Britain*, 1724–7

Isle of Rona

When any of them comes to Lewis, which is seldom, they are astonished to see so many people. They much admire grey-hounds and are mightily pleased at the sight of horses; and one of them observing a horse to neigh, asked if that horse laughed at him.

Martin Martin, *A Description of the Western Islands of Scotland*, 1703 – of 1695

Rona . . . is of so rocky a soil that it appears to be just a pavement. I was told, however, that it has a great deal of grass in the interstices.

James Boswell, *Journal of a Tour to the Hebrides with Samuel Johnson*, 1773 (1785)

Rum (and Eigg and Muck)

Those islands which sound like a new cocktail – Rum, Eigg and Muck.

H.V. Morton, *In Search of Scotland*, 1929

St Andrews

He wanted to mount the steeples, but it could not be done. There are no good inscriptions here. Bad Roman characters he naturally mistook for half-Gothic, half-Roman. One of the steeples, which he was told was in danger, he wished not to be taken down; 'for,' said he, 'it may fall on some of the posterity of John Knox – and no great matter!' Dinner was mentioned. JOHNSON. 'Ay, ay; amidst all these sorrowful scenes, I have no objection to dinner.'

James Boswell, *Journal of a Tour to the Hebrides with Samuel Johnson*, 1773 (1785)

Would you like to see a city given over,
Soul and body to a tyrannizing game?
If you would, there's little need to be a rover,
For St Andrew's is the abject city's name.

R.F. Murray, 'The City of Golf', *The Scarlet Gown*, 1891

St Kilda

High from the summit of a craggy cliff,
Hung o'er the deep, such as amazing frowns
On utmost Kilda's shore, whose lonely race
Resign the setting sun to Indian worlds.

James Thomson, *The Seasons, Spring*, 1728

But O, o'er all, forget not Kilda's race,
  On whose bleak rocks which brave the wasting tides,
Fair Nature's daughter, Virtue, yet abides!
  Go, just as they, their blameless manners trace!
Then to my ear transmit some gentle song
  Of those whose lives are yet sincere and plain,
Their bounded walks the ragged cliffs along,
  And all their prospect but the wintry main.
With sparing temperance, at the needful time,
  They drain the sainted spring or, hunger-pressed,
Along the Atlantic rock undreading climb,
  And of its eggs despoil the Solan's nest.
Thus blest in primal innocence they live,
  Sufficed and happy with that frugal fare
Which tasteful toil and hourly danger give.
  Hard is their shallow soil, and bare;
Nor ever vernal bee was heard to murmur there!

William Collins, 'Ode on the popular superstitions of the Highlands', *c.* 1749

Selkirk

There was something in the irregular square of Selkirk, the Fountain and the town hall that made me think of the decayed towns abroad.

Dorothy Wordsworth, *Journal*, 15 September 1822

Shetland

This Shetland is an Isle under the Scotish dominion, environed with other Islets, and the same is nipped with frost and chilly cold, lying open also on every side unto bitter stormes; the inhabitants whereof, like as those of Island use in steede of bread-corne, dried fish and the same braied and beaten, which we call Stockfish.

William Camden, *Britain*, 1610
(Philemon Holland's translation)

This country produces little horse, commonly called shelties, and they are very sprightly, though the least of their kind to be seen anywhere; they are lower in stature than those of Orkney, and it is common for a man of ordinary strength to lift a sheltie from the ground: yet this little creature is able to carry double. The black are esteemed to be the most hardy, but the pied ones seldom prove so good: they live many times till thirty years of age, and are fit for service all the while. These horses are never brought into the house, but exposed to the rigour of the season all year round; and when they have no grass feed upon sea-ware, which is only to be had at the tide of ebb.

Martin Martin, *A Description of the Western Islands of Scotland*, 1703

Skye

A native of this isle requires treble the dose of physic that will serve one living in the south of Scotland for a purge; yet an islander is easier purged in the south than at home. Those of the best rank are easier wrought on by purging medicines, than the vulgar.

Martin Martin, *A Description of the Western Islands of Scotland*, 1703

Several of both sexes have a quick vein of poesy, and in their language (which is very emphatic) they compose rhyme and verse, both which powerfully affect the fancy. . . .

The ignorance of vices is more powerful among those than all the precepts of philosophy are among the Greeks. For they are to this day happily ignorant of many vices that are practised in the learned and polite world. I could mention several, for which they have not as yet got a name, or so much as a notion of them.

Ibid.

Mrs Mackinnon told me that last year when the ship sailed from Portree for America, the people on shore were almost distracted when they saw their relations go off; they lay down on the ground and tumbled, and tore the grass with their teeth. This year there was not a tear shed. The people on shore seemed to think they would soon follow. This is a mortal sign.

James Boswell, *Journal of a Tour to the Hebrides with Samuel Johnson*, 1773 (1785)

Their weather is not pleasing. Half the year is deluged with rain. From the autumnal to the vernal equinox a dry day is hardly known, except when the showers are suspended by a tempest. Under such skies can be expected no great exuberance of vegetation. Their winter overtakes their summer, and their harvest lies upon the ground drenched with rain. The autumn struggles hard to produce some of our early fruits. I gathered gooseberries in September; but they were small, and the husk was thick.

Samuel Johnson, *Journey to the Western Isles of Scotland*, 1775

Cuillin Hills

When you come suddenly for the first time on the Coolins you mouth opens and you really do gasp. Imagine Wagner's 'Ride of the Valkyries' frozen in stone and hung up like a colossal screen against the sky. It seems as if Nature when she hurled the Coolins up into the light of the sun said: 'I will make mountains which shall be the essence of all that can be terrible in mountains.'

H.V. Morton, *In Search of Scotland*, 1929

Isle of Staffa

Fingal's Cave

There is a beautiful cave called Fingal's; which proves that nature loves Gothic architecture.

Horace Walpole, Letter the Rev. William Cole, 28 May 1774

One may compare the surface of the Island to a roof – this roof is supported by grand pillars of basalt standing together as thick as honeycombs. The finest thing is Fingal's Cave – it is entirely hollowing out of Basalt Pillars. Suppose now the Giants who rebelled against Jove had taken a whole Mass of black Columns and bound them together like bunches of matches – and then with immense Axes had made a cavern in the body of these columns – of course the roof and floor must be composed of the broken ends of the Columns – such is Fingal's Cave, except that the Sea has done the work of excavations and is continually dashing there – so that we walk along the sides of the cave on the pillars which are left as if for convenient Stairs – the roof is arched somewhat gothic wise and the length of some of the entire side pillars is 50 feet. – About the island you might seat an army of Men each on a pillar.

John Keats, Letter to Thomas Keats, 23–26 July 1818

We saw, but surely in the motley crowd,
Not One of us has felt the far-famed sight;
How *could* we feel it? each the other's blight,
Hurried and hurrying, volatile and loud.
O for those motions only that invite
The Ghost of Fingal to his tuneful Cave
By the breeze entered, and wave after wave
Softly embosoming the timid light!
And by *one* Votary who at will might stand
Gazing, and take into his mind and heart,
With undistracted reverence, the effect
Of those proportions where the almighty hand
That made the worlds, the sovereign Architect,
Has deigned to work as if with human Art!

William Wordsworth, 'Cave of Staffa', *Itinerary Poems of 1833, Yarrow Revisited and Other Poems*, 1835

Stirling

Stirling, in the evening, with a blown-out storm in the sky and the air drenched with the melancholy of autumn, is like a chapter of Malory. . . . Edinburgh is like an old soldier who has entered public life; Stirling is like an old soldier living in a house full of the trophies of his youth.

H.V. Morton, *In Search of Scotland*, 1929

Talisker (Isle of Skye)

Talisker is the place, beyond all that I have seen, from which the gay and the jovial seem utterly excluded; and where the hermit might expect to grow old in meditation, without possibility of disturbance or interruption.

Samuel Johnson, *Journey to the Western Isles of Scotland*, 1775

Tiree

A granite comma in the Atlantic.

BBC Television News, 28 February 1979

The Trossachs

. . . A place called the Trossachs, the Borrodale of Scotland & the only thing which really beats us – You must conceive the Lake of Keswick pushing itself up, a mile or two, into Borrodale, winding round Castle Crag, & in & out among all the nooks and promontories – & you must imagine all the mountains more *detachedly* built up, a general Dislocation – every rock it's own precipice, with Trees young and old – & this will give you some faint Idea of the Place – of which the character is extreme intricacy of effect produced by very simple means – one rocky high Island, four or 5 promontories, & a Castle Crag, just like that in the Gorge of Borrodale but not so large.

S.T. Coleridge, Letter to Mrs S.T. Coleridge, 2 September 1803

The Trossachs . . . are definitely unfair and should be abolished in the interests of more distant places. The Trossachs are like a traveller's sample of Scottish scenery. They remind me of those small tins of biscuits which firms send out beautifully packed to indicate a range of manufactures. If you like them you can order larger quantities.

The synopsis of Scotland known as the Trossachs can be, and no doubt is, taken by Americans in a hurry.

H.V. Morton, *In Search of Scotland*, 1929

River Tweed

and Till

Tweed said to Till
'What gars ye rin sae still?'
Till said to Tweed:
'Though ye rin wi' speed
And I rin slaw
Whar ye droon ae man
I droon twa.'

Anon., *Two Rivers*

Waft me, some muse, to Tweed's inspiring stream,
Where all the little Loves and Graces dream;
Where, slowly winding, the dull waters creep,
And seem themselves to own the power of sleep;
Where on the surface, lead, like feathers swims;
There let me bathe my yet unhallow'd limbs.

Charles Churchill, *The Prophecy of Famine*, 1763

Cauld licht and tumblin' cloods. It's queer
There's never been a poet here.

Hugh McDiarmid (C.M. Grieve), 'North of the Tweed', from *To Circumjack Cencrastus*, 1930

Wick

Certainly Wick in itself possesses no beauty: bare, grey shores, grim grey houses, grim grey sea: not even the gleam of red tiles; not even the greenness of a tree. . . . In Wick I have never heard anyone greet his neighbour with the usual 'Fine day' or 'Good morning.' Both come shaking their heads, and both say, 'Breezy, breezy!' And such is the atrocious quality of the climate that the remark is almost invariably justified by the fact.

The streets are full of the highland fishers, lubberly, stupid, inconceivably lazy, and heavy to move. You bruise against them, tumble over them, elbow them against the wall – all to no purpose; they will not budge; and you are forced to leave the pavement every step.

Robert Louis Stevenson, Letter to his mother, 11 September 1868

Zetland (Lerwick)

Mr Collector Ross tells me, that from the King's books it appears that the quantity of spirits, tea, coffe, tobacco, snuff, and sugar, imported annually into Lerwick for the consumption of Zetland, averages at sale price, £20,000 yearly at the least. Now the inhabitants of Zetland, men, women, and children, do not exceed 20,000 in all, and the proportion of foreign luxuries seems monstrous, unless we allow for the habits contracted by the seamen in their foreign trips. Tea, in particular, is used by all ranks, and porridge quite exploded.

Sir Walter Scott, Diary, 5 August 1814, in Lockhart, *Life of Scott*, 1838

A worse and most horrid opinion prevails, or did prevail, among the fishers – namely, that he who saves a drowning man will receive at his hands some deep wrong or injury. Several instances were quoted today in company, in which the utmost violence had been found necessary to compel the fishers to violate this inhuman prejudice. It is conjectured to have arisen as an apology for rendering no assistance to the mariners as they escaped from a shipwrecked vessel, for these isles are infamous for plundering wrecks. A story is told of a crew of a stranded vessel who were warping themselves ashore by means of a hawser which they had fixed to the land. The islanders (of Unst, I believe) watched their motions in silence, till an old man reminded them that if they suffered these sailors to come ashore, they would consume all their winter stock of provisions. A Zetlander cut the hawser, and the poor wretches, twenty in number, were all swept away. This is a tale of former times – the cruelty would not now be active.

Sir Walter Scott, Diary, 6 August 1814, in Lockhart, *Life of Scott*, 1838

GREAT BRITAIN – WALES

A Welshman and an Englishman disputed
Which of their lands maintained the greatest state;
The Englishman the Welshman quite confuted
Yet would the Welshman naught his brags abate.
'Ten cooks,' quoth he, 'In Wales one wedding sees.'
'True,' quoth the other, 'each man toasts his cheese.'

Henry Parrot, *c.* 1613

All that I heard him say of it was, that instead of bleak and barren mountains, there were green and fertile ones; and that one of the castles in Wales would contain all the castles that he had seen in Scotland.

James Boswell, quoting Samuel Johnson, *Life of Johnson*, October 1774

In Wales – they make calling one another Liar's &c – necessary vent-holes to the sulphureous Fumes of the Temper!

S.T. Coleridge, Letter to Robert Southey, 13 July 1794

'The cheapest country in England!' How much people are deceived at a distance! – its cheapness is all a flim-flam, and nothing remains as it used to be, but its glorious scenery.

Thomas Moore, Letter to Miss Dalby, 1812

I have . . . been made sensible by Wordsworth of one grievous defect in the structure of the Welsh valleys; too generally they take the *basin* shape – the level area at their foot does not detach itself with sufficient precision from the declivities that surround them.

Thomas de Quincey, *Autobiography*, 1834–53

Here is a theme that never fails,
To write or talk upon.
The Undersigned has been in Wales,
Jonah was but in One –

Thomas Hood, quoted in Henry Crabb Robinson, *Diary*, 26 July 1836

'Tis said, O Cambria, thou hast tried in vain
To form great poets, and the cause is plain.
Ap-Jones, Ap-Jenkins, and Ap-Evans sound
Among thy sons, but no Apollos found.

Anon., in *Epigrams Ancient and Modern*, ed. Rev. John Booth, 1863

Mother of holy fire! Mother of holy dew!
Thy children of the mist, the moor, the mountain side,
These change not from thine heart, these to thine heart allied:
These, that rely on thee, as blossoms on the blue.
O passionate dark faces, melancholy's hue!
O deep, gray eyes, so tragic with the fires they hide!
Sweet Mother, in whose light these live! thou dost abide,
Star of the West, pale to the world: these know thee true.
No alien hearts may know that magic, which acquaints
Thy soul with splendid passion, a great fire of dreams;
Thine heart with lovelier sorrow, than the wistful sea.
Voices of Celtic singers and of Celtic Saints
Live on the ancient air: their royal sunlight gleams
On moorland Merioneth and on sacred Dee.

Lionel Johnson, *Wales*, 1890

*We can trace almost all the disasters of English history to the influence of Wales.

Evelyn Waugh, *Decline and Fall*, 1928

Later, when I have finished this letter, I'll walk down the lane. It will be dark then; lamps will be lit in the farmhouses, and the farmers will be sitting at their fires, looking into the blazing wood and thinking of God knows what littlenesses, or thinking of nothing at all but their own animal warmth.

But even this, grey as it is and full of the noise of sanitating water, and full of the sight of miserably wet fields, is better than the industrial small towns. I passed them in the bus coming down here, each town a festering sore on the body of a dead country, half a mile of main street with its Prudential, its Co-op, the Star, its cinema and pub. On the pavements I saw nothing but hideously pretty young girls with cheap berets on their heads and paint smudged over their cheeks; thin youths with caps and stained fingers holding their cigarettes; women, all breast and bottom, hugging their purses to them and staring in at the shop windows; little colliers, diseased in mind and body as only the Welsh can be, standing in groups outside the Welfare Hall. I passed the rows of colliers houses, hundreds of them, each with a pot of ferns in the window, a hundred jerry-built huts built by a charitable corporation for the men of the town to breed and eat in.

All Wales is like this. I have a friend who writes long and entirely unprintable verses beginning, 'What are you, Wales, but a tired old bitch?' and 'Wales my country, Wales my sow.'

Dylan Thomas, Letter to
Pamela Hansford Johnson, Llangain, October 1933

The more I see of Wales, the more I think its a land completely peopled by perverts. I don't exclude myself, who obtain a high & soulful pleasure from telling women, old enough to be my mother, why they dream of two-headed warthogs in a field of semen.

Dylan Thomas, Letter to
Pamela Hansford Johnson, October 1934

Each section of the British Isles has its own way of laughing, except Wales which doesn't.

Stephen Leacock, *Humour,* 1935

I can still remember Dylan Thomas, drunk as a lord, yelling scornfully in the streets of Soho: 'Land of my fathers! They can bloody well keep it!'

James Kirkup, *One Man's Russia,* 1968 before 1953

Within the whispering gallery of St Paul's
The merest whisper travels round the walls,
But in the parts where I was born and bred
Folks hear things long before they're even said.

A.G. Prys-Jones, 'Quite So', *A Little Nonsense*, 1954

There are still parts of Wales where the only concession to gaiety is a striped shroud.

Gwyn Thomas, *Punch,* 18 June 1958

In Wales there are jewels
To gather, but with the eye
Only. A hill lights up
Suddenly; a field trembles
With colour and goes out
In its turn; in one day
You can witness the extent
Of the spectrum and grow rich

With looking. Have a care;
This wealth is for the few
And chosen. Those who crowd
A small window dirty it
With their breathing, though sublime
And inexhaustible the view.

R.S. Thomas, 'The Small Window', *Selected Poems 1946–1968*, 1973

This is the scarred land where the soil
is scorched almost beyond recall.
This is the valley of the Tawe, where a river
the colour of rust gropes through black banks
of slag towards a sea fouled, as always, by man.

Strangers ruined this landscape. Their greed
made the first metal industry here flourish;
packed the harbour, quay to quay
with Horn-weathered windjammers; brought
a million tons of copper to flow –
a blinding river of liquid wealth –
from glowing furnace after furnace.

But the strangers never settled here,
near the smoking desert of their making;
they preferred the gracious living
and the softer landscapes of England.
They came just to rape a timeless beauty;
to warp and buckle men with breaking toil;
to make money and leave to loot elsewhere. . . .

They are long gone, just shadows in history,
but their marks remain, scarring the land,
to remind us of the past again and again.

Bryn Griffiths, 'Scarred Landscape', *Scars,* 1969

Hooray for English culture
To Wales it's such a blessing
Tuneless songs and tasteless jokes
And blowsy bags undressing.

Harri Webb, 'Progress', *The Green Desert*, 1969

Welsh

our wildest beasts that breed
Upon our mightie wastes, or on our mountaines feed,
Were farre more sooner tam'd, then heere our Welsh-
men were:
Besides, in all the world no nation is so deere
As they unto their owne; that here within this ile,
Or else in forraine parts, yea, forced to exile,
The noble Britain still his countryman releeves;
A patriot, and so true, that it to death him greeves
To heare his Wales disgrac't: and on the Saxons swords
Oft hazardeth his life, ere with reprochful words
His language or his leeke hee'le stand to heare abus'd.
Besides, the Britain is so naturallie infus'd
With true poetick rage, that in their measures, art
Doth rather seeme precise, than comlie; in each part
Their metre most exact, in verse of th'hardest kind.
And some to riming be so wondrously inclin'd,
Those numbers they will hit, out of their genuine vaine,
Which many wise and learn'd can hardly ere attaine.

Michael Drayton, *Poly-Olbion*, 'The Sixt Song', 1612

The way to make a Welch-man thirst for blisse
And say his prayers dayly on his knees:
Is to perswade him, that most certaine 'tis,
The Moone is made of nothing but greene Cheese.

And hee'l desire of God no greater boone,
But place in heaven to feed upon the Moone.

John Taylor, *Epigram, in The Sculler*, 1612, *All the Works of John Taylor*, 1630

The older the welshman the more madman.

James Howell, *British Proverbs Englished*, in *Lexicon Tetraglotton . . . with another Volume of the Choicest Proverbs*, 1659

Sais Sais y gach yn ei bais,
Y Cymro glan y gach allan.
(The Saxon shites in his breech
The cleanly Briton in the hedge.)

Old Welsh proverb, quoted in *ibid.*

They value themselves much upon their antiquity: The antient race of their houses, and families, and the like; and above all, upon their antient heroes: their King Caractacus Owen ap Tudor, Prince Lewellin, and the like noblemen and princes of British extraction; and as they believe their country to be the pleasantest and most agreeable in the world, so you cannot oblige them more, than to make them think you believe so too.

Daniel Defoe, *A Tour through the Whole Island of Great Britain*, 1724–7

The Welch are said to be so remarkably fond of cheese, that in cases of difficulty their midwives apply a piece of toasted cheese to the *janua vitae*, to attract and entice the young Taffy, who on smelling it makes the most vigorous efforts to come forth.

Francis Grose, *A Classical Dictionary of the Vulgar Tongue*, 1785

All subtle feelings are discerned by Welsh eyes when untroubled by any mental agitation. . . . I may observe that there is human nature and Welsh nature.

George Meredith, *Sandra Belloni*, 1864

*'The Welsh,' said the Doctor, 'are the only nation in the world that has produced no graphic or plastic art, no architecture, no drama. They just sing,' he said with disgust, 'sing, and blow down wind instruments of plated silver.'

Evelyn Waugh, *Decline and Fall*, 1928

Why do I take to the Welsh? It cannot be that they are amoral. It cannot be that they have the highest rate of illegitimacy in the Three Kingdoms. Nor can it be that they are free and easy and that they have 'no complaints.' I know: they do not have to be superior to everyone else. There are no cold, superior Welshmen. Yes, after much cogitation I have discovered why I am attracted by Welshmen. And their women are charming too. No one is afraid them. No one is afraid to marry them.

There are few bachelors in Wales whereas in Ireland, with a population of less than four million, there are five hundred thousand bachelors. Why? Don't ask me. I am biassed; but this is certain: no one ever heard of a Welshman dying as one of the ancient leaders of the Irish did, 'from an excess of women.'

Oliver St John Gogarty, *It isn't this time of year at all*, 1954

We were a people taut for war; the hills
Were no harder, the thin grass
Clothed them more warmly than the coarse
Shirts our small bones.
We fought, and were always in retreat,
Like snow thawing upon the slopes
Of Mynydd Mawr; and yet the stranger
Never found our ultimate stand
In the thick woods, declaiming verse
To the sharp prompting of the harp.

Our kings died, or they were slain
By the old treachery at the ford.
Our bards perished, driven from the halls
Of nobles, by the thorn and bramble.

We were a people bred on legends,
Warming our hands at the red past.
The great were ashamed of our loose rags
Clinging stubbornly to the proud tree
Of blood and birth, our lean bellies
And mud houses were a proof
Of our ineptitude for life.

We were a people wasting ourselves
In fruitless battles for our masters,
In lands to which we had no claim,
With men for whom we felt no hatred.
We were a people, and are so yet.
When we have finished quarrelling for crumbs
Under the table, or gnawing the bones
Of a dead culture, we will arise,
Armed, but not in the old way.

R.S. Thomas, 'Welsh History', *Song at the Year's Turning*, 1956

Dai K lives at the end of a valley. One is not quite sure
Whether it has been drowned or not. His Mam
Loves him too much and his Dada drinks.
As for his girlfriend Blodwen, she's pregnant. So
Are all the other girls in the village – there's been a Revival.
After a performance of Elijah, the mad preacher
Davies the Doom has burnt the chapel down.
One Saturday night after the dance at the Con Club,
With the Free Wales Army up to no good in the back lanes,
A stranger comes to the village; he is of course,

God, the well known television personality. He
 succeeds
In confusing the issue, whatever it is, and departs
On the last train before the line is closed.
The colliery blows up, there is a financial scandal
Involving all the most respected citizens: the Choir
Wins at the National. It is all seen, naturally,
Through the eyes of a sensitive boy who never grows
 up.
The men emigrate to America, Cardiff, and the moon.
 The girls
Find rich and foolish English husbands. Only daft
 Ianto
Is left to recite the complete works of Sir Lewis Morris
To puzzled sheep before throwing himself over
The edge of the abandoned quarry. One is not quite
 sure
Whether it is fiction or not.

Harri Webb, 'Synopsis of the Great Welsh Novel', *The Green Desert*, 1969

Réné Cutforth said that the Welsh were Mediterraneans in the rain.

Nancy Banks-Smith, in *Guardian*, 17 October 1979

Abergeley

Abergeley is a large Village on the Sea Coast – Walking on the sea sands – I was surprized to see a number of fine Women bathing promiscuously with men and boys – *perfectly* naked! Doubtless the citadels of their Chastity are so impregnably strong, that they need not the ornamental Outworks of Modesty. But, seriously speaking, where sexual Distinctions are least observed, Men & Women live together in the greatest purity. Concealment sets the Imagination a working, and, as it were, *cantharidizes* our desires.

S.T. Coleridge, Letter to Henry Martin, 22 July 1794

Aberystwyth

The perfect town for the unambitious man.

Wynford Vaughan-Thomas, *Trust to Talk*, 1980

Anglesey

May the inhabitants be like the land they live in; which appears worse than it is, seemingly barren and really fruitful.

Thomas Fuller, *History of the Worthies of England*, 1662

The Roman Mona is the Mona Lisa of islands.

Christopher Wordsworth, *Observer Colour Magazine*, 24 August 1980

Barry

'But Barry is a dull place. Do you know Barry? Well, it's a one-eyed Godforsaken town, made out of odds and ends stuck down anywhere, all new houses, docks, coal tips, and railway sidings, and nowhere to go. It's best to stay aboard in Barry.'

H.M. Tomlinson, *The Sea and the Jungle*, 1912

Breconshire

Brecknockshire is a meer inland county, as Radnor is; the English jestingly (and I think not very improperly) call it Breakneckshire: 'Tis mountainous to an extremity, except on the side of Radnor, where it is somewhat more low and level.

Daniel Defoe, *A Tour through the Whole Island of Great Britain*, 1724–7

Caernarvon Castle

Which Castle I confesse to bee of no use at all but for the gaole of the Cowntry, and that by usurpacion.

The havn ys a barrd havn skant safe for fysher boats.

Sir John Harington, Letter to the Earl of Salisbury, 15 November 1609

Caernarvonshire

Old Lady: In faith, for little England
You'ld venture an emballing: I my selfe
Would for *Carnarvanshire.*

William Shakespeare, *King Henry the Eight*, *c.* 1612–13

Cardiff

Oh I'm proud to be a citizen of Cardiff
The finest spot upon the map of Wales
We've the City 'All, the Arms Park, and Brains
 Breweries
Where they makes the beer they calls the Prince of
 Ales.
But now they're trying to alter all our signposts
And make us live in streets we cannot say
I don't mind the Pakistanis and the coloureds
But I wish the bloody Welsh would stay away. . . .

Gareth Jones, *Welsh and Proud of It*, 1974

Cardiganshire

Dear Tommy, please, from far, sciatic Kingsley
Borrow my eyes. The darkening sea flings Lea

And Perrins on the cockled tablecloth
Of mud and sand. And, like a sable moth
A cloud against the glassy sun flutters his
Wings. It would be better if the sun is
Shut. Sinister dark over Cardigan
Bay. No good is abroad. I unhardy can
Hardly bear the din of No-good wracked dry on
The pebbles. It is time for the Black Lion
But there is only Buckley's unfrisky
Mild. Turned again Worthington. Never whisky.
I sit at the open window, observing
The salty scene and my Playered gob curving
Down to the wild, umbrella'd, and french lettered
Beach, hearing rise slimy from the Welsh lechered
Caves the cries of the parchs and their flocks. I
Hear their laughter sly as gonococci.

Dylan Thomas, Verse Letter to T.W. Earp, 21 September 1944

Carmarthen

Carmarthen, a large Town, all white-washed, – the Roofs of the Houses all white-washed! a great Town in a Confectioner's shop, on Twelfth cake Day or a huge Show piece at a distance.

S.T. Coleridge, Letter to Mrs S.T. Coleridge, 16 November 1802

Chirk Castle

The Castle though ancient and in a good form is yet not well situated for the pencil.

J.M.W. Turner, *Diary of a Tour in Part of Wales*, 1792

Denbigh

I shall be loth to leave Denbigh – 'tis such an admirable *Thinking-Place*.

Hester Lynch Thrale/Piozzi, *Thraliana*, September 1794

At Denbigh is a ruined Castle – it surpasses every thing I could have conceived – I wandered there an hour and a half last evening. Two well drest young men were walking there – Come – says one – I'll play my flute – 'twill be romantic! Bless thee for the thought, Man of Genius & Sensibility! I exclaimed – and pre-attuned my heartstring to tremulous emotion. He sat adown (the moon just peering) amid the most awful part of the Ruins – and – romantic Youth! struck up the affecting Tune of *Mrs Casey!*

S.T. Coleridge, Letter to Robert Southey, 13 July 1794

Denbigh is a taking picturesque town. Seen from here, as Henry Kerr says, it is always beautiful. The limekiln under a quarried cliff on this side of the town is always sending out a white smoke and this, and the grayer smoke of Denbigh, creeping upon the hill, what with sun and wind give fairy effects which are always changing.

Gerard Manley Hopkins, *Journal*, 4 February 1875

Denbighshire (Llandulas)

It is a highly geological country. Everyone in Wales has black spittle and whenever he meets you he says '*borra-da*' and spits. I was frightened at first, but after a time I became accustomed to it. Also I discovered that everyone's manners are so good that when you say, 'Am I going the right way to Llandulas?' they always say 'yes.' This courtesy led me many miles astray.

Evelyn Waugh, *Diary*, 25 January 1925

Dolgellau

If you ever go to Dolgellau
Don't stay at the Lion Hotel
There's nothing to put in your belly,
And no one to answer the bell.

Anon., quoted in *The Times*, 6 May 1978, with a note that things have changed for the better!

Ffestiniog

By fair Festiniog, mid the Northern Hills,
The vales are full of beauty, and the heights,
Thin set with mountain sheep, show statelier far
Than in the tamer South. There the stern round
Of labour rules, – a silent land sometimes
Loud with the blast that buffets all the hills
Whereon the workers toil, in quarries hewn
Upon the terraced rocksides. Tier on tier,
Above the giddy depths, they edge and cling
Like flies to the sheer precipice as they strike
The thin cleft slate. For solace of their toil
Song comes to strengthen them, and songlike verse
In the old Cymric measures.

Sir Lewis Morris, 'Llyn y Morwynion', *Songs of Britain*, 1887

Holyhead

Lo here I sit at holy head,
With muddy ale and mouldy bread:
I'm fastened both by wind and tide,
I see the ships at anchor ride.
All Christian vittals stink of fish,
I'm where my enemyes would wish. . . .
on this bleaky shore,

Where loudest winds incessant roar,
Where neither herb nor tree will thrive,
Where Nature hardly seems alive.

Jonathan Swift, *Holyhead,* 25 September 1727

Holywell

Barraud and I walked over to Holywell and bathed at the well and returned very joyously. The sight of the water in the well as clear as glass, greenish like beryl or aquamarine, trembling at the surface with the force of the springs, and shaping out the five foils of the well quite drew and held my eyes to it. . . . The strong unfailing flow of the water and the chain of cures from year to year all these centuries took hold of my mind with wonder at the bounty of God in one of His saints, the sensible thing so naturally and gracefully uttering the spiritual reason of its being (which is all in true keeping with the story of St. Winifred's death and recovery) and the spring in place leading back the thoughts by its spring in time to its spring in eternity: even now the stress and buoyancy and abundance of the water is before my eyes.

Gerard Manley Hopkins, *Journal,* 8 October 1874

Landore

It came to pass in days of yore
The Devil chanced upon Landore.
Quoth he, 'By all this fume and stink
I can't be far from home, I think.'

Anon.

Llandaff

A learned Prelate late dispos'd to laffe,
Hearing me name the Bishop of Landaffe:
You should says he, advising well hereon,
Call him Lord *Aff:* for all the land is gone.

Sir John Harrington, *Of the Bishopricke of Landaffe,* late sixteenth century

Llangathen (Dyfed)

'Tis now the raven's bleak abode;
'Tis now th'apartment of the toad;
And there the fox securely feeds;
And there the poisonous adder breeds,
Conceal'd in ruins, moss and weeds;
While ever and anon there falls
Huge heaps of hoary, moulder'd walls. . . .
A little rule, a little sway,
A sun-beam in a winter's day
Is all the proud and mighty have
Between the cradle and the grave.

John Dyer, *Grongar Hill,* 1727

Llantrisant

Llantrisant is now best known as the home of the Royal Mint, called disparagingly by employees of the old Mint in London, 'the hole with the Mint'.

Tim Jones, *The Times,* 3 May 1982

Laugharne (near)

Now we're with my mother and father in —— where everyone goes into the pubs sideways, and the dogs piss only on backdoors, and there are more unwanted babies shoved up the chimnies than there are used french letters in the offertory boxes. It's a mean place, but near Laugharne where we will go next week.

Dylan Thomas, Letter to Vernon Watkins, 27 July 1944

Merionethshire

The inhabitants, who for the most part wholy betake themselves to breeding & feeding of cattaile, and live upon white meates, as butter, cheese &c. . . . are for stature, cleere complexion, goodly feature, & lineaments of body inferiour to no nation in Britain: but they have an ill name among their neighbours, for being to forward in the wanton love of women, and that proceeding from their idlenesse.

William Camden, *Britain,* 1610
(Philemon Holland's translation)

*Merionethshire, the land of all that is beautiful in nature, and all that is lovely in woman.

Thomas Love Peacock, *Crotchet Castle,* 1831

Milford Haven

That Milford, which this ile her greatest port doth call.

Michael Drayton, *Poly-Olbion,* 'The Fift Song', 1612

In respect of Milford Haven all the Havens under the Heavens are inconsiderable.

John Taylor, *A Short Relation of a Long Journey,* 1653

near Mold

I continued along the great road; and, within two miles of *Mold,* hung long over the charming vale which opens with exquisite beauty from *Fron,* . . . *Cambria* here lays aside her majestic air, and condescends to assume a gentler form, in order to render less violent her approaching union with her *English* neighbour. It were to be wished she had acted with more moderation, and not outshone it at the rate, the most partial *Saxon* must allow it to have done.

Thomas Pennant, *Tours in Wales,* 1773–6

Montgomery

The Castle

Upon this Primrose hill,
Where, if Heav'n would distill
A shoure of raine, each severall drop might goe
To his owne primrose, and grow Manna so;
And where their forme and their infinitie
Make a terrestriall Galaxie,
As the small starres doe in the skie:
I wake to finde a true Love; and I see
That 'tis not a mere woman, that is shee,
But must, or more, or lesse than woman bee.

John Donne, *The Primrose, Being at Montgomery Castle, Upon the Hill, on which it is Situate, c.* 1613

Pembrokeshire

A part of this county is peopled by Flemings, placed there by King Henry the First, who was no less politic than charitable therein; for such Flemings, being driven out of their own country by an irruption of the ocean, were fixed here to defend the land given them against the Welch; and their country is called Little England beyond Wales. This mindeth me of a passage betwixt a Welch and English-man, the former boasting Wales in all respects beyond England; to whom the other returned, 'He had heard of an England beyond Wales, but never of a Wales beyond England.'

Thomas Fuller, *History of the Worthies of England,* 1662

Penmaen Pool

Who long for rest, who look for pleasure
Away from counter, court or school
O where live well your lease of leisure
But here at, here at Penmaen Pool.

You'll dare the Alp, you'll dart the skiff –
Each sport has here its tackle and tool:
Come, plant the staff by Cadair cliff;
Come, swing the skulls on Penmaen Pool. . . .

And all the landscape under survey,
At tranquil turns, by nature's rule,
Rides repeated topsyturvy
In frank, in fairy Penmaen Pool. . . .

Then come who pine for peace or pleasure
Away from counter, court or school,
Spend here your measure of time and treasure
And taste the treats of Penmaen Pool.

Gerard Manley Hopkins, *Penmaen Pool,* 1876

Penmaenmawr

Jenkin: . . . 'Is not *Pen-maen-maur,* and *Craig-Eriri* as good sound as *Adlas* every whit of him?
Evan: . . . 'Is caulld the *Pritish Aulpes,* Craig-Eriri, a very sufficient Hills.
Jenkin: . . . By got, we will play with him Hills for Hills, for sixteene and forty s'illings, when he dares.

Ben Jonson, *For the Honour of Wales – a Masque,* 1640

and Plinlimmon

Ev'n on the cliffy Height
Of *Penmenmaur,* and that Cloud-piercing Hill,
Plinlimmon, from afar the Traveller kens
Astonish'd, how the Goats their shrubby Brouze
Gnaw pendent; nor untrembling canst thou see,
How from a scraggy Rock, whose Prominence
Half overshades the Ocean, hardy Men,
Fearless of rending Winds, and dashing Waves,
Cut Sampire, to excite the squeamish Gust
Of pamper'd luxury.

John Philips, *Cyder,* 1708

Now good Mister Spictatur of *Crete Prittain,* you must know it, there iss in Caernarvonshire a fery Pig Mountain, the Clory of all Wales, which iss named *Penmainmaure,* and you must also know, it iss no great Journey on Foot from me; but the Road is stony and bad for Shoes. Now there is upon the Forehead of this Mountain a very high Rock, (like a Parish Steeple) that cometh out a huge deal over the Sea; so when I am in my Melancholies, and I do throw myself from it, I do desire my fery good Friend to tell me in his Spectatur, if I shall be cure of my griefous Loses; for there is the Sea clear as the Glass, and ass creen as the Leek. Then likewise, if I be drown, and preak my Neck, if Mrs. Gwinifred will not lose me afterwards. . . . Davyth ap Shenkyn.

Joseph Addison, *Spectator,* no.227, 20 November 1711

Our Caernarvonshire Hills looked very respectable after seeing both Alps & Appenines; we agreed that Penmanmawr was about the size of Vesuvius, & looked not unlike it one Evening from Bangor Ferry, when I shewed it Caecilia as a light Cloud covered its Top, & told her that it represented the Smoke issuing out of the Crater cleverly enough, & so it did.

Hester Lynch Thrale/Piozzi, *Thraliana,* September 1787

Rhymney (etc.)

Oh, what can you give me?
Say the sad bells of Rhymney.
Is there hope for the future?
Cry the brown bells of Merthyr.
Who made the mine owner?
Say the black bells of Rhondda.
And who robbed the miner?
Cry the grim bells of Blaina.
They will plunder willy-nilly
Say the bells of Caerphilly.
They have fangs, they have teeth,
Shout the loud bells of Neath.
To the South, things are sullen,
Say the pink bells of Brecon.
Even God is uneasy,
Say the moist bells of Swansea.
Put the vandals in court!
Cry the bells of Newport.
All would be well if-if-if
Say the green bells of Cardiff.
Why so worried, sisters, why?
Sing the silver bells of Wye.

Idris Davies, *Gwalia Deserta*, no. xv, 1938

The Severn Bridge

Two lands at last connected
Across the rivers wide
And all the tolls collected
On the English side.

Harri Webb, 'Ode to the Severn Bridge', *The Green Desert*, 1969

Snowdon

Leave to Robert Browning
Beggars, fleas and vines;
Leave to squeamish Ruskin
Popish Apennines,
Dirty stones of Venice
And his gas-lamps seven;
We've the stones of Snowdon
And the lamps of heaven.

Charles Kingsley, *The Invitation*, in a letter to Thomas Hughes, 1856

Swansea

Swansea still stands where it did. No one has blown up the churches. The Watch Committee still stands on its one leg and hands its glass eye round from member to member.

Dylan Thomas, Letter to Trevor Hughes, January 1933

GREECE

Graecia capta ferum victorem cepit et artes intulit agresti Latio.
(Greece, taken captive, captured her savage conqueror, and carried her arts into clownish Latium.)

Horace, *Epistles*, Bk II, epis. i, l. 156, *c.* 19 BC

Strabo, in the ninth book of his Geography, compares Greece to the picture of a man, . . . the breast lies open from those Acroceraunian hills in Epirus to the Sunian promontory in Attica; Pagae and Megara are the two shoulders; that Isthmus of Corinth the neck; and Pelopponesus the head. If this allusion hold, 'tis sure a mad head; Morea may be Moria [Folly]; and to speak what I think, the inhabitants of modern Greece swerve as much from reason and true religion at this day, as that Morea doth from the picture of a man.

Robert Burton, *Anatomie of Melancholie*, 1621

That famous Greece where learning flowrisht most,
Hath of her muses long since left to boast,
Th'unletter'd Turke, and rude barbarian trades,
Where Homer sang his lofty Iliads,

Michael Drayton, *Elegy to Master George Sandys*, 1621

Hail, Nature's utmost boast! unrivalled Greece!
My fairest reign! where every power benign
Conspired to blow the flower of human-kind,
And lavish'd all that genius can inspire: –
Clear sunny climates, by the breezy main,
Ionian or Aegean, temper'd kind;
Light, airy soils; a country rich and gay;
Broke into hills with balmy odours crown'd,
And, bright with purple harvest, joyous vales:
Mountains and streams, where verse spontaneous
  flow'd;
Whence deem'd by wondering men the seat of gods,
And still the mountains and the streams of song:
All that boon Nature could luxuriant pour
Of high materials, and my restless arts
Frame into finish'd life. How many states,
And clustering towns, and monuments of fame,
And scenes of glorious deeds, in little bounds!
From the rough tract of bending mountains, beat
By Adria's here, there by Aegean waves;
To where the deep-adorning Cyclade Isles
In shining prospect rise, and on the shore
Of farthest Crete resounds the Lybian Main.

James Thomson, *Liberty*, 1734–6

Cold is the heart, fair Greece! that looks on Thee,
Nor feels as Lovers o'er the dust they loved;
Dull is the eye that will not weep to see
Thy walls defaced, thy mouldering shrines removed
By British hands, which it had best behoved
To guard those relics ne'er to be restored: –

Curst be the hour when from their isle they roved,
And once again thy hapless bosom gored,
And snatched thy shrinking Gods to Northern climes
abhorred!

Lord Byron, *Childe Harold's Pilgrimage,* Canto the Second, 1812

And yet how lovely in thine age of woe,
Land of lost Gods and godlike men, art thou!
Thy vales of evergreen, thy hills of snow,
Proclaim thee Nature's varied favourite now:
Thy fanes, thy temples to thy surface bow,
Commingling slowly with heroic earth,
Broke by the share of every rustic plough:
So perish monuments of mortal birth,
So perish all in turn, save well-recorded *Worth:* . . .

Yet are thy skies as blue, thy crags as wild;
Sweet are thy groves, and verdant are thy fields,
Thine olive ripe as when Minerva smiled,
And still his honied wealth Hymettus yields;
There the blithe Bee his fragrant fortress builds,
The free-born wanderer of thy mountain-air;
Apollo still thy long, long summer gilds,
Still in his beam Mendeli's marbles glare:
Art, Glory, Freedom fail – but Nature still is fair.

Where'er we tread, 'tis haunted, holy ground;
No earth of thine is lost in vulgar mould,
But one vast realm of Wonder spreads around,
And all the Muse's tales seem truly told,
Till the sense aches with gazing to behold
The scenes our earliest dreams have dwelt upon;
Each hill and dale, each deepening glen and wold
Defies the power which crushed thy temples gone:
Age shakes Athena's tower, but spares gray Marathon.

Ibid.

Every principal city of GREECE occupies its peculiar plain, surrounded in a most remarkable manner by a natural wall of mountains: and, . . . the mere name of any *Grecian* city, by this circumstance of association, will convey with it, whenever it is mentioned, a correct, although an imaginary picture of its appearance and situation; especially to the minds of travellers who have once seen any similar instance of this nature. The country is naturally distributed into a series of distinct craters, each containing a spacious and level area, admirably adapted to the purposes of maintaining and defending as many different colonies. . . . It may easily be imagined, without much description, what scenes for the painter such a country must afford – what subjects for poetry it must contain: heaven and earth seem to be brought together: the mountain-tops appear shining above the clouds, in regions of ineffable light, as thrones for immortal beings; and the clouds, collected into stupendous volumes of inconceivable splendour and of every possible form, come rolling around the bases of the mountains, as if bringing the majesty of their celestial conductors towards the earth. Under the influence of so many sublime impressions, the human mind becomes gifted as by inspiration, and is by nature filled with poetical ideas. The Muses have ever made such scenes their favourite abode; and it is upon this account that they have haunted *Helicon* and *Parnassus,* and all the heights and depths, the vales, and the rocks, and the woods, and the waters, of GREECE: – nor can an example be adduced, where, in any country uniformly flat and monophanous, like *Scythia* or *Belgium,* the fire of imagination has ever kindled. . . . *Homer* himself, had he been a native of oriental *Tahtary,* cradled and brought up under the impressions made by such scenery, and under the influence of such a climate, would never have been a poet.

E.D. Clarke, *Travels in Various Countries,* 4th edn, 1818

In the plans of *Grecian* cities . . . Nature has herself supplied, upon a most stupendous scale, what Art would otherwise more humbly have contrived. In various parts of Greece, where the labours of man have been swept away, – where time, barbarians, nay, even earthquakes, and every other moral and physical revolution, have done their work, an eternal city seems still to survive; because the *Acropolis,* the *Stadium,* the *Theatre,* the *Sepulchres,* the *Shrines,* and the *votive receptacles,* are so many 'sure and firm-set' rocks; slightly modified, indeed, by the hand of man, but upon which the blast of desolation passes like the breath of a zephyr.

Ibid.

The isles of Greece, the isles of Greece!
Where burning Sappho loved and sung,
Where grew the arts of war and peace,
Where Delos rose, and Phoebus sprung!
Eternal summer gilds them yet,
But all, except their sun, is set.

Lord Byron, *Don Juan,* 1819–24

It is the only place I ever was contented in.

Lord Byron, Letter to Edward John Trelawney, 15 June 1823

The spirit of Greece, passing through and ascending above the world, hath so animated universal nature, that the very rocks and woods, the very torrents and wilds burst forth with it.

Walter Savage Landor, *Scipio Polybius and Panaetius – Imaginary Conversations,* 1824–53

On desperate seas long wont to roam,
Thy hyacinth hair, thy classic face,
Thy Naiad airs, have brought me home
To the glory that was Greece
And the grandeur that was Rome.

Edgar Allan Poe, *To Helen,* 1831

A French engineer showed us the skeleton of a map of Greece, which was then preparing under the direction of the French Geographical Society, exhibiting an excess of mountains and deficiency of plain, which surprised even those who had travelled over every part of the kingdom.

J.L. Stephens, *Incidents of Travel in the Russian and Turkish Empires,* 1839

La Grèce est le pays au monde où le mal marche le plus vite à la suite du bien.
(Greece is the country where bad follows most quickly after good.)

Edmond About, *La Grèce contemporaine,* 1854

Contrast between the Greek isles & those of the Polynesian archipelago. The former have lost their virginity. The latter are fresh as at their first creation. The former look worn, and are meagre, like life after enthusiasm has gone. The aspect of all of them is sterile and dry. Even Delos whose flowers rose by miracle in the sea, is now a barren moor, & to look upon the bleak yellow of Patmos, who would ever think that a god had been there.

Herman Melville, *Journal of a Visit to Europe and the Levant,* 26 December 1856

The governing idea of Hellenism is spontaneity of consciousness; that of Hebraism, strictness of conscience.

Matthew Arnold, *Culture and Anarchy,* 1869

Except the blind forces of Nature, nothing moves in this world which is not Greek in its origin.

Sir Henry James Main, *Village Communities in the East and West,* Lecture, 1875

Good God, Ellen, the Grecian Archipelago! Can't you see it in your mind's eye, a group of exquisite islands in a turquoise setting? Ugh! Cold, storm, sleety grey, pitching and rolling, misery, headaches, horrors of universal belchings! A moment's respite in the Dardanelles enables me to write to you: soon we shall be in the sea of Marmora, reputed, as I learn for the first time, the coldest and windiest in the world. However, I am at least quit of Athens, with its stupid classic Acropolis and smashed pillars.

George Bernard Shaw, Letter to Ellen Terry, 12 October 1899

When eras die, their legacies
Are left to strange police.
Professors in New England guard
The glory that was Greece.

Clarence Day, from *Thoughts on Death,* 1928

Everything in Greece takes just twice as long as it would anywhere else. In the country they just do not use time at all.

Evelyn Waugh, *Diary,* 1 January 1927

Marvellous things happen to one in Greece – marvellous *good* things which can happen to one nowhere else on earth. Somehow, almost as if He were nodding, Greece still remains under the protection of the Creator. Men may go about their puny, ineffectual bedevilment, even in Greece, but God's magic is still at work and, no matter what the race of men may do or try to do, Greece is still a sacred precinct – and my belief is it will remain so until the end of time.

Henry Miller, *The Colossus of Maroussi,* 1942

Entering Greece is like entering a dark crystal; the form of things becomes irregular, refracted. Mirages suddenly swallow islands and if you watch you can see the trembling curtain of the atmosphere. Once in the shadow of the Albanian hills you are aware of this profound change. It haunts you while you live there, this creeping refraction of light altering with the time of day, so that you can fall asleep in a valley and wake up in Tibet, with all the landmarks gone.

Lawrence Durrell, 'A Landmark Gone', *c.* 1942, in *Spirit of Place,* 1969

When you look down and see the first Greek islands, you are surprised by the difference from Italy, whose dense plantings of parched yellow fields you have so short a time before left behind. Here is a paler, purer, soberer country, which seems both wild and old and quite distinct from anything farther west. The sea is absolutely smooth, sometimes violet, sometimes blue, with a softness of water-colour, glistening in patches with a fine grain of silver; and the islands of all sizes, in bulbous or oblong shapes – blobs and round-bottomed bottles and the contours of plump roast fowl – seem not to rise out of the water but to be plaqued on it like cuff-links on cuffs or to lie scattered like the fragments of a picture-puzzle on a table with a blue cloth cover. These islands are a dry terra-cotta – quite unlike the deep earthy clay tints to which one has been accustomed in Italy – almost the color of too well-cooked liver, and the vegetation looks like gray lichens. The marblings on the looping beaches set up a feeling of uncanny familiarity which refers itself, as one recognises in a moment, to the patterns on the ancient Greek vases made out of this very soil. Even on the large islands and the mainland, there are visible little cultivation and few plainly cut ribbons of roads, and the country, after humanized Italy, seems grander and more mysterious. The haze of the fawn-colored foreground shades farther away into the blue, where the mountains stand dim and serene. These are the 'shadowy mountains' of Homer. . . .

There is a special apparent lightness of substance

and absence of strong color which characterizes Greece and sets it off from other countries.

Edmund Wilson, *Europe without Baedeker,* 1947

All but the most insensitive blossom out in a land which is so obviously our origin and which still holds nearly everything that, in our noblest moments, we wish to return to or to find. Nobility is the word. The landscape is held in an austerity of light and there is none of the Latin waste of beauty: the ingredients used are basic – light, rocks, dark sea, an incandescent sky – with a bare minimum of accessories, trees, fields or streams or towns, that make it possible for human habitation; and of these, the buildings of men are either subordinate or unimportant, and the things of nature are spaced with an aristocratic elegance, as if their rarity were not necessity but choice. The people too have that natural aristocracy which will dispense with luxuries, comforts, and even necessities for an abstract cause. They are the only nation I know where a beautiful mouth is frequent; where the peasants answer a question with a look of intelligence (this is so in Tuscany also); and where the dullness of clothes and poverty of houses is unimportant because of a living exuberance, the spiritual fountain. This no doubt is the secret of courage.

Freya Stark, *The Coasts of Incense,* 1953

We . . . set off . . . north again, poorer for knowing so little of the earthy myths and miraculous facts, the kings and suppliants, the tyrants and tyrannicides, the oligarchies and the clashes of those minute and disunited nations throughout Greece that, like a lens the wrong way round, compress the huge blurred issues of world wars into a small bright compass.

Kevin Andrews, *Athens,* 1967

Fifth-century Athenian democracy was expensive, something you had to fight for, but the memory of it was a saleable commodity – something you could always make a profit of in bad times, and in Greece bad times are chronic. Since 146 B.C. Greece has been selling foreigners the Age of Perikles, and this is what meets the traveller on arrival.

Ibid.

Greeks

We are lovers of the beautiful yet simple in our tastes, and we cultivate the mind without loss of manliness.

Thucydides, *The Peloponnesian War, c.* 400 BC, trans. Benjamin Jowett

Equo ne credite, Teucri.
Quidquid id est, timeo Danaos et dona ferentis.
(Men of Troy, trust not the horse! Be it what it may, I fear the Danaans, though their hands proffer gifts.)

Virgil, *Aeneid, c.* 29–19 BC

Natio Comoeda est.
(They are a nation of actors.)

Juvenal, *Satires,* Satire iii, *c.* AD 100–110

When Greek meets Greek then comes the tug of war.
– Popular misquotation of:
When Greeks joyn'd Greeks, then was the tug of war.

Nathaniel Lee, *The Rival Queens,* 1677

Troylus: The Greeks are strong, & skilful to their strength,
Fierce to their skill, and to their fiercenesse Valiant.

William Shakespeare, *Troylus and Cressida, c.* 1601–2

I like the Greeks, who are plausible rascals, with all the Turkish vices without their courage. – However some are brave and all are beautiful, very much resembling the busts of Alcibiades the women not quite so handsome.

Lord Byron, Letter to Henry Drury, 3 May 1810

We are all Greeks.

Percy Bysshe Shelley, Preface to *Hellas,* 1821

Few things can be less tempting or dangerous than a Greek woman of the age of thirty.

John Carne, *Letters from the East,* 1830

For the Greeks lookt mainly, and almost entirely, at the outward, at that which could be brought in distinct and definite forms before the eye of the Imagination. To this they were predisposed from the first by their exquisite animal organization, which gave them a lively susceptibility of every enjoyment the outward world could offer, but which at the same time was so muscular and tightly braced as not to be overpowered and rendered effeminate thereby: and this their natural tendency to receive delight from the actual enjoyment of the outward world found everything in the outward world best fitted to foster and strengthen it. The climate and country were such as to gratify every appetite for pleasurable sensation, without enervating or relaxing the frame, or allowing the mind to sink into an Asiatic torpour. They rewarded industry richly: but they also called for it, and would not pamper sloth. By its physical structure Greece gave to its inhabitants the hardihood of the mountaineer. . . . But the Greek was not shut in by his mountains. Whenever he scaled a height the sea spread out before him, and wooed him to come into her arms, and to let her bear him away to some of the smiling islands she encircles. . . . He had the two great stimulants to enterprise before him. The voice of the Mountains and the voice of the Sea. . . . The sea enlarged the range and scope of his thoughts, which the mountains might have hemmed in.

J.C. and A. Hare, *Guesses at Truth,* 3rd edn, 1847

We need never despair of a people who have intelligence and are at the same time vain.

Edmond About, *La Grèce contemporaine*, 1854

To tell the truth, the Greeks like none but the Greeks. If they like foreigners, it is in the same way that the sportsman loves game.

Edmond About, *Greece and the Greeks of the Present Day*, 1855

Any Englishman having the usual knowledge of ancient Greek will be able to read the Athenian papers with ease.

Murray's Guide, nineteenth century, quoted by Jan Morris, *Travels*, 1976

I have a feeling that all Greeks are going to be rather like him: very friendly and gentle with hair too low on the forehead.

Evelyn Waugh, *Diary*, 29 December 1926

They were the first comers in the fields of thought and literature. When they arrived at fairly obvious reflections upon life and love, upon war, fate or manners, they coined them into the slogans or epigrams for which their language was so well adapted, and thus preserved the patent rights for all time. Hence their reputation. Nobody ever told me this at school. I have thought it all out in later life.

Sir Winston Churchill, *My Early Life*, 1930

A wise Athenian declared to me, 'All the faults in the world are concentrated in this bloody country, but no one can say we're not alive!'

Kevin Andrews, *Athens*, 1967

What landscape-tasters the ancient Greeks were! They chose sites like a soldier chooses cover. The basic elements were always the same, southern exposure, cover from the prevailing wind, height for coolness and to defeat the humidity of the littoral.

Lawrence Durrell, *Sicilian Carousel*, 1977

The blue infinity of sky and the white marble were the keynotes of the Greek imagination; somehow one associates the Roman with the honey-coloured or the dun.

Ibid.

Argos

If *Athens*, by arts, by military talents, and by costly solemnities, became 'one of the *Eyes* of GREECE,' there was in the humanity of *Argos*, and in the good feeling frequently displayed by its inhabitants, a distinction which comes nearer to the *heart*. Something characteristic of the people may be observed even in a name given to one of their Divinities; for they worshipped a '*God of Meekness*.'

E.D. Clarke, *Travels in Various Countries*, 4th edn, 1818

Arakhova

The village of *Arracovia* is rich in comparison with *Castri*. It contains two hundred and fifty houses, inhabited by *Albanians*, and by *Greeks*, '*without a Turk*' among them. This expression, '*without a Turk*' is throughout *Greece* a saying of exultation; and it is never uttered but with an expression of triumph and gladness.

E.D. Clarke, *Travels in Various Countries*, 4th edn, 1818

Athens

behold,
Where on the *Aegean* shore a City stands
Built nobly, pure the air, and light the soil,
Athens the eye of *Greece*, Mother of Arts
And Eloquence, native to famous wits
Or hospitable, in her sweet recess,
City or Suburban, studious walks and shades.

John Milton, *Paradise Regain'd*, 1671

The mass of every people must be barbarous where there is no printing . . . the boasted Athenians were . . . barbarians.

Samuel Johnson, in Boswell, *Life of Johnson*, 31 March 1772

Much greater hardships and perils than it can be the lot of any traveller in European Turkey to undergo, would be at once recompensed and forgotten on arriving at Athens – you there perceive an agreeable change in the aspect of all around you: the Turk appears to have lost his ferocity, and to have put on a new character, ornamented by the virtues of humanity, kindness and an easy affability to which he attains in no other quarter of the Mahometan world. After having been constantly on your guard against the outlaws of the land or sea, you feel that you may throw aside all unpleasant apprehensions, and, free from the cumbrous attendance of soldiers and servants, indulge in the contemplation of Athens.

John Cam Hobhouse, *A Journey through Albania and Other Provinces of Turkey*, 1813 (of 1809)

A place which I think I prefer on the whole to any I have seen.

Lord Byron, Letter to Mrs Catherine Gordon Byron, 20 July 1810

I am living in the Capuchin Convent, Hymettus before me, the Acropolis behind, the temple of Jove to my right, the Stadium in front, the town to the left, eh, Sir, there's a situation, there's your picturesque! nothing like that, Sir, in Lunnun, no not even the Mansion House.

Lord Byron, Letter to Francis Hodgson, 20 January 1811

Ancient of days! august Athena! where,
Where are thy men of might? thy grand in soul?
Gone – glimmering through the dream of things that were:
First in the race that led to glory's goal,
They won, and passed away – is this the whole?
A schoolboy's tale, the wonder of an hour!
The warrior's weapon and the Sophist's stole
Are sought in vain, and o'er each mouldering tower,
Dim with the mist of years, grey flits the shade of power.
Son of the Morning, rise! approach you here!
Come, but molest not yon defenceless Urn:
Look on this spot – a Nation's sepulchre!
Abode of Gods, whose shrines no longer burn. . . .

Lord Byron, *Childe Harold's Pilgrimage*, Canto the Second, 1812

Athens appears as a forsaken habitation of *holiness*.

E.D. Clarke, *Travels in Various Countries*, 4th edn, 1818

Athens arose: a city such as vision
Builds from the purple crags and silver towers
Of battlemented cloud, as in derision
Of kingliest masonry: the ocean-floors
Pave it: the evening sky pavilions it;
Its portals are inhabited
By thunder-zoned winds, each head
Within its cloudy wings with sunfire garlanded,
A divine work! Athens diviner yet
Gleamed with its crest of columns, on the will
Of man, as on a mount of diamond set;
For thou wert, and thine all-creative skill
Peopled with forms that mock the eternal dead
In marble immortality, that hill
Which was thine earliest throne and latest oracle.

Percy Bysshe Shelley, *Ode to Liberty*, 1820

'Let there be light!' said Liberty;
And, like sunrise from the sea,
Athens arose! – Around her born,
Shone, like mountains in the morn,
Glorious states; – and are they now
Ashes, wrecks, oblivion? . . .

Another Athens shall arise
And to remoter time
Bequeath, like sunset to the skies
The splendour of its prime;
And leave, if naught so bright may live,
All earth can take or heaven can give.

Percy Bysshe Shelley, *Hellas*, 1821

The reader perhaps trembles at the name of Athens, but let him take courage. I promise to let him off easily.

J.L. Stephens, *Incidents of Travel in the Russian and Turkish Empires*, 1839

Solitude, silence, and sunset are the nursery of sentiment. I sat down on a broken capital of the Parthenon; the owl was already flitting among the ruins. I looked up at the majestic temple and down at the ruined and newly-regenerated city, and said to myself, 'Lots must rise in Athens!' I traced the line of the ancient walls, ran a railroad to the Piraeus, and calculated the increase on 'up-town lots' from building the king's palace near the Garden of Plato. Shall I or shall I not 'make an operation' in Athens? The court has removed here, the country is beautiful, climate fine, government fixed, steamboats are running, all the world is coming, and lots must rise. I bought (in imagination) a tract of good tillable land, laid it out in streets, had my Plato, and Homer, and Washington Places, and Jackson Avenue, built a row of houses to improve the neighbourhood where nobody lived, got maps lithographed, and sold off at auction. I was in the right condition to 'go in,' for I had nothing to lose; but unfortunately, the Greeks were very far behind the spirit of the age, knew nothing of the beauties of the credit system, and could not be brought to dispose of their consecrated soil 'on the usual terms,' *ten per cent down, balance on bond and mortgage;* so, giving up the idea, at dark I bade farewell to the ruins of the Acropolis, and went to my hotel to dinner.

Ibid.

When, then, I came to Athens, and saw that it was a humbug, I hailed the fact with a sort of gloomy joy. I stood in the Royal Square, and cursed the country which has made thousands of little boys miserable. They have blue stripes on the new Greek flag; I thought bitterly of my own.

W.M. Thackeray, *Punch in the East*, 1845

I have never seen a town in England which may be compared to this; for though Herne Bay is a ruin now, money was once spent upon it, and houses built; here, beyond a few score of mansions comfortably laid out, the town is little better than a rickety agglomeration of larger and smaller huts, tricked out here and there with the most absurd cracked ornaments and cheap attempts at elegance. But neatness is the elegance of poverty, and these people despise such a home-y ornament. I have got a map with squares, fountains, theatres, public gardens and Places d'Othon marked out; but they only exist in the paper capital – the wretched tumble-down wooden one boasts of none.

W.M. Thackeray, *Journey from Cornhill to Cairo*, 1845

Athens, the marvellous city that in all things ran ahead of her envious and sullen contemporaries. . . . Civilisation, not as a word, not as an idea, but as a thing, but as a power, was known in Athens.

Thomas de Quincey, *The Chinese Question in 1857*

Corfu is after all a dead place, and Athens a consolation for lost happiness. There is nothing alive in the Parthenon. You feel this acutely when you wander round the ancient Greek theatre with a small and vulgar crowd of English, Americans and Germans, and their pettifogging sentiments. Once, no doubt, Ajax took his farewell of the sun in that theatre while a people that understood listened. I have no use for these decaying twigs of antiquity except when I can build my nest of them. The ancient Greeks were a fine people, but that does not enable the modern mountain-goat to jump off its own shadow. So it spends its life, and imagines it succeeds, never having tasted reality. Ancient ruins are really only a sauce to heighten the enjoyment of those who relish flat, low, dull modern life.

Sir Walter Raleigh, Letter to L.R., 9 April 1898
(Mountain-goat – a family name for the cultured, hotel-haunting British spinster.)

Athens should be taken early in life if one wants to accept its despotism. After seeing Egypt and Syria, Italy and Japan, Greece shrinks; and after living in French Gothic and Michael Angelo Renaissance, Greek art has less to say to the simple-minded Christian. . . . At bottom Athens was always a fraud, and Aristophanes and Socrates and the rotten and impudent scepticism and cynicism and sophism of the schools expressed the character of the place very much more successfully than the artists ever succeeded in expressing religious majesty in Zeus or religious emotion in the Parthenon. . . . Athens leaves me cool.

Henry Adams, Letter to Charles Milnes Gaskell, 23 April 1898

To people with delicate ears a stay in Athens is torture. For some reason this roughly-paved town is a vast sounding-board which the ever-prevalent dust fails to deaden, and like all Southern Europeans the Greek not only loves noise but never stops making it. The car and tram drivers seem to take their hooters as a child does its rattle, for a delightful toy, that may sometimes serve the further purpose of attracting someone's attention; consequently they never stop hooting. To complete the agony, when modern ideas of traffic first reached Athens a few years ago, some bright person made a corner in hooters, and persuaded the authorities to insist on their all hooting on the same note. I cannot quite account for the almost unbearably irritating effect of this unison, – yet after all, I can. Fancy living in a wood with no birds in it but hysterical cuckoos. Well, that would be exactly the same sort of thing, and I shall never forget the hideous sound of that massed band of unison motor horns as heard from the top of Lycabettus, the fantastic rock that rises out of Athens like a lighthouse.

Ethel Smyth, *A Three-legged Tour in Greece*, 1925

and Chicago

In Athens I saw dovecotes, solariums, verandahs floating without support, rabbits sunning themselves on the roofs, goats kneeling before icons, turkeys tied to the door-knobs. Everybody had flowers, not just flower-pots. A door might be made of Ford fenders, and look inviting. A chair might be made of gasoline tins, and be pleasant to sit on. There were bookshops where you could read about Buffalo Bill or Jules Verne or Hermes Trismegistus. There was a spirit here which a thousand years of misery had not squelched. Chicago's South Side on the other hand, is like a vast, unorganized lunatic asylum. Nothing can flourish here but vice and disease. I wonder what the great Emancipator would say if he could see the glorious freedom in which the black man moves now. He made them free, yes – free as rats in a dark cellar.

Henry Miller, *The Air-conditioned Nightmare*, 1945

Athens would be unrecognizable if a large part of it were not for sale. Its whole commercial aspect is an eloquent medium (if not the only one) for the expression of the national spirit.

Kevin Andrews, *Athens*, 1967

If it's beauty you want, go to Italy, go to the Cotswolds, go to a museum: don't come to Athens, where something else may happen.

Ibid.

Acropolis

Acropolis – blocks of marble like sticks of Wenham ice – or like huge cakes of wax. – Parthenon elevated like cross of Constantine. Strange contrast of rugged rock with polished temple. At Stirling – art & nature correspond. Not so at Acropolis.

Herman Melville, *Journal of a Visit to Europe and the Levant*, 8 February 1857

It is thirty years . . . since I first drove up the road to Athens, and I find little change. The suburbs have extended somewhat, and the olive groves have shrunk, and the hills are even barer than before, but nothing marks the progress of the age unless it be the overthrow of the fine old Venetian walls of the Acropolis. I regret these as much as if they had pulled down the Parthenon itself.

Wilfred Scawen Blunt, Diary, 20 November 1888, *My Diaries*, 1919

It's a lovely spot. We have got all Athens in our arc of fire.

Paratroop Officer, Remark to Lord Moran, December 1944, quoted in *Winston Churchill, The Struggle for Survival*, 1966

A thing of beauty that is a joy once or twice, and afterwards a standing reproach.

Cyril Connolly, *The Condemned Playground*, 1945

Above the low roofs of Athens the Acropolis rises on its pedestal of rock: astonishing, dramatic, divine, with at the same time the look of a phantom.

Edmund Wilson, *Europe without Baedeker*, 1947

Son et Lumière at the Acropolis is a predictable and grandiose repetition of everything we've ever heard – the white elephant indulging in its swan-song. In a land where sun, moon, cloud and rain have presumably not changed since these structures were built to harmonize with a natural but highly varied illumination, floodlighting is superfluous except in so far as it accomplishes the impossible and turns the Parthenon into a stale biscuit.

Kevin Andrews, *Athens*, 1967

And now on the Acropolis we have, if not the real thing, the pure thing, which some people like better: a monument that never existed in history.

Ibid.

Those who tiptoe round the Acropolis today in their thousands hardly realise that they are looking at something like an empty barn.

Lawrence Durrell, *Sicilian Carousel*, 1977

The Parthenon is a monument to slavery. . . . It is built by slaves.

Edward Bond, in interview with Melvin Bragg, *The South Bank Show*, LWT, 4 May 1980

The Adytum, or Grotto of Pan

It seems ill suited to the stories which caused it to be considered as the scene of *Apollo's* amours with *Creusa*, and as a place of residence for *Pan:* but when the mind is completely subdued by superstition, it is seldom burdened by any scruples as to *probability*.

E.D. Clarke, *Travels in Various Countries*, 4th edn, 1818

Mount Athos

The monasteries . . . are like so many little fortresses in the midst of the most sublime solitudes.

E.D. Clarke, *Travels in Various Countries*, 4th edn, 1818

The Holy Mountain Athos, station of a faith where all the years have stopped.

Robert Byron, *The Station*, 1928

Attica

Tourist, spare the avid glance
  That greedy roves the sight to see:
Little here of 'Old Romance,'
  Or picturesque of Tivoli.
No flushful tint the sense to warm –
Pure outline pale, a linear charm.
The clear-cut hills carved temples face,
Respond, and share their sculptural grace.
'Tis art and nature lodged together,
  Sister by sister, cheek to cheek,
Such Art, such Nature and such weather,
  The All-in-All seems here a Greek.

Herman Melville, from *Timoleon*, 1891

Boeotia

the towns that lie like slain
Upon the wide Boeotian plain;

Arthur Hugh Clough, *Mari Magno, The Lawyer's First Tale*, 1861

Corfu/Kerkira

A very clean and rather attractive town. It reminded me of Brighton.

Evelyn Waugh, *Diary*, 9 January 1927

Corinth/Korinthos

Corinth, the *Gibraltar* of the Peloponnesus. . . .

E.D. Clarke, *Travels in Various Countries*, 4th edn, 1818

The Acrocorinthos

The stupendous rock of the *Acrocorinthus*, . . . was . . . very aptly named by an antient Oracle (and in times when the art of war was incapable of giving it the importance it might now possess) one of the *horns* which a conqueror ought to lay hold upon, in order to secure that valuable *heifer*, the *Peloponnesus*.

E.D. Clarke, *Travels in Various Countries*, 4th edn, 1818

Standing on the Isthmus commanding the Adriatic and Aegean Seas; receiving in one hand the riches of Asia, and in the other those of Europe; distributing them to every quarter of the then known world, wealth followed commerce, and then came luxury and extravagance to such an extent that it became a proverb, 'It is not for every man to go to Corinth.'

J.L. Stephens, *Incidents of Travel in the Russian and Turkish Empires,* 1839

Isthmus of Corinth, Carneta or Canetto, ancient Cromyon

A miserable hamlet, consisting of only six houses, called Carneta or Canetto, upon the site of the antient Cromyon. Its wretched inhabitants, a set of sickly-looking people, in the midst of a very bad air, had never seen a glove, and expressed the utmost astonishment at seeing a person take one off his hand.

E.D. Clarke, *Travels in Various Countries,* 4th edn, 1818

Crete/Kriti

The women generally wear linen breeches, as men do, and boots after the same manner, and their linen coats no longer than the middle of their thighs, and are insatiably inclined to venery; such is the nature of the soil and climate. The ancient Cretans were such notable liars, that the Heathen poet Epimenides, yea, and the apostle Paul, in his epistle to Titus, did term them to have been 'ever liars, evil beasts, and slow bellies;' whence sprung these proverbs; as *Cretense mendacium;* and, *Cretisandum est cum Cretensibus.*

The Candiots are excellent good archers, surpassing all the oriental people therein, couragious and valiant upon the sea, as in former times they were; and they are naturally inclined to singing; so that commonly after meat, man, wife, and child, of each family, will, for the space of an hour, sing with such an harmony, as is wonderful melodious to the hearer; yea, and they cannot forgo the custom of it.

William Lithgow, *Rare Adventures and Painfull Peregrinations,* 1614/32

Mount Ida is the highest mountain in Creta; and by the computation of shepherd's feet amounteth to six miles of height: It is overclade even to the top with cypress trees, and good store of medicinable herbs; insomuch, that the beasts which feed thereupon have their teeth gilded like to the colour of gold.

Ibid.

The valley of Suda . . . is twenty Italian miles long, and two of breadth; and I remember, as I descended to cross the valley, and pass the haven, I thought the whole plain resembled to me a green sea; and that was only by reason of infinite olive-trees growing there, whose boughs and leaves overtop all other fructiferous trees in that plain. The villages, for loss of ground, are all built upon the skirts of rocks upon the south side of the valley; yea, and so difficult to climb them, and so dangerous to dwell in them, that I thought their lives were in like peril, as he who was adjoined to sit under the point of a two-handed sword, and it hanging by the hair of a horse's tail.

Ibid.

*The people of Crete unfortunately make more history than they can consume locally.

'Saki', H.H. Munro, *The Jesting of Arlington Stringham,* 1911

Delphi/Castri

In its present condition, there is not in all *Lapland* a more wretched village than Castri.

E.D. Clarke, *Travels in Various Countries,* 4th edn, 1818

Delphi, I should think perhaps the Greekest thing of all. It comes nearest to being serious, and is charming; a transparent and elegant fraud that no one more than half believed in except when it suited them, but that was artistically satisfactory and socially perfect.

Henry Adams, Letter to Elizabeth Cameron, 20 April 1898

Demetriado/Parir

These miserable islanders are a kind of silly poor people, which, in their behaviour, shewed me the necessity they had to live, rather than any pleasure in their living.

William Lithgow, *Rare Adventures and Painfull Peregrinations,* 1614/32

Dhilos/Delos

Delos, of a most barren aspect, however flowery in fable. but desolate impact.

Herman Melville, *Journal of a Visit to Europe and the Levant,* 23 December 1856

A bleak impressive little island, a sort of ghostly city of ruins and marble fragments.

Logan Pearsall Smith, Letter to Mrs Berenson, 4 May 1926

Kalymnos

In Kalymnos the infant's paint-box has been at work again on the milky slopes of the mountain. Carefully, laboriously it has squared in a churchyard, a monastery, and lower down repeated the motif: a church, a monastery, a town; then, simply for the sake of appropriateness, a harbour with a shelf of bright craft at anchor, and the most brilliant, the most devastatingly brilliant houses. Never has one seen anything like it – the harbour revolving slowly round one as one comes in. Plane after stiff cubistic plane of pure colour. The mind runs up and down the web of vocabulary looking for a word which will do justice to it. In vain.

Lawrence Durrell, *Reflections on a Marine Venus,* 1953

Kephallinia/Cephalonia

We sayled close by Cephalenia, triangular in forme, one hundred and sixtie miles in circumference: the Mountaynes intermixed with profitable Valleyes, and the Woods with Champian. Unwatered with Rivers, and poore in Fountaines, but abounding with Wheate, Honey, Corents, Manna, Cheese, Wooll, Turkeyes, excellent Oyle, incomparable (though not long lasting) Muscadines, and Powder for the dying of Scarlet: This growes like a blister on the leafe of the holy Oke, a little shrub, yet producing Acornes: being gathered, they rub out of it a certaine dust, that converteth after a while into wormes, which they kill with Wine when they begin to quicken. Amongst her many harbours, Argostoli is the principall, capacious enough for a Navie. The Inhabitants of this Iland are Grecians, the Venetians their Sovereignes.

George Sandys, 1616, in *Purchas his Pilgrimes,* 1625

Knossos

Knossos is of course immensely interesting historically, but it is all on a small scale, and gives no aesthetic pleasure, and Evans is repainting and reconstructing it in a gaudy style of bad taste which gives it something of the look of his hideous house on Boar's Hill.

Logan Pearsall Smith, Letter to Mrs Berenson, 20 May 1926

Lesbos

Marble was her lovely city
And so pleasant was its air
That the Romans had no pity
For a Roman banished there;
Lesbos was a singing island
And a happy home from home
With the pines about its highland
And its crescent faint with foam.
Lady make a nota bene
That Love's lyric fount of glee
Rose in marbled Mytilene
Channelled by the purple sea.
Sappho sang to her hetairai,
And each lovely lyricist
Sappho's singing emulated;
And this point must not be missed:
Women were emancipated
Long before the Christian era.
Long before the time of Christ.
Then not only were they equal
To their menfolk but themselves;
And the lovely lyric sequel
Lives on all our learned shelves.
Yes: we may be fairly certain,
As results of this release
Sappho's was, with all its Girton
Girls, the fairest Isle of Greece.

Oliver St John Gogarty, 'The Isles of Greece: Lesbos', *Collected Poems,* 1951

Mani

When God finished making the world all He had left was stones, and He made the Mani last of all.

Greek old man, quoted Kevin Andrews, *The Flight of Ikaros,* 1959

Macedon (in part now Yugoslavia)

compared with Monmouth, Wales

Fluellen: I tell you Captain, if you looke in the Maps of the Orld, I warrant you sall finde in the comparisons betweene *Macedon & Monmouth,* that the situations looke you, is both alike. There is a River in *Macedon,* & there is also moreover a River at *Monmouth,* it is call'd Wye at *Monmouth*: but it is out of my praines, what is the name of the other River: but 'tis all one, tis alike as my fingers is to my fingers, and there is Salmons in both.

William Shakespeare, *Henry the Fifth, c.* 1598–9

The dogs in this country, as in many parts of Macedonia, wear body-clothes; and these animals afforded us the last remaining traces of the Macedonian costume.

E.D. Clarke, *Travels in Various Countries,* 4th edn, 1818

Marathon Lake

We found it overgrown with tall reeds and bulrushes, but well suited, by its unfathomable depth of water and mud, to confirm the probability of the fact related concerning it; and capable, at this day, of engulphing the most numerous army that might attempt its passage.

E.D. Clarke, *Travels in Various Countries,* 4th edn, 1818

Missolonghi/Mesolongion

The Situation of Messolonghi is not unknown to you; – The Dykes of Holland when broken down are the Deserts of Arabia for dryness in comparison.

Lord Byron, Letter to Charles Hancock, 5 February 1824

The whole was a mass of new-made ruins – of houses demolished and black with smoke – the tokens of savage and desolating war. . . . It was a cheerless place, and reminded me of Communipaw in bad weather. It had no connexion with the ancient glory of Greece, no name or place on her historic page, and no hotel where we could get a breakfast.

J.L. Stephens, *Incidents of Travel in the Russian and Turkish Empires*, 1839

Mycenae

Except that the art was in certain ways much higher, Mycenae is uncommonly like a ruined castle *quelconque* on the Dee or the Don. It is the citadel of a highland chief whose tastes are developed by contact with Indian Moguls. I was glad to clear my mind about it. Homer became easy, and even a little modern, as though he knew rather less about his ancient predecessors than I did.

Henry Adams, Letter to Elizabeth Cameron, 20 April 1898

Nauplia (Temple of Aesculapius)

The Temple of Aesculapius, a sort of Greek Carlsbad, though so Greek, and – oh, so little German! We passed the day there, lunching under the olive-trees, and dozing in their shade; rambling over the ruins, and wondering how much better the Greeks understood health-resorts than we.

Henry Adams, Letter to Elizabeth Cameron, 20 April 1898

Nemea

A song in the valley of Nemea:
Sing quiet, quite quiet here.

Song for the brides of Argos
Combing the swarms of golden hair:
Quite quiet, quiet there.

Under the rolling comb of grass,
The sword outrusts the golden helm.

Agamemnon under tumulus serene
Outsmiles the jury of skeletons:
Cool under cumulus the lion queen:

Only the drum can celebrate,
Only the adjective outlive them.

A song in the valley of Nemea:
Sing quiet, quiet, quiet here.

Tone of the frog in the empty well,
Drone of the bald bee on the cold skull,

Quiet, Quiet, Quiet.

Lawrence Durrell, 'Nemea', from *A Private Country*, 1943

Olympus

and Mount Athos

In that country are right great mountains toward the end of Macedonia. And among other there is one that men call Olympus, that departs Macedonia and Thrace; and it is high above the clouds. There is also another hill that men call Athos; and that is so high that the shadow thereof reaches unto Lempny [Lemnos] the which is there from near seventy-seven mile. Above on those hills is the air so clear and so subtle that men may feel no wind there; and therefore may no beast ne fowl live there, so is the air dry. And men say in those countries that philosophers some time went up on those hills and held to their noses sponges moisted with water for to catch air, for the air there was so dry. And also above on these hills in the powder they wrote letters with their fingers, and at the year end they went again and found the same letters that they had written the year before als fresh as they were on the first day without any default. And therefore it seems well that these hills pass the clouds to the pure air.

John Mandeville, *The Book of John Mandeville*, *c.* 1360

Above these mountains proud Olympus tow'rs,
The parliamental seat of heavenly pow'rs.

Lady Mary Wortley Montagu, *Verses Written in the Chiosk at Pera, Overlooking Constantinople*, 26 December 1718

Mount Parnassus

Oh, thou Parnassus! whom I now survey,
Not in the phrenzy of a dreamer's eye,
Not in the fabled landscape of a lay,
But soaring snow-clad through thy native sky,
In the wild pomp of mountain-majesty!
What marvel if I thus essay to sing?
The humblest of thy pilgrims passing by
Would gladly woo thine Echoes with his string.

Though from thy heights no more one Muse will wave
her wing. . . .

Happier in this than mightiest Bards have been.
Whose fate to distant homes confined their lot,
Shall I unmoved behold the hallowed scene,
Which others rave of, though they know it not?
Though here no more Apollo haunts his Grot,
And thou, the Muses' seat art now their grave,
Some gentle Spirit still pervades the spot,
Sighs in the gale, keeps silence in the Cave,
And glides with glassy foot o'er yon melodious wave.

Lord Byron, *Childe Harold's Pilgrimage,* Canto the First, 1812

Upon Parnassus going to the fountain of Delphi (Castri) in 1809 – I saw a flight of twelve Eagles – (Hobhouse says they are Vultures – at least in conversation) and I siezed the Omen. – On the day before, I composed the lines to Parnassus – (in Childe Harold) and on beholding the birds – had a hope – that Apollo had accepted my homage. –

Lord Byron, *Detached Thoughts,* 1821–2

Every schoolboy knows how hard it is to write poetry, but few know the physical difficulties of climbing the poetical mountain itself. . . . Perhaps, after all, I had a lucky escape; for, if the Greek tradition be true, whoever sleeps on the mountain becomes an inspired poet or a madman, either of which, for a professional man, is a catastrophe to be avoided.

J.L. Stephens, *Incidents of Travel in the Russian and Turkish Empires,* 1839

on Parnassus Mount
You take a mule to climb, and not a muse.

Elizabeth Barrett Browning, *Aurora Leigh,* 1856

I reached the top of Parnassus: for half an hour I saw the whole of Greece below me, a vision of incredible beauty, all its rusty headlands and misty seas and Olympus (which they call Olybus because mp = b) in the far north and *everything* in fact somewhere in sight: and crocus and scylla, incredibly blue ones, on the edge of the snow. When we came off the top, my guide wrapped me in a blanket and I fell asleep and woke after an hour with an icy wind and have been suffering from a miserable cough ever since: but one must be prepared to sacrifice something for trespassing on the Gods.

Freya Stark, Letter, 18 June 1939, in *The Coasts of Incense,* 1953

Paros

The Iland Paros, celebrated by Poets for the fine Marble growing there.

Fynes Moryson, *An Itinerary,* 1617

Rhodes

From the number of the appellations which it bore at different periods, *Rhodes* might have at last received the name of the *poly-onomous* island.

E.D. Clarke, *Travels in Various Countries,* 4th edn, 1818

Rhodes, where history lies sleeping.

Freya Stark, *Beyond Euphrates,* 1951

In Rhodes the days drop as softly as fruit from trees. Some belong to the dazzling ages of Cleobolus and the tyrants, some to the gloomy Tiberius, some to the crusaders. They follow each other in scales and modes too quickly almost to be captured in the nets of form.

Lawrence Durrell, *Reflections on a Marine Venus,* 1953

The island of Rhodes is about as far out as you can get in Europe.

Harry Kurnitz, Letter to Groucho Marx, 21 October 1959

Samos

The Capudan Pasha reasoned wih the people of Samos upon the propriety of their paying for a Turkish frigate which was wrecked upon their territory; 'because the accident would not have happened unless their island had been in the way.'

E.D. Clarke, *Travels in Various Countries,* 4th edn, 1818

Samothrace (and the Troad)

Methley and I pored over the map together; we agreed that whatever may have been the exact site of Troy, the Grecian camp must have been nearly opposite to the space betwixt the islands of Imbros and Tenedos: but Methley reminded me of a passage in the Iliad in which Neptune is represented as looking at the scene of action before Ilion from above the island of Samothrace. Now Samothrace, according to the map, appeared to be not only out of all seeing distance from the Troad, but to be entirely shut out from it by the intervening Imbros, a larger island, which stretches its length right athwart the line of sight from Samothrace to Troy. Piously allowing that the dread Commotor of our globe might have seen all mortal doings, even from the depths of his own cerulean kingdom, I still felt that if a station were to be chosen from which to see the fight, old Homer, so material in his ways of thought, so averse from all haziness and overreaching, would have *meant* to give the god for his station some spot within reach of men's eyes from the plains of Troy. I think that this testing of the poet's words by map and compass may have shaken a little of my faith in the completeness of his knowledge. Well, now I had come; there to the south was Tenedos, and here at my side was Imbros, all right, and according to the map, but aloft over Imbros, – aloft in a far away heaven was Samothrace, the watch-tower of Neptune!

Sŏ Homer had appointed it, and so it was: the map was correct enough, but could not, like Homer, convey *the whole truth*. Thus vain and false are the mere human surmises and doubts which clash with Homeric writ!

Nobody, whose mind had not been reduced to the most deplorably logical condition, could look upon this beautiful congruity betwixt the Iliad and the material world, and yet bear to suppose that the poet may have learned the features of the coast from mere hearsay; now then, I believed – now I knew that Homer had *passed along here* – that this vision of Samothrace overtowering the nearer island was common to him and to me.

A.W. Kinglake, *Eothen*, 1844

Scio

Its appearance is very singular: six or eight miles from the shore is a lofty chain of barren and purple rocks, which shut out all view of the interior, and the space between these and the sea is covered with delightful gardens and verdure, which inclose the town on every side, except towards the main.

The fine climate of this isle, the profusion of delicious fruits, the beauty of its women, and the friendly and hospitable character of the people, caused it to be preferred by travellers to any other of the Greek islands. In the evening when the setting sun was resting on the craggy mountains and the rich gardens at their feet, the shores and the shaded promenades around the town were filled with the Greek population, among which were multitudes of the gay and handsome women of Scio, distinguished for their frank and agreeable manners.

John Carne, *Letters from the East*, 1830

River Styx

In pouring rain we came down towards the Styx, and when the sun came out we saw it, a small pastoral torrent, green water among boulders under plane trees. It was nice to find it so easy and friendly.

Freya Stark, Letter, 2 June 1939, in *The Coasts of Incense*, 1953

Syra

The town of Syra is built upon the summit of a lofty hill, so remarkable for its conical form that it may be compared to a vast sugar-loaf covered with houses.

E.D. Clarke, *Travels in Various Countries*, 4th edn, 1818

Entering Syra harbor, I was struck again by the appearance of the town on the hill. The houses seemed clinging round its top, as if desperate for security, like ship-wrecked men about a rock beaten by billows.

Herman Melville, *Journal of a Visit to Europe and the Levant*, 23 December 1856

The Greek, of any class, seems a natural dandy. His dress, though a laborer, is that of a gentleman of leisure. . . . Some of the poorest sort present curious examples of what may be called the decayed picturesque.

Ibid., 25 December 1856

Salonica/Thessaloniki

Went into the Bazaar. Quite large, but filthy. Streets all narrow, like cow lanes. & smelling like barn-yards. Very silent. Women muffled about the face. All old. No young. Great numbers of Jews walking in long robes & pelisses. Also Greeks mixed with the Turks. Aspect of streets like those of Five Points. Rotten houses. Smell of rotten wood.

Herman Melville, *Journal of a Visit to Europe and the Levant*, 6 December 1856

Duckworth, the English resident, came off early. Talked with him. Said he had been *a day's shooting in the Vale of Tempe*. – Ye Gods! whortleberrying on Olympus.

Ibid.

Thessaly

THESSALY was the *Yorkshire* of Antient *Greece*, as to its country and its inhabitants. A vulgar adage in *England*, maintaining that '*if a halter be cast upon the grave of a Yorkshireman, he will rise and steal a horse;*' and the saying, '*Do not put Yorkshire upon us,*' as deprecating fraud; espress the aphorisms antiently in use respecting the *Thessalians*, who were notorious for their knavish disposition; insomuch that base money was called *Thessalian coin*, and a cheating action *Thessalian treachery*.

E.D. Clarke, *Travels in Various Countries*, 4th edn, 1818

Thira (formerly Santorin)

I found it a fantastic spot. Picturesque, or romantic, is too mild a term; the cliff-scenery and the colours of the sea and land made one catch one's breath. Under a bleak northern sky it would be a horrific kind of place; drenched in the glittering light of May it was fabulously beautiful. . . . Santorin is surely a vision which can disappoint nobody.

Norman Douglas, *Looking Back,* 1933

Tiryns

Tiryns, where Art seems to have rivalled Nature in the eternity of her existence.

E.D. Clarke, *Travels in Various Countries,* 4th edn, 1818

Zante/Zakinthos

The islanders are Greeks, a kind of subtle people and great dissemblers; . . . I was credibly informed here by the better sort, that this little isle maketh yearly (besides oil and wine) only of currants, one hundred and sixty thousand zechins . . . a rent or sum of money which these silly Islanders could never afford, (they being not above sixty years ago, but a base beggarly people, and an obscure place), if it were not for some liquorish lips here in England of late, who forsooth can hardly digest bread, pasties, broth, and (*verbi gratia*) bag-puddings, without these currants. And as these rascal Greeks becoming proud of late with this slavish expence, contemn justly this sensual prodigality, I have heard them often demand the English, in a filthy derision, what they did with such liquorish stuff, and if they carried them home to feed their swine and hogs withal. A question indeed worthy of such a female traffick; the inference of which I suspend: there is no other nation, save this, thus addicted to that miserable isle.

William Lithgow, *Rare Adventures and Painfull Peregrinations,* 1614/32

The houses of this Towne are built with stone, such as is digged out of the Rockie side of the Mountaine. They are somewhat lower than I have observed in other Townes: their Roofes are somewhat flatte according to the forme of the Italian Building, with a prettie round stone inserted into the middle of the out-side, which maketh the House there somewhat like to the broad Thrumbe Caps, that some of the olde women of the West parts of England, were wont to weare for some twentie yeeres since. . . . I could see no glasse windows in their houses, but all Lattice made of Firre which I observe to be generally used amongst them. Which Lattice leaves in the summer time they doe commonly take of, and then, seeing they are Greekes, and merrie Greekes too, they may be very properly said to keepe open houses. Now concerning their lowe houses, the reason they build them so lowe is, because of the manifold Earthquakes which doe as much share this Iland as any other place in the World. The Earthquakes are so frequent with them that sometimes they feel ten of them in a month.

Thomas Coryat, 1612, in *Purchas his Pilgrimes,* 1625

In habit they imitate the Italians, but transcend them in their revenges, and infinitely lesse civill. They will threaten to kill a Merchant that will not buy their Commodities, and make more conscience to breake a Fast, then to commit a Murther. . . . He is weary of his life that hath a difference with any of them, and will walke abroad after day-light.

George Sandys, 1610, in *Purchas his Pilgrimes,* 1625

Zitza

Monastic Zitza! from thy shady brow,
Thou small, but favoured spot of holy ground!
Where'er we gaze – around – above – below, –
What rainbow tints, what magic charms are found!
Rock, river, forest, mountain, all abound,
And bluest skies that harmonize the whole:
Beneath, the distant Torrent's rushing sound
Tells where the volumed Cataract doth roll
Between those hanging rocks, that shock yet please the soul.

Amidst the grove that crowns yon tufted hill
Which, were it not for many a mountain nigh
Rising in loftier ranks and loftier still,
Might well itself be deemed of dignity,
The Convent's white walls glisten fair on high:
Here dwells the caloyer, nor rude is he,
Nor niggard of his cheer; the passer by
Is welcome still; nor heedless will he flee
From hence, if he delight kind Nature's sheen to see.

Lord Byron, *Childe Harold's Pilgrimage,* Canto the Second, 1812

GREENLAND (Denmark)

. . . as we sayled along the coast the fogge brake up, and we discovered the land, which was the most deformed rockie and mountainous land that ever we saw: The first sight whereof did shew as if it had beene in forme of a sugar-loafe, standing to our sight above the cloudes, for that it did shew over the fogge like a white liste in the skie, the tops altogether covered with snow, and the shoare beset with yce a league off into the Sea, making such yrkesome noyse as that it seemed to be the true patterne of desolation, and after the same our Captaine named it, The land of Desolation.

John Janes Marchant (1585), in Richard Hakluyt, *Principal Navigations . . . of the English Nation,* 1598–1600

. . . it was very high, and it looked very blew. . . .

Henry Morgan (1586), in Richard Hakluyt, *Principal Navigations . . . of the English Nation*, 1598–1600

The Land of Groenland is a very high, ragged and mountainous Countrey, being all alongst the Coast broken Ilands, making very many good Rivers and Bayes, into some of which I entred, sayling up the same the space of ten or twelve English leagues, finding the same very navigable, with great abundance of fish of sundrie sorts. The land also in all places wheresoever I came, seemed to be very fertile, according to the Climate wherein it lyeth: for betweene the Mountaynes was most pleasant Plaines and Valleyes, in such sort as if I had not seene the same, I could not have beleeved, that such a fertile Land in shew could bee in these Northerne Regions.

James Hall, 1605, in *Purchas his Pilgrimes*, 1625

Greenland is a place in Nature nothing like unto the Name: for certainly there is no place in the World, yet knowne and discovered that is lesse greene then it.

Robert Fotherby, 1622, in *Purchas his Pilgrimes*, 1625

Bread Beere and Wine we had none. As for meate, our greatest and chiefest feeding was the Whale Fritters, and these mouldie too, the loathsomest meate in the world. For our venison 'twas hard to finde, but a great deale harder to get: and for our third sort of provision, the Beares; 'twas a measuring cast which should be eaten first, Wee or the Beares, when we first saw one another; and we perceived by them, that they had as good hopes to devoure us as wee to kill them.

Edward Pellham, *Gods Power and Providence Shewed in the Miraculous Preservation and Deliverance of Eight Englishmen, etc.*, 1631

As Men in *Green-land* left beheld the *Sun*
From their Horizon run;
And thought upon the sad half year
Of Cold and Darkness they must suffer there.
So on my parting Mistress did I look. . . .

Abraham Cowley, 'The Parting', in *The Mistress, or Several Copies of Love Verses*, 1647

For Greenland is a barren place,
A land where grows no green,
But ice and snow, and the whale-fish blow,
And the daylight's seldom seen, brave boys!
And the daylight's seldom seen!

Anon., from *The Greenland Fishery*, 1794

From Greenland's icy mountains
From India's coral strand
Where Afric's sunny fountains
Roll down their golden sand;
From many an ancient river,
From many a palmy plain,
They call us to deliver
Their land from error's chain.

Reginald Heber, 'Before a Collection for the Society for Propagating the Gospel', *Poems*, 1842

Greenland's icy mountains are fascinating and grand
And wondrously created by the Almighty's command;
And the works of the Almighty there's few can understand
Who knows but it might be a part of Fairyland?

Because there are churches of ice, and houses glittering like glass
And for scenic grandeur there's nothing can it surpass,
Besides there's monuments and spires, also ruins
Which serve for a safe retreat from the wild bruins. . . .

The icy mountains they're higher than a brig's topmast
And the stranger in amusement stands aghast
As he beholds the water flowing off the melted ice
Adown the mountain sides, that he cries out, Oh! how nice.

William McGonagall, *Greenland's Icy Mountains, Poetic Gems*, 1890

Greenland white and Iceland green! The general unfairness of things.

William Sansom, *Blue Skies Brown Studies*, 1961

Greenlanders

As concerning the people, they are (as I doe suppose) a kinde of Samoites, or wandring Nation travelling in the Summer time in Companies together, first to one place, and having stayed in that place a certayne time in hunting and fishing for Deere and Seales with other fish, streight they remove themselves with their Tents and baggage to another. They are men of a reasonable stature being browne in colour, very like to the people of the East and West Indies. They be very active and warlike, as we did perceive in their Skirmishes with us, using their Slings and Darts very nimbly. They eat their meate raw, or a little perboyled either with bloud, Oyle, or a little water which they doe drinke. They apparrell themselves in the skinnes of such beasts as they kill, but especially with Seales skins and fowle skins, dressing the skins very soft and smooth, with the haire and feathers on, wearing in Winter the haire and feather sides inwards, and in Summer outwards. Their Weapons are Slings, Darts, Arrowes, having their Bowes fast tyed together with sinewes; their Arrowes have but two feathers, the head of the same being for the most part of bone, made in manner and forme of a Harping Iron. . . . What knowledge they have of God I cannot certainly say, but I suppose them to be Idolaters, worshipping the Sunne.

James Hall, 1605, in *Purchas his Pilgrimes,* 1625

A stunted, stern, uncouth, amphibious stock
Hewn from the living marble of the rock
Or sprung from mermaids, and in ocean's bed
With orcs and seals in sunless caverns bred,
They might have held, from unrecorded time
Sole patrimony in that hideous clime,
So lithe their limbs, so fenced their frames to bear
The intensest rigours of the polar air;
Nimble and muscular and keen to run
The rein-deer down a circuit of the sun;
To climb the slippery cliffs, explore their cells,
And storm and sack the sea-birds citadels;
In bands, through snows, the mother-bear to trace
Slay with their darts the cubs in her embrace,
And while she licked their bleeding wounds to brave
Her deadliest vengeance in her inmost cave.
Train'd with inimitable skill to float
Each, balanced, in his bubble of a boat,
With dexterous paddle, steering through the spray,
With poised harpoon to strike his lunging prey
As though the skiff, the seaman, car and dart
Were one compacted body, by one heart
With instinct, motion, pulse, empower'd to ride
A human Nautilus upon the tide;
Or with a fleet of Kayaks to assail
The desperation of the stranded whale,
When wedg'd twixt jagged rocks he writhes and rolls
In agony among the ebbing shoals,
Washing the waves to foam, until the flood
From wounds like geysers seems a bath of blood,
Echo all night dumb – pealing to his roar
Till morn beholds him slain along the shore.

James Montgomery, *Greenland,* 1819

GRENADA

These people, upon hearing we were bound to Grenada, said, 'Oh, Grenada all gone, no Grenada now.' This inducing further enquiry, we learnt that the chief town called St George's, had recently been entirely destroyed by fire. . . .

William Hickey, *Memoirs,* 1749–1809

Grenada, the only place I ever left, after no matter how short a residence without a particle of regret.

Ibid.

I like the Grenadans much; they have a picture of an island, they give turtle, porter, and champagne in abundance and perfection, they lend horses, and send pines and pomegranates on board your ship, in short they are right pleasant Christians; . . . one thing only did I find fault with, but that one thing is, I am sorry to say, a mountain. Gentlemen of Grenada and the Grenadines as far as Cariacou, where are your wives? where are your heirs? you will say the fashion is Persian and that they are within the veils; you will say that there are just forty ladies in the island! it may be so, but show them, gentlemen, to the world and put to silence the moralities of Englishmen and Barbadians. Of Grenada alone I can say that I never saw a single lady all the while I was in it.

H.N. Coleridge, *Six Months in the West Indies* (in 1825), 1827

The head-quarters of the world for fruit.

Anthony Trollope, *The West Indies and the Spanish Main,* 1859

Grenada, immemorially has been as funny a word in Trinidad as Wigan is in England.

V.S. Naipaul, *The Middle Passage,* 1962

Grenadines (from the air)

As the air cleared, the entire archipelago of the Grenadines appeared: innumerable islets scattered across the sea from horizon to horizon, and seeming as they slid slowly southwards, to writhe and change shape and turn over: violoncellos, scissors, earwigs, pairs of braces, old boots, cogwheels, armadillos, palettes, wishbones, oak leaves, boomerangs and bowler hats, all of them hanging mysteriously in a blue dimensionless dream. Haloed at the surface with pale green water, their pedestals, visible until they were obscured by darkness, sank sharply to the bottom of the sea.

Patrick Leigh Fermor, *The Traveller's Tree,* 1951

GUADELOUPE

The hills succeeded each other in a soft interlock of curves and all the outlines were blurred by the shapes of trees. Palms and bananas opened their heavy fans overhead. . . . These low hills are called *mornes* in the French islands, and as we advanced farther among them, isolated huts appeared in clearings on their flanks. . . . These green slopes, hemmed in by their Garden of Eden forests, have an almost miraculous beauty. In the extending shadows of the late-afternoon sunlight they appeared as idyllic and eternal as the clearings in a rather sad heaven.

Patrick Leigh Fermor, *The Traveller's Tree,* 1951

GUATEMALA

There was but one side to politics in Guatemala. Both parties have a beautiful way of producing unanimity of opinion, by driving out of the country all who do not agree with them.

J.L. Stephens, *Incidents of Travel in Central America Chiapas and Yucatan,* 1841

. . . that alien, point-blank, green and actual Guatemala.

Wallace Stevens, 'Arrival at the Waldorf', *Parts of a World,* 1942

I'd never heard of this bloody place Guatemala until I was in my seventy-ninth year.

Sir Winston Churchill, Remark 28 June 1954, in Lord Moran, *Winston Churchill, The Struggle for Survival,* 1966

Antigua (formerly Santiago de Guatemala/La Ciudad Vieja)

This city of Guatemala, called by the Spaniards Santiago, or St. James of Guatemala, is seated in a valley, which is not above two miles and a half broad, for the high mountains do keep it close in; but in length towards the South Sea it continues a wide and champaign country, opening itself broader a little beyond that town, which to this day is called la Ciudad Vieja, or the Old City, standing somewhat above three miles from Guatemala. . . . The Chiefest mountains which straighten in this city and valley are two, called volcanoes, the one being a volcano of water, and the other a volcano or mountain of fire, termed so by the Spaniards, though very improperly a volcano may be said to contain water. . . . These two famous mountains stand almost the one over against the other, on each side of the valley. That of water hanging on the south side almost perpendicularly over the city; the other of fire standing lower from it, more opposite to the old city.

Thomas Gage, *The English-American . . . or, A New Survey of the West Indies,* 1648 (of 1630s)

If only the Conquistadores had come, say, eighty years earlier! Then Antigua might have been filled with lovely Gothic ruins.

Mr and Mrs Maudsley, *A Glimpse at Guatemala,* 1899

There is nothing grand at Antigua; but there is much that is charming; much that is surprising and queer; much – indeed everything – that is picturesque and romantic in the most extravagantly eighteenth century style. Piranesis confront you at every corner; there is hardly a back garden without its Hubert Robert or its Panini. Wherever one looks fantastic ruins fill the foreground and behind them rise, not modest Alban hills, not poor little Soracte, but gigantic volcanoes, as high as Monte Rosa, and almost as shapely as Fuji-yama. It is a thousand pities that his pilgrimage never took Childe Harold as far as Guatemala.

Aldous Huxley, *Beyond the Mexique Bay,* 1934

Between Antigua and Quezaltenango

For the first time we saw fields of wheat and peach-trees. The country was poetically called Europa; and though the Volcano de Agua still reared in full sight its stupendous head, it resembled the finest part of England on a magnificent scale.

J.L. Stephens, *Incidents of Travel in Central America Chiapas and Yucatan,* 1841

Lake Atitlan

Lake Como, it seems to me, touches the limit of the permissibly picturesque; but Atitlan is Como with the additional embellishment of several immense volcanoes. It is really too much of a good thing.

Aldous Huxley, *Beyond the Mexique Bay,* 1934

All this time in spite of sharp descents the road was climbing, eventually coming out onto a ridge or mountain crest along which it continues till, suddenly, at a certain point you see Lake Atitlan below you. This is the best view of it. Nothing can ever come up to this first moment of seeing it below you at its widest expanse, two thousand feet down, unruffled, blue as a peacock's breast, and rising to a high horizon across fifteen miles of water, with three magnificent volcanoes, San Pedro and Toliman together, so that from certain places they look to be one volcano, and this Atitlan. It is a view that qualifies beyond argument to be one of the wonders of the world, though not altogether or entirely pleasant because its very calm is a little sinister and threatening.

Sacheverell Sitwell, *Golden Wall and Mirador,* 1961

Guatemala City

The morning air was the most pure and invigorating I ever breathed. Situated in the 'Tierras templadas,' or temperate regions, on a table-land five thousand feet above the sea, the climate of Guatimala is that of perpetual spring, and the general aspect reminded me of the best class of Italian cities. It is laid out in blocks of from three to four hundred feet square, the streets parallel and crossing each other at right angles. The houses, made to resist the action of earthquakes, are of only one story, but very spacious, with large doors and windows, protected by iron balconies. In the centre of the city stands the Plaza, a square of one hundred and fifty yards on each side, paved with stone, with a colonnade on three sides; on one of these stands the old vice-regal palace and hall of the Audiencia; on another are the cabildo and other city buildings; on the third the custom-house and palace of the ci-devant Marquisate of Aycinena; and on the fourth side is the Cathedral, a beautiful edifice, in the best style of modern architecture, with the archiepiscopal palace on one side, and the College de Infantes on the other. In the centre is a large stone fountain, of imposing workmanship, supplied with pipes from the mountains about two leagues distant; and the area is used as a market-place. The churches and convents correspond with the beauty of the plaza, and their costliness and grandeur would attract the attention of tourists in Italy or Spain. . . .

. . . I have seldom been more favourably impressed with the first appearance of any city. . . .

J.L. Stephens, *Incidents of Travel in Central America Chiapas and Yucatan,* 1841

Guatemala may still be regarded as the capital of all the isthmus territories. They fabricate there not only priests and wax images, but doctors and lawyers, and all those expensive luxuries for the production of which the air of a capital is generally considered necessary.

Anthony Trollope, *The West Indies and the Spanish Main,* 1859

The market at Guatemala is the only place where I have seen reality outdoing a Dutch still life.

Aldous Huxley, *Beyond the Mexique Bay,* 1934

Guatemala City, an extremely horizontal place, is like a city on its back. Its ugliness, which is a threatened look (the low morose houses have earthquake cracks in their façades; the buildings wince at you with fright lines), is ugliest on those streets where, just past the last toppling houses, a blue volcano's cone bulges. I could see the volcanoes from the window of my hotel room. I was on the third floor, which was also the top floor. They were tall volcanoes and looked capable of spewing lava. Their beauty was undeniable; but it was the beauty of witches. The rumbles from their fires had heaved this city down.

Paul Theroux, *The Old Patagonian Express,* 1979

Huehuetenango

It suddenly occurred to me that it was unreasonable that an electric train should be rumbling through a subway immediately beneath us in Huehuetenango. I got up, grinning politely at our hosts, and, balancing the liquid in my glass, went to the door. The lamps in the plaza jogged about like spots in front of my eyes, and then, coming through the muffled din . . . I heard a noise like very heavy furniture being moved about in uncarpeted rooms somewhere in space. The world shifted slightly, softened, rippled, and there was an aerial tinkling of shattered glass. I felt a brief unreasoning stab of the kind of panic that comes when in a nightmare one suddenly begins a fall into endless darkness. . . .

'A quiet evening,' I remarked. 'With just one small earthquake thrown in.'

'A tremor, not an earthquake,' Calmo said. 'An earthquake must last at least half a minute. This was a shaking of secondary importance.'

There was a pause while he translated his next sentence into English. He then said: 'Sometimes earthquakes may endure for a minute, or even two minutes. In that case it is funny. . . . No, not funny, I mean very serious.'

Norman Lewis, *The Changing Sky,* 1959

Rabinal

Rabinal . . . hath all that heart can wish for pleasure and life of man. It inclineth rather to heat than cold, but the heat is moderate and much qualified with the many cool and shady walks. There is not any Indian fruit which is not there to be found. There are, besides the fruits of Spain, such as oranges, lemons, sweet and sour, citrons, pomegranates, grapes, figs, almonds, and dates. Only wheat is lacking. . . . For flesh, the town hath beef, mutton, kid, fowls, turkeys, quails, partridges, rabbits, pheasants; for fish it hath a river running by the houses, which yieldeth plenty both great and small.

Thomas Gage, *The English-American . . . or, A New Survey of the West Indies, 1648 – of 1630s*

Sierra Madre

Before us the great Sierra Madre, the natural bulwark of Central America, the grandeur and magnificence of the view disturbed only by the distressing reflection that we had to cross it.

J.L Stephens, *Incidents of Travel in Central America Chiapas and Yucatan,* 1841

GUIANAS

See also under Guyana and Surinam

The Empire of Guiana is directly East from Peru towards the Sea, and lieth under the Equinoctial line, and it hath more abundance of golde then any part of Peru, and as many or moe great Cities then ever Peru had when it flourished most . . . and I have bene assured by such of the Spaniards as have seene Manoa the Imperial Citie of Guiana, which the Spaniards call El Dorado, that for the greatnesse, for the riches, and for the excellent seat, it farre exceedeth any of the world, at least of so much of the world as is knowen to the Spanish Nation; it is founded upon a lake of salt water of 200. leagues long like unto Mare Caspium.

Sir Walter Ralegh, *The Discovery of Guiana*, 1595, in Richard Hakluyt, *Principal Navigations . . . of the English Nation*, 1598–1600

Guiana, whose rich feete are mines of golde,
Whose forehead knockes against the roofe of Starres,
Stands on her tip-toes at faire England looking
Kissing her hand, bowing her mightie breast,
And every sign of all submission making,
To be her sister, and the daughter both
Of our most sacred Maide: whose barrennesse
Is the true fruite of vertue, that may get,
Beare and bring forth anew in all perfection,
What heretofore savage corruption held
In barbarous Chaos; and in this affaire
Become her father, mother, and her heire.

George Chapman, 'De Guiana Carmen Epicum', 1596, in Richard Hakluyt, *Principal Navigations . . . of the English Nation*, 1598–1600

GULF STREAM

The Gulf Stream and the other great ocean currents are the last wild country there is left.

Ernest Hemingway, *Esquire*, April 1936, in *By-Line*, 1968

Cuba and the Gulf Stream

The biggest reason you live in Cuba is the great, deep blue river, three-quarters of a mile to a mile deep and sixty to eighty miles across, that you can reach in thirty minutes from the door of your farmhouse, riding through beautiful country to get to it, that has, when the river is right, the finest fishing I have ever known.

When the Gulf Stream is running well, it is a dark blue and there are whirlpools along the edges.

Ernest Hemingway, *Holiday*, July 1949, in *By-Line*, 1968

GUYANA

When I settle out of England, and take to the colonies for good and all, British Guiana shall be the land of my adoption. . . . At home there are prejudices against it, I know. They say that it is a low, swampy, muddy strip of alluvial soil, infested with rattlesnakes, gallinippers, and musquitoes as big as turkey-cocks; that yellow-fever rages there perennially; that the heat is unendurable; that society there is as stagnant as its waters; that men die as soon as they reach it; and when they live are such wretched creatures that life is a misfortune. . . . There never was a land so ill-spoken of, – and never one that deserved it so little. . . .

If there were but a snug secretaryship vacant there – and these things in Demerara are very snug – how I would invoke the goddess of patronage; how I would nibble around the officials of the Colonial Office; how I would stir up my friends' friends to write little notes to their friends! For Demerara is the Elysium of the tropics – the West Indian happy valley of Rasselas – the one true and actual Utopia of the Caribbean Seas – the Transatlantic Eden.

Anthony Trollope, *The West Indies and the Spanish Main*, 1859

The form of government is a mild despotism, tempered by sugar.

Ibid.

'And what is the prevailing disease of the colony?' I asked him.
'Dropsy with the black men,' he answered; 'and brandy with the white.'

Ibid.

This very fantastic and unhealthy land.

Lafcadio Hearn, Letter to Elizabeth Bisland, July 1887

Indians

The Indians, I learned later, are a solitary people, and it takes many hours heavy drinking to arouse any social interest in them. In fact, the more I saw of the Indians, the greater I was struck by their similarity to the English. They like living with their own families at great distances from their neighbours; they regard strangers with suspicion and despair; they are unprogressive and unambitious, fond of pets, hunting, and fishing; they are undemonstrative in love, unwarlike, morbidly modest; their chief aim seems to be on all occasions to render themselves inconspicuous; in all points, except in their love of strong drink, and perhaps in their improvidence, the direct opposite of the negro.

Evelyn Waugh, *Ninety-two Days*, 1934

Guyanese

Inhospitable, reactionary and lethargic except when predatory.

V.S. Naipaul, *The Middle Passage*, 1962

Slavery, the land, the latifundia, Bookers, indenture, the colonial system, malaria: all these have helped to make a society that is at once revolutionary and intensely reactionary, and have made the Guianese what he is: slow, sullen, independent though deceptively yielding, proud of his particular corner of Guiana, and sensitive to any criticism he does not utter himself. When the Guianese face goes blank and the eyes are fixed on you, you know that receptivity has ceased and that you are going to be told what the speaker believes you want to hear. It is hard to know what the Guianese are thinking; but if you make up your mind in advance you will find much corroboration.

Ibid.

Georgetown (formerly Demarara)

I believe I am beginning to write absurdities: it is so hot that rain-clouds form in one's head.

Lafcadio Hearn, Letter to Elizabeth Bisland, July 1887

Broad streets with detached wood buildings. Some quite considerable villas. Sordid emporiums. Scotto-Flemish town hall in matchboarding and cast iron. . . . General impression of Georgetown that I don't mind how soon I leave it. Too diffuse.

Evelyn Waugh, *Diary,* 23 December 1932

Georgetown is a white wooden city. One would like to sketch it on rough dark grey paper, using black ink, and thick white paint, to suggest the lightness and fragility of the two-storeyed buildings, a fragility most apparent at night, when light comes through verandas on the top floor, through windows, through open lattice-work, and the effect is of those chinese ivory palace-miniatures lit up from within. The city was founded by the British, but escaped being built by them.

V.S. Naipaul, *The Middle Passage,* 1962

H

HAITI (and Dominican Republic = Hispaniola)

The Countrie-men called the Iland of Hispaniola, Ayti and Quisqueya, which signifieth Roughnesse, and a great Countrie. The figure of it is like a Chestnut leafe. . . .

Antonio de Herrera, 1601, in *Purchas his Pilgrimes,* 1625

The chiefest of all the islands of this New World, . . . is called Hispaniola and formerly by the natives Haiti, which lamenteth the loss of at least three millions of Indians murdered by her new masters of Spain. This island is the biggest as yet discovered in all the world. It is in compass about 1,500 miles, and enjoyeth a temperate air, a fertile soil, and rich mines, and it trades much in amber, sugar, ginger, hides, and wax. It is reported for certain that here in twenty days herbs will ripen and roots also and be fit to be eaten. It yieldeth in nothing to Cuba, but excelleth in three things especially. First in the fineness of the gold, which is here more pure and unmixed. Secondly, in the increase of the sugar, one sugar cane here filling twenty, and sometimes thirty measures. And thirdly in the goodness of the soil for tillage, the corn here yielding an hundred fold.

This country is so replenished with swine and cattle that they become wild among the woods and mountains, so that ships that want provisions go ashore here, where it is little inhabited, and kill cattle and wild swine till they have a plentiful provision. Much of this country is not inhabited by reason that the Indians are quite consumed.

Thomas Gage, *The English-American . . . or, A New Survey of the West Indies,* 1648 (of 1630s)

Hear are a sort of Vagabons that are saved from the gallowes in Spaine and the king doth send them heare: Thes goe by the name of Cow killers, and indeed it is thayer trad . . . If it were not for theas Cowkillers and the Negors the spaniyards were not abell to hould up his hand against any ennemie, for the spaniyards are soe roten with the pox and soe lothegic that they cannot goe 2 mile but they are redie to die.

Henry Whistler, 18 April 1655, in C.H. Firth (ed.), *The Narrative of General Venables,* 1900

I don't much mind naked savages dancing round fires, performing dreadful rites, but I strongly object to them if they wear frock-coats and silk hats.

Richard Curle, *Wanderings – A Book of Travel and Reminiscence,* 1920

Tomorrow I go to Haiti. They say the President is a *Perfect Dear*!

Ronald Firbank, Postcard to Osbert Sitwell, in Sitwell's, *Noble Essences or Courteous Revelations,* 1950

Smart life in Haiti – the dazzling white tropical suits, the dark heads and hands – resembles a photographic negative. Only white chauffeurs at the wheel of the grand limousines are absent to complete the illusion.

Patrick Leigh Fermor, *The Traveller's Tree,* 1951

The Taxi-driver from Port au Prince airport offered me voodoo, folk-dancing, cock-fighting, gambling, Haitian women, Dominican women, Spanish women, women on women, men on men, and other, less mentionable delicacies. When I showed no appetite for any of them, he tried another line – a trip up into the mountains, five thousand feet above the sea. A hotel was all I wanted for the moment, and when he at last took me to one I found a Bible on the bedside table. Haiti has something for everybody.

But Haiti has very little for the Haitians.

Nicholas Wollaston, *Red Rumba,* 1962

I have seldom been in a country that charmed me more or left me feeling so depressed, and a 'joke' that a sad intellectual in Port au Prince told me stays in the mind, 'God may have had to make us black, but why did he also have to make Haiti?'

Mark Frankland, 'Haiti: Suicide in the Sun', *Observer,* 17 July 1977

It is the destiny of the people of Haiti to suffer.

President Duvalier, quoted by V.S. Naipaul, *The Return of Eva Peron,* 1980

Peu de Chose

We passed through a village called Peu de Chose, full of ghostly black versions of French grandees with white

Napoleon beards, panama hats, spats and Malacca canes.

Norman Lewis, *The Changing Sky,* 1959

Port au Prince

The destitute of Port au Prince camp out in one of the world's most terrific *bidonvilles,* a kind of slum Venice in which the canals are open drains.

Norman Lewis, *The Changing Sky,* 1959

Cape Tiburon

Cape Tiburon lyeth sliding downe to the Seaward, and maketh a sharpe cliffe like the snout of a Tiburon or sharke-fish; and upon the top thereof it appeareth like white wayes with certaine gullets or dreines upon it, which are caused by the passage of the water from the mountaines in the Winter time.

A Second Ruttier, in Richard Hakluyt, *Principal Navigations . . . of the English Nation,* 1598–1600

HAWAII (USA)

O, how my spirit languishes
To step ashore in the Sanguishes. . . .

Robert Louis Stevenson, Letter to Sidney Colvin, 16 October 1888

The Sandwich Islands do not interest us very much; we live here, oppressed with civilisation, and look for good things in the future.

Robert Louis Stevenson, Letter to Mrs Adelaide Boodle, 6 April 1889

No alien land in all the world has any deep, strong charm for me, but that one; no other land could so longingly and beseechingly haunt my sleeping and waking, through half a lifetime, as that one has done. Other things leave me, but it abides.

Mark Twain, Speech quoted in New York *Sun,* 4 April 1889

The Sandwich Islands remain my idea of the perfect thing in the matter of tropical islands. I would add another storey to Mauna Loa's 16,000 feet if I could, and make it particularly bold and steep and craggy and forbidding and snowy; and I would make that volcano spout its lava-floods out of its summit instead of its sides; but aside from these non-essentials I have no corrections to suggest. I hope these will be attended to; I do not wish to have to speak of it again.

Mark Twain, *More Tramps Abroad,* 1897

In what other land save this one is the commonest form of greeting not 'Good day,' nor 'How d'ye do,' but 'Love'? That greeting is *Aloha* – love, I love you, my love to you. . . . It is a positive affirmation of the warmth of one's own heart-giving.

Jack London, 'My Hawaiian Aloha', 1916, in *ibid.*

Hawaii is a paradise – and I can never cease proclaiming it; but I must append one word of qualification: *Hawaii is a paradise for the well-to-do.* It is not a paradise for the unskilled labourer from the mainland, nor for the person without capital from the mainland. . . . It must be remembered that Hawaii is very old . . . comparatively. When California was a huge cattle ranch, for hides and tallow . . . Hawaii was publishing newspapers and boasting schools of higher learning. . . . The shoestring days are past. The land and industries of Hawaii are owned by old families and large corporations, and Hawaii is only so large.

Ibid.

Hawaiians

We found all the Women of these Islands but little influenced by interested motives in their intercourse with us, as they would almost use violence to force you into their Embrace regardless whether we gave them any thing or not, and in general they were as fine girls as any we had seen in the south Sea Islands.

David Samwell, *Journal,* 31 January 1778

But a diversion the most common is upon the Water, where there is a very great Sea and surf breaking upon the Shore. The Men sometimes 20 or 30 go without the Swell of the Surf, & lay themselves flat upon an oval piece of plank about their size and breadth, they keep their legs close on the top of it, & their arms are us'd to guide the plank, they wait the time for the greatest Swell that sets on Shore, & altogether push forward with their Arms to keep on its top, it sends them in with a most astonishing Velocity, & the great art is to guide the plank so as always to keep in a proper direction on the top of the Swell, & as it alters its direction. If the Swell drives him close to the rocks before he is overtaken by its break he is much praised. On first seeing this very dangerous diversion I did not conceive it possible but that some of them must be dashed to mummy against the sharp rocks, but just before they reach the shore, if they are very near, they quit the plank, & dive under till the Surf is broke, when the piece of plank is sent many yards by the force of the Surf from the beach. The greatest number are generally overtaken by the break of the swell, the force of which they avoid, diving and swimming under the water out of its impulse. By such like exercises these men may be said to be almost amphibious.

James King, *Journal,* March 1779

Honolulu

I had fancied that in going to the Sandwich Islands, I was going to an uncivilized, heathen place. Imagine then my disappointment at finding an ordinary looking city, with pavements and electric lights and telephones all over the place. Actually, I have not since found a place where the telephone was in such general use. People telephoned invitations to visit or ride, and telephoned when they were ready, when about to start; and when they arrived, they telephoned home to that effect, and so on.

Lilian Leland, *Travelling Alone, A Woman's Journey Round the World,* 1890

Somebody said to me, when I told them I was going round the world that I would find Honolulu 'up to sample.' It most certainly is.

Alfred Viscount Northcliffe, *My Journey Round the World* (August 1921), 1923

'Pep' is its motto, 'Zip' its watchword.

Crosbie Garstin, *The Dragon and the Lotus,* 1928

I have several old sea-faring friends who visited Honolulu away back in the seventies or eighties, and at the mere mention of the place their mouths twitch and their eyes light up.

'Honolulu! Yes, I was there in the little *Minerva,* God knows how long ago. We came up from the Gilberts against the nor east Trades. It was a jolly spot! Every house wide open and everybody gave hops and picnics. Sat out eleven dances running with the same girl under one of those pink shower-trees and swore to love her till Doomsday. I was a midshipman then and everything was deuced romantic – a warm starry night and the scent of oleanders all about – you know how it is. Honolulu!'

Or, 'Ornolulu! Cripes, yes! Was there in the 'ull whaler, *Mary Fulton,* 'ome-bound from the Bering. Snow, ice, misery, an' stinkin' little Eskimos – then all of a sudden-like them there islands – a mass o' flowers an' fruit, an' everybody laughin'. I got a skinful, slept out under a bush all night and woke up next mornin' fair smothered, like a corpse in them there ginger blossoms. The Kanaka girls 'avin' their fun. An' not a cent gone from my pockets, sir, not a cent. Everybody smilin' an' go as you please. Why, I've seen the bloomin' king sittin' in a saloon in 'is pyjamas, playin' poker with the whaler captains. I 'ave, so 'elp me! 'Ornolulu!'

Ibid.

Kealakekua Bay

The setting sun was flaming upon it, a Summer shower was falling, and it was spanned by two magnificent rainbows. Two men who were in advance of us rode through these and for a moment their garments shone with a more than regal splendour. Why did not Captain Cook have taste enough to call his great discovery the Rainbow Islands? These charming spectacles are visible to you at every turn; they are common in all the islands; they are visible every day and frequently at night also – not the silvery bow we see once in an age in the States, by moonlight, but barred with all bright and beautiful colours, like the children of the sun and rain. . . . What the sailors call 'rain dogs' – little patches of rainbow – are often seen drifting about in these latitudes, like stained cathedral windows.

Mark Twain, *Roughing It,* 1872

Kilauea Crater

Here was a vast perpendicular-walled cellar, nine hundred feet deep in some places, thirteen hundred in others, level-floored, and *ten miles in circumference!* . . . There was a heavy fog over the crater and it was splendidly illuminated by the glare from the fires below. The illumination was two miles wide and a mile high perhaps; and if you ever, on a dark night and at a distance, beheld the light from thirty or forty blocks of distant buildings all on fire at once, reflected strongly against overhanging clouds, you can form a fair idea of what this looked like. . . .

The 'cellar' was tolerably well lighted up. For a mile and a half in front of us, and half a mile on either side, the floor of the abyss was magnificently illuminated; beyond these limits the mists hung down their gauzy curtains and cast a deceptive gloom over all that made the twinkling fires in the remote corners of the crater seem countless leagues removed – made them seem like the camp-fires of a great army far away. . . . You could not compass it – it was the idea of eternity made tangible – and the longest end of it made visible to the naked eye. . . .

The greater part of the vast floor of the desert under us was as black as ink, and apparently smooth and level; but over a mile square of it was ringed and streaked and striped with a thousand branching streams of liquid and gorgeously brilliant fire! It looked like a colossal railroad map of the State of Massachusetts done in chain lightning upon a midnight sky.

Mark Twain, *Roughing it,* 1872

Molokai

The place as regards scenery, is grand, gloomy, and bleak. Mighty mountain walls descending sheer along the whole face of the island into a sea unusually deep; the front of the mountain ivied and furred with clinging forest, one viridescent cliff: about halfway from east to west, the low, bare, stony promontory edged in between the cliff and ocean; the two little towns (Kalawao and Kalaupapa) seated on either side of it, as bare almost as bathing machines upon a beach; and the population – gorgons and chimeras dire.

Robert Louis Stevenson, Letter to Sidney Colvin, June 1889

HONDURAS

Tegucigalpa

Above the river stands the President's palace, a fantastic child's fort, with turrets and battlements and sentries dozing over their bayonets, and apologies to Balmoral, New Delhi, Saint Pancras and the Alhambra. It was hard to believe that any serious President could have the face to live in such a sugar-plum castle.

Nicholas Wollaston, *Red Rumba,* 1962

HONG KONG

A barren Island with hardly a House upon it.

Lord Palmerston, Letter to Sir Charles Elliot, 21 April 1841

More was to be learned by a visit to the Chinese Museum I saw in Boston, than could be seen, at the expense of leather to the amount of a new pair of boots, in trudging around promiscuously in Hong Kong. One thing did strike me – i.e. that the Chinese have a peculiar odour (not of Sanctity) about them – something like that hovering about a coffin, an empty one, of course, may be the new velvet imparts it to the article, and their calico clothing is perhaps the cause for the Chineys. Any how *It is there.*

Edward Yorke McCauley, Diary, 27 July 1853, *With Perry in Japan,* 1942

What is the secret of this sudden and enormous growth in population and trading importance, of a barren rock? This must be among the first questions of a stranger. Hong Kong itself, he sees at a glance, produces nothing but granite boulders and the thinnest scrub, – beneath the hottest of suns, and least healthy of climates. The city of Victoria, with its Cathedral and Episcopal palace, its Government House, and Supreme Court, with all its Merchants' palatial houses, is perhaps the very last spot, on all the coast of China, where a sensible man would have thought of placing house or home, if the choice had been left to himself. Victoria Peak rises 1,200 feet above the level of the sea, and stretches its solid bulk across the whole line of the city, effectually shutting out the south-west breeze, – and all the cool air to be had during six months of a most oppressive summer when everyone gasps for want of that needful aliment. From this arid rock many go home sick every year, with spleens much larger than their fortunes; and not a few remain, to have their bones laid in six feet of Chinese earth, in the 'Happy Valley,' where an English cemetery has been located.

Sir Rutherford Alcock, *The Capital of the Tycoon,* 1863

Hong Kong for all the world like some Spanish or Italian town with its white terraces, and coloured venetians, nestling in masses of dark green foliage at the foot of the bare rugged peak.

Harry de Windt, *From Pekin to Calais by Land,* 1889

All Hong-Kong is built on the sea-face; the rest is fog. One muddy road runs for ever in front of a line of houses which are partly Chowringee and partly Rotherhithe.

Rudyard Kipling, *From Sea to Sea,* 1889

Vice must be pretty much the same all the world over, but if a man wishes to get out of pleasure with it, let him go to Hong Kong.

'Of course things are out and away better at 'Frisco,' said my guide, 'but we consider this pretty fair for the Island.'

Ibid.

and Canton

Hong Kong and Canton are as close to each other as lips are to teeth.

Chinese saying, probably early twentieth century, quoted in O.M. Green, *Discovering China,* n.d.

(Perhaps applying the old Chinese saying 'When the lips are gone, the teeth are cold', to mean that if Hong Kong is not controlled by China, Canton is in danger.)

Hong Kong illuminated . . . is wonderful. Imagine a giant Monte Carlo with a hundred times as many lights!

Alfred Viscount Northcliffe, *My Journey Round the World* (November 1921), 1923

Its leading characters are wise and witty,
Their suits well-tailored, and they wear them well,
Have many a polished parable to tell
About the *mores* of a trading city.

Only the servants enter unexpected,
Their silent movements make dramatic news;
Here in the East our bankers have erected
A worthy temple to the Comic Muse.

Ten thousand miles from home and What's-Her-Name
A bugle on this late Victorian hill
Puts out the soldier's light; off-stage a war

Thuds like the slamming of a distant door:
Each has his comic role in life to fill,
Though life be neither comic nor a game.

W.H. Auden, 'A Voyage, IV. Hong Kong', December 1938 in *Journey to a War*, 1939

In one of my books I have claimed to recognise immediately an island of the first water, as diamond merchants recognise a diamond. Hong Kong is in that class.

Compton Mackenzie, *All Over the Place*, 1948

British Hong Kong dangles freakishly from the great underbelly of Communist China like some small but surprising anatomical monstrosity.

Dennis Bloodworth, *Chinese Looking Glass*, 1967

The city . . . appears at the foot of its radiant mountains: it blazes like a great flower of light with neon stamens and petals of floodlit stone.

James Kirkup, *Streets of Asia*, 1969

'Hong Kong subscribes,' one distinguished public official observed to me, 'to Victorian economic principles: these are the only economic principles that have ever actually *succeeded.*'

Jan Morris, 'Anglo-China', *Travels*, 1976

You may not like it. . . . We don't ask you to like it. We don't *expect* you to like it. But you must admit it *works.*

Jan Morris, quoting her European guide, in *ibid.*

Had they a message for me to take back to England, I enquired?

'Yes,' they said in chorus. 'Don't stop us showing how well we can do in Hong Kong.' I encountered a slightly different attitude from one of the young British at our party the next night.

'It's got to be stopped, it's got to be stopped,' he said.

'What's this?' I asked, fearing some frightful scandal was about to be revealed.

'All this money-making has got to be stopped,' he said. 'It's not healthy for them. They mustn't be allowed to go on running things this way.'

Edward Heath, *Travels, People and Places in My Life*, 1977

The usual life-saving hours are from 9 am to 6.30 pm on week days. During week-ends at the more popular and bigger beaches . . . the life-saving hours are extended – from 8.00 am to 7.30 pm.

Hong Kong Tourist Association Leaflet number 8, 1977

Suggestions on how to make the most of your visit . . . see a Chinese sentimental or Kung Fu movie. . . . Photograph members of the Royal Hong Kong Police directing traffic from pagoda rostrums. . . . See Deep Water Bay where 'Love is a Many Splendoured Thing' was filmed. . . . For an unusual meal try Mongolian Hot Pot. . . . Look into China from the Lok Ma Chau border post. . . . Have your fortune told with the aid of a small bird.

'Exciting Things to Do in Hong Kong', *Hong Kong Tourist Association Information Leaflet number 3*, 1977

A borrowed place living on borrowed time.

Anon, quoted in *The Times*, 5 March 1981

HUNGARY

Thes hungrours be good men of warre and hath contynually warre with the turkes, thei be people of a myddle stature and robustuos and of an hard conversation.

Roger Barlow, *A Brief Summe of Geographie*, *c.* 1540

The Hungarians have ever been theftuous, treacherous, and false; so that one brother will hardly trust another, which infidelity among themselves, and distracted deceitful governors, was the chief cause of their overthrow and subjection under infidels. . . .

Now as for the soil of Hungary, and kingdom itself, and for the goodness of it, it may be termed the granary of Ceres, the garden of Bacchus, the pasturage of Pan, and the richest beauty of Sylvan; for I found the wheat here growing higher than my head, the vines overlooking the trees, the grass justling with my knees,and the high sprung woods threatening the clouds; surely, if I should enter on particulars here, I have more subject to work upon than any kingdom that ever I saw.

William Lithgow, *Rare Adventures and Painfull Peregrinations*, 1614/32

Arms and freedom have ever been the ruling, though too often the unsuccessful, passion of the Hungarians, who are endowed by nature with a vigorous constitution of soul and body.

Edward Gibbon, *The Decline and Fall of the Roman Empire*, 1776–88

Hungarians! Save the world! Renew the stories
Of men who against hope repell'd the chain,
And make the world's dead spirit leap again!
On land renew that Greek exploit, whose glories
Hallow the Salaminian promontories,
And the Armada flung to the fierce main.

Matthew Arnold, *Sonnet to the Hungarian Nation*, 1849

Amanda: . . . I know what the Hungarians are too.
Elyot: What are they?
Amanda: Very wistful. It's all those pretzles I shouldn't wonder.
Elyot: And the Poostza; I always felt the Poostza was far too big, Danube or no Danube.

Noel Coward, *Private Lives*, 1930

The Magyar aristocrat is unlike any of us who dwell in Nordic climes: he has no false shame about himself. It is not necessary to remind him that he is a noble, for he is so absolutely convinced of it that he makes no attempt to persuade you. He knows that the aristocrat is . . . a distinct sociological species.

Walter Starkie, *Raggle-Taggle*, 1933

In Hungary is the strongest, most pervasive nationalism in Europe. In the chauvinism sweepstakes the Hungarians beat even the Poles. A little story is relevant. The proud father of an eight-year-old schoolgirl entering a geography class bought her a globe. She surveyed it and burst into tears. 'Papa,' she wailed, 'I want a globe with only Hungary on it.'

John Gunther, *Inside Europe*, 1938 edn

suddenly uprose hungary
and she gave a terrible cry
"no slave's unlife shall murder me
for i will freely die"

she cried so high thermopylae
heard her and marathon
and all prehuman history
and finally The UN

"be quiet little hungary
and do as you are bid
a good kind bear is angary
we fear for the quo pro quid"

uncle sam shrugs his pretty
pink shoulders you know how
and he twitches a liberal titty
and lisps "i'm busy right now"

so rah-rah-rah democracy
let's all be as thankful as hell
and bury the statue of liberty
(because it begins to smell)

e.e. cummings, *Thanksgiving*, 1956

It is not enough to be Hungarian – one must also have talent.

Slogan seen in Toronto office, Alistair Horne, *Canada and the Canadians*, 1961

Hungarians form not only a local clique but also a world-wide conspiracy, third in importance only to homosexuals and Roman Catholics. A homosexual Roman Catholic Hungarian cannot posibly have a worry in the world, he will fall on his feet wherever he may find himself.

George Mikes, *Boomerang – Australia Rediscovered*, 1968

If you have a Hungarian for a friend you don't need any enemies.

Hungarian Proverb, quoted by Alexander Korda, in John Masters, *Pilgrim Son*, 1971

To be a Hungarian is a permanent joy.

Joseph Wechsberg, *The Lost World of the Great Spas*, 1979

Budapest

The *Danube* separates the two cities, in other respects one. Buda is upon an eminence above the western, and Pest below upon the eastern bank. Pest is a very large and handsome city. . . . The streets are full of shops; and there are two theatres: there is also a handsome theatre at Buda. We were quite surprised by the magnificence of these two cities, of which so little is known in other parts of Europe. Pest, situate in a plain, is adorned with public edifices, erected in a style of grandeur and elegance: it also boasts of a University; although as little heeded by the Universities of England, as Cambridge and Oxford are by its Hungarian Professors.

E.D. Clarke, *Travels in Various Countries*, 4th edn, 1818

In Budapest there is nothing but what the people and a natural brightness in the air make of it. Here things are what they seem; atmosphere is everything, and the atmosphere is almost one of illusion. Budapest lives, with a speed that thrusts itself, not unattractively, upon one at every moment. . . . The people, with their sombre, fiery, and regular faces have the look of sleepy animals about to spring.

Arthur Symons, *Cities*, 1903

Life in Budapest moves to a more rapid rhythm than elsewhere in Europe, as though every moment of the day had unlimited possibilities of emotional excitement.

Walter Starkie, *Raggle-Taggle*, 1933

I had heard Budapest described as the most beautiful city in Europe. It is strange and dramatic, to be sure, but there is something rather barbaric about it. It wants to belong to the West, but one remembers the Mongolians and the Turks. It is a mixture of baroque and Gothic, a spiky and hispid city: churches with high, sharp spires, minarets with needles like stings. An element of the goblinesque: the porcupine dome of the Parliament House, which stretches along the Danube its weighty and enormous length; the ubiquitous unendearing cupids; the curious pronglike shaft in front of the Matyas Church, on which a bulging mass of these cupids seem swarming like torpid bees, an exercise in the same kind of baroque bad taste as the monument to the Plague in Vienna, with its gruesome mess of tangled corpses.

Edmund Wilson, 'Notes from a European Diary', 1963–4, in *Europe without Baedeker,* 1967 edn

Debrecen

The people of Debrecen are hard-headed, democratic burghers of the Flemish type.

Walter Starkie, *Raggle-Taggle,* 1933

between Bakabanya and Schemnitz

The principal part of the road from Bakabanya to Schemnitz exhibits that grandeur of scenery which is represented by the best pictures of Gaspar Poussin: but some respects of it display the richer and milder dispositions of landscape characteristic of the works of Claude.

E.D. Clarke, *Travels in Various Countries,* 4th edn, 1818

River 'Tibiscus'

It is three parts water, and two parts fish.

Daniel Defoe, *A Tour through the Whole Island of Great Britain,* 1724–7

I

ICELAND

Iceland is the best land on which the sun shines.
Icelandic proverb

Of Island to write is little nede,
Save of Stock-fish.
Anon, *The Libel of English Policy, c.* 1437, in Richard Hakluyt, *Principal Navigations of the English Nation,* 1598–1600

Island . . . seemes afarre off, like winter clouds.
Dithmar Blefkens, *His Voyages . . .* , 1563, in *Purchas his Pilgrimes,* 1625

CHAP. XLII
Concerning Owls

There are no owls of any kind in the whole island.
Nils Horrebow, *The Natural History of Iceland,* 1758
(This is the full text of the chapter concerned.)

Strange Isle! a moment to poetic gaze
Rise in thy majesty of rocks and bays
Glens, fountains, caves, that seem not things of earth
But the wild shapes of some prodigious birth,
As if the Kraken, monarch of the sea
Wallowing abroad in his immensity
By polar storms and lightning shafts assailed
Wedg'd with ice-mountains here had fought and fail'd,
Perish'd – and in the petrifying blast,
His hulk became an island rooted fast;
– Rather, from ocean's dark foundations hurl'd
Thou art a type of his mysterious world
Buoy'd on the desolate abyss to show
What wonders of creation hide below.
James Montgomery, *Greenland,* 1819

I may mention in passing that an Icelandic bog is not good riding, and that the loose stones on the edge of a lava-field is like my idea of a half-ruined Paris barricade.
William Morris, Letter to his wife, 11 August 1871

I dreamed very distinctly this morning that I had come home again, and that Webb was asking me what sort of climate we had in Iceland; I cried out, 'atrocious!' and waking therewith heard the rain pattering on the tent.
William Morris, *Journal of Travel in Iceland,* 16 August 1871

Surely I have gained a great deal, and it was no idle whim that drew me here, but a true instinct for what I needed.
William Morris, Letter, 1873, in J.W. Mackail, *The Life of William Morris,* 1899

Alone in Iceland you are alone indeed, and the homeless, undisturbed wilderness gives something of its awful calm to the spirit. It was like listening to noble music, yet perplexed and difficult to follow. If the Italian landscape is like Mozart; if in Switzerland the sublimity and sweetness correspond in art to Beethoven; then we may take Iceland as the type of nature of the music of the moderns – say Schumann at his oddest and wildest.
Miss Oswald, *By Fell and Fjord,* 1882

The reason for hereness seems beyond conjecture,
There are no trees, or trains, or architecture
Fruits and greens are insufficient for health
And culture is limited by lack of wealth,
The tourist sights have nothing like Stonehenge
The literature is all about revenge.
And yet I like it, if only because this nation
Enjoys a scarcity of population
And cannot rise to many bores or hacks
Or paupers, or poor men paying Super-Tax.
Louis MacNeice, Letter to Graham and Anne Shepard, Reykjavik, 16 August 1936, in Louis MacNeice and W.H. Auden, *Letters from Iceland,* 1937

Fortunate island,
Where all men are equal
But not vulgar – not yet.
W.H. Auden, *Iceland Revisited,* 1964

There is something allegorical about the very fact of Iceland, something that puts most visitors in mind of still remoter grandeurs – Dantean visions of heaven or hell, or classical conceptions of Elysium, improbably transplanted to these icy realms with asphodels among the glaciers. This is an island of absolutes, where nothing is blurred, and sometimes it feels less like a country than a prophecy, a mystery play, or a topsy-turvy sort of Utopia.
James Morris, 'Iceland', *Places,* 1972

Icelanders

There are many of the Iselanders very proud and high minded, especially by reason of the strength of body which they have. I saw an Iselander, who easily put an Hamburg Tunne full of Ale to his mouth, drinking off it as if hee had had but one small measure.

Both Sexes in Iseland have the same habite, so that by the garments you shall not easily discerne whether it bee Man or Woman. . . . The Women-kinde there are very beautifull, but ornaments are wanting.

The whole Nation of the Islanders is much given to Superstitions, and they have Spirits familiarly serving them. For they onely are fortunate in Fishing, who are raised up by night of the Devill to goe a fishing.

. . . The Parents teach their male Children (even from their child-hood) letters and the Law of that Iland, so that very few men are found throughout the whole Iland, but they know Letters, and many Women use our letters and have also other characters, with the which they express some whole words of theirs, which words can hardly bee written with our letters. They give themselves to hardnesse, and fishing from their Infancie; for all their life consists in Fishing. They exercise not Husbandrie, because they have no Fields, and the greatest part of their foods consisteth in Fish, unsaverie Butter, Milke and Cheese. In stead of Bread they have Fish bruised with a Stone. Their Drinke is Water or Whay. So they live many yeeres, without medicine or Physitian. Many of them live till they bee one hundred and fiftie yeeres old. . . .

While they drinke, they sing the heroicall acts of their ancestors, not with any certaine composed order or melodie, but as it commeth in every mans head. Neither is it lawfull for any one to rise from the Table to make water, but for this purpose the daughter of the house, or another maid or woman attendeth alwayes at the Table, watchfull if any becken; to him that beckeneth shee gives the chamber-pot under the Table with her owne hands; the rest in the meane while grunt like Swine, least any noise bee heard. The water being powred out, hee washeth the Bason, and offereth his service to him that is willing, and he is accounted uncivill who abhorreth this fashion. They entertaine them that come unto them with a kisse, and they behond and looke each on other, if paradventure they may see Lice creeping on their garments, which greatly trouble them for want of linnen: if they see any, each taketh them from the other and as often as he taketh away one, so often doth he thanke him, with his head discovered, and this they doe one to the other, as long as they see one.

By night the Master of the house, with all his family, his wife and children lye in one room, covered with a cloth made of Wooll which they make. And the like clothes they lap under them, without straw or hay put under. All of them make water in one chamber-pot, with the which in the morning they wash their face, mouth, teeth, and hands; they allege many reasons thereof, to wit, that this makes a faire face, maintaineth the strength, confirmeth the sinewes in the hands, and preserveth the teeth from putrifaction.

Dithmar Blefkens, *His Voyages . . .*, 1563, in *Purchas his Pilgrimes*, 1625

Their commodities were greene fish, and Island lings and stockfish, and a fish which is called Scatefish: of all which they had great store. They had also kine, sheep and horses, and hay for their cattell, and for their horses. Wee saw also their dogs. Their dwelling houses were made on both sides with stones, and wood layd crosse over them, which was covered over with turfes of earth, and they are flat on the tops, and many of these stood hard by the shore. Their boates were made with wood and yron all along the keele like our English boates: and they had nayles for to nayle them withall, and fish-hookes and other things for to catch fish as we have here in England. They had also brasen kettles, and girdles and purses made of leather, and knoppes on top of them of copper, and hatchets, and other small tooles as necessary as we have. They drie their fish in the Sun, and when they are dry, they packe them up in the top of their houses.

Henry Morgan (1586), in Richard Hakluyt, *Principal Navigations . . . of the English Nation*, 1598–1600

Pistol: Pish for thee, Island dogge: thou prickeard cur of Island.

William Shakespeare, *Henry the Fift*, *c.* 1598–9

As most other nations, they have a strong propensity to their native place, though one might think they would find more pleasure in other countries.

Nils Horrebow, *The Natural History of Iceland*, 1758

A very characteristic feature of the race is the eye, dark and cold as a pebble – the mesmerist would despair at the first sight.

Richard Burton, *Ultima Thule*, 1895

They get up unexpectedly late in Iceland.

James Morris, 'Iceland', *Places*, 1972

A geyser

He comes, he comes: th'infurate Geyser springs
Up to the firmament on vapoury wings;
With breathless awe the mounting glory view;
While waiting clouds his steep ascent pursue.
But lo! a glimpse; – refulgent to the gale,
He starts all naked through the riven veil;
A fountain-column, terrible and bright,
A living, breathing, moving form of light:
From central earth to heaven's meridian thrown
The mighty apparition towers alone,
Rising as though for ever he could rise
Storm and resume his palace in the skies.

All foam and turbulence and wrath below;
Around his beams the reconciling bow; . . .
While mist and spray, condensed to sudden dews
The air illumine with celestial hues.
As if the bounteous sun were raining down
In richest gems of his imperial crown.
In vain the spirit wrestles to break free
Foot-bound to fathomless captivity;
A power unseen, by sympathetic spell
For ever working, – to his flinty cell
Recalls him from the ramparts of the spheres;
He yields, collapses, lessens, disappears;
Darkness receives him in her vague abyss
Around whose verge light froth and bubbles hiss.

James Montgomery, *Greenland,* 1819

Mount Hekla

High in the frozen north where Hecla glows
And melts in torrents his coeval snows;
O'er isles and oceans sheds a sanguine light,
Or shoots red stars amid the ebon night;
When, at his base entombed, with bellowing sound
Fell Giesar roared, and struggling shook the ground;
Pour'd from red nostrils, with her scalding breath,
A boiling deluge o'er the blasted heath;
And, wide in air, in misty volumes hurl'd
Contagious atoms o'er the alarm'd world.

Erasmus Darwin, 'The Economy of Vegetation', *The Botanic Garden,* 1791

Herdholt

Just think, though, what a mournful place this is – Iceland I mean – setting aside the pleasure of one's animal life there: the fresh air, the riding and rough life, and feeling of adventure – how every place and name marks the death of its short-lived eagerness and glory; and withal so little is the life changed in some ways: . . . But Lord! what littleness and helplessness has taken the place of the old passion and violence that had place here once – and all is unforgotten; so that one has no power to pass it by unnoticed: yet that must be something of a reward for the old life of the land, and I don't think their life now is more unworthy than most people's elsewhere, and they are happy enough by seeming. Yet it is an awful place: set aside the hope that the unseen sea gives you here, and the strange threatening change of the blue spiky mountains beyond the firth, and the rest seems emptiness and nothing else: a piece of turf under your feet, and the sky overhead, that's all; whatever solace your life is to have must come out of yourself or these old stories, not over hopeful themselves.

William Morris, *Journal of Travel in Iceland,* 6 August 1871

Reykjavik

The town now lying ahead is a commonplace-looking little town of wood principally; but there are pretty-looking homesteads on some of the islands off it, and the bright green of their home-meads is a great relief to us after all the grey of the sea, and the ice-hills. . . . Ashore we go and land in a street of little low wooden houses, pitched, and with white sash frames; the streets of black volcanic sand; little ragged gardens about some of the houses growing potatoes, cabbages, and huge stems of angelica: not a very attractive place, yet not very bad, better than a north-country town in England.

William Morris, *Journal of Travel in Iceland,* 14 July 1871

Even Reykjavik, where more than a third of the Icelanders live, is recognisably a fish-port still. . . . The trawlers chug in and out of town as familiar as suburban buses, the trucks bounce out of the docks, loaded deep with herring, and the stink of the fish-factory at the end of the quay hovers perpetually over that end of town. – 'Mm,' say the Icelanders appreciatively, 'the *money-smell*. . . . '

James Morris, 'Iceland', *Places,* 1972

INDIA

In India are many divers countries; and it is called India because of a water that runs through that land, the which men call Inde. In that water men find eels thirty foot long. And folk that dwell near that water are ill coloured, yellow and green. . . . Men of India are of that condition that they pass not commonly out of their own land, for they dwell under a planet that is called Saturn.

John Mandeville, *The Book of John Mandeville, c.* 1360

But lest this remote countrey should seem like an earthly Paradise without any discommodities: I must needes take notice there of many Lions, Tygres, Wolves, Jackals (which seeme to be wild Dogs) and many other harmefull beasts. In their Rivers are many Crocodiles, and on the Land over-growne Snakes, with other venimouse and pernicious Creatures. In our houses there we often meete with Scorpions, whose stinging is most sensible and deadly, if the patient have not presently some Oyle that is made of them, to anoint the part affected, which is a present cure. The aboundance of Flyes in those parts doe likewise much annoy us, for in the heate of the day their numberlesse number is such as that we can be quiet in no place for them, they are ready to cover our meate as soone as it is placed on the Table, and therefore wee have men that stand on purpose with Napkins to fright them away when as wee are eating: in the night likewise we are much disquieted with Musquatoes, like our Gnats, but somewhat lesse: and in their great Cities, there are such aboundance of bigge hungrie Rats, that they often bite a man as he lyeth on his bed.

Edward Terry, 1616, in *Purchas his Pilgrimes*, 1625

The nations of India discover a domineering taste for fooleries of that class which run into the barbaresque. Their religion is made up of fooleries.

Thomas de Quincey, *Translation of Kant on National Character in Relation to the Sense of the Sublime and Beautiful*, 1824

The conquest of India by Bacchus might afford scope for a very brilliant poem of the fancy and the understanding.

Samuel Taylor Coleridge, *Table Talk*, 4 September 1835

Some general conversation, after dinner, about India, in the course of which Lord Clare gave no very agreeable idea either of the country itself or of the society there. A great want of beautiful scenery, all being so flat; and even where elevated, being but an ascending series of flats. The society very much of the same description.

Thomas Moore, *Diary*, 12 April 1837

He died of an abscess of the liver – of India in fact.

Emily Eden, Letter, 1838, in *Up the Country*, 1866

There is surely no country in the world where in the midst of such starvation there is so much waste; certainly none where the expense of it all is borne so wholly and directly by the poor.

Wilfred Scawen Blunt, *Ideas About India*, 1885

Famine is the horizon of the Indian villager. Insufficient food is the foreground.

Anon., quoted *Ibid.*

This is indeed India! The land of dreams and romance, of fabulous wealth and fabulous poverty, of splendour and rags, of palaces and hovels, of famine and pestilence, of genii and giants and Aladdin lamps, of tigers and elephants, the cobra and the jungle, the country of a hundred nations and a hundred tongues, of a thousand religions and two million gods, cradle of the human race, birthplace of human speech, mother of history, grandmother of legend, great-grandmother of Tradition, whose yesterdays bear date with the mouldering antiquities of the rest of the nations – the one sole country under the sun that is endowed with an imperishable interest for alien prince and alien peasant, for lettered and ignorant, wise and fool, rich and poor, bond and free, the one land that *all* men desire to see, and having seen once, by even a glimpse, would not give that glimpse for the shows of all the rest of the globe combined.

Mark Twain, *More Tramps Abroad*, 1897

A despotism of office-boxes tempered by an occasional loss of keys.

Lord Lytton, quoted in Wilfred Scawen Blunt, *India Under Ripon*, 1909

Wellington is reported to have said that he never knew a good-tempered man in India.

Sir Henry Morton Stanley, *Autobiography*, 1909

The arts of littleness are tragically lacking in India; there is scarcely anything in that tormented land which fills up the gulf between the illimitable and the inane, and society suffers in consequence. What isn't piety is apt to be indecency. What isn't metaphysics is intrigue.

E.M. Forster, 'Adrift in India', 1922, in *Abinger Harvest*, 1938

*There are some exquisite echoes in India; there is the whisper round the dome at Bijapur; there are the long, solid sentences that voyage through the air at Mandu, and return unbroken to their creator. The echo in a Marabar cave is not like these, it is entirely devoid of distinction. Whatever is said, the same monotonous noise replies, and quivers up and down the walls until it is absorbed into the roof. 'Boum' is the sound as far as the human alphabet can express it, or 'bou-oum,' or 'ou-boum,' – utterly dull. Hope, politeness, the blowing of a nose, the squeak of a boot, all produce 'boum.'

E.M. Forster, *A Passage to India*, 1924

One voyage to India is enough; the others are merely repletion.

Sir Winston Churchill, *My Early Life*, 1930

India rarely changes and rarely forgets.

F. Yeats Brown, *Bengal Lancer*, 1930

It is quite possible that India is the real world, and that the white man lives in a madhouse of abstractions. . . . Life in India has not yet withdrawn into the capsule of the head. It is still the whole body that lives. No wonder the European feels dreamlike: the complete life of India is something of which he merely dreams. . . . I did not see one European in India who really lived there. They were all living in Europe, that is, in a sort of bottle filled with European air. One would surely go under without the insulating glass wall; one would be drowned in all the things which we Europeans have conquered in our imagination.

C.G. Jung, *The Dreamlike World of India*, 1939

Externally the place has not changed . . . outside the carriage windows (the rather dirty windows) it unrolls as before – monotonous, enigmatic, and at moments sinister. . . . And this changelessness in her is called by some observers, 'the real India.' I don't myself like the phrase 'the real India.' I suspect it. It always makes me prick up my ears. But you can use it if you want to, either for the changes in her, or for the unchanged. 'Real' is at the service of all schools of thought.

E.M. Forster, 'India Again,' 1946, in *Two Cheers for Democracy*, 1951

Well, India is a country of nonsense.

M.K. Gandhi, before 1948, quoted in V.S. Naipaul, *An Area of Darkness*, 1964

For here where men as fungi burgeon
And each crushed puffball dies in dust
This plethoric yet phantom setting
Makes yours remote so that even lust
Can take no tint nor curve on trust
Beyond these plains' beyondless margin.

You are north-west but what is Western
Assurance here where words are snakes
Gulping their tails, flies that endemic
In mosque and temple, morgue and jakes,
Eat their blind fill of man's mistakes
And yet each carcase proves eternal?

Here where the banyan weeps her children
Where pavements flower with wounds and fins
And kite and vulture hold their vigil
Which never ends, never begins
To end, this world which spins and grins
Seems a mere sabbath of bacilli. . . .

So cast up here this India jolts us
Awake to what engrossed our sleep;
This was the truth and now we see it,
This was the horror – it is deep;
The lid is off, the things that creep
Down there are we, we were there always.

Louis MacNeice, *Letter from India*, 1947

I like the evening in India, the one magic moment when the sun balances on the rim of the world, and the hush descends, and ten thousand civil servants drift homeward on a river of bicycles, brooding on the Lord Krishna and the cost of living.

James Cameron, *News Chronicle*, 22 February 1957, in *What a Way to Run the Tribe*, 1968

The first thing in India that strikes a foreign visitor's eye is the pleasant fact that Indian birds and beasts are not in the least afraid of Indian human beings. Age-long experience has given them a well-justified confidence that their human co-inhabitants of the sub-continent will not slaughter them; but they are not grateful to Mankind for their immunity from the risk of being slain by human hands. They do not know that they owe this to a tabu which Indian Man has voluntarily imposed upon himself. Indian birds and beasts evidently imagine that they enjoy god-given animal rights, and that Man is constrained, willy nilly, to respect these rights as part of the divine ordering of the Universe. . . .

Indian human beings, too, possess animal rights, of course; but, in this animal raj, humans are definitely second-class citizens. In American parlance, they are 'under-privileged.' In the animal hierarchy, humans rank as non-Brahmins, but they do not enjoy the benefit of being a scheduled caste. No allowances are made for them. . . .

And life is also a curse for the animals themselves; for the cow's divine right is merely a right to live. It is not a right to enjoy a decent livelihood. And it is no fun being a demigoddess if you do not know where to turn for your next meal. . . . There is no provision for the pursuit of happiness in the Indian animals' bill of rights.

Arnold Toynbee, *East to West*, 1958

The outer and inner worlds . . . coexist; the society only pretends to be colonial; and for this reason its absurdities are at once apparent. Its mimicry is both less and more than a colonial mimicry. It is the special mimicry of an old country which has been without a native aristocracy for a thousand years, and has learned to make room for outsiders, but only at the top. The mimicry changes, the inner world remains constant: this is the secret of survival. . . . Yesterday the mimicry was Mogul: tomorrow it might be Russian or American; today it is English.

V.S. Naipaul, *An Area of Darkness*, 1964

It was my eye that had changed. I had seen Indian villages: the narrow, broken lanes with green slime in the gutters, the choked back-to-back mud houses, the jumble of filth and food and animals and people, the baby in the dust, swollen-bellied, black with flies, but wearing its good-luck amulet. I had seen the starved child defecating at the roadside while the mangy dog waited to eat the excrement. I had seen the physique of the people of Andrha, which had suggested the possibility of an evolution downwards, wasted body to wasted body. Nature mocking herself, incapable of remission. Compassion and pity did not answer; they were refinements of hope. Fear was what I felt. Contempt was what I had to fight against; to give way to that was to abandon the self I had known. Perhaps in the end it was fatigue that overcame me. For abruptly, in the midst of hysteria, there occurred periods of calm, in which I had grown to separate myself from what I saw

Ibid.

The British Raj

Is India free? And does she wear her plum'd

And jewell'd turban with a smile of peace?
Or do we grind her still?

William Cowper, *The Task*, Book IV, 'The Winter Evening', 1783–4 (pub. 1785)

Description of the young English sent out there
Animated with all the avarice of age, and all the impetuous ardour of youth, they roll in, one after another, wave after wave, while nothing presents itself to the view of the unhappy natives, except an interminable prospect of new flights of voracious birds of passage, with appetites insatiable for a food which is continually wasting under their attacks. Every other conqueror, Arab, Tartar, or Persian, has left behind him some monument, either of royal splendour or of useful beneficience. England has erected neither churches, nor hospitals, nor schools, nor palaces. If to-morrow we were expelled from Hindostan, nothing would remain to indicate that it had been possessed during the inglorious period of our dominion by any better tenants than the ourang-outang or the tiger.

Edmund Burke, Speech in the House of Commons, 1 December 1783

The English laws are the great Charter of the Indian people.

Edmund Burke, Letter to Lord Loughborough, *c.* 17 March 1796

The British Government in India is a phenomenon; and it will not answer to apply to it, in its present state, either the rules which guide other governments, or the reasoning upon which these rules are founded.

Duke of Wellington, Dispatch to Colonel Murray, 13 October 1803

If Gwalior belonged to Scindiah, it must be given up; and I acknowledge that whether it did, or did not, I should be inclined to give it to him. I declare that when I view the treaty of peace, and its consequences, I am afraid it will be imagined that the moderation of the British Government in India has a strong resemblance to the ambition of other governments.

Duke of Wellington, Dispatch to Major Malcolm, 29 January 1804

George wonders every day how we are allowed to keep this country a week.

Emily Eden, Letter, 21 June 1841, in *Letters from India*, 1872

The English did not calculate the conquest of the Indies. It fell to their character.

R.W. Emerson, *English Traits*, 1856

The key of India is London.

Benjamin Disraeli, Speech in the House of Lords, on the evacuation of Candahar, 5 March 1881

The apologists of British rule boast that they have given India peace, and peace doubtless is a noble gift; but it has given her far more than this. What really deserves all Indian thanks, and is indeed an inestimable acquisition, because it contains within it the germs of a reconquest of all the rest, is that it has given her liberty of thought. This is a new possession which India never had, and never perhaps would have had, but for English influences, and it is difficult not to see in it a gift undesigned, but which, like the last treasure issuing from Pandora's box, is destined to transform the curse of conquest into the blessing of hope.

Wilfred Scawen Blunt, *Ideas About India*, 1885

We wonder whether the traveller shall some day inspect, with unconcerned composure, the few scraps of stone and iron which may indicate the British occupation of India. . . . Yet perhaps, if that unborn critic of remote posterity would remember that 'in the days of the old British' the rice crop had been more abundant, the number of acres under cultivation greater, the population larger, and the death-rate lower, than at any time in the history of India – we should not be without a monument more glorious than the pyramids.

Sir Winston Churchill, *The Malakand Field Force*, 1898

It is only when you get to see and realise what India really is, – that she is the strength and greatness of England – it is only then that you feel that every nerve a man may strain, every energy he may put forward, cannot be devoted to a nobler purpose than keeping tight the cords that hold India to ourselves.

Lord Curzon, Viceroy of India, 1899–1905, in *Plain Tales from the Raj*, 1975

Our title to India depends on a first condition, that our being there is profitable to the Indian nations; and on a second condition, that we can make them see and understand it to be profitable.

W.E. Gladstone, quoted in Wilfred Scawen Blunt, *India Under Ripon*, 1909

About South Africa he [Winston Churchill] told how he had dined with Moore, the Natal Premier, a little while ago, and how Moore had said to him apropos of what was going on in India: 'Well, Churchill, I suppose you'll have to bleed them soon; there's nothing like it. Next time they have a demonstration ride them down, and if that isn't enough pour in a volley. You'll bleed a few thousands of them, but it will be better for them in the long run; there's nothing like bleeding.' Winston did not talk as much about India as I had hoped, but he said: 'If they ever unite against us and put us in coventry all round, the game would be up. If they could agree to have nothing at all to do with us the whole thing would collapse.'

Wilfred Scawen Blunt, Diary, 5 September 1909, *My Diaries*, 1919

I cannot help thinking, from all I have heard and seen, that the task of governing India will be made easier if we, on our part, infuse into it a wider element of sympathy.

King George V (when Prince of Wales), Speech at the Guildhall, 17 May 1906

India expects every man to do his doti.

Sir Edwin Lutyens, Motto for India, *c.* 1920, quoted in Mary Lutyens, *Sir Edwin Lutyens,* 1980

India is an autocracy without an autocrat. Its rule combines the disadvantages of absolute monarchy with the impersonality and irresponsibility of democratic officialdom.

H.G. Wells, *A Short History of the World,* 1922

It makes me sick when I hear the Secretary of State saying of India '*she* will do this and *she* will do that.' India is an abstraction. . . . India is no more a political personality than Europe. India is a geographical term. It is no more a united nation than the Equator.

Sir Winston Churchill, Speech at the Albert Hall, 18 March 1931

For many generations the British treated India as a kind of enormous country-house (after the old English fashion) that they owned. They were the gentry owning the house and occupying the desirable parts of it, while the Indians were consigned to the servants' hall and pantry and kitchen. As in every proper country-house there was a fixed hierarchy in those lower regions – butler, housekeeper, cook, valet, maid, footman, etc. – and strict precedence was observed among them. But, between the upper and lower regions of the house there was, socially and politically, an impassable barrier. The fact that the British Government should have imposed this arrangement upon us was not surprising; but what does seem surprising is that we, or most of us, accepted it as the natural and inevitable ordering of our lives and destiny. We developed the mentality of a good country-house servant.

Jawaharlal Nehru, *An Autobiography,* 1936

G. Lowes Dickinson is reported by E.M. Forster, in his recent life of him, to have once said about India: 'And, *why* can't the races meet? Simply because the Indians *bore* the English. *That* is the simple adamantine fact.'

Ibid.

That absurd phrase: 'The unchanging East.' It is the British predominant class who will not change. . . . The British Empire is . . . only democratic in pretence. It is, in actual fact, a timid yet greedy governing class, clamped upon possibilities far greater than itself.

H.G. Wells, *Travels of a Republican Radical in Search of Hot Water,* 1939

Even the Englishman is not settled in India; he is really condemned to serve his term there and to make the best of it. Hence all those hopeful, jolly, eager, energetic, powerful voices issue from people who are thinking and dreaming of spring in Sussex.

C.G. Jung, *The Dreamlike World of India,* 1939

The railway stations in the blinding sun;
the spilling, milling, spawning, gibbering mob;
the twisted half-mad shapes with sores that run;
the flies; the silent, huddled forms which gob
the betel-juice where they think fit; the smell;
the everlasting dogs; the beggar's whine;
the third-class, multi-coloured, heaving hell;
those blatant furtive squattings all along the line:
foul bazaars which reek and rot
and creep and crawl as day grows hot;
women who hold with lightest grip,
plum-bloom babies at their hip;
the buffalo black – vile, padding beast –
whose back's a scurf of old, dry yeast,
the train which threads the trembling way
through god-like hills at break of day,
past fold on mighty fold of brown,
up to the snows' eternal crown;
girls with ankles jewel-hung
who use their hands to scrape up dung;
the Taj Mahal serene and proud,
so beautiful, so white, a shroud; . . .
villages of mud and slime
the afterbirth, forgotten from the womb of time:
the Royal Hotel, – or Cecil – the Empress – or Green's;
the club cantonment and the bungalow;
the lordly ones in state; their would-be queens;
the world of the bottle, the stare, the pained 'hello;'
the well-kept lawns, nostalgic English flowers;
the bearers and the dhobis and the chowkidars
the shadowed ease; the slow, unruffled hours;
those leisured, velvet evenings, filled with diamond stars.

Harold Hugh Tilley, *The Indian Scene,* in R.N. Currey and R.V. Gibson, (eds) *Poems from India,* 1946

They left no noble monuments behind and no religion save a concept of Englishness as a desirable code of behaviour – of chivalry, it might be described, tempered by legalism – which in Indian minds can be dissociated from the fact of English rule, the vulgarities of racial arrogance, or the position of England today. . . . This consciousness of Englishness will survive because it was the product of fantasy, a work of national art; it will outlast England; . . . the Raj was an expression of the English involvement with themselves rather than with the country they ruled. It is not, properly, an imperialist attitude. It points, not to the good or evil of British rule in India, but to its failure.

V.S. Naipaul, *An Area of Darkness,* 1964

As soon as the English mind came in contact with the Hindu's, which was a very different kind of mind, it completely lost its temper, and so became incapable of dispassionate analysis. But the display of temper was at least spectacular, like fireworks.

Nirad C. Chaudhuri, 'On Understanding the Hindus,' *Encounter,* June 1965

Indians

There are no Capons amongst them but men.

Edward Terry, 1616, in *Purchas his Pilgrimes,* 1625

They delight much in Musicke, and have many stringed and wind Instruments, which never seemed in my eare to bee any thing but discord.

Ibid.

For the stature of these Easterne Indians, they are like us, but generally very streight, for I never beheld any in those parts crooked. They are of a tawnie or Olive colour, their haire blacke as a Raven, but not curl'd. They love not a man or woman that is very white or faire, because that (as they say) is the colour of Lepers common amongst them. Most of the Mahometans, but the Moolaes (which are their Priests) or those that are very old and retyred, keepe their chinnes bare, but suffer the haire on their upper lip to grow as long as Nature will feed it. They usually shave off all the haire from their heads, reserving only a Locke on the Crowne for Mahomet, to pull them into Heaven.

Ibid.

In Indostan every man literally may be said to be the master of his fortune. Great talents, unawed by scruples of conscience, seldom fail of success.

Robert Orme, *Historical Fragments of the Mogul Empire,* 1659

Amongst the sooty *Indians;* . . .
where Wives are forc'd
To live no longer when their Husbands dye:
Nay, what's yet worse, to share 'em whil'st they live
With many Rival Wives. . . .

William Wycherley, *The Plain-Dealer,* 1676

I mean the 'moral' of my Indian experience to be, that it is the most picturesque population with the ugliest scenery, that ever was put together.

Emily Eden, Letter, 5 November 1837, in *Up the Country,* 1866

I must do the Hindus the justice to say that they make as many holidays out of one year as most people do out of ten.

Ibid.

It is a curious people. With them, all life seems to be sacred except human life. Even the life of vermin is sacred, and must not be taken. The good Jain wipes off a seat before using it, lest he cause the death of some valueless insect by sitting down on it. It grieves him to have to drink water, because the provisions in his stomach may not agree with the microbes. Yet India invented Thuggery and Suttee. India is a hard country to understand.

Mark Twain, *More Tramps Abroad,* 1897

An Indian, inasmuch as he is really Indian, does not think, at least not what we call 'think.' *He rather perceives the thought.* He resembles the primitive in this respect. I do not say that he *is* primitive, but that the process of his thinking reminds me of the primitive way of thought-production.

C.G. Jung, *What India can Teach Us,* 1939

Intellectually the European mind was outraged by the Hindus precisely in those three principles which were fundamental to its approach to life, and which it had been applying with ever greater strictness since the Renaissance: that of reason, that of order, and that of measure.

Nirad C. Chaudhuri, 'On Understanding the Hindus', *Encounter,* June 1965

The Indian people want to live without putting in anything beyond the minimum amount of exertion, bodily or mental, without any continuous demand on their will power, and without the strain on the mind imposed by a positive goal of achievement. No Indian government can ignore this basic proclivity of theirs.

Nirad C. Chaudhuri, Article of 1966, quoted by himself, *Spectator,* 12 January 1980

Premature adulthood is one of the saddest things about India, but, . . . I seem to detect that actual adulthood in India has a compensatory touching innocence about it.

Ved Mehta, *Portrait of India,* 1970

Indians love to reduce the prosaic to the mystic.

Jan Morris, *Destinations,* 1980

Being Hindu means never having to say you're sorry.

Gita Mehta, *Karma Cola,* 1980

Agra

There is also another Bazare or Markett, which, although not soe Commendable, yett much frequented and allowed of, not onely heere but all India over, namely the Common Stewes, of which there bee in divers places of Agra. Each of them every eveninge is like a faire, where they resort, make their bargaines, take and choose the whores sittinge and lyeinge on their Cotts att their balcones and doores. Theis are called Manganaes.

Peter Mundy, *Travels in Europe and Asia,* 1632

I believe the best plan is, as I heard an Agra lady say the other day, 'not to think of the hot winds till they come, nor to mention them, but to keep all your strength to try and live through them.'

Emily Eden, Letter, 4 January 1840, in *Letters from India,* 1872

Taj Mahal

This Kinge [Shah Jehan] is now buildinge a Sepulchre for his late deceased Queene Tage Moholl, . . . whome hee dearely affected. . . . There is alreadye about her Tombe a raile of gold. The buildinge is begun and goes on with excessive labour and cost, prosecuted with extraordinary dilligence, Gold and silver esteemed comon Mettall, and Marble but as ordinarie stones. Hee intends, as some thinck, to remove all the Cittie hither, cawseinge hills to be made levell because they might not hinder the prospect of it, places appoynted for streets shopps, etts. dwellings, commaunding Marchants, shopkeepers, Artificers, to Inhabit, where they begin to repaire and called by her name, Tage Gunge.

Peter Mundy, *Travels in Europe and Asia,* 1632

White, like a spectre seen when night is old
Yet stained with hues of many a tear and smart,
Cornelian, blood-stone, matched in callous art:
Aflame, like passion, like dominion cold,
Bed of imperial consorts whom none part
For ever (domed with glory, heart to heart)
Still whispering to the ages, 'Love is bold
And seeks the height, though rooted in the mould:'
Touched, when the dawn floats in an opal mist
By fainter blush than opening roses own;
Calm in the evening's lucent amethyst;
Pearl-crowned, when midnight airs aside have blown
The clouds that rising moonlight faintly kissed;
– An aspiration fixed, a sigh made stone.

H.G. Keene, 'The Taj', *Peepul Leaves,* 1879

Prepared to admire, you are also aware of the defects alleged against the Taj – the rigidity of its outlines, the lack of shadow upon its unbroken front and flanks, and the coloured inlaying said to make it less a triumph of architectural than of mosaic work, an illustration somewhat too striking and lavish of what is declared of the Moguls, that 'they designed like giants, and finished like jewellers.'

Sir Edwin Arnold, *India Revisited,* 1886

As the Englishman leaned out of the carriage he saw first an opal-tinted cloud on the horizon, and, later, certain towers. The mists lay on the ground, so that the splendour seemed to be floating free of the earth; and the mists rose in the background, so that at no time could everything be seen clearly. Then as the train sped forward, and the mists shifted, and the sun shone upon the mists, the Taj took a hundred new shapes, each perfect and each beyond description. It was the Ivory Gate through which all good dreams come; it was the realisation of the gleaming halls of dawn that Tennyson sighs of; it was veritably the 'aspiration fixed,' the 'sigh made stone' of a lesser poet; and over and above concrete comparisons, it seemed the embodiment of all things pure, all things holy, and all things unhappy. That was the mystery of the building.

Rudyard Kipling, *From Sea to Sea,* 1897

You cannot keep your enthusiasms down, you cannot keep your emotions within bounds when that soaring bubble of marble breaks upon your view. But these are not *your* enthusiasms and emotions – they are the accumulated emotions and enthusiasms of a thousand fervid writers who have been slowly and steadily storing them up in your heart day by day and year by year all your life; and now they burst out in a flood and overwhelm you, and you could not be a whit happier if they were all your very own. By and by you sober down, and then you perceive that you have been drunk on the smell of somebody else's cork. For ever and ever the memory of my distant first glimpse of the Taj will compensate me for creeping around the globe to have that great privilege.

Mark Twain, *More Tramps Abroad,* 1897

Seen in the first pale flush of sunrise, with a cool wind stirring the treetops in the adjacent gardens, it has the fragile delicacy of a soap bubble; no other building I have ever seen has conveyed to me quite that degree of airy grace, of absolute purity. It demands a strenuous effort on the visitor's part, however, to enjoy it privately. At every turn he is beset by a horde of cringing, smarmy mendicants chanting facts and figures and whining for alms. Historians assert that Shah Jehan built the Taj to commemorate his wife Mumtaz Mahal, called the Ornament of the Palace, but if you believe the ceaseless patter of the guides, Lord Curzon, onetime Viceroy of India, deserves the lion's share of the credit. 'Lord Curzon's lamp, sahib – presented by Lord Curzon at a cost of five thousand rupees,' they jabber. 'All these fountains donated by Lord Curzon . . . ninety thousand rupees. . . . Lord Curzon gave these steps out of his own pocket – twelve thousand rupees, sahib . . . this pool gift of noble Lord Curzon . . . rupees . . . Curzon . . . rupees.' We backed out through the beautiful red sandstone gate bestowing a pox on the noble lord, grateful nonetheless for that first moment of revelation.

S.J. Perelman, *Westward Ha!,* 1948

Amanda: . . . and the Taj Mahal. How was the Taj
Mahal?

Elyot: (looking at her): Unbelievable, a sort of dream.
Amanda: That was the moonlight I expect, you must have seen it in the moonlight.
Elyot: (never taking his eyes off her face): Yes, moonlight is cruelly deceptive.
Amanda: And it didn't look like a biscuit box did it? I've always felt that it might. . . .

Noel Coward, *Private Lives*, 1930

That's my pudding!

Penelope Lee, to herself, on first seeing the Taj, February 1968

Of course I've known for years our marriage has been a mockery. My body lying there night after night in the wasted moonlight. I know now how the Taj Mahal must feel.

Alan Bennett, *Habeas Corpus*, 1973 (Mrs Wicksteed speaking)

Robin Day . . . and I travelled together to see the Taj Mahal a couple of years ago, which gave rise to a notable exchange. . . . I said that since his wife was not with him I claimed the right to be her surrogate and ask him a question she would have been entitled to put if she had been present in person. He gravely accepted my claim, and bade me ask. 'Darling,' I said, waving a hand at Shah Jehan's creation, 'do you love me so much that if I were to die you would build something like this in *my* memory?' Robin considered the question carefully. Then, 'Only if I could get it off tax,' he replied.

Bernard Levin, 'The Difference a Day Makes', *The Times*, 16 October 1980

The Banian Tree

The Figtree, not that kind for Fruit renown'd,
But such as at this day to *Indians* known
In *Malabar* or *Decan* spreds her Armes
Braunching so broad and long, that in the ground
The bended Twigs take root, and Daughters grow
About the Mother Tree, a Pillard shade
High overarch't, and echoing Walks between
There oft the *Indian* Herdsman, shunning heate
Shelters in coole, and tends his pasturing Herds
At Loopholes cut through thickest shade. . . .

John Milton, *Paradise Lost*, 1667

Baroda

Intensely Indian it was, and crumbly, and mouldering, and immemorially old, to all appearance. And the houses – oh, indescribably quaint, and curious they were, with their fronts an elaborate lace-work of intricate and beautiful wood-carvings, and now and then further adorned with rude pictures of elephants and princes and gods done in shouting colours; and all the ground-floors along these cramped and narrow lanes occupied as shops – shops unbelievably small, and impossibly packed with merchantable rubbish, and with nine-tenths-naked natives squatting at their work of hammering, pounding, brazing, soldering, sewing, designing, cooking, measuring out grain, grinding it, repairing idols – and then the swarm of ragged and noisy humanity under the horses' feet and everywhere and the pervading reek and fume and smell! It was all wonderful and delightful. . . .

I wonder how old the town is. There are patches of building – massive structures, monuments, apparently – that are so battered and worn, and seemingly so tired and so burdened with the weight of age, and so dulled and stupefied with trying to remember things they forgot before history began, that they give one the feeling that they must have been a part of original Creation.

Mark Twain, *More Tramps Abroad*, 1897

Barrackpore

The day before yesterday the rain came down very much as if the river had got up and out of its bed, and was walking about the park.

Emily Eden, Letter, 19 July 1836, in *Letters from India*, 1872

Benares

Bennaras . . . is a great Towne, and great store of Cloth is made there of Cotton, and Shashes for the Moores. In this place they bee all Gentiles, and be the greatest Idolaters that ever I saw. To this Towne come the Gentiles of Pilgrimage out of farre Countries. Here alongst the waters side, bee very many faire houses, and in all of them, or for the most part they have their Images standing, which bee evill favoured, made of stone and wood, some like Lyons, Leopards, and Monkies, some like Men and Women, and Peacockes, and some like the Divell with foure armes & foure hands. They sit crosse legged, some with one thing in their hands, and some another, and by breake of day and before, there are men and women which come out of the Towne and wash themselves in Ganges. And there are divers old men, which upon places of earth made for the purpose, sit praying, and they give the people three or foure strawes, which they take and hold them betweene their fingers when they wash themselves: and some sit to marke them in the foreheads, and they have in a cloth a little Rice, Barlie, or money, which, when they have washed themselves, they give to the old men which sit there praying. Afterwards they goe to divers of their Images, and give them of their Sacrifices. And when they give, the old men say certaine prayers, and then is all holy.

Ralph Fitch, *The Voyage,* 1583–91, in *Purchas his Pilgrimes,* 1625

Of all the Citties and Townes that I have seene in India, none resembles so much those of Europe as this Banaroz doth a distance off, by reason of the many great and high Spires that are in it, which belong to the Pagodes or Hindoo Churches. Also when wee came into it, wee found it wondrous populous, good buildings, paved streets, but narrow and Crooked.

Peter Mundy, *Travels in Europe and Asia,* 1632

We went in a large party to the town in carriages; when the streets grew too narrow for carriages, we got on elephants; when the elephants stuck fast, we tried tonjauns; and when the streets contracted still further, we walked; and at last, I suppose, they came to a point, for we came back. . . . Prout would go mad in a brown outline frenzy on the spot – the buildings are so very beautiful for his style.

Emily Eden, Letter, 22 November 1837, in *Up the Country,* 1866

Benares was not a disappointment. It justified its reputation as a curiosity. It is on high ground, and overhangs a curve of the Ganges. It is a vast mass of building, compactly crusting a hill, and is cloven in all directions by an intricate confusion of cracks which stand for streets. Tall, slim minarets and beflagged temple-spires rise out of it and give it picturesqueness, viewed from the river. The city is as busy as an ant-hill, and the hurly-burly of human life swarming along the web of narrow streets reminds one of the ants. The sacred cow swarms along too, and goes whither she pleases and takes toll of the grain-shops, and is very much in the way, and is a good deal of a nuisance, since she must not be molested.

Benares is older than history, older than tradition, older even than legend, and looks twice as old as all of them put together. From a Hindoo statement quoted in Rev Mr Parker's compact and lucid 'Guide to Benares,' I find that the site of the town was the beginning-place of the Creation. It was merely an upright 'lingam' at first, no larger than a stove-pipe, and stood in the midst of a shoreless ocean. This was the work of the god Vishnu. Later he spread the lingam out till its surface was ten miles across. Still it was not large enough for the business; therefore he presently built the globe around it. Benares is thus the centre of the earth This is considered an advantage.

Mark Twain, *More Tramps Abroad,* 1897

The city fascinated me and repelled me, like Yoga, like India.

It was no good pretending the repulsion did not exist: Benares is an incarnation of the Hindu mind, full of shocks and surprises. You cannot view her through the eyes of the flesh, or if you do you will want to shut them. Her real life burns in the Unconscious.

F. Yeats Brown, *Bengal Lancer,* 1930

Bengal

I hold that a constitution adapted to Bengal can hardly be adapted to any other climate under heaven.

Emily Eden, Letter, 7 September 1837, in *Letters from India,* 1872

So rich a shade, so green a sod
Our English fairies never trod!
Yet who in Indian bowers has stood,
But thought on England's 'good greenwood!' . . .
And breath'd a prayer, (how oft in vain!)
To gaze upon her oaks again?

Reginald Heber, 'An Evening Walk in Bengal', *Poems,* 1842

Bengal sits sodden astride the Tropic of Cancer.

Geoffrey Moorhouse, *Calcutta,* 1971

Bengalis

The Sepoys seem to me to be much finer soldiers than our people, partly from being so tall and upright and then . . . I am convinced that brown is the natural colour for man – black and white are unnatural deviations and look shocking. I am quite ashamed of our white skins.

Emily Eden, Letter, 2 April 1836, in *Letters from India,* 1872

George says he is sure that the staring *round* look which everybody's eyes have here, is not, as is always supposed, occasioned by the heat and by the shrinking of the eyelids, but by the knack they have of wondering at everything.

Emily Eden, Letter, 8 August 1836, in *Letters from India,* 1872

The physical organization ofthe Bengalee is feeble even to effeminacy. He lives in a constant vapour bath. His pursuits are sedentary, his limbs delicate, his movements languid. During many ages he has been trampled upon by men of bolder and more hardy breeds. Courage, independence, veracity, are qualities to which his constitution and situation are equally unfavourable. His mind bears a singular analogy to his body. It is weak even to helplessness, for purposes of manly resistance; but its suppleness and its tact move the children of sterner climates to admiration not unmingled with contempt. All those arts which are the natural defences of the weak are more familiar to this subtle race than to the Ionian of the time of Juvenal, or to the Jew of the dark ages. What the horns are to the buffalo, what the paw is to the tiger, what the sting is to the bee, what beauty, according to the old Greek song, is to woman, deceit is to the Bengalee. Large promises, smooth excuses, elaborate tissues of circumstantial falsehood, chicanery, perjury, forgery, are the weapons, offensive and defensive, of the people of the Lower Ganges.

T.B. Macaulay, 'Warren Hastings', October 1841, *Critical and Historical Essays*, 1843

Bengalis call themselves the French of the East.

Ved Mehta, *Portrait of India*, 1970

Bhilai

Next, another troupe, now of adults, comes onto the stage. They are led by a lady with a flushed face, who continually dabs at her forehead as she explains, in precise, formal Hindi, that the words of the number they are going to sing were written by a Russian engineer at the plant. The group sings, in chorus, 'Bhilai steel plant is famous for its steel, but this is not the only thing the plant is famous for. It is famous for the friendship between the Indian people and the Soviet people.' For some reason the words have been set to the tune of 'It's a Long Long way to Tipperary.'

Ved Mehta, *Portrait of India*, 1970

Bhutan

Nothing that a Buthia possesses is his own; he is at all times liable to lose it if it attracts the cupidity of anyone more powerful than himself. . . . There never was, I fancy, a country in which the doctrine of 'might is right' formed more completely the whole and sole law and custom of the land than it does in Bhutan.

British Envoy, 1864,
quoted Ved Mehta, *Portrait of India*, 1970

Bombay

Above all things it seems strange to me . . . that such a thing as this, which was expected to be one of the best parts of the Queen's portion, should not be better understood; it being, if we had it, but a poor place and not really so as was described to our King in the draught of it, but a poor little Island; whereas they made the King and Lord Chancellor and the other learned men about the King believe that that and other Islands which are near it were all one piece; and so the draught was drawn and presented to the King, and expected to prove so when our men came thither; but it is quite otherwise.

Samuel Pepys, *Diary*, 5 September 1663

It is at Bombay that the smell of All Asia boards the ship miles off shore, and holds the passenger's nose till he is clear of Asia again.

Rudyard Kipling, *From Tideway to Tideway*, 1892

Royal and Dower-royal, I the Queen
  Fronting thy richest sea with richer hands –
A thousand mills roar through me where I glean
  All races from all lands.

Rudyard Kipling, *The Song of the Cities*, 1893

BOMBAY! A bewitching place, a bewildering place, an enchanting place – the Arabian nights come again!

Mark Twain, *More Tramps Abroad*, 1897

A great fine, Italian-looking Anglo-Oriental city, situated on an island in a beautiful bay.

Alfred Viscount Northcliffe, *My Journey Round the World* (January 1922), 1923

*The huge city which the West had built and abandoned with a gesture of despair.

E.M. Forster, *A Passage to India*, 1924

The Anglo-Indian style of architecture of the past fifty years is not interesting, but it gives a peculiar character to Bombay, as if one had already seen it somewhere else.

C.G. Jung, *The Dreamlike World of India*, 1939

They tell the story of the Sikh who, returning to India after many years, sat down among his suitcases on the Bombay docks and wept. He had forgotten what Indian poverty was like.

V.S. Naipaul, *An Area of Darkness*, 1964

Calcutta

One of the most wicked Places in the Universe.

Robert Clive, Letter to George Greville, *c.* 1765

As awkward a place as can be conceived; and so very irregular that it looks as if all the houses had been thrown up in the air, and fallen down again by accident as they now stand: people keep constantly building; and every one who can procure a piece of ground to build a house upon, consults his own taste and convenience, without any regard to the beauty or regularity of the town: besides the appearance of the best houses is spoiled by the little straw huts, and such sort of encumbrances, which are built by the servants for themselves to sleep in: so that all the English part of the town, which is the largest, is a confusion of very superb and very shabby houses, dead walls, straw huts, warehouses, and I know not what.

Jemima Kindersley, *Letters from Teneriffe, Brazil, etc.*, 1777

It is a truth that, from the western extremity of California to the eastern coast of Japan, there is not a spot where judgement, taste, decency and convenience, are so grossly insulted as in that scattered and confused chaos of houses, huts, sheds, streets, lanes, alleys, windings, gullies, sinks and tanks, which, jumbled into an undistinguished mass of filth and corruption, equally offensive to human sense and health, compose the capital of the English Company's Government in India. The very small portion of cleanliness which it enjoys is owing to the familiar intercourse of hungry jackals by night, and ravenous vultures, kites, and crows by day. In like manner it is indebted to the smoke raised in public streets, in temporary huts and sheds, for any respite it enjoys from mosquitoes, the natural productions of stagnant and putrid waters.

William MacIntosh, *Travels in Europe, Asia and Africa*, 1782

Go where the maiden on a marriage plan goes,
Consign'd for wedlock to Calcutta's quay,
Where woman goes for mart, the same as mangoes,
And think of me. . . .

Thomas Hood, *Lines to a Lady on her Departure for India*, 1824

Calcutta is altogether (in the part of it inhabited by Europeans) very like the houses in St John's Wood.

Emily Eden, Letter, 26 June 1836, in *Letters from India*, 1872

It sometimes strikes me that we Europeans are mad people sent out here because we are dangerous at home, and that our black keepers are told never to lose sight of us, and the ingenious creatures never do.

Emily Eden, Letter, 17 June 1837, in *Letters from India*, 1872

What a damp furnace Calcutta is.

The Hon. F.H. Eden, Letter, 17 October 1837, in Emily Eden, *Letters from India*, 1872

Find if you can a more uninviting spot than Calcutta. . . . It unites every condition of a perfectly unhealthy situation. . . . The place is so bad by nature that human efforts could do little to make it worse; but that little has been done faithfully and assiduously.

Sir George Trevelyan, *Letters of a Competition Wallah*, 1864

There is only one city in India. Bombay is too green, too pretty, and too strugglesome; and Madras died ever so long ago. Let us take off our hats to Calcutta, the many-sided, the smoky, the magnificent, as we drive in over the Hughli Bridge in the dawn of a still February morning. We have left India behind us at Howrah Station, and now we enter foreign parts. No, not wholly foreign. Say rather too familiar. . . . 'Why, this is London! This is the docks. This is Imperial. This is worth coming across India to see!'

Then a distinctly wicked idea takes possession of the mind: 'What a divine – what a heavenly place to *loot!* . . . adorned, docked, wharfed, fronted, and reclaimed by Englishmen, existing only because England lives, and dependent for its life on England. All India knows of the Calcutta Municipality; but has any one thoroughly investigated the Big Calcutta Stink? There is only one. Benares is fouler in point of concentrated, pent-up muck, and there are local stenches in Peshawar which are stronger than the B.C.S.; but, for diffused, soul-sickening expansiveness, the reek of Bombay beats both Benares and Peshawar. Bombay cloaks her stenches with a veneer of assafoetida and tobacco; Calcutta is above pretence. There is no tracing back the Calcutta plague to any one source. It is faint, it is sickly and it is indescribable; . . . it is certainly not an Indian smell. It resembles the essence of corruption that has rotted for the second time – the clammy odour of blue slime. And there is no escape from it. . . . The thing is intermittent. Six moderately pure mouthfuls of air may be drawn without offence. Then comes the seventh wave and the queasiness of an uncultivated stomach. If you live long enough in Calcutta you grow used to it. The regular residents admit the disgrace, but their answer is: 'Wait till the wind blows off the Salt Lakes where the sewage goes, and *then* you'll smell something.' That is their defence!

Rudyard Kipling, *City of Dreadful Night*, 1888

If the city thought less about itself as a metropolis and more as a midden, its state would be better.

Ibid.

and Simla

Thus the midday halt of Charnock – more's the pity! –
Grew a city
As the fungus sprouts chaotic from its bed
So it spread –
Chance-directed, chance-erected, laid and built
On the silt –
Palace, byre, hovel – poverty and pride –
Side by side;
And, above the packed and pestilential town
Death looked down.
Let the city Charnock pitched on – evil day! –
Go Her way
Though the Argosies of Asia at her doors
Heap their stores,
Though Her enterprise and energy secure
Income sure,

Though 'out-station orders punctually obeyed,'
Swell her trade –
Still, for rule, administration, and the rest,
Simla's best.

Rudyard Kipling, *A Tale of Two Cities*, 1891

Me the Sea-captains loved, the River built,
Wealth sought, and Kings adventured life to hold.
Hail England! I am Asia – Power on silt,
Death in my hands, but Gold!

Rudyard Kipling, 'A Song of the English', *The Song of the Cities*, 1893

This is a very great city and at night with a grey fog and cold wind it almost allows one to imagine that it is London. I shall always be glad to have seen it – for the same reason Papa gave for being glad to have seen Lisbon – namely – 'that it will be unnecessary ever to see it again.'

Winston Churchill, Letter to his mother, 23 December 1896

Enough to make a doorknob mushy.

Mark Twain, *More Tramps Abroad*, 1897

William Hunter wrote home to his fiancée, 'Imagine everything that is glorious in nature combined with all that is beautiful in architecture and you can faintly picture to yourself what Calcutta is.' He was of course in love and he'd just arrived from Peckham.

Dennis Kincaid, *British Social Life in India*, 1938

The road to world revolution lies through Peking, Shanghai and Calcutta.

Anon., attributed to Lenin, but wrongly so, according to Geoffrey Moorhouse, *Calcutta*, 1971

In Calcutta you are still not quite out of India; for, though Calcutta looks like Pimlico if you keep your line of vision tilted to the second storey, one glance at street level brings India back incarnate in her cows.

Arnold Toynbee, *East to West*, 1958

At first, I felt that I could accept Calcutta, that it wasn't as bad as I had thought it would be. But now I know I cannot accept Calcutta. . . . The perception that Calcutta forces upon me is not of the fact of death – which perhaps I can accept – but the process of dying, possibly the dying of an entire population, for Calcutta's spreading poverty, like the slow strangulation of the Hooghly River, foreshadows something more frightening than personal death: it foreshadows racial extinction. . . . Feeling near hysteria, I ask myself how the species could have reached such a point of degradation and yet have adapted itself to that degradation, for the adaptation seems to show only how the will to survive bends us downward.

Ved Mehta, *Portrait of India*, 1970

In Calcutta actors are always dying.

Satyajit Ray, quoted Ved Mehta, *Portrait of India*, 1970

In a sense, Calcutta is a definition of obscenity.

Geoffrey Moorhouse, *Calcutta*, 1971

It is quite impossible to forget or ignore Calcutta's imperial past, for the city has been pickled in its origins.

Ibid.

Everyone knows about Calcutta. Everyone has seen its tall tenements stuffed with disease, its rioting millions in the battened streets, its children sprawled dead or alive on the midnight pavement. If there is one name that stands for misery, it is the name of this fearful and astonishing city – 'Calcutta,' as Mr Eugene Fodor's guide expresses it, 'Vigorous, Vibrant, Versatile.'

James Morris, 'Calcutta', *Places*, 1972

On the first day the city seemed like a corpse on which the Indians were feeding like flies; then I saw its features more clearly, the obelisks and pyramids in Park Street Cemetery, the decayed mansions with friezes and columns, and the fountains in the courtyards of these places: nymphs and sprites blowing on dry conches, who, like the people living under them in gunny sacks, are missing legs and arms. . . .

The best description of Calcutta is Todger's corner of London in Chapter IX of *Martin Chuzzlewit*. . . . Calcutta was Dickensian (perhaps more Dickensian than London ever was).

Paul Theroux, *The Great Railway Bazaar*, 1975

Cambay

Cambay . . . stands by the Sea, encompassed with a strong bricke wall, the houses high, and faire, the streets paved in a direct Line with strong gates at the end of each, the Bazar large; about the citie are such infinite numbers of Munkeyes, leaping from house to house, that they doe much mischiefe, and untyling the houses, are readie to braine men as they passe in the streets with the stones that fall. On the South is a goodly garden with a Watch-tower of an exceeding height; on the North are many faire Tankes.

William Finch, Journal, 1611, in *Purchas his Pilgrims*, 1625

Coonoor (and Ostaramund)

The scenery of them 'ere 'ills is very grand, *i.e.* on the *edges:* but the centre is like a bad sham Cumberland.

Edward Lear, Letter to Lord Carlingford, 28 March 1875

Darjeeling

Darjeeling is an exceedingly pretty place, unlike anything I have seen before. It is laid in terraces on the side of the mountain. Looking down from the hotel, the streets form an interlaced and zigzag pattern. I should never know how to get to any given house in the place. It is like one of those labyrinth puzzles that you try to get to the centre of without crossing a line. The safest way is to do as Alice did in the 'Looking-Glass House,' turn your back to a place, and presently you find yourself walking in at the front door. . . .

I like India better for having seen Darjeeling.

Lilian Leland, *Travelling Alone, A Woman's Journey Round the World,* 1890

At the railway station in Darjeeling you find plenty of cab-substitutes – open coffins, in which you sit, and are then borne on men's shoulders up the steep roads into the town.

Mark Twain, *More Tramps Abroad,* 1897

Imagine Margate, Filey, and Bognor Regis, wholly roofed in red corrugated iron; distorted into a phantasmagoria of chalets and chateaux, such as even they have yet to achieve; vomited into the tittups of an Indian hill-town; and then lifted bodily on to a long spur, a promontory rising from a sea of depths that seem to pierce the very core of the world; overseen by the white throne of God, a continent on end, trees, cliffs, and shores of snow five miles high, as the eye travels up them to the blue vault above; and still preserving all the inevitable accessories of our national life: the exclusive clubs, the Anglican, Scottish, and Roman Catholic churches, the Tudor Hotel, the seaside milliners, and the polo-ground in the bottom of a tea-cup; streets without motors, but municipally railed; rickshaws pulled and pushed by crowds of ragged Mongols; tiny ponies with saddles like high-chairs for children who can scarcely walk; all the races of the Himalayas: Nepali women with their huge necklaces of gold beads and red flannel, like Lord Mayors' chains; the elfin Lepchas and Sikkimese; emigrant Tibetans, mottled lumps of turquoise in the men's ears, the women's chests hung with enormous rhomboid charm-boxes, silver and jewelled; the clouds, as the morning advances, closing in, arriving mysteriously from both above and below, till the last glimpse of Kanchenjunga is obscured behind a wall of mist, the valleys themselves are lost, and at last, thank God, even Darjeeling is invisible but for the two nearest villas and their front gardens; such is the conflict of joy and horror at the first sight of Anglo-Himalaya.

Robert Byron, *First Russia then Tibet,* 1933

'Do you get much snow here in the winter?' G. opened politely.
'Oh! quantities,' was the reply.
'How marvellous everything must look!'
'Yes; and you know, it's such wonderful snow.'
'Oh, is it? How?'
The parson leaned forward confidentially: ' . . . *wonderful* for snowballs,' he whispered.

Ibid.

That left the rest of the day to kill in Darjeeling, never at any time a place of intense or varied distraction. It wore an air typical now of most hill stations established during the spacious administrative days, of forlorn desuetude, not unlike that of Bognor Regis in November, only here one knew that the season, such as it was, would never return; the paint would continue to peel, the weeds to grow on the gravel, the terraced roads to crumble and fall, with greater and greater frequency and less and less inconvenience, into the valley below. In its heyday it must always have been a reasonably good example of how the world's most sublime natural situations can be chosen for the world's most frightful town planning.

James Cameron, *Point of Departure,* 1967

Darjeeling . . . is all smallness. It is small physically, of course, . . . but it is still smaller figuratively. It is the most deliberately diminutive town I know, as though it is always trying to make itself less substantial still. . . . When I arrived there for the first time I found it swirled all around by cloud. It felt curiously private and self-contained – like a childish fancy, I thought, a folly, a town magically reduced in scale and shut off from the world by vapour: but then as to a crash of drums in a *coup de théâtre,* a gap momentarily appeared in the ever-shifting clouds, and there standing tremendously in the background, their snows flushed pink with sunlight, attended by range upon range of foothills and serenely surveying the expanse of the world, stood the divine mass of the Himalayan mountains.

I saw Darjeeling's point, and cut myself down to size.

James Morris, 'Darjeeling', *Places,* 1972

Delhi

Delhi, where I stayed ten days a making Delhineations of the Delhicate architecture as is all impressed on my mind as inDelhibly as the Dehliterious quality of the water of that city.

Edward Lear, Letter to Lord Carlingford, 24 April 1874

It is the most uncertain-minded of cities in the world. It is like a fidgety girl who will first sit here, and there, then somewhere else, and fifty square miles of ground and twenty thousand ruins tell where it has rested. The modern Delhi is like the capricious girl grown up – charming, capricious, imperial. But also, like so many grown up and charming ladies, Delhi is a city with a past.

John Foster Fraser, *Round the World on a Wheel,* 1899

The Viceroy took me one afternoon to see the new Delhi. It was very wonderful seeing it with him who had invented it all, and though I knew the plans and drawings I didn't realise how gigantic it was till I walked over it. They have blasted away hills and filled up valleys, but the great town itself is as yet little more than foundations. The roads are laid out that lead from it to the four corners of India, and down each vista you see the ruins of some older imperial Delhi. A landscape made up of empires is something to conjure with.

Gertrude Bell, Letter to her family,
18 February 1916

Magnificent! It will certainly make the finest ruin of the lot.

Georges Clemenceau, remark on being shown New
Delhi by the Viceroy, 1921,
quoted in John Masters, *Pilgrim Son,* 1971

Delhi is a glorified Harrogate . . . not quite as 'refained' and about twenty times duller. Apart from the Lutyens buildings, as imposing as uncomfortable – which is what I expected, having been in his houses – there is absolutely nothing.

Julian Phillipson, Letter to James Agate, in Agate's,
Ego 7, 1945

Driving through the tremendous hexagonal parks and plazas that crisscross New Delhi, one has to admit that New Delhi is certainly crisscrossed with tremendous hexagonal parks and plazas. The perspectives are overpowering – endless tree-lined boulevards sweeping up to gigantic official buildings, grandiose monuments that dominate mile-long vistas, everywhere a sense of organized planning that offers a sardonic contrast to the confusion of the politicians behind the façade.

S.J. Perelman, *Westward Ha!,* 1948

The streets were wide and grand, the roundabouts endless: a city built for giants, built for its vistas, for its symmetry: a city which remained its plan, unquickened and unhumanized, built for people who would be protected from its openness, from the whiteness of its light, to whom the trees were like the trees on an architect's drawing, decorations, not intended to give shade: a city built like a monument.

V.S. Naipaul, *An Area of Darkness,* 1964

A city that offers a stimulant to the present and future, and is always interesting to all mankind.

Sikh Guide, on 1965 bus tour of Delhi, quoted
Ved Mehta, *Portrait of India,* 1970

Delhi is not just a national capital, it is one of the political ultimates, one of the prime movers. It was born to power, war, and glory. It rose to greatness not because holy men saw visions there but because it commanded the strategic routes from the Northwest, where the conquerors came from, into the rich flatlands of the Ganges delta. Delhi is a soldiers' town, a politicians' town, a journalists' diplomats' town. It is Asia's Washington, though not so picturesque, and lives by ambition, rivalry and opportunism.

Jan Morris, *Destinations,* 1980

Delhi is the capital of the losing streak. It is the metropolis of the crossed wire, the missed appointment, the puncture, the wrong number.

Ibid.

The Red Fort
If there is a paradise on the face of the earth, it is this, oh! it is this, oh! it is this!

Inscription, Hall of Private Audience

Dum Dum

On Sunday a thunderstorn. . . . There was a powder magazine at Dumdum (the idea of living near Dumdum!) struck that afternoon, and poor Dumdum made such a noise that it would have been glad to be deaf deaf.

Emily Eden, Letter, 17 June 1837,
in *Letters from India,* 1872

Etawah

The Barbers of this place are much spoken of for their neatenesse in Shaveinge and artificiall Champinge. The latter is a kinde of Custome used all India over, att tyme of rest especiallye, which is to have their bodies handled as wee knead in England, but this is with gripeing their hands; and soe they will goe all over a mans body as hee lyes along, vizt. Armes, shoulders, back, thighes, leggs, feete and hands. Then will they pull and winde you in such a manner that they will almost make every joint to crack, but without paine. Then will they dobb you, which is thumpinge with their fists (as Children beat upon a board when they would imitate a Drumme). This they doe a long tyme together, varyinge from one tyme to an other; and this is here accompted to bee verie healthfull. Also the oyle of Chambelee [*chambeli,* jasmine] of this place is much esteemed for goodness and Cheapnes, with which men, but especially weomen, annoynt their heads dayly, and their bodies when they wash (which is verie often); accompted also verie wholsome.

The place it selfe, exceptinge the residence of a Governour and what afore mentioned, is of little esteeme, scarce any bazure, nor a good streete.

Peter Mundy, *Travels in Europe and Asia,* 1632

Fatephur Sikri

The Cittie of Futtapore . . . is encompassed with a faire high wall of bigg square redd stone. In my opinion it was the only place that might any way resemble our European Citties, for conformitie of stately buildinges. Now it lyes in a manner of a heape. . . .

Peter Mundy, *Travels in Europe and Asia,* 1632

Fatephur Sikri, that forsaken city full of wondrous buildings, which rises like an enchantment out of the waste.

Norman Douglas, *Looking Back,* 1933

Goa

The Citie of Goa, is the Metropolitan or chiefe Citie of all the Orientall Indies, where the Portugals have their traffique, where also the Vice-roy, the Arch-bishop, the Kings Counsell, and Chancerie have their residence, and from thence are all places in the Orientall Indies, governed and ruled. . . . It is an Iland wholly compassed about with a River, and is above three miles great, it lieth within the Coast of the Firme Land, so that the Iland, with the Sea coast of the Firme Land, doe both reach as farre each as other into the Sea. . . . The Towne is well built with faire houses and streets, after the Portugall manner, but because of the heate they are somewhat lower. They commonly have their Gardens and Orchards at the back-side of their houses, full of all kind of Indian fruits: as also the whole Iland through, they have many pleasant Gardens and Farmes, with houses to play in, and trees of Indian fruits, whether they goe to sport themselves, and wherein the Indian women take great delight. The Towne hath in it all sorts of Cloysters and Churches as Lisbon hath, onely it wanteth Nunnes, for the men cannot get the women to travell so farre, where they should be shut up, and forsake Venus.

John Huighen van Linschoten, 1583, in *Purchas his Pilgrimes,* 1625

It is a fine Citie, and for an Indian Towne very faire.

Ralph Fitch, 1583–91, in *Purchas his Pilgrimes,* 1625

Goans think they are very Latin.

Ved Mehta, *Portrait of India,* 1970

Gwalior

We went this evening to see the Fort and Palace, and very beautiful it was, so like Bluebeard's abode.

Emily Eden, Letter, 11 January 1840, in *Up the Country,* 1866

When one sees Gwalior, one finds it hard to believe that Nature did not deliberately site and shape this fort for Man's convenience.

Arnold Toynbee, *East to West,* 1958

Himalayas

See also under Tibet

above Simla

They were to be a revelation of 'all might, majesty, dominion and power, henceforth, and for ever,' in colour, form, and substance indescribable.

Rudyard Kipling, *Something of Myself,* 1937 – of 1880s

This vertical desert.

James Cameron, *Daily Mail,* 22 October 1962, in *What a Way to Run the Tribe,* 1968

Hyderabad

Hyderabad is like a great flower bed.

Wilfred Scawen Blunt, *India Under Ripon,* 1909 – of 1883

Jeypore/Jaipur

Jeypore is sometimes extolled as the finest specimen of a native city, European in design, but Oriental in structure and form, that is to be seen in the East. The 'rose-red city' over which Sir Edwin Arnold has poured the copious cataract of a truly Telegraphese vocabulary struck me, when I was in India, as a pretentious plaster fraud.

Hon. George Curzon, *Persia and the Persian Question,* 1892

And the city itself is a curiosity. Any Indian city is that, but this one is not like any other that we saw. It is shut up in a lofty turreted wall; the main body of it is divided into six parts by perfectly straight streets that are more than a hundred feet wide; the blocks of houses exhibit a long frontage of the most taking architectural quaintnesses, the straight lines being broken everywhere by pretty little balconies, pillared and highly ornamented, and other cunning and cosy and inviting perches and projections, and many of the fronts are curiously pictured by the brush, and the whole of them have the soft rich tint of strawberry ice-cream. One cannot look down the far stretch of the chief street and persuade himself that these are real houses and that it is all out of doors – the impression that it is an unreality, a picture, a scene in a theatre is the only one that will take hold.

Mark Twain, *More Tramps Abroad,* 1897

Jodhpur

This is the land of heroism, where deeds which would have been brutal elsewhere have been touched with glory. In Europe heroism has become joyless or slunk to museums: it exists as a living spell here. The civilization of Jodhpur, though limited has never ceased to grow. It has not spread far, or excelled in the arts, but it is as surely alive as the civilization of Agra is dead. Not as a poignant memory does it touch the heart of the son or the stranger. And when it does die, may it find a death complete and unbroken; may it never survive archaeologically, or hear, like Delhi, the trumpets of an official resurrection. One would wish for the sand to close in on the city, and the purple stones to show more frequently than they do through the soil; for the desert to resume the life it gave, and unobserved by men, take back the dragon's crown.

E.M. Forster, *Adrift in India,* 1914

Kalimpong

Kalimpong strayed up and down along the hill road, neat and trim here; vague and sprawling there. A hundred and fifty years is no time at all in the history of India, yet it is everything; in a century and a half no place escaped the subtle mark of the Raj, not Kalimpong itself. Here was the final transition, the ultimate fining-out of Imperial suburbia into the frontier wastes.

James Cameron, *Point of Departure,* 1967

Kanchenjunga (seen from Darjeeling)

Petrified melodrama.

James Cameron, *Point of Departure,* 1967

Kashmir

Who has not heard of the Vale of CASHMERE
With its roses the brightest that earth ever gave,
Its temples and grottos, and fountains as clear
As the love-lighted eyes that hang over their wave?

Thomas Moore, *Lalla Rookh,* 1817

Often the vale below is half-veiled by cloud, and one sees only a green patch here and there, or a suggestion of water: but all around the white mountains stand, holding Kashmir on their hips – peak after peak, ridge after ridge, with Nangar Parbat supreme on the northern flank to set the scale of them all. Kashmir is, as I say, a place like no other: yet even from such a vantage point, high up there in the snow and the sun, its character is curiously negative. It could not possibly be anywhere else: but it might, so it often seemed to me in the hush of those high places, be nowhere at all.

One can judge it only by itself. The fascination of Kashmir is essentially introspective, a mirror-pleasure in which the visitor may see his own self picturesquely reflected, adrift in his shikara among the blossoms and the kingfishers. It is no place for comparisons. Paradise, here as everywhere, is in the mind.

James Morris, 'Kashmir', *Places,* 1972

There was a touching pathos, I thought, to the Kashmiri style. 'How do you like your life?' I asked one new acquaintance there, when we had progressed into intimacy. 'Excellent,' he replied, with a look of inexpressible regret, 'I love every minute of it' – and he withdrew a cold hand from the recesses of his cloak, and waved it listlessly in the air to illustrate his enjoyment.

Ibid.

Kedgeree

Kedgeree is a pretty place – about two inches of bank, then a little jungle and an old ruin of a house that a former postmaster lived in, a little thatched bungalow which the present less well-paid man inhabits, a flag-staff which acts as a semaphore, and then a few native huts. Mrs Rousseau, the postmistress sent me a basket of fruit and vegetables. I wish she would come herself as she must want to see another European woman. I suspect her husband must be the original Rousseau. It is just the place he would have chosen to live in – utterly out of the reach of human kind. If he and his wife happen to dislike each other, it must be a delightful position to be in.

Emily Eden, Letter, 7 August 1837, in *Letters from India,* 1872

Kozhikode (formerly Calicut)

The gentilmen and marchantes of Calicut acustometh oftentimes in token of grete love among them, and to encrese more love betwene them to chaunge ther wifes one with another, and in ther language thei speke one to another and on this maner, My frende and brother, many yeres we have had company together and I thinke more conversation and love ther can not be amonge frendes, wherfore I wil, if it be your pleasure, in ernest token of the amitie betwene us to chaunge wifes, you to take plesaure with myne and I with yours. Unto the which the other answereth that it is of trouth and that he is content to do as he wil have him. And so he goeth home to his hous and calleth his wife onto him and saith to her, Hit is so as ye knowe this our frende of long contynuance we have ben frendes, and now in token of more amitie I am content that you shal go with him and to fulfylle his wylle, and he is content that his wyfe shal come to me to perfourme the same. Then she answereth and saithe Sir, I thinke ye do but jeste, then he swereth by his deores that he jesteth not, but that he speketh ernest, then she saith if it be so let us go, and so she departes with his frende, and when he cometh to his house incontynent he sendeth him his wyfe.

Roger Barlow, *A Brief Summe of Geographie*, c. 1540
(Deores = dears.)

Ladakh

Climate arid. The atmosphere like dry ice. . . . To think about Ladakh at all is to experience a sort of disorientation.

Ved Mehta, *Portrait of India*, 1970

Leh (in Ladakh)

'The problems are there,' an imposing-looking officer says, striding into the room. 'But there is nothing to acclimation that mental posture won't take care of. It's the mental posture that counts. "One," you say to yourself, "I'm going to like this place," and, two, you like the place.'

Ved Mehta, *Portrait of India*, 1970

Madura

When I had seen Madura I felt that I had at last seen a temple of Babylon in all its glory, and understood what the worship of Apis might have been in Egypt.

Wilfred Scawen Blunt, *Ideas About India*, 1885

Mahabalipuram

A monochrome world that has all the indulgence of colour,
A still world whose every harmonic is audible,
Largesse of spirit and stone;
Created things for once and for all featured in full while for once and never
The creator who is destroyer stands at the last point of land
Featureless; in a dark cell, a phallus of granite, as abstract
As the North Pole; as alone.

But the visitor must move on and the waves assault the temple,
Living granite against dead water, and time with its weathering action
Make phrase and feature blurred;
Still from today we know what an avatar is, we have seen
God take shape and dwell among shapes, we have felt
Our ageing limbs respond to those ageless limbs in the rock
Reliefs. Relief is the word.

Louis MacNeice, *Mahabalipuram*, 1948

Malabar people

The Malabares . . . have a speech by themselves, and their Countrey is divided into many Kingdomes, they goe all naked onely their privie members covered, the Women likewise have but a cloth from their Navell downe to their knees, all the rest is naked, they are strong of limbes, and verie arrogant and proud, of colour altogether blacke, yet verie smooth both of haire and skinne, which commonly they anoynt with Oyle, to make it shine; they weare their haire as long as it will grow, tyed on the top or crowne of their heads with a Lace, both men and women: the lappes of their Eares are open, and are so long that they hang downe to their shoulders, and the longer and wider they are, the more they are esteemed among them, and it is thought to be a beautie in them. Of Face, Bodie and Limbes, they are altogether like men of Europe, without any difference, but onely in colour, the men are commonly verie hairie, and rough upon the brest, and on their bodies, and are the most Leacherous and unchaste Nation in all the Orient, so that there are verie few women Children among them, of seven or eight yeeres old, that have their Maidenheads: They are verie readie to catch one from another, though it bee but for a small Penie.

John Huighen van Linschoten, 1583,
in *Purchas his Pilgrimes*, 1625

Marhatta Country

'Camp in the Province of Loo'
This country into which I have come to visit my posts on the Marhattas frontiers is worse than that which you curse daily. It is literally not worth fighting for.

Duke of Wellington, Dispatch to Major Monro,
8 October 1799

Marhattas
The Marhattas are but little in the habit of adhering to truth.

Duke of Wellington, Dispatch to the Hon.
M. Elphinstone, 26 January 1804

A people proud and jealous as the Chinese, vain and unpolished as the Americans, and as tyrannical and perfidious as the French.

Thomas Duer Broughton, *Letters Written in a Maratha Camp*, 1813

Madras

Fort St George, nearby
I was much pleased with the beautiful prospect this

place makes off at Sea. For it stands in a plain Sandy spot of Ground, close by the shore, the Sea sometimes washing its Walls, which are of Stone and high, with Half-Moons and Flankers, and a great many Guns mounted on the Battlements: so that what with the Walls and fine Buildings within the Fort, the large Town of Maderas without it, the Pyramids of the English Tombs, Houses and Gardens adjacent, and the variety of fine trees scattered up and down, it makes as agreeable a Landskip as I have any where seen.

William Dampier, *Voyages and Descriptions*, 1699 – of 1690

Just as I got my head above the companion ladder, I felt an indescribably unpleasant sensation, suddenly, as it were, losing the power of breathing, which alarmed me much; for I supposed it to be the forerunner of one of those horrid Indian fevers of which I had heard so much during our voyage.

Whilst worried by this idea, my friend Rogers, whose watch it was, said to me, 'Well, Bill, what do you think of this? How do you like the delightful breeze you are doomed to spend you life in?' Enquiring what he meant, I found that what had so surprised and alarmed me was nothing more than the common land wind, blowing as usual at that hour directly offshore, and so intensely hot that I could compare it only to standing within the oppressive influence of the steam of a furnace.

William Hickey, *Memoirs*, 1749–1809

There is something uncommonly striking and grand in this town, and its whole appearance charms you from novelty, as well as beauty. Many of the houses and public buildings are very extensive and elegant – they are covered with a sort of shell-lime which takes a polish like marble, and produces a wonderful effect. – I could have fancied myself transported into Italy, so magnificently are they decorated, yet with the utmost taste. . . .

The free exercise of all religions being allowed; the different sects seem to vie with each other in ornamenting their places of worship, which are in general well built, and from their great variety, and novel forms afford much gratification, particularly when viewed from the country, as the beautiful groups of trees intermingle their tall forms and majestic foliage with the white chunam and rising spires, communicating such harmony, softness and elegance to the scene, as to be altogether delightful; and rather resembling the images that float on the imagination after reading fairy tales, or the Arabian Nights entertainment, than any thing in real life; in fact Madras *is* what I conceived Grand Cairo to be, before I was so unlucky as to be undeceived.

Eliza Fay, *Original Letters from India* (13 April 1780), 1817

Clive kissed me on the mouth and eyes and brow,
  Wonderful kisses, so that I became
Crowned above Queens – a withered beldame now,
  Brooding on ancient fame.

Rudyard Kipling, *The Song of the Cities*, 1893

Madras is . . . the poorest of the great Presidencies. Recently an English scientist, to test this out, picked several groups of albino rats, all the same age, sex and weight, segregated each group, and gave each group the diet of different Indian communities. Eighty days later, the rats were weighed. The rat eating the normal Sikh diet weighed 235 grams; Pathan diet, 230 grams; Mahratta diet, 220 grams; Gurkha diet, 200 grams; Kanarese diet, 185 grams; Bengali diet, 180 grams; Madrasi diet, 155 grams.

John Gunther, *Inside Asia*, 1939

Noodeean

We . . . are now at Noodeean – evidently a corruption of Noodleland, or the land to which we noodles should come.

Emily Eden, Letter, 24 January 1839, in *Up the Country*, 1866

The Native States (under the Raj)

The territories of the native princes are for the most part not the most fertile tracts of India; and one cannot avoid a suspicion that their comparative poverty has been the cause of their continued immunity from annexation.

Wilfred Scawen Blunt, *Ideas About India*, 1885

*They are the dark places of the earth, full of unimaginable cruelty, touching the Railway and Telegraph on one side, and, on the other, the days of Haroun-al-Raschid.

Rudyard Kipling, *The Man Who Would be King*, 1888

Nepal

and Bhutan and Sikkim

Nepal, Bhutan, Sikkim, Three Pendants on India's Himalayan necklace.

Ved Mehta, *Portrait of India*, 1970

It's where the scene is, man! The word was out all over Europe, so here we are!

Bill Digby, American beatnik, quoted J. Anthony Lucas, *New York Times*, and from there by Ved Mehta, *Portrait of India*, 1970

Patna

A very longe Bazare with trees on each side (which is much used in theis part). It hath above 200 of Grocers or Druggists, and of severall druggs a world. It is the greatest Mart of all this Countrie.

Peter Mundy, *Travels in Europe and Asia,* 1632

G went to see the jail and the opium godowns, which he said were very curious. There is opium to the value of 1,500,000L in their storehouses, and Mr T says that they wash every workman who comes out; because the little boys even, who are employed in making it up, will contrive to roll about in it, and that the *washing* of a little boy well rolled in opium is worth four annas, (or sixpence) in the bazaar, if he can escape to it.

Emily Eden, Letter, 7 November 1837, in *Up the Country,* 1866

Poona

Poona is an uninteresting place, without a vestige of Eastern colour. It stands in a bare plain, feebly relieved by a river bordered with Acacia trees, and some shapeless hills of trappe formation. Great macadamized roads run everywhere, and modern buildings of debased Gothic with meaningless belfries and inscriptions to Sir Bartle Frere dot the landscape. Barracks, of course, and factory chimneys abound, and institutions of all sorts. The climate is, however, a healthy one.

Wilfred Scawen Blunt, *India Under Ripon,* 1909 – of 1883

Rishikish

Rishikish . . . where the Maharishi Mahesh Yogi once received the Beatles in an air-conditioned bungalow built on the proceeds of Western adulation, and where there is a township totally given to spirituality and alms, vividly decorated with green and red cast-ironwork, dominated by a Victorian clocktower, looking and feeling like a cross between Blackpool and Lourdes.

Geoffrey Moorhouse, *Calcutta,* 1971

Rivers

A great Indian river, at low water, suggests the familiar anatomical picture of a skinned human body, the intricate mesh of interwoven muscles and tendons to stand for water-channels, and the archipelagoes of fat and flesh inclosed by them to stand for the sand bars.

Mark Twain, *More Tramps Abroad,* 1897

Scinde

Peccavi (I have Scinde/sinned).

Sir Charles Napier, Dispatch after the victory of Hyderabad in Scinde, 1843

and Oudh

'Peccavi – I've Scinde,' wrote Lord Ellen so proud.
More briefly Dalhousie wrote – '*Vovi* – I've Oude.'

Anon., *Punch,* 22 March 1856

('Lord Ellen' was Lord Ellenborough, Governor General of India, 1841–4, and responsible for the annexation of Scinde. Lord Dalhousie, who in 1856 annexed Oudh, was Governor General 1847–56.)

In order properly to appreciate dust you must go by train across the desert of Sinde.

Gertrude Bell, Letter to her family, 11 February 1916

Shahzadpur

Here at Shawzaadpore is great store of the best paper made, and from thence sent to other parts; also Pintadoes or chints. It is finely seated on the River Ganges, a great place and populous. In some kinde it may bee compared to Constantinople, standinge on manie hills, which lye alongst the River side; but it wants greatnes and state. There is one streete in it above the rest that deserves notice and Commendations; For, besides that it is verie longe and straight, it hath a rowe of trees on each side before the doores, whose topps meete alofte, soe that you seeme to bee in a faire longe Arbour walke. . . . In conclusion, it is a dainty seate.

Peter Mundy, *Travels in Europe and Asia,* 1632

Sikkim

Sikkim . . . is stuck between Bhutan and Nepal like a postage stamp.

Ved Mehta, *Portrait of India,* 1970

Simla

There never was such delicious weather, just like Mr Wodehouse's gruel, 'cool but not too cool.'

Emily Eden, Letter, 29 April 1838, in *Up the Country,* 1866

The 'Queen's Ball' came off yesterday with great success. . . . Twenty years ago no European had ever been here, and there we were, with the band playing the 'Puritani' and 'Masaniello' and eating salmon from Scotland, and sardines from the Mediterranean and observing that St Cloup's potage à la Julienne was perhaps better than his other soups, and that some of the ladies sleeves were too tight according to the overland fashions for March, &c., and all this in the face of those high hills, some of which have remained untrodden since the creation, and we 105 Europeans being surrounded by at least 3,000 mountaineers, who, wrapped up in their hill blankets, looked on at what we call our polite amusements, and bowed to the ground, if a European came near them. I sometimes wonder they do not cut all our heads off, and say no more about it.

Emily Eden, Letter, 25 May 1839,
in *Up the Country,* 1866

It is inconceivable and consequently very English! – to have a capital as Simla is, entirely of tin roofs . . . if one was told monkeys had built it all one could only say 'What wonderful monkeys – they must be shot in case they do it again.'

Sir Edwin Lutyens, Letter, 1912,
in Christopher Hussey, *The Life of Sir Edwin Lutyens,* 1953

It is not the Himalayas or any sort of mountain place at all, but a freak of woods and ridges with houses pouring down their steepness like lava, dilapidated, Victorian, and corrupted by turret and pagoda fancies. There is a funny reminiscence of Venice I could not pin down, till I realized it was the absence of cars and the crowd padding on foot with rickshaws like gondolas calling out as they slip along.

Freya Stark, Letter, 27 May 1945,
in *Dust in the Lion's Paw,* 1961

The ridge sparkled with electric light, and in the lamplit darkness the town centre defined itself more clearly: an English country town of fairyland, of mock-mock styles, the great ecclesiastical building asserting the alien faith, the mean-fronted shops, ornately gabled, out of which nightcapped, night-gowned men might have appeared holding lanterns or candles: a grandiloquent assertion of a smallness and cosiness that never were. But it was not what I had expected. . . . Simla will never cease to be Kipling's city: a child's vision of Home, doubly a fairyland. India distorts and enlarges; with the Raj it enlarged upon what was already a fantasy.

V.S. Naipaul, *An Area of Darkness,* 1964

On the sharp white foothills of the Himalayas there still exists this dim memory of Matlock Spa.

Robert Robinson, *Robinson's Travels – Lucknow to the Hills,* BBC Television, 19 December 1979

Sardah/formerly Surdah

We stopped at Surder to take in some sheep. We ought to have been there two days ago. . . . G said last night, when we again failed in landing there, that it seemed to him Absurder rather than Surder. He made another good pun today. How our intellects are weakened by the climate.

Emily Eden, Letter, 28 October 1837,
in *Up the Country,* 1866
('G' is George Eden, later Earl of Auckland, the Governor General.)

Uttar Pradesh

It would not be inappropriate to describe Uttar Pradesh as the centre of the stage on which the drama of Indian history has been played. . . . Uttar Pradesh has reflected and interpreted the significance of the most important events in the country's history, though it has not actually staged many.

State Guidebook to Uttar Pradesh, quoted
Ved Mehta, *Portrait of India,* 1970

INDIAN OCEAN

The Injian Ocean sets an' smiles
  So sof', so bright, so bloomin' blue;
There arn't a wave for miles and miles
  Excep' the jiggle from the screw.

Rudyard Kipling, *For to Admire,* 1894

at Bagamoyo
The Indian Ocean here has the texture, and no doubt the specific gravity, of warm, very salty soup and is infested with a thousand slimy things.

Alan Moorhead, *The White Nile,* 1960

INDONESIA

The people there hearing our Countries are cold, have asked us if wee beat Pepper in our Morter, that we playster our wales with to make our houses warme.

Edmund Scot, *A Discourse of Java,* 1602–5,
in *Purchas his Pilgrimes,* 1625

They delight very much in Playes, and singing, but they have the worst voyces that one shall heare any people have.

Ibid.

No one who has ever been in these countries can be ignorant of the practice here called *amoc,* which means that an Indian intoxicated with opium rushes into the street with a drawn dagger in his hand, and kills everybody he meets, especially Europeans, till he is himself either killed or taken. This happened at Batavia three times while we were there to my knowledge, and much oftener, I believe. . . . So far, however, from being an accidental madness which drove them to kill whomsoever they met without distinction of persons, the three people that I knew of, and I have been told all others, had been severely injured, chiefly in love affairs, and first revenged themselves on the party who had injured them. It is true that they had made themselves drunk with opium before they committed this action; and when it was done rushed into the streets, foaming at the mouth like mad dogs, with their drawn *criss* or dagger in their hands: but they never attempted to hurt any one except those who tried or appeared to them to try to stop or seize them.

Sir Joseph Banks, *Journal of the Rt Hon Sir Joseph Banks,* 1768–71

The dominating fact about the islands is that, like Croesus and John D. Rockefeller, Jr., they are rich. They are the Big Loot of Asia.

John Gunther, *Inside Asia,* 1939

All the 'new nations' are at grips with the problem of forging a national identity, of inculcating common reflexes and a consciousness of mutual solidarity among divergent human groups penned inside more or less artificial and accidental frontiers. All their regimes employ, with varying degrees of success, the same familiar recipes long ago developed by European nationalist movements: education in the service of patriotism, the daily celebration of the cult of national leadership, national heroes, national symbols and national myths, and permanent mobilisation against an indispensable common enemy. The exotic transposition of the myths and magic formulas of the deified race or nation sometimes prevents us from recognising the old familiar face of *l'Europe des patries.* In this respect, Indonesia is no exception, but simply an extreme case. Nowhere else has the subordination of every other interest and concern to this unique preoccupation been carried to such obsessive, disconcerting and ruinous lengths. Almost every single manifestation of this feverish nationalism, every one of the slogans it has culled from all the ideologies of the world, can be found elsewhere; but the combination forms an incomparable orgy of synthetic emotions. In so far as a collective psychosis controlled by a charismatic leader is accessible to reason, the case of Indonesia deserves analysis.

Herbert Luethy, 'Indonesia Confronted', *Encounter,* December 1965

In the long run, Indonesia is paying more and more dearly for its illusion of receiving everything, while giving nothing, and robbing everyone.

Ibid.

as seen from off Singapore
*The low blue *blancmange* of Indonesia.

Paul Theroux, 'A Deed Without a Name', in *Sinning with Annie,* 1975

Ambon/Amboina

Amboyna sitteth as Queene between the Iles of Banda and the Moluccas; hee is beautified with the fruits of severall Factories, and dearely beloved of the Dutch: which the better to declare, they say they would give thirtie millions there were no Cloves but on that Iland onely. Neptune is her darling, and entertayned in her very bosome, it seemeth that the Water and the Earth are agreed together in unitie: for at the bottome of the Bay, with one hundred Pioners in seven dayes, of one Iland it may be made two.

Humphrey Fitzherbert, Letter to the East India Company, in *Purchas his Pilgrimes,* 1625

Bali

We drove for three hours straight across Bali, through village after village, without passing a soul on the roads, and in some villages without seeing a single face. It was the most extraordinary sensation, like journeying in a dream through the landscape, which bore every sign of recent habitation, but from which every soul had vanished. . . . And a lovely land it is! with some twenty equally beautiful and different scenes, which repeat over and over in astonishing and unpredictable rhythms. In this inhabited end of Bali there are very few trees, only coconut palms, bamboo, and an occasional enormous tree some four or five yards in diameter when all of its extra roots are considered. One of the lovely views is an almost open plain of rice fields, a few palms and one enormous tree of this sort, squatting in a thoroughly primeval fashion in the midst of the fragile rice and slender palm stems. There are gorges, any one of which would be listed as a 'beauty spot' at home, unbelievably rough and jagged but with the rough lines all blurred by a light, coarse grass. There are the rice fields themselves, with half a dozen characteristic but different aspects – those which are almost on a level, whose principal charm is the great variation in the same texture and color as one small plot ripens an hour or a day behind the other, but all the varying shades remain within the same narrow range, and the flooded fields, which actually do mirror the sky, and the steep terraces, where the roots of each stalk stand out like sharp patterns along the edge. Up above 2,500 feet, the landscape loses almost all tropical feeling. Spare brown fields covered with bracken and edged with scanty windbreaks of very sparsely covered trees make it look like western park land.

Margaret Mead, Letter from Oeboed, Bali, 29 April 1936

Some of the visitors who had inscribed their names had been unable to refrain from bursting into song. The most poignant item in the book was a series of stanzas, the first three of which began:

Oh noble breasts of Bali
Erect and proud you stand . . .

Ye beauteous breasts of Bali
To which the children cling . . .

and, finally:

Oh laughing breasts of Bali
That youth aspires to climb. . . .

Cedric Belfrage, *Away from It All*, 1936

Even to a visitor from California Bali seems beautiful.

Comment in a hotel visitors' book, quoted *ibid.*

In Bali I saw the only happy large community I have seen in my life.

Geoffrey Gorer, *Bali and Angkor*, 1936

Bantam/Banten (now ruinous)

Bantam is not a place to recover men that are sicke, but rather to kill men that come thither in health.

Edmund Scot, *A Discourse of Java*, 1602–5, in *Purchas his Pilgrimes*, 1625

Jakarta (formerly Batavia)

The Dutch (always true to their commercial interests) seemed to have pitched upon this situation entirely for the convenience of water-carriage, which indeed few, if any, towns in Europe enjoy in a higher degree. Few streets in the town are without canals of considerable breadth, running through, or rather stagnating in them. These canals are continued for several miles round the town, and with five or six rivers, some of which are navigable thirty or forty or more miles inland, make the carriage of every species of produce inconceivably cheap. . . . The streets are broad and handsome and the banks of the canals in general planted with rows of trees. A stranger on his first arrival is very much struck with these, and often led to observe how much the heat of the climate must be tempered by the shade of the trees and coolness of the water . . . but a very short residence will show him that the inconveniences of the canals far over-balance any convenience he can derive from them in any but a mercantile light. Instead of cooling the air, they contribute not a little to heat it, especially those which are stagnant, as most of them are, by reflecting back the fierce rays of the sun. In the dry season these stink most abominably, and in the wet many of them overflow their banks, filling the lower storeys of the houses near them with water. When they clean them, which is very often, as some are not more than three or four feet deep, the black mud taken out is suffered to lie upon the banks, that is, in the middle of the street, till it has acquired a sufficient hardness to be conveniently laden into boats. This mud stinks intolerably.

Sir Joseph Banks, *Journal of the Rt Hon Sir Joseph Banks*, 1768–71

We see Japan everywhere, but it is Japan without the fun.

Henry Adams, Letter to Elizabeth Cameron, 26 August 1891

Batavia is yet another variation of Europe in the Far East – this time Holland.

Alfred Viscount Northcliffe, *My Journey Round the World*, 1923

The first thing I noticed about Indonesia was that everyone seemed to be smiling and to look about sixteen years old. The second was that the capital, which was of Dutch creation, had an almost aggressive lack of character. Unlike Singapore, it is not even pretentious. It is simply a soulless imitation of Dutch architecture back home, which straggles without visible rhyme or reason along a dank depression between the mountains and the sea: an administrative convenience built by men who wanted to be reminded of their mother country. Today it is like a dead tooth from which the nerve has been extracted.

James Mossman, *Rebels in Paradise*, 1961

Java

Java is famous for its mountains, jungle, lakes, volcanoes, mud lakes, geysers, tropical plants, foliage, coffee, cocoa, tea, rice, sago, tapioca, vanilla, cocaine, cloves and other spices. With the exception of coffee, cocaine, and vanilla, I've seen all these things in other places.

Alfred Viscount Northcliffe, *My Journey Round the World*, 1923

A world in which Man coaxes Nature with inexhaustible love and labour, instead of coercing her as he does in Australia and North America. In Java I am in the same world as in Lombardy or in Holland.

Arnold Toynbee, *East to West*, 1958

Javanese

The Javans, are generally exceeding proud, although extreame poore, by reason that not one amongst an hundred of them will worke. The Gentlemen of this Land are brought to be poore by the number of Slaves that they keepe, which eate faster than their Pepper or Rice groweth. . . . The Chinese, . . . like Jewes live crooching under them, but rob them of their wealth, and send it for China.

Edmund Scot, *A Discourse of Java*, 1602–5, in *Purchas his Pilgrimes*, 1625

I did not personally find the Javanese very sympathetic; despite their fertility they gave somehow the impression of being a race of old and exhausted people, only half alive. This impression may I think be due partly to their religion, and to the abysmal poverty of the greater number. Poverty, especially uncomplaining and voluntary poverty, is numbing and repulsive anywhere; and Mohammedanism is the most deadening of all creeds. A purely personal point which prevented me enjoying their company was the question of size; I do not like being among people who appear smaller and weaker than I am, unless they have corresponding superiority elsewhere; I dislike the company of those I feel to be my inferiors.

Geoffrey Gorer, *Bali and Angkor,* 1936

Macassar

The distractions of Macassar at any time, and particularly during the rainy season, are hardly such as to earn it the reputation of a spa. True, there is a famous old harbour where, by scaling a barbed-wire fence, you may catch a glimpse of some quaint native prahus, and for lovers of sixteenth-century Portuguese forts, there is a passable sixteenth-century Portuguese fort; but the town, a huddle of bleak and pungent alleys, does not twine itself around the heart and the population seemed merely an Asiatic version of a West Virginia mining community. As for the Dutch contingent, a cross-section of which we reveled with at a social club called the Harmonie, it was less than the gayest society in memory. Most of the men bore a chilling resemblance to either Baldur von Schirach or Himmler; their ladies, with minor exceptions, were cumbrous, hostile, and notably devoid of chic.

S.J. Perelman, *Westward Ha!,* 1948

Moti (Moluccas)

The Dutch hath one onely Factorie upon this Iland, which is called by the same name, it yeeldeth but little fruit, and venteth lesse Merchandize: here Venus and Voluptuousness have their habitation through idlenesse. Thus much by the report of others, for I was not there to see it my selfe.

Humphrey Fitzherbert, Letter to the East India Company, in *Purchas his Pilgrimes,* 1625

'Puloway' (Ai, Banda Islands)

Pooloway is the Paradice of all the rest, entermitting pleasure with profit. There is not a tree on that Iland but the Nutmeg, and other delicate Fruits of superfluitie; and withall, full of pleasant walkes, so that the whole Countrey seemes a contrived Orchard with varieties. They have none but raine-water, which they keepe in Jarres and Cisternes, or fetch it from the above-named Ilands, which is their onely defect. The sea shoare is so steepe, that it seemeth, Nature meant to reserve this Iland particularly to her selfe.

Humphrey Fitzherbert, Letter to the East India Company, in *Purchas his Pilgrimes,* 1625

Savu

The women . . . are far from handsome, and have a kind of sameness of features among them which might well account for the chastity of the men, for which virtue this island is said to be remarkable.

Sir Joseph Banks, *Journal of the Rt Hon Sir Joseph Banks,* 1768–71

Siau

Siau was small but wealthy. Its inhabitants looked out at the world with tolerant unenvious eyes. Its rows of neat wooden houses with their good tiled roofs and carved stairways, its homely market-places and mellow stone bridges carrying its unpaved streets out into the nutmeg groves beyond, all expressed a quiet confidence, and even perhaps a mildly patronising feeling for an outside world whose only obvious virtue was its craving for seasoned food.

James Mossman, *Rebels in Paradise,* 1961

Sumatra

'This is the island of hope,' said an official of the provincial government who received us. 'It has only ten million inhabitants, and already it produces nearly half the revenue of the Indonesian Republic.'

Arnold Toynbee, *East to West,* 1958

Ternate and Tidore

the Iles
Of *Ternate* and *Tidore,* whence Merchants bring
Thir spicie Drugs.

John Milton, *Paradise Lost,* 1667

IRAN

Persia consists of two parts: a desert with salt, and a desert without salt.

Old saying, quoted Hon. George Curzon, *Persia and the Persian Question,* 1892

Persia is the most named land of all asia.

Roger Barlowe, *A Brief Summe of Geographie, c.* 1540

To travell in this countrey is not onely miserable and uncomfortable for lacke of townes and villages to harbour in when night commeth, and to refresh men with wholesome victuals in time of need, but also such scarsitie of water, that sometime in three dayes journey together, is not to be found any drop fit for man or beast to drinke, besides the great danger we stand in for robbing by these infidels, who doe account it remission of sinnes to wash their hands in the blood of one of us. Better it is therefore in mine opinion to continue a beggar in England during life, then to remaine a rich Merchant seven yeeres in this Countrey, as some shall well find at their comming hither.

Laurence Chapman (1568), in Richard Hakluyt, *Principal Navigations . . . of the English Nation,* 1598–1600

Unhappie *Persea,* that in former age
Hast bene the seat of mighty Conquerors. . . .

Christopher Marlowe, *Tamburlaine,* Part 1, *c.* 1587

Persia, a country imbarred with mountains, open to the sea, and in the middle of the world.

Francis Bacon, *Of the True Greatness of the Kingdom of Britain, c.* 1606

Followed, it is said, by two millions of *men,* Xerxes, the descendant of Cyrus, invaded Greece. Thirty thousand *soldiers,* under the command of Alexander the Son of Philip, who was intrusted by the Greeks with their glory and revenge, were sufficient to subdue Persia.

Edward Gibbon, *The Decline and Fall of the Roman Empire,* 1776–88

What do we know of it now that we have traversed its length? This much – I speak for myself: I have been most wofully disappointed. Instead of being one of the happiest countries under the sun, 'the garden of verdure and fruit trees, and rose-bushes haunted by nightingales,' I find it to be the worst-governed, the worst-cultivated, and the most ill-watered country in the world! The Persian upland is more like a true desert than any inhabited country I know of.

H.M. Stanley, *My Early Travels and Adventures* (July 1870), 1895

Talk to a Greek Minister about his country, and he will tell you his country is great and prospering, and immediately his imagination runs away with him, and he speaks of the regeneration of Europe or Asia, through Greek influence! A Persian Minister is addicted to the same style of language. He is always going to do great things, but all the while he wastes his talents in getting a better position by purchase, and when he has acquired it, he devotes his talents to amassing money, and it is then 'Every man for himself,' and 'Allah for Persia.'

Ibid.

A typical English village consists of detached and often picturesque cottages, half hidden amid venerable trees. A typical Persian village is a cluster of filthy mud huts, whose outline is a crude combination of the perpendicular and the horizontal, huddled within the protection of a decayed mud wall.

Hon. George Curzon, *Persia and the Persian Question,* 1892

Well in this country the men wear flowing robes of green and white and brown, the women lift the veil of a Raphael Madonna to look at you as you pass; wherever there is water a luxuriant vegetation springs up and where there is not there is nothing but stone and desert. Oh the desert round Teheran! miles and miles of it with nothing, *nothing* growing; ringed in with bleak bare mountains snow crowned and furrowed with the deep courses of torrents. I never knew what desert was till I came here; it is a very wonderful thing to see; and suddenly in the middle of it all, out of nothing, out of a little cold water, springs up a garden. Such a garden! trees, fountains, tanks, roses and a house in it, the houses which we heard of in fairy tales when we were little: inlaid with tiny slabs of looking-glass in lovely patterns, blue tiled, carpeted, echoing with the sound of running water and fountains. Here sits the enchanted prince, solemn, dignified, clothed in long robes. He comes down to meet you as you enter, his house is yours, his garden in yours, better still his tea and fruit are yours. . . . Your magnificence sits down and spends ten minutes in bandying florid compliments through an interpreter while ices are served and coffee, after which you ride home refreshed, charmed, and with many blessings on your fortunate head. And all the time your host was probably a perfect stranger into whose privacy you had forced yourself in this unblushing way. Ah, we have no hospitality in the west and no manners.

Gertrude Bell, Letter to Horace Marshall, 18 June 1892

and Iraq

There's little difference between Persia and Mesopotamia, except that in the one the wilderness is set upright and in the other it's laid flat.

Gertrude Bell, Letter to her father, 13 July 1918

Resignation is essential here, if one does not wish to live in a condition of perpetual fury.

Vita Sackville-West, *Passenger to Teheran,* 1926

I found myself thinking, not for once of Persia in her natural beauty, but of Persia as the ideal state, of the opportunities of a wise and idealistic dictator. Would it not be possible for this vast, majestic, and under-populated country to shut itself off from the miseries of the world, and, self-contained, to concentrate solely upon the well-being of its own inhabitants? That would indeed be a new venture in government, a bold and revolutionary programme.

Vita Sackville-West, *Twelve Days,* 1928

Here is what I am told is a typically Persian story. A merchant was doing very well in the bazaar. When his son grew up he took him into partnership. The son cheated the father till he reduced him to bankruptcy. Mr. M, who told me, says he went some time after to visit the old man, now reduced to great poverty, and was told the whole story – only the old man was just bursting with pride over the intelligence of his son.

Freya Stark, Letter, 7 May 1930, *Beyond Euphrates,* 1951

The start of a journey in Persia resembles an algebraical equation: it may or may not come out.

Robert Byron, *The Road to Oxiana,* 1937

I have made my country young, and myself old.

His Imperial Majesty Reza Shah Pahlevi, attrib., before 1944

Rothstein, the Soviet Ambassador in Teheran, . . . told me . . . that he had come to the conclusion that Persia was 'fundamentally sound.' Asked to give the reason for this view, he found an almost unanswerable one. 'They will take money from anyone,' he explained, 'from the British today and from the Russians tomorrow, or from the French or the Germans, or anybody else. But they will never do anything for the money. You may buy their country from them six times over, but you will never get it. Therefore I say Persia can never go under. Persia is fundamentally sound.'

John Gunther, *Inside Asia,* 1939

No, Persia wasn't all depressing. Beautiful Isfahan and Shiraz. Wicked, pompous, oily British. Nervous, cunning, corrupt and delightful Persian bloody bastards. Opium no good. Persian vodka made of beetroot, like stimulating sockjuice, very enjoyable. Beer full of glycerine and pips. Women veiled or unveiled ugly, or beautiful and entirely inaccessible, or hungry. The lovely camels who sit on their necks and smile. I shan't go there again.

Dylan Thomas, Letter to J.M. Brinnin, 12 April 1951

There are some countries in which, at every visit, one recaptures the magic of a first arrival; Greece, Italy and Persia are such to me. However often, misted with sand, I leave the hot borders of Iraq and climb the Paitak pass, and through the cliff-gate of Sar-i-Pul, come on to plains where the larks sing over nests hidden in flowers; and see slow clear rivers under bridges bent like bows; the tumbled mountains of Kermenshah and poppy fields of Kangevar; the Asadabad pass and its grassy shoulders where the sun seems to lay a separate mantle of gold on top of the green; and the high gentle wave of Elvand south from Hamadan – however often I may see them, I think there will always be that tightening at the heart which comes with the remoteness of beauty, just beyond the possible footsteps of men.

Freya Stark, *Beyond Euphrates,* 1951

Plato, in one of his myths, imagines that civilization has been wiped out, many times over, by repeated catastrophes. The cities in the lowlands have been obliterated, and, each time, civilization has been set going again, from the beginning, by unsophisticated highlanders who have come through the catastrophes unscathed and have descended from their mountains to repopulate the plains. Plato's myth is Iran's history; only, in Iran, the catastrophes have been, not Nature's work, but Man's. . . . In Iran the latent antagonism between Cain and Abel is visible on the surface.

Arnold Toynbee, *East to West,* 1958

Iran is rich enough to support revolution as an industry.

Shimon Peres, quoted by Donald Trelford, 'It's not so Easy being a Jew', *Observer,* 20 April 1980

Iranians

These persons are comely and of good complexion, proude and of good courage, esteeming themselves to bee best of all nations, both for their religion and holinesse, which is most erroneous, and also for all other their fashions. They be martial, delighting in faire horses and good harnesse, soone angrie, craftie and hard people.

Anthony Jenkinson (1563), in Richard Hakluyt, *Principal Navigations . . . of the English Nation,* 1598–1600

in the area of Isfahan

They ride on horse-backe for the most part, on horse-backe they fight with the Enemie, they execute all Affaires as well publike as private on horse-backe, they goe from place to place on horse-backe, they buy and sell, and on horse-backe they conferre and talke with one another; and the difference betweene the Gentleman and the slave is, that the slave never rideth, nor the Gentleman never goeth on foote. Besides, the nature of the people is arrogant seditious, deceitfull, and very unquiet, but that the fiercenesse of their nature is much restrayned by the Kings severe government. To sensualitie they are much inclined, having three sorts of women, as they terme them, viz. honest women, halfe honest women and Courtezans; and yet they chastise no offence with like extremitie as Adulterie, and that as well in the halfe honest woman, as in the honest. Last of all they are full of craftie stratagems, and are breakers of their promise (a vice that is very inbred in all Barbarians.) Not content with any mans government long: and lovers of Novelties.

John Cartwright, 1603, in *Purchas his Pilgrimes,* 1625

Now concerning the natives: they are generally well-limbed and straight; the zone they live in makes them tawny; the wine cheerful; opium salacious. The women paint; the men love arms; all affect poetry; what the grape inflames, the law allays, and example bridles. The Persians allow no part of their body hair except the upper lip, which they wear long and thick and turning downwards. . . .

The Persians had this character of old, *cunctorum hominum sunt mitissimi,* of all men the most civil; which disposition they reserve unto this day, being generally of a very gentle and obliging nature – facetious, harmless in discourse, and little inquisitive after exotic news; seldom exceeding this demand: if such and such a country have good wine, fair women, serviceable horses, and well-tempered swords. . . . At meals they are the merriest men alive: no people in the world have better stomachs, drink more freely, or more affect voracity; yet are harmlessly merry: a mixture of meat and mirth excellently becoming them. Jovial in a high degree; especially when the courtesans are in company. The men account that for good manners which we thought barbarous, when, in compliment or rather squalid wantonness, they would overcharge their mouths with pelo, and by an affected laughter exonerate their chops, throwing the overplus into the dish again, and as a symbol of goodwill (sur-reverence) offer others to eat what they had chewed formerly.

Sir Thomas Herbert, *Some Years Travell,* 1628

A Persian's heaven is easily made,
'Tis but black eyes and lemonade.

Thomas Moore, *The Twopenny Post Bag,* 1813

The Persians are the Asiatic Frenchmen. They are good poets, courteous, and of tolerably refined taste. They are not rigorous followers of Islam; and they allow their own voluptuous tendencies a pretty latitudinarian interpretation of the Koran.

Thomas de Quincey, *Translation of Kant on National Character in Relation to the Sense of the Sublime and Beautiful,* 1824

It takes two Jews to rob an Armenian, two Armenians to rob a Persian.

Tiflis proverb, quoted Harry de Windt, *A Ride to India,* 1891

The Persian character presents many complex features, elsewhere rarely united in the same individual. They are an amiable and polished race, and have the manners of gentlemen. They are vivacious in temperament, intelligent in conversation, and acute in conduct. If their hearts are soft, which is, I believe, undeniable, there is no corresponding weakness of the head. On the other hand, they are consummate hypocrites, very corrupt, and lamentably deficient in stability or courage. They stand in the sharpest contrast to the peoples who surround them, the truculent Kurd, the haughty Afghan, the sullen Turk, the listless Hindu. With none of these do they share many common characteristics. . . . Whilst, as individuals, they present many attractive features, as a community, they are wholly wanting in elements of real nobility or grandeur. With one gift only can they be credited on a truly heroic scale. . . . I allude to their faculty for what a Puritan might call mendacious, but what I prefer to style imaginative utterance. This is inconceivable and enormous. . . . I am convinced that a true son of Iran would sooner lie than tell the truth; and that he feels twinges of desperate remorse when, upon occasions, he has thoughtlessly strayed into veracity. Yet they are an agreeable people – agreeable to encounter, agreeable to associate with, perhaps not least agreeable to leave behind. . . . There remain three attributes of the Persian character which lead me to think that that people are not yet, as has been asserted, wholly 'played out'; that they are neither sunk in the sombre atrophy of the Turk, nor threatened with the ignoble doom of the Tartar. . . . These are their irrepressible vitality; an imaginativeness long notorious in the East, and capable of honourable utilisation; and, in spite of occasional testimony to the contrary, a healthy freedom from deep-seated prejudice or bigotry. History suggests that the Persians will insist upon surviving themselves; present indications are that they will gradually absorb the accomplishments of others.

Hon. George Curzon, *Persia and the Persian Question,* 1892

They treat a motor exactly as though it were a pack-animal.

Vita Sackville-West, *Passenger to Teheran,* 1926

Abadan

It was no surprise to learn that, apart from pigmented natives who did the white-skins' manual toil, only two forms of animal life were found in the Gulf in any profusion: white men, mostly Britishers, and sharks. The sharks were there for what they could get. Their pickings consisted of an occasional limb off a sahib driven by heat and golf-course shortage to the madness of swimming, or even sometimes the entire corpse of a whiteskin for whom carrying the burden had proved too much, or who had gone out forgetting his topee. The white men were there to carry the burden.

Cedric Belfrage, *Away from It All,* 1936

I am now sitting contemplating the beauties of

civilization – a forest of tall chimneys, an expanse of iron aluminium-painted tanks, a belching column of smoke which burns year in and year out – the Anglo-Persian oil port: . . . looking south the great river flows quiet and flat between palm groves just as the Sumerians saw it: and looking north it might be Glasgow except for the sun.

Freya Stark, Letter, 31 March 1937, in *The Coasts of Incense,* 1953

I am writing this in a tasty, stifflipped, liverish, British Guest House in puking Abadan on, as you bloody well know, the foul blue boiling Persian buggering Gulf. And lost, God blast, I gasp between gassed vodkas, all crude and cruel fuel oil, all petroleum under frying heaven, benzola bitumen, bunkers and tankers, pipes and refineries, wells and derricks, gushers and super-fractionators and shaft-el-Arab and all. . . .

Abadan is inhabited almost entirely by British – or so it seems. There are thousands of young British in the bachelor quarters, all quietly seething. Many snap in the heat of their ingrowing sex and the sun, and are sent back, baying to Britain. Immediately, their places are taken by fresh recruits: young well-groomed pups with fair moustaches and briar pipes, who, in the soaking summer, soon age, go bristled about, chain-smoke damp hanging fags, scream blue on arak, toss themselves trembly all sleepless night in the toss-trembling bachelors' quarters, answer the three-knock knock at the midnight door, see before them in the hot moonlight wetmouthed Persian girls who ask, by custom, for a glass of water, invite the girls in, blush, stammer, grope, are lost. These old-young men are shipped back also, packed full with shame and penicillin.

Dylan Thomas, Letter to an American friend, 1951

Abbasabad

. . . this accursed spot where they sell cigar-holders of green soapstone and the men wear red blouses, seemed the peak of misery.

Robert Byron, *The Road to Oxiana,* 1937

Baluchistan (in part Pakistan)

The coast-line of Baluchistan is six hundred miles long. On it there is one tree, a sickly, stunted-looking thing, near the telegraph station of Gwadar, which serves as a landmark to native craft and a standing joke to the English sailor. Planted some years since by a European, it has lived doggedly on, to the surprise of all in this arid soil. The tree of Baluchistan is as well known to the mariner in the Persian Gulf as Regent Circus or the Marble Arch to the London cabman.

Harry de Windt, *A Ride to India,* 1891

I drank to the dregs the dismal vision of Persian Baluchistan. 'When God made Baluchistan, He laughed.' And He must have laughed again when He made the Horn of Arabia.

Arnold Toynbee, *East to West,* 1958

Bushire

At a distance, and seen from the harbour, Bushire is not unlike Cadiz. Its Moorish buildings, the whiteness of its houses and blueness of the sea, give it, on a fine day, a picturesque and taking appearance, speedily dissipated, however, on closer acquaintance; for Bushire is indescribably filthy. The streets are mere alleys seven or eight feet broad, knee-deep in dust or mud, and as irregular and puzzling to a stranger as the maze at Hampton Court.

Harry de Windt, *A Ride to India,* 1891

On the southern side, . . . the town was formerly fortified by a high wall with twelve towers, and bastions and two gates. . . . The last time that this wall was repaired was in 1838, when Mohammed Shah rebuilt it, to withstand a possible attack from the English, who had occupied Kharak island in that year. It has since fallen to pieces, and is now a model of nineteenth century Persian fortification.

Hon. George Curzon, *Persia and the Persian Question,* 1892

Gilan

The Air is so unwholsom, that the People cry of him that is sent to command there; *Has he robb'd, stol'n, or murther'd, that the king sends him to Guilan?*

J.B. Tavernier, *The Six Voyages . . . through Turkey into Persia . . . made English by J.P.,* 1677

Gula Hek

Are we the same people I wonder when all our surroundings, associations, acquaintances are changed? Here that which is me, which womanlike is an empty jar that the passer by fills at pleasure is filled with such wine as in England I had never heard of, now the wine is more important than the jar when one is thirsty, therefore I conclude, cousin mine, that it is not the person who danced with you at Mansfield St. that writes to you to-day from Persia – Yet there are dregs, English sediments at the bottom of my sherbet, and perhaps they flavour it more than I think.

Gertrude Bell, Letter to Horace Marshall, 18 June 1892

Ormuz/Hormuz

It was a great miracle to see the Mountaines of Ormus, all of Salt, and as hard as a Flint stone: and this Salt is very good for divers diseases. All the Iland is salt, and the very ground where the Towne doth stand is salt: which is the cause of the excessive heat that is there. From eight of the clocke in the morning untill the Sunne goe downe, it is not possible for any body, that is not used to the Countrey, to passe either with shooes or barefoot, where the Sunne doth lie, it is so extreme hot. The Swine in Ormus have clawes of a quarter of an ell long, and some longer.

John Newbery, 1581, in *Purchas his Pilgrimes,* 1625

Ormus is an Iland in circuit about five and twentie or thirtie miles, and is the dryest Iland in the world: for there is nothing growing in it but onely Salt; for their water, wood, or victuals, and all things necessary come out of Persia, which is about twelve miles from thence.

Ralph Fitch, *The Voyage,* 1583–91, in *Purchas his Pilgrimes,* 1625

Isfahan

Hispahan is the noblest Citie of this Kingdome: and, though it lye but in one and thirtie degrees and a halfe of Northerly latitude; yet, by reason of the subtile piercing ayre, the cold is sharper, then by the climate or situation one would imagine. Now, in all this Kingdome you can scarse see any print of Antiquitie: all the houses being of unburned bricke, or earth rammed up betweene two boards; too slight stuffe to last many dayes, much lesse many yeeres.

Don Garcia Silva Figueroa, 1619, in *Purchas his Pilgrimes,* 1625

I . . . believe that it will long remain in my mind connected with a profoundly blue sky, clear air, dusky groves, gorgeous temples of pleasure, lofty minars and egg-shaped domes. My wishes are that Isfahan may never be worse than it is . . . for the city has fulfilled my dream of the Orient, though it is but a shadow of its former self.

H.M. Stanley, *My Early Travels and Adventures* (July 1870), 1895

'He who has not been to Isfahan has not seen half the world,' is the boasted saying of a Persian writer.

Ibid.

Their niggardliness and closeness in business matters are illustrated by a story told by Malcolm (Sketches of Persia Chap xiii), which has been crystallised into the saying that 'The merchant of Isfahan will put his cheese into a bottle, and rub his bread on the outside to give it a flavour.'

Hon. George Curzon, *Persia and the Persian Question,* 1892

The beauty of Isfahan steals on the mind unawares. You drive about, under avenues of white tree-trunks and canopies of shining twigs; past domes of turquoise and spring yellow in a sky of liquid violet-blue; along the river patched with twisting shoals, catching that blue in its muddy silver, and lined with feathery groves where the sap calls across bridges of pale toffee brick, tier on tier of arches breaking into piled pavilions; overlooked by lilac mountains, by the Kuh-i-sufi shaped like Punch's hump and by other ranges receding to a line of snowy surf; and before you know how, Isfahan has become indelible, has insinuated its image into that gallery of places which everyone privately treasures. . . .

From the XIth century, architects and craftsmen have recorded the fortunes of the town, its changes of taste, government, and belief. The buildings reflect these local circumstances; it is their charm, the charm of most old towns. But a few illustrate the heights of art independently, and rank Isfahan among those rarer places like Athens or Rome, which are the common refreshment of humanity.

Robert Byron, *The Road to Oxiana,* 1937

Isfahan is like a pale torquoise, its tree stems white, its sky light blue, a lovely skiey light about it all. In the fields around are huge circular towers like keeps, merely built to house innumerable pigeons. The whole of Isfahan gives the feeling of a great deal of labour and loveliness and thought spent on the light, airy, evanescent side of things. It was fun going about the bazaars where the carpets, miniatures and stamped patterned coverlets are made by tiny boys with long eyelashes bending over their fine brushes and bright paints.

Freya Stark, Letter, 28 April 1943, in *Dust in the Lion's Paw,* 1961

Jask

Here lies buried one Captain *Shilling,* unfortunately slaine, by the insulting *Portugall;* but that his bones want sence and expression, they would tell you the earth is not worthy his receptable, and that the people are blockish, rude, treacherous and indomitable.

Sir Thomas Herbert, *A Relation of Some Yeares Travell . . . Begunne 1626,* 1634

Kadamgh

The name means 'the place of the step,' the tradition being that the Imam Reza halted here on his way to Tus, and, in order to convince the local fire-worshippers of his superiority, left the imprint of his foot upon a black stone, which became a *ziarat gah,* or place of pilgrimage, ever afterwards. Over the sacred spot a mosque was raised. . . . The mosque stands on a raised platform at the upper end of a large garden, which has once been beautifully laid out in terraces, with flower beds, and tanks, and channels of running water, and which, though in a state of hopeless decay, is still overshadowed by considerable trees. Inside the mosque is a single chamber, entered by a coffered archway, and covered by a large dome. The sacred stone is inside; nor is it surprising to find that the Prophet's foot-marks are of more than ordinary size. All these great men had huge feet. I have seen Mohammed's footprint in the Mosque of Omar at Jerusalem, and Buddha's footprint on the summit of Adam's Peak in Ceylon; and in view of their prodigious magnitude I was surprised at the modesty of the Imam Reza in having been content with, comparatively speaking, so temperate a measurement.

Hon. George Curzon, *Persia and the Persian Question,* 1892

Kotal-i-Pir-i-Zan (or Pass of the Old Woman, near village of Dasht-i-Arzen)

The ascent is steep and joyless; but it is as nothing compared with the descent on the other side, which is long, precipitous, and inconceivably nasty. This is the famous Kotal-i-Pir-i-zan, or Pass of the Old Woman.

Some writers have wondered at the origin of the name. I feel no such surprise. On the contrary, I admire the apposite felicity of the title. For, in Persia, if one aspired by the aid of a local metaphor, to express anything that was peculiarly uninviting, timeworn, and repulsive, a Persian old woman would be the first and most forcible simile to suggest itself.

Hon. George Curzon, *Persia and the Persian Question,* 1892

Luristan

I spent a fortnight in that part of the country where one is less frequently murdered. . . . The Lurs, like the little girl with the curl, are very nice when they are nice, but when they are not they are horrid – and one rarely knows which it is going to be. There is an anxious interval when one comes to a strange tribe, and waits to see.

Freya Stark, *The Valleys of the Assassins,* 1934

Stealing is the national art. The Lurs appear to pride themselves on it more than on anything else. In the days of the Crusades it is recorded that they were so expert in escalading walls that Saladin, thinking them a dangerous people, used to put them in the advance of his attacks so as to exterminate them if possible. . . . 'There is no one like us for stealing in the world,' said Keram.

Ibid.

Mazanderan

Bengal in the rains, Demerara in the wet season, Bombay in the monsoon – these were the recollections that suggested themselves to my mind; and yet I think Mazaneran far more unpleasant than either.

James Fraser, *A Winter's Journey,* 1838 – of 1834

Meshed/Mashad

Perhaps the most extraordinary feature of Meshed life, . . . is the provision that is made for the material solace of the [pilgrims] during their stay in the city. In recognition of the long journeys which they have made, of the hardships which they have sustained, and of the distances by which they are severed from family and home, they are permitted, with the connivance of the ecclesiastical law and its officers, to contract temporary marriage during their sojourn in the city. There is a permanent population of wives suitable for the purpose. . . . In other words a gigantic system of prostitution, under the sanction of the Church, prevails in Meshed. There is probably not a more immoral city in Asia.

Hon. George Curzon, *Persia and the Persian Question,* 1892

I was on the look-out for coffins of defunct Shias on their way to the great necropolis of Meshed; and from the descriptions of previous travellers recognised the ghastly burden as soon as I saw it. Some that I passed were wrapped in black felt, and slung on either side of donkeys. One man, however, was carrying a very long coffin in front of him on his saddle-bow, and must have had moments of strange emotion. Sometimes a regular corpse-caravan is met, which has been chartered to convey so many score of departed Shias to their final resting-place. But as frequently an amateur carrier is encountered, who, to pay the expenses of his own journey, and leave a little for amusement at the end, contracts to carry the corpse of some wealthier fellow-citizen or friend.

Ibid.

Persepolis

Is it not passing brave to be a King,
And ride in triumph through *Persepolis*?

Christopher Marlowe, *Tamburlaine,* Part 1, *c.* 1587

. . . the piles of fall'n Persepolis . . .
Whence flits the twilight-loving bat at eve,
And the deaf adder wreathes her spotted train,
The dwellings once of elegance and art.
Here temples rise, amid whose hollow'd bounds
Spires the black pine, while thro' the naked street

Once haunt of tradeful merchants, springs the grass:
Here columns heap'd on prostrate columns, torn
From their firm base, increase the mould'ring mass.
Far as the sight can pierce, appear the spoils,
Of sunk magnificence! a blended scene
Of moles, fanes, arches, domes and palaces,
Where, with his brother Horror, Ruin sits!

Thomas Wharton, *Pleasures of Melancholy*, 1745

Just ahead rose what looked like a lot of battered ninepins on the top of a shaky table. This was Persepolis.

John Foster Fraser, *Round the World on a Wheel*, 1899

The space, the sky, the hawks, the raised-up eminence of the terrace, the quality of the Persian light, all give to the great terrace a sort of springing airiness, a sort of treble, to which the massive structure of bastion and archways plays a corrective bass. It is only when you draw near that you realise how massive that structure really is.

Vita Sackville-West, *Twelve Days*, 1928

Qom/Kum

Apparently . . . the good folk of Kum are without honour in their own country; for there is a Persian proverb that says: 'A dog of Kashan is better than a noble of Kum, albeit a dog is better than a man of Kashan.'

Hon. George Curzon, *Persia and the Persian Question*, 1892

A wonderful series of hills and mountains are around it – of the colour of lava and the formation of vitrified waves. To the north-west of Kûm, at the distance of a couple of farsakhs, is an isolated group of lofty peaks, whose Persian title means, 'Away – return no more.' . . . We looked intensely at the city – the city, alas, for those poets who sacrifice truth to style, who under the mask of fiction, disguise the living reality. There is nothing worthy of the name of a city here, except a city of the dead, who lie in unnumbered thousands around.

It is mainly a wilderness of ruins covering an area of about two square miles. There are numbers of mausoleums scattered outside the city, and many a lacquered dome rises above the flat-roofed houses. Scanty tufts of foliage may be seen here and there, amid the waste, and a rather dense growth surrounds the holy shrine and gilded dome of Fatima. For about a mile and a half from Kûm stretch its cornfields, its gardens of melons, pistachios, &c., various canauts leading from the 'Mountain of the Talisman,' 'Kûh-e-Telesm,' and from the hills of the 'Away, return no more,' there flows a stream, about two yards wide, and six inches deep. . . .

I wandered through the bazaars, ruined streets and lanes of Kûm, and saw acres of prostrate houses, and walls and mosques. Kûm is a hotbed of bigotry, despite its desolation. It is the home of indolence, unthrift, and superstition. It is a rendezvous of dead sheeahs. To obtain the happy distinction of laying their bones close to the beloved Fatima, those who can afford it pay large sums. . . . The Mollahs of Kûm permit no intoxicating liquors to be made in their city, which is the very palladium of the Sheeah religion.

H.M. Stanley, *My Early Travels and Adventures* (June 1870), 1895

Resht

Resht bears the unpleasant reputation of being the most unhealthy city in Persia. Its very name, say the natives, is derived from the word *rishta*, 'death'. 'If you wish to die,' says a proverb of Irak, 'go to Resht!'

Harry de Windt, *A Ride to India*, 1891

Shiraz

When Shiraz was Shiraz, Cairo was one of its suburbs.

Old saying

Here art magick was first hatched; here Nimrod for some time lived; here Cyrus, the most excellent of Heathen Princes, was born; and here (all but his head, which was sent to Pisigard) intombed. Here the Great Macedonian glutted his avarice and Bacchism. Here the first Sibylla sung our Saviour's incarnation. Hence the Magi are thought to have set out towards Bethlehem, and here a series of 200 Kings have swayed their scepters.

Sir Thomas Herbert, *Some Yeares Travel into Asia*, 1634

The Shirazi are a people whose thoughts dwell upon passionate love, and shades of trees. They are a people of sleepy eyes and melting moods.

H.M. Stanley, *My Early Travels and Adventures* (July 1870), 1895

Shiraz has been called the 'Paris of Persia,' from the cheerful, sociable character of its people as compared with other Persian cities; also, perhaps, from the beauty and coquetry (to use no other term) of its women.

Harry de Windt, *A Ride to India*, 1891

Shiraz, in the words of its own singer, Sadi, 'turns aside the heart of the traveller from his native land.'

Hon. George Curzon, *Persia and the Persian Question*, 1892

between Shiraz and Bushire
Now there are certain things all men should do as an

experiment – fall in love, fall overboard, get vaccinated, get into debt, have a tooth drawn, float a company, visit Holloway, run an opera, be a Parliamentary candidate and endeavour to run the state, and die. These, however, are only ten accepted truisms to complete the circle of existence. The eleventh, and most heroic, is to descend the Kotals from Shiraz to Bushire with a bicycle.

John Foster Fraser, *Round the World on a Wheel,* 1899

Sistan

Not long ago, Marjoribanks paid a first visit to Sistan. To gratify his appetite for modern street-planning, the terrified local authorities built a whole new town, Potemkin-wise, whose walls, though festooned with electricity, enclosed nothing but fields. A lorry preceded him by a day, bearing children's clothes. Next morning, the school assembled dressed like a French kindergarten. The monarch drove up, stopped long enough to sack the local schoolmaster because the children's clothes were backward, and drove on; but not before the clothes had been whisked off the children and bundled back into the lorry, to precede him at the next place. Persia is still the country of *Haji Baba.*

Robert Byron, *The Road to Oxiana,* 1937
(Marjoribanks = The Shah. Byron had been warned against criticism of the regime while in the country, and advised to write of the ruler under a pseudonym.)

Tabas

The Persian for 'get lost' is 'go to Tabas.'

The Economist, 3 May 1980
(in the aftermath of the American rescue débâcle at the end of April)

Tabriz

Money trolls about in that place more than any other part of Asia.

J.B. Tavernier, *The Six Voyages . . . through Turkey into Persia . . . made English by J.P.,* 1677

The features of Tabriz are a view of plush-coloured mountains, approached by lemon-coloured foothills; a drinkable white wine and a disgusting beer; several miles of superb brick-vaulted bazaars; and a new municipal garden containing a bronze statue of Marjoribanks in a cloak.

Robert Byron, *The Road to Oxiana,* 1937
(Marjoribanks: see note under Sistan above.)

Teheran

Seated is Tyroan in the midst of a large level or plain. The Houses are of white bricks hardened by the Sun. The City has about 3,000 Houses, of which the Duke's and the Buzzar are the fairest; yet neither to be admired. The Market is divided into two; some part thereof is open and other part arched. A Rivolet in two branches streams through the Town, serving withal both Grove and Gardens, who for such a favour, return a thankful tribute to the Gardiner. The inhabitants are pretty stately, the Women lovely, and both curious in novelties; but the jealousies of the men confine the temper of the weaker sex; yet by that little they adventured at, one might see *vetutis rebus gliscit voluntas.*

Sir Thomas Herbert, *Some Yeares Travel into Asia,* 1634

It has one advantage over almost every Oriental city: it is too far removed from the sea to be the resort of the Levantine.

H.M. Stanley, *My Early Travels and Adventures* (June 1870), 1895

and the Qanats

There seems to be no lack of water in Teheran. . . . It is . . . artificially supplied by 'connaughts,' or subterranean aqueducts flowing from mountain streams, which are practically inexhaustible. In order to keep a straight line, shafts are dug every fifty yards or so, and the earth thrown out of the shaft forms a mound, which is not removed. Thus a Persian landscape, dotted with hundreds of these hillocks, often resembles a field full of large ant-hills.

Harry de Windt, *A Ride to India,* 1891

We are in a city which was born and nurtured in the East, but is beginning to clothe itself at a West-End tailor's. European Teheran has certainly become, or is becoming; but yet, if the distinction can be made intelligible, it is being Europeanised upon Asiatic lines.

Hon. George Curzon, *Persia and the Persian Question,* 1892

If ever you have seen an Asiatic in a white shirt and frock-coat and patent-leather shoes for the first time, you have some conception of Teheran as it looks today. It is Asia struggling into the white shirt of European civilization.

John Foster Fraser, *Round the World on a Wheel,* 1899

Teheran itself, except for the bazaars, lacks charm; it is a squalid city of bad roads, rubbish-heaps, and pariah dogs; crazy little victorias with wretched horses; a few pretentious buildings, and mean houses on the verge of collapse. But the moment you get outside the city everything changes. For one thing, the city remains definitely contained within its mud rampart, there are no straggling suburbs, the town is the town and the country is the country, sharply divided. For another thing, the city is so low that at a little distance it is scarcely visible; it appears as a large patch of greenery, threaded with blue smoke. I call it a city, but it is more like an enormous village.

Vita Sackville-West, *Passenger to Teheran,* 1926

Teheran is a city I liked particularly, neither western nor eastern, but with a character of its own, colourless but clear, like water – and I do not mean the Teheran drinking water, which at that time ran in open gutters through the streets and was not clear at all. . . .

Freya Stark, *Beyond Euphrates,* 1951 – of 1931

Teheran, a boom town grafted onto a village, is a place of no antiquity and little interest, unless one has a particular fascination for bad driving and a traffic situation twenty times worse than New York's. . . . In spite of its size and apparent newness it retains the most obnoxious features of a bazaar, as Dallas does, and Teheran has all the qualities of that oil-rich Texas city: the spurious glamour, the dust and heat, the taste for plastic, the evidence of cash.

Paul Theroux, *The Great Railway Bazaar,* 1975

Yazd-e-Khvāst

Yezdi-Ghazt, towering shadowy and indistinct over the moonlit plain. . . . As we rode . . . through the semi-darkness caused by the shadow of the huge mass of boulders and mud on which the town is situated, the effect was extraordinary. It was like a picture by Gustave Doré; and, looking up at the weird city with its white houses, queer-shaped balconies, and striped awnings, standing out clear and distinct against the starlit sky, gave one an uncomfortable, uncanny feeling . . . although the hour was yet early, not a light was visible, not a sound to be heard. It was like a city of the dead.

Daylight does not improve the appearance of Yezdi-Ghazt. . . . The system of drainage . . . is simple, the sewage being thrown over, to fall, haphazard, on the ground immediately below. I nearly had a practical illustration during my examination. . . . I . . . ascended a steep rocky path, at the summit of which a wooden drawbridge leads over a deep abyss to the gate of the city. This bridge is the only access to Yezdi-Ghazt, which is, so to speak, a regular fortress-town. . . . The houses are of stone, two-storied, and mortised into the rock, which gives them the appearance from below, as if a touch would send them toppling over, while a curious feature is that none of their windows looks inwards to the street – all are on the outside wall facing the desert. . . . The present population are a continual source of dread to the neighbouring towns and villages, on account of their lawlessness and thieving proclivities, and mix very little with any of their neighbours who have given the unsavoury city the Turkish nickname of 'Pokloo Kalla,' or 'Filth Castle.'

Harry de Windt, *A Ride to India,* 1891

Yezd-i-Khast, that fantastic grey eyrie overhanging a chasm. Pierre Loti compared it to the abode of sea-birds; Gobineau to a .bee-hive. On one side it is flush with the plain, but on the other it rises sheer up from a dry river-bed, a skeleton-covered cliff of a town, pierced with windows like the eye-sockets of a skull, and beetling with wooden balconies and platforms that threaten to fall at any moment into the canyon below. It is difficult to see where the natural rock ends and the houses begin. The whole structure seems to be hooked and hitched together, in defiance, as Pierre Loti rightly said, of all laws of equilibrium and common sense; rickety, ramshackle, crazy, yet of untraceable antiquity. No architect hitched it there; it grew, as though the rock had sprouted upward, as though the original rock-dwellings had produced and transformed themselves into the semblance of sun-baked hovels. An air of uncompromising violence hangs about it. Its inhabitants must surely differ from other men.

Vita Sackville-West, *Twelve Days,* 1928

IRAQ

Politically . . . we rushed with the business with our usual disregard for a comprehensive political scheme. We treated Mesop. as if it were an isolated unit, instead of which it is part of Arabia, its politics indissolubly connected with the great and far reaching Arab question, which presents indeed, different facets as you regard it from different aspects, and is yet always and always one and the same indivisible block.

Gertrude Bell, Letter to her family, 27 April 1916

The Ark and all the rest become quite comprehensible when one sees Mesopotamia in flood time.

Gertrude Bell, Letter to her family, 26 May 1916

The prime fact of Mesopotamian history is that in the XIIIth century Hulagu destroyed the irrigation system; and that from that day to this Mesopotamia has remained a land of mud deprived of mud's only possible advantage, vegetable fertility. It is a mud plain, so flat that a single heron, reposing on one leg beside some rare trickle of water in a ditch, looks as tall as a wireless aerial. From this plain rise villages of mud and cities of sand. The rivers flow with liquid mud. The air is composed of mud refined into a gas. The people are mud-coloured; they wear mud-coloured clothes, and their national hat is nothing more than a formalised mud-pie. Baghdad is the capital one would expect of this divinely favoured land. It lurks in a mud fog; when the temperature drops below 110, the residents complain of the chill, and get out their furs. For only one thing is it now justly famous: a kind of boil which takes nine months to heal, and leaves a scar.

Robert Byron, *The Road to Oxiana*, 1937

It is extraordinary what a mixture of indiscipline and patience has been produced by centuries of injustice in a country where a basis of physical violence underlies everything from the climate downwards.

Freya Stark, Letter, 21 May 1937,
in *The Coasts of Incense*, 1953

On a dusty April day we left Baghdad – the air like damp under-wear and the tired spring colours of Iraq, jade, green, white sky, pale sand, melting into each other with a charm of fragile horizontal lines like those faint pencil marks drawn by artists round sketches of sheep, perhaps, with a man in an Abba before them. It is the secret of Iraq – that it looks so much more like a sketch than a photograph: a point or two is marked and the rest left fluid in dust.

Freya Stark, *Dust in the Lion's Paw*, 1961 – of 1943

Everyone agrees that Iraq is not fit to govern itself (might be said of lots of countries in Europe too). I think the Iraqis themselves agree in this: the difference is that they don't care so frightfully much about being well governed. It is rather peculiar of us to be so particular about it don't you think?

Freya Stark, Letter, 6 March 1930,
in *Beyond Euphrates*, 1951

Do you call to mind that our Bible notion of Hell is derived from the Babylonian – i.e. the fire and brimstone of Middle Eastern oil?

Freya Stark, Letter, 20 April 1944,
in *Dust in the Lion's Paw*, 1961

I generally felt bored and frustrated when I had to spend a night with Iraqi officials – for which I blamed myself, since my hosts were friendly and extremely hospitable. But their preoccupation was with Iraqi politics about which I knew little and cared less, while my interest in the tribes appeared to them incomprehensible or even sinister. . . . A suburbia covering the length and breadth of Iraq was the Utopia of which they dreamed.

Wilfred Thesiger, *The Marsh Arabs*, 1964 – of 1951–8

The story of Mesopotamia is, after all, a story of irrigation.

Gavin Young, *Return to the Marshes*, 1977

Iraqis

Capt. C.E. says the standard of vitality is much higher than in Europe; the people here pull through operations which he would not dare to attempt at home. Their nervous system is much more solid. They don't suffer from shock.

Gertrude Bell, Letter to her family, 25 January 1918

The Iraqi has not the haughty beauty of the Syrian: more the sort of pleasantness of the Venetian compared to Rome or Tuscany. Nose wide at nostril and slightly tilted: eyebrows inclined to meet: three-cornered face: lovely dark brown hair with wave in it seems typical.

Freya Stark, Notebook, 1 November 1929,
in *Beyond Euphrates*, 1951

I remember an old man, in a village on the Adil, saying to me, 'My son has a good job with the Government in Basra. We are poor, as you can see. I spent much money keeping him in Amara during the ten years he was at school. Later I thought he would look after us. We were happy with him when he was a child; he is our only son. Now he never comes near us or helps us. This education is a bad thing, Sahib, it steals our children.'

Wilfred Thesiger, *The Marsh Arabs*, 1964

'Alī al Gharbī

A bitter wind tears the river's cheek;
A sky cloud-massed;
And long grey hills that thrust up shoulders vast
As Cumbrian fells; barges, a monitor;
And, by the brimming edge, mud towers that lift
Like seagirt castles, wrapt with flying drift;
A hawk, two crows, of gulls a screaming score;
And fading into distance, sole 'twixt here
And Kut, a branching tree; and palms that stand
Wind-cuffed, scarce ten in all, a draggled band;
Three more trees near;
Where desert was, a marsh most foul and bleak!
And this is Ali Gharbi!
Our Mesopotamian Derby!
Change here for Sinn and Hanna and Sannaiyat
For bullets scream and cannons crash and riot,
And enter our enchanted land of pain
Which whoso enters comes not forth again
Save bearing eyes that hold, while living last,
Remembrance of past grief that is not past,
That stare, when things once seen to memory start,
Amid all fairest glories dazed and blind
Since here you leave behind
Childhood's gay, innocent heart
Here, where Earth's bravest slaughter and are slain.

Edward Thompson, 'Ali Gharbi', Winter 1915–16,
in *Collected Poems*, 1930

Babylon (ancient)

How many miles to Babylon?
Threescore miles and ten.

Can I get there by candle-light?
Yes, and back again.
If your heels are nimble and light,
You may get there by candle-light.

Songs for the Nursery, 1805

Babylon is fallen, is fallen, that great city.

The Bible, Revelation, 14: 8

MYSTERY, BABYLON THE GREAT, THE MOTHER OF HARLOTS AND ABOMINATIONS OF THE EARTH.

The Bible, Revelation, 17: 5

Baghdad

All the ground on which Babylon was spread, is left now desolate, nothing standing in that Peninsula, betweene the Euphrates and the Tigris, but onely part, and that a small part, of the great Tower. The Towne, which is now called Bagdat, and is on the other side of Tigris, towards Persia (onely a small Suburbe in the Peninsula) but removed from any stirpe of the first; to which men passe ordinarily by a Bridge of Boats, which every night is dissolved, for feare either of the Arabs, or some storme upon the River, which might carrie away the Boats, when there were no helpe readie. The buildings are after the Morisco fashion, low, without stories; and the Castle where the Bassa is resident, is a great vast place, without beautie or strength, either by Art, or Nature; the people somewhat more abstinent from offending Christians, then in other parts, through the necessitie of the trade of Ormus: upon which standeth both the particular and publike wealth of the State.

Sir Anthony Sherley, 1599,
in *Purchas his Pilgrimes*, 1625

We shall, I trust, make it a great centre of Arab civilisation, a prosperity; that will be my job, partly, I hope, and I never lose sight of it.

Gertrude Bell, Letter to her father, 10 March 1917

An eclipse seen from Baghdad
I hadn't been asleep long when I woke up to find the Great Bear staring me in the face. I lie looking north. It was very strange to see the Great Bear shining so brilliantly in the full moon of Ramadhan and while I wondered half asleep what had happened I realized that the whole world was dark, and turning round saw the last limb of the moon disappearing in a total eclipse. So I lay watching it, a wonderful sight the disc just visible, a dull and angry copper colour. In the bazaar a few hundred yards away everyone was drumming with sticks on anything that lay handy, to scare away the devil which hid the moon, and indeed they ultimately succeeded, for after a long, long time the upper limb of the moon re-appeared and the devil drew slowly downwards, angry still with deep red tongues and wreaths projecting from his copper coloured body and before I had time to sleep again the Ramadhan moon had once more extinguished the shining of the Bear.

But as for people who read of these things in their almanacs and know to a minute when to expect them, I think nothing of them and their educated sensations.

Gertrude Bell, Letter to her family, 6 July 1917

A long flat city in a flat land.

Freya Stark, Letter of 1929, in *Beyond Euphrates*, 1951

The English colonial community there
Baghdad colony has not been as bad as you prophesied: rather like a cathedral town involved in Edgar Wallace. They put me down as Edgar Wallace undiluted and the cathedral part has been disapproving.

Freya Stark, Letter, 6 March 1930,
in *Beyond Euphrates*, 1951

I had no very clear preconceived picture of Baghdad, and my experience of Arab towns had been limited to brief sojourns in North Africa. My first impression was that what the western colonial powers could do to a city in the way of desecration, was nothing to what the Arabs themselves could do when they got going. . . . It is perhaps the least favourable time for many centuries for a stranger to see Baghdad; the moment of transition from an eastern to a western culture that has as yet little meaning for the bulk of the people.

I have noticed that there is a longitudinal line east of which the squalor created by building appears as great as that of demolition. . . .

Gavin Maxwell, *A Reed Shaken by the Wind*, 1957

'They have only two words for everything,' said Thesiger, '*moderne* and *démodé*, and what isn't the first is the second.'

Ibid.

Basra

Basora in times past was under the Arabians, but now is subject to the Turke. But some of them the Turke cannot subdue, for that they hold certaine Ilands in the River Euphrates, which the Turke cannot winne of them. They be Thieves all and have no settled dwelling, but remove from place to place with their Camels, Goates, and Horses, Wives and Children and all. They have large blew Gownes, their Wives eares and noses are ringed very full of rings of Copper and Silver, and they weare rings of Copper about their legs.

Basora standeth neere the Gulfe of Persia, and is a

Towne of great trade of Spices and Drugs which come from Ormus.

Ralph Fitch, *The Voyage,* 1583–91, in *Purchas his Pilgrimes,* 1625

Basra was about the hottest place on earth in summer . . . the place where the fable of frying eggs on the street came true.

Cedric Belfrage, *Away from It All,* 1936

Birs Nimrud (formerly Borsippa and reputed Babel)

Here also are yet standing the ruines of the olde tower of Babel, which being upon a plaine ground seemeth a farre off very great, but the nerer you come to it, the lesser and lesser it appeareth; sundry times I have gone thither to see it, and found the remnants yet standing above a quarter of a mile in compasse, and almost as high as the stonework of Paul's steeple in London, but it sheweth much bigger. The bricks remaining in this most ancient monument be halfe a yard thicke, and three quarters of a yard long, being dried in the sunne onely, and betweene every course of bricks there lieth a course of mattes made of canes, which remaine sound and not perished, as though they had bene layed within one yeere.

John Eldred (1583), in Richard Hakluyt, *Principal Navigations . . . of the English Nation,* 1598–1600

We motored . . . to Birs Nimrud which is supposed to be the Tower of Babel, and I need not say isn't (because, partly, there wasn't one, and partly because the one there wasn't was not in that place; but I fear you'll fail to understand me!).

Gertrude Bell, Letter to her father, 18 April 1918

Euphrates (at Ramadi)

There is no river to be compared to him.

Gertrude Bell, Letter to her family, 25 February 1911

We were off early next day and went up river to Qulat Sabib – it was a delicious warm day and the river was delightful. I don't know why it should be as attractive as it is. The elements of the scene are extremely simple but the combination still makes a wonderfully attractive result. Yet there's really nothing – flat, far-stretching plain coming down to the river's edge, thorn covered, water-covered in the flood in the lower reaches, a little wheat and millet stubble in the base fields, an occasional village of reed-built houses and the beautiful river craft, majestic on noble sails or skimming on clumsy paddles. The river bends and winds, curves back on itself almost and you have the curious apparition of a fleet of white sails rising out of the thorny waste, now on one side of you, now the other. And by these you mark where your cruise must be, where the river divides wilderness from wilderness.

Gertrude Bell, Letter to her family, 1 January 1917

Hīt

From the ruines of old Babylon wee set forwards to Aleppo; travelling for the most part through the Desart Arabia. Having spent three dayes and better, from the ruines of old Babylon, we came to a Towne, called Ait, inhabited onely with Arabians, but very ruinous. Neere unto which Towne is a Valley of Pitch very marvellous to behold, and a thing almost incredible, wherein are many Springs, throwing out aboundantly a kind of blacke substance like unto Tarre and Pitch, which serveth all the Countries thereabouts to make staunch their Barkes and Boats; every one of which Springs maketh a noise like a Smiths Forge, in puffing and blowing out the matter, which never ceaseth night nor day, and the noyse is heard a mile off, swallowing up all weighty things that come upon it. The Moores call it, The mouth of Hell.

John Cartwright, 1603, in *Purchas his Pilgrimes,* 1625

Kurds

The Curdies, . . . some thinke to be a remnant of the ancient Parthians. This rude people are of a goodly stature, and well proportioned, and doe never goe abroad without their Armes, as Bowes and Arrowes, Scimitarre and Buckler, yea and at such time, when a man for age is ready to goe downe to his grave. They doe adore and worship the Devill, to the end hee may not hurt them or their Cattell, and very cruell are they to all sorts of Christians; in which regard, the Countrey which they inhabite, is at this day Termed Terra Diaboli, the Land of the Divell. They participate much of the nature of the Arabians, and are as infamous in their Latrocinies and robberies, as the Arabians themselves. They live under the commandement of the great Turke, but with much freedome and libertie.

John Cartwright, 1603, in *Purchas his Pilgrimes,* 1625

Kut

The mud-strips green with lettuce, red with stacks
Of liquorice; shattered walls and gaping caves;
Beyond, the shifting sands, and jackals' tracks;
The dirging wind, the wilderness of graves.

Edward Thompson, 'The River-front, Kut', in *Collected Poems,* 1930

Marsh country (round the Shatt al Arab)

Memories of that first visit to the Marshes have never left me: firelight on a half-turned face, the crying of geese, duck flighting in to feed, a boy's voice singing somewhere in the dark, canoes moving in procession down a waterway, the setting sun seen crimson through the smoke of burning reedbeds, narrow waterways that wound still deeper into the Marshes. A naked man in a canoe with a trident in his hand, reed houses built upon water, black, dripping buffaloes that looked as if they had calved from the swamp with the first dry land. Stars reflected in dark water, the croaking of frogs, canoes coming home at evening, peace and continuity, the stillness of a world that never knew an engine. Once again I experienced the longing to share this life, and to be more than a mere spectator.

Wilfred Thesiger, *The Marsh Arabs,* 1964 – of 1951

Sitting in the Euphrates *mudhifs,* I always had the impression of being inside a Romanesque or Gothic Cathedral, an illusion enhanced by the ribbed roof and the traceried windows at either end, through which bright shafts of light came to penetrate the gloom of the interior. Both on the Euphrates and on the Tigris the *mudhifs* represented an extraordinary architectural achievement with the simplest possible materials; the effect of enrichment, given by the reed patterns, came entirely from functional methods of construction. Historically, too, they were important. Long familiarity with houses such as these may well have given man the idea of imitating their arched form in mud bricks, as the Greeks later perpetuated wooden techniques in stone. Buildings similar to these *mudhifs* have been part of the scene in Southern Iraq for five thousand years and more. Probably within the next twenty years, certainly within the next fifty, they will have disappeared for ever.

Ibid.

We left the palm groves and the stretches of dry land behind us, and soon the horizon was flat and bare, and the yard high stubble of burnt reeds and bulrushes through which the ill-defined watercourses ran was paler than the blue-grey horizon sky. Very far away in front of us a few dark specks showed the last of the palm-groves before the edge of the permanent marsh. The earth seemed flat as a plate and stretched away for ever before us, vast, desolate and pallid; pale bulrush stubble standing in water that reflected a vast pale sky, against which strained here and there the delicate shape of a long reed bent before the wind, the silhouette urgent as the keening of a violin. As the gusts grew stronger and ruffled the water among the reeds into flurries of small ripples, it tore a chorus of strange sounds from the stiff, withered sedge stumps, groans and whistles, bleats and croaks, and loud crude sounds of flatulence; if the devils of Hieronymus Bosch could speak from the canvas this would be the babel of their tongues, these the derisive notes of the trumpets at their backsides.

There was no colour anywhere, and the grey sky, unbroken by hill or tree, seemed as immense as from a small boat far out at sea. Occasionally a flight of pelicans would sail majestically by, riding the wind on stiff outstretched wings, rigid and bulky in body as seaplanes; and once a flock of white ibis drifted past very high up, to fan out into a wheeling kaleidoscope of white petals on the great empty sky. It was in some way a terrible landscape, utterly without human sympathy, more desolate and inimical than the sea itself, except, perhaps, when it breaks in winter on a long shingle beach and the land behind it is flat. Here in the limbless stubble of pale bulrush one felt that no sheltering ship could sail nor human foot walk, and there seemed no refuge for any creature whose blood was warm.

Gavin Maxwell, *A Reed Shaken by the Wind,* 1957

Shethatha

None of these Arabs had ever seen snow. The Mudir of Shethatha told me that the people there when they woke and saw it lying on the ground, thought it was flour.

Gertrude Bell, Letter to her family, 4 March 1911

River Tigris ('Eden', above the ruins of Nineveh)

This Patriarch . . . wished us before we departed, to see the Iland of Eden, but twelve miles up the River, which hee affirmed, was undoubtedly a part of Paradise.

This Iland lies in the heart of the River Tygris, and is (as we could ghesse) in circuit ten English miles, and was sometimes walled round about with a wall of strong defence, as appeares by the ruinous foundation of Bricke which there remayneth. And howsoever the beautifull Land of Eden is now forgotten in these parts with those flourishing Countries of Mesopotamia, Assyria, Babylonia, and Chaldaea, being all swallowed up into meere Barbarisme, yet this Iland still retaynes the name of the Ile of Eden.

John Cartwright, 1603, in *Purchas his Pilgrimes,* 1625

There was a place,
Now not, though Sin, not Time first wraught the change,
Where Tigris at the foot of Paradise
Into a Gulf shot underground, till part
Rose up a fountain by the Tree of Life.

John Milton, *Paradise Lost,* 1667

IRELAND

Ireland is dim where the sun goeth on settle.
King Alfred, early English translation of his version of Orosius, *Geography of Europe*, c. 600, quoted by C.M. Doughty, *Travels in Arabia Deserta*, 1888

Icham of Irlande
Ant of the holy land of Irlande
Gode sir, pray ich ye
For of Saynte charite
Come and daunce wyt me
In Irlaunde.

Anon., thirteenth century

Ireland . . . separated from the rest of the known world, and in some sort to be distinguished as another world.
Giraldus Cambrensis, *The Topography of Ireland*, c. 1186–7

Irelande that holsome grounde.
John Rastell, *Interlude of the Four Elements*, c. 1518

Poor Ireland, worse and worse.
George Dowdall, Archbishop of Armagh, 1558, quoted in D.B. Quinn, *The Elizabethans and the Irish*, 1966

Within the compasse of this land,
no poysonyng beast doth live,
To Adder, Snake, nor Crocadile,
no respitte doeth it give.
Whereby the same repast maie take
to feede his appetite:
But with a deadly percyng blowe,
eche vermine it doeth smite
As sone as thei doe touch the grounde
even by and by thei dye:
And hope of longer life to live
from every one doeth flye. . . .
O holie sainct, O holie man,
O man of God I saie;
O Patricke chiefe of all these karne,
If speake to thee I maie,
What moved thee, the wriglyng Snake,
and other wormes to kill?
What caused thee on sillie beastes
to woorke thy cruell will?
What thyng incenst thee so to strike,
them with thy heavie hande?
When as thou lettest more spitefull beastes,
within this fertile lande.
Thou smotest the Serpentes venimous,
and Furies didst subverte;
And yet the footers of the boggs,
couldst thou no whit converte?
Couldst thou not bring them to thy bende,
nor bowe them like a Bowe?
Doeth not the Parsone teache his Clarke
his duetie for to knowe?

John Derricke, *The Image of Irelande*, 1581

Sick Ireland is with a strange warr possest
Like to an Ague; now raging, now at rest;
Which time will cure: yet it must doe her good
If she were purg'd, and her head vayne let blood.

John Donne, *Loves Warre*, c. 1594

Whylome, when IRELAND florished in fame
Of wealths and goodnesse, far above the rest
Of all that beare the *British* Islands name,
The Gods then us'd (for pleasure and for rest)
Oft to resort there-to, when seem'd them best:
But none of all there-in more pleasure found,
Then *Cynthia:* that is soveraine Queene profest
Of woods and forrests, which therein abound
Sprinkled with wholsom waters, more then most on
ground.

Edmund Spencer, *The Faerie Queene*, 1596

They say it is the fatall destiny of that land, that no purposes, whatsoever are ment for her good, wil prosper and take good effect: which, whether it proceede from the very genius of the soyle, or influence of the starrs, or that Almighty God hath not yet appoynted the time of her reformacion, or that he reserveth her in this unquiet state still, for some secret scourge, which shall by her come unto England, it is hard to be knowne, but yet much to be feared.

Edmund Spenser, *A Veue of the Present State of Ireland*, 1596

The North

Ffor that parte of the northe sometyme was as populous and plentifull as any parte in England. . . . Suer it is yett a moste bewtifull and sweete Country as any is under heaven, seamed thoroughout with many godly rivers, replenished with all sortes of fishe most aboundantlie: sprinkled with verie many sweete Ilandes and goodlie lakes, like little inland seas, that will carrie even shippes upon theire waters, adorned with goodlie woodes, fitt for building of houses and shipes so commodiouslie, as that if some princes in the world had them, they would soone hope to be lordes of all the seas, and er longe of all the worlde: also full of verie good portes and havens, opening uppon England and Scotland, as invitinge us to come unto them, to see what excellent commodities that Countrie can afforde, besides the soyle it selfe most fertile, fitt to yelde all kynde of fruit that shal be comitted there unto. And lastlie the heavens most milde and temperate, though some what more moyste then the partes towardes the West.

Ibid.

Welch: Captaine *Macmorrice*, I thinke, looke you,

under your correction, there is not many of your Nation.

Irish: Of my Nation? What ish my Nation? Ish a Villaine, and a Basterd, and a Knave, and a Rascall. What ish my Nation? Who talkes of my Nation?

Seventeenth Century

He that would England win
Must with Ireland first begin.

Proverb quoted in John Ray, *A Compleat Collection of English Proverbs*, 1670

The land of Ire.

Sir Robert Cecil, Letter to the Lord Admiral, 8 October 1600

The Spaniard and others have reported a long time since that, if the Princes of England knew what a jewel Ireland were, they needed not to seek the discovery of foreign countries to settle in.

Sir George Carew, *Plan for the Reformation of Ireland*, 1603

This island . . . is endowed with so many dowries of nature, considering the fruitfulness of the soil . . . and especially the race and generation of men, valiant, hard and active, as it is not easy, no not upon the continent, to find such confluence of commodities, if the hand of man did join with the hand of God.

Francis Bacon, *Considerations Touching the Plantation in Ireland*, 1606

Now, as well the aire as the ground is excessive moist, whence it is that very many there be sore troubled with loosenesse and rhewmes, but strangers especially: yet for the staying of the same, they have an *Aqua Vitae* [Uske bah] of the best which inflameth a great deale lesse, and drieth much more than ours.

William Camden, *Britain*, 1610
(Philemon Holland's translation)

And this I dare avow, there are more rivers, lakes, brooks, strands, quagmires, bogs and marshes in this country than in all Christendom besides; for travelling there in the winter all my daily solace was sink-down comfort; whiles, boggy-plunging deeps kissing my horses belly; whiles, over-mired saddle, body and all; and often or ever set a-swimming, in great danger, both I and my guides of our lives; that for cloudy and fountain-bred perils, I was never before reducted to such a floating labyrinth, considering that in five months' space I quite spoiled six horses, and myself as tired as the worst of them.

William Lithgow, *Rare Adventures and Painfull Peregrinations*, 1614/32

The houses of the Irish Cities, as Corke, Galoway and Lymrick (the fairest of them for building) are of unwrought free stone, or flint, or unpolished stones, built some two stories high, and covered with tile. The houses of Dublin and Waterford, are for the most part of timber, clay and plaster, yet are the streetes beautifull, and the houses commodious within, even among the Irish, if you pardon them a little slovenlinesse, proper to the Nation. In generall, the houses very seldome keepe out raine, the timber being not well seasoned, and the walles being generally combined with clay only, not with morter of lime tempered. The Irish have some quarries of Marble, but only some few Lords and Gentlemen bestow the cost to polish it. Many Gentlemen have Castles built of free stone unpolished, and of flints, or little stones, and they are built strong for defence in times of rebellion, for which cause they have narrow staires, and little windowes, and commonly they have a spatious hall joyning to the Castle, and built of timber and clay, wherein they eate with their Family. Neither are many of these gentle mens houses void of filth, and slovenlinesse. For other Irish dwellings, it may be said of them, as Caesar said of the old Brittaines houses. They call it a Towne, when they have compassed a skirt of wood, with trees cut downe, whether they may retire themselves and their cattle. For the meere barbarous Irish either sleepe under the canopy of heaven, or in cabbines watled, and covered with turfe.

Fynes Moryson, *An Itinerary*, 1617

Ireland for these many yeares hath been the receptacle of our English runnagates, that for their mis-led lives in England, do come running over into Ireland, some for murther, some for theft, some that have spent themselves in ryot and excesse, are driven over for debt, some come running over with other mens goods, some with other mens wives, but a great number now lately, that are more hurtfull than all the rest, and those be Recusants.

B. Rich, *The Irish Hubbub*, 1617

No more like *Ireland* brag, her harmless Nation
Fosters no venom since that *Scots'* Plantation.

John Cleveland, *The Rebell Scot*, *c.* January 1644

Mr Butler was now all full of his high discourse in praise of Ireland. . . . But so many lies I never heard in praise of anything as he told of Ireland.

Samuel Pepys, *Diary*, 28 July 1660

Eighteenth Century

I reckon no man is throughly miserable unless he be condemnd to live in Ireland.

Jonathan Swift, Letter to Ambrose Philips, 30 October 1709

I must be bold to say, that People in that Kingdom do very ill understand Raillery. I can railly much safer here with a great Minister of State or a Dutchess, than I durst do there with an Attorney or his Wife.

Jonathan Swift, Letter to Archbishop King, 10 April 1711

Ireland is not Paradise.

Jonathan Swift, Letter to Alexander Pope, 30 August 1716

I will define Ireland a Region of good eating and drinking, of tolerable Company, where a Man from England may sojourn some years with Pleasure, make a Fortune, and then return home, with the spoyls he has got by doing us all the Mischeif he can, and by that make a Merit at Court.

Jonathan Swift, Letter to John Gay, 20 November 1729

Some queries proposed to the consideration of the public:

Whether there be upon earth any Christian or civilised people so beggarly wretched and destitute, as the common Irish?

Whether, nevertheless, there is any other people whose wants may be more easily supplied from home?

Whether, if there was a wall of brass a thousand cubits high round their kingdom, our natives might not nevertheless live cleanly and comfortably, till the land and reap the fruits of it? . . .

Whether there be any country in Christiandom more capable of improvement than Ireland?

Whether we do not live in a most fertile soil and temperate climate, and yet whether our people in general do not feel great want and misery?

Whether any countrymen are not readier at finding excuses than remedies?

Whether the natural phlegm of this island needs any additional stupefier?

Whether all spirituous liquors are not, in truth, opiates? . . .

Whether the maxim, 'What is everybody's business is nobody's business,' prevails in any country under the sun more than in Ireland?

Whether we are the only people who starve in the market of plenty? . . .

Whose fault is it if poor Ireland continues poor?

George Berkeley, *The Querist,* 1735

This island is a region of dreams and trifles.

George Berkeley, Letter to Lord Percival, 1742

Dear Erin, how sweetly thy green bosom rises!
  An emerald set in the ring of the sea.
Each blade of thy meadows my faithful heart prizes,
  Thou queen of the west, the world's cushla ma-chree.

John Philpot Curran, *Cushla ma-Chree,* late Eighteenth Century
(Cushla ma-chree = darling of my heart.)

England and Ireland may flourish together. The world is large enough for us both. Let it be our care not to make ourselves too little for it.

Edmund Burke, Letter to Samuel Span, Esq., 1778

He had a kindness for the Irish nation, and thus generously expressed himself to a gentleman from that country, on the subject of an UNION which artful politicians have often had in view – 'Do not make an union with us, Sir. We should unite with you, only to rob you. We should have robbed the Scotch, if they had had any thing of which we could have robbed them.'

Samuel Johnson, quoted in Boswell, *Life of Johnson,* 12 October 1779

He, I know not why, shewed upon all occasions an aversion to go to Ireland, where I proposed to him that we should make a tour. JOHNSON. 'It is the last place where I should wish to travel.' BOSWELL. 'Should you not like to see Dublin, Sir?' JOHNSON. 'No, Sir! Dublin is only a worse capital.' BOSWELL. 'Is not the Giant's Causeway worth seeing?' JOHNSON. 'Worth seeing? yes; but not worth going to see.'

James Boswell, *Life of Johnson,* 12 October 1779

That Ireland would . . . come to make a figure amongst the nations, is an Idea which has more of the ambition of individuals in it, than of a sober regard to the happiness of a whole people. But if a people were to sacrifice solid quiet to empty glory, as on some occasions they have done, under the Circumstances of Ireland, *she* most assuredly, never would obtain that independent glory, but would certainly lose all her Tranquillity, all her prosperity, and even that degree of Lustre which she has by the very free and very honourable connexion she enjoys with a Nation the most splendid and the most powerful upon Earth. Ireland *constitutionally* is independent – *Politically* she never can be so. It is a struggle against Nature.

Edmund Burke, Letter to the Rev. Thomas Hussey, 18 May 1795

Nineteenth Century

O Paddy dear, an' did ye hear the news that's goin' round?
The shamrock is by law forbid to grow on Irish ground!
No more St. Patrick's Day we'll keep, his colour can't be seen,
For there's a cruel law agin the wearin' o' the Green!
I met wid Napper Tandy, and he took me by the hand,
And he said, 'How's poor ould Ireland, and how does she stand?'
She's the most disthressful country that iver yet was seen,
For they're hangin' men an' women there for the wearin' o' the Green.

The Wearin' o' the Green, street ballad, later added to by Dion Boucicault, *c.* 1800

Arm of Erin! prove strong, but be gentle as brave,
And, uplifted to strike, still be ready to save,
Nor one feeling of vengeance presume to defile
The cause or the men of the Emerald Isle.

William Drennan, *Erin, c.* 1800
(Drennan in his 1815 introduction to the poem denied claims that this was the first appearance of the phrase 'Emerald Isle' which he ascribed to 'Erin to Her Own Tune', 'a party song written without rancour of party in 1795'.)

There came to the beach a poor exile of Erin. . . .
He sang the bold anthem of *Erin go bragh.*

Thomas Campbell, *The Exile of Erin,* 1800
(Erin go bragh = Ireland for ever.)

When my country takes her place amongst the nations of the earth – then and not till then – let my epitaph be written.

Robert Emmett, Speech when condemned to death, 19 September 1803

The moment the very name of Ireland is mentioned, the English seem to bid adieu to common feeling, common prudence and common sense, and to act with the barbarity of tyrants and the fatuity of idiots.

Sydney Smith, *Peter Plymley Letters,* No. 2, 1807

Erin, the tear and the smile in thine eyes,
Blend like the rainbow that hangs in thy skies!
Shining through sorrow's stream,
Saddening through pleasures beam,
Thy suns with doubtful gleam,
Weep while they rise.

Erin, thy silent tear shall never cease,
Erin, thy languid smile ne'er shall increase,
Till, like the rainbow's light
Thy various tints unite,
And form in heaven's sight
One arch of peace!

Thomas Moore, 'Erin! The Tear and the Smile in thine Eyes', *Irish Melodies,* 1807–35

A beautiful country, sir, to live out of!

Thomas Moore, Remark attributed by Sir Rutherford Alcock, *The Capital of the Tycoon,* 1863

Our history, for many centuries past, is creditable neither to our neighbours nor ourselves, and ought not to be read by any Irishman who wishes either to love England, or to feel proud of Ireland.

Thomas Moore, Appendix to *Intolerance, a Satire,* 1809

To Scotland, Ireland is akin
In drinking, like as twin to twin, –
When other means are all adrift,
A liquor-shop is Pat's last shift,
Till reckoning Erin round from store to store,
There is one whisky shop in four.

Thomas Hood, *Ode to J.S. Buckingham Esq.,* 1835

Ireland may be regarded as the first English colony and as one which because of its proximity is still governed exactly in the old way. The people itself has got its peculiar character from this, and despite all their Irish nationalistic fanaticism, the fellows feel that they are no longer at home in their own country. Ireland for the Saxon! That is now being realised. The Irishman knows he cannot compete with the Englishman. . . . By consistent oppression they have been artificially converted into an utterly demoralised nation, and now fulfil the notorious function of supplying England, America, Australia, etc., with prostitutes, casual labourers, pimps, thieves, swindlers, beggars, and other rabble.

Friedrich Engels, Letter to Karl Marx, 1836

In all countries, more or less, paupers may be discovered, but an entire nation of paupers is what was never seen until it was shown in Ireland.

Gustave de Beaumont, *Ireland,* 1839

The bane of England and the opprobrium of Europe.

Benjamin Disraeli, Speech, 9 August 1843, referring to Ireland

As there is more rain in this country than in any other, and as, therefore, naturally, the inhabitants should be inured to the weather, and made to despise an inconvenience which they cannot avoid, the travelling conveyances are arranged so that you may get as much practice in being wet as possible.

W.M. Thackeray, *The Irish Sketch Book of 1842,* 1843

I don't know how it is, but throughout the country the men and the landscapes seem to be the same, and one and the other seem ragged, ruined, and cheerful.

Ibid.

You hear of the Limerick fairies, and the Donegal fairies, and the Tipperary fairies, and the fairies of two adjoining counties have their faction fights, just like the inhabitants themselves.

J.G. Kohl, *Ireland, Dublin, the Shannon, Limerick, Cork, and the Kilkenny Races . . . ,* 1843

Erin go Bragh! A far better anthem would be, Erin go bread and cheese, Erin go cabins that will keep out the rain, Erin go pantaloons without holes in them! What folly to be making eternal declarations about governing yourselves.

Sydney Smith, *Fragment on the Irish Roman Catholic Church, c.* 1844

Ugly spectacle: sad health: sad humour: a thing unjoyful to look back upon. The whole country figures in my mind like a ragged coat; one huge beggar's gaberdine, not patched or patchable any longer.

Thomas Carlyle, *Journal,* 11 November 1849

Ireland really *is* my problem; the breaking point of the huge suppuration which all British and all European society now is. Set down in Ireland, one might at least feel, '*Here* is thy problem: In God's name what wilt thou do with it?'

Thomas Carlyle, *Journal,* 17 May 1849

That domestic Irish giant named of Despair.

Thomas Carlyle, *Latter-Day Pamphlets,* No. 3, 1850

The fairies, the whole pantheon of Irish demigods are retiring, one by one from the habitations of man to the distant islands where the wild waves of the Atlantic raise their foaming crests, to render their fastnesses inaccessible to the schoolmaster and the railroad engineer.

W.R. Wilde, *Irish Popular Superstitions,* 1852

Ireland never was contented.
Say you so? You are demented
Ireland was contented when
All could use the sword and pen
And when Tara rose so high
That her turrets split the sky
And about her courts were seen
Liveried angels robed in green
Wearing, by St Patrick's bounty
Emeralds, big as half the county.

W.S. Landor, *Ireland Never Was Contented,* 1853

They do nothing in Ireland as they would elsewhere. When the Dublin mail was stopped and robbed my brother declares that a sweet female voice was heard behind the hedge, exclaiming, 'Shoot the gintlemen then, Patrick dear!'

Sydney Smith, quoted by Lady Holland, *Memoir of Sydney Smith,* 1855

arriving from the west

There lay the green shore of Ireland, like some coast of plenty. We could see towns, towers, churches, harvests; but the curse of eight hundred years we could not discern.

R.W. Emerson, *English Traits,* 1856

Justice for Ireland! rends the sky
  Shouted by many a Popish traitor
Justice for Ireland! too we cry,
  'Hang every agitator.'

Anon., 'On Erin', in *Epigrams Ancient and Modern,* 1863

I have somewhere seen it remarked that Ireland would be a very nice country, if they would only sweep it out, and make the beds about once a fortnight.

G.A. Sala, *My Diary in America in the Midst of War,* 1865

I have a sad misgiving that the religion of Ireland lies as deep at the root of all its sorrows, even as English misgovernment and Tory villainy.

Charles Dickens, Letter, 1846, in Forster, *Life of Dickens,* 1872–3

O Irlande, grand pays du Shillelagh et du bog,
Ou les patriotes vont toujours ce qu'on appelle le whole hog.

Anon, *A l'Irlande, par Victor Hugo,* quoted in G.W.E. Russell, *Collections and Recollections, 1898,* as a parody of Hugo on the occasion of passage of Forster's coercion Act, January 1881

*'Tis Ireland gives England her soldiers, her generals, too.

George Meredith, *Diana of the Crossways,* 1885

*Order is an exotic in Ireland. It has been imported from England, but it will not grow. It suits neither soil nor climate.

J.A. Froude, *The Two Chiefs of Dunboy,* 1889

*The functions of the Anglo-Irish government were to do what ought not to be done, and to leave undone what ought to be done.

Ibid.

There are some who will welcome with delight the idea of solving the Irish question by doing away with the Irish people. There are others who will remember that Ireland has extended her boundaries and that we now have to reckon with her not only in the Old World, but in the New.

Oscar Wilde, *Sententiae,* 1919 – from writings of the 1880s

Soon after I had relinquished the Kingdom of God, I began to take a real interest in the Kingdom of Ireland.

J.M. Synge, *Autobiography* (from his Notebooks), *c.* 1896–8

Thy sorrow and the sorrow of the sea,
Are sisters; the sad winds are of thy race:
The heart of melancholy beats in thee,
And the lamenting spirit haunts thy face,
Mournful and mighty Mother!

Lionel Johnson, *Ireland,* 1897

Down thy valleys, Ireland, Ireland,
    Down thy valleys green and sad,
Still thy spirit wanders wailing,
    Wanders wailing, wanders mad.

Long ago that anguish took thee,
    Ireland, Ireland, green and fair,
Spoilers strong in darkness took thee,
    Broke thy heart and left thee there.

Down thy valleys, Ireland, Ireland,
    Still thy spirit wanders mad;
All too late they love that wronged thee,
    Ireland, Ireland, green and sad.

Sir Henry Newbolt, 'Ireland, Ireland', *The Island Race*, 1898

Twentieth Century

Irish history is for Englishmen to remember and for Irishmen to forget.

Anon, early twentieth century (?), quoted in M.J. MacManus, *Irish Cavalcade*, 1939

The Irish bull is always pregnant.

Sir John Pentland Mahaffy, attrib. remark, defining the Irish 'Bull' as distinct from similar verbal fooleries in other tongues

Italy, at least, has two things to balance its miserable poverty and mismanagement: a lively intellectual movement and a good climate. Ireland is Italy without these two.

James Joyce, Letter to Stanislaus Joyce, 13 November 1906

If you want to interest him in Ireland, you've got to call the unfortunate island Kathleen ni Hoolihan and pretend she's a little old woman.

G. Bernard Shaw, *John Bull's Other Island*, 1907

The seeming needs of my fool-driven land.

W.B. Yeats, 'All Things Can Tempt Me' – *The Green Helmet and Other Poems*, 1910

Ireland is a little Russia in which the longest way round is the shortest way home, and the means more important than the end.

George Moore, *Ave*, 1911

Nothing in Ireland lasts long except the miles.

Ibid.

(An Irish mile is 2240 yards – an English mile 1760 yards.)

This lovely land that always sent
Her writers and artists to banishment
And in a spirit of Irish fun
Betrayed her own leaders, one by one. . . .

Oh Ireland my first and only love
Where Christ and Caesar are hand in glove!
O lovely land where the shamrock grows!
(Allow me, ladies, to blow my nose).

James Joyce, *Gas from a Burner*, 1912

Romantic Ireland's dead and gone.
It's with O'Leary in the grave.

W.B. Yeats, 'September 1913', *Responsibilities*, 1914

*Ireland is the old sow that eats her farrow.

James Joyce, *Portrait of the Artist as a Young Man*, 1916

*I belong to the *faubourg Saint-Patrice* called Ireland for short.

James Joyce, *Ulysses*, 1922

Ireland is to my mind something like the bottom of an aquarium, with little people in crannies like prawns.

D.H. Lawrence, Letter to Lord and Lady Glenavy, Scandicci, 21 October 1927

some comparisons

If you want to make me homesick, remind me of the Thuringian Fichtelgebirge, of the broad fields and delicate airs of France, of the Gorges of the Tarn, of the Passes of the Tyrol, of the North African desert, of the Golden Horn, of the Swedish lakes, or even of the Norwegian fiords, where I have never been except in imagination, and you may stir that craving in me as easily – probably more easily – as in any exiled native of those places. It was not until I went back to Ireland as a tourist, that I perceived that the charm of my country was quite independent of the accident of my having been born in it, and that it could fascinate a Spaniard or an Englishman more powerfully than an Irishman, in whose feeling for it there must always be a strange anguish, because it is a country where he has been unhappy, and where vulgarity is vulgar to him. And so I am a tolerably good European in the Nietzschean sense, but a very bad Irishman in the Sinn Fein or Chosen People sense.

G. Bernard Shaw, Preface to *Immaturity*, 1930

When we get Home Rule everyone in Ireland will do as he likes, and those who don't will be made to do it.

Attributed to an Irish Labour Leader, and quoted by Stephen Leacock, *Humour*, 1935

I come from an island, Ireland, a nation
Built upon violence and morose vendettas.
My diehard countrymen like drayhorses
Drag their ruin behind them.
Shooting straight in the cause of crooked thinking
Their greed is sugared with pretence of public spirit.
From all which I am an exile.

Louis MacNeice, *Eclogue from Ireland*, 1936

This is a land of Autolycuses. Monty put down his spectacles, and they were at once picked up. I left my best stick, . . . in the hotel cloakroom, and never saw it again. . . . And the man who eats at the next table has had his horse stolen. But the charm excuses the dishonesty; one reads this nation's poverty in its smiling eyes.

James Agate, *Ego 3,* 10 August 1936

Nobody can betray Ireland: it does not give him the chance; it betrays him first.

Oliver St John Gogarty, *As I Was Going Down Sackville Street,* 1937

Three great inventions came from Ireland – the invention of soda water, whereby whiskey outdoes champagne, the invention of the pneumatic tyre whereby was made possible the evolution of an engine to scale the blue, and the invention of the system whereby disease is made to support patient, nurse and doctor, and horses to carry hospitals!

Ibid.

'Ireland' has come to be as deadly and as degenerating an incantation as 'Freedom' was in the days of the Virgin Queen. Virgins have done a deal of harm in this island. And marriage does nothing to soften their dissatisfaction with life. It cannot be all the fault of the men. It must be the hardness of our women that is driving men to politics. A little slogan formed itself in my mind, a cry to the women of Ireland: 'More petting, less politics.'

Ibid.

Why do we like being Irish? Partly because
  It gives us a hold on the sentimental English
As members of a world that never was,
  Baptised with fairy water;
And partly because Ireland is small enough
  To be still thought of with a family feeling,
And because the waves are rough
  That split her from a more commercial culture;
And because one feels that here at least one can
  Do local work which is not at the world's mercy
And that on this tiny stage with luck a man
  Might see the end of one particular action.
It is self-deception of course;
  There is no immunity in this island either;
A cart that is drawn by somebody else's horse
  And carrying goods to somebody else's market.

Louis MacNeice, *Autumn Journal,* 1938

Now Ireland has her madness and her weather still.

W.H. Auden, *In Memory of W.B. Yeats,* 1939

SPENSER'S IRELAND
has not altered
  a place as kind as it is green,
  the greenest place I've never seen.

Marianne Moore, 'Spenser's Ireland', *What Are Years,* 1941

The Irish Literary Revivalists . . . sought in Ireland the kind of dignity and the kind of health that the industrialised world, the modern world, had lost; the Ireland they loved had an enormous West Coast and no Northeast corner.

Conor Cruise O'Brien, *Writers and Politics,* 1965

If you begin in Ireland, Ireland remains the norm; like it or not.

Elizabeth Bowen, *Pictures and Conversations,* 1975

Ireland seems to me the right size for a country, the truly contemporary size, the size at which regionalism becomes nationhood.

Jan Morris, 'Do You Think He Should Have Gone Over', *Travels,* 1976

I remember arriving home from Baltistan last year and feeling that I'd come from the Third World to some dotty Fourth World consisting only of Ireland.

Dervla Murphy, *A Place Apart,* 1978

Love is never defeated, and I could add, the history of Ireland proves that.

Pope John Paul II, Speech in Galway, 30 September 1979

Education in Ireland is synonymous with religion, and religion is synonymous with politics.

Belfast schoolgirl, quoted by Jack Pizzey, 'The Madonna and the Drum', *Listener,* 24 April 1980

Irish

Hibernicis ipsis Hibernior.
(More Irish than the Irish.)

Unknown, Proverb

If an Irishman be a good man, there is no better; if he be a bad man, there is no worse.

Giraldus Cambrensis, *Topography of Ireland,* c. 1185–6

As the northern men loveth fight, also the southern, falseness; they strutteth to strength, these to sleights; they to stalwartness, these to treason.

Unknown, *Of Ireland, c.* 1425

The people are thus inclined: religious, frank, amorous, ireful, sufferable of infinite pains, very vainglorious, many sorcerers, excellent horsemen, delighted with wars, great almsgivers, passing in hospitality. The lewder sort, both clerks and laymen, are sensual and overloose in living. The same, being virtuously bred up or reformed, are such mirrors of holiness and austerity that other nations retain but a shadow in comparison of them. . . . Greedy of praise they be and fearful of dishonour.

Richard Stanyhurst, in Holinshed, *Chronicle*, 1577

Lenity were better to be used than severe meanes. Truly the generall nature of all countrys not fully conquered is plainly against it. For untyll by tyme they fynde the sweetenes of dew subjection, it is impossible that any gentle meanes shoolde putt owt the freshe remembrance of their loste liberty. And that the Irish man is that way as obstinate as any nation, withe whome no other passion can prevaile but feare, besydes their storye whiche plainly painte it out, their manner of lyfe wherein they choose rather all filthiness then any law, and their owne consciences who beste know their owne natures, give sufficient proofe of. For under the son there is not a nation, whiche live more tiranniously then they doe one over the other.

Sir Philip Sidney, *A Discourse on Irish Affairs*, 1577

My soul doth detest their wild shamrock manners.

John Derrick, *The Image of Irelande*, 1581

I mervailde in my mynde,
  and there upon did muse:
To see a Bride of heavenlie hewe,
  an ouglie Feere to chuse.
This bride it is the Soile,
  the Bridegroome is the Karne,
With writhed glibbes like wicked sprits,
  with visage rough and stearne.
With sculles upon their poules,
  in stead of civill Cappes:
With speares in hand and swordes by sides
  to beare of after clappes,
With Jackettes long and large,
  which shroude simplicitie:
Though spitefull dartes which thei do beare
  importe iniquitie.
Their shirtes be verie straunge
  not reachyng paste the thie:
With pleates on pleates thei pleated are,
  as thicke as pleates maie lye.
Whose sleves long trailing doune,
  almoste unto the Shoe:
And with a Mantell commonlie,
  the Irishe karne doe goe.
Now some emongest the reste,
  doe use an other weede:
A coate I meane, of strange device
  which fancie first did breede.
His skirtes be verie shorte
  with pleates set thicke about,
And Irish trouzes more to put
  their straunge protractours out.

Ibid.

The uncivil kerns of Ireland.

William Shakespeare, *Henry VI part 2, c.* 1589–92

Now for our Irish wars:
We must supplant those rough rug-headed kerns,
Which live like venom where no venom else
But only they have privilege to live.

William Shakespeare, *Richard II, c.* 1595–6

The cheifest abuses which are nowe in that realme are growne from the English, that are now much more lawlesse and lycentious then the very wild Irish: so that as much care as was then by them had to reform the Irish, so much and more must nowe be used to reforme them.

Edmund Spenser, *A Veue of the Present State of Ireland*, 1596

For the Irish man, I assure you, feares the government noe longer then he is within fight or reach.

Ibid.

compared with the Russians

Wild Irish are as civil as the Russes in their kind,
Hard choice which is the best of both, each bloody, rude, and blind.

George Turberville, *Tragicall Tales*, 1587

Seventeenth Century

I never found in the remote shires of England and Wales either the gentry more kind in their fashion or entertainment, or the merchants and townsmen and women more civil in behaviour, or the mean sort and peasants more loving and serviceable, where they are honestly used, throughout all the five provinces.

Sir John Harington, *A Short View*, 1605

And to speake in generall of them all, this Nation is strong of bodie, and passing nimble, stout and haughty in heart, for wit quicke, martiall, prodigall, and carelesse of their lives, enduring travail, cold and hunger, given to fleshly lust, kind and curteous to strangers, constant in love, in enmitie implacable, light of beleefe, greedie of glory, impacient of abuse and injurie. If they bee bad you shall nowhere meete with worse: if they bee good, you can hardlie finde better.

William Good, in William Camden, *Britain*, 1610 (Philemon Holland's translation)

When they be hunger-bitten in time of dearth, they disdaine not to devour raw flesh, after they have pressed out the blood thereof: and for to concoct and digest it, they swill and powre downe the throat Uskebah draught after draught. They let their kine bloud also, which when it is growne to a gelley and strewed over with butter, they eat with good appetite.

Ibid.

This oppression did of force and necessity make the

Irish a crafty people; for such as are oppressed and live in slavery are ever put to their shifts.

Besides, all the common people have a whining tune or accent in their speech, as if they did still smart or suffer some oppression. And this idleness, together with fear of imminent mischiefs, which did continually hang over their heads, have been the cause that the Irish were ever the most inquisitive people after news, of any nation in the world.

Sir John Davies, *Discoverie of the true Causes why Ireland was never entirely Subdued,* 1612

And for my clothing in a mantle goe
And feed on *Sham-roots,* as the Irish doe.

George Wither, *Abuses Stript and Whipt,* 1613

The other as goodly sight I saw was women traveling, or toiling at home, carrying their infants about their necks, and laying their dugs over their shoulders, would give suck to the babes behind their backs, without taking them in their arms. Such kind of breasts, methinketh, were very fit to be made money-bags for East or West Indian merchants, being more than half a yard long, and as well wrought as any tanner, in the like charge, could ever mollify such leather.

William Lithgow, *Rare Adventures and Painfull Peregrinations,* 1614/32

The wild and (as I may say) meere Irish, inhabiting many and large Provinces, are barbarous and most filthy in their diet. They skum the seething pot with an handfull of straw, and straine their milke taken from the Cow through a like handfull of straw, none of the cleanest, and so clense, or rather more defile the pot and milke. They devoure great morsels of beefe unsalted, and they eat commonly Swines flesh, seldom mutton, and all these pieces of flesh, as also the intralles of beasts unwashed, they seeth in a hollow tree, lapped in a raw Cowes hide, and so set over the fier, and therewith swallow whole lumps of filthy butter. Yea (which is more contrary to nature) they will feede on Horses dying of themselves, not only upon small want of flesh, but even for pleasure.

Fynes Moryson, *An Itinerary,* 1617

Those wild Irish.

Robert Burton, *Anatomie of Melancholie,* 1621

I much admire, that never an eminent Irish native grew in England to any greatness; so many English have prospered in that country. But, it seems, we love to live there, where we may command; and they care not to come where they must obey.

Thomas Fuller, *History of the Worthies of England,* 1662

Eighteenth Century

Now we Irish men are apt to think something & nothing are next neighbours.

George Berkeley, *Commonplace Book, c.* 1708

I always cry shame at the ladies of Ireland, who never walk at all, as if their legs were of no use, but to be laid aside.

Jonathan Swift, *Journal to Stella,* May 1711

The most eating, drinking, wrangling, quarrelsome country that ever I saw. There is no keeping the peace among them.

Sir John Stanley, Letter to Jonathan Swift, Dublin, 20 November 1713

A servile race in folly nursed,
Who truckle most when treated worst.

Jonathan Swift, *On the Death of Dr. Swift,* 1731

We . . . in this island are growing an odd and mad people. We were odd before, but I was not sure of our having the genius necessary to become mad.

George Berkeley, Letter to Sir John James, 30 June 1736

Whether it be from the heaviness of the climate or from the Spanish or Scythian blood that runs in their veins, or whatever else may be the cause there still remains in the natives of this island a remarkable antipathy to labour.

George Berkeley, *A Word to the Wise,* 1749

The negroes in our plantations have a saying 'If negro was not negro Irishman would be negro!'

Ibid.

'The Irish are not in a conspiracy to cheat the world by false representations of the merits of their countrymen. No, Sir; the Irish are a FAIR PEOPLE; – they never speak well of one another.'

Samuel Johnson, in Boswell, *Life of Johnson,* 18 February 1775

As to the natural history of the Irish species, they are only remarkable for the thickness of their legs, especially those of plebeian females.

Richard Twiss, *Tour in Ireland,* 1776

I do not like Ireland. The family pride which reigns here produces the worst effects – They are in general proud and mean, the servile respect that is universally paid to people of quality disgusts me, and the minute attention to propriety stops the growth of virtue. As a nation I do not *admire* the Irish, I never before felt what it was to love my country; but now I have a value for it built on rational grounds, and my feelings concur to fix it. I never see an English face without feeling tenderness. In short I should not chuse this kingdom for my residence, if I could subsist any where else.

Mary Wollstonecraft, Letter to
Everina Wollstonecraft, 4 March 1787

The Irish men are reckoned terrible heart stealers – but I do not find them so very formidable.

Mary Wollstonecraft, Letter to
Everina Wollstonecraft, 11 May 1787

The Protestants of Ireland are just like the Catholicks – the Cat looking out of the Window and the Cat looking in at the Window. The difference of being in or out of power is the only difference between them; and power is a very corrupting thing; especially low and jobbish power – This makes the Protestants a triffle worse – as servility makes the Catholicks a little worse on the other hand.

Edmund Burke, Letter to Richard Burke Jr,
20 March 1792

The people of our island are by nature penetrating, sagacious, artful and comic.

John Philpot Curran, attrib. probably late
Eighteenth Century, quoted Frank Mathew,
Ireland, 1905

Nineteenth Century

For dear is the Emerald Isle of the ocean,
  Whose daughters are fair as the foam of the wave,
Whose sons unaccustom'd to rebel commotion,
  Tho' joyous, are sober, – tho' peaceful, are brave.

Horace and James Smith, *Rejected Addresses,* 1812

The Irish *when* good are perfect.

Lord Byron, Letter to Lady Melbourne,
1 October 1813

John remarked upon the misnomer of *settlers* applied to the Irish, who are always unsettling both at home and abroad.

Thomas Moore, *Journal,* 3 August 1823

There is perpetual kindness in the Irish cabin – butter-milk, potatoes – a stool is offered or a stone is rolled that your honour may sit down and be out of the smoke, and those who beg everywhere else seem desirous to exercise free hospitality in their own houses. Their natural disposition is turned to gaiety and happiness: while a Scotchman is thinking about the term-day, or if easy on that subject, about hell in the next world – while an Englishman is making a little hell in the present, because his muffin is not well roasted – Pat's mind is always turned to fun and ridicule. They are terribly excitable, to be sure, and will murder you on slight suspicion, and find out next day that it was all a mistake, and that it was not yourself they meant to kill, at all at all.

Sir Walter Scott, Diary, 21 November 1825,
in Lockhart, *Life of Scott,* 1838

Every Irishman, the saying goes, has a potato in his head.

Augustus Hare, *Guesses at Truth,* 1827

Talking of Ireland, he [Samuel Rogers] enumerated the long list of distinguished men whom she has poured into England. Believed the Irish to be beyond most other people in *genius,* but behind them in *sense.*

Thomas Moore, *Diary,* 25 September 1832

The Irish hate our free and fertile isle. They hate our order, our civilization, our enterprising industry, our sustained courage, our decorous liberty, our pure religion. This wild, reckless, indolent, uncertain, and superstitious race, have no sympathy with the English character. Their fair ideal of human felicity is an alternation of clannish broils and coarse idolatry. Their history describes an unbroken cycle of bigotry and blood.

Benjamin Disraeli, Letter to *The Times,* 1836

I am beginning to find out now, that a man ought to be forty years in the country instead of three months, and *then* he wouldn't be able to write about it. I wonder who *does* understand the place? not the natives certainly, for the two parties so hate each other, that neither can view the simplest proceeding of the other without distrusting, falsifying and abusing it. And where in the midst of all the lies that all tell, is a stranger to seek for truth?

W.M. Thackeray, Letter to
Mrs Carmichael-Smyth, 25–30 September 1842

I have discovered the origin of the Irish as well as that of the Scotch. The Irish are from a tribe of Arabs, the most distinguished in the desert, whose women, for many thousand years have been famous for their beauty, and the men likewise for their strong attachments.

Lady Hester Stanhope, in Charles Meryon, *Memoirs
of the Lady Hester Stanhope,* 1845

The aboriginal peasantry . . . were in an almost savage state. They never worked till they felt the sting of hunger. They were content with accommodation inferior to that which, in happier countries, was provided for domestic cattle. Already the potato, a root which can be cultivated with scarcely any art, industry, or capital, and which cannot be long stored, had become the food of the common people. From a people so fed diligence and forethought were not to be expected.

T.B. Macaulay, *History of England,* 1849–61
– of late seventeenth century

The Irish . . . were distinguished by qualities which tend to make men interesting rather than prosperous.

Ibid.

Ah, you always detect a little of the Irish fossil, the potato, peeping out in an Irishman.

Sydney Smith, quoted by Lady Holland, *Memoir of Sydney Smith,* 1855

A gulf, certainly, does appear to yawn between the Gorilla and the Negro. The woods and wilds of Africa do not exhibit an example of any intermediate animal. But . . . a creature manifestly between the gorilla and the negro is to be met with in some of the lowest districts of London and Liverpool. . . . It comes from Ireland, whence it has contrived to migrate; it belongs, in fact, to a tribe of Irish savages: the lowest species of the Irish Yahoo. When conversing with its kind it talks a sort of gibberish. It is, moreover, a climbing animal, and may sometimes be seen ascending a ladder laden with a hod of bricks. . . . The somewhat superior ability of the Irish Yahoo to utter articulate sounds, may suffice to prove that it is a development and not, as some imagine, a degeneration of the gorilla.

Punch, October 1862

The Irish . . . always ready to react against the despotism of fact.

Henri Martin, *Histoire de France depuis les temps les plus reculés jusqu'en 1789,* 4th edn, 1865

The Irishman is an imaginative being. He lives on an island in a damp climate, and contiguous to the melancholy ocean. He has no variety of pursuit. There is no nation in the world that leads so monotonous a life as the Irish, because their only occupation is the cultivation of the soil before them. These men are discontented because they are not amused.

Benjamin Disraeli, Earl of Beaconsfield, Speech on Aylesbury Hustings, 1868

*Their treason is a fairy tale, and their sedition is a child talking in its sleep.

Benjamin Disraeli, *Lothair,* 1870

There are surely bad races and good races . . . and the Irish belong to the category of the impossible.

Henry James, Letter to Mrs Henry James Sr, 7 February 1881

A random remark connecting Irishmen and beer, brought this nugget of information out of him –

'They don't drink it, sir. They *can't* drink it, sir. Give an Irishman lager for a month, and he's a dead man. An Irishman is lined with copper, and the beer corrodes it. But whiskey polishes the copper, and is the saving of him, sir.'

Mark Twain, *Life on the Mississippi,* 1883

The Irish are difficult for us to deal with. For one thing the English do not understand their innate love of fighting and blows. If on either side of an Irishman's road to Paradise shillelahs grew, which automatically hit him on the head, yet he would not be satisfied.

Alfred Lord Tennyson, in conversation, 1887, in *Alfred Lord Tennyson, a Memoir, by his Son,* 1897

What captivity was to the Jews, exile has been to the Irish. America and American influence has educated them.

Oscar Wilde, Book Review, *Pall Mall Gazette,* 13 April 1889

On our way home we renewed our argument as applied especially to the Irish. 'They ought to have been exterminated long ago,' said Gerald, 'but it is too late now.'

Wilfred Scawen Blunt, *Diary,* 7 August 1892, quoting Gerald Balfour, later chief Secretary for Ireland

Are not young Irish geniuses as plentiful as blackberries?

Oscar Wilde, quoted by Katharine Tynan, *Twenty-Five Years,* 1913 – before 1900

Twentieth Century

When I was younger I had a friend to whom I gave myself freely. . . . He was Irish, that is to say he was false to me.

James Joyce, Letter to Nora Barnacle, 29 August 1904

Oh, the dreaming! the dreaming! the torturing, heart-scalding, never satisfying dreaming, dreaming, dreaming, dreaming! . . . An Irishman's imagination never lets him alone, never convinces him, never satisfies him; but it makes him that he cant face reality nor deal with it nor handle it nor conquer it: he can only sneer at them that do. . . . He cant be intelligently political. . . . If you want to interest him in Ireland youve got to call the unfortunate island Kathleen ni Hoolihan and pretend shes a little old woman. It saves thinking. It saves working. It saves everything except imagination, imagination, imagination: and imagination's such a torture that you cant bear it without whisky.

G. Bernard Shaw, *John Bull's Other Island,* 1904

An Irishman's heart is nothing but his imagination.

Ibid.

I tell you, an Irish peasant's industry is not human: it's worse than the industry of a coral insect.

Ibid.

The Irish, when they are bad, they are the worst; but when they are good, oh! I love them; they are so soft.

Remark by German traveller, quoted by Frank Mathew, *Ireland*, 1905

There is no Irish race any more than there is an English race or a Yankee race. There *is* an Irish climate, which will stamp an immigrant more deeply and durably in two years, apparently, than the English climate will in two hundred.

G. Bernard Shaw, Preface to *John Bull's Other Island*, 1907

For the great Gaels of Ireland
Are the men that God made mad,
For all their wars are merry,
And all their songs are sad.

G.K. Chesterton, *The Ballad of the White Horse*, 1911

A nation of brilliant failures, the Irish, who are too poetical to be poets.

Max Beerbohm?, quoted in Luther Munday, *A Chronicle of Friendships*, 1913

Democratic principles are unsuited to Ireland. . . . The Irish like priests and believe in the power of priests to forgive them their sins and to change God into a biscuit. They are only happy in convents and monasteries. The only reason that the Irish would tolerate home rule would be if they were given permission to persecute someone, that is the Roman Catholic idea of liberty. It always has been and always will be.

George Moore, Letter to Edward Marsh, 3 August 1916

The English and the Irish are very much alike, except that the Irish are more so.

James Dunne, in conversation during the Irish troubles, quoted by J.M. and M.J. Cohen, *The Penguin Dictionary of Modern Quotations*, 1971

The quiet Irishman is about as harmless as a powder magazine built over a match factory.

James Dunne, in conversation during the Irish troubles, *ibid.*

and Swedes

*'You disapprove of the Swedes?'
'Yes, sir.'
'Why?'
'Their heads are too square, sir.'
'And you disapprove of the Irish?'
'Yes, sir.'
'Why?'
'Because they are Irish, sir.'

P.G. Wodehouse, *The Small Bachelor*, 1927

The Anglo-Irish were the best Irish but I can see very little future for them as the present belongs to that half-crazy Gaeldom which is growing dominant about us.

George Russell, Letter to W.B. Yeats, 23 May 1932 – *Letters from A.E.*, 1961

A fighting race who never won a battle, a race of politicians who cannot govern themselves, a race of writers without a great one of native strain, an island race who have yet to man a fleet for war, for commerce, or for the fishing banks and to learn how to build ships, a pious race excelling in blasphemy, who feel most wronged by those they have first injured, who sing of love and practise fratricide, preach freedom and enact suppression, a race of democrats who sweat the poor, have a harp for an emblem and no musicians, revelled on foreign gold and cringed without it, whose earlier history is myth and murder, whose later, murder, whose tongue is silver and whose heart is black, a race skilled in idleness, talented in hate, inventive only in slander, whose land is a breeding-ground of modern reaction and the cradle of western crime.

Tom Penhaligon, *The Impossible Irish*, Dedication, 1935

Every St Patrick's day every Irishman goes out to find another Irishman to make a speech to.

Shane Leslie, *American Wonderland*, 1936

Politics is the chloroform of the Irish People, or, rather, the hashish.

Oliver St John Gogarty, *As I Was Going Down Sackville Street*, 1937

Why does every educated Irishman regret that he is Irish?

Ibid.

The Irish, whose other creed is Hate.

Rudyard Kipling, *Something of Myself*, 1937

Anglo-Irish I was born and Anglo-Irish I wish to be, for was it not a fact that the Anglo-Irish have always been the salt of the British Empire? Nowadays it is the fashion to make us dwindle into West Britons, flitting pathetically in a vague Limbo between Gael and Anglo-Saxon; but like all other Anglo-Irish I was deeply conscious of my Irish nationality: for what is nationality but the earth one springs from and the sky above?

Walter Starkie, *The Waveless Plain*, 1938

Irish poets, learn your trade,
Sing whatever is well made,
Scorn the sort now growing up
All out of sort from toe to top,
Their unremembering hearts and heads
Base-born products of base beds.

Sing the peasantry, and then
Hard-riding country gentlemen,
The holiness of monks, and after
Porter-drinkers' randy laughter;
Sing the lords and ladies gay
That were beaten into the clay
Through seven heroic centuries;
Cast your mind on other days
That we in coming days may be
Still the indomitable Irishry.

W.B. Yeats, *Under Ben Bulben,* V, 4 September 1938

They are an amazing lot. They are exactly like the Hungarians but they all speak fluent English.

Hungarian Journalist, reporting first reactions to the Irish to his compatriots in the 1930s, quoted by George Mikes, *English Humour for Beginners,* 1980

You should never praise one Irishman to another Irishman.

Oliver St John Gogarty, *It Isn't this Time of Year at all,* 1954

There is in Ireland a kind of third person which, though married, is sexless. The male of the species is more a churchman than a layman; and the female of the species is more churchman than the male.

Ibid.

*To marry the Irish is to look for poverty.

J.P. Donleavy, *The Ginger Man,* 1956

This is a dark dark world, and that is why the Irish are always half-lit.

Adlai Stevenson, remark, before 1965, quoted in Leon Harris, *The Fine Art of Political Wit,* 1965

Pat: He was an Anglo-Irishman.
Meg: In the blessed name of God what's that?
Pat: A Protestant with a horse.

Brendan Behan, *The Hostage,* 1958

Irishness is not primarily a question of birth or blood or language: it is the condition of being involved in the Irish situation, and usually of being mauled by it.

Conor Cruise O'Brien, *Writers and Politics,* 1965

Joyce: The proudest boast of an Irishman is – I paid back my way.

Tom Stoppard, *Travesties,* 1975

The luck of the Irish is a wish more than a characteristic.

Jan Morris, 'Do You Think He Should Have Gone Over', *Travels,* 1976

The great thing about this country is – there's always somebody who doesn't care.

Anon. American journalist retired to Ireland and quoted by Alistair Cooke, *The Americans,* 1979

Letting the Irish shoot first is what we call the 'Irish Dimension.'

SAS soldier, quoted in Tony Geraghty, *Who Dares Wins,* 1980

Antrim (Northern Ireland)

No spot of earth where men have so fiercely for ages of time
Fought and survived and cancelled each other,
Pict and Gael and Dane, McQuillan, Clandonnel, O'Neill,
Savages, the Scot, the Norman, the English,
Here in the narrow passage and the pitiless North, perpetual
Betrayals, relentless, resultless fighting.
A random fury of dirks in the dark: a struggle for survival
Of hungry blind cells of life in the womb.
But now the womb has grown old, her strength has gone forth; a few red carts in a fog creak flax to the dubs,
And sheep in the high heather cry hungrily that life is hard; a plaintive peace; shepherds and peasants.

We have felt the blades meet in the flesh in a hundred ambushes
And the groaning blood bubble in the throat;
In a hundred battles the heavy axes bite in the deep bone,
The mountain suddenly stagger and be darkened.
Generation on generation we have seen the blood of boys
And heard the moaning of women massacred,
The passionate flesh and nerves have flamed like pitchpine and fallen
And lain in the earth softly dissolving.
I have lain and been humbled in all these graves, and mixed new flesh with the old and filled the hollow of my mouth
With maggots and rotten dust and ages of repose, I lie here and plot the agony of resurrection.

Robinson Jeffers, *Antrim,* 1931

Aran Islands

The absence of the heavy boot of Europe has preserved to these people the agile walk of the wild animal, while the general simplicity of their lives has given them many other points of physical perfection. Their way of life has never been acted on by anything much more artificial than the nests and burrows of the creatures that live round them, and they seem, in a certain sense, to approach more nearly to the finer types of our aristocracies – who are bred artificially to a natural ideal – than to the labourer or citizen, as the wild horse resembles the thoroughbred rather than the hack or the cart-horse. Tribes of the same natural development are, perhaps, frequent in half-civilized countries; but here a touch of the refinement of old societies is blended, with singular effect, among the qualities of the wild animal.

J.M. Synge, *The Aran Islands,* 1911

The islands of Aran where the air is truly delightful and where there are so many stones to split that it is a real pleasure.

James Joyce, Letter to Lucia Joyce, Paris, 28 March 1935

'Arlo Hill' (Mt Galtymore)

Eftsoones the time and place appointed were,
Where all, both heavenly Powers, and earthly wights,
Before great Nature's presence should appeare,
For triall of their Titles and best Rights;
That was, to weet, upon the highest hights
Of *Arlo-hill* (Who knows not *Arlo-hill?*)
That is the highest head (in all mens sights)
Of my old father *Mole,* whom Shepheards quill
Renowned hath with hymnes fit for a rurall skill. . . .
(Beeing of old the best and fairest Hill
That was in all this holy-Islands hights).

Edmund Spenser, *The Faerie Queene,* 1596

Nath'lesse, *Diana,* . . .
also quite forsooke
All those faire forrests about Arlo hid,
And all that Mountaine, which doth over-looke
The richest champian that may else be rid,
And the faire *Shure* in which are thousand Salmons bred.

Ibid.

Armagh (Northern Ireland)

An Italian Frier comming of old into Ireland, and seeing at Armach this their diet and nakednesse of the women, . . . is said to have cried out,
Civitas Armachana, Civitas vana,
Carnes crudae, mulieres nudae.
Vaine Armach City, I did thee pity,
Thy meates rawnes, and womens nakednesse.

Fynes Moryson, *An Itinerary,* 1617

This County of Armagh . . . excepting its cursed roads, and want of downs to ride on, is the best part I have seen of Ireland.

Jonathan Swift, Letter to William Richardson, 23 October 1736

Arranmore

Oh! Arranmore, lov'd Arranmore,
How oft I dream of thee,
And of those days when, by thy shore,
I wandered young and free.
Full many a path I've tried, since then,
Through pleasure's flowery maze,
But ne'er could find the bliss again
I felt in those sweet days.

Thomas Moore, 'Oh! Arranmore, Lov'd Arranmore', *Irish Melodies,* 1807–35

Athlone (en route to, from Ballymacky)

I pedalled on towards Athlone through slashing rain across brown miles of harvested bog – looking like a child's dream of a world made of chocolate.

Dervla Murphy, *A Place Apart,* 1978

Rivers Avon and Avoca (between Rathdrum and Arklow, county Wicklow)

There is not in the wide world a valley so sweet
As that vale in whose bosom the bright waters meet;
Oh! the last rays of feeling and life must depart,
Ere the bloom of that valley shall fade from my heart.

Yet it *was* not that Nature had shed o'er the scene
Her purest of crystal and brightest of green;
'Twas *not* her soft magic of streamlet or hill,
Oh! no, – it was something more exquisite still.

'Twas that friends, the belov'd of my bosom, were near,
Who made every dear scene of enchantment more dear,
And who felt how the best charms of nature improve,
When we see them reflected from looks that we love.

Sweet vale of Avoca! how calm could I rest
In thy bosom of shade with the ones I love best,
Where the storms that we feel in this cold world should cease,
And our hearts, like thy waters, be mingled in peace.

Thomas Moore, *The Meeting of the Waters,* 1807

Ballyshannon

Adieu to Belashanny where I was bred and born;

Go where I may, I'll think of you, as sure as night and morn,
The kindly spot, the friendly town, where everyone is known,
And not a face in all the place but partly seems my own;
There's not a house or window, there's not a field or hill,
But east or west, in foreign lands, I'll recollect them still.
I leave my warm heart with you, though my back I'm forced to turn –
So adieu to Belashanny and the winding banks of Erne!

William Allingham, *Belashanny Songs Ballads and Stories*, 1877

River Barrow (near Carlow)

Wheel, Barrow, wheel thy winding course. . . .

Anon., quoted Thomas Moore, *Journal*, 30 July 1823

Belfast (Northern Ireland)

The Lord in His Mercy be good to Belfast
The grief of the exile she soothed as he passed.

Old Ballad

They call Belfast the Irish Liverpool. If people are for calling names, it would be better to call it the Irish London at once – the chief city of the kingdom at any rate. It looks hearty, thriving and prosperous, as if it had money in its pockets, and roast-beef for dinner: it has no pretensions to fashion, but looks mayhap better in its honest broadcloth than some people in their shabby brocade. The houses are as handsome as at Dublin, with this advantage, that the people seem to live in them.

W.M. Thackeray, *The Irish Sketch Book of 1842*, 1843

Other Irish towns may present more picturesque forms to the eye. But Belfast is the only large Irish town in which the traveller is not disgusted by the loathsome aspect and odour of long lines of human dens far inferior in comfort and cleanliness to the dwellings which, in happier countries, are provided for cattle. No other large Irish town is so well cleaned, so well paved, so brilliantly lighted. The place of domes and spires is supplied by edifices, less pleasing to the taste, but not less indicative of prosperity, huge factories, towering many stories above the chimneys of the houses, and resounding with the roar of machinery.

T.B. Macaulay, *History of England*, 1849–61

A fine place, with rough people.

Charles Dickens, Letter, 1858, in Forster, *Life of Dickens*, 1872–3

The folk that live in Black Belfast, their heart is in their mouth,
They see us making murders in the meadows of the South.
They think a plough's a rack they do, and cattle-calls are creeds
And they think we're burnin' witches when we're only burnin' weeds.

G.K. Chesterton, 'Me Heart', *The Flying Inn*, 1914

See Belfast, devout and profane and hard,
Built on reclaimed mud, hammers playing in the shipyard,
Time punched with holes like a steel sheet, time
Hardening the faces, veneering with a grey and speckled rime
The faces under the shawls and caps:
This was my mother-city, these my paps.
Country of callous lava cooled to stone,
Of minute sodden haycocks, of ship-sirens' moan,
Of falling intonations. . . .

Louis MacNeice, *Valediction*, January 1934

Belfast, a city that every good Dubliner, except myself, despises and reviles.

James Joyce, Letter to Lucia Joyce, Paris, 1 June 1935 (writing in Italian)

While Dublin is obviously a capital, though a seedy and impoverished one, Belfast is mean and provincial. Too many of its shops are branches of well-known London emporiums, the whole place is depressing, and the note is a dull opinionativeness. The things which struck me most were the number of swans and newsboys, the out-of-the-wayness of the obviously unwanted Parliament House, and the age of the taxi-cabs. The one in which we made the tour of the city was fusty with old leather, smelling of all the funerals I have ever attended. Intellectually the place is as backward as Spain.

James Agate, *Ego 3*, 15 August 1936

Red brick in the suburbs, white horse on the wall,
Eyetalian marbles in the City Hall:
O stranger from England, why stand so aghast?
May the Lord in His mercy be kind to Belfast.

This jewel that houses our hopes and our fears
Was knocked up from the swamp in the last hundred years;
But the last shall be first and the first shall be last:
May the Lord in His mercy be kind to Belfast.

We swore by King William there'd never be seen
An all-Irish parliament at College Green,
So at Stormont we're nailing the flag to the mast:
May the Lord in His mercy be kind to Belfast.

O the bricks they will bleed and the rain it will weep,
And the damp Lagan fog lull the city to sleep;
It's to hell with the future and live on the past:
May the Lord in His mercy be kind to Belfast.

Maurice James Craig, *Ballad to a Traditional Refrain*, in John Montague (ed.), *Faber Book of Irish Verse*, 1974

It is impossible to be gloomy for long in Belfast. I was feeling rather depressed one afternoon when I turned a corner and saw on a gable-end the familiar NO POPE HERE. And underneath, in different coloured paint, LUCKY OLD POPE!

Dervla Murphy, *A Place Apart*, 1978

There is a story that when incoming jets throttle back for the approach to Belfast's Aldergrove Airport, the pilots tell their passengers to put their watches back to local time – 1690.

Quoted by Russell Miller, *Sunday Times*, 27 April 1980

Blarney

There is a stone there
That whoever kisses,
Oh! he never misses
  To grow eloquent.
'Tis he may clamber
To a lady's chamber
Or become a member
  Of Parliament.

Francis Sylvester Mahony (Father Prout), *The Groves of Blarney* (lines added to R.A. Milliken's poem of the same title), *c.* 1830s

Sir Walter scrambled to the top of the castle, and kissed with due faith and devotion, the famous *Blarney stone*, one salute of which is said to emancipate the pilgrim from all future visitations of *mauvaise honte*.

J.G. Lockhart, *Life of Scott* (1825), 1838

Boyne River

Such was the Boyne, a poor inglorious stream,
That in Hibernian vales obscurely strayed,
And unobserved in wild meanders played;
Till by your lines and Nassau's sword renowned,
Its rising billows through the world resound,
Where'er the hero's godlike acts can pierce,
Or where the fame of an immortal verse.

Joseph Addison, *Letter from Italy to the Right Honourable Lord Halifax*, 1701

In Belfast they are of opinion that the Battle of the Boyne took place last Saturday week; actually, it happened two hundred and fifty years ago [in 1690].

M.J. MacManus, *Irish Cavalcade*, 1939

The Burren (Co. Clare)

There is not wood enough to hang a man, nor water enough to drown him, nor earth enough to bury him in.

Oliver Cromwell, attrib., *c.* 1649–50

Castlepatrick

For I come from Castlepatrick and me heart is on me
  sleeve,
But a lady stole it from me on St Gallowglass's Eve.

G.K. Chesterton, 'Me Heart', *The Flying Inn*, 1914

Connaught

. . . No hissinge serpent there doth 'bide
noe toade, nor spider, adder nor yet snake
noe stinging venom'd thinge may there partake
the sweetes and pleasures of that happy soyle
there they doe live without or care or toyle
they neither plant, nor sowe, nor till the ground
nor with a hedge their own encompass rounde
all things are common, there they nothing wante
they feele no penurie or pynchinge scante.

Gervase Markham, *A Newe Metamorphosis*, *c.* 1600

Connemara

There are few things in the world more delightful than a drive at sunset, in a bright autumn evening, among the mountains and lakes of Connemara. A friend of ours describes the air of his favourite place by saying it is like breathing champagne.

Harriet Martineau, *Letters from Ireland*, 1852

West of the Shannon may be said,
Whatever comes into your head;
But you can do, and chance your luck
Whatever you like West of the Suck.

There's something sleeping in my breast
That wakens only in the West;
There's something in the core of me
That needs the West to set it free.

And I can see that river flow
Beside the town of Ballinasloe
To bound a country that is worth
The half of Heaven, the whole of Earth. . . .

As often as I take the road
Beyond the Suck, I wish to God
That it were but a one-way track
Which I might take and not come back.

Oliver St John Gogarty, 'Connemara', *Collected Poems*, 1951

Cork

The third County hath the name of the City Corke, consisting almost all of one long streete, but well knowne and frequented, which is so compassed with rebellious neighbours, as they of old not daring to marry their Daughters to them, the custome grew and continues to this day, that by mutuall marriages one with another, all the Citizens are of kinne in some degree of Affinity.

Fynes Moryson, *An Itinerary*, 1617

The citizens of Cork are all akin.

Attributed to Camden by Thomas Fuller, Sermon, 1654

Cork indeed was a place of trade, but for some years past is gone to decay, and the wretched merchants, instead of being dealers, are dwindled to pedlars and cheats.

Jonathan Swift, Letter to Lady Brandreth, 30 June 1732

The Scene of Corke is ever the same: dull, insipid, and void of all Amusement: . . . The Butchers are as greasy, the Quakers as formal, & the Presbeyterians as holy & full of the Lord as usual: All Things are in statu quo: even the Hogs and Piggs gruntle in the same cadence as of yore.

Earl of Orrery, Letter to Jonathan Swift, 15 March 1737

The approach to Cork by Glanmire magnificent; a sort of sea avenue up to the town, with beautiful banks on each side, studded over with tasteful villas; gives a 'note of preparation,' however, which Cork itself by no means comes up to.

Thomas Moore, *Journal*, 1 August 1823

Donaghadee (Northern Ireland)

I've never gone to Donaghadee,
That vague far townlet by the sea;
In Donaghadee I shall never be:
Then why do I sing of Donaghadee.

Thomas Hardy, 'Donaghadee', *Human Shows*, 1925

Donegal (en route to, from Sligo)

A country that *might* all be very beautiful, but is not so, is bare, gnarled, craggy, and speaks to you of sloth and insolvency. 'When every place was no place, and Dublin was a shaking bog;' Irish phrase for the beginning of time.

Thomas Carlyle, *Reminiscences of My Irish Journey in 1849*, 1882

Co. Down (Northern Ireland)

A land that floweth with milk and honey, a fertile soil truly if there be any in Europe, whether it be manured to corn or left to grass. There is timber, stone, plaster, and slate commodious for building everywhere abundant, a country full of springs, rivers, and lakes, both small and great, full of excellent fish and fowl.

Thomas Smith, *A letter sent by I.B. Gentlemen unto his very frende Mayster R.C. Esquire*, c. 1571

Drogheda

It hath pleased God to bless our endeavour at Drogheda.

Oliver Cromwell, Dispatch to the Speaker of the English House of Commons, 1649

Dublin

This town of Dublin is rather ill-inhabited than seated; the people of good natural abilities, but corrupted some with a wild, some with a loose life; and, indeed, there is almost nothing in this country but it is either savage or wanton. They have hitherto wanted nothing more than to be kept in fear, which (by God's grace) they shall not want hereafter. They are inclined, more than any nation I have seen to superstitions, which surely have crept in between ignorance and liberty. In their hospitalities there is fully as much unhandsomeness as plenty. For their general parts, their bodies are active, and their minds are rather secret than nimble.

Sir Henry Wotton, Letter to John Donne, (?) 1599

This is the roiall City and seat of Ireland, a famous towne for Merchandize, the chiefe Court of Justice, in munition strong, in buildings gorgeous, in Citizens populous. . . . Seated it is in a right delectable and holesome place: for to the South yee have hils mounting up aloft, Westward an open champion ground, and on the East the sea at hand and in sight: The River *Liffy* running downe at North-East affordeth a safe roade and harbour for ships. By the river side, are certaine Wharfes or Kaies, as we tearme them, whereby the violent force of the water might be restrained.

William Camden, *Britain*, 1610
(Philemon Holland's translation)

No men in Dublin go to Taverns who are worth sitting with.

Jonathan Swift, Letter to Charles Ford, 16 August 1725

This town . . . I believe is the most disagreeable place in Europe, at least to any but those who have been accustomed to it from their youth, and in such a case I suppose a jail might be tolerable.

Jonathan Swift, Letter to Knightly Chetwode, 23 November 1727

The most hospitable city I ever passed through.

Mary Wollstonecraft, *Letters Written During a Short Residence in Sweden, etc.*, 1796

Ireland will be the richest country in the world for its capital is always doubling (dublin).

Washington Irving, in notes of his expenses, 1805

Och, Dublin City, there is no doubtin',
Bates every city upon the say;
'Tis there you'll see O'Connell spoutin',
An' Lady Morgan makin' tay;
For 'tis the capital of the finest nation,
Wid charmin' pisintry on a fruitful sod,
Fightin' like divils for conciliation,
An' hatin' each other for the love of God.

Anon., *Dublin City,* old ballad revised by Charles James Lever, 1820s

A handsomer town, with fewer people in it, it is impossible to see on a summer's day.

W.M. Thackeray, *The Irish Sketch Book of 1842,* 1843

You see more ragged and wretched people here than I ever saw anywhere else. *En revanche*, the women are really very handsome – quite in the lowest class – as well at Cork as here.

Queen Victoria, Letter to her uncle, 6 August 1849

Sad reflexions upon Dublin, and the animosities that reign in its hungry existence – *Not* now the 'Capital' of Ireland; has Ireland any Capital, or *where* is its future Capital to be? Perhaps Glasgow or Liverpool is its real 'capital city' just now!

Thomas Carlyle, *Reminiscences of My Irish Journey in 1849,* 1882

My intention was to write a chapter of the moral history of my country and I chose Dublin for the scene because that city seemed to me the centre of paralysis.

James Joyce, Letter to Grant Richards, 5 May 1905

When you remember that Dublin has been a capital for thousands of years, that it is the 'second' city of the British Empire, that it is nearly three times as big as Venice it seems strange that no artist has given it to the world.

James Joyce, Letter to Stanislaus Joyce, 18 September 1905

and James Joyce's 'Ulysses'

Ulysses . . . is a revolting record of a disgusting phase of civilisation; but it is a truthful one; and I should like to put a cordon round Dublin; round up every male person in it between the ages of 15 and 30; force them to read it; and ask them whether on reflection they could see anything amusing in all that foul mouthed, foul minded derision and obscenity. . . . I have walked those streets and known those shops and have heard and taken part in those conversations. I escaped from them to England at the age of twenty; and forty years later have learnt from the books of Mr. Joyce that Dublin is still what it was, and young men are still drivelling in slackjawed blackguardism just as they were in 1870. It is, however, some consolation to find that at last somebody has felt deeply enough about it to face the horror of writing it all down and using his literary genius to force people to face it. In Ireland they try to make a cat cleanly by rubbing its nose in its own filth. Mr. Joyce has tried the same treatment on the human subject. I hope it may prove successful.

G. Bernard Shaw, Letter to Sylvia Beach, 10 October 1921

Humptydump Dublin squeaks through his norse,
Humptydump Dublin hath a horrible vorse
And with all his kinks english
Plus his irismanx brogues
Humptydump Dublin's grandada of all rogues.

James Joyce, Rhyme written to advertise publication of *Haveth Childers Everywhere,* 1932

Grey brick upon brick,
Declamatory bronze
On sombre pedestals –
O'Connell, Grattan, Moore –
And the brewery tugs and the swans
On the balustraded stream
And the bare bones of a fanlight
Over a hungry door
And the air soft on the cheek
And porter running from the taps
With a head of yellow cream
And Nelson on his pillar
Watching his world collapse. . . .

She is not an Irish town,
And she is not English,
Historic with guns and vermin
And the cold renown
Of a fragment of Church latin,
Of an oratorical phrase.
But oh the days are soft,
Soft enough to forget
The lesson better learnt,
The bullet on the wet
Streets, the crooked deal,
The steel behind the laugh,
The Four Courts burnt.

Fort of the Dane

Garrison of the Saxon
Augustan capital
Of a Gaelic nation,
Appropriating all
The alien brought,
You give me time for thought
And by a juggler's trick
You poise the toppling hour –
O greyness run to flower,
Grey stone, grey water,
And brick upon grey brick.

Louis MacNeice, *The Closing Album, I: Dublin,* August–September 1939

It is the best thing that Orangemen ever built.

Oliver St John Gogarty, *It Isn't this Time of Year at all,* 1955

It is a city where you can see a sparrow fall to the ground, and God watching it.

Conor Cruise O'Brien, attrib.

'Enjoy yourself now!' everybody says in Dublin, and they mean enjoy yourself *notwithstanding*.

Jan Morris, *Travels,* 1976

The most instantly talkative city in Europe.

V.S. Pritchett, 'Conversation', *Sunday Times Weekly Review*, 2 July 1978

Georgian Dublin has been preserved by a cocoon of poverty.

Desmond Guinness, *Georgian Dublin,* 1979

Dublin: Details
Behold a proof of Irish Sense!
  Here Irish wit is seen
When nothing's left that's worth defence
  We build a magazine.

Jonathan Swift, Epigram, *c.* 1737

Merrion Square
. . . Merrion Square, the Harley Street of Dublin, which the wags called 'The Valley of the Shadow of Death.'

Oliver St John Gogarty, *It Isn't this Time of Year at all,* 1954

Trinity College
It is a paradise in the oriental sense of the word, that is to say, a place surrounded by a high wall.

Walter Starkie, *The Waveless Plain,* 1938

'The Silent Sister,' as Dublin University was called in Oxford and Cambridge. . . .

Oliver St John Gogarty, *It Isn't this Time of Year at all,* 1954

Mount Errigal (Co. Donegal)

I remarked to a native that I thought from its shape it was of volcanic origin. He replied, 'Ah, not at all, it's that way since the memory of man.'

Frank Mathew, *Ireland,* 1905

Erris

Few but sportsmen and poor-law officials know much about Erris.

Harriet Martineau, *Letters from Ireland,* 1852

Galway Bay

If you ever go across the sea to Ireland
It may be at the closing of the day
You can sit and watch the moon rise over Claddagh
And watch the sun go down on Galway Bay.

Arthur Colahan, *Galway Bay,* 1947

Galway

When it is stated that, throughout the town of Galway, you cannot get a cigar which costs more than twopence, Londoners may imagine the strangeness and remoteness of the place.

W.M. Thackeray, *The Irish Sketch Book of 1842,* 1843

Straight steep streets, remarkable old city; how in such a stony country it exists! Port wine and Spanish and French articles inwards, cattle outwards and scantlings of corn; no *other* port for so many miles of country; *enough* of stony country, even that will make a kind of feast.

Thomas Carlyle, *Reminiscences of My Irish Journey in 1849,* 1882

Claddagh
Claddagh as like Madagascar as England. A kind of charm in that poor savage freedom.

Ibid.

The difficulty seems to lie in the absence of a middle class of society. The people are, in this, like the buildings.

Harriet Martineau, *Letters from Ireland,* 1852

O the crossbones of Galway,
The hollow grey houses,
The rubbish and sewage,
The grass-grown pier,
And the dredger grumbling
All night in the harbour:
The war came down on us here.

Louis MacNeice, *The Closing Album, IV: Galway,* August–September 1939

Lough Garagarry (Mangarton Mount Killarney, ends Glen na Cloghereen)

O'Donoghue's Ink Bottle.

Traditional, so called from the darkness of its waters

The Giant's Causeway

'But where, if you please, is the Causeway?'

'That's the Causeway before you,' says the guide.

'Which?'

'That pier which you see jutting out into the bay right ahead.'

'*Mon dieu!* and I travelled a hundred and fifty miles to see *that!*'

I declare, upon my conscience, the barge moored at Hungerford Market is a more majestic object and seems to occupy as much space. . . .

And now, by force of money, having got rid of the sea and land beggars, you are at liberty to examine the wonders of the place. . . . The solitude is awful. . . . It looks like the beginning of the world, somehow: the sea looks older than in other places, the hills and rocks strange, and formed differently from other rocks and hills – as those vast dubious monsters were formed who possessed the earth before man. The hill-tops are shattered into a thousand cragged fantastical shapes; the water comes swelling into scores of little strange creeks, or goes off with a leap, roaring into those mysterious caves yonder, which penetrate who knows how far into our common world. The savage rock-sides are painted of a hundred colours. Does the sun ever shine here? When the world was moulded and fashioned out of formless chaos, this must have been the *bit over* – a remnant of chaos! Think of that! – it is a tailor's simile.

W.M. Thackeray, *The Irish Sketch Book of 1842*, 1843

Glen Lough (Co. Donegal)

Here is a wild and unlettered and un-French-lettered country, too far from Andera, a village you can't be too far from. Here are gannets and seals and puffins flying and puffing and playing a quarter of a mile outside my window where there are great rocks petrified like the old Fates and destinies of Ireland, and smooth white pebbles under and around them like the souls of the dead Irish. There's a huge echo. You shout and the dead Irish answer from behind the hill. I've forced them into confessing that they're sad, grey, lost, forgotten, dead and damned forever.

Dylan Thomas, Letter to Bert Trick, *c.* July 1935

Kerry

Lyne quoted to me Lord Bellamont's description of Kerry, 'All acclivity and declivity, without the intervention of a single horizontal plane; the mountains all rocks, and the men all savages.'

Thomas Moore, *Journal*, 6 August 1823

and Cork

When the glass is up to thirty
Cork and Kerry will be dirty;
When the glass is high O very
There'll be rain in Cork and Kerry;
When the glass is low, O Lork!
There'll be rain in Kerry and Cork.

E.V. Lucas and C.L. Graves, 'Rhyming Reminders', in *England Day By Day*, 1903

Kildare

Kildare, as I entered it, looked worse and worse: one of the wretchedest wild villages I ever saw; and full of ragged beggars this day (Sunday), – exotic altogether, 'like a village in Dahomey,' men and Church both. Knots of worshipping people hung about the streets, and every-where around them hovered a harpy-swarm of clamorous mendicants, men, women, children: – a village *winged*, as if a flight of harpies had alighted in it!

Thomas Carlyle, *Reminiscences of My Journey in Ireland in 1849*, 1882

Kilkenny

That antient and delightful City is not so remarkable for a splendid outside as for intrinsic Worth the rich Marble that covers the Houses and even the streets not being distinguishable by the Eye from the vilest stone untill by Tryall you have discover'd it's Hardness and the Pollish & Lustre it is capable of receiving.

George Berkeley, Letter to Samuel Molyneux, 26 November 1709

Killarney (near)

Funeral overtaken by us; the 'Irish howl' – totally disappointing, there was no sorrow whatever in the tone of it. A pack of idle women, mounted on the hearse as many as could, and the rest walking, were hoh-hohing with a grief quite evidently hired, and not worth hiring.

Thomas Carlyle, *Reminiscences of My Irish Journey in 1849*, 1882

Kinsale (and Cork, en route between)

When I complained to an Irish soldier of the length of the miles between Kinsale and Cork, he acknowledged the truth of my observation; but archly added, that though they were *long*, they were but *narrow*.

Philip Thicknesse, *A Year's Journey through France and Spain*, 1789

River Liffey

There was the Liffey, rolling down the lea.

Edmund Spenser, *The Faerie Queene*, 1589–96

Limerick (Dublin and Cork)

Limerick was, Dublin is, and Cork shall be
The finest city of the three.

Quoted by Dean Hole in 1859 as 'The Old Prophecy'

*The City of *Limerick*, the siege of which was begun by his majesty king *William* himself, the year after I went into the army – lies, an' please your honours, in the middle of a devilish wet, swampy country. – 'Tis quite surrounded, said my uncle Toby, with the *Shannon*, and is, by its situation, one of the strongest fortified places in *Ireland*. –

I think this is a new fashion, quoth Dr. *Slop*, of beginning a medical lecture.

Laurence Sterne, *Tristram Shandy*, vol. v, 1761

I remember nothing good but the pigs and gloves; and nothing pleasant but the women, who were quite delightful, and as wicked as they were pretty: or as women could wish to be.

Charles James Napier (1827), in Sir William Napier, *Life and Opinions of General Charles James Napier*, 1857 – of *c.* 1790s

Charles Kemble's story of the Irishman mulcted in 5l. for beating a fellow, and saying, 'What, five pounds! Well (turning to the patient), wait till I get you in Limerick, where *bating* is *cheap*, and I'll take it out of you.'

Thomas Moore, *Diary*, 26 February 1830

Justly celebrated for its Hooks, it is far more to be admired for its Eyes, for although the former are the best in all the world, the latter are much more killing.

Samuel Hole as 'An Oxonian', *A Little Tour in Ireland*, 1859

Listowel

The place seemed like a scene at a country theatre, once smartly painted by the artist; but the paint has cracked in many places, the lines are worn away, and the whole piece only looks more shabby for the flaunting strokes of the brush which remain.

W.M. Thackeray, *The Irish Sketch Book of 1842*, 1843

Newtown Limavaddy (en route to)

Mountains stretch'd around,
  Gloomy was their tinting,
And the horses hoofs
  Made a dismal clinting;
Wind upon the heath
  Howling was and piping,
On the heath and bog,
  Black with many a snipe in;
Mid the bogs of black
  Silver pools were flashing,
Crows upon their sides
  Picking were and splashing;
Cockney in the car
  Closer folds his plaidy,
Grumbling at the road
  Leads to Limavaddy.

Through the crashing woods
  Autumn brawled and blustered,
Tossing round about
  Leaves the hue of mustard;
Yonder lay Lough Foyle,
  Which a storm was whipping,
Covering with mist
  Lake and shores, and shipping.
Up and down the hill
  (Nothing could be bolder)
Horse went with a raw
  Bleeding on his shoulder.
'Where are horses changed?'
  Said I to the laddy
Driving on the box:
  'Sir, at Limavaddy.'

W.M. Thackeray, 'Peg of Limavaddy', in *The Irish Sketch Book of 1842*, 1843

Londonderry (Northern Ireland)

The city of Londonderry is the most compact, regular, well built town, that I have seen in the King's Dominions, the town house (no mean structure) stands in the midst of a square piazza from which there are four principal streets leading to as many gates. It is a walled town, and has walks all round the walls planted with trees, as in Padua. The Cathedral is the prettiest in Ireland. My house is a fashionable thing, not five years old, and cost eleven hundred pounds. The Corporation are all good churchmen, a civil people, and throughout English, being a colony from London. I have hardly seen a more agreeable situation, the town standing on a peninsula in the midst of a fine spreading lake, environed with green hills, and at a distance the noble ridge of Ennishawen mountains and the mighty rocks of Maghilligan form a most august scene. There is indeed much of the *gusto grande* in the laying out of this whole country, which recalls to mind many prospects of Naples and Sicily.

George Berkeley, Letter to Lord Percival, 8 June 1724

On the highest ground stood the Cathedral, a church which, though erected when the secret of Gothic architecture was lost, and though ill qualified to sustain a comparison with the awful temples of the middle ages, is not without grace and dignity.

T.B. Macaulay, *History of England*, 1849–61

'Mole' (etc.)

(The Ballahoura Mountains and the Galties. 'Mulla' is the source of the river Awbeg, and 'Armulla' Spenser's invented name for its valley.)

Old father *Mole*, (*Mole* hight that mountain gray,
That walls the Northside of *Armulla* dale)
He had a daughter fresh as floure of May,
Which gave that name unto that pleasant vale;
Mulla the daughter of old *Mole*, so hight
The Nimph, which of that water course hath charge,
That springing out of *Mole*, doth run downe right
To *Buttevant*, where spreading forth at large,
It giveth name unto that auncient Cittie,
Which *Kilnemullah* cleped is of old:
Whose ragged ruines breed great ruth and pittie,
To travailers, which it from far behold.

Edmund Spenser, *Colin Clout's Come Home Againe*, 1595

Mourne (mountains of)

Where the Mountains o' Mourne sweep down to the sea.

William Percival French, Song, *The Mountains of Mourne*, *Chronicles and Poems of Percy French*, 1922

Munster

Out of every corner of the woods and glens they came, creeping forth upon their hands, for their legs could not bear them; they looked like anatomies of death, they spake like ghosts crying out of their graves; they did eat the dead carrions, happy where they could find them, yea, and one another soon after insomuch as the very carcasses, they spared not to scrape out of their graves; and if they found a plot of water-cresses or shamrocks, there they flocked as to a feast for a time, yet not able long to continue therewithall, that in short space there were none almost left; and a most populous and plentiful country suddenly left void of man and beast; yet sure in all that war, there perished not many by the sword, but all by the extremity of famine.

Edmund Spenser, *A Veue of the Present State of Ireland*, 1596, on the effects of the Munster Wars

Pool-a-Phooka

Yesterday we went to Pool-a-Phooka, the Leap of the Goblin Horse. What is that, do you suppose? Why, a cleft in the mountains, down and through which the river Liffey (not very long born from the earth) comes leaping and roaring. Cold veal pies, champagne, etc., make up the enchantment.

Edward Fitzgerald, Letter to Bernard Barton, 17 August 1843

Passage West (Co. Cork)

The town of Passage is both large and spacious,
And situated upon the say
'Tis nate and decent and quite adjacent
To come from Cork on a summer's day;
There you may slip in to take a dipping,
Fornent the shipping that at anchor ride.
Or in a wherry cross o'er the ferry
To Carrigaloe on the other side.

Mud cabins swarm in this place so charming,
With sailor garments hung out to dry;
And each abode is snug and commodious
With pigs melodious in their straw-built sty.
Tis there the turf is, and lots of murphies,
Dead sprats and herrings, and oyster-shells;
Nor any lack, O! of good tobacco –
Though what is smuggled by far excels.

There are ships from Cadiz, and from Barbadoes,
But the leading trade is in whiskey punch;
And you may go in where one Molly Bowen
Keeps a nate hotel for a quiet lunch.
But land or deck on, you may safely reckon,
Whatever country you came hither from,
On an invitation to a jollification,
With a parish priest that's called 'Father Tom.'

Of ships there's one fixed for lodging convicts
A floating 'stone jug' of amazing bulk;
The hake and salmon, playing at bagammon,
Swim for diversion all around this 'hulk';
There 'Saxon' jailors keep grave repailors
Who soon with sailors must anchor weigh

From the emerald island ne'er to see dry land
Until they spy land in sweet Botany Bay.

Francis Sylvester Mahony (Father Prout), *The Attractions of a Fashionable Irish Watering Place*, *c.* 1830s

Rathcoole

In the space of three days Rathcoole has disappeared from my memory.

W.M. Thackeray, *The Irish Sketch Book of 1842,* 1843

Rathdrum

Rathdrum, like, as I found later, most towns in Ireland, reminded me strongly of Shoreham.

Evelyn Waugh, *Diary,* August 1924

Roundwood (The Devil's Glen)

You may get as much out of an hour's walk there as out of the best hour's extempore preaching.

W.M. Thackeray, *The Irish Sketch Book of 1842,* 1843

Shandon (Cork and River Lee)

With deep affection
And recollection
I often think on
Those Shandon bells,
Whose sounds so wild would,
In the days of childhood,
Fling round my cradle
Their magic spells –
On this I ponder
Wher'er I wander,
And thus grow fonder,
Sweet Cork, of thee;
With the bells of Shandon
That sound so grand on
The pleasant waters
Of the river Lee.

Francis Sylvester Mahony (Father Prout), *The Bells of Shandon, c.* 1830s

River Shannon

The spacious Shenan spreading like a sea.

Edmund Spenser, *The Faerie Queene*, Canto xi, 1596

River Slaney (near Enniscorthy)

Before dinner had a most delicious walk by myself along the banks of the river Slaney, which, for two or three miles out of the town, are full of beauty, and this sunny evening was quite worthy of them. It was likewise delightful to me to be *alone* in such a scene, for it is only alone I can enjoy Nature thoroughly; men and women disturb such scenes dreadfully.

Thomas Moore, *Diary,* 25 August 1835

Slievenea (Co. Kerry)

There is in one of the southern districts a group of rocky hills, called in the neighbourhood the Slievenamora Mountains (but I doubt if any map so designates them), so bleak, lonely, and isolated, that they look like an accidental heap thrown down carelessly into creation's lap after the rest of the world was made.

They show no signs of continuity with the plain they stand on. There is no gradation of earth and stone, no trees or shrubs on their sides, no tufts of rushes or coarse grass, like those close to their base, to tell of a common soil or a geological connection. Artificial mounds of rockwork, fantastically raised in a garden, may give a miniature notion of this unearthly-looking mass. But it is unique almost in its dreary and seemingly purposeless existence.

T.C. Grattan, *Beaten Paths and Those Who Trod Them,* 1862

Tipperary

and the Shannon

I never yet saw in Ireland a spot of earth two feet wide, that had not in it something to displease. I think I was once in your county, Tipperary, which is like the rest of the whole kingdom, a bare face of nature, without houses or plantations; filthy cabins, miserable, tattered, half-starved creatures, scarce in human shape; one insolent, ignorant, oppressive squire to be found in twenty miles riding; a parish church to be found only in a summer-day's journey, in comparison of which, an English farmer's barn is a cathedral; a bog of fifteen miles round; every meadow a slough, and every hill a mixture of rock, heath, and marsh; and every male and female, from the farmer inclusive to the day-labourer, infallibly a thief, and consequently a beggar, which in this island, are terms convertible. The Shannon is rather a lake than a river, and has not the sixth part of the stream that runs under London bridge. There is not an acre of land in Ireland turned to half its advantage; yet it is better improved than the people: and all these evils are effects of English tyranny.

Jonathan Swift, Letter to Dean Brandreth, 30 June 1732

It's a long way to Tipperary, it's a long way to go;
It's a long way to Tipperary, to the sweetest girl I know!

Good-bye, Piccadilly, farewell, Leicester Square,
It's a long way to Tipperary, but my heart's right there!
Harry Williams and Jack Judge, *It's a Long Way to Tipperary*, 1912

Ulster

Ulster will fight; Ulster will be right.
Lord Randolph Churchill, Letter, 7 May 1886

My experience in the Cape Colony leads me to believe that the Ulster question is one which would soon settle itself.
Cecil Rhodes, Letter to Charles Stuart Parnell, 19 June 1888

Valentia

The finest Sea I have seen is at Valentia (Ireland), without any wind and seemingly without a Wave, but with the momentum of the Atlantic behind it, it dashes up into foam – blue diamond it looked like – all along the rocks – like ghosts playing at Hide and Seek.
Alfred Lord Tennyson, in Edward Fitzgerald, *Some Recollections of Tennyson's Talk*, *c.* 1852–3

Wexford

Pray observe the inhabitants about Wexford; they are old English; see what they have particular in their manners, names, and language: magpies have always been there, and no where else in Ireland, till of late years. They say the cocks and dogs go to sleep at noon, and so do the people.
Jonathan Swift, *Journal to Stella*, July 1711

Your description of it is excellent; clean sheets, but bare walls.
Ibid., September 1711

ISRAEL (and Palestine)

And Israel shall be a proverb and a byword among all people.
The Bible, I Kings 9: 7

The land of repromession, that men call the Holy Land. . . .
John Mandeville, *The Book of John Mandeville*, *c.* 1360–2

A Land that flowed with Milke and Honey: in the middest as it were of the habitable World, and under a temperate Clime. Adorned with beautiful Mountaynes, and luxurious Valleys; the Rockes producing excellent Waters: and no part emptie of delight or profit.
George Sandys, 1610, in *Purchas his Pilgrimes*, 1625

That miracle of countries, the Holy Land.
Robert Burton, *Anatomie of Melancholie*, 1621

How comely are thy *Tents*, O *Israel!*
(Thus he began) what conquests they foretel!
Less fair are *Orchards* in their *Autumn* pride,
Adorn'd with *Trees* on some fair *Rivers* side.
Less fair are *Valleys* their green mantles spread!
Or *Mountains* with tall *Cedars* on their head!
'Twas *God* himself (thy *God* who must not fear?)
Brought thee from *Bondage* to be *Master* here.
Slaughter shall wear out these; new *Weapons* get;
And *Death* in triumph on thy darts shall sit.
When *Judahs Lyon* starts up to his prey,
The *Beasts* shall hang their *Ears* and creep away.
When he lies down the *Woods* shall silence keep,
And dreadful *Tygers* tremble at his *sleep*.
Thy *Cursers, Jacob*, shall twice *cursed* be;
And he shall bless *himself* that blesses *Thee*.
Abraham Cowley, *Davideis, A Sacred Poem of the Troubles of David*, 1656

I cannot forbear to mention . . . an observation which is very obvious to all who visit the Holy Land, viz., that almost all passages and histories related in the gospels are represented by them that undertake to show where everything was done, as having been done most of them in grottoes; and that, even in such cases where the condition and circumstances of the actions themselves seem to require places of another nature. . . . Wherever you go, you find almost everything is represented as done underground.
Henry Maundrell, *Journey . . . to Jerusalem, 1697*, 1703

Palestine, . . . a territory scarcely superior to Wales, either in fertility or extent.
Edward Gibbon, *The Decline and Fall of the Roman Empire*, 1776–88

The first thought or impression which I remember as occurring on my entrance into the Holy Land was one of pleasure that it was so like home.
Harriet Martineau, *Eastern Life Past and Present*, 1848

Stones of Judea. We read a good deal about stones in Scriptures. . . . Monuments and memorials are set up of stones; men are stoned to death; the figurative seed falls in stony places; and no wonder that stones should so largely figure in the Bible. Judea is one accumulation of stones – Stony mountains & stony plains; stony torrents & stony roads; stony walls & stony fields; stony houses & stony tombs; stony eyes & stony hearts. Before you and behind you are stones. Stones to right &

stones to left. In many places laborious attempt has been made, to clear the surface of these stones. You see heaps of stones here & there; and stone walls of immense thickness are thrown together, less for boundaries than to get them out of the way. But in vain; the removal of one stone only serves to reveal there stones still larger, below it. It is like mending an old barn; the more you uncover, the more it grows. . . . To account for this abundance of stones, many theories have been stated; *My* theory is that long ago, some whimsical King of the country took it into his head to pave all Judea, and entered into contracts to that effect; but the contractor becoming bankrupt mid-way in his business, the stones were only dumped on the ground, & there they lie to this day.

Herman Melville, *Journal of a Visit to Europe and the Levant,* January 1857

The word Palestine always brought to my mind a vague suggestion of a country as large as the United States. I do not know why, but such was the case. I suppose it was because I could not conceive of a small country having so large a history.

Mark Twain, *The Innocents Abroad,* 1869

Monotonous and uninviting as much of the Holy Land will appear to persons accustomed to the almost constant verdure of flowers, ample streams, and varied surface of our own country, we must remember that its aspect to the Israelites after the weary march of forty years through the desert must have been very different.

Mark Twain, quoting anon. writer in 'Life in the Holy Land', *ibid.*

'Then once more I bowed my head. It is no shame to have wept in Palestine. I wept when I saw Jerusalem, I wept when I lay in the starlight at Bethlehem, I wept on the blessed shores of Galilee. My hand was no less firm on the rein, my finger did not tremble on the trigger of my pistol when I rode with it in my right hand, along the shore of the blue sea (weeping). My eye was not dimmed by those tears, nor my heart in aught weakened. Let him who would sneer at my emotion close this volume here, for he will find little to his taste in my journeyings through the Holy Land.'

He never bored but he struck water.

William C. Grimes, quoted, with comment, by Mark Twain, *ibid.*

('Grimes' is probably Twain's invention.)

A bare limestone country of little natural beauty.

Charles M. Doughty, *Travels in Arabia Deserta,* 1888

This is the land that flowed with milk and honey. As a matter of fact it flows now chiefly with stones.

Lilian Leland, *Travelling Alone, A Woman's Journey Round the World,* 1890

We are here today to lay the foundation stone of the house which is to shelter the Jewish nation.

Theodor Herzl, Speech at Conference at Basle, 1897

In Palestine we do not propose even to go through the form of consulting the wishes of the present inhabitants of the country . . . the four Great Powers are committed to Zionism. And Zionism, be it right or wrong, good or bad, is rooted in age-long traditions, in present needs, in future hopes, of far profounder import than the desires and prejudices of the seven hundred thousand Arabs who now inhabit that ancient land. . . . So far as Palestine is concerned, the Powers have made no statement of fact which is not admittedly wrong, and no declaration of policy which at least in the letter, they have not always intended to violate.

Arthur Balfour, Memorandum to the Cabinet, 1919

There will be trouble in Palestine.

Alfred Viscount Northcliffe, *My Journey Round the World,* 1923

The futility – not to mention the danger – of Balfour's messing himself up with things between Arabs and Jews is beyond castigation. There's bound to be unnecessary trouble there – before long.

Rudyard Kipling, Letter to Rider Haggard, 31 March 1925

The nations which have put mankind and posterity most in their debt have been small states – Israel, Athens, Florence, Elizabethan England.

William Ralph Inge, *The State Visible and Invisible – Outspoken Essays,* 2nd Series, 1922

Definition of a Zionist, or rather of Zionism: 'When two Jews send a third Jew at the expense of a fourth to Palestine.'

Sir Robert Bruce Lockhart, *Diary,* 13 May 1933

When Arthur Balfour launched his scheme for peopling Palestine with Jewish immigrants, I am credibly informed that he did not know there were Arabs in the country.

W.R. Inge, Dean of St Paul's, *Evening Standard,* before 1939, quoted in Michael Bateman, *This England – Selections from the New Statesman,* 1969

Senator Austin . . . said to me: 'You are in a bad mess in Palestine.' It was a very good dinner, excellent champagne, and I said gaily, 'Oh, not really. I could settle it if I were a Dictator.' 'I'll make you a Dictator,' he said: 'Now what do you do?' 'I look round and settle on a principle,' said I, 'and then I don't *wobble*. And the principle is, if you agree, that people should be consulted about the immigrants who go into their countries.' 'Well,' said the Senator, 'I come from Vermont and we're an independent people: I wouldn't quarrel with that.' 'Not with all that tea in Boston harbour,' I said, 'you couldn't, could you?' So we settled the Palestine question.

Freya Stark, Letter, 28 December 1943, in *Dust in the Lion's Paw,* 1961

One thing they always tell you in Israel: the one about its being not a melting pot, but a pressure cooker. Now, on Passover Eve, it begins to steam.

James Cameron, *News Chronicle,* 15 April 1954, in *What a Way to Run the Tribe,* 1968

In Israel, in order to be a realist, you must believe in miracles.

David Ben-Gurion, Comment on CBS–TV, 5 October 1956

When I was a child, in my own mind, I always thought a Jew was a person whose back is bent, who is always afraid, who is always on the run, who is always absorbing blows. Israel has straightened the backbone of every Jew – every Jew consciously or otherwise walks taller than he did before Israel was created. . . . He is serene and unafraid, the look of the persecuted has gone from his face.

Rabbi Usher Kirshblum, Thames Television interview, quoted Maldwyn A. Jones, *Destination America,* 1976

'A Professor at the Hebrew University wrote a study likening Israel to a new-born child whose womb is thousands of years old.'

Yahya Rabah, quoted by Jonathan Dimbleby, *The Palestinians,* 1979

They tell a story about the Zionist who came to Israel for the first time and saw that Jews were really working the land by themselves. He turned to his friends: 'You know all the lies I was preaching? I find they're really true.'

Amos Avriel, in James McNeish, *Belonging,* 1980

Anywhere else I am at the mercy of the government. It is very simple. *I want to be in a country where I can defend myself when I am attacked.*

Ada Sereni, in James McNeish, *Belonging,* 1980

Here we are in the holy land of Israel – a Mecca for tourists.

David Vine, *Superstars,* BBC 1, quoted *Private Eye,* 29 February 1980

Jews and Israelis

I saw all Israel scattered upon the hills, as sheep that have not a shepherd.

The Bible, I Kings 22:17

The hills stand about Jerusalem: even so standeth the Lord round about his people, from this time forth for evermore.

The Book of Common Prayer, Psalms 125:2

Behold an Israelite indeed, in whom is no guile!

The Bible, St John 1:47

Shylock: . . . I am a *Jewe:* Hath not a *Jew* eyes? hath not a *Jew* hands, organs, dementions, sences, affections, passions, fed with the same foode, hurt with the same weapons, subject to the same diseases, healed by the same meanes, warmed and cooled by the same Winter and Sommer as a Christian is: if you pricke us doe we not bleede? if you tickle us, doe we not laugh? if you poison us doe we not die? and if you wrong us shall we not revenge? if we are like you in the rest, we will resemble you in that. . . . The villanie you teach me I will execute, and it shall goe hard but I will better the instruction.

William Shakespeare, *The Merchant of Venice,* *c.* 1596–7

It is for the most part now inhabited by Moores and Arabians: those possessing the Valleyes, and these the Mountaynes. Turkes there be few, but many Greekes, with other Christians, of all Sects and Nations, such as impute to the place an adherent holinesse. Here be also some Jewes, yet inherit they no part of the Land, but in their owne Countrey doe live as Aliens; a people scattered throughout the whole World, and hated by those amongst whom they live; yet suffered as a necessary mischiefe: subject to all wrongs and contumelies, which they support with an invincible patience. Many of them have I seene abused; some of them beaten: yet never saw I Jew with an angry countenance. They can subject themselves unto times, and to whatsoever may advance their profit. In generall they are worldly wise, and thrive wherever they set footing.

George Sandys, 1610, in *Purchas his Pilgrimes,* 1625

The Jews are the least of any people that I know addicted to a military life.

Tobias Smollett, *Travels through France and Italy,* 1766

The Jewish religion was admirably fitted for defence, but it was never designed for conquest.

Edward Gibbon, *The Decline and Fall of the Roman Empire,* 1776–88

While Israel's sons, by scorpion curses driven
Outcasts of earth and reprobates of heaven
Through the wide world in friendless exile stray
Remorse and shame sole comrades of their way,
With dumb despair their country's wrongs behold
And, dead to glory, only burn for gold.

Reginald Heber, *Palestine,* a Prize Poem, 1803

Triumphant race, and did your power decay?
Failed the bright promise of your early day?

Ibid.

A people still, whose common ties are gone;
Who, mixed with every race, are lost in none.

George Crabbe, *The Borough,* 1810

The condition of the Jews in Palestine is . . . insecure. . . . There is little national feeling or enthusiasm among them; though there are some exceptions, where these exist in an intense degree. . . . Yet it is an interesting sight to meet with a Jew wandering with his staff in his hand, and a venerable beard sweeping his bosom, in the rich and silent plain of Jericho. . . . Did a spark of the love of this country warm his heart, his feelings must be exquisite: but his spirit is suited to his condition.

John Carne, *Letters from the East,* 1830

Yes, I am a Jew, and when the ancestors of the Right Honourable Gentleman were brutal savages in an unknown island mine were priests in the Temple of Solomon.

Benjamin Disraeli, attrib., reply to Daniel O'Connell, 1835

*The Jews are among the aristocracy of every land; if a literature is called rich in the possession of a few classic tragedies, what shall we say to a national tragedy lasting for fifteen hundred years, in which the poets and the actors were also the heroes.

George Eliot, *Daniel Deronda,* 1874–6

From the beginning the Christian was the theorizing Jew; consequently the Jew is the practical Christian.

Karl Marx, *The Capacity of the Present-Day Jews and Christians to Become Free,* 1884

No Jew was ever foolish enough to turn Christian unless he was a clever man.

Israel Zangwill, *Children of the Ghetto,* 1892

Jedes Land hat die Juden, die es verdient.
(Every country has the Jews that it deserves.)

Karl Emil Franzos, *Schlüssel zur neueren Geschichte der Juden,* before 1904

Hebrew: *n.,* A male Jew, as distinguished from the Shebrew, an altogether superior creation.

Ambrose Bierce, *The Cynic's Word Book,* 1906

Why humanity has hated Jews, I have come to the conclusion, is that the Jews have always taken religion – since the great days, that is, and used it for their own personal and private gratification, as if it were a thing administered to their own importance and well-being and conceit. This is the slave-trick of the Jews – they use the great religious consciousness as a trick of personal conceit. This is abominable. With them the conscious ego is the absolute, and God is a name they flatter themselves with. – When they have learned again pure reverence to the Holy Spirit, then they will be free and not slaves before men. Now, a Jew cringes before men, and takes God as a Christian takes whiskey, for his own self-indulgence.

D.H. Lawrence, Letter to S.S. Koteliansky, 3 July 1917

The existence and differentiation of the Jewish people, as a race ethnically, and as a nation politically, is as much a fact as the existence of coal, or diamonds.

Hilaire Belloc, *The Jews,* 1922

I don't like 'Ebrews. They work harder; they're more sober; they're honest, and they're everywhere.

John Galsworthy, *Loyalties,* 1922

The Jews generally give value. They make you pay; but they deliver the goods. In my experience, the men who want something for nothing are invariably Christians.

G. Bernard Shaw, *Saint Joan,* 1923

If my theory of relativity is proven successful, Germany will claim me as a German, and France will declare that I am a citizen of the world. Should my theory prove untrue, France will say that I am a German, and Germany will declare that I am a Jew.

Albert Einstein, Address at the Sorbonne, Paris, *c.* 1922

To be a Jew is a destiny.

Vicki Baum, *And Life Goes on,* 1931

I met a Jewish friend of mine the other day and he asked me, 'What is going to happen to the Jews?' I told him I had rather he had asked me a different question, 'What is going to happen to mankind?'

'But *my* people – ' he began.

'That,' said I, 'is exactly what is the matter with them.'

H.G. Wells, *Travels of a Republican Radical in Search of Hot Water,* 1939

To the Christian the Jew is the incomprehensibly obdurate man, who declines to see what has happened; and to the Jew the Christian is the incomprehensibly daring man, who affirms in an unredeemed world that its redemption has been accomplished.

Martin Buber, *Paths in Utopia,* 1949

There is only one race greater than the Jews – and that is the Derby.

Victor Sassoon, attrib., quoted in Alan Jenkins, *The Rich Rich,* 1978

*Never call a Jew a Jew unless you can be sure of making him lose his temper by doing so.

Kingsley Amis, *One Fat Englishman,* 1963

Now that's another thing that you sense – a street Arab. I am of a Semitic background – I *assume* I'm Jewish. A lot of Jews who think they're Jewish are not – they're switched babies.

Lenny Bruce, 'The Jews', in *The Essential Lenny Bruce,* 1973 – before 1966

*A Jewish man with parents alive is a fifteen-year-old boy, and will remain a fifteen-year-old boy till they die.

Philip Roth, *Portnoy's Complaint,* 1969

I would say that history proves certain things about us. For some reason – I don't know why, – we are chosen. You might say discriminated against. I'm not boasting, I'm stating it as a fact. And if it is so, if there is any connection between this discrimination and this land, then the only reason to live here is in order to make it a fact – to consummate it.

Uzi Davidson, in James McNeish, *Belonging,* 1980

Palestinians

Write down
I am an Arab.
You usurped my grandfather's vineyards
& the plot of land I used to plough
I & all my children
& you left us
  & all my grandchildren
nothing but these rocks . . . so
your government
will it take them too as rumour has it?
So be it.
  Write down at the top of the first page:
  I do not hate people.
  I steal from no-one.
However
  if I am hungry
  I will eat the flesh of my usurper.
Beware beware of my hunger
& of my anger.

Mahmoud Darwish, 'Identity Card' – from *Leaves of the Olive Tree,* 1964, trans. Ian Wedde and Fawwaz Tuqan

There was no such thing as a Palestinian people . . . it is not as though there was a Palestinian people and we came and threw them out and took their country away from them. They did not exist.

Golda Meir, quoted in interview with Frank Giles, *Sunday Times,* 15 June 1969

At no time have the people of Palestine exercised undisputed and independent political control over all the area known in modern times as Palestine.

This stark fact of history, once grasped, begins to give us a hint of the dimensions of the Palestinian tragedy. It also shows why the two contending forces of today, Zionism and Palestinian Arab nationalism, have collided with such terrific force: each held out to its people the hope of establishing a state that would no longer be the colony, protectorate or sphere of influence of outsiders.

John K. Cooley, *Green March, Black September,* 1973

The Jews of the Arab World.

Anon., quoted Lord Bethell, *Guardian,* 23 March 1981

From a variety of standpoints to say that a Palestinian State is politically viable is only to say that the problems associated with its creation *may* be preferable to those that attend its absence.

Ian Lustig, *Guardian,* 23 March 1981

There is already a Palestinian State and its name is Jordan.

Israeli Saying

El Azariyeh/Bethany

By the dim light of a taper we descended very cautiously, by twenty-five slippery steps, to the reputed sepulchre of Lazarus, or El Azariyeh, as both tomb and village are now called. . . . It is a wretched cavern, every way unsatisfactory, and almost disgusting.

I have never been so painfully impressed as to-day with the importance of the advice not to allow mere topographical controversies to rob one of the delightful and precious influences which these sacred stones ought to afford.

W.M. Thomson, *The Land and the Book,* 1859

Caesarea

Caesarea is, in some respects, the most interesting site on the earth to the missionary.

W.M. Thomson, *The Land and the Book,* 1859

Canaan

A land flowing with milk and honey; unto the place of the Canaanites, and the Hittites, and the Amorites, and the Perizzites, and the Hivites, and the Jebusites.

The Bible, Exodus 3:8

Dan (and Beersheba)

*I pity the man who can travel from *Dan* to *Beersheba,*

and cry, 'Tis all barren – and so it is; and so is all the world to him who will not cultivate the fruits it offers.

Laurence Sterne, *A Sentimental Journey through France and Italy*, 1768

From a little mound here in the plain issues a broad stream of limpid water and forms a large shallow pool, and then rushes furiously onward, augmented in volume. This puddle is an important source of the Jordan. Its banks, and those of the brook, are respectably adorned with blooming oleanders, but the unutterable beauty of the spot will not throw a well-balanced man into convulsions, as the Syrian books of travel would lead one to suppose.

Mark Twain, *The Innocents Abroad*, 1869

Dead Sea

Divers authors have reported that nothing will sink into it, of any reasonable weight, as dead men, or carcasses of beasts; but by experience I found the contrary; for it beareth nothing at all, yea, not the weight of a feather, nor the pile of withered grass, but it will sink therein, with the which my hands made sundry trials. . . . The water itself is of a blackish colour, and at some times in the year, there are terrible shapes and shows of terror in it, as I was informed at Jericho, by the Arabian inhabitants there. . . .

This contagious and pestilential lake of Sodom, resembleth much (as may be supposed) that infernal gulf of hell; but in my opinion, I hold it to be the purgatory of Papists; for they say *Limbus Patrum* is near, or in the second room to hell, which I think must needs be Sodom; for although it be not hell itself, yet I am perswaded it is a second hell, having, (as some report), no bottom.

William Lithgow, *Rare Adventures and Painfull Peregrinations*, 1614/32

Th' Asphaltick Pool.

John Milton, *Paradise Lost*, 1667

I bathed in the Dead Sea. The ground covered by the water sloped so gradually, that I was not only forced to 'sneak in,' but to walk through the water nearly a quarter of a mile, before I could get out of my depth. When at last I was able to attempt to dive, the salts held in solution made my eyes smart so sharply, that the pain I thus suffered, joined with the weakness occasioned by want of food, made me giddy and faint for some moments; but I soon grew better. I knew beforehand the impossibility of sinking in this buoyant water; but I was surprised to find that I could not swim at my accustomed pace: my legs and feet were lifted so high and dry out of the lake, that my stroke was baffled, and I found myself kicking against the thin air, instead of the dense fluid upon which I was swimming. The water is perfectly bright and clear; its taste detestable. After finishing my attempts at swimming and diving, I took some time in regaining the shore, and, before I began to dress, I found that the sun had already evaporated the water which clung to me, and that my skin was thickly encrusted with salts.

A.W. Kinglake, *Eothen*, 1844

from the eastern side

The sea was spread out before me, motionless as a lake of molten lead. . . . The sand is not bright like that of an Atlantic or Mediterranean beach, but of a dirty, dark brown. The water is exceedingly clear and transparent, but its taste and smell are a compound of all that is bad. . . .

Before I left Jerusalem I had resolved not to bathe in it, on account of my health; . . . but, on the point of turning up among the mountains, I could resist no longer. My clothes seemed to come off of their own accord, and before Paul had time to ask me what I was going to do, I was floating on its waters. Paul and the Arabs followed, and, after splashing about for a while, we lay like a parcel of corks upon its surface.

John Lloyd Stephens, *Incidents of Travel in Egypt, etc.*, 1837

Ride over mouldy plain to Dead Sea – Mountains on both sides – Lake Como – all but verdure. – foam on beach & pebbles like slaver of mad dog – smarting bitter of the water, – carried the bitter in my mouth all day – bitterness of life – thought of all bitter things – Bitter is it to be poor & bitter to be reviled, & Oh bitter are these waters of Death, thought I. – Old boughs tossed up by water – relics of pick-nick – nought to eat but bitumen & ashes with desert of Sodom apples washed down with water of Dead Sea. . . . – Barrenness of Judea. Whitish mildew pervading whole tracts of landscape – bleached – leprosy – encrustation of curses – old cheese – bones of rocks, – crunched, knawed and mumbled – mere refuse & rubbish of creation – like that laying outside of Jaffa Gate – all Judea seems to have been accumulations of this rubbish. – You see the anatomy – compares with ordinary regions as skeleton with living & rosy man.

Herman Melville, *Journal of a Visit to Europe and the Levant*, January 1857

The Dead Sea is but the Jordan's highway to heaven. Purified from every gross and earthly alloy, it is called back to the skies by the all-attracting sun, emblem of that other resurrection, when Christ shall come in the clouds. . . . May we thus be drawn from earth to heaven.

W.M. Thomson, *The Land and the Book*, 1859

Lake Galilee/Sea of Tiberias

There she lay, the Sea of Galilee. Less stern than

Wastwater – less fair than gentle Windermere – she had still the winning ways of an English lake.

A.W. Kinglake, *Eothen*, 1844

Travellers going to Tabarea (Tiberias) should be warned what the place is like, that they may not be deluded, as we were, with pleasant visions of rest by the lake-side; but take their survey, and ride away again, before they are made ill by the oppression of the atmosphere.

Harriet Martineau, *Eastern Life Past and Present*, 1848

If these unpeopled deserts, these rusty mounds of barrenness, that never, never do shake the glare from their harsh outlines, and fade and faint into vague perspective; that melancholy ruin of Capernaum; this stupid village of Tiberias, slumbering under its six funereal plumes of palms; yonder desolate declivity where the swine of the miracle ran down into the sea, and doubtless thought it was better to swallow a devil or two and get drowned into the bargain than have to live longer in such a place; this cloudless, blistering sky; this solemn, sailless, tintless lake, reposing within its rim of yellow hills and low, steep banks, and looking just as expressionless and unpoetical (when we leave its sublime history out of the question), as any metropolitan reservoir in Christendom – if these things are not food for to rock me to sleep, mother, none exist, I think.

Mark Twain, *The Innocents Abroad*, 1869

Gaza (to Beit Jibrin; Israeli occupied zone)

It is a full fair city and full of riches and of folk.

John Mandeville, *The Book of John Mandeville, c.* 1360

It stands upon a hill surrounded with valleyes; and those again well-nigh environed with hills, most of them planted with all sorts of delicate fruits. The building meane, both for forme and matter: the best but low, of rough stone, arched within, and flat on the top including a quadrangle: the walls surmounting their roofes, wrought through with pot-sheards to catch and strike downe the refreshing winds, having spouts of the same, in colour, shape and sight, resembling great Ordnance. Others covered with mats and hurdles; some built of mud; amongst all, not any comely or convenient. Yet there are some reliques left, and some impressions, that testifie a better condition: for divers simple roofes are supported with goodly Pillars of Parian marble, some plaine, some curiously carved. A number broken in pieces doe serve for thresholds, jambs of doores, and sides of windowes, almost unto every beggarly Cottage.

George Sandys, 1610, in *Purchas his Pilgrimes*, 1625

In reality, Philistia closely resembles some of the most beautiful regions of our own glorious West. True it lacks our fine forests, and misses our charming country-houses, with their orchards; but that is owing to the inhabitants.

W.M. Thomson, *The Land and the Book*, 1859

Jaffa

The appearance of Jaffa is singular, being situated on so steep a declivity, that the houses almost climb over each other up the face of the hill.

John Carne, *Letters from the East*, 1830

Joppa is certainly antidiluvian – a port before the Flood. It has no antiquities worth speaking of – It is too ancient.

Herman Melville, *Journal of a Visit to Europe and the Levant*, January 1857

Jaffa stands on an eminence to whose slopes the houses appear to cling like a cluster of grey snail shells, on account of the colour of the stone wherewith they are built.

H.M. Stanley, *My Early Travels and Adventures* (January 1870), 1895

The streets of Jaffa are narrow and are composed of four equal parts of donkey, camel, native and mud.

Lilian Leland, *Travelling Alone, A Woman's Journey Round the World*, 1890

Jericho

Ancient Jericho is not very picturesque as a ruin. When Joshua marched around it seven times, some three thousand years ago, and blew it down with his trumpet, he did the work so well and so completely that he hardly left enough of the city to cast a shadow. . . . Its site will always remain unoccupied; and yet it is one of the very best locations for a town we have seen in Palestine.

Mark Twain, *The Innocents Abroad*, 1869

Jerusalem

The Lord doth build up Jerusalem: and gather together the outcasts of Israel.

The Book of Common Prayer, Psalms 147:2

By the waters of Babylon we sat down and wept: when we remembered thee, O Sion. . . .
How shall we sing the Lord's song in a strange land?
If I forget thee, O Jerusalem; let my right hand forget her cunning.
If I do not remember thee, let my tongue cleave to the

roof of my mouth: yea if I prefer not Jerusalem in my mirth.

The Book of Common Prayer, Psalms, 137:1

For they shall see eye to eye, when the Lord shall bring again Zion. Break forth into joy, sing together, ye waste places of Jerusalem: for the Lord hath comforted his people, he hath redeemed Jerusalem.

The Bible, Isaiah 52:8

Much lies waste; the old buildings (except some few) all ruined, the new contemptible. None exceed two stories: the under no better then Vaults; the upper arched above, and standing upon Arches, being well confirmed against fire, as having through out no combustible matter: the Roofes flat, and covered with Plaister. Inhabited it is by Christians out of their devotion; and by Turks, for the benefite received by Christians, otherwise perhaps it would be generally abandoned.

George Sandys, 1611, in *Purchas his Pilgrimes,* 1625

All the Citizens are either Tailors, Shoomakers, Cookes, or Smiths (which Smiths make their keyes and lockes not of Iron, but of wood), and in generall poore rascall people, mingled of the scumme of divers Nations, partly Arabians, partly Moores, partly the basest inhabitants of neighbour Countries, by which kind of people all the adjoyning Territorie is likewise inhabited. The Jewes in Turky are distinguished from others by red hats, and being practicall, doe live for the most part upon the sea-coasts, and few or none of them come to this Citie, inhabited by Christians that hate them, and which should have no traffique, if the Christian Monasteries were taken away. Finally the Inhabitants of Jerusalem at this day are as wicked as they were when they crucified our Lord. . . .

Fynes Moryson, *Itinerary,* 1617

Thrice sacred Sion, sometimes blaz'd abroad,
To be the mansion of the living God;
For prophets, oracles, apostles dear,
And godly kings, who rais'd great glory here;
Where Aaron's rod, the ark, and tables two,
And Manna's pot, fire of sacrifice so
From heaven that fell, were all inclos'd in thee,
Containing near what not contain'd could be. . . .

William Lithgow, *Rare Adventures and Painful Peregrinations,* 1614/32

from the direction of Bethlehem
It looked so small, and yet lay spread out before me so distinctly that it seemed as if I ought to perceive the inhabitants moving through the streets and hear their voices humming in my ears. I saw that it was walled all around and that it stood alone in an extensive waste of mountains, without suburbs or even a solitary habitation beyond its walls. There were no domes, steeples, or turrets to break the monotony of its aspect, and even the mosques and minarets made no show. . . . It was tame and vacant. There was nothing in its appearance that afforded me a sensation; it did not even inspire me with melancholy; and I probably convict myself when I say that the only image it presented to my mind was that of a city larger and in better condition than the usual smaller class of those within the Turkish dominion. . . . One thing only particularly struck me – its exceeding stillness.

John Lloyd Stephens, *Incidents of Travel in Egypt, etc.,* 1837

The pavement is the worst I ever walked on; – worse than Cologne; worse than my native city of Norwich.

Harriet Martineau, *Eastern Life Past and Present,* 1848

As in the army of the Crusaders, the word Jerusalem! was repeated from mouth to mouth; but we, who consider ourselves civilised and superior beings, repressed our emotions; we were above showinn that we participated in the feelings of our barbarous companions. As for myself, I would have got off my horse, and walked barefooted towards the gate, as some did, if I had dared; but I was in fear of being laughed at for my absurdity, and therefore sat fast in my saddle. At last I blew my nose and I rode on slowly towards the Bethlehem gate.

Hon. Robert Curzon, *Visits to Monasteries in the Levant,* 1849

How it affects one to be cheated in Jerusalem.

Herman Melville, *Journal of a Visit to Europe and the Levant,* January 1857

The color of the whole city is grey & looks at you like a cold grey eye in a cold old man – its strange aspect in the pale olive light of the morning.

Ibid.

No country will more quickly dissipate romantic expectations than Palestine – particularly Jerusalem. To some the disappointment is heart sickening. . . .

Is the desolation of the land the result of the fatal embrace of the Deity? Hapless are the favorites of heaven.

In the emptiness of the lifeless antiquity of Jerusalem the emigrant Jews are like flies that have taken up their abode in a skull.

Ibid.

Jerusalem the golden
With milk and honey blessed
Beneath thy contemplation,
Sink heart and voice oppressed.

John Mason Neale, Translation, 1858, of *The Rhythm of Bernard de Morlaix,* Twelfth Century

The appearance of the city is peculiar. It is as knobby with countless little domes as a prison door is with bolt-heads. Every house has from one to half a dozen of these white plastered domes of stone, broad and low, sitting in the centre of, or in a cluster upon the flat roof. Wherefore, when one looks down from an eminence, upon the compact mass of houses (so closely crowded together in fact, that there is no appearance of streets at all, and so the city looks solid), he sees the knobbiest town in the world, except Constantinople. It looks as if it might be roofed, from centre to circumference, with inverted saucers. . . .

Mark Twain, *The Innocents Abroad*, 1869

from the Jaffa gate side
And this is Jerusalem which we see at the distance of a mile from us! This mass of masonry on the brow of a hill, half hidden by those barrack-like buildings and groups of dead walls and modern cottages, with bits of wretched battlemented wall appearing at intervals, and enclosing those uninteresting houses beyond? Oh!

H.M. Stanley, *My Early Travels and Adventures* (January 1870), 1895

The Jebusite,
That, maugre all God's promises could do,
The chosen People never conquer'd quite;
Who therefore lived with them,
And that by formal truce and as of right,
In metropolitan Jerusalem.

Coventry Patmore, *The Unknown Eros*, 1877

One's first impression of Jerusalem is extremely interesting, but certainly not pleasing.

Gertrude Bell, Letter to her father, 13 December 1899

You begin to be in Jerusalem before you know it, very suddenly round a corner, and in a minute there is before you the City set on a hill, like many another Oriental grey stone city. Seventy-five thousand people in it – and some mighty queer ones.

Alfred Viscount Northcliffe, *My Journey Round the World* (February 1922), 1923

It is an astonishing place. Words fail me. I can't begin to describe it. There is a mad balance (preserved by Brit Govt.) between ancient and utter loveliness and mod. bestial commercial enterprise – in fact they cancel out. i.e. between the two you may say there is no real Jerusalem at all. There is also a mad confusion of religions, all worshipping and scrapping at the same shrines.

Eric Gill, Letter to Graham Carey, 5 April 1934

The beauty of Jerusalem in its landscape can be compared with that of Toledo. The city stands in the mountains, a scape of domes and towers enclosed by crenellated walls and perched on a table of rock above a deep valley. As far as the distant hills of Moab the contours of the country resemble those of a physical map, sweeping up the slopes in regular, stratified curves, and casting grand shadows in the sudden valleys. Earth and rock reflect the lights of a fire-opal. Such an essay in urban emplacement, whether accidental or contrived, has made a work of art. . . .

Yet Jerusalem is more than picturesque, more than shoddy in the style of so many Oriental towns. There may be filth, but there is no brick or plaster, no crumbling and discolourment. The buildings are wholly of stone, a whitish cheese-like stone, candid and luminous, which the sun turns to all tones of ruddy gold. Charm and romance have no place. All is open and harmonious. The associations of history and belief, deep-rooted in the first memories of childhood, dissolve before the actual apparition. The outpourings of faith, the lamentations of Jew and Christian, the devotion of Islam to the holy Rock, have enshrouded the *genius loci* with no mystery. That spirit is an imperious emanation, evoking superstitious homage, sustained thereby perhaps, but existing independently of it. Its sympathy is with the centurions rather than the priests. And the centurions are here again. They wear shorts and topees, and answer, when addressed, with a Yorkshire accent.

Robert Byron, *The Road to Oxiana*, 1937

Jerusalem will remain undivided for all generations until the end of the world.

Menachem Begin, *Observer*, 'Sayings of the Week', 1 October 1978

Jerusalem is not just for living. Jerusalem is *being*.

Nurit Shiloh, in James McNeish, *Belonging*, 1980

Districts and details

Calvary/Church of the Holy Sepulchre
The circumstance that most perplexes every traveller is, to account for Mount Calvary's having been formerly without the city. It is at present not a small way within; and in order to shut it out, the ancient walls must have made the most extraordinary and unnecessary curve imaginable. Its elevation was probably always inconsiderable, so that there is little to stagger one's faith in the lowness of its present appearance. The exclusion of Calvary must have deprived the ancient city of a considerable space of habitable ground, of which, from the circumscribed nature of its site, there could have been little to spare. But tradition could not err in the identity of so famous a spot: and the smallest scepticism would deprive it of all its powerful charm.

John Carne, *Letters from the East*, 1830

A Protestant, familiar with the Holy Scriptures, but

ignorant of tradition and the geography of modern Jerusalem, finds himself a good deal 'mazed' when he first looks for the sacred sites. The Holy Sepulchre is not in a field without the walls, but in the midst, and in the best part of the town under the roof of the great church which I have been talking about. It is a handsome tomb of oblong form, partly subterranean, and partly above ground, and closed in on all sides except the one by which it is entered. You descend into the interior by a few steps, and there find an altar with burning tapers. This is the spot held in greater sanctity than any other in Jerusalem. When you have seen enough of it, you feel perhaps weary of the busy crowd, and inclined for a gallop; you ask your Dragoman whether there will be time before sunset to send for horses and take a ride to Mount Calvary. Mount Calvary, Signor? – eccolo! it is *upstairs – on the first floor.* In effect you ascend, if I remember rightly, just thirteen steps, and then you are shown the now golden sockets in which the crosses of our Lord and the two thieves were fixed. All this is startling, but the truth is, that the city, having gathered round the Sepulchre (the main point of interest), has gradually crept northward, and thus in great measure are occasioned the many geographical surprises that puzzle the 'Bible Christian.'

A.W. Kinglake, *Eothen*, 1844 – of *c.* 1835

To think of Christ and Christianity in the midst of this church is like having a reverie of sunrise from a mountain-top when one is looking at a puppet-show.

Harriet Martineau, *Eastern Life Past and Present*, 1848

The Holy Sepulchre. No Jew allowed in Church of H.S. – ruined dome – confused & half-ruinous pile. – Laberithys & terraces of mouldy grottoes, tombs, & shrines. Smells like a dead-house. dingy light. – At the entrance, in a sort of grotto in the wall a divan for Turkish policemen, where they sit cross-legged & smoking, scornfully observing the continuous troops of pilgrims entering & prostrating themselves before the anointing-stone of Christ, which veined with streaks of a mouldy red looks like a butcher's slab. Near by is a blind stair of worn marble ascending to the reputed Calvary where among other things the showman point show you by the smoky light of old pawnbrokers lamp of dirty gold, the hole in which the cross was fixed & and through a narrow grating as over a cole-cellar, point out the rent in the rock! On the same level near by is a kind of gallery, railed with marble, overlooking the entrance of the church: and here almost every day I would hang, looking down upon the spectacle of the scornful Turks on the divan, & the scorned pilgrims kissing the stone of the anointing. – The door of the church is like that of a jail – a grated window in it. – The main body of the church is that overhung by the lofty and ruinous dome whose fallen plastering reveals the meagre skeleton of beams & laths a sort of plague stricken splendor reigns in the painted & mildewed walls around. In the midst of all stands the Sepulchre; a church in a church. It is of marbles, richly sculpted in parts & bearing the faded aspect of age. From its porch issue a garish stream of light, upon the faces of the pilgrims who crowd for admittance into a space which will hold but four or five at a time. First passing a wee vestibule where is shown the stone on which the angel sat, you enter the tomb. It is like entering a lighted lanthorn. Wedged & half-dazzlled, you stare for a moment on the ineloquence of the bedizened slab, and glad to come out, wipe your brow glad to escape as from the heat & jam of a show-box. All is glitter & nothing is gold. A sickening cheat. The countenances of the poorest & most ignorant pilgrims would seem tacitly to confess it as well as your own.

Herman Melville, *Journal of a Visit to Europe and the Levant*, January 1857

By far the most interesting half-acre on the face of the earth.

W.M. Thomson, *The Land and the Book*, 1859

The reputed sepulchre of the Son of God is no place for Soulless criticism.

Ibid.

When one stands where the Saviour was crucified, he finds it all he can do to keep it strictly before his mind that Christ was not crucified in a Catholic Church. He must remind himself every now and then that the great event transpired in the open air, and not in a gloomy candle-lighted cell in a little corner of a vast church, upstairs – a small cell all bejewelled and bespangled with flashy ornamentation, in execrable taste.

Mark Twain, *The Innocents Abroad*, 1869

There is a green hill far away,
  Without a city wall,
Where the dear Lord was crucified,
  Who died to save us all.

Cecil Frances Alexander, *There is a Green Hill*, 1870

Turks guard the door to keep Christians from fighting.

Lilian Leland, *Travelling Alone, A Woman's Journey Round the World*, 1890

The Middle East threat is to the oily places, not the holy places.

Shimon Peres, quoted Donald Trelford, 'It's Not So Easy Being a Jew', *Observer*, 20 April 1980

Mount of Olives

These are the monuments shewn us upon the Mount of Olives. First, the print of the left foot of our Saviour, in an immoveable stone, which he made when he ascended to heaven. The Guardiano told us further, that the right foot's print was taken away by the Turks, and detained by them in the temple of Solomon; but who can think our Saviour trod so hard at his ascension as to have left the impression of his feet behind him?

William Lithgow, *Rare Adventures and Painfull Peregrinations,* 1614/32

On the descent of Olivet is shown the spot where Christ wept over Jerusalem: tradition could not have selected a more suitable spot.

John Carne, *Letters from the East,* 1830

River Jordan

Nor shall I ever forget . . . the indescribable feeling of disappointment at the Jordan.

W.M. Thomson, *The Land and the Book,* 1859

The Jordan valley was a vast flat of cracked, brown-baked plaster of Paris between two distant mountain ranges. . . .

A pot-holed track led across it to where a brown stream flowed between banks of mud. . . . We stood on the bank and James said it was where John baptised Jesus. We asked how he knew this was the place and he said he ought to know, the guides in Jerusalem all agreed on a place every year, and this year this was it. It had only been changed six times in the past five years, to the best of his recollection.

Cedric Belfrage, *Away from It All,* 1936

What public relations can do for a river.

Henry Kissinger, Remark on visiting a disappointing trickle of Jordan river, quoted Donald Trelford, *Observer,* 20 April 1980

Nazareth/Nasirah

No place in Palestine satisfied me more entirely than Nazareth. Much as one's associations require, it is all there; and one's first and constant emotion here is of thankfulness that Jesus was reared amidst such natural beauty.

Harriet Martineau, *Eastern Life Past and Present,* 1848

There is a sort of latent beauty and appropriateness in the arrangement by which He who made *all things out of nothing* should himself come forth to the world *out of a place that had no history.* The idea here tempts one to linger upon it and expatiate.

W.M. Thomson, *The Land and the Book,* 1859

. . . clinging like a white washed wasps nest to the hillside.

Mark Twain, *The Innocents Abroad,* 1869

Mount Tabor

Many yeeres since there was a Monasterie there inhabited by Popish Friers, but being molested by the Arabs, tooke away the holinesse with them, and left the Mountaine behind them; yet still they call this Mount Tabor, in Italian, Monte Santo, that is, the Holy Mountaine: as if there were some inherent holinesse in the Mountaine.

William Biddulph, 1601, in *Purchas his Pilgrimes,* 1625

Tel Aviv

If Tel Aviv were in Russia, the world would be raving over its planning and architecture, its smiling communal life, its intellectual pursuits, and its air of youth enthroned. But the difference from Russia is, that instead of being still only a goal for the future, these things are all an accomplished fact.

Robert Byron, *The Road to Oxiana,* 1937

The physical and mental effervescence in the streets of Tel Aviv is something unlike anything I have ever felt in any other country. It reminded me of the busy buzz of productive ecstasy on the running-board of a hive on a perfect summer day and hundreds of happy bees stream in and out of the hive on the communal business of finding nectar and storing honey.

Leonard Woolfe, *The Journey Not the Arrival Matters,* 1969

ITALY

Ahi serva Italia, di dolore ostello,
Nave senze nocchiere in gran tempesta,
Non donna di provincia, ma bordello!

Ah, slavish Italy! thou inn of grief!
Vessel without a pilot in loud storm!
Lady no longer of fair provinces,
But brothel-house impure!

Dante, *Purgatorio, c.* 1310–21 (H.F. Cary's translation, 1814)

Sixteenth Century

Suffer not your sonnes to passe the Alpes: for they shall exchange for their forraine travell . . . but others vices for their own virtues, Pride, Blasphemy and Atheisme for Humilitie Reverence and Religion.

William Cecil, Lord Burleigh, *Precepts or Directions for the Well-Ordering . . . of a Man's Life . . . to his Sonne,* 1637 – written before 1598

A paradise inhabited with devils.

Sir Henry Wotton, Letter to Lord Zouche, 25 June 1592

Italy, the Paradice of the earth, and the Epicures heaven, how doth it forme our yong master? It makes him to kis his hand like an ape, cringe his necke like a starveling, and play at hey passe repasse come aloft when he salutes a man. From thence he brings the art of atheisme, the art of epicurising, the art of whoring, the art of poysoning, the art of Sodomitrie. The onely probable good thing they have to keepe us from utterly condemning it, is that it maketh a man an excellent Courtier, a curious carpet knight: which is by interpretation, a fine close leacher, a glorious hipocrite. It is nowe a privie note amongst the better sort of men, when they would set a singular marke or brand on a notorious villaine, to say, he hath beene in *Italy*.

Thomas Nashe, *The Unfortunate Traveller*, 1594

Italy worthily called the Queene of Nations, can never be sufficiently praised, being most happy in the sweete Ayre, the most fruitfull and pleasant fields, warme sunny hils, hurtlesse thickets, shaddowing groves, Havens of the Sea, watering brookes, baths, wine, and oyle for delight, and most safe forts or defences as well of the sea as of the Alpes. Neither is any part of Europe so inhabited, more adorned with Cities and Castles, or to be compared thereunto for tillage and husbandry.

Fynes Moryson, *An Itinerary*, 1617

And being now in *Italy, that great limbique of working braines*, he must be very circumspect in his cariage, for she is able to turne a *Saint* into a *Devill* and deprave the best natures, if one will abandon himselfe to pleasure, and become a prey to dissolut courses & wantonnes, the *Italian*, being the *greatest embracer of pleasures*, and the greatest *Courtier of Ladies* of any other. Here he shall find vertue and vice, love and hatred, Atheisme and Religion in their extremes; being a witty contemplative people; and *Corruptio optimi est pessima. Of your best wines you make your tartest vinegar. . . .*

She is the prime climat of Complement, which oftentimes puts such a large distance, twixt the tongue and the heart, that they are seldome relatives, but they often give the lye one to another; some will offer to kisse the hands which they wish were cut off, and would be content to light a candle to the Devill, so they may compasse their owne ends: Hee is not accounted essentially wise, who openeth all the hopes of his breast to any.

The *Italians* are for the most part of a speculative complexion . . . *and he is accounted little lesse than a foole who is not melancholy once a day; they are only bountifull to theire betters, from whom they may expect a greater benefit; To others the purse is closest shut, when the mouth openeth widest, nor are you like to get a cup of wine there unlesse your grapes be knowne to be in the wine-presse.*

James Howell, *Instructions for Forren Travell*, 1650

Travellers do nothing else but run up & downe to see sights, that come into *Italy*.

John Evelyn, *Diary*, June 1645

Nature's darling.

Richard Lassels, *An Italian Voyage, or a Compleat Journey through Italy*, 1679

That Nation, which hath civilized the whole world and taught Mankind what it is to be a Man.

Richard Lassels, *An Italian Voyage*, 1679

Eighteenth Century

Lust chose the Torrid Zone of *Italy*,
Where Blood ferments in Rapes and Sodomy:
Where swelling Veins o'erflow with livid Streams,
With Heat impregnate from *Vesuvian* Flames:
Whose flowing Sulphur forms Infernal Lakes,
And humane Body of the Soil partakes.
There Nature ever burns with hot Desires,
Fann'd with Luxuriant Air from Subterranean Fires:
Here undisturb'd in Floods of Scalding Lust,
Th'Infernal King reigns with Infernal Gust.

Daniel Defoe, *The True-Born Englishman*, 1701

For wheresoe'er I turn my ravished eyes,
Gay gilded scenes and shining prospects rise,
Poetic fields encompass me around,
And still I seem to tread on classic ground;
For here the muse so oft her harp has strung
That not a mountain rears its head unsung,
Renowined in verse each stately thicket grows,
And every stream in heavenly numbers flows.

Joseph Addison, *Letter from Italy to the Right Honourable Lord Halifax*, 1701

How has kind Heaven adorned the happy land,
And scattered blessings with a wasteful hand!
But what avail her unexhausted stores,
Her blooming mountains and her sunny shores,
With all the gifts that heaven and earth impart,
The smiles of nature and the charms of art,
While proud oppression in her valleys reigns,
And tyranny usurps her happy plains?
The poor inhabitant beholds in vain
The reddening orange and the swelling grain:
Joyless he sees the growing oils and wines,
And in the myrtle's fragrant shade repines:
Starves in the midst of nature's bounty curst
And in the loaden vineyard dies for thirst.

Ibid.

One seldom finds in Italy a spot of ground more agreeable than ordinary, that is not covered with a convent.

Joseph Addison, *Remarks on Several Parts of Italy, in the Years 1701, 1702, and 1703*, 1705

Ah, poor Italia! what a bitter cup
Of vengence hast thou drain'd! Goths, Vandals, Huns,
Lombards, barbarians, broke from every land, –

How many a ruffian form hast thou beheld!
What horrid jargons heard, where rage alone
Was all thy frighted ear could comprehend!
How frequent by the red inhuman hand,
Yet warm with brother's, husband's, father's blood,
Hast thou thy matrons and thy virgins seen
To violation dragg'd, and mingled death!
What conflagrations, earthquakes, ravage, floods,
Have turn'd thy cities into stony wilds;
And succourless and bare, the poor remains
Of wretches forth to Nature's common cast!
Added to these, the still continued waste
Of inbred foes, that on thy vitals prey,
And, double tyrants, seize the very soul.

James Thomson, *Liberty*, 1734–6

In Italy they seem to have found out how hot their climate is, but not how cold; for there are scarce any chimneys, and most of the apartments painted in fresco; so that one has the additional horror of freezing with imaginary marble.

Horace Walpole, Letter to Richard West, 22 March 1740

Mr Walpole says, our memory sees more than our eyes in this country.

Thomas Gray, Letter to Richard West, May 1740

Italia, nurse of every softer art,
Who, feigning to refine, unmans the heart;
Who lays the realms of Sense and Virtue waste;
Who mars while she pretends to mend our taste;
Italia, to complete and crown our shame,
Sends us a fiend, and Legion is his name.
The farce of greatness without being great,
Pride without power, titles without estate,
Souls without vigour, bodies without force,
Hate without cause, revenge without remorse,
Dark, mean revenge, murder without defence,
Jealousy without love, sound without sense,
Mirth without humour, without wit grimace,
Faith without reason, Gospel without grace,
Zeal without knowledge, without nature art. . . .

Charles Churchill, *The Times*, 1764

Could Nature's beauties satisfy the breast,
The sons of Italy were surely blest.

Oliver Goldsmith, *The Traveller*, 1765

I do assure you the climate of Italy affects me much. It inflamed my hot desires, and now it keeps my blood so warm, that I have all day long such spirits as a man has after having taken a cheerful glass.

James Boswell, Letter to John Johnston of Grange, 19 July 1765

Give what scope you please to your fancy, you will never imagine half the disagreeableness that *Italian* beds, *Italian* cooks, *Italian* post-horses, *Italian* postilions, and *Italian* nastiness offer to an *Englishman*, in an autumnal journey; much more to an *English* woman.

Samuel Sharp, *Letters from Italy*, 1767

A man who has not been in Italy, is always conscious of an inferiority, from his not having seen what it is expected a man should see. The grand object of travelling is to see the shores of the Mediterranean.

Samuel Johnson, in Boswell, *Life of Johnson*, 11 April 1776

*Travelling is the ruin of all happiness! There's no looking at a building here after seeing Italy.

Fanny Burney (Mme D'Arblay), *Cecilia*, 1782

Nothing is so little animated by the sight of living creatures as an Italian prospect.

Hester Lynch Piozzi, *Observations . . . in the Course of a Journey*, 1789

It is a sort of Native land to us all; as our earliest ideas are from the antient Italy, and some of our pleasantest amusements from the modern.

Edmund Burke, Letter to Friedrich Ludwig Wilhelm Meyer, after 8 May 1791

For all those circumstances that render that classical country illustrious, the seat of great men – the theatre of the most distinguished actions – the exclusive field in which the elegant and agreeable arts have loved to range – what country can be compared with Italy? to please the eye, to charm the ear, to gratify the enquiries of a laudable curiosity, whither would you travel? In every bosom whatever, Italy is the second country in the world – of all others, the surest proof that it is the first.

Arthur Young, *Travels . . . [in] . . . France* (27 December 1789), 1792

Nineteenth Century

Italy is well deserving the character it has acquired of being the Garden of Europe – and of being likewise the abode of poverty, villainy – filth and extortion. A Traveller pays dearly for the intellectual pleasures it furnishes, by suffering from bad accomodations in dirty inns – from the impositions of innkeepers servants &c – from wretched carriages, roguish drivers, corrupt custom house officers in short a combination of rogues of every class.

Washington Irving, *Journal*, 22 April 1805

in fair Italia's bowers,
Where, ling'ring yet, the ghost of ancient wit
Midst modern monks profanely dares to flit,

And pagan spirits, by the pope unlaid,
Haunt every stream and sing through every shade.

Thomas Moore, 'To the Honourable W.R. Spencer, from Buffalo, upon Lake Erie', *Poems relating to America,* 1806

Italy is my Magnet.

Lord Byron, Letter to Annabella Milbanke, 20 April 1814

Italia, Italia, O tu cui feo la sorte,
Dono infelice di bellezza, ond' hai
Funesta dote d'infiniti guai
Che in fronte scritti per gran doglia porte.

Vicenzo da Filicaja, *Italia, c.* 1707

Italia! oh Italia! thou who hast
The fatal gift of beauty, which became,
A funeral dower of present woes and past,
On thy sweet brow is sorrow plough'd by shame,
And annals graved in characters of flame.

Lord Byron, *Childe Harold's Pilgrimage,* Canto the Fourth, 1816

Italy! Italy! thou who'rt doomed to wear
The fatal gift of beauty and possess
The dower funest of infinite wretchedness
Written upon thy forehead by despair.

Henry Wadsworth Longfellow, 'To Italy', *Poetical Works* 1851

There are *two* Italies – one composed of the green earth and transparent sea, and the mighty ruins of ancient time, and aerial mountains, and the warm and radiant atmosphere which is interfused through all things. The other consists of the Italians of the present day, their works and ways. The one is the most sublime and lovely contemplation that can be conceived by the imagination of man; the other is the most degraded, disgusting and odious. What do you think? Young women of rank actually eat – you will never guess what – *garlick!*

Percy Bysshe Shelley, Letter to Leigh Hunt, 22 December 1818

Thou Paradise of exiles, Italy!

Percy Bysshe Shelley, *Julian and Maddolo,* 1819

Italy is the place for you, the very place – the Paradise of exiles, the retreat of Pariahs.

Percy Bysshe Shelley, Letter to Thomas Medwin, 17 January 1820

The features of an Italian landscape are very peculiar. The bold and the grand are constantly blended with the soft and the beautiful.

Henry Matthews, *Diary of an Invalid,* 1820

If ever there was one region blessed beyond all others, and made by nature for the special enjoyment of the most favoured of her creatures, that region is Italy! Let her fortresses and her cells, her despots and her monks tell her sad story, and explain how suns may shine, and soils may teem – in vain!

Lady Morgan, *Italy,* 1820

Kennst du das Land, wo die Citronen blühn
Im dunkeln Laub die Gold-Orangen glühn,
Ein sanfter Wind vom blauen Himmel weht.
Die Myrte still und hoch der Lorbeer steht.

J. W. von Goethe, *Wilhelm Meister* (Mignon's Song), 1821

Knowst thou the land where the lemon-trees bloom,
Where the gold orange glows in the deep thicket's gloom,
Where a wind ever soft from the blue heaven blows,
And the groves are of laurel and myrtle and rose?

Thomas Carlyle's translation, 1824

O Italy, how beautiful thou art:
Yet I could weep – for thou are lying alas,
Low in the dust; and we admire thee now
As we admire the beautiful in death.
Thine was a dangerous gift, when thou wert born,
The gift of beauty. Would thou hadst it not;
Or wert as once, among the caitiffs vile
That now beset thee, making thee their slave!
Would they had loved thee less, or feared thee more!
– But why despair? Twice hast thou lived already;
Twice shone among the nations of the world,
As the sun shines among the lesser lights of heaven.

Samuel Rogers, *Italy,* 1822–34

There is a technical description of the chief towns in Italy, which those who learn the Italian grammar are told to get by heart – *Genoa la superba, Bologna la dotta, Ravenna l'antica, Firenze la bella, Roma la santa.* Some of these I have seen, and others not; and those that I have not seen seem to me the finest. Does not this list convey as good an idea of these places as one can well have? It selects some one distinct feature of them, and that the best. Words may be said, after all, to be the finest things in the world. Things themselves are but a lower species of words, exhibiting the grossness and details of matter. Yet, if there be any country answering to the description or idea of it, it is Italy; and to this theory I must add, the Alps are also a proud exception.

William Hazlitt, *Notes of a Journey through France and Italy,* 1826

The popular superstition of Italy is the offspring of the climate, the old associations, the manners, and the very names of the places. It is pure paganism, undisturbed by any anxiety about orthodoxy, or animosity against heretics. Hence, it is much more good-natured, and pleasing to a traveller's feelings, and certainly not a whit less like the true religion of our dear Lord than the gloomy idolatry of the Spaniards.

Samuel Taylor Coleridge, *Table Talk,* 25 July 1831

I never was in such a country as this – one can count upon nothing neither upon expenses time nor means of conveyance and as for the people – goodness take me out from amongst them and trust me for ever again troubling them with my presence unless I have time and money in abundance and even then an urgent motive only would tempt me to re-enter the country – To travel in or through Italy several things are necessary, your pockets should be full of money, your mind full of patience, and time no object without these requisites no one should travel in Italy, otherwise he is sure to be disgusted with the people and their continual exactions. Their exactions are in proportion as they see you pressed for time.

John Webster, *Notes of a Journey from London to Constantinople . . . ,* 1836

Fair Land! Thee all men greet with joy; how few
Whose souls take pride in freedom, virtue, fame,
Part from thee without pity dyed in shame:
I could not – while from Venice we withdrew,
Led on till an Alpine strait confined our view
Within its depths, and to the shore we came
Of Lago Morto, dreary sight and name,
Which o'er sad thoughts a sadder colouring threw.
Italia! on the surface of thy spirit,
(Too aptly emblemed by that torpid lake)
Shall a few partial breezes only creep? –
Be its depths quickened; what thou dost inherit
Of the world's hopes, dare to fulfil; awake,
Mother of Heroes, from thy death-like sleep!

William Wordsworth, *Memorials of a Tour in Italy, 1837,* 1842

Italien ist ein geographischer Begriff.
(Italy is a geographical expression.)

Prince Metternich, Letter, 19 November 1849

If Italy is famous at present for any two things, it is for political uneasiness and *minestra.*

Leigh Hunt, *Autobiography,* 1850

You learn for the first time in this climate, what colours really are. No wonder it produces painters. An English artist of any enthusiasm might shed tears of vexation, to think of the dull medium through which blue and red come to him in his own atmosphere, compared with this. . . . A red cap in Italy goes by you, not like a mere cap, much less anything vulgar or butcher-like, but like what it is, an intense specimen of the colour of red.

Ibid.

To the American, especially if he be of an imaginative temper, Italy has a deeper charm. She gives him cheaply what gold cannot buy for him at home, a Past at once legendary and authentic, and in which he has an equal claim with every other foreigner. In England he is a poor relation, whose right in the entail of home traditions has been docked by revolution; . . . but Rome is the mother country of every boy who has devoured Plutarch or taken his daily doses of Florus. Italy gives us antiquity with good roads, cheap living, and above all, a sense of freedom from responsibility.

James Russell Lowell, *Leaves from My Journal in Italy and Elsewhere,* 1854

Is not one chief charm of the land, that it is changeless without being Chinese?

Ibid.

Oh, woman-country, wooed, not wed,
Loved all the more by earth's male-lands
Laid to their hearts instead!

Robert Browning, 'By the Fireside', *Men and Women,* 1855

Italy, my Italy!
Queen Mary's saying serves for me –
  (When fortune's malice
  Lost her – Calais) –
Open my heart and you will see
Graved inside of it, 'Italy.'

Robert Browning, *De Gustibus,* 1855

    And now, my Italy.
Alas, if we could ride with naked souls
And make no noise, and pay no price at all,
I would have seen thee sooner, Italy, –
For still I have heard thee crying through my life,
Thou piercing silence of extatic graves,
Men call that name!

Elizabeth Barrett Browning, *Aurora Leigh,* 1856

*'In Italy is she really?' said Flora, 'with the grapes and figs growing everywhere and lava necklaces and bracelets too that land of poetry burning mountains, picturesque beyond belief though if the organ-boys come away from the neighbourhood not to be scorched nobody can wonder being so young and bringing their white mice with them most humane, and is she really in that favoured land with nothing but blue about her and dying gladiators and Belvederas though Mr F himself did not believe for his objection when in spirits was that the images could not be true there being no medium between expensive quantities of linen badly got up and all in creases and none whatever, which certainly does not seem probable though perhaps in consequence of the extremes of rich and poor which may account for it. . . .

'Venice Preserved too,' said she, 'I think you have been there is it well or ill preserved for people differ so and Macaroni if they really eat it like the conjurors why not cut it shorter, you are acquainted . . . acquainted I believe with Mantua what *has* it got to do with Mantua-making for I never have been able to conceive?'

Charles Dickens, *Little Dorrit,* 1857–8

How I feel Goethe's greatness in this place! Here in Italy one feels that all time spent out of Italy by tourists in France, Germany, Switzerland, etc., etc., is – human life being so short – time misspent. Greece and parts of the East are the only other places to go to.

Matthew Arnold, Letter to his mother, 5 June 1865

Lump the whole thing! say that the Creator made Italy from designs by Michael Angelo!

Mark Twain, *The Innocents Abroad,* 1869

Italian dirt, though unpleasant, . . . is the product not of a brutal revolt against decency, but of an easy-going indolence. It is, as Heine somewhere says, 'grossartiger Schmutz.' The squalor of an Italian town surrounds monuments of incomparable beauty, and somehow does not seem altogether out of harmony with them.

Leslie Stephen, *The Playground of Europe,* 1871

The great aggregation of beautiful works of art in the Italian cities strikes the visitor nowadays (so far as present Italy is concerned) as the mere stock-in-trade of an impecunious but thrifty people.

Henry James, 'Italy Revisited,' 1877, in *Portraits of Places,* 1883

Land of us all that have loved thee dearliest
  Mother of men that were lords of man
    Whose name in the world's heart works as a spell
My last song's light, and the star of mine earliest.

A.C. Swinburne, 'Spring in Tuscany', *Poems and Ballads,* Second Series, 1878

I can honestly say that if I was told at this moment that I was dying, not my first, not my second, but certainly my third thought would be that I should never see Italy again.

Mrs Henry Fawcett, *Orient Line Guide,* 1885

Henry James would always remember & remark on the hideous things. 'I always think of Italy & see the waiters flopping among the flies.'

Logan Pearsall Smith, *Diary,* July 1896

Twentieth Century

'What do people do here?' I once asked at a little town between Rome and Naples; and the man with whom I talked, shrugging his shoulders, answered curtly, '*C'è miseria*' – there's nothing but poverty. The same reply could be given in towns and villages without number throughout the length of Italy.

George Gissing, *By the Ionian Sea,* 1901

entered from the St Gotthard
To young Adams this first plunge into Italy passed Beethoven as a piece of accidental education. Like music it differed from other education in being, not a means of pursuing life, but one of the ends attained. Further, on these lines, one could not go. It had but one defect – that of attainment. Life had no richer impression to give; it offers barely half-a-dozen such, and the intervals seem long.

Henry Adams, *The Education of Henry Adams,* 1906

The past of Italy belongs to all lands which have felt the reverberations of that gorgeous procession. An Englishman in Italy stands upon soil that for century after century has bequeathed to him, among so many thousand others, his own share of its richness, and if he carries with him a single grain of golden dust, it may well be to Italy that he owes it.

Percy Lubbock, *Elizabeth Barrett Browning in her Letters,* 1906

Italy against the outlay of ¼ of her revenue has an impoverished illiterate population, medieval sanitation, a terrible accumulation of taxes, and an army and navy which would probably fetch a few hundred pounds in a lottery.

James Joyce, Letter to Stanislaus Joyce, 6 November 1906

How incomparably the old coquine of an Italy is the most beautiful country in the world – of a beauty (and an interest and complexity of beauty) so far beyond any other that none other is worth talking about.

Henry James, Letter to Mrs Wharton, 11 August 1907

One doesn't (any longer) so much want to live in that unspeakable country as to feel, whenever one will, well on the way to it.

Henry James, Letter to Madame Wagniere, 22 December 1909

One must love Italy if one has lived there. It is so non-moral. It leaves the soul so free. Over these countries, Germany and England, lies the gloom of the dark moral judgement and condemnation and reservation of the people. Italy does not judge.

D.H. Lawrence, Letter to A.W. McLeod, 26 April 1913

One begins to realise how old the real Italy is, how man-gripped and how withered. England is far more wild and savage and lonely, in her country parts. Here since endless centuries man has tamed the impossible mountain side into terraces, he has quarried the rock, he has fed his sheep among the thin woods, he has cut his boughs and burnt his charcoal, he has been half domesticated even among the wildest fastnesses. This is what is so attractive about the remote places, the Abruzzi, for example. Life is so primitive, so pagan, so strangely heathen and half-savage. And yet it is human life. And the wildest country is half humanised, half brought under. It is all conscious. Wherever one is in Italy, either one is conscious of the present, or of the mediaeval influences, or of the far mysterious gods of the early Mediterranean. Wherever one is, the place has its conscious genius. Man has lived there and brought forth his consciousness there and in some way brought that place to consciousness, given it expression, and really, finished it. The expression may be Proserpine or Pan, or even the strange 'shrouded gods' of the Etruscans or the Sikels, none the less it is an expression. The land has been humanised, through and through: and we in our own tissued consciousness bear the results of this humanisation. So that for us to go to Italy and to *penetrate* into Italy is like a most fascinating act of self-discovery – back, back down the old ways of time. Strange and wonderful chords awake in us, and vibrate again after many hundreds of years of complete forgetfulness.

And then – and then – there is a final feeling of complete sterility. It is all worked out. It is all known: *connu, connu!*

Norman Douglas, *Old Calabria,* 1915

It is essentially a land of blue and its derivatives – cool, intellectual tints. The azure sea follows you far inland with its gleams. Look landwards from the water – purple Apennines are ever in sight. And up yonder, among the hills, you will rarely escape from the celestial hues.

Speaking of these mountains in a general way, they are bare masses whose coloration trembles between misty blue and mauve according to distance, light, and hour of day. As building-stone, the rock imparts a grey-blue tint to the walls. The very flowers are blue; it is a peculiarity of limestone formation, hitherto unexplained, to foster blooms of this colour. Those olive coloured slopes are of a glaucous tone.

Norman Douglas, *Alone,* 1921

I can never make a poem about Italy. About Italy you do, you address, bless and say adieu. Adieu Italy beautiful Italy adieu.

Gertrude Stein, 'Land of Nations', *Geography and Plays,* 1922

Italy is so tender – like cooked macaroni – yards and yards of soft tenderness, ravelled round everything.

D.H. Lawrence, *Sea And Sardinia,* 1923

Talk of the hanging gardens of Babylon, all Italy, apart from the plains, is a hanging garden. For centuries upon centuries, man has been patiently modelling the surface of the Mediterranean countries, gently rounding the hills and graduating the big slopes into the almost invisible levels of terraces. Thousands of square miles of Italy have been lifted in human hands, piled and laid back in tiny little flats, held up by drystone walls, whose stones came from the lifted earth. It is the work of many, many centuries. . . . Man, feeling his way sensitively to the fruitfulness of the earth, has moulded the earth to his necessity without violating it.

D.H. Lawrence, *Flowery Tuscany,* 1927, in *Phoenix,* 1936

Italy is now the Sick Land of Europe, a fever patient, flushed with a hectic resemblance to health, and still capable of convulsive, but not of sustained violence. She declines. She has fallen out of the general circle of European development; she is no longer a factor in progressive civilisation. . . . She has murdered or exiled all her Europeans.

H.G. Wells, 'What is Fascism?', 9 February 1927, in *The Way the World is Going,* 1928

Democracy in the French or English sense has never existed in Italy. If there was no outstanding figure the power fell into the hands of the secret societies, who after their fashion, again, represented the principle of minority rule. In Italy the democratic façade was never anything more than a façade; if it ever became anything more, anarchy inevitably followed. The great Italian individual's qualities issue forth in a marvellous earth-bound realism of the spirit. He finds the necessities of political life just as natural as the mother finds the needs of her little children.

Count Keyserling, *Europe,* 1928

An immense quantity of the earth's surface in Italy is wasted by nature, serves no useful purpose save to impress the unaccustomed eye. . . . The eye can discover in the distance naught but a dreamy, hazy, ideal beauty conceived on a terrifying scale. If beauty and terror are the desiderata of the artist, here he has them, incredibly combined.

Arnold Bennett, *Journal* (1929), 1930

Italy today is far more Etruscan in its pulse than Roman: and will always be so. The Etruscan element is like the grass of the field and the sprouting of corn, in Italy: it will always be so. Why try to revert to the Latin-Roman mechanism and suppression?

D.H. Lawrence, *Etruscan Places,* 1932

Of all the Italian people that ever lived, the Etruscans were surely the least Roman. Just as, of all the people that ever rose up in Italy, the Romans of ancient Rome were surely the most un-Italian, judging from the natives of to-day.

Ibid.

Mussolini . . . has muscled into all the guidebooks in Rome. . . . At the end of every guidebook in English one expects to see the famous lines of Browning slightly changed by official order, 'Open my heart and you will see graven inside it, "Il Duce."'

James Thurber, *My World and Welcome to It,* 1942

I am bound to say, if the House will forgive the metaphor, that the Allied High Command have approached the Italian mainland like an old man approaching a young bride, fascinated, sluggish, and apprehensive.

Aneurin Bevan, Speech, House of Commons, December 1943

We shall continue to operate on the Italian donkey at both ends – with a carrot and with a stick.

Sir Winston Churchill, Reply at Press Conference in USA, May 1943, when asked how Italy would be treated

What one feels always in Italy is an extraordinary and direct mingling of freshness and repose, as though all life were sunset and sunrise, winter and spring.

Charles Morgan, *Reflections in a Mirror,* 1944

This country has made an *art* of being vanquished.

Anon. exasperated American, Remark to Freya Stark, 1945, in *Dust in the Lion's Paw,* 1961

Since the year 476 the history of Italy has been one long chronicle of dishonour. Down to 1860 the country was almost constantly under foreign rule, and all its local governments were grounded upon oppression tempered by assassination. In World War I it ratted on its allies, and in World War II it ratted again. Such is the heir and assign of the Rome of Caesar and Augustus.

H.L. Mencken, 'Minority Report', *H.L. Mencken's Notebooks,* 1956

The Italian way of life down the centuries attracted people who wanted to take a holiday from their national virtues. In the heart of every man, whenever he is born, whatever his education and tastes, there is one small corner which is Italian, that part that finds regimentation irksome, the dangers of war frightening, strict morality stifling, that part which loves frivolous and entertaining art, admires larger-than-lifesize solitary heroes, and dreams of an impossible liberation from the strictures of a tidy existence.

Luigi Barzini, *The Italians,* 1964

Foreign diplomats in Rome disconsolately say, 'Italy is the opposite of Russia. In Moscow nothing is known, yet everything is clear. In Rome everything is public, there are no secrets, everybody talks, things are at times flamboyantly enacted, yet one understands nothing.'

Ibid.

The virtues necessary to become the head of anything, in Italy, head of a convent, a municipal kennel, a vegetable market Mafia, a secondary railway station, or the mayor of a mountain village, are such that could, in most other countries, easily make a man foreign minister, the alcove favourite of the queen, the chief of staff, or the president of the republic.

Ibid.

Very little counts for less in Italy than the state.

Peter Nichols, *Italia, Italia,* 1973

Can it be that from the waist down Italy is a different creature? Is the famous boot shape really an elegantly shod hoof, and the top a normal Western country?

Ibid.

All dwellers in the Teutonic north, looking out at the winter sky, are subject to spasms of a nearly irresistible pull, when the entire Italian peninsula from Trieste to Agrigento begins to function like a lodestone. The magnetism is backed by an unseen choir, there are roulades of mandolin strings in the air; ghostly whiffs of lemon blossom beckon the victims south and across the Alpine passes. It is Goethe's Law and is ineluctable as Newton's or Boyle's.

Patrick Leigh Fermor, *A Time of Gifts,* 1977

You've heard the one about the Italian tanks. They've even got reversing lights on them.

David Frost, quoted by Thomson Prentice in *Daily Mail,* 21 May 1979

Political parties in Italy repeat themselves like broken gramophone records.

Professor Pedarotti, in Interview on BBC *Newsnight,* 4 August 1980

Italians

Early

Who is ignorant of the vanity and arrogance of the Romans? a nation nursed in sedition, cruel, untractable, and scorning to obey, unless they are too feeble to resist. When they promise to serve, they aspire to reign; if they swear allegiance, they watch the opportunity of revolt; yet they vent their discontent in loud clamours, if your doors or your counsels are shut against them. Dexterous in mischief, they have never learned the science of doing good. Odious to earth and heaven, impious to God, seditious among themselves, jealous of their neighbours, inhuman to strangers, they love no one, by no one are they beloved; and, while they wish to inspire fear, they live in base and continual apprehension. They will not submit; they know not how to govern; faithless to their superiors, intolerable to their equals, ungrateful to their benefactors, and alike impudent in their demands and their refusals. Lofty in promise, poor in execution: adulation and calumny, perfidy and treason, are the familiar acts of their policy.

St Bernard of Clairvaux, translated by Edward Gibbon, in *The Decline and Fall of the Roman Empire*, 1776–88

. . . for the men you shall have there, although some in deede be excellentlie lerned, yett are they all given to soe counterfeit lerning, as a man shall learne of them more false groundes of thinges, then in anie place ells that I doe knowe for from a tapster upwardes they are all discoursers. In fine, certaine quallities, as Horsemanshipp, Weapons, Vauting, and such like, are better there then in those other countries, for others more sounde they doe little excell neerer places.

Sir Philip Sidney, Letter to Robert Sidney, *c.* 1578

The Italians make little difference between children and nephews or near kinsfoks; but so they be of the lump, they care not though they pass not through their own body.

Francis Bacon, *Essays*, 1598–1625

Seventeenth Century

I will ever magnifie and extoll the Italian for as courteous a man to a stranger as any man whatsoever in Christendome. For I have had a little experience in my travels of some of every principall nation of Christendome.

Thomas Coryate, *Crudities*, 1611

The soil is generally abundant in all things necessary for human life, and the people for the most part are both grave and ingenious, but wondrous deceitful in their actions; so unappeaseable in anger, that they cowardly murder their enemies rather than seek an honourable revenge, and so inclined to unnatural vices, that for bestiality they surpass the Infidels. The women of the better sort are slavishly infringed from honest and lawful liberty; they of the middle rank somewhat modest in carriage, witty in speech, and bountiful in affection; they of the vulgar kind are both ignorant, sluttish, and greedy; and, lastly, the worser dregs, their impudent courtesans, the most lascivious harlots in the world.

William Lithgow, *Rare Adventures and Painfull Peregrinations*, 1614/32

The Italians are so ravished with the beauty of their owne Countrey, as having by the sharpenesse of wit more then the true value of things, magnified and propounded to strangers admiration, each Brooke for a River, each vice for the neighbour vertue, and each poore thing, as if it were to be extolled above the Moone, they have thereby more wronged themselves then us. For we passing through Italy, though we find ourselves deceived in the fame of things, yet still we heare and see many things worthy to be observed; but of the Italians, holding Italy for a Paradice, very few sharpen their wits with any long voyage, and great part of them have not seene the Villages and Cities within ten miles of their dwellings. Hence it is that great part of the Italians have nothing to boast of but their naturall wit.

Fynes Moryson, *An Itinerary*, 1617

Why are Italians at this day generally so good poets and painters? Because every man of any fashion amongst them hath his mistress.

Robert Burton, *Anatomie of Melancholie*, 1621

Germany hath not so many drunkards, *England* Tobacconists, *France* dancers, *Holland* Mariners, as *Italy* alone hath jealous husbands.

Ibid.

They are generally indulgent of themselves, and great Embracers of Pleasure, which may proceed from the luscious rich Wines, and luxurious Food, Fruits, and Roots, where with the Country abounds; insomuch that in some Places, Nature may be said to be, *Lena sui, A Bawd to herself.* The Cardinal de Medici's Rule is of much Authority among them, *That there is no Religion under the Navel.* And some of them are of the Opinion of the Asians, who hold, that touching those natural Passions, Desires and Motions, which run up and down in the Blood, God Almighty, and his Handmaid Nature, did not intend they should be a Torment to us, but be used with Comfort and Delight.

James Howell, 'Letter to Capt. Francis Bacon, from Turin, 30 November 1621,' *Familiar Letters*, 1645

Some say, *The* Italian *loves no favour, but what's future.*

James Howell, 'Letter to Lord Viscount Rocksavage, Westminster, 22 March 1630', *Familiar Letters*, 1645

Eighteenth Century

Sallads, and Eggs, and lighter Fare
Tune the ITALIAN Spark's Guitar.

Matthew Prior, *Alma*, Canto iii, 1715–18

How tedious it is to deal with Italians. I never knew people so ready to promise and so slow to perform.

George Berkeley, Letter to Lord Percival, July 1720

The only thing the Italians shine in, is their reception of strangers.

Thomas Gray, Letter to Philip Gray, 9 October 1740

Could Nature's bounty satisfy the breast,
The sons of Italy were surely blest. . . .

But small the bliss that sense alone bestows,
And sensual bliss is all the nation knows.
In florid beauty groves and fields appear,
Man seems the only growth that dwindles here.
Contrasted faults through all his manners reign,
Though poor luxurious, though submissive, vain,
Though grave, yet trifling, zealous, yet untrue,
And even in penance planning sins anew.
All evils here contaminate the mind,
That opulence departed leaves behind.

Oliver Goldsmith, *The Traveller*, 1764

Italy is certainly the native country of this art: and yet, I do not find the people in general either more musically inclined, or better provided with ears than their neighbours.

Tobias Smollett, *Travels through France and Italy*, 1766

Of all the people I ever knew, the Italians are the most villainously rapacious.

Ibid.

Familiarities between man and wife are still connived at in this country however, provided they are carried on in private; but for a man to be seen hand in hand with his wife, in public, would not be tolerated.

John Moore, *A View of Society and Manners in Italy*, 1781

My idea of the Italians is, that they are an ingenious, sober people, with quick feelings, and therefore irritable; but when unprovoked, of a mild and obliging disposition, and less subject to avarice, envy, or repining at the narrowness of their own circumstances, and the comparative wealth of others, than most other nations.

Ibid.

Religion, in Italy, being nearly reduced to a shell, the fruit of which has long been given up to nations better disposed to taste its value, and consequently having little or nothing left but exterior, demands no particular consideration apart from the Italian manners; and to them it certainly gives a very strong tincture; their ceremonious practice of it throwing a deep shade of decency and solemnity over their ordinary conduct, and serving, in the eye of the world, as a useful contrast to their natural vivacity, and to irregularities springing from their warmth of temperament. Of their civil morality, if I may so express it, as professedly distinguished from religion, one may judge with tolerable certainty, if we admit this general principle, that to be, and to appear, are two things absolutely different; and that it is seldom men of the world are not obliged, for their own advantage, to show themselves different from what they really are. . . . It is observable . . . that when the Italians have to deal with each other, they know pretty well how far their own assurances and pretences will go; and what credit to give those they mutually receive. Now, it will be easily imagined, that the practice of dissembling their sentiments, and of continually holding a language that has little to do with their thoughts, must reduce those who, nevertheless, wish to display their wit and parts in conversation, to the necessity of talking much, without saying any thing, and of exhausting the chapter of indifferent trifles, and general observations. This every foreigner must have remarked, particularly at Rome; and cannot but have attributed to it the pompous insipidity of their conversations. Any one, the least used to them, foresees nearly what every man will say, that enters the room. This poverty of conversation, amidst a great deal of talking, is the most striking in those who have rank to support it, and who have their constant assemblies on certain fixed days. What makes all this the more provoking to a stranger, is that these persons are so far from wanting wit, or talents, that they fall into these habits from having too much of them.

William Beckford, *Dreams Waking Thoughts and Incidents*, 1783

Were the Inhabitants of Italy charming as their Country, all other Regions would be depopulated I think.

Hester Lynch Thrale/Piozzi, *Thraliana*, 1786

Whoever seeks to convince instead of persuade an Italian, will find he has been employed in a Sisyphean labour; the stone may roll to the top, but is sure to return and rest at his feet who had courage to try the experiment. Logic is a science they love not, and, I think, steadily refuse to cultivate; nor is argument a style of conversation they naturally affect.

Hester Lynch Thrale/Piozzi, *Observations and Reflections in the Course of a Journey*, 1789

Nineteenth Century

Gli Italiani tutti ladroni.
(The Italians are all robbers.)

Napoleon Bonaparte, Remark, in a loud voice, in public, to which a lady replied, 'Non tutti, ma buona parte,' ['Not all, but the most part'] in S.T. Coleridge, *Biographia Literaria*, 1817

The modern Italians seem a miserable people, without sensibility, or imagination, or understanding. Their outside is polished, and an intercourse with them seems to proceed with much facility, though it ends in nothing, and produces nothing. The women are particularly empty, and though possessed of the same kind of superficial grace, are devoid of every cultivation and refinement.

Percy Bysshe Shelley, Letter to William Godwin, 25 July 1818

Lord D.[illon] . . . praises the Italians for their intelligence, but says they have a total want of heart; no cordiality, no hospitality; a grave and reserved people; their dislike of *suggezione* or restraint, which shows itself even in their consideration for others, and in their phrase *Si leva l'incommodo,* when they are taking their leave of any one.

Thomas Moore, *Journal*, 19 October 1819

Their moral is not your moral – their life is not your life – you would not understand it – it is not English nor French – nor German – which you would all understand – the Conventual education – the Cavalier Servitude – the habits of thought and living are so entirely different – and the difference becomes so much more striking the more you live intimately with them – that I know now how to make you comprehend a people – who are at once temperate and profligate – serious in their character and buffoons in their amusements – capable of impressions and passions which are at once *sudden* and *durable* (what you find in no other nation) and who *actually* have *no society* (what we would call so) as you may see by their Comedies – they have no real comedy not even in Goldoni – and that is because they have no society to draw it from.

Lord Byron, Letter to John Murray,
21 February 1820

I wonder what figure these Italians will make in a regular row. I sometimes think that, like the Irishman's gun (somebody had sold him a crooked one), they will only do for 'shooting round a corner;' at least, this sort of shooting has been the late tenor of their exploits. And yet, there are materials in this people, and a noble energy, if well directed. But who is to direct them? No matter. Out of such times heroes spring. Difficulties are the hot-beds of high spirits, and Freedom the mother of the few virtues incident to human nature.

Lord Byron, *Ravenna Journal*, 8 January 1821

Subtle, discerning, eloquent, the slave
Of Love or Hate, for ever in extremes;
Gentle when unprovoked, easily won,
But quick in quarrel – through many a thousand
  shades
His spirit flits chameleon-like, and mocks
The eye of the observer.

Samuel Rogers, *Italy*, 1822–34

The genius of the Italians . . . is acute, profound, and sensual, but not subtle; hence what they think to be humorous is merely witty.

Samuel Taylor Coleridge, *Table Talk*, 23 April 1832

Talk of your Italians! why, they are extinguished by the Austrians because they don't blaze enough of themselves to burn the extinguisher. Only people who deserve despotism are forced to suffer it.

Edward Fitzgerald, Letter to F. Tennyson,
October 1841

. . . a people, naturally well-disposed, and patient, and sweet-tempered. Years of neglect, oppression and misrule, have been at work, to change their nature and reduce their spirit; miserable jealousies, fomented by petty Princes to whom union was destruction, and division strength, have been a canker at their root of nationality, and have barbarized their language; but the good that was in them ever, is in them yet, and a noble people may be, one day, raised up from these ashes. Let us entertain that hope!

Charles Dickens, *Pictures from Italy*, 1846

An Italian annoys you neither with his pride like an Englishman, nor with his vanity like a Frenchman. He is quiet and natural, self-possessed without wrapping himself up in a corner, and ready for cheerfulness without grimace. His frankness sometimes takes the air of a simplicity, at once misplaced and touching.

Leigh Hunt, *Autobiography*, 1850

In Italy, gentlemen do not look so much like gentlemen as in England, but there are greater numbers of women who look like ladies.

Ibid.

The air and life of Italy
Comes sharp into me and carves clear
My northern nature perfectly.

O what frank animals are here!
With beauty they have lived and had
Great offspring who make rich our sphere.

And Beauty was their mistress glad
She cannot die: but now she wears
The look that makes a people mad.

George Meredith, *Italy*, 1861

Through all Europe the movement is now towards science, and the Italian people is distinguished amongst all others by its scientific intellect – this is undoubtedly true; so that with the movement there now is among them there is no saying where they may go. They imitate the French too much, however; it is good for us to attend to the French, they are so unlike us, but not good for the Italians, who are a sister nation.

Matthew Arnold, Letter to his mother, 24 May 1865

I cannot but think this a mere fair-weather kingdom, 80,000 French, English, or Germans might, I am perfectly convinced, enter this country to-morrow, overrun it in three months, and hold it for ever against all opposition they would meet from within. The Piedmontese is the only virile element – he is like a country Frenchman – but he is a small leaven to leaven the whole lump. And the whole lump want back-bone, serious energy, and power of honest work to a degree that makes one impatient. I am tempted to take the professors I see in the schools by the collar, and hold them down to their work for five or six hours a day – so angry do I get at their shirking and inefficiency. They have all a certain refinement which they call civilisation, but a nation is really civilised by acquiring the qualities it by nature is wanting in; and the Italians are no more civilised by virtue of their refinement alone than we are civilised by virtue of our energy alone.

Matthew Arnold, Letter to his sister, 21 June 1865

We have the notion in our country that Italians never do heavy work at all, but confine themselves to the lighter arts, like organ-grinding, operatic singing, and assassination. We have blundered, that is plain.

Mark Twain, *A Tramp Abroad,* 1880

The more I see of them the more struck I am with their having no sense of the ridiculous.

Henry James, Letter to Mrs Fanny Kemble, 24 March 1881

I was very unfavourably impressed with the Italian tone in regard to international matters where the rights of non-European nationalities were at stake. The Italians, like the French and all the Latin races, seemed to me incapable of grasping the idea, which we in England at any rate admit in theory, if seldom in practice, that the nations outside the community of Christian civilization have any rights at all.

Wilfred Scawen Blunt, Diary, 1891, *My Diaries,* 1919

He talked the matter over with his nose. There are 5000 ways of looking at an egg and at least as many of tapping an Italian's nose.

Samuel Butler, *Further Extracts from Note-Books,* 1934 – before 1902

Twentieth Century

The Italian imagination is like a cinematograph.

James Joyce, Letter to Stanislaus Joyce, 7 December 1906

The men and women are faithful in marriage on the whole – but they have tribes of children. The butcher said to his wife one night 'You *were* going to have an infant, weren't you?' 'Yes you dolt,' she said. 'I had it this morning. There it is in the cradle.' And she went out to fetch some coal in. They are a spunky lot and of no soul or intellect. Its an awful relief to live among them.

D.H. Lawrence, Letter to Will Holbrook, January 1913

The men and women in Italy are natural enemies – it is very queer.

D.H. Lawrence, Letter to Mitchell Kennerly, 5 October 1913

The Italian people are called 'Children of the Sun.' They might better be called 'Children of the Shadow.' Their souls are dark and nocturnal.

D.H. Lawrence, *Twilight in Italy,* 1916

It is not a melancholy thing being one of them. It is not an interesting thing being one of them. It is not an exciting thing being one of them, it is not an important thing being all of them. It is an important enough thing being all of them. It is a pleasant thing being with them. It is not a pleasant thing expecting anything from them. It is not a disconcerting thing expecting anything from them. It is an agreeable thing knowing about them. It is an exciting thing first hearing about them. It is a delightful thing coming among them although it is a frightening thing the first seeing of them. It is a very pleasant thing living where they are living. It is a completely pleasant thing living where they are living. It is a troublesome thing waiting for any one of them. It is a troublesome thing waiting for them to go on finishing anything. It is not an exasperating, not a disconcerting thing waiting for any one of them.

They are certainly ones deciding something. They are certainly ones expecting anything. They are certainly ones not despairing in being ones being living. They are certainly ones not certain that they will be expecting anything. . . .

Gertrude Stein, 'Italians', *Geography and Plays,* 1922

It is not impossible to govern Italians. It is merely useless.

Benito Mussolini, attrib.

in Asmara, Ethiopia

When taxed with filth of town Italians say, 'We are in Africa.' Bad omen if they regard tropics as excuse for inferior hygiene. Reminded that they are race who have inhabited and created the slums of the world.

Evelyn Waugh, *Diary,* 31 August 1936

The trouble with Italy is that we have never allowed its inhabitants to leave the stage. Italian has to be the language of rhetorical superlatives – a language full of exaggerated gestures. Italy taught Europe how to act and how to sing in opera. Consequently, every Italian is a *primo tenore* who advances to the footlights and tickles the ears of the groundlings by his florid voice; or else he is always some poor devil of a Harlequin playing for ever the part of the clown.

Walter Starkie, *The Waveless Plain,* 1938

Is there any other country in Europe where the

character of the people seems to have been so little affected by political and technological change?

W.H. Auden, Introduction to Goethe's *Italian Journey*, 1962

The Italian social structure can be compared to the olive tree, that most Italian of all trees, which looks entirely different when seen from above from what it looks when seen from below. The leaves are glossy dark-green on top and powdery grey underneath. The faces of the Italians look flattering, smiling and kindly from above, but overbearing, insolent, pitiless from below. Foreigners are automatically promoted to be honorary members of the ruling class. They occupy a position of vantage. Theirs is the bird's-eye view of the olive tree.

Luigi Barzini, *The Italians*, 1964

Italian virtuosi have been famous for having produced floods of *trompe l'oeil, trompe* the mind, and *trompe* the heart.

Ibid.

There is an Italian saying that once people are born registered and baptised, they enjoy provisional liberty.

Peter Nichols, *Italia, Italia*, 1973

Their smiles and laughter are due to their habit of thinking pleasurably aloud about the pleasures of life. They have humanity rather than humour, and the real significance of the distinction is seldom understood.

Ibid.

By 1948 the Italians had begun to pull themselves together, demonstrating once more their astonishing ability to cope with disaster which is so perfectly balanced by their absolute inability to deal with success.

Gore Vidal, *Matters of Fact and Fiction*, 1977

Then one of the French ladies remarked on a clear note, '*Pour moi les Italiens du nord sont des hommes décafeinés.*'

Lawrence Durrell, *Sicilian Carousel*, 1977

Women

In generall it is said of Italian weomen: Son gazza a le porte, Sante in Chiesa, capre n'i giardini, Diavoli in casa, Angeli in strada, Sirene all fenestra. They are Magpyes at the doore, Saints in the Church, Goates in the garden, Divels in the house, Angels in the streete, and Syrens at the window.

Fynes Moryson, *Itinerary*, 1617

My desire to know the world made me resolve to intrigue a little while in Italy, where the women are so debauched that they are hardly to be considered as moral agents, but as inferior beings.

James Boswell, *Journal*, 10 January 1765

The women in Italy (so far as I have seen hitherto) are detestably ugly. They are not even dark and swarthy, but a mixture of brown and red, coarse, marked with the small pox, with pug-features, awkward, ill-made, fierce, dirty, lazy, neither attempting nor hoping to please.

William Hazlitt, *Notes of a Journey through France and Italy*, 1826

Men run the country, but women run men. Italy is, in reality, a crypto-matriarchy.

Luigi Barzini, *The Italians*, 1964

Italian Language

If one were to be worded to death, *Italian* is the fittest Language, in regard of the Fluency and Softness of it: for thro'out the whole Body of it, you have not a Word ends with a Consonant, except some few monosyllable Conjunctions and Prepositions, and this renders the Speech more smooth; which made one say, *That when the Confusion of Tongues happen'd at the Building of the Tower of* Babel, *if the* Italian *had been there,* Nimrod *had made him a Plaisterer.*

James Howell, 'Letter to Captain Francis Bacon, . . . 30 November 1621', in *Familiar Letters*, 1645

I love the language, that soft bastard Latin,
  Which melts like kisses from a female mouth.
And sounds as if it had been writ on satin,
  With syllables which breathe of the sweet South.

Lord Byron, *Beppo*, 1818

The Tuscan's siren tongue,
That music in itself, whose sounds are song,
The poetry of speech.

Lord Byron, *Childe Harold's Pilgrimage*, 1812–18

Rhyme o'erflows
Italian, which hath scarcely prose.

W.S. Landor, *Collection of 1846*, No. CCLXVII

I am very witty in Italian, though a little violent; and I need space.

Dylan Thomas, Letter to John Davenport, 29 May 1947

I love Italian, it's the most beautiful language to write in, but terribly hard for writers because you can't tell when you've written nonsense. In English you know right away.

W.H. Auden, Remark, 1953, quoted in Robin Maugham, *Escape from the Shadows*, 1972

There is no Italian word for privacy.

Peter Nichols, *Italia, Italia*, 1973

The Abruzzi

These impressive Abruzzi ridges that combined in so special a way hard temper with soft color – as if there were steel underneath blue silver, yet a blue so etherealized that one peak, with its pencilled veins of snow, seemed to merge into the slate-blue heavens.

Edmund Wilson, *Europe without Baedeker*, 1947

Agrigento (formerly Girgenti)

Plato, when he visited Sicily, was so much struck with the luxury of Agrigentum, both in their houses and their tables, that a saying of his is still recorded: that they built as if they were never to die, and eat as if they had not an hour to live.

Patrick Brydone, *A Tour through Sicily and Malta*, 1773

Girgenti as a landscape is Athens with improvements. Two thousand, or twenty-five hundred years ago, it must have been immensely charming, like Japan in its prime, but now it is a landscape with hardly ten lines of history, and no art.

Henry Adams, Letter to Elizabeth Cameron, 23 April 1899

When we were there we came across an American lady, seated on the steps of one [temple], in an attitude of despair. She complained, 'I'm tired of it, temple after temple, and all exactly alike.'

M. and C.H.B. Quennell, *Everyday Things in Archaic Greece*, 1931

It came in sight slowly, the famous city; at first as a series of suggestive shapes against the evening sky, then as half dissolved forms which wobbled in the heat haze to settle at last firmly into the cubist boxes of a modern city. . . . It became obvious that what was being unfolded before us and below us was a most remarkable site. Successive roundels led in a low spiral up to the top of the steep hillock upon which an Acropolis had perched, and where now two parvenu skyscrapers and an ignoble huddle of unwarranted housing did duty for the old city's centre. We had reached by now the commercial nexus of the new town, which lies a bit below the city, makeshift, and ugly. But the light was of pure opalescent honey, and the setting (I am sorry to labour the point) was Hymettus at evening with the violet city of Athens sinking into the cocoon of night. I tremble also to insist upon the fact that from the point of view of natural beauty and elegance of site Agrigento is easily a match for Athens on its hills. Just as the ocean throws up roundels of sand to form pools, so the successive ages of geological time had thrown up successive rounds of limestone, rising in tiers like a wedding-cake to the Acropolis. From the top one looks down as if into a pie-dish with two levels, inner and outer ridges. It is down there at the entrance to the city, that all the Temples are situated, like a protective screen, tricked out with fruit orchards, with sweeps of silver olives, and with ubiquitous almond trees, whose spring flowering has become as famous as the legendary town itself.

Lawrence Durrell, *Sicilian Carousel*, 1977

Albano

The young women . . . from Gensano and Albano, and that are known by their scarlet boddices and white head-dresses and handsome good-humoured faces, are the finest specimens I have ever seen of human nature. They are like creatures that have breathed the air of Heaven, till the sun has ripened them into perfect beauty, health and goodness.

William Hazlitt, *Notes of a Journey through France and Italy*, 1826

I have talked of the picturesque all my life: now at last, by way of a change, I see it.

Henry James, Letter to Alice James, 25 April 1873

Amalfi

The cathedral is in the least agreeable of those styles of architecture that were invented or adopted in the barbarous ages, when Grecian rules and proportions were forgotten. The steeple is one of the ugliest of its kind, and the portico has not even Gothic lightness. Two grand antique columns of red Egyptian granite placed at the entrance of the chancel make the deformity of the surrounding objects more visible.

Henry Swinburne, *Travels in the Two Sicilies in 1777–1780*, 1785

Sweet the memory is to me
Of the land beyond the sea,
Where the waves and mountains meet;
Where amid her mulberry-trees
Sits Amalfi in the heat,
Bathing ever her white feet
In the tideless, summer seas. . . .
Vanished like a fleet of cloud,
Like a passing trumpet-blast
Are those splendours of the past
And the commerce of the crowd!
Fathoms deep beneath the seas
Lie the ancient wharves and quays,
Swallowed by the engulfing waves;
Silent streets, and vacant halls,
Ruined roofs, and towers and walls;
Hidden from all mortal eyes

Deep the sunken city lies:
Even cities have their graves.

Henry Wadsworth Longfellow, *Amalfi*, 1875

Ancona

They have a proverb, one Peter in Rome, one Tower in Cremona, and one Haven in Ancona (for the excellency of them).

Fynes Moryson, *An Itinerary*, 1617

I said, that the Popes territory extendeth this way as high as Ancona, and these inhabiters of Marca are accounted a wicked generation, the greatest part of the cut-throtes and murtherers dispersed through Italy, being borne in this Country.

Ibid.

Ancona . . . stands on a promontory, and looks more beautiful at a distance than when you are in it.

Joseph Addison, *Remarks on Several Parts of Italy, in the Years 1701, 1702, and 1703*, 1705

The town seemed full of *trade stench and filth.*

Washington Irving, *Journal*, 19 April 1805

Filthy hole: like rotten cabbage. Thrice swindled.

James Joyce, Postcard to Stanislaus Joyce, 31 July 1906

As for Ancona I cannot think of it without repugnance. There is something Irish in its bleak gaunt beggarly ugliness.

James Joyce, Letter to Stanislaus Joyce, 7 August 1906

Anzio (formerly Antium)

Coriolanus: A goodly City is this *Antium.*

William Shakespeare, *Coriolanus*, *c.* 1607–8

Valle d'Aosta

The great ones, the giants of Alps, stood about us here and there in a cloudless sky, a burning serenity. Their immobility never seems to me static; it has a vitality that seems to us repose, like that of a humming top at rest on its axis, spinning along its orbit in space.

Freya Stark, *Traveller's Prelude*, 1950

Apennines

The Mount Appenine derived from the Alpes, runnes all the length of Italy, in the forme of a fishes backe bone, and almost in the midst devides it into two tracts.

Fynes Moryson, *An Itinerary*, 1617

The Appenines are not near so high, nor so horrible, as the Alps.

John Wilkes, Letter to his daughter, 1 February 1765

Listen, listen, Mary mine
To the whisper of the Apennine,
It bursts on the roof like the thunder's roar,
Or like the sea on a northern shore,
Heard in its raging ebb and flow
By the captives pent in the cave below.
The Apennine in the light of day
Is a mighty mountain, dim and grey
Which between the earth and sky doth lay;
But when night comes, a chaos dread
On the dim starlight then is spread,
And the Apennine walks abroad in the storm.

Percy Bysshe Shelley, *Passage of the Apennines*, 4 May 1818

We left Milan on the 1st of May, and travelled across the Apennines to Pisa. This part of the Apennine is far less beautiful than the Alps; the mountains are wide and wild, and the whole scenery broad and undetermined – the imagination cannot find a home in it.

Percy Bysshe Shelley, Letter to Thomas Love Peacock, 5 June 1818

Their character is of the least interesting sort of any mountains, being neither distinct nor wooded; but undulating, barren, and coarse; without any grandeur but what arises from an excess of that appearance. They lie in a succession of great doughy billows, like so much enormous pudding, or petrified mud.

Leigh Hunt, *Autobiography*, 1850

Appian Way

The Appian way . . . was more used by the noble Romans than any other in Italy, as it led to Naples, Baia, and the most delightful parts of the nation. It is indeed very disagreeable to be carried in haste over this pavement.

Joseph Addison, *Remarks on Several Parts of Italy, in the Years 1701, 1702, and 1703*, 1705

Aquila

The town looked as if it were constructed of hard panes of light and shade that made the most violent contrasts. Above white blinding sidewalkless streets stood façades built of local stone that had a richness despite their austerity, with their juxtaposed orange and sepia, burnt sienna and café au lait, neutral liver and greenish grey, that made a double scale of colors, one darkened and cold, one glowing. The tall doorways were impressively hooded with heavy ornamental architraves, and the windows, well-proportioned and brown-shuttered, were capped with a variety of pediments that resembled now triangular crests, now crowns with twin peaks, now coronets, and contributed to a standard of dignity that . . . attained something akin to grandeur. . . . Aquila had a unity and harmony which made it seem all to have been built in one piece like those wasps'-nests in the hills that had given her the creeps, but which here imposed themselves upon her and compelled her to respect and admire. This, she saw, was what architecture could do – not merely lay out a plan as at Washington, but dominate a whole city and actually provide the medium in which human beings lived.

Edmund Wilson, *Europe without Baedeker,* 1947

Arezzo

Arezzo is the first considerable town which succeeds to Florence. Its subtile air has been asserted to be peculiarly favourable to genius; and in fact, under many moral disadvantages, it has produced men of eminent talent from Maecenas to Petrarch.

Lady Morgan, *Italy,* 1820

Augusta (Sicily)

It was of extraordinary beauty this little oil port. A thousand tulips of light and coloured smoke played about its derricks and towers and drums – a forest of refineries whose beauty was made quite sinister by the fact that the whole was deserted. There was not a soul in the whole place, not a dog or a cat; there wasn't even a guard-post. Yet the light played about in it, the smoke gushed and spat, as if it were the very forge of the Titans, and a thousand invisible trolls were hard at work in it. Its beauty was quite breath-taking. I watched its diminishing perspective, reflected in the windows of the bus, and it seemed like a thousand wax-lights afloat on the waters of chaos. Two days later we were to pass it in daylight, and to have our ardour quenched by its hideous ugliness, its ungainly spider-like instruments.

Lawrence Durrell, *Sicilian Carousel,* 1977

Bagni di Lucca

When at Lucca we visited the springs at the Baths 14 miles distant, it is a sort of Matlock upon a large scale.

E.H. (Edward Hakewill, ? 1812–72), Letter to J.M.W. Turner, 24 August 1840

We had both of us, but he chiefly, the strongest prejudice against the Baths of Lucca, taking them for a sort of wasp's nest of scandal and gaming, and expecting to find everything trodden flat by the Continental English; yet I wanted to see the place, because it is a place to see after all. So we came, and were so charmed by the exquisite beauty of the scenery, by the coolness of the climate and the absence of our countrymen, political troubles serving admirably our private requirements, that we made an offer for rooms on the spot. . . . The air of this place seems to penetrate the heart, and not the lungs only; it draws you, raises you, excites you. Mountain air, without its keenness, sheathed in Italian sunshine, think what *that* must be! . . . What is peculiarly beautiful and wonderful is the variety of the shapes of the mountains. They are a multitude, and yet there is no likeness. None, except where the golden mist comes and transfigures them into one glory. For the rest, the mountain there wrapt in the chestnut forest is not like that bare peak which tilts against the sky, nor like that serpent twine of another which seems to move and coil in the moving coiling shadow.

Elizabeth Barrett Browning, Letter to Miss Mitford, 1849

Bari (and Francavilla)

At Bari and Francavilla, horse-flesh is said to be publicly sold in the market; and the tail left on, to shew the wretched purchasers what beast the meat belonged to. The wits among the populace nickname these shamble horses *Caprio ferrato,* i.e. a shod deer.

Henry Swinburne, *Travels in the Two Sicilies in 1777–1780,* 1785

Bergamo

What a black, dirty, stinking, dismal place! I stared at some well dressed people I met, wondering what they had to do there; thanking my stars that I was not an inhabitant of Bergamo; foolishly enough, as if it were the brick and mortar of a place that give felicity, and not the connexion formed from infancy and matured by habit.

Arthur Young, *Travels . . . [in] . . . France* (17 October 1789), 1792

Bitonto

It is next to impossible to sketch at Bitonto, from the violence of the half-savage crowd in every lowest stage of beggary or filth.

A.J.C. Hare, *Cities of Southern Italy,* 1883

Bologna

not far from hens iz Bononi, wher students yuz to kum, but il for us and therfor termd, Sepulcrum Anglorum.
Thomas Whythorne, *Autobiography, c.* 1576

Bologna . . . is built like a ship, whereof the *Torre d'Asinello* may go for the Main-Mast.
John Evelyn, *Diary*, May 1645

You know 'tis the third city in Italy for pictures: knowing that, you know all.
Horace Walpole, Letter to Richard West, 1739–40

Those who are not pleased with the entertainment they meet with at the inns in this city, it will be a difficult matter to please; they must be possessed of a degree of such nicety, both in their palates and temper, as will render them exceedingly troublesome to themselves and others, not only in their travels through Italy, but in the whole course of their journey through life.
John Moore, *A View of Society and Manners in Italy*, 1781

*On his arrival at this town, the first object which strikes the eye of a stranger, is a noble marble fountain, in the area before the Palazzo Publico. The principal figure is a statue of Neptune, eleven feet in height; one of his hands is stretched out before him, in the other he holds the Trident. The body and limbs are finely proportioned, the anatomy perfect, the character of the countenance severe and majestic. . . . The whole is the workmanship of Giovanni di Bologna, and is highly esteemed; yet there seems to be an impropriety in making water flow in streams from the breasts of the sea nymphs, or syrens.

Over the entrance of the Legate's palace, is a bronze statue of a Pope. The tiara, and other parts of the Papal uniform, are not so favourable to the sculptor's genius, as the naked simplicity in which Neptune appears. A female traveller, however, not extravagantly fond of the fine arts, would rather be observed admiring the sculptor's skill in imitating the folds of the sacerdotal robes, than his anatomical accuracy in forming the majestic proportions of the Sea Divinity.
Ibid.

The celebrated mart of lap-dogs and sausages.
William Beckford, *Dreams, Waking Thoughts and Incidents*, 1783

The fronts of the houses are built upon arcades. . . . In a country such as Italy it may be doubted whether such a mode of building is advisable – Among a revengeful people who seek satisfaction with the stilletto – these dark arcades afford the best of opportunities at night to lie in wait and wreak their vengeance on an unsuspecting adversary.
Washington Irving, *Journal*, 24 April 1805

Bologna you know – or do not know – is celebrated for the production of Popes – Cardinals – painters – & sausages – besides a female professor of anatomy – who has left there many models of the art in waxwork – some of them not the most decent.
Lord Byron, Letter to Augusta Leigh, 4 June 1817

I have just returned from a moonlight walk through Bologna. It is a city of colonnades, and the effect of the moonlight is strikingly picturesque. There are two towers here – one 400 feet high – ugly things, built of brick, which lean both different ways; and with the delusion of moonlight shadows, you might almost fancy that the city is rocked by an earthquake.
Percy Bysshe Shelley, Letter to Thomas Love Peacock, 9 November 1818

Bologna is to the middle ages, what Pompeii has been to antiquity – a monument of the manner of their domestic existence.
Lady Morgan, *Italy*, 1820

The leaning lump of brick at Bologna . . . looks like the chimney of a steam engine blown a little out of the perpendicular.
Henry Matthews, *Diary of an Invalid*, 1820

Wordsworth . . . has been all day very uncomfortable – annoyed by the length of the streets.
Henry Crabb Robinson, *Diary*, 7 June 1837

First thing at Bologna tried Bologna sausage on the principle that at Rome you go first to St Peter's.
Herman Melville, *Journal of a Visit to Europe and the Levant*, 30 March 1857

The medieval nobles built towers just for pure swank, to see who should have the tallest, till a town like Bologna must have bristled like a porcupine in a rage, or like Pittsburgh with chimney-stacks – but square ones.
D.H. Lawrence, *Etruscan Places*, 1932

the Square of San Petronio
The square of San Petronio with its colour as if sunset were built into the walls.
Freya Stark, *Traveller's Prelude*, 1950

Una Città a misura dell'uomo.
(A city to the measure of man.)
Municipio slogan, quoted by John Ardagh, *The Tale of Five Cities*, 1979

Bolzano (formerly Bozen)

I got unwell at Botzen – Bellzebubbotzenhofe, as I called it on account of its horrid row of bells and bustle.
Edward Lear, Letter to Chichester Fortescue, 13 September 1871

Buffaloria (formerly Sybaris)

Lenormant praises the landscape hereabouts as of 'incomparable beauty'; unfortunately I saw it in a sunless day, and at unfavourable moments I was strongly reminded of the Essex coast – grey, scrubby flats, crossed by small streams, spreading wearily seaward. One had only to turn inland to correct this mood; the Calabrian mountains, even without sunshine, had their wonted grace. Moreover, cactus and agave, frequent in the foreground, preserved the southern character of the scene. This great plain between the hills and the sea grows very impressive; so silent it is, so mournfully desolate, so haunted with memories of vanished glory.

George Gissing, *By the Ionian Sea,* 1901

Calabria

A well-known Italian senator has declared that the story of south Italy is, was, and will be, the story of malaria; and the greater part of Calabria will certainly remain an enigma to the traveller who ignores what is meant by this plague.

Malaria is the key to the correct understanding of the landscape; it explains the inhabitants, their mode of life, their habits, their history.

Norman Douglas, *Old Calabria,* 1915

Calabria is not a land to traverse alone. It is too wistful and stricken; too deficient in those externals that conduce to comfort. Its charms do not appeal to the eye of romance, and the man who would perambulate Magna Graecia as he does the Alps would soon regret his choice. . . . The joys of Calabria are not to be bought, like those of Switzerland for gold.

Ibid.

One of the charms of a journey through Calabria is that it sets in continual antithesis the coast and the mountain.

Walter Starkie, *The Waveless Plain,* 1938

The Campagna di Roma

An undulating flat . . . where few people can live; and where for miles and miles there is nothing to relieve the terrible monotony and gloom. Of all kinds of country that could, by possibility, lie outside the gates of Rome, this is the aptest and fittest burial-ground for the Dead City. So sad, so quiet, so sullen; so secret in its covering up of great masses of ruin, and hiding them; so like the waste places into which men possessed with devils used to go and howl, and rend themselves, in the old days of Jerusalem.

Charles Dickens, *Pictures from Italy,* 1846

Campania

Here the beautie of all the World is gathered as it were into a bundle.

Fynes Moryson, *An Itinerary,* 1617

Campania . . . has been described as Eden which produces poverty.

Peter Nichols, *Italia, Italia,* 1973

Capri

This isle reunites such a variety of beauties and advantages that it is a matter of wonder to me, why so few of our mysanthropic countrymen resort to it; a man of an indolent philosophical cast would here be suited with a scene for meditation and solitary enjoyments; the temperature of the air and the excellence of the fruits would secure his health; and the delightful scenery round him would dispel his cares, and give an even cheerful flow to his spirits.

Henry Swinburne, *Travels in the Two Sicilies in 1777–1780,* 1785

I am very sick of Capri: it is a stewpot of semi-literary cats.

D.H. Lawrence, Letter to Catherine Carswell, Capri, 5 February 1920

The place is full of fairies.

F. Scott Fitzgerald, Letter to Maxwell Perkins, Capri, 31 March 1925

I am quite drunk. I am told that this is Capri; though as I remember Capri was quieter.

F. Scott Fitzgerald, Letter to John Peale Bishop, Capri, March 1925

Capri is not the place for moralizing.

Norman Douglas, *Footnote on Capri,* 1952

At this moment Capri is in danger of developing into a second Hollywood, and that, it seems, is precisely what it aspires to become.

Ibid.

Capri out of season is not only quiet but moribund. There is nowhere to go, no one to see, nowhere to eat except for two crummy restaurants . . . in fact the whole thing is a bugger. . . . Capri in inverno non me piace e sono troppo stanco of not being comfortable.

Noel Coward, Letter, quoted in Cole Lesley, *Life of Noel Coward,* 1976

The Piazza will never cease to be a surprising edifice, four-sided, miniature, smoothly paved like the floor of a stage and no bigger than a stage: that baroque church takes most of one side, the rose and green colour-washes and cafe blinds filling the others, and in the lamplight all of it as chalky and cheeseclothy as floodlit scenery. There are other stage-sets – the Place de la Contrescarpe in Paris and the Plaza in little Andorra – but none so perfectly miniature, so prettily perfect as this life-size Caprese fabrication. No one can enter and cross it without an appearance of entrance and exit. And in any case the walk-ons and bit players of a Capri night, all dressed up in island summer-wear, are theatrical in themselves.

William Sansom, *Blue Skies, Brown Studies,* 1961

The Blue Grotto
*Passion was stilled here; love was silenced; the chastened solemnity, the purity of its mysterious divinity had no affinity with the fevered dreams and sensuous sweetness of mortal desires. . . . The boat paused in the midst of the still violet lake-like water. Where he lay at her feet he looked upwards at her through the ethereal light that floated round them, and seemed to sever them from earth. . . . Would to God I could die now!

Ouida, *Idalia,* 1867

Capua

This City is newly built, but if you goe out of the Gates to St Maries Church towards Naples upon the South-West side of the Towne, there you shall see a Colossus, and a Cave, and many Monuments of old Capua among the Orchards: the delicacies of which Citie were of old so famous, as we reade, that the Army of Hanibal grew effeminate thereby.

Fynes Moryson, *An Itinerary,* 1617

Rose at 6; & standing at the door of a Macaroni-shop saw it in every stage of the process. Every shop being lighted by the door, all are laid open as by the Diable Boitu. First came a lawyer's, a man in a broad hat & black habit among many writings in close conversation, with him. – Then a lottery office numbers crouding to hear their fate, a country-man coming out with a handful of copper-money, & joy in his eyes – then a cook-shop, fish & sallad displayed, & a little officer at breakfast with a silver fork – then the macaroni shop, where it was selling by the weight, then the next, where it was making, & hanging from the ceiling, like sheets in a printer's warehouse, then a coffee-house where two men muffled in their cloaks were drinking off rapidly their coffee, all this in the little town of Capua.

Samuel Rogers, *Italian Journal,* 19 March 1815

At Capua . . . we found none of those seducing luxuries, which enervated the soldiers of Hannibal.

Henry Matthews, *Diary of an Invalid,* 1820

Carrara

This Towne . . . is famous for the marble, which is much preferred before other, as well for the exceeding whiteness of some stones, as for the length of pillars and tables digged thence. . . . When I beheld the beauty of Men and Weomen in these parts, which seemed to me greater than in any other part of Italy, I remembered the Patriark Jacob, who laid party coloured rods in the watering troughes, when the Ewes were in heat, to make them bring party coloured lambs: and I thought by the same reason and force of nature, that they who digged these white marbles, might have a more beautifull race.

Fynes Moryson, *An Itinerary,* 1617

Tell that fat fellow Chantrey that I did think of him, *then* (but not for the first nor the last time) of the thousands he had made out of those marble craigs which only afforded me a sour bottle of wine and a sketch; but he deserves everything which is good, though he did give me a fit of the spleen at Carrara.

J.M.W. Turner, Letter to George Jones, 13 October 1828

Catania

The bishop's revenues are considerable, and arise principally from the sale of snow, the snow on mount Ætna. One small portion of which, lying on the north of the mountain, is said to bring him in upwards of 1000.*l.* a year; for Ætna furnishes snow and ice, not only to the whole island of Sicily, but likewise to Malta, and a great part of Italy, and makes a very considerable branch of commerce; for even the peasants in these hot countries regale themselves with ices during the summer heats; and there is no entertainment given by the nobility, of which these do not always make a principal part: a famine of snow, they themselves say, would be more grievous, than a famine of either corn or wine. It is a common observation amongst them, that without the snows of mount Ætna, their island could not be inhabited; so essential has this article of luxury become to them.

Patrick Brydone, *A Tour through Sicily and Malta,* 1773

The immediate environs of the town are extremely pleasant, but notwithstanding the lively appearance of the fruit-trees in blossom, which made the country look as if it were powdered, the number and extent of the beds of lava are so great, that I soon found the landscape excessively gloomy and disagreeable.

Henry Swinburne, *Travels in the Two Sicilies in 1777–1780,* 1785

The cathedral . . . is dedicated to St Agatha the Saint

who has Catania under her peculiar protection. . . . I was mentioning to a Sicilian servant at the Inn my opinion that St Agatha was rather careless of her charge when in 1693 she suffered a torrent of Lava to overwhelm the largest and finest part of Catania. He shook his head and said the saint was not to blame. The people of Catania had been very wicked and inattentive to their devotions when St Agatha determined to give them a lesson she therefor permitted the Lava to run over *a part* of Catania, that the other part might see from what miseries she had preserved them and take warning accordingly.

Washington Irving, *Journal*, 12 February 1805

Catanzaro (and Marina di Catanzaro)

The sun was setting when I alighted at the Marina, and as I waited for the branch train my eyes feasted upon a glory of colour which made me forget aching weariness. All around lay orchards of orange trees, the finest I had ever seen, and over their solid masses of dark foliage, thick hung with ripening fruit, poured the splendour of the western sky. It was a picture unsurpassable in richness of tone; the dense leafage of deepest, warmest green glowed and flashed, its magnificence heightened by the blaze of the countless golden spheres adorning it. Beyond, the magic sea, purple and crimson as the sun descended upon the vanishing horizon. Eastward, above the slopes of Sila, stood a moon almost at its full, the yellow of an autumn leaf, on a sky soft-flushed with rose.

In my geography it is written that between Catanzaro and the sea lie the gardens of the Hesperides.

George Gissing, *By the Ionian Sea*, 1901

One of the citizens in describing the past, said to me: 'In those days it was *la città dei tre V – Venti, Velluti, e nostro protettore, San Vitaliano'* (the city of the three V's – wind, velvet, and our patron-saint, Vitaliano).

Walter Starkie, *The Waveless Plain*, 1938

Chaos

We saw to our left a small cottage perched on a headland with two wind-bent pines outside it – the whole hanging there over the sea, as if outside the whole of the rest of nature. There was no other sign of human habitation, save this desolate and memorable little cottage. With the black sunlight, it looked deeply, tragically significant, as if it were the backdrop for a play. Hardly anybody paid attention to the scene, but Roberto, with an air of sadness, announced over the speaker: 'The birthplace of Pirandello. A little hamlet called Chaos!'

Lawrence Durrell, *Sicilian Carousel*, 1977

Civitâ Vecchia

This Civita Vecchia is the finest nest of dirt, vermin, and ignorance we have found yet, except that African perdition they call Tangier, which is just like it. The people here live in alleys two yards wide which have a smell about them which is peculiar, but not entertaining. It is well the alleys are not wider, because they hold as much smell now as a person can stand, and of course, if they were wider they would hold more, and then the people would die. These alleys are paved with stone, and carpeted with deceased cats, and decayed rags, and decomposed vegetable-tops, and remnants of old boots, all soaked with dish-water, and the people sit around on stools and enjoy it. . . . This is the first Italian town I have seen which does not appear to have a patron saint. I suppose no saint but the one that went up in the chariot of fire could stand the climate.

Mark Twain, *The Innocents Abroad*, 1869

between Civitâ Vecchia and Rome
I cannot fancy what these people think as to honesty or whether they have a dispensation from the Pope to rob Travellers?

John Webster, *Notes of a Journey from London to Constantinople . . .*, 1836

Como

More pleased, my foot the hidden margin roves
Of Como, bosomed deep in chestnut groves.

William Wordsworth, *Descriptive Sketches*, 1791–2, pub. 1793

And Como! thou, a treasure whom the earth
Keeps to herself, confined as in a depth
Of Abyssinian privacy. I spake of thee
Of thee, thy chestnut woods, and garden plots
Of Indian corn tended by dark-eyed maids;
Thy lofty steeps, and pathways roofed with vines,
Winding from house to house, from town to town,
Sole link that binds them to each other; walks,
League after league, and cloistral avenues,
Where silence dwells if music be not there: . . .
ye have left
Your beauty with me, a serene accord
Of forms and colours, passive, yet endowed
In their submissiveness with power as sweet
And gracious almost, might I dare to say,
As virtue is, or goodness; sweet as love.

William Wordsworth, *The Prelude*, 1805 (text of 1850)

This lake exceeds any thing I ever beheld in beauty, with the exception of the arbutus islands of Killarney. It is long and narrow, and has the appearance of a mighty river, winding among the mountains and the forests. . . .

This shore of the lake is one continued village, and the Milanese nobility have their villas here. The union of culture and the untameable profusion and loveliness of nature is here so close, that the line where they are divided can hardly be discovered.

Percy Bysshe Shelley, Letter to Thomas Love Peacock, 20 April 1818

This Eden of Lombardy.

Lady Morgan, *Italy,* 1820

The defect of the Lake of Como is, that it is out-built, and that whatever is false in taste or grotesque in selection, is to be found, choaking up spots of the most exquisite natural beauty, and disfiguring buildings of the handsomest architecture. Upon the heights which overhang the Garuo, or Villa d'este, stands the city of Saragossa (I believe), executed in cut and painted deal, and erected by a former proprietor in honor of the triumphs of the Army of Italy; although, seen from the Lake, it is readily mistaken for a baby-house.

Ibid.

The day has been spent on the lake, and so much exquisite pleasure I never had on water. The tour or rather excursion we have been making surpasses certainly all I have ever seen, and Wordsworth asserts the same. . . . But the pleasure can hardly be recorded, it consisting in the contemplation of scenes absolutely indescribable by words, and in sensations for which no words have ever been invented.

Henry Crabb Robinson, *Diary,* 29 August 1820

Como dry must be interesting enough; Como flooded is a marvel. What else is Venice? And here is a Venice at the foot of high mountains, and *all* in the water, no streets or squares; a fine even depth of three feet and a half or so for navigators.

Hilaire Belloc, *The Path to Rome,* 1902

Cosenza

. . . if one can disregard the evil smells which everywhere catch one's breath – Cosenza has wonders and delights which tempt to day-long rambling. To call the town picturesque is to use an inadequate word; at every step, from the opening of the main street at the hill-foot up to the stern mediaeval castle crowning its height, one marvels and admires. So narrow are the ways that a cart drives the pedestrian into shop or alley; two vehicles (but perhaps the thing never happened) would with difficulty pass each other. As in all towns of Southern Italy, the number of hair-dressers is astonishing, and they hang out the barber's basin – the very basin (of shining brass and with a semicircle cut out of the rim) which the Knight of La Mancha took as substitute for his damaged helmet.

George Gissing, *By the Ionian Sea,* 1901

Cotrone

The common type of face at Cotrone is coarse and bumpkinish; ruder, it seemed to me, than faces seen at any point of my journey hitherto. A photographer had hung out a lot of portraits, and it was a hideous exhibition; some of the visages attained an incredible degree of vulgar ugliness. This in the town which still bears the name of Croton. The people are all more or less unhealthy; one meets peasants horribly disfigured with life-long malaria. There is an agreeable cordiality in the middle classes; business men from whom I sought casual information, even if we only exchanged a few words in the street, shook hands with me at parting. I found no one who had much good to say of his native place.

Ibid.

I was surprised to discover as sunny and smiling a town as I had seen in South Italy. I . . . came to the conclusion that Gissing's mind was prejudiced against the place because he had been stricken down there by malaria.

Walter Starkie, *The Waveless Plain,* 1938

Cremona

The town is thinly peopled; but exquisitely clean, perhaps for that very reason.

Hester Lynch Thrale/Piozzi, *Observations . . . in the Course of a Journey,* 1789

Dolomites

The Dolomites . . . recall quaint Eastern architecture, whose daring pinnacles derive their charm from a studied defiance of the sober principles of stability. The Chamonix aiguilles, as I have said, inevitably remind one of Gothic cathedrals; but in their most daring moments they appear to be massive, immovable, and eternal. The Dolomites are strange adventurous experiments, which one can scarcely believe to be formed of ordinary rock. They would have been fit background for the garden of Kubla Khan.

Leslie Stephen, *The Playground of Europe,* 1871

In a letter . . . I describe the Dolomites as 'finicky', which seems a peculiar adjective . . . but there is a lot of detail about them which makes them look, beside the Alps, as a Japanese garden might look beside the old trees of an English park. To me, the great and simple lines of the granite are ever the most satisfying: yet the Dolomites have a domestic loveliness; old age can walk about in their meadows, where no distance is too unmanageable. . . . few countries in the world look more happy or more beautiful.

Freya Stark, *The Coasts of Incense,* 1953

Elba

Lucky Napoleon!

Dylan Thomas, Letter to Bill and Helen McAlpine, 26 July 1947

The heat! Old Elbanites on their flayed and blistered backs whimper about the heat. Sunblack webfooted waterboys, diving from cranes, bleed from the heat. Old scorched mineral-miners, fifty years in the fire, snarl at the heat as they drag the rusty trolleys naked over the skeleton piers. . . . Oh, oh, oh, the heat! It comes round corners at you like an animal with windmill arms.

Dylan Thomas, Letter to Margaret Taylor, 3 August 1947

Mount Etna

To conclude of Aetna, the gross Papists hold it to be their purgatory.

William Lithgow, *Rare Adventures and Painfull Peregrinations,* 1614/32

the shatter'd side
Of thundering *Aetna,* whose combustible
And fewel'd entrals thence conceiving Fire,
Sublim'd with Mineral fury, aid the Winds
And leave a singed bottom all involv'd
With stench and smoak. . . .

John Milton, *Paradise Lost,* 1667

Aetna and all the burning Mountains find
Their kindled Stores with inbred Storms of Wind
Blown up to Rage, and roaring out complain
As torn with inward Gripes and torturing Pain.
Lab'ring they cast their dreadful Vomit round,
And with their melted Bowels spread the Ground;
Down their scorcht Sides destructive Torrents flow,
And form a Red Metallick Sea below.
And while the Deluge in its lawless Course
Frightful advances with resistless Force,
Fragments of Rocks, Trees, once the Mountain's Pride,
And Heaps of Oar roll down th'incumber'd Tyde:
Till in the Main it disembogues its Waves,
Outroars the Deep, and fills its hollow Caves.

Sir Richard Blackmore, *Prince Arthur,* 4th edn, revised 1714

Many parts of this region are surely the most heavenly spots upon earth; and if Aetna resembles hell within, it may with equal justice be said to resemble paradise without. It is indeed a curious consideration, that this mountain should reunite every beauty and every horrour; and, in short, all the most opposite and dissimilar objects in nature.

Patrick Brydone, *A Tour through Sicily and Malta,* 1773

The most beautiful part of the scene is certainly the mountain itself; the island of Sicily, and the numerous islands lying round it. All these, by a kind of magic in vision, that I am at a loss to account for, seem as if they were brought close round the skirts of Ætna; the distances appearing reduced to nothing.

Ibid.

Alone! –
On this charr'd, blacken'd melancholy waste,
Crown'd by the awful peak, Etna's great mouth.

Matthew Arnold, *Empedocles on Etna,* 1852

from the air
It looked like a toy – but a rather dangerous one.

Lawrence Durrell, *Sicilian Carousel,* 1977

Etna . . . spat out a mouthful of hot coals, and then dribbled a small string of blazing diamonds down her chin.

Ibid.

Ferrara

Tis in a word a durty Towne, & though the Streetes be large they remaine illpav'd.

John Evelyn, *Diary,* May 1645

The Soil is abandoned and uncultivated, nor were there hands enough so much as to mow their Grass, which we saw withering in their Meadows, to our no small Wonder. We were amazed to see so rich a Soil thus forsaken of its Inhabitants; and much more when we passed through that vast Town, which, by its Extent, shews what it was about an Age ago, and is now so much deserted, that there are whole Sides of Streets without Inhabitants; and the Poverty of the Place appears signally in the Churches, which are mean, and poorly adorned: for the Superstition of Italy is so ravenous, and makes such a Progress in this Age, that one may justly take the Measures of the Wealth of any Place from the Churches. . . . But to return to *Ferrara:* I could not but ask all I saw, how it came, that so rich a Soil was so strangely abandoned? Some said, the Air was become so unhealthy, that those who stay in it were very short-lived: But it is well known, that fourscore years ago it was well peopled, and the ill Air is occasioned by the want of Inhabitants; for there not being People to drain the Ground, and to keep the Ditches clean, this makes that there is a great deal of Water that lies on the Ground and rots, which infects the Air in the same Manner, as is observed in that vast and rich, but uninhabited Champaign of *Rome*. So that the ill Air is the Effect, rather than the Cause, of the dispeopling of the Pope's Dominions. The true Cause is the Severity of the Government, and the heavy Taxes and frequent Confiscations.

Gilbert Burnet, *Some Letters Containing an Account of what seemed Remarkable in Travelling . . .*, 1687

My pen was just upon the point of praising its cleanliness . . . till I reflected there was nobody to dirty it.

Hester Lynch Piozzi, *Observations . . . in the Course of a Journey*, 1789

Of all the places I have seen in Italy, it is the one by far I should most covet to live in. It is the *ideal* of an Italian city, once great, now a shadow of itself. Whichever way you turn, you are struck with picturesque beauty and faded splendours, but with nothing squalid, mean, or vulgar. The grass grows in the well-paved streets. You look down long avenues of buildings, or of garden walls, with summer-houses or fruit-trees projecting over them, and airy palaces with dark portraits gleaming through the grated windows – you turn, and a chapel bounds your view one way, a broken arch another, at the end of the vacant, glimmering, fairy perspective. You are in a dream, in the heart of a romance; you enjoy the most perfect solitude, that of a city which was once filled with 'the busy hum of men,' and of which the tremulous fragments at every step strike the sense, and call up reflection. In short, nothing is to be seen of Ferrara, but the remains, graceful and romantic, of what it was – no sordid object intercepts or sullies the retrospect of the past.

William Hazlitt, *Notes of a Journey through France and Italy*, 1826

More solitary, more depopulated, more deserted, old Ferrara than any city of the solemn brotherhood! The grass so grows up in the silent streets, that any one might make hay there, literally, while the sun shines. But the sun shines with diminished cheerfulness in grim Ferrara; and the people are so few who pass and repass through the places, that the flesh of the inhabitants might be grass indeed, and growing in the squares.

Charles Dickens, *Pictures from Italy*, 1846

Florence

Ma quell'ingrato popolo maligno,
  che discese di Fiesole ab antico
  e tiene ancor del monte e del macigno . . . ,
Vecchia fama nel mondo li chiama orbi,
  gente avara, invidiosa e superba:
  da' lor costumi fa che tu ti forbi.

(But that ungrateful, malignant people, who of old came down from Fiesole, and still savours of the mountain and the rock, . . . Old report on earth proclaims them blind, a people avaricious, envious and proud: Look that you cleanse yourself of their customs.)

Dante, *Inferno*, Canto xv, *c.* 1300

Of the Florentines, though most courteous, yet sparing, other Italians jeast, saying, that when they meete a man about dinner time, they aske Vos' Signoria ha desinato, Sir, have you dined? and if he answer, I, they replie, as if they would have invited him to dinner: but if he answere no, they reply Andate Signor, ch' e otta, Goe Sir, for it is high time to dine. They thinke it best to cherish and increase friendship by metings in Market places and Gardens, but hold the table and bed unfit for conversation, where men should come to eate quickly, and sleepe soundly.

Fynes Moryson, *An Itinerary*, 1617

A City so beautiful that the great Emperor Charles V. said, *That she was fitting to be shown and seen only upon Holidays*.

James Howell, 'Letter to Sir J.C., from Florence, 1 November 1621', *Familiar Letters*, 1645

Here is the prime Dialect of the *Italian* spoken, tho' the Pronuncuation be a little more guttural than that of *Sienna*, and that of the Court of *Rome*, which occasions the Proverb:

Lingua Toscana in bocca Romana.
The Tuscan Tongue sounds best in a Roman Mouth.

The people here generally seem to be more generous and of a higher comportment than elsewhere, very cautious and circumspect in the Negotiation; whence ariseth the Proverb:

Chi ha da far con Tosco
Non bisogna che sia Losco.
Who dealeth with a Florentine,
Must have the use of both his Ey'n.

Ibid.

As, by the absence of the great duke, Florence is become in a manner a country town I believe there never were a set of people so peaceable, and such strangers to scandal. 'Tis the family of love, where everybody is paired, and go as constantly together as parroquets. Here nobody hangs or drowns themselves; they are not ready to cut one another's throats about elections or parties; don't think that wit consists in saying bold truths, or humour in getting drunk. But I shall give you no more of their characters, because I am so unfortunate as to think that their encomium consists in being the reverse of the English, who in general are either mad, or enough to make other people so.

Horace Walpole, Letter to the Hon. H.S. Conway, 25 September 1740

The diversions of a Florentine Lent are composed of a sermon in the morning, full of hell and the devil; a dinner at noon, full of fish and meager diet; and, in the evening, what is called a Conversazione, a sort of assembly at the principal people's houses, full of I cannot tell what.

Thomas Gray, Letter to Mrs Gray, his mother, 19 March 1740

Yesterday, with violent rains, there came flouncing down from the mountains such a flood, that it floated the whole city. The jewellers on the Old Bridge removed their commodities, and in two hours after the bridge was cracked. The torrent broke down the quays, and drowned several coach horses, which are kept here in stables underground. We were moated into our house all day, which is near the Arno, and had the miserable spectacles of the ruins that were washed along with the hurricane. There was a cart with two oxen not quite dead, and four men in it drowned: but what was ridiculous, there came tiding along a fat hay-cock, with a hen and her eggs, and a cat.

Horace Walpole, Letter to Richard West, November 1740

I am astonish'd at the profusion of fine things We meet with in Every part of this City, & at the poverty of the inhabitants; they are a new Set of beings to Me, & quite a new Study.

David Garrick, Letter to the Duke of Devonshire, 30 November 1763

We had need of inspiration, I think, since nothing else would have tempted us over such dreary, uninteresting hillocks as rise from the banks of the Arno. The hoary olive is their principal vegetation; so that Nature, in this country, seems in a withering decrepit state, and may not unaptly be compared to 'an old woman clothed in grey.'

William Beckford, *Dreams Waking Thoughts and Incidents,* 1783

Merciful powers! what a set harbour within its walls!

Ibid.

The circumstance that strikes one at Florence, is the antiquity of the principal buildings; every thing one sees considerable, is of three or four hundred years standing: of new buildings there are next to none; all here remind one of the Medicis: there is hardly a street that has not some monument, some decoration, that bears the stamp of that splended and magnificent family. How commerce could enrich it sufficiently to leave such prodigious remains, is a question not a little curious; for I may venture, without apprehension, to assert, that all the collected magnificence of the House of Bourbon, governing for eight hundred years twenty millions of people, is trivial, when compared with what the Medicis family have left, for the admiration of succeeding ages, sovereigns only of the little mountainous region of Tuscany, and with not more than a million of subjects.

Arthur Young, *Travels . . . [in] . . . France* (1 December 1789), 1792

But Arno wins us to the fair white walls,
Where the Etrurian Athens claims and keeps
A softer feeling for her fairy halls:
Girt by her theatre of hills, she reaps
Her corn, and wine, and oil – and Plenty leaps
To laughing life, with her redundant Horn.
Along the banks where smiling Arno sweeps
Was modern Luxury of Commerce born,
And buried Learning rose, redeemed to a new Morn.

Lord Byron, *Childe Harold's Pilgrimage,* Canto the Fourth, 1818

Of all the fairest Cities of the Earth
None is so fair as Florence. 'Tis a gem
Of purest ray; and what a light broke forth,
When it emerged from darkness! Search within
Without; all is enchantment! 'Tis the Past
Contending with the Present; and in turn
Each has the mastery.

Samuel Rogers, *Italy,* 1822–34

Many of the narrower streets are like lofty paved courts, cut through a solid quarry of stone. . . . Florence is like a town that has survived itself. It is distinguished by the remains of early and rude grandeur; it is left where it was three hundred years ago. Its history does not seem brought down to the present period.

William Hazlitt, *Notes of a Journey through France and Italy,* 1826

There is no such thing as justly describing the fine things that we have seen today. . . . Art has here brought fiction so near upon the verge of reality, that the line between them is too nice to be drawn by words.

J.P. Cobbett, *Journal of a Tour in Italy,* 1830

In Florence itself the common people are well to do. They are, perhaps, the least agreeable people to deal with in Italy; self-opinionated, independent, and lazy, they can often scarcely be brought to work at all; and, when they do, it is in their own way, and at their own time. They love their ease, and they enjoy it: they are full of humour and intelligence, though their conceit often acts as a drawback on the latter.

Mary Shelley, *Rambles in Germany and Italy,* 1844

and Pisa

I leave with unreverted eye the towers
  Of Pisa pining o'er her desert stream.
Pleasure (they say) yet lingers in thy bowers
  Florence, thou patriot's sigh, thou poet's dream!
O could I find thee as thou once wert known
  Thoughtful and lofty, liberal and free!
But the pure spirit from thy wreck hath flown,
  And only Pleasure's phantom dwells with thee.

W.S. Landor, *Collection of 1846,* no. CCI

Magnificently stern and sombre are the streets of beautiful Florence; and the strong old piles of building make such heaps of shadow, on the ground and in the river, that there is another and different city of rich forms and fancies, always lying at our feet.

Charles Dickens, *Pictures from Italy,* 1846

Brute-force shall not rule Florence! Intellect
May rule her, bad or good, as chance supplies, –
But intellect it shall be!

Robert Browning, *Luria,* 1846

Florence is beautiful, as I have said before, and must say again and again, most beautiful. The river rushes through the midst of its palaces like a crystal arrow, and it is hard to tell, when you see all by the clear sunset, whether those churches, and houses, and windows, and bridges, and people walking, in the water or out of the water, are the real walls and windows, and bridges, and people, and churches.

Elizabeth Barrett Browning, Letter to Mr Boyd, 1847

Of course it *is* very dead in comparison [with Paris] but it's a beautiful death, and what with the lovely climate, and the lovely associations, and the sense of repose, I could turn myself on my pillow, and sleep on here till the end of my life; only be sure that *I shall do no such thing*.

Elizabeth Barrett Browning, Letter, 1852

It was for this country I was predestined, for I found everything just as I expected.

Matthew Arnold, Letter to his wife, 23 May 1865

and the Arno

It is popular to admire the Arno. It is a great historical creek with four feet in the channel and some scows floating around. It would be a very plausible river if they could pump some water into it. They all call it a river, and they honestly think it *is* a river do these dark and bloody Florentines. They even help out the delusion by building bridges over it. I do not see why they are too good to wade.

Mark Twain, *The Innocents Abroad,* 1869

Everything about Florence seems to be coloured with a mild violet, like diluted wine.

Henry James, Letter to Henry James Sr, 26 October 1869

She sat in the sunshine beside her yellow river like the little treasure-city that she has always seemed, without commerce, without other industry than the manufacture of mosaic paper-weights and alabaster Cupids, without actuality, or energy, or earnestness, or any of those rugged virtues which in most cases are deemed indispensable for civic robustness; with nothing but the little unaugmented stock of her mediaeval memories, her tender-coloured mountains, her churches and palaces, pictures and statues.

Henry James, 'Italy Revisited,' 1877, in *Portraits of Places,* 1883

At Florence, then, this time, the Newgate-like palaces were rightly hateful to me; the old shop and market-streets rightly pleasant; the inside of the Duomo a horror, the outside a Chinese puzzle. All sacred art, – frescoes, tempera, what not, mere zero, as they were to the Italians themselves; the country round, dead wall and dusty olive; the whole, a provocation and weariness, except for one master, M. Angelo.

John Ruskin, *Praeterita,* 1885–9

In the distant plain lay Florence, pink and gray and brown, with the rusty huge dome of the cathedral dominating its center like a captive balloon, and flanked on the right by the smaller bulb of the Medici chapel and on the left by the airy tower of the Palazzo Vecchio; all around the horizon was a billowy rim of lofty blue hills, snowed white with innumerable villas. After nine months of familiarity with this panorama, I still think, as I thought in the beginning, that this is the fairest picture on our planet, the most enchanting to look upon, the most satisfying to the eye and the spirit. To see the sun sink down, drowned in his pink and purple and golden floods, and overwhelm Florence with tides of color that make all the sharp lines dim and faint and turn the solid city to a city of dreams, is a sight to stir the coldest nature, and make a sympathetic one drunk with ecstasy.

Mark Twain, *Autobiography* (1892), 1924

Florence is the home of those who cultivate with an equal ardour Mah-jongg and a passion for Fra Angelico. Over tea and crumpets they talk, if they are too old for love themselves, of their lascivious juniors; but they also make sketches in water colour and read the Little Flowers of St Francis.

Aldous Huxley, *Along the Road,* 1925

When I first went to Florence, I had only a confused impression that this Italian city was full of English ladies; and that they were all Theosophists.

G.K. Chesterton, *Autobiography,* 1937

Firenze the most damned of Italian cities, wherein is place neither to sit, stand, nor walk. . . . Truly this town cast out its greatest writer, and a curse of discomfort has descended and lasted six hundred years.

Ezra Pound, *Guide to Kulchur,* 1938

It still has sparks of the old Renaissance genius but no longer the material around them to burst into flames.

Peter Nichols, *Italia, Italia,* 1973

Districts and details

Mosciano/Scandicci, near Florence
I am awfully sick of it here, on the beautiful hills above Florence, drinking chianti in our marble shanty, sick of vini and contadini and bambini, and sicker still when I go, bumbly with mosquito bites, to Florence itself, which is a gruelling museum.

Dylan Thomas, Letter to T.W. Earp, 11 July 1947

Michelangelo's David
The David is as if a large mass of solid marble fell upon one's head, to crush one's faith in great names. It looks like an awkward overgrown actor at one of our minor theatres, without his clothes: the head is too big for the body, and it has a helpless expression of distress.

William Hazlitt, *Notes of a Journey through France and Italy,* 1826

Michelangelo's David is the presiding genius of Florence. Not a shadow of doubt about it. Once and for all, Florence. So young: sixteen, they say. So big: and stark naked. Revealed. Too big, too naked, too exposed. Livid, under today's sky. The Florentine! The Tuscan pose – half self-conscious all the time. Adolescent. Waiting. The tense look. No escape. The Lily. Lily or iris, what does it matter? Whitman's Calamus, too.

D.H. Lawrence, 'David', *Phoenix,* 1936

Giotto's Tower

Giotto's tower,
The lily of Florence blossoming in stone.

Henry Wadsworth Longfellow, 'Giotto's Tower', *Sonnets,* 1866

The Duomo
In my way home, I looked into the cathedral, an enormous fabric, inlaid with the richest marbles, and covered with stars and chequered work, like an old-fashioned cabinet. The architect seems to have turned his building inside out; nothing in art being more ornamented than the exterior, and few churches so simple within.

William Beckford, *Dreams Waking Thoughts and Incidents,* 1783

Under the shadow of a stately Pile,
The dome of Florence, pensive and alone,
Nor giving heed to aught that passed the while,
I stood, and gazed upon a marble stone,
The laurelled Dante's favourite seat. A throne,
In just esteem, it rivals; though no style
Be there of decoration to beguile
The mind, depressed by thought of greatness flown.
As a true man, who long had served the lyre,
I gazed with earnestness, and dared no more.
But in his breast the mighty Poet bore
A Patriot's heart, warm with undying fire.
Bold with the thought, in reverence I sate down
And, for a moment, filled that empty throne.

William Wordsworth, *Memorials of a Tour in Italy, 1837,* 1840–1, pub. 1842

At Pisa we say, 'How Beautiful!' here we say nothing; it is enough if we can breathe. The mountainous marble masses overcome us as we look up – we feel the weight of them on the soul.

Elizabeth Barrett Browning, Letter to Mr Boyd, 1847

Florence is the most enchanting place I know in the world. . . . The Cathedral outside (not inside) is to my feeling the most beautiful church in the world, and it always looks to me like a hen gathering its chickens under its wings, it stands in such a soft, lovely way, with Florence round it.

Matthew Arnold, Letter to his sister, 13 October 1879

The Ponte-Vecchio

Taddeo Gaddi built me. I am old;
  Five centuries old. I plant my foot of stone
  Upon the Arno, as St. Michael's own
  Was planted on the dragon. Fold by fold
Beneath me as it struggles, I behold
  Its glistening scales. Twice hath it overthrown
  My kindred and companions. Me alone
  It moveth not, but is by me controlled.
I can remember when the Medici
  Were driven from Florence; longer still ago
  The final wars of Ghibelline and Guelf.
Florence adorns me with her jewelry;
  And when I think that Michael Angelo
  Hath leaned on me, I glory in myself.

Henry Wadsworth Longfellow, *The Old Bridge at Florence,* 1874

Uffizi Palace
'It's as bad as too much pain: it gets to be pain at last.' Heard this broken latter part of sentence from wearied lady coming from Uffizi Palace. – She was talking no doubt about excess of pleasure in these galleries.

Herman Melville, *Journal of a Visit to Europe and the Levant,* 24 March 1857

Fondi

Take note of Fondi, in the name of all that is wretched and beggarly. . . . How the gaunt dogs that sneak about the miserable streets, come to be alive, and undevoured by the people, is one of the enigmas of the world.

Charles Dickens, *Pictures from Italy*, 1846

Frascati

Frascati, as one turns in and out of its streets, opening suddenly on vague glimpses, as if cut by the sides of a frame, is like a seaside village; and one cannot help imagining the wash of waves, instead of the grassy plain of the Campagna, at the end of those coiling streets.

Arthur Symons, *Cities*, 1903

Genoa

It is proverbially said of this City; Montagne senza legni, Mar senza pesci, huomini senza fede, donne senza vergogna, Mori bianchi, Genoa superba: That is, Mountaines without wood, Sea without fish, Men without faith, Weomen without shame, white Moores, Genoa the proud.

Fynes Moryson, *An Itinerary*, 1617

The proudest for Buildings of any I met withal; yet the People go the plainest of any other, and are also most parsimonious in their Diet: they are the subtillest, I will not say the most subdolous Dealers: they are wonderful wealthy, specially in Money. . . .

In the time of Louis XI of France . . . when she would have given herself up to him for Protection, K. *Lewis* being told that *Genoa* was content to be his, he answer'd, *She should not be his long, for he would give her up to the Devil, and rid his hands of her.*

Indeed the Genowaies have not the Fortune to be so well belov'd as other People in *Italy;* which proceeds, I believe, from their Cunningness and Overreachings in bargaining, wherein they have something of the Jew.

James Howell, 'Letter to Sir J.C., from Florence, 1 November 1621', *Familiar Letters*, 1645

The Citty is built in the hollow or bossome of a Mountaine, whose ascent is very steepe, high & rocky; so as from the Lanterne, & Mole, to the hill it represents the Shape of a Theater; the Streetes & buildings so ranged one above the other; as our seates are in Playhouses: but by reason of their incomparable materials, beauty and structure: never was any artificial sceane more beautifull to the eye of the beholder; nor is any place certainely in the World, so full for the bignesse of well designed and stately Palaces; . . . indeeds this beautifull Citty is more stayn'd with such horrid acts of revenge and murthers, than any one place in Europ, or haply the World besides where there is a political government; which renders it very unsafe to strangers: This makes it a gally matter to carry a knife about one whose poynt is not broken off.

John Evelyn, *Diary*, 17 October 1644

I never beheld any thing more amiable. Only figure to yourself a vast semicircular bason, full of fine blue sea, and vessels of all sorts and sizes, some sailing out, some coming in, and others at anchor; and all round it palaces and churches, peeping over one another's heads, gardens and marble terrases full of orange and cypress trees, fountains, and trellisworks covered with vines, which altogether compose the grandest of theatres. This is the first coup d'oeil.

Thomas Gray, Letter to Richard West, 21 November 1739

It has the face of business.

Tobias Smollett, *Travels through France and Italy*, 1766

It is not without reason that Genoa is called *La superba*. The city itself is very stately; and the nobles are very proud. Some few of them may be proud of their wealth: but, in general, their fortunes are very small. . . . If a Genoese nobleman gives an entertainment once a quarter, he is said to live upon the fragments all the rest of the year.

Ibid.

The Genoese were anciently renowned for their craftiness and want of faith – and the present generation prove that they have inherited in these respects the qualities of their ancestors. It is a saying in Italy that 'It takes six Christians to cheat a Jew and six Jews to cheat a genoese but a genoese Jew is a match for the devil himself.'

Washington Irving, *Journal*, 23 December 1804

A grand but gloomy disagreeable city, owing to the houses being very high, and the streets so narrow you might almost shake hands across them out of the window.

Eliza Fay, *Original Letters from India* (17 June 1779), 1817

The gardens are everywhere in the same style, all neat and trim, like a desert island in a pastry cook's shop, with garnish and frippery enough to please a Dutchman.

Eliza Fay, *Original Letters from India* (28 June 1779), 1817

As a capital, the great defect of Genoa is the deficiency of outlets or suburbs. Venice only has fewer facilities than Genoa, for the citizens to partake of the benefits of air and exercise. Built against rocky acclivities on the edge of the bay; shut in by mountains, and almost inaccessible by land, it appears to strangers a sort of prison.

Lady Morgan, *Italy,* 1820

Proud city, that by the Ligurian sea
  Sittest as at a mirror, lofty and fair;
And towering from thy curving banks in air,
Scornest the mountains that attend on thee;
Why, with such structures, to which Italy
  Has nothing else, though glorious, to compare,
  Hast thou not souls with something like a share,
Of look, heart, spirit, and ingenuity?
Better to bury at once ('twould cost thee less)
  Thy golden sweating heaps, where cramped from
    light
They and their pinch'd fasts ply their old distress
  Thy rotting wealth, unspent, like a thick blight,
Clouds the close eyes of these: dark hands oppress
  With superstition those: – and all is night.

Leigh Hunt, *To Genoa,* 1823

This is by no means a city that would strike an Englishman as being agreeable to *dwell* in. We cannot help acknowledging the grandeur for which it has been so reputed; but, at the same time, there are, mingled in the display of magnificence by which we are surrounded, some circumstances which render the general effect of the city far more dismal than delightful. . . . The houses in every street are immensely high, and the streets are, excepting only a few of them, so very narow that there is not sufficient room for a carriage to pass. They are not what we should call *streets* at all, but rather long *alleys.* In these alleys you may sometimes fancy yourself shut out from day-light in the day-time; so lofty are the houses around, and so far back have you to throw your head to get a peep at the sky. The influence of habit, prejudice out of the question, is such, that it is impossible for an Englishman not to prefer his LONDON to such a place as GENOA.

J.P. Cobbett, *Journal of a Tour in Italy, etc.,* 1830

The Genoese manner . . . is exceedingly animated and pantomimic; so that two friends of the lower class conversing pleasantly in the street, always seem on the eve of stabbing each other forthwith. And a stranger is immensely astonished at their not doing it.

Charles Dickens, Letter to John Forster, 20 July 1844

What a sad place Italy is! a country gone to sleep, and without a prospect of waking again! I never shall forget, as long as I live, my first impressions of it, as I drove through the streets of Genoa . . . I thought that of all the mouldy, dreary, sleepy, dirty, lagging, halting, God-forgotten towns in the wide world, it surely must be the very uttermost superlative. It seemed as if one had reached the end of all things – as if there were no more progress, motion, advancement, or improvement of any kind beyond; but here the whole scheme had stopped centuries ago, never to move on any more, but just lying down in the sun to bask there, 'till the Day of Judgement.

I have a great interest in it now; and walk about, or ride about, the town, when I go there, in a dreamy sort of way which is very comfortable. I seem to be thinking, but I don't know what about – I haven't the least idea. I can sit down in a church, or stand at the end of a narrow Vico, zig-zagging uphill like a dirty snake: and not feel the least desire for any further entertainment.

Charles Dickens, Letter to Count D'Orsay, 7 August 1844

I jumped up, hurried on my clothes, and went on deck; a clear moonlight revealed enough of the scene to show its admirable beauty; and I remained gazing from the silver sea to the mountains, and the white masses of buildings shining at their feet, till I got pinched with cold, and retired, remembering that probably I, and certainly Genoa, would be in that place tomorrow.

Fanny Kemble (Mrs Butler), *A Year of Consolation,* 1847

On becoming intimate with Genoa, I found that it possesses multitudes of handsome women; and what surprised me, many of them with beautiful northern complexions. But an English lady told me, that for this latter discovery I was indebted to my short sight.

Leigh Hunt, *Autobiography,* 1850

Took omnibus (2 sous) to end of harbor. Light house (300 feet high) Ascended. Superb view. Sea coast to south. Promontory. All Genoa & her forts before you. The heigtth & distances of these forts, their outlying loneliness. The bleackness, the savageness of glens between, seem to make Genoa rather the capital and fortified camp of Satan: fortified against the Archangels.

Herman Melville, *Journal of a Visit to Europe and the Levant,* 12 April 1857

The people here live in the heaviest, highest, broadest, darkest, solidest houses one can imagine. Each one might 'laugh a siege to scorn.' A hundred feet front and a hundred high is about the style, and you go up three flights of stairs before you begin to come upon signs of occupancy. Everything is stone, and stone of the heaviest – floors, stairways, mantels, benches, everything. The walls are four to five feet thick. The streets generally are four to five to eight feet wide, and as crooked as a corkscrew. You go along one of these gloomy cracks and look up and behold the sky like a mere ribbon of light, far above your head, where the tops of the tall houses on either side of the street bend almost together. You feel as if you were at the bottom of some tremendous abyss, with all the world far above you. You wind in and out, and here and there, in the most mysterious way, and have no more idea of the points of the compass than if you were a blind man. You can never persuade yourself that these are actually streets, and the frowning, dingy, monstrous houses dwellings, till you see one of these beautiful, prettily -dressed women emerge from them – see her emerge from a dark, dreary looking den that looks dungeon all over, from the ground away halfway up to heaven. And then you wonder that such a charming moth could come from such a forbidding shell as that. The streets are wisely made narrow, and the houses heavy, and thick, and stony, in order that the people may be cool in this roasting climate. And they are cool and stay so.

Mark Twain, *The Innocents Abroad,* 1869

There may be prettier women in Europe, but I doubt it.

Ibid.

Genoa is the queerest place in the world, and even a second visit helps you little to straighten it out. In the wonderful, crooked, twisting, climbing, soaring, burrowing Genoese alleys, the traveller is really up to his neck in the old Italian sketchability. . . . Genoa is the crookedest and most incoherent of cities; tossed about on the sides and crests of a dozen hills, it is seamed with gullies and ravines that bristle with those innumerable palaces for which we have heard from our earliest years that the place is celebrated. These great edifices, with their mottled and faded complexions, lift their big ornamental cornices to a tremendous height in the air, where, in a certain indescribably forlorn and desolate fashion, overtopping each other, they seem to reflect the twinkle and glitter of the warm Mediterranean. Down about the basements, in the little, dim, close alleys, the people are for every moving to and fro, or standing in their cavernous doorways or their dusky, crowded shops, calling, chattering, laughing, scrambling, living their lives in the conversational Italian fashion. For a long time I had not received such an impression of human agglomeration. I had not for a long time seen people elbowing each other so closely, or swarming so thickly out of populous hives.

Henry James, 'Italy Revisited', 1877,
in *Portraits of Places,* 1883

La Superba is worthy of her name, but not shining today. Rain since yesterday afternoon, and she looks like Portsmouth with the storm-signal flying.

George Meredith, Letter to Mrs Marie Meredith,
15 September 1882

O epic-famed, god-haunted Central Sea,
Heave careless of the deep wrong done to thee
When from Torino's track I saw thy face first flash on me.

And multimarbled Genova the Proud,
Gleam all unconscious how, wide-lipped up-browed,
I first beheld thee clad – not as the Beauty but the Dowd.

Out from a deep-delved way my vision lit
On housebacks pink, green ochreous – where a slit
Shoreward 'twixt row and row revealed the classic blue through it.

And there across waved fishwives' high-hung smocks,
Chrome kerchiefs, scarlet hose, darned underfrocks;
Often since when my dreams of thee, O Queen, that frippery mocks:

Whereat I grieve, Superba! . . . Afterhours
Within Palazzo Doria's orange bowers
Went far to mend these marrings of thy soul-subliming powers.

But, Queen, such squalid undress none should see,
Those dream-endangering eyewounds no more be
Where lovers first behold thy form in pilgrimage to thee.

Thomas Hardy, *Genoa and the Mediterranean,*
March 1887

The untidiest port in the world.

Robert Byron, *First Russia then Tibet,* 1933

Genoa initiated me into Italian life. Now that I have known it for twenty years, it has been associated in my mind with all the different phases of Italian history. Genoa gives me what Goethe called 'a sense of the past and present as being one: a conception which infuses a spectral element into the present.' Whenever in my mind I try to conjure up in a flash the exquisite loveliness of Italy, I see before me the vision of Genoa from the sea. It is a sunny morning and we are moored outside the harbour. In the clear air the city rises like a gigantic jewel glittering in its rugged Alpine setting. In the distance the bright-hued buildings soaring tier by tier give the impression of having been honeycombed out of the Ligurian mountains. From the boat it looks like a fantastic city of the Genii, created by magic power – a dream city evoked by the caprice of a wizard who might with a sudden Satanic impulse cast it hurtling into the calm waters at its feet.

Walter Starkie, *The Waveless Plain,* 1938

The dock-front of Genoa is marvellous. Such heat and colours and dirt & noise and loud wicked alleys with all the washing of the world hanging from the high windows.

Dylan Thomas, Letter to his parents, 5 May 1947

Mount Grivola

One shouldn't be frivolous
On places like Grivolas.

W.P. Ker, Quip, 1913, quoted by Freya Stark,
Traveller's Prelude, 1950

Herculaneum

We saw the theatre at Herculaneum, which had been buried sixteen centuries; and passed under vaults to view it by torch-light; – while wandering about the galleries, I was of course obliged to express surprise and pleasure; but in truth I wished myself away, for there were neither singers nor dancers, nor pretty women there, and I never had any taste for antiques.

Michael Kelly, *Reminiscences*, 1826

Ischia

The island Inarime is an epitome of the whole earth containing within the compass of eighteen miles, a wonderful variety of hills, vales, ragged rocks, fruitful plains, and barren mountains, all thrown together in a most romantic confusion. The air is, in the hottest season, constantly refreshed by cool breezes from the sea. The vales produce excellent wheat and Indian corn, but are mostly covered with vineyards intermixed with fruit-trees. Besides the common kinds, as cherries, apricots, peaches, &c., they produce oranges, limes, almonds, pomegranates, figs, water-melons, and many other fruits unknown to our climates, which lie every where open to the passenger. The hills are the greater part covered to the top with vines, some with chestnut groves, and others with thickets of myrtle and lentiscus. The fields in the northern side are divided by hedge-rows of myrtle. Several fountains and rivulets add to the beauty of this landscape, which is likewise set off by the variety of some barren spots and naked rocks. But that which crowns the scene is a large mountain rising out of the middle of the island, (once a terrible volcano, by the ancients called Mons Epomeus). Its lower parts are adorned with vines and other fruits; the middle affords pasture to flocks of goats and sheep; and the top is a sandy pointed rock, from which you have the finest prospect in the world, surveying at one view, besides several pleasant islands, lying at your feet, a tract of Italy about three hundred miles in length, from the promontory of Antium to the Cape of Palinarus: the greater part of which hath been sung by Homer and Virgil, as making a considerable part of the travels and adventures of their two heroes. . . . The inhabitants of this delicious isle, as they are without riches and honours, so they are without the vices and follies that attend them; and were they but as much strangers to revenge as they are to avarice and ambition, they might in fact answer the poetical notions of the golden age. But they have got, as an alloy to their happiness, an ill habit of murdering one another, on slight offences. . . . By the sole secret of minding our own business, we found a means of living securely among those dangerous people.

George Berkeley, Letter to Alexander Pope, 22 October 1717

The girls in the northern villages of Ischia . . . are mostly plain, but here in the Nitroli region you may see many of rare beauty – nymph-like creatures, flower-loving, soft-voiced, with flashing Maenad eyes. Their good looks have been attributed to the fact that they wash their *household linen* in warm mineral water.

Norman Douglas, *Summer Islands, Ischia and Ponza*, 1931

I thought I saw a man-o'war
Making from Naples Bay;
I looked again and saw it was
The Isle of Ischia.
Poor thing, I said, poor silly thing,
It can't get under way.

That is how Lewis Carroll might have put it if he had seen Ischia and Procida from our plane when he was writing Sylvie and Bruno.

Arnold Toynbee, *Between Niger and Nile*, 1965

Itri

The old town of Itri, like a device in pastry. . . .

Charles Dickens, *Pictures from Italy*, 1846

Italian Lakes

So I went on till I got to the lake, and there I found a little port about as big as a dining room (for the Italian lakes play at being little seas. They have little ports, little lighthouses, little fleets for war, and little custom-houses, and little storms and little lines of steamers. Indeed, if one wanted to give a rich child a perfect model or toy, one could not give him anything better than an Italian lake).

Hilaire Belloc, *The Path to Rome*, 18902

Maggiore

The Italian lakes have that in them and their air which removes them from common living. Their beauty is not the beauty which each of us sees for himself in the world; it is rather the beauty of a special creation; the expression of some mind. To eyes innocent, and freshly noting our great temporal inheritance – I mean to the eyes of a boy and girl just entered upon the estate of this glorious earth, and thinking themselves immortal, this shrine of Europe might remain for ever in the memory; an enchanted experience, in which the single sense of sight had almost touched the boundary of music. They would remember these lakes as the central emotion of their youth. To mean men also, who, in spite of years and of a full foreknowledge of death, yet attempt nothing but the satisfaction of sense, and pride themselves upon the taste and fineness with which they achieve this satisfaction, the Italian lakes would seem a place for habitation, and there such a man might build his house contentedly. But to ordinary Christians I am sure there is something unnatural in this beauty of theirs, and they find it in either a paradise only to be won by a much longer road or a bait and veil of sorcery, behind which lies great peril. Now, for all we know, beauty beyond the world may not wear this double aspect; but to us on earth – if we are ordinary men – beauty of this kind has something evil. Have you not read in books how men when they see even divine visions are terrified? So as I looked at Lake Major in its halo I also was afraid, and I was glad to cross the ridge and crest of the hill and to shut out that picture framed all round with glory.

Hilaire Belloc, *The Path to Rome,* 1902

Lecce

Lecce seems as large as Florence in extent but houses lower not a spout or supporter to the balustrade, or balcony but wrought in the grotesque figure of some animal or otherwise carved horses men griffins bears &c supporting the Balcony of the Benedictines church with a round window somewhat Gothic stone handsome and well coloured. In no part of Italy such a general gusto of Architecture. . . . They seem to show some remains of the spirit & elegant genius of the Greeks formerly inhabited these parts.

George Berkeley, *Journal,* 27 May 1717

Lecce . . . has the reputation of being, to the rest of the kingdom, what Thebes was to Greece, and a native of Lecce is said to be distinguishable from his fellow-subjects, by the heaviness of his manner, and the dulness of his apprehension. I dare not be so rash as to pronounce upon this point . . . but I cannot suspect a city to be the sea of stupidity, that has an academy of Belles Lettres, and where some of the Muses at least met with very sincere and successful admirers.

Henry Swinburne, *Travels through the Two Sicilies in 1777–1780,* 1785

Lerici

Lerici is wild and retired, with a bay and rocky eminences; the people suited to it, something between the inhabitants of sea and land.

Leigh Hunt, *Autobiography,* 1850

Leghorn/Livorno

The Duke [of Florence] made this place as it were a sanctuary to offenders, upon whom he used to impose for punishment, either to dwell there for ever, or at least for some yeeres, and to adde one or more houses to the building: so as the City was not faire and populous, but it was filled with Citizens guilty of crimes, and of no civill conversation. My self hearing that they were such men, perhaps out of a prejudicate opinion, did thinke their lookes barbarous, which made me looke more warily to my selfe, and to those things I had with me.

Fynes Moryson, *An Itinerary,* 1617

Leghorne is the neatest, cleanest and pleasantest place that I have seene, their houses painted without side in Stories, Landskipps, etc., with various Coulors, makeing a verie delightfull shewe.

Peter Mundy (before 1620), *The Travels of Peter Mundy,* 1907

Here is in Ligorne . . . such a concourse of Slaves, consisting of Turkes, Mores and other Nations, as the number and confusion is prodigious; some buying, others selling; some drinking, others playing, some working, others sleeping, fighting, singing, weeping & a thousand other postures and Passions; yet all of them naked, & miserably Chayn'd, with a Canvas onely to hide their shame: Here was now a Tent erected, where any idle fellow, weary of that trifle, might stake his liberty against a few Crownes; which if lost (at Dice or other hazard) he was immediately chaynd, & lead away to the Gallys, where he was to serve a tearme of Yeares, but whence they seldome returned; and many sottish persons would in a drunken bravado trye their fortune. The houses of this neate Towne are very uniforme, and excellently paynted a fresca on the out wales, being the representation of many of their Victories against the Turkes.

John Evelyn, *Diary,* 21 October 1644

Perhaps the most interesting sight in Leghorn is the English burying-ground.

Henry Matthews, *The Diary of an Invalid,* 1820

A thriving, business-like, matter-of-fact place, where idleness is shouldered out of the way by commerce.

Charles Dickens, *Pictures from Italy,* 1846

Leghorn is a polite Wapping, with a square and a theatre.

Leigh Hunt, *Autobiography,* 1850

Locarno

for fair Locarno smiles
Embowered in walnut slopes and citron isles.

William Wordsworth, *Descriptive Sketches,* 1791–2, pub. 1793

Lombardy

Lucentio: fruitfull *Lumbardie,*
The pleasant garden of great *Italy.*

William Shakespeare, *The Taming of the Shrew,* c. 1593–4

Surely such is the fertility of this country, that I thinke

no Region or Province under the Sunne may compare with it. For it is passing plentifully furnished with all things, tending both to pleasure and profit, being the very Paradise, and Canaan of Christendome. For an Italy is the garden of the world, so is Lombardy the garden of Italy, and Venice the garden of Lombardy. It is wholly plaine, and beautified with such abundance of goodly rivers, pleasant meadowes, fruitfull vineyardes, fat pastures, delectable gardens, orchards, woodes, and what not, that the first view thereof did even refocillate my spirits, and tickle my senses with inward joy. To conclude this introduction to Lombardy, it is so fertile a territory, that . . . the butter thereof is oyle, the dew hony, and the milk nectar.

Thomas Coryate, *Crudities*, 1611

When I pass'd through some parts of *Lombardy*, among other things, I observ'd the Physiognomies and Complexions of the People, Men and Women; and I thought I was in *Wales*, for divers of them have a cast of countenance and a nearer resemblance with our Nation than any I ever saw yet: And the reason is obvious; for the *Romans* having been near upon three hundred years among us, where they had four Legions (before the *English* Nation or Language had any being) by so long a coalition and tract of time, the two Nations must needs copulate and mix: insomuch that I believe there is yet remaining in *Wales* many of the *Roman* Race, and divers in *Italy* of the *British*. Among other resemblances one was in their Prosody, and vein of Versifying or Rhyming, which is like or *Bards*, who hold Agnominations, and enforcing of consonant Words or Syllables one upon the other, to be the greatest Elegance.

James Howell, 'Letter to Christopher Jones, Esq., . . . Naples, 8 October 1621', *Familiar Letters*, 1645

Tis astonishing how like these Lombards are to our Welch People! the low ones in particular: I saw a Signor Curàto the other day at the Country Seat of an agreeable Family near Milan – I could not keep from looking at the Man, & expecting him to speak Welch: his long straight Hair, ruddy Colour, & coarse Manners all contributed to make one stare at the striking Resemblance; but 'tis amazing that the slyness of Shopkeepers, & the quiet tho' cutting Replies of the ordinary People, should be so very similar in Nations who never proposed each other as Patterns of Imitation – It comes in my head while I write, that Howell too was struck with the Likeness and mentions it in his Letters.

Hester Lynch Thrale/Piozzi, *Thraliana*, 1784

Beneath is spread like a green sea
The waveless plain of Lombardy
Bounded by the vaporous air
Islanded by cities fair.

Percy Bysshe Shelley, *Lines Written among the Euganian Hills*, October 1818

The cities of Lombardy are all like large country houses: walking out of their gates you seem to be stepping from a door or window that opens on a trim and beautiful garden, where mulberry-tree is married to mulberry by festoons of vines, and where the maize and sunflower stand together in rows between patches of flax and hemp.

J.A. Symonds, *Sketches and Studies in Italy and Greece*, 1874

Loretto

It is of little circuit, and lieth in length from East to the West, so narrow; ass it hath almost but one street in the bredth, and all the houses of this streete are Innes, or Shops of them that sell Beades to number prayers. . . . Upon the dores of this Church, famous for mens superstitious worship, these verses are written:

Illotus timeat quincunque intrara, Sacellum,
 In terris nullum sanctius orbis habet.
Enter not here unwashed of any spot,
For a more holy Church the world hath not.

Fynes Moryson, *An Itinerary*, 1617

The Holy Chapel of Loretto, all the world knows, was originally a small house in Nazareth, inhabited by the Virgin Mary, in which she was saluted by the Angel, and where she bred our Saviour. After their deaths, it was held in great veneration by all believers in Jesus, and at length consecrated into a chapel, and dedicated to the Virgin. . . . This sanctified edifice was allowed to sojourn in Galilee as long as that district was inhabited by Christians; but when infidels got possession of the country, a band of angels, to save it from pollution, took it in their arms, and conveyed it from Nazareth to a castle in Dalmatia. This fact might have been called in question by incredulous people, had it been performed in a secret manner; but, that it might be manifest to the most short-sighted spectator, and evident to all who were not perfectly deaf as well as blind, a blaze of celestial light, and a concert of divine music, accompanied it during the whole journey; besides, when the angels, to rest themselves, set it down in a little wood near the road, all the trees of the forest bowed their heads to the ground, and continued in that respectful posture as long as the Sacred Chapel remained among them. But, not having been entertained with suitable respect at the castle above mentioned, the same indefatigable angels carried it over the sea, and placed it in a field belonging to a noble lady, called Lauretta, from whom the Chapel takes its name. This field happened unfortunately to be frequented at that time by highwaymen and murderers; a circumstance with which the angels undoubtedly were not acquainted when they placed it there. After they were better informed, they removed it to the top of a hill belonging to two brothers, where they imagined it would be perfectly secure from the dangers of robbery or assassination; but the two brothers, the proprietors of the ground, being equally enamoured of their new visitor, became jealous of each other, quarrelled, fought, and fell by mutual wounds. After this final catastrophe, the angels in waiting finally removed the holy Chapel to the eminence where it now stands, and has stood these four hundred years, having lost all relish for travelling.

John Moore, *A View of Society and Manners in Italy,* 1781

Lucca

There is a notable little active Republic towards the midst of *Tuscany,* call'd *Lucca,* which in regard she is under the Emperor's Protection, he dares not meddle withal, tho' she lie as a Partridge under a Faulcon's Wings, in relation to the Grand Duke. . . . There is no State that winds the Penny more nimbly and makes quicker Returns.

James Howell, 'Letter to Sir J.C., from Florence, 1 November 1621', *Familiar Letters,* 1645

Happy for me that the environs of Lucca were so beautiful; since I defy almost any city to contain more ugliness within its walls. Narrow streets and dismal alleys; wide gutters and cracked pavements; everybody in black, according with the gloom of their habitations, which however are large and lofty enough of conscience; but having all grated windows, they convey none but dark and dungeon-like ideas. My spirits fell many degrees upon entering this sable capital.

William Beckford, *Dreams Waking Thoughts and Incidents,* 1783

This is the Ilam gardens of Europe; and whoever has seen that singular spot in Derbyshire belonging to Mr Port, has seen little Lucca in a convex mirror.

Hester Lynch Thrale/Piozzi, *Observations . . . in the Course of a Journey,* 1789

The common people of Lucca have the reputation of being great tricksters. They have a saying, 'Sono un Luchese, ma vi sono de' buoni e cattivi al mio paese.' – 'I am a Luchese, but there are good, as well as bad, in my country.' Aretin the satirist, 'yclept 'the Bitter Tuscan,' and who hated Lucca for some slight shewn to him, said, that when their best actress was acting with energy, she always threw one, or both of her arms, out of the republic; meaning it was so contemptibly small.

Michael Kelly, *Reminiscences,* 1826

Hitherto, all architecture, except fairy-finished Milan, had depended with me for its delight on being partly in decay. . . .

Here in Lucca I found myself suddenly in the presence of twelfth century buildings, originally set in such balance of masonry that they could all stand without mortar; and in material so incorruptible, that after six hundred years of sunshine and rain, a lancet could not now be put between their joints.

Absolutely for the first time I now saw what mediaeval builders were, and what they meant. I took the simplest of façades for analysis, that of Santa Maria Foris-Portam, and thereon literally *began* the study of architecture.

John Ruskin, *Praeterita,* 1885–9

At Lucca, an enthusiastic sightseer once asked Mr Ruskin, 'What is the finest thing to see in Lucca?' The answer was: – 'Oh, the clouds, you know.'

Mrs Henry Fawcett, *Orient Line Guide,* 1885

The town of Lucca . . . is the neatest, the regularest, the exactest, the most fly-in-amber little town in the world, with its uncrowded streets, its absurd fortifications, and its contented silent houses – all like a family at ease and at rest under its high sun. It is as sharp and trim as its own map, and that map is as clear as a geometrical problem. Everything in Lucca is good.

Hilaire Belloc, *The Path to Rome,* 1902

Mantua

This Citie is marveilous strong, and walled round with faire bricke wals, wherein there are eight gates, and is thought to be foure miles in compasse: the buildings both publique and private and very sumptuous and magnificent: their streets straite and very spacious. Also I saw many stately Pallaces of a goodly height: it is most sweetly seated in respect of the marvailous sweete ayre thereof, the abundance of goodly meadows, pastures, vineyards, orchards, and gardens about it. For they have such store of gardens about the Citie, that I thinke London which both for frequencie of people, and multitude of howses doth thrise exceed it, is not better furnished with gardens.

Thomas Coryate, *Crudities,* 1611

and the way there from Verona

The country between this beautiful town and Mantua, presents one continued grove of dwarfish mulberries, among which start up innumerable barren hills. Now and then a knot of poplars diversify their craggy summits, and sometimes a miserable shed. Mantua itself rises out of a morass formed by the Mincio, whose course, in most places is so choked up with reeds, as to be scarcely discernible. It requires a creative imagination to discover any charms in such a prospect, and a strong prepossession not to be disgusted with the scene where Virgil was born. . . . I abandoned poetry and entered the city in despair.

William Beckford, *Dreams Waking Thoughts and Incidents,* 1783

It is a *lady's* town.

Hester Lynch Thrale/ Piozzi, *Observations . . . in the Course of a Journey*, 1789

Retrospect of Mantua, with its dome, & spires & towers; the first spires I have seen in Italy – a long line just above the waters of its lake – more like a dutch town than any other.

Samuel Rogers, *Italian Journal*, 8 April 1815

If ever a man were suited to his place of residence, and his place of residence to him, the lean apothecary and Mantua came together in a perfect fitness of things. It may have been more stirring then, perhaps. If so, the Apothecary was a man in advance of his time, and knew what Mantua would be, in eighteen hundred and forty-four. He fasted much, and that assisted him in his foreknowledge.

Charles Dickens, *Pictures from Italy*, 1846

I have seen many ruins and of every period. . . . I have seen great cities dead or in decay. . . . But over none, it seemed to me, did there brood so profound a melancholy as over Mantua; none seemed so dead or so utterly bereft of glory; now here was desolation more pregnant with the memory of splendour, the silence nowhere so musically rich with echoes. . . . It is through Mallarmé's *creux néant musicien* that one walks in Mantua.

And not in Mantua alone. For wherever the Gonzaga lived, they left behind them the same pathetic emptiness, the same pregnant desolation, the same echoes, the same ghosts of splendour.

Aldous Huxley, *Along the Road*, 1925

Marguzzo (and the Alps)

We ariv'd at night to *Marguzzo*, an obscure village at the end of the Lake, & very foote of the Alpes which now rise as it were suddainly, after some hundred of miles of the most even Country in the World, & where there is hardly a stone to be found, as if nature had here swept up the rubbish of the Earth in the Alpes, to forme and cleare the Plaines of *Lumbardy*.

John Evelyn, *Diary*, May 1646

Merano

The country is wonderful. Mountains, holding up cups of snow to the fiery sun, who glares on them in vain. The peasantry are a noble race: pious, and with a strong smell. Priests abound and soap flies before them. . . . Nothing can be grander than the colossal mountains of porphyry and dolomite shining purple and rosy, snow-capped here and there, with some tumultuous river noising below, and that eternal stillness overhead, save when some great peak gathers the thunders and bellows for a time.

George Meredith, Letter to Frederick A. Maxse, 26 July 1861

Menaggio (the view across the lake)

As I sit writing in the garden under a magnolia I look across to Varenna in the sun, and the 'Sourmilk Gill' coming into the lake close by it; and the grand jagged line of mountains that bound the lake towards Colico, almost snowless in August, stand glittering now like the Oberland range. You never saw anything so calculated to make you drunk.

Matthew Arnold, Letter to Walter Arnold, 5 May 1873

Messina

This place is vastly dirty. Dirtyissimo.

Edward Lear, Letter to Lady Waldegrave, 13 April 1866

The countless shacks made me think of a mushroom town which had sprung up in the night during a gold-rush. The sight of Messina was an index to the mentality of the people. When I compare the Sicilian with the South Italian, I find that the latter expresses the thoughts and impulses that bubble up within him in a wealth of gestures and gesticulations. The Sicilian, on the other hand, is more of a fatalist, and there is in him a certain gravity of demeanour which we associate with the Arabs. How can the Sicilian help being a fatalist when he sees around him the debris of such a disaster as the earthquake of 1908? Nature, the Steward of God, gave him a paradise to dwell in, but in compensation, to convince him of the vanity of all that beauty, God, with one fell blow, laid it in ruins about him.

Walter Starkie, *The Waveless Plain*, 1938

Straits of Messina (the 'Fata Morgana' seen from Reggio)

Sometimes, but rarely, it exhibits a very curious phaenomenon, vulgarly called *La Fata Morgana*. . . . To produce this pleasing deception, many circumstances must concur, which are not known to exist in any other situation. The spectator must stand with his back to the east, in some elevated place behind the city, that he may command a view of the whole bay; beyond which the mountains of Messina rise like a wall, and darken the background of the picture. The winds must be hushed; the surface quite smoothed; the tide at its height; and the waters pressed up by currents to a great elevation in the middle of the channel. All these events coinciding, as soon as the sun surmounts the eastern hills behind Reggio, and rises high enough to form an angle of forty-five degrees on the water before the city, – every object existing or moving at Reggio will be repeated a thousand-fold upon this marine looking-glass; which, by its tremulous motion, is, as it were, cut into facets. Each image will pass rapidly off in succession, as the day advances, and the stream carries down the wave on which it appeared.

Thus the parts of this moving picture will vanish in the twinkling of an eye. Sometimes the air is at that moment so impregnated with vapours, and undisturbed by winds, as to reflect objects in a kind of aerial screen, rising about thirty feet above the level of the sea. In cloudy, heavy weather, they are drawn on the surface of the water, bordered with fine prismatical colours.

Henry Swinburne, *Travels in the Two Sicilies in 1777–1780,* 1785

Milan

and Lombardy from the roof of Milan Cathedral

There I observed the huge suburbs, which are as bigge as many a faire towne, and compassed about with ditches of water: there also I beheld a great part of Italy, together with the lofty Apennines. . . . The Territory of Lombardy which I contemplated round about from this Tower, was so pleasant an object to mine eyes, being replenished with such unspeakable variety of all things, both for profit and pleasure, that it seemeth to me to be the very Elysian fields, so much decantated and celebrated by the verses of Poets, or the Temple or Paradise of the world. For it is the fairest plain, extended about some two hundred miles in length that ever I saw, or ever shall if I should travell over the whole habitable world: insomuch that I said to myself that this country was fitter to be an habitation for the immortal Gods then for, mortall men.

Thomas Coryate, *Crudities,* 1611

Milan is striking – the Cathedral superb – the city altogether reminds me of Seville – but a little inferior.

Lord Byron, Letter to John Murray, 15 October 1816

Milanese . . . a vagrant tribe, whose industry and enterprise carry them from the *Lake of Como* to the remotest regions of the earth. They are seen in all countries; even in *Lapland.*

E.D. Clarke, *Travels in Various Countries,* 4th edn, 1816

The people here, though inoffensive enough, seem both in body and soul a miserable race. The men are hardly men; they look like a tribe of stupid and shrivelled slaves, and I do not think that I have seen a gleam of intelligence in the countenance of man since I passed the Alps. The women in enslaved countries are always better than the men; but they have tight-laced figures, and figures and mien which express (O how unlike the French!) a mixture of the coquette and prude which reminds me of the worst characteristics of the English. Everything but humanity is in much greater perfection here than in France.

Percy Bysshe Shelley, Letter to Thomas Love Peacock, 20 April 1818

Milan was entered by us with anticipations the most gracious; which, contrary to ordinary experience, were surpassed by the events. The very name of this city, as I write it, awakens feelings which the impartiality of veracious narrative should distrust.

Lady Morgan, *Italy,* 1820

and Antwerp

Milan always affected my imagination as representing the splendour and wealth of the middle age – the noble, grandiose splendour and wealth, as Antwerp represents the bourgeois splendour and wealth.

Matthew Arnold, Letter to his wife, 25 June 1865

Milan . . . has seemed prosaic and winterish as if it were on the wrong side of the Alps.

Henry James, Letter to Mrs Fanny Kemble, 24 March 1881

Beastly Milano, with its imitation hedgehog of a Cathedral, and its hateful town Italians, all socks and purple cravats and hats over the ear, did for me.

D.H. Lawrence, Letter to Lady Cynthia Asquith, 23 October 1913

When I first saw Milan, at the beginning of May [1945], it looked like a slice of Hell. Some of the shabby green trams were running and some of the inhabitants were going about their routines, but the whole place seemed stunned and stopped, and the bloodless under-nourished people, wrapped in any old cloth that could protect their skins, seemed to have been reduced, in the course of the German oppression, the bombings by the allies, and the embittered civil war, to a condition of permanent strain. The children, especially, were appalling: they had acquired, as they were growing up, expressions of indignation and apprehension which were now as much a part of their faces as malnutrition was of their bones.

Edmund Wilson, *Europe without Baedeker,* 1947

Milan is a giant, nightmare city. The snow & rain had just ceased before we arrived – a day or two before. The immensely long, wide streets, which run the entire length of the city, or seem to, were bakingly hot &

dusty, clanking with great, packed, racing trams, buzzing with little toy motor bikes; there were stop-me-&-buy-one bicycle boys selling, not ice-cream, but bottles of Chianti, & set-faced sinister armed policemen.

Dylan Thomas, Letter to his parents, 11 April 1947

When you observe things more closely, in Milan, even the things which want to appear foreign, extremely efficient and modern, the powerful businessmen, the aerial skyscrapers reflecting the passing clouds in their hundreds of windows, the elevated autostrade running along on concrete crutches, the complex industrial plants apparently invented by mad engineers or science-fiction writers, you begin to notice that many things are a little too much and too emphatically what they are supposed to be. In fact, Milan, in its newer quarters, is a little more like Zürich, Dusseldorf, and Madison Avenue than Zürich, Dusseldorf, or Madison Avenue themselves. You are in Italy after all.

Luigi Barzini, *The Italians,* 1964

Italy's answer to Birmingham.

Anon.

The Cathedral

How glorious that Cathedral is! worthy almost of standing face to face with the snow Alps; and itself a sort of snow dream by an artist architect, taken asleep in a glacier!

Elizabeth Barrett Browning, Letter, 1851

The Cathedral is an awful failure. Outside the design is monstrous and inartistic. The over-elaborated details stuck high up where no one can see them; everything is vile in it; it is, however, imposing and gigantic as a failure, through its great size and elaborate execution.

Oscar Wilde, Letter to his mother, 25 June 1875

. . . the beautiful city with its dominant frost-crystalline Duomo. . . .

John Ruskin, *Praeterita,* 1885–9

Modena

An ill-built, melancholy place, all of brick. . . .

Thomas Gray, Letter to Mrs Gray, his mother, 9 December 1739

At one short post from Parma, the little village of Saint Ilario places the traveller beyond the Parmesan confines, and within the frontier of the sovereign of Modena, or, as the Italians contemptuously call his Highness, *'Il Duchino,' the little Duke.* This event is notified by an unusual display of military force; besides the ordinary civil administration of power and impediment. His Imperial Highness Francesco the Fourth is a very warlike Prince: and though, by rising early, he might quit his own States to breakfast with the Duchess of Parma, and return in good time for dinner at Modena; yet he keeps up a military armament so formidable, that his Ducato is known by no other name at present, in Italy, than that of *'Il Regno de' Dragoni.'*

Lady Morgan, *Italy,* 1820

Naples

See Naples and die.

Italian proverb

The *Neapolitane* carrieth the bloodiest mind, and is the most fleering murderer: whereupon it is growen to a common proverbe, *Ile give him the Neapolitan shrug,* when one intends to play the villaine, and make no boast of it.

Thomas Nashe, *The Unfortunate Traveller,* 1594

Naples, the Paradise of Italy,
As that is of earth.

John Fletcher (and Philip Massinger?), *The Double Marriage, c.* 1621

A City swelling with all Delight, Gallantry and Wealth; and truly, . . . This is a delicate luxurious City, fuller of true-bred Cavaliers than any place I saw yet. The Clime is hot, and the Constitutions of the Inhabitants more hot.

The Neapolitan is accounted the best Courtier of Ladies and the greatest embracer of Pleasure of any other People; . . . a Proverb they have in *Italy* for this People

Napolitano
Largo di bocca, stretto di mano.
The Neapolitans
Have wide Mouths, but narrow Hands.

They make strong masculine Promises, but female Performances (*for deeds are Men but words are Women*), and if in a whole *flood* of Compliments one find a *drop* of *Reality,* 'tis well. The first acceptance of a Courtesy is accounted the greatest Incivility that can be amongst them, and a ground for a Quarrel; as I heard of a *German* Gentleman that was baffled for accepting only one Invitation to a Dinner.

James Howell, 'Letter to Sir T.H. Knight, from Naples, 1 October 1621', *Familiar Letters,* 1645

The very winter here is a summer, ever fruitefull, & continually pregnant, so as in the midst of February we had Melons, Cheries, Abricots and many other sorts of fruite: The building of the Citty is for the quantity the most magnificent of Europe, the streetes exceeding large, well paved, having many Vaults, and conveyances under them for the sullage which renders them very sweete and cleane even in the midst of winter: . . . The Women are generally well featur'd but excessively libidinous; the Country people so jovial and addicted to Musick, that the very husbandmen almost universally play upon the guitarr, singing and composing songs in prayse of their Sweetehearts, & will go to the field commonly with their fiddle; they are merry, Witty, and genial; all which I much attribute to the excellent quality of the ayre.

John Evelyn, *Diary*, 8 February 1645

Prospects are the natural ornaments of this kingdom.

George Berkeley, Letter to Lord Percival, 6 April 1717

My wonder still increased on entering the city, which I think, for number of people, outdoes both Paris and London. The streets are one continued market, and thronged with populace so much that a coach can hardly pass. The common sort are a jolly lively kind of animals, more industrious than Italians usually are; they work till evening; then take their lute or guitar (for they all play) and walk about the city, or upon the sea-shore with it, to enjoy the fresco. One sees their little brown children jumping about stark naked, and the bigger ones dancing with castanets, while others play on the cymbal to them. Your maps will show you the situation of Naples; it is on the most lovely bay in the world, and one of the calmest seas: It has many other beauties besides those of nature.

Thomas Gray, Letter to Mrs Gray, his mother, 14 June 1740

I went little into company at Naples, and remember solely that the Neapolitan ladies resembled country chamber-maids. I was there during Lent when there are no public entertainments. During my stay at Naples I was truly libertine. I ran after girls without restraint. My blood was inflamed by the burning climate, and my passions were violent. I indulged them; my mind had almost nothing to do with it. I found some very pretty girls. I escaped all danger.

James Boswell, Letter to J-J Rousseau, Lucca, 3 October 1765 (original in French)

It is hard to say, whether the view is more pleasing from the singularity of many of the objects, or from the incredible variety of the whole. You see an amazing mixture of the antient and modern; some rising to fame, and some sinking to ruin. Palaces reared over the tops of other palaces, and antient magnificence trampled under foot – by modern folly. – Mountains and islands that were celebrated for their fertility, changed into barren wastes, and barren wastes into fertile fields and rich vineyards. Mountains sunk into plains, and plains swelled into mountains. Lakes drunk up by volcanos, and extinguished volcanos turned into lakes. The earth still smoking in many places; and in others throwing out flame. – In short, Nature seems to have formed this coast in her most capricious mood; for every object is a *lusus naturae*. She never seems to have gone seriously to work; but to have devoted this spot to the most unlimited indulgence of caprice and frolic.

Patrick Brydone, *A Tour through Sicily and Malta*, 1773

Provisions are here plentiful and cheap, therefore the lower class of people work but little; their delight is to bask in the sun and to do nothing. Persons of a middle rank pass too much of their time in coffee-houses, and places of public resort; few pursue their callings with the zeal and activity we are wont to meet with in the professional men of colder countries. Gluttony is a much more predominant vice than ebriety, of which instances are extremely rare. In the female sex, the passion for finery is almost superior to all others, and notwithstanding any effect the genial warmth of the climate may have on the constitution of a Neapolitan woman, I doubt whether she would not nine times out of ten prefer a present to a lover.

Henry Swinburne, *Travels in the Two Sicilies in 1777–1780*, 1785

Nothing, I will venture to affirm, is less true than that the Neapolitans are soft and effeminate; nor are they even voluptuous, in the more elegant sense in which that word is usually understood. They are fiery, and sensual, in a high degree, and during the prevalence of the siroc wind, extremely relaxed and indolent. But, their general tone of character is rough, harsh, and impetuous, even, in higher life; in the lower, gross, barbarous, and violent; choleric and vindictive in both. What undiscerning eyes may have mistaken for politeness, is nothing but the habitual cringe of adulation to the iron rod of arbitrary power. But let me do the Neapolitans justice: they want not feeling or generosity; and would but the church and the state emancipate them from that superstition and ignorance; which one hath been no less fond than the other, of converting into an engine of power; the Neapolitans, with a genius and sensibility which no person can deny them, would soon become a gallant and respectable nation.

William Beckford, *Dreams Waking Thoughts and Incidents*, 1783

Which town at last is not a large one, but full as an egg.

Hester Lynch Thrale/Piozzi, *Observations . . . in the Course of a Journey*, 1789

The most populous of cities relative to its size, whose luxurious inhabitants seem to dwell on the confines of paradise and hell-fire.

Edward Gibbon, *Memoirs of his Life*, 1796

It is a country of fiddlers and poets, whores and scoundrels.

Horatio Lord Nelson, Dispatch to Lord St Vincent, 20 September 1798

I sha'nt go to Naples. It is but the second best sea-view, and I have seen the first and third, viz. Constantinople and Lisbon (by the way, the last is but a river-view; however, they reckon it after Stamboul and Naples, and before Genoa), and Vesuvius is silent, and I have passed by Ætna.

Lord Byron, Letter to Thomas Moore, 11 April 1817

On entering Naples, the first circumstance that engaged my attention was an assassination. A youth ran out of a shop, pursued by a woman with a bludgeon, and a man armed with a knife. The man overtook him, and with one blow in the neck, laid him dead in the road. On my expressing the emotions of horror and indignation which I felt, a Calabrian priest, who travelled with me, laughed heartily, and attempted to quiz me, as what the English call a flat.

Percy Bysshe Shelley, Letter to Thomas Love Peacock, 22 December 1818

The first impression given of the Neapolitan population, on a general and rapid view of all classes, as they are seen in the streets and the vineyards . . . is that of a people created out of the elements of their own brilliant and fervid region, for whom the word *genius* was invented, a people whose character is as volcanic as their soil! The fires of Vesuvius seem to circulate in their veins; the brilliancy of their skies is reflected in their imagination. Their organs are more acute and their impressions more vivid than those of other nations; and their over-abundant vitality, uncalled on by their torpid institutes, bursts forth as it can, and wastes itself in shrill sounds, rapid movements, and vivacious gestures that render the language superfluous which they are called upon to second or assist.

Lady Morgan, *Italy*, 1820

Naples! thou heart of man which ever pantest
  Naked beneath the lidless eye of heaven!
Elysian City which to calm enchantest
  The mutinous air and sea: they round thee, even
  As sleep round Love, are driven!
  Metropolis of a ruined Paradise
    Long lost, late won, and yet but half regained!
  Bright altar of the bloodless sacrifice
    Which armed Victory offers up unstained
    To Love, the flower-enchained!
Thou which wert once, and then did cease to be,
Now art, and henceforth ever shall be, free,
  If Hope, and Truth, and justice can avail,
    Hail, hail, all hail!

Percy Bysshe Shelley, Ode to Naples, 1820

This region surely is not of the earth.
Was it not dropt from Heaven?

Samuel Rogers, *Italy*, 1822–34

As we came through the suburbs of this city, and coming into the city itself, the people were swarming; I never saw such multitudes; the place seemed to be fairly *leaping alive;* twas enough to make a Malthusian fall down with affright.

J.P. Cobbett, *Journal of a Tour in Italy, etc.*, 1830

And what if it is Naples . . . I won't be imposed upon by a name.

R.W. Emerson, *Journal*, 12 March 1833

A little incident occurred to me which gave a pretty good idea of the people I was amongst. In the widest street, 'Strada di Toledo' at 1 o'clock p.m. a youth of about 16 years attempted to deprive me of my pkt Handkerchief, which he had already extracted from my pocket and thrown to another party. I turned round in time to get my Handkerchief but not to catch the thief who run to the other side of the street and there stood. Now in London they will pick your pocket but scarcely under the same circumstances. Here the people behind me of whom there were many did not attempt to stop him. I was apprised at Rome of the propensity of the people of Naples for their neighbours Hfs. but I was not prepared for such tricks in broad day and in the sight of hundreds of well dressed people. I complained to a countryman here of the apathy of the bystanders. His reply was 'It is a rule here that nobody interferes with his neighbours calling.'

John Webster, *Notes of a Journey from London to Constantinople* . . ., 1836

compared with Rome, Pisa and Florence

A poet might introduce Naples as Martha, and Rome as Mary. A Catholic may think Mary's the better employment; but even a Catholic, much more a protestant, would prefer the table of Martha. . . . It is the only place in Italy that has seemed to me to have the same sort of vitality which you find in all the great English ports and cities. Rome and Pisa are dead and gone; Florence is not dead but sleepeth; while Naples overflows with life.

T.B. Macaulay, *Journal*, 3 January 1839

What would I give that you should see the lazzaroni as they really are – mere squalid, abject, miserable animals for vermin to batten on; slouching, slinking, ugly, shabby, scavenging scarecrows! And oh the raffish counts and more than doubtful countesses, the noodles and the blacklegs, the good society! And oh the miles of miserable streets, and wretched occupants.

Charles Dickens, Letter, 1845, in Forster, *Life of Dickens*, 1872–3

This is the negation of God erected into a system of government.

W.E. Gladstone, Letter to the Earl of Aberdeen on the state of Naples, 1851

That is the view, of all the views of the world, that will stay longest with me. For the same reason that I prefer driving through the country to seeing sights in the towns I prefer, infinitely prefer as a matter of *pleasure,* Naples to Rome; . . . Capri in front, and the Sorrento peninsula girdling the bay: never can anything give one, of itself, without any trouble on one's own part, such delectation as that.

Matthew Arnold, Letter to his mother, 5 June 1865

'See Naples and die.' Well, I do not know that one would necessarily die after merely seeing it, but to attempt to live there might turn out a little differently.

Mark Twain, *The Innocents Abroad,* 1869

I conceived at Naples a tenfold deeper loathing than ever of the hideous heritage of the past – and felt for a moment as if I should like to devote my life to laying rail-roads and erecting blocks of stores on the most classic and romantic sites. The age has a long row to hoe.

Henry James, Letter to William James, 27 December 1869

and Etna

When Etna basks and purrs
Naples is more afraid
Than when she shows her Garnet Tooth –
Security is loud.

Emily Dickinson, *c.* 1869
(who must have meant Vesuvius)

The treatment of the dead shows the character of this idolatrous and self-seeking people in its saddest aspect. When the funeral of a friend passes, a Neapolitan will exclaim with characteristic selfishness, 'Salute a noi' – 'Health to ourselves' – without thought of the departed.

A.J.C. Hare, *Cities of Southern Italy,* 1883

How horrible civilized man is. All day the spectacle of these Neapolitans in their modern slop clothes has been to me a nightmare; all nature is defiled by them. What countenance of filthy passions! What abominations to the senses! what foul rubbish heaps! what stenches!

Wilfred Scawen Blunt, Diary, 23 April 1891, *My Diaries,* 1919

The museum is full as you know, of lovely Greek bronzes. The only bother is that they all walk about the town at night.

Oscar Wilde, Letter to Ernest Dowson, 11 October 1897

In Naples the insolence of the mercenary fraternity has attained to such an unexampled pitch that the traveller is often tempted to doubt whether such a thing as honesty is known.

Karl Baedeker, *Guide to Southern Italy,* 1890

I have rarely entered a strange city without a certain apprehension;, but no city ever filled me with such terror as Naples. Those long streets of tall, mean houses, from which narrow alleys climbed the hill, and descended to the harbour, in row after row of meaner and not less tall houses, all with their little iron balconies, over which clothes and linen draggled, all with their crowded, squalid, patched, and coloured throngs of restless life; the cracking of whips, the clatter of wheels and of horses' hoofs on the uneven stones; the thud of the cow-bell, the sharper tinkle of the goat-bell, as the creatures wander about the streets or wait at the doors of houses; the rattling of boot-blacks' brushes, the petulant whine of beggars, the whole buzz of that humming, half-obliterated Neapolitan, with its punctuation of gestures; the rush and bustling of those side-walks, after the courteous and ample leisure of Rome; something sordid in the very trees on the sea-front, second-rate in the aspect of the carriages that passed, and of the people who sat in them; the bare feet, rags, rainbow-coloured dirt, sprawling and spawning poverty of Santa Lucia, and not of Santa Lucia alone; the odour of the city; and then the indiscoverable length and extent of it, the ways that seemed to lead in whatever direction I wanted to go, and then ended suddenly, or turned aside in another direction; the darkness up the hill, and the uncertainty of all those new, as yet unknown, roads: that, as I turned away from the sea, when night began to come down upon it, mounted to my head like some horrible fume, enveloping me with disgust, possessing me with terror. I have got a little accustomed to it now, I know my way through those streets, which are, after all, simple enough in their arrangement; I have come to see certain advantages, even, in the turning of all this dirt and poverty out into the sun; I find it a touching tribute to cleanliness that every other poor person whom you see is hunting for his own or his neighbour's vermin; but, all the same, I think my first impression is likely to last.

I do not think that the Neapolitans are more vivacious or intend to be more objectionable than other people, but they are poor, naturally untidy; they live in the street because there is sun and air in the street, and it does not occur to them that there is anything in human nature to hide. They have an absolute, an almost ingenuous lack of civilisation, and after seeing the Neapolitans I have more respect for civilisation.

Arthur Symons, *Cities,* 1903

He said that the progress of sanitation in Naples (where up to a few years ago there were no privies at all) was very much hindered by the fact that a company paid the corporation 300000 francs a year for the right to remove human excrement. Another company pay 100,000 for right to remove dog excrement. (Same thing in Constantinople, Aleppo, etc.) Dog excrement sent to U.S.A. for preparing kid gloves, etc. Nothing like it for that.

Arnold Bennett, *Journal,* 10 October 1911

The head of a hospital at Naples tells me that stomach diseases are more prevalent there than in any other part of Europe, and the stomach, whatever sentimentalists may say to the contrary, being the true seat of the emotions, it follows that a judicious system of dieting might work wonders upon their development. Nearly all Mediterranean races have been misfed from early days; that is why they are so small. I would undertake to raise the Italian standard of height by several inches, if I had control of their nutrition for a few centuries. I would undertake to alter their whole outlook upon life, to convert them from utilitarians into romantics – were such a change desirable. For if utilitarianism be the shadow of starvation, romance is nothing but the vapour of repletion.

Norman Douglas, *Old Calabria,* 1915

Beware of the fat Neapolitan. He is fat from prosperity, from dining off his leaner brothers.

Ibid.

Whoever it was who said (I believe it was Nelson), 'See Naples and die,' perpetrated one of the greatest hoaxes in history. Or perhaps I am unlucky when I go there.

Geoffrey Harmsworth, *Abyssinian Adventure,* 1935

And everybody who has passed the age of puberty seems to be busy making more children: the town is full of pregnant women and of women with wretched little babies that have sores all over their faces or are covered with the pink mottlings of disease. The Neapolitans seem to me sometimes to have as little relation to people as small octopi crabs and molluscs brought in by the marine tide. . . . But the life here is rank and flamboyant, and even in death it exults in the flesh. I have never seen a city in which funerals seem to figure in so important a way. Where so many human beings are begotten many must be constantly dying, and they like to make a fete of death.

Edmund Wilson, *Europe without Baedeker,* 1947

Neapolitans still reproduce what must be the nearest equivalent to life in classical times. Naples is one of the great tests. Some people hate it and some people love it. I think that people who do not like Naples are afraid of something.

Peter Nichols, *Italia, Italia,* 1973

and Capri and Vesuvius
I liked Capri best, – going up Vesuvius it was a bit dusty and that, and it spoilt your shoes.

Schoolboy, returned from school trip to Naples, interviewed on radio, 12 July 1980

I think it was Gore Vidal who said that he lived in a beautiful house to the south of Naples because it was the best place to observe the end of the world.

Peter Nichols, 'Italy – a Special Report', *The Times,* 27 October 1981

Lake Nemi

The lake of Nemi lies in a very deep bottom, so surrounded on all sides with mountains and groves, that the surface of it is never ruffled with the least breath of wind, which, perhaps, together with the clearness of its waters, gave it formerly the name of Diana's looking-glass.

Speculumque Dianae. Virgil.

Joseph Addison, *Remarks on Several Parts of Italy, in the Years 1701, 1702, and 1703,* 1705

Nicolosi (slopes of Etna)

We found a degree of wildness and ferocity in the inhabitants of this mountain that I have not observed any where else. It put me in mind of an observation the Padre della Torre (the historiographer of mount Vesuvius) told me he had often made in the confines of Naples; that in the places where the air is most impregnated with sulphur and hot exhalations, the people are always most wicked and vicious. Whatever truth there may be in the observation, the people about Nicolosi at least seem to confirm it. The whole village flocked round us, and the women in particular abused us exceedingly.

Patrick Brydone, *A Tour through Sicily and Malta,* 1773

Orvieto

Sudden view of Orvieto in midst of amphitheatre of hills. Unsurpassed. Like a show mushroom grown there.

Arnold Bennett, *Journal,* 21 April 1914

Otranto

I did not even know that there was a castle of Otranto. When the story was finished, I looked into the map of the kingdom of Naples for a well-sounding name, and that of Otranto was very sonorous.

Horace Walpole, Letter to the Right Hon. Elizabeth Lady Craven, 27 November 1786

Padua

and Pisa
Lucentio: for I have *Pisa* left,

And am to *Padua* come, as he that leaves
A shallow plash, to plunge him in the deepe,
And with sacietie seekes to quench his thirst.

Willam Shakespeare, *The Taming of the Shrew*, *c.* 1595–6

Faire *Padua,* nurserie of Arts.

Ibid. (Lucentio)

A fertile nursery, and sweete emporium and mart town of learning.

Thomas Coryate, *Crudities*, 1611

Padua is the most melancholy city of Europe, the cause only arising of the narrow passage of the open streets, and of the long galleries, and dark ranges of pillars, that go all where on every hand of you through the whole streets of the town. The scholars here in the night commit many murders against their private adversaries, and too often executed upon the strangers and innocent, and all with gun-shot or else with stilettoes. For beastly sodomy, it is as rife here as in Rome, Naples, Florence, Bullogna, Venice, Ferrara, Genoa, Parma not being exempted, nor yet the smallest village of Italy: A monstrous filthiness, and yet to them a pleasant pastime, making songs, and singing sonnets of the beauty and pleasure of their *bardassi*, or buggered boys.

William Lithgow, *Rare Adventures and Painfull Peregrinations*, 1614/32

Here one sees the Decays of a vast City, which was once one of the biggest of all *Italy:* the Compass is the same that it was, but there is much uninhabited Ground in it, and Houses there go almost for nothing. The Air is extreme good; and there is so great a Plenty of all things except Money, that a little Money goes a great way. The University here, tho' so much supported by the *Venetians*, that they pay fifty Professors, yet sinks extremely: There are no Men of any great Fame now in it; and the Quarrels among the Students have driven away most of the Strangers that used to come and study here; for it is not safe to stir abroad here after Sun-set. The Number of Palaces here is incredible; and tho' the Nobility of *Padua* is almost quite ruined, yet the Beauty of their ancient Palaces shews what they once were. The *Venetians* have been willing to let the ancient Quarrels, that were in all those conquer'd Cities, continue still among them; for while one kills another, and the Children of the other take their Revenges afterwards, both come under the *Bando* by this means, and the Confiscation goes to the Senate.

Gilbert Burnet, *Some Letters Containing an Account of what Seemed Remarkable in Travelling . . .*, 1687

I am at Padua like a Mouse in a Parmasan cheese.

Lady Mary Wortley Montagu, Letter to Wilhelmina Tichborne, 15 June 1759

The Franciscan church, dedicated to St. Antonio, the great patron of this city, was the place we were first led to by the Cicerone of our inn. The body of this holy person is inclosed in a sarcophagus, under an altar in the middle of the chapel, and is said to emit a very agreeable and refreshing flavour. Pious Catholics believe this to be the natural effluvia of the saint's body; while heretics assert, that the perfume (for a perfume there certainly is) proceeds from certain balsams rubbed on the marble every morning, before the votaries come to pay their devotions. I never presume to give an opinion on contested points of this kind; but I may be allowed to say, that if this sweet odour really proceeds from the holy Franciscan, he emits a very different smell from any of the brethren of that order whom I ever had an opportunity of approaching.

John Moore, *A View of Society and Manners in Italy*, 1781

The University of Padua is a dying taper.

Edward Gibbon, *Memoirs of his Life*, 1796

In thine halls the lamp of learning
Padua, now no more is burning;
Like a meteor, whose wild way
Is lost over the grave of day,
It gleams betrayed, and to betray.

Percy Bysshe Shelley, *Lines Written among the Euganian Hills*, October 1818

Palermo

catacombs of the Capuchins

This morning we went to see a celebrated convent of Capuchins, about a mile without the city; it contains nothing very remarkable but the burial-place, which indeed is a great curiosity. This is a vast subterraneous apartment, divided into large commodious galleries, the walls on each side of which are hollowed into a variety of niches, as if intended for a great collection of statues; these niches, instead of statues, are all filled with dead bodies, set upright upon their legs, and fixed by the back to the inside of the nich: their number is about three hundred: they are all dressed in the clothes they usually wore, and form a most respectable and venerable assembly. The skin and muscles, by a certain preparation, become as dry and hard as a piece of stock-fish; and although many of them have been here upwards of two hundred and fifty years, yet none are reduced to skeletons; the muscles, indeed, in some appear to be a good deal more shrunk than in others; probably because these persons had been more extenuated at the time of their death.

Here the people of Palermo pay daily visits to their deceased friends, and recal with pleasure and regret the scenes of their past life: here they familiarize themselves with their future state, and chuse the company they would wish to keep in the other world. It is a common thing to make choice of their nich, and to try if their body fits it, that no alterations may be necessary after they are dead; and sometimes, by way of a voluntary penance, they accustom themselves to stand for hours in these niches. . . .

I am not sure if this is not a better method of disposing of the dead than ours. These visits must prove admirable lessons of humility; and I assure you, they are not such objects of horror as you would imagine: they are said, even for ages after death, to retain a strong likeness to what they were when alive; so that, as soon as you have conquered the first feeling excited by these venerable figures, you only consider this as a vast gallery of original portraits, drawn after the life, by the justest and most unprejudiced hand. It must be owned that the colours are rather faded; and the pencil does not appear to have been the most flattering in the world; but no matter, it is the pencil of truth, and not of a mercenary, who only wants to please.

Patrick Brydone, *A Tour through Sicily and Malta*, 1773

and the sirocco

I found the climate of Sicily warmer and more oppressive than that of Naples; indeed, when the sirocco blows, it is almost insupportable. . . . Such is the opinion which the natives have of its baleful influence, that I once heard a Palermatan dilettante say, when obliged to allow that some music composed by his favourite Pigniotti was bad – 'Well, I suppose I must admit it bad; but perhaps he composed it during the sirocco!'

Michael Kelly, *Reminiscences*, 1826

Piacenza

The Cathedral is among the rudest . . . in Italy.

Lady Morgan, *Italy*, 1820

A brown, decayed, old town, Piacenza is. A deserted, solitary, grass-grown place, with ruined ramparts; half-filled-up trenches, which afford a frowzy pasturage to the lean kine which wander about them: and streets of stern houses, moodily frowning at the other houses over the way. The sleepiest and shabbiest of soldiery go wandering about, with the double curse of laziness and poverty, uncouthly wrinkling their misfitting regimentals; the dirtiest of children play with their impromptu toys (pigs and mud) in the feeblest of gutters; and the gauntest of dogs trot in and out of the dullest of archways, in perpetual search of something to eat which they never seem to find.

Charles Dickens, *Pictures from Italy*, 1846

Piedmont

I observed that many of their women and children goe onely in their smocks and shirts in divers places of the countrey without any other apparrell at all by reason of the extreme heat of the clymate: and many of their children which doe weare breeches, have them so made, that all the hinder parts of their bodies are naked, for the more coolenesse of the ayre.

Thomas Coryate, *Crudities*, 1611

This country of Piemont is a marvellous fruitful and plain country, and wonderfully populous, like to the river-sides of Arno round about Florence; insomuch, that a Venetian demanding a Piemont cavalier, What Piemont was? replied, It was a town of three hundred miles in circuit; meaning of the habitations and populosity of the soil.

William Lithgow, *Rare Adventures and Painfull Peregrinations*, 1614/32

Avenge, O Lord, thy slaughter'd saints, whose bones
Lie scatter'd on the Alpine mountains cold;
Ev'n them who kept thy truth so pure of old
When all our Fathers worshipt Stocks and Stones,
Forget not: in thy book record their groanes
Who were thy Sheep, and in their antient Fold
Slayn by the bloody Piemontese that roll'd
Mother with Infant down the Rocks. . . .

John Milton, *Sonnet – On the Late Massacher in Piedmont*, May 1655, *Poems*, 1673

A lady of a great house in Piedmont, having four sons, makes no scruple to declare, that the first shall represent the family, the second enter into the army, the third into the church, and that she will breed the fourth a gamester.

Tobias Smollett, *Travels through France and Italy*, 1766

The Piedmontese are really charming people, so simple and kindly. Only I wish they weren't all counts.

Edward Lear, Letter to Chichester Fortescue, 31 July 1870

Pisa

Pisa renowned for grave Citizens.

William Shakespeare, *The Taming of the Shrew*, *c.* 1595–6

Pisa is a fine old city, that strikes you with the same veneration you would feel at sight of an ancient temple, which bears the marks of decay, without being absolutely dilapidated.

Tobias Smollett, *Travels through France and Italy*, 1766

A large, disagreeable city, almost without inhabitants.

Percy Bysshe Shelley, Letter to Thomas Love Peacock, 5 June 1818

I was very much stricken at Pisa with the resemblance which the quays of that city bear to those of Dublin . . . yet, of all places in Italy, I left Pisa with least regret; its sombre appearance, and want of amusement, did not at all suit my mercurial spirits.

Michael Kelly, *Reminiscences,* 1826

Pisa has a look of elegant tranquillity, which is not exactly *dullness,* and pleases me particularly.

Anna Jameson, *Diary of an Ennuyée,* 1826

Oh, it is so beautiful and so full of repose, yet not *desolate;* it is rather the repose of sleep than of death. . . . The worst of Pisa is, or would be to some persons, that, socially speaking, it has its dullnesses; it is not lively like Florence, not in that way.

Elizabeth Barrett Browning, Letter to Mrs Martin, 1846

Let the reader imagine a small white city, with a tower leaning at one end of it, trees on either side, and blue mountains for background; and he may fancy he sees Pisa, as the traveller sees it in coming from Leghorn. Add to this, in summer-time, fields of corn on all sides, bordered with hedgerow trees, and the festoons of vines, of which he has so often read, hanging from tree to tree; and he may judge of the impression made upon an admirer of Italy, who is in Tuscany for the first time.

In entering the city, the impression is not injured. What looked white in the distance remains as pure and fair on closer acquaintance. . . .

The first novelty that strikes you, after your dreams and matter-of-fact have recovered from the surprise of their introduction to one another, is the singular fairness and new look of houses that have been standing hundreds of years. This is owing to the dryness of the Italian atmosphere. Antiquity refuses to look ancient in Italy. It insists upon retaining its youthfulness of aspect. The consequence at first is a mixed feeling of admiration and disappointment; for we miss the venerable. The houses seem as if they ought to have sympathized more with humanity, and were as cold and as hard-hearted as their materials. But you discover that Italy is the land, not of the venerable, but the beautiful; and cease to look for old age in the chosen country of Apollo and the Venus.

Leigh Hunt, *Autobiography,* 1850 – of 1822

Pisa, *vituperio delle genti,* in point of laxativeness and deadly weariness.

Richard Burton, *Wanderings in West Africa,* 1863

and the Arno

In the hour of evening, under a wintry sky amid whose darkly massed vapours a young moon is peering down upon this maddened world, I wander alone through deserted roadways towards that old solitary brick-tower. Here I stand and watch the Arno rolling its sullen waves. In Pisa, at such an hour, the Arno is the emblem of Despair. Swollen with melted snow from the mountains, it has gnawed its miserable clay banks and now creeps along, leaden and inert, half solid, like a torrent of liquid mud – irresolute whether to be earth or water; whether to stagnate here for ever at my feet, or crawl onward yet another sluggish league into the sea. So may Lethe look or Styx: the nightmare of a flood.

Norman Douglas, *Alone,* 1921

The Leaning Tower

The Campanile . . . stands alone on the right side of the Domo or Cathedrall, strangely remarkable for this, that the beholder would expect every moment when it should fall; being built exceedingly declining by a rare adresse of the imortal Architect: and really I take it to be one of the most singular pieces of workmanship in the World; how it is supported from immediately falling would puzzle a good Geometrician.

John Evelyn, *Diary,* 20 October 1644

The Cathedral, – a venerable pile of party-coloured marble. The first impression of this style of building is unfavourable; but this may be the mere effect of novelty. One seldom likes what one is not accustomed to.

The leaning tower at first sight is quite terrific, and exceeds expectation. . . . Upon the whole it is a very elegant structure; and the general effect is so pleasing, that, – like Alexander's wry neck, – it might well bring leaning into fashion amongst all the towers in Christendom.

Henry Matthews, *The Diary of an Invalid,* 1820

Like most things connected in their first associations with school-books and school-time, it was too small. I felt it keenly.

Charles Dickens, *Pictures from Italy,* 1846

The group of buildings, clustered on and about this verdant carpet: comprising the Tower, the Baptistery, the Cathedral, and the Church of the Campo Santo: is perhaps the most remarkable and beautiful in the whole world; and from being clustered there, together, away from the ordinary transactions and details of the town, they have a singularly venerable and impressive character. It is the architectural essence of a rich old city, with all its common life and common habitations pressed out, and filtered away.

Ibid.

I know not whether my first sensation at the sight of the Leaning Tower, was admiration of its extreme beauty, or astonishment at its posture.

Leigh Hunt, *Autobiography,* 1850

Walked at once to the Duomo. . . . One end of it looks like coral grottoes in sea, – pearl diver. pillars in tiers. . . . Baptistery like dome set on ground. Wonderful pulpit of marble. – Campanile like pine poised just ere snapping. You wait to hear crash.

Herman Melville, *Journal of a Visit to Europe and the Levant,* 23 March 1857

Pompeii

A brilliant day – Went to Pompeii, winding along the shore & round Vesuvius, thro' Villages, one half desolated & rebuilt, (Torre del Grece) one (Portici) built unknowingly over a town swallowed up & lost in liquid lava that has hardened into stone. Passed thro' fields of indurated lava & among the richest gardens, the mountain, like a gloomy tyrant above, sending forth his displeasure, & seeming only to withhold destruction from those who lived beneath him – We had no intimation of what was coming – when, alighting at a small door, we descended a few paces, & found ourselves in the forum, the columns of its portico standing, & on some of them scrawled by the people names, a horse galloping in red chalk – then came the theatres, the basilica, the temples, the streets – after passing the Apothecary's, who can stand at the fountain – Ganimede – where the three ways meet paved with lava – & look up & down near the oil-merchant's door & the miller's, & not feel a strange & not unpleasing sadness. Who can walk thro' the better houses – one of these is bounded by Vesuvius itself – particularly those in the borgo, their baths, & courts & gardens unmoved? or stand near the gateway & look down the street of tombs, one by one, so vast, & of marble so white, so ornamented, so entire – What an idea do they give us of the Via Appia?

Samuel Rogers, *Italian Journal,* 20 February 1815

I stood within the city disinterred
  And heard the autumnal leaves like light footfalls
Of spirits passing through the streets; and heard
  The mountain's slumberous voice at intervals
  Thrill through those roofless halls. . . .
  Around me gleamed many a bright sepulchre
Of whose pure beauty, Time, as if his pleasure
  Were to spare Death, had never made erasure.

Percy Bysshe Shelley, *Ode to Naples,* 1820

The walls of these little cabinets are frequently painted in frescoes, the birds, beasts, and flowers sometimes well executed; the pavement in the better and larger houses is of many-coloured mosaics; but, except in one superior mansion, called the house of Sallust, we did not observe one room long enough to contain an English bed.

Lady Morgan, *Italy,* 1820

Nothing is wanting but the inhabitants. Still, a morning's walk through the solemn silent streets of Pompeii, will give you a livelier idea of their modes of life, than all the books in the world. They seem, like the French of the present day, to have existed only *in public.*

Henry Matthews, *Diary of an Invalid,* 1820

Others even regret that the houses are not repaired and inhabited – but this would very soon destroy the identity and antiquity of the place.

John Webster, *Notes of a Journey from London to Constantinople . . . ,* 1836

On the 9th of February, Sir Walter went to Pompeii. . . . I was sometimes enabled to call his attention to such objects as were the most worthy of remark. To these observations, however, he seemed generally nearly insensible, viewing the whole and not the parts, with the eye, not of an antiquary, but a poet, and exclaiming frequently – 'The City of the Dead,' without any other remark.

Sir William Gell, quoted by J.G. Lockhart, *Life of Sir Walter Scott,* 1838 – of 1832

Pompeii like any other town. Same old humanity. All the same whether one be dead or alive. Pompeii comfortable sermon. Like Pompeii better than Paris.

Herman Melville, *Journal of a Visit to Europe and the Levant,* 18 February 1857

The ghastly suburb of Pompeii repeats, like a remote echo, the very note of Naples. Pompeii, though you will find it large enough when you follow all the intersections of its abrupt, crossing ways, remains in the memory like a toy city, or a cabinet in a museum.

Arthur Symons, *Cities,* 1903

and Messina

It was Goethe who, speaking of Pompeii, said that of the many catastrophes which have afflicted mankind, few have given greater pleasure to posterity. The same will never be said of Messina.

Norman Douglas, *Old Calabria,* 1915

Pompeii that was at one time the Beverly Hills of Italy. . . . Philadelphia comes nearer approaching it than any big city I know of.

Will Rogers, *Letters of a Self-Made Diplomat to his President,* 1927

It is true that much of the town was crowded and rectilinear, the small plain windowless houses lining the streets monotonous and unornamental; to live in them must have been like living in one of a row of bathing huts.

Rose Macaulay, *Pleasures of Ruins,* 1953

Pontine Marshes (near Rome)

The short, but pathetic reply, made to an inquiring

traveller, is well known. – 'How do you manage to live here?' said he, to a group of these animated spectres – 'We die!'

Henry Matthews, *Diary of an Invalid*, 1820

Radicofani

I began to despair of magical adventures, since none happened at Radicofani, which nature seems wholly to have abandoned. Not a tree, not an acre of soil, has she bestowed upon its inhabitants, who would have more excuse for practising the gloomy art than the rest of mankind. I was very glad to leave their black hills and stony wilderness behind.

William Beckford, *Dreams Waking Thoughts and Incidents*, 1783

Bleak Radicofani! escaped with joy –

William Wordsworth, *Memorials of a Tour in Italy, 1837*, 1840–1, pub. 1842

Ravenna

Ravenna itself preserves perhaps more of the old Italian manners than any City in Italy – it is out of the way of travellers and armies – and thus they have retained more of their originality. – They make love a good deal, – and assassinate a little.

Lord Byron, Letter to Lady Byron, 20 July 1819

Inhabitants somewhat savage – rather treacherous and highly inflamed by politics. Fine fellows, though, – good materials for a nation. Out of chaos God made a world, and out of high passions comes a people.

Lord Byron, *Ravenna Journal*, 5 January 1821

Ravenna, where Robert positively wanted to go to live once, has itself put an end to all those yearnings. The churches are wonderful: holding an atmosphere of purple glory, and if one could just live in them, or in Dante's tomb – well, otherwise, keep me from Ravenna. The very antiquity of the houses is white-washed, and the marshes on all sides send up stenches new and old, till the hot air is sick with them.

Elizabeth Barrett Browning, Letter, 1848

Ravenna was my personal circus. It was what I came for. . . . The Ravenna churches with their mosaics . . . are a revelation of what can be done by an old civilisation when the gold-bug breaks down, and empires expire.

Henry Adams, Letter to Elizabeth Cameron, 15 July 1896

We ended in Ravenna and felt the splendour of Rome dying among barbarians in a way that I never felt again until I reached the ruins of the Levant.

Freya Stark, *Traveller's Prelude*, 1950

Reggio Calabria

I could have desired no happier incident for the close of my journey; by lucky chance this visit to the museum had been postponed till the last morning, and, as I idled through the afternoon about the Via Plutino, my farewell mood was in full harmony with that in which I had landed from Naples upon the Calabrian shore. So hard a thing to catch and to retain, the mood corresponding perfectly to an intellectual bias – hard, at all events, for him who cannot shape his life as he will, and whom circumstance ever menaces with dreary harassment. Alone and quiet, I heard the washing of the waves; I saw the evening fall on cloud-wreathed Etna, the twinkling lights come forth upon Scylla and Charybdis; and, as I looked my last towards the Ionian Sea, I wished it were mine to wander endlessly amid the silence of the ancient world, to-day and all its sounds forgotten.

George Gissing, *By the Ionian Sea*, 1901

Rome

Ancient

Civis Romanus Sum.
(I am a Roman citizen.)

Marcus Tullius Cicero, *In Verrem*, v, lvii, 147

Augustus Caesar when he had many diverse waies both beautified and strengthened or fensed the citie of Rome, and had also for many yeres to come, as moche as in hym laie, made the same suer and safe from all daungiers, being proude thereof not without cause, he would often saie: I found Rome made but of Bricke, and I will leave it of Marble.

Nicholas Udall (trans.), *The Apothegmes of Erasmus*, 1564

Rome onely might to Rome compared bee,
And onely Rome could make great Rome to tremble.

Edmund Spenser, *The Ruines of Rome by Bellay*, Complaints, 1591

The queen of nations, absolutely great.

William Alexander, Earl of Stirling, *Doomsday*, The Sixth Hour, St. 77, *c.* 1614, pub. 1637

A people, who, while they were poor, robbed mankind; and as soon as they became rich, robbed one another.

Samuel Johnson, in James Boswell, *Life of Johnson*, 1756

I have already found such a fund of entertainment for a mind somewhat prepared for it by an acquaintance with the Romans, that I am really almost in a dream. Whatever ideas books may have given us of the greatness of that people, their accounts of the most flourishing state of Rome fall infinitely short of the picture of its ruins. I am convinced there never existed such a nation, and I hope for the happiness of mankind that there never will again.

Edward Gibbon, Letter to Edward Gibbon Sr, 9 October 1764

It appears to me that nothing romantic or poetical can coexist with what is Roman. . . . The Romans were a blunt, flat people.

Walter Savage Landor, Letter to Southey, 30 November 1809

Vile in its origin, barbarous in its institutions, a casual association of robbers and of outcasts became the destiny of mankind.

Lady Morgan, *Italy,* 1820

The Romans would never have had time to conquer the world if they had been obliged to learn Latin first of all.

Heinrich Heine, *Das Buch le Grand,* in *Reisebilder,* 1826–31

If the Romans had been better acquainted with the laws of hydraulics they would not have constructed all the aqueducts that surround the ruins of their cities; they would have made a better use of their power and their wealth. If they had invented the steam-engine, perhaps they would not have extended to the extremities of their empire those long artificial ways which are called Roman roads. These things are the splendid memorials at the same time of their ignorance and of their greatness.

A people that left no other vestige than a few leaden pipes in the earth and a few iron rods on its surface might have been more the master of nature than the Romans.

Alexis de Tocqueville, *Democracy in America,* the second part, 1840

The barbarians who broke up the Roman empire did not arrive a day too soon.

R.W. Emerson, 'Considerations by the Way', *Conduct of Life,* 1860

The mere names in Roman history make my blood warm.

George Gissing, *By the Ionian Sea,* 1901

It is easy to speak of the Empire and to say that it established its order from the Tyne to the Euphrates; but when one has travelled alone and on foot up and down the world, and seen its vastness and its complexity, and yet everywhere the unity even of bricks in their courses, then one begins to understand the name of Rome.

Hilaire Belloc, *Hills and the Sea,* 1906

The Roman people were military. They had no love for ships. The sea terrified them: their expansion was by land and their horror of the sea explains much of their history.

Hilaire Belloc, *Esto Perpetua,* 1906

Everybody knows that the ancient world ran down into the completed Roman Empire as into a reservoir, and everybody knows that the modern world has flowed outwards from that reservoir by various channels.

Ibid.

Proverbs

Neque protinus uno est Condita Roma die.
(Rome was not built in a day.)

Pietro Angelo Manzolli (Palingenius, pseud.), *Zodiacus Vitae,* xii, 460

Chi Asino va a Roma, Asino se ne torna.
(If an Asse at Rome doe sojourne,
As Asse he shall from thence returne.)

Fynes Moryson, 'Of Travelling in General', *An Itinerary,* 1617

All roads lead to Rome.

Traditional

At Florence you think; at Rome, you pray; at Venice, you love; at Naples, you look.

Italian proverb, quoted Maurice Baring, *Round the World in any Number of Days,* 1913

Dove è il Papa, ivi è Roma.
(Where the Pope is, there is Rome.)

Italian proverb

When at Rome, do as the Romans do.

Traditional

Sixteenth Century

Thou stranger, which for *Rome* in *Rome* here seekest,
And nought of *Rome* in *Rome* perceiv'st at all,
These same olde walls, olde arches which thou seest,
Olde Palaces, is that which *Rome* men call.
Behold what wreake, what ruine, and what wast,
And how that she, which with her mightie powre
Tam'd all the world, hath tam'd herselfe at last,
The pray of time, which all things doth devowre.
Rome now of *Rome* is th'onely funerall,
And onely *Rome* of *Rome* hath victorie;
Ne ought save *Tyber* hastning to his fall
Remaines of all: O worlds inconstancie.

That which is firme doth flit and fall away,
And that is flitting, doth abide and stay. . . .

All that which *Aegypt* whilome did devise,
All that which *Greece* their temples to embrave,
After th'Ionicke, Atticke, Doricke guise,
Or *Corinth* skil'd in curious workes to grave:
All that *Lysippus* practike art could forme,
Apelles wit, or *Phidias* his skill,
Was wont this auncient Citie to adorne,
And the heaven it selfe with her wide wonders fill;
All that which *Athens* ever brought forth wise,
All that which *Afrike* ever brought forth strange,
All that which *Asie* ever had of prise,
Was here to see. O mervelous great change:
Rome living was the worlds sole ornament,
And dead, is now the worlds sole moniment.

Edmund Spenser, *The Ruines of Rome by Bellay,* Complaints, 1591

Note by the waye that it is the use in *Rome,* for all men whatsoever to weare their haire short: which they doe not so much for conscience sake, or any religion they place in it, but because the extremitie of the heate is such there, that if they should not doe so, they should not have a haire left on their heads to stand upright when they were scared with sprights.

Thomas Nashe, *The Unfortunate Traveller,* 1594

If thou doost but lend half a looke to a *Romans* or *Italians* wife, thy porredge shall be prepared for thee, and cost thee nothing but thy lyfe. Chance some of them break a bitter iest on thee, and thou retortst it severely, or seemest discontented: goe to thy chamber, and provide a great blanket, for thou shall be sure to be visited with guests in a mask the next night, when in kindnes and courtship thy throat shall be cut, and the doers returne undiscovered. Nothing so long of memorie as a dog, these *Italians* are old dogs, & will carrie an iniurie a whole age in memorie: I have heard of a boxe on the eare that hath been revenged thirtie yeare after.

Ibid.

Hate and debate Rome through the world hath spread
Yet Roma, *amor* is if backward read;
Then is it strange Rome hate should foster? No!
For out of backward love all hate doth flow.

Sir John Harington, *Epigram,* late sixteenth century

Of Rome, in short, this is my opinion, or rather indeed my most assured knowledge, that her delights on earth are sweet, and her judgements in heaven heavy.

Sir Henry Wotton, Letter to Lord Zouche, 8 May 1592

Eighteenth Century

Our days at present like those in the first chapter of Genesis consist only of the evening and the morning; for the Roman noons are as silent as the midnights of other countries.

Joseph Addison, Letter to Mr Wortley Montagu, 7 August 1701

Here domes and temples rise in distant views
And opening palaces invite my muse.

Joseph Addison, Letter from Italy to the Right Honourable Lord Halifax, 1701

By the remains one sees of Roman grandeur in their structures, 'tis evident that there must have been more pains taken to destroy those piles than to raise them. They are more demolished than any time or chance could have effected. I am persuaded that in an hundred years Rome will not be worth seeing; tis less so now than one would believe.

Horace Walpole, Letter to Richard West, 7 May 1740

There is a horrid Thing called the mal'aria that comes to Rome every summer, and kills one, and I did not care for being killed so far from Christian burial.

Horace Walpole, Letter to the Hon. Henry Seymour Conway, 5 July 1740

What is more curious than all the Antiquitys . . . is that there is litterally no money in the whole Town, where they follow Mr Law's System and live wholly upon Paper. . . . They go to market with paper, pay the Lodgings with paper, and, in short, there is no Specie to be seen, which raises the prices of every thing to the utmost extravagance, no body knowing what to ask for their goods.

Lady Mary Wortley Montagu, Letter to her husband, 23 November 1740

I hardly slept the night before I arriv'd there with the thoughts of seeing it – my heart beat high, my imagination expanded itself, and my Eyes flash'd again, as I drew near the *Porta del Popolo;* but the moment I enter'd it, I fell at once from my Airy Vision & Utopian Ideas into a very dirty ill looking *place,* (as they call it) with three crooked streets in front, terminated inded at this End with two tolerable Churches – what a disappointment! my Spirits sunk & it was with reluctance that I was drag'd in the afternoon to see the Pantheon – but my God, what was my Pleasure and Surprize! – I never felt so much in my life as when I entered that glorious Structure: I gap'd, but could not speak for 5 Minutes – It is so very noble, that it has not been in the Power of Modern Frippery, or Popery (for it is a Church you know) to extinguish Its grandeur and Elegance – Here I began to think myself in *Old* Rome, & when I saw the ruins of the famous amphitheatre – . . . then I felt my own littleness – & was convinced that the Romans were as much superiour to the Moderns in Every thing, as

Vespasian's Amphitheatre was to Broughton's – it is impossible, my dear Colman, to have any Idea of these things from any Prints that have been made of 'em, – all modern performances look better upon paper, but these Ruins are not to be conceiv'd, but *by the sensible and true Avouch of your own Eyes*. Tho I am pleas'd, much pleas'd with Naples, I have such a thirst to return to Rome, as cannot possibly be slak'd till I have drank up half the Tiber, which, in it's present state, is but a scurvy draught neither. It is very strange that so much good poetry should be thrown away upon such a pitiful River; it is no more comparable to our Thames, than our modern Poets are to their Virgils and Horaces.

David Garrick, Letter to George Colman, 24 December 1763

As I was walking along the streets of Rome, which are very little different from those of any other city, I said to myself, 'Was the Epistle of St. Paul to the Romans written to the inhabitants of this city? And did I use to be so terrified by it?'

James Boswell, Letter to J.-J. Rousseau, 3 October 1765

It was at Rome, on the 15 of October 1764, as I sat musing amidst the ruins of the Capitol, while the bare-footed fryars were singing vespers in the Temple of Jupiter, that the idea of writing the decline and fall of the city first started in my mind.

Edward Gibbon, *Memoirs of his Life*, 1796

Nineteenth Century

As we approach Rome, Antient Italy rushes on the Imagination. Italy has had two lives! Can it be said of any other Country?

Samuel Rogers, *Italian Journal*, 22 November 1814

The capital of the vanished world.

Percy Bysshe Shelley, Letter to Thomas Love Peacock, 20 November 1818

Oh, Rome! my Country! City of the Soul!
The orphans of the heart must turn to thee,
Lone Mother of dead Empires! and control
In their shut breasts their petty misery.
What are our woes and sufferance? Come and see
The cypress – hear the owl – and plod your way
O'er steps of broken thrones and temples – Ye!
Whose agonies are evils of a day –
A world is at our feet as fragile as our clay.

The Niobe of nations! there she stands,
Childless and crownless, in her voiceless woe;
An empty urn within her withered hands,
Whose holy dust was scattered long ago;
The Scipios' tomb contains no ashes now;
The very sepulchres lie tenantless
Of their heroic dwellers: dost thou flow,
Old Tiber! through a marble wilderness?
Rise, with thy yellow waves, and mantle her distress. . . .
Alas, for Earth, for never shall we see
That brightness in her eye she bore when Rome was free!

Lord Byron, *Childe Harold's Pilgrimage*, Canto the Fourth, 1818

I've stood upon Achilles' tomb
And hear Troy doubted; time will doubt of Rome.

Lord Byron, *Don Juan*, 1819–24

You pass over miles of a barren common, much like Hounslow Heath; and when, at last, you arrive at the gate of the Eternal City, the first impression is, I think, a feeling of disappointment. . . . We were soon in the *Piazza di Spagna*, – the focus of fashion, and the general resort of the English. Some travellers have compared it to Grosvenor-Square; – but the Piazza di Spagna is little more than an irregular open space, a little less nasty than the other piazzas in Rome, because the habits of the people are in some measure restrained by the presence of the English. Still, there is quite enough left to make me believe the Romans the nastiest people in Christendom, – if I had not seen the Portuguese. The English swarm everywhere. We found all the inns full. It seemed like a country town in England at an assizes.

Henry Matthews, *Diary of an Invalid*, 1820

Go thou to Rome, – at once the Paradise,
The grave, the city, and the wilderness.

Percy Bysshe Shelley, *Adonais*, 1821

I am in Rome! Oft as the morning-ray
Visits these eyes, waking at once I cry,
Whence this excess of joy? What has befallen me?
And from within a thrilling voice replies
Thou art in Rome! A thousand busy thoughts
Rush on my mind, a thousand images;
And I spring up as girt to run a race!

Samuel Rogers, *Italy*, 1822–34

In Rome, around it nothing strikes the eye, nothing rivets the attention but ruins, the fragments of what has been; the past is like a *halo* forever surrounding and obscuring the present!

William Hazlitt, *Notes of a Journey through France and Italy*, 1826

This *Terra Pictura*.

J.M.W. Turner, Letter to George Jones, 13 October 1828

The effect of every part is so vast and overpowering – there is such an air of greatness and repose cast over the whole, and, independent of what one knows from history, there are such traces of long sorrow and humiliation, suffering, punishment and decay, that one has a mixture of feelings, partly such as those with which one would approach a corpse, and partly those which would be excited by the sight of the spirit which had left it.

John Henry Newman, Letter to Frederic Rogers, 5 March 1833

We began, in a perfect fever, to strain our eyes for Rome; and when, after another mile or two, the Eternal City appeared, at length, in the distance; it looked like – I am half afraid to write the word – like LONDON!!! There it lay, under a thick cloud, with innumerable towers, and steeples, and roofs of houses, rising up into the sky, and high above them all, one Dome. I swear, that keenly as I felt the seeming absurdity of the comparison, it was so like London, at that distance, that if you could have shown it me, in a glass, I should have taken it for nothing else.

Charles Dickens, *Pictures from Italy,* 1846

Oh! Rome, tremendous, who, beholding thee,
Shall not forget the bitterest private grief
That e'er made havoc of one single life?

Fanny Kemble (Mrs Butler), *A Year of Consolation,* 1847

Rome disappoints me much; I hardly as yet
understand, but
Rubbishy seems the word that most exactly would suit it.
All the foolish destructions, and all the sillier savings,
All the incongrous things of past incompatible ages,
Seem to be treasured up here to make fools of present
and future.
Would to Heaven the old Goths had made a cleaner
sweep of it!
Would to Heaven some new ones would come and
destroy these churches!
However, one can live in Rome, as also in London.
Rome is better than London, because it is other than
London. . . .
Rome disappoints me still; but I shrink and adapt
myself to it.
Somehow a tyrannous sense of a superincumbent
oppression
Still, wherever I go, accompanies ever, and makes me
Feel like a tree (shall I say?) buried under a ruin of
brickwork.
Rome, believe me my friend, is like its own Monte
Testaceo,
Merely a marvellous mass of broken and castaway
wine-pots.
Ye gods! what do I want with this rubbish of ages
departed,
Things that nature abhors, the experiments that she
has failed in?
What do I find in the Forum? An Archway and two or
three pillars.
Well, but St Peter's? Alas, Bernini has filled it with
sculpture!
No one can cavil, I grant, at the size of the great
Coliseum.
Doubtless the notion of grand and capacious and
massive amusement,
This the old Romans had; but tell me, is this an idea?
Yet of solidity much, but of splendour little is extant:
'Brickwork I found thee, and marble I left thee!' their
Emperor vaunted;
'Marble I thought thee, and brickwork I find thee!' the
Tourist may answer.

Arthur Hugh Clough, *Amours de Voyage,* 1849

O Land of Empire, art and love!
What is it that you show me?
A sky for Gods to tread above,
A soil for pigs below me!
O in all place and shape and kind
Beyond all thought and thinking,
The graceful with the gross combined,
The stately with the stinking! . . .
O richly soiled and richly sunned,
Exuberant, fervid, and fecund!
Are these the fixed condition
On which may Northern pilgrim come
To imbibe thine ether-air, and sum
Thy store of old tradition?
Must we be chill, if clean, and stand
Foot-deep in dirt in classic land?

Arthur Hugh Clough, 'Oh Land of Empire, Art and Love', *c.* 1849

At Rome may everything be bought
But honesty, there vainly sought:
For other kinds of costly ware
The pontif opens a bazaar.
If you have lost your soul you may
Procure a better . . . only pay.
If you have any favourite sin,
The price is ticketed . . . walk in.
For a few thousand golden pieces
Uncles may marry here their nieces;
The pontif slips the maiden sash
And winks, and walks away the cash.
Naples, so scant of blushes sees
And blushes at such tricks as these
Until a ghostly father saith,
Behold my sons! the ancient faith!
This ancient faith brought faithful Gauls
In guise of friends to scale the walls
Of manfull Rome; and Louis' word
Unsheath'd Christina's tarnisht sword.

W.S. Landor, *Last Fruit,* No. CXLV, 1853

*Of course our first pilgrimage was to St Peter's. What

a walk! Under what noble shadows does one pass; how great and liberal the houses are, with generous casements and courts, and great grey portals which giants might get through and keep their turbans on. Why, the houses are twice as tall as Lamb Court itself; and over them hangs a noble dinge, a venerable mouldy splendour. Over the solemn portals are ancient mystic escutcheons – vast shields of princes and cardinals, such as Ariosto's knights might take down; and every figure about them is a picture by himself. At every turn there is a temple; in every court a brawling fountain. Besides the people of the streets and houses, and the army of priests black and brown, there's a great silent population of marble. There are battered gods tumbled out of Olympus and broken in the fall, and set up under niches and over fountains; there are senators namelessly, noselessly, noiselessly seated under archways, or lurking in courts and gardens. And then, besides these defunct ones, of whom these old figures may be said to be the corpses, there is the reigning family, a countless carved hierarchy of angels, saints, confessors of the latter dynasty which has conquered the court of Jove. . . .

I think I have lost sight of St Peter's haven't I? Yet it is big enough. How it makes your heart beat when you first see it! Ours did as we came in at night from Cività Vecchia, and saw a great, ghostly, darkling dome rising solemnly up into the grey night, and keeping us company ever so long as we drove, as if it had been an orb fallen out of heaven with its light put out. As you look at it from the Pincio, and the sun sets behind it, surely that aspect of earth and sky is one of the grandest in the world. I don't like to say that the façade of the church is ugly and obtrusive. As long as the dome overawes, that façade is supportable. You advance towards it – through, oh, such a noble court! with fountains flashing up to meet the sunbeams; and right and left of you two sweeping half-crescents of great columns; but you pass by the courtiers and up to the steps of the throne, and the dome seems to disappear behind it. It is as if the throne was upset, and the king had toppled over.

W.M. Thackeray, *The Newcomes*, 1853–5

To leave Rome will fill me with a barbarian complacency. I don't pretend to have a rag of sentiment about Rome. It is a palimpsest Rome – a watering-place written over the antique – and I haven't taken it as a poet should, I suppose; only let us speak the truth, above all things. I am strongly a creature of association, and the associations of the place have not been favourable to me.

Elizabeth Barrett Browning, Letter to Miss Mitford, 10 May 1854

Any one who has remarked how grandly the Romans do nothing will be slow to believe them an effete race. Their style is as the colossal to all other, and the name of Eternal City fits Rome also, because time is of no account in it. The Roman always waits as if he could afford it amply, and the slow centuries move quite fast enough for him. Time is to other races the field of a taskmaster, which they must painfully till; but to the Roman it is an entailed estate, which he enjoys and will transmit. The Neapolitan's laziness is that of a loafer; the Roman's is that of a noble.

James Russell Lowell, *Leaves from my Journal in Italy and Elsewhere*, 1854

*Here, it seemed to Little Dorrit that a change came over the Marshalsea spirit of their society, and that Prunes and Prism got the upper hand. Everybody was walking about St. Peter's and the Vatican on somebody else's cork legs, and straining every visible object through somebody else's sieve. Nobody said what anything was, but everybody said what the Mrs Generals, Mr Eustace, or somebody else said it was. The whole body of travellers seemed to be a collection of voluntary human sacrifices, bound hand and foot, and delivered over to Mr Eustace and his attendants, to have the entrails of their intellects arranged according to the taste of that sacred priesthood. Through the rugged remains of temples and tombs and palaces and sěnate halls and theatres and amphitheatres of ancient days, hosts of tongue-tied and blindfolded moderns were carefully feeling their way, incessantly repeating Prunes and Prism, in the endeavour to set their lips according to the received form. Mrs General was in her pure element. Nobody had an opinion. There was a formation of surface going on around her on an amazing scale, and it had not a flaw of courage or honest free speech in it.

Charles Dickens, *Little Dorrit*, 1857–8

More imagination wanted *at* Rome than at home to appreciate the place.

Herman Melville, *Journal of a Visit to Europe and the Levant*, 1857

*When we have once known Rome, and left her where she lies, like a long-decaying corpse, retaining a trace of the noble shape it was, but with accumulated dust and fungous growth overspreading all its more admirable features; – left her in utter weariness, no doubt of her narrow, crooked, intricate streets, so uncomfortably paved with little squares of lava that to tread over them is a penitential pilgrimage, so indescribably ugly, moreover, so cold, so alley-like, into which the sun never falls, and where a chill wind forces its deadly breath into our lungs; – left her, tired of the sight of those immense, seven-storied, yellow-washed hovels, or call them palaces, where all that is dreary in domestic life seems magnified and multiplied, and weary of climbing those staircases, which ascend from a ground floor of cook-shops, cobblers' stalls, stables, and regiments of cavalry, to a middle region of princes, cardinals, and ambassadors, and an upper tier of artists, just beneath the unattainable sky; – left her, worn out and shivering at the cheerless and smoky fireside, by day, and feasting with our own substance the ravenous little populus of a Roman bed, at night; – left her, sick at heart of Italian trickery, which has uprooted whatever faith in man's integrity had endured till now, and sick at stomach of sour bread, sour wine, rancid butter, and bad cookery, needlessly bestowed on evil meats; – left her, disgusted with the pretence of Holiness and the reality of Nastiness, each equally omnipresent; – left her, half lifeless from the languid atmosphere, the vital principle of which has been used up long ago, or corrupted by myriads of slaughters; left her, crushed down in spirit with the desolation of her ruin, and the hopelessness of her future; – left her, in short, hating her with all our might, and adding our individual curse to the Infinite Anathema which her old crimes have unmistakeably brought down; – when we have left Rome in such mood as this, we are astonished by the discovery, by and by, that our heartstrings have mysteriously attached themselves to the Eternal City, and are drawing us thitherward again, as if it were more familiar, more intimately our home, than even the spot where we were born!

Nathaniel Hawthorne, *Transformation, The Marble Faun*, 1860

Everyone soon or late comes round by Rome.

Robert Browning, *The Ring and the Book*, v. 296, 1868–9

At last, for the first time – I live! It beats everything: it leaves the Rome of your fancy – your education – nowhere. It makes Venice, Florence – Oxford – London – seem like little cities of pasteboard. I went reeling and moaning through the streets in a fever of enjoyment. In the course of four or five hours I traversed almost the whole of Rome and got a glimpse of everything – the Forum, the Coliseum (stupendissimo)! the Pantheon, the Capitol, St Peter's, the Column of Trajan, the Castle of St Angelo – all the Piazza's and ruins and monuments. The effect is something indescribable. For the first time I know what the picturesque is. In St Peter's I stayed some time. It's even beyond its reputation. It was filled with foreign ecclesiastics – great armies encamped in prayer on the marble plains of its pavement – an inexhaustible physiognomical study. To crown my day, on my way home, I met his Holiness in person – driving in prodigious purple state – sitting dim within the shadows of his coach with two uplifted benedictory fingers – like some dusky hindoo idol in the depths of its shrine. Even if I should leave Rome tonight I should feel that I have caught the keynote of its operation on the senses. I have looked along the grassy vista of the Appian Way and seen the topmost stonework of the Coliseum sitting shrouded in the light of heaven, like the edge of an Alpine chain. I've trod the Forum and I have scaled the Capitol. I've seen the Tiber hurrying along, as swift and dirty as history! From the high tribune of a great chapel of St Peter's I have heard in the papal choir a strange old man sing in a high shrill unpleasant soprano. I've seen troops of little tonsured neophytes clad in scarlet, marching and countermarching and ducking and flopping, like poor little raw recruits for the heavenly host. In fine, I've seen Rome, and I shall go to bed a wiser man than I last rose – yesterday morning.

Henry James, Letter to William James, Rome, 30 October 1869

Nothing can be more depressing to those who really value Rome than to meet Englishmen hunting in couples through the Vatican galleries, one looking for the number of the statue in the guide-book, the other *not* finding it; than to hear Americans describe the Forum as the dustiest heap of old ruins they had ever looked upon; or say, when asked their opinion of the Venus de Medici, that they 'guess they are not particular gone on stone gals;' or, of the Coliseum, that 'it will be a handsome building when it is *finished;*' . . .

A.J.C. Hare, *Walks in Rome*, 1871

'And what,' cries Cupid, 'will save us?'
  Says Apollo: '*Modernise Rome!*'
What inns! Your streets, too, how narrow!
  Too much of palace and dome!

Matthew Arnold, *New Rome*, 1873

  Yea, from the very soil of silent Rome,
You shall grow wise; and, walking, live again
  The lives of buried peoples, and become
  A child by right of that eternal home,
Cradle and grave of empires, on whose walls,
The sun himself subdued to reverence falls.

John Addington Symonds, 'Southward Bound', *Many Many Moods*, 1878

Time's central city, Rome.

Thomas Hardy, *Rome: Building a New Street in the Ancient Quarter*, April 1887

Twentieth Century

Rome is a sea in which many worlds have gone down, and its very pavement is all in waves; so that to drive through these narrow streets, and across these broad squares, in which there is no footway over which a wheel may not drive, is like rocking in a boat on slightly uneasy water.

Arthur Symons, *Cities*, 1903

Every road does not lead to Rome, but every road in Rome leads to eternity.

Ibid.

For the rest, Italy was mostly an emotion, and the emotion naturally centred in Rome. . . . Rome was the worst spot on earth to teach nineteenth-century youth what to do with a twentieth-century world . . . for no one, priest or politician, could honestly read in the ruins of Rome any other certain lesson than that they were evidence of the just judgements of an outraged God against all the doings of man. This moral unfitted Rome for every sort of useful activity; it made Rome a gospel of anarchy and vice; the last place under the sun for educating the young; yet it was, by common consent, the only spot that the young – of either sex and every race – passionately, perversely, wickedly loved. . . . Two great experiments of Western civilization had left there the chief monuments of their failure, and nothing proved that the city might not still survive to express the failure of a third. . . . The tourist . . . went on repeating to himself the eternal question: – Why! Why!! Why!!! – . . . No one had ever answered the question to the satisfaction of any one else; yet every one who had either head or heart, felt that sooner or later he must make up his mind what answer to accept. Substitute the word America for the word Rome, and the question became personal.

Henry Adams, *The Education of Henry Adams,* 1906

Rome reminds me of a man who lives by exhibiting to travellers his grandmother's corpse.

James Joyce, Letter to Stanislaus Joyce, 25 September 1906

There was once upon a time an Englishwoman who came out to Rome to live there. She was the wife of a scholar who had rooms in the Vatican itself, and she herself lived in a neighbouring Palazzo. She was asked by one of her compatriots whether she liked Rome. She said it was a great come-down after what she had been used to.

'And where,' asked the second Englishwoman, 'used you to live in England?'

'Surbiton,' she answered.

Maurice Baring, *Round the World in Any Number of Days,* 1913

It rains persistently in soft, warm showers. Rome is mirthless.

There arises, before my mind's eye, the vision of a sweet old lady friend who said to me, in years gone by: 'When next you go to Rome, please let me know if it is still raining there.'

Norman Douglas, *Alone,* 1921

In Rome you have to do as the Romans do, or get arrested.

Geoffrey Harmsworth, *Abyssinian Adventure,* 1935

Competition for the inspiration of literary works has always been keen among Roman ruins.

Rose Macaulay, *Pleasures of Ruins,* 1953

*Rome's just a city like anywhere else. A vastly overrated city, I'd say. It trades on belief just as Stratford trades on Shakespeare.

Anthony Burgess, *Inside Mr Enderby,* 1963

Rome, Italy, is an example of what happens when the buildings in a city last too long.

Andy Warhol, *The Philosophy of Andy Warhol (From A to B and Back Again),* 1975

Rome is the only European capital which each year must spend millions of pounds restoring ruins – restoring them at least to their state of ruin of 100 years ago.

George Armstrong, in *Guardian,* 9 August 1979

Districts and Details

The Colosseum

While stands the Coliseum, Rome shall stand;
When falls the Coliseum, Rome shall fall;
And when Rome falls – the World.

Lord Byron, *Childe Harold's Pilgrimage,* Canto the Fourth, 1818

and the Baths of Caracalla

The Coliseum is a thing about which it's useless to talk: it must be seen and felt. But as a piece of the picturesque – a province of it – it is thoroughly and simply delightful. . . . I betook myself to the almost equal ruins of the Baths of Caracalla. It was the hour of sunset and I had them all to myself. They are a collection of perfectly mountainous masses of brick-work, to the right of the Appian Way. Even more than the Coliseum I think they give you a notion of the Roman *scale.* Imagine a good second class mountain in reduced circumstances – perforated and honeycombed by some terrestrial cataclysm – and you'll have an idea of these terrific ruins.

Henry James, Letter to Alice James, 7 November 1869

The neighbourhood of the Colisseum is like an old cemetery with broken columns of temples and slabs. You know the Colisseum from Pictures. While we were in the middle of it, looking at it all round gravely from a sense of duty, I heard a voice from London on one of the lowest gallery say: – The Colisseum –

Almost at once two young men in serge suits and straw hats appeared in an embrasure. They leaned on the parapet and then a second voice from the same city clove the calm evening, saying:

– Whowail stands the Colisseum Rawhm shall stand
When falls the Colisseum Rawhm sh'll fall
And when Rawhm falls the world sh'll fall –
but adding cheerfully:
– Kemlong, 'ere's the way aht –

James Joyce, Letter to Stanislaus Joyce, 7 August 1906

The Coliseum is surely one of the most famous structures in the world. Even they who have never been to the spot would recognise it from those myriad reproductions – especially, one would think, an Italian. Nevertheless, while thus discoursing, a man came up to us, a well-dressed man, who politely inquired:

'Could you tell me the name of this *castello?*'

I am glad to think that some account of the rich and singular flora of the Coliseum has been preserved by Deakin and Sebastiani, and possibly by others. I could round off their efforts by describing the fauna of the Coliseum. The fauna of the Coliseum – especially after 11 p.m. – would make a readable book; readable but hardly printable.

Norman Douglas, *Alone,* 1921

I walked around the old Madison Square Garden, which, so unlike the American building, embodied, in its grimness and grandeur, a human attitude that made it an official mask.

Edmund Wilson, *Europe without Baedeker,* 1947

Tarpeian Rock

The Tarpeian Rock is now of so small a fall that a man would think it no great matter for his diversion to leap over it.

Gilbert Burnet, *Letters Containing an Account of What seemed most remarkable in travelling through Switzerland, Italy, . . . ,* 3rd edn, 1708

The Tarpeian rock we all agreed was high and steep enough to break either the late Bp. Burnet's or any man else's neck who should try the experiment by leaping down.

George Berkeley, *Journal,* 15 January 1717

Trevi Fountain

* . . . where some sculptor of Bernini's school had gone absolutely mad in marble.

Nathaniel Hawthorne, *Transformation, The Marble Faun,* 1860

Pilate's House

I was at *Pontius Pilates* house and pissed against it.

Thomas Nashe, *The Unfortunate Traveller,* 1594

Vatican City

Today, on coming out of the Vatican Gallery, Greek Gods and the Roman middle-classes in my brain, all marble to make the contrast worse, I found that the Vatican Gardens were open to the Bohemian and Portuguese pilgrims. I at once spoke both languages fluently, explained that my English dress was a form of penance, and entered that waste desolate park, with its faded Louis XIV gardens, its sombre avenues, its sad woodland. The peacocks screamed, and I understood why tragedy dogged the gilt feet of each pontiff. But I wandered in exquisite melancholy for an hour. One Philippo, a student, whom I culled in the Borgia room, was with me: not for many years has love walked in the Pope's pleasaunce.

Oscar Wilde, Letter to Robert Ross, 27 April 1900

A Baroque State the size of Hyde Park.

Patrick O'Donovan, *Observer,* 13 August 1978

St Peter's

St. Peter's seldom answers expectation at first entering it, but enlarges itself on all sides insensibly, and mends upon the eye every moment.

Joseph Addison, *Remarks on Several Parts of Italy, in the Years 1701, 1702, and 1703,* 1705

St Peters is in its proportions much to be admired, but the Popish arrangements must be shunned off.

Mrs Bousquet, *Diary,* 1765

The church would have produced a still greater effect, had it been detached entirely from the buildings of the Vatican. It would then have been a masterpiece of architecture, complete in all its parts, entire and perfect; whereas at present, it is no more than a beautiful member attached to a vast undigested and irregular pile of building.

Tobias Smollett, *Travels through France and Italy,* 1766

In the sqare of St Peter's there are about three hundred fettered criminals at work, hoeing out the weeds that grow between the stones of the pavement. Their legs are heavily ironed, and some are chained two by two. They sit in long rows, hoeing out the weeds, dressed in parti-coloured cloths. Near them sit or saunter, groups of soldiers, armed with loaded muskets. The iron discord of those innumerable chains clanks up into the sonorous air, and produces, contrasted with the musical dashing of the fountains, and the deep azure beauty of the sky, and the magnificence of the architecture around, a conflict of sensations allied to madness. It is the emblem of Italy – moral degradation contrasted with the glory of nature and the arts.

Percy Bysshe Shelley, Letter to Thomas Love Peacock, 6 April 1819

As a whole St Peter's is fit for nothing but a ballroom, and it is a little too gaudy even for that.

John Ruskin, Letter to the Rev. Thomas Dale, 31 December 1840

and Niagara Falls

It is very common for people to say that they are disappointed in the first sight of St. Peter's; and one hears much the same about Niagara. I cannot help thinking that the fault is in themselves; and that if the church and the cataract were in the habit of giving away their thoughts with that rash generosity which characterizes tourists, they might perhaps say of their visitors, 'Well, if *you* are those Men of whom we have heard so much, we are a little disappointed, to tell the truth!' The refined tourist expects somewhat too much when he takes it for granted that St. Peter's will at once decorate him with the order of imagination, just as Victoria knights an alderman when he presents an address. . . . It would be wiser, perhaps, for him to consider whether, if Michael Angelo had had the building of *him*, his own personal style would not have been more impressive.

James Russell Lowell, *Leaves from My Journal in Italy and Elsewhere*, 1854

That is a grand and solemn place, the gigantic arms inviting the concourse of all the children of men; but it is an impious work – architecture, swagger, human prowess, human greatness. . . . The face of Christ has been more defiled by our praise than by spittle – for we have not praised him but ourselves.

Eric Gill, *Autobiography*, 1940

It seems to be the only architectural work of Man which has exactly fulfilled its object. . . . It must receive, as its natural furniture, such myriads that the crowd of them shall be a symbol of the Church itself – and this with plenitude and without strain. It must have about it the note of complete success, although it deals with a spiritual and social fact beyond the power of human measurement.

Hilaire Belloc, *Places*, 1942

The vastness struck me as so uniform, so remorseless, as to be self-annihilating, like the vastness of stellar statistics, whose zeros our tiny minds accept so lightly, like necklaces of nothings. What is marvellous about a sky-high ceiling when the walls are remote as horizons? The inflation was insufficiently selective. Gigantic marble popes like vertical gray clouds jutted from niches as high overhead as housetops; church-size chapels, one after another, slowly rotated into view around the colossal piers; living men walked and talked together as if on the open street. Reverence was not in the air. The ghostly presences of so many commemorated ecclesiastical princes melted together into a faceless, sumptuous ambience that seemed to invite, urbanely, by way of devotion, if any was desired – a kind of secondary pantheism. The most majestic and most vast basilica in Christendom so successfully aped the scale of Creation that it seemed to me to deliver, like certain dreadful natural landscapes, a crushing comment on human insignificance. *Vanity, vanity* each overweening vault declared, in polished syllables of porphyry and gilt. If I found space for any holy emotion in this maelstrom of artificial immensity, it was pity for the dizzy workmen who had risked their lives in its construction.

John Updike, 'Mea Culpa', in *Assorted Prose*, 1965

Ronciglione

A little town like a large pig-sty.

Charles Dickens, *Pictures from Italy*, 1846

River Rubicone

This river that makes so great a figure in history is nothing more than a muddy stream that we would hardly dignify with the name of a brook in America. Indeed I have been exceedingly disappointd in the classic streams of Italy that have been so often sung by the poets; I have found them generally yellow dirty & turbid and the nymphs must surely have been mere drabs that inhabited them.

Washington Irving, *Journal* 21 April 1805

San Lorenzo

San Lorenzo is a town built on the summit of a hill, in consequence of the ravages of the *malaria* in the old town, situated in the valley below. It looks like a large alms-house, or else like a town that has run away from the plague and itself, and stops suddenly on the brow of a hill to see if the Devil is following it.

William Hazlitt, *Notes of a Journey through France and Italy*, 1826

San Remo

At San Remo, as the Italian coast draws to a close it gathers up on its lovely bosom the scattered elements of its beauty and heart-broken at ceasing to be that land of lands, it exhales towards the blind insensate heavens a rapturous smile, more poignant than any reproach. There is something hideous in having at such a place to get back into one's carriage.

Henry James, Letter to Henry James Sr, 18 January 1870

Sardinia

One of the most neglected spots in Europe.

Arthur Young, *Travels . . . [in] . . . France*, 1792

To be in central Sardinia is to live among people who have rejected every element of what is proudly called European civilisation: the Phoenicians were there and the Romans and the Byzantines, and the Genoese and the Spaniards and the Piedmontese and now the Italians, and it is as though they had never been. They have all been rejected.

Peter Nichols, *Italia, Italia*, 1973

The real fugitive from justice in Sardinia in the words of a communist deputy from the island, Ignazio Pirastu, was the state.

Ibid.

Scylla and Charybdis

Between Scylla and Charybdis.

Greek proverb

'Hello, doctor, what are you doing up here at this time of night? – What do you want to see this place for?'

'What do *I* want to see this place for? Young man, little do you know me or you wouldn't ask such a question. I wish to see *all* the places that's mentioned in the Bible.'

'Stuff – this place isn't mentioned in the Bible.'

'It ain't mentioned in the Bible! – *this* place ain't – well now, what place *is* this, since you know so much about it?'

'Why, it's Scylla and Charybdis.'

'Scylla and Cha – confound it, I thought it was Sodom and Gomorrah!'

Mark Twain, *The Innocents Abroad,* 1869

Siena

Siena
Di tre cose e piena:
Torri, campane,
E figli di putane.
(Siena has plenty of three things: towers, bells, and sons of whores.)

Florentine saying, quoted by Norman Douglas, *Alone,* 1921

The situation of Sienna is most pleasant, upon a high hill, and the forme not unlike to an earthen vessell, broad in the bottom, and narrow at the mouth, which narrow part lies towards the West. . . . In the center of the City lies a most faire Marketplace, in the forme of an Oyster.

Fynes Moryson, *An Itinerary,* 1617

This famous Citty stands on several rocky Hills, which makes it uneven, has an old ruin'd Wall about it, over-grown with *Caper* shrubbs: but the Air is incomparable, whence divers passe the heates of Summer there; Provisions cheape, the Inhabitants Courteous and the Italian purely spoken. The Citty at a little distance presents the Traveller with an incomparable Prospect, occasion'd by the many playne brick Towers, which (whilst it was a Free state) were erected for defence. . . .

The Piazza, . . . being made with descending steps much resembles the figure of an Escalop-shell, with the white ranges of Paving intermix'd with the incomparable brick . . . & with which generally the towne is well paved, which renders it marvailously cleane.

John Evelyn, *Diary,* 31 October 1644

There is nothing in this city so extraordinary as the cathedral, which a man may view with pleasure after he has seen St. Peter's, though it is quite of another make, and can only be looked upon as one of the master-pieces of Gothic architecture. When a man sees the prodigious pains and expence that our forefathers have been at in these barbarous buildings, one cannot but fancy to himself what miracles of architecture they would have left us, had they only been instructed in the right way.

Joseph Addison, *Remarks on Several Parts of Italy, in the Years 1701, 1702, and 1703,* 1705

'tis old, and very smug, with very few inhabitants.

Horace Walpole, Letter to Richard West, 22 March 1740

Of Sienna I can say nothing from my own observation, but that we were indifferently lodged in a house that stunk like a privy, and fared wretchedly at supper.

Tobias Smollett, *Travels through France and Italy,* 1766

Here my duty of course was to see the cathedral, and I got up much earlier than I wished, in order to perform it. I wonder that our holy ancestors did not choose a mountain at once, scrape it into tabernacles, and chisel it into scripture stories. It would have cost them almost as little trouble as the building in question, which may certainly be esteemed a masterpiece of ridiculous taste and elaborate absurdity. The front, encrusted with alabaster, is worked into a million of fretted arches and puzzling ornaments. There are statues without number, and relievos without end or meaning. The church within is all of black and white marble alternately; the roof blue and gold, with a profusion of silken banners hanging from it; and a cornice running above the principal arcade, composed entirely of bustos representing the whole series of sovereign pontiffs, from the first bishop of Rome to Adrian the fourth. . . . I hardly knew which was the nave, or which the cross aisle, of this singular edifice so perfect is the confusion of its parts. The pavement demands attention, being inlaid so curiously as to represent a variety of histories taken from holy writ, and designed somewhat in the style of that hobgoblin tapestry which used to bestare the walls of our ancestors. Near the high altar stands the strangest of pulpits, supported by polished pillars of granite, rising from lions' backs, which serve as pedestals. In every corner of the place some chapel or other offends or astonishes you.

William Beckford, *Dreams Waking Thoughts and Incidents,* 1783

Sienna is a fine old town, but more like a receptacle of the dead than the residence of the living. 'IT WAS,' might be written over the entrance to this, as to most of the towns in Italy. The magnificence of the buildings corresponds but ill with the squalidness of the inhabitants; there seems no reason for crowding the streets so close together when there are so few people in them.

William Hazlitt, *Notes of a Journey through France and Italy*, 1826

It is like a bit of Venice, without the water.

Charles Dickens, *Pictures from Italy*, 1846

There was what they called a Carnival in progress; but, as its secret lay in a score or two of melancholy people walking up and down the principal street in common toy-shop masks, and being more melancholy, if possible, than the same sort of people in England, I say no more of it.

Ibid.

The air is as fresh as English air, without English dampness and transition; yes, and we have English lanes with bowery tops of trees, and brambles and blackberries, and not a wall anywhere, except the walls of our villa.

Elizabeth Barrett Browning, Letter to Miss Isa Blagden, 1850

The lovely city of my love
Bathes deep in the sun-satiate air
That flows round no fair thing more fair
Her beauty bare . . .
O gracious city well-beloved,
  Italian, and a maiden crowned,
Siena, my feet are no more moved
  Towards thy strange-shapen-mountain-bound:
But my heart in me turns and moves,
O lady loveliest of my loves
Toward thee to lie before thy feet.

A.C. Swinburne, 'Siena', *Songs Before Sunrise*, 1871

I had a bad weary headache at Siena; and the cathedral seemed to me every way absurd – over-cut, over-striped, over-crocketed, over-gabled, a piece of costly confectionery, and faithless vanity.

John Ruskin, *Praeterita*, 1885–9

The land in the world, I suppose, least like New South Wales.

Henry James, Letter to the Countess of Jersey, Siena, 11 June 1892

Sicily

The sun is the father of the ragged.

Sicilian proverb

In some circumstances these banditti are the most respectable of the island; and have by much the highest and most romantic notions of what they call their point of honour. That, however criminal they may be with regard to safety in general; yet, with respect to one another, and to every person to whom they have once professed it, they have ever maintained the most unshaken fidelity. The magistrates have often been obliged to protect them, and even pay them court, as they are known to be perfectly determined and desperate; and so extremely vindictive, that they will certainly put any person to death who has ever given them just cause of provocation. On the other hand, it never was known that any person who had put himself under their protection, and shewed that he had confidence in them, had cause to repent of it, or was injured by any of them, in the most minute trifle; but on the contrary, they will protect him from impositions of every kind. For these reasons, most travellers chuse to hire a couple of them from town to town; and may thus travel over the whole island in safety.

Patrick Brydone, *A Tour through Sicily and Malta*, 1773

The lower class of Sicilians generally seem to take it for granted, that a stranger thinks them both silly and knavish. In numberless instances they have begun their conversations with me by defending themselves against suspicions which I had not given the least hint of my entertaining; I am assured that at first a Sicilian is easily duped, but when once he has learnt experience at this cost, grows quickly a master in the art, able to retaliate with interest upon those that had over-reached him. . . . The Sicilian . . . has no interval of humanity, when once he has abandoned himself to wickedness.

Henry Swinburne, *Travels in the Two Sicilies in 1777–1780*, 1785

The fatigue of ascending Etna is the only thing that has not been exaggerated in it – & of Sicily in generall all is exaggerated grossly except the abominableness of the Government, & the vice & abject wretchedness of the people.

S.T. Coleridge, Letter to Mrs S.T. Coleridge, 12 December 1804

In England we have no idea what a Sicilian flea is.

John Henry Newman, Letter to Harriet Newman, 25 April 1833

Coleridge . . . [said] . . . that Sicily was an excellent school of political economy; for, in any town there, it only needed to ask what the government enacted, and reverse that, to know what ought to be done; it was the most felicitously opposite legislation to anything good and wise. There were only three things which the government had brought into that garden of delights, namely, itch, pox, and famine.

R.W. Emerson, *English Traits*, 1856 – of 1833

Like Sicily extremely – a good on-the-brink feeling – one hop and you're out of Europe: nice, that.

D.H. Lawrence, Letter to Lady Cynthia Asquith, Taormina, 25 March 1920

There is in the Sicilian, as in the Andalusian, a great deal of Arab solemnity as a background to Italian vivacity.

Walter Starkie, *The Waveless Plain,* 1938

'Surely,' said I, 'it would be easy to put down the Mafia here if the Government placed power in the hands of one efficient man.'

'If you lived in Sicily,' replied the custodian, 'you would not say that. Only a Sicilian knows the ramifications, the never-ending subtleties of the Mafia which follows every Sicilian as closely as the shadow does the body.'

Ibid.

Sicily is the schoolroom model of Italy for beginners, with every Italian quality and defect magnified, exasperated and brightly coloured.

Luigi Barzini, *The Italians,* 1964

Thrown down almost in mid-channel like a concert grand, it had a sort of minatory, defensive air. From so high one could see the lateral tug of the main deep furling and unfurling its waters along those indomitable flanks of the island. . . . It looked huge, and sad, and slightly frustrated, like a Minoan bull – and at once the thought clicked home. Crete, Cyprus! It was like them, an island of the mid-channel – the front line of defence against the huge seas combing up from Africa. Perhaps even the vegetation echoed this as it does in Crete? I felt at once reassured; as if I had managed to situate the island more clearly in my mind. Magna Graecia!

Lawrence Durell, *Sicilian Carousel,* 1977

In a sense all our thinking about the Mediterranean crystallised around the images planted here by the Greeks – in this Greater Greece, so aptly named. In Sicily one sees that the Mediterranean evolved at the same rhythm as man, they both evolved together. One interpreted itself to the other, and out of the interaction, Greek culture was first born.

Ibid.

I have heard it said that Sicilians can't use the telephone because they need both hands to talk with.

Anon.

Spezzia

Spezzia wheels the blue sea into the arms of the wooded mountains.

Elizabeth Barrett Browning, Letter to Miss Mitford, 1849

Since it has become prosperous Spezia has grown ugly. The place is filled with long, dull stretches of dead wall and great raw expanses of artificial land. It wears that look of monstrous, of more than Occidental, newness, which distinguishes all the creations of the young Italian state.

Henry James, 'Italy Revisited', 1877, in *Portraits of Places,* 1883

Spoleto

Of the wine, Martiall thus writes;

De Spoletanis quae sunt curiosa lagenis.
Malveris, quam si musta Falerna hibas.
If with Spoleto bottels once you meet,
Say that Falerno must is not so sweet.

Fynes Moryson, *An Itinerary,* 1617

Spoleto, I think the most romantic city I ever saw. There is here an aqueduct of astonishing elevation, which unites two rocky mountains, – there is the path of a torrent below, whitening the green dell with its broad and barren track of stones, and above there is a castle, apparently of great strength and of tremendous magnitude, which overhangs the city, and whose marble bastions are perpendicular with the precipice. I never saw a more impressive picture; in which the shapes of nature are of the grandest order, but over which the creations of man, sublime from their antiquity and greatness seem to predominate.

Percy Bysshe Shelley, Letter to Thomas Love Peacock, 20 November 1818

Spoleto is a handsome town, delightfully situated, and has an appearance (somewhat startling in Italy) as if life were not quite extinct in it.

William Hazlitt, *Notes of a Journey through France and Italy,* 1826

Stromboli

Stromboli is ever at work, and for ages past has been looked upon as the great light-house of these seas.

Patrick Brydone, *A Tour through Sicily and Malta,* 1773

Taormina

Were I to name a place that possesses every grand and beauteous qualification for the forming of a picture; a place in which I should wish to employ the powers of a Salvator or a Poussin, Taormina should be the object of my choice. – Every thing belonging to it is drawn in a large sublime style; the mountains tower to the very clouds, the castles and ruins rise on mighty masses of perpendicular rock, and seem to defy the attacks of mortal enemies; Etna with all its snowy and woody sweeps fills half the horizon; the sea is stretched out upon an immense scale and occupies the remainder of the prospect.

Henry Swinburne, *Travels in the Two Sicilies in 1777–1780,* 1785

Taormina in itself is one of the most beautiful spots in the world. I've seen most of the great landscapes, including the slopes of Fujiyama and Kilauea and Orizaba and Popocatapetl and Turquino. They are all divine, but the Greek is the only man who ever lived that could get the whole value out of his landscape, and add to it a big value of his own. His share counts for almost as much as the share of nature. The wretch was so complete an artist that big or little was equally easy for him to handle, and he took hold of Etna just as easily as he did of the smallest lump of gold or silver to make a perfect coin.

Henry Adams, Letter to Elizabeth Cameron, 23 April 1899

Here one feels as if one had lived for a hundred thousand years. What it is that is so familiar I don't know. You remember Stopford said Sicily had been waiting for me for about 2000 years: must be the sense of that long wait. Not that Sicily waited for me alone –

She waits for each and other,
She waits for all men born.

– What for? To rook them, overcharge them, to diddle them and do them down. Capri is an unhatched egg compared to this serpent of Trinacria.

D.H. Lawrence, Letter, 31 March 1920, quoted in Norman Douglas, *Looking Back,* 1934

I have seen many different kinds of traveller arrive in Taormina – idle travellers, lying travellers, proud, vain, and splenetic travellers – but no sooner do they mount to the Greek theatre in face of Ætna than all their eccentricities disappear, and they become nothing but Lotos-eating travellers. Taormina should be let out by the Italian Government, as an open-air asylum for Anglo-Saxons who live their lives according to the adage 'Time is money.' It would soon cure their restless efficiency. Nobody ever looks at a clock in Taormina.

Walter Starkie, *The Waveless Plain,* 1938

How pleasant . . . to dawdle the length of that main street, – like walking the bridge of a Zeppelin . . . the whole thing has been anchored in mid-heaven, at a thousand feet, and up here the air is still and calm. The white curtains in my hotel-room breathed softly in and out, like the lungs of the universe itself.

Lawrence Durrell, *Sicilian Carousel,* 1977

Taranto

In Taranto it is always afternoon. 'The Tarentines,' says Strabo, 'have more holidays than workdays in the year.'

Norman Douglas, *Old Calabria,* 1915

Taranto today gallantly proclaims to the world its greatness as a seaport, but its blocks of modern apartments, its big harbour full of ships, seemed pathetically unreal to the lonely traveller dreaming of Greater Greece. The proud fishermen and patient husbandmen looked on these modern buildings with as much stupefaction as though they had been set there in the night by the genie of Aladdin's lamp.

Walter Starkie, *The Waveless Plain,* 1938

Falls of Terni

No description can give a more lively idea of the impression which the first sight of it makes upon the spectator, than the exclamation of Wilson the painter, overheard by Sir Joshua Reynolds, who happened to be on the spot. Wilson stood for a moment in speechless admiration, and then broke out, with, – '*Well done,* Water, by G—!'

Henry Matthews, *Diary of an Invalid,* 1820

If this noble and interesting object have a fault, it is that it is too slender, straight, and accompanied with too few wild or grotesque ornaments. It is the Doric, or at any rate the Ionic, among waterfalls.

William Hazlitt, *Notes of a Journey through France and Italy,* 1826

Terracina (near, between Rome and Naples)

The man, who had no money in his pocket, might formerly dismiss all fear of robbers; – but in these days, an empty purse is no longer a security. These modern desperadoes carry men away even from their homes, for the sake of the ransom, which they think they may extort for their liberation. We are told that two men were lately kidnapped from this neighbourhood, and taken up into the mountains. The friends of one sent up nearly the sum that was demanded; – the other had no friends to redeem him. The robbers settled the affair, in the true spirit of that cold-blooded savage disposition, that has leisure to be sportive in its cruelty. They sent the first man back without his ears; detaining these, as a set-off against the deficiency in the ransom; – and the other poor fellow was returned in *eight pieces!* – So much for Italian government. An edict has lately been issued against ransoms, as operating to encourage kidnapping.

Henry Matthews, *Diary of an Invalid,* 1820

River Tiber

Sometimes to gentle Tiber I retire,

And the famed river's empty shores admire,
That, destitute of strength, derives its course
From thrifty urns and an unfruitful source,
Yet sung so often in poetic lays
With scorn the Danube and the Nile surveys.

Joseph Addison, *Letter from Italy to the Right Honourable Lord Halifax,* 1701

A river that ancient Rome made more considerable than any merit of its own could have done: However, it is not contemptibly small, but a good handsome stream; very deep, yet somewhat of a muddy complexion.

Thomas Gray, Letter to Mrs Gray, his mother, 2 April 1740

The Tiber frightens me.

James Joyce, Postcard to Stanislaus Joyce, 31 July 1906

Tivoli

Altogether Tivoli has left an agreeable impression. . . . By the bye, Wordsworth called the Cascadelles 'nature's waterworks.'

Henry Crabb Robinson, *Diary,* 13 May 1837

I shall not say anything about Tivoli. A waterfall in type is likly to be a trifle stiffish.

James Russell Lowell, *Leaves from My Journal in Italy and Elsewhere,* 1854

Lake Trasimene

It struck me as not unlike Windermere in character and scenery, but I have seen other lakes since, which have driven it out of my head.

William Hazlitt, *Notes of a Journey through France and Italy,* 1826

Tre Fontane

After siesta we took a taxi and drove along dusty and dull and very bad roads to Tre Fontane – the place where Paul's head jumped three times after being cut off, at each place producing a fountain. There are three churches, and if they locate the fountains, Paul's head must have very considerably bounded.

Arnold Bennett, *Journal,* 5 February 1926

Trento

to Trenta then I kam,
which iz the first of Italy, az thar doth go the fam.
in which sitty the langwages indiffrent ar to all,
Both Alman and Italien, eevn az on toong doth fall.

Thomas Whythorne, *Autobiography, c.* 1576

Trieste

Trieste is the rudest place I have ever been in. It is hardly possible to exaggerate the incivility of the people.

James Joyce, Letter to Stanislaus Joyce, 12 July 1905

*And trieste, ah trieste ate I my liver.

James Joyce, *Finnegans Wake,* 1939

'We are the furthest limit of Latinity,' the Mayor of Trieste exclaimed to me one day, 'the southern extremity of Germanness.' Triestini love this sort of hyperbole.

Jan Morris, *Destinations,* 1980

Turin

The prospect of Turin is a company of dirty red flat howses, few or no steeples onely four towres coverd with Tin of the dukes palace.

Richard Symonds, *Notebooks,* 1649, quoted in *Travels of Peter Mundy,* 1907

'Tis really by far one of the prettiest cities I have seen – not one of your large straggling ones, that can afford to have twenty dirty suburbs, but clean and compact, very new and very regular. The king's palace is not of the proudest without, but of the richest within; painted, gilt, looking-glassed, very costly, but very tawdry; in short, a very popular palace.

Horace Walpole, Letter to Richard West, 11 November 1739

After eight days journey through Greenland, we arrived at Turin. . . . The city is not large, as being a place of strength and consequently confined within its fortifications; it has many beauties and some faults; among the first are streets all laid out by the line, regular uniform buildings, fine walks that surround the whole, and in general a good lively, clean appearance: but the houses are of brick plaistered, which is apt to want repairing; the windows of oiled paper, which is apt to be torn; and every thing very slight, which is apt to tumble down. There is an excellent Opera, but it is only in the Carnival: Balls every night, but only in the Carnival: Masquerades too, but only in the Carnival. This Carnival lasts only from Christmas to Lent; one half of the remaining part of the year is passed in remembering the last, the other in expecting the future Carnival.

Thomas Gray, Letter to Richard West, 16 November 1739

There was here many fine women. The counts and other pretty gentlemen told me whenever I admired a lady, 'Sir, you can have her. It would not be difficult.' I thought at first they were joking, and waggishly amusing themselves with a stranger. But I at last discovered that they were really in earnest and that the manners here were so openly debauched that adultery was carried on without the least disguise. I asked them, 'But why then do you marry?' 'Oh, it's the custom; it perpetuates families.'

James Boswell, *Journal,* 8 January 1765

This being the first Italian city for beauty that I have seen, I have been all eyes today. Some travellers have represented it as the prettiest town in Europe, and the Strada di Po the finest street. I hurried to it with eagerness. I was in the middle of it, asking for it. *Questa, questa!* replied an officer, holding up his hands, as if to point out an object of great beauty which I did not see, and in truth I saw it not. It is strait and broad, and nearly regular. Two rows of brick barns might be so equally. The houses are of ugly obfuscated brick; a few have stucco, and that old and dirty; the scaffold holes in the walls of all the rest are left unfilled; some of them enlarged by time, and several courses of bricks between those holes, not pointed, which has as bad an effect; the windows are narrow and poor; some with iron balconies – some without; the arcades, for there is a row on each side of the street, would be destructive of beauty, if it was here: the arches are plaistered, which patches the line with white: and through them are exhibited nothing but poor shops that incumber their spans with all sorts of lumber; the lamps are fifty or sixty yards asunder. In a word, there are fifty streets at London to which this cannot be compared. If those who have travelled in Italy think this street fine, what am I to meet with in other towns.

Arthur Young, *Travels . . . [in] . . . France* (26 September 1789), 1792

It is built in the form of a star, with a large stone in its centre, on which you are desired to stand, and see the streets all branch regularly from it, each street terminating with a beautiful view of the surrounding country, like spots of ground seen in many of the old-fashioned parks in England, where the etoile and vista were the mode. . . . Model of elegance, exact Turin! . . . This charming town is the *salon* of Italy.

Hester Lynch Thrale/Piozzi, *Observations . . . in the Course of a Journey,* 1789

Notwithstanding the undeniable beauty of this little city of palaces, the sin of incompleteness is every where conspicuous.

Lady Morgan, *Italy,* 1820

My arrival at Turin was the first and only moment of intoxication I have found in Italy. It is a city of palaces.

William Hazlitt, *Notes of a Journey through France and Italy,* 1826

Turin is a noble city, like a set of Regent streets made twice as tall.

Leigh Hunt, *Autobiography,* 1850

Turin is more regular than Philadelphia. Houses all one cut, one color, one height. City seems all built by one contractor.

Herman Melville, *Journal of a Visit to Europe and the Levant,* 10 April 1857

This is a remarkably agreeable place. A beautiful town, prosperous, thriving, growing prodigiously, as Genoa is; crowded with busy inhabitants; full of noble streets and squares. The Alps, now covered deep with snow, are close upon it, and here and there seem almost ready to tumble into the houses. The contrast this part of Italy presents to the rest is amazing. Beautifully made railroads admirably managed; cheerful, active people; spirit, energy, life, progress.

Charles Dickens, Letter, 1853, in Forster, *Life of Dickens,* 1872–3

In the matter of roominess it transcends anything that was ever dreamed of before, I fancy. It sits in the middle of a vast dead-level, and one is obliged to imagine that land may be had for the asking, and no taxes to pay, so lavishly do they use it.

Mark Twain, *A Tramp Abroad,* 1880

Turin is not a city to make, in vulgar parlance, a fuss about, and I pay an extravagant tribute to subjective emotion in speaking of it as ancient. . . . Relatively speaking, Turin is diverting; but there is, after all, no reason in a large collection of shabbily stuccoed houses, disposed in a rigidly rectangular manner, for passing a day of deep, still gaiety. The only reason, I am afraid, is the old superstition of Italy – that property in the very look of the written word, the evocation of a myriad images, that makes any lover of the arts take Italian satisfactions upon easier terms than any other. Italy is an idea to conjure with, and we play tricks upon our credulity even with such inferior apparatus as is offered to our hand at Turin.

Henry James, 'Italy Revisited', 1877, in *Portraits of Places,* 1883

Turin is a very large city, rectangular in form and spirit.

Arnold Bennett, *Journal 1929,* 1930

Tuscany

I knew a young English-woman, who, having grown up

in Tuscany, thought the landscapes of her native country insipid, and could not imagine how people could live without walks in vineyards. To me, Italy had a certain hard taste in the mouth. Its mountains were too bare, its outlines too sharp, its lanes too stony, its voices too loud, its long summer too dusty. I longed to bathe myself in the grassy balm of my native fields.

Leigh Hunt, *Autobiography,* 1850

Wherein lies that particular salt of Tuscan speech? In its emphasis, its air of finality. They are emphatic rather than profound. Their deepest utterances, if you look below the surface, are generally found to be variants of one of those ancestral saws or proverbs wherewith the country is saturated. Theirs is a crusted charm. A hard and glittering sanity, a kind of ageless enamel, is what confronts us in their temperament. There are not many deviations from this Tuscan standard.

Norman Douglas, *Alone,* 1921

Vallombrosa

he stood and call'd
His Legions, Angel Forms, who lay intrans't
Thick as Autumnal Leaves that strow the Brooks
In *Vallombrosa,* where th'*Etrurian* shades
High overarch't imbowr; or scatterd sedge
Afloat, when with fierce Winds *Orion* arm'd
Hath vext the Red-Sea Coast, whose waves orethrew
Busiris and his *Memphian* Chivalry.

John Milton, *Paradise Lost,* 1667

How we enjoyed that great, silent, ink-black pine wood!

Elizabeth Barrett Browning, Letter, 1847

Venice

Pria Veneziani, poi Christiani.
(A Venetian first, and then a Christian.)

Old Proverb

Seventeenth Century

A Clock going with many wheels, and making small motions, sometimes out of order, but soon mended, and all without change or variety.

Sir Dudley Carleton, Letter to
Sir William Fleetwood, early seventeenth century

The best flesh-shambles in *Italie.*

John Day, *Humour Out of Breath,* 1608

That most glorious, renowned, and Virgin Citie of Venice, the Queene of the Christian world, that Diamond set in the ring of the Adriatique gulfe, and the most resplendent mirrour of Europe.

Thomas Coryate, *Crudities,* Epistle Dedicatorie, 1611

This incomparable city, this most beautifull Queene, this untainted virgine, this Paradise, this Tempe, this rich Diademe and most flourishing garland of Christendome: of which the inhabitants may as proudly vaunt, as I have read the Persians have done of their Ormus, who say that if the world were a ring, then should Ormus be the gemme thereof; the same (I say) may the Venetians speake of their citie and much more truely. The sight whereof hath yeelded unto me such infinite contentment (I must needes confesse) . . . that had there bin an offer made unto me before I took my iourney to Venice, eyther that foure of the richest mannors of Somersetshire (wherein I was borne) should be *gratis* bestowed upon me if I never saw Venice, or neither of them if I should see it; although certainly those mannors would do me much more good in respect of a state of livelyhood to live in the world, then the sight of Venice: yet notwithstanding I will ever say while I live, that the sight of Venice and her resplendent beauty, antiquities and monuments hath, by many degrees more contented my minde, and satisfied my desires, then those four Lordshippes could possibly have done.

Thomas Coryate, *Crudities,* 1611

For you must consider that neither the Venetian Gentlemen nor any others can ride horses in the streets of Venice as in other Cities and Townes, because their streets being both very narrow and slippery, in regard they are all paved with smooth brick, and joyning to the water, the horse would quickly fall into the river, and so drowne both himselfe and his rider. Therefore the Venetians do use Gondolaes in their streets, that is, in their pleasant channels. So that I now finde by mine owne experience that the speeches of a certaine English Gentleman (with whom I once discoursed before my travels) a man that much vaunted of his observations in Italy are utterly false. For when I asked him what principall things he observed in Venice, he answered me that he noted but little of the city. Because he rode through it in post. A fiction as grosse and palpable as ever was coyned.

Ibid.

This incomparable mansion is the only paragon of all the cities in the world.

William Lithgow, *Rare Adventures and Painfull Peregrinations,* 1614/32

The Venetians are of a variable disposition, very jealous, and some of them giving the use of their bodies freely without reward (but I think there be few such,) for they pleasantly scoff at our English women, that they give the fruit of love to their lovers for charity.

Fynes Moryson, *An Itinerary,* 1617

Though the flood or ebbe of the salt water be small, yet with that motion it carrieth away the filth of the City, besides that, by the multitude of fiers, and the situation open to all windes, the ayre is made very wholsome, whereof the Venetians bragge, that it agrees with all strangers complexions, by a secret vertue, whether they be brought up in a good or ill ayre, and preserveth them in their former health. And though I dare not say that the Venetians live long, yet except they sooner grow old, and rather seeme then truly be aged: I never in any place observed more old men, or so many Senators venerable for their grey haires and aged gravity.

Ibid.

Theis baits drawe many hither, some for Curiositie, others for Luxurie, there being wayes to gett, but many more to spend.

Peter Mundy, *Sundry Relations of Certaine Voyages,* July 1620

A common Saying that is used of this dainty City of *Venice:*

Venetia, Venetia, chi non te vede non te Pregia,
M chi t'ha troppo veduto *te Dispreggia.*

English'd and rhym'd thus . . .

Venice, Venice, *None* Thee *unseen can prize;*
Who hath seen too much will Thee *despise.*

James Howell, 'Letter to Robert Brown Esq, . . . from Venice, 12 August 1621', *Familiar Letters,* 1645

The best and most of their authors ascribe their first beginnings rather to chance or necessity, than counsel; which yet in my opinion will amount to no more than a pretty conjecture intenebrated by antiquity, for thus they deliver it: they say that among the tumults of the middle age, when the nations went about swarming like bees, Atylas, that great captain of the Hunnes, and scourge of the world (as he was styled) lying along with a numerous army at the siege of Aquileia, it struck a mighty affrightment and confusion into the nearer parts. Whereupon the best sort of the bordering people out of divers towns, agreed either suddenly, or by little and little (as fear will sometimes collect as well as distract) to convey themselves and their substance into the uttermost bosom of the Adriatick Gulf, and there possessed certain desolate islets, by tradition about seventy in number, which afterwards, (necessity being the mother of art) were tacked together with bridges, and so the city took a rude form, which grew civilized with time, and became a great example of what the smallest things well formented may prove.

They glory in this their beginning two ways. First, that surely their progenitors were not of the meanest and basest quality (for such having little to lose had as little cause to remove). Next, that they were timely instructed with temperance and penury (the nurses of moderation). And true it is, that as all things savour of their first principles, so doth the said Republic (as I shall afterwards show) even at this day; for the rule will hold as well in civil as in natural causes.

Sir Henry Wotton, Letter to the Marquis of Buckingham (?), 12 December 1622

Esto perpetua!
(Be thou perpetual!)

Pietro Sarpi, Dying apostrophe to Venice, 15 January 1623

You are now in a place where you may feed all your senses very cheap; I allow you the pleasing of your Eye, your Ear, your Smell and Taste; but take heed of being too indulgent of the fifth Sense. The Poets feign, that *Venus* the Goddess of Pleasure, and therefore call'd *Aphrodite,* was ingendred of the froth of the Sea (which makes Fish more salacious commonly than Flesh); it is not improbable that she was got and coagulated of that Foam which *Neptune* useth to disgorge upon those pretty Islands whereon that City stands.

James Howell, 'Letter to Mr. T. Lucy, . . . 15 January 1635', *New Volume of Familiar Letters,* 1647

. . . add the perfumers & Apothecaries, and the innumberable cages of Nightingals, which they keepe, that entertaines you with their melody from shop to shop, so as shutting your Eyes, you would imagine your selfe in the Country, when indeede you are in the middle of the Sea: besides there being neither rattling of Coaches nor trampling of horses, tis almost as silent as the field.

John Evelyn, *Diary,* June 1645

The *Venetians* apprehend so much from the active Spirits of a necessitous Nobility, that, to lay those asleep, they encourage them in all those things that may blunt and depress their Minds. . . .

Yet I must add one thing, that tho' *Venice* is the Place in the whole World, where Pleasure is most studied, and where the Youth have both the greatest Wealth, and the most Leisure to pursue it; yet it is the Place that I ever saw, where true and innocent Pleasure is the least understood: . . . As for the Pleasures of Friendship or Marriage, they are Strangers to them; for the horrible Distrust, in which they all live, of one another, makes that it is very rare to find a Friend in *Italy,* but most of all in *Venice:* And tho' we have been told of several Stories of celebrated Friendships there, yet these are now very rare. As for their Wives, they are bred to so much Ignorance, and they converse so little, that they know nothing but the dull Superstition on Holydays, in which they stay in the Churches as long as they can, and so prolong the little Liberty they have of going abroad on those Days, as Children do their Hours of Play. They are not employed in their domestick Affairs, and generally they understand no sort of Work; so that I was told, they were the insipidest Creatures imaginable. They are perhaps as vicious as in other Places, but it is among them downright Lewdness; for they are not drawn into it by the Entanglements of Amour, that inveigle and lead many Persons much farther than they imagined or intended at first; but in them the first Step, without any Preamble or Preparative is downright Beastliness.

Gilbert Burnet, *Some Letters Containing an Account of what seemed Remarkable in Travelling,* 1687

Eighteenth Century

It looks, at a distance, like a great town half floated by a deluge.

Joseph Addison, *Remarks on Several Parts of Italy, in the Years 1701, 1702, and 1703,* 1705

Our voyage-writers will needs have this city in great danger of being left, within an age or two, on the *terra firma;* and represent it in such a manner, as if the sea were sensibly shrinking from it, and retiring into its channel. I asked several, and among the rest, Father Coronelli, the state's geographer, of the truth of this particular; and they all assure me, that the sea rises as high as ever, though, the great heaps of dirt it brings along with it are apt to choke up the shallows, but that they are in no danger of losing the benefit of their situation, so long as they are at the charge of removing these banks of mud and sand. One may see abundance of them above the surface of the water, scattered up and down, like so many little islands, when the tide is low; and they are these that make the entrance for ships difficult to such as are not used to them, for the deep canals run between them, which the Venetians are at a great expence to keep free and open.

Ibid.

O happy streets! to rumbling wheels unknown,
No carts, no coaches shake the floating town!

John Gay, *Trivia,* 1716

The seeming god-built city! which my hand
Deep in the bosom fixed of wondering seas.
Astonished mortals sailed with pleasing awe
Around the sea-girt walls, by Neptune fenced,
And down the briny street, where on each hand,
Amazing seen amid unstable waves,
The splendid palace shines, and rising tides,
The green steps marking, murmur at the door.
To this fair queen of Adria's stormy gulf,
The mart of nations! long obedient seas
Rolled all the treasure of the radiant East.
But now no more. . . .

James Thomson, *Liberty,* Part IV, 1736

It is so much the established fashion for every body to live their own way, that nothing is more ridiculous than censuring the actions of another. This would be terrible in London, where we have little other diversion; but for me, who never found my pleasure in malice I bless my destiny that has conducted me to a part where people are better employed than in talking of the affairs of their acquaintance.

Lady Mary Wortley Montagu, Letter to Lady Pomfret, 6 November 1739

There is no great City so proper for the retreat of Old Age as Venice.

Lady Mary Wortley Montagu, Letter to Lady Bute, 5 December 1758

This Venice is the most particular Place in the whole world – it glares upon you at first, & inchants You, but living a Month here (like the honey moon) brings you to a temperate consideration of things, & you long for your terra firma liberty again! – I am tired to death; tho I have seen here such sights I had no conception of but in Fairy land, & have seen the Visions of the Arabian Night realiz'd by the Venetian *Regate*; . . . which plainly shew'd, that the Contrivers were as little formidable in war and Politicks, as they were superiour to all the World as Managers of a Puppet-Shew.

David Garrick, Letter to George Colman, Venice, 12 June 1764

Of all the towns in Italy, I am the least satisfied with Venice; Objects which are only singular without being pleasing, produce a momentary surprize which soon gives way to satiety and disgust. Old and in general ill built houses, ruined pictures, and stinking ditches dignified with the pompous denomination of Canals; a fine bridge, spoilt by two Rows of houses upon it, and a large square decorated with the worst Architecture I ever yet saw, such are the colours I should employ in my portrait of Venice; a portrait certainly true in general, tho' perhaps you should attribute the very great darkness of the shades to my being out of humour with the place.

Edward Gibbon, Letter to Dorothea Gibbon, 22 April 1765

In the midst of the waters, free, indigent, laborious, and inccessible, they gradually coalesced into a republic.

Edward Gibbon, *The Decline and Fall of the Roman Empire,* 1776–88

In the evening there generally is, on St Mark's Place, such a mixed multitude of Jews, Turks, and Christians; lawyers, knaves, and pick-pockets; mountebanks, old women, and physicians; women of quality, with masks; strumpets barefaceed; and, in short, such a jumble of senators, citizens, gondoleers, and people of every character and condition, that your ideas are broken, bruised, and dislocated in the crowd, in such a manner, that you can think, or reflect, on nothing; yet this being a state of mind which many people are fond of, the place never fails to be well attended, and, in fine weather, numbers pass a great part of the night there.

When the piazza is illuminated, and the shops, in the adjacent streets, are lighted up, the whole has a brilliant effect; and as it is the custom for the ladies, as well as the gentlemen, to frequent the cassinos and coffee-houses around, the Place of St Mark answers all the purposes of either Vauxhall or Ranelagh.

John Moore, *A View of Society and Manners in Italy,* 1781

No city in the world has less affinity with the country than Venice.

Ibid.

I had been so often forewarned of the amazement with which I should be struck at first sight of this city, that when I actually did see it, I felt little or no amazement at all. You will behold, said those anticipators, a magnificent town . . . standing in the middle of the sea. Well; this, unquestionably is an uncommon scene; and there is no matter of doubt that a town, surrounded by water, is a very fine sight; but all the travellers that have existed since the days of Cain will not convince me, that a town, surrounded by land, is not a much finer. Can there be any comparison, in point of beauty, between the dull monotony of a watery surface, and the delightful variety of gardens, meadows, hills, and woods?

If the situation of Venice renders it less agreeable than another city, to behold at a distance, it must render it, in a much stronger degree, less agreeable to inhabit. For you will please to recollect, that, instead of walking or riding in the fields, and enjoying the fragrance of herbs, and the melody of birds; when you wish to take the air here, you must submit to be paddled about, from morning to night, in a narrow boat, along dirty canals; or, if you don't like this, you have one resource more, which is, that of walking in St. Mark's Place.

These are the disadvantages which Venice labours under with regard to situation; but it has other peculiarities, which, in the opinion of many, overbalance them, and render it, on the wole, an agreeable town.

Ibid.

I have been told that the Venetians are remarkably spirited; and so eager in the pursuit of amusement as hardly to allow themselves any sleep. . . . This may be very true, and yet I will never cite the Venetians as examples of vivacity. Their nerves unstrung by disease and the consequence of early debaucheries, allow no natural flow of lively spirits, and at best but a few moments of false and feverish activity. The approaches of rest, forced back by an immoderate use of coffee, render them weak and listless to like any active amusement, and the facility of being wafted from place to place in a gondola, adds not a little to their indolence. In short, I can scarcely regard their Eastern neighbours in a more lazy light; and am apt to imagine, that instead of slumbering less than any other people, they pass their lives in one perpetual doze.

William Beckford, *Dreams Waking Thoughts and Incidents,* 1783

'Tis certain my beloved town of Venice ever recalls a series of eastern ideas and adventures. I cannot help thinking St. Mark's a mosque, and the neighbouring palace some vast seraglio, full of arabesque saloons, embroidered sofas, and voluptuous Circassians.

Ibid.

Never was locality so subservient to the purposes of pleasure as in this city; where pleasure has set up her airy standard.

Hester Lynch Thrale/Piozzi, *Observations . . . in the Course of a Journey,* 1789

This town cannot be a wholesome one, for there is scarcely a possibility of taking exercise.

Ibid.

Expected to see a gay clean-looking town, with quays on either side of the canals, but was extremely disappointed; the houses are in the water, and look dirty and uncomfortable on the outside; the innumerable quantity of gondolas, too, that look like swimming coffins, added to the dismal scene, and,. I confess, Venice on my arrival struck me with horror rather than pleasure.

Elizabeth Lady Craven, *A Journey thrugh the Crimea to Constantinople,* 1789

Luxury here takes a turn much more towards enjoyment than consumption; the sobriety of the people does much, the nature of their food more. . . . If cheapness of living, *spectacles,* and pretty women, are a man's objects in fixing his residence, let him live at Venice; for myself, I think I would not be an inhabitant to be Doge, with the power of the Grand Turk. Brick and stone, and sky and water, and not a field nor a bush even for fancy to pluck a rose from! My heart cannot expand in such a place: an admirable monument of human industry, but not a theatre for the feelings of a farmer!

Arthur Young, *Travels . . . [in] . . . France* (1 November 1789), 1792

Nineteenth Century

Once did she hold the gorgeous East in fee;
  And was the safeguard of the West: the worth
  Of Venice did not fall below her birth,
Venice, the eldest Child of Liberty.
She was a maiden City, bright and free;
  No guile seduced, no force could violate;
  And, when she took unto herself a mate,
She must espouse the everlasting Sea.

And what if she had seen those glories fade,
  Those titles vanish, and that strength decay;
Yet shall some tribute of regret be paid
  When her long life hath reach'd its final day:
Men are we, and must grieve when even the Shade
  Of that which once was great is pass'd away.

William Wordsworth, *On the Extinction of the Venetian Republic,* 1802

It has always been (next to the East) the greenest island of my imagination.

Lord Byron, Letter to Thomas Moore, 17 November 1816

Venice . . . is my head, or rather my *heart*-quarters.

Lord Byron, Letter to Thomas Moore, 11 April 1817

I stood in Venice, on the Bridge of Sighs;
A palace and a prison on each hand:
I saw from out the wave her structures rise
As from the stroke of the enchanter's wand:
A thousand years their cloudy wings expand
Around me, and a dying Glory smiles
O'er the far times, when many a subject land
Look'd to the winged Lion's marble piles,
Where Venice sate in state, throned on her hundred isles!
She looks a sea Cybele, fresh from ocean,
Rising with her tiara of proud towers
At airy distance, with majestic motion,
A ruler of the waters and their powers:
And such she was; – her daughters had their dowers
From spoils of nations, and the exhaustless East
Pour'd in her lap all gems in sparkling showers.
In purple was she robed, and of her feast
Monarchs partook, and deem'd their dignity increased.

In Venice Tasso's echoes are no more,
And silent rows the songless gondolier;
Her palaces are crumbling to the shore,
And music meets not always now the ear:
Those days are gone – but Beauty still is here.
States fall, arts fade – but Nature doth not die,
Nor yet forget how Venice once was dear,
The pleasant place of all festivity,
The revel of the earth, the masque of Italy! . . .

Before St Mark still glow his steeds of brass,
Their gilded collars glittering in the sun;
But is not Doria's menace come to pass?
Are they not *bridled?* – Venice, lost and won,
Her thirteen hundred years of freedom done,
Sinks like a seaweed into whence she rose!
Better be whelm'd beneath the waves, and shun,
Even in destruction's depth, her foreign foes,
From whom submission wrings an infamous repose.

Lord Byron, *Childe Harold's Pilgrimage,* Canto the Fourth, 1816

Underneath day's azure eyes
Ocean's nursling, Venice lies
A peopled labyrinth of walls,
Amphitrite's destined halls,
Which her hoary sire now paves
With his blue and beaming waves . . .
Sun-girt city, thou hast been
Ocean's child, and then his queen
Now is come a darker day
And thou soon must be his prey,
If the power that raised thee here
Hallow so thy watery bier.
A less drear ruin then than now,
With thy conquest-branded brow
Stooping to the slave of slaves
From thy throne among the waves
Wilt thou be when the seamew
Flies, as once before it flew,
O'er thine isles depopulate,
And all is in its ancient state,
Save where many a palace gate
With green sea-flowers overgrown
Like a rock of ocean's own,
Topples o'er the abandoned sea
As the tides change sullenly. . . .
Those who alone thy towers behold
Quivering through aerial gold,
As I now behold them here,
Would imagine not they were
Sepulchres, where human forms,
Like pollution-nourished worms
To the corpse of greatness cling,
Murdered, and now mouldering.

Percy Bysshe Shelley, *Lines Written among the Euganian Hills,* October 1818

I swam from Lido right to the end of the Grand Canal – including its whole length – besides that space from Lido the Canal's entrance (or exit) by the statue of Fortune – near the Palace and coming out finally at the end opposite Fusina and Maestre – staying in half an hour & – I know not what distance more than the other two – & swimming easy – the whole distance computed by the Venetians at four and a half of Italian miles. – I was in the sea from half past 4 – till a quarter past 8 – without touching or resting. – I could not be much fatigued having had a *piece* in the forenoon – & taking another in the evening at ten of the clock.

Lord Byron, Letter to John Cam Hobhouse, 25 June 1818

Mourn not for Venice; though her fall
  Be awful, as if Ocean's wave
Swept o'er her, she deserves it all,
  And Justice triumphs o'er her grave.
Thus perish ev'ry King and State,
  That run the guilty race she ran,

Strong but in ill, and only great
By outrage against God and man!
Thomas Moore, *Rhymes of the Road,* 1819

The Piazzetta of St. Mark, with its extraordinry Ducal Palace, and the fantastical church, and the gaudy clock opposite, altogether makes a most barbaric appearance. . . . The disenchantment one meets with at Venice, – the Rialto so mean – the canals so stinking!
Thomas Moore, *Journal,* 8 October 1819

As a city, even when seen, it still appears rather a phantom than a fact.
Lady Morgan, *Italy,* 1820

There is a glorious City in the Sea,
The Sea is in the broad, the narrow streets
Ebbing and flowing; and the salt sea-weed
Clings to the marble of her palaces.
No track of men, no footsteps to and fro
Lead to her gates. The path lies o'er the Sea
Invisible; and from the land we went,
As to a floating City – steering in,
And gliding up her streets as in a dream,
So smoothly, silently – by many a dome,
Mosque-like and many a stately portico,
The statues ranged along an azure sky;
By many a pile in more than Eastern pride,
Of old the residence of merchant-kings;
The fronts of some, though Time had shattered them
Still glowing with the richest hues of art,
As though the wealth within them had run o'er.
Samuel Rogers, *Italy,* 1822–34

Dangerous and sweet-tongued Venice.
Ibid.

For an hour and a half, that it takes you to cross from the last point of land to this Spouse of the Adriatic, its long line of spires, towers, churches, wharfs, is stretched along the water's edge, and you view it with a mixture of awe and incredulity. A city built in the air would be something still more wonderful; but any other must yield the palm to this for singularity and imposing effect. If it were on the firm land it would rank as one of the first cities in Europe for magnificence, size, and beauty; as it is, it is without a rival. . . . If a parallel must be found for it, it is . . . like Genoa shoved into the sea. Genoa stands *on* the sea, this *in* it. The effect is certainly magical, dazzling, perplexing. You feel at first a little giddy: you are not quite sure of your footing on the deck of a vessel. You enter its narrow, cheerful canals, and find that instead of their being scooped out of the earth, you are gliding amidst rows of palaces and under broad arched bridges, piled on the sea-green wave. You begin to think that you must cut your liquid way in this manner through the whole city, and use oars instead of feet. You land, and visit quays, squares, market-places, theatres, churches, halls, palaces; ascend tall towers, and stroll through shady gardens, without being once reminded that you are not on *terra firma*. . . . Venice is loaded with ornament, like a rich city-heiress with jewels. It seems the natural order of things. Her origin was a wonder: her end is to surprise. The strong, implanted tendency of her genius must be to the showy, the singular, the fantastic. Herself an anomaly, she reconciles contradictions, liberty with aristocracy, commerce with nobility, the want of titles with the pride of birth and heraldry. A violent birth in nature, she lays greedy, perhaps ill-advised, hands on all the artificial advantages that can supply her original defects. Use turns to gaudy beauty; extreme hardship to intemperance in pleasure. From the level uniform expanse that forever encircles her, she would obviously affect the aspiring in forms, the quaint, the complicated, relief and projection. The richness and foppery of her architecture arise from this: its stability and excellence probably from another circumstance counter-acting this tendency to the buoyant and the fluttering, *viz.*, the necessity of raising solid edifices on such slippery foundations, and of not playing tricks with stone-walls upon the water. Her eye for colours and costume she would bring with conquest from the East. The spirit, intelligence, and activity of her men, she would derive from their ancestors: the grace, the glowing animation and bounding step of her women, from the sun and mountain-breeze! The want of simplicity and severity in Venetian taste seems owing to this, that all here is factitious and the work of art: redundancy again is an attribute of commerce, whose eye is gross and large, and does not admit of the *too much;* and as to irregularity and want of fixed principles, we may account by analogy at least for these, from that element of which Venice is the nominal bride, to which she owes her all, and the very essence of which is caprice, uncertainty, and vicissitude!
William Hazlitt, *Notes of a Journey through France and Italy,* 1826

It seems like being both *in town* and *at sea,* at one and the same time.
J.P. Cobbett, *Journal of a Tour in Italy,* 1830

A city for beavers.
Ralph Waldo Emerson, *Journal,* June 1833

Nothing in the world that you have ever heard of Venice, is equal to the magnificent and stupendous reality. The wildest visions of the Arabian Nights are nothing to the piazza of St Mark, and the first impression of the inside of the church. The gorgeous and wonderful reality of Venice is beyond the fancy of the wildest dreamer. Opium couldn't build such a place, and enchantment couldn't shadow it forth in a vision. . . . It has never been rated high enough. It is a thing you would shed tears to see. When I came *on board* here last night (after a five miles' row in a gondola; which somehow or other I wasn't at all prepared for); when, from seeing the city lying, one light, upon the distant water, like a ship, I came plashing through the silent and deserted streets; I felt as if the houses were reality – the water, fever-madness. But when, in the bright, cold, bracing day, I stood upon the piazza this morning, by Heaven the glory of the place was insupportable! And diving down from that into its wickedness and gloom – its awful prisons, deep below the water; its judgement chambers, secret doors, deadly nooks, where the torches you carry with you blink as if they couldn't bear the air in which the frightful scenes were acted; and coming out again into the radiant, unsubstantial Magic of the town; and diving in again, into vast churches and old tombs, – a new sensation, a new memory, a new mind came upon me. Venice is a bit of my brain from this time.

Charles Dickens, Letter, 1844,
in Forster, *Life of Dickens,* 1872–3

But close about the quays and churches, palaces and prisons: sucking at their walls, and welling up into the secret places of the town: crept the water always. Noiseless and watchful: coiled round and round it, in its many folds, like an old serpent: waiting for the time, I thought, when people should look down into its depths for any stone of the old city that had claimed to be its mistress.

Charles Dickens, *Pictures from Italy,* 1846

How light we go, how soft we skim,
And all in open moonlight swim!
Bright clouds against, reclined I mark
The white dome now projected dark,
And, by o'er-brilliant lamps displayed,
The Doge's columns and arcade;
Over still waters mildly come
The distant laughter and the hum.
How light we go, how softly! Ah,
Life should be as the Gondola!

Arthur Hugh Clough, *Dipsychus, c.* 1850

I have been between heaven and earth since our arrival at Venice. The heaven of it is ineffable. Never had I touched the skirts of so celestial a place. The beauty of the architecture, the silver trails of water up between all that gorgeous colour and carving, the enchanting silence, the moonlight, the music, the gondolas – I mix it all up together, and maintain that nothing is like it, nothing to equal it, not a second Venice in the world. Do you know when I came first I felt as if I could never go away. But now comes the earth side. Robert, after sharing the ecstasy, grows uncomfortable, and nervous, and unable to eat or sleep. . . . Alas for these mortal Venices – so exquisite and so bilious!

Elizabeth Barrett Browning, Letter to Miss Mitford,
4 June 1851

Well might it seem that such a city had owed its existence rather to the rod of the enchanter, than the fear of the fugitive; that the water which encircled her had been chosen for the mirror of her state, rather than the shelter of her nakedness; and that all which in nature was wild or merciless – Time and Decay, as well as the waves and tempests, had been won to adorn her instead of to destroy, and might still spare, for ages to come, that beauty which seemed to have fixed for its throne the sands of the hour-glass as well as those of the sea.

John Ruskin, *The Stones of Venice,* 1851–3

The fact is, with reverence be it spoken, that whereas Rogers says 'There is a glorious city in the Sea,' a truthful person must say 'There is a glorious city in the Mud.' It is startling at first to say so, but it goes well enough with marble, 'Oh Queen of Marble and of Mud.'

John Ruskin, Letter to Charles Eliot Norton,
May 1859

What a funny old city this Queen of the Adriatic is! Narrow streets, vast, gloomy marble palaces, black with the corroding damp of centuries and all partly submerged; no dry land visible anywhere, and no side-walks worth mentioning; if you want to go to church, to the theatre, or to a restaurant, you must call a gondola. It must be a paradise for cripples, for verily a man has no use for legs here.

For a day or two the place looked so like an overflowed Arkansas town because of its currentless waters laving the very doorsteps of all the houses, and the cluster of boats made fast under the windows, or skimming in and out of the alleys and by-ways, that I could not get rid of the impression that there was nothing the matter here but a spring freshet, and that the river would fall in a few weeks, and leave a dirty high-water mark on the houses, and the streets full of mud and rubbish.

Mark Twain, *The Innocents Abroad,* 1869

White swan of cities, slumbering in thy nest
  So wonderfully built among the reeds
  Of the lagoon, that fences thee and feeds,
  As sayest thy old historian and thy guest!
White water-lily, cradled and caressed
  By ocean streams, and from the silt and weeds
  Lifting thy golden filaments and seeds,
Thy sun-illumined spires, thy crown and crest!
White phantom city, whose untrodden streets
  Are rivers, and whose pavements are the shifting
  Shadows of the palaces and strips of sky;
I wait to see thee vanish like the fleets
  Seen in mirage, or towers of cloud uplifting
  In air their unsubstantial masonry.

Henry Wadsworth Longfellow, *Venice,* 1876

The back streets of Venice would be all the better for a little diluted carbolic acid.

G.A. Sala, *Paris Herself Again,* 1879

It is a great pleasure to write the word; but I am not sure there is not a certain impudence in pretending to add anything to it. Venice has been painted and described many thousands of times, and of all the cities in the world it is the easiest to visit without going there.

Henry James, 'Venice', 1882,
in *Portraits of Places,* 1883

If we were asked what is the leading colour at Venice we should say pink, and yet, after all, we cannot remember that this elegant tint occurs very often. It is a faint, shimmering, airy, watery pink; the bright sea-light seems to flush with it, and the pale whitish-green of lagoon and canal to drink it in. There is, indeed in Venice a great deal of very evident brickwork, which is never fresh or loud in colour, but always burnt out, as it were, always exquisitely mild. There are certain little mental pictures that rise before the sentimental tourist at the simple mention, written or spoken, of the places he has loved. When I hear, when I see, the magical name I have written above these pages, it is not of the great Square that I think, with its strange basilica, and its high arcades, nor of the wide mouth of the Grand Canal, with the stately steps and the well-poised dome of the Salute; it is not of the low lagoon, nor the sweet Piazzetta, nor the dark chambers of St Mark's. I simply see a narrow canal in the heart of the city – a patch of green water and a surface of pink wall. The gondola moves slowly; it gives a great, smooth swerve, passes under a bridge, and the gondolier's cry, carried over the quiet water, makes a kind of splash in the stillness. A girl is passing over the little bridge, which has an arch like a camel's back, with an old shawl on her head, which makes her look charming; you see her against the sky as you float beneath. The pink of the old wall seems to fill the whole place; it sinks even into the opaque water. Beneath the wall is a garden, out of which the long arm of a white June rose – the roses of Venice are splendid – has flung itself by way of spontaneous ornament. On the other side of this small water-way is a great shabby facade of Gothic windows and balconies – balconies on which dirty clothes are hung and under which a cavernous-looking doorway opens from under a low flight of slimy water-steps. It is very hot and still, the canal has a queer smell, and the whole place is enchanting.

Ibid.

My Venice, like Turner's, had been chiefly created for us by Byron; but for me there was also the pure childish passion of seeing boats float in clear water. The beginning of everything was in seeing the gondola-beak come actually inside the door at Daniele's, when the tide was up, and the water two feet deep at the foot of the stairs; and then, all along the canal sides, actual marble walls, rising out of the salt sea, with hosts of little brown crabs on them, and Titians inside.

John Ruskin, *Praeterita,* 1885–9

Hare and Murray for common sense, and Mr Ruskin for uncommon sense will be the best guides here.

Mrs Henry Fawcett, *Orient Line Guide,* 1885

Those who are very energetic in the way of walking exercise, will . . . probably prefer to take Venice after having undergone a good deal of fatigue in other places.

Ibid.

The charm of Venice grows on me strangely; at first I had no real personal impression: and then one rainy day, when the wind, with the sound of bells in it, blew up the Grand Canal, and everything was half blotted in a veil of rain, I suddenly felt all the melancholy charm – the charm of silence and beauty and decay. The strangest thing is to go at night, as we often do in our little boat, up the Grand Canal, & then turn in anywhere, and lose ourselves in the blackness and silence. The great palaces are so high that these little canals seem almost like subterranean rivers, save for the strip of sky and the vague stars above. Sometimes we come suddenly, round a corner, on a square with yellow lights & footsteps & music. Then we glide away into the darkness till at last we come out by the Grand Canal again.

In the afternoons we go out on the lagoon – that is almost the most wonderful of all. A great stretch of grey, windless, waveless water, so still that the boats are either mirrored in it, or when they move, trail long diverging furrows across its surface. To the North you can see the wintry Alps, to the South is the Adriatic, and you hear the sound of the surf beating on the Lido shores, but within the lagoon there is a grey enchanted quiet, with the domes and towers of Venice & the faint sound of its bells.

Logan Pearsall Smith, Letter to his mother,
15 November 1895 in John Russell, *Portrait of Logan Pearsall Smith,* 1950

Twentieth Century

When I went to Venice – my dream became my address.

Marcel Proust, Letter to Madame Strauss,
c. May 1906 – of 1900

It has become a phrase, almost as meaningless as Arcadia. And indeed it is difficult to think of Venice as being quite a real place, its streets of water as being exactly real streets, its gondolas as being no more than the equivalent of hansoms, its union of those elsewhere opposed sentiments of the sea, the canal, the island, walled and towered land, as being quite in the natural order of things. I had had my dreams of Venice, but nothing I had dreamed was quite as impossible as what I found. . . . The Doge's palace looked exactly like beautifully painted canvas, as if it were stretched on frames, and ready to be shunted into the wings for a fresh 'set' to come forward. Yes, it is difficult to believe in Venice, most of all when one is in Venice.

I do not understand why anyone paints Venice, and yet everyone who paints, paints Venice. But to do so is to forget that it is itself a picture, a finished, conscious work of art. You cannot improve the picture as it is, you can add nothing, you need arrange nothing. Everything has been done, awaits you, enchants you, paralyses you; the artistic effect of things as they are is already complete: it leaves, or should leave you, if you have artistic intentions upon it, helpless. Mere existence, at Venice, becomes at once romantic and spectacular: it is like living in a room without a blind, in the full sunlight. A realist, in Venice, would become a romantic, by mere faithfulness to what he saw before him.

Arthur Symons, *Cities,* 1903

The great *genre* picture which is Venice.

Ibid.

Venice now lies like a sea-shell on the shores of the Adriatic, deserted by the wonderful organism that once inhabited it.

Logan Pearsall Smith, *Life and Letters of Sir Henry Wotton,* 1907

I'm glad to find that you dislike Venice because I thought it detestable when we were there, both times – once it might be due to insanity but not twice, so I thought it must be my fault.

Virginia Woolf, Letter to Vanessa Bell, 25 April 1913

and USA

Let the beauty of Venice be a sort of zenith to us, beyond which there is no seeing. Let Lincoln Cathedral fan her wings in our highest heaven, like an eagle at our pitch of flight. We can do no more. We have reached our limits of beauty. But these are not the limits of all beauty. They are not the limit of all things: only of *us*. Therefore St Mark's need be no reproach to an American. It isn't *his* St Mark's. It is ours. And we like crabs ramble in the slack waters and gape at the excess of our own glory. Behold our Venice, our Lincoln Cathedral like a dark bird in the sky at twilight. And think of our yesterdays! What would you not give, O America, for our yesterdays? Far more than they are worth, I assure you. What would not *I* give for your tomorrows.

D.H. Lawrence, 'America Listen to Your Own', *New Republic,* 15 December 1920

. . . abhorrent, green, slippery city. . . .

D.H. Lawrence, 'Pomegranate', 1920, *Birds, Beasts and Flowers,* 1923

I was surprised to find what pleasure it gave me to be in Venice again. It was like coming home, when sounds and smells which one had forgotten stole upon one's senses; and certainly there is no place like it in the world: everything there is better in reality than in memory. I first saw it on a romantic evening after sunset in 1900, and I left it on a sunshiny morning, and I shall not go there again.

A.E. Housman, Letter to his sister, Mrs E.W. Symons, 23 June 1926

The whole of Venice . . . was one vast explosion of cut-throat competition in luxury and swagger; that was why Ruskin had gone about it cursing and lamenting, and inventing strange theories to excuse himself for yielding to its charm.

Desmond MacCarthy, *Experience,* 1935

The bathing, on a calm day, must be the worst in Europe: water like hot saliva, cigar-ends floating into one's mouth, and shoals of jelly-fish.

Robert Byron, *The Road to Oxiana,* 1937

Venice . . . is at once so stately and so materialist, like a proud ghost that has come back to remind men that he failed for a million.

Rebecca West, *Black Lamb and Grey Falcon,* 1942

Wonderful city, streets full of water, please advise.

Robert Benchley, Telegram/Cable, attributed, *c.* 1947

Venice never loses that magic of appearing as if for the first time.

Freya Stark, *Traveller's Prelude,* 1950

Really, Venice is excessively ugly in the rain: it looks like King's Cross.

Sir John Gielgud, Remark, 1953, quoted in Cecil Beaton, *The Strenuous Years,* 1973

Venice at dawn . . . wobbling in a thousand fresh-water reflections, cool as a jelly. It was as if some great master, stricken by dementia, had burst his whole colour-box against the sky, to deafen the inner eye of the world. Cloud and water mixed into each other, dripping with colours, merging, overlapping, liquefying, with steeples and balconies and roofs floating in space, like the fragments of history touched with the colours of wine, tar, ochre, blood, fire-opal, and ripening grain. The whole at the same time being rinsed softly back at the edges into a dawn sky as softly as circumspectly blue as a pigeon's egg.

Lawrence Durrell, *Bitter Lemons,* 1957

Near the celebrated Lido where the breeze is fresh and free
Stands the ancient port of Venice called the City of the Sea.

All its streets are made of water, all its homes are brick
and stone,
Yet it has a picturesqueness which is justly all its own.

Here for centuries have artists come to see the vistas
quaint,
Here Bellini set his easel, here he taught his School to
paint.

Here the youthful Giorgione gazed upon the domes and
towers,
And interpreted his era in a way which pleases ours.

A later artist, Tintoretto, also did his paintings here,
Massive works which generations have continued to
revere.

Still to-day come modern artists to portray the
buildings fair
And their pictures may be purchased on San Marco's
famous Square.

When the bell notes from the belfries and the
campaniles chime
Still today we find Venetians elegantly killing time

In their gilded old palazzos, while the music in our ears
Is the distant band at Florians mixed with songs of
gondoliers.

Thus the New World meets the Old World and the
sentiments expressed
Are melodiously mingled in my warm New England
breast.

John Betjeman, 'Longfellow's Visit to Venice', in *Collected Poems,* 1958

She was never loved. She was always the outsider, always envied, always suspected, always feared. She fitted into no convenient category of nations. She was the lion who walked by herself.

James Morris, *Venice,* 1960

A wholly materialist city is nothing but a dream incarnate. Venice is the world's unconscious.

Mary McCarthy, *Venice Observed,* 1961

Venice is like eating an entire box of chocolate liqueurs at one go.

Truman Capote, *Observer,* 'Sayings of the Week', 26 November 1961

At the best of times there is something precarious about the city.

Richard Mayne, 'Italian Notebook', *Encounter,* October 1964

Venice was created by logic as little as it excited logic in its admirers; if anything it made them impatient with everything they had known before; they began to think it absurd to build cities on land. We must never forget the illogical sea that was always present under the window, at the side of the *calle,* shining in the distance, separating the islands, rising and falling in a rhythm that made little of men and logic; and the reviving air that seeped through the closed windows, quickly mending the effect of a dissipated night. While this strange city invited dissipation it also stirred health, which is why the historians can never decide whether she was really debauched in the eighteenth century or a happy, well-functioning little state to her last day. What would be a debauched life in a land-city is a different affair in Venice.

Maurice Rowdon, *The Fall of Venice,* 1970

The whole course of Venetian art can be seen as a blissful attempt to define Venetian light, until with Tiepolo in the eighteenth century there is only the light left. There is no subject any longer, not even much of a feeling: just the fullness of the light, glittering, searching, flooding everything.

Ibid.

Nothing of its original purpose survives today, it's all tourists and tankers. . . . it remains a freak city, the only one in Europe to have remained basically unchanged for five hundred years; besides the unchanged eighteenth century decor there is the unique water-life which makes a profound appeal to every castaway from amniotic fluid. . . . The effects of light alone are an earthly paradise.

Cyril Connolly, *The Evening Colonnade,* 1973

Venice is the supreme example of how men correct and exploit nature and nature cooperates or submits. (And, like Naples, Venice is a test; those who claim to dislike it usually blame the tourists but what they really mean is that they cannot stomach a dream come true.)

Peter Nichols, *Italia, Italia,* 1973

Venice, like a drawing room in a gas station, is approached through a vast apron of infertile industrial flatlands, criss-crossed with black sewer troughs and stinking of oil, the gigantic sinks and stoves of refineries and factories, all intimidating the delicate dwarfed city beyond. . . . The lagoon with its luminous patches of oil slick, as if hopelessly retouched by Canaletto, has a yard-wide tidewrack of rubble, plastic bottles, broken toilet seats, raw sewage, and that bone white factory froth the wind beats into drifts of foam. The edges of the city have succumbed to industry's erosion, and what shows are the cracked back windows and derelict posterns of water-logged villas, a few brittle Venetian steeples, and farther in, but low and almost visibly sinking, walls of spaghetti-colored stucco and red roofs over which flocks of soaring swallows are teaching pigeons to fly.

Paul Theroux, *The Great Railway Bazaar,* 1975

Who wants a Renaissance Disneyland, anyway, with entrance fees only the very rich can afford?

Private Eye, No. 440, 27 October 1978

Venetians . . . know all too well that they are 'picturesque;' in Venice one never loses the sense that life is being staged for the onlooker.

Jonathan Raban, *Arabia through the Looking Glass,* 1979

For six days last week Venice looked like a blocked sink.

Caption to photograph in *Sunday Times,* 25 December 1979

Districts and details

The Arsenal

I went with a freind to see the famous Arsenall, a place of about two myles in compasse, walled round, haveinge but one entrance for a Gally to goe in or out, there being within water for two or three hundred to ride afloate. Here is alsoe about one hundred great roomes open att both ends for building new Gallyes, where were some on the Stocks; from thence to the place where they cast Ordnance: Then to great Store howses, of which there are many full of the said Ordinance, ready mounted on Carriages. In others were Gunns dismounted, others full of Carriages ready made, others with bullets piled in seemely order. Wee were likewise shewed where they made Anchors, Cables and ropes, Rudders, Oares, Masts, yards, all sort of Iron for gallies, ground saltpeter, Planck, Sawyers, etts., with ware howses where every one of the aforementioned lay ready made. Then went Wee upp staires, where were very faire halls, hung on both sides with Armour from the head to the Knees, others with swords, Musketts Pikes and Targetts to a very great number; other halls with munition for fifty Gallies; in each Hall their being fifty pertitions, and in every of them soe many Guns with match, swords, Pikes, etts. sufficient for one Gallie. In other halls were sailes ready made for soe many gallies, and as some spend, there are others made new in their roomes, which are sowen by weomen, of whome there were att present greate Companies att worke. Divers other things there were worth notice which to perticularize would require much tyme, As sondry sorts of auncient Armes, also compleat Armours of certen famous men, reserved there for a Monument; All theis, with the aforesaid kept cleane and in Excellent good Order. Then were wee brought to the Bucentero, a vessell like a Gallye, but shorter, thicker and higher, whereon is shewed the uttermost of Art for carved Worke, that being over layed with Gold, soe that when shee is in the Water, shee appeares to be all of pure gold. . . . In this vessell goeth the Duke and Nobillitie of Venice to marrie the Sea, an auncient Custome observed every yeare on Assention Day. . . .

Peter Mundy, *Sundry Relations of Certaine Voyages,* 27 July 1620

Palace of the Doges

There is near unto the Dukes Palace a very faire prison, the fairest absolutely that ever I saw. . . . I think there is not a fairer prison in all Christendome. . . .

Thomas Coryate, *Crudities,* 1611

The nobleness of the Staircases, the Riches of the Halls, and the Beauty of the whole Building, are much prejudiced by the Beastliness of those that walk along, and that leave their Marks behind them, as if this were rather a common House of Office, than so noble a Palace.

Gilbert Burnet, *Some Letters Containing an Account of what seemed Remarkable in Travelling . . . ,* 1687

Thunder and rain! O dear, O dear!
But see, a noble shelter here,
This grand arcade where our Venetian
Has formed of Gothic and of Grecian
A combination strange, but striking,
And singularly to my liking.

Arthur Hugh Clough, *Dipsychus,* Scene VII, 'The Interior Arcade of the Doge's Palace', *c.* 1850

If Venice is no longer Venice, as every body says, one can however see what was not seen before – at least in the way one would like.

Samuel Rogers, *Italian Journal,* 17 October 1814

Gondolas

The gondolas themselves are things of a most romantic and picturesque appearance; I can only compare them to moths of which a coffin might have been the chrysalis.

Percy Bysshe Shelley, Letter to Thomas Love Peacock, 8 October 1818

The Lido

What now? the Lido shall it be?
That none may say we didn't see
The ground which Byron used to ride on,
And do I don't know what beside on.

Arthur Hugh Clough, *Dipsychus, c.* 1850

Rialto

It is almost time to talk of the Rialto, said to be the finest single arch in Europe, and I suppose it is so; very beautiful too, when looked on from the water, but so dirtily kept, and deformed with mean shops, that passing over it, disgust gets the better of every other sensation. The truth is, our dear Venetians are nothing less than cleanly; St. Mark's Place is all covered over in a morning with chicken-coops, which stink one to death; as nobody I believe thinks of changing their baskets: and all about the Ducal palace is made so very offensive by the resort of human creatures for every purpose most unworthy of so charming a place, that all enjoyment of its beauties is rendered difficult to a person of any delicacy; and poisoned so provokingly that I do never cease to wonder that so little police and proper regulation are established in a city so particularly lovely, to render her sweet and wholesome.

Hester Lynch Thrale/Piozzi, *Observations . . . in the Course of a Journey*, 1789

St Mark's

And above this gallery, and over the great doore of the Church, be foure horses of brasse, guilded over, very notable for antiquity and beauty; and they are so set, as if at the first step they would leape into the market place. . . . And all the parts of these horses being most like the one to the other, yet by strange art, both in posture of motion, and otherwise, they are most unlike one to the other.

Fynes Moryson, *An Itinerary,* 1617

O beautiful, beneath the magic moon,
To walk the watery way of palaces!
O beautiful, o'ervaulted with gemmed blue,
This spacious court; with colour and with gold,
With cupolas, and pinnacles, and points,
And crosses multiplex, and tips and balls
(Wherewith the bright stars unreproving mix,
Nor scorn by hasty eyes to be confused);
Fantastically perfect this low pile
Of oriental glory; these long ranges
Of classic chiselling, this gay flickering crowd,
And the calm Campanile. Beautiful!

Arthur Hugh Clough, *Dipsychus, c.* 1850

On these still summer days the fair Venetians float about in full bloom like pond lilies. . . . On the canals of Venice all vehicles are represented. Omnibus, private coach, light gig, or sulky, pedler's cart, hearse. – You at first think it a freshet, it will subside, not permanent – only a temporary condition of things. – St Mark's at sunset. gilt mosaics, pinnacles, looks like a holyday affair. As if the Grand Turk had pitched his pavilion here for a summer's day. 800 years! Inside the precious marbles, from extreme age, look like a mural of rare old soaps. – have an unctuous look. Fairly steamed with old devotions as refectories with old dinners. – In Venice nothing to see for the Venetian. – Rather be in Venice on rainy day than in other capital on fine one.

Herman Melville, *Journal of a Visit to Europe and the Levant,* 5 April 1857

I do not think it, nobody can think it, beautiful, and yet I never was more entertained by any building.

T.B. Macaulay, Letter, 1856, in Sir G.O. Trevelyan, *Life and Letters of Lord Macaulay*, 1876

One lingers about the Cathedral a good deal, in Venice. There is a strong fascination about it – partly because it is so old, and partly because it is so ugly. Too many of the world's famous buildings fail of one chief virtue – harmony; they are made up of a methodless mixture of the ugly and the beautiful; this is bad; it is confusing, it is unrestful. One has a sense of uneasiness, of distress, without knowing why. But one is calm before St Mark, one is calm within it, one would be calm on top of it, calm in the cellar; for its details are masterfully ugly, no misplaced and impertinent beauties are intruded anywhere; and the consequent result is a grand harmonious whole, of soothing, entrancing, tranquillising, soul-satisfying ugliness. One's admiration of a perfect thing always grows, never declines; and this is the surest evidence to him that it *is* perfect. St Mark is perfect. To me it soon grew to be so nobly, so augustly ugly, that it was difficult to stay away from it, even for a little while. Every time its squat domes disappeared from my view, I had a despondent feeling; whenever they reappeared, I felt an honest rapture – I have not known any happier hours than those I daily spent in front of Florian's, looking across the Great Square at it. Propped on its long row of low thick-legged columns, its back knobbed with domes, it seemed like a vast warty bug taking a meditative walk.

Mark Twain, *A Tramp Abroad,* 1880

If Venice, as I say has become a great bazaar, this exquisite edifice is now the biggest booth.

Henry James, 'Venice', 1882, in *Portraits of Places,* 1883

Women of

Iago: In Venice, they do let Heaven see the prankes
They dare not shew their Husbands.
Their best Conscience,
Is not to leav't undone, but kept unknowne.

William Shakespeare, *Othello*, 1604–5

The Venetians say 'The first handsome woman that ever was made, was made of Venice glasse.'

James Howell, *Familiar Letters* (1 June 1621), 1645

The women *kiss* better than those of any other nation – which is notorious – and is attributed to the worship of images and the early habit of osculation induced thereby.

Lord Byron, Letter to John Murray, 25 March 1817

It is a very good place for women – I have a few like every one else. . . . The City however is decaying daily and does not gain in population.

Lord Byron, Letter to Samuel Rogers, 3 March 1818

She was, in truth, the wonder of her sex,
At least in Venice – where with eyes of brown,
Tenderly languid, ladies seldom vex
An amorous gentle with a needless frown;
Where gondolas convey guitars by packs,
And Love at casements climbeth up and down,
Whom for his tricks and custom in that kind,
Some have considered a Venetian blind.

Thomas Hood, *Bianca's Dream,* 1827

Verona

Romeo:
There is no world without *Verona* walles,
But Purgatorie, Torture, hell it selfe:
Hence banished, is banisht from the world,
And worlds exile in death.

William Shakespeare, *Romeo and Juliet, c.* 1594–5

This most faire City is built in the forme of a Lute. . . . It hath a pure aire, and is ennobled by the civility and auncient Nobility of the Citizens, who are indued with a chearfull countenance, magnificent mindes, and much inclined to all good literature.

Fynes Moryson, *An Itinerary,* 1617

Certainly this Citty deserv'd all those Elogies Scaliger has honour'd it with, for in my opinion, tis situated in one of the most delightfullst places that ever I came in, so sweetly mixed with risings, & Vallies, so Elegantly planted with Trees, on which *Bacchus* seems riding as it were in Triumph every *Autumn,* for the Vines reach from tree to tree; & here of all places I have travell'd in *Italy* would I fix preferable to any other, so as well has that learned Man given it the name of the very Eye of the World.

John Evelyn, *Diary,* May 1646

The Veronese Nobillity . . . say, God has reserv'd Glory to himselfe and permitted Pleasure to the persuit of Man.

Lady Mary Wortley Montagu, Letter to Lady Bute, 24 July 1755

Love no child's play in this town. The day before yesterday a man in a fit of jealousy stilotted his wife & her lover, his friend. . . .

Samuel Rogers, *Italian Journal,* 14 October 1814

Juliet's Tomb
I have been over Verona. . . . Of the truth of Juliet's story, they seem tenacious to a degree, insisting on the fact – giving a date (1303), and showing a tomb. It is a plain, open, and partly decayed sarcophagus, with withered leaves in it, in a wild and desolate conventual garden, once a cemetery, now ruined to the very graves. The situation struck me as being very appropriate to the legend, being blighted as their love. I have brought away a few pieces of the granite, to give to my daughter and my nieces.

Lord Byron, Letter to Augusta Leigh, 7 November 1816

The House of the Capulets
It was natural enough to go straight from the Market-place, to the House of the Capulets, now degenerated into a most miserable little inn. Noisy vetturini and muddy market-carts were disputing possession of the yard, which was ankle-deep in dirt, with a brook of splashed and bespattered geese; and there was a grim-visaged dog, viciously panting in a doorway, who would certainly have had Romeo by the leg, the moment he put it over the wall, if he had existed, and been at large in these times. . . . The house is a distrustful jealous-looking house as one would desire to see, though of a very moderate size.

Charles Dickens, *Pictures from Italy,* 1846

I must not yet say more of Verona, than that, though truly Rouen, Geneva and Pisa have been the centres of thought and teaching to me, Verona has given the colouring to all they taught. She has virtually represented the fate and beauty of Italy to me; and whatever concerning Italy I have felt, or been able with any charm or force to say, has been dealt with more deeply, and said more earnestly for her sake.

John Ruskin, *Praeterita,* 1885–9

Juliet's home-town, I suppose some would call it. The phrase takes the edge off romance, and I designed it to do so, determined as I am somehow to vent my rage at being shown Juliet's house, a picturesque and untidy tenement, with balconies certainly too high for love, unless Juliet was a trapeze acrobat, accustomed to hanging downwards by her toes.

This was not Juliet's house, for the sufficient reason that so far as authentic history knows, there never was any Juliet.

Arnold Bennett, *Journal 1929,* 1930

At Verona, an American in Auden's compartment said to his companion, 'Hey, didn't Shakespeare live here?' at which Auden observed loudly, 'Surely it was Bacon.'

Charles Osborne, *W.H. Auden,* 1980 – of 5 September 1951

Vesuvius

With much difficulty I reached to the top of Mount Vesuvius, in which I saw a vast aperture full of smoak, which hindered the seeing its depth and figure. I heard within that horrid gulf certain odd sounds, which seemed to proceed from the belly of the mountain; a sort of murmuring, sighing, throbbing, churning, dashing (as it were) of waves, and between whiles, a noise, like that of thunder or cannon, which was constantly attended with a clattering, like that of tiles falling from the tops of houses on the streets.

George Berkeley, Bishop of Cloyne, 'Extract of a Letter from Naples', *Philosophical Transactions,* 1717

Then on foot to Vesuvius. Monstrous mounting. Smoke; saw hardly anything.

James Boswell, *Journal,* 14 March 1765

If I had not been ashamed to have gone away from Naples without going up, I should certainly not have given myself the trouble.

Charles Howard Earl of Carlisle, *c.* 1768
quoted in Geoffrey Trease, *The Grand Tour,* 1967

I had a peep very far into the crater. The sides seemed all lava and scoria, with very little variety in the flints, closed at bottom by an impenetrable screen of smoke. I have seen old ruined coalpits, that afford a tolerable idea of this volcanic kettle.

Henry Swinburne, *Travels in the Two Sicilies in 1777–1780,* 1785

Vesuvius, vomitting fire, and pouring torrents of red hot lava down its sides, was the only object visible; and *that* we saw plainly in the afternoon thirty miles off, where I asked a Franciscan friar, If it was the famous volcano? 'Yes,' replied he, 'that's our mountain, which throws up money for us, by calling foreigners to see the extraordinary effects of so surprising a phaenomenon.'

Hester Lynch Thrale/Piozzi, *Observations . . . in the Course of a Journey,* 1789

Went up Mount Vesuvius – its furrowed & channelled sides – channelled by floods of lava – Sunshine. A hazy morning. No cloud. Wind North East. Mounted a small horse at Portici. A mountain road, rough & stony. A church. A vineyard wall – a cottage – a cross – Lizards sunning themselves among the stones. . . . Descended into a valley of cinders, & now what stood before us but a black Mountain, a Mountain of Cinders – travellers ascending & descending like small white spots – Atrio dei Cavalli – Left our horses at the foot of it & gained the summit; & as you drew near it, sulphur-stains appeared on every side, & smoke rose here & there; & the ashes felt warm to the feet. – Proceeded to the crater; nor heard nor saw any thing till we had gained the utmost height that intercepted all sight & sound; then we looked down a small but dismal hollow, an inclined plane beyond which appeared the gulph, the opposite side of which, black & sulphurous, rose precipitately, & considerably above the nearer side. Then it was that we heard & saw – & we descended to the edge of the gulph – The noise was not continual, but by fits – The silence that came continually, rendering it still more awful – a noise now deep & hollow, like the rolling & dashing of waters, or of a metallic fluid, much heavier & harder than water – now sharp & clattering like that of a Forge such as Virgil places in Etna – Volcani Domus – & now like the explosion of great Ordnance, or of thunder among mountains – the noise instantly followed by a discharge of large substances, most of them red hot, many of which fell back into the abyss, & many against the sides with a violent crash – & some at our feet & behind us. In the air they appeared like shells thrown by an enemy, & the danger was not small my two guides continually pulling me by the arm, & crying, 'Andiamo, Signor.' – Those that fell near us were lighted cinders, near a foot square, & red as when dropping or shot out from a fire. The sound increasing, & a greater explosion having taken place, & the wind shifting against us, we retired to our first position, above a hundred yards from the crater, when another still greater succeeded, throwing vast cinders even to the place we had reached. From the extreme edge it was indeed most horrid, the substances continually thrown half-way up resembling in the darkness lumps or masses of red flesh, like so many drops or 'gouts of blood,' & now & then a flame lighting up, as it were, the darkness. Stood awhile on the brow of the mountain, now looking down on Herculaneum & Pompei & Stabia & now on the horrid gulph. It was an awful & an interesting thing to connect them in one's mind, the Sun shining on the Sea & the shore, on Portici, Resina, Torre del Greco, Castello del Mare – Annonciata – all so lovely & smiling so near the mouth that may devour them all.

Samuel Rogers, *Italian Journal,* 23 February 1815

Vesuvius is, after the glaciers, the most impressive exhibition of the energies of nature I ever saw. It has not the immeasurable greatness, the overpowering magnificence, nor, above all, the radiant beauty of the glaciers; but it has all their character of tremendous and irresistible strength. From Resina to the hermitage you wind up the mountain, and cross a vast stream of hardened lava, which is an actual image of the waves of the sea, changed into hard black stone by inchantment. The lines of the boiling flood seem to hang in the air, and it is difficult to believe that the billows which seem hurrying down upon you are not actually in motion. This plain was once a sea of liquid fire. . . . On the summit is a kind of irregular plain, the most horrible chaos that can be imagined; riven into ghastly chasms, and heaped up with tumuli of great stones and cinders, and enormous rocks blackened and calcined, which had been thrown from the volcano upon one another in terrible confusion. In the midst stands the conical hill from which volumes of smoke, and the fountains of liquid fire, are rolled forth for ever. The mountain is at present in a slight state of eruption; and a thick, heavy white smoke is perpetually rolled out, interrupted by enormous columns of an impenetrable black bituminous vapour, which is hurled up, fold after fold, into the sky, with a deep hollow sound, and fiery stones are rained down from its darkness, and a black shower of ashes fell even where we sat. The lava, like a glacier, creeps on perpetually, with a crackling sound as of suppressed fire. There are several springs of lava; and in one place it gushes precipitously over a high crag, rolling down the half-molten rocks and its own overhanging waves; a cataract of quivering fire. We approached the extremity of one of the rivers of lava; it is about twenty feet in breadth and ten in height; and as the inclined plane was not rapid, its motion was very slow. We saw the masses of its dark exterior surface detach themselves as it moved, and betray the depth of the liquid flame. In the day the fire is but slightly seen; you only observe a tremulous motion in the air, and streams and fountains of white sulphurous smoke.

At length we saw the sun sink between Capreae and Inarime, and, as the darkness increased, the effect of the fire became more beautiful. We were, as it were, surrounded by streams and cataracts of the red and radiant fire; and in the midst, from the column of bituminous smoke shot up into the air, fell the vast masses of rock, white with the light of their intense heat, leaving behind them through the dark vapour trains of splendour. We descended by torch-light, and I should have enjoyed the scenery on my return, but they conducted me, I know not how, to the hermitage in a state of intense bodily suffering.

Percy Bysshe Shelley, Letter to Thomas Love Peacock, 22 December 1818

Excursion to Vesuvius. – My surgeon warned me against this ascent, but I was resolved to go. To leave Naples, without seeing Vesuvius, would be worse, than to die at Naples, after seeing Vesuvius.

Henry Matthews, *Diary of an Invalid*, 1820

We had some conversation with the hermit who lived on the mountain; he was a Frenchman, and said to have been formerly a hairdresser in London; whether this be fact or not, I cannot say; the subject was much too delicate to touch upon with a recluse in such a situation. The mountain seemed in a most villainous humour, emitting flames and large bodies of lava. I soon had enough of it, and was right glad to find myself once more at Portici, with a supper of red mullet, &c. before me.

Michael Kelly, *Reminiscences*, 1826

The Neapolitans call the crater, '*La cucina del diavolo*' (The devil's kitchen). I asked our guide what he supposed was doing underneath. 'No doubt,' said he, 'it is the devils cooking macaroni.'

J.P. Cobbett, *Journal of a Tour in Italy, etc.*, 1830

The red hot ashes were falling in showers; and the noise and fire, and smoke, and sulphur, made me feel as if I were dead drunk. To which effect, the trembling crust of ground beneath my feet, contributed, no doubt.

It is a tremendous sight. Awful and terrible indeed. Between the stately moon, and the fire, and the black smoke, and the white Snow, and the red going-down of the Sun, there was a combination of Lights and Shadows upon it, such as I could never have imagined. It is more terrible than Niagara: the effect of which (to me at least) is peacefully and gently solemn, as the happy deaths of ten thousand people, without pain or blood, might be. But the two things are as different in the impressions they produce as – in short as fire and water are, which I suppose is the long and the short of it.

Charles Dickens, Letter to Emile de la Rue, 23 and 25 February 1845

The first sight of the Alps had been to me as a direct revelation of the beneficent will in creation. Long since in the volcanic powers of destruction, I had been taught by Homer, and further forced by my own reason to see, if not the personality of an Evil Spirit, at all events the permitted symbol of evil, unredeemed; wholly distinct from the conditions of storm, or heat, or frost, on which the healthy courses of organic life depended. In the same literal way in which the snows and Alpine roses of Lauterbrunnen were visible Paradise, here, in the valley of ashes and throat of lava, were visible Hell. If thus in the natural, how else should it be in the spiritual world? . . . The common English Traveller, if he can gather a black bunch of grapes with his own fingers, and have his bottle of Falernian brought to him by a girl with black eyes, asks no more of this world, or the next; and declares Naples a Paradise. But I knew from the first moment when my foot furrowed volcanic ashes, that no mountain form or colour could exist in perfection, when everything was made of scoria, and that blue sea was to be little boasted of, if it broke on black sand.

John Ruskin, *Praeterita*, 1885–9

Vesuvius don't talk – Aetna don't. One of them said a syllable, a thousand years ago, and Pompeii heard it and hid forever. She couldn't look the world in the face afterward, I suppose. Bashful Pompeii! . . .

Emily Dickinson, Letter to Mr Theodore Holland, 1885

If Vesuvius does not frighten those who live under it, is it likely that Hell-fire should frighten any reasonable person?

Samuel Butler, *Note-Books*, 1912

Viareggio

Viareggio, dead at this season, is a rowdy place in summer; not rowdy, however, after the fashion of Margate. There is a suggestive difference between the two. . . . Set Viareggio down at the very gate of Rome and fill it with the scum of Trastevere: the difference would still be there. It might be more noisy than Margate. It would certainly be less blatant.

As for myself, I hate Viareggio at all seasons, and nothing would have brought me here but the prospect of visiting the neighbouring Carrara mines. . . .

For this is a modern town built on a plain of mud and sand, a town of heartrending monotony, the least picturesque of all cities in the peninsula, the least Italian. It has not even a central piazza! You may conjure up visions of Holland and detect something of an old-world aroma, if you stroll about the canal and harbour where sails are now flapping furiously in the north wind; you may look up to the snow-covered peaks, and imagine yourself in Switzerland, and then thank God you are not there; of Italy I perceive little or nothing. The people are birds of prey; a shallow and rapacious brood who fleece visitors during those summer weeks and live on the proceeds for the rest of the year.

Norman Douglas, *Alone,* 1921

Vicenza

On the left hand of the bridge which leadeth into the citie from Padua, I told sixteene pretty water-mils, which are very commodious to the citie: it is thought to be about some foure miles in compasse with the suburbes, being seated in a plaine at the foot of the hill Bericus, and built in that manner that it representeth the figure of a Scorpion. For it extendeth itselfe much more in length than breadth. And about the West end it is so slender and narrow, that it resembleth the taile of a Scorpion.

Thomas Coryate, *Crudities,* 1611

Viterbo

The *Black Eagle* inn at VITERBO is the best house we have met with on this road: and that is not saying *much* for it. In a dining-room, which resembles (not in *cleanliness*) one of the largest English farm-house kitchens, the walls are covered by the scribblings of travellers. This is the case in many of the inns. It is amusing to read what some have left behind them. There is not consolation enough at the *Black Eagle* to have prevented our comfort-hunting countrymen from being very querulous here.

'Wm. Arnold, John Righton, Henry Colbrook:
'three fools for leaving English comfort for the
'sake of seeing greater fools than themselves.'

J.P. Cobbett, *Journal of a Tour in Italy, etc.*, 1830

A somnolent mountain hamlet out of a Schubert operetta.

S.J. Perelman, *Westward Ha!,* 1948

Volterra

Volterra, a sort of inland island, still curiously isolated and grim.

D.H. Lawrence, *Etruscan Places,* 1932

IVORY COAST

The Ivory Coast, an important division of French West Africa, some years ago elected a distinguished Negro lawyer, Victor Biaka-Boda, as a senator to Paris. Mr Biaka-Boda returned to his constituency in 1950 to do some electioneering, and disappeared out in the bush. All efforts to trace him failed. On March 30, 1953, he was officially declared dead by a court sitting at Bouafle which, on inspecting the evidence, decided that he had been eaten by cannibals. '*Debris humain*' was the proof. There are cases innumerable in the world of senators feasting with the constituents, but this must surely be the only instance on record of constituents feasting on a senator.

John Gunther, *Inside Africa,* 1955

Grand Bassam

Grand Bassam . . . is for connoisseurs of decay.

Richard West, *The White Tribes of Africa,* 1965

J

JAMAICA

This Isle is a marveilous fertil Isle, & is as a garden or store house for divers parts of the maine. It is full of plaine champion ground, which in the rest of the Indies we have not seene: it aboundeth with beeves and Cassavi, besides most pleasant fruits of divers sorts. We have not found in the Indies a more pleasant and holsome place.

Sir Anthony Sherley (1597), in Richard Hakluyt, *Principal Navigations . . . of the English Nation*, 1598–1600

Jamaica, an island then considered as one of the most unhealthy in the West Indies, or in the world.

William Hickey, *Memoirs*, 1749–1809

It is one of the few sores on our huge and healthy carcase; and the sore has been now running so long, that we have almost given over asking whether it be curable.

Anthony Trollope, *The West Indies and the Spanish Main*, 1859

and Tenerife, etc.

When Columbus was ordered by Isabel la Catolica to describe the appearance of Jamaica, he crushed a sheet of paper in his hand, and partially opening it out upon the table, told Her Majesty that the crumpled paper would show it better than his words could tell. The same would serve for Madeira, Tenerife, Fernando Po, and almost all these outlying islands of West Africa, which contrast strongly with the flat coralline formations of the eastern coast.

Richard Burton, *Wanderings in West Africa*, 1863

We had, close over our port bow, the most beautiful island in the world. It is useless to deny it, and to declare you know a better island. Can't I see Jamaica now? I see it most plain. It descends abruptly from the meridian, pinnacles and escarpments trembling in the upper air with distance and delicate poise, and comes down in rolling forests and steep verdant slopes, where facets of bare rock glitter, to more leisurely open glades and knolls; and then, being not far from the sea, drops in sheer cliffs to where the white combers pulse. It is a jewel which smells like a flower.

H.M. Tomlinson, *The Sea and the Jungle*, 1912

*'My dear wife . . . is taking a trip to the West Indies.'
'Jamaica?'
'No, she went of her own free will.'

P.G. Wodehouse, *Uncle Dynamite*, 1948

We have neither Summer nor Winter
Neither Autumn nor Spring

We have instead the days
When gold sun shines on the lush green canefields—
Magnificently

The days when the rain beats like bullets on the roofs
And there is no sound but the swish of water in the gullies
And trees struggling in the high Jamaica winds.

Also there are the days when the leaves fade off the guango trees
And the reaped canefields lie bare and fallow in the sun.

But best of all there are the days when the mango and the logwood blossom.

When the bushes are full of the sound of bees and the scent of honey
When the tall grass sways and shivers to the slightest breath of air
When the buttercups have paved the earth with yellow stars
And beauty comes suddenly and the rains have gone.

H.D. Carberry, 'Nature', in [ed.] John Figueroa, *Caribbean Voices – Dreams and Visions*, 1966

Kingston

Of all the towns that I ever saw, Kingston is perhaps, on the whole, the least alluring, and is the more absolutely without any point of attraction for a stranger than any other. . . . Kingston on the map, – for there is a map even of Kingston – looks admirably well. The streets all run in parallels. There is a fine, large square, plenty of public buildings, and almost a plethora of places of worship. Everything is named with propriety, and there could be no nicer town anywhere. But this word of promise to the ear is strangely broken when performance is brought to the test. More than half the streets are not filled with houses. Those which are so filled, and those which are not, have an equally ragged, disreputable, and bankrupt appearance. The houses are mostly of wood, and are unpainted, disjointed, and going to ruin. Those which are built with brick not unfrequently appear as though the mortar had been diligently picked out from the interstices . . . The street is neither paved nor macadamized, nor prepared for traffic in any way. In dry weather it is a bed of sand, and in wet weather it is a watercourse. Down the middle of this the unfortunate pedestrian has to wade, with a tropical sun on his head; and this he must do in a town which, from its position, is hotter than almost any other in the West Indies.

Anthony Trollope, *The West Indies and the Spanish Main,* 1859

It would be idle to pretend that Kingston is an attractive city. It is bigger and uglier than any other town in the British West Indies. The centre resembles the nastiest of London outskirts and the outskirts are equal to the most dreary of West Indian slums. It was a relief to discover, after a few days, that it is quite unrepresentative of the rest of this beautiful island.

Patrick Leigh Fermor, *The Traveller's Tree,* 1951

The slums of Kingston are beyond description. Even the camera glamorises them, except in shots taken from the air. Hovels of board and cardboard and canvas and tin lie choked together on damp rubbish dumps behind which the sun sets in mocking splendour. More respectable, and on drier ground are the packing-case houses, the tiniest houses ever built, suggesting a vast arrested community given over to playing in grubby dolls' houses. Then there are the once real houses packed to bursting point, houses so close in streets so narrow that there is no feeling of openness. Filth and rubbish are disgorged everywhere; everywhere there are puddles; on the rubbish dumps latrines are forbidden by law.

V.S. Naipaul, *The Middle Passage,* 1962

The North East Coast

There are unfounded complaints that hotels have bought up all the white sand beaches, leaving only black sand for Jamaicans: a neat symbol of the racial resentment tourism is exciting.

V.S. Naipaul, *The Middle Passage,* 1962

JAPAN

This nation is the delight of my soul.

St Francis Xavier, attrib.

The extreame part of the knowen world unto us is the noble Iland Giapan, written otherwise Japon and Japan. This Island standeth in the East Ocean, beyond all Asia, betwixt Cathayo and the West Indies . . . the travaile thither, both for civill discord, great pyracie and often shipwracks is very dangerous. This countrey is hillie and pestered with snow, wherefore it is neither so warme as Portugall, nor yet so wealthy, so far as we can learne, wanting oyle, butter, cheese, milke, egges, sugar, honey, vinegar, saffron, cynamon, and pepper. Barley-branne the Ilanders doe use in stead of salt; medicinable things holsome for the bodie they have none at all. Nevertheless in the Iland sundry fruites doe growe, not much unlike the fruites of Spaine: and great store of Silver mynes are therein to be seene. The people are tractable, civill, wittie, courteous, without deceit, in vertue and honest conversation exceeding all other nations lately discovered, but so much standing upon their reputation, that their chiefe Idole may be thought honour. The contempt thereof causeth among them much discord and debate, manslaughter and murther: . . . They live chiefely by fish, hearbes and fruites, so healthfully that they die very old . . . No man is ashamed there of his povertie, neither be their gentlemen therefore lesse honoured of the meaner people, neither will the poorest gentleman there match his child with the baser sort for any gaine, so much do they make more account of gentry than of wealth. The greatest delight they have is in armour. . . . They feede moderately, but they drinke largely.

R. Willes (*c.*1565), in Richard Hakluyt, *Principal Navigations . . . of the English Nation,* 1598–1600

The Countrey of Japan is very large and spacious, consisting of severall Ilands and pettie Provinces; it is Mountainous and craggie, full of Rockes and stonie places, so that the third part of this Empire is not inhabited or manured; neither indeed doth it affoord that accomodation for Inhabitants which is needfull, or that fatnesse and conveniencie for the growth of Corne, Fruit, and small grayne as is requisite; which causeth the people to select the choycest and plainest parts and places of the land both to till and dwell in. The Climate is temperate and healthie not much pestred with infectious or obnoxious ayres, but very subject to fierce windes, tempestuous stormes, and terrible Earth-quakes, insomuch that both Ships in the harbour have beene over-set, and driven a shore by the furie of the one, and Houses on the land disjoynted and shaken to pieces by the fearefull trembling of the other.

Arthur Hatch, *A Letter touching Japan,* 1623, in *Purchas his Pilgrimes,* 1625

Japan is essentially a country of paradoxes and anomalies, where all – even familiar things – put on new faces, and are curiously reversed. Except that they do not walk on their heads instead of their feet, there are few things in which they do not seem, by some occult law, to have been impelled in a perfectly opposite direction, and a reversed order. They write from top to bottom, from right to left, in perpendicular instead of horizontal lines; and their books begin where ours end, thus furnishing examples of the curious perfection this rule of contraries has attained. Their locks, though imitated from Europe, are all made to lock by turning the key from left to right. The course of all sublunary things appears reversed. Their day is for the most part our night; and this principle of antagonism crops out in the most unexpected bizarre way in all their moral being, customs and habits. I leave to philosophers the explanation – I only speak to the facts. There old men fly kites while the children look on; the carpenter uses his plane by drawing it *to* him, and their tailors stitch *from* them; they mount their horses from the off-side – the horses stand in the stables with their heads where we place their tails, and the bells to their harness are always on the hind quarters instead of the front; ladies black their teeth instead of keeping them white, and their anti-crinoline tendencies are carried to the point of seriously interfering not only with grace of movement but with all locomotion, so tightly are the lower limbs, from the waist downwards, girt round with their garments; – and, finally, the utter confusion of sexes in the public bath-houses, making that correct, which we in the West deem so shocking and improper, I leave as I find it – a problem to solve.

Sir Rutherford Alcock, *The Capital of the Tycoon*, 1863

I had indeed long given up looking at temples in Japan; for after seeing one or two, it is like looking at successive negroes – nothing but a familiarity of acquaintance, which you do not desire, can enable you to distinguish any difference between them.

Ibid.

A double pleasure rewards the pioneer who is the first to penetrate into the midst of a new people. Besides the rare exhilaration felt in treading soil virgin to alien feet, it acts like mental oxygen to look upon and breathe in a unique civilization like that of Japan. To feel that for ages millions of one's own race have lived and loved, enjoyed and suffered and died, living the fullness of life, yet without the religion, laws, customs, food, dress, and culture which seems to us to be the vitals of our social existence, is like walking through a living Pompeii.

W.E. Griffis, *The Mikado's Empire*, 1876

There is no blacker page in history than the exactions and cruelties practised against Japan by the diplomatic representatives of the natives called Christian – in the sense of having the heaviest artillery. In their financial and warlike operations in Japan, the foreign ministers seem to have acted as if there was no day of judgement.

Ibid.

The actual government of Japan is despotism tempered by assassination.

Anon., quoted *ibid.*

An Imperial throne founded on an exploded religious fiction, a State religion receiving an outward homage from those who ridicule it, scepticism rampant among the educated classes, and an ignorant priesthood lording it over the lower classes; an Empire with a splendid despotism for its apex, and naked coolies for its base, a bald materialism its highest creed and material good its goal, reforming, destroying, constructing, appropriating the fruits of Christian civilisation, but rejecting the tree from which they spring – such are among the contrasts and incongruities everywhere!

Isabella Bird, *Unbeaten Tracks in Japan*, 1880

Japan offers as much novelty perhaps as an excursion to another planet.

Ibid.

This is a child's country. Men, women and children are taken out of the fairy books. The whole show is of the nursery. Nothing is serious; nothing is taken seriously. All is toy; sometimes, as with the women, badly made and repulsive; sometimes laughable, as with the houses, gardens and children; but always taken from what La Farge declares to have been the papboats of his babyhood. I have wandered, so to express it, in all the soup-plates of forty-eight years' experience, during the last week, and have found them as natural as Alice found the Mock Turtle. Life is a dream, and in Japan one dreams of the nursery.

Henry Adams, Letter to John Hay, 9 July 1886

It is so strange to be in a clean land, and stranger to walk among dolls' houses. Japan is a soothing place for a small man.

Rudyard Kipling, *From Sea to Sea*, 1889

Japan is a great people. Her masons play with stone, her carpenters with wood, her smiths with iron, and her artists with life, death, and all the eye can take in. Mercifully she has been denied the last touch of firmness in her character which would enable her to play with the whole round world. We possess that— We, the nation of the glass flower-shade, the pink worsted mat, the red and green china puppy dog, and the poisonous Brussels carpet. It is our compensation.

Ibid.

The land of disappointments.

Old resident in Japanese Service, quoted in Basil Hall Chamberlain, *Things Japanese*, 1890

Old Japan was like an oyster: – to open it was to kill it.

Basil Hall Chamberlain, *ibid.*

At first, the sense of existence here is like that of escaping from an almost unbearable atmospheric pressure into a rarefied, highly oxygenated medium. That feeling continues: in Japan the law of life is not as with us, – that each one strives to expand his own individuality at the expense of his neighbour's. But on the other hand how much one loses. Never a fine inspiration, a deep emotion, a profound joy, or a profound pain, – never a thrill, or, as the French say so much better than we, a *frisson*.

Lafcadio Hearn, Letter to Basil Hall Chamberlain, 1891

Le Japon, voyez-vous, c'est une traduction mal faite. (Japan, you see, is a bad translation.)

Resident Diplomat, quoted by Henry Norman, *The Real Japan*, 1892

Give as little foothold as possible to foreigners.

Herbert Spencer, Letter to Baron Kaneko Kentaro, 1892

I think we have thrown Japan morally backward a thousand years: she is going to adopt our vices, (which are much too large for her).

Lafcadio Hearn, Letter to Basil Hall Chamberlain, 14 January 1893

General Descharmes talked much of Japan, where he was military instructor for some years, and in glowing terms of their success in the war with China. He declares them to have *le diable dans le corps* for fighting, and that it would take a European power all it knew to beat them. 'I would not,' he said, 'undertake to land an army in Japan with less than 60,000 men, all Frenchmen.'

Wilfred Scawen Blunt, Diary, 14 October 1894, *My Diaries*, 1919

The development of the mathematical faculty in the race – unchecked and unmollified by our class of aesthetics and idealisms – ought to prove a serious danger to western civilization at last. At least it seems to me that here is a danger. . . . Imagine a civilization on western lines with cold calculation universally substituted for ethical principle! The suggestion is very terrible and very ugly. One would prefer even the society of the later Roman Empire.

Lafcadio Hearn, Letter to Basil Hall Chamberlain, February 1895

Etiquette is the Kaiser of Japan.

Douglas Sladen, *Queer Things About Japan*, 1903

One used to speak of Japan as a kind of dolls house . . . It is a very tragic dolls house – much more tragic than Ibsen's.

Ibid.

I saw the native home in Japan as a supreme study in elimination—not only of dirt, but the elimination of the insignificant. So the Japanese house naturally fascinated me and I would spend hours taking it all to pieces, and putting it together again. I saw nothing meaningless in the Japanese home and could find very little added in the way of ornament because all *ornament* as we call it, they get out of the way. The necessary things are done by bringing out and polishing the beauty of the simple materials they used in making the building. Again, you see, a kind of cleanliness.

At last I had found one country on earth where simplicity, as natural, is supreme. The floors of these Japanese homes are all made to live on – to sleep on, to kneel and eat from, to kneel upon soft silken mats and meditate upon. On which to play the flute, or to make love. . . . Strangely enough, I found this ancient Japanese dwelling to be a perfect example of the modern standardising I had myself been working out.

Frank Lloyd Wright, *An Autobiography*, 1979 – of *c.* 1914

Japan, a country combining a feverish proficiency in many of the habits of advanced civilisation with uncompromising relics of feudal crystallisation.

George Curzon, Marquess of Kedleston, *Tales of Travel*, 1923

As to Japan, the understanding of nature of its inhabitants is so inordinately great, that they have subjugated their surroundings aesthetically; in the same way as a patch of colour can determine and change the meaning of a picture, the Japanese, by deliberately inserting his particular existence into surrounding nature has transferred the keynote of the latter completely into himself.

Count Herman Keyserling, *America Set Free*, 1930

Sometimes it looks as if Japan were created as a satire on and for Western civilization.

Lincoln Steffens, *Autobiography*, 1931

Japan is the product of art but not its material. From every feature – you might say from every line – human ingenuity has drained the essence, till what one sees is not a stretch of pebbly road, among rice fields in which the peasants are at work, so much as a complete colour print by Hiroshige . . . .All landscapes acquire the character of their inhabitants, and the Japanese is no exception to this rule, indeed a striking proof of its validity.

Peter Quennell, *A Superficial Journey from Tokyo to Peking*, 1932

Japan, land of high romance, whose emergence from feudalism and rise to the status of a great Power is still the wonder of the modern world . . . the Ultima Thule of Asia.

'Government Railways', *An Official Guide to Japan*, 1933

Japan does not disappoint the stranger; she corrects his fancies, perhaps a little grimly, and then begins to enrich him with her truths.

Edmund Blunden, 'Japanese Moments', in *The Mind's Eye, Essays*, 1934

Japan has never been sweet sixteen.

John Gunther, *Inside Asia*, 1939

A case might be made out for Japan as a Pandora's box.

Ibid.

It's so far away . . . and then you have to eat all that raw fish, drink tepid rice wine and live in cardboard houses. . . . And someone told me the toilet seats are much too small for my bottom. . . . Besides, I can't distinguish one Japanese from another . . . .

W.H. Auden, quoted by Nicholas Nabokov, in Charles Osborne, *W.H.Auden*, 1980 – of 1952

I feel that there is a possibility that here in Japan, where the old order of the East overlaps with that of the West as nowhere else, and the hand and the machine work side by side, a new synthesis, which is needed by us all, may take place for the first time. It will require a long gestation, and it will be the work of many men, but a good start has been made.

Bernard Leach, Diary, 1953, *A Potter in Japan*, 1960

I feel that we in the West need to know, to respect, and even to love what I am having such a unique opportunity of experiencing each day. Time simply flows through the senses from an inner life which all the turmoil of outward Westernization has not yet destroyed. Voiceless beauty; the almost empty room, the exquisite adjustment of things, the colour of the green tea in its bowl, the lie of the chop-sticks on their rest, the writing on the wall of the recess, the white light through paper 'shoji' and the shadows of bamboo leaf upon it. I could go on indefinitely but it has to be lived in to be really felt.

Bernard Leach, Diary, 26 March 1953, *A Potter in Japan*, 1960

For my part, I greatly hope that Japan will not work out her foreign policy in terms of her actual and potential military power. Because of Japan's social and political structure, I doubt whether she can become militarized without becoming militaristic . . . .It seems to me that it is by their economic skills, not their military prowess, that the Japanese people can best assure security and welfare both for themselves and for their neighbours in the Pacific.

Professor W.MacMahon, in *English Mainichi*, quoted D.J. Enright, *The World of Dew*, 1955

In the past assassination has been Japan's substitute for public opinion.

D.J. Enright, *The World of Dew*, 1955

Japan is the testing-ground of humanism. An excess of man and an insufficiency of man's means: if your faith in man survives this test, it is impregnable.

Ibid.

'In Japan, burglary is a profession,' Mr Shima said, 'It is often hereditary. Some men take great pride in being good burglars.' I had a feeling he was trying to tell us something . . . .

'I do not think this guy is a depraved bad character,' he said. 'He is only a burglar. But it is very unfortunate he did not manage to steal anything, the first time. It means he will persist in trying to crack your joint, because he has lost face.'

When I told this to Mr Shima, he gloomily nodded agreement. 'Now he has failed twice,' he pointed out. 'He will become still more desperate. He may try to kill you. On the other hand,' Mr. Shima added, more hopefully, 'he may decide to kill himself, out of chagrin.'

I said I desired neither to be killed by a persistent burglar, nor to have his suicide on my conscience. 'How would it be,' I suggested, 'if I left something out for him to steal? Would he take it and not return?'

Mr Shima shook his head. 'He would guess you wanted him to do that,' he said. 'So it would not get him back his face.'

There were times when Mr Shima seemed to have a very negative approach to things.

Alexander Campbell, *The Heart of Japan*, 1962

Japan enchants me. Japan has the instant effect upon me of making it imperative to write of it, to convey something of that strange nervous atmosphere to those who think of the country in terms of Madame Butterfly on the one side or Pearl Harbor on the other . . . as though it had not in fact been done a hundred times before, as though oneself was the first to be beguiled by the subtle flavour of the place. Just a little more study, I felt, just the experience of one more month and it could be done. Of course it never will.

James Cameron, *Point of Departure*, 1967

The light in Japan is always slightly peculiar, different from the light in any other country I know. It has the strange, oblique intensity that often lends subjects a tranced look and gives landscapes momentarily the appearance of being immobilized under glass. I like to think that this quality of the light that both animates and hypnotizes Japanese scenes is due to Japan's curious slanting position on the globe: certainly the fact that in Japan the land is never far from seas, lakes and rivers, must contribute to these impressions of luminous clarity. Indeed it might be said that Japan is more water than air, more sea than land.

James Kirkup, *Japan Behind the Fan*, 1970

I find things more interesting than people, and Japan is above all else a land of things.

Ibid.

Once upon a time, everyone thought that Japan consisted only of Mount Fuji, a peak inhabited entirely by geisha.

James Kirkup, *Heaven Hell and Hara-Kiri*, 1974

According to a popular Japanese saying, the four most fearsome things in human life are: earthquake, thunder, fire and father.

Ibid.

From the air Siberia looks like cold nothing. The Sea of Japan looks like wet nothing. But Japan itself, as soon as you catch your first glimpse of it, immediately looks like something. Even geographically it's a busy place.

Immediately you are impressed by the wealth of detail – an impression that will never leave you for as long as you are there. Only a tenth of the land is useful for anything. The remaining nine-tenths, when you look down on it, is a kind of corduroy velvet: country so precipitously convoluted that the rivers flowing through it look like the silver trails of inebriated slugs. The useful tenth is inhabited, cultivated, and industrialised with an intensity that boggles the Occidental mind. I had never seen anything like it in my life.

Seen from high up, the basic agricultural pattern of the western countries is of accumulated squares. America looks like a patchwork quilt; France is like another quilt, but with smaller patches; Britain like yet another quilt with smaller patches still. The basic agricultural pattern of Japan is of proliferating brain cells. Everywhere a rice paddy can possibly be put, a rice paddy has been put, even if it is only the size of a table napkin.

Merging with this nervous tissue, like bionic grafts, are the areas of urban habitation, and industry. One hundred and ten million people live and work down there, most of them in conurbations which to the stratospheric eye look like infinitely elaborate printed circuits. You can tell straight away before you even touch the ground, that in Japan there is nowhere anybody can hide. They're all in it together.

Clive James, 'Postcard from Japan', *Observer*, 4 June 1978

Japanese

The Inhabitantes shewe a notable witte, and an incredible pacience, in sufferinge, labour and sorowes. They take great and diligent care lest, either in worde or deede, they shoulde shewe either feare, or dulnesse of mynde, and lest they should make any man (whosoever he be) partaker of their trowbles and wantes. They covet exceedingly honour and prayse; and povertie with them bringeth no damage to the nobilitie of bloude. They suffer not the least iniurie in the worlde to passe unrevenged. For gravitie and curtesie they gyve not place to the Spainardes. They are generally affable and full of compliments. They are very punctuall in the entertayning of strangers, of whom they will curiously inquyre even tryfles of forreyne people, as of their maners, and such like thinges. They will as soone lose a limbe as omit one ceremonie in welcoming a friend.

Anon., *The First Booke of Relations of Modern States*, sixteenth century

The people of this Iland of Iapon are good of nature, curteous above measure and valiant in warre: their iustice is severely executed without any partialitie upon transgressors of the law. They are governed in great civilitie. I meane, not a land better governed in the world by civill policie. The people be verie superstitious in their religion, and are of divers opinions.

Will Adams, *To my Unknowne Friends and Countri-men*, 22 October 1611

The people of Japan affect brevitie.

John Saris, *Journal*, 1613, in *Purchas his Pilgrimes*, 1625

The eighth [of July] three *Japonians* were executed, *viz.* two men and one woman: . . . which done, every man that listed (as very many did) came to trie the sharpenesse of their cattans upon the corps, so that before they left off, they had hewne them all three into peeces as small as a mans hand, and yet notwithstanding did not then give over, but placing the peeces one upon another, would try how many of them they could strike through at a blow; and the peeces are left to the fowles to devoure.

Captain Saris, *His Arrival at Firando and his Intertaynment*, 1613

They blow their Noses with a certaine sofft and tough kind off paper which they carry aboutt them in small peeces, which having used, they Fling away as a Fillthy thing, keeping handkercheifes off lynnen to wype their Faces and hands.

Peter Mundy, *Travels in Europe and Asia*, 1637

The People of this Nation, especially the Women, die

with strange constancy and assurance, without any the least emotion of sorrow or weakness.

Francis Caron, trans. Roger Manley, *A True Description of Japan*, 1663

The Japanese are in general intelligent and provident, free and unconstrained, obedient and courteous, curious and inquisitive, industrious and ingenious, frugal and sober, cleanly, good-natured and friendly, upright and just, trusty and honest, mistrustful, superstitious, proud, and haughty, unforgiving, brave and invincible.

Charles Peter Thunberg, *Travels in Europe Africa and Asia . . . Between 1770 and 1779*, 1795

The Japanese may be regarded partially as the Englishmen of the Oriental world; but hardly for any other qualities than their firmness – which degenerates into obstinacy – their courage, and their contempt of death. In all other respects they show few marks of the grand English style of mind.

Thomas de Quincey, *Translation of Kant on National Character in Relation to the Sense of the Sublime and Beautiful*, 1824

It I were asked to give in a few words the conclusion to which I have been led as to the kind and degree of civilisation attained by the Japanese, without taking account of the various qualifications and reservations already touched upon, I should say that theirs was a material civilisation of a high order, in which all the industrial arts were brought to as great perfection as could well be attainable without the aid of steam-power and machinery – an almost unlimited command of cheap labour and material supplying apparently many counterbalancing advantages. Their intellectual and moral pretensions, on the other hand, compared with what has been achieved in the more civilised nations of the West during the last three centuries, must be placed very low; while their capacity for a higher and better civilisation than they have yet attained, should be ranked, I conceive, far before that of any other Eastern nation, not excepting the Chinese.

Sir Rutherford Alcock, *The Capital of the Tycoon*, 1863

In moral character the *average* Japanese is frank, honest, faithful, kind, gentle, courteous, confiding, affectionate, filial, loyal. Love of truth for its own sake, chastity, temperance are not characteristic virtues.

W.E. Griffis, *The Mikado's Empire*, 1876

The Japanese are the most irreligious people that I have ever seen – their pilgrimages are picnics, and their religious festivals fairs.

Isabella Bird, *Unbeaten Tracks in Japan*, 1880

It is singular that the Japanese, who rarely commit a solecism in taste in their national costume, architecture, or decorative art, seem to be perfectly destitute of perception when they borrow ours.

Ibid.

If you think we are worked by strings,
Like a Japanese marionette,
You don't understand those things:
It is simply Court etiquette.

Sir William Schwenk Gilbert, *The Mikado*, 1885

From before the time when they began to leave records of their actions the Japanese have been a nation of importers, not of merchandize, but of ideas.

Percival Lowell, *The Soul of the Far East*, 1888

They grew old young, and have remained much the same age ever since. What they were centuries ago, that at bottom they are today. Take away the European influence of the last twenty years, and each man might be his own great-grandfather.

Ibid.

The sense of self grows more intense as we follow the wake of the setting sun, and fades steadily as we advance into the dawn. America, Europe, the Levant, India, Japan, each is less personal than the one before. We stand at one end of the scale, the far Orientals at the other. If with us the I seems to be of the very essence of the soul, then the soul of the Far East may be said to be Impersonality.

Ibid.

The Japanese should have no concern with business.

Rudyard Kipling, *From Sea to Sea*, 1889

The Japanese have never had a philosophy of their own. Formerly they bowed down before the shrine of Confucius. They now bow down before the shrine of Herbert Spencer.

Basil Hall Chamberlain, *Things Japanese*, 1890

The Japanese have done with their past. They want to be somebody else and something else than what they have been and still partly are.

Ibid.

Surely, for happiness, gentleness, and sobriety, for soft-voiced and always smiling chatter, for the blessed faculty of inhaling healthful enjoyment from the simplest things . . . no other country can even profess to show the match of a festival crowd in Japan . . . Police in such a throng, it seems to us, can have no more to do than the lilies of the valley.

Major General Palmer, R.E., in *Japan Daily Mail*, quoted *ibid.*

The different ways of thinking and the difficulties of the language render it impossible for an educated Japanese to find pleasure in the society of a European. Here is an astounding fact. The Japanese child is as close to you as a European child – perhaps closer and sweeter because infinitely more natural and naturally refined. Cultivate his mind, and the more it is cultivated the farther you push him from you. Why? – Because here the race antagonism shows itself. As the Oriental thinks naturally to the left, where we think to the right, the more you cultivate him the more he will think in an opposite direction from you.

Lafcadio Hearn, Letter to Ellwood Hendrick, November 1892

Imagine people having no sentiment of light – of blue – of infinity! And they cannot feel possibly the beauty of their own day as you or I do. I think of the comparison of Fuji to a white half-open inverted fan, hanging in the sky: of course it is pretty; it is even startlingly real; – but what sentiment is there in it? What feeling do mountains give this people?

Lafcadio Hearn, Letter to Basil Hall Chamberlain, 27 January 1894

A race primitive as the Etruscan before Rome was, or more so, adopting the practices of a larger civilization under compulsion.

Lafcadio Hearn, Letter to Basil Hall Chamberlain, March 1895

Under all the amazing self-control and patience, there exists an adamantine something very dangerous to reach.

Lafcadio Hearn, *Out of the East*, 1895

There are plenty of Japanese houses which, when secured for the night would hardly stand a drunken man leaning against them. An Englishman's house may be his castle: a Japanese's house is his bedroom, and his bedroom is his passage.

Douglas Sladen, *Queer Things About Japan*, 1903

The Japanese is cremated for the same reason that he dies a Buddhist monk: he is in such a mortal fright of immortality that he wants to make extinction as sure as possible.

Ibid.

The Japanese, whose *grande passion* is bathing, use water at higher temperatures – 110 – 120 Fahrenheit – than physicians in Europe consider healthful. No one however will be injured by taking baths of between 100 and 104 Fahrenheit, unless he have a weak heart, or be liable to congestion. Owing to some unexplained peculiarity of the climate, hot baths are found by almost all Europeans in Japan to suit them better than cold. It is advisable to pour hot water over the head from time to time, and strong persons may advantageously end up with a cold douche. . . . The Japanese have the habit, to us disagreeable, of getting into the same bath one after another, or even at the same time: but it is a breach of etiquette to discolour the water by the use of soap. They soap themselves outside.

Basil Hall Chamberlain and W.B.Mason, *Handbook for Travellers in Japan*, 1913

The Japanese are superficially polite and have the art of leg-pulling carried to a degree.

Alfred Viscount Northcliffe, *My Journey Round the World*, 1923

Brilliance – the cynical brilliance of the West . . . – is not a common commodity in Japan. On arriving, I had pictured the Japanese as a sharp-witted, uncannily acute race, endowed by nature with every superficial gift. At a first acquaintance, the very opposite proved true; hesitating, tongue-tied, and always nervous, they suggested a people of adolescents, alternatively assertive and depreciatory, prone to sudden collapses and odd recoveries, to spurts of rudeness and long intervals of embarrassment, over-eager, over-calculating, over-polite. . . . I noticed the extreme slowness of their mental processes and the agony it obviously cost them to come to a decision. Time – a Japanese must have time; and the structure of the Japanese spoken language seems to favour the habit of thinking slowly, for instance a conventional ejaculation, roughly equivalent to 'Look here now!' which used to preface instructions and commands, is like knocking on a door before you enter so that the inmate may have the opportunity to wake up.

Emphatically they are industrious rather than clever; whereas the Chinese, in the ordinary business of life, are cynical, quick-witted, but apathetic. The Japanese possess the virtue of perseverance; yet their perseverance has its curious limitations. For so energetic a race they are strangely feminine, and when they collapse it is with awful unexpectedness.

Peter Quennell, *A Superficial Journey through Tokyo and Peking*, 1932

The touch of ceremony – . . . you cannot elude it – in Japan where vice itself is ceremonial.

Ibid.

The loyalty of a Japanese is no news. It is only from those who are offended with Japanese pride that the notion of untrustworthy Nippon is circulated. . . . The Japanese are not Orientals.

Edmund Blunden, 'Japanese Moments', *The Mind's Eye, Essays*, 1934

How courteous is the Japanese;
He always says, 'Excuse it, please'
He climbs into his neighbor's garden,
And smiles, and says, 'I beg your pardon';
He bows and grins a friendly grin,

And calls his hungry family in;
He grins, and bows a friendly bow;
'So sorry, this my garden now.'

Ogden Nash, 'Fellow Creatures, II: The Japanese', in *I'm a Stranger Here Myself*, 1938

. . . no one in the world is so unintelligent as a single Japanese, and no one so bright as two.

John Gunther, *Inside Asia*, 1939

and Chinese

The Japanese are men in armour, carrying a machine-gun; the Chinese men in undershirts, wondering when it is going to rain. If you ask a Japanese to choose between spending the rest of his life on an island with either a Chinese or an Englishman, he will pick the Chinese, who would presumably become his slave; the Chinese confronted with a similar choice, would almost certainly pick the Englishman, who he assumes might be educated to become his equal. The Japanese are fanatics. The Chinese are almost indescribably reasonable.

John Gunther, *Inside Asia*, 1939

The Japanese, whose game is what I may call to make hell while the sun shines . . . .

Sir Winston Churchill, Speech in the House of Commons, 27 January 1942

Ambiguity interests the Japanese a good deal more than does logic.

D.J. Enright, *The World of Dew*, 1955

For the sake of its very existence every race has built up a more or less complicated system of behaviour; however fanciful that system, at the heart of it is a piece of sound common sense—the recognition that we are all human. The Japanese may be unique in that their unusually complicated system of behaviour is based not on a recognition of humanity but on a proud and yet pathetic denial of it. It may strike the outsider that they adopted precisely those ideals which by nature they were least fitted to fulfil.

Ibid.

Like Napoleon and other militarists in the past, the Japanese in the Second World War made history not for themselves, but for unintended beneficiaries.

Arnold Toynbee, *East to West*, 1958

Considering what a proud, undefeated people the Japanese were, and that practically all their great cities and towns except Kyoto, were burnt out by incendiary bombing, it is amazing the way they have picked themselves up, shaken off the dust, raised their eyebrows saying 'Shi kata ga nai' (It cannot be helped), and gone on with their non-military reconstruction. That feeling is genuine and widespread and I have heard the remark several times, 'It would have been worse if we had won'.

Bernard Leach, *A Potter in Japan, 1953–4*, 1960

'We've never had a strike, you know,' he added. 'Not even immediately after the war, when the unions were making the most of their new freedom, and there were strikes everywhere . . . .' He laughed. 'The President of the company says he sometimes wishes we *did* have a strike.'

'Why?' I asked.

'So that both the management and the workers could learn through personal experience just how unprofitable strikes always are!'

Alexander Campbell, *The Heart of Japan*, 1962

The Japanese assimilate rather than imitate.

James Kirkup, *These Horned Islands*, 1962

The Japanese have almost as big a reputation for cruelty as have young children.

Dennis Bloodworth, *Chinese Looking Glass*, 1967

The Japanese when they are alone, are like the sea when no one is looking at it. It is more than ever sea, sea pure and simple, as the Japanese when foreigners are not present. I am sad because I shall never know the Japanese like that – in their pure state like the ocean when no one is looking at it.

James Kirkup, *Japan Behind the Fan*, 1970

Sexual titillations and attachments are an accepted part of life on the packed Japanese underground and overhead trains. This is now so common that no one would dream of objecting to sexual advances from a stranger; if the attentions are unwelcome one simply turns away. This is one of the reasons why the rush hour in big cities gets progressively worse: people are enjoying themselves too much.

James Kirkup, *Heaven, Hell and Hara-Kiri*, 1974

As in sex, the Japanese do not care for extended encounters: 'in and out' is their motto in love and war – another example of national insecurity.

Ibid.

The Japanese are a great people. They cannot and should not be satisfied with a world role which limits them to making better transistor radios and sewing machines, and teaching other Asians how to grow rice.

Lee Kwan Yew, Remark to Richard Nixon, 1965, quoted in Richard Nixon, *The Real War*, 1980

There must be something in the Japanese character that saves them from the despair Americans feel in similar throes of consuming. The American, gorging himself on merchandise, develops a sense of guilty self-consciousness; if the Japanese have these doubts they do not show them. Perhaps hesitation is not part of the national character, or perhaps the ones who hesitate are trampled by the crowd of shoppers – that natural selection that capitalist society practices against the reflective. The strong impression I had was of a people who acted together because of a preconceived plan: a people programmed. You see them queuing automatically in the subway, naturally forming lines at ticket counters and machines, and it is difficult to avoid the conclusion that the people all have printed circuits. But my assessment changed with time . . .

Paul Theroux, *The Great Railway Bazaar*, 1975

The Ainu

The 'hairy Ainos', as these savages have been called, are stupid, gentle, good-natured, and submissive. They are a wholly distinct race from the Japanese. In complexion they resemble the people of Spain and Southern Italy, and the expression of the face and the manner showing courtesy are European rather than Asiatic. If not taller, they are of a much broader and heavier make than the Japanese; the hair is jet black, very soft, and on the scalp forms thick, pendant masses, occasionally wavy, but never showing any tendency to curl. The beard, moustache, and eyebrows are very thick and full, and there is frequently a heavy growth of stiff hair on the chest and limbs. The neck is short, the brow high, broad, and massive, the nose broad and inclined to flatness, the mouth wide but well formed, the line of the eyes and eyebrows perfectly straight, and the frontal sinuses well marked. Their language is a very simple one. They have no written characters, no literature, no history, very few traditions, and have left no impression on the land from which they have been driven.

Isabella Bird, *Unbeaten Tracks in Japan*, 1880

My friend Frank Iwama said one of the most embarrassing moments in his life occurred when an Ainu woman on Hokkaido went up to him, and asked him indignantly: 'What is it that is peculiar about us? Why do Japanese people look at us as if we were freaks?' She had tattooed round her lips and chin an enormous blue mustache, and a blue beard.

Alexander Campbell, *The Heart of Japan*, 1962

Women

Women never hang themselves, but, as may be expected, suicide is more common among women than among men . . . .In these cases they usually go out at night, and after filling their capacious hanging sleeves with stones, jump into a river or well.

Isabella Bird, *Unbeaten Tracks in Japan*, 1880

But how sweet the Japanese woman is! – all the possibilities of the race for goodness seem to be concentrated in her.

Lafcadio Hearn, Letter to Basil Hall Chamberlain, 1891

I do not generally admire Japanese women; they have no figures, to speak of, and look as if a bee had stung them in the eye.

Crosbie Garstin, *The Dragon and the Lotus*, 1928

Language

It has always seemed a grave reflection on the Japanese character, that their language, with the exception of the word 'fool' – and 'countryfied fool' is extremely strong – should contain no opportunities for invective.

Peter Quennell, *A Superficial Journey through Tokyo and Peking*, 1932

Foreign literature seems refreshing after their own; and this contrast, considerably to my surprise, was once voiced by a student in his essay, a young man whose behaviour was not ingratiating and usually short and sullen to the point of rudeness: 'I think that the English language,' ran his thesis, 'is the expression of the English people as well as the Japanese language is that of the Japanese. The English people are creative like a fountain jumping up toward Heaven eternally. Therefore the English language is always fresh and pure. The Japanese people are rather mechanical like a rat coming out of a hole. Therefore the Japanese language is hesitating.'

Ibid.

The Japanese language is such that by the time you know it sufficiently well for your knowledge to make any vital difference, it is probable that you will be too enervated – if indeed you are nothing worse than enervated – to write about the Japanese people. You may not even notice them any more.

D.J. Enright, *The World of Dew*, 1955

Food and Drink

It is the man who drinks the first cup of saké, then the second cup of saké drinks the first; then it is the saké that drinks the man.

Old proverb

Pork and tough fowls for meat, and rice for vegetables, eggs for milk (butter and milk being both unknown luxuries here), with an occasional pigeon for *entremet*, may support life even under the barbarous handling of a Japanese or Chinese cook – twin brothers in capacity and instinct; but I am satisfied there must be a limit somewhere in sanitary conditions. The total deprivation of beef and mutton must in time be a serious detriment to the English constitution. . . . Have my readers ever realised what it is for months or years never to taste *beef* or *mutton*?

Sir Rutherford Alcock, *The Capital of the Tycoon*, 1863

Here, remember, the people *really* eat lotuses: they form a common article of diet.

Lafcadio Hearn, Letter to Page M.Baker, August 1891

If ever I want to be reminded of Japan I shall chew a mouthful of burnt straw and immediately I shall be back in the Tokyo Express drinking saki.

Crosbie Garstin, *The Dragon and the Lotus*, 1928

There is a saying that the Chinese eat with their stomachs and the Japanese with their eyes.

Bernard Leach, *A Potter in Japan, 1953–4*, 1960

Another Hokkaido brand . . . advertised itself for the international market as 'Finest quality whisky made from genuine imported Scottish grapes.'

Charles A.Fisher, *Three Times a Guest*, 1979

Aso-Umi Lagoon *(near Monju, the Ama-no-hashidate, 'Floating Bridge of Heaven')*

Ama-no-hashidate (Floating Bridge of Heaven). View from Kasamatsu Park: connoisseurs in the art of viewing scenery like to look at the scene from between the legs, which makes Ama-no-hashidate appear as if it were suspended in mid-air, it is claimed.

Official Guide Book

Atami

The spas of Atami are not gay as a place of residence.

Sir Rutherford Alcock, *The Capital of the Tycoon*, 1863

Atami is a pleasure city that clings to a steep hillside overlooking the curve of a blue bay. The express trains that dash between Tokyo and Osaka stop at Atami, then vanish into a hole in the mountainside, with their loads of *zaibatsu* millionaires and Japanese politicians. Atami is full of 'hotels for couples', and its narrow streets swarm with ugly, bald little men and pretty girls. The shops all sell as a souvenir a fat-bellied beaver made of wood, with enormous testicles. The beaver is the Japanese symbol of virility.

Alexander Campbell, *The Heart of Japan*, 1962

Fujiyama

As time goes on, he becomes an infatuating personality.

Isabella Bird, *Unbeaten Tracks in Japan*, 1880

Fujiyama . . . gathers in its skirts from the surrounding plain and rises, plumed with white, across the sky – faultless, utterly symmetrical. 'Like a fan', said the student who showed me his poem; like some majestic and inimitable commonplace, conceived for the delight of mediocrity, since it is banal and supremely beautiful all at once. How unfortunate have been the Japanese in their great mountain!

Peter Quennell, *A Superficial Journey through Tokyo and Peking*, 1932

I once started to climb it, in company with about a million Japanese, but it was so unpleasantly like scrambling up a pile of coke that I gave up after five minutes.

James Kirkup, *These Horned Islands*, 1962

The sacred rubbish dump.

James Kirkup, *Japan Behind the Fan*, 1970

Mt Fuji is a valuable classic property, which Japan is proud of, and matches well with Tomei highway.

Inscription on back of Japanese picture postcard, quoted Charles A. Fisher, *Three Times a Guest*, 1979

Fukui

I shall never forget my emotions, in that sudden first glimpse of the city embowered in trees, looming across the plain, amidst the air laden with snow-flakes, and seen in the light reflected from storm-clouds. There were no spires, golden-vaned; no massive pediments, façades, or grand buildings such as strike the eye on beholding a city in the western world. I had formed some conception of Fukui while in America: something vaguely grand, mistily imposing—I knew not what. I now saw simply a dark, vast array of low-roofed houses, colossal temples, gables, castle-towers, tufts of bamboo, and groves of trees. This was Fukui.

W.E. Griffis, *The Mikado's Empire*, 1876

Hakodate

It is the realisation of all a sailor's dreams of a harbour.

Sir Rutherford Alcock, *The Capital of the Tycoon*, 1863

A single look at Hakodate itself makes one feel that it is Japan all over. The streets are very wide and clean, but the houses are mean and low. The city looks as if it had just recovered from a conflagration. The houses are nothing but tinder. The grand tile roofs of some other cities are not to be seen. There is not an element of permanence in the wide and windy streets. It is an increasing and busy place; it lies for two miles along the shore, and has climbed the hill till it can go no higher; but still houses and people look poor. It has a skeleton aspect too, which is partially due to the number of permanent 'clothes-horses' on the roofs. Stones, however, are its prominent feature. Looking down upon it from above, you see miles of grey boulders, and realise that every roof in the windy capital is 'hodden doun' by a weight of paving stones. Nor is this all. Some of the flatter roofs are pebbled all over like a courtyard, and others, such as the roof of this house for instance, are covered with sod and crops of grass, the two latter arrangements being precautions against risks from sparks during fires. These paving stones are certainly the cheapest possible mode of keeping the roofs on the houses in such a windy region, but they look odd.

Isabella Bird, *Unbeaten Tracks in Japan*, 1880

Hiroshima

At the station exit, my bundle in hand,
Early the winter afternoon's wet snow
Falls thinly round me, out of a crudded sun.
I had forgotten to remember where I was.
Looking about, I see it might be anywhere –
A station, a town like any other in Japan,
Ramshackle, muddy, noisy, drab; a cheerfully
Shallow permanence: peeling concrete, little, 'Atomic
Lotion, for hair fall-out,' a flimsy department-store;
Racks and towers of neon, flashy over tiled and tilted
  waves
Of little roofs, shacks cascading lemons and
  persimmons,
Oranges, dark red apples; shanties awash with
  rainbows
Of squid and octopus, shellfish, slabs of tuna, oysters,
  ice;
Ablaze with fans of soiled nude-picture books
Thumbed abstractedly by schoolboys, with
  second-hand looks.
The river remains unchanged, sad, refusing
  rehabilitation.
In this long, wide, empty official boulevard
The new trees are still small, the office blocks
Basely functional, the bridge a slick abstraction.
But the river remains unchanged, sad, refusing
  rehabilitation.

In the city centre, far from the station's lively squalor,
A kind of life goes on, in cinemas and hi-fi coffee bars,
In the shuffling racket of pin-table palaces and
  parlours,
The souvenir-shops piled with junk, kimonoed
  kewpie-dolls,
Models of the bombed Industry Promotion Hall,
  memorial ruin
Tricked out with glitter-frost and artificial pearls.
Here atomic peace is geared to meet the tourist trade.
Let it remain like this, for all the world to see,
Without nobility or loveliness, and dogged with shame
That is beyond all hope of indignation. Anger, too, is
  dead.
And why should memorials of what was far
From pleasant have the grace that helps us forget?

In the dying afternoon, I wander dying round the Park
  of Peace.
It is right, this squat, dead place, with its left-over air
Of an abandoned International Trade and Tourist
  Fair . . .

James Kirkup, 'No More Hiroshimas', *These Horned Islands*, 1962

The ferocious paradoxes of the place were symptoms partly of the baffling character of the Japanese, partly of the traumatic reaction of a community well aware that it had been made the guinea-pig of the most cold-blooded and terrible physical experiment in history (since the Japanese were as aware as everyone else that they were atom-bombed *after* their attempts to sue for peace). We had found the awesome sight of a Hiroshima that was now even bigger than it had been before the bomb, far richer and more prosperous, the chilling fact that the bomb had become Hiroshima's incontestable asset, exploited with a terrifying kind of business-like hysteria by a people whose minds, among the survivors, had been scarred into a compulsion to disguise, distort, forget.

James Cameron, *Point of Departure*, 1967

Hokkaido

The northernmost island of an archipelago seems always to have some special value. Sumatra is Indonesia's island of hope; Hokkaido is Japan's island of expectation. In Hokkaido today one can already see the Japan of the future.

Arnold Toynbee, *East to West*, 1958

'In Tokyo,' said the deputy governor scornfully, 'they think there is nothing up here but bears, codfish, and snow.'

Alexander Campbell, *The Heart of Japan*, 1962

The Inland Sea

Appropriately enough the entrance to Japan is through the narrow and fiord-like Inland Sea, scattered thick with a thousand islands of distinctive beauty that proclaim themselves at first sight as Japanese. They suggest the islands of an exquisite wash drawing, steep volcanic eminences fledged with pines, dark crests two-dimensional and clear-cut – at a distance they seem to float above the haze that hangs as smooth as milk across the water. They are more beautiful than any Grecian archipelago, of every shape, every size and degree of fantasy. And nature slowly unwinds her improvization, like an artist with two hands unwinding a scroll.

Peter Quennell, *A Superficial Journey through Tokyo and Peking*, 1932

Ise

If the most celebrated cathedrals of Europe were situated in the Black Forest, and were all simple wooden structures resembling very large but plain log cabins, Christianity would approximate to Shinto in its aesthetic appeal.

Alexander Campbell, *The Heart of Japan*, 1962

Kaisuiyokui

Kaisuiyoki is abominable. Why do the Japanese deliberately pick out bathing resorts where the bottom is all jagged rocks and stones? – as at Oisi? And why, oh why, do they prefer such damnable places to smooth velvety beaches of sand? Is it only because of their rare artistic perception of the beauty of stones?

Lafcadio Hearn, Letter to Basil Hall Chamberlain, 27 August 1891

Kobé

between Kobé and Osaka, seen from the train

But the countryside was the thing that made us open our eyes. Imagine a land of rich black soil, very heavily manured, and worked by the spade and hoe almost exclusively, and if you split your field (of vision) into half-acre plots, you will get a notion of the raw material the cultivator works on. But all I can write will give you no notion of the wantonness of neatness visible in the fields; of the elaborate system of irrigation, and the mathematical precision of the planting. There was no mixing of crops, no waste of boundary in footpath, and no difference of value in the land. The water stood everywhere within ten feet of the surface, as the well-sweeps attested. On the slopes of the foot-hills each drop between the levels was neatly riveted with unmortared stones, and the edges of the water-cuts were faced in like manner. The young rice was transplanted very much as draughts are laid on the board; the tea might have been cropped garden box; and between the lines of the mustard the water lay in the drills as in a wooden trough, while the purple of the beans ran up to the mustard and stopped as though cut with a rule.

On the seaboard we saw an almost continuous line of towns variegated with factory chimneys; inland, the crazy-quilt of green, dark-green and gold. Even in the rain the view was lovely, and exactly as Japanese pictures had led me to hope for. Only one drawback occurred to the Professor and myself at the same time. Crops don't grow to the full limit of the seed on heavily worked ground dotted with villages except at a price.

'Cholera?' said I, watching a stretch of well-sweeps.

'Cholera,' said the Professor. 'Must be, y'know. It's all sewage irrigation.'

Rudyard Kipling, *From Sea to Sea*, 1889

This comes from Kobé . . . the European portion of which is a raw American town. We walked down the wide, naked streets, between houses of sham stucco, with Corinthian pillars of wood, wooden verandahs and piazzas, all stony grey beneath stone grey skies, and keeping guard over raw green saplings miscalled shade trees. In truth Kobé is hideously American in externals. Even I, who have only seen pictures of America, recognised at once that it was Portland, Maine.

Ibid.

Kyoto

In Kioto the streets are almost as clean as the floors.

Lilian Leland, *Travelling Alone, A Woman's Journey Round the World*, 1890

Kyoto is as good as Glasgow for excursions.

Douglas Sladen, *Queer Things About Japan*, 1903

Kyoto, – or for that matter, any Japanese city – is a barfly's Valhalla.

Truman Capote, 'The Duke in His Domain,' 1956 in *The Dogs Bark*, 1974

Temple of all earth's towns; of all the bell
Far-heard clear-calm whatever thunders roll!

Edmund Blunden, 'Voice of Kyoto', *A Hong-Kong House*, 1962

Nagasaki

The harbor at Nangasaque is the best in all Japon, wheare there may 1,000 seale of shipps ride land lockt, and the greatest shipps or caricke sin the world may goe in and out at pleasure and ride before the towne within a cables length of the shore in 7 or 8 fathom water at least, yt being a greate cittie and many rich marchantes dwelling in it, . . . yt being one of the fairest and lardgest harbours that eaver I saw, wherinto a man may enter in and goe out with shipping at all tymes, the wind serving, without helpe of boate or penisse.

Richard Cocks, Letter to the East India Company, 10 March 1620

The 4th of June, of pleasant memory to Etonians, opened the port of Nagasaki to our rain-drenched party . . . even under a cloudy sky the entrance was not devoid of beauty. Island after island comes into view as the bay is entered, many very picturesque in form. As the ship moves further up the bay, the town of Nagasaki is seen lying at the farther end, clustering at the foot of a range of hills, and creeping no inconsiderable distance up the wooded sides. *Decima* to the right fixes the eye – a low, fan-shaped strip of land, dammed out from the waters of the bay, the handle being towards the shore, and truncated. One long wide street, with two-storied houses on each side, built in European style, gives an air of great tidiness; but they looked with large hollow eyes into each others interiors, in a dismal sort of way, as if they had been so engaged for six generations at least, – and were quite weary of the view. A conscious sense of the inevitable monotony of life passed within its boundaries leaves one little disposed to admire even the trimness and cleanliness of all around.

Sir Rutherford Alcock, *The Capital of the Tycoon*, 1863

The Lourdes of the Atomic Age.

Murray Sayle, quoted by Auberon Waugh, *Spectator*, 24 September 1980

Naha (Okinawa)

We walked through the town of Napa, the streets were all paved with granite, cut in all manners of shapes, with the edges neatly fitting each other, the houses are low, and the tiles, cemented together, presenting a very tidy appearance; every house is walled around seven or eight feet high, and none have a direct entrance, but by a zig-zag path round little walls & fences, which though very good for the purpose of keeping off the spy, upon which system the Govt. is founded, suggests difficulties in getting an easy access home after partaking of the compliments of the season on a New Years day, and in no way reconcileable wth the object of latch keys – the walls with their regularity of appearance (like the streets) with the large quantity of trees and plants peeping over them, give the whole a *home-ey* sort of look, as though there might be something inside the establishments, that would be good for the inner man.

Edward Yorke McAuley, Diary, 20 August 1853, *With Perry in Japan*, 1942

Nikko

The Japanese proverb says *Nikko wo minai uchi wa kekko to iu na* – until you have seen *Nikko*, do not say *Kekko i.e.* grand or splendid.

Douglas Sladen, *Queer Things About Japan*, 1903

Okinawa

Okinawa is the keystone of the Pacific in the free world's fight against the spread of Communism.

Handbook of the American Third Marine Division

Approached on a sunny day, in a calm sea, the island looks like a luscious pear laid on soft, crinkly blue paper.

Alexander Campbell, *The Heart of Japan*, 1962

Osaka

In trade it is a Chicago. In situation it is a Venice.

John Foster Fraser, *Round the World on a Wheel*, 1899

Ryukyu Islands

The Ryukyu Islands, the tail to the rocket of Japan . . .

George Woodcock, *Asia, Gods and Cities*, 1966

Tokyo (formerly Edo/Yedo)

About 3 a clock in the after nowne there hapned an exceading earthquake in this citty of Edo in Japon, which contynewed, from the begyning to the end, about the eight part of an hower; but about the halfe tyme it was soe extreame that I thought the howse would have falne down on our heads, and so was glad to run out of doares without hat or shewes, the tymbers of the howse making such a nois and cracking that it was fearefull to heare. It began by littell and littell, and so encreased till the middell, and in lyke sort went away againe.

Richard Cocks, *Diary*, 30 August 1616

We went rowndabout the kyngs castell or fortresse, which I do hould to be much more in compas then the citty of Coventry.

Richard Cocks, *Diary*, 7 September 1616

The general shape of Tokyo is that of an egg, with the point to the South the butt to the North. The yolk of this egg is the castle, or O Shiro, a work of vast proportions.

W.E. Griffis, *The Mikado's Empire*, 1876

No view of Tôkiyô, leaving out the impression produced by size, is striking, indeed there is a monotony of meanness about it. . . . As a city it lacks concentration. Masses of greenery, lined or patched with grey, and an absence of beginning or end, look suburban rather than metropolitan. Far away in the distance are other grey patches; you are told that those are still Tôkiyô, and you ask no more. It is a city of 'magnificent distances' without magnificence.

Isabella Bird, *Unbeaten Tracks in Japan*, 1880

The street signs do little to relieve the monotony of the low, grey houses, nor do the shops (except the toy-shops which are gorgeous) make much show, with their low fronts half-concealed by curtains. Confectioners usually display a spiked white ball a foot and a half in diameter; *sake*-dealers a cluster of cypress trimmed into a sphere; the sellers of the crimson pigment with which women varnish their lips a red flag; goldbeaters a great pair of square spectacles, with gold instead of glass; druggists and herbalists a big bag resembling in shape the small ones used in making their infusions; kite-makers a cuttle-fish; sellers of cut flowers a small willow tree; dealers in dried and salt fish, etc. two fish, coloured red, and tied together by the gills with straw, indicating that they can supply the gifts which it is usual to make to betrothed persons; but the Brobdignagian signs in black, red, and gold, which light up the streets of Canton, are too 'loud' and explicit for Japanese taste, which prefers the simple and symbolical.

Ibid.

Mr Lowell, as an artist in words, does not add what we, simple recorders of facts are bound to do, that with so much to appeal to the eye, Tokyo has not a little that appeals to the nose.

Basil Hall Chamberlain, *Things Japanese*, 1890

There is no Japan like Tokyo.

Lafcadio Hearn, Letter to Sentarō Nishida, January 1895

In this Tokyo, this detestable Tokyo there are no Japanese impressions to be had except at rare intervals. To describe to you the place would be utterly impossible, – more easy to describe a province. Here the quarter of the foreign embassies, looking like a well-painted American suburb; – nearby an estate with quaint Chinese gates several centuries old; a little further square miles of indescribable squalor; – then miles of military parade-ground trampled into a waste of dust, and bounded by hideous barracks; – then a great park full of really weird beauty, the shadows all black as ink; – then square miles of streets of shops, which burn down once a year,—then more squalor; – then rice fields and bamboo groves; – then more streets. All this not flat but hilly – a city of undulations. Immense silences – green and romantic – alternate with quarters of turmoil and factories and railroad stations. Miles of telegraph-poles looking at a distance like enormous fine-tooth combs, make a horrid impression. Miles of water-pipes, – miles and miles and miles of them – interrupt the traffic of the principal streets: they have been trying to put them underground for seven years . . . . Streets melt under rain, water-pipes sink, water-pipe holes drown spreeing men and swallow up playful children; frogs sing amazing songs in the street. – To think of art or time or eternity in the dead waste and muddle of this mess is difficult.

Lafcadio Hearn, Letter to Ellwood Hendrick, August 1897

Honestly I do not see how the people in Tokyo live. They do not seem to manufacture anything except university graduates; and it is only a port in name, because there is barely enough water for a junk. University students are the curse of Japan; they are the turbulent soshi who are at the root of every disturbance.

'What are Soshi?' I asked a British Consul in Japan.

'People who have too much education and too little to eat.'

Douglas Sladen, *Queer Things About Japan*, 1903

That street was typical of the modern Tokyo – not of its main arteries, mushroom offices and towering apartment stores, but of the Tokyo which lies always around the corner, an easy stone's throw from the bright lights and the grinding trams. Vague and slatternly, a sprawling skyline of wooden houses overlooked by a massive procession of telegraph poles that marched – or rather staggered – up its slope, linked together by loose wires in a drooping curve . . . These telegraph poles, as though conscious of their superiority, never take the trouble to stand straight. Like street bullies, their hands deep in their pockets, they lurch drunkenly over the cowering shabby roofs and lean at affected angles on strong supports. The old Japan is changing in their shadow; the future belongs to them and all they symbolize. The squalor of the new 'progressive' city has the effect of a perpetual sardonic sneer.

Peter Quennell, *A Superficial Journey through Tokyo and Peking*, 1932

Then I saw for the first time the true beauty of Tokyo, and of all Japanese cities. They are only beautiful at night, when they become fairylands of gorgeous neon: towers and sheets and globes and rivers of neon, in stunning profusion, a wild razzle-dazzle of colours and shapes and movements, fierce and delicate, restrained and violent against the final afterglow of sunset. As the sky's darkness deepened, the piercing, eye-singeing emeralds and rubies and blinding diamond-whites, the pinks, mauves, blues and lemons blazed out with fevered intensity and abandon; at the top of pinnacles of glittering glass and steel, enormous searchlights revolved, sweeping the city with long white arms in stroking gestures of mechanical affection. Millions of windows were exploding with light. Down dark alleys, big round red lanterns and long, cylindrical ones like concertinas shed a subdued radiance outside small eating-shops.

James Kirkup, *These Horned Islands*, 1962

Tokyo is also the city where one encounters at its most intense, its most vital and its most vulgar the kind of society that has resulted from the double impact of industrialization and the West. Japanese society is a kind of conglomerate, in which borrowings from many places at many times are fossilized and united by the cement of Japanese tradition. The writing and much of the surviving religious and courtly ceremonial came from China. The present political constitution is basically British. The beer and the beer halls which one finds in every city are German. The uniform of the students is that of Hapsburg Austria, and the middy-blouses of the high-school girls date from Victorian England. The cake shops, when they are not Japanese are most often French in style, the coffee bars are Italian – innocent emanations of *La Dolce Vita* – and the fashions in western dress are American. As for art, the styles run all the way from the French impressionists to the most recent schools of New York and Italy, and often we would be impressed against our better judgements by the meticulous faithfulness with which Japanese painters had imitated such masters as Monet, Matisse, and Picasso.

At first we were bewildered at the very incongruity of this mixture of the strange and the familiar, and then amazed at the zest for having the best of both worlds which seems to be the most outstanding characteristic of the modern Japanese.

George Woodcock, *Asia, Gods and Cities*, 1966

Frequent outbreaks of fire constitute one of the greatest perils to life in Japan. In Tokyo, burning houses are given the poetic name of 'the flowers of Edo.'

James Kirkup, *Heaven, Hell and Hara-Kiri*, 1974

Yamada (the Geku Shrine near there)

The impression produced by the whole resembles that made upon the minds of those who have made the deepest researches into Shinto—there is nothing, and all things, even the stately avenues of the Gekû, lead to NOTHING.

Isabella Bird, *Unbeaten Tracks in Japan*, 1880

Yezo

Yezo is to the main island of Japan what Tipperary is to an Englishman . . . . Nobody comes here without meeting with something queer, and one or two tumbles.

Isabella Bird, *Unbeaten Tracks in Japan*, 1880

Yokohama

Earthquake, October 1884

While the quaking was going on the fancy came to me that it was a laugh rippling over Mother Earth. Today, being gloomy, it seems more like a sigh heaving her bosom . . . . They say the more you see of earthquakes, the less you like them. I think I like them less.

Lilian Leland, *Travelling Alone, A Woman's Journey Round the World*, 1890

Took a walk in the village of Yokohama. It is a very interesting little place. The houses are all of wood very neat and clean, no windows but now and then a sliding door with paper in the sashes instead of glass. Each house had a store adjoining it, built of wood and covered over with about an inch thick of lime cement, which as the buildings are far apart, is sufficiently fire-proof for all Japanese purposes.

Edward Yorke McCauley, Diary, 18 March 1854, *With Perry in Japan*, 1942

A favorite threat of atrabilious Frenchmen, blustering Russians, and petty epaulet-wearers of all sorts, when their demands were refused, was to strike their flag, go on board a man-of-war, and blow up the native town. Yokohama still stands, having survived bombardments in five languages.

W.E. Griffis, *The Mikado's Empire*, 1876

Yokohama does not improve on further acquaintance. It has a dead-alive look. It has irregularity without picturesqueness, and the grey sky, grey sea, grey houses, and grey roofs look harmoniously dull.

Isabella Bird, *Unbeaten Tracks in Japan*, 1880

JORDAN

Nowhere more than in Jordan have I felt a sense that this is where the world began.

Edward Heath, *Travels, People and Places in My Life*, 1977

I had been wary of coming to Jordan. I hadn't liked the look of its Gross National Product.

Jonathan Raban, *Arabia through the Looking Glass*, 1979

Being all right is *the* Jordanian habit of mind.

Peter Skelton, quoted *ibid.*

and the Palestinians

I believe in a Palestinian homeland. It's called Jordan.

Shimon Peres, quoted by Donald Trelford, 'It's Not So Easy Being a Jew', *Observer*, 20 April 1980

Amman

'No! No! No!' she said. 'You don't understand! Amman is not a city of a million people, it is a city of a hundred couples!'

Gabriela Durra, quoted by Jonathan Raban, *Arabia through the Looking Glass*, 1979

Primed to expect almost anything now, I walked down the steps of the hotel loggia into Switzerland. Amman was a mossy, alpine rock-garden. Its folded hills were packed solid with little stone chalets, but these houses looked more as if they had been quarried from the rock than built on it. They took their colours from the surrounding stone: pink, lime-green, oxide-blue, pale, creamy grey. If one squinted for a moment, there were no houses at all; just a pastel-coloured abstract of rocky outcrops and crevices. Every crag and knobble held a stunted tree, like a Japanese *bonsai*. There were little cedars, baby olives, and eucalyptus trees growing at queer angles on rosy pinnacles of bare stone. A shaly patch of waste ground at my feet was bright with periwinkles and daisies. The hills were cross-hatched with zig-zag streets and twisty mountain paths. Even the air was alpine – bright and biting, without a trace of that putrescent smell which I had thought was an essential ingredient in every Arab city . . . . Minarets . . . there must be minarets . . . . I looked for them, and found a few hidden away in the crooks of the hills, where they looked quaint and curious, like picturesque relics of some old superstitious sect. The Roman amphitheatre in front of the hotel looked more at home here than the mosques.

Jonathan Raban, *Arabia through the Looking Glass*, 1979

Bethlehem

But thou, Beth-lehem Ephratah, though thou be little among the thousands of Judah, yet out of thee shall he come forth unto me that is to be ruler in Israel.

The Bible, Micah 5:2

Bethlehem is the pleasantest village in all Judea.

William Lithgow, *Rare Adventures and Painfull Peregrinations*, 1614/32

Earth has many a noble city,
Bethlehem thou dost all excel.

Rev. Edward Caswall, *Earth has Many a Noble City* (A translation of Prudentius' *O Sola Magnarum Urbium*, 4th century.)

We went to Bethlehem too; and saw the apocryphal wonders there.

W.M. Thackeray, *Journey from Cornhill to Cairo*, 1845

Here we see a lot more tombs and altars, and pictures of the crucifixion, the tombs of the parents of Mary, the room where Jesus was born, the spot where his cradle rested, and the room occupied by St Jerome. Some of these people appear to have tombs in Judea, a city tomb and a country tomb, and a tomb at a fashionable seaside resort. Indeed their saintly remains are scattered about in the most promiscuous manner.

Lilian Leland, *Travelling Alone, A Woman's Journey Round the World*, 1890

The atmosphere of the place was almost as revealing a commentary on the practical application of Christianity as its namesake town in America where the guns and high explosives are made.

Arriving there was like arriving at a Barnum and Bailey fairground. Walking across the courtyard to the church we were attacked by a swarm of vendors of mother-of-pearl crucifixes and other souvenirs . . . . Inside were many more tarbooshed Arab hawkers and guides waiting for business. After all the Christian churches I had seen in my life, I had had to come to the birthplace of Jesus to see for the first time a score of men wearing hats in one. Tourists had scrawled their names over every available inch of the walls and pillars.

Downstairs, in a crypt, was what was said to be the actual manger in which Jesus was born. A policeman sat by it, keeping guard.

Cedric Belfrage, *Away from It All*, 1936

Men of

They are ever distinguished in the great feasts at Jerusalem, by their fierce and lawless manners, and if any row occurs they are sure to have a hand in it. It is asserted in this country that there is something in the water of certain places which renders the people sturdy, hard, and fearless; and it is curious enough that people of this character have ever been connected with Bethlehem.

W.M. Thomson, *The Land and the Book*, 1859

El Khalil / Hebron

In the city of Hebron are the graves of the patriarchs Adam, Abraham, Isaac and Jacob and of their wives Eve, Sarah, and Rebecca, and they are in the hanging of the hill . . . And there, a little beside, is a cave in a rock, where Adam and Eve were dwelling when they were driven out of Paradise; and there gat they their childer.

John Mandeville, *The Book of John Mandeville*, *c.* 1360

Jericho

I have observed that travellers generally, when they arrive at any place of extraordinary interest, find the right glow of feeling coming over them precisely at the proper moment. I never had any difficulty in Italy . . . but in a country like this, a man is thrown upon his own resources; and, notwithstanding the interest attached to the name of Jericho, I found it a hard matter to feel duly excited.

John Lloyd Stephens, *Incidents of Travel in Egypt, etc.*, 1837

Petra

Match me such marvel save in Eastern clime
A rose-red city – 'half as old as time'!

J.W. Burgon, *Petra*, 1845

What a mixture of wild romance with the daily life of a city! It was now like Jinnee land; and it seemed as if men were too small ever to have lived here. . . . The longer we staid, and the more mountain temples we climbed to, the more I felt that the inhabitants, among their other peculiarities, must have been winged.

Harriet Martineau, *Eastern Life Past and Present*, 1848

We rode on and soon got into the entrance of the defile which leads to Petra. The Bab es Sik is a passage about half a mile long and in places not more than 8 ft. wide; the rocks rise on either side straight up 100 ft. or so, they are sandstone of the most exquisite red and sometimes almost arch overhead. The stream runs between filling all the path, though it used to flow through conduits and the road was paved; oleanders grew along the stream and here and there a sheaf of ivy hung down over the red rock. We went on in ecstasies until suddenly between the narrow opening of the rocks, we saw the most beautiful sight I have ever seen. Imagine a temple cut out of the solid rock, the charming façade supported on great Corinthian columns standing clear, soaring upwards to the very top of the cliff in the most exquisite proportions and carved with groups of figures almost as fresh as when the chisel left them – all this in the rose red rock, with the sun just touching it and making it look almost transparent. As we went on the gorge widened, on either side the cliffs were cut out into rock tombs of every shape and adorned in every manner, some standing, columned, in the rock, some clear with a pointed roof, some elaborate, some simple, some capped with pointed pyramids, many adorned with a curious form of stair high up over the doorway. . . . The gorge opened and brought us out into a kind of square between the cliffs with a rude cut theatre in it and tombs on every side. We went on and got into a great open place the cliffs widening out far on every side and leaving this kind of amphitheatre strewn over with mounds of ruins. And here we camped under a row of the most elaborate tombs, three stories of pillars and cornices and the whole topped by a great funeral urn. They are extremely rococo, just like the kind of thing you see in a Venetian church above a seventeenth century Doge leaning on his elbow, but time has worn them and weather has stained the rock with exquisite colours – and, in short, I never liked Bernini so well! . . . It is like a fairy tale city, all pink and wonderful.

Gertrude Bell, Journal letter to her father,
29 March 1900

I have now got the geography of Petra familiarly, and feel I can see the old main street beside the stream, banked up with an embankment of great sandstone blocks and covered with bridges, and in the low middle ground all the houses, a temple and acropolis on a small southern height, and the cliffs all around worked into façades of tombs. They must have been a horrid rich commercial people, all out for display, and with a very coarse taste in their sculpture: the older tombs are the best, just decorated with a sort of parapet and a plain door; but the later Greek and Roman effendis went in for columns, urns, pediments and all the worst Mid-Victorian ornament.

Freya Stark, Letter, 31 March 1933,
in *Beyond Euphrates*, 1951

JUAN FERNANDEZ / MAS-A-TIERRA (Chile)

Alexander Selkirk's sojourn here from 1704–8 inspired Defoe's description of Crusoe's imaginary island

The woods which covered most of the steepest hills were free from all bushes and underwood, and afforded an easy passage through every part of them; and the irregularities of the hills and precipices, in the northern part of the Island, necessarily traced out by their various combinations a great number of romantic vallies; most of which had a stream of clearest water running through them, that tumbled in cascades from rock to rock, as the bottom of the valley, by the course of the neighbouring hills, was at any time broken into a sharp descent: Some particular spots occurred in these vallies, where the shade and fragrance of the contiguous woods, the loftiness of the overhanging rocks, and the transparency and frequent falls of the neighbouring streams, presented scenes of such elegance and dignity, as would perhaps with difficulty be rivalled in any other part of the globe. It is in this place, perhaps, that the simple productions of unassisted nature may be said to excel all the fictitious descriptions of the most animated imagination.

George Anson (Richard Walter and Benjamin Robins), *A Voyage Round the World, 1740–4*, 1748

K

KENYA

Kenya should no longer be known as 'A Place in the Sun for Shady People'.

It is true that there are still any amount of people out there who have earned for the Colony the right to ask the question: 'Are you married, – or do you live in Kenya?' And in Nairobi I must say, I ran into the grandest assortment of 'types' that I have encountered in any capital. Still, every one of these will tell you:

'Oh, *this* isn't Kenya!'

What Kenya is, I can't say; I never could bring that Colony into focus. I think it is a state of mind more than anything else.

Negley Farson, *Behind God's Back*, 1940

Come to Kenya, where the Zoo looks at you, and not you at the Zoo!

Tourist poster (?), quoted in James Agate, *Ego 9*, 22 July 1946

I heard a critic from a neighbouring country, speaking of Mombasa's and Nairobi's ambitious social halls, say with some asperity:

'In Kenya they believe parquet floors to be a cure for soil erosion!'

Elspeth Huxley, *The Sorcerer's Apprentice*, 1948

It's the land of the living here. The land of the living.

Kenya Scot, quoted by Richard West, *The White Tribes of Africa*, 1965

In Kenya any eccentricity gets blamed on the altitude.

Richard West, *The White Tribes of Africa*, 1965

and Tanzanians

President Nyerere of Tanzania calls Kenya the 'Man Eat Man Society.' With even more accuracy Kenyans describe Tanzania as the 'Man Eat Nothing Society.'

Stephen Glover, *Daily Telegraph*, 24 June 1982

Kenyans

and the British

Of the eight Britons on EXCO, three have lived in Kenya for twenty-five years or longer, and think of themselves as Kenyan more than British. One told me, 'I am more an African than any damned Kikuyu.'

John Gunther, *Inside Africa*, 1955

Kikuyu – English attitudes to them

Most Britons in Kenya despise Kikuyus; I heard one settler say with perfect seriousness, 'There are no Kikuyus in the Nairobi football team. Something must be wrong with a man who doesn't go in for football.' Another said, 'We have educated the Kukes much too fast. They should have had two hundred years, not forty, to jump from barbarism to the present. They are no more fit for government than to be pilots of jet aircraft. They read Shakespeare in the most *filthy* huts.'

John Gunther, *Inside Africa*, 1955

Indians

I heard one British official complain, 'All Indians say "Yes, *but–*" to everything and they are litigious even before breakfast.'

John Gunther, *Inside Africa*, 1955

There is a violence and exuberance about the white Kenyans which recall the age of Tom Jones. One of the most pro-African of the whites I met admitted that he quite frequently beat his servants. When one of his several dogs howled too loudly he cheerfully kicked its head in a way that would horrify kindly people in England. Yet he is not a cruel man, He and his wife are extremely friendly with the Africans – 'I felt at home immediately I came out here. The Africans are so like the Irish' – and indeed he himself is rather African in his outlook. A neighbour recalled, 'We had a cock-fight in the drawing-room one night. When my wife got back there were blood and feathers all over the place. She was furious.' No wonder.

Richard West, *The White Tribes of Africa*, 1965

The Great North Road (out of Nairobi)

The Great North Road, which has the surface of a moderately rough laundry board . . . .

John Gunther, *Inside Africa*, 1955

Mambrui

The twentieth century has passed Mambrui by. So,

indeed, have all the other centuries; it is a place severed from time and circumstance as if embedded in a never-ending dream.

Elspeth Huxley, *The Sorcerer's Apprentice*, 1948

Mombasa

At Mombasa we reach the true Africa of the Victorian illustrations . . . . The town has charm and smells like Morocco.

Cyril Connolly, *The Evening Colonnade*, 1973

Nairobi

It is impossible that a town will not play a part in your life; it does not even make much difference whether you have more good or bad things to say of it, it draws your mind to it by a mental law of gravitation. The luminous haze on the sky above the town at night, which I could see from some places on my farm, set my thoughts going, and recalled the big cities of Europe . . . .

During all my time, Nairobi was a medley place, with some fine new buildings, and whole quarters of old corrugated iron shops, offices, and bungalows, laid out with long rows of eucalyptus trees along the bare dusty streets . . . . And it was a live place, in movement like running water, and in growth like a young thing, it changed from year to year, and while you were away on a shooting safari . . . . Nairobi said to me: 'Make the most of me and of time. *Wir kommen nie wieder so jung* – so undisciplined and rapacious – *zusammen*.' Generally I and Nairobi were in very good understanding, and at one time I drove through the town and thought: There is no world without Nairobi's streets.

Karen Blixen, *Out of Africa*, 1937

Nairobi is the Paris of the East African coast – of all Africa below Cairo.

Negley Farson, *Behind God's Back*, 1940

Nairobi has passed without time to gather the least moss of tradition from the status of a pioneer market-town to that of the commercial – and, now, political – capital of a region inhabited by thirteen million people. Such forced growth could bring no grace or dignity, only a sort of hectic boom-town vitality which at its best may stimulate and at its worst depress by a kind of pretentious self-sufficiency.

This is among the Europeans. The population of roughly 100,000 is compounded of six parts African to three parts Indian to one part European. Yet Nairobi strikes one mainly as an Indian city.

Elspeth Huxley, *The Sorcerer's Apprentice*, 1948

Nairobi is like a balloon floating high aloft but stationary, where Europeans are overworked, well-meaning and important, and the rest of East Africa a distant blur. Everyone has his own ideas of what is going on down below, but no one can actually see it happening, or has the time to descend and find out.

Ibid.

I was also impressed by a peculiar phenomenon that I encountered several times at formal dinner parties; gentlemen do not go to the toilet after separating from the ladies, but walk out on the lawn, and in the equatorial darkness stand in a row facing a hedge or garden wall, and there relieve themselves while murmuring a low toast, 'To Africa.'

John Gunther, *Inside Africa*, 1955

Nairobi is the safari capital of the world.

Ibid.

Ngong Hills

The geographical position and the height of the land combined to create a landscape that had not its like in all the world. There was no fat on it and no luxuriance anywhere; it was Africa distilled up through six thousand feet, like the strong and refined essence of a continent. The colours were dry and burnt, like the colours in pottery. The trees had a light delicate foliage, the structure of which was different from that of the trees in Europe; it did not grow in bows or cupolas, but in horizontal layers, and the formation gave to the tall solitary trees a likeness to the palms, or a heroic and romantic air like fullrigged ships with their sails furled, and to the edge of a wood a strange appearance as if the whole wood were faintly vibrating. Upon the grass of the great plains the crooked bare old thorn-trees were scattered and the grass was spiced like thyme and bog-myrtle; in some places the scent was so strong, that it smarted in the nostrils. All the flowers that you found on the plains, or upon the creepers and liana in the native forest, were diminutive like flowers of the downs – only just in the beginning of the long rains a number of big, massive heavy-scented lilies sprang out of the plains. The views were immensely wide. Everything that you saw made for greatness and freedom, and unequalled nobility.

The chief feature of the landscape, and of your life in it, was the air. Looking back on a sojourn in the African highlands, you are struck by your feeling of having lived for a time up in the air. The sky was rarely more than pale blue or violet, with a profusion of mighty, weightless, ever-changing clouds towering up and sailing on it, but it had a blue vigour in it, and at a short distance it painted the ranges of hills and the woods a fresh deep blue. In the middle of the day the air was alive over the land, like a flame burning; it scintillated, waved and shone like running water, mirrored and doubled all objects, and created great

Fata Morgana. Up in this high air you breathed easily, drawing in a vital assurance and lightness of heart. In the highlands you woke up in the morning and thought: Here I am, where I ought to be.

Karen Blixen, *Out of Africa*, 1937

KOREA

The dust of Korea was worse than any dust normally experienced by human kind; it combined the properties of emery-powder and poison gas, for not only did it tear and rasp at the throat, but at the same time introduced into the respiratory passages a concentrate of pestilential bacilli from the reeking paddies.

James Cameron, *Point of Departure*, 1967

The sun seemed abruptly to leap into the sky and the heat came pouring down. And with the heat the smell; it rose off the fields almost visibly as the morning grew. Although as one's experience of Korea lengthened the first revulsion dulled, the smell remained as a background for all other sensations. This characteristic of Korea, – the hand-fertilizing of the paddies with domestic ordure – was of course by no means unique in the East, but it is a fact that here it reached an especial concentration of evidence. I have never known a country where there was a more lively and thriving commerce in human excrement, even throughout the continent of Asia, which always seems to Europeans excessively reluctant to part with its sewage.

Ibid.

The Koreans have been called 'the Irish of the East,' but this is an insult to the Irish.

James Kirkup, *Streets of Asia*, 1969

No matter how many times I give the same speech the words seem new to me . . . like Eisenhower in 1952: 'If elected in November,' the Great Golfer read dutifully from a text plainly new to him, 'I will go to . . . *Korea?*' The voice and choler rose on the word 'Korea.' No one had told him about the pledge.

Gore Vidal, *Matters of Fact and Fiction*, 1977

Korea hangs like a lumpy phallus between the sprawling thighs of Manchuria and the Sea of Japan. Roughly the size of England and Scotland, it was, in 1950, the home of about twenty million people, most of whom lived in the south. The peninsula has sometimes been called 'the Hermit Kingdom,' and most visitors have been only too happy to leave it alone. Sebald had crossed it six times in the 1930's. He had thought that it was 'a nation of sad people – oppressed, unhappy, poor, silent, and sullen,' and he hadn't changed his mind since. A Korean proverb for the country runs: 'Over the mountains, mountains.' The hills in fact seem interminable. They are also dun-colored, granitic, steep, and speckled here and there with boulders, scrub oaks, and stunted firs. In the valleys, streams meander past rice paddies, walled cities, and pagodas fingering drab skies from terraced slopes. The landscape is colorless. There are almost no flowers. The hillsides are gouged with thousands of dells and gorges, many deep enough to conceal battalions of troops. It is ideal terrain for guerrilla fighting.

William Manchester, *American Caesar*, 1979

Seoul (South)

Lying between chill sheets that night in my icy room, I tried to organize my first impressions of Seoul. In the back of my mind I felt that the place reminded me of somewhere I had been before. The impression of gloom and darkness and wildness could not be dispelled. Many of the streets had been quite black, lit only now and then by faint lights from the windows of shops, so that I was aware always of the intense blackness of the sky, the coruscation of the winter stars. The dimly lit street cars and buses were crammed to the doors, and everywhere there was the curiously clanging, grumbling tone of Korean speech. From time to time I was reminded of northern Japanese towns in winter time – Akita, Aomori, Niigata or Sapporo. But then it flashed into my mind that what Seoul really reminded me of was the Arctic: the bare, freezing desolations on the outskirts of Kiruna and Narvik.

James Kirkup, *Streets of Asia*, 1969

L

LAOS

The major said: 'If you wish to suggest that, in the sense of building railways and roads, France did little or nothing for Laos, then I agree. In other ways – and I say this proudly – we preserved it with our neglect . . . . It was a wonderful country; and if you want to see what it will be like in a few years' time, just go and have a look at Siam. Of course, the Viets may take it over. In any case, the charm we've known is a thing of the past. As for the future, you might say it's a toss-up between the strip-tease and the political lecture.'

Norman Lewis, *The Changing Sky*, 1959

Kennedy turned the conversation to Laos. De Gaulle observed that the countries of South East Asia did not offer a good terrain for western troops, nor indeed for western politics. Unlike India and Japan which were 'real' nations, these were 'fictitious' nations, and neutralization was the best solution. The French experience had been that exerting influence in South East Asia and taking military action there were almost incompatible.

Arthur M.Schlesinger, *One Thousand Days*, 1965
(account of Kennedy's meeting with De Gaulle
in Paris, 31 May 1961)

Only one journalist ever understood Laos and she was fired by her own news agency because the true reports she filed were not as acceptable as the fiction filed by everyone else. How can one explain a country where three armies, Right, Left, and Neutralist, are locked in vague battle over the misty plains; where the main industry, opium-growing, is backed by the CIA; where the capital can be shelled by its own police in an attack on the army (or maybe the other way round, I cannot remember); where the peace talks began over a fancy-dress party at which the US Ambassador was attired, if my memory is correct, as Sinbad the Sailor?

Richard West, *Victory in Vietnam*, 1974

Laos, a river bank, had been overrun and ransacked; it was one of America's practical jokes, a motiveless place where nothing was made, everything imported; a kingdom with baffling pretensions to Frenchness. What was surprising was that it existed at all, and the more I thought of it, the more it seemed like a lower form of life, like the cross-eyed planarian or squashy amoeba, the sort of creature that can't die even when it is cut to ribbons.

Paul Theroux, *The Great Railway Bazaar*, 1975

Luang Prabang

Glimpsed from the road above it, through the golden mohur and the bamboo fronds, Luang Prabang, on its tongue of land where the rivers met, was a tiny Manhattan – but a Manhattan with holy men in yellow in its avenues, with pariah dogs, and garlanded pedicabs carrying somnolent Frenchmen nowhere, and doves in its sky.

Norman Lewis, *The Changing Sky*, 1959

For those not familiar with Luang Prabang it can be placed only by saying that Siam was behind, Burma over one shoulder and Viet Nam the other, and China straight ahead.

James Cameron, *Point of Departure*, 1967

Ah yes, monsieur, Cambodia was a paradise once, but now one has to come to Luang Prabang. It is the last paradise left.

Richard West, quoting a Cambodian drinking
companion, in *Victory in Vietnam*, 1974

Vientiane

Vientiane is exceptional, but inconvenient. The brothels are cleaner than the hotels, marijuana is cheaper than pipe tobacco, and opium easier to find than a cold glass of beer.

Paul Theroux, *The Great Railway Bazaar*, 1975

'LAPLAND' (Norway, Sweden, Finland, North of)

The Finns and Laplands are acquainted well
With such-like Spirits, and Winds to Merchants sell;
Making their Cov'nant, when and how they please
They may with prosp'rous Weather cross the Seas;
As thus: They in a Handkerchief fast tie
Three Knots, and loose the First, and by and by
You find a gentle Gale blow from the Shore;
Open the Second, it increaseth more,

To fill the Sails: when you the third unty
The intemperate Gusts grow vehement and high.

Thomas Heywood, *The Hierarchy of the Blessed Angels*, 1635

The Laplanders, when they would sell a Wind,
Wafting to Hell, bag up the Phrase, and bind
It to the Barque, which at the Voiage end
Shifts Poop, and breeds th' Cholic in the Field.

John Cleveland, *The King's Disguise*, 1647

Not so the sons of Lapland: wisely they
Despise th'insensate barbarous trade of war;
They ask no more than simple Nature gives;
They love their mountains, and enjoy their storms.
No false desires, no pride-created wants,
Disturb the peaceful current of their time,
And through the restless, ever-tortured maze
Of pleasure or ambition bid it rage.
Their rendeer form their riches. These their tents,
Their robes, their beds, and all their homely wealth
Supply, their wholesome fare and cheerful cups.
Obsequious at their call, the docile tribe
Yield to the sled their necks, and whirl them swift
O'er hill and dale, heap'd into one expanse
Of marbled snow, or, far as eye can sweep,
With a blue crust of ice unbounded glazed.

James Thomson, *The Seasons – Winter*, 1726

Extreme cold has diminished the stature and congealed the faculties of the Laplanders; and the Arctic tribes, alone among the sons of men, are ignorant of war, and unconscious of human blood: an happy ignorance, if reason and virtue were the guardians of their peace!

Edward Gibbon, *The Decline and Fall of the Roman Empire*, 1776–88

'And now that you've seen Helsinki,' the man from the Finnish Tourist Office said, 'how would you like to visit Lapland?'

'Why?' I inquired.

'Because,' he said, 'you will see nothing like it anywhere. For the first time you will come to real grips with the mysterious forces of the North. You will see vast trackless wilds of virgin forests and naked hills, strapping spruces, sunny summits, bristling birches, earthy bots, matted moss, stilted cranes, frosty forests, boggy bilberries, fertile fields, whining willows, turbulent tundra, ranting reindeer, lonely Laplanders, lusty log-rollers, wily wolves, fidgety foxes, bumbling bears, countless caves, piny paradises, raging rivers, shining streams, windy wastelands, dazzling dam sites, haughty herdsmen, doughty dogs, salty salmon, harried herrings, carefree cattle, steaming saunas, fearless fodder, mushy marshlands, towering timber, swollen swamps, fragrant firs, fetching fountainheads, mucky mire, misty meadows, stunted sycamores, and muted minks.'

'How many marks for the dollar?' I inquired.

'Three hundred and forty to the dollar,' my man said.

'Good, I'll go.'

Art Buchwald, *I Chose Caviar*, 1957

Lapps

Between North Cape and Cape Grace

The whole Countrey in a manner is either Lakes or Mountaines, which towards the Sea side are called Tondro, because they are all of hard and craggie Rocke, but the inland parts are well furnished with Woods, that grow on the hill sides, the lakes lying between. Their dyet is very bare and simple. Bread they have none, but feed onely upon Fish and Fowle . . . .

The whole Nation is utterly unlearned, having not so much as the use of any Alphabet, or Letter among them. For practice of Witch-craft and Sorcerie, they passe all Nations in the World. Though for the inchanting of ships that sayle along their Coast (as I have heard it reported) and their giving of winds good to their friends, and contrary to other, whom they meane to hurt by tying of certayne knots upon a Rope (somewhat like to the Tale of Aeolus his wind-bag) is a very Fable, devised (as may seeme) by themselves, to terrifie Saylers for comming neere their Coast. Their Weapons are the Longbow, and Hand-gunne, wherein they excell, aswell for quicknesse to charge and discharge, as for neernesse at the Marke, by reason of their continuall practice (whereto they are forced) of shooting at wild-fowle. Their manner is in Summer time to come down in great companies to the Sea-side. . . . and there to fish for Cod, Salmon, and But-fish. . . . When their fishing is done, their manner is to draw their Carbasses, or Boats on shoare; and there to leave them with the Keele turned upwards, till the next Spring-tyde. Their travell too and fro is upon Sleds, drawne by the Olen Deere: which they use to turne a grazing all the Summer time, in an Iland called Kilden (of a very good Soyle compared with other parts of that Countrey) and toward the Winter time, when the Snow beginneth to fall, they fetch them home againe, for the use of their Sled.

Dr Giles Fletcher, *A Treatise of Russia, etc.*, 1589, in *Purchas his Pilgrimes*, 1625

Every individual who has visited Lapland must have remarked one characteristic common to all the Lapps; namely, their mild and pacific disposition. When inflamed by spirituous liquor, their intoxication betrays itself by acts of intemperance; but never by anger, malice, or cruelty. It is manifested only in an elevation of spirits, amounting indeed to madness; in shouting, jumping, and laughing; in craving for drams, with hysteric screams, until they fall senseless to the ground;

in a total disregard of all that belongs to them, offering any thing they possess for brandy; in raging lust, and total violation of all decency in their conduct; suffering at the same time, kicks, cuffs, and blows, insults and provocations of any kind, without the smallest irascibility. When sober, they are as gentle as lambs; and the softness of their language, added to their effeminate tone of voice, remarkably corresponds with their placable disposition. It might be supposed that they had borrowed this meekness of character (as it has been sometimes remarked of shepherds) from the animals to whose care their whole lives are dedicated: for the rein-deer is, of all quadrupeds, the most gentle and harmless.

E.D. Clarke, *Travels in Various Countries*, 1824

Laplanders are best enjoyed at a distance. Their clothes of leather are put on them as infants and added to them as they grow, in pieces.

Lilian Leland, *Travelling Alone, A Woman's Journey Round the World*, 1890

LEBANON

These most pleasant territories are inhabited by wicked people, but God sent us a faire wind, by which we escaped from them, into whose Ports, if we had been driven, they would have taken all just and unjust occasions to extort money from us, if they did us no worse harme.

Fynes Moryson, *An Itinerary*, 1617

Few persons new to the climate of Syria escape a rash of some description . . . .

Charles Meryon, *Memoirs of the Lady Hester Stanhope*, 1845

These most theologic hills.

R.B. Cunningham Graham, *Mogreb-el-Acksa*, 1898

To be a Levantine is to live in two worlds or more at once, without belonging to either; to be able to go through all the external forms which indicate the possession of a certain nationality, religion, or culture, without actually possessing it. It is no longer to have a standard of values of one's own, not to be able to create, but only to imitate; and so not even to imitate correctly, since that also needs a certain individuality. It is to belong to no community, and to possess nothing of one's own. It reveals itself in lostness, pretentiousness, cynicism and despair.

Albert H. Hourani, *Syria and Lebanon; A Political Essay*, 1946

My Lebanon, which I drew at times so close around me, was a cloak of many colours. Beirut was Levantine to the heart, astute, multilingual, many-minded, and with an element of sheer bawdy wickedness. Tripoli up north beyond the great headland that came out from the mountain and plunged to the sea, was Sunni, fanatic, austere. Tyre and Sidon slept in the sand by the sea. The people of the plain were not the people of the mountain a mile away. The Maronite was no Druze who had in common with the strange Nusairiya only the element of a secret faith restricted to the inner circle of the elders. You passed from one nation to another while going round a bend in the road.

Albion Ross, *Journey of an American*, 1957

Lebanon is too conspicuous and successful an example of political democracy and economic Liberalism to be tolerated in a region that has turned its back on both systems.

Charles Issawi, in L.Binder (ed.), *Politics in Lebanon*, 1966

The monument which characterizes the ethics of Lebanon is . . . the government-operated Casino du Liban, where dollars change hands on the throw of the dice or a turn of the wheel.

Joseph Malone, *The Arab Lands of Western Asia*, 1973

. . . an open forum . . . the country of all the Arabs . . . the only country where an Arab wherever he came from, could feel completely at home.

Kamal Salibi, *Crossroads to Civil War*, 1976

Why should we kid ourselves? This is parvenu nation. We never fought for our independence. We never had a state.

Edouard Saab, quoted by James Markham, *New York Times*, 10 April 1976

There's a story about Lebanon: God made the world in six days, but he worked especially hard on the seventh to create Lebanon. The people of the world objected. Why, God, should such a small country have everything – mountains, beaches, and lovely weather? God answered: but I gave the country its eternal punishment – the Lebanese people.

Lina Mikdadi, 'Letter from Beirut', in the *Guardian*, 21 May 1979

Jokes at the expense of the confessional system abound. One tells of a Maronite officer visiting a platoon remaining inactive on the front line in Palestine in 1948. He asks the lieutenant, a Greek Catholic, why the platoon is not engaged in combat. 'One of our men was just killed,' the lieutenant replies, 'and we are waiting for three Maronites, two Sunni's, two Shi'ites, two Greek Orthodox and one Druze to be killed before we resume action.'

David C. Gordon, *Lebanon the Fragmented Nation*, 1980

The Druses

where the tempest rives the hoary stone
The wintry tops of giant Lebanon.
Fierce, hardy, proud, in conscious freedom bold,
Those stormy seats the warrior Druses hold:
Erom Norman blood their lofty line they trace
Their lion courage proves their generous race.
They, only they, while all around them kneel
In sullen homage to the Thracian steel,
Teach their pale despot's waning Moon to fear
The patriot terrors of the mountain spear.
Yes, valorous chiefs, while yet your sabres shine
The native guard of feeble Palestine,
Oh, ever thus, by no vain boast dismay'd
Defend the birthright of the cedar shade!

Reginald Heber, *Palestine, a Prize Poem*, 1803

Baalbec

At Balbec, as at other eastern ruins, a traveller must luxuriate on the pleasures of imagination, for he will get no luxury more substantial.

John Carne, *Letters from the East*, 1830

Baalbeck is the triumph of stone; of lapidary magnificence on a scale whose language, being still the language of the eye, dwarfs New York into a home of ants. The stone is peach-coloured, and is marked in ruddy gold as the columns of St. Martin-in-the-Fields are marked in soot. It has a marmoreal texture, not transparent, but faintly powdered, like bloom on a plum. Dawn is the time to see it, to look up at the Six Columns, when peach-gold and blue air shine with equal radiance, and even the empty bases that uphold no columns have a living, sun-blest identity against the violet deeps of the firmament. Look up, look up; this quarried flesh, these thrice-enormous shafts, to the broken capitals and the cornice as big as a house, all floating in the blue. Look over the walls, to the green groves of white-stemmed poplars; and over them to the distant Lebanon, a shimmer of mauve and blue and gold and rose. Look along the mountains to the void: the desert, that stony, empty sea. Drink the high air. Stroke the stone with your own soft hands. say goodbye to the West if you own it. And then turn, *tourist*, to the East.

Robert Byron, *The Road to Oxiana*, 1937

Beirut

Since the close of the thirteenth century, few signal events have happened to vary the monotony of her story. But . . . it was here that St. George killed the dragon; exactly when, or what particular dragon I know not, but he *must* have killed him, for he has never been seen since that time, and all agree he is dead.

W.M. Thomson, *The Land and the Book,* 1859

I live here in clear sunshine among damned fools.

James Elroy Flecker, Letter to John Mavrogordato, 10 December 1911

Beirut's a hole to live in but a fine place to get out of.

James Elroy Flecker, Letter to Frank Savery, 10 January 1912

A profound carelessness pervaded the life of Beirut, an empirical, striated disorder and randomness.

John Knowles, *Double Vision: American Thoughts Abroad*, 1964

The Beiruti knows the ways of the West, but it is a small time West although he likes to think of his style as sophisticated and cosmopolitan.

Morroe Berger, *The Arab World Today*, 1964

An artificial Babel.

Henry Tanner, *New York Times*, 9 June 1976

The frequent crises in Beirut, the fighting, the curfew, the bombings, just like the personal attacks one experienced, all seemed to become a matter of routine. A colleague – psychologist – likened us to the frog in a famous experiment, who is put in a pan over a flame. The temperature is increased, but slowly enough so that the frog is given the feeling that while it is hot, he can jump off at any time – until, of course, he is cooked to death. Some of us have jumped off the pan.

David C. Gordon, *Lebanon, the Fragmented Nation*, 1980

Beka'a Valley

The Beka'a is I think the boundary between the Levant and Asia. Where the tiled roofs end and the flat roofs become general, and the Christian churches have no bells, is the beginning; and it is roughly separated from the Mediterranean world by a curtain of wastelands, of which the Syrian-Iraqi desert is the easiest to cross.

Freya Stark, *Beyond Euphrates*, 1951

Litani River

Once upon a geological time the Litani was rushing to mingle his waters with the Jordan's. But then he suddenly changed his mind and swerved off at right-angles westward in search of the Mediterranean. If man-made frontiers were as old as natural ones, you might have fancied that Litani had shied away from Israel and had turned at an angle of ninety degrees in order to keep within the bounds of his native land, the Lebanese Republic.

Arnold Toynbee, *East to West*, 1958

Mount Lebanon (and the cedars)

When we arrived at the place where the cedars grew, we saw but twenty-four in all, growing after the manner of oak trees, but a great deal taller, straighter, and greater, and the branches grow so straight and interlocking, as though they were kept by art . . . . Although that, in the days of Solomon, this mountain was overclad with forests of cedars, yet now there are but only these, and, nine miles westward thence, seventeen more . . . . This mountain . . . is beautified with all the ornaments of nature, as herbage, tillage, pasturage, fructiferous trees, fine fountains, good corns, and absolutely the best wines produced upon the earth.

William Lithgow, *Rare Adventures and Painfull Peregrinations*, 1614/32

After having been told so often that they are ragged and ugly, I am agreeably disappointed in them. There are about 400 of them, some very fine old trees, grass and flowers growing under them – a heavenly camping ground. At this moment it is too delicious: a low sun, birds singing in the great branches and the pale brown, snow-sprinkled hills gleaming behind. We are extremely happy.

Gertrude Bell, Letter to her father, 5 June 1900

Tripoli

This towne standeth under a part of the mountain of Libanus two English miles distant from the port; on the side of which port, trending in forme of an halfe Moone, stand five blocke houses or small forts, wherein is some very good artillery, and the forts are kept with about an hundred Janisaries. Right before this towne from the seaward is a banke of moving sand, which gathereth and increaseth with the Westerne winds, in such sort that, according to an old prophecie among them, this banke is like to swallow up and overwhelm the towne: for every yere it increaseth and eateth up many gardens, although they use all policy to diminish the same and to make it firme grounde. The city is about the bignesse of Bristow, and walled about, though the walles be of no great force. The chiefe strength of the place is in a Citadell, which standeth on the south side within the walles, and overlooketh the whole towne, and is strongly kept with two hundred Janisaries and good artillery. A river passeth thorow the midst of the city, wherewith they water their gardens and mulbery trees, on which there grow abundance of silke wormes, wherewith they make great quantity of very white silke, which is the chiefest naturall commodity to be found in and about this place.

John Eldred (1583), in Richard Hakluyt, *Principal Navigations . . . of the English Nation*, 1598–1600

Tyre

Tyre the crowning city, whose merchants are princes.

The Bible, Isaiah 23:8

I and certain Armenians went to visit this decayed towne, and found the most famous ruines here that the World from memory can afforde, and a delicious encircling harbour, inclosed within the middle of the towne, fitt to receive small barkes, frigates, and galleons: the compassing fore-face being all of squared marble and alabaster stones; the houses used to stand on pillars of the same stones, the infinite number thereof may as yet be (above and below the sands) perspectively beheld. There be only 19 fine houses here, which are Moores.

William Lithgow, *Rare Adventures and Painfull Peregrinations*, 1614/32

As she now is, and has long been, Tyre is God's witness; but great, powerful and populous, she would be the infidel's boast.

W. M. Thomson, *The Land and the Book*, 1859

I have seen old ships sail like swans asleep,
Beyond the village which men still call Tyre.

James Elroy Flecker, *The Old Ships*, 1915 – before 1914

LESOTHO

Basutoland is the Switzerland of South Africa, and very appropriately, is the part of South Africa where the old inhabitants, defended by their hills, have retained the largest measure of freedom.

James Bryce, *Impressions of South Africa*, 1897

Whoever feels for the native, and cares for his future, must wish a fair chance for the experiment that is now being tried in Basutoland of letting him develop in his own way, shielded from the rude pressure of the whites.

Ibid.

An American agricultural engineer visited Basutoland recently, and exclaimed, 'This is the most *beautiful* erosion I have ever seen!'

John Gunther, *Inside Africa*, 1955

If Basutoland has a profile, it is that of a blue saw.

Ibid.

LIBERIA

Mrs Stowe's most frouzy paradise.
Richard Burton, *Wanderings in West Africa*, 1863

The weak point of a knowing African, even in the Land of Freedom, is that he is perpetually outwitting himself.
Ibid.

There is a distinctly Stuart air about the civilization of the Liberian Coast.
Graham Greene, *Journey without Maps*, 1936

All hail, Liberia, hail!
All hail, Liberia, hail!
This glorious land of liberty shall long be ours,
Tho' new her name, green be her fame,
And mighty be her powers.
In joy and gladness with our hearts united,
We'll shout the freedom of a land benighted.
Long live Liberia, happy land,
A home of glorious liberty by God's command.

All hail, Liberia, hail!
All hail, Liberia, hail!
In union strong success is sure we cannot fail
With God above our rights to prove.
We will o'er all prevail.
With heart and hand our country's cause defending.
We'll meet the foe with valour unpretending.
Long live Liberia, happy land,
A home of glorious liberty by God's command.
Liberian Anthem, quoted by Graham Greene, *ibid.*

In the field of *political* corruption Liberia has had some wonderful distinctions. One President of the Republic (not Mr Tubman) got 243,000 votes in a certain election, though only 15,000 persons were privileged to vote. That is really laying it on. It might have happened in Missouri. But not even in Missouri would any politician have quite dared to do what one Liberian candidate for office did in the early 1940's just for fun – he dressed a monkey in a frock coat, took him to the polls, and let him 'vote'.
John Gunther, *Inside Africa*, 1955

Liberia (bad communications plus bad government) offers an extraordinary example of what can be done in the names of Freedom and Democracy when released slaves are turned loose on native Africans who until the said released slaves appeared on the scene had had the good fortune to remain free.
Norman Lewis, *The Changing Sky*, 1959

Liberians

Krumen, near the Cape of Palms
Their appearance struck me as grotesque. Conceive the head of a Socrates upon the body of the Antinous or Apollo Belvidere. A more magnificent development of muscle, such perfect symmetry in the balance of grace and strength, my eyes had never yet looked upon. But the faces! except when lighted up by smiles and good humour – expression to an African face is all in all – nothing could be more unprepossessing. The flat nose, the high cheek-bones, the yellow eyes, the chalky-white teeth pointed like the shark's, the muzzle projecting as that of a dog-monkey, combine to form an unusual amount of ugliness. To this somewhat adds the tribe mark, a blue line of cuts half-an-inch broad, from the forehead-scalp to the nose-tip; in some cases it extends over both lips to the chin; – whence they are called Blue-noses, like our North American friends, not however because inactivity precludes circulation, – whilst a broad arrow or wedge pointed to the fore, and also blue, occupies each temple, just above the zygomata. The marks are made with a knife, little cuts into which the oily smoke of a gum is rubbed. Their bodies are similarly ornamented with stars, European emblems, as anchors, &c., especially with broad double lines down the breast and other parts.
Richard Burton, *Wanderings in West Africa*, 1863

In Sierra Leone, in the bright electric Hill Station, one was conscious under the fans beside the iced drinks of how the land had been subdued; but even in the capital town of Liberia one was aware only of a settlement, a very chancy settlement that might be wiped out at any time by yellow fever. White and black they were living here for a short while on the surface of the land, but Africa had the last say, and it said it in the form of rats and ants, of the forest swallowing up the little pits the Dutch prospectors had made and abandoned. There is not so much virginity in the world that one can afford not to love it when one finds it.
Graham Greene, *Journey without Maps*, 1936

Monrovia

'I understand you can no longer obtain the Russian cigarette in London,' he murmured, helping himself liberally to the whisky. 'Of course in Monrovia we can still manage to get them. At our parties they form a course in themselves.'

'At the end?' asked my companion.

'Oh no. After the fish and before the salad the lights are lowered, and each guest quietly smokes one cigarette.'
Col. Davis, 'The Dictator of Grand Bassa', quoted in Barbara Greene, *Land Benighted*, 1938

The ex-slaves who were the original settlers here built Monrovia in the time-improved image they carried in their minds of the American South. They built with a touching and preposterous affection for Greek columns, porticoes, pilasters and decorative staircases, and a century of Liberian sun and rain has reduced their creations to splendidly theatrical shacks. The bright, slapped-on paint no longer serves to keep up pretence, although Van Gogh would have been in his element here among all the sun-tamed reds and blues and browns . . . . It was Monrovia that taught me the beauty and interest of corrugated iron as a building material, when suitably painted, with its rhythmical troughs of shade. And in Monrovia it is in lavish use.

By night, especially if there is moonlight to put back a little of the colour, the effect is strikingly romantic. The city becomes fragile, its buildings cracked and seamed with the pale internal light of Halloween candles.

Norman Lewis, *The Changing Sky*, 1959

LIBYA

The land of Libya . . . because of over mickle heat is barren and bears no manner of fruit.

John Mandeville, *The Book of John Mandeville*, *c.* 1360

All the Numidians being most ignorant of Naturall, Domesticall, and Commonwealth matters, are principally addicted unto Treason, Trecherie, Murther, Theft and Robberie. This Nation, because it is most slavish, will right gladly accept of any service among the Barbarians, be it never so vile or contemptible . . . . Likewise the Inhabitants of Libya live a brutish kind of life; who neglecting all kinds of good Arts and Sciences, doe wholy apply their minds unto theft and violence. Never as yet had they any Religion, and Lawes, or any good forme of living; but alwaies had, and ever will have a most miserable and distressed life. There cannot any trechery or villanie be invented so damnable, which for lucres sake they dare not attempt. They spend all their dayes either in most lewd practices, or in hunting, or else in warfare; neither weare they any shooes nor garments.

John Leo, on Africa, in *Purchas his Pilgrimes*, 1625

That triumph of imagination, the Libyan Association.

Hilaire Belloc, *The Modern Traveller*, 1898

Is Libya viable? Of course not, unless it manages to stay united and continues to receive foreign aid. Its future, like that of any child, depends on how well it is brought up. Give it names, give it food, give it schooling, and it can develop. This, the newest member of the family of nations, has a useful role to fulfil, and there is no inherent reason why it cannot do so. If it is frail, give it a brace. As a matter of fact it is walking quite briskly already. Libya does not cost very much, and North Africa needs a free country here. The cost of preserving Libya will be less than surrendering it to chaos or to Communism.

John Gunther, *Inside Africa*, 1955

M

MADAGASCAR

Magastar, one of the greatest and richest Isles of the World, three thousand miles in circuit, inhabited by Saracens, governed by foure old men.

Marco Polo (1320), in *Purchas his Pilgrimes*, 1625

MADEIRA

Madera . . . doth rise to him that commeth in the Northnortheast part upright land in the west part of it, and very high: and to the Southsoutheast a low long land, and a long point, with a saddle thorow the middest of it, standing in two and thirtie degrees: and in the West part, many springs of water running downe from the mountaine, and many white fieldes like unto corne fields, & some white houses to the Southeast part of it: and the toppe of the mountain sheweth very ragged, if you may see it, and in the Northeast part there is a bight or bay as though it were a harborow: Also in the said part, there is a rocke a little distance from the shoare, and over the sayd bight you shall see a great gappe in the mountain.

Richard Hakluyt, *Principal Navigations . . . of the English Nation*, 1598–1600

The Island of *Madera* . . . is famous through all our *American* settlements for its excellent wines, which seem to be designed by Providence for the refreshment of the inhabitants of the Torrid Zone.

George Anson (Richard Walter and Benjamin Robins), *A Voyage Round the World, 1740–4*, 1748

The climate is so fine that any man might wish it was in his power to live there under the benefits of English laws and liberty.

Sir Joseph Banks, *Journal of the Rt. Hon. Sir Joseph Banks*, September 1768

I should think the situation of Madeira the most enviable on the whole earth. It ensures almost every European comfort together with almost every tropical luxury. Any degree of temperature may be enjoyed between Funchal and the Ice House. The seasons are the youth, maturity, and old age of a never ending, still beginning spring.

H.N. Coleridge, *Six Months in the West Indies, in 1825*, 1826

Madeira . . . has, and ever will have, one terrible drawback besides extensive humidity. The ennui which it breeds is peculiar; it makes itself felt during a few hours' stay. Little islands are all large prisons: one cannot look at the sea without wishing for the wings of the swallow. This, with usual sense of confinement, combines the feeling of an hospital, or a sick-bay, and one soon sighs to escape from its dreary volcanic rocks. Game is well-nigh shot off, except a few resident partridges . . . . In the season there are balls, concerts, teafights; out of the season, nothing. The theatre is built, but rarely speaks; the opera has to take root; the Turkish bath is unknown; indeed, there is not a bath on the island. Even the English club-rooms are closed at night. I should feel in such a place like a caged hawk; or, to speak more classically, like a Prometheus with the Demon Despair gnawing at my heart.

Richard Burton, *Wanderings in West Africa*, 1863

Madeira is a prison, and a cockneyfied prison: a prison in which you meet 'Town' to boot.

Ibid.

Madeira is the home of wineries,
And extremely expensive embroidered fineries.
I seem to sense a relation tender
Between vintner and embroidery vendor.
Free sample sippings of the grape
Inflate the tourist to a shape
In which, by the time he's embroiled in the embroidery
  imbroglio
He will pay for a dozen doilies the price of an authentic
  First Folio.

Ogden Nash, 'Madeira', in *Everyone but Thee and Me*, 1964

Madeirans

The inhabitants of the towns are more ill favoured than the country people, and often pale and lean. The men wear French clothes, commonly black, which do not seem to fit them, and have been in fashion in the polite world about half a century ago.

George Forster, *A Voyage Round the World*, 1777

The common people of this country are of a tawny colour and well-shaped, though they have large feet, owing perhaps to the efforts they are obliged to make in climbing the craggy paths of this mountainous country.

Ibid.

I could not but observe that the sane residents long settled at Madeira are thin, pale, sub-green-tinted like East Indians, and wearing the regular tropical look. However fit may be the Madeiran atmosphere for men with one lung or a bittock of a lung, it is by no means so well suited to those with a healthy pair. And the fact is that the English constitution cannot thrive without a winter.

Richard Burton, *Wanderings in West Africa*, 1863

Swarthy skins, flat faces, round, stout contours, bon-sens expression, and a wondrous waddle, are here the rule.

Ibid.

Funchal

The town of Funchal stretches along the margin of the bay for nearly a mile and a half, but it is barely a third of that size in breadth in any part. It is by no means so dirty as the Portuguese like, but the English residents are so influential here, that they have been able to exercise a tyranny of cleanliness, which the natives sullenly endure at the hazard of catching colds . . . . The Portuguese ladies in Madeira never wash their faces, and complain that the English destroy their fine complexions by too much water. Dry rubbing is the thing.

H.N. Coleridge, *Six Months in the West Indies, in 1825*, 1826

The town, in fact, is one huge caravanserai, all for hire.

Richard Burton, *Wanderings in West Africa*, 1863

We called at Funchal. Madeira rises out of the dark blue water, an unconvincing, an overstated island. Her gorges and terraces are arbitrarily and improbably disposed. Wisps of cloud pose self-consciously about her peaks. From a grey prosaic beach land soars straight up like a backcloth: a backcloth in the old, the anxiously romantic manner. In the steep and extortionate town, oxen pull sledges through the cobbled streets, deliberately quaint. Morris Cowleys are also to be seen. Indeed, the place has a slightly colonial atmosphere: one feels the need for a Residency. The inhabitants wear buskins, and for the most part carry in their hands a long, black demonic-looking fish, curled in a loop, its tail stuck through its mouth. Madeira contrives to be at once drab and gaudy, at once matter of fact and artificial: like a musical comedy in rehearsal.

Peter Fleming, *Brazilian Adventure*, 1933

The shabby notorious town.

Graham Greene, *Journey without Maps*, 1936

MALAWI

*What did we Africans do to deserve such a poor place to live?

'Dr Hastings Osbong', in Paul Theroux, *Jungle Lovers*, 1971

*It was half-past six, the spectacle of the sun rehearsing its disappearance usual in Malawi: the sun did not drop whole and round behind the earth, but rather broke like an egg low in the sky, making a fiery bloody omelette at the sharp rim of the sky's base. It was this wide thing, not the sun, that set scrap by scrap.

Paul Theroux, *Jungle Lovers*, 1971

MALAYA

The Malay Peninsula, with the climate of a perpetual Turkish bath.

Sir Frank Swettenham, *British Malaya*, 1906

I have come to believe that every country where a man cannot live naked in all seasons, is condemned to work, to war, and to the hampering restraint of moral codes.

R.H. Bruce Lockhart, *Memoirs of a British Agent*, 1932

The most prosaic of all oriental countries.

James Kirkup, *Tropic Temper*, 1963

The Malayan countryside is rather like a rich feast, with a little too much of everything good.

George Woodcock, *Asia, Gods and Cities*, 1966

Malays

The Countrey fast without the Towne belongeth to the Malayos, which is a kind of proud people. They goe naked with a cloth about their middle, and a little roll of cloth about their heads.

Ralph Fitch, *The Voyage*, 1583–91, in *Purchas his Pilgrimes*, 1625

When we were leaving the ship Rogers cautioned me respecting the women, saying, 'Take care of yourself, Bill; the Malays are a dangerous and revengeful people, and you, who are by nature of an amorous disposition, will be looking after the girls, in which case, should any of the men discover you, certainly you will have one of their *creeses* up to the hilt in your guts.' As he said this with great gravity, and I was utterly ignorant of the habits or prejudices of the people I was going amongst, I resolved to keep clear of all amours, and have as little as possible to do with the Malays.

William Hickey, *Memoirs*, 1749–1809

Piracy is well suited to the wild and desperate character

of the Malays, and it may be considered their national profession.

Henry Ellis, *Journal of an Embassy to China*, 1817

Even in his most unregenerate days the Malay dearly loved a real picnic.

Sir Frank Swettenham, *British Malaya*, 1906

The Malay is loyal, for loyalty is part of his creed. He is hospitable, generous, extravagant, a gambler, a cox-comb. He is of fair and quick intelligence, a ready imitator, good at most games and likes to excel, but more inclined to admire the greater skill of a rival than to be jealous of it. He is reserved with strangers, cordial and sympathetic to his friends; he has a strong sense of humour, and makes an excellent companion, equally ready to talk or be silent. As a casual acquaintance he is politely uncommunicative; he will ask a few questions: but seldom give direct answers. Once you have gained his confidence he will probably make no concealments, taking a pleasure in telling you all he can. If he knows you well, he will be almost sure to borrow money from you, and he will seldom find it possible to repay the debt; but he will hold himself ready to undertake any service on your behalf, and you will probably realize in time that the obligation is rather on your side.

Ibid.

and the Chinese community

It was said in Malaysia that if the Chinese as a community became Muslims, the Malays would become Buddhists.

V.S. Naipaul, *Among the Believers*, 1981

Kuala Lumpur

Big City . . . . Le nom de cette ville . . . . Nous croyons entendre: *'l'Impure'* Et nous en restons la.

Jean Cocteau, *Mon Premier Voyage – Tour du Monde en 80 Jours*, 1948 – of 1936

First impressions of Kuala Lumpur. Brighton Pavilion gone mad in a rather dull way, and with nothing like the exquisite treasures. The dumpy Edwardian-Moorish red-brick official buildings look as if they had been constructed from some rich child's bumper box of bricks. The Public Works Department has the temerity to floodlight them . . . Originally a primitive Chinese trading centre, Kuala Lumpur has developed into a colonial city as suburban as Wimbledon.

James Kirkup, *Tropic Temper*, 1963

This sprawling city, where building had not even begun to keep pace with the influx of people since it was metamorphosed from a rubber-opulent provincial town into the capital of one of the richest countries of Asia. A successful metropolis needs either a dramatically planned centre, or a historical tradition made manifest in its buildings. But in Malaya it is Singapore that has the dramatic planning, and Malacca that has the historical tradition. Kuala Lumpur, like the makeshift capitals of so many of the new countries, has neither; it grew so rapidly with the events of the last decade that before anyone had decided what a capital city should be like it has already become too large for effective planning to be feasible.

George Woodcock, *Asia, Gods and Cities*, 1966

Malacca

Whoever is Lord of Malacca has his hand on the throat of Venice.

Tomé Pires, in Armando Cortesao (ed), *The Suma Oriental of Tomé Pires*, 1944 – written 1512–15

Malacca is a Place of no great Trade, yet here are several Moors Merchants always residing here. These have Shops of Wares, such as come from Surrat, and the Coast of Coromandel and Bengal. The Chinese also are seated here, who bring the Commodities of their Country hither, especially Tea, Sugar-candy, and other Sweet-meats. Some of them keep Tea-houses, where for a Stiver, a Man has near a Pint of Tea, and a little Porrenger of Sugar-candy, or other Sweet-meats, if he pleases. Others of them are Butchers: their chief Flesh is Pork, which you may have very reasonably, either fresh or salted: Neither are you desired to take any particular Piece, but they will cut a Piece at one Place, and the like at another, either fat or lean, as you would have it. Others among these Chinese are Tradespeople; and they are all in general very industrious, but withal extraordinary Gamesters: and if they can get any to play with them, all Business must submit to that.

William Dampier, *Voyages and Descriptions*, 1699

Penang

Penang is one of the most beautiful seaside places I have ever seen. It is the Bay of Cannes, with the Estérel heights behind it . . . . But it is a very big Bay of Cannes.

Alfred Viscount Northcliffe, *My Journey Round the World* (December 1921), 1923.

Penang has a certain Sicilian air. It is a sort of Palermo, lacking indeed the architecture and the orange groves, those characteristically Mediterranean amenities, but rich in a tropical wealth of wicker huts and naked children, of coco palms and jungle.

Aldous Huxley, *Jesting Pilate*, 1926

If ever you want a perfect honeymoon spot, a place

where scenery and climate fuse to produce unadulterated witchery, where life has the tremulous sweetness of a plucked lute string and darkness falls all too soon, go to the Hotel Plaza in New York. Of all the lethargic, benighted, somnolent fleabags this side of Hollywood, the port of Georgetown on the island of Penang is the most abysmal.

S. J. Perelman, *Westward Ha!*, 1948

A sweating, heavy-bottomed Englishman in Bermuda shorts sat beside us on the ferry. 'Don't expect too much of Penang,' he jundered. 'Fine-looking place, Pearl of the damned Orient, all that sort of thing. But it's been going downhill ever since *we* gave it up. The trade's finished. Just a damned backwater.' He looked round at me with mildly fanatical eyes. 'Bloody clip joint, too,' he muttered, for my hearing only.

George Woodcock, *Asia, Gods and Cities*, 1966

Ah, Penang! All the vice of the East reduced to a pocket edition. v. convenient.

Duncan Fallowell, Postcard to Justin Wintle, 10 November 1980

Waterfalls near the town

Up on the hillside the voice of the water was saying something, but I was too sleepy to listen; and on the top of the hill lay a fat cloud just like an eiderdown quilt tucking everything in safely . . .

I looked and beheld that I could not give in words the genius of the place . . . See now, go to the very worst of Zola's novels and read there his description of a conservatory. That was it.

Rudyard Kipling, *From Sea to Sea*, 1889

MALDIVE ISLANDS

They are divided into thirteene Provinces, which they call Atollons, which is a naturall partition according to the scituation of the places. Forasmuch as every Atollon is separated from others, and contaynes in it selfe a great multitude of small Iles; it is admirable to behold, how that each of these Atollons are invironed round with a huge ledge of Rockes. The Atollons are all after a sort circular or ovall, having each of them thirtie leagues, some a little more, some a little lesse, and lye all one at the end of the other: from the North to Susans, they almost touch one another: there are betweene two channels of the Sea, the one large, the other exceeding narrow. Being in the middest of an Atollon, you shall see about you a great ledge of Rockes, which impale and defend the Iles, against the impetuousnesse of the Sea. But it is a very fearfull thing even to the most couragious to approach to this ledge, and see the waves come afarre off and breake furiously on every side. For I assure you, as a thing which I have seene a thousand times, that the surge or billow is greater then a House, and as white as Cotton: so that you shall view round about you as it were a very white Wall, especially when the Sea is loftie.

Now within each of these Cantons, is almost an infinite number of Ilands, both smal and great.

François Pyrard de Laval (1602), in *Purchas his Pilgrimes*, 1625

People of

As for the men they can swimme well, which in those parts of the Sea preserves them daily, and to speake truly, they are as it were halfe fishes, they are so used to the Sea, whither they goe daily either swimming, or roading or waling. I have seene them many times within the ledge of Rockes, where the Sea is calme, runne swimming after the fishes, which they have suddenly perceived bathing themselves, and have taken them in their course. And this is usuall. And yet they fail not often to lose their Barkes, notwithstanding all their dexteritie.

François Pyrard de Laval (1602), in *Purchas his Pilgrimes*, 1625

The people are above measure superstitious, and addicted to their Religion: but yet extremely given to women, wanton and riotous. There is nothing commoner than Adulteries, Incest and Sodomie, notwithstanding the rigour of their Lawes and Penalties: As for simple Fornication, there is nothing more ordinarie: they count it not a sinne, neither their Wives, nor Daughters which are not married, make it no great matter to yeeld themselves to their Friends, and after (which is very execrable) to evacuate their Fruit by making an abortion, or destroy their children which are not legitimate. The women are strangely impudent, and the men are not lesse vitious (but they cannot be more) and very effeminate. All their desire is to procure (if they can) some Receit, that they may better content their Wives, and be more strong to exercise their Fornications. I thinke they spend all their goods on this; hereof they continually speake, and are very dissolute in their words, and almost never stirre from their Wives, of whome they have pluralitie, to three, which is the cause they cannot satisfie each of them: also the Aire of the Countrey is hot, and exhales part of their spirits and courage: and also their continually softening their flesh in water, and that the most part eate Opium, or Aphion, as they call it, which tipples, intoxicates and duls them.

Ibid.

MALI

Timbuctoo

To that impracticable place Timbuctoo,

where Geography finds no one to oblige her
With such a chart as may be safely stuck to.

Lord Byron, *Don Juan*, 1819–24

MALTA

It is a whole Rock cover'd with very little Earth.

Lady Mary Wortley Montagu, Letter to the Abbé Conti, 31 July 1718

The industry of the Maltese in cultivating their little island is inconceivable. There is not an inch of ground lost in any part of it; and where there was not soil enough, they have brought over ships and boats loaded with it from Sicily, where there is plenty and to spare. The whole island is full of inclosures and free-stone, which gives the country a very uncouth and very barren aspect; and, in summer, reflects such light and heat, that it is exceedingly disagreeable and offensive to the eyes.

Patrick Brydone, *A Tour through Sicily and Malta*, 1773

I consider Malta as a most important outwork to India.

Horatio Lord Nelson, Dispatch to H. Addington, 28 June 1803

Adieu, ye joys of La Valette!
Adieu, sirocco, sun and sweat!
Adieu, thou palace rarely enter'd!
Adieu, ye mansions where – I've ventured!
Adieu, ye cursed streets of stairs!
(How surely he who mounts you swears!) . . .
And now, O Malta! since thou'st got us,
Thou little military hothouse!
I'll not offend with words uncivil
And wish thee rudely at the Devil
But only stare from out my casement,
And ask, for what is such a place meant?

Lord Byron, Farewell to Malta, 26 May 1811

You know Malta, where there is more magnificence than comfort.

Sir Walter Scott, Letter to James Skene, 25 November 1831, in Lockhart, *Life of Scott*, 1838

When I was in Malta, all animated nature was discordant! The very cats caterwauled more horribly and pertinaciously there than I had ever heard elsewhere. The children will stand and scream inarticulately at each other for an hour together, out of pure love to dissonance. The dogs are deafening, and so throughout . . . . I have hardly gotten rid of the noise yet.

No tongue can describe the moral corruption of the Maltese when the island was surrendered to us. There was not a family in it in which a wife or a daughter was not a kept mistress. A marquis of ancient family applied to Sir Alexander Ball to be appointed his valet. 'My valet!' said Ball, 'what can you mean, Sir?' The marquis said, he hoped he would then have the honour of presenting petitions to his Excellency. 'Oh, that is it, is it!' said Sir Alexander; 'my valet, Sir, brushes my clothes, and brings them to me. If he dared to meddle with matters of public business, I should kick him downstairs.' In short, Malta was an Augean stable, and Ball had all the inclination to be a Hercules.

Samuel Taylor Coleridge, *Table Talk*, 16 April 1834

And so we arrived at Malta. Did you ever hear of one of those eating houses, where, for a certain fee, the guest has the right to make one thrust with a fork into a huge pot, in which the whole dinner is bubbling, getting perhaps a bit of boilet meat, or a potato, or else nothing? Well, when the great cauldron of war is seething, and the nations stand round it striving to fish out something to their purpose from the mess, Britannia always has a great advantage in her trident. Malta is one of the titbits she has impaled with that awful implement.

James Russell Lowell, *Leaves from My Journal in Italy and Elsewhere*, 1854

To many people however Malta ought to be a charming winter residence: for there is every variety of luxury, animal, mineral and vegetable – a Bishop and daughter, pease and artichokes, works in marble and fillagree, red mullet, and Archdeacon, Mandarin Oranges, Admirals and Generals, Marsala Wine 10d. a bottle – religious processions, poodles, geraniums, balls, bacon, baboons, books and what not.

Edward Lear, Letter to Lady Waldegrave, 13 February 1866

Malta is a strange place – a dry, bath-brick island that glares and sets your teeth on edge and is so dry that one expects oneself to begin to crackle.

D. H. Lawrence, Letter to Catherine Carswell, 28 May 1920

Maltese

The peasants or natural inhabitants . . . are of the African complexion, tawny, and sunburnt; and their language like to the Barbarian speech, without any great difference, both tongues being a corrupt Arabic . . . . These rural Malteze are extremely bent, in all their actions, either to good or evil: wanting fortitude of mind, and civil discretion, they cannot temper the violent humours of their passions; but as the headstrong tide, so the dispositions run to the superfluous excess of affections.

They follow the Roman Church, though ignorant of the way; and their women are lovey fair, going with their faces covered with black veils, and much inclined to licentiousness; their beauties being borrowed from art more than from nature.

William Lithgow, *Rare Adventures and Painfull Peregrinations*, 1614/32

As Malta is an epitome of all Europe, and an assemblage of the younger brothers, who are commonly the best, of its first families, it is probably one of the best academies for politeness in this part of the globe; besides, where every one is entitled by law as well as custom, to demand satisfaction for the least breach of it, people are under a necessity of being very exact and circumspect, both with regard to their words and actions.

Patrick Brydone, *A Tour through Sicily and Malta*, 1773

The Maltese a dark, light limbed people – the women 5/10ths ugly – of the remainder 4/5ths would be ordinary but that they look so *quaint* – and 1/10th perhaps may be called quaint-pretty. The prettiest resemble pretty Jewesses in England. – They are the noisiest race under Heaven, & Valetta the noisiest place–:–sudden shot-up explosive *Bellows* – no cries you ever heard in London would give you the faintest Idea of it.

S.T. Coleridge, Letter to Mrs S.T. Coleridge, 5 June 1804

. . . there was something about the appearance of the people that told you – 'here you are in a place of safety.'

John Webster, *Notes of a Journey from London to Constantinople . . .*, 1836

Neither rats nor Jews can exist in Malta. The Maltese are too much for them.

Admiral of the Fleet, Lord Fisher, *Memories*, 1919

Gozo

As Gozzo is supposed to be the celebrated island of Calypso, you may believe we expected something very fine; but we were disappointed. It must either be greatly fallen off since the time she inhabited it, or the archbishop of Cambray, as well as Homer, must have flattered greatly in their painting.

Patrick Brydone, *A Tour through Sicily and Malta*, 1773

Its Coast scenery may truly be called pomskizillious and gromphibberous, being as no words can describe its magnificence.

Edward Lear, Letter to Lady Waldegrave, 13 April 1866

Valletta

The Harbour at Valetta is narrow as the neck of a Bottle in the entrance; but instantly opens out into a Lake with tongues of Land, capes, one little Island, &c, &c, where the whole Navy of England might lie as in a Dock in the worst of weathers – all around it's banks in the form of an amphitheatre rise the magnificent Houses of Valetta, and it's two over-the-water Towns Bormola & Floriana (which are to Valetta what the Borough is to London) – the Houses all lofty & built of white free-stone, something like Bath, only still whiter & *newer*-looking, yet the windows from the prodigious Thickness of the walls being all out of sight, the whole appeared to me as Carthage to Aeneas, a proud City well nigh, but not quite finished.

S.T. Coleridge, Letter to Mrs S.T. Coleridge, 5 June 1804

Fortifications near Valetta

They have likewise invented a kind of ordnance of their own, unknown to all the world besides. For we found, to our no small amazement, that the rocks were not only cut into fortifications, but likewise into artillery to defend those fortifications; being hollowed out in many places into the form of immense mortars. The charge is said to be about a barrel of gunpowder over which they place a large piece of wood, made exactly to fit the mouth of the chamber. On this they heap a great quantity of cannon balls, shells or other deadly materials; and when an enemy's ship approaches the harbour, they fire the whole into the air, and they pretend it produces a very great effect, making a shower for two or three hundred yards round that would sink any vessel.

Patrick Brydone, *A Tour through Sicily and Malta*, 1773

MARQUESAS ISLANDS

Typee

In telling of Typee, the Garden of Eden, I want to lay special stress on this one thing: if ever there was a Garden of Eden, it was right here in this valley. Nowhere else in the world is the climate so perfect, nowhere else in the world can be found the myriads of delicious fruits, nowhere else is there such a provision of wild cattle, goat, turkey, and chicken, to say nothing of the different species of ducks, cranes, storks, and pigeons. One thing that struck me as strange was that the thousands and thousands of pure white doves which soared and floated over our heads showed absolutely no fear of us. It was evident they had never been molested.

Martin Johnson, *Through the South Seas with Jack London*, 1913 (of 1907)

Marquesans

The Inhabitants, to speak of them in general, are the most beautifull race of people I ever beheld – of a great number of men that fell under my inspection, I did not observe a single one either remarkably thin or disagreeably corpulent, but they were all in fine Order & exquisitely proportioned. We saw very few of their Women, but what were seen, were remarkably fair for the situation of their Country and very beautifull – The Men are punctuated (or as they call it tattowed) from head to foot in the prettiest manner that can be conciev'd.

Charles Clerke, *Log of the Proceedings of . . . His Majesty's Ship Resolution*, 1774

They are peculiarly cleanly in regard to the egesta. At the Society Islands, the wanderer's eyes and nose are offended every morning, in the midst of a path, with the natural effects of a sound digestion: but the natives of the Marquesas, are accustomed after the manner of our cats, to bury the offensive objects in the earth. At Taheitee, indeed, they depend on the friendly assistance of rats, who greedily devour these odoriferous dainties; nay, they seemed to be convinced that their custom is the most proper in the world; for their witty countryman, Tupaya (Tupia), found fault with our want of delicacy, when he saw a little building, appropriated to the rites of Cloacina, in every house in Batavia.

George Forster, *A Voyage Round the World*, 1777

The native strength of their constitutions is no way shown more emphatically than in the quantity of sleep they can endure. To many of them, indeed, life is little else than an often interrupted and luxurious nap.

Herman Melville, *Typee*, 1846

It is all a swindle: I chose these isles as having the most beastly population, and they are far better and far more civilised than we. I know one old chief Ko-o-amua, a great cannibal in his day, who ate his enemies even as he walked home from killing 'em, and he is a perfect gentleman, and exceedingly amiable and simple-minded: no fool though.

Robert Louis Stevenson, Letter to Sidney Colvin, July 1888

Polynesian women were notoriously uninhibited, and early European visitors were quick to take advantage of their easy-going attitudes. The people of the Marquesas advanced the ingenious notion that the white race consisted solely of men, who had to travel all the way to the Marquesas in order to have intercourse with women; only their voracious sexual appetite could account for repeated and otherwise inexplicable visits by Europeans.

Claude Nigel Davies, *Voyagers to the New World*, 1979

MARSHALL ISLANDS

Bikini

So we came to Bikini: a typical Pacific coral atoll, several tiny islands, surrounding a lagoon twenty miles long by ten miles wide. The main island, drawing close on the starboard bow, was so precisely the conventional picture of a South Sea Island that it might have been the jacket of a very old novel.

James Cameron, *Point of Departure*, 1967

MARTINIQUE

Martinique is France. Arriving from Trinidad you feel you have crossed not the Caribbean, but the English Channel.

V.S. Naipaul, *The Middle Passage*, 1962

St Pierre (before its destruction by Mont Pelée in 1902)

Upon the whole, St. Pierre is a pretty and civilized town undoubtedly,but scarcely deserving the extravagant commendations which are usually lavished upon it. It has attained the acme of good looks; it can hardly be made more spacious or more convenient in any respect than it is; it is neat and Frenchy,and it cannot be more

H. N. Coleridge, *Six Months in the West Indies, in 1825*, 1826

Imagine old New Orleans, the dear quaint part of it, young and idealized as a master-artist might idealize it, – made all tropical, with narrower and brighter streets; all climbing up the side of a volcanic peak to a tropical forest, or descending in terraces of steps to the sea – fancy our Creole courts filled with giant mangoes and columnar palms (a hundred feet in height sometimes); and everything painted in bright colours, and everybody in a costume of more than Oriental picturesqueness – and astonishments of half-breed beauty – and a grand tepid wind enveloping the city in one perpetual perfumed caress. – Fancy all this and you may have a faint idea of the sweetest, queerest, darlingest little city in the Antilles: – I love it as if it were a human being.

Lafcadio Hearn, Letter to Elizabeth Bisland, July 1887

MAURITANIA

Mauritania a province that hathe been gretelie named by cosmographours past, for thei take this place for the ende of the worlde.

Roger Barlow, *A Brief Summe of Geographie*, *c.* 1540

But Mauretania's giant-shadows frown
From mountain-cliff to coast descending sombre down.
Lord Byron, *Childe Harold's Pilgrimage*, Canto the Second, 1812

To describe Mauretania one needs only to employ the word 'desert'. The inhabitants are mostly Moors, who in olden days were avid and successful slave traders; every year they descended into Senegal, and reaped a crop of human loot. Mauretania has important deposits of iron ore. Also it has exactly two secondary schools.
John Gunther, *Inside Africa*, 1955

As a political entity Mauretania is insignificant. It has about one million inhabitants, who occupy an area of desert which is one-tenth the size of the United States. Its borders follow compass bearings, straight lines on a map, and were laid down after heated argument between two ministries of the same government, the government of imperial France. Its annual rainfall varies between four inches and none, but the great majority of its people still manage to live by stock raising. Nouakchott was originally the site of a Foreign Legion fort, and it still looks more like a camp than a town. The sea is five miles away, but there is no port. The sand blows across the streets and piles up between the shacks of the metropolis; sweeping it into heaps is about the only source of steady employment that the city can offer.
Patrick Marnham, *Fantastic Invasion*, 1980

MAURITIUS

It is a daintie Island of good refreshing for homeward bound shipps, and (in my opinion of an Island not Inhabited) it is the best provided for mans use of any other under the Sunne hitherto found out.
Peter Mundy, *Travels in Europe and Asia*, 1634

This is, by heavens, a Paradise, and not without angels.
Theodore Hook, Letter to Charles Mathews, 24 March 1814

The sloping plain of the Pamplemousses, interspersed with houses, and coloured by the large fields of sugar-cane of a bright green, composed the foreground. The brilliancy of the green was the more remarkable, because it is a colour which generally is conspicuous only from a very short distance. Towards the centre of the island, groups of wooded mountains rose out of this highly-cultivated plain; their summits, as so commonly happens with ancient volcanic rocks, being jagged into the sharpest points. Masses of white clouds were collected around these pinnacles, as if for the sake of pleasing the stranger's eye. The whole island, with its sloping border and central mountains, was adorned with an air of perfect elegance; the scenery, if I may use such an expression, appeared to the sight harmonious.
Charles Darwin, *Journal . . . During the Voyage . . . of H.M.S.Beagle*, 1832–6

What there is of Mauritius is beautiful. You have undulating wide expanses of sugar-cane – a fine fresh green and very pleasant to the eye; and everywhere else you have a ragged luxuriance of tropic vegetation of vivid greens of varying shades, a wild tangle of underbrush, with graceful tall palms lifting their crippled plumes high above it; and you have stretches of shady dense forest, with limpid streams frolicking through them, continually glimpsed and lost, and glimpsed again in the pleasantest hide-and-seek fashion; and you have some tiny mountains, some quaint and picturesque groups of toy-peaks, and a dainty little vest-pocket Matterhorn; and here and there and now and then a strip of sea with a white ruffle of surf breaks into the view.

That is Mauritius; and pretty enough. The details are few, the massed result is charming but not imposing; not riotous, not exciting; it is a Sunday landscape. Perspective, and the enchantments wrought by distance, are wanting. There are no distances; there is no perspective, so to speak. Fifteen miles as the crow flies is the usual limit of vision. Mauritius is a garden and a park combined. It affects one's emotions as gardens and parks affect them. The surface of one's spiritual deeps are pleasantly played upon, the deeps themselves are not reached, not stirred.
Mark Twain, *More Tramps Abroad*, 1897

Island under French control – which means a community which depends upon quarantine for its health, not upon sanitation.
Ibid.

The first year they gather shells; the second year they gather shells and drink; the third year they do not gather shells.
– said of Immigrants to Mauritius.
Ibid.

MEDITERRANEAN

The grand object of travelling is to see the shores of the Mediterranean.
Samuel Johnson, in Boswell, *Life of Johnson*, 11 April 1776

from Albaro
I never saw . . . yet in anything, picture, book, or vestal boredom, such awful, solemn, impenetrable blue, as in that same sea. It has such an absorbing, silent, deep, profound effect, that I can't help thinking it suggested the idea of Styx. It looks as if a draught of it, only so

much as you could scoop up on the beach in the hollow of your hand, would wash out everything else, and make a great blue blank of your intellect.

Charles Dickens, Letter, 1844, in Forster, *Life of Dickens*, 1872–3

I don't like sunshine. I would like a Mediterranean life in a northern climate.

W.H. Auden, Remark, 1953, quoted in Robin Maugham, *Escape from the Shadows*, 1972

MEXICO

The Spanyards have notice of seven cities which old men of the Indians shew them should lie towards the Northwest from Mexico. They have used and use dayly much diligence in seeking of them, but they cannot find any one of them. They say that the witchcraft of the Indians is such, that when they come by these townes they cast a mist upon them, so that they cannot see them.

Henry Hawks, in Richard Hakluyt, *Principal Navigations . . . of the English Nation*, 1598–1600

The Mexican towns we had visited, were in no manner of life different upon this frontier from those of central Mexico. The impression had been of a fixed stagnancy amounting to a slow national decay; the cause, a religious enslavement of the mind, preventing education, communication, and growth, giving rise to bigotry, hypocrisy, political and social tyranny, bad faith, priestly spoliation, and, worst of all, utter degradation of labor.

Frederick Law Olmsted, *A Journey through Texas*, 1857

Napoleon has no right to Mexico. Mexico may deserve a licking. That is possible enough. Most people do. But nobody has any right to lick Mexico except the United States. We have a right, I flatter myself, to lick the entire continent, including ourselves, any time we want to.

Charles F. Browne, *Artemus Ward (His Travels) Among the Mormons*, (1863), 1865

Poor Mexico, so far from God, and so near to the United States!

Porfirio Diaz, attrib.

Good-bye – if you hear of my being stood up against a Mexican wall and shot to rags, please know that I think that a pretty good way to depart this life. It beats old age, disease, or falling down the celler steps. To be a Gringo in Mexico – ah, that is euthanasia!

Ambrose Bierce, Letter, 1 October 1913

Yes, U.S.A., you do put a strain on the nerves. Mexico puts a strain on the temper. Choose which you prefer. Mine's the latter. I'd rather be in a temper than pulled taut . . . .

The old people had a marvellous feeling for snakes and fangs down here in Mexico. And after all, Mexico is only the sort of solar plexus of North America. The great paleface overlay hasn't gone into the soil half an inch. . . . It's a queer continent. The anthropologists may make what prettiness they like out of the myths. But come here, and you'll see that the gods bit. There is none of the phallic preoccupation of the old Mediterranean. Here they hadn't even got as far as hot-blooded sex. Fangs and cold serpent folds, and bird-snakes with fierce cold blood, and claws . . . .

And this is what seems to me the difference between Mexico and the United States. And this is why, it seems to me Mexico exasperates, whereas the U.S.A. puts an unbearable tension on one. Because here in Mexico the fangs are still obvious. Everybody knows the gods are going to bite within the next five minutes. While in the United States, the gods have had their teeth pulled out, and their claws cut, and their tails docked, till they seem like real mild lambs. Yet all the time, inside it's the same old dragon's blood. The same old American dragon's blood.

And that discrepancy of course, is a strain on the human psyche.

D.H. Lawrence, 'Au Revoir U.S.A.', *Laughing Horse* No. 8, 1923, *Phoenix*, 1936

*'It is a country where men despise sex, and live for it,' said Ramon. 'Which is suicide.'

D.H. Lawrence, *The Plumed Serpent*, 1926

Mexico has a faint, physical smell of her own, as each human being has. And this is a curious, inexplicable scent, in which there are resin and perspiration, and sunburned earth, and urine, among other things.

D.H. Lawrence, *Mornings in Mexico*, 1927

In their desire to escape from the horrors of industrial reality, – to escape from, and at the same time to find a remedy for, them – some American thinkers have run forward into the revolutionary future; others back into the pre-industrial past. But in Mexico the pre-industrial past still exists, is contemporary with the industrial depression across the border . . . . Since the depression, books on Mexico have been almost as numerous, I should guess, as books on Russia. The Marxes flee Northwards, the [William] Morrises towards the South . . . . Morris gave his contemporaries *News from Nowhere*; his successors give us news from Mexico.

Aldous Huxley, *Beyond the Mexique Bay*, 1934

After Mexico I shall always associate balconies and politicians – plump men with blue chins wearing soft hats and guns on their hips. They look down from the official balcony in every city all day long with nothing to do but stare with the expression of men keeping an eye on a good thing.

Graham Greene, *The Lawless Roads*, 1939

No hope anywhere: I have never been in a country where you are more aware all the time of hate. Friendship there is skin deep – a protective gesture. That motion of greeting you see everywhere upon the street, the hands outstretched to press the other's arms, the semi-embrace – what is it but the motion of pinioning to keep the other man from his gun? There has always been hate, I suppose, in Mexico, but now it is the official teaching: it has superseded love in the school curriculum. Cynicism, a distrust of men's motive, is the accepted ideology.

Ibid.

Violence came nearer – Mexico is a state of mind.

Ibid.

*Juarez had lived and died. Yet was it a country with free speech, and the guarantee of life, liberty, and the pursuit of happiness? A country of brilliantly muralled schools, and where even each little cold mountain village had its stone open-air stage, and the land was owned by its people free to express their native genius? A country of model farms: of hope? – It was a country of slavery, where human beings were sold like cattle, and its native peoples, the Yaquis, the Papagos, the Tomasachics, exterminated through deportation, or reduced to worse than peonage, their lands in thrall or the hands of foreigners . . . . All this spelt *Porfirio Diaz*: *rurales* everywhere, *jefes politicos*, and murder, the extirpation of liberal political institutions, the army an engine of massacre, and instrument of exile . . . . Yet the banality stood: that the past was irrevocably past. And conscience had been given man to regret it only in so far as that might change the future. For man, every man, even as Mexico, must ceaselessly struggle upward.

Malcolm Lowry, *Under the Volcano*, 1947

It is a land of violence. Thunder and avalanches in the mountains, huge floods and storms on the plains. Volcanoes exploding. The earth shaking and splitting. The woods full of savage beasts and poisonous insects and deadly snakes. Knives are whipped out at a word. Whole families are murdered without any reason. Riots are sudden and bloody and often meaningless. Cars and trucks are driven into each other or over cliffs with an indifference which is half suicidal. Such an energy in destruction. Such an apathy when something has to be mended or built. So much honour in despair. So much weary fatalism toward poverty and disease. The shrug of the shoulders and the faint smile of cynicism. No good. Too late. It's gone. Finished. Broken. They're all dead. Ignore it. Use the other door. Sleep in another room. Throw it in the gutter. Tie the ends together with string. Put up a memorial cross.

What is cooking in there, with such ominous sounds, nobody now alive will ever know. A new race and a new culture, certainly. Perhaps an entirely different kind of language. But whatever it may be, it is cooking. And it will go on doing so, mysteriously, noisily, furiously, through all the bad times that are coming.

Christopher Isherwood, *The Condor and the Cows*, 1949

Mexico is a violent country that has been at peace over forty years. But one is conscious here, as one is in Peru, of a continuing underlying vocation of violence. One feels, indeed, that the Mexicans themselves are aware of it and determined that it shall never break out again as in the bloody time of upheaval that began four years before the First World War and that continues to dominate Mexican public life.

Brian Crozier, 'Latin American Journey', *Encounter*, February 1965

In Mexico, the air grew so oppressive, the sinister totem-Stalinism of that most subtly totalitarian of states so intolerable, that instead of the easy drive North I had promised myself, I did twenty hours flat out to Laredo, and practically kissed the chiliburger-littered macadam of the Customs shed.

Keith Botsford, 'Yanqui Gringo', *Encounter*, September 1965

When I visit Mexico, I feel the same exhilaration that I feel when I visit, say, Western Pakistan. Here is a country whose population is racially diversified yet socially and culturally united. When I see this, I hope that I am having a pre-view of what the whole world – including even the Teutonic-speaking parts of North America and Europe – is going to be like eventually. I can only hope that the Latin-American and Islamic freedom from race-prejudice is 'the wave of the future.'

Arnold Toynbee, 'The Racial Solution', *Encounter*, September 1965

Few countries on earth have greater cause to be xenophobic.

Paul Theroux, *The Old Patagonian Express*, 1979

Mexicans

The people of the countrey are of a good stature, tawny coloured, broad faced, flat nosed, and given much to drinke both wine of Spaine and also a certeine kind of wine which they make with hony of Magueiz and roots, and other things which they use to put into the same. They call the same wine Pulco. They are soone drunke, and given much to beastlinesse, and void of all goodnesse. In their drunkennesse they use and commit Sodomy; and with their mothers and daughters they have their pleasures and pastimes. Whereupon they are defended from the drinking of wines, upon paines of money, aswell he that selleth the wines as the Indian that drinketh the same. And if this commaundement were not, all the wine in Spaine and in France were not sufficient for the West Indies onely.

They are of much simplicity, and great cowards, voide of all valour, and are great witches. They use divers times to talke with the divell, to whom they do certeine sacrifices and oblations: many times they have bene taken with the same, and I have seene them most cruelly punished for that offence. . . .

They say, that they came of the linage of an olde man which came thither in a boat of wood, which they call a canoa. But they cannot tell whether it were before the flood or after, neither can they give any reason of the flood, nor from whence they came.

Henry Hawks (1572), in Richard Hakluyt, *Principal Navigations . . . of the English Nation*, 1598–1600

At first, I confess, almost everybody in the republic looks like a home-made cigar. But when your eyes become properly focussed it is difficult to remember having thought of so cheap a comparison . . . You cannot but admit, after becoming used to the type, that there is among all classes an extraordinary amount of beauty.

Charles Macomb Flandrau, *Viva Mexico*, 1908

An honest Mexican is one who *stays* bought.

Anon. joke, quoted by John Gunther, *Inside U.S.A.*, 1947

Acapulco

The port of *Acapulco* is by much the securest and finest in all the northern parts of the *Pacific* Ocean, being, as it were, a bason surrounded by very high mountains: but the town is a most wretched place, and extremely unhealthy, for the air about it is so pent up by the hills, that it has scarcely any circulation. The place is besides destitute of fresh water, except what is brought from a considerable distance, and is in all respects so inconvenient, that except at the time of the mart, whilst the *Manila* galeon is in the port, it is almost deserted.

George Anson (Richard Walter and Benjamin Robins), *A Voyage Round the World, 1740–4*, 1748

Campeche (Indians of)

They are generally well-shaped, of a middle Size; streight and clean Limbed. The Men more spare, the Women plump and fat, their Faces round and flat, their Foreheads low, their Eyes little, their Noses of a middle Size, somewhat flattish; full Lips, pretty full but little Mouths; white Teeth, and their Colour of a dark tawny, like other Indians. They sleep in Hammocks made with small Cords like a Net, fastned at each End to a Post. Their Furniture is but mean, viz. Earthen Pots to boil their Maiz in, and abundance of Callabashes. They are a very harmless Sort of People; kind to any Strangers; and even to the Spaniards, by whom they are so much kept under, that they are worse than Slaves: nay, the very Negroes will domineer over them; and are countenanced to do so by the Spaniards. This makes them very melancholly and thoughtful: however they are very quiet, and seem contented with their Condition, if they can tolerably subsist: But sometimes when they are imposed on beyond their Ability, they will march off whole Towns, Men, Women, and Children together, as is before related.

William Dampier, *Voyages and Descriptions*, 1699 – of 1676

Chichen Itza (etc.)

Chichen Itza and Mitla and Palenque, the enormous tombstones of history.

Graham Greene, *The Lawless Roads*, 1939

The pyramids of Mexico, – at Teotihuacan and Uxmal and Chichen-Itza – are clearly the efforts of people aspiring to make mountains; they match the landscape and in places mock it. The god-king must demonstrate that he is capable of duplicating divine geography, and the pyramids were the visible proof of this attempt.

Paul Theroux, *The Old Patagonian Express*, 1979

Chololla

Cholalla . . . is a Citie of twenty thousand housholds within the wals; and in the suburbs as much more. It sheweth outwards very beautifull, and full of Towers, for there are as many Temples as dayes in the yeare, and every Temple has his Tower. Our men counted foure hundred Towers. The men and women are of good disposition, well favoured, and very wittie. The women are Goldsmiths and also Carvers, the men are warriers, and light fellowes, and good Maisters for any purpose: they goe better apparelled then any other Indians yet seene.

Francis Lopez de Gomara, *c.* 1552, in *Purchas his Pilgrimes*, 1625

Ejutla (en route to)

Our road wound across vast hills, bare and utterly dry

– the grandiose emblems of a perfect hopelessness. A magnificent landscape; but one looks at it with a sinking heart; there is something profoundly horrifying in this immense, indefinite not-thereness of the Mexican scene.

Aldous Huxley, *Beyond the Mexique Bay*, 1934

Mexico City

It is situated in the middest of a lake of standing water, and environed round about with the same, saving in many places, going out of the Citie, are many broad wayes through the said lake or water. This lake and Citie, is environed also with great mountaines round about, which are in compasse above thirtie leagues and the saide Citie, and lake of standing water, doeth stand in a great plaine in the middest of it . . . . The said Citie of Mexico hath the streetes made very broad, and right, that a man being in the high place, at one ende of the street, may see at least for a good mile forward, and in all the one part of the streets in the North part of their Citie, there runneth a pretie lake of very cleare water, that every man may put into his house as much as he will, without the cost of any thing, but of the letting in. Also there is a great cave or ditch of water, that commeth through the Citie, even unto the high place, where come every morning at the break of the day twentie or thirty Canoas, or troughes of the Indians, which bring in them all maner of provision for the Citie, which is made and groweth in the Countrey, which is a very good commoditie for the inhabitants of the place . . . . The weather is there alwayes very temperate, the day differeth but one houre of length all the yere long. The fields and the woods are alwayes greene. The woods full of popinjays, and many other kinde of birds, that make such an harmonie of singing, and crying, that any man will rejoice to heare it. In the fields are such odoriferous smels of flowers and hearbs that it giveth great content to the senses.

Robert Tomson (1558), in Richard Hakluyt, *Principal Navigations . . . of the English Nation*, 1598–1600

The situation of this city is much like that of Venice, but only differs in this, that Venice is built upon the sea-water, and Mexico upon a lake, which seeming one, is indeed two. One part is standing water; the other ebbeth and floweth according to the wind that bloweth. The part which standeth is wholesome, good, and sweet, and yieldeth store of small fish. That part which ebbeth and floweth is of saltish, bitter, and pestiferous water, yielding no kind of fish, small or great. The sweet water standeth higher than the other, and falleth into it, and reverteth not backward, as some conceive it doth. The salt lake containeth fifteen miles in breadth, and fifteen in length, and more than five and forty in circuit; and the lake of sweet water containeth even as much, so that the whole lake containeth much about a hundred miles . . . .

Their buildings are with stone and brick, very strong, but not high, by reason of the many earthquakes, which would endanger their houses, if they were above three storeys high. The streets are very broad; in the narrowest of them three coaches may go, and in the broader six may go in the breadth of them, which makes the city seem a great deal bigger than it is. In my time it was thought to be of betweene thirty and forty thousand Spaniards, who are so proud and rich that half the city was judged to keep coaches . . . . It is a by-word that at Mexico four things are fair; that is to say, the women, the apparel, the horses, and the streets. But to this I add the beauty of the coaches of some of the gentry . . . for they spare no silver, nor gold, nor precious stones, nor cloth of gold, nor the best silks from China to enrich them. And to the gallantry of their horses the pride of some doth add the cost of bridles and shoes of silver.

The streets of Christendom must not compare with those in breadth and cleanness, but especially in the riches of the shops which do adorn them. Above all, the goldsmiths' shops and works are to be admired. The Indians, and the people of China that have been made Christians and every year come thither, have perfected the Spaniards in that trade.

Thomas Gage, *The English-American . . . or, A New Survey of the West Indies*, 1648 – of 1626

I have grown rather tired of reading in magazines that 'the city of Mexico resembles a bit of Paris' – particularly as the City of Mexico doesn't in the least resemble a bit of Paris. It resembles absolutely nothing in the wide world except itself. To criticise it as having most of the objectionable features and few of the attractions of a great city would be unfair; but first telling myself that I *am* unfair, I always think of it in those terms. In truth it is a great and wonderful city and it grows more wonderful every day; also, I am inclined to believe, more disagreeable . . . . When it finally burst upon me in all its shallow brilliancy, I felt that I was no longer in Mexico, but without the compensation of seeming to be somewhere else. I certainly did not seem to be in Paris . . . . It remained extremely interesting – geographically, historically, architecturally – but it was oddly lacking in the one quality everybody is led to believe it has in a superlative degree – . . . the City of Mexico lacks the indefinable quality that makes one either desirous of putting on one's best clothes, or regretful that one has not better clothes to put on. . . . The place has upon one – it has at least upon me – the effect of something new and indeterminate and mongrel, which for a city founded in 1522 is a decidedly curious effect to exert.

Charles Macomb Flandrau, *Viva Mexico*, 1908

This city doesn't feel *right* – feels like a criminal plotting his next rather mean crime.

D.H. Lawrence, *c.* 1924, quoted in Graham Greene, *The Lawless Roads*, 1939

It is a stunningly grand centre, with a scatter of abysmal squalor round its hems, like a mother who keeps herself in style at the expense of her children.

William McIlvanney, 'The Tartan Trail to Argentina', *Observer*, 28 May 1978

Nuevo Laredo

They called this Nuevo Laredo to distinguish it from the town in Texas, but as so often happens the son looked older than the father, more acquainted with the seamy side of life.

Graham Greene, *The Lawless Roads*, 1939

Oaxaca to Puebla

The journey from Oaxaca to Puebla is so frightful that its frightfulness describes, so to speak, a full circle and comes out at the other end of the qualitative barometer as a joke.

Aldous Huxley, *Beyond the Mexique Bay*, 1934

Palenque (ruined city of)

Here were the remains of a cultivated, polished and peculiar people, who had passed through all the stages incident to the rise and fall of nations; reached their golden age, and perished, entirely unknown. The links which connected them with the human family were severed and lost, and these were the only memorials of their footsteps upon earth . . . often we imagined a scene of unique and gorgeous beauty and magnificence, realizing the creations of Oriental poets, the very spot which fancy would have selected for the 'Happy Valley' of Rasselas. In the romance of the world's history nothing ever impressed me more forcibly than the spectacle of this once great and lovely city, overturned, desolate, and lost; discovered by accident, overgrown with trees for miles around, and without even a name to distinguish it.

J.L. Stephens, *Incidents of Travel in Central America, Chiapas and Yucatan*, 1841, 1842

Popocatapetl

The name indeed of the colossal mountain which dominates the city of Mexico is not very easy to pronounce, and it is well to adopt the mnemonic formula invented by an American traveller (was it General Grant, or the late Commodore Wyse?) 'Pop the cat in the kettle.' There you have 'Popocatapetl' in the twinkling of a tongue.

G.A. Sala, *America Revisited*, 1882

Puebla

Puebla, in the eighteenth century, developed a style of domestic architecture all its own. The model was that Andalusian classic of which you may see such admirable specimens at San Fernando, near Cadiz, and at Ronda and Arcos; but the Pueblans embroidered on this originally austere architectural scheme till it became something altogether new, something extravagant and wholly fantastic.

Pueblan houses are tall . . . and are built, in the ordinary Spanish way, round an arcaded patio. Their originality lies in the façades they turn towards the street. They are made of brick, alternating with brilliant yellow-and-white or blue-and-white *azulejos*. In many cases the bricks are arranged in elaborate herring-bone patterns, with a bright tile at the centre of each diamond or lozenge thus formed. The colours, in their pied gaiety, have something mediaeval about them; but all of the forms are incongruously neo-Roman. The proportions (and how rare this is in Mexico!) are classically correct. Classical too, are the heavily carved stone cornices, the stone escutcheons over the entrance doors, the stone frames round each window. It is as though Sir Christopher Wren had dressed up as Benozzo Gozzoli. The effect is extremely queer; but also, which is more remarkable, extremely charming.

Aldous Huxley, *Beyond the Mexique Bay*, 1934

Puebla was the only Mexican town in which it seemed to me possible to live with some happiness. It had more than the usual beauty: it had grace. Something French seemed to linger there from Maximilian's time.

Graham Greene, *The Lawless Roads*, 1939

Tabasco (El Frontera/Puerto Obregon)

El Frontera itself was out of sight round a river bend: three or four aerials stuck up into the blazing sky from among the banana groves and the palm-leaf huts: it was like Africa seeing itself in a mirror across the Atlantic. Little islands of lily plants came floating down from the interior, and the carcasses of old stranded steamers held up the banks.

Graham Green, *The Lawless Roads*, 1939

Taxco

Taxco is a sort of Mexican Saint-Paul largely inhabited

by artists and by those camp-followers of the arts whose main contribution to the cause of Intellectual Beauty consists in being partially or completely drunk for several hours each day. In the eighteenth century, Borda, the mining millionaire, built for Taxco one of the most sumptuous churches in Mexico – one of the most sumptuous and one of the most ugly. I have never seen a building in which every part, down to the smallest decorative detail, was so consistently ill-proportioned. Borda's church is an inverted work of genius.

Aldous Huxley, *Beyond the Mexique Bay*, 1934

Vera Cruz

In this towne of Vera Cruz within these twenty yeres, when women were brought to bed, the children new born incontinently died; which is not so now in these dayes, God be thanked.

This towne is inclined to many kinde of diseases, by reason of the great heat, and a certeine gnat or flie which they call a musquito, which biteth both men and women in their sleepe; and assoone as they are bitten, incontinently the flesh swelleth as though they had bene bitten with some venimous worme. And this musquito or gnat doth most follow such as are newly come into the countrey. Many there are that die of this annoyance.

This towne is situated upon the river aforesayd, and compassed with rivers of divers maners and sorts, and many fruits, as orenges and limons, guiaves and divers others, and birds in them, popinjayes both small and great, and some of them as big as a raven and their tailes as long as the taile of a fezant. There are also many other kinde of birds of purple colour, and small munkeys, marvellous proper.

Henry Hawks (1572), in Richard Hakluyt, *Principal Navigations . . . of the English Nation*, 1598–1600

The Castle of San Juan de Ulua . . . contains a permanent exhibit of Veracruz's past, a pictorial record of invasions, punitive missions and local military defeats. It was that most Mexican of enthusiasms – humiliation as history. . . . Veracruz is known as 'the heroic city'. It is a poignant description: in Mexico a hero is nearly always a corpse.

Paul Theroux, *The Old Patagonian Express*, 1979

Villahermosa

I went and saw the Chief of Police, a big blond cheery creature with curly hair, dressed too tightly in white drill with a holster at his fat hip. He laughed aloud when he saw my passport, putting an arm round my shoulder with that false Mexican camaraderie. 'That's fine,' he said, 'fine. You've come home. Why, everybody in Villahermosa is called Greene – or Graham.'

'Are there English people in the town then?'

'No, no,' he said. 'The Greenes are Mexican.'

Graham Greene, *The Lawless Roads*, 1939

Yucatan (also in part Guatemala and Belize)

This Realme of Yucatan was full of inhabitants; for that it was a Countrie in every respect wholesome, and abounding in plentie of victuals, and of fruites more then Mexico; and singularly exceeded for the abundance of Honie and Waxe there to be found, more then in any quarter of the Indies, which hath beene seene unto this present . . . . The people of that Countrie were the most notable of all the Indies, as well in consideration of their policie, and prudencie, as for the uprightnesse of their life, verily worthy the training of the knowledge of God: amongst whom there might have beene builded great Cities by the Spanish, in which they might have lived as in an earthly Paradise, if so be they had not made themselves unworthy, because of their exceeding covetousnesse, hard hartednesse, and heinous offences: as also unworthy they were of other moe blessings a great many which God had set open in these Indies.

Bartholomew de las Casas, 1542, in *Purchas his Pilgrimes*, 1625

Yucatan received the name from . . . the first discoverers asking the place, the Indian answering tectetan, tectetan, that is, I understand you not, which they understood of the proper appellation, and corruptly called the place Yucatan.

Garcilasso de la Vega, *c.*1580, in *Purchas his Pilgrimes*, 1625

MEXICO, GULF OF

Echo beyond the Mexique Bay.

Andrew Marvell, *Bermudas*, *c.* 1650

The Gulf of Mexico was flat and dark blue and finely wrinkled by a steady breeze. It was as though we were gliding over an endless expanse of blue morocco leather, over the sumptuous, royal binding of some enormous folio. A book, I thought, as I looked over the rail. And what is written within? *Quien sabe*?

Aldous Huxley, *Beyond the Mexique Bay*, 1934

MINORCA (Spain)

Minorca in general has one astounding historical quality. History becomes *alive* there . . . . One may be strolling along a Spanish street of low adobe houses and dust, of acacias in bloom and the smell of oil frying over charcoal, and suddenly stop arrested by a chorus piped in high children's voices, English words sounding from laughing brown faces: 'All fall down'. And there in the dust are several dark-skinned Minorcan children certainly falling down. They have been playing ring-a-ring-o'-roses. The first lines of the old plague-song turned nursery rhyme were sung in *menorquín* dialect, the last line in English. Yet the English . . . sailed away in the first decade of the nineteenth century . . . and they have not been back since.

William Sansom, *Blue Skies, Brown Studies*, 1961

MONACO

The present Prince of Monaco lives almost always at Paris, so that the palace looked desolate, like the house of a Scots laird who lives in England.

James Boswell, *Journal*, 15 December 1765

If, having passed no customs barrier, you find that the streets seem to have received a Hollander's scrubbing, and the post boxes to have been repainted overnight with Swiss-clean silver, and each blade of grass in the park gives the sensation of a nursery gardener's personal attention, and there is less garden space than usual – then you are in the Principality of Monaco . . . . Fantastic, giddy, dizzy, crazy, enchanting – supremely artificial and without the vegetation that softens similar extravagancies along the rest of the coast. Cyclamen faience balconies, turquoise urns, gold moorish tiles, a sunbaked hotel called Balmoral, the whorled icing of the Casino with its elegant lavender lamps on Suicide Terrace and its brown, hushed inside. And the Gas Works, the Palace, the Beer Factory – it is all still there, whoever owns it.

William Sansom, *Blue Skies, Brown Studies*, 1961

'Safe,' he repeated. 'You see – it's so small. Europe, the outside world is getting bigger and harder to understand every day – but here we have limits, reasonable limits within which a man can live.'

Ibid.

Monte Carlo

The first visit to Monte Carlo must be a sort of event in the life of anyone with imagination . . . .

On the whole I was disappointed, by the exterior aspects of the town. It lacks spaciousness, and since it is in the absolute control of one autocratic authority, spaciousness is what it ought not to have lacked. Some of the villas however, with their white paint and general air of being toys, are *excessivement chic*. The casino is all right in its florid, heavy way – but what a chance for an architect, on that site over the sea! The whole town had an air of being Parisian, but not quite Parisian enough.

Arnold Bennett, *Journal*, 26 January 1904

Whoever wants to see flowers and trees on their best behaviour, must come to Monte Carlo, where the spick-and-span Riviera note is at its highest development. Not a leaf is out of place; they have evidently been groomed and tubbed and manicured from the hour of their birth. And yet – is it possible? Lurking among all this modern splendour of vegetation, as though ashamed to show their faces, may be discerned a few lowly olive trees. Well may they skulk! For these are the Todahs and Veddahs, the aboriginals of Monte Carlo, who peopled its sunny slopes in the long-forgotten days of rustic life – once lords of the soil, now pariahs. What are they doing here? And how comes it that the eyesore has not yet been detected and uprooted by those keen-sighted authorities that perform such wonders in making the visitor feel at home, and hush up with miraculous dexterity everything in the nature of a public scandal.

Norman Douglas, *Alone*, 1921

Here in Monte Carlo, where we have to take amusement seriously, there is not much to laugh at.

Anthony Burgess, *Observer*, 28 May 1978

In Monte Carlo, and especially among tax exiles, one does not choose friends. It's a bit like being in prison. You talk to the people you're thrown in with.

'Taki', *Spectator*, 20 December 1980

MONGOLIA

Outer Mongolia . . . is such *terra incognita* that Tibet is practically Coney Island by comparison

John Gunther, *Inside Asia*, 1939

Mongols

Tea even fails to thaw completely their reserve.

James Gilmour, *Among the Mongols*, 1884

I was sadly disappointed, I must own, in the Mongolian Tartar. I had pictured him a wild, fierce-looking fellow, bristling with knives and firearms, and leading a wild, romantic existence, of which privation and danger formed a daily part. I found him a mild, stupid-looking individual, lazy, good-tempered, dirty – not to say filthy – in appearance and habits, and addicted to petty theft when there was no fear of being found out.

The men are of middle size, muscular and stoutly built, with thick lips and small beady black eyes. Naturally fair, the combined effects of sun, argol smoke and last, but not least, dirt give to most of them the hue of the negro. Their women are plain, and, as a rule, virtuous.

Harry de Windt, *From Pekin to Calais by Land*, 1889

They have bitten very widely into history, though the bite is not deep.

John Gunther, *Inside Asia*, 1939

Gobi Desert

The Great Hungry Desert.

Chinese name, quoted Harry de Windt, *From Pekin to Calais by Land*, 1889

I retired to my cart about five o'clock for a rest . . . and fell asleep. The sun was low in the heavens when I awoke and looked out of the little window. All traces of vegetation had vanished . . . on the far side of the sand-hills the sea, or what appeared so exactly like it, that I had to rub my eyes to make sure I was not dreaming. There it was; the great grey waste looking exactly as it does when lit up at sunset, by the rays of the setting sun after a hot summer's day in England. The low yellow sand-hills, too, heightened the illusion, and stood out clear and distinct against the grey expanse and level, unbroken horizon.

Harry de Windt, *From Pekin to Calais by Land*, 1889

Ulan Bator (formerly Ourga)

Ourga can scarcely be called a city in the true acceptance of the term. Its Mongol name, 'Ta Huren', or 'The Encampment,' better describes the huge cluster of tents that compose the Mongolian capital, dwellings precisely similar in shape and size to those in the desert, save that here they are surrounded by rough wooden palisades, eight to ten feet in height, as a protection against the thieves and marauders who in the caravan season nightly infest the streets . . . .

At a short distance Ourga presents the appearance of some huge fair. The white tents, blue and gold temples, and gaudy prayer-flags, gave us at first sight a pleasing impression of the place, which was, however, speedily dispelled on closer acquaintance with its dismal-looking streets, deserted save by beggars and dogs, and the hideous customs practised day and night by its strange population.

Harry de Windt, *From Pekin to Calais by Land*, 1889

It was Petroff who first called my attention to a faint sickly odour I had noticed on and off all the afternoon during our peregrinations, a hot pungent smell as of decaying matter, which I had detected in my bedroom at the Consulate the day before, and which seemed to pursue one everywhere in and about Ourga. 'You had better light a cigarette,' said the colonel, offering me his case. 'It is always worse on these damp evenings.'

'Do you mean to say the Consul has not told you of our Golgotha,' he continued, as soon as we were fairly alight. . . . 'Why, it is the sight of the place. There is just time before dinner; we will ride home that way.'

I was no longer surprised after my visit to 'Golgotha' . . . where hundreds of corpses lay rotting above ground, that the city of Ourga did not smell as sweet as one could wish. My only surprise is, after visiting the spot in question, that plague is not always raging in a city where the inhabitants never dream of burying their dead, but carry them to a spot not three hundred yards from the gates, and there let them slowly decompose in the open air.

It would be impossible to imagine a more horrible spectacle than met our eyes on arriving at Golgotha, an open space or cleft between two low green hillocks just outside Ourga, a valley literally crammed with corpses in every stage of decomposition, from the bleached bones of skeletons that had lain there for years, to the disfigured, shapeless masses of flesh that had been living beings but a few days or hours ago. The moon shed a pale. unearthly light over the grinning skulls and grey upturned faces of the dead, some of whom lay stark and stiff, just as they had been left by their friends, others with their blue shrouds ragged and torn, with disfigured faces and twisted limbs, lying in the horribly grotesque positions in which the dogs or wolves had dragged them. Near us was the body of a woman that had lain there but a few hours, Petroff said, judging from the clean and untorn appearance of her shroud. A little further off a number of huge dogs were fighting and snarling over the remains of a child. Overhead great carrion birds were flapping their huge black wings, occasionally swooping down, with a hoarse croak, to bury beak and talon in some newly arrived corpse. The very ground we trod on was composed of human bones which crunched under our ponies' feet as we rode a short distance up the narrow, ghastly defile. The stench was awful. I can never think of the place even now without a shudder, and devoutly wish I had never seen it. The Mongol is, at any rate, free from an evil which always more or less threatens us of superior civilization – that of being buried alive.

Ibid.

MONTSERRAT

The negros here have an Irish accent, which grafted on negro English forms the most diverting jargon I ever heard in my life.

H.N. Coleridge, *Six Months in the West Indies, in 1825*, 1826

I have had a chance also to experience some of the

extraordinary physical aspects of this island, which, no matter how well they are explained, you still don't quite believe. I've had three weeks to get used to a world in which the temperature shifts from five minutes to five minutes, in which you may have your own private rainstorm beating down, and half a mile away in three directions, you see the bluest sky and the calmest sea and sunlight resting on the hilltops. The formation of the mountains changes all the time, as the shifting clouds bring out the different patterns, and no one knows whether it will rain here or there or nowhere at all in the next ten minutes as the sea suddenly turns winedark and threatening from your viewpoint, floating on its surface. On no island I have ever lived has there been such a simultaneity of microclimates, all visible at once.

Margaret Mead, Letter from Montserrat, 2 September 1966

MOROCCO

A visit to Morocco must be considered as an Epilogue, or preface to *a tour through Spain.*

H. O'Shea, *A Guide to Spain,* 1865

In Morocco the prevailing tone is greyish white, men's clothes, and houses, towns, bushes, tall umbelliferae, nodding like ghosts in autumn, all are white; white sands upon the shore, and in the Sahara, and over all a white and saddening light, as if the sun was tired with shining down for ever on the unchanging life.

R.B. Cunningham Graham, *Mogreb-el-Acksa,* 1898

Morocco is a cold country with a hot sun.

Marshal Louis Hubert Gonzalve Lyautey, attrib.

Marshal Lyautey in his blunt way divided Morocco into two parts – 'Maroc Utile,' and the rest of the country.

John Gunther, *Inside Africa*, 1955

Morocco, too, in her day, has been, like Britain, an 'Ultima Thule', marooned at the extremity of the civilised world.

Arnold Toynbee, *Between Niger and Nile*, 1965

Morocco is like a tree nourished by roots deep in the soil of Africa which breathes through foliage rustling to the winds of Europe. Yet Morocco's existence is not only vertical. Horizontally it looks to the East, with which it is bound by ties of religion and culture. Even if we wished to sever those ties – and we do not wish to, – it would be impossible.

King Hassan II of Morocco, *Le Défi*, translated Anthony Rhodes as *The Challenge*, 1979

Moroccans

Consider whether, if all the world were regulated by a duly-elected county council, all chosen from a properly qualified, and democratic, well-educated, pious electorate, and all men went about minding each other's business – with fornication, covetousness, evil concupiscence, adultery, and murder quite unknown, and only slander and a little cheating left to give a zest to life – they would be happier upon the whole than are the unregenerate Moors, who lie and steal, fight, fornicate, and generally behave as if blood circulated in their veins and not sour whey?

R.B. Cunningham Graham, *Mogreb-el-Acksa,* 1898

The Arab dress in windy weather teaches one what women undergo in petticoats upon a boisterous day, but still their pains are mitigated by the fact that generally men are near at hand to look at them whereas we could not expect to find admiring ladies on the bleak limestone plain.

Ibid.

A Tunisian is a Tunisian, but a Moroccan can be a lot of things.

John Gunther, *Inside Africa*, 1955

Arabs in the Kasbah Country of the High Atlas
Around a sharp bend sat a row of crouching Arabs, and I reflected for the fortieth time that these can be the most fixed and immobile people on earth. They might have been white rocks, stone markers to keep us from going off the cliff. Then I saw that they were not Arabs at all; they *were* white rocks.

John Gunther, *Inside Africa*, 1955

Casablanca

At Casa Blanca . . . Consuls abound, of course, so do hyenas – that is outside the town – but both are harmless and furnish little sport.

R.B. Cunningham Graham, *Mogreb-el-Acksa,* 1898

Up to the time that we contemplated making this picture, I had no idea that the city of Casablanca belonged exclusively to Warner Brothers.

Groucho Marx, Letter to Warner Brothers, *c.* 1941
(Warners tried to stop the Marx brothers using the name Casablanca in a film title, to protect their investment in *Casablanca*, the Bogart/ Bergman vehicle)

Fez

This city of Fez is situate upon the bodies and twice

double sloping faces of two hills, like to Granada in Andalusia in Spain, the interval or low valley between both (through which the torrid river of Murraheba runneth southward) being the centre and chief place, is the most beautiful and populous part of the city; the situation of which, and of the whole, is just set under the tropic of Cancer.

Over which river, and in this bottom, there are sixty-seven bridges of stone and timber, each of them being a passage for open streets on both sides. The interval consisteth of two miles in length, and half a mile broad; wherein, besides five Chercaffs, or market-places, there are great palaces, magnificent mosques, colleges, hospitals, and a hundred palatiate taverns, the worst whereof may lodge a monarch's train. Most part of all which buildings are three and four stories high, adorned with large and open windows, long galleries, spacious chambers, and the streets being covered above, betwixt these plainset fabrics, have large lights cut through the textured tops everywhere; in whose lower shops or rooms are infinite merchandise, and ware of all sorts, to be sold.

The people of both kinds are cloathed in long breeches and bare ankles, with red or yellow shoes, shod with iron on the heels, and on the toes with white horn; and wear on their bodies long robes of linen or dimity, and silken waistcoats of divers colours . . . . The women here go unmasked abroad, wearing on their heads broad and round caps, made of straw or small reeds, to shade their faces from the sun; and damnable libidinous, being prepared both ways to satisfy the lust of their luxurious villains; neither are they so strictly kept as the Turkish women, marching where they please.

There are twelve thousand allowed brothel-houses in this town, the courtesans being neatly kept, and weekly well looked to by physicians; but worst of all, in the summer-time, they openly licentiate three thousand common stews of sodomitical boys; nay, I have seen at mid-day, in the very market-places, the Moors buggering these filthy carrions, and, without shame of punishment, go freely away . . . .

The two hills on both sides of the planured city, east and west, are overclad with streets and houses of two stories high, being beautified also with delicate gardens, and on their extreme sloping parts, with numbers of mosques and watch-towers; on which heights, and about the town, there stand three hundred wind-mills, most part whereof pertain to the mosques, and the two magnificent colleges erected for the education of children in the Mahometan law . . . .

This city aboundeth in all manner of provision fit for man or beast, and is the goodliest place of all north Afric, containing an hundred and twenty thousand fire-houses, and in them a million of souls. Truly this is a world of a city, and may rather second Grand Cairo, than subjoin itself to Constantinople, being far superior in greatness to Aleppo. For these are the four greatest cities that ever I saw, in the world, either at home or abroad.

William Lithgow, *Rare Adventures and Painfull Peregrinations*, 1614/32

Fez,
Where all is Eden, or a wilderness.

There the large olive rains its amber store
In marble fonts; there grain and flower and fruit
Gush from the earth until the land runs o'er;
But there too many a poison-tree has root,
And midnight listens to the lion's roar,
And long, long deserts scorch the camel's foot
Or heaving whelm the helpless caravan.
And as the soil is, so the heart of man.

Lord Byron, *Don Juan*, 1819–24

If you like your romance dark, Fez is probably the most romantic city on earth. It might have been dreamed up by Edgar Allan Poe – almost sinister in its secretiveness, a twisted city, warped and closed.

John Gunther, *Inside Africa*, 1955

Marrakesh

Fez is Europe but closed; Marrakesh is Africa, but open. Fez is black, white, and grey; Marrakesh is red.

John Gunther, *Inside Africa*, 1955

The bus to Marrakesh, Morocco,
Traverses landscapes simply socko.
The agricultural economy
Suggests the Book of Deuteronomy.
The machine has not replaced the mammal,
And everything is done by camel.
I hope I'll never learn what flesh
I ate that day in Marrakesh,
But after struggling with a jawful
I thought it tasted humpthing awful.

Ogden Nash, 'Morocco', in *Everything but Thee and Me*, 1964

and Mazaghan, etc.
How large a part, I thought, the light of the African sun plays in the infinite horror of African cities, as I have seen them, and yet how greatly it varies! There are the white lights that play on Oran, city of half-castes and mean whites on the eternal fringe of things; the scintillating, quivering images of the dried salt lakes that constitute an unreal approach to the desert city of Tozeur, lying under the grape-bloom edges of the sky, where it touches the sand; even in so distant Marrakesh, in many repects the ideal African city of water-lawns, cool, pillared palaces and orange groves, situated in a superb oasis between two snow-capped ranges, the strong rays momentarily expose an age-old squalor lying only just under the surface; while, not far

from Marrakesh, in Mazaghan, that city the very name of which sounds as though it contained within it the rolling of drums for executions, a curious yellow light runs like grease over the broken stone houses, and over the great Atlantic waves themselves, pounding so endlessly upon the deserted, thick yellow sands.

Osbert Sitwell, *Escape with Me*, 1939

Tangier

The white walls of Tangiers glitter on the opposite coast, resting like a snow-wreath, on dark mountains.

Richard Ford, *A Handbook for Travellers in Spain*, 3rd edn, 1855

Tangier the White . . . posted like a sentinel on the most northern part of Africa.

Pierre Loti (trans. W. P. Baines), *Morocco*, 1914

It was the nearest thing to the Glamorous East I had seen outside of the Fox Westwood Hills lot. You had to wonder whether in such a case the movies were any longer borrowing from life, or it was life now that took its cue from Hollywood, trying to live up to the reputation the films had given it.

The movies could not have done it better than Tangier did it.

Cedric Belfrage, *Away from It All*, 1936

I was a bit disappointed that the city didn't seem as beautiful as it used to. I remember such wonderful coloured walls – very pale blue and pink and white, like marshmallow.

Cecil Beaton, *The Strenuous Years*, 1973 – of 1949

For anybody inclined to be a crook, Tangier . . . offers a setting almost too perfect to be believed, although four different codes of law are in force.

John Gunther, *Inside Africa*, 1955

It is uncertain . . . whether Tangier was named after the fruit, or vice versa. Actually tangerines are called mandarins in Tangier.

Ibid.

Women of

I have caught a glimpse of the faces of several Moorish women (for they are only human, and will expose their faces for the admiration of a Christian dog when no male Moor is by), and I am full of veneration for the wisdom that leads them to cover up such atrocious ugliness.

Mark Twain, *The Innocents Abroad*, 1869

Tarudant

As the Sherif explained, 'the town looks like a silver cup dropped in a tuft of grass.' This, as I did not see it, I take on trust, believing perhaps that Moses had died happier had he not had the view from Pisgah's summit over the plains of Canaan.

R. B. Cunningham Graham, *Mogreb-el-Acksa*, 1898

Telouet

I have various images of Telouet. The last and most enduring is after a great snowfall when more than four thousand sheep and goats in the surrounding mountains were buried and killed by suffocation. When the snows thawed and the carcases were exposed every vulture, kite and raven congregated on Telouet. As the sun went down the air was dark with them as with a swarm of locusts; they homed for Telouet in their thousands, like starlings to Trafalgar Square, till the branches of the trees broke under them, till the battlements of the castle were foul with their excreta, and still, as the last of the light went, the black wings were thronging to alight and jostle their neighbours. It was on that night that, listening to the jackals howling, I became lost in the castle, and found my torch shining upon white but manacled bones in a dungeon. With the turbulent history of Telouet they could have been either a hundred or less than five years old.

Gavin Maxwell, *Lords of the Atlas*, 1966

Tindoof

I urged the old Persian . . . to tell of . . . the Oasis of Tindoof, which he described by smoothing his hand upon the sand to show the flatness of it, and then said, 'Tindoof walou,' that is, in Tindoof, nothing; though he confessed it is the mouth of Timbuctoo.

R. B. Cunningham Graham, *Mogreb-el-Acksa*, 1898

MOUNTAINS

Mountains interposed
Make enemies of nations who had else
Like kindred drops been mingled into one.

William Cowper, 'The Timepiece', *The Task*, 1785

Horror constitutes beauty in a rocky country.

Hester Lynch Thrale Piozzi, *Observations . . . in the Course of a Journey*, 1789

I live not in myself, but I become
Portion of that around me; and to me
High mountains are a feeling, but the hum
Of human cities torture . . .

Lord Byron, *Childe Harold's Pilgrimage*, Canto the Third, 1816

I believe it is Doctor Clarke who advises travellers never to see a mountain without going to the top of it.

J. R. Planché, *A Descent of the Danube from Ratisbon to Vienna During the Autumn of 1827*, 1828

Ages are thy days,
Thou grand expressor of the present tense,
And type of permanence!
Firm ensign of the fatal Being,
Amid these coward shapes of joy and grief,
That will not bide the seeing.
Hither we bring
Our insect miseries to the rocks;
And the whole flight, with pestering wing,
Vanish, and end their murmuring, –
Vanish beside these dedicated blocks . . .

R. W. Emerson, 'Monadnoc', *Poems*, 1846

Mountains are the beginning and the end of all natural scenery.

John Ruskin, *Modern Painters*, 1843–60

Above all young traveller, take my advice, and never, *never*, be such a fool as to go up a mountain, a tower, or a steeple. I have tried it. Men still ascend eminences, even to this day, and descending, say they have been delighted. But it is a lie. They have been miserable the whole day. Keep you down: and have breakfast while the asinine hunters after the picturesque go braying up the hill.

W. M. Thackeray, 'Wanderings of Our Fat Contributor', *Punch*, August 1844

Surely there never was a more glorious dumb creature of God than a snow mountain; in its awful calmness it almost looks intelligent.

M. F. Tupper, *Paterfamilias' Diary of Everybody's Tour*, 1856

Did any man know of any good befalling him from going up a mountain; always excepting Albert Smith, who we are told, has realized half a million by going up Mont Blanc? If a man can go up his mountains in Piccadilly, it may be all very well; in so doing he perhaps may see the sun rise, and be able to watch nature in her wildest vagaries. But as for the true ascent – the nasty, damp, dirty, slippery, boot-destroying, shin-breaking, veritable mountain! Let me recommend my friends to let it alone, unless they have a gift for making a million in Piccadilly. I have tried many a mountain in a small way, and never found one to answer. I hereby protest that I will never try another.

Anthony Trollope, *The West Indies and the Spanish Main*, 1859

In all mountain scenery there is no effect so impressive as the appearance of a great peak unexpectedly . . . . Such a view never loses its power, and is never forgotten. At one moment there was before the eyes nothing but a blank wall of rock or snow, or a curtain of dull mist; the next you stand face to face with one of the grandest objects of nature; it is, apparently, close to you, even above you; and as the gaze wanders upwards, over ice and crag and snow, to the culminating summit, you believe almost that the majestic form has just risen to its place, and that it is aware of your presence.

Woolmore Wigram, *Memoirs*, 1908 – of 1862

I used to fancy that everybody would like clouds and rocks as well as I did, if once told to look at them; whereas after fifty years of trial, I find that it is not so, even in modern days; having long ago known that, in ancient ones, the clouds and mountains which have been life to me, were mere inconvenience and horror to most of mankind.

John Ruskin, *Praeterita*, 1885–9

Our critics, curiously enough, repeat in substance Mr Ruskin's original taunt, that we regard the mountains as greased poles. I must confess that a natural and incurable denseness of understanding does not enable me to feel the sting of this taunt . . . I do not perceive the enormity or sin of climbing poles.

A. F. Mummery, *My Climbs in the Alps and Caucasus*, 1905 – of 1893

To climb is to exchange the rapture of first love and the adoration of the unknown for the companionable friendship founded on knowledge and understanding. Like Moses, the mountaineer can see the promised land but can never set foot in it, for the mountain that he climbs is not the mountain which he worships from afar.

Arnold Lunn, *Mountains of Youth*, 1925 – of 1909

No, I can't do with mountains at close quarters – they are always in the way, and they are so stupid, never moving and never doing anything but obtrude themselves.

D. H. Lawrence, Letter to Lady Cynthia Asquith, 23 October 1913

To live in mountains is like living with someone who always talks at the top of his, or it may be her, voice.

Leonard Woolf, *Beginning Again*, 1964

Mountains are complacent edifices. They make man sorry if he tries to exploit them.

Peter Nichols, *Italia, Italia*, 1973

People ask me, 'Why did you go and buy a mountain?' and I say, 'To keep it clean.'

Robert Redford, Interview with Alexander Walker, quoted *Evening Standard*, 12 March 1980

MOZAMBIQUE

Mozambique is a curious mixture – Shangri La with a bullwhip behind the door.

John Gunther, *Inside Africa*, 1955

The coelocanth, oldest of fish, still lurks in the Gulf of Mozambique. Some wags say that Mozambique is a coelocanth trying to change itself suddenly into a salmon.

Richard West, *The White Tribes of Africa*, 1965

Limpopo River (and in Zimbabwe and South Africa)

The great grey-green, greasy Limpopo River, all set about with fever-trees.

Rudyard Kipling, 'The Elephant's Child', *Just So Stories*, 1902

Lourenço Marques

South Africans and Southern Rhodesians troop to Mozambique on holiday. 'Of course, it wouldn't seem much to you.' they often said, 'but for us it seems marvellously continental.' They used the word 'continental' in just the same way as the English do, meaning Latin, warm, spicy, relaxed and erotic. Lourenço Marques is the only town I have been to in Africa that really seems like Europe. The South Africans on holiday wear the same kind of awkward, bemused look as the English on holiday in Spain: the men in blazers and flannels, the women in head-scarves and sun-red necks; the jokes about garlic and 'Mozambique belly'; the prevailing sense of naughtiness . . . . The Southern Rhodesians go rather to Beira up the coast, which they have turned into a kind of hot Blackpool.

Richard West, *The White Tribes of Africa*, 1965

N

NAMIBIA (also South-West Africa)

Is South-West Africa a 'country'? I asked this question of a leading official and got the answer, 'Frankly, no one really knows.'

John Gunther, *Inside Africa*, 1955

Walvis Bay

'Ever been to Walvis Bay?'
I asked him where it was.
'Why, that's where the whales go to make love!'
'Nonsense!'
'Absolutely! I've seen them at it! Though what the hell fun *they* get out of it, I don't know!'

Negley Farson, *Behind God's Back*, 1940

Desert, near Walvis Bay
On my first evening, when a port official had led me to the edge of the desert, and asked me to look at it, I asked him what lay above, below, and out beyond us.

'Nothing!' he said, with a note of hysteria in his voice. 'It's just miles, and miles, and miles – and MILES! – of Sweet Fanny Adams!'

Ibid.

Windhoek

There are only five miles of paved road in all South-West Africa. And Windhoek has all of them.

This hilly capital is God's gift to the picture postcard industry. Its sky is just that incredible blue. Its buff Government buildings rest on impossibly green hills. They have red roofs. And nearly everywhere you look in Windhoek, there are beds of scarlet geraniums and purple bougainvillea, while even the grave-yard, which is one of the show-places of the town, is laid out with vistas of cypress and classic urns . . . .

A newcomer usually finds it difficult to breathe, in the baking summer at this height of over 5,500 feet. But the winters are cold. The two castles built on two hills overlooking Windhoek have baronial fireplaces of hewn stone.

Both the castles, amply turreted, were built by the same man; a German baron, one of the old 'aristos' whose epoch ended with the last war. One was for himself, the other he built for his wife. He called upon her every morning. But before doing so, he always sent his 'boy' across with a card, to see if it was convenient to receive him.

Negley Farson, *Behind God's Back*, 1940

NATIONS

The nations are as a drop of a bucket, and are accounted as the small dust of the balance.

The Bible, Isaiah 38:15

A nation is not a body, the figure of which is to be represented by the human body; but is like a body contained within a circle, having a common center, in which every radius meets; and that center is formed by representation.

Thomas Paine, *The Rights of Man*, Part II, 1792

The entire man is, so to speak, to be seen in the cradle of the child. The growth of nations presents something analogous to this; they all bear some marks of their origin; and the circumstances which accompanied their birth and contributed to their rise, affect the whole term of their being.

Alexis de Tocqueville, *Democracy in America*, 1835

Nations touch at their summits.

Walter Bagehot, *The English Constitution*, 1867

Nations are but enlarged schoolboys.

James Anthony Froude, *Oceana, or England and Her Colonies*, 1886

It is from a nation's holidays that one can best judge its character.

Douglas Sladen, *Queer Things About Japan*, 1903

Nationalism as catching in the Middle East as measles.

Freya Stark, *Beyond Euphrates*, 1951

A nation should be like an audience in some great theatre – 'in the theatre,' said Victor Hugo, 'the mob becomes a people,' – watching the drama of its own history . . . that sacred drama must to all mature eyes and ears become the greatest of parables.

W.B.Yeats, *Commentary on the Three Songs – Poetry*, December 1934

Nations being the largest organized groups are from a psychological point of view clumsy, stupid, and amoral monsters like those huge saurians with an incredibly small brain. They are inaccessible to reasonable argument, they are suggestible like hysterical patients, they are childish and moody, helpless victims of their emotions. They are caught in every swindle, called slogans, they are stupid to an amazing degree, they are greedy, reckless, and blindly violent, like a rhino suddenly aroused from sleep. They persevere in every nonsense, in every emotion and resentment, in every prejudice, far beyond the psychological moment, and they get ensnared by the cheapest of all obvious tricks. Most of the time they live in dreams and primitive illusions usually rigged out as 'isms.' As long as they can feed on open ground in an undisturbed way they are sleepy and harmless. But if their food gets scarce and they begin to migrate and to encroach upon neighbouring territory, they resort to violence. They are not to be convinced that human beings have evolved much better methods in many thousands of years and that these individual men believe in reason and intelligence.

C.G.Jung, *Psychology and National Problems*, Lecture, 14 October 1936

Nations are known for the things they are not. Russia for its soul; Germany for its *Gemutlichkeit*; France for its logic; Spain for its religious compassion – and the United States for its efficiency.

Harry Roskolenko, *When I was Last on Cherry Street*, 1965

Nations talk about what they lack; America is talking about peace, Germany about unity, France about glory, Russia about freedom, and India about food.

James Reston, *New York Times*, 15 December 1965

NATURE

Nature never disappoints; the humbug is always found in the arts, literature, ruins, &c. &c.

Thomas Moore, *Journal*, 12 November 1819

Let us not flatter ourselves overmuch on account of our human victories over nature. For each such victory it takes its revenge on us . . . at every step we are reminded that we by no means rule over nature like a conqueror over a foreign people.

Friedrich Engels, *The Part Played by Labour in the Transition from Ape to Man*, 1876 published 1896

How strange that Nature does not knock, and yet does not intrude!

Emily Dickinson, Letter to Mrs J.S. Cooper, 1880

But Nature is 'old-fashioned,' perhaps a Puritan.

Emily Dickinson, Letter to Mrs J.S. Cooper, 1883

Nature is a foolish place to look for inspiration in, but a charming one in which to forget one ever had any.

Oscar Wilde, Letter to E.W. Godwin, April 1885

Nature will not be admired by proxy.

Sir Winston Churchill, *The Malakand Field Force*, 1898

Nature's way of dealing with unhealthy conditions is unfortunately not one that compels us to conduct a solvent hygiene on a cash basis. She demoralizes us with long credits and reckless overdrafts, and then pulls us up cruelly with catastrophic bankruptcies.

G.Bernard Shaw, Preface to *Heartbreak House*, 1919

Nature worship is a product of good communications. In the seventeenth century all sensible men disliked wild nature . . . . Poets responded to the invitation of the engineers.

Aldous Huxley, *Beyond the Mexique Bay*, 1934

NETHERLANDS

Seventeenth Century

This country was heretofore called *Batavia*, and the inhabitants *Batávi*, which are mentioned by Caesar and Tacitus. They were in times past accounted a very sottish and foolish people, even as the Boeotians were amongst the ancient Graacians. But in this age they deserve not to be so esteemed. For they are as ingenious both for all manuary arts, and also for the ingenuous disciplines, as any people whatsoever in all Christendome: which a man that liveth amongst them may easily perceive. The name of Batavia was commonly in use til the yeare of our Lord 860. at what time there hapend such an exceeding inundation as overflowed a great part of the country, and did so scowre and wash the very bowels of the earth, that it hath bene ever since . . . hollow and spungie. For which cause the old name of *Batavia* was afterward changed to Holland, which is so called *quasi* hollow land, or *quasi* Hol-land. For hol in the Flemish tongue doth signifie as much as our word hole.

Thomas Coryate, *Crudities*, 1611

For policies, industries, strong towns, and fortifications, it is the mirror of virtue and the garden of Mars; yea, and the light of all Europe, that he who hath exactly trod it may say he hath seen the map of the whole universe.

William Lithgow, *Rare Adventures and Painfull Peregrinations*, 1614/32

The Duke of Alva . . . [said] . . . That the Inhabitants of this Country were the nearest Neighbours to Hell (the greatest Abyss) of any People upon Earth, because they dwell lowest: Most of that ground they tread, is plucked, as it were, out of the very Jaws of *Neptune*, who is afterwards penn'd out by high Dikes, which are preserved with incredible Charge; insomuch that the chief *Dike-Grave* here, is one of the greatest Officers of Trust in all the Province, it being in his power to turn the whole Country into a Salt-lough when he list, and so to put *Hans* to swim for his Life; which makes it to be one of the chiefest Parts of his Litany, *From the Sea, the Spaniard, and the Devil, the Lord deliver me.*

James Howell, 'Letter to my Brother, 1 April 1617', *Familiar Letters*, 1645

Holland, that scarce deserves the name of *Land*,
As but th'Off-scouring of the *Brittish Sand*;
And so much Earth as was contributed
By *English Pilots* when they heav'd the Lead;
Or what by th'Oceans slow alluvion fell,
Of shipwrackt Cockle and the Muscle-shell;
This indigested vomit of the Sea
Fell to the *Dutch* by just Propriety.
Glad then as Miners that have found the Oar,
They with mad labour fish'd the *Land* to *Shoar*;
And div'd as desperately for each piece
Of Earth, as if't had been of *Ambergreece*; . . .
How did they rivet, with Gigantick Piles,
Thorough the Center their new-catched Miles;
And to the stake a strugling Country bound,
Where barking Waves still bait the forced Ground;
Building their *watry Babel* far more high
To reach the *Sea*, then those to scale the *Sky*.
Yet still his claim the Injur'd Ocean laid,
And oft at Leap-frog ore their Steeples plaid: . . .
The Fish oft-times the Burger dispossest,
And sat not as a Meat but as a Guest; . . .
Nature, it seem'd, asham'd of her mistake,
Would throw their Land away at *Duck* and *Drake* . . .
Who best could know to pump an Earth so leak
Him they their *Lord* and *Country's Father* speak.
To make a *Bank* was a great *Plot of State*;
Invent a *Shov'l* and be a *Magistrate*.

Andrew Marvell, *The Character of Holland*, *c.* 1653

The soil of the whole Province of *Holland* is generally flat, like the sea in a calm, and looks as if after a long contention between land and water, which it should belong to, it had at length been divided between them.

Sir William Temple, *Observations upon the United Provinces of the Netherlands*, 1672

Holland is a country, where the earth is better than the air, and profit more in request than honour; where there is more sense than wit; more good nature than good humour; and more wealth than pleasure; where a man would choose rather to travel than to live; shall find more things to observe than to desire; and more persons to esteem than to love.

Ibid.

Ay, ay, I have made the tourè of *Holland*, but it was èn postè, derè was no staying for me, . . . for de Gentleman can no more live derè den de Toad in *Ir'land* . . . .

William Wycherley, *The Gentleman-Dancing-Master*, 1672

A CUNTRY that Draws fifty foot of Water
In which Men live, as in the Hold of Nature;
And when the Sea dos in upon them break
And drown a Province, dos but Spring a Leak;
That always Ply the Pump, and never think
They can be Safe, but at the Rate they sink;
That live as if they have been Run on Ground
And when they dy, are cast away and Drownd;
That dwel in Ships like Swarms of Rats, and Prey
Upon the Goods all Nations Fleets Convey
And, when their Merchants are Blown up and Crackt,
Whole Towns are cast away in Storms and wrackt;
That feed like Canibals on other Fishes
And serve their Coussen Germans up in Dishes:
A Land that Rides at Anchor, and is moord
In which they do not live, but go abourd.

Samuel Butler, *Description of Holland*, before 1680

Eighteenth Century

Frogs there
'Dutch nightingales' as they are known at Paris.

Richard Steele, *Tatler*, No. 236, 12 October 1710

Sure nothing can be more agreable than travelling in Holland. The whole Country appears a large Garden, the roads all well pav'd, shaded on each side with rows of Trees and border'd with large Canals full of Boats passing and repassing. Every 20 paces gives you the prospect of some villa and every 4 hours a large Town, so surprizingly neat, I am sure you would be charm'd with them.

Lady Mary Wortley Montagu, Letter to Jane Smith, 5 August 1716

I have been assured by a curious friend of mine of great veracity, who had lived many *Winters* in *Holland*, that nothing is more common than for hot pudding to freeze in that cold country.

Peter Ludlow, Letter to Jonathan Swift, 10 September 1718

Adieu! canaux, canards, canaille.

Voltaire, attrib.

Or, where the Rhine
Branch'd out in many a long canal extends,
From every province swarming, void of care,
Batavia rushes forth; and as they sweep,
On sounding skates, a thousand different ways,
In circling poise, swift as the winds, along,
The *then gay* land is madden'd all to joy.

James Thomson, *The Seasons – Winter*, 1726

Farewell to Leyden's lovely bound,
The Belgian Muse's sober seat;
Where, dealing frugal gifts around
To all the favourites at her feet,
She trains the body's bulky frame
For passive, persevering toils;
And lest, from any prouder aim,
The daring mind should scorn her homely spoils,
She breathes maternal fogs to damp its restless flame.

Farewell the grave, pacific air,
Where never mountain zephyr blew:
The marshy levels lank and bare,
Which Pan, which Ceres never knew:
The Naiads, with obscene attire,
Urging in vain their urns to flow;
While round them chaunt the croaking choir,
And haply soothe some lover's prudent Browe,
Or prompt some restive bard and modulate his lyre.

Farewell, ye nymphs, whom sober care of gain
Snatched in your cradles from the god of Love:
She rendered all his boastful arrows vain;
And all his gifts did he in spite remove.
Ye too, the slow-eyed fathers of the land,
With whom dominion steals from hand to hand,
Unowned, undignified by public choice,
I go where Liberty to all is known,
And tells a monarch on his throne,
He reigns not but by her preserving voice.

O my loved England, when with thee
Shall I sit down, to part no more?
Far from this, pale, discoloured sea,
That sleeps upon the reedy shore . . .

Mark Akenside, 'On Leaving Holland', 1744, in *Odes on Several Subjects*, 1745

Nothing can be more disagreeable than the heap of Dirt & Mud & Ditches & Reeds, which they here call a Country, except the silly Collection of shells, & clipt evergreens which they call a Garden.

David Hume, Letter to John Home of Ninewells, 16 March 1748

Holland, at first view, appears to have some pretensions to polite learning. It may be regarded as the great emporium, not less of literature, than of every commodity. Here, though destitute of what may be properly called a language of their own, all the languages are understood, cultivated, and spoken. All useful inventions in arts, and new discoveries in science, are published here almost as soon as at the places which first produced them. Its individuals have the same faults however with the Germans, of making more use of their memory, than their judgement . . . . A Dearth of wit in France or England, naturally produces a scarcity in Holland . . . . They wait till something new comes out from others, examine its merits, and reject it, or make it reverberate through the rest of Europe.

After all, I know not whether they should be allowed any national character for polite learning. All their taste is derived to them from neighbouring nations, and that in a language not their own. They somewhat resemble their brokers, who trade for immense sums, without having any capital.

Oliver Goldsmith, *An Enquiry into the Present State of Polite Learning in Europe*, 1759

To men of other minds my fancy flies,
Embosom'd in the deep where Holland lies,
Methinks her patient sons before me stand,
Where the broad ocean leans against the land,
And, sedulous to stop the coming tide,
Lift the tall rampire's artificial pride . . .
While the pent ocean, rising o'er the pile,
Sees an amphibious world beneath him smile.
The slow canal, the yellow blossom'd vale,
The willow tufted bank, the gliding snail,
The crowded mart, the cultivated plain,
A new creation, rescued from his reign.
Thus while around the wave-subjected soil
Impels the native to repeated toil,
Industrious habits in each bosom reign,
And industry begets a love of gain.
Hence all the good from opulence that springs,
With all those ills superfluous treasure brings,
Are here display'd. Their much-lov'd wealth imparts
Convenience, plenty, elegance, and arts;
But view them closer, craft and fraud appear,
Even liberty itself is bartered here.
At gold's superior charms all freedom flies,
The needy sell it, and the rich man buys:
A land of tyrants and a den of slaves,
Here wretches seek dishonourable graves,
And calmly bent, to servitude conform,
Dull as their lakes that slumber in the storm.

Oliver Goldsmith, *The Traveller*, 1764

To Holland, where politeness ever reigns,
Where primitive sincerity remains,
And makes a stand; where Freedom in her course
Hath left her name, though she hath lost her force
In that as other lands; where simple Trade
Was never in the garb of Fraud array'd;
Where Avarice never dared to shew his head
Where, like a smiling cherub, Mercy, led
By Reason, blesses the sweet-blooded race;
And cruelty could never find a place;
To Holland for that charity we roam,
Which happily begins and ends at home.

Charles Churchill, *The Times*, 1764

The minute neatness of the villages, their red roofs, and the lively green of the meadows which shade them, corresponded with the ideas I had formed of Chinese prospects; a resemblance which was not diminished upon viewing on every side the level scenery of enamelled meadows, with stripes of clear water across them, and innumerable barges gliding busily along.

William Beckford, *Dreams Waking Thoughts and Incidents*, 1783

Nineteenth Century

A Dutch town soon becomes fatiguing to a traveller, particularly after having visited the gayer cities of Europe. There is a sameness in the houses – streets, people, manners &c that in a little time satiates curiosity.

Washington Irving, *Journal*, 2 October 1805

Old William of Orange talked of dying in 'the last ditch' of his dingy country. It is lucky I can swim, or I suppose I should not well weather the first. But let us see. I have heard hyaenas and jackalls in the ruins of Asia; and bull-frogs in the marshes, – besides wolves and angry Mussulmans. Now, I should like to listen to the shout of a free Dutchman.

Lord Byron, *Journal*, November 1813

Certainly no country exhibits such a succession of water, trees & shipping so agreably mixed up together as Holland, & the trees are just now of the liveliest verdure. Such a country in other hands would have been intolerable.

Samuel Rogers, *Italian Journal*, 30 April 1815

The public clocks in most of the towns of Holland strike the hour twice, – once half an hour before, and again at the correct time. Custom renders this less inconvenient than might have been supposed. But I have heard even the natives admit, when approving of the practice, that they themselves are sometimes deceived, though to be half an hour out in the calculation of time is considered by them as an instance of great heedlessness.

Charles Tennant, *A Tour, etc.*, 1824

Fancy has never yet, in any of her flights, alighted upon the marshy flats of Holland.

Ibid.

Holland is perhaps the only country which you gain nothing by seeing. It is exactly the same as the Dutch landscapes of it.

William Hazlitt, *Notes of a Journey through France and Italy*, 1826

The repetition of the same objects, and the extent of *home* view, become at last oppressive . . . What is the use of seeing a hundred windmills, a hundred barges, a hundred willow-trees, or a hundred herds of cattle at once? Any one specimen is enough, and the others hang like a dead-weight on the traveller's patience. Besides there is something lumpish and heavy in the aspect of the country; the eye is clogged and impeded in its progress over it by dams and dykes, and the marshy nature of the soil damps and chills imagination . . . The towns and villas in Holland are unrivalled for neatness, and an appearance of wealth and comfort. All the way from Utrecht to Amsterdam, to the Hague, to Rotterdam, you might fancy yourself on Clapham Common.

Ibid.

Holland and the Netherlands ought to be seen once, because no other country is like them. Everything is artificial. You will be struck with the combinations of vivid greenery, and water, and building; but everything is so distinct and rememberable, that you would not improve your conception by visiting the country a hundred times over. It is interesting to see a country and a nature *made*, as it were, by man, and to compare it with God's nature.

If you go, remark (indeed you will be forced to do so in spite of yourself), remark, I say, the identity (for it is more than proximity) of a disgusting dirtiness in all that concerns the dignity of, and reverence for, the human person; and a persecuting painted cleanliness in everything connected with property. You must not walk in their gardens; nay, you must hardly look into them.

The Dutch seem very happy and comfortable, certainly; but it is the happiness of *animals*. In vain do you look for the sweet breath of hope and advancement among them.

In fact, as to their villas and gardens, they are not to be compared to an ordinary London merchant's box.

Samuel Taylor Coleridge, *Table Talk*, 4 May 1830

As a nation the most ancient ally, the *alter idem* of England, the best deserving of the cause of freedom and religion and morality of any people in Europe.

Samuel Taylor Coleridge, *Table Talk*, 15 August 1831

Compared with Greece and Italy – Holland is but a platter-faced, cold gin-and-water country, after all! . . . and a heavy, barge-built, web-footed race are its inhabitants.

Sir F.B. Head, *Bubbles from the Brunnens of Nassau*, 1834

Never come into Holland . . . . The roads all paved – inns dirty, and dearer than the dearest in England – country frightful beyond all belief; no trees but willows – no fuel but turf; all the people uglier than Mcauley.

Sydney Smith, Letter to Lady Grey, 12 May 1837

If you only fancy the very worst country for hunting in the whole world, except for otter dogs, you will have it exactly. Every highway is a canal; and as for lanes and bridle-roads, they are nothing but ditches.

Thomas Hood, *Up the Rhine*, 1840

Holland, a country which, between its carillons and its canals might be described by a punster as 'wringing wet.'

Ibid.

What wounds one's feelings in Holland is the perpetual consciousness that the country has no business there at all. You see it all below the level of the water, soppy, hideous, and artificial; and because it exists against nature, nobody can exist there except at a frightful expense, which is very well for the natives, who may be thankful to live on any terms, but disagreeable for foreigners, who do not like to pay twice as much as elsewhere for being half as comfortable . . . . In Holland what is most disagreeable is the climate; you live in a constant smell of ooze, at least in summer, – hot ooze when in the sun, cold ooze when you go under the trees. The pleasant moment is when you get on the open beach, at Schevening, for instance, with the waves tumbling and the wind whistling; but even then you cannot help feeling that the sea ought, if it had its right, to be *over* the beach and rolling across the country for miles inland.

Matthew Arnold, Letter to Miss Arnold, 19 June 1859

I have at last done my Holland: you won't be surprised to hear that I did it in two days, and was glad to rush home on the first pretence, after (as usual) seeing nothing I cared the least about. The Country itself I had seen long before in Dutch Pictures, and between Beccles and Norwich: the Towns I had seen in Picturesque Annuals, Drop Scenes, etc.

Edward Fitzgerald, Letter to George Crabbe, 4 August 1863

In no other country do the keels of the ships float above the chimneys, and nowhere else does the frog, croaking from among the bulrushes, look down upon the swallow on the house-top.

Anon. quoted by John W. Forney, *Letters from Europe*, 1867

Twentieth Century

Holland it seems is not a country of villages, but of compact, clean towns, standing scattered over a great waste of grass like the sea.

Hilaire Belloc, *Hills and the Sea*, 1906

My love for plane geometry prepared me to feel a special affection for Holland. For the Dutch landscape has all the qualities that make geometry so delightful. A tour in Holland is a tour through the first book of Euclid. Over a country that is the ideal plane surface of the geometry books, the roads and the canals trace out the shortest distances between point and point.

Aldous Huxley, *Along the Road*, 1925

We went for a day or two into Holland (Amster- and Rotter- dam) which is the most unreal country under the wet heavens! Never conceived how absolutely artificial it is in every way till I saw the farmers making it by dredging it out of the canals.

Rudyard Kipling, Letter to Rider Haggard, 15 February 1925

Imaginary interiors. . . . No wonder they took shape in painting terms! Ever since those first hours in Rotterdam a three-dimensional Holland had been springing up all round me and expanding into the distance in conformity with another Holland which was already in existence and in every detail complete. For, if there is a foreign landscape familiar to English eyes by proxy, it is this one; by the time they see the original, a hundred mornings and afternoons in museums and picture galleries and country houses have done their work. These confrontations and recognition-scenes filled the journey with excitement and delight. The nature of the landscape itself, the colour, the light, the sky, the openness, the expanse and the detail of the towns and the villages are leagued together in the weaving of a miraculously consoling and healing spell. Melancholy is exorcised, chaos chased away and wellbeing, alacrity of spirit and a thoughtful calm take their place.

Patrick Leigh Fermor, *A Time of Gifts*, 1977 – of 1933

A flat country partitioned with a symmetry so emphatic as to be rather charming. But the flatness is overdone; privacy and surprise – surely the two prime qualities in a civilized landscape – are almost wholly excluded. Holland looks rather dull to me.

Peter Fleming, *One's Company*, 1934

Whenever I go to Holland, I feel at once that I have reached the apotheosis of bourgeois society. The food, the comfort, the cleanliness, the kindliness, the sense of age and stability, the curious mixture of beauty and bad taste, the orderliness of everything including even nature and the sea – all this makes one realize that here on the shores of the dyke-controlled Zuider Zee one has found the highest manifestation of the complacent civilization of the middle classes. I have felt something of the same thing in Sweden and Denmark, but I do not think that the Scandinavians have ever reached quite the heights of domestication and complacency attained by the Dutch . . . . I am sure that I should feel suffocated if I had to live my life in the feather-bed civilization of Delft or The Hague. Yet there is in life a great deal to be said for it and for a short time it is very pleasant to feel that one is in a really civilized country from which nature has been expelled by something more efficacious than a fork. At any rate I prefer the tradition of comfortable civilization in the Netherlands to that of Teutonic sentimental savagery across the border.

Leonard Woolf, *Downhill All the Way*, 1967

Dutch

Seventeenth Century

The Dutch, whom Wealth, (not Hatred) doth divide . . .

Ben Jonson, 'Ode Allegorical', prefixed to Hugh Holland, *Pancharis*, 1603

Spungie hydroptique Dutch.

John Donne, *On His Mistris,* before 1635

The *Hollander* slower . . . , more surly and respectless of Gentry and Strangers, homely in his clothing, of very few words, and heavy in action; which may be well imputed to the quality of the Soil, which works so strongly upon the Humours, that when People of a more vivacious and nimble Temper come to mingle with them, their Children are observ'd to partake rather of the Soil than the Sire: and so it is in all Animals besides.

James Howell, 'A Survey of the Seventeen Provinces, Antwerp, 1 May 1622', *Familiar Letters*, 1645

The time they there spend, is in eating well, in drinking much, and prating most. For the truth is, the compleatest drinker in Europe is your English Gallant. There is no such Consumer of liquor as the Quaffing off of his Healths. Time was the Dutch had the better of it; but of late he hath lost it by prating too long over his pot . . . . So the one is drunk sooner, the other longer. As if striving to recover the wager, the Dutchman would still be the perfectest soker.

Anon., *A Brief Character of the Low Countries*, 1660

But it was pretty news came the other day so fast, of the Dutch fleets being in so many places, that Sir W. Batten at table cried, 'By God!' says he, 'I think the Devil shits Dutchmen!'

Samuel Pepys, *Diary*, 19 July 1667

In general, all appetites and passions seem to run lower and cooler here, than in other countries where I have conversed. Avarice may be excepted. And yet that shall not be so violent, where it feeds only upon industry and parsimony, as where it breaks out into fraud, rapine, and oppression. But quarrels are seldom seen among them, unless in their drink, revenge rarely heard of, or jealousy known. Their tempers are not airy enough for joy, or any unusual strains of pleasant humour, nor warm enough for love. This is talked of, sometimes, among the younger men, but as a thing they have heard of, rather than felt; and as a discourse that becomes them, rather than affects them. I have known some among them, that personated lovers well enough; but none that I ever thought were at heart in love; nor any of the women, that seemed at all to care, whether they were so or no. Whether it be, that they are such lovers of their liberty, as not to bear the servitude of a mistress, any more than that of a master; or, that the dulness of their air renders them less susceptible of more refined passions; or, that they are diverted from it by the general intention every man has upon his business, whatever it is, (nothing being so mortal an enemy of love, that suffers no rival, as any bent of thought another way).

Sir William Temple, *Observations upon the United Provinces of the Netherlands*, 1672

This Country and People, who are well, when they are not ill; and pleas'd when they are not troubled.

Sir William Temple, *ibid.*

Dutchmen! . . . that have no soul for anything but Gain, that have no Pleasure but Interest or the Bottle; but in Affairs of Love, go to the most sacred part of it more brutally than the most sordid of their four-footed Brethren: nay, they are so far from the Warmth of Love, that thro their Phlegmatick Mass there is not Fire enough to give 'em a vigorous Apetite, so far are they from the Fineness of vehement Passion.

Aphra Behn, Letter, c. 1666 in *The History of the Life and Memoirs of Mrs Behn, by One of the Fair Sex* (Charles Gildon?), 1718

Well may they boast themselves an ancient Nation;
For they were bred e'er Manners were in fashion.

'Satyr on the Dutch, written by Mr Dryden in the Year 1662' in *Poems on Affairs of State*, iii, 1704 (But in fact this couplet was added in this edition to lines from Dryden's Prologue to *Amboyna*, 1673, and authorship is uncertain.)

Eighteenth Century

When a man happens to break in *Holland*, they say of him that *he has not kept true Accompts*. This phrase, perhaps, among us, would appear a soft or humourous way of speaking, but with that exact Nation it bears the highest Reproach; for a Man to be mistaken in his Calculation of his Expence, in his Ability to answer future Demands, or to be impertinently sanguine in putting his Credit to too great Adventure, are all Instances of as much Infamy, as with gayer Nations to be failing in Courage or common Honesty.

Richard Steele, *Spectator*, No. 174, 19 September 1711

They are mistaken who imagine that a *Dutchman* can't love; for tho they are generally more phlegmatick than other Men, yet it sometimes happens that Love does penetrate their Lump, and dispense an enlivening Fire, that destroys its graver and cooler Considerations.

Charles Gildon (?), *The History of the Life and Memoirs of Mrs Behn, by One of the Fair Sex*, 1718

The Dutch are like a knot of sharpers among a parcel of honest gentlemen, who think they understand play, and are bubbled of their money. I love them for the love they have to their country; which however, is no virtue in them, because it is their private interest, which is directly contrary in England.

Jonathan Swift, Letter to Francis Grant, 23 March 1734

The modern Dutch man is quite a different creature from him of former times, he in every thing imitates a French man but in his easy disengagd air which is the result of keeping polite company, the Dutch man is vastly ceremonious and is perhaps exactly what a French man might have been in the reign of Lewis the 14th. Such are the better bred but the downright Hollander is one of the oddest figures in Nature. Upon a head of lank hair he wears a half cock'd Narrow leav'd hat lacd with black ribbon, no coat but seven waistcoats and nine pairs of breeches so that his hips reach almost up to his arm pits. This well cloathd vegetable is now fit to see company or make love but what a pleasing creature is the object of his appetite why she wears a large friez cap with a deal of flanders lace and for every pair of breeches he carries she puts on two petticoats, is it not surprising how things should ever come close enough to make it a match. When I spoke of love I was not to be understood in a – in short I was not to be understood at all, a Dutch Lady burns nothing about her Phlegmatick admirer but his Tobacco. You must know Sr every woman carries in her hand a Stove with coals in it which when she sits she snugs under her petticoats and at this chimney Dozing Strephon lights his pipe. I take it that this continual smoaking is what gives the man the ruddy healthfull complexion he generally wears, by draining his superfluous moisture while the woman deprivd of this amusement overflows with such visciditys as teint the complexion and gives the paleness of visage which Low fenny grounds and moist air conspire to cause.

Oliver Goldsmith, Letter to the Reverend Thomas Contarine, *c.* 6 May 1754

There is no people in the universe so free from low spirits or the affectation of them as the Dutch. They cannot endure anything that looks being pensive without a cause; and as for low spirits, they laugh at them.

David Dalrymple, Letter to James Boswell, 11 April 1764

A people whose souls are so little tuned to joy.

John Wilkes, Letter to his daughter, 25 December 1767

Very slight authority would persuade me there was a period when Holland was all water, and the ancestors of the present inhabitants fish. A certain oysterishness of eye, and flabbiness of complexion, are almost proofs sufficient of this aquatic descent: and pray tell me for what purpose are such galligaskins as the Dutch burthen themselves with contrived, but to tuck up a flouncing tail, and thus cloak the deformity of their dolphin-like terminations?

William Beckford, *Dreams Waking Thoughts and Incidents*, 1783

Amphibious wretches, speedy be your fall,
May man *un*dam you, and God damn you all!

Edward, first Baron Thurlow, Lord Chancellor, attrib., *c.* 1780

The children in Holland take pleasure in making
What children in England take pleasure in breaking.

Old rhyme

Nineteenth Century

The first thing that strikes a stranger upon entering this town (or in fact any other place in Holland) is the extreme cleanliness of the houses. The rage for cleaning and scowring amounts almost to a folly in Holland – you are incommoded by it perpetually. We ran several risks of being drenched by servant maids who were washing windows which to all appearance were not in the least soiled or dusty. The climate and situation of Holland renders this cleanliness necessary – otherwise from the humidity of the air and the dampness of the soil they would be subjected to intermittents and overrun with vermin. What originally arose from necessity has gradually become a habit and has so strongly engrafted itself in the dutch character that tho removed to a country and climate completely different, it will still prevail for several generations – We have proofs sufficient of the truth of this in America.

Washington Irving, *Journal*, 30 September 1805

Bland called. – He says Dutch society (he has been in Holland) is second-hand French; but the women are like women every where else. This is a bore: I shoud like to see them a little *un*like; but that can't be expected.

Lord Byron, *Journal*, 7 December 1813

One cause . . . will discover a Dutchman in any quarter of the globe, viz. the inordinate desire of accumulating wealth . . . . It seems as if it were the first feeling inculcated in infancy, and the only one which did not weaken with old age. But . . . in every speculation in which a Dutchman is concerned there must be a certainty of *some* profit. A sure basis must be seen for protection against loss, before any calculation of profit is commenced; and . . . this may be called the Dutchman's creed, – 'Small gains, and little risk.'

Charles Tennant, *A Tour, etc.* 1824

An enraged Dutchman, particularly amongst the lower classes, is proverbially as dangerous as a wild beast.

Ibid.

In matters of commerce, the fault of the Dutch
Is offering too little and asking too much.

George Canning, Despatch in cipher to the English Ambassador in Holland, 31 January 1826

*In the case of beseiging they open all their slowces, and the Dutch being amphibbyus, all the enemy is drowndid xcept themselves.

Thomas Hood, *Up the Rhine*, 1840 (Martha Penny writing)

in Indonesia

Who do you think is my typical Dutchman? – I meet him everywhere, and he is odious; but yesterday, all through a very hot, dusty, day on the railroad, we had the society of women of the Dutch species, and they were another revelation. A very distinguished middle-aged woman . . . overwhelmed us with three daughters . . . . I never understood how flesh could be pitchforked onto girls, till then; and how clothes could be stuck over the flesh. The effect of square corsets was wonderful . . . . On the whole I want to see no more Dutch colonies. While willing to admit that the only ultimate object of our race is to be born, to feed, and incidentally to die, the world so organised fails to interest me, and industry devoted solely to the purpose is distinctly a bore.

Henry Adams, Letter to Elizabeth Cameron, 26 August 1891

National traits can't hide themselves. The Dutch owe their comparatively small place in the world very largely to their national meanness . . . . They are a hardy folk. A breakfast passed my window this morning composed of raw herrings, pancakes and treacle, cheese with caraway seeds in it, and a fine glass of iced beer, foaming atop.

Alfred Viscount Northcliffe, *My Journey Round the World* (December 1921, en route to Java on a Dutch ship), 1923

I was remarking to the captain on the extreme cleanliness of his ship, which was typically Dutch, I said. To which he responded in his broken English –

'It is a pity we Dutch do nott allretty so often wash the corpse (body) as we do the house front.'

Ibid.

Women

The Women (as I have heard some Hollanders confesse) not easily finding a Husband, in respect of this disparity of the Sexes in number, commonly live unmarried till they be thirty yeeres old, and as commonly take Husbands of twenty yeeres age, which must needs make the Women more powerful in generation. And the Women not onely take young Men to their Husbands, but those also which are most simple and tractable: so as by the foresaid priviledge of Wives to dispose goods by their last will, and by the contracts in respect of their Dowry, (which to the same end use to be warily drawne,) they keepe their Husbands in a kind of awe, and almost alone, without their Husbands intermedling, not onely keepe their shops at home, but exercise trafficke abroade. My selfe have heard a Wife make answere to one asking for her Husband, that he was not at home, but had newly asked her leave to goe abroade . . . I may boldly say, that the Women of these parts, are above all other truly taxed with this unnatural domineering over their Husbands.

Fynes Moryson, *An Itinerary*, 1617

A Gentleman told me, that the Women of this Country, when they are deliver'd, there comes out of the Womb, a living Creature besides the Child, call'd *Zucchie*, likest a *Bat* of any other Creature, which the Midwives throw into the Fire, holding Sheets before the Chimney lest it should fly away.

James Howell, 'Letter to Sir John Smith, Knight', 10 April 1623

The women are handsome and allow of great freedom, but are esteemed more chaste than they appear.

Sir John Reresby, *Travels* (before 1689), 1813

I could make a shift to bear the brutality of men if the other sex made me amends; but i'faith they are cold to such a degree, that neither love nor wine can thaw them . . . . By signs and other notions, I can make shift to tell them what I would eat and drink; but I cannot, with all that my eyes can speak, with all that my fingers can express, make the women understand my meaning so as to relieve my more pressing necessities . . . if love be a deity there are no such damn'd atheists in the world as in this strange climate. . . . Those few here that pretend to own his power, pay their oblations to him with as ill a will, as a breaking tradesman pays his taxes to the government. It does not come from any generous principle within, the heart has no share in the sacrifice, and the soul, which in other countries loves to assist and go along with the body on these occasions is as unconcerned here as a tradesman's rake-hell prentice at a Quakers meeting.

Thomas Brown, *A Letter from a Gentleman in Holland to His Friend in England*, *c.*1692

It was truly ludicrous to talk in Dutch to a whore. This scene was to me a rarity as great as peas in February.

James Boswell, *Journal*, 26 May 1764

Amsterdam

In some Places, as in *Amsterdam*, the Foundation costs more than the Superstructure, for the Ground being soft, they are constrain'd to ram in huge stakes of Timber (with Wool about it to preserve it from Putrefaction) till they come to a firm Basis; so that, as one said, Whosoever could see *Amsterdam* under ground should see a huge Winter-Forest.

James Howell, 'A Survey of the Seventeen Provinces, Antwerp, 1 May 1622', *Familiar Letters*, 1645

As for the art off Painting and the affection off the people to Pictures, I thincke none other goe beeyond them, there having bin in this Country many excellent Men in thatt Facullty, some att presentt, as Rimbrantt, etts, All in generall striving to adorne their houses, especially the outer or streete roome, with costly peeces, Butchers and bakers not much inferiour in their shoppes, which are Fairely sett Forth, yea many tymes blacksmithes, Coblers, etts. will have some picture or other by their Forge and in their stalle. Such is the generall Notion, enclination and delight that these Countrie Natives have to Paintings.

Peter Mundy, *Travels in Europe and Asia*, 1640

It was on a Sunday morning about 11, that I purposely went to the Bourse (after the sermons were ended) to see their Dog-market, which lasts till two after-noone. I do not looke on the structure of this Exchange to be comparable to that of Sir Tho: Greshams in our Citty of Lond: yet in one respect it exceeds, that ships of considerable burthen ride at the very key continguous to it; and realy it is by extraordinary industry, that as well this Citty, as almost generaly the Townes of Holland are so accomodated with Grafts, Cutts, Sluces, Moles & Rivers, that nothing is more frequent then to see a whole Navy of Marchands & others environ'd with streetes & houses, every particular mans Barke, or Vessell at anker before his very doore, and yet the streetes so exactly straite, even, & uniforme that nothing can be more pleasing, especialy, being so frequently planted and shaded with the beautifull lime trees, which are set in rowes before every mans house, affording a very ravishing prospect.

John Evelyn, *Diary*, August 1641

Sure when *Religion* did it self imbark,
And from the *East* would *Westward* steer its Ark,
It struck, and splitting on this unknown ground,
Each one thence pillag'd the first piece he found:
Hence *Amsterdam, Turk-Christian-Pagan-Jew*,
Staple of Sects and Mint of Schisme grew;
That *Bank of Conscience*, where not one so strange
Opinion but finds Credit, and Exchange.
In vain for *Catholicks* our selves we bear;
The *universal Church* is onely there.
Nor can Civility there want for *Tillage*,
Where wisely for their *Court* they chose a *Village*.
How fit a Title clothes their *Governours*,
Themselves the *Hogs* as all their Subjects *Bores*!

Andrew Marvell, *The Character of Holland*, c. 1653

Had long a full view of Amsterdam, its roofs & towers intermixed with masts – less in the water than Venice, & rather running along a green level shore. – Went up & down the streets. Plate glass in the windows Magnificence of the Merchant's houses – ... The shops richly furnished & from their neatness, & the brightness of the window-panes not to mention the proprete of the figures within, in may respects surpassing most in London, & far those of every City, not excepting Paris –

The Dutch, by planting trees wherever water ran, have given a chearful charm to a Morass – Canals they love to a madness – they make them where they don't find them – along the side of every road – round every villa – every one has a canal of his own & builds as near the public canal as he can – & thro' every orchard, & garden.

Samuel Rogers, *Italian Journal*, 28 April 1815

Every building in this magnificent city stands upon enormous piles, and it was in allusion to this forest foundation, that Erasmus, when he first visited Amsterdam, observed, 'that he had reached a city, the inhabitants of which lived like crows upon the tops of trees.'

Charles Tennant, *A Tour, etc.*, 1824

Amsterdam did not answer our expectations; it is a kind of paltry, rubbishy Venice.

William Hazlitt, *Notes of a Journey through France and Italy*, 1826

On a desolate marsh overhung by fogs and exhaling diseases, a marsh where there was neither wood nor stone, neither firm earth nor drinkable water, a marsh from which the ocean on one side and the Rhine on the other were with difficulty kept out by art, was to be found the most prosperous community in Europe. The wealth which was collected within five miles of the Stadhous of Amsterdam would purchase the fee-simple of Scotland.

T. B. Macaulay, *History of England*, 1849–61

Postcard from my secretary, Alan Dent, who is on holiday in Amsterdam:

DEAR JAAMS,

I think u would not mooch like this place. It is ver wicked but also ver dirty. It suits me well because I am ver mooch both.

your – Jock.

James Agate, *Ego 3*, 16 August 1936

The Dutchmen are their own best pals
They're satisfied with their own canals
So their galleries lack one major menace –
Those everlasting views of Venice.

Ogden Nash, 'Amsterdam, Rotterdam and the Hague', in *Everyone but Thee and Me*, 1964

Bergen op Zoom

On this side I entered the City, where be many poore houses built in the forme of a Lutes necke, which being added to the City almost of a round forme, make the whole City much like unto a Lute.

Fynes Moryson, *An Itinerary*, 1617

Brock (near Amsterdam)

Went in an open carriage along canals to Brock, a village like a succession of scenes in a new comic opera – the houses as painted yesterday – almost all wood & in various colours – the windows bright – the courts pebbled in mosaic figures – the public walks (all foot-ways) swept & smooth as in a pleasure-ground.

Samuel Rogers, *Italian Journal*, 28 April 1815

Brock . . . is a little village so remarkable for the neatness of its appearance, as probably to be unique throughout the world . . . . Remarkable as are the Dutch for the cleanliness of their dwellings, this village, even amongst themselves, is considered as a curiosity, and, in fact, it is nothing short of the burlesque . . . . At the entrance into the village is posted up the ancient *lex scripta*, requiring that every rider, on passing through, should dismount and lead the animal by its nose; and that no person should smoke in any part of the village without a guard over the ball of the pipe, in order to prevent the ashes from falling out, on pain of forfeiture of the pipe in question.

Charles Tennant, *A Tour, etc.*, 1824

Delft

It is a most sweet town with bridges and a river in every street.

Observing that in every house of entertainment there hangs in every room a poor-man's box and desirous to know the reason thereof, it was told me that it is their custom to confirm all bargains by putting something into the poor people's box, and that that binds as fast as anything.

We saw likewise the Guesthouse, where it was very pleasant to see what neat preparation there is for the poor. We saw one poor man a-dying there.

After we had seen all, we light by chance of an English house to drink in, where we were very merry discoursing of the town and the thing that hangs up like a bushell in the Stathouse, which I was told is a sort of punishment for some sort of offenders to carry through the streets of the town over his head, which is a great weight.

Samuel Pepys, *Diary*, 18 May 1660

That great parent of pottery.

William Beckford, *Dreams Waking Thoughts and Incidents*, 1783

In this excellent city, though it is outside Eden, you may, when the wind is in the right quarter, receive in distant and rare appeals, the scent and air of Paradise; the soul is filled . . . .

And to think that you can get to a place like that for less than a pound.

Hilaire Belloc, *Hills and the Sea*, 1906

Delft is the most charming town in the world. It is one of the neat cities: trim, small, packed, self-contained. A good woman in early middle age, careful of her dress, combed, orderly, not without a sober beauty, – such a woman on her way to church of a Sunday morning is not more pleasing than Delft. It is on the verge of monotony yet still individual; in one style, yet suggesting many centuries of activity. There is a full harmony of many colours, yet the memory the place leaves is of a united, warm, and generous tone. Were you suddenly put down in Delft you would know very well that the vast and luxuriant meadows of Holland surrounded it, so much are its air, houses, and habits those of men inspired by the fields.

Ibid.

Dordrecht/Dort

The buildings of this Towne, both publique and private, sacred and civill, are very beautifull, being built all with bricke, and garnished with those kind of pretie battlements that are so much used in the Batavian Cities. Their streets also are of a notable length and breadth, in number many and paved with bricke as those of Gorcom . . . .

Out of those foure Rivers that inviron the Towne round about, and make it an Iland, there are some pretie armes derived into the Towne, which doe make certaine inferiour rivers that are very commodious to the inhabitants. Over one of them that runneth through the middle of the towne, there are many pretie Bridges, but two especially very faire. Whereof one is of Timber, the fairest wooden Bridge that I saw in Germany, saving that of Heidelberg. For it is so broad that three Cartes may passe ioyntly together over it. On both sides of this bridge there lyeth great abundance of shippes. The other is of stone, the edges whereof are finely rayled with yron rayles contrived in curious workes.

Thomas Coryate, *Crudities*, 1611

The forme of the City resembles a Galley, the length whereof lies from the East to the West.

Fynes Moryson, *An Itinerary*, 1617

Dordrecht, or Dort, a quaint, characteristic town, that looked like an old acquaintance, its features being such as are common on the pictorial Dutch tiles.

Thomas Hood, *Up the Rhine*, 1840

Grave

When the Archduke did raise his siege from Grave, the then secretary came to Queen Elizabeth; and the Queen, having intelligence first, said to the secretary, *Wot you what? The Archduke is risen from the Grave.* He answered, *What, without the trumpet of the Archangel?* The Queen replied; *Yes, without sound of trumpet.*

Francis Bacon, *Apothegmes . . . collected by Francis Lord Verulam . . .* , 1625

The Hague

I remember not to have seene a more pleasant village then this: great part of the houses are fairly built of bricke, though many of them in by-streetes be covered with thatch, and some few are stately built of free-stone. The village hath the forme of a Crosse, and upon the East side comming in from Leyden, there is a most pleasant Grove, with many wild walkes like a maze, and neerer the houses is another very pleasant walke, set round with willowes.

Fynes Moryson, *An Itinerary*, 1617

The Hague is a most neat place in all respects. The houses so neat in all places and things as possible . . . . And indeed I cannot speak enough of the gallantry of the town. Everybody of fashion speak French or Latin, or both. The women, many of them very pretty and in good habitt, fashionable, and black spots.

Samuel Pepys, *Diary*, 14–15 May 1660

The Hague is Hampton-Court turned into a large town.

William Hazlitt, *Notes of a Journey through France and Italy*, 1826

At the Hague whence I write there is nothing which need detain an Englishman (who has seen everything in his own country).

Sydney Smith, Letter to Lady Grey, 12 May 1837

*The king lives at the Ha-gue and I'll be bound it's haguish enuf for Holland is a cold marshy flatulint country and lies so low they're only saved by being dammed.

Thomas Hood, *Up the Rhine*, 1840 (Martha Penny writing)

The Hague is a town of 70,000 people, with a number of streets of excellent houses, bordered with fine trees. I never saw a city where the well-to-do classes seemed to have given the whole place so much of their own air of wealth, finished cleanliness, and comfort; but I never saw one, either, in which my heart would have so sunk at the thought of living.

Matthew Arnold, Letter to Miss Arnold, 12 June 1859

between Katwyk-sur-Rhin and The Hague

The country through which I now passed is extremely rich and pretty, being the only part of Holland which I had yet seen with a tendency towards undulation.

Charles Tennant, *A Tour, etc.*, 1824

Middelburg

I am in the midst of the worst humourd people.

Sir Philip Sidney, Letter to Lord Burghley, 11 December 1585

Nijmegen

If you were with me in this Town you would be ready to receive visits from your Nottingham friends. No 2 places were ever more ressembling; one has but to give the Maese the name of the Trent and there is no distinguishing the prospects: the Houses, like those of Nottingham, built one above another and intermixd in the same manner with Trees and Gardens. The Tower they call Julius Caesar's has the same situation with Nottingham Castle, and I can't help fancying I see from it the Trent field, Adboulton, etc,. places so well known to us. 'Tis true the fortifications make a considerable difference.

Lady Mary Wortley Montagu, Letter to Sarah Chiswell, 13 August 1716

The elevation on which this town is built is a range of high land stretching round like the side of a great basin, with a large sweep towards the north as far as the eye can carry. In another respect, also, the basin is not an inappropriate comparison, for it seems as if Nature had here kindly interposed a barrier against the further progress of the waters, and as if tired with her monotonous labours, she had said, 'Here will I finish Holland;' and raising herself out of the reach of Holland's swampy flats, had commenced another work called 'Germany.'

Charles Tennant, *A Tour, etc.*, 1824

and Germany, between Ostend and Cologne
And onward thro' those dreary flats
We move, with scanty space to sit on.
Flanked by stout girls with steeple hats,
And waists that paralyse a Briton –

By many a tidy little town,
Where tidy little Fraus sit knitting;
(The men's pursuits are, lying down,
Smoking perennial pipes, and spitting).

Charles Stuart Calverley, 'Dover to Munich', in *Verses and Translations*, 1861

Rotterdam

en route to, through the canals

We had abundant leisure to observe the picturesque craft, with their high cabins, and cabin-windows well furnished with flower-pots and frows, – in fact, floating houses – while the real houses scarcely above the water-level, looked like so many family arks that had gone only ashore, and would be got off next tide. These dwellings of either kind looked scrupulously clean, and particularly gay; the houses, indeed, with their bright, pea-green doors and shutters, shining, bran new, as if by common consent, or some clause in their lease, they had all been freshly painted within the last week. But probably they must thus be continually done in oil to keep out the water, – the very Dryads, to keep them dry, being favoured with a coat, or rather pantaloons, of sky-blue or red, or some smart colour, on their trunks and lower limbs. At times, however, nothing could be seen but the banks, till perchance you detected a steeple and a few chimneys, as if a village had been sowed there, and was beginning to come up. The vagaries of the perspective, originating in such an arrangement, were rather amusing. For instance, I saw a ruminating cow apparently chewing the top of a tree, a Quixotic donkey attacking a windmill, and a wonderful horse, quietly reposing and dozing with a weathercock growing out of his back. Indeed it is not extravagant to suppose that a frog, without hopping, often enjoys a bird's eye view of a neighbouring town. So little was seen of the country, that my aunt, in the simplicity of her heart, inquired seriously, 'Where's Holland?' 'It ought to be hereabouts, madam,' said the yellow-face, 'if it wasn't swamped in the night.' 'Swamped indeed!' said the red-face; 'it's sinful to mistrust Providence, but renounce me, if I could live in such a place without an everlasting rainbow overhead to remind me of the Promise.' 'They'd be drowned tomorrow, sir,' said the captain, 'if they wasn't continually driving piles, and building dams, like so many beavers on two legs.' 'They have all the ways of beavers, sure enough,' chimed in my uncle, 'and, egad!' pointing to a round-sterned fellow at work on the bank, 'they have the same breadth of tail.'

Thomas Hood, *Up the Rhine*, 1840

We arived late at Roterdam, where was at that time their annual Mart or Faire, so furnish'd with pictures (especially Landscips, and Drolleries, as they call those clownish representations) as I was amaz'd: some of these I bought and sent into England. The reason of this store of pictures, and their cheapnesse proceeded from their want of Land, to employ their Stock; so as 'tis an ordinary thing to find, a common Farmor lay out two, or 3000 pounds in this Commodity, their houses are full of them, and they vend them at their Kerams'es to very greate gaines.

John Evelyn, *Diary*, 13 August 1641

All the streets are pav'd with broad stones, and before the meanest artificer's doors, seats of various colour'd marbles, and so neatly kept that I'll assure you I walk'd allmost all over the Town Yesterday, incognito, in my slippers without receiving one spot of Dirt, and you may see the Dutch maids washing the Pavement of the street with more application than ours do our bed chambers. The town seems full of people with such busie faces, all in motion, that I can hardly fancy that it is not some celebrated fair, but I see 'tis every day the same. 'Tis certain no Town can be more advantagiously situated for Commerce. Here are 7 large Canals on which the merchant ships come up to the very doors of their Houses. The shops and warehouses are of a surprizing neatness and Magnificence, fill'd with an incredible Quantity of fine Merchandize, and so much cheaper than what we see in England, I have much adoe to perswade me selfe I am still so near it. Here is neither Dirt nor Beggary to be seen. One is not shock'd with those loathsome Cripples so common in London, nor teiz'd with the Importunitys of idle Fellows and Wenches that chuse to be nasty and lazy. The common Servants and little shop Women here are more nicely clean than most of our Ladys, and the great variety of neat dresses (every Woman dressing her Head after her own Fashion) is an additional pleasure in seeing the Town.

Lady Mary Wortley Montagu, Letter to Lady Mar, 3 August 1716

Rotterdam is remarkedly clean: the Dutch even wash the outside brick-work of their houses.

Mary Shelley, *History of a Six Weeks' Tour* (8 September 1814), 1817

There is in this town a peculiarity in most of the buildings . . . the peculiarity is in erecting the buildings so much out of the perpendicular, that to a stranger, at first sight, they seem to be in imminent danger of falling; but on further observation it is evident that this is not matter of accident, but of design . . . under the idea that the building is preserved from damp by thus more effectually throwing off the water from the foundation, and . . . it is only the front of the building which is out of the perpendicular; the front being here the last part of the work, and in little or no degree contributing to the support of the fabrick.

Charles Tennant, *A Tour, etc.*, 1824

Before me lie dark waters,
In broad canals and deep,
Whereon the silver moonbeams
Sleep, restless in their sleep:
A sort of vulgar Venice
Reminds me where I am, –
Yes, yes, you are in England,
And I'm at Rotterdam

Thomas Hood, *To* *****, 1840

The sweep of Rotterdam seen from the river, wrapt in smoke, with its towers and spires, and brick houses breaking through, with masts of ships everywhere, reminds one very much of London; in fact, the great towns of Holland remind one constantly of one side of England – its commercial side; but never does one feel more the splendid variety of England, that it has so much more than its mere commercial side; and even its commercial side it has on a scale so prodigious that this has a grandiosity of its own which in Holland is nowhere to be found.

Matthew Arnold, Letter to Miss Arnold, 19 June 1859

Utrecht

I groaned with the idea of living all winter in so shocking a place.

James Boswell, Letter to John Johnston of Grange, 23 September 1763

At Utrecht you begin to have a sniff of dry, wholesome air, and the trees look as if they stood in real ground, and the grass as if it was not growing in the water.

Matthew Arnold, Letter to his sister, 19 June 1859

Vlissingen (Flushing)

Uppon Thursdai we came into this town drivin to land at Ramekins becaws the wynd began to ryse in such sort as our masters durst not anker before the town, and from thence came with as durty a waulk as ever poor governor entred his charge withall. I fynd the people very glad of me, and promis my self as much surety in keeping this town as popular goodwill gotten by light hopes . . . may breed me, for indeed the garrison is far to weak to command by authority which is pitty for how great a jewel this is to the crown of England and the Queenes safety I need not wryte it to your Lordeshippe who knows it so well, yet I must neede sai the better I know it the more I fynd the preciowsnes of it.

Sir Philip Sidney, Letter to the Earl of Leicester, Flushing, 22 November 1585

The situation of this towne is very memorable. For it is built in the forme of a pitcher, which is slender at both the endes, and wide in the middle. In regard whereof the name of the towne is derived from the Dutch word, *Flessche*, which signifieth a pitcher. For indeed he that shall rightly consider the forme of the building thereof will say that it doth very neare represent the fashion of a pitcher. For I for mine owne part observed the site of it, and found it very correspondent to the mould of a pitcher, the endes being slender, the middle long. Which is the reason that the inhabitants doe represent the figure of a pitcher in their flagges and banners that are advanced at the tops of the mastes in their ships.

Thomas Coryate, *Crudities*, 1611

And now me thought the Seane was infinitely chang'd, to see so prety and neate a towne in the frontier: Here we first went to view the Pr: of Oranges house and garden, the Wales whereof are washed with Neptune continualy; after that the State-house, which are generally in all the Low countries magnificently built.

John Evelyn, *Diary*, 22 July 1641

NETHERLANDS ANTILLES

Curaçao

Curaçao: the long barren island, shaped like a ship hit broadside by a gale – it seems to be listing. On the west, the land slopes up gently to a central range of sharp-peaked hills; on the east, it falls steeply away to the shore. Almost no vegetation and hardly any houses, until you round the cape and see Willemstad. The toy-like prettiness of the town makes you gasp. It is absurdly gay; orange, crimson, scarlet, parrot green and canary yellow. I don't know if this architecture is typical of the Caribbean, but it is extremely individual: ridiculous little classical porches, window-frames decorated with bold slapdash festoons of colour, an air of mock grandeur, of Negro high spirits, and something of the decor of the Russian ballet.

Christopher Isherwood, *The Condor and the Cows*, 1949

NEW CALEDONIA (France)

Those people approach nearer the dress of Adam before he sewed the fig leaves together, than any we have seen before.

William Wales, *Journal*, 5 September 1774

The dress of these our good friends is somewhat singular – when we found them they were totally naked to the Penis, which was wrapt up in leaves, and whatever you gave them, or they by any means attain'd; was immediately apply'd there; nor wou'd they care one farthing for any article of dress, that cou'd not in some form be made to contribute to the decorating that favourite part. I gave one of them one day a stocking – he very deliberately pull'd it on there – I then gave him a string of Beads, with it he ty'd the stocking up – I then presented him with a medal, which he immediately hung to it – in short, let that noble part be well decorated and fine, they're perfectly happy, and totally indifferent about the state of all the rest of the Body.

Charles Clerke, *Log of the Proceedings of . . . His Majesty's Ship Resolution*, 1774

NEW GUINEA

'God made the country,' said Cowper, in his rather too blank verse. In New Guinea he would have had his doubts.

Aldous Huxley, *Do What You Will*, 1929

Bird-shaped island, with secretive bird-voices
Land of apocalypse, where the earth dances,
The mountains speak, the doors of the spirit open,
And men are shaken by obscure trances.

J.P.McAuley, 'New Guinea', in *A Vision of Ceremony*, 1956

On a map, it resembles an obese, gigantic buzzard.

William Manchester, *American Caesar*, 1979

Sepik River

He took us to our first 'black water,' which is the loveliest thing the Sepik has to offer. The Sepik itself is a wide, monotonous and rather dirty yellow river, remarkable only for its varying load of drifting islands which have detached themselves from the half-submerged fen lands and have drifted out through some waterway and finally will float out to sea. But into these fens lead what the native call *barets* – and you must all learn this word, because I know of no English one to describe them. They are like canals. Often the natives have either cut them entirely, or widened them, or changed them. They flow from inland lakes into the Sepik, when the Sepik is low, and sometimes when the Sepik is in flood from its mountain sources hundreds of miles higher up, the *barets* flow backwards into the inland lakes. The water in them, unless too much of the Sepik has gotten in, is black, coal black, and shining with a dull lustre, and tasting like lily-stems and sun-heated oil. And the lake to which we came, through a *baret*, was all black, polished like a mirror, with faraway mountains ringing it all about and on its shining surface floated pink and white lotuses, lying in patches of thousands, their pads still and fixed, on the black water, while among them stood, as if posed for a portrait, white ospreys, and blue herons. It is all as ordered, as simple in its few contrasting themes, as a Japanese print, and the lack of miscellaneous, only half-congruent notes makes it seem unreal. It was before sunrise, when we slid into the centre of the lake and the black irregular arms of water stretched away among further and further patches of lotuses, seeming almost to meet the mountains, and there was no human thing there except ourselves. It is the best this country has to offer, and very, very good.

Margaret Mead, Letter from Tchambuli, 1 February 1933

NEW ZEALAND

Was this Country settled by an Industrus people they would very soon be supply'd not only with the necessarys but many of the luxuries of life.

Captain James Cook, *Journal*, March 1770

That rude chaotic country.

George Forster, *A Voyage Round the World*, 1777

Perhaps in future ages, when the maritime powers of Europe lose their American colonies, they may think of making new establishments in more distant regions; and if it were ever possible for Europeans to have humanity enough to acknowledge the indigenous tribes of the South Sea as their brethren, we might have settlements which would not be defiled with the blood of innocent nations.

Ibid., November 1773

I believe we were all glad to leave New Zealand. It is not a pleasant place. Amongst the natives there is absent that charming simplicity which is found at Tahiti; and the greater part of the English are the very refuse of society. Neither is the country itself attractive. I look back to but one bright spot, and that is Waimate with its Christian inhabitants.

Charles Darwin, *Journal . . . During the Voyage . . . of H.M.S.Beagle*, 1832–6

New Zealand is destined to a giant's career. It is a youthful Hercules that will throttle the snakes about its cradle. The climate, not too relaxing, the soil, the waters, the interconnexion between the noblest children of civilisation, and by very much the noblest race of savages in the world . . . compose a body of inauguration for this enterprise which wears a promise hardly within the compass of disappointment. The long infancy of all other colonies will be spared to this.

Thomas de Quincey, *The Opium Question with China in 1840*

The day was the perfection of New Zealand weather,

which is the perfection of all climates – hot, but rarely sultry; bright, but not glaring, from the vivid green with which the earth is generally clothed.

Bishop George Augustus Selwyn, Journal Letter, 13 November 1843

I believe I have now acquired the two greatest requisites for bushmen in New Zealand, *viz.*, the capability of walking barefoot, and the proper method of cooking and eating fern root.

Thomas Brunner, *Journal of an Expedition to the Interior of the Middle Island*, (21 October 1847), 1848

One of the great evils of New Zealand travelling is the scarcity of portable food.

Percy Smith, *Notes of a Journey from Taranaki to Mokau, etc.*, 1858

New Zealand seems far better adapted to develop and maintain in health the physical than the intellectual nature.

Samuel Butler, *A First Year in Canterbury Settlement*, 1863

near Christchurch
On the morning after I arrived, for the first time in my life I saw a sheep killed. It is rather unpleasant, but I suppose I shall get as indifferent to it as other people are by and by. To show you that the knives of the establishment are numbered, I may mention that the same knife killed the sheep and carved the mutton we had for dinner.

Ibid.

A mountain here is only beautiful if it has good grass on it. Scenery is not scenery – it is 'country' . . . If it is good for sheep, it is beautiful, magnificent, and all the rest of it; if not, it is not worth looking at.

Ibid.

On their first few experiences of one of those New Zealand rivers people dislike them extremely, they then become callous to them, and are as unreasonably foolhardy as they were before timorous; they then generally get an escape from drowning or two, or else they get drowned in earnest.

Ibid.

The great drawback to New Zealand, – or I should more properly say to travelling in New Zealand, – comes from the feeling that after crossing the world and journeying over so many miles, you have not at all succeeded in getting away from England. When you have arrived there you are, as it were, next door to your own house, and yet you have a two months barrier between yourself and your home.

Anthony Trollope, *Australia and New Zealand*, 1873

Lo! Here where each league hath its fountains
In isles of deep fern and tall pine,
And breezes snow-cooled on the mountains,
Or keen from the limitless brine,
See men to the battlefield pressing
To conquer one foe – the stern soil,
Their kingship in labour expressing,
Their lordship in toil.

William Pember Reeves, *N.Z.*, 1893

If it would not look too much like showing off, I would tell the reader where New Zealand is. For he is as I was: he thinks he knows.

Mark Twain, *More Tramps Abroad*, 1897

The first thing that strikes an Englishman about the landscape of New Zealand is the absence of atmosphere. The jagged hills stand out sharp against the clear sky like a photograph seen through a stereoscope. There are no half-lights, no melting mist or wreathing haze, no vague distances.

Maurice Baring, *Round the World in Any Number of Days*, 1913

The longer I live the more I turn to New Zealand. I thank God I was born in New Zealand. A young country is a real heritage, though it takes time to recognise it. But New Zealand is in my very bones. What wouldn't I give to have a look at it!

Katherine Mansfield, Letter to the Hon. Dorothy Brett, 19 March 1922

New Zealand! I've never seen so much to eat as I saw in New Zealand. Meat! Meat! Meat! Tea! Tea! Tea!

Alfred Viscount Northcliffe, Interview with the *Sydney Sun*, 7 September 1921, in *My Journey Round the World*, 1923

These islands;
the remnant peaks of a lost continent,
roof of an old world, molten droppings
from earth's bowels, gone cold;
ribbed with rock, resisting the sea's corrosion
for an age, and an age to come. Of three races
the home: two passing in conquest
or sitting under the leaves, or on shady doorsteps
with quiet hands, in old age, childless.
And we, the latest: their blood on our hands: scions
of men who scaled ambition's
tottering slopes, whose desires
encompassed earth and heaven: we have prospered
greatly,
we, the destined race, rulers of conquered isles,
sprouting like bulbs in warm darkness, putting out
white shoots under the wet sack of Empire.

A.R.D.Fairburn, 'Album Leaves', in *Dominion*, 1938

To the young man I would say:

Get out! Look sharp, my boy,
before the roots are down,
before the equations are struck,
before a face or a landscape
has power to shape or destroy.
This land is a lump without leaven,
a body that has no nerves.
Don't be content to live in
a sort of second grade heaven
with first-grade butter, fresh air,
and paper in every toilet;
becoming a butt for the malice
of those who have stayed and soured,
staying in turn to sour,
to smile, and savage the young.
If you're enterprising and able,
smuggle your talents away,
hawk them in livelier markets
where people are willing to pay.
If you have no stomach for roughage,
if patience isn't your religion,
if you must have sherry with your bitters,
if money and fame are your pigeon,
if you feel that you need success
and long for a good address,
don't anchor here in the desert –
the fishing isn't so good:
take a ticket for Megalopolis,
don't stay in this neighbourhood!

A.R.D. Fairburn, 'I'm Older than You, Please Listen', in *Strange Rendezvous*, 1941

There is nothing soft about New Zealand, the country. It is very hard and sinewy, and will outlast many of those who try to alter it.

John Mulgan, *Report on Experience*, 1947

Half-gallon Quarter-acre Pavlova Paradise.

Title of book by Austin Mitchell, 1972

What I couldn't understand was why this wingless night-grubber had ever been chosen as New Zealand's national image. It was a bad move. New Zealanders should never have called themselves *Kiwis*. Perhaps it has been the Kiwi aspect of New Zealand life and character that encouraged visitors in the past to call them dull. Though not a unique native of the country, the glorious albatross would have been my first choice.

J.B. Priestley, *A Visit to New Zealand*, 1974

Compared to England it is like the week after a bloodless and smiling revolution.

Ibid.

The seasons blur, they lack the humours of the Old World.

James McNeish, *As For the Godwits*, 1977

'You know,' I suddenly said to our friends, 'we have been here for three weeks, travelling all over the country and we have never heard the words "New Zealand" mentioned. At home it is always "Australia and New Zealand" in one breath. Here New Zealand has never cropped up. How do you account for that?' There was a long pause.

'Perhaps because it is irrelevant,' volunteered one of our Australian escorts.

Edward Heath, *Travels, People and Places in My Life*, 1977

You are now landing in New Zealand. Everybody is requested to put their watches back ten years.

Anon.

If an English butler and an English nanny sat down to design a country, they would come up with New Zealand.

Anon.

Terrible Tragedy in the South Seas. Three million people trapped alive!

Tom Scott, Apocryphal newspaper headline, *New Zealand Listener*, April 1979

A little piece of Victoriana in the Antipodes.

Tony Simpson, in a letter, 1980

New Zealanders

A few expressions were not familiar to me. When we should say in England 'Certainly not,' it is here 'No fear,' or 'Don't *you* believe it.' When they want to answer in the affirmative they say 'It is *so*,' 'It does *so*.' The word 'hum', too, without pronouncing the *u*, is in amusing requisition. I perceived that this stood either for assent, or doubt, or wonder, or a general expression of comprehension without compromising the hummer's own opinion, and indeed for a great many more things than these; in fact, if a man did not want to say anything at all he said 'hum-hum.' It is a very good expression, and saves much trouble when its familiar use has been acquired. Beyond these trifles I noticed no Yankeeism, and the conversation was English in point of expression. I was rather startled at hearing one gentleman ask another whether he meant to wash this year, and receive the answer 'No.' I soon discovered that a person's sheep are himself. If his sheep are clean, he is clean. He does not wash his *sheep* before shearing, but *he* washes; and, most marvellous of all, it is not his sheep which lamb, but he 'lambs down' himself.

Samuel Butler, *A First Year in Canterbury Settlement*, 1863

New Zealand is the land of British family mysteries. On

occasion heirs to titles and fortunes have been unearthed here. But the New Zealanders certainly don't like titles. I should think, first, because in the mind of each of them there is the desire for a Utopia – a land of equality, and secondly, because they have had some very bad specimens of titled people here. Even now each town has its little coterie of well-born remittance men – those who live upon doles from England.

Alfred Viscount Northcliffe, *My Journey Round the World* (August 1921), 1923

Super-Suburbia of the Southern Seas,
Nature's – and Reason's – true Antipodes,
Hail, dauntless pioneers, intrepid souls,
Who cleared the Bush – to make a lawn for bowls,
And smashed the noble Maori to ensure
The second-rate were socially secure!
Saved by the Wowsers from the Devil's Tricks,
Your shops, your pubs, your minds all close at six.
Your battle-cry's a deep, contented snore,
You voted Labour, then you worked no more.
The Wharfies' Heaven, the gourmet's Purgat'ry:
Ice-cream on mutton, swilled around in tea!

A Maori fisherman, the legends say,
Dredged up New Zealand in a single day.
I've seen the catch, and here's my parting crack –
It's under-sized; for God's sake throw it back!

Wynford Vaughan-Thomas, *Farewell to New Zealand*

Oh, they crossed the Upper and Under Dogs
To produce this Island Race, Sir
A Society neither Up nor Down
With a puzzled Look on its Face, Sir.

'Whim Wham', 'Pioneer Stock', in *Whim Wham Land*, 1942

That we may never lack two Sundays in a week
One to rest and one to play
That we may worship in the liturgical drone
Of the race-commentator and the radio raconteur
That we may avoid distinction and exception
Worship the mean, cultivate the mediocre
Live in a state house, raise forcibly-educated children
Receive family benefits, and standard wages and a pension
And rest in peace in a state crematorium
Saint Allblack
Saint Monday Raceday
Saint Stabilisation
Pray for us.

From all foreigners, with their unintelligible cooking
From the vicious habit of public enjoyment
From kermesse and carnival, high day and festival
From pubs cafés bullfights and barbecues
From Virgil and vintages, fountains and fresco-painting
From afterthought and apperception
From tragedy, from comedy
And from the arrow of God
Saint Anniversaryday
Saint Arborday
Saint Labourday
Defend us.

When the bottles are empty
And the keg runs sour
And the cinema is shut and darkened
And the radio gone up in smoke
And the sports-ground flooded
When the tote goes broke
And the favourite scratches
And the brass bands are silenced
And the car is rusted by the roadside
Saint Fathersday
Saint Mothersday
Saint Happybirthday
Have mercy on us.

And for your petitioner, poor little Jim,
Saint Hocus,
Saint Focus
Saint Bogus
And Saint Billy Bungstarter
Have mercy on him.

M.K. Joseph, 'Secular Litany', *Imaginary Islands*, 1955

I remembered that Jung had suggested somewhere that the soul of a conquered people enters, and tends to dominate, the unconscious of their conquerors . . . . Would I find that among younger and perhaps more sensitive and imaginative New Zealanders, no longer aware of the British background, perhaps deliberately rejecting the British heritage to affirm their New Zealand nationality, the Maoris would seem more and more important, their traditions and history and way of life, their legends and arts, filling and then enriching a vacancy, a new blankness intolerable to the upper levels of the unconscious and consciousness alike?

J.B. Priestley, *A Visit to New Zealand*, 1974

In New Zealand, as in Italy, two countries of comparably short national life, the greatest crime is held to be self-criticism. We are free to criticise others at will, we may even invite others to criticise us, since such criticism may easily be ignored as foreign. But we must never criticise ourselves. This is the ultimate sin.

James McNeish, *As For the Godwits*, 1977

Maoris

When they attack they work themselves up into a kind

of artificial courage, which does not allow them time to think much.

Sir Joseph Banks, *Journal of the Rt Hon Sir Joseph Banks* (30 November 1769), 1768–71

The bones were clearly human; upon them were evident marks of their having been dressed on the fire; the meat was not entirely picked off them, and on the grisly ends, which were gnawed, were evident marks of teeth; and they were accidentally found in a provision basket. On asking the people what bones they were, they answered; 'The bones of a man.' – 'And have you eaten the flesh?' – 'Yes.' – 'Have you none of it left?' – 'No.''Why did you not eat the woman we saw to-day in the water?' – 'She was our relation.' – 'Whom, then, do you eat?' – 'Those who are killed in war.'

Ibid., 16 January 1770

and the English

An Englishman here said to the Bishop the other day, 'I find your Lordship's words in one of your Journals fully verified, where you say that the Maories are the most covetous people you ever met with.' To which the Bishop added, 'But you have only quoted half my sentence, for I said further, "except the English."'

Charles Abraham, *Journal of a Walk from Auckland to Taranaki*, 1855

It is very difficult to make the New Zealanders explain the nature of their religious belief. One superstition seems general with all the tribes respecting the formation of the world; or, rather, of their own island; for that is the place of the first importance in their estimation. They say a man, or a god, or some great spirit, was fishing in his war-canoe, and pulled up a large fish, which instantly turned into an island; and a lizard came upon that, and brought up a man out of the water by his long hair; and he was the father of all the New Zealanders.

Augustus Earle, *Narrative of a Residence in New Zealand in 1827*, 1832
(version of the Legend of Maui)

and European music

I had brought my violin from Sydney, on which I used to play occasionally. The New Zealanders generally expressed the greatest dislike to it; and my companions used to rally me much on the subject, saying it was not that the savages did not like music, but it was my discordant playing that frightened them away; which might be true. It was, however, a useful discovery for us all; as I often took that method of civilly driving them out of our house when we grew tired of their company.

Ibid.

Looking at the New Zealander one naturally compares him with the Tahitian; both belonging to the same family of mankind. The comparison, however, tells heavily against the New Zealander. He may perhaps be superior in energy, but in every other respect his character is of a much lower order. One glance at their respective expressions brings conviction to the mind that one is a savage, the other a civilised man .... No doubt the extraordinary manner in which tatooing is here practised gives a disagreeable expression to their countenances. The complicated but symmetrical figures covering the whole face, puzzle and mislead an unaccustomed eye: it is moreover probable, that the deep incisions, by destroying the play of the superficial muscles, give an air of rigid inflexibility. But, besides this, there is a twinkling in the eye which cannot indicate anything but cunning and ferocity.

Charles Darwin, *Journal . . . During the Voyage . . . of H.M.S.Beagle*, 1832–6

The two cardinal virtues of good humour and patience are indispensable to the traveller in New Zealand, who wishes to move with any comfort, the first is particularly acceptable to the natives, who are naturally of a joyous and good-humoured temperament, and who abhor a *tangata riri*, as they call an irritable man; combined, they enable a man to get along smoothly, amidst delays which he must inevitably encounter, with a race who do not value time themselves, and cannot understand the importance which we attach to it.

John Johnson, *Notes from a Journal*, December 1846

One of the permanent difficulties in the way of a complete pacification of New Zealand is the Maories' innate love of fighting, for mere fighting's sake.

Herbert Meade, *A Ride through the Disturbed Districts of New Zealand* (January 1865), 1870

In humours and cussedness, as in passion and casuistry, the modulation of the voice and the care of natural children, the Maori bests us. By so far and much further. We no longer regard him as different, which he is, but as backward, which is insulting .... We know, still, very little about him. We, the average, we. We know in fact rather less about the Maori than the Anglo-Indians knew about the Indian before the fall of the Raj. We know that we have softened him and we are proud of it, though we use another word. We say integrate. This was our aim and this we have achieved, the politicians and New Zealand House say, as if we had done it all and done it all ourselves. We have softened him.

James McNeish, *As For the Godwits*, 1977

Auckland

I regard Auckland as being the representative city of New Zealand. . . . Dunedin is a Scotch town and

Christchurch an English town, here planted, – and Wellington is a chosen site for a parliament; – but Auckland is redolent of New Zealand . . . . It may be well to notice here the fact that as Auckland considers herself to be the cream of New Zealand, so does New Zealand consider herself to be the cream of the British Empire. The pretension is made in, I think, every British colony that I visited . . . . But the New Zealander among John Bulls is the most John-Bullish. He admits the supremacy of England to every place in the world, only he is more English than any Englishman at home, He tells you that he has the same climate, – only somewhat improved . . . .

Anthony Trollope, *Australia and New Zealand*, 1873

Last, loneliest, loveliest, exquisite, apart –
On us, on us the unswerving season smiles.
Who wonder 'mid our fern why men depart
To seek the Happy Isles!

Rudyard Kipling, *The Song of the Cities*, 1893

Christchurch

It was Junior England all the way to Christchurch – in fact, just a garden. And Christchurch is an English town, with an English park annex, and a winding English brook just like the Avon – and named the Avon; but from a man, not from Shakespeare's river . . . . It is a settled old community, with all the serenities, the graces, the conveniences, and the comforts of the ideal home-life. If it had an Established Church and social inequality it would be England all over again with hardly a lack.

Mark Twain, *More Tramps Abroad*, 1897

As to the appearance of Christchurch architecturally, I confess I was disappointed. Of course I know that the day was vile as regards its weather and no place will look well in drizzling rain and driving gale. But still, I saw that the usual mean wooden buildings, interspersed with pretentious edifices of stucco-covered brick, were here, as in Wellington and Auckland, the regular style, and I was disappointed, because I had great hopes of Christchurch developing into a fine modern city when I was here before, and it seems to me (I hope its citizens will forgive me for saying so, but I don't suppose they will) to have become somewhat slipshod and down-at-heel in appearance.

F.T. Bullen, *Advance Australasia*, 1907

It looks as if it might have been lent to New Zealand by the Anglican Church – at its best . . . . It represents a dream carried 13,000 miles, down into the Antipodes, and subtly changing as soon as it began to be realized.

J.B.Priestley, *A Visit to New Zealand*, 1974

Canterbury

On this great plain the eye
Sees less of land than sky,
And men seem to inhabit here
As much the cloud-crossed hemisphere
As the flat earth. Trains travel fast and straight,
And travellers early or late
Think of their destination
More than of pasture, wheatfield, wayside station.
Here birds and winds fly free,
And tree is miles from tree
Except where in dark ranks they muster
Against the gales or cluster
Befriending lonely farms.
Tired tramps and trampers fare
Sadly along the endless roads, but the hare
Is lucky, and the magpie, black and white
Highwayman with his shout.
Sounds are soon dead being echoless
In the vast emptiness,
Though thunder and the ocean roar
Carry, on calm days, far:
And some sounds hardly ever rest:
The sound of wind from nor'east or nor'west
And three great rivers with proud Maori names
Chafing worn shingle till the ocean tames
Their wildness. This is my holy land
Of childhood. Trying to comprehend
And learn it like the features of a friend,
Sight rides on power-poles and tops of trees
From the long eastern beaches and loud seas
League after league
Till definition fades in bluish vague
Distance: then dreams begin
To see in vision colourless and thin
Beyond the western foothills lost
The huge and desolate ranges of the Coast.

Basil Dowling, *Canterbury*, 1949

Mount Cook

No one can mistake it. If a person says he *thinks* he has seen Mount Cook, you may be quite sure that he has not seen it. The moment it comes into sight the exclamation is, 'That is Mount Cook!' – not 'That *must* be Mount Cook!' There is no possibility of mistake.

Samuel Butler, *A First Year in Canterbury Settlement*, 1863

Dunedin

The people are Scotch. They stopped here on their way from home to heaven – thinking they had arrived.

Mark Twain, *More Tramps Abroad*, 1897

There is something about Dunedin that appeals very strongly to the visitor fresh from home, and I think that something may be summed up in the word 'weather.' During the winter at any rate Dunedin can compete successfully with us in Britain in the matter of atmospheric uncertainty of conditions and disagreeableness. It is no uncommon thing to get five or six samples of weather in almost the same number of hours, each vieing with the other which shall be the most unpleasant. It is a strenuous climate, and it breeds strenuous folk as it always did, and therefore it is that Dunedin strikes the visitors from Britain as being homely.

F.T. Bullen, *Advance Australasia,* 1907

I couldn't help feeling that what had once been a noble attempt to create a South Pacific Edinburgh, with the best of it still there, had been leased more recently to Ohio and Southern California . . . . I was troubled by a vague feeling that the city must have been governed alternatively by wise men and blockheads.

J.B. Priestley, *A Visit to New Zealand,* 1974

Dusky Bay

The climate of Dusky Bay is, I must own, its greatest inconvenience, and can never be supposed a healthy one. During the whole of our stay, we had only one week of continued fair weather, all the rest of the time the rain predominated. But perhaps the climate was less noxious to Englishmen, than to any other nation, because it is analogous to their own.

George Forster, *A Voyage Round the World,* 1777

Invercargill

The Last Lamp-post in the World.

Quoted by Rudyard Kipling, *Something of Myself,* 1937 – of 1891

Mocatoa

The place is like the inside of a brown cup, with a small ledge just inside the rim.

Charles Abraham, *Journal of a Walk from Auckland to Taranaki,* 1855

Napier

I once asked a native what sort of road it was from Napier to Wairoa; he described it simply by holding up one hand with the fingers outstretched and running the forefinger of the other hand up and down them, and we found his description correct. Lofty ranges, on the summit of which crops out a hard shelly conglomerate, and deep glens constitute the character of the country.

Lt Col. J.H.H. St John, *Pakeha Rambles through Maori Lands,* 1873

The feature which was most impressive was a precipitous cliff, which, only about fifty yards from the shore end of the pier, rose a sheer 300 feet into the air, as if defying all further ingress to the country. A good road wound around the base of this cliff – as good a road, indeed, as any we can boast of at home – and I noticed presently that a low, concrete sea-wall had begun to skirt it. Then the side-walk of asphalt was planted at intervals of about six or seven yards with the beautiful Norfolk Island pine, a species of araucaria, but not nearly so grotesque as the 'monkey puzzle' tree. As we walked on the cliff to shoreward sloped downward, and gave pretty views of houses perched here and there amid embowering foliage, until presently we turned a corner, and lo! I was in Tunbridge Wells, at the corner of the Pantiles looking towards the Pump Room. The illusion was almost perfect, in spite of the many wooden houses which alternate with the stucco-fronted ones here, as elsewhere in New Zealand . . . . The town wears an air of solid prosperity, but it is quite sedate and satisfied in its appearance, as if bustle and growth were neither looked for or, indeed, much desired.

F.T.Bullen, *Advance Australasia,* 1907

Nelson

There was certainly a sleepiness about the place when regarded with commercial eyes. But though sleepy, it seemed to be happy . . . . Every house was neat and pretty. The site is, I think, as lovely as that of any town I ever saw. Merely to breathe there, and to dream, and to look around was a delight. Nobody seemed to be either rich or poor, – to be either great or humble. They have their own Parliament House, and their own parliament, and manage themselves after a sleepy, fat, and plentiful, rather than prosperous fashion, which is not without its advantages in the world . . . . I was very much in love with Nelson during the few hours that I passed there; but it is not the place to which I would send a young man to make a fortune.

Anthony Trollope, *Australia and New Zealand,* 1873

Poverty Bay

The Bay . . . I have named *Poverty Bay* because it afforded us no one thing we wanted.

Captain James Cook, *Journal,* 11 October 1769

Ohinemutu

The whole scene strikes the visitor as being almost of an

unearthly character – the large cauldrons, the smaller springs, in fierce ebullition, often sending up jets of boiling water, the heated streams running in every direction, the sulphurous vapour tainting the air – the feeling that in an instant he might be engulphed, and suffer a horrible death, leaves an impression that no one who has visited Ohinemutu, will readily forget.

John Johnson, *Notes from a Journal*, January 1847

Ohinemutu, a settlement on the southern shore of the lake, built in the very midst of the hot springs, which surround what is considered by one who has also seen those of Iceland, the largest geysers in the world, and an infinite number of hot springs; so that, except during a strong southerly breeze, the inhabitants live in a perpetual cloud of steam . . . .

The whole village is built on a thin crust of rock and soil, roofing over one vast boiler. Hot springs hiss and seethe in every direction; some spurting upwards and boiling with the greatest fury, others merely at an agreeable warmth. From every crack and crevice spurt forth jets of steam or hot air, and the open bay of the lake itself is studded far and near with boiling springs and bubbling steam-jets. So thin is the crust on which these men have built their little town and lived for generations, that in most places, after merely thrusting a walking-stick into the ground beneath our feet, steam instantly followed its withdrawal.

Nature is here the public cook. Food is boiled by being hung in a flaxen basket in one of the countless boiling pools; nature also finding salt. Stewing and baking are performed by simply scraping a shallow hole in the earth, wherein to place the pot, and covering it up again to keep the steam in; or by burying the food between layers of fern and earth in one of the hot-air passages.

Herbert Meade, *A Ride through the Disturbed Districts of New Zealand* (December 1864), 1870

Of all the queer places I ever saw in my life, Ohinemutu is certainly the queerest; . . . Everything is of course pervaded by a brimstony flavour which soon however ceases to be noticed; and the effects of the atmosphere and of the baths are visible in the shiny skins and bad teeth of the inhabitants . . . .

Starting from the *whare-runanga* . . . we were introduced *seriatim* to some of the peculiarities of the place . . . . A little further on, a brook, brawling down a slight incline, and partly concealing itself under the misty steam always hanging over it, was bridged by some rough flag-stones; a few steps beyond this on each side yawned a deep black hole emitting a concentration of stinks, and disclosing a central mass of fetid boiling mud in a state of constant agitation, the orifice in the middle being every now and then closed and covered by a huge bubble which, bursting with a 'B-b-b-lobb' let out a fresh collection of stenches; it was just as if all the rotten eggs in New Zealand were being cracked at one and the same moment.

Lt Col. J.H.H. St John, *Pakeha Rambles through Maori Lands*, 1873

Otago Mountains (from Lindis Pass)

They had a very narrow range of colour, that afternoon, from yellow ochre to something between raw sienna and raw umber. Their texture suggested anything from a roughened bronze to a well-worn and weathered light fur-coat. To declare their aspect unfriendly would be an understatement. Apparently they had heard some vague rumours about a species like ours, making a little dust below, and were now waiting for us to go just as quickly as we had arrived.

J.B. Priestley, *A Visit to New Zealand*, 1974

Oxford

Why it should be called Oxford I do not know.

Samuel Butler, *A First Year in Canterbury Settlement*, 1863

Pahiatua

Pahiatua is a hard name to rhyme and harder still for rhythm. It's about the hardest name for poetic purposes that I've struck yet – except perhaps, 'Oorgntsumeballow' in New South Wales. Pahiatua is pronounced Pah-hie-ah-tua, I suppose, but I am doubtful as to which syllable the accent is on. Some people sound five syllables, some only four; others say 'Pahtua'.

I met a British (cockney) new-chum on the road and asked him how to pronounce it, He fixed his eyeglass and said 'Aw! Paw-hee-aw-tew-aw. Aw!' A local man said it was 'Piertua'. I next asked an Irish Swagman. He said, 'Oh yes, to be sure, "Pahey-tooey,"' So we'll let it go at 'Pahey-tooey'. He said it quick and pronounced the 'a' as in bad.

Henry Lawson, *First Impressions of Pahiatua*, 1894

Palmerston North

Palmerston North came really as a surprise. Owing to the fact that it lies upon a perfectly level plain it is not nor can it be picturesque; indeed it might, only the word sounds unkind, be called straggling. It certainly does cover a very large area for its population, and those responsible for its laying-out, have been most generous in the matter of streets. Also wherever there are any public buildings they are as usual in the North Island of the prevailing construction, stucco-covered brick. I have often wondered what could have become of all the plasterers when stucco went out in England. I know now: they came to New Zealand, and here they revel in their favourite medium, imitating stone to their heart's content.

F.T. Bullen, *Advance Australasia*, 1907

Rimutaka

In our school-days we were taught on Virgil's authority that Eolus dwelt in a cave: had the poet lived in these times and visited New Zealand he would have made the God's habitat on the top of a hill, and that hill would have been Rimutaka.

Lt Col. J.H.H. St John, *Pakeha Rambles through Maori Lands*, 1873

Rotorua

Spirit of Picnics, here should thy temple be.

Charles Heaphy, *Expedition to the South West of Nelson*, 1846

Over all Roturoa there is a faint aroma, not at all disagreeable, from the geysers, steam holes and other rather alarming manifestations of the nearness of Hell. The most astounding hole on this course is the short Sodom and Gomorrah hole. Here you play over a hundred yards of fissures out of which comes reeking sulphurous steam. I looked down one tiny volcano top, and it was filled with seething, boiling, gurgling, and bubbling mud. (I got a three at this hole, using my famous 'old gent'.)

Alfred Viscount Northcliffe, *My Journey Round the World* (August 1921), 1923

South Island

The South Island, mainly populated by Scots, their sheep, and the Devil's own high winds . . . .

Rudyard Kipling, *Something of Myself*, 1937 – of 1891

It reminds you of Switzerland at *one-half* the price.

Airline advertisement, 1980

Mount Tangariwa

Tangariwa, the mountain that 'has the same shape from *every* point of view.' That is the common belief in Auckland. And so far it has – from every point of view except thirteen . . . .

Mark Twain, *More Tramps Abroad*, 1897

Te Tarata

Imagine a shelving slope descending gradually to the margin of the lake in an uneven series of steps for some hundred and fifty feet, bounded on each side by low scrub-bush, and culminating at the top in an open crater, whence rolls out cloud after cloud of white steam. The steps appear from the height to be now white, and now purple contrasting strongly with the azure hues of the basins, and glistening under the hot sun whose rays dance on the thin film of water constantly trickling down. At irregular intervals on the grades are pools; – pools! the word is a profanation; they are alabaster basins filled with molten silver, blue as the vault of heaven, over whose gracefully-recurved lips pours down with a gentle murmur a never ceasing flow derived from the boiling contents of the crater above.The more we gazed upon the scene, the more difficult it was to realise it, till at length one bold attempt was made at comparison, and H – –exclaimed that this must be the abode of the Queen of the Naiads as it would be depicted by Grieve and Telbin in a transformation scene.

Lt Col. J.H.H. St John, *Pakeha Rambles through Maori Lands*, 1873

(Near Lake Rotomahana. This lake was destroyed by the eruption of Tarawera Mountain in 1886. The unusual sinter terraces disappeared at the same time.)

Lake Taupo

A lake out of another and better world.

J.B. Priestley, *A Visit to New Zealand*, 1974

River Waiho

Walked on, with very hot sun, over dry fern-hills, where we expected a . . . want of water; but, just as the party were beginning to be thirsty, we came suddenly upon the Waiho (Thames), rushing like an arrow, through the middle of the barren country, with a bright blue stream, full of life, and sparkling with purity. It is a river worthy to be named as it is; but as yet it has no Eton or Richmond on its banks. Still its name brought to mind all the most happy passages of my life.

Bishop George Augustus Selwyn, Journal Letter, 24 December 1843

A fresh breeze of wind soon carried us to the bottom of the bay, where we found a very fine river, broad as the Tames at Greenwich, though not quite so deep . . . the Captain [Cook] was so much pleased with it that he resolved to call it the Thames.

Sir Joseph Banks, *Journal of the Rt Hon Sir Joseph Banks* (14 November 1769), 1768–71

Waikarimoana

It may be laid down as an axiom that whenever the tourist in New Zealand arrives at a hill christened 'Gentle Annie' he may prepare himself for a breather; there was no exception to the rule as far as concerned the 'Gentle Annie' of Waikarimoana, and it was uncommonly hot work getting up to the top.

Lt Col. J.H.H. St John, *Pakeha Rambles through Maori Lands*, 1873

Waimakiriri River

How one would like, too, to come occasionally across some little *auberge* with its *vin ordinaire*, and refreshing fruit!

Samuel Butler, *A First Year in Canterbury Settlement*, 1863

Waimate

When I looked at this whole scene I thought it admirable. It was not merely that England was brought vividly before my mind; yet, as the evening drew to a close, the domestic sounds, the fields of corn, the distant, undulating country with its trees might well have been mistaken for our fatherland: nor was it the triumphant feeling at seeing what Englishmen could effect; but rather the high hopes inspired for the future of this fine island.

Charles Darwin, *Journal . . . During the Voyage . . . of H.M.S.Beagle*, 1832–6

Waitara

The mountain in all its glorious diadem of snow, sending down such healthy bracing breezes day and night as speedily restored our strength, and added to the *bush* appetite that we had brought with us. Instead of the old proverb, 'Good wine needs no *bush*' the Bishop always reads it, 'Good bush needs no wine'; and certainly its effects are lasting and most exhilarating – I have been quite ashamed of my appetite.

Charles Abraham, *Journal of a Walk from Auckland to Taranaki*, 1855

Wellington

Wellington is also the seat of the National Joke of New Zealand . . . . The National Joke of New Zealand, which has not been immortalized yet is that you can always tell a Wellingtonian by the way in which he grabs his hat when going round a corner.

Sometimes you'll hear it on the boat coming over.

Henry Lawson, *New Zealand from an Australian's Point of View*, 1893

Wellington has a good harbour, bold scenery, splendid climate and perhaps the most Liberal Government and the biggest building in the world. The Government will make the biggest blunder by-and-bye, and the building would make the biggest fire.

Ibid.

Back again in what the New Zealanders proudly call the Empire City, oblivious entirely of the misnomer. It is a beautiful little city, a well-groomed and orderly city, fully worthy of its position and is prospering in a very high degree. But to call it the Empire City is to ape the flapdoodle of the United States citizens, who, like the average users of forceful adjectives, see nothing incongruous or ridiculous in calling a collection of shacks a city, and cannot call a magnificent aggregation like New York or Philadelphia anything else. I would not, for a great deal say anything that could even seem derogatory of Wellington. It is a place worthy of the utmost love and admiration of its citizens. In its surroundings it is peculiarly happy. They are romantic, picturesque in the extreme, which qualities, in days not so far distant, constituted a serious drawback to the city's expansion.

F.T. Bullen, *Advance Australasia*, 1907

While it is quite true that occasionally the city experiences three days' steady rain without a break, it is false to say that dirty or windy weather is anything like normal – in fact it would be truer to say that such climatic conditions are abnormal. Earthquakes do occur undoubtedly, but so infrequently and of such slight importance that they are practically ignored . . . . Indeed, taken altogether, Wellington, apart from the delightful character of its citizens, is one of the most desirable places to live in that is to be found in the whole world, in my opinion.

Ibid.

Before sailing from London, five people told me that you can always tell a Wellington man because he holds on his hat when he walks round the corner of a street because the wind blows round the corners. Everybody in the ship coming out to whom I mentioned New Zealand told me the story again, until at last I thought of having a small placard hanging round my neck with 'I know how to tell a Wellington man,' or 'Please don't tell me the story of the Wellington man and the wind; I know it.'

Maurice Baring, *Round the World in Any Number of Days*, 1913

NICARAGUA

There is no man which is able worthily and sufficiently

to speake of the fertilitie, healthsomenesse, prosperitie,. and frequencie, of those Nations that there were.

Bartholomew de Las Casas, 1542, in *Purchase his Pilgrimes*, 1625

The country is so pleasing to the eye, and so abounding in all things necessary that the Spaniards call it Mohamed's paradise. Among other flourishing trees here groweth one of that nature that a man cannot touch any of its branches but it withereth presently. It is as plentiful of parrots as our country of England is of crows; turkeys, fowls, quails and rabbits are ordinary meat there. There are many populous Indian towns, . . . and especially two cities of Spaniards. One is Leon, a bishop's seat, and the other Granada, which standeth upon a lake [Nicaragua] of fresh water which hath about 300 miles in compass, and having no intercourse with the ocean, doth yet continually ebb and flow.

Thomas Gage, *The English-American . . . or, A New Survey of the West Indies*, 1648 – of 1630s

I observed more than the usual number of crosses. The people of Nicaragua are said to be the worst in the republic. The inhabitants of the other states always caution a stranger against them, and they are proportionally devout.

J.L. Stephens, *Incidents of Travel in Central America Chiapas and Yucatan*, 1841

I was going on, when a respectable-looking gentleman stopped me, with many apologies for the liberty, and asked for a medio, sixpence. I gave him one, which he examined, and handed back, saying, 'No corre,' 'it does not pass.' It was always, in paying money, a matter of course to have two or three pieces returned, and this I sometimes resisted; but as in this land everything was al reverso, it seemed regular for beggars to be choosers, and I gave him another.

Ibid.

Every country has the writers she requires and deserves, which is why Nicaragua, in two hundred years of literacy, has produced one writer – a mediocre poet.

Paul Theroux, *The Old Patagonian Express*, 1979

Leon

This city of Leon is very curiously built, for the chief delight of the inhabitants is in their houses, in the pleasure of the country adjoining, and in the abundance of all things for the life of man more than in any extraordinary riches which are not so much enjoyed there as in other parts of America. They are contented with fine gardens, with variety of singing birds, and parrots, with plenty of fish and flesh, which is cheap, and with gay houses, and so lead a delicious, lazy, and idle life, not aspiring much to trade and traffic, though they have near unto them the lake, . . . which to them might be very commodious for any dealing and rich trading in Peru or to Mixco, if their spirits would carry them so far. The gentlemen of this city are almost as vain and fantastical as are those of Chiapa. And especially from the pleasure of this city is all that province of Nicaragua called by the Spaniards, Mahomet's Paradise.

Thomas Gage, *The English-American . . . or, A New Survey of the West Indies*, 1648 – of 1630s

It had the appearance of old and aristocratic respectability, which no other city in Central America possessed. The houses were large, and many of the fronts were full of stucco ornaments; the plaza was spacious, and the squares of the churches and the churches themselves magnificent. It was the seat of a bishopric, and distinguished for the costliness of its churches and convents, its seats of learning, and its men of science, down to the time of its revolution against Spain; but in walking through its streets I saw palaces in which nobles had lived dismantled and roofless, and occupied by half-starved wretches, pictures of misery and want; and on one side an immense field of ruins, covering half the city.

J.L. Stephens, *Incidents of Travel in Central America Chiapas and Yucatan*, 1841

Managua

Managua Nicaragua is a wonderful town.

Song, 1930s, an Andrews Sisters hit

The most attractive feature of Managua is the habit its people have, in the evening, of bringing their rocking-chairs out on to the pavement. It is impossible to walk more than a few yards down a street, for at almost every front door one is stopped by a family circle, all bobbing up and down in their chairs, and forcing one to step out into the traffic. But one doesn't complain, for it is a friendly and aesthetic custom.

Nicholas Wollaston, *Red Rumba*, 1962

The heat in Managua is devastating. It's more than just a matter of temperature, it's another element – a hot liquid clinging to you, encasing you, through which you have to move. It moulds your face, slips down your shirt, chokes in your throat, smothers you; and if there's a wind it doesn't cool you, but merely presses the heat harder against you.

Ibid.

Masaya (volcano of)

Hanging midway, impressed with the solitude and the

extraordinary features of a scene upon which so few human eyes have ever rested, and the power of the great Architect who has scattered his wonderful works over the whole face of the earth, I could not but reflect, what a waste of the bounties of Providence in this favoured but miserable land! At home this volcano would be a fortune; with a good hotel on top, a railing round to keep children from falling in, a zigzag staircase down the sides, and a glass of iced lemonade at the bottom. Cataracts are good property with people who know how to turn them to account. Niagara and Trenton Falls pay well, and the owners of volcanoes in Central America might make money out of them by furnishing facilities to travellers. This one could probably be bought for ten dollars, and I would have given twice that sum for a rope and a man to hold it.

J.L. Stephens, *Incidents of Travel in Central America Chiapas and Yucatan*, 1841

RIVER NIGER

His brother Niger too, and all the floods
In which the full-form'd maids of Afric lave
Their jetty limbs . . .

James Thomson, *The Seasons – Summer*, 1727

The Niger, as has been well observed, is not a lottery in which men may win fortunes, but a field of labour in which they may earn them.

Richard Burton, *Wanderings in West Africa*, 1863

NIGERIA

Oliver Howard has died, of fever, in Nigeria. What a gratuitous mischance. There was no call whatever for him to go to these malignant countries, no necessity of money or his profession, only a perverse desire for that worst madness which possesses young Englishmen, the sport of arbitrary power in wild countries, with the occasional chance of shooting black men – this is what attracted him.

Wilfred Scawen Blunt, Diary, 28 September 1908, *My Diaries*, 1919

Nigeria is a place where the best is impossible but where the worst never happens.

Old saying, quoted *The Economist*, 18 April 1953

God did not make Nigeria. The British did.

His Highness Oba Adeniji Adela II of the Royal House of Addo, principal chief of Lagos, Attrib.

West and East Nigeria are as different as Ireland from Germany. The North is as different from either as China.

Obafemi Awolowo, quoted by John Gunther, *Inside Africa*, 1955

I met a British official in the interior, He had a thin brittle voice, profound erudition, and hands like little puddings. He said, 'You must remember that this is a mad country – *quite* mad!'

John Gunther, *Inside Africa*, 1955

In the beginning God created the Universe. Then He created the moon, the stars and the wild beasts of the forests. On the sixth day he created the Nigerian. But on the seventh day while God rested, the Nigerian invented noise.

Anthony Enahoro, *How to Be A Nigerian*, 1966

Hausas

. . . the civilised, commerce-loving, and industrious Hausas, . . . whose intellectual capacity H.M. Stanley has aptly emphasized by describing them as 'the only Central African people who value a book.'

Sir George T. Goldie, Introduction to Seymour Vandeleur, *Campaigning on the Upper Nile and Niger*, 1898

Ibos

The Heebos, in their persons, are tall and well formed, many of the women symmetrically so.

Captain John Adams, *Remarks on the Country Extending from Cape Palmas to the River Congo*, 1823

Abeokuta

The first aspect of Abeokuta was decidedly remarkable. The principal peculiarity was the fantastic breaking of the undulating plain by masses of grey granite – the rose-coloured is not easily seen – between twenty and thirty in number, sometimes rising two hundred and fifty to three hundred feet above the lower levels. White under the sun's glare, and cast in strange forms – knobs, pinnacles, walls, backbones, scarps, and logans – they towered over the patches of dark trees at their bases and the large brown villages, or rather towns, which separated them. There was a long dorsum which nearly bisected the town from north to south, and which lay like a turtle's neck between the scattered lines of habitations. The schorl, the sandstone formations, and the iron conglomerates were thrown into shade by these masses protruded from below . . . . In some places the habitations seemed as close packed as cells in a honeycomb; in others they were broken by bush, whose growth is encouraged because fire-engines are unknown. The ground was exceedingly complicated. Our guides pointed out to us the sites of the chief towns, Ake, and Ikija Bagura and Owu, the Rock Olumo – 'the builder,' or capitolium – and other places which a few minutes afterwards were forgotten. A line of denser and more regular trees marks the course of the river, and blue distance, rolling here and there in long waves, broken by dwarf cones and subsiding into a mysteriously hazed horizon, formed a charming prospect after our confinement in the trough-like river.

Richard Burton, *Abeokuta and the Camaroons Mountains*, 1863

The Yoruba at Abeokuta

This is a race equally regardless of the past and reckless of the future, with whom the present is ever all in all, and actual life the 'be-all and end-all of all things:' their brains are in matters of novelty marble to receive and wax to retain: nothing, if to be permanent, can be done in a hurry, or, rather, without a long delay: they forget all that has not been impressed upon them by many repetitions, and they regard what Englishmen call a 'business-like manner' with a supreme contempt. 'He does half who does quickly,' should be the Anglo-African's rule.

Ibid.

Baragu (on the Ogun river)

Our hosts were perfectly civil and obliging, and so were our hostesses – rather too much so I could prove, if privileged to whisper into the reader's ear. But what would Mrs. Grundy say?

Richard Burton, *Abeokuta and the Camaroons Mountains*, 1863

Benin

Beware and take heed of the Bight of Benin
Where few come out though many go in.

Anon.

Bonny River

This African Styx.

Richard Burton, *Wanderings in West Africa*, 1863

They cannot afford to reject any kind of provisions, and after a year or two amongst the people, even a European would, I suspect, look somewhat queerly upon a fat little black boy.

Ibid.

Bonny! Well, come inside the bar and anchor off the factories: seaward there is the foam of the bar gleaming and wicked white against a leaden sky, and what there is left of Breaker Island. In every other direction you will see the apparently endless walls of mangrove, unvarying in colour, unvarying in form, unvarying in height, save from perspective. Beneath and between you and them lie the rotting mud waters of Bonny River, and away up and down river, miles of rotting mud waters fringed with walls of rotting mud mangrove-swamp. The only break in them – one can hardly call it a relief to the scenery – are the gaunt black ribs of the old hulks, once used as trading stations, which lie exposed at low water near the shore, protruding like the skeletons of great unclean beasts who have died because Bonny water was too strong for them.

Raised on piles from the mud shore you will see the white-painted factories and their great store-houses for oil; each factory likely enough with its flag at half mast, which does not enliven the scenery either, for you know it is because somebody is 'dead again.' Throughout and over all is the torrential downpour of the wet-season rain, coming down night and day with its dull roar. I have known it rain six mortal weeks on Bonny River, just for all the world as if it were done by machinery . . .

When your eyes are drinking in the characteristics of Bonny scenery you notice a peculiar smell – an intensification of that smell you noticed when nearing Bonny, in the evening, out at sea. That's the breath of the malarial mud, laden with fever, and the chances are, you will be down to-morrow. If it is near evening time now, you can watch it becoming incarnate, creeping and crawling and gliding out from the side creeks and between the mangrove-roots, laying itself upon the river, stretching and rolling in a kind of grim play, and finally crawling up the side of the ship to come on board and leave its cloak of moisture that grows green mildew in a few hours over all.

Mary Kingsley, *Travels in West Africa*, 1897

Good heavens! what an awful accident. We've gone and picked up the Styx.

Ibid.

Coastal scenery, travelling eastward from Lagos

Nothing is more simple than to sketch the view as seen from the sea. Above, an azure space based upon a band of dull and bright greens, resting upon a thin line of golden sand, and in the foreground a little deeper ultramarine than in the air. In the rainy season, change the blue above to a heavy mass of clouds, reposing upon the land, and the blue below to a brown olive. Where a river gap exists it will be denoted by an uneven notch in the land, and as a rule the proper right point, that is to say, the western, will be somewhat higher than the other.

Richard Burton, *Wanderings in West Africa*, 1863

Lagos

In July you must die,
August go you must;

In September remember,
October it's all over.

Old rhyme describing rainy season, quoted by Richard Burton, *Wanderings in West Africa*, 1863

. . . The British Consulate, like that at Fernando Po, a corrugated iron coffin or plank-lined morgue, containing a dead consul once a year . . . .

Richard Burton, *Wanderings in West Africa*, 1863

The site of the town, four miles from the entrance, is detestable; unfortunately, there is no better within many a league . . . . The first aspect is as if a hole had been hollowed out in the original mangrove forest that skirts the waters, where bush and dense jungle, garnished with many a spreading tree, tall palms, and matted mass of fetid verdure, rise in terrible profusion around.

Ibid.

Most African cities which are not yet altogether absorbed by the twentieth century have prevailing colours, caused in part by architecture, in part by local costumes. Marrakesh is a pink city, Ibadan is tin-coloured, Khartoum ochre, and Accra white. The colour of Lagos is, I should say, indigo.

John Gunther, *Inside Africa*, 1955

There is a greeting card on sale in Lagos which is sent to children who are about to take examinations. It reads: 'He who climbs well deserves a push.'

Patrick Marnham, *Fantastic Invasion*, 1980

Nupe (Old Kingdom of)

A black Byzantium.

S.F. Nadel, Title of Book, 1942

Oshogbo

Oshogbo . . . is an amazing, eccentric town, perhaps the only place in the world which has a petrol station of real artistic interest. The Esso petrol station has been transformed by a local sculptor. The local sculptor didn't like the hideous Esso petrol station. So he built cement sculptures around it. The one I liked best was of cars being filled with petrol.

John Heilpern, *Conference of the Birds*, 1977

NORTH AND SOUTH

The *Jewes* their beds, and offices of ease,
Plac't *North* and *South*, for these cleane purposes;
That mans uncomely froth might not molest
Gods wayes and walks, which lie still East and West.

Robert Herrick, *North and South*, 1647

Ask where's the North? At York, 'tis on the Tweed;
In Scotland, at the Orcades; and there,
At Greenland, Zembla, or the Lord knows where:
No creature owns it in the first degree,
But thinks his neighbour farther gone than he.

Alexander Pope, *An Essay on Man*, Epistle ii, 1733

So far from thinking that the primitive inhabitants of the world lived in a Southern climate, where Paradise spontaneously arose, I am led to infer, from various circumstances, that the first dwelling of man happened to be a spot like this, which led him to adore a sun so seldom seen: for this worship, which probably preceded that of demons or demi gods, certainly never began in a southern climate, where the continual presence of the sun prevented its being considered as a good; or rather the want of it never being felt, this glorious luminary would carelessly have diffused its blessings without being hailed as a benefactor. Man must therefore have been placed in the north, to tempt him to run after the Sun, in order that the different parts of the earth might be peopled.

Mary Wollstonecraft, *Letters Written During a Short Residence in Sweden, etc.*, 1796

NORTH SEA

The same old thing. A grey-green expanse of smudgy waters grinning angrily at one with white foam-ridges, and over all a cheerless, unglowing canopy, apparently made of wet blotting paper . . . .

It isn't for nothing that the North Sea is also called the German Ocean.

Joseph Conrad, 'Poland Revisited', 1915, *Notes on Life and Letters*, 1921

NORWAY

If that country could be brought to maintain a million more of inhabitants, Norway might defy the world . . . but it is much under-handed now.

Samuel Taylor Coleridge, *Table Talk*, 3 January 1834

November always seemed to me the Norway of the year.

Emily Dickinson, Letter to Dr and Mrs J.G. Holland, 1864

Norway is a hard country: hard to know, hard to shoot over, and hard – very hard – to fall down on: but hard to forsake and harder to forget.

J.A. Lees, *Peaks and Pines, Another Norway Book*, 1899

I would not enter Norway again for all the firs in Scandinavia. The blight of temperance has settled on the place. Half the towns have prohibition laws. The only art work of any consequence is Rodin's 'Man with the Key,' and if there's anything but insipidity in any of the national music, I have yet to detect it. Cold, clean living, and scenery have killed the place – if it ever lived. Like Switzerland it is ruined by tidiness and order . . . . No one would want to lust with these Puritan dummies whose only word is a scream when you get a hand as far as the tapes of their drawers. I'd a sight rather have Wednesday afternoon in pouring rain in Macclesfield. At least you could have a quick success in the lobby of the Mechanics' Institute.

Archie Grant of Stroud, Gloucestershire, Letter to a friend, 1912, quoted in Alan Wykes (ed.), *Abroad*, 1973

Little Norway is land of large taxes.

William Sansom, *Blue Skies, Brown Studies*, 1961

Norwegians

The Norwegian peasants possess much spirit and fire in their manner, are frank, open, and undaunted, yet not insolent; never fawning to their superiors, yet paying proper respect to those above them.

Their principal mode of salute is by offering their hand; and when we gave them or paid them a trifle, the peasants, instead of returning thanks by word or by a bow, shook our hands with great frankness and cordiality.

William Coxe, *Travels into Poland, Russia, Sweden, etc.*, 4th edn, 1792

The Norwegians appear to me a sensible, shrewd people, with little scientific knowledge, and still less taste for literature; but they are arriving at the epoch which precedes the introduction of arts and sciences.

Mary Wollstonecraft, *Letters Written During a Short Residence in Sweden, etc.*, 1796

Sincerity, honesty and freedom from conventional cant are the chief national virtues . . . . The outward forms of politeness are very little observed.

Karl Baedeker, *Norway and Sweden*, 1879

They are the kindest people in Europe but they frighten me to death.

Sir Edmund Gosse, Letter to Maurice Baring, 12 August 1899

The expression *en norsk Nordmand fra Norge*, 'a Norwegian Norseman from Norway,' was commonly used to qualify the stiffness of the people from Christiana, who irritated the easy-mannered Danes by seeming, in childish phrase, to have 'swallowed a poker.'

Edmund Gosse, *Two Visits to Denmark*, 1911 – of 1874

'The Norwegians,' one of my Scandinavian friends once put it, 'are, like their landscape, rather vertical.'

John Gunther, *Inside Europe*, 1938 edn

Bergen

Reaching Bergen we fail to find it particularly attractive. Everything is fishy. You eat fish and drink fish and smell fish and breathe fish. The bill of fare is made up of it, the water tastes of it, the air is full of it.

Lilian Leland, *Travelling Alone, A Woman's Journey Round the World*, 1890

Fredericstadt (pine woods nearby)

The pine and fir woods, left entirely to nature, display an endless variety; and the paths in the wood are not entangled with fallen leaves which are only interesting whilst they are fluttering between life and death. The grey cobweb-like appearance of the aged pines is a much finer image of decay; the fibres whitening as they lose their moisture, imprisoned life seems to be stealing away. I cannot tell why, – but death, under every form, appears to me like something getting free – to expand in I know not what element; nay I feel that this conscious being must be as unfettered, have the wings of thought, before it can be happy.

Mary Wollstonecraft, *Letters Written During a Short Residence in Sweden, etc.*, 1796

The Whirlpool Maelstrom *opposite North Folden Fjord*

Turn the broad helm, the fluttering canvas urge
From Maelstrome's fierce innavigable surge.
– 'Mid the lorn isles of Norway's stormy main,
As sweeps o'er many a league his eddying train,
Vast watery walls in rapid circles spin.
And deep-ingulph'd the demon dwells within;
Springs o'er the fear-froze crew with harpy-claws,
Down his deep den the whirling vessel draws;
Churns with his bloody mouth the dread repast,
The booming waters murmuring o'er the mast.

Erasmus Darwin, 'The Economy of Vegetation', *The Botanic Garden*, 1791

North Cape

I thincke it to bee the uncomfortablest country and most inconvenient For the liffe of Man off any other part off the world thatt is inhabited, yeilding little or Nothing fitting For his sustenance or Comffort.

Peter Mundy, *Travels in Europe and Asia*, 1641

Arctic Sea from the North Cape

The 'Open Polar Sea,' as seen from the North Cape,

eight hundred feet above it, the sunlight softened by a passing cloud, suggested limitless 'cobwebby gray velvet, with the tender bloom like cold gravy,' with just a glistening satiny finish.

Lilian Leland, *Travelling Alone, A Woman's Journey Round the World*, 1890

Oslo (formerly Christiana)

As we approached Christiana, the country was more wild and hilly, but still very fertile and agreeable; and about two miles from the town we came to the top of a mountain and burst upon as fine a view as I ever beheld. From the point on which we stood in raptures, the grounds, laid out in rich enclosures, gradually sloped to the sea; below us appeared Christiana, situated at the extremity of an extensive and fertile valley, forming a semi-circular bend along the shore of a most beautiful bay, which being enclosed by hills, uplands, and forests, had the appearance of a large lake. Behind, before, and around, the inland mountains of Norway rose on mountains covered with dark forests of pines and fir, the inexhaustible riches of the north. The most distant summits were capped with eternal snow. From the glow of the atmosphere, the warmth of the weather, the variety of the productions, and the mild beauties of the adjacent scenery, I could scarcely believe that I was nearly in the 60th degree of northern latitude.

William Coxe, *Travels into Poland, Russia, Sweden, etc.*, 4th edn, 1792

Christiana is a clean, neat city; but it has none of the graces of architecture, which ought to keep pace with the refining manners of a people.

Mary Wollstonecraft, *Letters Written During a Short Residence in Sweden, etc.* , 1796

Only when you see the provincialism of Oslo do you appreciate the wonderfulness of Ibsen.

Arnold Bennett, *Journal 1929*, 1930

One of our ambassadors described it to me as 'Six Suburbs in Search of a Centre.'

R.H. Bruce Lockhart, *My Europe*, 1952

East Rusoer

The view of this wild coast, as we sailed along it, afforded me a continual subject for meditation . . . . The images fastened on me, and the world appeared a vast prison. I was soon to be in a smaller one . . . for no other name can I give to Rusoer. It would be difficult to form an idea of the place if you had never seen one of these rocky coasts . . . . We saw about two hundred houses crowded together under a very high rock . . . still higher appearing above. Talk not of Bastilles! To be born here was to be bastilled by nature – shut out from all that opens the understanding or enlarges the heart. Huddled one behind another, not more than a quarter of the dwellings even had a prospect of the sea. A few planks formed passages from house to house, which you must often scale, mounting steps like a ladder, to enter.

Mary Wollstonecraft, *Letters Written During a Short Residence in Sweden, etc.*, 1796

Sogne Fjord

More or less everywhere along the fjord there is one consistent picture, representative of all mountain-fjords in summertime. It is a vertical one: one views it up and down. In the centre, and taking up most of the picture, rises the immediate massed cliffside, furred with dark green fir-trees, one or two thousand feet or more of rock. At the top, patches of snow – and glimpses above of higher mountains bellying up snow and dark granite against the distant sky like the giant black and white rump of a celestial panda. Now whizz the eye down to the bottom where a very small patch of bright yellow-green or emerald shines out – the fields of the lonely village with their dicing of painted houses. In the immediate foreground, the bottle-green glass of the tree-reflecting fjord-water.

Suppose this up-and-down strip of a picture to be two foot high – sky, snowline, tall mountain-side, farm, water – then only about one small inch will be represented by the yellow-green glint of human life. It is awe-inspiring, pathetic, and warming. It is like watching, and feeling for, the odyssey of a small green insect trying to climb a window-pane. Proportions viewed from the boat-deck, or from another farmer's eye from the opposite side of the fjord, are somersaulted – the village becomes a toy and only the vertiginous mountain-side of real size.

William Sansom, *Blue Skies, Brown Studies*, 1961

Spitzbergen

When . . . we first came to the Foreland of *Spitzbergen*, the foot of these mountains looked like fire, and the topps of them were covered with foggs; the snow was marbel'd, and looked as if it were boughs and branches of trees, and gave as bright and glorious a gloss or shining to the air or skies as if the sun had shin'd. When the mountains look thus fiery, a hard storm generally ensues.

Frederick Martens (trans.), 'Voyage to Spitzbergen', in *An Account of Several Late Voyages and Discoveries to the South and West, etc.*, 1694

from the sea
The view was indeed beautiful; blue sea, with glittering patches of drift-ice, and straight ahead, the mountains after which Spitsbergen is named, sharp-pointed peaks with snow on their upper flanks, rather as if the top four thousand feet of the Alps had been cut off and transplanted to the Arctic Ocean.

Julian Huxley, *Memories*, 1970

Tonsberg (and Moss, between)

It was often beautiful; but seldom afforded those grand views, which fill, rather than soothe, the mind.

Mary Wollstonecraft, *Letters Written During a Short Residence in Sweden, etc.*, 1796

Trondheim

and Bodo, coast between
The scenery becomes more Arthurian as we get further north . . . the mountains on the starboard bow like a Doré engraving.

Evelyn Waugh, *Diary*, July 1934

Its natives are in a sub-category of their own: outspoken, kindly, remarkable for sustained loyalty between peaks of emotional turmoil . . . . They are the only people in Norway who will tell you they are busy, dismiss you, and then spend two hours in sleep. Among all their fellow countrymen they are the most easily understood by Englishmen.

Philip Caraman, *Norway*, 1969

O

OCEAN / SEA

The burden of the desert of the sea.
The Bible, Isaiah 21:1

He maketh the deep to boil like a pot.
The Bible, Job 41:31

All the rivers run into the sea; yet the sea is not full.
The Bible, Ecclesiastes 1:7

He that will learn to pray, let him go to Sea.
George Herbert, *Jacula Prudentum*, 1640

Let him who knows not how to pray, go to sea.
John Ray, *English Proverbs*, 4th edn, 1768

He goes a great voyage that goes to the bottom of the sea.
H.G. Bohn, *Hand-Book of Proverbs*, 1855

To be master of the sea is an abridgement of a monarchy . . . he that commands the sea is at great liberty, and may take as much and as little of the war as he will.
Francis Bacon, *Essays*, 1597–1625

That great fishpond, the sea.
Thomas Dekker, *The Honest Whore*, 1604

The Sea
That shuts still as it opes, and leaves no tracts
Nor prints of precedent for poor men's facts.
George Chapman, *Bussy d'Ambois*, 1607

Thus shoulde Man at once loose halfe his Inheritance, if the Art of Navigation did not inable him to manage this untamed Beast, and with the Bridle of the Winds, and Saddle of his Shipping to make him serviceable. Now for the services of the Sea, they are innumerable; it is the great Purveyor of the Worlds Commodities to our use, Conveyor of the Excesse of Rivers, Uniter by Traffique of al Nations; it presents the eye with diversified Colours and Motions, and is as it were with rich Brooches, adorned with various Ilands; it is an open field for Merchandize in Peace, a pitched field for the most dreadfull fights of Warre; yeelds diversitie of Fish and Fowle for diet, Materials for Wealth, Medicine for Health, Simples for Medicines, Pearles and other Jewels for Ornament, Amber and Ambergrise for delight, the wonders of the Lord in the Deepe for instruction, variety of Creatures for use, multiplicity of Natures for Contemplation, diversity of accidents for admiration, compendiousness to the way, to full bodies healthfull evacuation, to the thirsty earth fertile moysture, to distant friends pleasant meeting, to weary persons delightfull refreshing; to studious and religious minds a Map of Knowledge, Mystery of Temperance, Exercise of Continence, Schoole of Prayer, Meditation, Devotion and Sobrietie: refuge to the distressed, Portage to the Merchant, passage to the Traveller, Customes to the Prince, Springs, Lakes, Rivers, to the Earth; it hath on it Tempests and Calmes to chastise the Sinnes, to exercise the faith of Sea-men; manifold affections in it selfe, to affect and stupefie the subtilest Philosopher; sustaineth moveable Fortresses for the Souldier, mayntayneth (as in our Iland) a Wall of defence and waterie Garrison to guard the State; entertaines the Sunne with vapours, the Moone with obsequiousnesse, the Starres also with a naturall Looking-glasse, the Soyle with supplenesse, the Rivers with Tydes, the Hils with moysture, the Valleyes with fertilitie; contayneth most diversified matter for Meteors, most multiforme shapes, most various, numerous kindes, most immense, difformed, deformed, unformed Monsters; Once (for why should I longer detayne you?) the Sea yeelds Action to the bodie, Meditation to the Minde, the World to the World, all parts thereof to each part, by this Art of Arts, Navigation.
Samuel Purchas, *Hakluytus Posthumus, or Purchas his Pilgrimes*, 1625

Why was the sea made salt? Because, I think
If fresh, the fishes every drop would drink.
Timotheus Polus (d. 1632),

I love the sea; she is my fellow-creature.
Francis Quarles, *Emblems*, 1635

Sir Andrew Freeport . . . has usually some sly way of jesting . . . he calls the Sea the *British Common*.
Richard Steele, *Spectator*, no. 2, 2 March 1711

Ocean exhibits, fathomless and broad,
Much of the power and majesty of God.
William Cowper, *Retirement*, 1781

I took a young woman once with me to the coast of Sussex, who at twenty-seven years old, and a native of England had never seen the sea; nor any thing else indeed ten miles out of London: – And well, child! said I, are you not much surprised? – 'It is a fine sight, to be sure,' replied she coldly, 'but,' – but what? you are not disappointed are you? – 'No, not disappointed, but it is not what I expected when I saw the ocean.' Tell me then, pray good girl, and tell me quickly, what did you expect to see? *'Why I expected,'* with a hesitating accent, *'I expected to see a great deal of water.'*

Hester Lynch Thrale/Piozzi, *Observations . . . in the Course of a Journey*, 1789

In ocean's pearly haunts, the waves beneath
Sits the grim monarch of insatiate Death;
The shark rapacious with descending blow
Darts on the scaly brood that swims below;
The crawling crocodiles beneath that move,
Arrest with rising jaw the tribes above;
With monstrous gape sepulchral whales devour
Shoals at a gulp, a million in an hour.
– Air, earth, and ocean, to astonish'd day
One scene of blood, one mighty tomb display!
From Hunger's arms the shafts of Death are hurl'd,
And one great Slaughter-house the warring world!

Erasmus Darwin, *Origin of Society*, 1789–91

Past are three summers, since she first beheld
The ocean; all around the child await
Some exclamation of amazement here.
She coldly said, her long-lasht eyes abased,
Is this the mighty ocean? is this all?

Walter Savage Landor, *Gebir*, 1798

Far-spooming Ocean.

John Keats, *Endymion*, 1818

Roll on, thou deep and dark blue Ocean – roll!
Ten thousand fleets sweep over thee in vain;
Man marks the earth with ruin – his control
Stops with the shore; – upon the watery plain
The wrecks are all thy deed, nor doth remain
A shadow of man's ravage, save his own,
When, for a moment, like a drop of rain,
He sinks into thy depths with bubbling groan –
Without a grave – unknelled, uncoffined,
and unknown.

His steps are not upon thy paths, – thy fields
Are not a spoil for him, – thou dost arise
And shake him from thee; the vile strength he wields
For earth's destruction thou dost all despise,
Spurning him from thy bosom to the skies –
And send'st him, shivering in thy playful spray
And howling, to his Gods, where haply lies
His petty hope in some near port or bay,
And dashest him again to Earth: – there let him lay . . .

Thou glorious mirror, where the Almighty's form
Glasses itself in tempests; in all time,
Calm or convulsed – in breeze, or gale, or storm –
Icing the Pole, or in the torrid clime
Dark-heaving – boundless, endless, and sublime–
The image of Eternity – the throne
Of the Invisible; even from out thy slime
The monsters of the deep are made – each Zone
Obeys thee – thou goest forth, dread, fathomless,
alone.

And I have loved thee, Ocean! and my joy
Of youthful sports was on thy breast to be
Borne, like thy bubbles, onward: from a boy
I wantoned with thy breakers – they to me
Were a delight; and if the freshening sea
Made them a terror – 'twas a pleasing fear.
For I was, as it were, a Child of thee,
And trusted to thy billows far and near,
And laid my hand upon thy mane, – as I do here.

Lord Byron, *Childe Harold's Pilgrimage*, Canto the Fourth, 1818

There is something in being near the sea, like the confines of eternity. It is a new element, a pure abstraction. The mind loves to hover on that which is endless, and forever the same . . . . I wonder at the sea . . . that vast Leviathan, rolled round the earth, smiling in its sleep, waked into fury, fathomless, boundless, a huge world of water-drops – Whence is it, whither goes it, is it of eternity or of nothing?

William Hazlitt. *Notes of a Journey through France and Italy*, 1826

And Thou, vast Ocean! on whose awful face
Time's iron feet can print no ruin trace.

Robert Montgomery, *The Omnipresence of the Deity*, 1828

3° N Lat, E Long 9°
Here we are becalmed, the sea looking like a plate of silver that has been cleaned by a remarkably good under-butler. He has not left a spot on it.

Emily Eden, Letter, 10 February 1836, in *Letters from India*, 1872

You sea! I resign myself to you also – I guess what you
mean,
I behold from the beach your crooked inviting fingers,
I believe you refuse to go back without feeling of me,
We must have a turn together, I undress, hurry me out
of sight of the land,
Cushion me soft, rock me in billowy drowse,
Dash me with amorous wet, I can repay you.
Sea of stretch'd ground-swells,
Sea breathing broad and convulsive breaths,
Sea of the brine of life and of unshovell'd yet
always-ready graves,

Howler and scooper of storms, capricious and dainty sea,
I am integral with you, I too am of one phase and of all phases.

Walt Whitman, 'Song of Myself', *Leaves of Grass*, 1855–81

'Tis a noble and friendly power, and seemed to say to me, 'Why so late & slow to come to me? Am I not here always, thy proper summer home? Is not my voice thy needful music; my breath, thy healthful climate, in the heats; my touch, thy cure? Was ever building like my terraces? Was ever couch so magnificent as mine? Lie down on my warm ledges and learn that a very little hut is all you need. I have made thy architecture superfluous, and it is paltry beside mine. Here are twenty Romes and Ninevahs, and Karnacs in ruins altogether, obelisk and pyramid and Giants' Causeway here they all are prostrate or half piled.'

And behold the sea, the opaline, plentiful & strong, yet beautiful as the rose or the rainbow, full of food, nourisher of men, purger of the world, creating a sweet climate, and in its unchangeable ebb and flow and in its beauty at a few furlongs, giving a hint of that which changeth not and is perfect.

Ralph Waldo Emerson, *Journals*, 1856

The monotony of a long sea voyage is such that people eat for pastime.

Charles Mackay, *Life and Liberty in America, 1857–8*, 1859

There are certain things – a spider, a ghost,
The income-tax, gout, an umbrella for three –
That I hate, but the thing that I hate the most
Is a thing they call the SEA.

Lewis Carroll, 'A Sea Dirge', *Phantasmagoria*, 1869

Consider the sea's listless chime:
Time's self it is, made audible, –
The murmur of the earth's own shell.
Secret continuance sublime
Is the sea's end: our sight may pass
No furlong further. Since Time was
This sound hath told the lapse of time . . . .
Gather a shell from the strown beach
And listen at its lips: they sigh
The same desire and mystery,
The echo of the whole sea's speech.
And all mankind is thus at heart
Not anything but what thou art:
And Earth, Seas, Man, are all in each.

Dante Gabriel Rossetti, 'The Sea-Limits', *Poems*, 1870

To me the sea is never sane. It has too much to do with the moon to be quite compos mentis.

G.A. Sala, *America Revisited*, 1882

It is virtually impossible to keep out of the fresh air; this is perhaps the leading difference between life at sea and life on shore.

W.J. Loftis, *Orient Line Guide*, 1885

At sea with low and falling glass, soundly sleeps a callous ass;
Only while it's high and rising, timely rests a careful wise one.

Anon., *Ibid.*

J'aime la mer comme on aime tout *être* capricieux et qui vous fait souffrir. (I love the sea as one loves any capricious being who makes one suffer.)

Carolus Duran, quoted by Wilfred Scawen Blunt, *Diary*, 17 October 1892

The difference between a river and the sea, is that the river looks fluid, the sea solid – usually looks as if you could step out and walk on it.

Mark Twain, *More Tramps Abroad*, 1897

Old Indefatigable
Time's right-hand man, the sea.

W.E. Henley, 'Rhymes and Rhythms: xiv, to J.A.C.', *Poems*, 1898

The sea is at its best at London, near midnight, when you are within the arms of a capacious chair, before a glowing fire, selecting phases of the voyages you will never make. It is wiser not to try to realize your dreams. There are no real dreams. For as to the sea itself, love it you cannot. Why should you? I will never believe again the sea was ever loved by anyone whose life was married to it. It is the creation of Omnipotence, which is not of human kind and understandable, and so the springs of its behaviour are hidden. The sea does not assume its royal blue to please you. Its brute and dark desolation is not raised to overwhelm you; you disappear then because you happen to be there. It carries the lucky foolish to fortune, and drags the calculating wise to the strewn bones.

H.M.Tomlinson, *The Sea and the Jungle*, 1912

It is the drawback of all sea-side places that half the landscape is unavailable for purposes of human locomotion, being covered by useless water.

Norman Douglas, *Alone*, 1921

Apart from nature, geometry's all there *is*: . . . Geometry belongs to man. Man's got to assert himself against Nature, all the *time* . . . . I hate sunsets and flowers. And I loathe the *sea*. The sea is formless. . . .

W.H. Auden, quoted as 'Weston', in Christopher Isherwood, *Lions and Shadows*, 1938

God made the land and filled it with His music,
Blessed it with blossom, gave it spring and fall,

Gave to it life and love, and tears and laughter,
But to the sea He gave no thought at all.

From poem in a Sunday paper, quoted by James Agate, *Ego 8*, 1946

The waters of the world are sovereign Powers.

Jan Morris, 'On Wateriness', *Travels*, 1976

OMAN

The heat was so intense that it burned the marrow in the bones; the sword in its scabbard melted like wax, and the gems which adorned the handle of the dagger were reduced to coal . . .

In the plains the chase became a matter of perfect ease,
For the desert was filled with roasted gazelles.

Abd-er-Razzak, *Narrative of the Journey of*, May 1442, quoted in R.H. Major (ed.), *India in the Fifteenth Century*, 1857

Muscat

In the months of August and September, it is here so incredible hot and scorching that I am not able to express the condition strangers are in, being as if they were in boiling Cauldrons or in sweating-tubs, so that I have known many who were not able to endure the heat would jump into the sea and remain there till the Heat of the day be over.

John Struys, *The Voyages of John Struys*, done out of the Dutch by John Morison, 1684 – of 1673

The Muskat Arabs are remarkable for their Humility and Urbanity.

Alexander Hamilton, *A New Account of the East Indies*, 1727

The ship's crews of men-of-war are never allowed to land in the town of Muscat, for fear of the possible consequences of their hilarity.

Hon. George Curzon, *Persia and the Persian Question*, 1892

It was of the people of Muscat that the English ship's captain being instructed, on visiting strange places, to make a report of the manners and customs of the inhabitants, penned the famous saying: 'As to manners they have none; and their customs are beastly.'

Ibid.

Muscat was the realisation of a pirate's lair as imagined by any schoolboy: a crescent of white houses huddled in a cove with high cliffs projecting on either side which completely hid the town till a ship was right opposite the entrance. The cliffs on either side, as the ship came dead-slow into the cove, were painted with the names of British men o' war and the dates they had called there, going back more than a hundred years . . . . The place was clearly designed by Allah as a centre for piracy and slave-running.

Cedric Belfrage, *Away from It All*, 1936

P

PACIFIC ISLANDS

and see under individual headings

The immense Pacific smiles
Round ten thousand little isles
– Haunts of violence and wiles.

James Montgomery, *A Voyage Round the World, Works,* 1841

The first experience can never be repeated. The first love, the first sun-rise, the first South Sea Island, are memories apart, and touched a virginity of sense.

R.L. Stevenson, *In the South Seas,* 1889

attitudes to Europeans
I believe all natives regard white blood as a kind of talisman against the powers of hell. In no other way can they explain the unpunished recklessness of Europeans.

R.L. Stevenson, *ibid.* 1889

God's best – at least God's sweetest works – Polynesians.

Robert Louis Stevenson, Letter to Charles Baxter, 10 May 1889

The South Seas swarm with laughable satires on everything civilised, and especially on every known standard of morality. They flourished in outrageous defiance of every known moral, economical, social and sanitary law, until morality and economy were taught them, and then they went, promptly and unanimously to the devil. Nine in every ten perished of virtue, among all the islands and races, little and big; and they go on perishing with an unanimity quite conclusive. I do not undertake to draw a moral from their euthanasia. Only the wise draw morals, and I am one of the foolish. . . .

Henry Adams, Letter to Henry Cabot Lodge, 4 August 1891

between Singapore and Java (South China Sea)
I wish the novelists who write about the islands we are passing would say a little more about the heat and perspiration, and a little less about the waving palms and the dusky queens.

Alfred Viscount Northcliffe, *My Journey Round the World,* 1923

The South Seas! Coral atolls plumed with swaying palms. Fantastic friezes of coloured clouds. Majestic mountains out of a silken sea. Verdant valleys bowered in blossoms. Dappled shadows vibrant with mystic quiet or pulsing with chanted harmonies tuned to the staccato beat of split bamboo and the muffled throb of great gourd drums. Leafy temples echoing the rhythmic pad of bare brown feet – pagan figures majestically swaying in some barbaric rite of old Polynesia.

Shipping line travel brochure, quoted
Cedric Belfrage, *Away from It All,* 1936

Most of what the American and Australian publics thought they knew about the isles of the Southwest Pacific had been invented by movie scriptwriters. Even as the Japanese were pictured as a blinky-eyed, toothy Gilbert and Sullivan race, so the South Seas was an exotic world where lazy breezes whispered in palm fronds, and Sadie Thompson seduced missionaries, and native girls dived for pearls wearing fitted sarongs, like Dorothy Lamour. In reality the proportions of the women there were closer to those of duffel bags.

William Manchester, *American Caesar,* 1979

PACIFIC OCEAN

That great sea, miscalled the Pacific.

Charles Darwin, *Journal . . . During the Voyage . . . of H.M.S. Beagle,* 1832–6

The Pacific is even a nastier ocean than I had imagined, very much nastier than the Atlantic.

The Marchioness of Dufferin and Ava, *My Canadian Journal* (13 August 1876), 1891

The Pacific licks all other oceans out of hand.

Robert Louis Stevenson, Letter to W.E. Henley, October 1879.

In three voyages out of five, the North Pacific, too big to lie altogether idle, too idle to get hands about the business of a storm, sulks and smokes like a chimney. . . .

Rudyard Kipling, *From Tideway to Tideway,* 1892

The power that rules the Pacific . . . is the power that rules the world.

Senator Albert J. Beveridge, Speech, 1900

The Pacific is exactly like any other ocean, and so far quite cool, cooler than Carlton Gardens.

Alfred Viscount Northcliffe, *My Journey Round the World* (August 1921), 1923

. . . Here from this mountain shore, headland beyond
stormy headland plunging like dolphins through the
blue seasmoke
Into pale sea – look west at the hill of water: it is half
the planet: this dome, this half-globe, this bulging
Eyeball of water, arched over to Asia,
Australia and white Antarctica: those are the eyelids
that never close; this is the staring unsleeping
Eye of the earth; and what it watches is not our wars.

Robinson Jeffers, *The Eye*, 1941

PAKISTAN

Baluchistan

I had, up to the time of my visit, often wondered, that with India so near, Baluchistan should have been so long allowed to remain the *terra incognita* it is. My surprise ceased on arrival at Kelat. It is impossible to conceive a more monotonous or uninteresting journey, from a traveller's point of view, than that from the sea to Quetta.

Harry de Windt, *A Ride to India*, 1891

Bannu

There'th nothing but thtones and thniperth here.

English infantry major, quoted F. Yeats Brown, *Bengal Lancer*, 1930 – of 1905

Karachi

Kurrachee looked like Surbiton trying to be imposing.

John Foster Fraser, *Round the World on a Wheel*, 1899

The vision of an American city in the Middle West expanded below us.

Robert Byron, *First Russia then Tibet*, 1933

Karachi, the Americans say, 'is half the size of Chicago cemetery and twice as dead.'

Freya Stark, Letter, February 1945, in *Dust in the Lion's Paw*, 1961

Lahore

Lahore is one of the greatest Cities of the East. . . . The castle or Towne is inclosed with a strong bricke wall, having thereto twelve faire gates, nine by land, and three openings to the River: the streets faire and well paved, the inhabitants most Baneans and handicrafts men; all white men of note lying in the Suburbs. The buildings are faire and high, with bricke and much curiositie of carved windowes and doores: most of the Gentiles doores of sixe or seven steps ascent, and very troublesome to get up, so built for more securitie, and that passengers should not see into their houses. The castle is seated on Ravee, a goodly River which falleth into Indus.

William Finch, *Journal*, 1610, in *Purchas his Pilgrimes*, 1625

The goodly city of Lahore in *India*, one of the largest Cities of the whole universe.

Thomas Coryate, *Letter to Maister L.W. from India*, 1615

Lahore is a sort of glorified Kensington Gardens. There seem to be no streets, only avenues. The borders are lined with flowers, and all the buildings are palaces.

John Foster Fraser, *Round the World on a Wheel*, 1899

The growling, flaring, creed-drunk city.

Rudyard Kipling, *Something of Myself*, 1937 – of 1880s

Because this new Lahore rises out of the decrepitude of the chaotic old city, and not, like Karachi, from a barren desert, one experiences there a feeling of the compression of time, or perhaps rather of the dissolution of the normal sequences of progress. A new class of hard-jowled business men in English-cut suits has arisen; they fill the chrome-plated modern cafés in the centre of the city, and personify the era of the construction sites and the American and Italian cars parked in serried ranks under the aristocratic trees of The Mall. But the older world of the poor still lives in the nineteenth century or in some even older and less definable past. It was the constant juxtaposition of these two ways of life, representing in objective terms two completely different stages of social evolution, that dominated one's impressions of Lahore.

George Woodcock, *Asia, Gods and Cities*, 1966

. . . A city that was familiar: it matched a stereotype in my memory. My image of the Indian city derives from Kipling, and it was in Lahore that Kipling came of age as a writer. Exaggerating the mobs, the vicious bazaar, the color and confusion, the Kipling of the early stories and *Kim* is really describing Lahore today. . . .

Paul Theroux, *The Great Railway Bazaar*, 1975

The North West Frontier

For the North
Guns always – quietly – but always guns.

Rudyard Kipling, *One Viceroy Resigns: Lord Dufferin to Lord Lansdowne*, 1888

Quetta

Quetta is, from everything but a strategical point of view, dull and uninteresting. It is an English garrison town, and all is said. The usual nucleus of scandal, surrounded by dances, theatricals, polo, flirtation, drink and – divorce. Are they not all alike from Gibraltar to Hong Kong?

Harry de Windt, *A Ride to India,* 1891

Jack Barrett went to Quetta
  Because they told him to.
He left his wife at Simla
  On three-fourths his monthly screw.
Jack Barrett died at Quetta
  Ere the next month's pay he drew.

Jack Barrett went to Quetta.
  He didn't understand
The reason of his transfer
  From the pleasant mountain-land.
The season was September,
  And it killed him out of hand.

Rudyard Kipling, *The Story of Uriah,* 1886

PANAMA

Fish, fruits, and herbage for salads are more plentiful in Panama than flesh, and the cool water of the *coco* [nut] is the women's best drink, though chocolate also, and much wine from Peru abound. The Spaniards in this city are much given to sin, looseness, and venery especially, and they make the Blackamoors (who are many, rich, and gallant) the chief objects of their lust. It is held to be one of the richest places in all America.

Thomas Gage, *The English-American . . . or, A New Survey of the West Indies,* 1648 – of 1630s

A few hasty rambles through its ruined convents and colleges and grass-grown plazas – a stroll on its massive battlements, lumbered with idle cannon, of the splendid bronze of Barcelona – were all that I could accomplish in a short stay of a day and a half . . . .The city was already half American. The native boys whistled Yankee Doodle through the streets, and Señoritas of the pure Castilian blood sang the Ethiopian melodies of Virginia to their guitars. Nearly half the faces seen were Americans, and the signs on the shops of all kinds appeared in our language. . . .
Panama is one of the most picturesque cities on the American Continent. Its ruins – if those could be called ruins which were never completed edifices – and the seaward view from its ramparts, on a bright morning, would ravish the eye of an artist. Although small in limit, old, and terribly dilapidated, its situation and surroundings are of unsurpassable beauty. There is one angle of the walls where you can look out of a cracked watch-tower on the sparkling swells of the Pacific, ridden by flocks of snow-white pelicans and the rolling canoes of the natives – where your vision, following the entire curve of the Gulf, takes in on either side nearly a hundred miles of shore.

Bayard Taylor, *Eldorado, or Adventures in the Path of Empire,* 1850

The main street is composed almost entirely of hotels, eating-houses and 'hells'. The old ruined houses have been patched up with whitewash and paint, and nothing remains unaltered but the cathedral. This building is in what I believe is called the 'early Spanish' style, which in the colonies is more remarkable for the tenacity with which the mud bricks hold together, than for any architectural advantages. The principal features in connection with these ancient churches are the brass bells they contain, many of which are of handsome design; and these bells are forced on the notice of the visitor to Panama, inasmuch as being now all cracked, they emit a sound like that of a concert of tin-pots and saucepans. At the corner of every street is a little turreted tower, from the top of which a small boy commences at sunrise to batter one of these discordant instruments, whilst from the belfries of the cathedral there issues a peal, to which, comparatively speaking, the din of a boiler manufactory is a treat. If these bells fail to bring the people to church, at all events they allow them no peace out of it.

Frank Marryat, *Mountains and Molehills,* 1855

The country through which we pass is very beautiful. But it will not do to trust it much, because it breeds fevers and other unpleasant disorders at all seasons of the year. Like a girl we most all have known, the Isthmus is fair but false.

Charles F. Browne, *Artemus Ward (his Travels) among the Mormons* (1863),1865

Panama means the canal even more than Honduras means bananas.

Nicholas Wollaston, *Red Rumba,* 1962

The Bridge between the Oceans.

Local slogan,

I don't want to enter History. I want to enter the Canal Zone.

General Omar Torrijos, quoted by Graham Greene, 'The Country with Five Frontiers', *New York Review of Books,* 17 February 1977

The Panamanians are not romantic. There is a hard cynical streak which you can find in their popular songs – 'Your love is a yesterday's newspaper,' and the slogans on the beautifully painted buses – 'Don't get dressed because you are not going.'

Graham Greene in *ibid.*

That well-known collectors' item, that controversial but beguiling example of diplomatic craftmanship, the Panama situation . . . .The Panama situation is a late classic of the imperial form. It possesses all the true imperial elements: a distant and tremendous dominant power, an anxious settler community, a subject people united only by resentment, dubious historical origins, a sleazy tropical setting, above all a specific raison d'être.

Jan Morris, *Destinations,* 1980

Panama Canal

I took the Canal Zone and . . . while the debate goes on, the canal does also.

Theodore Roosevelt, attrib.

It is the greatest liberty Man has ever taken with Nature.

James Bryce, *South America,* 1912

'Want to know the trouble with these people?' said an American political officer at the embassy. 'They can't decide whether the Canal is a government department, or a company, or an independent state.'

Paul Theroux, *The Old Patagonian Express,* 1979

The Canal . . . was bred by Big Stick out of Manifest Destiny, two thoroughbreds of American assertion.

Jan Morris, *Destinations,* 1980

Whenever I crossed the unmarked frontier out of the Republic of Panama into the Canal Zone, I felt I was taking a retrograde step out of reality into pretense.

Ibid.

Chagres

The town of Chagres deserves notice, inasmuch as it is the birthplace of a malignant fever that became excessively popular among the Californian emigrants, many of whom have acknowledged the superiority of this malady by giving up the ghost, a few hours after landing. Most towns are famous for some particular manufacture, and it is the fashion for visitors to carry away a specimen of the handicraft; so it is with Chagres. It is composed of about fifty huts, each of which raises its head from the midst of its own private malaria, occasioned by the heaps of filth and offal, which putrefying under the rays of a vertical sun, choke up the very doorway.

Frank Marryat, *Mountains and Molehills,* 1855

Colón

A rose by any other name would smell as sweet, and Colon or Aspinwall will be equally vile however you call it. It is a wretched, unhealthy, miserably situated, but thriving little American town, created by and for the railway and the passenger traffic, which comes in here both from Southampton and New York . . . . I can say nothing in its favour. My only dealing there was with a washerwoman, and I wish I could place before my readers a picture of my linen in the condition in which it came back from that artist's hands. I confess that I sat down and shed bitter tears.

Anthony Trollope, *The West Indies and the Spanish Main,* 1859

PARAGUAY

*'So you have already been to Paraguay?' said Candide. 'Indeed I have,' replied Cacambo. 'I was once a servant in the College of the Assumption, so I know how the reverend fathers govern as well as I know the streets of Cadiz. It's a wonderful system they have. There are thirty provinces in their kingdom, and it is more than three hundred leagues across. The reverend fathers own the whole lot, and the people own nothing: that's what I call a master-piece of reason and justice. I don't think I have ever seen such godlike creatures as the reverend fathers. They fight the kings of Spain and Portugal over here and give them absolution in Europe. In this country they kill Spaniards, and in Madrid they send them to Heaven. Delightful, isn't it?'

Voltaire, *Candide,* 1758

Nothing ever happens in Paraguay – it just rolls along.

United States official, quoted by John Gunther, *Inside South America,* 1967

This landlocked shoebox of a country,

John Gunther, *Inside South America,* 1967

Asunción

Asunción . . . is both a mudhole and a charming small metropolis . . . .The people of Asunción represent typical elements in the national character. They are violently chauvinist, but not xenophobic; foreigners are liked. They have a stolid inflexibility like Finns or Turks, but are capable of fierce excesses of sudden wrath. Almost all are decent, frugal, humble, honest, clean; motorists seldom bother to lock their cars. No racial problem exists at all; nobody thinks anybody is inferior because his skin is dark.

John Gunther, *Inside South America,* 1967

Guayra

Somehow, I like those countries, which, as the province

of Guayra and Paraguay, appear to have no future, and of which the charm is in the past It pleases me to think that the sharp business men of times gone by, patting their stomachs (the prison of their brain), predicted great advancement, and were all deceived. For then it seems as if the prognostications of to-day's schemes may also fail, and countries which they have doomed to progress still remain as in Guayra, their towns deserted, with but the broken spire of some old church emerging from the verdure of the tropics, as the St. Paul's Rocks rise sheer out of the sea. If there is charm in the unknown, there is at least as great a charm in the forgotten, and the Salto de Guayra is one of the most forgotten corners of the earth.

R.B. Cunninghame Graham, *A Vanished Arcadia*, 1901

PATAGONIA (Argentina/Chile)

The curse of sterility is on the land.

Charles Darwin, *Journal . . . During the Voyage . . . of H.M.S. Beagle*, 1832–6

In calling up images of the past, I find the plains of Patagonia frequently cross before my eyes: yet these plains are pronounced by all to be the most wretched and useless. They are characterised only by negative possessions; without habitations, without water, without trees, without mountains, they support only a few dwarf plants. Why then – and the case is not peculiar to myself – have these arid wastes taken so firm possession of my mind? . . . The Plains of Patagonia are boundless, for they are scarcely practicable, and hence unknown: they bear the stamp of having thus lasted for ages, and there appears no limit to their duration through future time. If, as the ancients supposed, the flat earth was surrounded by an impassable breadth of water, or by deserts heated to an intolerable excess, who would not look at these last boundaries to man's knowledge with deep but ill-defined sensations.

Charles Darwin, *Voyage of the Beagle*, 1839

'Well,' said a friend at my elbow, 'I suppose you would not care to go to Patagonia again?'

I glanced at the scene before me, and as certain unpleasant memories which it called forth passed through my mind, I answered, shuddering, and with decided emphasis, 'By Jove, no!'

Julius Beerbohm, *Wanderings in Patagonia, or Life Among the Ostrich Hunters*, 1879

I believe that we have here the secret of the persistence of Patagonian images and their frequent recurrence in th minds of many who have visited that gray, monotonous, and in one sense eminently uninteresting region. It is not the effect of the unknown. It is not imagination: it is that nature in these desolate scenes . . . moves us more deeply than in others.

W. H. Hudson, *Idle Days in Patagonia*, 1893

Il n'y a plus que la Patagonie, la Patagonie, qui convienne à mon immense tristesse . . . .
(Patagonia, and only Patagonia, now, is in accord with my great sadness.)

Blaise Cendrars, *La Prose du Transsiberien et de la Petite Jehanne de France*, 1913

Patagonia, a wool-and-mutton factory . . . .
Sophisticates in Buenos Aires think of Patagonia and its austere steppes as a kind of Siberia . . . .

John Gunther, *Inside South America*, 1967

The poet lived . . . alone in a two-roomed hut. He had been a teacher of literature in Buenos Aires. He came down to Patagonia forty years back and stayed . . . His fingers gripped my arm. He fixed me with an intense and luminous stare.

'Patagonia!' he cried. 'She is a hard mistress. She casts her spell. An enchantress! She folds you in her arms and never lets go.'

Bruce Chatwyn, *In Patagonia*, 1977

Patagonians

at Port Famine
Here inhabit a kinde of strange Canibals, short of body, not above five or six spans high, and very strong and thicke made: their mouthes are very bigge, and reach almost to their eares; they eate their meate in a manner raw, for they doe nothing but scorch it a little in the fire, and so eate it, and with the bloud that runneth from their mouthes, they smeare all their faces, and their breasts, and lay yong feathers on their bodies to the bloud that clingeth to their skinnes like Glue.

Anthony Knivet, 1601, in *Purchas his Pilgrimes*, 1625

The Patagonians of humans first
Discovered Communism, and were cursed
Through all the centuries to stay the same.

Roy Campbell, *Flowering Rifle*, Book III, 1938

Isla de los Estados

Though *Terra del Fuego* had an aspect extremely barren and desolate, yet this island of *Staten-land* far surpasses it, in the wildness and horror of its appearance: It seeming to be entirely composed of inaccessible rocks, without the least mixture of earth or mold between them. These rocks terminate in a vast number of ragged points, which spire up to a prodigious height, and are all of them covered with everlasting snow: the points themselves are on every side surrounded with frightful precipices, and often overhang in a most astonishing manner; and the hills which bear them, are generally separated from each other by narrow clefts, which appear as if the country had been rent by earthquakes; for these chasms are nearly perpendicular, and extend through the substance of the main rocks, almost to their very bottoms: so that nothing can be imagined more savage and gloomy, than the whole aspect of this coast.

George Anson (Richard Walter and Benjamin Robins), *A Voyage Round the World, 1740–1*, 1748

PERSIAN GULF

No arm of the sea has been, or is of greater interest alike to the geologist and archeologist, the historian and geographer, the merchant and the student of strategy, than the inland water known as the Persian Gulf.

Sir Arnold Wilson, *The Persian Gulf*, 1928

The Persian Gulf is the arsehole of the world, and Basra is eighty miles up it.

Harry Hopkins, remark to a British General, *c.*1941, quoted by John Masters, *The Road Past Mandalay*, 1961

(But Eric Partridge, *A Dictionary of Catch Phrases*, 1977, p.266 quotes another version: 'You know the old saying: the Persian Gulf's the arsehole of the world – and Shaiba's half-way up it', and notes that this is an RAF catchphrase from the 1920s, when there was a transit camp at *Sha'aiba*, and that the RAF have claimed the A of W distinction for several other 'hell-hole' stations.)

The jugular of the West.

The Shah of Iran, attrib., 1970s

PERU

Seeing an Indian Fisherman at the mouth of a River, foure of the Spaniards went ashore farre from the place where he was, being good runners and swimmers to take him.

The Indian marvailing what kinde of creature the Ship under saile might be, was taken in the mids of his muse and carried a shipboord. They asked him by signes and words (being somewhat refreshed after that dreadfull surprize and bearded sight) what Countrie that was, and how called. The Indian not understanding what they demanded, answered and told them his proper name, saying Beru, and added another word, saying Pelu: as if he should have said, if yee aske me what I am, my name is Beru, and if you ask me whence, I was in the River, Pelu being the common name of a River in that language. The Christians conceived that hee had understood them, and answered to the purpose; and from that time Anno 1515. or 1516. they called by the name of Peru that great and rich Empire.

Garcilasso de la Vega, *c.* 1580, in *Purchas his Pilgrimes*, 1625

Peru is divided as it were into three parts, long and narrow, which they call Lanos, Sierras, and Andes; the Lanos runs alongst the Sea coast; the Sierras be all hils, with some vallies; and the Andes be steepe and craggie Mountaines. The Lanos or Sea coast, have some ten leagues in breadth, in some parts lesse, and in some parts a little more. The Sierra containes some twenty leagues in breadth: and the Andes as much sometimes more, sometimes lesse. They run in length from North to South, and in breadth from East to West. . . . It never raines upon the coast or Lanos, although there fals some-times a small dew, which they call Guarua, and in Castill Mollina, the which sometimes thickens, and fals in certaine drops of water, yet it is not troublesome, nor such as they need any covering. Their coverings are of mats with a little earth upon them which is sufficient. Upon the Andes it raines in a manner continually, although it be sometimes more cleere then other. In the Sierra which lies betwixt both the extreames, it raineth in the same season as it doth in Spaine, which is from September unto April, but in the other season, the time is more cleere, which is when the Sunne is farthest off and the contrary when it is neerest . . . .

That which they call Sierra, causeth Vallies, where as it opens, which are the best dwellings of Peru. . . . Beyond the Citie of Cusco . . . the two ridges of Mountaines separate themselves one from the other, and in the midst leave a Playne and large Champaigne, which they call the Province of Callao, where there are many Rivers, and great store of fertile Pastures: there is also that great Lake of Titicaca.

Joseph Acosta, *c.* 1588, in *Purchas his Pilgrimes*, 1625

as the larger Province of the Old Spanish Empire

Mendoza, that was vice-roy of Peru was wont to say: *That the government of Peru was the best place that the King of Spain gave, save that it was some–what too near Madrid.*

Apothegmes . . . collected by Francis Lord Verulam . . ., 1625

I would not change my native land
For rich Peru with all her gold.

Rev. Isaac Watts, D.D., *Praise for Birth and Education in a Christian Land*, *Works*, 1753 – before 1748

I cannot say I liked the very little I saw of Peru.

Charles Darwin, *Journal . . . During the Voyage . . . of H.M.S. Beagle*, 1832–6

and Ecuador

We went on to see Dr Porros, who works at the

Ministry of Foreign Affairs. A very amusing man. In his office there is a map of Peru which seems to confirm all the Ecuadorean accusations of land-grabbing; the Peruvian frontier has moved northward and westward right up to the Andes, like a rising tide. When I remarked on this to Dr Porros, he laughed and said: 'Ah – you mustn't take that too seriously. What else can you expect in the Ministry of Foreign Affairs? We love the Ecuadoreans, so we want to come closer to them. We believe in *rapprochement.*'

Christopher Isherwood, *The Condor and the Cows,* 1949

Peru, it may be fairly said, is the only nation in the world which lived basically for a long period on bird manure.

John Gunther, *Inside South America,* 1967

'Times are bad in Peru,' a man said, 'even the anchovy has left our waters and swum away.'

Paul Theroux, *The Old Patagonian Express,* 1979

The only way to handle a Peruvian is to agree with his pessimism.

Paul Theroux, *The Old Patagonian Express,* 1979

Incas

They were certainly an impressive people. But they fill me, personally, with a kind of horror. I find them, as we used to say during the Evelyn Waugh period, madly ungay.

Christopher Isherwood, *The Condor and the Cows,* 1949

Arequipa

One must place Tunis or Trebizond in the valley of Zermatt to get an impression of Arequipa as it stands, encircled by snow fields and massive towers of rock.

James Bryce, *South America,* 1912

Callao

Callao is a filthy, ill-built, small seaport. The inhabitants, both here and at Lima, present every imaginable shade of mixture between European, Negro, and Indian blood. They appear a depraved, drunken set of people. The atmosphere is loaded with foul smells, and that peculiar one, which may be perceived in almost every town within the tropics, was here very strong.

Charles Darwin, *Journal . . . During the Voyage . . . of H.M.S. Beagle,* 1832–6

Cuzco

Wandering through its streets one is possessed every moment by the sense of how much has happened in a place where nowadays nothing seems to happen . . . .

The long grey mouldering streets and houses of Spanish Cuzco, the ancient walls of primitive Peruvian Cuzco, defying time better than the convents and the churches, each calling up contrasted races and civilizations, the plazas too vast for the shrunken population, the curious sense of two peoples living side by side in a place from which the old life has vanished, and into which no new life has come, the sense of utter remoteness from the modern world, all these things give to Cuzco a strange and dreamy melancholy, a melancholy all the deeper because there was little in its past that one could wish restored.

James Bryce, *South America,* 1912

There is no sense in my trying to describe Cuzco; I should only be quoting from the guide-book. . . . What remains with you is the sense of a great outrage, magnificent but unforgivable. The Spaniards tore down the Inca temples and grafted splendid churches and mansions on to their foundations. This is one of the most beautiful monuments to bigotry and sheer stupid brutality in the whole world.

Christopher Isherwood, *The Condor and the Cows,* 1949

One could say that it is as though, not Communist China had occupied Lhasa but Catholic Spain, and not long after the reign of Ferdinand and Isabella; that there are Spanish structures upon the Tibetan buildings, that miscegenation has taken place and there is a half-breed population of Mongol with Iberian; at which point we may not bother ourselves as to whether the draught animals – except that neither draws a vehicle and both are beasts of burden – are yaks or llamas.

Sacheverell Sitwell, *Golden Wall and Mirador,* 1961

en route to Cuzco

Up here, you become overwhelmingly aware of the presence of the Indians. Cuzco was the capital of the Inca empire, and the *puna,* despite conquest and expropriation, is still their native land. You see them, singly or in groups, all over the plain. Some of them are working on patches of arable field, others watch their herds of cows, sheep, llamas and vicunas. In the extraordinary clarity of the atmosphere, every living figure seems significant and dramatic; the skirts of the Indian women, brilliant pink, deep orange or red, are visible as sharp spots of colour even in the farthest distance. These people, like the Chinese peasants, have an uncanny air of belonging to their landscape – of being, in the profoundest sense, its inhabitants. It would hardly surprise you to see them emerging from or disappearing into the bowels of the earth.

Christopher Isherwood, *The Condor and the Cows,* 1949

Iquitos

Iquitos is called 'Peru's Atlantic Port,' although it lies 2,300 miles from the sea.

John Gunther, *Inside South America,* 1967

The dogs look healthy, so that, as one local observer put it, 'You know that the people have enough food.'

Ibid.

Lima

Lima is neere as big as London within the walls: the houses are of Lome baked, for want of Stone.

John Ellis, 1593, in *Purchas his Pilgrimes,* 1625

One is at first surprised to find the houses extremely low, many of one storey and hardly any (save a few new residences on the outskirts) exceeding two stories, and to be told that they are built of bricks, or more commonly of cane and reeds plastered with mud. It is commonly said that in Lima a burglar needs nothing more than a bowl of water and a sponge to soften the plaster, and a knife to cut the canes. But the reason is apparent, when one remembers that no place on the West coast has suffered more from earthquakes.

James Bryce, *South America,* 1912

For more than half the year Lima has a peculiar climate. It is never cold enough to have a fire, but usually cold enough to make you wish for one. It never rains, but it is never dry; that is to say, it is not wet enough to make one hold up an umbrella, yet wet enough to soak one's clothes.

Ibid.

The main thing to say about Lima even today, is that it was the dominant Spanish city in South America for three hundred years. It still has the overtones of an imperial metropolis, and it still utterly dominates Peru, so much so that it is sometimes ironically called 'a city searching for a country.'

John Gunther, *Inside South America,* 1967

Few great cities in the world look more plundered and bankrupt than Lima. It is the look of Rangoon, the same heat and colonial relics and corpse-odours: the imperial parades have long ago marched away from its avenues and left the spectators to scavenge and beg. Ever since Mexico, the description, 'formerly an important Spanish city, famous for its architecture' made me stiffen in apprehension, but no city had fallen as far as Lima. Like a violated tomb in which only the sorry mummy of withered nationalism was left, and just enough religion to console a patient multitude with the promise of happier pickings beyond the grave. . . .

Paul Theroux, *The Old Patagonian Express,* 1979

Miraflores

The houses in Miraflores are mostly villas in casino style, in uninhibited dreaming of Monte Carlo. Or it is no more than a natural affinity for probably neither architects nor owners have visited the Principality in person, or seen the public buildings of the Société des Bains de Mer. But there are moments, many of them, when Monte Carlo seems the architectural ideal, however remote and distant.

Sacheverell Sitwell, *Golden Wall and Mirador,* 1961

Macchu Picchu

We come upon permanence: the rock that abides and
the word:
the city upraised like a cup in our fingers,
all hands together, the quick and the dead and the
quietened; death's
plenitude holding us here, a bastion, the fullness
of life like a blow falling, petals of flint
and the perduring rose, abodes for the sojourner.
a glacier for multitudes, breakwater in Andes.

Pablo Neruda, 'The Heights of Macchu Picchu', – *Canto General,* 1950, trans. Ben Belitt, *Selected Poems of Pablo Neruda,* 1961

en route to Macchu Picchu

What a breath-taking place! You seem to be climbing into a larger world, a landscape built by titans in a fit of sheer megalomania. From the narrow saddleback on which the ruined city stands, the precipices plunge headlong into the raging brown river, fifteen hundred feet below. Looking up makes you even giddier than looking down, for all around the valley are black snow-streaked mountains looming over you through the driving clouds, and right ahead, at the end of the ridge, towers an appalling berg of rock, like the fragments of a fallen moon. This is called Huayna Picchu. The Incas, who must have been able to climb like flies, built a watch-tower on top of it, to guard the approach to the citadel.

Christopher Isherwood, *The Condor and the Cows,* 1949

This is the most stupendous approach there has ever been, to something which in its own right is perhaps the most startlingly dramatic archaeological site in either the Old or the New World. For the setting is enough, is almost too much in itself. It is nearly too good to be believed that there should be something to see here.

Sacheverell Sitwell, *Golden Wall and Mirador,* 1961

There are certain places, among them some of the most impressive and beautiful in the world, that call for only a single dose, repeated perhaps the next morning. If nothing else, it is a tribute to their potency. Even the Parthenon, even the paintings in the Prado, are not to be seen each day, and every day. Macchu Picchu, which is certainly among the wonders of both Americas, and a dual artifact of nature and of man, has hidden itself away, and it is not its intention that we should spend too long a time looking at it. We should come to it, preferably from far away, admire it, and move on. . . . The greatest achievements of the human spirit are not for perpetual repetition. If they stale, they stale badly, and it is only after long silence or absence that they become fresh again. Macchu Picchu, sited in one of the most astounding landscapes in the world is not, and never was, a work of art. It is a historical relic in marvellous and unaccountable preservation and, once seen, curiosity is satisfied and one can go away.

Ibid.

PHILIPPINES

It was my fortune to be in company with one Diego Gutieres, who was the first Pilot that ever went to that countrey of the Phillippinas. He maketh report of many strange things in that Countrey, aswell riches as other, and saith, if there bee any Paradise upon earth, it is in that countrey: and addeth, that sitting under a tree, you shal have such sweet smels, with such great content and pleasure, that you shall remember nothing, neither wife, nor children, nor have any kinde of appetite to eate or drinke, the odoriferous smels wil be so sweete.

Henry Hawks (1572), in Richard Hakluyt, *Principal Navigations . . . of the English Nation,* 1598–1600

*'What th' divvle ar-re th' Ph'lippeens,' says he. 'Is it a festival,' says he, 'or a dhrink?' he says. 'Faith, 'tis small wondher ye don't know,' says I, 'f'r'tis mesilf was weak on it a year ago,' I says. 'Th' Ph'lippeens is an issue,' says I, 'an' islands,' says I, 'an' a public nuisance,' I says. . . .

Finlay Peter Dunne, *Mr Dooley's Philosophy,* 1900

The presence of Americans in these islands is simply one of the results, in logical sequence, of great national prosperity, and in remote consequences is likely to transcend in importance anything recorded in the history of the world since the discovery of America. To doubt the wisdom of the United States remaining in these islands is to doubt the stability of republican institutions.

Arthur MacArthur, *c.* 1901, quoted by William Manchester, *American Caesar,* 1979

The finest group of islands in the world, its strategic position is unexcelled by that of any other position on the globe.

Ibid.

In spite of my affection for America, I have sometimes felt a touch of the same irritation as my fellow Dutchmen, Frenchmen, and Britons, at hearing my American friends confidently assert that America has done better by the Philippines than the rest of us Westerners have done by those Asian and African countries that have been temporarily under our rule. My glimpse of the Philippines has changed my feelings about this. The American boast is a proud one, but I believe it is no more than the plain truth.

Arnold Toynbee, *East to West,* 1958

Three hundred years in the convent and fifty years in Hollywood.

Anon, quoted Brian Eads, *Observer,* 6 April 1980 – the commonest shorthand for the Philippines' cultural inheritance from Spanish and American colonialism

Filipinos

The Filipino is treacherous and deceitful. Besides we want his country.

St Louis Post Dispatch, c. 1898, quoted in Richard West, *Victory in Vietnam,* 1974

We have bought ten million Malays at two dollars a head unpicked, and nobody knows what it will cost to pick them.

Thomas B.Reed, *c.* December 1898, in reference to US purchase of the Philippines, quoted in W.A. Robinson, *Thomas B. Reed, Parliamentarian,* 1930

Capul

The people of this island go almost all naked and are tawny of colour. The men weare onely a stroope about their wastes, of some kinde of linnen of their owne weaving, which is made of plantan leaves, and another stroope comming from their backe under their twistes, which covereth their privie parts, and is made fast to their girdles at their navels.

These people use a strange kinde of order among them, which is this. Every man and man-childe among them hath a nayle of Tynne thrust quite through the head of his privie part, being split in the lower ende and rivetted, and on the head of the nayle is as it were a crowne: which is driven through their privities when they be yong, and the place groweth up againe, without any great paine to the child: and they take this nayle out and in as occasion serveth: and for the truth thereof we our selves have taken one of these nailes from a sone of one of the kings which was of the age of ten yeeres, who did weare the same in his privie member.

This custome was granted at the request of the women of the country, who finding their men to be given to the fowle sinne of Sodomie, desired some remedie against that mischiefe, and obteined this before named of the magistrates. . . . These people wholly worship the devill, and oftentimes have conference with him, which appeareth unto them in most ugly and monstrous shape.

Francis Pretty (1588), in Richard Hakluyt, *Principal Navigations . . . of the English Nation,* 1598–1600

Corregidor

Intrinsically it is but a barren war-worn rock, hallowed as so many places by death and disaster. Yet it symbolizes within itself that priceless, deathless thing, the honor of a nation. Until we lift our flag from its dust we stand unredeemed before mankind. Until we claim again the ghastly remnants of its last gaunt garrison, we can but stand humble supplicants before Almighty God. There lies our Holy Grail.

Douglas MacArthur, Statement of 6 May 1943, on first anniversary of the fall of Corregidor to the Japanese, in Douglas MacArthur, *A Soldier Speaks,* 1965

Manila

Quiapo

Quiapo is the teeming traditional shopping district of Manila. Unlike the commercial centres in Makati and Cubao, Quiapo has no swank. It is unpretentiously proletarian, one large bargain emporium.

In Quiapo you will find such hard-to-get items as ancient, scratchy phonograph records and military surplus equipment, like knives, canteens, and jackets. Its sidewalks are lined with stalls that sell pictures of movie idols, shoestring, combs, stain removers, nail clippers, brassieres.

The Manila Visitor, Edition iv, 1977

Rizal Park

Rizal Park is an essential pause for those worn down by metropolitan frenzy. . . . In the early mornings Rizal Park is a place of ritual for worshippers of physical fitness. If you're up to it join the joggers who huff and puff around the dewy turf for a few laps. If this is too strenuous, simply watch the fascinating slow-motion calisthenics performed by aging Chinese and Kung Fu practitioners.

Witness the changing of the guard at the Rizal monument. Not as colorful and pompous as Buckingham's but the Philippine Marine sentries, nevertheless, perform the ritual with snap and precision.

The monument honors Dr José P. Rizal, the national hero. It was once fashionable to execute those who dared defy the Spanish crown in the park, and Rizal himself faced the firing squad here in 1898. . . .

Evening adds a romantic touch to the park, as lovers meet in their usual trysts. . . .

If all that walking around has made you hungry, have a sandwich and iced fruit juice at a unique café beside the central fountain. The waiters and the rest of the café staff are deaf-mutes. You have to write down your order legibly on a piece of paper.

Like we said, there's more to do in Rizal Park than just stroll, sit in the grass or feed the pigeons.

Ibid.

POLAND

When God made Poland he sent to the Poles some reason and the feet of a gnat, but even this little was taken away by a woman.

Polish proverb, in Selwyn Gurney Champion (ed.), *Racial Proverbs,* 1938

If you except Crakaw, and the greater Cities, the building in these parts is poore, being of meere dirt in the Villages, and of timber and clay in the better townes, the houses being covered with straw, or tiles of wood, and the gentlemens houses be farre distant one from another, and of no beauty.

Fynes Moryson, *An Itinerary,* 1617

Poland was but a breakfast.

Edmund Burke, Letter to Henrich von Burcke, post 17 January 1774, referring to the aggressive designs of Russia

Poland . . . a country in which it is difficult to imagine or to exaggerate, the extent as well as variety of human wretchedness!

Sir N.W. Wraxall, *Memoirs of the Courts of Berlin, etc.,* 1779

Polish liberty may be considered as the source of Polish wretchedness; and Poland appears to me, as far as I can judge by the specimens which fell under my observation, of all countries, the most distressed.

William Coxe, *Travels into Poland, Russia, Sweden, etc.,* 1792

'Happy Englishmen!' exclaimed the King, 'your house is raised, and mine is yet to build.'

Stanislaus Augustus of Poland, quoted *ibid.*

Poor Poland! They go on sadly there.

S.T. Coleridge, Letter to Robert Southey, 13 July 1794

Et ces gueux la appellent cette pays une patrie!
(And those beggars call that country a fatherland!)

Napoleon, attrib., *c.* 1812, on hearing Poles boasting of their country, quoted by J.L. Stephens, *Incidents of Travel in the Russian and Turkish Empires,* 1839

Poland left for Russia's lunch
Upon the side-board, snug reposes.

Thomas Moore, *The Fudge Family in Paris,* 1818

She, like the eagle, will renew her age.

Thomas Campbell, *Lines on Poland,* 1831

The nations may not be trod out, and quite
Obliterated from the world's great page –
The nations that have filled from age to age
Their place in story. They who in despite
Of this, a people's first and holiest right,
In lust of unchecked power, or brutal rage,
Against a people's life such warfare wage,
With man no more, but with the Eternal fight.
They who break down the barriers He hath set,
Break down what would another time defend
And shelter their own selves; they who forget
(For the indulgence of the present will)
The lasting ordinances, in the end
Will rue their work, when ill shall sanction ill.

Charles Chenevix Trench, *Poland,* 1831

How long, O God, shall men be ridden down,
And trampled under by the last and least
Of men? The heart of Poland hath not ceased
To quiver, tho' her sacred blood doth drown
The fields, and out of every smouldering town
Cries to Thee, lest brute Power be increased
Till that o'ergrown Barbarian in the East
Transgress his ample bound to some new crown: –
Cries to Thee, 'Lord, how long shall these things be?
How long this icy-hearted Muscovite
Oppress the region? Us, O Just and Good,
Forgive, who smiled when she was torn in three;
Us, who stand now, when we should aid the right –
A matter to be wept with tears of blood!'

Alfred Lord Tennyson, 'On the Result of the late Russian Invasion of Poland', *Poems,* 1833 (later, simply 'Poland')

That advanced outpost of western civilization.

Joseph Conrad, 'A Note on the Polish Problem', in *Notes on Life and Letters,* 1921

and Ireland
There are certain things in this world that are at once intensely loved and intensely hated. They are naturally things of a strong character and either very good or very bad. They generally give a good deal of trouble to everybody; and a special sort of trouble to those who try to destroy them. But they give most trouble of all to those who try to ignore them. Some hate them so insanely as to deny their very existence; but the void made by that negation continues to exasperate those who have made it, till they are like, men choked with a vacuum. They declare that it shall be nameless and then never cease to curse its name. This curious case is perhaps best illustrated by examples. One example of it is Ireland. Another is Poland.

G.K. Chesterton, *Generally Speaking,* 1928

The soul of Poland is indestructible . . . she will rise again like a rock, which may for a spell be submerged by a tidal wave, but which remains a rock.

Sir Winston Churchill, Speech in the House of Commons, 1 October 1939

The Russian armies now stand before the gates of Warsaw. They bring the liberation of Poland in their hands. They offer freedom, sovereignty, and independence to the Poles.

Sir Winston Churchill, Speech in the House of Commons, 2 August 1944

There is something exhausting about communist countries (even if the Poles are there), as if the Marxist-Leninist system never planned to have enough oxygen.

J.B. Priestley, *A Visit to New Zealand,* 1974

Poland is a vast and flat land where the winds blow very hard in any direction, and when this happens not only the hats fly away, the heads also.

Mieczyslaw Rakowski, quoted in interview by Oriana Fallaci, *The Times,* 23 February 1982

Poles

Poland is a large and mighty kingdom, powerful in horsemen, and populous of strangers, being charged with a proud nobility, a familiar and manly gentry, and a ruvidous vulgarity. They are all, for the most part, of square and thick bodies, having bull-necks, great thighs and legs, grim and broad faces, and commonly their shaven heads are finely covered with overthwarting strokes of crooked shables; for they, and the Armenians of Asia, are of stature and thicknesse the biggest and grossest people the world affordeth.

William Lithgow, *Rare Adventures and Painfull Peregrinations,* 1614/32

The Poles seem a lively people and use much action in their ordinary conversation. Their common mode of saluting is to incline their heads, and to strike the breast with one of their hands, while they stretch the other towards the ground; but when a common person meets a superior, he bows his head almost to the earth, waving at the same time his hand, with which he touches the bottom of his leg near the heel of the person to whom he pays his obeisance. The men of all ranks generally wear whiskers, and shave their heads, leaving only a circle of hair upon the crown. The summer dress of the peasants consists of nothing but a shirt and drawers of coarse linen, without shoes or stockings, with round caps or hats. The women of the lower class wear upon their heads a wrapper of white linen, under which their hair is braided and hangs down in two plaits. I observed several of them with a long piece of white linen hanging round the side of their faces, and covering their bodies below the knees: this singular kind of veil makes them look as if they were doing penance.

The dress of the higher orders, both men and women, is uncommonly elegant. That of the gentlemen is a waistcoat with sleeves, over which they wear an upper robe of a different colour, which reaches down below the knee, and is fastened round the waist with a sash or girdle; the sleeves of this upper garment are in warm weather tied behind the shoulders: a sabre is a necessary part of their dress as a mark of nobility. In the summer the robe, &c, is of silk; in winter, of cloth, velvet, or stuff, edged with fur. They wear fur caps or bonnets, and buskins of yellow leather, the heels of which are plated with iron or steel. The dress of the ladies is a simple polonaise, or long robe edged with fur.

William Coxe, *Travels into Poland, Russia and Sweden, etc.*, 1792

The general dissolution of morals among the upper orders, is not one of the least extraordinary and characteristic features of the capital and country. . . . Neither Petersburgh nor Naples can surpass Warsaw in these respects. All the principles which bind society together, and which purify and perpetuate it, appear to me to be relaxed among the Poles.

Sir N.W. Wraxall, *Memoirs of the Courts of Berlin, etc.*, 1779

The Poles are the worst and most dangerous kind of deceivers, for they succeed in deceiving themselves.

Sir Robert Bruce Lockhart, *Diary*, 6 January 1944

There are few virtues which the Poles do not possess and there are few errors which they have ever avoided.

Sir Winston Churchill, Speech in the House of Commons, after the Potsdam Conference, 1945

I began to realise why the Poles were so dour and icy: they had been several times through hell, and war had steeled their hearts against everything. They had become so hard that now nothing could hurt them again.

James Kirkup, *One Man's Russia*, 1968

River Bug

For many centuries the banks of the Bug have been the battle-ground of the Russians and Poles. In the time of Boleslaus the Terrible, the Russians were defeated there with great slaughter, and the river was so stained with blood that it has retained ever since the name of the *Horrid*.

J.L. Stephens, *Incidents of Travel in the Russian and Turkish Empires*, 1839

Cracow

Of all the Cities, Crakaw is the chiefe, where the King and his Councell reside. It is seated in a plaine, having mountaines on all sides, but somewhat distant, and it is compassed with two walles of stone and a dry ditch. The building is very faire, of free stone foure roofes hye but covered with tiles of wood for the most part. It is of a round forme, but somewhat longer from the East to the West. In the midst of the City is a large market place quadrangular, wherein is the Cathedrall Church, and in the midst of the market place is the Senate house for the City, about which are many shops of Merchants. Upon the East side of the City is the King's Castle, seated on a hill; being faire, and high built, almost quadrangular, but somewhat more long then broad, and lying open on the South side without any building above the wall. . . . Upon the East side of this City, where this Castle is seated, lie foure suburbes; namely the Jewes little City, and Cagmen, which is divided by the river Vistula, from the other two, called Stradam and the Stewes. And Stradam belongs to the City, but the rest have their own Magistrates and priviledges. Towards the South and South-west, lies the suburb Garbatz, belonging to the City, which of late was burnt in the civill war. . . . On the North side are the suburbs Biskop, and Clepart, which have their own Magistrates.

Fynes Moryson, *An Itinerary*, 1617

The salt mines of

Thus cavern'd round in Cracow's mighty mines,
With crystal walls a gorgeous city shines;
Scoop'd in the briny rock long streets extend
Their hoary course, and glittering domes ascend;
Down the bright steps, emerging into day,
Impetuous fountains burst their headlong way,
O'er milk-white vales in ivory channels spread,
And wondering seek their subterraneous bed.
Form'd in pellucid salt with chissel nice,
The pale lamp glimmering through the sculptured ice,
With wild reverted eyes fair Lotta stands,
And spreads to heaven, in vain, her glassy hands;
Cold dews condense upon her pearly breast,
And the big tear rolls lucid down her vest.

Far gleaming o'er the town transparent fanes
Rear their white towers, and wave their golden vanes;
Long lines of lustres pour their trembling rays,
And the bright vault returns the mingled blaze.

Erasmus Darwin, 'The Economy of Vegetation', *The Botanic Garden*, 1791

Cracow stands in an extensive plain, watered by the Vistula, which is broad but shallow: the city and its suburbs occupy a vast tract of ground, but are so thinly peopled, that they scarcely contain 16,000 inhabitants. The great square in the middle of this town is very spacious; and has several well-built houses, one richly furnished and well inhabitated, but most of them now either untenanted, or in a state of melancholy decay. Many of the streets are broad and handsome but almost every building bears the most striking marks of ruined grandeur: the churches alone seem to have preserved their original splendour. . . . The effects of cannon, grape, and musket-shot, are still discernible on the walls and houses. In a word, Cracow exhibits the remains of a magnificent capital in ruins: from the number of fallen and falling houses one would imagine it had lately been sacked and that the enemy had left it only yesterday. The town is surrounded with high walls of brick, strengthened by round and square towers of whimsical shapes in the antient style of fortification.

William Coxe, *Travels into Poland, Russia, Sweden, etc.*, 1792

The Square, immense in its solitude, was full to the brim of moonlight. The garland of lights at the foot of the houses seemed to burn at the bottom of a bluish pool. I noticed with infinite satisfaction that the unnecessary trees the municipality insisted upon sticking between the stones had been steadily refusing to grow. They were not a bit bigger than the poor victims I could remember. Also, the paving operations seemed to be exactly at the same point at which I left them forty years before. There were the dull, torn up patches on that bright expanse, the piles of paving material looking ominously black, like heads of rocks on a silvery sea. Who was it that said Time works wonders? What an exploded superstition! As far as those trees and these paving-stones were concerned, it had worked nothing. The suspicion of the unchangeableness of things already vaguely suggested to my senses by our rapid drive from the railway station, was agreeably strengthened within me.

Joseph Conrad, 'Poland Revisited', 1915, in *Notes on Life and Letters*, 1921

But what gives Cracow a sort of sharp outline of spires and turrets against the background of history is the fact that it is a seat of culture on the edge of the uncultivated wilds. The city, like the nation, is a sort of out-post, and the contrast is of the sort that belongs to capes and islands and the edges of things. That balance of the mind that we call philosophy is here balanced on the edge of an abyss. . . . The Germans who do not carry learning lightly, and the Slavs who do not carry it at all, press upon that more slender and subtle experiment with the weight of less living things.

G.K. Chesterton, *Generally Speaking*, 1928

Danzig/Gdansk

The City of Dantzke is a very faire City, and howsoever few ages past they had not any houses built of stone, yet at this time, many were built of free-stone, and the rest of bricke, with great beauty and magnificence, being sixe or seven roofes high. And they had publike gardens for sports, banquets, and exercises, which are very pleasant. They have a very faire Senate-house, called Hoff, that is, the Court; and the Citizens have a strange fashion, to put off their hats when they passe by it. From the market place being round . . . to the gate Hochethore (being richly engraved) lieth a very faire street (called Longgasse) and leads up towards the Mountaines hanging over the City. . . . There is a faire water conduit, vulgarly called Wasserkunst, where by a mill the waters are drawne up into a cesterne, from whence they are carried by pipes into all the streetes and private houses; besides that many Citizens have their private wels.

Fynes Moryson, *An Itinerary*, 1617

The houses are in general lofty, and in an antique taste. In most of the streets are planted trees, which at this season of the year afford an agreeable shade; but which in the winter must be found very inconvenient, and ought to be removed.

Sir N.W. Wraxall, *A Tour Round the Baltic*, 1775

The broad avenue between this city and one of its pleasure-suburbs has two roadways separated by a continuous lawn of well-tended green grass. I was startled to see a tram running over this lawn. Then only did I notice that there was a double set of tramlines between the two roadways, and that grass had been grown between and on either side of the rails. This device made all the difference to the appearance of the avenue. The desert is arid, but less arid than a double set of gravelled tramlines, and not more dusty. Someone had thought of the device. He possessed imagination. And the city council, his employers, had the wit to consent to bear the slight expense of his imagination. Rare.

Arnold Bennett, *Journal 1929*, 1930

Warsaw

This metropolis seems to me, like the Republic of which it is the nominal head, to unite the extremes of civilization and of barbarism, of magnificence and wretchedness, of splendor and misery; but, unlike all other great cities of Europe, these extremes are not softened, approximated, and blended by any intermediate gradations. The middle orders of men, who every where else form the most numerous class of citizens, the most useful, and the most industrious, appear hardly to have any existence here. Palaces and sheds, the mansions of the great, and the cottages of the poor, compose exclusively the larger portion of Warsaw. It is like an assemblage of nobles and slaves, of lords and vassals, such as the darkness of the middle ages, when feudal tyranny prevailed universally, might have exhibited; but which, happily for mankind, is now nowhere to be seen except in Poland. . . .

As I walk through the streets of Warsaw, and survey the buildings around me, I am tempted to imagine myself in some scattered and half ruined village.

Sir N.W. Wraxall, *Memoirs of the Courts of Berlin, etc.*, 1779

Warsaw
Famous for mines of salt and yokes of iron.

Lord Byron, *Don Juan*, 1819–24

I think one sees more pretty women in five minutes in Warsaw than in half-an-hour in any other European capital, London thrown in.

Harry de Windt, *From Pekin to Calais by Land*, 1889

Odours can haunt one even as tunes. One morning in my luxurious apartment in the Hotel Bristol in Warsaw I was suddenly taken frightfully ill with nausea. The recollection of a visit the day before to the dreadful Trefna Jatka, a tenemount house occupied by over one thousand families of very poor Jews, and of the dreadful smells in many of the rooms I had entered, had suddenly swept over me. I thought that this was a sign of particular sensitiveness on my part, and was feeling rather proud of my delicacy of feeling, when Mr Whitehead, the manager of a big lace factory in the Polish capital, told me that after a walk down the Jewish quarter in Lublin, at the end of which he had been taken ill, he was seized every day for three weeks with a violent fit of vomiting when he recalled his sensations in that awful ghetto. This, by the way, *en passant*, may illustrate the shameful treatment to which the Jews are subjected in the Russian Empire.

Robert Harborough Sherard, *My Friends the French*, n.d.

Somebody once said that if you take a handful of Warsaw soil and squeeze it, the blood will run from it.

Alicya Iwanska, remark in Peter Batty's documentary TV film *Battle for Warsaw* – BBC tv, 30 May 1981

Palace of Culture and Science
The awfulness of . . . war still seemed to hang over Warsaw. It hung over the ludicrous Palace of Culture and Science too – the wedding-cake architecture that was a gift from Stalin to the heroic citizens of Warsaw. Those citizens have a sharp sense of the ridiculous and they say that the best view of Warsaw is from the top of this monstrous edifice, because then you cannot see it.

James Kirkup, *One Man's Russia*, 1968

view of park from Europejski Hotel
From the window of my hotel I could see the park – at night surely the darkest in Europe and the least unfrequented.

Ibid.

PORTUGAL

When the King of Spain conquered Portugal, he gave special charge to his lieutenant that the soldiers should not spoil, lest he should alienate the hearts of the people. The army also suffered much scarcity of victual. Whereupon the Spanish soldiers would afterwards say: That they had won the King a Kingdom, as the Kingdom of Heaven useth to be won, by fasting and abstaining from that that is another man's.

Francis Bacon, *Apothegmes . . . collected by Francis Lord Verulam . . .*, 1625

I am very happy here, because I loves oranges, and talk bad Latin to the Monks, who understand it as it is like their own. And I goes into society (with my pocket-pistols) and I swims in the Tagus all across at once, and I rides on an ass or a mule and swears Portuguese, and have got a diarrhoea, and bites from the mosquitoes. But what of that? Comfort must not be expected by folks that go a pleasuring.

Lord Byron, Letter to the Rev. F. Hodgson, 16 July 1809

Oh, Christ! it is a goodly sight to see
What heaven hath done for this delicious land!
What fruits of fragrance blush on every tree!
What goodly prospects o'er the hills expand!

Lord Byron, *Childe Harold's Pilgrimage*, Canto the First, 1812

Portugal, the western terminus of Rome's conquests, remains to the present day the most Roman of Latin countries. Her language approaches nearest to the speech of the ancient mistress of the world. Her people still preserve the sturdiness and perseverance, often degenerating into dogged obstinacy; the turbulent love of liberty; the materialism and unartistic spirit; the conservatism and love of routine; the superstition and the lust of territorial aggrandisement which distinguished the former conquerors of the world. Even in the present day, the traveller in Portugal sees with astonishment the domestic life of Rome, her poetry and literature, her arts and sciences; and the archaic form of civilization has extended even to the Brazil.

Richard Burton, *Explorations of the Highlands of the Brazil,* 1869

One of the most novel sights to me in Portugal were the hedges of the corn-fields, which were composed of aloes and geraniums.

J.R. Planché, *Recollections and Reflections,* 1872

Wet or fine the air of Portugal has a natural happiness in it, and the people of the country should be as happy and prosperous as any people in the world.

H.G. Wells, *A Year of Prophesying,* 1925

Nowhere else in Europe has one so strong a feeling of a country in pawn to capital held abroad.

Ibid.

If there is one slice of Christendom, one portion of Europe which was made by the sea more than another, Portugal is that slice, that portion, that belt. Portugal was made by the Atlantic.

Hilaire Belloc, *Places,* 1942

This 'little America' aspect of Lisbon contrasts rather naively with the rest of Portugal, like a figure out of drawing in a primitive painting. Yet just this naivete comes to seem, after a time, typically Portuguese. This small country with its variety of climates and mixture of racial strains, is an assiduous copyist, mimic, and borrower. Any sizable Portuguese town looks like a superstitious bride's finery – something old, something new, something borrowed, and something blue. Portugal has its 'little Versailles,' in the pink palace of Queluz (with a miniature Dutch canal added); its Balmoral, in the Scottish-baronial Pena Palace. It has its 'little Switzerland,' in the northern province of the Minho; its bit of Africa, in the southern Algarve. . . . Portugal got its characteristic *azulejos* (painted tiles) from the Arabs and then subjected them to a Dutch influence. Its painters copied the Flemish, and its furniture makers the English and the French. . . . It is only in the far north, in the Minho and the 'lost' provinces of Tras-os-Montes (Beyond the Mountains), that you find a pure architecture – the Portuguese baroque, done in granite and severe white plaster, and decorated with gold – that is unlike anything else in the world.

Mary McCarthy, Letter from Portugal, February 1955, in *On the Contrary*, 1962

Portuguese

Strip a Spaniard of all his virtues, and you have a Portuguese.

Spanish proverb

The Portuguese had need to have the stomachs of ostriches to digest the loads of savoury viands with which they cram themselves. Their vegetables, their rice, their poultry, are all stewed in the essence of ham, and so strongly seasoned with pepper and spices, that a spoonful of peas, or a quarter of an onion, is sufficient to set one's mouth in a flame. With such a diet, and the continual swallowing of sweetmeats, I am not surprised at their complaining so often of head-aches and vapours.

William Beckford, Letter, 9 November 1787, in *Sketches of Spain and Portugal,* 1834

No beggars equal those of Portugal for strength of lungs, luxuriance of sores, profusion of vermin, variety and arrangement of tatters, and dauntless perseverance.

William Beckford, Letter, 28 November 1787, *ibid.*

They have no public spirit, and consequently no national character. An Englishman or a Frenchman may be distinguished in foreign countries by an air and manners peculiar to his nation, and which he would attempt in vain to disguise; but any meagre, swarthy man may pass for a Portuguese.

Robert Semple, *Journey to Spain,* 1805

There exists in the people of Portugal an unconquerable love of their ease, which is superior even to their fear and detestation of the enemy. Neither will they, or their magistrates, or the Government, see that the temporary indulgence of this passion for tranquillity must occasion the greatest misfortunes to the state and hardships to the individuals themselves; and no person in the country likes to have his tranquillity and habits disturbed for any purpose, however important, or to be the instrument of disturbing those of others. Thus every arrangement is defeated. . . .

Duke of Wellington, Dispatch to Charles Stuart Esq., 3 January 1811

There is something very extraordinary in the nature of the people of the Peninsula. I really believe them, those of Portugal particularly, to be the most loyal and best disposed, and the most cordial haters of the French, that ever existed: but there is an indolence, and a want even of the power of exertion in their disposition and habits, either for their own security, that of their country, or of their allies, which baffles all our calculations and efforts.

Duke of Wellington, Dispatch to Charles Stuart Esq., 16 June 1811

Huxley told me a story of Wellington, When Wellington was asked, apropos of the mistakes of military commanders, what was the worst order he had ever heard of as being given by a G.O.C., he said it was: 'Soldiers, remember that you are Portuguese.'

Arnold Bennett, *Journal,* 11 February 1927

A nation swoln with ignorance and pride,
Who lick yet loathe the hand that waves the sword
To save them from the wrath of Gaul's unsparing Lord.

Lord Byron, *Childe Harold's Pilgrimage,* Canto the First, 1812

'The Spaniards,' says Dr Southey, 'despise the Portuguese: the Portuguese hate the Spaniards.' The Spaniards in their national songs, threaten the Portuguese with invasion: the Portuguese content themselves with defying the Spaniards. 'Strip a Spaniard of all his virtues, and you make a good Portuguese of him,' says the Spanish proverb. 'I have heard it more truly said,' says Dr Southey, 'add hypocrisy to a Spaniard's vices, and you have the Portuguese character.'

Josiah Conder, *The Modern Traveller,* vol. 19, 1830

*The Portuguese and the English have always been the best of friends because we can't get no Port Wine anywhere else.

Captain Frederick Marryat, *Peter Simple,* 1834

The Spaniards are too proud to work and too lazy to steal – therefore they only cheat; the Portuguese are not too proud or lazy to procure a subsistence in any way they can get it, – therefore they sometimes work, sometimes steal, and always cheat. Generally I think they are more amiable and inoffensive than the Spaniards, who did not impress me favourably in that respect. I saw a good deal of vulgar rowdyism in Spain, but none in Portugal. The dirtiest and laziest vagrants among the Portuguese seemed at least disposed to be friendly and obliging. The worst feature about them is their noses, which are frightfully long, thick, and ill adapted to any purpose that I know of, unless it may be snuffling up the foul odours that fill the streets.

Ross Browne, *An American Family in Germany,* 1866

We must always remember, with reference to the Portuguese, that they were the original civilisers of Africa. They had the bad luck, if I may say so, to get only the coast, to be on the fringe, and never to have penetrated to the high healthy plateau at the back.

Cecil Rhodes, Speech to shareholders of the Chartered Company, 18 January 1895

This is Portuguese all over – indolence, piousness, poverty, impotence.

Mark Twain, *More Tramps Abroad,* 1897

Mr Asquith was much amused by an Army Order which he had actually seen in print, to the effect that the Portuguese were not to be referred to as Ruddy Geese, but as Our Ancient Allies.

Edward Marsh, *A Number of People,* 1939 – of 1917

The rich in Portugal are said to be the richest in Europe. As you watch them in the hotels – silent, like sharks, endlessly masticating, with their medicines before them – you form a new conception of what cold selfishness can be. Strangely it is not the peasants on their donkeys . . . or the workers . . . who look foreign to American eyes; it is the moneyed classes who appear to be of a different breed. The lowering heavy darkness of the moneyed classes seems to be as much a state of mind or soul as a physical appearance. The thick skin, the somnolent, heavy-lidded gaze, are perhaps a kind of protection against fellow-feeling. The difference between rich and poor is so extreme in Portugal that it seems to have formed a carapace over the rich making them torpid and incurious.

Mary McCarthy, Letter from Portugal, February 1955, in *On the Contrary,* 1962

If there is no Portuguese word for blarney, there should be.

Richard West, *The White Tribes of Africa,* 1965

Cintra/Sintra

It unites in itself all the wildness of the Western Highlands with the verdure of the South of France.

Lord Byron, Letter to Mrs Catherine Gordon Byron, 11 August 1809

Lo! Cintra's glorious Eden intervenes
In variegated maze of mount and glen. . . .
The horrid crags, by toppling convent crowned,
The cork-trees hoar that clothe the craggy steep,
The mountain-moss by scorching skies imbrowned,
The sunken glen, whose sunless shrubs must weep,
The tender azure of the unruffled deep,
The orange tints that gild the greenest bough,
The torrents that from cliff to valley leap,
The vine on high, the willow branch below,
Mixed in one mighty scene, with varied beauty glow.

Lord Byron, *Childe Harold's Pilgrimage,* Canto the First, 1812

I should compare it with Malvern – but to the heights of Malvern must be added some hundred feet of perpendicular rock.

Henry Matthews, *The Diary of an Invalid,* 1820

Estoril

Most Americans shun Lisbon and huddle together in a sort of stockade in Estoril, which is an ugly little beach resort, with a casino, and houses painted blue and cream, like so many filling stations.

Mary McCarthy, Letter from Portugal, February 1955, in *On the Contrary,* 1962

Lisbon

Dined with Captain Lambert and his father-in-law and had much talk of Portugall from whence he is lately come, and he tells me that it is a very poor, dirty place – I mean the City and Court of Lisbone. That the King is a very rude and simple fellow; and for reviling of somebody a little while ago and calling of him cuckold, was run into the cods with a sword, and had been killed had he not told them that he was their king. That there is no glass windows, nor will have any; which makes sport among our merchants there, to talk of an English factor that being newly come thither, he writ unto England that glasse would be a good commodity to send thither, &c. That the King hath his meat sent up by a dozen of lazy guards and in pipkins; sometimes to his own table – and sometimes nothing but fruits, and now and then half a hen. And that now the Infanta is become our Queene, she is come to have a whole hen or goose to her table – which is not ordinary.

Samuel Pepys, *Diary,* 17 October 1661

The more one is acquainted with Lisbon, the less it answers the expectations raised by its magnificent appearance from the river. Could a traveller be suddenly transported without preparation or prejudice to many parts of this city, he would reasonably conclude himself traversing a succession of villages awkwardly tacked together, and overpowered by massive convents. The churches in general are in a woful taste of architecture, the taste of Borromini, with crinkled pediments, furbelowed cornices and turrets, somewhat in the style of old-fashioned French clock-cases, such as Boucher designed with many a scrawl and flourish to adorn the apartments of Madame de Pompadour.

William Beckford, Letter, 30 June 1787, in *Sketches of Spain and Portugal,* 1834

The filth of this city is indeed astonishing; every thing is thrown into the street, and all the refuse of the kitchen, and dead animals are exposed to these scorching suns. I believe these Portuguese would throw one another out, and 'leave the dead to bury the dead,' if it were not the interest of the priests to prevent them.

In wet weather the streets of Lisbon are very agreeable: if you walk under the houses you are drenched by the waterspouts; if you attempt the middle, there is a torrent; would you go between the two, there is the dunghill. When it rains hard some of the streets are like rivers.

Robert Southey, *Letters Written During a Journey in Spain,* 1797

*I expressed surprise to one person that they should have ventured to raise houses to such a height in a town so lately overthrown by an earthquake.

'It is because it has been so lately overthrown,' he replied, 'that we venture: for as other capitals in Europe deserve an earthquake as much as Lisbon, and none of them have been alarmed with more than the first symptoms hitherto, it is reasonable to believe that they will all have their turn, according to their deserts; and, of course, it will be a long time before it comes round to Lisbon again.'

John Moore, *Mordaunt,* 1800

What beauties doth Lisboa first unfold!
Her image floating on that noble tide,
Which poets vainly pave with sands of gold. . . .

But whoso entereth within this town,
That, sheening far, celestial seems to be,
Disconsolate will wander up and down,
Mid many things unsightly to strange ee;

For hut and palace show like filthily:
The dingy denizens are reared in dirt;
Ne personage of high or mean degree
Doth care for cleanliness of surtout or shirt,
Though shent with Egypt's plague, unkempt,
unwashed, unhurt.

Poor, paltry slaves! yet born 'midst noblest scenes –
Why, Nature, waste thy wonders on such men?

Lord Byron, *Childe Harold's Pilgrimage,* Canto the First, 1812

Doghood and Priesthood are certainly the most thriving trades in Lisbon.

Henry Matthews, *The Diary of an Invalid,* 1820

The trouble with Lisbon is that it is not quite different enough. It may have seemed so once, . . . but today Bournemouth has reached out and muffled it in bourgeois sameness, even down to days of sea-fog.

Cyril Connolly, 'When Frontiers Fell Like Nine-pins', 1966, in *The Evening Colonnade,* 1973

Oporto (from the sea)

A beautiful Scene verily it was! – & *is!* – The High land of Portugal, & the Mountain land behind it, & behind that fair Mountains with blue Pyramids & Cones. By the Glass I could distinguish the larger Buildings in Oporto, a scrambling City, part of it seemingly walls washed by the Sea, part of it upon Hills at first view, it looked much like a vast Brick kilnery in a sandy clayey Country, on a hot summer afternoon; seen more distinctly, it gave the nobler idea of a ruined City in a Wilderness, it's Houses & Streets lying low in ruins under it's ruined walls, & a few Temples & Palaces standing untouched.

S.T. Coleridge, Letter to Robert Southey, 16 April 1804

Sao Vicente, C. de / Cape St Vincent

Cape St.Vincent . . . presented itself to my eyes the first thing when I came upon deck in the morning, clear, solitary, blind-looking, feeling, as it were, the sea air and solitude for ever, like something between stone and spirit. It reminded me of a couplet written not long before, of

Ghastly castle, that eternally
Holds its blind visage out to the lone sea.

Such things are beheld in day-dreams, and we are almost surprised to find them real.

Leigh Hunt, *Autobiography*, 1850

PUERTO RICO

The Towne consisteth of many large streets, the houses are built after the Spanish manner, of two stories height onely, but very strongly, and the roomes are goodly and large, with great doores in stead of windowes for receit of aire, which for the most part of the day wanteth never. For about eight in the morning there riseth ordinarily a fresh breeze (as they call it) and bloweth till foure or five in the afternoone, so that their houses all that while are very coole, of all the artificiall day the space from three in the morning till sixe, is the most temperate, so that then a man may well indure some light clothes upon him; from sixe till the breeze rise is very soultering, from five in the afternoone hottest of all the rest till midnight, which time also is held dangerous to be abroad, by reason of the Serenaes (they call them) which are raynie dewes. . . . The Towne in circuit is not so bigge as Oxford, but very much bigger then all Portsmouth within the fortifications, and in sight much fayrer. In all this space there is very little lost ground; for they have beene still building. . . . The Cathedrall Church is not so goodly as any of the Cathedrall Churches in England, and yet it is faire and handsome; two rowes of proportionable pillars, make two allies besides the middle walke, and this all along up to the high Altar. It is darker then commonly Countrie Churches in England. For the windowes are few and little, and those indeed without glasse (whereof there is none to be found in all the Towne) but covered with Canvas, so that the most of the light is received by the doores, the greatest whereof is just in the West end to the Seaward, so that out of it a man walking in the Church may behold the ships riding in a very faire Harbour. . . .

The rest of this little Iland (at least halfe a league in length) is for the most Woods complaining of the want of dressing and industrie, yet are they all youthfully greene, and none without some fruit or other, but so strange as would pose the professors of that skill in England: and in these woods Horses and Oxen grow fat, if they be suffered to rest. Therein be also some large inclosures carefully dressed, not unlike to our manner of dressing Hop-yards, and every hillocke laden with the fruites of the Countrie. Lemmons or rather Lymes, and the goodliest Oranges that ever I saw are ordinarily to be found where no man set them.

George, Earl of Cumberland, 1596, in *Purchas his Pilgrimes*, 1625

It is a kind of lost love-child, born to the Spanish Empire and fostered by the United States.

Nicholas Wollaston, *Red Rumba*, 1962

The Puerto Ricans, their dues – what's their eccentricity? They love garbage, oh yeah.

'They love garbage! Are you kidding? Puerto Ricans, they bring it from Puerto Rico! And they take the garbage and they have it on a string – they won't let people throw it away. They put it on the street like flowers. Puerto Rican garbage. There it is. They disperse it. Ya think they throw it away? No, change it around, different neighborhoods. Nice garbage. Puerto Rican garbage. Roll in it, and love it, and hug and kiss it.'

Lenny Bruce, 'The Jews', in *The Essential Lenny Bruce*, 1973 – before 1966

Q

QATAR

Doha

It was at that moment in the evening when the low sun goes squashy in the Gulf and coats everything with a soft thick light the colour of broom. It gilded the wailing six-lane highway. It gilded the sandy roadside where I walked. It gilded the long trail of garbage – the crushed Pepsi cans, discarded Frigidaires, torn chunks of motor tyre, cardboard boxes, broken fan-belts lying in the dust like snakes, the building rubble, polystyrene packing-blocks, and a rather long-dead goat. So many cars had been junked at the side of the road, and reared, rusting, on their axles, that it seemed legitimate to wonder whether people here threw Pepsi cans out of cars or cars out of Pepsi cans. There were ruins, but they were not picturesque: squalid little rectangles of mud whose walls had fallen out, leaving a pathetic detritus in view – a few stained and ripped cushions, a child's graffito, a wrecked tricycle. . . .

It looked more like the scene of a recent civil war than a utopian city-state. Yet there was something about it which I recognized – the careless absent-mindedness of the very rich. No one leaves more squalor in his wake than a passing millionaire: some hireling will clear up the mess afterwards, and to be tidy is to reveal a streak of mean thrift. Really lavish waste is one of the most certain of all signs of wealth. . . .

Down over the hump of Mr Moon's flyover I could see the bits of the city that one was supposed to notice. They looked as if a rich man had been making a hobby of them. The national museum was a castellated wedding-cake, creamy and toothsome in the sunset. The Qatar Monetary Agency was a giant gold ingot, its tinted windows taking their colour from the hammered sea. Around the harbour-front, the Corniche looped in a wide sweep past the moored yachts, the fishing dhows, cranes, container trucks and ships' funnels. It was, if one squinted a little and held one's nose, a lovely little golden city on the sea; and as the fairy-lights came up on the minarets, Doha gleamed and twinkled as prettily as if it had quite forgotten where it was and had mistaken the Gulf for the Riviera.

Jonathan Raban, *Arabia through the Looking Glass*, 1979

R

RED SEA

The water of this red see is not redde of his owne kynde, the colour of it is by reson of the costes and the botom of it which be redde grounde, and with contynually betyng and dasshing of the water upon the costes and incresyng of it and decresyng, it maketh the water redde. Notwithstonding ther be other opynyons, but this is the trouthe for as many as hathe sene it do affyrme the same.

Roger Barlow, *A Brief Summe of Geographie, c.* 1540

That exaggerated bugbear the Red Sea.

Harry de Windt, *From Pekin to Calais by Land,* 1889

REUNION

Passing Isle de Bourbon. Broken-up skyline of volcanic mountains in the middle. Surely it would not cost much to repair them, and it seems inexcusable neglect to leave them as they are.

Mark Twain, *More Tramps Abroad,* 1897

ROMANIA

No country is kinder to the wanderer who has good legs.

Walter Starkie, *Raggle-Taggle,* 1933

There is a cruel little joke about Rumania. 'Mania' means madness. 'Klepto-mania' means madness to steal. 'Rumania' means madness to steal applied to a nation.

John Gunther, *Inside Europe,* 1938 edn

I asked one professor, a historian, if he did not feel oppressed by the lack of liberty. He answered: 'Freedom has very rarely been a choice for us. We have learned to live with oppressors. There is a Rumanian proverb which says "The head that is bowed is not cut off." . . . ' I suggested that the Poles seemed nowadays to have won themselves a fair measure of freedom. 'But the Poles are different from us,' he said. 'They react to oppression with audacity. The Rumanian reaction is silence and cunning. You know the phrase of James Joyce.'

'What about exile – '

'I had left that word unspoken.'

Maurice Cranston, 'A Rumanian Notebook', *Encounter,* November 1963

Romanians

The Roumanians impressed me very forcibly by their skill in repartee. At table with these companions I heard again and again epigrams that would have disgraced no Byzantine Greeks of the best period. I felt all the time that my only chance to keep up the good name of Ireland abroad for wit was somehow or other to spirit back from the Elysian Fields the shadowy form of the late Provost of Trinity College, Dr.Mahaffy.

Walter Starkie, *Raggle-Taggle,* 1933

Bucharest

In passing through the streets, our carriages were subject to a continual and extraordinary concussion; being dragged over the trunks of trees, and other large logs of timber, placed transversely, instead of pavement, as in the road from *Petersburg* to *Moscow;* forming a kind of raft floating upon liquid mud, which, as the timber sank with the weight upon it, sprang up through the interstices. All these pieces of wood were loose; and being thus put into motion, the whole seemed like a broken floating bridge, between the disjointed parts of which there was apparently danger of being buried.

E.D. Clarke, *Travels in Various Countries,* 1818

Bucharest is the town of one street, one church and one idea.

Roumanian proverb, quoted Walter Starkie, *Raggle-Taggle,* 1933 (of the street then called calea Victoriei)

Carr: Bucharest.
Tzara: Oh, yes. Yes. The Paris of the Balkans . . .
Carr: Silly place to put it, really. . . .

Tom Stoppard, *Travesties,* 1975

Huedin

What we want here is a couple of saxophones and a few good brothels.

Citizen of Huedin, quoted by Walter Starkie, *Raggle-Taggle,* 1933

Temeswar

All the inhabitants of Temeswar are affected by the bad air, so that a healthy-looking person is hardly to be seen among them. Born says, that, when he was here, he 'fancied himself in the realms of death, inhabited by carcasses in fine tombs, instead of men.'

E.D. Clarke, *Travels in Various Countries,* 1818
(quoting Born, *Travels in the Bannat,* 1777)

Transylvania

Poverty reigns in Transylvania, but it is a distinguished poverty.

Walter Starkie, *Raggle-Taggle,* 1933

RUSSIA / USSR

The Soyle of the Countrey for the most part is of a sleight sandie mold, yet very much different one place from another, for they yeeld of such things as grow out of the earth. The Country Northwards, towards the parts of Saint Nicholas & Cola, and North-East towards Siberia, is all very barren, and full of desart Woods by reason of the Clymate, and extremitie of the cold in Winter time. . . . The whole Countrey differeth very much from it selfe, by reason of the yeere: so that a man would marvaile to see the great alteration and difference betwixt the Winter and the Summer in Russia. The whole Countrey in the Winter lyeth under Snow, which falleth continually, and is sometimes of a yard or two thicke, but greater towards the North. The Rivers and other waters are all frozen up, a yard or more thicke, how broad or swift soever they bee: and this continueth commonly five Moneths, viz. from the beginning of November, till towards the end of March, what time the snow beginneth to melt. So that it would breed a frost in a man to looke abroad at that time, and see the winter face of that Countrey. The sharpenesse of the ayre you may judge of by this: for that water dropped downe or cast up into the ayre, congealeth into Ice before it come to the ground. In the extremitie of Winter, if you hold a Pewter dish or pot in your hand, . . . your fingers will freeze fast unto it, and draw of the skinne at the parting. When you passe out of a warme roome into a cold, you shall sensibly feele your breath to waxe starke, and even stifeling with the cold, as you draw it in and out. Divers not onely that travell abroad, but in the very Markets, and streets of their Townes, are mortally pinched and killed withall: so that you shall see many drop downe in the Streets, many Travellers brought into the Townes sitting dead and stiffe in their Sleds. Divers lose their Noses, the tippes of their Eares, and the balls of their Cheekes, their Toes, Feete, &c. Many times (when the winter is very hard and extreame) the Beares and Wolves issue by troupes out of the woods driven by hunger, and enter the Villages, tearing and ravening all they can finde: so that the Inhabitants are faine to flee for safeguard of their lives. And yet in the Summer time you shall see such a new hew and face of a Countrey, the Woods (for the most part which are all of Firre and Birch) so fresh and so sweet, the Pastures and Meadowes so greene and well growne, (and that upon the sudden) such varietie of Flowers, such noyse of Birds, (specially of Nightingales, that seeme to be more loud and of a more variable note then in other Countries) that a man shall not lightly travell in a more pleasant Countrey. And this fresh and speedy growth of the Spring there seemeth to proceed from the benefit of the Snow: which all the Winter time being spred over the whole Countrey as a white robe, and keeping it warme from the rigour of the Frost, in the Spring time (when the Sunne waxeth warme, and dissolveth it into water) doth so throughly drench and soake the ground, that is somewhat of a sleight and sandie mold, and then shineth so hotly upon it againe, that it draweth the Hearbs and Plants forth in great plentie and varietie, in a very short time.

Dr Giles Fletcher, *A Treatise of Russia,* 1589,
in *Purchas his Pilgrimes,* 1625

The streets of their Cities and Townes in stead of paving, are planked with Firre trees, plained and layd even close the one to the other. Their houses are of wood without any lime or stone, built very close and warme with Firre trees plained and piled one upon another. They are fastned together with dents or notches at every corner, and so clasped fast together. Betwixt the trees or timber they thrust in mosse (whereof they gather plenty in their Woods,) to keepe out the aire. Every house hath a paire of staires that lead up into the chambers out of the yard or street after the Scottish manner. This building seemeth farre better for their Countrey, then that of stone and bricke: as being colder and more dampish then their woodden houses, specially of Firre, that is a dry and warme wood. . . . The greatest inconvenience of their woodden building is the aptnesse for firing, which happeneth very oft, and in very fearefull sort, by reason of the drinesse and fatnesse of the Firre, that being once fired, burneth like a Torch, and is hardly quenched till all bee burnt up.

Ibid.

The state and forme of their government is plaine tyrannicall. . . .

Dr Giles Fletcher, *Of the Russe Commonwealth,* 1591

Angelo: This will last out a night in *Russia*
When nights are longest there.

William Shakespeare, *Measure for Measure, c.* 1604–5

And then walked into the fields as far almost as Sir G.

Whitmore's all the way talking of Russia – which he says is a sad place; and though Mosco is a very great city, yet it is, from the distance between house and house, and few people compared with this – and poor sorry houses, the Emperor himself living in a wooden house – his exercise only flying a hawke at pigeons and carrying pigeons ten or twelve miles off and then laying wagers which pigeon shall come soonest home to her house. All the winter within doors, some few playing at Chesse but most drinking their time away. Women live very slavishly there. And it seems, in the Emperor's Court no room hath above two or three windows, and those the greatest not a yard wide or high – for warmth in winter time. And that the general cure for all disease there is their sweating-houses – or people that are poor, they get into their ovens, being heated, and there lie. Little learning among things of any sort – not a man that speaks Latin, unless the Secretary of State by chance.

Samuel Pepys, *Diary,* 16 September 1664

Eighteenth Century

I know of but one nation who could attempt the conquest of China, with any probability of success, and that is Russia; but the territories of that empire are so extensive, in this quarter of the world, as to exceed even the bounds of ambition itself; and the Russians seem to entertain no desire of extending them further.

John Bell, *A Journey from St Petersburg to Pekin, 1719–1722,* 1763

I cannot avoid beholding the Russian empire as the natural enemy of the more western parts of Europe, as an enemy already possessed of great strength, and, from the nature of the government, every day threatening to become more powerful. . . . The Russians are now at that period between refinement and barbarity, which seems most adapted to military achievement, and if once they happen to get a footing in the western parts of Europe, it is not the feeble efforts of the sons of effeminacy and dissention, that can serve to remove them. The fertile valley and soft climate will ever be sufficient inducements to draw whole myriads from their native desarts, the trackless wild, or snowy mountain.

Oliver Goldsmith, *The Citizen of the World,* 1760–1

Agriculture can never flourish in a nation where the husbandman possesses no property.

Catherine the Great, before 1796, attributed by J.L. Stephens, *Incidents of Travel in the Russian and Turkish Empires,* 1839

When one reflects of the immense magnitude of this empire, one is lost in the idea.

Sir N.W. Wraxall, *A Tour Round the Baltic,* 1775

Russia is always defeated, but never beaten.

Old saying

Russia is not a state, but a world.

Czarist proverb

Nineteenth Century

In whatever country we seek for original genius, we must go to *Russia* for the talent of imitation. This is the acme of Russian intellect; the principle of all Russian attainments. The Russians have nothing of their own; but it is not their fault if they have not every thing that others invent. Their surprising powers of imitation exceed all that has been hitherto known. The meanest Russian slave is sometimes able to accomplish the most intricate and the most delicate works of mechanism; to copy, with single hand, what has demanded the joint labours of the best workmen in France or England. Although untutored, they are the best actors in the world.

E.D. Clarke, *Travels in Various Countries,* 4th edn, 1816

The principal articles of diet are the same everywhere – *grease* and *brandy*. The horrors of a Russian kitchen are inconceivable; and there is scarcely a bed in the whole empire that an English traveller would venture to approach, if he were aware of its condition.

Ibid.

Most faithful Russia – faithful to whoe'er
Could plunder best and give him amplest share;
Who, ev'n when vanquish'd, sure to gain his ends,
For want of *foes* to rob, made free with *friends,*
And, deepening still by amiable gradations,
When foes were stript of all, then fleec'd relations!

Thomas Moore, *The Fudge Family in Paris,* 1818

and Turkey

It seems that the Cannibals of Europe are going to eating one another once again. A war between Russia and Turkey is like the battle of the Kite and the Snake. Whichever destroys the other leaves a destroyer the less for the world.

Thomas Jefferson, Letter to John Adams, 1 June 1822

The power of Russia is still more formidable, when it is considered that the army is composed of hardy, bold, enterprising, and needy men; who, go where they will, must be better off, either as to climate or productions than at home.

Captain John Dundas Cochrane, *Narrative of a Pedestrian Journey through Russia, etc.,* 1824

There are at the present time two great nations in the world, which started from different points, but seem to tend toward the same end. I allude to the Russians and the Americans. . . . Each of them seems marked out by the will of Heaven to sway the destinies of half the globe.

Alexis de Tocqueville, *Democracy in America*, 1835

I will exalt your name as a politician forever if you will contrive to persuade me that we have nothing to fear from the domineering Russia – It is not the present fuss made about her that makes me tremble, but I have always been afraid that she was the Power kept in pickle to overwhelm Europe just as men were beginning to settle into a better state than the World has yet seen – If she were out of the question we should do very well.

Edward FitzGerald, Letter to W.M. Thackeray, 29 November 1838

Other nations have endured oppression; the Russian nation loved it and loves it still.

Marquis de Custine, *The Empire of the Czar*, 1843 – of 1839

A word of truth dropped in Russia is a spark that may fall on a barrel of gunpowder.

Marquis de Custine, *Ibid.*

To an American, Russia is an interesting country. . . . Like our own, Russia is a new country, and in many respects resembles ours. It is true that we began life differently. Russia has worked her way to civilization from a state of absolute barbarism, while we sprang into being with the advantage of all the lights of the Old World. Still, there are many subjects of comparison, and even of emulation between us.

J.L. Stephens, *Incidents of Travel in the Russian and Turkish Empires*, 1839

All over Russia Princes are as plenty as pickpockets in London.

Ibid.

That empire indeed, though less extensive than at present, was the most extensive that had ever obeyed a single chief. The dominions of Alexander and of Trajan were small when compared with the immense area of the Scythian desert. But in the estimation of statesmen that boundless expanse of larch forest and morass, where the snow lay deep during eight months of every year, and where a wretched peasantry could with difficulty defend their hovels against troops of famished wolves, was of less account than the two or three square miles into which were crowded the counting houses, the warehouses, and the innumerable masts of Amsterdam.

T.B. Macaulay, *History of England*, 1849–61 – of the seventeenth century

Russia has two generals in whom she can confide – Generals Janvier and Fevrier.

Nicholas I of Russia, attrib., *Punch*, 10 March 1855

Of all hard-named generals that caused much distraction
And poor Boney's hopes so ill-naturedly cross'd
The hardest of all and the *keenest* in action
That Russia produces is General *Frost*.

Anon., nineteenth century

Russia has two faces, an Asiatic face which looks always towards Europe, and a European face which looks always towards Asia.

Benjamin Disraeli, Earl of Beaconsfield, attrib.

in Asia

I hold it as a principle that in Asia the duration of peace is in direct proportion to the slaughter you inflict upon the enemy. The harder you hit them the longer they will be quiet afterwards.

General Skoboleff, quoted by the Hon. G. N. Curzon, *Russia in Central Asia*, 1889

Russia . . . the country where one would least like to live.

Matthew Arnold, *A Word More About America*, 1885

I remember once reading the remark that 'In Russia the discipline of the camp is substituted for the order of the city; martial law is the normal condition of life.'

Hon. G.N. Curzon, *Russia in Central Asia*, 1889

I am not one of those who hold that Russian policy has, either for a century or for half a century, or for a less period, been animated by an unswerving and Machiavellian purpose. . . . So far from regarding the foreign policy of Russia as consistent, or remorseless, or profound, I believe it to be a hand-to-mouth policy, a policy of waiting upon events, of profiting by the blunders of others, and as often committing the like herself.

Ibid.

No return tickets are issued to a punitive foray of Cossacks. Advance is inexorably followed by annexation. *'J'y suis, j'y reste,'* is the watchword of the Russian vanguard. There is no likelihood of 'making it so hot' for Russia that for the sake of peace, or economy, or men's lives, she will waver or fall back. A hornet's nest raised about her head is followed not by a hasty withdrawal of the intruding member, but by a wholesome extermination of the insects. . . .

It would be unfair, however, both to Russian character and to Russian policy, to suggest that it is owing solely to prudential reasons, that there is no visible antagonism to her sway. . . . So far as I was able to ascertain, Russian dominion is not only accepted by, but is acceptable to the bulk of her Asiatic subjects, and . . . the ruling class, though feared, is also personally esteemed. Russia unquestionably possesses a remarkable gift for enlisting the allegiance and attracting even the friendship of those whom she has subdued by force of arms, a faculty which is to be attributed as much to the defects as to the excellence of her character.

Ibid.

The conquest of Central Asia is a conquest of Orientals by Orientals, of cognate character by cognate character. It is the fusing of strong with weaker metal, but it is not the expulsion of an impure by a purer element. Civilised Europe has not marched forth to vanquish barbarian Asia. This is no nineteenth century crusade of manners or morals; but barbarian Asia, after a sojourn in civilised Europe, returns upon its former footsteps to reclaim its own kith and kin.

Ibid.

I remember once being told in Russia that the only really scientific table of statistics which the Government had issued for some years was one relating to the consumption of *vodka* and its effects upon the national mortality. The population was divided into three classes: the moderate drinkers, the excessive drinkers, and the total abstainers; and it was triumphantly demonstrated by the returns that the first named were rewarded with the longest span of life; a result which was as warmly welcomed by the Excise Department as it was acceptable to the consuming public.

Hon. George Curzon, *Persia and the Persian Question*, 1892

Russia is omnipotence. . . . Who can ever penetrate that polar mystery? . . . Russia is impenetrable, and any intelligent man will deal with her better, the less closely he knows her.

Henry Adams, Letter to Brooks Adams, 5 June 1895

Russia is rotten before it is ripe.

Nineteenth-century saying

Rossiya – rodina slonov.
(Russia is the homeland of elephants.)

Old Russian proverb, quoted by Eric de Mauny, *Russian Prospect*, 1969

Twentieth Century

Of course Russia is what we know! There is no sense in supposing that it is modern or American or economical. But it may still come out very much ahead on a hundred years' stretch. Its scale is so enormous that it is bound to dwarf its neighbours, and with such mass and momentum, speed is a subordinate element.

Any way, it is a question of mathematics and of forces and strains; and wisdom or knowledge is useless. Fate rules in these parts. One is fatalist by necessity.

Henry Adams, Letter to John Hay, 26 August 1901

In Russia everything is large and everything is loud.

Arthur Symons, *Cities*, 1903

Our government wants no better than to help Russia, but you might as well try to reason with an insane Irishman full of whiskey.

Henry Adams, Letter to Elizabeth Cameron, 28 February 1904

*Don't you forget what's divine in the Russian soul – and that's resignation.

Joseph Conrad, *Under Western Eyes*, 1911

Eliminate all notions of castles, Rhine country, feudal keeps, and stone houses in general. Think of an endless plain, a sheet of dazzling snow in winter, an ocean of golden corn in summer, a tract of brown earth in autumn, and now in the earliest days of spring an expanse of white melting snow with great patches of brown earth and sometimes green grass appearing at intervals, and further patches of half-melted snow of a steely-grey colour sometimes blue as they catch the reflection of the dazzling sky in the sunlight. In the distance on one side the plain stretches to infinity, on the other you may see the delicate shapes of a brown, leafless wood, the outlines soft in the haze. If I had to describe Russia in three words I should say a plain, a windmill and a church. The church is made of wood and is built in Byzantine style with a small cupola and a minaret. It is painted red and white, or white and pale-green. Sometimes the cupola is gilt. The plain is dotted with villages.

Maurice Baring, *What I Saw in Russia*, 1913

The whole secret of avoiding bothers in Russia is not to bother people who do not wish to be bothered. If you do what you wish to do quietly nobody interferes with you. If you ask you will probably be told it is impossible – it is in theory, but not in practice.

Ibid.

Woollen underwear is recommended.

Karl Baedeker *Russia, with Teheran, Port Arthur and Peking*, 1914

An old Russian General once said to me, 'Russia first declares war and then prepares for it.'

Denis Garstin, *Friendly Russia*, 1915

I think of the country as 'the Land of Nitchevo' – of 'never mind.'

Ibid.

No nation might have had so large an influence on the

perpetual wranglings of Europe as Russia. No nation has been more indifferent to the world's doings outside her borders, and unless civilization has the effect of turning a peaceful people into a warlike race, there is no reason why the Russians should change their national trait and threaten the peace of Europe.

The bear, they say, is only dangerous when her cubs are attacked, and the bear is the symbol of Russia.

Ibid.

Russia seems to me now the positive pole of the world's spiritual energy, and America the negative pole.

D.H. Lawrence, Letter to S.S. Koteliansky, 3 July 1917

I have been over into the future, and it works.

Lincoln Steffens, Remark, after visiting Russia, 1919

I reflect upon the destruction and cruelty upon which the ancient splendour was built: the poverty, drunkenness, prostitution, in which life and health were uselessly wasted; I think of all the lovers of freedon who suffered in Peter and Paul: I remember the knoutings and pogroms and massacres. By hatred of the old I become tolerant of the new, but I cannot like the new on its own account.

Yet I reproach myself for not liking it. It has all the characteristics of vigorous beginnings. It is ugly and brutal, but full of constructive energy and faith in the value of what it is creating. In creating new machinery for social life it has no time to think of anything beyond machinery. When the body of the new society has been built, there will be time enough to think about giving it a soul – at least so I am assured. . . . I wonder whether it is possible to build a body first, and then afterwards inject the requisite amount of soul. Perhaps – but I doubt it.

Bertrand Russell, Journal Letter, 13 May 1920, in *Autobiography*, 1968

Friends of Russia here think of the dictatorship of the proletariat as merely a new form of representative government, in which only working men and women have votes, and the constituencies are partly occupational, not geographical. They think that 'Proletariat' means 'proletariat' but 'Dictatorship' does not quite mean 'dictatorship'. This is the opposite of the truth. When a Russian Communist speaks of Dictatorship, he means the word literally, but when he speaks of the proletariat, he means the word in a Pickwickian sense. He means the 'class-conscious' part of the proletariat, *i.e.*, the Communist Party.

Bertrand Russell, *The Practice and Theory of Bolshevism*, 1920

Communism is Soviet power plus electrification of the whole country.

Lenin, Remark to a Party conference, November 1920

I know very little of Russia. Simbirsk, Kazan, Petersburg, exile in Siberia and that is nearly all.

Lenin, Remark to Gorki, quoted in Maxim Gorki, *Days with Lenin*, 1932

Russia will certainly inherit the future. What we already call the greatness of Russia is only her pre-natal struggling.

D.H. Lawrence, Foreword to Leo Shestov's *All Things are Possible*, 1920

Russia is a country that buries its troubles. Your criticism is your epitaph. You simply say your say, and then you're through.

Will Rogers, before 1935 quoted Alistair Cooke, *One Man's America*, 1973

What one knows before one goes to Russia is not worth knowing. In Russia one learns a new truth a minute.

Hubert Griffith, *Seeing Soviet Russia*, 1932

I repeat that the bare spare life of modern Russia – with all its thoughts and its aims bent so drivingly on the future – is life in a romantic land.

Ibid.

The atmospheric oppression of a land where the only truths are the class war and the machine, and where all culture must be subservient to those ends, is alleviated by the novelty – one might even say eccentricity – that results. The air is mixed with laughing-gas. But it is a stifling air.

Robert Byron, *First Russia, then Tibet*, 1933

I had expected to find a new Russia stirring in its sleep and ready to awaken to Cosmopolis, and I found it sinking deeper into the dope-dream of Sovietic self-sufficiency.

H.G. Wells, *An Experiment in Autobiography*, 1934

The U.S.S.R. owes it to herself to prove to us the Communist ideal is not an Anthill Utopia.

André Gide, *Message to the Congress of Soviet Workers*, 1935

There is not a more interesting country in the world today to visit than Soviet Russia, and I find travelling there perfectly safe and pleasant. . . . Tomorrow I leave this land of hope and return to our Western countries of despair.

George Bernard Shaw, inscription in hotel guest book, 1930s, quoted in Harry M. Geduld (ed.), *The Rationalization of Russia by George Bernard Shaw*, 1964

Intourist provides cheap tickets into a plausible future.

Graham Greene, *Journey without Maps*, 1936

That other and more powerful League of Nations – the Soviet Union.

John Gunther, *Inside Europe,* 1938 edn

I cannot forecast to you the action of Russia. It is a riddle wrapped in a mystery inside an enigma; but perhaps there is a key. That key is Russian national interest.

Sir Winston Churchill, Speech in London, 1 October 1939

In Russia it is dangerous to be a coward.

Josef Stalin, Remark of November 1943, quoted in Lord Moran, *Winston Churchill, The Struggle for Survival,* 1966

The primeval tomtom still beats while the atom bomb ticks. Russia is straddling the centuries, in victory more than ever pounding backward to Peter the Great and racing to overtake Henry Ford . . . before she has caught up with Thomas Jefferson.

Anne O'Hare McCormick, *Harper's Magazine,* May 1946

Russia fears our friendship more than our enmity. The Soviet Dictatorship could not stand free intercourse with the West. We must make Moscow fear our enmity more than our friendship.

Sir Winston Churchill, Remark, 19 July 1951, quoted in C.L. Sulzberger, *A Long Row of Candles: Memoirs and Diaries,* 1969

The P.M. is less sure about things today. It appears that when he pleaded with Ike that Russia was changed, Ike spoke of her as a whore, who might have changed her dress, but who should be chased from the streets. Russia, according to Ike, was out to destroy the civilised world.

Lord Moran, *Winston Churchill, The Struggle for Survival,* 1966 – of 5 December 1953

Soviet taste seems in a variety of ways to have fixed upon the British sea-side lodging house at the turn of the century as the beau ideal of progressive socialism,

René McColl, *Just Back from Russia,* 1954

The Soviets will almost never say frankly that you can't visit such and such a factory or else that they don't want you to. There is always a far-fetched excuse. Favourites: 'The factory is closed for repairs.' 'The manager has been called away from the factory, and the assistant manager has gone with him.' 'The manager, the assistant manager, the chief engineer and the general supervisor have become suddenly ill.'

The most uproarious excuse of all was when some westerners had arranged to visit an artists' school in Soviet Central Asia. They were told at the last moment that they could not go after all, because 'the building is being unexpectedly whitewashed.'

Ibid.

Travellers to Venice often remark on the vivid scents of that city. The public places of Russia, terminals and department stores, restaurants and theatres, also have a reek instantly recognisable. And Miss Ryan, taking her first sniff of it said, 'Boy, I wouldn't want a bottle of this. Old socks, and a million yawns.'

Truman Capote, *The Muses Are Heard,* 1957

The first question everyone asks you on your return from the Soviet Union is: 'Were you followed?' Every Western tourist likes to think he was. There is really no fun going to a police state, if you're not followed by someone. In the Hotel Metropole in Moscow I had the feeling I was always being watched, but it was always by other tourists who thought I was *watching them.*

Art Buchwald, *More Caviar,* 1958

*Ideas in modern Russia are machine-cut blocks coming in solid colors; the nuance is outlawed, the interval walled up, the curve grossly stepped.

Vladimir Nabokov, *Pale Fire,* 1962

The juggernaut just doesn't jug.

Adlai Stevenson, Comment on Russia, 1962

If Russia didn't cover such a large part of the earth's surface and if there weren't so many Russians, this country would be one long laugh.

British resident of Moscow in the 1930s, quoted by John Gunther, *Inside Russia Today,* 1962 edn

There are no experts on the Soviet Union, only varying degrees of ignorance.

Former US Ambassador to Moscow, quoted Erik de Mauny, *Russian Prospect,* 1969

Everybody who has been in the Soviet Union for any length of time has noticed their concern with the United States: we may be the enemy, but we are the admired enemy, and the so-called good life is the to-be-good life for them. During the war, the Russian combination of dislike and grudging admiration for us, and ours for them, seemed to me like the innocent rivalry of two men proud of being large, handsome, and successful. But I was wrong. They have chosen to imitate and compete with the most vulgar aspects of American life, and we have chosen, as in the revelations of the CIA bribery of intellectuals and scholars, to say, 'But the Russians do the same thing,' as if honor were a mask that you put on and took off at a costume ball. They condemn Vietnam, we condemn Hungary. But the moral tone of giants with swollen heads, fat fingers pressed over the atom bomb, staring at each other across the forests of the world, is monstrously comic.

Lillian Hellman, *An Unfinished Woman,* 1969

The Soviet Union has often been referred to as a monolith. It is no longer a monolith in the true sense, but at most a crumbling replica of one, like a taxidermist's mammoth inflicted with moth and other symptons of slow decay.

Erik de Mauny, *Russian Prospect,* 1969

There is a saying in the Soviet Union for the sort of occasion when a sudden silence falls. People do not say 'an angel is passing,' but '*rodilsya militsionair*' – 'a policeman has been born.'

Ibid.

What is philosophy?
Philosophy is a black cat in a dark room.
What is Marxist philosophy?
Marxist philosophy is a dark room in which you are looking for a black cat – only there is no cat.
What is Marxist–Leninist philosophy?
Marxist–Leninist philosophy is a dark room in which you are looking for a black cat and there is no cat, but every so often you shout: 'I've got it! I've got it!'

Soviet joke, quoted *ibid.*

'Do not say "Russia",' Zhatenko admonishes me. 'It reminds me of pre-Revolutionary times. We now have the Soviet Union. . . . '
'Do not say "Siberia", because it reminds me of pre-Revolutionary times,' he says. 'Now there are simply the western, eastern, northern and southern areas of the Soviet Union.'

Ved Mehta, *Portrait of India,* 1970

The cold of this country has a freakish quality. Each moment outdoors is a confrontation with a vast antagonistic force. . . . Winter lays hands on you in October, takes command of you, throttles you straight through until April. . . . Irrationally resentful, you begin to take the punishment personally, and by late February – after the January thaw fails to appear – you recognise traces of persecution anxiety. . . . Always you are conscious of living in a land where *nature has gone wrong* and appeals do not lie to justice or reason. . . .

Although worse than I had imagined, the brutalization of political life is also less important because it is subsidiary to climate, geography and mood, the chief oppressors of everyday life. . . .

The elements are hostile here; this is the *fons et origo* of hulking buildings, strident newspapers and absent amenities – of everything that village-bred, disaster-fearing men (for these are the kind who control all public reactions as well as rule) make ponderous, laborious and inimical to public amusement. Where life is a struggle to fend off such giant forces, why build cafés to serve aperitifs or coffee? No matter that even more northerly countries are far less grim; in Russia, encumbered by backwardness, the environment is *perceived* as hostile. With their mothers' milk children are given to understand that their hot, cramped homes are love, but that the world outside is essentially unfriendly to human habitation.

George Feifer, *Moscow Farewell,* 1976

I have begun to sense what Russian writers have long revealed: that this is a place where the human spirit is made to struggle, thereby becoming fuller as well as more repressed.

Ibid.

The brain is ill-equipped to comprehend the meaning of a nation that encompasses eleven time zones.

Hedrick Smith, *The Russians,* 1977

Russia . . . is an information vacuum.

Ibid.

A country that since 1914 has lost, as a result of two world wars, a civil war, famine, and various 'purges', perhaps up to 60 million citizens, must define 'unacceptable damage' differently from the United States which has known no famines or purges, and whose deaths from all the wars waged since 1775 are estimated at 650,000 – fewer casualties than Russia suffered in the 900-day siege of Leningrad in World War II alone.

Richard Pipes, 'Why the Soviet Union Thinks it could Fight and Win a Nuclear War', *Commentary,* July 1977

This is one of the two great states of the world. We either live with her or we die with her.

James Callaghan, in the House of Commons, quoted in *The Times,* 19 May 1978

. . . the famous one about life in Russia being like life at an English public school but with politics taking the place of sex.

V.S. Prichett, quoting Isaiah Berlin, 'Conversation', *Sunday Times Weekly Review,* 2 July 1978

The first characteristic of the Soviet Union is that it always adopts the attitude of bullying the soft and fearing the strong. The second characteristic of the Soviet Union is that it will go in and grab at every opportunity.

Deng Xiaoping, Interview, *Time,* 5 February 1979

What comes out above all is a vivid projection of what old hands know to be the most striking feature of the Soviet system (and the hardest to convey to outsiders); the fundamental, the irremediable *silliness* behind the more familiar brutality and nastiness and general fee-fi-fo-fum. This makes the book something special.

Edward Crankshaw, Review of Nora Beloff's *No Travel Like Russian Travel, Observer,* 4 November 1979

My opinion of the Russians has changed most drastically in the last week.

President Jimmy Carter, Remark in ATV interview, following the Soviet invasion of Afghanistan, January 1980

The basic rule of Soviet behaviour was laid down years ago by Lenin: Probe with bayonets. If you encounter steel, withdraw. If you encounter mush, continue. The question is which will the Soviets encounter: steel or mush?

Richard M. Nixon, *The Real War,* 1980

When they go to take a bite out of the world, the Soviets are not fussy eaters.

Ibid.

You have Jesus Christ Super-star, we have Lenin Super-Tsar.

Russian youth to American visitor, Remark, quoted *Ibid.*

Russians

They are right foul folk and fell and full of malice.

John Mandeville, *The Book of John Mandeville, c.* 1360

Upon this coast be the scythas which receveth straungers lovingly and after thei kylleth them and ete them and drynke bloude myngled with mylke. Thei be evyl people and liveth pastorally, for the most parte of the lond is good and abundant of pasture.

Roger Barlow, *A Brief Summe of Geographie, c.* 1540

They bee naturally given to great deceit, except extreame beating did bridle them. They bee naturally given to hard living as well in fare as in lodging. I heard a Russian say, that it was a great deal merrier living in Prison than foorth, but for the great beating.

Richard Chancellor, *A Letter . . . touching his Discoverie of Moscovia,* 1553, in *Purchas his Pilgrimes,* 1625

The Russie men are round of bodies, fully fac'd,
The greatest part with bellies bigge that overhang the waste,
Flat headed for the most, with faces nothing faire,
But browne, by reason of the stove, and closenesse of the aire:
It is their common use to shave or els to sheare
Their heads, for none in all the land long lolling locks doth weare,
Unlesse perhaps he have his sovereigne prince displeas'd,
For then he never cuts his haire, untill he be appeas'd. . . .
Their garments be not gay, nor handsome to the eye,
A cap aloft their heads they have, that standeth very hie,
Which Colpack they do terme. They weare no ruffes at all:
The best have collers set with pearle, which they Rubasca call.
Their shirts in Russie long, they worke them downe before,
And on the sleeves with coloured Silks, two inches good and more.
Aloft their shirts they weare a garment jacket wise
Hight Onoriadka, and about his burlie waste he tyes
His portkies, which in stead of better breeches be:
Of linnen cloth that garment is, no codpiece is to see.
A paire of yarnen stocks to keepe the colde away,
Within his boots the Russie weares, the heeles they underlay
With clouting clamps of steele, sharpe pointed at the toes,
And over all a Shuba furd, and thus the Russie goes.
Well butned is the Shube, according to his state,
Some Silke, of Silver other some: but those of poorest rate
Do weare no Shubs at all, but grosser gownes to sight,
That reacheth downe beneath the calfe, and that Armacha hight:
These are the Russies robes. . . .
The colde is rare, the people rude, the prince so full of pride,
The Realme so stored with Monks and nunnes, and priests on every side:
The maners are so Turkie like, the men so full of guile,
The women wanton, Temples stuft with idols that defile
The Seats that sacred ought to be, the customes are so quaint,
As if I would describe the whole, I feare my pen would faint.
In summe, I say I never saw a prince that so did raigne,
Nor people so beset with Saints, yet all but vile and vaine.
Wilde Irish are as civill as the Russies in their kinde,
Hard choice which is the best of both, ech bloody, rude and blinde.

George Turberville, Verse Letter, 1568, in Richard Hakluyt, *Principal Navigations . . . of the English Nation,* 1598–1600

A people passing rude, to vices vile inclinde,
Folke fit to be of Bacchus traine, so quaffing is their kinde.
Drinke is their whole desire, the pot is all their pride,
The sobrest head doth once a day stand needfull of a guide.
If he to banket bid his friends, he will not shrinke
On them at dinner to bestow a douzen kindes of drinke:
Such licour as they have, and as the countrey gives,

But chiefly two, one called Kvas, whereby the Mousike
lives.
Small ware and waterlike, but somewhat tart in taste,
The rest is Mead of honie made, wherewith their lips
they baste.
And if he goes unto his neighbour as a guest,
He cares for litle meate, if so his drinke be of the best.

Ibid.

As touching the naturall habit of their bodies, they are for the most part of a large size, and of very fleshly bodies: accounting it a grace to be somewhat grosse and burley, and therefore they nourish and spread their Beards, to have them long and broad. But for the most part they are very unweldy, and unactive withall. Which may be thought to come partly of the Climate, and the numbnesse which they get by the cold in Winter, and partly of their Dyet that standeth most of Roots, Onions, Garlike, Cabbage, and such like things that breed grosse humours, which they use to eate alone, and with their other meates.

Their Dyet is rather much, than curious. At their Meales they beginne commonly with a Chark, or small cup of Aqua-vitae (which they call Russe Wine) and then drinke not till towards the end of their Meales, taking it in largely, and all together with kissing one another at every pledge. And therefore after dinner there is no talking with them, but every man goeth to his bench to take his after-noones sleepe, which is as ordinary with them as their nights rest. . . . To drinke drunke, is an ordinary matter with them every day in the Weeke. Their common Drinke is Mead, the poorer sort use water, and a thin Drinke called Quasse, which is nothing else (as wee say) but water turned out of his wits, with a little Bran mashed with it.

This Dyet would breed in them many Diseases, but that they use Bath-stoves, or Hot-houses in stead of all Physicke, commonly twice or thrice every Weeke. . . . These two extremities, specially in the Winter, of heate within their Houses, and of extreme cold without, together with their Dyet, maketh them of a darke and sallow complexion, their skinnes being tanned and parched both with cold and with heat: specially the women, that for the greater part are of farre worse complexions than the men. . . .

The Russe because that he is used to both these extremities of heate and of cold, can beare them both a great deale more patiently than strangers can doe. You shall see them sometimes (to season their bodies) come out of their Bath-stoves all on a froth, and fuming as hote almost as a Pigge at a Spit, and presently to leape into a River starke naked, or to powre cold water all over their bodies, and that in the coldest of all the Winter time.

Dr Giles Fletcher, *A Treatise of Russia*, 1589, in *Purchas his Pilgrimes*, 1625

. . . As for the truth of his word, as some say, the Russe neither beleeveth any thing that another man speaketh, nor speaketh any thing himselfe worthy to bee beleeved. These qualities make them very odious to all their Neighbours, specially to the Tartars, that account themselves to be honest and just, in comparison of the Russe.

Ibid.

The oppression and slavery is so open, and so great, that a man would marvell, how the Nobilitie and People should suffer themselves to be brought under it, while they had any meanes to avoide and repulse it: or being so strengthned as it is at this present, how the Emperours themselves can be content to practise the same, with so open injustice and oppression of their Subjects, being themselves of a Christian profession. By this it appeareth how hard a matter it were to alter the state of the Russe Government as it now standeth.

Ibid.

Yet God hath a great plage in store for this people; what shal we saye? The naturall disposicion of this nacion was so wicked and viell, that if the old Emperowr had not haeld so hard a hand and sever government over them, he could never have lived so longe, for their treacherous and treasonable praectices and still discovered.

Sir Jerome Horsey, *A Relacion Abstracted out of . . . his Travells*, *c.* 1590

The muscovite women esteem none loving husbands except they beat their wives.

Thomas Fuller, *The Holy State and the Profane State*, 1642

And as some say, they are not well contented, unless their *Husbands* give them beating, being like *Spaniels*, the more they are beaten, the better they love.

Richard Blome, *A Geographical Description of the Four Parts of the World*, 1670

And 'mong the *Cossacks* had been bred,
Of whom we in *Diurnals* read,
That serve to fill up Pages here,
As with their Bodies Ditches there.

Samuel Butler, *Hudibras*, Part I, Canto II, 1663

Eighteenth Century

The Russian peasants appeared in general a large coarse hardy race, and of great bodily strength. Their dress is a round hat or cap with a very high crown, a coarse robe of drugget (or in winter of sheep-skin with the wool turned inwards reaching below the knee and bound round the waist by a sash, trowsers of linen almost as thick as sack-cloth, a woollen flannel cloth wrapped round the leg, instead of stockings, sandals woven from strips of a pliant bark, and fastned by strings of the same materials, which are afterwards twined round the leg, and serve as garters to the woollen or flannel wrappers. In warm weather the peasants frequently wear only a short coarse shirt and trowsers.

Their cottages are built in the same manner as those of Lithuania; but larger, and somewhat better provided with furniture and domestic utensils: they are of a square shape; formed of whole trees, piled upon one another and secured at the four corners where their extremities meet, with mortises and tenons. The interstices between these piles are filled with moss. Within the timbers are smoothed with the axe, so as to form the appearance of wain-scot; but without are left with bark in their rude state. The roofs are in the penthouse form, and generally composed of the bark of trees or shingles, which are sometimes covered with mould or turf.

William Coxe, *Travels into Poland, Russia, Sweden, etc.,* 1792

I must own I was astonished at the barbarism in which the bulk of the people still continue. I am ready to allow that the principal nobles are as civilized , and as refined in their entertainments, mode of living, and social intercourse, as those of other European countries. But there is a wide difference between polishing a nation, and polishing a few individuals. The merchants and peasants still universally retain their beards, their national dress, their original manners; and, what is most remarkable, the greatest part of the merchants and burghers of the large towns, even the citizens of Petersburgh and Moscow, resemble, in their external appearance and general mode of living, the inhabitants of the smallest village.

Ibid.

I hate the Russians.

Horatio Lord Nelson, Letter to Captain Ball, 21 January 1799

Grattez le Russe et vous trouverez le Tartare.
(Scratch a Russian and you will find a Tartar.)

French proverb, attributed variously to Joseph de Maistre, Napoleon and the Prince de Ligne

Scratch a Russian and you get a Tatar; scratch a Tatar and you get – a Tatar.

Old proverb

Nineteenth Century

The picture of Russian manners varies little with reference to the Prince or the peasant. The first nobleman in the empire, when dismissed by his Sovereign from attendance upon his person, or withdrawing to his estate in consequence of dissipation and debt, betakes himself to a mode of life little superior to that of brutes. You will then find him, throughout the day, with his neck bare, his beard lengthened, his body wrapped in a sheep's skin, eating raw turnips, and drinking *quass;* sleeping one half of the day, and growling at his wife and family the other. The same feelings, the same wants, wishes, and gratifications, then characterize the nobleman and the peasant; and the same system of tyranny, extending from the throne downwards, through all the bearings and ramifications of society even to the cottage of the lowest boor, has entirely extinguished every spark of liberality in the breasts of a people composed entirely of slaves. They are all, high and low, rich and poor, alike servile to superiors; haughty and cruel to their dependants; ignorant, superstitious, cunning, brutal, barbarous, dirty, mean. The Emperor canes the first of his grandees; princes and nobles cane their slaves; and the slaves, their wives and daughters. Ere the sun dawns in Russia, flagellation begins; and throughout its vast empire, cudgels are going, in every department of its population, from morning until night.

E.D. Clarke, *Travels in Various Countries,* 4th edn, 1816

Old Russian nobility
Of all the Europeans, they bear the greatest resemblance to the Neapolitans.

Ibid.

In matters of affection the Russians are the gentlest wild beasts that are to be seen on earth, and their well-concealed claws unfortunately divest them of none of their charms.

Marquis de Custine, *The Empire of the Czar,* 1843 – of 1839

An inordinate, a boundless ambition, the kind of ambition that can take root only on the misery of an entire nation is astir in the hearts of the Russians. . . . To cleanse himself of his impious sacrifice of all public and personal liberty, the kneeling slave dreams of world domination. . . . The Russian people will surely become incapable of anything except the conquest of the world. I always return to this expression, because it is the only one that can explain the excessive sacrifices imposed here upon the individual by society.

Marquis de Custine, *ibid.*

The silent Russians . . . I believe to be worth something: are they not even now drilling, under much obloquy, an immense, semi-barbarous, half-world from Finland to Kamtschatka, into rule, subordination, civilization, – really in an old Roman fashion; speaking no word about it; quietly hearing all manner of vituperative Able Editors speak!

Thomas Carlyle, *Past and Present,* 1843

*Some people . . . may be Rooshans, and others may be

Prooshans; they are born so and will please themselves. Them which is of other naturs thinks different.

Charles Dickens, *Martin Chuzzlewit,* 1843–4 (Mrs Gamp speaking)

Russian diplomats in London in 1698

The strangers spoke no civilised language. Their garb, their gestures, their salutations, had a wild and barbarous character. The ambassador and the grandees who accompanied him were so gorgeous that all London crowded to stare at them, and so filthy that nobody dared to touch them. They came to the court balls dropping pearls and vermin.

T.B. Macaulay *History of England,* 1849–61

No one can love or understand the Russian people who does not love orthodoxy.

Feodor Dostoevsky, attrib.

*It is easier for a Russian to become an atheist than for anyone else in the world.

Feodor Dostoevsky, *The Idiot,* 1866 (Prince Myshkin speaking)

Nihilism in Russia will never be laid at rest until an Emperor comes, bold enough to trust the people and chance the hatred of the nobles. He may be assassinated, but he will be the saviour of Russia. The Russians do not ask for much. Their men of thought, who are their men of action in domestic politics, ask for a graduated scale of liberty. Their moderation must have struck you.

Alfred Lord Tennyson, in conversation, 1888, *Alfred Lord Tennyson, a Memoir, by his Son,* 1897

The Russian Cossack . . . that cheery, hospitable race, – better fellows than whom it would, as a rule, be hard to meet.

Harry de Windt, *From Pekin to Calais by Land,* 1889

The extreme frankness and amiability of Russian manners cover a genuine *bonhomie* and a good-humoured *insouciance,* which render it easy for them to make friends and which disarm the suspicion even of a beaten foe. The Russian fraternises in the true sense of the word. He is guiltless of that air of conscious superiority and gloomy hauteur, which does more to inflame animosity than cruelty may have done to kindle it, and he does not shrink from entering into social and domestic relations with alien or inferior races. His own unconquerable carelessness renders it easy for him to adopt a *laissez-faire* attitude towards others, and the tolerance with which he has treated the religious practices, the social customs, and the local prejudices of his Asiatic fellow-subjects is less the outcome of diplomatic calculation than it is of ingrained *nonchalance.*

Hon. G.N. Curzon, *Russia in Central Asia,* 1889

*The Russian is a delightful person till he tucks in his shirt. As an Oriental he is charming. It is only when he insists on being treated as the most easterly of western peoples instead of the most westerly of easterns that he becomes a racial anomaly extremely difficult to handle.

Rudyard Kipling, 'The Man Who Was', in *Life's Handicap,* 1891

I hope for the Russian invasion of the West. When the Russians have, after the conquest, reached the point of writing poems like Gautier's 'Nombril' . . . it will then be time for the Chinese to conquer the world.

Lafcadio Hearn, Letter to Basil Hall Chamberlain, 18 February 1893

There is a curious reservation in the communicativeness of a Russian. He will tell you all you wish to know (and more) of himself and of his family, but once touch upon his country, or his Government, and he is dumb.

Gertrude Bell, 'Safar Nameh', *Persian Pictures,* 1894

Make ye no truce with Adam-zas – the Bear that walks like a Man!

Rudyard Kipling, *The Truce of the Bear,* 1898

Twentieth Century

When the Russian is cruel, he is cruel just as the barbarian always is, because he is indifferent to pain, his own or another's. He does not spare because he would not complain.

Arthur Symons, *Cities,* 1903

I like the Russian people, but I abhor the Russian system of government, and I cannot trust the word of those at the head.

Theodore Roosevelt, 1905, quoted in Thomas A. Bailey, *America Faces Russia,* 1950

I asked a Little Russian gentleman what the main differences were between Little Russians and Big Russians, and he said the Little Russians were more decent people but far lazier than the Big Russians; that the Little Russian was so lazy, that he would say to his wife, 'Little wife, say "woa" to my horse: I have a pain in my tongue.'

Maurice Baring, *What I Saw in Russia,* 1913

Their character (that of the great Russians) has been influenced not only by a long history of feudal despotism, but also by the gloomy forests, the unresponsive soil, the rigorous climate, and especially the enforced inactivity of the long winters. Even the educated Russian gives comparatively little response to the actual demands of life; he is more or less the victim of fancy and temperament, which sometimes lead him to a despondent slackness, sometimes to emotional outbursts. Here we have the explanation of the want of organization, the disorder, and the waste of time which strikes the western visitor to Russia.

Karl Baedeker, *Guide to Russia,* 1914

We imagine that because England is politically free it is a free country. Any form of freedom that is not countenanced by our conventions we call licence, and licence, we say, is wrong. Thus it came about that I found myself living among a people who, to the English mind were politically in a position of abject slavery, which is abhorrent to all good Britishers, and socially in a state of complete licence, which to us is more abhorrent still.

Denis Garstin, *Friendly Russia,* 1915

Get this into your head once for all: if the Czar doesn't knout them, they'll knout themselves.

John Pentland Mahaffy, Remark quoted by Oliver St John Gogarty, *It Isn't this Time of Year at all,* 1954

You will still come up against it if you accuse any Russian of being a lady or a gentleman.

G. Bernard Shaw, *On the Rocks,* Preface, 1934

The Russian has always conceived of progress as a mass-advance towards an immediate millennium, rather than as a succession of steps taken by gifted individuals towards objective truth. While no country has produced more theorists on the theme of human betterment, their concern has always been with the prompt delivery rather than with the quality of the perfection supplied.

Robert Byron, *First Russia, then Tibet,* 1933

A peasant queues up to see Lenin's body in the Red Square mausoleum, comes out again. 'What did you think of him?' a friend asks. Reply: 'He's just like us, dead, but not yet buried.'

John Gunther, *Inside Europe,* 1938 edn

Everybody has always underrated the Russians. They keep their own secrets alike from foe and friends.

Sir Winston Churchill, Speech in the House of Commons, 23 April 1942

We are dealing with people who are unpredictable and, at times, they are just practically inexplicable, so far as we are concerned.

Dwight D. Eisenhower, quoted from Press Conference in *New York Times,* 24 January 1957

Surely the right course is to test the Russians, not the bombs.

Hugh Gaitskell, *Observer,* 'Sayings of the Week', 23 June 1957

The Russians train; they do not dare educate.

Max Lerner, 'Four Fallacies of Our Schools', *The Unfinished Country,* 1959

I bought me a fur hat, fur coat, and fur-lined galoshes, all for forty dollars. Back on the street, wearing my new outfit, it came to me why the bear was the symbol of Russia. The only way a Russian could survive the winter was to dress like a bear.

Harpo Marx, *Harpo Speaks,* 1961

The Russian people can be angels one minute and devils the next, and . . . more than any other I know in the world, give constantly the note of striving for fulfilment, and have so much force, discipline, and faith, in spite of their bleak totalitarian surroundings.

John Gunther, *Inside Russia Today,* rev. edn, 1962

The Russians are devout believers in an eye for an eye, or if possible two.

Ibid.

An interesting example of modern Soviet terminology is that alcoholics are called 'partial suicides.'

Ibid.

The Russians seemed to me a nation of sheep – angry sheep, but nevertheless sheep, and in sheep's clothing.

James Kirkup, *One Man's Russia,* 1968

I was never at any time in any doubt about the Russian people's sincere desire for peace. They were always talking about it and expressing their hatred of war. . . . No other people express themselves so strongly about the need for peace except the Japanese. Their sincerity and utter honesty of mind in this matter are deeply impressive. They seize every opportunity they can find to impress upon foreigners this fundamental passion for peace and hatred of war. In this I found them truly admirable and an example to the rest of the world's nations.

Ibid.

Sooner or later . . . one reaches the conclusion that the main difficulty in knowing the Russians as they really are stems from the fact that they themselves do not know what they are. As soon as a totalitarian country is able to express itself freely, it not only discovers that it is different from what it appeared to be, but it *becomes* different. The 'ghost' reality of unexpressed wishes, hates, and hopes acquires finally the necessary self-expression and self-consciousness.

Arrigo Levi, former Moscow correspondent of *Corriera della Sera,* quoted by Erik de Mauny, *Russian Prospect,* 1969

Russians puzzle us, we puzzle them. Their pride is the pride of poor people, the manners they require from others must be more elegant than ever could have been known at Versailles. And in so many ways their recent social customs have run counter to ours: they are, for example, romantic and dawn-fogged about sex, and I often find the talk about love and fidelity too high-minded for my history or my taste.

Lillian Hellman, *An Unfinished Woman*, 1969 of 1944

Russians have always had a deep love of their country, but now they are in love with each other.

Ibid.

I've had what they call in diplomacy an exchange of views, but I've never had with any Russians what you and I would call a conversation.

Sargent Shriver, quoted Hedrick Smith, *The Russians*, 1977

Nor can foreigners spend much time in Russia without having their livers threatened by vodka. For centuries, Russians have been flooding Westerners with vodka as a form of hospitality which conveniently numbs the travelers' critical faculties.

Hedrick Smith, *The Russians*, 1977

Russians are conoisseurs of the cold.

Ibid.

At times pulling the wool over foreigners' eyes approaches a national sport. 'We do it naturally,' a bright young government consultant on foreign policy admitted to me one evening in the privacy of his apartment. 'It is to our advantage. Deceit is a compensation for weakness, for a feeling of inferiority before foreigners. As a nation we cannot deal with others equally. Either we are more powerful or they are. And if they are, and we feel it, we compensate by deceiving them. It is a very important feature of our national character.'

Ibid.

'Friends are the one thing we have which are all our own,' a mathematician confided. 'They are the one part of our lives where we can make our own choice completely for ourselves. We cannot do that in politics, religion, literature, work. Always, someone above influences our choice. But not with friends. We make that choice for ourselves.'

Ibid.

Fifteen years ago Peter Fleming who knew and loved Russia and the Russians as well as could any sane westerner observed to me that every people had their own technique of lying. 'Latins and Arabs lie to please; the British to cover up,' he remarked, 'but only the Russians lie without any discernible motive and often to their detriment. It's a way of life.'

Alastair Horne, 'Intourist and the Big Lie', *Spectator*, 1 December 1979

And what do Soviet people say about 'rotting capitalism'? 'It may be rotting, but what a lovely smell!' – and they inhale voluptuously.

Vladimir Bukovsky, 'My Life as a Dissenter', in *To Build a Castle,* trans. Michael Scammell, 1979

They can't accept a big concession. They've got to extort it from you.

Henry Kissinger, Television interview with Michael Parkinson, BBC, 21 November 1979 (on the psychology of negotiating with the Russians)

To most Americans, the Russian experience is . . . incomprehensible. The illusion is widespread that because the Soviet way of life is unnatural to Americans, it is unnatural to Russians; that if only the Soviet people were exposed to the ways of the West, they would quickly change. The Westerner believes the Soviet system is bound to change simply because people cannot live that way. But they do, and this is the point that the West must grasp. We can hope that the Soviet system eventually changes, but we act at our peril if we expect it to change and base our policies on that expectation.

Richard Nixon, *The Real War*, 1980

River Alma

In two nations annals graven, thou art now a deathless name
And a star for ever shining in their firmament of fame.

Many a great and ancient river, crowned with city, tower and shrine
Little, streamlet, knows no magic, boasts no potency like thine. . . .

O thou river! dear for ever to the gallant, to the free,
Alma, roll thy waters proudly, proudly roll them to the sea.

Richard Chenevix Trench, *Alma, c.* 1855

Altan Bulak (formerly Maimatchin)

Of all the celebrated places I have seen, and which have nothing to support their celebrity, Maimatchin is the most eminent. It is a small, ill-built, mud town, with four narrow, mud-paved streets, running at right angles, containing, during the fair, from twelve to fifteen hundred men and boys, for the female sex are prohibited. The houses are without windows, and there is a total absence of everything that can interest even the most ignorant or careless. . . . The absence of windows may be pardonable . . . but to the absence of the fair sex is mainly attributable that dreadful degeneracy which is said to pervade all ranks of society among them.

Captain John Dundas Cochrane, *Narrative of a Pedestrian Journey through Russia, etc.*, 1824

Amu Darya / Oxus

But the majestic river floated on,
Out of the mist and hum of that low land,
Into the frosty starlight, and there moved,
Rejoicing, through the hush'd Chorasmian waste,
Under the solitary moon; – he flowed
Right for the polar star, past Orgunjè,
Brimming, and bright, and large; then sands begin
To hem his watery march and dam his streams,
And split his currents; that for many a league
The shorn and parcelled Oxus strains along
Through beds of sand and matted rushy isles –
Oxus, forgetting the bright speed he had
In his high mountain-cradle in Pamere,
A foil'd circuitous wanderer – till at last
The long'd for dash of waves is heard, and wide
His luminous home of waters opens, bright
And tranquil, from whose floor the new-bathed stars
Emerge, and shine upon the Aral Sea.

Matthew Arnold, *Sohrab and Rustum,* 1853

The Oxus, that famous river that, like the Euphrates and the Ganges, rolls its stately burden down from a hoar antiquity through the legends and annals of the East.

Hon. G.N. Curzon, *Russia in Central Asia,* 1889

Armenia

The *Armenians* are almost as grave as the *Turks,* and they have all the boorishness of *Dutchmen;* insomuch, that this is a common saying with *European* merchants in *Constantinople;* 'A sportive *Armenian* is as awkward as a dancing bear.'

E.D. Clarke, *Travels in Various Countries,* 4th edn, 1816

Notwithstanding that my master, the Padre Pasquale Aucher . . . assured me 'that the terrestrial Paradise had been certainly in *Armenia,*' I went seeking it – God knows where – did I find it? Umph! Now and then, for a minute or two.

Lord Byron, *Detached Thoughts,* 1821

Archangel

The Country by report suteable to thatt little which wee have here seene, *viz.*, vast wast with greatt wildernesses, woods, Marishes, (No travelling through the Country without a speciall passe, No nott to places here adjoyning. . . .)

Peter Mundy, *Travels in Europe and Asia,* 1641

Asov

'Englishmen,' said the old *Commandant,* as he approached the shore, to welcome our arrival, *'are the only travellers who would come to Azof, if it could be avoided.'*

E.D. Clarke, *Travels in Various Countries,* 4th edn, 1816

Astrakhan

In reaching Astrakhan one is plunged into the atmosphere of the East. On the quays there is an infinite quantity of booths containing every kind of fruit and a coloured herd of people living in the dust and the dirt, splendidly squalid, noisy as parrots, and busy doing nothing like wasps.

Maurice Baring, *What I Saw in Russia,* 1913

Astrakhan seemed to me more like hell than anything I had ever imagined. The town water-supply was taken from the same part of the river into which ships shot their refuse. Every street had stagnant water which bred millions of mosquitoes; every year one third of the inhabitants had malaria. There was no drainage system but a vast mountain of excrement at a prominent place in the midst of the town. Plague was endemic. . . . The flies were so numerous that at meal-time a table-cloth had to be put over the food, and one had to insert one's hand underneath and snatch a mouthful quickly. The instant the table-cloth was put down it became completely black with flies so that nothing of it remained visible. The place is a great deal below sea-level, and the temperature was 120 degrees in the shade. The leading doctors of the place were ordered by the Soviet officials who accompanied us to hear what Haden Guest had to say about combating malaria. . . . He gave them an admirable lecture on the subject at the end of which they said: 'Yes, we know all that but it is very hot.'

Bertrand Russell, *Autobiography,* 1968 of 1920

Atchinsk

Atchinsk is, if not the largest, decidedly the most taking town we saw in Siberia. It has a population of about ten thousand, and is built on the summits of five or six low hills. The grassy hollows between these are used as common land, where cattle, pigs, and geese roam about at will. The cheerfull aspect of the place, when compared with other Siberian towns, is partly due to the fact that the soil is of a much lighter colour, and nearly all the wooden buildings are painted white or grey, picked out with bright colours. The immediate neighbourhood of Atchinsk, too, is free of forest. The town stands in the middle of a large grass plain watered by the Chulim river – a plain composed of large enclosed grass meadows, where, as we drove by that bright sunshiny morning, cattle and sheep were browsing, knee deep in rich, luxuriant pasture, and wild flowers. Atchinsk is the one bright spot of that weary journey – an oasis of flowers and sunshine in the dark, dreary desert of gloom and monotony lying between Tomsk and Irkoutsk.

Harry de Windt, *From Pekin to Calais by Land,* 1889

Lake Baikal

village of Monshafskaya

It was just like being at the seaside in England . . . a wooden jetty, with a lighthouse at the end, ran out for a distance of fifty yards into the lake, forming a small harbour in which lay moored a number of small fishing-boats and two large black hulks, prison barges, waiting to be towed back to Listvenitz for a fresh convoy. Such was the scene from our rest-house on the hill. Has the reader ever seen the village of Clovelly in Devonshire? If so, let him substitute pines for oak and beech-trees, unpaved paths for cobbled streets, wooden huts for stone houses, and he has seen Monshafskaya as I saw it that bright August morning, when for the first time I looked on the waters of the Holy Sea of Siberia, for by this name alone is Lake Baikal known by the natives inhabiting its shores. To call it a lake to a Siberian is an insult.

Harry de Windt, *From Pekin to Calais by Land,* 1889

Lake Baikal derives its name of Holy Sea from the fact that Our Saviour, when visiting this part of Asia, is supposed to have mounted to the summit of Olkon, an island about sixty miles long by fifteen broad, in the middle of the lake, and surveyed the surrounding countries. Having blessed the land on the north and west, He turned to the south-west, and, stretching out His hands, cried, '*Beyond this shall be desolation.*'

Ibid.

That strange, scimitar-shaped marvel, Lake Baikal.

Erik de Mauny, *Russian Prospect,* 1969

Baku

. . . Bachu, neere unto which towne is a strange thing to behold. For there issueth out of the ground a marveilous quantitie of oile, which oile they fetch from the uttermost bounds of all Persia: it serveth all the countrey to burne in their houses.

This oyle is blacke, and is called Nefte: they use to carry it throughout all the Countrey upon kine & asses, of which you shall oftentimes meet with foure or five hundred in a company. There is also by the said town of Bachu another kind of oyle which is white and very precious: and it is supposed to be the same that here is called Petroleum. There is also not far from Shamaky, a thing like unto tarre, and issueth out of the ground, whereof we have made the proofe, that in our ships it serveth well in the stead of tarre.

Geffrey Ducket (1574), in Richard Hakluyt, *Principal Navigations . . . of the English Nation,* 1598–1600

New Baku may well be called the Paris of the Caspian.

H.M. Stanley, *My Early Travels and Adventures* (May 1870), 1895

The smell of oil, . . . from the moment you enter until you leave Baku, there is no getting away from. Although the wells are fully three miles away, the tablecloths and napkins were saturated with it, and the very food one ate had a faint sickly flavour of naptha. 'I bathed in the Caspian once last summer,' said Mr. B – despairingly, 'and did not get the smell out of my skin for a week, during which time my friends forbade me their houses! Mon Dieu! Quel pays!'

Harry de Windt, *A Ride to India,* 1891

Baku, with its chimnies and cisterns and refineries, with its acres of rails outside the station covered with tank-cars, its grimy naptha-besprinkled streets, its sky-high telegraph poles and rattling tramcars, its shops for every article under the sun, its Persian ruins and its modern one-storeyed houses, its shabby conglomeration of peoples, its inky harbour, its canopy of smoke, and its all-pervading smells – Baku, larger, more pungent, and less inviting than ever.

Hon. George Curzon, *Persia and the Persian Question,* 1892

Balaclava

The wild gigantic landscape, towards its southern extremity surrounding the town; its mountains, ruins, and harbour; its houses covered by vines and flowers, or overshadowed by thick foliage of mulberry and walnut trees; make it altogether enchanting.

E.D. Clarke, *Travels in Various Countries,* 1816

Bukhara

The nineteenth century can scarcely be considered as yet to have got a firm hold upon Bokhara.

Hon. G.N. Curzon, *Russia in Central Asia,* 1889

Where the British soldier is ordered to pile arms and to stand at ease, the Bokharan sits down on the ground. Some years ago the drill contained a movement of a most interesting character which has since been abandoned. At a given signal the soldiers lay down upon their backs, and kicked their heels in the air. This was copied from the action of Russian troops in one of the earlier engagements, where, after crossing a river, they were ordered to lie down and shake the water out of their big top-boots. The retreating Bokhariots saw the manoeuvre and attributed to it a magical share in the Russian victory.

Ibid.

Caspian Sea

In order to form an idea of the salineness of the Caspian, I drank some of the water, then opened a flask of Dead Sea water I had with me, and tasted that, but I must confess that I did not observe any very great difference between the two waters. I thought one was as salty as the other.

H.M. Stanley, *My Early Travels and Adventures* (May 1870), 1895

Caucasus

Bolingbroke: Oh who can hold a fire in his hand
By thinking on the frostie *Caucasus?*

William Shakespeare, *Richard the Second, c.* 1595–6

compared with the Alps
The Alps incline you to altruism; you take off your hat . . . and . . . promise the wide hills . . . that henceforth you will be a good man. The Caucasus don't do that. They frighten you; their scowl makes you shiver.

John Foster Fraser, *Round the World on a Wheel,* 1899

Travellers who quit the beaten track should be provided with rugs, a lantern, an air-cushion, rubber overshoes, an alarum-clock, pins and needles, thread, string, straps, preserved meats, condensed meat (all these obtainable in Odessa), bread (seldom obtainable in the mountains and never good) or biscuits, tea, sugar, quinine, opiates, vaseline, carbolic acid, bandages, soap, matches, candles, insect powder, wrapping paper, and writing materials. All these may be obtained in Tiflis, and all except the preserves in Vladivkazak. – Those who mean to ascend any of the higher mountains should import a tried guide from the Alps; the natives, except at Mt. Kazbek and Mt. Ararat, cannot be depended upon, and should not be used except as porters. . . . Besides the ordinary mountaineering requisites, the traveller should have a tent for nightquarters, a sleeping bag, an axe for cutting wood, a hammer, nails for the boot-soles, some spirits of wine and charcoal for making a fire where there is no wood, and torches. Wine should be renounced, and tea taken instead. Spirits should not be used except in urgent cases.

Karl Baedeker, *Russia, with Teheran, Port Arthur and Peking,* 1914

Crimea

Fevers are so general during the summer, throughout the *Peninsula,* that it is hardly possible to avoid them . . . such is the dangerous nature of the climate to strangers, that Russia must consider the country as a cemetery for the troops which are sent to maintain its possession.

E.D. Clarke, *Travels in Various Countries,* 1816

Whether Paradise is formed from the plans of the south coast of the Crimea, or *vice versa,* I don't know, but they must be from the same design.

John Foster Fraser, *Round the World on a Wheel,* 1899

East Cape, Bering Straits – Mys Dezhneva

The end of the end of the world.

Harry de Windt, *From Paris to New York by Land,* 1904

Ekaterinburg

Hard by the town of Ekaterinburg, by the side of the Great Post-Road to Siberia, is a large stone pillar, on one side of which is carved the word 'Europe,' upon the other 'Asia,' and this marks the boundary between the two quarters of the globe. . . . The base of the pillar is covered with inscriptions, letters rudely carved by those who have there looked their last on their native land. It is the custom to make a halt and allow the exiles to bid good-bye, many of them for ever, to Europe.

Harry de Windt, *From Pekin to Calais by Land,* 1889

Estonia

I once told a Russian how much I liked Estonia. 'Ah,' he smiled, 'now I can see you are anti-Soviet.'

Michael Binyon, *The Times,* 30 May 1980

Tallinn, formerly Reval
It's our little piece of the West.

Anon Russian, quoted, *ibid.*

Georgia

Nobility is cheap in Georgia. There is only one rank, and that is prince.

John Foster Fraser, *Round the World on a Wheel,* 1899

Harkov

The Palace of Industry . . . lies on the outskirts of the place, and when complete will form a circle of skyscrapers, joined by bridges, in the middle of an empty plain. Even now, with only one-fifth of its circumference built, its appearance is that of an industrial 'folly', whose architect has tried to go one better than Stonehenge.

Robert Byron, *First Russia, then Tibet,* 1933

Irkutsk

On my approach to the capital early in the morning, a thick fog hovering on the Angara precluded a view of it, till I reached the monastery near the river; coasting which I suddenly observed, over the dense atmosphere, the churches beautifully reflecting the sun's ray from their tin or copper casings. . . . Irkutsk indeed scarcely deserves the name of city, except for its public buildings, which are good. . . . The streets are wide, and run at right angles, but there are in some of them gaps of two and three hundred yards without a building. There are, however many fine points of view, and when it is considered that Irkutsk has been raised into a government and city only within these forty years, its progress towards improvement must be acknowledged. The houses are for the greater part of wood, though many are of brick. . . . Of the churches there are at least a dozen, which not a little contribute to the splendour of its appearance.

Captain John Dundas Cochrane, *Narrative of a Pedestrian Journey through Russia, etc.*, 1824

One was constantly being assailed in Irkoutsk by mysterious individuals with documents which they wished delivered to their friends in Europe.

Harry de Windt, *From Pekin to Calais by Land,* 1889

Irkutsk presents, at first sight, an untidy, unfinished appearance. Like most Siberian towns, its buildings are a strange mixture of squalor and grandeur. The majority are of brick, for since the great fire of 1879 a law has been passed forbidding the construction of any more wooden dwellings. The consequence is that the greater part of the city presents a patch-work appearance, the lofty mansion of a millionaire gold-miner, with it conservatories and gardens, often standing next door to the dilapidated wooden hovel of some peasant with half its roof off, which has been partially saved from the flames. One's first feeling on walking through the streets is one of intense depression, for a more melancholy-looking city does not exist. The streets, though wide and regular, give one the idea of being continually up for repair. . . . Although much care is lavished on the architecture and decoration of the buildings, the streets are apparently left to look after themselves.

The 'Grande Rue' is the principal street . . . which would not disgrace a European city. . . . The principal shops are situated here, but though one may buy almost anything in this far-away corner of the globe, from an English steam-plough to a Parisian bonnet, there is no outward or visible sign in any of the windows of the goods sold within. Merely a roughly painted board over the doorway indicating the name and business of the proprietor. . . . To the nakedness of the shop-windows, perhaps, among other reasons may be attributed the dismal appearance the place presents. Perhaps, too, the black roads, total absence of trees or gardens, or indeed of colour of any kind, has much to do with the sense of depression that fastens on one after ever so short a residence in any Siberian town. I cannot say exactly why, but one's only thought, after a couple of days was invariably, 'When shall I get away?' . . . sunshine only served to reveal more plainly the dirty, unwashed appearance which everything, including the natives, presented.

Ibid.

By the time I crossed the frontier from Mongolia into Irkutsk the temperature was so low you would have required to get down on your hands and knees to see it. . . . Irkutsk is set, apparently, in the middle of a million miles of snow; it is the kind of place whose citizens might well take their holidays at the Pole.

James Cameron, *Point of Departure,* 1967

Kaliningrad (formerly Konigsberg)

This is a vast city . . . it contains fifty thousand inhabitants, exclusive of eight thousand soldiers; but it is a great collection of houses and streets without elegance, beauty, or order: the buildings are in a vile taste, and mostly antique.

Sir N.W. Wraxall, *A Tour Round the Baltic,* 1775

Kalmucks

Of all the inhabitants of the *Russian* empire, the *Calmucks* are the most distinguished by peculiarity of feature and manners. In personal appearance they are athletic and revolting. Their hair is coarse and black, their language harsh and guttural. . . . The Cossacks alone esteem them, and intermarry with them. This union sometimes produces women of very great beauty;

although nothing is more hideous than a *Calmuck*. High, prominent, and broad cheek-bones; very little eyes, widely separated from each other; a flat and broad nose; coarse, greasy, jet-black hair; scarcely any eye-brows; and enormous prominent ears; compose no very inviting countenance. . . . The stories related of their placing pieces of horse-flesh under the saddle, in order to prepare them for food, are true. They acknowledged that this practice was common among them during a journey, and that a stake so dressed became tender and palatable. . . . The greatest part of their life is spent in amusement. . . . They deem a residence in houses so insupportable, that to be shut up in the confined air of a close apartment, even for a short time, when under the necessity of going into towns, . . . is considered by them with a degree of horror. . . . The venereal disease causes great ravages. . . . They give to this disorder a name very expressive of the estimation in which they hold their mode of life, by calling it 'The house disease.'

E.D. Clarke, *Travels in Various Countries,* 4th edn, 1816

Kamchatka (natives of)

Being much fatigued with rowing the Kamtschadale resigned himself to his fate & would work no longer, & being pressed to it by the Gentleman he seriously told him that he would cut his own Throat sooner than bear such hardships much longer (this agrees with the character given of the Kamtschadales by Crashininnicoff who says that they are all prone to Suicide).

David Samwell, *Journal,* June 1779

The whole race indeed, look like beings better qualified to extinguish than propagate the human species.

Captain John Dundas Cochrane, *Narrative of a Pedestrian Journey through Russia, etc.,* 1824

Koriak Tribespeople

Although the wandering Koriaks treat their animals with kindness, their cruelty to women is proverbial. Unlike the Kamchatdales and their nearer neighbours, they are extremely jealous, and very often kill their wives on a mere suspicion of infidelity, the more often that they have a right to slay them if really guilty. No Koriak's wife is ever permitted by her lord to beautify herself, or even wash, for fear of attracting the notice of others. To make assurance doubly sure these northern Othellos from time to time compel their wretched women to cover their entire bodies with a thick coating of rancid oil, which effectually keeps even the most amorous lover at a safe distance. When the Koriaks, male or female, become old and unfit for work, they are killed by their family, being allowed the privilege of choosing whether they shall be stoned to death, or have their throats cut. Part of a Koriak youth's education is learning to give the *coup de grace* as painlessly as possible.

Harry de Windt, *From Pekin to Calais by Land,* 1889

A Kamchatdale may be smelt a mile off, their bodies exuding a strong smell of fish, on which they subsist, eaten raw; but they are friendly, hospitable fellows.

Harry de Windt, *ibid.*

Khabarovsk

I lingered, talking to a fierce captain about the declining Soviet birth rate.

'What about family planning?' I asked.

'We are trying to stop it!'

'Are you succeeding?'

'Not yet. But I think we can increase production.'

Paul Theroux, *The Great Railway Bazaar,* 1975

Kiev

The Jerusalem of Russia.

Old nickname, quoted by Karl Baedeker, *Russia, with Teheran, Port Arthur and Peking,* 1914

The mother of all Russian towns.

Old saying, quoted *ibid.*

It stands at a great height, on the crest of an amphitheatre of hills, which rise abruptly in the middle of an immense plain, apparently thrown up by some wild freak of nature, at once curious, unique, and beautiful. The style of its architecture is admirably calculated to give effect to its peculiar position; and after a dreary journey over the wild plains of the Ukraine, it breaks upon the traveller with all the glittering and gorgeous splendour of an Asiatic city. For many centuries it has been regarded as the Jerusalem of the North, the sacred and holy city of the Russians; and, long before reaching it, its numerous convents and churches, crowning the summit, and hanging on the sides of the hill, with their quadrupled domes, and spires, and chains, and crosses, gilded with ducat gold and glittering in the sun, gave the whole city the appearance of golden splendour. The churches and monasteries have one large dome in the centre, with a spire surmounted by a cross, and several smaller domes around it, also with spires and crosses connected by pendant chains, and gilded so purely that they never tarnish.

J.L. Stephens, *Incidents of Travel in the Russian and Turkish Empires,* 1839

By its position overlooking the river Kieff reminded me of Quebec and, if Quebec has perhaps the finer site, the picturesqueness of the Kieff architecture is more than sufficient compensation.

R.H. Bruce Lockhart, *Memoirs of a British Agent,* 1932

Kolyma

With respect to the salubrity of the town and district of Kolyma, I fear it cannot be highly extolled, being subject to the ravages of many diseases, among which the leprosy, apoplexy, venereal, and scurvy are the most dangerous. . . . The complaints called *diable au corps,* and imerachism must also be specified; the former is a most extraordinary one, and consists in an idea that the body of the patient is possessed with one or more devils, attended with incessant hiccoughs. The parties afflicted with it are generally most delicate and interesting in their appearance; and it is seldom indeed that any individual is cured. . . . Imerachism . . . carries with it an air of merriment, as it by no means affects the health of the person, though it subjects him to the most violent paroxysms of rage, fear, and mortification. Whatever is said or done in the presence of an imerach, will be repeated by him at the moment, however indecorous, improper, or violent the act may be.

Captain John Dundas Cochrane, *Narrative of a Pedestrian Journey through Russia, etc.,* 1824

Klaipeda (formerly Memel)

I asked if there were any objects of curiosity at Memel. 'There is not any thing that I know of,' said the second brother, 'except a pot-ash manufactory, and you may see a better one at Dantzic: the ships at the quay are our finest sight.'

Sir N.W. Wraxall, *A Tour Round the Baltic,* 1775

Kutais

My first view of it embraced a broken-down bridge, a church in process of construction, two other churches glorious in green paint and swelling domes, a multitude of houses and trees, the latter so numerous that they hide more than one half of the town from first view.

It was in this town I first began to enjoy life in the Caucasus. I found myself in good society. There were hotels, one of which might compete with any in Paris for the excellence of its cuisine. This was the Hotel de France, kept by a Frenchman, and fronted the great square of the city. Kutais is intensely civilised, and glories in its refinement and taste. It claims to be the Lyons of the Caucasus – not in manufactures, but in wealth, cleanliness, position, influence; Tiflis, of course, being the Paris of the Caucasus. Every afternoon, when the coolness of the day has begun, every dame and gentle girl in the town begin their promenade, in imitation of the mode which prevails in Western Europe. Then begins, and continues until nightfall, the by-play of full feathered coquettes. I calmly contemplate all this while sitting in an iron chair in the Grand Square.

H.M. Stanley, *My Early Travels and Adventures* (May 1870), 1895

Lady

We were agreeably surprised, even in this remote place, to meet with some English strong beer; and no less pleased to see our supper served in dishes of our countryman Wedgewood's cream-coloured ware. The luxury of clean straw for our beds was no small addition to these comforts.

William Coxe, *Travels into Poland, Russia, Sweden, etc.,* 1792

Leningrad / St Petersburg

Every thing is on a vast and colossal scale, resembling that of the empire itself. The public buildings, churches, monasteries, and private palaces of the nobility, are of an immense size, and seem as if designed for creatures of a superior height and dimensions to man.

Sir N.W. Wraxall, *A Tour Round the Baltic,* 1775

I am told, that the style of loveliness here, is not a little different from ours; and that in order to possess any pre-eminent degree of it, a woman must weigh at least two hundred weight.

Ibid.

As I walked about this metropolis I was filled with astonishment upon reflecting that so late as the beginning of this century, the ground on which Petersburg now stands was only a vast morass occupied by a few fishermen's huts.

William Coxe, *Travels into Poland, Russia, Sweden, etc.,* 1792

As no stranger can stay in Petersburgh without permission, neither can he leave without it; and, to obtain this, he must advertise three times in the Government Gazette, stating his name, address, and intention of leaving the empire; and as the Gazette is only published twice a week, this formality occupies eight days. One of the objects of this is to apprize his creditors, and give them an opportunity of securing their debts; and few things show the barbarity, and imperfect civilisation of the Russians more clearly than this; making it utterly impossible for a gentleman to spend a winter in St. Petersburgh and go away without paying his landlord.

J.L. Stephens, *Incidents of Travel in the Russian and Turkish Empires,* 1839

No more effective illustration could be furnished of the Janus-like character of this huge political structure, with its vast unfilled courts and corridors in the east, and, as Peter the Great phrased it, its northern window looking out upon Europe, than the outward appearance of its two principal cities, the one a Western plagiarism, the other an Asiatic original.

Hon. G.N. Curzon, *Russia in Central Asia,* 1889

St. Petersburg . . . with its architecture borrowed from Italy, its amusements from Paris, and its pretentiousness from Berlin. . . .

Ibid.

It is, in truth a far more beautiful city than Moscow. . . . But even in summer, in the season of the white nights, St Petersburg always seemed to me cold and grey. Beneath its lovely exterior its heart was chill. Never at any time did it inspire me with the same friendly affection as Moscow.

R.H. Bruce Lockhart, *Memoirs of a Secret Agent,* 1932

Paris itself has not boulevards so wide and so straight. A plan of the city looks like a proposition in Euclid. But whereas Paris with its trees and lights is all graciousness and decorative effect, St. Petersburg from the beginning must have given the impression of a barracks. And it is now, to the outward and superficial sight, a barracks that has fallen upon evil days.

Hubert Griffith, *Seeing Soviet Russia,* 1932

Leningrad is grey, under lowering skies – or where the stucco is not grey, it is painted the colour of stale mustard. . . . 'Be Paris and Berlin together!' seems to have said its first owner, forgetting that its latitude lies north of the Hebrides.

Ibid.

Since Russians demand of architecture colour, ornament, and, above all, a prodigious scale, Western forms are made to serve these ends, heightened by a kind of emphatic eccentricity which is often fantastic in the manner of John Martin or Rex Whistler, but never quaint in the manner of Nuremberg. Thus Leningrad is a city not of architectural units but of architectural landscapes, and landscapes which, if so hackneyed a distinction may be applied to so unusual a subject, are romantic rather than formal, despite their groves of pillars and boscage of applied trophies. The merit of this immense ostentation is its patent honesty. The national megalomania, combined with a sure instinct for bold, frank design, leaves no room for petty vulgarity. Its expression may be conscious, and have become, in latter years, allusive. But it is never inhibited, like Milan railway station. To walk about the streets of Leningrad is to enjoy more good building, more general and more immediately apprehensible, than is provided by any of the world's large capitals.

Robert Byron, *First Russia, then Tibet,* 1933

It is as if this city had been built by another people who had no connection with Moscow or Kiev. It is a silent, lonely beauty.

Lillian Hellman, *An Unfinished Woman,* 1969 – of 1944

The skeleton is still imperial, even if much of the skin is missing.

John Gunther, *Inside Russia Today,* 1962 edn

Parisian blacks and greys predominate, but suddenly, here and there, the hot Italian palette intervenes: a palace of bitter green, of brilliant ochre, pale blue, orange. . . . Peter the Great who is given high marks by the current regime because he introduced the sciences to Russia, would probably approve the myriad television aerials that have settled like a swarm of metal insects on the roofs of his once imperial city.

Truman Capote, *The Muses are Heard,* 1957

This is essentially a European city, almost without any trace of the Orient or Byzantium. The dignified eighteenth-century buildings of French-Italianate style remind one of Versailles, of Vienna's Schonbrunn and Belvedere Palaces, of Salzburg's Residenz, Heilbronn and Schloss Mirabell, of the parks and palaces of Lazienki and Belvedere in Warsaw, of Berlin's Schloss Charlottenburg and Schloss Bellevue. But even more, Leningrad reminded me of an English city I know well, the city of Bath, which has the same timeless, tranquil air, the lovely rivers, canals and bridges, the superb eighteenth-century architecture and the gentle radiance of Leningrad light. Leningrad is Bath on a grand scale.

James Kirkup, *One Man's Russia,* 1968

Remember . . . St Petersburg is Russian – but it is not Russia.

Russian friend, Remark to Lesley Blanch, *Journey into the Mind's Eye,* 1968

There it was, intact, or reconstructed with infinite love and care by its inhabitants: The 'Queen of the North' standing proudly on the shores of the Neva and the Neva's many confluents and those canals dug by Czar Peter to make it look like another Amsterdam. Splendid, spacious, airy, curiously absent-minded, yet the most extraordinary city human beings have ever conceived and built! Parallel only, but on a much grander scale to such jewels as Venice before its present decline, or to Pekin, I suppose, at the time of the Ming Empire.

Nicholas Nabokov, *Bagázh,* 1975

'More Leningraders expired d-during the Nine Hundred Days' (the Wehrmacht siege of 1941–43) 'than Americans in their w-wars combined. I m-mean all the wars in the history of your country, including the Civil W-war.'

He stated this as dry fact, perhaps implying that Leningrad's tortured political history – the purges and bloody retributions, execution and exile of hundreds of thousands of her best people, including the best Communists – cannot be understood without a grasp of the tragedies that were *not* self-imposed. This is an underlying theme of much that he says about Soviet – and tsarist – rule: cruel acts of nature visited upon Russia sustain an atmosphere and mentality that encourage the politics of masochism.

George Feifer, *Moscow Farewell,* 1976 (quoting a Russian friend)

Lithuania

It is inconceivable how few are the wants of the Lithuanian peasants! Their carts are put together without iron; their bridles and traces are generally plaited from the bark of trees, or composed merely of twisted branches. They have no other instrument but a hatchet, to construct their huts, cut out their furniture, and make their carts. Their dress is a thick linen shirt and drawers, a long coarse drugget coat, or a sheepskin cloak, a round black felt cap lined with wool, and shoes made from the bark of trees. Their huts are built of trunks of trees heaped on each other, and look like piles of wood in wharfs, with penthouse roofs.

William Coxe, *Travels into Poland, Russia, Sweden, etc.,* 1792

'Lucomoria'

They say that to the men of Lucomoria chaunceth a marveilous thing and incredible: For they affirme, that they die yeerely at the xxvi. day of November, being the feast of S. George among the Muscovites: and that at the next spring about the xxiii day of Aprill, they revive againe as doe Frogges.

Giles Fletcher (1588), in Richard Hakluyt, *Principal Navigations . . . of the English Nation,* 1598–1600

Malmish

A small neat town with a growling postmaster.

Captain John Dundas Cochrane, *Narrative of a Pedestrian Journey through Russia, etc.*, 1824

Minsk

Minsk is one of the better class of Lithuanian towns, being the chief town of the government of Minsk, but very dirty and irregular. The principal street terminates in a large open square of grass and mean wooden huts. From this another street goes off at right angles, containing large houses, and joining with a second square, where some of the principal buildings are of brick. From this square several streets branch off, and enter a crowd of wooden hovels irregularly huddled together, and covering a large piece of ground. The churches are heavily constructed, and in a style peculiar to Lithuania, their gable ends fronting the street, and terminated at each corner by a square spire, with a low dome between them. The population is half Catholic and half Jewish, and the Jews are of the most filthy and abject class.

J.L. Stephens, *Incidents of Travel in the Russian and Turkish Empires,* 1839

between Minsk and Smolewitzo

In various parts of the forest we observed a circular range of boards fixed to several trees about twelve feet from the ground, and projecting three in breadth from the trunk. Upon inquiry, we were informed, that upon any great hunting party, ladders were placed against these scaffoldings, and that when any person is closely pursued by a bear, he runs up the ladder, and draws it up after him: the bear, although an excellent climber, is stopped in his ascent by the projection of the boards.

William Coxe, *Travels into Poland, Russia, Sweden, etc.,* 1792

Moscow

Little Mother Moscow.

Traditional nickname, quoted by Karl Baedeker, *Russia, with Teheran, Port Arthur and Peking,* 1914

The Citie of Mosco is great, the houses for the most part of wood, and some of stone, with windowes of Iron, which serve for Summer time. There are many faire Churches of stone, but more of wood, which are made hot in the Winter time. The Emperours lodging is in a faire and large Castle, walled foure square of Bricke, high, and thicke, situated upon an Hill, two miles about, and the River on the South-west side of it, and it hath sixteene gates in the walls, and as many Bulwarkes. His Palace is separated from the rest of the Castle, by a long wall going North and South, to the River side. In his Palace are Churches, some of stone, and some of wood, with round Towres fairely gilded. In the Church doores, and within the Churches are Images of Gold: the chiefe Markets for all things are within the said Castle, and for sundry things, sundry Markets, and every Science by it selfe. And in the

Winter there is a great Market without the Castle, upon the River being frozen, and there is sold Corne, earthen Pots, Tubs, sleds, &c. The Castle is in circuit two thousand and nine hundred paces.

Anthony Jenkinson, *The First Voyage,* 1557, in *Purchas his Pilgrimes,* 1625

A city so irregular, so uncommon, so extraordinary, and so contrasted, had never before claimed my astonishment. The streets are in general exceedingly long and broad: some of them are paved; others, particularly those in the suburbs, are formed with trunks of trees, or are boarded with planks like the floor of a room; wretched hovels are blended with large palaces; cottages of one story stand next to the most superb and stately mansions. Many brick structures are covered with wooden tops; some of the wooden houses are painted; others have iron doors and roofs. Numerous churches presented themselves in every quarter, built in a peculiar style of architecture; some with domes of copper, others of tin, gilt, or painted green, and many roofed with wood. In a word, some parts of this vast city have the appearance of a sequestered desert, other quarters of a populous town; some of a contemptible village, others of a great capital.

William Coxe, *Travels into Poland, Russia, Sweden, etc.,* 1792

Moscow is in every thing extraordinary; as well in disappointing expectation, as in surpassing it; in causing wonder and derision, pleasure and regret. . . . Numerous spires, glittering with gold, amidst burnished domes and painted palaces, appear in the midst of an open plain, for several versts before you reach this gate. Having passed, you look about, and wonder what is become of the city, or where you are; and are ready to ask, once more, How far is it to *Moscow?* They will tell you, 'This is *Moscow!*' and you behold nothing but a wide and scattered suburb, huts, gardens, pig-sties, brick walls, churches, dunghills, palaces, timber-yards, warehouses, and a refuse, as it were, of materials sufficient to stock an empire with miserable towns and miserable villages. One might imagine all the States of EUROPE and ASIA had sent a building, by way of representative to *Moscow:* and under this impression the eye is presented with deputies from all countries, holding congress: timber-huts from regions beyond the ARCTIC; plastered palaces from SWEDEN and DENMARK, not white-washed since their arrival; painted walls from the TIROL; mosques from CONSTANTINOPLE; Tahtar temples from BUCHARIA; pagodas, pavilions, and virandas, from CHINA; cabarets from SPAIN; dungeons, prisons, and public offices, from FRANCE; architectural ruins from ROME; terraces, and trellises from NAPLES; and warehouses from WAPPING.

E.D. Clarke, *Travels in Various Countries,* 4th edn, 1816

It is said that the Empress Cathrine used to call *Moscow* her little haughty republic.

Ibid.

Ils ne m'aiment pas beaucoup, . . . je ne suis pas à la mode à Moscou.
(They don't like me much, . . . I'm not in fashion at Moscow.)

Catherine the Great, quoted in *Lettres et Pensées du Prince du Ligne,* quoted *ibid.*

What a tremendous spectacle! These are Scythians indeed.

Napoleon, watching the burning of Moscow by the Russians, 1812

We gave five or six hours to a stroll through this wonderful city, a city of white houses and green roofs, of conical towers that rise one out of another like a foreshortened telescope; of bulging gilded domes, in which you see, as in a looking-glass, distorted pictures of the city; of churches which look, outside, like bunches of variegated cactus (some branches crowned with green prickly buds, others with blue, and others with red and white) and which, inside, are hung all round with *eikons* and lamps, and lined with illuminated pictures up to the very roof; and, finally, of pavement that goes up and down like a ploughed field, and *drojky*-drivers who insist on being paid thirty per cent. extra to-day, 'because it is the Empress's birthday.'

Lewis Carroll, *Diary,* August 1867

Moscow is . . . next to Constantinople, the earthly paradise of the sight-seer.

Harry de Windt, *From Pekin to Calais by Land,* 1889

Moscow is essentially a city of bells and churches.

Ibid.

. . . the Oriental irregularity and bizarre beauty of Moscow, an Eastern exotic transplanted to the West, an inland Constantinople, a Christian Cairo.

Hon. G.N. Curzon, *Russia in Central Asia,* 1889

For pleasure, one ought to come here early in life, and especially before visiting Constantinople and Ravenna; one ought to start from Petersburg and pass down through here to Kiev and Roumania, and so to Byzantium and the rest and best; but anyway I've got it done, and it leaves a queer taste like caviar and vodka, semi-barbarous and yet *manqué.* Even barbarism is sometimes weak. The Kremlin is more than half barbarous, but it is not strong; it is Byzantium barbarised. The bulbous domes are weak. The turnip with its root in the air is not so dignified as the turnip with its root in the earth. The architecture is simply ignorance. The builders built in 1600 as they built in

1200 because they knew no more. They had no building-stone. Gold was their only idea of splendor. Crude blue and green was all their decoration when they had to stop on red. They had no fund of taste in themselves; no invention or sense of form or line or color. Where on earth did our tenth-century French get all these? Charlemagne was about on a line with Ivan the Terrible who reigned here somewhere about seven hundred years afterwards, and I can see no ghost of a reason why art should have had seven hundred years of wonderful wealth after Charlemagne, and should have stayed dead after Ivan. . . . but the more I see of Russia, the more terrific the business of Russianising becomes. Moscow is, *à la fin de la fin, une ville manquée.*

Henry Adams, Letter to Elizabeth Cameron, 21 August 1901

In the vast village of Moscow the buildings are all built broad, not high, because there is so much space to cover. The public squares, unpaved, and surrounded by a little rim of cobbles, are as big as meadows. . . . Colours shriek and flame; the Muscovite eye sees only by emphasis and by contrast; red is completed either by another red or by a bright blue. There are no shades, no reticences, no modulations. . . . The houses are painted red or green or blue; the churches are like the temples of savage idols, tortured into every unnatural shape and coloured every glaring colour. Bare feet, osier-sandals, and legs swathed in rags, pass to and fro among the top-boots of the middle classes, the patent leather boots of the upper classes, like the inner savagery of a race still so near barbarism, made evident in that survival of the foot-gear of primitive races.

Nothing in Moscow is quite like anything one has seen anywhere else; and no two houses, all of which are so unlike the houses in any other country, are quite like one another. Their roofs are almost invariably painted green, and the water-pipes make a sort of green edging round the house-front. But the colours of the houses are endless: green, pink, blue, brown, red, chocolate, lilac, black even, rarely two of the same colour side by side, and rarely two of so much as the same general shape. Every shop has its walls painted over with rude pictures of the goods to be found inside; the draper has his row of clothed dummies, the hatter his pyramid of hats, the green-grocer his vegetables, the wine-seller his many-coloured bottles. Fruit-stalls meet one everywhere, and from the flower-like bouquet of fruits under their cool awnings there is a constant, shifting glow, the yellows and reds of apples, the purple of plums, the green and yellow of melons, and the crisp, black-spotted pink of melons sliced. And in these coloured streets, which in summer flame with the dry heat of a furnace, walk a multitude of coloured figures, brighter than the peasants of a comic opera; and the colours of their shirts and petticoats and handkerchiefs and bodices flame against the sunlight.

Set in such a frame, itself at all points so strange in shape and colour, the Kremlin and the churches with their glittering domes, on which the symbolical Russian cross has made a footstool of the crescent, are but the last in a series of shocks with which this inexhaustible city greets one. All Moscow is distorted by eccentricity; the hand of a madman is visibly upon it. . . . The Kremlin is like the evocation of an Arabian sorcerer, called up out of the mists and snows of the North. . . . Russian architecture which seems to proceed from an imaginary assumption to an impossible conclusion, has no standard of beauty to which its caprices of line can appeal, but presents itself rather as a wildly inhuman grotesque, without root in nature or limitation in art.

Arthur Symons, *Cities,* 1903

If ever a city expressed the character and peculiarities of its inhabitants, that city is Moscow.

Karl Baedeker, *Russia, with Teheran, Port Arthur and Peking,* 1914

Moscow in winter, a crystallized city of the Arabian Nights, all aglitter in the crisp air, with golden domes and minarets, cupolas and turret-tops, with white walls for palaces, red walls for the enemy to assail, thick snow lying partly on the roofs, sledges breaking trail after a new fall, the black horses, and massive drivers, dark and gallant against the white streets, plunging along, and snorting out their breath in trailing clouds of glory; or Moscow in summer with the blazing sun to coax the colours out, as it coaxes out the lizards in the south, and peasants too, to sit in little groups beside the Moskva river eating red melons to the eternal plaint of the fruit sellers on the bridge, 'Grooshi sleevi, yabloki, gospoda!' or chewing great handfuls of sunflower seed in contemplative fashion, spitting out the husks as some folk clear their throat, before speaking – whichever it is, Moscow in the tremendous, brilliant winter, or in the more human, lazy summer, it is equally beautiful, and the sympathy for beauty of those who live there one feels to be very real. It is, some say, the inspiration of art in Russia, as it is the inspiration of their holy faith.

Denis Garstin, *Friendly Russia,* 1915

I felt that if I were condemned to live there for long, I should go mad. . . . People glanced over their shoulders at dinner to see whether the servants were listening; . . . dinner-parties were given indeed, but every guest arrived rather as though he had just escaped a lion in the street. . . . I got the impression of a population furtively slinking along the walls; a people cowering away; a nation whose aspirations had been trimmed to a dead level, as a hedge. There was beggary, the depth to which one might sink, but no height, beyond that dead level, to which one might rise.

V. Sackville-West, *Passenger to Teheran,* 1926

Moscow is again, as the Russian poet said, the heart of Russia; even if the heart is broken.

G.K. Chesterton, *Generally Speaking,* 1928

Leningrad is a city of Rastrelli and the European architects of the Baroque period. Moscow was built by architects who lived in an age when architects were the private property of their owners, and when, as happened in the case of the amazing St. Basil Cathedral, they were liable to have their eyes put out at the end of their labours for fear they should later create anything more beautiful.

Hubert Griffith, *Seeing Soviet Russia,* 1932

The Red Capital in winter is a silent place. Like black ghouls on the soundless snow the Muscovites went their way, hatted in fur, lamb, leather, and velvet, each with a great collar turned up against the wind that sweeps down the river from the east. With bent heads they hurried past, impervious to collision with one another, or myself, as though desensitized by a decade of mass-living. Farther on, at the corner by the bridge, stood a line of hackney sledges, whose owners, the rearguard of capitalism, sat huddled in their portentous blue coats. . . . This, at last, was Red Russia; this horde of sable ghosts the Bolshevists, the cynosure of an agitated world. It was more than Russia, it was the capital of the Union, the very pulse of proletarian dictatorship, the mission-house of Dialectical Materialism.

Robert Byron, *First Russia, then Tibet,* 1933

The difference between Moscow and Leningrad is the difference in visible terms between the historic alternatives that have always confronted the Russian State: sufficiency from within or attraction from without. At present the balance is in favour of the former, and Moscow is again the capital.

Ibid.

Moscow I found greatly changed – even from the air this was visible; not set and picturesque, a black-and-gold barbaric walled city-camp about a great fortress, as I had seen it first in 1914; nor definitely shabby, shattered and apprehensive as I had seen in the time of Lenin, but untidily and hopefully renascent. There was new building going on in every direction, workers' dwellings, big groups of factories, and, amidst the woods, new *datchas* and country clubs. No particular plan was apparent from the air; it looked like a vigorous, natural expansion such as one might see in the most individualistic of cities.

H.G. Wells, *An Experiment in Autobiography,* 1934

Moscow is a depressing place. To me its atmosphere is somehow suggestive of servants' bedrooms.

Peter Fleming, *One's Company,* 1934

Moscow was always an ugly city except for the Kremlin Red Square and a few merchant sections, but now it is much uglier, as if Los Angeles had no sun and no grass. The city sprawls around, is inconvenient and haphazard with brash new buildings pushing against the old, as if bright mail order teeth were fitted next to yellowed fangs. There is a brutality about modern architecture in America, but in Moscow the brutality is mixed with something idiot-minded, as if their architects could loll about, giggling, poking fun at each other at a tipsy party given in honour of nothing.

Lillian Hellman, *An Unfinished Woman,* 1969 – of 1944

The centre of Moscow is a series of great deserts linked to one another by thin fringes of buildings.

René McColl, *Just Back from Russia,* 1954

It did look like the other side of the moon should look – gray, flat, and spooky.

Harpo Marx, *Harpo Speaks,* 1961

Everybody in Moscow seemed to be concentrating on what he was doing, even when he was doing nothing.

Ibid.

The whole country has a fixation on shoes. Moscow is a city where, if Marilyn Monroe should walk down the street with nothing on but shoes, people would stare at her feet first.

John Gunther, *Inside Russia Today,* 1962

*He wondered how many of the people they passed were walking for the same reason as themselves, that the public street was the only private place to talk. All over Moscow the streets must have been alive with communal intimacy. Two by two the talkers walked, passing, overtaking, and intersecting as if the city were some vast, complex cloister.

Michael Frayn, *The Russian Interpreter,* 1966

Moscow, I saw at once, is Horrorsville.

James Kirkup, *One Man's Russia,* 1968

It was lovely to walk in the fresh, cool air of morning in the empty streets: what a relief it was not to see any Russians with their ungainly bodies and surly faces! Moscow is at its most beautiful when there are no people about; in this respect it is just the exact opposite of Japan, where a street devoid of people is a street devoid of beauty and grace. Without people, Japan would be nothing. Without people, Russia is finally something, a place of calm loveliness.

Ibid.

Exciting it may be, industrious, creative, durable, packed with power and force, but it is still a kind of automaton among cities, regulated to the uttermost inch, devoid of the priceless asset of freedom, and governed in the last analysis by the harshest type of fear.

John Gunther, *Twelve Cities,* 1969

A dusty overgrown village from the last century, on which has been superimposed an angular, futuristic modern metropolis.

Erik de Mauny, *Russian Prospect,* 1969

It is the smells of a strange city that gradually lure one into its inner mysteries, and in Moscow these were rich, strange and various, especially in summer: a blend of low-grade petrol fumes, cheap calico, black *mahorka* tobacco, disinfectant, the warm yeasty odour of freshly-baked bread, and the slightly acrid smell of tar when the water-cart has passed. Then as the days lengthened and the dry breath of the surrounding plains invaded the city, the *topol* or white poplar shed its fluffy seeds upon the air, where they slowly sank to gather in great bleached drifts along the pavement edge, like a parody of snowfalls past or still to come.

Ibid.

A city landscape wanting neon and city life, as if square miles of squat buildings had been abandoned at the first November snows.

George Feifer, *Moscow Farewell,* 1976

What world capital can compare to the rambling village called Moscow when the spring sun shines and the smell of earth makes you free as Huck Finn? The dust won't rise for hours. The Kremlin is Disneyland on a lavender horizon.

Ibid.

The Russians have a saying . . . 'Moscow is downhill from all the Russias,' meaning that the best of everything flows down into Moscow.

Hedrick Smith, *The Russians,* 1977

The exterior landscape of Moscow is one of grandiose façades.

Ibid.

The Kremlin

. . . The Kremlin in which all the reminiscences of Moscow's past are united.

. . . 'There is nothing above Moscow,' says the proverb, 'except the Kremlin, and nothing above the Kremlin except Heaven.'

Karl Baedeker, *Russia, with Teheran, Port Arthur and Peking,* 1914

A curious irony has dowered the creed of utilitarianism with this edifice as the symbol of outward power. While collective man sits within, the walls deny him and the domes laugh aloud. Fantastic one has always known it to be from photographs. But the reality embodies fantasy on an unearthly scale – a mile and a half of weathered, rose-coloured brick in the form of a triangle that rises uphill from its base along the river. These airy walls, which in places attain a height of forty feet, are hedged with deep crenellations, cloven and coped in white stone after the Venetian fashion. Their impalpable tint and texture might suggest rather the protection of some fabled kitchen-garden than the exigencies of medieval assault. But from their mellow escarpments bursts a succession of nineteen towers, arbitrarily placed, and exhibiting such an accumulation of architectural improbability as might have resulted had the Brobdingnagians, during a game of chess, suddenly built a castle for Gulliver with the pieces. . . . Within the walls, rose a white hill, as it were a long table covered with a cloth of snow, lifting up to the winter sky the residences of those vanished potentates, Tsar and God: to the west the two palaces, nineteenth-century Russo-Venetian, cream-coloured against the presage of snow in the sky; the little Italian palace of the fifteenth century, whose grey-stone façade of diamond rustications conceals the tiny apartments of the early Tsars; and then the Cathedrals: that of the Annunciation, with nine orange-domes; that of the Dormition, where the coronations took place, with five helm-shaped domes; and that of the Archangel Michael, whose central bulb stands high above its four smaller companions; nineteen domes in all, each finished with a cross, most of them thinly gilt; and then, higher than all, the massive belfry, crowned with a flat onion; yet still overtopped by the ultimate cupola of the tower of Ivan Veliki, colossal in solitude, the climax of this Caesaropapist fantasia. I looked down to the river below me; I looked up to the sky; I looked to the right and I looked to the left: horizontally and vertically, towers and domes, spires, cones, onions, crenellations, filled the whole view. It might have been the invention of Dante, arrived in a Russian heaven.

Robert Byron, *First Russia, then Tibet,* 1933

There it stands for all that is secretive and sinister in the Russian character.

Lord Moran, *Winston Churchill, The Struggle for Survival,* 1966

My first impression of Moscow was of violent impact – a feeling so intense that, seeing the Kremlin for the first time, I wanted to swallow it in one great gulp. This was the real blood and bones of Russia – of Muscovy, of Pushkin's Golden-Headed Moscow.

The Kremlin! What words can conjure up this fabulous conglomeration of palaces, churches, prisons, treasure-houses, belfries, gilded cupolas, pinnacles and crimson walls? Its terror, its legends, its loveliness are like nothing else in all the world. No life, I felt, would be long enough to know it in all its aspects. Seeing it rising, sumptuous and barbaric, archetypal Russia, shimmering above the grey waters of the Moskva river, my degree of possessive, lovers' greed was such that my mouth watered.

Over the years the Kremlin's beauty has never staled

for me. No other building or site compares and, for me, it remains the eighth wonder of the world.

Lesley Blanch, *Journey into the Mind's Eye,* 1968

Lenin's mausoleum
In their determination that Lenin should sleep his last sleep surrounded by no single thing that either in its shape or colour should bear resemblance to the traditional Chapel in a Cathedral, the architects and designers have been forced back upon Modernity – and Modernity has produced something that has a slight resemblance to a Berlin Cinema-Palace. One leaves the poor dead figure where it has set up its everlasting rest in the red glare of its Cinema-cottage, and goes out into the night with one's aesthetic sensibilities unawakened.

Hubert Griffith, *Seeing Soviet Russia,* 1932

University of Moscow
I have never seen a building so lacking in humanity. It suggested an enormous termitary of cement.

James Kirkup, *One Man's Russia,* 1968

Nakhodka

The town is quite nobly sited on an inlet among hills and sea mountains, but, with its glum buildings, broken roads and sad blocks of workers' flats, it gave an impression of unspeakable joylessness and dreariness. There was a large number of drunks staggering about the streets. The people looked simply brutish and uncouth, and I did not see a single smartly dressed person.

James Kirkup, *One Man's Russia,* 1968

The Siberian port of Nakhodka in December gives the impression of being on the very edge of the world, in an atmosphere that does not quite support life. . . . There are lights burning, but they are like lighthouse beacons positioned to warn people who stray near Nakhodka that it is a place of danger and there is only emptiness beyond it. The subzero weather makes it odorless and not a single sound wrinkles its silence. It is the sort of place that gives rise to the notion that the earth is flat.

Paul Theroux, *The Great Railway Bazaar,* 1975

Novgorod

The melancholy ideas excited by the present appearance of Novgorod have been felt by all travellers. Who has not heard the ancient saying, which prevailed in the days of its greatness?

QUIS CONTRA DEOS, ET MAGNAM NOVOGORDIAM?
Who can resist the Gods and great Novgorod?

E.D. Clarke, *Travels in Various Countries,* 4th edn, 1816

Novgorod . . . resembles in size and charm an English cathedral city such as Salisbury, the centre of a large agricultural district, and built round a Kremlin instead of a close.

Robert Byron, *First Russia, then Tibet,* 1933

Odessa

Odessa is remarkable for the superior flavour of its mutton.

E.D. Clarke, *Travels in Various Countries,* 1816

I have not felt so much at home for a long time as I did when I 'raised the hill' and stood in Odessa for the first time. It looked just like an American city; fine broad streets, and straight as well; low houses (two or three stories), wide, neat, and free from any quaintness of architectural ornamentation; locust trees bordering the sidewalks (they call them acacias); a stirring business-look about the streets and the stores; fast walkers; a familiar *new* look about the houses and everything; yea, and a driving and smothering cloud of dust that was so like a message from our own dear native land that we could hardly refrain from shedding a few grateful tears and execrations in the old time-honoured American way. Look up the street, or down the street, this way or that, we saw only America . . . and then we came upon a church and a hack-driver, and presto! – the illusion vanished! The church had a slender-spired dome that rounded inward at its base, and looked like a turnip turned upside-down, and the hackman seemed to be dressed in a long petticoat without any hoops.

Mark Twain, *The Innocents Abroad,* 1869

Odessa is the dingiest, most dog-eared city I saw in the USSR; it looks as if mold were growing all over it.

John Gunther, *Inside Russia Today,* 1962 edn

Okhotsk

In spite of the attentions and hospitality heaped upon me by the inhabitants of Okotsk, I could not regret my departure. It has such a sameness – so little to be seen – so little to interest – and, what was worse than all, so much scandal circulating there, that every thing done in Irkutsk and St Petersburg was sure to be known in a very short time.

Captain John Dundas Cochrane, *Narrative of a Pedestrian Journey through Russia, etc.,* 1824

Okhotsk may literally be called the end of the world.

Harry de Windt, *From Pekin to Calais by Land,* 1889

River Okota

Lord Byron swam the Hellespont, and John Cochrane

the Okota. Of the two feats, mine was surely the most difficult: his lordship was neither fatigued, hungry, nor cold, nor compelled to his undertaking; while I had each and all of those evils to contend with.

Captain John Dundas Cochrane, *Narrative of a Pedestrian Journey through Russia, etc.*, 1824

Perm

I reached the city at midnight, exceedingly worn out. The police, mistaking me for a horse, gave me a stable for a lodging.

Captain John Dundas Cochrane, *Narrative of a Pedestrian Journey through Russia, etc.*, 1824

Petropavlosk – Kamchatski

The hills about the Bay rising with a gentle ascent & covered with Trees afford many prospects equal and not unlike to Mount Edgecumbe near Plymouth. There is one View here that excells any I ever met with, which is that of the Summit of a very high Mountain far inland that is covered with Snow, which rising beyond some Hills of moderate height covered with Verdure presents through the Vally a most delightful and grand Picture, exhibiting the Image of Summer and Winter at one View.

David Samwell, *Journal*, August 1779

St Peter and St Paul's, the chief city of the peninsula of Kamchatka, contains forty-two dwellings, besides fifteen edifices belonging to the government, an old church, and the foundation of a new one. Among the public buildings are to be reckoned magazines for bread, for powder, for sailors, for convicts, for wine, and for arms; a guard-house, smithy, hospital, chancery, school, and a building for the chief and his assistant. All, however, with the exception of the hospital, sailors' barracks, and school, are, at best, like the rest of the city, but emblems of misery and wretchedness. I have never seen, even on the banks of the Frozen Sea, so contemptible a place, hardly meriting the name of a village, much less that of a city; yet such is the place which has been so eulogised from one end of the world to the other. The erection of hospitals, of schools, of churches, and the diffusion of happiness and knowledge have been extravagantly vaunted of in magazines and reviews, in defiance of the most lamentable facts of a very opposite description.

Captain John Dundas Cochrane, *Narrative of a Pedestrian Journey through Russia, etc.*, 1824

If an anti-communist Hollywood film director were to dream up the worst Russian set he could think of, I don't think he could outdo the reality of Petropavlovsk. The mud and filth, the condition of the roads and sidewalks, the fleet of chalets sinking into the bog, assuming distorted shapes as they slowly go down, the corpses of the animals on the side-roads, – side roads that give the impression of having been shelled.

René McColl, *Just Back from Russia*, 1954

Pushkin (formerly Zarsko-Selo)

Zarsko-Selo . . . is the completest triumph of barbarous taste that I have seen in these northern kingdoms. The situation is low, commanding hardly any natural advantages to claim such a preference. It is very large, and the front extends to a great length, as there is only one story besides the ground floors. In defiance of common sense, as well as of the weather and the climate, all the capitals of the pillars, the statues, and many other parts of the external structure are gilt: the eye indeed, meets scarcely any thing else than gilding, in the apartments within. One room is decorated with a very singular and uncommon style of magnificence, the sides of the apartment being composed entirely of amber, on which are disposed festoons, and other ornaments of the same curious production. Its transparency, and the consciousness of its rarity, have a fine effect.

Sir N.W. Wraxall, *A Tour Round the Baltic*, 1775

The palace of Tsarkoselo . . . is built of brick, plastered over . . . and it is entirely covered, in a most barbarous taste, with columns, and pilasters, and cariatides, stuck between the windows. All of these, in the true style of Dutch gingerbread, are gilded. The whole of the building is a compound of what an architect ought to avoid, rather than to imitate.

E.D. Clarke, *Travels in Various Countries*, 4th edn, 1816

As we proceeded there suddenly rose to the south-east a tremendous blaze, the cause of which it seemed difficult to conjecture. At first I imagined it might be, as I had often seen in England, a blazing bonfire, with a group of mirthful rustics revelling round it. But the scene grew soon too terrific to allow of so simple a solution, the flame rising to a prodigious height, and the smoke rolling into a beautiful dark arch on the clear sky. Immense masses of fire, and sparks at intervals exploded and separated like a rocket.

We continued to gaze as we advanced, till, on reaching the beautiful town of Tzarsko Selo, the source was, indeed, but too apparent; it was the Emperor's favourite palace, wrapped in an inextinguishable flame. I had looked forward with hope to the survey of so celebrated an edifice. . . . It was midnight; parties of men surrounded the wasting pile. All, however, was order and regularity; not a voice was heard amid the thousands of people employed. The Emperor was present, evidently impressed with extreme regret, and . . . continued to give directions with perfect coolness. . . .

Being excessively fatigued, and finding my individual exertions perfectly useless towards checking the progress of the flames, I retired to the gardens, where I passed a couple of restless hours on a bed of moss, amid herbs and flowers, whose sweet perfumes were as yet unvanquished by the fire or smoke. Some demon hovered over me, and my dreams presented the probable incidents of my journey, in all the horrors which imagination could shadow forth. I arose, and returned to the scene of devastation, now evidently increasing, and appearing to defy the numerous engines pouring upon it from all sides.

Captain John Dundas Cochrane, *Narrative of a Pedestrian Journey through Russia, etc.*, 1824

Riga

The city of Riga itself, is a most disagreeable one: the buildings being crowded together, and surrounded by fortifications which prevent a possibility of alteration, or amendment in this respect. The houses are all high, and the streets very narrow, ill paved, and very dirty. The suburbs are as large as the place itself, and are possessed by native Russians; the municipal privileges of Riga, which are rigidly maintained, excluding them from the capacity of exercising any trade within its walls.

Sir N.W. Wraxall, *A Tour Round the Baltic,* 1775

There *was* something decayed, 'Parisian,' rather shocking in an old-fashioned way about the place . . . a kind of aristocratic Brighton to which one slipped away from a Duchess's bed with someone from the theatre, someone to be described in terms of flowers and pink ribbons, chocolates and champagne in the slipper, of black silk stockings and corsets. All the lights in Riga were dimmed by ten: the public gardens were quite dark and full of whispers, giggles from hidden seats, excited rustles in the bushes. One had the sense of a whole town on the tiles. It was fascinating, it appealed immensely to the historical imagination, but it certainly wasn't something new, lovely and happy.

Graham Greene, *Journey without Maps,* 1936

Samarkand

Then shal my native city *Samarcanda*
And christall waves of fresh *Iaertis* streame,
The pride and beautie of her princely seat,
Be famous through the furthest continents,
For there my Pallace royal shal be plac'd:
Whose shyning Turrets shal dismay the heavens,
And cast the fame of *Ilions* Tower to hell.

Christopher Marlow, *Tamburlane the Great,* Part II, *c.* 1588

and Bukhara

In all other parts of the world light descends upon earth. From holy Samarkand and Bukhara, it ascends.

Old proverb, quoted by John Gunther, *Inside Russia Today,* 1962 edn

I have hazarded the statement that the Righistan of Samarkand was originally, and is still even in its ruin, the noblest public square in the world. I know of nothing in the East approaching it in massive simplicity and grandeur; and nothing in Europe, save perhaps on a humbler scale – the Piazza di San Marco at Venice – which can even aspire to enter the competition. No European spectacle indeed can adequately be compared with it, in our inability to point to an open space in any Western city that is commanded on three of its four sides by Gothic cathedrals of the finest order.

Hon. G.N. Curzon, *Russia in Central Asia,* 1889

For lust of knowing what should not be known,
We take the golden road to Samarkand.

James Elroy Flecker, *Hassan,* 1913

Sevastopol

Sevastopol we found full of things that did not interest. Sullen fortifications, threatening batteries, gaunt barracks, slimy docks, deadly mines, bastions, earthworks, hospitals, and cemeteries are its stock-in-trade. No one, except an undertaker can be jovial in such a place. The town is overrun with military and naval authorities, whose occupation, the whole day long, is to salute one another.

John Foster Fraser, *Round the World on a Wheel,* 1899

I am afraid we disapproved of Sevastopol *in toto.* The pink-and-white town, nestling in ridges between creeks of vivid blue; glimpses of white alleys with their riotous patches of colouring; the warm, sweet scents that came down these alleys from the banks of flowers – all these did not appeal to our aesthetic soul. For a time we tried to people the town with soldiery and the horrors of war, to pander to our lust for sensations – held those barren hills Russian, those with English troops, and annihilated thousands on various slopes; but bathos would creep in.

Denis Garstin, *Friendly Russia,* 1915

Drove with Jumbo Wilson, Alex and the Chiefs of Staff to Sebastopol. We got out of the cars after leaving Balaclava, when the C.I.G.S. pulled out a map, which he studied attentively for some time; then he gave it back to his A.D.C. and pointed to the valley below us.

'That's where the Light Brigade charged.' But I noticed that no one was paying any attention to his discourse; they were all looking intently at a skull, a thigh bone and some ribs scattered on the ground. One of them touched the skull with his foot.

'Can you,' he whispered, 'tell if it is a Russian or a German skull?'

Lord Moran, Diary, 7 February 1945, in *Winston Churchill, The Struggle for Survival,* 1966

Siberia

In Siberia, 100 miles is ordinary distance, 100 roubles an ordinary sum, but a day without sunshine is extraordinary.

Old proverb

In the end of the Region of these Tartars, is a Countrey reaching to the furthest North, called Darknesse, because the most part of the Winter moneths, the Sunne appeares not, and the Ayre is thicke and darkish, as betimes in the morning with us. The men there are pale and great, have no prince, and live like beasts.

Marco Polo, 1320, in *Purchas his Pilgrimes,* 1625

But what is this? Our infant Winter sinks,
Divested of his grandeur, should our eye
Astonish'd shoot into the Frigid Zone,
Where for relentless months continued Night
Holds o'er the glittering waste her starry reign.
There, through the prison of unbounded wilds,
Barr'd by the hand of Nature from escape,
Wide roams the Russian exile. Nought around
Strikes his sad eye, but deserts lost in snow;
And heavy-loaded groves; and solid floods,
That stretch, athwart the solitary vast,
Their icy horrors to the Frozen Main;
And cheerless towns far distant, never bless'd,
Save when its annual course the caravan
Bends to the golden coast of rich Cathay,
With news of human-kind. Yet there life glows;
Yet cherish'd there, beneath the shining waste,
The furry nations harbour: – tipp'd with jet,
Fair ermines, spotless as the snows they press;
Sables, of glossy black; and, dark-embrown'd,
Or beauteous freak'd with many a mingled hue,
Thousands besides, the costly pride of courts.
There, warm together press'd, the trooping deer
Sleep on the new-fallen snows; and, scarce his head
Raised o'er the happy wreath, the branching elk
Lies slumbering sullen in the white abyss. . . .
There through the piny forest, half absorb'd,
Rough tenant of these shades, the shapeless bear,
With dangling ice all horrid, stalks forlorn,
Slow-pac'd, and sourer as the storms increase;
He makes his bed beneath th' inclement drift,
And, with stern patience, scorning weak complaint,
Hardens his heart against assailing want.

James Thomson, *The Seasons – Winter,* 1726

There is . . . so little of interest in Siberia, so little to be seen, that it is hardly possible to form an interesting work on that topic, unless the traveller be a botanist or naturalist, or otherwise versed in the mysteries of science. Siberia is, in fact, one immense wilderness, whose inhabitants are so scattered, that five or six hundred miles are passed by the traveller without seeing an individual, much less any cultivation, or any works of man at all worthy of description. The manners, customs, and dress of most of the inhabitants are the same. The severity of the climate is in most places co-equal, and in general, productive of the same results. The matter of interest is to be compressed into so small a space; and all that I may be said to have done, may consist in the fact of showing others, that a man may go where he chooses.

Captain John Dundas Cochrane, *Narrative of a Pedestrian Journey through Russia, etc.,* 1824

In Siberia's wastes
  The Ice-wind's breath
Wounded like the toothed steel;
Lost Siberia doth reveal
  Only blight and death.

Blight and death alone.
  No Summer shines
Night is interblent with Day.
In Siberia's wastes always
  The blood slackens, the heart pines.

In Siberia's wastes
  No tears are shed,
For they freeze within the brain.
Nought is felt but dullest pain,
  Pain acute, yet dead;

Pain as in a dream,
  When years go by
Funeral-paced, yet fugitive
When man lives, and doth not live,
  Doth not live – nor die.

In Siberia's wastes
  Are sands and rocks.
Nothing blooms of green or soft,
But the snow-peaks rise aloft
  And the gaunt ice-blocks.

And the exile there
  Is one with those;
They are part, and he is part,
For the sands are in his heart,
  And the killing snows.

James Clarence Mangan, 'Siberia', in the *Nation,* 18 April 1846

I found the prisons of Siberia clean and comfortable.

Harry de Windt, *From Pekin to Calais by Land,* 1889.

Picture the neighbourhood of Aldershot with its undulating pine-clad hills suddenly transplanted into the depths of the black country lying around Newcastle-on-Tyne. For stone buildings, let him substitute filthy, tumble-down houses of unpainted wood, almost undistinguishable at a distance from the dark, greasy soil around them. People these villages with dirty, wild-looking men clad in sheepskins and gaudy-coloured rags, and still dirtier half-naked women. Conceive a sickly smell (peculiar to Asiatic Russia) of old skins, wood, smoke, turpentine, and sewage, and a Siberian landscape is before you.

Ibid.

You can take the whole of the United States of America, from Maine to California and from Lake Superior to the Gulf of Mexico, and set it down in the middle of Siberia, without touching anywhere the boundaries of the latter's territory; you can then take Alaska and all the countries of Europe, with the exception of Russia, and fit them into the remaining margin like the pieces of a dissected map. After having thus accommodated all of the United States, including Alaska, and the whole of Europe, except Russia, you will still have more than 300,000 miles of Siberian territory to spare. In other words, you will still have unoccupied in Siberia an area half as large again as the Empire of Germany.

George Kennan, *Siberia and the Exile System,* 1891

On the whole, I am satisfied that America has no future in the Pacific. She can turn south, indeed, but after all, the west coast of South America offers very little field. Her best chance is Siberia. Russia will probably go to pieces; she is rotten and decrepit to the core, and must pass through a bankruptcy, political and moral. If it can be delayed another twenty-five years, we could Americanise Siberia, and this is the only possible work that I can see still open on a scale equal to American means.

Henry Adams, Letter to Henry Cabot Lodge, 4 August 1891

Imagine a barren, snow-clad Sahara absolutely uninhabited for the first six hundred miles, and then sparsely peopled by the filthiest race in creation, and you may faintly realise the region traversed by my expedition for nearly two months of continuous travel from the last Russian outpost to Bering Straits. Place a piece of coal sprinkled with salt on a white tablecloth, a few inches off it scatter some lump sugar, and it will give you in miniature a very fair presentment of the scenery. The coal is the bleak coast-line continually swept clear of snow by furious gales; the sugar, sea-ice, and the cloth the frozen beach over which we journeyed for over 1600 miles. . . . Fair and foul weather in the Arctic reminded me of some beautiful woman, bejewelled and radiant amid lights and laughter, and the same divinity landing dishevelled, pale, and seasick from the deck of a Channel steamer.

Harry de Windt, *From Paris to New York by Land,* 1904

Siberians tell a joke against themselves, that reveals something of their attitude to Siberia: 'It's a place where 100 roubles is not money, 1,000 kilometres is no distance, and half a litre of vodka is no drink.'

Eric Newby, 'In the Land of Ghenghis Khan', *Observer,* 1 October 1978

The Steppes en route to Moscow

These steppes have their own very personal kind of beauty, in which the monotony of their apparent endlessness is after all only that monotony which is an element of all fine style, in nature as well as in art.

Arthur Symons, *Cities,* 1903

Sredni-Kolymsk

The most pitiable characteristic about Sredni-Kolymsk is perhaps the morbid influence of the place and its surroundings on the mental powers. . . . Indeed, I can safely state that, with three exceptions, there was not a perfectly sane man or woman amongst all the exiles I saw here.

'A couple of years usually makes them shaky,' said an official, 'and the strongest-minded generally become childish when they have been here for five or six.'

'But why is it?' I asked.

My friend walked to the window, and pointed to the mournful street, the dismal hovels, and frozen river darkening in the dusk.

'That,' he said, 'and the awful silence. Day after day, year after year, not a sound. I have stood in that street at mid-day and heard a watch tick in my pocket.'

Harry de Windt, *From Paris to New York by Land,* 1904

The Crim Tartars

For person and complexion they have broade and flatte visages, of a tanned colour into yellow and blacke, fierce and cruell lookes, thinne haired upon the upper lippe, and pitte of the chinne, light and nimble bodied, with short legges, as if they were made naturally for horsemen: whereto they practise themselves from their childhood, seldome going afoot about anie businesse. Their speech is verie sudden and loude, speaking as it were out of a deepe hollowe throate. When they sing you would thinke a kowe lowed, or some great bandogge howled. Their greatest exercise is shooting, wherein they traine up their children from their verie infancie, not suffering them to eate till they have shot neere the marke within a certaine scantling. They are the very same that sometimes were called Scythae Nomades, or the Scythian shepheards, by the Greekes and Latines.

Giles Fletcher (1588), in Richard Hakluyt, *Principal Navigations . . . of the English Nation,* 1598–1600

So a wilde *Tartar* when he spies
A man that's handsome, valiant, wise,
If he can kill him, thinks t'inherit
His Wit, his Beauty, and his Spirit.

Samuel Butler, *Hudibras,* 1663–78

Tchuktchi (people of the Russian far north-east)

When a Tchuktchi gets drunk, his first impulse is to get a rifle and shoot. He prefers a white man to practise upon, but if there are none handy he will kill anybody, even his mother, without compunction, and be very sorry for it when he is sober.

Harry de Windt, *From Paris to New York by Land,* 1904

Tobolsk

Tobolsky, from the number and rank of the exiled, is become a large and populous city, full of shops, and containing theatres, besides other places of public amusement. Its inhabitants, above two thousand versts from *Moscow,* have booksellers, masquerades, French hotels, and French wines, with the porter and beer of England. Those who have resided there, either as officers on duty, as travellers, or as exiles, give the highest accounts of its gaiety and population. An officer of considerable rank in the Russian service told us, he would rather have the half of his pay and live at *Tobolsky,* than the whole of it in residence at *Petersburg.* . . . This is no subject of wonder. *Tobolsky* is admirably adapted to the Russian taste . . . it is the very temple of *Bacchus* and *Indolence.*

E.D. Clarke, *Travels in Various Countries,* 4th edn, 1816

Tobolsk is distinctly the prettiest town in Siberia. . . . On first appearance one is reminded not a little of Gibraltar.

Harry de Windt, *From Pekin to Calais by Land,* 1889

Ukraine

We passed through the Ukraine, which depressed me in spite of its rich black soil, for I remembered how before the war I had stayed there in the magnificent hospitality of Polish friends, riding, dancing, laughing; living at a fantastic rate in that fantastic oasis of extravagance and feudalism, ten thousand horses on the estate, eighty English hunters, and a pack of English hounds; a park full of dromedaries; another park, walled in, full of wild animals kept for sport; Tokay of 1750 handed round by a giant; cigarettes handed round by dwarfs in eighteenth century liveries; and where was all that now? Gone, as it deserved to go; the house razed to the ground till it was lower than the wretched hovels of the peasants, the estate parcelled out, cut in half by the new Polish frontier, the owner dead with his brains blown out, and his last penny gambled away in Paris.

V. Sackville-West, *Passenger to Teheran,* 1926

Ural Mountains

Thence to Bisserkaya Krepost, over eighteen miles of uncultivated country, after which I gently ascended a considerable elevation into the bosom of the Ural mountains, where not a vestige of cultivation exists besides young firs and birch. The sun was exceedingly cold on the summit. At noon I stopped at the last European station, called Kirgishantsky Krepost, and at the last European residence, where I dined. The good people had resolved I should not leave the paramount quarter of the globe with any trace of dissatisfaction, as young children continually presented me with wild strawberries and cream; the strawberries were of excellent flavour, and it is the custom of these poor people to present the traveller with such fruit during the season. I received the present, standing with one foot in Asia and the other in Europe, surrounded on all sides by lofty mountains, covered, however, with nothing but brush-wood.

Captain John Dundas Cochrane, *Narrative of a Pedestrian Journey through Russia, etc.,* 1824

Verkhoyansk

Loyal Russians call Verkhoyansk the heart of Siberia. Political exiles have another name for the place also commencing with the letter H, which I leave to the reader's imagination.

Harry de Windt, *From Paris to New York by Land,* 1904

Vitebsk

Do you think I have come so far to conquer these miserable huts?

Napoleon, before marching on to Moscow, attrib.,1812

Volga River

'What does the Volga look like?' is the question, I

suppose people wish to have answered. My answer to that is that in various parts of its course the Volga reminds me of almost every river I have ever seen, from the Dart to the Liao-he, and from the Neckar to the Nile.

Maurice Baring, *What I Saw in Russia,* 1913

Yakutia

Yakutia is the enormous backyard of Russia.

Erik de Mauny, *Russian Prospect,* 1969

Yakutsk

Again settled in Yakutsk, I had time to walk about and see all that is worth seeing. If my former opinion of it was bad, it is now worse; the only alteration being, that some of the churches and the monastery have been white-washed. There are about a dozen respectable-looking houses, the inmates of which are not even on speaking terms with one another.

Captain John Dundas Cochrane, *Narrative of a Pedestrian Journey through Russia, etc.,* 1824

A more lifeless, depressing city does not exist on the face of this planet. Even Siberians call this the end of the world.

Harry de Windt, *From Paris to New York by Land,* 1904

The end of the line except that there is no line to be the end of.

Erik de Mauny, quoted Hedrick Smith, *The Russians,* 1977

Yalta

Yalta is called the Brighton of Russia. It is not that.

John Foster Fraser, *Round the World on a Wheel,* 1899

Yalta is one of the most obviously beautiful places I have ever seen. A town of white houses that struggle for a foothold between the great green heights and the blue sea, it has often been compared to Monte Carlo and the inhabitants, having been infected with our disease of calling one place by the name of another, continually think fit to advertise it as Russia's Riviera.

When I came back to live there, I found it had a personality no European town could ever acquire.

Denis Garstin, *Friendly Russia,* 1915

Zachiversk (near River Indigurka, area of modern Tyugyuren, Sikerin and Bertes)

Of all the places I have ever seen, bearing the name of a city or town, this is the most dreary and desolate; my blood froze within me as I beheld and approached the place. . . . I have, during my service in the navy, and during a period when seamen were scarce, seen a merchant ship with sixteen guns and only fifteen men, but I never before saw a town with only seven inhabitants. . . . The planner or proposer of this site for a town might deserve punishment, but certainly less than that of being made its perpetual commander.

Captain John Dundas Cochrane, *Narrative of a Pedestrian Journey through Russia, etc.,* 1824

RWANDA
(and Burundi, formerly Ruanda-Urundi)

A fierce mountainous bastion, with great crenellated ramparts, the last refuge of strange men, whose physical and psychical contrasts at the same time separate and unite them . . . in the very heart of Africa, a tenacious survival of Biblical times, with their shepherd kings and cruel and patriarchal customs . . . a lost world where life continues untroubled to the peaceful voice of nature.

Official Government Handbook (?), quoted by Art Buchwald, *I Chose Caviar,* 1957

That African Switzerland.

Negley Farson, *Behind God's Back,* 1940

S

ST HELENA

The Iland of S. Helena, where the Portugals use to relieve themselves.

Thomas Cavendish (1588), in Richard Hakluyt, *Principal Navigations . . . of the English Nation,* 1598–1600

The Ile is very even and delightful above, and gives a large prospect into the Ocean. Tis a saying with the Sea-men, a man there has his choice, whether he will break his heart going up, or his necke comming downe, either wish bestowing more oicundity then comfort.

Sir Thomas Herbert, *A Relation of Some Yeares Travaile, begunne Anno 1626,* 1634

Never saw itt more greene and Flourishing in grasse and trees then Now att present. . . . Never soe Many lemmons, having Now Found among the woodes Many other trees Not formerly knowne by them, Most bending with their burthens, on whome beesides the Multitude off well coulloured ripe ones were as Many greene and smalle, and Many More blossomes; the Cattle allsoe Never in better case: all this alofft. . . . For from the place where wee rode, which was on the Northwest side, there is hardly such another Ragged, steepy, stony, high, Cragged, rocky, barren, Desolate and Comfortlesse coaste to bee seene, all the way uppe suteable in Most places. But above the ground is of excellentt Mold, all though For the Most part in very high round, rising, small hills, steepy ascentts and Discentts, payneffull and Difficultt to bee travelled; beetweene each these swellings a Running water; commonly Few playnes; the higher the land the better ground; here and there groves and woodes off small trees, and in other places thicketts off Shrubbes, weedes and Fearnes, harbours for hogges as the rockes for the goates; All the rest yeilding good grasse; allsoe some Mints, Malloes, purcelane, a kind off Camomill smelling very sweet are here to bee Found.

Peter Mundy, *Travels in Europe and Asia,* 1638

That poor, but healthy place.

William Dampier, *Voyages and Descriptions,* 1699

I certainly never left a place in which I had resided a fortnight with so little regret as I did St Helena. The comforts it affords are few indeed.

William Hickey, *Memoirs,* 1749–1809

Insects there are . . . a few, and one species of snail, which inhabits only the tops of the highest ridges, and has probably been there ever since their original creation. . . . For my part I confess I feel more wonder at finding a little snail on the top of the ridges of St Helena, than in finding people upon America, or any other part of the globe.

Sir Joseph Banks, *Journal of the Rt Hon Sir Joseph Banks* (May 1771), 1768–71

Judge if I did not rejoice at the sight of this romantic Island; though its appearance from the sea is very unpromising, – inaccessible rocks, and stupendous crags frowning every side but one, nor is there any anchorage except at that point. – The town is literally an ascending valley between two hills, just wide enough to admit of one street. The houses are in the English style, with sashed windows, and small doors. Here are back-gardens, but no gardens; which makes the place intensely hot for want of a free circulation of air; but when you once ascend *Ladder Hill* the scene changes, and all seems enchantment. The most exquisite prospects you can conceive burst suddenly on the eye – fruitful vallies, – cultivated hills and diversified scenery of every description. The inhabitants are obliging and attentive, indeed, remarkably; so altogether I find it a most welcome resting place.

Eliza Fay, *Original Letters from India* (24 September 1782), 1817

At first I thought it rather extensive, but it seemed to diminish as we approached.

Count de las Cases, *Journal of the Private Life and Conversations of the Emperor Napoleon at St Helena* (15 October 1815), 1824

In this accursed island (*isola maladetta*), . . . there is neither sun nor moon to be seen for the greatest part of the year. Constant rain and fog. It is worse than Capri.

Napoleon, remark, 19 April 1816, quoted Barry O'Meara, *Napoleon in Exile, A Voice from St Helena,* 1822

'Everything is judged by comparison in this world,' said the Emperor; 'The island of Elba, which a year ago, was thought so disagreeable, is a paradise compared to St Helena. As for this Island, it may set all future regret at defiance.'

Napoleon, quoted Count de las Cases, *Journal of the Private Life and Conversations of the Emperor Napoleon at St Helena* (20 February 1816), 1824

'How far is St. Helena from the field of Austerlitz?'
You couldn't hear me if I told – so loud the cannon roar.
But not so far for people who are living by their wits.
(*'Gay go up' means 'Gay go down' the wide world o'er!*)

'How far is St. Helena from an Emperor of France?'
I cannot see – I cannot tell – the Crowns they dazzle so.
The Kings sit down to dinner, and the Queens stand up to dance.
(*After open weather you may look for snow!*)

'How far is St. Helena from the Capes of Trafalgar?'
A longish way – a longish way – with ten year more to run.
It's South across the water underneath a falling star.
(*What you cannot finish you must leave undone!*)

'How far is St. Helena from the Beresina ice?'
An ill way – a chill way – the ice begins to crack.
But not so far for gentlemen who never took advice.
(*When you can't go forward you must e'en come back!*)

'How far is St. Helena from the field of Waterloo?'
A near way – a clear way – the ship will take you soon.
A pleasant place for gentlemen with little left to do.
(*Morning never tries you till the afternoon!*)

Rudyard Kipling, 'A St. Helena Lullaby', *Rewards and Fairies,* 1910

ST KITTS (formerly St Christopher)

The first and best earth that ever was inhabited by Englishmen amongst the heathen cannibals in America.

? 1667. Quoted in V. S. Naipaul, *The Middle Passage,* 1963

The ruggedness of this central cluster only renders the contrast of the cultivated lands below more striking, and the entire prospect is so charming, that I could not help agreeing with the captain's clerk, who said he wondered that Colon, who was so delighted with this island as to give it his own name, should not have made a full stop upon its shores. I do not uphold the pun, but upon the whole it was well enough for a hot climate and a captain's clerk.

H.N. Coleridge, *Six Months in the West Indies in 1825,* 1826

ST LUCIA

The first approach to this island from the south offers the most striking combination of various kinds of scenery that I have ever seen. Two rocks, which the gods call Pitons, and men Sugar-loaves, rise perpendicularly out of the sea, and shoot to a great height in parallel cones which taper away towards the summit like the famous spires of Coventry. These rocks, which are feathered from the clouds to the waves with evergreen foliage, stand like pillars of Hercules on either side of the entrance into a small but deep and beautiful bay. A pretty little village or plantation appears at the bottom of the cove; the sandy beach stretches like a line of silver round the blue water, and the cane fields form a broad belt of vivid green in the back ground. Behind this, the mountains, which run north and south throughout the island, rise in the most fantastic shapes, here cloven into steep-down chasms, there darting into arrowy points, and every where shrouded or swathed, as it were, in wood, which the hand of man will probably never lay low. The clouds, which within the tropics are infallibly attracted by any woody eminences, contribute greatly to the wildness of the scene; sometimes they are so dense as to bury the mountains in darkness; at other times they float transparently like a silken veil; frequently the flaws from the gulleys perforate the vapors and make windows in the smoky mass, and then again, the wind and the sun will cause the whole to be drawn upwards majestically like the curtain of a gorgeous theatre.

H.N. Coleridge, *Six Months in the West Indies in 1825,* 1827

Castries

Architecturally speaking, Castries seems to be the victim of a curse. It is always catching fire and being burnt to the ground. . . . It seems to be a magnet for Acts of God, and the ugliness of the town has thus nothing intentional and perverted about it.

It looked merely as if the inhabitants, sceptical of the permanence of their handiwork, had got tired of building it up again.

Patrick Leigh Fermor, *The Traveller's Tree,* 1951

EL SALVADOR

El Salvador is known affectionately as the Ruhr of Central America, but I can't believe the Ruhr is anything like so exciting. In El Salvador eighty-two per cent of the population is born illegitimate, seventeen per cent of the women who enter hospital are found to have syphilis, and the second most popular cause of death, after gastritis, is homicide. Over the whole country, lost in ethereal mists of wealth, privilege and nepotism, swim the Fourteen Families.

Nicholas Wollaston, *Red Rumba,* 1962

San Salvador

San Salvador, prone to earthquakes, was not a pretty

place; it sprawled, it was noisy, its buildings were charmless, and in the glare of headlights were buoyant particles of dust. Why would anyone come here? 'Don't knock it,' an American in San Salvador told me. 'You haven't seen Nicaragua yet!'

Paul Theroux, *The Old Patagonian Express,* 1979

Santa Ana

The town looked Godforsaken; in fact it was comfortable. It was a nice combination of attributes. In every respect, Santa Ana, the most Central American of Central American towns, was a perfect place – perfect in its pious attitudes and pretty girls, perfect in its slumber, its coffee-scented heat, its jungly plaza, and in the dusty elegance of its old buildings whose whitewash at nightfall gave them a vivid phosphorescence. Even its volcano was in working order.

Paul Theroux, *The Old Patagonian Express,* 1979

SAMOA

It is suggested to me that you might like to know what will be my future society. Three consuls, all at loggerheads with one another, or at the best in clique of two against one; three different sects of missionaries, not upon the best of terms; and the Catholics and Protestants in a condition of unhealable ill-feeling as to whether a wooden drum should or should not be beaten to announce the time of school. The native population very genteel, very songful, very agreeable, very good-looking, chronically spoiling for a fight. . . . As for the white population of (technically) 'The Beach', I don't suppose it is possible for any person not thoroughly conversant with the South Seas to form the smallest conception of such a society, with its grog-shops, its apparently unemployed hangers-on, its merchants of all degrees of respectability and the reverse.

Robert Louis Stevenson, Letter to E.L. Burlingame, 13 July 1890

If you want a lecture on Samoan politics, I am in a fair way to be able to give you one; for though I loathe the very word, and of all kinds of politics detest most those of islands, I am just soaked with the stuff here, where the natives are children, full of little jealousies and intrigues, and the foreigners are rather worse than the natives. The three foreign powers have made a mess, and the natives are in it.

Henry Adams, Letter to Elizabeth Cameron, 12 October 1890

If you wish to go there you will have no trouble about finding it if you follow the directions given by Robert Louis Stevenson to Dr Conan Doyle and to Mr J.M. Barrie. 'You go to America, cross the continent to San Francisco, and then it's the second turning to the left.'

Mark Twain, *More Tramps Abroad,* 1897

In the South Seas the Creator seems to have laid himself out to show what he *can* do.

Rupert Brooke, *Letters from America, 1913,* 1916

Samoans

I believe that ennui is the chief cause of their wars.

Henry Adams, Letter to Elizabeth Cameron, 15 December 1890

The natives are the next thing conceivable to Highlanders before the forty-five.

Robert Louis Stevenson, Letter to J.M. Barrie, 5 December 1892

Manu'a

The three islands of Manu'a are independent, and are ruled over by a little slip of a half-caste girl of about twenty, who sits all day in a pink gown, in a little white European house, with about a quarter of an acre of roses in front of it, looking at the palm-trees on the village street, and listening to the surf. This, so far as I could discover, was all she had to do. 'This is a very dull place,' she said.

Robert Louis Stevenson, Letter to Henry James, 7 July 1894

Tau

There is the most peculiar sensation one gets here from even a few hours in a native house, a different taste in the mouth, a sense of heavy, almost sticky heat, a feeling as if one's skin were going to fly off in thin gossamer layers and a curious buzzing inside one's head, mostly from the strain of listening. I don't know exactly what is responsible for it, possibly the food and sitting cross-legged and the flies.

Margaret Mead, Letter from Samoa, 11 December 1925, in *Letters from the Field, 1925–75,* 1977

SAUDI ARABIA

The most part of these deserts is neither fit for herbage or tillage, being covered over with a dry and a thick sand, which the wind transporteth whither it listeth, in heaps and mountains, that often intercept and indanger fatigued travellers. The inhabitants here are few; so are their cities; their dwellings being in sequestrate dens, and hair-cloth tents: the most of their wealth consisteth in camels, dromedaries, and goats.

William Lithgow, *Rare Adventures and Painfull Peregrinations*, 1614/32

The people generally are addicted to theft, rapine, and robberies; hating all sciences, mechanical or civil: they are commonly all of the second stature, swift of foot, wicked, and seditious, boisterous in speech, of a tawny colour, boasting much of their tribal antiquity and noble gentry; notwithstanding their garments are born with them from the bare belly, their food also like to their ruvid condition, and as savagely tame, I protest, as the four-footed citizens of Libya.

Ibid.

When Colonel Lawrence visited Doughty, he asked him how he came to go to Arabia. The reply made by the author of *Arabia Deserta* was that he went there 'in order to rescue English Prose from the slough into which it had fallen.'

I have this from Colonel Lawrence, and as near as I can remember, those were the words used.

Wyndham Lewis, *Blasting and Bombardiering*, 1937

Kleenex is a good deal more important in modern Arabia than the camel.

Helga Graham, *Arabian Time Machine*, 1978

Riyadh

One does not often see a whole city being built at one moment, but this is what is happening here.

Arnold Toynbee, *East to West*, 1958

SENEGAL

Dakar

Dakar was the Baudelaire of *L'Invitation au Voyage*, when it was not the René Clair of *Le Million*.

Graham Greene, *Journey without Maps*, 1936

Dakar has been fittingly called 'the boomingest boom town on the continent.' It is a real city, in the European manner, and resembles a smaller Casablanca; we have come a long way from West Coast towns like Lagos and Accra, which are camps made of mud and tin, or the shabby, disgraceful squalor of Monrovia. Dakar is somewhat tawdry at the edges like any provincial town built practically overnight, and looks like a Florida real-estate development; its harbour is one of the most important in Africa, but it has no substantial hinterland; it lives on government, the sea, and peanuts. . . . The joke is that Dakar is being fitted out to be the capital of France, if the French are beaten in World War III.

John Gunther, *Inside Africa*, 1955

The climate is not only better than most in Africa but better than that of France. . . . The Africans there have learned the old French skill of simultaneously shrugging the shoulders, raising both hands with fingers extended outwards in a sign of bewilderment, smoking a Gauloise, pouting the lower lip, and driving a car. They have inherited the French love of notices telling you what not to do. I particularly liked the scrawl on the wall of a back street in Dakar: 'Défense de stationner et d'uriner.'

Richard West, *The White Tribes of Africa*, 1965

The true prostitutes of Dakar are the taxi-drivers.

Cyril Connolly, *The Evening Colonnade*, 1973

SIERRA LEONE

I have travelled east, I have travelled west, north and south, ascended mountains, dived in mines, but I never knew and never heard mention of so villainous or iniquitous a place as Sierra Leone. I know not where the Devil's Poste Restante is, but the place surely must be Sierra Leone.

Captain Chamier, *Life of a Sailor*, 1833

No statistical writer has yet tried to give the minutest fraction representing the chance of (even) a surgeon's return from S'a Leone.

Medical Gazette, 14 April 1838, quoted by Richard Burton, *Wanderings in West Africa*, 1863

The 'Red Grave,' as this portion of the great cemetery of the Anglo-Saxon race is called.

Richard Burton, *Wanderings in West Africa*, 1863

The Hamitic Sodom and Gomorrah.

Richard Burton, *Explorations of the Highlands of Brazil*, 1869

Sierra Leone, charming as it is, has a sort of Christy Minstrel air about it.

Mary Kingsley, *West African Studies*, 1899

People of Sierra Leone

The S'a Leone man is handier than his Southern brother, he can mend a wheel, make a coffin, or cut your hair, operations which in other places must remain wanted. Yet no one – at least if not a perfect greenhorn on the coast – will engage him in any capacity. In civility and respectfulness, he is far below the Brazilian or the Cuban emancipado. He has learned a 'trick or two:' even a black who has once visited Sierra Leone is considered spoiled for life, as if he spent a year in England.

Richard Burton, *Wanderings in West Africa,* 1863

The Sierra Leone man is an inveterate thief; he drinks, he gambles, he intrigues, he over-dresses himself, and when he has exhausted his means, he makes master pay for all. With a terrible partiality for summonsing and enjoying himself thoroughly in a court of law, he enters into the spirit of the thing like an attorney's clerk.

Ibid.

Freetown

Nothing can be viler than the site selected for Freetown; the fifteenth century would have chosen a better. This capital of the unhappy colony lies on the north coast of the S'a Leone Peninsula, on a gentle declivity, a narrow shelving ledge of diluvium washed from the higher levels, and forming in places dwarf facets and little basins. The sandstone is so soft and friable, that it readily absorbs the deluging torrents of rain, and as readily returns them to the air in the shape of noxious vapours. The lowest houses are besprinkled by the water-spray. . . . On the heights above the settlement there is doubtless room for cool and healthy country seats, where the European exiles might be comparatively safe from dysentery and yellow fever. . . . But the effects of original sin in site are terribly lasting in these lands; they descend from generation to generation. It is far easier in the Tropics to build than to unbuild, which involves rebuilding. The great gift of Malaria is utter apathy, at once its evil and its cure, its bane and its blessing. Men come out from Europe with the fairest prospect, if beyond middle age, of dying soon.

Richard Burton, *Wanderings in West Africa,* 1863

Freetown . . . at first was just an impression of heat and damp; the mist streamed along the lower streets and lay over the roofs like smoke. Nature, conventionally grand, rising in tree-covered hills above the sea and the town, a dull uninteresting green, was powerless to carry off the shabby town. One could see the Anglican cathedral, laterite bricks and tin with a square tower, a Norman church built in the nineteenth century, sticking up out of the early morning fog. . . .

Tin roofs and peeling posters and broken windows in the public library and wooden stores, Freetown had a Bret Harte air without the excitement, the saloons, the revolver shots or the horses. . . .

This was an English capital city. England had planted this town, the tin shacks, and the Remembrance Day posters, and had then withdrawn up the hill-side to smart bungalows, with wide windows and electric fans and perfect service. . . . They had planted their seedy civilization and then escaped from it as far as they could. Everything ugly in Freetown was European: the stores, the churches, the Government offices, the two hotels; if there was anything beautiful in the place it was native: the little stalls of the fruit-sellers which went up after dark at the street corners, lit by candles; the native women rolling home magnificently from church on a Sunday morning, the cheap European cottons, the deep coral or green flounces, the wide straw hats, dignified by the native bearing, the lovely roll of the thighs, the swing of the great shoulders. They were dressed for a garden party and they carried off cheap bright grandeur in the small back-yards among the vultures as nature couldn't carry off Freetown.

Graham Greene, *Journey without Maps,* 1936

The beauty and charm of everything enchant me. I mill about in a state of pleasure with God. What a good job He has done here with people, skins, gestures, expressions, voices, dramas, the air, the light, the landscape, the trees, the flowers, the sea. Freetown markets, streets, traffic, charm.

Michael Kelly, 'A Winter Journal – Just a Touch of the Africas', *Literary Review,* no. 14, 18 April–1 May 1980

SINGAPORE

Wee came to the entraunce of the straightts of Sincapura. . . . Wee wentt 4 or 5 leagues, all the way on both hands soe full of Creekes, passages and Ilands, as I never saw the like, especially on the starboard side, the little Iles lying like soe many Haicocks laid close together, all overgrowne with trees.

Peter Mundy, *Travels in Europe and Asia,* 1637

Singapore a vision of green hills and red dust, a sickly odour of pepper, cocoa, nut-oil, and drains.

Harry de Windt, *From Pekin to Calais by Land,* 1889

People in Singapur are dead-white – as white as Naaman – and the veins on the backs of their hands are painted in indigo.

It is as though the Rains were just over, and none of the womenfolk had been allowed to go to the hills. Yet no one talks about the unhealthiness of Singapur. A man lives well and happily until he begins to feel unwell. Then he feels worse because the climate allows him no chance of pulling himself together – and then he dies.

Rudyard Kipling, *From Sea to Sea,* 1889

Hail, Mother! East and West must seek my aid
Ere the spent hull may dare the ports afar,
The second doorway of the wide world's trade
Is mine to loose or bar.

Rudyard Kipling, *The Song of the Cities,* 1893

I hear that a year or two back there was a mutiny in Singapore of which we heard practically nothing. A local native regiment got loose and started murdering people, rushing up and down the streets asking everybody if he was English. Those who said 'Yes,' had their throats cut at once. One English wag said that he was Irish. They let him, and the others who followed his example, alone. Presently, one of His Majesty's ships came round the corner, and I understand that the bluejackets did their work very thoroughly indeed. . . . The mutineers seemed to have special aversion to golfers, who were surprised to find themselves being murdered in the bunkers.

Alfred Viscount Northcliffe, *My Journey Round the World* (December 1921), 1923

Field Marshall Lord Roberts once said the history of the world would be decided at Singapore one day.

John Gunther, *Inside Asia,* 1939

I have never made any predictions, except things like saying Singapore would hold out. What a fool and a knave I should have been to say it would fall!

Sir Winston Churchill, Speech in the House of Commons, 2 July 1942

The first impression of Singapore as we slide in is that it is about the greenest place that I have ever seen. It is like entering Dartmouth on a muggy August afternoon.

Harold Nicholson, *Journey to Java,* 1957

That modern apology for a Romantic Eastern Port.

Paul Scott, *India: a Post-Forsterian View,* Lecture to the Royal Society of Literature, 1968

*In such a small place, an island with no natives, everyone a visitor, the foreigner made himself a resident by emphasising his foreignness.

Paul Theroux, *Saint Jack,* 1973

Singapore . . . possesses a mingled allure of the rapacious, the aggressive, the repellent and the extraordinary that any true pilgrim would relish. . . . It is the last of the city-states – or perhaps, gnomically speaking, the first.

No Florence, though, or Mantua. Flat, steamy, thickly humid, the island lies there in its hot seas, fringed with mangrove swamps, and from the air it looks as it always did, a slightly desperate place that ought to be uninhabited. It looks like an invented place, and so of course it is.

Jan Morris, 'The City-State', *Travels,* 1976

'You do a lot of travelling,' said my friend, 'so tell me, is Singapore a good idea?'

Ibid.

Raffles Hotel

I had expected something straight out of Somerset Maugham, paneled in mahogany and full of aquiline-featured cads involved in desperate intrigues with the wives of neighbouring planters. What I saw instead was a double row of tables reminiscent of a Childs Restaurant, flanking a dance-floor that cried out for a mother-of-pearl jukebox to complete its utter commonplaceness. The people about us may have been cads, but their skins had been tanned by gin and bitters rather than fierce tropical suns. At noon the room began to take on the aspect of a New Jersey beach hotel; comfortable bourgeois families exchanged condolences about the servant problem and their children slid up and down the dance floor, whooping and pinching each other. It was very disillusioning, and whether it was due to travel fatigue, or the four gimlets I had taken, or the end of my boyhood dream, it made me want to cry.

S.J. Perelman, *Westward Ha!,* 1948

SOMALIA

British Somaliland is the only country I know where you see camels walking in the sky and goats climbing trees. This of course, is the effect of the mirage, and not the result of exposing your head to the sun. Zeila floats in the sky in just the same way for many miles before you reach this strange jumble of Arabian, Turkish, Egyptian and Portuguese architecture.

Geoffrey Harmsworth, *Abyssinian Adventure,* 1935

The sight of blood makes them literally drunk and they massacre their enemies mercilessly. They are not however cruel. They kill quickly and never make their victims suffer. In short, if one must be killed in Africa it is preferable for the operation to be performed by a doubat, or in general by a Somali. They never think of torturing their enemies as do Ethiopians, Danakils, or Issas, whose sadistic cruelty surpasses by far that of the most notorious Chinese executioners.

Edmund Demaitre, 'With the Lions of Juba', in *Abyssinian Stop Press,* 1936

The Somalis are independent people unused to any sort of central government, unaccustomed to any form of direct taxation, and intensely suspicious of the foreigner, the white man, and the Christian. The only forms of national sport are raiding one's neighbour's camels, seizing his water supplies, and emasculating his males.

J. Darrell Bates, 'The Somaliland Protectorate', *Corona,* May 1953

Mogadishu

Everything at Mogadiscio is sane and orderly, . . . neat and white. It is all a little like the old White City by day and Act II of a pre-war musical comedy by night. There are stucco replicas of Roman triumphal arches. Government House, the home of General Graziani, is white, too, and looks like an old Moorish palace. The gates are guarded by two splendid *Dubats*, an aristocratic tribe notable for their fine physique and good looks, in green and gold uniforms, carrying huge curved swords. There are two open-air cinemas, a fascist club, a tennis club (where they play by electric light), a modernistic war memorial, a wireless station, one or two expensive European shops, and an assortment of corrugated iron stores selling everything under the sun, kept by prosperous-looking Indian and Arabian merchants. The streets are well surfaced (the town was tidied up a year or two ago for the visit of King Victor Emmanuel), and most of them are named after Mussolini and members of the Italian Royal Family.

Geoffrey Harmsworth, *Abyssinian Adventure*, 1935

Mogadiscio, the capital, is variously spelt Mukdisha, Magadisho, Mukdishu, Mogadisho, Mogadaxo, and Mogadischo. The legend is that this is the place to which Mussolini sent Italians whom he *really* wanted to get rid of.

John Gunther, *Inside Africa*, 1955

SOUTH AFRICA

The news from Africa is absorbingly interesting for the moment. Good will come, I suppose, of this disaster, because it will lead to a more thorough subjugation of the Zulus, and to a more speedy extension of the Englishry as far as the climate will let them extend – that is, about up to the Tropic of Capricorn. And, unattractive as the raw Englishry is, it is good stuff, and, always supposing it not to deteriorate but to improve, its spread is the spread of future civilisation.

Matthew Arnold, Letter to Miss Arnold, January, 1879

It is apt to be forgotten that the Cape was not occupied with a view to the establishment of a European Colony in our present sense of the word. The Dutch took it that they might plant a cabbage-garden: the English took it that they might have a naval station and half-way house to India.

James Bryce, *Impressions of South Africa*, 1897

There have never been any traditions of violence, still less of crime in South Africa, except as against the natives.

Ibid.

By far the most interesting features in the history of South Africa have been the relations to one another of the various races that inhabit it.

Ibid.

Here in this land, where nature unconfined
Taunts the great desert of the human mind. . . .

Roy Campbell, *The Golden Shower*, 1926

South Africa, renowned far and wide
For politics and little else beside:
Where, having torn the land with shot and shell,
Our sturdy pioneers as farmers dwell,
And, 'twixt the hours of strenuous sleep, relax
To shear the fleeces or to fleece the blacks:
Where every year a fruitful increase bears
Of pumpkins, cattle, sheep, and millionaires –
A clime so prosperous both to men and kine
That which were which a sage could scarce define;
Where fat white sheep upon the mountains bleat
And fatter politicians in the street;
Where lemons hang like yellow moons ashine
And grapes the size of apples load the vine;
Where apples to the weight of pumpkins go
And donkeys to the height of statesmen grow,
Where trouts the size of salmon throng the creeks
And worms the size of magistrates – the beaks;
Where the precocious tadpole, from his bog,
Becomes a journalist ere half a frog;
Where every shrimp his proud career may carve
And only brain and muscle have to starve.
The 'garden colony' they call our land,
And surely for a garden it was planned:
What apter phrase with such a place could cope
Where vegetation has so fine a scope,
Where *weeds* in such variety are found
And all the rarest *parasites* abound,
Where pumpkins to professors are promoted
And turnips into Parliament are voted.
Where else do men by vegetating vie
And run to seed so long before they die?

Roy Campbell, *The Wayzgoose*, 1928

South Africa is spinning on a hub of gold.

Negley Farson, *Behind God's Back*, 1940

When old settlers say, 'One has to understand the country,' what they mean is 'You have to get used to our ideas about the native.' They are saying, in effect, 'Learn our ideas, or otherwise get out; we don't want you.'

Doris Lessing, *The Grass is Singing*, 1950

In racial matters the Union today is a kind of shabby cross between Germany in 1933 and backwoods Tennessee in the 1880's.

John Gunther, *Inside Africa*, 1955

One editor told me proudly, 'To survive, we must be supermen. This is a country fit for none but heroes.'

Ibid.

Anybody so tactless as to mention that Brazil is an

infinitely pleasant, civilized, and happy country, is, of course, ruled out of bounds as a crank or 'traitor'. Or the remark will be made that there are not enough white genes in South Africa to make a Brazil. If fusion should ever occur, the resulting mixture will not be 'coffee-coloured,' but something darker.

Ibid.

Ever since I can remember I have been struck by the profound quality of melancholy which lies at the heart of the physical scene in Southern Africa. I recollect clearly asking my father once: 'Why do the vlaktes and Koppies always look so sad?' He replied with unexpected feeling: 'The sadness is not in the plains and hills but in ourselves.'

Laurens van der Post, *The Lost World of the Kalahari,* 1958

In South Africa the white man's fear has been so stimulated, so empowered, that our country can be aptly compared to Sparta, where the ruling invaders worshipped Fear, and built a temple to Fear because they knew their whole form of government was largely maintained by Fear!

Mary Benson, 'Twelve Years! It's Nothing! – A Letter to James Baldwin', May 1965

It is easy, indeed dangerously easy, to enter a social set in which everybody is against the regime. This produces a quite unjustified sense of optimism about the future.

The kind of South African who votes for the United Party is eager to tell you that his is not a police State. Maybe. It is, however, the only English-speaking country to which I have been where people habitually lower their voices when talking politics in a public place.

Richard West, *The White Tribes of Africa,* 1965

What one misses most in Africa are interesting towns, country walks, safe swims, imaginative cooking, bookshops, news-stands and somewhere to go in the evening. But a Polish expatriate told me that after two or at most three trips to Europe the homesickness for South Africa grows stronger than the pull in the opposite direction; the sun and emptiness, the brown landscape flecked with patches of livid green that one sees from the air, become indispensable, the tidiness and perfection of Europe seem over-crowded and over done. Perhaps Africa is like bilharzia: after you have had it twice you can't take the treatment any more.

Cyril Connolly, *The Evening Colonnade,* 1973

The light in South Africa . . . replaces architecture.

Ibid.

There is to South Africa a strong suggestion of the bull ring – the cruelty of it, the splendor, the mixed emotion of revulsion, loyalty and admiration, the absoluteness of sun and shade, the glare of the arena, the hissing, cheering crowd, and, approaching all the time, dreaded but desired, the Moment of Truth to end it all. In this mise-en-scène the part of the bull is played by the Afrikaner traditionalist, the modern Voortrekker.

Jan Morris, Article of 1977, in *Destinations,* 1980

The policies of neo-apartheid sound infinitely cold, crafty, and greedy. Coldness and craft and greed are there, obviously, but there are also other forces at work. Fear is one: fear of the internal and external consequences of the provocation constituted by racial apartheid. The need to find a substitute for this seems to be felt as keenly as is the need to produce synthetic petrol, as insurance against sanctions. ('Our Chemistry Department,' I was told at Potchefstroom, 'can make petrol out of anything black.')

Conor Cruise O'Brien, 'The Guilt of Afrikanerdom', *Observer,* 29 July 1979.

South Africans

Fancy, a whole nation of *lower* middle-class Philistines!

Olive Schreiner, before 1920, quoted in William Plomer, *Cecil Rhodes,* 1933

If you talk with many thinking people down in the Union (particularly those of English extraction) you will find that occasionally one will admit that the attitude of the white man towards the native *is* based upon fear. You may do anything you like to him, but he is still there – by the millions.

His capacity for suffering, his vitality, his faith that one day things must come all right for him, are indestructible. They shame you. What *are* you going to do with him? In Africa, the black man, by his very presence, has made the white man do mean things. Demean himself. And the white man hates him for it. . . .

'It is absurd,' growled the young engineer, 'to think that the native has taken everything that has happened to him, and then forgot. You will find this look of resentment, however skilfully it may be veiled, throughout Africa.'

Negley Farson, *Behind God's Back,* 1940

When a white man in Africa by accident looks into the eyes of a native and sees the human being (which it is his chief preoccupation to avoid), his sense of guilt, which he denies, fumes up in resentment, and he brings down the whip.

Doris Lessing, *The Grass is Singing,* 1950

Afrikaaners

Left Cape Town on the 8th of June [1852]. Boers along

the road are very kind, and great rogues. Have very small regard for truth, and if one swears he is doing you a favour you may take his oath as meaning that he is cheating you. Their talk is entirely on rix dallers, scaap, guilders, Uithaalder, paarde, moi dick vrowen etc. They are more like Jews than any people I know. . . . The follies of men make the world interesting. What a dull drivelling affair it would be if the Universe were regulated according to the dicta of heavy Dutch Predikants, for instance. Who would not wish to escape from a chaos of everlasting humdrum – schaap rix dallers, moi dik vrowen, etc.

David Livingstone, *Private Journals,* 1852

The emigrant Boers, who despise the law of benevolence enuntiated in the declaration that God hath made of one blood all the nations of the Earth, are themselves becoming as degraded as the natives whom they despise. A slave population everywhere works the ruin and degradation of the free class which employs it.

David Livingstone, Letter to Arthur Tidman, 26 April 1872

He is deeply religious; profoundly ignorant; dull, obstinate, bigoted; uncleanly in his habits; hospitable, honest in his dealings with the whites, a hard master to his black servant; lazy, a good shot, good horseman, addicted to the chase; a lover of political independence, a good husband and father; not fond of herding together in towns, but liking the seclusion and remoteness and solitude and empty vastness and silence of the velt; a man of mighty appetite, and not delicate about what he appeases it with – well satisfied with pork, and Indian corn and biltong, requiring only that the quantity shall not be stinted; willing to ride a long journey to take part in a rude all night dance interspersed with vigorous feeding and boisterous jollity, but ready to ride twice as far for a prayer meeting; proud of his race's achievements in South Africa – its bold plunge into hostile and uncharted deserts in search of free solitudes unvexed by the pestering and detested English, also its victories over the natives and the British; proudest of all, of the direct and effusive personal interest which the deity has always taken in its affairs. He cannot read, he cannot write; he has one or two newspapers, but he is apparently not aware of it; until latterly he had not schools, and taught his children nothing; news is a term which has no meaning to him, and the thing itself he cares nothing about. He hates to be taxed and resents it. He has stood stock still in South Africa for two centuries and a half, and would like to stand still till the end of time, for he has no sympathy with Uitlander notions of progress. He is hungry to be rich, for he is human; but his preference has been for riches in cattle, not in fine clothes and fine houses, and gold and diamonds. The gold and diamonds have brought the godless stranger within his gates, also contamination and broken repose, and he wishes that they had never been discovered.

Mark Twain, *More Tramps Abroad,* 1897

First catch your Boer, then kick him.

Mark Twain, 'Pudd'nhead Wilson's New Calendar', *ibid.*

The most peculiar and characteristic type that the country has produced is the Boer of the eastern plateau. . . . These men . . . have retained a passion for solitude that even today makes them desire to live many miles from any neighbour, a sturdy self-reliance, a grim courage in the face of danger, a sternness from which the native races have often had to suffer. The majesty of nature has not stimulated in them any poetical faculty. But her austerity, joined to the experience of their race, has contributed to make them grave and serious, closely bound to their ancient forms of piety, and prone to deem themselves the special objects of divine protection.

James Bryce, *Impressions of South Africa,* 1897

*'Well ye see 'tis this way,' said Mr Dooley. 'Ye see th'Boers is a simple, pasthral people that goes about their business in their own way, raisin' hell with ivrybody. . . . '

Finlay Peter Dunne, *Mr Dooley's Philosophy,* 1900

You cannot govern South Africa by trampling on the Dutch.

Cecil Rhodes, after the siege of Kimberley, quoted W.T. Stead, *Last Will . . . of C.J. Rhodes,* 1902

He was profoundly religious, with the language of piety always on his lips, and yet deeply sunk in matter. Without imagination, he had the habits of a recluse and in a coarse way the instincts of a poet. He was extremely narrow in a bargain, and extremely hospitable. With a keen sense of justice, he connived at corruptions, and applauded oppression. A severe moral critic, he was often lax, and sometimes unnatural in his sexual relations. He was brave in sport and battle, but his heroics always had a mercantile basis, and he would as soon die for an ideal as it is commonly understood, as sell his farm for a sixpence. There were few virtues or vices which one could deny him utterly or with which one could credit him honestly. In short the typical Boer to the typical observer became a sort of mixture of satyr, Puritan, and successful merchant, rather interesting, rather distasteful, and wholly incomprehensible. . . . And yet the phenomenon is perfectly normal. . . . He is the ordinary backward countryman, more backward and more of a countryman than is usual in our modern world. . . . At the root of all his traits lies a meagre imagination.

John Buchan, *The African Colony,* 1903

No man who has lived much with the people can regard them without a little aversion, a strong liking, and a large and generous respect.

Ibid.

They were the most good-hearted enemy I have fought against in the four continents in which it has been my fortune to see Active Service.

Sir Winston Churchill, *My Early Life*, 1930

The Afrikaner's altar is his biggest weapon, his nuclear bomb, his firing-squad. For three centuries the history of the Afrikaner people has been one long *via dolorosa*. There is nothing that the enemy fears so much as an Afrikaner who prays.

Rev. G.J.J. Boshoff, Sermon, 1960

Blacks

Aboriginal peoples

With the officers I had good discourse, perticularly of the people at the Cape of Good Hope – of whom they of their own knowledge do tell me these one or two things, *viz.*, that when they come to age, the men do cut off one of the stones of each other, which they hold doth help them to get children the better and to grow fat. That they never sleep lying, but always sitting upon the ground. That their speech is not so articulate as ours, but yet understand one another well. That they paint themselfs all over with the grease the Dutch sell them (who have a fort there).

Samuel Pepys, *Diary*, 30 December 1662

Mild, melancholy, and sedate, he stands,
Tending another's flock upon the fields,
His father's once, where now the White Man builds
His home, and issues forth his proud commands,
His dark eye flashes not; his listless hands
Lean on the shepherd's staff; no more he wields
The Libyan bow – but to th'oppressor yields
Submissively his freedom and his lands.
Has he no courage? Once he had, – but lo!
Harsh Servitude hath worn him to the bone.
No enterprise? Alas! the brand, the blow,
Have humbled him to dust – even *hope* is gone!
'He's a base-hearted hound – not worth his food' –
His master cries – 'he has no *gratitude!*'

Thomas Pringle, *African Sketches*, 1834

South Africa is a country of black men, – and not of white men. It has been so; it is so; and it will continue to be so.

Anthony Trollope, *South Africa*, 1878

Well, I have made up my mind that there must be class legislation, that there must be Pass Laws and Peace Preservation Acts, and that we have got to treat natives, when they are in a state of barbarism, in a different way to ourselves. We are to be lords over them. These are my politics on native affairs, and these are the politics of South Africa. Treat the natives as a subject people as long as they continue in a state of barbarism and communal tenure; be the lords over them and let them be a subject race – and keep the liquor from them.

Cecil Rhodes, Speech. 1888, quoted in
W.T. Stead, *Last Will . . . of C.J. Rhodes*, 1902

That there should be little community of ideas, and by consequence little sympathy, between such a race and the whites is no more than any one would expect . . . but the traveller in South Africa is astonished at the strong feeling of dislike and contempt – one might almost say of hostility – which the bulk of the whites show to their black neighbours.

James Bryce, *Impressions of South Africa*, 1897

After a hundred years of merciless battering at the hands of the white man, the native is still, as a racial group, the least corrupted form of humanity in South Africa.

Leonard Barnes, *Caliban in Africa? or the New Boer War*, 1932

The Negro does not need a home. He can sleep under a tree.

Dr Daniel F. Malan, in *Time*, 5 May 1952

Bushmen

The Bushman . . . is the last wild thing in human form.

Negley Farson, *Behind God's Back*, 1940

Bloemfontein

The stranger looking at Bloemfontein, and forgetting for a while that it is the capital of a country or the seat of a Bishop, will behold a pretty quiet smiling village with willow trees all through it, lying in the plain, – with distinct boundaries, most pleasing to the eye.

Anthony Trollope, *South Africa*, 1878

As it is one of the smallest, so it is one of the neatest, and, in a modest way, best appointed capitals in the world. . . . It looks, and one is told it is, the most idyllic community in Africa.

James Bryce, *Impressions of South Africa*, 1897

Bophutha-Tswana

I don't know if you have ever unrolled a map of Bophuta-Tswana? Even cartographically that independent State shows signs of mental strain. It looks less like a country than it does like a colony of bacilli under the microscope: a cluster of disconnected blobs of assorted sizes. Even to look at it makes you feel a bit queazy: to be deemed to be a citizen of such an artifact would make you sick.

Conor Cruise O'Brien, 'Metamorphoses of Apartheid', *Observer,* 22 July 1979

Cape of Good Hope

This Cape is a most stately thing and the fairest Cape we saw in the whole circumference of the Earth.

Sir Francis Drake, in Richard Hakluyt, *Principal Navigations . . . of the English Nation,* 1598–1600

I am too old and the seas are too long, for me to double the Cape of Good Hope.

Francis Bacon, Lord Verulam, *Memorial of Access,* 1622

The Cape of Good Hope is situated in a temperate climate, where the excesses of heat and cold are rarely known; and the *Dutch* inhabitants, who are numerous, and who here retain their native industry, have stock'd it with a prodigious plenty of all sort of food and provisions; most of which, either from the equality of the seasons, or the peculiarity of the soil, are more delicious in their kind than can be met with elsewhere: So that by these, and by the excellent water which abounds there, this settlement is the best provided of any in the known world, for the refreshment of seamen after long voyages.

George Anson (Richard Walter and Benjamin Robins), *A Voyage Round the World, 1740–4,* 1748

The Cape is a good acquisition – but for us there is no Cape of good hope.

Edmund Burke, Letter to the Rev. Thomas Hussey, 27 September 1795

And now there's Africa in sight. . . . It looked very much like the Cape of Good Hope in a Map. . . . And there is the great Table Mountain with others ranged beside it, rugged, handsome, and dead.

Hon. F.H. Eden, Letter, 14 December 1835, in Emily Eden, *Letters from India,* 1872

Farewell, terrific shade! though I go free
Still of the powers of darkness art thou Lord:
I watch the phantom sinking in the sea
Of all that I have hated or adored.

The prow glides smoothly on through seas
  quiescent:
But where the last point sinks into the deep
The land lies dark beneath the rising crescent,
And night, the Negro, murmurs in his sleep.

Roy Campbell, 'Rounding the Cape', *Adamastor,* 1930

Cape Town

It . . . consists of about a thousand houses, neatly built of brick, and in general whitened over. The streets in general are broad and commodious, all crossing each other at right angles. In the chief of them is a canal, on each side of which is a row of oak trees, which flourish tolerably well, and yield an agreeable shade to walkers. Besides this there is another canal running through the town, but the slope of the ground is so great that both have to be furnished with sluices, at intervals of little more than fifty yards.

Sir Joseph Banks, *Journal of the Rt Hon Sir Joseph Banks* (April 1771), 1768–71

Had I been inclined for a wife,I think this is the place of all others I have seen, where I could have best suited myself.

Ibid.

The whole Town may be consider'd as one great Inn fitted up for the reception of all comers and goers. Upon the whole there is perhaps not a place in the known World that can equal this in affording refreshments of all kinds to Shipping.

Captain James Cook, *Journal,* April 1771

The rocks are rather grand in a rough way and the town looks white and Dutch-like, and clean, which is, I believe, a most deceptious appearance.

Emily Eden, Letter, 14 December 1835, in *Letters from India,* 1872

Capetown in truth is not of itself a prepossessing town. It . . . is not especially dirty, – but it is somewhat ragged. The buildings are not grand, but there is no special deficiency in that respect. The scenery around is really fine, and the multiplicity of banks and of Members of Parliament, – which may be regarded as the two most important institutions the Colonies produce, – seemed to argue prosperity. But the town is not pleasing to a stranger. . . . 'It is a beastly place you know,' one Capetown gentleman said to me.

'Oh no!' said I, in that tone which a guest is obliged to use when the mistress of a house speaks ill of anything at her own table. 'No, no; not that.'

But he persisted. 'A beastly place,' – he repeated. 'But we have plenty to eat and plenty to drink, and manage to make out life pretty well. The girls are as pretty as they are any where else, and as kind – and the brandy and soda as plentiful.'

Anthony Trollope, *South Africa,* 1878

Hail! Snatched and bartered oft from hand to hand,
  I dream my dream, by rock and heath and pine,
Of Empire to the northward. Ay, one land
  From Lion's Head to Line!

Rudyard Kipling, *The Song of the Cities,* 1893

*Seen from the sea, if you can look past the docks without seeing them, it is an enchanting place – though perhaps its charm is chiefly centred in its mountain.

Gertrude Page, *Jill's Rhodesian Philosophy, – or the Dam Farm,* 1910

Table Mountain
Lofty Table Mountain with its beautiful table cloth of fleecy clouds.

David Livingstone, Letter to Janet and Agnes Livingstone, 30 March 1841

Durban

Durban is a neat and clean town. One notices this without having his attention called to it.

Mark Twain, *More Tramps Abroad,* 1897

Durban is mostly one long street 'West Street.' With slight differences in architecture, say about windows and doors and more verandahs, it might pass for an Australian town, heat, dust, and all – or say, as it is, but without the heat, for a New Zealand city. There's a good deal of corrugated iron about.

Henry Lawson, *Durban,* 1900

*Durban is a modern Garden of Eden beside the sea. I do not know how to describe it. There is a certain passionate, lurid, riotous, luxuriant revelry about its colouring, which, I understand, is a grotesque contradiction to the sedate and staid parochialism of its inhabitants, and that defies description. . . . Yet I do not know if I like Durban. Almost I think I do not. Perhaps we British of the homely northern Island, cannot by nature quite attune ourselves to an over-luxuriant richness of colour. Perhaps the moist, warm atmosphere, which is almost tropical, suits ill with the strong, stern blood of a northern race. I should distrust Durban as, if I were a man, I should distrust a woman who was so beautiful that she cast a spell over my senses and drained my manhood.

Gertrude Page, *Jill's Rhodesian Philosophy, – or the Dam Farm,* 1910

Durban was plastered with notices. On hotels, on restaurants, on public baths, on urinals, on cemeteries, – on everything that might serve a human need, were inscribed the same words, 'Reserved for Europeans.' It was like a foretaste of what Hitler's world might be when he had finished setting it up.

E.R. Dodds, *Missing Persons,* 1977 – of 1942

East London

Such was the character of the place [that] I was told by more than one voice that vessels were sent there on purpose to be wrecked. . . . 'She was intended to come on shore,' was said by all voices that day in East London, as to the vessel that was still lying among the breakers, while men were at work upon her to get out the cargo. 'They know that ships will drag their anchor here; so, when they want to get rid of an old tub, they send her to East London.'

Anthony Trollope, *South Africa,* 1878

Ermelo

My chief recollection of Ermelo is of a talk with a deputation of neighbouring farmers on the subject of cattle diseases. One admirable old man explained his perplexity. 'Formerly,' he said, 'we used to be told that diseases came from on High. Now we are told that some are from on High, and some are our own fault. But which is which? Personally,' he concluded, 'I believe that Providence is a good deal to blame for them all.'

John Buchan, *The African Colony,* 1903

Fort Elizabeth (Algoa Bay)

Fort Elizabeth, as I walked away from the quay, up to the club where I took up my residence, seemed to be as clean, as straight, and as regular as a first class American little town in the State of Maine.

Anthony Trollope, *South Africa,* 1878

Georgetown

I swore that it was the prettiest village on the face of the earth, – the prettiest village at any rate that I had ever seen. . . . George will probably resent the description. . . . George considers itself to be a town. . . . In George the houses are all . . . away from the road. They have trees around them. And they are quaint in their designs, many of them having been built by Dutch proprietors and after Dutch patterns. And they have an air of old-fashioned middle-class comfort, – as though the inhabitants all ate hot roast mutton at one o'clock as a rule of their lives. As far as I could learn they all did.

Anthony Trollope, *South Africa,* 1878

Johannesburg

It is a busy, eager, restless, pleasure-loving town.

James Bryce, *Impressions of South Africa,* 1897

An extended brickfield is the first impression: a prosperous powder-factory is the last. . . .

Formerly she was a mixture of every European capital, plus a little of the Dutch dorp: now she is English in essence, the most English of all South African towns.

John Buchan, *The African Colony*, 1903

People who have the best time in Johannesburg are the visitors. . . . They look at Johannesburg from all angles, in much the same way as they would besiege a celebrated statesman at a press conference. They ask crucial questions without getting emotionally involved in the town's preoccupations.

I have often tried to put myself in this position, to approach Johannesburg with the attitude of a disengaged visitor. Unfortunately for me I cannot succeed in doing this. I am a part of Johannesburg. The most I can do is regard myself as someone who has, unwittingly, volunteered to become the guinea pig in some incredible experiment by a quack scientist.

Nathaniel Nakasa, *Johannesburg, Johannesburg*, before 1965, in *South African Writing Today*, ed. N. Gordimer and L. Abrahams, 1967

If there is any place in the world where love has died, it is here.

Mary Benson, 'Twelve Years! It's Nothing! – A Letter to James Baldwin', May 1965 – in *ibid.*

The first impressions were: of an airport Inquiries desk which, when asked how to find a Suburban address answered, 'That's a bleddy silly question'; the conductor of the airport bus who deliberately and sneeringly gave £5 worth of change in silver; the racial segregation of public lavatories, park benches and lifts; the hotel porter who said insolently and incorrectly, 'You left you key up in your room, man. You'd better go up and fetch it'; the airline office which lost and has not yet found my mail for the last month; the dank bars for (white) men only; the piano-infested hotel lounges; a cinema whose ceiling and walls are decorated to give the impression of sitting outdoors at night in Disney's medieval Germany under twinkling stars and surrounded by gabled houses and castles, also with lights in their latticed windows. These were some of the things I noticed during the first hours in Johannesburg. I wrote in my diary, 'Manchester under Fascism.' It was a spurious judgement, for Jo'burg is comparable to no other city, while Dr Verwoerd's regime is not, yet, fascist.

Richard West, *The White Tribes of Africa*, 1965

As for purchasable women, Johannesburg was gruffly secretive about its accommodations (yet, since this was home, could it ever be secretive enough?).

Lionel Abrahams, 'Fruits of the Earth', in *South African Writing Today*, ed. N. Gordimer and L. Abrahams, 1967

There it stands ringed by its yellow mine dumps, like stacks of its own excreta, the richest city in Africa, but altogether without responsibility. It is the ultimate money city. Its only raison d'être is gold, and its pavements are literally impregnated with the stuff.

Jan Morris, *Destinations*, 1980 – article of 1977

The city on the Reef looked luridly beautiful in the setting sun, El Greco's Toledo, with a whiff of brimstone.

Conor Cruise O'Brien, 'Metamorphoses of Apartheid', *Observer*, 22 July 1979

Kimberley

The pit is 250 feet deep, nearly circular, though after a while the eye becomes aware of the fact that it is oblong. At the top the diameter is about 300 yards of which 250 cover what is technically called 'blue' – meaning diamondiferous soil. Near the surface, and for some way down, the sides are light brown. . . . Below this everything is blue, all the constructions in the pit having been made out of some blue matter which at first sight would seem to have been carried down for the purpose. But there are other colours on the wall which give a peculiar picturesqueness to the mines. The top edge as you look at it with your back to the setting sun is red with the gravel of the upper reef, while below, in places, the beating of rain and running of water has produced peculiar hues, all of which are a delight to the eye.

As you stand at the edge you will find high-raised boxes at your right hand and at your left, and you will see all round the margin crowds of such erections, each box being as big as a little house, and higher than most of the houses in Kimberley. These are the first recipients for the stuff that is brought up out of the mine. And behind these . . . are the whims by means of which the stuff is raised, each whim being worked by two horses. . . . As this is going on round the entire circle it follows that there are wires starting everywhere from the rim and converging to a centre at the bottom, on which the buckets are always scudding through the air. They drop down and creep up not altogether noiselessly but with a gentle trembling sound which mixes itself pleasantly with the murmur from the voices below. And the wires seem to be the strings of some wonderful harp, – aerial or perhaps infernal, – from which the beholder expects that a louder twang will soon be heard. . . . The mine is seen best in the afternoon and the visitor looking at it should stand with his back to the setting sun. . . . The most peculiar phase of the mine, as you gaze into its one large pit, is the subdivision into claims and portions. Could a person see the sight without having heard any word of explanation, it would be impossible, I think, to conceive the meaning of all those straight cut narrow dikes, of those mud walls all at right angles to each other, of those square separate pits, and again of those square upstanding blocks, looking like houses without doors or windows. You can see that nothing on earth was ever less level than the bottom of the bowl . . . as though some diabolically ingenious architect had contrived a house with 500 rooms, not one of which should be on the same floor, and to and from none of which should there be a pair of stairs or a door or a window. In addition to this it must be imagined that the architect had omitted the roof, in order that the wires of the harp above described might be brought into every chamber. The house has then been furnished with picks, shovels, planks, and a few barrels, populated with its black legions, and there it is for you to look at. . . .

I must add also that a visitor to Kimberley should, if possible, take an opportunity of looking down upon the mine by moonlight. It is a weird and wonderful sight, and may almost be called sublime in its peculiar strangeness.

Anthony Trollope, *South Africa,* 1878

When I am in Kimberley, I often go and sit on the edge of the De Beers Mine, and I look at the blue diamondiferous ground, reaching from the surface a thousand feet down the open workings of the mine, and I reckon up the value of diamonds in the 'blue' and the power conferred by them. In fact, every foot of ground means so much power. This I cannot do with your gold reefs.

Cecil Rhodes, before 1902, remarks quoted in Hans Sauer, *Ex Africa,* 1937

Next to Mr Rhodes, to me the most interesting convulsion of nature in South Africa was the diamond-crater. The Rand gold-fields are a stupendous marvel, and they make all other gold-fields small, but I was not a stranger to gold-mining; the velt was a noble thing to see, but it was only another and lovelier variety of our Great Plains; the natives were very far from being uninteresting, but they were not new; and as for the towns, I could find my way without a guide through most of them, because I have learned the streets, under other names, in towns just like them in other lands; but the diamond mine was a wholly fresh thing, a splendid and absorbing novelty. Very few people in the world have seen the diamond in its home. It has but three or four homes in the world, whereas gold has a million. It is worth while to journey around the globe to see anything which can truthfully be called a novelty, and the diamond mine is the greatest and most restricted novelty which the globe has in stock.

Mark Twain, *More Tramps Abroad,* 1897

The 'Big Hole' at Kimberley . . . has been called the 'womb' of South Africa.

John Gunther, *Inside Africa,* 1955

Natal

Take the downs at Brighton, and there is Natal, I believe.

Cecil Rhodes, Letter to his mother, 1870

Oudtshoorn

I wish some of my readers would write the name of the village in order that they may learn the amount of irritation which may be produced by an unfortunately awkward combination of letters.

Anthony Trollope, *South Africa,* 1878

Pretoria

I was assured . . . that the climate of Pretoria was one which required great care from its inhabitants. It is subject to very violent storms, and deaths from lightning are not uncommon. The hailstorms, when they come, are very violent, the stones being so large as not unfrequently to batter the cattle to death. . . . 'What does a man do if he is out on the veld?' I asked when I heard these frightful stories. 'Put his saddle over his head,' was the answer. . . . 'But if he have not a saddle?' 'Ah, then indeed, he would be badly off.' . . . I could not however learn that people were often killed. I therefore accepted the Pretorian hailstones with a grain of salt.

Anthony Trollope, *South Africa,* 1878

Rustenberg (Transvaal)

The Boerish Eden, Magaliesberg.

David Livingstone, Letter to William Thompson, 14 May 1854

Soweto

There is nowhere else in the world like Soweto. It is something like a disused exhibition, something like a construction camp, and something like a slum. With a population of more than a million – twice the size of Johannesburg itself – Soweto is one of the great cities of Africa, but it does not feel like a city at all, for it has no center. . . . There is no focus to Soweto, no complex of stores and offices, no cathedral tower or television mast: it is like a haggard dream, in which one is always on the edge of somewhere, but never ever gets there.

Jan Morris, *Destinations,* 1980 – article of 1977

The South African Tourist Bureau have issued a revised handout for visitors to Johannesburg, one paragraph of which reads: 'Soweto Tour. Duration: 3½ hours (approx). See Soweto first-hand, the home of a million happy Blacks. Compare its quaint, box-style houses with the palatial homes of Dusky Millionaires. Marvel at the fantastic gardens into which the house-proud community pour their creative souls. You will enjoy the sight of Sports Fields, Soccer Stadiums, Public Libraries, Croquet Lawns, and Community Centres. Above all, laugh at the antics of the eager Black kiddies as they sport in the sparkling waters of the Municipal Swimming Pool.'

Christopher Logue, 'True Stories', *Private Eye,* 15 August 1980 (quoting *South African Tourist Board Pamphlet,* March 1980)

Stellenbosch

As good Americans, when dead, go to Paris, so do good Dutchmen while still alive go to Stellenbosch, – and more especially good Dutchwomen, for it is a place much affected by widows.

Anthony Trollope, *South Africa,* 1878

Table Bay

The Bay of Soldania and all about the Cape is so healthfull and fruitfull, as it might grow a Paradise of the World; it well agrees with English bodies, for all but one in twentie dayes recovered, as at the first day they set forth. They had then in June, Snow upon the hills, the weather warmish. The countrey is mixed, Mountaines, Plaines, Medowes, Streames, the Woods as if they were artificially planted for order. There is free stone to build with, plentie of fish and fowle, wild Geese, Partriches and Duckes, Antilopes, Deere, Rivers. They had thirtie nine Beeves, one hundred and fifteene sheepe for a little Brasse cut out of two or three old Kettles. . . . The people are loving, afraid at first by reason of the unkindnesse of the Dutch (which came there to make traine Oyle, who killed and stole their Cattell) and at our returne more kind: of middle size, well limmed, very nimble and active. They dance in true measure all naked, only weare a short Cloke of sheepe or Seale skinnes to their middle, the hairie side inward, a Cap of the same, and a kind of Rats skinne about their privities; some had a Sole on their feet tyed about; their neckes were adorned with greasie Tripes, which sometimes they would pull off and eat raw. . . . The Womens habit is as the Mens. They were shame-fac't at first; but at our returne homewards they would lift up their Rat-skinnes and shew their privities. Their breasts hang to the middle, their haire curles. Copper with them is Gold; Iron, Silver; their Houses little Tents in the field, of skins, moveable at pleasure, their Language with doubling the tongue in their throat. There is a high hill, called the Table, overcovering all the adjoyning Territories one hundred miles.

Rev. Patrick Copland, *Tractate,* 1611–14, in *Purchas his Pilgrimes,* 1625

Transkei

The birth of apartheid's first child.

Anon., quoted by Nicholas Ashford, *The Times,* 26 October 1978

The Veld

Cecil Rhodes liked to spend time there, 'Alone with the Alone.'

J.G. Lockhart and C.M. Woodhouse, *Rhodes,* 1963

in sight of the Magaliesberg
There is something extraordinarily delicate and remote about the vista; it might be a mirage, did not the map bear witness to its reality. It is not unlike a child's conception of the landscape of Bunyan, a road running straight through a mystical green country, with the hilltops of the Delectable Mountains to cheer the pilgrim.

John Buchan, *The African Colony,* 1903

There is one feature of the high veld which has not had the attention it deserves – I mean the wind – and with the wind go all manner of tin cans, trundling from one skyline to another with a most purposeful determination. Somewhere, – S.S.W. I should put the direction – there must be a Land of Tin-cans, where in some sheltered valley all the *debris* of the veld has come to anchor.

Ibid.

SOUTH AMERICA

See also under individual countries

Our confederacy must be viewed as the nest from which all America, North and South is to be peopled. We should take care too, not to think it for the interest of that great continent to press too soon on the Spaniards. Those countries cannot be in better hands. My fear is that they are too feeble to hold them till our population can be sufficiently advanced to gain it from them piece by piece.

Thomas Jefferson, Letter to Archibald Stuart, 25 January 1786

I called the New World into existence to redress the balance of the Old.

George Canning, The King's Message, 12 December 1826
(on Great Britain's recognition of the rebellious Spanish Colonies there)

The freedom of the New World is the hope of the universe.

Simon Bolivar, attrib.

America is ungovernable for us. Those who serve the revolution plough the sea. The only thing to do in America is to emigate. This country will infallibly fall into the hands of an unbridled crowd of petty tyrants almost too small to notice and of all colours and races.

Simon Bolivar, Letter to General Flores, 9 November 1830

*'Prepare our little circle in Paris for the birth of another South American Republic. One more or less, what does it matter? They may come into the world like evil flowers on a hotbed of rotten institutions. . . . Late in the afternoon, the mob, disappointed in their hopes of loot, made a stand in the narrow streets to the cries of "Viva la Libertad! Down with Feudalism!" (I wonder what they imagine Feudalism to be?) "Down with the Goths and Paralytics." . . . Nobody in the town has any real power, except the railway engineers.'

Joseph Conrad, *Nostromo,* 1904

South America is bounded at its northern end by an isthmus and at its southern by a strait. . . . An isthmus and a strait are, to the historical geographer and to the geographical historian, the most interesting things with which geographical science has to deal.

James Bryce, *South America,* 1912

In Latin America . . . eloquence comes by nature, and seems to become a part of thought itself.

Ibid.

It is undeniable, since nations cannot escape their ancestry, that the grandmother of South America is Spain.

Philip Guedalla, *Argentine Tango,* 1932

My deepest impression is that we have been travelling through an empire in the final stage of its dissolution. True, its provinces have all revolted long since and established their independence. Even the last outward forms of Madrid's domination have disappeared. But the new republics aren't yet really free, really integrated. They haven't yet become nations.

If they felt truly free and integrated, they surely wouldn't be so suspicious of each other. It would be natural for them to enter into a close federation. All of them have the same cultural background. All of them, except Brazil, speak the same language. I believe that their mutual suspicions are founded on their memories of the Spanish empire. They are terribly afraid of finding themselves, once again, under some central authority. They daren't surrender any of their sovereign power.

In order to become nations, they must cease to be colonies.

Christopher Isherwood, *The Condor and the Cows,* 1949

*Self-removal to South America was the traditional climax of an evasive career.

Kingsley Amis, *Lucky Jim,* 1954

The discovery of America was a disaster for Spain, and possibly for Europe as well. It was a pity that things did not happen otherwise. America should have been discovered by the English, which is what might have happened if Ferdinand and Isabel had locked up Columbus in a lunatic asylum where he belonged. That formidable reservoir of human energy which went west and mastered a continent in a generation should have invaded the southern shores of the Mediterranean, from Tangiers to the Bosphorus. The Spanish-American nations would today be Spanish-African; the whole of America would be an English-speaking continent; and France, free in Europe, would have spread her culture from Paris to Moscow in peace.

Salvador de Madariaga, *Latin America,* 1962

Modern Latin America, for better or for worse, far from being romantic or remote, is very much a part of the world the rest of us live in. A colleague of mine once said, 'You make South America sound like Golders Green.' Parts of it are. Parts of it are like Liberia. Uruguay is as different from Paraguay as Britain is from Albania; Argentina is more like Australia than it is like Peru; Mexico is like nowhere except Mexico. But none of it is in the least like the stereotype which the rest of the world has come to accept.

J. Halchro Ferguson, *Latin America,* 1963

We are the good; you are the neighbour.

South American quip, quoted by John Gunther, *Inside South America,* 1967

There can be no preservation of the status quo in Latin America.

Robert F. Kennedy, *To Seek a New World,* 1968

South America was a problem in geography that could only be understood if one kept moving: to stay put was to be baffled. People complained of the barbarism of the places, but as far as I was concerned they were not barbarous enough.

Paul Theroux, *The Old Patagonian Express,* 1979

South Americans

My inquiries show that the typical Latin American

lacks confidence in his potency but is eager to prove it on every possible occasion.

Professor J. Mayone Stycos, 'Sex and the Argentine Man', *Atlas*, March 1964

Much of our North American rancour, our imperialism, our sense of superiority, all of which they quite properly resent, comes down to this: that *they have failed in our dream.* To us it seems so easy, that dream. Then we are brought face to face with the fact that they don't want any part of it. They have dreams of their own. They are romantic heroes all, and they think of the Yankees, who made a mad republic out of mystical notions of human progress and divine providence, as crass materialists. It is too much.

Keith Botsford, 'Yanqui Gringo', *Encounter*, September 1965

Few South Americans have ulcers.

John Gunther, *Inside South America,* 1967

'You must not judge people by their country,' a lady advised me. 'In South America, it is always wise to judge people by their altitude.'

Paul Theroux, *The Old Patagonian Express*, 1979

Andes

The features in the scenery of the Andes which struck me most, as contrasted with the other mountain chains with which I am acquainted, were, – the flat fringes sometimes expanding into narrow plains on each side of the valleys; the bright colours, chiefly red and purple, of the utterly bare and precipitous hills of porphyry; the grand and continuous wall-like dykes; the plainly divided strata which, where nearly vertical, formed the picturesque and wild central pinnacles, but where less inclined composed the great massive mountains on the outskirts of the range; and lastly, the smooth conical piles of fine and bright-coloured detritus which sloped up at a high angle from the base of the mountains, sometimes to a height of more than 2000 feet.

Charles Darwin, *Journal . . . During the Voyage . . . of H.M.S. Beagle*, 1832–6

SPAIN

Thou shalt make castels than in Spayne,
And dreme of joye, al but in vayne.

Geoffrey Chaucer, *Romaunt of the Rose*, *c.* 1370

All evil comes from Spain; all good from the north.

Sir Thomas Chaloner, Letter from Florence, 1597, 'A common proverb in every man's mouth'

. . . rich without men, confident without reason, proud and adventurous without meanes sufficient. . . .

Laurence Keymis (1596), in Richard Hakluyt, *Principal Navigations . . . of the English Nation,* 1598–1600

Seventeenth Century

They have hotter daies in *Spain* than we have here, but our daies are longer; and yet we are hotter in our business here, and they are longer about it there.

John Donne, Letter to Sir Robert Carr, 1624

A Spaniard was censuring to a French gentleman the want of devotion amongst the French; in that, whereas in Spain, when the Sacrament goes to the sick, any that meets with it turns back and waits upon it to the house whither it goes; but in France they only do reverence, and pass by. But the French gentleman answered him; *There is reason for it; for here with us Christ is secure amongst his friends; but in Spain there be so many Jews and Maranos, that it is not amiss for him to have a convoy.*

Francis Bacon, *Apothegmes . . . collected by Francis Lord Verulam. . . .*, 1625

As one saith in a brave kind of expression, *the sun never sets in the Spanish dominions, but ever shines on one part or other of them.*

Francis Bacon, *An Advertisement Touching an Holy Warre,* 1629

In Spain you lose experience; 'Tis a climate
Too hot to nourish arts; the nation proud,
And in their pride unsociable; the court
More pliable to glorify itself
Than do a stranger grace: if you intend
To traffic like a merchant, 'twere a place
Might better much your trade; but as for me
I soon took surfeit on it.

John Ford, *Love's Sacrifice,* 1633

The warme Sun . . . is somewhat too liberall of his beames here; which makes the ground more barren, and consequently to be a kind of wildernesse in comparison of *France,* if you respect the number of people, the multitude of Townes, Hamlets, and Houses: for about the third part of the continent of *Spaine* is made up of huge craggie Hils and Mountaines, amongst which one shall feele in some places more difference in point of temper of heat and cold in the ayre, then 'twixt winter and summer under other Climes. But where Spaine hath water and Valleis there she is extraordinarily fruitfull, *such blessings humility carieth alwayes with her.* So that Spain yieldeth to none of her neighbours in perfection of any thing, but only in *plenty;* which I believe was the ground of a Proverbe they have amongst them, *No ay cosa mala en Espana, sino lo que habla,* there is nothing ill in Spaine, but that which speakes.

James Howell, *Instructions for Forren Travell,* 1650

Now for some Ages had the Pride of *Spain*
Made the Sun shine on half the World in vain:
Whilst she bid War to all that durst supply
The place of those her Cruelty made Dye.
Of Nature's bounty Men forbore to Tast,
And the best Portion of the Earth lay wast.
From the new World her Silver and her Gold
Came, like a Tempest, to confound the Old.
Feeding with these the brib'd Elector's hopes,
Alone she gave us Emperors and Popes;
With these accomplishing her vast designs,
Europe was shaken with her *Indian* Mines.
When *Britain* looking with a just disdain
Upon this gilded Majesty of *Spain,*
And knowing well that Empire must decline,
Whose chief support and sinews are of Coin;
Our Nations solid Virtue did oppose,
To the rich troublers of the Worlds repose.

Edmund Waller, 'Of a War with Spain, and a Fight at Sea', *Poems,* 7th edn,1705 – *c.* 1650s

Here we fell into talk with Sir St. Fox; and among other things, of the Spanish manner of walking, when three are together; and showed me how, which was pretty, to prevent differences.

Samuel Pepys, *Diary,* 14 March 1667

The *Spanish* Proverb says, Excuses neither satisfie Creditors nor the injur'd; the wounds of Honour must have blood and wounds. . . .

William Wycherley, *The Gentleman-Dancing-Master,* 1672

Eighteenth Century

Pride, the first Peer, and President of Hell,
To his share Spain, the largest Province, fell.
The subtile Prince thought fittest to bestow
On these the Golden Mines of *Mexico;*
With all the Silver Mountains of *Peru;*
Wealth which would in wise hands the World undo:
Because he knew their Genius to be such;
Too lazy and too Haughty to be Rich.
So proud a People, so above their Fate,
That if reduc'd to beg, they'll beg in State.
Lavish of Money, to be counted Brave,
And proudly starve, because they scorn to save.
Never was Nation in the World before,
So very rich, and yet so very Poor.

Daniel Defoe, *The True-Born Englishman,* 1701

Spain gives us pride – which Spain to all the Earth
May largely give, nor fear herself a dearth –
Gives us that jealousy, which, born of fear
And mean distrust, grows not by nature here;
Gives us that superstition, which pretends
By the worst means to serve the best of ends;
That cruelty, which, stranger to the brave,
Dwells only with the coward and the slave;
That cruelty, which led her Christian bands
With more than savage rage o'er savage lands,
Bade them, without remorse, whole countries thin,
And hold of nought, but mercy, as a sin.

Charles Churchill, *The Times,* 1764

Spain flourished as a province, and has declined as a kingdom. Exhausted by the abuse of her strength, by America and by superstition. . . .

Edward Gibbon, *The Decline and Fall of the Roman Empire,* 1776–88

Thou that hast wasted earth, and dar'd despise
Alike the wrath and mercy of the skies,
Thy pomp is in the grave, thy glory laid
Low in the pits thine avarice has made.

William Cowper, *Charity,* 1781

A whale stranded upon the coast of Europe.

Edmund Burke, Speech in the House of Commons, (originally 'A whale stranded upon the sea shore of Europe.')

Nineteenth Century

Oh,lovely Spain, renowned, romantic Land!
Where is that standard which Pelagio bore
When Cava's traitor-sire first called the band
That dyed thy mountain streams with Gothic gore?
Where are those bloody banners which of yore
Waved o'er thy sons, victorious to the gale,
And drove at last the spoilers to their shore?
Red gleamed the Cross, and waned the Crescent pale,
While Afric's echoes thrilled with Moorish matrons' wail.

Teems not each ditty with the glorious tale?
Ah! such, alas! the hero's amplest fate!
When granite moulders and when records fail,
A peasant's plaint prolongs his dubious date.
Pride! bend thine eye from Heaven to thine estate,
See how the Mighty shrink into a song!
Can Volume, Pillar, Pile preserve thee great?
Or must thou trust Tradition's simple tongue,
When Flattery sleeps with thee, and History does thee wrong?

Awake, ye Sons of Spain! awake! advance!
Lo! Chivalry, your ancient Goddess, cries,
But wields not, as of old, her thirsty lance,
Nor shakes her crimson plumage in the skies:
Now on the smoke of blazing bolts she flies,
And speaks in thunder through yon engine's roar:

In every peal she calls – 'Awake! arise!'
Say, is her voice more feeble than of yore,
When her war-song was heard on Andalusia's shore?

Lord Byron, *Childe Harold's Pilgrimage,* Canto the First, 1812

Each day cloudless, and the air like a furnace. The heat of the moon is unpleasant at night. *Quel pays!*

Benjamin Disraeli, *Home Letters, 1830–1,* 1885

Whoever wishes to be well acquainted with the morbid anatomy of governments, whoever wishes to know how great states may be made feeble and wretched, should study the history of Spain.

T.B. Macaulay, 'The War of Succession in Spain', *Edinburgh Review,* January 1833, *Critical and Historical Essays,* 1843

There is no country in Europe which it is so easy to overrun as Spain; there is no country which it is more difficult to conquer.

Lord Macaulay, *ibid.*

Fortunate indeed was it, according to a Castilian preacher, that the Pyrenees concealed Spain when the Wicked One tempted the Son of Man by an offer of all the kingdoms of the world, and the glory of them. . . . It was but the other day that a foreigner was relating in a *tertulia,* or conversazione of Madrid, the well-known anecdote of Adam's revisit to the earth. The narrator explained how our first father on lighting in Italy was perplexed and taken aback; how on crossing the Alps into Germany, he found nothing that he could understand – how matters got darker and stranger at Paris, until, on his reaching England he was altogether lost, confounded and abroad, being unable to make out any thing. Spain was his next point, where, to his infinite satisfaction, he found himself quite at home, so little had things changed since his absence, or indeed since the sun at its creation first shone over Toledo.

Richard Ford, *Gatherings from Spain,* 1846

From the earliest period down to the present all observers have been struck with this *localism* as a salient feature in the character of the Iberians. . . . Spain is to-day, as it always has been, a bundle of small bodies tied together by a rope of sand. . . . The much-used phrase *Españolismo* expresses rather a 'dislike of foreign dictation,' and the 'self-estimation' of Spaniards, *Españoles sobre todos,* than any real patriotic love of country, however highly they rate its excellence and superiority to every other one under heaven: this opinion is condensed in one of those pithy proverbs which, no-where more than in Spain, are the exponents of popular sentiment: it runs thus, '*Quien dice España, dice todo,*' which means, 'Whoever says Spain, says every-thing.'

Ibid.

The *Alameda,* or church show, and the bull-fight, are the chief relaxations. These will be best enjoyed in the Southern provinces, the land also of song and dance, of bright suns and eyes, wholesale love making, and of not the largest female feet in the world.

Richard Ford, *A Handbook for Travellers in Spain,* 3rd edn, 1855

Spain is not a land of fleshly comforts, or of social sensual civilization. *Oh! dura tellus Iberiae!* – God there sends the meat, and the evil one cooks: – there are more altars than kitchens – *des milliers de prêtres et pas un cuisinier.*

Ibid.

Men have no idea of time in any country that is or has been connected with Spain.

Anthony Trollope, *The West Indies and the Spanish Main,* 1859

Spain is also the land of the man, of the gun, and of the rod.

H. O'Shea, *A Guide to Spain,* 1865

The whole country [is] a vast agglomeration of mountains, comparable to a gigantic pyramid half-way severed. . . . These lofty ranges, were they seen from a balloon, would give one the idea of the mighty skeleton or carcase of a ship-wrecked leviathan world, whose bones protrude through the tawny skin and verdant soil. These intersect the surface in every sense, and have been most effective in creating differences of race, laws, history, each province being a totally different metal – the gold being represented, we shall suppose, by the bright, sunny Andalusian; iron by the hardy, industrious Catalan-Aragonese; copper by the humble Asturian, &c. To coin these into a single kingdom has been the work of generations, and the amalgamation is not as yet consummated.

Ibid.

Spain must be in a manner explained by the East, and never by the North, as it too often is.

Ibid.

I am she that set my seal upon the nameless
  West worlds of seas;
And my sons as brides took unto them the tameless
  Hesperides
Till my sins and sons through sinless lands dispersed
  With red flame shod
Made accurst the name of man, and thrice accursed
  The name of God.

A.C. Swinburne, 'The Litany of Nations', *Songs Before Sunrise,* 1871

He who would really see Spain, must go prepared to rough it, must be unembarrassed by a courier, must be content with humble inns, coarse fare, windows often glassless, vehicles always jolting, and above all must put all false Anglican pride in his pocket, and treat every Spaniard, from the lowest begger upwards, as his equal. He must take Spain as he finds her; she is not likely to improve; she does not wish to improve; the only way of finding pleasure in her is to take her as she is, without longing for her to be what she is not. The Spanish standard of morals, of manners, of religion, of duty, of all the courtesies which are due from one person to another, however wide apart their rank, is a very different and in most of these points, a much higher standard than the English one, and, if an English traveller will not at least endeavour to come up to it, he had much better stay at home.

It is also necessary at once to lay aside all false expectations as to what one will find, Spain is *not* a beautiful country. If a traveller expects to find the soft charm and luxuriant loveliness of Italy, life in Spain will be a constant disappointment: no hope can possibly be more misplaced. Spain is not the least like Italy: it has not even the beauty of the greater part of France. Beyond the Asturias and the valleys near the Pyrenees, there is not a tree worth speaking of in the Peninsula. There is scarcely any grass; the shrubs may even be counted; except when the corn is out, which here lasts such a short time, there is hardly any vegetation at all. Those who wish to find beauty must only look for beauty of an especial kind – without verdure, or refinement.

A.J.C. Hare, *Wanderings in Spain,* 1873

A very concentration of dulness, stagnation, and ugliness.

Ibid.

I think Spain a hole, and . . . I only want to get out of it. . . . I am mortified to find how little even my wisdom has of logic, for I must own that, in spite of everything, Spain does amuse me. Every day with perfect regularity a sky so blue that one can scoop it out with a spoon; a sun so glorious that the shadows are palpably black; a dry, crisp air that tightens all one's muscles and makes life easy; and a good natured, dirty people who are always good natured if one does not insult them. . . . We know about ten words of Spanish and converse fluently all day. In short, this is a country of non-sequiturs. Every thing is upside down and wrong end first, but I think it suits an American palate, for the climate is American, and as no one pretends to being anything, our American amour-propre has a vacation. . . .

Henry Adams, Letter to Charles Milnes Gaskell, 24 October 1879

Twentieth Century

Spain is an absurd country and metaphysically impossible; absurdity is her nerve and mainstay. Her turn to prudence will denote the end.

Angel Ganivet, quoted in James Morris, *The Presence of Spain,* 1964

Occident all Spain the taste.

Gertrude Stein, 'In the Grass (On Spain)', *Geography and Plays,* 1922

Spain is an overflow of sombreness . . . a strong and threatening tide of history meets you at the frontier.

Wyndham Lewis, 'A Soldier of Humour', *The Wild Body,*1927

As it seems to me the past develops, continuous, and is alive in Spain; like a seed still promising good things, whereas in so much of the West the seeds have perished.

Hilaire Belloc, *Many Cities,* 1928

Men, when they travelled in Spain during the sixteenth century, were nearly always in a bad temper. And they had cause to be.

W. Somerset Maugham, *Don Fernando,* 1935

But still the Spaniard's empire on this earth
Has been in height as ours in sweeping girth
And, perpendicular as ours is level
Affords less room or foothold for the devil.
His mission is to save as ours to clutch
And there's no country that we owe so much,
Who conquering more great powers than we have small
Has twenty times averted Europe's fall
As now she stands between us and the hell
Which no godless democracy could quell. . . .
Spain has mostly battled with the strongest
And in their rout her history's the longest.

Roy Campbell, *Flowering Rifle,* Book II, 1938

In Spain, where Lenin thought his way was clear,
If anywhere within the human sphere.

Ibid.

While Spain repudiates the breed that barters
And owns the sway of heroes, saints, and martyrs.

Ibid.

The one Spanish word that no foreigner can avoid learning is *mañana* – 'tomorrow' (literally, 'the morning'). . . . In Spain nothing from a meal to a battle ever happens at the appointed time. As a general rule things happen too late, but just occasionally – just so that you shan't even be able to depend on their happening late – they happen too early.

George Orwell, *Homage to Catalonia,* 1938

Spain is the very native land of carnage and of the

saints. Of those who martyrise and those who are martyred.

Hilaire Belloc, *Places,* 1942

Spanish civilisation is built upon a dread of and antipathy to Nature. In the huddling together of their houses and streets, in the intensity of their town life lies an anxiety to escape from the emptiness of the surrounding spaces. Every little pueblo feels itself beleaguered by the deadly boredom of the sun-drenched sierras and plains and, since the centrifugal forces that are so strong in Northern countries such as England simply do not exist here, Spaniards are driven to living pell-mell on top of one another in a manner not seen anywhere else except in Arab lands. Hence the warmth and animation of social life, but hence too, when disagreements arise, the bitterness.

Gerald Brenan, *The Face of Spain,* 1950

The Spanish economic system is like a game of musical chairs, in which there are only half as many seats as there are performers.

Ibid.

There is never any doubt, then, that one has arrived in Spain. . . . There is a faint sound of drums, a smell of crude olive-oil, and current of strong, leaking electricity.

Anthony Carson, *A Train to Tarragona,* 1957

A cloud of dust, left in the air when a great people went galloping down the highroad of history.

Jose Ortega y Gasset, quoted by James Morris, *The Presence of Spain,* 1964

God gave us a country we must fight like a lion.

Anon Spanish farmer, quoted by Laurie Lee, *As I Walked Out One Summer Morning,* 1969

A country that has sold its soul for cement and petrol and can only be saved by a series of earthquakes. Oh for more taste, less greed! Is there any Spain left? Perhaps only in Estremadura.

Cyril Connolly, *The Evening Colonnade,* 1973

Spaniards

Three Spaniards, four opinions.

Spanish proverb

The Spanish in America

The Spaniards doe sucke from the Indians the whole substance of their bodies, because they have nothing else in their houses. They make them spit bloud: They exhibite them to all dangers: They lay upon them sundry and intollerable travailes: and more then all this, They loade them with torments, beatings, and sorrowings: to be briefe, they spoile and consume a thousand manner of wayes.

Bartholomew de las Casas, 1542, in *Purchas his Pilgrimes,* 1625

Of all nacons under heaven, I suppose, the Spaniard is the most mingled, most uncerten and most bastardlie.

Edmund Spenser, *A Veue of the Present State of Ireland,* 1596

Seventeenth Century

The high-minded Spaniard, and their high-topped mountains, have an infused contention together; the one, through arrogant ambition, would invade the whole earth, to enlarge his dominions; the other, by steep swoln height, seem to threaten the heavens to pull down Jupiter from his throne. As I take it, the Spaniard being of a low stature, borroweth his high-minded breast from the high-topped mountains; for the one in quality, and the other in quantity, are extraordinarily similar.

William Lithgow, *Rare Adventures and Painfull Peregrinations,* 1614/32

The Spaniard is of a spare diet, and temperate, if at his own cost he spend; but if given *gratis,* he hath the longest tusks that ever played at table.

Ibid.

The Spaniard is a bad servant, but a worse master.

Thomas Adams, *Sermons,* 1629

He is a great servant of Ladies, nor can he be blam'd, for, as I said before, he comes of a *Goatish* race; yet he never brags of, nor blazes abroad his doings that way, but is exceedingly careful of the repute of any Woman (a Civility that we much want in *England*). . . . The *Spaniard* is not so smooth and oily in his Compliment as the *Italian;* and tho' he will make strong protestations, yet he will not swear out Compliments like the *French* and *English.*

James Howell, 'Letter to . . . Lord Colchester . . . Madrid, 1 February 1623', *Familiar Letters,* 1645

In Spaine he must be much more carefull of his diet, abstemious from fruit, more reserved and cautelous in his Discours, but entertaine none at all touching *Religion,* unlesse it be with *Silence;* a punctual repaiger of visits, extraordinary humble in his comportments, for the *Spaniards,* of all other love to be respected at their own homes, and cannot abide an insolent carriage in a Stranger; On the other side, Courtesie and *Morigeration,* will gain mightily upon them

James Howell, *Instructions for Forren Travell,* 1650

There was never a Spaniard that thought any one laugh'd at him.

William Wycherley, *The Gentleman-Dancing-Master,* 1672

Blackamoor: Hold up your head, hold up your head, Sir, a stooping *Spaniard,* Malo.
Monsieur: True, a *Spaniard* scorns to look upon the ground.

Ibid.

Now in *Spain,* he is wise enough that is grave, politick enough, that says little; and honourable enough that is jealous.

Ibid.

Fetherfool: . . . this fine thin sharp Air of *Madrid* has a most notable Faculty of provoking an Appetite: Prithee let's to the Ordinary. . . .
Blunt: Why, how now, what's the Door shut upon us?
Fetherfool: And reason, *Ned,* 'tis Dinner-time in the Ambassador's Kitchen, and should they let the savoury Steam out, what a world of *Castilians* would there be at the door feeding upon't. – Oh there's no living in *Spain* when the Pot's uncover'd.
Blunt: Nay, 'tis a Nation of the finest clean Teeth –
Fetherfool: Teeth! Gad an they use their swords no oftner a Scabbard will last an age.

Aphra Behn, *The Rover, Part ii, or The Banish'd Cavaliers,* 1681

Eighteenth Century

The very mention of horns is an insult, and the sight of them makes their blood boil. As their constitution may be said to be made up of the most combustible ingredients, and prone to love in a degree that natives of more northern latitudes can have no idea of, the custom of embracing persons of the other sex, which is used on many occasions by foreigners, sets the Spaniards all on fire. They would as soon allow a man to pass the night in bed with their wives or daughters, as suffer him to give them a kiss, and indeed, I believe the ladies themselves would look upon that favour as a certain prelude to others of greater consequence. Next to accusing a Spaniard of wearing horns, nothing can give him such offence, as to suspect him of having an issue.

Henry Swinburne, *Travels through Spain in the Years 1775 and 1776,* 1779

All these nights past we have heard the people singing doleful ditties under our windows, to the sound of a guitar, which they strike with their nails, without any notion of air, but merely as a kind of an accompaniment, sometimes high, sometimes low, but very coarse and monotonous. I can compare their music to nothing so well as to the beating of a frying-pan, to call down a swarm of bees.

Ibid.

It is said that the Spaniards, being a mixed people, descending from the Goths, Moors, Jews, and ancient Spaniards, borrowed their superstition from the Jews; melancholy from the Moors; pride from the Goths; and from the original Spaniards, a desire and thirst after the first of all earthly blessings – LIBERTY.

Philip Thicknesse, *A Year's Journey through France and Spain,* 1789

The Spaniards are most obstinately attached to their old customs. I heard of two men who left a manufactory at Guadalaxara because the Proprietor of it chose to introduce wheelbarrows. 'No,' they said, 'they were Spaniards, and it was only fit for beasts to draw carriages!'

Robert Southey, *Letters Written During a Journey in Spain,* 1797

Nineteenth Century

*'Since the Spaniards are so prone to follow the example of Friars,' said I, 'it is a pity that some societies of *working* friars are not established.'

John Moore, *Mordaunt,* 1800

They are really children in the art of war, and I cannot say that they do anything as it ought to be done, with the exception of running away and assembling again in a state of nature.

Duke of Wellington, Dispatch to Viscount Castlereagh, 25 August 1809

I am afraid that the Spaniards will bring us all to shame yet. . . . The Cortes appear to suffer under the national disease in as great a degree as the other authorities, that is, boasting of the strength and power of the Spanish nation, till they are seriously convinced they are in no danger, and then sitting down quietly and indulging their national indolence.

Duke of Wellington, Dispatch to the Right Hon. H. Wellesley, 2 December 1810

I am afraid that the *utmost* we can hope for is, *to teach them how to avoid being beat.* If we can effect that object, I hope *we* might do the rest.

Duke of Wellington, Dispatch, 18 August 1812

Lascelles Hoppner . . . spoke of the low order or mass of the Spaniards as being a fine people; very honourable, & seeming to disregard money, being willing to do anything from kindness. The men of this degree fine figures, – the women genteel and airy, but rather pretty than handsome. Both sexes have much natural grace. A painter has nothing to do but imitate what he sees perpetually, – groupes of picturesque figures, – attitudes always striking to the eye of an Artist. The Cloak and other parts of the dress what a painter would attempt to conceive. – The people are spirited & gay without the frivolity of the French. They are very religious, & this substantially as it influences their morals.

Joseph Farington, *Diary,* 18 April 1810

Such the ungentle sport that oft invites
The Spanish maid, and cheers the Spanish swain.
Nurtured in blood betimes, his heart delights
In vengeance, gloating on another's pain.
What private feuds the troubled village stain!
Though now one phalanxed host should meet the foe,
Enough, alas! in humble homes remain,
To meditate 'gainst friend the secret blow,
For some slight cause of wrath, whence Life's warm
stream must flow.

Lord Byron, *Childe Harold's Pilgrimage,* Canto the First, 1812

The Spaniards are less influenced in their habits, and even their political opinions, by their government, than any other people in existence.

Josiah Conder, *The Modern Traveller,* Vol. 18, 1830

The genius of the Spanish people is exquisitely subtle, without being at all acute; hence there is so much humour and so little wit in their literature.

Samuel Taylor Coleridge, *Table Talk,* 23 April 1832

While other nations were putting away childish things, the Spaniard still thought as a child and understood as a child. Among the men of the seventeenth century, he was the man of the fifteenth century or of a still darker period, delighted to behold an *Auto de fe,* and ready to volunteer on a Crusade.

T.B. Macaulay, 'The War of the Succession in Spain', *Edinburgh Review,* January 1833, *Critical and Historical Essays,* 1843

The Spaniards, who are not to be driven with a rod of iron, may be led by a straw.

Richard Ford, *A Handbook for Travellers in Spain,* 3rd edn, 1855

Never forget that the Spaniard is of a very high caste, and a gentleman by innate aristocracy, proud as Lucifer and combustible as his matches.

Ibid.

Spaniards are bad fellow-travellers; the Spaniard, at least, of the western hemisphere. They seize the meats upon the table somewhat greedily; their ablutions are not plentiful; and their timidity makes them cumbersome. That they are very lions when facing an enemy on terra firma. I do not doubt. History, I believe, tells so much for them. But half a gale of wind lays them prostrate, at all hours except feeding-time.

Anthony Trollope, *The West Indies and the Spanish Main,* 1859

Twentieth Century

If the people of Spain have one common trait it is pride, and, if they have another, it is common sense, and if they have a third, it is impracticality. Because they have pride, they do not mind killing, feeling that they are worthy to give this gift. As they have common sense they are interested in death, and do not spend their lives avoiding the thought of it and hoping it does not exist only to discover it when they come to die. This common sense that they possess is as hard and dry as the plains and mesas of Castilla and it diminishes in hardness and dryness as it goes away from Castilla. At its best it is combined with a complete impracticality. In the south it becomes picturesque; along the littoral it becomes mannerless and Mediterranean; in the north, in Navarra and Aragon, there is such tradition of bravery that it becomes romantic, and along the Atlantic coast, as in all countries bounded by a cold sea, life is so practical that there is no time for common sense. Death, to people who fish in the cold parts of the Atlantic ocean is something that may come at any time, that comes often, and is to be avoided as an industrial accident; so that they are not preoccupied with it, and it has no fascination for them.

Ernest Hemingway, *Death in the Afternoon,* 1932

If I am not mistaken here is the secret of the greatness that was Spain. In Spain it is men that are the poems, the pictures, and the buildings. Men are its philosophies. They lived, these Spaniards of the Golden Age; they felt and did; they did not think. Life was what they sought and found, life in its turmoil, its fervour and its variety. Passion was the seed that brought them forth, and passion was the flower they bore. But passion alone cannot give rise to a great art. In the arts, the Spaniards invented nothing. They did little in any of those they practised but give a local colour to a virtuosity they borrowed from abroad. . . . Their pre-eminence was great, but it lay in another direction: it was a pre-eminence of character. In this I think they have been surpassed by none and equalled only by the ancient Romans. It looks as though all the energy, all the originality, of this vigorous race had been disposed to one end and one end only, the creation of man. It is not in art that they excelled, they excelled in what is greater than art – in man. But it is thought that has the last word.

W. Somerset Maugham, *Don Fernando,* 1935

Long before I got to know Spain, I used to think of Death as a Spaniard

Arthur Koestler, *Dialogue With Death – Spanish Testament,* 1937

I would sooner be a foreigner in Spain than in most countries. How easy it is to make friends in Spain! . . . I defy anyone to be thrown as I was among the Spanish working class – I ought perhaps to say the Catalan working class, for apart from a few Aragonese and Andalusians I mixed only with Catalans – and not be struck by their essential decency; above all, their straightforwardness and generosity. A Spaniard's generosity, in the ordinary sense of the word, is at times almost embarrassing. . . . And beyond this there is generosity in a deeper sense, a real largeness of spirit, which I have met with again and again in the most unpromising circumstances.

George Orwell, *Homage to Catalonia,* 1938

In Spain the dead are more alive than the dead of any other country in the world.

Federico Garcia Lorca, 'The Duende: Theory and Divertissement', *Poet in New York,* 1940, Appendix 6, trans. Ben Belitt

The Spaniards have no sense of equity. They live by a tribal or client system which makes it a moral duty for them to favour their friends at the expense of the State and to penalise their adversaries. That is the first law of this country.

Gerald Brenan, *The Face of Spain,* 1950

A mysterious change comes over some Spaniards in the presence of death and suffering. These things seem to draw out of them some deep approval, as if their own death-instincts had been unloosed and given vicarious satisfaction. It is not sadism or love of cruelty, but a sort of fascinated absorption in what they regard as the culminating moment of existence. They unite themselves to it as the voyeur may do to the spectacle of another person's orgasm. I have seen this attitude displayed on many different occasions in Spanish life, including some of the most important and sacred, and have noted that the prelude to it is often a numbing of the ordinary responses. When, for example, they are put in the position of witnessing some act of which they would normally disapprove, both the wish and the power to intervene are atrophied. This is a feature which struck me very strongly during the early days of the Spanish Civil War.

Gerald Brenan, *South from Granada,* 1957

The Spaniards . . . with their hot, empty cruelty, their pride like wind on the stomach, like heartburn.

James Kirkup, *These Horned Islands,* 1962

The Spaniards are negative individualists. There is nothing very constructive to their jealous egotism.

James Morris, 'The Spanish Helmet', *Encounter,* October 1964

The master illusion of Spain is the conviction that the Spaniards are a people different, when they are only a people separate.

James Morris, *The Presence of Spain,* 1964

Spanish women

Touching their Women, Nature hath made a more visible distinction 'twixt the two Sexes here than elsewhere; for the Men for the most part are swarthy and rough, but the Women are of a far finer mould; they are commonly little: and whereas there is a Saying that makes a compleat Woman, let her be *English* to the neck, *French* to the waste, and *Dutch* below; I may add, for hands and feet let her be *Spanish,* for they have the least of any. They have another saying, A *Frenchwoman* in a dance, a *Dutchwoman* in the kitchen, an *Italian* in a window, an *England-woman* at board, and the *Spanish* a-bed. . . . After thirty they are commonly past Child-bearing, and I have seen Women in *England* look as youthful at fifty as some here at twenty-five. Money will do miracles here, in purchasing the favour of Ladies, or anything else; tho' this be the Country of Money, for it furnisheth well near all the World besides, yea their very Enemies, as the *Turk* and *Hollander;* insomuch that one may say, the *Coin* of *Spain* is as *Catholic* as her *King.*

James Howell, 'Letter to . . . Lord Colchester, from Madrid, 1 February 1623', *Familiar Letters,* 1645

There is a quality which gives a certain finish to Spanish women, and which is unique in them. It is a sort of smiling irony, which seems to penetrate the whole nature: the attitude of one who is aware of things, not unsatisfied with them, decided in her own point of view, intelligent enough to be tolerant of the point of view of others, without coquetry or self-consciousness; in fact, a small, complete nature, in which nothing is left vague or uneasy.

Arthur Symons, *Cities,* 1903

The bashful Spaniardess apparently finds the amorous Spaniard so menacing to her virtue
That she has to employ a duenna so that he shan't duennacing to her virtue.

Ogden Nash, 'These Latins', in *Many Long Years Ago,* 1945

Spanish language

Sonorous Castilian, in which, as Charles V. said, 'God ought alone to be addressed in prayer.'

Richard Ford, *A Handbook for Travellers in Spain,* 3rd edn, 1855

It was George Borrow who said that the Spanish language was greater than its literature.

W. Somerset Maugham, *Don Fernando,* 1935

Spanish food

I must frankly own that the only possible practical knowledge I have yet learnt, is to confirm P.'s theory of the *eatability* of cats, by the custom of this country. In the kitchen at Espinosa, M. remarked to me in Spanish that the cat was a very large one, and Mambrino immediately inquired if we eat cats in England. As you may suppose, an exclamation of surprise was the answer: . . . Why, said Mambrino, the night you were at Villafranca we had one for supper that weighed seven pounds.

Robert Southey, *Letters Written During a Journey in Spain,* 1797

Mambrino's account of the cat-eating is confirmed: I was playing with one last night, and the lady told me she was obliged to confine it in the house lest the neighbours should steal and eat it.

Ibid.

Spaniards think of a meal as of a religious service. Just as the introit leads up to the gradual, so the soup introduces the omelette, the omelette paves the way for the fish – in which there is about as much variety as there is between one collect and another – and the fish ushers in the clinching part of the meal, – the veal cutlet or beef steak. But an Englishman will find absolutely no cause for grumbling till he has been living in a Spanish hotel for at least a month.

Gerald Brenan, *The Face of Spain,* 1950

Aguilar de la Frontera

'This is a wretched place,' said the bus driver. 'Nothing but poverty and hunger. Why, it's *más feo que Dios,* uglier than God.'

Gerald Brenan, *The Face of Spain,* 1950

Alcolea (near Córdoba)

The Guadalquivir is crossed by the noble bridge of dark marble, built by Charles III., at *Alcolea.* This is so fine that the Spaniards say that the French, when they saw it, asked if it were not made in France.

Richard Ford, *A Handbook for Travellers in Spain,* 3rd edn, 1855

Algeciras

Modern rectangular common-place Algeciras. . . .

Richard Ford, *A Handbook for Travellers in Spain,* 3rd edn, 1855

Alicante (and Benidorm)

Alicante, a purely mercantile place, is much addicted to smuggling, especially on the wild coast near Benidorm.

Richard Ford, *A Handbook for Travellers in Spain,* 3rd edn, 1855

The town-hall has some sort of an appearance, but without any determined style or definable effect.

H. O'Shea, *A Guide to Spain,* 1865

Almería

'Do you know what other Spaniards call it? They call it *el culo de España,* 'the bum of Spain', and though I regard that as an insult to me personally, because it is directed at my city, I must admit that they're not far wrong.'

Gerald Brenan, *South from Granada,* 1957

Almeria is like a bucket of whitewash thrown down at the foot of a bare, greyish mountain

Ibid.

Andalusia

Andalusia's maids
Nurst in the glowing lap of soft Desire.

Lord Byron, *Childe Harold's Pilgrimage,* Canto the First, 1812

Aragón

Arragon, a disagreeable province, is inhabited by a disagreeable people. Obstinacy, indeed, is the characteristic of the *testarudo* natives, who are said to drive nails into walls with their heads, into which, when anything is driven, nothing can get it out. They have however a certain Spartan simplicity, and are fine, vigorous, active men, warlike, courageous, and enduring to the last.

Richard Ford, *A Handbook for Travellers in Spain,* 3rd edn, 1855

The name alone is enough to fill a man with delight and to magnify him with the story of twelve hundred years.

Hilaire Belloc, *Many Cities,* 1928

The Aragonese are a cold, serious, obstinate, daring race.

H. O'Shea, *A Guide to Spain,* 1865

Val d'Aran

Hemingway has written that in the Spanish shadow of the Pyrenees, which Republican militia men and civilians began to crawl out of in March by way of the Val d'Aran, military positions could be held by 'determined graduates of any good girls' finishing school.'

James Thurber, *My World and Welcome to It,* 1942

Asturias

The roads in the Asturias, much like those of Gallicia, savour more of the age of Adam than of Macadam.

Richard Ford, *A Handbook for Travellers in Spain*, 3rd edn, 1855

The season for travelling in Asturias is spring, summer, or not at all.

H. O'Shea, *A Guide to Spain*, 1865

Avila

Avila is a city in which it should be pleasant to linger. There is nothing much to do there and little to see. The walls, greatly restored, are like the walls of an old city in a book of hours. The neat, round towers placed at regular intervals look like the trim curls of a seventeenth century peruke. . . . A silent city. There are many streets in which you may stand for an hour without seeing a passer-by.

W. Somerset Maugham, *Don Fernando*, 1935

Avila is a miniature Jerusalem that must have been transported to Castile from Palestine on angel's wings.

Arnold Toynbee, *Between Niger and Nile*, 1965

Badajoz

A dull unsocial town.

Richard Ford, *A Handbook for Travellers in Spain*, 1855

Barbastro (and Lérida)

Previously I had seen Barbastro in brief glimpses, and it had seemed to me simply a part of the war – a grey, muddy, cold place, full of roaring lorries and shabby troops. It seemed entirely different now. Wandering through it I became aware of pleasant tortuous streets, old stone bridges, wine shops with great oozy barrels as tall as a man, and intriguing semi-subterranean shops where men were making cartwheels, daggers, wooden spoons, and goatskin water-bottles. I watched a man making a skin bottle and discovered with great interest, what I had never known before, that they are made with the fur inside, and the fur is not removed, so that you are really drinking distilled goat's hair. I had drunk out of them for months without knowing this. And at the back of the town there was a shallow jade-green river, and rising out of it a perpendicular cliff of rock, with houses built into the rock, so that from your bedroom window you could spit straight into the water a hundred feet below. Innumerable doves lived in the holes in the cliff. And in Lerida there were old crumbling buildings upon whose cornices thousands upon thousands of swallows had built their nests, so that at a little distance the crusted pattern of nests was like some florid moulding of the rococo period. It was queer how for nearly six months past I had had no eye for such things. With my discharge papers in my pocket I felt like a human being again, and also a little like a tourist. For almost the first time I felt that I was really in Spain, in a country that I had longed all my life to visit. In the quiet back streets of Lerida, and Barbastro I seemed to catch a momentary glimpse, a sort of far-off rumour of the Spain that dwells in everyone's imagination. White sierras, goatherds, dungeons of the Inquisition, Moorish palaces, black winding trains of mules, grey olive trees and groves of lemons, girls in black mantillas, the wines of Malaga and Alicante, cathedrals, cardinals, bull-fights, gypsies, serenades – in short, Spain. Of all Europe it was the country that had had most hold upon my imagination.

George Orwell, *Homage to Catalonia*, 1938

Barcelona

This city is a sweet spot; the air excels in purity, and much excels in mildness, the boasted climate of Montpellier. Except in the dog-days, you may here have green pease all the year round.

Henry Swinburne, *Travels through Spain in the Years 1775 and 1776*, 1779

The Fandango, as danced at Barcelona

Our evening ended with a ball, where we had for the first time the pleasure of seeing the Fandango danced. It is odd and entertaining enough, when they execute with precision and agility all the various footings, wheelings of the arms, and crackings of the fingers; but it exceeds in wantonness all the dances I ever beheld. Such motions, such writhings of the body and positions of the limbs, as no modest eye can look upon whithout a blush! A good Fandango lady will stand five minutes in one spot, wriggling like a worm that has just been cut in two.

Ibid.

To all but commercial travellers a few days will suffice.

Richard Ford, *A Handbook for Travellers in Spain*, 3rd edn, 1855

Of society, which is after all the least interesting feature in a country, there is little.

H. O'Shea, *A Guide to Spain*, 1865

When Charles V., in 1519, came here, he wished to be received, not as a King, but as one of the former counts; 'for,' said he, 'I would rather be Count of Barcelona than King of the Romans.'

Ibid.

It was the first time that I had ever been in a town where the working class was in the saddle. Practically every building of any size had been seized by the workers and was draped with red flags or with the red and black flag of the Anarchists; every wall was scrawled with the hammer and sickle and with the initials of the revolutionary parties; almost every church had been gutted and its images burnt. Churches here and there were being systematically demolished by gangs of workmen. Every shop and café had an inscription saying that it had been collectivized; even the bootblacks had been collectivized and their boxes painted red and black. Waiters and shopwalkers looked you in the face and treated you as an equal. . . . Down the Ramblas, the wide central artery of the town where crowds of people streamed constantly to and fro, the loudspeakers were bellowing revolutionary songs all day and far into the night. And it was the aspect of the crowds that was the queerest thing of all. In outward appearance it was a town in which the wealthy classes had practically ceased to exist.

George Orwell, *Homage to Catalonia,* 1938 – of December 1936

There was the startling change in the social atmosphere – a thing difficult to conceive unless you have actually experienced it. When I first reached Barcelona I had thought it a town where class distinctions and great differences of wealth hardly existed. Certainly that was what it looked like. 'Smart' clothes were an abnormality, nobody cringed or took tips, waiters and flower-women and bootblacks looked you in the eye and called you 'comrade'. I had not grasped that this was mainly a mixture of hope and camouflage. . . . Now things were returning to normal.

Ibid.

The worst of being wanted by the police in a town like Barcelona is that everything opens so late.

Ibid.

Barcelona Cathedral
I went to have a look at the cathedral – a modern cathedral, and one of the most hideous buildings in the world. It has four crenellated spires exactly the shape of hock bottles. Unlike most of the churches in Barcelona it was not damaged during the revolution – it was spared because of its 'artistic value' people said. I think the Anarchists showed bad taste in not blowing it up when they had the chance, though they did hang a red and black banner between its spires.

Ibid.

It takes all kinds of cities to make Barcelona. It takes among others a Roman city, a Gothic city, a maritime city, and a city of cosmopolitan pleasure. And the odd thing is that none of them at first sight looks particularly Spanish. . . . This is the last of the old Barcelonas, the new city, which surrounds them like a wrench gripping a nut.

Kenneth Tynan, 'Barcelona', 1959, in *Tynan Right and Left,* 1967

Basques

Les Basques sont un petit peuple qui saute et danse au sommet des Pyrénées.
(The Basques are a little people who leap and dance on top of the Pyrenees.)

Voltaire, attrib.

The Basque, as being the head of the Iberian family, is naturally prejudiced in favour of his country and himself; ultra local, he rarely quits even his parish, and therefore overrates his own ignorance as much as he underrates the intelligence of others. If the Castellano sees double in his own favour, the Basque sees quadruple, and his power of vision is keen in all that concerns himself and his interests, for in his limited scope, *self* forms the foreground and emphatic feature of his parochial picture; but *self* being placed so near, stands forward in too large a scale and in too bright colour; and as his eye for perspective is as defective as it is for proportion, every thing and person beyond his boundary appears too diminutive and subordinate.

Richard Ford, *A Handbook for Travellers in Spain,* 3rd edn, 1855

Like other Highlanders, they are grievously afflicted with genealogy and goitre.

Ibid.

They are good soldiers, especially when under the immediate and exclusive orders of a countryman. . . . Though deficient in the works of imagination, taste, and art, they are excellent mathematicians, learned scholars, and stout reasoners. Physically they are a very superior race, tall, muscular, well-proportioned, wiry, and swift-footed. Fair hair and blue eyes are frequent. . . . The women are very handsome, stand and walk like queens, fair-complexioned, and with magnificent long hair, worn in *trenzas* hanging over the back. They are reserved and haughty before strangers. Their claims to be the descendants of Noah and Tubal, the most noble race in the world, and of the pure and earliest nobility, are prominent features in their character.

H. O'Shea, *A Guide to Spain,* 1865

The Basque proverb says, –
Arraina eta arroza
Heren egunac carazes, campora deragoza.
'Fish and guests after the third day stink, and must be cast out of the house.'

Richard Burton, *Explorations of the Highlands of the Brazil,* 1869

Any description of the Basques must begin with their language, just as any introduction to their homeland starts with those arcane road signs, for the Basques more than anyone depend upon their language for their existence as a race.

James Morris, 'Basque Country', *Places,* 1972

Burgos

Most like some aged king it seemed to me,
Who had survived his old regality,
Poor and deposed, but keeping still his state
In all he had before of truly great;
With no vain wishes and no vain lament,
But his enforced leisure well content
To soothe with meditation, books and prayer:
For all was sober and majestic there.

Richard Chenevix Trench, *Recollections of Burgos, c.* 1850

I one asked him [the Duke of Wellington] whether in the case of Burgos, the government at home had been to blame for that insufficiency. 'Not in the least,' was the reply. 'It was all my own fault. The place was very like a hill-fort in India. I had got into a good many of these, and I thought I could get into this. The French, however, had a devilish clever fellow there, one Le Breton, and he fairly kept me out.'

Lord Ellesmere, *On the Life and Character of the Duke of Wellington,* 1852

Tourists . . . are apt to pass by this city without visiting it. The well-merited reputation of dullness and desolation of this backward provincial capital, and its second-rate hotels, have undoubtedly contributed to this indifference; but as in Spain the past alone is to be sought, we advise them to put up with the above, and not miss Burgos.

H. O'Shea, *A Guide to Spain,* 1865

From being the first place generally visited in Spain, Burgos has been greatly overrated by most travellers. It is not a picturesque place, and its new houses and white quays along the banks of the Arlanzon have the look of a very inferior Bordeaux.

Augustus Hare, *Wanderings in Spain,* 1885

Burgos typifies what is another characteristic of Spain, and that is the endless fertility of architectural adventure: the flowering of stone.

Hilaire Belloc, *Places,* 1942

Convent of Miraflores, near Burgos
The convent of Miraflores . . . looks at a distance as Eton chapel would look if placed on a bare wind-stricken height.

Ibid.

Cáceres

Caceres is the capital of its swinish district. . . . The climate, like the bacon is delicious. . . . Caceres is full of feudal architecture – of baronial massive houses decorated with granite doorways, and armorial bearings. Heraldry and hams indeed run riot here.

Richard Ford, *A Handbook for Travellers in Spain,* 3rd edn, 1855

Cádiz

The Towne of it selfe was a very beautifull towne, and a large, as being the chiefe See of the Bishop there, and having a good Cathedrall Church in it, with a right goodly Abbey, a Nunnery, and an exceeding fine Colledge of the Jesuites, and was by naturall situation, as also by very good fortification, very strong, and tenable enough in all mens opinions of the better judgement. Their building was all of a kinde of hard stone, even from the very foundation to the top, and every house was in a manner a kinde of a Fort or Castle, altogether flat-roofed in the top, after the Turkish manner, so that many men together, and that at ease, might walke thereon; having upon the house top, great heapes of weighty stones piled up in such good order, as they were ready to be throwne downe by every woman most easily upon such as passed by, and the streetes for the most part so exceeding narrow (I think to avoid the intollerable great heat of the Sun) as but two men or three at the most together, can in any reasonable sort march thorow them, no streete being broader commonly then I suppose Watling streete in London to be. The towne is altogether without glasse, excepting the Churches, yet with faire comely windowes, and with faire grates of Iron to them, and have very large folding leaves of wainscot, or the like. It hath very few Chimnies in it, or almost none at all: it may be some one chimney in some one or other of the lower out-roomes of least account, serving for some necessary uses, either to wash in, or the like, or else, now and then, perchance for the dressing of a dish of meate, having as it should seeme unto me, alwayes a greater care and respect how to keepe themselves from all kinde of great heate, then how to provide for any store of great roste.

The Voyage to Cadiz, 1596, in Samuel Purchas, *Purchas his Pilgrimes,* 1625

Except the *Calle Ancha,* all the streets are narrow, ill-paved, and insufferably stinking. They are all drawn in strait lines, and most of them intersect each other at right angles. The swarms of rats that in the nights run about the streets are innumerable, whole droves of them pass and repass continually, and these their midnight revels are extremely troublesome to such as walk late. The houses are lofty, with each a vestibule, which being left open till night, serve passengers to retire to; this custom, which prevails throughout Spain, renders these places exceedingly offensive. In the middle of the house is a court like a deep well, under which is generally a cistern, the breeding-place of gnats and mosquitos; the ground-floors are ware-houses, the first stories compting-house or kitchen, and the principal apartment up two pair of stairs. The roofs are flat, covered with an impenetrable cement, and few are without a *mirador* or turret, for the purpose of commanding a view of the sea. Round the parapet-wall at top are placed rows of square pillars, meant either for ornament, according to some traditional mode of decoration, or to fix awnings to, that such as sit there for the benefit of the sea-breeze may be sheltered from the rays of the sun; but the most common use made of them, is to fasten ropes for drying linen upon. High above all these pinnacles, which give Cadiz a most singular appearance, stands the tower of signals; here flags are hung out on the first sight of a sail, marking the size of the ship, the nation it belongs to, and if a Spanish Indiaman, the port of the Indies it comes from. The city is divided into twenty-four quarters, under the inspection of as many commissioners of police, and its population is reckoned at one hundred and forty thousand inhabitants, of which twelve thousand are French, and at least as many more Italians.

Henry Swinburne, *Travels through Spain in the Years 1775 and 1776,* 1779

Cadiz, sweet Cadiz! is the most beautiful town I ever beheld, very different from our English cities in every respect except cleanliness (and it is as clean as London) but still beautiful and full of the finest women in Spain, the Cadiz belles being the Lancashire witches of their land. . . . I beg leave to observe that Intrigue here is the business of life, when a woman marries she throws off all restraint, but I believe their conduct is chaste enough before. – If you make a proposal which in England would bring a box on the ear from the meekest of virgins, to a Spanish girl, she thanks you for the honour you intend her, and replies 'wait till I am married, & I shall be too happy.' – This is literally and strictly true.

Lord Byron, Letter to Mrs Catherine Gordon Byron, 11 August 1809

All have their fooleries – not alike are thine,
Fair Cadiz, rising o'er the dark blue sea!
Soon as the Matin bell proclaimeth nine,
Thy Saint-adorers count the Rosary:
Much is the VIRGIN teased to shrive them free
(Well do I ween the only virgin there)
From crimes as numerous as her beadsmen be;
Then to the crowded circus forth they fare:
Young, old, high, low, at once the same diversion share.

Lord Byron, *Childe Harold's Pilgrimage,* Canto the First, 1812

The lower orders have borrowed from foreigners many vices not common in the inland towns of temperate and decent Spain. Cadiz, as a residence, is but a sea-prison; the water is bad, and the climate, during the *Solano* wind, (its sirocco), detestable; then the mercury in the barometer rises six or seven degrees, and the natives are driven almost mad, especially the women: the searching blast finds out everything that is wrong in the nervous constitution. The use of the knife is so common during this wind, that courts of justice make allowances for the irritant effects, as arising from electrical causes, the passing over heated deserts. . . . The invalid will find the soft, moist air somewhat relaxing; but the city is well ventilated by fresh breezes, and the sea is an excellent scavenger.

Richard Ford, *A Handbook for Travellers in Spain,* 3rd edn, 1855

As the witty Frenchman said, 'ici les lettres de change sont les belles lettres.'

H. O'Shea, *A Guide to Spain,* 1865

The Spaniards call Cadiz, 'Una taza de plata,' a silver cup.

R.B. Cunninghame Graham, *Mogreb-el-Acksa,*1898

Not to be born would be best, or being born, to live at Cadiz.

Cyril Connolly, *The Condemned Playground,* 1945

Cartagena

The best Port upon the *Mediterranean;* for what Ships and Gallies get in thither, are shut up as it were in a Box from the violence and injury of all Weathers; which made *Andrea Doria,* being ask'd by *Philip* II. which were his best Harbours? he answer'd, *June, July,* and *Carthagena; meaning that any Port is good in those two Months, but Carthagena* was good any time of the year.

James Howell, 'Letter to Sir John North, Knight, Malamocco, 30 April 1621', *Familiar Letters,* 1645

The port of Cartagena is the completest I ever saw, formed by the hand of Nature in the figure of a heart.

Henry Swinburne, *Travels through Spain in the Years 1775 and 1776,* 1779

Castile (and Aragón)

A Castilia y Aragón
Otro mundo dió Colón.

(To Castile and Aragon, Columbus gave another world.)

Epitaph to Columbus in the Cathedral at Seville

Satan met his ancient friend
With more hauteur, as might an old Castilian
Poor noble meet a mushroom rich civilian.

Lord Byron, *Vision of Judgement,* 1822

Self, indeed, is the centre of Castilian gravity; bred and born among difficulties, obstacles, and privations, under a fierce sun, and on a hard soil, the wild weed of strong rank nature grows up harsh and unyielding. Here *man* is to be seen in his unsophisticated, untamed state, in all his native *individual force;* for here everything is personal, and the very antithesis of our social, corporate, fusing political combinations. Fond of *law,* and respectful in keeping it, he is not; for, disgusted at the limping pace and frequent ophthalmia of slow and venal *justice,* the splendid rage of the people rushes to conclusions, and taking the law and knife in its own hands, acts often as judge, jury, and executioner too; for they do not measure their oriental vengeance and retaliation by scruples, moral or arithmetical: but the Castilian is not addicted to mean, dishonourable crimes. . . .

The Castilians, from their male and trustworthy character, are still Robur Hispaniae (Flor ii 17,9), they constitute the virility, vitality, and heart of the nation, and the sound stuff of which it has – if ever – to be reconstructed. . . . However degenerated the pigmy aristocracy, the sinewy muscular forms of the brave peasants, true children of the Goth, are no unfitting framework of a vigorous and healthy, although uneducated mind. . . . The ancient qualities are *gravedad, lealtad, y amor de Dios,* self respect, love of God, and loyalty.

The genuine old Castilian is true to his king, his faith and to himself; his religion having a tendency to run into bigotry, his loyalty into subserviency; he hates foreign dictation, clings to the ways of his ancestors, thinks Spain the first kingdom in the world, the Castiles its first provinces, and himself the first of its population. No wonder therefore, that these peasants, as Addison said of those in the Georgics, toss about even manure with an air of dignity. . . .

Richard Ford, *A Handbook for Travellers in Spain,* 3rd edn, 1855

The Castilians have a classical non-perception of landscape, and a singular antipathy to trees.

Ibid.

Coming from the South, the first thing that strikes us when we walk in the streets is the sibilant sound of the Castilian accent. There is a continued subdued hissing as from snakes. But listen not for sounds, but for words. Then one will hear, like shots fired off at intervals, a stream of *No No No Nada Nada Nada.*These people seem to be always refusing or rejecting something. If the language of Provence used to be known as the *langue d'oc* and that of France as the *langue d'oil* and that of Italy as the *langue de si,* then decidely Spanish should be called the *langue de no.*

Gerald Brenan, *The Face of Spain,* 1950

between Castro de la Ventosa and Villafranca, on the high road to Compostella

The bee-hives here are made of part of the trunk of a tree, hollowed, about three feet high, and covered with a slate. *Sit mihi fas audita loqui.* An Englishman told me that going behind a posada by moonlight, he saw one of these hollow pieces of wood with its stone cover, and mistook it for a sort of necessary convenience, the want of which is the greatest inconvenience our countrymen feel either in Spain or in Edinburgh. A caricature of the Englishman's mistake upon the occasion, would amuse the Spaniards, for he was in the worst possible trim for making a speedy retreat, when he took off the cover, and out came the bees upon him.

Robert Southey, *Letters Written During a Journey in Spain,* 1797

Catalonia

Catalonia is undoubtedly the best cultivated, the richest, and most industrious province, or principality in Spain; and the king, who has the SUN FOR HIS HAT (for it always shines in some part of his dominions), has nothing to boast of, equal to Catalonia.

Philip Thicknesse, *A Year's Journey through France and Spain,* 1789

The Catalans are neither French nor Spaniards, but a distinct people, both in language, costume, and habits; indeed, their roughness and activity are enough to convince the traveller that he is no longer in high-bred, indolent Spain. Your republican who thinks rudeness a proof of equality and independence, inspires every well-bred gentleman with a desire to have as little to do with him as possible.

Richard Ford, *A Handbook for Travellers in Spain,* 3rd edn, 1855

The women fit to marry and breed Catalans are generally on a large scale; and neither handsome nor amiable. . . .

Ibid.

The Catalans are the most industrious, business-like, enterprising people in Spain; they are the Scotch of this country, as the Andalusians are the Irish, and the Asturians the Welsh. They are sober, laborious, honest, enthusiastic for progress, proud of their own, looking up to France for example and competition, and down on the surrounding provinces with contempt and pity. Wherever there is trade, fabrics, enterprise, there you are sure to find Catalans; in England, in America, in the East, they have everywhere, and in all ages and times carried their insatiable love of enterprise and activity. They are vehement, austere, revengeful, and generally not capable of great feeling or lasting friendship, and egotism seems to be a pivot around which all their actions turn. They are besides destitute of stability in their own political principles, and have sold themselves always to the highest bidder; but it must not be forgotten that in their hearts and souls they are neither Spaniards nor French, they are Catalans; and in their eyes, there is only one Cataluña, and Barcelona is its prophet. Their religion reaches superstition; their activity degenerates into feverish craving; their love of liberty has led them to bloodshed, excesses and rapine. They hold the commerce of Spain in their hands, and have been justly defined, as a province, the Spanish Lancashire. Cataluña has been always the centre of rebellion, the focus of republicanism and democracy; it is the feeder of Spain, its stomach, which is the centre and cause of all disease in the great body. They are patient and daring soldiers, excellent sailors, and model smugglers and guerrilleros. The dress is plain and unpicturesque. The women . . . who are not a handsome race, but strong, masculine, angular, and rough diamonds, wear a tight boddice, short dress, and an unbecoming handkerchief *mocado,* on their heads, which is generally red.

H. O'Shea, *A Guide to Spain,* 1865

It sounds an odd thing to say of eager Catalonia – but it is true – that here, if anywhere in the world, there is peace.

Hilaire Belloc, *Many Cities,* 1928

Chiclana

Chiclana is . . . a sort of medical Botany Bay, to which the Andalusian faculty transports those many patients whom they cannot cure. . . .

Richard Ford, *A Handbook for Travellers in Spain,* 3rd edn, 1855

Córdoba

The narrow streets, or rather alleys, so well adapted to give shade in summer, when the heat here is almost insupportable, are an unaltered relic of the Moorish dominion, under which Cordova was the successful rival of Bagdad and Damascus. Utterly devoid of picturesqueness, they have a more thoroughly African appearance than those of any other town in Spain. One threads one's way between interminable whitewashed walls, their scanty windows guarded by heavy iron bars, over a pebbly pavement so rough that it is like the bed of a torrent, littered with straw from the burdens of innumerable donkeys. There are no shops apparent, no animation whatever, nor any sign of life in the houses, and the few silent figures you pass are only miserable beggars wrapped in their mantas, generally lying on steps in the sun, almost too inert to extend their hands for charity, an occasional veiled lady gliding by to mass, or a majo, who goes swiftly along, erect upon his tall mule. Cordova is like a city of the dead; yet it looks modern and fresh, for every mark of antiquity is effaced by the coating of whitewash which clothes everything, and which makes the building of a thousand years ago indistinguishable from that of yesterday. . . . At Cordova Spanish idleness reaches its climax.

Augustus Hare, *Wanderings in Spain,* 1873

The Great Mosque

Nothing can be more striking than the first step into this singular rather than beautiful edifice. To acquire some idea of it, you must represent to yourself a vast gloomy labyrinth, like what the French are so fond of in their gardens, a fine *quincunx.* It is divided into seventeen iles, or *naves,* (each about twenty feet wide) by rows of columns of various marbles, viz. blue with white veins, yellow, red, red veined with white, gray, and Granadine and African green. . . . It is scarce possible to ascertain the exact number of columns in the mosque as they originally stood, because great changes have been made, many taken away, displaced, or built up in the walls of chapels, and several added when the choir was erected in the center of the whole. . . . Many chapels stuck up in various parts between the pillars, interrupt the enfilade, and block up the passage. . . . I can imagine no *coup d'oeil* more extraordinary than that taken by the eye when placed in such spots of the church as afford a clear reach down the iles, at right angles, uninterrupted by chapels and modern erections. Equally wonderful is the appearance, when you look from the points that give you all the rows of pillars and arches in an oblique line. It is a most puzzling scene of confusion.

Light is admitted by the doors, and several small cupolas; but nevertheless the church is dark and awful: people walking through this chaos of pillars seem to answer the romantic ideas of magic, inchanted knights, or discontented wandering spirits.

Henry Swinburne, *Travels through Spain in the Years 1775 and 1776,* 1779

Corunna

Other places attract the eye of a traveller, but Coruna takes his attention by the nose. My head, still giddy from the motion of the ship, is confused by the multiplicity of novel objects . . . the dress of the people . . . the projecting roofs and balconies on the houses . . . the filth of the streets, so strange and so disgusting to an Englishman; but what is most strange, is to hear a language which conveys to me only the melancholy reflection, that I am in a land of strangers.

Robert Southey, *Letters Written During a Journey in Spain,* 1797

We passed by a little island, seven leagues from Coruna, and one of our fellow passengers who knew the country observed, on pointing it out to us, that it was only inhabited by *hares* and *rabbits.* A Swede, (who had a little before obliged me with a lecture on the pronunciation of the English language) made a curious blunder in his reply, confounding the vowels *a* and *o;* 'As for de vimmin,' said he, 'dey may be very good – but de robers I should not like at all.'

Ibid.

The Costa del Sol

This is the Costa del Sol, variously known as the Coca Cola Coast and the Costa Mierda, for which a genteel translation would be the Coast of Dung.

Kenneth Tynan, 'The Rising Costa del Sol', 1963, in *Tynan Right and Left,* 1967

Daimiel

Daimiel turned out to be white, dusty and undistinguished. It has dull little streets, a dull little square and an air of profound boredom. Spaniards express the fact that they are bored, not by opening their mouths in a yawn, but by closing them firmly and allowing their faces to sag and collapse, and the streets and cafés of Daimiel were full of these collapsed and expressionless faces.

Gerald Brenan, *The Face of Spain,* 1950

Daroca

The town formerly occupied the hills for safety, but has now crept down into the vale for shelter.

Joseph Townsend, *Journey through Spain,* 1786–7

River Duero (at Tordesillas)

We crossed the Duero at Tordesillas by a noble bridge. One of the Latin historians says, that the water of this river made the Roman soldiers, who drank of it, melancholy; and if they drank nothing else, we may believe him.

Robert Southey, *Letters Written During a Journey in Spain,* 1797

Elche

Elche . . . has more of the idea Africa than Africa itself, and is the most splendid oasis in a singularly dismal desert. Generally, African travellers complain of the Spanish deserts as being deserts without any oases at all.

Augustus Hare, *Wanderings in Spain,* 1885

The Escorial

It might indeed, supposing it were three times as large, be made the new poor-law union of the Peninsula.

Richard Ford, *A Handbook for Travellers in Spain,* 3rd edn, 1855

'This grandest and gloomiest failure of modern times.'

Anon., quoted by Fergusson, *History of the Modern Styles of Architecture,* 1862

It is so profoundly curious that it must of necessity be visited, though it is so utterly dreary and so hopelessly fatiguing a sight, that it requires the utmost Christian patience to endure it. Well may Theophile Gautier exclaim, that whatever the other ills and trials of life may be, one may console oneself by thinking that one might be at the Escorial, and that one is not.

Augustus Hare, *Wanderings in Spain,* 1873

Philip II not only dedicated it to St Lawrence but built it in the shape of a gridiron. . . . Señor Junoy, the distinguished Catalan writer said to me with great imaginative insight: 'It seems so cold, and yet it is so ardent.' Philip's gridiron, almost like Pickwick's warming pan, was a cover for hidden fire. The very coldness of the surroundings accentuates that contained intensity. . . . Nobody had ever told me . . . that the Spanish King had done something altogether unique and even unnatural when he built in such a place and in such a style his grim gridiron of stone. Nobody had made me understand that he built a palace almost on the top of a mountain, far away upon naked and sterile heights only approached by rocky and ruinous roads like mountain passes. He had built a palace where anyone else would have built a hermitage.

G.K. Chesterton, *Tom Jones and the Escorial,* 1926

I salute it: the supreme monument of human permanence in stone; the supreme symbol of majesty. . . . In time it must at last be gone as must, for that matter, the pyramids; but it seems to me that works of this mighty sort are like dents inflicted on the armour of time. . . .

Hilaire Belloc, *Places,* 1942

This web of faith was drawn so tautly true
That suns are proud its rectitudes to burnish,
And the sierra for its rule to furnish
Pythagorean empires in the blue.
The lines, though airy gossamer and lace,
Dethroned the peaks with their pre-answered prayer:

For what the stars concede to us of space
And what the clouds abandon of the air
Is all pure architecture. The enraptured
Fabric is pinnacled with soaring notions.
By means of stone (with forests, peaks, and oceans)
Worlds in the web of symmetry are captured.
Stone thews the conquering purpose of the line.
When a proud people has decreed its altars,
The mountains move. Fulfilment rarely falters
That dawned in faith – the faith of this design.
Its consummation can be seen the better
Where the stone wrestles, and the ranges yield,
Surrendering the skies they used to shield
And reaching rocky arms for it to fetter.

Roy Campbell, *On the Architect's Designs for the Escorial,* after 1939

After the guide had expatiated for several minutes on the smallness and austerity of Philip II's own bedroom, an American lady ventured the question: 'You mean he was a democrat?'

Anthony Powell, *Messengers of Day,* 1978

Estremadura

The shepherds are mere brutes, like the animals with whom they live, and in whose skins they are clothed. They refute those pastorals in which the sentiments of civilization are placed in the mouths of the veriest clods of earth.

Richard Ford, *A Handbook for Travellers in Spain,* 3rd edn, 1855

It is mostly very flat, and consists of boundless, trackless plains, with villages, like happy days, 'few and far between', and an indolent, simple, pastoral, ignorant population, given exclusively to pasturing and rearing swine. The cities are very poor, and lack objects of interest to the tourist. The want of roads, wretched accommodation, and absence of subjects of interest to attract tourists have made us write so brief a description of its towns. However, the very features of this country, its loneliness and silence, its unexplored natural history, may tempt some tourists of a peculiar class and disposition.

H. O'Shea, *A Guide to Spain,* 1865

Galicia

This province of galesia is a londe of grete mountaynes and metelie provided of corne, wyne and vitalle. The people be somewhat rude and enclyned to robbyng and discention, and in it is moche tymbre for shippis and housys.

Roger Barlow, *A Brief Summe of Geographie, c.* 1540

In your life you never saw anything *so bad* as the Galicians; and yet they are the finest body of men, and the best movers I have seen.

Duke of Wellington, Dispatch, 10 December 1812

In Fray Gerundio's satirical newspaper on the Constitution of Spain, published some years ago, the first article ran thus: 'All those who are born in Spain are Spaniards, and the Gallegos besides.'

H. O'Shea, *A Guide to Spain,* 1865

Gironella

This is a fortified city, and well built, but every house has the appearance of a convent; I was going to say a gaol.

Philip Thicknesse, *A Year's Journey through France and Spain,* 1789

Granada

The Mores believe Granada Ly's
Directly under Paradise
And that they differ both no more
Than th'upper Roomes do from the Floure.

Samuel Butler, *Poetical Thesaurus – History,* before 1680

No wonder the Moors regretted Granada; no wonder they still offer up prayers to God every Friday for the recovery of this city, which they esteem a terrestrial paradise.

Henry Swinburne, *Travels through Spain in the Years 1775 and 1776,* 1779

The walls and gates of the town, very few parts excepted, are demolished or built up, and the city is open on all sides. Most of the streets are narrow and dirty. To the lanes and alleys the common people retire to perform the most filthy of nature's functions: but they do it with much decency, having by long practice acquired great expertness in casting their cloak like a net, so as to fall exactly round at a proper distance from the body. Though it is common enough to find them squatted down in the streets, you never see any body make water publicly, for when pressed, they always retire behind a door, into an entry, or to some secret corner.

Henry Swinburne, *Travels through Spain in the Years 1775 and 1776,* 1779

The Moors' once affluent and beautiful capital, the Damascus of the West.

Josiah Conder, *The Modern Traveller,* Vol. 18, 1830

Que no ha visto Granada
No ha visto nada.

Quoted H. O'Shea, *A Guide to Spain,* 1865

Long before railway days, I knew some ladies, who being delayed for a few days between two steamers at Malaga, determined to reach Granada, though it was only possible to spend one day there. Day and night, though in feeble health, they rode on in ever-increasing exhaustion. At last, on the summit of a desolate mountain, their strength altogether gave way, and they felt it impossible to proceed further. But just then, a solitary traveller approached from the other side of the pass – the path was so narrow, so hemmed in by precipices, that it was impossible to linger – there was no time for many words, but as the stranger passed, he exclaimed, 'Go on, go on, it is alike the Paradise of Nature and of Art,' – and they took courage and went on, and found it, as so many thousands of travellers have done since, the most perfectly beautiful place in the world.

Augustus Hare, *Wanderings in Spain,* 1873

To my mind Granada ranks with the *first*-class places.

Henry Adams, Letter to Charles Milner Gaskell, 21 November 1879

Granada became known as *la tierra del ochavico,* the land of the farthing, because almost nothing in it cost more than that.

Gerald Brenan, *South from Granada,* 1957

The Alhambra

It may disappoint those who, fonder of the present and a cigar than of the past and the abstract, arrive heated with the hill, and are thinking of getting back to an ice, a dinner, and a siesta. . . . Few airy castles of illusion will stand the prosaic test of reality, and nowhere less than in Spain.

Richard Ford, *A Handbook for Travellers in Spain,* 3rd edn, 1855

The Alhambra, the Acropolis, the Windsor Castle of Granada. . . .

Ibid.

I saw the Alhambra in a steady drizzle, and it seemed to me shoddy and bedraggled, like a gipsy girl sitting under a damp hedge.

Gerald Brenan, *South from Granada,* 1957

Grazalema

Grazalema is plastered like a martlet-nest on the rocky hill, and can only be approached by a narrow ledge. . . . The wild women, as they wash their parti-coloured garments in the bubbling stream, eye the traveller as if a perquisite of their worthy mates.

Richard Ford, *A Handbook for Travellers in Spain,* 3rd edn, 1855

Griteru (and Bamonde)

I should think Griteru the worst place in Europe, if we were not now at Bamonde.

Robert Southey, *Letters Written During a Journey in Spain,* 1797

Guadix

Observe the extraordinary character of the environs. The whole country about the town resembles a sea, whose waves have suddenly been transformed into solid substances. The hillocks rise up fantastically into conical and pyramidal shapes: their marly sides are excavated into caves, the homes of the troglodyte poor. No wonder some are called *los dientes de la Vieja,* although they are more like the teeth of a petrified colossal crocodile, than of an old woman.

Richard Ford, *A Handbook for Travellers in Spain,* 3rd edn, 1855

Guipuzcoa

In the parage of bylbo is the province of byskay, and sant sebastian is in the province of lepuzcua, it is mountayne contreis and hathe little corne and wyne but that as is brought to them from other partes. Thei have plentie of woodes and make many shippis, the people be colerike and soone steryd to angre and where thei overcome thei be very cruell but at the first brunt if thei be manfully resisted ther hartes be soone overcome. Thei be good maryners and occupie moche the see.

Roger Barlow, *A Brief Summe of Geographie, c.* 1540

Ibiza

Every year the Spanish police decide that they must cut down on the floating population of escapists, who regard the island as a slightly more accessible Tahiti, and a purge takes place. Deportation is usually carried out on grounds of moral insufficiency. . . . Annually Ibiza's Bohemian plant is pruned back to the roots, and with each new season it produces a fresh crop.

Norman Lewis, *The Changing Sky,* 1959

La Mancha

All the Mancha before us seems to be a bare

corn-country, ugly and tedious beyond expression. For my part, unless it be to look out at a venta, or peep about for an adventure at the meeting of the cross-roads, I intend sleeping all the way to Madrid.

Henry Swinburne, *Travels through Spain in the Years 1775 and 1776,* 1779

The traveller is sickened with the wide expanse of monotonous steppes, over which nought but the genius of Cervantes could have thrown any charm, gilding, as it were, its unendurable misery and dulness.

The towns are few, poverty-stricken, and without a particle of comfort or interest: the mud-built villages, the abodes of under-fed, ill-clothed, labourers: besides the want of water, fuel is so scarce that dry dung is substituted, as in the East. . . . The *Manchego* is honest, patient, and hardworking when there is any one to hire him; and his affections are more developed than his reason. Temperate, brave, and moral, he is attached and confiding when kindly used and honestly dealt with; reserved and stern when he suspects ill-treatment and injustice.

Richard Ford, *A Handbook for Travellers in Spain,* 3rd edn, 1855

León

There is no Appearance of Commerce, Manufactures, or Industry. The Houses are low, built of brick and Mud and Pebble stones from the fields. No Market worth notice. Nothing looks either rich or chearfull but the Churches and Churchmen.

John Adams, *Diary,* 6 January 1780

It is but a large agricultural village, silent and backward. . . . Leon now lies in torpid lethargy, shrouded in the magnificence of her past, and taking, it would appear, an eternal siesta, under the shade of her glorious cathedral.

H. O'Shea, *A Guide to Spain,* 1865

Loeches

I remember spending a day and a night at Loeche and seeing the people paddling together in their oleaginous tanks. I likewise remember the scenery as something grand, gloomy and peculiar.

Henry James, Letter to Thomas Sergeant Perry, 15 August 1867

Los Angeles (near Madrid)

The last relay is at *Los Angeles,* 'The Angels,' where Devils would not live could they help it.

Richard Ford, *A Handbook for Travellers in Spain,* 3rd edn, 1855

Madrid

Quien te quiere, no te sabe;
Quien te sabe, no te quiere.
(He who likes thee does not know thee;
He who knows thee does not like thee.)

Pedro da Costa Perestrello

El aire de Madrid es tan sotil
Que mata a un hombre, y no apaga a un candil.
(The air which will not extinguish a candle puts out a man's life.)

Quoted by Richard Ford, *A Handbook for Travellers in Spain,* 3rd edn, 1855

A most excellent air; a pleasant site, but the inhabitants are slovens, and the streets uncleanly kept.

Robert Burton, *Anatomy of Melancholy,* 1621

The walking is very unpleasant, as the streets have no flag stones: the general fault of the streets is their narrowness. In one of them it was with difficulty I kept myself so near the wall as to escape being crushed by a carriage; a friend of M. had a button on his breast torn off by a carriage in the same place: accidents must have been frequent here, for it is called, The Narrow Street of Dangers. *La Calle angusta de los peligros.*

Robert Southey, *Letters Written During a Journey in Spain,* 1797

Madrid, as a residence, is disagreeable and unhealthy, alternating between the extremities of heat and cold, or, according to the adage, with 3 months of winter and 9 of hell, *tres meses de invierno y nueve del inferno.*

Richard Ford, *A Handbook for Travellers in Spain,* 1855

Upstart Madrid, raised in a morbid hour to suit the purpose of a selfish vow.

H. O'Shea, *A Guide to Spain,* 1865

Madrid is nothing but a French town, on the walls of which, as on the Bordeaux and Paris shops might be written 'aqui se halla Español.'

Ibid.

It may truly be affirmed that as God worked six days, and rested on the seventh, Madrileños rest the six, and on the seventh . . . go to the bull-fight.

Ibid.

At best Madrid is a hole but in rainy weather it is a place fit only to drown rats in.

Henry Adams, Letter to Charles Milner Gaskell, 21 November 1879

Madrid is a sad city, particularly at night. Otto said all great cities look plague-like in a war, much worse than small towns or country villages.

Lillian Hellman, *An Unfinished Woman* (28 October 1937), 1969

Madrid, like a live eye in the Iberian mask
Asks help from heaven and receives a bomb.
Doom makes the night her eyelid, but at dawn
Drawn is the screen from the bull's-eye capital.
She gazes at the Junker angels in the sky
Passionately and pitifully. Die
The death of the dog, O Capital City, still
Sirius shall spring up from the kill.

George Barker, 'Elegy on Spain', *Lament and Triumph*, 1940

One cannot contemplate the size of Madrid nor the scale of life that prevails in it without some misgivings. Here is a city of nearly a million and a quarter inhabitants built in a wilderness and manufacturing next to nothing. Philip II chose the site for no other reason than that it was at the geographic centre of Spain, the point to which you would have to attach the string if you hung its cardboard replica horizontally from the ceiling. As a friend of mine once remarked, it was designed as the observation point in a centrally organized prison.

Gerald Brenan, *The Face of Spain*, 1950

Every few yards one meets a one-armed or one-legged man. Some have no legs at all and creep along on all fours, wearing a sort of boot on their hands. I am told that many of these cripples are *mutilados de guerra*, but not all. . . . Spaniards are very careless of their safety and shed their limbs with the facility of crabs.

Ibid.

As the symbol of ancient Spain was the great Cathedral, today it is the monstrous Bank. There are perhaps more enormous banks to the mile in Madrid than anywhere on earth, like temples to some powerful god who has not yet shown up.,

James Cameron, *News Chronicle*, 1 March 1954, in *What a Way to Run the Tribe*, 1968

In winter especially she seems a capital half-frozen in the attitudes of a past generation. . . . Upon Madrid herself change has fallen like a pile of concrete.

James Morris, 'The Spanish Helmet', *Encounter*, October 1964

River Manzanares

Except when swollen by the mountain snows, the Manzanares is so shallow, that if a cockle should attempt to navigate it, he must inevitably run aground.

Robert Southey, *Letters Written During a Journey in Spain*, 1797

This anatomy, which has the form of a river without the circulation.

Richard Ford, *A Handbook for Travellers in Spain*, 3rd edn, 1855

It is entitled a river by courtesy, because it has bridges – superfluous luxuries – which many real simple streams in Spain have not. The dilemma here has been whether to sell a bridge or buy water; but in this land of anomalies, rivers often want water and bridges, while bridges want water and rivers. . . . Whenever it rains, the stranger should run quickly down to see the river before it is gone. In summer the rivulet is scarcely as wide as its name is long, and they say the bed was once *watered*, when Ferd. VII passed it, to prevent his being annoyed by the dust.

Ibid.

Below, in the hollow, dribbles the Manzanares, which can scarcely be called a river, and which has been compared by Tirso de Molina to that dreariest of things, a university town during the long vacation.

Como Alcalá y Salamanca,
  Teneis y no sois Colegio,
Vacaciones en Verano
  Y curso solo en Invierno.

Augustus Hare, *Wanderings in Spain*, 1885

Málaga

'You're leaving us very soon,' said Doña María Luisa. 'Are you tired of Málaga already?'

I protested vehemently. Málaga, I said, was an earthly paradise.

'Aha,' said Don Carlos, laughing, 'you know the saying *Paradiso habitado por demonious*, A paradise inhabited by devils. That describes us completely. When you're with Malagueños, keep your eyes open.'

Gerald Brenan, *The Face of Spain*, 1950

When I told him that I had a house near Málaga, he said that he knew it must have the best climate in Spain because once, when he was visiting the town in winter, he found eight bishops staying there.

Ibid.

Montserrat

It stands single, towering over an hilly country, like a pile of grotto work or Gothic spires.

Henry Swinburne, *Travels through Spain in the Years 1775 and 1776*, 1779

It seems as if vast torrents of water, or some violent convulsion of nature, had split the eastern face of

Montserrat, and formed in the cleft a sufficient platform to build the monastery upon. The Llobregat roars at the bottom, and perpendicular walls of rock, of prodigious height, rise from the water edge near half-way up the mountain. Upon these masses of white stone rests the small piece of level ground which the monks inhabit. Close behind the abbey, and in some parts impending over it, huge cliffs shoot up in a semicircle to a stupendous elevation; their summits are split into sharp cones, pillars, pipes, and other odd shapes, blanched and bare; but the interstices are filled up with forests of evergreen and deciduous trees and plants. Fifteen hermitages are placed among the woods; nay, some of them on the very pinnacles of the rocks, and in cavities hewn out of the loftiest of these pyramids. The prospect is not only astonishing, but absolutely unnatural. These rocks are composed of limestones of different colours, glued together by a sand, and a yellow calcareous earth. In some parts they consist of freestone and white quartz, mixed with some touchstone. There may perhaps be reason to suspect fire to have been a principal agent in the formation of this insulated mountain.

Ibid.

It is called *Montserrat*, or *Mount Scie*, by the Catalonians, words which signify a cut or *sawed mountain;* and so called, from its singular and extraordinary form; for it is so broken, so divided, and so crowned with an infinite number of spiring cones, or PINE heads, that it has the appearance, as a distant view, to be the work of man; but upon a nearer approach, to be evidently raised by HIM alone to whom nothing is impossible. It looks indeed, like the first rude sketch of God's work; but the design is great, and the execution such, that it compels all men who approach it to lift up their hands and eyes to heaven, and to say, – Oh, God! – HOW WONDERFUL ARE ALL THY WORKS!

Philip Thicknesse, *A Year's Journey through France and Italy*, 1789

It rises an isolated grey mass, chiefly of pudding-stone. . . . The outline is most fantastic, consisting of cones, pyramides, buttresses, nine-pins, sugar-loaves, which are here jumbled by nature in a sportive mood.

Richard Ford, *A Handbook for Travellers in Spain*, 3rd edn, 1855

from Manresa

Beyond the river are ranges of olive-clad hills, above which, as we were drawing in the afternoon, uprose in mid-air a glorious vision, lifted high into the sky: pinnacles, spires, turrets, sugar-loaves, pyramids of faint-grey rocks, so wonderful that it was almost impossible to believe them a reality and not a phantasmagoria – the mountains of Monserrat.

Augustus Hare, *Wanderings in Spain*, 1873

Murcia

El cielo y el suelo buenos, el entre-suelo malo.
(The sky and the soil are good: all between them is bad.)

Luis de Belluga, Bishop of Murcia, attributed, *c.* 1300

The complexion of the Murcian is sallow, often livid: he is gloomy, choleric, hypochondriacal. Hepatic diseases are prevalent here, which are attributed to the want of exercise, bad food, of which *pimiento* always forms a principal ingredient, the excessive use of iced water, which is carried, even among the common people, to the pitch of a mania, and excess of sleep. The inhabitants go to bed early, rise late, and their *siesta* is two hours long.

Josiah Conder, *The Modern Traveller*, Vol. 18, 1830

This Dunciad province.

Richard Ford, *A Handbook for Travellers in Spain*, 3rd edn, 1855

This petrified nation is really a European curiosity, and ought to be walled in, and admittance granted on certain days of the year with tickets. . . . They all are, however, a good-natured honest people, fond of their country, their backwardness, their clergy, and pimiento; and not the less piquant for that. . . . This marmot, vegetable people.

H. O'Shea, *A Guide to Spain*, 1865

There is little or no art at Murcia; books and snow are alike unknown; where the body melts into water the mind cannot be active or strong. . . . The sooner, therefore, that the tourist leaves this frying pan the better.

Ibid.

Navarre

The highlanders of Navarre are remarkable for their light, active, physical forms, their temperate habits, endurance of hardships and privation, individual bravery, and love of perilous adventure; the pursuits of the chase, smuggling, with a dash of robbery, form their moral education.

Richard Ford, *A Handbook for Travellers in Spain*, 3rd edn, 1855

Old Castile (between Agreda and Soria)

Now the traveller has re-entered the bald regions of Old Castile, and the best thing is to get out of them again as quickly as possible.

Richard Ford, *A Handbook for Travellers in Spain*, 3rd edn, 1855

Orihuela

There is a Spanish proverb in favour of [Orihuela]. . . . *Si llove, aytrigo en Orihuela, y si no llove aytrigo en Orihuela:* 'If it rains there is plenty of wheat in Orihuela, and if it does not rain there is still plenty of wheat in Orihuela.'

Henry Swinburne, *Travels through Spain in the Years 1775 and 1776,* 1779

Pamplona

Long before we reached it, we could see the rock-built Pamplona, its brown towers and walls standing out as if embossed against the delicate pale pink of the snow-tipped mountains, and rising from the long reaches of the dead green Cuenca, as the surrounding plain is called, the cup which contains the precious 'key of Navarre,' and which here closely resembles the Roman Campagna in its desolation and colouring.

Augustus Hare, *Wanderings in Spain,* 1885

Pyrenees

The Pyrenees look much more Homeric than the Alps.

Alfred Lord Tennyson, Remark, 1874, in *Alfred Lord Tennyson, a Memoir, by his Son,* 1897

Roncesvalles

A small hamlet with a great name.

Richard Ford, *A Handbook for Travellers in Spain,* 3rd edn, 1855

Ronda

Undoubtedly on the long highways of a thinly-peopled land, accidents may occur, as Spanish gentlemen who have met with misfortunes in troubled times will take to the road. But robbery is the exception, rather than the rule, in Spain; and latterly precautions have been so increased that some ingenuity must be displayed in managing to get waylaid and pillaged – not that to the very ambitious for such events, or to the imprudent or incautious, the thing is altogether impossible. The experiment might be tried with prospect of success in Andalucia, taking Ronda as the centre of a robbing radius.

Richard Ford, *A Handbook for Travellers in Spain,* 3rd edn, 1855

There is but one Ronda in the world, and this *Tajo,* cleft as it were by the scimitar of Roldan, forms, when the cascade is full, as we have seen it, and as it ought to be seen, its heart and soul. The scene, its noise and movement, baffle pen and pencil, and, like Wilson at the Falls of Terni, we can only exclaim, 'Well done, rock and water, by Heavens!'

Ibid.

Salamanca

Mr. Johnson persisted in advising me to go to Spain. I said it would divert him to get a letter from me dated at Salamanca. 'I love the University of Salamanca,' said he, 'for when the Spaniards were in doubt if they should conquer the West Indies, the University of Salamanca gave it as their opinion that they should not.'

James Boswell, *Boswell's London Journal,* 28 July 1763

Gastronomy never was an Iberian science, and if Salamanca has produced 100,000 doctors, it never has reared one good cook. The food for body and mind, however copious in quantity, is unsatisfactory in quality.

Richard Ford, *A Handbook for Travellers in Spain,* 3rd edn, 1855

Travellers in the early spring will observe the quantities of pet lambs in the streets of Salamanca, generally decorated with bunches of red worsted. By a curious custom a general slaughter of these takes place on Good Friday upon the doorsteps – the little creatures being executed by their own mistresses, who stab them in the throat.

Augustus Hare, *Wanderings in Spain,* 1885

To judge it as it should be judged, one must not come in by the common road or rail from the direction of north or east. One must come in across the river from the south.

The great University of the Middle Ages, the rival of Oxford and of Paris, the dominating towers, the characteristic saffron stone of the hill – all these stand out before you on the journey northward from the Guadarrama mountains. . . .

Here, as in a hundred other cases, it is from the Roman approach that one sees the European meaning.

Hilaire Belloc, *Many Cities,* 1928

Salamanca is an agreeable place to linger in. It has a noble square, with arches all round it, and here towards evening the whole population perambulates, the men in one direction, the girls in the other, so that they may ogle one another as they pass. The town hall, with its plateresque façade, is rose-coloured. The mass of the cathedral, seen from a little distance, is fine; it seems to be planted on the ground with a sort of solid arrogance; but when you approach you are repelled by its ugly reddish brown and the florid decoration. The interior is overwhelmingly magnificent. There are huge, lofty pillars that tower to a height that seems hardly believable. The choir is surrounded by elaborate bas-reliefs. It is all so grand and sumptuous, it reminds you of a Lord Mayor's banquet; it suggests a ceremonial, assured, opulent religion, and you ask yourself what solace in trouble the stricken heart could hope to find there.

W. Somerset Maugham, *Don Fernando,* 1935

Santiago

Santiago is built on an uneven, irregular site: thus while the convent of *San Francisco* lies in a hole, the cathedral occupies a slope in the heart of the city, and indeed it was the origin of its life; and from this centre, many veins of streets diverge, and the apostle's tomb is as the web of a spider's nest, in which strange and foolish flies are caught. The town is damp, cold, full of arcades, fountains, and scallop-shells; it has a sombre look, owing to the effect of humidity on its granite materials. From the constant rain this holy city is irreverently termed *El orinal de España,* therefore everybody carries an umbrella: the peasants also add a stick, for their love of broils is not damped.

Richard Ford, *A Handbook for Travellers in Spain,* 3rd edn, 1855

The Cathedral
The architecture is luxuriant, but its heroic grandeur prevents it from being tiresome and the perfect balance of the decorative motives gives an impression of an almost classic severity. It is like a purple patch in Chapman's *Homer.*

W. Somerset Maugham, *Don Fernando,* 1935

Seville

A Strange Ceremony. I was told thatt when the King of Spaine cometh thatt way and is to enter the Citty, they make a bridge for him thatt hee may com over the walls and not through any of the gates; for, through which gate so ever the King enters, all goods, Merchandize, etts., which shall either bee imported or exported through the same, shall bee Custom free, which would bee a great losse and hinderance to the Citty: soe the King is pleased to com over the walls as aforementioned.

Peter Mundy, *Travels,* 1615

and Cadiz
Fair is proud Seville; let her country boast
Her strength, her wealth, her site of ancient days;
But Cadiz, rising on the distant coast,
Calls forth a sweeter, though ignoble praise.
Ah, Vice! how soft are thy voluptuous ways!
While boyish blood is mantling, who can 'scape
The fascination of thy magic gaze?
A Cherub-Hydra round us dost thou gape,
And mould to every taste thy dear delusive shape.

Lord Byron, *Childe Harold's Pilgrimage,* Canto the First, 1812

'Quien no ha visto a Sevilla,
No ha visto a meravilla.'
He who has not at Seville been,
Has not, I trow, a wonder seen.

Quoted by Richard Ford, *A Handbook for Travellers in Spain,* 3rd edn, 1855

Seville is the alma mater of the bull-fight.

Ibid.

Infants produce small scandal in Seville; they may be only the result of having eaten of the lily, which is sacred to the Virgin.

Augustus Hare, *Wanderings in Spain,* 1873

The oven of Spain.

Popular saying (?), quoted *ibid.*

Seville, more than any city I have ever seen, is the city of pleasure. . . . It has the constant brightness, blitheness, and animation of a city in which pleasure is the chief end of existence, and an end easily attained, by simple means within every one's reach. It has sunshine, flowers, and expressive river, orange-groves, palm trees, broad walks leading straight into the country, beautiful, ancient buildings in its midst, shining white houses, patios and flat roofs and vast windows, everything that calls one into the open air, and brings light and air to one, and thus gives men the main part of their chances of natural felicity. . . . it is concentrated, and yet filled to the brim; it has completely mastered its own resources.

Arthur Symons, *Cities,* 1903

Seville lights up for a feast-day as a face lights up with a smile.

Ibid.

Sierra Nevada

El Picacho de la Veleta, the Watchpoint
This eternal rampart of the lovely Vega is very impressive: the sharp mother-of-pearl outline cuts the blue sky; clear and defined, yet mysteriously distant, size, solitude, and sublimity are its characteristics. The adventurous are advised to scale the heights, and win the favours of this cold beauty, and she will be melted by such daring.

Richard Ford, *A Handbook for Travellers in Spain,* 3rd edn, 1855

seen from Granada
Through the bare network of the plane trees, we could see far above us the snow banks of the Sierra Nevada, like a great double bed which no one had slept in.

Gerald Brenan, *The Face of Spain*, 1950

The Somosierra (between Madrid and Burgos)

Dreary now becomes the face of nature, the heat in summer is terrific; green as a colour, and water as a liquid are curiosities; it is just the place to send a patient who is afflicted with hydrophobia.

Richard Ford, *A Handbook for Travellers in Spain*, 3rd edn, 1855

Tarifa

The crumbling walls of Tarifa might be battered with its oranges, which although the smallest, as beyond comparison the sweetest in Spain.

Richard Ford, *A Handbook for Travellers in Spain*, 3rd edn, 1855

Tarragona

We've travelled far, and beef has become mutton, chicken partridge – I should hardly know now if you gave me pork to eat. This is a sad state of things only balanced by the beauties of nature and the antiquities of man, upon which I would discourse if you would listen, but to tell the truth it is the food one thinks of more than anything abroad. When I tell you that the W.C. opposite our room has not been emptied for 3 days, and you can there distinguish the droppings of Christian, Jew, Latin and Saxon – you can imagine the rest. This is Tarragona.

Virginia Woolf, letter to Lytton Strachey, Tarragona, 1 September 1912

Tarragona has a cathedral that is grey and austere, very plain, with immense, severe pillars; it is like a fortress; a place of worship for headstrong, violent, and cruel men. The night falls early within its walls and then the columns in the aisles seem to squat down on themselves and darkness shrouds the Gothic arches. It terrifies you. It is like a dungeon.

W. Somerset Maugham, *Don Fernando*, 1935

Toledo

Toledo is the strangest city you can imagine in point of situation; something like Durham or Richmond in Yorkshire, but not equal to either in beauty, as it is totally bare of wood.

Henry Swinburne, *Travels through Spain in the Years 1775 and 1776*, 1779

Toledo is a museum, the Pompeii of Spain, and its former 200,000 inhabitants seem to be taking their siesta rather than to have departed from it for ever. Its steepleless churches, crumbling palaces, dilapidated walls, are so picturesquely grouped, have such individuality, colouring, and relief, that it seems as if some great painter, say Salvator Rosa, or Turner, had been allowed to realise here the Irishman's idea of *building* ruins.

H. O'Shea, *A Guide to Spain*, 1865

At a distance the town rises grandly, not distinguished by any one marked feature or building, except its great Alcazar, which is chiefly of the last century, but an irregular line of towers, battlemented walls, and ancient houses, crowning the black precipitous rocks, which rise abruptly from the yellow Tagus, and backed by rugged hills, scorched and parched into every shade of orange and brown by the tropical sunshine. The general views of Toledo have no beauty, but are solemn and affecting beyond those of all other places, so huge and historical does it stand, without any vegetation whatever, girdled in from the living world by the indescribable solitude of its utterly desolate hills.

Augustus Hare, *Wanderings in Spain*, 1873

Toledo looked to me much more like Jerusalem than Jerusalem ever looked like most pictures of it. It has a wall crowning a hill whose steep sides have an indefinable look of a ruin and even a rubbish-heap. It is in the sort of country that is spotted with hardy olives or striped with hardy vines. It has that look that we never know in the rich rain and deep grasses of our northern islands – the look of vegetation being an exception.

G.K. Chesterton, *The Tradition of Toledo*, 1926

. . . burn, with Athens and with Rome,
A sacred city of the mind.

Roy Campbell, *Toledo*, July 1936

And round Toledo's shattered walls,
Where, like a crater on the moon,
The desecrated grandeur sprawls. . . .

Roy Campbell, 'The Hoopoe', *Talking Bronco*, 1946

Like Fez it reeks of the Middle Ages: like Lhasa, of monks.

Gerald Brenan, *The Face of Spain*, 1950

Torremolinos

This is the capital of what has been sourly described as

'Nescafé Society.' Is your marriage about to collapse? Do you seek friends as lost as yourself? Would you bend a law or two for a puff of marijuana imported from Morocco? Does a barfly life, spiced with amateur orgies, appeal to your notion of holiday? If so, and if you do not mind wading through the debris of broken glass left at dawn by feuding couples, Torremolinos is your place. This is an open township, inbred and amoral after which the next stop is Tangier, followed by a suicidal leap from some high peak in the Canary Islands.

Kenneth Tynan, 'The Rising Costa del Sol', 1963, in *Tynan Right and Left,* 1967

Valencia

specifically Villareal, near Castellón
Un paradiso habitado por demonios.
(A paradise inhabited by fiends.)

Quoted by G.A. Sala, *Paris Herself Again,* 1879

The Valencians say:

Carne es verdura;
Verdura es aqua;
Hombres son mugeres,
Y mugeres nada.

(The meat is greens, the greens are water, the men are women, and the women nothing.)

H. O'Shea, *A Guide to Spain,* 1865

One of the noblest Cities in all *Spain,* situate in a large Vega, or Valley, above sixty miles compass: here are the strongest Silks, the sweetest Wines, the excellentest Almonds, the best Oils, and beautiful'st Females of all Spain, for the prime Courtesans in *Madrid* and elsewhere are had hence. The very brute Animals make themselves Beds of Rosemary, and other fragrant Flowers hereabouts; and when one is at Sea, if the Wind blow from the Shore, he may smell this Soil before he come in sight of it, many Leagues off, by the strong odoriferous Scent it casts. As it is the most pleasant, so it is also the temperat'st Clime of all *Spain;* and they commonly call it the second *Italy,* which made the *Moors,* whereof many thousands were disterr'd and banish'd hence to *Barbary,* to think that Paradise was in that part of the Heavens which hung over this City.

James Howell, 'Letter to Dr Fr. Mansel, from Valentia, 1 March 1620', *Familiar Letters,* 1645

Various and overpowering are the stinks that rise up in every corner. . . . The houses are filthy, ill-built and ruinous; and most of the churches are tawdry, and loaded with barbarous ornaments both without and within. . . . In all, the judicious observer will be disgusted with loads of garlands, pyramids, broken pediments, and monstrous cornices – a taste too Gothic and trifling for any thing but the fruit of a mountebank's booth, or a puppet-show in a fair.

Henry Swinburne, *Travels through Spain in the Years 1775 and 1776,* 1779

We shall leave Valencia to-morrow, being heartily tired of our quarters. The climate is mild and pleasant, but there is something faintish and enervating in the air. Every thing we eat is insipid, and void of substance; the greens, wine and meat, seem the artificial forced productions of continual waterings and hot-beds. . . . Here a man may labour for an hour at a piece of mutton, and when he has tired his jaws, find he has been only chewing the *idea* of a dinner. The meat, as soon as cut into, yields abundance of gravy, and may be said to bleed a second time to death, for nothing remains but a mere withered *caput mortuum,* as our servants know by woful experience. Vegetables, with the finest outward shew imaginable, taste of nothing but water. This washy quality seems also to infect the bodies and minds of the Valencians: they are largely built, and personable men, but flabby and inanimate. Scarce any society is kept up amongst them, though the salubrity of the climate, and reasons of oeconomy induce several very considerable families to make this city the place of their abode. In some strange way or other they spend very large incomes, without doing themselves the least credit. Their chief expence lies in servants, mules, and equipages; low, obscure amours often consume the best part of their fortunes.

Ibid.

Valencia, in spite of its opulence and the affability of its inhabitants, is far from being an amusing town, – at least to a Frenchman. . . .

Josiah Conder, *The Modern Traveller,* Vol. 18, 1830

In darker shades of character the Valencians resemble both their Celtiberian and Carthaginian ancestors; they are superstitious, cunning, perfidious, vindictive, sullen and mistrustful, fickle and treacherous. Theirs is a sort of *tigre singe* character; one of cruelty allied with frivolity; so blithe, so smooth, so gay, yet empty of all good; nor can even their pleasantry be trusted, for, like the Devil's good humour, it depends on their being pleased; at the least rub, they pass, like the laughing hyena, into a snarl and bite: nowhere is assassination more common; they smile, and murder while they smile.

Richard Ford, *A Handbook for Travellers in Spain,* 3rd edn, 1855

The principal features of character are, superstition; revengeful, relentless spirit, *ni olvido ni perdono;* love of pleasure, dancing, making love, sipping the delicious cool *horchata de chufas,* a local drink. The people are laborious, persevering, generally honest; fond of bright colours and pomp; in violent love or hatred, sullen and mistrustful. Crime, arising from jealousy, envy, family dissension, and tavern brawls, is frequent, and attended with hyena-like fierceness, watchful of good opportunity, thirsty of blood, not gold. The escopeta and trabuco are used with wonderful precision by the labourers, who seldom go without one, as *ultima ratio,* or timely advertisements about wages, and mere trifles. They are withal lively, imaginative, very intelligent, enterprising, and the upper classes most polished and agreeable, of unbounded charity and generosity. The darker shades of their character would be considerably brightened up by interior light, as all is night still in their minds, and education would correct and refine the conditions of their fine, nervous temperament, excited and irritated by the burning sun, and checked by nought and none. To the stranger they are affable, kindhearted, and have pride in showing off their cities, their huerta, their dress, and even their expeditious way of suppressing their intimate enemies.

H. O'Shea, *A Guide to Spain,* 1865

It is, with its ill-assorted medley of old and new, its often tasteless modernisation surrounding (and all too often engulfing) elegant seventeenth and eighteenth century houses, its tendency to disintegrate into dusty squares that have the air of building lots, an untidy town.

Rose Macaulay, *Fabled Shore,* 1949

The wart on the Mediterranean lip.

Anon., quoted by Kenneth Tynan, 'The Judicious Observer will be Disgusted', in *The Sound of Two Hands Clapping,* 1975

Mrs Ryan, a woman whose lion-hearted chic nothing can daunt, offered me one or two comments on the place. 'Valencia,' she said, 'lets you make your own choices. It preserves its own pride and lets you preserve yours. And it doesn't matter what you wear because God knows you aren't going to meet anyone!' She can still mime what she describes as 'that special, unforgettable *look* you get from Spanish friends when you tell them you're going on vacation to Valencia.' It is a look of stunned incredulous grief.

Ibid. (quoting Mrs John Barry Ryan III)

I haven't yet mentioned the smell in the streets, which on warm days conjures up an image of several thousand veteran turbot trapped in an avalanche of guano.

Ibid.

Pittsburgh without the air pollution

Anon, American, quoted *ibid.*

The tourist explosion, I believe, is already creating a new breed of European tourist – the anti-tourist, with appetites quite different from those of his predecessors. . . . Valencia, where a noisy and majestic ugliness stands sentinel, ever ready to repel outsiders, is one of the few places that come close to fulfilling all our demands. . . . Some people go on vacation to meet strangers, others go to meet themselves. For this group, Valencia, world hub of anti-tourism, is the predestined haven and hiding-place.

Ibid.

near Valencia

Our pleasurable ideas were a little ruffled by the sight of some hundreds of women in their villages, sitting in the sun, lousing each other, or their husbands and children. When a young woman condescends to seek for lice in a man's head, it is supposed that the last favours have been granted by the fair one, or at least that he may have them for the asking.

Henry Swinburne, *Travels through Spain in the Years 1775 and 1776,* 1779

Valladolid

The inhabitants are genuine old Castilians, grave, formal, honourable, and bores of the *first class.*

Richard Ford, *A Handbook for Travellers in Spain,* 3rd edn, 1855

Vélez

A white town sliding down a steep hill.

Gerald Brenan, *The Face of Spain,* 1950

Vigo

We merely touched at Vigo, which looked fruitful, rolled up in a hot mist.

Alfred Lord Tennyson, Letter Diary, 21 August 1859, in *Alfred Lord Tennyson, a Memoir, by his Son,* 1897

Yegen

With its grey box-shaped houses of a battered Corbusier style, all running down the hill and fusing into one another, and its flat clay roofs and small smoking chimneys, it suggested something that had been made out of the earth by insects.

Gerald Brenan, *South from Granada,* 1957

SUDAN

Report says that the Mahdi sent Sheikh el Obeid (the *man* not the *city*) to tell him to come to Obeid (the *city* not the *man*), and devoted himself to God's service, as a dervish. The Sheikh el Obeid (the *man* not the *city*) does not see it for he is very rich (I know it is a horrid nuisance, these names, but I did not give them). It would be a charity to execute the man, for those who are perplexed, and end the difficulty. We cannot execute the city.

General Charles George Gordon, *Journal,* 16 October 1884

I forget how many days we passed in the 'Sudd', where there is nothing in ken but 'green beds of growing rushes where no leaf blooms or blushes.' . . . There was a story that Lady Cromer's maid on the third or fourth day of this had said to her mistress, 'How long, my Lady, must we tarry in this shrubbery?' but as I was told afterwards that Lady Cromer had never been in the Sudd, it must have been someone else's maid.

Edward Marsh, *A Number of People,* 1939 – of 1908

Politically the Sudan is, I think, the most exciting country we saw in all Africa, with the possible exception of Nigeria. This is not a nation half-dead at birth, like Libya. It has the intense virility of something newly born and its vibrant will to live derives from sound old roots. The Sudan sounds a note unlike any we have met in Africa so far – of animation, confidence, and spontaneity. It is crowded with zest to get ahead; it boils and sparkles with euphoria. I even heard a youthful Sudanese say, 'Our country is going to be like the United States; we will try to combine here the best of both Africa *and* Europe.' On a different level he went on enthusiastically, 'We want more than just good roads, good schools, good hospitals. We want good *movies* too!'

John Gunther, *Inside Africa,* 1955

The South (under the British)

DC's in the south were nicknamed 'Bog Barons'. One senior official told me, 'Of course we sent the *clever* lads to the northern provinces. The south is no place for a *clever* man. Anybody clever would go crazy. For the south we had to have stolid chaps, but, by Jove, what good chaps they were!'

John Gunther, *Inside Africa,* 1955

Sudanese

The Nubian is interesting in his appearance and character; his figure is tall, thin, sinewy, and graceful, possessing what would be called in civilized life an uncommon degree of gentility; his face is rather dark, though far removed from African blackness; his features are long and aquiline, decidedly resembling the Roman; the expression of his face mild, amiable, and approaching to melancholy.

John Lloyd Stephens, *Incidents of Travel in Egypt etc.,* 1837

These miserable people do not understand energy, and the Ramadan increases their incapacity.

Sir Samuel Baker, *Ismailia,* 1874

One Sudanese told me, 'Most Moslems do not become Communists easily.' Then he used an unexpected adjective: 'We do not care for an ideology so *emaciated*.'

John Gunther, *Inside Africa,* 1955

The Bari Tribe

I had always expected trouble with the Baris, as I had known them during my former journey as a tribe of intractable savages. The Austrian missionaries had abandoned them as hopeless, after many efforts, and a great expenditure of money and energy.

The natives had pulled down the mission house, and they had pounded and ground the bright red bricks into the finest powder, which mixed with grease formed a paint to smear their naked bodies. Thus the only results of many years' teaching were the death of many noble men . . . and . . . the missionary establisment itself was converted into an external application for the skin: the house of God was turned into 'pomade divine.' This was a result that might have been expected by any person who had practical experience of the Baris.

Sir Samuel Baker, *Ismailia,* 1874

The women are not absolutely bad-looking.

Ibid.

The Dinka

When you are gazing at a grown-up Dinka man in all his glory, you realize that clothes were invented by pre-Fall Man for fun, and not either for utility or for prudery. In this climate, clothes are useless, and, as for prudery, a Dinka man's clothes do not cater for that. Picture to yourself a slim male figure, about six feet six inches tall, with a glossy black skin. He is standing on one stilt-like leg, with the other leg drawn up and resting on the straight leg, stork-fashion. From his close crisp hair a plume of feathers rises erect. On his arms he wears heavy brass armlets; on his ankles he wears elegant brass anklets. Round his middle he wears gay-coloured stays that rise to a point between his shoulder-blades, but do not come down below his hips. In his hand he carries a bow or alternatively a couple of spears and a narrow wooden shield. For the rest, he is as Nature made him.

Arnold Toynbee, *Between Niger and Nile,* 1965

Equatoria

When you have got the ink that has soaked into blotting paper out of it, then slavery will cease in these lands.

General Gordon, *c.* 1879, on leaving Equatoria, quoted in Lytton Strachey, *Eminent Victorians,* 1918

Khartoum

A more miserable, filthy and unhealthy place, can hardly be imagined.

Sir Samuel Baker, *The Albert Nyanza, Great Basin of the Nile,* 1866

Khartoum was . . . rebuilt by Kitchener in 1899. He laid it out – with what magisterial self-righteousness and confidence! – in the shape of a Union Jack.

John Gunther, *Inside Africa,* 1955

As I was getting out of a bus the conductor said to me in a confidential tone

'I say, what does that mean? "Sack of Khartoum?" What does "Sack of Khartoum" mean?'

'It means,' said I, 'that they've taken Khartoum and played hell with it all round.' He understood that and thanked me, whereon we parted.

Samuel Butler, *Notebooks,* 1912

River Nile (in Sudan)

From his two springs, in Gojam's sunny realm,
Pure-welling out, he through the lucid lake
Of fair Dambea rolls his infant stream.
There, by the Naiads nursed, he sports away
His playful youth, amid the fragrant isles,
That with unfading verdure smile around.
Ambitious thence, the manly river breaks;
And gathering many a flood, and copious fed
With all the mellowed treasures of the sky,
Winds in progressive majesty along;
Through splendid kingdoms now devolves his maze,
Now wanders wild o'er solitary tracts
Of life-deserted sand; till, glad to quit
The joyless desert, down the Nubian rocks,
From thundering steep to steep, he pours his urn,
And Egypt joys beneath the spreading wave.

James Thomson, *The Seasons – Summer,* 1727

Omdurman (Battle of, 1898)

A white gunboat, seeing our first advance, had hurried up the river in the hopes of being of some assistance. From the crow's nest its commander, Beatty, watched the whole event with breathless interest. Many years passed before I met this officer or knew that he had witnessed our gallop. When we met, I was First Lord of the Admiralty and he the youngest Admiral in the Royal Navy. 'What did it look like?' I asked him. 'What was your prevailing impression?' 'It looked,' said Admiral Beatty, 'like plum duff: brown currants scattered about in a great deal of suet.'

Sir Winston Churchill, *My Early Life,* 1930

Sennar (the weather there)

I call it *hot,* when a man sweats at rest, and excessively on moderate motion. I call it *very hot,* when a man, with thin or little clothing, sweats much, though at rest. I call it *excessive hot,* when a man in his shirt, at rest, sweats excessively, when all motion is painful, and the knees feel feeble, as if after a fever. I call it *extreme hot,* when the strength fails, a disposition to faint comes on, a straitness is found round the temples, as if a small cord were drawn round the head, the voice impaired, the skin dry, and the head seems more than ordinary large and light. This, I apprehend, denotes death at hand.

James Bruce, *Travels to Discover the Source of the Nile . . . 1768–1773,* 1790

The Sudd

Some evil spirit appears to rule in this horrible region of everlasting swamp. . . . No dependence can ever be placed on this cursed river. The fabulous Styx must be a sweet rippling brook, compared to this horrible creation. . . . The water being pent up by enormous dams of vegetation, mixed with mud and half-decayed matter, forms a chain of lakes at slightly varying levels. The sudden breaking of one dam would thus cause an impetuous rush of stream that might tear away miles of country, and entirely change the equilibrium of the floating masses.

Sir Samuel Baker, *Ismailia,* 1874

Tarfawi (formerly Terfowey: Nubian Desert, near)

We had no sooner got into the plain than we felt great symptoms of the Simoom; and about a quarter before twelve, our prisoner first, and then Idris, cried out, The simoom! the simoom! My curiosity would not suffer me to fall down without looking behind me. About due south, a little to the east, I saw the coloured haze as before. It seemed now to be rather less compressed, and to have with it a shade of blue. The edges of it were not defined as those of the former, but like a very thin smoke, with about a yard in the middle tinged with those colours. We all fell upon our faces, and the simoom passed with a gentle ruffling wind. It continued to blow in this manner till near three o'clock; so we were all taken ill that night, and scarcely strength was left us to lead the camels and arrange the baggage.

James Bruce, *Travels to Discover the Source of the Nile . . . 1768–1773,* 1790

SURINAM

*I must say thus much of it; that certainly had his late Majesty, of sacred Memory, but seen and known what a vast and charming World he had been Master of in that Continent, he would never have parted so easily with it to the *Dutch.* 'Tis a Continent whose vast Extent was never yet known, and may contain more noble Earth than all the Universe beside; for, they say, it reaches from East to West one way as far as *China,* and another to *Peru:* it affords all things both for Beauty and Use; 'tis there eternal Spring, always the very Months of *April, May,* and *June;* the Shades are perpetual, the Trees bearing at once all degrees of Leaves and Fruit, from blooming Buds to ripe Autumn: Groves of Oranges, Lemons, Citrons, Figs, Nutmegs, and noble Aromaticks, continually bearing their Fragrancies. The Trees appearing all like Nosegays adorn'd with Flowers of different kinds, some are all White, some Purple, some Scarlet, some Blue, some Yellow; bearing at the same Time, ripe Fruit, and blooming Young, or producing every Day new. The very Wood of all these Trees has an intrinsick Value above common Timber; for they are, when cut, of different Colours, glorious to behold, and bear a price considerable, to inlay withal. Besides this, they yield rich Balm, and Gums; so that we make our Candles of such an aromatick Substance, as does not only give a sufficient Light, but, as they burn, they cast their Perfumes all about. Cedar is the common firing, and all the Houses are built with it. The very Meat we eat, when set on the Table, if it be native, I mean of the Country, perfumes the whole Room; especially a little Beast called an *Armadilly,* a thing which I can liken to nothing so well as a *Rhinoceros;*'tis all in white Armour, so jointed, that it moves as well in it, as if it had nothing on: this Beast is about the bigness of a Pig of six Weeks old. But it were endless to give an account of all the divers wonderful and strange Things that Country affords, and which we took a very great delight to go in search of; tho those Adventures are oftentimes fatal, and at least dangerous.

Aphra Behn, *Oroonoko, or the Royal Slave, c.* 1678

In Surinam Holland is Europe; Holland is the centre of the world. Even America recedes. . . . Surinam feels only like a tropical, tulipless extension of Holland; some Surinamers call it Holland's twelfth province.

V.S. Naipaul, *The Middle Passage,* 1962

Coronie

A landscape which had never ceased to be unreal, because the scene of an enforced and always temporary residence; the slaves kidnapped from one continent and abandoned on the unprofitable plantations of another, from which there could never more be escape: I was glad to leave Coronie, for, more than lazy Negroes, it held the full desolation that came to those who made the middle passage.

V.S. Naipaul, *The Middle Passage,* 1962

SWAZILAND

In all Africa there is no more vividly African place than Swaziland.

James Morris, 'Swaziland', *Places,* 1972

Swaziland indeed is almost like an exhibition country, clothed in that meticulous decorum which the British brought to their possessions and protectorates everywhere. Its two principal towns, Mbabane and Manzini, are trim garden settlements, with prominent post offices and cosy places for coffee. Its central landscapes are mountainous, dotted here and there with hygienic-looking kraals. Its southern regions are flat ranchlands, hot and empty, prickled with scrub. Its western reaches are covered with a particularly disciplined kind of forest – one of the largest man-made forests on earth, scrupulously categorized in blocks, and functionally centred upon a large sawmill. Swaziland is a layered, staked sort of country, logically disposed, as though it has been organized for demonstration purposes.

Ibid.

SWEDEN

Cromwell: You met with a barren country and very cold.
Whitelocke: The remoter parts of it from the Court are extreme barren; but at Stockholm and Upsal, and most of the great towns, they have store of provisions; but fat beef and mutton in the winter time is not so plentiful with them as in the countries more southerly; and their hot weather in summer as much exceeds ours, as their cold doth in winter.
Cromwell: That is somewhat troublesome to endure; but how could you pass over their very long winter nights?
Whitelocke: I kept my people together and in action and recreation, by having music in my house, and encouraging that and the exercise of dancing which held them by the ears and eyes, and gave them diversion without any offence. And I caused the gentlemen to have disputations in Latin, and declamations upon words which I gave them.

Cromwell: Those were very good diversions and made your house a little academy.

Bulstrode Whitelocke, *Journal of the Swedish Embassy,* 3 July 1654

Signor Pietro, a famous *Musitian,* who had ben long in *Sweden* . . . told me the heate some part in summer was as excessive as the Cold in winter in Sweden; so cold he affirm'd, that the streetes of all the townes are desolate, no creature stirring in them for many moneths, all the inhabitants retiring to their stoves.

John Evelyn, *Diary,* 23 September 1680

There is a profusion of dishes at the entertainments in this country, but no taste in the arrangement or disposition of them. The table groans beneath a number of covers, which are all brought in at once, and then are left to cool during a ceremonious meal of at least two hours. But, the prologue to this play is even worse. Before they sit down to dinner, the company commonly take bread and butter, which they wash down with a glass of brandy; a fashion that prevails not only among persons of condition, but extends even to the ladies, as well as to the men. I must own that I cannot reconcile myself to a custom, which, though it doubtless originated from the extreme rigor of the climate, is only worthy of the Muscovites.

Sir N.W. Wraxall, *A Tour Round the Baltic,* 1775

The polite arts have made their way into Sweden.

William Coxe, *Travels into Poland, Russia, Sweden, etc.,* 1792

Sweden appeared to me the country in the world most proper to form the botanist and natural historian; every object seemed to remind me of the creation of things, of the first efforts of sportive nature. When a country arrives at a certain stage of perfection it looks as if it were made so, and curiosity is not excited.

Mary Wollstonecraft, *Letters Written During a Short Residence in Sweden etc.,* 1796

Brandy the bane of this country.

Ibid.

I have a great respect for former Sweden. So zealous as it was for Protestantism! – And I have always fancied it more like England than many Countries; – & according to the Map, many of the names have a strong resemblance to the English.

Jane Austen, Letter to Francis Austen, 3 July 1813

The extraordinary sight of men employed in knitting stockings, so common in Sweden, is, perhaps, not to be seen elsewhere.

E.D. Clarke, *Travels in Various Countries,* 1824

English travellers in Sweden are liable to disorders caused by obstructed perspiration, being frequently attacked with sore throats, fevers, rheumatism, &c. The blood, which almost boils during the day, becomes suddenly chilled after sun-set. If you ask the inhabitants, whose diet consists principally of salted provisions, how they escape these disorders; they will answer, 'that they preserve their health by drinking brandy, morning and evening.'

Ibid.

Mrs W. said that Sweden is a great knife and fork country. They think too much about eating she said.

Virginia Woolf, *Diary,* 8 September 1922

Sweden seems to me to be the most comfortable country in Europe – and the least cosy.

Kathleen Nott, *A Clean, Well-Lighted Place,* 1961

In most countries I can think of, nature keeps its distance, at the end of a long journey, and high and icy and frowning up in the sky. In Sweden it seems to be delivered to your door-step by some co-operative; I know no other way of describing the mixture of the wild with planning.

Ibid.

Everything about modern Sweden is superbly functional, particularly the beautiful blondes at the Ambassadeur and other top night-clubs in Stockholm.

Charles Graves, *The Rich Man's Guide to Europe,* 1966

Suicide elsewhere is an affair of the heart. Here it is a professional set-back.

Lars Forssel, quoted by Peter Ackroyd, 'No Garrets in Sweden', *Spectator,* 1 March 1980

Swedes

The Swedes were very just in performing their agreements, and regarded their advantages not more than all other princes and states do; and as they were a wise and subtle people, so they would find those no children with whom they were to deal, and that the Swedes were but men.

Bulstrode Whitelocke, *Journal of the Swedish Embassy in 1653 and 1654,* 1855

They are more apt to sit down with a superficial Knowledge than pursue their Studies to any Degree. They are much better qualified for a Life of Labour and Fatigue than of Art and Curiosity.

Thomas Salmon, *A New Geographical and Historical Grammar,* 1751

But it must be their stars, not the zephyrs gently stealing on their senses which here lead frail women astray. – Who can look at these rocks, and allow the voluptuousness of nature to be an excuse for gratifying the desires it inspires? We must, therefore, find some other cause besides voluptuousness, I believe to account for the conduct of the Swedish and American country girls; for I am led to conclude, from all the observations I have made, that there is always a mixture of sentiment and imagination in voluptuousness, to which neither of them have much pretension. . . . The manners of Stockholm are refined, I hear, by the introduction of gallantry; but, in the country, romping and coarse freedoms, with coarse allusions, keep the spirits awake.

Mary Wollstonecraft, *Letters Written During a Short Residence in Sweden, etc.*, 1796

The situation of the servants in every respect, particularly that of the women shews how far the Swedes are from having a just conception of rational equality. They are not *termed* slaves; yet a man may strike a man with impunity because he pays him wages. . . . Still the men stand up for the dignity of man, by oppressing the women.

Ibid.

The most liberal hospitality to strangers is the distinguishing characteristic of the Swedes: it is a virtue which they sometimes carry to such an excess, as even to prove troublesome to travellers from the delay it occasions. But such examples occur only among persons of boorish habits and of low education. The real Swedish gentleman is an honour to his country and to mankind.

E.D. Clarke, *Travels in Various Countries,* 1824

If ever there was a Yankeer than Yankee, he's a Swede. . . . The further I came north, the more like New England everything grew to look, so that I thought myself travelling forward and back between Boston and Quebec.

Henry Adams, Letter to Elizabeth Cameron, 10 September, 1901

The Swede is, surely, the human blackbird, with his copious, rich and liquid voice, in a language that reaches the extreme of voluptuous volubility.

Edmund Gosse, *Two Visits to Denmark,* 1911

It is a curious fact, of which I can think of no satisfactory explanation, that enthusiasm for country life and love of natural scenery are strongest and most widely diffused precisely in those European countries which have the worst climate and where the search for the picturesque involves the greatest discomfort. . . . As for Scandinavia – it is well known that there is no part of the world, excluding the tropics, where people so freely divest themselves of their clothing. The Swedish passion for nature is so strong that it can only be adequately expressed when in a state of nature. 'As souls unbodied,' says Donne, 'bodies unclothed must be to taste whole joys.' Noble, nude and far more modern than any other people in Europe, they sport in the icy waters of the Baltic, they roam naked in the primeval forest.

Aldous Huxley, *Along the Road*, 1925

It's odd how much the Scandinavians scrape, scent, gurgle, and clean at night considering the results next morning: as hard as a board, and as gray as a scullery pail.

Virginia Woolf, Letter to Vanessa Bell, 9 April 1927

It is a curious thing, and I wonder whether my experience is that of everybody else, or exceptional, or unique. I can recall at this moment only three Swedish acquaintances who were not either freaks or frauds. Has latitude something to do with it? Their lore and literature are full of hyperborean abruptness and exaggeration; irresponsible stuff, streaked with emotionalism and a kind of elfish canniness.

Norman Douglas, *Looking Back,* 1933

The folk who live in Scandinavia
Are famous for their odd behavia.
They have the frigidest of climates
And avoid their bellicose fellow-primates.
Though salesmen cluster at the door,
They don't want anybody's war.
It isn't that they put on airs;
They merely mind their own affairs.

Ogden Nash, 'Fellow Creatures, III: The Northerners', in *I'm a Stranger Here Myself,* 1938

Swedish children always look as if they were the offspring of the moon rather than of the sun and it takes them some time to be done brown – several summers.

Kathleen Nott, *A Clean, Well-Lighted Place,* 1961

The Swedes have good taste, damn them!

Anon., quoted *ibid.*

The Swedes were in those days, and still are, more civilized than most Europeans. Their civilization was their own. It was a little too self-conscious, too antiseptic and sterilized and municipalized for my taste, but it was refreshingly alive and vigorous. The Scandinavians have a passion for knowledge and for asking questions, and we were always having to try and satisfy this thirst for information in our cousins and their children and friends, in naked strangers whom we met on the rocks of Bohusland or in fully clothed strangers whom we met in trains, steamers, trams and buses. 'Do you belong to the Church of England?' 'Do you believe in God?' 'What is the constitution of the Stock Exchange?' 'Can you divorce your wife in England if she is insane?' This conscientious, relentless, somewhat humourless pursuit of knowledge occasionally filled me with despair – Virginia used to say that in similar circumstances a look would sometimes cross my face which made her fear that I would stand up and howl like a child of three, suddenly aware that the bottom has dropped out of its world.

Leonard Woolf, *Beginning Again,* 1964 – of 1911

Long before I visited Sweden for the first time, I had built up a composite portrait of the average Swede. He was withdrawn and spasmodic, reserved on the surface but explosive beneath it, veering between troughs of depression and fits of abandon. He was a pacifist, a socialist, an alcoholic and a hiker. He swam nude and tended to commit suicide during the long winters. Like many other popular misconceptions (e.g. that the French are greedy and the Spanish stoical), this turned out to be fairly close to the truth.

Kenneth Tynan, 'The Fiesta Route', in *The Sound of Two Hands Clapping,* 1975

'The Swedes,' a Norwegian had said to me, 'are Germans who look like human beings.'

Peter Ackroyd, 'No Garrets in Sweden', *Spectator,* 1 March 1980

The Arctic Circle

Coming by train, you realise that the Arctic Circle really is a natural phenomenon, a belt of no-man's – and no-tree's-land. However, the Swedes leave you in no doubt. The *Polarkreis* is marked out with white stones, like a widely spaced set of gleaming dentures.

Kathleen Nott, *A Clean, Well-Lighted Place,* 1961

Bole

Here the houses are no longer painted red, as is common all over Sweden, towards the south. They are literally log-houses; consisting of the mere timber laid together hewn with an axe, the only tool used in building, and without a nail in any part of them. Every man is his own carpenter and builder; working without saw, plane, chisel, nails, or hammer. Many new houses had been constructed here: we saw one which was building. The trunks of trees are piled longitudinally, and fitted at the corners by a sort of dove-tail work. All these buildings, viewed from a little distance, resemble piles of timber heaped for exportation.

E.D. Clarke, *Travels in Various Countries,* 1824

Gothenburg

Gothenburg is a clean airy town, and having been built by the Dutch, has canals running through each street, and in some of them there are rows of trees that would render it very pleasant were it not for the pavement which is intolerably bad.

Mary Wollstonecraft, *Letters Written During a Short Residence in Sweden, etc.,* 1796

The commerce of Gothenburg is of high importance to Sweden; and there is, perhaps, no place in Europe where the benefits to be derived from commerce are more eagerly sought for, than among the inhabitants of this city. Every other consideration is absorbed in the pursuit; commerce alone engrossing all the employment, thoughts, and hopes of each individual. Iron and fish are the principal exports. Among the imports, English porter is a very considerable article; and the privilege of importing it is extended to no other town in Sweden. The consumption of porter here is very great, owing to the number of workmen employed in the fishery, oil-trade, &c.

E.D. Clarke, *Travels in Various Countries,* 1824

Halleberg

The antiquities of Halleberg next claimed our attention: it was once the *Holy Mountain* of *Westro-Gothland* . . . . A fearful precipice rises perpendicularly behind a thick grove of trees, which appear to have been self-planted among the broken rocks at its base. . . . The tradition of the inhabitants concerning this place maintains, that the giants of old, who inhabited this country, when they wished to hasten their departure for *Valhall,* (that future site of happiness where all the Northern nations expected to carouse full goblets of ale with the Gods,) or, when any of them were seized with a *taedium vitae,* used to repair, in complete armour, to the brink of the precipice, whence, leaping down, they were dashed to pieces, and immediately made partakers of *Elysium.*

E.D. Clarke, *Travels in Various Countries,* 1824

Leksand

It looked faintly suburban like an Englishman's idea of Canada.

Kenneth Tynan, 'The Fiesta Route', in *The Sound of Two Hands Clapping,* 1975

Lund

Lund is esteemed the most antient town in Sweden, according to an old proverb, that when our Saviour was born, Lund was in its glory.

William Coxe, *Travels into Poland, Russia, Sweden, etc.,* 1792

Orebro

The town . . . consists of one street, almost a mile in length. Several of the better houses, and almost all the others, are covered with turf; which grows to such a height, that it appears fit for mowing, and presents the extraordinary sight of sloping meadows, sheltering the inhabitants of a whole town beneath their verdure.

E.D. Clarke, *Travels in Various Countries,* 1824

Scania and Smaland

The peasants of Scania and Smaland are civil and humble to obsequiousness, grateful for the donation of a third part of a halfpenny, and infinitely less uncivilized and barbarous, than one would be tempted to suppose, from the appearance of every object around them. I saw a number of very pretty forms among the women, who used to crowd round the carriage at every post-house; and I must own that I distributed my schellings more in proportion to their beauty, than to their age, infirmities, or poverty. Such is the enchantment of this captivating endowment, that I attempted in vain to resist its influence; my head condemned me, but my heart counteracted all its dictates, and warped my benevolence in compliance with its own preferences.

Sir N.W. Wraxall, *A Tour Round the Baltic,* 1775

Stockholm

The island which Whitelocke viewed this day (May 22 1654) and many other greater and smaller islands, upon which are buildings, do make up this city, which by some is resembled for the situation of it unto the City of Venice, which stands as this doth upon several islands in the sea. The waters are great and deep about this city, which is compassed with mountains, except only where they give way to the passage of the waters. The town, in the prospect of it, seems to be as in the midst of the circuit of the mountains, and as it were composed of divers pieces, each of them apart making a good town, and so appear as several villages separated by the many arms of water, or by the Lake Mälaren, which come hither to meet one another, and make the large and deep water; and it seems to be the diameter of the mountains, and now all plain, by carrying away the earth of a hill within it, and the stones there-with filling up ditches and uneven grounds, and serving for foundations for their buildings, and to make their streets even and handsome: so that now it is all level as if no hill had ever been. . . . It is too, in the view of it, pleasant and noble for the situation; and the grounds about it are dry and wholesome, yet fruitful. The streets are some of them large, others more narrow; most of them are straight, the houses being equally advanced and set together. In the heart of the city they are for the most part built of stone or brick, making the fairer show by their height of four or five stories. . . . taken altogether, from the prospect of the mountains upon the churches, castle, houses, waters and ships, the town appears noble and beautiful.

Bulstrode Whitelocke, *Journal of the Swedish Embassy in 1653 and 1654,* 1855

Almost in every point of view, the local situation of Stockholm is injudicious in itself, and improper for the capital of the kingdom. Policy, plenty, and commerce, seem all to dictate another part of Sweden, as much more eligible.

Sir N.W. Wraxall, *A Tour Round the Baltic,* 1775

I have seen no town with whose situation I was so much struck as with that of Stockholm, for its singular and romantic scenery. This capital, which is very long and irregular, occupies, beside two peninsulas, seven small rocky islands, scattered in the Maeler, in the streams which issue from that lake, and in a bay of the Baltic. A variety of contrasted and enchanting views are formed by numberless rocks of granite rising boldly from the surface of the water, partly bare and craggy, partly dotted with houses, or feathered with wood. The harbour is an inlet of the Baltic: the water is of such depth that ships of the largest burthen can approach the quay, which is of considerable breadth, and lined with spacious buildings and warehouses. At the extremity of the harbour several streets rise one above another in the form of an amphitheatre; and the palace, a magnificent building, crowns the summit. Towards the sea, about two or three miles from the town, the harbour is contracted into a narrow strait, and, winding among high rocks, disappears from the sight; and the prospect is terminated by distant hills overspread with forest. It is far beyond the power of words, or of the pencil, to delineate these singular views. . . . Excepting in the suburbs, where several houses are of wood painted red, the generality of the buildings are of stone, or brick stuccoed white. . . . The traveller who is fond of the picturesque in nature, will be charmed with many delightful points of view; but with none more than that from an eminence in the South suburbs, called the Mount of Moses. From this enchanting spot, the spectator commands a bird's-eye view, almost unparalleled in its kind, of the city and its various isles, of the harbour, the channel, and the lake Maeler, forming an assemblance of rocks, houses, wood, ships, and water, in all the variety of rugged, beautiful, and romantic scenery.

William Coxe, *Travels into Poland, Russia, Sweden, etc.,* 1792

The street in which we lodged was close to the great square called the *Nordermalm,* or *North Place;* . . . This square may be considered as affording a concentration of almost every thing worth seeing in Stockholm; and, if we were to judge from external appearance only, we should say, that there are few things in Europe to vie with the colossal greatness which it exhibits: but when we found, upon a closer examination, that, as at Petersburg, the semblances and show of architecture consisted for the most part, of white-washed edifices, built either of bricks, or, what is worse, of lath and plaster, not having half the durability even of Bernasconi's cement; mere wood and mortar, tricked out to look like Corinthian pillars and stone walls; we could not but consider such pageantry as only one degree removed from the pasteboard and painted scenery of a common playhouse. With due allowance made for these deficiencies, the streets of Stockholm might remind a traveller of the streets of Rome; excepting that the windows are without balconies.

E.D. Clarke, *Travels in Various Countries,* 1824

Winter has decided to pass the summer here.

Spanish Ambassador to Sweden, remark, 1835
recorded by Henry Wadsworth Longfellow, in
Samuel Longfellow (ed.), *Life,* 1886

Stockholm is many degrees warmer, dryer, and cheerfuller than Petersburg, and has one, or even two, excellent Rembrandts, and a cleverly arranged Zoo, where the beasts seem very fat and well fed, and generally resemble the people in ways. . . . They all drink like Vikings and take four bottles as a mere horn.

Henry Adams, Letter to Elizabeth Cameron,
1 September 1901

and Venice

Whoever invented the phrase about Stockholm, which calls it 'the Venice of the North,' seems to me, upon reflection, to have got things wrong. . . . Venice is queenly, Stockholm is homely. . . . The beauty of Stockholm where you get it, is from without. The city is remembered years after the traveller has left it; but remembered less for its content or for its monuments than for the nature around it. As your ship moves away from Venice, you look back on a distant vision of splendour, man-made and a triumph for a man. As your ship moves away from Stockholm, you look back upon something grey which mixes with the undistinguished hills around.

Nevertheless Stockholm contains this secret of the north, *mystery:* Stockholm has produced in the past and will, I think, recover in the future, legends or episodes which touch on things beyond the world – but things of the night: winter things.

Hilaire Belloc, *Places,* 1942

First impressions of Stockholm Paradise, second Limbo. Girls very pretty and not disfigured by paint and hairdressing. All look sexually and socially satisfied.

Evelyn Waugh, *Diary,* 18 August 1947

'It is not a city at all,' he said, with intensity. 'It is ridiculous of it to think of itself as a city. It is simply a rather larger village, set in the middle of some forests and some lakes. You wonder what it thinks it is doing there, looking so important.'

Ingmar Bergman, quoted in interview by James
Baldwin, *Nobody Knows My Name,* 1964 – in 1960

Trollhaetta (condition of the people)

In this part of Sweden we never had the satisfaction to observe any thing like comfort or cleanliness. In this respect they are certainly inferior to the Danes. A close and filthy room, crowded with pale, swarthy, wretched-looking children, sprawling upon a dirty floor, in the midst of the most powerful stench, were the usual objects that presented themselves to our notice. It is therefore marvellous that, in spite of all these obstacles, the Swedish peasants afterwards attain to a healthy maturity, and appear characterized by a sturdiness of form, and the most athletic stature. Many of them seem to belong to a race of giants, with nerves of iron. . . . There is a cast of countenance so universally prevalent, that it may be called *family likeness* . . . . The men have a long and pale face, rather bony, with a high forehead and long chin, and an expression which is the very opposite to ferocity in their eyes; and stout muscular limbs. The women, although there be some exceptions, are generally not handsome. Upon the whole they compose a hardy active people, hitherto undebilitated by any refinement or luxury.

E.D. Clarke, *Travels in Various Countries,* 1824

Umeå

In approaching the town, the view of it is not like anything seen in the other parts of Europe: it may be described by comparing it to a number of large boxes, or deal-cases, some of which are painted red, standing by the water-side, as if ready for exportation.

E.D. Clarke, *Travels in Various Countries,* 1824

Uppsala

The town is situated in a vast plain, open on all sides, and at present covered with grain: but the houses are mostly composed of wood, nor is there one public or private edifice of stone to be found in the place. Like most other seats of learning, Upsal is lonely, silent, and dull; but clean; and contains numerous gardens within its walls. There is an observatory, and a theatre: both, however, are mean. Upsal is not renowned for good cheer. The provisions, wine, and other accommodations of that nature, hold out no temptations to an

Epicurean. Fruits, except the berry tribe, we cannot expect to find in the sixtieth degree of northern latitude.
Sir N.W. Wraxall, *A Tour Round the Baltic,* 1775

Upsala, which stands in the beginning of an open plain fertile in grain and pasture, is a small, but very neat town, containing, exclusive of the students, about 3000 inhabitants. The ground plot is extremely regular: it is divided into two almost equal parts by the small river Sala; and the streets are drawn at right angles from a central kind of square; a few of the houses are built with brick and stuccoed; but the generality are constructed with trunks, smoothed into the shape of planks, and painted red, and the roofs are covered in with turf. Each house has its small court-yard, or garden.
William Coxe, *Travels into Poland, Russia, Sweden, etc.,* 1792

SWITZERLAND

Point d'argent, point de Suisse.
(No money, no Swiss.)
Jean Racine, *Les Plaideurs* , 1668 (said to have been the actual words of Swiss hired troops in 1521, on leaving the service of Francis I, because they had not received their pay)

Ilz ont force beaux lacs et force sources d'eau,
Force prez, force bois. J'ai du reste (Belleau)
Perdu le souvenir, tant ilz me firent boire.
(They have many fine lakes and many springs, meadows and woods. Beyond that, Belleau, I've forgotten: they made me drink so much.)
Joachim du Bellay, *Les Regrets,* 1558

They bragge of their ancient temperance, and say, that excesse came into the Commonwealth, together with the accepting of military stipends from forraigne Princes.
Fynes Moryson, *An Itinerary,* 1617

Eighteenth Century

I believe this is the first letter that was ever sent you from the . . . top of the highest mountain in Switzerland, where I am now shivering among the eternal frosts, and snows. . . . I assure you, I can hardly keep my ink from freezing in the middle of the dog-days. I am here entertained with the prettiest variety of snow-prospects that you can imagine, and have several pits of it before me that are very near as old as the mountain itself: for in this country it is as lasting as marble. I am now upon a spot of it, which they tell me fell about the reign of King Charlemain, or King Pepin.
Joseph Addison, *Tatler,* No.93, 1709

The Lord loves Switzerland, and will save many who might not be suitable for the congregation.
James Hutton, *Memoirs,* 1856 – of 1748

*As Francis the First of *France* was one winterly night warming himself over the embers of a wood fire, and talking with his first minister of sundry things for the good of the state – it would not be amiss, said the king, stirring up the embers with his cane, if this good understanding between ourselves and *Switzerland* was a little strengthened – There is no end, Sire, replied the minister, in giving money to these people – they would swallow up the treasury of France – Poo! poo! answered the king – there are more ways, Mons. *le Premier,* of bribing states, besides that of giving money – I'll pay *Switzerland* the honour of standing godfather for my next child – Your majesty, said the minister, in so doing, would have all the grammarians in *Europe* upon your back – *Switzerland,* as a republick being a female, can in no construction be godfather – She may be godmother, replied Francis hastily – so announce my intentions by a courier tomorrow morning.
Laurence Sterne, *Tristram Shandy,* Vol. iv, 1761

I remember after making the tour of Savoy and the Lower Valais, every woman we met in Switzerland appeared an angel.
Patrick Brydone, *A Tour through Sicily and Malta,* 1773

That country which a Philosopher would perhaps prefer to the rest of Europe.
Edward Gibbon, Letter to Dorothea Gibbon, 3 July 1775

O happier SWITZERLAND! – as yet 'tis thine
To see bright Liberty triumphant shake
Her radiant Aegis on thy craggy shrine,
And dip her pinions in thy silver lake!

Not on its fertile banks, or through the street
Of busy Zuric, does the squalid crew
Of useless beggary the traveller meet,
Wound his reluctant ear, and shock his view;

But Plenty breathes an universal gale,
And liberal Commerce every want supplies,
For equal her unfetter'd powers prevail,
Urge the quick step, and animate the eyes.
Anna Seward, *Alpine Scenery,* 1785

I lived in Switzerland among the Alps at twenty six, under a bitter domestic calamity. I found their solitudes soothe me as nothing else would – I have loved solitude more since.
William Beckford, Letter of 1820s, quoted in Cyrus Redding, *Memoirs of William Beckford,* 1859 – of 1786

The Derbyshire of Europe.
Hester Lynch Thrale/Piozzi, *Observations . . . in the Course of a Journey,* 1789

We are now . . . upon the point of quitting these most sublime and beautiful parts; and you cannot imagine the melancholy regret which I feel at the idea. . . . I have looked upon, and as it were conversed with, the objects which this country has presented to my view so long, and with such increasing pleasure, that the idea of parting with them oppresses me with a sadness similar to what I have always felt in quitting a beloved friend. . . . Ten thousand times in the course of this tour I have regretted the inability of my memory to retain a more strong impression of the beautiful forms before me; again and again, in quitting a fortunate station, have I returned to it with the most eager avidity, in the hope of bearing away a more lively picture. At this moment, when many of these landscapes are floating before my mind, I feel a high enjoyment in reflecting that perhaps scarcely a day of my life will pass in which I shall not derive some happiness from these images.

William Wordsworth, *Descriptive Sketches Taken During a Pedestrian Tour,* 1790

Every object in Switzerland has more than gratified our expectations, except the glaciers.

William Coxe, *Travels in Switzerland,* 1791

Nineteenth Century

Two Voices are there; one is of the sea,
One of the mountains; each a mighty Voice:
In both from age to age thou didst rejoice,
They were thy chosen music, Liberty!
There came a Tyrant, and with holy glee
Thou fought'st against him; but hast vainly striven;
Thou from thy Alpine holds at length art driven,
Where not a torrent murmurs heard by thee.
Of one deep bliss thine ear hath been bereft:
Then cleave, O cleave to that which still is left;
For, high-souled Maid, what sorrow would it be
That mountain Floods should thunder as before,
And Ocean bellow from his rocky shore,
And neither awful Voice be heard by thee!

William Wordsworth, 'Thoughts of a Briton on the Subjugation of Switzerland', *Poems in Two Volumes,* 1807

One slides down the snow as the Gauls used to do; with this difference, that instead of a shield one has nothing better than what nature has given all of us, to slide on.

Stratford Canning, Letter to his mother, 1 October 1815

I look upon Switzerland as an inferior sort of Scotland.

Sydney Smith, Letter to Lord Holland, August 1815

It is a country to be in for two hours, or two hours and a half, if the weather is fine, and no longer. Ennui comes on the third hour, and suicide attacks you before night. There is no *resource whatever* for passing the time, except looking at lakes and hills which is over immediately.

Henry Lord Brougham, Letter to Thomas Creevey, 15 August 1816

Travellers have certainly done no good to Switzerland.

Henry Matthews, *Diary of an Invalid,* 1820

The more one sees of Switzerland, the more one is pleased with the country, and the less one is pleased with the inhabitants.

Ibid.

Switzerland is a curst selfish, swinish country of brutes, placed in the most romantic region of the world. I never could bear the inhabitants, and still less their English visitors.

Lord Byron, Letter to Thomas Moore, 19 September 1821

By way of N.B., let me offer a hint to the traveller, that in all his bargains in Switzerland he may never leave any opening for an extra charge.

Charles Tennant, *A Tour, etc.,* 1824

Switzerland is certainly a wonderful country and very attractive, but I think no more so than the Pyrenees. Sweet as it is, the flats of East and West Ham look to *us* sweeter. . . . I also hope our circulation of books and tracts has been useful, and the establishment of at least one library at Brienz, for the use of the labouring classes.

Elizabeth Fry, in *Memoir of the Life of Elizabeth Fry,* 1848 – of 1839

Do you ask my opinion of Switzerland? . . . in the investigation of the assertion that the Swiss mountains are beautiful; with a certain amount of clouds, a sunset, a cheerful companion, a contented stomach, I think it perfectly true; but with too many clouds, or none at all, with a glaring noonday sun, alone, or tearing up a hill after dinner, I think it perfectly false.

Arthur Penrhyn Stanley, Letter to Canon Hugh Pearson, 1840

One may form an idea of the mountains and lakes of Switzerland by magnifying Primrose Hill and the Serpentine respectively, but a glacier is without a type in our country.

G.F. Weston, *Journal of a Tour in Europe and the East,* 1894 – of 1844

and Canada

It struck me suddenly how utterly different the impression of such a scene would be, if it were in a strange land, and in one without history; how dear to the feeling is the pine of Switzerland, compared to that of Canada.

John Ruskin, *Diary,* 19 April 1846

Saw Blanc, he was very sulky, kept his nightcap on, doff'd it one morning when I was knocked up out of bed to look at him at four o'clock, the glance I gave did not by any means repay me for the toil of travelling to see him. Two other things I *did* see in Switzerland, the stateliest bits of landskip I ever saw, one was a look down on the valley of Lauterbrunnen while we were descending from the Wengern Alp, the other a view of the Bernese Alps: don't think that I am going to describe them. Let it suffice that I was so satisfied with the size of crags that (Moxon being gone on before in vertigo and leaning on the arm of the guide) I *laughed* by myself. I was satisfied with the size of crags, but mountains, great mountains disappointed me.

Alfred Lord Tennyson, Letter to Edward Fitzgerald, 12 November 1846

*I assure you, Mr Dombey, Nature intended me for an Arcadian. I am thrown away in society. Cows are my passion. What I have ever sighed for, has been to retreat to a Swiss farm, and live entirely surrounded by cows – and china.

Charles Dickens, *Dombey and Son,* 1847–8 (Mrs Skewton speaking)

It was touching to listen to the talk of these secluded mountaineers. The good hostess, even the servant maids, hung about H., expressing such tender interest for the slave. All had read Uncle Tom. And it had apparently been an era in their life's monotony, for they said, 'O, madam, do write another! Remember, our winter nights here are *very* long!'

Harriet Beecher Stowe, *Sunny Memories of Foreign Lands,* 1853

How beautiful it is! How pleasant! How great and affable too, the landscape is! It's delightful to be in the midst of such scenes – the ideas get generous reflections from them. I don't mean to say my thoughts grow mountainous and enormous like the Alpine chain yonder – but, in fine, it is good to be in the presence of this noble nature. It is keeping good company; keeping away mean thoughts.

W.M. Thackeray, Letter to William Bradford Reed, 21 July 1853

Talking of Switzerland: Well, what are they doing now in the irritable little republic? They say a change in the hour of shutting the gates convulsed the whole canton of Geneva. . . . You remember —'s answer, when they sent him a decree that he could not be permitted to fire *in* the republic? 'Very well,' said he, 'It makes no sort of difference to me; I can very easily fire *over* the republic.'

Sydney Smith, quoted by Lady Holland, *Memoir of Sydney Smith,* 1855

Switzerland is, I fear, a romance of natural beauty wedded to a reality of human ugliness.

M.F. Tupper, *Paterfamilias' Diary of Everbody's Tour,* 1856

Swiss toleration is a self-interested virtue.

Ibid.

I was thinking, as I walked here yesterday, why it was that I am so especially fond of Switzerland, as distinguished from other countries; and I find the reason to be that I am so peculiarly sociable (provided only that people don't talk to me). In all other countries the masses of the people are collected in cities, . . . but in Switzerland the mass of the people is dispersed through the whole country.

John Ruskin, Letter, 30 May 1858

The land of wooden houses, innocent cakes, thin butter soup, and spotless little inn bedrooms with a family likeness to dairies.

Charles Dickens, 'Travelling Abroad', in *The Uncommercial Traveller,* 1861

We have been through Switzerland, where I climbed some of the highest peaks with a spy-glass – a method I find very agreeable, and which spares honest sole-leathers. I am thinking of getting up an achromatic-telescope Alpine Club, to which none will be admitted till they have had two fits of gout, authenticated by a doctor's bill.

James Russell Lowell, Letter to Thomas Hughes, November 1873

Of all the joys in life, none is greater than the joy of arriving on the out-skirts of Switzerland at the end of a long dusty day's journey from Paris. The true epicure in refined pleasures will never travel to Basle by night. He courts the heat of the sun and the monotony of French plains, – their sluggish streams and never-ending poplar-trees, – for the sake of the evening coolness and the gradual approach to the great Alps, which await him at the close of the day.

John Addington Symonds, *Sketches and Studies in Italy and Greece,* 1874

Switzerland is simply a large, humpy, solid rock, with a thin skin of grass stretched over it.

Mark Twain, *A Tramp Abroad,* 1880

As . . . [Mont Blanc] passed out of sight at last, an old Englishman settled himself in his seat and said –

'Well, I am satisfied. I have seen the principal features of Swiss scenery – Mont Blanc and the goitre – now for home!'

Ibid.

To Switzerland, the land of lakes and snow,
And ancient freedom of ancestral type,
And modern innkeepers who cringe and bow,
And venal echoes, and Pans paid to pipe!
See I am come. . . .

This is the birthplace of all sentiment,
The fount of modern tears . . .

Wilfred Scawen Blunt, *A New Pilgrimage*, xxi, 1889 – of 1886

Europe . . . persistently ignores the existence of Switzerland, that most instructive patent museum of politics, apparently only because she is a small country and people go there to see lakes and climb mountains.

James Bryce, *The American Commonwealth*, 1888

I rejuvenate in Switzerland and senescate (if there is no such verb, there ought to be) in London.

Thomas Henry Huxley, Letter to Sir J.D. Hooker, 24 September 1889

I am told . . . that safety is the great feature of travel in Switzerland. It is quite plain that you can't be permitted to have your blood run cold here; you must go to the Yosemite Valley for that.

Lilian Leland, *Travelling Alone, A Woman's Journey Round the World*, 1890

Duchess of Berwick: Dear girl! She is so fond of photographs of Switzerland. Such a pure taste I think.

Oscar Wilde, *Lady Windermere's Fan*, 1892

I knew so well . . . straight into what a purgatory you were all running. The high Swiss mountain inn, the crowd, the cold, the heat, the rain, the Germans, the scramble, the impossible rooms, and the still more impossible everything else – the hope deferred, the money misspent, the weather accurst: these things I saw written on your azure brows even while I perfidiously prattled with your prattle. The only thing was to let you do it – for one can no more come between a lady and her Swiss hotel, than between a gentleman and his wife.

Henry James, Letter to Edmund Gosse, 22 August 1894

Petkoff: Are you Emperor of Switzerland?
Bluntschli: My rank is the highest known in Switzerland: I am a free citizen.

George Bernard Shaw, *Arms and the Man*, 1898

I don't like Switzerland: it has produced nothing but theologians and waiters; Amiel and *Obermann* are types of sterility. I attribute it all to the lack of physical beauty in the race: they are shapeless, colourless, grey of texture, and without form. The beautiful races are the great races: here they are like cavemen: no impulse born of the splendour of physical perfection has ever filled them; their cattle have more expression. *Je m'en ennuie, je m'en ennuie.*

Oscar Wilde, Letter to Louis Wilkinson, 2 March 1899

Twentieth Century

Nor let us be too hard upon the just but anxious fellow that sat down dutifully to paint the soul of Switzerland upon a fan.

Hilaire Belloc, *The Path to Rome*, 1902

Rousseau raved of noble savages: he showed us how to discover beauty in Switzerland – the beauty of a coloured photograph. Yes; and long may Switzerland with its sham honey, sham wine, sham coffee, sham cigars, and sham Wilhelm Tell – with its inhabitants whose manners and faces reflect their sombre and craggy mountains – long may it continue to attract, and wholly absorb, the superbly virile energies of our own upper-better-middle classes! Thanks, Rousseau; thanks for not living in Italy.

Norman Douglas, *Siren Land*, 1911

I walked across Switzerland and am cured of that little country for ever. The only excitement in it is that you can throw a stone a frightfully long way down – that is forbidden by law.

D.H. Lawrence, Letter to Lady Cynthia Asquith, 23 October 1913

Switzerland is a small, steep country, much more up and down than sideways, and is all stuck over with large brown hotels built in the cuckoo-clock style of architecture. Every place that the land goes sufficiently sideways a hotel is planted, and all the hotels look as though they had been cut out by the same man with the same scroll saw.

Ernest Hemingway, *Toronto Star Weekly*, 4 March 1922, in *By-Line*, 1968

Paris swarms with fairies and I've grown to loathe it and prefer the hospital-like air of Switzerland where nuts are nuts and coughs are coughs.

F. Scott Fitzgerald, Letter to Edmund Wilson, summer 1930

A radiant hospitable country, to which I hope now constantly to return, a bower of bourgeois bliss with its pre-war standards of health and courtesy, the complex land of Rousseau and Calvin, where all Nature cries 'Forgive yourself!' and Man, defiant, answers 'Never!'

Cyril Connolly, 'Homage to Switzerland', 1946, in *Ideas and Places*, 1953

It's not that awful – know what the fella said – In Italy for thirty years under the Borgias they had warfare, terror, murder, bloodshed, but they produced Michelangelo, Leonardo da Vinci, and the Renaissance. – In Switzerland they had brotherly love, they had 500 years of democracy and peace, and what did that produce, – the cuckoo clock.

Orson Welles as Harry Lime, in *The Third Man*, 1949

I believe that an additional reason why people are so fond of Switzerland is because so many people have been so fond of Switzerland, and that it is the human interest of past events, thoughts, and deeds in particular places which produces a subsequent attraction to those places.

G.R. de Beer, *Travellers in Switzerland,* 1949

The Swiss managed to build a lovely country around their hotels.

George Mikes, *Down with Everybody,* 1951

Exquisite postal service. No bothersome demonstrations, no spiteful strikes. Alpine butterflies. Fabulous sunsets – just west of my window, spangling the lake, splitting the crimson sun! Also, the pleasant surprise of a metaphorical sunset in charming surroundings.

Vladimir Nabokov, Interview, October 1971

*Was it not, after all, La Rochefoucauld in his *Maximes* who had it that in Zurich in Spring in wartime a gentleman is hard put to find a vacant seat for the spurious spies peeping at police spies spying on spies eyeing counter-spies *what a bloody country even the cheese has got holes in it.*

Tom Stoppard, *Travesties,* 1975

*If I may quote La Rochefoucauld, 'Quel pays sanguinaire, même le fromage est plein des trous.'

Ibid.

Carr: My dear Tristan, to be an artist *at all* is like living in Switzerland during a world war.

Ibid.

The Alps were rising, and in the sheerest places wide-roofed chalets were planted, as close to the ground as mushrooms and clustered in the same way at various distances from gravity-defying churches. Many of the valleys were dark, the sun showing only farther up on cliff faces and at the summits. At ground level the train passed fruit farms and clean villages and Swiss cycling in kerchiefs, calendar scenes that you admire for a moment before feeling an urge to move on to a new month.

Paul Theroux, *The Great Railway Bazaar,* 1975

I expressed anxiety to my neighbour about an expedition I was proposing to make up into the Alps the next day. A terrible accident in which a cable had broken on the French side had just led to the death of many people in the cars it was carrying. 'You have no need to worry,' she said. 'You see, in Switzerland we never use our cables for more than four years. Then we take them down and replace them – and sell the old ones to the French.'

Edward Heath, *Travels, People and Places in My Life,* 1977

Switzerland . . . is like a giant, cloud-topped tureen, its rim ringed by the molten candles of the Alps, its bowl criss-crossed with serpentine super-highways skirting soupy lakes – the Afghanistan of continental capitalism, at once awesomely impregnable, and crushingly claustrophobic.

Alan Brien, *Sunday Times,* 24 February 1980
(on the vision of Switzerland in Alain Tanner's film, *Messidor*)

Swiss

We see the Switzers last well, notwithstanding their diversity of religion and of cantons. For utility is their bond, and not respects.

Francis Bacon, *Essays,* 1597–1625

To make the best Advantages
Of others Quarrels, like the *Swiss:*
And out of foreign Controversies,
By aiding both Sides, *fill their Purses.*

Samuel Butler, *Hudibras,* Part III, Canto III, 1678

The inhabitants of the country are as great curiosities as the country itself. They generally hire themselves out in their youth, and if they are musquet-proof till about fifty, they bring home the money they have got, and the limbs they have left, to pass the rest of their time among their native mountains. One of the gentlemen of the place, who is come off with the loss of an eye only, told me, by way of boast, that there were now seven wooden legs in his family: and that for these four generations, there had not been one in his line that carried a whole body with him to the grave. I believe you will think the style of this letter a little extraordinary: but the *Rehearsal* will tell you that 'people in clouds must not be confined to speak sense'; and I hope that we that are above them may claim the same privilege.

Joseph Addison, *Tatler,* No.93, 1709

Where the bleak Swiss their stormy mansions tread,
And force a churlish soil for scanty bread;
No product here the barren hills afford,
But man and steel, the soldier and his sword.
No vernal blooms their torpid rocks array,
But winter lingering chills the lap of May;
No Zephyr fondly sooths the mountain's breast,
But meteors glare and stormy glooms invest.
Yet still, even here, content can spread a charm,
Redress the clime and all its rage disarm.
Though poor the peasant's hut, his feasts though small,
He sees his little lot, the lot of all;
Sees no contiguous palace rear its head
To shame the meanness of his humble shed;
No costly lord the sumptuous banquet deal
To make him loath his vegetable meal;
But calm, and bred in ignorance and toil,

Each wish contracting fits him to the soil.
Cheerful at morn he wakes from short repose,
Breasts the keen air, and carrols as he goes;
With patient angle trolls the finny deep,
Or drives his ventrous plough-share to the steep;
Or seeks the den where snow tracks mark the way,
And drags the struggling savage into day.
At night returning, every labour sped,
He sits him down the master of a shed;
Smiles by his cheerful fire, and round surveys
His childrens looks, that brighten at the blaze:
While his lov'd partner, boastful of her hoard,
Displays her cleanly platter on the board;
And haply too some pilgrim, thither led,
With many a tale repays the nightly bed.
Thus every good his native wilds impart,
Imprints the patriot passion on his heart,
And even those hills, that round his mansion rise,
Enhance the bliss his scanty fund supplies.
Dear is that shed to which his soul conforms,
And dear that hill which lifts him to the storms;
And as a child, when scaring sounds molest
Clings close and closer to the mother's breast,
So the loud torrent, and the whirlwind's roar,
But bind him to his native mountains more.

Oliver Goldsmith, *The Traveller,* 1764

The common people of Switzerland are far more intelligent than the same rank of men in any other country.

William Coxe, *Travels in Switzerland,* 2nd edn, 1791

The intrepid Swiss who guards a foreign shore,
Condemned to climb his mountain-cliffs no more
If chance he hears the song so sweet so wild
His heart would spring to hear it when a child,
Melts at the long-lost scenes that round him rise,
And sinks a martyr to repentant sighs.

Samuel Rogers, *The Pleasures of Memory,* 1792

To a Swiss, a gay Frenchman in company said
'Your soldiers are forced, Sir, to fight for their bread,
Whilst for honour alone, the French rush to the field –
So your motives, to ours, Sir, must certainly yield.'
'By no means,' cried the other, 'pray why should you boast?
Each fights for the thing he's in need of the most.'

Anon., Nineteenth Century

Continually since I have been in Switzerland have I been struck with the similarity in sentiment and manners between the Swiss and the Americans – It is impossible this nation can always be kept under, the love of liberty burns too strongly in their bosoms.

Washington Irving, *Journal,* 8 May 1805

Switzerland is the Scotland of Europe; a land that supplies servants – a land to be boasted of by its inhabitants, and quitted. The Swiss, like the Scotch, are all of good families and of old families; I should much like to see a person from either nation of a bad family, or of a new family.

T.J. Hogg, *Two Hundred and Nine Days on the Continent,* 1827

The fondness of the Swiss for gunpowder on interesting occasions, is one of the drollest things.

Charles Dickens, Letter to John Forster, 12 July 1846

Don't be hard upon the Swiss. They are a thorn in the sides of European despots, and a good wholesome people to live near Jesuit-ridden kings on the brighter side of the mountains. My hat shall ever be ready to be thrown up, and my glove ever ready to be thrown down for Switzerland.

Charles Dickens, Letter to W.S. Landor, 22 November 1846

The Swiss fleece you with admirable gravity.

George Meredith, Letter to F.M. Evans, 9 July 1861

I wish that all men of the same class, in England and elsewhere, were as independent, well-informed, and trustworthy as Swiss mountaineers!

Leslie Stephen, *The Playground of Europe,* 1871

I understand the anger which some people feel against the Swiss when they travel in that country, though I will always hold that it is monstrous to come into a man's country of your own accord, and especially into a country so free and so well governed as is Switzerland, and then to quarrel with the particular type of citizen that you find there.

Hilaire Belloc, *The Path to Rome,* 1902

These Swiss, who, after all, in the intervals of passing dishes to stately guests in hotel-refectories, have a national life of their own; who indeed have shown more skill and commonsense in the organisation of posts, hotels, and military conscription, than any other nation; so much so, that one gazes and wonders how on earth a race so thick-headed and tedious could ever have done it.

Arnold Bennett, *Paris Nights,* 1913

The Swiss are inspired hotel-keepers. Some centuries since, when a stranger strayed into one of their valleys, their simple forefathers would kill him and share out the little money he might have about him. Now they know better. They keep him alive and writing cheques.

C.E. Montague, *The Right Place,* 1924

If it be true that we are the most backward, conservative, stiff-necked, self-righteous, smug, and churlish of all European nations, this would mean that in Switzerland the European is truly at home in his geographical and psychological centre. There he is attached to the earth, unconcerned, self-reliant, conservative, and backward – in other words, still intimately connected with the past, occupying a neutral position between the fluctuating and contradictory aspirations and opinions of the other nations or functions. That wouldn't be a bad role for the Swiss: to act as Europe's centre of gravity.

C.G. Jung, *The Swiss Line in the European Spectrum*, 1928, trans. R.F.C. Hull

A new idea for the Swiss is always something of a risk; it is like an unknown, dangerous animal, which must, if possible, be circumvented or else approached with extreme caution. (This, I may add, accounts for the remarkably poor intuitive capacity of the Swiss.)

Ibid.

*The Swiss . . . are not a people so much as a neat clean solvent business

William Faulkner, *Intruder in the Dust*, 1948

I greatly admired Switzerland and the nation itself, not merely the scenery and the towns; but the Swiss are very stand-offish; one can hardly have a Swiss friend, because as they have to live on foreigners, I suppose they dislike them. That would be the same case with the Mexicans. They chiefly live on Americans, on American tourists, and I don't think anybody likes to be a hotel keeper, even though there's nothing dishonourable about it.

Jorge Luis Borges, Interview with Ronald Christ, July 1966, *Paris Review*, winter-spring 1967

The only nation I've ever been tempted to feel really racist about are the Swiss – a whole country of phobic handwashers living in a giant Barclays Bank.

Jonathan Raban, *Arabia through the Looking Glass*, 1979

Alps

Unpast *Alpes* stop me, but I'll cut through all
And march, the *Muses Hannibal.*

Abraham Cowley, 'The Motto', in *Miscellanies*, 1656

When one considers the Height of those Hills, and the Chain of so many of them together, and their Extent . . . he will be afterwards apt to imagine, . . . that these cannot be the primary productions of the Author of Nature, but are the vast Ruines of the first World, which at the Deluge broke here into so many Inequalities.

Gilbert Burnet, *Some Letters Containing an Account of what Seemed most Remarkable in Travelling through Switzerland, . . . &c., 1685 and 1686*, 1687

To enable a man to describe rocks and precipices, it is absolutely necessary that he pass the Alps.

George Berkeley, Letter to Alexander Pope, 1 May 1714

near the Grande Chartreuse en route to Geneva

In our little journey up to the Grande Chartreuse, I do not remember to have gone ten paces without an exclamation, that there was no restraining; Not a precipice, not a torrent, not a cliff, but is pregnant with religion and poetry. There are certain scenes that would awe an atheist into belief, without the help of other argument. One need not have a very fantastic imagination to see spirits there at noon-day: You have Death perpetually before your eyes, only so far removed, as to compose the mind, without frighting it.

Thomas Gray, Letter to Richard West, 16 November 1739

Such uncouth rocks and such uncomely inhabitants! my dear West, I hope I shall never see them again!

Horace Walpole, Letter to Richard West, 11 November 1739

I now began to be really among the Alps. Jacob said, 'If one were to transport these mountains to Holland, they wouldn't stay there. The watery earth could not support them. They would sink at once.'

James Boswell, *Journal*, 4 January 1765 (quoting his Swiss servant, Jacob Hanni)

On arriving near the Alps, it appeared that I had formed a very erroneous idea of the route, having always supposed that we had only one mountain to pass, and that the rest of the way was level ground; instead of which, when we came to Pont de Beauvoisin (50 miles from Lyons, and the barrier between France and Savoye) we heard the agreeable news, that we had a hundred and twelve miles to travel tho' a chain of mountains, to the great Mont Cenis.

Eliza Fay, *Original Letters from India* (14 June 1779), 1817

Surely the immediate sensation conveyed to the mind by the sight of such tremendous appearances must be in every traveller the same, a sensation of fulness never experienced before, a satisfaction that there is something great to be seen on earth – some object capable of contenting even fancy.

Hester Lynch Piozzi, *Observations . . . in the Course of a Journey*, 1789

Pass St Jean Maurienne. . . . The mountains now relax their terrific features: they recede enough, to offer to the willing industry of the poor inhabitants something like a valley; but the jealous torrent seizes it with the hand of despotism, and like his brother tyrants, reigns but to destroy. On some slopes vines: mulberries begin to appear; villages increase; but still continue rather shapeless heaps of inhabited stones than ranges of houses; yet in these homely cots, beneath the snow-clad hills, where natural light comes with tardy beams, and art seems more sedulous to exclude than admit it, peace and content, the companions of honesty, may reside; and certainly would, were the penury of nature the only evil felt; but the hand of despotism may be more heavy. In several places the view is picturesque and pleasing: inclosures seem hung against the mountain sides, as a picture is suspended to the wall of a room. The people are in general mortally ugly and dwarfish.

Arthur Young, *Travels . . . [in] . . . France* (23 December 1789), 1792

But lo! the Alps, ascending white in air
Toy with the sun and glitter from afar.

William Wordsworth, *Descriptive Sketches*, 1791–2, pub. 1793

I had once given to these sketches the title of Picturesque, but the Alps are insulted in applying to them that term. Whoever, in attempting to describe their sublime features, should confine himself to the cold rules of painting, would give his reader but a very imperfect idea of those emotions which they have the irresistible power of communicating to the most impassive imaginations. The fact is, that controuling influence, which distinguishes the Alps from all other scenery, is derived from images which disdain the pencil. Had I wished to make a picture of this scene, I had thrown much less light into it. But I consulted nature and my feelings. The ideas excited by the stormy sunset I am here describing owed their sublimity to that deluge of light, or rather of fire, in which nature had wrapped the immense forms around me: any intrusion of shade, by destroying the unity of the impression, had necessarily diminished it's grandeur.

William Wordsworth, Note to *Descriptive Sketches*, 1793

Above me are the Alps,
The Palaces of Nature, whose vast walls
Have pinnacled in clouds their snowy scalps,
And throned Eternity in icy halls
Of cold Sublimity where forms and falls
The Avalanche – the thunderbolt of snow!
All that expands the spirit, yet appals,
Gather around these summits, as to show
How Earth may pierce to Heaven, yet leave vain man below.

Lord Byron, *Child Harold's Pilgrimage*, Canto the Third, 1812

Every thing indeed has fallen perhaps a little short of my expectations, but the Alps alone. They have exceeded them, & whenever they appear, they affect me as much as if I was seeing them for the first time. – I may almost say, as if I had never heard of them.

Samuel Rogers, *Italian Journal*, 19 September 1814

Pinnacles of snow, intolerably bright, part of the chain connected with Mont Blanc, shone through the clouds at intervals on high. I never knew – I never imagined what mountains were before. The immensity of these aerial summits excited, when they suddenly burst upon the sight, a sentiment of ecstatic wonder, not unallied to madness. And remember this was all one scene, it all pressed home to our regard and our imagination. Though it embraced a vast extent of space, the snowy pyramids which shot into the bright blue sky seemed to overhang our path; the ravine, clothed with gigantic pines, and black with its depth below, so deep that the very roaring of the untameable Arve, which rolled through it, could not be heard above – all was as much our own, as if we had been the creators of such impressions in the minds of others, as now occupied our own. Nature was the poet, whose harmony held our spirits more breathless than that of the divinest.

Percy Bysshe Shelley, *History of a Six Weeks' Tour*, 1817

Who first beholds those everlasting clouds,
Seed-time and harvest, morning noon and night,
Still where they were, steadfast, immovable;
Those mighty hills, so shadowy, sublime,
As rather to belong to Heaven than Earth –
But instantly receives into his soul
A sense, a feeling, that he loses not
A something that informs him 'tis an hour
Whence he may date henceforward and for ever.
To me they seemed the barriers of a World,
Saying, Thus far, no further! . . .
And still and still I felt as if I gazed
For the first time.

Samuel Rogers, *Italy*, 1822–34

Let no one imagine that the crossing the Alps is the work of a moment, or done by a single heroic effort – that they are a huge but detached chain of hills, or like the dotted line we find in the map. They are a sea or an entire kingdom of mountains. . . . Any one, who is much of an egotist, ought not to travel through these districts; his vanity will not find its account in them; it will be chilled, mortified, shrunk up: but they are a noble treat to those who feel themselves raised in their own thoughts and in the scale of being by the immensity of other things, and who can aggrandise and piece out their personal insignificance by the grandeur and eternal forms of nature! It gives one a vast idea of Buonaparte to think of him in these situations.

William Hazlitt, *Notes of a Journey through France and Italy*, 1826

Would that I had been born a mountaineer, to have

held intercourse with the fairies, and to have looked forth every morning of my life upon the majesty of the wonderful 'Sons of Earth.' And the earth has reason to be proud of such sons as the Swiss mountains. If a man be disappointed at the apparent elevation of the Alps, let him ascend their lower basements, and enter into their rocky wonders, peering down into their tremendous abysses, or gazing up to the abodes of the chamois and eagle; then, if he come down and still complain of their not answering his previous expectations, he had better return home as quickly as he can, go to bed, and *enjoy* himself there for a fortnight.

Thomas Dyke, *Travelling Memoirs During a Tour . . . 1832,* 1834

The Alps oppressed his spirits like whispers implying painful mysteries or threatening news. The lines of great mountains have a mathematics of their own; they are hieroglyphics. By those who apprehend them in part, but only in part, they are regarded with aversion. To him they were perplexing and distressing, as the minor key eminently was in music; for he felt there was a deep significance in them: but they would neither reveal what they meant nor let him alone. . . . I took him to one more Alpine view. . . . After a long silence he looked up and said, 'I pray to Heaven I may never see mountains *of this sort* again.' I turned on my heel and walked home; and his wife, on his return, accused him of having insulted my mountains.

Aubrey de Vere, *Recollections,* 1897 – of Sir Henry Taylor, in 1843

The whole descent between Andermatt . . . and Altdorf, William Tell's town . . . is the highest sublimation of all you can imagine in the way of Swiss scenery. Oh God! what a beautiful country it is! How poor and shrunken, beside it, is Italy in its brightest aspect!

Charles Dickens, Letter to John Forster, 15 June 1845

Fast, fast, by my window
The rushing winds go
Towards the ice-cumbered gorges
The vast fields of snow.
There the torrents drive upward
Their rock-strangled hum,
And the avalanch thunders
The hoarse torrent dumb.
I come, O ye mountains –
Ye torrents, I come.

Matthew Arnold, *Parting,* in Letter to A.H. Clough, 23 September 1849

The ALPS! It was the first time I had seen mountains. They had a fine sultry look, up aloft in the sky, – cold, lofty, and distant. I used to think that mountains would impress me but little; that by the same process of imagination reversed by which a brook can be fancied a mighty river, with forest instead of verdure on its banks, a mountain could be made a molehill, over which we step. But one look convinced me to the contrary. I found I could elevate better than I could pull down; and I was glad of it. . . . I seemed to meet for the first time a grand poetical thought in a material shape, – to see a piece of one's book-wonders realized, – something very earthly, yet standing between earth and heaven, like a piece of the antediluvian world looking out of the coldness of ages. . . . The first sight of the Alps . . . startles us like the disproof of a doubt, or the verification of an early dream, – a ghost, as it were, made visible by daylight and giving us an enormous sense of its presence and materiality.

Leigh Hunt, *Autobiography,* 1850

But there were the Alps! I repeated to myself: these are the Alps – the Alps! How wild were my emotions! I felt ready to leap from the vehicle, to clap my hands, and shout aloud, The Alps – The Alps! I realised that I was in Switzerland.

Henry P. Tappan, *A Step from the New World to the Old and Then Back Again,* 1851

We had the most byooootiful ride yesterday from Basel going through a country which I suppose prepares one for the splendider scenery of the Alps; kind good-natured little mountains, not too awful to look at, but encouraging in appearance, and leading us gradually up to the enormities which we're to contemplate in a day or two.

W.M. Thackeray, Letter to Mrs Brookfield, 19 July 1851

A clergyman wrote in the visitors' book at the Mer de Glace, Chamouni, something to the following effect: 'No one can view this sublime scene, and deny the existence of God,' under which Shelley, using a Greek phrase, wrote, 'P.B. Shelley, Atheist,' thereby proclaiming his opinion to all the world.

E.J. Trelawney, *Records of Shelley, Byron, and the Author,* 1858

Every one should see the Alps once, to know what they are.

Matthew Arnold, Letter to his sister, 6 August 1858

Our lives are Swiss –
So still – so Cool –
Till some odd afternoon
The Alps neglect their Curtains
And we look farther on!

Italy stands the other side!
While like a guard between –
The solemn
The siren Alps
Forever intervene!

Emily Dickinson, [Untitled], *c.*1859

My first sight of the Alps has raised odd feelings. Here at last seems something more than earth, and visible, if not tangible. They have the whiteness, the silence, the beauty and mystery of thoughts seldom unveiled within us, but which conquer earth when once they are. In fact they have made my creed tremble. – Only for a time. They have merely dazzled me with a group of symbols. Our great error has been (the error of all religion, as I fancy) to raise a spiritual system in antagonism to Nature. What though yonder Alp does touch the Heavens? Is it a rebuke to us below? In you and me there may be lofty virgin points, pure from what we call fleshiness. And so forth.

George Meredith, Letter to Frederick A. Maxse, 26 July 1861

*Carry your fevers to the Alps, you of minds diseased; not to sit down in sight of them ruminating, for bodily ease and comfort will trick the soul and set you measuring our lean humanity against yonder sublime and infinite; but mount, rack the limbs, wrestle it out among the peaks; taste danger, sweat, earn rest; learn to discover, ungrudgingly that haggard fatigue is the fair vision you have to run to earth, and that rest is your uttermost reward.

George Meredith, *The Adventures of Harry Richmond,* 1870

Nothing is more delightful than fine weather in the Alps; but as a general rule, the next thing to it is bad weather in the Alps.

Leslie Stephen, *The Playground of Europe,* 1871

What were the feelings with which they were regarded when theologians treated them as puzzling phenomena, only to be fully explained when we understood the origin of evil?

Ibid.

After all the Alps are best. I say this deliberately, and I think I have a right to pronounce an opinion. If you do not yet know Switzerland, you have a joy to come which will last longer than anything which the Arts can give.

John Addington Symonds, Letter to Horatio F. Brown, 25 May 1873

There is probably no pleasure equal to the pleasure of climbing a dangerous Alp; but it is a pleasure which is confined strictly to people who can find pleasure in it.

Mark Twain, *A Tramp Abroad,* 1880

The Alps are easily too many for me.

Henry James, Letter to John Addington Symonds, London, 22 February 1884

the Alps first seen from Schaffhausen

There was no thought in any of us for a moment of their being clouds. They were clear as crystal, sharp on the pure horizon sky, and already tinged with rose by the sinking sun. Infinitely beyond all that we had ever thought or dreamed, – the green walls of lost Eden could not have been more beautiful to us; not more awful, round heaven, the walls of sacred Death.

John Ruskin, *Praeterita,* 1885–9

and the Simplon Pass

More and more deeply every hour, in retracing Alpine paths, – by my fireside, – the wonder grows on me, what Heaven made the Alps for, and gave the chamois its foot, and the gentian its blue, – yet gave no one the heart to love them. And in the Alps, why especially that mighty central pass was so divinely planned, yet no one to pass it but against their wills, till Napoleon came, and made a road over it.

Nor often, since with any joy; though in truth there is no such piece of beauty and power, full of human interest of the most strangely varied kind, in all the mountain scenery of the globe, as that traverse, with its two terminal cities, Geneva and Milan; its two lovely lakes of approach, Leman and Maggiore; its two tremendous valleys of vestibule, the Valais and the Val d'Ossola; and its own, not desolate nor terrible, but wholly beautiful, upper region of rose and snow.

Ibid.

In the mountain kingdom of which I claimed possession by the law of love, in first seeing it from the Col de la Faucille, the ranges of entirely celestial mountain, the 'everlasting clouds' whose glory does not fade, are arranged in clusters of summits definitely distinct in form, and always recognisable, each in its own beauty, by any careful observer who has once seen them on the south and north. Of these, the most beautiful in Switzerland, and as far as I can read, or learn, the most beautiful mountain in the world, is the Jungfrau of Lauterbrunnen. Next to her, the double peaks of the Wetterhorn and Wellhorn, with their glacier of Rosenlaui; next to these, the Aiguille de Bionnassay, the buttress of Mont Blanc on the south-west; and after these loveliest, the various summits of the Bernese, Chamouni and Zermatt Alps, according to their relative power, and the advantage of their place for the general observer. Thus the Blumlis Alp, though only ten thousand feet high, has far greater influence than the Mont Combin, which is nearly as high as Mont Blanc, but can only be seen with difficulty, and in no association with the lowlands.

Ibid.

Adieu, white brows of Europe! sovereign brows,
  That wear the sunset for a golden tiar.
With me in memory shall your phantoms house
  For ever, whiter than yourselves, and higher.

Sir William Watson, 'The Alps', in *Poems,* 1892

The dear old Sierras, after all, are infinitely finer with their freshness, their beauty, their absolute and wholesome rudeness and sincerity, and I never knew before how I really loved them, and how they have taken such a hold on my life; here everything is grand and spectacular – but in the very heart of the wilderness there is a suspicion of drains and the smell of French cooking comes in at your window, with the breath of the pines.

Bret Harte, Letter to his Wife, 25 August 1895

the Alps first seen from the Jura

There below me, thousands of feet below me, was what seemed an illimitable plain; at the end of that world was an horizon, and the dim bluish sky that overhangs an horizon

There was brume in it and thickness. One saw the sky beyond the edge of the world getting purer as the vault rose. But right up – a belt in that empyrean – ran peak and field and needle of intense ice, remote, remote from the world. Sky beneath them, and sky above them, a steadfast legion, they glittered as though with the armour of the immovable armies of Heaven. Two days' march, three days' march away, they stood up like the walls of Eden. I say it again, they stopped my breath. I had seen them. . . .

To what emotion shall I compare this astonishment? So, in first love one finds that *this* can belong to *me* . . . .

These, the great Alps, seen thus, link one in some way to one's immortality. . . . Let me put it thus: that from the height of Weissenstein I saw, as it were, my religion.

Hilaire Belloc, *The Path to Rome,* 1902

The dogma of the Total Depravity of man, on which Calvin laid such stress, cannot stand uncontradicted in view of the fact that a beautiful landscape has power to *evoke,* spontaneously, such noble thoughts and such hallowed aspirations. The Divinity which is *in* man is stirred to life when confronted by the divinity in nature. Hence, I say, that the best refutation of Calvin's doctrine is a ramble among the Alps or a boating excursion on the lake.

D.T. Holmes, *A Scot in France and Switzerland,* 1910 – of 1906

To know, to feel, to understand the Alps, is to know, to feel, to understand humanity. . . . Only the Alps have these deep tragic contrasts, washing out the soul, as tragedy does, with pity and terror. The Alps are international, European, humanitarian.

Frederic Harrison, *My Alpine Jubilee,* 1908

I hate the Alps on principle.

James Elroy Flecker, Letter to Edward Marsh, 1 December 1913

A range of mountains may not be the Alps, and yet have a career.

C.E. Montague, *The Right Place,* 1924

Lives there a man with nose so dead that . . . he could not smell the Alps from Mulhouse or Grenoble?

Ibid.

He looked out at the Alps. He said, 'They say if the Swiss had designed these mountains, um, they'd be rather flatter.'

Paul Theroux, *The Great Railway Bazaar,* 1975

Baden

The Baths . . . are famous for medicine, and are in number thirty, seated on each side the Brooke, which divideth them into Bethora the great and the little. In the great, divers Bathes are contained under one roofe of a faire house, and without the gate are two common to the poore. These waters are so strong of brimstone, as the very smoake warmeth them that come neere, and the waters burne those that touch them. Of these one is called the Marques Bath, and is so hot, as it will scald off the haire of a Hogge: many having no disease but that of love, howsoever they feign sickenesse of body, come hither for remedy, and many times find it. Weomen come hither as richly attired as if they came to a marriage: for Men, Weomen, Monkes, and Nunnes, sit all together in the same water, parted with boords, but so as they may mutually speake and touch, and it is a rule here to shun all sadnes, neither is any jealousie admitted for a naked touch. The waters are so cleere as a penny may be seene in the bottome, and because melancholy must be avoided, they recreate themselves with many sports, while they sit in the water; namely at cards, and with casting up and catching little stones, to which purpose they have a little table swimming upon the water, upon which sometimes they doe likewise eate. These Bathes are very good for Weomen that are barren. They are also good for a cold braine, and a stomacke charged with rhume; but are hurtfull for hot and dry complexions, and in that respect they are held better for Weomen than for Men.

Fynes Moryson, *An Itinerary,* 1617

The poor people put a Cheat upon strangers, bringing them to sell (as they pretend) *fossile Dice,* which they say, they dig out of the Earth naturally so figured and marked. But I am well assured, such as they brought us were artificial Dice, and if they dig'd them out of the Earth, they first buried them there themselves.

John Ray, *Travels through the Low Countries, etc.,* 1663

The streets short, twisting and steep – very, *very* old-fashioned.

Dorothy Wordsworth, *Journal,* 3 August 1820

Basle

Surely it is exceeding sweetly situate, having on one side of the Rhine a pleasant plaine that yeeldeth great abundance of wine and corne, but especially corne; on the other side hils, in number three, whereon one part of the Citie standeth. Also the ayre of this City is esteemed as sweet and comfortable as in any Citie of the whole World, as a certaine English Gentleman told me that soiourned in the University for learning sake at the time of my being there, who affirmed that it was the most delectable place for ayre that ever he lived in. Again, it is as finely watered as ever I saw a Citie, partly with goodly rivers, and partly with pleasant springs or fountaines that doe incessantly flow out of delicate conduits.

Thomas Coryate, *Crudities,* 1611

The first noble carowsing that I saw in Germany was at mine Inne at Basil. Where I saw the Germanes drink helter skelter very sociably, exempting my selfe from their liquid impositions as well as I could.

Ibid.

The *Rhine* maketh a Crook before it, and the Town is situated on a rising Ground, which hath a noble Effect on the Eye, when one is on the Bridge, for it looketh like a Theatre.

Gilbert Burnet, *Some Letters Containing an Account of What Seemed Remarkable in Travelling . . . ,* 1687

I arrived at Basle, as I supposed about twelve at noon; but was much surprised to find that all the clocks in the town actually struck one: and, on inquiry, I was informed, that they constantly go an hour faster than the real time. . . . There is a . . . reason given for this strange custom which seems the most probable. It is well known that the choirs of cathedrals are constructed towards the east: that of Basle declines somewhat from this direction; and the sun-dial, which is placed upon the outside of the choir, and by which the town-clock is always regulated, partakes of this declination: a circumstance which, according to the celebrated Bernoulli, occasions a variation from the true time of above five and forty minutes.

William Coxe, *Travels in Switzerland,* 2nd edn, 1791

This is a remarkably neat town; but it lies beyond the confines of the picturesque.

William Hazlitt, *Notes of a Journey through France and Italy,* 1826

But Basel at night! with a full moon waking the river and sending up straight beams from the heavy clouds that overhung it. We saw this from the bridge. The river runs so strong that it keeps the bridge shaking. Then we walked about the place and first of all had the adventure of the little Englishwoman with her hat off. We went through great spacious streets and places dead still and came to fountains of the clearest black water through which pieces of things at the bottom gleamed white. We got up to a height where a bastion-shaped vertical prominence shaded with chestnut trees looked down on the near roofs, which then in moonlight were purple and velvety and edged along with ridges and chimneys of chalk white. A woman came to a window with a candle and some mess she was making, and that was gone and there was no light anywhere but the moon. We heard music indoors about. We saw the courtyard of a charming house with some tree pushing to the windows and a fountain. A church too of immensely high front all dead and flush to the top and next to it three most graceful flamboyant windows. Nothing could be more taking and fantastic than this stroll.

Gerard Manley Hopkins, *Journal,* 6 July 1868

Bellinzona

They call this place the Swiss key of Italy.

M.F. Tupper, *Paterfamilias' Diary of Everybody's Tour,* 1856

Bern

en route to

What Ruskin said of the scenery on the road to Bern – some thirty years ago – is equally true of it to-day. Its 'mountain spirit throwing into it a continual succession of slope and dale,' being interpreted into cyclist language, means that it is somewhat hilly, but not tediously so.

A.R. Sennett, *Fragments from Continental Journeyings,* 1905 – of 1898

The most faire City Berne hath the name of Beares in the Dutch tongue, because Berthold Duke of Zeringen, being to build the Citie, and going forth to hunt, thought good to give it the name of the first beast he should meete and kill. And there being a Wood of Oakes in the very place where the Citie was to be built, the workemen cutting the same for the building of the Citie did sing this Rime in Dutch:

Holtz lass dich hawen gern:
Die stat muss heissen Bern.
Wood let us willingly cut thee:
this Citie must Bern named be.

They write, that the ground whereupon the City is built, was of old called the Sacke and that the Citie thereupon was built in the forme of a sacke.

Fynes Moryson, *An Itinerary,* 1617

The canton of Berne ordered all the impressions of Helvetius's Esprit and Voltaire's Pucelle to be seized. The officer of justice employed by them came into the council and said,'*Magnifiques seigneurs, après toutes les recherches possibles, on n'a pû trouver dans toute la ville que très peu de l'Esprit, et pas une Pucelle.*'

Horace Walpole, Letter to George Montagu, 5 January 1766

The foreigner who prefers the constant intercourse of company to a more tranquil society, will chuse the residence of Berne rather than that of any other town in Switzerland.

William Coxe, *Travels in Switzerland,* 2nd edn, 1791

There is a beautiful order, a solidity, a gravity, in this city, which strikes at first sight and never loses its effect. The houses are of one grey hue, and built of stone. They are large and sober, but not heavy, or barbarously elbowing each other.

Dorothy Wordsworth, *Journal,* 5 August 1820

If here things were reduced to a small scale, you would have a step up from the river to the town, from the latter to the table land of the valley, and from this last a few steps up to the distant and surrounding mountains.

John Webster, *Notes of a Journey from London to Constantinople . . . ,1836*

Bernese

The Men are generally sincere, but heavy: They think it necessary to correct the Moisture of the Air with liberal Entertainments; and they are well furnish'd with all necessary Ingredients; for as their Soil produces good Cattle, so their Lakes abound in Fish, and their Woods in Fowl; the Wine is also light and good. The Women are generally employ'd in their domestick Affairs; and the Wives even of the chief Magistrates of *Bern,* look into all the Concerns of the House and Kitchen, as much as the Wives of the meanest Peasants. Men and Women do not converse promiscuously together; and the Women are so much amused with the Management at Home, and enter so little into Intrigues, that among them, as an eminent Physician there told me, *they know not what Vapours are,* which he imputed to the Idleness and Intrigues that abound elsewhere; whereas, he said, among them the Blood was cleansed by their Labour; and as that made them sleep well, so they did not amuse themselves with much thinking, nor did they know what Amours were. The third Adultery is punished with Death; which is also the Punishment of the fifth Act of Fornication.

Gilbert Burnet, *Some Letters Containing an Account of What Seemed Remarkable in Travelling . . . ,* 1687

Nothing can be more absurd than the cap of a *Bernoise,* for it answers no purpose of utility, with a broad, starched, black lace frill standing up all round it, in which she flits about as with the wings of a dragon-fly; though this is a very bad comparison, for the rest of her dress gives her figure such a heavy Dutch look, that no wings could support it. . . . With a delicacy of complexion that rivals the fair faces of England, there is a robustness almost amounting to clumsiness in their figures, which is irreconcilable with the graces. Madame Roland, in characterizing the beauty of the women of Bern, says wittily enough; 'C'est le *rosbif* des Anglais pour les estomacs à toute épreuve.'

Henry Matthews, *Diary of an Invalid,* 1820

Bernese Oberland

The mountain ranges, as any series or body of inanimate like things not often seen, have the air of persons and of interrupted activity.

Gerard Manley Hopkins, *Journal,* 9 July 1868

Proceeding along the road that runs across the Bernese Oberland from Montreux on Lake Geneva to Interlaken in the region of the Jungfrau, a friend of mine of great geographical sensitivity but simple mind rolls down the window of his car at a certain point near a village called Saanemoser, carefully scrapes his throat, and then spits. The reason, he informs his passengers, is that at this point the fluid so released is equally likely to flow down various streams to the Rhone and the Mediterranean or to augment the Rhine and eventually the North Sea.

John Kenneth Galbraith, *Economics, Peace and Laughter,* 1971

Brienz

Brienz on our Brienzer See
From Interlaken every day
A steamer seeks, and at our pier
Lets out a crowd to see things here;
Up a steep path they pant and strive;
When to the level they arrive,
Dispersing, hither, thither, run,
For all must rapidly be done,
And seek, with questioning and din,
Some the cascade, and some the inn;
The waterfall, for if you look
You find it printed in the book
That man or woman, so inclined,
May pass the very fall behind,
So many feet there intervene,
The rock or flying jet between;
The inn, 'tis also in the plan,
For tourist is a hungry man,
And a small *salle* repeats by rote

A daily task of *table d'hote,*
Where broth and meat, and country wine,
Assure the strangers that they dine;
Do it they must while they have power,
For in three-quarters of an hour
Back comes the steamer from Brienz,
And with one clear departure hence
The quietude is more intense.

Arthur Hugh Clough, *Mari Magno – The Lawyer's First Tale,* 1861

Chillon

Lake Leman lies by Chillon's walls:
A thousand feet in depth below
Its massy waters meet and flow;
Thus much the fathom-line was sent
From Chillon's snow-white battlement,
  Which round about the wave inthrals:
A double dungeon wall and wave
Have made – and like a living grave
Below the surface of the lake
The dark vault lies wherein we lay,
We heard it ripple night and day;
  Sounding o'er our heads it knock'd.

Lord Byron, *The Prisoner of Chillon,* 1816

The scene is almost as despicable as dismal. It is not a place to fear, or admire, or love, or even hate – but simply to *dislike.* Instead of dark ponderous towers, inculcating the ancient predominance of might over virtuous constancy, suggestive of power and heroic suffering, I saw a squalid building of white-washed brickwork, prodigal in unpicturesque angles, and surmounted by low pepper-box turrets, having the air of a provincial house of correction or union work-house.

Sir T.N. Talfourd, *Vacation Rambles,* 1844

The insupportable solitude and dreariness of the white walls, and towers, the sluggish moat and drawbridge, and the lonely ramparts I never saw the like of. But there is a courtyard inside; surrounded by prisons, oubliettes, and old chambers of torture; so terrifically sad, that death itself is not more sorrowful. And oh! a wicked old Grand Duke's bedchamber upstairs in the tower, with a secret staircase down into the chapel where the bats are wheeling about; and Bonnivard's dungeon; and a horrible trap whence prisoners were cast out into the lake; and a stake all burnt and crackled up, that still stands in the torture-ante-chamber to the salon of justice(!) – what tremendous places! Good God, the greatest mystery in all the earth, to me, is how or why the world was tolerated by its Creator through the good old times, and wasn't dashed to fragments.

Charles Dickens, Letter, 1846, in Forster, *Life of Dickens,* 1872–3

We visited the dungeons, wishing only that Byron had not set the bad example of cutting his name on a column.

M.F. Tupper, *Paterfamilias' Diary of Everybody's Tour,* 1856

I took the steamer and made pilgrimage to the dungeons of the Castle of Chillon, to see the place where poor Bonnivard endured his dreary captivity 300 years ago. I am glad I did that, for it took away some of the pain I was feeling on the prisoner's account. His dungeon was a nice, cool, roomy place, and I cannot see why he should have been so dissatisfied with it.

Mark Twain, *A Tramp Abroad,* 1880

At the castle of Chillon we walked through the lower storeys of the dungeons. 'We could turn this into a gymnasium,' Willie said.

On the way back to the hotel Willie leaned forward to me, 'Do you think the man who lived there thought of it as a retreat?' he enquired. 'You see, I know all about ivory towers. An ivory tower is a place into which a man will retire to think of the world in general and himself in particular.'

Robin Maugham, *Conversations with Willie,* 1978
('Willie' is Somerset Maugham.)

Chur / Coire

The queer little old town of Coire – a Roman town, which looks not ruined or wasted, but actually *shrivelled* by time.

Sir T.N. Talfourd, *Vacation Rambles,* 1844

Clarens

Clarens has *no* aspect of the 'birth-place of love'; it is a long, dull, bricky village, stretching along the breast of a scantily-wooded hill – steep enough for weariness, but not for romance.

Sir T.N. Talfourd, *Vacation Rambles,* 1844

Davos

The place? Although they call it Platz,
  I will be bold and state my view;
It's not a place at all – and that's
  The bottom verity, my Dew.

There are, as I will not deny,
  Innumerable inns; a road;
Several Alps indifferent high;
  The snow's inviolable abode;

Eleven English parsons, all
  Entirely inoffensive; four

True human beings – what I call
  Human – the deuce a cipher more;

A climate of surprising worth;
  Innumerable dogs that bark;
Some air, some weather, and some earth;
  A native race – God save the mark! –

A race that works, yet cannot work,
  Yodels, but cannot yodel right,
Such as, unhelped with rusty dirk,
  I vow that I could wholly smite.

A river that from morn till night
  Down all the valley plays the fool;
Not once she pauses in her flight,
  Nor knows the comfort of a pool,

But still keeps up, by straight or bend,
  The selfsame pace she hath begun –
Still hurry, hurry, to the end –
  Good God, is that the way to run?

If I a river were I hope,
  That I should better realise
The opportunities and scope
  Of that romantic enterprise.

I should not ape the merely strange,
  But aim besides at the divine;
And continuity and change
  I still should labour to combine.

Robert Louis Stevenson, Letter to A.G. Dew-Smith, November 1880

Many as are the drawbacks of spending one's life at Davos, it has, aesthetically and sensually, the greatest pleasures which an epicure can hope for. All the Appennines, from Consuma to La Vernia, through Rieti, Aquila, Sulmona, Tivoli, have not a single line of beauty in them equal to what lies about us everywhere in this region. The beauty here, of line and profile, is so overwhelmingly rich, that artists cannot deal with it.

John Addington Symonds, Letter to Mrs Ross, *c.* November 1889

and Klosters

Klosters was nice, actually, though I don't ski and have no intentions of embarking on a sport where they give you morphine and splints when you buy the basic equipment. Just above Klosters is Davos, the Magic Mountain Country. All the sanitoria have runners on the streets and God help you, if you cough twice they throw a net over you.

Harry Kurnitz, Letter to Groucho Marx, 8 January 1956

Eiger Glacier (station)

The Eiger glacier station soon came under our notice, and made us feel that the whole thing was a desecration. . . . Not only mountaineers, but all travellers of just taste, must surely feel that this railway is a desecration of nature; something like a merry-go-round in Westminster Abbey.

Walter Larden, *Recollections of an Old Mountaineer,* 1910 – of 1906

Fribourg

On all sides the descent to the town is extremely steep: in one place the streets even pass over the roofs of the houses. Many of the edifices are raised in regular gradation like the seats of an amphitheatre: many overhang the edge of a precipice in such a manner that on looking down, a weak head would be apt to turn giddy; and an unfortunate lover, repulsed in his suit, might instantly put an end to his pains, by taking a leap from the parlour window.

William Coxe, *Travels in Switzerland,* 3rd edn, 1791

Gelmer (fall of the)

Across the valley too we saw the fall of the Gelmer – like milk chasing round blocks of coal; or a girdle or long purse of white weighted with irregular black rubies, carelessly thrown aside and lying in jutty bends, with a black clasp of the same stone at the top – for those were the biggest blocks, squared, and built up, as it happened, in lessening stories, and the cascade enclosed them on the right and left hand with its foam; or once more like the skin of a white snake square-pied with black.

Gerard Manley Hopkins, *Journal,* 19 July 1868

Geneva

The town seems to me marvellous unpleasant, and the French a badly grounded people.

Sir Henry Wotton, Letter to Lord Zouche, Geneva, 22 August 1593

The Inhabitants of that Town, methinks, are made of another Paste, differing from the affable Nature of those People I had convers'd withal formerly; . . . *Geneva* . . . Lies like a Bone 'twixt three Mastiffs, the Emperor, the *French* King, and the Duke of *Savoy:* they all three look upon the Bone, but neither of them dare touch it singly, for fear the other two would fly upon him.

James Howell, 'Letter to Mr Tho. Bowyer, from Lions, 5 December 1621', *Familiar Letters,* 1645

Glance, Glorious Geneve, Gospell-Guiding Gem;
Great God Governe Good Geneves Ghostly Game.

William Lithgow, *Rare Adventures and Painfull Peregrinations,* 1614/32

''Tis a strong, well fortified Citty, part of it built on a rising ground; the houses are not despicable, but the high pent-houses (for I can hardly call them Cloysters) being all of wood; thro which the people passe drie, & in the shade winter & summer, do esceedingly deforme the fronts of the buildings. Here are aboundance of Booke-sellers, but Ill Impressions: These with Watches (of which store are made here), Chrystal, & excellent Screw'd Gunns, are the staple commodities: & all Provisions are good and cheape.

John Evelyn, *Diary,* July 1646

Geneva is too well known to be much insisted on. . . . There is an universal Civility, not only towards Strangers, but towards one another, that reigns all the Town over, and leans to an Excess: So that in them one sees a Mixture of a *French* Openness, and an *Italian* Exactness; there is indeed a little too much of the last.

Gilbert Burnet, *Some Letters Containing an Account of What Seemed Remarkable in Travelling . . .* ,1687

This Place is exactly like an English Country Town, the Prospects very pretty to any Eye that had not seen Naples or Genoa.

Lady Mary Wortley Montagu, Letter to her husband, 22 October 1741

This little Republic has an air of the Simplicity of Old Rome in its earliest Age. The Magistrates toil with their own Hands, and their Wives litterally dress their Dinners against their return from their little Senate. Yet without dress or Equipage, 'tis as dear living here for a stranger as in Places where one is oblig'd to both, from the price of all sort of provision, which they are forc'd to buy from their Neighbours, having allmost no Land of their own.

Lady Mary Wortley Montagu, Letter to her husband, 5 November 1741

Why suicide is more frequent in Great Britain and Geneva than elsewhere, would be a matter of curious investigation. For it appears very extraordinary, that men should be most inclined to kill themselves in countries where the blessings of life are best secured. There must be some strong and peculiar cause for an effect so preposterous.

Before coming here, I was of opinion, that the frequency of suicide in England, was occasioned in a great measure by the stormy and unequal climate, which, while it clouds the sky, throws also a gloom over the minds of the natives. – To this cause, foreigners generally add, that of the use of coal, instead of wood, for fuel. . . . But neither can account for the same effect at Geneva.

John Moore, *A View of Society and Manners in Italy, Switzerland, Germany, etc.,* 1779

Geneva is such an atom of a state as not to be divisible.

Ibid.

The Genevese are also much inclined to Puritanism. It is true that from habit they dance on a Sunday, but as soon as the French government was abolished in the town, the magistrates ordered the theatre to be closed, and measures were taken to pull down the building.

Mary Shelley, Letter, 1 June 1816

There is nothing in it . . . which can repay you for the trouble of walking over its rough stones. The houses are high, the streets narrow, many of them on the ascent, and no public building of any beauty to attract your eye, or any architecture to gratify your taste. The town is surrounded by a wall, the three gates of which are shut exactly at ten o'clock, when no bribery (as in France) can open them.

Ibid.

I should like the window to open onto the Lake of Geneva, – and there I'd sit and read all day like the picture of somebody reading.

John Keats, Letter to Fanny Keats, 13 March 1819

In talking of Geneva, and the sort of miniature scale everything is upon there, Lord L[ansdowne] said, that one time when he was passing there, they had contrived to get up a little Catholic Question, a cession having been made to them from Savoy, of a village (Cologne, I believe), which made it necessary to discuss the privileges of these Catholic subjects, &c. &c. Talleyrand's quizzing the Genevese, by saying that geographers had quite forgot in enumerating the parts of the world, Europe, Asia, &c. &c., to add a fifth part, Geneva.

Thomas Moore, *Journal,* 15 January 1823

Geneva is, I think, a very neat and picturesque town, not equal to some others we had seen, but very well for a Calvinistic capital. . . . I was not altogether delighted with the manners and appearance of the inhabitants. Their looks may be said to be moulded on the republican maxim, that 'you are no better than they,' and on the natural inference from it, that 'they are better than you.' They pass you with that kind of scrutinizing and captious air, as if some controversy was depending between you as to the form of religion or government.

William Hazlitt, *Notes of a Journey through France and Italy,* 1826

This is a dull sky-and-water atmosphere, after the blue

sweaters of the south; and the English locust of course prevails in it.

Arthur Hugh Clough, Letter to F.T. Palgrave, 7 August 1849

The climate of the Valley of Geneva is not at any season of the year a very perfect one, except in two or three sheltered nooks like Montreuil; while in winter it is boisterous and glacial enough to make a white bear curse the north pole, and wish himself at the equator.

John W. De Forest, *European Acquaintance*, 1858

The delightful city where accurate time-pieces are made for the rest of the world, but whose own clocks never give the correct time of day by any accident.

Mark Twain, *A Tramp Abroad*, 1880

A little canton four miles square, and which did not wish to be six miles square! A little town, composed of a cluster of water-mills, a street of penthouses, two wooden bridges, two dozen of stone houses on a little hill, and three or four perpendicular lanes up and down the hill. The four miles of acreage round, in grass, with modest gardens, and farm-dwelling houses; the people, pious, learned, and busy, to a man, to a woman – to a boy, to a girl of them; progressing to and fro mostly on their feet, and only where they had business. And this bird's nest of a place, to be the centre of religious and social thought, and of physical beauty, to all living Europe! . . . this inconceivable point of patience.

John Ruskin, *Praeterita*, 1885–9

Calvin's Hideaway.

Noel Coward, quoted in Cole Lesley, *The Life of Noel Coward*, 1976

Geneva! My mind flows back to a day in 1916 when I was standing down there, in front of a triumphal arch put up to celebrate the three hundred and eightieth anniversary of Calvin's first arrival in the city. 'Since that man came here,' said Monsieur Nivelle deliberately and emphatically, 'this place has never been the same again.' 'But anyway,' he went on to console himself, 'that vulgar electric light along the lake-side has been cut off thanks to this war.'

Arnold Toynbee, *Between Niger and Nile*, 1965

This city of wealth by stealth.

Robert Morley, *More Morley*, 1978

near Geneva

What will be the morning glory, when at dusk thus
gleams the lake?
Light by light puts forth Geneva: what a land – and, of
the land,
Can there be a lovelier station that this spot where now
we stand?

Robert Browning, *La Saisiaz*, 1878 – of 1877

All the women were like used-up men, and all the men like a sort of fagged dogs. But the good, genuine, grateful Swiss recognition of the commonest kind word – not too often thrown at them by our countrymen – made them quite radiant. I walked the greater part of the way, which was like going up the Monument.

Charles Dickens, Letter from Chamonix, 20 October 1853, in Forster, *Life of Dickens*, 1872–3

Lake of Geneva / Lac Leman

'Do not the mountains drop sweetness? the hills run with milk and honey, and the valleys stand thick with corn?' [wrote St Bernard of Clairvaux, but] when travelling by the Lake of Geneva, after having passed a whole day in riding along its shore, in the evening, when his companions were speaking about 'the Lake,' he enquired, 'what lake?' to their no little surprise.

James Cotter Morison, *The Life and Times of St Bernard, Abbot of Clairvaux*, 1863 – of 1125

Clear, placid Leman! thy contrasted lake,
With the wild world I dwelt in, is a thing
Which warns me, with its stillness, to forsake
Earth's troubled waters for a purer spring.

Lord Byron, *Childe Harold's pilgrimage*, Canto the Third, 1816

Lake Leman woos me with its crystal face,
The mirror where the stars and mountains view
The stillness of their aspect in each trace
Its clear depth yields of their far height and hue:
There is too much of man here, to look through
With a fit mind the might which I behold.

Ibid.

and Mont Blanc

'Twas at this instant – while there glow'd
This last, intensest gleam of light –
Suddenly, through the opening road,
The valley burst upon my sight!
That glorious valley, with its Lake,
And Alps on Alps in clusters swelling,
Mighty, and pure, and fit to make
The ramparts of a Godhead's dwelling.

I stood entranc'd – as Rabbins say
This whole assembled gazing world
Will stand upon that awful day,
When the Ark's Light, aloft, unfurl'd
Among the opening clouds shall shine,
Divinity's own radiant sign!

Mighty Mont Blanc, thou wert to me,
That minute, with thy brow in heaven,
As sure a sign of Deity
As e'er to mortal gaze was given.

Nor ever, were I destin'd yet
To live my life twice o'er again,
Can I the deep felt awe forget,
The dream, the trance that rapt me then.

Thomas Moore, *Rhymes on the Road,* 1819

There is an idea here, too, that people are occasionally made despondent and sluggish in their spirits by this great mass of still water, Lake Leman,

Charles Dickens, Letter to John Forster, 3 October 1846

'Ce n'est pas très gai le Lac. Et puis toute cette histoire de ce Monsieur Calvin. Non. Ce n'est pas très gai. Tout de même. . . . '
(It's not very jolly, The Lake. And then there's all this business about Mr Calvin. No. It's not very jolly. All the same. . . .)

General de Gaulle, Remark to Harold Macmillan, quoted Alistair Horne, *A Savage War of Peace,* 1977

'My wife,' he says deadpan, 'Tells me I like it; She tells me I like it a lot.'

Norman Krasna, quoted by Michael Pye, *Sunday Times,* 19 February 1978

Giessbach Falls

You are amazed at the power of so small a stream, which falls, as if of many tons weight, with a noise of thunder, and see the deep-coloured hills beyond the lake, and its dark-blue waters below them, through a crystal veil, where the water is unbroken, and through a brilliant drapery of drops where it is divided; reminding you of nature as seen through the medium of Shelley's poetry, shrouded in some passages by a veil as radiant, and as pure, and variegated in others, by gushing and irradiated fancies, like the glistening water-drops which are here ever passing away and ever renewed.

Sir T.N. Talfourd, *Vacation Rambles,* 1844

The Giessbach falls like heaps of snow or like laces of shining rice. The smaller falls in it shew gaily sprigged, fretted, and curled edges dancing down, like the crispest endive.

Gerard Manley Hopkins, *Journal,* 13 July 1868

Glaciers

When we were on the glacier, the scene was very solemn; we could almost fancy ourselves out of the world, hemmed in as we were with mountains, and upon an immense body of ice: it was so awful that we were not sorry to quit it, for scenes of civilised life; in which, though perhaps curiosity might be less gratified, more comfort was to be obtained.

Thomas Pennington, *Continental Excursions,* 1809 – of 1787

The glaciers themselves fell far short of my expectation, though certainly vast and wonderful objects. . . . Conceive narrow arms of a tempestuous sea, rushing down in the hollow between stupendous rocks, and suddenly arrested in its fury by a mighty frost, and you have them before your eyes. But I fondly expected that the congealed billows would present all the *eclat* to the sight of pure ice, and imagined them sparkling in the sunbeams with the most radiant lustre. No such thing, my dear girl!

Thomas Sedgewick Whalley, Letter to Fanny Sage, 6 October 1784

In my opinion glaciers, though they are fine things with accompaniments, do not do any better by themselves than the base of Handel's music would do without the other parts.

Charlton Byam Wollaston, Letter to his mother, 24 August 1791

The story that the Mer de Glace resembles the sea suddenly frozen in a storm is all nonsense. From Montanvert it looks rather like a magnified white ploughed field.

Albert Smith, *The Story of Mont Blanc,* 1860 – of 1838

the Rhône Glacier, seen from the Grimsel
. . . Lying like a glove with its palm downward, and the fingers crooked and close, – a gauntlet of ice which centuries ago Winter threw down in defiance to the Sun.

Henry Wadsworth Longfellow, *Journal,* 16 July 1836

Glion

Glion? – Ah, twenty years, it cuts
All meaning from a name!
White houses prank where once were huts.
Glion, but not the same!

And yet I know not! All unchanged
The turf, the pines, the sky!
The hills in their old order ranged;
The lake with Chillon by!

Matthew Arnold, *Obermann Once More,* 1867

and the Dent du Midi
The Dent du Midi now uprears
His proud tiara through the mist,
The sacred crown whose triple tiers
Are walls of Titan amethyst. . . .

Here would I dream away long years
  Till with the mountains I was one,
Knowing not loves or hates or fears,
  Standing immutably alone.

James Elroy Flecker, *Glion – Noon,* July 1904

From Glion when the sun declines
  The world below is clear to see:
I count the escalading pines
  Upon the rocks of Meillerie.

Like a dull bee the steamer plies
  And settles on the jutting pier.
The barques, strange sailing butterflies,
  Round idle headlands idly veer.

The painted sceneries recall
  Such toil as Canaletto spent
To give each brick upon each wall
  Its due proportion of cement.

Yet rather seem those lands below
  From Glion at the close of day
As vivid as a cameo
  Graved by the poet Gautier.

James Elroy Flecker, *Glion – Evening,* July 1904

One can see France and it sort of hallows the surrounding Helvetic air.

James Elroy Flecker, Letter to Frank Savery, 14 August 1913

Glovelier

Glovelier is a place of no excellence whatever, and if the thought did not seem extravagant I should be for putting it to the sword and burning it all down.

Hilaire Belloc, *The Path to Rome,* 1902

Mount Grimsel

No situation can exceed the solitary horror of the scenery on the top of the Grimsel. Its appearance resembled the inside of a mine, and seemed as if the bowels of the earth had been violently rent asunder.

William Coxe, *Travels in Switzerland,* 2nd edn, 1791

Grindelwald

The Vale of Grindelwald first opens on the view in form of a large deep basin, at the upper side of which a Glacier appears to be lying upon a gentle declivity at the base of a mountain, no lovely object as seen from that distance! It resembles a mass of dingy snow remaining in a hollow after a hasty spring-thaw.

Dorothy Wordsworth, Journal, 10 August 1820

Grisons

I took my course through the Grisons to Geneva, leaving a discreet country in my opinion too soon.

Sir Henry Wotton, Letter to Lord Zouche, 22 August 1593

  Among those hilly regions where, embraced
In peaceful valés, the happy Grisons dwell;
Oft, rushing sudden from the loaded cliffs,
Mountains of snow their gathering terrors roll.
From steep to steep, loud-thundering down they come,
A wintry waste in dire commotion all;
And herds, and flocks, and travellers, and swains,
And sometimes whole brigades of marching troops,
Or hamlets sleeping in the dead of night,
Are deep beneath the smothering ruin whelm'd.

James Thomson, *The Seasons – Winter,* 1726

Gstaad

Gstaad is an up and coming Kitzbuhel, not too high, not too enclosed – a mountain village open to the sun, surrounded by fir-woods and fat pastures. . . . The whole ambience has that exquisite stimulation of a mountain resort assured of a future.

Cyril Connolly, 'Homage to Switzerland', 1946, in *Ideas and Places,* 1953

All of what I call my serious books have been written there; no place in the world is so efficient. One works until one is tired and then, either in euphoria or frustration, goes skiing or walking. Neither of these recreations occupies the mind; I have never heard of anyone who was mentally so retarded that he could not be taught to ski and I've encountered quite a few who could not conceivably be taught anything else. So to fill the vacuum one continues to ponder and by the next day you often have something more to say. The rich, dividing about equally between those who are functional illiterates and those who have heard I'm a Bolshevist, leave me entirely alone.

John Kenneth Galbraith, *Economics, Peace and Laughter,* 1971

Handeck

He was a very patriotic Irishman. Whatever I said in praise of the scenery around us he seemed to regard as a distinct aspersion on Ireland 'What can you compare here,' he demanded, 'with the mountains of Wicklow?' 'Perhaps,' I replied, 'one might name the mountains of the Mont Blanc range.' 'Oh!' he replied, 'they are out of all reason! I am after walking along the Chamouni Valley for three days, and I only saw four of those mountains! Sure in Wicklow I have counted as many as eight of them in three hours!'

Aubrey de Vere, *Recollections,* 1897 – of 1839

Interlaken

Interlaken, spoilt I trow by having become a very Cheltenham of fashionable English.

M.F. Tupper, *Paterfamilias' Diary of Everybody's Tour*, 1856

The Jungfrau

The Yung frau . . . is the highest of this range – heard the Avalanches falling every five minutes nearly – as if God was pelting the Devil down from Heaven with snow balls – from where we stood on the Wengren Alp – we had all these in view on one side – on the other the clouds rose from the opposite valley curling up perpendicular precipices – like the foam of the ocean of Hell during a Springtide. . . . Arrived at the Grindenwald – dined – mounted and rode again to the higher Glacier – twilight – but distinct – very fine Glacier – like a *frozen hurricane* – Starlight – beautiful – but a devil of a path – never mind – got safe in – a little lightning – but the whole of the day as fine in point of weather – as the day on which Paradise was made – Passed *whole woods of withered pines – all withered* – trunks stripped and barkless – branches leafless – done by a single winter – their appearance reminded me of me and my family.

Lord Byron, *Alpine Journal*, 23 September 1816

I crossed the Wengern Alp, which, on its ascent and from its summit, brought me face to face with the Jungfrau. It was, indeed, a most solemn interview. . . . In its vastness, and its intense whiteness and brilliancy, it made me think continually of the 'great white throne' in the Apocalypse.

Andrew P. Peabody, *Reminiscences of European Travel*, 1868 – of 1866

the Silberhorn

The mountains and in particular the Silberhorn are shaped and nippled like the sand in an hourglass and the Silberhorn has a subsidiary pyramidal peak naped sharply down the sides. Then one of their beauties is in nearly vertical places the fine pleatings of the snow running to or from one another, like the newness of lawn in an alb and sometimes cut off short as crisp as celery.

There are round one of the heights of the Jungfrau two ends or falls of a glacier. If you took the skin of a white tiger or the deep fell of some other animal and swung it tossing high in the air and then cast it out before you it would fall and so clasp and lap round anything in its way just as this glacier does and the fleece would part in the same rifts: you must suppose a lazuli under-flix to appear. The spraying out of one end I tried to catch but it would have taken hours: it was this which first made me think of a tiger-skin, and it ends in tongues and points like the tail and claws: indeed the ends of the glaciers are knotted or knuckled like talons.

Gerard Manley Hopkins, *Journal*, 13 July 1868

Murren faces the Jungfrau. This glorious creature is your one object of interest from morning to night. It seems so near that you could fancy a stone could be thrown across to it. Between you and it is a broad valley: but so deep, and with sides so precipitous, that it is entirely out of sight. So the Jungfrau *vis-à-vis*-es you frankly through the bright sweet intervening air. And then she has such moods; such unutterable smiles, such inscrutable sulks, such howls of rage suppressed, such thunder of avalanches, such crown of stars. One evening our sunset was the real rose-pink you have heard of so much. It fades, you know, into a death-like chalk-white. That is the most *awful* thing. A sort of spasm seems to come over her face, and in an instant she is a corpse, rigid, and oh so cold! Well, so she died, and you felt as if a great soul had ebbed away into the Heaven of Heavens: and thankful, but very sad, I went up to my room. I was reading by candle-light, for it gets dark immediately after sunset, when A. shrieked to me to come to the window. What a Resurrection – so gentle, so tender – like that sonnet of Milton's about his dead wife returning in vision! The moon had risen; and there was the Jungfrau – oh chaste, oh blessed saint in glory everlasting! Then all the elemental spirits that haunt crevasses, and hover around peaks, all the patient powers that bear up the rock buttresses, and labour to sustain great slopes, all streams and drifts, and flowers and vapours, made a symphony, a time most solemn and rapturous. It was there, unheard, perhaps, I will not deny it; but there nevertheless. A young Swiss felt it, and with exquisite delicacy, feeling his way, as it were, to some expression, however inadequate, he played a sonata of Schumann, and one or two of the songs, such as the *Fruhlingsnacht* . . . . The abyss below was a pot of boiling blackness, and on to this, and down into this, and all over this, the moonlight fell as meal falls on to porridge from nimbly sifting fingers. Moon-meal! that was it.

Thomas Edward Brown, Letter, 18 October 1874

Oft as the Maiden Mount, sublime in her purity yonder,
Veiled in a glory of snow, musing I mark from below,
Not uprear'd from the valley, methinks was the radiant wonder;
Rather a hill of the sky silently sank from on high.

Handley Carr Glyn Moule, *To the Jungfrau*, 1901

Jura *(in part French)*

With all my Tory prejudice (I mean, principle), I have to confess that one great joy of Swiss – above all,

Jurassic Swiss – ground to me, is in its effectual, not merely theoretic, *liberty*. Among the greater hills, one can't always go just where one chooses, – all around is the too far, or too steep, – one wants to get to this, and climb that, and can't do either – but in Jura one can go every way, and be happy everywhere. . . . All Switzerland is there in hope and sensation, and what was less than Switzerland was in some sort better, in its meek sincerity and healthy purity.

John Ruskin, *Praeterita*, 1885–9

Lakes

Horrid pots of blue paint.

Walter Pater, quoted by Michael Levey, *The Case of Walter Pater*, 1978 – of before 1894

Lausanne

My passion for my wife or mistress (Fanny Lausanne) is not palled by satiety and possession of two years. I have seen her in all seasons and in all humours, and though she is not without faults, they are infinitely overbalanced by her good qualities. Her face is not handsome, but her person and everything about her has admirable grace and beauty; she is of a very cheerful and sociable temper, without much learning she is endowed with taste and good-sense, and though not rich the simplicity of her education makes her a very good oeconomist; she is forbid by her parents to wear any expensive finery, and though her limbs are not much calculated for walking, she has not yet asked me to keep her a Coach.

The only disagreeable circumstance is the increase of a race of animals with which this country has been long infested, and who are said to come from an island in the Northern Ocean.

Edward Gibbon, Letter to Lord Sheffield, 1 October 1765

Lausanne has nothing but its situation to recommend it.

Charles Tennant, *A Tour, etc.*, 1824

Of the little town he spoke in his next letter as having its natural dulness increased by the fact of its streets going up and down hill abruptly and steeply like the streets in a dream.

John Forster, quoting Charles Dickens (1846), in *Life of Dickens*, 1872–3

*Lord Curzon paused at the doorway of his apartment and surveyed it: 'How ghastly!' he sighed. He walked towards the window, pulled aside the yellow cretonne curtain, and gazed across to the lights of Evian. 'How positively ghastly!' he repeated.

Harold Nicolson, *Some People*, 1927

Here we are at Le Touquet with Vittel at the other side of the road and all surrounded by Beaugency, Śpa and the half dozen other places we said we were going to. Greetings to you both from this synthethic pleasure resort.

James Joyce, Postcard to Mr and Mrs George Turner, 12 August 1939, from Grand Hotel de la Paix, Lausanne

And yet Lausanne today is not what it was; it is with Lucerne the smuggest of Swiss cities, the most sport- and tourist-ridden; there is too much tennis and golf and exiled royalty, it's all too much of a *Musée Bourgeoise;* one wants, as in so many Swiss towns, to let loose some Senegalese, some French sailors or workmen, some drunken American women, some props and pillars of moral worthlessness, someone to walk on the grass or spit in the funicular.

Cyril Connolly, *Ideas and Places*, 1953 – of 1946

Leuk / Leukerbad

Those baths remove fat, and also skin-diseases. The patients remain in the great tanks hours at a time. A dozen gentlemen and ladies occupy a tank together, and amuse themselves with rompings and various games. They have floating desks and tables, and they read or lunch, or play chess in water that is breast-deep. The tourist can step in and view this novel spectacle if he chooses. There is a poor box, and he will have to contribute. There are several of these big bathing-houses, and you can always tell when you are near one of them by the romping noises and shouts of laughter that proceed from it. The water is running water, and changes all the time, else a patient with ringworm might take the bath with only a partial success, since while he was ridding himself of his ringworm he might catch the itch.

Mark Twain, *A Tramp Abroad*, 1880

Locarno

Locarno! spreading out in width like Heaven,
How dost thou cleave to the poetic heart,
Bask in the sunshine of the memory. . . .

William Wordsworth, *The Prelude*, 1805 (text of 1850)

Lucerne

I can foresee, within the perspective of but a few years, the town of Lucerne consisting of a row of symmetrical hotels round the foot of the lake, its old bridges destroyed, an iron one built over the Reuss, and an acacia promenade carried along the lake shore, with a

German band playing under a Chinese temple at the end of it, and the enlightened travellers, representatives of European civilisation, performing before the Alps, in each afternoon summer sunlight, in their modern manner, the Dance of Death.

John Ruskin, *Modern Painters,* V, 1856

What a charming toy-shop it is.

M.F. Tupper, *Paterfamilias' Diary of Everybody's Tour,* 1856

Macucagna (the Pizzo Bianco)

This is my mountain.

William Paton Ker, Remark shortly before collapsing and dying upon it, 17 July 1923

Martigny

The Houses in this Country are all built of firr boards plain'd within, low & seldom of above one storie: the People very Clownish, & rustickly clad, after a very odd fashion, for the most part in blew cloth, very whole and warme, nor with almost any variety or distinction, twixt the gentlemen & common sort, by a law of their Country, being exceedingly frugal: so as I saw not one begger among them; add to this their greate honestie and fidelitie, though exacting enough for what they part with. . . . Every man gos with a sword by his side, & the whole Country well disciplind, & indeede impregnable, which made the *Romans* have so ill successe against them; one lusty Swisse, at their narrow passages sufficient to repell a Legion. . . . I looke upon this Country to be the safest spot of all *Europ,* neither Envyed, nor Envying, nor are any of them rich, nor poore; but live in greate Simplicity and tranquilitie.

John Evelyn, *Diary,* May 1646

The Matterhorn

Committed thus and in other ways to the Matterhorn, the condition of my mind regarding it might be fitly compared to one of those uncheerful tenements often seen in the neighbourhood of London, where an adventurous contractor has laid the foundations, run up the walls, fixed the rafters, but stopped short, through bankruptcy, without completing the roof. As long as the Matterhorn remained unscaled, my Alpine life could hardly be said to be covered in.

John Tyndall, *Hours of Exercise in the Alps,* 1871 – of 1862

Not unapparent that the Matterhorn is like a Greek galley stranded, a reared-up rostrum – the sharp quains or *arrêtes,* the gunwales, the deck of the forecastle looking upon Zermatt, the figurehead looking the other way reaching up in the air, the cutwater and ram descending and abutting on a long reef – the gable-length of the mountain.

Gerard Manley Hopkins, Journal, 21 July 1868

Its strange form, its august isolation, and its majestic unkinship with its own kind, make it, so to speak, the Napoleon of the mountain world. 'Grand, gloomy and peculiar,' is a phrase which fits it as aptly as it fitted the great captain.

Mark Twain, *A Tramp Abroad,* 1880

The Matterhorn was too much of an Egyptian obelisk to please me.

John Ruskin, *Praeterita,* 1885–9

When I got back from the Matterhorn, I was asked by Gussfeldt, who was in Zermatt, how I found it. 'Difficult,' I said, without hesitation. 'Thank God!' he exclaimed, 'at last here's someone brave enough to call the Matterhorn difficult.'

Julius Kugy, *Alpine Pilgrimage,* 1934 – of 1886

Thirty-two years since, up against the sun,
Seven shapes, thin atomies to lower sight,
Labouringly leapt and gained thy gabled height,
And four lives paid for what the seven had won.

They were the first by whom the deed was done,
And when I look at thee my mind takes flight
To that day's tragic feat of manly might,
As though, till then, of history thou hadst none.

Yet ages ere men topped thee, late and soon
Thou didst behold the planets lift and lower;
Saw'st, maybe, Joshua's pausing sun and moon.
And the betokening sky when Caesar's power
Approached its bloody end; yea, even that Noon
When darkness filled the earth till the ninth hour.

Thomas Hardy, *Zermatt To the Matterhorn,* June-July 1887

It reminds me at the moment of a gaunt, cold, lonely old maid; but that beautiful fleecy cloud has the same softening effect that a chiffon scarf gives. I suppose . . . great heights must be lonely, and therefore, after all, it may be happier to mingle with the crowd.

Eileen Montague Jackson, quoting her mother, 1925, in *Switzerland Calling,* 1927

No! The Matterhorn is not a mountain. It is a large hatchet made of obsidian that cuts the blue sky.

Haruko Ichikawa, *Japanese Lady in Europe,* 1932

*He has in fact got a job. . . . He is working with Harry Fisher's design group. . . . They are designing the Alps. . . . Howard's whole body is full of a genial electric warmth. In just six and a half hours he has produced the Matterhorn. . . . It's a real young man's mountain of course. He never does anything quite so bold again or quite so fast.

Michael Frayn, *Sweet Dreams*, 1973
(Howard is in Heaven, after a car-crash here.)

Meiringen

I steered into the main street, but there I found such a yelling and roaring as I had never heard before, and very damnable it was; as though men were determined to do common evil wherever God has given them a chance of living in awe and worship.

For they were all bawling and howling with great placards and tickets, saying, 'This way to the Extraordinary Waterfall; that way to the Strange Cave. Come with me and you shall see the never-to-be-forgotten Falls of the Aar,' and so forth. So that my illusion of being alone in the roots of the world dropped off me very quickly, and I wondered how people could be so helpless and foolish as to travel about in Switzerland as tourists and meet with all this vulgarity and beastliness.

Hilaire Belloc, *The Path to Rome*, 1902

Mont Rigi

Along the route, at different intervals are wooden crosses, on which are nailed little wooden pictures, representing some period of the sufferings of our Saviour, and these I remarked are generally placed where the ascent is most fatiguing. For what purpose, and by whom these are erected, must be too apparent to need remark, but that the cunning Capuchins should have instilled into the minds of these *ignorantacci* the firm belief that these are the identical spots where our Saviour rested himself when he bore the cross upon his shoulder over Mount Rigi, is perhaps worthy of being noticed, as an extraordinary instance of fanaticism, in an enlightened state of Europe, and in the nineteenth century. . . . The man and the woman expressed with so much seriousness their perfect credence in this . . . that . . . I therefore only listened, and expressed my surprise that I should never before have heard that our Saviour had climbed Mount Rigi, at which, these two deluded souls seemed no less amazed than I was.

Charles Tennant, *A Tour, etc.*, 1824

Monte Rosa

Monte Rosa, occasionally seen at the extremity of the valley, is a mere white heap, with no more form in it than a haycock after a thunder-shower.

John Ruskin, quoted in E.T. Cook *Life of Ruskin*, 1911 – of 1845

Ouchy

. . . the freedom, the ease, the *primitive* solitude of dear little Ouchy.

Edward Gibbon, Letter to Lady Elizabeth Foster, 8 November 1792

The Pisse Vache Falls (near Martigny)

Having crossed the Trient, a turbid torrent, which issues from a narrow and obscure glen, remarkable for its rugged and romantic scenery, we arrived at the Pisse-Vache, a cataract much noticed by travellers. The characteristic beauty of this fall is, that it seems to burst from a cleft in the middle of the rock, through hanging shrubs that start abruptly from the crevices, and forms a perpendicular column of water about two hundred feet in height. The body of water being very ample, and the elevation not so considerable as to reduce it entirely into spray, render the effect very striking.

William Coxe, *Travels in Switzerland*, 2nd edn, 1791

Pontresina

The only manner in which I could obtain sufficient nourishment was by attending two tables d'hôte, one after the other.

Oscar Browning, *Memories of Sixty Years*, 1910 – of 1867

River Rhône

The Rhene had in times past one more strange property then any river in the whole world, that I could either heare or reade of in any history whatsoever, sacred or prophane, that whensoever any infants were cast into his channell (a thing that hath sometimes hapned) if they were begotten out of lawfull wedlocke, the river as a iust revenger of the mothers polluted bed would presently swallow it up in his swift streame; but if he found them to be begotten in the honest and chaste couple of marriage, he would gently and quietly conveigh them upon the toppe of the water, and restore them unto the trembling hands of the wofull mother, yeelding safety unto the silly babe as the most true testimony of the mothers impolluted chastity.

Thomas Coryate, *Crudities*, 1611

But the Rhone flows like one lambent jewel; its surface is nowhere, its ethereal self is everywhere, the iridescent rush and translucent strength of it, blue to the shore and radiant to the depth.

Fifteen feet thick, of not flowing, but flying water; not water, neither – melted glacier, rather, one should call it; the force of the ice is with it, and the wreathing of the clouds, the gladness of the sky, and the continuance of Time.

Waves of clear sea are, indeed, lovely to watch, but they are always coming or gone, never in any taken shape to be seen for a second. But here was one mighty wave that was always itself, and every fluted swirl of it, constant as the wreathing of a shell. No washing away of the fallen foam, no pause for gathering of power, no helpless ebb of discouraged recoil; but alive through bright day and lulling night, the never-pausing plunge, and never-fading flash, and never-hushing whisper, and, while the sun was up, the ever-answering glow of unearthly aquamarine, ultramarine, violet-blue, gentian-blue, peacock-blue, river-of-paradise blue, glass of a painted window melted in the sun, and the witch of the Alps flinging spun tresses of it forever from her snow. . . . And in the midst of all the gay glittering and eddied lingering, the noble bearing by of the midmost depth, so mighty, yet so terrorless and harmless, with its swallows skimming instead of petrels, and the dear old decrepit town as safe in the embracing sweep of it as if it were set in a brooch of sapphire.

John Ruskin, *Praeterita,* 1885–9

Schaffhausen

At the first entrance of the old city gates, you cannot but be rouzed and say to yourself, 'here is something which I have not seen before, yet I hardly know what.'

Dorothy Wordsworth, *Journal,* 1 August 1820

The Virgin-Mountain, wearing like a Queen,
A brilliant crown of everlasting snow,
Sheds ruin from her sides; and men below
Wonder that aught of aspect so serene
Can link with desolation. Smooth and green,
And seeming at a little distance, slow,
The waters of the Rhine; but on they go
Fretting and whitening, keener and more keen;
Till madness seizes on the whole wide Flood,
Turned to a fearful Thing whose nostrils breathe
Blasts of tempestuous smoke – wherewith he tries
To hide himself, but only magnified;
And doth in more conspicuous torment writhe,
Deafening the region in his ireful mood.

William Wordsworth, *Illustration: The Jungfrau and the Fall of the Rhine near Schaffhausen,* 1821, pub. 1822

It was exceedingly sultry at the falls of Schaffhausen. These were very impressive, but to escape the sun we were glad to take refuge in a shed, pervaded by an atrocious odour of decayed cheeses, or some such horror. 'This is my usual luck,' says Tennyson, 'I never go to see anything which is very impressive, without encountering something mean or repulsive. Now, this sublime cataract, and this disgusting stench, will for ever dwell together in my memory.' He went on to say that the unpleasant odours of London were as offensive as those of Paris, but that the latter were more pungent, piercing like the point of a lance; and then he added with grave emphasis, 'It is an age of lies, and also an age of stinks.'

Alfred Lord Tennyson, a Memoir, by his Son, 1897 – of 1869

The Schreckhorn

Aloof, as if a thing of mood and whim;
Now that its spare and desolate figure gleams
Upon my nearing vision, less it seems
A looming Alp-height than a guise of him
Who scaled its horn with ventured life and limb,
Drawn on by vague imaginings, maybe,
Of semblance to his personality
In its quaint glooms, keen lights, and rugged trim.

At his last change, when Life's dull coils unwind,
Will he, in old love, hitherward escape,
And the eternal essence of his mind
Enter this silent, adamantine shape,
And his low voicing haunt its slipping snows
When dawn that calls the climber dyes them rose?

Thomas Hardy, *The Schreckhorn, – with thoughts of Leslie Stephen,* June 1897

I was beginning to think that the Schreckhorn had an absurd reputation, but the hour of arête from the saddle to the top made me alter my opinion. It's a capital bit of rock climbing, a razor edge going quite steep down, snow on one side and rock on the other, not quite solid, so that you have to take the greatest care, and with a couple of very fine bits of climbing in it. It raises the Schreckhorn into the first class among mountains, though it's rather low down in its class.

Gertrude Bell, Letter to her father, August 1901

Schwytz (and Bern)

By antique fancy trimmed – though lowly, bred
To dignity – in thee, O SCHWYTZ! are seen
The genuine features of the golden mean;
Equality by Prudence governed,
Or jealous Nature ruling in her stead;
And, therefore, art thou blest with peace serene
As that of the sweet fields and meadows green
In unambitious compass round thee spread.
Majestic BERNE, high on her guardian steep,
Holding a central station of command,
Might well be styled this noble body's HEAD:
Thou, lodged 'mid mountainous entrenchments deep,

Its HEART; and ever may the heroic Land
Thy name, O SCHWYTZ, in happy freedom keep!

William Wordsworth, 'The Town of Schwytz', *Memorials of a Tour on the Continent in 1820,* 1821, pub. 1822

Seewen

Some of our party were reminded . . . of the complaint made by the French, that, when stationed in this country, they could neither procure a mistress nor a spy.

Dorothy Wordsworth, *Journal,* 19 August 1820

Simplon Pass

Brook and road
Were fellow-travellers in this gloomy Pass
And with them did we journey several hours
At a slow step. The immeasurable height
Of woods decaying, never to be decayed,
The stationary blasts of waterfalls,
And in the narrow rent, at every turn,
Winds thwarting winds, bewildered and forlorn,
The torrents shooting from the clear blue sky,
The rocks that muttered close upon our ears,
Black drizzling crags that spake by the wayside
As if a voice were in them, the sick sight
And giddy prospect of the raving stream,
The unfettered clouds, and region of the heavens,
Tumult and peace, the darkness and the light –
Were all like workings of one mind, the features
Of the same face, blossoms upon one tree
Characters of the great Apocalypse,
The types and symbols of Eternity,
Of first, and last, and midst, and without end.

William Wordsworth, *The Simplon Pass, c.*1799, pub. 1845

Our dinner at Simplon is worth recording; after vain attempts to demolish the remains of some venerable cow, we feasted on a dish of fritters, so delicate and tempting in appearance that they would have graced the table of an Alderman. We of course congratulated ourselves upon having found such young and tender chickens upon the top of Mont Simplon, when suddenly my Father exclaimed, 'Clara, you have been eating frogs.'

Clarissa Trant, *Journal,* 5 April 1815

The Simplon is magnificent in its nature and its art – both God & Man have done wonders – to say nothing of the Devil – who must certainly have had a hand (or a hoof) in some of the rocks & ravines through and over which the works are carried.

Lord Byron, Letter to John Murray, 15 October 1816

Ascended the Simplon which baffles all description. A road, carried up into the very clouds, over torrents and precipices; nothing was ever like it. At the last stage, before we reached the barrier on the summit, walked on by myself, and saw such a scene by sunset as I shall never forget. The mighty panorama of the Alps, whose summits there, indistinctly seen, looked like the top of gigantic waves, following close upon each other; the soft lights falling on those green spots which cultivation has conjured up in the midst of this wild scene: the pointed top of the Jungfrau, whose snows were then pink with the setting sun; all this was magnificent to a degree that quite over-powered me, and I alternately shuddered and shed tears as I looked upon it. Just, too, as we arrived near the snows on the very summit, the moon rose beautifully over them, and gave a new sort of glory to the scene.

Thomas Moore, *Journal,* 27 September 1819

The top itself, so wild, and bleak, and lonely, is a thing *by* itself, and not to be likened to any other sight. The cold was piercing; the north wind high and boisterous; and when it came driving into our faces, bringing a sharp shower of little points of snow and piercing it into our very blood, it really was, what it is often said to be, 'cutting,' – with a very sharp edge too. . . .

The cold in Switzerland, since, has been something quite indescribable. My eyes are tingling tonight, as one may suppose cymbals to tingle when they have been lustily played.

Charles Dickens, Letter to Mrs Charles Dickens, 23 November 1844

Solothurn / Soleure (and Fribourg)

These are two of the chief of the Popish *Cantons* after *Lucern:* and one sees in them a Heat and Bigotry beyond what appears either in *France* or *Italy.* Long before they come within the Church Doors they kneel down in the Streets when Mass is saying in it. The Images are also extreme gross. In the chief Church of *Solothurn* there is an image of God the Father, as an old Man with a great black Beard, having our Saviour on his Knees, and a Pigeon over his Head.

Gilbert Burnet, *Some Letters Containing an Account of What Seemed Remarkable in Travelling . . . ,* 1687

At twelve I waited on Monsieur de Barthes. He complained much of his situation. He said that Soleure was divided in politics. The French party hates the Spanish; and they live ill together. He complained much of the Swiss, who he said had lost their morals and had no longer their attachment to the French nation. He called them a dull, mean people. He said, 'We prefer the noble hatred of the English to that of the Swiss, who hate us like snakes.' He said, 'Un de ces paysans sur sa rude montagne vous dirait que le Roi de

France peut lui lecher le cul.' I must say this in English. The Swiss are now very little in the interest of France. The vulgar are taught to despise that renowned monarchy; so that it is common enough for 'a peasant on his rude mountain to bid the King of France kiss his backside.'

James Boswell, *Journal,* 28 November 1764

The public prison, newly constructed, is a solid edifice of stone, and is well adapted to the purpose of the building. . . . Although the penal laws are severe in theory, yet the judicial sentences, in criminal affairs, are so remarkably mild, that a prisoner, on his acquittal, wrote the following inscription on the wall of his cell: 'He who is inclined to rob, and escape hanging, let him rob in the Canton of Soleure.'

William Coxe, *Travels in Switzerland,* 2nd edn, 1791

Great Saint Bernard Pass (and convent)

*Seen from those solitudes, and from the Pass of the Great Saint Bernard, which was one of them, the ascending Night came up the mountain like a rising water. When it at last rose to the walls of the convent of the Great Saint Bernard, it was as if that weather-beaten structure were another Ark, and floated on the shadowy waves.

Charles Dickens, *Little Dorrit,* 1857–8

*'We have had, of course,' said the young lady, who was rather reserved and haughty, 'to leave the carriages and fourgon at Martigny. And the impossibility of bringing anything that one wants to this inaccessible place, and the necessity of leaving every comfort behind, is not convenient.'

'A savage place, indeed,' said the insinuating traveller.

The elderly lady, who was a model of accurate dressing, and whose manner was perfect, considered as a piece of machinery, here interposed a remark in a low soft voice.

'But like other inconvenient places,' she observed, 'it must be seen. As a place much spoken of, it is necessary to see it.'

'Oh! I have not the least objection to seeing it, I assure you, Mrs. General,' returned the other carelessly.

Ibid.

St Gotthard Pass

The scenery everywhere was most exquisite, but of the great *pass* I shall say nothing – it was like standing in the presence of God when He is terrible. The tears overflowed my eyes. I think I never *saw* the sublime before.

Elizabeth Barrett Browning, Letter, 1851

Through the St Gothard artery all Germania is now pouring, like frothing beer through neck of bottle, all the hotels, all the steamboats, compact of her progeny, resolute to see, careless of being a sight.

George Meredith, Letter to Miss Louisa Lawrence, 8 September 1882

From a point not far from the St. Gotthard Pass the head waters of the Rhine, the Rhone, the Po and the Danube are all within the landscape that you see. Here you are placed at a seat of command whence there radiate the wires that give order and animation to armies too great and too widely deployed to be seen with the bodily eye at one time. From here there go about their multifarious business the threads of governing force that are not to rest from their august patrol of Europe till they obtain their discharge into seas whose other sides are America, Africa and Asia.

To see Nature holding so many reins in one hand gives a wonderful lift to your mind. All going well it is lifted into that rare and happy state in which the senses seem to borrow for the moment the longer range of imagination, or else imagination borrows the vivid urgency of bodily sense.

C.E. Montague, *The Right Place,* 1924

St Moritz

The patients at St. Moritz put me in mind of that Eastern prince whose physician induced him to kick a football under the impression that it contained a charm. The sagacious doctor knew that faith has a dynamic power unpossessed by knowledge. Through the agency of this power he stirred the prince to action, caused him to take wholesome exercise, and thus cured him of his ailments. At St. Moritz the water is probably the football.

John Tyndall, *Hours of Exercise in the Alps,* 1871 – of 1864

and Tarasp

If St Moritz is, as Mr Stephen thinks, the limbo of Switzerland set apart for the world – that is, for kings, millionaires and people who travel with couriers – Tarasp is its purgatory, providentially created for the class whom the flesh has rendered unfit for such Alpine paradises as Grindelwald, or even Pontresina.

Douglas Freshfield, *Italian Alps,* 1875 – of 1866

and Davos

The village of St Moritz is one of the dirtiest, the most untidy, the most irregularly and badly built in the whole valley; and I should say, from certain unsavoury smells which assail one in sundry quarters, very badly drained. . . . Davos is a dull dreary, monotonous mountain valley, and an American who had spent a winter in the place assured me that, 'to save his life, he would not pass another there.'

J. Burney Yeo, *Health Resorts,* 1882 – of 1869

St. Moritz acts like one of those flytraps to be seen in old-fashioned inns, which do not indeed diminish the swarm of intrusive insects, but profess at least to confine them to one spot. And if any district were to be selected into which the cockneyism of the surrounding Alps might be drained as into a reservoir, certainly no better selection could be made than St. Moritz. The upper valley of the Inn is one of the very few Alpine districts which may almost be called ugly. The high bleak level tract, with monotonous ranges of pine forests at a uniform slope, has as little of the picturesque as can well be contrived in the mountains. Even in the great peaks there is a singular want of those daring and graceful forms, those spires, and domes, and pinnacles, which give variety and beauty to the other great mountain masses. I should rejoice if it could be made into the Norfolk Island of the Alps, and all kings, cockneys, persons travelling with couriers, Americans doing Europe against time, Cook's tourists and their like, commercial travellers, and especially that variety of English clergyman which travels in dazzling white ties and forces church services upon you by violence in remote country inns, could be confined within it to amuse or annoy each other. Meanwhile, though this policy has not been carried out, it is gratifying that a spontaneous process of natural selection has done something of the kind. Like flies to like; the cockney element accumulates like the precious metal in the lodes of rich mines.

Leslie Stephen, *The Playground of Europe,* 1871

It's too rich and too black and too white, like living in a wedding cake. I should soon want some nice cheap plebeian mud.

Earl of Desart, *A Page from the Past,* 1932 – of 1908

Tucked away in the Engadine Valley, shut in by snow-capped mountains and unspoiled by civilization is a small town called St Moritz. Here for over 100 years the nomadic tribes of Europe have come for the winter to find grazing lands for their herds of Rolls Royces, Cadillacs and Mercedes Benzes. These nomadic tribes are shy people by nature, and avoid being interviewed by anthropologists and newspapermen. . . .

The St Moritzers, as we shall call them (the scientific name is E Pluribus Unum).

Art Buchwald, *More Caviar,* 1958

St Moritz, the heart of the broken-limb country, where a man must prove himself first on skis and then on a stretcher.

Art Buchwald, *I Chose Caviar,* 1957

St Pierre *('The last, dirtiest, and most wretched village of the Valais' – Tennant)*

The only observation, as far as I could learn, with which my guide was honoured by Bonaparte, was when he descended, dripping wet, from his mule, at the village of St Pierre, where, in a wretched little habitation, which my guide pointed out to me as we passed by, Bonaparte took up his lodgings for the night. There, doffing his three-cornered hat to shake off the rain, he held it forth, exclaiming in his usual hurried manner, '*Voici! ce que j'ai fait sur vos montagnes, – j'ai gâté mon chapeau neuf – bah! j'en trouverai un autre de l'autre côté.*'

Charles Tennant, *A Tour, etc.,* 1824

Thun (Unterseen, Interlaken)

I was entranced by that lake of Thun. And our drive of two miles after we landed, through Unterseen to Interlaken was lovely; yet I can scarcely say I was delighted by it; for then, after my feelings on the lake, I began to be oppressed with beauty, and to cry to Nature, 'Hold, enough!'

Martha Macdonald Lamont, *Impressions, Thoughts and Sketches . . . in France and Switzerland,* 1844

Thusis

We have been a week in this singularly lovely place – a place that almost reconciles us to Switzerland. . . . I don't know that I quite agree with you in pronouncing this (with admirable lucidity on your part) an *odious* country; but somehow I grudge it more than a measured experience and doubt that of my own free will I shall ever come here again. So much the worse for *you!* – Thusis cries out – and I think that if I could give you some faint picture of Thusis you would say yes.

Henry James, Letter to Grace Norton, 8 August 1872

Undervelier

They cook worse in Undervelier than any place I was ever in, with the possible exception of Omaha, Neb.

Hilaire Belloc, *The Path to Rome,* 1902

The Valais (en route to Sion)

The richness of the soil . . . prevents labour by almost spontaneously producing the fruits of the earth. In fact the people assist nature very little.

William Coxe, *Travels in Switzerland,* 2nd edn, 1791

cretins and idiots of the Valais

It has been asserted also that the people very much

respect these idiots, and even consider them as *blessings from Heaven;* which is strongly contradicted by others. Upon my questioning some gentlemen of this country, at the baths of Leuk, they treated the notion as absurd and false . . . but . . . having since that time repeatedly inquired among the lower ranks I am convinced that the common people esteem them as blessings. They call them 'Souls of God, without Sin,' and many parents prefer these idiot children to those whose understandings are perfect.

Ibid.

The *Cretins* are sad disgusting objects. I was prepared to expect the *goitre.* . . . It would seem as if nature in these regions could not help breaking out into excrescences, as well in the animate, as in the inanimate part of her creation.

Henry Matthews, *Diary of an Invalid,* 1820

Place me somewhere in the Valais, 'mid the mountains
west of Binn,
West of Binn, and east of Savoy, in a decent kind of inn,
With a peak or two for climbing, and a glacier to
explore, –
Any mountains will content me, though they've all
been climbed before –
Yes! I care not any more
Though they've all been done before,
And the names they keep in bottles may be numbered
by the score.

Though the hand of Time be heavy: though your
ancient comrades fail:
Though the mountains you ascended be accessible by
rail:
Though your nerve begin to weaken, and you're gouty
grown and fat,
And prefer to walk in places that are reasonably flat –
Though you grow so very fat
That you climb the Gorner Grat
Or perhaps the Little Scheideck, – and are rather
proud of that:
Yet I hope that till you die
You will annually sigh
For a vision of the Valais with the coming of July,
For the Oberland or Valais and the higher, purer air,
And the true delight of living, as you taste it only there!

A.,D. Godley, *Switzerland, Second Strings,* 1902

Vevey

Vevey . . . is Paradise, and I don't see how the people there and at Lausanne can have the impudence to suppose that they can go to Heaven after death.

Edward Lear, Letter to Chichester Fortescue, July 1861

Vevey. . . . A different climate. Mild, *sec.* I bought a Swiss cigar, and we got into a tiny Swiss tram. Had the Swiss feeling. Feeling much intensified when, in the waiting room of the funicular, we found a vast musical box, which I caused to play for 10 centimes. . . .

I was so anxious to see the panorama this morning that I slept badly. I thought it wonderful, but I was disappointed because it seemed so small. I had expected something much bigger. Well, it has been 'growing' on me all day. . . . My opinion of this panorama is going up every minute. . . . Below us cloud effects on lake continually changing. Really the scene is enchantingly beautiful. We see Vevey as though from a balloon.

Arnold Bennett, *Journal,* 14 December 1908

Wallenstadt Lake

If, indeed, I were bound to select one lake above all others, preserving the attributes of its order, and possessing them in the greatest perfection, I should prefer this to all others I have seen.

Sir T.N. Talfourd, *Vacation Rambles,* 1844

Wengern Alp

Surely the Wengern Alp must be precisely the loveliest place in this world. To hurry past it, and listen to the roar of the avalanches, is a very unsatisfactory mode of enjoyment; it reminds one too much of letting off crackers in a cathedral. The mountains seem to be accomplices of the people who charge fifty centimes for an echo. But it does one's moral nature good to linger there at sunset or in the early morning, when tourists have ceased from travelling, and the jaded cockney may enjoy a kind of spiritual bath in the soothing calmness of the scenery.

Leslie Stephen, *The Playground of Europe,* 1871

Perhaps the Wengern Alp pleased me somewhat less than in old years, but it is too much beset with tourists, beggars, and places of entertainment.

Matthew Arnold, Letter to his mother, 13 August 1871

Wettingen (near Baden)

About a mile from Baden, where the Limmat flows with the greatest rapidity, we shot under the bridge of Wettingen with such ferocity, that in the moment of admiring its bold projection on one side, I imperceptibly found myself on the other.

William Coxe, *Travels in Switzerland,* 2nd edn, 1791.
(This was the wooden bridge, 240 feet long and 20 feet above the water, the work of Grubenman, the self-taught architect.)

Zermatt

It is a grand view but I could never care for it. . . . I am very glad to have seen it, but, if I can help it, nothing shall ever induce me to see it again.

Augustus Hare, *Memorials of a Quiet Life*, 1872 – of 1854

An English gentleman who had lived some years in this region said it was the cradle of compulsory education.

Mark Twain, *A Tramp Abroad*, 1880

Wonderfully soothing all the great sights are. They attempt nothing, they force nothing. There the peaks climb the sky and fence the world, and they fence you and bid you climb without a word to you, and their strong beauty puts all small thoughts to a quiet death, you feel as if you had passed something and were on the other side.

Edward Benson, Archbishop of Canterbury, *Diary*, 27 August 1889

The whole of Zermatt had a busy, prosperous temple-atmosphere, dedicated to the service of the mountains.

Freya Stark, *Traveller's Prelude*, 1950 – of 1923

Zürich

The habits of the Citizens doe in some things differ from the attyre of any nation that ever I saw before. For all the men doe weare round breeches with codpeeces. So that you shall not finde one man in all Zurich, from a boy of ten yeares old to an old man of the age of a hundred yeares, but he weareth a Codpeece. Also all their men doe weare flat caps and ruffe bandes. For I could not see one man or boy in the whole City weare a falling band. Many of their women especially maides doe use a very strange and phantasticall fashion with their haire that I never saw before, but the like I observed afterwards in many other places of Switzerland, especially in Basil. For they plait it in two very long locks that hang down over their shoulders half a yard long. And many of them doe twist it together with prety silke ribbands or fillets of sundry colours.

The beds of the Innes of this City and of all the other Helvetian and German Cities are very strange, such as I never saw before. The like being in the private houses of every particular Citizen as I heard. For evere man hath a light downe, or very soft feather bedde laid upon him which keepeth him very warme, and is nothing offensive for the burden. For it is exceeding light, and serveth for the coverled of the bedde.

Thomas Coryate, *Crudities*, 1611

The Citizens have a custome that when they goe forth against the enemy, they place the Ministers or Pastors in the front, or where they may partake the danger.

Fynes Moryson, *An Itinerary*, 1617

One sees here the true ancient Simplicity of the *Switzers*, not corrupted with Luxury or Vanity. Their Women not only do not converse familiarly with Men, except those of their near Kindred, but even in the Streets do not make any Returns to the Civility of Strangers; for it is only Strangers that put off their Hats to Women, but they make no Courtesies: and here, as in all *Switzerland*, Women are not saluted, but the Civility is expressed by taking them by the Hand.

Gilbert Burnet, *Some Letters Containing an Account of What Seemed Remarkable in Travelling . . .*, 1687

Among their sumptuary laws, the use of a carriage in the town is prohibited to all sorts of persons except strangers: and it is almost inconceivable that in a place so commercial and wealthy luxury should so little prevail.

At Zuric the original Swiss spirit of independence prevails more than in any of the large towns in this country.

William Coxe, *Travels in Switzerland*, 2nd edn, 1791

The houses are certainly far too numerous for picturesque effect, not to speak of their unquiet hues: but the character of the Lake, so large and ample, is of free chearfulness; and from that cause it is not *disturbed* by buildings which amongst the lakes of the North of England would be the ruin of all repose. *I* complained not of *patchiness* or *spottiness;* it was pleasure enough for me to think how numerous the families who enjoy at evening and morning in their dwellings and pretty gardens the beauties of the Lake, while I had distant glimpses of the higher mountains, inviting the fancy to solitudes and retirements of pastoral life.

Dorothy Wordsworth, *Journal*, 3 August 1820

The town of Zurich has long been dignified with the honourable appelation of the Athens of Switzerland, and has probably produced more celebrated men than all the other towns of Switzerland put together.

Charles Tennant, *A Tour, etc.*, 1824

Never was I thoroughly warm there except once in a café.

Matthew Arnold, Letter to his wife, 26 February 1886

Zurich: incongruous image! Straightway I was transported from this harmonious desolation of Ferento; . . . and found myself glancing over a leaden lake and wandering about streets full of ill-dressed and ungracious folk; escaping thence further afield, into featureless hills encrusted with smug, tawdry villas and drinking-booths smothered under noisome horse-chestnuts and Virginia creepers. How came they to hit upon the ugliest tree, and the ugliest creeper, on earth? Infallible instinct! Zurich: who shall sum up thy merciless vulgarity? . . .

Fearsome town! Its ugliness is of the active kind; it grips you by the throat and sits on your chest like a nightmare.

Norman Douglas, *Alone,* 1921

*Zurich is not unlike an American city. . . . In Zurich there was a lot besides Zurich – the roofs up-led the eyes to tinkling cow-pastures, which in turn modified hilltops further up – so life was a perpendicular starting off to a postcard heaven.

F. Scott Fitzgerald, *Tender is the Night,* 1939

*The bustling metropolis of swiftly gliding trams and greystone banking houses, of cosmopolitan restaurants on the great stone banks of the swiftly-gliding snot-green (mucus mutandis) Limmat River, of jewelled escapements and refugees of all kinds.

Tom Stoppard, *Travesties,* 1975

SYRIA

What a country this is! I fear I shall spend the rest of my life travelling in it. Race after race, one on top of the other, the whole land strewn with the mighty relics of them. We in Europe are accustomed to think that civilization is an advancing flood that has gone steadily forward since the beginning of time. I believe we are wrong. It is a tide that ebbs and flows, reaches a high water mark and turns back again. Do you think that from age to age it rises higher than before? I wonder – and I doubt.

Gertrude Bell, Letter to Florence Lascelles, 9 April 1905

The north of Syria seems scarce Arab at all – half the people with fairish hair and blue eyes: said to be descendants of Crusaders, but anyway they might be sturdy peasants in the Alps. It is lovely to drive over that great open country rolling away in emptiness near the hills and then in great red strips of ploughed earth and corn: people riding over it with droves of horses, Arab but a little stockier than the delicate creatures of Iraq – and everywhere you see dotted here and there and rising out of the haze against the mountain ranges old mounds of nameless cities. There is a feeling of incredible age here, an easy country over which armies have marched since the first days of mankind. Usually near the mound some little village lingers – looking, in all the country between Homs and Aleppo, like a camp of tents from the conical fashion of their beehive domed huts, little square mud affairs with a door and a few window holes, very cool they say in summer. They are not beautiful, but look amusing, sticking like teeth against the skyline as they lean up against the more ancient mounds.

Freya Stark, Letter, 31 May 1937, in *The Coasts of Incense,* 1953

Syrians

She doted upon the Assyrians, her neighbours, captains and rulers clothed most gorgeously, horsemen riding upon horses, all of them desirable young men.

The Bible, Ezekiel 23:12

Syrians – sterile in invention, by an easy imitation may become smatterers in the liberal arts.

Charles M. Doughty, *Travels in Arabia Deserta,* 1888

Aleppo

The City is nothing lesse than well fortified, but most pleasantly seated, having many sweet gardens. The aire was so hot, as me thought I supped hot broth, when I drew it in; but it is very subtile, so as the Christians comming hither from Scanderona, (a most unhealthfull place, having the aire choaked with Fens), continually fall sicke, and often die.

Fynes Moryson, *An Itinerary,* 1617

Aleppo is thoroughly Oriental in this . . . : that the poets of Islam have made a fantastic mirage of it, and particularly of its river – so called. . . .

But the river of Aleppo is (if I may say so without too much offending the guardian spirits of the place) a narrow, dirty ditch, stagnant, foul with refuse: almost a drain; and there is very little of it at that.

Hilaire Belloc, *Places,* 1942

Alexandretta / Scanderoon (old port of Aleppo)

Scandarone or Allexandretta is the Sea port of Alleppo, some three dayes Journie distant. It is very unwholsome by reason of the huge high hills hindringe the approach of the Sunne Beames, untill nine or ten a Clocke in the morning, lyeinge in a great Marsh full of boggs, foggs and Froggs, the Topps of the Mountaines continually covered with Snowe, aboundinge with wild beasts, as Lyons, Wylde Boares, Jacalls, Porcupines, etc.

Peter Mundy, *Sundry Relations of Certaine Voyages. . . . etc.,* (before 1620), 1907

The Crac des Chevaliers

Most perfect of medieval fortresses (and model for every sandcastle ever built).

Peter Wilsher, *Sunday Times,* 30 December 1979

Damascus

Damascus is a faire city and full of good merchandise. . . . There is nowhere such another city of gardens and of fruit. In that city also is wonder mickle folk; and it is well walled about with a double wall. In that city also dwell many physicians; and there used St Paul some time the craft of physic before that he was converted.

John Mandeville, *The Book of John Mandeville, c.* 1360

The Turkes say, that their Prophet Mahomet was once at Damascus, and that when he saw the pleasant situation of it, and beheld the stately prospect of it, excelling all others that hee saw before; refused to enter into the Citie, lest the pleasantnesse thereof should ravish him, and move him there to settle an Earthly Paradise, and hinder his desire of the heavenly Paradise.

William Biddulph, 1600, in *Purchas his Pilgrimes,* 1625

Now may we see *Damascus* lofty towers,
Like to the shadowes of *Pyramides,*
That with their beauties grac'd the Memphion fields:
The golden stature of their feathered bird,
That spreads her wings upon the citie wals,
Shall not defend it from our battering shot.
The townes-men maske in silke and cloath of gold,
And every house is as a treasurie.
The men, the treasure, and the towne is ours.

Christopher Marlowe, *Tamburlaine,* Pt 1, *c.*1587

A large round mountain in front prevented us from catching a glimpse at it, till, on turning a point of the rock, it appeared suddenly at our feet. . . . The domes and minarets of the sacred city rose out of the heart of a forest of gardens and trees, which was twelve miles in circumference. Four or five small rivers ran through the forest and the city, glittering at intervals in the sun; and to form that vivid contrast of objects in which Asiatic so much excels European scenery, the plain was encircled on three of its sides, by mountains of light and naked rocks.

John Carne, *Letters from the East,* 1830

The greatest luxuries the city contains are the coffee-houses; many of these are built on the bosom of the river, and supported by piles. The platform of the coffee-house is raised only a few inches above the level of the stream; the roof is supported by slender rows of pillars, and it is quite open on every side; innumerable small seats cover the floor, and you take one of these and place it in the position you like best; the river, whose surrounding banks are covered with wood, rushes rapidly by, close to your feet. Near the coffee-houses are one or two cataracts several feet high, with a few trees growing out of the river beside them; and the perpetual sound of their fall, and the coolness they spread around, are exquisite luxuries in the sultry heat of day. At night, when the lamps, suspended from the slender pillars, are lighted, and Turks, of different ranks, in all the varieties of their rich costume, cover the platform, just above the surface of the river, on which, and on its foaming waterfalls, the moonlight rests, and the sound of music is heard, you fancy that if ever the Arabian Nights' enchantments are to be realized, it is here.

Ibid.

This 'Holy' Damascus, this 'earthly paradise' of the Prophet, so fair to the eyes that he dared not trust himself to tarry in her blissful shades – she is a city of hidden palaces, of copses, and gardens, and fountains, and bubbling streams. The juice of her life is the gushing and ice-cold torrent that tumbles from the snowy sides of Anti-Lebanon. Close along on the river's edge through seven sweet miles of rustling boughs and deepest shade, the city spreads out her whole length; as a man falls flat, face forward on the brook, that he may drink, and drink again; so Damascus, thirsting for ever, lies down with her lips to the stream, and clings to its rushing waters.

A.W. Kinglake, *Eothen,* 1844 – of *c.*1835

Whilst I was at Damascus I had my quarters at the Franciscan convent there; and very soon after my arrival I asked one of the monks to let me know something of the spots that deserved to be seen: I made my inquiry in reference to the associations with which the city had been hallowed by the sojourn and adventures of St Paul. 'There is nothing in all Damascus,' said the good man, 'half so well worth seeing as our cellars.'

Ibid.

What was . . . curious was the atmosphere of the rascally Syrian town, made of Moslem scoundrels, Christian thieves, and Jew moneylenders, all of types that blanch Chicago white. Yet what bores one in Chicago, intensely amused me in Damascus. They cheated me out of my eye-lids, stole my letters, lied ten times to the word, and made me live like a swine, and I only laughed.

Henry Adams, Letter to Elizabeth Cameron, 24 March 1898

Lovely with almond-blossom and flooded water
With wind-flushed sheen of swaying orchard-meadows;
With azure starred of infrequent grape hyacinth;
Meshed blue with the fig-groves' wintry haze;
Ruddy with budded apricot; snowy with apple –
Damascus now into April glory awakening.

Edward Thompson, 'Damascus Orchards', *Collected Poems,* 1930

Damascus is . . . a symbol. One might call it a bunch of symbols. It is a symbol of the permanent physical conditions that run throughout history; the permanent geographical limits of human settlement, government and war.

Hilaire Belloc, *Places,* 1942

the street called Straight

The street called Straight is straighter than a corkscrew, but not as straight as a rainbow. St Luke is careful not to commit himself; he does not say it is the street which *is* straight, but the 'street which is *called* Straight.' It is a fine piece of irony; it is the only facetious remark in the Bible, I believe.

Mark Twain, *The Innocents Abroad,* 1869

Hama

This towne of Hammah is fallen and falleth more and more to decay, and at this day there is scarse one half of the wall standing, which hath bene very strong and faire: but because it cost many mens lives to win it, the Turke will not have it repaired; and hath written in the Arabian tongue over the castle gate, which standeth in the midst of the towne, these words; Cursed be the father and the sonne that shall lay their hands to the repairing hereof.

John Eldred (1583), in Richard Hakluyt, *Principal Navigations . . . of the English Nation,* 1598–1600

Homs

Homs is not much of a place, but such as it is, it has a character of its own. It is all built of black tufa and the best houses have inner courtyards with a simple but very excellent decoration of white limestone let into the black either in patterns or in straight courses like the Pisan building. Moreover the minarets of the mosques and tall slender towers, for spire, for all the world like an Italian campanile, like the towers of San Gimignano, except that they are capped with a whole cupola, very pretty and decorative.

Gertrude Bell, Letter to her stepmother, 10 March 1905

Jabal Druz

Imagine a very huge giant emptying out giant-size sackfuls of big basalt boulders, as a child might empty out paper-bagfuls of monkey nuts. Make the top of the heap rise five or six thousand feet above seal level, and sprinkle the higher altitudes of the boulder dump with dwarf oaks. That is the best notion that I can give you of the Jabal Druz. Here and there the cones of volcanoes stand up in the distance.

Arnold Toynbee, *East to West,* 1958

Palmyra

I wonder if the wide world presents a more singular landscape. It is a mass of columns, ranged into long avenues, grouped into temples, lying broken on the sand or pointing one long solitary finger to Heaven. Beyond them is the immense Temple of Baal; the modern town is built inside it and its rows of columns rise out of a mass of mud roofs. And beyond all is the desert, sand and white stretches of salt and sand again, with the dust clouds whirling over it and the Euphrates five days away. It looks like the white skeleton of a town, standing knee deep in the blown sand.

Gertrude Bell, Journal-Letter to her family, 20 May 1900

Not that Palmyra is much in itself. Colonnades of fine pillars with horrid little brackets, it appears, where the bourgeois donor placed his edifying bust.

James Elroy Flecker, Letter to Frank Savery, 10 January 1912

On looking closer this architecture presents a puzzle: it is Roman surely? but there is something not quite Roman about it; there are mistakes that the Roman builders would not have made. Indeed, the Romans did not build it, no; Arabs built it, dazzled by what they had seen or heard of the Roman models. . . . It lacks the grand solidity of Roman building, and the Roman sense of proportion is notably absent. But I like Palmyra. It is very feminine; it is gay, whimsical, and a little meretricious. It seems to have drunk the desert sun, and to have granted free passage to all the desert winds with a wanton insouciance. Palmyra is a Bedouin girl laughing because she is dressed up as a Roman lady.

Vita Sackville-West, *Twelve Days,* 1928

Water in landscape is like eyes in a face, when the lids close, the expression of life departs; and so it has departed from the lands around Palmyra, whose fields, I am told, can still be seen from the air, under a dead skin of sand.

Freya Stark, *The Coasts of Incense,* 1953 – of 1935

T

TAHITI

Notwithstanding nature hath been very bountifull to it yet it doth not produce any one thing of intrinsick Value or that can be converted into an Article of trade, so that the value of the discovery consists wholy in the refreshments it will always afford to Shipping in their passage through these seas.

Captain James Cook, *Journal*, July 1769

The houses, or rather dwellings of these people are admirably adapted to the continual warmth of the climate. They do not build them in villages or towns, but separate each from the other, according to the size of the estate the owner of the house possesses. They are always in the woods; and no more ground is cleared for each house than is just sufficient to hinder the dropping off the branches from rotting the thatch with which they are covered, so that you step from the house immediately under shade, and that the most beautiful imaginable. No country can boast such delightful walks as this; for the whole plains where the people live are covered with groves of breadfruit and cocoanut trees without underwood. These are intersected in all directions by the paths which go from one house to the other, so that the whole country is one shade, than which nothing can be more grateful in a climate where the sun has so powerful an influence. The houses are built without walls, so that the air, cooled by the shade of the trees, has free access in whatever direction it happens to blow . . . nothing more than a thatched roof of the same form as in England, supported by three rows of posts or pillars, one on each side, and one in the middle. The floor was covered some inches deep with soft hay, upon which here and there were laid mats for the convenience of sitting down. This is almost the only furniture, as few houses have more than one stool, the property of the master of the family, and constantly used by him: most are entirely without the stool. These houses serve them chiefly to sleep in and make their cloth, etc; they generally eat in the open air under the shade of the nearest tree, if the weather is not rainy. The mats which serve them to sit upon in the daytime are also their beds at night; the cloth which they wear in the day serves for covering; and a little wooden stool, a block of wood, or bundle of cloth for a pillow. Their order is generally this: near the middle of the room sleep the master of the house and his wife, and with them the rest of the married people; next to them the unmarried women; next to them again, at some small distance, the unmarried men; the servants (*toutous*) generally lie in the open air, or if it rains, come just within shelter.

Sir Joseph Banks, *Journal of the Rt Hon Sir Joseph Banks* (1769), 1768–71

It must . . . be allowed to be a very beautiful Island, and appears, no doubt, to great advantage after a long Voyage. I remember well that England does so, and run no risk in asserting that Otahitee would make but an indifferent appearance if placed beside it.

William Wales, *Journal*, 31 August 1773

We could not but compare this happy country to Mahomed's Paradise, where the appetite is never cloyed by being gratified.

George Forster, *A Voyage Round the World*, 1777

How I abominate Mr Banks and Dr Solander, who routed the poor Otahetians out of the centre of the ocean, and carried our abominable passions amongst them! not even that poor little speck could escape European restlessness.

Horace Walpole, Letter to the Rev. William Cole, 15 June 1780

The land appeared as uneven as a piece of crumpled paper.

Sydney Parkinson, *A Journal of a Voyage to the South Seas*, 1784

Poor Omai the savage said, when about to return to Otaheite – *No horse there! no ass! no cow, no golden pippins, no dish of tea! – Ah, missey! I go without every thing – I always so content there though.*

Hester Lynch Thrale/Piozzi, *Observations . . . in the Course of a Journey*, 1789

The island to which every voyager has offered up his tribute of imagination.

Charles Darwin, *Journal . . . During the Voyage . . . of H.M.S. Beagle*, 1832–6

J.C. should have appeared in Taheiti.

Herman Melville, *Journal of a Visit to Europe and the Levant*, 1857

Tahiti is lovely; the climate is perfect; we have made a

sort of home here; and I never shall meet another spot so suitable to die in. The world actually vanishes here. . . . Man somehow got here, I think about a thousand years ago, and made a society which was on the whole the most successful the world ever saw, because it rested on the solidest possible foundation of no morals at all.

Henry Adams, Letter to Elizabeth Cameron, 19 April 1891

Tahiti is a true Crusoe island.

Henry Adams, Letter to Elizabeth Cameron, 3 May 1891

and Roratonga
Roratonga gives you a kind of foretaste of the whole charm and beauty of the South Seas. It is the appetizer, the *hors-d'oeuvre*, not the whole meal. Tahiti is the whole thing; the real thing; the thing one has dreamt about all one's life; the thing which made Stevenson leave Europe for ever. All tellers of fairy tales, and all poets from Homer downwards have always imagined the existence of certain *Fortunate* islands which were so full of magic and charm that they turned man from his duty and from all tasks . . . and held him a willing captive.

Maurice Baring, *Round the World in Any Number of Days*, 1913

Everything grows wild in Tahiti. Nobody seems to bother about gardening, still less of weeding. It is not only the lilies who do not toil and spin, but the gardeners also. The unaided results of Nature are so prodigious that the imagination is staggered to think of what might be done supposing an energetic gardener were let loose in these islands and allowed to try experiments. He would produce such a garden as the world has never seen – and very likely spoil the island.

Ibid.

Very pretty to look at, but I didn't want to stay, not one bit. Papeete is a poor sort of place, mostly Chinese, natives in European clothes, and fat. . . . I never want to *stay* in the Tropics. There is a sort of sickliness about them, smell of cocoa-nut oil and sort of palm-tree, reptile nausea. . . . These are supposed to be the earthly paradises: these South Sea Isles. You can have 'em.

D.H. Lawrence, Letter to Mary Cannan, 31 August 1922

Tahiti, Tahiti,
Tahiti, Tahiti,
Sieh die Cocoa Cuties, mitaus noddings on.
Hier a Leaf, da a Leaf,
Hinten a Coral Reef.
Dass iss doch kein Climate für a mittelaged Mann.

Kurt M. Stein, 'Vor a Gauguin Picture zu Singen', *Gemixte Pickles*, 1927

Only Keats could fairly have reproduced its glamour, its atmosphere of romance.

Tourist brochure quoting Beatrice Grimshaw, quoted Cedric Belfrage, *Away from It All*, 1936

compared with Fiji
You couldn't but feel that, if the Pacific islands had to be run either like Paris or like London, Paris was preferable.

Cedric Belfrage, *Away from It All*, 1936

European imperialism long ago made Tahiti a distant suburb of Paris, the missionaries made it a suburb of Christ's kingdom, and the radio made it a suburb of Los Angeles.

Ibid.

The American girl . . . looked very thoughtful at lunch, and finally said: 'I know why it is I like this place so much. It reminds me of Seattle.'

Ibid.

The trouble with Tahiti is that it is devoted almost exclusively to 'Con.' It really is thrown at you all the time and this is 'ow you say très gentil if you happen to like it . . . there is a cafe here on the port called Vaimar's where one can sit watching all the cons watching all the cons watching all the cons go by. It is picturesque, but fairly dull. . . . The petites Tahitiennes spend most of their time when not being rogered in emitting little squeaks. This is rather boring, however I have my ear plugs.

Noel Coward, Letter, 7 March 1962, quoted in Cole Lesley, *The Life of Noel Coward*, 1976

France spoils Tahiti: partly because of prestige reasons but mostly for love. Tahiti accepts France's adoration with a slight yawn and with the bored air of a great and spoiled beauty.

As a French friend, living here, put it:

'Tahiti is listed as an underdeveloped territory. This is nonsense. Tahiti is spoilt, pampered and overdeveloped. Indeed, Tahiti and the United States are the only two overdevelopment territories in the world, struggling with all the horrid difficulties of overdevelopment. But France, it seems, wants it that way. Very well, as long as the phrase Income Tax is not uttered, France will be permitted to stay and pay homage.'

George Mikes, *Boomerang – Australia Rediscovered*, 1968

Tahitians

In the article of food these happy people may almost be said to be exempt from the curse of our forefathers; scarcely can it be said that they earn their bread by the sweat of their brow, when their chief sustenance, breadfruit, is procured with no more trouble than that of climbing a tree, and pulling it down. Not that the trees grew here spontaneously, but, if a man, in the course of his life planted ten such trees (which, if well done, might take the labour of an hour, or thereabouts), he would as completely fulfil his duty to his own as well as future generations, as we, natives of less temperate climates, can do by toiling in the cold of winter to sow, and in the heat of summer to reap, the annual produce of our soil.

Sir Joseph Banks, *Journal of the Rt Hon Sir Joseph Banks* (1769), 1768–71

They are certainly as cleanly a people as any under the sun; they all wash their whole bodies in running water as soon as they rise in the morning, at noon, and before they sleep at night. . . . As for their lice, had they the means only they would certainly be as free from them as any inhabitants of so warm a climate could be. . . . Eating lice is a custom which none but children, and those of the inferior people can be charged with.

Ibid.

The superior women are in every respect as large as Europeans, but the inferior sort are in general small owing possibly to their early amours which they are more addicted to then their superiors.

Captain James Cook, *Journal*, July 1769

One ought not to be too severe upon these people when they do commit a thieft, sence we can hardly charge them with any other Vice, Incontency in the unmarried people can hardly be called a Vice sence neither the State nor Individuals are the least injured by it. . . . In short the more one is acquainted with these people the better one likes them, to give them their due I must say they are the most obligeing and benevolent people I ever met with.

Ibid., September 1773

Their natural levity hinders them from paying attention long to any one thing. You might as well undertake to fix mercury, as to keep their mind steady on the same subject.

John Reinhold Forster, *Observations Made During a Voyage Round the World*, 1778

The women have an open, cheerful countenance, a full, bright, and sparkling eye; the face more round than oval; the features arranged with uncommon symmetry, and heightened and improved by a smile which beggars all description. The rest of the body above the waist, is well proportioned, included in the most beautiful soft outline, and sometimes extremely feminine.

Ibid.

'These Voyages (pointing to the three large volumes of *Voyages to the South Sea*, which were just come out) *who* will read them through? A man had better work his way before the mast, than read them through; they will be eaten by rats and mice, before they are read through. There can be little entertainment in such books; one set of Savages is like another.' BOSWELL. 'I do not think the people of Otaheite can be reckoned Savages.' JOHNSON. 'A dog or a cat can swim.' BOSWELL. 'They carve very ingeniously.' JOHNSON. 'A cat can scratch, and a child with a nail can scratch.'

James Boswell, *Life of Johnson*, 15 June 1784

There is a mildness in the expression of their countenances which at once banishes the idea of a savage, and an intelligence which shows that they are advancing in civilisation. The common people, when working, keep the upper part of their bodies quite naked, and it is then that the Tahitians are seen to advantage. They are very tall, broad shouldered, athletic, and well-proportioned. It has been remarked that it requires little habit to make a dark skin more pleasing and natural to the eye of a European than his own colour. A white man bathing by the side of a Tahitian was like a plant bleached by the gardener's art compared with a fine dark green one, growing vigorously in the open fields. Most of the people are tatooed, and the ornaments follow the curvature of the body so gracefully that they have a very elegant effect. . . . Here, though fashion is far from immutable, every one must abide by that prevailing in his youth. An old man has thus his age for ever stamped on his body, and he cannot assume airs of a young dandy.

Charles Darwin, *Journal . . . During the Voyage . . . of H.M.S Beagle*, 1832–6

This is a much better place for children than any I have hitherto seen in these seas. The girls (and sometimes the boys) play a very elaborate kind of hopscotch. The boys play horses exactly as we do in Europe; and have very good fun on stilts, trying to knock each other down, in which they do not often succeed. The children of all ages go to Church, and are allowed to do what they please, running about the aisles, stealing mamma's bonnet and publicly sitting on it, and at last going to sleep in the middle of the floor. I forgot to say that the whips to play horses, and the balls to roll about the church – at least I never saw them used elsewhere – grow ready made on trees; which is rough on toy-shops.

Robert Louis Stevenson, Letter to Thomas Archer, November 1888

I never saw a people that seemed so hopelessly bored as the Tahitians.

Henry Adams, Letter to Elizabeth Cameron, 12 February 1891

The Europeans walking about in their white clothes do

not look like Europeans you see in Ceylon, all washed out and wearied from the heat and strain; they look as if they were enjoying life, as if they were happy where they were. They have, moreover, a peculiar expression – not self-satisfied, or supercilious, but *certain* – on their faces, which seems to say: '*Please, please,* do not argue with us about our life; we *know*.'

Maurice Baring, *Round the World in Any Number of Days*, 1913

It's too fascinating at first sight. And Gauguin *grossly* maligned these ladies. – Oh, I know all that about expressing their primitive souls by making their bodies squat and square. But it's blasphemy.

Rupert Brooke, Letter to Edward Marsh, 16 January 1914, quoted in Edward Marsh, *A Number of People*, 1939

Eimeo

On the lofty and broken pinnacles white massive clouds were piled up, which formed an island in the blue sky, as Eimeo itself did in the blue ocean. The island, with the exception of one small gateway is completely encircled by a reef. At this distance a narrow, but well-defined brilliantly white line was alone visible, where the waves first encountered the wall of coral. The mountains rose abruptly out of the glassy expanse of the lagoon included within this narrow white line, outside which the heaving waters of the ocean were dark-coloured. The view was striking: it may aptly be compared to a framed engraving, where the frame represents the breakers, the marginal paper the smooth lagoon, and the drawing the island itself.

Charles Darwin, *Journal . . . During the Voyage . . . of H.M.S. Beagle*, 1832–6

Papeete

Papeete is one of those ideal spots which have no fault except that of being insupportable. . . . The town is different from anything I ever saw in the long catalogue of towns I have met and has an expression of lost beatitude quite symbolic of Paradise, apart from its inhabitants. As for its inhabitants, I cannot imagine why I should be so worried by them, but I am; and yet they are more amusing than we had a right to expect. My chief trouble is the pervasive half-castitude that permeates everything; a sickly, whitey-brown or dirty white complexion that suggests weakness, disease, and a combination of the least respectable qualities, both white and red. . . . Even when I forget the half-breeds and the cottages, and go swimming, so to speak in the blue and purple light, I never lose consciousness of a sort of restless melancholy that will not explain why it should want to haunt a spot that by rights ought to be as gay as a comic opera.

Henry Adams, Letter to Elizabeth Cameron, 23 February 1891

A city so gay that I can only compare it by calling it the Paris of the South Sea islands.

Martin Johnson, *Through the South Seas with Jack London*, 1913 – of 1907

Papeete . . . reminded me much more of my birthplace, Siklos, a sleepy and dusty little village in South Hungary, than of the romance of the South Pacific.

George Mikes, *Boomerang – Australia Rediscovered*, 1968

TAIWAN (formerly Formosa)

Formosa is a noble Island, and produces many valuable Commodities, as well for the Sustenance of Mankind as for Pleasure and Luxury.

Alexander Hamilton, *A New Account of the East Indies*, 1727

The Religion of Teywon is purely Pagan. They all worship the Sun and Moon, and the Stars their Children. Some worship the first living Thing they see in the Morning, except a Lizard.

Ibid.

An unsinkable aircraft-carrier and submarine tender.

Douglas Macarthur, Statement on the importance of Formosa to U.S. security, 27 August 1950, quoted in Douglas Macarthur, *A Soldier Speaks*, 1965

Keelung

I am an amateur of sad harbours. I have my own cherished collection of seedy seaports, among which Port Said and Port Swettenham have always held pride of place. But my heart throbbed with fresh pleasure and excitement when I first saw Keelung: this was the seediest, most fascinating of all, a kind of low-life Venice of the Orient.

James Kirkup, *Streets of Asia*, 1969

TANZANIA (formerly Tanganyika)

Northern Tanzania is complete in itself, it is one of the most beautiful countries in the world, the climate is excellent, the people delightful; the animals unique. Ideally there should be one huge animal empire here which would include the Serengeti, the Ngorongoro Crater reserves, the game regions contiguous to both, and some of the other craters together with Lake Evasi. With its variety of plains, lakes and mountains, all under one administration, it could become the largest protected area in the world, a sanctuary financed by all the institutions with an interest in it, both American and European.

President Nyerere is the most enlightened and wild-life conscious of all African rulers, he appreciates both the aesthetic and scientific arguments. I was delighted by a story that when informed how much the scenery of the Serengeti mattered to us he replied: 'When I was in Scotland I was always being told how beautiful the weather was, the moorlands, the heather; I could not agree, but I decided it meant something to you which I would never understand – it is the same with the Serengeti.'

Cyril Connolly, *The Evening Colonnade*, 1973

as Tanganyika

Arusha was a hot-bed of British settlers' discontent. . . . 'The Mandate has been just one long succession of blunders . . . a complete fiasco. The very idea of a Mandate is wrong. Civilisation is built up on pride of race – and, when you have a Mandate, you have no pride of race. A man can live here all his life, a foreigner, and never become a naturalised Englishman. We're all hybrids.

'A man in a Mandate is like a mule – he has no pride of ancestry and no hope for posterity.'

Negley Farson, *Behind God's Back*, 1940

Arusha

To have intercourse with natives would be considered eccentric, and it is easier to be eccentric in Bournemouth than in Arusha.

Norman Douglas, *Looking Back*, 1933

Arusha with its scarlet cannas and Nandi flame trees, bamboos, banana, cassia, coffee . . . a tropical Washington.

Cyril Connolly, *The Evening Colonnade*, 1973

Dar es Salaam

It is no wonder that the early Arabs called Dar es-Salaam the 'Haven of Peace.'

Negley Farson, *Behind God's Back*, 1940

Dar es Salaam lies like a dormant bush-baby curled round a blue bay fringed with coconuts and flamboyants. Brightly painted yachts are moored upon a silky ocean, tamarisks and lush greenery half conceal white-fronted houses, a red sun sinks behind darkly silhouetted palm-fronds, a moon comes up as yellow as a Cheshire cheese and many twinkling lights leap and waver on a sleepy sea.

Elspeth Huxley, *Forks and Hope*, 1964

The heat and damp give Dar es Salaam an air of sweet decay which strikes African after the brisk highlands of Kenya. The plaster rots, the tin rusts and damp spreads like a stain over the side of the new flats. A cooking fire blazes in the third storey tenement opposite. The mood is of working-class Athens or middle-class Bombay. It is far less British than Kenya. In Margot's excellent restaurant the dandified French-trained African waiter suggests, 'Why don't you try our Tournedos Stroganov. It's Madame's creation, and I think I can guarantee that you'll go away rejuvenated.' The multi-racial juke-box bars are a far cry from the solemn strip club of Nairobi. Two Liberians, two Germans and their girls chat in English. Then the girls break into a fight. The argument is yelled in Swahili, but the final insults are yelled in English, 'You fuckee bush girl!' It is a very agreeable city.

Richard West, *The White Tribes of Africa*, 1965

An engineer who is building a cement works in Dar es Salaam said, 'Trying to build a cement works here is like farting against thunder. . . .'

Ibid.

Mount Kilimanjaro

Far away in the distance the august mountain Kilimanjaro shone in the upper air like a vast celestial mould of Christmas pudding streaked with frozen rivers of brandy-butter.

Edward Marsh, *A Number of People*, 1939 – of 1908

People who live in its charmed area – both European and Africans – have a strong, almost mystical feeling about it, calling it 'the mountain' as if there could be no other mountain. I heard phrases like 'Good chap, that ranger – soundest man with elephants on the mountain,' or 'Ghastly bore of a fellow – can't understand what *he*'s doing on the mountain.'

John Gunther *Inside Africa*, 1955

From an . . . African I heard . . . 'God came from this mountain, and *is* the mountain.'

Ibid.

Mikindani Harbour

This harbour has somewhat of the shape of a bent bow or the spade on a playing-card, the shaft of the arrow being the entrance in.

David Livingstone, *Last Journals*, 27 March 1866

Moshi (Mount Kilimanjaro)

In all Africa there can scarcely be a lusher, greener spot

than the slopes of this enormous mountain. In every untended corner, plant life wells up like a green fountain; lofty forest trees mingle with exotic wattle; crops spring with vigour from the moist earth; even from the faces of precipices, ferns and creepers peer. A deep, rich, volcanic soil, a lavish rainfall, snows and glaciers that feed clear stone-hopping streams, a genial sun to warm the soil – Kilimanjaro has everything. Narrow earth roads wind among steep gorges, and over the tree-tops you glimpse the huge plain below stretching away to the purple-furrowed hills of Paré, the white-rimmed lake of Jipé, and the far blue horizon.

Elspeth Huxley, *The Sorcerer's Apprentice*, 1948

Serengeti

This is by far the greatest collection of plains-dwelling animals left in the world today. It is a microcosm of what most of East and Central Africa was like little more than half a century ago, a surviving pocket, a remembrance of one of the greatest sights the world has every known. This is all we have left.

Elspeth Huxley, *Forks and Hope*, 1964

How can one convey the power of Serengeti? It is an immense, limitless lawn, under a marquee of sky; the grasses ripen at different seasons and force the herds sometimes to the boundaries (where they are poached) sometimes to the centre. This is the origin of the vast migration, now in full swing. The light is dazzling, the air delectable: kopjes rise out of the grass at far intervals, some wooded; the magic of the unraped American prairie here blends with the other magic of the animals as they existed before man. There is a lightening of the spirit, a sense of atonement, of being able to compound at last for the endless cycle of vanity and greed to which they have been subjected. Nature's world of beauty and justice without cruelty or compassion. Descriptions are useless because they must fall back on catalogues, photographs fare little better. I print: 'There is nothing the matter with Northern Tanzania' on my notebook and leave it at that.

Cyril Connolly, *The Evening Colonnade*, 1973

Tabora

For those fortunate enough to be unfamiliar with this town I should say that it is the country's sole railway-junction, and that of all the God-forgotten places in East Africa it is the most inexpressibly deadly.

I say this in no particular spirit of criticism. It is merely my opinion that if there was a rock-bottom fundament of the world, this was it.

James Cameron, *Point of Departure*, 1967

Zanzibar

It is not worth while to go round the world to count the cats in Zanzibar.

Henry David Thoreau, *Walden*, Conclusion, 1854

I am surprised at the combined folly and brutality of civilized husbands, who, anxious to be widowers, poison, cut the throats, or smash the skulls of their better halves. The thing can be as neatly and quietly, safely and respectably effected by a few months of African air at Zanzibar.

Sir Richard Burton, *Zanzibar, City Island and Coast*, 1857 (published 1872)

It might be called Stinkibar rather than Zanzibar.

David Livingstone, Journal, 2 March 1866

When the flute is played in Zanzibar all Africa east of the Lakes must dance.

Arab proverb, quoted John Gunther, *Inside Africa* 1955

Zanzibar . . . is as relaxing as a Turkish bath.

Alan Moorhead, *The White Nile*,1960

THAILAND (formerly Siam)

On the map it looks rather like an octopus with one tentacle dangling into Malaya towards Singapore.

John Gunther, *Inside Asia*, 1939

Do you come from Boston, Massachusetts, or Boston, England? Are you familiar with the Lincolnshire fens? Have you visited the English or the Continental Holland, or the waterlaced hinterland of Venice? Keep the dykes and canals; change the turnip-fields and pastures into a green-gold sea of ripening rice; magnify this landscape several hundredfold, and you will be viewing Thailand with your mind's eye.

Arnold Toynbee, *East to West*, 1958

And then I think of Siam, which by the almost miraculous cunning of its rulers escaped enslavement by the West, only to become through liberty and prosperity hardly more than a fun-fair mirror reflection of the U.S.A.

Norman Lewis, *The Changing Sky*, 1959

Guinness . . . mixed with Benedictine, has become a favourite aphrodisiac in Siam.

Ibid.

Their good-fortune as a nation has, in fact, been largely due to their ability to turn their easy-going nature into a political weapon and to exploit on a grand scale the answer that turns away wrath. . . .

An Indian U.N. official in Bangkok told me, with the admiration of a man who knew the shrewd intricacies of traditional oriental diplomacy, 'Never underestimate the Thais. Whatever happens in the world, they will come out on top.'

George Woodcock, *Asia, Gods and Cities*, 1966

and the Chinese there
We don't mind who holds the head of the cow providing we can milk it.

Chinese proverb, quoted in D. Insor, *Thailand, a Political Social and Economic Analysis*, 1963

Bangkok

The Chinese do the heavy work in Bangkok and the Siamese let them – proving the moral superiority of the former and the mental superiority of the latter, consciousness of which is evident on every smiling face.

Crosbie Garstin, *The Dragon and the Lotus*, 1928

Bangkok is stuck as thick with pagodas as a duff with plums.

Ibid.

and other cities of the Far East
It is impossible to consider these populous modern cities of the East without a certain malaise. They are all alike, with their straight streets, their arcades, their tramways, their dust, their blinding sun, their teeming Chinese, their dense traffic, their ceaseless din. They have no history and no traditions. Painters have not painted them. No poets, transfiguring dead bricks and mortar with their divine nostalgia, have given them a tremulous melancholy not their own. They live their own lives, without associations, like a man without imagination. They are hard and glittering and as unreal as a backcloth in a musical comedy. They give you nothing. But when you leave them it is with a feeling that you have missed something, and you cannot help thinking that they have some secret that they have kept from you. And though you have been a trifle bored, you look back upon them wistfully; you are certain that they have after all something to give you which, had you stayed longer, or under other conditions, you would have been capable of receiving. For it is useless to offer a gift to him who cannot stretch out a hand to take it. But if you go back, the secret still evades you and you ask yourself whether, after all, their only secret is not that the glamour of the East enwraps them. Because they are called, Rangoon, Bangkok, or Saigon, because they are situated on the Irrawaddy, the Menam, or the Mekong, those great turbid rivers, they are invested with the magic spell that the ancient and storied East has cast upon the imaginative West.

W. Somerset Maugham, *The Gentleman in the Parlour*, 1930

The royal Wat is not a wat but a city of wats; it is a gay, coloured confusion of halls and pagodas, some of them in ruins, some with the appearance of being brand-new; there are buildings, brilliant of hue though somewhat run to seed, that look like monstrous vegetables in the kitchen-gardens of the djinn; there are structures made of tiles and encrusted with strange tile flowers, three of them enormous, but many small ones, rows of them, that look like the prizes in a shooting-gallery at a village fair in the country of the gods. It is like a page of *Euphues* and you are tickled to death at the sesquipedalian fancy that invented so many sonorous, absurd, grandiloquent terms.

Ibid.

From the very beginning I was charmed by Bangkok, and I propose to be aggressively syrupy about it in the most buckeye travelogue manner. I liked its polite, gentle, handsome people, its temples, flowers, and canals, the relaxed and peaceful rhythm of life there. Apart from its shrill and tumultuous central thoroughfare swarming with Chinese and Indian bazaars, it struck me as the most soothing metropolis I had thus far seen in the East. Its character is complex and inconsistent; it seems at once to combine the Hannibal, Missouri, of Mark Twain's boyhood with Beverly Hills, the Low Countries, and Chinatown. You pass from populous, glaring streets laden with traffic into quiet country lanes parelleled by canals out of a Dutch painting; a tree-shaded avenue of pretentious mansions set in wide lawns abruptly becomes a bustling row of shops and stalls, then melts into a sunny village of thatched huts among which water-buffalo graze. The effect is indescribably pleasing; your eye constantly discovers new vistas, isolated little communites around every corner tempting you to explore them.

S.J.Perelman, *Westward Ha!*, 1948

As Calcutta smells of death and Bombay of money, Bangkok smells of sex, but this sexual aroma is mingled with the sharper whiffs of death and money.

Paul Theroux, *The Great Railway Bazaar*, 1975

An immeasurable flatness, a pancake, but a pancake in a spiked frying-pan; for, at regular intervals the flatness is interrupted, or rather pierced, by tall conglomerations of cement and glass that invariably consist of banks or hotels, modernity coming up for air in a soup of timeless shackdom. Not unlike, in fact, most cities in hot countries without much money.

Justin Wintle, Letter, 1980

TIBET

While the eye is dazzled with colour and form of such intensity and glitter, and on such a scale, that it seems as though our drab and commonplace planet had been exchanged for the moon or some other heavenly body, an unwilling, clandestine fear lurks in the shadows of the stranger's being, as though he were threatened with gradual but total extinction, with that cessation of being or becoming which Buddhism teaches to be the goal of man and his perfection.

Robert Byron, *First Russia then Tibet*, 1933

'Oh for a tree!' groaned M. from the depths of a temperament that finds beauty only in luxuriance. 'What a country for motor-racing!' murmured G. 'I shall tell Segrave.' 'Well, it won't see me again,' replied M. sharply, 'till there's a wagon-lit.'

Ibid.

Tibet seems to be the countersign for a world-wide community who have this much in common at least – they know that there is something more to life than is summed up in the empirical knowledge of the high priests of logic and science.

Henry Miller, *The Air-conditioned Nightmare*, 1945

Butter (like bones and silence) constitutes one of the most characteristic features of Tibet.

Fosco Mariani, *Secret Tibet*, trans. Eric Mosbacher, 1954

The highest, bleakest, coldest, remotest, most inhospitable country in the world; a great soaring place fifteen times the size of England, where the depths of the valleys were higher than the summits of the Alps, a country where you were either a slave or a demigod; the final stronghold of the dead days of Asia.

James Cameron, *Point of Departure*, 1967

Tibetans

Next unto them are the people of Tebet, men which were wont to eate the carkasses of their deceased parents: that for pities sake, they might make no other Supulchre for them, then their owne bowels. Howbeit of late they have left off this custome, because that thereby they became abominable and odious unto all other Nations. Notwithstanding, unto this day they make fine Cups of the Skulls of their parents, to the end, that when they drinke out of them, they may amidst all their jollities and delights, call their dead parents to rememberance. This was told mee by one that saw it. The said people of Tebet have great plentie of gold in their Land. Whosoever therefore wanteth gold, diggeth til he hath found some quantitie, and then taketh so much thereof as will serve his turne, hee layeth up the residue within the earth: because if he should put it into his Chest or Storehouse, he is of opinion that God would withold from him all other gold within the earth. I saw some of those people, being very deformed creatures.

Friar William of Rubruck, 1253, in *Purchas his Pilgrimes*, 1625

The diseased and sinister Tibetan imagination ... revels in bones, blood and death – all the pleasures of the slaughterhouse. Nothing pleases it more than the thought of troops of demons engaged in liturgical rites among dismembered parts of the human body, skeletons and entrails, disporting themselves in lakes of blood, using skulls as sacred symbols. The Tibetan mind enjoys the macabre, delights in the revolting, intoxicates itself with tortures described with voluptuous relish and realism.

Fosco Mariani, *Secret Tibet*, trans. Eric Mosbacher, 1954

It was incidentally also against Tibetan social usage, at least among the proletariat, to wash at any time between birth and death, a decision readily understandable in a people who live in conditions of such climatic acerbity, but one which nevertheless tended to make their company oppressive.

James Cameron, *Point of Departure*, 1967

Mount Everest

Mount Everest is very easy to climb, only just a little too high.

André Roche, *Observer*, 'Sayings of the Week', 25 January 1953

We've knocked the bastard off!

Sir Edmund Hillary, after the first ascent to the summit, 29 May 1953

If by some fiat I had to restrict all this writing to one sentence, this is the one I would choose: The summit of Mt. Everest is marine limestone.

John McPhee, *Basin and Range*, 1981

Himalayas

Cities of the Aryan soul.

F. Yeats Brown, *Bengal Lancer*, 1930

It is not my habit to moralise on the smallness of man. But the Himalayas do induce a sense of it. They are out of scale to a degree which evokes something like fear – the sort of feeling, I imagine, that might beset one in the depths of the ocean, however safe the submarine.

Robert Byron, *First Russia then Tibet*, 1933

When you fly, even high, over the Himalayas, the cold comes through the floor of the plane and shoots up your leg like an electric shock.

Arnold Toynbee, *Between Niger and Nile*, 1965

Lhasa

If the palace had exceeded my expectations, the town as far fell short of them. There is nothing striking, nothing pleasing in its appearance. The habitations are begrimed with smut and dirt. The avenues are full of dogs. . . . In short, everything seems mean and gloomy and excites the idea of something unreal. Even the mirth and laughter of the inhabitants I thought dreamy and ghostly.

Thomas Manning, Journal, 1811, *Journey of Mr Thomas Manning To Lhasa*, 1876

*I travelled for two years in Tibet . . . and amused myself by visiting Lhassa and spending some days with the head Lama.

'Sherlock Holmes', in Sir Arthur Conan Doyle, *The Empty House*, 1903

TIERRA DEL FUEGO (Argentina/Chile)

Tierra del Fuego may be described as a mountainous land, partly submerged in the sea, so that deep inlets and bays occupy the place where valleys should exist. The mountain sides, except on the exposed western coast, are covered from the water's edge upwards by one great forest. The trees reach to an elevation of between a thousand and fifteen hundred feet, and are succeeded by a band of peat, with minute Alpine plants; and this again is succeeded by the line of perpetual snow which, according to Captain King, in the Strait of Magellan, descends to between 3000 and 4000 feet. To find an acre of level land in any part of the country is most rare. I recollect only one little flat piece near Port Famine, and another of rather larger extent near Goeree Roads. In both places, and everywhere else, the surface is covered by a thick bed of swampy peat. Even within the forest, the ground is concealed by a mass of slowly putrefying vegetable matter, which, from being soaked with water, yields to the foot.

Charles Darwin, *Journal . . . During the Voyage . . . of H.M.S. Beagle*, 1832–6

The atmosphere . . . in this climate, where gale succeeds gale, with rain, hail, and sleet, seems blacker than anywhere else. In the Strait of Magellan, looking due southward from Port Famine, the distant channels between the mountains appeared from their gloominess to lead beyond the confines of the world.

Ibid.

'It is beautiful,' she said, looking from the farm at the black line where the grass ended and the trees began. 'But I wouldn't want to come back.'

'Neither would I,' I said.

Bruce Chatwyn, *In Patagonia*, 1977

Fuegians

They are perhaps as miserable a set of People as are this day upon earth.

Captain James Cook, *Journal*, 16 January 1769

I could not have believed how wide was the difference between savage and civilised man; it is greater than between a wild and domesticated animal, inasmuch as in man there is a greater power of improvement.

Charles Darwin, *Journal . . . During the Voyage . . . of H.M.S. Beagle*, 1832–6

How little can the higher powers of the mind be brought into play: what is there for imagination to picture, for reason to compare, for judgement to decide upon? To knock a limpet from a rock does not require even cunning, that lowest power of the mind. Their skill in some respects may be compared to the instinct of animals; for it is not improved by experience. . . . There is no reason to believe that the Fuegians decrease in number; therefore we must suppose that they enjoy a sufficient share of happiness, of whatever kind it may be, to render life worth having. Nature, by making habit omnipotent, and its effects hereditary, has fitted the Fuegian to the climate and the productions of his miserable country.

Ibid.

It is certainly true, that when pressed in winter by hunger, they kill and devour their old women before they kill their dogs; the boy being asked by Mr Low why they did this, answered, 'Doggies catch otters, old women no.' This boy described the manner in which they are killed by being held over smoke and thus choked; he imitated their screams as a joke, and described the parts of their bodies which are considered best to eat.

Ibid.

Yaghan Indians

What shall we think of a people who defined 'monotony' as 'an absence of male friends?' Or, for 'depression', used the word that described the vulnerable phase in a crab's seasonal cycle, when it has sloughed off its old shell and waits for another to grow? Or who derived 'lazy' from the Jackass Penguin? Or 'adulterous' from the hobby, a small hawk that flits here and there, hovering motionless over its next victim?

Bruce Chatwyn, *In Patagonia*, 1977

TONGA

Both men and Women are of a Common size with Europeans and their Colour is that of a lightish Copper and more uniformly so than the Inhabitants of Otaheite and the Society Isles. Some of our gentlemen were of the opinion these were a much handsomer race, others again mentioned a contrary opinion of which number I was one, be this as it will, they have a good shape and regular features, and are active brisk and lively; the

Women in particular, who are the merriest creatures I ever met with and will keep chattering by ones side without the least invitation or consideration whether or no they are understood provided one does but seem pleased with them.

Captain James Cook, *Journal*, October 1773

During our stay here we had a constant Intercourse with the Women both on board the Ships and on Shore, & the price was a Shirt or a Hatchet for the Night; they were brought to us & the Bargain made by their Fathers, Brothers or some Friend or Relation. . . . They are of a very amorous Complexion & highly deserving of what they got.

David Samwell, *Journal*, June 1777

Chastity is by no means the reigning Virtue of these Isles, the good Lasses readily contributed their Share to our Entertainment, and render'd our Bill of Fare compleat.

Charles Clerke, *Journal*, July 1777

TRINIDAD

This yland of Trinidad hath the forme of a sheephooke, and is but narrow.

Sir Walter Ralegh, *The Discovery of Guiana*, 1595, in Richard Hakluyt, *Principal Navigations . . . of the English Nation*, 1598–1600

In our land
Sin is not deep
And bends before the truth
Asking repentantly for pardon:
In our land
The ugly stain
That blotted Eden garden
Is skin deep only.

Harold M. Telemaque, 'In Our Land', in John Figueroa (ed.), *Caribbean Voices*, 1966

General impression of Trinidad that I don't want to see it again.

Evelyn Waugh, *Diary*, 20 December 1932

In this world I know there are millions of whites
Who appreciate the coloured man's rights,
And has a desire and willingness
To aid in his pursuit of happiness.
A white man would love a Negro to the core
As a brother, but not a brother-in-law.
So these mixed marriages in my opinion,
Is the cause of all this racial discrimination.

'Attila the Hun', Calypso, quoted Patrick Leigh Fermor, *The Traveller's Tree*, 1951

'I'm a second-rater,' a successful American businessman said to an Englishman, who told it to me. 'But this is a third-rate place and I'm doing well. Why should I leave?'

V.S. Naipaul, *The Middle Passage*, 1962

There is no set way in Trinidad of doing anything. Every house can be a folly. There is no set way of dressing, or cooking, or entertaining. Everyone can live with whoever he can get, wherever he can afford. Ostracism is meaningless; the sanctions of any clique can be ignored. It is in this way, and not in the way of the travel brochure, that the Trinidadian is a cosmopolitan. He is adaptable; he is cynical; having no rigid social conventions of his own, he is amused by the conventions of others. He is a natural anarchist, who has never been able to take the eminent at their own valuation. He is a natural eccentric, if by eccentricity is meant the expression of one's own personality, unhampered by fear of ridicule, or the discipline of a class. If the Trinidadian has no standards of morality, he is without the greater corruption of sanctimoniousness, and can never make pleas for intolerance in the name of piety. . . . Everything that makes the Trinidadian an unreliable, exploitable citizen makes him a quick, civilized person whose values are always human ones, whose standards are only those of wit and style.

As the Trinidadian becomes a more reliable and efficient citizen, he will cease to be what he is.

Ibid.

A small country like ours only has principles.

Dr Eric Williams, *Observer*, 'Sayings of the Week', 27 June 1965

Port of Spain

Port of Spain. What a legendary and romantic town the syllables evoke! . . . On landing this shroud of purple is blown to ribbons in a second. The ugly carcase of the Trinidadian capital is laid bare. Dismal barracks and Victorian red-brick buildings appear, and churches built in servile imitation of English models of the time of Pusey and Ruskin. The bleak streets echo with the clatter of trams, and the prevailing weather alternates between damp and debilitating heat, when the glare scorches the eyeballs like quick-lime and the wind drives the dust along the thoroughfares in hot volleys of grape-shot, and a grey and all-obliterating deluge. At these moments the town and the lamp-posts and bricks and tram-lines, faintly looming through the downpour, are indistinguishable from Glasgow in December. Suburbs and slums trail away for miles. They are replaced here and there by trim white blocks of workers' flats, which are healthy but hideous. Then the slums resume their sway.

And yet . . . Port of Spain possesses a forcefulness and a vulgarity that are almost pleasing. It is a large and startlingly cosmopolitan town. The streets blaze with milk-bars, drug stores, joints and picture-palaces, and almost everybody on the pavement chews gum.

Patrick Leigh Fermor, *The Traveller's Tree*, 1951

Today I am a stranger in the city myself. Port of Spain is bigger, brighter, noisier and better-educated than it was when I was at school there between 1939 and 1948. Then, in spite of the war and the United States base, it felt like a place at the rim of the world.

V.S. Naipaul, *The Loss of El Dorado*, 1969

The Pitch Lake

A ropeway goes down from the pitch lake to the sea. Its buckets, at the moment, dangle idly; as of everything else, the world has an excess of asphalt. No work is being done at the lake, and the telpher wires, stretched tightly across the sky, serve only as convenient perches for innumerable black pelicans. They sit there like a passage of semi-quavers on a mile-long expanse of ruled paper. We seemed to be landing at the foot of a gigantic page of Liszt.

Aldous Huxley, *Beyond the Mexique Bay*, 1934

The Pitch Lake of Trinidad sounds satanic, and, indeed, it is; but not exactly in the seething, Phlegethonic fashion that one might suppose. It is the blankness, the emptiness, the boredom of this expanse that fills the observer with horror. It has the colour and texture of a gramophone record a hundred and fourteen acres in extent, channelled and broken up by a network of cracks, where the surface softens into black treacle treacherously covered by a thin wrinkled skin. It is one of the hottest places in the world.

Patrick Leigh Fermor, *The Traveller's Tree*, 1951

TRISTAN DA CUNHA

There is something really terrific in the appearance of this island as you approach the shore. The sea breaks with violence over rocks which are just rising above water, and the whole extent of beach is whitened with surf. It is unsafe for any other than whale boats to attempt landing here. On quitting the boat, I found a road, formed of black lava, cut down the cliff, along which the islanders had brought their boat. The cliff is about fifty feet high, and at its summit there is an extended plain, reaching to the foot of a mountain; and this plain is covered with a coarse kind of grass, called by the settlers *Tussek*, which grows in clusters, and is as strong as a small reed. Arriving at the village, which consists of half a dozen houses, covered with thatch made of this native grass, I found two women, and a number of children, who were all equally delighted to see a stranger amongst them. The houses, and all around them, had an air of comfort, cleanliness, and plenty, truly English; and which was highly gratifying to my feelings, from the contrast it formed to those I had lately seen in South America.

Augustus Earle, *Narrative of a Residence on the Island of Tristan d'Acunha, in 1824*, 1832

Snore in the foam; the night is vast and blind;
The blanket of the mist about your shoulders,
Sleep your old sleep of rock, snore in the wind,
Snore in the spray! the storm your slumber lulls,
His wings are folded on your nest of boulders
As on their eggs the grey wings of your gulls.

No more as when, so dark an age ago,
You hissed a giant cinder from the ocean,
Around your rocks you furl the shawling snow
Half sunk in your own darkness, vast and grim,
And round you on the deep with surly motion
Pivot your league-long shadow as you swim.

Why should you haunt me thus but that I know
My surly heart is in your own displayed,
Round whom such leagues in endless circuit flow,
Whose hours in such a gloomy compass run –
A dial with its league-long arm of shade
Slowly revolving to the moon and sun. . . .

Your strength is that you have no hope or fear,
You march before the world without a crown,
The nations call you back, you do not hear,
The cities of the earth grow grey behind you,
You will be there when their great flames go down
And still the morning in the van will find you.

You march before the continents, you scout
In front of all the earth; alone you scale
The mast-head of the world, a lorn look-out,
Waving the snowy flutter of your spray
And gazing back in infinite farewell
To suns that sink and shores that fade away. . . .

Your path is but a desert where you reap
Only the bitter knowledge of your soul:
You fish with nets of seaweed in the deep
As fruitlessly as I with nets of rhyme –
Yet forth you stride, yourself the way, the goal,
The surges are your strides, your path is time.

Roy Campbell, 'Tristan da Cunha', *Adamastor*, 1930

TUNISIA

Rain is the best governor.

Tunisian proverb, quoted John Gunther, *Inside Africa*, 1955

In the courtyard of a modern office building I saw a

sign, 'Religious and Political Discussion Forbidden in this Area.'

John Gunther, *Inside Africa*, 1955

Ancient

Delenda est Carthago.
(Carthage must be destroyed.)

Marcus Porcius Cato, in Plutarch, *Life of Cato*, *c.* AD 100

She was of *Carthage*, not of *Tunis*.
This *Tunis* Sir was *Carthage*.

William Shakespeare, *The Tempest*, *c.* 1611–12

Carthage had not desired to create, but only to enjoy: therefore she left us nothing.

Hilaire Belloc, *Esto Perpetua*, 1906

On a day while spring was still calm upon the Mediterranean and before the great heats had come, I sat in a small simple restaurant, French in management and cooking, half-way up a slope that overlooked the Tunisian Sea. Save for the modest house attached to the place, for one or two villas surrounded by deep gardens, for a small halt (rather than a station) upon a local tramway, there was little habitation around me. One great French road went up the hill behind. No vehicle moved upon it.

In the spring sunlight of that noon the Angelus bell from a church upon the height broke the silence, but for the rest it was an empty place enough, with no hint of the past. . . .

That hill, that bay, were the Hill and the Bay of Carthage.

Hilaire Belloc, *Many Cities*, 1928

Sousse / Susa

Susa . . . lay in its glittering garb of whitewash – houses, walls, and roofs all drenched and crusted with the same unmitigated and blinding hue – looking like some great sea-mew preening its snowy plumage on the shore.

George Curzon, Marquess of Kedleston, *Tales of Travel*, 1923

Tozeur

It was in Tozeur, I remember, that when I remarked to a friend in English that the buildings of the town precisely resembled slums, my Arab guide turned round and delightedly said, 'Oui, c'est ça: tout le monde a dit qu'il ressemble beaucoup aux "slooms"!'

Osbert Sitwell, *Escape with Me*, 1939

TURKEY

Neither is the Art of Cookery greater in Turkey than with us in Wales, for Toasting of Cheese in Wales, and seething of Rice in Turkey, will enable a man freely to profess the Art of cookery.

Fynes Moryson, *An Itinerary*, 1617

Turkey is not Prey at least for them . . . [the Russians] . . . whose motions are sometimes indeed precipitate, but seldom alert. The Nature of the Turkish frontier provinces (an immense Ditch Fosse if I may call it so) of Desart, is a defence made indeed at in great measure the expense of mankind, but still it is a great defence. . . .

I don't wish well to [Turkey]. Any people but the Turks so seated as they are would have been cultivated in 300 years, but they grow more gross in the very native soil of civility and Refinement.

Edmund Burke, Letter to Adrian Henrich von Borcke, post 17 January 1774

Know ye the land where the cypress and myrtle
  Are emblems of deeds that are done in their clime,
Where the rage of the vulture, the love of the turtle
  Now melt into sorrow, now madden to crime? . . .
Where the virgins are soft as the roses they twine,
And all save the spirit of man is divine?

Lord Byron, *The Bride of Abydos*, 1813

Turkish tobacco is mild and their horses entire – two things as they should be.

Lord Byron, *Journal*, December 1813

Lamentable indeed would be the event of Turkey becoming dependent upon Russia! still more so of seeing the Russian flag hoisted upon the towers of Constantinople. The expressive words of *Bonaparte*, 'DIEU ME GARDE DES RUSSES!' ought to be adopted as a motto for the *arms* of *Turkey*.

E.D. Clarke, *Travels in Various Countries*, 4th edn, 1818

O Turkey! how mild are thy manners,
  Whose greatest and highest of men
Are all proud to be rhymers and scanners,
  And wield the poetical pen!

Thomas Hood, *Poetry, Prose, and Worse*, 1836

Nouse avons sur les bras un homme malade – un homme gravement malade.
We have on our hands a sick man, a very sick man [the sick man of Europe – the declining Ottoman Empire].

Nicholas I of Russia, quoted by Sir G.H. Seymour, in Letter to Lord John Russell, 11 January 1853

I wish Europe would let Russia annihilate Turkey a

little – not much, but enough to make it difficult to find the place again, without a divining-rod or a diving bell.
Mark Twain, *The Innocents Abroad*, 1869

Monotonous, colourless, lifeless, unsubdued by a people whose thoughts travel no further than the next furrow, who live and die and leave no mark upon the great plains and the barren hills – such is central Asia, of which this country is a true part. And that is why the Roman roads make so deep an impression on one's mind. They impressed the country itself, they implied a great domination, they tell of a people that overcame the universal stagnation.
Gertrude Bell, Letter to her family, 7 May 1907

I am sure the first idea of a Turkish mosque came to someone who saw two cypress trees, one on either side of a small round hill.
Freya Stark, Letter, 12 February 1940, in *Dust in the Lion's Paw*, 1961

from the air
Europe slides by like a giant suburban golf-course. . . . It isn't until one crosses the Bosphorus and is over Turkey that one gets into the rough – a landscape of red boulders, creased and furrowed like badly wrapped parcels.
Jonathan Raban, *Arabia through the Looking Glass*, 1979

Before World War I Turkey was known as the 'Sick Man of Europe'; now it is almost a terminal case.
Richard Nixon, *The Real War*, 1980

Turks

Turkes are ful of brags
And menace more than they can wel performe.
Christopher Marlowe, *Tamburlaine*, Part 1, *c.* 1587

The women are of a low stature, thick and round of growth, going seldom abroad, . . . they are fearful and shame-faced abroad, but lascivious within doors, and pleasing in matters of incontinency; and they are accounted most beautiful who have the blackest brows, the widest mouths and the greatest eyes. . . .

The Turks . . . are of the second stature of man, and robust of nature, circumspect and courageous in all their attempts, and no way given to industry or labour, but are wonderful avaricious and covetous of money above all the nations of the world. They never observe their promises, unless it be with advantage, and are naturally prone to deceive strangers; changing their conditional bargains, as time giveth occasion to their liking! They are humble one to another, but especially to their superiors, before whom they do not only great homage, but also keep great silence, and are wonderful coy during the time of their presence. They are extremely inclined to all sorts of lascivious luxury, and generally addicted, besides all their sensual and incestuous lusts, unto sodomy, which they account as a dainty to digest all their other libidinous pleasures. They hold that every one hath the hour of his death wrote upon his fore-brow, and that none can escape the good or evil hour predestined for them. This ridiculous error makes them so bold and desperate, yea, and often, to run headlong into the most inevitable dangers: They are not much given to domestic pastimes, as chess, cards, dice and tables; but abroad and in travel, they are exceeding kind disposers of their meat and drink to any stranger without exception. The better sort of their women are sumptuously attired, and adorned with pearls and precious stones, and some of them are accustomed to turn their hands and hair into a red colour, but especially the nails of their hands and feet; and are wont to go to bathe themselves in stoves twice a-week, as well as men.
William Lithgow, *Rare Adventures and Painfull Peregrinations*, 1614/32

The Turks . . . are as excessively addicted to smoke, as Dutchmen are to the pot.
Ibid.

I must not forget to note their jealousy, wherein a Turk exceeds an Italian as far as he us; the cause is polygamy, which makes the husband guilty of insufficient correspondence, and therein fearful that his wife may seek a further satisfaction; therefore their women go muffled all but the eyes.
Henry Blount, *A Voyage into the Levant*, 1634

You will find among the Turks far more dead saints than living ones.
Henry Maundrell, *A Journey from Aleppo to Jerusalem*, 1697

But what can you expect from such a country as this, from which the muses have fled, from which letters seem eternally banished, and in which you see, in private scenes, nothing pursued as happiness, but the refinements of an indolent voluptuousness, and where those who act upon the publick theatre live in uncertainty, suspicion and terror. Here pleasure, to which I am no enemy when it is properly seasoned and of a good composition, is surely of the cloying kind. Veins of wit, elegant conversation, easy commerce, are unknown among the Turks; and yet they seem capable of all these, if the vile spirit of the government did not stifle genius, damp curiosity, and suppress an hundred passions, that embellish and render life agreeable. The luscious passion of the Seraglio is the only one almost that is gratified here to the full, but it is blended so with the surly spirit of despotism in one of the parties, and with the dejection and anxiety which this spirit produces in the other, that to one of my way of thinking it cannot appear otherwise than as a very mixed kind of enjoyment. The women here are not indeed, so closely confined as many have related; they enjoy a high degree of liberty even in the bosom of servitude, and they have methods of evasion and disguise that are very favourable to gallantry; but after all, they are still under uneasy apprehensions of being discovered; and a discovery exposes them to the most merciless rage of jealousy, which is here a monster that cannot be satiated but with blood.

Lady Mary Wortley Montagu, Letter to Alexander Pope, 1 September 1717

They are good people, but perfectly useless.

Horatio Lord Nelson, Letter to Commodore Troubridge, 7 September 1799

In England the vices in fashion are whoring & drinking, in Turkey, Sodomy & smoking, we prefer a girl and a bottle, they a pipe and pathic. – They are sensible people.

Lord Byron, Letter to Henry Drury, 3 May 1810

The Turks are the last people on earth who deserve to be called hypocrites in their religion.

E.D. Clarke, *Travels in Various Countries*, 4th edn, 1818

compared with Russians

Some few murmured out the word *Salaam*: upon this our Captain congratulated us; adding, 'The *welcome* of a *Turk*, and the *farewell* of a *Russian*, are pleasing sounds.'

E.D. Clarke, *Travels in Various Countries*, 1816

They have no past; they are not an historical people; they exist only in the present.

Samuel Taylor Coleridge, *Table Talk*, 1 January 1823

The beauty of the Turks is peculiar; the features have a general bluntness, without 'points or angles.' The thick and heavy eyebrow covers a full, round, and dark eye; the nose straight, and the chin round, with a very handsome mouth. They walk extremely erect; and their large limbs, their slow pace, and flowing garments, give them a very majestic air. They will sit on benches spread with soft carpets, in the open air, a great part of the day; . . . nothing can exceed their indolence: they hold a string of beads in their hands of different colours, to play with like children, from mere inanity of thought, during the intervals of smoking.

From the extreme tranquillity and regularity of their lives, and their freedom from strong passions, derangement is a very rare circumstance with this people.

John Carne, *Letters from the East*, 1830

Will they ever be civilized? I think not. Such a fine country ought to be in better hands.

John Webster, *Notes of a Journey from London to Constantinople*, 1836

Oh, these Turks are luxurious dogs. Chibouks, coffee, hot baths, and as many wives as they please. What a catalogue of human enjoyments!

J.L. Stephens, *Incidents of Travel in the Russian and Turkish Empires*, 1839

The Turks are a sufficiently intelligent people, and cannot help feeling the superiority of strangers.

Ibid.

A real Turk is a manly, though rather violent, kind-hearted being, and, if he has confidence in you, very easy to deal with.

Lady Hester Stanhope, Letter to Mr Webb, October 1827, in Charles Meryon, *Memoirs of the Lady Hester Stanhope*, 1845

The Turks have spoilt the best part of their customs and feelings by aping our ideas of civilization. Where formerly was to be seen a race of brave, and in many points highly civilized, men, now are a lot of bad imitation Franks, whose costume, manners, and customs, are a clumsy rehearsal of what they have seen among the renegades and refugees of all nations, who, mostly labouring under difficulties which made their stay at home disagreeable, have come to sojourn with them. They have copied to a nicety all the follies and debauchery of the class of men they have chosen as patterns, retaining none of the good moral precepts and practices of Islam, but only its superstition and bigotry.

Mansfield Parkyns, *Life in Abyssinia*, 1853

What energy can be expected of a people with no heels to their shoes?

Lord Palmerston, quoted by Evelyn Ashley, *The Life of . . . Lord Palmerston*, 1876 – before 1865

The Turk, man as well as woman, is still unawakened; the mind, here, does not exist; there is only the animal and its instinct. The people, their cloistered women, and their homeless dogs in possession, are all alike creatures of instinct. They do not reason; they make arbitrary rules; and then fight or submit. . . . The Turk has no pity, and it is pity which civilises.

Arthur Symons, *Cities*, 1903

I have fallen a hopeless victim to the Turk; he is the most charming of mortals and some day, when I have a little more of his language, we shall be very intimate friends, I foresee.

Gertrude Bell, Letter to her family, 21 April 1905

The Turks . . . I hate them because I am a modern civilised man. Catholics should and do love them. Why is Turkey rotten? Why is the Turk an inefficient gentleman? Islam? Nonsense: not entirely. Simply because he thinks middle age and is middle age. Saladin and Richard were both very near each other.

They talked the same language. They both believed in Aristotle. But Saladin is still Saladin – arguing with a twist – because his *Aristotle* was translated for him and he never learnt Latin at the Renaissance. Richard is now King George V.

James Elroy Flecker, Letter to Frank Savery, July 1913

The epithet popularly associated with the Turk in the English mind is 'unspeakable': and the inevitable reaction against the popular prejudice takes the form of representing the Turk as 'the perfect gentleman' who exhibits all the virtues which the ordinary Englishman lacks. Both these pictures are fantastic.

Arnold Toynbee and Kenneth P. Kirkwood, *Turkey*, 1926

A humorless soldierly people whose arts are courage, honor, and bloodletting.

Nelson Algren, *Who Lost an American?*, 1963

Ankara (formerly Angora)

Angora . . . was then a gaunt and sordid hole.

Norman Douglas, *Looking Back*, 1933 – of 1895

Antioch

One feels about Antioch that if it were to extend again over its now empty lanes, to reach its ancient limits, and to rebuild the full circuit of its walls, it would not be a resurrection, but a natural return. It it as though a man had gone on a long journey and left his household on board wages, and shut up three-quarters of the rooms, and left but a little income for general upkeep, but might be expected to come home.

There is no town on which I feel more curious as to its future.

Hilaire Belloc, *Places*, 1942

Agri Dagi / Mount Ararat

On the top of this Mountaine did the Arke of Noah rest, as both Jewes, Turkes and Armenians affirmed. Some Friers of Saint Gregories Monasterie told us, that even at this day some part of the Arke is yet to be seene on the top of this Mountaine, if any could ascend thither, but the way (as they say) is kept by Angels, so that whosoever shall presume to goe up (as once a Brother of that Monasterie did) shall be brought downe in the night season, from the place which hee had gayned by his travaile in the day time before.

John Cartwright, 1603, in *Purchas his Pilgrimes*, 1625

But see, where Persia's beauteous clime extends,
How gloriously diluvian Ararat
Hath pinnacled his rocky beak in clouds. . . .
Time cannot mar his glory, grand he swells
As when the Ark was balanced on his brow.

Robert Montgomery, *Satan*, 1830

The best season for the ascent is August and September. Rugs, cooking utensils, tea, red wine, rice, and two bags of coal must be carried. Information may be had from the frontier officer or from the village-chief at Araluikh. Each porter receives 5rb. for the whole excursion. – As the traveller may possibly be molested by the nomadic Kurds, he is advised to take a revolver and procure an escort of Cossacks from the frontier officer.

Karl Baedeker, *Russia with Teheran, Port Arthur, and Peking*, 1914

Broussa

There is an authentic smack of Paradise about Broussa.

Norman Douglas, *Looking Back*, 1933

Dardanelles (Ancient Hellespont)

The straight Hellespont between
The Sestos and Abydos of her breasts.

John Donne, *Elegie, Love's Progresse*, *c.* 1590s

Since I have seen this streight, I find nothing improbable in the adventure of Leander or very wonderfull in the Bridge of Boats of Xerxes. 'Tis so narrow, 'tis not surprizing a young Lover should attempt to swim it or an Ambitious King try to pass his Army over it. But then tis so subject to storms, 'tis no wonder the Lover perish'd and the Bridge was broken.

Lady Mary Wortley Montagu, Letter to the Abbe Conti, 31 July 1718

The water of the Hellespont is the most important channel of water in the world. . . . The most famous war of all time was fought, not for any human Helen, but to control that channel.

John Masefield, *Gallipoli*, 1916

Sestos and Abydos
This morning I *swam* from *Sestos* to *Abydos*, the immediate distance is not above a mile but the current renders it hazardous, so much so, that I doubt whether Leander's conjugal powers must not have been exhausted in his passage to Paradise.

Lord Byron, Letter to Henry Drury, 3 May 1810

For sixty miles (its whole length) it presents a continued succession of new beauties, and in the hands of Europeans, particularly English, improved as country seats, would make one of the loveliest countries in the world.

J.L. Stephens, *Incidents of Travel in the Russian and Turkish Empires*, 1839

Sestos

A naked point on the European side, so ugly compared with all around it as to attract particular attention, projects into the strait, and here are the ruins of Sestos; here Xerxes built his bridge of boats to carry over his millions to the conquest of Greece; and here, when he returned with the wreck of his army, defeated and disgraced, found his bridge destroyed by a tempest, and, in his rage, ordered the chains to be thrown into the sea, and the waves to be lashed with rods. From this point, too, Leander swam the Hellespont for love of Hero, and Lord Byron and Mr Ekenhead for fun. Nearly opposite, close to the Turkish fort, are the ruins of Abydos. Here Xerxes, and Leander, and Lord Byron, and Mr Ekenhead landed.

Ibid.

About 11 A.M. entered the Helespont. Gentle wind from the north. Clear & fine. The new castles of Europe & Asia on either hand. Little difference in the aspect of the continents. Only Asia looked a sort of used up – superannuated.

Herman Melville, *Journal of a Visit to Europe and the Levant*, 10 December 1856

It was a Miasma that brought about the Dardanelles Adventure.

Admiral of the Fleet Lord Fisher, *Memories*, 1919

Gallipoli

Callipolis maketh a faire shew a-farre off; but entred, is nothing lesse then it promised.

George Sandys, 1610, in *Purchas his Pilgrimes*, 1625

Istanbul (formerly Constantinople and Ancient Byzantium)

The streetes of this Citie are narrow, and shadowed with pentises of wood, and upon both sides the way is raised some foot high, but of little breadth, and paved for men and women to passe, the middest of the street being left low and unpaved, and no broader, then for the passage of Asses or beasts loaded. In many places of the streetes lye carcasses, yea sometimes the bodies of dead men, even till they be putrified, and I thinke this uncleanlinesse of the Turks (who otherwise place Religion in washing their bodies, and keeping their apparrell, especially their Tulbent pure and cleane) is the chiefe cause that this Citie, though most pleasantly seated, yet above all the Cities of the world is continually more or lesse infected with the plague.

Fynes Moryson, *An Itinerary*, 1617

This Citie by destinie appointed, and by nature seated for Soveraigntie . . . stands on a Cape of Land, neere the entrance of the Bosphorus. In forme triangular, on the East-side washed with the same, and on the North-side with the Haven, adjoyning on the West to the Continent. Walled with bricke and stone, intermixed orderly, having foure and twentie gates and posternes; whereof five doe regard the Land, and nineteene the water, being about thirteene miles in circumference. Than this there is hardly in nature a more delicate Object, if beheld from the Sea or adjoyning Mountaines; the loftie and beautifull Cypresse Trees so intermixed with the buildings, that it seemeth to present a Citie in a Wood to the pleased beholders. Whose seven aspiring heads (for on so many hils and no more they say it is seated) are most of them crowned with magnificent Mosques, all of white Marble, round in forme, and coupled above; being finished on the top with gilded Spires, that reflect the beames they receive with a marvellous splendor; some having two, some foure, some sixe adjoyning Turrets, exceeding high, and exceeding slender; Tarrast aloft on the out-side like the mayne top of a ship, and that in severall places equally distant.

George Sandys, 1610, in *Purchas his Pilgrimes*, 1625

Truly, I may say of Constantinople, as I said once of the world, in the Lamentado of my second pilgrimage:

A painted whore, the mask of deadly sin,
Sweet fair without, and stinking foul within.

For indeed outwardly it hath the fairest show; and inwardly, the streets being narrow, and most part covered, the filthiest and most deformed buildings in the world. The reason of its beauty is, because being situate on moderate prospective heights, the universal tectures afar off yield a delectable show, the covertures being erected like the back of a coach after the Italian fashion, with guttered tile. But being entered within, there is nothing but a stinking deformity, and a loathsome contrived place; without either internal domestic furniture, or the external decorations of fabricks extended like a palace. Notwithstanding that, for its situation, the delicious wines, and temperate climate, the fertile circumjacent fields, the Hellespont sea, and pleasant Asia on the other side; it may truly be called the paradise of the earth.

William Lithgow, *Rare Adventures and Painfull Peregrinations*, 1614/32

For me, Ile only say of *Constantinople*, that for an Imperial seat, 'tis one of the noblest Cities I ever saw, situated on two seas, with its two feet *Colossean*, treading on *Asia* and *Europe*, nor did I ever see truer bravery or greater Gallantry than there, every one wearing such various coloured silks, with swelling Turbans, and flowing garments, as their streets appear just like *Tulipp* Gardens, whilst ours, (with so many wearing black) appear just like *mortuary* houses, all mourning for the dead.

Richard Flecknoe, *A Relation of Ten Yeares Travells*, 1654 – of 1647

The pleasure of going in a Barge to Chelsea is not comparable to that of rowing up on the Canal of the Sea here, where for 20 miles together down the Bosphorus the most Beautifull variety of Prospects present themselves. The Asian side is covered with fruit trees, villages and the most delightfull Landscapes in nature. On the European side stands Constantinople, situate on Seven Hills. The unequal heights make it seem as Large again as it is (tho' one of the Largest Citys in the world), Shewing an agreeable mixture of Gardens, Pine and Cypress trees, Palaces, Mosques and publick buildings, rais'd one above another with as much Beauty and appearance of Symetry as your Ladyship ever saw in a Cabinet adorn'd by the most skilfull hands, Jars shewing themselves above Jars, mix'd with Canisters, babys and Candlesticks. This is a very odd Comparison, but it gives me an exact image of the thing.

Lady Mary Wortley Montagu, Letter to Lady Bristol, 10 April 1718

The harbour of Constantinople, which may be considered as an arm of the Bosphorus, obtained, in a very remote period, the denomination of the *Golden Horn*. The curve which it describes might be compared to the horn of a stag, or, as it should seem, with more propriety, to that of an ox.

Edward Gibbon, *The Decline and Fall of the Roman Empire*, 1776–88

Constantinople had been left naked and desolate, without a prince or a people. But she could not be despoiled of the incomparable situation which marks her for the metropolis of a great empire; and the genius of the place will ever triumph over the accidents of time and fortune.

Ibid. (referring to the Turkish conquest of Constantinople in 1453)

Essentially the great question remains: Who will hold Constantinople?

Napoleon, Letter to the Marquis de Caulaincourt, May 1808

The walls of the Seraglio are like the walls of Newstead Gardens only higher, and much in the same *order*, but the ride by the walls of the city on the land side is beautiful, imagine, four miles of immense triple battlements covered with *Ivy*, surmounted with 218 towers, and on the other side of the road Turkish burying grounds (the loveliest spots on earth) full of enormous cypresses, I have seen the ruins of Athens, of Ephesus, and Delphi, I have traversed great part of Turkey and many other parts of Europe and some of Asia, but I never beheld a work of Nature or Art, which yielded an impression like the prospect on each side, from the Seven Towers to the End of the Golden Horn.

Lord Byron, Letter to Mrs Catherine Gordon Byron, 28 June 1810

I might have shared with Russia the possession of the Turkish empire. We had oftener than once entertained the idea, but Constantinople was always the obstacle that opposed its execution. The Turkish capital was the grand stumbling block between us. Russia wanted it, and I could not resign it. Constantinople is an Empire of itself. It is the real keystone of power; for he who possesses it may rule the world.

Napoleon, quoted by Count de las Cases, *Journal of the Private Life and Conversations of the Emperor Napoleon at St Helena*, (April 1816), 1824

After what has been said of the external grandeur of this wonderful city, the Reader is perhaps ill prepared for a description of the interior; the horror, the wretchedness, and filth of which are not to be conceived. Its streets are narrow, dark, ill paved, and full of holes and ordure. In the most abominable alleys of *London*, or of *Paris*, there is nothing so revolting. They more resemble the interior of common sewers than public streets. . . .

View the exterior of *Constantinople*, and it seems the most opulent and flourishing city in *Europe*: examine its interior, and its miseries and deficiencies are so striking, that it must be considered the meanest and poorest metropolis of the world. . . . Never was there a people in possession of such advantages, who either knew or cared so little for their enjoyment.

E.D. Clarke, *Travels in Various Countries*, 1816

Each villa on the Bosphorus looks a screen
New painted or a pretty opera scene.

Lord Byron, *Don Juan*, 1819–24

Can this beautiful city, rich with the choicest gifts of heaven, be pre-eminently the abode of pestilence and early death? . . . where, year after year, the angel of death stalks through the streets, and thousands and tens of thousands look him calmly in the face, and murmuring 'Allah, Allah, God is merciful,' with a fatal trust in the Prophet, lie down and die? We enter the city, and these questions are quickly answered. A lazy, lounging, and filthy population; beggars basking in the sun, and dogs licking their sores; streets never cleaned but by the winds and rains; immense burying-grounds all over the city; tombstones at the corners of the streets; graves gaping ready to throw out their half-buried dead, and the whole approaching to one vast charnel-house, dispel all illusions, and remove all doubts, and we are ready to ask ourselves if it be possible that, in such a place, health can ever dwell.

J.L. Stephens, *Incidents of Travel in the Russian and Turkish Empires*, 1839

Nowhere else does the sea come so home to a city.
A.W. Kinglake, *Eothen*, 1844

Perhaps as you make your difficult way through a steep and narrow alley, shut in between blank walls, and little frequented by passers, you meet one of those coffin-shaped bundles of white linen that implies an Ottoman lady.
Ibid.

I did not see the Golden Horn at Constantinople, nor hear it blown, probably on account of the fog.
W.M. Thackeray, *Punch in the East*, 1845

Passed between wall & Golden Horn through Greek and Jew quarters, and came outside the land wall in view of Sweet Waters, which run inland & end in beautiful glades. Rode along the land wall. By this wall Constantinople was taken by the Turks & the last of the Constantines fell in their defence. . . . Here fell the soldiers of Constantine – sowed in corruption & raised in potatoes.
Herman Melville, *Journal of a Visit to Europe and the Levant*, 14 December 1856

The water clear as Ontario – the banks natural quays, shelving off like those of a canal. Large vessels go close along the shore. – The palaces of the Sultan – the pleasure-houses – palaces of ambassadors – The white foam breaks on these white steps as on long lines of coral reefs. One peculiarity is the introduction of ocean into inland recesses. Ships anchor at the foot of ravines, deep among green basins, where the only canvass you would look for would be tents. – A gallery of ports & harbors, formed by the interchange of promontory & bay. Many parts like the Highlands of the Hudson, magnified. Porpoises sport in the blue; & large flights of pigeons overhead go through evolutions like those of armies. The sun shining on the palaces. View from the heights of Buuydereh. . . . No wonder the Czars have always coveted the capital of the Sultans. No wonder the Russian among his firs sighs for these myrtles.
Ibid.

Constantinople makes a noble picture.

But its attractiveness begins and ends with its picturesqueness. From the time one starts ashore till he gets back again, he execrates it. . . . it was, – well, it was an eternal circus. People were thicker than bees in those narrow streets, and the men were dressed in all the outrageous, outlandish, idolatrous, extravagant, thunder-and-lightning costumes that ever a tailor with the delirium tremens and seven devils could conceive of. There was no freak in dress too crazy to be indulged in; no absurdity too absurd to be tolerated; no frenzy in ragged diabolism too fantastic to be attempted. No two men were dressed alike. It was a wild masquerade of all imaginable costumes.
Mark Twain, *The Innocents Abroad*, 1869

As we steamed down the Bosphorus the Russian ship's mate, who talked some English he had learned in Japan, described what might be done with such a position in the hands of a European Power, the continuous streets, the railways, the electric light, etc. Thank Heaven, it is still in its old-fashioned way.
Wilfred Scawen Blunt, Diary, 26 September 1895, *My Diaries*, 1919

If it were not for the beauty of the situation the place would be an unredeemed hole.
Henry Adams, Letter to Elizabeth Cameron, 29 April 1898

Water flows through the city, purifying it; light floods it, making it over again, hourly. It lies between the water and the sky, in a great luxurious abandonment to the light. Seen from the Bosphorus at sunset, Stamboul rises like a great cloud, silhouetted against pure gold, and no more substantial than a cloud; its edges are cut into patterns of domes and minarets and cypresses, above luminous banks of cloud; it hangs there, lifted and burning, wholly a part of the sky. Around the point of the Seraglio, there is pure sea, with sails and islands; on the right, naked from the sunset, the walls and square window-holes of Pera, rising up solidly out of the land.

Sunrise, as I see it from the height of Pera, brings out all the colours of Stamboul, like water washing over veined marble. The whole city, washed by the light, whitens and reddens, every window grows distinct, and the balcony of every minaret. On the water the boats seem to crawl over steel-blue oil. A few thin spires of smoke rise slowly, forming into clouds of sombre fleece above the minarets. The light seems to draw a curtain back slowly over Kassim Pacha; below, the cypresses and half of the valley are still cold. . . .

The sunset was brief, and the water has grown dull, like slate. Stamboul fades to a level mass of smoky purple, out of which a few minarets rise black against a grey sky with bands of orange fire. Last night, after a golden sunset, a fog of rusty iron came down, and hung poised over the jagged level of the hill. The whole mass of Stamboul was like black smoke; the water dim grey, a little flushed, and then like pure light, lucid, transparent, every ship and every boat sharply outlined in black on its surface; the boats semed to crawl like flies on a lighted pane.
Arthur Symons, *Cities*, 1903

Stamboul, seen from the old bridge at evening, goes up like a mountain to the domes and lances of the Suleimanie. It lies with its feet in the water, like Venice; out of the water rise brown masts and spars, with furled sails, the lines fitting together into exquisite patterns; and this great, dim, coloured mass, in which certain dull reds, greys, and faint blues catch the eye, harmonises into a kind of various brown, like some rich, veined wood. . . . The streets of Stamboul climb and zigzag; to walk in them is to crawl like a maggot in rotting cheese.

Ibid.

Society here is worse than that of a small cathedral town in England.

James Elroy Flecker, Letter, 1910

Constantinople is a city where the Oriental loses his virtues and the Occidental adds to his vice.

Caleb Frank Gates, *Not to Me Only*, 1940

There can never have been such a site for a huge metropolis. The shore of Asia is crowded with buildings and mosques and minarets. . . . Our ship makes a sweep towards it, and in that moment we see before and in front of us the opening of the Golden Horn, and one after another all the Imperial Mosques of Istanbul standing against and upon the skyline. . . . It is the most sensational revelation: one after another of these great domes as in a panorama, they stand there on the sky-line like huge kettle-drums with something menacing and martial in their air, and in that moment it is more of a capital than any other city, more than London, or than Rome, or Paris: much vaster than Venice which in comparison is but a few churches and palaces upon the water at water level, or even it could be said, at water-lily level, for the Salute apart, which like a huge shell stands upon its own steps or platform that could be self-formed of pale madrepores or coral, the Venetian buildings rise from a height no higher than the pavement.

In this moment Istanbul is alone and tremendous. No water city can compare to it; no other city of the Orient climbs upon its seven hills above a trident or triple lane of calmed and inland waters. It must be the most wonderful site for a great capital there has ever been.

Sacheverell Sitwell, *Arabesque and Honeycomb*, 1957

Istanbul does possess, as you can feel from the deck of your ship, the arrogance of the very old: like the rudeness of an aged actor whose prime was long ago, whose powers have failed him, but who struts about still in cloak and carnationed buttonhole, snubbing his inferiors. . . . It is only when you get closer that you realize the illusion of it, just as you observe, if he leans too close to you on the sofa, the creases of despair around the actor's mouth.

Jan Morris, *Destinations*, 1980

The Seraglio

The palace of the Seraglio, the cloister with marble pillars, the hall of the ambassadors, the impenetrable gate guarded by eunuchs and ichoglans, have a romantic look in print; but not so in reality. Most of the marble is wood, almost all the gilding is faded, the guards are shabby, the foolish perspectives painted on the walls are half cracked off. The place looks like Vauxhall in the day-time.

W.M. Thackeray, *Journey from Cornhill to Cairo*, 1845

Once, when my hostess was visiting the Serai, a helpful Turkish guide drew her attention to a ceiling, decorated in the rococo style.

'C'etait fait,' he said proudly, 'par Monsieur Rococo lui-meme.'

Lord Kinross, *Europa Minor*, 1956

Mosque of Sophia

There is the best kirk of the world and the fairest, and it is of Saint Sophia.

John Mandeville, *The Book of John Mandeville*, *c.* 1360

Owing to its peculiar form St: Sophia viewed near to, looks as partly underground; as if you saw but the superstructrure of some immense temple, yet to be disinterred. You step *down* to enter. The dome has a kind of dented appearance, like crown of old hat. Must inevitably cave in one of these days. Within dome has appearance (from its flatness) of an immense sounding board. A firmament of masonry. The interior a positive appropriation of space.

Herman Melville, *Journal of a Visit to Europe and the Levant*, 17 December 1856

It is the rustiest old barn in heathendom.

Mark Twain, *The Innocents Abroad*, 1869

Izmir (formerly Smyrna)

The town is at the end of the bay, and where for a little it stretches along a declivity, it looks, from the lowness of the houses, their flat roofs red-tiled like a field of broken pottery.

Herman Melville, *Journal of a Visit to Europe and the Levant*, 20 December 1856

the 'Mediterranean race' there

It speaks no language though it will chatter with you in half a dozen, it has no native land though it is related by marriage to all Europe, and with the citizens of each country it will talk to its compatriots and itself as 'we'; it centres round no capital and is loyal to no government though it obeys many. Cheerful careless contented hospitable to a fault, it may well be all, for it is divested of all natural responsibilities, it has little to guard and little to offer but a most liberal share in its own inconceivably hugger mugger existence. Kindness is its distinctive quality, as far as I have sampled it, and I hope I may have many opportunities of sampling it further.

Gertrude Bell, Letter to her family, November 1899

Trabzon/Trebizond

*When we saw Trebizond lying there in its splendid bay, the sea in front and the hills behind, the cliffs and ravines which held the ancient citadel, and the white Turkish town lying along the front and climbing up the hill, it was like seeing an old dream change its shape, as dreams do, becoming something else, for this did not seem the capital of the last Byzantine empire, but a picturesque Turkish port and town with a black beach littered with building materials, and small houses and mosques climbing the hill, and ugly buildings along the quay.

Rose Macaulay *The Towers of Trebizond*, 1956

*Then, between sleeping and waking, there rose before me a vision of Trebizond: not Trebizond as I had seen it, but the Trebizond of the world's dreams, of my own dreams, shining towers and domes shimmering on a far horizon, yet close at hand, luminously enspelled in the most fantastic unreality, yet the only reality, a walled and gated city, magic and mystical, standing beyond my reach yet I had to be inside, an alien wanderer yet at home, held in the magic enchantment; and at its heart, at the secret heart of the city and the legend and the glory in which I was caught and held, there was some pattern that I could not unravel, some hard core that I could not make my own, and, seeing the pattern and the hard core enshrined within the walls, I turned back from the city and stood outside it, expelled in mortal grief.

Ibid.

Troy

High barrows without marble or a name,
A vast, untilled, and mountain-skirted plain,
And Ida in the distance, still the same,
And old Scamander (if 'tis he) remain.
The situation seems still formed for fame.
A hundred thousand men might fight again
With ease; but where I sought for Ilion's walls,
The quiet sheep feeds, and the tortoise crawls.

Lord Byron, *Don Juan*, 1819–24

If there be a spot of ground on earth in which the historical, and the poetical, and the fabulous are so beautifully blended together that we would not separate them even to discover the truth, it is before us now.

J.L. Stephens, *Incidents of Travel in the Russian and Turkish Empires*, 1839

U

UGANDA

I had travelled through tropical forests in Cuba and India, and had often before admired their enchanting, yet sinister luxuriance. But the forests of Uganda, for magnificence, for variety of form and colour, for profusion of brilliant life – plant, bird, insect, reptile, beast – for the vast scale and awful fecundity of the natural processes that are beheld at work, eclipsed, and indeed effaced, all previous impressions. One becomes, not without a secret sense of aversion, the spectator of an intense convulsion of life and death. Reproduction and decay are locked struggling in infinite embraces. In this glittering equatorial slum huge trees jostle one another for room to live; slender growths stretch upwards – as it seems in agony – towards sunlight and life. The soil bursts with irrepressible vegetations. Every victor, trampling on the rotting mould of exterminated antagonists, soars aloft, only to encounter another host of aerial rivals, to be burdened with masses of parasitic foliage, smothered in the glorious blossoms of creepers, laced and bound and interwoven with interminable tangles of vines and trailers. Birds are as bright as butterflies; butterflies are as big as birds. . . . The telegraph-wire runs northwards to Gondoroko through this vegetable labyrinth. Even its poles had broken into bud.

Sir Winston Churchill, *My African Journey*, 1908

In Uganda the arguments for state ownership and employment of the natural resources of the country seem to present themselves in their strongest and most formidable array. . . . It would be hard to find a country where the conditions were more favourable than in Uganda to a practical experiment in State Socialism.

Ibid.

Almost for the first time in Africa I got the impression that this was a country where Africans were happy.

John Gunther, *Inside Africa*, 1955

Sir John Gray describes its history as being like 'a crime to which there have been no eye-witnesses'.

Alan Moorhead, *The White Nile*, 1960

Uganda was a few years ago a naked people, now they are all decently clad . . . but there is a tendency, wherever English authority is relaxed among them, to revert to their old terrible habits.

Daily Telegraph, *c.*1 October 1892, quoted Wilfred Scawen Blunt, *My Diaries*, 1919

Albert Nyanza

This point is destined to become the capital of Central Africa.

Sir Samuel Baker, *Ismailia*, 1874

Kampala

Kampala is a Baganda cosmopolis – in which the English are shop or bank employees.

Negley Farson, *Behind God's Back*, 1940

Like Rome and Lisbon, Kampala is built on seven hills. 'How refreshing,' one Briton told us, 'to see a view in Africa that has an end!'

John Gunther, *Inside Africa*, 1955

Kabalega Falls/formerly Murchison Falls

They are . . . quite the *pièce de résistance* of Equatoria.

Seymour Vandeleur, *Campaigning on the Upper Nile and Niger*, 1898

The most exciting single incident in the Nile's long journey to the sea.

Rennie Bere, quoted in Alan Moorhead, *The White Nile*, 1960

The whole pent-up volume of the river dashes out of a ravine like a burst water-main; it is really more of an explosion of water than a fall, and it can exert a curious mesmerism on the mind if one stands there and watches for a while.

Alan Moorhead, *Ibid.*

Lake Victoria (at Jinja)

'The Germans have a queer idea,' a man on the hotel veranda told us. 'You know what scientific chaps they are. Well, one of their geologists has discovered that

Lake Tanganyika lies 1,200 feet below shallow Lake Victoria – you know this lake is never more than 250 feet deep at any place. Well – this is the German's idea – the barrier of flats between the two lakes is only inconsiderable. It would only require a slight change to DRAIN Lake Victoria . . . just a few blasts of dynamite . . . and BANG! goes Lake Victoria!'

'What do you think would happen to Egypt then?' he ruminated. 'Wake up some morning, the poor Gippies, and find there just *was* no Nile! No Nile in Egypt! Grandiose idea, isn't it.'

He took another suck at his pipe: 'The hell of it is, that German geologist was right – it *could* be done. In 1926 the Egyptian Government sent some archaeologists to Tanganyika who confirmed this.'

Negley Farson, *Behind God's Back*, 1940

'You could put all Ireland into the middle of that lake – an' still not be able to see it from the shore. I've sometimes thought of trying it!' he said dreamily.

Ibid.

There is a mysterious and disturbing atmosphere about the lake. One feels here very strongly the primitiveness of Africa, its overwhelming multiplicity in emptiness.

Alan Moorhead, *The White Nile*, 1960

URUGUAY

I will call my book *The Purple Land*; for what more suitable name can one find for a country so stained with the blood of her children?

W.H. Hudson, *The Purple Land*, 1885

Whoever wishes to have something by which to distinguish Uruguay from its many sister republics, the size and character of which are unfamiliar to us in Europe, may learn to remember that it is the smallest of the South American states, and that it has neither mountains, nor deserts, nor antiquities, nor aboriginal Indians. Nevertheless it is by no means a country to be described by negatives, but has . . . a marked character of its own. . . .

With an area of only 72,000 square miles, as against 1,134,000 in Argentina, and 3,208,000 in Brazil, Uruguay seems like a garden plot between two vast estates. But she is a veritable garden. There is hardly an acre of useless ground within her borders.

James Bryce, *South America*, 1912

There are seventy stanzas in the Uruguay national anthem, which fact may account for the Uruguay standing army.

Franklin P. Adams, attrib.

Arriving in Uruguay, you get the vague feeling that you have lost your way; you realise soon enough that it is not you who should not be there at all, but Uruguay. The country, you feel, should not be in South America, but somewhere in Europe. What to do with DP's (Displaced Persons) was an enormous problem after the last war; the problem of DC's (Displaced Countries) if not so pressing, is even harder to solve. Uruguay, it seems to me, should emigrate, and settle somewhere between Belgium and Holland.

George Mikes, *Tango: A Solo Across South America*, 1961

The Denmark of Latin America

Anon., quoted John Gunther, *Inside South America*, 1967

What does Uruguay need most?
1. More Uruguayans.
2. One economist.
3. Vitality.

What runs Uruguay?
1. Anybody close enough to a minister to be able to ask a favor of his secretary on the telephone.

John Gunther, *Inside South America*, 1967

Montevideo

I sat down on a bench beside the sea or river – for some call it one thing, some the other, and the muddied line and freshness of the water, and the uncertain words of geographers, leave one in doubt as to whether Montevideo is situated on the shores of the Atlantic, or only near the Atlantic and on the shores of a river one hundred and fifty miles wide at its mouth.

W.H. Hudson, *The Purple Land*, 1885

Tolosa

They seemed to be a rather listless set in Tolosa, and when I asked them what they were doing to make a livelihood, they said they were *waiting*.

Ibid.

UNITED STATES OF AMERICA

Colonial America

God hath sifted a whole Nation that he might send Choice Grain over into this Wilderness.

William Stoughton, *New England's True Interest; . . . a Sermon*, 1670

While we are, as I may call it, *Scouring* our Planet, by *clearing America* of Woods, and so making this side of our Globe reflect a brighter Light to the Eyes of Inhabitants in *Mars* or *Venus*, why should we, in the Sight of

Superior Beings, darken its People? Why increase the Sons of *Africa*, by planting them in *America*, where we have so fair an Opportunity, by excluding all Blacks and Tawneys, of increasing the lovely White and Red? But perhaps I am partial to the Complexion of my Country, for such Kind of Partiality is natural to Mankind.

Benjamin Franklin, *Observations Concerning the Increase of Mankind*, 1751

America is more wild and absurd than ever.

Edmund Burke, Letter to Lord Rockingham, 9 September 1769

I observ'd to them that Nations as well as Individuals, had their different Ages, which challeng'd a different Treatment. . . . you have sometimes no doubt given your Son a whipping; and I doubt not, but it was well merited and did him much good: yet you will not think proper at present to employ the birch: the Colonies are no longer in their Infancy, but yet I say to you, they are still in their Nonage and Dr Franklyn wishes to emancipate them too soon from their mother country.

David Hume, Letter to William Strahan, 1 March 1774

The next Augustan age will dawn on the other side of the Atlantic. . . . At last some curious traveller from Lima will visit England and give a description of the ruins of St Paul's.

Horace Walpole, Letter to Sir Horace Mann, 12 June 1775

Young man, there is America – which at this day serves for little more than to amuse you with stories of savage men and uncouth manners; yet shall, before you taste of death, show itself equal to the whole of that commerce which now attracts the envy of the world.

Edmund Burke, Speech on Conciliation with America, 22 March 1775

Independence

Driven from every corner of the earth, freedom of thought, and the right of private judgement in matters of conscience direct their course to this happy country as their last asylum.

Samuel Adams, Speech, Philadelphia, 1 August 1776

You cannot conquer America.

William Pitt, Earl of Chatham, Speech, House of Lords, 18 November 1777

I think that a young State, like a young Virgin, should modestly stay at home, and wait the Application of Suitors for an Alliance with her; and not run about offering her Amity to all the World; and hazarding their Refusal. . . . Our Virgin is a jolly one; and tho at present not very rich, will in time be a great Fortune, and where she has a favourable Predisposition, it seems to me well worth cultivating.

Benjamin Franklin, Letter to Charles W.F. Dumas, 22 September 1778

Liberty has still a continent to exist in.

Horace Walpole, *Letter to the Countess of Upper Ossory*, 17 February 1779

What can be the Ground of Malice of so many against America?

John Adams, *Diary*, 28 February 1781

E pluribus Unum.

(One from many. /From many, one)

Motto used on the title page of the *Gentleman's Journal*, January 1692

Motto for the Seal of the United States, proposed originally on 10 August 1776 by a committee composed of Benjamin Franklin, John Adams and Thomas Jefferson, and adopted 20 June 1782. The motto was added to certain coins in 1796. The actual selection of the motto has been claimed for Pierre Eugene du Simitière, a Swiss artist, who was employed by the committee, shortly after the Declaration of Independence, to submit a design for the seal – a design which was not accepted.

Here [in America] individuals of all nations are melted into a new race of men.

Michael Guillaume Jean de Crèvecoeur, *Letters from an American Farmer*, 1782

A great revolution has happened – a revolution made, not by chopping and changing of power in any of the existing states, but by the appearance of a new state, of a new species, in a new part of the globe. It has made as great a change in all the relations and balances, and gravitations of power, as the appearance of a new planet would in the system of the solar world.

Edmund Burke, Note, *Detached Papers*, 1782, and *Works*, 1852

Thirteen staves and ne'er a hoop will not make a barrel.

Peletiah Webster, *A Dissertation on the Political Union and Constitution of The Thirteen United States of North America*, 1783

Others object to the *Bald Eagle*, as looking too much like a *Dindon*, or Turkey. For my own part, I wish the Bald Eagle had not been chosen as the Representative of our Country; he is a bird of bad moral Character; he does not get his living honestly; you may see him perch'd on some dead Tree, near the river where, too lazy to fish for himself, he watches the Labour of the Fishing-Hawk; and, when that diligent Bird has at last taken a Fish, and is bearing it to his Nest for the support of his Mate and Young Ones, the Bald Eagle pursues him, and takes it from him. With all this Injustice he is never in good Case; but, like those among Men who live by Sharping and Robbing, he is generally poor, and often very lousy. Besides, he is a rank Coward; the little *KingBird*, not bigger than a Sparrow, attacks him boldly and drives him out of the District. He is therefore by no means a proper Emblem for the brave and honest Cincinnati of America, who have driven all the *Kingbirds* from our Country; though exactly fit for that Order of Knights, which the French call *Chevaliers d'Industrie*.

I am, on this account not displeas'd that the Figure is not known as a Bald Eagle, but looks more like a Turk'y. For in Truth the Turk'y is,in comparison, a much more respectable Bird, and withal a true original Native of America. He is, though a little vain and silly, it is true, but not the worse emblem for that, a Bird of Courage, and would not hesitate to attack a Grenadier of the British Guards, who should presume to invade his FarmYard with a *red* coat on.

Benjamin Franklin, Letter to Mrs Sarah Bache, 26 January 1784

I tremble for my country when I reflect that God is just.

Thomas Jefferson, *Notes on the State of Virginia*, 1784–5

The independence of America, considered merely as a separation from England, would have been a matter but of little importance, had it not been accompanied by a revolution in the principles and practise of governments. She made a stand, not for herself only, but for the world, and looked beyond the advantages herself could receive. . . .

As America was the only spot in the political world, where the principles of universal reformation could begin, so also it was the best in the natural world. An assemblage of circumstances conspired not only to give birth, but to add gigantic maturity to its principles.

The scene which that country presents to the eye of a spectator, has something in it which generates and encourages great ideas. Nature appears to him in magnitude. The mighty objects he beholds, act upon his mind by enlarging it, and he partakes of the greatness he contemplated. Its first settlers were emigrants from different European nations, and of diversified professions of religion, retiring from governmental persecutions of the old world, and meeting in the new, not as enemies, but as brothers. The wants which necessarily accompany the cultivation of a wilderness, produced among them a state of society, which countries, long harassed by the quarrels and intrigues of governments, had neglected to cherish. In such a situation, man becomes what he ought. He sees his species, not with the inhuman idea of a natural enemy, but as kindred; and the example shows to the artificial world, that man must go back to nature for information.

Thomas Paine, *The Rights of Man*, Part II, 1792

The Government of the United States is not, in any sense, founded upon the Christian religion.

George Washington, Treaty with Tripoli, 1795

And ne'er shall the sons of Columbia be slaves,
While the earth bears a plant,or the sea rolls its waves.

Robert Treat Paine, *Adams and Liberty*, 1798

Our country is too big for union, too sordid for patriotism, too democratic for liberty.

Fisher Ames, Letter to Thomas Dwight, 26 October 1803

Nineteenth Century

All that creation's varying mass assumes
Of grand or lovely, here aspires and blooms:
Bold rise the mountains, rich the gardens glow,
Bright lakes expand, and conquering rivers flow;
But mind, immortal mind, without whose ray,
This world's a wilderness, and man but clay,
Mind, mind alone, in barren, still repose,
Nor blooms, nor rises, nor expands, nor flows.
Take Christians, Mohawks, democrats, and all
From the rude wig-wam to the congress-hall,
From man the savage, whether slav'd or free,
To man the civiliz'd, less tame than he, –
'Tis one dull chaos, one unfertile strife
Betwixt half-polish'd and half-barbarous life;
Where every ill the ancient world could brew
Is mix'd with every grossness of the new;
Where all corrupts, though little can entice,
And nought is known of luxury, but its vice!

Thomas Moore, 'To the Honourable W.R.Spencer, from Buffalo, upon Lake Erie', *Poems relating to America*, 1806

Bonaparte hates our government because it is a living libel on his. The English hate us because they think our prosperity filched from theirs.

Thomas Jefferson, Letter to William Duane, 13 November 1810

'Tis the star-spangled banner, O! long may it wave
O'er the land of the free and the home of the brave!

Francis Scott Key, 'The Star-Spangled Banner', published in the *Baltimore Patriot*, 20 September 1814

The prospect in regard to America is not consoling. That power will always hang on the skirts of Great Britain unless there should be some change in her own situation.

Duke of Wellington, Dispatch to Earl Bathurst, 22 February 1814

The less we have to do with the amities or enmities of Europe the better. Not in our day, but at no distant one, we may shake a rod over the heads of all, which may make the stoutest tremble. But I hope our wisdom will grow with our power, and teach us, that the less we use our power the greater it will be.

Thomas Jefferson, Letter to Thomas Leiper, 12 June 1815

Our country! In her intercourse with foreign nations, may she always be in the right; but our country, right or wrong.

Stephen Decatur, Toast given at Norfolk, Virginia, April 1816

Dilke, whom you know to be a Godwin perfectibility Man, pleases himelf with the idea that America will be the country to take up the human intellect where England leaves off – I differ there with him greatly – A country like the united states whose greatest Men are Franklins and Washingtons will never do that – They are great Men doubtless but how are they to be compared with those of our countreymen Milton and the two Sidneys – The one is a philosophical Quaker full of mean and thrifty maxims the other sold the very Charger who had taken him through all his Battles. Those Americans are great but they are not sublime Men – the humanity of the United States can never reach the sublime.

John Keats, Letter to George Keats, 14-31 October 1818

This great spectacle of human happiness.

Sydney Smith, *Essays: Waterton's Wanderings*, 1825

I know of few things more fatiguing for a continuance, than fine scenery. . . . At all events we had not much fatigue of this kind to complain of in any part of America, for, take it all in all, a more unpicturesque country is hardly to be found anywhere.

Captain Basil Hall, *Travels in North America*, 1829

The United States form another England, without its unbearable taxes, its insolent game laws, its intolerable dead-weight, and its treadmills.

William Cobbett, *Rural Rides – Eastern Tour*, 19 April 1830

My country, 'tis of thee,
Sweet land of liberty,
Of thee I sing;
Land where my fathers died,
Land of the pilgrims' pride,
From every mountain side
Let freedom ring.

Samuel Francis Smith, *America* (first printed in a broadside in connection with an Independence Day celebration by the Boston Sabbath School Union, 4 July 1831)

Those who meditate leaving Europe and going to America to work, and toil, and build a fortune, might as well also leave their *poetry* behind. It will not be supposed that I mean their books, but their poetry of *expectation*.

Calvin Colton, *Manual for Emigrants to America*, 1832

The American spring is by no means so agreeable as the American autumn; both move with faltering step and slow; but this lingering pace, which is delicious in autumn, is most tormenting in the spring. In the one case, you are about to part with a friend, who is becoming more gentle and agreeable at every step, and such steps can hardly be made too slowly; but in the other you are making your escape from a dreary cavern, where you have been shut up with black frost and biting blasts, and where your best consolation was being smoke-dried.

Mrs Frances Trollope, *Domestic Manners of the Americans*, 1832

Had America every attraction under heaven that nature and social enjoyment can offer, this electioneering madness would make me fly it in disgust

Ibid.

Can there ever be any thorough national fusion of the Northern and Southern States? I think not. In fact, the Union will be shaken almost to dislocation whenever a very serious question between the States arises. The American Union has no *centre*, and it is impossible now to make one. The more they extend their borders into the Indians' land, the weaker will the national cohesion be. But I look upon the States as splendid masses to be used, by and by, in the composition of two or three great governments.

Samuel Taylor Coleridge, *Table Talk*, 4 January 1833

The possible destiny of the United States of America – as a nation of a hundred millions of freemen – stretching from the Atlantic to the Pacific, living under the laws of Alfred, and speaking the language of Shakespeare and Milton, is an august conception. Why should we not wish to see it realized? America would then be England viewed through a solar microscope; Great Britain in a state of glorious magnification! How deeply to be lamented is the spirit of hostility and sneering which some of the popular books of travels have shown in treating of the Americans! They hate us, no doubt, just as brothers hate; but they respect the opinion of an Englishman concerning themselves ten times as much as that of a native of any other country on earth.

Samuel Taylor Coleridge, *Table Talk*, 10 April 1833

America is a fine country and to people of middling circumstances a paradise but the spirit of change is too active, the blast of unlimited democracy too furious to make it agreeable to the classes who happen to be exempted by circumstances from labor. In a regular democracy there should be no property.

Charles Francis Adams, *Diary*, 19 February 1834

Nothing is more embarrassing in the ordinary intercourse of life than this irritable patriotism of the Americans. A stranger may be well inclined to praise many of the institutions of their country, but he begs permission to blame some things in it, a permission that is inexorably refused. America is therefore a free country in which, lest anybody should be hurt by your remarks, you are not allowed to speak freely of private individuals or of the state, of the citizens or of the authorities, of public or of private undertakings, or, in short, of anything at all except, perhaps, the climate and the soil; and even then Americans will be found ready to defend both as if they had co-operated in producing them.

Alexis de Tocqueville, *Democracy in America*, 1835

The deference of the Americans to the laws has been justly applauded; but it must be added that in America legislation is made by the people and for the people. Consequently, in the United States the law favors those classes that elsewhere are most interested in evading it.

Ibid.

No power on earth can prevent the increasing equality of conditions . . . from leading every member of the community to be wrapped up in himself. . . . And no one can foretell into what disgrace and wretchedness they would plunge themselves lest they should have to sacrifice something of their own wellbeing to the prosperity of their fellow-creatures.

Ibid.

Mr Madison remarked to me that the United States had been 'useful in proving things before held impossible.'

Harriet Martineau, *Society in America*, 1837

The pride and delight of Americans is their quantity of land. I do not remember meeting with one to whom it had occurred that they had too much. . . .

The possession of land is the aim of all action, generally speaking, and the cure for all social evils, among men in the United States. If a man is disappointed in politics or love – he goes and buys land. If he disgraces himself he betakes himself to a lot in the West. If the demand for any article of manufacture slackens, the operatives drop into the unsettled lands. If a citizen's neighbours rise above him in the towns, he takes himself where he can be monarch of all he surveys.

Ibid.

If destruction be our lot we must ourselves be its author and finisher. As a nation of free men, we must live through all time or die by suicide.

Abraham Lincoln, Speech in Springfield, Illinois, 27 January 1838

America, thou half-brother of the world;
With something good and bad of every land.

Philip James Bailey, *Festus*, 1839

The passion of love is not felt with the same intensity by either sex in this country as even in France; still less so than in England, and with nothing approaching to the ardour with which this passion burns in Portugal, in Spain, and in Italy.

J.S.Buckingham, *The Slave States of America, 1839*, 1842

Various as is the climate, in such an extensive region, certain it is that, in one point, that of *excitement* it has, in every portion of it, a very pernicious effect.

Captain Frederick Marryat, *A Diary in America*, 1839

Nature is excessively fond of drapery in America. I have never yet fallen in with a naked rock.

Ibid.

In your vast unoccupied territory, a fruitful soil presents its attractions to those individuals in whom Acquisitiveness and Ambition predominate. . . . In your political institutions, Self-esteem and Love of Approbation find unlimited scope. . . . Some persons appear to conceive liberty to consist in the privilege of unlimited exercise of the animal propensities. The head of Liberty stamped on the earlier medals, commemorative of the French Revolution, is the very personification of this idea. She is a female figure with a villainously small, low, and retreating forehead, deficient moral organs, and ample development of the base and posterior regions of the brain, devoted to the propensities. Her hair is flying back in loose disorder, and her countenance expresses vivacity and passion, but neither morality nor wisdom. The same figure appears on the earlier coins of the United States. Liberty, as I should draw her, would possess large moral and intellectual organs, with moderate propensities. I should arrange her hair in simple elegance, and imprint serene enjoyment, benignity, and wisdom on her brow. She should represent moral liberty, or the unlimited freedom to accomplish all that is good, and the absence of every desire to do evil. Such alone is the liberty after which you should aspire.

George Combe, *Notes . . . during a Phrenological Visit, 1838–40*, 1841

The aspect of American society is animated because men and things are always changing, but it is monotonous because all these changes are alike.

Alexis de Tocqueville, *Democracy in America, the second part*, 1840

If ever America undergoes great revolutions,they will be brought about by the presence of the black race on the soil of the United States; that is to say, they will owe their origin, not to the equality, but to the inequality of condition.

Ibid.

I hear Morpeth is going to America, a resolution which I think very wise, and what I should certainly carry into execution myself, if I were not going to heaven.

Sydney Smith, Letter to Lady Grey, 24 August 1841

An English tourist in the United States admits the superiority of our thunder and lightning.

J.L. Stephens, *Incidents of Travel in Central America, Chiapas, and Yucatan*, 1841

I believe there is no country, on the face of the earth, where there is less freedom of opinion on any subject in reference to which there is a broad difference of opinion, than in this.

Charles Dickens, Letter to John Forster, 24 February 1842

I still reserve my opinion of the national character – just whispering that I tremble for a radical coming here, unless he is a radical on principle, by reason and reflection, and from the sense of right. I fear that if he were anything else, he would return home a tory. . . . I say no more on that head for two months from this time, save that I do fear that the heaviest blow ever dealt at liberty will be dealt by this country, in the failure of its example to the earth.

Ibid.

Thou, O my country, hast thy foolish ways,
Too apt to purr at every stranger's praise.

Oliver Wendell Holmes, *An After-Dinner Poem*, 1843

*'Why, I was a-thinking, sir,' returned Mark, 'that if I was a painter, and was called upon to paint the American Eagle, how should I do it?'

'Paint it as like an Eagle as you could, I suppose.'

'No,' said Mark. 'That wouldn't do for me sir. I should want to draw it like a Bat, for its short-sightedness; like a Bantam, for its bragging; like a Magpie, for its honesty; like a Peacock, for its vanity; like an Ostrich, for its putting its head in the mud, and thinking nobody sees it – '

'And like a Phoenix, for its power of springing from the ashes of its faults and vices, and soaring up anew into the sky!' said Martin. 'Well, Mark, let us hope so.'

Charles Dickens, *Martin Chuzzlewit*, 1844

*'Lord love you, sir,' he added, 'they're so fond of Liberty in this part of the globe, that they buy her and sell her, and carry her to market with 'em. They've such a passion for Liberty, that they can't help taking liberties with her. That's what it's owing to.'

Ibid.

America is a country of young men.

R.W. Emerson, *Essays – Old Age*, 1844

. . . Our manifest destiny to overspread the continent allotted by Providence for the free development of our yearly multiplying millions.

John O'Sullivan, *U.S.Magazine and Democratic Review*, July 1845

I never use the word 'Nation' in speaking of the United States; I always use the word 'Union,' or 'Confederacy.' We are not a Nation, but a Union, a confederacy of equal and sovereign States.

John C. Calhoun, Letter to Oliver Dyer, 1 January 1849

Thou, too, sail on, O Ship of State
Sail on, O Union, strong and great!
Humanity with all its fears,
With all the hopes of future years,
Is hanging breathless on thy fate! . . .
Sail on, nor fear to breast the sea!
Our hearts, our hopes are all with thee,
Our hearts, our hopes, our prayers, our tears,
Our faith triumphant o'er our fears,
Are all with thee, – are all with thee!

Henry Wadsworth Longfellow, *The Building of the Ship*, 1849

This is a glorious country. It has longer rivers and more of them, and they are muddier and deeper and run faster, and rise higher, and make more noise and fall lower and do more damage than anybody else's rivers. It has more lakes and they are bigger and deeper and clearer and wetter than those of any other country. Our railway cars are bigger and run faster and pitch off the track oftener, and kill more people than all other railway cars in any other country. Our steamboats carry bigger loads, are longer and broader, burst their boilers oftener and send up their passengers higher and the captains swear harder than the captains in any other country. Our men are bigger and longer and thicker; can fight harder and faster, drink more mean whisky, chew more bad tobacco, than in every other country.

American newspaper, 1850

There is less that is wrong here on the whole, though less that is great.

Arthur Hugh Clough, Letter, 14 December 1852

It was the brave Columbus
  A sailing o'er the tide,

Who notified the nations
  Of where I would reside!

Emily Dickinson, 1852

I think you have beyond all question the happiest and best country going.

Arthur Hugh Clough, Letter to Charles Eliot Norton, 29 August 1853

England, we who know America agree, is more endurable because of one's knowledge of America as a refuge.

Ibid.

There, I thought, in America, lies nature sleeping, overgrowing, almost conscious, too much by half for men in the picture, and so giving a certain *tristesse*, like the rank vegetation of swamps and forests seen at night, steeped in dews and rains, which it loves; and on it man seems not to make much impression. There, in that great sloven continent, in the high Alleghany pastures, the sea-wide sky-skirted prairie, still sleeps and murmurs and hides the great mother, long since driven away from the trim hedge-rows and over cultivated garden of England. And, even in England, I am quite too sensible of this. Every one is on his good behaviour and must be dressed for dinner at six.

R.W. Emerson, *English Traits*, 1856

The drawback of writing letters from these parts is that the subject is so supremely disagreeable. Over a thousand miles of railroad I have not seen a beautiful prospect – only swamp, sand, pines, wood cabins or villages and negroes reposing here and there – on the Alabama river a view about as mournful as if it was a tributary to the Styx, on this Mississippi the same dreariness on a wider scale, in the taverns dirt stenches dreadful swearing in the bars gongs banging night and day to plentiful filthy meals, every mans and womans knife in the mouth or the dish alternately. . . . I can hardly bear it. I do not mind about spitting any more: but the gentlemen very very many of them blow their noses with their fingers and only use their pocket handkerchiefs for dessert. I don't like to write about the country and what I see in it. . . . I see a sort of triumphant barbarism, a sordid greed everywhere and an extravagance quite as astounding, well its a fact the boat shakes so that it shakes the sentences out of my head. All profits of all businesses immensely high.

W.M. Thackeray, Letter to the Rev. Whitwell Elwin, 28 January-23 March 1856

It is our misfortune that all the towns of the Republic are alike, or differ in scarcely anything else than in natural position or wealth. Our Federal Union has been also architectural.

Frederick Law Olmsted, *A Journey through Texas*, 1857

to an Irishman
The refuge of his race, the home of his kindred, the heritage of his children and their children . . . a sort of half-way stage to heaven.

Thomas Colley Grattan, *Civilized America*, 1859

The government and social life of the people there . . . afford the most interesting phenomenon which we find as to the new world; – the best means of prophesying . . . what the world will next be, and what men will next do.

Anthony Trollope, *The West Indies and the Spanish Main*, 1859

No author, without a trial, can conceive of the difficulty of writing a romance about a country where there is no shadow, no antiquity, no mystery, no picturesque and gloomy wrong, nor anything but a commonplace prosperity, in broad and simple daylight, as is happily the case with my dear native land.

Nathaniel Hawthorne, *Transformation, The Marble Faun*, 1860

To the States or any one of them, or any city of the
  States,
  Resist much, obey little,
Once unquestioning obedience, once fully enslaved,
Once fully enslaved, no nation, state, city of this earth,
  ever afterward resumes its liberty.

Walt Whitman, 'To the States', from *Leaves of Grass*, 1860

Sail, sail thy best, ship of Democracy
Of value is thy freight, 'tis not the Present only,
The Past is also stored in thee.
Thou holdest not the venture of thyself alone, not of the
  Western continent alone,
Earth's *résumé* entire floats on thy keel O ship,
  is steadied by thy spars, . . .
With all their ancient struggles, martyrs, heroes, epics,
  wars,
  thou bear'st the other continents.

Walt Whitman, *Thou Mother with Thy Equal Brood*, Sec. 4, 1872

O America because you build for mankind, I build for
  you.

Walt Whitman, *By Blue Ontario's Shore*, 1855

America is the only place where man is full-grown!

O.W. Holmes, *The Professor at the Breakfast-Table*, 1860

A song for our banner? The watchword recall
Which gave the Republic her station:
'United we stand – divided we fall!'
It made and preserves us a nation!
The union of lakes, the union of lands –

The union of states none can sever –
The union of hearts, the union of hands –
And the Flag of our Union for ever!
George Pope Morris, *The Flag of our Union*, *c*.1860

Our Union is river, lake, ocean and sky:
Man breaks not the medal when God cuts the die!
O.W. Holmes, *Brother Jonathan's Lament for Sister Caroline*, 1861

A diagnosis of our hist'ry proves
Our native land a land its native loves;
Its birth a deed obstetric without peer,
Its growth a source of wonder far and near.
To love it more behold how foreign shores
Sink into nothingness beside its stores;
Hyde Park at best – though counted ultra-grand –
The 'Boston Common' of Victoria's land.
R.H. Newell (Orpheous C. Kerr), 'National Hymn, by Ol-v-r W-nd-l H-lmes', *The Rejected National Hymns*, August 1861

I myself think that people in general have no notion what widely different nations will develop themselves in America in some fifty years, if the Union breaks up. Climate and mixture of race will then be enabled fully to tell, and I cannot help thinking that the more diversity of nation there is on the American continent the more chance there is of one nation developing itself with grandeur and richness. It has been so in Europe. What should we all be if we had not one another to check us and to be learned from? Imagine an English Europe! How frightfully *borné* and dull! Or a French Europe either, for that matter.
Matthew Arnold, Letter to his sister, 28 January 1861

We rejoice that they are weakened, not because we derive gratification from their mortification, or desire to take advantage of their misfortunes, but because they both over-estimated and abused their strength, and because this over-estimate and this abuse were bad for them as well as disturbing to us.
Walter Bagehot, 'English Feeling Towards America', *The Economist*, 28 September 1861 (The 'weakening' was the secession of the Confederate States and the beginning of the American Civil War.)

We can now understand the answer of an American architect who was asked the difference between a federation and a union. 'Why,' he said, 'a federation is union with a top to it.'
Walter Bagehot, 'The American Constitution at the Present Crisis', *National Review*, October 1861

Humboldt justly ridiculed the 'maddest natural philosopher,' who compared the American continent to a female figure – long, thin, watery, and freezing at the 58th, the degrees being symbolic of the year at which woman grows old.
Richard Burton, *The City of the Saints*, 1861

Columbia, Columbia, to glory arise,
The queen of the world and the child of the skies!
Thy genius commands thee; with rapture behold,
While ages on ages thy splendors unfold.
Timothy Dwight, *Columbia*, 1861

Gigantic daughter of the West
We drink to thee across the flood. . . .
For art not thou of English blood?
Alfred Lord Tennyson, 'Hands All Round', first published in *The Examiner*, 1862

The traveller who desires to tell his experience of North America must write of people rather than of things.
Anthony Trollope, *North America*, 1862

America means opportunity, freedom, power.
Ralph Waldo Emerson, 'Public and Private Education', November 1864, *Uncollected Lectures*, 1932

While European genius is symbolised by some majestic Corinne crowned in the capitol in Rome, American genius finds its true type in the poor negro soldier lying in the trenches by the Potomac with his spelling book in one hand and his musket in the other.
Ralph Waldo Emerson, 'Books', December 1864, *Uncollected Lectures*, 1932

To attempt to describe any phase of American manners without frequent reference to the spittoon is impossible. It would be like the play of Hamlet with the part of Hamlet omitted.
G.A.Sala, *My Diary in America in the Midst of War*, 1865

She of the open soul and open door,
With room about her hearth for all mankind.
J.R. Lowell, *Commemoration Ode*, 1865

When you have made your picture of petrified New England life, left aground like a boulder near the banks of the Merrimac, does the Mississipian or the Minnesotian or the Pennsylvanian recognise it as American society? We are a nation of provinces, and each province claims to be the court.
John W. de Forest, 'The Great American Novel', *The Nation*, 9 January 1868.

For some reason or other, the European has rarely been able to see America except in caricature. . . . We do not ask to be sprinkled with rosewater, but may perhaps fairly protest againt being drenched with the rinsings of an unclean imagination.
J.R. Lowell, 'On a Certain Condescension in Foreigners', *Atlantic Monthly*, January 1869

Our society distributes itself into Barbarians, Philistines, and Populace; and America is just ourselves, with the Barbarians quite left out, and the Populace nearly.
Matthew Arnold, *Culture and Anarchy*, Preface, 1869

The ancients considered the pillars of Hercules the head of navigation and the end of the world. The information the ancients didn't have was very voluminous. Even the prophets wrote book after book and epistle after epistle, yet never once hinted at the existence of a great continent on our side of the water; yet they must have known it was there, I should think.
Mark Twain, *The Innocents Abroad*, 1869

I hate this shallow Americanism which hopes to get rich by credit, to get knowledge by raps on midnight tables, to learn the economy of the mind by phrenology, or skill without study, or mastery without apprenticeship.
Ralph Waldo Emerson, 'Success', *Society and Solitude*, 1870

America is American: that is incontestable.
Henry James, Letter to Grace Norton, 20 May 1870

And thou America,
Thy offspring towering e'er so high, yet higher thee above all towering,
With Victory on thy left, and at thy right hand Law;
Thou Union holding all, fusing, absorbing, tolerating all,
Thee, ever thee, I sing.
Walt Whitman, *Song of the Exposition*, 1871

The depravity of the business classes of our country is not less than has been supposed, but infinitely greater. The official services of America, national, state, and municipal, in all their branches and departments, except the judiciary, are saturated in corruption, bribery, falsehood, mal-administration; and the judiciary is tainted. The great cities reek with respectable as much as non-respectable robbery and scoundrelism. . . . I say that our New World democracy . . . is, so far, an almost complete failure.
Walt Whitman, *Democratic Vistas*, 1871

American life storms about us daily, and is slow to find a tongue.
Ralph Waldo Emerson, 'Letters and Social Aims', *Poetry and Imagination*, 1876

I once heard it argued – so low have we fallen – in my own college, I am sorry to own it, by Englishmen, that it was a good thing for us that we have lost the United States. There are some subjects on which there can be no argument, and to an Englishman this is one of them.
Cecil Rhodes, *A Draft of Some of my Ideas*, *c.*1877, in W.T. Stead, *Last Will . . . of C.J. Rhodes, etc.*, 1902

The only American institution which has yet won my respect is the rain. One sees it is a new country, they are so free with their water.
Robert Louis Stevenson, Letter to Sidney Colvin, August 1879

The United States – bounded on the north by the Aurora Borealis, on the south by the procession of the equinoxes, on the east by primeval chaos, and on the west by the Day of Judgement.
John Fiske, Toast at a dinner in Boston, before 1900

My country need not change her gown,
Her triple suit as sweet
As when 'twas cut at Lexington,
And first pronounced 'a fit.'

Great Britain disapproves, 'the stars';
Disparagement discreet, –
There's something in their attitude
That taunts her bayonet.
Emily Dickinson, *c.*1881

While travelling in America, never cease to bear the cardinal fact in mind, that this is a wholesale, and not a retail country.
G.A. Sala, *America Revisited*, 1882

I am lost in wonder and amazement. It is not a country, but a world. . . . The West I liked best. The people are stronger, fresher, saner than the rest. They are ready to be taught. The surroundings of nature have instilled in them a love of the beautiful, which but needs development and direction. The East I found a feeble reflex of Europe; in fact, I may say that I was in America for a month before I saw an American.
Oscar Wilde, quoted in *St Louis Daily Globe-Democrat*, under heading 'Speranza's Gifted Son', 26 February 1882

America is one long expectoration.
Oscar Wilde, Newspaper interview during his visit to America, 1882

It is the best country for a Rothschild I ever knew.
Matthew Arnold, Letter to his sister, 15 November 1883

Though I have kind invitations enough to visit America, I could not, even for a couple of months, live in a country so miserable as to possess no castles.
John Ruskin, *Praeterita*, 1885–9

. . . the capital defect of life over here: namely, that compared with life in England it is so uninteresting, so without savour and without depth.
Matthew Arnold, Letter to Sir Mountstuart Grant Duff, 29 July 1886

Our country has liberty without licence, and authority without despotism.

James Cardinal Gibbons, Address at Rome, 25 March 1887

English people are far more interested in American barbarism than they are in American civilization. . . . They have been known to prefer Buffaloes to Boston. Why should they not? The cities of America are inexpressibly tedious. The Bostonians take their learning too sadly: culture with them is an accomplishment rather than an atmosphere; their 'Hub' as they call it, is the paradise of prigs. Chicago is a sort of monster-shop, full of bustle and bores. Political life at Washington is like political life in a suburban vestry. Baltimore is amusing for a week, but Philadelphia is dreadfully provincial; and though one can dine in New York, one could not dwell there.

Oscar Wilde, 'The American Invasion', *Court and Society Review*, March 1887

America has never quite forgiven Europe for having been discovered somewhat earlier in history than itself

Oscar Wilde, 'The American Man', *Court and Society Review*, April 1887

The play of their institutions suggests . . . the image of a man in a suit of clothes which fits him to perfection, leaving all his movements unimpeded and easy; a suit of clothes loose where it ought to be loose, and sitting close where its sitting close is an advantage; a suit of clothes able, moreover, to adapt itself naturally to the wearer's growth, and to admit of all enlargements as they successively rise.

Matthew Arnold, *Civilization in the United States*, 1888

America is a Commonwealth of commonwealths, a Republic of republics, a State which, while one, is nevertheless composed of other States even more essential to its existence than it is to theirs.

James Bryce, *The American Commonwealth*, 1888

America excites an admiration which must be felt on the spot to be understood.

Ibid.

The settlers have generally moved along parallels of latitude, and we have therefore the curious result that the characteristics of the older states have propagated themselves westward in parallel lines, so that he who travels from the Atlantic to the Rocky Mountains will find fewer differences to note than he who, starting from Texas, travels north to Manitoba.

Ibid.

Centre of equal daughters, equal sons,
All, all alike endear'd, grown, ungrown, young or old,
Strong, ample, fair, enduring, capable, rich,
Perennial with the Earth, with Freedom, Law and
  Love,
A grand, sane, towering, seated Mother,
Chair'd in the adamant of Time.

Walt Whitman, *America*, 1888

I do not think America is a good place in which to be a genius. A genius can never expect to have a good time anywhere, if he is a genuine article, but America is about the last place in which life will be endurable at all for an inspired writer of any kind.

Samuel Butler, *Notebooks, c.* 1890

America's hatred of England is the hoop round the forty-four staves of the Union.

John Hay, Remark, 1890s, quoted
Rudyard Kipling, *Something of Myself*, 1937

Bismarck, when asked what was the most important fact in modern history, replied: 'The fact that North America speaks English.'

Sir Gurney Benham, *Benham's Book of Quotations*, 1948

Republic of the West,
  Enlightened, free, sublime,
Unquestionably best
  Production of our time.

The telephone is thine,
  And thine the Pullman car,
The caucus, the divine
  Intense electric star.

To thee we likewise owe
  The venerable names
Of Edgar Allan Poe
  And Mr Henry James.

In short it's due to thee
  Thou kind of Western star,
That we have come to be
  Precisely what we are.

But every now and then,
  It cannot be denied,
You breed a kind of men
  Who are not dignified,

Or courteous or refined,
  Benevolent or wise,
Or gifted with a mind
  Beyond the common size,

Or notable for tact,
  Agreeable to me,
Or anything, in fact,
  That people ought to be.

James Kenneth Stephen, *On a Rhine Steamer*, 1891

The only place in Ireland that a man can make his fortune in is in America.

Irish Bull quoted by Marie Ann de Bovet, *Three Months Tour in Ireland*, 1891

In America the President reigns for four years, and Journalism governs for ever and ever.

Oscar Wilde, *The Soul of Man under Socialism*, 1891

*Perhaps after all America never has been discovered. . . . I myself would say that it had merely been detected.

Oscar Wilde, *The Picture of Dorian Gray*, 1891

Of course America had often been discovered before, but it had always been hushed up.

Oscar Wilde, attrib.

Wide open and unguarded stand our gates,
And through them presses a wild, motley throng –
Men from the Volga and the Tartar steppes,
Featureless faces from the Huang-Ho,
Malayan, Scythian, Teuton, Kelt and Slav,
Flying the Old World's poverty and scorn;
These bringing with them unknown Gods and rites,
Those, tiger passions here to stretch their claws.
In street and alley, what strange tongues are these,
Accents of menace alien to our air,
Voices that once the Tower of Babel knew!
O Liberty, white Goddess! Is it well
To leave the gates unguarded?

Thomas Bailey Aldrich, *The Unguarded Gates*, 1892

America! America!
God shed His grace on thee
And crown thy good with brotherhood
From sea to shining sea!

Katherine Lee Bates, *America the Beautiful*, 1893

Lady Caroline: There are a great many things you haven't got in America, I am told, Miss Worsley. They say you have no ruins, and no curiosities.
Mrs Allonby: What nonsense! They have their mothers and their manners.

Oscar Wilde, *A Woman of No Importance*, 1892

*It was wonderful to find America, but it would have been more wonderful to miss it.

Mark Twain, *Pudd'nhead Wilson's Calendar*, 1897

*It is by the goodness of God that in our country we have those three unspeakably precious things: freedom of speech, freedom of conscience, and the prudence never to practise either of them.

Mark Twain, 'Pudd'nhead Wilson's New Calendar', in *More Tramps Abroad*, 1897

and the Philippines, 1898

'I have already,' a troubled American said when the Philippines were delivered into his hands, 'more country than I can love.'

C.E. Montague, *The Right Place*, 1924

My country, 'tis of thee
Sweet land of felony
Of thee I sing
Land where my father fried
Young witches and applied
Whips to the Quaker's hide
And made him spring.

Ambrose Bierce, quoted in Richard O'Connor, *Ambrose Bierce*, 1968

A great broad blackness with two or three small points of light struggling and flickering in the universal black of ignorance, crudity, conceit, tobacco-chewing, ill-dressing, unmannerly manners and general barbarity.

Ambrose Bierce, quoted in W. Blair and Hamlin Hill (eds), *America's Humor*, 1978

Twentieth Century

The great advantage, it seems to me, that America possesses over the Old World, is its material and moral plasticity. Even among the giant structures of this city, one feels that there is nothing rigid, nothing oppressive, nothing inaccessible to the influence of changing conditions. If the buildings are Cyclopean, so is the race that reared them. The material world seems as clay on the potter's wheel, visibly taking on the impress of the human spirit; and the human spirit, as embodied in this superbly vital people, seems to be visibly thrilling to all the forces of civilisation.

William Archer, *America Today*, 1900

The United States is a self-conscious, clearly defined, and heroically vindicated idea, in whose further vindication the whole world is concerned . . . .The United States of America, let us say, is a rehearsal for the United States of Europe, nay, of the world.

Ibid.

*'Th' enthusyasm iv this counthry, Hinnissy, always makes me think iv a bonfire on an ice-floe. It burns bright so long as ye feed it, an' it looks good, but it don't take hold, somehow, on th' ice.'

Finley Peter Dunne, *Mr Dooley's Philosophy*, 1900

*Behold th' land iv freedom, where ivry man's as good as ivry other man, on'y th' other man don't know it.

Finley Peter Dunne, 'The New York Custom House', *Mr Dooley's Opinions*, 1901

My ardours for emprize nigh lost
Since life has bared its bones to me,
I shrink to seek a modern coast
Whose riper times have yet to be;

Where the new regions claim them free
From that long drip of human tears
Which peoples old in tragedy
Have left upon the centuried years.

For, winning in these ancient lands,
Enchased and lettered as a tomb,
And scored with prints of perished hands,
And chronicled with dates of doom,
Though my own Being bear no bloom
I trace the lives such scenes enshrine.
Give past exemplars present room,
And their experience count as mine.

Thomas Hardy, 'On an Invitation to the United States', *Poems of Past and Present*, 1901

I am still unconvinced about America, & don't believe an unfêted pilgrim would find it so pleasant. If one has escaped from a monster, one does not like to think it a painted monster, & so I still believe that it does breathe flame!

Logan Pearsall Smith, Letter to Mrs Berenson, 17 January 1903

I was thinking this morning that the United States Republic has substituted an aristocracy of commercial cleverness for the old forms of aristocracy. It is said that every man has an equal chance in the U.S., and he has. But commercial aptitude, with as little honesty as possible, is the only thing that will be of use to him. And everything is so arranged that the 'risen' can trample on those who have not risen.

Arnold Bennett, *Journal*, 5 November 1904

I found my native land, after so many years, interesting, formidable, fearsome, and fatiguing, and much more difficult to see and deal with in any extended and various way than I had supposed. . . . It is an extraordinary world, an altogether huge 'proposition', as they say there, giving one, I think, an immense impression of material and political power; but almost cruelly charmless in effect, and calculated to make one crouch, ever afterwards, as cravenly as possible, at Lamb House, Rye.

Henry James, Letter to Paul Harvey, Rye, 11 March 1906

America has a new delicacy, a coarse, rank refinement.

G.K. Chesterton, *Charles Dickens*, 1906

Every time Europe looks across the Atlantic to see the American eagle, it observes only the rear end of an ostrich.

H.G. Wells, *America*, 1907

There, to stay in any American hotel is to suffer penance for sin unrepented of – and the punishment is fully adequate.

F.T. Bullen, *Advance Australasia*, 1907

As for America, it is the ideal fruit of all our youthful hopes and reforms. Everybody is fairly decent, respectable, domestic, bourgeois, middle-class, and tiresome. There is absolutely nothing to revile except that it's a bore.

Enfin! we made it so.

Henry Adams, Letter to Charles Milnes Gaskell, 17 December 1908

The American Constitution, one of the few modern political documents drawn up by men who were forced by the sternest circumstances to think out what they really had to face, instead of chopping logic in a university class-room.

G. Bernard Shaw, Preface to *Getting Married*, 1908

*America is God's Crucible, the great Melting-Pot where all the races of Europe are meeting and re-forming! Here you stand, good folk, think I, when I see them at Ellis Island, here you stand in your fifty groups, with your fifty languages and histories, and your fifty blood hatreds and rivalries. But you won't be long like that brothers, for these are the fires of God you've come to – these are the fires of God. A fig for your feuds and vendettas! Germans and Frenchmen, Irishmen and Englishmen, Jews and Russians – into the Crucible with you all! God is making the American. . . .

No, the real American has not yet arrived. He is only in the Crucible, I tell you – he will be the fusion of all races, perhaps the coming superman.

Israel Zangwill, *The Melting Pot*, 1908

But the glory of the present is to make the future free,
We love our land for what she is, and what she is to be.

Oh, it's home again and home again, America for me!
I want a ship that's westward bound to plough the
rolling sea
To the blessed Land of Room Enough beyond the
ocean bars
Where the air is full of sunlight and the flag is full of
stars.

Henry Van Dyke, *America for Me*, June 1909

What this country needs – what every country needs occasionally – is a good hard bloody war to revive the vice of patriotism on which its existence as a nation depends.

Ambrose Bierce, Letter, 15 February 1911

I think of American cities as enormous agglomerations in whose inmost dark recesses innumerable elevators are constantly ascending and descending, like the angels of the ladder.

Arnold Bennett, *Those United States*, 1912

America was established not to create wealth but to

realize a vision, to realize an ideal – to discover and maintain liberty among men.

Woodrow Wilson, Address, Chicago, 12 February 1912

I remember somebody once saying to me a long time ago, that the Americans had attained to luxury by jumping over comfort. I think this is true.

Maurice Baring, *Round the World in Any Number of Days*, 1913

America is a tune. It must be sung together.

Gerald Stanley Lee, *Crowds*, 1913

America is a young country with an old mentality

George Santayana, *Winds of Doctrine: Studies on Contemporary Opinion*, 1913

Your newspapers are too big, and your lavatory paper's too small.

Ernest Bevin, on his first visit to the USA in 1915, when asked for his views on America by newsmen, quoted in Alistair Horne, *Canada and the Canadians*, 1961

America lives in the heart of every man everywhere, who wishes to find a region where he will be free to work out his destiny as he chooses.

Woodrow Wilson, Speech, New York, 17 May 1915

Our whole duty, for the present, at any rate, is summed up in the motto America first.

Woodrow Wilson, Speech, New York, 20 April 1915

'A country without conversation,' said a philosopher. 'The big land has a big heart,' wrote a kindly scholar; and by the same post from another critic, 'that land of crushing hospitality!' 'It's hell, but it's fine,' an artist told me. 'El Cuspidorado,' remarked an Oxford man brilliantly. But one wiser than all the rest wrote, 'Think gently of the Americans. They are so very young; and so very anxious to appear grown up; and so very lovable.' This was more generous than the unvarying comment of ordinary English friends when they heard of my purpose, 'My God!' And it was more precise than those nineteen several Americans, to each of whom I said, 'I am going to visit America,' and each of whom replied, after long reflection, 'Wal! it's a great country.'

Rupert Brooke, *Letters from America*, 1916

Wake up America!

Augustus P. Gardner, Speech, 16 October 1916

The United States is like a gigantic boiler. Once the fire is lighted under it, there is no limit to the power it can generate.

Sir Edward Grey, *c.*1916 quoted in Christopher Hassall, *Edward Marsh*, 1954

I may get killed for America – but I'm going to die for myself.

F. Scott Fitzgerald, Letter to Mrs Richard Taylor, 10 June 1917

America . . . is the prize amateur nation of the world. Germany is the prize professional nation.

Woodrow Wilson, Speech to Officers of the Fleet, August 1917

I tell you, fellow citizens, that the war was won by the American spirit. . . . You know what one of our American wits said, that it took only half as long to train an American army as any other, because you only had to train them to go one way.

Woodrow Wilson, Speech, Kansas City, 6 September 1919

Sometimes people call me an idealist. Well that is the way I know I am an American. America is the only idealistic nation in the world.

Woodrow Wilson, Address at Sioux Falls, 8 September 1919

White America assumes, inevitably and frighteningly, the Red Indian nature – little by little.

D.H. Lawrence, Letter to E.H. and Achsah Brewster, May 1921

This America is an amazing place – I don't really believe that it exists; or rather I feel that it will burst one day like a great bubble, & leave no trace behind it. I can't see that it has any meaning, anything really to show in the final account – no thought, no literature, no style, no education. But I must say I do like the ice-cream.

Logan Pearsall Smith, Letter to James Whitall, 7 November 1921

If material life could be made perfect, as (in a very small way) it was perhaps for a moment among the Greeks, would not that of itself be a most admirable achievement? . . . And possibly on that basis of perfected material life, a new art and philosophy would grow unawares, not similar to what we call by those names, but having the same relation to the life beneath which art and philosophy amongst us ought to have had, but never had. You see, I am content to let the past bury its dead. It does not seem to me that we can impose on America the task of imitating Europe.

George Santayana, Letter to Logan Pearsall Smith, 1921

You are right in your impression that a number of persons are urging me to come to the United States. But why on earth do you call them my friends?

G. Bernard Shaw, Letter to Oswald Garrison Villard, 4 August 1921

Oh, America, the sun sets in you.
Are you the grave of our day?

D.H. Lawrence, 'The Evening Land', 1922, *Birds Beasts and Flowers*, 1923

The glorious bards of Massachusetts seem
To want to make New Hampshire people over
They taunt the lofty land with little men.
I don't know what to say about the people.
For art's sake one could almost wish them worse
Rather than better. How are we to write
The Russian novel in America
As long as life goes so unterribly?
There is the pinch from which our only outcry
In literature to date is heard to come.
We get what little misery we can
Out of not having cause for misery.
It makes the guild of novel writers sick
To be expected to be Dostoievskis
On nothing worse than too much luck and comfort.

Robert Frost, *New Hampshire*, 1923

'Tis not too late to build our young land right,
Cleaner than Holland, courtlier than Japan,
Devout like early Rome, with hearths like hers.
Hearths that will recreate the breed called man.

Vachel Lindsay, 'To Reformers in Despair', *Collected Poems*, 1923

Here the general average of intelligence, of knowledge, of competence, of integrity, of self-respect, of honour, is so low that any man who knows his trade, does not fear ghosts, has read fifty good books, and practices the common decencies, stands out as brilliantly as a wart on a bald head, and is thrown willy nilly into a meager and exclusive aristocracy. And here, more than anywhere else that I know or have heard of, the daily panorama of human existence, of private and communal folly – the unending procession of governmental extortions and chicaneries, of commercial brigandages and throat-slittings, of theological buffooneries, of aesthetic ribaldries, of legal swindles, and harlotries, of miscellaneous rogueries, villainies, imbecilities, grotesqueries, and extravagancies, – is so inordinately gross and preposterous, so perfectly brought up to the highest conceivable amperage, so steadily enriched with an almost fabulous daring and originality, that only the man who was born with a petrified diaphragm can fail to laugh himself to sleep every night, and to awake every morning with all the eager unflagging expectation of a Sunday school superintendent touring the Paris peep-shows.

H.L. Mencken, 'On Being an American', in *Prejudices*, Third Series, 1923

The United States to my eye is incomparably the greatest show on earth. It is a show which avoids diligently all the kinds of clowning which tire me most quickly – for example royal ceremonials, the tedious hocus pocus of *haut politique*, the taking of politics seriously – and lays chief stress upon the kinds which delight me unceasingly – for example, the ribald combats of demagogues, the exquisitely ingenious operations of master rogues, the pursuit of witches and heretics, the desperate struggles of inferior men to claw their way into Heaven. . . . Human enterprises which, in all other Christian countries, are resigned despairingly to an incurable dullness – things that seem devoid of exhilarating amusement by their very nature – are here lifted to such vast heights of buffoonery that contemplating them strains the midriff almost to breaking.

Ibid.

Nowhere in the world is superiority more easily attained, or more eagerly admitted. The chief business of the nation, as a nation, is the setting up of heroes, mainly bogus.

Ibid.

America is still a government of the naive, by the naive, and for the naive. He who does not know this, nor relish it, has no inkling of the nature of his country.

Christopher Morley, *Inward Ho!*, 1923

It is impossible to read in America, except in the train, because of the telephone. Everyone has a telephone, and it rings all day and most of the night. This makes conversation, thinking, and reading out of the question, and accordingly these activities are somewhat neglected.

Bertrand Russell, *Impressions of America*, 1924

The business of America is business.

Calvin Coolidge, Speech before the Society of American Newspaper Editors, 17 January 1925

. . . America itself, the still unravished bride of silences. The great continent, its bitterness, its brackish quality, its vast glamour, its strange cruelty. Find this, Americans and get it into your bones. The powerful, unyielding breath of America, which Columbus sniffed, even in Europe, and which sent the Conquistadores mad. National America is a gruesome sort of fantasy. But the unvarnished *local* America still waits vast and virgin as ever, though in process of being murdered. . . .

A man in America can only *begin* to be American. After five hundred years there are no *racial* white Americans. They are only national, woebegone, or strident. After five hundred years more there may be the developing nucleus of a true American race. If only men, some few, trust the American passion that is in them, and pledge themselves to it.

But the passion is not national. No man who doesn't feel the last anguish of tragedy – *and beyond that* – will ever know America, or begin, even at the beginning's beginning, to be American.

D.H. Lawrence, Review of *In the American Grain* by William Carlos Williams, *Nation*, 14 April 1926, and *Phoenix*, 1936

Q: If you find so much that is unworthy of reverence in the United States, then why do you live here?
A: Why do men go to zoos?

H.L. Mencken, 'Catechism', in *Prejudices*, Fifth Series, 1926

"next to of course god america i
love you land of the pilgrims' and so forth oh
say can you see by the dawn's early my
country 'tis of centuries come and go
and are no more what of it we should worry
in every language even deafanddumb
thy sons acclaim your glorious name by gorry
by jing by gee by gosh by gum
why talk of beauty what could be more beautiful than these heroic happy dead
who rushed like lions to the roaring slaughter
they did not stop to think they died instead
then shall the voice of liberty be mute?"

He spoke. And drank rapidly a glass of water

e.e.cummings, 'next to of course god america i' – *is 5*, 1926

We have all learnt America in picture theatres; and it is distinctly unfortunate that we have learnt it wrong.

Philip Guedalla, *Conquistador*, 1927

American muse, whose strong and diverse heart
So many men have tried to understand
But only made it smaller with their art
Because you are as various as your land.

Stephen Vincent Benét, 'Invocation', *John Brown's Body*, 1928

The American system of rugged individualism.

Herbert Clark Hoover, Speech, New York City, 22 October 1928; also in *The New Day*, 1934

America is fundamentally the land of the overrated child.

Count Hermann Keyserling, *America Set Free*, 1929

In America . . . where law and custom alike are based upon the dreams of spinsters.

Bertrand Russell, *Marriage and Morals*, 1929

I regard America as peculiarly indifferent to fact.

Bertrand Russell, Letter, 3 January 1930, in *America*, 1973

We shall not make Britain's mistake. Too wise to try to govern the world, we shall merely own it. Nothing can stop us.

Ludwell Denny, *America Conquers Britain*, 1930

A Bad Thing: America was thus clearly top nation, and History came to a.

W.C. Sellar and R.J. Yeatman, *1066 and All That*, 1930

The most amazing feature of American life is its boundless publicity. Everybody has to meet everybody, and they even seem to enjoy this enormity. To a central European such as I am, this American publicity of life, the lack of distance between people, the absence of hedges or fences round the gardens, the belief in popularity, the gossip columns of the newspapers, the open doors in the houses (one can look from the street right through the sitting-room and the adjoining bedroom into the backyard and beyond), the defencelessness of the individual against the onslaught of the press, all this is more than disgusting, it is positively terrifying. You are immediately swallowed by a hot and all-engulfing wave of desirousness and emotional incontinence. You are simply reduced to a particle in the mass, with no other hope or expectation than the illusory goals of an eager and excited collectivity. You just swim for life, that's all. You feel free – that's the queerest thing – yet the collective movement grips you faster than any old gnarled roots in European soil would have done. Even your head gets immersed. There is a peculiar lack of restraint about the emotions of an American collectivity. You see it in the eagerness and in the bustle of everyday life, in all sorts of enthusiasm, in orgiastic sectarian outbursts, in the violence of public admiration and opprobrium. The overwhelming influence of collective emotions spreads into everything. If it were possible, everything would be done collectively, because there seems to be an astonishingly feeble resistance to collective influences.

C.G. Jung, *The Complications of American Psychology*, 1930

Have you ever compared the skyline of New York or any great American city with that of a Pueblo like Taos? And did you see how the houses pile up to towers towards the centre? Without conscious imitation the American unconsciously fills out the spectral outline of the Red Man's mind and temperament

Ibid.

Intellectually I know that America is no better than any other country; emotionally I know she is better than every other country.

Sinclair Lewis, Interview in Berlin, 29 December 1930

The European traveller in America is struck by two peculiarities: first, the extreme similarity of outlook in all parts of the U.S. (except the old South), and second the passionate desire of each locality to prove that it is peculiar and different from every other. The second of these is, of course, the cause of the first . . . .

When one considers the difference between a Norwegian and a Sicilian, and compares it with the lack of difference between a man from say, North Dakota and a man from Southern California, one realises the immense revolution in human affairs which has been brought about by man's becoming the master instead of the slave of his physical environment. Norway and Sicily both have ancient traditions; they had pre-Christian religions embodying man's reactions to the climate and when Christianity came, it inevitably took very different forms in the two countries. The Norwegian feared ice and snow; the Sicilian feared lava and earthquakes. Hell was invented in a Southern climate; if it had been invented in Norway it would have been cold. But neither in South Dakota nor in Southern California is Hell a climatic condition; in both it is a stringency in the money market. This illustrates the unimportance of climate in modern life.

Bertrand Russell, 'Modern Homogeneity', 1930, in *In Praise of Idleness and Other Essays*, 1935

God bless America.

Irving Berlin, Title of song, first sung in public by Kate Smith, in broadcast on Armistice Day, 11 November 1930

I have fallen in love with American names,
The sharp names that never get fat,
The snakeskin titles of mining claims,
The plumed war-bonnet of Medicine Hat,
Tucson and Deadwood and Lost Mule Flat.

Seine and Piave are silver spoons,
But the spoonbowl-metal is thin and worn,
There are English counties like hunting-tunes
Played on the keys of a postboy's horn,
But I will remember where I was born.

I will remember Carquinez Straits,
Little French Lick and Lundy's Lane,
The Yankee ships and the Yankee dates
And the bullet-towns of Calamity Jane.
I will remember Skunktown Plain.

I will fall in love with a Salem tree
And a rawhide quirt from Santa Cruz,
I will get me a bottle of Boston sea
And a blue-gum nigger to sing me blues.
I am tired of loving a foreign muse.

Rue des Martyrs and Bleeding-Heart-Yard,
Senlis, Pisa, and Blindman's Oast
It is a magic ghost you guard
But I am sick for a newer ghost,
Hamburg, Spartanburg, Painted Post . . .

I shall not rest quiet in Montparnasse.
I shall not lie easy at Winchelsea.
You may bury my body in Sussex grass,
You may bury my tongue at Champmedy.
I shall not be there. I shall rise and pass.
Bury my heart at Wounded Knee.

Stephen Vincent Benét, *American Names*, 1931

I feel that you are justified in looking into the future with true assurance, because you have a mode of living in which we find the joy of life and the joy of work harmoniously combined. Added to this is the spirit of ambition which pervades your very being, and seems to make the day's work like a happy child at play.

Albert Einstein, *New Year's Greeting*, 1931

*America is the last abode of romance and other medieval phenomena.

Eric Linklater, *Juan in America*, 1931

For the most part the climate throughout the continent seems to have been one which tended to produce a high nervous tension in the living beings subjected to it, even the savages, not only from its sudden changes, but from some quality which we do not know. . . . The Red Indians' nervous systems were unstable and they were of a markedly hysterical make-up, peculiarly susceptible to suggestion.

James Truslow Adams, *The Epic of America*, 1931

God's Own Country (Western Division) as opposed to God's Own Country (England).

Ford Madox Ford, *Return to Yesterday*, 1932

I claim that this country has been built by speculation, and further progress must be made in that line.

Richard Whitney, Statement to the Senate Banking Committee, *c.*1932

I sometimes think that the saving grace of America lies in the fact that the overwhelming majority of Americans are possessed of two great qualities – a sense of humor and a sense of proportion.

Franklin D. Roosevelt, Address in Savannah, Georgia, 18 November 1933

Self-help and Self-control are the essence of the American tradition.

Franklin D. Roosevelt, State of the Union Message, 3 January 1934

The more the traveller sees of this continent . . . the less he succeeds in understanding it. But there is this consolation. The more he sees of it, the more he ought to understand why he cannot understand it.

A.G. Macdonell, *A Visit to America*, 1935

The Hygienic Theory of the United States appears to be based on a remarkable notion. Anyone who can afford to buy a first-class ticket is automatically assumed to be free from all contagious infection.

Ibid.

The truth of the matter is, and I record it with misgiving, reluctance, and a sense of imminent calamity, that the American does not like strangers to say that America is a new country. He himself will say it, over and over again, but it is as much as your life is worth to say it yourself. It is risky even to agree with him when he says it. In fact it is safer either to say nothing at all in answer to him, or to confine yourself to a muttered reference to Karlsefne or Leif Ericson.

It is a peculiar business, the American attitude to Antiquity. Of all the citizens of the world there is no one so alive as the American to the values of modernity, so fertile in experiment, so feverish in the search for something new. There is nothing, from Architecture to Contract Bridge, from the Immortality of the Soul to the Ventilation of Railroad-Cars, from Golf to God that he does not pounce upon and examine critically to see if it cannot be improved. And then, having pulled it to pieces, mastered its fundamental theory, and reassembled it in a novel and efficient design, he laments bitterly because it is not old

Ibid.

America is the greatest of opportunities and the worst of influences.

George Santayana, *The Last Puritan*, 1935

In the United States there is more space where nobody is than where anybody is. That is what makes America what it is.

Gertrude Stein, *The Geographical History of America*, 1936

Europe makes heroes of the scrapped. America scraps her heroes.

Shane Leslie, *American Wonderland*, 1936

The American sign of civic progress is to tear down the familiar and erect the monstrous.

Ibid.

The most characteristic thing in America, mechanical America, is that it can make poetry out of material things. America's poetry is not in literature, but in architecture.

Oliver St John Gogarty, *As I Was Going Down Sackville Street*, 1937

Going South always seems to me rather desolate and fatal and uneasy. This is no exception. Going North is a safe dull feeling.

F. Scott Fitzgerald, Letter to Ernest Hemingway (on a train, heading south), 5 June 1937

The United States is the greatest single achievement of European civilization.

R.B. Mowat, *The United States of America*, 1938

France was a land, England was a people, but America, having about it still the quality of the idea, was harder to utter – it was the graves at Shiloh, and the tired, drawn, nervous faces of its great men, and the country boys dying in the Argonne for a phrase that was empty before their bodies withered. It was a willingness of the heart.

F. Scott Fitzgerald, *The Crack-Up*, 1945 (pre 1940)

The Arsenal of Democracy.

This phrase was first used by Jean Monnet, in conversation with Justice Felix Frankfurter, who was so taken with it that he persuaded Monnet not to use it any more, but rather to let the President use it, which Roosevelt did in 1940

In England, if something goes wrong – say, if one finds a skunk in the garden – he writes to the family solicitor, who proceeds to take the proper measures; whereas in America, you telephone the fire department. Each satisfies a characteristic need; in the English, love of order, and legalistic procedure; and here in America what you like is something vivid, and red, and swift.

Alfred North Whitehead, Remark, 30 August 1941, *Dialogues of A.N. Whitehead as Recorded by Lucien Price*, 1954

And stylites America, squatting on the poles
Of the rugged or the dogged individual, is lost
Worse than all whales in water or lost souls.
Liberty has nothing to do with a good post.
The terrible Pharaohs gibber on the peaks of success
And John Brown inhabits the concept of freedom:
Liberty usually leads to a tomb of duress.

Her prison is the future. This, she cannot escape,
The immense feminine who wears her heart on her
sleeve,
The negro polishing her shoes, and on the nape
Of her gold neck Capital riding. Who will believe
That all tomorrows grow in the grit of her hand
And God supplicates at her knee for pardon
Because his jokes are more than she can understand?

Thus rocked to sleep between Pacific and Atlantic
The hundred and thirty million, simple as children,
Resting their heads on the Rockies and their frantic
Anxiety on inefficient education, widen
The innocent mouth of the world to take their kiss,
As primitive as liberals and passionate anthropoids,
It is this that the real inheritor of the world is.

George Barker, *Third American Ode*, 1941

The Land was ours before we were the land's,
She was our land more than a hundred years
Before we were her people. She was ours
In Massachusetts, in Virginia,
But we were England's still colonials,

Possessing what we still were unpossessed by,
Possessed by what we now no more possessed.
Something we were withholding made us weak
Until we found out that it was ourselves
We were withholding from our land of living,
And forthwith found salvation in surrender.
Such as we were we gave ourselves outright
(The deed of gift was many deeds of war)
To the land vaguely realising westward
But still unstoried, artless, unenhanced
Such as she was, such as she would become.

Robert Frost, 'The Gift Outright', *A Witness Tree*, 1942

I like it here, just because it is the Great Void where you have to balance without handholds.

W.H. Auden, Letter to Naomi Mitchison, 1942 – quoted in Charles Osborne, *W.H. Auden*, 1980

The combination of a hatred of war and militarism with an innocent delight in playing soldiers is one of the apparent contradictions of American life that one has to accept.

D.W. Brogan, *The American Character*, 1944

America is no place for an artist: to be an artist is to be a moral leper, an economic misfit, a social liability. A corn-fed hog enjoys a better life than a creative writer, painter or musician. To be a rabbit is better still.

Henry Miller, *The Air-conditioned Nightmare*, 1945

I have never been able to look upon America as young and vital, but rather as prematurely old, as a fruit which rotted before it had a chance to ripen. The word which gives the key to the national vice is waste.

Ibid.

The United States is a country unique in the world because it was populated not merely by people who live in it by the accident of birth, but by those who willed to come here.

John Gunther, *Inside U.S.A.*, 1947

The forests of America, however slighted by man, must have been a great delight to God, because they were the best He ever planted.

John Muir, quoted *ibid.*

I went a hundred miles north into the Berkshires. It was April. . . . Was I in England? Almost, but not quite. That was again and again to be my sensation, and in the Arizona desert I was to feel that I was almost but not quite in India, and in the Yosemite valley that it was not quite Switzerland. America is always throwing out these old-world hints, and then withdrawing them in favour of America.

E.M. Forster, 'The United States', 1947, in *Two Cheers for Democracy*, 1951

America is rather like life. You can usually find in it what you look for. . . . It will probably be interesting, and it is sure to be large.

Ibid.

Count Hermann Keyserling once said truly that the greatest American superstition was belief in facts.

John Gunther, *Inside U.S.A.*, 1947

Here, in the first gaunt years of the Atomic Age, lies a country, a continental mass, more favoured by man and nature than any other in history, now for the first time attempting with somewhat faltering steps to justify its new station as a mature world power. Here, beyond anything else on the whole earth, is a country blessed by an ideal geography and almost perfect natural frontiers, by incalculable bulk and wealth and variety and vitality, by a unique and indeed unexampled heritage in democratic ideas and principles – and a country deliberately founded on a good idea.

Ibid.

There are no generalizations in American politics that vested selfishness cannot cut through.

Ibid.

In the law courts, they have to prove *me* wrong!

Central European refugee, quoted *ibid.*

It is all part of the American tragedy – that, in the one remaining country where necessities are cheap, where a room and food and wine and clothes and cigarettes and travel are within everyone's reach, to be poor is still disgraceful. The American way of life is one of the most effective the world has known, but about the end of life Americans are more in the dark than any people since the Gauls of Tacitus.

Cyril Connolly, 'American Injection', 1947, in *Ideas and Places*, 1953

The virtue of American civilization is that it is unmaterialistic. . . . The strongest argument for the un-materialistic character of American life is the fact that we tolerate conditions that are, from a materialistic point of view, intolerable. What the foreigner finds most objectionable in American life is its lack of basic comfort. No nation with any sense of material well-being would endure the food we eat, the cramped apartments we live in, the noise, the traffic, the crowded subways and buses. American life, in large cities at any rate, is a perpetual assault on the senses and the nerves: it is out of asceticism, out of unworldliness precisely, that we bear it.

Mary McCarthy, 'America the Beautiful', September 1947, in *On the Contrary*, 1962

The real English social revolution occurred, not in England, but in America; and . . . the United States stands to England in the relation of England's own modern history, as if the first French Republic had been detached and set up in another country, where it was able to prosper in a material way far more than it could have done at home, while the old regime in France continued fighting the old kind of wars with its neighbours and adapting itself, as it had to, to moderate industrial development.

Edmund Wilson, *Europe without Baedeker*, 1947

*That impersonal insensitive friendliness that takes the place of ceremony in that land of waifs and strays.

Evelyn Waugh, *The Loved One*, 1948

One happy afternoon when God was feeling good He sat down and thought up a beautiful country, and He called it the U.S.A.

From the film *Forever in Love*, quoted by James Agate, *Ego 9*, 1948

In American justice the suspect is considered guilty until he is proved innocent, but in society the opposite applies.

Cecil Beaton, *Portrait of New York*, 1948

If we ever pass out as a great nation, we ought to put on our tombstone 'America died of the delusion that she had moral leadership.'

Will Rogers, *The Autobiography of Will Rogers*, 1949

In America nature is autocratic, saying 'I am not arguing, I am telling you.'

Erik H. Erikson, *Childhood and Society*, 1950

Whatever America hopes to bring to pass in the world must first come to pass in the heart of America.

Dwight D. Eisenhower, Inaugural Address, 20 January 1953

America is a large friendly dog in a small room. Every time it wags its tail it knocks over a chair.

Arnold Toynbee, *News Summaries*, 14 July 1954

Baseball is an allegorical play about America, a poetic, complex and subtle play of courage, fear, good luck, mistakes, patience about fate and sober self-esteem (batting average). It is impossible to understand America without a thorough knowledge of baseball.

Saul Steinberg, 'Chronology', 1954, in Harold Rosenberg, *Saul Steinberg*, 1978

More and more in American restaurants, advertising has taken over the menu. You are sold on the meal before you have even started.

Cecil Beaton, *It Gives Me Great Pleasure*, 1955

Missing lunch in America is not like missing lunch in France.

Norman Krasna, Letter to Groucho Marx, 3 August 1955

America, which has the most glorious present still existing in the world today, hardly stops to enjoy it, in her insatiable appetite for the future.

Anne Morrow Lindbergh, 'The Beach at My Back', in *Gift from the Sea*, 1955

. . . Supposing someone would ask him why he came to America, he would reply: 'To continue my life-long search for naked women in wet mackintoshes.'

J.M. Brinnin, quoting Dylan Thomas, in *Dylan Thomas in America*, 1956 (of 1950)

'I guess that's the way with Americans,' he remarked. 'If it's big, it's gotta be good; and if it's only good, you gotta make it bigger.'

James Morris, *Coast to Coast*, 1956

Blue go up & blue go down
to light the lights of Dollartown.

Nebuchadnezzar had it so good?
wink the lights of Hollywood.

I never think, I have so many things,
flash the lights of Palm Springs. . . .

I have the blind staggers
call the lights of Niagara.

We shall die in a palace
shout the black lights of Dallas.

I couldn't care less, my favorite son,
fritter the lights of Washington. . . .

I cannot quite focus
cry the lights of Las Vegas.

I am a maid of shots & pills
swivel the lights of Beverly Hills. . . .

I am all satisfied love & chalk
mutter the great lights of New York. . . .

Here comes a scandal to light you to bed.
Here comes a cropper. That's what I said.

John Berryman, 'American Lights Seen from Off Abroad', in *His Thoughts Made Pockets as the Plane Buckt*, 1958

The family which takes its mauve and cerise, air-conditioned, power-steered and power-braked automobile out for a tour passes through cities that are badly paved, made hideous by litter, blighted buildings, billboards and posts for wires that should long since have been put underground. They pass on into a countryside that has been rendered largely invisible by commercial art. . . . They picnic on exquisitely packaged food from a portable icebox by a polluted stream and go on to spend the night at a park which is a menace to public health and morals. Just before dozing off on an air mattress, beneath a nylon tent, amid the stench of decaying refuse, they may reflect vaguely on the curious unevenness of their blessings. Is this, indeed, the American genius?

John Kenneth Galbraith, *The Affluent Society*, 1958

*America is so big, and everyone is working, digging, bulldozing, trucking, loading, and so on, and I guess the sufferers suffer at the same rate.

Saul Bellow, *Henderson the Rain King*, 1959

Walking . . . is an un-American activity.

Lord Kinross, *The Innocents at Home*, 1959

America as I travelled across it became increasingly a United States of Suburbia.

Ibid.

When I first arrived in the States a shrewd American said to me: 'A European coming to America for the first time, should skip New York and fly direct to Kansas. Start from the Middle. The East will only mislead you.'

Ibid.

We live in a welfare state which seeks to put a floor below which no one sinks, but builds no ceiling to prevent man from rising.

Henry Cabot Lodge Jr, *News Reports*, 18 September 1959

My fellow Americans: ask not what your country can do for you, ask what you can do for your country. My fellow citizens of the world: ask not what America can do for you, but what together we can do for the freedom of man.

John Fitzgerald Kennedy, Inaugural Address, 20 January 1961

America is a hurricane, and the only people who do not hear the sound are those fortunate if incredibly stupid and smug White Protestants who live in the centre, in the serene eye of the big wind.

Norman Mailer, *Advertisements for Myself*, 1961

The happy ending is our national belief.

Mary McCarthy, 'America the Beautiful: The Humanist in the Bathtub', in *On the Contrary*, 1961

We are a nation of twenty million bathrooms, with a humanist in every tub.

Ibid.

This monster of a land, this mightiest of nations, this spawn of the future, turns out to be the macrocosm of microcosm me. . . . From start to finish I found no strangers. . . . For all of our enormous geographic range, for all of our sectionalism, for all our interwoven breeds drawn from every part of the ethnic world, we are a nation, a new breed. Americans are much more American than they are Northerners, Southerners, Westerners, or Easterners. And descendants of English, Irish, Italian, Jewish, German, Polish, are essentially American. This is not patriotic whoop-de-do; it is carefully observed fact. California Chinese, Boston Irish, Wisconsin German, yes, and Alabama Negroes, have more in common than they have apart. And this is the more remarkable because it has happened so quickly. It is a fact that Americans from all sections and of all racial extractions are more alike than the Welsh are like the English, the Lancashireman like the Cockney, or for that matter, the Lowland Scot like the Highlander. It is astonishing that this has happened in less than two hundred years, and most of it in the last fifty. The American identity is an exact and provable thing.

John Steinbeck, *Travels with Charley*, 1962

American cities are like badger holes ringed with trash.

Ibid.

A tasteless, efficient equalitarian society, created by the European poor.

William Toye, *A Book of Canada*, 1962

*Not a future. At least not in Europe. America's different of course, but America's really only a kind of Russia.

Anthony Burgess, *Honey for the Bears*, 1963

Every European visitor to the states, I think, receives the impression that nowhere else in the world is real poverty – admittedly, rarer here than anywhere else – so cheerless, sordid, and destitute of all grace. . . . In Europe the rich man and the poor man were thought of as being two different kinds of men: the poor man might be an inferior kind, but he was a man; but here the poor man was not, as such, a man, but a person in a state of poverty, from which, if he were a real man, he would presently extricate himself.

W.H. Auden, *The Dyer's Hand and Other Essays*, 1963

The United States has to move very fast to even stand still.

John Fitzgerald Kennedy, *Observer*, 'Sayings of the Week', 21 July 1963

We would like to live as we once lived, but history will not permit it.

John Fitzgerald Kennedy, Speech, Fort Worth, November 1963

A country in which, spiritually speaking, there are no

workers, only candidates for the hand of the boss's daughter.

James Baldwin, *The Fire Next Time*, 1963

The world is not a big Red sea in which this country is being scuttled, but a vast arena of political upheaval, in which the quest for freedom, ever stronger, has overthrown the colonial empires of the past. It isn't a tidy world, nor is it a secure one. But it is one for which the United States set the revolutionary example.

Frank Church, Speech in US Senate, 12 January 1965

from the air
Am tucked up solicitously for the night, but am still able to see out of the window, my goodness me, no sleep with a view like that. America sliding by, 650 miles an hour, airspeed, with 150 miles an hour tail wind; 800 miles an hour over the ground – no cloud. Cities, gleaming, glowing ravishments slide under us six miles down, lines of phosphorescence scored at right angles to each other. Moon and snow. Stars, perceptibly wheeling. More molten cities. Body understands that America is crust of earth with fire inside, must break out somewhere, hence these scores, these right-angled lava cracks, these chess-board patterns of luminosity (with here and there a wink of veritable incandescence like the white spark on a red coal), but all soft as the tiny lights of a shock cradle. Garish street lamps, Christmas decorations, traffic signals, window displays, sky signs, now softened, softened. Body lines up jet-hole with city – sees it swallow a whole street six miles long in seconds, how to take the children to school, scoop! three blocks of run-down houses, park, Motel, Motel, Motel, parking lot, cemetery, jump the sparking traffic lights, scoop! Drugstore, Charlies Cheeseburgers, Eats, Frolic Fashion House, Beautician, Physician, Mortician, Realty, News Office
WinnDixie MountjoyToyTownSurplusWarStock
CrossroadsChurchofChrist(Airconditioning)Square!
MayoraltyFireStationPoliceStationHowardJohnson
Square!LightsLightsLightsSquare!LightsLightsLights
RiverSquare! All sucked in and blown out, scooped up, hurled back, august, imperial, god-like, America, oh from up here and at this power, even unto weeping, America The —

William Golding, 'Body and Soul', in *The Hot Gates and Other Occasional Pieces*, 1965

The Great Society asks not how much, but how good; not only how to create wealth, but how to use it; not only how fast we are going, but where we are headed. It proposes as the first test for a nation: the quality of its people.

Lyndon B. Johnson, State of the Union Message, 4 January 1965

For this is what America is all about. It is the uncrossed desert, and the unclimbed ridge. It is the star that is not reached, and the harvest that's sleeping in the unplowed ground.

Lyndon B. Johnson, Inaugural Address, 20 January 1965

We have some impatience with prosaic, everyday things of life – I think those hurt us. That sort of whimsical patience that other countries may have – that's really painful to endure: to be minor. We leap for the sublime. You might almost say American literature and culture begins with *Paradise Lost*. I always think there are two great symbolic figures that stand behind American ambition and culture. One is Milton's Lucifer and the other is Captain Ahab: these two sublime ambitions that are doomed and ready, for their idealism, to face any amount of violence.

Robert Lowell, quoted by A. Alvarez, 'A Talk with Robert Lowell', *Encounter*, February 1965

This country can seduce God. Yes, it has that seductive power, – the power of dollarism.

Malcolm X, *Malcolm X Speaks*, 1965

The U.S., perhaps, cannot 'lead': for that she is, paradoxically, far too powerful.

John Mander, 'Mexico City to Buenos Aires', *Encounter*, September 1965

After all, this is a nation that, except for a hard core of winos at the bottom and a hard crust of artistocrats at the top, has been going gloriously middle class for two decades.

Tom Wolfe, *The Kandy-Colored Tangerine-Flake Streamline Baby*, 1965

I asked why so many Argentines disliked the United States. The reply came with a rush – 'Envy!'

John Gunther, *Inside South America*, 1967

No one should be required to see America for the first time.

Anon., quoted by Ashley Montagu on the *Today Show*, 23 February 1967

Nehru . . . described America as a country which one should never go to for the first time.

Woodrow Wyatt, Review of Sarvenpalli Gopal, *Jawaharlal Nehru, 1947–1956*, in the *Sunday Times*, 27 January 1980

Unless drastic reforms are made we must accept that fact that every four years the United States will be up for sale, and the richest man or family will buy it.

Gore Vidal, *Reflections upon a Sinking Ship*, 1969

The civilization whose absence drove Henry James to Europe.

Gore Vidal, *Two Sisters: A Memoir in the Form of a Novel*, 1970

Nothing that you say about the whole country is going to be true.

Alistair Cooke, *Alistair Cooke's America*, 1973

Don't read your reviews,
A*M*E*R*I*C*A:
you are the only land.

John Updike, 'Notes to a Poem', *Picked Up Pieces*, 1976

In America a man's home is not his castle but merely a 'gigantic listening device with a mortgage.'

Tom Wolfe, quoting remark overheard, 'The Intelligent Coed's guide to America', 1976, in *Mauve Gloves and Madmen, Clutter and Vine*, 1976

What distinguishes America is not its greater or lesser goodness, but simply its unrivalled power to do that which is good or bad.

Mark Frankland, *Observer*, 6 November 1977

We really are 15 countries, and it's really remarkable that each of us thinks we represent the *real* America. The Midwesterner in Kansas, the black American in Durham – both are certain they are the real America. And Boston just *knows* it is.

Maya Angelou, quoted in *Time Magazine*, 24 April 1978

I begin to think that America *is* an entertainment industry.

Russell Davies, *Observer Review*, 5 March 1978

Could that last American frontier be an amusement park?

Nicholas von Hoffman, 'America on the Run', *Spectator*, 23 September 1978

It's interesting that more European communities have managed to survive in a pure form in America, and not in Europe.

Ruth Prawer Jhabvala, Interview with Melinda Camber Porter, *The Times*, 13 July 1978

Then, in an obvious pitch to ethnic groups, in which his support is eroding, he claimed that the U.S. is 'not a melting pot. We are more like a pot of minestrone.'

President Jimmy Carter, quoted *Time Magazine*, 20 August 1979

Columbus and his successors, one might say, did not discover America; they discovered the land-mass upon which America was to be constructed.

J.H. Parry, *The Discovery of South America*, 1979

'Well, well, well,' a man said to me. A regular Babbitt he was. He even slapped me on the back. 'Twenty years since you bin home, eh? Well, well, well, what do you think of America?'

And I am looking at all those great wheels of cheese, mountains of salads, running rivers of the fruit of all the world – plus oceans of beef, ham, pork, turkey, and chicken – and I say: 'If I were America's dad, I'd smack its arse, and send it to bed with no supper.'

Stanley Reynolds, 'America's Drooling Class', *Guardian*, 17 November 1979

No more is Chicago the hog butcher of the world, nor is Pittsburgh its forge, nor Detroit a tourist attraction. They go to Japan to look at the factories and they come here to see Mickey Mouse. We make the movies, the Germans make the steel. That's the American apprehension as the Eighties begin, but a nation that lives on mineral water is sober enough to control its destiny.

Nicholas von Hoffman, 'America's Plastic Decade', *Spectator*, 5 January 1980

It has always been an urgent necessity in America to filter the popular voice through political institutions, in place of the social habits which filter it, at an earlier stage, in Europe.

Henry Fairlie, 'The Populism of Mr Reagan', *Spectator*, 29 March 1980

André Malraux once commented to me that the United States was 'the only nation ever to become the most powerful in the world without seeking to.'

Richard Nixon, *The Real War*, 1980

Not long ago I asked Dr. Edward Teller, the nuclear physicist who is often called 'the father of the hydrogen bomb,' what he thought things would be like in the United States in the year 2000. He thought for a long while, and then replied that he believed there was a 50 per cent chance that the United States would not be in existence. I asked whether he meant physically or as a system of government. He said, 'Either – or both.'

Ibid.

America is a vast conspiracy to make you happy.

John Updike, 'How to Love America and Leave it at the Same Time', *Problems*, 1980

Americans

Eighteenth Century

It is a wealthy people
Who sojourn in this land;
Their churches all with steeples
Most delicately stand:

Their houses like the gilly
  Are painted white and gay
They flourish like the lily
  In North Americay.

On Turkeys fowls and fishes,
  Most frequently they dine;
With well replenished dishes
  Their tables always shine.
They crown their feasts with butter,
  They eat, and rise to pray
In silks their ladies flutter
  In North Americay.

Anon. New England patriot, *American Taxation*, 1765

Then join hand in hand, brave Americans all, –
By uniting we stand, by dividing we fall!

John Dickinson, 'Liberty Song', first published in *Boston Gazette*, 18 July 1768

A people who are still, as it were, but in the gristle, and not yet hardened into the bone of manhood.

Edmund Burke, Second Speech on Conciliation with America, 19 April 1774

I am not a Virginian, but an American.

Patrick Henry, Speech in the Virginia Convention, September 1774

Sir, they are a race of convicts, and ought to be thankful for any thing we allow them short of hanging.

Samuel Johnson, in Boswell, *Life of Johnson*, 1775

If I were an American as I am an Englishman while a foreign troop was landed in my country I never would lay down my arms, – never! never! never!

William Pitt, Earl of Chatham, Speech, 18 November 1777

Put none but Americans on guard tonight.

George Washington, attributed, Remark, based on his circular letter to regimental commanders, 30 April 1777

I am willing to love all mankind, *except an American.*

Samuel Johnson, in Boswell, *Life of Johnson*, 15 April 1778

Our citizenship in the United States is our national character. Our citizenship in any particular state is only our local distinction. By the latter we are known at home, by the former to the world. Our great title is AMERICANS – our inferior one varies with the place.

Thomas Paine, *The American Crisis*, 19 April 1783

My God! how little do my country men know what precious blessings they are in possession of, and which no other people on earth enjoy. I confess I had no idea of it myself. While we shall see multipled instances of Europeans going to live in America, I will venture to say no man now living will ever see an instance of an American removing to settle in Europe and continuing there.

Thomas Jefferson, Letter to James Monroe, Paris, 17 June 1785

The truth is the people have ever governed in America: all the might of the royal governors and councils, even backed with fleets and armies, have never been able to get the advantage of them, who have always stood by their houses of representatives in every instance and carried all their points; and no governor ever stood his ground against a representative assembly – as long as he governed by their advice he was happy; and as soon as he differed from them he was wretched and soon obliged to retire.

John Adams, *A Defence of the Constitution of Government of the United States of America*, 1787

It has frequently been remarked that it seems to have been reserved to the people of this country, by their conduct and example, to decide the important question, whether societies of men are really capable or not of establishing good government from reflection and choice, or whether they are forever destined to depend for their political constitutions on accident and force.

Alexander Hamilton, *The Federalist*, 1787

Providence has been pleased to give this one connected country to one united people – a people descended from the same ancestors, speaking the same language, professing the same religion, attached to the same principles of government, very similar in their manners and customs, and who, by their joint counsels, arms, and efforts, fighting side by side throughout a long and bloody war, have nobly established general liberty and independence.

This country and this people seem to have been made for each other, and it appears as if it was the design of Providence, that an inheritance so proper and convenient for a band of brethen, united to each other by the strongest ties, should never be split into a number of unsocial, jealous, and alien sovereignties.

John Jay, *The Federalist*, 1787

Nineteenth Century

He said he should be afraid to go to America without understanding english. I told him the Americans were a strange set of fellows that run about all parts of the world without caring to learn the language before hand.

Washington Irving, *Journal*, 19 August 1804

All the men in America make money their pursuit.

Richard Parkinson, *A Tour of America*, 1805

The American people, dispersed over an immense territory, abounding in all the means of commercial greatness, to whom an opportunity was presented at an early period of adapting their government to their circumstances, followed the manifest order of nature, when they adopted a free, republican, commercial federation.

Charles T. Ingersoll, *Inchiquin*, 1810

There is one thing in the Americans which . . . I have . . . *kept back* to the last moment. It has presented itself several times; but I have turned from the thought, as men do from thinking of any mortal disease that is at work in their frame. It is not covetousness; it is not niggardliness; it is not insincerity; it is not enviousness, it is not cowardice, above all things; it is DRINKING. Aye, and that too, amongst but too many men, who, one would think, would loath it. You can go into hardly any man's house without being asked to drink wine or spirits, even *in the morning*. They are quick at meals, are little eaters, seem to care little about what they eat, and never talk about it. This, which arises out of the universal abundance of good and even fine eatables, is very amiable. You are here disgusted with none of those *eaters by reputation* that are found, especially among *the Parsons*, in England: fellows that *unbutton* at it. Nor do the Americans *sit and tope much after dinner*, and talk on till they get into nonsense and *smut*, which last is a sure mark of a silly and, pretty generally, even of a base mind. But, they *tipple*; and the infernal spirits they tipple too! . . . The Americans preserve their gravity and quietness and good-humour even in their drink; and so much the worse. It were far better for them to be as noisy and quarrelsome as the English drunkards; for then the odiousness of the vice would be more visible, and the vice itself might become less frequent.

William Cobbett, *A Year's Residence in the United States of America*, 1817–19

I am to the full as much of a Philoyankeist as you are. I doubt if there ever was an instance of a new people conducting their affairs with so much wisdom, or if there ever was such an extensive scene of human happiness and prosperity.

Sydney Smith, Letter to Francis Jeffrey, 23 November 1818

Whenever an American requests to see me – (which is *not* unfrequently) I comply – 1stly. because I respect a people who acquired their freedom by firmness without excess – and 2dly. because these transatlantic visits . . . make me feel as if talking with Posterity from the other side of the Styx.

Lord Byron, *Detached Thoughts*, 1821–2

The most striking circumstance in the American character which had come under my notice was the constant habit of praising themselves, their institutions and their country, either in downright terms, or by some would-be indirect allusions, which were still more tormenting. I make use of this sharp-edged word, because it really was exceedingly teasing, while we were quite willing and ready to praise all that was good, and also to see every thing, whether good or bad, in the fairest light, to be called upon so frequently to admit the justice of such exaggerations. It is considered, I believe, all over the world, as bad manners for a man to praise himself or his family. Now, to praise one's country appears, to say the least of it, in the next degree of bad taste.

Captain Basil Hall, *Travels in North America*, 1829

It often appeared to me that the old women of a state made the laws, and the young men broke them.

Mrs Frances Trollope, *Domestic Manners of the Americans*, 1832

'Law!' echoed another gentleman of Vernon, 'this is a free country, *we have no laws here*, and we want no foreign power to tyrannise over us.'

Ibid.

Other nations have been called thin-skinned, but the citizens of the United States have, apparently, no skins at all; they wince if a breeze blows over them, unless it be tempered with adulation.

Ibid.

I am inclined to think this most vile and universal habit of chewing tobacco is the cause of a remarkable pecularity in the male physiognomy of Americans; their lips are almost uniformly thin and compressed. At first I accounted for this upon Lavater's theory, and attributed it to the arid temperament of the people; but it is too universal to be so explained; whereas the habit above mentioned, which pervades all classes (excepting the literary) well accounts for it, as the act of expressing the juices of this loathsome herb, enforces exactly that position of the lips, which gives this remarkable peculiarity to the American countenance.

Ibid.

Discomposed by head ache from indigestion. I eat too fast. This is a fault of all Americans and springs from hurry of habit. Most of the dyspepsia for which the country is peculiar springs from it.

Charles Francis Adams, *Diary*, 17 December 1833

The Americans are not a race of French agility, and therefore cannot be expected to show that pliant politeness towards women, which depends, in a great degree upon this peculiar quality; they are not easily excitable, and consequently, not versatile in conversation; they therefore cannot show that quick politeness which depends upon this inventive brightness of the moment; but they are essentially polite, ready to serve a woman, of whatever class, and to show the greatest regard to the female sex in general.

Francis Lieber, *The Stranger in America*, 1835

I know of no country . . . where the love of money has taken stronger hold on the affections of men and where a profounder contempt is expressed for the theory of the permanent equality of property. But wealth circulates with inconceivable rapidity, and experience shows that it is rare to find two succeeding generations in the full enjoyment of it.

Alexis de Tocqueville, *Democracy in America*, 1835

If an American were condemned to confine his activity to his own affairs, he would be robbed of one half of his existence.

Ibid.

In this Country . . . men seem to live for action as long as they can and sink into apathy when they retire.

Charles Francis Adams, *Diary*, 15 April 1836

The Americans have many virtues, but they have not Faith and Hope.

Ralph Waldo Emerson, *Nature, Addresses and Lectures: Man the Reformer*, 1836

An American, by his boasting of the superiority of the Americans generally, but especially in their language, once provoked me to tell him that 'On that head the least said the better, as the Americans presented the extraordinary anomaly of a *people without a language*.' That they had mistaken the English language for baggage (which is called *plunder* in America), and had stolen it.

Samuel Taylor Coleridge, *Letters Conversations and Recollections*, ed. Thomas Allsop, 1836

The civilisation and the morals of the Americans fall far below their own principles.

Harriet Martineau, *Society in America*, 1837

They are better educated by providence than by men.

Ibid.

One of the first directions in which Americans have indulged their taste, and indicated their refinement, is in the preparation and care of their burial-places. . . . Living men are comparatively scarce, and the general mind dwells more upon the past and the future, (of both which worlds death is the atmosphere,) than in the present. By various influences death is made to constitute a larger element in their estimate of collective human experience, a more conspicuous object in their contemplation of the plan of Providence than it is to, perhaps, any other people. As a natural consequence, all arrangements connected with death occupy much of their attention, and engage a large share of popular sentiment.

Harriet Martineau, *Retrospect of Western Travel*, 1838

The 4th of July, the sixty-first anniversary of American Independence. Pop-pop-bang-pop-pop-bang-bang-bang! Mercy on us! how fortunate it is that anniversaries come only once a year. Well, the Americans may have great reason to be proud of this day, and of the deeds of their forefathers, but why do they get so confoundedly drunk? why, on this day of independence, should they become so *dependent* upon posts and rails for support? . . . There is something grand in the idea of a national intoxication. In this world, vices on a grand scale dilate into virtues: he who murders one man is strung up with ignominy; but he who murders twenty thousand has a statue to his memory, and is handed down to posterity as a hero. A staggering individual is a laughable, and sometimes a disgusting spectacle; but the whole of a vast continent reeling, offering a holocaust of its brains for mercies vouchsafed, is an appropriate symbol of gratitude for the rights of equality and the *levelling spirit* of their institutions.

Captain Frederick Marryat, *Diary in America*, 1839

There is no part of the world perhaps, where you have more difficulty in obtaining permission to be alone, and indulge in a reverie, than in America. The Americans are as gregarious as school-boys and think it an incivility to leave you by yourself. Every thing is done in crowds and among a crowd. They even prefer a double bed to a single one, and I have often had the offer to sleep with me made out of real kindness.

Ibid.

The men are generally tall and slender in figure, more frequently above five feet ten inches than below it, and rarely exceeding three feet in circumference about the waist; the arms are long, the legs small, the chest narrow, the form not so frequently erect, as slightly stooping, arising from carelessness of gait and hurry in walking; the head is small, but the features are long, the complexion pale, the eyes small and dark, the hair straight, the cheeks generally smooth or without whiskers or beard, and the whole expression and deportment is grave and serious. The women of America are not so tall in stature as the women of Europe generally, being oftener below five feet four inches than above it; of slender figure, without the fullness or rotundity and flowing lines of the Medicean statue, imperfect development of bust, small hands and feet, small and pretty features, pale complexions, dark eyes, a mincing gait, delicate health, and a grave rather than a gay or animated expression. If the men seem to be marked by a general uniformity of standard in personal appearance, the women are still more alike.

J.S. Buckingham, *The Slave States of America, in 1839*, 1842

The people of America are too busy, and too much engrossed with preparations for the future, to devote much of the present to the habits which make so many corpulent men in England, and which cause the tendency to be transmitted hereditarily, like the gout, from generation to generation.

Ibid.

An American, instead of going in a leisure hour to dance merrily at some place of public resort, as the fellows of his class continue to do throughout the greater part of Europe, shuts himself up at home to drink. He thus enjoys two pleasures; he can go on thinking of his business and can get drunk decently by his own fireside.

Alexis de Tocqueville, *Democracy in America, the second part*, 1840

The Americans, in their intercourse with strangers, appear impatient of the smallest censure and insatiable of praise.

Ibid.

I accost an American sailor and inquire why the ships of his country are built so as to last for only a short time; he answers without hesitation that the art of navigation is every day making such rapid progress that the finest vessel would become almost useless if it lasted beyond a few years. In these words, which fell accidentally, and on a particular subject, from an uninstructed man, I recognise the general and systematic idea upon which a great people direct all their concerns.

Ibid.

To evade the bondage of system and habit, of family maxims, class opinions, and, in some degree, of national prejudices; to accept tradition only as a means of information, and existing facts only as a lesson to be used in doing otherwise and doing better; to seek the reason of things for oneself, and in oneself alone; to tend to results without being bound to means, and to strike through the form to the substance – such are the principal characteristics of what I shall call the philosophical method of the Americans.

But if I go further and seek among these characteristics the principal one, which includes almost all the rest, I discover that in most of the operations of the mind each American appeals only to the individual effort of his own understanding.

America is therefore one of the countries where the precepts of Descartes are least studied and are best applied. Nor is this surprising. The Americans do not read the works of Descartes, because their social condition deters them from speculative studies; but they follow his maxims, because this same social condition naturally disposes their minds to adopt them.

Ibid.

The Americans inherit the cerebral organisation of the three British nations, in whom the organs of Combativeness, Destructiveness, Self-esteem, and Firmness, the elements of pugnacity and warlike adventure, are largely developed. In them this endowment is accompanied by a restless activity of mind which finds natural and agreeable vent in war, and by a degree of intelligence which renders them capable equally of individual enterprise and of combination in action. . . . Here then we have a people of naturally pugnacious dispositions, reared in the admiration of warlike deeds, imperfectly instructed in the principles on which the real greatness of nations is founded, possessed of much mental activity, impelled by all the fervour of youth, and unrestrained by experience.

George Combe, *Notes . . . during a Phrenological Visit, in 1838–40*, 1841

A Scotchman with whom . . . we became acquainted . . . remarked to me that the only way to know the Americans thoroughly is to 'count siller' with them, *anglice*, to deal with them.

Ibid.

It would be well, there can be no doubt, for the American people as a whole, if they loved the Real less, and the Ideal somewhat more.

Charles Dickens, *American Notes*, 1842

The Yankee is one who, if he once gets his teeth set on a thing, all creation can't make him let go.

Ralph Waldo Emerson, *Journals*, 1842

I am quite serious when I say that it is *impossible*, following them in their own direction, to caricature that people. I lay down my pen in despair sometimes when I read what I have done, and find how it halts behind my own recollection.

Charles Dickens, Letter to Jane Welsh Carlyle, 7 January 1844

'Well, I declare!' I overheard the snuff-coloured gentleman say, 'but we air a greater people than I thought for!'

'I knowd it,' said a long Yankee from Maine; 'we're born to whip universal nature. The Europeans can't hold a candle to us already e'en a'most.'

Alexander Mackay, *The Western World . . . in 1846–7*, 1849

'Then you have a longer line of ancestors than most of your fellow-countrymen can boast of,' I observed.

'We don't vally these things in this country,' said he in reply. 'It's what's above ground, not what's under, that we think on.'

Ibid.

'We have had many quarrels with you,' said a lady to me once in Washington, 'but we are proud of our descent from the English! We court the French when it suits our purpose, but,' she added, with great emphasis, 'we would not be descended from them on any account.'

Ibid.

Aye, they have a great population, viz. 21 millions of the greatest bores that the moon ever saw.

David Livingstone, Letter to Mr and Mrs N. Livingstone, 26 September 1852.

There's a rush and activity of life quite astounding, a splendid recklessness about money which has in it something admirable too. Dam the money says every man. He's as good as the richest for that day. . . . There's a beautiful affection in this country, immense tenderness, romantic personal enthusiasm, and a kindliness and serviceableness and good nature which is very pleasant and curious to witness for us folks at home, who are mostly ashamed of our best emotions and turn on our heel with a laugh sometimes when we are most pleased and touched. If a man falls into a difficulty a score of men are ready to help. . . . I tell you it's a grand country entirely. The young blood beating in its pulses warms one, like the company of young men in England. I don't know what I wouldn't do if I were ten years younger.

W.M. Thackeray, Letter to Albany Fonblanque, 4 March 1853

'Well now, I declare I know'd it; we air a great people, and bound to be tolerable troublesome to them kings.'

Anon. Maine Yankee to William Edward Baxter, *America and the Americans*, 1855

The Americans, of all nations at any time upon the earth, have probably the fullest poetical nature. The United States themselves are essentially the greatest poem. In the history of the earth hitherto, the largest and most stirring appear tame and orderly to their ampler largeness and stir. Here at last is something in the doings of man that corresponds with the broadcast doings of the day and night.

Walt Whitman, Preface to *Leaves of Grass*, 1855

The American is only the continuation of the English genius into new conditions, more or less propitious.

R.W.Emerson, *English Traits*, 1856

They set up a President only to attack and vilify him, just as some African savages make an idol that they may kick and cuff while they pretend to pray to it.

Charles Mackay, *Life and Liberty in America, 1857–8*, 1859

If the gentlemen would but shake hands less, and the ladies would shake hands a little more, America would be perfectly delightful.

Ibid.

Good Americans, when they die, go to Paris.

Thomas Appleton (1812–84), quoted in O.W. Holmes, *Autocrat of the Breakfast-Table*, 1858

Every American owns all America.

O.W. Holmes, *The Professor at the Breakfast-Table*, 1859

If the Americans were not bumptious, how unlike would they be to the parent that bore them!

Anthony Trollope, *The West Indies and the Spanish Main*, 1859

We impatient Americans! If we came on the wires of the telegraph, yet, on arriving, every one would be striving to get ahead of the rest.

Ralph Waldo Emerson, *Journals*, 1859

There is one other grand ruling characteristic of the Southerner, which I here state as a fact, without pretending to state it clearly, and without undertaking to account for it, only observing that it is far more decided than the difference of climate merely would warrant. It is intensity of impulse – willfullness. Every wish of the Southerner is for the moment at least, more imperative than of the Northerner, every belief more undoubted, every hate more vengeful, every love more fiery. Hence, for instance, the scandalous fiend-like street fights of the South. If a young man feels offended with another, he does not incline to a ring and a fair stand-up set to, like a young Englishman; he will not attempt to overcome his opponent by logic; he will not be content to vituperate, or to cast ridicule upon him; he is impelled straightway to kill him with the readiest deadly weapon at hand, and with as little ceremony and pretense of fair combat as the loose organisation of the people against violence will allow. He seems crazy for blood.

Frederick Law Olmsted, *A Journey in the Back Country*, 1860

America breeds . . . people by the thousands, who appear to live eternally on the edge of resentment, and to be as inflammable as tinder. It is dangerous to deal with them in badinage, irony, sarcasm, or what we call 'chaff.' Before the expiration of the first day I had noted that their high spirits scarcely brooked a reproof, or contradiction, the slightest approach to anything of the kind exciting them to a strange heat.

Sir Henry Morton Stanley, *Autobiography*, 1909 – of 1860

American politicians have been sometimes called, in allusion to a phrase of the puritan times, *waiters upon the people*.

Walter Bagehot, *The Economist*, 4 January 1862

In his mind he is quicker, more universally intelligent, more ambitious of general knowledge, less indulgent of stupidity and ignorance in others, harder, sharper, brighter with the surface brightness of steel, than is an Englishman; but he is more brittle, less enduring, less malleable, and I think less capable of impressions. The mind of the Englishman has more imagination, but that of the American more incision. The American is a great observer, but he observes things material rather than things social or picturesque. . . . In his aspirations the American is more constant than an Englishman, – or I should rather say he is more constant in aspiring. Every citizen of the United States intends to do something.

Anthony Trollope, *North America*, 1862

After dinner, if all that I hear be true, the gentlemen occasionally drop into the hotel bar and 'liquor-up.' Or rather this is not done specially after dinner, but without prejudice to the hour at any time that may be found desirable. I have also 'liquored up,' but I cannot say that I enjoy the process. I do not intend hereby to accuse Americans of drinking much, but I maintain that when they do drink, they drink in the most uncomfortable manner that the imagination can devise.

Ibid.

The Americans as a rule live in an atmosphere which is almost unbearable by an Englishman. To this cause, I am convinced, is to be attributed their thin faces, their pale skins, their unenergetic temperament, – unenergetic as regards physical motion, – and their early old age. The winters are long and cold in America, and mechanical ingenuity is far extended. These two facts together have created a system of stoves, hot-air pipes, steam-chambers, and heating apparatus, so extensive that from autumn till the end of spring, all inhabited rooms are filled with the atmosphere of a hot oven. An Englishman fancies that he is to be baked, and for a while finds it impossible to exist in the air prepared for him.

Ibid.

The difficulty of creating a strong government in America is almost insuperable. The people, in the first place, dislike government, not this or that administration, but government in the abstract, to such a degree that they have invented a quasi political theory, proving that government, like war or harlotry, is a 'necessary evil.' Moreover, they have constructed a machinery in the shape of states, specially and deliberately calculated to impede central action, to stop the exercise of power, to reduce government, except so far as it is expressed in arrests by the parish constable, to an impossibility. They have an absolute parliament, and though they have a strong executive it is, when opposed to the people, or even when in advance of the people, paralysed by a total absence of friends. To make this weakness permanent they have deprived even *themselves* of absolute power, have first forbidden themselves to change the Constitution except under circumstances which never occur, and have then, through the machinery of the common schools, given to that Constitution the moral weight of a religious document.

Walter Bagehot, *The Economist*, 29 April 1865

Both the French and Italians dislike the Americans, and call them a *nation mal élevée*, and so they are: such awful specimens as I was in the Coliseum with! and by moonlight too.

Matthew Arnold, Letter to his sister, 21 June 1865

The vastness of the land absorbs nearly all the vice and immorality of America . . . with industry and conduct, anybody may emphatically become anything he wants to be: and even when you stumble on the threshold, you may go 'further up', and gather yourself together.

G.A. Sala, *My Diary in America in the Midst of War*, 1865

Our Pilgrim stock wuz pithed with hardihood.

James Russell Lowell, *The Biglow Papers*, Series II, No. 6, 1867

We Americans have got suppled into the state of melioration.

R.W. Emerson, *Journal*, 1867

The Englishmen I have met not only kill but bury in unfathomable depths, the Americans I have met. A set of people less framed to provoke national self-complacency than the latter it would be hard to imagine. There is but one word to use in regard to them – vulgar; vulgar, vulgar. Their ignorance – their stingy, grudging, defiant attitude towards everything European – their perpetual reference of all things to some American standard or precedent which exists only in their own unscrupulous wind-bags – and then our unhappy poverty of voice, of speech and of physiognomy – these things glare at you hideously. On the other hand, we seem a people of *character*, we seem to have energy, capacity and intellectual stuff in ample measure. What I have pointed out as our vices are the elements of the modern man with *culture* quite left out. It's the absolute and incredible lack of *culture* that strikes you in common travelling Americans

Henry James Letter to Mrs Henry James Sr, 13 October 1869

Our American people cannot be taxed with slowness in performance, or in praising their performance.

Ralph Waldo Emerson, 'Success', *Society and Solitude*, 1870

Lords of an empire wide as Shakespeare's soul,
Sublime as Milton's immemorial theme,
And rich as Chaucer's speech, and fair as Spenser's
  dream.

Sydney Dobell, 'America', *Poetical Works*, 1875

Our leading men are not of much account and never have been, but the average of the people is immense, beyond all history. . . . We will not have great individuals or great leaders, but a great average bulk, unprecedentedly great.

Walt Whitman, *Specimen Days* (1879), 1882

That which in England we call the Middle Classes is in America virtually the nation.

Matthew Arnold, *A Word About America*, 1882

The Americans are certainly great hero-worshippers, and always take their heroes from the criminal classes.

Oscar Wilde, Letter to Norman Forbes-Robertson, 19 April 1882

American youths are pale and precocious, or sallow and supercilious, but American girls are pretty and charming, little oases of pretty unreasonableness in a vast desert of practical common sense. . . . Every American girl is entitled to have twelve young men devoted to her. . . . The men are entirely given to business; they have, as they say, their brains in front of their heads. . . . Every man when he gets to the age of twenty-one is allowed to vote, and thereby immediately acquires his political education. The Americans are the best politically educated people in the world. It is well worth one's while to go to a country which can teach us the beauty of the word FREEDOM and the value of the thing LIBERTY.

Oscar Wilde, *Impressions of America*, Lecture, 1883

'April 19. This morning struck into the region of full goatees – sometimes accompanied by a moustache, but only occasionally.'

It was odd to come across this thick crop of an obsolete and uncomely fashion; it was like running suddenly across a forgotten acquaintance whom you had supposed dead for a generation. The goatee extends over a wide extent of country; and is accompanied by an iron-clad belief in Adam and the biblical history of creation, which has not suffered from the assaults of the scientists.

Mark Twain, *Life on the Mississippi*, 1883

Until I went to the United States I had never seen a people with institutions which seemed expressly and thoroughly suited to it. I had not properly appreciated the benefits proceeding from this cause.

Matthew Arnold, *A Word More About America*, 1885

The American man is the very Don Quixote of common sense, for he is so utilitarian that he is absolutely unpractical.

Oscar Wilde, 'The American Man', in *Court and Society Review*, April 1887

In America the young are always ready to give to those who are older than themselves the full benefits of their inexperience.

Oscar Wilde, 'The American Invasion', in *Court and Society Review*, March 1887

The American man marries early, and the American woman marries often; and they get on extremely well together. . . . On the whole the great success of marriage in the States is due partly to the fact that no American man is ever idle, and partly to the fact that no American wife is considered responsible for the quality of her husband's dinners. In America, the horrors of domesticity are almost unknown.

Oscar Wilde, 'The American Man', in *Court and Society Review*, April 1887

We must not . . . take her statesmen as types of the highest or strongest American manhood. The national qualities come out fully in them but not always in their best form.

James Bryce, *The American Commonwealth*, 1888

Let there be no misunderstanding about the matter. I love this People. . . . They are bleeding-raw at the edges, almost more conceited than the English, vulgar with a massive vulgarity which is as though the Pyramids were coated with Christmas-cake sugar-works. Cocksure they are, lawless, and as casual as they are cocksure; but I love them, and I realised it when I met an Englishman who laughed at them. . . .

'I admit everything,' said I. 'Their Government's provisional; their law's the notion of the moment; their railways are made of hairpins and match-sticks, and most of their good luck lives in their woods and mines and rivers and not in their brains; but for all that they be the biggest, finest, and best people on the surface of the globe! Just you wait a hundred years and see how they'll behave when they've had the screw put on them and have forgotten a few of the patriarchal teachings of the late Mister George Washington. Wait till the Anglo-American-German-Jew – the Man of the Future – is properly equipped.'

Rudyard Kipling, *From Sea to Sea*, 1889

Your women shall scream like peacocks when they talk and your men neigh like horses when they laugh. You shall call 'round' 'raound,' and 'very' 'varry' and 'news' 'noose' till the end of time. You shall be governed by the Irishman and the German, the vendors of drinks and the keepers of vile dens, that your streets may be filthy in your midst and your sewage arrangements filthier.

Rudyard Kipling, Letter to the *Pioneer Mail*, Allahabad, India, 13 November 1889

(Kipling's 'seven-fold curse on America', provoked by American piracy of his books, was omitted from the later compilation of these letters, *From Sea to Sea* – see the *Bookman*, ix, p. 29.)

Mrs Allonby: They say, Lady Hunstanton, that when good Americans die, they go to Paris.
Lady Hunstanton: Indeed? And when bad Americans die, where do they go to?
Lord Illingworth: Oh, they go to America.
Kelvil: I am afraid you don't appreciate America, Lord Illingworth. It is a very remarkable country, especially considering its youth.
Lord Illingworth: The youth of America is their oldest tradition. It has been going on now for three hundred years. To hear them talk one would imagine they were in their first childhood. As far as civilisation goes, they are in their second.

Oscar Wilde, *A Woman of No Importance*, 1893

There isn't a single human characteristic that can be safely labeled as 'American!'

Mark Twain, *What Paul Bourget Thinks of Us*, 1895

We are a conquering race. We must obey our blood and occupy new markets and if necessary new lands.

Senator Albert J. Beveridge, Speech, 27 April 1898, quoted in C.G. Bowers, *Beveridge in the Progressive Era*, 1932

'Th' American nation in th' Sixth Ward is a fine people,' he says. 'They love th' eagle,' he says, 'on the back iv a dollar.'

Finley Peter Dunne, *Mr Dooley in Peace and War*, 1898

The American tramp is a distinct species. He is a man of iron constitution. Therefore, on principle, he refuses to drink water – for fear he should rust.

John Foster Fraser, *Round the World on a Wheel*, 1899

Twentieth Century

We're a great people. We are that. And the best of it is, we know we are.

Finley Peter Dunne, *Mr Dooley Remembers*, Philip Dunne (ed.), 1963 – pre-1919

From the very beginning our people have markedly combined practical capacity for affairs with power of devotion to an ideal. The lack of either quality would have rendered the other of small value.

Theodore Roosevelt, Speech, Philadelphia, 22 November 1902

From the old-world point of view, the American had no mind; he had an economic thinking-machine which could work only on a fixed line. The American mind exasperated the European as a buzz-saw might exasperate a pine forest. The English mind disliked the French mind because it was antagonistic, unreasonable, perhaps hostile, but recognised it as at least a thought. The American mind was not a thought at all; it was a convention, superficial, narrow, and ignorant; a mere cutting instrument, practical, economical, sharp, and direct.

Henry Adams, *The Education of Henry Adams*, 1906

Alien, *n*. An American sovereign in his probationary state.

Ambrose Bierce, *The Cynic's Word Book*, 1906

The willpower of the Americans astonished me . . . the determination that has transformed a handful of immigrants into a powerful nation; the industry which has made it great and wealthy, and the wisdom which is leading it onward to a glorious and assured future.

Count Vay de Vaya, *The Inner Life of the United States*, 1908

The psychological peculiarities of the Americans exhibit features that would be accessible to psychoanalysis, since they point to intense sexual repression. The reasons for repression are to be sought in the specifically American complex, namely living together with lower races, more particularly the Negroes. Living together with barbarous races has a suggestive effect on the laboriously subjugated instincts of the white race and drags it down. Hence strongly developed defensive measures are necessary, which manifest themselves in the particular aspects of American culture.

C.G. Jung, Abstract of talk by Jung, by Otto Rank, 1910

American society is a sort of flat, fresh-water pond which absorbs silently, without reaction, anything which is thrown into it, and its one merit is that it pretends to be nothing else. It does not cant. A few score of individuals, – counting women, perhaps a few hundred, – all more or less neurasthenic, try to create, and are desperate because society swallows passively whatever is thrown at it, but never even splashes when hit. It regards itself much like a pig in a stye. Its business is to eat refuse. It is even afraid to approve, or, – for that matter, – to disapprove beyond your bromide formula of knowing what it likes, – which it doesn't.

Henry Adams, Letter to Royal Cortissoz, 20 September 1911

We have a great ardor for gain; but we have a deep passion for the rights of man.

Woodrow Wilson, Speech, New York, 6 December 1911

*He held too, in his enlightened way, that Americans have a perfect right to exist. But he did often find himself wishing Mr Rhodes had not enabled them to exercise that right in Oxford.

Max Beerbohm, *Zuleika Dobson*, 1911

The rough broad difference between the American and the European business man is that the latter is anxious to leave his work, while the former is anxious to get to it.

Arnold Bennett, *Those United States*, 1912

The American race seems to have developed two classes, and only two, the upper-middle, and the lower-middle. Their faces are very distinct. The upper-class head is long, often fine about the forehead, and eyes, and very clearly outlined. The eyes have an odd tired pathos in them – mixed with the friendliness that is so admirable, – as if of a perpetual never quite successful effort to understand something. It is like the face of an only child who has been brought up in the company of adults. I am convinced it is partly due to the endeavour to set their standards by the habits and culture of older nations. But the mouth of such men is their most typical feature. It is small, tight, and closed downwards at the corners, the lower lip very slightly protruding. It has little expression in it, and no curves. There the Puritan comes out. But no other nation has a mouth like this. It is shared to some extent by the lower classes; but their mouths tend to be wider, and more expressive. Their foreheads are meaner, and their eyes hard, but the whole face rather more adaptive, and in touch with life. These, anyhow, are the types which strike one in the eastern cities. And there are intermediate varieties, as of the genial business-man, with the narrow forehead, and the wide, smooth – the too wide, and too smooth – lower face. Smoothness is the one unfailing characteristic. Why do American faces hardly ever wrinkle? Is it the absence of a soul? It must be. For it is less true of the Bostonian than of the ordinary business American, in whose life exhilaration and depression take the place of joy and suffering.

Rupert Brooke, *Letters from America*, 1913

All his life he jumps into the train after it has started and jumps out before it has stopped; and he never once gets left behind, or breaks a leg.

George Santayana, *Character and Opinion in the United States*, 1920

The American . . . seems to bear lightly the sorrowful burden of human knowledge. In a word, he is young. . . . The American has never yet had to face the trials of Job.

Ibid.

The one woman who never gives herself is your free woman, who is always giving herself. America affects me like that.

D.H. Lawrence, Letter to Harriet Monroe, 23 September 1922

The truth is, that the majority of non-Anglo-Saxon immigrants since the Revolution, like the majority of Anglo-Saxon immigrants before the Revolution, have been, not the superior men of their native lands, but the botched and unfit: Irishmen starving to death in Ireland, Germans unable to weather the *Sturm und Drang* of the post Napoleonic reorganisation, Italians weed-grown on exhausted soil, Scandinavians run to all bone and no brain, Jews too incompetent to swindle even the barbarous peasants of Russia, Poland, and Roumania. Here and there among the immigrants, of course, there may be a bravo, or even a superman – *e.g.* the ancestors of Volstead, Ponzi, Jack Dempsey, Schwab, Daugherty, Debs, Pershing – but the average newcomer is, and always has been, simply a poor fish.

H.L.Mencken, 'On Being an American', in *Prejudices*, Third Series, 1923

Any man with a superior air, the intelligence of a stockbroker, and the resolution of a hat-check girl, – in brief, any man who believes in himself enough, and with sufficient cause, to be called a journeyman – can cadge enough money, in this glorious commonwealth of morons, to make life soft for him.

Ibid.

Americans are enormously adaptable: perhaps because inwardly, they are not adjusted at all to their environment. They are never American as a chipmunk is, or as an Indian is: only as a Ford car, or as the Woolworth building.

D.H. Lawrence, Letter to Kyle Crichton, 28 September 1925

*Vital race, that – sublime disregard of the law themselves, and a strong sence of moral turpitude in others.

John Galsworthy, *Escape*, 1926

Hospitality in America is genuine and warm-hearted, and carried on with that relentless efficiency with which they handle hogs in Chicago. . . . On you go, propelled by relentless machinery like the hog down the Chicago chute, with this difference, that sheer explosive kindliness is the propelling power.

Crosbie Garstin, *The Dragon and the Lotus*, 1928

Americans are getting like a Ford car – they all have the same parts, the same upholstering and make exactly the same noises.

Will Rogers, *Autobiography*, 1928

We don't know what we want, but we are ready to bite somebody to get it.

Ibid.

I've seen Kentuckians who hated whisky, Virginians who weren't descended from Pocahontas, Indianians who hadn't written a novel . . . spendthrift Yankees, cold-blooded Southerners, narrow-minded Westerners.

Professor Kenneth B. Murdock, Speech before the New England Society of Cleveland and the Western Reserve, 1928

*The Americans, who are the most efficient people on earth . . . have invented so wide a range of pithy and hackneyed phrases that they can carry on an amusing and animated conversation without giving a moment's reflection to what they are saying and so leave their minds free to consider the more important matters of big business and fornication.

W. Somerset Maugham, *Cakes and Ale*, 1930

*There won't be any revolution in America,' said Isidore. Nikitin agreed. 'The people are too lean. They spend all their time changing their shirts and washing themselves. You can't feel fierce and revolutionary in a bathroom.'

Eric Linklater, *Juan in America*, 1931

There is nothing the matter with Americans except their ideals. The real American is all right; it is the ideal American who is all wrong.

G.K. Chesterton, *New York Times*, 1 February 1931, reprinted in *Sidelights*, 1932

Most Americans are born drunk. . . . They have a sort of permanent intoxication from within, a sort of invisible champagne. . . . Americans do not need to drink to inspire them to do anything.

G.K. Chesterton, *New York Times*, 1 February 1931, 28 June 1931

The Americans are a queer people; they can't rest.

Stephen Leacock, *A Neighbor Looks at America*, in Fred. J. Ringel (ed.), *America as Others See It*, 1932

You simply cannot hang a millionaire in America.

Bourke Cockran, quoted Shane Leslie, *American Wonderland*, 1936

I am told on every hand that the American school system does not educate: that it only smears the courses on the men. They emerge like luggage after a well planned tour covered with labels but with very little acquirement within. The Universities are largely the gifts of the very rich, handed back to the middle class.

Shane Leslie, *American Wonderland*, 1936

This generation of Americans has a rendezvous with destiny.

Franklin D. Roosevelt, Speech accepting renomination, 27 June 1936

I begin to perceive that Americans regard food as something to sober up with.

James Agate, *Ego 3*, 5 May 1937

It is the custom of good Americans to bestow, somewhat in the Chinese fashion, a kind of posthumous nobility upon their ancestors; to transform the farmers and small tradesmen from whom they are almost all descended into scions of great, historic English houses.

Logan Pearsall Smith, *Unforgotten Years*, 1938

In America everybody is, but some are more than others. I was more than others.

Gertrude Stein, *Everybody's Autobiography*, 1938

There are no second acts in American lives.

F. Scott Fitzgerald, Notes to uncompleted *The Last Tycoon*, 1941

When you consider how indifferent Americans are to the quality and cooking of the food they put into their insides, it cannot but strike you as peculiar that they should take such pride in the mechanical appliances they use for its excretion.

W. Somerset Maugham, *A Writer's Notebook*, 1949 – of 1941

I met the French journalist 'Pertinax' . . . and asked him how he liked America. 'A desert,' he said. 'They are lost, not in space, but in time.' He blew off his finger-tips into the outer darkness. 'They detest us all, but you British more because they feel themselves inferior. *Ce n'est pas une civilisation.*' 'But the future,' said I. 'They may be growing into a *civilisation.* How long do you think it will take?' 'I don't know – five hundred years perhaps. It is of no interest.' He shrugged his shoulders, lifted his chin and dismissed the whole continent.

Freya Stark, Letter, 2 January 1944, in *Dust in the Lion's Paw*, 1961

The fat, puffy, wattle-faced man of forty-five who has turned asexual is the greatest monument to futility that America has created. He's a nymphomaniac of energy, accomplishing nothing. He's an hallucination of the Paleolithic man. He's a statistical bundle of fat and jangled nerves for the insurance man to convert into a frightening thesis. He sows the land with prosperous, restless, empty-headed, idle-handed widows, who gang together in ghoulish sororities where politics and diabetes go hand in hand.

Henry Miller, *The Air-conditioned Nightmare*, 1945

A Pueblo chieftain once confided to me that he thought all Americans (the only white men he knew) were crazy, and the reasons he gave for this view sounded exactly like a description of people who were possessed.

C.G. Jung, *After the Catastrophe*, 1946, trans. R.F.C. Hull

Many an immigrant arrived in this country with the most materialistic expectations, hoping not to escape from a world in which a man was the sum of his circumstances, but to become a new sum of circumstances himself. But this hope was self-defeating: the very ease with which new circumstances were acquired left insufficient time for a man to live into them. . . . The new American . . . camped out in his circumstances, as it were, and was never assimilated to them. And for the native American, the great waves of internal migration had the same result. The homelessness of the American migrant in geography and on the map of finance, is the whole subject of the American realists of our period. European readers see in these writers only violence and brutality. They miss not only the pathos but the nomadic virtues associated with it, generosity, hospitality, equity, directness, politeness, simplicity of relations – traits which, together with a certain gentle timidity (as of very *unpracticed* nomads), comprise the American character. Unobserved also is a peculiar nakedness, a look of being shorn of everything, that is very curiously American, corresponding to the square wooden desolation of a frontier town and the bright thinness of the American light. The American character looks always as if it had just had a rather bad haircut, which gives it, in our eyes at any rate, a greater humanity than the European, which even among its beggars has an all too professional air.

The openness of the American situation creates the pity and the terror; status is not protection; life for the European is a career; for the American, it is a hazard.

Mary McCarthy, 'America the Beautiful', September 1947, in *On the Contrary*, 1962

The immense popularity of American movies abroad demonstrates that Europe is the unfinished negative of which America is the proof. . . . America is indeed a revelation though not quite the one that was planned. Given a clean slate, man, it was hoped, would write the future. Instead he has written his past. This past, inscribed on billboards, ball parks, dance halls, is not seemly, yet its objectification is a kind of disburdenment. The past is at length outside. It does not disturb us as it does Europeans, for our relation with it is both more distant and more familiar. We cannot hate it for to hate it would be to hate poverty, our eager ancestors, and ourselves.

If there were time, American civilization could be seen as a beginning, even a favourable one, for we have only to look around us to see what a lot of sensibility a little ease will accrue. The children surpasss the fathers, and Louis B. Mayer cannot be preserved intact in his descendants. . . . Unfortunately, as things seem now, posterity is not around the corner.

Ibid.

American officials in South America

The North American official is every inch a business man. He represents his Government just as he would represent a private firm. The President's photograph above his desk is simply a picture of the Boss. 'What can I do for you?' he asks, and the offer is as genuine as his excellent teeth. He is all ready for business. He has goods to sell – the best goods in the world – and he will give you plenty of whisky while you make up your mind about buying them. The U.S. Constitution, for example – that's a product he can highly recommend. He knows it inside out and will explain to you exactly how it works, with sincere technical enthusiasm, as though it were a refrigerating plant. His frankness is very attractive. It will only become sinister if and when he develops into a conscious technocrat, ruthlessly determined to make the world safe for iceboxes. . . . Meanwhile he goes cheerfully ahead with his promoting, and secretly rather despises the devious ways of the professional diplomats. Why beat about the bush? Why fuss with a lot of protocol? And why the hell talk French?

Christopher Isherwood, *The Condor and the Cows*, 1949

The making of an American begins at that point where he himself rejects all other ties, any other history, and himself adopts the vesture of his adopted land.

James Baldwin, 'Many Thousands Gone', 1951, *Notes of a Native Son*, 1955

It always strikes me that Americans are the only people who remind me of Russians. You don't object to my saying that? Americans are so generous, energetic. And underneath all that brag they have such a wishing to be loved, they want to be petted, like dogs and children, and told that they are just as good and even better than the rest of us. Well, Europeans are inclined to agree with them. But they simply won't believe it. They go right on feeling inferior and far away. Alone. Like Russians. Precisely.

Anon. Norwegian, met by Truman Capote in Russia, and quoted in *The Muses are Heard*, 1954

Whatever else an American believes, or disbelieves about himself, he is absolutely sure he has a sense of humor.

E.B. White, 'Some Remarks on Humor', *The Second Tree from the Corner*, 1954

It is possible to believe in progress as a fact without believing in progress as an ethical principle; but in the catechism of many Americans, the one goes with the other.

Norbert Wiener, *The Human Use of Human Beings*, 1954

Americans are not materialistic in the money sense: they are too generous and wasteful, too idealistic for that. Yet their idealism is sometimes curiously lacking in the spiritual values. They have an abiding belief in their ability to control reality by purely spiritual means.

Cecil Beaton, *It Gives Me Great Pleasure*, 1955

Perhaps the most revolting character that the United States ever produced was the Christian business man.

H.L. Mencken, *Minority Report – H.L. Mencken's Notebooks*, 1956

American children develop national characteristics disconcertingly early. This is the land of opportunism, and the children realize it soon.

James Morris, *Coast to Coast*, 1956

The thing that impresses me most about America is the way parents obey their children.

Duke of Windsor, *Look*, 5 March 1957

An American who can make money, invoke God, and be no better than his neighbor, has nothing to fear but truth itself.

Marya Mannes, *More in Anger*, 1958

An American is either a Jew, or an anti-Semite, unless he is both at the same time.

Jean-Paul Sartre, *Les Séquestrés d'Altona / The Condemned of Altona*, 1959

We are an obsessively moral people, but our morality is a team morality.

Edgar Z. Friedenberg, 'The Impact of the School', *The Vanishing Adolescent*, 1959

So much of learning to be an American is learning not to let your individuality become a nuisance.

Ibid.

As the psychiatrist helps Americans to get to know themselves, so does the Public Relations man help them to get to know other Americans.

Lord Kinross, *The Innocents at Home*, 1959

In the modern world, we Americans are the old inhabitants. We first had political freedom, high industrial production, an economy of abundance.

Paul Goodman, *Growing up Absurd*, 1960

That's why they don't like Americans anywhere. That's why we have lost the world completely – because we fucked all of their mothers for chocolate bars. And don't you forget it, Jim. Don't ever forget that.

Lenny Bruce, 'The Dirty-Word Concept', before 1966, in *The Essential Lenny Bruce*, 1973

Between the Americans and the British . . . there exists profound natural antipathy, as between cats and dogs.

Pamela Frankau, *Pen to Paper*, 1961

. . . that small fame which comes upon any young American who makes a great deal of money in a hurry.

Norman Mailer, *Advertisements for Myself*, 1961

We are all American at puberty; we die French.

Evelyn Waugh, *Diary*, July 1961

[Americans] expect to eat and stay thin, to be constantly on the move and ever more neighborly . . . to revere God and be God.

Daniel J. Boorstin, *Newsweek*, 26 February 1962

Never have people been more the masters of their environment. Yet never has a people felt more deceived and disappointed. For never has a people expected so much more than the world could offer.

Daniel J. Boorstin, Introduction to *The Image*, 1962

The old South which the Southerner idealized, which he may still be found idealizing today and which the Northerner has come to idealize, too, was mostly located in time in the eighteenth century; and in geography especially in eastern Virginia, colonial, and post-Revolutionary, that powerful and wealthy society, self-confident and self-contained and ruled by a few hundred families who were themselves pretty nearly autonomous.

Edmund Wilson, *Patriotic Gore*, 1962

If one compares Americans with Europeans, one might say, crudely and too tidily, that the mediocre American is possessed by the Present, and the mediocre European is possessed by the Past.

W.H. Auden, 'The American Scene', in *The Dyer's Hand and Other Essays*, 1963

Frustrate a Frenchman, he will drink himself to death; an Irishman, he will die of angry hypertension; a Dane, he will shoot himself; an American, he will get drunk, shoot you, then establish a million dollar aid program for your relatives. Then he will die of an ulcer.

Stanley Rudin, *New York Times*, 22 August 1963

The people of the United States are at the present time dominated and driven by two kinds of officially propagated fear: fear of the Soviet Union and fear of the income tax.

Edmund Wilson, *The Cold War and the Income Tax*, 1963

The typical American believes that no necessity of the soul is free and that there are precious few, if any, which cannot be bought.

Joseph Wood Krutch, 'The European Visitor', *If You Don't Mind My Saying So*, 1964

Everybody is in analysis. It's the dominant mode for the American interpretation of reality.

A. Alvarez, 'A Talk with Robert Lowell', *Encounter*, February 1965

Loneliness: It is a continual, almost palpable quality

which the country gives off like a heat shimmer. It is no less present in the utter separateness and indifference of city life, the blank size of the buildings, the self-sufficiency of the different ethnic ghettoes, than in the deserts and mountains of the South-west. It is not made less for an instant by that terrible friendliness, mass produced, pre-packaged, frozen, that coos at you from every T.V. screen and bill-board. Rather, this false cosiness – instant Doris Day – accentuates the loneliness precisely because it is mass produced, a convention as chilling and formal as diplomatic protocol. Perhaps it is this style of friendliness without human sympathy that helps to make the Americans so wary of any organized welfare: in a certain light – that, perhaps cast by a million television screens – social benevolence looks much like contempt.

A. Alvarez, 'American After-thoughts', *Encounter*, June 1965

Sitting at the table doesn't make you a diner unless you eat some of what's on that plate. Being here in America doesn't make you an American. Being born here in America doesn't make you an American.

Malcolm X, *Malcolm X Speaks*, 1965

What is it that distinguishes the American Man from his counterparts in other climes; what *is* it that makes him so special? He is quietly affirmative. He is trustworthy, loyal, helpful, friendly, courteous, kind, obedient, cheerful, thrifty, brave, clean and reverent.

John Updike, 'Anywhere is Where you Hang Your Hat', *Assorted Prose*, 1965

Like almost everyone outside the US and not a few in it, I had always been greatly alarmed by the Americans. For many years they had been putting the wind up the world by actions of terrifying charity and menacing goodwill, but especially did they scare me, since the more I alienated myself from everything they did internationally the more I seemed to get mixed up with them personally.

The American nation is unprecedented in history: so rich, so strong, so vulnerable, so generous, so blind, so bountiful, so clumsy, so kind, so perilous, so unmanageable in their simple-minded craftiness, the brutal innocence of their lethal benevolence. Nobody but the Americans could have invented a President who posed as a peasant to conceal the expert ruthlessness that concealed the fact that he was a peasant all the time. Nobody ever knocked people about like the Americans to establish the warmth of their own hearts. (I recalled the genuinely tender consideration with which the army in Viet Nam provided artificial limbs for the children whose legs they had blown off.) The Americans were the people with whose good intentions the road to hell was so painstakingly paved.

James Cameron, *Point of Departure*, 1967

We have earned the slogan, 'Yanks, go home!'

Edmund Wilson, Preface to *Europe Without Baedeker*, 1967 edn

Americans think of themselves collectively as a huge rescue squad on twenty-four-hour call to any spot on the globe where dispute and conflict may erupt.

Eldridge Cleaver, 'Rallying Round the Flag', *Soul on Ice*, 1968

. . . christ, Americans are childish in many ways and about as subtle as a Wimpy bender: but in the long run it doesn't make any difference. They just turn on the power.

Tom Wolfe, 'The Mid-Atlantic Man', in *The Pump House Gang*, 1968

The land of the dull and the home of the literal.

Gore Vidal, *Reflections upon a Sinking Ship*, 1969

Whatever the noteworthy aspects of the American system of diplomatic representation, it produces an exceptionally large number of men who are qualified, in their own view, to comment on its shortcomings.

John Kenneth Galbraith, *Economics, Peace and Laughter*, 1971

Americans are, so to speak, canted toward the future.

Frances Fitzgerald, *Fire in the Lake*, 1972

Americans ignore history, for to them everything has always seemed new under the sun. The national myth is that of creativity and progress, of a steady climbing upward into power and prosperity, both for the individual and for the country as a whole. Americans see history as a straight line and themselves standing at the cutting edge of it as representatives for all mankind. They believe in the future as if it were a religion; they believe that there is nothing they cannot accomplish, that solutions wait somewhere for all problems, like brides.

Ibid.

Richard Crossman . . . [said] . . . that it took an Englishman a long time to fight for a liberty but once he had it nobody could take it away, but that we in America fought fast for liberty and could be deprived of it in an hour.

Lillian Hellman, *Scoundrel Time*, 1976

We are a people who do not want to keep much of the past in our heads. It is considered unhealthy in America to remember mistakes, neurotic to think about them, psychotic to dwell on them.

Ibid.

I hear America swinging,
The carpenter with his wife or the mason's wife, or even
the mason,

The mason's daughter in love with the boy next door,
who is in love with the boy next door to him,
Everyone free, comrades in arms together, freely
swinging. . . .

Peter de Vries, *I Hear America Swinging*, 1976

Americans . . . generally think of language as some arcane disease of the throat.

Peter Ackroyd, *Spectator*, 1 October 1977

A peculiarity of American sexual mores is that those men who like to think of themselves as exclusively and triumphantly heterosexual are convinced that the most masculine of all activities is not tending to the sexual needs of women but watching other men play games. I have never understood this aspect of my countrymen but I suppose there is a need for it (bonding?), just as the Romans had a need to see people being murdered. Perhaps there is a connection between the American male's need to watch athletes and his fatness: according to a W.H.O. report the American male is the world's fattest and softest; this might explain why he also loves guns – you can always get your revolver up.

Gore Vidal, *Matters of Fact and Fiction*, 1977

A society where mistresses are rare, expensive, and difficult.

Nicholas von Hoffman, 'America on the Run', *Spectator*, 21 September 1978

. . . the American conviction that one should not kick a man when he is up. . . .

Henry Fairlie, *Spectator*, 24 May 1980

For Europeans the fascination is singular. Americans are the people we might have been. . . . The mirror we look into is deliciously and disturbingly distorted.

Trevor Fishlock, *Americans and Nothing Else*, 1980

Americans emerge from the womb groping for a steering wheel.

Ibid.

The seventies . . . was . . . the disease decade, when Americans learned their destiny was to be medical patients. . . . It was the seventies which changed having a baby from a natural act to a medical emergency.

Nicholas von Hoffman, 'America's Plastic Decade', *Spectator*, 5 January 1980

It bewilders Americans to be hated.

Lance Morrow, quoted · *Observer*, 'Sayings of the Week', 13 January 1980

A well-known psychiatric joke declares that the cure for severe depression has been discovered: it is to fly to the United States, where you will be diagnosed instead as a schizophrenic.

Peter Sedgewick, *Sunday Times*, 27 January 1980

All Americans born between 1890 and 1945 wanted to be movie stars.

Gore Vidal, 'Scott's Case', *New York Review of Books*, 1 May 1980

Americans are now defensively aware of their history: they are in transit from a Ptolemaic to a Copernican view of themselves, and a scaling down of their range and ambitions in the world. The diminution, even the implicit insult of the process is painful.

Time Magazine, 7 July 1980

The key to a coherent understanding of Americans may lie in knowing that from the beginning they have kept two sets of books: their history and their myth. They have always intertwined, of course, but they differ radically in purpose and content. The myth has always been the engine of the future.

Ibid.

American Women

In the evening we were conversing again with the Lyons merchant concerning america; he was very inquisitive about our manners – and of course about our women. We assured him that they did not come short of the european ladies in respect to personal charms – and that they were remarkable for their affectionate fidelity to their husbands – This last eulogium produced a true Frenchmans remark – 'Mon dieu,' said he '*c'est un pays malheureux pour les garçons*'. 'Certainement' said C—— 'il faut se marier la.'

Washington Irving, *Journal*, 19 May 1805

They fade at an earlier age than in England; but, till then, they are as beautiful as the women in *Cornwall*, which contains, to my thinking, the prettiest women in our country.

William Cobbett, *A Year's Residence in the United States of America*, 1817–19

I certainly believe the women of America to be the handsomest in the world, but as surely do I believe that they are the least attractive.

Mrs Frances Trollope, *Domestic Manners of the Americans*, 1832

In circumstances where an English woman would look proud, and a French woman *nonchalante*, an American lady looks grim.

Ibid.

A great unknown pleasure remains to be experienced

by the Americans in the well-modulated, gentle, healthy, cheerful voices of women. It is incredible that there should not, in all time to come, be any other alternative than that which now exists, between a whine and a twang. When the health of the American woman improves, their voices will improve. In the meantime, they are unconscious how the effect of their remarkable and almost universal beauty is injured by their mode of speech.

Harriet Martineau, *Society in America*, 1837

An American girl scarcely ever displays that virginal softness in the midst of young desires or that innocent and ingenuous grace which usually attend the European woman in the transition from girlhood to youth. It is rare that an American woman, at any age, displays childish timidity or ignorance. Like the young women of Europe, she seeks to please, but she knows precisely the cost of pleasing. If she does not abandon herself to evil, at least she knows that it exists; and she is remarkable rather for purity of manners than for chastity of mind.

Alexis de Tocqueville, *Democracy in America, the second part*, 1840

For myself, I have entertained on sundry occasions that sort of feeling for an American woman which the close vicinity of an unclean animal produces. . . . If there be two of them they talk loudly together, having a theory that modesty has been put out of court by women's rights. But though not modest, the woman I describe is ferocious in her propriety. She ignores the whole world around her, and as she sits with raised chin and face flattened with affectation she pretends to declare aloud that she is positively not aware that any man is even near her. She speaks as though to her in her womanhood, the neighbourhood of men was the same as that of dogs or cats. . . . But her own face always gives her the lie. In her assumption of indifference she displays her nasty consciousness, and in each attempt at would-be propriety is guilty of an immodesty.

Anthony Trollope, *North America*, 1862

Lady Caroline: . . . Why can't they stay in their own country? They are always telling us it is the Paradise of Women.
Lord Illingworth: It is, Lady Caroline. That is why, like Eve, they are so extremely anxious to get out of it.
Lady Caroline: Who are Miss Worsley's parents?
Lord Illingworth: American women are wonderfully clever at concealing their parents.

Oscar Wilde, *A Woman of No Importance*, 1893

There a woman takes to the telephone as women in more decadent lands take to morphia.

Arnold Bennett, *Those United States*, 1912

Every American woman has two souls to call her own, the other being her husband's.

James Agate, *Ego 3*, 15 May 1937

American female energy is increased enormously by the fact that they don't mind being middle aged.

Freya Stark, Letter, 23 December 1943, in *Dust in the Lion's Paw*, 1961

The dream of the American male is for a female who has an essential languor which is not laziness, who is unaccompanied except by himself, and who does not let him down. He desires a beautiful, but comprehensible creature who does not destroy a perfect situation by forming a complete sentence.

E.B. White, 'Notes on our Time', *The Second Tree from the Corner*, 1954

Blacks

It is not good to be a Negro in the land of the free and the home of the brave.

Rudyard Kipling, *From Sea to Sea*, 1889

'You must repudiate separation,' I said. 'no peoples have ever yet endured the tension of intermingled distinctness.'

'May we not become a peculiar people – like the Jews?' he suggested. 'Isn't that possible?'

H.G. Wells, quoting his conversation with Booker T. Washington, *The Future in America*, 1906

The American negro was said to be made up of many different negroes: Jamaican, South American, etc. To-day he looks as though he were made up of many different whites.

Shane Leslie, *American Wonderland*, 1936

. . . the great Negro race which alone keeps America from falling apart.

Henry Miller, *The Colossus of Maroussi*, 1942

The economic situation of the Negroes in America is pathological.

Gunnar Myrdal, *An American Dilemma*, 1944

Not long ago, but before World War II was over, a young Negro girl was asked how she would punish Hitler. Answer: 'Paint him black and bring him over here.'

Walter Winchell, *New York Daily Mirror*, 26 March 1945

One of the things that makes a Negro unpleasant to white folk is the fact that he suffers from their injustice. He is thus a standing rebuke to them.

H.L. Mencken, *Minority Report – H.L. Mencken's Notebooks*, 1956

The Negro problem is a white man's problem.
Franz Schoenberner, *Confessions of a European Intellectual*, 1946

I know Negroes who prefer the South and white Southerners, because 'at least there, you don't have to play any guessing games!' The guessing games referred to have driven more than one Negro into the narcotics ward, the madhouse, or the river.
James Baldwin, 'Fifth Avenue, Uptown', 1960, *Nobody Knows My Name*, 1964

Here's how the world looks to the American Negro; he's a convict rioting in a corrupt prison.
Lenny Bruce, 'Blacks', before 1966, in *The Essential Lenny Bruce*, 1973

To be a Negro in America is to hope against hope.
Martin Luther King, *Chaos or Community*, 1967

To be black and conscious in America is to be in a constant state of rage.
James Baldwin, quoted by Joan Didion, *The White Album*, 1979

Indians

Lo, the poor Indian! whose untutor'd mind
Sees God in clouds, or hears him in the wind;
His soul proud Science never taught to stray
Far as the solar walk or milky way;
Yet simple nature to his hope has giv'n,
Behind the cloud-topt hill, an humbler Heav'n; . . .
To be, contents his natural desire;
He asks no Angel's wing, no Seraph's fire;
But thinks, admitted to that equal sky,
His faithful dog shall bear him company.
Alexander Pope, *Essay on Man*, 1732

The aboriginal inhabitants of these countries I have regarded with the commiseration their history inspires.
Thomas Jefferson, Second Inaugural Address, 4 March 1805

An Indian has his knowledge for use, & it only appears in use. Most white men that we know have theirs for talking purposes.
Ralph Waldo Emerson, *Journals*, 1857

* – What do you mean by the *provisional* races, Sir? – said the divinity-student, interrupting him.

Why, the original bipeds, to be sure, – he answered, – the red-crayon sketch of humanity laid on the canvas before the colours for the real manhood were ready.

I hope they will come to something yet, – said the divinity-student.

Irreclaimable, Sir, – irreclaimable – said the little Gentleman. – Cheaper to breed white men than domesticate a nation of red ones. When you can get the bitter out of a partridge's thigh, you can make an enlightened commonwealth of Indians. A provisional race, Sir – nothing more. Exhaled carbonic acid for the use of vegetation, kept down the bears and catamounts, enjoyed themselves scalping and being scalped, and then passed away, or are passing away, according to the programme.
Oliver Wendell Holmes, *The Professor at the Breakfast Table*, 1859

Unless they shall be treated as a truly Christian community would treat a band of orphan children providentially thrown on its hands, the aborigines of this country will be practically extinct within the next fifty years. . . . It needs but little familiarity with the actual, palpable aborigines to convince any one that the poetic Indian of Cooper and Longfellow – is only visible to the poet's eye. To the prosaic observer the average Indian of the woods and prairies is a being who does little credit to human nature, – a slave of appetite and sloth, never emancipated from the tyranny of one animal passion save by the more ravenous demands of another. As I passed over those magnificent bottoms of the Kansas which form the reservations of the Delawares, Potawatamies, etc., constituting the very best corn-lands on earth, and saw their owners sitting around the doors of their lodges at the height of the planting season, and in as good, bright, planting weather as sun and soil ever made, I could not help saying, 'These people must die out – there is no help for them. God has given this earth to those who will subdue and cultivate it, and it is vain to struggle against His righteous decree.'
Horace Greeley, *An Overland Journey from New York to San Francisco in . . . 1859*, 1860

He is, I am aware, at a painful discount just at present, and I confess that his nobility is, in the main, nonsense, and he himself, a nuisance.
G.A. Sala, *My Diary in America in the Midst of War*, 1865

The only good Indian I ever saw was a dead Indian.
General Philip Henry Sheridan, Remark at Old Fort Cobb, Indian Territory, January 1869, when introduced to a chief called Old Toch-a-way as a 'good Indian', according to Edward M. Ellis

It isn't worth while, in these practical times, for people to talk about Indian poetry – there never was any in them – except the Fenimore Cooper Indians. But *they* are an extinct tribe that never existed. I know the Noble Red Man. I have camped with the Indians; I have been on the warpath with them, taken part in the chase with them – for grasshoppers; helped them steal cattle; I have roamed with them, scalped them, had them for breakfast. I would gladly eat the whole race if I had a chance.

Mark Twain, *The Innocents Abroad*, 1869

Alabama

Alabama . . . seems to have a bad name even among those who reside in it.

J.S. Buckingham, *The Slave States of America, 1839*, 1842

Alaska

Seward's Ice-box.

Anon. term of derision, at the time of the purchase of Alaska, 1867

Where the short-legged Esquimaux
Waddle in the ice and snow,
And the playful polar bear
Nips the hunter unaware . . .
Polar dock where Nature slips
From the ways her icy ships;
Land of fox and deer and sable
Shore end of our western cable,
Let the news that flying goes
Thrill through all your arctic floes. . . .
Know you not what fate awaits you
Or to what the future mates you?
All ye icebergs make salaam, –
You belong to Uncle Sam!
On the spot where Eugene Sue
Led his wretched wandering Jew,
Stands a form whose features strike
Russ and Esquimaux alike.
He it is whom skalds of old
In their Runic rhymes foretold!
Lean of flank and lank of jaw,
See the real Northern Thor!
See the awful Yankee leering
Just across the Straits of Behring.
On the drifted snow, too plain,
Sinks his fresh tobacco stain
Just beside the deep inden-
Tation of his Number 10. . . .

Bret Harte, *An Arctic Vision*, 1867

In summer a land of sound – a land echoed with the voices of birds, the ripple of running water, the mournful music of the waving pine branch; in winter a land of silence, its great rivers glimmering in the moonlight, wrapped in their shrouds of ice, its still forests rising weird and spectral against the auroral-lighted horizon, its nights so still that the moving streamers across the Northern skies seem to carry to the ear a sense of sound!

General Sir William Butler, *The Great Lone Land*, 1872

Southern Alaska is the Switzerland of America.

Harry de Windt, *From Paris to New York by Land*, 1904

Albany (New York)

Albany is an excessively dull place and combines filth and heat to a great degree. But it seems to be thriving and prosperous. As a situation for commercial advantage it may be good, but nobody would ever wish to pass a whole day there a second time, when travelling merely for pleasure.

Charles Francis Adams, *Diary*, 8 August 1826

They told me that I saw Albany; but I was by no means sure of it. This large city lay in the landscape like an anthill in a meadow.

Harriet Martineau, *Retrospect of Western Travel*, 1838

Alexandria (north of La Grange and Canton, above St Louis)

I missed Alexandria; was told it was under water, but would come up to blow in the summer.

Mark Twain, *Life on the Mississippi*, 1883

Amarillo (Texas)

De vedder out here I do not like. De rain vas all vind, and de vind vas all sand.

German settler, quoted by John Gunther, *Inside U.S.A.*, 1947

Amherst

The Amherst heart is plain and whole and permanent and warm.

Emily Dickinson, Letter to Professor J.K. Chickering, 1885

Anaheim (California)

We drove through the clean and well-kept avenues and streets, scenting Rhineland on every side; and indeed, this Anaheim itself, is nothing less than a bit of Germany, dropped down on the Pacific Coast. It has little in common with Los Angeles the dirty.

James F. Rusling, *Across America*, 1874 – of 1866

Anchorage (Alaska)

. . . This most unwelcoming outpost of the American way of life. . . . There was a poster saying that the Anchorage Thespians would be performing *The Rainmaker*. At once this gave me the feeling of a little hothouse of amateur-arty gossip and intrigue, improbably lost in snowy wildernesses, efficiently central-heated.

James Kirkup, *These Horned Islands*, 1962

Our stop at Anchorage . . . enabled us to stretch our legs and reorganize our stomachs. So far as I could make out through the darkness the entire surroundings were heavily snowbound, though the log-cabin-style airport was overpoweringly hot, and I was a trifle disconcerted to observe two very tough-looking Arctic frontiersmen, each with revolvers on both hips, and distinctly heard one say to the other: 'Say, why don't we go get a glass of milk.' Clearly, like the old grey mare, the frontier wasn't what it used to be.

Charles A. Fisher, *Three Times a Guest*, 1979 – of 1961

Arkansas

from the Mississippi
The scenery was by this time very wild. These hundreds of miles of level woods, and turbid, rushing waters, and desert islands, are oppressive to the imagination. Very few dwellings were visible. We went ashore in the afternoon, just for the sake of having been in Arkansas. We could penetrate only a little way through the young cotton-wood and the tangled forest, and we saw nothing.

Harriet Martineau, *Retrospect of Western Travel*, 1838

*The creation state, the finishin-up country. . . . Then its airs – just breathe them, and they will make you snort like a horse.

'Jim Doggett', in Thomas Bangs Thorpe, *The Big Bear of Arkansas*, 1841

I met a traveller from Arkansas
Who boasted of his state as beautiful
For diamonds and apples. 'Diamonds
And apples in commercial quantities?'
I asked him, on my guard. 'Oh yes,' he answered,
Off his. The time was evening in the Pullman
'I see the porter's made your bed,' I told him.

Robert Frost, *New Hampshire*, 1923

Arkansas has its own popular motto and it is this: 'I've never seen nothin', I don't know nothin', I hain't got nothin', and I don't want nothin'.' . . . It (Arkansas) just grew out of seepage. . . . A belt of mud prevented Arkansas from having a port and denied to her a metropolis, a civilisation, and a history. A people who were willing to foot it a hundred miles through the muck to get nowhere founded Arkansas and achieved their aim. . . . No stream can rise higher than its source and Arkansas has proved it. . . . Few can read in Arkansas, and those who can, do not.

C.L. Edson, Essay in *The Nation*, 1930s

Arkansas City (on the Mississippi)

We asked a passenger who belonged there what sort of a place it was. 'Well,' said he, after considering, and with the air of one who wishes to take time and be accurate, 'It's a hell of a place.' A description which was photographic for exactness.

Mark Twain, *Life on the Mississippi*, 1883

Athens (Georgia)

Georgia may be one of the few places on earth where trees are treated anthropomorphically. At the summit of a steep cobblestone side street in Athens, Georgia, stands a tree with property rights. It owns itself. 'For and in consideration of the great love I bear this tree and the great desire I have for its protection for all time,' says a marker attached to a fence that surrounds it, 'I convey entire possession of itself and all land within eight feet of the tree on all sides.' The legacy took effect in 1875, on the death of the tree's unusual admirer, one William H. Jackson.

E.J. Kahn Jr, *New Yorker*, 6 February 1978

Atlanta

I heard it said that the 'architecture' of Atlanta is rococola.

John Gunther, *Inside U.S.A.*, 1947

When I pray 'Thy Kingdom come on earth,' I mean I want Atlanta to look like heaven.

Andrew Young (when a Congressman), quoted *Time Magazine*, 27 August 1979

'The City too busy to hate,' – a slogan coined, or at least repeated today, by a people too short-sighted to notice.

Simon Winchester, 'Atlanta, a Dream Turned Sour', *Sunday Times Magazine*, 16 August 1981

Atlantic City

That monstrosity aptly described by C.D. Warner as 'having been cut out with a scroll saw' – Atlantic City. (May I never! never! behold anything resembling it again!)

Lafcadio Hearn, Letter to Elizabeth Bisland, 1889

Oscar Wilde called the Atlantic Ocean 'disappointing.' Out-of-season Atlantic City . . . is complete and summary disillusion.

James Agate, *Ego 3*, 15 May 1937

What they wanted was Monte Carlo. They didn't want Las Vegas. What they got was Las Vegas. We always knew they would get Las Vegas.

Stuart Mendelson of the *Philadelphia Journal*, on the introduction of legalized gambling to Atlantic City, quoted by Michael Leapman, *The Times*, 29 May 1978

Augusta (Georgia)

A queer little rustic city called Augusta – a great broad street 2 miles long – old quaint looking shops – houses with galleries – ware-houses – trees – cows and negroes strolling about the side walks – plank roads – a happy dirty tranquillity generally prevalent.

W.M. Thackeray, Letter to Kate Perry, 14–16 February 1856

I never saw so many cows in my life, – at least in the streets of an inhabited town. . . . An innocent life. Plenty of fodder. The consciousness that you have done your duty to society by giving it an ample supply of nice, new milk, and there an end. . . . If there be a metempsychosis, I think that I should like to be a cow, at Augusta, in the State of Georgia.

G.A. Sala, *America Revisited*, 1882

Austin (Texas)

It reminds one somewhat of Washington; Washington *en petit*, seen through a reversed glass.

Frederick Law Olmsted, *A Journey through Texas*, 1857

Avon (New York)

It is a straggling, ugly little place, and not any of their 'Romes, Carthages, Ithacas, or Athens,' ever provoked me so much. This Avon flows sweetly with nothing but whiskey and tobacco juice.

Mrs Frances Trollope, *Domestic Manners of the Americans*, 1832

Azusa

Azusa, in case you don't know, has a drugstore where you can buy straw hats for horses and also for people.

Groucho Marx, Letter to Thornton Delahanty, 14 June 1945

The Bad Lands (South Dakota)

A part of hell with the fires burnt out.

General Custer, attrib., *c.* 1874

The Badlands look as you might expect the moon to look, if it were hot, a parched picture of the earth in exploding wrath. It is as if it were the devil's own bit of the planet and he had stabbbed and slashed with some great knife until all fertility drained away from yawning wounds. South Dakota . . . has skilfully turned it into a tourist attraction, thus making the best of a badlands job.

Douglas Reed, *Far and Wide*, 1951

They deserve this name. They are like the work of an evil child. Such a place the Fallen Angels might have built as a spite to Heaven, dry and sharp, desolate and dangerous, and for me filled with foreboding. A sense comes from it that it does not like or welcome humans

John Steinbeck, *Travels with Charley*, 1962

Baltimore

This is the dirtiest Place in the World.

John Adams, *Diary*, 8 February 1777

*I expect some parts of Fells Point would suit Mr Dickens fust rate. It's old as the Hills, and crooked as a ram's horn, and a body can hear jest as much bad English there as he could among the cockneys of London, and can find sum fancy caracters, male and female, that would do honour to St Giles's or to any other romantic corner of the British metropolis.

William T. Thompson, *Major Jones's Sketches of Travel . . .*, 1848

*You are the gastronomic metropolis of the Union. Why don't you put a canvasback duck on the top of the Washington column? Why don't you get that lady off from the Battle Monument and plant a terrapin in her place? Why will you ask for other glories when you have soft crabs? No, Sir, – you live too well to think as hard as we do in Boston. Logic comes to us with the salt-fish of Cape Ann; rhetoric is born of the beans of Beverly; but *you* – if you open your mouths to speak, Nature stops them with a fat oyster, or offers a slice of the breast of your divine bird, and silences all your aspirations.

Oliver Wendell Holmes, *The Professor at the Breakfast-Table*, 1859

It is more like an English town than most of its transatlantic brethren, and the ways of its inhabitants are English. . . . The country looks as hunting country should look, whereas no man that ever crossed a field after a pack of hounds would feel the slightest wish to attempt that process in New England, or New York.

Anthony Trollope, *North America*,1862

This is one of the places where Butler carried it with a high hand during the war, and where the ladies used to spit when they passed a Northern soldier. They are very handsome women, with an Eastern touch in them, and dress brilliantly. . . . They are a bright responsive people likewise, and very pleasant to read to.

Charles Dickens, Letter to his sister-in-law, 29 January 1868, quoted in Forster, *Life of Dickens*, 1872–3

Baton Rouge

Baton Rouge was clothed in flowers like a bride – no, much more so; like a greenhouse. For we were in the absolute South now – no modifications, no compromise, no half-way measures. . . .

Sir Walter Scott is probably responsible for the Capitol Building; for it is not conceivable that this little sham castle would ever have been built if he had not run the people mad, a couple of generations ago, with his mediaeval romances. The South has not yet recovered from the debilitating influence of his books

Mark Twain, *Life on the Mississippi*, 1883

Biloxi (Mississippi)

The only town which gave me a genuine and pleasant surprise was Biloxi, Mississippi.

Henry Miller, *The Air-conditioned Nightmare*, 1945

Boston

compared with Philadelphia
Philadelphia with all its Trade, and Wealth, and Regularity, is not Boston. The Morals of our People are much better, their Manners are more polite, and agreeable – they are purer English. Our Language is better, our Persons are handsomer, our Spirit is greater, our Laws are wiser, our Religion is superior, our Education is better. We exceed them in every Thing, but in a Markett, and in charitable public foundations.

John Adams, *Diary*, 9 October 1774

Boston is the Bristol, New York, the Liverpool, and Philadelphia, the London of America.

Henry Wallsey, *An Excursion to the United States of North America in 1794*, 1796

I hate the purse proud ostentation of the City of Boston. It is not the pride I like, it is not mine. . . . I am an aristocrat, but not of Boston.

Charles Francis Adams, *Diary*, 4 September 1824

Nobody can live in this climate without considerable resources.

Charles Francis Adams, *Diary*, 25 February 1833

Boston is perhaps as aristocratic, vain and vulgar a city, as described by its own 'first people', as any in the world. Happily, however, Boston has merits which these people know not of.

Harriet Martineau, *Society in America*, 1837

Development of the Brain in the Inhabitants of Boston. . . . Here the female head is in general beautifully developed in the moral and intellectual departments, and the natural language of the countenance is soft, affectionate and rational. In the men, also, large moral and intellectual organs are very general, but Benevolence and Veneration are more frequently large than Conscienciousness. The cerebral organization of this people, taking them all in all appears really to have been enlarged in the moral and intellectual regions by long cultivation, added to the influence of a favourable stock.

George Combe, *Notes . . . during a Phrenological Visit . . . in 1838–40*, 1841

When I got into the streets upon this Sunday morning, the air was so clear, the houses were so bright and gay; the signboards were painted in such gaudy colours; the gilded letters were so very golden; the bricks were so very red, the stone was so very white, the blinds and area railings were so very green, the knobs and plates upon the street doors so very marvellously bright and twinkling; and all so slight and unsubstantial in appearance – that every thoroughfare in the city looked exactly like a scene in a pantomime. . . . The suburbs are, if possible, even more unsubstantial looking than the city. The white wooden houses (so white that it makes one wink to look at them), with their green jalousie blinds, are so sprinkled and dropped about in all directions, without seeming to have any root at all in the ground; and the small churches and chapels are so prim, and bright, and highly varnished, that I almost believed the whole affair could be taken up piecemeal like a child's toy, and crammed into a little box.

Charles Dickens, *American Notes*, 1842

*If a man could walk edgeways, he mought possibly git through a square or two of Boston 'thout gittin nocked off the side-walk more'n a dozen times. Why, they ain't much wider than the space between the rows of a pea-patch and then they are so twistified, that its as much as a common sized body can do to keep both feet in the same street at the same time. And then what makes it worse, is the way the Boston people walks. They all go dashin along like they was gwine to die, and hadn't but a few hours left to settle their bisness.

William T. Thompson, *Major Jones's Sketches of Travel*, 1848

'What we want in Boston,' said he, 'is *territory* to build on. If we were as flush of it as they are here, we would make them sing small in the city way, that's a fact.'

Alexander Mackay, *The Western World*, 1849

A Boston man is the East wind made flesh.

Thomas Appleton, attrib.

See Boston and die! see the State Houses, old and new, the caterpillar wooden bridges crawling with innumerable legs across the flats of Charles; see the Common, – largest park, doubtless in the world, – with its files of trees planted as if by a drill-sergeant, and then for your *nunc dimittis*!

James Russell Lowell, *A Moosehead Journal*, 1853

Mrs. ——— says Boston ladies suffer in their health through the endless trouble of keeping servants doing things properly and nicely.

Arthur Hugh Clough, Letter, 10 January 1853

*Boston State-House is the hub of the solar system. You couldn't pry that out of a Boston man if you had the tire of all creation straightened out for a crow-bar.

O.W. Holmes, *The Autocrat of the Breakfast Table*, 1857–8

In Boston the onus lies upon every respectable person to prove that he has not written a sonnet, preached a sermon, or delivered a lecture.

Charles Mackay, *Life and Liberty in America, 1857–8*, 1859

*That's all I claim for Boston, – that it is the thinking centre of the continent, and therefore of the planet.
– And the grand emporium of modesty, – said the divinity-student, a little mischievously.

Oliver Wendell Holmes, *The Professor at the Breakfast-Table*, 1859

We say the cows laid out Boston. Well, there are worse surveyors.

Ralph Waldo Emerson, *Conduct of Life – Wealth*, 1860

Boston has a right to be proud of what it has done for the world of letters. It is proud; but I have not found that its pride was carried too far

Anthony Trollope, *North America*, 1862

Boston's a hole, the herring-pond is wide.

Robert Browning, *Mr Sludge, 'The Medium'*, 1864

Boston is one of the grandest, sure-footedst, clear-headest, comfortablest cities on the globe. Onlike ev'ry other large city I was ever in, the most of the hackmen don't seem to hav bin speshully intended by natur for the Burglery perfession, and its about the only large city I know of where you don't enjoy a brilliant opportunity of bein swindled in sum way, from the Risin of the sun to the going down thereof. There4 I say, loud and continnered applaus for Boston!

Charles F. Browne ('Artemus Ward'), *Boston*, 1865

What impression does the first glimpse of America make on a stranger? Absolutely that of a large box full of German toys. I saw the state of Massachusetts to begin with from Boston harbour. The shows were wonderfully toy-like – everything spick and span, and shining and new-looking. Trim, chalet-looking wooden houses, painted in all kinds of gay colours, dotted about like ornaments on a twelfth-cake. Toy trees, slim in the stem, straight in the branches, light and feathery in foliage; toy road, serpentine, dazzling, sparkling; the kind of roads you see in a Valentine, with a lady and a gentleman meandering towards the Temple of Hymen in the middle distance. Toy carriages: so crank and slender and brightly varnished are they – they all look as though they were made of painted tin; toy fences and palisades, and curious little toy churches, with bright green jalousies to the windows, and wooden steeples. Only give me the run of Mr Cremer's toy warehouse in Regent street, and I would build you up a model of the environs of Boston in half an hour. As a background you must have a sky not *quite* Italian blue . . . – a Sèvres porcelain sky, in fact. Let this sky be thoroughly clear from cloud or murk; let the air be as clear as a silver bell, – a wry, high-toned rarefied atmosphere, not bracing, however, but stimulating, lung-lifting, pulse-inclining, stringing your nerves to a degree of tension which is perhaps not very salutary, and of which the reaction may be languor, exhaustion, and ennui. Make the outlines clear of every object sharply defined; make the shadows cast by the sun clear and incisive, and in their texture luminous, instead of (as in our umbrageousness) heavy and woolly. Do this, *pictor ignotus*, and with your toy houses, toy gardens, toy fences, toy trees, and toy carriages, you may get up a suburban Boston to the very life.

G.A. Sala, *My Diary in America in the Midst of War*, 1865

Boston looks like a town that has been paid for ; Boston has a balance at its bankers.

Ibid.

The rocky nook with hill-tops three
  Looked eastward from the farms,
And twice each day the flowing sea
  Took Boston in its arms.

Ralph Waldo Emerson, *Boston*, 1873

Boston is a state of mind

Mark Twain, attributed; also attributed to Emerson and Thomas G. Appleton

Talking of (Boston) . . . as very little less holy than

Jerusalem, and as the home of all the good and great people outside of Palestine

William Dean Howells, *A Chance Acquaintance*, 1873

Crush up a sheet of letter-paper in your hand, throw it down, stamp it flat, and that is a map of old Boston.

Walt Whitman, *Specimen Days* (1 May 1881), 1882

Makes me think of the glints we get (as in Symonds' books) of the jolly old Greek cities. Indeed there is a good deal of the Hellenic in B., and the people are getting handsomer too – padded out, with freer motions, and with color in their faces. I never saw (although this is not Greek) so many *fine*-looking gray-haired women.

Ibid.

*The Bostonian who leaves Boston ought to be condemned to perpetual exile.

William Dean Howells, *The Rise of Silas Lapham*, 1885

I have learned enough never to argue with a Bostonian.

Rudyard Kipling, *From Sea to Sea*, 1889

I come from the city of Boston
The home of the Bean and the cod,
Where Cabots speak only to Lowells,
And Lowells speak only to God.

Samuel C. Bushnell, *Boston*, *c.*1905

and New York and Philadelphia
In Boston they ask, How much does he know? In New York, How much is he worth? In Philadelphia, Who were his parents?

Mark Twain, *What Paul Bourget thinks of Us*, 1897

The finality of Boston is a quantitive consequence. The capacity of Boston, it would seem, was just sufficient, but no more than sufficient, to comprehend the whole achievement of the human intellect up, let us say, to the year 1875 A.D. Then an equilibrium was established. At or about that year Boston filled up. . . . It is the peculiarity of Boston's intellectual quality that she cannot unload again.

H.G. Wells, *The Future in America*, 1906

Of Boston I refuse to say anything. I dislike the Hill as much as the Hill dislikes me. It was in those days – and I daresay it still is – an architectural imitation of the intellectual suburb of London called Hampstead, N.W. It still had imitation English writers, imitation disagreeable old gentlemen who wrote articles in imitation of those in London *Athenaeum* and imitation formidably disagreeable Duchesses who sat about in rooms whose furniture scantily imitated that of their English predecessors. . . . It had of course William James. But do you believe that one just man could have saved *that* Gomorrah? I do not. And the accent! . . . When a real Boston man used to approach me uttering sounds like those of a brick-throated bull-frog it used to occur to me that if the Cabots really had the ear of the Almighty, He must bitterly have regretted that He ever invented the vocal organs of humanity.

Ford Madox Ford, *Return to Yesterday*, 1932 – of 1906

Only Bostonians can understand Bostonians and thoroughly sympathize with the inconsequences of the Boston mind.

Henry Adams, *The Education of Henry Adams*, 1907

One day, through the primeval wood,
A calf walked home, as good calves should;
But made a trail all bent askew,
A crooked trail, as all calves do. . . .
This forest trail became a lane,
That bent and turned and turned again. . . .
And this, before men were aware,
A city's crowded thoroughfare; . . .
And men two centuries and a half
Trod in the footsteps of that calf.

Sam Walter Foss, 'The Calf-Path', *The Simple Speller*, 1907

Within an hour or so I had been familiarised by Bostonians with a whole series of apparently stock jokes concerning, and against, Boston, such as that one hinging on the phrase, 'Cold roast Boston,' and that other one about the best thing in Boston being the five o'clock train to New York. (I do not vouch for the hour of departure). Even in Cambridge, a less jocular place, a joke seemed to be imminent, to the effect that, though you could always tell a Harvard man, you could not tell him much.

Arnold Bennett, *Those United States*, 1912

Boston prides itself on virtue and ancient lineage – it doesn't impress me in either direction. It is musty, like the Faubourg St. Germain. I often want to ask them what constitutes the amazing virtue they are so conscious of.

Bertrand Russell, Letter to Margaret Llewellyn Davies, 12 April 1914

It is not age which killed Boston, for no cities die of age; it is the youth of other cities.

W.L. George, *Hail Columbia*, 1921

Let us erect in the Basin a lofty fountain.
Suckled on ponds, the spirit craves a watery mountain.

Wallace Stevens, 'Boston without a Notebook', *New England Verses*, 1923

On another occasion a guest at a White House reception eased up to the President and remarked: 'Mr President, I'm from Boston.'

His blue eyes rested only briefly on her as he said: 'You'll never get over it.'

Ishbel Ross, *Grace Coolidge and her Era*, 1962 – of 1920s

And here's to the City of Boston
The town of the cries and the groans,
Where the Cabots can't see the Kabotschniks,
And the Lowells won't speak to the Cohns.

Franklin P. Adams, *On the Aristocracy of Harvard, Revised*

I was prepared to like Boston.

When I came up on deck to catch my first glimpse of the shore line I was immediately disappointed. Not only disappointed I might say but actually saddened. The American coast looked bleak and uninviting to me. I didn't like the look of the American house; there is something cold and austere, something barren and chill about the architecture of the American home. It was *home*, with all the ugly, evil, sinister connotations which the word contains for a restless soul. There was a frigid, moral aspect to it, which chilled me to the bone.

Henry Miller, *The Air-conditioned Nightmare*, 1945

I have just returned from Boston. It is the only thing to do if you find yourself up there.

Fred Allen, Letter to Groucho Marx, 12 June 1953

The man in the story . . . approached St Peter and at the Pearly Gates presented his credentials and petition to enter. Saint Peter asked him where he was from, and when informed 'BOSTON', hesitated, then said, 'Well, your record is spotless, and you may come in, but I don't think you will like it here.'

A 'Guide at a Glance' of Historic Boston, 1970s

and Harvard University

William F. Buckley Jr once remarked that he would rather be governed by the first 100 names in the Boston telephone book than by the faculty of Harvard University.

Richard Nixon, *The Real War*, 1980

Mount Auburn

Have you ever been to Mount Auburn? If not, you can form but slight conception of this 'City of the Dead.' It seems as if nature had formed this spot with a distinct idea in view of its being a resting-place for her children, where, wearied and disappointed, they might stretch themselves beneath the spreading cypress, and close their eyes.

Emily Dickinson, Letter to Mrs A.P. Strong, 8 September 1846

Bunker Hill monument

Hundreds of the 'tall chimneys' in our manufacturing districts have quite as imposing an appearence as has Bunker's Hill monument.

Alexander Mackay, *The Western World*, 1849

Bunker Hill

Our Fathers being weary
Laid down on Bunker Hill;
And tho' full many a morning,
Yet they are sleeping still. . . .

Emily Dickinson, Valentine Letter to Mr William Howland, 1852

Faneuil Hall

Cradle of American Liberty.

James Otis, attrib., *c.* 1760's

Buffalo

Of all the thousand and one towns I saw in America, I think Buffalo is the queerest looking; it is not quite so wild as Lockport, but all the buildings have the appearance of having been run up in a hurry, though every thing has an appearance of great pretension; there are porticos, columns, domes and colonnades, but all in wood. Every body tells you there, as in all their other new-born towns, and every body believes, that their improvement, and their progression, are more rapid, more wonderful than the earth ever before witnessed; while, to me, the only wonder is, how so many thousands, nay millions of persons, can be found, in the nineteenth century, who can be content so to live. Surely this country may be said to spread rather than to rise.

Mrs Frances Trollope, *Domestic Manners of the Americans*, 1832

Buffalo is as undesirable a place of residence as any in the free states. It is the rendezvous of all manner of persons; the passage through which fugitives pass from the States to Canada, from Canada to the States, and from Europe and the Eastern States into the wild West. Runaway slaves come here, and their owners come in hopes of recapturing them. Indian traders, land speculators, and poor emigrants come here, and the most debased Indians, the half-civilised, hang about the outskirts. No influence that the mass of respectable inhabitants can exert can neutralize the effects of a floating population like this; and the place is unavoidably a very vicious one. A sufficient proof of this is that ladies cannot walk beyond the streets without the protection of a gentleman.

Harriet Martineau, *Retrospect of Western Travel*, 1838

A forefinger of stone, dreamed by a sculptor, points to the sky.
It says: This way! this way!

Four lions snore in stone at the corner of the shaft.
They too are the dream of a sculptor.
They too say This way!

The street cars swing at a curve.
The middle class passengers witness low life.
The car windows frame low life all day in pictures.

Two Italian cellar delicatessens sell red and green
peppers.
The Florida bananas furnish a burst of yellow.
The lettuce and the cabbage give a green.

Boys play marbles in the cinders.
The boys' hands need washing.
The boys are glad; they fight among each other.

A plank bridge leaps the Lehigh Valley railroad.
Then acres of steel rails, freight cars, smoke,
And then . . . the blue lake shore
. . . Erie with Norse blue eyes . . . and the white sun.

Carl Sandburg,'Slants at Buffalo, New York', in *Cornhuskers, 1918*

and Niagara

Within the town of Buffalo
Are prosy men with leaden eyes.
Like ants they worry to and fro
(Important men in Buffalo).
But only twenty miles away
A deathless glory is at play:
Niagara, Niagara. . . .

Within the town of Buffalo
Are stores with garnets, sapphires, pearls,
Rubies, emeralds aglow, –
Opal chains in Buffalo,
Cherished symbols of success.
They value not your rainbow dress: –
Niagara, Niagara.

The shaggy meaning of her name
This Buffalo, this recreant town,
Sharps and lawyers prune and tame;
Few pioneers in Buffalo;
Except young lovers flushed and fleet
And winds halooing down the street:
'Niagara, Niagara.' . . .

Above the town a tiny bird,
A shining speck at sleepy dawn,
Forgets the ant-hill so absurd,
This self-important Buffalo.
Descending twenty miles away
He bathes his wings at break of day –
Niagara, Niagara.

Vachel Lindsay, 'Niagara', *Collected Poems*, 1923

I feel I had there a fuller glimpse into the real old U.S. than ever before. I was really interested, and the real Buffalos at home were much nicer than I had expected. . . . Why doesn't somebody write your *Cranford*? Buffalo is a sort of Cranford.

D.H. Lawrence, Letter to Mrs Bessie Freeman, August 1923

Buncombe County (North Carolina)

This is for Buncombe.

Felix Walker, Speech in the United States Congress, 1820, a speech intended to impress his constituents – hence the origin of 'Bunkum'

Butte (Montana)

'Butte Is the Black Heart of Montana.'

This is the toughest, bawdiest town in America, with the possible exception of Amarillo, Texas. Also it is something that Amarillo is not, and something so singular that the shock persists long after a visit – a town almost literally dying on its feet.

Butte 'a mile high, a mile deep,' built on the 'richest hill on earth,' and generally described as the greatest mining camp ever known, lies in a ragged and bleached cup of hills on a spur of the divide. By night it has a certain inferno-like magnificence, with lights appropriately copper-coloured – I heard it called 'the only electric-lit cemetery in the United States.' By day it is one of the ugliest places I have ever seen. The mine dumps, heaps of slag that nobody removes, line the hills; there is hardly any vegetation, since fumes from open hearth smelting in the old days seared and poisoned the living green; the frowsy streets are faced with slovenly and dilapidated ancient tenements. . . . The gallows frames show where the mines are, and underneath are not less than 2,700 miles of winzes, shafts, and tunnels; the town sits crazily on a shaky and sagging crust of ore; underground, practically every other inch is metal.

John Gunther, *Inside U.S.A.*, 1947

Butte stands in open country, on the edge of the hills, like a scab on a fair skin, dominated by the worst excrescences of the profit motive.

James Morris, *Coast to Coast*, 1956

Cairo

At the junction of the two rivers, on ground so flat and low and marshy, that at certain seasons of the year it is inundated to the housetops, lies a breeding-place of fever, ague, and death; vaunted in England as a mine of Golden Hope, and speculated in, on the faith of monstrous representations to many people's ruin. A dismal swamp, on which the half-built houses rot away: cleared here and there for the space of a few yards; and teeming then with rank unwholesome vegetation, in whose baleful shade, the wretched wanderers who are tempted hither, droop, and die, and lay their bones; the hateful Mississippi circling and eddying before it, and turning off upon its southern course a slimy monster hideous to behold: a hotbed of disease, an ugly sepulchre, a grave uncheered by any gleam of promise, a place without one single quality in earth or air or water, to commend it: such is this dismal Cairo.

Charles Dickens, *American Notes*, 1842

It by no means follows that because one Cairo can stand ankle deep in the sands of the desert, another could do so up to the knees in the marshes of Ohio.

Alexander Mackay, *The Western World*, 1849

I had heard some ludicrous accounts of Cairo, for instance, at the mouth of the Ohio, but was fairly shocked with amusement, to see it in sober detail composed of, item, one house, leaning every way, uncertain of the softest spot to fall; item, one shanty, labeled 'telegraph office;' item, four flat-boats, high and dry, labeled 'boarding,' 'milk' etc.; item, four ditto, afloat labeled 'post office,' etc. Compared with such a town as this, our craft, with its vast population and regal splendour, should rank a great metropolis. . . .

Frederick Law Olmsted, *A Journey through Texas*, 1857

The place is situated exacly at the point at which the Ohio and the Mississippi meet, and is, I should say, merely guessing on the matter, some ten or twelve feet lower than the winter level of the two rivers. . . . Who were the founders of Cairo, I never ascertained? They are probably buried fathoms deep in the mud, and their names will no doubt remain a mystery to the latest ages.

I cannot tell what was the existing population of Cairo. I asked one resident, but he only shook his head and said that the place was about 'played out.' And a miserable play it must have been.

Anthony Trollope, *North America*, 1862

California

Our generall called this countrey, Nova Albion, and that for two causes: the one in respect of the white bankes and cliffes, which ly towardes the sea: and the other, because it might have some affinitie with our Country in name, which sometime was so called.

There is no part of earth here to bee taken up, wherein there is not some speciall likelihood of gold or silver

The Famous Voyage of Sir Francis Drake, 1589, in Richard Hakluyt, *Principal Navigations . . . of the English Nation*, 1598–1600

Of late years, the *Jesuits*, encouraged and supported by a large donation from the Marquis *de Valero*, a most munificent bigot, have fixed themselves upon the place, and have established a very considerable mission . . . they already make a considerable quantity of wine, resembling in flavour the inferior sorts of *Madera*.

George Anson (Richard Walter and Benjamin Robins), *A Voyage Round the World, 1740–4*, 1748

The attraction and superiority of California are in its days. It has better days, and more of them, than any other country.

R.W. Emerson, *Journal*, 1871

All scenery in California requires distance to give it its highest charm.

Mark Twain, *Roughing It*, 1872

first sight of, travelling west
I am usually very calm over the displays of nature, but you will scarce believe how my heart leaped at this. It was like meeting one's wife. I had come home again.

Robert Louis Stevenson, *Across the Plains*, 1892 – of 1879

California is an Italy without its art. There are subjects for the artist, but it is universally true that the only scenery which inspires utterance is that which man feels himself the master of. The mountains of California are so gigantic that they are not favorable to art or poetry. There are good poets in England, but none in Switzerland. There the mountains are too high. Art cannot add to nature.

Oscar Wilde, quoted in 'Art and Aesthetics', *Denver Tribune*, 13 April 1882

The climate . . . is, according to the Californians, perennial spring; but eulogy in this direction reached its acme when an enthusiastic writer declared the climate of California to be 'eminently favourable to the cure of gunshot wounds.'

G.A. Sala, *America Revisited*, 1882

'I understand that you are going to stay some time in California. Do you mind my giving you a little advice? I am speaking now of towns that are still rather brusque in their manners. When a man offers you a drink accept at once, and then stand drinks all round. I don't say that the second part of the programme is as necessary as the first, but it puts you on a perfectly safe footing. Above all, remember that where you are going you must never carry anything. The men you move among will do that for you. They have been accustomed to it. It is in some places, unluckily, a matter of life and death as well as daily practice to draw first. I have known really lamentable accidents occur from a man carrying a revolver when he did not know what to do with it. Do you understand anything about revolvers?'

'N–no,' I stammered, 'of course not.'

'Do you think of carrying one?'

'Of course not. I don't want to kill myself.'

'Then you are safe. But remember you will be moving among men who go heeled, and you will hear a good deal of talk about the thing and a great many tall stories. You may listen to the yarns, but you must not conform to the custom however much you may feel tempted. You invite your own death if you lay your hand on a weapon you don't understand. No man flourishes a revolver in a bad place. It is produced for one specified purpose and produced before you can wink.' . . .

When he had departed it struck me that, in the language of the East, 'he might have been pulling my leg.' But there remained no doubt whatever as to his skill with the weapon he excused so tenderly.

Rudyard Kipling, *From Sea to Sea*, 1889

Remember that the men who stocked California in the 50's were physically and as far as regards certain tough virtues, the pick of the earth. . . . To this nucleus were added all the races of the Continent – French, Italian, German, and, of course, the Jew. The result you shall see in large-boned, deep-chested, delicate handed women, and long, elastic, well-built boys. It needs no little golden badge . . . to mark the native son of the Golden West. . . . Him I love because he is devoid of fear, carries himself like a man, and has a heart as big as his boots.

Ibid.

When a tree takes a notion to grow in California nothing in heaven or on earth with stop it.

Lilian Leland, *Travelling Alone, A Woman's Journey Round the World*, 1890

California, more than any other part of the Union, is a country by itself, and San Francisco a capital.

James Bryce, *The American Commonwealth*, 1901

Southern California . . . which however the real C, I believe much repudiates, has completely bowled me over – such a delicious difference from the rest of the U.S. do I find in it. (I speak of course all of nature and climate, fruits and flowers; for there is absolutely nothing else, and the sense of the shining social and human inane is utter.) The days have been mostly here of heavenly beauty, and the flowers, the wild flowers just now in particular, which fairly *rage*, with radiance, over the land, are worthy of some purer planet than this.

Henry James, Letter to Mrs William James, 5 April 1905

East is East, and West is San Francisco. . . . Californians are a race of people; they are not merely inhabitants of a state.

O. Henry, *A Municipal Report*, before 1910

It's a shame to take this country away from the rattlesnakes.

D.W. Griffith, attrib.

California is a queer place – in a way, it has turned its back on the world, and looks into the void Pacific. It is absolutely selfish, very empty, but not false, and at least, not full of false effort. . . . It's sort of crazy-sensible. Just the moment: hardly as far ahead as *carpe diem.*

D.H. Lawrence, Letter to J.M. Murry, 24 September 1923

Yes, I have walked in California,
And the rivers there are blue and white.
Thunderclouds of grapes hang on the mountains.
Bears in the meadows pitch and fight.
(*Limber, double-jointed lords of fate,*
Proud native sons of the Golden Gate.)
And flowers burst like bombs in California,
Exploding on tomb and tower.
And the panther-cats chase the red rabbits,
Scatter their young blood every hour.
And the cattle on the hills in California
And the very swine in the holes
Have ears of silk and velvet
And tusks like long white poles.
And the very swine, big-hearted,
Walk with pride to their doom
For they feed on the sacred raisins
Where the great black agates loom.
Goshawfuls are Burbanked with the grizzly bears.
At midnight their children come clanking up the stairs.
They wriggle up the canyons,
Nose into the caves.
And swallow the papooses and the Indian braves.
The trees climb so high the crows are dizzy
Flying to their nests at the top.
While the jazz-birds screech, and storm the brazen beach
And the sea-darts turn flip-flop.
The solid Golden Gate soars up to Heaven.
Perfumed cataracts are hurled
From the zones of silver snow
To the ripening rye below,
To the land of the lemon and the nut
And the biggest ocean in the world.
While the native sons, like lords tremendous,
Lift up their heads with chants sublime,
And the band-stands sound the trombone, the saxophone and xylophone
And the whales roar in perfect tune and time.
And the chanting of the whales in California
I have set my heart upon.
It is sometimes a play by Belasco
Sometimes a tale of Prester John.

Vachel Lindsay, 'The Golden Whales of California, I: A Short Walk along the Coast', *Collected Poems*, 1923

I met a Californian who would
Talk California – a state so blessed,
He said, in climate, none had ever died there
A natural death, and Vigilance Committees
Had had to organize to stock the graveyards
And vindicate the state's humanity.
'Just the way Steffanson runs on,' I murmured,
'About the British Arctic. This is what comes
Of being in the market with a climate.'

Robert Frost, *New Hampshire*, 1923

I attended a dinner the other morning given for the Old Settlers of California. No one was allowed to attend unless he had been in the State 2 and one half years.

Will Rogers, *The Illiterate Digest*, 1924

This state, in its early days, was peopled by a hardy and adventurous folk, including many fugitives from justice, and in consequence life there was full of charm. But of late it has been overrun by retired country bankers, cattle-dealers, and other such petty rogues from the Middle West, and the old charm has vanished. Los Angeles, its largest city, is run by Christian business men. Any visitor suspected of harboring radical economic views is clubbed by the police, and sent to jail. The courts of California are the worst in the United States. Just outside pious Los Angeles is Hollywood, a colony of moving picture actors. Its morals are those of Port Said.

H.L. Mencken, *Americana*, 1925

California is a great place . . . if you happen to be an orange.

Fred Allen, attrib.

Give me men to match my mountains.

Inscription in State Capitol, Sacramento, quoted John Gunther, *Inside U.S.A.*, 1947

*They are a very decent generous lot of people out here and *they don't expect you to listen.* Always remember that, dear boy. It's the secret of social ease in this county. They talk entirely for their own pleasure. Nothing they say is designed to be heard.

Evelyn Waugh, *The Loved One*, 1948 (Sir Francis Hinsley speaking)

Even suicide is cheaper out here. The California motorist will, on the average, knock off three pedestrians a month.

Groucho Marx, Letter to Abel Green, 11 February 1949

California, that advance post of our civilisation, with its huge aircraft factories, TV and film studios, automobile way of life . . . its flavourless cosmopolitanism, its charlatan philosophies and religions, its lack of anything old and well-tried, rooted in tradition and character.

J.B. Priestley, 'They Come from Inner Space', *Thoughts in the Wilderness*, 1957

If California had been in the middle, and the Middle West on this far side, I don't believe anyone would have bothered to come so far.

Freya Stark, Letter, 20 February 1944, in *Dust in the Lion's Paw*, 1961

Northern California

We who were born here, and our parents also felt a strange superiority over newcomers, barbarians, *forestieri*, and they, the foreigners, resented us and even made a rude poem about us:

The miner came in forty-nine,
The whores in fifty-one.
And when they got together,
They made a Native Son.

John Steinbeck, *Travels with Charley*, 1962

California, where the twentieth century is a burning and a shining neon light, and where, anyway, cows are rarely seen out-of-doors nowadays.

Malcolm Muggeridge, *Observer*, 11 April 1965

California is a tragic country – like Palestine, like every Promised Land.

Christopher Isherwood, *Exhumations*, 1966

Southern California, I found, is a veritable paradise of statuspheres.

Tom Wolfe, Introduction to *The Pump House Gang*, 1968

. . . the various landscapes of California – Switzerland and Burgundy and Yorkshire and Scotland and Spain.

Alistair Cooke, *Alistair Cooke's America*, 1973

The law against sodomy goes back fourteen hundred years to the Emperor Justinian, who felt that there should be such a law because, as everyone knew, sodomy was a principal cause of earthquake.

'Sodomy' gets them. For elderly, good-hearted audiences I paraphrase; the word is not used. College groups get a fuller discussion of Justinian and his peculiar law, complete with quotations from Procopius. California audiences living on or near the San Andreas fault laugh the loudest – and the most nervously. No wonder.

Gore Vidal, *Matters of Fact and Fiction*, 1977

California is not for me: too fruity and nutty by half.

George Gale, 'I Like it Here', *Spectator*, 23 September 1978

A wet dream in the mind of New York.

Erica Jong, *How to Save Your Own Life*, 1978

It struck me why there are so many pulled muscles among joggers in Beverly Hills, where any man on foot used to be picked up by the police as a suspicious character: a lot of the people who are running in California these days have never walked.

'Talk of the Town', *New Yorker*, 28 May 1979

It used to be that a travelling man could make his calls in California with no worries to distract him except earthquakes, rockslides, flash floods, droughts, motorcycle gangs, and the possibility of being stuck in an elevator with one of those people who keep saying 'far out,' and 'mellow.' Those carefree days are over. Now that California has a gasoline shortage, the scheming starts even before you leave New York.

Ibid.

A society in which a sense of history is continually sacrificed to a dream of the future.

A. Alvarez, *Observer*, 21 October 1979 (in a review of Joan Didion's *The White Album*)

An analyst I know says that what makes Californians – and not them only – so bewitched is hearing people say 'have a nice everything' in a voice that implies 'I hope your colon drops out'. 'Thank you for calling the Crabgrass Hotel,' intone the operators, before they put you on permanent hold, the telephonic equivalent of a life support machine.

Eric Korn, 'Remainders', *Times Literary Supplement*, 11 April 1980

Q: Why does it take six Californians to change a light bulb?
A: One to turn the switch on and off, one to change the bulb, and four to share the experience.

Anon.

the California trail
As we neared the California trail, the white coverings of the many emigrant and transport wagons dotted the landscape, giving the trail the appearance of a river running between great meadows, with many ships sailing on its bosom.

Horace Greeley, *An Overland Journey from New York to San Francisco . . . in 1859*, 1860

Cambridge (Massachusetts)

I mourn when I am at Cambridge, but I think there are a few places where I could be happier.

Charles Francis Adams, *Diary*, 22 September 1824

Cambridge – our dear detestable common Cambridge.

Henry James, Letter to Grace Norton, 26 September 1870

Town of Cambridge, rather slatternly.

Arnold Bennett, *Journal*, 27 October 1911

the Cambridge ladies who live in furnished souls
are unbeautiful and have comfortable minds
(also,with the church's protestant blessings
daughters,unscented shapeless spirited)
they believe in Christ and Longfellow,both dead,
are invariably interested in so many things—
at the present writing one still finds
delighted fingers knitting for the is it Poles?
perhaps. While permanent faces coyly bandy
scandal of Mrs. N and Professor D
. . . the Cambridge ladies do not care,above
Cambridge if sometimes in its box of
sky lavender and cornerless,the
moon rattles like a fragment of angry candy

e.e. cummings, 'Sonnets – Realities', *Tulips & Chimneys*, 1922

Harvard University
This celebrated institootion of learnin is pleasantly situated in the Bar-room of Parker's in School Street.

Charles F. Browne ('Artemus Ward'), *Boston*, 1865

Portland: Does every boy in Boston *have* to go to Harvard?
Fred: It isn't compulsory. If you know the right people you can get out of it.

Fred Allen, *Treadmill to Oblivion*, 1954

Campton (Kentucky)

De Camptown ladies sing dis song
  Doo dah! doo dah!
De Camptown racetrack five miles long
  Oh! doo dah day!
I come down dah wid my hat caved in
  Doo dah! doo dah!
I go back home wid a pocket full of tin
  Oh! doo dah day!

Stephen Collins Foster, *Gwine to Run All Night; or, De Camptown Races*, 1850

Cape Cod

But the ship ryding here in no good harborow and with all the weather doubted, the Master stood off again into the sea, southwardly, and soone after found himself embayed with a mightie Headland, where Coming to an ancre within a legue of the shoare, Captayne Gosnoll comaunded the shallop to be trymmed out and went a shore, where he perceaved this Headland to be parcell of the Mayne and sondry Islandes lying amost rownd about yt, whereupon thus satisfied he repayred abourd agayne, where during the tyme of his absence which was not above 6. howres, he found the shippe so furnished with excellent Cod-fish which they had hauled that they were compelled to throw numbers of them over-bourd againe, in so much yt left this belief in them all that in this season namely Aprill and Maie there maie upon this Coast in this height (as I said of about 43.) be as good fishing and in as great plentie as in the newfound land, and they were the more probably confirm'd herein by the sculls of Mackarells, Herrings, Cod, and other Fish, which they dailie saw as they went and came from the shoare: the place besides where they tooke these Codds being but in 7. faddome water and within lesse then a league of the shoare. . . . This headland therefore they called Cape-Cod.

William Strachey, *The Historie of Travell into Virginia Britania*, *c.* 1612

Cape Girardeau (Missouri)

Uncle Mumford said that Cape Girardeau was the Athens of Missouri.

Mark Twain, *Life on the Mississippi*, 1883

Cape Prince of Wales (Alaska)

There is probably no place in the world where the weather is so persistently vile as on this cheerless portion of the earth's surface. In winter furious tempests and snow, in summer similar storms, accompanied by rain, sleet, or mist, are experienced here five days out of the seven. If by accident a still, sunlit day does occur, it is called a 'weather-breeder,' for dirtier weather than before is sure to be lurking behind it. A howling south-wester on the English coast would be looked upon here as a moderate gale. While walking on the beach one day I was lifted clean off my feet by the wind, although the day was locally called rather a pleasant one.

Harry de Windt, *From Paris to New York by Land*, 1904

Carolina

The gentleman who asked if one required a revolver in Carolina . . . was answered, 'You may be here one year, and you may be here two, and never want it; but when you do want it, you'll want it very bad.'

Mary Kingsley, *Travels in West Africa*, 1897

Alas! Carolina! Carolina! Fair land of my birth,
Thy fame will be wafted from the mountain to the sea
As being the greatest educational centre on earth,
At the cost of men's blood thro' thy 'one X' whiskey.
Two very large elephants thou hast lately installed,
Where thy sons and thy daughters are invited to come,
And learn to be physically and mentally strong,
By the solemn proceeds of thy 'innocent' rum.

J. Gordon Coogler, *Alas! Carolina!*, 1897
(Elephants = State universities.)

North Carolina

North Carolina has less alien blood per square inch than any other State in the Union. That is one good reason why she has less writers, less painters, less sculptors, and above all, less musicians, than practically any other State of equal resource: certainly any other State of equal bombast.

Carolina Magazine of the State University, *c.* 1925, quoted in H.L. Mencken, *Americana*, 1925

compared with Virginia and South Carolina
North Carolina has been referred to as 'The valley of humility between two mountains of conceit.' (Virginia and South Carolina).

Harry Golden, *For 2¢ Plain*, 1958

South Carolina

The ruling intellect of the State has now, as it originally had, more than that of any other American community, a profound conviction, that God created men to live in distinct classes or castes, one beneath another, one subject to another.

Frederick Law Olmsted, *Journey in the Seaboard Slave States*, 1856

Carson City (Nevada)

My informants declared that in and about Carson a dead man for breakfast was the rule; besides accidents perpetually occurring to indifferent or to peace-making parties, they reckoned per annum fifty murders. In a peculiar fit of liveliness an intoxicated gentleman will discharge his revolver in a ball-room, and when a 'shyooting' begins in the thin-walled frame houses, those not concerned avoid bullets and splinters by jumping into their beds. During my three days' stay at Carson City I heard of three murders. A man 'heavy *on* the shoulder,' who can 'hit out straight from the hip,' is a valuable acquisition.

Richard Burton, *The City of the Saints*, 1861

They shoot folks here somewhat, and the law is rather partial than otherwise to first-class murderers.

Charles F. Browne, *Artemus Ward (His Travels) Among the Mormons, 1863*, 1865

It was a wooden town. . . . The main street consisted of four or five blocks of little white frame stores, which were too high to sit down on, but not too high for various other purposess, in fact, hardly high enough. They were packed close together, side by side as if room were scarce in that mighty plain.

Mark Twain, *Roughing It*, 1872

Central City (Colorado)

Every class and profession is represented in Colorado. The lawyers are too many for such a narrow compass. They are an uneasy, restless set of men, who are continually exciting the people. Nightly they hold forth about some political question, as if that bowl in which Central City lies composed the world. Dickens or a Thackeray could find new characters in Colorado lawyers. Their sign-boards, bearing the title of 'Attorney and counsellor-at-law,' swaying to and fro, meet you at every step. Another class is too largely represented, composed of effeminate clerks. Every vacancy is filled, and they know it well, yet they persist in standing idle all the day, loafing at the street corners, impressing the superficial traveller that times are dull in Colorado. Times are not dull in Colorado, or in any part of the west, to those who are ready to engage in manual labour.

H.M. Stanley, *My Early Travels and Adventures* (August 1867), 1895

The Victorianism of the place is its present fortune. Shop names are written in ornate lettering; houses that would hardly deserve a second glance in some dingy London outskirt are displayed as historic attractions. The Old West, which seems so very old to the western American, smacks strongly of Aunt Agatha to the wandering Englishman. Central City is a museum piece, interesting enough as a memorial to the mining pioneers, but stultified and stuffed.

James Morris, *Coast to Coast*, 1956

Charleston (South Carolina)

Charles-town is, in the north, what Lima is in the south; both are Capitals of the richest provinces of their respective hemispheres. . . .

Hector St John de Crèvecoeur, *Letters from an American Farmer*, 1782

It more resembles a West Indian than an American city – from the number of wooden buildings painted white, the large verandas and porticos of the more stately mansions of brick, and the universal prevalence of broad verandas, green Venetian blinds, and other provisions to secure coolness and shade. The shops have none of the exterior elegance or display which characterize those of Broadway, in New York, or Chestnut street in Philadelphia; but are literally stores, like those on Pearl-street and Pine street, in the first-named city.

J.S. Buckingham, *The Slave States of America in 1839*, 1842

Its natives and regular residents are seldom the victims of the acute diseases which it inflicts upon the stranger; but, judging from their appearance, they look as if they had all once been very ill, and were in a state of chronic convalescence.

Alexander Mackay, *The Western World*, 1849

It was pleasant to find an American city not wearing the appearance of having all been built yesterday. The atmosphere, charged with an unusual dampness in consequence of the low position of the town on coast and river bank, helps materially to deepen the marks of the years; soon discoloring the paint upon the house and facilitating the progress of the green moss, which here is ever creeping over the northern side of walls and roofs. The whole town looks picturesquely dingy, and the greater number of buildings have assumed something of the appearance of European antiquity.

John Milton Mackie, *From Cape Cod to Dixie*, 1864

Charleston is a beautiful memory, a corpse whose lower limbs have been resuscitated.

Henry Miller, *The Air-conditioned Nightmare*, 1945

In . . . [Charleston] . . . you actually have to pin a man to the mat before you can talk business to him. And if he happens to be a good business man, this chap from Charleston, the chances are that he is also a fanatic about something unheard of. His face registers changes of expression, his eyes light up, his hair stands on end, his voice swells with passion, his cravat slips out of place, his suspenders are apt to come undone, he spits and curses, he coos and prances, he pirouettes now and then. And there's one thing he never dangles in front of your nose – his time-piece. He has time, oodles of time. And he accomplishes everything he chooses to accomplish in due time, with the result that the air is not filled with dust and machine oil, and cash register clickings.

Ibid.

Charleston sums up this tragedy of the South. It is a lovely city, warm and graceful; but over it hangs a pall of obsession, distorting thoughts and perverting motives, turning almost every conversation into a rude clash of prejudices. The mind of educated Charleston is dominated first by the endless conceits of pedigree; secondly (and more horribly) by the task of maintaining total white supremacy.

James Morris, *Coast to Coast*, 1956

Death on the Atlantic.

Anon.

Chattahoochee River (Alabama/Georgia)

Out of the hills of Habersham,
Down the valleys of Hall,
I hurry amain to reach the plain;
Run the rapid and leap the fall,
Split at the rock, and together again
Accept my bed, or narrow or wide,
And flee from folly on every side
With a lover's pain to attain the plain,
Far from the hills of Habersham,
Far from the valleys of Hall.

Sidney Lanier, *The Song of the Chattahoochee*, 1877

Chattanooga

Missionary Ridge overlooks Chattanooga, and few will envy it.

William Manchester, *American Caesar*, 1979

Chesapeake Bay

This is the famous Chesipiacke Bay. . . . Indeed it is a goodly Bay, and a fairer, not easily to be found.

William Strachy, *A. . . . reportory of the Wracke and Redemption of Sir Thomas Gates*, 1610, in *Purchas his Pilgrimes*, 1625

Cheyenne

Cheyenne is a kind of iron pivot bound in buckskin.

John Gunther, *Inside U.S.A.*, 1947

Chicago

The Indians used to say the first white man that lived in Chicago was a negro.

Nehemiah Matson, *Pioneers of Illinois*, 1882

The city is situated on both sides of the Chicago river, a sluggish, slimy stream, too lazy to clean itself, and on both sides of its north and south branches, upon a level piece of ground, half dry and half wet, resembling a salt marsh, and containing a population of 20,000. There was no pavement, no macadamised streets, no drainage, and the three thousand houses in which the people lived, were almost entirely small timber buildings, painted white, and this white much defaced by mud.

John L. Peyton, *Over the Alleghanies*, 1869 – of *c.* 1863

Then lift once more thy towers on high,
And fret with spires the western sky,
To tell that God is still with us,
And love is still miraculous.

John Greenleaf Whittier, *Chicago*, 1871
(with reference to the great fire of 1871)

I . . . like it in spite of lake-wind sharpness and prairie flatness, damp tunnels, swinging bridges, hard water, and easy divorces. . . . A lady from the East lately said of it, very charmingly, 'It is New York with the heart left in.' I do not deny that the genuine Chicagoan has well learned the prayer of the worthy Scotchman, 'Lord gie us a guid conceit o' oursels!' and that the prayer has been abundantly answered.

Grace Greenwood (Sara Clarke Lippincott), *New Life in New Lands*, 1873

It grows on Independence Days and Sabbath Days, and all days. It grows o' nights. Its enterprise, daring and vigilance storm the land and fetter the sea, defy and override physical laws and circumvent nature. A great part of the west side of the city seems to me to have been heaved up out of the mud by a benevolent earthquake. . . . All this rapid change and progress is as mysterious as it is marvellous, till you know a regular genuine Chicagoan, and see him go about his business with a drive, a devotion, a matchless economy of time and means, which stop just short of hurry and greed, – of the desperate and the sordid. The very struggle which the men of Chicago have always waged against adverse natural conditions has been to a degree ennobling, and has lifted their lives above the commonplace. It is essentially heroic; it is something titanic; it is more creation than development.

Ibid.

This is a great uninteresting place.

Matthew Arnold, Letter to Miss Arnold, 23 January 1884

Chicago . . . perhaps the most typically American place in America.

James Bryce, *The American Commonwealth*, 1888

Chicago seemed a great and gloomy city. I remember having subscribed, let us say sixpence, towards its restoration at the period of the fire; and now when I beheld street after street of ponderous houses and crowds of comfortable burghers, I though it would be a graceful act for the corporation to refund that sixpence, or, at the least, to entertain me to a cheerful dinner.

Robert Louis Stevenson, *Across the Plains*, 1892 – of 1879

The wondrous prairie city in the State of Illinois has been as Aaron's rod and has swallowed up all the other marvels.

G.A. Sala, *America Revisited*, 1882

That astonishing Chicago – a city where they are always rubbing the lamp, and fetching up the genii, and contriving and achieving new impossibilities. It is hopeless for the occasional visitor to try to keep up with Chicago – she outgrows his prophecies faster than he can make them. She is always a novelty; for she is never the Chicago you saw when you passed through the last time.

Mark Twain, *Life on the Mississippi*, 1883

Where was the architecture of the great city – the 'Eternal City of the West'? Where was it? Hiding behind these shameless signs? A vacant block would come by. Then enormous billboards planted there stood up grandly, had it all their own way, obliterating everything in nothing. That was better. Chicago! Immense gridiron of dirty, noisy streets. . . . Heavy traffic crossing both ways at once, managing somehow; torrential noise.

A stupid thing, that gridiron: conflicting currents of horses, trucks, street cars grinding on hard rails, mingling with streams of human beings in seeming confusion. Clamor! But habit was in the movement making it expert and so safe enough. Dreary – dim – smoked. Smoked dim and smoking. A wide, desolate, vacant strip ran along the waterfront over which the Illinois Central trains puffed, shrieked, and ground incessantly, cutting the city off from the lake.

Terrible! This grinding and piling up of blind forces. If there was logic here, who could grasp it?

To stop and think in the midst of this would be to give way to terror. The grey, soiled river, with its mist of steam and smoke, was the only beauty. And that smelled to heaven.

Frank Lloyd Wright, *An Autobiography*, 1979 – of 1887

I have struck a city, – a real city, – and they call it Chicago. The other places do not count. San Francisco was a pleasure-resort as well as a city, and Salt Lake was a phenomenon. This place is the first American city I have encountered. It holds rather more than a million people with bodies, and stands on the same sort of soil as Calcutta. Having seen it, I urgently desire never to see it again. It is inhabited by savages. Its water is the water of the Hughli, and its air is dirt. Also it says it is the 'boss' town of America.

I do not believe that it has anything to do with this country.

Rudyard Kipling, *From Sea to Sea*, 1889

SATAN: *(impatiently) to NEW-COMER*: The trouble with you Chicago people is, that you think you are the best people down here; whereas you are merely the most numerous.

Mark Twain, 'Pudd'nhead Wilson's New Calendar', in *More Tramps Abroad*, 1897

Nothing missed by these Chicago papers. If world came to an end tomorrow *Tribune* would come out day after with illustrations and an interview with God Almighty.

John Foster Fraser, *Round the World on a Wheel*, 1899

Got talking to man about my travels; mentioned Parthenon by moonlight. 'Yes,' he said, 'it may be all right, but guess it's not so big as our Masonic Temple.'

Ibid.

I am already (after 17 days of the 'Great Middle West') rather spent and weary, weary of motion and chatter, and oh, of such an unimagined dreariness of *ugliness* (on many, on most sides!) and of the perpetual effort of trying to 'do justice' to what one doesn't like. If one could only damn it and have done with it! So much of it is rank with good intentions. . . . This Chicago is huge, *infinite* (of potential size and form, and even of actual) black, smoky, *old*-looking, very like some preternaturally *boomed* Manchester or Glasgow lying beside a colossal lake (Michigan) of hard pale green jade, and putting forth railway antennae of maddening complexity and gigantic length.

Henry James, Letter to Edward Warren, 19 March 1905

And then suddenly Chicago is a dark smear under the sky.

H.G. Wells, *The Future in America*, 1906

So it goes on mile after mile – Chicago. . . . It was like a prolonged, enlarged mingling of the south side of London with all that is bleak and ugly in the Black Country. It is the most perfect presentation of nineteenth century individualistic industrialism I have ever seen – in its vast, its magnificent squalor; it is pure nineteenth century; it had no past at all before that; in 1800 it was empty prairie, and one marvels for its future.

Ibid.

It is a veritable Babel of languages. It would seem as if all the millions of human beings disembarking year upon year upon the shores of the United States were unconsciously drawn to make the place their headquarters. Chicago is the land of promise to all malcontents and aimless immigrants. . . . Nowhere else has immigration assumed such huge proportions.

Monsignor Count Vay de Vaya and Luskod, *The Inner Life of the United States*, 1908

Because it is so laden with soot, the air of Chicago is a great mystifier and beautifier. Atmospheric effects may be seen there that are unobtainable without the combustion of soft-coal. Talk, for example, as much as you please about the electric sky-signs of Broadway – not all of them together will write as much poetry in the sky as in the single word 'Illinois' that hangs without a clue to its suspension in the murky dusk over Michigan Avenue. The visionary aspects of Chicago are incomparable

Arnold Bennett, *Those United States*, 1912

Chicago. . . . A mushroom and a suburb of Warsaw.
Ibid.

Chicago is stupefying . . . an Olympian freak, a fable, an allegory, an incomprehensible phenomenon . . . monstrous, multifarious, unnatural, indomitable, puissant, preposterous, transcendent . . . throw the dictionary at it!
Julian Street, *Abroad at Home*, 1914

Hog Butcher for the World,
Tool Maker, Stacker of Wheat,
Player with Railroads and the Nation's Freight
  Handler;
Stormy, husky, brawling,
City of the Big Shoulders.

They tell me you are wicked, and I believe them; for I
  have seen your painted women under the gas lamps
  luring the farm boys.
And they tell me you are crooked, and I answer: Yes, it
  is true I have seen the gunmen kill and go free to kill
  again.
And they tell me you are brutal, and my reply is: On
  the faces of women and children I have seen the
  marks of wanton hunger.
And having answered so I turn once more to those who
  sneer at this my city, andI give them back the sneer
  and say to them:
Come and show me another city with lifted head
  singing so proud to be alive and coarse and strong
  and cunning.
Flinging curses amid the toil of piling job on job, here is
  a tall bold slugger set vivid against the little soft
  cities;
Fierce as a dog with tongue lapping for action, cunning
  as a savage pitted against the wilderness,
    Bareheaded,
      Shovelling,
      Wrecking,
      Planning,
      Building, breaking, rebuilding,
Under the smoke , dust all over his mouth, laughing
  with white teeth,
Under the terrible burden of destiny laughing as a
  young man laughs,
Laughing even as an ignorant fighter laughs who has
  never lost a battle,
Bragging and laughing that under his wrist is the pulse,
  and under his ribs the heart of the people,
        Laughing!
Laughing the stormy, husky, brawling laughter of
  Youth, half-naked, sweating, proud to be Hog
  Butcher, Tool Maker, Stacker of Wheat, Player with
  Roads and Freight Handler to the Nation.
Carl Sandburg, 'Chicago', from *Chicago Poems*, 1916

and some comparisons with elsewhere
Venice is a dream of soft waters, Vienna and Bagdad
  recollections of dark spears and wild turbans: Paris
  is a thought in Monet grey on scabbards, fabrics,
  façades; London is a fact in fog filled with the
  moaning of transatlantic whistles; Berlin sits amid
  white scrubbed quadrangles and torn arithmetics
  and testaments; Moscow brandishes a flag and repeats a dance figure of a man who walks like a
  bear.
Chicago fished from its depths a text: Independent
  as a hog on ice . . .
Carl Sandburg, 'The Windy City', in *Slabs of the Sunburnt West*, 1922

In the years following the publication of the *Chicago Poems* (Carl) Sandburg used to say publicly, 'Here is the difference between Dante, Milton, and me. They wrote about hell and never saw the place. I wrote about Chicago after looking the town over for years and years.'
Harry Golden, *Carl Sandburg*, 1961

There is no peace in Chicago. it is a city of terror and light, untamed.
W.L. George, *Hail Columbia*, 1921

It rained and fogged in Chicago and muddy-flowing people oozed thick in the canyon-beds of the streets. Yet it seemed to me more alive and more real than New York.
D.H. Lawrence, Letter to Mrs Bessie Freeman, August 1923

I say God's Chicago, for who else will own it, complete it, and gather it to be the perfect city upon earth? Chicago has all the possibilities of becoming the earth's final city, the Babylon of the Plains.
Shane Leslie, *American Wonderland*, 1936

If one got behind Michigan Avenue, one had the feeling that Chicago had been, and to some extent still was, a whited sepulchre. Insulls and Rockefellers had lived on the whited exterior. Inside were the dead men's bones of the slums.
M. Philips Price, *America After Sixty Years*, 1936

Chicago gave me a snowstorm, and this morning I walked for an hour on the crisp surface in a world which must be parks and sheets of water in summer: Greek temples scattered about and skyscrapers in the background, and the lake with blocks of ice making a white horizon. Inside the hotel it is like the Balkans grown prosperous – square, squat females with furs and loud cordial voices telling everybody's business in the lounge.
Freya Stark, Letter, 9 January 1944, in *Dust in the Lion's Paw*, 1961

This is the greatest and most typically American of all cities. New York is bigger and more spectacular and can outmatch it in other superlatives, but it is a 'world' city, more European in some respects than American. Chicago . . . gives above all the sense that America and the Middle West are beating upon it from all sides.

John Gunther, *Inside U.S.A.*, 1947

Chicago is as full of crooks as a saw with teeth.

Ibid.

I reel, I sway, I am utterly exhausted
Should you ask me when Chicago was founded I could
only reply I didn't know it was losted.

Ogden Nash, 'Ask Daddy, he won't know',
The Family Re-union, 1951

In spite of the many friends who showed me hospitality, I had the feeling that one could be lonelier in this wind-seared town than anywhere else on earth.

Cecil Beaton, *It Gives Me Great Pleasure*, 1955

Yes, Chicago was a town where nobody could ever forget how the money was made. It was picked up from floors still slippery with blood, and if one did not protest and take a vow of vegetables, one knew at least that life was hard, life was in the flesh and in the massacre of the flesh – one breathed the last agonies of beasts. So something of the entrails and the secrets of the gut got into the faces of native Chicagoans. A great city, a strong city with faces tough as leather and hide and pavement, it was also a city where the faces took on the broad beastiness of ears which were dull enough to ignore the bleatings of the doomed, noses battered enough to smell no more the stench of every unhappy end, – mouths – fat mouths or slit mouths – ready to taste the gravies which were the reward of every massacre, and eyes, simple pig eyes, which could look the pig truth in the face. In any other city they would have found technologies to silence the beasts with needles, quarter them with machines, lull them with Musak. . . . But in Chicago they did it straight, they cut the animals right out of their hearts – which is why it was the last of the great American cities, and people had great faces, carnal as blood, greedy, direct, too impatient for hypocrisy, in love with honest plunder.

Norman Mailer, *Miami and the Siege of Chicago*, 1968

and comparisons

Chicago is the great American city. New York is one of the capitals of the world, and Los Angeles is a constellation of plastic, San Francisco is a lady, Boston has become Urban Renewal, Philadelphia and Baltimore and Washington blink like dull diamonds in the smog of Eastern Megalopolis, and New Orleans is unremarkable past the French Quarter. Detroit is a one-trade town, Pittsburgh has lost its golden triangle, St Louis has become the golden arch of the corporation, and nights in Kansas City close early. The oil depletion allowance makes Houston and Dallas naught but checkerboards for this sort of game. But Chicago is a great American city. Perhaps it is the last of the great American cities.

Ibid.

'I Will' is the unofficial slogan of Chicago: or 'I Will', as the columnist Max Royko once suggested, 'If I Don't Get Caught.'

James Morris, 'Chicago', *Places*, 1972

Sometimes the twin strains of Chicago, the colossal and the cultivated, are blended in a scene or an institution. This produces a flavour altogether unique to this city – which is, of course, a great capital without a nation, a Vienna that never had an Empire. It is, I think, essentially a saltless flavour – bland, fleshy perhaps. One misses intellectual Jews in this city, or sardonic Yankees. The wide pale lake, though it has its perilous gales, its ships direct from Europe, even its modest tides, is distinctly not the open sea, but looks as though its water would be soft and slithery to the touch. The blustering winds carry no tang, the water-front spray leaves no tingle on the face. The posh apartment blocks on the Edgewater shore, complete with their marinas, striped umbrellas and private beaches, are like segments of Beirut deposited upon the edge of the Caspian. The conversation of Chicago lacks edge, and tends towards the exhortatory monologue.

Ibid.

Chicago is never tired.

Ibid.

The city that works.

Quoted in *The Economist*, 3–9 March 1979, as
'recently traditional', without source

Nelson Algren says living there is like being married to a woman with a broken nose: there may be lovelier lovelies, but never a lovely so real.

Quoted by Stephen Fay, *Sunday Times*,
13 January 1980

O'Hare Airport

O Mother O'Hare, big bosom for our hungry poets, pelvic saddle for our sexologists and Open Classroom theorists – O houri O'Hare, who keeps her Perm-O-Pour Stoneglow thighs ajar to receive a generation of frustrated and unreadable novelists –

But wait a minute. It may be too early for the odes. Has it ever been duly noted that O'Hare, which is an airport outside Chicago, is now the intellectual center of the United States?

Curious, but true. There at O'Hare, on any day, Monday through Friday, from September to June, they sit . . . in row after Mies van der row of black vinyl and stainless-steel sling chairs . . . amid soaring walls of plate glass . . . from one tenth to one third of the literary notables of the United States. In October and April, the peak months, the figure goes up to one half.

Masters and Johnson and Erica Jong, Kozol and Rifkin and Hacker and Kael, Steinem and Nadar, Marks, Hayden and Mailer, Galbraith and Heilbronner, and your bearmarket brothers in the PopEco business, Lekachman & Others – which of you has not hunkered down lately in the prodigious lap of Mother O'Hare!

And why? Because they're heading out into the land to give lectures. . . . Giving lectures in the heartland is one of the lucrative dividends of being a noted writer in America. . . . All the skyways to Lecture-land lead through O'Hare Airport. In short, up to one half of our intellectual establishment sits outside Chicago between planes.

At a literary conference at Notre Dame, I . . . ran into a poet who is noted for his verse celebrating the ecology, née Nature. He lives in a dramatic house nailed together completely from uncut pieces of hickory driftwood, perched on a bluff overlooking the crashing ocean. . . . I remarked that this must be the ideal setting in which to write about the ecological wonders. 'I wouldn't know,' he said. 'I do all my writing in O'Hare.'

Tom Wolfe, 'The Intelligent Coed's Guide to America', in *Mauve Gloves and Madmen, Clutter and Vine*, 1976

The Stockyards

The Vision of Gore which I beheld at the Chicago Stockyards rises up before me. . . . The wooden floors were slippery with blood; and that which perhaps made me feel more nervous and uncomfortable was the astonishing and ghastly variety of expression on the countenances of the slaughtered pigs. Utter amazement, mild remonstrance, indignant expostulation, profound dejection, dogged stolidity, profound and contemptuous indifference, placid tranquillity, abject terror, and imbecile hilarity, were pictured in these upturned snouts and half-closed eyes. The scene reminded you with the ugliest possible closeness, of going over a field of battle, after the fray, and when the plunderers of the dead have done their work.

G.A. Sala, *America Revisited*, 1882

Cincinnati

The sight of bricks and mortar was really refreshing, and a house of three stories looked splendid. . . . But alas! the flatness of reality after the imagination has been busy! I hardly know what I expected to find in this city, fresh risen from the bosom of the wilderness, but certainly it was not a little town, about the size of Salisbury, without even an attempt at beauty in any of its edifices, and with only just enough of the air of a city to make it noisy and bustling.

Mrs Frances Trollope, *Domestic Manners of the Americans*, 1832

It seems hardly fair to quarrel with a place because its staple commodity is not pretty, but I am sure I should have liked Cincinnati much better if the people had not dealt so very largely in hogs. The immense quantity of business done in this line would hardly be believed by those who had not witnessed it. . . . If I determined upon a walk up Main-street, the chances were five hundred to one against my reaching the shady side without brushing by a snout fresh dripping from the kennel; when we had screwed up our courage to the enterprise of mounting a certain noble-looking sugar-loaf hill, that promised pure air and a fine view, we found the brook we had to cross at its foot, red with the streams from a pig slaughter-house; while our noses, instead of meeting 'the thyme that loves the hill's green breast,' were greeted by odours that I will not describe, and which I heartily hope my readers cannot imagine; our feet that on leaving the city had expected to press the flowery sod, literally got entangled in pigs' tails and jawbones: and thus the prettiest walk in the neighbourhood was interdicted for ever.

Ibid.

She is enthroned upon a high platform, – one of the rich bottoms occurring on the Ohio, which expands the traveller's notions of what fertility is. Behind her are hills, opening and closing, receding and advancing; here glowing with the richest green pasturage, and there crested and ribbed by beeches which seem transplanted from some giant land. . . . The hillsides reminded me of the Castle of Indolence, of the quiet paths of Eden, of the shades that Una trod, of Windsor Forest, – of all that my memory carried about undulating woodlands: but nothing would do; no description that I am acquainted with is rich enough to answer what I saw on the Ohio.

Harriet Martineau, *Society in America*, 1837

There is a prevalent superstition in Cincinnati that the hindermost citizen will fall into the clutches of the Devil. The wholesome fear of this dire fate, secret, or acknowledged with more or less candour, actuates the whole population. A ceaseless energy pervades the city and gives its tone to everything. A profound hurry is the marked characteristic of the place. I found it difficult to take any repose or calm refreshment, so magnetic is the air. 'Now then Sir!' everything seems to say. Men smoke and drink like locomotives at a relay-house. They seem to sleep only like tops, with brains in steady whirl. There is no pause in the tumultuous life of the streets. The only quiet thing I found was the residence of Mr Longworth – a delicious bit of rural verdure, lying not far from the heart of the town, like a tender locket heaving on a blacksmith's breast.

What more need be said of Cincinnati? Bricks, hurry, and a muddy roar make up the whole impression. The atmosphere, at the time of our visit, was of damps, coal-smoke, chilly and dirty, almost like that of the same season in Birmingham.

Frederick Law Olmsted, *A Journey through Texas*, 1857

As we began to ascend from the level of the outskirts of the town we were greeted by a rising flavour in the air, which soon grew into a strong odour, and at last developed itself into a stench that surpassed in offensiveness anything that my nose had ever hitherto suffered. . . . It was the odour of hogs going up to the Ohio heavens; – of hogs in a state of transit from hoggish nature to clothes-brushes, saddles, sausages, and lard. . . . Let the visitors to Cincinnati keep themselves within the city, and not wander forth among the mountains. It is well that the odour of hogs should ascend to heaven and not hang heavy over the streets; but it is not well to intercept that odour in its ascent.

Anthony Trollope, *North America*, 1862

compared with other American towns
It has become a very smoky place of late years, with quite the climate of the manufacturing towns of England, but its situation is beautiful, and it has more look of age and solidity than most American towns. What strikes me so much in them all is, what is the truth, that they are so unfinished; they are like a new quarter still in the builders' hands, with roads half made and in a frightful state, and with heaps of rubbish and materials not yet cleared away.

Matthew Arnold, Letter to Mrs Cropper, 7 February 1884

Mrs Trollope's bazaar
This bazaar is the great deformity of the city. Happily it is not very conspicuous, being squatted down among houses nearly as lofty as the summit of its dome. . . . It is built of brick, and has Gothic windows, Grecian pillars, and a Turkish dome, and it was originally ornamented with Egyption devices, which have, however, all disappeared under the brush of the whitewasher.

Harriet Martineau, *Retrospect of Western Travel*, 1838

It is composed of many varieties of architecture, but I think that the order under which it must be classed is the *preposterous*.

Captain Frederick Marryat, *A Diary in America*, 1839

Cleveland (Ohio)

and the typical American
In the towns and cities you find the typical American everywhere. His expression is mild, bland, pseudo-serious and definitely fatuous. He is usually dressed in a cheap, ready-made suit, his shoes shine, a fountain pen and pencil in his breast pocket, a brief case under his arm – and of course he wears glasses, the model changing with the changing styles. He looks as if he were turned out by a university with the aid of a chain store cloak and suit house. One looks like the other, just as the automobiles, the radios, and the telephones do. This is the type between 25 and 40. After that age we get another type – the middle aged man who is already fitted with a set of false teeth, who puffs and pants, who insists on wearing a belt though he should be wearing a truss. He is a man who eats and drinks too much, smokes too much, sits too much, talks too much, and is always on the edge of a breakdown. Often he dies of heart failure in the next few years. In a city like Cleveland, this type comes to apotheosis. So do the buildings, the restaurants, the parks, the war memorials. The most typical American city I have struck thus far. Thriving, prosperous, active, clean, spacious, sanitary, vitalized by a liberal infusion of foreign blood and by the ozone from the lake, it stands out in my mind as the composite of many American cities. Possessing all the virtues, all the prerequisites for life, growth, blossoming, it remains, nevertheless, a thoroughly dead place – a deadly, dull, dead place.

Henry Miller, *The Air-conditioned Nightmare*, 1945

I know of no other metropolis with quite so impressive a record in the practical application of good citizenship to government.

John Gunther, *Inside U.S.A.*, 1947

Clinton (Iowa)

At Clinton the Mississippi was reached. . . . The bridge spanning it looks as though made a couple of sizes too big and then cut down. On the Iowa side it does not begin crossing from the ground; it is perched high up in the air, and you get to it by a slanting, heaving platform running sideways on the bank. On reaching the top you discover the bridge slopes the whole way till it rests on the soil of Illinois. It is clearly a bridge that has been cut in two. Americans have big ideas, and they thought the Mississippi twice as broad as it is.

John Foster Fraser, *Round the World on a Wheel*, 1899

Colorado

Colorado, the most spectacular of the mountain states, lives on many things – scenery, beet, sugar, gold, molybdenum, livestock, tourists, and tuberculosis. As to this last I heard an ungentle and tasteless Coloradan complain, 'Some fiend in human form discovered that rest, not altitude, was the best cure for t.b., and so the tuberculosis cases don't come to Colorado so much any more, and the economy of the state suffered terribly as a result, so I suppose you could say that t.b. is killing us, not the patients.'

John Gunther, *Inside U.S.A.*, 1947

This state has more sunshine and more bastards than any place on earth.

Utilities executive, on being sentenced to jail by Judge Ben Lindsay, quoted *ibid.*

Colorado River

From the heart of the mighty mountains strong-souled for my fate I came,
My far-drawn track to a nameless sea through a land without a name; . . .
I stayed not, I could not linger; patient, resistless, alone,
I hewed the trail of my destiny deep in the hindering stone.

Sharlot M. Hall, *Song of the Colorado*, c. mid nineteenth century

Columbia (South Carolina)

One would think that in selecting a site for their capital, fertility in the circumjacent region would be a *sine qua non* with any people. But not so with the Carolinians, who, in order to have it in as central a position as possible, have placed it in the midst of one of the most barren districts of the state. Luckily, its limited population renders it easy of supply, for it is difficult to see how a large population could subsist on such a spot, unless they could accommodate themselves to pine cones as their chief edible.

Alexander Mackay, *The Western World in 1846–7*, 1849

Columbus (Georgia)

By a law of the State of Georgia it was arranged that sixty days should elapse, after this portion of land reserved for the city was completely surveyed, before any of the building lots could be sold. These lots were to consist of half an acre each, and the whole five miles square was to be distinctly marked out in streets on paper, and being numbered and lettered accordingly, they were to be advertised for sale over the whole Union. These sixty days were considered sufficient to enable adventurers, settlers, land-speculators, merchants, and all others so disposed, to come to the spot preparatory to the auction.

The project took like wildfire: and the advantages of the new city being loudly proclaimed over the land, people flocked from all quarters to see and judge of it themselves. We arrived, fortunately, just in the nick of time to see the curious phenomenon of an embryo town – a city as yet without a name, or any existence in law or fact, but crowded with inhabitants, ready to commence their municipal duties at the tap of an auctioneer's hammer.

Captain Basil Hall, *Travels in North America* (31 March 1828), 1829

I had seen in no place since I left Washington, so much gambling, intoxication, and cruel treatment of servants in public, as in Columbus. This, possibly, was accidental; but I must caution persons, travelling for health or pleasure, to avoid stopping in the town.

Frederick Law Olmsted, *Journey in the Seaboard Slave States*, 1856

Columbus (Ohio)

I suppose that the high-water mark of my youth in Columbus, Ohio, was the night the bed fell on my father.

James Thurber, 'The Night the Bed Fell', *The Thurber Carnival*, 1945

Columbus is a town in which almost anything is likely to happen and in which almost everything has.

James Thurber, 'More Alarms at Night', *The Thurber Carnival*, 1945

Columbus is the world capital of the motorcycle life. This statement, I find, comes as a surprise and an annoyance . . . to a lot of people in Columbus.

Tom Wolfe, *The Pump House Gang*, 1968

Concord

By the wide bridge that arched the flood,
  Their flag to freedom's breeze unfurled,
Here once the embattled farmers stood,
  And fired the shot heard round the world.

R.W. Emerson, *Concord Hymn*, 19 April 1836

I have travelled a good deal in Concord.

Henry David Thoreau, *Walden, or Life in the Woods*, (1845–7), 1854

Walden Pond

In such a day, in September or October, Walden is a perfect forest mirror, set round with stones as precious to my eye as if fewer or rarer. Nothing so fair, so pure, and at the same time so large, as a lake, perchance, lies on the surface of the earth. Sky water. It needs no fence. Nations come and go without defiling it. It is a mirror which no stone can crack, whose quicksilver will never wear off, whose gilding Nature continually repairs; no storms, no dust, can dim its surface ever fresh; – a mirror in which all impurity presented to it sinks, swept and dusted by the sun's hazy brush, – this the light dust-cloth, – which retains no breath that is breathed on it, but sends its own to float as clouds high above its surface, and be reflected in its bosom still.

Henry David Thoreau, *Walden, or Life in the Woods*, (1845–7), 1854

Connecticut

. . . Connecticut as a state, and the last one expected to yield its steady habits (which were essentially bigoted in politics as well as religion).

Thomas Jefferson, Letter to Marquis de la Fayette, 14 May 1817

Connect-de-coot, the leetle yellow spot dat make de clock-peddler, de school master, and de senator. De first, give you time; the second tell you what to do with him; and de sird make your law and your civilization.

Alexis de Tocqueville, Speech, 1839, quoted in W.C. Fowler, *The Ministers of Connecticut in the Revolution*, 1876

The warm, the very warm, heart of 'New England at its best', such a vast abounding Arcadia of mountains and broad vales and great rivers and large lakes and white villages embowered in prodigious elms and maples. It is extraordinarily beautiful and graceful and idyllic – for America.

Henry James, Letter to Sir T.H. Warren, 29 May 1911

Little Connecticut, with but 4800 square miles of area, lies just outside New York City, and is made up, in almost equal parts, of golf links and squalid factory towns. There is a university called Yale at New Haven. The people of Connecticut, in the early days, were very sharp traders – in fact swindlers. They made nutmegs of wood, and sold them in New York. The nickname, Nutmeg State, clings to this day.

H.L. Mencken, *Americana*, 1925

Connecticut River

from the top of Mount Holyoke

The view from the summit of Mount Holyoke . . . is really splendid. . . . The top is 880 feet above the level of the river Connecticut which winds about in the alluvial land below in a very fantastic style. This pretty stream was visible in a northern direction for many miles, in gorges amongst the hills; but, on turning to the south, we could discover only a few touches of it here and there, which to the naked eye seemed merely patches of smoke; but when viewed through a pocket telescope, these glimpses looked like bits of some immense looking-glass, shivered to pieces and cast among the trees.

Captain Basil Hall, *Travels in North America*, 1829 – of 4 October 1827

There is a great river this side of Stygia,
Before one comes to the first black cataracts
And trees that lack the intelligence of trees.

In that river, far this side of Stygia,
The mere flowing of the water is a gayety,
Flashing and flashing in the sun. On its banks,

No shadow walks. The river is fateful,
Like the last one. But there is no ferryman.
He could not bend against its propelling force.

It is not to be seen beneath the appearances
That tell of it. The steeple at Farmington
Stands glistening and Haddam shines and sways.

It is the third commonness with light and air,
A curriculum, a vigor, a local abstraction . . .
Call it, once more, a river, an unnamed flowing,

Space-filled, reflecting the seasons, the folk-lore
Of each of the senses; call it, again and again,
The river that flows nowhere, like a sea.

Wallace Stevens, 'The River of Rivers in Connecticut', *Inventario V*, 1953

Cornell

The Cornell Campus is on top of a steep hill, with a long, thin, ice-cold lake below it, into which run streams through spectacular – or, as the Americans say, scenic, – gorges; these gorges are used by the students for suicide.

Louis MacNeice, *The Strings are False*, *c.* 1940, pub. 1965

'Crossline' (Ohio)

With the exception of such cities as Chicago, St. Louis, and Cincinnati, settlers can hardly be said to have chosen their own localities. These have been chosen for them by the originators of the different lines of railway. And there is nothing in Europe in any way like to these western railway settlements. In the first place the line of the rails runs through the main street of the town, and forms not unfrequently the only road. . . . At Crossline . . . I did find a street in which there was no railroad, but it was deserted and manifestly out of favour with the inhabitants. . . . As the whole place is dependent on the railway, so is the railway held in favour and beloved. The noise of the engine is not disliked, nor are its puffings and blowings held to be unmusical. . . . It has been taken to them all as a domestic animal; no one fears it, and the little children run about almost among its wheels. It is petted and made much of on all sides, and as far as I know, it seldom bites or tears.

Anthony Trollope, *North America*, 1862

Dallas

and Fort Worth
Dallas is a baby Manhattan; Fort Worth is a cattle annex.

John Gunther, *Inside U.S.A.*, 1947

'Its Place In the Sun,' cried the *Dallas Morning News*, 'Gets Bigger All the Time.'

J.B. Priestley, *Journey Down a Rainbow*, 1955

Deer Isle (Maine)

It is an island that nestles like a suckling against the breast of Maine, but there are many of those. The sheltered darkling water seems to suck up light, but I've seen that before. The pine woods rustle and the wind cries over open country that is like Dartmoor. Stonington, Deer Isle's chief town, does not look like an American town at all in place or in architecture. Its houses are layered down to the calm waters of the bay. This town very closely resembles Lyme Regis on the coast of Dorset, and I would willingly bet that its founding settlers came from Dorset or Somerset or Cornwall. . . . The coastal people below the Bristol Channel are secret people, and perhaps magic people. There's aught behind their eyes, hidden away so deep that perhaps even they do not know they have it. And that same thing is so in Deer Islers. To put it plainly, this Isle is like Avalon; it must disappear when you are not there.

John Steinbeck, *Travels with Charley*, 1962

De Kalb (Illinois)

It is an odd experience to be in De Kalb, Illinois, in the very corn-crib of America, and have some coventional-looking housewife . . . come up to you and ask: 'Is there much tripling going on in New York?'

'Tripling?'

Tripling turns out to be a practice, in De Kalb, anyway, in which a husband and wife invite a third party – male or female, but more often female – over for an evening of whatever, including polymorphous perversity, even the practices written of in the one-hand magazines, such as *Hustler*, all the things involving tubes, and hoses and tourniquets and cups, and double-jointed sailors.

Tom Wolfe, 'The Me Decade and the Third Great Awakening', in *Mauve Gloves and Madmen, Clutter and Vine*, 1976

Delaware

and Kansas
Kansas was once the butt of many a senatorial gibe, but all that ended when John J. Ingalls in 1873 took his seat in the upper chamber. To a Delaware Senator who risked criticism of Kansas, Senator Ingalls flashed back: 'Mr President, the gentleman who has just spoken represents a state which has two counties when the tide is up – and only three when it is down.'

Edwin Boykin (ed.), *The Wit and Wisdom of Congress*, 1961

This is a small and measly state, owned by a single family, the Du Ponts. They made their money manufacturing explosives. Now they spend it quarreling among themselves. Most of Delaware is but two or three feet above sea-level. It has no large city, and no person of any consequence has lived in it for half a century.

H.L. Mencken, *Americana*, 1925

Denver (Colorado)

I apprehend that there have been, during my two weeks sojourn, more brawls, more fights, more pistol shots with criminal intent in this log city of one hundred and fifty dwellings, not three-fourths completed, nor two-thirds inhabited, nor one-third fit to be, than in any community of no greater numbers on earth.

Horace Greeley, *An Overland Journey from New York to San Francisco . . . in 1859*, 1860

between Denver and Golden City
Meanwhile, as we rode, the passengers enlivened the hour by pointing out the various localities renowned in the brief history of Denver, and by giving graphic descriptions of the incidents which rendered such places notorious. 'See here,' cried one, 'there is a tree on which fifteen men have been hung; just beyond is the tree which D.M. and C.I. were strung up for murdering poor L----n; here is a hollow where the d---dest fight took place you ever saw between, etc.; and there, just round that bluff, some lucky chaps picked up a nugget weighing fifty-six ounces.'

H.M. Stanley, *My Early Travels and Adventures* (August 1867), 1895

. . . cash! why they create it here.
Walt Whitman, *Specimen Days, 1879*, 1882

At Denver I met the most interesting people I have ever seen.
'Rough and ready, I suppose?'
'Ready but not rough. They were polished and refined compared with the people I met in large cities further East. Yes, I *did* see the common people. I spent a night in a silver mine. I dined with the men down there. They were great strong, well-formed men, of graceful attitude and free motion. Poems every one of them. A complete democracy under ground. I find people less rough and coarse in such places. There is no chance for roughness. The revolver is their book of etiquette. This teaches lessons that are not forgotten.'
Oscar Wilde, quoted in the *Morning Herald*, Halifax, Nova Scotia, under title 'The Apostle of Beauty in Nova Scotia', 10 October 1882

The air is so refined that you can live without much lungs.
Shane Leslie, *American Wonderland*, 1936

The remarkable thing about Denver is its ineffable closedness; when it moves, or opens up, it is like a Chippendale molting its veneer. This is not to say that Denver is reactionary. No – because reaction suggests motion, whereas Denver is immobile. . . . Denver is Olympian, impassive, and inert. It is probably the most self-sufficent, isolated, self-contained and complacent city in the world.
John Gunther, *Inside U.S.A.*, 1947

Des Moines (Iowa)

Des Moines has the largest per capita ice cream consumption in America.
The second largest gold-fish farm in the world is located within seventy miles of Des Moines.
The best pair of overalls made on the American Continent came from Iowa
There is no group of two and a half million people in the world who worship God as Iowans do.
Harangue by Professor of Iowa State College, quoted in H.L. Mencken, *Americana*, 1925

In Des Moines I was shown the front page of the issue of the local paper that recorded the sinking of the *Titanic*. A big black streamer headline announced the loss of the ship accross the top of the page; but directly beneath it there was a second headline almost as big, almost as black, announcing with satisfaction: 'No Des Moines Passengers Aboard.'
James Morris, *Coast to Coast*, 1956

Detroit

The country round Detroit is as flat as can be imagined. . . . A lady of Detroit once declared, that if she were were to build a house in Michigan, she would build a hill first.
Harriet Martineau, *Society in America*, 1837

It is a large, well-built, half-finished city. . . . It is . . . neither pleasant nor picturesque at all. I will not say that it is uncivilized, but it has a harsh, crude, unprepossessing appearance. . . . I do not think it well to recommend any Englishman to make a special visit to Detroit, who may be wholy uncommercial in his views and travel in search of that which is either beautiful or interesting.
Anthony Trollope, *North America*, 1862

If Detroit was not naturally one of the prettiest cities on the American continent, art, capital, and the home-loving instincts of its somewhat cosmopolitan population could not fail to make it such. Its charming and almost unique situation, its temperate climate, clear, sparkling atmosphere, with its numerous parks and squares, noble avenues, and spacious public buildings, its picturesque walks and drives, added to the generous hospitality of its citizens, and the excellence of its hotel accommodation, combine to make it one of the most attractive and really enjoyable cities on the American continent.
S.W. Silver & Co., *Handbook to Canada*, 1881

When I had been round the Ford works – or that part of them which is comprised in the Fordson factory – I felt like the Queen of Sheba, of whom it is recorded that when she had seen Solomon's Temple and palaces, there was no more spirit left in her. To be sure these buildings are not temples and palaces, but if absolute completeness, and perfect adaptation of means to end justify the word, they are in their own way works of art, and they have the artistic quality of stirring the imagination till it falls back exhausted.
J.A. Spender, *Through English Eyes*, 1928

*Detroit lay across the river, a mile away, like a huge pincushion stuck full of lights.
Eric Linklater, *Juan in America*, 1931

The capital of the new planet – the one, I mean, which will kill itself off – is of course, Detroit. I realized that the moment I arrived.
Henry Miller, *The Air-conditioned Nightmare*, 1945

If Detroit is right . . . there is little wrong with the American car, that is not wrong with the American public.
John Keats, *The Insolent Chariots*, 1958

Dixon (Illinois)

It is one of those places at which great beginnings have been made, but as to which the deities presiding over new towns have not been propitious. Much of it has been burnt down, and more of it has never been built up.

Anthony Trollope, *North America*, 1862

Duluth (Minnesota)

The zenith city of the unsalted seas.

James Proctor Knott, Speech in the House of Representatives, 27 January 1871

The radiant, sea-fronting, hillside city of Duluth.

Sinclair Lewis, attrib.

America's air-conditioned city, in the Hay Fever Haven of America.

Anon., from a booster pamphlet, quoted by John Gunther, *Inside U.S.A*, 1947

Dummerston (Vermont, en route to)

It was beautiful beyond expression, nature's boldest sketch in black and white, done with a Japanese disregard of perspective, and daringly altered from time to time by the restless pencils of the moon.

Rudyard Kipling, *In Sight of Monadnock*, 1892

Eagle Pass (on the Rio Grande, Texas)

When he returned, he said it had been the most respectable funeral he ever saw on the Rio Grande.

'Was there a sermon preached?' I asked, thinking the chaplain of the post probably officiated.

'Oh, no, there ain't no parson here; there weren't no ceremonies, but they had a coffin fixed up for him; first time I ever saw a coffin out in this country.'

Frederick Law Olmsted, *A Journey through Texas*, 1857

Ellsworth (Kansas)

The population of the town of Ellsworth is estimated, according to the latest census, at forty men, four women, eight boys and seven girls. There are also fourteen horses, and about twenty-nine and one half dogs. There is neither a cow, hog, cat, nor chicken around, but there are plenty of rattlesnakes, copperheads, gophers, owls, mice, and prairie dogs within the limits of the town. As Ellsworth is part and parcel of this great and progressive country, it is also progressive – for no sooner has the fifth house begun to erect its stately front above the green earth, than the population is gathered in the three saloons above-mentioned, to gravely discuss the propriety of making the new town a city, and of electing a mayor. . . . As houses are only built of rough boards, the new town has quite a rough appearance. The men are rough, the women and children are also rough, and they have a certain rough hospitality, geniality and kindness, which is beyond criticism.

H.M. Stanley, *My Early Travels and Adventures* (May 1867), 1895

El Paso

The city of the Four C's – Climate, Cotton, Cattle, Copper.

John Gunther, *Inside U.S.A.*, 1947

El Reno (Oklahoma)

On my travels I had breakfast at a place called El Reno in Oklahoma. There was a large sign at the station saying El Reno is good enough for us. We believe you would like it. After that I was not surprised that they believe in God and the Democratic Party.

Bertrand Russell, Letter to Charles Sanger, 29 December 1929, in *Bertrand Russell's, America*, ed. B. Feinberg and R. Kastrils, 1973

Fargo (North Dakota)

If you will take a map of the United States and fold it in the middle, eastern edge against western, and crease it sharply, right in the crease will be Fargo. On double-page maps sometimes Fargo gets lost in the binding. That may not be a very scientific method for finding the east-west middle of a country, but it will do. But beyond this, Fargo to me is brother to the fabulous places of the earth, kin to those magically remote spots mentioned by Herodotus and Marco Polo and Mandeville. From my earliest memory, if it was a cold day, Fargo was the coldest place on the continent. If heat was the subject, then at that time the papers listed Fargo as hotter than any place else, or wetter or drier, or deeper in snow. . . . I must admit that when I passed through Moorhead, Minnesota, and rattled across the Red River into Fargo on the other side, it was a golden autumn day, the town as traffic-troubled, as neon-plastered, as cluttered and milling with activity as any other up-and-coming town of forty-six thousand souls.

John Steinbeck, *Travels with Charley*, 1962

Florida

The Floridians when they travell, have a kind of herbe

dried, who with a cane and an earthen cup in the end, with fire and the dried herbs put together, doe sucke thorow the cane the smoke thereof, which smoke satisfieth their hunger, and therewith they live foure or five days without meat or drinke, and this all the Frenchmen used for this purpose: yet do they holde opinion withall, that it causeth water and fleame to void from their stomacks. The commodities of this land are more then are yet knowen to any man: for besides the land itself, whereof there is more than any king Christian is able to inhabit, it flourisheth with medow, pasture ground, with woods of Cedar and Cypres, and other sorts, as better can not be in the world. They have for apothecary herbs, trees, roots, and gummes great store. . . . Golde and silver they want not. . . . Of unicornes they have many.

Voyage of Sir John Hawkins, 1565, in Richard Hakluyt, *Principal Navigations . . . of the English Nation*, 1598–1600

Florida . . . does beguile and gratify me – giving me my first and last (evidently) sense of the tropics, or à peu pres, the subtropics, and revealing to me a blandness in nature of which I had no idea.

Henry James, Letter to Edmund Gosse, 16 February 1905

A few things for themselves,
Convolvulus and coral,
Buzzards and live-moss,
Tiestas from the keys,
A few things for themselves,
Florida, venereal soil,
Disclose to the lover. . . .

Wallace Stevens, 'O Florida, Venereal Soil', *Revue, The Dial*, July 1922

As I went farther and farther north and it got colder I was aware of more and more advertising for Florida real estate and, with the approach of the long and bitter winter, I could see why Florida is a golden word. As I went along I found that more and more people lusted toward Florida and that thousands had moved there and more thousands wanted to and would. The advertising, with a side look at Federal Communications, made few claims except for the fact that what they were selling was in Florida. Some of them went out on a limb and promised that it was above tide level. But that didn't matter; the very name Florida carried the message of warmth and ease and comfort. It was irresistible.

John Steinbeck, *Travels with Charley*, 1962

Florida (Missouri)

I was born the 30th of November, 1835, in the almost invisible village of Florida, Monroe County, Missouri. . . . The village contained a hundred people and I increased the population by 1 per cent. It is more than many of the best men in history could have done for a town.

Mark Twain, *Autobiography (c.*1897–1910), 1924

Frankfort (Kentucky)

Frankfort is the capital of Kentucky, and is as quietly dull a little town as I ever visited. . . . The legislature of the State was not sitting when I was there, and the grass was growing in the streets.

Anthony Trollope, *North America*, 1862

Fredericksburg

It was really comfortable to get into a place where the eye could rest here and there on a house above a year old, or which did not look as if it were just out of the carpenter's shop. I absolutely saw in Fredericksburg two houses with green moss on the roof. The streets too, were completed, and the dwellings of the inhabitants within gunshot of one another, which was sociable after Washington.

Captain Basil Hall, *Travels in North America* (31 January 1828), 1829

Gary (Indiana)

Gary, I believe, is called after a steel magnate named Judge Gary, and I presume the adjective 'garish' is also from that derivation. And if it was originally coined to describe the town, or the Judge either, for that matter, it has acquired an altogether erroneous mildness of meaning.

A.G. Macdonell, *A Visit to America*, 1935

Georgia

My native State! My cherish'd home!
  Hallow'd alike by smile and tear,
May glory o'er thee build her dome,
  And fame her temples rear:
I love thee for thy burning sky
  'Neath which my feet have ever trod
I love thee for the forms that lie
  Cold, cold beneath thy sod.

'R.M.C.', 'Georgia', *Augusta Mirror*, 1839

In the small towns of the country, however, we found the hospitality of the residents all that we could desire, and more than we could enjoy.

J.S. Buckingham, *The Slave States of America, 1839*, 1842

and South Carolina
Where northward as you go
The Pines for ever grow;
Where southward if you bend
Are pine-trees without end;
Where, if you travel west,
Earth loves the pine-tree best;
Where eastward if you gaze
Through long, unvaried ways,
Behind you and before
Are pine-trees evermore.

Charles Mackay, *Life and Liberty in America, 1857–8*, 1859

There the liberated lower orders of whites have borrowed the worst commercial bounderism of the Yankee and superimposed it upon a culture that, at bottom, is but little removed from savagery. Georgia is at once the home of the cotton-mill sweater and of the most noisy and vapid sort of chamber of commerce, of the Methodist parson turned Savonarola and of the lynching bee. A self-respecting European, going there to live, would not only find intellectual stimulation utterly lacking; he would actually feel a certain insecurity, as if the scene were the Balkans, or the China Coast. . . . There is a state with more than half the area of Italy and more population than either Denmark or Norway, and yet in thirty years it has not produced a single idea.

H.L. Mencken, 'The Sahara of the Bozart', in *Prejudices*, Second Series, 1921

Oh, Georgia booze is mighty fine booze,
The best yuh ever poured yuh,
But it eats the soles right offen yore shoes,
For Hell's broke loose in Georgia.

Stephen Vincent Benét, *The Mountain Whippoorwill*, 1925

Driving around the state, one sometimes gets the impression that there are more churches than houses. . . . Wherever one goes in Georgia, one senses the impact of faith on the lives of its citizens. There cannot be many other places where one is likely to be confronted by a billboard that says 'God Makes House Calls'.

E.J. Kahn Jr, *New Yorker*, 6 February 1978

Gloucester (Massachusetts)

The population of the Peninsula is homogeneous. There is probably no individual beyond Gloucester whose parentage may not be referred to a particular set of people, at a particular date in English history. It has great wealth of granite and fish. It is composed of granite; and almost its only visitors are fish.

Harriet Martineau, *Society in America*, 1837

Grand Canyon

To stand upon the edge of this stupendous gorge is to enjoy in a moment compensation for years of uneventful life.

John L. Stoddard, *Grand Canyon – Lectures, c.* 1900

Leave it as it is. You cannot improve on it. Keep it for your children, your children's children, and for all who come after you as the one great sight which every American should see.

Theodore Roosevelt attrib., on visiting the Grand Canyon, 1903

The Grand Canyon gets less like Dawlish as one looks at it after breakfast, twenty Matterhorns blazing with alpine glow and situated many feet below one.

Harold Nicolson, *Diary*, 1 April 1933

I thought I could imagine a better Grand Canyon did I? Well, cried Reality, take a look at this – and oh boy! – you ain't seen nothing yet. . . . I have heard rumours of visitors who were disappointed. The same people will be disappointed at the Day of Judgement. . . . The Colorado river, which is powerful, turbulent, and so thick with silt that it is like a saw, made it . . . but you feel when you are there that God gave the Colorado river its instructions. . . . If I were an American I should make my remembrance of it the final test of men, art, and policies. I should ask myself: is this good enough to exist in the same country as the Canyon? How would I feel about this man, this kind of art, these political measures, if I were near that Rim? Every member or officer of the Federal Government ought to remind himself with triumphant pride, that he is on the staff of the Grand Canyon.

J.B. Priestley, *Midnight on the Desert*, 1937

When you come to the Grand Canyon it's as though Nature were breaking out in supplication. . . . It's mad, completely mad, and at the same time so grandiose, so sublime, so illusory that when you come upon it for the first time, you break down and weep with joy. *I* did, at least. For over thirty years I had been aching to see this huge hole in the earth. Like Phaestos, Mycenae, Epidauros, it is one of the few spots on this earth which not only come up to expectation but surpass it.

Henry Miller, *The Air-conditioned Nightmare*, 1945

Suppose yourself walking on a Surrey common near Bagshot. There are a good many fir trees around, the soil is sandy, and the prospect rather dull. Suddenly the common stops and you are standing without any warning on the brink of a precipice which is one mile deep. One mile into the tortured earth it goes, the other side of the chasm is miles away, and the chasm is filled with unbelievable deposits of rock which resemble sphinxes draped in crimson shawls. . . . It is the most astounding natural object I have ever seen. It frightens. There are many colours in it besides crimson, – strata of black and of white, and rocks of ochre and pale lilac. And the Colorado River itself is, when one gets down to it, still more sinister, for it is muddy white and very swift, and it rages like an infuriated maggot between precipices of granite, gnawing at them and cutting the Canyon deeper. It was strange, after two days amongst these marvels and terrors, to return to the surface of the earth, and go bowling away in a bus between little fir trees.

E.M. Forster, 'The United States', 1947, *Two Cheers for Democracy*, 1951

Those who write about the Canyon generally begin by saying that it is indescribable; then they undertake to describe it.

Joseph Wood Krutch, *Grand Canyon*, 1958

Two young men . . . who stood beside the parapet at the edge of the rim, across the terrace from the hotel. They peered fearfully down into the mile-deep chasm.

'Supposing one of us fell in?' one breathed.

His friend replied gallantly, 'The other would be *heart-broken*!'

Ethel Mannin, *An American Journey*, 1967

Maybe the Grand Canyon . . . was God's main purpose, and once they were done, it was a piddling afterthought to make Adam and Eve and the billions of scattering ants we now call 'the human family.' Look at the Grand Canyon long enough and you are in danger not so much of total misanthropy, as of a fixed, stony indifference to our world and its inhabitants.

Alistair Cooke, *The Americans*, 1979

The one place on earth for which no description can prepare you.

John Carter, *The Times*, 17 November 1979

It is a chameleon of a canyon.

Trevor Fishlock, *Americans and Nothing Else*, 1980

Grand Rapids (Michigan)

Wild roved the Indians once
On the banks of the Grand River,
And they built their little huts
Down by that flowing river.
In a pleasant valley fair,
Where flows the river rapid,
An Indian village once was there,
Where now stands Grand Rapids.

Indians have left and gone
Beyond the Mississippi.
They called the river Owashtenong
Where stands this pleasant city.
Louis Campau the first white man
Bought land in Grand Rapids.
He lived and died an honored man
By people of Grand Rapids.

When Campau came to the valley
No bridge was across the river;
Indians in their light canoes
Rowed them o'er the water.
Railroads now from every way
Run through the city, Grand Rapids;
The largest town in west Michigan
Is the city of Grand Rapids.

Julia A. Moore, *Grand Rapids*, 1876

Grand Rapids makes America's furniture, and I suspect the movement of the American rocking chair is based on the rapidity of the Falls.

Shane Leslie, *American Wonderland*, 1936

'Oh, that's very Grand Rapids!' has become a standard criticism for bad furniture, though few people stop to realize that most of the good tables and chairs in America originate from this vilified town in Michigan.

Coming from the airport, I had the impression that Grand Rapids looked like an American city seen in lithographs of the turn of the century. It had a curiously anachronistic air about it, and reminded me, for some reason or other, of those old-fashioned drawings of Uncle Sam as a long-goateed gentleman in a red-white-and-blue morning coat. Some of the buildings had the ugly superannuated quality of industrial revolution warehouses – that is, until someone informed me that the city was to a large proportion Dutch. Then, when I noticed that every other house's name began with a 'van', everything suddenly looked like a Dutch painting, and the houses like those along the waterways in Holland.

Cecil Beaton, *It Gives Me Great Pleasure*, 1955

The Great Dismal Swamp

Fancy cannot picture to itself a more repulsive or desolate region. Not that nature is here without power; but her powers are applied to hideous production. There is something awful, as well as repulsive, in the scene. It is desolation in the lap of luxuriance – it is solitude in a funereal garb.

Alexander Mackay, *The Western World*, 1849

Great Lakes

See also under Canada

The lakes in America are cold, cumbrous, uncouth, and uninteresting; intended by nature for the conveyance of cereal produce, but not for the comfort of travelling men and women.

Anthony Trollope, *North America*, 1862

These lakes, called 'Great' with reason, are the fresh-water Mediterranean of the western hemisphere, as has nicely been said. They are the Middle West's equivalent of a coastline.

John Gunther, *Inside U.S.A.*, 1947

and Lake Erie in particular

One extraordinary thing about them, as de Tocqueville noted a century ago, is that unlike almost all European lakes they are not walled in – they merge flatly into the plains and prairie. But do not think that they cannot be angry! I have seen weather on Lake Erie that made the China Sea seem calm. Normally one does not associate such turbulent outburst of nature with a mechanical civilization, but Lake Erie is also the greatest industrial waterway in the world, a lake almost as big as Palestine with a cordon of railways drawn tight around it like a noose.

Ibid.

Lake Huron/Lake Michigan – view from Fort Holmes

I can compare it to nothing but what Noah might have seen, the first bright morning after the deluge. Such a cluster of little paradises rising out of such a congregation of waters, I can hardly fancy to have seen elsewhere. The capacity of the human eye seems here suddenly enlarged, as if it could see to the verge of the watery creation. Blue, level waters appear to expand for thousands of miles in every direction; wholly unlike any aspect of the sea. Cloud shadows, and specks of white vessels, at rare intervals, alone diversify it. Bowery islands rise out of it; bowery promontories stretch down into it; while at one's feet lies the melting beauty which one almost fears will vanish in its softness before one's eyes; the beauty of the shadowy dells and sunny mounds, with browsing cattle and springing fruit and flowers. Thus, and no otherwise, would I fain think did the world emerge from the flood. I was never before so unwilling to have objects named. The essential unity of the scene seemed to be marred by any distinction of its parts.

Harriet Martineau, *Society in America*, 1837

Lake Michigan

The sun was going down. We watched the sunset, not remembering that the refraction above the fresh waters would probably cause some remarkable appearance. We looked at one another in amazement at what we saw. First, there were three gay, inverted rainbows between the water and the sun, then hidden behind a little streak of cloud. Then the sun emerged from behind this only streak of cloud, urn-shaped; a glistering golden urn. Then it changed, rather suddenly, to an enormous golden acorn. Then to a precise resemblance, except being prodigiously magnified, of Saturn with his ring. This was the most beautiful apparition of all. Then it was quickly narrowed and elongated till it was like the shaft of a golden pillar; and then it went down square. Long after its disappearance, a lustrous, deep crimson dome, seemingly solid, rested steadily on the heaving waters. An inexperienced navigator might be pardoned for making all sail towards it; it looked so real.

Ibid.

When I see the waves of Lake Michigan toss in the bleak snow storm, I see how small & inadequate the common poet is.

Ralph Waldo Emerson, *Journals*, 1855–6

Green Bay (Wisconsin)

First Man: It's a real nice place.
Second Man: What's nice about it? Only things ever come out of Green Bay is the Packers and ugly whores.
First Man: Now, wait just one minute, you son of a bitch. My wife is from Green Bay.
Second Man: She is? What position she play?

John Steinbeck, quoted in a letter to John Kenneth Galbraith, in Galbraith, *Economics, Peace and Laughter*, 1971

Green County (Wisconsin)

Here, not anywhere in Switzerland, is the Swiss cheese capital of the world. Its atmosphere is, indeed, much more Swiss than anything I ever saw in Zurich or Geneva. Swiss from the old country sent emissaries here many years ago, who tested one Wisconsin area after another, until they found a place where conditions of soil and water most closely resembled those in Switzerland itself. Then they moved over and have lived happily here ever since. The smallest whisper in Green County is still a yodel.

John Gunther, *Inside U.S.A.*, 1947

Greenville (Maine)

Greenville (a little village which looks as if it had dripped down from the hills and settled in the hollow at the foot of the lake). . . .

James Russell Lowell, *A Moosehead Journal*, 1853

Griggsville (Illinois)

One place had such an ugly name that I refused to lecture there. It was called Grigsville. Supposing I had founded a school of Art there – fancy 'Early Grigsville.'

Imagine a School of Art teaching 'Grigsville Renaissance.'

Oscar Wilde, *Impressions of America*, 1883

Harmony (Pennsylvania)

When Rapp the harmonist embargoed marriage
In his harmonious settlement (which flourishes
Strangely enough as yet without miscarriage,
Because it breeds no more mouths than it nourishes,
Without those sad expenses which disparage
What Nature naturally most encourages),
Why called he 'Harmony' a state sans wedlock?
Now here I have got the preacher at a deadlock,
Because he either meant to sneer at harmony
Or marriage by divorcing them thus oddly.

Lord Byron, *Don Juan*, 1819–24

Harpers Ferry

Jefferson pronounced it the finest scenery he had seen – but he was a Virginian.

Frederick Law Olmsted, *Journey through Texas*, 1857

Highway 66

*Highway 66 is the main migrant road. 66 – the long concrete path across the country, waving gently up and down on the map, from the Mississippi to Bakersfield – over the red lands and the gray lands, twisting up into the mountains, crossing the Divide and down into the bright and terrible desert, and across the desert to the mountains again, and into the rich California valleys.

66 is the path of a people in flight, refugees from the dust and shrinking land, from the thunder of tractors and shrinking ownership, from the desert's slow northward invasion, from the twisting winds that howl up out of Texas, from the floods that bring no richness to the land and steal what little richness is there. From all of these the people are in flight, and they come into 66 from the tributary side roads, from the wagon tracks and the rutted country roads, 66 is the mother road, the road of flight.

John Steinbeck, *The Grapes of Wrath*, 1939

Hollywood

see also under Los Angeles

'Now folks, stop and think. If you tell a Frenchman, a German, or an Italian that you live in Pasadena, he won't know what you mean. But tell him you live in Hollywood, and watch his eyes light up! All the world knows Hollywood. All the world wants to come to it. You can go to the naked savage living in darkest Africa, to the untutored Aborigine, who bites raw meat with his sharpened teeth, so that the blood runs down his chin, and you can say to him, 'I live in Hollywood,' and what will he say? He will reply, 'Yes boss, I'se thinking of movin' there myself.' (Much laughter).

Hollywood real estate agent, quoted in Collinson Owen, *The American Illusion*, 1929

A trip through a sewer in a glass-bottomed boat.

Wilson Mizner, quoted Alva Johnson, *The Incredible Mizners*, 1953 – before 1933

The people are unreal. The flowers are unreal, they don't smell. The fruit is unreal, it doesn't taste of anything. The whole place is a glaring, gaudy, nightmarish set, built up in the desert.

Ethel Barrymore, Remark after working in Hollywood in 1932, quoted in Hollis Alpert, *The Barrymores*, 1965

California has given Art its Calvary.

Shane Leslie, *American Wonderland*, 1936

Charles Laughton . . . talked a lot about Hollywood and how film-actors take their art more seriously than their colleagues in the theatre: 'The nearest thing to the atmosphere of the studio is a monastery.' This entirely contradicts my notion of Hollywood as a bathing-pool where the Claudette Colberts spend their non-filming time taking headers into milk.

James Agate, *Ego 3*, 8 February 1937

Hollywood is a place where people from Iowa mistake each other for stars.

Fred Allen, attrib., 1941

A town where inferior people have a way of making superior people feel inferior.

Dudley Field Malone, attrib.

*It's a mining town in lotus land.

F. Scott Fitzgerald, *The Last Tycoon*, 1941

*At the worst I accepted Hollywood with the resignation of a ghost assigned to a haunted house.

Ibid.

*Under the moon the back lot was thirty acres of fairyland – not because the locations really looked like African jungles and French chateaux and schooners at anchor and Broadway at night, but because they looked like the torn picture books of childhood, like fragments of stories dancing in an open fire. I never lived in a house with an attic, but a back lot must be something like that, and at night of course, in an enchanted distorted way, it all comes true.

Ibid.

earthquake

*We didn't get the full shock, like at Long Beach,

where the upper storeys of the shops were spewed into the streets and small hotels drifted out to sea – but for a full minute our bowels were one with the bowels of the earth – like some nightmare attempt to attach our navel cords again and jerk us back to the womb of creation.

Ibid.

Tomorrow I will discover Sunset Boulevard. Eurythmic dancing, ball room dancing, tap dancing, artistic photography, ordinary photography, lousy photography, electro-fever treatment, internal douche treatment, ultra-violet ray treatment, elocution lessons, psychic readings, institutes of religion, astrological demonstrations, hands read, feet manicured, elbows massaged, faces lifted, warts removed, fat reduced, insteps raised, corsets fitted, busts vibrated, corns removed, hair dyed, glasses fitted, soda jerked, hangovers cured, headaches driven away, flatulence dissipated, business improved, limousines rented, the future made clear, the war made comprehensible, octane made higher, and butane lower, drive in and get indigestion, flush the kidneys, get a cheap car wash, stay awake pills and go to sleep pills. Chinese herbs are very good for you, and without a Coca-cola life is unthinkable. From the car window it's like a strip-teaser doing the St Vitus's dance - a corny one.

Henry Miller, *The Air-conditioned Nightmare*, 1945

My own attitude to Hollywood was that authors should keep away, unless of exceptionally sound constitution. . . . I agreed with the author who always went to see the film of his last book in order to get the plot for his next. . . . The Vatican has endured for almost two thousand years on the definition of salvation. Hollywood hopes to last as long on the definition of sex.

Cecil Roberts, *And so to America*, 1946

The only way to avoid Hollywood is to live there.

Igor Stravinsky, attrib.

Hollywood is nothing more than a suburb of the Bronx, both financially and from the point of view of talent.

John Gunther, *Inside U.S.A.*, 1947

You never meet anyone in Hollywood except by appointment.

Grace Kelly, later Princess Grace of Monaco, quoted Cecil Beaton, *It Gives Me Great Pleasure*, 1955

Hollywood is a suburb of Los Angeles, or vice versa, depending upon your point of view.

Cecil Beaton, *It Gives Me Great Pleasure*, 1955

Hollywood is a place where there is no definition of your worth earlier than your last picture.

Murray Kempton, 'The Day of the Locust', *Part of Our Time*, 1955

Hollywood money isn't money. It's congealed snow, melts in your hand, and there you are.

Dorothy Parker, Interview, *Writers at Work*, First Series, 1958

The convictions of Hollywood and television are made of boiled money.

Lillian Hellman, *An Unfinished Woman*, 1969

When Gertrude Stein returned to New York after a short sojourn in Hollywood somebody asked her . . . 'What is it like – out there?'

To which, with little delay, and the minimum of careful thought the sage replied . . . 'There *is* no "There" – there.'

David Niven, *Bring on the Empty Horses*, 1975

It is well to remember what these very rich movie men were like, since I doubt they have changed. . . . Hollywood lived the way the Arabs are attempting to live now, and while there is nothing strange about people vying with each other for great landed estates, there is something odd about people vying with each other for better bathrooms. It is doubtful that such luxury has ever been associated with the normal acts of defecating or bathing oneself. It is even possible that feces are not pleased to be received in such grand style and thus prefer to settle in the soul.

Lillian Hellman, *Scoundrel Time*, 1976

The one thing that you simply have to remember all the time that you are there is that Hollywood is an Oriental city. As long as you do that you might survive. If you try to equate it with anything else you'll perish.

Olivia de Havilland, quoted by Dirk Bogarde, *Snakes and Ladders* 1978

Franklin Avenue

In the [late sixties] I was living in a large house in a part of Hollywood that had once been expensive and was now described by one of my acquaintances as a 'senseless-killing neighbourhood.'

Joan Didion, *The White Album*, 1979

The place makes everyone a gambler. Its spirit is speedy, obsessive, immaterial. The action itself is the art form, and is described in aesthetic terms: 'A very imaginative deal,' they say, or, 'He writes the most creative deals in the business.' There is in Hollywood, as in all cultures in which gambling is the central activity, a lowered sexual energy, an inability to devote more than token attention to the preoccupations of the society outside. The action is everything, more consuming than sex, more immediate than politics; more important always than the acquisition of money, which is never, for the gambler, the true point of the exercise.

Ibid.

Hollywood, the Versailles of Los Angeles.

Jan Morris, *Destinations*, 1980

A dreary industrial town controlled by hoodlums of enormous wealth.

S.J. Perelman, quoted on radio after Perelman's death, on 18 October 1979

Hoover Dam, (Boulder, Colorado)

I walked across the marble star map that traces a sidereal revolution of the equinox and fixes forever, the Reclamation man had told me, for all time and for all people who can read the stars, the date the dam was dedicated. The star map was, he said, for when we were all gone and the dam was left. I had not thought much of it when he said it, but I thought of it then, with the wind whining and the sun dropping behind a mesa with the finality of a sunset in space. Of course that was the image I had seen always, seen it without quite realizing what I saw, a dynamo finally free of man, splendid at last in its absolute isolation, transmitting power and releasing water to a world where no one is.

Joan Didion, *The White Album*, 1979

Houston

It is bigger than Dallas and supposed to be much rougher and tougher. Somebody up there told me that a Gracious Living sort of woman arrived in Houston and asked where she could find a nice restaurant, with shaded lights, wine, soft music: 'Sorry lady,' said the Houstonian, 'this is strictly a whisky and trombone town.'

J.B. Priestley, *Journey Down a Rainbow*, 1955

Every time I go from down-town Houston out to the Shamrock Hotel, I read my favourite notice: *Turn Right on Next Block for Perfection.* I believe it has something to do with oiling or cleaning cars, but that doesn't matter. Half the people in these cities are turning, or about to turn, on next block for perfection. There it is, they believe, just round the corner. Not something a litle better, nor much better, than what they already have or are – but *Perfection.*

Ibid.

In Houston the air was warm and rich and suggestive of fossil fuel. . . .

Joan Didion, *The White Album*, 1979

Hudson River

*The Hudson River is like old October and tawny Indians in their camping places long ago; it is like long pipes and old tobacco; it is like cool depths and opulence; it is like the shimmer of liquid green on summer days.

Thomas Wolfe, *Of Time and the River.*1935

Humboldt River (Nevada)

The Humboldt, all things considered, is the meanest river of its length on earth . . . its water . . . is about the most detestable I ever tasted. . . . I thought I had seen barrenness before . . . but . . . here, on the Humboldt, famine sits enthroned, and waves his sceptre over a dominion expressly made for him. . . . I am sure no one ever left it without a sense of relief and thankfulness.

Horace Greenley, *An Overland Journey from New York to San Francisco . . . in 1859,* 1860

A 'river' in Nevada is a sickly rivulet which is just the counterpart of the Erie canal in all respects save that the canal is twice as long and four times as deep. One of the pleasantest and most invigorating exercises one can contrive is to run and jump across the Humboldt river till he is overheated, and then drink it dry.

Mark Twain, *Roughing It*, 1872

Idaho

I asked an Idaho patriot why potatoes were so big. Answer: 'We fertilize 'em with cornmeal, and irrigate with milk.'

John Gunther, *Inside U.S.A.*, 1947

Illinois

The Grand Prairie

The resemblance to the sea, which some of the prairies exhibited, was really most singular. I had heard of this before, but always supposed the account exaggerated. There is one spot in particular, near the middle of the Grand Prairie . . . where the ground happened to be of the rolling character alluded to, and where, excepting in the article of colour – and that was not widely different from the tinge of some seas, – the similarity was so very striking, that I almost forgot where I was. This deception was heightened by a circumstance which I had often heard mentioned, but the force of which, perhaps, none but a seaman could fully estimate; I mean, the appearance of the distant insulated trees, as they gradually rose above the horizon, or receded from our view. They were so exactly like strange sails heaving in sight, that I am sure, if two or three sailors had been present, they would almost have agreed as to what canvass these magical vessels were carrying.

Captain Basil Hall, *Travels in North America*, 1829

This climate and people are a new test for the wares of a man of letters. All his thin watery matter freezes; 'tis only the smallest portion of alcohol that remains good.

Ralph Waldo Emerson, *Journals*, 1856

The Illinois prairies . . . repel the idea of being new to civilized life and industry – . . . they, with their borders of trees and belts of timber, reminded the traveler rather of the parks and spacious fields of an old country like England – . . . you were constantly on the involuntary look-out for the chateaux, or at least the humbler farmhouses, which should diversify such a scene.

Horace Greeley, *An Overland Journey from New York to San Francisco . . . in 1859*, 1860

He who has not seen corn on the ground in Illinois or Minnesota, does not know to what extent the fertility of land may go, or how great may be the weight of cereal crops.

Anthony Trollope, *North America*, 1862

O you who lose the art of hope,
Whose temples seem to shrine a lie,
Whose sidwalks are but stones of fear,
Who weep that Liberty must die,
Turn to the little prairie towns,
Your higher hope shall yet begin.
On every side awaits you there
Some gate where glory enters in . . .

Vachel Lindsay, 'The Gospel of Beauty, II: The Illinois Village', in *Collected Poems*, 1923

and Iowa
There's talk says Illinois
Is there says Iowa

Archibald MacLeish, 'Colloquy for the States', *A Time to Act*, 1943

Illinois did a fair autumn day for us, crisp and clean. We moved quickly northward, heading for Wisconsin through a noble land of good fields and magnificent trees, a gentleman's countryside, neat, and white-fenced and I would guess subsidized by outside income. It did not seem to me to have the thrust of land that supports itself and its owner. Rather it was like a beautiful woman who requires the support and help of many faceless ones just to keep going. But this fact does not make her less lovely – if you can afford her.

John Steinbeck, *Travels with Charley*, 1962

Independence (Missouri)

Independence, as everybody knows, is Mr Truman's home base. The president's attitude to it may be guessed from his remark to me that Kansas City is 'one of its suburbs.'

John Gunther, *Inside U.S.A., 1947*

Indiana

Blest Indiana! in whose soil
Men seek the sure rewards of toil,
And honest poverty and worth
Find here the best retreat on earth,
While hosts of Preachers, Doctors, Lawyers,
All independent as wood-sawyers,
With men of every hue and fashion,
Flock to the rising 'hoosier' nation.

John Finley, *The Hoosier's Nest, published as the Address of the Carrier of the Indianapolis Journal*, 1 January 1833

I asked the Scotchman what was his objection to Indiana? 'Objection,' he replied with a strong Highland accent; 'objection, did ye say? There is no objection but to its over-fruitfulness. The soil is so rich, the climate so delicious, that the farmer has no adequate inducement to work. The earth produces its fruits too readily. The original curse presses too lightly . . . here in Indiana, Illinois, and away to the West, as far as you can go, man gains his bread too easily to remain virtuous.'

Charles Mackay, *Life and Liberty in America, 1857–8*, 1859

I come from Indiana, the home of more first-rate second-class men than any State in the Union.

Thomas R. Marshall, *Recollections*, 1925

The Hoosier State of Indiana!

John W. Davis, Toast at the Jackson dinner at Indianapolis, 8 January 1933

The brighter they were, the sooner they came.

George Ade, referring to the 'bright' men who came from Indiana, before 1944

Indianapolis

Indianapolis . . . proved to have a certain French atmosphere – but in terms rather of some extravagant Paris exhibition of the early nineteen hundreds.

Lord Kinross, *The Innocents at Home*, 1959

Iowa

'It is so wet that a man can't live any more than a year or two without getting web footed.'

Quoted Lilian Leland, *Travelling Alone, A Woman's Journey Round the World*, 1890

Three millions yearly for manure
but not one cent for literature

Ellis Parker Butler, before 1937

Iowa, a really fecund state, throws its corn over into Nebraska and Illinois, and its old folks all the way to California.

John Gunther, *Inside U.S.A.*, 1947

Jackson (Mississippi)

I heard it said in Jackson . . . that 'if you shoot a Republican, out of season, the fine will be ten dollars and costs.'

John Gunther, *Inside U.S.A.*, 1947

Kalamazoo (Michigan)

A quaint place quaintly named.

Edmund Yates, *Recollections and Experiences,* 1884.

Yes, Kalamazoo is a spot on the map
And the passenger trains stop there
And the factory smokestacks smoke
And the grocery stores are open Saturday nights
And the streets are free for citizens who vote
And inhabitants counted in the census.
Saturday night is the big night.
Listen with your ears on a Saturday night in
Kalamazoo
And say to yourself: I hear America, I hear, *what* do I
hear? . . .
Kalamazoo kisses a hand to something far off.
Kalamazoo calls to a long horizon, to a shivering silver
angel, to a creeping mystic what-is-it.
'We're here because we're here,' is the song of
Kalamazoo.
'We don't know where we're going but we're on our
way,' are the words.
There are hound dogs of bronze in the public square,
hound dogs looking far beyond the public square. . . .
And the children grow up asking each other, 'What can
we do to kill time?'
They grow up and go to the railroad station and buy
tickets for Texas, Pennsylvania, Alaska.
'Kalamazoo is all right,' they say. 'But I want to see the
world.'
And when they have looked the world over they come
back saying it is all like Kalamazoo.

Carl Sandburg, 'The Sins of Kalamazoo', in *Smoke and Steel,* 1920

Kansas

Oh, they chew tobacco thin in Kansas,
Oh, they say that drink's a sin in Kansas.

Kansas folksong, quoted by John Gunther, *Inside U.S.A.*, 1947

There are men who are born to go to Kansas, men born to take a bee line to an axe.

Ralph Waldo Emerson, *Journals* 1857

It takes three log houses to make a city in Kansas, but they begin *calling* it a city as soon as they have staked out the lots.

Horace Greeley, *An Overland Journey from New York to San Francisco . . . in 1859*, 1860

It is an old saying on the plains, and one which has been repeatedly proven to be true – viz., that 'A man without a horse has no business on the prairie.'

H.M. Stanley, *My Early Travels and Adventures* (May 1867), 1895

Kansas used to believe in Populism and free silver. It now believes in hot summers and a hot hereafter.

Julian Street, *Abroad at Home*, 1914

This is the coldest state in the Union.

F. Scott Fitzgerald, Letter to Mrs Edward Fitzgerald, winter 1919

And we felt free in Kansas
From any sort of fear,
For thirty thousand tramps like us
There harvest every year.

She stretches arms for them to come,
She roars for helpers then,
And so it is in Kansas
That tramps, one month, are men

Vachel Lindsay, 'Kansas', *Collected Poems*, 1923

Kansas had better stop raising corn, and begin raising hell.

Mary Lease, attrib.

To understand why people say, 'Dear old Kansas!' is to understand that Kansas is no mere geographical expression, but a state of mind, a religion, and a philosophy in one.

Carl Becker, quoted in Ladd Haystead, *If the Prospect Pleases*, 1945

Kansas is the child of Plymouth Rock.

William Allen White, *Autobiography*, 1946

A kind of gravity point for American democracy.

John Gunther, *Inside U.S.A.*, 1947

Kansas City

It is the most religious city in the State; it is the Boston of the west. Her churches are legion; they embrace all the denominations. The family and general reading book of the people is the Holy Bible. The streets of this religious city are huge furrows in the hills, and are sunk to the depth of fifty feet and over. The cliff-like walls rise frowningly above the street pedestrians. Behind them on the river bank, stands the city, stretching its skeleton arms even into Kansas State. The houses appear to be built without regard to order; some are built on stilts, others on rocks, others are situated on perpendicular bluffs – this latter class probably from a desire for views. The city possesses a public square. To-day it is most forlorn, planted with scraggy-looking shrubs. Ten years hence it will have undergone a magical transformation. There will be shade trees, grass plats and parterres of flowers. So they say, though to-day it seems doubtful.

H.M. Stanley, *My Early Travels and Adventures* (July 1867), 1895

Kansas City not only calls itself 'The Heart of America' (it is almost the geographical dead centre), but 'America's Most Beautiful City'. This is a touch of hyperbole which need not be taken too seriously in a country where civic pride can become almost a religious ecstasy. There are men in America who would die for their cities, just as there used to be those who would die for a faith.

Collinson Owen, *The American Illusion*, 1929

It isn't necessary to have relatives in Kansas City to be unhappy.

Groucho Marx, Letter to Goodman Ace, 18 January 1951

Ev'rythin's up to date in Kansas City.
They've gone about as fur as they c'n go!
They went and built a skyscraper seven stories high –
About as high as a buildin' orta grow.
Ev'rythin's like a dream in Kansas City.
It's better than a magic-lantern show.
Y' c'n turn the radiator on whenever you want some heat,
With ev'ry kind o' comfort ev'ry house is all complete,
You c'n walk to privies in the rain an' never wet yer feet –
They've gone about as fur as they c'n go!
Yes, sir!
They've gone about as fur as they c'n go!

Oscar Hammerstein II, 'Kansas City', *Oklahoma*, 1943

When I write, I aim in my mind not toward New York but toward a vague spot a little to the east of Kansas.

John Updike, *Picked Up Pieces*, 1976

The Western Prairies
Another peculiarity of the prairie is, in places, its seeming horizontality, whereas it is never level: on an open plain, apparently flat as a man's palm, you cross a long ground-swell which was not perceptible before, and on its further incline you come upon a chasm wide and deep enough to contain a settlement. . . . Over the rolling surface . . . lay a tapestry of thick grass already turning to a ruddy yellow under the influence of approaching autumn. The uniformity was relieved by streaks of livelier green in the rich soils of the slopes, hollows, and ravines, where the water gravitates: . . . The silvery cirri and cumuli of the upper air flecked the surface of earth with spots of dark cool shade, surrounded by a blaze of sunshine, and by their motion, and as they trooped and chased one another, gave a peculiar liveliness to the scene; while here and there a bit of hazy blue distance, a swell of the sea-like land upon the far horizon gladdened the sight – every view is fair from afar. Nothing, I may remark is more monotonous, except perhaps the African and Indian jungle, than those prairie tracts, where the circle of which you are the centre has but about a mile of radius; it is an ocean in which one loses sight of land. You see as it were the ends of the earth, and look around in vain for some object upon which the eye may rest: it was the sublimity of repose so suggestive in the sandy deserts, and the perpetual motion so pleasing in the aspect of the sea.

Richard Burton, *The City of the Saints*, 1861

Kentucky

That beautiful region which was soon to verify its Indian appellation of the dark and bloody ground.

C.J. Latrobe, *The Rambler in North America, 1832-3*, 1835. (The Cherokee word 'kentucke' meant simply a meadow or prairie.)

A dashing Kentuckian intimates to you the richness of the soil; saying 'If you plant a nail at night, 'twill come up a spike next morning.'

Harriet Martineau, *Society in America*, 1837

The sun shines bright in the old Kentucky home.

S.C. Foster, Song, *My Old Kentucky Home*, 1852

Here spreads, for hundreds of miles before you, an immense natural park, planted, seeded to sward, drained, and kept up, by invisible hands, for the delight and service of man. Travel where you will for days, you find always the soft, smooth sod, shaded with oaks and beeches noble in age and form, arranged in vistas and masses, stocked with herds, deer, and game. Man has squatted here and there over the fair heritage, but his shabby improvements have the air of poachers' huts amidst this luxuriant beauty of nature. It is landscape gardening on the largest scale.

Frederick Law Olmsted, *A Journey through Texas*, 1857

The song birds are the sweetest
  in Kentucky;

The thoroughbreds are the fleetest
in Kentucky;
Mountains tower proudest,
Thunder peals the loudest,
The landscape is the grandest,
And politics the damnedest,
in Kentucky.
Judge James H. Mulligan, Song, late 19th century

Here's a health to old Kentucky,
Where the fathers, through the years,
Hand down the courtly graces,
To the sons of cavaliers;
Where the golden age is regnant,
And each succeeding morn
Finds 'the corn is full of kernels,
And the colonels full of 'corn'.'
William J. Lampton, *To Old Kentucky*, late 19th century

*Talk about th' Boer war an'th' campaign in the Ph'lippeens! Whin Kentucky begins f'r to shoot up her fav'rite sons they'll be more blood spilled thin thim two play wars'd spill between now an' th' time when Ladysmith's relieved f'r th' las' time an' Agnyaldoo is r-run up a three on th' outermost corner iv Hoar County, state iv Luzon. They'se rale shootin' in Kentucky, an' whin it begins ivrybody takes a hand. 'Tis th' on'y safe way. If ye thry to be an onlooker an' what they calls a non-combatant 'tis pretty sure ye'll be taken home to ye'er fam'ly lookin' like a cribbage-board. So th' thing f'r ye to do is be wan iv th' shooters ye'ersilf, load up ye'er gun an' whale away f'r th' honor iv ye'er counthry.
Finley Peter Dunne, *Mr Dooley's Philosophy*, 1900

Heaven is a Kentucky of a place.
From *Kentucky* in the American Guide Series, 1938

It is shaped, as that celebrated Kentuckian Irvin S. Cobb once said, like a camel lying down.
John Gunther, *Inside U.S.A.*, 1947

Whatever their moral characteristics may be, these Kentuckians are a very noble-looking race of men; their average height considerably exceeds that of Europeans, and their countenances, excepting when disfigured by red hair, which is not unfrequent, extremely handsome.
Mrs Frances Trollope, *Domestic Manners of the Americans*, 1832

Kentuckians . . . really do look unlike all other people.
Harriet Martineau, *Society in America*, 1837

*Have you seen the Kentuckians? said I. . . . They *are* on a scale that will please you, I guess; whopping big fellows them, I tell you; half horse, half alligator, with a touch of the airthquake.
T.C. Haliburton, *The Clockmaker, or the Sayings and Doings of Samuel Slick*, second series, 1838

Laredo (Texas)

It was a rainy night in Laredo – not late, and yet the place seemed deserted. A respectable frontier-town, sprawling at the very end of the Amtrak line, it lay on a geometric grid of bright black streets on a dirt bluff that had the clawed and bulldozed look of a recent quarry. . . . In Spanish I said, 'It is quiet here.' . . .
'Laredo,' said the taxi driver. He shrugged.
'Where are all the people?'
'The other side.'
'Nuevo Laredo?'
'Boys' Town,' he said. The English took me by surprise, the phrase tickled me. He said, now in Spanish again, 'There are one thousand prostitutes in the Zone.'
It was a round number, but I was convinced. And that of course explained what had happened to this city. After dark, Laredo slipped into Nuevo Laredo, leaving the lights on. It was why Laredo looked respectable, even genteel, in a rainswept and mildewed way: the clubs, the bars, the brothels, were across the river. The red light district was ten minutes away, in another country.
Paul Theroux, *The Old Patagonian Express*, 1979

Las Vegas

If you aim to leave Las Vegas with a small fortune, go there with a large one.
Anon. American saying

Las Vegas . . . is a man-made paradise, the fallen Adam in the arms of a neon serpent. . . . This is Playland as Eden, essentially infantile, but it entrances many bored people, including lots of foreigners.
Robert Mazzocco, 'Letter from Las Vegas', *New York Review of Books*, 15 September 1977

It is highwayman and whore on the desert road, a city both veneer and venereal, dedicated to waste and excess, heartless and without a heart; a town where, probably, nothing good or worthwhile has ever happened, nor ever will. . . . As I set off I did not look back in case I was struck into salt.
Trevor Fishlock, *Americans and Nothing Else*, 1980

Leadville (Colorado)

I was told that if I went there they would be sure to

shoot me or my travelling manager. I wrote and told them that nothing they could do to my travelling manager would intimidate me. They are miners – men working in metals, so I lectured them on the Ethics of Art. I read them passages from the Autobiography of Benvenuto Cellini, and they seemed most delighted. I was reproved by my hearers for not having brought him with me. I explained that he had been dead for some little time, which elicited the enquiry 'Who shot him?' They afterwards took me to a dancing saloon where I saw the only rational method of art criticism I have ever come across. Over the piano was printed a notice

PLEASE DO NOT SHOOT THE PIANIST HE IS DOING HIS BEST

The mortality among pianists in that place is marvellous. Then they asked me to supper, and having accepted, I had to descend a mine in a rickety bucket in which it was impossible to be graceful. Having got into the heart of the mountain I had supper, the first course being whisky, the second whisky and the third whisky.

I went to the theatre to lecture and I was informed that just before I went there two men had been seized for committing a murder, and in that theatre they had been brought onto the stage at eight o'clock in the evening, and then and there tried and executed before a crowded audience.

But I found these miners very charming and not at all rough.

Oscar Wilde, Lecture, *Impressions of America*, 1883

Lexington (Kentucky)

Should you come to Lexington, leave your best thoughts behind. The theories you have most revolved, the results that are to you most certain, pack them close away, and give them no airing here. Your mind must stifle, if your body thrives. Apart from slavery too, but here a product of it, there is that throughout the South, in the tone of these fine fellows, these otherwise true gentlemen, which is very repugnant – a devilish, undisguised, and recognised contempt for all humbler classes. It springs from their relations with slaves, 'poor whites,' and tradespeople, and is simply incurable. A loose and hearty blasphemy is also a weakness of theirs, but is on the whole far less repulsive. God is known to be forgiving, but slighted men and slaves hanker long for revenge.

Frederick Law Olmsted, *A Journey through Texas*, 1856

Lockport (New York)

Lockport is beyond all comparison, the strangest looking place I ever beheld. As fast as half a dozen trees were cut down, a *factory* was raised up; stumps still contest the ground with pillars and porticos are seen to struggle with rocks. It looks as if the demon of machinery, having invaded the peaceful realms of nature, had fixed on Lockport as the battle-ground on which they should strive for mastery.

Mrs Frances Trollope, *Domestic Manners of the Americans*, 1832

Long Island

*It was a matter of chance that I should have rented a house in one of the strangest communities in North America. It was on that slender riotous island which extends itself due east of New York – and where there are, among other natural curiosities, two unusual formations of land. Twenty miles from the city a pair of enormous eggs, identical in contour and separated only by a courtesy bay, jut out into the most domesticated body of salt water in the Western hemisphere, the great wet barnyard of Long Island Sound. They are not perfect ovals . . . but their physical resemblance must be a source of perpetual wonder to the gulls that fly overhead. To the wingless a more interesting phenomenon is their dissimilarity in every particular except shape and size.

F. Scott Fitzgerald, *The Great Gatsby*, 1926

Los Alamos (New Mexico)

This is a lovely country for farming. Think of twenty-nine thousand acres in one farm. Then take a breath and think of sixty thousand acres in one farm. Then take more breath and think of thirty miles in one farm.

Lilian Leland, *Travelling Alone, A Woman's Journey Round the World*, 1890

After the visit I found myself wondering about two things. The first is, do all, no, a great many, of the people who live in this city, which has a destructive purpose at its very heart, suffer from it, feeling guilty, corrupted, or at least uneasy? Hiroshima and Nagasaki came directly out of these lovely mesas. The second thing is this. Setting aside all questions of the Laboratory and its purposes, does Los Alamos represent more or less what socialism would achieve if it had its head, plenty of money, and a clean slate? I can't help fearing it may: the be-done-good-to-or-else paternalism, the standardisation and model planning, the virtuousness of everything that leads only to the ghastly feeling of being institutionalised for life.

Jacquetta Hawkes, *Journey Down a Rainbow*, 1955

Los Angeles

And see under Hollywood

A sort of Naples here.

Oscar Wilde, Letter to Norman Forbes-Robertson, 27 March 1882

Nineteen suburbs in search of a metropolis.

H.L. Mencken, *Americana,* 1925

Los Angeles is famous for three things: first as a city where more suckers are strung, and more wallets are extracted than in any other city of like size in America. Second as a city where the marriage relation is made ridiculous and where sex-stimulation is at the maximum. Third as a city where there are more religious vagaries, more cults and isms, more psychic manifestations and delusions, more commercialized miracles, and more flagrant deceptions in the name of the gentle child Jesus, than in any other city, possibly, in the entire world. Los Angeles is fertile soil for every kind of impostor that the face of the earth has been cursed by. The suckers all come here sooner or later, and the whole twelve months is open season.

Bob Shuler's Magazine, c. 1925, quoted *ibid.*

Thought is barred in this city of Dreadful Joy, and conversation is unknown.

Aldous Huxley, *Jesting Pilate,* 1926

I had been warned many times by American friends that I must expect to find a mushroom town filled to overflowing with exquisitely beautiful young ladies. My first impression was that Los Angeles is a toadstool town filled to overflowing with centenarians. . . . I discovered afterwards, of course, that these are the Middle-Westerners, who have come to Los Angeles to die and find that it is a good deal harder than they expected.

A.G. Macdonell, *A Visit to America,* 1935

The violet hush of twilight was descending over Los Angeles as my hostess, Violet Hush, and I left its suburbs headed towards Hollywood. In the distance a glow of huge piles of burning motion-picture scripts lit up the sky. The crisp tang of frying writers and directors whetted my appetite. How good it was to be alive, I thought, inhaling deep lungfuls of carbon monoxide.

S.J. Perelman, 'Strictly from Hunger', 1937, in *The Most of S.J. Perelman,* 1959

It is hereby earnestly proposed that the U.S.A. would be much better off if that big, sprawling, incoherent, shapeless, slobbering civic idiot in the family of American communities, the City of Los Angeles, could be declared incompetent and placed in charge of a guardian like any individual mental defective.

Westbrook Pegler, *New York World-Telegram,* 22 November 1938

*Not a pretty girl, for there are none of those in Los Angeles – one girl can be pretty, but a dozen are only a chorus.

F. Scott Fitzgerald, *The Last Tycoon,* 1941

Is it true what they say about Los Angeles, that Los
 Angeles is erratic,
That in the sweet national symphony of common sense
 Los Angeles is the static?
Yes it is true, Los Angeles is not only erratic, not only
 erotic,
Los Angeles is crotchety, centrifugal, vertiginous,
 esoteric and exotic.
Many people blame the movies and the movie makers
 for Los Angeles's emotional rumpus,
But they are mistaken, it is the compass.
Certainly Los Angeles is a cloudburst of nonsequiturs,
 and of logic a drouth,
But what can you expect of a city that is laid out east
 and west instead of north and south? . . .
That is why the Los Angeles mind does not function in
 the normal true and tried ways,
Because their city runs east and west instead of north
 and south so they approach every decision sideways.
The only solution is for Los Angeles to pivot,
And I imagine the Chamber of Commerce will replace
 the divot.

Ogden Nash, 'Don't Shoot Los Angeles', in *Good Intentions,* 1942

If you tilt the whole country sideways, Los Angeles is the place where everything loose will fall.

Frank Lloyd Wright, attrib.

Less a city than a perpetual convention.

George Sessions Perry, *Saturday Evening Post,* 15 December 1945, quoted John Gunther, *Inside U.S.A.,* 1947

A circus without a tent.

Carey McWilliams, *Southern California Country,* 1946

It was more like Egypt – the suburbs of Cairo or Alexandria – than anything in Europe. We arrived at the Bel Air Hotel – very Egyptian with a hint of Addis Ababa in the smell of the blue gums.

Evelyn Waugh, *Diary,* 6 February 1947

A fine mist hovered over the City of the Walking Dead as we swung up over the Cahuenga Pass and pointed our radiator emblem toward San Francisco. Hirschfield leaned out and stared pensively at the myriad twinkling lights of Los Angeles.

'You know,' he said at length, 'somebody once called this town Bridgeport with palms. But I'll tell you something about it just the same.'

'What's that?' I asked, never taking my foot off the throttle.

'I'd rather be embalmed here than any place I know,' he said slowly. He turned up the collar of his trench coat and lit a cigarette, and in the flare of the match I saw that his tiny pig eyes were bright with tears.

S.J. Perelman *Westward Ha!* 1948

The town is like an advertisement for itself; none of its charms are left to the visitor's imagination.

Christopher Isherwood, *The Condor and the Cows,* 1949

*A big hard-boiled city with no more personality than a paper cup.

Raymond Chandler, *The Little Sister,* 1949

It was the first time I had seen a highway city, which was to be the model for the rest of our cities. Los Angeles is the avant-garde city of parody in architecture and even in nature (canyons and palm trees). Difficult to draw, a trap – like portraying clowns.

Saul Steinberg, 'Chronology' (of 1950), in Harold Rosenberg, *Saul Steinberg,* 1978.

If the whole human conglomeration of Los Angeles seems like an incandescent bubble, reflecting shapes and lights and tints, but with only frail substance of its own, Hollywood is its glittering inner filament.

Douglas Reed, *Far and Wide,* 1951

*When I got home I mixed a stiff one and stood by the open window in the living room and sipped it and listened to the ground swell of the traffic on Laurel Canyon Boulevard and looked at the glare of the big, angry city hanging over the shoulder of the hills through which the boulevard had been cut. Far off the banshee wail of police or fire sirens rose and fell, never for very long completely silent. Twenty-four hours a day somebody is running, somebody else is trying to catch him. Out there in the night of a thousand crimes people were dying, being maimed, cut by flying glass, crushed against steering wheels or under heavy car tyres. People were being beaten, robbed, strangled, raped, and murdered. People were hungry, sick, bored, desperate with loneliness or remorse or fear, angry, cruel, feverish, shaken by sobs. A city no worse than others, a city rich and vigorous and full of pride, a city lost and beaten and full of emptiness.

Raymond Chandler, *The Long Goodbye,* 1953

You need a car in Los Angeles like you need your liver.

Transworld Getaway Guide, 1975–6

Back East, people think of us as running around dressed in chartreuse sequins and walking raspberry-dyed poodles.

Los Angeles politician, quoted *ibid.*

A sense of humor is required to savour the special qualities of Los Angeles.

Ibid.

The last time I saw Dorothy Parker, Los Angeles had been on fire for three days. As I took a taxi from the studio I asked the driver, 'How's the fire doing?' 'You mean,' said the Hollywoodian, 'the holocaust.'. The style, you see, must come as easily and naturally as that. I found Dorothy standing in front of her house, gazing at the smoky sky; in one hand she held a drink, in the other a comb which absently she was passing through her short straight hair. As I came toward her she gave me a secret smile. 'I am combing,' she whispered, 'Los Angeles out of my hair.' But of course that was not possible. The ashes of Hollywood are still very much in our hair.

Gore Vidal, *Matters of Fact and Fiction,* 1977

The world's most celebrated suburb of nowhere.

Time Magazine, 4 July 1977

It would be Hans Anderson if it wasn't so terribly Grimm.

John Armstrong, quoted in Anthony Powell, *Messengers of Day,* 1978

Leaving Los Angeles is like giving up heroin.

David Puttnam, *Radio Times,* 21–27 October 1978

The city's layout is a tangle of circumferences which have lost contact with their centres.

Clive James, 'Postcard from L.A.', *Observer,* 10 June 1979

. . . one of those weeks when Los Angeles seemed most perilously and breathtakingly itself, a cartoon of natural disaster. . . .

Joan Didion, *The White Album,* 1979

It's a town like any other town filled with walking people, filled with the arts, filled with glamour and degradation. It has everything. It is in most ways America in microcosm, but more it is the cutting edge of America. What happens here happens five years before anywhere else in America. We send the style to the rest of the country.

Harlan Ellison, BBC radio programme, *On the Town, Los Angeles,* 20 February 1980

and San Francisco

They say that in San Francisco there is less than meets the eye: in Los Angeles there is far more.

Jan Morris, *Destinations,* 1980

'Say,' they told me, 'there was a cop here from England only the other day – he was *dazzled* by the level of crime we have here.'

Ibid., quoting source at Police Headquarters, Los Angeles

Los Angeles Airport
Bump, rumble, rumble, lights! lights! Los Angeles. Time? Enter Belshazzar's hall. Body finds hall moving slowly, but they can't fool body. Body knows the movement is the world turning to catch up. More halls, enough for whole dynasties of Belshazzars. Soul will enjoy this when it catches up. More halls, *Mene, mene*. . . . Tunnels, fountains, lights, music, palms, lights, more halls – they would have to put *Mene, mene* out by roneograph, or use the public-address system. *A message for Mr Belshazzar!* Am delirious I think. Find broom supporting man in centre of hundredth hall. Body asks broom politely 'Which way is out, Bud?' Broom answers politely, 'Don't arst me Bud, we just built it.' More halls.

William Golding *The Hot Gates and Other Occasional Pieces*, 1965

Beverly Hills
Beverly Hills . . . is a caricature of a stockbroker's suburb, enlivened by illusions of greater grandeur.

James Morris, *Coast to Coast*, 1956

Watts
There is really no mystery about why Watts revolted. It was the protest by a group of people maddened by their own wretchedness in the midst of unparalleled prosperity.

The Times, 20 June 1966

Louisville (Kentucky)

Louisville has interminable, ragged, nasty suburbs, and lacks edifices – in other respects it is a good specimen of a brisk and well-furnished city. . . . It owes its position to the will of Nature, who stops here, with rapids, the regular use of the river.

Frederick Law Olmsted, *A Journey through Texas*, 1856

It is another great town, like all the others, built with high stores, and great houses, and stone-faced blocks. I have no doubt that all the building speculations have been failures, and that the men engaged in them were all ruined. But there as the result of their labour, stands a fair great city on the southern banks of the Ohio.

Anthony Trollope, *North America*, 1862

Lowell (Masschusetts)

Lowell . . . already looks like a younger Manchester.

George Combe, *Notes . . . during a Phrenological Visit, in 1838–40*, 1841

Those indications of its youth which first attract the eye, give it a quaintness and oddity of character. . . . It was a very dirty winter's day, and nothing in the whole town looked old to me, except the mud, which in some parts was almost knee-deep, and might have been deposited there on the subsiding of the waters after the Deluge. In one place there was a new wooden church, which, having no steeple, and being yet unpainted, looked like an enormous packing case without any direction upon it. In another there was a large hotel, whose walls and colonnades were so crisp, and thin, and slight, that it had exactly the appearance of being built with cards. . . . when I saw a baby of some week or ten days old in a woman's arms at the street corner, I found myself unconsciously wondering where it came from: never supposing for an instant that it could have been born in such a young town as that.

Charles Dickens, *American Notes*, 1842

Lowell is the realization of a commercial Utopia.

Anthony Trollope, *North America*, 1862

Low Freight

An Irish railroad gang, coming on a lake in Arkansas that the French had named L'Eau Froid, struggled awhile, and left it on the map as Low Freight.

Alistair Cooke, *Alistair Cooke's America*, 1973.

Lubbock (Texas)

Nobody minds
Dust storms in Lubbock;
They don't create havoc,
Just hubbubbock.
But I'm so full
Of Holy Texas
I'll be hallowed ground
When they annex us.

Ogden Nash, 'The Dust Storm, or I've got Texas in my Lungs', in *The Private Dining Room*, 1952

Macon (Georgia)

I am in a great big rambling shambling village which they call a city here.

W.M. Thackeray, Letter to Anne and Harriet Thackeray, 22–24 February 1856

Mackinaw (Michigan)

The island is so healthy that, according to the commandant, people who want to die must go somewhere else. . . . I asked about the climate; the answer was, 'We have nine months winter, and three months cold weather.'

Harriet Martineau, *Society in America*, 1837

I enquired . . . if people lived to a good old age in the islands; his reply was quite American – 'I guess they do; if people want to die here – they're obliged to go elsewhere.'

Captain Frederick Marryat, *A Diary in America,* 1839

Maine

Maine is as dead, intellectually, as Abyssinia. Nothing is ever heard from it.

H.L. Mencken, *Americana,* 1925

'Don't ever ask directions of a Maine native,' I was told.

'Why ever not?'

'Somehow we think it is funny to misdirect people and we don't smile when we do it, but we laugh inwardly. It is our nature.'

John Steinbeck, *Travels with Charley,* 1962

Malibu

Malibu tends to astonish and disappoint those who have never before seen it, and yet its very name remains, in the imagination of people all over the world, a kind of shorthand for the easy life. I had not before 1971 and will probably not again live in a place with a Chevrolet named after it.

Joan Didion, *The White Album,* 1979

Manitou (Colorado)

At Manitou are iron and soda springs. It is a strictly temperance place. There is a sign on a refreshment house there which is almost as pathetic as it is honest. It reads thus: 'Barley water and bad cigars'.

Lilian Leland, *Travelling Alone, A Woman's Journey Round the World,* 1890

Marias River (Montana)

I deturmined to give it a name and in honour of Miss Maria Wood called it Maria's River. It is true that the hue of the waters of this turbulent and troubled stream but illy comport with the pure celestial virtues and amiable qualifications of that lovely fair one; but on the other hand it is a noble river . . . and . . . will become one of the most interesting branches of the Missouri.

Meriwether Lewis, *c.* 8 June 1805, quoted in note to Elliott Coues (ed.), *History of the Expedition under the Command of Lewis and Clark,* 1965

Marin County (California)

It is an area of high wooded hills, of sandy beaches and attractive houses, cliff-hanging from steep hillsides, or lining the waterfront. There is a saying 'Live in Marin County and park your car in the attic.'

Ethel Mannin, *An American Journey,* 1967

Martha's Vineyard

I live at the top of old West Chop
In a house with a cranky stove,
And when I swim I risk life and limb
On the pebbles that line the cove –
Where the waves wish-wash, and the foghorn blows,
And the blow-fish nibble at your toes-oes-oes,
The blow-fish nibble at your toes. . . .

Ogden Nash, 'Martha's Vineyard', in *Versus,* 1949

Maryland

At present, my chief study is West-Indian history. You would not think me very ill-natured if you knew all I feel at the cruelty and villainy of European settlers – But this very morning I found that part of the purchase of Maryland from the savage proprietors (for *we* do not massacre, *we* are such good Christians as only to cheat) was a quantity of vermilion and a parcel of Jews-harps!

Horace Walpole, Letter to Richard Bentley, 4 August 1755

The manners of Maryland are somewhat peculiar. They have but few Merchants. They are chiefly Planters and Farmers. The Planters are those who raise Tobacco and the Farmers such as raise Wheat &c. The Lands are cultivated, and all sorts of Trades are exercised by Negroes, or by transported Convicts, which has occasioned the Planters and Farmers to assume the Title of Gentlemen and they hold their Negroes and Convicts, that is all labouring People and Tradesmen, in such Contempt, that they think themselves a distinct order of Beings. Hence they will never suffer their Sons to labour or learn any Trade, but they bring them up in Idleness or what is worse in Horse Racing, Cock Fighting, and Card Playing.

John Adams, *Diary*, 22 February 1777

The despot's heel is on thy shore, Maryland!

James Ryder Randall, *Maryland, My Maryland,* April 1861

Maryland looks like a squat leftward-pointing pistol with a jaggedly divided butt.

John Gunther, *Inside U.S.A.,* 1947

They were represented as a gigantic, gun-powder race of men, exceedingly expert at boxing, biting, gouging, and other branches of the rough-and-tumble mode of warfare, which they had learned from their prototypes and cousins german, the Virginians, to whom they have ever borne considerable resemblance. Like them, too, they were great roisters, much given to revel on hoe-cake and bacon, mint-julep and apple-toddy; whence their newly-formed colony had already acquired the name of Merryland; which, with a slight modification, it retains to the present day.

Washington Irving, *The History of New York from the Beginning of the World. . . . by Diedrich Knickerbocker,* 1809

*I have a fancy that those Marylanders are just about near enough to the sun to ripen well.

Oliver Wendell Holmes, *The Professor at the Breakfast-Table,* 1859

Massachusetts

The State of Massachusetts is made up of the enterprise of its inhabitants.

Charles Francis Adams, *Diary,* 21 September 1835

Massachusetts has a good climate, but it needs a little anthracite coal.

Ralph Waldo Emerson, *Journals,* 1857–8

There has always been something a little difficult between myself and Massachusetts, some incompatibility.

H.G. Wells, *The Way the World is Going,* 1928

Memphis (Tennessee)

The little town is situated at the most beautiful point of the Mississippi; the river here is so wide as to give it the appearance of a noble lake; an island covered with lofty trees divides it, and relieves by its broad mass of shadow the uniformity of its waters. The town stretches in a rambling, irregular manner along the cliff from the Wolf river, one of the innumerable tributaries of the Mississippi, to about a mile below it. Half a mile more of the cliff beyond the town is cleared of trees, and produces good pasture for horses, cows and pigs; sheep they had none. At either end of this space the forest again rears its dark wall and seems to say to man, 'so far shalt thou come, and no farther!' Courage and industry, however, have braved the warning. Behind this long street the town straggles back into the forest, and the rude path that leads to the more distant log dwellings becomes wilder at every step. The ground is broken by frequent water-courses, and the bridges that lead across them are formed by trunks of trees thrown over the stream, which support others of smaller growth that are laid across them. These bridges are not very pleasant to pass, for they totter under the tread of a man, and tremble most frightfully beneath a horse or a waggon; they are, however, very picturesque. The great height of the trees, the quantity of pendant vine branches that hang amongst them; and the variety of gay plumaged birds, particularly the small green parrot, made us feel we were in a new world.

Mrs Frances Trollope, *Domestic Manners of the Americans,* 1832

we stopped at Memphis, the port of Tennessee
And wondered why they gave it such a name of old renown
A dreary, dingy, muddy, melancholy town.

Charles Mackay, 'Down the Mississip', in *Life and Liberty in America, 1857–8, 1859*

It is a beautiful city, nobly situated on a commanding bluff overlooking the river. The streets are straight and spacious, though not paved in a way to incite distempered admiration. No, the admiration must be reserved for the town's sewerage system, which is called perfect; a recent reform, however. . . .

Mark Twain, *Life on the Mississippi,* 1883

Memphis . . . was experienced, above all other cities on the river, in the gracious office of the Good Samaritan.

Ibid.

Miami

and Brighton UK
America doubtless suffers from too much Miami on the brain. Britain, however, seems to suffer even more gravely from too much Brighton on the soul.

Irving Kristol, 'The View from Miami', *Encounter,* November 1963

Miami Airport
If it is true that all buildings stand in physical and mathematical relation to the beings that made them, then Miami Airport has those anatomical defects to be expected of an electronic brain. Many things are altogether omitted as though certain faculties are no longer working.

Sacheverell Sitwell, *Golden Wall and Mirador,* 1961

Miami Beach

That Heliogabaluslike organism, Miami Beach. . . .

John Gunther, *Inside U.S.A.,* 1947

Over hundreds, then thousands of acres, white sidewalks, streets and white buildings covered the earth where the jungle had been. Is it so dissimilar from covering your poor pubic hair with adhesive tape for fifty years? The vegetal memories of that excised jungle haunted Miami Beach in a steam-pot of miasmas.

Ghosts of expunged flora . . . rose right up through the baked asphalt and into the heated air which entered the lungs like a hand slipping into a rubber glove. . . . the sensation of breathing, then living, was not unlike being obliged to make love to a 300-pound woman who has decided to get on top. . . .

For ten miles, from the Diplomat to the Di Lido, above Hallandale Beach Boulevard down to Lincoln Mall, all the white refrigerators stood, piles of white refrigerator six and eight and twelve stories high, twenty stories high, shaped like sugar cubes and ice-cube trays on edge, like mosques and palaces, shaped like matched white luggage and portable radios, stereos, plastic compacts and plastic rings, Moorish castles shaped like waffle irons, shaped like the baffle plates on white plastic electric heaters, and cylinders like Waring blenders, buildings looking like giant op art and pop art paintings, and sweet wedding cakes, cottons of kitsch and piles of dirty cotton stucco, yes, for ten miles.

Norman Mailer, *Miami and the Siege of Chicago*, 1968

Miami Beach is a rich sandbar with a drawbridge, and in no sense part of the main.

Gore Vidal, *Reflections upon a Sinking Ship*, 1969

Michigan

Milton must have travelled in Michigan before he wrote the garden parts of 'Paradise Lost.'

Harriet Martineau, *Society in America*, 1837

Citizens of Atlantic cities say they miss their grand rocks and hills, and the sea, 'that symbol of the infinite.' But Lake Michigan is a respectable bit of water; and the prairie has a beauty and even a grandeur of its own. If a cornfield of several thousand acres is not a 'symbol of the infinite,' I should like to know what is.

Grace Greenwood (Sara Clarke Lippincott), *New Life in New Lands*, 1873

'The Mid West'

There, in the Mississippi Valley, beyond a question, and in a very brief time, will be cities and towns to rival any in the world in population, in commercial enterprise, and in the productions of art, in the refinements of cultivated life and manners, and I fear, in *luxury*.

Calvin Colton, *Manual for Emigrants to America*, 1832

In the Western settlements we may behold democracy arrived at its utmost limits. In these states, founded offhand and as it were by chance, the inhabitants are but of yesterday. Scarcely known to one another, the nearest neighbours are ignorant of each other's history. In this part of the American continent, therefore, the population has escaped the influence not only of great names and great wealth, but even of the natural aristocracy of knowledge and virtue. None is there able to wield that respectable power which men willingly grant to the remembrance of a life spent in doing good before their eyes. The new states of the West are already inhabited, but society has no existence among them.

Alexis de Tocqueville, *Democracy in America*, 1835

In good time the Western bottom lands will spontaneously grow poets. The American mind will be brought to maturity along the chain of the great lakes, the banks of the Mississippi, the Missouri, and their tributaries, in the far Northwest. There on the rolling plains, will be formed a republic of letters, which, not governed like that on our seaboard, by the great literary powers of Europe, shall be free indeed. For there character is growing up with a breadth equal to the sweep of the great valleys; dwarfed by no factitious ceremonies or usages, no precedents or written statutes, no old superstition or tyranny. The winds sweep unhindered from the lakes to the gulf, from the Alleghanies to the Rocky Mountains; and so do the thoughts of the Lord of the Prairies. He is beholden to no man being bound neither head nor foot. He is an independent world himself, and speaks his own mind. Some day he will make his own books as well as his own laws. He will not send to Europe for either pictures or opinions. He will remain on his prairie, and all the arts of the world will come and make obeisance to him, like the sheaves in his fields. He will be the American man, and beside him there will be none else.

J. Milton Mackie, *From Cape Cod to Dixie*, 1854

The Corn Belt is a gift of the gods – the rain god, the sun god, the ice god, and the gods of geology.

J. Russell Smith, *North America*, 1925

I used to think, as many others think, that the Middle West is supremely ignorant. I was wrong. The Middle West is supremely wise. It goes on its own way, hating no man, and fearing no man, and saying, as Shakespeare's Corin said 'The greatest of my pride is to see my ewes graze and my lambs suck.'

It knows very little about Europe, even though so many thousands of the farmers are first generation immigrants from Scandinavia. . . .

The Mississippi Valley takes them and makes them into Americans, because the Mississippi Valley is America. The cities of the East, and of the long Pacific slope are important, but they are not the heart of the country. They talk more, and mean less. They travel the world and broaden their minds, but when the ill winds begin to blow it is not the East and West that stand unshakeable. It is that Valley in the middle that cannot be conquered.

A.G. Macdonell, *A Visit to America*, 1935

I do not like the provinces, particularly in the USA where they are provincial by so many thousand miles. . . . The Middle West seems to me an Eliot landscape where the spiritual air is 'thoroughly small and dry.' If I stay here any longer, I shall either take to . . . mysticism . . . or buy a library of pornographic books.

W.H. Auden, Letter to Ursula Niebuhr, 1941, quoted in Charles Osborne, *W.H. Auden*, 1980

Nobody can possibly understand the Middle West who has not, for fun or profit, once looked through the catalogue of a great mail order company.

John Gunther, *Inside U.S.A.*, 1947

The Midwest is exactly what one would expect from a marriage between New England puritanism and *rich* soil.

Ibid.

Milk River (Montana)

The water has a peculiar whiteness, such as might be produced by a tablespoonful of milk in a dish of tea, and this circumstance induced us to call it Milk River.

History of the Expedition under the Command of Lewis and Clark, 8 May 1805

Milwaukee

Milwaukee and its environs provided a grey landscape, drawn with hard lines and great attention to detail. It struck me that the American scene was not one to be painted in Impressionist terms, but with the painstaking precision of the primitives.

Cecil Beaton, *It Gives Me Great Pleasure*, 1955

In Milwaukee, Phew! They used to walk out and walk *towards* me. Milwaukee I had such grief, man – Milwaukee, that's like Grey Line *en mass*. Yeah. Really got rank, the people there, with me, you know. Oh, it was really grim in Milwaukee. The club was right next to the river, and even *that* started to look good. . . .

Now I get there, and the first thing that scares me to death, they've got a six-thirty dinner show. Six-thirty at night, people go to a nightclub?

Lenny Bruce, 'Performing and the Art of Comedy', in *The Essential Lenny Bruce*, 1973

Minneapolis

and St Anthony, the bridge between them

The suspension bridge which connects Minneapolis with St Anthony . . . is a fit type of the enterprise of the people. . . . I was struck with the answer given by the young man who took the toll, in reply to my inquiry as I returned, if my coming back wasn't included in the toll paid going over? 'No,' he said, in a very good-natured way, 'we don't know anything about coming back: it's all go-ahead in this country.'

Christopher C. Andrews, *Minnesota and Dakota*, 1856

When I was born, St Paul had a population of three persons, Minneapolis had just a third as many. The then population of Minneapolis died two years ago; and when he died he had seen himself undergo an increase, in forty years, of fifty-nine thousand nine hundred and ninety-nine persons. He had a frog's fertility.

Mark Twain, *Life on the Mississippi*, 1883

and St Paul

Minneapolis and St Paul . . . are nicknamed the Twin Cities. They are divided by the Mississippi River, and united by the belief that the inhabitants of the other side of the river are inferior.

Trevor Fishlock, *Americans and Nothing Else*, 1980

Minnehaha Park

The Falls of Minnehaha
Flash and gleam amoung the oaktrees
Laugh and leap into the valley . . .
From the waterfall he named her
Minnehaha Laughing Water.

Henry Wadsworth Longfellow, *The Song of Hiawatha*, 1855

Minnehaha, laughing water. Such I believe is the interpretation. The name in this case is more imposing than the fall. It is a pretty little cascade, and might do for a picnic in fine weather, but it is not a waterfall of which a man can make much when found so far away from home.

Anthony Trollope, *North America*, 1862

Minnesota

I have lived in Minnesota . . . for thirteen years, a western Scandanavia where the birds sing in Swedish, the wind sighs its lullabyes in Norwegian, and the snow and rain beat against the windows to the tune of a Danish dirge.

Journal of the American Medical Association (?), *c.* 1925, quoted in H.L. Mencken, *Americana*, 1925

Mississippi

Mississippi will drink wet and vote dry – so long as any citizen can stagger to the polls.

Will Rogers, attrib.

Man is one of the toughest of animated creatures. Only the anthrax bacillus can stand so unfavourable an environment for so long a time. All other mammals would succumb quickly to what man endures almost without damage. Consider, for example, the life of a soldier in the front line – or the life of anyone in Mississippi.

H.L. Mencken, 'Minority Report', *The Notebooks of H.L. Mencken*, 1956

Even Mississippi, on some remote tomorrow, may reach the estate of Poland between the two World Wars.

Ibid.

Mississippi River

What has four eyes and cannot see? – The Mississippi River.

American Negro riddle, quoted Archer Taylor, *English Riddles from Oral Tradition*, 1951

confluence of the Mississippi and Missouri Rivers

The most striking circumstance observable at this confluence, is the difference in colour and purity of the two rivers. The Missouri is nearly as thick as peas soup, of a dirty, muddy, whitish colour, while the Mississippi, above the confluence, is of a clear light blue, not unlike that of the deep sea, or the Rhone at Geneva. At some places it looked like the Tweed, when it has got a slight tinge of the moors; but when a glass of it was taken up, it always appeared as clear as any spring water. If a glass of the Missouri were, however, dipped up in like manner, it was perfectly turbid, worse than the rain puddles on a highway road, and in a few moments a stratum of mud was formed in the bottom of the tumbler. The surface of the Mississippi, above the confluence was clear of drift wood, while that of its companion was all covered over with half-burnt logs, trees with their branches torn off, and great rafts, or floating islands of timber, drifted from the interior, sweeping and swirling along at a furious rate.

The Missouri enters the Mississippi from the westward, nearly at right angles to it; and such is the impetuosity of its current, that it fairly drives the Mississippi over to the left or eastern bank. There were literally not above ten or twelve yards of clear water on that side of the river, while the rest was muddy. The line of actual contact was particularly interesting. It seemed as if the dirty Missouri had insinuated itself under the clear Mississippi; for we saw it boiling up at a hundred different places. First a small, curdling white spot, not bigger than a man's hand, made its appearance near the surface. This rapidly swelled and boiled about, till in a few seconds it suddenly became as large as a steam-boat, spreading itself on all sides in gigantic eddies, or whirlpools, in a manner that I hardly know how to describe, but which was amazingly striking. At other places *the two* currents ran along side by side, without the least intermixture like oil and water. But this separation never continued long and the contaminating Missouri soon conquered the beautiful Mississippi.

Captain Basil Hall, *Travels in North America*, 1829

between the mouths of the Ohio and Missouri

The velocity of the river at some places in this interval was so great, that we had the utmost difficulty in making headway against it. There was one point in particular, called by the uncivil name of the 'Hanging-dog,' which cost us so much trouble to pass that our worthy captain almost lost his temper, and said, in answer to some question I put very innocently, respecting the rate of going, – 'Why sir, this is the most scandalous bit of river that ever any man had to come up!'

Ibid.

I never beheld a scene so utterly desolate as this entrance of the Mississippi. Had Dante seen it, he might have drawn images of another Bolgia from its horrors. One only object rears itself above the eddying waters; this is the mast of a vessel long since wrecked in attempting to cross the bar, and it still stands, a dismal witness of the destruction that has been, and a boding prophet of that which is to come. . . . For several miles above its mouth the Mississippi presents no objects more interesting than mud banks, monstrous bulrushes, and now and then a huge crocodile luxuriating in the slime. . . . At no one point was there an inch of what painters call a second distance.

Mrs Frances Trollope, *Domestic Manners of the Americans*, 1832

The valley of the Mississippi is, on the whole, the most magnificent dwelling-place prepared by God for man's abode; and yet it may be said that at present it is but a mighty desert.

Alexis de Tocqueville, *Democracy in America*, 1835

If there be excess of mental luxury in this life, it is surely in a voyage up the Mississippi, in the bright and leafy month of May.

Harriet Martineau, *Retrospect of Western Travel*, 1838

In England, rivers are all males –
For instance, Father Thames.
Whoever in Columbia sails,
Finds them Ma'amselles or Dames;

For there the softer sex presides,
Aquatic, I assure ye;
And Mrs Sippi rolls her tides
Responsive to Miss Souri.

James Smith (?), before 1839

Never perhaps, in the records of nations was there an instance of such unvarying and unmitigated crime as is to be collected from the history of the turbulent and blood-stained Mississippi. The stream itself appears as if appropriate for the deeds which have been committed. . . . There are no pleasing associations connected with this great common sewer of western America.

Captain Frederick Marryat, *A Diary in America*, 1839

But what words shall describe the Mississippi, great father of rivers, who (praise be to Heaven) has no young children like him! An enormous ditch, sometimes two or three miles wide, running liquid mud, six miles an hour: its strong and frothy current choked and obstructed everywhere by huge logs and whole forest trees: now twining themselves together in great rafts, from the interstices of which a sedgy lazy foam works up, to float upon the water's top; now rolling past like monstrous bodies, their tangled roots showing like matted hair; now glancing singly like giant leeches; and now writhing round and round in the vortex of some small whirlpool, like wounded snakes. The banks low, the trees dwarfish, the marshes swarming with frogs, the wretched cabins few and far apart, their inmates hollow-cheeked and pale, the weather very hot, mosquitoes penetrating into every crack and crevice of the boat, mud and slime on everything: nothing pleasant in its aspect, but the harmless lightning which flickers every night upon the dark horizon.

Charles Dickens, *American Notes*, 1842

The Mississippi Valley, in fact, with all its 6,000 miles of uninterrupted steamboat navigation, is a great wilderness of unexplored fertility, into which a few men have crept like ants into a pantry. We give it a vast importance in our thoughts, but it is an entirely prospective one.

Frederick Law Olmsted, *A Journey through Texas*, 1857

Oh the hapless river! in its early run
Clear as molten crystal, sparkling in the sun;
Ere the fierce Missouri rolls its troublous tide
To pollute the beauty of his injured bride;
Like a bad companion poisoning a life,
With a vile example and incessant strife, –
So the Mississippi, lucent to the brim,
Wedded to Missouri, takes her hue from him;
And is pure no longer, but with sullen haste
Journeys to the ocean, a gladness gone to waste. . . .

Charles Mackay, 'Down the Mississip', *Life and Liberty in America, 1857–8*, 1859

south of Memphis

Weary were the forests, dark on either side,
Weary were the marshes stretching far and wide:
Weary were the wood-piles strewn on either bank;
Weary were the cane-groves, growing wild and dank –
Weary were the tree-stumps, charred and black with fire;
Weary was the wilderness, without a house or spire;
Weary were the log-huts, built upon the sand;
Weary were the waters, weary was the land;
Weary was the cabin with its gilded wall,
Weary was the deck we trod, – weary – weary all –
Nothing seemed so pleasant to hope for or to keep,
Nothing in the wide world so beautiful as sleep
As we journeyed Southward in our lazy ship
Dawdling idling loafing down the Mississipp.

Ibid.

. . . fit for everything except to drink and wash in. . . .

Charles Mackay, *Life and Liberty in America, 1857–8* 1859

and Missouri

Some geographers have proposed to transfer to the Missouri, on account of its superior length, the honour of being the real head of the Mississippi; they neglect, however, to consider the direction and the course of the stream, an element which must enter largely in determining the channels of great rivers. It will, I hope, be long before the great ditch wins the day from the glorious Father of Waters.

Richard Burton, *The City of the Saints*, 1861

'The London *Times* is one of the greatest powers in the world – in fact I don't know anything which has much more power – except perhaps the Mississippi.'

Abraham Lincoln, quoted in William Howard Russell, *My Diary North and South*, 1862

The basin of the Mississippi is the Body of the Nation. . . . As a dwelling place for civilised man it is by far the first upon our globe.

Editor's Table, *Harpers Magazine*, February 1863

Still more appalling is the prospect revealed to us by some American patriots. Their statistical prophecies about the Mississippi valley have given me occasional nightmares. Conceive of a gigantic chess-board many hundreds of miles in length and breadth, with each square so like its neighbours that any two might be changed in the night without its inhabitants detecting the difference; suppose each square to be inhabited by several millions of human beings as like the denizens of an ant-hill; all of them highly educated persons brought up under school boards and public meetings and church organisations, with no political or social grievances; and, in short, as somebody calls them, intelligent and godfearing citizens. The imagination fairly recoils from the prospect in horror. We long to believe that some earthquake may throw up a few mountain-ranges and partition off the country, so as to give its wretched inhabitants a chance of developing a few distinctive peculiarities.

Leslie Stephen, *The Playground of Europe*, 1871

It is by far the most important stream on the globe. . . . Only the Mediterranean Sea has play'd some such part in history, and all through the past, as the Mississippi is destined to play in the future.

Walt Whitman, *Specimen Days* (1879), 1882

The Mississippi is a just and equitable river; it never tumbles one man's farm overboard without building a new farm just like it for that man's neighbour. This keeps down hard feelings.

Mark Twain, *Life on the Mississippi*, 1883

If you will throw a long, pliant apple-paring over your shoulder, it will pretty fairly shape itself into an average section of the Mississippi River; that is, the nine or ten hundred miles stretching from Cairo, Illinois, southward to New Orleans.

Ibid.

The loneliness of this solemn, stupendous flood is impressive – and depressing. League after league, and still league after league, it pours its chocolate tide along, between its solid forest walls, its almost untenanted shores, with seldom a sail or a moving object of any kind to disturb the surface and break the monotony of the blank, watery solitude; and so the day goes, the night comes, and again the day – and still the same, night after night, and day after day – majestic, unchanging sameness of serenity, repose, tranquillity, lethargy, vacancy – symbol of eternity, realisation of the heaven pictured by priest and prophet, and longed for by the good and thoughtless.

Ibid.

Nature herself seems to have designed the Mississippi Basin as she has designed the unbroken levels of Russia, to be the dwelling-place of one people.

James Bryce, *The American Commonwealth*, 1888

Ol' man river, dat ol' man river,
He must know sumpin, but don't say nothin',
He just keeps rollin', he keeps on rollin' along

Oscar Hammerstein, *Ol' Man River, Showboat*, 1927

It remains what it always was, – a kind of huge rope, no matter with what knots and frayings, tying the United States together. It is the Nile of the Western Hemisphere.

John Gunther, *Inside U.S.A.*, 1947

The Mississippi, . . . with its paddle boats, ferries and hoot owls, is the most haunted river in the world.

Cecil Beaton, *It Gives Me Great Pleasure*, 1955

Missouri

The catch-words of this state are 'Show me,' indicative of doubt and mistrust.

J. Kenneth Ferrier, *Crooks and Crime*, 1928

To the West, to the West, to the land of the free,
Where the mighty Missouri rolls down to the sea
Where a man is a man, even though he must toil
And the poorest may gather the fruits of the soil.

Anon. ballad, recalled in old age by Andrew Carnegie, quoted by Samuel Gompers, *Seventy Years of Life and Labor*, 1925

Missouri River

see also under Mississippi

The Missori is, perhaps, different in appearance and character from all other rivers in the world: there is a terror in its manner which is sensibly felt, the moment we enter its muddy waters from the Mississippi.

George Catlin, *Letters and Notes on . . . North Americans*, 1841

Big Muddy.

Anon.

between St Joseph and Atchison

Its muddiness is beyond all description; its color and consistency are those of thick milk porridge; you could not discern an egg in a glass of it. A fly floating in a tea-cup of this dubious fluid an eighth of an inch below the surface would be quite invisible. . . . I have not yet learned to like it.

Horace Greeley, *An Overland Journey from New York to San Francisco . . . in 1859*, 1860

At ten we reached Omaha and crossed the Missouri – such an extremely muddy river, it excites no desire to bathe in it.

The Marchioness of Dufferin and Ava, *My Canadian Journal* (3 August 1876), 1891

This outlaw hippopotamus, this mud-foaming behemoth of rivers. . . .

John Gunther, *Inside U.S.A.*, 1947

at Bismark, North Dakota

Someone must have told me about the Missouri River at Bismark, North Dakota, or I must have read about it. In either case, I hadn't paid attention. I came on it in amazement. Here is where the map should fold. Here is the boundary between east and west. On the Bismark side it is eastern landscape, eastern grass, with the look and smell of eastern America. Across the Missouri on the Mandan side, it is pure west, with brown grass and water scorings and small outcrops. The two sides of the river might well be a thousand miles apart.

John Steinbeck, *Travels with Charley*, 1962

A sense comes from it that it does not like or welcome humans.

Ibid.

Mobile

I have never once thought of work in connection with the word Mobile. *Not anybody working.* A city surrounded with shells, the empty shells of by-gone fiestas. Bunting everywhere, and the friable relics of yesterdays's carnival. Gaiety always in retreat, always vanishing, like clouds brushing a mirror. In the centre of this glissando, Mobile itself, very prim, very proper, Southern and not Southern, listless but upright, slatternly yet respectable, bright but not wicked. Mozart for the Mandolin. Not Segovia feathering Bach. Not grace and delicacy so much as anaemia. Fever coolth, Musk. Fragrant ashes.

Henry Miller, *The Air-conditioned Nightmare*, 1945

Mojave Desert

The Mojave is a big desert and a frightening one. It's as though nature tested a man for endurance and constancy to prove whether he was good enough to get to California.

John Steinbeck, *Travels with Charley*, 1962

Montana

Montana's real trouble . . . is that her graveyards aren't big enough.

Arthur Fisher, in Ernest Gruening (ed.), *These United States, A Symposium*, 1923

Montana place names have a healthy nostalgic tang. One range of hills is the Scratch Gravel Mountains and one mine is called Molly Muck-a-Chuck-New York; a town was once called Copperopolis. Among gulches there are Seven Up Pete, Buttermilk Jim (near the interesting town of Boulder), Ready Cash, and Never Sweat; among Creeks are Fool Hen, Keep Cool, Navy Time, and Try Again.

John Gunther, *Inside U.S.A.*, 1947

I am in love with Montana. . . . Montana seems to me to be what a small boy would think Texas is like from hearing Texans.

John Steinbeck, *Travels with Charley*, 1962

It's the kind of country where men are expected to walk tall. I just said I was English and slunk around as I usually do.

John Hurt, quoted in interview in *Evening Standard*, 14 December 1979

Monterey (California)

It is only dull in the sense that Nice and Pisa are dull cities.

Bayard Taylor, *Eldorado, or Adventures in the Path of Empire*, 1850 (of 1849)

Monterey is a place where there is no summer or winter, and pines and sand and distant hills and a bay all filled with real water from the Pacific. You will perceive that no expense has been spared. . . . The population of Monterey is about that of a dissenting chapel on a wet Sunday in a strong Church neighbourhood. They are mostly Mexican and Indian – mixed.

Robert Louis Stevenson, Letter to Sidney Colvin, September 1879

They fish for tourists now, not pilchards, and that species they are not likely to wipe out.

John Steinbeck, *Travels with Charley*, 1962

Muncie (Indiana)

In viewing this sober, hopeful, well-meaning city, caught in its institutional conflicts, caught between past and future, and not knowing which way to move, one recalls now and again Tawney's characterization of the ruling class in Europe after the French Revolution; ' . . . they walked reluctantly backwards into the future, lest a worse thing should befall them.'

Robert S. Lynd and Helen Merrell Lynd, *Middletown in Transition*, 1937

Middletown is *against* the reverse of the things it is for.

Ibid.

There is no area of Middletown's life, save religion, where symbol is more admittedly and patently divorced from reality than in government, and no area where the functioning of an institution is more enmeshed in undercover intrigue and personalities.

Ibid.

Middletown is a marrying city.

Ibid.

If Rip van Winkle went to sleep 50 years ago and returned to Muncie today, he would not have too many adjustment problems.

Theodore Caplow, quoted in *Time*, 16 October 1978

Nachitoches (and Alexandria)

I was told that there was more morality, and more immorality in Nachitoches than in almost any other place of its size in the United States; and that in Alexandria, a town some distance below it, on Red River, there was about as much immorality, without any morality at all.

Frederick Law Olmsted, *Journey in the Seaboard Slave States*, 1856

Nantucket

The Little Grey Lady.

Old sailors' name

A singular custom prevails here among the women, at which I was greatly surprised; and am really at loss to account for the original cause that has introduced in this primitive society so remarkable a fashion, or rather so extraordinary a want. They have adopted these many years the Asiatic custom of taking a dose of opium every morning; and so deeply rooted is it, that they would be at a loss how to live without this indulgence; they would rather be deprived of any necessary than forego their favourite luxury. This is much more prevailing among the women than the men . . . though the sheriff . . . has for many years submitted to this custom. He takes three grains of it every day after breakfast, without the effects of which, he often told me, he was not able to transact any business.

Hector St John de Crèvecoeur, *Letters from an American Farmer*, 1782

Idleness is the most heinous sin that can be committed in Nantucket.

Ibid.

Nantucket is a curious place. The poverty of the spot, its utter nakedness and the rich subsistence it affords through the active disposition of its citizens are worthy of philosophical consideration. Siasconset is the Nahant of this Community. Originally a fishing settlement, the huts were gradually deserted by their original tenants and taken by the comfortable citizens for the purpose of affording clear air and change of scene for the two summer months. They are all of a similar construction, of one story and protected from the external air by shingles over boards. They are rarely painted and probably cost five or six hundred dollars to build. The houses are placed within a very few feet of each other and the people when there make a sort of general society. There is a primitive simplicity about this whole thing which I have met with nowhere else. A simplicity which is amusing to imagine although perhaps not agreeable to practise. Everybody in the settlement must of course be aware of every body's daily doings. The gossip must all be of each other's domestic matters with the usual modicum of scandal.

Charles Francis Adams, *Diary*, 18 September 1835

I was pleased with the civility of the people, their freedom from pomp and the kindness which they manifested. One old captain Myrick especially drew me aside and expressed so much very plain but honest respect for our name that I felt as I always do upon such occasions that there is some compensation to a public man for his trials and mortifications.

Charles Francis Adams, *Diary*, 19 September, 1835

*Nantucket! Take out your map and look at it. See what a real corner of the world it occupies; how it stands there away off shore, more lonely than the Eddystone lighthouse. Look at it – a mere hillock and elbow of sand; all beach without a background. There is more sand there than you would use in twenty years as a substitute for blotting paper. Some gamesome wights will tell you that they have to plant weeds there, they don't grow naturally; that they import Canada thistles; that they have to send beyond seas for a spile to stop a leak in an oil cask; that pieces of wood in Nantucket are carried about like bits of the true cross in Rome; that people there plant toadstools before their houses, to get under the shade in summer time; that one blade of grass makes an oasis, three blades in a day's walk a prairie; that they wear quicksand shoes, something like Laplander snowshoes; that they are so shut up, belted about, every way inclosed, surrounded and made an utter island of by the ocean, that to their very chairs and tables, small clams will sometimes be found adhering, as to the backs of sea turtles. But these extravagances only show that Nantucket is no Illinois.

Herman Melville, *Moby Dick*, 1851

Nantucket is . . . almost part and parcel of the ocean; as much in league with the waters as Venice, its very buildings seasoned with tar and the salt winds.

James Morris, *Coast to Coast*, 1956

Nashville

The Dimple of the Universe.

Anon., quoted by John Gunther, *Inside U.S.A.*, 1947

The Protestant Vatican of the South.

Ibid.

The Athens of Dixie

Ibid.

The city like so many in America seemed empty and lifeless in its heart when the working day was done. . . . For a European it takes time to adjust to the back-to-front nature of many American towns. You have to travel away from the hub and out along the spokes to find restaurants and entertainment and attractive housing.

Trevor Fishlock, *Americans and Nothing Else*, 1980

Nebraska

We were at sea – there is no other adequate expression – on the plains of Nebraska. . . . It was a world almost without a feature; an empty sky, an empty earth; front and back, the line of the railway stretched from horizon to horizon, like a cue across a billiard board; on either hand, the green plain ran till it touched the skirts of heaven. Along the track, innumerable wild sunflowers, no bigger than a crown-piece, bloomed in a continuous flower-bed; grazing beasts were seen upon the prairie at all degrees of distance and diminution; and, now and again we might perceive a few dots beside the railroad which grew more and more distinct, as we drew nearer till they turned into wooden cabins, and then dwindled and dwindled in our wake until they melted into their surroundings, and we were once more alone upon the billiard-board. The train toiled over this infinity like a snail; and being the one thing moving it was wonderful what huge proportions it began to assume in our regard. It seemed miles in length, and either end of it within but a step of the horizon. Even my own body or my own head seemed a great thing in that emptiness. I note the feeling the more readily as it is the contrary of what I have read of in the experience of others. Day and night above the roar of the train, our ears were kept busy with the incessant chirp of grasshoppers – a noise like the winding up of countless clocks and watches, which began after a while to seem proper to that land.

Robert Louis Stevenson, *Across the Plains*, 1892 – of 1879

I met a Nebraskan in Hong Kong, and he asked me what I thought of his native State. I told him I thought it was a case of having too much of a good thing. . . . My impression of Nebraska is twin steel rails running dead straight for ever and ever across a dead level plain of dead maize.

Crosbie Garstin, *The Dragon and the Lotus*, 1928

Nevada

Nevada was discovered many years ago by the Mormons, and was called Carson county. It only became Nevada in 1861, by Act of Congress. There is a popular tradition that God Almighty created it; but when you come to see it . . . you will think differently. Do not let that discourage you though. The country looks something like a singed cat, owing to the scarcity of shrubbery, and also resembles that animal in the respect that it has more merits than its personal appearance would seem to indicate.

Mark Twain, *Washoe – Information Wanted, – San Francisco Golden Era*, 22 May 1864

Nevada has no intellectual life. The members of the divorce colony occupy themselves by playing golf, watching the calendar, and practising adultery.

H.L. Mencken, 'Notes for Foreign Students', *Americana*, 1925

Nevada calls itself, 'The Cyclone-Cellar of the Tax-Weary.'

Douglas Reed, *Far and Wide*, 1951

Newark (New Jersey)

'This is the great champagne manufactory of America,' said a New Yorker, sitting by me.

'Champagne manufactory?' I repeated, not exactly comprehending him.

'The best cider in the country is made here,' he added, 'and by far the greater portion of the best champagne, which we import, comes from Newark.'

Alexander Mackay, *The Western World*, 1849

New England

New England is a legitimate child of *Old* England, although in its minority it became undutiful, and broke the bonds of parental restraint. . . . It is England and Scotland again in miniature and in childhood – not so mature not so much crowded, and with less of the refinements and luxuries of overgrown estates.

Calvin Colton, *Manual for Emigrants to America*, 1832

I believe no one attempts to praise the climate of New England.

Harriet Martineau, *Retrospect of Western Travel*, 1838

There was the usual aspect of newness on every object of course. All the buildings looked as if they had been built and painted that morning, and could be taken down on Monday with very little trouble.

Charles Dickens, *American Notes*, 1842

Those New England States, I do believe, will be the noblest country in the world in a little while. They will be the salvation of that very great body with a very little soul, the rest of the United States; they are the pith and marrow, heart and core, head and spirit of that country.

Fanny Kemble (Mrs Butler), *A Year of Consolation*, 1847

I saw but one drunken man through all New England, and he was very respectable. He was, however, so uncommonly drunk that he might be allowed to count for two or three.

Anthony Trollope, *North America*, 1862

*The frosty rocks, where nutmaigs am made outn' maple, an' whar wimmen paints clock-faces an' pints shoe' paigs, an' the men invents rat-traps, mantraps, an' new fangled doctrins fur the aid ove the devil.

'Sut Lovingood', in G.W. Harris, *Yarns Spun by a Nat'ral born Durn'd Fool*, 1867

. . . a simple pastoral, germ-state of society . . . forever gone. Never again shall we see that union of perfect repose in regard to outward surroundings and outward life with that intense activity of the inward and intellectual world, that made New England. . . . the vigorous, germinating seed-bed for all that has since been developed of politics, laws, letters, and theology, through New England to America, and through America to the world.

Harriet Beecher Stowe, *Oldtown Folks*, 1869

How condescending to descend
And be of buttercups the friend
In a New England Town.

Emily Dickinson, *c.* 1873

There is a sumptuous variety about the New England weather, that compels the admiration – and regret. The weather is always doing something there; always attending strictly to business; always getting up new designs and trying them on the people to see how they will go. But it gets through more business in spring than in any other season. In the spring I have counted one hundred and thirty-six different kinds of weather inside of four-and-twenty hours.

Mark Twain, 'The Weather', Speech at dinner of New England Society, New York, 22 December 1876

I . . . am seeing, feeling, how agreeable it is, in the maturity of age, to revisit the long neglected and long unseen land of one's birth – especially when that land affects one as such a living and breathing and feeling and moving great monster as this one is. It is all very interesting and quite unexpectedly and almost uncannily delightful and sympathetic – partly or largely, from my intense impression (all this glorious golden autumn, with weather like tinkling crystal and colours like molten jewels) of the sweetness of the country itself, this New England rural vastness, which is all that I've seen.

Henry James, Letter to Edmund Gosse, 27 October 1904

Resistance to something was the law of New England nature; . . . the New Englander . . . in his long struggle with a stingy or hostile universe had learned also to love the pleasure of hating; his joys were few. . . . The chief charm of New England was harshness of contrasts and extremes of sensibility – a cold that froze the blood and a heat that boiled it – so that the pleasure of hating – one's self if no rarer victim offered – was not its rarest amusement; but the charm was a true and natural child of the soil, not a cultivated weed of the ancients.

Henry Adams, *The Education of Henry Adams*, 1906

The very smell and sentiment of the American summer's end . . . mingle for me with the assault of forest and lake and of those delicious orchardy, yet rocky vaguenesses and 'nowheres,' which are the note of what is sweetest and most attaching in dear old American, or particularly New England scenery. It comes back to me as with such a magnificent beckoning looseness – in relieving contrast to the consummate tightness (a part too, oddly, of the very wealth of effect) *du pays d'ici*.

Henry James, Letter to William James, Rye, 17 August 1909

The New England shopkeepers and theologians never really developed a civilization; all they ever developed was a government.

H.L. Mencken, 'The Sahara of the Bozart', in *Prejudices*, Second Series, 1921

The swaggering underemphasis of New England

Heywood Broun, *Collected Edition*, 1941

New England is a finished place. Its destiny is that of Florence or Venice, not Milan, while the American empire careens onward towards its unpredicted end. . . . It is the first American section to be finished, to achieve stability in its conditions of life. It is the first old civilization, the first permanent civilization in America.

Bernard DeVoto, *New England: There She Stands – Forays and Rebuttals*, 1936

The most serious charge which can be brought against New England is not Puritanism but February.

Joseph Wood Krutch, 'February', *The Twelve Seasons* 1949

A certain New Englander was once working in his garden when a parson walked by and congratulated him on what God and he had wrought together as evidenced in such a commendable yield. 'Yep,' the man said, 'and you should have seen it when God had it all to himself.'

Erik H. Erikson, *Identity, Youth and Crisis*, 1968

New Englanders

I like them extremely well, but I do not wish to have any business transactions with them, if I could avoid it, lest to use their own phrase, 'they should be too smart for me.'

It is by no means rare to meet elsewhere, in this working-day world of ours, people who push acuteness to the verge of honesty, and sometimes, perhaps, a little bit beyond; but, I believe, the Yankee is the only one who will be found to boast of doing so. It is by no means easy to give a clear and just idea of a Yankee; if you hear his character from a Virginian, you will believe him a devil; if you listen to it from himself, you might fancy him a god – though a tricky one; Mercury turned righteous and notable. . . . In acuteness, cautiousness, industry, and perseverance, he resembles the Scotch; in habits of frugal neatness, he resembles the Dutch; in love of lucre he doth greatly resemble the sons of Abraham, but in frank admission and superlative admiration of his own peculiarities, he is like nothing on earth but himself.

Mrs Frances Trollope, *Domestic Manners of the Americans*, 1832

The great vice of this New England people is their adoration of Mammon. And rooted as it is in the character, the tree has now attained immense luxuriance and bids fair to overshadow us all.

Charles Francis Adams, *Diary*, 6 October 1833

We have always been taught to look upon the people of New England as a selfish cunning set of fellows, that was fed on fox ears and thistle tops; that cut their wisdom teeth as soon as they were born; that made money by their wits, and held on to it by nature; that called cheatery mother-wit; that hung onto political power because they had numbers; that raised up manufactures to keep down the South and West; and in fact, had so much of the devil in all their machinery, that they could neither lead nor drive, unless the load was going into their own cribs. But I assure you gentlemen, I begin to think different of you, and I think I see a good many good reasons for so doing.

I don't mean that because I eat your bread and drink your liquor that I feel so. No: that don't make me see clearer than I did. It is your habits, and manners, and customs; your industry; your proud independent spirits; your hanging onto the eternal principles of right and wrong; your liberality in prosperity and your patience when you are ground down by legislation, which, instead of crushing you, whets your invention to strike a path without a blaze on a tree to guide you; and above all your never-dying deathless grip to our great Constitution. These are the things that make me think that you are a mighty good people. (Here I had to stop a while).

Davy Crockett, *Tour to the North and Down East . . . in 1834*, 1835

*The Yankees see further ahead than most folks; they can een a most see round tother side of a thing; indeed, some on them have hurt their eyes by it, and sometimes I think that's the reason such a sight of them wear spectacles.

T.C. Haliburton, *The Clockmaker, or the Sayings and Doings of Samuel Slick*, first series, 1836

The oration was by an ex-senator of the United States. It consisted wholly of an elaboration of the transcendant virtues of the people of New England. . . . He told his hearers of the superiority of their physical, intellectual, and moral constitution to that of their brethren of the middle and southern States, to that of Europeans, and all other dwellers in the earth; a superiority which forbade their ever being understood and appreciated by any but themselves. He spoke especially of the intensity of the New England character, as being a hidden mystery from all but natives.

Harriet Martineau, *Society in America*, 1837

'Why, our people,' said he, 'can turn their hand a'most to any thing, from whippin' the universe to stuffin' a mosquito.'

Alexander Mackay, *The Western World*, 1849

'Here,' said Mr D—— in explanation, 'they call all Yankees who come from the North. But if you ask a New Yorker who are the Yankees, he will refer you to New England. In many parts of New England, again, you will be referred to Boston, as their *locus in quo*, but the Bostonians decline the honour of harbouring them, and refer you to the rural districts of New Hampshire. And without entering into nice distinctions as to what constitutes a Yankee, there is no doubt that it is in the last-mentioned localities that the most genuine specimens are to be found.'

Ibid.

It is generally considered that the inhabitants of New England, the Yankees properly so called, have the American characteristics of physiognomy in the fullest degree. The lantern jaws, the thin and lithe body, the dry face on which there has been no tint of the rose since the baby's long-clothes were first abandoned, the harsh, thick hair, the thin lips, the intelligent eyes, the sharp voice with the nasal twang – not altogether harsh, though sharp and nasal, – all these traits were supposed to belong especially to the Yankee.

Anthony Trollope, *North America*, 1862

You can always tell the Irish,
  You can always tell the Dutch
You can always tell a Yankee;
  But you cannot tell him much.

Eric Knight, *All Yankees are Liars*, before 1943

Cape Newenham

Captain Cook with great politeness told Mr Williamson that the Cape which he was on shou'd be called after the name of any friend of his. It was therefore nam'd in honour of Sir Edwd Newenham of Ireland.

James King, *Journal*, 17 July 1778

New Hampshire

Up in the mountains of New Hampshire God Almighty has hung out a sign to show that there he makes men.

Daniel Webster, attrib.

If two New Hampshiremen aren't a match for the devil, we might as well give the country back to the Indians.

Stephen Vincent Benét, *The Devil and Daniel Webster – 13 O'clock*, 1937

Emerson said, 'The God who made New Hampshire
Taunted the lofty land with little men.'
Another Massachusetts Poet said
'I go no more to summer in New Hampshire.
I've given up my summer place in Dublin.'
But when I asked to know what ailed New Hampshire
She said she couldn't stand the people in it,
The little men (it's Massachusetts speaking).
And when I asked to know what ailed the people,
She said, 'Go read your own books and find out.'

Robert Frost, *New Hampshire*, 1923

It's . . .
. . . restful just to think about New Hampshire.
At present I am living in Vermont.

Ibid.

From Portland . . . the road climbed northwards into the steeper landscape of New Hampshire, its forest flaring and glowing in an extravaganza of hot colour above the blue lakes, cold as steel. Ranging up the mountainsides were flames of scarlet and crimson and orange, maples and oaks, as it were, devouring the white trunks of the birches and the evergreen trees. Beneath them cinder-pink leaves smouldered over the earth like embers, seeming to kindle the undergrowth to an even fiercer blaze. It was a spectacle, showy and a trifle outrageous, characteristic of a continent with an indigenous trend to extremes.

Lord Kinross, *The Innocents at Home*, 1959

New Haven (Connecticut)

Many of its streets . . . are planted with rows of grand old elm-trees; and the same natural ornaments surround Yale College, an establishment of considerable eminence, and reputation. The various departments of this institution are erected in a kind of park or common in the middle of the town, where they are dimly visible among the shadowing trees. The effect is very like that of an old cathedral yard in England; and when their branches are in full leaf must be extremely picturesque. Even in the winter-time, these groups of well-grown trees, clustering among the busy streets and houses of a thriving city, have a very quaint appearance: seeming to bring about a kind of compromise between town and country; as if each had met the other half way, and shaken hands upon it, which is at once novel and pleasant.

Charles Dickens, *American Notes*, 1842

It looked to me like a town spending the summer months in the country.

Alexander Mackay, *The Western World*, 1849

Here's to the town of New Haven
The home of the Truth and the Light,
Where God talks to Jones in the very same tones
That He uses with Hadley and Dwight.

F.S. Jones, *On the Democracy of Yale*

New Jersey

The semi-colon of the Eastern seaboard – that's modern New Jersey.

Irvin S. Cobb, *Some United States*, 1926

A raucous little state.

John Gunther, *Inside U.S.A.*, 1947

New Mexico

Supposing one fell onto the moon, and found them talking English, it would be something the same as falling out of the open world, plump down here in the middle of America. 'Here' means New Mexico, the Southwest, wild, and woolly and artistic and sagebrush desert.

It is all rather like comic opera played with solemn intensity. All the wildness and woolliness and westernity and motor-cars and art and sage and savage are so mixed up, so incongruous, that it is a farce and everybody knows it. But they refuse to play it as farce. The wild and woolly section insists on being heavily dramatic, bold and bald, on purpose; the art insists on being real American, and artistic; motor-cars insist on being thrilled, moved to the marrow; highbrows insist on being ecstatic; Mexicans insist on being Mexicans, squeezing the last black drop of macabre joy out of life; and Indians wind themselves in white cotton sheets like Hamlet's father's ghost, with a lurking smile.

Everybody smirks at everybody else, and says tacitly: 'Go on, and do your little stunt, and I'll do mine,' and they're like the various troupes in a circus, all performing at once, with nobody for Master of Ceremonies.

D.H. Lawrence, 'Indians and Englishmen', *The Dial*, February 1923; *Phoenix* 1936

New Mexico has an austere and planetary look that daunts and challenges the soul.

Elizabeth Shepley Sergeant, in Ernest Gruening (ed.), *These United States, A Symposium*, 1923

New Mexico, one of the United States, part of the USA. New Mexico, the picturesque reservation and playground of the Eastern States, very romantic, old Spanish, Red Indian, desert mesas, pueblos, cowboys, penitentes, all that film-stuff. Very nice, the great South-West, put on a sombrero and knot a red kerchief round your neck, to go out in the great free spaces!

That is New Mexico wrapped in the absolutely hygienic and shiny mucous-paper of our trite civilization. That is the New Mexico known to most of the Americans who know it at all. But break through the shiny sterilized wrapping, and actually *touch* the country and you will never be the same again.

I think New Mexico was the greatest experience from the outside world that I have ever had. It certainly changed me for ever. Curious as it may sound, it was New Mexico that liberated me from the present era of civilization, the great era of material and mechanical development. . . . The moment I saw the brilliant, proud morning shine high up over the deserts of Santa Fe, something stood still in my soul, and I started to attend. . . . For a *greatness* of beauty I have never experienced anything like New Mexico. . . . It had a splendid silent terror, and a vast far-and-wide magnificence which made it way beyond mere aesthetic appreciation. Never is the light more pure and overweening than there, arching with a royalty almost cruel over the hollow uptilted world. For it is curious that the land which has produced modern political democracy at its highest pitch should give one the greatest sense of overweening, terrible proudness and mercilessness: but so beautiful, God! so beautiful! . . . Just day itself is tremendous there. It is so easy to understand that the Aztecs gave hearts of men to the sun.

D.H. Lawrence, 'New Mexico', *Survey Graphic*, May 1931; *Phoenix*, 1936

New Mexico . . . looks like the uplands of Luristan only less inhabited.

Freya Stark, Letter, 28 January 1944, in *Dust in the Lion's Paw*, 1961

On the licence plates in New Mexico it reads: 'the Land of Enchantment.' And that it is, by God! There's a huge rectangle which embraces parts of four states – Utah, Colorado, New Mexico and Arizona – and which is nothing but enchantment, sorcery, illusionismus, phantasmagoria. Perhaps the secret of the American continent is contained in this wild, forbidding, and partially unexplored territory. It is the land of the Indian par excellence. Everything is hypnagogic, cthonian, and super-celestial. Here Nature has gone Gaga and Dada. Man is just an irruption, like a wart or a pimple. Man is not wanted here. Red men, yes, but then they are so far removed from what we think of as man that they seem like another species.

Henry Miller, *The Air-conditioned Nightmare*, 1945

Actually, of course, Texas is no bigger than New Mexico. It only appears bigger because it is spread out so much thinner. The mean average thickness of New Mexico from sunshine to sea level is 5600 feet. The higher you go into the mountains the meaner it gets. . . . Mashed down and rolled out to the same thinness as Texas, New Mexico would reach all the way from Yalta to the Atlantic Charter with enough lapover to flap in the Texas wind. On the other hand, at the thickest point in Texas, an average New Mexico screwbilled angleworm could bore through to the bottom in one wriggle. . . .

Fourscore years before the first Texas cowboy scuffed a high-heeled boot on Plymouth Rock, a Mr. Coronado of Spain was eating corn off the cob in New Mexico and mailing home post-cards of five-storied Pueblo tourist courts marked 'Come on over, the climb is fine.' . . .

New Mexico has plains so flat that the State Highway Department has to put up signs to show the water which way to run when it rains; yet the mountains are so steep that the bears which inhabit them have all developed corkscrew tails so that they can sit down once in a while without sliding off into Texas. . . .

Snow falls so deep in New Mexico's mountains that it takes 40,000 automobile loads of Texas hot air each summer to melt it. . . .

New Mexico is game country too. If all the deer horns in the state were clustered together into one giant hatrack, it would make a good place for Texans to hang their hats when not talking through them. . . .

The charge that half the voters in New Mexico are sheep is erroneous. By and large, the votes are no sheeper here than they are in Jersey City. But the sunshine is, 365 days of the year, and twice on Sundays.

S. Omar (The Tentmaker) Barker of Tecolotenos, New Mexico, in *El-Paso Herald-Post*, quoted John Gunther, *Inside U.S.A.*, 1947

New Orleans

There is on the globe one single spot, the possessor of which is our natural and habitual enemy. It is New Orleans, through which the produce of three eighths of our territory must pass to market.

Thomas Jefferson, Letter to Robert R. Livingston, US Minister to France, 18 April 1802

I will hold New Orleans in spite of Urop and all hell.

Andrew Jackson, 1812

New Orleans presents very little that can gratify the eye of taste.

Mrs Frances Trollope, *Domestic Manners of the Americans*, 1832

All was very new, very foreign in its aspect. Many of the ladies in the streets wore caps or veils instead of bonnets; the negroes who passed shouted their very peculiar kind of French; and every thing seemed to tell us that we had plunged into the dog-days. I never before knew how impressions of heat can be conveyed through the eye. The intensity of glare and shadow in the streets, and the many evidences that the fear of heat is the prevailing idea of the place, affect the imagination even more than the scorching power of the sun does the bodily frame.

Harriet Martineau, *Retrospect of Western Travel*, 1838

My strongest impression of New Orleans is, that while it affords an instructive study, and yields some enjoyment to a stranger, it is the last place in which men are gathered together where one who prizes his humanity would wish to live.

Ibid.

It was dusk ere we came in sight of the city, and seen from a little distance through the uncertain twilight, it looked like a dark and ponderous exhalation surging slowly from the swamps around it.

Alexander Mackay, *The Western World*, 1849

'Sure there's no other town in the whole country where you'll find green peas in the month of January.'

Ibid.

I found New Orleans remarkably dull and healthy. . . . The rain came down, 'not from one lone cloud,' but as if a thousand cisterns had been stove in at once. In half an hour after a shower commenced, the streets were navigable.

Bayard Taylor, *Eldorado, or Adventures in the Path of Empire*, 1850

What little I have seen of this I like perhaps better than any town in the Union. There are pictures on the Quays: there are old French houses: there are streets which look for all the world like Havre – the sweet kind French tongue is spoken in the shops and I felt quite a liking for the negro who drove me from the station for calling out in good French to a brother driver. There is capital ordinaire Claret for dinner – The faces are not Yankee faces, with their keen eager narrow eyes, there are many fat people – these are interesting facts.

W.M. Thackeray, Letter to Anne and Harriet Thackeray, 7–10 March 1856

I doubt if there is a city in the world, where the resident population has been so divided in its origin, or where there is such a variety in the tastes, manners, habits, and moral codes of the citizens. Although this injures civic enterprise – which the peculiar situation of the city greatly demands to be directed to means of cleanliness, convenience, comfort, and health – it also gives a greater scope to the working of individual enterprise, taste, genius, and conscience; so that nowhere are the higher qualities of man – as displayed in generosity, hospitality, benevolence, and courage – better developed, or the lower qualities, liking him to a beast less interfered with, by law or the action of public opinion.

Frederick Law Olmstead, *Journey in the Seaboard Slave States*, 1856

New Orleans . . . reminds the European traveller of Havre or Boulogne-sur-Mer. From the admixture of people speaking the English language it is most like Boulogne; but the characteristics of the streets, and of the architecture are more like those of Havre.

Charles Mackay, *Life and Liberty in America, 1857–8*, 1859

The Levee sloped down with a noble breadth to the river, and stretched for miles up and down in front of the city, and was crowded with the cargoes of the hundreds of vessels which lay broadside to it. In some places the freights lay in mountainous heaps, but the barrels and hogsheads and cotton bales covered immense spaces, though arranged in precise order; and, with the multitudes of men – white, red, black, yellow, – horses, mules, and drays and wagons, the effect of such a scene, with its fierce activity and new atmosphere upon a raw boy from St Asaph, may be better imagined than described. . . .

The soft, balmy air, with its strange scents of fermenting molasses, semi-baked sugar, green coffee, pitch, Stockholm tar, brine, of mess-beef, rum and whiskey-drippings, contributed a great deal towards imparting the charm of romance to everything I saw. The people I passed appeared to me to be nobler than any I had yet seen. They had a swing of the body wholly un-English, and their facial expressions differed from those I had been accustomed to. . . . These people knew no master, and had no more awe of their employers than they had of their fellow-employees.

Sir Henry Morton Stanley, *Autobiography*, 1909 – of 1859

I am very weary of New Orleans. The first delightful impression it produced has vanished. The city of my dreams bathed in the gold of eternal summer, and perfumed with the amorous odours of orange-flowers, has vanished like one of those phantom cities of Spanish America, swallowed up centuries ago by earthquakes, but reappearing at long intervals to deluded travellers. What remains is something horrible like the tombs here, – material and moral rottenness which no pen can do justice to. You must have read some of those mediaeval legends in which an amorous youth finds the beauiful witch he has embraced all through the night crumble into a mass of calcined bones and ash in the morning. Well, I feel like such a one.

Lafcadio Hearn, Letter to H.E. Krehbiel, February 1881

'See Naples and die,' says the proverb. My view of things is that you should see Canal-street, new Orleans, and then try to live as much longer as ever you can.

G.A. Sala, *America Revisited*, 1882

There is no architecture in New Orleans, except in the cemeteries.

Mark Twain, *Life on the Mississippi*, 1883

It is the most congenial city in America that I know of and it is due in large part, I believe, to the fact that here at last on this bleak continent the sensual pleasures assume the importance which they deserve. It is the only city in America where, after a lingering meal, accompanied by good wine and good talk, one can still stroll at random through the French quarter and feel like a civilized human being.

Henry Miller, *The Air-conditioned Nightmare*, 1945

Newport (Rhode Island)

The climate is like that of Italy north of Rome. . . . The land is pleasantly diversified with hills, vales, and rising grounds. Here are also some amusing rocky scenes. There are not wanting several fine rivulets and groves. The sea, too, mixed with capes and adjacent islands, makes very delightful prospects. . . . The town is prettily built, contains about five thousand souls, and hath a very fine harbour. The people industrious, and though less orthodox, I cannot say they have less virtue (I am sure they have more regularity) than those I left in Europe. They are indeed a strange medley of different persuasions, which nevertheless all agree in one point, viz. that the Church of England is the second best.

George Berkeley, Letter to Lord Percival, 28 March 1729

To me Newport could never be a place charming by reason of its own charms. That it is a very pleasant place when it is full of people, and the people are in spirits and happy, I do not doubt. But then the visitors would bring, as far as I am concerned, the pleasantness with them. The coast is not fine. . . . In another hundred years or so, Rhode Island may be, perhaps, as pretty as the Isle of Wight.

Anthony Trollope, *North America*, 1862

. . . where idleness ranks among the virtues.

Oscar Wilde, Letter to Charles Eliot Norton, Newport, *c.* 15 July 1882

There is, I think, a far more intimate fondness between Newport and its frequenters than that which in most American watering-places consecrates the somewhat mechanical relation between the visitors and the visited. This relation here is for the most part slightly sentimental.

Henry James, 'Newport', 1870, in *Portraits of Places*, 1883

New York

Nineteenth Century

The renowned and ancient city of Gotham.

Washington Irving, *Salmagundi*, 11 November 1807 (the earliest reference found to New York City as Gotham, a nickname possibly derived from the proverb about the 'wise men of Gotham'; see Gotham, Great Britain)

Dews are very prevailing during the nights of the summer season. Their pernicious effects, however, can be easily prevented by avoiding improper exposure.

Anon., *The Picture of New York*, 1828

Never let the poor and destitute emigrant stop at New York – it will be his ruin.

Calvin Colton, *Manuel for Emigrants to America*, 1832

Here was a great city of busy people. Yet in this city there seemed little of the character of a fixed population and little of the external appearance of happiness or content. The Houses look as if they had been built upon too small a scale for the present necessity. And as if contrivances of every kind had been put in requisition to supply the defects. Then the activity of competition glares in every street. Here is a livery stable built of half burnt bricks and clay mortar painted to imitate a Roman temple, there a two story wooden tenement announces the Café des Mille colonnes. One man advertises his blacking in large chalk capitals upon the wooden fences of every vacant lot and another man builds a house to the clouds that *his* painted letters may be seen for half a mile glaring over the intervening houses. Then such an intermixture of fashion and poverty. The spot where all the trade of the town is carried on is the residence of most of its wealthy men. Here is a great house and there a ginshop, or a tailor's or a grocery. Such is the character of New York. The old families which were an aristocracy have given way. The new ones are coming forward on the strength of wealth suddenly acquired and which in all probability will be as suddenly lost. Adventurers dash in for the spoils and the thousand and one bloodsuckers who are found in the haunts of a corrupt city. I should never be anxious to live in such a city.

Charles Francis Adams, *Diary*, 11 November 1834

A bulger of a place it is. The number of the ships beat me all hollow, and looked for all the world like a big clearing in the West, with the dead trees all standing.

Davy Crockett, *Tour to the North and Down East . . . in 1834*, 1835

The first aspect of the city on the side of the East River, strikingly resembles that of Amsterdam. High, irregular, red brick fabrics, with innumerable masts, extending over a space of two miles in length, and half-shading the houses from the eye, characterise both.

George Combe, *Notes . . . during a Phrenological Visit in 1838–40*, 1841

When I arrived for the first time at New York, by that part of the Atlantic Ocean which is called the East River, I was surprised to perceive along the shore, at some distance from the city, a number of little palaces of white marble, several of which were of classic architecture. When I went the next day to inspect more closely one which had particularly attracted my notice, I found that its walls were of whitewashed brick, and its columns of painted wood. All the edifices that I had admired the night before were of the same kind.

Alexis de Tocqueville, *Democracy in America, the second part*, 1840

There is one quarter, commonly called the Five Points, which in respect of filth and wretchedness, may be safely backed against Seven Dials, or any other part of famed St Giles's . . . these narrow ways, diverging to the right and left, and reeking everywhere with dirt and filth. Such lives as are led here, bear the same fruits here as elsewhere. The coarse and bloated faces at the doors, have counterparts at home, and all the wide world over. Debauchery has made the very houses prematurely old. See how the rotten beams are tumbling down, and how the patched and broken windows seem to scowl dimly, like eyes that have been hurt in drunken frays. Many of those pigs live here. Do they ever wonder why their masters walk upright in lieu of going on all-fours? and why they talk instead of grunting?

Charles Dickens, *American Notes*, 1842

The Americans are justly very proud of it, and its residents passionately attached to it . . . a young New Yorker, who had been in Europe for more than a year, was in the same sleigh with me. 'There goes the old city!' said he in his enthusiasm, as we entered Broadway; 'I could almost jump out and hug a lamp-post!'

Alexander Mackay, *The Western World*, 1849

In both visits to America I have found the effects of the air here the same. I have a difficulty in forming the letters as I write them down on this page – in answering questions, in finding the most simple words to form the answers. A Gentleman asked me how long I had been in New York – I hesitated and then said a week – I had arrived the day before – I could not gather my thoughts together readily enough to be able to reply to him – hardly know what is said am thinking of something else nothing definite, with an irrepressible longing to be in motion. I sleep 3 hours less than in England, making up however with a heavy long sleep every 4th night or so. Talking yesterday with a very clever man (T Appleton of Boston) he says the effect upon him on his return from Europe is the same – There is some electric influence in the air & sun here which we don't experience on our side of the globe. Under this Sun people cant sit still people can't ruminate over their dinners dawdle in their studies and be lazy and tranquil – they must keep moving, rush from one activity to another, jump out of sleep and to their business, have lean eager faces – I want to dash into the street now. At home after breakfast I want to read my paper leisurely and then get to my books and work. . . . Yesterday as some rain began to fall I felt a leaden cap taken off my brain pan and began to speak calmly and reasonably, & not wish to quit my place.

W.M. Thackeray, Letter to Mrs Carmichael-Smyth, 16–20 November 1855

*A great city, Sir – replied the Little Gentleman, – a very opulent, splendid city. A point of transit of much that is remarkable, and of permanence for much that is respectable. A great money-centre. San Francisco with the mines above ground, – and some of 'em under the side-walks. I have seen next to nothing *grandiose*, out of New York, in all our cities. It makes 'em all look paltry and petty. Has many elements of civilization. May stop where Venice did, though, for aught we know . . . all that did not make Venice the brain of Italy.

Oliver Wendell Holmes, *The Professor at the Breakfast-Table*, 1859

In New York City, the common bats fly only at twilight. Brick-bats fly at all hours.

George Dennison Prentice, *Prenticeana*, 1860

New York is a sucked orange.

R.W. Emerson, *Conduct of Life: Culture*, 1860

I have two faults to find with it. In the first place there is nothing to see; and in the second place there is no method of getting about to see anything.

Anthony Trollope, *North America*, 1862

City of orgies, walks and joys,
City whom that I have lived and sung in your midst
  will one day make you illustrious,
Not the pageants of you, not your shifting tableaus,
  your spectacles repay me,
Not the interminable rows of your houses, nor the ships
  at the wharves,
Nor the processions in the streets, nor the bright
  windows with goods in them,
Nor to converse with learn'd persons, or bear my share
  in the soiree or feast;
Not those, but as I pass O Manhattan, your frequent
  and swift flash of eyes offering me love,
Offering response to my own – these repay me,
Lovers, continual lovers, only repay me.

Walt Whitman, 'City of Orgies', *Leaves of Grass*, 1860–7

I was asking for something specific and perfect for my
  city,
Whereupon lo! up sprang the aboriginal name.
Now I see what there is in a name, a word, liquid, sane,
  unruly, musical self-sufficient,
I see that the word of my city is that word from of
  old. . . .
The beautiful city, the city of hurried and sparkling
  waters! the city of spires and masts!
The city nested in bays! my city!
The city of such women, I am mad with them! I will
  return after death to be with them!
The city of such young men, I swear I cannot live
  happy without I often go talk, walk, eat, drink, sleep
  with them!

Walt Whitman, 'Manhattan', *Leaves of Grass*, 1860–71

More and more too, the *old name* absorbs into me – MANNAHATTA, 'the place encircled by many swift tides and sparkling waters.' How fit a name for America's great democratic island city! The word itself, how beautiful! how aboriginal! how it seems to rise with tall spires, glistening in sunshine, with such New World atmosphere, vista and action!

Walt Whitman, *Goodbye My Fancy*, 10 May 1879

The shape of Manhattan island was like that of a sole, with its head at Harlem, and its tail at the Castle garden: the backbone being represented by Broadway, and the continuous line of ships fringing the wharves along the East River and the Hudson River respectively, figuring the lateral small bones of the fish.

G.A. Sala, *America Revisited*, 1882

It is altogether an extraordinary growing, swarming, glittering, pushing, chattering, good-natured, cosmopolitan place, and perhaps in some ways the best imitation of Paris that can be found (yet with a great originality of its own).

Henry James, Letter to George du Maurier, 17 April 1883

There are only about four hundred people in New York society.

Ward McAllister, Interview with Charles H. Crandall, in the *New York Tribune*, 1888

Speaking of New York, . . . he said that it was impossible to have a picturesque address there.

Logan Pearsall Smith, quoting Henry James, Letter to his sister Alys, 14 May 1888

That frightful cyclone of electricity and machinery called New York.

Lafcadio Hearn, Letter to Elizabeth Bisland, 1889

It was not a city. It was a theatre. It was a huge fair. Bunting of all nationalities and of no nationality was flaunting over the streets. Poles of liberty accentuated the 'Rights of Man.' Bands of Music preceded processions of a dozen boys bearing flags and tattered targets. Irish was spoken in the wharves, German in the saloons, French in the restaurants. But the chiefest feature in this polyglot city was its boyhood. A boy in heart, but a man, and a very shrewd one, in head!

Dion Boucicault, 'Leaves from a Dramatist's Diary', *North American Review*, August 1889

This city drives me crazy, or, if you prefer, crazier; and I have no peace of mind or rest of body till I get out of it. Nobody can find any body, nothing seems to be anywhere, everything seems to be mathematics and geometry and enigmatics and riddles and confusion worse confounded: architecture and mechanics run mad. One has to live by intuition and move by steam. I think an earthquake might produce some improvement. The so-called improvements in civilization have apparently resulted in making it impossible to see, hear, or find anything out. You are improving yourselves out of the natural world. . . . I am sorry not to see you, but since you live in hell what can I do?

Lafcadio Hearn, Letter to Joseph Tumson, 1889

The more one studied it, the more grotesquely bad it grew – bad in its paving, bad in its streets, bad in its street-police, and but for the kindness of the tides, would be worse than bad in its sanitary arrangements. No one as yet had approached the management of New York in a proper spirit; that is to say, regarding it as the shiftless outcome of squalid barbarism and reckless extravagance. No one is likely to do so, because reflections on the long, narrow pig-trough are construed as malevolent attacks against the spirit and majesty of the American people, and lead to angry comparisons.

Rudyard Kipling, *From Tideway to Tideway*, 1892

Oh mighty city of New York! you are wonderful to
  behold,
Your buildings are magnificent, the truth be it told,
They were the only thing that seemed to arrest my eye,
Because many of them are thirteen storeys high. . . .

And there's also ten thousand rumsellers there
Oh! wonderful to think, I do declare!
To accommodate the people of that city therein
And to encourage them to commit all sorts of sin. . . .

And with regard to New York and the sights I did see
One street in Dundee is more worth to me
And believe me, the morning I sailed from New York
For bonny Dundee, my heart it felt light as a cork.

William McGonagall, 'Jottings of New York', *Poetic Gems*, 1890

Twentieth Century

This is the first sensation of life in New York – you feel that the Americans have practically added a new dimension to space. They move almost as much on the perpendicular as on the horizontal plane. When they find themselves a little crowded, they simply tip a street on end and call it a skyscraper.

William Archer, *America Today* 1900

*Nearly all th' most foolish people in th' country an' minny iv th' wisest goes to Noo York. Th' wise people ar-re there because th' foolish wint first. That's th' way th' wise men make a livin'.

Finley Peter Dunne, 'Some Political Observations', *Mr Dooley's Opinions*, 1901

New York is too strenuous for me; it gets on my nerves.

Ambrose Bierce, Letter, 5 October 1904

New York is appalling, fantastically charmless and elaborately dire.

Henry James, Letter to W.E. Norris, 15 December 1904

Vulgar of manner, overfed,
Overdressed and underbred;
Heartless, Godless, hell's delight,
Rude by day and lewd by night;
Bedwarfed the man, o'er grown the brute,
Ruled by Jew and prostitute;
Purple-robed and pauper-clad,
Raving, rotting, money-mad;
A squirming herd in Mammon's mesh,
A wilderness of human flesh;
Crazed with avarice, lust and rum,
New York, thy name's Delirium.

Byron R. Newton, *Owed to New York*, 1906

departure by sea
Suddenly as I looked back at the skyscrapers of lower New York a queer fancy sprang into my head. They reminded me quite irresistibly of piled-up packing cases outside a warehouse. I was amazed I had not seen the resemblance before. I could really have believed for a moment that that was what they were, and that presently out of these would come the real thing, palaces and noble places, free, high circumstances, and space and leisure, light and fine living for the sons of men.

H.G. Wells, *The Future in America*, 1906

It is all, absolutely, an expression of things lately and currently *done*, done on a large impersonal stage, and on the basis of inordinate gain.

Henry James, *The American Scene*, 1907

*We plant a tub and call it Paradise. . . . New York is the great stone desert.

Israel Zangwill, *The Melting Pot*, 1908

*To Europe she was America, to America she was the gateway of the earth. But to tell the story of New York would be to write a social history of the world.

H.G. Wells, *The War in the Air*, 1908

New York in truth is a city of many beauties and with a reckless prodigality she has done her best to obscure them all.

Charles Whibley, *American Sketches*, 1908

*If there ever was an aviary overstocked with jays it is that Yaptown-on-the-Hudson, called New York. . . . 'Little ole New York's good enough for us' – that's what they sing.

O. Henry, *Gentle Grafter: A Tempered Wind*, 1908

*What else can you expect from a town that's shut off from the world by the ocean on one side and New Jersey on the other?

Ibid.

*Far below and around lay the city like a ragged purple dream, the wonderful, cruel, enchanting, bewildering, fatal, great city.

O. Henry, *Strictly Business: The Duel*, 1910

*Well, little old Noisyville-on-the-Subway is good enough for me.

Ibid.

At the centre of the first cross-roads, I saw a splendid and erect individual, flashing forth authority, gaiety, and utter smartness in the gloom. Impossible not to believe that he was the owner of all the adjacent ground, disguised as a cavalry officer on foot.

'What is that archduke?' I inquired.

'He's just a cop.'

I knew then that I was in a great city.

Arnold Bennett, *Those United States*, 1912

We burst startlingly into a very remarkable deep glade – on the floor of it long, and violent surface-cars, a few open shops, and bars with commissionaires at the doors, vehicles dipping and rising out of holes in the ground, vistas of forests of iron pillars, on the top of which ran deafening, glittering trains, as on a tight-rope; above all that, a layer of darkness; and above the layer of darkness enormous moving images of things in electricity – a mastodon kitten, playing with a ball of thread, an umbrella in a shower of rain, siphons of soda-water being emptied and filled, gigantic horses galloping at full speed, and an incredible heraldry of chewing-gum . . . sky-signs.

Ibid.

In New York the earth seems to spin more quickly round its axis.

Herbert Beerbohm Tree, 'Impressions of America', *The Times*, 9 September 1916

Who that has known thee but shall burn
  In exile till he came again
To do thy will, O stern
Moon of the tides of men!

John Reed, *Proud New York*, 1917

*New York's a small place when it comes to the part of it that wakes up just as the rest is going to bed.

P.G. Wodehouse, 'The Aunt and the Sluggard', *My Man Jeeves*, 1919

New York looks as ever: stiff, machine-made, and against nature. It is so mechanical there is not the sense of death.

D.H. Lawrence, Letter to S.S. Koteliansky, 14 March 1924

I carry the place around the world in my heart but sometimes I try to shake it off in my dreams.

F.Scott Fitzgerald, Letter to Marya Mannes, October 1925

The great big city's a wondrous toy
Just made for a girl and boy
We'll turn Manhattan
Into an isle of joy.

Lorenz Hart, *Manhattan*, 1925

The life of the city, it must be confessed, is as interesting as its physical aspect is dull. It is, even more than London or Paris, the modern Babylon. . . . All the colossal accumulated wealth of the United States, the greatest robber nation in history, tends to force itself at least once a year through the narrow neck of the Manhattan funnel. To that harsh island come all the thieves of the Republic with their loot . . . At no time and place in modern times has harlotry reached so delicate and yet so effusive a development; it becomes, in one form or another, one of the leading industries of the town. New York, indeed, is the heaven of every man with something useless and expensive to sell.

H.L. Mencken, 'Totentanz', in *Prejudices*, Fourth Series, 1925

Every great wave of popular passion that rolls up on the prairies is dashed to spray when it strikes the hard rocks of Manhattan.

Ibid.

*I think this city is full of people wanting inconceivable things.

John Dos Passos, *Manhattan Transfer*, 1925

The city of dreadful height.

James Bone, Description of New York, in *Manchester Guardian*

*Over the great bridge, with the sunlight through the girders making a constant flicker upon the moving cars, with the city rising up across the river in white heaps and sugar lumps all built with a wish out of non-olfactory money. The city seen from the Queensboro Bridge is always the city seen for the first time, in its first wild promise of all the mystery and the beauty in the world.

F. Scott Fitzgerald, *The Great Gatsby*, 1926

New York is a good spot to stop away from.

Crosbie Garstin, *The Dragon and the Lotus*, 1928

New York is not all bricks and steel. There are hearts there too, and if they do not break, then they at least know how to leap. It is the place where all the aspirations of the Western World meet to form one vast master aspiration, as powerful as the suction of a steam dredge. It is the icing on the pie called Christian Civilization.

H.L. Mencken, *Prejudices*, Sixth Series, 1928

Seen here in New York is the same architectural insignificance due to the national blind-spot found all the way from coast to coast except bigger and better insignificance. The insignficance we had seen all along the line had some rights. None here. Here in the greatest metropolis of the U.S.A., in ambitious, but fatal variety, is the same deadly monotony where the building is concerned. Man-eating skyscrapers, all tall, but seeking false monumental mass for 1929 riveted steel skeletons, nineteenth century architecture. Not twentieth. The utter contradiction of structure and idea is what is most distinctive everywhere in New York.

Frand Lloyd Wright, *An Autobiography*, 1979 – of 1929

*'We certainly do lead the world in architecture,' said Professor Timson. 'Architecture, I take it, is the natural artistic expression of a young nation. Youth wants to build, and Manhattan Island kind of looks as though we've done what we wanted.' . . .

But what kind of youth could build like this? Some Titan's brood, or the nurselings of Brobdingnag. Was blind Polyphemus sent to stud, and did he cover Irish giantesses? Else how came this race that built forty storeys high to show it had done with teething?

Eric Linklater, *Juan in America*, 1931

*The mortal Andes of Manhattan.

Ibid.

At night . . . the streets become rhythmical perspectives of glowing dotted lines, reflections hung upon them in the streets as the wistaria hangs its violet racemes on its trellis. The buildings are a shimmering verticality, a gossamer veil, a festive scene-drop hanging there against the black sky to dazzle, entertain, amaze.

Frank Lloyd Wright, *The Disappearing City*, 1932

Tips are of an appallingly high scale in this city and must by no means be omitted if efficient attention is desired. If, however, the traveller does not intend again to visit the establishment the formality may be omitted.

Baedeker, *New York*, alleged quote from an early addition, quoted by Ford Madox Ford, *Return to Yesterday*, 1932

*On one of those nights of frozen silence when the cold is so intense that it numbs one's flesh, and the sky above the city flashes with one deep jewelry of cold stars, the whole city, no matter how ugly its parts may be, becomes a proud, passionate, Northern place: everything about it seems to soar upward with an aspirant, vertical, glittering magnificence to meet the stars. One hears the hoarse notes of the great ships in the river, and one remembers suddenly the princely girdle of proud, potent tides that bind the city, and suddenly New York blazes like a magnificent jewel in its fit setting of sea, and earth, and stars.

There is no place like it, no place with an atom of its glory, pride, and exultancy. It lays its hand upon a man's bowels; he grows drunk with ecstasy; he grows young and full of glory, he feels that he can never die.

Thomas Wolfe, *From Death to Morning*, 1935

It was a grey frost-bitten city which I had not seen for fifteen years. I visioned the new skyscrapers: buildings I could not imagine or recall. But it was a different New York. The everlasting scream of rivets and building machinery had stopped, and in spite of the trams the streets were fairly quiet. It was like Babel the morning after the building had to stop. And, curiously enough, the same curse of languages had descended. Every time the car stopped I heard a new tongue. New York is not an American city. It is like an enormous waiting-room in a railway depot fixed between the two hemispheres. The streets were half deserted. Broadway lay like a broken-down firework piece on the morning after the Fourth.

Shane Leslie, *American Wonderland*, 1936 – of 1934

A harlot amongst cities.

Bourke Cockran, quoted *ibid.*

I . . . wonder what it is in the New York air that enables me to sit up till all hours of the night in an atmosphere which in London would make a horse dizzy, but here merely clears the brain.

James Agate, *Ego 3*, 9 May 1937

Looking over New York as the sun was setting, Ben Hecht said to me: 'I always call that a Jewish Sunset. I call it that because all the smoke you see, which makes the body of the sunset, comes out of chimneys owned by Jews. So I call it a Jewish sunset.' And it had indeed a Jewish look: a sort of fulminating Old Testament heaviness and brooding beauty.

Wyndham Lewis, *Blasting and Bombardiering*, 1937

Now, very slowly, the famous New York skyline comes through the mist. At first it looks like one of those scenes in stencilled cardboard fashionable in the London theatre just after the War. Here I have the same experience as Mr Bergeret's little dog, Riquet: 'As I approach an object I grow less.' Soon the spectacle becomes overwhelmingly grand: I am now no size at all.

James Agate, *My American Journey*, 1938

*The magnificent facade of the homeland, the harbour of New York. . . .

F. Scott Fitzgerald, *Tender is the Night*, 1939

New York . . . seemed to me one of the most exciting cities in the world: the blueness of the sky floated about its pencil buildings, and shops, taxis, all human affairs seemed to go in deep canyon-beds of natural erosion rather than among the excrescences constructed by men. It is the only town where one's looks are drawn all the time away from the ground into the sky: the huge buildings are not too close together; they keep their individuality like the towers of San Gimignano or Bologna, and from the shadow of the streets you look to their sunlight and the long vistas of the avenues, and would not be surprised to see clouds trailing about their summits.

Freya Stark, *Dust in the Lion's Paw*, 1961 – of 1943

The River groans with green and crimson eyes,
And, like the monster-haunted Amazon,
Bellows and groans from alligator-throat,
Night passes. And Manhattan's mountains rise
Pale in the pearl-white dawn – chaste calm remote.
The lurid blatant beast with dark has gone.

Edward Thompson, 'East River, Brooklyn', from *100 Poems by Edward Thompson*, 1944

To the image of stark, grim ugliness which Boston had created was added a familiar feeling of terror. Sailing around the Battery from one river to the other, gliding close to the shore, night coming on, the streets dotted with scurrying insects, I felt as I had always felt about New York – that it is the most horrible place on God's earth. No matter how many times I escape, I am brought back like a runaway slave, each time detesting it, loathing it, more and more.

Henry Miller, *The Air-conditioned Nightmare*, 1945

In New York beautiful girls can become more beautiful
by going to Elizabeth Arden,
And getting stuff put on their faces and waiting for it to
harden,
And poor girls with nothing to their names but a letter
or two can get rich and joyous
From a brief trip to their loyous.
So I can say with impunity
That New York is a city of opportunity.

It also has many fine theatres and hotels,
And a lot of taxis, buses, subways and els,
Best of all, if you don't show up at the office or at a tea
nobody will bother their head,
They will just think you are dead.
That's why I really think New York is exquisite.
And someday I'm going to pay it a visit.

Ogden Nash, 'A Brief Guide to New York', in *Many Long Years Ago*, 1945

It is a city designed for pickpockets, the most romantic aspects of the city being on the summits of towering buildings where the architects burst into reminiscences of Ur of the Chaldees, the Hanging Gardens of Babylon, the campaniles, domes and porticos of Italy and here and there the patios of Spain, the mosques and minarets of the East. So that one is ever looking upwards from the geometrical plan of traffic-filled avenues to a sky filled with fantasy.

Cecil Roberts, *And So to America*, 1946

This rocky island, this concrete Capri.

Cyril Connolly, 'American Injection', 1947, in *Ideas and Places*, 1953

If one need never descend below the fortieth floor, New York would seem the most beautiful city in the world, its skies and cloudscapes are tremendous, its southern latitude is revealed only in its light (for vegetation and architecture are strictly northern); here one can take in the Hudson, the East river, the mid-town and down-town colonies of skyscrapers, Central Park and the magnificent new bridges and curving arterial highways and here watch the evening miracle, the lights going on all over these frowning termitaries against a sky of royal-blue velvet only to be paralleled in Lisbon or Palermo. A southern city with a southern pullulation of life, yet with a northern winter imposing a control; the whole nordic energy and sanity of living crisply enforcing its authority for three of the four seasons on the violet airy babel of tongues and races; this tension gives New York its unique concentration and makes it the supreme metropolis of the present.

Ibid.

If Paris is the setting for a romance, New York is the perfect city in which to get over one, to get over anything. Here the lost *douceur de vivre* is forgotten and the intoxication of living takes its place.

Ibid.

A hundred times I have thought, New York is a catastrophe, and fifty times: it is a beautiful catastrophe.

Le Corbusier, 'The Fairy Catastrophe', in *When the Cathedrals were White*, 1947

New York City isn't a melting pot, it's a boiling pot.

Thomas E. Dewey, in conversation with John Gunther, *Inside U.S.A.*, 1947

New York is simply an island full of clip joints.

Anon. Philadelphian, quoted by John Gunther, *Inside U.S.A.*, 1947

New York City, the incomparable, the brilliant star city of cities, the forty-ninth state, a law unto itself, the Cyclopean paradox, the inferno with no out-of-bounds, the supreme expression of both the miseries and the splendors of contemporary civilization, the Macedonia of the United States. It meets the most severe test that may be applied to definition of a metropolis – it stays up all night. But also it becomes a small town when it rains.

John Gunther, *Inside U.S.A.*, 1947

From the moment a New Yorker is confronted with almost any large city of Europe, it is impossible for him to pretend to himself that his own city is anything other than an unscrupulous real-estate speculation.

Edmund Wilson, *Europe Without Baedeker*, 1947

I particularly like New York on hot summer nights when all the . . . uh, superfluous people are off the streets.

Tennessee Williams, Remark, 1948, quoted by Gore Vidal, *Matters of Fact and Fiction*, 1977

On any person who desires such queer prizes, New York will bestow the gift of loneliness and the gift of privacy.

E.B. White, *Here is New York*, 1949

It can destroy an individual, or it can fulfil him, depending a good deal on luck. No one should come to New York to live unless he is willing to be lucky.

Ibid.

Of all targets, New York has a certain clear priority. In the mind of whatever perverted dreamer might loose the lightning, New York must hold a steady, irresistible charm.

Ibid.

A haven as cosy as toast, cool as an icebox and safe as skyscrapers.

Dylan Thomas, 1950, quoted J.M. Brinnin, *Dylan Thomas in America*, 1956

There seems at first sight to be no reality at all in the life here: it is all an enormous facade of speed and efficiency and power behind which millions of little individuals are wrestling, in vain, with their own anxieties.

Dylan Thomas, Letter to his parents, 26 February 1950

New Yorkers are inclined to assume it will never rain and certainly not on New Yorkers.

Brooks Atkinson, *Once Around the Sun*, 1951

It looked like a pagan banner planted on a Christian rampart.

Douglas Reed, *Far and Wide*, 1951

the importance of not beginning there

Having traced the root and stem of America, the traveller will study with more understanding the exotic fruit that has been grafted on at the top, an alien growth on an American stalk.

Ibid.

Manhattan is a haven for the ambitious.

James Morris, *Coast to Coast*, 1956

New York attracts the most talented people in the world in the arts and professions. It also attracts them in other fields. Even the bums are talented.

Edmund Love, Introduction to *Subways are for Sleeping*, 1957

Here personality tends to be overridden by category, as in the more rigid European societies it is overridden by class. Who your parents were is indeed of no consequence; but what you do counts more than what you are.

Lord Kinross, *The Innocents at Home*, 1959

But the classic view of the New York skyline – this time the downtown skyline of Wall Street – is from the Brooklyn waterfront. Here, on my third evening in New York, I look across the river . . . to see range upon range of towers, racing upwards to a chaotic variety of heights, yet so compressed as to make an orderly form out of the chaos. I was reminded of the serried church-towers of San Gimignano, multiplied and blown up to a colossal scale – and indeed I have since noticed that San Gimignano provides a favourite subject for American painters in Italy. But these were not church-towers. They were towers filled with men. And to what purpose? Was New York, perhaps, the City of Dreamless Spires?

Ibid.

There is no greenery; it is enough to make a stone sad.

Nikita Krushchev, Remark during visit, October 1960

And there, unmistakably it is: the familiar Manhattan look: A pettish, slightly resentful frown, as if a great promise had somehow not quite been fulfilled. In the midst of prosperity, people look as if they had been robbed.

Kenneth Tynan, 'A Memoir of Manhattan', 1960, in *Tynan Right and Left*, 1967

A city whose living immediacy is so urgent that when I am in it I lose all sense of the past.

Ibid.

New York is the greatest city in the world – especially for my people. Where else, in this grand and glorious land of ours, can I get on a subway, sit in any part of the train I please, get off at any station above 110th Street, and know I'll be welcome?

Dick Gregory, *From the Back of the Bus*, 1962

The faces in New York remind me of people who played a game and lost.

Murray Kempton, quoting Lane Adams's daughter, 'Is This All?', *America Comes of Middle Age*, 1963

One of the few charms that Manhattan has for me is its nearly complete freedom from one of the most annoying of American habits: impertinent curiosity about other people's affairs.

Sir Denis Brogan, in *Encounter*, June 1964

It is a city where everyone mutinies but no one deserts.

Harry Hershfield, Interview, *New York Times*, 5 December 1965

I love short trips to New York; to me it is the finest three-day town on earth.

James Cameron, *Witness*, 1966

Ah, New York. I was there and I liked it very much – I said to myself: 'Well, I have made this; this is my work.'

Jorge Luis Borges, Interview with Ronald Christ, July 1966, in *Paris Review*, 1967

'Of course, a city like New York is obsolete,' he said. 'People will no longer concentrate in great urban centres for the purpose of work. New York will become a Disneyland, a pleasure dome.'

Marshall McLuhan, quoted by Tom Wolfe, 'What if He is Right?', in *The Pump House Gang*, 1968

You know, it's funny on Saturday in New York, especially on one of those Indian Summer days – God, somehow Culture just seems to be in the air, like part of the weather, all of the antique shops on Madison Avenue, with a little blaze of golden ormolu here, and a little oxblood-red leathery marquetry there, and the rugs hung up in the second-floor display windows – rich! – a Bakhtiari with a little pale yellow setting off the red – and the galleries, God, gallery after gallery, with the pristine white walls of Culture, the black wooden floors, and the Culture buds, a little Renoirish softness in the autumn faces.

Tom Wolfe, 'Bob and Spike', in *The Pump House Gang*, 1968

I think that New York is not the cultural centre of America, but the business and administrative centre of American culture.

Saul Bellow, radio interview, *Listener*, 22 May 1969

I remember *not* being surprised or overwhelmed by New York. I found it the way I expected it to be: a kind of immense vertical mess (Edmund Wilson used to call it real estate gone mad) set upon a square horizontal order.

Nicolas Nabokov, *Bagazh*, 1975

If you're a Rockefeller, New York is really your town. Can you imagine?

Andy Warhol, *The Philosophy of Andy Warhol (From A to B and Back Again)*, 1975

Hemingway described literary New York as a bottle full of tapeworms trying to feed on each other.

John Updike, *Picked Up Pieces*, 1976

She has become a wicked and wild bitch in her old age has Manhattan, but there is still no sensation in the world quite like walking her sidewalks. Great surges of energy sweep all around you; the air fizzes like champagne, while always there is a nervous edge of fear and whispered distant promises of sudden violence.

Tom Davies, 'Intimations of Violence', *Observer Review*, 11 November 1979

New York is a city of strong flavours, of gasps and not sighs. It feeds you on mustard and tabasco sauce and makes you mainline on adrenalin. It is not possible to be neutral about it. It has a thumping heart. . . . Almost everything you have heard about it is largely true.

Trevor Fishlock, *Americans and Nothing Else*, 1980

New York's like a disco, but without the music.

Elaine Stritch, *Observer*, 'Sayings of the Week', 17 February 1980

Districts and Details

Broadway

Every body appears to be in motion, and every thing else. The carriages rattle through the streets: the carts dance as if they were running races with them; the ladies trip along in all the colours of the rainbow; and the gentlemen look as though they actually had something to do. They all walk as if they were in a hurry, and on my remarking this to my uncle, he replied in his usual sarcastic manner, 'Yes, they all seem as if they were running away from an indictment'. I did not comprehend what he meant.

James Kirke Paulding, *The New Mirror for Travellers*, 1828

A description of Broadway – O Lord is that describing America? It's a mole or a pimple on the great Republican body, or a hair of his awful beard and no more

W.M. Thackeray, Letter to Albany Fonblanque, 4 March 1853

It is a street *sui generis*, combining in itself the characteristics of the Boulevard des Italiens at Paris, and of Cheapside or Fleet Street in London, with here and there a dash of Whitechapel or the Minories; and here and there a dash of Liverpool and Dublin. It is longer, more crowded, and fuller of buildings than the Boulevard des Italiens: it is as bustling as Cheapside; and more than all, it has a sky above it as bright as the sky of Venice. Its aspect is thoroughly Parisian.

Charles Mackay, *Life and Liberty in America, 1857–8*, 1859

New York's (perhaps the world's)great thoroughfare.

Walt Whitman, *Specimen Days* (April 1879), 1882

Give my regards to Broadway.

George M. Cohan, Title and refrain of popular song, 1904

What a glorious garden of wonders this would be, to any one who was lucky enough to be unable to read.

G.K. Chesterton, Remark on first seeing Broadway, in his *What I saw in America*, 1923

and Piccadilly Circus, in London

I took a considerable delight in the dancing illuminations of Broadway – in Broadway. Everything there is suitable to them, the vast interminable thoroughfare, the toppling houses, the dizzy and restless spirit of the whole city. It is a city of dissolving views, and one may almost say a city in everlasting dissolution. But I do not especially admire a burning fragment of Broadway stuck up opposite the old Georgian curve of Regent Street. I would as soon express sympathy with the Republic of Switzerland by erecting a small Alp with imitation snow in the middle of St. James's Park.

Ibid.

When you are away from old Broadway you are only camping out.

George M. Cohan, quoted in Fred. J. Ringel (ed.), *America as Americans See It*, 1932

*If I have all the tears that are shed on Broadway by guys in love, I will have enough salt water to start an opposition to the Atlantic and Pacific, with enough left over to run the Great Salt Lake out of business.

Damon Runyon, 'Tobias the Terrible', *More than Somewhat*, 1937

Broadway . . . is tawdry, like a film-producer's notion of the Place Clichy, with a hint of Shepherd's Bush.
James Agate, *Ego 3*, 3 May 1937

Brooklyn
Only the Dead Know Brooklyn.
Thomas Wolfe, title of story, in *From Death to Morning*, 1935

In the midst of life we are in Brooklyn.
Anon., quoted Shane Leslie, *American Wonderland*, 1936

The Bronx
The bronx?
No thonx.
Ogden Nash, in *New Yorker*, 1931

Central Park

and Hyde Park, London
A man who strolls in Hyde Park after nightfall may possibly find himself in the police court next morning. (It would largely depend on what kind of lady he met, and what sort of adventures attract him.) But the man who strolled in Central Park after nightfall would almost certainly find himself in the morgue.
Collinson Owen, *The American Illusion*, 1929

Central Park . . . is a smaller and shabbier Hampstead Heath, with bits of the Serpentine and Rotten Row thrown in. Not a single flower, and the grass brown and patchy. The astonishing thing is still the skyscrapers; the Park is the crater of which they are the walls. From far away and in the near distance they are enormously impressive; when one gets right under them they vanish and one regains one's normal size.
James Agate, *Ego 3*, 3 May 1937

If you should happen after dark
To find yourself in Central Park
Ignore the paths that beckon you
And hurry, hurry to the zoo
And creep into the tiger's lair.
Frankly you'll be safer there.
Ogden Nash, in *Everyone but Thee and Me*, 1964

Central Park, a stretch of brown vegetation which runs through the centre of Manhattan, is the least 'natural' area in the world. New York must have been built to afford some kind of relief from it. At night it looks like a dry jungle; during the day it resembles a bomb crater which is slowly putting up shoots. The lakes in the middle of it smell disagreeably, and on a summer's stroll beside them I brushed against two large water rats. Perhaps they were looking for babies to kill.
Peter Ackroyd, *Spectator*, 1 October 1977

Greenwich Village
Greenwich village is the Coney Island of the soul.
Maxwell Bodnheim, quoted in Allen Churchill, *The Improper Bohemians*, 1959

The internment camp of Manhattan nonconformity.
Kenneth Tynan, 'A Memoir of Manhattan', 1960, in *Tynan Right and Left*, 1967

Harlem
Negroes and Puerto Ricans get on well together by and large. One Puerto Rican told me this was natural because his people want to get Americanized as quickly as possible, and the Negroes represent Anglo-Saxon culture!
John Gunther, *Inside U.S.A.*, 1947

Park Avenue
This is where wealth is so swollen that it almost bursts.
Collinson Owen, *The American Illusion*, 1929

The Rockefeller Center
That sinister Stonehenge of economic man, the Rockefeller Center.
Cyril Connolly, 'American Injection', 1947, in *Ideas and Places*, 1953

Statue of Liberty
Not like the Brazen giant of Greek fame
With Conquering limbs astride from land to land,
Here at our sea-washed, sunset gates shall stand
A mighty woman with a torch, whose flame
Is the imprisoned lightning, and her name
Mother of Exiles. From her beacon-hand
Glows world-wide welcome: her mild eyes command
The air-bridged harbour that twin cities frame.
'Keep, ancient lands, your storied pomp!' cries she
With silent lips, 'Give me your tired, your poor,
Your huddled masses yearning to breathe free
The wretched refuse of your teeming shore,
Send these, the homeless, tempest tossed to me,
I lift my lamp beside the golden door!'
Emma Lazarus, *The Colossus*, 1883

*I was made by a Dago and presented to the American people on behalf of the French Government for the purpose of welcomin' Irish immigrants into the Dutch city of New York.
O. Henry, *Sixes and Sevens: The Lady Higher Up*, 1911

It is fine, – until you get near enough to see its clumsiness. A hand fell on my shoulder, and a voice said, 'Look hard at that, young man! That's the first time you've seen Liberty – and it will be the last until you turn your back on this country again.'
Rupert Brooke, *Letters from America*, 1913

One time here in New York, I played at a big benefit to get a statue of Liberty for Russia. Now can you imagine Russia with a statue of liberty? We don't even know if they want one or not. If they do want one we will loan them ours. Ours has got its back turned on us at the present time, showing us that our liberty is behind us.

Will Rogers, *Autobiography*, 1928

The statue of Liberty, a big girl who is obviously going to have a baby.The Birth of a Nation, I suppose.

James Agate, *Ego 3*, 3 May 1937

The Statue of Liberty stood forward, floodlit white. In my mood of momentary dejection, she seemed to be wearing a jewelled Crown of Thorns. But I knew this was not so.

Lord Kinross, *The Innocents at Home*, 1959

Niagara Falls (US/Canadian border)

I felt as if approaching the very residence of the Deity.

Thomas Moore, Letter to his mother, 24 July 1804

'Did the Falls answer your expectations?'

The best answer on this subject I remember to have heard of was made by a gentleman who had just been at Niagara, and on his return was appealed to by a party he met on the way going to the Falls, who naturally asked him, if he thought they would be disappointed. 'Why, no,' said he: 'Not unless you expect to witness the sea coming down from the moon.'

Captain Basil Hall, *Travels in North America*, 1829

I felt as it were, staggered and confused, and at times experienced a sensation bordering on alarm – I did not well know at what – a strong mysterious sort of impression that something dreadful might happen. At one moment I looked upon myself as utterly insignificant, in the presence of such a gigantic moving, thundering body – and in the next, was puffed up with a sort of pride and arrogant satisfaction, to think that I was admitted into such company, and that I was not altogether wasting the opportunity: at others I gave up the reins of my imagination altogether, and then tried to follow, but with no great success, some of the innumerable trains of wild and curious reflections which arose in consequence. . . . More than once I really almost forgot where I was, and became more than half unconscious that I saw millions on millions of tons of water dashing down before me at every second, at the distance of only a few yards; – and even ceased to recollect that the sound I heard came from the greatest cascade in the world. Still, however, in spite of these abstractions, – which I made no attempt to restrain, – I was all the while sensible that something very delightful was passing. . . . It may help to give some idea of the extravagant length to which the over-indulged fancy can carry the dreamer on such occasions, to mention that once for some seconds, I caught myself thinking that I had fairly left this lower world for the upper sky, – that I was traversing the Heavens in company with Sir Isaac Newton, – and that the Sage was just going to tell me about the distance of the fixed stars.

Ibid.

The amazing Fall that is naturally made by the Almighty, is caused by the source of the River S Lawrence, in which its passage runs from Lake Erie into Lake Ontario. The cataract is called the Falls of Niagara. It is uncertainly said that it is the largest and noblest in the world. It is about one hundred and thirty feet perpendicular, and it runs like a horseshoe. It can pour its waters into the Atlantic Ocean. When any of the persons visits the Falls, I think he is amazing at seeing it, that makes him attack it, and when he is imprudent, to go and fall violently into it. It is useless for the Falls to run continually, yet it makes those who are delighted to see its curiosity. It is said, that one of the Indians slept in a canoe, which was bound to the root of a tree with a rope. When a white man saw him asleep, he rejoiced that he broke the rope out of the root; and when the canoe was afloat, the Indian opened his eyes, and immediately took his oar and rowed; but he left it: so he was fond of drinking some spirituous liquors, and when the Falls swallowed up the canoe, which fell down, his limbs were all broken, and perished.

'Of the Cataract, by a young man of eighteen years of age, born deaf and dumb', quoted *ibid.*

Who does not know that dreadful gulf where Niagara falls,
Where eagle unto eagle screams, to vulture vulture calls;
Where down beneath, Despair and Death in liquid darkness grope,
And upward, on the foam there shines a rainbow without Hope;
While, hung with clouds of Fear and Doubt, the unreturning wave
Suddenly gives an awful plunge, like life into the grave. . . .

Thomas Hood, *The Fall*, 1832

I wept with a strange mixture of pleasure and of pain, and certainly was, for some time, too violently affected in the *physique* to be capable of much pleasure. . . .

Exactly at the Fall, it is the Fall and nothing else you have to look upon; there are not, as at Trenton, mighty rocks and towering forests, there is only the waterfall; but it is the fall of an ocean.

Mrs Frances Trollope, *Domestic Manners of the Americans*, 1832

To offer an idea of Niagara by writing of hues and

dimensions is much like representing the kingdom of Heaven by images of jasper and topazes.

Harriet Martineau, *Retrospect of Western Travel*, 1838

Flow on for ever in thy glorious robe
Of terror and of beauty; God hath set
His rainbow on thy forehead, and the cloud
Mantles around thy feet. And he doth give
Thy voice of thunder power to speak of Him
Eternally – bidding the lip of man
Keep silence, and upon thy rocky altar pour
Incense of awe-struck praise.

Mrs Sigourney, *Niagara*, 1854, but published before 1839

As I stood on the brink above the Falls, continuing for a considerable time to watch the great mass of water tumbling, dancing, capering, and rushing wildly along, as if in a hurry to take the leap and delighted at it, I could not help wishing that I too had been made of such stuff, as would have enabled me to have joined it; with it to have rushed innocuously down the precipice; to have rolled uninjured into the deep unfathomable gulf below, or to have gamboled in the atmosphere of spray, which rose again in a dense cloud from its recesses. For about half an hour more I continued to watch the rolling waters, and then I felt a slight dizziness and a creeping sensation come over me – that sensation arising from strong excitement, and the same, probably, that occasions the bird to fall into the jaws of the snake. This is a feeling which, if too long indulged in becomes irresistible, and occasions a craving desire to leap into the flood of rushing waters. It increased upon me every minute; and retreating from the brink, I turned my eyes to the surrounding foliage, until the effect of the excitement had passed away. I looked upon the waters a second time, and then my thoughts were directed into a very different channel. I wished myself a magician, that I might transport the Falls to Italy, and pour their whole volume of waters into Mount Vesuvius; witness the terrible conflict between the contending elements, and create the largest steam-boiler that ever entered into the imagination of man.

Captain Frederick Marryat, *A Diary in America*, 1839

Then when I felt how near my Creator I was standing, the first effect, and the enduring one – instant and lasting – of the tremendous spectacle, was Peace. Peace of Mind, tranquillity, calm recollections of the Dead, great thoughts of Eternal Rest and Happiness; nothing of gloom or terror. Niagara was at once stamped upon my heart, an Image of Beauty; to remain there, changeless and indelible, until its pulses cease to beat, for ever. . . .

I think, in every quiet season now, still do those waters roll and leap, and roar and tumble all day long: still are the rainbows spanning them, a hundred feet below. Still when the sun is on them, do they shine and glow like molten gold. Still, when the day is gloomy, do they fall like snow, or seem to crumble away like the front of a great chalk cliff, or roll down the rock like dense white smoke. But always does the mighty stream appear to die as it comes down, and always from its unfathomable grave arises that tremendous ghost of spray and mist which is never laid: which has haunted this place with the same dread solemnity since Darkness brooded on the deep, and that first flood before the Deluge – Light – came rushing on Creation at the word of God.

Charles Dickens, *American Notes*, 1842

The reader who is acquainted with the localities of London, may, from the following illustration form some faint idea of the magnitude of Niagara. Let him suppose a ledge of rock, nearly as lofty as its towers, commencing at Westminster Abbey, and after running down Whitehall, turning, at Charing Cross, into the Strand, and continuing on to Somerset House. Let him then suppose himself on Waterloo Bridge, whence every point of the mighty precipice could be seen. Let him lastly suppose an immense volume of water falling over the whole of it, with the exception of a portion extending, say, from the Home Office to the Admiralty, which is left dry, – and he may have some notion of the extent of the great cataract. The tumbling and foaming mass extending from Somerset House to the Admiralty, would, with the bend at Charing Cross, occupy the place of the Horseshoe, or Canada Fall; the dry rock, between the Admiralty and the Home Office, that of the precipice of Goat Island; and the continuation of the cataract, between the Home Office and the Abbey, that of the American Fall.

Alexander Mackay, *The Western World*, 1849

At Niagara, I noticed that as quick as I got out of the wetting of the Fall, all the grandeur changed into beauty. You cannot keep it grand, it is so quickly beautiful.

Ralph Waldo Emerson, *Journals*, 1856

There is no caprice or rage about it; – nothing but the triumphant song of gravitation.

Charles Mackay, *Life and Liberty in America, 1857–8*, 1859

My feelings . . . were not so much those of astonishment as of an overpowering sense of the Law, mingled with a delicious pleasure.

Ibid.

Nothing ever disappointed me less than the Falls of Niagara – but my raptures did not truly commence for the first half-day. Their charms grow upon one like the conversation of a brilliant man.

Anthony Trollope, *The West Indies and the Spanish Main*, 1859

I came across an artist at Niagara who was attempting to draw the spray of the waters. 'You have a difficult subject,' said I. 'All subjects are difficult,' he replied, 'to a man who desires to do well.' 'But yours, I fear, is impossible,' I said. 'You have no right to say so till I have finished my picture,' he replied.

Anthony Trollope, *North America*, 1862

To realize Niagara you must sit there until you see nothing else than that which you have come to see. You will hear nothing else, and think of nothing else. At length you will be at one with the tumbling river before you. You will find yourself among the waters as though you belonged to them. The cool green liquid will run through your veins, and the voice of the cataract will be the expression of your own heart. You will fall as the bright waters fall, rushing down into your new world with no hesitation and with no dismay; and you will rise again as the spray rises, bright, beautiful, and pure. Then you will flow away in your course to the uncompassed, distant, and eternal ocean.

Ibid.

A lively French-Canadian, gossiping to me about Niagara, remarked, 'It is a horror. It is a Barnum Museum with a vente a l'encan. It is full of brigands who ask you to buy. I am asked to buy the skull of Le General Brock. I am asked to buy the sword of Monsieur de Salaberry. He not kill here. I am ask to buy, what you call, a racoon: and horror of horrors, one miserable, he say, 'Sare, you buy one piece of the Pantaloon of Mr Sam Patch, who jump over the Fall and break his neck.'

G.A. Sala, *My Diary in America in the Midst of War*, 1865

And was this all? . . . These were the Falls of Niagara. *They looked comparatively small, and the water looked dingy* . . .

A Swiss watchmaker observed that he was very glad 'de beautiful ting was going.' He looked upon it as some kind of clockwork arrangement, which would run down and be wound up again. Everybody knows the story of the 'cute Yankee who called it 'an almighty water privilege.' It *is* one, and would turn all the mill-wheels in the world. 'Here creation's done its d . . . dest,' remarked another, and quoth a fifth, 'I guess this hyar suckles the ocean-sea considerable.'

Ibid.

from the Canadian side

The perfect taste of it is the great characteristic. It is not in the least monstrous; it is thoroughly artistic, and, as the phrase is, thought out. In the matter of line it beats Michel Angelo. . . . If the line of beauty had vanished from the earth elsewhere, it would survive on the brow of Niagara. . . . The genius who invented it was certainly the first author of the idea that order, proportion, and symmetry are the conditions of perfect beauty. He applied his faith among the watching and listening forests, long before the Greeks proclaimed theirs in the measurements of the Parthenon. Even the roll of the white batteries at the base seems fixed and poised and ordered, and in the vague middle zone of the difference between the flood as it falls and the mist as it rises you imagine a mystical meaning – the passage of body to soul, of matter to spirit, of human to divine.

Henry James, 'Niagara', 1871, in *Portraits of Places*, 1883

I was disappointed with Niagara – most people must be disappointed with Niagara. Every American bride is taken there, and the sight of the stupendous waterfall must be one of the earliest, if not the keenest disappointments in American married life.

Oscar Wilde, *Impressions of America*, Lecture, 1883

I had to visit Niagara fifteen times before I succeeded in getting my imaginary Falls gauged to the actuality and could begin to sanely and wholesomely wonder at them for what they were, not what I had expected them to be. When I first approached them it was with my face lifted towards the sky, for I thought I was going to see an Atlantic ocean pouring down thence over cloud-vexed Himalayan heights, a sea-green wall of water sixty miles front and six miles high: and so, when the toy reality came suddenly into view – that be-ruffled little wet apron hanging out to dry – the shock was too much for me, and I fell with a dull thud. Yet slowly, surely, steadily, in the course of my fifteen visits, the proportions adjusted themselves to the facts, and I came at last to realise that a waterfall a hundred and sixty-five feet high and a quarter of a mile wide was an impressive thing. It was not a dipperful to my vanished great vision, but it would answer.

Mark Twain, *More Tramps Abroad*, 1897

We slipped into a gaunt, Saturday-to-Monday kind of town, where the people in the streets were all trippers, and the shops sold nothing but mugs with inscriptions, pens of white bone, with little holes to which you applied one eye, twisted your face into contortions, and thought you were looking at views; catch-penny trinkets, twopenny-halfpenny shows, and whole stacks of photographs. We were at Niagara Falls. . . .

There has been enough laudation already of the Niagara falls to make them conceited.

John Foster Fraser, *Round the World on a Wheel*, 1899

Endlich fortissimo!
(At last fortissimo!)

Gustav Mahler, on visiting Niagara, in 1908, quoted in K.Blaukopf, *Gustav Mahler*, 1969

It is merely a great deal of water falling over some cliffs. But it is very remarkably that.

Rupert Brooke, *Letters from America*, 1913

I could not get out of my mind the thought of a friend, who said that the rainbows over the Falls were like the arts, and beauty, and goodness, with regard to the stream of life – caused by it, thrown up on its spray, but unable to stay or direct or affect it, and ceasing when it ceased.

Ibid.

Niagara gave me no emotion.

Bertrand Russell, Letter to Lucy Donnelly, 6 June 1914, in *Bertrand Russell's America*, 1973

I saw the white water at night too, lit up by two (or whatever it was) billion candle power: vulgarity to make the forces of nature play parlour tricks.

Freya Stark, Note of 5 February 1929, in *Beyond Euphrates*, 1951

Niagara is really some waterfall. It falls over like a great noisy beard made of cotton wool, veiled by spray and spanned by rainbows.

Harold Nicolson, *Diary*, 31 January 1933

A traveller's first duty in America is to visit Niagara, and his second is to record impressions as fleeting as the waters.

Shane Leslie, *American Wonderland, 1936*

*'I thought your wife's name was Frances.'
'Well, it isn't. It's Niagara.'
'What a peculiar name.'
'Her parents spent their honeymoon at the Niagara Falls hotel.'
'Niagara is a town in America, is it not?'
'Not so much a town as a rather heavy downpour.'

P.G.Wodehouse, *Full Moon*, 1947

The reporters asked me what I thought of them. . . . 'I saw them before you were born. I came here first in 1900.' 'Do they look the same?' 'Well,' I replied, 'the principle seems the same. The water still keeps falling over.'

Sir Winston Churchill, *Closing the Ring*, 1952

The roar of Niagara is the Delphian voice of the great spaces of North America.

Osbert Sitwell, *'The Four Continents*, 1954

Nome (Alaska)

Then we climbed the cold creeks near a mission
That is run by the agents of God,
Who trade Bibles and Prayer-books to heathen
For ivory, seal-skins and cod.
At last we were sure we had struck,
But alas! for our hope of reward,
The landscape from sea-beach to sky-line
Was staked in the name of the Lord!

Sam Dunham, *The Goldsmith of Nome*, *c.*1900

You will find a magic city
On the shore of Bering Strait,
Which shall be for you a station
To unload your arctic freight.
Where the gold of Humboldt's vision
Has for countless ages lain
Waiting for the hand of labour
And the Saxon's tireless brain.

Sam Dunham, *c.* 1900

Cape Nome derives its name from the Indian word '*No-me*,' which signifies in English, 'I don't know.' In former days, when whalers anchored here to trade, the invariable answer given by the natives to all questions put by the white men was '*No-me*', meaning that they did not understand, and the name of the place was thus derived.

Harry de Windt, *From Paris to New York by Land*, 1904

Nome city impressed me at first as being a kind of squalid Monte Carlo. There is the same unrest, the same feverish quest for gold and the same extravagance of life as in the devil's garden on the blue Mediterranean. On landing I was struck with the number of well-dressed men and women who rub shoulders in the street with the dilapidated-looking mining element. In the same way, palatial banks and prim business houses are incongruously scattered amongst saloons and drinking bars.

Ibid.

Norfolk (Virginia)

This Norfolk, the capital of Virginia, is a most strange place; nothing to be seen in the streets but dogs and negroes, and the few ladies that *pass for white* are to be sure the most unlovely pieces of crockery I ever set my eyes upon.

Thomas Moore, Letter to his mother, 7 November 1803

Norfolk is a dirty, low, ill-arranged town, nearly divided by a morass. It has a single creditable public building, a number of fine private residences, and the polite society is reputed to be agreeable, refined, and cultivated, receiving a character from the families of the resident naval officers. It has all the immoral and disagreeable characteristics of a large seaport, with very few of the advantages that we should expect to find as a relief to them. . . . If a deadly, enervating pestilence had always reigned here, this Norfolk could not be a more miserable, sorry little sea-port town than it is.

Frederick Law Olmsted, *Journey in the Sea-board Slave States*, 1856

Northampton (Massachusetts)

Few cities turn upon their neighbours greater floods of polished virginity at commencement time each year than does Northampton.

Hampshire Gazette, *c.*1925, quoted H.L. Mencken, *Americana*, 1925

North Platte (Nebraska)

The town of North Platte, which is the present terminus of the line, is of but eight months' growth, and deserves mention. . . . Every gambler in the Union seems to have steered his course for North Platte, and every known game under the sun is played here. The days of Pike's Peak and California are revived. Every house is a saloon, and every saloon is a gambling den. Revolvers are in great requisition. Beardless youths imitate to the life the peculiar swagger of the devil-may-care bull-whacker and blackleg, and here, for the first time they try their hands at the 'Mexican monte,' 'high-low-jack,' 'strap,' 'rouge-et-noir,' 'three-card-monte,' and that satanic game, 'chuck-a-luck,' and lose their all. 'Try again, my buck; nothing like 'sperience; you are cuttin' your eye-teeth now; by-and-by you will be a pioneer.' Such are the encouraging words shouted to an unfortunate young man by the sympathising bystanders. On account of the immense freighting done to Idaho, Montana, Utah, Dacotah, and Colorada, hundreds of bull-whackers walk about and turn the one street into a perfect Babel. Old gamblers who revelled in the glorious days of 'flush times,' in the gold districts, declare that this town outstrips all yet.

H.M. Stanley, *My Early Travels and Adventures* (May 1867), 1895

Oakland (California)

And you have 'the hills back of Oakland!' God what would I not give to help you range them, the dear old things! Why, I know every square foot of them from Walnut Creek to Niles Cañon. Of course they swarm with ghosts, as do all places out there, even the streets of San Francisco; but I and my ghosts always get on well together. With the female ones my relations are sometimes a bit better than they were with the dear creatures when they lived.

Ambrose Bierce, Letter, 21 October 1903

Ohio

Ohio is most the only country I know on where folks are saved that trouble, and there the freshets come jist in the nick of time for 'em, and sweep all the crops right up in a heap for 'em, and they have nothin to do but take it home and house it; and sometimes a man gets more than his own crop, and finds a proper swad of it all ready piled up, only a little wet or so; but all countries aint like Ohio.

T.C. Haliburton, *The Clockmaker, or the Sayings and Doings of Samuel Slick*, first series, 1836

Ohio was not at all as I had pictured it. We were now on those great plains which stretch unbroken to the Rocky Mountains. The country was flat like Holland, but far from being dull. All through Ohio, Indiana, Illinois, and Iowa, or for as much as I saw of them from the train, and in my waking moments, it was rich and various and breathed an elegance peculiar to itself. The tall corn pleased the eye; the trees were graceful in themselves, and framed the plain into long aerial vistas; and the clean, bright, gardened townships spoke of country fare, and pleasant summer evenings on the stoop. It was a sort of flat paradise; but, I am afraid, not unfrequented by the devil. That morning dawned with such a freezing chill as I have rarely felt; a chill that was not perhaps so measurable by instrument, as it struck home upon the heart and seemed to travel with the blood. Day came in with a shudder.

Robert Louis Stevenson, *Across the Plains*, 1892 – of 1879

Ohio is the farthest west of the east and the farthest north of the south.

Louis Bromfield, attrib.

Ohio State University lies in a region of literacy and slurred enunciation, literary tradition and careless diction, vivid vocabulary and flat pronunciation. There the words 'Mary' and 'marry' are pronounced the same as 'merry', and there, too, Gudda is spoken ('Where's he gudda go? What's he gudda do?'), which results from a partial immobility of the lips in speaking. (A stone-deaf lip-reader instantly identified me, not many years ago, as a native of Ohio, Indiana, or Illinois. 'You say most words as if you were saying "King",' she said.)

James Thurber, *The Thurber Album*, 1952

Ohio River

There is an extreme beauty in the Ohio river . . . it appears deeply embedded in the wild forest scenery thro' which it flows. The whole stream is alive with small fresh-water turtle, who play on the surface of its clear water; while the most beautiful varieties of the butterfly tribe cross over from one side to the other, from the slave-States to the free – their liberty at all events, not being interfered with, as, on the free side it would be thought absurd to catch what would not produce a cent: while on the slaves', their idleness and indifference to them are their security.

Captain Frederick Marryat, *A Diary in America*, 1839

and Mississippi
There is little that is picturesque on the great lines of travel, for the Ohio and Mississippi are but monstrous drains.

Charles Mackay, *Life and Liberty in America, 1857–8*, 1859

Ohio River towns
The towns, almost without exception, are repulsively ugly and out of keeping with the tone of mind inspired by the river. Each has had its hopes, not yet quite abandoned, of becoming the great mart of the valley, and has built in accordant style its one or two tall brick city blocks, standing shabby-sided alone on the mud slope to the bank, supported by a tavern, an old store-house, and a few shanties. These mushroom cities mark only a night's camping-place of civilisation.

Frederick Law Olmsted, *A Journey through Texas*, 1857

I am glad that I had the chance to see these Ohio towns, this Mahoning River, which looks as if the poisonous bile of all humanity had poured into it, though in truth it may contain nothing more evil than the chemicals and waste products of the mills and factories. I am glad I had the chance to see the color of the earth here in winter, a color not of age and death, but of disease and sorrow. Glad I could take in the rhinoceros-skinned banks that rise from the river's edge, and in the pale light of a wintry afternoon reflect the lunacy of a planet given over to rivalry and hatred. Glad I caught a glimpse of those slag heaps which look like the accumulated droppings of sickly prehistoric monsters which passed in the night.

Henry Miller, *The Air-conditioned Nightmare*, 1945

Oklahoma

This state is chiefly given over to oil-drilling. It was settled largely by persons who left the East for the East's good, and remains turbulent and barbarous to this day. Its politicians are almost unanimously thieves. Its towns bear such Indian names as Okmulgee, Pawhuska, Tahlequah and Comanche. In Oklahoma the American frontier is gasping out its last breath.

H.L. Mencken, *Americana*, 1925

*Okie use' to mean you was from Oklahoma. Now it means you're scum.

John Steinbeck, *The Grapes of Wrath*, 1939

It is part of the High Plains, wide and flat. If you raise your arms, they touch the sky, and if you spread them, they reach the end of the earth.

Douglas Reed, *Far and Wide*, 1951

Here, a town was two streets of bungalows, a lumber-yard, a grocery store, an American flag, and, a moment later, prairie. . . . I wondered what it must be like to be born in a place like this, where only the foreground – the porch, the storefront, the main street – mattered. The rest was emptiness, or did it only seem that way to me because I was a stranger, passing through on a train? I had no wish to stop. The Oklahoman or Texan celebrates his freedom and speaks of the confinement of the New Yorker; but these towns struck me as confining to a suffocating degree. There was a pattern of defensiveness in the way they were laid out, as if they had simply sprung out of a common fear. And the pattern? It was that of a circle of wagons – wagons without wheels, which had been parked there for no better reason than that there were others already there. The land was vast, but the houses were in huddles, regarding the neighbours and the narrow street, their backs turned to the immense spaces of the prairie.

Paul Theroux, *The Old Patagonian Express*, 1979

Oklahoma City

Oklahoma City, an improvised, shanty sort of place, with its edges buried under thousands of derelict cars and mounds of scrap metal, looking as if its civilisation, like a hurriedly knitted sweater, were now unravelling.

J.B. Priestley, *Journey Down a Rainbow*, 1955
(of the view from the train)

Omaha (Nebraska)

Be it known that Omaha, notwithstanding its beautiful location, its enterprise, its George Francis Train, and its desire to become connected with St Louis by rail at the earliest possible period, yet truth compels me to say . . . that no town on the Missouri River is more annoyed, even afflicted by moving clouds of dust and sand – when the wind is up – than Omaha. It is absolutely terrific. The lower terrace along the river is a waste of fine sand, which is blown about in drifts, and banked up against the houses, like snow in a wintry storm. For two or three days people have been obliged to shut themselves up in their houses for protection from the sand. But Omaha is a wide-awake, energetic town, and is beautifully located, on the second high terrace from the river, with a cordon of hills which are mantled with country residences, among which the State capitol with its small cupola is the most conspicuous building.

H.M.Stanley, *My Early Travels and Adventures* (September 1867), 1895

Omaha, Nebraska, was but a halting-place on the road to Chicago, but it revealed to me horrors that I would not willingly have missed. The city to casual investigation seemed to be populated entirely by Germans, Poles, Slavs, Hungarians, Croats, Magyars, and all the scum of the Eastern European States, but it must have been laid out by Americans. No other people would cut the traffic of a main street with two streams of railway lines, each some eight or nine tracks wide, and cheerfully drive tram-cars across the metals. Every now and again they have horrible railway-crossing accidents at Omaha, but nobody seems to think of building an over-head bridge. That would interfere with the vested interests of the undertakers.

Rudyard Kipling, *From Sea to Sea*, 1889

Red barns and red heifers spot the green
grass circles around Omaha – the farmers
haul tanks of cream and waggon loads of cheese.

Shale hogbacks across the river at Council
Bluffs – and shanties hang by an eyelash to
the hill slants back around Omaha.

A span of steel ties up the kin of Iowa and
Nebraska across the yellow, big-hoofed Missouri
River.

Omaha, the roughneck, feeds armies,
Eats and swears from a dirty face.
Omaha works to get the world a breakfast.

Carl Sandburg, 'Omaha', in *Smoke and Steel*, 1920

Omaha is a large, cheerful, modern town. The streets are wide, and the buildings plain, solid, and of a reasonably low altitude. The people are either busy or anxious to be busy. There are no idle rich, for the simple reason that no one who was rich enough to be idle would live of his own free will in Omaha.

A.G. Macdonell, *A Visit to America*, 1935

Oregon

Oregon is seldom heard of. Its people believe in the Bible, and hold that all radicals should be lynched. It has no poets and no statesmen.

H.L. Mencken, *Americana*, 1925

The green damp England of Oregon.

Alistair Cooke, *Alistair Cooke's America*, 1973

Oregon . . . a pleasant, homogeneous, self-contained state, filled with pleasant, homogeneous, self-contained people, overwhelmingly white, Protestant, and middle class. Even the working class was middle class.

Arthur M. Schlesinger Jr, *Robert Kennedy and His Times*, 1978

The Ozarks (Missouri)

The Ozarks are the Poor White Trash citadel of America.

John Gunther, *Inside U.S.A.*, 1947

Palm Beach (Florida)

An example of what God would do if He had money.

Ronald Hastings, *Daily Telegraph*, 15 September 1977

Palm Beach looks like hell on wheels, Rolls Royce of course, where every face is lifted, and many of the jewels, where in winter they sleep in their sables, where life's a ball, a party, but don't drop dead on the dance floor – not without a photographer, because the only really dead people in Palm Beach are those whose pictures no longer appear in the two local papers.

Ibid.

Pennsylvania

Why should the *Palatine Boors* be suffered to swarm into our settlements and, by herding together, establish their Language and Manners, to the Exclusion of ours? Why should *Pennsylvania*, founded by the *English*, become a Colony of *Aliens*, who will shortly be so numerous as to Germanize us instead of our Anglifying them, and will never adopt our Language or Customs any more than they can acquire our Complexion?

Benjamin Franklin, *Observations Concerning the Increase of Mankind*, 1751

I have never felt any great regard for Pennsylvania. It has always had in my estimation a low character for commercial honesty, and a certain flavour of pretentious hypocrisy.

Anthony Trollope, *North America*, 1862

and the prairies
Pennsylvania, with its rocky gorges and woodland scenery, reminded me of Switzerland. The prairie reminded me of a piece of blotting paper.

Oscar Wilde, *Impressions of America*, Lecture, 1883

Why Pennsylvania Was Settled
Penn refused to pull his hat off

Before the king and therefore sat off
Another country to light pat on
Where he could worship with his hat on.
C.G. Bombaugh, M.A., M.D., *Gleanings for the Curious*, 1890

I have been in Pennsylvania,
In the Monongahela and the Hocking Valleys.

In the blue Susquehanna
On a Saturday morning
I saw the mounted constabulary go by,
I saw the boys playing marbles.
Spring and the hills laughed.

And in places
Along the Appalachian chain,
I saw steel arms handling coal and iron,
And I saw white cauliflower faces
Of miners' wives waiting for the men to come home
from the day's work.

I made colour studies in crimson and violet
Over the dust and domes of culm at sunset.
Carl Sandburg, 'Pennsylvania', in *Smoke and Steel*, 1920

No other State can match this (California)
for place-names rich in rhyme and rhythm.
Los Angeles Times

Out upon you, California!
Tuneful titles do adorn ya –
More than does your megalomania –
But, before you make your boast,
Upstart of our Western Coast!
Lend an ear to Pennsylvania:

Philadelphia – most colonial
Of our true Colonial Dames –
Curtsying, leads the ceremonial
March of quaint and State-ly names:
Bethlehem, Emmaus, Kingsessing,
Lititz, Darby, Conoquenessing,
Conshohocken, Tulpehocken,
King of Prussia, Shackamaxon,
Aliquippa, Lackawaxen,
Conestoga, Quakake, Trappe,
Punxsutawney, Hokendauqua,
Catawissa, Catasauqua,
Lundy's Lane, Paoli, Gap.

Now then, take another breath;
Start again with Nazareth,
Nesquehoning and Chicora,
Tomb, Two Taverns, Tuscarora,
Gipsy, Bird in Hand, Lyndora,
Add Mauch Chunk and Equinunk:
Add the urban Manajunk;
Hickory Corners, Hickory Hill,
Juniata, Phoenixville,
Gwynedd Valley, Hazlebrook,
Maxatawney, Ontelaunee,
Sabbath Rest, Glenolden, Nook,
Gold, Lycoming,
Wissinoming,
Mustard, Muse, Morganza, Muff –
Oh, but surely that's enough!

Here are place-names 'rich in rhythm' –
And they're not so poor in rhyme;
Haven't I convinced you with 'm?
No? I could if I had time.
T. A. Daly, 'Pennsylvania Places', *Late Lark Singing*, 1946

Pennsylvanians tend to take the fascinating form of clouds. If the Middle Atlantic states have a psycho-history, it is that Puritanism skipped over them on its way west.
John Updike, *Picked Up Pieces*, 1976

Peoria (Illinois)

and New England
Since a detachment of Dullards came over with the Pilgrims in the *Mayflower* and made a favourable report of the country, their increase by birth, immigration, and conversion has been rapid and steady. . . . The intellectual center of the race is somewhere about Peoria, Illinois, but the New England Dullard is the most shockingly moral.
Ambrose Bierce, *The Devil's Dictionary*, 1906 (definition of Dullard)

Will it play in Peoria?
Traditional political query about a suggested course of action, Peoria being the classically average town of middle America, quoted in 'American Diary', *The Times*, 6 October 1978

Philadelphia

But this I will say for the good Providence of God, that of all the many places I have seen in the world, I remember not one better seated; so that it seems to me to have been appointed for a town, whether we regard the rivers; or the conveniency of the coves, docks, springs; the loftiness and soundness of the land; and the air, held by the people of these parts to be very good.
William Penn, *General Description of Pennsylvania*, 1683

The question eagerly put to me by every one in Philadelphia is, 'Don't you think the city *greatly improved*?' They seem to me to confound *augmentation* with *improvement*. It always was a fine city, since I first knew it; and it is very greatly augmented.

William Cobbett, *A Year's Residence in the United States of America*, 1817–19

There is another show at Philadelphia which combines a little of the terrible: this is the practice of young boys and gentlemen, rolling hoops on the pavements. Armies of these almost grown men take possession of the sidewalks and drive the people into the open streets. It is the only city where young gentlemen roll hoops.

Mrs Anne Royall, *Mrs Royall's Pennsylvania*, 1829

I returned home to dinner, on the whole pleased with the appearance of Philadelphia. There is something solid and comfortable about it, something which shows *permanency*. Every thing looks neat, the steps are white, the entries clean, the carriages nice, the houses bright. All this betokens perhaps too nice attention to the minutiae of life, but the effect upon the eyes of strangers cannot be denied to be cheerful and inviting. I think I should like to live in Philadelphia very well. It seems to me to combine many of the essentials to mere bodily enjoyment and not a few of those of the mind. New York is all display, Baltimore is upstart, Washington is fashion and politics, Boston is unbending rigidity. I think Philadelphia has neither of these faults. Perhaps the greatest might be tameness, but that is almost equally shared with all our American Cities.

Charles Francis Adams, *Diary*, 13 November 1834

The climate of Philadelphia destroys musical instruments imported from England.

George Combe, *Notes . . . during a Phrenological Visit in 1838–40*, 1841

The first idea which strikes you when you arrive in Philadelphia, is that it is Sunday: every thing is so quiet, and there are so few people stirring: but by the time that you have paraded half a dozen streets, you come to a conclusion that it must be Saturday, as that day is, generally speaking, a washing day. Philadelphia is so admirably supplied with water from the Schuykill water-works that every house has it laid on from the attic to the basement; and all day long they wash windows, doors, marble steps, and pavements in front of the houses. Indeed they have so much water that they can afford to be very liberal to passers by.

Captain Frederick Marryat, *A Diary in America*, 1839

It is a handsome city, but distractingly regular. After walking about it for an hour or two, I felt that I would have given the world for a crooked street. The collar of my coat appeared to stiffen, and the brim of my hat to expand, beneath its quakery influence. My hair shrunk into a sleek short crop, my hands folded themselves upon my breast of their own calm accord, and thoughts of taking lodgings in Mark Lane over against the Market Place, and of making a large fortune by speculations in corn, came over me involuntarily.

Charles Dickens, *American Notes*, 1842

. . . a great, flat, overbaked brick-field. . . .

Alexander Mackay, *The Western World*, 1849

The whole place is formal, precise, and unattractive, leaving no impression upon the mind of the traveller, but that of a weary sameness and provoking rectangularity. . . .

The colour of Philadelphia – the Quaker city, the city of Brotherly Love, or, according to the disparaging assertion of New Yorkers, the city of 'brotherly love and riots,' . . . is fiery-drab wherever you turn – fiery-drab houses, fiery-drab pavements, fiery-drab chapels, and fiery-drab churches.

Charles Mackay, *Life and Liberty in America, 1857–8*, 1859

*Oh, Philadelphia? – Waterworks, – killed by the Croton and Cochituate; – Ben Franklin, – borrowed from Boston; David Rittenhouse, – made an orrery; Benjamin Rush, – made a medical system: – both interesting to antiquarians; – great Red-river raft of medical students, – spontaneous generation of professors to match; – more widely known through the Moyamensing hose-company, and the Wistar parties; – for geological section of the social strata, go to *The Club*. – Good place to live in, – first-rate market, – tip-top peaches. – What do we know about Philadelphia, except that the engine-companies are always shooting each other?

Oliver Wendell Holmes, *The Professor at the Breakfast-Table*, 1859

and New York

A right-angled parallelogramical city, such as are Philadelphia and the new portion of New York, is from its very nature odious to me. . . . I prefer a street that is forced to twist itself about.

Anthony Trollope, *North America*, 1862

When I was last there it seemed to me that it reminded me of the Byzantine Empire – without of course the latter's one redeeming quality: the aesthetic halo of crime which surrounds it in the perspective of History.

Logan Pearsall Smith, Letter to Mrs Costelloe, 2 November 1886, in John Russell, *Portrait of Logan Pearsall Smith*, 1950

My impression of the old families of Philadelphia Quakers was that they had all the effeteness of a small aristocracy. Old misers of ninety would sit brooding over their hoard while their children of sixty or seventy waited for their death with what patience they could command. Various forms of mental disorder appeared common. Those who must be accounted sane were apt to be very stupid.

Bertrand Russell, *Autobiography*, 1967 – of 1896

I liked poor dear queer flat comfortable Philadelphia almost ridiculously (for what it is – extraordinarily *cossu* and materially civilized).

Henry James, Letter to Edmund Gosse, Palm Beach, 16 February 1905

If you're off to Philadelphia in the morning,
You mustn't take my stories for a guide.
There's little left, indeed, of the city you will read of,
And all the folk I write about have died. . . .

If you're off to Philadelphia this morning,
And wish to prove the truth of what I say,
I pledge my word you'll find the pleasant land behind
Unaltered since Red Jacket rode that way.
Still the pine-woods scent the noon; still the catbird sings his tune;
Still autumn sets the maple-forest blazing;
Still the grape-vine through the dusk flings her soul-compelling musk;
Still the fire-flies in the corn make night amazing!
They are there, there, there with Earth immortal
(Citizens, I give you friendly warning).
The things that truly last when men and times have passed,
They are all in Pennsylvania this morning!

Rudyard Kipling, 'Philadelphia', *Rewards and Fairies*, 1910

Exaggeration is always the frame of American humour. For instance, the story that Philadelphia is so comfortably behind the times that a postman was said to have been shot in the streets after being mistaken for a Confederate soldier.

Shane Leslie, *American Wonderland*, 1936

Imagine Birmingham encircled with a ring of Streatham-like suburbs and set down in the middle of Surrey.

James Agate, *Ego 3*, 25 May 1937

On the whole I'd rather be in Philadelphia.

W.C.Fields, attributed reply when asked what he would like inscribed on his tombstone. Also reported as 'even this is better than playing Philadelphia.'

Only the rich remember the past,
The strawberries once in the Apennines,
Philadelphia that the spiders ate.

Wallace Stevens, *Arcades of Philadelphia the Past*, 1939

Philadelphia, a metropolis sometimes known as the City of Brotherly Love, but more accurately as the City of Bleak November Afternoons.

S.J. Perelman, *Westward Ha!*, 1948

In Boston, the saying goes, people ask, 'What do you know?' – not 'What do you do?' as in Chicago, or 'What have you got?', as in New York. In Philadelphia they ask, 'Who was your father?'

Lord Kinross, *The Innocents at Home*, 1959

*In the midst of moderation, amplitude and fecundity did the settlers found their city; . . . ease, won with ease, was the lot of Monopolis. The ironic gods now looked down on the City of Moderation and forthwith planned their jest – how to bring about excess? Here then was the jest: out of moderation's very heart excess had been created – too much moderation.

Owen Wister, from an unfinished novel, quoted Nathaniel Burt, *The Perennial Philadelphians*, 1963

Philadelphia, the home of respectability, and the city of respectable homes.

Saying, quoted Nathaniel Burt, *The Perennial Philadelphians*, 1963

Strangers . . . bring with them . . . two highly developed Philadelphia myths: for as the city lies caught between its two rivers, so the fact lies caught between its two fictions.

These two myths might be labeled the 'Dead Burg' myth and the 'Fox-hunting Aristocracy' myth; the one the idea that Philadelphia is utterly lacking in gaiety, a town of Quaker slowness and sobriety; the other that it is the citadel of an extremely frosty upper class almost wholly devoted to snobbishness and horses. Like many myths, both of these are based on solid fact.

There is no doubt, for instance, that Philadelphia has the least rewarding night life of almost any city in the world. It is an axiom that Philadelphia has 'no good restaurants,' and that its boites are lively as wet flannel, its theater spotty and secondhand. It is not Fun; it is the Salesman's Graveyard.

Nathaniel Burt, *The Perennial Philadelphians*, 1963

There used to be a time when people didn't really believe in Philadelphia, especially in the 'twenties and 'thirties and in New York. . . . When people heard stories of the kind of thing that still existed there, they didn't like it and refused to accept it. Typical was the reaction of one of the more brittle female members of New York's Algonquin group. Caught by mischance at a Philadelphia dinner party during the 'thirties, she went around muttering, 'Moss, moss on everything!'

Ibid.

Independence Hall

Independence Hall . . . provides a graceful example of

that American architectural style which might be defined as 'delayed William and Mary.'

Lord Kinross, *The Innocents at Home*, 1959

Pittsburgh

'Sir,' said the custom-house officer at Leghorn, 'your papers are forged! there is no such place in the world! Your vessel must be confiscated!' The trembling captain laid before the officer a map of the United States, – directed him to the Gulf of Mexico, – pointing out the mouth of the Mississippi, led him 1000 miles up it, to the mouth of the Ohio, – and thence another 1000 to Pittsburgh. 'There, Sir, is the port whence my vessel cleared out.' The astonished officer, before he saw the map, would as soon have believed that this ship had been navigated from the moon.

Clay's speeches, quoted in Harriet Martineau, *Retrospect of Western Travel*, 1838

Pittsburgh is like Birmingham in England; at least its townspeople say so. Setting aside the streets, the shops, the houses, waggons, factories, public buildings, and population, perhaps it may be. It certainly has a great quantity of smoke hanging about it.

Charles Dickens, *American Notes*, 1842

P S Pitsburg is a 1 horse town. A.W.

Charles Browne (Artemus Ward), in *The Cleveland Plain Dealer*, 1858

Pittsburgh is the Merthyr-Tydvil of Pennsylvania, – or perhaps I should better describe it as an amalgamation of Swansea, Merthyr-Tydvil, and South Shields. It is without exception the blackest place which I ever saw.

Anthony Trollope, *North America*, 1862

The country round Pittsburgh is full of natural gas, which you see here and there towering into the air in a clear flame through an orifice in the ground; this gas they have lately conducted to the works and made to do the work of coal; no more coal is used, and there is no smoke. As a consequence, Pittsburgh, from having been a town in the Black Country, has become a seemly place.

Matthew Arnold, Letter to Miss Arnold, 26 July 1886

Plains (Georgia)

In parts of the state removed from Carter country, it has been jokingly suggested that to expedite traffic it would make sense to have the whole of Plains packed up and moved to the Atlanta Stadium's parking lot, which is seldom full, and is much closer to the Atlanta airport than Plains is.

E.J. Kahn Jr, *The New Yorker*, 6 February 1978

South Platte River (Nebraska)

We came to the shallow, yellow, muddy South Platte with its low banks and its scattering flat sand-bars and pigmy islands – a melancholy stream straggling through the centre of the enormous flat plain, and only saved from being impossible to find with the naked eye by its sentinel rank of scattering trees standing on either bank. The Platte was 'up' they said – which made me wish I could see it when it was down, if it could look any sicker and sorrier.

Mark Twain, *Roughing It*, 1872

A mile wide, an inch deep, stand it on end and it will reach to heaven, so muddy that the catfish have to come up to sneeze.

Anon., quoted *Life*, 30 August 1943, and John Gunther, *Inside U.S.A.*, 1947

Plymouth (Massachusetts)

It was somewhere along here that the pilgrims landed at Plymouth, and began to people this part of the world: and a hard time they must have had of it in this barren country. However, I suppose it was all right. If they had had fine land, they would have had less necessity to work hard; and bring up their children to industry, and give them such cute teaching as makes them know how to make ducks and drakes out of us out yonder, when they come among us.

Davy Crockett, *Tour to the North and Down East . . . in 1834*, 1835

Plymouth is a somewhat flourishing town even at this day, but its principal pride is its historical recollections. As the place upon which a few pious conscientious men founded a State which with all it's deviations yet bears much of the primitive stamp, it will ever be memorable. To think of landing here on the 22d of December without a shelter and three thousand miles from what was once a beloved home. The idea as I stood upon the burying place which is high and overlooks the harbour made me shiver. Yet even I could do as much with a sufficient motive.

Charles Francis Adams, *Diary*, 14 September 1835

As we drew near the coast, I anxiously watched the character of the scenery, trying to view it with the eyes of the first emigrants. It must have struck a chill to their hearts; – so bare, so barren, so wintry. The firs grew more and more stunted, as we approached the sea; till, as one of my companions observed, they were ashamed to show themselves any smaller, and so turned into sand.

Harriet Martineau, *Society in America*, 1837

Plymouth Rock
The Blarney Stone of New England.

Anon. Irish orator at a public banquet, quoted by Charles Mackay, *Life and Liberty in America, 1857–8*, 1859

Portland (Maine)

Oh happy Portlanders, if they only know their own good fortune! They get up early, and go to bed early. The women are comely and sturdy, able to take care of themselves without any fal-lal of chivalry; and the men are sedate obliging, and industrious. . . . All was, or seemed to be, sleek, orderly, and unobtrusive. Probably of all modes of life that are allotted to man by his Creator, life such as this is the most happy. One hint, however for improvement I must give, even to Portland! It would be well if they could make their streets of some material harder than sand.

Anthony Trollope, *North America*, 1862

Lake Providence (Louisiana)

Mr H. . . . referred in a sort of casual way – and yet significant way – to 'the fact that the life policy in its simplest form is unknown in Lake Providence – they take out a mosquito policy besides.' He told many remarkable things about these lawless insects. Among others, said he had seen them try to *vote*. Noticing that this statement seemed to be a good deal of a strain on us, he modified it a little: said he might have been mistaken as to that particular, but knew he had seen them around the polls 'canvassing.'

Mark Twain, *Life on the Mississippi*, 1883

Reno

The biggest little city in the world.

Anon. American saying

Rhode Island (and Texas)

Texas could wear Rhode Island as a watch fob.

Pat Neff, former Governor of Texas, quoted by John Gunther, *Inside U.S.A.*, 1947

Richmond (Virginia)

Richmond, the capital of Virginia, is a small, but certainly a very pretty town, if its people would only content themselves with having it so. It is a weakness of theirs to be constantly making the largest possible draughts upon the admiration of the visitor, by extorting his assent to the fidelity of comparisons which would be amongst the very last to present themselves to his own mind. He is reminded, for instance, that the prospect which it commands is very like the view obtained from the battlements of Windsor Castle; and to those who have never been at Windsor, or who, having been there, have never seen Richmond, the comparison may certainly hold good.

Alexander Mackay, *The Western World*, 1849

It is a genial city; that is enough for me.

G.A. Sala, *America Revisited*, 1882

Richmond, a city whose tragic and pathetic history, of which one is reminded by everything that one sees there, always gets on my nerves with a particular dejection. True, the history is some fifty years old, but it is always with me when I am there, making solemn eyes at me.

Ambrose Bierce, Letter, 25 April 1912

Broad-streeted Richmond . . .
The trees in the streets are old trees used to living with
  people,
Family trees that remember your grandfather's name.

Stephen Vincent Benét, *John Brown's Body*, 1927

and Jamestown, Virginia
It is a singular fact that within a radius of 8 miles the whole saga of the British experiment in North America is encompassed, omitting Canada. Within this brief distance, across the events of one hundred and seventy-four years, the English settlers came to Jamestown in 1607 to conquer the American continent; and at Yorktown, in 1781, were driven from it, in defeat. . . . Considering the width and depth of this vast continent . . . it is a caprice of history that the first step and the last step in Britain's experiment on that vast scene should be located within some fifteen miles of each other.

Cecil Roberts, *And So to America*, 1946

Rochester (New York)

The very streets seemed to be starting up of their own accord, ready-made, and looking as fresh and new, as if they had been turned out of the workmen's hands but an hour before – or that a great boxfull of new houses had been sent by steam from New York, and tumbled out onto the half-cleared land. The canal-banks were at some places still unturfed: the lime seemed hardly dry in the masonry of the aqueduct, in the bridges, and in the numberless great saw-mills and manufactories. In many of the buildings the people were at work below stairs, while at the top the carpenters were busy nailing on the planks of the roof. . . . Several streets were nearly finished, but had not as yet received their names; and many others were in the reverse position, being named, but not commenced . . . these half-finished, whole-finished, and embryo streets were crowded with people, carts, stages, cattle, pigs, far beyond the reach of numbers . . . it occurred to us, several times, within the immediate limits of the inhabited town itself, in streets too, where the shops were opened, and all sorts of business actually going on, that we had to drive, first on one side, and then on the other, to avoid the stumps of an oak, or a hemlock, or a pine-tree, staring us full in the face . . . the same fir which might be waving about in full life and vigour in the morning, should be cut down, dragged into daylight, squared, framed, and before night be hoisted up to make a beam or rafter to some tavern or factory or store, at the corner of a street, which twenty-four hours before had existed only on paper, and yet which might be completed, from end to end within a week afterwards.

Captain Basil Hall, *Travels in North America*, 1829

Rochester is one of the most famous of the cities built on the Jack and the Bean-stalk principle. There are many splendid edifices in wood; and certainly more houses, warehouses, factories and steam-engines than ever were collected together in the same space of time; but I was told by a fellow-traveller that the stumps of the forest are still to be found firmly rooted in the cellars.

Mrs Frances Trollope, *Domestic Manners of the Americans*, 1832

Men of Rochester, I am glad to see you. I am glad to see your noble city. Gentlemen, I saw your falls, which I am told are one hundred and fifty feet high. This is a very interesting fact. Gentlemen, Rome had her Caesar, her Scipio, her Brutus, but Rome in her proudest days had never a waterfall a hundred and fifty feet high. Gentlemen, Greece had her Pericles, her Demosthenes, and her Socrates, but Greece in her palmiest days had never a waterfall a hundred and fifty feet high. *Men of Rochester, Go On!*

Daniel Webster, ascribed by Stephen Leacock, *Essays and Literary Studies*, 1919 but probably a parody of Webster's manner, by Leacock himself

Rockbridge County's Natural Bridge

The most sublime of Nature's works. . . .

If the view from the top be painful and intolerable, that from below is delightful in an equal extreme. It is impossible for the emotions arising from the sublime to be felt beyond what they are here; so beautiful an arch, so elevated, so light, and springing as it were up to heaven, the rapture of the spectator is really indescribable!

Thomas Jefferson, *Notes on Virginia*, 1782

Reply made by a gentleman of Virginia to a silly question by a lady. 'Who made the Natural Bridge?' – 'God knows, madam.'

Harriet Martineau, *Society in America*, 1837

Rocklin (California)

Rocklin is celebrated – and by certain bad people, ridiculed – all over this part of the foot-hills for the superabundance of its juvenile population. If one makes any inquisitive remarks about this fact, the Rocklinite addressed will either blush or grin, according to his temperament, and say, 'It's the glorious climate.'

Thomas Stevens, *Around the World on a Bicycle*, 1887

Rocky Mountains

The Rocky Mountains, with their grand aromatic forests, their grassy glades, their frequent springs, and dancing streams of the brightest, sweetest water, their pure, elastic atmosphere, and their unequalled game and fish, are destined to be a favourite resort and home of civilised man. I never visited a region where physical life could be more surely prolonged or fully enjoyed.

Horace Greeley, *An Overland Journey from New York to San Francisco . . . in 1859*, 1860

No, partner – if you want to see scenery see the Rockies: that's something to look at! Even the sea's afraid of them mountains, – ran away from them: you can see four thousand feet up where the sea tried to climb before it got scared!

American gold prospector in British Guiana, Remark to Lafcadio Hearn, quoted in Letter to Elizabeth Bisland, July 1887

Rome (New York)

'What place are we now approaching?' I demanded of a fellow-traveller. 'Rome,' said he. 'I live to Rome myself; it's gettin – to be quite a place.' I thought it was high time that Rome did so.

Alexander Mackay, *The Western World*, 1849

Mount Rushmore

The brow of lonely Mount Rushmore has been fashioned into the likeness of four American presidents. This is described as 'the greatest sculptural feat ever attempted by mankind.' The late Mr Gutzon Borglum used a steeplejack's cradle and a roadmender's electric drill or something like it. I could not imagine how he kept the sense of line and proportion, suspended in space and carving the mountainside with something less than a high-precision tool. Unkind falls of rock may have forced him to re-arrange the group of the four huge granite heads, six thousand feet above sea level. They have a somewhat compressed appearance and Theodore Roosevelt looks rather like a man who tries to see what goes on between the heads of Washington, Jefferson and Lincoln.

Douglas Reed, *Far and Wide*, 1951

Sacramento (California)

Sacramento is built on the banks of the river, from the encroachment of which it is as often drowned as its sister city is burnt. The houses are gaily painted, and the American flag waves in every direction; the streets are wide, and some trees that have been left standing in the town give it a cheerful appearance.

It is an American town at the first glance; an immense quantity of signboards stare at you in every direction, and if anything would induce a man to purchase 'Hay and Grain,' 'Gallego Flour,' 'Goshen Butter,' or any other article for which he has no want, it would be the astounding size of the capital letters, in which these good things are forced upon his notice.

Every other house is an hotel or boarding-house, for with few exceptions every one is put out to 'livery,' as it were in Sacramento; and in hard times, when cash is scarce, one half of the population may be said to feed the other half gratuitously, or on credit, which amounts to the same thing, thus affording a beautiful illustration of mutual support and confidence.

Sacramento is terribly dusty; the great traffic to and from the mines grinds three or four inches of the top soil into a red powder, that distributes itself everywhere; it is the dirtiest dust I ever saw, and is never visited by a shower until the rainy season sets in, and suddenly converts it into a thick mud.

Frank Marryat, *Mountains and Molehills*, 1855

St Augustine (Florida)

I am stopping for two or three days at the 'oldest city in America' – two or three being none too much to sit in wonderment at the success with which it has outlived its age.

Henry James, Letter to Edmund Gosse, 18 February 1905

St Louis (Missouri)

In point of heat St Louis certainly approaches the nearest to the Black Hole of Calcutta of any city that I have sojourned in. . . . The flies, on a moderate calculation, are in many parts fifty to the square inch. . . . I was day and night so melting away that I expected, like some of the immortal half-breeds of Jupiter, to become a tributary stream to the Mississippi.

Captain Frederick Marryat, *A Diary in America*, 1839

In the old French portion of the town, the thoroughfares are narrow and crooked, and some of the houses are very quaint and picturesque: being built of wood, with tumbledown galleries before the windows, approachable by stairs, or rather ladders from the street. There are queer little barbers' shops and drinking-houses too, in this quarter; and abundance of crazy old tenements with blinking casements, such as may be seen in Flanders. Some of these ancient habitations with high garret gable-windows perking into the roofs, have a kind of French shrug about them; and being lop-sided with age, appear to hold their heads askew, besides, as if they were grimacing in astonishment at the American improvements.

Charles Dickens, *American Notes*, 1842

It fuses northern and southern qualities, perhaps native and foreign ones, to perfection, rendezvous the whole stretch of the Mississippi and Missouri rivers, and its American electricity goes well with its German phlegm.

Walt Whitman, *Specimen Days* (1879), 1882

'Account for it? There ain't any accounting for it, except that if you send a damned fool to St Louis, and you don't tell them he's a damned fool *they'll* never find it out. There's one thing sure – if I had a damned fool I should know what to do with him: ship him to St Louis – it's the noblest market in the world for that kind of property.'

Mark Twain, quoting unidentified elderly resident of Hannibal, Missouri, *Life on the Mississippi*, 1883

The first time I ever saw St Louis, I could have bought it for six million dollars, and it was the mistake of my life that I did not do it. It was bitter now to look abroad over this domed and steepled metropolis, this solid expanse of bricks and mortar stretching away on every hand into dim, measure-defying distances, and remember that I had allowed that opportunity to go by.

Mark Twain, *Life on the Mississippi*, 1883

St Louis interests me very much; it is very dirty, certainly, and in the buildings there is the want of anything beautiful which in all the American towns depresses me, but it is an old place, and a mixed place, and it looks like both of these, and escapes the profound *Gemeinheit* of the ordinary American city thereby.

Matthew Arnold, Letter to Miss Arnold, 1 February 1884

Meet me in St. Louis, Louis,
meet me at the fair,

Don't tell me the lights are shining
any place but there;
We will dance the Hoochee Koochee,
I will be your tootsie wootsie;
If you will meet me in St. Louis, Louis,
meet me at the fair.

Andrew B. Sterling, Chorus of *Meet Me in St. Louis*, 1945

St Loüis which is called a city, but which is a foul, stinking corpse rising up from the plain like an advertisement of Albrecht Durer's 'Melancholia'. Like its twin-sister, Milwaukee, this great American city creates the impression that architecture itself has gone mad. The true morbidity of the American soul finds its outlet here. Its hideousness is not only appalling, but suffocating. The houses seem to have been decorated with rust, blood, tears, sweat, bile, rheum, and elephant dung.

Henry Miller, *The Air-conditioned Nightmare*, 1945

St Michael (Alaska)

St. Michael is now a military reservation, where even the sale of beer or claret is strictly prohibited. . . . But although the liquor law was enforced with severity ashore, its infringement afloat was openly winked at by the authorities. . . . It was even whispered that 'Hootch' (a fiery poison akin to 'Tanglefoot') was manufactured at the barracks, and retailed by the soldiers to the natives, the very class for whose protection against temptation the prohibitive law was framed.

'All my men are intoxicated,' the Commandant at St. Michael was said to have exclaimed. 'So I suppose I had better get drunk myself.'

Harry de Windt, *From Paris to New York by Land*, 1904

St Paul (Minnesota)

St. Paul is a wonderful town. It is put together in solid blocks of honest brick and stone, and has the air of intending to stay. Its post-office was established thirty-six years ago; and by and by, when the postmaster received a letter, he carried it to Washington, horseback, to inquire what was to be done with it. Such is the legend. . . .

Mark Twain, *Life on the Mississippi*, 1883

Salt Lake City (Utah)

This is the place.

Brigham Young, 2 July 1847

Salt Lake City was healthy – an extremely healthy city. They declared there was only one physician in the place and he was arrested every week regularly and held to answer under the vagrant act for having 'no visible means of support.'

Mark Twain, *Roughing It*, 1872

Salt Lake City . . . is as plain-sailing, downright, straightforward, unpoetical and ugly a place as any other 'Gentile' American town of from twenty-five thousand to thirty thousand inhabitants.

G.A. Sala, *America Revisited*, 1882

On polygamy Oscar grew epigrammatic, saying that while Salt Lake City's 'execrable architecture' was bad enough, the place robbed life of romance – 'for the romance of life is that one can love so many people and marry but one.'

Lloyd Lewis and Henry Justin Smith, *Oscar Wilde Discovers America*, 1936

The Tabernacle

The Tabernacle is in the shape of a soup-kitchen.

Oscar Wilde, *Impressions of America* Lecture, 1883.

The Tabernacle . . . is rather like a whale; indeed very much like a whale. The roof looks just like a whale stranded.

John Foster Fraser, *Round the World on a Wheel*, 1899

This remarkable Tabernacle . . . looks like an immense black mushroom – Brigham Young is said to have got the idea from his umbrella.

Crosbie Garstin, *The Dragon and the Lotus*, 1928

Mormon women

I was touched. My heart was wiser than my head. I warmed towards these poor, ungainly, and pathetically homely creatures, and as I turned to hide the generous moisture in my eyes, I said, 'No – the man that marries one of them has done an act of Christian charity which entitles him to the kindly applause of mankind, not their harsh censure – and the man that marries sixty of them has done a deed of open-handed generosity so sublime that the nations should stand uncovered in his presence, and worship in silence.'

Mark Twain, *Roughing It*, 1872

Great Salt Lake (Utah)

That inland briny sea, which apparently has no business there.

Richard Burton, *The City of the Saints*, 1861

I had heard strange accounts of its buoyancy. It was said to support a bather as if he were sitting in an arm-chair, and to float him like an unfresh egg. My experience differs in this point from that of others. There was no difficulty in swimming nor indeed in sinking. After sundry immersions of the head, in order to feel if it really stang and removed the skin, like a mustard plaster, – as described – emboldened by the detection of so much hyperbole, I proceeded to duck under with open eyes, and smarted 'for my pains.' The sensation did not come on suddenly; at first there was a sneaking twinge, then a bold succession of twinges, and lastly a steady honest burning like what follows a pinch of snuff in the eyes. There was no fresh water at hand, so scrambling upon the rock I sat there for half an hour, presenting to Nature the ludicrous spectacle of a man weeping flowing tears.

Ibid.

And 'Have faith,' said the commercial traveller as he walked into water heavy as quicksilver. 'Walk!' I walked, and I walked till my legs flew up and I had to walk as one struggling with a high wind, but still I rode head and shoulders above the water. It was a horrible feeling, this inability to sink. Swimming was not much use. You couldn't get a grip of water, so I e'en sat me down and drifted like a luxurious anemone among the hundreds that were bathing in that place. You could wallow for three-quarters of an hour in that warm sticky brine and fear no evil consequences; but when you came out you were coated with white salt from top to toe. And if you accidentally swallowed a mouthful of the water, you died. This is true, because I swallowed half a mouthful and was half-dead in consequence.

Rudyard Kipling, *From Sea to Sea*, 1889

The largest inland body of salt water in the world, of no use, even for suicide.

Cecil Roberts, *And So to America*, 1946

San Antonio (Texas)

In the day San Antonio is more Mexican than American, not quite genuine Mexican (it is far too clean for that) but picture postcard Mexican. . . . The San Antonio river is wound cunningly through the town like a pattern on a Valentine (does it make a heart?) with little waterfalls and ferny banks. . . . you have the sensation in San Antonio by day of the world being deliciously excluded.

Graham Greene, *The Lawless Roads*, 1939

San Francisco

The appearance of San Francisco at night, from the water, is unlike anything I ever beheld. The houses are mostly of canvas, which is made transparent by the lamps within, and transforms them, in the darkness, to dwellings of solid light. Seated on the slopes of its three hills, the tents pitched among the chaparral to the very summits, it gleams like an amphitheatre of fire. Here and there shine out brilliant points, from the decoy-lamps of the gaming-houses; and through the indistinct murmur of the streets comes by fits the sound of music from their hot and crowded precincts. The picture has in it something unreal and fantastic; it impresses one like the cities of the magic lantern, which a moving of the hand can build or annihilate.

Bayard Taylor, *Eldorado, or Adventures in the Path of Empire*, 1850 of September 1849

When I had climbed the last sand-hill, riding in towards San Francisco, and the town and harbour and crowded shipping again opened to the view, I could scarcely realize the change that had taken place during my absence of three weeks. The town had not only greatly extended its limits, but seemed actually to have doubled its number of dwellings since I left. High up on the hills, where I had seen only sand and chaparral, stood clusters of houses; streets which had been merely laid out, were hemmed in with buildings and thronged with people; new warehouses had sprung up on the water side, and new piers were creeping out toward the shipping; the forest of masts had greatly thickened; and the noise, motion, and bustle of business and labour on all sides were incessant. Verily, the place was in itself a marvel. To say that it was daily enlarged by from twenty to thirty houses may not sound very remarkable after all the stories that have been told; yet this, for a country which imported both lumber and houses, and where labor was then $10 a day, is an extraordinary growth. The rapidity with which a ready-made house is put up and inhabited, strikes the stranger in San Francisco as little short of magic. He walks over an open-lot in his before-breakfast stroll – the next morning, a house complete, with a family inside, blocks up his way. He goes down to the bay and looks out on the shipping – two or three days afterward a row of storehouses, staring him in the face, intercepts the view.

Ibid.

I went on deck, in the misty daybreak, to take a parting look at the town and its amphitheatric hills. As I turned my face shorewards, a little spark appeared through the fog. Suddenly it shot up into a spiry flame, and at the same instant I heard the sound of gongs, bells and trumpets, and the shouting of human voices. The calamity, predicted and dreaded so long in advance, that men ceased to think of it, had come at last – San Francisco was on fire! The blaze increased with fearful rapidity. In fifteen minutes, it had risen into a broad, flickering column, making all the shore, the misty air and the water ruddy as with another sunrise. The sides of new frame houses, scattered through the town, tents high up on the hills, and the hulls and listless sails of vessels in the bay, gleamed and sparkled in the thick atmosphere. Meanwhile the roar and tumult swelled, and above the clang of gongs and the cries of the populace, I could hear the crackling of blazing timbers, and the smothered sound of falling roofs. I climbed into the rigging and watched the progress of the conflagration. As the flames leaped upon a new dwelling, there was a sudden whirl of their waving volumes – an embracing of the frail walls in their relentless clasp – and, a second afterwards, from roof and rafter and foundation-beam shot upwards a jet of fire, steady and intense at first, but surging off into spiral folds and streamers, as the timbers were parted and fell.

Ibid. – of late 1849

We have arrived at the moment of the great June Fire of 1850, and San Francisco is again in ashes! . . . although four hundred houses have been destroyed, they were but of wood or thin sheet iron, and the 'devouring element' has made a clean sweep of everything, except a few brick chimneys and iron pots. Everybody seems to be in good humour . . . so soon as the embers cool, the work of rebuilding will commence.

I found it amusing the next day to walk over the ground and observe the effects of the intense heat on the articles which were strewed around. Gun-barrels were twisted and knotted like snakes; there were tons of nails welded together by the heat, standing in the shape of the kegs which had contained them; small lakes of molten glass of all the colours of the rainbow; tools of all descriptions from which the wood-work had disappeared, and pitch-pots filled with melted lead and glass. Here was an iron house that had collapsed with the heat, and even an iron fire-proof safe that had burst under the same influence; spoons, knives, forks and crockery were melted up together in heaps; crucibles even had cracked; preserved meats had been unable to stand this second cooking, and had exploded in every direction. The loss was very great by this fire, as the houses destroyed had been for the most part filled with merchandise; but there was little time wasted in lamentation, the energy of the people showed itself at once in action, and in forty-eight hours after the fire the whole district resounded to the din of busy workmen.

Frank Marryat, *Mountains and Molehills*, 1855

On entering one of these saloons the eye is dazzled almost by the brilliancy of chandeliers and mirrors. The roof, rich with gilt-work, is supported by pillars of glass; and the walls are hung with French paintings of great merit, but of which female nudity forms alone the subject. The crowds of Mexicans, Miners, Niggers, and Irish bricklayers through which with difficulty you force a way, look dirtier (although there is no need of this) from contrast with the brilliant decorations. . . . Amidst all the din and turmoil of the crowd, and the noisy music that issues from every corner, two or three reports of a pistol will occasionally startle the stranger, particularly if they should happen to be in his immediate vicinity, and a bullet should (as is not uncommon) whistle past his head and crack the mirror on the other side of him. There is a general row for a few moments, spectators secure themselves behind pillars and under the bar; there is a general exclamation of 'don't shoot,' which means of course 'don't shoot till we get out of the way;' but after the first discharges the excitement settles down, and the suspended games are resumed. A wounded man is carried out, but whether it is a 'monte' dealer who has shot a player, or one gentleman who has drawn on another gentleman in the heat of altercation, one does not learn that night, but it will appear in the morning paper; if the former it will be headed '*Murderous affray*,' if the latter, 'Unfortunate *difficulty*.' There are different names for the same thing even in a democratic colony.

Ibid.

Serene, indifferent of Fate
Thou sittest at the Western Gate

Upon thy heights so lately won
Still slant the banners of the sun;

Thou seest the white seas strike their tents
O Warder of two Continents! . . .

Thou drawest all things, small or great
To thee beside the Western gate.

O Lion's whelp, that hidest fast
In jungle growth of spire and mast

I know thy cunning and thy greed
Thy hard high lust and wilful deed,

And all thy glory loves to tell
Of specious gifts material

Drop down, O fleecy Fog and hide
Her sceptic sneer, and all her pride!

Bret Harte, *San Francisco from the Sea*, *c.* 1860

Many of the citizens of San Francisco remember the Sabbath-day to keep it jolly.

Charles F. Browne, *Artemus Ward (His Travels) Among the Mormons* (1863), 1865

'Everybody turns up here. They're bound to do it.'

Old acquaintance to G.A. Sala, *America Revisited*, 1882

Choose a place on one of the huge throbbing ferry-boats, and when you are midway between the city and the suburb, look around. The air is fresh and salt, as if you were at sea. On the one hand is Oakland, gleaming white among its gardens. On the other, to seaward, hill after hill is crowded and crowned with the palaces of San Francisco; its long streets lie in regular bars of darkness, east and west, across the sparkling picture; a forest of masts bristles like bulrushes about its feet. . . . What enchantment of the Arabian Nights can equal this evocation of a roaring city, in a few years of a man's life, from the marshes and the blowing sand. Such swiftness of increase, as with an overgrown youth, suggests a corresponding swiftness of destruction. . . . Next, perhaps, in order of strangeness to the rapidity of its appearance is the mingling of the races that combine to people it. The town is essentially not Anglo-Saxon; still more essentially not American. The Yankee and the Englishman find themselves alike in a strange country. There are none of those touches – not of nature, and I dare scarcely say of art, – by which the Anglo-Saxon feels himself at home in so great a diversity of lands. Here, on the contrary, are airs of Marseilles and of Pekin. The shops along the streets are like the consulates of different nations. The passers-by vary in features like the slides of a magic lantern.

Robert Louis Stevenson, *San Francisco*, 1883

San Francisco is a really beautiful city. China town, peopled by Chinese labourers is the most artistic town I have ever come across. The people, – strange melancholy Orientals, whom many people would call common, and they are certainly very poor – have determined that they will have nothing about them that is not beautiful. In the Chinese restaurant, where these navvies meet to have supper in the evening, I found them drinking tea out of china cups as delicate as the petals of a rose-leaf, whereas at the gaudy hotels I was supplied with a delf cup an inch and a half thick. When the Chinese bill was presented it was made out on rice paper, the account being done in Indian ink as fantastically as if an artist had been etching little birds on a fan.

Oscar Wilde, *Impressions of America*, Lecture, 1883

San Francisco is a mad city – inhabited for the most part by perfectly insane people whose women are of remarkable beauty.

Rudyard Kipling, *From Sea to Sea*, 1889

*I suppose in about a fortnight we shall be told that he has been seen in San Francisco. It is an odd thing, but everyone who disappears is said to be seen at San Francisco. It must be a delightful city, and possess all the attractions of the next world.

Oscar Wilde, *The Picture of Dorian Gray*, 1891

I'd never set foot in San Francisco. Of all the Sodoms and Gomorrahs in our modern world, it is the worst. There are not ten righteous (and courageous) men there. It needs another quake, another whiff of fire – and – more than all else – a steady trade wind of grapeshot. . . . That moral penal colony of the world.

Ambrose Bierce, Letter 25 June 1907

San Francisco is essentially a night city, and, next to Paris, I should say it was the gayest night city in the world. . . . The microbe of gaiety . . . is in the air of the place.

Maurice Baring, *Round the World in Any Number of Days*, 1913

As for Frisco itself, it looked hopeless. Hundreds of tons of the wreckage had been cleared away, but hundreds of tons still remained. Some few buildings had already been erected. Most of them were stores, little wooden affairs, knocked together until better could be built. The fire and quake had ruined the pavements, and the streets were nothing but great pools of water and mud. A man was actually drowned in one of these pools while walking down Market Street. There were constant deaths by accidents; walls, frail and fissured, had a trick of collapsing and letting down their bushels of brick and stone on the heads of such as were in the streets; the street-car service was badly muddled, and several persons were killed while riding the precarious conveyances. . . . wages were sky-high; yet workmen still complained and struck for more. At the time I was there, the bricklayers, who were getting ten dollars a day, struck for twelve dollars and a half.

Martin Johnson, *Through the South Seas with Jack London*, 1913

Not by the earthquake daunted
Nor by new fears made tame,
Painting her face and laughing
Plays she a new-found game.
Here on her half-cool cinders
'Frisco abides in mirth,
Planning the wildest splendor
Ever upon the earth. . . .

God loves this rebel city,
Loves foemen brisk and game,
Tho', just to please the angels.
He may send down his flame.
God loves the golden leopard
Tho' he may spoil her lair,
God smites, yet loves, the lion.
God makes the panther fair.

Dance then wild guests of 'Frisco,
Yellow, bronze, white and red!
Dance by the golden gateway –
Dance tho' he smite you dead!

Vanchel Lindsay, 'The City that will not Repent', *Collected Poems*, 1923

The first thing that strikes the stranger in San Francisco is that it is built not upon fourteen hills but upon about ten thousand ladders.

A.G. Macdonell, *A Visit to America*, 1935

'The greatness of Rome is somehow associated – whether correctly or not – with the fact that it was built on seven hills. How much greater, then, should San Francisco be, standing on fourteen hills?' ... The answer, so it seemed to me, surely must be 'Twice.'

American Railroad Guide, with comments by A.G. Macdonell, *A Visit to America*, 1935

San Francisco is a city of charming people and hideous buildings, mostly erected after the earthquake in the style of 1910, with a large Chinatown in which everything is fake – except the Chinese – with a tricky humid climate (though sunny in winter), and a maddening indecision in the vegetation – which can never decide if it belongs to the North or the South and achieves a Bournemouth compromise.... Yet San Francisco and its surroundings ... probably represent the most attractive all-the-year-round alternative to Europe which the world can provide.

Cyril Connolly, 'American Injection', 1947, in *Ideas and Places*, 1953

*' ... I been down and out myself. In Frisco. Nobody picked me up in no taxi either. There's one stony-hearted town.'
'San Francisco,' I said mechanically.
'I call it Frisco,' he said. 'The hell with them minority groups ... '

Raymond Chandler, *The Long Goodbye*, 1953

San Francisco is perhaps the most European of all American cities.

Cecil Beaton, *It Gives Me Great Pleasure*, 1955

A city on hills has it over flat-land places. New York makes its own hills with craning buildings, but this gold and white acropolis rising wave on wave against the blue of the Pacific sky was a stunning thing, a painted thing, like a picture of a mediaeval Italian city which can never have existed.... Over the green higher hills to the south, the evening fog rolled like herds of sheep coming to cote in the golden city.

John Steinbeck, *Travels with Charley*, 1962

from Yerba Buena Island
When you emerge from the tunnel you are confronted with an unobstructed view of San Francisco.... and my first reaction was one of dismay. I did not want San Francisco to look like that, a cross between Manhattan and Chicago.

Ethel Mannin, *An American Journey*, 1967

In San Francisco, Broadway is 'the strip,' a combination of Macdougal Street in Greenwich Village and strip row on 'East Bal'more' in Baltimore. It is about four blocks long, an agreeably goofy row of skin-show nightclubs, boho caves, saturated in black paint, with names like 'Mother's', featuring light-projection shows, monologuists, *intime* jazz shows with brooding Negroes on the bass, and 'colourful' bars with names like Burp Hollow. There is one tree on Broadway. It is about three inches in diameter, about 12 feet tall, and has 342 minute leaves on it and a tin anti-urine sleeve around the bottom.

Tom Wolfe, 'The Put-Together Girl', in *The Pump House Gang*, 1968

When you get tired of walking around San Francisco, you can always lean against it.

Transworld Getaway Guide, *San Francisco*, 1975–6

San Francisco is beautiful in the way a young girl in an absolutely crazy miniskirt is beautiful.

Ibid.

Few cities create such a wake of expectation as San Francisco. You get the impression that if the place were chosen as the setting for the Second Coming the citizens would be pleased but not surprised.

Edward Mace, 'Far out in the West', *Observer*, 11 June 1978

Santa Monica

..., The most characteristic Santa Monica effect, that air of dispirited abandon which suggests that the place survives only as illustration of a boom gone bankrupt, evidence of some irreversible flaw in the laissez-faire small-business ethic.

Joan Didion, *The White Album*, 1979

Saranac Lake (Adirondack Mountains, New York)

A bleak, blackguard, beggarly climate, of which I can say no good, except that it suits me and some others of the same or similar persuasions whom (by all rights) it ought to kill. It is a form of Arctic St Andrews, I should imagine; and the miseries of forty degrees below zero, with a high wind, have to be felt to be appreciated. The greyness of the heavens here is a circumstance eminently revolting to the soul; I have near forgot the aspect of the sun.

Robert Louis Stevenson, Letter to Miss Ferrier, April 1888

Saratoga (New York)

It is a very ugly situation in a sandy soil and covering with dust all the men and horses.... What the devil is the use of going to such a spot for pleasure, when our country affords so many beautiful spots where you are not constantly surrounded by stumps of trees and hillocks of sand, without verdure and with incessant monotony. I think in this wide country, not a quarter of which I have seen however, no uglier place could have been pitched upon as the scene of dashing high life for two months out of the twelve.

Charles Francis Adams, *Diary*, 9 August 1826

You make acquaintances there whom you do not necessarily know, or who do not know you elsewhere.

Alexander Mackay, *The Western World*, 1849

'An Lor lub yer, . . . Saratoga's dreffel for gentility, *and gemblemens can get drinks all day Sunday*.'

Anon. waiter, quoted in G.A. Sala, *My Diary in America in the Midst of War*, 1865

I glanced gloomily forth from either side of the barouche, to see if Saratoga looked anything like a watering-place. To my mind it didn't; it had more the appearance of Jersey City, gone a short way out of town – say to Peckham-Rye – and much overtaken by dust.

G.A. Sala, *My Diary in America in the Midst of War*, 1865

As they sit with their white hats tilted forward, and their chairs tilted back, and their feet tilted up, and their cigars and toothpicks forming various angles with these various lines, I seem to see in their faces a tacit reference to the affairs of the continent. They are obviously persons of experience – of a somewhat narrow and monotonous experience, certainly; an experience of which the diamonds and laces which their wives are exhibiting hard by are, perhaps, the most substantial and beautiful result; but, at any rate, they have *lived*, in every fibre of the will. . . . They are hard nuts, which have grown and ripened as they could. When they talk among themselves, I seem to hear the cracking of the shells.

If the men are remarkable, the ladies are wonderful. Saratoga is famous, I believe, as the place of all places in America, where women adorn themselves most, or as the place, at least, where the greatest amount of dressing may be seen by the greatest number of people. Your first impression is therefore of the – what shall I call it? – of the abundance of petticoats. Every woman you meet, young and old, is attired with a certain amount of richness, and whatever good taste may be compatible with such a mode of life. You behold an interesting, and indeed a quite momentous spectacle; the democratisation of elegance.

Henry James, 'Saratoga', 1870 in *Portraits of Places*, 1883

Savannah (Georgia)

I chose the situation for the town upon an high ground, forty feet perpendicular above high-water mark; the soil dry and sandy, the water of the river fresh, and springs coming out of the side of the hill. I pitched upon this place, not only for the pleasantness of the situation, but because, from the above-mentioned and other signs, I thought it healthy; for it is sheltered from the western and southern winds by vast woods of pine-trees, many of which are an hundred and few under seventy feet high. An Indian nation who knew the nature of this country chose the same spot for its healthiness.

James Edward Oglethorpe, Letter, 20 February 1733

It stands upon a terrace about forty feet higher than the river and presents the appearance of an agglomeration of rural hamlets and small towns. If four-and-twenty villages had resolved to hold a meeting, and had assembled at this place, each with its pump, its country church, its common, and its avenue of trees, the result would have been a facsimile of Savannah.

Charley Mackay, *Life and Liberty in America, 1857–8*, 1859

Savannah is a living tomb about which there still clings a sensuous aura as in old Corinth.

Henry Miller, *The Air-conditioned Nightmare*, 1945

Schenectady (New York)

Schenectady! There are throughout the North five hundred Schenectadys feeding like one. A broad, dusty main thoroughfare, bordered with trees and irregularly paved. No three houses of the same size together; but the same types of many-windowed factory, tumble-down shanty, shingle villa whitewashed, and packing-case-looking shop of dun brick, repeated over and over again *ad nauseam*. To the whitewashed shingle villas green venetians. No knockers to the doors; but bell-pulls, and name-plates, electro-silvered. At some gates, a ragged, dirty negress, dully babbling with an Irish help – not ragged she, but dirtier. High steps, or 'stoops' to the private houses, and towards evening the entire family sitting, standing, or lounging thereupon: the father, spectacles on nose, reading the local newspaper, in which there is nothing to read save advertisements, eight lines of telegraphic despatches, mostly apocryphal, and sixteen lines of editorial, setting forth how the local's contemporary – if it have one – is a liar and scoundrel, and that it's brother-in-law suffered two years in the penitentiary for stealing a horse; the young ladies, in grand evening toilette, staring other young ladies who may happen to pass, out of countenance; mamma, grandmamma, and two or three maiden aunts, or acidulated cousins, knitting socks for the sanitary Commission; and the younger branches of the family yelling over contested candy, beating upon drums, or – if any of them are girls, and above six years old, fanning themselves and twirling their skirts in imitation of their elders. I dare say were you rude enough to peep through the window at the table laid out for supper, you would find there was Pie. To this, add the jangling of half-a-dozen pianofortes, and the familiar strains of the waltz from *Faust.*

G.A. Sala, *My Diary in America in the Midst of War,* 1865

Seattle (Washington)

Its streets are so steep, like those of San Francisco, that you practically need spikes in your shoes, and its politics are almost as spectacular as the scenery.

John Gunther, *Inside U.S.A.*, 1947

Seattle is a comparatively new-looking city that covers an old frontier town like frosting on a cake.

Winthrop Sargeant, in *New Yorker*, 26 June 1978

'The South'

The South, the poor South!

John C. Calhoun, last words, 1850

Dis world was made in jis' six days,
An' finished up in various ways.
Look away! look away! look away! Dixie land!
Dey den made Dixie trim and nice,
And Adam called it 'Paradise'.
Look away! look away! look away! Dixie land! . . .
Den I wish I was in Dixie! Hooray! Hooray!
In Dixie land, I'll take my stand,
And lib and die in Dixie,
Away, away,
Away down south in Dixie.

Daniel Decatur Emmet, *I Wish I Was in Dixie's Land,* 1859

A southerner talks music.

Mark Twain, *Life on the Mississippi*, 1883

'Everything is changed down here since the war, for better or for worse; but you'll find people down here born grumblers, who see no change except the change for the worse. There was an old negro woman of this sort. A young New Yorker said in her presence, 'What a wonderful moon you have down here!' She sighed and said, 'Ah, bless yo' heart, honey, you ought to seen dat moon befo' de waw!''

Ibid. (quoting unidentified speaker)

In the South, the war is what A.D. is elsewhere: they date from it.

Ibid.

Alas! for the South, her books have grown fewer –
She never was much given to literature.

J. Gordon Coogler, 'Alas! for the South!', *Purely Original Verse*, 1897

Down there a poet is now almost as rare as an oboe-player, a dry-point etcher, or a metaphysician. It is, indeed, amazing to contemplate so vast a vacuity. . . . Nearly the whole of Europe could be lost in that stupendous region of fat farms, shoddy cities, and paralyzed cerebrums: one could throw in France, Germany and Italy and still have room for the British Isles. And yet, for all its size and all its wealth, and all the 'progress' it babbles of, it is almost as sterile, artistically, intellectually, culturally, as the Sahara Desert. There are single acres in Europe that house more first-rate men than all the states south of the Potomac; there are probably single square miles in America.

H.L. Mencken, 'The Sahara of the Bozart', in *Prejudices*, Second Series, 1921

The old South was ploughed under. But the ashes are still warm.

Henry Miller, *The Air-conditioned Nightmare*, 1945

We Southerners are of course a mythological people.

Jonathan Daniels, *A Southerner Discovers the South,* 1943

The blacks are the weak and the flexible backbone of this decapitated region of America.

Henry Miller, *The Air-conditioned Nightmare*, 1945

The South has preaching and shouting, the South has grits, the South has country songs, old mimosa traditions, clay dust, Old Bigots, New Liberals – and all of it, all of that old mental cholesterol, is confined to the Sunday radio.

Tom Wolfe, *The Kandy-Colored Tangerine-Flake Streamline Baby*, 1965

Southerners say that their speech is so measured that before a southern girl can explain that she won't, she already has.

Trevor Fishlock, *Americans and Nothing Else*, 1980

Springfield (Illinois)

In this, the City of my Discontent,
Sometimes there comes a whisper from the grass,
'Romance, Romance – is here. No Hindu town
Is quite so strange. No Citadel of Brass
By Sinbad found, held half such love and hate;
No picture-palace in a picture-book
Such webs of Friendship, Beauty, Greed and Fate!'
In this, the City of my Discontent,

Down from the sky, up from the smoking deep
Wild legends new and old burn round my bed
While trees and grass and men are wrapped in sleep.
Angels come down, with Christmas in their hearts,
Gentle, whimsical, laughing, heaven-sent;
And, for a day, fair Peace have given me
In this the City of my Discontent!

Vachel Lindsay, 'Springfield Magical', *Collected Poems*, 1923

Staten Island (and surroundings)

We were lying off Staten Island, a beautiful *orné* landscape with spires, villas, hills, and woods. 'Just like Richmond,' I said to some one by me, 'and not a single Mohican running about!' This precious speech has got into the newspapers here.

Matthew Arnold, Letter to Miss Arnold, October 1883

Stockton (California)

Stockton has no miners any more, and no celebrity, except as being the place where the State insane asylum is located. But that celebrity is broad and well established; so much so, that when one is in California and tells a person he thinks of going to Stockton, the remark must be explained, or an awkward report may get out.

Mark Twain, 'California Experience', *Choice Humorous Works of Mark Twain*, 1877

Swanee River

Way down upon de Swanee ribber,
Far, far away,
Dere's wha' my heart is turning ebber,
Dere's wha' de old folks stay.

Stephen Collins Foster, *Old Folks at Home*, 1851

Syracuse (New York)

At five o'clock we arrived at Syracuse. I do detest these old names vamped up. Why do not the Americans take the Indian names? They need not be so very scrupulous about it; they have robbed the Indians of Everything else.

Captain Frederick Marryat, *A Diary of America*, 1839

Tahoe Lake (California/Nevada)

People say that Tahoe means 'Silver Lake' – 'Limpid Water' – 'Falling Leaf' – Bosh. It means grasshopper soup, the favourite dish of the Digger tribe – and of the Pi-utes as well.

Mark Twain, *The Innocents Abroad*, 1869

Taos (New Mexico)

There it is then, the pueblo, as it has been since heaven knows when. And the slow dark weaving of the Indian life going on still, though perhaps more waveringly. And oneself, sitting there on a pony, a far-off stranger, with gulfs of time between me and this. And yet, the old nodality of the pueblo still holding, like a dark ganglion, spinning invisible threads of consciousness. A sense of dryness, almost a weariness about the pueblo. And a sense of the inalterable. It brings a sort of sick feeling over me, always, to get into the Indian vibration. Like breathing chlorine.

D.H. Lawrence, 'Taos', *The Dial*, March 1923; *Phoenix*, 1936

Tennessee

Our Country, south and west of Hatteras
Abounds in charming feminine flatteras.
Sweet talk is scant by Lake Cayuga,
But in Tennessee, they chatta nougat.

Ogden Nash 'Is it True what they say about Dixie, or Is it Just the Way they say it?' in *The Private Dining Room*, 1952

Texas

The province of Techas will be the richest state of our Union without any exception.

Thomas Jefferson, Letter to James Monroe, 15 May 1820

The state of Texas is part of Mexico and is on the frontier between that country and the United States. In the course of the last few years the Anglo-Americans have penetrated into this province, which is still thinly peopled; they purchase land, they produce the commodities of the country, and supplant the original population. It may easily be foreseen that if Mexico takes no steps to check this change, the province of Texas will very shortly cease to belong to that government.

Alexis de Tocqueville, *Democracy in America*, 1835

If I owned Texas and Hell, I would rent out Texas and live in Hell.

General Philip P. Sheridan, spoken at Officers' Mess at Fort Clark, Texas, in 1855

We saw the land lying idle; we took it. This to other

nations is all that we can say. Which one of them can cast the first stone? . . . Since an English plough first broke the virgin sward of the sea-slope of Virginia, Saxons have not entered upon so magnificent a domain. . . . Texas has an arcadian preeminence of position among our States, and an opulent future before her, that only wanton mismanagement can forfeit.

Frederick Law Olmsted, *A Journey through Texas*, 1857

'G.T.T.,' (gone to Texas), was the slang appendage, within the reader's recollection, to every man's name who had disappeared before the discovery of some rascality. Did a man emigrate thither, everyone was on the watch for the discreditable reason to turn up.

Ibid.

Other states were carved or born,
Texas grew from hide to horn.

Berta Hart Nance, *c.* 1930

Texas seemed to be half Mexico already – and half Will Rogers.

Graham Greene, *The Lawless Roads*, 1939

I like the story, doubtless antique, that I heard near San Antonio. A child asks a stranger where he comes from, whereupon his father rebukes him gently, 'Never do that son. If a man's from Texas, he'll tell you. If he's not, why embarrass him by asking?'

John Gunther, *Inside U.S.A.*, 1947

Texas reminded me a good deal of Argentina. . . . The similarities are, indeed, extraordinary: cattle culture, absentee ownership, vast land holdings by semifeudal barons, a great preoccupation with weather, an underdeveloped middle class, interminable flatness and open spaces, and fierce political partisanship and nationalism.

Ibid.

Here was a society dominated entirely by the masculine principle. Why were so many of these women at once so arch and so anxious? There was nothing wrong with them as women. Superficially, everything seemed blazingly right with them. But even here in these circles, where millionaires apparently indulged and spoilt them, giving them without question or stint what women elsewhere were for ever wistfully hoping for, they were haunted by a feeling of inferiority, resented, but never properly examined and challenged. They lived in a world so contemptuous and destructive of real feminine values that they had to be heavily bribed to remain in it. All those shops, like the famous Neiman-Marcus store (a remarkable creation) here in Dallas, were part of the bribe. They were still girls in a mining camp. And to increase their bewilderment, perhaps their despair, they are told they are living in a matriarchy.

J.B. Priestley, *Journey Down a Rainbow*, 1955

Texas, in the eyes of its inhabitants and in maps supplied to visitors, occupies all of the North American continent but a fraction set aside for the United States, Canada, and Mexico.

Lord Kinross, *The Innocents at Home*, 1959

Once you are in Texas it seems to take forever to get out, and some people never make it. . . .

Writers facing the problem of Texas find themselves floundering in generalities, and I am no exception. Texas is a state of mind, Texas is an obsession. Above all, Texas is a nation in every sense of the word. And there's an opening covey of generalities. A Texan outside of Texas is a foreigner. My wife refers to herself as the Texan that got away. . . . Texas is the only state that came into the Union by treaty. It retains the right to secede at will. We have heard them threaten to secede so often that I formed an enthusiastic organization – The American Friends for Texas Secession. This stops the subject cold. They want to be able to secede but they don't want anyone to want them to.

Like most passionate nations, Texas has its own private history based on, but not limited by, facts. The tradition of the tough and versatile frontiersman is true but not exclusive. It is for the few to know that in the great old days of Virginia there were three punishments for high crimes – death, exile to Texas, and imprisonment, in that order. And some of the deportees must have descendants.

John Steinbeck, *Travels with Charley*, 1962

They're really concerned with 'bawls' – they got ninety-year-old men biting rattle-snakes' heads off!

Lenny Bruce, 'The Jews', before 1966, in *The Essential Lenny Bruce*, 1973

Troy (New York)

Troy, like a modern academy, is classical, as well as commercial, having Mount Olympus on one side, and Mount Ida in its rear.

Captain Frederick Marryat, *A Diary of America*, 1839

Tucson (Arizona)

Tucson we found to be a sleepy old town, of a thousand or so inhabitants, that appeared to be trying its best to take things easy, and succeeds in doing so. . . . It is reputed to be some two hundred years old, and its appearance certainly justifies its reputation.

James F. Rusling, *Across America*, 1874 – of 1866

As likeable a little city as you will find in a desert. . . . It is white, bright, and lively, full of big hotels, banks, fine shops, pleasant homes. Its roof-line is low, which gives blessed relief in America; a man's head is in the air, and instead of canyonesque cliffs, it has the wide desert sky for roof and dark distant mountains for background. In the lemon-coloured dusk and velvet night, its myriad twinkling lights, in pink and violet and mauve and rose, take on a quality of enchantment which the same hues quite lack in the sombre abysses of Broadway or Madison street. It is a little Montmartre in the desert, with its night-clubs, open-air dancing, restaurants, filling-stations, cabin-camps, and used car lots, all strung with vari-coloured illuminations.

Douglas Reed, *Far and Wide*, 1951

Utah

Let the Mormons have the territory to themselves – it is worth very little to others.

Horace Greeley, *An Overland Journey From New York to San Francisco . . . in 1859*, 1860

Jews in Utah, being non-Mormons, are theoretically subject to classification as Gentiles, which gives rise to the well-known remark that 'Utah is the only place in the world where Jews are Gentiles.'

John Gunther, *Inside U.S.A.*, 1947

Vermont

A Sunday-school teacher asked a child . . . 'In what state were mankind left after the fall?' – 'In the state of Vermont.'

Harriet Martineau, *Society in America*, 1837

This is the native State of the Hon. Mr Coolidge. Otherwise it is a vacuum. It consists mainly of hills.

H.L. Mencken, *Americana*, 1925

and New Hampshire

Anything I can say about New Hampshire
Will serve almost as well about Vermont,
Excepting that they differ in their mountains.
The Vermont mountains stretch extended straight;
New Hampshire mountains curl up in a coil.

Robert Frost, *New Hampshire*, 1923

Archibald MacLeish . . . said it reminded him of the New Yorker visiting Vermont who said, 'There are so many rocks here. Where did they come from? Do you grow rocks in Vermont?' The Vermont farmer replied, 'The rocks were brought here by the great glacier.' The New Yorker said, 'What became of the glacier?' The Vermonter said, 'It went back to get more rocks.'

John Gunther, *Inside Asia*, 1939

The summer like a rajah dies
And every widowed tree
Kindles for Congregational eyes
An alien suttee.

Ogden Nash, 'Kipling's Vermont', in *The Private Dining Room*, 1952

Mount Vernon (Virginia)

If you haven't been to the sweet Mount Vernon, then I *will* tell you how on one soft spring day we glided down the Potomac in a painted boat, and jumped upon the shore – how hand in hand we stole along up a tangled pathway till we reached the tomb of General George Washington, how we paused beside it, and no one spoke a word, then hand in hand, walked on again, not less wise or sad for that marble story; how we went within the door – raised the latch he lifted when he last went home – thank the Ones in Light that he's since passed through a brighter wicket! Oh, I could spend a long day, if it did not weary you, telling of Mount Vernon.

Emily Dickinson, Letter to Dr and Mrs J.G. Holland, spring 1854

Considering the circumstances and history of the place, the position of Mount Vernon, as I saw it, was very remarkable. It lay exactly between the lines of the two armies. The pickets of the Northern army had been extended beyond it, not improbably with the express intention of keeping a spot so hallowed within the power of the northern Government. But since the war began it had been in the hands of the seceders. In fact it stood there in the middle of the battlefield, on the very line of division between loyalty and secession. And this was the spot which Washington had selected as the very heart and centre, and safest rallying homestead of the united nation which he left behind him.

Anthony Trollope, *North America*, 1862

Vicksburg (and Natchez)

In Vicksburg and Natchez, in my time, ice was jewellery; none but the rich could wear it.

Mark Twain, *Life on the Mississippi*, 1883

Virginia

We found shoal water, where we smelt so sweet and so strong a smell, as if we had been in the midst of some delicate garden abounding with all kinds of odoriferous flowers, by which we were assured that the land could not be far distant.

Philip Amadas or Arthur Barlow, *The First Voyage Made to North America*, 2 July 1584, in Richard Hakluyt, *Principal Navigations . . . of the English Nation*, 1598–1600

We have discovered the maine to be the goodliest soyle under the cope of heaven, so abounding with sweete trees, that bring such sundry, rich and pleasant gummes, grapes of such greatnesse, yet wilde, as France, Spaine, nor Italie have no greater, so many sorts of Apothecarie drugs, such severall kindes of flaxe, & one kinde like silke, the same gathered of a grasse, as common there as grasse is here. And now within these few dayes we have found here Maiz or Guinie wheate. . . . Besides that, it is the goodliest and most pleasing territorie of the world: for the continent is of an huge and unknowen greatnesse, and very well peopled and towned, though savagely, and the climate so wholsome, that we had not one sicke since we touched the land here. To conclude, if Virginia had but horses and kine in some reasonable proportion, I dare assure my selfe being inhabited with English, no realme in Christendome were comparable to it. For this already we finde, that what commodities soever Spaine, France, Italy, or the East partes doe yeeld unto us, in wines of all sortes, in oyles, in flaxe, in rosens, pitch frankensence, corrans, sugers, and such like, these parts doe abound with the growth of them all, but being Savages that possesse the land, they know no use of the same.

Ralph Lane (1585), in Richard Hakluyt, *Principal Navigations . . . of the English Nation*, 1598–1600

This Maine is the goodliest Continent that ever we saw, promising more by farre then we any way did expect: for it is replenished with faire fields, and in them fragrant Flowers, also Medowes, and hedged in with stately Groves, being furnished also with pleasant Brookes, and beautified with two maine Rivers that (as wee judge) may haply become good harbours, and conduct us to the hopes men so greedily doe thirst after.

Gabriel Archer, *The Relation of Captain Gosnold's Voyage*, 1602, in *Purchas his Pilgrimes*, 1625

Seagull: Come boyes, *Virginia* longs till we share the rest of her Maidenhead.
Spendall: Why is she inhabited already with any English?
Seagull: A whole Country of English is there man, bred of those that were left there in 79. They have married with the Indians, and make 'hem bring forth as beautiful faces as any we have in England: and therefore the Indians are so in love with 'hem, that all the treasure they have, they lay aside at their feete.
Scapthrift: But is there such treasure there, Captaine, as I have heard?
Seagull: I tell thee, Gold is more plentifull there then Copper is with us: and for as much redde Copper as I can bring, Ile have thrice the waight in Golde. Why man all their dripping pans, and their Chamber Pottes are pure Gold; and all the Chaines with which they chaine up their streetes, are massie Golde; all the Prisoners they take, are fetterd in Gould: and for Rubies and Diamonds, they goe forth on holydayes and gather 'hem by the Sea-shore, to hang on their childrens Coates, and stick in their Cappes, as commonly as our children weare Saffron guilt Brooches, and groates with hoales in 'hem.
Scapthrift: And is it a pleasant Countrie withall?
Seagull: As ever the sunne shinde on: temperate and full of all sorts of excellent viands; wilde Boare is as common there, as our tamest Bacon is here: Venison, as Mutton. And then you shall live freely there, without Sergeants, or Courtiers, or Lawyers, or Intelligencers, onely a few industrious Scots perhaps, who indeed are disperst over the face of the whole earth.

George Chapman, Ben Johnson and John Marston, *Eastward Hoe*, 1605

Ile to *Virginia* like some cheating Bankrout, and leave my Creditor ith' suddes.

S.S., *The Honest Lawyer*, 1606

Virginia,
Earth's onely paradise.

Where nature hath in store,
Fowle, venison and fish,
  And the fruitfull'st soyle
Without your toyle,
Three harvests more,
All greater than you wish.

And the ambitious vine
Crownes with his purple masse,
  The Cedar reaching hie
  To kisse the sky,
The Cypresse, pine
And use-full Sassafras

To whose, the golden age,
Still natures lawes doth give,
  No other cares that tend,
  But them to defend
From winters age
That long there doth not live.

When as the luscious smell
Of that delicious land,
  Above the seas that flowes,
  The cleere wind throwes,
Your hearts to swell
Approaching the deere strand.

In kenning of the shore
(Thanks to God first given,)
  O you the happy'st men,
  Be frolicke then,
Let cannons roare,
Frighting the wide heaven.

And in regions farre
Such heroes bring ye foorth,
  As those from whom we came,
  And plant our name,
Under that starre
Not knowne unto our north.

Michael Drayton, *To the Virginian Voyage*, 1606

The Summer is hot as in Spaine; the Winter cold as in France or England. The heate of Summer is in June, July, and August, but commonly the coole Breeses asswage the vehemencie of the heate. The chiefe of Winter is halfe December, January, February, and halfe March. The cold is extreame sharpe, but heere the Proverbe is true, That no extreme continueth long. . . . The winds here are variable but the like Thunder and Lightning to purifie the Aire, I have seldome either seene or heard in Europe. . . . The Countrie is not mountainous nor yet low, but such pleasant plaine Hils and fertile Vallies, one prettily crossing another, and watered so conveniently with their sweete Brookes and Christall Springs, as if Art it selfe had devised them.

Captain John Smith, *The Description of Virginia*, 1607, in *Purchas his Pilgrimes*, 1625

Easily you may see that the good things of Virginia are naturall and her owne, the bad accidental and our owne; and consequently if wee amend our selves, Virginia will soone be amended. The boady there is sound; to cut the haire, avoide the excrements, paire the nailes, wash away sweat and dust, and to cure other like accidents of negligence, or impenitent and unprofitable diligence, is a worke feasible and facile also to industrious and unanimous workemen.

Intelligence from Virginia, 1624, in *Purchas his Pilgrimes*, 1625

All the rich endowments of Virginia, her Virgin-portion from the creation nothing lessened, are wages for all this worke: God in wisedome having enriched the Savage Countries, that those riches might be attractives for Christian suters, which there may sowe spirituals and reape temporals.

A Discourse on Virginia, 1625, in *Purchas his Pilgrimes*, 1625

I am not a Virginian but an American.

Patrick Henry, Speech, Continental Congress, 5 September 1774

On the whole, I find nothing anywhere else, in point of climate, which Virginia need envy to any part of the world

Thomas Jefferson, Letter to Martha Jefferson Randolph, 31 May 1791

The good Old Dominion, the blessed mother of us all.

Thomas Jefferson, *Thoughts on Lotteries*, February 1826

A Virginian gentleman told me that ever since he had married, he had been accustomed to have a negro girl sleep in the same chamber with himself and his wife. I asked for what purpose this nocturnal attendance was necessary? 'Good heaven,' was the reply, 'If I wanted a glass of water during the night, what would become of me?'

Mrs Frances Trollope, *Domestic Manners of the Americans*, 1832

Dilapidated, fenceless, and trodden with war as Virginia is, wherever I move across her surface, I find myself roused to surprise and admiration. What capacity for products, improvements, human life, nourishment and expansion. Everywhere that I have been in the Old Dominion, (the subtle mockery of that title now!) such thoughts have fill'd me. The soil is yet far above the average of any northern States. And how full of breadth the scenery, everywhere distant mountains, everywhere convenient rivers. Even yet prodigal in forest woods, and surely eligible for all the fruits, orchards and flowers. The skies and atmosphere most luscious, as I feel certain, from more than a year's residence in the State, and movements hither and yon. I should say very healthy as a general thing. Then a rich and elastic quality by night and by day. The sun rejoices in his strength, dazzling and burning, and yet, to me, never unpleasantly weakening. It is not the panting tropical heat, but invigorates. The north tempers it. The nights are often unsurpassable. Last evening (Feb. 8), I saw the first of the new moon, the outlined old moon clear along with it; the sky and air so clear, such transparent hues of colour, it seem'd to me I had never really seen the new moon before. It was the thinnest cut crescent possible. It hung delicate just above the silky shadow of the Blue Mountains. Ah, if it might prove an omen and a prophecy for this unhappy State.

Walt Whitman, *Specimen Days* (9 February 1864), 1882

Virginia, where charm is laid on so thick you could saw it off in chunks and export it. . . . Shout at Virginia, shake it, slap its face, jump on it – Virginia will open one eye, smile vaguely, and go to sleep again.

William Golding, *The Hot Gates and Other Occasional Pieces*, 1965

Virginia City (Nevada)

Virginia is very wild, but I believe it is now pretty generally believed that a mining city must go through with a certain amount of unadulterated cussedness, before it can settle down and behave itself in a conservative and seemly manner.

Charles F. Browne, *Artemus Ward (His Travels) Among the Mormons* (1863), 1865

Virginia was a busy city of streets and houses above ground. Under it was another busy city, down in the bowels of the earth, where a great population of men thronged in and out among the intricate maze of tunnels and drifts, flitting hither and thither under a winking sparkle of lights, and over their heads towered a vast web of interlocking timbers that held the walls of the gutted Comstock apart. These timbers were as large as a man's body, and the framework stretched upward so far that no eye could pierce its top through the closing gloom. It was like peering upwards through the cracked ribs and bones of some colossal skeleton. Imagine such a framework two miles long, sixty feet wide, and higher than any church spire in America. Imagine this stately lattice-work stretching down Broadway, from the St. Nicholas to Wall street, and a Fourth of July Procession, reduced to Pigmies, parading on top of it and flaunting their flags, high above the pinnacle of Trinity steeple.

Mark Twain, *Roughing It*, 1872

Wabash River (Indiana)

When an Eastern man is cheated by a Hoosier he is said to be *Wabashed.*

R.W. Emerson, *Journal*, 1860

Oh the moonlight's fair tonight along the
Wabash,
From the fields there comes the breath of new-mown
hay;
Thro' the sycamores the candle lights are gleaming,
On the banks of the Wabash far away.

Paul Dresser, *On the Banks of the Wabash*, 1897

Washington (District of Columbia)

That Indian swamp in the wilderness.

Thomas Jefferson, *c.* 1789, attrib., quoted in Alastair Cooke, *America*, 1973

'Tis evening now; beneath the western star
Soft sighs the lover through his sweet segar,
And fills the ears of some consenting she
With puffs and vows, with smoke and constancy.
The patriot, fresh from Freedom's councils come,
Now pleas'd retires to lash his slaves at home;
Or woo, perhaps, some black Aspasia's charms,
And dream of freedom in his bondmaid's arms.
In fancy now, beneath the twilight gloom,
Come, let me lead thee o'er this 'second Rome!'
Where tribunes rule, where dusky Davi bow,
And what was Goose-Creek once is Tiber now: –
This embryo capital, where Fancy sees
Squares in morasses, obelisks in trees;
Which second-sighted seers, ev'n now, adorn
With shrines unbuilt, and heroes yet unborn.
Though nought but woods, and J———n they see,
Where streets should run, and sages *ought* to be.

Thomas Moore, 'To Thomas Hume, Esq., M.D., from the City of Washington', *Poems relating to America*, 1806

. . . the whole affair . . . looks as if some giant had scattered a box of his child's toys at random on the ground.

Captain Basil Hall, *Travels in North America* (29 December 1827) 1829

The dead calm which is so often felt in Washington and leaves a man more tired in the morning than he was the night before.

Charles Francis Adams, *Diary*, 8 July 1834

Luckily for me this was a true Washington day. Mild and hazy with the relaxing, enervating feeling which is characteristic of the climate. . . . I . . . took a walk almost to the Capitol hill. The Pennsylvania Avenue looks now far more like a Street and the place begins to concentrate, but every thing wears the appearance of poverty and of want of permanency.

Charles Francis Adams, *Diary*, 18 November 1834

Washington is no place for persons of domestic tastes. Persons who love dissipation, persons who love to watch the game of politics, and those who make a study of strong minds under strong excitements, like a season at Washington; but it is dreary to those whose pursuits and affections are domestic.

Harriet Martineau, *Retrospect of Western Travel*, 1838

The town looks like a large straggling village reared in a drained swamp.

George Combe, *Notes . . . during a Phrenological Visit in 1838–40*, 1842

In democratic communities the imagination is compressed when men consider themselves; it expands indefinitely when they think of the state. Hence it is that the same men who live on a small scale in cramped dwellings frequently aspire to gigantic splendor in the erection of their public monuments.

The Americans have traced out the circuit of an immense city on the site which they intend to make their capital, but which up to the present time is hardly more densely peopled than Pontoise, though, according to them, it will one day contain a million inhabitants. They have already rooted up trees for ten miles around lest they should interfere with the future citizens of this imaginary metropolis. They have erected a magnificent palace for Congress in the center of the city and have given it the pompous name of the Capitol.

Alexis de Tocqueville, *Democracy in America, the second part*, 1840

It is sometimes called the City of Magnificent Distances but it might with greater propriety be termed the City of Magnificent Intentions. . . . Spacious avenues that begin in nothing and lead nowhere; streets, mile long, that only want houses, roads, and inhabitants; public meetings that need but a public to be complete; and ornaments of great thoroughfares, which only lack great thoroughfares to ornament – are its leading features. One might fancy the season over and most of the houses gone out of town forever with their masters.

Charles Dickens, *American Notes*, 1842

Washington may be called the head-quarters of tobacco-tinctured saliva.

Ibid.

*Washington City, with the great umbrella top of the Capitol loomin' up into the heavens, grand, gloomy, and peculiar.

William T. Thompson, *Major Jones's Sketches of Travel*, 1848

Here . . . is to be seen in constant whirl the balance-wheel, such as it is, of the most complicated political machine on earth. . . .

Alexander Mackay, *The Western World*, 1849

The place has a Wiesbaden air – there are polities and gaieties straggling all over it.

W.M. Thackeray, Letter to Kate Perry, 7–14 February 1853

I . . . found the capital still under the empire of King Mud. . . . Were I to say that it was intended to be typical of the condition of the government, I might be considered cynical.

Anthony Trollope, *North America*, 1862

It contains, certainly, some notable public buildings, but they are scattered far and wide, with all kinds of incongruous environments, producing upon the stranger a perplexed impression that the British Museum has suddenly migrated to the centre of an exhausted brickfield, where rubbish may be shot; or that St. Paul's Cathedral, washed quite white, and stuck upon stone stilts, has been transferred to the middle of the Libyan desert, and called a Capitol. There is a perpetual solution of continuity at Washington. There is no cohesion about Pennsylvania Avenue. Its houses are Hudibras' story of the Bear and the fiddle – begun and broke off in the middle. It is an architectural conundrum which nobody can guess, and in which I candidly believe there is no meaning. The Vitruviuses and Palladios of America have perpetrated a vast practical joke, and called it Washington. It is the most 'bogus' of towns – a shin-plaster in brick and mortar, and with a delusive frontispiece of marble. The inhabitants seem to be very fond of building houses, but when they have run up three or four stories which threaten to attain the altitude of the Tower of Babel, the confusion of tongues sets in; the builders abandon their work; but, nothing disheartened, erect three or four stories of fresh houses elsewhere. It is said of those patrons of the drama who habitually avail themselves of half-price, that they have seen nothing but *dénouements*. Washington, on the contrary, is a collection of first acts without any catastrophes. . . . Washington will be, I have no doubt, some day uproariously splendid; but at present it isn't anything. It is in the District of Columbia and the State of the Future.

G.A. Sala, *My Diary in America in the Midst of War*, 1865

The United States is the only great country in the world which has no capital.

James Bryce, *The American Commonwealth*, 1888

It is a place where a court might be created, did anyone wish to create it.

Ibid.

Everywhere except in Washington, Americans were toiling for the same object. Every one complained of surroundings, except where, as at Washington, there were no surroundings to complain of.

Henry Adams, *The Education of Henry Adams*, 1906

In 1868 Washington stood outside the social pale. No Bostonian had ever gone there.

Ibid.

The whole effect of Washington is a want of concentration, of something unprehensile and apart. It is on, not in, the American process. The place seems to me to reflect, even in its sound and physical forms, that dispersal of power, that evasion of a simple conclusiveness, which is the peculiar effect of that ancient compromise, the American Constitution.

H.G. Wells, *The Future in America*, 1906

Washington talks about herself and about almost nothing else. . . . It is in positive quest of an identity of some sort, much rather, that Washington goes forth, encumbered with no ideal of avoidance or escape: it is about herself *as* the City of Conversation precisely that she incessantly converses: adorning the topic of moreover with endless ingenuity and humour. But that, absolutely, remains the case, which thus becomes one of the most thorough, even if probably one of the most natural and of the happiest cases of collective self-consciousness that one knows. The spectacle as it at first met my senses, was that of a numerous community in ardent pursuit of some workable conception of its social self, and trying meanwhile intelligently to talk itself, and even this very embarrassment, into a *subject* for conversation.

Henry James, *The American Scene*, 1907

This other and better world than California.

Ambrose Bierce, Letter, 29 November 1910

General effect of Washington. A plantation of public edifices amid a rather unkempt growth of streets.

Arnold Bennett, *Journal*, 17 October 1911

Things get very lonely in Washington sometimes. The real voice of the great people of America sometimes sounds faint and distant in that strange city. You hear politics until you wish that both parties were smothered in their own gas.

Woodrow Wilson, Speech in St Louis, 5 September 1919

*Washington he found was instantly recognisable as a national capital. Its architecture was dignified and official. There were open spaces well-gardened and overlooked by numerous statues. Clearly its growth had never been straitened by commercial pressures, but was moulded by art and taught in lordly ways. . . . Anyone would recognise Washington as a capital city, but no one would guess that it was the American capital, for it looked European. There was little of the towering rectangularity of New York or Chicago or Detroit but plenty of handsome curves, balconies, dignity happily rounded and often sustained by portly columns.

Eric Linklater, *Juan in America*, 1929

Washington cherishes an independence which is beyond alliances.

Shane Leslie, *American Wonderland*, 1936

There are a number of things wrong with Washington. One of them is that everyone has been too long away from home.

Dwight D. Eisenhower, Statement at Presidential press conference, 11 May 1955

The more I observed Washington, the more frequently I visited it, and the more people I interviewed there, the more I understood how prophetic L'Enfant was when he laid it out as a city that goes around in circles.

John Mason Brown, *Through These Men*, 1956

Washington isn't a city, it's an abstraction.

Dylan Thomas, Remark to interviewer, 1950, quoted in J.M. Brinnin, *Dylan Thomas in America*, 1956

The tendency to make the capital a catch-all for a variety of monuments to honor the immortals, the not-so-immortals, the greats, the near-greats, and the not-so-greats must stop. We must be on our guard lest the nation's capital come to resemble an unplanned cemetery.

Hugh Scott, Comment when US Senator for Pennsylvania, 10 September 1960

A city of southern efficiency and northern charm.

John Fitzgerald Kennedy, quoted by William Manchester, *Portrait of a President*, 1962

People only leave by way of the box, – ballot or coffin.

Senator Claiborne Pell, on Washington life, *Vogue*, 1 August 1963

It was, bar nowhere, the fullest place I ever saw. It swarmed, it surged, it seemed at times to seethe with earnest, determined people, leaping in and out of enormous cars, bounding urgently up the steps of hotels and secretariats, grasping glasses of milk with their eyes on their wrist watches.

James Cameron, *Points of Departure*, 1967 – of 1946

I spent four months in Washington in 1967. Perhaps the strangest four months in my life. I had the life of an immigrant in a country where normally there is no immigration – like Norway, for instance, or Albania. I lived in Georgetown in a house that looked like a Norwegian palace, fortunately belonging to a zoologist who specialized in Gorillas – a perfect occasion to read as much as I wanted about them, including the fact that the elderly gorilla loses interest in social life, becomes a loner and follows the tribe from a certain distance. One of the most attractive things about the Smithsonian was its stationery. I made many drawings on it, exploiting the excellent logo.

Saul Steinberg, 'Chronology', in Harold Rosenberg, *Saul Steinberg*, 1978

As a political capital it makes all others seem provincial, while remaining itself provincial in all other respects. The life of Washington (I am not counting its black majority of course, nor its tens of thousands of minor bureaucrats and secretaries and the like) is the life of politics. Observing Washington is like looking at the inside of a clock for the first time; you cannot see the time for the workings of the wheels. Here it all is: wheels, cogs, checks, balances, the power of the mainspring of elective democracy – politics in places other than Washington is either second-rate, or secret, or both. To visit, certainly, but not to live in. Its courts come and go; and in this respect it is an hotel.

George Gale, 'I Like it Here', *Spectator*, 23 September 1978

Arlington National Cemetery

Fame's Camping Ground.

Inscription on triumphal arch

The Capitol

After much menutial search for an eligible situation, prompted, I may say, from a fear of being prejudiced in favour of a first opinion, I could discover no one so advantageously to greet the congressional building as is that on the West End of Jenkins Heights, which stands as a pedestal waiting for a monument.

Major Pierre Charles L'Enfant, Report to George Washington, 28 June 1791

In the swathed Senate Chamber I noticed two holland-covered objects that somehow reminded me of my youth and of religious dissent. I guessed that the daily proceedings of the Senate must be opened with devotional exercises, and these two objects, seemed to me to be proper – why, I cannot tell – to the United States Senate; but there was one point that puzzled me.

'Why,' I asked, 'do you have *two* harmoniums?'

'Harmoniums, Sir!' protested our guide, staggered. 'Those are roll-top desks.'

If only the floor could have opened and swallowed me up, as it opens and swallows up the grand piano at the Thomas concerts in Chicago.

Arnold Bennet, *Those United States*, 1912

The Capitol buildings look like a version of St. Peter's and the Vatican turned out by a modern firm.

Shane Leslie, *American Wonderland*, 1936

Library of Congress

The Library of Congress . . . seems to have been consecrated to the purpose of flirtation.

Alexander Mackay, *The Western World*, 1849

President's Square – statue of George Washington

Of all the statues on horseback which I ever saw, either in marble or bronze, this is by far the worst and most ridiculous. The horse is most absurd, but the man sitting on the horse is manifestly drunk.

Anthony Trollope, North America, 1862

The Pentagon

The Pentagon, that immense monument to man's subservience to the desk.

Sir Oliver Frank, *Observer*, 'Saying of the Week', 30 November 1952

Potomac

All quiet along the Potomac to-night.

Ethel Lynn Beers, 'All quiet Along the Potomac', *Harper's Weekly*, 1861. (General George B. McLellan, commander of the army of the Potomac, is also said to have originated this Phrase, and to have exasperated public opinion, which was eager for action, by its constant repetition.)

Washington Monument

Saw Washington monument. Phallic. Appalling. A national catastrophe, – only equalled by the Albert Memorial. Tiny doll-like people waiting to go into it.

Arnold Bennett, *Journal*, 17 October 1911

The White House

We have private houses in London considerably larger. . . . The President's House is nice to look at, but it is built on marshy ground, not much above the levels of the Potomac, and is very unhealthy. I was told that all who live there become subject to fever and ague, and that few who now live there have escaped it altogether. This comes of choosing the site of a new city, and decreeing that it shall be built on this or that spot. Large cities, especially in these latter days, do not collect themselves in unhealthy places. Men desert such localities or at least do not congregate at them when their character is once known. But the poor President cannot desert the White House. He must make the most of the residence which the nation has prepared for him.

Anthony Trollope, *North America*, 1862

A spell of fine soft weather. I wander about a good deal, sometimes at night under the moon. Tonight took a long look at the President's house. The white portico – the palace-like, tall, round columns, spotless as snow – the walls also – the tender and soft moonlight, flooding the pale marble, and making peculiar faint languishing shades, not shadows – everywhere a soft transparent, hazy, thin, blue moon-lace, hanging in the air – the brilliant and extra-plentiful clusters of gas, on and around the facade, columns, portico, etc., – everything so white, so marbly pure and dazzling, yet soft – the White House of future poems, and of dreams and dramas, there in the soft and copious moon – the gorgeous front, in the trees, under the lustrous flooding moon, full of reality, full of illusion – the forms of the trees, leafless, silent, in trunk and myriad angles of branches under the stars and sky – the White House of the land, and of beauty and night – sentries at the gates, and by the portico, silent, pacing there in blue overcoats – stopping you not at all, but eyeing you with sharp eyes, whichever way you move.

Walt Whitman, *Specimen Days* (24 February 1863), 1882

About all the public saloons – the State apartments I suppose I may call them, without offending the dignity of a Republican simplicity – there is a bare and uncomfortable look, something between that of a waiting room at a railway terminus, the drawing room at an hotel, and the *foyer* of an opera-house. . . . The prevailing desolation is as handsome as upholstery can make it, but it lacks solemnity, it lacks associations of historical interest.

G.A. Sala, *My Diary in America in the Midst of War*, 1865

Washington State

There is a great deal in the remark of the discontented traveller: 'When you have seen a pine forest, a bluff, a river, and a lake, you have seen all the scenery of western America. Sometimes the pine is three hundred feet high, and sometimes the rock is, and sometimes the lake is a hundred miles long. But it's all the same don't you know. I'm getting sick of it.'

Rudyard Kipling, *From Sea to Sea*, 1889

'The West'

Go West, young man, and grow up with the country.

Horace Greeley, *Hints toward Reforms*, 1850

So infinitestimal did I find the knowledge of Art, West of the Rocky Mountains, that an art patron – who in his day had been a miner – actually sued the railway company for damages because the plaster cast of the Venus di Milo, which he had imported from Paris, had been delivered minus the arms. And, what is more surprising still, he gained his case and the damages.

Oscar Wilde, *Impressions of America*, Lecture, 1883

The West may be called the most distinctively American part of America because the points in which it differs from the East are the points in which America as a whole differs from Europe.

James Bryce, *The American Commonwealth*, 1888

What the Mediterranean Sea was to the Greeks, breaking the bond of custom, offering new experiences, calling out new institutions and activities, that the ever retreating Great West has been to the eastern United States directly, and to the nations of Europe more remotely.

F.J. Turner, *The Significance of the Frontier*, 1893

Oh give me a home where the buffalo roam.

Dr Brewster Higley, *Home on the Range*,

Out where the handclasp's a little stronger,
Out where the smile dwells a little longer,
That's where the West begins.

Arthur Chapman, 'Out Where the West Begins' – *. . . and other Small poems of a Big Country*, 1916

Only remember – West of the Mississippi it's a little more look, see, act. A little less rationalize, comment, talk.

F. Scott Fitzgerald, Letter to Andrew Turnbull, summer 1934

In the West the past is very close. In many places, it still believes it's the present.

John Masters, *Pilgrim Son*, 1971

Desert, west of the Rockies

We left the snowy Wind River Mountains and Uinta Mountains behind, and sped away, always through splendid scenery but occasionally through long ranks of white skeletons of mules and oxen – monuments of the huge emigration of other days. . . . It was the loneliest land for a grave. . . . On damp murky nights, these scattered skeletons gave forth a soft, hideous glow, like very faint spots of moonlight starring the vague desert. It was because of the phosphorus in the bones. But no scientific explanation could keep a body from shivering when he drifted by one of those ghostly lights, and knew that a skull held it.

Mark Twain, *Roughing It*, 1872

Pacific West Coast

What can we do with the western coast, a coast of 3,000 miles, rockbound cheerless, uninviting, and not a harbour on it? What use have we for such a country? I will never vote one cent from the public treasury to place the Pacific Ocean one inch nearer Boston than it is now.

Daniel Webster, quoted in Nancy Wilson Ross, *Farthest Reach*, 1944

The shattered water made a misty din.
Great waves looked over others coming in,
And thought of doing something to the shore
That water never did to land before.
The clouds were low and hairy in the skies,
Like locks blown forward in the gleam of eyes.
You could not tell and yet it looked as if
The shore was lucky in being backed by cliff,
The cliff in being backed by continent:
It looked as if a night of dark intent
Was coming, and not only a night, an age.
Someone had better be prepared for rage.
There would be more than ocean-water broken
Before God's last *Put out the Light* was spoken.

Robert Frost, 'Once by the Pacific', from *West Running Brook*, 1928

West Point

In this beautiful place: the fairest among the fair and lovely Highlands of the North River: shut in by deep green heights and ruined forts, and looking down upon the distant town of Newburgh, along a glittering path of sunlit water, with here and there a skiff, whose white sail often bends on some new tack as sudden flaws of wind come down upon her from the gullies in the hills: hemmed in, besides, all round with memories of Washington, and events of the revolutionary war: is the military school of America.

Charles Dickens, *American Notes*, 1842

Winnetka, Illinois

My fellow man I do not care for.
I often ask me, What's he there for?
The only answer I can find.
Is, reproduction of his kind.
If I'm supposed to swallow that,
Winnetka is my habitat.

Ogden Nash, 'A Bas Ben Adhem', in *Many Long Years Ago*, 1945

Wisconsin

Wisconsin has always boasted of raising the largest crops of talking humanity.

Bayard Taylor, *Eldorado, or Adventures in the Path of Empire*, 1850

Woodsville (New Hampshire)

Woodsville's a place of shrieks and wandering lamps
And cars that shock and rattle – and *one* Hotel.

Robert Frost, 'North of Boston', from *A Hundred Collars*, 1916

Worcester (Massachusetts)

Among other personal shortcomings . . . I seem to have been endowed at birth by a Bad Fairy with a paucity of visual imagination which amounts practically to a squint. . . . To those who go about picturing new scenes in their imagination for every novel they read, this may sound a little incredible . . . [and] . . . this limitation of mine might not be so cramped in its effect if the few visual images which I have were not confined almost exclusively to street scenes in Worcester, Massachusetts, the fortunate city which gave me birth and fostered me till I was seventeen. Now, Worcester, Massachusetts is a splendid city, with an excellent school system and a wide range of manufacturing interests but it is not the ideal locale for the *Chanson de Roland* or the adventures of Ivanhoe. It does not have the bucolic atmosphere essential to a complete feeling for the Wessex of Hardy. . . . No amount of travelling or sightseeing can shift me from this visual inertia. I have been in Venice, but the Venice of bookland is to me simply King Street flooded with water. . . .

Robert Benchley, 'Mind's Eye Trouble', *Around the World*, 1952

Yellowstone Park

Canyon of the Yellowstone River, Wyoming
That inspection began with curiosity and finished in terror, for it seemed that the whole world was sliding in chrysolite from under my feet. I followed with the others round the corner to arrive at the brink of the cañon: we had to climb up a nearly perpendicular ascent to begin with, for the ground rises more than the river drops. Stately pine woods fringe either lip of the gorge, which is – the Gorge of the Yellowstone.

All I can say is that, without warning or preparation, I looked into a gulf seventeen hundred feet deep, with eagles and fish-hawks circling far below. And the sides of that gulf were one wild welter of colour – crimson, emerald, cobalt, ochre, amber, honey splashed with port-wine, snow-white, vermilion, lemon, and silver-grey, in wide washes. The sides did not fall sheer, but were graven by time and water and air into monstrous heads of kings, dead chiefs, men and women of the old time. So far below that no sound of its strife could reach us, the Yellowstone River ran – a finger-wide strip of jade-green. The sunlight took those wondrous walls and gave fresh hues to those that nature had already laid there. Once I saw dawn break over a lake in Rajputana and the sun set over the Oodey Sagar amid a circle of Holman Hunt hills. This time I was watching both performances going on below me – upside down, you understand – and the colours were real! The cañon was burning like Troy town; but it would burn for ever, and, thank goodness, neither pen nor brush could ever portray its splendours adequately. The Academy would reject the picture for a chromo-lithograph.

Rudyard Kipling, *From Sea to Sea*, 1889

Norris Geyser Basin
'What I say,' shrieked the old lady *apropos* of matters theological, 'and what I say more, after having seen all that, is that the Lord has ordained a Hell for such as disbelieve His gracious works.'

Ibid.

'I drive blame cur'ous kinder folk through this place,' said he. 'Blame cur'ous. Seems a pity that they sould ha' come so far just liken Norris Basin to Hell. Guess Chicago would ha' served 'em, speaking in comparison, jest as good.'

Ibid.

It is my opinion that we enclose and celebrate the freaks of our nation and of our civilization. Yellowstone National Park is no more representative of America than is Disneyland.

John Steinbeck, *Travels with Charley*, 1962

Yosemite Valley (California)

The *fall* of the Yosemite, so called, is a humbug. . . . At present the little stream that leaps down the Yosemite, and is all but shattered to mist by the amazing descent, looks like a tapeline let down from the cloud-capped height to measure the depth of the abyss.

Horace Greeley, *An Overland Journey from New York to San Francisco . . . in 1859*, 1860

looking up the face of El Capitan

That first full gaze up the opposite height! Can I ever forget it? The valley is here scarcely half a mile wide, while its northern wall of mainly naked, perpendicular granite is at least four thousand feet high – probably more. But the modicum of moonlight that fell into this awful gorge gave to that precipice a vagueness of outline, an indefinite vastness, a ghostly or weird spirituality. Had the mountain spoken to me in audible voice, or begun to lean over with the purpose of burying me beneath its crushing mass, I should hardly have been surprised.

Ibid.

Arrived here Wednesday afternoon. Since then we have passed a year or two in the amusement of climbing the face of cliffs three thousand feet high, and standing on their edge afterwards. This sensation certainly takes away one's breath, if that is its object, and at last I have struck on the edge business, leaving it to the baronet on the principle that his son may just as well succeed now as later to the baronetcy. I prefer to break my own neck short of three thousand feet, not requiring so much time as the Britisher for reflection in the air.

Henry Adams, Letter to Elizabeth Cameron, 4 November 1888

Fort Yuma

Fort Yuma is probably the hottest place on earth. The thermometer stays at one hundred and twenty in the shade there all the time – except when it varies and goes higher. . . . There is a tradition (attributed to John Phenix) that a very very wicked soldier died there, once, and of course went straight to the hottest corner of perdition – and the next day he telegraphed back for his blankets.

Mark Twain, *Roughing It*, 1872

V

VANUATU (formerly New Hebrides)

They seemed most pleased with Marbled Paper & some of them immediately converted it, before our Eyes into a Covering for the only part which is covered about them.

William Wales, *Journal*, 22 July 1774

Some had taken it into their heads that the Natives of this Island were Sodomites. This opinion they grounded on one of the Natives endeavouring to entice certain of our People into the Woods for a purpose I need not mention. . . . No person had been attempted who had not either a softness in his features or whose employment it was to carry bundles of one kind or other which is the Office of their own Women, and of this sort was the Instance I am going to relate. The Man who carried Mr Foster's Plant Bag had, I was told, been two or three times attempted, and he happening to go into the Bushes on some occasion or other whilst we were set down drinking our Cocoa-nuts &c. I pointed it out to the Natives who sat round us, with a sort of sly look and *significant action* at the same time, on which two of them jump'd up and were following him with great glee; but some of our Party bursting out into a laugh, those who were by (suspecting it I suppose) called *Erramange! Erramange!* (Its a Man! Its a Man!) on which the other returned, very much abashed on the Occasion.

William Wales, *Journal*, 13 August 1774

Tana / Tanna

I must confess I have been often led to think the Feats which Homer represents his heros as performing with their Spears a little too much of the marvellous to be admitted into a Heroic Poem, I mean when confined within the straight stays of Aristotle; nay even so great an advocate for him as Mr Pope, acknowlidges them to be *Surprising*. But sence I have seen what these people can do with their wooden ones; and them badly pointed and not of a very hard nature either, I have not the least exception to any one passage in that Great Poet on this account. But if I can find fewer exceptions I can find infinite number more beauties in him as he has, I think scarce an action, circumstance or discription of any kind whatever relateing to a spear, which I have not seen and recognised amongs the People, as their whirling motion and whistling noise as they fly. Their quivering motion as they stick in the ground when they fall. Their meditating their aim when they are going to throw and their shaking them in their hand as they go along, &ca &ca.

William Wales, *Journal*, August 1774

As I happened to hum a song, many of them eagerly intreated me to sing to them, and though not one of us was properly acquainted with music, yet we ventured to gratify their curiosity, and in fact, offered them a great variety of different airs. Some German and English songs, especially of the more lively kind, pleased them very much; but Dr Sparman's Swedish tunes gained universal applause; from which it appeared that their judgement of music was not influenced by the same rules which regulate the taste of other countries.

George Forster, *A Voyage Round the World*, 1777

Volcano

At noon we reached the edge of the crater. Just as we got there, there came a tremendous explosion, and away we ran, guides and all. When we recovered our courage, we crept up to the edge, and looked down nearly half a mile into what looked like hell. Out of the bowels of the earth were thrown huge boulders, which spent their force and fell back with hideous reverberations into the pit whence they came; and away at the bottom, the farthest down I have ever seen – and I believe it is the bottom-most point to which one can see – were two boiling lakes of lava, and when an explosion came, the lava would be thrown spattering against the encrusted crater sides, nearly to the top, and then run in thousands of rivers of liquid fire back to the bottom. The rumblings and explosions were deafening. I had to leave the edge of the crater, for there was stealing over me the overwhelming desire to jump off and to the bottom of the two twin lakes of molten death – a desire that everyone has experienced when looking down from a vast elevation.

Martin Johnson, *Through the South Seas with Jack London*, 1913 – of 1907

'How can I describe these people in my diary?' Mrs London asked.

'Worse than naked, and let it go at that,' Jack replied.

Ibid.

'Where do you keep your wife?' he dropped his voice to ask. I said I hadn't one to keep. He whispered: 'I keep mine so far off that if she goes a yard further she'll be coming back.' I asked where this advantageous spot might be, and he roared: 'New Hebrides. I tried South Africa, but it didn't wash.'

James Agate, *Ego 2*, 15 April 1936

VENEZUELA

This morning, very early, I went up on deck – and there was South America. Its mountains rose up sheer and solemn out of the flat sea, thrown into massive relief by tremendous oblique shafts of light from the rising sun. The gorges were deep in crimson shadow, and the ridges were outlined in dazzling gold. The town of La Guaira lay scattered over the slopes and along the shore. It was very still. . . . And already you could smell the land. A harsh disturbing smell, after the cleanness of the sea. A smell which presaged the long journey ahead of us with all its excitements and fatigues. The smell of an alien civilization, a foreign language, other faces and different food. A smell which made my dim mental pictures of the expected continent suddenly sharp and three-dimensional and real. A smell which somehow conveyed to the mind, more instantly and powerfully than any word or image the obvious but staggering fact that South America actually exists – that it is down here, all the time, every day of our lives. . . . Caskey, who by now had joined me at the rail, said without hesitation that it was garlic.

Christopher Isherwood, *The Condor and the Cows*, 1949

. . . This pioneer democracy, built
on foundations, not of rock, but blood hard as rock.

Robert Lowell, 'Caracas I', *Notebook*, 1970

Caracas

Caracas has a bad reputation. Venezuelans are not liked by their fellow Latin Americans. Why? There must be some reason for so universal a sentiment. And there is: Caracas is brash, bustling, and successful, and doesn't hesitate to let you know it. In the cant phrase, she's been 'Americanised.' She is, probably, the most 'modern' city in Latin America – sharp and clean where Buenos Aires and Santiago, the boom towns of fifty years ago, are shabby-genteel, smudged, rickety.

John Mander, 'Mexico City to Buenos Aires', *Encounter*, September 1965

This is one of the most astonishing cities I have ever seen. . . . It looks as Manhattan might look if bits of suburban White Plains, N.Y., or fields near Greenwich, Connecticut, lay between Forty-second Street and the Battery, The city does not have a center or focal point. It expands like a hand with fingers constantly stretching out and grabbing bits of hill or valley.

John Gunther, *Inside South America*, 1967

Orinoco River

The great river of Orenoque or Baraquan hath nine branches which fall out on the North side of his own maine mouth: on the South side it hath seven other fallings into the sea, so it disemboqueth by sixteene armes in all, betweene Ilands and broken ground, but the Ilands are very great, many of them as bigge as the Isle of Wight, and bigger, and many lesse. From the first branch on the North, to the last of the South, it is at least 100 leagues, so as the rivers mouth is 300 miles wide at his entrance into the sea, which I take to be farre bigger then that of Amazones.

Sir Walter Ralegh, *The Discovery of Guiana* 1595), in Richard Hakluyt, *Principal Navigations . . . of the English Nation*, 1598–1600

'The Mountain of Crystal' (Angel Falls)

When it grew towards sunneset, we entred a branch of a river that fell into Orenoque called Winicapora: where I was enformed of the mountaine of Christall, to which in trueth for the length of the way, and the evill season of the yeere, I was not able to march, nor abide any longer upon the joùrney: wee saw it afarre off and it appeared like a white Church-tower of an exceeding height. There falleth over it a mighty river which toucheth no part of the side of the mountaine, but rusheth over the toppe of it, and falleth to the ground with so terrible a noyse and clamor, as if a thousand great bels were knockt one against another. I thinke there is not in the world so strange an over-fall, nor so wonderful to behold: Berreo told me that there were Diamonds and other precious stones on it, and that they shined very farre off.

Ibid.

VIRGIN ISLANDS (USA)

The Virgines are little Ilands not inhabited; some thinke for want of water, some thinke that is no cause, and that there is store of water. They are very barren and craggie. . . . Among these many scattered Ilands there is one called the Bird-Iland, by reason of the incredible store of Fowle. So stored is it with plenty of Fowle, that never was English Dovecoat more willing to yeelde her increase then that hillocke, for you may take with your hands onely, as much as you will to the filling of Bushels and Quarters.

George, Earl of Cumberland, 1596, in *Purchas his Pilgrimes*, 1625

St Thomas

It is a Niggery-Hispano-Dano-Yankee-Doodle place; in which, perhaps, the Yankee-Doodle element, declaring itself in nasal twang and sherry cobblers, seems to be of the strongest flavour; as undoubtedly will be the case in many of these parts as the years go on revolving.

Anthony Trollope, *The West Indies and the Spanish Main*, 1859

Men who settle at St Thomas have most probably roughed it elsewhere unsuccessfully.

Ibid.

As veritable a Dutch-oven for cooking fever in, with as veritable a dripping-pan for the poison when concocted in the tideless basin below the town, as man ever invented.

Charles Kingsley, *At Last, A Christmas in the West Indies*, 1871

Very fair and full of promise
Lay the island of St Thomas:
Ocean o'er its reefs and bars
Hid its elemental scars;
Groves of cocoanut and guava
Grew above its fields of lava.
So the gem of the Antilles, –
'Isles of Eden,' where no ill is, –
Like a great green turtle slumbered
On the sea that it encumbered.

Then said William Henry Seward
As he cast his eye to leeward,
'Quite important to our commerce
Is this island of St Thomas.'

Said the Mountain ranges, 'Thank'ee
But we cannot stand the Yankee
O'er our scars and fissures poring,
In our very vitals boring,
In our sacred caverns prying,
All our secret problems trying, –
Digging, blasting with dynamite
Mocking all our thunders! Damn it!
Other lands may be more civil
But our lava crust if we will.'

Bret Harte, 'St Thomas', *A Geographical Survey*, 1868

The Danish influence is felt everywhere. It is especially noticeable in the gabled and shingled houses and the clean white cobbles, the massive and brightly painted buildings, the statues, and coats of arms, and the names of streets and towns. The capital has a childish and Scandinavian aspect which is very strange indeed. On top of this strangeness comes the American influence. . . . The result of this compounding of elements is a fascinating elfo-African atmosphere: Santa Claus in robes of scarlet and fur, but equipped as well with a grass skirt and wreath of hibiscus, sipping, with evident relish, Coca-Cola through a straw.

Patrick Leigh Fermor, *The Traveller's Tree*, 1951

VIETNAM

Vietnam as a whole is a country analogous, in size and shape and historical terms, to Norway, assuming that Norway were a country turned back-to-front, with its coast on the east instead of the west. They are both elongated, wasp-waisted territories with bulges in both north and south, flanked by sea on one side and mountains on the other, geographically associated with neighbours who have frequently threatened their independence. The northern borders of both Vietnam and Norway march with those of a major power that is now Communist, but which, in an imperialist past, sought to dominate them. Their southern extremities reach into waters contended over by other nations. Both the Norwegians and the Vietnamese have long and enduring and individual cultures, which have been preserved in the face of many political vicissitudes. They are of almost identical size – 125,000 square miles, which is almost half again as big as Britain.

From here the analogy breaks down in human terms; there are four million Norwegians and some thirty million Vietnamese. And in no circumstances would it be possible to mistake these citizens for each other.

James Cameron, *Witness*, 1966 (paraphrasing remarks by William Warbey, MP)

Through the hours of daylight practically nothing whatever moved on four wheels on the roads of North Vietnam: hardly a car or a truck; from the air, in the sunlight, it must have looked as though the country had no wheeled transport at all. That, of course, was the idea. It was the roads and the bridges that were being bombed; it was held to be no longer safe, after sunrise, to be near either. Furthermore it was the illusion that was important; there was a kind of aesthetic importance in creating illusions, and there were, of course, two. One was that North Vietnam is a growing and progressive industrial nation. The other was that, between sunrise and sunset, it was inhabited by nobody at all.

Ibid.

I regard the war in Indochina as the greatest military, political, economic, and moral blunder in our national history.

US Senator George McGovern, quoted in *The Congressional Record*, 22 June 1970

The U.S. First Infantry Division has carved its divisional insignia with defoliants in a stretch of jungle – a giant poisonous graffito. . . .

Frances Fitzgerald, *Fire in the Lake*, 1972

The French and the Americans tried to stop the revolution, and in doing so they created an interregnum of violence unparalleled in Vietnamese history. In the end the Vietnamese may reject them and their intervention as an organism rejects a foreign body. As one Vietnamese scholar told a Frenchman, 'If you want so much to be in Vietnam, just wait a bit and perhaps in your next reincarnation you will be born Vietnamese.'

Ibid.

It has often been said by people who should know better that South Vietnam was a poor, peace-loving country; it used to be, on the contrary, a rich, war-loving country, which is why the people are now so shocked by their present condition of beggary.

Richard West, *Victory in Vietnam*, 1974

My mother thinks Vietnam is somewhere near Panama.

US Marine, just before dying of wounds on a helicopter in Vietnam, quoted by John Pilger, *Do you remember Vietnam?*, ATV Network production, 3 October 1978

Vietnam was as much a laboratory experiment as a war.

John Pilger, *Do You Remember Vietnam?*, ATV Network production, 3 October 1978

I used to see Vietnam as a war rather than a country.

Ibid.

Vietnamese

They are a very white people, because there it begins to bee cold, low of Stature, flat Nosed and little Eyed, with a very few hayres on their Chins, and Mustachoes: none at all on their Cheekes, the hayre of the Head they weare long like Women, tyed up with a blacke silke hayre-lace, and weare a flat Cap upon them. They weare Cloath breeches made very levell, and a short Robe above them, like a Master of the Chambers of Accounts.

Monsieur de Monfart, *c.* 1604, in *Purchas in Pilgrimes*, 1625

All Annamites talk as though they had cleft palates.

Crosbie Garstin, *The Dragon and the Lotus*, 1928

*To take an Annamite to bed with you is like taking a bird: they twitter and sing on your pillow.

Graham Greene, *The Quiet American*, 1955

No people in the world have been so continuously at war as these small people of Vietnam. . . . Someone or other was, at almost any recorded period, attempting to swallow Vietnam; it is a most curious and interesting historical fact that no one ever contrived permanently to succeed. Much of this fact may be accounted for by the singular resilience and continuity of the Vietnamese, who are, despite the graceful and beguilingly diffident tactfulness of their demeanour, among the toughest and most unanswerable people on earth. It is a fact that, surrounded by all this charm, all this almost irresistable accommodation of character, one can too easily overlook the basically iron factor in their political nature. A Vietnamese told me the other day: 'You overrate this quality of sweetness in the Indo-Chinese nature; we are brutal at heart. At least to each other. What is going on in the south of the country couldn't otherwise be conceivable.'

James Cameron, *Witness*, 1966

North Vietnamese

They're just a bunch of shits. Tawdry, filthy shits.

Richard Nixon, quoted by Anthony Sampson in Review of Nixon's Memoirs, *Observer*, 11 June 1978

Along Bay

The islands grew nearer, innumerable crags, cones and pillars, rising to three and four hundred feet, assuming every shape and form. There were islands that took on grotesque human profiles, others that looked like crouching frogs, sugar loaves and ships under sail. There were prehistoric monoliths, church spires, crenelated Border towers, twin towers like those of Notre Dame de Paris, towers which leaned like that of Pisa, vast Roman triumphal arches and Egyptian pyramids. It was as though the architectural giants of the world, grown senile, eaten with age and weather, had been dumped down here to crumble quietly away. Close they stood, weary tower leaned towards corroded arch across passages so narrow one might jerk a stone across. Their bases were undermined by sea-wear, they seemed to be toppling one upon the other, millions of tons of rock reeling wearily this way and that. A thick scabrous cement of oysters plastered their bases. Their sheer flanks were gnawed with fantastic holes and grottoes, like air-bubbles in faulty metal. Their tops were shaggy with palmettoes and trailing vines.

Crosbie Garstin, *The Dragon and the Lotus*, 1928

Can Tho (in the Mekong Delta)

'I want to see the day,' one adviser informed me, 'when every peasant is saving up for a second Honda. I want to make this a real, get-up-and-go, greedy society.'

Richard West, *Victory in Vietnam*, 1974

Da Nang (formerly Tourane)

There are places of which the only point is the arrival; they promise the most fantastic adventures of the spirit and give you no more than three meals a day and last year's films. They are like a face full of character that intrigues and excites you, but that on closer acquaintance you discover is merely the mask of a vulgar soul. Such is Tourane.

W. Somerset Maugham, *The Gentleman in the Parlour*, 1930

It must be the curse of the Chams that has doomed Danang to be first a war town and then an oil town: from Armageddon to Abu Dhabi, from Hell to Shell.

Richard West, *Victory in Vietnam*, 1974

Danang was pushed next to the sea and all the land around it had been stripped of trees. If ever a place looked poisoned, it was Danang.

Paul Theroux, *The Great Railway Bazaar*, 1975

Haiphong

It always was, for Vietnam, a dreary place; it had none of the meretricious corrupt luxury of Saigon or the torpid grace of Hanoi or the rural dignity of Hué and Dalat; it was a sort of Oriental Swansea.

James Cameron, *Witness*, 1966

Hanoi

At Hanoi I found nothing much to interest me. . . . The French tell you it is the most attractive town in the East, but, when you ask them why, answer that it is exactly like a town, Montpellier, or Grenoble, in France.

W. Somerset Maugham, *The Gentleman in the Parlour*, 1930

I had not been here for 12 years or so. . . . It was then what the French made of all their colonial garrison towns: a sort of provençal prefecture with Asian overtones; the French were said to create their colonies of boulevards and brothels.

James Cameron, *Evening Standard*, 7 December 1965; *What a Way to Run the Tribe*, 1968

Ho Chi Minh City (formerly Saigon)

My little party was amazed to discover that we were in a miniature Paris – wide boulevards, fine shops as in the Rue de la Paix, and a palace of tremendous size, wider than Fontainebleau.

Alfred Viscount Northcliffe, *My Journey Round the World* (December 1921), 1923

As we drove into the town, it became plain that Saigon was, in fact, an achievement, unique, a French city flowering alone out of a tropical swamp in the farthest corner of Asia. Once there, within its narrow confines, it is as though, in the manner of the polite fiction adopted by embassies the world over, you stood upon the actual soil of France.

Osbert Sitwell, *Escape with Me*, 1939

Saigon did not straggle into the countryside. The edges of the city were sharply defined, stopping suddenly where the vivid green of the rice lands surrounding the urban mass began. The air above the city was thick with pollution so that from a distance it appeared that the closely massed buildings lay beneath a gigantic yellowish-brown dome. The pollution was so thick that it had semblance of solidity making it appear much more than a cloud.

Milton Osborne, *Before Kampuchea*, 1979

and Hanoi
The difference between these two cities is the difference between New York and Shrewsbury.

John Pilger, *Do You Remember Vietnam?*, ATV Network production, 3 October 1978

Hué

Hué is a pleasant little town with something of the leisurely air of a cathedral city in the West of England.

W. Somerset Maugham, *The Gentleman in the Parlour*, 1930

between Hué and Da Nang, Ashau Valley
No picture could duplicate the complexity of the beauty: over there, the sun lighted a bomb scar in the forest, and next to it smoke filled the bowl of a valley; a column of rain from one fugitive cloud slanted on another slope, and the blue gave way to black green, to rice green on the flat fields of shoots, which became, after a strip of sand, an immensity of blue ocean. The distances were enormous and the landscape was so large it had to be studied in parts, like a mural seen by a child. . . .

We were on the fringes of the bay that was green and sparkling in bright sunlight. Beyond the leaping jade plates of the sea was an overhang of cliffs and the sight of a valley so large it contained sun, smoke, and rain and cloud – all at once – independent quantities of color. I had been unprepared for this beauty; it surprised and humbled me in the same degree as the emptiness had in rural India. Who has mentioned the fact that the heights of Vietnam are places of unimaginable grandeur? . . . We should have known all along that the French would not have colonized it, nor would the Americans have fought so long, if such ripeness did not invite the eye to take it.

Paul Theroux, *The Great Railway Bazaar*, 1975

The Montagnard Peoples

One legend says that at the beginning of time a dog , a buffalo and a woman were arguing which should drink first at a river, when the dog killed and ate the buffalo and then mated the woman, to start the Montagnard race. Another legend, of greater political acumen, says that when all the world's peoples crawled out of holes in the ground, the Montagnards were not fast enough and lost their share of good land.

Richard West, *Victory in Vietnam*, 1974

Qui Nhon

One American in Qui Nhon, a lugubrious construction worker, said to me once: 'There's a captain I know who's done two tours of duty and he regards this country with passionate hatred, I mean hatred. He's really worked at it. He says, and I've got to kind of agree with him, that the only solution to this country is to withdraw all the Americans, and then to plaster the whole goddam place with nukes. Then after it was all over he'd take up an airplane with two monkeys, a male and a female, attached to two parachutes. And just before throwing them out of the plane he'd say: 'This time, don't fuck it up!'

Richard West, *Victory in Vietnam*, 1974

Thanh Hoa province (south of Hanoi, en route to)

It was a landscape of almost wildly theatrical beauty. . . . The Vietnamese countryside . . . in certain conditions, is wholly bizarre. It is a plain studded with strange little precipitous mountains, as though a shower of enormous meteorites had become embedded in the land; it is a geological phenomenon I do not understand; once before I had seen it in the South Chinese province of Kwangsi; in the light of the full moon it is eerie beyond expression; it is like living in the heart of a seventeenth-century Oriental water-colour.

James Cameron, *Witness*, 1966

W

THE WEST

Ex oriente lux, ex occidente lex.
(From the East, light, from the West, law.)
Anon. Latin proverb

And stepping westward seemed to be
A kind of *heavenly* destiny.
William Wordsworth, *Stepping Westward*, 3 June 1805

WEST INDIES

See also under individual islands

I become daily more and more convinced that all the West India Islands will remain in the hands of the people of colour, and a total expulsion of the whites will sooner or later take place. It is high time we should foresee the bloody scenes which our children certainly, and possibly ourselves (south of the Potomac) have to wade through, and try to avert them.
Thomas Jefferson, Letter to James Monroe, 14 July 1793

I like a ball in the West Indies better than in England. True it is you perspire, but then you have not to undergo the triumph of superior frigidity in your partner; she perspires in precise analogy with yourself, lifts and relifts the cambric toties quoties, as the Papists say, while ever doth the orient humour burst forth at intervals upon her ivory cheek, and gravitate in emulous contrafluence with your own. . . . It is my advice not to drink much; restrain yourself till twelve o'clock or so, and then eat some cold meat and absorb a pint of porter cup, which is perfectly innoxious to the system, and more restorative to the animal spirits than punch, wine, or sangaree. Above all, do not be persuaded to swallow any washy tea; it gives neither strength nor vivacity, but rather impairs both, and makes you excessively uncomfortable.
H.N. Coleridge, *Six Months in the West Indies, in 1825*, 1826

Life in the West Indies has its pleasures and its pains, like opium. The former are drinking porter and having common of turtle sans stint et sans nombre; the latter are perspiration, mosquitos, and the yawny-drawly way in which the men converse.
Ibid.

The West Indies I behold
Like the Hesperides of old
– Trees of life with fruits of gold.

No – a curse is on their soul
Bonds and scourges, tears and toil
Man degrade and earth despoil.
James Montgomery, 'A Voyage Round the World', *Works*, 1841

Oh, what stars they are, those in that western tropical world! How beautiful a woman looks by their light, how sweet the air smells, how gloriously legible are the constellations of the heavens!
Anthony Trollope, *The West Indies and the Spanish Main*, 1859

They were valued only for the wealth which they yielded, and society there has never assumed any particularly noble aspect. There has been splendour and luxurious living, and there have been crimes and horrors, and revolts and massacres. There has been romance, but it has been the romance of pirates and outlaws. The natural graces of life do not show themselves under such conditions. There has been no saint in the West Indies since Las Casas, no hero, unless philonegro enthusiasm can make one out of Toussaint. There are no people there in the true sense of the word, with a character and purpose of their own.
James Anthony Froude, *The English in the West Indies*, 1887

The most immediately conspicuous difference between the British Colonies of the Caribbean and the Spanish American republics is a difference in the women's clothes. Sartorially the colonies are bits of the English provinces with their provinciality raised to the *n*th power.
Aldous Huxley, *Beyond the Mexique Bay*, 1934

Everywhere in Havana there hangs the perfume of cigar smoke. Cuba is lucky in this, her characteristic smell, it is agreeable and sophisticated. Every one of the islands has, for me, its own special scent. In Curaçao the air is heavy with oil fumes, in Barbados you are never far from the sweet thick odour of the cane juice, while the smaller islands like Grenada or St Vincent float in a subtle aroma of spices or the pungent reek of the piles of arrowroot stacked for the grinding mill. In the evening I strolled across Central Park to buy cigars.

Dane Chandos, *Isles to Windward*, 1955

In West Indian towns history seems dead, irrelevant. Perhaps it is because the past is so unimaginable; perhaps it is the light; perhaps it is because so much is makeshift and new and the squalor so wholly contemporary.

V.S. Naipaul, *The Middle Passage*, 1962

Lesser Antilles

I was altogether unprepared for their beauty and grandeur. For hundreds of miles, day after day, the steamer carried us past a shifting diorama of scenery which may be likened to Vesuvius and the Bay of Naples, repeated again and again with every possible variation of the same type of delicate loveliness.

Charles Kingsley, *At Last, A Christmas in the West Indies*, 1871

Each outer line trends upwards so surely towards a single focus; each whole is so sharply defined between its base-line of sea and its background of sky, that, like a statue, each island is compact and complete in itself, an isolated and self-dependent organism; and therefore, like every beautiful statue it looks much smaller than it is. So perfect this isolation seems, that one fancies, at moments, that the island does not rise out of the sea, but floats upon it; that it is held in place, not by the roots of the mountains, and deep miles of lava-wall below, but by the cloud which has caught it by the top, and will not let it go. Let that cloud but rise and vanish, and the whole beautiful thing will be cast adrift; ready to fetch away before the wind.

Ibid.

Y

YEMEN (South)

They are of small stature and meagre muscular development; their faces are hairless and covered with a slight down, their expression degenerate and slightly dotty, an impression which is accentuated by their loping, irregular gait.

Evelyn Waugh, *Remote People*, 1931
(in USA *They Were Still Dancing*)

The Cuba of the Arabian peninsula.

Richard Nixon, *The Real War*, 1980

Aden

Aden . . . is situated under the foote of an unfruitfull mountaine, a place where I should scarce have looked for a Towne, but it is set there for strength, where it is very defencible, and not by any enemie easily to be wonne, if the defendants within be men of resolution, and so that it be formerly victualled and provided of munition; and to Sea-ward, though it be in a manner drie at low-water, there stands an high Rocke somewhat larger than the Tower of London, which is not by enemies to be in hast ascended, by reason it is so steepe . . . this Rocke is so walled, flankered, and furnished with Ordnance, as it seemeth to me, it may command both the Towne and Roade.

Nicholas Downton, *Journal*, 1610, in *Purchas his Pilgrimes*, 1625

The Coal-hole of the East.

Richard Burton, *Lake Regions of Central Africa*, 1860

Aden should mean oven. Only the camels seemed baked enough to suit it.

Henry Adams, Journal Letter to Elizabeth Cameron, 29 September 1891

I would as soon throw myself to the sharks as live in that arid, salty hell. That Rimbaud should have endured it, should have endured the Hotel de l'Univers, is a real tribute to the horrors of Aden; for it was to be expected that Rimbaud, with that perversity which made him renounce literature at the age of nineteen, should inflict upon himself a sojourn in precisely the most repulsive corner of the world he could find.

Vita Sackville-West, *Passenger to Teheran*, 1926

You can have no idea of what a sunset is in Aden. Imagine one half of the sky a luminous green – I can't tell you how luminous, like green water when you are in it and looking through it to the sun: and this green shoots up fanlike in rays towards the other half of sky where night is lying already, deep blue. Above the sea along the horizon are pink ripples of cloud; the sea heaves with the sweep of the coast past the mouth of Aden bay, with flat lights on it as it catches the west. And half bathed in the light, half black in their own volcanic shadows, the rocks of Aden stand up like dolomites, so jagged and old. . . . There is a feeling of gigantic and naked force about it all, and one thinks what it was when these hills were boiling out their stream of fire, hissing them into the sea, and wonders at anything so fragile as man living on these ancient desolations.

Freya Stark, *The Coasts of Incense*, 1953

Mocha / Mokha

The towne for the most part built with bricke and stone fairely playstered over with Playster of Paris: the building flat-roofed some two stories high, with Tarrises on the top, whereon they build Summer houses of Canes and Mats, in which they rest in the nights and passe the first quarter of the day, having at that time a fresh breese from the Sea; all the rest of the day so hot, that men cannot well endure any clothes, not so much as a shirt. It lyeth levell alongst the Sea-side, being about two miles from the North to South. There are many faire houses and three principall Moschees; the streets kept cleane, each mans doore every morning and evening watered and swept, seeming liker sandie bowling allies then streets: no filth suffered to be cast abroad, but carried to a place appointed scowred by the Sea: In fine, I have not lightly seene, a sweeter, cleaner, better governed Towne then this Mocha.

Edward Heynes, *Journal* 1618, in *Purchas his Pilgrimes*, 1625

Mukalla

This is a charming little town to look at, rather like a picture by Carpaccio, only white.

Freya Stark, Letter, 19 January 1935, in *The Coasts of Incense*, 1953

YUGOSLAVIA

Belgrade

There ride before the Cittie thirty-five floatinge milles, theire Cables of withes, and theire Anchors greate basketts filled full of stones, makeinge as faire a shewe afarr of as they were handsome within, in all things resembling a howse, saveinge the forepart, which was shipp shapen, built on a greate Barge, the building being neatly contrived, each tymber beinge squared and wrought, haveinge no Iron worke, all fastned with wooden pinns, there being an other small boate to uphold the other end of the Axeltree whereon the water wheel turneth, which are att least eight yards broad, I meane that part or outer circle which the water turneth, in regard of the soft motion of the Streame, and a small bridge to passe from the Mill to the lesser boate. Theie are made aloft in the Country, and sent downe with the Currant. The river is abundant in fish as Sturgeons, Carpes, Pikes, etts., which are soe cheape as is almost incredible.
The first of June, 1620. Wee went to see the Cittie, being scituate on a poynte where the River Saba runneth into Danubius which is nothing neere halfe soe broad, but of a farre more swifter course. The Cittie conteynes about 2000 howsholds, whereof sixty or seventy are Jewes, the rest Christians and Turkes: generally made of Boards, both walls and rooffe (Churches, Besistenes, bathes and Canes excepted), which are built of Stone. Howsoever, those wooden buildings make a faire shewe being very handsomely contrived.
The 2nd. June, 1620. The Castle is next worth notice (if not cheife): it standeth within the Cittie on the very pointe which the Two Rivers make shewinge without to bee a very great, faire and stronge thinge, being very much beautifyed with Turretts, bulwarks, battlements and watch Towers round about, wherein is as it were an other Cittie, haveinge Churches, Bathes etts., all the dwellers Turkes.

Peter Mundy, *Sundry Relations of Certaine Voyages*, *c.* 1640

The sunset sky against which I first saw Belgrade, was like a crimson and orange and purple moth, barred with colours as hard and clear as enamel. Belgrade stood heaped white on its hill, all its windows on fire with light; a long white mound, set there in a semi-circle above water and a great plain, with a point of land running down into the water. Beyond the city, as you enter Servia, there are valleys in which the trees grow as thick as grass, bulrushes tufted with white wool along the river-courses, great fields of melons with their dry stalks, and often a kind of English scenery, a monotony of tilled plenty.

Arthur Symons, *Cities*, 1903

Belgrade reminded me at one time of Moscow, at another of some white Spanish city. The whole place is made by the crossing of straight lines: I never saw a curve. Few of the houses have more than two storeys; the streets are broad, mountainously paved; and when I came into it at night there was a white nocturnal silence over everything. . . . Oxen with huge branching horns move slowly through the streets, drawing long, narrow wooden carts; or lie down to rest, as the men do at midday, with their heads on the stones with which they are paving the streets. The town is like a great village, ready made; and one can imagine it being harnessed to those oxen, and carted bodily away, and the flat, dreary country which lies all round lapsing into its original dry barrenness.

Ibid.

Belgrade is blessed as few cities are with natural beauty, lying high on the confluence of two great rivers, Danube and Save; but it is like a pretty peasant girl with the carriage of a queen and the raiment of a dirty beggar.

John Gunther, *Inside Europe*, 1938 edn

In the middle of the night the train pulled into Belgrade station, which is always as stimulating an experience as arriving in Stockton-on-Tees.

James Cameron, *Point of Departure*, 1967

An odd mixture of a continental capital and an eastern village.

E.R. Dodds, *Missing Persons*, 1977 – of 1917

Dubrovnik (formerly Ragusa)

Another account was told us, how in the Dukedome of Regusa in the Adriatique (a State which is little, but more ancient they say then Venice, and is called the mother of Venice) and the Turkes lie round about it – that they change all the officers of their guard, for fear of conspiracy, every 24 houres, so that nobody knows who shall be Captain of the guard tonight; but two men come to a man, and lay hold of him as a prisoner and carry him to the place; and there he hath the keys of the garrison given him, and he presently issues his orders for the night's Watch; and so always from night to night.

Samuel Pepys, *Diary*, 11 January 1662

Montenegro

They rose to where their sovran eagle sails,
They kept their faith, their freedom on the height,
Chaste, frugal, savage, arm'd by day and night
Against the Turk; whose inroad nowhere scales
Their headlong passes, but his footstep fails,
And red with blood the Crescent reels from fight
Before their dauntless hundreds, in prone flight

By thousands down the crags and thro' the vales.
O smallest among peoples! rough rock-throne
Of Freedom! warriors beating back the swarm
Of Turkish Islam for five hundred years,
Great Tsernogora! never since thine own
Black ridges drew the cloud and brake the storm
Has breathed a race of mightier mountaineers.

Alfred Lord Tennyson, 'Montenegro', *Nineteenth Century*, 1 May 1877

Nis

Nis is the Clapham Junction of South-East Europe. People have been stuck there for ever.

James Cameron, *Point of Departure*, 1967

Rovinj / Rovingo

I did not a little wonder when I observed every second or third person of this City to halt and be lame of one foot, which made me remember the Citizens of Islebe in Germany, and in the Province of Saxony, where almost all the men have wry neckes; whereof I knew the cause, mainly because they used daily to dig in mines, with their neckes leaning to one side; but of this common lamenes of the Inhabitants of Rovingo, I could not learne any probable cause, except it were the foule disease of lust, raigning in those parts, which I rather thought likely, because the lamenesse was common to weomen as men.

Fynes Moryson, *An Itinerary*, 1617

Pola / Pula

Pola is a queer old place.

James Joyce, Letter to Stanislaus Joyce, 19 January 1905

Servian Forest

Endless and endless now on either side, the tall oaks closed in their ranks, and stood gloomily lowering over us, as grim as an army of giants with a thousand years' pay in arrear.

A.W. Kinglake, *Eothen*, 1844 – of *c.* 1835

Serbia (under the Turks)

There are few countries less infested by 'lions' than the provinces on this part of your route; you are not called upon to 'drop a tear' over the tomb of 'the once brilliant' anybody, or to pay your 'tribute of respect' to any thing dead or alive; there are no Servian or Bulgarian litterateurs with whom it would be positively disgraceful not to form an acquaintance; you have no staring, no praising to get through: the only public building of any interest that lies on the road is of modern date, but is said to be a good specimen of oriental architecture; it is a pyramidical shape, and is made up of thirty thousand skulls contributed by the rebellious Servians in the early part (I believe) of this century; I am not at all sure of my date, but I fancy it was in the year 1806 that the first skull was laid. I am ashamed to say that in the darkness of the early morning, we unknowingly went by the neighbourhood of this triumph of art, and so basely got off from admiring 'the simple grandeur of the architect's conception,' and 'the exquisite beauty of the fretwork.'

A.W. Kinglake, *Eothen*, 1844 – of *c.* 1835

The Moslem quarter of a city is lonely and desolate; you go up, and down, and on, over shelving and hillocky paths through the narrow lanes walled in by blank, windowless dwellings; you come out upon an open space strewed with the black ruins that some late fire has left; you pass by a mountain of castaway things, the rubbish of centuries, and on it you see numbers of big, wolf-like dogs lying torpid under the sun, with limbs outstretched to the full, as if they were dead; storks or cranes, sitting fearless upon the low roofs, look gravely down upon you; the still air that you breathe is loaded with the scent of citron and pomegranate rinds scorched by the sun, or (as you approach the Bazaar) with the dry, dead perfume of strange spices. You long for some signs of life, and tread the ground more heavily, as though you would wake the sleepers with the heel of your boot; but the foot falls noiseless upon the crumbling soil of an eastern city, and Silence follows you still. Again and again you meet turbans, and faces of men, but they have nothing for you – no welcome – no wonder – no wrath – no scorn – they look upon you as we do upon a December's fall of snow – as a 'seasonable,' unaccountable, uncomfortable work of God that may have been sent for some good purpose – to be revealed hereafter.

Ibid.

Split

It recalls Naples, because it also is a tragic and architecturally magnificent sausage-machine, where a harried people of mixed race have been forced by history to run for centuries through the walls and cellars and sewers of ruined palaces, and have now been evicted by a turn of events into the open day, neat, and slick, and uniform, taking to modern clothes and manners with the adaptability of oil, though at the same time they are set aside for ever from the rest of the world by the arcana of language and thoughts they learned to share while they scurried for generations close pressed through the darkness.

Rebecca West, *Black Lamb and Grey Falcon*, 1942

Z

ZAIRE (formerly Belgian Congo)

*Heart of Darkness.

Joseph Conrad, Title of story, 1902

*'I always ask leave in the interests of science to measure the crania of those going out there,' he said. 'And when they come back too?' I asked. 'Oh I never see them,' he remarked, 'and moreover, the changes take place inside you know.'

Joseph Conrad, *Heart of Darkness*, 1902

'Well, so long!' called back the young German, as he took the wheel of his battered, box-body Ford. 'I tell you one thing to remember about the Congo – what the White Ants don't get the White Fathers will!'

Negley Farson, *Behind God's Back*, 1940

Every nation has a right to its own War of the Roses.

Anon. comment, in 1962, on the Congolese Civil War, quoted by A.M. Schlesinger, *One Thousand Days*, 1965

Some of these journalists comfort themselves with re-reading Conrad's *Heart of Darkness*. 'Ten minutes of it before breakfast and I can face the day,' said a colleague on one of the London dailies. It is still the definitive work on what it feels like to be in the Congo.

Richard West, *The White Tribes of Africa*, 1965

The Congo vaccinated me for good against that entire continent.

George Gale, 'I Like it Here', *Spectator*, 23 September 1978

One feels obliged to re-emphasize just what an incredible arrangement this was. The Congo had not been taken as a colony by Belgium, nor was Leopold to rule it as king of the Belgians. A brand-new state had been created essentially by fiat out of a vast African territory, unbeknown to the overwhelming majority of the people who lived there. And a private individual, whom an even greater number of those people had never heard of, had been given that state to own personally and had been made its king. 'The sovereignty of the Congo is invested in the person of the Sovereign,' a Belgian lawyer of the time wrote. 'His will can be resisted by no juridical obstacle whatsoever.' Leopold II could say with more justification than Louis XIV did: *'L'état c'est moi.'* Leopold himself, somewhat later, put it even more bluntly: 'My rights over the Congo are to be shared with none; they are the fruit of my own struggle and expenditure . . . the King was the founder of the state; he was its organizer, its owner, its absolute sovereign.' Perhaps an American newspaperman at that time summed up this peculiar situation most succinctly: 'He possesses the Congo just as Rockefeller possesses Standard Oil.'

Peter Forbath, *The River Congo*, 1978 (referring to the status conferred under the Berlin Act of 26 February 1885)

Zaire's got to be great. I've never seen so many Mercedes.

Muhammad Ali, Remark, 1979, quoted Patrick Marnham, *Fantastic Invasion*, 1980

Zaireans / Congolese

In the management of a bargain I should back the Congoese native against Jew or Christian, Parsee or Banyan, in all the round world. Unthinking men may perhaps say cleverness at barter, and shrewdness in trade, consort not with their unsophisticated condition and degraded customs. Unsophisticated is the very last term I should ever apply to an African child or man in connection with the knowledge of how to trade. . . . I have seen a child of eight do more tricks of trade in an hour than the cleverest European trader on the Congo could do in a month. . . . Therefore when I write of a Congo native, whether he is of the Bakongo, Byyanzi, or Bateké Tribes, remember to associate him with an almost inconceivable amount of natural shrewdness, and power of indomitable and untiring chaffer.

Henry Morton Stanley, *The Congo*, 1885

Pigmies

You do not believe your first pigmy when you see him.

Negley Farson, *Behind God's Back*, 1940

Boende

The phrase for 'white man' in the local language is *Lolema djola feka feka*, which means 'the bat that flies hard without knowing where it is going.'

John Gunther, *Inside Africa*, 1955

Kinshasa (formerly Leopoldville)

It has big warehouses stacked like packing cases along the river, broad businesslike streets, one skyscraper (ten stories) known as 'Le Building', and no charm. . . . It reflects strongly the Belgian national character. People are hard-headed, hard-working, frugal, bourgeois, and successful. There is no nonsense about aesthetics. Leopoldville puts forth a note of practicality, commerce, and good will. It reminded me of Belgium immediately after the war, when Brussels was a thriving metropolis while Paris still lay in the abyss.

John Gunther, *Inside Africa*, 1955

Kisangani (formerly Stanleyville)

Nothing could be more quintessentially the heart of tropical Africa than Stanleyville, but it has the liveliness and efficiency of a miniature Antwerp.

John Gunther, *Inside Africa*, 1955

Zaire River (formerly River Congo)

I wish I had some of the assurance possessed by others, but I am oppressed with the apprehension that after all it may turn out that I have been following the Congo; and who would risk being put into a cannibal pot and converted into black man for it?

David Livingstone, *Journal*, 1873
(on the headwaters of the Congo, while
searching for those of the Nile)

*It had become a place of darkness. But there was in it one river especially, a mighty big river, that you could see on the map, resembling an immense snake uncoiled, with its head in the sea, its body at rest curving afar over a vast country, and its tail lost in the depths of the land. And as I looked at the map of it in a shop-window, it fascinated me as a snake would a bird – a silly little bird.

Joseph Conrad, *Heart of Darkness*, 1902

*Going up that river was like travelling back to the earliest beginnings of the world, when vegetation rioted on the earth, and the big trees were kings. An empty stream, a great silence, an impenetrable forest. The air was warm, thick, heavy, sluggish. There was no joy in the brilliance of sunshine. The long stretches of the waterway ran on, deserted, into the gloom of overshadowed distances. On silvery mudbanks hippos and alligators sunned themselves side by side. The broadening waters flowed through a mob of wooded islands; you lost your way on that river as you would in a desert and butted all day long against shoals, trying to find the channel, till you thought yourself bewitched and cut off for ever from everything you had known once – somewhere – far away – in another existence perhaps. There were moments when one's past came back to one, as it will sometimes when you have not a moment to spare to yourself; but it came in the shape of an unrestful and noisy dream, remembered with wonder amongst the overwhelming realities of this strange world of plants, and water and silence. And this stillness of life did not in the least resemble a peace. It was the stillness of an implacable force brooding over an inscrutable intention. It looked at you with a vengeful aspect. I got used to it afterwards.

Ibid. (Marlow speaking)

*The earth seemed unearthly. We are accustomed to look upon the shackled form of a conquered monster, but there – there you could look at a thing monstrous and free. It was unearthly, and the men were – No, they were not inhuman. Well, you know, that was the worst of it – this suspicion of their not being inhuman. It would come slowly to one. They howled, and leaped, and spun, and made horrid faces; but what thrilled you was just the thought of their humanity – like yours – the thought of your remote kinship with this wild and passionate uproar. Ugly. Yes, it was ugly enough; but if you were man enough you would admit to yourself that there was in you just the faintest trace of a response to the terrible frankness of that noise, a dim suspicion of there being a meaning in it which you – you so remote from the night of first ages – could comprehend.

Ibid. (Marlow speaking)

Then I saw the Congo, creeping through the black,
Cutting through the jungle with a golden track.

Vachel Lindsay, 'The Congo', in *Collected Poems*, 1914

The Congo is another river, like the Amazon, which lends itself to fine writing. But, for most people, it is just one everlasting, uneventful, unbearable wall of green.

Negley Farson, *Behind God's Back*, 1940

The Congo is the circulatory system of the Congo.

John Gunther, *Inside Africa*, 1955

Congo: the two sudden syllables beat on the imagination like the beat of a jungle drum, calling up nightmare visions of primeval darkness, unfathomable mystery, dreadful savagery. No other word has quite that power; no other symbol stands more vividly for the myth and magic of Africa than the fabulous river those two barbaric syllables name. And for hundreds and hundreds of years, from the time *Congo* first entered the geography and literature of Western civilization in the fifteenth century, this has been so.

Peter Forbath, *The River Congo*, 1978

I . . . had fallen into a conversation with a young Zairois official, a government veterinarian. . . . At one point in our aimless, friendly chatter, I happened to refer to the river as the Congo. His expression stiffened and he corrected me pointedly, calling it the Zaire. I was surprised, and apologised but took the opportunity to question him on what I regarded as the foolishness of the name change. No, it was not foolish, he replied firmly. 'You will understand me, my friend, when I say that *Congo* is a very heavy word. It is a word far too heavy for a people like ourselves to bear in this modern age. When I was a student in Europe, I never liked to say I was Congolese. I pretended I was Guinean. Because there in Europe, and also in your America and, yes, even here in Africa, *Congo* has come to stand for all the things we are now struggling so hard to leave behind, for all the savage and primitive things of our past.'

Ibid.

ZAMBIA (fomerly Northern Rhodesia)

Northern Rhodesia, which lives mostly on copper, is like a Texas millionaire – somewhat dull and perhaps uncouth, but rich.

John Gunther, *Inside Africa*, 1955

Lusaka

The capital, Lusaka, looks like a Wild West set in early, shabby movies.

John Gunther, *Inside Africa*, 1955

Ndola

If Salisbury is Surbiton superimposed on Africa, then the copper belt is its Scunthorpe.

Richard West, *The White Tribes of Africa*, 1965

ZIMBABWE (formerly Southern Rhodesia)

They are calling the new country Rhodesia, that is from the Transvaal to the Southern end of Tanganyika; the other name is Zambesia. I find that I am human, and should like to be living after my death; still, perhaps if that name is coupled with the object of England everywhere, and united, the name may convey the discovery of an idea which ultimately led to the cessation of all wars and one language throughout the world.

Cecil Rhodes, Letter to W.T. Stead, 1891

The visit to Windsor must have been the occasion when the Queen asked Rhodes what he had been doing since she had last seen him. 'I have added two provinces to Your Majesty's dominions,' he replied, 'Ah,' said the Queen, I wish some of my Ministers, who take away my provinces, would do as much.'

J.G. Lockhart and C.M. Woodhouse, *Rhodes*, 1963 – of 1894

'My North.'

Cecil Rhodes, 1890 quoted Gordon le Sueur, *Cecil Rhodes, the Man and his Work*, 1913

They can't take it away from me, can they? You never heard of a country's name being changed . . . ?

Cecil Rhodes, *c.* 1896 after the Jameson Raid, quoted in Stuart Cloete, *African Portraits*, 1946

Rhodesia is the right name for that land of piracy and pillage, and puts the right stain upon it.

Mark Twain, *More Tramps Abroad*, 1897

*Farming is not at all a scientific process in Rhodesia: you can grow lots of things by chiefly looking at niggers. They do all the work, and the farmer rides about on a nice horse, with a gun, and makes his fortune.

Gertrude Page, *Jill's Rhodesian Philosophy – or the Dam Farm*, 1910

*It was a wilderness and a desert – a vast untamed country, inhabited by uncivilised beings, which gripped and held the imagination.

'Do you think we ought to be here?' I asked the Soldier-man lightly. 'I feel as if we were intruding.'

'Intruding upon what?'

'Intruding upon someone else's world. This belongs to Bushmen and dwellers in caves and huts. You and I . . . we . . . we savour too much of motor omnibuses and dreadnoughts and aeroplanes.'

He laughed and rode forward, – a goodly figure of a man, with crisp black hair, and clear blue eyes, and the hall-mark of Britain's best.

At the top of a ridge, where we could see farthest, he drew rein, and looked at the far-reaching, far-spreading prospect, with eyes that loved it.

'Isn't that good,' he said. 'Whether we are intruders or not, we have at least brought it appreciation at last. How does it strike you?'

'Oh I like it,' I told him. 'It appeals powerfully, It's all new and fresh, and young and untried. It's like going back to the Creation. You and I are looking at a world God has just made, and wondering what is going to happen in it. Nothing at all has happened yet, you see, so no one can tell. I hope God is going to try another plan altogether, don't you? One in which duty won't always be something detestable; and where goodness isn't almost always dullness; and where little children will stop little much longer, and miss out the tiresome, awkward years altogether, and where one can be quite sure that dogs and horses go to heaven.

Ibid.

*When I saw the word 'Rhodesia' written across a lovely shade of pink, I said, 'That is the place for Jill.'

Ibid.

Rhodesian history flows upward from the Cape.

John Gunther, *Inside Africa*, 1955

Whatever occurs in that sullen land, I am heartily glad not to be there to witness it.

Richard West, *The White Tribes of Africa*, 1965

A suburb masquerading as a nation.

Anon., 1960s

Everything is fine in Rhodesia.

Ian Smith, quoted *Observer*, 'Sayings of the Week', 16 September 1979

To me it's always seemed perfectly simple. If you don't like black people don't come and live in Africa.

Sir Roy Welensky, attrib.

A combination of the Wild West and Tunbridge Wells.

Doris Lessing, quoted by John Archer in *Listener*, 8 May 1980

Zimbabweans

The Matabele

The Matabele were indeed as murderous a race of savages as ever lived, and their defeat was a moral as well as a political necessity. It is well to protect the aborigine; but when he is armed with a dozen assegais and earnestly desires your blood it is safer to shoot him or drive him further afield.

John Buchan, *The African Colony*, 1903

The Whites

The history of the whites in Southern Rhodesia is comparable to the first three parts of Wagner's *Ring of the Niebelungen*. They came in search of gold, overthrew the existing race by cunning and treachery, and now behave as though cursed by the Niebelung curse. The parallel could be pursued, but falls down in two respects: we have still to wait for the twilight of the gods, and Mr Ian Smith makes a shabby Siegfried.

Richard West, *The White Tribes of Africa*, 1965

Bulawayo

'Look at that – all homes; and all the result of an idle thought.'

Cecil Rhodes, quoted Gordon le Sueur, *Cecil Rhodes, the Man and his Work*, 1913

A dull town with flower shops.

Evelyn Waugh, *Diary*, 14 February 1931

Gwelo

The first sign that we were close upon Gwelo came from the sight of a number of white men in shirt-sleeves running across a meadow – an unusual sight in South Africa, which presently explained itself as the English inhabitants engaged in a cricket match. Nearly the whole town was either playing or looking on.

James Bryce, *Impressions of South Africa*, 1897

The Matopo Hills (grave of Cecil Rhodes)

Sliding down the rock, which has something of the texture and even the appearance of a flat-iron, I thought that only a true megalomaniac, who nevertheless must on occasion have experienced neurotic insecurities, would choose for his grave a setting so majestically isolated and immovable.

John Gunther, *Inside Africa*, 1955

Mtali

White ants are one of the four plagues of South Central Africa (the other three are locusts, horse-sickness, and fever; some add a fifth – the speculators in mining shares). . . . I was taken to see the public library at Mtali, and found they had destroyed nearly half of it. . . . We spent weary hours in trying to get them out of our food-boxes, being unable to fall in with the local view that they ought to be eaten with the meat they swarm over, as a sort of relish to it.

James Bryce, *Impressions of South Africa*, 1897

Salisbury *(now Harare City)*

Street-lamps now light people to their homes along paths where four years ago lions were still encountered. The last lion recoiling in dismay from the first street-lamp would be a good subject for a picture to illustrate the progress of Mashonaland.

James Bryce, *Impressions of South Africa*, 1897

One does not see many Africans in Salisbury; fewer it seemed than in London. There are black porters in the larger shops, and the white Shop-girls are abominably rude to them. They are also rather rude to their white customers, for they are at pains to demonstrate that under God all white men were created equal. The well-paid plumber who comes out to work in a private house, expects to sit down in the dining room with the family. He has a black, ill-paid assistant who squats outside. Here, as in England, the Champions of the colour bar are the classes whose modest skills many negroes can master. . . .

The visitor to Rhodesia sees as little of the native as a visitor to the United States sees of the very poor. (But in Rhodesia the natives are proportionally more numerous than the destitute in America.)

Evelyn Waugh, *A Tourist in Africa* (21 March 1959), 1960

The Mayor is very proud of the orderliness of Salisbury: 'Really it's just like Surbiton, Surbiton set in Africa. The average Salisbury man is not a wild westerner.'

Richard West, *The White Tribes of Africa*, 1965

It's okay, I guess – but it's too far from town.

Larry Fellows of the *New York Times*, at the time of UDI, attributed

Umtali

Come to Umtali and get bombed.

Slogan on White Rhodesian T-shirt, quoted by John Humphrys, 'Mugabe and the Whites', *Listener*, 6 March 1980

Victoria Falls (border with Zambia)

We proceeded next morning, 9th August 1860, to see the Victoria Falls. Mosi-oa-tunya is the Makololo name, and means smoke-sounding; Seongo, or Chongwe, meaning the Rainbow, or the place of the Rainbow, was the more ancient term they bore.

David and Charles Livingstone, *Narrative of an Expedition to the Zambesi and its Tributaries*, 1865

Above and Beyond

WORLD / EARTH

The earth is the lord's and the fullness thereof; the world and they that dwell therein.

The Bible, Psalms 24:1

TO THE MOST HIGH, MOST MIGHTY, AND MOST ANCIENT, Producer Seducer and Abuser of Mankind, the World.

Most Potent and Powerfull *Imposture*, take it not amisse that I a poore worme of your own breeding, doe (in waie of retribution) give you here the encrease of my Tallent, which I have beene almost 60 yeeres a gathering. It was told me that when I first came to visit you, that I cri'd and Waw'ld, and that when I leave you, I shall sigh and grone: and ever since I knew you, I have loved you so well for the good parts I have seen in you that I should verie willingly be glad to change you for a better.

John Taylor ('The Water Poet'), Dedication to *All the Workes of John Taylor*, 1630

The world's a book writ by the *eternal art*
Of the great Maker; printed in man's heart;
'Tis falsely printed though divinely penned,
And all the errata will appear at the end.

Francis Quarles, *Divine Fancies*, 1632

The created world is but a parenthesis in eternity.

Sir Thomas Browne, *Christian Morals* (before 1682), 1716

Above the smoke and stirr of this dim spot,
Which men call Earth. . . .

John Milton, *A Mask, Presented at Ludlow-Castle*, 1634

Had you the world on your chessboard, you could not fit all to your mind.

George Herbert, *Jacula Prudentum*, 1640

This opacous earth, this punctual spot.

John Milton, *Paradise Lost*, Book viii, 1667

O Earth, how like to Heav'n, if not preferrd
More justly, Seat worthier of Gods, as built
With second thoughts, reforming what was old!
For what God after better worse would build?
Terrestrial Heav'n, danc't round by other Heav'ns
That shine, yet bear thir bright officious Lamps,
Light above Light, for thee alone, as seems,
In thee concentring all thir precious beams
Of sacred influence: As God in Heav'n
Is Center, yet extends to all, so thou
Centring receav'st from all those Orbs; in thee,
Not in themselves, all thir known vertue appeers
Productive in Herb, Plant, and nobler birth
Of creatures animate with gradual life
Of Growth, Sense, Reason, all summ'd up in Man.

John Milton, *Paradise Lost*, Book ix, 1667

This world is like Noah's Ark
In which few men but many beasts embark.

Samuel Butler, *The World*, before 1680

If all the world were paper,
And all the sea were ink,
And all the trees were bread and cheese,
What should we do for drink?

Anon., seventeenth century

See, how the Earth has gain'd that very place,
Which, of all others in the boundless space,
Is most convenient, and will best conduce
To the wise ends requir'd for Nature's use.
You, who the Mind and Cause Supreme deny,
Nor on his aid to form the World rely,
Must grant, had perfect wisdom been employ'd
To find, through all the interminable void,
A seat most proper, and which best became
The earth and sea, it must have been the same.
Now who can this surprising fact conceive,
Who this event fortuitous believe,
That the brute Earth, unguided, should embrace
The only useful, only proper place,
Of all the millions in the empty space?

Sir Richard Blackmore, *The Creation*, Book I, 1712

The world is a great wilderness where mankind have wandered and jostled each other about from the creation. Some have removed by necessity and others by choice. One nation has been fond of seizing what another was tired of possessing; and it will be difficult to point out the country which is to this day in the hands of its first inhabitants.

Henry St John, Viscount Bolingbroke, *Reflections Upon Exile*, 1716

As it is my establish'd Opinion That this Globe of ours is no better than a Holland Cheese and the Walkers about in it Mites, I possess my Mind in patience, let what will happen, and should feel tolerably easy tho a great Rat came and eat halfe of it up.

Lady Mary Wortley Montagu, Letter to Lady Mar, February 1725

The world is a country which nobody ever yet knew by description; one must travel through it one's self to be acquainted with it.

Lord Chesterfield, Letter to this Son, 2 October 1747

*'To what end was this world formed?' said Candide. 'To infuriate us,' replied Martin.

Voltaire, *Candide*, 1759

*If this is the best of all possible worlds, then where are the others?

Ibid.

In short, my dear Sir, we must take the world, and the things in it, as they are; it is a dirty world, but, like France, has a vast number of good things in it.

Philip Thicknesse, *A Year's Journey through France and Spain*, 1789

'Still alive and still bold,' shouted Earth:
'I grow bolder, and still more bold.
The dead fill me ten thousand fold
Fuller of speed and splendour and mirth
I was cloudy and sullen and cold,
Like a frozen chaos uprolled,
Till by the spirit of the mighty dead
My heart grew warm: I feed on whom I fed.'

Percy Bysshe Shelley, *Written on Hearing . . . of the Death of Napoleon*, 1821

Juan . . .
Had seen the world, which is a curious sight
And very much unlike what people write.

Lord Byron, *Don Juan*, 1819–24

The Earth with its scarred face is the symbol of the Past; the Air and Heaven, of Futurity.

Samuel Taylor Coleride, *Table Talk*, 2 June 1824

This world is very odd, we see;
We do not comprehend it;
But in one fact can all agree
God won't and we can't mend it.

Arthur Hugh Clough, *Dipsychus*, *c.* 1850

Oh the Earth was *made* for lovers

Emily Dickinson, 1850

Earth being so good, would Heaven seem best?

Robert Browning, 'The Last Ride Together', *Men and Women*, 1855

The earth, that is sufficient,
I do not want the constellations any nearer,
I know they are very well where they are,
I know they suffice for those who belong to them.

Walt Whitman, *Song of the Open Road, 1*, 1856

We were looking towards the higher Alps, and Tennyson said that perhaps this earth and all that is on it – storms, mountains, cataracts, the sun and the skies – are the Almighty: in fact, such is our petty nature, we cannot see Him, but we see his Shadow, as it were, a distorted shadow.

Alfred Lord Tennyson, a Memoir, by his Son, 1897 – of 1869

*The true mystery of the world is the visible, not the invisible.

Oscar Wilde, *Picture of Dorian Gray*, 1891

The world, it would appear, is a vast class-room, and its Creator but a professor of political economy, apparently unable to carry out his theories with effect. Therefore, to us, the Western Europeans, he has turned for help, and upon us devolved the task of extirpating all those peoples upon whom he tried his 'prentice hand. On us he laid injunctions to increase at home, and to the happier portions of the world to carry death under the guise of life unsuitable to those into whose lands we spread.

R.B. Cunninghame Graham, *A Vanished Arcadia*, 1901

We are told that when Jehovah created the world he saw that it was good. What would he say now?

G. Bernard Shaw, 'Maxims for Revolutionists', *Man and Superman*, 1901–3

The world is a gaming table so arranged that all who enter the casino must play and all must lose more or less heavily in the long run, though they win occasionally by the way.

Samuel Butler, *Note-Books*, 1912

The world is so big, and I am so small,
I do not like it at all at all.

Woodrow Wilson, quoted by Adlai Stevenson, in Leon Harris, *The Fine Art of Political Wit*, 1965

Earth's the right place for love:
I don't know where it's likely to go better.

Robert Frost, *Birches*, 1916

One real world . . . is enough.

George Santayana, Preface to *Egotism in German Philosophy*, 1916

Gyrate, old Top, and let who will be clever;
The mess we're in is much too deep to solve.
Me for a quiet life, while you, as ever,
Continue to revolve.

Bert Leston Taylor, 'To a Well-known Globe', *The So-Called Human Race*, 1922 – before 1921

Man makes a great fuss
About this planet
Which is only a ball-bearing
In the hub of the universe. . . .

Christopher Morley, 'The Hubbub of the Universe', *Translations from the Chinese*, 1922

I am for world-control of production and of trade and transport, for a world coinage, and the confederation of mankind. I am for the Super-State, and not for any League. Cosmopolis is my city, and I shall die cut off from it.

H.G. Wells, *A Year of Prophesying*, 1925

'I quite realized,' said Columbus
'That the earth was not a rhombus,
But I *am* a little annoyed
To find it an oblate spheroid.'

E. Clerihew Bentley, *More Biography*, 1929

What you cannot find on earth is not worth seeking.

Norman Douglas, attrib.

This is the way the world ends
Not with a bang but a whimper.

T.S. Eliot, *The Hollow Men*, 1925

Superficially the world has become small and known. Poor little globe of earth, the tourists trot round you as easily as they trot round the Bois or round Central Park. There is no mystery left, we've been there, we've seen it, we know all about it. We've done the globe, and the globe is done.

D.H. Lawrence, 'New Mexico', *Survey Graphic May 1931; Phoenix*, 1936

It's hard to keep straight in a world that's so round.

Dame Madge Kendal, Interview, quoted in James Agate, *Ego 2*, 1936

I cannot bring a world quite round,
Although I patch it as I can.

Wallace Stevens, *The Man with The Blue Guitar*, 1937

The world only exists in your eyes – your conception of it. You can make it as big or as small as you want to.

F. Scott Fitzgerald, *The Crack-Up*, 1945

What's wrong with this world is, it's not finished yet. It is not completed to that point where man can put his final signature to the job and say, 'It is finished. We made it, and it works.'

William Faulkner, Address, Wellesley, Massachusetts, 8 June 1953

The most incomprehensible thing about the world is that it is incomprehensible.

Alfred Einstein, quoted in Obituary, 19 April 1955

I have no particular *objection* to the earth, but I wouldn't go so far as to call myself its friend.

Caption to Cartoon by J.B. Handelsman, *New Yorker*, 5 April 1982

MOON

With how sad steps, O Moon, thou climb'st the skies,
How silently, and with how wan a face!

Sir Philip Sidney, *Astrophel and Stella – Sonnet XXI*, 1591

Dull: What was a month old at Cain's birth, that's not five months old yet?
Holofernes: Dictyanna, goodman Dull; Dictyanna, goodman Dull.
Dull: What is Dictyanna?
Nathaniel: A title to Phoebe, to Luna, to the moon.

William Shakespeare, *Love's Labours Lost, c.* 1594–5

The moon, the governess of floods.

William Shakespeare, *A Midsummer Night's Dream, c.* 1595–6

Some of our men of good credit that were in this last voiage to Guinea, affirme earnestly that in the night season, they felt a sensible heat to come from the beames of the moone.

Richard Hakluyt, *Principal Navigations . . . of the English Nation*, 1598–1600

In Moungan' Park there is a deer
Silver horns and golden ear:
Neither fish, flesh, feather or bone
In Moungan's Park he walks alone.

– The Moon.

Irish (Westmeath) riddle, quoted Archer Taylor, *English Riddles from Oral Tradition*, 1951

My face is pale
And full and fair;
And round it,
Beauty spots there are.
By day indeed,
I seem less bright,
And only seen,

Sometimes at Night
And when the Sun
Is gone to Bed
I then begin
To shew my Head.

– The Moon

A New Riddle-Book; or, A Whetstone for Dull Wits, eighteenth century

Doth the moon care for the barking of a dog?

Robert Burton, *Anatomie of Melancholie*, 1621

Soon as the evening shades prevail
The moon takes up the wondrous tale
And nightly, to the listening earth
Repeats the story of her birth.

Joseph Addison, 'Ode', *Spectator*, No. 456, 23 August 1712

Some thought it mounted to the Lunar Sphere,
Since all things lost on Earth, are treasur'd there.
There heroes' Wits are kept in pondrous Vases,
And Beaus' in *Snuff-boxes* and *Tweezer-Cases*.
There broken Vows, and Death-bed Alms are found,
And Lovers' Hearts with Ends of Riband bound;
The Courtier's Promises, and Sick Man's Pray'rs,
The Smiles of Harlots, and the Tears of Heirs,
Cages for Gnats, and Chains to Yoak a Flea;
Dry'd Butterflies, and Tomes of Casuistry.

Alexander Pope, *The Rape of the Lock*, Canto V, 1722

Meanwhile the Moon,
Full-orb'd and breaking through the scatter'd clouds,
Shows her broad visage in the crimson'd east.
Turn'd to the Sun direct, her spotted disk –
Where mountains rise, umbrageous vales descend,
And caverns deep, as optic tube descries,
A smaller earth, – gives us his blaze again,
Void of its flame, and sheds a softer day.
Now through the passing cloud she seems to stoop,
Now up the pure cerulean rides sublime.
Wide the pale deluge floats, and streaming mild
O'er the sky'd mountain to the shadowy vale,
While rocks and floods reflect the quivering gleam,
The whole air whitens with a boundless tide
Of silver radiance, trembling round the world.

James Thomson, *The Seasons – Autumn*, 1730

The moon, like a flower,
In heaven's high bower
With silent delight
Sits and smiles on the night.

William Blake, 'Night', *Songs of Innocence*, 1789

Art thou pale for weariness
Of climbing heaven, and gazing on the earth,
Wandering companionless
Among the stars that have a different birth, –
And ever changing, like a joyless eye
That finds no object worth its constancy?

Percy Bysshe Shelley, *To the Moon*, 1820

And like a dying lady, lean and pale,
Who totters forth, wrapt in a gauzy veil,
Out of her chamber, led by the insane
And feeble wanderings of her fading brain,
The moon arose upon the murky earth,
A white and shapeless mass.

Percy Bysshe Shelley, *The Waning Moon*, 1820

He sighed; the next resource is the full moon
Where all sighs are deposited, and now
It happened luckily the chaste orb shone
As clear as such a climate will allow,
And Juan's mind was in the proper tone
To hail her with the apostrophe, 'Oh thou!'
Of amatory egotism the *Tuism*,
Which further to explain would be a truism.

But lover, poet, or astronomer,
Shepherd or swain, whoever may behold,
Feel some abstraction when they gaze on her.
Great thoughts we catch from thence (besides a cold
Sometimes, unless my feelings rather err);
Deep secrets to her rolling light are told.
The ocean' tides and mortals' brains she sways
And also hearts, if there be truth in lays.

Lord Byron, *Don Juan*, Canto xvi, 1819–24

If you go expressly to look at the moon, it becomes tinsel.

R.W. Emerson, *Journal*, 1836

The Moon – who does not love the silver moon,
In all her fantasies and all her phases?
Whether full-orb'd in the nocturnal noon,
Shining in all the dewdrops on the daisies,
To light the tripping fairies in their mazes,
Whilst stars are winking at the pranks of Puck;
Or huge and red, as on brown sheaves she gazes;
Or new and thin, when coin is turn'd for luck; –
Who will not say that Dian is a Duck?

Thomas Hood, *Love and Lunacy*, 1839

Sometimes she riseth from her shroud
Like the pale apparition of a sun.

Thomas Hood, *A Poetical Fragment*, before 1845

Moonlight is sculpture, sunlight is painting.

Nathaniel Hawthorne, *Notebook*, 1838

A lifeless solitude – an angry waste,
Searing our alien eyes with horrors bare;
No fertilising cloud – no genial air
To mitigate its savageness of breast;
The light itself all undiffusive there;
Motionless terror clinging to the crest

Of steepmost pinnacles; as by despair
Unfathomable caverns still possessed!
How shall we designate such world forlorn?
What nook of heaven abhors this portent dark?
Lo! Where the *Moon* reveals her gentle ray,
Waking the nightingale and poet's lay;
Speeding the voyager's return;
And lighting furtive kisses to their mark.

John Swanwick Drennan, 'On the Telescopic Moon', *Poems and Sonnetts*, 1895

The moon, that traveller's friend, a companion to the solitary man, like the blazing hearth of Northern climates, rose behind the filmy tree-tops and made us hail the gentle light. We have not the same feeling for the stars, or even the planets, though Jupiter and Venus give more light than does the Crescent in England; they are too distant, to far above us, whilst the Moon is of the earth, earthy, a member of our body physical, the complement of our atom.

Richard Burton, *Explorations of the Highlands of the Brazil*, 1869

That gentle Moon, the lesser light, the Lover's lamp,
  the Swain's delight,
A ruined world, a globe burnt out,
  a corpse upon the road of night.

Sir Richard Burton, *The Kasidah*, 1880

That it was in fact cloudless, appeared from the unbroken disc of the full moon, which, if I may venture to say so, had a kind of silly expression, as though it were a bad imitation of the sun, totally unable to keep the darkness in order.

Set in that strange gloom the moon looked wan and miserable enough; the lingering sunlight showed by contrast that she was but a feeble source of illumination; and, but for her half-comic look of helplessness, we might have sympathized with the astronomers who tell us that she is nothing but a vast perambulating tombstone, proclaiming to all mankind in the words of the familiar epitaph, 'As I am now, you soon shall be!' To speak after the fashion of early mythologies, one might fancy that some supernatural cuttlefish was shedding his ink through the heavens to distract her, and that the poor moon had but a bad chance of escaping his clutches.

Leslie Stephen, *The Playground of Europe*, 1894 edn

The innocent moon, which nothing does but shine,
Moves all the labouring surges of the world.

Francis Thompson, *Sister Songs*, 1895

Total eclipse of the moon last night. At 7.30 it began to go off. At total – or about that – it was like a rich rosy cloud with a tumbling surface framed in the circle and projecting from it – a bulge of strawberry-ice, so to speak. At half-eclipse the moon was like a gilded acorn in its cup.

Mark Twain, *More Tramps Abroad*, 1897 (journal entry of 4 September 1895)

I would not be the Moon, the sickly thing,
To summon owls and bats upon her wing;
For when the noble sun is gone away,
She turns his night into a pallid day.

She hath no air, no radiance of her own,
That world unmusical of earth and stone.
She wakes her dim, uncoloured, voiceless hosts,
Ghost of the sun, herself the sun of ghosts.

The mortal eyes that gaze too long on her
Of Reason's piercing ray defrauded are.
Light in itself doth feed the living brain;
That light, reflected, but makes darkness plain.

Mary Coleridge, 'In dispraise of the Moon', *Poems*, 1908 (before 1907)

*The moon, like a gardenia in the night's button-hole – but no! why should a writer never be able to mention the moon without likening her to something else – usually something to which she bears not the slightest resemblance? . . . The moon, looking like nothing whatsoever but herself, was engaged in her old and futile endeavour to mark the hours correctly on the sun-dial at the centre of the lawn.

Max Beerbohm, *Zuleika Dobson*, 1911

'What do you think of it, Moon,
  As you go?
Is Life much, or no?'
'O, I think of it, often think of it
  As a show
God ought surely to shut up soon,
  As I go.'

Thomas Hardy, 'To the Moon', *Moments of Vision*, 1917

The moon? It is a griffin's egg,
Hatching tomorrow night.
And how the little boys will watch
With shouting and delight
To see him break the shell and stretch
And creep across the sky.
The boys will laugh. The little girls,
I fear, may hide and cry.
Yet gentle will the griffin be,
Most decorous and fat,
And walk up to the Milky Way
And lap it like a cat.

Vachel Lindsay, 'Yet Gentle will the Griffin Be', *Collected Poems*, 1923

Oh Moon, when I look on thy beautiful face,
Careering along through the boundaries of space,
The thought has quite frequently come to my mind,
If ever I'll gaze on thy glorious behind.

Anon.

who knows if the moon's
a balloon,coming out of a keen city
in the sky—filled with pretty people?
(and if you and i should

get into it,if they
should take me and take you into their balloon,
why then
we'd go up higher with all the pretty people

than houses and steeples and clouds:
go sailing
away and away sailing into a keen
city which nobody's ever visited,where

always
it's
Spring)and everyone's
in love and flowers pick themselves

e.e. cummings, *& [AND]*, 1925

Moonshine is all moonshine to me.

Logan Pearsall Smith, *Last Words – All Trivia*, 1933

The moon is the mother of pathos and pity.

Wallace Stevens, 'Lunar Paraphrase', *Harmonium*, 1931

The light of the moon is unkind.

Walter Starkie, *Raggle-Taggle*, 1933

High over France, a full moon, cold and exciting
Like one of those dangerous flatterers we meet and love
When we are utterly wretched, returns our stare. . . .

W.H. Auden, *Dover*, August 1937

The moon follows the sun like a French
Translation of a Russian poet.

Wallace Stevens, *Variations on a Summer Day*, 1940

The moon, fancy's rear-vision mirror.

Vladimir Nabokov, *Speak Memory*, 1967

Treading the soil of the moon, palpitating its pebbles, tasting the panic and splendour of the event, feeling in the pit of one's stomach the separation from terra – these form the most romantic sensations an explorer has ever known.

Vladimir Nabokov, in *New York Times*, 21 July 1969

The moon is a desert. I have seen deserts.

W.H. Auden, Remark on the occasion of the Americans landing on the moon, 1969

I loved the moon, – until they trod on it.

Hair, 1969, line ad-libbed into the London production at the Shaftesbury Theatre

I do remember that when we were on the surface of the moon the thought came to me that here were two people who were farther away from home than anyone had ever been before, but we had a larger audience watching, paying attention to our every movement, than any people had had before.

Buzz Aldrin, Interview with Ludovic Kennedy, for BBC TV, *Change of Direction*, printed in *Listener*, 6 March 1980

SUN

and moon and earth

Timon: The Sunnes a Theefe, and with his great attraction
Robbes the vaste Sea. The Moones an arrant Theefe,
And her pale fire, she snatches from the Sunne.
The Seas a Theefe, whose liquid Surge, resolves
The Moone into Salt tears. The earth's a Theefe,
That feeds and breeds by a composture stolne
From gen'rall excrement: each thing's a Theefe.

William Shakespeare, *Timon of Athens, c.* 1607–8

I came from beyond the ocean
I drink water out of the sea
I lighten many a nation
And give myself to thee.

– The Sun.

Jamaican riddle, quoted Archer Taylor, *English Riddles from Oral Tradition*, 1951

What goes round the house, and in the house, and never touches the house?

– The Sun.

Old Nova Scotia riddle, quoted Archer Taylor, *English Riddles from Oral Tradition*, 1951

Busie old foole, unruly Sunne
Why dost thou thus,
Through windowes, and through curtaines call on us?

John Donne, *The Sunne Rising, c.* 1605

For thus the Sun is the eye of the World; and he is indifferent to the Negro, or the Cold Russian, to them that dwell under the line, and them that stand near the Tropicks, the scalded Indian, or the poor boy that shakes at the foot of the Riphean hills . . . and some have only a dark day and a long night from him, snow and white cattel, a miserable life, and a perpetual harvest of Catarrhes and Consumptions, apoplexies and dead palsies; but some have splendid fires, and aromatick spices, rich wines, and well-digested fruits, great wit and great courage; because they dwell in his eye, and look in his face, and are the Courtiers of the Sun and wait upon him in his Chambers of the East.

Jeremy Taylor, *B. Taylor's Opuscula*, 1678

See, how th'indulgent father of the day
At such due distance does his beams display,
That he his heat may give to sea and land,
In just degrees, as all their wants demand!
But had he, in th'unmeasurable space,
Of ether, chosen a remoter place;
For instance, pleas'd with that superior seat
Where Saturn, or where Jove, their course repeat;
Or had he happen'd farther yet to lie
In the more distant quarters of the sky;
How sad, how wild, how exquisite a scene
Of desolation had this planet been!

Sir Richard Blackmore, *The Creation*, Book I, 1712

Who in this Bowling Alley bowld the Sun?
Who made it always when it rises set:
To go at once both down, and up to get?

Edward Taylor, 'The Preface', *God's Determinations*, before 1728

I begin to be of opinion that the sun is grown old; it is certain he does not ogle with so much spirit as he used to do, or our planet has made some slip unperceived by the mathematicians.

Lady Mary Wortley Montagu, Letter to Lady Pomfret, 17 May 1740

. . . Oh, never may I, while I lift this brow
Believe in any god *less* like a god than thou.

Leigh Hunt, *Ode to the Sun*, 1850

It rises – passes – on our South
Inscribes a simple Noon –
Cajoles a Moment with the Spires
And infinite is gone.

Emily Dickinson, *c.* 1865

UNIVERSE

This wide machine, the universe regard,
With how much skill is each apartment rear'd!
The Sun a globe of fire, a glowing mass,
Hotter than melted flint or fluid glass,
Of this our system holds the middle place.
Mercurius, nearest to the central Sun,
Does in an oval orbit circling run;
But rarely is the object of our sight
In solar glory sunk, and more prevailing light.
Venus the next, whose lovely beams adorn
As well the dewy eve as opening morn,
Does her fair orb in beauteous order turn.
The globe terrestrial next, with slanting poles,
And all its ponderous load, unwearied rolls.
Then we behold bright planetary Jove,
Sublime in air, through his wide province move;
Four second planets his dominion own,
And round him turn, as round the Earth the Moon.
Saturn revolving in the highest sphere
With lingering labour finishes his year.
Yet is this mighty system, which contains
So many worlds such vast ethereal plains,
But one of thousands which compose the whole,
Perhaps as glorious, and of worlds as full.

Sir Richard Blackmore, *The Creation*, Book II, 1712

Something inherently mean in action! even the creation of the universe disturbs my idea of the Almighty's greatness.

Samuel Taylor Coleridge, Notebook, December 1801

Nothing puzzles me more than time and space; and yet nothing troubles me less.

Charles Lamb, Letter to Thomas Manning, 2 January 1810

Though the earth and the heavens were to disappear, there are other worlds, which roll afar; the light of other stars shines upon them; and the sky, which mantles them is garnished with other stars. Is it presumptuous to say that the moral world extends to these distant and unknown regions?

Rev. Thomas Chalmers, D.D., *A series of Discourses on the Christian Revelation . . . in Connection with the Modern Astronomy*, 1817

Let us interrogate the great apparition, that shines so peacefully around us.

Ralph Waldo Emerson, Introduction to *Nature*, 1836

That which once existed in intellect as pure law has now taken body as Nature. It existed already in the mind in solution; now, it has been precipitated, and the bright sediment is the world.

Ralph Waldo Emerson, *The Method of Nature*, 1841

The whole firmament was suddenly irradiated by the coruscations of the Aurora Borealis. It was so vivid in its brightness, and so rapidly changeful in its hues – from green to red, amber and purple, and back again through the whole gamut of colour that the scenery of the river was for a while eclipsed by the grander scenery of the skies. By that glorious light our voyage down the St Lawrence became a kind of triumphant procession in which the heavens as well as the earth and the waters seemed to bear their part. . . .

It seemed as if the banners of eternity were waved in the clear blue firmament by angelic hands, and as if aerial hosts of cherubim and seraphim were doing battle in some great undefinable cause of liberty and right: or perhaps – for imagination was unusually vagrant at the time, and roamed whither it pleased –

these electric ebullitions were but the tentaculae of the great Earth-Monster floating in the ocean of Space, as the medusae float in the clear waters of the western Seas. Nay, might they not be the respirations of that sublime Mother and Bona Dea, upon whose epidermis man is but an insect, and his proudest works but the scraping and piling up of the exudation of her cuticle?

Charles Mackay, *Life and Liberty in America, 1857–8*, 1859 (of the Aurora Borealis seen from the St Lawrence River, Canada)

It is inconceivable that the whole Universe was merely created for us who live in this third-rate planet of a third-rate sun.

Alfred Lord Tennyson, *Alfred Lord Tennyson, a Memoir, by his Son*, 1897

The universe is but a kaleidoscope within the mind of the so-called thinking being, who is himself a curiosity without a cause, an accident conscious of the great accident around him, and who amuses himself with it so long as the phenomenon of his vision lasts.

Henri Frederic Amiel, *Journal*, 19 March 1868, trans. Mrs Humphrey Ward

Who knows but that I may soon be pegging out claims for England in Jupiter?

Hubert Harvey, Comment when mortally wounded in Matabeleland, 1896

A man said to the universe:
'Sir, I exist!'
'However,' replied the universe,
The fact has not created in me
A sense of obligation.'

Stephen Crane, *A Man Said to the Universe – War is Kind*, 1899

To think of those stars, that you see overhead at night, those vast worlds which we can never reach. I would annex the planets if I could; I often think of that. It makes me sad to see them so near and yet so far.

Cecil Rhodes, quoted in W.T. Stead, *Last Will and Testament of C.J. Rhodes, etc.*, 1902

I accept the universe is reported to have been a favourite utterance of our New England transcendentalist, Margaret Fuller; and when some one repeated this phrase to Thomas Carlyle, his sardonic comment is said to have been, 'Gad, she'd better.'

William James, *The Varieties of Religious Experience*, 1902

The Universe, so far as we can observe it, is a wonderful and immense engine; its extent, its order, its beauty, its cruelty, make it alike impressive. If we dramatize its life and conceive its spirit, we are filled with wonder, terror and amusement, so magnificent is that spirit, so prolific, inexorable, grammatical and dull.

George Santayana, *The Life of Reason*, 1905

The cosmos is a gigantic fly-wheel making 10,000 revolutions a minute. Man is a sick fly taking a dizzy ride on it. Religion is the theory that the wheel was designed and set spinning to give him the ride.

H.L. Mencken, *Prejudices*, Third Series, 1922

The conclusion forced upon me in the course of a life devoted to natural science is that the universe as it is assumed to be in physical science is a spiritual universe in which spiritual values count for everything.

J.S.Haldane, *The Sciences and Philosophy*, 1929

The universe is not hostile, nor yet is it friendly. It is simply indifferent.

John Haynes Holmes, *The Sensible Man's View of Religion*, 1933

My theology, briefly is that the universe was dictated, but not signed.

Christopher Morley, attrib.

It is impossible to imagine the universe run by a wise, just and omnipotent God, but it is quite easy to imagine it run by a board of gods. If such a board actually exists it operates precisely like the board of a corporation that is losing money.

H.L.Mencken, *Minority Report – H.L.Mencken's Notebooks*, 1956

For travelers going sidereal
The danger they say is bacterial.
I don't know the pattern
On Mars or on Saturn
But on Venus it must be venereal.

Robert Frost, *For Travelers going Sidereal*, c. 1962

Nature it seems is the popular name
for milliards and milliards and milliards
of particles playing their infinite game
of billiards and billiards and billiards.

Piet Hein, *Atomyriades – Grooks*, 1966

I'm not very interested in other planets. I like them where they are, in the sky.

W.H.Auden, Interview with Michael Newman, in the *Paris Review*, Spring 1974

POSTSCRIPT

I suggested that she take a trip round the world. 'Oh, I know,' returned the lady, yawning with ennui, 'but there's so many other places I want to see first.'

S.J. Perelman, *Westward Ha!*, 1948

Of Paradise can I not speak properly, for I have not been there.

John Mandevile, *The Book of John Mandevile*, *c.* 1360

Index of Places and Peoples

Including buildings and other minor headings

Index of Persons Quoted